# Drugs Used In Psychiatry

This guide contains color reproductions of some commonly prescribed major psychotherapeutic drugs. This guide mainly illustrates tablets and capsules. A † symbol preceding the name of the drug indicates that other doses are available. Check directly with the manufacturer. *(Although the photos are intended as accurate reproductions of the drug, this guide should be used only as a quick identification aid.)*

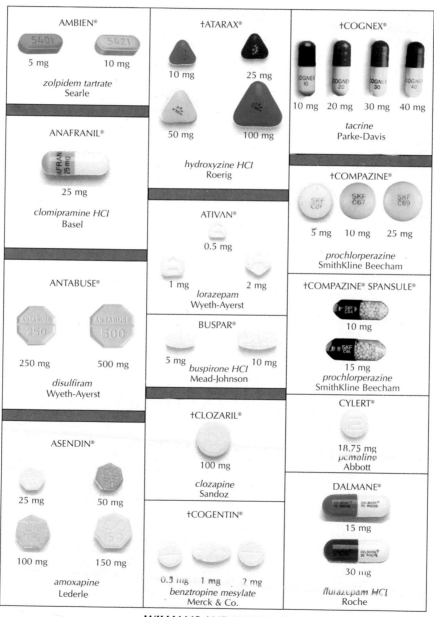

AMBIEN®
5 mg    10 mg
*zolpidem tartrate*
Searle

ANAFRANIL®
25 mg
*clomipramine HCl*
Basel

ANTABUSE®
250 mg    500 mg
*disulfiram*
Wyeth-Ayerst

ASENDIN®
25 mg    50 mg
100 mg    150 mg
*amoxapine*
Lederle

†ATARAX®
10 mg    25 mg
50 mg    100 mg
*hydroxyzine HCl*
Roerig

ATIVAN®
0.5 mg
1 mg    2 mg
*lorazepam*
Wyeth-Ayerst

BUSPAR®
5 mg    10 mg
*buspirone HCl*
Mead-Johnson

†CLOZARIL®
100 mg
*clozapine*
Sandoz

†COGENTIN®
0.5 mg    1 mg    2 mg
*benztropine mesylate*
Merck & Co.

†COGNEX®
10 mg    20 mg    30 mg    40 mg
*tacrine*
Parke-Davis

†COMPAZINE®
5 mg    10 mg    25 mg
*prochlorperazine*
SmithKline Beecham

†COMPAZINE® SPANSULE®
10 mg
15 mg
*prochlorperazine*
SmithKline Beecham

CYLERT®
18.75 mg
*pemoline*
Abbott

DALMANE®
15 mg
30 mg
*flurazepam HCl*
Roche

**WILLIAMS AND WILKINS©**

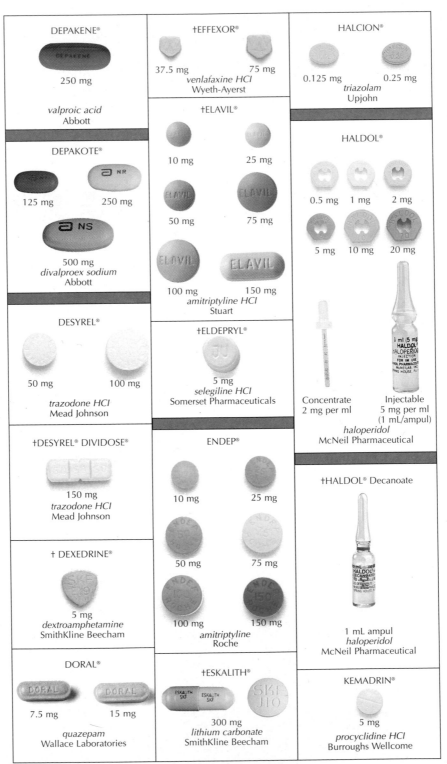

**DEPAKENE®**

250 mg

*valproic acid*
Abbott

**DEPAKOTE®**

125 mg          250 mg

500 mg
*divalproex sodium*
Abbott

**DESYREL®**

50 mg          100 mg

*trazodone HCl*
Mead Johnson

**†DESYREL® DIVIDOSE®**

150 mg
*trazodone HCl*
Mead Johnson

**† DEXEDRINE®**

5 mg
*dextroamphetamine*
SmithKline Beecham

**DORAL®**

7.5 mg          15 mg

*quazepam*
Wallace Laboratories

**†EFFEXOR®**

37.5 mg          75 mg
*venlafaxine HCl*
Wyeth-Ayerst

**†ELAVIL®**

10 mg          25 mg

50 mg          75 mg

100 mg          150 mg
*amitriptyline HCl*
Stuart

**†ELDEPRYL®**

5 mg
*selegiline HCl*
Somerset Pharmaceuticals

**ENDEP®**

10 mg          25 mg

50 mg          75 mg

100 mg          150 mg
*amitriptyline*
Roche

**†ESKALITH®**

300 mg
*lithium carbonate*
SmithKline Beecham

**HALCION®**

0.125 mg          0.25 mg
*triazolam*
Upjohn

**HALDOL®**

0.5 mg    1 mg    2 mg

5 mg    10 mg    20 mg

Concentrate          Injectable
2 mg per ml          5 mg per ml
                     (1 mL/ampul)
*haloperidol*
McNeil Pharmaceutical

**†HALDOL® Decanoate**

1 mL ampul
*haloperidol*
McNeil Pharmaceutical

**KEMADRIN®**

5 mg
*procyclidine HCl*
Burroughs Wellcome

**WILLIAMS AND WILKINS©**

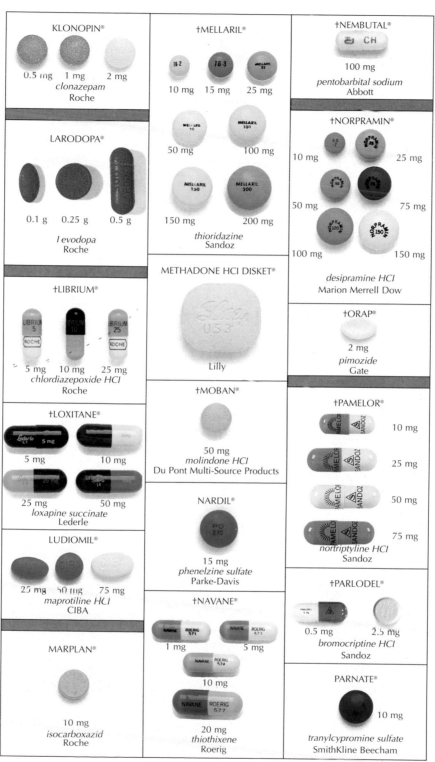

**KLONOPIN®**

0.5 mg · 1 mg · 2 mg
*clonazepam*
Roche

**LARODOPA®**

0.1 g · 0.25 g · 0.5 g
*levodopa*
Roche

**†LIBRIUM®**

5 mg · 10 mg · 25 mg
*chlordiazepoxide HCl*
Roche

**†LOXITANE®**

5 mg · 10 mg
25 mg · 50 mg
*loxapine succinate*
Lederle

**LUDIOMIL®**

25 mg · 50 mg · 75 mg
*maprotiline HCl*
CIBA

**MARPLAN®**

10 mg
*isocarboxazid*
Roche

**†MELLARIL®**

10 mg · 15 mg · 25 mg
50 mg · 100 mg
150 mg · 200 mg
*thioridazine*
Sandoz

**METHADONE HCl DISKET®**

Lilly

**†MOBAN®**

50 mg
*molindone HCl*
Du Pont Multi-Source Products

**NARDIL®**

15 mg
*phenelzine sulfate*
Parke-Davis

**†NAVANE®**

1 mg · 5 mg
10 mg
20 mg
*thiothixene*
Roerig

**†NEMBUTAL®**

100 mg
*pentobarbital sodium*
Abbott

**†NORPRAMIN®**

10 mg · 25 mg
50 mg · 75 mg
100 mg · 150 mg
*desipramine HCl*
Marion Merrell Dow

**†ORAP®**

2 mg
*pimozide*
Gate

**†PAMELOR®**

10 mg
25 mg
50 mg
75 mg
*nortriptyline HCl*
Sandoz

**†PARLODEL®**

0.5 mg · 2.5 mg
*bromocriptine HCl*
Sandoz

**PARNATE®**

10 mg
*tranylcypromine sulfate*
SmithKline Beecham

**WILLIAMS AND WILKINS©**

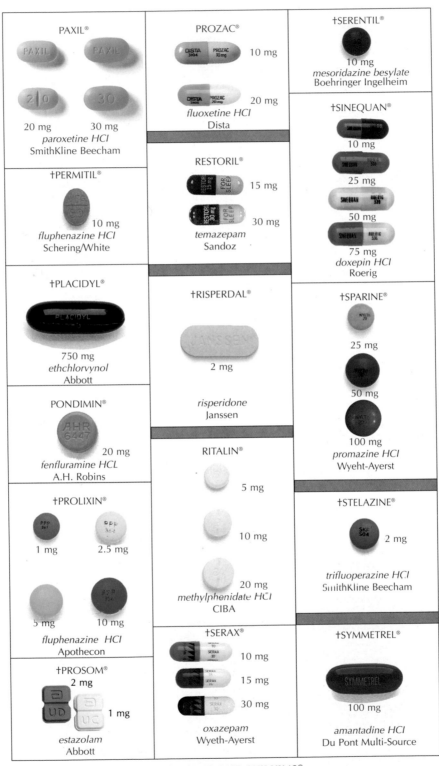

PAXIL®

20 mg          30 mg
paroxetine HCl
SmithKline Beecham

†PERMITIL®
10 mg
fluphenazine HCl
Schering/White

†PLACIDYL®
750 mg
ethchlorvynol
Abbott

PONDIMIN®
20 mg
fenfluramine HCL
A.H. Robins

†PROLIXIN®
1 mg          2.5 mg
5 mg          10 mg
fluphenazine HCl
Apothecon

†PROSOM®
2 mg
1 mg
estazolam
Abbott

PROZAC®
10 mg
20 mg
fluoxetine HCl
Dista

RESTORIL®
15 mg
30 mg
temazepam
Sandoz

†RISPERDAL®
2 mg
risperidone
Janssen

RITALIN®
5 mg
10 mg
20 mg
methylphenidate HCl
CIBA

†SERAX®
10 mg
15 mg
30 mg
oxazepam
Wyeth-Ayerst

†SERENTIL®
10 mg
mesoridazine besylate
Boehringer Ingelheim

†SINEQUAN®
10 mg
25 mg
50 mg
75 mg
doxepin HCl
Roerig

†SPARINE®
25 mg
50 mg
100 mg
promazine HCl
Wyeht-Ayerst

†STELAZINE®
2 mg
trifluoperazine HCl
SmithKline Beecham

†SYMMETREL®
100 mg
amantadine HCl
Du Pont Multi-Source

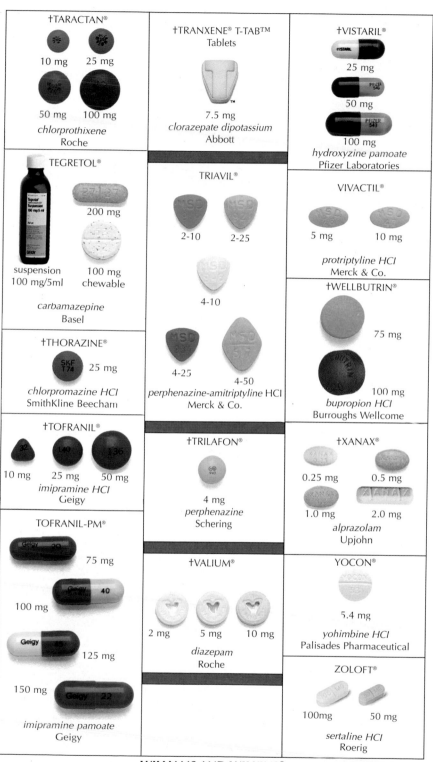

†TARACTAN®

10 mg  25 mg

50 mg  100 mg

chlorprothixene
Roche

TEGRETOL®

200 mg

suspension
100 mg/5ml

100 mg
chewable

carbamazepine
Basel

†THORAZINE®

25 mg

chlorpromazine HCl
SmithKline Beecham

†TOFRANIL®

10 mg  25 mg  50 mg

imipramine HCl
Geigy

TOFRANIL-PM®

75 mg

100 mg

125 mg

150 mg

imipramine pamoate
Geigy

†TRANXENE® T-TAB™
Tablets

7.5 mg
clorazepate dipotassium
Abbott

TRIAVIL®

2-10  2-25

4-10

4-25  4-50

perphenazine-amitriptyline HCl
Merck & Co.

†TRILAFON®

4 mg
perphenazine
Schering

†VALIUM®

2 mg  5 mg  10 mg

diazepam
Roche

†VISTARIL®

25 mg

50 mg

100 mg
hydroxyzine pamoate
Pfizer Laboratories

VIVACTIL®

5 mg  10 mg

protriptyline HCl
Merck & Co.

†WELLBUTRIN®

75 mg

100 mg
bupropion HCl
Burroughs Wellcome

†XANAX®

0.25 mg  0.5 mg

1.0 mg  2.0 mg

alprazolam
Upjohn

YOCON®

5.4 mg

yohimbine HCl
Palisades Pharmaceutical

ZOLOFT®

100mg  50 mg

sertaline HCl
Roerig

**WILLIAMS AND WILKINS©**

# KAPLAN AND SADOCK'S
# SYNOPSIS OF
# PSYCHIATRY

## Behavioral Sciences

## Clinical Psychiatry

### SEVENTH EDITION

# KAPLAN AND SADOCK'S
# SYNOPSIS OF PSYCHIATRY

## Behavioral Sciences

## Clinical Psychiatry

### SEVENTH EDITION

## HAROLD I. KAPLAN, M.D.

Professor of Psychiatry, New York University School of Medicine;
Attending Psychiatrist, Tisch Hospital, the University Hospital
of the New York University Medical Center;
Attending Psychiatrist, Bellevue Hospital;
Consultant Psychiatrist, Lenox Hill Hospital, New York, New York

## BENJAMIN J. SADOCK, M.D.

Professor and Vice Chairman, Department of Psychiatry,
New York University School of Medicine;
Attending Psychiatrist, Tisch Hospital, the University Hospital
of the New York University Medical Center;
Attending Psychiatrist, Bellevue Hospital;
Consultant Psychiatrist, Lenox Hill Hospital, New York, New York

## JACK A. GREBB, M.D.

Clinical Associate Professor of Psychiatry, College of Medicine,
University of Illinois at Chicago, Chicago, Illinois

### Williams & Wilkins

BALTIMORE • PHILADELPHIA • HONG KONG
LONDON • MUNICH • SYDNEY • TOKYO

A WAVERLY COMPANY

Editor: David C. Retford
Managing Editor: Molly L. Mullen
Copy Editor: Joan Welsh
Designer: Norman W. Och
Illustration Planner: Lorraine Wrzosek
Production Coordinator: Barbara J. Felton

Copyright © 1994
Williams & Wilkins
428 East Preston Street
Baltimore, Maryland 21202, USA

Accurate indications, adverse reactions, and dosage schedules for drugs are provided in this book, but it is possible that they may change. The reader is urged to review the package information data of the manufacturers of the medications mentioned.

*Printed in the United States of America*

First Edition 1972
  Spanish
Second Edition 1976
  Italian
Third Edition 1981
  Portuguese
  Spanish
Fourth Edition 1985
  Portuguese
  Spanish
Fifth Edition 1988
  Portuguese
  Spanish
Sixth Edition 1991
  Greek
  Portuguese
  Spanish

**Library of Congress Cataloging-in-Publication Data**
Kaplan, Harold I.
    Kaplan and Sadock's synopsis of psychiatry : behavioral sciences, clinical psychiatry / Harold I. Kaplan, Benjamin J. Sadock, Jack A. Grebb—7th ed.
        p.    cm.
    Rev. ed. of: Synopsis of psychiatry. 6th ed. c1991.
    Includes bibliographical references and index.
    ISBN 0-683-04530-X
    1. Mental illness. 2. Psychiatry. I. Sadock, Benjamin J. II. Grebb, Jack A. III. Kaplan, Harold I. Synopsis of psychiatry. IV. Title. V. Title: Synopsis of psychiatry.
    [DNLM: 1. Mental Disorders. WM 100 K172k 1994]
RC454.K35 1994
616.89—dc20
DNLM/DLC                                                           93-27556
for Library of Congress                                           CIP

95  96  97  98
4  5  6  7  8  9  10

Dedicated to Nancy Barrett Kaplan
and
Virginia Alcott Sadock
and
to our families and friends

# ☐ Preface

This is the seventh edition of *Kaplan and Sadock's Synopsis of Psychiatry*; the first edition was published in 1972. The appearance of this edition—so soon after the sixth edition, published in 1991—was brought about by the publication of the fourth edition of *Diagnostic and Statistical Manual of Mental Disorders* (DSM-IV) by the American Psychiatric Association. DSM-IV revamped, once again, the psychiatric nosology. This edition of *Synopsis* is consistent with the new nosology. Indeed, it is one of the first psychiatric textbooks that relies on the new terminology completely and that includes the current DSM-IV diagnostic criteria for all mental disorders.

Frequent revisions of *Synopsis* have been necessary to keep up with the steady expansion of the body of knowledge in behavioral science and psychiatry. New advances have been made in the neural sciences, particularly in the areas of neurochemistry, neurophysiology, psychoimmunology, and psychoendocrinology. New data about the diagnosis and the treatment of mental disorders, particularly in the area of psychopharmacology, are presented in detail.

The eclectic and multidisciplinary approach that is the hallmark of all our books is also implemented in this edition. Accordingly, biological, psychological, and sociological factors are integrated and presented as they affect the person in health and in disease. We repeat what we wrote in the preface to the sixth edition:

Modern psychiatry must emphasize the humane and compassionate aspects of medicine; this textbook is dedicated to the humanism that is unfortunately often lost in technically based modern medical education, training, and practice. Of equal importance, the interactions between medical school faculty and students require a high level of mutual empathic concern if America is to avoid producing computerlike robotic physicians. . . . If taught properly, with quality and sensitivity, psychiatry should be a dramatic and continuing reminder to all in medicine of its mission—the diagnosis, treatment, and elimination of pain, suffering, and disease through the treatment of the whole patient.

## SOCIOPOLITICAL ISSUES

Medicine in the United States is undergoing a dramatic change. The introduction of the American Health Security Bill in 1993 has fueled intense debate about the future of medicine. Psychiatry is likely to be affected adversely, since prejudice toward mental illness has always existed in many quarters—political policy makers, insurance companies, the general public, and, sadly, the medical profession itself. The reality is that mental illness is a fact of life

that must be dealt with by society at large, as well as by the medical profession.

All medical textbooks, including our own, have an obligation to provide a forum for the discussion of some of the new sociopolitical forces that affect medical practice. Decisions are now being made that involve diverse issues affecting physicians and patients: managed care; third-party insurance reimbursement for medical care, including psychiatric care; Medicare and Medicaid; the use, classification, and definition of controlled substances; the use of triplicate prescriptions; homosexual men and women in the military; poverty, homelessness, and deinstitutionalization; and the working conditions and the number of hours on duty of medical house staff are only a few of the current sociopolitical issues.

Unfortunately, most physicians, because of the nature of their medical education, are poorly prepared to deal with the socioeconomics of health care delivery. But now they are being forced to become involved, as a result of the American Health Security Bill and the current domestic controversy about the delivery and the quality of medical care, including psychiatry.

Medical schools have an obligation to educate physicians in sociopolitical areas. Toward that end, we have made observations about controversial areas. Psychiatrists, who are involved in the humane aspect of medical care, have a special obligation to become knowledgeable about all issues that affect the physical and psychological well-being of their patients. We hope that other medical textbooks will also exercise their editorial prerogatives in those areas.

## DECADE OF THE BRAIN

By presidential proclamation, 1990–1999 was declared the decade of the brain. Many studies regarding the human brain are being conducted at the National Institutes of Health, particularly the National Institute of Mental Health. As the presidential proclamation states:

Over the years, our understanding of the brain—how it works, what goes wrong when it is injured or diseased—has increased dramatically. However, we still have much more to learn. The need for continued study of the brain is compelling: millions of Americans are affected each year by disorders of the brain ranging from neurogenetic diseases to degenerative disorders such as Alzheimer's, as well as stroke, schizophrenia, autism, and impairments of speech, language, and hearing.

A new era of psychiatric discovery is dawning. We hope that this textbook contributes to that new era of discovery and leads to a continued improvement in the diagnosis and treatment of mental disorders.

## CHANGES IN THIS EDITION

**Format.** This edition has 344 more pages than the previous edition because of the inclusion of more written material, illustrations, and tables, including all the tables from DSM-IV. The color illustrations of all the major drugs currently used in psychiatry in their various dosage forms have been expanded to include all the latest drugs available in the United States. The psychotherapeutic drug identification guide has been one of the more popular features of *Synopsis*. To keep the book from becoming too large, we have limited the references to the major books, monographs, and articles. And we have used small type in some sections to conserve space.

**DSM-IV.** The mental disorders discussed in this textbook are consistent with the nosology of the fourth edition of the American Psychiatric Association's *Diagnostic and Statistical Manual of Mental Disorders* (DSM-IV), which is being published in 1994. Many psychiatrists have reservations about the DSM-IV nosology; in several sections of this book, those objections are clearly stated. Such terms as "neurosis" and "psychosomatic" are used in this book, even though those terms are not a part of the official nosology.

The inclusion of the DSM-IV nosology and diagnostic criteria means that almost every section dealing with clinical disorders has undergone a thorough and extensive revision. For example, DSM-IV no longer uses the term "organic mental disorders." An entirely new chapter in this textbook—"Delirium, Dementia, and Amnestic and Other Cognitive Disorders"—has been written to reflect that change. Similarly, the topic of psychoactive substance-induced organic mental disorders—the term used in the revised third edition of DSM (DSM-III-R)—is now covered in Chapter 12, "Substance-Related Disorders," which is the DSM-IV classification. The entire textbook has been reorganized to reflect the DSM-IV organization, and new chapters, such as "Relational Problems" and "Problems Related to Abuse or Neglect," have been added.

DSM-IV is now the law of the land; accordingly, it is strictly adhered to in this book. However, DSM-IV is a manual on nosology; it is *not* a textbook. *Synopsis* and other textbooks on psychiatry cover the entire field of psychiatry, not just nosology.

**New and revised areas.** The first chapter, on the doctor-patient relationship, has been expanded to include a discussion of interviewing techniques. Chapter 2, "Human Development Throughout the Life Cycle," has been revised to include discussions of the psychological aspects of pregnancy and childbirth. The subject of fetology and fetal life has been expanded to reflect new advances in that area. Section 2.7, "Thanatology: Death and Bereavement," includes a discussion of physician-assisted suicide. A review and critique of President Bill Clinton's American Health Security Bill, sent to Congress in 1993, is included in Section 4.9, "Socioeconomic Aspects of Health Care." For the first time, the theories of Erik Erikson and Jean Piaget appear as separate sections in this edition. Chapter 3, "The Brain and Behavior," has been updated to provide coverage of the fields of neurochemistry, neurophysiology, and psychoendocrinology; a new section, "Behavioral Genetics," has been added. Chapter 11, "Neuropsychiatric Aspects of Human Immunodeficiency Virus (HIV) Infection and Acquired Immune Deficiency Syndrome (AIDS)," has been updated, and Section 7.3, "Medical Assessment in Psychiatry," has been added. Other extensively changed areas include geriatric psychiatry, brain-imaging techniques, ethics in psychiatry, neuropsychiatric tests and rating scales, the role of laboratory tests in psychiatry, behavioral medicine, and the psychiatric aspects of immunology.

**Childhood disorders.** The chapters on child and adolescent psychiatry have been heavily rewritten. As in the adult areas, the new organization is based on DSM-IV. The new chapters include "Assessment, Examination, and Psychological Testing," "Mental Retardation," "Learning Disorders," "Mood Disorders and Suicide," and "Schizophrenia with Childhood Onset."

**Biological therapies.** A major change introduced in the sixth edition of *Synopsis* is continued in this edition. Drugs used in the treatment of mental disorders are classified and discussed pharmacologically, rather than as antidepressants, antipsychotics, and the like. We use that unique format to provide the student with an understanding not only of the general principles of psychopharmacology but also of the use of each psychotherapeutic drug according to its pharmacological activity as a discrete drug, rather than as one of a family of drugs. This edition adds information about the uses, cautions, interactions, and dosages of drugs and includes information on the drugs most recently introduced in the United States. Chapter 33, "Biological Therapies," also includes information about drugs not yet on the market. A tinted page contains an index to guide the reader to the section where each of the drugs used in psychiatry is discussed.

## TEACHING SYSTEM

This textbook forms one part of a comprehensive system we have developed to facilitate the teaching of psychiatry and the behavioral sciences. At the head of the system is *Comprehensive Textbook of Psychiatry*, which is global in depth and scope; it is designed for and used by psychiatrists, behavioral scientists, and all workers in the mental health field. *Kaplan and Sadock's Synopsis* is a relatively brief, highly modified, original, and current version useful for medical students, psychiatric residents, practicing psychiatrists, and mental health professionals. Another part of the system is *Study Guide and Self-Examination Review for Kaplan and Sadock's Synopsis of Psychiatry*, which consists of multiple-choice questions and answers; it is designed for students of psychiatry and for clinical psychiatrists who require a review of the behavioral sciences and general psychiatry in preparation for a variety of examinations. The questions are modeled after and consistent with the new format used by the National Board of Medical Examiners and the Federation of State Medical

Boards' United States Medical Licensing Examination. Other parts of the system are the pocket handbooks: *Pocket Handbook of Clinical Psychiatry*, *Pocket Handbook of Psychiatric Drug Treatment*, and *Pocket Handbook of Emergency Psychiatric Medicine*. Those books cover the diagnosis and the treatment of psychiatric disorders, psychopharmacology, and psychiatric emergencies, respectively, and are compactly designed and concisely written to be carried in the pocket by clinical clerks and practicing physicians, whatever their specialty, to provide a quick reference. Finally, *Comprehensive Glossary of Psychiatry and Psychology* provides simply written definitions for psychiatrists and other physicians, psychologists, students, other mental health professionals, and the general public.

Taken together, those books create a multipronged approach to the teaching, study, and learning of psychiatry.

## THE FUTURE OF PSYCHIATRY

The publication of this book coincides with seismic changes in the delivery of health care in this country that are likely to affect the field of psychiatry. For example, managed-care programs are attempting to limit mental health benefits in an effort to control costs. Some proposals curtail the number of outpatient visits for psychotherapy to 5 to 20 sessions a year. Although some types of psychotherapy can be conducted within that framework, other types of psychotherapy, particularly insight-oriented psychotherapies, require frequent visits over an extended period. In addition, before a patient can be referred to a psychiatrist, many health maintenance organizations (HMOs) require that a primary care physician (the so-called gatekeeper) see the patient for several weeks before the referral; during that time, pharmacotherapy, rather than psychotherapy, is administered. Drugs, rather than psychotherapy, will become the treatment of choice, in spite of the fact that many studies have found the superior efficacy of drugs used in conjunction with psychotherapy in the treatment of most mental disorders, particularly depressive disorders. In addition, persons who are emotionally well make fewer general medical visits than do persons with emotional disorders; the result is savings in the overall cost of general medical care.

We believe that managed-care oversight of psychiatric treatment will undermine the doctor-patient relationship. It can destroy the psychotherapeutic process, which requires confidentiality, trust, independent judgment, and freedom from external bureaucratic constraints to be effective. We believe that prejudice toward psychiatry and fear of mental illness are largely responsible for those limitations.

## ACKNOWLEDGMENTS

A new author, Jack Grebb, M.D., has joined us. A distinguished clinician and scholar, Dr. Grebb helped in the conceptualization, the writing, and the implementation of every aspect of this textbook.

We thank our contributing editors: Glen Gabbard, M.D., Rebecca Jones, M.D., Peter Kaplan, M.D., Caroly Pataki, M.D., and Virginia A. Sadock, M.D. Each made major contributions that were of immeasurable value.

Others who helped us were Norman Sussman, M.D., Richard Perry, M.D., Eugene Rubin, M.D., and Clifford Feldman, M.D. We express our appreciation to Jay E. Kantor, Ph.D., Research Associate Professor of Humanities at New York University School of Medicine, for his help in the ethics section of the book. We also thank Nancy B. Kaplan, James Sadock, Victoria Sadock, and Phillip Kaplan, M.D., for their help.

Justin Hollingsworth played a key role in assisting us in all aspects of our work. His prodigious efforts were extremely important. Laura Marino and Lynda Abrams Zittell, M.A., were also of great help.

In addition, we thank our close friend, Joan Welsh, who has done outstanding editorial work for this book, as she has done in the past for other books. We also thank Dorice Vieira, Head of Educational Services of the Frederick L. Ehrman Medical Library of the New York University School of Medicine, for her valuable assistance in this project.

We also take this opportunity to acknowledge those who have translated this and other works into foreign languages. Current translations include Italian, French, Portuguese, Spanish, Indonesian, and German, in addition to a special Asian and international student edition of *Synopsis*.

We thank Robert Cancro, M.D., Professor and Chairman of the Department of Psychiatry at New York University School of Medicine, who participated as Senior Contributing Editor of this edition. Dr. Cancro's commitment to psychiatric education and psychiatric research is recognized throughout the world. He has been a source of great inspiration and friendship to us and has contributed immeasurably to this and previous books.

Finally, we thank our publishers, Williams & Wilkins, for their cooperation in every aspect of this textbook.

Harold I. Kaplan, M.D.
Benjamin J. Sadock, M.D.
Jack A. Grebb, M.D.

New York University Medical Center
New York, New York
February 1994

# Contents

# The Doctor-Patient Relationship and Interviewing Techniques

The physician has many tools with which to diagnose, manage, and treat patients' disorders. The tools range from in-depth laboratory investigations to highly sophisticated radiographic procedures. Although medical schools and residencies provide training grounds for the acquisition of complex and essential skills, one such skill is often treated superficially. The capacity to develop an effective doctor-patient relationship requires a solid appreciation for the complexities of human behavior and a rigorous education in the techniques of talking and listening to people. To diagnose, manage, and treat an ill person's disorder, the physician must learn to listen. For many physicians—trained to be, first and foremost, active, aggressive, and in control—the act of listening may take on the mantle of an uncomfortable passivity. One of the supreme tasks of any medical training center is to help the physician acquire skills of active listening, both to what the physician and the patient are saying and to the undercurrents of the unspoken feelings between the two. A physician who is continually monitoring not only the content of the interaction (what the patient and the doctor say) but also the process (what the patient or the doctor may not say but conveys in a variety of other ways) is a physician who realizes that communication between two people occurs on several levels at once. A physician who is sensitive to the effects that history, culture, environment, and psychology have on that relationship is a physician who is working with a multifaceted patient, not a disease syndrome. When the art and the technique of active listening are not emphasized, respected, and conveyed, physicians fail to be trained in the rudiments of establishing a relationship with their patients, and patient care is the inevitable loser.

## BIOPSYCHOSOCIAL MODEL

George Engel has been the most prominent proponent of the biopsychosocial model of disease, which stresses an integrated systems approach to human behavior and disease. The biopsychosocial model is derived from general systems theory. The biological system emphasizes the anatomical, structural, and molecular substrate of disease and its effects on the patient's biological functioning; the psychological system emphasizes the effects of psychodynamic factors, motivation, and personality on the experience of illness and the reaction to it; and the social system emphasizes cultural, environmental, and familial influences on the expression and the experience of illness. Engel

postulated that each system affects and is affected by every other system. Engel's model does not assert that medical illness is a direct result of a person's psychological or sociocultural makeup but, rather, encourages a comprehensive understanding of disease and treatment. A dramatic example of Engel's conception of the biopsychosocial model was a 1971 study of the relation between sudden death and psychological factors. After investigating 170 sudden deaths over about six years, he observed that serious illness or even death may be associated with psychological stress or trauma. Among the potential triggering events Engel listed are the following: the death of a close friend, grief, anniversary reactions, loss of self-esteem, personal danger or threat and the letdown after the threat has passed, and reunions or triumphs.

The doctor-patient relationship is a critical component of the biopsychosocial model. All physicians must not only have a working knowledge of the patient's medical status but also be familiar with how the patient's individual psychology and sociocultural milieu affect the medical condition, the emotional responses to the condition, and involvement with the doctor.

## ILLNESS BEHAVIOR

*Illness behavior* is the term used to describe a patient's reactions to the experience of being sick. Some describe aspects of illness behavior as the sick role. The *sick role* is the role that society ascribes to the sick person because he or she is ill. Characteristics of the sick role include such factors as being excused from certain responsibilities and being expected to want to obtain help to get well. Edward Suchman described five stages of illness behavior: (1) *the symptom experience stage*, in which a decision is made that something is wrong; (2) *the assumption of the sick role stage*, in which a decision is made that one is sick and needs professional care; (3) *the medical care contact stage*, in which a decision is made to seek professional care; (4) *the dependent-patient role stage*, in which a decision is made to transfer control to the doctor and to follow prescribed treatment; and (5) *the recovery or rehabilitation stage*, in which a decision is made to give up the patient role.

Illness behavior and the sick role are affected by a person's previous experience with illness and by a person's cultural beliefs about disease. The influence of culture on the reporting and the presentation of symptoms must be evaluated. The relation of illness to family processes, class status, and ethnic identity are also important. The person's and the culture's attitudes about dependency and helplessness greatly influence how and if a person asks for help, as do such psychological factors as personality type and the personal meaning attributed to the experience of being ill. For instance, different persons react to illness in different ways, depending on their habitual modes of thinking, feeling, and behaving. Some persons experience illness as overwhelming loss, whereas others see in the same illness a challenge to be overcome or a punishment for something they feel guilty about. Table 1–1 lists essential areas to be addressed in the assessment of illness behavior and questions that are helpful in making that assessment.

## MODELS OF THE DOCTOR-PATIENT RELATIONSHIP

The doctor-patient relationship has a number of potential models. Often, neither the doctor nor the patient is fully conscious of choosing one or another model. The models most often derive from the personalities, expectations, and needs of both the doctor and the patient. The fact that the personalities, the expectations, and the needs are largely unspoken and may be different for doctor and patient may lead to miscommunication and disappointment for both participants in the relationship. The doctor must be consciously aware of which model is operating with which patient and be able to shift models, depending on the particular needs of specific patients and on the treatment requirements of specific clinical situations.

### Specific Models

Models of the doctor-patient relationship include the active-passive model, the teacher-student (or parent-child, guidance-cooperation) model, the mutual participation model, and the friendship (or socially intimate) model.

The *active-passive model* implies the complete passivity of the patient and the taking over by the physician that necessarily results. In that model the patient assumes virtually no responsibility for his or her own care and takes no part in

**Table 1–1**
**Assessment of Individual Illness Behavior**

Prior illness episodes, especially illnesses of standard severity (childbirth, renal stones, surgery)
Cultural degree of stoicism
Cultural beliefs concerning the specific problem
Personal meaning or beliefs about the particular problem

Specific questions to ask to elicit the patient's explanatory model:

1. What do you call your problem? What name does it have?
2. What do you think caused your problem?
3. Why do you think it started when it did?
4. What does your sickness do to you? How does it work?
5. How severe is it? Will it have a short or long course?
6. What do you fear most about your sickness?
7. What are the chief problems that your sickness has caused for you?
8. What kind of treatment do you think you should receive? What are the most important results you hope to receive from treatment?
9. What have you done so far to treat your sickness?

Table from M Lipkin Jr: Psychiatry and medicine. In *Comprehensive Textbook of Psychiatry*, ed 5, H I Kaplan, B J Sadock, editors, p 1280. Williams & Wilkins, Baltimore, 1989.

treatment. The model is appropriate when a patient is unconscious, immobilized, or delirious.

In the *teacher-student model* the dominance of the physician is assumed and emphasized. The role of the physician is paternalistic and controlling; the role of the patient is essentially one of dependence and acceptance. That model is often observed during a patient's recovery from surgery.

The *mutual participation model* implies equality between doctor and patient; both participants require and depend on each other's input. The need for a doctor-patient relationship based on a model of mutual, active participation is most obvious in the treatment of such chronic illnesses as renal failure and diabetes, in which a patient's knowledge and acceptance of treatment ramifications are critical to the success of the treatment. The model may also be effective in subtle situations—for example, in pneumonia.

The *friendship model* of the doctor-patient relationship is generally considered dysfunctional if not unethical. It most often represents a primary, underlying psychological problem in the physician, who may have an emotional need to turn the care for the patient into a relationship of mutual sharing of personal information and love. The model often involves indeterminate perpetuation of the relationship, rather than an appropriate ending, and a blurring of boundaries between professionalism and intimacy.

### General Considerations

Gaining conscious insight into the relationship between physicians and patients requires constant evaluation. The better understanding that doctors have of themselves, the more secure they feel, and the better able they are to modify destructive attitudes. Doctors need to empathize but not to the point of assuming the burdens of their patients or unrealistically fantasizing that only they can be the patients' saviors. They should be able to leave behind the problems of their patients when away from the office or the hospital and not use their patients as substitutes for an intimacy or a relationship that may be missing in their personal lives. Otherwise, they will be handicapped in their efforts to help sick people, who need sympathy and understanding but not sentimentality and overinvolvement.

The physician is prone to some defensiveness, partly with good reason, for many innocent doctors have been sued, attacked, and even killed because they did not give some patients the satisfaction they desired. Consequently, the physician may assume a defensive attitude toward all patients. Although such rigidity may create the image of thoroughness and efficiency, it is frequently inappropriate. Greater flexibility leads to a responsiveness to the subtle interplay between the two persons. It also assumes a certain tolerance for the uncertainty present in any clinical situation with any patient. The doctor must learn to accept the fact that, as much as he or she may wish to control everything in the care of a patient, that wish can never be fully realized. In some situations a disease cannot be controlled, and death cannot be prevented, no matter how conscientious, competent, or caring a physician is.

Physicians must also avoid sidestepping issues that they find difficult to deal with because of their own sensitivities, prejudices, or peculiarities when those issues are important to the patient.

A medical student insisted on questioning a patient about

her relationship with her 23-year-old son. The playback of a tape-recorded interview revealed that the patient wished to talk about her problems with her husband. When the patient was later interviewed by the supervising doctor, she said: "The medical student was a nice fellow, but I could see that he was having trouble with his mother. It made me understand my own son more."

In such a complex interaction as the doctor-patient relationship, mistakes are usually not disastrous to the relationship if they are relatively infrequent. When the patient senses interest, enthusiasm, and goodwill on the part of the interviewer, the patient is apt to tolerate considerable inexperience.

## INTERVIEWING

One of the most critical tools a physician has is the ability to interview effectively. A skillful interview is able to gather the data necessary to understand and treat the patient and in the process to increase the patient's understanding of and compliance with the physician's advice. Every interview has three main components, all of which require special techniques and skills: the beginning of the interview, the interview itself, and the closing of the interview.

Ekkehard Othmer and Sieglinde Othmer described an interview as taking place in four dimensions—establishing rapport, assessing the patient's mental status, using specific techniques, and diagnosing—with the interviewing process progressing through seven stages. Table 1–2 and Figure 1–1 summarize their conceptualization of an ideal interview. They stress that the order of completion of the interview tasks is determined by following the patient's needs; the order is not necessarily the order outlined in Table 1–2. In general, an interviewer must convey an attitude that is nonjudgmental, interested, concerned, and kind; otherwise, potentially crucial information may not be obtained.

Many factors influence both the content and the process of the interview: (1) The patient's personality and character style significantly influence reactions and the emotional context in which the interview unfolds. (2) Various clinical situations—including whether the patient is seen on a general hospital ward, on a psychiatric ward, in the emergency room, or as an outpatient—shape the type of questions asked and the recommendations offered. (3) Technical factors—such as telephone interruptions, the use of an interpreter, note taking, and the room's physical space and comfort—affect the interview. (4) The timing of the interview in the patient's illness, be it in the most acute stage or during a remission, influences the interview's content and process. (5) The interviewer's style, orientation, and experience have a significant influence on the interview. Even the timing of interjections, such as "uh-huh," can influence what a patient does or does not say and when, as the patient tries unconsciously to follow the subtle leads and cues provided by the doctor.

Every interview has two major technical goals: recognition of the psychological determinants of behavior and symptom classification. Othmer and Othmer described goals as encompassing two styles of interviewing: the insight-oriented or psychodynamic style and the symptom-oriented or descriptive style. *Insight-oriented interviewing*

**Table 1–2**
**Seven Phases of the Interview and the Four Components**

| Phase | Rapport | Mental Status | Technique | Diagnosis |
|---|---|---|---|---|
| 1. Warm-up | Put patient at ease, set limits | Observe appearance, psychomotor function, speech, thinking, affect, orientation, memory | Select productive questions | Note diagnostic clues from patient's behavior |
| 2. Screening of the problem | Empathize with suffering, become a compassionate listener | Explore mood, insight, memory, judgment | Open with broad screening questions | Classify the chief complaint; assess symptoms, severity, course, stressors; list differential diagnoses |
| 3. Follow-up of preliminary impressions | Become an ally, make shifts in topics clear | Assess speed of thinking, ability to shift sets | Shift topics, progress from open-ended to closed-ended questions | Verify or exclude diagnostic impressions |
| 4. Confirmatory history | Show expertise, interest, thoroughness, and leadership | Evaluate responsibility, judgment, remote memory | Follow-up, shift topics, handle defenses | Assess course, effects on social life, family and medical history |
| 5. Completion of data base | Motivate for testing | Test mental status functions | Fill in gaps, follow up clues, reconcile inconsistencies | Exclude unlikely disorders |
| 6. Feedback | Secure acceptance of diagnosis | Discuss mental status findings, explore interest in help | Explain disorders and treatment options | Establish diagnosis and prognosis |
| 7. Treatment contract | Assume the authority role and assure compliance | Make inferences about insight, judgment, and compliance | Discuss treatment contract | Predict treatment effects |

Table from E Othmer, S C Othmer: *The Clinical Interview Using DSM-III-R*, p 246. American Psychiatric Press, Washington, 1989. Used with permission.

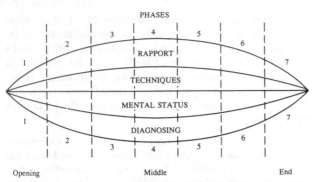

**Figure 1–1.** The seven phases of the standard interview. The opening or beginning of the interview consists of one phase (1). The middle phase or interview proper is subdivided into four phases (2 to 5). The end phase or closing of the interview is subdivided into two phases (6 and 7). (Figure from E Othmer, S C Othmer: *The Clinical Interview Using DSM-III-R*, p 13. American Psychiatric Press, Washington, 1989. Used with permission.)

tends to emphasize the eliciting and the interpretation of unconscious conflicts, anxieties, and defenses; the *symptom-oriented approach* emphasizes the classification of the patient's complaints and dysfunctions as defined by specific diagnostic categories. The approaches are not mutually exclusive and, in fact, can be compatible. The patient's diagnosis can be described as precisely as possible by eliciting such details as the patient's symptoms, course of illness, and family history and by understanding the patient's personality, developmental history, and unconscious conflicts.

## Psychiatric versus Medical-Surgical Interviews

### Similarities

FUNCTIONS OF THE INTERVIEW, COPING MECHANISMS, AND PSYCHOLOGICAL VERSUS MEDICAL SYMPTOMS. Mack Lipkin, Jr., described three functions of the medical interview: to assess the nature of the problem, to develop and maintain a therapeutic relationship, and to communicate information and implement a treatment plan (Table 1–3). Those functions are exactly the same as those of psychiatric and surgical interviews. Also universal are the predominant coping mechanisms, both adaptive and maladaptive. Those mechanisms include such reactions as anxiety, depression, regression, denial, anger, and dependency (Table 1–4). Those reactions must be anticipated, recognized, and addressed by every physician if any treatment or intervention is to be effective. Many psychiatric problems present as medical illnesses, and, conversely, many medical and surgical problems present with psychiatric symptoms. For that reason alone, all physicians must recognize the importance of obtaining a comprehensive biopsychosocial history for each of their patients.

PSYCHOGENIC SYNDROMES AND MEDICAL SYNDROMES WITH PSYCHIATRIC PRESENTATIONS. Lipkin defined psychogenic syndromes as "illnesses presenting as medical problems but characterized by strong evidence to suggest that the dominant role in the timing, etiology, and nature of the syndrome is that of psychological or social events, rather than biological ones." Examples include somatization dis-

order, factitious disorder with predominantly physical signs and symptoms, pain disorder, and hypochondriasis. Medical problems that can present with psychiatric symptoms include acquired immune deficiency syndrome (AIDS) (depression, anxiety, cognitive deficits), multiple sclerosis (personality changes, mood swings, depression), and hypothyroidism (irritability, depression, paranoia, delusions, hallucinations).

**Differences.** A psychiatric patient must often contend with stresses and pressures different from those suffered by the patient who does not have a psychiatric disorder. Those stresses include the stigma attached to being a psychiatric patient (it is more acceptable to have a medical or surgical problem than to have a mental problem); difficulties in communicating because of disorders in thinking, which can include delusions, hallucinations, and disorganized thought processes; and oddities of behavior and impairments of insight and judgment that make compliance with treatment particularly difficult. Because psychiatric patients often find it difficult to describe fully what is going on, the physician must be prepared to obtain information from other sources. Family members, friends, and the spouse can provide critical pieces of information about the patient—such as past psychiatric history, responses to medication, and precipitating stresses—that the patient may not be able to provide.

Psychiatric patients may not be able to tolerate a traditional interview format, especially in the most acute stages of a disorder. For instance, a psychiatric patient suffering from increased agitation, paranoia, or depression may not be able to sit for 30 to 45 minutes of discussion or questioning. In that case the physician must be prepared to conduct multiple brief interactions over a period of time—sitting or standing with the patient for as long as the patient is able, then stopping and returning when the patient appears able to tolerate more.

Physicians must be particularly prepared to use their powers of observation with psychiatric patients who are not able to communicate well verbally. The specific skills include observations of the patient's general appearance, behavior, and body language and how all those factors provide diagnostic clues.

Many nonpsychiatric physicians see psychiatric patients. Studies show that about 60 percent of all patients with mental disorders visit a nonpsychiatric physician during any six-month period and that patients with mental disorders are twice as likely to visit a primary care physician as are other patients. Nonpsychiatric physicians should be knowledgeable about the special problems of psychiatric patients and the specific techniques used to treat them.

## Establishing Rapport

Establishing rapport is the first step of an interview, and interviewers often use their own empathic responses to facilitate the development of rapport. Othmer and Othmer defined the development of rapport as encompassing six strategies: (1) putting the patient and the interviewer at ease; (2) finding the pain and expressing compassion; (3) evaluating the patient's insight and becoming an ally; (4) showing expertise; (5) establishing authority as a physician and therapist; and (6) balancing the roles of empathic listener, expert, and authority.

As part of a strategy for increasing rapport, Othmer and Othmer developed a checklist (Table 1–5) that enables

**Table 1–3**
**Three Functions of the Medical Interview**

| Functions | Objectives | Skills |
|---|---|---|
| I. Determining the nature of the problem | 1. To enable the clinician to establish a diagnosis or recommend further diagnostic procedures, suggest a course of treatment, and predict the nature of the Illness | 1. Knowledge base of diseases, disorders, problems, and clinical hypotheses from multiple conceptual domains: biomedical, sociocultural, psychodynamic, and behavioral<br>2. Ability to elicit data for the above conceptual domains (encouraging the patient to tell his or her story; organizing the flow of the interview, the form of questions, the characterization of symptoms, the mental status examination)<br>3. Ability to perceive data from multiple sources (history, mental status examination, physician's subjective response to patient, nonverbal cues, listening at multiple levels)<br>4. Hypothesis generation and testing<br>5. Developing a therapeutic relationship (function II) |
| II. Developing and maintaining a therapeutic relationship | 1. The patient's willingness to provide diagnostic information<br>2. Relief of physical and psychological distress<br>3. Willingness to accept treatment plan or a process of negotiation<br>4. Patient satisfaction<br>5. Physician satisfaction | 1. Defining the nature of the relationship<br>2. Allowing the patient to tell his or her story<br>3. Hearing, bearing, and tolerating the patient's expression of painful feelings<br>4. Appropriate and genuine interest, empathy, support, and cognitive understanding<br>5. Attending to common patient concerns over embarrassment, shame, and humiliation<br>6. Elicitation of the patient's perspective<br>7. Determining the nature of the problem (function I)<br>8. Communicating information and recommending treatment (function III) |
| III. Communicating information and implementing a treatment plan | 1. The patient's understanding of the nature of the illness<br>2. The patient's understanding of suggested diagnostic procedures<br>3. The patient's understanding of the treatment possibilities<br>4. Achievements of consensus between physician and patient over the above items 1 to 3<br>5. Achievement of informed consent<br>6. Improve coping mechanisms<br>7. Life-style change | 1. Determining the nature of the problem (function I)<br>2. Developing a therapeutic relationship (function II)<br>3. Establishing the differences in perspective between physician and patient<br>4. Educational strategies<br>5. Clinical negotiations for conflict resolutions |

Table from A Lazare, J Bird, M Lipkin Jr, S Putnam: Three functions of the medical interview: An integrative conceptual framework. In *The Medical Interview,* M Lipkin Jr, S Putnam, A Lazare, editors, p 103. Springer, New York, 1989. Used with permission.

the interviewer to recognize and refine the problems in establishing rapport.

In one survey of 700 patients, the patients substantially agreed that physicians do not have the time or the inclination to listen and to consider the patient's feelings, that

**Table 1–4**
**Predictable Reactions to Illness**

| Intrapsychic | Clinical |
|---|---|
| Lowered self-image → loss → grief | Anxiety |
| Threat to homeostasis → fear | Denial |
| Failure of (self) care → | Depression |
|   helplessness, hopelessness | Bargaining and blaming |
| Sense of loss of control → shame | Regression |
|   (guilt) | Isolation |
| | Dependency |
| | Anger |
| | Acceptance |

Table from M Lipkin Jr: Psychiatry and medicine. In *Comprehensive Textbook of Psychiatry,* ed 5, H I Kaplan, B J Sadock, editors, p 1280. Williams & Wilkins, Baltimore, 1989.

physicians do not have enough knowledge of the emotional problems and socioeconomic background of the patient's family, and that physicians increase the patient's fear by giving explanations in technical language. Psychosocial and economic factors exert a profound influence on human relations, so the physician should have as much understanding as possible of the patient's subculture.

The failure of the physician to establish good rapport with the patient accounts for much of the ineffectiveness in care. The presence of rapport implies that understanding and trust between doctor and patient are present. Differences in social, intellectual, and educational status can interfere seriously with rapport. Understanding—or not understanding—the patient's beliefs, use of language, and attitudes toward illness influences the character of the physician's examination.

Evaluating the social pressures in the patient's early life helps the doctor better understand the patient. Emotional reactions, healthy or unhealthy, are the result of a constant interplay of biological, sociological, and psychological forces. Each stress leaves behind some trace of its influence

**Table 1–5**
**Checklist**

The following checklist allows clinicians to rate their skills in establishing and maintaining rapport. It helps them detect and eliminate weaknesses in interviews that failed in some significant way.

| | Yes | No | N/A |
|---|---|---|---|
| 1. I put the patient at ease. | ___ | ___ | ___ |
| 2. I recognized the patient's state of mind. | ___ | ___ | ___ |
| 3. I addressed the patient's distress. | ___ | ___ | ___ |
| 4. I helped the patient warm up. | ___ | ___ | ___ |
| 5. I helped the patient overcome suspiciousness. | ___ | ___ | ___ |
| 6. I curbed the patient's intrusiveness. | ___ | ___ | ___ |
| 7. I stimulated the patient's verbal production. | ___ | ___ | ___ |
| 8. I curbed the patients' rambling. | ___ | ___ | ___ |
| 9. I understood the patient's suffering. | ___ | ___ | ___ |
| 10. I expressed empathy for the patient's suffering. | ___ | ___ | ___ |
| 11. I tuned in on the patient's affect. | ___ | ___ | ___ |
| 12. I addressed the patient's affect. | ___ | ___ | ___ |
| 13. I became aware of the patient's level of insight. | ___ | ___ | ___ |
| 14. I assumed the patient's view of the disorder. | ___ | ___ | ___ |
| 15. I had a clear perception of the overt and the therapeutic goals of treatment. | ___ | ___ | ___ |
| 16. I stated the overt goal of treatment to the patient. | ___ | ___ | ___ |
| 17. I communicated to the patient that I am familiar with the illness. | ___ | ___ | ___ |
| 18. My questions convinced the patient that I am familiar with the symptoms of the disorder. | ___ | ___ | ___ |
| 19. I let the patient know that he or she is not alone with the illness. | ___ | ___ | ___ |
| 20. I expressed my intent to help the patient. | ___ | ___ | ___ |
| 21. The patient recognized my expertise. | ___ | ___ | ___ |
| 22. The patient respected my authority. | ___ | ___ | ___ |
| 23. The patient appeared fully cooperative. | ___ | ___ | ___ |
| 24. I recognized the patient's attitude toward the illness. | ___ | ___ | ___ |
| 25. The patient viewed the illness with distance. | ___ | ___ | ___ |
| 26. The patient presented as a sympathy-craving sufferer. | ___ | ___ | ___ |
| 27. The patient presented as a very important patient. | ___ | ___ | ___ |
| 28. The patient competed with me for authority. | ___ | ___ | ___ |
| 29. The patient was submissive. | ___ | ___ | ___ |
| 30. I adjusted my role to the patient's role. | ___ | ___ | ___ |
| 31. The patient thanked me and made another appointment. | ___ | ___ | ___ |

Table adapted from E Othmer, S C Othmer: *The Clinical Interview Using DSM-III-R*, p 46. American Psychiatric Press, Washington, 1989. Used with permission.

and continues to manifest itself throughout life in proportion to the intensity of its effect and the susceptibility of the particular human being. Those stresses and strains should be determined to the extent possible. The significant point may not be the stress itself but the person's reactions to it.

The establishment of genuine rapport also depends on a basic understanding of such complex interpersonal factors as transference and countertransference.

**Transference.** *Transference* is generally defined as the set of expectations, beliefs, and emotional responses that a patient brings to the doctor-patient relationship. They are based not necessarily on who the doctor is or how the doctor acts in reality but, rather, on persistent experiences the patient has had with other important authority figures throughout life.

TRANSFERENTIAL ATTITUDES. The patient's attitude toward the physician is apt to be a repetition of the attitude he or she has had toward authority figures. The attitude may range from one of realistic basic trust, with an expectation that the doctor has the patient's best interest at heart, through one of overidealization and even eroticized fantasy to one of basic mistrust, with an expectation that the doctor will be contemptuous and potentially abusive. A patient may expect the doctor to do something—for example, prescribe medication or perform surgery—and can accept a doctor's care as

sufficient and competent only if those actions occur. Inherent in that attitude is the patient's role as a passive recipient in relation to the doctor's role as an active bestower of help. A patient in whom those expectations are established feels uncomfortable if the doctor has different expectations. Another patient may be active and expect to participate fully in treatment and, correspondingly, feels at odds with a doctor who does not want patient participation.

ROLE OF THE PSYCHIATRIST VERSUS THE NONPSYCHIATRIC PHYSICIAN. In many respects the role of a psychiatrist is different from that of a nonpsychiatric physician, and yet many patients expect the same from the psychiatrist as they do from other physicians. If they expect a doctor to take action, give advice, and prescribe medication to cure an illness, they may well expect the same interaction with a psychiatrist and be disappointed or angry if it does not occur. Transference reactions may be strongest with psychiatrists for a number of reasons. For example, in intensive insight-oriented psychotherapy the encouragement of transference feelings is an integral part of treatment. In some types of therapy, a psychiatrist is more or less neutral. The more neutral or less known the psychiatrist is, the more a patient's transferential fantasies and concerns are mobilized and projected onto the doctor. Once the fantasies are stimulated and projected, the psychiatrist can help patients gain insight into how those fantasies and concerns affect all the important relationships in their lives. Although a nonpsychiatrist does not use or even need to understand transference attitudes in that intensive way, a solid understanding of the power and the manifestations of transference is necessary for optimal treatment results in any doctor-patient relationship.

The doctor's words and deeds have a power far beyond the commonplace because of his or her unique authority and the patient's dependence on the doctor. How a particular physician behaves and interacts has a direct bearing on the patient's emotional and even physical reactions. One patient repeatedly had high blood pressure readings when examined by a physician he considered cold, aloof, and stern. He had normal blood pressure readings, however, when seen by a doctor he regarded as warm, understanding, and sympathetic.

**Countertransference.** Just as the patient brings transferential attitudes to the doctor-patient relationship, doctors themselves often have countertransferential reactions to their patients. Countertransference may take the form of negative feelings that are disruptive to the doctor-patient relationship, but it may also encompass disproportionately positive, idealizing, or even eroticized reactions. Just as patients have expectations for physicians—for example, competence, lack of exploitation, objectivity, comfort, and relief—physicians often have unconscious or unspoken expectations of patients. Most commonly, patients are thought of as good patients if their expressed severity of symptoms correlates with an overtly diagnosable biological disorder, if they are compliant and generally nonchallenging with treatment, if they are emotionally controlled, and if they are grateful. If those expectations are not met, the patient may be blamed and experienced as unlikable, unworkable, or bad.

DISLIKING A PATIENT.    A physician who actively dislikes a patient is apt to be ineffective in dealing with him or her. Emotion breeds counteremotion. For example, if the physician is hostile, the patient becomes hostile; the physician then becomes even angrier than before, and the relationship deteriorates rapidly. If the physician can rise above such emotions and handle the resentful patient with equanimity, the interpersonal relationship may shift from one of mutual overt antagonism to one of at least increased acceptance and grudging respect. Rising above such emotions involves being able to step back from the intense countertransferential reactions and to dispassionately explore why the patient is reacting to the doctor in such an apparently self-defeating way. After all, the patient needs the doctor, and the hostility ensures that the needed help will not occur. If the doctor can understand that the patient's antagonism is in some ways defensive or self-protective and most likely reflects transferential fears of disrespect, abuse, and disappointment, the doctor may be less angry and more empathic than otherwise.

Doctors who have strong unconscious needs to be all-knowing and all-powerful may have particular problems with certain types of patients. The patients may be difficult for most physicians to handle, but—if the physician is as aware as possible of his or her own needs, capabilities, and limitations—the patients will not be threatening. Such patients include the following: those who appear to repeatedly defeat attempts to help them (for example, patients with severe heart disease who continue to smoke or drink), those who are perceived as uncooperative (for example, patients who question or refuse treatment), those who request a second opinion, those who fail to recover in response to treatment, those who use physical or somatic complaints to mask emotional problems (for example, patients with somatization disorder, pain disorder, hypochondriasis, or factitious disorders), those with chronic cognitive disorders (for example, patients with dementia of the Alzheimer's type), and those who are dying or in chronic pain (for example, patients who represent a professional failure and are, thus, a threat to the physician's identity and self-esteem).

SEXUALITY AND THE PHYSICIAN.    Physicians are bound to like some patients more than others. However, if the physician feels a strong attraction to a patient and is tempted to act on the attraction, stepping back and dispassionately assessing the situation are essential. In some medical specialties in which the doctor-patient relationship is not particularly intimate or intense, the prohibition against romantic involvement with patients may not be strong. In other specialties, however, especially psychiatry, the ethical and even legal prohibition is important. The doctor is a powerful figure in this country's culture and may trigger many unconscious fantasies of being rescued, taken care of, and loved. Doctors themselves may have their own unconscious fantasies of being and needing to be all-powerful, rescuing, and lovable. Those fantasies are inherently unrealistic and dehumanizing and are inevitably disappointed. The disappointments, if realized in a romantic relationship between the doctor and the patient, can be destructive, especially for the patient. Patient-therapist sex is discussed further in Chapter 52.

Another aspect of sexuality as it pertains to countertransference issues relates to asking patients about sexual issues and obtaining a sexual history. A reluctance to do so may reflect the physician's own anxiety about sexuality or even an unconscious attraction toward the patient. Moreover, the omission of those questions generally tells patients that the doctor is uncomfortable with the subject, thus leading to an inhibition about discussing any number of other sensitive subjects.

SELF-MONITORING OF COUNTERTRANSFERENCE FEELINGS.    Countertransference feelings do not always have to be perceived in negative terms. They also have the potential, if recognized and analyzed, to help the doctor better understand the patient who has stimulated the feelings. For instance, if a doctor feels bored and restless when with a particular patient and has ascertained that the boredom is not secondary to his or her own preoccupations, the doctor may surmise that the patient is speaking about trivial or insignificant concerns to avoid real and potentially disturbing concerns.

PHYSICIANS AS PATIENTS.    A special example of countertransference issues occurs when the patient being treated is a physician. Problems that can arise in that situation include an expectation that the physician-patient will take care of his or her own medications and treatment and the treating physician's fear of criticism of his or her skills or competence. Ill physicians are notoriously poor patients, most likely because physicians are trained to be in control of medical situations and to be the masters in the doctor-patient relationship. For a physician, being a patient may mean giving up control, becoming dependent, and appearing vulnerable and frightened—tendencies that most physicians are professionally trained to suppress. Physician-patients may be reluctant to become what they perceive as burdens to overworked colleagues, or they may be embarrassed to ask pertinent questions for fear of appearing ignorant or incompetent. Physician-patients may stimulate fear in the treating physicians who see themselves in the patient, an attitude that can lead to denial and avoidance on the part of the treating physician.

## Beginning the Interview

How a physician begins an interview provides a powerful first impression to patients, and the manner in which a doctor opens communication with a patient has potentially powerful effects on how the remainder of the interview proceeds. Patients are often anxious on first encounters with physicians, feeling both vulnerable and intimidated. A physician who can establish rapport quickly, put the patient at ease, and show respect is well on the way to conducting a productive exchange of information. That exchange is critical to formulating a correct diagnosis and to establishing treatment goals.

The physician should initially make sure that he or she knows the patient's name and that the patient knows the physician's name. The physician should introduce himself or herself to any other people who are present with the patient. If relatives or friends accompany the patient, the physician should ascertain whether the patient would like them to be present during the initial interview. If the patient states an emphatic desire for the presence of another person during the initial interview, that request should be respected, as the other person's presence may alleviate the patient's anxiety about the interview. It may also help gain the trust of significant people in the patient's life, people who may be essential to the patient's continued compliance with and acceptance of the doctor. However, the physician should also attempt to speak to the patient individually to make sure that the patient has a chance to say anything he or she may not want to say in front of others. One way to do that is to see the patient along with a family member or friend first and then say: "I very much appreciate speaking with you both and getting all your thoughts and input about what is going on with Mr. X. At this point, let me give Mr. X a chance to speak with me alone, since he and I are going to work together closely in the coming weeks. If you would like to meet together with me again in the future, I would be happy to arrange such a meeting."

Patients have the right to know the position and the professional status of the persons involved with their care. For example, medical students should introduce themselves as such, not as doctors, and physicians should make it clear whether they are consultants (called in by another physician to see the patient), covering for another physician, or involved in the interview to teach students, rather than to treat the patient.

## Opening Questions

Once the introductions and other initial assessments have been made, a useful and appropriate opening remark is, "Can you tell me about the troubles that bring you in today?" or "Tell me about the problems you have been having." Following up that remark with a second one—such as, "What other problems have you been experiencing?"—often elicits further information that the patient was reluctant to give initially. It also indicates to the patient that the doctor is interested in hearing as much as the patient wants to say.

A less directive approach is to ask the patient, "Where shall we start?" or "Where would you prefer to begin?" If a patient has been referred by another doctor for consultation, the initial remarks can indicate that the consulting doctor already knows something about the patient. For example, the consulting doctor may say, "Your doctor has told me something about what has been troubling you [for example, cardiovascular symptoms or depression], but I'd like to hear from you in your own words about what is troubling you."

Most patients do not speak freely unless they have privacy and are sure that their conversations cannot be overheard. A physician who makes sure at the beginning of an interview that such factors as privacy, quiet, and the lack of interruptions are attended to conveys to the patient that what the patient has to say is important and worthy of serious consideration.

A patient may appear frightened or resistant at the beginning of an interview and may not want to answer questions. If that seems to be the case, the physician may comment on that impression directly in a gentle and supportive way, encouraging the patient to talk about his or her feelings regarding the interview itself. Acknowledging the patient's anxiety may be the first step in delineating what the anxiety is about and can enable the physician to offer appropriate reassurance. An example of what could be said is, "I can't help but notice that you seem to be feeling anxious about talking with me, and I wonder if there is anything I can do or any question I can answer that will make it easier for you." Or "I know that it can be difficult or frightening to talk to a doctor, especially one you have never met before, but I would like to make it as comfortable for you as possible. Is there anything that you can put your finger on that is making it tough for you to talk to me?"

Another important initial question is, "Why now?" The physician should be clear about why the patient has chosen that particular time to ask for help. The reason may be a simple as that it was the first available appointment time. Very often, however, people seek out doctors as the result of particular events in their lives that have led to an increase in stress. Those stressful events may be thought of as precipitants and are often significant contributors to the patient's current problems. Examples of stressful precipitants include real or symbolic losses (for example, death and separations), milestone events (for example, significant birthdays), and physical changes (for example, the initiation of a new diet or a new drug). Physicians who are unaware of such stresses in a person's life may miss unspoken fears and questions that can compromise the patient's care and well-being.

## Interview Proper

In the interview proper the physician discovers in detail what is troubling the patient. The physician must do so in a systematic way that facilitates the identification of relevant problems in the context of an ongoing empathic working alliance with the patient.

**Content versus process.** The *content* of an interview is literally what is said between the doctor and the patient: the topics discussed, the subjects mentioned. The *process* of the interview is what is occurring nonverbally between the doctor and the patient: what is happening in the interview beneath the surface. Process involves feelings and reactions that are unacknowledged or unconscious. For example, a patient may use body language to express feelings he or she cannot express verbally—a clenched fist or nervous tearing at a tissue in the face of an apparently calm outward demeanor. A patient may shift the interview away from an anxiety-provoking subject onto a neutral topic without realizing that he or she is doing so. A patient may return again and again to a particular topic, regardless of what direction the interview appeared to be taking. Trivial remarks and apparently casual asides may reveal serious underlying concerns—for example, "Oh, by the way, a neighbor of mine tells me that he knows someone with the same symptoms as my son, and that person has cancer."

### Specific interviewing techniques

OPEN-ENDED VERSUS CLOSED-ENDED QUESTIONS. Interviewing any patient involves a fine balance between allowing the patient's story to unfold at will and obtaining the necessary data for diagnosis and treatment. Most experts on interviewing agree that the ideal interview is one in which the interviewer begins with broad open-ended questioning, continues by becoming specific, and closes with detailed direct questioning.

The early part of the interview is generally the most open-ended, in that the physician allows the patient to speak as much as possible in his or her own words. A closed-ended question or directive question is one that asks for specific information and that does not allow the patient many options in answering. Too many closed-ended questions, especially in the early part of an interview, can lead to a restriction of the patient's responses. Sometimes directive questions are necessary to obtain important data, but, if they are used too often, the patient may think that information is to be given only in response to direct questioning by the doctor. An example of an open-ended question is, "Can you tell me more about that?" A closed-ended question, if the patient states that he or she has been feeling depressed, might be, "Your mother died recently, didn't she?" That question can be answered only by a "yes" or a "no," and the mother's death may or may not be the reason the patient is depressed. More information is likely to be obtained if the doctor responds with, "Tell me more about what you're feeling and what you think may be causing it."

Closed-ended questions, however, can be effective in generating specific and quick responses about a clearly delineated topic. Closed-ended questions have been shown to be effective in eliciting information about the absence of certain symptoms (for example, auditory hallucinations and suicidal ideation). Closed-ended questions have also been found to be effective in assessing such factors as the frequency, the severity, and the duration of symptoms. Table 1–6 summarizes some of the pros and cons of open-ended and closed-ended questions.

REFLECTION. In the technique of reflection, the doctor repeats to the patient in a supportive manner something that the patient has said. The purpose of reflection is twofold: to assure the doctor that he or she has correctly understood what the patient is trying to say and to let the patient know that the doctor is perceiving what is being said. It is an empathic response meant to allow the patient to know that the doctor is both listening to the patient's concerns and understanding them. For example, if the patient is speaking about fears of dying and the effects of talking about those fears with his or her family, the doctor may say, "It seems that you are concerned with becoming a burden to your family." That reflection is not an exact repetition of what the patient has said but, rather, a paraphrase that indicates that the doctor has perceived what the patient is trying to say.

FACILITATION. The doctor helps the patient continue in the interview by providing both verbal and nonverbal cues that encourage the patient to keep talking. Nodding one's head, leaning forward in one's seat, and saying, "Yes, and then. . .?" or "Uh-huh, go on" are all examples of facilitation.

SILENCE. Silence can be used in many ways in normal conversations, even to indicate disapproval or disinterest. However, in the doctor-patient relationship, silence may be constructive; in certain situations it may allow the patient to contemplate, to cry, or just to sit in an accepting, supportive environment where the doctor makes it clear that not every moment must be filled with talk.

CONFRONTATION. The technique of confrontation is meant to point out to a patient something that the doctor thinks the patient is not paying attention to, is missing, or is in some way denying. Confrontation must be done in a skillful way, so that the patient is not forced to become hostile and defensive. The confrontation is meant to help the patient face

**Table 1–6**
**Pros and Cons of Open-Ended and Closed-Ended Questions**

| Aspect | Broad Open-Ended Questions | Narrow Closed-Ended Questions |
|---|---|---|
| 1. Genuineness | High<br>They produce spontaneous formulations | Low<br>They lead the patient |
| 2. Reliability | Low<br>They may lead to nonreproducible answers | High<br>Narrow focus; but they may suggest answers |
| 3. Precision | Low<br>Intent of question is vague | High<br>Intent of question is clear |
| 4. Time efficiency | Low<br>Circumstantial elaborations | High<br>May invite yes or no answers |
| 5. Completeness of diagnostic coverage | Low<br>Patient selects the topic | High<br>Interviewer selects the topic |
| 6. Acceptance by patient | Varies<br>Most patients prefer expressing themselves freely; others become guarded and feel insecure | Varies<br>Some patients enjoy clear-cut checks; others hate to be pressed into a yes or no format |

Table from E Othmer, S C Othmer: *The Clinical Interview Using DSM-III-R*, p 55. American Psychiatric Press, Washington, 1989. Used with permission.

whatever needs to be faced in a direct but respectful way. For example, a patient who has just made a suicidal gesture but is telling the doctor that it was not serious may be confronted with the statement, "What you have done may not have killed you, but it's telling me that you are in serious trouble right now and that you need help so that you don't try suicide again."

CLARIFICATION. In clarification the doctor attempts to get details from the patient about what the patient has already said. For example, the doctor may say: "You are feeling depressed. When is it that you feel most depressed?"

INTERPRETATION. The technique of interpretation is most often used when the doctor states something about the patient's behavior or thought that the patient may not be aware of. The technique follows up on the doctor's careful listening to the underlying themes and patterns in the patient's story. Interpretations usually help clarify interrelationships that the patient may not have been seeing. The technique is a sophisticated one and should generally be used only after the doctor has established some rapport with the patient and has a reasonably good idea of what some of the interrelationships are. For example, the doctor may say: "When you talk about how angry you are that your family has not been supportive, I think you're also telling me how worried you are that I won't be there for you either. What do you think?"

SUMMATION. Periodically during the interview, the doctor can take a moment and briefly summarize what the patient has said thus far. Doing so assures both the patient and the doctor that the information the doctor has heard is the same as what the patient has actually said. For example, the doctor may say, "OK, I just want to make sure that I've gotten everything right up to this point. . . ."

EXPLANATION. The doctor explains the treatment plan to the patient in easily understandable language and allows the patient to respond and ask questions. For example, the doctor may say: "It is essential that you come into the hospital now because of the seriousness of your condition. You will be admitted tonight through the emergency room, and I will be there to make all the arrangements. You will be given a small dose of medication that will make you sleepy. The medication is called triazolam (Halcion), and the dose you will be getting is 0.125 mg. I will see you again first thing in the morning, and we'll go over all the procedures that will be required before anything else happens [etc., etc.]. . . . Now, what are your questions? I know you must have some."

TRANSITION. The technique of transition allows the doctor to convey the idea that enough information has been obtained on one subject; it encourages the patient to continue on to another subject. For example, the doctor may say: "You've given me a good sense of that particular time in your life. It would be good now if you told me a bit more about an even earlier time in your life."

SELF-REVELATION. Limited, discreet self-disclosure by the physician may be useful in certain situations. The physician should feel natural and communicate a sense of self-comfort. Conveying that sense may involve answering questions from the patient about whether the physician is married and where he or she comes from. However, a doctor who practices self-revelation excessively is using the patient to fulfill certain unfilled needs in his or her own life and is abusing the role of physician. If the doctor feels that some piece of information will help the patient be more comfortable, the doctor can decide in each case whether to be self-revealing. It depends on whether the information will further the patient's care or whether it will provide nothing useful. Even if the doctor decides that self-revelation is not warranted, he or she should be careful not to make the patient feel embarrassed for asking.

For example, the doctor may say: "I'm not sure whether you are really asking if I'm married. Let's talk about it a little more, so that I can understand why that information is important to you. Maybe it has more to do with some concerns you have about my commitment to your care." Or "I am married, but let's talk a little about why it was important for you to know that. If we talk about it, I'll have a bit more information about who you are and what your concerns are regarding me and my involvement in your care." Perhaps the important point here is not to take questions from patients at face value alone. Many questions, especially personal ones, convey not just natural curiosity about the doctor but also hidden concerns that should not be ignored.

POSITIVE REINFORCEMENT. The technique of positive reinforcement allows the patient to feel comfortable in telling the doctor anything, even about such things as noncompliance with treatment. The doctor encourages the patient to feel that the doctor will not be upset by whatever the patient has to say and thereby facilitates an open exchange. For example, the doctor may say: "I appreciate your telling me that you have stopped taking your medication. Can you tell me what the problem was with the medication? The more I know what's going on with you, the better I'll be able to treat you in a way that you will feel comfortable with."

REASSURANCE. Truthful reassurance of a patient can lead to increased trust and compliance and can be experienced as an empathic response of a concerned physician. False reassurance, however, is essentially lying to the patient and can badly impair the patient's trust and compliance. False reassurance is often given in the desire to make a patient feel better, but, once a patient knows that the doctor has not told the truth, the patient is not likely to accept or believe truthful reassurance. In an example of false reassurance, a patient with a terminal illness asks, "Am I going to be all right, doctor?" and the doctor responds, "Of course, you'll be all right; everything is fine." In an example of truthful reassurance the doctor responds: "I am going to do everything I can to make you feel as comfortable as possible, and part of being comfortable is for you to know as much as I know about what is going on with you. We both know that what you have is serious. I'd like to know exactly what you think is happening to you and to clarify any questions or confusion you have."

ADVICE. In many situations it is not only acceptable but desirable for the physician to give advice to a patient. To be effective and to be perceived as empathic, rather than as inappropriate or intrusive, the advice should be given only after the patient is allowed to talk freely about whatever the problem is, so that the physician has an adequate information base from which to make suggestions. At times, after the doctor has listened carefully to a patient, it is clear that the patient does not, in fact, want advice as much as an objective, caring, nonjudgmental ear. Giving advice too quickly can lead the patient to feel that the doctor is not really listening but, rather, is responding either out of anxiety or from the belief that the doctor inherently knows better than the patient what should be done in a particular situation. In an example of advice given too quickly, the patient states, "I cannot take this medication; it's bothering me," and the physician responds: "Fine. I think you should stop taking it, and I'll start you on something new." A more appropriate response is the following: "I'm sorry to hear that. Tell me what about the medication is bothering you, so that I have a better idea of what we may do to make you feel more comfortable." In another example the patient states, "I've really been feeling down lately," and the doctor responds, "Well, I think in that case it would be a good idea for you to go out and really do some things that are fun, like going to the movies or walking in the park." In that case a more appropriate and helpful response is the following: "Tell me what you mean by 'feeling down.' The more I know about what you're feeling, the more likely it will be that I can help."

**Interviewing psychotic patients.** Psychotic patients often have limited insight, are more concrete than abstract in their thinking, and are not always psychologically minded or introspective. In fact, many psychotic patients experience insight and introspection as frightening and threatening, because their perceptions are distorted and they are unable to integrate certain feelings, fantasies, and ideas about themselves without decompensating (becoming more psychotic than before). Their internal psychological makeup is fragile or vulnerable, and certain psychological insights can impose too much stress for them to bear. If a psychotic person can tolerate certain degrees of insight and introspection, they should be encouraged, although for the most part the physician's role with a psychotic person is supportive, rather than insight-oriented. The support, in part, involves increasing the patient's ability to reality-test (to differentiate between fantasy and reality). Insight-oriented interventions often trigger disturbing fantasies. Psychotic patients often experience what has been termed the "need-fear dilemma," in which they experience both an overwhelming loneliness and need for contact with others and a profound fear that contact with others is dangerous, overwhelming, and destructive.

Specific therapy techniques to be used with psychotic patients involve the following: (1) Do not attempt to talk patients out of delusional beliefs. (2) Do not laugh at bizarre, psychotic material that may sound funny but is clearly not meant to be funny. (3) Maintain a certain formality with the patients, so that they do not feel threatened by what is perceived as frightening closeness. (4) Focus on concrete, day-to-day survival and social skills. (5) Decrease pressure on the patients to achieve more than they may feel capable of achieving (including answering interview questions). (6) Structure the interview sessions so that the patients know what to expect and are not left, for instance, with long periods of silence if those periods seem to increase anxiety. (7) Be sensitive to how easily humiliated or shamed the patients may feel over relatively minor inadequacies (such as the inability to remember a past medication).

## Concluding the Interview

The doctor wants the patient to leave the interview feeling understood and respected and feeling that all the pertinent and important information has been conveyed to an informed, empathic listener. To that end, the doctor should give the patient a chance to ask questions and should let the patient know as much as possible about the plans for the future. The doctor should thank the patient for sharing the necessary information and let the patient know that the information conveyed has been helpful in clarifying the next steps. Any prescription of medication should be clearly and simply spelled out, and the doctor should ascertain whether the patient understands the prescription and how to take it. The doctor should make another appointment or give a referral and some indication about how the patient can reach help quickly if it is necessary before the next appointment.

## COMPLIANCE

*Compliance*, also known as adherence, is the degree to which a patient carries out the clinical recommendations of the treating physician. Examples of compliance include keeping appointments, entering into and completing a treatment program, taking medications correctly, and following recommended changes in behavior or diet. Compliance behavior depends on the specific clinical situation, the nature of the illness, and the treatment program. In general, about one third of all patients comply with treatment, one third sometimes comply with certain aspects of treatment, and one third never comply with treatment. An overall figure assessed from a number of studies indicates that 54 percent of patients comply with treatment at any given time. One study found that up to 50 percent of hypertensive patients do not follow up at all with treatment and that 50 percent of those who do follow up leave treatment within one year.

In an attempt to understand why such a high percentage of patients fail to comply regularly, researchers have investigated a number of variables. For example, an increased complexity of the regimen, plus an increased number of required behavioral changes, appears to be associated with noncompliance. Psychiatric patients also exhibit a higher degree of noncompliant behavior than do medical patients. However, there is no clear association between compliance and the patient's sex, marital status, race, religion, socioeconomic status, intelligence, or educational level. Compliance is increased by such physician characteristics as enthusiasm, permissiveness, age, experience, time spent talking to the patient, and short waiting room time.

The doctor-patient relationship or what has been termed the doctor-patient match is the most important factor in compliance issues. When the doctor and the patient have different priorities and beliefs, different styles of communication (including a different understanding of medical advice), and different medical expectations, the patient's compliance diminishes. Compliance can be increased if the physician explains the value to the patient of a particular treatment outcome and explains that following the recommendation will produce that outcome. Compliance can also increase if the patients know the names and the effects of each drug they are taking. A highly significant factor in compliance seems to be the patient's subjective feeling of distress or illness, as opposed to the doctor's often objective medical estimate of the disease and the required therapy. Patients must believe that they are ill. Thus, asymptomatic patients, such as those with hypertension, are at greater risk for noncompliance than are patients with symptoms. Simply stated, when there are problems in communication, compliance decreases; when there is effective communication, coupled with close patient supervision and the patient's subjective sense of satisfaction that the doctor has met expectations, compliance increases. Studies have shown that noncompliance is associated with doctors who are perceived as rejecting and unfriendly. Noncompliance is also associated with asking a patient for information without giving feedback and with failing to explain a diagnosis or the cause of the presenting symptoms. A doctor who is aware of the patient's belief system, feelings, and habits and who enlists the patient in establishing a treatment regimen will increase compliant behavior.

Strategies suggested to improve compliance include asking patients directly to describe what they themselves believe is wrong with them, what they believe should be done, what they understand about what the doctor believes should be done, and what they believe to be the risks and the benefits of following the prescribed treatment. Common errors are patients' not taking medications as often or as long as they are supposed to and not taking the right number of pills or treatments. Patients are generally noncompliant if they have to take more than three types of medications a day or if their medications must be taken more than four times a day. Purely verbal instructions by the doctor or the presentation of treatment prescriptions to the patient in the few hours immediately before being discharged from the hospital is associated with increased error and noncompliance. Elderly persons who may have trouble hearing or reading small type may become noncompliant if they cannot hear the verbal instructions or read the prescription labels. In those instances, it is helpful to print the instructions on a piece of paper, ask the patient to read them back, ask if the patient has any questions, and ask the patient to explain when specifically and in what amounts the medication is to be taken. Sometimes, instead of making errors, patients deliberately change the treatment regimen—for example, by not showing up for appointments or by taking medications in a manner different from that recommended. In those instances, in which there may be competing pressures from the family or work or a lack of understanding about the details of the doctor's advice, the doctor needs to negotiate a compromise with the patient, what has been termed a patient contract. In that case, the doctor and the patient together specify what they can expect from each other. Implicit in that approach is the idea that the contract can be renegotiated, and the patient can be assured that suggestions can be made by either the doctor or the patient to improve compliance.

## SPECIFIC ISSUES

### Fees

Before an ongoing relationship with a patient can be established, the physician must address certain issues. For instance, the matter of payment or fees must be openly discussed from the beginning: the doctor's charges, whether the doctor is willing to accept insurance company payments directly (known as assignment), the doctor's policy concerning payment for missed appointments, and whether the doctor uses a sliding scale based on ability to pay. Discussing those questions and any other questions about fees from the beginning of the relationship between doctor and patient can minimize misunderstanding later.

### Confidentiality

The doctor should discuss the extent and the limitations of confidentiality with the patient, so that the patient is clear about what can and cannot remain confidential. As much as one must legally and ethically respect a patient's confidentiality, confidentiality in some situations may be either partially or wholly broken. The doctor must make the patient aware of those situations to avoid mistrust. For instance, if a patient makes clear that he or she intends to harm another person violently, the doctor has a legal responsibility to warn the intended victim. Other examples of issues related to confidentiality involve the patient's medical record and who has access to it; the extent of the information required by particular insurance companies (which may be highly detailed); and the degree, if any, to which a patient's case will be used in teaching medical students, residents, or others. In all such situations the patient must give prior permission for the use of the medical records.

### Use of Supervisors

It is both commonplace and necessary for doctors in training to receive supervision from experienced physicians. In large teaching hospitals that is the norm, and most patients are aware of it. If a young doctor is receiving supervision from a senior physician, the patient should know that from the beginning. Informing the patient is particularly important in psychiatry, in which the supervision of individual psychotherapy cases is a routine and established practice and in which the psychiatric resident is required to present verbatim accounts of an entire therapy session (process notes) to a senior supervisor. If a patient is curious about the level of the treating doctor's experience, the doctor or medical student should respond honestly and not mislead the patient. If the doctor is less than truthful and the patient discovers that later, the relationship between the doctor and the patient may become untenable.

### Session Length and Missed Appointments

Patients need to be informed about the doctor's policies regarding the length of each session and the issue of missed appointments. Psychiatrists, for example, generally see patients in regularly scheduled blocks of 20 to 45 minutes; at the end of that time, it is expected that the patient will accept the fact that the session is over. Nonpsychiatric physicians may schedule somewhat differently, putting aside 30 minutes to an hour for an initial visit and then perhaps scheduling patient visits every 15 to 20 minutes for follow-up appointments. A psychiatrist who is treating a psychotic inpatient may determine that the patient cannot tolerate a lengthy session and may decide to see the patient in a series of 10-minute sessions throughout the day. Whatever the doctor's policy is, the patient must be made aware of it, so that misunderstandings do not occur.

The same can be said for the doctor's policy on missed appointments, about which the patient must be informed. Some doctors deal with the issue of missed appointments by asking the patient to give 24 hours' notice to avoid being billed for a missed session. Other doctors bill for missed sessions regardless of notice. Still other doctors decide on a case-by-case basis, perhaps stating a 24-hour rule but making exceptions when warranted. Some doctors state that, if they receive notice and can fill the vacated time with another patient, they will not charge for the missed appointment; other doctors do not charge for missed appointments at all. The decision is up to the individual physician, but the patient must know the doctor's policy in advance, so that an informed decision can be made about whether to accept the policy or to choose another doctor.

## Doctor-Patient Interaction Between Scheduled Appointments

What is the doctor's obligation to be available to patients in between scheduled appointments? Is it incumbent on the physician to be available 24 hours a day? Once a patient enters into a contract to receive care from a particular physician, it is the physician's responsibility to have a mechanism in place by which the patient can receive help if an emergency occurs outside the time of scheduled appointments. The patient should be explicitly informed what that mechanism is, whether it is an emergency phone number or a covering physician. If a physician is going to be away for any length of time, coverage by another physician must be obtained, and the patient must be informed how to reach the covering doctor. The patient should know that the doctor will be available between appointments to answer pressing questions and that, if necessary, extra appointments can be scheduled.

Within those general parameters, however, physicians must make their own individual decisions about their availability to specific patients. In some cases the doctor may have to place firm limits on availability between sessions. For instance, patients who repeatedly call at all hours with concerns that are best addressed in the context of a regularly scheduled appointment should be gently but definitely encouraged to bring up their concerns only during scheduled sessions. The doctor in such a case may reassure the patient that all concerns will be addressed and that, if there is not enough time during the regularly scheduled time, another appointment can be made but that nonemergency concerns will be postponed until the appointment.

## Continuing Care

Many events can disrupt the continuity of the doctor-patient relationship; some of those events are routine (such as when residents end training and move on to another hospital); others are out of the ordinary and thus unpredictable (such as when physicians become ill and can no longer take care of their patients). The patient must be assured that, regardless of what occurs in the course of a particular doctor-patient relationship, the patient's care will be ongoing. If the doctor is a resident and will be serving as the patient's doctor for a finite time, the doctor should be explicit about that at the beginning of treatment. At the same time, the resident can make clear to the patient that, when he or she moves on, the patient's care will continue, albeit with a new doctor. It may help the patient's sense of continuity if the departing resident introduces the incoming resident to the patient.

A complex situation arises when physicians become ill and are unable to continue caring for patients. If the physicians know in advance that they are going to have to interrupt therapy, clear arrangements for referral to other physicians can be made. Although there are arguments for

both revealing and not revealing the physicians' illnesses to patients, it seems best to inform patients truthfully why the doctors are discontinuing therapy. That information should be conveyed in as calm and nonthreatening a way as possible. The risk in not telling patients the truth is that many patients may have fantasies to explain why a doctor has stopped seeing them, including the fear that something about them made the doctor want to leave. Nontruthfulness in the situation also encourages the view that being ill is something shameful or frightening and that doctors who cannot discuss or handle their own illnesses should not expect patients to be able to. However, it is not the role of patients to take care of their doctors; informing patients should not carry with it any sense that a doctor's illness is the patient's burden.

## Difficult Patients

Some types of patients require particular skill on the part of any physician. Those patients can create undue stress if they are not managed effectively. Inherent in the management of all those patients is the doctor's understanding of the covert emotions, fears, and conflicts that the patient's overt behavior represents. An appropriate understanding of what is hidden behind a particular patient's difficult behavior can lead the doctor away from responding with anger, contempt, or anxiety and toward responding with helpful interventions.

**Histrionic.** Histrionic patients are often seductive with doctors out of an unconscious need for reassurance that they are still attractive even if ill and out of fear that they will not be taken seriously unless they are found to be sexually desirable. They often appear overly emotional and intimate in their interactions with doctors. The physician needs to be calm, reassuring, firm, and nonflirtatious. The patients do not really want to seduce the physician, but they may not know any other way to get what they feel they need.

**Demanding and dependent.** Demanding and dependent patients need a tremendous amount of reassurance and yet are often resistant to any and all such offers. They are the patients who are most likely to make repeated, urgent calls in between scheduled appointments and to demand that the doctor provide special attention. They often become angry or frightened if they perceive that the doctor is not taking their concerns seriously. The doctor must be prepared to set necessary limits within the context of an expressed willingness to listen and to care for the patient.

**Demanding and impulsive.** Demanding and impulsive patients have a difficult time delaying gratification and may demand that their discomfort be eliminated immediately. They are easily frustrated and may become petulant or even angry and aggressive if they do not get what they want as soon as they want it. The patients may impulsively do something self-destructive if they feel thwarted by the doctor and may appear manipulative and attention seeking. What they may be feeling underneath the surface manifestations includes the fear that they will never get what they need from others and, thus, must act in that inappropriately aggressive way. They can be particularly difficult patients for any doctor to treat; the doctor must set firm, nonangry limits from the outset, defining clearly acceptable and unacceptable behavior. The patients must be treated with respect and care but must be held responsible for their actions.

**Narcissistic.** Narcissistic patients act as though they are superior to everyone around them, including the doctor. They have a tremendous need to appear perfect and are contemptuous of others, whom they perceive to be imperfect. They may be rude, abrupt, arrogant, or demeaning. They may initially overidealize the physician in their need to have their doctor be as perfect as they are, but the overidealization may quickly turn to disdain when they discover that the doctor is human. Underneath their surface arrogance, the patients often feel inadequate, helpless, and empty, and they fear that others will see through them.

**Obsessive and controlling.** Obsessive and controlling patients are orderly, punctual, and overconcerned with detail. They often appear unemotional, even aloof, especially with regard to anything potentially disturbing or frightening. They may be resistant to any perceived control on the part of the doctor, as they have such a strong need of their own to be in control of everything in their environment. Underneath, the patients are often frightened of losing control and of being dependent and helpless. Physicians must be prepared to strengthen the patients' sense of control by including them as much as possible in their own care and treatment. Doctors should explain in detail what is going on and what is being planned.

**Hypervigilant and paranoid.** Hypervigilant and paranoid patients fear that people want to hurt them and are out to do them harm. The patients may misperceive cues in their environment to the degree that they see conspiracies in neutral events. They are critical, evasive, and suspicious. They are often called grievance seekers, because they tend to blame others for everything bad that happens in their lives. They are extremely mistrustful and may question everything that the doctor says needs to be done. The doctor must remain somewhat formal, albeit always respectful and courteous, with the patients, as expressions of warmth and empathy are often viewed with suspicion ("what does he want from me?"). As with obsessive patients, the doctor should be prepared to explain in detail every decision and planned procedure and should react nondefensively to the patients' suspicions.

**Isolated and solitary.** Termed schizoid personalities, isolated and solitary patients appear detached and reclusive and do not appear to need or want much contact with other human beings. Intimate contact with a doctor is viewed with distaste by the patients, who would prefer to take care of themselves entirely on their own if they could. The doctor should treat the patients with as much respect for privacy as possible and should not expect them to respond to the doctor's concern in kind.

**Complaining, martyrlike, and passive-aggressive.** Complaining, martyrlike, and passive-aggressive patients appear to communicate solely through a litany of complaints and disappointments. They often covertly blame others for all their problems, and they make others feel guilty about not doing or caring enough. They are often not able to express angry feelings directly and, thus, express them indirectly or passively by being late for appointments or not making their payments on time. They often perceive themselves as being extremely self-sacrificing and as being taken advantage of by others, who are seen as selfish. The patients may unconsciously believe that the only way to be taken seriously or to be cared for or loved is to be sick. The doctor must be patient and tolerant with the patients, as difficult as they can sometimes be. Doctors should take such patients' concerns seriously but without encouraging the sick role; firm limits must be set on the doctor's availability (as with overly dependent patients). At the same time, doctors should reassure the patients that they will listen to them during frequent, regularly scheduled appointments. The doctor must often be involved with the patient's family; family members are dealing with the patient's difficult style every day and are likely to be angry, frustrated, and guilty themselves.

**Sociopathic and malingering.** Sociopathic patients are those described in psychiatric terminology as antisocial personalities; they do not appear to experience appropriate guilt and, in fact, may not even be consciously aware of what it means to be guilty. On the surface they may appear charming, socially adept, and intelligent, but they have over many years perfected the behaviors they know to be appropriate, and they perform almost as an actor would. They often have histories of criminal acts, and they get by in the world through lying and manipulation. They are often self-destructive, harming not only others but themselves in perhaps an unacknowledged expression of self-punishment. Sociopathic patients often malinger, which is the term for consciously feigning illness for some clear secondary gain (for example, to obtain drugs, to get a bed for the night, or to hide out from people pursuing them). Obviously, they do get sick, just as nonsociopathic people do, and, when they are sick, they need to be cared for in the same ways that others do. The doctor must treat them with respect but with a heightened sense of vigilance. The patients can inspire fear in others, often legitimately so, as many have violent histories. Doctors who feel threatened by patients should unashamedly seek assistance and not feel compelled to see the patients alone. Firm limits must be set on behavior (for example, no drugs in the hospital and no sexual activity with other patients), and the consequences of transgressing must be firmly stated and adhered to (for example, discharge from the hospital if the patient is medically stable, isolation if not). If inappropriate behavior is discovered, the patients must be confronted directly and nonangrily, and they must be held responsible for their actions.

## SPECIFIC STRESSES ON PHYSICIANS

A trained physician not only has learned the knowledge base and the techniques of the profession but also must confront, resolve, and incorporate a number of significant attitudinal issues involved in becoming a skilled and effective physician. Those issues encompass the ideals of balancing compassionate concern with dispassionate objectivity; the wish to relieve pain and distress with the ability to make difficult, often painful decisions; and the desire to cure or control with the acceptance of the limits on what one can realistically accomplish. Learning to balance those interrelated aspects of the physician's role is essential in allowing the doctor to withstand, in a graceful and life-affirming way, daily work that involves the continual confrontation of illness, pain, sadness, fear, suffering, vulnerability, and death. A lack of balance can lead a physician to feel overwhelmed, depressed, and burnedout. A sense of futility and failure can begin to permeate the physician's attitude, setting the stage for anger and frustration about one's profession, patients, and self. Many physicians are at risk for that lack of balance because of particular personality and coping styles prevalent among those drawn to the practice of medicine. For instance, many medical students are perfectionistic, controlling, and obsessive. Those traits can be adaptive for physicians if balanced with healthy doses of self-knowledge, humility, humor, and kindness. If the balance is absent, many physicians travel the path of dispassion at the expense of compassion, willingness to be in charge at the expense of being supportive, and they have a diminished capacity to tolerate the limits of what one can realistically and honestly accomplish.

## References

Balint M: *The Doctor, the Patient, and the Illness*. International Universities Press, New York, 1964.

Billings J A, Stoeckle J D: *The Clinical Encounter: A Guide to the Medical Interview and Case Presentation*. Year Book Medical, Chicago, 1989.

Bishop J: Guidelines for a nonsexist (gender-sensitive) doctor-patient relationship. Can J Psychiatry *37*: 62, 1992.

Engel G L: The clinical application of the biopsychosocial model. Am J Psychiatry *137*: 535, 1980.

Freud S: The dynamics of transference. In *Standard Edition of the Complete Psychological Works of Sigmund Freud*, vol 12 p 99. Hogarth Press, London, 1958.

Freud S: Recommendations to physicians practicing psychoanalysis. In *Standard Edition of the Complete Psychological Works of Sigmund Freud*, vol 12 p 109. Hogarth Press, London, 1958.

Hall J A, Dornan M C: What patients like about their medical care and how often they are asked: A meta-analysis of the satisfaction literature. Soc Sci Med *27*: 935, 1988.

Korsch B, Negrete V: Doctor-patient communication. Sci Am *227*: 66, 1972.

Lane F E: Utilizing physician empathy with violent patients. Am J Psychother *40*: 448, 1986.

Leigh H, Reiser M F: *The Patient: Biological, Psychological, and Social Dimensions of Medical Practice*. Plenum, New York, 1980.

Leon R L: *Psychiatric Interviewing: A Primer*, ed 2. Elsevier, New York, 1989.

Lipkin M Jr: Psychiatry and medicine. In *Comprehensive Textbook of Psychiatry*, ed 5, H I Kaplan, B J Sadock, editors, p 1280. Williams & Wilkins, Baltimore, 1989.

Lipkin M Jr, Putnam S, Lazare A, editors: *The Medical Interview*. Springer, New York, 1989.

Mishler, E G, Clark J A, Ingelfinger J, Simon M P: The language of attentive patient care: A comparison of two medical interviews. J Gen Intern Med *4*: 325, 1989.

Omer H: Enhancing the impact of therapeutic interventions. Am J Psychother *44*: 218, 1990.

Othmer E, Othmer S C: *The Clinical Interview Using DSM-III-R*. American Psychiatric Press, Washington, 1989.

Quill T: Partnerships in patient care: A contractual approach. Ann Intern Med *98*: 228, 1983.

Reiser D E, Rosend D H: *Medicine as a Human Experience*. University Park Press, Baltimore, 1984.

Reiser D E, Schroder A K: *Patient Interviewing: The Human Dimension*. Williams & Wilkins, Baltimore, 1984.

Roter D L, Hall J A: Studies of doctor-patient interaction. Annu Rev Public Health *10*: 163, 1989.

Shea S C: *Psychiatric Interviewing: The Art of Understanding*. Saunders, Philadelphia, 1988.

Silver A, Weiss D: Paternalistic attitudes and moral reasoning among physicians at a large teaching hospital. Acad Med *67*: 62, 1992.

Stoffelmayr B, Hoppe R B, Weber N: Facilitating patient participation: The doctor-patient encounter. Prim Care *16*: 265, 1989.

Walsh J M, McPhee S J: A systems model of clinical preventive care: An analysis of factors influencing patient and physician. Health Educ Q *19*: 157, 1992.

West C: Reconceptualizing gender in physician-patient relationships. Soc Sci Med *36*: 57, 1993.

Wilson J: Patients' wants vs. patients' interests. J Med Ethics *12*: 127, 1986.

# Human Development Throughout the Life Cycle

## 2.1 / Overview of the Life Cycle and Normality

Systematic study of the life cycle began in the early 20th century as an outgrowth of psychiatry's concern with the course of personality development. Initial formulations examined the role of internal psychological events and the effects of childhood development on the adult personality. Subsequent conceptualizations extended the focus of interest to include the influence of interpersonal processes and the nature of change throughout life. Recently, the biological substrate of behavior has been emphasized because of new findings in neural science. The charting of the life cycle (the life course, as it is sometimes called) is essential to a complete understanding of human behavior and in predicting the difficulties that arise during human development.

### ASSUMPTIONS

#### Epigenetic Principle

The fundamental assumption of life-cycle theory holds that development occurs in successive clearly defined stages. According to the epigenetic principle, each stage follows on the one before, and each must be satisfactorily passed through for development to proceed smoothly. If a stage is not resolved, all subsequent stages reflect that failure in the form of physical, cognitive, social, or emotional maladjustment.

#### Crisis Points

Another basic assumption in life-cycle theory is that each stage is characterized by a crisis point that must be negotiated successfully. A crisis requires the person to adapt. It is a biopsychosocial event in that it consists of the interaction of biological, psychological, and social factors. Each stage has one or more events or crisis points

that distinguish it from stages that either preceded it or will follow it.

Life-cycle study lies within the boundaries of developmental psychology and involves such diverse elements as biological maturity, psychological capacity, adaptive techniques, defense mechanisms, symptom complexes, role demands, social behavior, cognition, perception, language development, and interpersonal relationships. The various models of the life cycle describe the major developmental phases but emphasize different elements. Taken together, however, the models show that there is an order in the course of human life, despite the fact that each person's life is unique. As Theodore Lidz, a major exponent of life-cycle theory, commented: "The journey from the womb to adulthood and then through maturity into old age is lengthy, circuitous, and beset by countless contingencies."

No common language clearly defines the stages of the life cycle, and no standard vocabulary describes the major developmental phases. A phase of the cycle may be described by various terms, including stage, season, period, era, epoch, and life stage. Those terms are conceptually congruent in general and can be used interchangeably.

### CONTRIBUTIONS TO LIFE-CYCLE THEORY

#### Sigmund Freud

Work on the human life cycle has been shaped by a handful of highly influential sources; however, the dominant work on the subject is the developmental scheme introduced by Sigmund Freud in 1905 in *Three Essays on the Theory of Sexuality*. Freud's theory, which focused on the childhood period, was organized around his libido theory. According to Freud, childhood phases of development correspond to successive shifts in the investment of sexual energy to areas of the body usually associated with eroticism: the mouth, the anus, and the genitalia. He discerned developmental periods that were accordingly classified as follows: oral phase, birth to 1 year; anal phase, ages 1 to 3 years; and phallic phase, ages 3 to 5 years.

Freud also described a fourth period, latency, which extends from ages 5 and 6 years until puberty. Latency is marked by a diminution of sexual interest, which is reactivated at puberty. The basic outlook expressed by Freud was that the successful resolution of the childhood phases is essential to normal adult functioning. By comparison, what happens in adulthood is of relatively little consequence. Freud's theories are discussed thoroughly in Section 6.1.

## Freud's Followers

Many followers of Freud modified or built on his conceptualizations while adhering to his focus on sexual energy as the quality that distinguishes the stages of development. Karl Abraham, for example, subdivided the phases of psychosexual development. He divided the oral period into sucking and biting phases and the anal phase into destructive-expulsive and mastering-retaining phases. He linked certain adult personality types to difficulties in resolving one of those specific periods.

Melanie Klein adhered to Freud's basic formulations; however, she saw developmental events as occurring more rapidly than Freud did. She also believed that aggressive drives, rather than sexual drives, are preeminent during the earliest phase of development.

## Carl Gustav Jung

Carl Gustav Jung viewed external factors as playing an important role in personal growth and adaptation. He described the process of individuation as the growth and expansion of personality that occurs through realizing and learning what one intrinsically is. According to Jung, libido is every possible manifestation of psychic energy; it is not limited to sexuality or to aggression but includes the religious or spiritual urges and the drive to seek a clear or deep understanding of the meaning of life.

## Harry Stack Sullivan

Harry Stack Sullivan approached the issue of the life cycle by stating that human development is largely shaped by external events, specifically by social interaction. His influential model of the life cycle states that each phase of development is marked by a need for interaction with certain other people. The quality of that interaction influences the personality. Sullivan distinguished the stages or eras of normal development as follows:

1. Infancy, birth to the beginning of language (1½ to 2 years)
2. Childhood, language to the need for peers (2 to 5 years)
3. Juvenile era, the need for peers and the beginning of formal education to preadolescence (5 to 9 years)
4. Preadolescence, the beginning of the capacity for intimate relationships with peers of the opposite sex or the same sex until genital maturity (9 to 12 years)
5. Adolescence, the eruption of true genital interest to the patterning of sexual behavior
6. Maturity, the establishment of a fully human or mature repertoire of interpersonal relationships, the development of self-respect, and the capacity for intimate and collaborative relationships and loving attitudes.

## Erik Erikson

Erik Erikson accepted Freud's theory of infantile sexuality but also saw developmental potentials at all stages of life. Erikson constructed a model of the life cycle consisting of eight stages that extend into adulthood and old age. The stages are summarized as follows:

Stage 1. Trust versus mistrust
Stage 2. Autonomy versus shame and doubt
Stage 3. Initiative versus guilt
Stage 4. Industry versus inferiority
Stage 5. Ego identity versus role confusion
Stage 6. Intimacy versus isolation
Stage 7. Generativity versus stagnation
Stage 8. Ego integrity versus despair

Erikson's five childhood psychosocial stages of trust, autonomy, initiative, industry, and identity correlate with Freud's psychosexual stages. In addition, Erikson added three stages—intimacy, generativity, and integrity—that extend beyond young adulthood into old age. Those eight stages have both positive and negative aspects, have specific emotional crises, and are affected by the interaction of the person's biology, culture, and society. Each stage has two possible outcomes, one positive or healthy and the other negative or unhealthy. Under ideal circumstances, the crisis is resolved when the person achieves a new and higher level of functioning at the positive end of the stage. According to Erikson, most persons do not achieve perfect positive polarity but fall more toward the positive pole than toward the negative pole. Erikson's theories are discussed in depth in Section 6.3.

## Jean Piaget

Another major model is Jean Piaget's theory of cognitive (intellectual) development. By conducting intensive studies of the way children think and behave, Piaget formulated a theory of cognition, which he divided into four stages—sensorimotor, preoperational thought, concrete operations, and formal operations. Piaget's theories are discussed in depth in Section 4.1.

## Daniel Levinson

Daniel Levinson and his coworkers at Yale University focused on personality development over the life course. In a major study they set out to clarify the issues and the characteristics of male personality development in early and middle adulthood. A total of 40 men were studied; their ages at the start of the investigation ranged from 35 to 45 years. The resulting observations caused Levinson to postulate a new scheme of the adult phases of the life cycle. He suggested that the life cycle is composed of four major eras, each lasting about 25 years, with some overlap, so that a new era is starting as the previous one is ending. Levinson was able to identify a typical age of onset—that is, the age at which an era usually begins. The evolving sequence of eras and their age spans described by Levinson are childhood and adolescence, birth to 22 years; early adulthood, 17 to 45 years; middle adulthood, 40 to 65 years; and late adulthood, 65 years and beyond. Levinson also identified four- to five-year transitional periods between eras that function as boundary zones during which a person terminates the outgoing era and initiates the incoming one.

## George Vaillant

George Vaillant and his group studied a cohort of men for more than 35 years, starting when they were freshmen at Harvard University. A happy childhood was found to correlate significantly with positive traits in middle life, manifested by few oral-dependent traits, little psychopathology, the capacity to play, and good object relations.

Vaillant noted that a hierarchy of ego mechanisms was constructed as the men advanced in age. Defenses were organized along a continuum that reflected two aspects of the personality: immaturity versus maturity and psychopathology versus mental health. He found that the maturity of the defenses was related to both psychopathology and objective adaptation to the external environment. Moreover, the defensive style shifted as a person matured.

Vaillant concluded that adaptive styles mature over the years and that the maturation depends more on development from within than on changes in the interpersonal environment. He also corroborated Erikson's model of the life cycle.

## Bernice Neugarten

Bernice Neugarten and her group have been among the few workers to study the psychology of the life cycle in women, in addition to men. In particular, she has found that most women successfully adapt to the various crisis points of marriage, pregnancy, childbirth, and the menopause. She has also studied issues of work, leisure, retirement, and grandparenting.

## NORMALITY IN PSYCHIATRY

Psychiatrists have long made a concerted effort to define mental health and normality. In years past, they understood implicitly that mental health could be defined as the opposite of mental illness. With such an assumption, the absence of gross psychopathology was often equated with normal behavior. A number of recent trends have cast doubt on the usefulness of that assumption and have made it increasingly important for psychiatrists to provide precise concepts and definitions of mental health and normality.

The many theoretical and clinical concepts of normality seem to fall into four functional perspectives. Although each perspective is unique and has its own definition and description, the perspectives complement each other, and together they represent the totality of the behavioral science and social science approaches to normality. The four perspectives of normality, as formulated by Daniel Offer and Melvin Sabshin, are normality as health, normality as utopia, normality as average, and normality as process.

## Normality as Health

The first perspective is basically the traditional medical-psychiatric approach to health and illness. Most physicians equate normality with health and view health as an almost universal phenomenon. Behavior is assumed to be within normal limits when no manifest psychopathology is present. If all behavior were to be put on a scale, normality would encompass the major portion of the continuum, and abnormality would be the small remainder.

That definition of normality correlates with the traditional model of the doctor who attempts to free the patient from grossly observable signs and symptoms of disease. To that physician the lack of signs or symptoms indicates health. In other words, health in that context is a reasonable, rather than an optimal, state of functioning.

## Normality as Utopia

The second perspective conceives of normality as that harmonious and optimal blending of the diverse elements of the mental apparatus that culminates in optimal functioning. Such a definition clearly emerges when psychiatrists or psychoanalysts talk about the ideal person or when they discuss their criteria for successful treatment. That approach can be traced directly back to Freud, who, when discussing normality, stated, "A normal ego is like normality in general, an ideal fiction."

## Normality as Average

The third perspective is commonly used in normative studies of behavior and is based on the mathematical principle of the bell-shaped curve. That approach conceives of the middle range as normal and of both extremes as deviant. The normative approach based on that statistical principle describes each person in terms of general assessment and total score. Variability is described only within the context of total groups, not within the context of one person.

Although that approach is more commonly used in psychology and biology than in psychiatry, psychiatrists have recently been using standardized personality pencil-and-paper tests to a much larger extent than in the past. In the normality-as-average model, one assumes that the topologies of character can be statistically measured.

## Normality as Process

The fourth perspective stresses that normal behavior is the end result of interacting systems. On the basis of that definition, temporal changes are essential to a complete definition of normality. In other words, the normality-as-process perspective stresses changes or processes, rather than a cross-sectional definition of normality.

Investigators who subscribe to that approach can be found in all the behavioral and social sciences. Most typical of the concepts in that perspective are Erikson's conceptualization of epigenesis of personality development and the eight developmental stages essential in the attainment of mature adult functioning.

## Other Parameters of Normality

Efforts are increasing to develop empirical research in the area of normality. Along with their growing involvement in linking normality and social process, psychoanalysts are continuing their long-term interest in elucidating the vicissitudes of the normal psychopathology of everyday life. Psychoanalysts are increasingly demonstrating their interest in normal adaptation to the social environment. A summary of psychoanalytic concepts of normality is presented in Table 2.1–1.

Heinz Hartmann, a psychoanalyst, expanded on the concept of the ego, defined by Freud as the mediator between the id and the external world. The main function of the ego is to maintain a relation to the external world—that is, to help the organism test and adapt to reality. Hartmann described autonomous ego functions, present at birth, that are conflict-free—that is, uninfluenced by the internal psychic world. They include perception, intuition, comprehension, thinking, language, certain aspects of motor development, learning, and intelligence.

The concept of autonomous and conflict-free functions of the ego has intensified clinical exploration of the mechanisms whereby some persons lead relatively normal lives in the presence of extraordinary external experiential traumas. Discussing the average expectable environment, Hartmann provided a framework in which the molding of character structure in specific contexts can be easily understood.

Erikson's work also serves as a bridge linking normality to developmental stages and social process. His concept of crises at specific stages of life provides a framework of normal behavior and a cross-sectional analysis of behavior throughout life. Thus, he makes it possible to establish specific modes of adaptation.

## Table 2.1-1
### Psychoanalytic Concepts of Normality

| Theorist | Concept |
| --- | --- |
| Sigmund Freud | Normality is an ideal fiction. |
| Kurt Eissler | Absolute normality cannot be obtained because the normal person must be totally aware of his or her thoughts and feelings. |
| Melanie Klein | Normality is characterized by strength of character, the capacity to deal with conflicting emotions, the ability to experience pleasure without conflict, and the ability to love. |
| Erik Erikson | Normality is the ability to master the periods of life: trust vs. mistrust; autonomy vs. shame and doubt; initiative vs. guilt; industry vs. inferiority; identity vs. role confusion; intimacy vs. isolation; generativity vs. stagnation; and ego integrity vs. despair. |
| Laurence Kubie | Normality is the ability to learn by experience, to be flexible, and to adapt to a changing environment. |
| Heinz Hartmann | Conflict-free ego functions represent the person's potential for normality; the degree the ego can adapt to reality and be autonomous is related to mental health. |
| Karl Menninger | Normality is the ability to adjust to the external world with contentment and to master the task of acculturation. |
| Alfred Adler | The person's capacity to develop social feeling and to be productive is related to mental health; the ability to work heightens self-esteem and makes one capable of adaptation. |
| R. E. Money-Kryle | Normality is the ability to achieve insight into one's self, an ability that is never fully accomplished. |
| Otto Rank | Normality is the capacity to live without fear, guilt, or anxiety and to take responsibility for one's own actions. |

## Longitudinal Studies

The understanding of normality has been advanced by a number of longitudinal studies. For example, D. Offer and M. Sabshin studied a group of young adolescents throughout their high school years and identified three normal types of development: continuous growth, surgent growth, and tumultuous growth. Although persons typical of those types are different, they are placed along a continuum of normality. Offer and Sabshin formulated an operational definition of normality that is not absolute but, rather, descriptive of one type of middle-class adolescent population. The criteria best describing the teenagers are the following:

1. Almost complete absence of gross psychopathology, severe physical defects, and severe physical illness
2. Mastery of previous developmental tasks without serious setbacks
3. Ability to experience affects flexibly and to resolve their conflicts actively with reasonable success
4. Relatively good object relationships with parents, siblings, and peers
5. Feeling a part of a larger cultural environment and being aware of its norms and values

The developmental approach is also being used by Vaillant and others for adults. Studies of adaptation to marriage, parenthood, work, and leisure activities are increasingly prominent. Precise empirical studies are being conducted regarding developmental problems in the period of involution and decline.

A controversial view has been taken by Thomas Szasz, who believes that the concept of mental illness should be abandoned entirely. He also states that normality can be measured only in terms of what people do or do not do and that normality is actually a problem of ethics.

The development of geriatric psychiatry has moved in a normative direction. The deficit-focused orientation of early studies in gerontology has been replaced, to a significant extent, by a normative framework that asks, in effect, "How do elderly people cope with the adaptational tasks of their 60s, 70s, and beyond?"

**Table 2.1-2**
**A Synthesis of Developmental Theorists**

| Age (Years) | Margaret Mahler | John Bowlby | Sigmund Freud | Erik Erikson | Jean Piaget |
|---|---|---|---|---|---|
| 0–1 | Normal autistic phase (birth to 4 weeks)<br>• State of half-sleep, half-wake<br>• Major task of phase is to achieve homeostatic equilibrium with the environment<br><br>Normal symbiotic phase (3–4 weeks to 4–5 months)<br>• Dim awareness of caretaker, but infant still functions as though he or she and caretaker were in state of undifferentiation or fusion<br>• Social smile characteristic (2–4 months)<br><br>The subphases of separation-individuation proper:<br><br>First subphase: differentiation (5–10 months)<br>• Process of hatching from autistic shell (i.e., developing more alert sensorium that reflects cognitive and neurological maturation)<br>• Beginning of comparative scanning (i.e., comparing what is and what is not mother)<br>• Characteristic anxiety: stranger anxiety, which involves curiosity and fear (most prevalent around 8 months) | Phase I (birth to 8–12 weeks)<br>• Infant's ability to discriminate one person from another is limited to olfactory and auditory stimuli<br>• To any person in infant's vicinity, infant will:<br>—orient to that person<br>—have tracking movements of the eyes<br>—grasp and reach<br>—smile<br>—babble<br>—stop crying on hearing voice or seeing face<br>• Those behaviors, by influencing the adult's behavior, are likely to increase the time the baby is in proximity to mother (adult)<br><br>Phase II (8–12 weeks to 6 months or much later, according to circumstances)<br>• Continuation of phase I activities but most marked in relation to mother specifically<br><br>Phase III (6–7 months and continues throughout second and into third year)<br>• Attachment to mother figure evident<br>• Following departing mother<br>• Greeting her on her return<br>• Using her as base from which to explore<br>• Waning of friendly, undifferentiated responses to others | Oral phase (birth to 1 year)<br>• Major site of tension and gratification is the mouth, lips, tongue—includes biting and sucking activities | Basic trust vs. basic mistrust (oral sensory) (birth to 1 year)<br>• Trust is demonstrated by ease of feeding, depth of sleep, bowel relaxation<br>• Depends on consistency and sameness of experience provided by caretaker<br>• Second six months' teething and biting moves infant "from getting to taking"<br>• Weaning leads to "nostalgia for lost paradise"<br>• If basic trust is strong, child maintains hopeful attitude | Sensorimotor stage (birth to 2 years)<br>• Intelligence rests mainly on actions and movements coordinated under "schemata" (Schema is a pattern of behavior in response to a particular environmental stimulus.)<br>• Environment is mastered through *assimilation* and *accommodation.* (Assimilation is the incorporation of new environmental stimuli. Accommodation is the modification of behavior to adapt to new stimuli.)<br>• *Object permanence* is achieved by age 2 years. Object still exists in mind if it disappears from view: search for hidden object<br>• Reversibility in action begins |
| 1–2 | Second subphase: practicing (10–16 months)<br>• Beginning of this phase marked by upright locomotion—child has new perspective and also mood of elation | | Anal phase (1–3 years)<br>• Anus and surrounding area are major source of interest<br>• Acquisition of voluntary sphincter control (toilet training) | Autonomy vs. shame and doubt (muscular-anal) (1–3 years)<br>• Biologically includes learning to walk, feed self, talk<br>• Muscular maturation sets | |

2–3

- Mother used as home base
  - Characteristic anxiety: separation anxiety

Third subphase: rapprochement (16–24 months)
- Infant now a toddler—more aware of physical separateness, which dampens mood of elation
- Child tries to bridge gap between self and mother—concretely seen as bringing objects to mother
- Mother's efforts to help toddler often not perceived as helpful; temper tantrums are typical
- Characteristic event: rapprochement crisis: wanting to be soothed by mother and yet not being able to accept her help
- Symbol of rapprochement: child standing on threshold of door not knowing which way to turn in helpless frustration
- Resolution of crisis occurs as child's skills improve and child is able to get gratification from doing things

Fourth subphase: consolidation and object constancy (24–36 months)
- Child better able to cope with mother's absence and to engage substitutes
- Child can begin to feel comfortable with mother's absences by knowing she will return
- Gradual internalization of image of mother as reliable and stable
- Through increasing verbal skills and better sense of time, child can tolerate delay and endure separations

- Treating strangers with caution, alarm, withdrawal

Phase IV (from 24 months)
- Mother figure seen as independent
- Object seen as persistent in time and space
- More complex relationship with mother develops—partnership between mother and child develops, in which child acquires insight into mother's feelings and motives
- Child observes mother's behavior and what influences it

stage for holding on and letting go
- Need for outer control, firmness of caretaker before development of autonomy
- *Shame* occurs when child is overtly self-conscious because of negative exposure
- *Self-doubt* can evolve if parents overly shame child (e.g., about elimination)

Preoperational stage (2–7 years)
- Appearance of *symbolic* functions, associated with language acquisition.
- *Egocentrism:* child understands everything exclusively from own perspective
- Thinking is illogical and magical
- Nonreversible thinking with absence of conservation
—*Animism:* belief that inanimate objects are alive (i.e., have feelings and intentions)
—*Immanent justice:* belief that punishment for bad deeds is inevitable

*Continued*

**Table 2.1-2**
*continued*

| Age (Years) | Margaret Mahler | John Bowlby | Sigmund Freud | Erik Erikson | Jean Piaget |
|---|---|---|---|---|---|
| 3–4 | | | Phallic-oedipal phase (3–5 years)<br>• Genital focus of interest, stimulation, and excitement<br>• Penis is organ of interest for both sexes | Initiative vs. guilt (locomotor genital) (3–5 years)<br>• *Initiative* arises in relation to tasks for the sake of activity, both motor and intellectual | |
| 4–5 | | | • Genital masturbation is common<br>• Intense preoccupation with *castration anxiety* (fear of genital loss or injury)<br>• *Penis envy* (discontent with one's own genitals and wish to possess genitals of male) seen in girls in this phase<br>• *Oedipus complex* universal: child wishes to have sex with and marry parent of opposite sex and simultaneously be rid of parent of same sex | • *Guilt* may arise over goals contemplated (especially aggressive)<br>• Desire to mimic adult world; involvement in oedipal struggle leads to resolution through social role identification<br>• Sibling rivalry frequent | |
| 5–6 | | | Latency phase (from 5–6 years to 11–12 years)<br>• State of relative quiescence of sexual drive with resolution of oedipal complex<br>• Sexual drives channeled into more socially appropriate aims (i.e., schoolwork and sports) | | |
| 6–11 | | | • Formation of *superego*: one of three psychic structures in mind that is responsible for moral and ethical development, including conscience<br>• Other two psychic structures are *ego*, which is a group of functions mediating between the drives and the external environment, and the *id*, repository of sexual and aggressive drives | Industry vs. inferiority (latency) (6–11 years)<br>• Child is busy building, creating, accomplishing<br>• Receives systematic instruction and fundamentals of technology<br>• Danger of sense of inadequacy and inferiority if child despairs of tools, skills, and status among peers<br>• Socially decisive age | Concrete (operational) stage (7–11 years)<br>• Emergence of logical (cause-effect) thinking, including reversibility and ability to sequence and serialize<br>• Understanding of part and whole relationships and classifications<br>• Child able to take other's point of view<br>• Conservation of number, length, weight, and volume |

11+

- The id is present at birth, and the ego develops gradually from rudimentary structure present at birth

Genital phase (from 11–12 years)
- Final stage of psychosexual development—begins with puberty and the biological capacity for orgasm but involves the capacity for true intimacy

Identity vs. role diffusion (11 years through end of adolescence)
- Struggle to develop *ego identity* (sense of inner sameness and continuity)
- Preoccupation with appearance, hero worship, ideology
- *Group identity* (with peers) develops
- Danger of *role confusion*, doubts about sexual and vocational identity
- *Psychosocial moratorium*, stage between morality learned by the child and the ethics to be developed by the adult

Formal (abstract) stage (11 years through end of adolescence)
- Hypothetical-deductive reasoning, not only on basis of objects but also on basis of hypotheses or of propositions
- Capable of thinking about one's thoughts
- Combinative structures emerge, permitting flexible grouping of elements in a system
- Ability to use two systems of reference simultaneously
- Ability to grasp concept of probabilities

Table by Sylvia Karasu, M.D., and Richard Oberfield, M.D.

## Normal Child Development

Normal child development may be approached from a variety of perspectives. Melvin Lewis described normal childhood behavior as that that conforms to the expectations of the majority in a given society at a given time. According to Lewis, disordered behavior in a child is behavior that the majority of adults consider inappropriate in form, frequency, or intensity. Lewis pointed out that the criteria for such a judgment "are often nebulous," and different biases come into play that infuse the boundary between normal and abnormal.

Sigmund Freud described five psychosexual stages of child development—oral, anal, phallic, latency, and genital—derived from the analysis of adults with various types of psychopathology. On the basis of direct observations of children, other psychoanalysts elaborated on many of Freud's theories.

Anna Freud delineated aspects of normal growth and development in children and was interested in empirical research directed at helping to clarify how children cope with adaptive tasks. She described stages of development—such as dependence to independence, wetting to bladder control, self-involvement to companionship—that represent the movement from the immature infant to the complexity of the developed child.

Margaret Mahler studied early childhood object relations and made a significant contribution to the understanding of personality development. She described the separation-individuation process, resulting in a person's subjective sense of separateness from the world around him or her. The separation-individuation phase of development begins in the fourth or fifth month of life and is completed by age 3 years.

Jean Piaget's developmental psychology also influenced the study of the life cycle and had similarities to both psychoanalysis and academic disciplines. In deriving general principles from the intensive study of a relatively few children, Piaget used an approach resembling that of psychoanalytic inquiry. By concentrating on normal development and using structured tasks (for example, multiple experiments with each child), he used a scientific method. Piaget's stages of sensorimotor development, preoperational thinking, concrete operations, and formal operations have been a dominant theory of cognition and are discussed in detail in Section 4.1.

**Stages.** According to workers like Erikson and Piaget, the infant grows by predetermined steps through various stages. In that epigenetic view of development, each stage has its own characteristics and needs, and it must be negotiated successfully before it is possible to go on the next level. The sequence of stages is not automatic; rather, it depends on both central nervous system growth and life experiences. Ample evidence indicates that an unfavorable environment can delay some of the developmental stages; however, particularly favorable environmental stimulators can accelerate one's progress through the stages.

In view of the various models for conceptualizing the phases of development (Table 2.1–2), it has become customary to organize the developmental stages in chronological order as follows: infancy; toddler period; preschool period; school period or middle years; early, middle, and late adolescence; and early, middle, and late adulthood (old age). Each developmental stage is discussed in detail in the sections that follow.

### References

Adler L L, editor: *Cross-Cultural Research in Human Development.* Praeger, New York, 1989.
Colorusso C A, Nemiroff R A: *Adult Development: A New Dimension in Psychodynamic Theory and Practice.* Plenum, New York, 1981.
Erikson E: *Childhood and Society.* Norton, New York, 1959.
Freud A: *The Ego and the Mechanisms of Defense.* International Universities Press, New York, 1966.
Hartmann H: *Ego Psychology and the Problem of Adaptation.* International Universities Press, New York, 1958.
Kellam S E, Branch J D: *Mental Health and Going to School: The Woodlawn Program of Assessment, Early Intervention, and Evaluation.* University of Chicago Press, Chicago, 1975.
Kelley S J: Parenting stress and child maltreatment in drug-exposed children. Child Abuse Negl *16:* 317, 1992.
Lidz T: *The Person: His and Her Development Throughout the Life Cycle.* Basic Books, New York, 1976.
Maccoby E E: The role of gender identity and gender constancy in sex-differentiated development. New Dir Child Dev *47:* 5, 1990.
Notman M T: Menopause and adult development. Ann N Y Acad Sci *592:* 149, 1990.
Offer D, Sabshin M: *Normality and the Life Cycle.* Basic Books, New York, 1984.
Robins L N, Rutter M, editors: *Straight and Devious Pathways from Childhood to Adulthood.* Cambridge University Press, Cambridge, 1989.
Seiden A M: Psychological issues affecting women throughout the life cycle. Psychiatr Clin North Am *12:* 1, 1989.
Vaillant G E, editor: *Empirical Studies of Ego Mechanism and Defense.* American Psychiatric Association Press, Washington, 1986.
Werner E E: The children of Kauai: Resiliency and recovery in adolescence and adulthood. J Adolesc Health *13:* 262, 1992.
Wolff S: Attachment and morality: Developing themes with different values. Br J Psychiatry *156:* 266, 1990.

# 2.2 / Pregnancy, Childbirth, and Related Issues

## PREGNANCY

The pregnant woman undergoes marked biological, physiological, and psychological changes. Attitudes toward pregnancy reflect deeply felt beliefs about reproduction, the timing of the pregnancy—whether it has been planned and whether a baby is wanted—the quality of the woman's relationship with her husband, whether she is married, her age, her history, her sense of identity, and her reactions to prospective motherhood. The prospective father also faces psychological challenges as he anticipates fatherhood.

### Psychology of Pregnancy

In the psychologically healthy woman, pregnancy is one expression of her sense of self-realization and identity as a woman. Many women report that being pregnant is a creative experience that gratifies a fundamental narcissistic need in that another being is produced that is an extension of the self. Negative attitudes about pregnancy are often associated with the fear of childbirth or of the mothering role. Some women view pregnancy as a way of diminishing self-doubts about their femininity or as a means of reassuring themselves that they are able to conceive. During the pregnancy, particularly if it is a first pregnancy, the mother recapitulates early stages of her own development. Among those stages the process of separation-individuation from her mother is of major importance. Unconscious fears and fantasies associated with early pregnancy often center on the concept of fusion with her own mother. If her own mother was a poor role model, the woman's sense of maternal competence may be impaired, and a lack of confidence before and after the birth of her baby may result.

Psychological attachment to the fetus begins in utero, and by the beginning of the second trimester most women have a mental picture of the infant. The fetus is viewed as a separate being, even before being born, and is endowed with a prenatal personality. According to psychoanalytic theorists, the child-to-be is a blank screen on which the mother projects her hopes and fears. In rare instances those projections account for postpartum pathological states, such as the mother's wanting to harm the infant, who is viewed as a hated part of herself. Normally, however, giving birth to a child fulfills a woman's basic need to create and nurture life.

Fathers are also profoundly affected by pregnancy. Impending parenthood demands a synthesis of such developmental issues as gender role and identity, separation-individuation from the man's own father, sexuality, and, as Erik Erikson proposed, generativity. Pregnancy fantasies in men and wishes to give birth in boys are early identifications with the mother and wishes to be as powerful and creative as they perceive her to be. For some men, getting a woman pregnant is proof of their potency, a dynamic that plays a large part in adolescent fatherhood.

In general, the psychodynamics of pregnancy is based on the developmental history of the person. It is an event that also has psychodynamic implications for persons who relate to the pregnant woman, including parents, grandparents, the extended family, and friends.

## Pregnancy and Marriage

The prospective wife-mother and husband-father have to redefine their roles as a couple and as individual persons. They face readjustments in their relationships with friends and relatives, and they must deal with new responsibilities as caretakers to the newborn and to each other. Both parents may experience anxiety about their adequacy in the area of parenthood; one or both partners may be consciously or unconsciously ambivalent about the addition of the child to the family and about its effects on the dyadic relationship. The father may feel guilty about his wife's discomfort during pregnancy and parturition, and some men experience jealousy or envy of the experience of pregnancy. Accustomed to gratifying each other's dependency needs, the couple must attend to the unremitting needs of a new infant and developing child. Although most couples respond positively to those demands, some do not. Under

ideal conditions the desire to become a parent and to have a child should be a decision that is agreed on by both partners to meet a generative need for creative self-realization. Sometimes, however, parenthood is rationalized as a way to achieve intimacy in a conflicted marriage or to avoid having to deal with other life circumstance problems.

**Attitudes toward the pregnant mother.** In general, attitudes of others toward the pregnant mother reflect a variety of factors: intelligence, temperament, cultural practices, and myths of the society and the subculture into which both parents were born. Married men's responses to pregnancy are generally positive. For some men, however, reactions vary from a misplaced sense of pride that they are able to impregnate the woman to fear of increased responsibility and subsequent termination of the relationship. Small children react to a mother's obvious pregnancy with curiosity about the origin of babies, particularly about where the baby will exit and how it originally got there.

## Alternative Life-Style Pregnancy

Some lesbian couples choose to have one of them become pregnant through artificial insemination. In those instances, many of the same psychodynamics that apply to heterosexual couples are in evidence. Societal pressures against such arrangements may create stresses in the relationship between the partners; however, if the relationship between the two women is secure, they tend to bond strongly together as a family unit against that prejudice.

Similarly, some single, never-married women do not wish to marry but do want to become pregnant, and they do so through artificial or natural insemination. Although few in number, such women constitute a group who believe that motherhood is the absolute fulfillment of female identity, without which they view their lives to be incomplete and, in some cases, without meaning.

## Pregnancy and Sexual Behavior

The effects of pregnancy on sexual behavior vary among women. Some women experience an increased sex drive as pelvic vasocongestion produces an increased sexually responsive state. Others are more responsive than before the pregnancy because they no longer fear becoming pregnant. Some have diminished desire or lose interest in sexual activity altogether, either because of physical discomfort or because of a psychological mind-set that associates motherhood with asexuality. That association can also occur in men with a Madonna complex, who view pregnant women as sacred and not to be defiled by the sexual act. Some men find the pregnant body ugly. Either the man or the woman may erroneously regard intercourse as potentially harmful to the developing fetus and as something to be avoided for that reason. If a man has an extramarital affair during his wife's pregnancy, it usually occurs during the last trimester.

**Coital prohibitions.** Most obstetricians place no prohibitions on coitus during pregnancy. Some suggest that sexual intercourse cease four to five weeks antepartum. If bleeding occurs early in pregnancy, it is usually, though not invariably, followed by a spontaneous abortion. In those cases the obstetrician prohibits coitus on a temporary basis as a therapeutic measure. That abstinence may put a strain on the marriage. Maternal deaths resulting from forcibly blowing air into the vagina during cunnilingus have been reported, presumably resulting from air emboli in the placental-maternal circulation. That activity should be interdicted.

## Pregnancy and Medications

Teratogenic syndromes related to medication or drug use occur in pregnancy; however, only 2 to 3 percent of all fetal congenital anomalies are drug-induced. In spite of warnings, pregnant women take an average of 3.8 drugs per pregnancy, mostly prescription drugs. In general, the fetus is most vulnerable during the first trimester of pregnancy. Even though maternal blood and fetal blood are not exchanged, drugs pass through the placenta into the fetal capillaries. Psychotropic drugs, including sedatives and hypnotics, are used by about a third of all pregnant women. In addition, pregnant women take over-the-counter medications that are self-prescribed and difficult to monitor. The Food and Drug Administration (FDA) rates drugs in five categories of safety for use in pregnancy (Table 2.2–1).

**Medications and lactation.** Lactation is influenced by many factors. Nursing may be an ideal that some women feel they should meet, or it may be imposed by others—the husband, friends, relatives, or physicians. In those cases the woman may have guilt feelings if she chooses not to nurse or is unable to do so for physical reasons. There is no evidence of improved psychological or physical adjustment in breast-fed infants and children than in bottle-fed infants. Currently, more than 50 percent of babies are breast-fed; of that number about 30 percent of babies are breast-fed for three months or longer.

Many drugs can be transferred to the infant through breast milk. Although most drugs are generally compatible with breast feeding, some can produce signs and symptoms in the newborn infant (for example, antibiotics can produce rashes, and narcotics can produce sedation).

## Biology of Pregnancy

The first presumptive sign of pregnancy is the absence of menses for one week. Other presumptive signs are breast engorgement and tenderness, changes in breast size and shape, nausea with or without vomiting (morning sickness), frequent urination, and fatigue. A diagnosis can be made 10 to 15 days after fertilization by testing for human chorionic gonadotrophin (HCG), which is produced by the placenta. The definitive diagnosis requires a doubling of HCG levels, fetal heart sounds, and fetal movements. Ultrasound scanning can reveal a pregnant uterus as early as four weeks after fertilization.

## Stages of Pregnancy

Pregnancy is commonly divided into three trimesters, starting from the first day of the last menstrual cycle and ending with the delivery of a baby. The estimated date of confinement (EDC) is calculated by subtracting seven days from the first day of the last menses and adding nine months. Only about 10 percent of women are delivered on the EDC; the rest are delivered from one week early to one week late. The pregnant woman may experience considerable anxiety about various issues from one trimester to the next (Figure 2.2–1).

During the first trimester the woman must adapt to changes in her physical habitus. The enlarging uterus presses against the bladder and the rectum and can cause constipation and frequent urination. Rising estrogen levels may contribute to a decrease in libido in some women; others may avoid sex because they think their bodily change is unattractive.

A major event of the second trimester is quickening—the mother's perception of fetal movement that occurs between 16 and 20 weeks. Quickening reinforces the mother's mental picture of the child-to-be; many cultural beliefs relate the types of fetal movement to the sex of the baby and its personality. Such beliefs may create anxiety or depression in some women when those beliefs are at variance with their expectations. Most women, however, equate quickening with having a live fetus and find it an exhilarating experience that is commonly shared with the spouse. If other children are in the household, allowing them to feel the fetal movements helps them prepare for the new sibling and work through issues of sibling rivalry. As delivery approaches, practical issues relate to the arrival of the baby (for example, child care, baby clothes, and finances). In addition, preparations for the delivery and postnatal care are made (for example, notifying the doctor, getting to the hospital, the use of an anesthetic, and breast versus bottle feeding). Parents often worry about specific health issues, such as whether the infant will be deformed, but in many cases the worries are not verbalized. If one or both partners show increasing anxiety as the EDC approaches, that and other issues may be anxiety-provoking (for example, vaginal delivery versus a cesarean section) and should be discussed with the physician.

The third trimester is associated with physical discomfort for many women. All systems—cardiovascular, renal, pulmonary, gastrointestinal, and endocrine—have undergone profound changes that may produce a heart murmur, weight gain, exertional dyspnea, and heartburn (pyrosis). Some

**Table 2.2–1**
**FDA Rating of Drug Safety in Pregnancy**

| Category | Definition | Drug Examples |
|---|---|---|
| A | No fetal risks in controlled human studies | Folic acid, iron |
| B | No fetal risk in animal studies but no controlled human studies or fetal risk in animals but no risk in well-controlled human studies | Caffeine, nicotine, acetaminophen |
| C | Adverse fetal effects in animals and no human data available | Aspirin, haloperidol, chlorpromazine |
| D | Human fetal risk seen (may be used in life-threatening situation) | Lithium, tetracycline, ethanol |
| X | Proved fetal risk in humans (no indication for use, even in life-threatening situations) | Valproic acid, thalidomide |

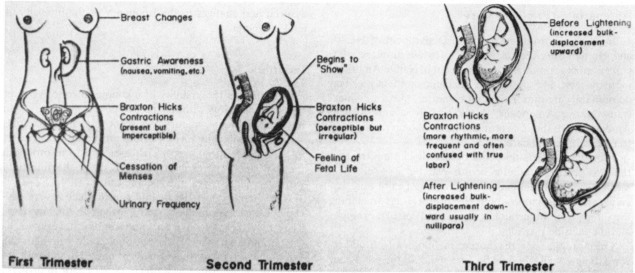

**First Trimester**          **Second Trimester**          **Third Trimester**

**Figure 2.2–1.** The symptoms most common to each trimester of pregnancy. The hormonally determined symptoms of pregnancy are often placed in the secondary service of emotional determinants. Thus, the nausea and vomiting of early pregnancy may become overly determined to the extent that hospitalization is required (hyperemesis gravidarum). Braxton-Hicks contractions are apparently physiological and occur throughout most of pregnancy. Usually imperceptible in early pregnancy and painless in midpregnancy, the contractions, although expulsively ineffective, are frequently and at times exasperatingly confused with true labor during the last weeks of pregnancy. Lightening occurs during the last weeks of pregnancy and is due to the downward descent and accommodation of the fetal head into the pelvic inlet. Upward displacement of the diaphragm by the encroaching uterus is correspondingly reduced, resulting in greater ease of respiration. With the downward displacement of the abdominal bulk, symptoms become targeted to the pelvic girdle, the lumbosacral area, and the lower extremities. Lightening is most obvious in first pregnancies and may not occur in multiparas until the onset of labor. (Figure from E C Mann, T N Armistead: Pregnancy and sexual behavior. In *The Sexual Experience*, B J Sadock, H I Kaplan, A M Freedman, editors, p 240. Williams & Wilkins, Baltimore, 1976. Used with permission.)

women require reassurance that those changes are not evidence of disease and that they will return to normal shortly after delivery—generally in four to six weeks.

## Psychopathology Associated with Pregnancy

Despite the tremendous physiological and psychological changes during pregnancy, most adult women without underlying psychopathology tolerate the process remarkably well. Teenage mothers do not fare as well as adults, and teenagers have an increased risk of suicide. Before the widespread availability of contraception and legal abortions, pregnant women had a high risk of suicide, especially when they were unwed and without social supports.

**Pica.** Pica is the repeated ingestion of nonnutritive substances, such as dirt, clay, starch, sand, and feces. It is an eating disorder most often seen in young children, but it is common in pregnant women in some subcultures, most notably among African-American women in the rural South, where the eating of clay or starch (for example, Argo) is seen in many pregnant women.

**Pseudocyesis.** Pseudocyesis is a rare condition in which a patient has the signs and symptoms of pregnancy—such as abdominal distention, breast enlargement, pigmentation, cessation of menses, and morning sickness. Pseudocyesis was first reported by Hippocrates; Mary Tudor, queen of England (1516–1558), allegedly had two episodes of pseudocyesis; and Sigmund Freud's patient Anna O. also suffered from pseudocyesis.

Pseudocyesis can occur at any age, and it has been reported in men, as well as in women. Male pseudocyesis is different from couvade, which occurs in some primitive cultures; in couvade, the father takes to his bed during or shortly after the birth of his child, as though he himself had given birth to the child.

The incidence of pseudocyesis has decreased over the past 50 years. It may be viewed as a psychosomatic disorder related to conversion symptoms. Unconscious mechanisms may include the restitution of a lost object or conflicts over gender role and generativity. The term "somatic compliance" is used to indicate that the body undergoes genuine physiological changes in response to unconscious needs and conflicts.

The treatment of pseudocyesis should be undertaken in concert with a gynecologist or a primary care physician. Negative results on pregnancy tests (plasma or urine HCG and abdominal ultrasound) often result in a reduction of symptoms when the results are communicated to the patient in a compassionate manner. Reality-based supportive psychotherapy is the treatment of choice. Some patients respond to antipsychotic medications if the belief is fixed and does not respond to reality testing.

## Hyperemesis Gravidarum

Hyperemesis gravidarum is differentiated from morning sickness in that vomiting is chronic, persistent, and frequent, leading to ketosis, acidosis, weight loss, and dehydration. Maternal or fetal death may ensue. The cause is unknown. Preexisting hepatorenal disease may predispose to the condition. Women with histories of anorexia nervosa or bulimia nervosa may be at risk.

## Antepartum (Prenatal) Care

In 1989, according to the U.S. Department of Health and Human Services, 21 percent of white mothers, 39.6 percent of black mothers, 42.1 percent of Native American mothers, and 40.5 percent of Hispanic mothers received no prenatal care during the first trimester. Mexican Americans, Native Americans, Alaskan natives, and African Americans are the four ethnic groups who are least likely to receive prenatal care.

Prenatal care should begin before conception, so that the prospective mother's health can be assessed. The mother can be examined to ensure fetal health and survival, and information about the use of drugs (including the interdiction of alcohol, tobacco, and coffee), exercise, and diet can be provided.

Once pregnancy is diagnosed, the mother's attitude toward the pregnancy should be assessed: Was the pregnancy planned? What are her values about having a child? Are children viewed as a burden or a joy? What are her husband's feelings? If she works, when does she plan to stop work? Does she plan to return to work; if so, when? How will a new baby affect the family's finances? Those and other questions can provide clues to the possible course of the pregnancy. Mothers who are under stress have a greater than usual risk of miscarriage, premature birth, and other complications. The risk of postpartum depression is increased if there is a history of depression in the mother or her family or if the mother had a previous postpartum psychiatric illness.

Prenatal care includes a variety of laboratory tests, such as a complete blood count (CBC), cultures for gonorrhea and chlamydia, Venereal Disease Research Laboratory (VDRL) tests, blood typing, rubella antibody tests, urinalysis, a Papanicolaou (Pap) test of the cervix, and a sickle cell screen for black patients. In general, follow-up visits are scheduled at one-month intervals until 28 weeks of pregnancy, at two-week intervals until 36 weeks, and then weekly until delivery. Danger signals requiring immediate obstetric attention include vaginal bleeding or other discharge, swelling of the face or the fingers, severe headache, blurred vision, abdominal pain, persistent vomiting, fever, dysuria, and changes in the frequency or the intensity of fetal movements.

## Infertility

Infertility is the inability of a couple to conceive after one year of coitus without the use of a contraceptive. In the United States, about 15 percent of married couples suffer from infertility. The cause is attributed to disorders in the woman in 60 percent of cases and to disorders in the man in 40 percent of cases. Tests in the infertility workup usually reveal the specific cause (Table 2.2–2).

The inability to have a child can produce severe psychological stress on one or both partners in the marriage. They may feel defective and undesirable, have low self-esteem, and become depressed. Some may grieve for the lost fantasized infant they can never have. No statistics are available on infertility as a precipitating factor in divorce, but it does play a role. In those couples in which one person (usually the woman) chooses adoption as an alternative choice but the other person (usually the man) is unwilling to do so, divorce may occur. Similarly, if one or both partners are unwilling to take advantage of assisted reproductive techniques (Table 2.2–3), the marriage may falter. Various clinics report that 20 to 50 percent of couples presently facing infertility can be helped.

Until recently, the onus for the failure to conceive was on the woman, and feelings of guilt, depression, and inadequacy frequently accompanied her perception of being barren. Current practice encourages simultaneous investigation of factors preventing conception in both the man and the woman. However, it is still frequently the woman who first presents for an infertility workup.

A thorough sexual history of the couple—including such factors as frequency of contact, erectile or ejaculatory dysfunction, and coital position—must be obtained. Frequently, conception is less likely simply because the woman rises to void, wash, or even douche immediately after coitus. Preference for coitus with the woman in the superior position is also not conducive to conception because of the lessened retention of semen.

A psychiatric evaluation of the couple may be advisable.

**Table 2.2–2**
**Tests in the Infertility Workup**

| Possible Cause | Test | Comments |
|---|---|---|
| Anovulation | Basal body temperature chart | Patient must do each morning |
| | Endometrial biopsy | Office procedure in late luteal phase |
| | Serum progesterone | Blood test |
| | Urinary ovulation detection kit | Home use at midcycle |
| Anatomical disorder | Hysterosalpingography | X-ray in proliferative phase |
| | Diagnostic laparoscopy | View external surfaces of internal structures |
| | Hysteroscopy | Visualize endometrial cavity |
| Abnormal spermatogenesis | Semen analysis | Normal value 20 million per mL, 2 mL volume, 60% motility |
| | Postcoital test | Midcycle timing |
| Immunological disorder | Antisperm antibodies | Male and female tested |

Table from C R B Beckmann, F W Ling, B M Barzansky, G W Bates, W N P Herbert, D M Laube, R P Smith: *Obstetrics and Gynecology for Medical Students*, p 353. Williams & Wilkins, Baltimore, 1992. Used with permission.

**Table 2.2–3**
**Assisted Reproductive Techniques**

| Method | Comments |
|---|---|
| Ovulation-inducing agents (clomiphene citrate) | Stimulates ovulation; may produce multiple births; used with anovulation or other endocrine problems |
| Induction of spermatogenesis | Spermatogenesis in about 20 percent of men with clomiphene may be stimulated |
| Artificial insemination | Donor sperm is injected into the uterine cavity or the fallopian tubes; the sperm of the husband may be used if healthy |
| Gamete intrafallopian transfer (GIFT) | Transfer of collected oocytes and sperm into the fallopian tubes; zygote may also be transferred (ZIFT); used for infertility from endometriosis |
| In vitro fertilization and embryo transfer (IVF-ET) | Transfer of developing embryos into the uterus after extracorporeal incubation of collected sperm with oocytes retrieved by laporoscopic surgery or by ultrasound-guided transvaginal aspiration; used when there is occlusion of the fallopian tubes |
| Surrogate mother | Surrogate mother may donate oocyte to host mother or may herself be inseminated and carry the baby to term; it is a highly controversial technique with unclear legal ramifications |

Data in part from Virginia Susman, M.D.: *Pregnancy* in *Behavioral Science for Medical Students*, F S Sierles, editor, p 119. Williams & Wilkins, Baltimore, 1993. Used with permission.

Marital disharmony or emotional conflicts around intimacy, sexual relations, or parenting roles can directly affect endocrine function and such physiological processes as erection, ejaculation, and ovulation. There is no evidence for any simple, causal relation between stress and infertility.

The stress of infertility itself in a couple who want children can lead to emotional disturbance. When a preexisting conflict gives rise to problems of identity, self-esteem, and guilt, the disturbance may be severe. It may manifest itself through regression; extreme dependence on the physician, the mate, or a parent; diffuse anger; impulsive behavior; or depression. The problem is further complicated if hormone therapy is being used to treat the infertility, because the therapy may temporarily increase depression in some patients.

People who have difficulty conceiving experience shock, disbelief, and a general sense of helplessness, and they develop an understandable preoccupation with the problem. Involvement in the infertility workup and the development of expertise about infertility can be a constructive defense against feelings of inadequacy and the humiliating, sometimes painful

aspects of the workup itself. Worries about attractiveness and sexual desirability are common. Partners may feel ugly or impotent, and episodes of sexual dysfunction and loss of desire are reported. Those problems are aggravated if a couple is scheduling their sexual relations according to temperature charts.

In addition, they are dealing with a narcissistic blow to their senses of femininity and masculinity. An infertile partner may fear abandonment or feel that the spouse is remaining in the relationship resentfully. Single people who are aware of their own infertility may shy away from relationships for fear of being rejected once their "defect" is known. Infertile people may have particular difficulty in their adult relationships with their own parents. The identification and the equality that come from sharing the experience of parenthood must be replaced by internal reserves and other generative aspects of their lives.

Professional intervention may be necessary to help infertile couples ventilate their feelings and go through the process of mourning their lost biological functions and the children they cannot have. Couples who remain infertile must cope with an actual loss. Couples who decide not to pursue parenthood may develop a renewed sense of love, dedication, and identity as a pair. Others may need help in exploring the options of husband or donor insemination, laboratory implantation, and adoption.

## Perinatal Loss

Perinatal loss is defined as death sometime between the 20th week of gestation and the first month of life. It includes spontaneous abortion (miscarriage), fetal demise, stillbirth, and neonatal death. In previous years, the intense bond between the expectant or new parent and the fetus or neonate was underestimated. Perinatal loss is now recognized as a significant trauma for both parents. Parents who experience such a loss go through a period of mourning much like that experienced when any loved one is lost.

Intrauterine fetal death can occur at any time during the pregnancy and is an emotionally traumatic experience. In the early months of pregnancy, the mother is usually unaware of fetal death and learns of it only from her doctor. Later in pregnancy, after fetal movements and heart tones have been present, the mother may be able to detect fetal demise. When given the diagnosis of fetal death, most women want the dead fetus removed; depending on the trimester, labor may be induced, or the patient may have to wait for the spontaneous expulsion of the uterine contents. Many couples view sexual relations during the period of waiting as not only undesirable but psychologically unacceptable.

Loss can also occur when a child is stillborn or when an antenatal diagnosis detects an abnormal fetus and an abortion is induced. As mentioned above, attachment to the unborn child begins before the birth, and grief and mourning can occur after a loss at any time. The grief experienced after a third-trimester loss, however, is generally greater than that experienced after a first-trimester loss. Some parents do not wish to view a stillborn child, and their wishes should be respected. Others wish to hold the stillborn, which can assist the mourning process. A subsequent pregnancy may diminish overt feelings of grief but does not eliminate the need to mourn. So-called replacement children are at risk for overprotection and future emotional problems.

## High-Risk Pregnancy

Women who become pregnant before age 16 or after age 35 have higher rates of maternal and infant mortality than do women age 20 to 29, who have the lowest rates. Patients younger than age 16 have the most complications. Women over age 35 are prone to eclampsia, hypertension of pregnancy, uterine leiomyomas, and chromosomal abnormalities. The risk of trisomy syndromes (for example, Down's syndrome) increases about seven times from age 35 to 45. In addition, women over 35 are more often delivered by cesarean section than vaginally in an effort to decrease infant morbidity. Other causes of high-risk pregnancy include metabolic disorders (for example, diabetes, cardiovascular diseases, and renal disease) and complicated pregnancy histories (for example, previous stillbirth or preterm infants).

## FAMILY PLANNING AND CONTRACEPTION

In today's society, with more and more women joining the work force because of either economic necessity or the desire for self-actualization and with relative freedom of sexual expression, postponing or avoiding pregnancy assumes an important role in the lives of many women. *Family planning* is the process of choosing when and if to bear children. *Contraception* is the prevention of fecundation or fertilization of the ovum; it is just one form of family planning.

The choice of a contraceptive method is a complex decision involving both the woman and her partner. Factors influencing the decision include the woman's age and medical condition, her access to medical care, and the couple's religious beliefs and need for spontaneity. The woman and her partner can weigh the risks and the benefits of the various forms of contraception and make their decision on the basis of their current life-style and needs. The success of contraceptive technology has enabled career-minded couples to delay childbearing into their 30s and 40s. Such a delay, however, may increase infertility problems. Consequently, many women with careers feel their biological clocks ticking and plan to have children in their early 30s to avoid the risk of not being able to have them at all. Table 2.2–4 provides information on current methods of contraception, and Figure 2.2–2 shows some contraceptive modalities.

## Induced Abortion

Induced abortion is the planned termination of a pregnancy. About 1.4 million abortions are performed in the United States each year—346 abortions for every 1,000 live births. In Western nations, most women who obtain abortions are young, unmarried, and primiparous; in underdeveloped nations, abortion is most common among married women with two or more children.

Fifty percent of abortions are performed under 8 weeks of gestation, 25 percent between 9 and 10 weeks, and 10 percent between 11 and 12 weeks. The remainder occur after 13 weeks, with 1 percent occurring after 21 weeks. Table 2.2–5 summarizes the most common abortion techniques.

Abortion has become an important philosophical and political issue in the United States; the country is sharply divided between pro-choice (pro-abortion) and pro-life (antiabortion) factions. Recent years have seen angry confrontations between antiabortion demonstrators and the patients and staffs of abortion clinics. The atmosphere of moral condemnation and intimidation may make the decision to terminate a pregnancy difficult. Nonetheless, recent studies have shown that most women who undergo a termination of pregnancy—particularly if they do so before the 12th week of gestation—do not suffer significant psychological sequelae. In fact, most of the women experience a sense of relief and have less of an emotional reaction than do those who maintain the pregnancy and give the baby up for adoption.

Second-trimester abortions are more psychologically traumatic than first-trimester abortions. The most common reason for late abortions is the discovery (through amniocentesis or ultrasound) of a severe abnormality in the fetus. Thus, late abortions usually involve the loss of a wanted child with whom the mother has already formed a bond.

Before the legalization of abortion in the United States in 1973, many women sought illegal abortions, often performed by untrained practitioners under unsterile condi-

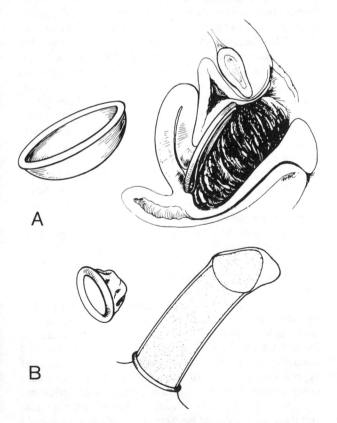

**Figure 2.2–2** Pictorial representation of certain contraceptive modalities. **A.** The intravaginal diaphragm and its correct position as viewed during coition. **B.** The condom before and after being unrolled onto the erect penis.

**Table 2.2–4**
**Current Methods of Contraception**

| Type | Method of Action | Effectiveness | Advantages | Disadvantages | Potential Complications |
|------|------------------|---------------|------------|---------------|-------------------------|
| Fertility awareness method (FAM); rhythm | Timed-abstinence; couple abstains 7 days before and after ovulation | Low | No cost or health risks; always available; no professional help required | Imposed coital timing (lack of spontaneity); continuous recording of menstrual cycle necessary; must learn to take basal body temperature and check cervical mucus | Essentially none |
| Withdrawal; coitus interruptus | Prevention of insemination | Low (but theoretically high) | No cost; always available; no professional help required | Regular coital use required; requires considerable attention and control by man, which may interfere with pleasure for both partners | Essentially none |
| Diaphragm | Rubber dome inserted into vagina; works as sperm barrier; used with spermicidal jelly; must be left in place for 6 hours after coitus (Figure 2.2–2) | Medium to high | Inexpensive | Regular coital use required; possible interference with enjoyment; requires professional fitting; not anatomically adaptable to everyone; repeated intercourse requires new application of spermicide | Essentially none but diaphragm can dislodge during coitus; used by 3.4 percent of women |
| Cervical cap | Rubber cap covers only cervical os; works as sperm barrier; works best with spermicidal jelly | Medium to high | Inexpensive; does not cover anterior vaginal wall, so may be more pleasurable for both partners; allows for repeated coitus without new application of spermicide | More difficult to fit and to insert than diaphragm; cannot be used if cervical lesions present | Essentially none but may dislodge during coitus |
| Contraceptive sponge | Polyurethane sponge with spermicide inserted into vagina before intercourse; must be left in place for 6 hours after coitus | Medium | Easy to insert into vagina; vaginal walls not covered; must be left in place for 6 hours after intercourse; can be used for 24 hours with repeated coitus | Must be removed after 24 hours or infection can develop | Chemical sensitivity to spermicide; sponge may break |

*Continued*

**Table 2.2–4**
*continued*

| Type | Method of Action | Effectiveness | Advantages | Disadvantages | Potential Complications |
|---|---|---|---|---|---|
| Intravaginal foams, creams, jellies, and suppositories | Spermicidal | Low | Inexpensive; generally available; most effective when used with condom | Regular coital use required; possible messiness; possible interference with enjoyment | Essentially none; possible allergies |
| Condom | Sperm barrier (a female condom made of polyurethane is placed in the vaginal space before coitus and acts as a sperm barrier) (Figure 2.2–2) | Medium | Inexpensive; latex condom protects against AIDS; generally available; no professional help required; decreased acquisition of coitally transmitted diseases | Regular coital use required; possible interference with enjoyment | Essentially none; may tear; 3 to 1,000 defective manufacture rate; allergy to latex is rare; used by 12.6 percent of couples |
| Intrauterine device (IUD) | Unknown (possibly prevents zygote implantation) | Medium | Inexpensive; only single decision required; not coitally connected; does not interfere with pleasure | Possible increase in bleeding and cramping; requires professional insertion; annual checkup required | Uterine perforation, pelvic infection, spontaneous expulsion; used by 10.2 percent of women |
| Oral (hormonal) | Prevention of ovulation (possible interference with sperm mobility); two types: (1) combined progesterone-estrogen, (2) progesterone only (minipill) | High (most commonly used method) | Inexpensive; potential absolute efficiency; not coitally connected | Possible side effects; daily ingestion; requires professional visit and prescription | Thromboembolism, hypertension, depression; used by 36.6 percent of women |
| Progestin implants (Norplant) | Suppresses ovulation; high change in cervical mucus | High | Effective for 5 years; no interference with spontaneity or pleasure | Requires minor surgery (local anesthesia) to implant and to remove | Menstrual irregularities, weight gain, headache |
| Postcoital hormonal method (RU–486) | Prevention of implantation of fertilized ovum | High | Cited as ideal contraceptive; can be used after coitus without contraception, after rape and incest | Not yet legal in United States, developed and used in France | Unknown |
| Male sterilization (vasectomy) | Surgical interruption of vas deferens so that sperm cannot travel from testes to penis | High | Failure very rare; 20-minute office procedure | Morbidity in 1 to 2% of patients includes infections, clots | Can be reversed in only 80% of cases; rare neurotic impotence reaction; used by 10.4% of men |

**Table 2.2–4**
*continued*

| Type | Method of Action | Effectiveness | Advantages | Disadvantages | Potential Complications |
|---|---|---|---|---|---|
| Female sterilization | Tubal ligation prevents transport of oocyte | High | Almost 100% protection; no impairment of sexual function or pleasure | More complex procedure than vasectomy; reversal is complicated and difficult | Surgical morbidity; used by 13.6 percent of women |

Table adapted and modified after data by Eugene C. Sandberg, M.D. Effectiveness is rated roughly as follows: low, more than 20 pregnancies for 100 women-years of use; medium, 1 to 20 pregnancies for 100 women-years of use; high, less than 1 pregnancy for 100 women-years of use.

tions. Considerable morbidity and mortality were associated with those illegal abortions. In addition, some women who were denied abortion chose suicide over continuation of an unwanted pregnancy. If the woman is forced to carry the fetus to term, the risk of infanticide, abandonment, and neglect of unwanted newborns is increased.

Abortion is also a significant experience for men. If the man has a significant relationship with the pregnant woman, he may wish to play an active role in the abortion, accompanying her to the hospital or abortion clinic and providing emotional support. Fathers may experience considerable grief over the termination of a wanted pregnancy. In general, however, most men are passive in preventing the unwanted pregnancy and in planning for and learning about abortion.

### Sterilization

Sterilization is a procedure that prevents a man or a woman from producing offspring. In a woman the procedure is usually salpingectomy, ligation of the fallopian tubes. It is a hospital procedure with low morbidity and low mortality. A man is usually sterilized by vasectomy, excision of part of the vas deferens. It is a simpler procedure than a salpingectomy and is performed in the physician's office. Voluntary sterilization, especially vasectomy, has become the most popular form of birth control in couples married for more than 10 years.

A small proportion of patients who elect sterilization may suffer a neurotic poststerilization syndrome. It may manifest itself through hypochondriasis, pain, loss of libido, sexual unresponsiveness, depression, and concerns about masculinity or femininity. One study of a group of women who regretted sterilization found they had chosen the procedure while in poor relationships, frequently with abusing husbands. Cases of regret are most prevalent when a new relationship has formed and the sterilized person wishes to bear a child with a new partner.

Psychiatric consultation can frequently separate patients seeking sterilization for psychotic or neurotic reasons from those who have made the decision after some time or thought.

Involuntary sterilization procedures have been performed to prevent the reproduction of traits considered genetically undesirable. There have been statutes allowing for the sterilization of hereditary criminals, sex offenders, syphilitic patients, mentally retarded persons, and epileptic patients. Some of those statutes have been declared unconstitutional. In recent years human rights and civil liberties groups have been challenging the legality and ethical standing of such sterilization procedures with increasing vigor.

The operative procedures for sterilization have assumed less importance than in the past because of the advent of contraceptives and the relative ease of obtaining abortions. Nonetheless, sterilization procedures are still chosen by men and women who, for a variety of reasons, want to permanently end their ability to produce children.

**Vasectomy.** In a vasectomy the man's vas deferens is ligated bilaterally, and a segment is removed. The procedure is done under local anesthesia in a doctor's office and takes about 20 minutes. The procedure can be reversed in 80 to 90 percent of cases. A few men experience a postvasectomy syndrome, consisting of decreased libido, impotence, identity confusion, and signs of depression. However, in such cases, most were previously depressed. In most cases of male sterilization, no negative psychological sequelae are experienced.

**Tubal ligation.** In women the fallopian tubes are cauterized by laparotomy. Reversal of the procedure is far less effective than is vasectomy in men. For a small proportion of women, a poststerilization syndrome consisting of hypochondria, pain, loss of libido, and doubt about female identity may develop. When that occurs, the woman generally had a preexisting psychopathological state.

Psychiatric consultation is of value before sterilization to evaluate the person's motivation for the procedure (for example, being coerced by a partner) and to rule out preexisting psychopathology, such as depression, that may lead to postoperative syndrome.

## CHILDBIRTH

The process of childbirth (parturition) is initiated by a host of complex hormonal and other biological events. Figure 2.2–3 gives an overview of the process, which is divided into three stages of labor.

According to the U.S. Department of Health and Human Services, 4,179,000 babies were born in the United States in 1990; the birth rate was 15.9 per 1,000 population. Advances in prenatal and perinatal care reduced the infant death rate to 8.9 per 1,000 live births in 1991 (down from 9.1 infant deaths per 1,000 live births in 1990 and 9.8 infant deaths per 1,000 live births in 1989). The United States ranks 22nd in infant mortality among the industrialized nations, according to the statistics for 1989. The fertility

**Table 2.2–5**
**Abortion Techniques**

| Type | Benefits | Risks |
| --- | --- | --- |
| Cervical dilation and evacuation of uterine contents by curettage or vacuum aspiration | Most commonly performed procedure for termination of pregnancy; can be done before 16 weeks gestation | Uterine perforation<br>Cervical incompetence<br>Adhesions<br>Hemorrhage<br>Infection<br>Incomplete removal of fetus and placenta |
| Menstrual aspiration (miniabortion) | Can be done within 1 to 3 weeks of missed period | Implanted zygote not removed<br>Uterine perforation (rare)<br>Failure to recognize ectopic pregnancy |
| Medical induction (cervical dilation with laminaria followed by high dose of IV oxytocin) | Can be used for second-trimester abortions | Water intoxication<br>Rupture of uterus, cervix, or isthmus |
| Intra-amniotic hyperosmotic solutions (salting out) | Can be used for second-trimester abortions | Hyperosmolar crisis<br>Heart failure<br>Peritonitis<br>Hemorrhage<br>Water intoxication<br>Myometrial necrosis<br>Accounts for only 2% of abortions |
| Prostaglandins (applied intravaginally, cervically, or intra-amniotically) | Noninvasive procedure | Expulsion of live fetus |

rate was 67.3 live births per 1,000 women aged 15 to 44 years, which is an increase over previous years. Provisional data by the U.S. Public Health Service indicate a continuation of an upward trend in the fertility rate, based on the number of live births per 1,000 women. The largest increases (6 to 8 percent) are occurring in the birth rates for teenagers and for women aged 35 to 44 years.

The overwhelming majority of babies are born in hospitals with physicians in attendance, but freestanding birthing centers with access to a hospital are an alternative for some couples. High-risk babies are best delivered in a hospital with a perinatal center, since they face the risk of neonatal morbidity and mortality.

The number of babies born by cesarean section has increased steadily—from about 5 percent in the 1960s to about 20 percent in the 1980s. Some of the increase is the result of physicians' fear of malpractice suits. That fear is understandable, because malpractice suits are emotionally traumatic for both patient and physician. Prolonged labor, which is sometimes hazardous to the fetus, is also avoided with a cesarean section. Analgesic drugs given to the mother during labor enter the fetal bloodstream and sedate the newborn infant. A drug that depresses the mother's nervous system affects the infant's sucking reflex, sometimes for a few days.

## Lamaze Method

Also known as natural childbirth, the Lamaze method originated with the French obstetrician Fernand Lamaze. Mothers are fully conscious during labor and delivery, and no analgesic or anesthetic is used. The expectant mother and father attend special classes, during which they are taught relaxation and breathing exercises designed to facilitate the birth process. Women who undergo such training often report minimal pain during labor and delivery.

## Premature Births

Childbirth is a potentially hazardous time for both mother and child. Although most premature infants develop normally, a premature birth increases the risk of dysfunction. About 30 percent of premature infants suffer from one or more of the following: mental retardation, behavior problems, emotional disorders, blindness, hearing deficits, movement disorders, and sensorimotor problems, such as dyslexia. Also, premature babies are at a greater than usual risk for child abuse. Prematurity occurs when the birth weight is under 2,500 grams or when the gestation period is less than 34 weeks. Prematurity is correlated with low socioeconomic status, poor maternal nu-

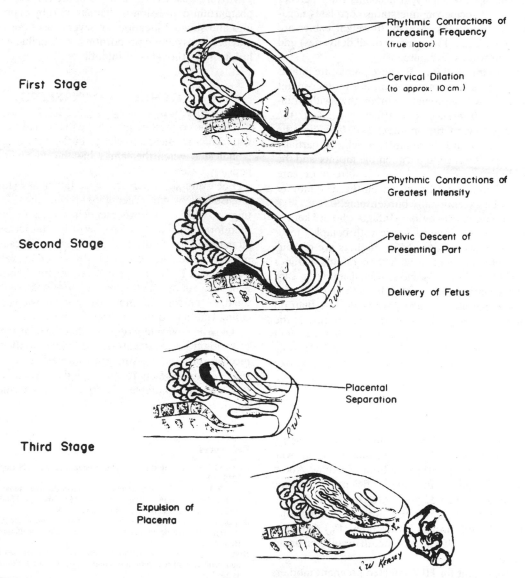

First Stage

Rhythmic Contractions of Increasing Frequency (true labor)

Cervical Dilation (to approx. 10 cm.)

Second Stage

Rhythmic Contractions of Greatest Intensity

Pelvic Descent of Presenting Part

Delivery of Fetus

Third Stage

Placental Separation

Expulsion of Placenta

**Figure 2.2–3.** Stages of labor. Prodromal events: Usually and fairly consistently, labor is preceded by the loss of a blood-tinged mucous plug from within the endocervix. That loss occurs in procursive relation to silent cervical effacement and cervical dilation. The loss of the cervical barrier to ascending infection usually presages the imminence of labor and is referred to as a bloody show. Occasionally, the first stage is preceded by premature rupture of the membrane. First stage: The first stage of labor is signaled by uterine contractions of a progressively frequent and regular order. Unlike false labor, true labor is characterized by contractions that are productive of increasing cervical effacement and dilation. Initially of short duration and occurring as much as 20 minutes apart, the intervals between contractions steadily decrease until the contractions recur every three to five minutes. Complete cervical dilation (10 cm) marks the end of the first stage of labor. The length of the first stage of labor is highly variable, depending primarily on the progression and the quality of labor. It is longer with primiparas than with multiparas, usually by some four to five hours. The usual primipara can ordinarily count on her first stage of labor lasting 12 to 14 hours. Second stage: The second stage is defined as that portion of labor transpiring between complete cervical dilation and the birth of the baby. Typically, the contractions during the second stage are of greatest frequency, intensity, and duration. The contractions occur every two to three minutes and last about one minute. During the second stage, the patient, with the descent of the presenting part through the completely dilated cervix and into the birth canal, begins using her abdominal muscles to bear down during each contraction. Her efforts are, in time, followed by crowning (appearance of the widest diameter of the presenting part through the vulvar ring) and by delivery. Some 95 percent of vaginal deliveries are vertex, with only 3 to 4 percent being breech and less than 1 percent being of the most unusual variety, such as face presentation. The second stage of labor is longer for primiparas than for multiparas. On the average, it entails a matter of an hour for primiparas; for multiparas, it may entail only a matter of minutes, usually not more than 30. Third stage: The terminal stage of labor begins immediately after the delivery of the infant and ends with the delivery of the placenta. It is generally of short duration, lasting less than 10 minutes. (Figure from E C Mann, T N Armistead: Pregnancy and sexual behavior. In *The Sexual Experience,* B J Sadock, H I Kaplan, A M Freedman, editors, p 242. Williams & Wilkins, Baltimore, 1976. Used with permission.)

trition, and teenage pregnancy; it accounts for 7 percent of all births. High socioeconomic status correlates negatively with infant mortality. Low-birth-weight babies are most common in blacks (13.2 percent of all deliveries) and least common in whites (5.7 percent).

**Mother-infant interaction.** Because premature infants have a weakened sensorimotor system, less mother-infant interaction occurs with a premature infant than with a full-term baby. That difference may affect *attachment* (the infant's feelings toward the mother) and *bonding* (the mother's feelings toward the infant), which are partially dependent on the interaction between the mother and the infant. In addition, premature babies require more care than full-term babies, and the strain on the new mother and father can be exceptionally burdensome.

**Neonatal intensive care units.** Infants who are kept in neonatal units receive intensive care with complex technological life-support systems. Most mothers are encouraged to have physical contact with their infants within a few hours of birth, but, in some neonatal intensive care units, mothers may not be able to hold their babies for several days. Generally, fathers participate less than do mothers, and both have little to do because the care of the infant is carried out by the neonatal intensive care unit staff. If possible, parents should be involved in nursing tasks and should be allowed to touch, clean, and stroke the neonates.

## AIDS

Mothers infected with the human immunodeficiency virus (HIV) can transmit the virus to their children, who can be infected in utero or through breast feeding. About 85 percent of acquired immune deficiency syndrome (AIDS) in children under 13 are contracted from infected mothers. In America most infected mothers are nonwhites who became infected through intravenous (IV) drug use. AIDS is among the top 10 causes of death in children under 5 years of age.

Since no treatment for HIV-infected pregnant mothers or infants is available, prevention is the best course. Education about the dangers of coitus without condom protection and the use of shared needles by substance abusers is essential.

### Postpartum Depression and Postpartum Psychosis

About 20 to 40 percent of women report some emotional disturbance or cognitive dysfunction in the postpartum period. Many experience postpartum blues, a normal state of sadness, dysphoria, frequent tearfulness, and clinging dependence. Those feelings, which may last several days, have been ascribed to the woman's rapid change in hormonal levels, the stress of childbirth, and her awareness of the increased responsibility that motherhood brings.

A similar syndrome has been described in the father who has mood changes during his wife's pregnancy or after the baby is born. Such a father is affected by several factors: added responsibility, diminished sexual outlet, decreased attention from his wife, and the belief that the child is a binding force in an unsatisfactory marriage.

In rare cases (1 to 2 in 1,000 deliveries) a woman's postpartum depression is characterized by depressed feelings and suicidal ideation. In severe cases the depression may reach psychotic proportions, with hallucinations, delusions, and thoughts of infanticide.

## GENETIC COUNSELING

Genetic counseling provides patients and their families with direct medical knowledge in the field of genetics. It is indicated when the family has the possibility of a genetically based disorder.

For example, a person whose father has Huntington's disease may be concerned about having the disease. Huntington's disease follows mendelian rules of inheritance; therefore, a person whose parent has the disorder has a 50 percent chance of having the disease. Because the age of onset varies, the longer one lives without becoming ill, the lower is the risk. A chemical test for determining the gene carriers of Huntington's disease was recently developed, so persons can now use that knowledge when deciding whether to have children.

Genetic counseling requires that the clinician be aware of a patient's level of maturity, individual conflicts, defense mechanisms, and ego strengths and weaknesses. The counselor has to be ready to deal with depression, anger, anxiety, and other complex emotions related to the issues at hand.

**References**

Annas G J: Protecting the liberty of pregnant patients. N Engl J Med *316*: 1213, 1987.
Apfel R J, Mazor M D: Psychiatry and reproductive medicine. In *Comprehensive Textbook of Psychiatry*, ed 5, H I Kaplan, B J Sadock, editors, p 1331. Williams & Wilkins, Baltimore, 1989.
Briggs G G, Freeman R K, Yaffee S J: *Drugs in Pregnancy and Lactation: A Reference Guide to Fetal and Neonatal Risk*. Williams & Wilkins, Baltimore, 1986.
Bryan J W, Freed F W: Abortion research: Attitudes, sexual behavior, and problems in a community college population. J Youth Adoles *22*: 1, 1993.
Cath S H, Gurwitt A R, Ross J M, editors: *Father and Child; Developmental and Clinical Perspectives*. Little, Brown, Boston, 1982.
Colman A, Colman L: *Pregnancy: The Psychological Experience.* Seabury, New York, 1973.
Connolly K J, Edelmann R J, Cooke I D, Robson J: The impact of infertility on psychological functioning. J Psychosom Res *36*: 459, 1992.
Cook R J: Abortion laws and policies: Challenges and opportunities. Int J Gynecol Obstet *3* (Suppl): 61, 1989.
Friedman R, Gradstein B: *Surviving Pregnancy Loss.* Little, Brown, Boston, 1982.
Group for the Advancement of Psychiatry: *The Joys and Sorrows of Parenthood.* Scribner's, New York, 1973.
Hechtman L: Teenage mothers and their children: Risks and problems: A review. Can J Psychiatry *34*: 569, 1989.
Hoffman N S: Stress factors related to antenatal testing during high-risk pregnancy. J Perinatol *10*: 195, 1990.
Mahler M S, Pine F, Bergman A: *The Psychological Birth of the Human Infant.* Basic Books, New York, 1975.
Matthews K A, Rodin J: Pregnancy alters blood pressure responses to psychological and physical challenge. Psychophysiology *29*: 232, 1992.
McCormick M C, Brooks-Gunn J, Shorter T, Holmes J H, Wallace C Y, Heagarty M C: Factors associated with smoking in low-income pregnant women: Relationship to birth weight, stressful life events, social support, health behaviors and mental distress. J Clin Epidemiol *43*: 441, 1990.
Molfese V J, Holcomb L C: Predicting learning and other developmental disabilities: Assessment of reproductive and caretaking variables. Birth Defects *25*: 1, 1989.
Rofe Y, Blittner M, Lewin I: Emotional experiences during the three trimesters of pregnancy. J Clin Psychol *49*: 3, 1993.

Rosett H L, Weiner L: *Alcohol and the Fetus: A Clinical Perspective.* Oxford University Press, New York, 1984.

Youngs D D, Ehrhardt A A: *Psychosomatic Obstetrics and Gynecology.* Appleton-Century-Crofts, New York, 1980.

Zhang J, Cai W: Risk factors associated with antepartum fetal death. Early Hum Dev *28:* 193, 1992.

# 2.3 / Prenatal Period, Infancy, and Childhood

The commonly accepted stages of early development are the prenatal period, infancy (birth to about 15 months), the toddler period (15 months to 2½ years), the preschool period (2½ to 6 years), and the middle years (6 to 12 years). Those stages are a continuum along which development proceeds; after birth there is rarely a clear-cut division between them.

Arnold Gesell described developmental schedules that outline the qualitative sequence of motor, adaptive, and personal-social behavior of the child from birth to 6 years. The milestones of development allow for a comparison of the development of a particular child and of a normative standard. Gesell's schedules are widely used in both pediatrics and child psychiatry. Table 2.3–1 details the sequence of normal behavioral development from birth to 6 years.

To fully understand development, one must be aware of the viewpoints of the major theorists. Sigmund Freud took a psychoanalytic stance. Erik Erikson modified that stance into a psychosocial view of eight stages or life chal-

**Table 2.3–1**
**Landmarks of Normal Behavioral Development**

| Age | Motor and Sensory Behavior | Adaptive Behavior | Personal and Social Behavior |
|---|---|---|---|
| Birth to 4 weeks | Hand to mouth reflex, grasping reflex<br>Rooting reflex (puckering lips in response to perioral stimulation), Moro reflex (digital extension when startled); sucking reflex, Babinski reflex (toes spread when sole of foot is touched)<br>Differentiates sounds (orients to human voice) and sweet and sour tastes<br>Visual tracking<br>Fixed focal distance of 8 inches<br>Makes alternating crawling movements<br>Moves head laterally when placed in prone position | Anticipatory feeding-approach behavior at 4 days<br>Responds to sound of rattle and bell<br>Regards moving objects momentarily | Responsiveness to mother's face, eyes, and voice within first few hours of life<br>Endogenous smile<br>Independent play (until 2 years)<br>Quiets when picked up<br>Impassive face |
| 4 weeks | Tonic neck reflex positions predominate<br>Hands fisted<br>Head sags but can hold head erect for a few seconds<br>Visual fixation, stereoscopic vision (12 weeks) | Follows moving objects to the midline<br>Shows no interest and drops objects immediately | Regards face and diminishes activity<br>Responds to speech<br>Smiles preferentially to mother |
| 16 weeks | Symmetrical postures predominate<br>Holds head balanced<br>Head lifted 90 degrees when prone on forearm<br>Visual accommodation | Follows a slowly moving object well<br>Arms activate on sight of dangling object | Spontaneous social smile (exogenous)<br>Aware of strange situations |
| 28 weeks | Sits steadily, leaning forward on hands<br>Bounces actively when placed in standing position | One-hand approach and grasp of toy<br>Bangs and shakes rattle<br>Transfers toys | Takes feet to mouth<br>Pats mirror image<br>Starts to imitate mother's sounds and actions |
| 40 weeks | Sits alone with good coordination<br>Creeps<br>Pulls self to standing position<br>Points with index finger | Matches two objects at midline<br>Attempts to imitate scribble | Separation anxiety manifest when taken away from mother<br>Responds to social play, such as pat-a-cake and peekaboo<br>Feeds self cracker and holds own bottle |
| 52 weeks | Walks with one hand held<br>Stands alone briefly | Seeks novelty | Cooperates in dressing |

*Continued*

**Table 2.3–1**
*continued*

| Age | Motor and Sensory Behavior | Adaptive Behavior | Personal and Social Behavior |
|---|---|---|---|
| 15 months | Toddles<br>Creeps up stairs | | Points or vocalizes wants<br>Throws objects in play or refusal |
| 18 months | Coordinated walking, seldom falls<br>Hurls ball<br>Walks up stairs with one hand held | Builds a tower of three or four cubes<br>Scribbles spontaneously and imitates a writing stroke | Feeds self in part, spills<br>Pulls toy on string<br>Carries or hugs a special toy, such as a doll<br>Imitates some behavioral patterns with slight delay |
| 2 years | Runs well, no falling<br>Kicks large ball<br>Goes up and down stairs alone<br>Fine motor skills increase | Builds a tower of six or seven cubes<br>Aligns cubes, imitating train<br>Imitates vertical and circular strokes<br>Develops original behaviors | Pulls on simple garment<br>Domestic mimicry<br>Refers to self by name<br>Says "no" to mother<br>Separation anxiety begins to diminish<br>Organized demonstrations of love and protest<br>Parallel play (plays side by side but does not interact with other children) |
| 3 years | Rides tricycle<br>Jumps from bottom steps<br>Alternates feet going up stairs | Builds tower of 9 or 10 cubes<br>Imitates a three-cube bridge<br>Copies a circle and a cross | Puts on shoes<br>Unbuttons buttons<br>Feeds self well<br>Understands taking turns |
| 4 years | Walks down stairs one step to a tread<br>Stands on one foot for five to eight seconds | Copies a cross<br>Repeats four digits<br>Counts three objects with correct pointing | Washes and dries own face<br>Brushes teeth<br>Associative or joint play (plays cooperatively with other children) |
| 5 years | Skips, using feet alternately<br>Usually has complete sphincter control<br>Fine coordination improves | Copies a square<br>Draws a recognizable man with a head, a body, limbs<br>Counts 10 objects accurately | Dresses and undresses self<br>Prints a few letters<br>Plays competitive exercise games |
| 6 years | Rides two-wheel bicycle | Prints name<br>Copies triangle | Ties shoelaces |

Table adapted from Arnold Gesell, M.D., and Stella Chess, M.D.

lenges. Jean Piaget's approach was cognitive. For the best understanding of human development, one should have a working knowledge of all three theories. They are not mutually exclusive; they seek to explain different dimensions of psychological growth; by accepting all three theories, one gains a rich appreciation of the developing child.

## PRENATAL PERIOD

After implantation, the egg begins to divide; at that time it is known as an *embryo*. Growth and development occur at a rapid pace; by the end of eight weeks, the shape is recognizably human, and it is known as a *fetus*.

Any view of mental disorders must consider the utero-placental environment of the fetus and its neurobiological substrate. The fetus maintains an internal equilibrium that interacts continually with the intrauterine environment with variable effects.

Prenatal events have great relevance to psychiatry because the development of the embryo and the fetus can go awry for a variety of causes and can affect future behavior in a variety of ways. For example, the person's genes exert their effects throughout life. By birth the person may

have a predisposition at the genetic level to the development of an abnormal state that can appear at any time during the life span. A predisposition to anxiety may be present because of a cerebral disorganization in utero that manifests itself in perceptual motor dysfunctions and impulse control problems later in life. Genetic factors may have delayed effects: Huntington's disease first becomes manifest in middle adulthood, and life events play no part in the development of the disease.

In general, most disorders are multifactorial—the result of a combination of effects, some of which may be additive. Damage at the fetal stage is usually more global than is damage after birth; rapidly growing organs are the most vulnerable. Boys are more vulnerable to developmental damage than are girls, and geneticists recognize the fact that, in humans and animals, females show a propensity for greater biological vigor than do males, possibly because of the female's second X chromosome.

### Fetal Life

A great deal of biological activity occurs in utero. A fetus is involved in a variety of behaviors that are necessary for adaptation outside the womb. For example, the fetus practices sucking behaviors by inserting its thumb or finger in its mouth; it folds and unfolds its body and eventually assumes a position in which its occiput is in an anterior vertex position, which is the position in which it exits the uterus. Some workers believe that the fetus determines the onset of labor; when it is psychobiologically ready to be born, it is born.

**Behavior.** Mothers are extraordinarily sensitive to prenatal motoric behavior. They describe their unborn babies as active or passive, as kicking vigorously or rolling around, as quiet when the mothers are active but as kicking as soon as the mothers try to rest.

The mother usually detects fetal movements at 16 to 20 weeks into the pregnancy. The fetus can be artificially set into total body motion by in utero stimulation of its ventral skin surfaces by the 14th week. The fetus may be able to hear by the 18th week, and it responds to loud noises with muscle contractions, movements, and an increased heart rate. Smell and taste are also developed at that time, and the fetus responds to substances that may be injected into the amniotic sac, such as contrast medium. Some reflexes present at birth exist in utero, including the grasp reflex, which appears at 17 weeks; Moro (startle) reflex, which appears at 25 weeks; and the sucking reflex, which appears at about 28 weeks.

**Development of the nervous system.** The nervous system arises from the neural plate, which is a dorsal ectodermal thickening that appears at about the 16th day of gestation. By the sixth week, part of the neural tube becomes the cerebral vesicle, which later becomes the cerebral hemispheres. The incidence of two forms of neural defects, anencephaly and spina bifida, is about 0.5 per 1,000 births.

The cerebral cortex begins to develop by the 10th week, but layers do not appear until the sixth month of pregnancy; the sensory cortex and the motor cortex are formed before the association cortex. In utero, some brain function has been detected by fetal encephalographic responses to sound. The weight of the human brain is about 350 grams at birth and 1,450 grams at full adult development; that is a fourfold increase, mainly in the neocortex. During fetal life and early infancy the number and the branching of dendrites and the number of synaptic junctions grow enormously. Uterine contractions may contribute to fetal neural development by causing the developing neural network to receive and transmit sensory impulses. Figure 2.3–1 shows the uterofetal relations as they develop during pregnancy.

### Transmission of Maternal Stress

The fetus is vulnerable and reacts to such stimuli as drugs and maternal stress. Animal studies have shown that maternal stress during pregnancy affects behavior in the offspring; the same effects are seen in humans. Maternal hormones cross the placenta, producing secondary effects in the fetus; if the mother is stressed, corticosteroids and other stress-related hormones may affect the cardiovascular system of the fetus, whose blood pressure is sensitive to external stimuli. Some correlation has been found between the mother's autonomic responses and the neonate's responses. Mothers with high anxiety levels are likely to produce babies who are hyperactive and irritable, have sleep disorders and low birth weight, and feed poorly.

### Prenatal Diagnosis

In many cases, genetic counseling depends on prenatal diagnosis. The diagnostic techniques used include amniocentesis (transabdominal aspiration of fluid from the amniotic sac), ultrasound examinations, X-rays, fetoscopy (the direct visualization of the fetus), fetal blood and skin sampling, chorionic villus sampling, and α-fetoprotein screening. In about 2 percent of the total number of women tested, the results are positive for some abnormality, including X-linked disorders, neural tube defects (detected by high levels of α-fetoprotein), chromosomal disorders (for example, trisomy 21), and various inborn errors of

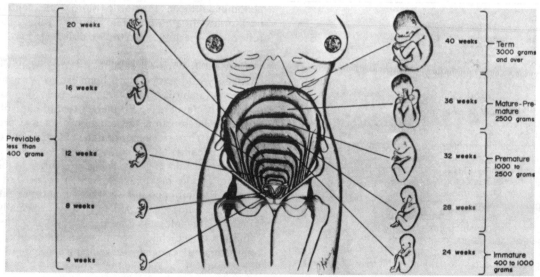

**Figure 2.3–1.** Uterofetal relations as they develop during pregnancy. (Figure from E C Mann, T N Armistead: Pregnancy and sexual behavior. In *The Sexual Experience,* B J Sadock, H I Kaplan, A M Freedman, editors, p 238. Williams & Wilkins, Baltimore, 1976.)

metabolism (for example, Tay-Sachs disease and lipoidoses).

Some diagnostic tests carry a risk; for example, about 5 percent of the women who undergo fetoscopy have miscarriages. Amniocentesis, which is usually performed between the 14th and the 16th week of pregnancy, causes fetal damage or miscarriage in fewer than 1 percent of women tested. Fully 98 percent of all prenatal tests in pregnant women reveal no abnormality in the fetus. Prenatal testing is recommended for women over 35 and for those with a family history of a congenital defect.

### Other Defects

Fetal alcohol syndrome affects about one third of all infants born to alcoholic mothers. The syndrome is characterized by (1) growth retardation of prenatal origin (height, weight); (2) minor anomalies, including microphthalmia, short palpebral fissures, midface hypoplasia, a smooth or short philtrum, and a thin upper lip; (3) central nervous system (CNS) manifestations, including microcephaly (head circumference below the third percentile), a history of delayed development, hyperactivity, attention deficits, learning disabilities, intellectual deficits, and seizures. The incidence of infants born with fetal alcohol syndrome was 0.4 per 1,000 live births in 1990, according to the U.S. Public Health Service.

Smoking during pregnancy is associated with lower-than-average infant birth weight. Infants born to mothers dependent on narcotics go through a withdrawal syndrome at birth. If the mother is exposed to severe radiation during the first 20 weeks of her pregnancy, the baby will be born

**Table 2.3–2**
**Causes of Human Malformations**
**Observed during the First Year of Life**

| Suspected Cause | Percentage of Total |
|---|---|
| Genetic | |
| Autosomal genetic disease | 15–20 |
| Cytogenetic (chromosomal abnormalities) | 5 |
| Unknown | 65 |
| Polygenic | |
| Multifactorial (genetic-environmental interactions) | |
| Spontaneous error of development | |
| Synergistic interactions of teratogens | |
| Environmental | |
| Maternal conditions: diabetes; endocrinopathies; nutritional deficiencies, starvation; drug and substance addictions | 4 |
| Maternal infections: rubella, toxoplasmosis, syphilis, herpes, cytomegalic inclusion disease, varicella, Venezuelan equine encephalitis, Parvovirus B 19 | 3 |
| Mechanical problems (deformations): abnormal cord constrictions, disparity in uterine size and uterine contents | 1–2 |
| Chemicals, drugs, radiation, hyperthermia | <1 |
| Preconception exposures (excluding mutagens and infectious agents) | <1 |

Table from R L Brent, D A Beckman: Environmental teratogens. Bull N Y Acad Med *66*: 125, 1990. Used with permission.

with gross deformities. Estimates are that 3 to 6 percent of all newborns have some sort of birth defect that is fatal at birth or that causes permanent disability. Table 2.3–2 lists malformations that occur during the first year of life.

Prenatal exposure to various medications can also result in abnormalities. Common drugs that have teratogenic effects include antibiotics (tetracycline [Achromycin]), phenytoin (Dilantin), progesterone-estrogens, lithium (Eskalith), and warfarin (Coumadin).

### INFANCY

The delivery of the fetus marks the start of infancy. The average newborn weighs about 3,400 grams (7½ pounds). *Small fetuses*, which are defined as those with a birth weight below the 10th percentile for their gestational age, occur in about 7 percent of all pregnancies. At the 26th to the 28th week of gestation, the prematurely born fetus has a good chance of survival. *Premature infants* are usually defined as those infants weighing between 1,000 and 2,500 grams. With each 100-gram increment of weight, beginning at about 1,000 grams, the infant has a progressively better chance of survival. A 36-week-old fetus has less of a chance of survival than does a 3,000-gram fetus born close to term.

*Postmature infants* are defined as infants born two weeks or more beyond the expected date of birth. Since pregnancy at term is calculated as being 40 weeks from the last menstrual period and since the exact time of fertilization varies, the incidence of postmaturity is high when based on menstrual history alone. The postmature baby typically has long nails, scanty lanugo hair, more than the usual amount of scalp hair, and increased alertness.

### Developmental Landmarks

**Newborn reflexes and survival systems.** Reflexes are present at birth. They include the rooting reflex (puckering of the lips in response to perioral stimulation), the grasp reflex, the plantar (Babinski) reflex, the knee reflex, the abdominal reflexes, the startle (Moro) reflex, and the tonic neck reflex. In a normal child the grasp reflex, the startle reflex, and the tonic neck reflex disappear by the fourth month.

Survival systems—breathing, sucking, swallowing, and circulatory and temperature homeostasis—are relatively functional at birth. However, the sensory organs are incompletely developed. Further differentiation of neurophysiological functions depends on an active process of stimulatory reinforcement from the external environment, such as touching and stroking the infant.

**Language and cognitive development.** At birth, infants are able to make noises, such as crying, but they do not vocalize until about 8 weeks. At that time, guttural or babbling sounds occur spontaneously, especially in response to the mother. The persistence and the further evolution of the child's vocalizations depend on parental reinforcement. Language development occurs in well-delineated stages, as outlined in Table 2.3–3.

According to Piaget, the infant is in the sensorimotor period of cognitive development (Table 2.3–4). By the end of that stage, (which has six substages), the infant has

**Table 2.3–3**
**Language Development**

| Age and Stage of Development | Mastery of Comprehension | Mastery of Expression |
|---|---|---|
| 0–6 months | Shows startle response to loud or sudden sounds<br>Attempts to localize sounds, turning eyes or head<br>Appears to listen to speakers, may respond with smile<br>Recognizes warning, angry, and friendly voices<br>Responds to hearing own name | Has vocalizations other than crying<br>Has differential cries for hunger, pain<br>Makes vocalizations to show pleasure<br>Plays at making sounds<br>Babbles (repeats a series of sounds) |
| 7–11 months<br>Attending to language stage | Shows listening selectivity (voluntary control over responses to sounds)<br>Listens to music or singing with interest<br>Recognizes "no," "hot," own name<br>Looks at pictures being named for up to one minute<br>Listens to speech without being distracted by other sounds | Responds to own name with vocalizations<br>Imitates the melody of utterances<br>Uses jargon (own language)<br>Has gestures (shakes head for no)<br>Has exclamation ("oh-oh")<br>Plays language games (pat-a-cake, peekaboo) |
| 12–18 months<br>Single-word stage | Shows gross discriminations between dissimilar sounds (bell *vs.* dog *vs.* horn *vs.* mother's or father's voice)<br>Understands basic body parts, names of common objects<br>Acquires understanding of some new words each week<br>Can identify simple objects (baby, ball, etc.) from a group of objects or pictures<br>Understands up to 150 words by age 18 months | Uses single words (mean age of first word is 11 months; by age 18 months, child is using up to 20 words)<br>"Talks" to toys, self, or others, using long patterns of jargon and occasional words<br>Approximately 25% of utterances are intelligible<br>All vowels articulated correctly<br>Initial and final consonants often omitted |
| 12–24 months<br>Two-word messages stage | Responds to simple directions ("Give me the ball")<br>Responds to action commands ("Come here," "Sit down")<br>Understands pronouns (me, him, her, you)<br>Begins to understand complex sentences ("When we go to the store, I'll buy you some candy") | Uses two-word utterances ("Mommy sock," "all gone," "ball here")<br>Imitates environmental sounds in play ("moo," "rrmm, rrmm," etc.)<br>Refers to self by name, begins to use pronouns<br>Echoes two or more last words of sentences<br>Begins to use three-word telegraphic utterances ("all gone ball," "me go now")<br>Utterances 26% to 50% intelligible<br>Uses language to ask for needs |
| 24–36 months<br>Grammar formation stage | Understands small body parts (elbow, chin, eyebrow)<br>Understands family name categories (grandma, baby)<br>Understands size (little one, big one)<br>Understands most adjectives<br>Understands functions (why do we eat, why do we sleep) | Uses real sentences with grammatical function words (can, will, the, a)<br>Usually announces intentions before acting<br>"Conversations" with other children, usually just monologues<br>Jargon and echolalia gradually drop from speech<br>Increased vocabulary (up to 270 words at 2 years, 895 words at 3 years) includes slang<br>Speech 50% to 80% intelligible<br>P, b, m articulated correctly<br>Speech may show rhythmic disturbances |
| 36–54 months<br>Grammar development stage | Understands prepositions (under, behind, between)<br>Understands many words (up to 3,500 at 3 years, 5,500 at 4 years)<br>Understands cause and effect (What do you do when you're hungry?, cold?)<br>Understands analogies (Food is to eat, milk is to _____) | Correct articulation of n,w,ng,h,t,d,k,g<br>Uses language to relate incidents from the past<br>Uses wide range of grammatical forms: plurals, past tense, negatives, questions<br>Plays with language: rhymes, exaggerates<br>Speech 90% intelligible, occasional errors in the ordering of sounds within words<br>Able to define words<br>Egocentric use of language rare<br>Can repeat a 12-syllable sentence correctly<br>Some grammatical errors still occur |

*Continued*

**Table 2.3–3**
*continued*

| Age and Stage of Development | Mastery of Comprehension | Mastery of Expression |
|---|---|---|
| 55 months on<br>True communication stage | Understands concepts of number, speed, time, space<br>Understands left and right<br>Understands abstract terms<br>Is able to categorize items into semantic classes | Uses language to tell stories, share ideas, and discuss alternatives<br>Increasing use of varied grammar; spontaneous self-correction of grammatical errors<br>Stabilizing of articulation of f,v,s,z,l,r,th, and consonant clusters<br>Speech 100% intelligible |

Table from M Rutter, L Hersov, editors: *Child and Adolescent Psychiatry*. Blackwell, London, 1985. Used with permission.

transformed reflexes into self-generated schemes of action that are the building blocks of cognition. The infant begins to interact with the environment, experiences feedback from its own body, becomes intentional in its actions, and, by the end of the second year of life, begins to use symbolic play and language.

**Emotional and social development.** By the age of 3 weeks, infants imitate the facial movements of adult caretakers. The baby opens its mouth and thrusts out its tongue in response to an adult who is doing the same. By the third and fourth months of life, those behaviors are easily elicited. The imitative behaviors are believed to be the precursors of emotional life in the infant. The smiling response occurs in two phases: the first phase is endogenous smiling, which occurs spontaneously within the first two months and is unrelated to external stimulation; the second phase is exogenous smiling, which is stimulated from the outside, usually by the mother, and occurs by the 16th week.

The stages of emotional development parallel those of cognitive development. Indeed, the caretaking person provides the major stimulus for both aspects of mental growth. The human infant is totally dependent on adults for survival. Through regular and predictable interaction, the infant's behavioral repertoire expands as a consequence of the caretakers' social responses to its behaviors (Table 2.3–5).

In the first year an infant's mood is highly variable and is intimately related to internal states, such as hunger. Toward the second two thirds of the first year, the infant's mood is increasingly related to external social cues (for example, a parent can get even a hungry infant to smile). When the infant is internally comfortable, a sense of interest and pleasure in the world and in its primary caretakers should prevail. The development of the infant's personal and social behavior is outlined in Table 2.3–1.

Freud described infancy as the oral stage of development, in which the mouth is the primary erogenous zone. Erikson described the period as the stage of basic trust versus basic mistrust. He expanded on Freud's view that, during the first months of life, the mouth is the most sensitive zone of the body. Infants incorporate—taking in food, a nipple, a finger. There is a hunger for nourishment and for stimulation of the sense organs and the whole surface of the skin. Depending on what happens between

**Table 2.3–4**
**Overview of Piaget's Sensorimotor Period of Cognitive Development**

| Age | Characteristics |
|---|---|
| 1. Birth–2 months | Uses inborn motor and sensory reflexes (sucking, grasping, looking) to interact and accommodate to the external world |
| 2. 2–5 months | Primary circular reaction—coordinates activities of own body and five senses (e.g., sucking thumb); reality remains subjective—does not seek stimuli outside of its visual field; displays curiosity |
| 3. 5–9 months | Secondary circular reaction—seeks out new stimuli in the environment; starts both to anticipate consequences of own behavior and to act purposefully to change the environment; beginning of intentional behavior |
| 4. 9 months–1 year | Shows preliminary signs of object permanence; has a vague concept that objects exist apart from itself; plays peekaboo; imitates novel behaviors |
| 5. 1 year–18 months | Tertiary circular reaction—seeks out new experiences; produces novel behaviors |
| 6. 18 months–2 years | Symbolic thought—uses symbolic representations of events and objects; shows signs of reasoning (e.g., uses one toy to reach for and get another); attains object permanence |

Table adapted from H P Ginsburg: Jean Piaget. In *Comprehensive Textbook of Psychiatry*, ed 4, H I Kaplan, B J Sadock, editors, p 179. Williams & Wilkins, Baltimore, 1985.

**Table 2.3–5**
**Emotional Development from Infancy Through Childhood**

| Age | Emotional Capacity and Expression |
|---|---|
| Birth | Pleasure, surprise, disgust, distress |
| 6–8 weeks | Joy |
| 3–4 months | Anger |
| 8–9 months | Sadness, fear |
| 12–18 months | Tender affection, shame (begins at 18 months) |
| 24 months | Pride |
| 3–4 years | Guilt, envy |
| 5–6 years | Insecurity, humility, confidence |

Data adapted from Joseph Campas at the University of Denver and from other researchers.

babies and mothers, who are also the bearers of the society's values, babies develop either a basic feeling of trust that their wants will be frequently satisfied or a sense that they are going to lose most of what they want.

During the second six months, the dominant social mode moves from getting to taking, manifested orally in biting. However, nursing infants learn that the nipple is removed if they bite. Weaning begins. Sorrow or nostalgia begins, too. But if basic trust is strong, infants develop a sense of optimism and hope, instead of a sense of pessimism and despair. Prolonged separation from the mother at that time can lead to depression, hospitalism, anaclitic depression, or a depressive tone that becomes part of the person's adult character structure.

## Temperamental Differences

There are strong suggestions of inborn differences and wide variability among individual infants in autonomic reactivity and temperament. Stella Chess and Alexander Thomas (husband and wife psychiatric collaborators) identified the following nine behavioral dimensions, from which reliable differences can be obtained:

1. Activity level—the motor component present in a given child's functioning
2. Rhythmicity—the predictability of such functions as hunger, feeding pattern, elimination, and the sleep-wake cycle
3. Approach or withdrawal—the nature of the response to a new stimulus, such as a new food, toy, or person
4. Adaptability—the speed and the ease with which a current behavior is able to be modified in response to altered environmental structuring
5. Intensity of reaction—the amount of energy used in mood expression
6. Threshold of responsiveness—the intensity level of stimulation required to evoke a discernible response to sensory stimuli, environmental objects, and social contacts
7. Quality of mood—pleasant, joyful, friendly behavior as contrasted with unpleasant, crying, unfriendly behavior
8. Distractibility—the effectiveness of extraneous environmental stimuli in interfering with or in altering the direction of ongoing behavior
9. Attention span and persistence—the length of time a particular activity is pursued by the child (attention span) and the continuation of an activity in the face of obstacles (persistence).

The ratings of individual children showed considerable stability over a 25-year follow-up period; however, some temperamental traits did not persist over time; that finding was attributed to genetic effects on personality. Some gene actions were discontinuous. There is a complex interplay among the initial characteristics of the infant, the mode of parental management, the child's subsequent behavior, and even the appearance of symptoms. Those connections support the concept of the importance of genetic endowment (nature) and environmental experience (nurture) on behavior.

## Attachment

Infants in the first months after birth become attuned to social and interpersonal interaction. They show a rapidly increasing responsivity to the external environment and an ability to form a special relationship with significant primary caretakers—that is, to form an attachment.

Ethologists have demonstrated, primarily in birds, that during a critical period shortly after birth the newborn becomes imprinted on a moving, sound-producing object. That bond elicits following behavior from the newborn. For all its undoubted importance, imprinting has not been demonstrated conclusively in human beings or in other primates.

**Harry Harlow.** Harry Harlow studied social learning and the effects of social isolation in monkeys. Harlow placed newborn rhesus monkeys with two types of surrogate mothers—one a wire-mesh surrogate and the other a wire-mesh surrogate covered with terry cloth. The monkeys preferred the terry cloth surrogates, which provided contact and comfort. When frightened, terry-cloth-raised monkeys showed intense clinging behavior and appeared to be comforted, whereas wire-mesh-raised monkeys gained no comfort and appeared to be disorganized. Both types of surrogate-reared monkeys were subsequently unable to adjust to life in a monkey colony and had extraordinary difficulty in learning to mate. When impregnated, the females failed to mother their young. Those behavioral peculiarities were attributed to the isolates' lack of mothering in infancy.

**John Bowlby.** John Bowlby studied the attachment of infants to mothers and concluded that early separation of infants from their mothers had severe negative effects on the children's emotional and intellectual development. He described attachment behavior, which develops during the first year of life; it is characterized by the maintenance of physical contact between the mother and the child when the child is hungry, frightened, or in distress.

**Social deprivation syndromes and maternal neglect.** Investigators, especially René Spitz, have long documented the severe developmental retardation that accompanies maternal rejection and neglect. Infants in institutions characterized by low staff-to-infant ratios and frequent turnover of personnel tend to display marked developmental retardation, even with adequate physical care and freedom from infection. The same infants, placed in adequate foster or adoptive care, undergo a marked acceleration in development.

**Fathers and attachment.** Babies become attached to fathers, as well as to mothers, but the attachment is different. Generally, mothers hold babies for caretaking, and fathers hold babies for purposes of play. Given a choice of either parent after separation, infants usually go to the mother, but if the mother is unavailable, they turn to the father for comfort.

**Stranger anxiety.** A fear of strangers is first noted in infants at about 26 weeks of age but does not develop fully until about 32 weeks (8 months). At the approach of a stranger, infants cry and cling to their mothers. Babies exposed to only one caretaker are more likely to have stranger anxiety than are those exposed to a variety of caretakers.

Separation anxiety, which occurs between 10 and 18 months of age, is related to stranger anxiety but is not identical to it. Separation from the person to whom the infant is attached precipitates separation anxiety. Stranger anxiety, however, occurs even when the infant is in the mother's arms. The infant learns to separate as it starts to crawl and move away from the mother, but the infant constantly looks back and frequently returns to the mother for reassurance.

Margaret Mahler described a developmental phase called symbiosis, during which the infant feels fused with the mother or the mother's breast. The phase extends from the age of 3 or 4 weeks to 4 or 5 months, at which point the separation-individuation phase begins. Individuation is characterized by the child's perception of himself or herself as a distinct person, separate from the mother.

### Effects of Infant Care

Clinicians are starting to view the infant as an important actor in the family drama, one who, in part, determines its course. The behavior of the infant controls the behavior of the mother, just as the mother's behavior modulates the infant's behavior. The calm, smiling, predictable, good infant is a powerful reward for tender maternal care. The jittery, irregular, irritable infant tries a mother's patience. If a mother's capacities for giving are marginal, such infant traits may cause her to turn away from her child and thus complicate the child's already inadequate beginnings.

**Parental fit.** The concept of parental fit concerns how well the mother or the father relates to the newborn or developing infant and takes into account temperamental characteristics of both parent and child. Each newborn has innate psychophysiological characteristics, which are known collectively as temperament. Chess and Thomas identified a range of normal temperamental patterns, from the difficult child at one end of the spectrum to the easy child at the other end. *Difficult children*, who make up 10 percent of all children, have a hyperalert physiological makeup. They react intensely to stimuli (cry easily at loud noises), sleep poorly, eat at unpredictable times, and are difficult to comfort. *Easy children*, who make up 40 percent of all children, are regular in eating, eliminating, and sleeping; are flexible; are able to adapt to change and to new stimuli with a minimum of distress; and are easily comforted when they cry. The other 50 percent of children are mixtures of those two types. The difficult child is harder to raise and places greater demands on the parent than does the easy child. Chess and Thomas used the term "goodness of fit" to characterize the harmonious and consonant interaction between a mother and a child in their motivations, capacities, and styles of behavior. Poorness of fit is characterized by dissonance between a parent and a child, which is likely to lead to distorted development and maladaptive functioning. The difficult child must be recognized because parents of such infants often have feelings of inadequacy and believe that something they are doing wrong accounts for the difficulty in sleeping and eating and the problems in comforting the child. In addition, a majority of difficult children have emotional disturbances later in life.

**Good-enough mothering.** Donald W. Winnicott provided a blend of Freudian and Kleinian thought in the form of a radically different developmental theory. Winnicott believed that the infant begins life in a state of unintegration, with unconnected and diffuse experiences, and that the mother provides the relationships that enable the infant's incipient self to emerge. The mother supplies a holding environment, within which the infant is contained and experienced. During the last trimester of pregnancy and for the first few months of the baby's life, the mother is in a state of primary maternal preoccupation, absorbed in fantasies about the baby and experiences with her baby. The mother need not be perfect, but she must provide good-enough mothering. She plays a vital role in bringing the world to the child and in offering empathic anticipations of the infant's needs. If the mother is able to resonate with the infant's needs, the baby can become attuned to its own bodily functions and drives that afford the basis for the gradually evolving sense of self.

## TODDLER PERIOD

The second year of life is marked by an acceleration of motor and intellectual development. The ability to walk confers on toddlers a degree of control over their own actions; that mobility enables children to determine when to approach and when to withdraw. The acquisition of speech profoundly extends their horizons. Typically, children learn to say "no" before they learn to say "yes." Toddlers' negativism plays a vital part in the development of independence. If persistent, however, oppositional behavior connotes a problem.

### Developmental Landmarks

**Language and cognitive development.** Learning language is a crucial task in the toddler period. Vocalizations become distinct, and the toddler has the ability to name a few objects and to make needs known in one or two words. Near the end of the second year and into the third year, toddlers sometimes use short sentences. They begin to reason and to listen to explanations that can help them tolerate delay. Toddlers create new behaviors from old ones (originality) and engage in symbolic activities (for example, using words and playing with dolls when the dolls represent something, such as a feeding sequence). Toddlers have variable capacities for concentration and self-regulation.

According to Piaget, the toddler period occurs during the sensorimotor stage of cognitive development (Table 2.3–4). By age 2 the child is beginning to make symbolic representations of events.

**Emotional and social development.** In the child's second year, affects of pleasure and displeasure become further differentiated. Observed are excited explorations, assertive pleasure, pleasure in discovery and in developing new behavior (for example, new games), including teasing and surprising or fooling the parent (for example, hiding). The toddler has capacities for an organized demonstration of love (for example, running up and hugging, smiling, and kissing the parent at the same time) and protest (for example, turning away, crying, banging, biting, hitting, yelling, and kicking). Comfort with family and apprehension with strangers may increase. Anxiety appears to be related to disapproval and the loss of a loved caretaker, and it can be disorganizing. Additional information appears in Table 2.3–1.

For Erikson, the toddler period is the stage of autonomy versus shame and self-doubt (specifically, 1 to 3 years). During the second and third years of life, children gain autonomy. Their challenge is to become separate, individual beings. They learn to walk, to eat by themselves, to control the anal sphincter, and to talk. The term "terrible twos" reflects the willfulness of children in that stage of development.

Freud described the period as the anal stage of development. The child retains or lets go of feces. Too rigorous toilet training can produce an overly compulsive personality who is orderly, meticulous, and selfish. Freud referred to those personality types as anal characters, marked by parsimony, punctuality, and perfectionism.

**Sexual development.** The forerunners of sexual differentiation are evident from birth, when parents start dressing and treating infants differently because of the expectations evoked by sex typing. Through imitation, reward, and coercion, the child assumes the behaviors that the culture defines as appropriate for its sexual role. The child exhibits curiosity about anatomical sex. If that curiosity is recognized as healthy and is met with honest and age-appropriate replies, the child acquires a sense of the wonder of life and is comfortable with its own role in it. If the subject of sex is taboo and the child's questions are rebuffed, shame and discomfort result. By the age of 2½ years, children have a sense of gender identity—that is, whether they are boys or girls. In general, play is determined by gender; boys play with guns, and girls play with dolls and dollhouses. However, cultural mores and social trends significantly influence children's choices of games and toys.

**Sphincter control and sleep.** The second year of life is a period of increasing social demands on the child. Toilet training serves as a paradigm of the family's general training practices; that is, the parent who is overly severe in the area of toilet training is likely to be punitive and restrictive in other areas as well. Control of daytime urination is usually complete by the age of 2½ years, and control of nighttime urination is usually complete by the age of 4 years. Bowel control is usually accomplished by the age of 4 years.

Toddlers may have sleep difficulties related to fear of the dark, which can often be managed by the use of a night-light. In general, most toddlers sleep about 12 hours a day, including a two-hour nap. Parents need to be aware that children at that age may need reassurance before going to bed and that the average 2-year-old takes about 30 minutes to fall asleep.

## Parenting

Parallel to the changing tasks for the child are changing tasks for the parents. In infancy, the major responsibility

for parents is to meet the infant's needs in a sensitive and consistent fashion, without anticipating and fulfilling all the needs so that the child never experiences tension. Some tension is desirable. The parental task in the toddler stage requires firmness about the boundaries of acceptable behavior and encouragement of the child's progressive emancipation. Parents must be careful not to be too authoritarian at that stage. Children must be allowed to operate for themselves and to learn from their mistakes. And they must be protected and assisted when the challenges are beyond their abilities.

During the toddler period, children are likely to struggle for the exclusive affection and attention of their parents. That struggle includes rivalry both with siblings and with one or another parent for the star role in the family. Although children are beginning to be able to share, they do so with reluctance. If the demands for exclusive possession are not effectively resolved, the result is likely to be jealous competitiveness in relations with peers and lovers. The fantasies aroused by the struggle lead to fear of retaliation and displacement of fear onto external objects. In an equitable, loving family, the child elaborates a moral system of ethical rights. Parents need to set realistic limits on the toddler's behavior, balancing between punishment and permissiveness.

## PRESCHOOL PERIOD

The preschool period is characterized by marked physical and emotional growth. Somewhere between 2 and 3 years of age, children reach half of their adult height. The 20 baby teeth are in place at the beginning of the stage, and by the end they begin to fall out. Children are ready to enter school by the time the stage ends at age 5 or 6. They have mastered the tasks of primary socialization—to control their bowels and urine, to dress and feed themselves, and to control their tears and temper outbursts, at least most of the time.

The term "preschool" for the age group of 2½ to 6 years may be a misnomer, because many of the children are already in schoollike settings, such as preschool nurseries and day-care centers. Many mothers must place their children in such nurseries or day-care centers. Preschool education can be of value; however, too great a stress on academic advancement beyond the capabilities of the child can be counterproductive.

### Developmental Landmarks

**Language and cognitive development.** In the preschool period, language expands, and the child uses sentences. Individual words have regular and consistent meanings at the beginning of the period. For Piaget, the preschool period is the preoperational phase (specifically, 2 to 7 years), during which children begin to think symbolically. In general, however, their thinking is egocentric, as in the sensorimotor period; they cannot place themselves in the position of another child and are incapable of empathy. Preoperational thought is also intuitive and prelogical; children in the preschool period do not understand cause-and-effect relations.

**Emotional and social behavior.** At the start of the preschool period, children can express such complex affects as love, unhappiness, jealousy, and envy at both preverbal and verbal levels. The child's emotions are still easily influenced by somatic events, such as tiredness and hunger. Although affects are still mostly at an egocentric level, the child's capacity for cooperation and sharing is emerging. Anxiety is related to the loss of a loved and depended-on person and to the loss of approval and acceptance. Although still potentially disorganizing, anxiety can be better tolerated than in the past.

Four-year-olds are learning to share and to have concern for others. Feelings of tenderness are sometimes expressed. Anxiety over bodily injury and the loss of a loved person's approval is sometimes disruptive.

By the end of the preschool period, children have many emotions that are relatively stable. Expansiveness, curiosity, pride, and a gleeful excitement related to the self and the family are balanced with coyness, shyness, fearfulness, jealousy, and envy. Shame and humiliation are evident. Capacities for empathy and love are developed but fragile and easily lost if competitive or jealous strivings intervene. Anxiety and fears are related to bodily injury and loss of respect, love, and emerging self-esteem. Guilt feelings are possible. Additional information appears in Table 2.3–1.

Children between ages 3 and 6 years are aware of the genitalia and of the differences between the sexes. In their play, doctor-nurse games allow children to act out their sexual fantasies. Their awareness of their bodies extends beyond the genitalia. They show a preoccupation with illness or injury, so much so that the period has been called the Band-Aid phase; every injury needs to be examined and taken care of by a parent.

Freud described the preschool period as the phallic stage of development; infancy represented the oral phase; toddlerhood, the anal stage. During the phallic stage, pleasure is connected with the genital area. It is the time of the Oedipus complex, when children have sexual impulses toward the opposite-sex parent and want to eliminate the same-sex parent—wishes for which punishment is expected (the talion principle). The punishment feared by boys is castration. Castration anxiety leads the boy to give up his mother as a love object, to repress his impulses toward her, to identify with his father, and in the process to form a superego. The Electra complex holds that the girl wishes to have the exclusive love of her father and to replace her mother; the daughter resolves the conflict by identifying with her mother. Lack of a penis is considered evidence of castration. Freud believed that a girl develops penis envy as a result and wants to possess her father in order to obtain his penis. The little girl's urge to marry the father and to have a baby represents the desire for a penis.

Observational research with children has yielded data that contradict some of Freud's theories of gender identity. Normatively, gender identity is a process that evolves over the first few years of life. It does not occur precipitously in boys with the resolution of the Oedipus complex, nor is penis envy a normal or universal determinant of female gender identity.

Erikson described this stage as the stage of initiative versus guilt (specifically, 3 to 5 years). At the age of 3, children move out into the world, where their learning becomes instructive; they grab with eagerness and curiosity. However, children take their first initiatives at home, where they express passionate interest in the parent of the opposite sex. Children experience disappointment during this stage and often try to wrest a place for themselves in the affection of their parents, especially if siblings are present.

Children develop a division between what they want and what they are told they should do. The division increases until a gap grows between the children's set of expanded desires, their exuberance at unlimited growth, and their parents' restrictions. They gradually turn those parental values into self-obedience, self-guidance, and self-punishment.

At the end of the preschool stage, the child's conscience (Freud's superego) is established. The development of a conscience sets the tone for the child's moral sense of right and wrong. Piaget proposed stages of moral development to parallel the stages of cognition. In the preoperational stage, children experience rules as absolute and as existing for their own sake. The children do not understand that there may be more than one point of view to a moral issue; a violation of the rules calls for absolute retribution—that is, the child has the notion of immanent justice.

Using Piaget's work as a starting point, Lawrence Kohlberg proposed three major stages of moral development, each with two substages. The preschool child operates at level 1, preconventional morality. At that level, moral reasoning is based on (a) a concrete punishment-obedience stance, in which whatever is punished is bad and external and powerful authority is the only criterion for morality, and (b) quid-pro-quo morality, in which "what I do for you must be reciprocated by what you do for me." Kohlberg's three stages are discussed in Section 2.4.

SIBLING RIVALRY. In the preschool period the child relates to others in new ways. The birth of a sibling (a common occurrence during the period) tests the preschool child's capacity for further cooperation and sharing. It may also evoke sibling rivalry, which is most likely to occur at that time. Sibling rivalry depends on child-rearing practices. Favoritism, for any reason, is a common outcome of such rivalry. Children who get special treatment because they are gifted, defective in some way, or of a preferred gender are likely to be the recipient of angry feelings from their siblings. Experiences with siblings may influence the growing child's relationships with peers and authority. If, for example, the needs of the new baby prevent the mother from attending the firstborn child's needs, a problem may result. If not handled properly, the displacement of the firstborn can be a traumatic event.

PLAY. In the preschool years the child begins to distinguish reality from fantasy, and play reflects that growing awareness. Games of "let's pretend" are popular and help test real-life situations in a playful manner. Dramatic play in which the child acts out a role, such as that of a housewife or a truck driver, is common. One-to-one play relationships advance to complicated patterns with rivalries, secrets, and two-against-one intrigues. Children's play behavior reflects their level of social development.

Between 3 and 6 years of age, growth can be traced

through drawings. The first drawing of a person is a circular line with marks for the mouth, the nose, and eyes; ears and hair are added later; next, arms and sticklike fingers appear; then legs. The last to appear is a torso in proportion to the rest of the body. The intelligent child is able to deal with details. Drawings express creativity throughout the child's development. They are representational and formal in early childhood, make use of perspective in middle childhood, and become abstract and affect-laden in adolescence. Drawings also reflect a person's body image concepts and sexual and aggressive impulses.

IMAGINARY COMPANIONS. Imaginary companions most often appear during the preschool years, usually in children with above-average intelligence and usually in the form of persons. Imaginary companions may also be things, such as toys that are anthropomorphized. Some studies indicate that up to 50 percent of children between the ages of 3 and 10 years have imaginary companions at one time or another. Their significance is not clear, but they are usually friendly, relieve loneliness, and reduce anxiety in the child. In most instances, imaginary companions disappear by age 12, but they may occasionally persist into adulthood.

## MIDDLE YEARS

During the middle years the child enters elementary school. The formal demands for academic learning and accomplishment become major determinants of further personality development.

### Developmental Landmarks

**Language and cognitive development.** In the middle years, language is used to express complex ideas with relations among a number of elements. Logical exploration tends to dominate fantasy, and the child shows an increased interest in rules and orderliness and an increased capacity for self-regulation. The ability to concentrate is well established by age 9 or 10.

From Piaget's perspective, the middle years are the stage of concrete operations, during which a child's conceptual skills develop and thinking becomes organized and logical. Toward the end of the period, the child begins to think in abstract terms.

Improved gross motor coordination and muscle strength enable the child to write with fluency and to draw artistically. The child is also capable of complex motor tasks and activities, such as tennis, gymnastics, golf, baseball, and skateboarding.

**Emotional and social behavior.** Freud called the middle years the latency period, resulting from resolution of the Oedipus complex and an assumed quiescence of the sexual drive. Oedipal resolution also accounts for superego development; the formation of the superego enables the child to make moral judgments. In recent years, evidence has shown that latency results from maturational changes in the brain. The child is now capable of increased independence, learning, and socialization. In contrast to Freud, recent theorists consider moral development a gradual, stepwise process spanning childhood, adolescence, and young adulthood. Children in latency are able to deal with

the emotional and intellectual demands that are being placed on them by the environment, particularly in the school.

According to Freud, a girl has identified with her mother. Instead of wanting her father as a love object, the daughter now directs her energy toward wanting somebody like him. However, it is still culturally acceptable for the girl to remain attached to her father during latency, although not with the same degree of emotional intensity.

In latency, both girls and boys make new identifications with other adults, such as teachers and counselors. Those identifications may so influence the girl that her goals of wanting to marry and have babies, as her mother did, may be combined with a desire for a career, postponed, or abandoned entirely.

Some girls in latency act as if they were still in the oedipal stage. A girl who is unable to identify with her mother or whose father is overly attached may become fixated at a 6-year-old level and, as a result, may fear men or women or both or become seductively close to them. In either case, she may not be seen as normal during the school-age years. A similar situation may occur in the boy who enters latency without having resolved his Oedipus complex. The boy may have been unable to identify successfully with his father because his father was aloof, brutal, or absent. Perhaps his mother prevented the boy from identifying with his father by being overprotective or by binding the son too closely to herself. As a result, the boy may enter latency with a variety of problems. The boy may be fearful of men, unsure of his sense of masculinity, or unwilling to leave his mother (which may be manifested by a school phobia), or he may lack initiative and be unable to master school tasks, which then present as academic problems.

The school-age period is a time in which peer interaction assumes major importance. Interest in relationships outside the family take precedence over those within the family. However, a special relationship exists with the same-sex parent, with whom the child identifies and who is now a role model. In the middle years the child idealizes the same-sex parent and wants to be like that parent.

Empathy and a concern for others begin to emerge early in the middle years; by the time children are 9 or 10, they have well-developed capacities for love, compassion, and sharing. They have a capacity for long-term, stable relationships with family, peers, and friends, including best friends. Although sexual feelings are repressed, emotions regarding sexual differences begin to emerge as either excitement or shyness with the opposite sex. The school-age child prefers to interact with children of the same sex. The period has also been referred to as a psychosexual and psychosocial moratorium—a lull between the preschool child's oedipal strivings and the adolescent's pubescent sexual impulses. The moratorium is characterized by an absence of overt sexual behavior, which, according to Freud, is sublimated and expressed in other abilities, such as sports, studies, and nonsexual peer activities.

CHUM PERIOD. Harry Stack Sullivan postulated that a chum or buddy is an important phenomenon during the school years. By about 10 years of age, the child develops a close same-sex relationship, which Sullivan believed is necessary for further healthy psychological growth. Moreover, Sullivan believed that an early harbinger of schizophrenia is the absence of a chum during the middle years of childhood.

SCHOOL REFUSAL.  In some children the refusal to go to school occurs at this time, generally as a result of separation anxiety. A fearful mother may transmit her own fear of separation to the child, or a child who has not resolved dependence needs panics at the idea of separation. School refusal is usually not an isolated problem; children with the problem typically avoid many other social situations.

Erikson's stage of industry versus inferiority occurs during the middle years. Children can become confident of their ability to use adult materials during the period of latency, when they are waiting, learning, and practicing to be providers. Or they can forsake the attempt, forsake industry itself, and come to the conclusion that they are inferior and cannot operate the things of the world. The stage runs from ages 6 to 11 years.

## OTHER ISSUES IN CHILDHOOD

### Development of Sex Roles

One's sex role is similar to one's gender identity; one sees oneself as male or female. The sex role also involves identification with culturally acceptable masculine or feminine ways of behaving; however, changing expectations in the society (particularly in the United States) of what constitutes masculine behavior and feminine behavior create ambiguity. By age 2½, two thirds of children know their own sex, and boys and girls identify themselves as such in almost 100 percent of cases.

Parents react differently to their male and female children. Independence, physical play, and aggressiveness are encouraged in boys; dependence, verbalization, and physical intimacy are encouraged in girls. However, roles are changing. Boys are now encouraged to be verbal about their feelings and to pursue traditionally girl interests; girls are now encouraged to pursue careers traditionally dominated by men and to participate in competitive sports. As society becomes more tolerant than in the past in its expectations of the sexes, roles become less rigid, and opportunities for boys and girls are increasing.

Biologically, boys are more aggressive motorically than are girls; however, parental expectations, particularly the expectations of fathers, reinforce that trait.

Sex differences also exist in play activities: boys play with guns and trucks; girls play with dolls and clothes. Those differences appear as early as 2 or 3 years of age and remain fairly constant. Boys are less tolerant of opposite-sex behavior by other boys (sissy behavior) than are girls who see other girls engage in opposite-sex behavior (tomboy behavior).

### Dreams and Sleep

Dreams in children can have a profound effect on behavior. During the child's first year of life, when the differentiation between reality and fantasy is not yet fully achieved, the dream may be experienced as if it were or could be true. The child has strong reactions to dreams; they are viewed either with pleasure or, as is most often reported, with fear. The dream content should be seen in connection with the child's life experience, developmental stage, mechanisms used during dreaming, and sex.

Disturbing dreams peak when the child is 3, 6, and 10 years old. The 2-year-old child may dream about being bitten or chased; at the age of 4, the child may have many animal dreams, and people are introduced who either protect or destroy. At age 5 or 6, dreams of being killed or injured, of flying and being in cars, and of ghosts become prominent, exposing the role of conscience, moral values, and increasing conflicts around those themes. In early childhood, aggressive dreams rarely seem to occur; instead, the dreamer is in danger, perhaps reflecting the child's dependent position. By about the age of 5, children realize that their dreams are not real; before that time, they believe that dreams are real events. By age 7, children know that dreams are created by themselves.

At certain periods a child wakes from sleep disturbed by the content of the dream and is extremely frightened; the child is unwilling to return to sleep unless comforted by a parent. *Pavor nocturnus* (night terror) is a severe form of fright in which the content of the dream overwhelms reality, so that the child remains frightened by the dream for an extended period. During night terror, which occurs during nonrapid eye movement (NREM) sleep stages 3 and 4, children remain in an in-between state from which they cannot be fully aroused. Children do not appear to recognize the people in the room, and, even though their eyes are open, the dream seems to continue.

Between the ages of 3 and 6 years, children normally want to keep the bedroom door open or a light on, so that they can either maintain contact with their parents or view the room in a realistic and nonfearful way. At times, children resist going to sleep to avoid dreaming. Disorders associated with falling asleep, therefore, are often connected with the dream experience. Rituals are set up as protective devices designed to make safe the withdrawal from the world of reality into the world of sleep.

Somnambulism (sleepwalking) may occur. Often, the content of the dream seems to release motor discharge, and children go to those persons and places that can offer them protection.

Periods of rapid eye movement (REM) take place about 60 percent of the time during the first few weeks of life, during which the infant sleeps two thirds of the time. Premature babies spend even more time asleep than do full-term babies. The sleep-wake cycle of newborns is about three hours long. Among adults the dream-to-sleep ratio is stable: 20 percent of sleeping time is spent dreaming. Even newborns have brain activity similar to that of the dreaming state. However, it is doubtful that dreaming is possible before speech—that is, before the existence of mental representation of the outside world.

### Spacing of Children

For women in the United States, 10 percent of conceptions that lead to live births are considered to be unwanted, and 20 percent are wanted but considered to be ill-timed. The implications of those figures are that some couples may be poorly prepared or may feel guilty about not wanting to be parents at that particular time. It is desirable to plan the pregnancy and to have mutual agreement on the spacing of children. The typical number of children in a present-day family is two, half the typical number at the beginning of the century. Repeated childbearing prevents adequate recuperation from the birth process and places the mother at risk for complications and injury. The new mother requires time to adapt; the period of adaptation may range from a few weeks to several months. The demands of other children at home can be taxing, and the family may be stressed beyond its capacity if those children are also young.

Studies of children from large families (four or five children) show that they are more likely to have conduct disorder and to have a slightly lower level of verbal intelligence than do children from small families. Decreased parental interaction and discipline may account for those findings.

## Birth Order

The effects of birth order are variable. Firstborn children are often more highly valued than are subsequent children, particularly if the firstborn is male. That is especially so in non-Western cultures, but it also occurs in the United States. Firstborns have been found to have higher intelligence quotients (I.Q.s) than their younger siblings, which may reflect the parents' having more time to interact with the firstborn child. Firstborn children appear to be more achievement-oriented than are subsequent children born to the same parents. As more children enter the family, the time for each child diminishes; prenatal stress may also increase as more children have to be cared for.

Second and third children have the advantage of their parents' previous experience. If children are spaced too closely together, however, there may not be enough lap time for each child. The arrival of new children in the family affects not only the parents but also the siblings. Firstborn children may resent the birth of a new sibling, who threatens their sole claim on parental attention. In some cases, such regressive behavior as enuresis or thumb sucking occurs.

In general, the oldest child achieves the most and is the most authoritarian, the middle child usually receives the least attention in the home and may develop strong peer relationships to compensate; and the youngest child may receive too much attention and be spoiled.

## Effects of Divorce on Children

Many children live in homes in which divorce has occurred. In 1992 approximately 30 percent of all children in America lived in homes in which one parent (usually the mother) was the sole head of the household. Sixty-one percent of all children born in any given year can expect to live with only one parent before they reach the age of 18 years. The age of the child at the time of the parents' divorce affects the child's reaction to the divorce. Immediately after the divorce, an increase in behavioral and emotional disorders appears in all age groups. Three-to-

6-year-old children do not understand what is happening, and those who do understand often assume that they are responsible for the divorce in some way. If divorce occurs when the child is between 7 and 12 years, school performance generally declines. Older children, especially adolescents, comprehend the situation and believe that they could have prevented the divorce had they intervened in some way—in effect, serving as surrogate marriage therapists—but they are still hurt, angry, and critical of their parents' behavior. Some children harbor the fantasy that their parents will be reunited at some future date. Such children show animosity toward a parent's real or potential new mate because they are forced to recognize that a reconciliation will not take place. Recovery from and adaptation to the effects of divorce usually take three to five years, but about one third of all children from divorced homes have lasting psychological trauma. Among boys, physical aggression is a common sign of distress. Adolescents tend to spend more time away from the parental home after the divorce. Suicide attempts may occur as a direct result of the divorce; one of the predictors of suicide in adolescence is the recent divorce or separation of the parents. Children who adapt well to divorce do so if each parent makes an effort to continue to relate to the child in spite of the child's anger. To facilitate recovery, the divorced couple must avoid arguing with one another and must show consistent behavior toward the child.

**Stepparents.** When remarriage occurs, the child must learn to adapt to the stepparent and the so-called reconstituted family. The adaptation is usually difficult, especially if the stepparent is nonsupportive or resentful of the stepchild or favors his or her own natural children. A natural child born to the new couple—a stepsibling—sometimes receives more attention than a stepchild and, as a result, is the object of sibling rivalry.

## Adoption

*Adoption* is defined as the process by which a child is taken into a family by one or more adults who are not the biological parents but are recognized by law as the child's parents. In 1981 an estimated 2.5 million persons under 18 years of age were adopted. Fifty-two percent of the children were adopted by persons not related to them by birth or marriage, and the remainder were adopted by relatives or stepparents. The majority of adopted children were born out of wedlock, and 40 percent of all such children were born to mothers between 15 and 19 years of age.

Adoptive parents most often tell their children of their status between the ages of 2 and 4 years to reduce the possibility that their children will learn of their adoption from extrafamilial sources, who may cause them to feel betrayed by their adoptive parents and abandoned by their biological parents.

Emotional and behavior disorders have been reported to be higher among adopted children than among nonadopted children; aggressive behavior, stealing, and learning disturbances are higher among adopted children than among nonadopted children. The later the age of adoption, the higher the incidence and the more severe the degree of behavior problems.

Throughout childhood and adolescence, children may be preoccupied with fantasies of two sets of parents. The adopted child may split the two sets of parents into good parents and bad parents. Adopted children usually have a strong desire to know their biological parents, and some children pattern themselves after their fantasies of their absent biological parents, creating a conflict with their adoptive parents. In most cases in which adopted children have sought out and met their biological parents (and vice versa), the experience has been generally positive, especially if the child is in late adolescence or early adulthood.

## Family Factors in Child Development

**Family stability.** Parents and children living under the same roof in harmonious interaction is the expected cultural norm in Western society. Within that framework, childhood development is expected to proceed most expeditiously. Deviations from that norm (for example, divorced and single-parent families) are associated with a broad range of problems in children, including (1) low self-esteem, (2) increased risk of child abuse, (3) increased incidence of divorce when they eventually marry, and (4) increased incidence of mental disorders, particularly depressive disorders and antisocial personality disorder as adults. Why some children from unstable homes are less affected than others (or even immune to those deleterious effects) is of great interest. Michael Rutter has postulated that vulnerability is influenced by sex (boys are more affected than girls), age (the older child is less vulnerable than the younger child), and the child's inborn personality characteristics. For example, children who have a placid temperament are less likely to be victims of abuse within the family than are hyperactive children; by virtue of their placidity, they may be less affected by the emotional turmoil surrounding them.

**Other family factors.** In childhood and adolescence the death of a parent is associated with adverse effects, such as an increase in later emotional problems, particularly a susceptibility to depression and divorce. That finding is in sharp contrast to separations that result from less traumatic events. For example, no evidence indicates that working mothers raise children who are less healthy than those raised by mothers in the home. Home caretakers can act as surrogate mothers, and in such cases the children do not become more attached to the caretaker than to the parent.

The role of day-care centers for children is under continuous investigation. Some studies show that children placed in day-care centers before the age of 5 years are less assertive and less effectively toilet trained than are home-reared children. Such studies need to take into account the quality of both the day-care center and the home from which the child comes. For example, the child from a disadvantaged home may be better off in a day-care center than is the child from an advantaged home. Similarly, a woman who wishes to leave the home to work for financial or other reasons and is unable to do so may resent being forced to remain in the home in a child-rearing role and, thus, may adversely affect the child.

PARENTING STYLES. Rutter described four types of parenting styles: (1) authoritarian, characterized by rigidity and strict rules, which can lead to depression in the child; (2) permissive, characterized by indulgence and no limit setting, which can lead to poor impulse control; (3) indifferent, characterized by neglect and lack of involvement, leading to aggressive behavior; and (4) reciprocal, characterized by shared decision making with behavior directed in a rational manner, which results in a sense of self-reliance.

In general, experimental studies indicate that the most effective parenting involves consistency and reward for good behavior and punishment for undesirable behavior, both of which should occur within the context of a warm, loving environment.

## References

Ainsworth M, Bell S M, Stayton D: Infant-mother attachment and social development: Socialization as a product of reciprocal responsiveness to signals. In *The Integration of the Child into a Social World*, M Richards, editor, p 7. Cambridge University Press, Cambridge, England, 1974.
Bowlby J: *Attachment and Loss*: vol I. *Attachment*. Basic Books, New York, 1969.
Brandt P, Magyary D, Hammond M, Barnard K: Learning and behavioral-emotional problems of children born preterm at second grade. J Pediatr Psychol *17*: 291, 1992.
Brodzinksy D M, Schechter D, editors: *The Psychology of Adoption*. Oxford University Press, New York, 1988.
Brodzinsky D M, Schechter D, Brodzinsky A M: Children's knowledge of adoption: Developmental change and implications for adjustment. In *Thinking about the Family: View of Parents and Children*, R Ashmore, D Brodzinsky, editors, p 43. Erlbaum, Hillsdale, N J, 1986.
Buka S L, Tsuang M T, Lipsitt L P: Pregnancy-delivery complications and psychiatric diagnosis: A prospective study. Arch Gen Psychiatry *50*: 151, 1993.
Butler J A: Child health and the family. Bull N Y Acad Med *65*: 285, 1989.
Call J D, editor: Normal development. In *Basic Handbook of Child Psychiatry*, J D Noshpitz, editor, vol 1, p 52. Basic Books, New York, 1979.
Call J D, Galenson E, Tyson R L, editors: *Frontiers of Infant Psychiatry*, vols. 1, 2. Basic Books, New York, 1983, 1984.
Chehrazi S, editor: *Psychosocial Issues in Day Care*. American Psychiatric Press, Washington, 1990.
Dworkin P H: Behavior during middle childhood: Developmental themes and clinical issues. Pediatr Ann *18*: 347, 1989.
Erikson E H: *Childhood and Society*, ed 2, Norton, New York, 1963.
Feldman H: The development of thinking skills in school age children. Pediatr Ann *18*: 356, 1989.
Field T: Individual and maturational differences in infant expressivity. New Dir Child Dev *44*: 9, 1989.
Greenspan S I: Normal child development. In *Comprehensive Textbook of Psychiatry*, ed 5, H I Kaplan, B J Sadock, editors, p 1695. Williams & Wilkins, Baltimore, 1989.
Greenspan S I, Greenspan N T: *First Feelings: The Emotional Care of Infants and Young Children*. Viking, New York, 1985.
Kohnstamm G A, Bates J E, Rothbart M K, editors: *Temperament in Childhood*. Wiley, New York, 1989.
Lewis M: Emotional development in the preschool child. Pediatr Ann *18*: 316, 1989.
Lidz T: *The Person: His and Her Development Throughout the Life Cycle*. Basic Books, New York, 1976.
Newcomb A F, Bukowski W M, Pattee L: Children's peer relations: A meta-analytic review of popular, rejected, neglected, controversial, and average sociometric status. Psychol Bull *113*: 99, 1993.
Parke R D: Social development in infancy: A 25-year perspective. Adv Child Dev Behav *21*: 1, 1989.
Tse W Y, Hindmarsh P C, Brook C G: The infancy-childhood-puberty model of growth: Clinical aspects. Acta Paediatr Scand Suppl *356*: 38, 1989.

# 2.4 / Adolescence

Adolescence, a time of variable onset and duration, is the period between childhood and adulthood. It is characterized by profound biological, psychological, and social developmental changes. The biological onset of adolescence is signaled by the rapid acceleration of skeletal growth and the beginnings of physical sexual development; the psychological onset is characterized by an acceleration of cognitive development and a consolidation of personality formation; socially, adolescence is a period of intensified preparation for the coming role of young adulthood.

In many cultures the onset of adolescence is clearly signaled by puberty rites, which usually involve the adolescent's performance of feats of strength and courage. In technologically advanced societies, however, the end of childhood and the requirements for adulthood are not clearly defined; the adolescent undergoes a more prolonged and, in some cases, confused struggle to attain independent adult status.

The end of adolescence occurs when the adolescent is accorded full adult prerogatives; the timing and the length of the end of adolescence vary among societies. In the United States the long period of specialized study required for professional roles often delays the age of self-support, the opportunity for marriage, and creative contributions to society—all attributes of the adult role.

Adolescence is commonly divided into three periods: (1) early (ages 11 to 14), (2) middle (ages 14 to 17), and (3) late (ages 17 to 20). However, those divisions are arbitrary; growth and development occur along a continuum that varies from person to person. One must distinguish between puberty, which is a physical process of change characterized by the development of secondary sex characteristics, and adolescence, which is largely a psychological process of change. Under ideal circumstances the processes are synchronous; when they do not occur simultaneously, as they often do not, the adolescent has to cope with that imbalance as an added stress.

## PUBERTY

The onset of puberty is triggered by the maturation of the hypothalamic-pituitary-adrenal-gonadal axes, leading to the secretion of sex steroids. That hormonal activity produces the manifestations of puberty, which are traditionally categorized as primary and secondary sex characteristics. The primary sex characteristics are those directly involved in coitus and reproduction: the reproductive organs and the external genitalia. The secondary sex characteristics include enlarged breasts and hips in girls and facial hair and lowered voices in boys. The increase in height and weight occurs earlier in girls than in boys; by age 12, girls are generally both taller and heavier than boys. Table 2.4–1 gives a summary of puberty changes.

Precocious or delayed growth, acne, obesity, and enlarged mammary glands in boys and small or overabundant breasts in girls are some deviations from the expected patterns of maturation. Although those conditions may not be medically significant, they often lead to psychological sequelae. Adolescents are sensitive to the opinions of their peers and are constantly comparing themselves with others. Any deviation, real or imagined, can lead to feelings of inferiority, low self-esteem, and loss of confidence. Girls are more sensitive to early physical manifestations of puberty than are boys. For example, tall girls feel more self-conscious about their height than do tall boys when they compare themselves with their peers.

### Age of Onset of Puberty

The age of onset varies, with girls entering puberty 12 to 18 months earlier than do boys. The average age is 11 for girls (with a range of 8 to 13) and 13 for boys (with a range of 10 to 14).

### Hormonal Changes

Sex hormones increase slowly throughout adolescence and correspond to bodily changes. Follicle-stimulating hormone (FSH) and luteinizing hormone (LH) also increase throughout adolescence, but LH is frequently elevated above adult values between ages 17 and 18. LH levels characteristic of adult functioning begin in late adolescence. From age 16 to 17, a large increase seems to occur in average testosterone levels, which then decrease to stabilize at the adult level. Testosterone is the hormone responsible for the masculinization of boys, and estradiol is the hormone responsible for the feminization of girls. Both hormones also influence central nervous system functioning, including mood and behavior. Decreased levels of estrogen may be associated with depressed mood (as happens in the premenstrual period in some women). High testosterone levels have been correlated with aggression and impulsivity in some men. In adolescent boys, testosterone levels correlate with libido and are manifested by sex drive, masturbation, and the drive for coitus. Adolescent girls are also influenced by androgens (produced by the adrenal gland) but to a much smaller extent than in boys. Sexual intercourse in girls is determined almost entirely by psychosocial factors; hormones have much less influence on girls than on boys.

Figure 2.4–1 presents an overview of the hormonal changes associated with adolescent development.

## PSYCHOSEXUAL DEVELOPMENT

Sigmund Freud referred to adolescence as the period in which the libido or sexual energy, which has remained latent during the preadolescent years, is revived. The sex drive is triggered by certain androgens, such as testosterone, which are at higher levels during adolescence than at

**Table 2.4–1**
**Pubertal Stages**

| Stage | Genital Development* | Pubic Hair Development | Breast Development† |
|---|---|---|---|
| | | Characteristics | |
| 1 | Testes, scrotum, and penis are about the same size and shape as in early childhood. | The vellus over the pubis is not further developed than over the abdominal wall (i.e., no pubic hair). | There is elevation of the papillae only. |
| 2 | Scrotum and testes are slightly enlarged. The skin of the scrotum is reddened and changed in texture. There is little or no enlargement of the penis at this stage. | There is sparse growth of long, slightly pigmented, tawny hair, straight or slightly curled, chiefly at the base of the penis or along the labia. | Breast bud stage. There is elevation of the breasts and papillae as small mounds. Areolar diameter is enlarged over that of stage 1. |
| 3 | Penis is slightly enlarged, at first mainly in length. Testes and scrotum are larger than in stage 2. | The hair is considerably darker, coarser, and more curled. It spreads sparsely over the pubis. | Breasts and areolae are both enlarged and elevated more than in stage 2 but with no separation of their contours. |
| 4 | Penis is further enlarged, with growth in breadth and development of glans. Testes and scrotum are larger than in stage 3; scrotum skin is darker than in earlier stages. | Hair is now adult in type, but the area covered is still considerably smaller than in the adult. There is no spread to the medial surface of the thighs. | The areolae and papillae form secondary mounds projecting above the contours of the breasts. |
| 5 | Genitalia are adult in size and shape. | The hair is adult in quantity and type, with distribution of the horizontal (or classically feminine) pattern. Spread is to the medial surface of the thighs but not up the linea alba or elsewhere above the base of the inverse triangle. | Mature stage. The papillae only project, with the areolae recessed to the general contours of the breasts. |

*For boys.
†For girls.
Table by R W Brunstetter, L B Silver: Normal adolescent development. In *Comprehensive Textbook of Psychiatry*, ed 4, H I Kaplan, B J Sadock, editors, p. 1609. Williams & Wilkins, Baltimore, 1985.

any other time of life. According to William Masters and Virginia Johnson, the peak of the male sex drive occurs between 17 and 18 years of age. The early adolescent vents libidinal urges most often through masturbation, a safe way to satisfy sexual impulses.

Because girls enter puberty two years earlier than do boys, they may begin dating and having sexual intercourse at an earlier age; however, adolescent girls are less sexually active than are boys of the same age. Boys are easily aroused by stimuli, and erections are frequent. For girls, the sexual impulse is closely associated with other feelings. Girls tend to view sex and love as related; boys find desire or lust and love to be separable.

Anna Freud described intellectualism and asceticism as the two defense mechanisms most commonly used by adolescents to deal with sexual drives. Intellectualization is manifested by involvement in ideas and books; asceticism is manifested by a retreat into grand ideas and a renunciation of bodily pleasures. Most adolescents struggle with the control of their libidinal drives. The early adolescent is still attached to the family and sometimes has a resurgence of oedipal feelings and even sexual fantasies about the opposite-sex parent. In general, those thoughts and feelings are repressed, and sexuality is directed outward; crushes, hero worship, and the idealization of movie and music stars are characteristic of that stage.

In middle adolescence, sexual behavior and experimentation with a variety of sexual roles are common. Masturbation occurs as a normal activity about equally in both sexes at that time; however, a strict religious upbringing

may engender strong feelings of guilt. Heterosexual crushes, often with an unattainable person of the same age or an older age, are common.

Homosexual experiences may also occur in middle adolescents, but they are usually transient. Many adolescents need reassurance about the normality of an isolated homosexual experience and confirmation that it is not an indication of a permanent homosexual orientation. For others, a homosexual orientation has already been predetermined by that time. Those adolescents (estimated to make up between 1 and 4 percent of all adolescent boys and 0.5 to 2 percent of all adolescent girls) may require counseling on how to deal with their sexual orientation.

Although many adolescents experiment with sex at an early age, recent surveys indicate that the average age for the first sexual intercourse in both sexes is 16 years. The trend in American society is toward greater and more frequent sexual activity at earlier ages than in the past. A decade ago, for example, the average age for the first sexual intercourse was 18, and only 55 percent of women had had sexual intercourse by that time. Currently, 80 percent of men and 70 percent of women have engaged in coitus by age 19.

### Menarche

The onset of menarche is one of the pubertal changes in girls. The current trend is toward an earlier age of menarche than in the past. In the 1920s in the United States,

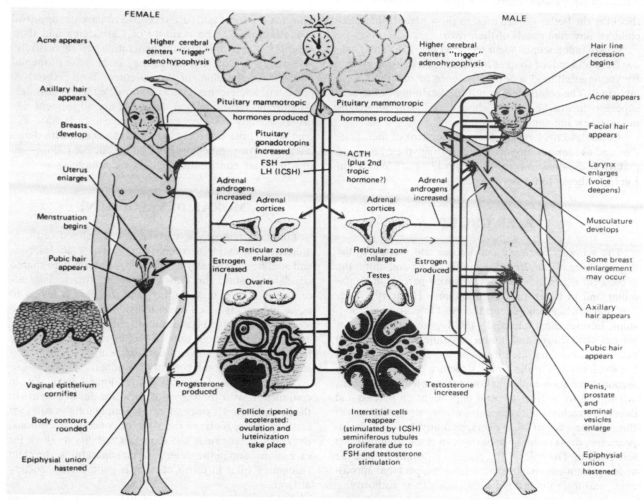

FEMALE  MALE

**Figure 2.4–1.** Effects of sex hormones on development in puberty. (Copyright 1965 by CIBA Pharmaceutical Company. Division of CIBA-GEIGY Corporation. Reproduced with permission from the Ciba Collections of Medical Illustrations, by Frank Netter, M.D. All rights reserved.)

the average age of menarche was 14.5 years; by the 1980s it had dropped to 13 years. Cultural attitudes toward the menarche vary from viewing it as a curse at one extreme to seeing it as a joyful affirmation of one's womanhood at the other extreme. Most adolescent girls still do not receive information on the menses from their parents. They rely on information from peers, schools, and the media. Menarche can be delayed by a variety of factors: poor nutritional status, excessive exercise—for example, marathon running—and psychological stress.

## COGNITIVE AND PERSONALITY DEVELOPMENT

According to Jean Piaget, at the beginning of adolescence, thinking becomes abstract, conceptual, and future-oriented; he termed it the stage of formal operations. At that time, many adolescents show remarkable creativity, which they express in writing, music, art, and poetry. Creativity is also expressed in sports and in the adolescent's interest in the world of ideas—humanitarian issues, morals, ethics, and religion. Keeping a personal diary is a common creative outlet during that period.

According to Erik Erikson, the major task of adolescence is to achieve ego identity, which he defined as the awareness of who one is and where one is going. Erikson described the normal struggle of adolescence as identity versus role confusion. *Identity* is a secure sense of self. *Confusion*, also called *identity diffusion*, is a failure to develop a cohesive self or self-awareness. Part of the resolution of the identity crisis is to move from being a dependent person to being an independent person. The initial struggles often revolve around the established concepts of sex roles and gender identification. Old techniques that the child used earlier to master separation may return.

Negativism reappears. "No, I can do it myself. Don't tell me how long my hair can be. Don't tell me how short my skirt can be." That negativism is a renewed attempt to tell, first, parents and then the world that the growing persons have minds of their own. Negativism becomes an active verbal way of expressing anger. Adolescents may seize almost any issue to show that they have minds separate from their parents' minds. Parents and adolescents may argue about the adolescents' choice of friends, peer groups, school plans and courses, and points of philosophy and etiquette. Members of each generation recall how clothes, hairstyles, and other external badges—the more shocking the better—were used to show parents that their children now had minds of their own.

Slowly, adolescents begin to blend many different values from all kinds of sources into their own existing values. By young adulthood a new conscience or superego is established. The compatibility and the flexibility of the new superego has to be able to change and grow to accommodate new life situations.

As adolescents begin to feel independent of their families and as families support and encourage their emerging maturity, the questions of "Who am I?" and "Where am I going?" begin to be answered.

## PEER GROUP

The school experience accelerates and intensifies the degree of separation from the family. More and more, the adolescent exists in a world with which parents are unfamiliar and in which they do not share. Home is a base. The real world is school, and the most important relationships, besides the adolescent's family, are with those persons of similar ages and interests. Adolescents attempt to establish a personal identity, separate from their parents but close enough to the family structure to be included. A second separation-individuation occurs when adolescents, attempting to be free, are still dependent on parents and deeply attached. Adolescents often view themselves through the eyes of their peers, and any deviation in appearance, dress code, or behavior can result in diminished self-esteem. The role of the parents is to understand the sudden, frequent changes in friendships, personal appearance, and interests but not to abrogate their authority.

## PARENTING

The concept of the generation gap between parents and children developed from the experience of being parents of adolescents. The gap represents the difference in life experiences and perceptions of life events. In addition to having to deal with the turmoil that accompanies adolescent development, parents of adolescents are usually middle-aged and have to make adjustments at that time to work, to marriage, and to their own parents. Many difficulties surround the adolescent's need to assume increased independence from the home, a move that can be threatening to parents who cannot let go and who need to maintain control of their children. Some parents may be unable to set limits on behavior; others act out their hidden or unconscious fantasies through the lives of their children. Superego lacunae (gaps or holes in the conscience) in the parent may engender similar lacunae in the child, and those gaps are then acted out. Moreover, the strong emerging sexuality of the adolescent may trigger anxiety in the parent. A few parents may be attracted to their opposite-sex offspring and then deal with the subsequent anxiety in maladaptive ways, such as getting angry (reaction formation).

In spite of the conclusions described above, most parents of adolescents report few major altercations. Most parents get along with their adolescent sons and daughters, who, for the most part, are receptive to parental approval and disapproval. The majority of adolescents and their parents are able to bridge the generation gap successfully. When they do not, that failure may be because of mental disorders in the child or the parent or both. About 20 percent of adolescents have a diagnosable mental disorder. Among the most common diagnoses are adjustment disorders; anxiety disorders and depressive disorders are also common. Those disorders are often associated with delinquent behavior, rebelliousness, and academic failure—all of which may contribute to family disharmony.

## MORAL DEVELOPMENT

For most people, developing a well-defined sense of morality is a major accomplishment of late adolescence and adulthood. *Morality* is defined as conformity to shared standards, rights, and duties. However, two socially accepted standards may conflict, and the person learns to make judgments based on an individualized sense of conscience. The person has a moral obligation to abide by established norms but only to the degree that they serve human ends. That stage of development internalizes ethical principles and the control of conduct.

Piaget described morality as developing gradually, in conjunction with the stages of cognitive development. In the preoperational stage, the child simply follows rules set forth by the parents; in the stage of concrete operations, the child accepts rules but shows an inability to allow for exceptions; and in the stage of formal operations, the child recognizes rules in terms of what is good for the society at large.

Lawrence Kohlberg integrated Piaget's concepts and described three major levels of morality. The first level is *preconventional morality,* in which punishment and obedience to the parent are the determining factors; the second level is *morality of conventional role-conformity,* in which the child tries to conform to gain approval and to maintain good relationships with others; and the third and highest level is *morality of self-accepted moral principles,* in which the child voluntarily complies with rules on the basis of a concept of ethical principles and makes exceptions to rules in certain circumstances.

## OCCUPATIONAL CHOICE

Occupational choice stems from the question, "Where am I going?" Both men and women need to feel independent, autonomous, and content with their vocational choices. The adolescent is beleaguered by peers, parents, teachers, and counselors, as well as subconscious forces, in attempting to decide on a vocation. Whether opportunities exist for further schooling certainly plays a role in the decision. Among college graduates, 30 percent go on to some type of postcollege graduate education. Those adolescents who are unable to continue schooling are severely hampered in establishing a satisfactory vocational identity. Many are fated for lives of economic and emotional depression.

The psychological basis for a sense of individual worth

as an adult rests on the acquisition of competence during adolescence. A sense of competence is acquired by experiencing success in a task that today's society views as important. The sustained motivation necessary for mastering a difficult work role is possible only when the adolescent has a likelihood of fulfilling that role in adult life and of having it respected by others.

## RISK-TAKING BEHAVIOR

Risk-taking behavior in adolescence involves alcohol, tobacco, and other substance use; promiscuous sexual activity—which is especially dangerous in view of the risk of acquired immune deficiency syndrome (AIDS)—and accident-prone behavior, such as fast driving, skydiving, and hang gliding. Most mortality statistics for teenagers cite accidents as the leading cause of death, with vehicular accidents accounting for about 40 percent of all teenage deaths. The reasons for risk-taking behavior are varied and relate to counterphobic dynamics, the fear of inadequacy, the need to affirm a masculine identity, and group dynamics, such as peer pressure. The behavior may also be a reflection of some adolescents' omnipotent fantasies, in which they view themselves as invulnerable to harm and injury. As adolescence proceeds, risk-taking behavior abates, and responsible decision-making activity occurs.

## ADOLESCENT TURMOIL

The normal adolescent does not progress through a tumultuous phase of rebelliousness, mood swings, and impulsiveness commonly known as adolescent turmoil. Erikson's identity crisis is a normal process; however, if it is not negotiated successfully, role confusion—such as running away, criminality, and severe mental illness—may result. Adolescent turmoil, therefore, should be distinguished from a diagnosable mental disorder.

## PREGNANCY

Each year about 1 million teenage girls become pregnant. Of that number, 600,000 give birth; the remainder — 400,000 (40 percent)—obtain abortions. The number of teenagers who are having sex is increasing. Boys generally have more sexual partners than do girls, and boys are less likely than are girls to seek emotional attachments with their sexual partners.

Teenage pregnancy is most common in nonwhite, low socioeconomic adolescent girls. Among those girls, prenatal care is low, which is a major contributing factor in maternal morbidity and mortality. Only one third of sexually active teenagers use contraceptives; most of them are uneducated about contraceptive use or are unwilling or unable to obtain contraceptives. Table 2.4–2 lists the reasons for contraceptive misuse or rejection.

In some subcultures, teenagers view pregnancy as a rite of passage into adulthood. The adolescent girl who is depressed, insecure about her attractiveness, or the child of a conflicted or divorced couple is more likely to become

**Table 2.4–2**
**Factors in the Misuse or Rejection of Contraceptives**

| Factors | Comments |
|---|---|
| Denial | The belief that pregnancy will not or cannot occur |
| Opportunism | Taking advantage of the opportunity (possibly unexpected) for coitus without regard for the consequences |
| Love | Coitus is driven by passionate enthusiasm with the expectation of marriage if pregnancy occurs |
| Guilt | Contraceptive use represents planned coitus, which engenders feelings of guilt |
| Embarrassment | Self-consciousness about using condom or inserting diaphragm in front of the partner |
| Entrapment | The desire to impregnate or to become pregnant to force the partner to become attached emotionally |
| Eroticism | The belief that contraceptive use decreases or interferes with erotic pleasure |
| Nihilism | The belief that contraceptives are ineffective or useless |
| Fear and anxiety | Coitus is associated with high levels of anxiety; fear of performance ability interferes with contraceptive use |
| Abortion | The belief that, if one gets pregnant, abortion can be obtained; therefore, a contraceptive is not needed |
| Education | The lack of education about effective contraceptive use from parents and school |
| Availability | Access to or cost of contraceptive prohibits its use |

pregnant than is the adolescent from a stable background.

The average adolescent mother is unable to care for her child, who is either placed in foster care or raised by the teenager's already overburdened parents or other relatives. Few girls marry the fathers of their children; the fathers, usually teenagers, are unable to care for themselves, much less the mothers of their children. If the couple do marry, they usually divorce.

### Abortion

Teenage girls often use abortion services. Almost all the girls are unwed mothers from low socioeconomic groups; their pregnancies resulted from sex with boys to whom they felt emotionally attached. Most teenagers elect to have abortions with their parents' consent; however, laws of mandatory parental consent put two rights into competition: the child's claim to privacy and the parent's need to know. Most adults believe that teenagers should have parental permission for an abortion. When parents refuse to give their consent, most states prohibit the parents' vetoing of the teenagers' decisions.

## PROSTITUTION

Teenagers constitute a large portion of all prostitutes, with estimates ranging up to 1 million teenagers involved in prostitution. Most adolescent prostitutes are girls, but boys are also involved as homosexual prostitutes. Most teenagers who enter into a life of prostitution come from broken homes or were abused as children. Many of the girls were victims of rape. Most teenagers ran away from home and were taken in by pimps and substance abusers; then the adolescents themselves became substance abusers. They are at high risk for AIDS, and many, up to 70 percent in some studies, are infected with the human immunodeficiency virus (HIV).

### END OF ADOLESCENCE

The end of adolescence occurs when the person begins to assume the tasks of young adulthood, which involve choosing an occupation and developing a sense of intimacy that leads, in most cases, to marriage and parenthood. Daniel Levinson described an early-adult transition between adolescence and adulthood in which the young person begins to leave home and live independently. That period sees a peaking of biological development, the assumption of new social roles, the socialization into those roles that involves learning skills and attitudes required to perform the roles well, and the eventual assumption of an adult self and life structure.

#### References

Adelson J B: The mystique of adolescence. In *Childhood Psychopathology,* S I Harrison, J F McDermott, editors, p. 214. International Universities Press, New York, 1972.
Blos P: *On Adolescence: A Psychoanalytic Interpretation.* Free Press, New York, 1962.
Brent D A, Johnson B, Bartle S, Bridge J: Personality disorder, tendency to impulsive violence, and suicidal behavior in adolescents. J Am Acad Child Adolesc Psychiatry *32:* 69, 1993.
Flanagan C A, Eccles J S: Changes in parents' work status and adolescents' adjustment at school. Child Dev *64:* 246, 1993.
Freud A: Adolescence. Psychoanal Study Child *13:* 255, 1958.
Garber J, Weiss B, Shanley N: Cognitions, depressive symptoms, and development in adolescents. J Abnorm Psychol *102:* 47, 1993.
Group for the Advancement of Psychiatry: *Normal Adolescence.* Group for the Advancement of Psychiatry, New York, 1968.
Lidz T: *The Person: His and Her Development Throughout the Life Cycle.* Basic Books, New York, 1976.
Looney J G, Oldham D G: Normal adolescent development. In *Comprehensive Textbook of Psychiatry,* ed 5, H I Kaplan, B J Sadock, editors, p 1710. Williams & Wilkins, Baltimore, 1989.
Murry V M: Incidence of first pregnancy among black adolescent females over three decades. Youth Soc *23:* 478, 1992.
Mussen P H, Conger J J, Kagan J: Adolescence. In *Essentials of Child Development and Personality.* Harper & Row, New York, 1984.
Newcomb M D: Life change events among adolescents. J Nerv Ment Dis *175:* 280, 1986.
Offer D, Ostrov E, Howard K I: The mental health professional concept of normal adolescents. Arch Gen Psychiatry *38:* 149, 1981.
Sarnoff C A: *Latency.* Aronson, New York, 1976.
Takanishi R: The opportunities of adolescence: Research, interventions, and policy. Am Psychol *48:* 85, 1993.
Vaughan V C, Litt I F: *Child and Adolescent Development.* Saunders, Philadelphia, 1990.

## 2.5 / Adulthood

Much of psychiatry is concerned with adulthood—that period of life when the person is presumed to be fully developed and mature and the time when the potential for personal fulfillment is at its peak. It is the longest part of the life cycle and is usually divided into three major periods: young or early adulthood (from age 20 to 40), middle adulthood (from age 40 to 65), and late adulthood or old age. This section is concerned with the tasks of early and middle adulthood, when the phenomena relating to marriage, child rearing, and work are most significant. The onset of adulthood varies from person to person. It is a time of great change—sometimes dramatic, at other times subtle, but always continuous.

### EARLY ADULTHOOD

Usually considered to begin at the end of adolescence (about age 20) and to end at age 40, early adulthood is characterized by the peaking of biological development, the assumption of major social roles, and the evolution of an adult self and life structure. The successful passage into adulthood depends on the satisfactory resolution of childhood and adolescent crises.

During late adolescence, the young person leaves home and begins to function independently. Relationships with the opposite sex become serious, and the quest for intimacy begins. The transitional period into early adulthood involves a variety of important events: high school graduation, starting a job or entry into college, and leaving home. The 20s are spent, for the most part, exploring options for occupation, marriage, or alternative relationships and making commitments in various areas. However, the choices made in the late teens and early 20s are tentative at best; the young adult may make several false starts before a lasting commitment is reached.

#### Developmental Tasks

During the early phase of adulthood, options for occupation and marriage (or other intimate relationships) are explored. For most young adults, selecting a mate and starting a family are of paramount importance.

Persons in their 30s also become increasingly concerned with achieving great authority, independence, and self-sufficiency. The primary goal of early adulthood is to become more autonomous and less dependent on the persons and institutions in one's life.

At about age 30 young adults are likely to feel a need to take life seriously. Many young adults ask themselves at that time whether the life they have is the one they really want. Daniel J. Levinson called that period of reappraisal the "age 30 transition." Some young people who feel that their lives are going well reaffirm their commitments and experience a smooth transition at that time. Others, however, may experience a major crisis, manifested by marital problems, job changes, and psychiatric symptoms, such as anxiety and depression. Levinson described developmental periods through all phases of adulthood (Figure 2.5–1).

Roger Gould reported a similar process among persons in their late 20s and early 30s who discover new talents, wishes, tendencies, and interests not previously appreciated or acknowledged. That awareness may bring out either disillusionment and depression or a new sense of self with a realistic appraisal of one's strengths and weaknesses.

**Erik Erikson.** Erik Erikson described the period between about age 20 and age 40 as the stage of intimacy versus self-absorption or isolation. Intimacy concerns the person's ability to form warm friendships and associations with others. In particular, intimacy concerns the person's capacity to be intimate in sexual relations, to combine love and sex. Sigmund Freud wrote of those unable to combine love and sex: where they love, they cannot desire, and where they desire, they cannot love.

The antithesis to intimacy is self-absorption or isolation. Unable to develop long-term relationships, the person does not marry and remains apart from others; self-absorption follows, with no attachments made to any social group.

**Carl Gustav Jung.** Carl Gustav Jung referred to the major task of adult development as individuation. Adults must see themselves as unique persons both apart from and part of society at large. Adults learn to recognize and to respect a value system that can withstand external pres-

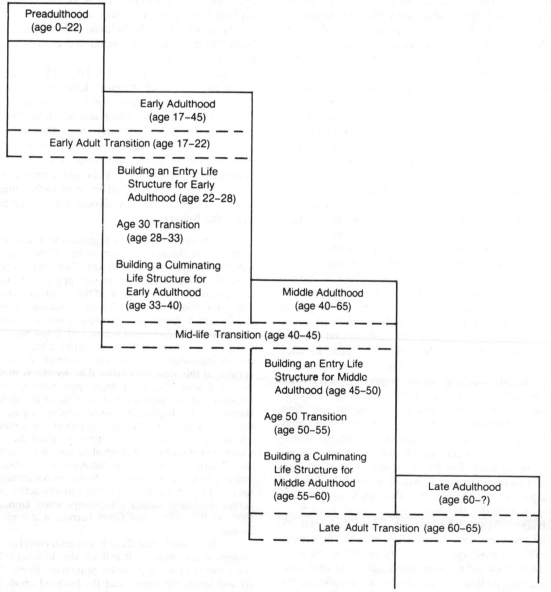

**Figure 2.5–1.** Developmental periods in the eras of early and middle adulthood. (Figure adapted by D J Levinson, W E Gooden from D J Levinson, C N Darrow, E B Klein, M H Levinson, B McKee: *The Seasons of a Man's Life.* Knopf, New York, 1978. Used with permission.)

sures. According to Jung, the person must not become a conformist who uncritically accepts social norms.

**Occupation.** Socioeconomic group, gender, and race affect the pursuit and the development of a particular occupational choice. Blue-collar workers generally enter the work force directly after high school; white-collar workers and professionals usually enter the work force after college or professional school.

A healthy adaptation to work provides an outlet for creativity, satisfactory relationships with colleagues, pride in accomplishment, and increased self-esteem. Job satisfaction is not wholly dependent on money. In contrast, maladaptation can lead to dissatisfaction with oneself and the job, insecurity, decreased self-esteem, anger, and resentment at having to work. Symptoms of job dissatisfaction are a high rate of job changes, absenteeism, mistakes at work, accident-proneness, and even sabotage.

Members of racial minorities are frequently burdened with low socioeconomic status, which limits their opportunities for rewarding and satisfying work. They frequently begin their 20s with hopes of becoming successful but are often disappointed in that endeavor later in life.

WOMEN AND WORK. Women often exhibit one of two patterns in their 20s: work for pay is the central component of their life structure, and family is absent or secondary; or marriage and family are primary, and career is absent or secondary. By their 30s, many women try to combine both patterns, usually with difficulty. Housewives and mothers face particular problems if they decide to work. They are expected to continue to take care of child rearing and housework, maintain the marital relationship, and at the same time deal with the demands of a career. In general, men are still not expected to juggle the roles of husband, father, and worker. Some changes are occurring in those gender expectations, but the changes are not sufficient to upset the stereotype of the working woman having to be Supermom and Superwife at the same time.

Ninety percent of all women have to work to support themselves. Economic necessity and personal desire now prompt the homemaker to enter the labor force, something that may not have been a consideration in the past. Dual-career families, in which both the husband and the wife have jobs, constitute more than 50 percent of all families. Employers who do not recognize family-oriented needs—such as flexible working hours, negotiable leaves, and shared or part-time jobs—contribute to family stress.

UNEMPLOYMENT. The effects of unemployment transcend those of loss of income; the psychological and physical tolls are enormous. The incidence of alcohol dependence, homicide, violence, suicide, and mental illness rises with unemployment. The person's core identity, which is often tied to occupation and work, is seriously damaged when a job is lost, whether it is through firing, attrition, or early or regular retirement.

**Marriage.** Most Americans marry in their mid-20s; however, the marriage rate is going down, and an increasing number of marriages in the United States end in divorce. Most divorced persons marry again—in most cases more successfully than the first time—which indicates that the marital unit still provides the means for sustained intimacy, perpetuating the culture, and gratifying interpersonal needs. In the 1990s nearly two thirds of all persons

in their 20s are married, and nearly three quarters of all persons in their 30s are married. Almost twice as many whites as blacks are married in the age range of 25 to 34.

The change in mores from a restrictive moral climate in the 1950s to a permissive moral climate in the 1990s is seen in the number of unmarried adults who live together (cohabitation). In the 1960s only 8 percent of couples lived together before marrying; currently, more than 50 percent of first marriages are preceded by cohabitation.

Despite the improvement in black-white relations over the past 20 years, the number of interracial marriages has not changed during that period. Interracial marriages still make up only 2 percent of all marriages. However, whites married to other groups, such as Asians, increased during that time, although exact figures are unavailable.

As Erikson noted, persons who reach adulthood in a state of continued role confusion are unable to establish the psychological state of intimacy that is necessary for marriage to occur and to occur successfully. Being in love, according to Freud, is irrational in that there is a loss of reality testing about the beloved. The two persons in love block out the rest of the world and are not accessible to group influences.

FORMS OF MARRIAGE. In the United States a high value is placed on marital stability, love, and happiness. Although most people marry for love, it is not possible to predict who will marry whom and which marriages will be successful. Most people marry within their own socioeconomic group to persons from their own neighborhoods. The decision to marry also hinges on group and family pressures. Most persons are expected to marry in their 20s.

David Reed, who studied emotional adjustment in marriage and the factors that account for marital happiness, wrote the following:

> Most studies concur that happiness in a marriage implies happiness in the general relationship. However, those who report very happy marriages tend to dwell on their relationship in surveys, and those who are unhappy tend to indicate external sources of stress. None of this research includes objective observation of actual behavior. In relations in which need satisfaction is measured, researchers are inconclusive as to how emotional adjustment is achieved. It has become popular to advocate communication and verbal confrontation as important ingredients in emotional adjustment in marriage. Advocates of this view proselytize that openness, more talking, increased sensitivity to feelings, personalizing of language symbols, and keeping the communication channels open all contribute to happiness. Some studies agree with this view. . . . However, other studies report that communication can disturb a relationship, particularly when there is an emphasis on verbal overkill. Complete openness can be destructive. There may be a secret intolerance of weakness or an inability to perceive accurately the emotional strength of one's spouse. In such a relationship the verbally active partner becomes the better fighter who always wins. Thus, conflict is never well handled, and fights become a chronic source of despair. . . .
>
> . . . [I]t is likely that there is a general correlation between happiness and stability. It is likely that in most relationships some form of success precedes general emotional fulfillment. By and large, this means that the husband needs to succeed in his role performance before there is an overwhelming concern with companionship. This is particularly true in disadvantaged families in which survival is an issue of far greater

importance than pleasure. Moreover, satisfaction should not be confused with bliss, for satisfaction may include overt hostility more than peaceful companship. . . .

Theodore Lidz has written extensively on marital interaction from a psychodynamic point of view. He stated that marital success is a combination of stability (the satisfaction of role perception and performance) and emotional adjustment (self-realization). Marriage demands a reorganization of the personalities of both partners. The spouses' egos must expand pertaining to their views of themselves, their partners, and the marriage relationship itself. Moreover, one's spouse should become one's alter ego when there is optimum mutuality of need satisfaction. Lidz noted that a prototype for an effective husband-wife relationship is the mutuality of the mother and the child.

Lidz also noted that each spouse needs to have some change at the superego level in order to cope with the spouse's id, an apparent reference to the modification of a value system that tolerates the basic emotional demands of a partner without necessarily giving in to the partner. The impulses that most need to be recognized in a relationship involve assertion and self-preservation. And both partners need to respect ego defenses. Lidz noted that there is often a transference of parental traits to one's spouse; that psychological factor is an important ingredient in dealing with dependence needs and the learning of social roles. He also indicated that within the marriage the spouses exchange parental roles whenever a life-cycle crisis places one or the other in an overdependent state. Marriage also involves a fusion of the original families of the spouses, a factor that brings role relationships back into play.

MARITAL PROBLEMS.    Although marriage tends to be regarded as a permanent tie, unsuccessful unions may be terminated, as indeed they are in most societies. In spite of that, many marriages that do not end in separation or divorce are disturbed.

In considering marital problems, the clinician is concerned not only with the persons involved but also with the marital unit itself. How any marriage works out relates to the partners selected, the personality organization or disorganization of each, the interaction between them, and the original reasons for the union. People marry for a variety of reasons—emotional, social, economic, and political, among others. One person may look to the spouse to meet unfulfilled childhood needs for good parenting. Another sees the spouse as someone to be saved from an otherwise unhappy life. Irrational expectations between spouses increase the risk of marital problems.

MARITAL THERAPY.    When families consist of grandparents, parents, children, and other relatives living under the same roof, assistance for marital problems can sometimes be obtained from a member of the extended family with whom one or both partners have rapport. However, with the contraction of the extended family in recent times, that source of informal help is no longer as accessible as it once was. Similarly, religion once played a more important role than it does now in the maintenance of family stability. Wise religious leaders are available to provide counseling; but they are not sought out to the extent that they once were, a reflection of the decline of religious influence for large segments of the population. Formerly, both the extended family and religion not only provided guidance for the couple in distress but also prevented dissolution of the marriage by virtue of the social pressure that the extended family and religion exerted on the couple to stay together. As family, religious, and societal pressures relaxed, legal procedures for relatively easy separation and divorce expanded. Concurrently, the need for formalized marriage counseling services developed.

Marital therapy is a form of psychotherapy for married people who are in conflict with each other. A trained person establishes a professional contract with the patient-couple and, through definite types of communication, attempts to alleviate the disturbance, reverse or change maladaptive patterns of behavior, and encourage personality growth and development.

In *marriage counseling,* only a particular conflict related to the immediate concerns of the family is discussed; marriage counseling is conducted in a much more superficial manner than is marital therapy and by persons with less training in psychotherapy. In *marriage therapy*, there is greater emphasis on restructuring the interaction between the couple—including, at times, an exploration of the psychodynamics of each partner. Both therapy and counseling emphasize helping the marital partners cope effectively with their problems.

**Parenthood.**    By age 30, most persons have established families and have to deal with a variety of parent-child problems. In addition to the economic burden of raising a child (estimated to be more than $100,000 for a middle-class family whose child goes to college), there are emotional costs as well. The child may reawaken conflicts in parents that they themselves had as children, or the child may have a chronic illness that challenges the emotional resources of the family. In general, men are more concerned with their work and advancement in their occupations than with child rearing. Women are more concerned about their role as mothers; however, that emphasis is changing dramatically for both sexes as more women enter the job market. At about age 35, women may dramatically change the course of their lives. As their children get older, they reenter the work force to resume their careers or to start a career for the first time.

Parenting in one's 20s and 30s has been described as a continuing process of letting go. The child must be allowed to separate from the parents and in some cases encouraged to do so. When parents are in their 20s, letting go involves the separation of the child who is starting school. School phobias and school refusal syndromes that are accompanied by extreme separation anxiety may have to be dealt with at that time. Often, a parent who is unable to let go of the child accounts for the situation. Some parents want their children to remain tightly bound to them emotionally. Family therapy in which those dynamics are explored may be necessary to resolve the problem.

As children get older and enter adolescence, the process of individuation assumes great importance. Peer relationships become crucial to the child's development, and overprotective parents who keep the child from developing friendships or allowing the child the freedom to experiment with friends that the parents disapprove of can interfere with the child's passage through adolescence. That does not mean that the parents exert no influence over their child. Guidance and involvement are crucial. However, parents must recognize that adolescents especially need parental approval; although rebellious on the surface, adolescents are much more tractable than they appear, provided the parents are not overbearing or generally punitive.

SINGLE-PARENT FAMILIES.   There are more than 30 million families with one or more children under the age of 18; of those families, 20 percent are single-parent homes in which a woman is the sole head of the household. Although the majority of those children are left in the care of their mothers who are awarded custody by the courts in divorce proceedings, other children are abandoned by their fathers. Among black families with one or more children under 18, almost 48 percent are headed by women with no spouse present.

Only 15 percent of divorced or separated women were awarded alimony. The rate of child-support awards ranged from 24 percent for never-married women to 72 percent for separated, married, or divorced women. Furthermore, some of those women who are awarded alimony or child support do not receive full or any payment. Consequently, most of the women are living under severe economic hardship and are forced to work to support themselves and their children. When mothers are forced to work after divorce or abandonment, their children are at risk for emotional problems, because the mothers cannot devote sufficient time to the care of the children. A small number of children in single-parent homes are precocious, their maturity fostered by having to take on increased responsibilities at a young age.

## MIDDLE ADULTHOOD

The ages used to define middle adulthood vary among theorists. Typically, the period spans the years from 40 to 65. Jung referred to age 40 as the noon of life. The task of terminating early adulthood involves a process of reviewing the past, considering how one's life has gone, and deciding what the future will be like. With regard to occupation, many persons begin to experience the gap between early aspirations and current achievements. They may wonder if the life-style and the commitments they chose in early adulthood are worth continuing. They may feel that they would like to live the remaining years in a different, more satisfying way, without knowing exactly how. As children grow up and leave home, the parental roles change; at that time, people also redefine their roles as husbands and wives.

Important gender changes occur in middle adulthood.

Many women, no longer needing to nurture young children, are able to release their energy into independent pursuits that require assertiveness and a competitive spirit, traits that were traditionally considered to be masculine. Alternatively, men in middle adulthood may develop qualities that enable them to express their emotions and recognize their dependence needs, traits that were traditionally considered to be feminine. The new balance of the masculine and the feminine may enable a person to relate more effectively than in the past to someone of the opposite sex. Jung recognized that process in men and women in the 1900s when he described the anima and the animus. *Anima* is the female side of a man. *Animus* is the male side of a woman. Both anima and animus exist to some degree in each gender, and an awareness of each is necessary for mental health.

## Developmental Tasks

Robert Butler described a number of underlying themes in middle adulthood that appear to be present regardless of marital and family status, gender, or economic level (Table 2.5–1). The themes include (1) aging, since changes in bodily functions are noticed in middle adulthood; (2) taking stock of one's accomplishments and setting goals for the future; (3) reassessing one's commitments to family, work, and marriage; (4) dealing with the new generation and relationships with one's children; (5) using accumulated power responsibly and ethically; (6) dealing with illness and death in one's parents; and (7) attending to all the above developmental tasks without losing one's capacity to experience pleasure or to engage in playful activity.

**Erik Erikson.**   Erikson described middle adulthood as the stage when the adult is characterized by generativity or stagnation. Erikson defined *generativity* as the process by which one guides the oncoming generation or improves society. It includes having and raising children, but wanting or having children does not ensure generativity. A childless person can be generative by helping others, by being creative, and by contributing to society. Parents have to be secure in their own identity to raise a child successfully.

**Table 2.5-1**
**Features Salient to Middle Life**

| Issues | Positive Features | Negative Features |
|---|---|---|
| Prime of life | Responsible use of power; maturity; productivity | Winner-loser view; competitiveness |
| Stocktaking: what to do with the rest of one's life | Possibility; alternatives; organization of commitments; redirection | Closure; fatalism |
| Fidelity and commitments | Commitment to self, others, career, society; filial maturity | Hypocrisy, self-deception |
| Growth-death (to grow is to die); juvenescence and rejuvenation fantasies | Naturality regarding body, time | Obscene or frenetic efforts (e.g., to be youthful); hostility and envy of youth and progeny; longing |
| Communication and socialization | Matters understood; continuity: picking up where left off; large social network; rootedness of relationships, places, and ideas | Repetitiveness; boredom; impatience; isolation; conservatism; confusion; rigidity |

Data from Robert N. Butler, M.D.

They cannot be preoccupied with themselves and act as if they were or wished to be the child in the family.

To be *stagnant* is to stop one's development. For Erikson, stagnation was anathema, and he referred to the adult who has no impulse to guide the new generation or who produces children without caring for them as being "within a cocoon of self-concern and isolation." Such persons are in great danger. Because they are unable to negotiate the developmental tasks of middle adulthood, they are unprepared for the next stage of the life cycle, old age, which places more demands on the psychological and physical capacities of the person than do all the preceding stages.

**George Vaillant.** In his longitudinal study of 173 men who were interviewed at five-year intervals after they graduated from Harvard, George Vaillant found a strong correlation between physical health and emotional health in middle age. In addition, those persons who had the poorest psychological adjustment during college years had a high incidence of physical illness in middle age. No single factor in childhood accounted for adult mental health; however, an overall sense of stability in the parental home predicted a well-adjusted adulthood. A close sibling relationship during the college years was correlated with emotional and physical well-being in middle age. In another study Vaillant found that childhood work habits correlated with adult work habits and that adult mental health and good interpersonal relationships were associated with the capacity to work in childhood.

## Sexuality

Sexuality in general is a major issue in midlife. Although William Masters and Virginia Johnson reported, as did Alfred Kinsey and others, that enjoyable sexual activity (including coitus) may continue well into old age, a decline in sexual functioning may occur. For some persons, however, the erroneous belief that vigorous sexual activity is the prerogative of youth is sufficient to interfere with their normal physiological sexual responses.

Fears and the reality of impotence are a common problem in middle-aged men. The most common cause of impotence in the middle years is not aging but excessive alcohol intake, drugs (such as tranquilizers and antidepressants), and stress with fatigue and anxiety; 90 percent of the cases of chronic impotence in middle adulthood are due to psychological causes, rather than organic causes.

Middle-aged women may also experience a decline in sexual functioning that is more related to psychological causes than to physical causes. Women do not reach their sexual prime until their mid-30s; consequently, they have a greater capacity for orgasm in middle adulthood than in young adulthood. Women, however, are more vulnerable than men to narcissistic blows to their self-esteem as they lose their youthful appearance, which is overvalued in today's society. During middle adulthood they may feel less sexually desirable than in early adulthood and, therefore, feel less entitled to an adequate sex life.

An inability to deal with changes in body image prompts many women and men to undergo cosmetic surgery in an effort to maintain their youthful appearance.

## Male and Female Climacterium

Middle adulthood is the time of the male and female climacterium, that period in life characterized by a decrease in biological and physiological functioning.

For women, the menopausal period is considered to be the climacterium and may start anywhere from the 40s to the early 50s. Bernice Neugarten studied that period and found that more than 50 percent of the women described the menopause as an unpleasant experience; however, a significant portion of the women believed that their lives had not changed in any significant way, and many women experienced no adverse effects. Because they no longer had to worry about becoming pregnant, several women reported feeling freer after the menopause than they had felt before its onset. Generally, the female climacterium has been stereotyped as a sudden or radical psychophysiological experience. However, it is more often a gradual experience as estrogen secretion decreases with changes in the flow, timing, and eventual cessation of the menses. Vasomotor instability (hot flashes) may occur, and the menopause may extend over a period of several years. Some women experience anxiety and depression, but usually one's premenopausal personality structure predisposes the person to the menopausal syndrome.

For men, the climacterium has no clear demarcation like the menopause. Male hormones stay fairly constant through the 40s and 50s. Nevertheless, men must adapt to a decline in biological functioning and overall physical vigor. The crisis can be mild or severe, characterized by a sudden drastic change in work or the marital relationship, severe depression, the increased use of alcohol or drugs, or a shift to an alternate life-style.

Normal turning points during middle age are usually mastered without distress. Only when life events are severe or unexpected—such as the death of a spouse, the loss of a job, or a serious illness—does the person experience an emotional disorder severe enough to warrant the term "midlife crisis." Men and women who are most prone to midlife crises tend to come from families characterized by one or more of the following during their adolescence: parental discord, withdrawal by the same-sex parent, anxious parents, and impulsive parents with a low sense of responsibility.

**Empty-nest syndrome.** Another phenomenon described in middle adulthood has been called the empty-nest syndrome, a depression that occurs in men and women when their youngest child is about to leave home. However, most parents perceive the departure of the youngest child as a relief, rather than a stress. If no compensating activities have been developed, particularly by the mother, some parents become depressed.

## Other Tasks of Middle Adulthood

As persons approach the age of 50, they clearly define what they want from work, family, and leisure. Men who have reached their highest level of advancement in work may experience disillusionment or frustration when they realize that they can no longer anticipate new work challenges. For the woman who has invested herself completely in the mothering role, this period of life leaves her with no suitable identity after the children leave home. Sometimes social rules become rigidly established; lack of freedom in life-style and a sense of entrapment may lead to depression and a loss of confidence. There may also be unique financial burdens in middle age, resulting from pressures to care for aged parents at one end of the spectrum and for one's own children at the other end.

Levinson described a transitional period between the ages of 50 and 55, during which a developmental crisis may occur if the person feels incapable of changing an intolerable life structure. Although no single event characterizes the transition, the physiological changes that begin to appear may have a dramatic effect on the person's sense of self. For example, the person may experience a decrease in cardiovascular efficiency that accompanies aging; but chronological age and physical infirmity are not linear. Those who exercise regularly, who do not smoke, and who eat and drink in moderation are able to maintain their physical health and emotional well-being.

Middle adulthood is the period when one frequently feels overwhelmed by too many obligations and duties, but it is also a time of great satisfaction for most persons. People have developed a wide array of acquaintances, friendships, and relationships. The satisfaction persons express about their network of friends predicts positive mental health. Some social ties, however, may be a source of stress if demands are made on the person that cannot be met or that assault the person's self-esteem. Power, leadership, wisdom, and understanding are most generally possessed by the middle-aged, and if one's health and vitality remain intact, it is truly the prime of life.

# DIVORCE

Divorce is a major crisis of adult life. Spouses often grow, develop, and change at different rates. One spouse may discover that the other is not the same as when they first married. In truth, both partners have changed and evolved, not necessarily in complementary directions. Frequently, one spouse blames a third person for alienation of affections and refuses to examine his or her own role in the marital problems. Certain aspects of marital deterioration and divorce seem to be related to specific qualities of middle life—the need for change, the weariness with acting responsibly, the fear of facing up to oneself. The following cases by Robert W. Butler are informative.

A 43-year-old woman was divorced after 21 years of marriage. She had brought up four children. She felt she had contributed to the material success of her husband, who received all the credit. She was bitter and hurt over his failure to appreciate her but saw that failure as his problem alone. She was dismayed when he pressed for a divorce. Neither wanted marital counseling. The end came quickly. They no longer even talked to each other. Neither of them could quite believe they were divorced.

Some men and women begin to seek a last fling or a last chance to experience something they feel they have missed. That phenomenon is not confined to heterosexual relationships.

Mary and Joan had lived together for 23 years. Their homosexuality was only part of their rich relationship together. They had lived through many painful public remarks. They had developed good relationships with their neighbors. Mary had always struggled with the possibility of trying a heterosexual relationship. At 44 she felt that she had little time left. An opportunity arose, and she seized the chance for a heterosexual affair. Joan was deeply hurt. Despite the long-standing success of their life together, they were not certain it would survive that development. They jointly sought therapeutic help.

## Types of Separation

Paul Bohannan, an anthropologist with expertise in marriage and divorce, described the types of separation that take place at the time of divorce.

**Psychic divorce.** In psychic divorce the love object is given up, and a grief reaction about the death of the relationship occurs. Sometimes a period of anticipatory mourning sets in before the divorce occurs. Separating from a spouse forces the person to become autonomous, to change from a position of dependence. The separation may be difficult to achieve, especially if both persons are used to being dependent on each other (as normally happens in marriage) or if one was so dependent as to be afraid or incapable of becoming independent. Most persons report such feelings as depression, ambivalence, and mood swings at the time of divorce. Studies indicate that the process of recovery from divorce takes about two years. At that time the ex-spouse may be viewed neutrally, and each spouse accepts his or her new identity as a single person.

**Legal divorce.** Legal divorce involves going through the courts so that each of the parties is remarriageable. Seventy-five percent of divorced women and 80 percent of divorced men remarry within three years of divorce. No-fault divorce, in which neither person is judged to be the guilty party in the divorce, has become the most widely used legal mechanism for divorce.

**Economic divorce.** The division of the couple's property between them and economic support for the wife are major concerns. Many men who are ordered by the courts to pay alimony or child support flout the law, creating a major social problem.

**Community divorce.** The social network of the divorced couple changes markedly. A few relatives and friends are retained from the community, and new ones are added. The task of meeting new friends is often difficult for divorced persons, who may realize how dependent they were on the spouse for social exchanges.

**Coparental divorce.** Coparental divorce is the separation of a parent from the child's other parent. Being a single parent is different from being a married parent.

## Custody

The parental-right doctrine is a concept in law that awards custody to the more fit natural parent and attempts to ensure that the best interest of the child is served. Most often, custody is awarded to the mother, but, in about 5 percent of cases, custody is awarded to the father.

The types of custody include (1) joint custody, in which the child spends equal time with each parent, which is becoming increasingly common; (2) split custody, in which siblings are separated and each parent has custody of one or more of the children; and (3) single custody, in which the children live solely with one parent, the other parent having rights of visitation that may be limited in some ways by the court.

Problems may surface in the parent-child relationship with the custodial parent or the noncustodial parent. The presence of the custodial parent in the home represents the reality of the divorce, and that parent may become the target of the child's anger. The parent under such stress may not be able to deal with the child's increased needs and anger.

The noncustodial parent must cope with limits placed on time spent with the child. That parent loses the day-to-day gratification and the responsibilities involved with parenting. Emotional distress is common in both the parent and the child. Joint custody offers a solution with some advantages; however, it requires a high degree of maturity on the part of the parents and can present some problems. Parents must separate their child-rearing practices from their postdivorce resentments, and they must develop a spirit of cooperation regarding the rearing of the child. They must also have the ability to tolerate frequent communication with an ex-spouse.

## Reasons for Divorce

Divorce tends to run in families and is highest in couples who marry as teenagers or come from different socioeconomic backgrounds. Every marriage is psychologically unique, and so is each divorce. If a person's parents were divorced, he or she may choose to resolve a marital problem in the same way, through divorce. Expectations of the spouse may be unrealistic. One partner may expect the other to act as an all-giving mother or as a magically protective father. The parenting experience places the greatest strain on a marriage. In surveys of couples with and without children, those without children reported getting more pleasure from the spouse than did those couples with children. Illness in the child creates the greatest strain of all, and in marriages in which a child has died through illness or accident, more than 50 percent end in divorce.

Other causes of marital distress are problems concerning sex and money. Both areas may be used as a means of control, and withholding sex or money is a means of expressing aggression. There is also less social pressure now than in the past to remain married. As previously discussed, the easing of divorce laws and the declining influence of religion and the extended family make divorce an acceptable course of action today.

**Extramarital intercourse.** Adultery is defined as voluntary sexual intercourse between a married person and someone other than his or her spouse. Studies report that, by middle age, 60 percent of men and 40 percent of women have had at least one extramarital affair. For men, the first extramarital affair is often associated with the wife's pregnancy, when coitus may be interdicted. Most of those incidents are kept secret from the spouse and, if known, rarely account for divorce. However, the infidelity may serve as the catalyst for basic dissatisfactions in the marriage to surface, which then may lead to its dissolution. Adultery may decline as potentially fatal sexually transmitted diseases, such as acquired immune deficiency syndrome (AIDS), serve as sobering deterrents.

## References

Arnstein R L: Overview of normal transition to young adulthood. Adolesc Psychiatry *16*: 127, 1989.

Arthur M B, Bailyn L, Levinson D J: *Working with Cancers.* Center for Research in Career Development, Columbia University, New York, 1984.

Christensen A, Pasch L: The sequence of marital conflict: An analysis of seven phases of marital conflict in distressed and nondistressed couples. Clin Psychol Rev *13*: 3, 1993.

Colarusso C A, Nemiroff R A: *Adult Development: A New Dimension in Psychodynamic Theory and Practice.* Plenum, New York, 1981.

Gould R L: Adulthood. In *Comprehensive Textbook of Psychiatry,* ed 5, H I Kaplan, B J Sadock, editors, p 1998. Williams & Wilkins, Baltimore, 1989.

Hornstein G A: The structuring of identity among midlife women as a function of their degree of involvement in employment. J Pers *54*: 551, 1986.

Howe M L, Brainerd C J: *Cognitive Development in Adulthood: Progress in Cognitive Development Research.* Springer, New York, 1988.

Kimmel D C: *Adulthood and Aging: An Interdisciplinary Developmental View.* Wiley, New York, 1974.

Krause N: Stress and sex differences in depressive symptoms among older adults. J Gerontol *41*: 727, 1986.

Levinson D J: A conception of adult development. Am Psychol *41*: 3, 1986.

Levinson D J, Damow C N, Klein E B, Levinson M H, McKeeb B: *The Seasons of a Man's Life.* Knopf, New York, 1978.

Lusski W: Effective elderly adjustment. J Am Geriatr Soc *34*: 764, 1986.

Matthews K A, Wing R R, Kuller L H, Meilahn E N, Kelscy S F, Costello E J, Caggiula A W: Influences of natural menopause on psychological characteristics and symptoms of middle-aged healthy women. J Consult Clin Psychol *58*: 345, 1990.

Nemiroff R A, Colarusso C A: Frontiers of adult development in theory and practice. J Geriatr Psychiatry *21*: 7, 1988.

Neugarten B L: *Personality in Middle and Late Life.* Atherton, New York, 1964.

Reed D M: Traditional marriage. In *The Sexual Experience,* B J Sadock, H I Kaplan, A M Freedman, editors, p 217. Williams & Wilkins, Baltimore, 1976.

Repetti R L: Short-term effects of occupational stressors on daily mood and health complaints. Health Psychol *12*: 125, 1993.

Roberts P, Newton P M: Levinsonian studies of women's adult development. Psychol Aging *2*: 154, 1987.

Vaillant G E: *Adaptation to Life.* Little, Brown, Boston, 1977.

Vaillant G E, Vaillant C O: Natural history of male psychological health: 12. A 45-year study of predictors of successful aging at age 65. Am J Psychiatry *147*: 31, 1990.

Van Gennep A: *The Rites of Passage.* University of Chicago Press, Chicago, 1960.

Westman M, Eden D: Excessive role demand and subsequent performance. J Org Behav *13*: 519, 1992.

Whitbourne S K: Personality development in adulthood and old age: Relationships among identity style, health, and well-being. Ann Rev Gerontol Geriatr 7: 189, 1987.

Woodruff S I, Conway T L: A longitudinal assessment of the impact of health-fitness status and health behavior on perceived quality of life. Percept Mot Skills *75*: 3, 1992.

# 2.6 / Late Adulthood (Old Age)

Late adulthood, also known as old age, usually means the phase of the life cycle beginning at age 65. The elderly population is the fastest growing age group in America; more people are living longer now than in the past, a phenomenon that Robert N. Butler called a triumph of survivorship, rather than a cause for despair. Gerontology— the study of aging—has become a new field of specialization. Gerontologists divide the aged into two groups:

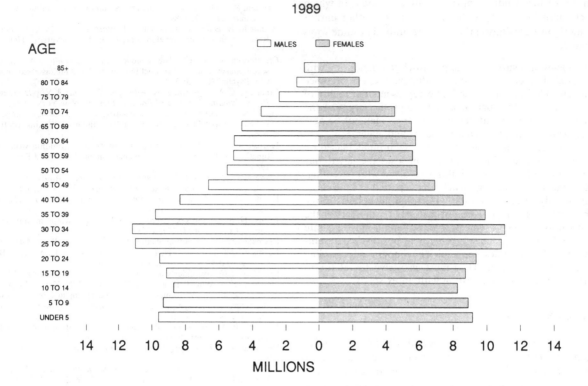

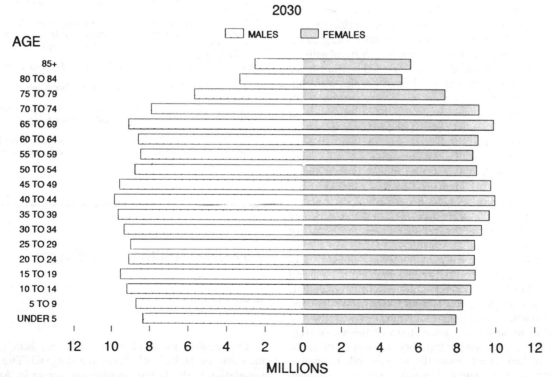

**Figure 2.6–1.**  U.S. population, by age and sex: 1989 and 2030. (Figure from U.S. Bureau of the Census: Estimates of the population of the United States, by single years of age, color, and sex: 1900 to 1959. In *Current Population Reports,* p 22. U S Government Printing Office, Washington, 1965; G Spencer: Projections of the population of the United States, by age, sex, and race: 1988 to 2080. In *Current Population Reports,* p 21. U S Government Printing Office, Washington, 1989; F W Hollman: U.S. population estimates, by age, sex, race, and Hispanic origin: 1989. In *Current Population Reports,* p 21. U S Government Printing Office, Washington, 1990.)

the young-old, ages 65 to 74, and the old-old, ages 75 and older. In addition, the population includes the well-old, who are healthy and do not suffer from any illness, and the sick-old, who have an infirmity that interferes with functioning and that requires medical or psychiatric attention. The health needs of those old adults have become enormous, and the role of the geriatric physician and psychiatrist has never been more important than it is now.

## DEMOGRAPHICS

In 1989 an estimated 31 million people in the United States were more than 65 years old. According to the U.S. Bureau of the Census, that figure will rise to more than 50 million persons over the age of 65 by the year 2030, a result of the aging of the baby-boom generation—those born between the years 1946 and 1964. Figure 2.6–1 shows the United States population by age and sex in 1989 and 2030.

## BIOLOGY OF AGING

The aging process is called senescence (from the Latin *senescere,* meaning to grow old) and is characterized by a gradual decline in the functioning of all the body's systems—cardiovascular, respiratory, genitourinary, endocrine, and immune, among others. However, the belief that old age is invariably associated with profound intellectual and physical infirmity is a myth. Most aged persons retain their cognitive ability and physical capacity to a remarkable degree.

An overview of the biological changes that accompany old age is given in Table 2.6–1. The various decrements listed do not occur in a linear fashion in all systems. Not all organ systems deteriorate at the same rate, nor do they follow a similar pattern of decline for all persons. Each person is genetically endowed with one or more vulnerable systems, or a system may become vulnerable because of environmental stressors or intentional misuse (for example, excessive ultraviolet exposure, smoking, alcohol). Moreover, not all organ systems deteriorate at the same time; a person does not disintegrate like the one-horse shay in Oliver Wendell Holmes's poem, "The Deacon's Masterpiece," which "went to pieces all at once." Rather, any one of a number of organ systems begins to deteriorate, which then leads to illness or death.

In general, the aging of a person is the aging of cells. The most commonly held theory is that each cell has a genetically determined life span, during which it can replicate itself a limited number of times before it dies. Structural changes in cells occur with age. In the central nervous system, for example, age-related cell changes occur in neurons, which show signs of degeneration. In senility (characterized by severe memory loss and a loss of intellectual functioning), signs of degeneration are much more severe and are known as neurofibrillary degeneration, seen most commonly in dementia of the Alzheimer's type.

Changes in the structure of deoxyribonucleic acid (DNA) and ribonucleic acid (RNA) are also found in aging cells; the cause has been attributed to genotypic programming, X-rays, chemicals, and food products, among others. There is probably no single cause of aging. All areas of the body are affected to some degree.

Genetic factors have been implicated in disorders that commonly occur in the aged, such as hypertension, coronary artery disease, arteriosclerosis, and neoplastic disease. Family studies indicate inheritance factors for breast and stomach cancer, colon polyps, and certain mental disorders of old age. Huntington's disease shows an autosomal dominant mode of inheritance with complete penetrance. The average age of onset is between 35 and 40, but cases have occurred as late as 70 years of age.

### Longevity

Longevity has been studied since the beginning of recorded history and has remained a topic of immense interest. The research about longevity reveals that a family history of longevity is the best indicator of a long life: almost half of the fathers of persons who live past 80 also lived past 80. However, many of the conditions leading to a shortened life can be prevented, ameliorated, or delayed with effective intervention. Heredity is but one factor—one that is beyond the person's control. Predictors of longevity that are within one's control include regular medical checkups, minimal or no caffeine or alcohol consumption, work gratification, and a perceived sense of the self as being socially useful in an altruistic role, such as spouse, teacher, mentor, parent, or grandparent. Diet and exercise are also associated with health and longevity.

### Life Expectancy

In the United States the average life expectancy has increased in every decade—from 48 years in 1900 to 75.5 years in 1991. The projected life expectancy at birth and at age 65 is indicated in Table 2.6–2.

Changes in morbidity and mortality have also occurred. Over the past 30 years, for example, there has been a 60 percent decline in mortality from cerebrovascular disease and a 30 percent decline in mortality from coronary artery disease. In contrast, mortality from cancer, which has a steep rise with age, has increased, especially from cancer of the lung, colon, stomach, skin, and prostate.

The prediction of mortality is important to actuaries and insurance companies, among others. All mortality formulas have flaws, but the one that has been most accepted is the law of human mortality. Proposed in 1825 by Benjamin Gompertz, the formula holds that mortality in a given population rises exponentially with the passage of time, and after age 30 the mortality rate doubles about every 8.5 years. The death rate in the United States for all ages is 860.3 deaths a year per 100,000 population from all causes. In the age group 65 to 74, it is 2,618.5 per 100,000; in the age group 74 to 85, it is 5,890 per 100,000; and in the age group 85 and over, it is 15,107.6 per 100,000.

Life expectancy at age 85 rose by 33 percent between 1960 and 1987, and by 2050 the population over age 85 is expected to rise from the current 1.2 percent to an estimated 5 percent of the total population. Figure 2.6–2 gives the projected growth in population by age group.

Accidents rank among the top seven causes of death in persons over age 65. Most fatal accidents are caused by falls, pedestrian incidents, and burns. Neurological and

**Table 2.6–1**
**Biological Changes Associated with Aging**

Cellular level
  Change in cellular DNA and RNA structures: intracellular organelle degeneration
  Neuronal degeneration in central nervous system, primarily in superior temporal precentral and inferior temporal gyri; no loss in brainstem nuclei
  Receptor sites and sensitivity altered
  Decreased anabolism and catabolism of cellular transmitter substances
  Intercellular collagen and elastin increase

Immune system
  Impaired T-cell response to antigen
  Increase in function of autoimmune bodies
  Increased susceptibility to infection and neoplasia
  Leukocytes unchanged, T lymphocytes reduced
  Increased erythrocyte sedimentation (nonspecific)

Musculoskeletal
  Decrease in height because of shortening of spinal column (two-inch loss in both men and women from the second to the seventh decade)
  Reduction in lean muscle mass and muscle strength; deepening of thoracic cage
  Increase in body fat
  Elongation of nose and ears
  Loss of bone matrix, leading to osteoporosis
  Degeneration of joint surfaces may produce osteoarthritis
  Risk of hip fracture is 10–25% by age 90
  Continual closing of cranial sutures (parietomastoid suture does not attain complete closure until age 80)
  Men gain weight until about age 60, then lose; women gain weight until age 70, then lose.

Integument
  Graying of hair results from decreased melanin production in hair follicles (by age 50, 50% of all persons male and female are at least 50% gray; pubic hair is last to turn gray)
  General wrinkling of skin
  Less active sweat glands
  Decrease in melanin
  Loss of subcutaneous fat
  Nail growth slowed

Genitourinary and reproductive
  Decreased glomerular filtration rate and renal blood flow
  Decreased hardness of erection, diminished ejaculatory spurt
  Decreased vaginal lubrication
  Enlargement of prostate
  Incontinence

Special senses
  Thickening of optic lens, reduced peripheral vision
  Inability to accommodate (presbyopia)
  High-frequency sound hearing loss (presbyacusis)—25% show loss by age 60, 65% by age 80
  Yellowing of optic lens
  Reduced acuity of taste, smell, and touch
  Decreased light-dark adaption

Neuropsychiatric
  Learning
    Takes longer to learn new material, but complete learning still occurs
    Intelligence quotient (I.Q.) remains stable until age 80
    Verbal ability maintained with age
    Psychomotor speed declines
  Memory
    Tasks requiring shifting attentions performed with difficulty
    Encoding ability diminishes (transfer of short-term to long-term memory and vice versa)
    Recognition of right answer on multiple-choice tests remains intact
    Simple recall declines
  Neurotransmitters
    Norepinephrine decreases in central nervous system
    Increased monoamine oxidase and serotonin in brain

Brain
  Decrease in gross brain weight, about 17% by age 80 in both sexes
  Widened sulci, smaller convolutions, gyral atrophy
  Ventricles enlarge
  Increased transport across blood-brain barrier
  Decreased cerebral blood flow and oxygenation

Cardiovascular
  Increase in size and weight of heart (contains lipofuscin pigment derived from lipids)
  Decreased elasticity of heart valves
  Increased collagen in blood vessels
  Increased susceptibility to arrhythmias
  Altered homeostasis of blood pressure
  Cardiac output maintained in absence of coronary heart disease

Gastrointestinal (GI) system
  At risk for atrophic gastritis, hiatal hernia, diverticulosis
  Decreased blood flow to gut, liver
  Diminished saliva flow
  Altered absorption from GI tract (at risk for malabsorption syndrome and avitaminosis)
  Constipation

Endocrine
  Estrogen levels decrease in women
  Adrenal androgen decreases
  Testosterone production declines in men
  Increase in follicle-stimulating hormone (FSH) and luteinizing hormone (LH) in postmenopausal women
  Serum thyroxine ($T_4$) and thyroid-stimulating hormone (TSH) normal, triiodothyronine ($T_3$) reduced
  Glucose tolerance test result decreases

Respiratory
  Decreased vital capacity
  Diminished cough reflex
  Decreased bronchial epithelium ciliary action

sensory defects are the major causes of accidents. Most falls result from cardiac arrhythmias and hypotensive episodes.

Some gerontologists consider death in very old persons (over 85) to be the result of an aging syndrome characterized by diminished elastic-mechanical properties of the heart, arteries, lungs, and other organs. Death results from trivial tissue injuries that would not be fatal to a younger person; accordingly, senescence is viewed as the cause of death.

## Race and Ethnicity

The proportion of elderly persons in the nonwhite and Hispanic population is smaller than in the white population but is increasing at a fast rate. That growth is the result

**Table 2.6–2**
**Projected Life Expectancy at Birth and Age 65, by Sex: 1990–2050 (in years)**

| Year | At birth | | | At age 65 | | |
|------|------|-------|------------|------|-------|------------|
| | Men | Women | Difference | Men | Women | Difference |
| 1990 | 72.1 | 79.0 | 6.9 | 15.0 | 19.4 | 4.4 |
| 2000 | 73.5 | 80.4 | 6.9 | 15.7 | 20.3 | 4.6 |
| 2010 | 74.4 | 81.3 | 6.9 | 16.2 | 21.0 | 4.8 |
| 2020 | 74.9 | 81.8 | 6.9 | 16.6 | 21.4 | 4.8 |
| 2030 | 75.4 | 82.3 | 6.9 | 17.0 | 21.8 | 4.8 |
| 2040 | 75.9 | 82.8 | 6.9 | 17.3 | 22.3 | 5.0 |
| 2050 | 76.4 | 83.3 | 6.9 | 17.7 | 22.7 | 5.0 |

Table from G. Spencer: Projections of the population of the United States, by age, sex and race: 1988 to 2080. In *Current Population Reports,* p 43. U S Bureau of the Census, Washington, 1989.

of a higher birth rate for nonwhites and Hispanics than for whites. Figure 2.6–3 shows the growth of the minority elderly population.

### Sex Ratios

On the average, women live longer than men and are more likely than men to live alone. The number of men per 100 women decreases sharply from age 65 to 85 (Figure 2.6–4).

### Geographic Distribution

Twenty-five percent of all aged persons in the United States reside in California, New York, and Florida. Florida has the largest proportion of those over 65, and Alaska has the smallest number of elderly persons. The state with the youngest population is Utah, with a median age of 25.7. Figure 2.6–5 shows the percent increase in population over age 65 from 1980 to 1989.

### Diet, Exercise, and Health

Diet and exercise play a role in a variety of chronic diseases of the elderly, such as arteriosclerosis and hypertension.

Hyperlipemia correlates with coronary artery disease and can be controlled by reducing body weight, decreasing the intake of saturated fat, and limiting the intake of cholesterol. Increasing the daily intake of dietary fiber can also help decrease serum lipoprotein levels.

Reduced salt intake (less than 3 grams a day) is associated with a lowered risk of hypertension. Hypertensive geriatric patients can often correct their condition by moderate exercise and decreased salt intake without the addition of drugs.

A regimen of daily moderate exercise (walking for 30 minutes a day) has been associated with a reduction in cardiovascular disease, a decreased incidence of osteoporosis, improved respiratory function, the maintenance of ideal weight, and a general sense of well-being. In many cases a disease process has been reversed and even cured

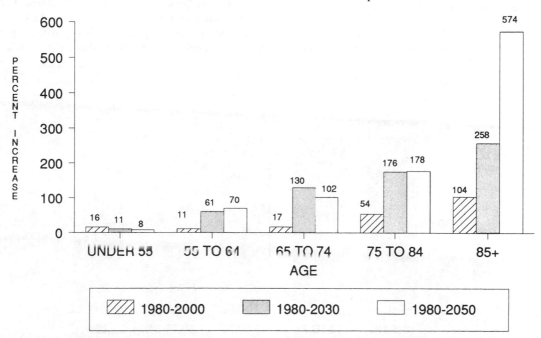

**Figure 2.6–2.** Projected growth in population, by age group: 1980–2050. (Figure from G Spencer: Projections of the population of the United States, by age, sex, and race: 1988 to 2080. In *Current Population Reports,* p 13. U S Government Printing Office, Washington, 1989.)

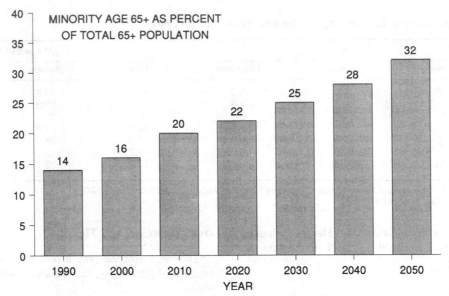

**Figure 2.6–3.** Growth of the minority elderly population: 1990–2050. (Figures computed by Donald G. Fowles, U.S. Administration on Aging, from data in G Spencer: Projections of the Hispanic population: 1983–2080. In *Current Population Reports,* p 12. U S Bureau of the Census, Washington, 1986. G Spencer: Projections of the population of the United States, by age, sex, and race: 1988 to 2080. In *Current Population Reports,* p 8. U S Government Printing Office, Washington, 1989.)

by diet and exercise, without additional medical or surgical intervention.

Table 2.6–3 lists the biological changes associated with diet and exercise. A comparison with Table 2.6–1 reveals that almost every biological change associated with aging is positively affected by diet and exercise.

## DEVELOPMENTAL TASKS

### Erikson's Stage of Integrity versus Despair and Isolation (over 65 years)

In Erik Erikson's eighth stage of the life cycle, the conflict is between integrity, the sense of satisfaction one feels reflecting on a life productively lived, and despair, the sense that life has had little purpose or meaning. It can be a contented period, a time to enjoy grandchildren, to contemplate one's major efforts, and perhaps to see the fruits of one's labors being put to good use by younger generations. As one aging scientist professed, "I can go on cheerfully so long as I remain convinced that cell division will continue indefinitely."

However, old age holds no peace, no contented backward look, Erikson wrote, unless one has lived beyond narcissism and into intimacy and generativity. Without generativity, the elderly have no sense of world order and no conviction of the calming idea that one's life has come at a time and in a segment of history when a person developed exactly as one did. Without that conviction, the

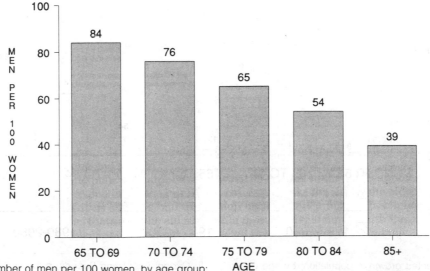

**Figure 2.6–4.** Number of men per 100 women, by age group: 1989. (Figure from F W Hollman: U.S. population estimates, by age, sex, race, and Hispanic origin: 1989. In *Current Population Reports,* p 11. U S Government Printing Office, Washington, 1990.)

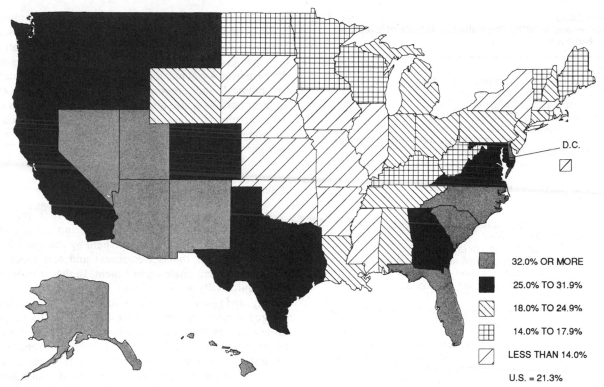

**Figure 2.6–5.** Percent increase in population 65+: 1980–1989. (Figure from E Byerly: State population and household estimates: July 1, 1989. In *Current Population Reports*, p 6. U S Government Printing Office, Washington, 1990.)

elderly have a fear of death, despair, and disgust. Misanthropes are classified in Erikson's scheme as those who have not achieved integrity and who are stuck in a state of despair.

## Maintenance of Self-Esteem

Heinz Kohut's theory of self psychology has special application to the elderly because of its emphasis on narcissism. Old persons must continually cope with narcissistic injury as they attempt to adapt to the biological, psychological, and social losses associated with the aging process. Self-esteem and self-sufficiency are continually at risk, particularly if the elderly person loses external sources of support.

The maintenance of self-esteem is a major task of old age. Self-esteem can be promoted by several factors: (1) economic security, which allows the person to secure the basic necessities of life; (2) supportive persons, who protect against isolation and allow dependence needs to be gratified; (3) psychological health, which allows mature coping and defense mechanisms to function; and (4) physical health, which enables the person to pursue productive or pleasurable activities. When all or any of those factors are affected adversely, the aged person is unable to maintain self-esteem; tension, anxiety, frustration, anger, and depression can result. In addition, the perceived changes in physical and psychological functioning cause aging persons to question their continued adequacy.

## Other Tasks of Old Age

Bernice Neugarten described the major conflicts of old age as related to having to give up one's position of au-

thority and evaluating one's former competence, achievements, and pleasures. For both sexes there is, as Neugarten described,

the yielding of a position of authority and the questioning of one's former competence; the reconciliations with significant others and with one's achievements and failures; the resolution of grief over the death of others and of the approaching death of self; the maintenance of a sense of integrity in terms of what one has been, rather than what one is; and concern over legacy and how to leave traces of oneself.

Daniel Levinson described a transitional period into old age between the ages of 60 and 65, which he termed the late adult transition. The physiological changes that accompany aging create feelings of physical decline and mortality. Those feelings are escalated by the increased incidence of illness and death among loved ones and friends. If persons are narcissistic and too heavily invested in the appearance of the body, they are liable to become overly preoccupied with death. Creative mental activity is a normal and healthy substitute for reduced physical activity.

According to Freudian theory, as the person matures, there is increasing control of the ego and the id, resulting in increased autonomy. A movement in the opposite direction (that is, a loss of autonomy or regression), permits primitive modes of function to emerge. Such regressions are associated with the aging process and account for such phenomena as the inability to distinguish external sensory perceptions from internal fantasies or the emergence of primitive aggressive or sexual drives. Regression of superego functions also occurs and can be manifested either by excessive guilt or, conversely, by the absence of guilt related to various conflicts and situations.

George Vaillant followed up a group of Harvard fresh-

**Table 2.6–3**
**Positive and Healthy Physiological Effects of Exercise and Nutrition**

Increases
  Strength of bones, ligaments, and muscles
  Muscle mass and body density
  Articular cartilage thickness
  Skeletal muscle ATP, CRP, K+, and myoglobin
  Skeletal muscle oxidative enzyme content and mitochondria
  Skeletal muscle arterial collaterals and capillary density
  Heart volume and weight
  Blood volume and total circulating hemoglobin
  Cardiac stroke volume
  Myocardial contractility
  Maximal C(A-V)O$_2$
  Maximal blood lactate concentration
  Maximal pulmonary ventilation
  Maximal respiratory work
  Maximal oxygen diffusing capacity
  Maximal exercise capacity as measured by the maximal oxygen intake, exercise time, and distance
  Serum high-density lipoprotein concentration
  Anaerobic threshold
  Plasma insulin concentration with submaximal exercise

Decreases
  Heart rate at rest and during submaximal exercise
  Blood lactate concentration during submaximal exercise
  Pulmonary ventilation during submaximal work
  Respiratory quotient during submaximal work
  Serum triglyceride concentration
  Body fatness
  Serum low-density lipoprotein concentration
  Systolic blood pressure
  Core temperature threshold for initiation of sweating
  Sweat sodium and chloride content
  Plasma epinephrine and norepinephrine with submaximal exercise
  Plasma glucagon and growth hormone concentrations with submaximal exercise
  Relative hemoconcentration with submaximal exercise in the heat

Table by E R Buskirk. In *Diet and Exercise: Synergism in Health Maintenance*, P L White, T Monderka, editors, p 133. American Medical Association, Chicago, 1982. Used with permission.

men into old age and found that emotional health at age 65 was related to the following factors: (1) having been close to one's brothers and sisters at college correlated with emotional well-being; (2) early traumatic life experiences, such as the death of a parent and parental divorce, did not correlate with poor adaptation in old age; (3) being depressed at some point between ages 21 and 50 did predict emotional problems at age 65; and (4) two personality traits—pragmatism and dependability—when present in the young adult, were associated with a sense of well-being at age 65.

## PSYCHOSOCIAL ASPECTS OF AGING

### Social Activity

Healthy elderly persons usually maintain a level of social activity that is only slightly changed from that of earlier years. For many, old age is a period of continued intellectual, emotional, and psychological growth. In some cases, however, physical illness or the death of friends and relatives may preclude continued social interaction. Moreover, as persons experience an increased sense of isolation, they may become vulnerable to depression. Growing evidence indicates that maintaining social activities is valuable for physical and emotional well-being. Contact with younger persons is also important because old persons can pass on cultural values and can provide care services to the younger generation and thereby maintain a sense of usefulness that contributes to self-esteem.

### Ageism

Ageism, a term coined by Robert N. Butler, refers to the discrimination toward old persons and the negative stereotypes about old age that are held by younger adults. Old persons may themselves resent and fear other old people and discriminate against them. In that scheme, old age is universally associated with loneliness, poor health, senility, and general weakness or infirmity. The experience of aged persons, however, does not consistently support those attitudes. For example, although 50 percent of young adults expect poor health to be a problem for those over 65, only 20 percent of those over 65 report health as a problem. Similarly, although 65 percent of young adults expect loneliness to be a problem for the aged, only 13 percent of old persons actually experience loneliness.

Old persons generally have a positive view of their health. Only about one third report that their health is fair or poor (Figure 2.6–6). Health problems, when they do exist, involve chronic conditions more often than acute conditions. More than four out of five people over the age of 65 have at least one chronic condition (Table 2.6–4).

### Countertransference

The feelings and attitudes that the physician has toward old persons stem from a variety of sources: countertransference, societal attitudes, and the attitudes projected by the patient about being old. Countertransference feelings about aging are determined by the physician's needs and past experiences, and they function on both a conscious level and an unconscious level. Physicians may have fears about their own old age or may have had conflicts about the aging or death of parents or grandparents. Physicians must be aware of those feelings, especially if negative views of aging exist. Some aged persons may act out the poor expectations held for them by the physician. Consequently, they may lose confidence in their abilities and appear to be what, in fact, they are not.

### Psychodynamics

Adaptation to aging also depends on the defense mechanisms used throughout adult life. The healthiest and most mature defenses include suppression, anticipation of reality, altruism, and humor. If acquired during early and middle adulthood, those defenses enable the aged person to cope with the vicissitudes of life in the most effective manner.

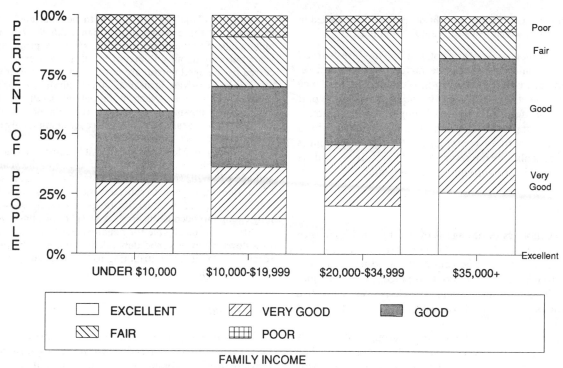

**Figure 2.6–6.** Self-assessment of health by income for people 65+: 1989. (Figure from National Center for Health Statistics: Current estimates from the National Health Interview Survey, 1989. In *Vital and Health Statistics,* p 11. U S Government Printing Office, Washington, 1990.)

*Mature defenses* are the normal adaptive mechanisms that are found in psychologically and physically healthy adults. *Suppression* is the conscious or semiconscious decision not to think about an impulse or conflict. It is normally coupled with *anticipation of reality,* which permits the person to plan realistically for future events (its antithesis is denial). *Altruism* is the provision of service to others and is related to Erikson's concept of generativity, which is characterized by the conviction that one's life has been purposeful. *Humor* is characterized by the ability to stand outside oneself and observe and comment on events and their incongruities and inconsistencies. Humor may also be expressed as playfulness.

In contrast to those mature defenses, a group of coping mechanisms seen in the aged are not as adaptive. They include

the following: (1) *denial,* in which external reality is negated; (2) *regression,* in which the person returns to an early level of functioning; (3) *counterphobia,* in which the person attempts to deny a fear by engaging in a dangerous or fearful activity; (4) *rigidity,* in which the person maintains habits or traits that are no longer useful or adaptive; (5) *exclusion of stimuli,* in which the person blocks out stimuli that may be upsetting or that require a response the old person is no longer capable of giving; (6) *selective memory,* in which the person remembers past events that may be more satisfying and full of accomplishment than current events; (7) *projection,* in which incompatible thoughts or feelings are externalized or directed toward the self from another person, which may cause paranoid ideation in severe cases; and (8) *reaction formation,*

**Table 2.6–4**
**Top 10 Chronic Conditions for People 65+, by Age and Race: 1989 (number per 1,000 people)**

| Condition | Age | | | | Race (65+) | | |
|---|---|---|---|---|---|---|---|
| | 65+ | 45 to 64 | 65 to 74 | 75+ | White | Black | Black as % of White |
| Arthritis | 483.0 | 253.8 | 437.3 | 554.5 | 483.2 | 522.6 | 108 |
| Hypertension | 380.6 | 229.1 | 383.8 | 375.6 | 367.4 | 517.7 | 141 |
| Hearing impairment | 286.5 | 127.7 | 239.4 | 360.3 | 297.4 | 174.5 | 59 |
| Heart disease | 278.9 | 118.9 | 231.6 | 353.0 | 286.5 | 220.5 | 77 |
| Cataracts | 156.8 | 16.1 | 107.4 | 234.3 | 160.7 | 139.8 | 87 |
| Deformity or orthopedic impairment | 155.2 | 155.5 | 141.4 | 177.0 | 156.2 | 150.8 | 97 |
| Chronic sinusitis | 153.4 | 173.5 | 151.8 | 155.8 | 157.1 | 125.2 | 80 |
| Diabetes | 88.2 | 58.2 | 89.7 | 85.7 | 80.2 | 165.9 | 207 |
| Visual impairment | 81.9 | 45.1 | 69.3 | 101.7 | 81.1 | 77.0 | 95 |
| Varicose veins | 78.1 | 57.8 | 72.6 | 86.6 | 80.3 | 64.0 | 80 |

Table from National Center for Health Statistics: Current estimates from the National Health Interview Survey, 1989. In *Vital and Health Statistics,* p 31. National Center for Health Statistics, Washington, 1990.

in which the unacceptable thought or impulse is expressed in opposite ways, which leads to prejudice and bias.

Defense mechanisms are not static. They are learned and can be unlearned; adaptive mature defenses can replace immature defenses, even in old age. The tendency of old persons to reminisce has been postulated to be part of a normal life-review process brought about by the realization of approaching death. It is characterized by a progressive return to consciousness of past experiences and, in particular, by the resurgence of unresolved conflicts that can be worked through and reintegrated.

## Socioeconomics

The economics of old age is of paramount importance to the aged themselves and to the society at large. In the United States about 75 percent of the aged have incomes below $10,000, and only about 10 percent have incomes above $20,000. About 3.5 million persons over age 65 live below the poverty level. Those over age 85 have the lowest incomes.

Women make up the largest single group of the elderly poor and are twice as likely as men to be poor (Figure 2.6–7). Black elderly women over 65 are five times more likely to be poor than are white elderly women.

The poor economic conditions of many aged persons have a direct effect on both their psychological health and their physical health. Figure 2.6–8 provides income sources for persons aged 65 and older. For many aged persons, worrying about money can become an obsessive preoccupation that interferes with their enjoyment of life. Obtaining proper medical care may be especially difficult if personal funds are not available or sufficient.

Medicare (Title 18) provides both hospital and medical insurance for those over age 65 (Figure 2.6–9). About 150 million bills are reimbursed under the Medicare program each year; but only about 40 percent of all medical expenses incurred by the aged person are covered under Medicare. The rest is paid by private insurance, state insurance, or personal funds. Some services—such as outpatient psychiatric treatment, skilled nursing care, physical rehabilitation, and preventive physical examinations—are covered minimally or not at all.

In addition to Medicare, the Social Security program pays benefits to persons over age 65 (over age 66 in the year 2009 and age 67 in 2027) and pays benefits at reduced rates from 62 on. Benefits payable to retired workers average about $500 a month. To qualify for benefits, the person must have worked long enough to become insured. A worker must have worked for 10 years to be eligible for benefits. Benefits are also paid to widows, widowers, and dependent children if the persons receiving benefits or contributing to Social Security die (survivor benefits).

## Retirement

For many old persons, retirement is a time for the pursuit of leisure and for freedom from the responsibility of previous working commitments. For others, it is a time of stress, especially if retirement results in economic problems or a loss of self-esteem. Ideally, employment after age 65 should be a matter of choice. With the passage of the Age Discrimination in Employment Act of 1967 and its amendments, forced retirement at age 70 has been virtually eliminated in the private sector, and it is not legal in federal employment.

Of those persons who voluntarily retire, a majority reenter the work force within two years. They do so for a

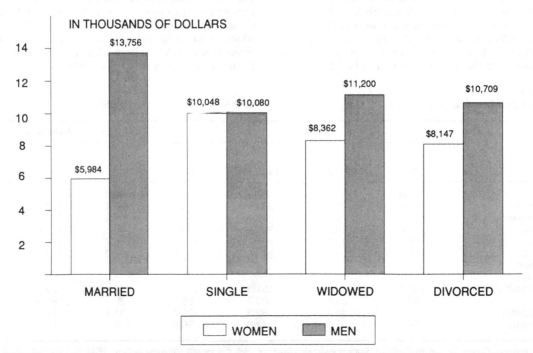

**Figure 2.6–7.** Median income of elderly men and women, by marital status: 1989. (Figure from the Congressional Research Service: *Current Population Survey,* p 14. U S Government Printing Office, Washington, 1990.)

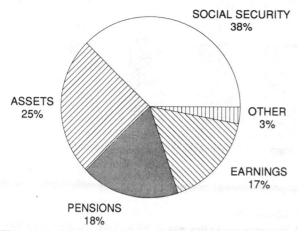

**Figure 2.6–8.** Income sources of persons age 65 + : 1988. (Figure from S Grad: *Income of the Population 65 or Over, 1988,* p 26. U S Government Printing Office, Washington, 1990.)

variety of reasons—negative reactions to being retired, feelings of being unproductive, economic hardship, and loneliness.

The amount of time spent in retirement has increased as the life span has nearly doubled since 1900. Figure 2.6–10 shows the time spent in retirement compared with other activities as part of the life cycle.

### Sexual Activity

An estimated 70 percent of men and 20 percent of women over age 60 are sexually active. Sexual activity is usually limited by the absence of an available partner. Longitudinal studies have found that the sex drive does not decrease as men and women age; in fact, some report an increase in sex drive. William Masters and Virginia Johnson reported sexual functioning of persons in their 80s. Expected physiological changes in men include a longer time period for erection to occur, decreased penile turgidity, and ejaculatory seepage; in women, decreased vaginal lubrication and vaginal atrophy are associated with lowered estrogen levels. Medications can also adversely

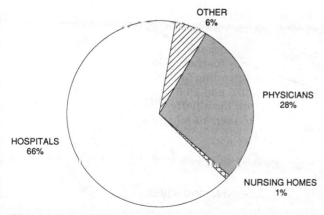

**Figure 2.6–9.** Where the Medicare dollar for the elderly goes: 1987. (Figure from D R Waldo, S T Sonnefeld, D R McKusick, R H Arnett III: Health expenditures by age group, 1977 and 1987. Health Care Finan Rev *10*: 98, 1989. Total exceeds 100 percent because of roundings.)

affect sexual behavior. A significant finding was that the more active one's sex life was in early adulthood, the more likely it is to be active in old age.

### Long-Term Care

Many aged patients who are infirm require institutional care. Although only 5 percent of the aged are institutionalized in nursing homes at any one time, about 35 percent of the aged require care in a long-term facility at some time during their lives (Figure 2.6–11). Elderly nursing home residents are mainly widowed women, and about 50 percent are over age 85.

Nursing home care costs are not covered by Medicare, and they range from $20,000 to $50,000 a year. About 20,000 long-term nursing care institutions are available in the United States—not enough to meet the need. Those elderly persons who do not require skilled nursing care can be managed in other types of health-related facilities, such as a center they attend during the daytime hours. However, the need for care far exceeds the availability of such centers. The American Health Security Bill proposed by President Bill Clinton includes extended care as one of its provisions but only after an acute illness or injury.

Outside institutions, care for the aged is provided by their children (primarily their daughters and daughters-in-law), their wives, and other women (Figure 2.6–12). Over 50 percent of those women also work in jobs outside the home, and about 40 percent care for their own children as well. In general, women end up as caretakers more often than do men because of cultural and societal expectations. According to the American Association of Retired Persons, those daughters with jobs spend an average of 12 hours a week providing care and currently spend about $120 a month for travel, telephone calls, special foods, and medication for the elderly.

## EMOTIONAL PROBLEMS OF THE AGED

Loss is the predominant theme that characterizes the emotional experiences of the aged. An elderly person must deal with the grief of multiple losses (death of a spouse, friends, family, and colleagues), change of work status and prestige, and decline of physical abilities and health. They expend enormous amounts of emotional and physical energy in grieving, resolving grief, and adapting to the changes that result from loss. Living alone is a major stress that affects about 10 percent of the elderly (Figure 2.6–13). Women account for more than 75 percent of all elderly persons living alone.

Depression is a maladaptive response to loss that in the elderly may mimic senile dementia. In addition to the classic signs of depression—such as appetite and sleep disturbances, loss of interest in outside events, self-deprecatory remarks, and thoughts that life is no longer worth living—the person may show memory impairment, difficulty in concentrating, poor judgment, and irritability.

The incidence of suicide in the aged is high (40 per 100,000 population). The suicide of aged persons is perceived differently by surviving friends and family members, depending on gender: men are thought to have been phys-

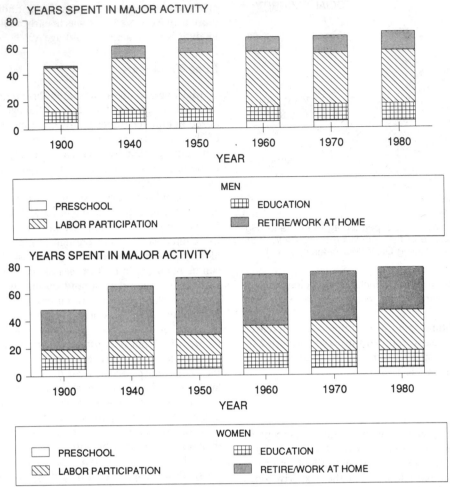

**Figure 2.6–10.** Life cycle distribution of major activities: 1900–1980. (Figures from U.S. Bureau of the Census: Educational attainment in the United States: March 1981 and 1980. In *Current Population Reports,* p 32. (median years of school for persons 25 years or older, 1940–1980). U S Government Printing Office, Washington, 1984; F Best: *Work Sharing: Issues, Policy Options, and Prospects,* p 8. Upjohn Institute for Employment Research, Kalamazoo, Mich, 1981; National Center for Health Statistics: Life tables. In *Vital Statistics of the United States,* p 48. U S Government Printing Office, Washington, 1990; U.S. Department of Labor, Bureau of Labor Statistics: *Worklife Estimates: Effects of Race and Education.* U S Government Printing Office, Washington, 1986.)

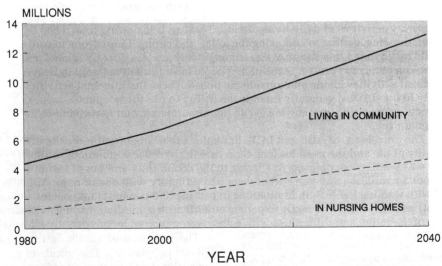

**Figure 2.6–11.** People age 65+ in need of long-term care: 1980–2040. (Figure from Manton, Soldo: Dynamics of health changes in the oldest old: New perspectives and evidence. Milbank Q *63*: 12, 1985.)

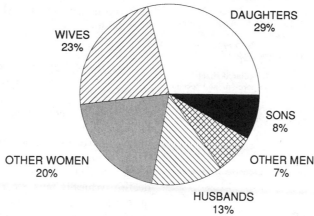

**Figure 2.6–12.** Caretakers and their relationship to the elderly care recipient: 1982. (Figure from Select Committee on Aging, U.S. House of Representatives: *Exploding the Myths: Caregiving in America*, p 60. U S Government Printing Office, Washington, 1987. Caretaker population includes primary and secondary caretakers.)

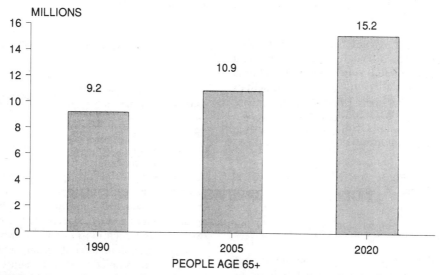

**Figure 2.6–13.** Projected increase in number of people 65 + living alone: 1990–2020. (Figure from Lewin: ICF estimates based on data from *Current Population Survey*, U S Government Printing Office, Washington, 1990; and the Brookings/ICF Long-Term Care Financing Model, 1990.)

ically ill, and women are thought to have been mentally ill.

The relation between good mental health and good physical health is clear in the elderly. Adverse effects on the course of chronic medical illness are correlated with emotional problems. An extensive discussion of psychiatric problems in the elderly appears in Chapter 50.

### References

*Aging America: Trends and Projections.* U S Government Printing Office, Washington, 1991.
Anderson J E, editor: *Psychological Aspects of Aging.* American Psychological Association, Washington, 1956.
Andrews G R: Cross-cultural studies: An important development in aging research. J Am Geriatr Soc *37*: 483, 1989.
Blair K A: Aging: Physiological aspects and clinical implications. Nurse Pract *15*: 14, 1990.
Bromley D B: The idea of ageing: An historical and psychological analysis. Compr Gerontol *2*: 30, 1988.
Busse E W, Pfeiffer E, editors: *Behavior and Adaptation in Late Life.* Little, Brown, Boston, 1969.
Butler R N: *Why Survive? Being Old in America.* Harper & Row, New York, 1975.
Butler R N, Lewis M I: *Aging and Mental Health; Positive Psychosocial and Biomedical Approaches,* ed 3. Mosby, St. Louis, 1982.
Cunningham W R, Brookbank J W: *Gerontology: The Psychology, Biology, and Sociology of Aging.* Harper & Row, New York, 1988.
Eisdorfer C, Lawbon M P: *The Psychology of Adult Development and Aging.* American Psychological Association, Washington, 1973.
Erikson E H, editor: *Adulthood.* Norton, New York, 1978.
Erikson E H, Erikson J M, and Kivnick H G: *Vital Involvement in Old Age.* Norton, New York, 1986.
Gutmann D: Psychoanalysis and aging: A development view. In *The Course of Life: Psychoanalytic Contributions toward Understanding Personality Development,* vol. 3, S I Greenspan, G H Pollock, editors, p 489. U S Department of Health and Human Services, Mental Healthy Study Center, Adelphi, Md, 1981.
Kenney R A: *Physiology of Aging: A Synopsis,* ed 2. Year Book Medical, Chicago, 1989.
Kohut H: *The Analysis of the Self.* International Universities Press, New York, 1971.
Nemiroff R A, Colarusso C A: *The Race Against Time: Psychotherapy and Psychoanalysis in the Second Half of Life.* Plenum, New York, 1985.
Pollock G M: Aging or aged: Development or pathology? In *The Course of Life: Psychoanalytic Contributions toward Understanding Personality Development,* vol. 3, S I Greenspan, G M Pollock, editors, p 549. U S Department of Health and Human Services, Mental Health Study Center, Adelphi, Md, 1981.
Pruchno R, Kleban M H: Caring for an institutionalized parent: The role of coping strategies. Psychol Aging *8*: 18, 1993.
Rinn W E: Mental decline in normal aging: A review. J Geriatr Psychiatry Neurol *1*: 144, 1988.

Sahey B J, Birkner K: Stress and aging. Int J Psychosom *35*: 49, 1988.

Schiavi R C, Schreiner-Engel P, Mandeli J, Schanzer H, Cohen E: Healthy aging and male sexual function. Am J Psychiatry *147*: 766, 1990.

Stoller E P, Forster E, Portugal S: Self-care responses to symptoms by older people: A health diary study of illness behavior. Med Care *31*: 24, 1993.

Uchino B N, Keicolt-Glaser J K, Cacioppo J T: Age-related changes in cardiovascular response as a function of a chronic stressor and social support. J Pers Soc Psychol *63*: 839, 1992.

West R L, Crook T H, Barron K L: Everyday memory performance across the life span: Effects of age and noncognitive individual differences. Psychol Aging *7*: 72, 1992.

# 2.7 / Thanatology: Death and Bereavement

An ongoing reality in the lives of most practicing physicians is a regular confrontation with death, dying, and grief. In most medical training programs, that reality is often inadequately addressed; as a result, the treatment of dying patients is often unnecessarily painful for all involved. *Thanatology* is the study of the processes involved in reactions to death, both in those who are dying and in those who are grieving. A related area of study concerns the reactions of caretakers to death and grief in their work with patients and how the caretakers learn to understand their own fears and sense of loss.

## MEANING OF DEATH

The reaction to death depends, in part, on the context. For instance, death may be experienced as timely or untimely. *Timely death* implies that one's expected survival and actual life span are approximately equal; essentially, one dies when one is expected to, and those left to grieve are not surprised by the death. In Erik Erikson's scheme of the life cycle, the last phase of life involves the conflict between integrity and despair. According to Erikson, a positive developmental resolution of the conflict in the face of inevitable death involves a sense of fulfillment, peace, and integrity, rather than a sense of failure, horror, and despair. A positive resolution is predicated, in Erikson's theory, on having successfully resolved the conflicts of the preceding adult developmental phases.

*Untimely death* implies an unexpected or premature death, and those left to grieve are in shock. Untimely death may refer to (1) the death of a young person, (2) sudden death, or (3) catastrophic death associated with violence or an accident and utter meaninglessness.

Death has also been described as intentional (suicide), unintentional (trauma or disease), and subintentional (substance abuse, alcohol dependence, cigarette smoking). Death may have multiple psychological meanings, both for the person who is dying and for society in general. In Susan Sontag's formulation, death may even take on the power of metaphor. For example, some persons view death as deserved punishment for what are perceived as immoral or sinful life-styles.

## SUDDEN DEATH OF PSYCHOGENIC ORIGIN

Emotional factors alone may be sufficient to trigger sudden death in certain persons not otherwise at risk. For instance, myocardial infarctions may follow sudden psychic stress. Voodoo death or death secondary to a hex occurs when a person who is thought to have the power to cause death psychically puts a curse on someone who believes in that person's power. In such instances, it is theorized that the hypothalamic-pituitary-adrenal axis and the autonomic nervous system become dysfunctional because of emotional stress, which causes the cessation of vital functions. Unless a folk healer removes the curse, a person under such a spell or hex may die.

## LEGAL ASPECTS OF DEATH

According to law, the physician must sign a death certificate that attests to the cause of death (for example, congestive heart failure or pneumonia). The physician must also classify death as being from natural, accidental, suicidal, homicidal, or unknown causes. Anyone who dies unattended by a physician must be examined by the appointed medical examiner, coroner, or pathologist, and an autopsy must be performed to determine the cause of death. In some cases a *psychological autopsy* is performed, in which the person's sociocultural and psychological background is examined retrospectively by interviewing friends, relatives, and doctors to determine whether a mental illness, such as a depressive disorder, was present. A determination can be made that a person died because he or she was pushed (murder) or because he or she jumped (suicide) from a high building. Each situation has clear medical and legal implications.

## REACTIONS TO IMPENDING DEATH

A number of researchers have studied reactions to death. One of the earliest and most useful organizations of reactions to impending death came from the psychiatrist and thanatologist Elisabeth Kübler-Ross. Seldom does any dying patient follow a regular series of responses that can be clearly identified; no established sequence is applicable to all patients. However, the following five stages proposed by Kübler-Ross are widely encountered.

### Stage 1—Shock and Denial

On being told that they are dying, patients have initial reactions of shock. The patients may appear dazed at first and then may refuse to believe the diagnosis or deny that anything is wrong. Some patients never pass beyond that stage and may go from doctor to doctor until they find one who supports their position. The degree to which denial is adaptive or maladaptive appears to depend on whether the patient continues to obtain treatment, even while denying the prognosis. In such cases, the physician must communicate to the patient and the patient's family, in a respectful and direct way, basic information about the illness, its prognosis, and the options for treatment. Inherent in effective communication is allowing for patients' emotional responses and reassuring them that they will not be abandoned.

## Stage 2—Anger

Patients become frustrated, irritable, and angry that they are ill. A common response is, "Why me?" They may become angry at God, their fate, a friend, or a family member; they may even blame themselves. The anger may be displaced onto the hospital staff members and the doctor, who are blamed for the illness. Patients in the stage of anger are difficult to treat. The doctor who has difficulty in understanding that anger is a predictable reaction and is really one of displacement may withdraw from the patient or transfer the patient to another doctor's care. The treatment of angry patients involves understanding that the anger being expressed cannot be taken personally. An empathic, nondefensive response can help defuse the patient's anger and can help the patient refocus on the deep feelings (for example, grief, fear, loneliness) that underlie the anger. Also, the physician should recognize that anger may represent patients' desires for control in a situation in which they feel completely out of control.

## Stage 3—Bargaining

Patients may attempt to negotiate with physicians, friends, or even God: in return for a cure, they will fulfill one or many promises, such as giving to charity and attending church regularly. Another aspect of bargaining is that the patients believe that, by their being good (compliant, nonquestioning, cheerful), the doctor will make them better. The treatment of such patients involves making it clear that they will be taken care of to the best of the doctor's abilities and that everything that can be done will be done, regardless of any action or behavior on the patients' part. The patient must also be encouraged to participate as a partner in the case and to understand that being a good patient means being as honest and straightforward as possible.

## Stage 4—Depression

In the fourth stage, patients show clinical signs of depression—withdrawal, psychomotor retardation, sleep disturbances, hopelessness, and, possibly, suicidal ideation. The depression may be a reaction to the effects of the illness on their lives (for example, the loss of jobs, economic hardship, helplessness, hopelessness, and isolation from friends and family), or it may be in anticipation of the loss of life that will eventually occur. If a major depressive disorder with vegetative signs and suicidal ideation develops, treatment with antidepressant medication or electroconvulsive therapy (ECT) may be indicated. All persons feel some degree of sadness at the prospect of their own deaths, and normal sadness does not require biological intervention. However, major depressive disorder and active suicidal ideation can be alleviated and should not be accepted as just a normal reaction to impending death. A person who suffers from major depressive disorder may be unable to sustain hope. Hope can alter longevity and can enhance the dignity and the quality of the patient's life.

## Stage 5—Acceptance

Patients realize that death is inevitable, and they accept the universality of the experience. Their feelings may range from a mood that is neutral to one that is euphoric. Under ideal circumstances, the patients resolve their feelings about the inevitability of death and are able to talk about death in the face of the unknown. Those persons who have strong religious beliefs and are convinced of a life after death can find comfort in the ecclesiastical belief: fear not death; remember those who have gone before you, and those who will come after.

## CARING FOR THE DYING PATIENT

Physicians' abilities to care compassionately and effectively for dying patients depend, in large part, on their awareness of their own attitudes toward death and dying. Some physicians have dysfunctional attitudes toward death and the dying patient that may be reinforced by their medical training. When training focuses almost entirely on the control and the eradication of disease at the expense of the care and the comfort of the person with disease, death and the dying patient become the enemy. In other words, death and the dying patient may become equated with failure and may thus reflect the doctor's inadequacy and limitations. When that occurs, it is no surprise that the dying patient is avoided or is experienced as a source of irritation, impatience, and fear.

Because of their extensive knowledge of the human body and their technical expertise in controlling many disease states, physicians may begin unconsciously to feel omnipotent and all-powerful with regard to preventing death. When those physicians confront death, they may feel threatened and defensive; their image of themselves has been badly injured. Those physicians view dying patients as painful reminders of their own fallibility.

Some physicians enter the practice of medicine because of their own unconscious fears of death. Those doctors unconsciously hope that, through the study and the mastery of medicine, they may achieve some control over their own mortality. Although those doctors must deal with dying patients, they may feel an inordinate amount of anxiety, coupled with a strong need to avoid the dying patients. Those physicians may attempt to deal with their underlying fear of death through extensive intellectualization; for instance, they may provide dying patients with minute and often unnecessary details about the day-to-day vicissitudes of the illness while sidestepping any discussion of the patients' fears, concerns, and feelings.

The major task of physicians caring for dying patients is to provide compassionate concern and continuing support. The hallmarks of appropriate care are visiting with the patients regularly, maintaining eye contact, touching appropriately, listening to what the patients have to say, and being willing to answer all questions in as respectful a way as possible. What is most important is to be tactfully honest. Most patients want their doctors to be truthful with them; for example, they prefer to know that they have cancer. Honesty, however, does not preclude hope. If 85 percent of patients with a particular disease die within five years, 15 percent are still alive after that time. Still, some patients do not want to know the facts of their illness. A doctor may ask patients how much they want to know about the illness and should respond to the patients' wishes.

The patient, the family, and the hospital staff members vary in the extent of their knowledge of the patient's illness. In one classification, four patterns of awareness may exist: *open awareness*, in which staff members, the family, and the patient are completely aware of the diagnosis, treatment, and prognosis of the illness; *mutual pretense awareness*, in which those same persons know but pretend not to know; *suspected awareness*, in which everyone knows except the patient, who suspects the truth; and *closed awareness*, in which everyone except the patient knows. Hospitals tend toward open awareness when it can be tolerated by all concerned; but some terminally ill patients may choose not to know the truth about their condition, and that wish should be respected. However, every attempt should be made, gently and respectfully, to encourage a dying patient and the family to speak openly with one another. Many times, what initially appeared to be a reluctance to talk about the impending death may, in fact, have been a fear of isolation or rejection or a perceived lack of courage.

Other factors need to be considered in caring for the dying patient. Pain management should be vigorous in the terminally ill. A dying patient needs to function as effectively as possible, given the illness. Doing so is made easier when the patient is relatively free of pain. The physician should use narcotics as liberally as they are needed and tolerated, so that the patient can attend to any business with a minimum of discomfort. In addition, physicians should not take personally the complaints of a patient who may be in the anger phase of dying and should help the members of the dying patient's family deal with their feelings about the patient's illness. For many patients, family members are the main source of emotional support and are far more available to and knowledgeable about the patient than is the doctor on the case.

### Family Interventions

The first step in working with the family of a dying patient is to develop an alliance with them. That can be accomplished by allowing the family members to talk about their own lives and stresses and by offering some understanding. The physician should try to assess to what degree the family members want direction or help and to what degree they prefer a sense of autonomy.

At times of great external stress, such as the impending death of a family member, family conflicts may intensify. A physician can help the family refocus attention on confronting the external stress, rather than on mutual blame and argument. Opening communication channels among family members can be helpful.

Family members may be reluctant to talk to dying patients about the impending death for fear of being too upset themselves or of upsetting the patients. Conversely, dying patients may be reluctant to talk about their own impending death for fear of burdening the family. In that situation a physician can let each party know what the others are feeling and can encourage discussion or even raise the topic when all parties are present.

## DEATH CRITERIA, DNR, AND LIVING WILLS

The *Uniform Determination of Death Act* states that "an individual who has sustained either (a) irreversible cessation of circulatory and respiratory functions, or (b) cessation of function of the entire brain, including the brain stem, is dead. A determination of death must be made in accordance with acceptable medical standards."

The physician must anticipate the wishes of patients and their families regarding the use of life-sustaining procedures. Moreover, the physician should discuss the patients' wishes with the family members and the patients while the patients are still competent. Patients may ask that their lives not be prolonged by artificial means (for example, "Do not resuscitate [DNR] if in extremis").

*Living wills* are legal documents in which patients give instructions to their physicians about withholding life-support measures. But physicians must use their best judgment, even in the absence of a living will. If major questions arise with regard to any of those decisions, the physician should consult the hospital administrator or lawyer. A sample living will and health care proxy is given in Table 2.7–1.

The American Medical Association states that doctors can withhold all means of life-prolonging medical treatment, including food and water, from patients in irreversible comas, provided adequate safeguards are taken to confirm the accuracy of the diagnosis. The decision is made in conjunction with the patient's family or legal guardians. In those cases the physician lets a terminally ill patient die; the physician does not intentionally cause death. Persons are brain-dead when they suffer irreversible cessation of the functions of the entire brain, including the brainstem, even if the heart and the lungs continue to function.

## EUTHANASIA

Physicians often walk a fine line between their responsibility to relieve suffering and their obligation to preserve life. The ethical and legal issues surrounding active and passive deprivation of life in severely ill patients are controversial. *Euthanasia,* the act of killing a hopelessly ill or injured person for reasons of mercy, may take one of two forms, either direct (active) or indirect (passive). Either form may be voluntary or nonvoluntary. In view of the technological advances that prolong life, coupled with limitations on resources required to sustain human life of acceptable quality, society will probably move increasingly in the direction of designing a legal framework within which euthanasia can be clarified.

### Physician-Assisted Suicide

The issue of physician-assisted suicide came to national attention in 1990, when Jack Kevorkian, a physician in Michigan, connected Janet Adkins, a victim of dementia of the Alzheimer's type, to a so-called suicide machine that enabled her to give herself an infusion of potassium chloride (KCL) that ended her life. Since then, Kevorkian has

**Table 2.7–1**
**Advance Directive Living Will and Health Care Proxy**

*Death is a part of life. It is a reality like birth, growth and aging. I am using this advance directive to convey my wishes about medical care to my doctors and other people looking after me at the end of my life. It is called an advance directive because it gives instructions in advance about what I want to happen to me in the future. It expresses my wishes about medical treatment that might keep me alive. I want this to be legally binding.*

*If I cannot make or communicate decisions about my medical care, those around me should rely on this document for instructions about measures that could keep me alive.*

*I do not want medical treatment (including feeding and water by tube) that will keep me alive if:*
- *I am unconscious and there is no reasonable prospect that I will ever be conscious again (even if I am not going to die soon in my medical condition), or*
- *I am near death from an illness or injury with no reasonable prospect of recovery.*

*I do want medicine and other care to make me more comfortable and to take care of pain and suffering. I want this even if the pain medicine makes me die sooner.*

*I want to give some extra instructions: [Here list any special instructions, e.g., some people fear being kept alive after a debilitating stroke. If you have wishes about this, or any other conditions, please write them here.]*

**The legal language in the box that follows is a health care proxy. It gives another person the power to make medical decisions for me.**

I name _____, who lives at _____ _____, phone number _____, to make medical decisions for me if I cannot make them myself. This person is called a health care "surrogate," "agent," "proxy," or "attorney in fact." This power of attorney shall become effective when I become incapable of making or communicating decisions about my medical care. This means that this document stays legal when and if I lose the power to speak for myself, for instance, if I am in a coma or have Alzheimer's disease.

My health care proxy has power to tell others what my advance directive means. This person also has power to make decisions for me, based either on what I would have wanted, or, if this is not known, on what he or she thinks is best for me.

If my first choice health care proxy cannot or decides not to act for me, I name _____, address ___, phone number _____, as my second choice.

I have discussed my wishes with my health care proxy, and with my second choice if I have chosen to appoint a second person. My proxy(ies) has(have) agreed to act for me.

I have thought about this advance directive carefully. I know what it means and want to sign it. I have chosen two witnesses, neither of whom is a member of my family, nor will inherit from me when I die. My witnesses are not the same people as those I named as my health care proxies. I understand that this form should be notarized if I use the box to name (a) health care proxy(ies).

Signature _____

Date _____

Address _____

Witness' signature _____

Witness' printed name _____

Address _____

Witness' signature _____

Witness' printed name _____

Address _____

Notary [to be used if proxy is appointed] _____

Table drafted and distributed by Choice In Dying, Inc.—the National Council for the Right to Die. Choice In Dying is a National not-for-profit organization which works for the rights of patients at the end of life. In addition to this generic advance directive, Choice In Dying distributes advance directives that conform to each state's specific legal requirements and maintains a national Living Will Registry for completed documents. Used with permission.

helped 19 other persons take their own lives. His license to practice medicine has been revoked, and he is facing a possible trial for murder in Michigan.

In the United States, physician-assisted suicide and euthanasia have been consistently opposed by the American Medical Association. The World Medical Association issued the following declaration on euthanasia in October 1987:

Euthanasia, that is the act of deliberately ending the life of a patient, even at his own request or at the request of his close relatives, is unethical. This does not prevent the physician from respecting the will of a patient to allow the natural process of death to follow its course in the terminal phase of sickness.

The New York State Committee on Bioethical Issues is also opposed to euthanasia but has stated that the physician has an obligation to provide effective treatment to relieve pain and suffering, even though the treatment may on occasion hasten death. The committee stated the following:

The principle of patient autonomy requires that physicians respect the decision of a patient who possesses decision-making capacity to forgo life-sustaining treatment. Life-sustaining treatment is defined as any medical treatment that serves to prolong life without reversing the underlying medical condition. Life-sustaining treatment includes, but is not limited to, mechanical ventilation, renal dialysis, blood transfusions, chemotherapy, antibiotics, and artificial nutrition and hydration.

Physicians are obligated to relieve pain and suffering and to promote the dignity and autonomy of dying patients in their care. This obligation includes providing effective palliative treatment even though it may occasionally hasten death. However, physicians should not perform euthanasia or participate in assisted suicide. Support, comfort, respect for patient autonomy, good communication, and adequate pain control may dramatically decrease the demand for euthanasia and assisted suicide. In certain carefully defined circumstances, it is humane to recognize that death is certain and suffering is great. However, the societal risks of involving physicians in medical interventions to cause patients' deaths is too great to condone active euthanasia or physician-assisted suicide.

In the Netherlands, physicians are allowed to participate in active euthanasia, provided certain conditions are met: (1) The patient must make repeated requests that are well-informed and enduring. (2) The patient's mental or physical condition must be considered incurable. (3) All other options for care must have been exhausted. (4) The assisting physician must have the agreement of another physician.

In the United States a group called the Hemlock Society actively promotes the practice of euthanasia. Its founder, Derek Humphrey, in his book *Final Exit*, gave explicit directions on suicide techniques. The book has been a bestseller in this country and abroad, attesting to the interest and the controversy surrounding the issue.

Some surveys among United States physicians have found 25 to 30 percent in favor of euthanasia; but the majority of United States physicians oppose the practice.

With the increase in technology and life-support systems and the increase in longevity, society will have to develop a comprehensive policy regarding euthanasia that is acceptable to patients, physicians, lawyers, and theologians, among others. Euthanasia is likely to be a source of continuing controversy for the foreseeable future.

## ATTITUDES TOWARD DEATH ACROSS THE LIFE CYCLE

The stages of children's emotional and cognitive development play a significant role in their perception, interpretation, and understanding of death. The ability of children to understand death reflects their ability to understand any abstract concept. Preschool children under age 5 years (Jean Piaget's preoperational phase) are animistic (they believe that everything, even an inanimate object, is alive) and are aware of death only in the sense that it is a separation similar to sleep. Between the ages of 5 and 10 years (concrete operations), children have a developing sense of inevitable human mortality; they fear that their parents will die and that they will be abandoned. At about age 9 or 10, children conceptualize death as something that can happen to a child, as well as to a parent.

Usually by puberty, children are able to conceptualize death as universal, irreversible, and inevitable, as do adults.

In contrast to parents from other parts of the world, middle-class parents in the United States tend to shield children from a knowledge of death. The air of mystery surrounding death in such instances may create irrational fears in children, which is just the opposite of what is intended.

Adolescents may be preoccupied with issues related to body image and control of the environment; thus, they may appear to focus on what adults perceive to be concerns more trivial than death itself. Treating dying adolescents may be difficult because of their intense need at times for independence and control.

Young adults, in Erikson's stage of intimacy versus isolation, are in the process of developing new, deep relationships. They may focus on the issues of never having the chance to marry or to have children and, therefore, may feel threatened by the potential isolation. Young adult parents fear that their untimely deaths will result in their children's growing up alone. They also fear that they will not experience the role of grandparent.

Middle-aged adults, in Erikson's stage of generativity versus stagnation, may feel frustrated in their hopes to become involved with the next generation and in their plans to enjoy hard-earned pleasure.

Elderly persons, facing the Erikson conflict between integrity and despair, must confront the increasing reality of their own mortality through the deaths of family members and friends.

Children with fatal illnesses create major emotional stresses on their caretakers, be they parents, relatives, hospital staff members, or physicians. A consistent, trusted person is essential in providing optimal care for the dying child. The separation of the child from its mother is as traumatic an event for the hospitalized child as the illness itself, perhaps even more so. As John Bowlby pointed out, having the mother or an equally valued and familiar caretaker room with the hospitalized child can help alleviate the child's anxiety and can facilitate necessary medical care.

## GRIEF, MOURNING, AND BEREAVEMENT

The terms "grief," "mourning," and "bereavement" apply to the psychological reactions of persons who survive a significant loss. *Grief* is the subjective feeling precipitated by the death of a loved one. The term is used synonymously with "mourning," although, in the strictest sense, *mourning* is the process by which grief is resolved; it is the societal expression of postbereavement behavior and practices. *Bereavement* literally means the state of being deprived of someone by death, and it refers to being in the state of mourning. Regardless of the fine points that differentiate those terms, sufficient similarities are present in the experience of grief and bereavement to warrant the experience as a syndrome that has signs, symptoms, a demonstrable course, and an expected resolution.

Grief can occur as the result of a variety of losses, in addition to the loss of a loved person. They include the loss of status, the loss of a national figure, and the loss of a pet. The expression of grief encompasses a wide range of emotions, depending on the cultural norms and expectations (for example, some cultures encourage or demand an intense display of emotions, whereas other cultures expect just the opposite) and on the circumstances of the loss (for example, a sudden unexpected death versus one that is clearly anticipated). *Grief work* is a complex psychological process of withdrawing attachment and working through the pain of bereavement. Grief and bereavement are discussed further in Chapter 30. Figure 2.7–1 summarizes one conceptualization of some of the recognizable and predictable manifestations of the phases of uncomplicated grief.

## Characteristics of Normal Grief

Uncomplicated grief is viewed as a normal response in view of the predictability of its symptoms and its course. Initial grief is often manifested as a state of shock that may be expressed as a feeling of numbness and a sense of bewilderment. That apparent inability to comprehend what has happened may be short-lived. It is followed by such expressions of suffering and distress as sighing and crying, although in Western cultures that expected feature of grief is less common among men than among women. Feelings of weakness, decreased appetite, weight loss, and difficulty in concentrating, breathing, and talking also appear. Sleep disturbances may include difficulty in falling asleep, waking up during the night, and awakening early. Dreams of the deceased person often occur, after which the dreamer awakens with a sense of disappointment in finding that the experience was only a dream.

Self-reproach is common, although it is less intense in normal grief than in pathological grief. Self-reproachful thoughts usually center on some relatively minor act of omission or commission toward the deceased. A phenomenon known as *survivor guilt* occurs in persons who are relieved that the death is someone else's and not their own. Survivors sometimes believe that they should have been the person who died and may (if the guilt persists) have difficulty in establishing new intimate relationships out of fear of betraying the deceased person. Forms of denial occur throughout the period of bereavement; often, the bereaved person inadvertently thinks or acts as if the loss had not occurred. Efforts to perpetuate the lost relationship are evidenced by an investment in objects that were treasured by the deceased person or that remind the grief-stricken person of the deceased (linkage objects).

A sense of the deceased person's presence may be so intense that it constitutes an illusion or a hallucination (for example, hearing the deceased person's voice or feeling the person's presence). In normal grief, however, the survivor realizes that the perception is not real. As part of what has been labeled *identification phenomena,* the survivor may take on the qualities, mannerisms, or characteristics of the deceased person to perpetuate that person in some concrete way. That maneuver can reach potentially

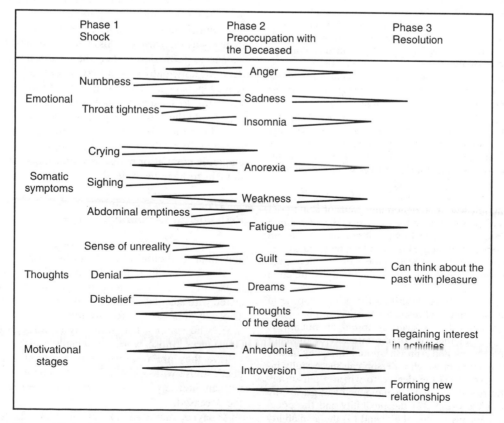

**Figure 2.7–1.** Phases of uncomplicated grief. (Figure from J T Brown, A Stoudemire: Normal and pathological grief. JAMA *250*: 378, 1983. Used with permission.)

pathological expression with the development of physical symptoms similar to those that were experienced by the deceased person or to ones suggestive of the illness of which the deceased person died.

John Bowlby hypothesized four stages of bereavement: *Stage 1* is an early phase of acute despair characterized by numbness and protest. Denial may be immediate, and outbursts of anger and distress are common. The stage may last moments to days and may be periodically revisited by the grieving person throughout the mourning process. *Stage 2* is a phase of intense yearning and searching for the deceased person. It is characterized by a physical restlessness and an all-consuming preoccupation with the deceased. The phase may last several months or even years in an attenuated form. In *Stage 3*, which has been described as a phase of disorganization and despair, the reality of the loss begins to sink in. A sense of going through the motions is dominant, and the grieving person appears to be withdrawn, apathetic, and listless. Insomnia and weight loss often occur, as does a feeling that life has lost its meaning. The grieving person constantly relives memories of the deceased; an associated inevitable feeling of disappointment occurs when the bereaved person recognizes that the memories are just memories. *Stage 4* is a phase of reorganization, during which the acutely painful aspects of grief begin to recede and the grieving person begins to feel like returning to life. The deceased person is now remembered with a sense of joy, as well as sadness, and the image of the lost person becomes internalized.

C. M. Parkes described five stages of bereavement: (1) *Alarm*—a stressful state manifested by physiological changes, such as a rise in blood pressure and heart rate—is somewhat similar to Bowlby's first stage of protest, fear, and anger. (2) *Numbness* is a state in which bereaved persons appear to be superficially unaffected by the loss but are, in reality, protecting themselves from feeling the acute distress produced by the loss. (3) In *pining* or searching the bereaved persons look for or are constantly reminded of the lost person. The illusions or hallucinations of the deceased person mentioned above (sometimes called pseudoillusions or pseudohallucinations because the bereaved person immediately recognizes them as such) may occur during the phase. The phase resembles Bowlby's second stage of yearning and searching for the lost figure. (4) In *depression*, bereaved persons feel hopeless about the future, cannot go on living, and tend to withdraw from family and friends. (5) In the final stage, *recovery and reorganization*, bereaved persons recognize that their lives will continue with new adjustments and different goals.

Eric Lindemann, after the 1944 Coconut Grove fire, described what he felt were pathognomonic signs of acute grief and emotional responses among the survivors. His description of their responses to shocking loss is considered a paradigm for grief reactions to situational loss. Lindemann's acute signs included somatic distress, preoccupation with the deceased, guilt, hostility, and an interruption in the ability to function positively.

Other investigators have described the grief response in terms of a general emotional response to crisis and have emphasized that the earliest, most acute symptoms are not always the best predictors of the type or the intensity of the later reactions. Ellen Bassuk and Ann Birk noted three key factors that affect the manner in which a person can successfully integrate a crisis event: (1) the degree to which a person acknowledges the reality of what has happened and grasps the consequences of the event, (2) the flexibility and the effectiveness of the person's coping skills, and (3) the availability of support and the willingness to use it.

## Length of Grief

Because people vary greatly in their expressions of grief, the signs, symptoms, and phases of mourning and bereavement are not as discrete as their characterizations may imply. Nevertheless, the manifestations of grief usually tend to subside over time. The length and the intensity of grief, especially the acute phases, can be shaped by the suddenness of the death. If death occurs without warning, shock and disbelief may last for a long time; if death has been long anticipated, much of the mourning process may have already occurred by the time death intervenes. Traditionally, grief lasts about six months to one year, as the grieving person experiences the calendar year at least once without the lost person. Some signs and symptoms of grief may persist much longer than one or two years, and a survivor may have various grief-related feelings, symptoms, and behavior throughout life. Eventually, however, normal grief resolves, and people return to a state of productivity and relative well-being. In general, the acute grief symptoms gradually lessen, and within one or two months the grieving person is able to eat, sleep, and return to functioning.

## Anticipatory Grief

*Anticipatory grief* is grief expressed in advance of a loss that is perceived as inevitable, as distinguished from grief that occurs at or after the loss. By definition, anticipatory grief ends with the occurrence of the anticipated loss, regardless of what reactions follow. Unlike conventional grief, which diminishes in intensity with the passage of time, anticipatory grief may either increase or decrease in intensity as the expected loss becomes imminent. In some instances, particularly when the occurrence of the loss is delayed, anticipatory grief may be expended, and the bereaved person shows few manifestations of acute grief when the loss occurs. Once anticipatory grief has been expended, the bereaved person may find it difficult to reestablish the prior relationship; that phenomenon is experienced with the return of persons long gone (for example, in combat or concentration camps) and of persons thought to have been dead.

## Pathological (Abnormal) Grief

For some people the course of grief and mourning is abnormal. Pathological grief can take a number of forms, ranging from grief that is absent or delayed to grief that is excessively intense and prolonged to grief that is associated with suicidal ideation or frank psychotic symptoms. Those at greatest risk for an abnormal grief reaction are those who suffer a loss suddenly or through horrific circumstances, those who are socially isolated, those who believe they are responsible (real or imagined) for the death, those with a history of traumatic losses, and those with an intensely ambivalent or dependent relationship to the deceased.

**Delayed, inhibited, or denied grief.** Delayed, inhibited, or denied grief is the absence of the expression of grief at the time of the loss, when it is ordinarily expected. In some instances, grieving is simply delayed until it can no longer be avoided.

Persons vary greatly in their need to hide their grief. Familial and cultural influences affect how the mourner behaves in public. The stiff upper lip admired by one group contrasts dramatically with the weeping, wailing, and fainting accepted by another group as the norm. Hence, gauging the extent of another's grief from outward appearances may be difficult unless one has some understanding of the person's background.

Grief that is inhibited or denied expression is potentially pathogenic because the bereaved person avoids dealing with the reality of the loss. A false euphoria may prevail, suggesting that bereavement is on a pathological course. Inhibited or denied grief reactions contain the seeds of such unfortunate consequences as experiencing persistent physical symptoms similar to those of the deceased person and unaccountable reactions on the anniversary of the loss or on occasions of significance to the deceased. Denied or inhibited grief may also be displaced to some other loss that, although seemingly insignificant in its own right, may symbolize the original loss. Overreaction to another person's trouble may be one manifestation of displacement.

Some relationships, regardless of their public appearances, are sufficiently negative to render reduced or absent grief a normal and appropriate response. In those cases the consequences of the death of a spouse or a parent may be decidedly positive for the survivor.

**Overidentification or psychosis in grief.** Other forms of abnormal grief occur when some of the aspects of normal grieving are distorted or intensified to psychotic proportions. Identifying with the deceased person, such as taking on certain admired traits or treasuring certain possessions, is normal; believing that one is the deceased or that one is dying of exactly what the deceased person died of (if, in fact, that is not true) is not normal. Hearing a fleeting, transient voice of the deceased person may be normal; persistent, intrusive, complex auditory hallucinations are not normal. Denial of certain aspects of the death is normal; denial that includes the belief that the dead person is still alive is not normal.

## Grief versus Depression

Both grief and depression may be manifested by sadness, crying, and tension expressed as either psychomotor retardation or psychomotor agitation. Decreased appetite, weight loss, insomnia, diminished sexual interest, and withdrawal from outside activities are also common to both conditions. However, as the loss becomes remote, the grief-stricken person usually shows shifts of mood from sadness to a normal state and finds increasing enjoyment in life's experiences. Self-blame generally centers on what was done or not done in relation to the lost person, whereas the self-accusations of depressed persons are likely to involve being bad, worthless, or even evil. The general demeanor of a grief-stricken person intuitively elicits sympathy, support, and consolation from others, to which the person shows some responsiveness and appreciation. In contrast, the complaints and the laments of the depressed

person may irritate and annoy listeners. In normal grief the response is accepted as appropriate and normal by both the grieving person and others; in depression the response readily conveys the idea that something is not right about what is going on.

People who have experienced previous depressions are likely to experience depression, rather than normal grief, at the time of a major loss; therefore, the bereaved person's clinical history may be helpful in judging a current reaction. Depressed persons threaten suicide more often than do grieving persons, who, except in unusual instances—for example, physically dependent and aged persons—do not seriously wish to die, even if they claim that life is unbearable. Marked feelings of worthlessness, extended functional impairment, and psychomotor retardation argue more for major depressive disorder than for uncomplicated bereavement. Frank psychotic symptoms, such as hallucinations and delusions, may be part of the clinical picture of major depressive disorder but not of normal grief.

The physician must determine when grief has become pathological and has evolved into major depressive disorder. Grief is a normal, albeit intensely painful, state that is responsive to support, empathy, and the passage of time. Major depressive disorder is potentially a medical emergency that requires immediate intervention to forestall a complication, such as suicide. Intervention may involve hospitalization or the use of antidepressant medication. Table 2.7–2 summarizes some of the distinguishing features of grief and major depressive disorder.

## Bereavement in Children

Bowlby also studied the bereavement process in children. The process is similar to that in adults, especially once the child is able to understand the irrevocability of death. The mourning process resembles that of separation in that there are three phases: protest, despair, and detachment. In the *protest phase* the child has a strong desire for the mother or other caretaker who died and cries for her return; in the *despair phase* the child begins to feel hopeless about her return, crying is intermittent, and withdrawal and apathy set in. In the *detachment phase* the child begins to relinquish some of the emotional attachment to the dead parent and to show a reawakening of interest in the surroundings.

In dealing with bereaved children, physicians should recognize the children's need to find a person who will substitute for the parent. The children may transfer their need for a parent to several adults, rather than to one. If no consistent person is available, severe psychological damage to the children may result, so that they no longer look for or expect intimacy in any relationship. The importance of managing grief reactions in children is highlighted by the increased evidence that depressive disorders and suicide attempts occur more frequently in adults who in early childhood experienced the death of a parent.

The question of whether children should attend funerals is a common one, and no hard and fast rule is available. Most child experts agree that, if the child expresses a desire to go, the wish should be respected; if the child is reluctant

**Table 2.7–2**
**Distinguishing Grief from Major Depressive Disorder***

| | Grief | Major Depressive Disorder |
|---|---|---|
| Time course | Intense symptoms ≤1–2 months | Longer |
| Suicidal ideation | Usually not present | Often present |
| Psychotic symptoms | Only transient visions or voice of the deceased | May have sustained depressive delusions |
| Emotional symptoms | Pangs interspersed with normal feelings | Continuous pervasive depressed mood |
| Self-blame | Related to deceased | Focused on self |
| Response to support and ventilation | Improvement over time | No change or worsening |

*Depressed symptoms are a pervasive part of the grief response, and a clear delineation—grief versus major depressive disorder—is not always possible.
Table from J L Levenson: Psychiatric aspects of medical practice. In *Clinical Psychiatry for Medical Students*, A Stoudemire, editor, p 543. Lippincott, Philadelphia, 1990. Used with permission.

or refuses to go, that should also be respected. In most circumstances it is probably best to encourage the child to attend so that the ritual is not enveloped in a frightening and distorted fantasy or mystery.

### Grief in Parents

Parents react to a child's death or to the birth of a malformed infant in stages similar to those that Kübler-Ross described in terminal illness: shock, denial, anger, bargaining, depression, and acceptance. The death of a child is often a more intense emotional experience than the death of an adult. Parental feelings of guilt and helplessness may be overwhelming; they may believe that somehow they did not protect their children and have unnaturally outlived them. Lost hopes, wishes, and fulfillments associated with a new generation cause additional pain. Manifestations of the grief may well last a lifetime.

A sudden death is often more traumatic than a prolonged death, because anticipatory grief can occur when death is expected. A parent may become overprotective toward the dying child or shower the child with gifts that were previously denied. The stress of dealing with a child's death may cause a marriage that has had conflicts to disintegrate. One parent may blame the other for the child's fatal illness, especially if the child's disease had a hereditary basis. The physician should be alert to those patterns of dissension. Some studies indicate that up to 50 percent of marriages in which a child dies or is malformed end in divorce.

### Psychodynamics

In 1917 Freud wrote in *Mourning and Melancholia* that normal grief (mourning) results from the withdrawal of the libido from its attachment to the lost object. In normal mourning the loss is clearly and unambivalently perceived, and the deceased person is eventually, through the grief work, internalized as a loving and loved object. In abnormal grief (melancholia) the lost object is not given up but is incorporated within the survivor's psyche as an object infused with negative feelings. Those negative feelings toward the deceased person are experienced as part of the self, and the survivor becomes depressed, has low self-esteem, feels worthless, and becomes self-accusatory, with possible delusional expectations of punishment. Freud's distinction between mourning and melancholia is still considered valid—that is, an exaggerated loss of self-esteem is not part of normal grieving.

Other psychoanalytic theorists have stressed the role of unconscious dynamics in grief reactions. The greater the role of unconscious and ambivalent factors (for example, anger toward the deceased), the greater is the likelihood of an abnormal grief reaction. Karl Abraham described the introjection of an ambivalently loved lost object and the subsequent direction of anger toward the introjected object.

### Grief and Medical Illness

Compelling evidence suggests that, during bereavement, the surviving person is in a vulnerable physical state of biological disequilibrium. Clinical evidence and research findings support the hypothesis that bereavement is a factor in the development of a wide range of physical and emotional disorders, including fatal illness. Comparisons of close relatives of deceased persons with relatives of living persons (matched for age, sex, and marital status) indicate that bereaved relatives have a much higher mortality rate during the first year of bereavement, the greatest risk being for widowed people. During bereavement, widows have a much higher consultation rate for all causes than they did before the loss of their spouses. Aged persons, in particular, tend to express their reactions in terms of somatic symptoms.

**Physician's role in grief.** The physician plays an important role in dealing with bereaved spouses, relatives, and friends. First, the physician may have to prepare the family for the probability that a loved one will die. In the event of the patient's death, the physician should encourage the family's ventilation of feelings. If that emotional expression is inhibited, in all likelihood the feelings will be expressed in an intense manner at a later date. Outcomes of bereavement are most favorable if the grief-stricken person can interact with others who share or empathize with their feelings of loss.

Persons in normal grief seldom seek psychiatric help, because they accept their reactions and behavior as appropriate. Accordingly, the attending physician should not routinely recommend that a bereaved person see a psychiatrist unless a markedly divergent reaction to the loss is noted. For example, under usual circumstances the bereaved person will not make a suicide attempt. Should a suicide be attempted, psychiatric intervention is indicated.

When professional assistance is sought, it usually involves a request for sleeping medication from the family physician. A mild sedative to induce sleep may be useful in some situations, but antidepressant medication or antianxiety agents are rarely indicated in normal grief. The bereaved person may have to go through the mourning process, however painful it is, for a successful resolution to occur. To narcotize the patient with drugs interferes with a normal process that ultimately can lead to a favorable outcome.

**Physicians' responses.** The reactions of a physician to dying patients often reflects underlying attitudes toward death. If a physician experiences death as a personal failure or a threat to a feeling of personal immortality, the dying patient is likely to be avoided. Sadness on the part of a physician in response to a patient's death is normal and expectable; but, if sadness or a sense of helplessness interferes with the physician's ability to provide optimal care, the physician needs to seek support, advice, or consultation from colleagues. Both excessive, inappropriate intervention and a complete withdrawal of hope can reflect the underlying imbalance in the physician's attitude toward accepting the inevitability of death.

### Grief Management and Therapy

Because grief reactions may develop into a depressive disorder or pathological mourning, specific counseling sessions for the bereaved are often valuable. Grief therapy is an increasingly important skill. In regularly scheduled sessions the grieving person is encouraged to talk about feelings of loss and about the deceased. Many bereaved persons have difficulty in recognizing and expressing angry or ambivalent feelings toward the deceased, and they must be reassured that those feelings are normal.

During grief therapy an attachment to the therapist usually occurs, that attachment provides the bereaved with temporary support until a sense of confidence about the future develops. The therapist gradually encourages the patient to take on new responsibilities and to develop a sense of autonomy. To do grief therapy, the therapist must be comfortable in dealing with the issues of death and dying and must be able to handle the patient's intense emotional reactions of sadness, anger, guilt, and self-denigration. In addition, grief therapy requires that the therapist be active and participate in the decision-making process with the patient, especially in decisions that guide the patient toward independence.

Grief therapy need not be conducted only on a one-to-one basis; group counseling is also effective. Self-help groups have value in certain cases. About 30 percent of widows and widowers report that they become isolated from friends, withdraw from social life, and, thus, experience feelings of isolation and loneliness. Self-help groups offer companionship, social contacts, and emotional support; they eventually enable their members to reenter society in a meaningful way.

Bereavement care and grief therapy have been most effective with widows and widowers. The necessity for that type of therapy stems, in part, from the contraction of the family unit. Previously, extended family members were able to provide the needed emotional support and guidance during the mourning period.

### HOSPICE MOVEMENT

A *hospice* is a domicile in which care is provided for dying patients; its primary emphasis is on the physical and psychological comfort of the terminally ill. Such care may also be provided in an institution or at home. The central concept of the hospice is the humanization of terminal care by helping dying patients and their families carry out final choices with dignity and control.

The hospice movement began in the early 1960s, when Dame Cicely Saunders established a small residential unit to care for the terminally ill. At present, about 1,800 such units are active in the United States. Most hospices are sponsored by hospitals or are affiliated with home health care agencies; some are approved by Medicare, which reimburses patients for hospice care with certain restrictions. Round-the-clock coverage is provided by a multidisciplinary team composed of physicians, psychiatrists, social workers, and trained volunteers.

A hospice program has many positive features. A supervised organized routine provides intensive care for both the patient and the family; the control of pain is a primary goal, and narcotics are given without the fear of addiction; and group support is provided for the patients, who are not as isolated as they are in general hospitals.

Because the bereavement process is a major focus, hospice care also helps prevent pathological grief from occurring in surviving family members. Several studies have indicated that hospice care has a more favorable effect than does standard hospital care on family members' abilities to cope and adapt. The *burned-out syndrome,* in which health care providers become uninterested and irritable with the terminally ill patients who require almost constant attention, is rarely seen. If the patient is in home hospice care, visiting nurses provide relief for overburdened family members.

Medicare pays for hospice care if the patient's doctor states that the patient has a life expectancy of six months or less. In one study by C. M. Parkes, however, predictions concerning the length of survival for patients referred to a hospice did not correlate with the actual length of survival. Doctors were able to state only that patients with incurable cancer would die within a relatively short time and could not be more precise than that. Unfortunately, current federal regulations do not provide for financing hospital care once federally sponsored hospice care has begun; thus, a patient who uses a hospice's care will not be insured on reentry to a hospital if the need arises.

The hospice movement is in its ascendancy, especially because it costs more to keep a terminally ill patient in a general hospital than it does to provide hospice benefits. It is also a more compassionate and humane method for treating preterminal and terminal patients than is general hospital care.

## AIDS Patients and the Hospice

People with acquired immune deficiency syndrome (AIDS) provide a special example of the need for greatly increased hospice care centers for terminally ill patients. The AIDS epidemic poses profound challenges to the medical care system, to the mental health care system, and to social service agencies, as well as to patients and their families. AIDS has a devastating effect on most areas of human functioning, and many patients are debilitated for long periods before death. Many patients' needs overwhelm the capabilities of their own social networks, just as the needs of AIDS patients are overwhelming the capacities of the existing traditional health care facilities. Furthermore, the incidence of the burned-out or chronic professional stress syndrome in caretakers of people with AIDS is high and presents a major challenge to the development and the maintenance of an adequate care system for those patients.

## References

Baker J E, Sedney M A, Gross E: Psychological tasks for bereaved children. Am J Orthopsychiatry 62: 105, 1992.

Bassuk E L, Birk A W: *Emergency Psychiatry: Concepts, Methods, and Practices*. Plenum, New York, 1984.

Conwell Y, Caine E D: Rational suicide and the right to die: Reality and myth. N Engl J Med 325: 1100, 1991.

Council on Ethical and Judicial Affairs: Current Opinions. American Medical Association, Chicago, 1992.

deWachter M M: Active euthanasia in the Netherlands. JAMA 262: 3316, 1989.

Gonda T A: Death, dying, and bereavement. In *Comprehensive Textbook of Psychiatry*, ed 5, H I Kaplan, B J Sadock, editors, p 1339. Williams & Wilkins, Baltimore, 1989.

Hinohara S: Sir William Osler's philosophy on death. Ann Intern Med 118: 639, 1993.

Horowitz M J: Depression after the death of a spouse. Am J Psychiatry 149: 579, 1992.

Humphrey D: *Final Exit: The Practicalities of Self-Deliverance and Assisted Suicide for the Dying*. Hemlock Society, Eugene, Ore, 1991.

Jeret J S: Discussing dying: Changing attitudes among patients, physicians, and medical students. Pharos 52: 15, 1989.

Kübler-Ross E: *On Death and Dying*. Macmillan, New York, 1969.

Kutscher A, Carr A, Kutscher L, editors: *Principles of Thanatology*. Columbia University Press, New York, 1987.

Leming M R, Dickinson G E: *Understanding Dying, Death and Bereavement*. Holt, Rinehart & Winston, New York, 1985.

Lindemann E: Symptomatology and management of acute grief. Am J Psychiatry 101: 141, 1945.

Ness D E, Pfeffer C R: Sequelae of bereavement resulting from suicide. Am J Psychiatry 147: 279, 1990.

Nuss W S, Zubenko G S: Correlates of persistent depressive symptoms in widows. Am J Psychiatry 149: 346, 1992.

Osterweis M, Solomon F, Green M, editors: *Bereavement: Reaction Consequences and Care*. National Academy Press, Washington, 1984.

Parkes C M, Weiss R S: *Recovery from Bereavement*. Basic Books, New York, 1983.

Roberts G, Owen J: The near-death experience. Br J Psychiatry 153: 607, 1988.

Rosner F, Rogatz P: Physician-assisted suicide: Committee on Bioethical Issues of the Medical Society of the State of New York. N Y State J Med 92: 388, 1992.

Saunders C M, Baines M: *Living with Dying: The Management of Terminal Disease*, ed 2. Oxford University Press, Oxford, 1989.

Speece M W, Brent S B: The acquisition of a mature understanding of three components of the concept of death. Death Stud 16: 211, 1992.

Stoudemire A, editor: *Clinical Psychiatry for Medical Students*. Lippincott, Philadelphia, 1990.

Tedeschi R G, Calhoun L G: Using the support group to respond to the isolation of bereavement. J Ment Health Counsel 15: 47, 1993.

Warren W G: *Death Education and Research: Critical Perspectives*. Haworth, New York, 1989.

Weiss L, Frischer L, Richman J: Parental adjustment to intrapartum and delivery room loss: The role of hospital-based support program. Clin Perinatol 16: 1009, 1989.

Zizook S, DeVaul R: Unresolved grief. Am J Psychoanal 45: 370, 1985.

# The Brain and Behavior

## 3.1 / Neuroanatomy and Neuropsychiatry

The human brain is the common denominator for all schools of thought regarding human behavior. Although the brain continues to mystify and inspire awe in both lay people and neuroscientists, the innovative techniques of contemporary basic and clinical psychiatric research are rapidly revealing the functional organization of the human brain.

A historical objective for neuroanatomy has been to relate specific regions of the brain to specific functions, but that objective has not been attained for the complex mental functions with which psychiatry concerns itself. The primary reason for difficulty in finding one-to-one neuroanatomical-behavioral correlations is that the brain operates by using complexes of systems within itself. For example, at the neuronal level, such a system may involve neurons in many layers of the cerebral cortex; at the whole brain level, such a system may involve groups of neurons in many regions of the brain. Although the knowledge of currently recognized systems is incomplete, the three major systems of particular relevance to psychiatry are the cortical-thalamic, the limbic-hypothalamic, and the basal ganglia.

The term "biological psychiatry" is sometimes used interchangeably with the term "neuropsychiatry." In current usage, however, the two terms have different connotations. *Biological psychiatry* emphasizes a neurochemical and neuropharmacological approach to psychiatric disorders. In contrast, *neuropsychiatry* emphasizes the many real and conceptual relations between neurology and psychiatry. Many, if not most, of the neurological disorders that affect the brain (in contrast to the neurological disorders that affect the peripheral nervous system or the spinal cord) have associated psychiatric symptoms that can mimic psychiatric disorders (Table 3.1–1). What is less obvious and less appreciated is that many psychiatric disorders have associated neurological symptoms or symptoms that can be conceptualized as being neurological. For example, the high prevalence of abnormal reflexes among schizophrenic patients is an instance of neurological signs

in a psychiatric disorder. Of potentially greater importance, however, are the potential insights gained into the pathophysiology of a psychiatric disorder by conceptualizing classic psychiatric symptoms (for example, lack of will to dress in the morning) as potentially being a classic neurological symptom (for example, a dressing apraxia).

Beyond those theoretical considerations are two clinically relevant reasons for a clinician working with psychiatric patients to understand neuroanatomy and to be familiar with the interface between neurology and psychiatry. First, many neurological disorders can present with psychiatric symptoms, and the psychiatric clinician must be knowledgeable about the approach to the differential diagnosis of such symptoms. Second, psychiatric clinicians are regularly called to consult on the psychiatric symptoms of neurologically and medically ill patients. An understanding of the underlying neuroanatomy, pathophysiology, and treatment approaches facilitates the formulation of accurate assessments and effective treatment plans.

### NEURONS

The basic functional unit of the nervous system is the *neuron* or *nerve cell,* of which the brain contains approximately $10^{11}$. Each neuron comprises four major areas: the cell body or soma, the axon, dendrites, and synapses (Figure 3.1–1). The *cell body* contains the nucleus and many other major elements of neural functioning. Each neuron generally has a single *axon,* which conducts the nerve impulse to some location removed from the cell body. Some neurons, termed *projection neurons,* have long axons and either relay information from the peripheral sensory receptors to the central nervous system (CNS) (*sensory neurons*) or relay motor activation signals from the brain to the muscles (*motor neurons*). In contrast, other neurons, termed *local circuit neurons* or *interneurons,* have short axons and relay information locally to neighboring neurons. At the distal end of the axon, the axon may branch and enlarge at its tips. Those terminal enlargements are called the *axon terminals* or *boutons* and are the sites of presynaptic neurotransmitter release. Most neurons have a great multiplicity of *dendrites,* which receive signals from other neurons and transmit them back to the cell body of their own neuron. Dendrites are unmyelinated and are usually profusely branched and studded with small protrusions, called *dendritic spines,* which are the actual sites of synaptic connection. Neurons with distinct axons and dendrites are called *bipolar cells,* although a number of basic arrangements of those processes are found in the brain (Figure 3.1–2).

**Table 3.1–1**
**Neurological Diseases That May Present**
**as Psychiatric Diagnoses by DSM-IV Criteria**

**Disorders usually first diagnosed in infancy, childhood, or adolescence**
Tourette's disorder
Subacute sclerosing panencephalitis
Vitamin deficiencies
Juvenile Huntington's disease
Acute intermittent porphyria

**Delirium, dementia, amnestic, and other cognitive disorders**
Dementia of the Alzheimer's type
Pick's disease
Dementia of frontal lobe
Vitamin $B_{12}$ deficiency
Normal pressure hydrocephalus
Metabolic diseases (thyroid disease, Cushing's disease, hypopituitarism)
Neurosyphilis
Intracranial pathology
Wilson's disease
Leukodystrophies
Neurodegenerative disorders
Chronic meningitis
Heavy metal poisoning (mercury, thallium, arsenic)

**Substance-related disorders**
Acute intermittent porphyria
Epilepsy
Multiple sclerosis
Metabolic diseases (thyroid disease, Cushing's disease, hypopituitarism, calcium abnormalities)
Infections (encephalitis, meningitis)

**Schizophrenia and other psychotic disorders**
Complex visual disorders (Balint's syndrome)
Lupus cerebritis
Alcoholic hallucinosis
Temporal lobe epilepsy
Parietal lobe disease
Amphetamine overdose
Huntington's disease
Inorganic mercury poisoning
Wilson's disease
Neurosyphilis
AIDS dementia
Neurodegenerative disorders
Acute intermittent porphyria
Niemann-Pick disease type II-C
Aphasia (Wernicke's and transcortical)
Delusional disorder (paranoia)
    Extrapyramidal disorders: Parkinson's disease, Huntington's disease, Wilson's disease, Sydenham's chorea, spinocerebellar degeneration, idiopathic basal ganglia calcification
    CNS infections: viral encephalitis, Cruetzfeldt-Jakob disease, cerebral malaria, syphilis, trypanosomiasis
    Demyelinating disease: multiple sclerosis, metachromatic leukodystrophy, adrenoleukodystrophy
    Epilepsy
    Neoplasms: temporal lobe, deep white matter lesions
    Cerebrovascular diseases
    Posttraumatic encephalopathy
    Degenerative diseases: Dementia of the Alzheimer's type, Pick's disease
    Miscellaneous: hydrocephalus, cerebral anoxia, Marchiafava-Bignami disease, inborn errors of metabolism ($G_{m2}$ gangliosidosis, Gaucher's disease type 1, Niemann-Pick disease type II-C), paraneoplastic limbic encephalitis
Psychotic disorder not otherwise specified

**Mood disorders**
Major depressive disorder
    Frontal lobe syndromes (trauma, postsurgical, tumors)

    Multiple sclerosis
    Huntington's disease
    Subcortical dementias
    Organic solvent inhalation
    Vitamin $B_{12}$ deficiency
    AIDS dementia
    Paraneoplastic limbic encephalitis
    Neurosyphilis
    Cerebrovascular diseases
    Parkinson's disease
    Progressive supranuclear palsy
    Calcification of basal ganglia
    Colloid cysts of third ventricle
    Pseudobulbar palsy
    Temporal lobe tumors
    Metabolic diseases (Cushing's disease, thyroid disease, hypopituitarism)
Bipolar I disorder
    Frontal lobe syndromes (trauma, postsurgical, tumors)
    Huntington's disease
    Multiple sclerosis
    Inorganic mercury poisoning (Mad Hatter syndrome)
    AIDS dementia
    Neoplasms (diencephalic, hypothalamic, and medial frontal)
    Cerebrovascular lesions (temporal, deep hemispheric)
    Thalamotomy
    Hemidecortication
    Postencephalitic Parkinson's disease
    Wilson's disease
    Epilepsy
    Neurosyphilis
    Pick's disease
    Viral encephalitis
    Klinefelter's syndrome
    Kleine-Levin syndrome
    Vitamin $B_{12}$ deficiency
    Cryptococcal meningitis
    Drugs

**Anxiety disorders**
Vitamin $B_{12}$ deficiency
Paraneoplastic limbic encephalitis
Huntington's disease
Dementias, frontal lobe disease
Neurosyphilis
Toxins (mercury, heavy metals)
Multiple sclerosis

**Somatoform disorders**
Multiple sclerosis
Frontal lobe dementia
Acute intermittent porphyria
Neurosyphilis

**Factitious disorders**
Multiple sclerosis
Acute intermittent porphyria
Subacute heavy metal poisoning
Epilepsy

**Dissociative disorders**
Amnestic syndromes
Transient global amnesia
Korsakoff's amnesia
Parietal lobe disorder

**Sexual and gender identity disorders**
Tumors of the hypothalamus or third ventricle
Medial temporal lobe diseases
Klüver-Bucy syndrome
Frontal lobe disorders

**Sleep disorders**
Hypothalamic disorders
Idiopathic narcolepsy
Dream anxiety disorder caused by apnea or medication
Sleep apnea
Restless legs syndrome
Periodic limb movements of sleep

**Table 3.1–1**
*Continued*

**Impulse control disorders not elsewhere classified**
    Meige's disease
    Temporal lobe epilepsy
    Calcification of basal ganglia
    Tourette's disorder
    Hypothalamic tumors
**Adjustment disorder**
    Frontal lobe disease
    Multiple sclerosis
**Psychological factors affecting medical condition**
    Parkinson's disease
    Huntington's disease
    Tourette's disorder
    Epilepsy

**AXIS II:**
    **Personality disorders**
        Huntington's disease
        Frontal lobe syndromes
        Encephalitis lethargica affecting the brainstem
        Viral encephalitis
        Wilson's disease
        Tourette's disorder

Table adapted from D Z Skuster, K B Digre, J J Corbett: Neurologic conditions presenting as psychiatric disorders. Psychiatr Clin North Am *15*: 311, 1992. Used with permission.

The final organizational component of neurons is the *synapse,* the specialized area of contact between two or more neurons. The nature of synapses is discussed in depth in Section 3.3. Each of the approximately $10^{11}$ neurons has $10^3$ to $10^4$ synaptic connections on its cell surface from as many as $10^3$ neurons.

## GLIA

The nonneuronal cells in the nervous system are the *glia,* which are also called the glial cells, the neuroglia, and the macroglia. Astrocytes, oligodendrocytes, ependymal cells, and microglia are the four types of glial cells in the CNS. Although the vast majority of research regarding the pathophysiology of psychiatric disorders focuses on neurons, an increasing number of research reports suggest that glial cells are much more actively involved in neuronal activity than is currently appreciated. For example, receptors for many neurotransmitters can be found on glial cells. Thus, most of the commonly used psychiatric drugs affect glial function, as well as neuronal function. Structural support for neurons is provided by the *astrocytes,* which are also the glial cells involved in the formation of CNS scars when neurons degenerate. Many studies of postmortem brain tissue from schizophrenic patients have attempted to find a correlation between glial scar tissue and the pathophysiological processes of schizophrenia. Myelin in the CNS is produced by the *oligodendrocytes,* which may also perform a nurturing role for neurons. The process of phagocytosis in the CNS involves both astrocytes and oligodendrocytes. The *ependymal cells* line the brain ventricles and the central canal of the spinal cord. The surface of the ependyma is usually covered with cilia, whose beating facilitates the movement of cerebrospinal fluid (CSF). Selected regions of ependymal cells and neurons of a few other regions synthesize and apparently secrete a class of molecules known as

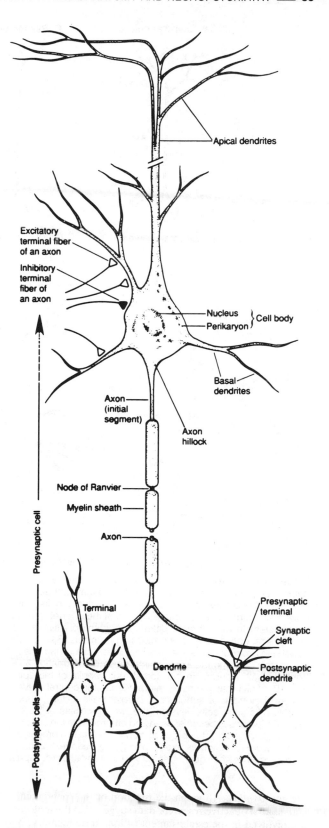

**Figure 3.1–1.** A neuron. (Figure from E R Kandel: Nerve cells and behavior. In *Principles of Neural Science,* ed 3, E R Kandel, J H Schwartz, T M Jessell, editors, p 19. Elsevier, New York, 1991. Used with permission.)

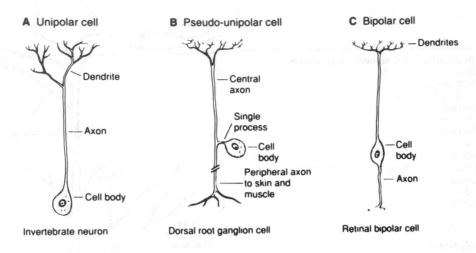

**A** Unipolar cell

Dendrite

Axon

Cell body

Invertebrate neuron

**B** Pseudo-unipolar cell

Central
axon

Single
process

Cell
body

Peripheral axon
to skin and
muscle

Dorsal root ganglion cell

**C** Bipolar cell

Dendrites

Cell
body

Axon

Retinal bipolar cell

**D** Three types of multipolar cells

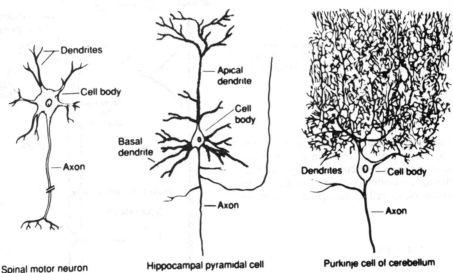

Dendrites

Cell body

Axon

Spinal motor neuron

Apical
dendrite

Cell
body

Basal
dendrite

Axon

Hippocampal pyramidal cell

Dendrites — Cell body

Axon

Purkinje cell of cerebellum

**Figure 3.1–2.** Types of neurons. Neurons can be classified as unipolar, bipolar, or multipolar, according to the number of processes that originate from the cell body. **A.** Unipolar cells, which have a single process, are characteristic of the invertebrate nervous system. In invertebrates, different segments of a single axon serve as receptive surfaces or releasing terminals. **B,C.** Bipolar cells have two processes: the dendrite, which carries information toward the cell, and the axon, which transmits information away from the cell. Neurons in the dorsal root ganglia of the spinal cord (**B**), which carry sensory information to the central nervous system, belong to a subclass of bipolar cells called pseudo-unipolar. As such cells develop, the two processes of the embryonic bipolar cell become fused and emerge from the cell body as a single process. That process then splits into two processes, both of which function as axons, one going peripherally to skin or muscle, the other going centrally to the spinal cord. Bipolar cells of the retina (**C**) or of the olfactory epithelium represent typical bipolar cells. **D.** Multipolar cells, which have an axon and many dendritic processes, are the most common type of neuron in the mammalian nervous system. Three examples show the large diversity of shape and organization. The spinal motor neuron innervates skeletal muscle fibers. The pyramidal cell has a pyramid-shaped cell body. Dendrites emerge from both the apex (the apical dendrite) and the base (the basal dendrites). Pyramidal cells are found in the hippocampus and throughout the cerebral cortex. The Purkinje's cell of the cerebellum is characterized by its rich and extensive dendritic tree in one plane. The structure is designed to accommodate an enormous synaptic input. (Figure from E R Kandel: Nerve cells and behavior. In *Principles of Neural Science,* ed 3, E R Kandel, J H Schwartz, T M Jessell, editors, p 33. Elsevier, New York, 1991. Used with permission.)

the *ependymins*. Although the function of the ependymins is still an area of active research, data suggest that the molecules are involved in the establishment of long-term memory, perhaps by facilitating or regulating synaptogenesis.

## Blood-Brain Barrier

The blood-brain barrier is a semipermeable barrier between the blood vessels and the brain. The blood-brain barrier is so constructed that many polar molecules are unable to pass from the blood to the brain. The following areas of the brain, however, do not have a blood-brain barrier: the pituitary gland, the median eminence, the area postrema, the preoptic recess, the paraphysis, the pineal gland, and the endothelium of the choroid plexuses.

The endothelial cells, the basement membrane, and the glia constitute the main components of the blood-brain barrier. The ability of a molecule to pass from the blood into the brain is based on its concentration gradient between brain and blood, its permeability, and the presence of an active transport mechanism for the molecule. Its permeability is a function of its molecular size, electrical charge, and lipid solubility. Active transport systems of relevance to psychiatry include active transports for glucose (of relevance to position emission tomography [PET] scanning techniques) and monocarboxylic acids (of relevance to the lactate infusion test for panic disorder). Another mechanism that affects blood-brain permeability is the activation or the antagonism of the neurotransmitter receptors found on the brain microvessels. They include α-adrenergic, β-adrenergic, dopamine, histamine, and various peptide receptors.

## CENTRAL, PERIPHERAL, AND AUTONOMIC NERVOUS SYSTEMS

The *central nervous system* (CNS) consists of the brain and the spinal cord. The *peripheral nervous system* consists of the cranial nerves, the spinal nerves, and the peripheral ganglia. The peripheral nervous system conveys sensory information to the CNS and conducts motor commands from the CNS. The *autonomic nervous system* innervates the internal organs. Sensory receptors in the peripheral organs also relay sensory information back to the CNS. The autonomic nervous system is divided into its sympathetic and parasympathetic components, which are generally set up as having antagonistic or balancing effects on organ systems.

### CNS Development

A brief overview of the development of the mature CNS provides a degree of insight into the functional systems that appear later in development. In development the neural tube constitutes the embryonic nervous system. The neural tube contains three primary divisions: the prosencephalon, the mesencephalon, and the rhombencephalon (Figure 3.1–3). The prosencephalon eventually develops into the cerebral cortex, the striatum, the amygdala, the hippocampus, the thalamus, the hypothalamus, and the epithalamus. In the adult, complex brain functions (for example, emotions and sensory perceptions) involve multiple areas of the brain that were, in fact, a single region early in development.

**Neuronal migration.** In contrast to what one may intuitively think, all cortical neurons begin their life cycle near the cerebral ventricles during gestation and then migrate to their final locations. For the cerebral cortex, the first step in development is the formation of radial glial cells projecting up through what will later become the cerebral cortex. Developing cortical neurons then migrate along those radial glial guides and, for poorly understood reasons, stop at specific spots along the radial glia and complete their development into mature neurons, sending out both dendritic trees and axons. Neuroscientists interested in psychiatric disorders are giving an increasing amount of attention to that level of CNS development. Data suggest that the movement of neurons along the radial glial cells is tightly programmed. Throughout development, the regulation of gene expression, including both turning on and turning off specific developmental genes, is carefully orchestrated. Interference with any of those stages in development, either because of genetic mutations or be-

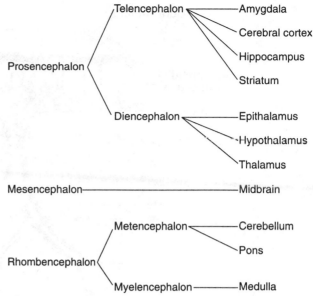

**Figure 3.1–3.** Development from the neural tube to mature brain structures.

cause of environmental events, may lead to subtle differences in brain development and potent effects on mature brain functioning.

Another aspect of neuronal development involves the establishment of synaptic contacts between neurons. As neurons migrate, develop, and extend axons and dendrites, they also form synaptic contacts with other neurons. Several types of data support the hypothesis that the establishment of those synaptic contacts follows a specific plan. However, at subsequent times in development, a process known as *synaptic pruning* or *synaptic elimination* occurs. Some investigators hypothesize that a possible pathophysiological mechanism for schizophrenia is the failure of a sufficient degree of synaptic pruning to occur, thus leaving the person with an overly connected and perhaps inefficient or incoherent set of neurons.

## OVERALL BRAIN STRUCTURE

In the CNS, gray matter contains the neuronal cell bodies, whereas white matter consists mainly of myelinated neuronal axons. The three areas of gray matter are the cerebral cortex, the cerebellar cortex, and the subcortical cerebral and cerebellar nuclei. The right and left cerebral hemispheres are connected by the corpus callosum and other small commissural tracts. The cerebral cortex itself is heavily folded with gyri (convolutions) and fissures (sulci or grooves). The brainstem comprises the medulla oblongata, the pons, and the mesencephalon.

### Meninges

The *meninges* (Figure 3.1–4) cover the brain and the spinal cord. The outermost and strongest of the coverings is the *dura mater,* which is attached to the inside of the skull. Below the dura mater are the *arachnoid* and the *pia mater*; the pia mater is attached to the surface of the brain. The *subarachnoid space,* which is filled with CSF, lies between the arachnoid and the pia mater.

Three neurological conditions involving the meninges are

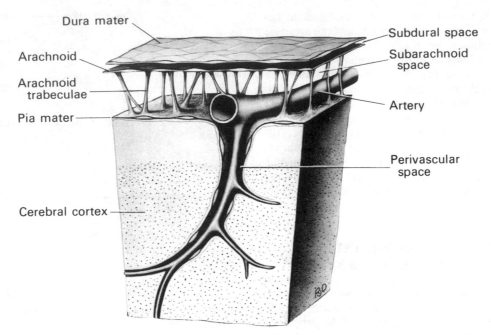

**Figure 3.1–4.** Diagram of the meninges, showing the relation of the membranes to the subarachnoid and perivascular spaces. (Figure from M B Carpenter, J Sutin: *Human Neuroanatomy*, p 16. Williams & Wilkins, Baltimore, 1983. Used with permission.)

important to consider in the differential diagnoses of patients presenting with psychiatric symptoms. The relatively gradual onset (weeks) of depression, personality changes, and cognitive decline can be symptoms of a *subdural hematoma*. A subdural hematoma usually results from trauma that tears a vein and causes a relatively slow accumulation of blood beneath the dura mater. In contrast, the much more rapid onset of classic neurological symptoms (for example, headache and loss of consciousness) can be caused by an *epidural hematoma,* which usually results from trauma that tears an artery. An epidural hematoma is a life-threatening and rapid accumulation of blood between the dura mater and the skull. *Meningitis* is an infection and inflammation of one or more of the meningeal layers.

## Ventricular System

Cerebrospinal fluid (CSF) is contained in the hollow cavities within each cerebral hemisphere. Those cavities constitute the ventricular system (Figure 3.1–5). A lateral ventricle in each hemisphere is divided into the anterior horn, the central part, the posterior horn, and the temporal horn. The two lateral ventricles join to a single third ventricle through the interventricular foramina of Monro. The third ventricle joins the fourth ventricle through the cerebral aqueduct.

Structural brain imaging techniques, such as computed tomography (CT) and magnetic resonance imaging (MRI), have been used to study the ventricular system in patients with psychiatric disorders. Particularly in studies of schizophrenic patients, there have been many reports of cerebral ventricular enlargement not caused by hydrocephalus. In those studies the enlargement of the cerebral ventricular space is thought to reflect the presence of less than usual brain tissue, although it is not known whether the decreased amount of brain tissue is due to the failure of the brain to develop normally or to an abnormal degeneration of neurons.

## Cerebrospinal Fluid

Normal adults have approximately 125 mL of CSF. Approximately 500 mL of CSF are produced daily; therefore, the total volume of CSF is replaced about four times daily. CSF is produced by the choroid plexuses in the lateral ventricles and within the brain parenchyma itself (Figure 3.1–5). *Hydrocephalus* results from a disorder of CSF drainage that causes CSF pressure to increase. Dilated ventricles on CT and MRI brain scans can indicate its presence.

**Normal pressure hydrocephalus.** Normal pressure hydrocephalus, first described in 1956, is caused by the blockage of CSF drainage over the convexities of the cerebral cortex. The clinical features are progressive dementia, a gait disturbance, and urinary incontinence. Normal pressure hydrocephalus is a treatable but relatively uncommon type of dementia. Additional psychiatric symptoms can be depression, apathy, and an akinetic mute state. The major abnormal objective findings are enlarged cerebral ventricles on a CT or MRI scan in the presence of normal CSF pressure. The MRI or CT scan of a patient with normal pressure hydrocephalus differs from the scan of an Alzheimer's disease patient by the presence of normal or compressed cerebral gyri, rather than the presence of atrophied gyri, which are seen in Alzheimer's disease. Patients with normal pressure hydrocephalus also have periventricular edema, resulting from the infusion of CSF into the surrounding tissues. The treatment of choice is to shunt the CSF from the ventricular space to either the cardiac atrium or the peritoneal space. Reversal of the dementia and the associated signs and symptoms is sometimes dramatic after treatment.

## CEREBRAL CORTEX

The primary input pathways of the cerebral cortex contain visual, auditory, and somatosensory information and

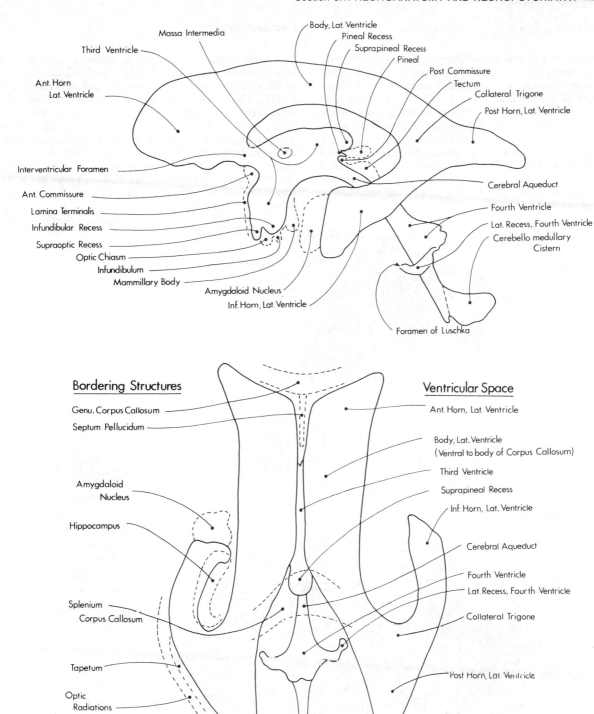

**Figure 3.1–5.** Lateral (above) and dorsal (below) views of the ventricles and the choroid plexus. The dashes show the approximate positions of some of the important structures that border on the ventricular space. (Figure from D E Haines: *Neuroanatomy: An Atlas of Structures, Sections, and Systems,* ed 2, p 42. Urban & Schwarzenberg, Baltimore, 1987. Used with permission.)

project primarily to the occipital, temporal, and parietal cortices, respectively. The primary, observable output functions derive from the primary motor area, the premotor area, and Broca's area and result in the movement of specific muscles, coordinated muscle movement, and speech, respectively.

The cerebral cortex, containing about 70 percent of the neurons in the CNS, is a thin layer of gray matter that covers the surfaces of the cerebral hemispheres. The cerebral cortex contains both projection neurons, which have long axons that project to distant sites, and interneurons, which have relatively short axons that project to local neurons.

## Anatomy

The four lobes of the cerebral cortex are the frontal, temporal, parietal, and occipital lobes (Figures 3.1–6 to 3.1–10). Some neuroanatomists conceptualize the limbic system as a fifth lobe of the cerebral cortex. The right and left cerebral hemispheres are separated by the longitudinal cerebral fissure at the midline. The frontal lobe is separated from the parietal lobe by the central sulcus (fissure of Rolando). The temporal lobes are demarcated from the frontal lobes by the lateral cerebral sulcus (fissure of Sylvius). The occipital lobe, located at the posterior end of the brain, is separated from the parietal lobe by an imaginary line running down from the parieto-occipital sulcus.

## Cytoarchitecture

The differential arrangement of neuron layers within the cortex is referred to as the cortical cytoarchitecture. There are six classically recognized layers in the cerebral cortex (Figure 3.1–11). The neurons and their processes can be displayed in brain tissue by using a variety of histological staining procedures. In silver staining procedures (for example, Golgi's stain) the myelin that surrounds selective cell bodies, axons, and some of the largest dendrites are stained. Aniline dyes (for example, Nissl's stains) stain the ribonucleotides (Nissl substance) and reveal only the cell bodies of neurons. In contrast to the selective staining of Golgi's stain, Weigert's stain for myelin reveals all myelin.

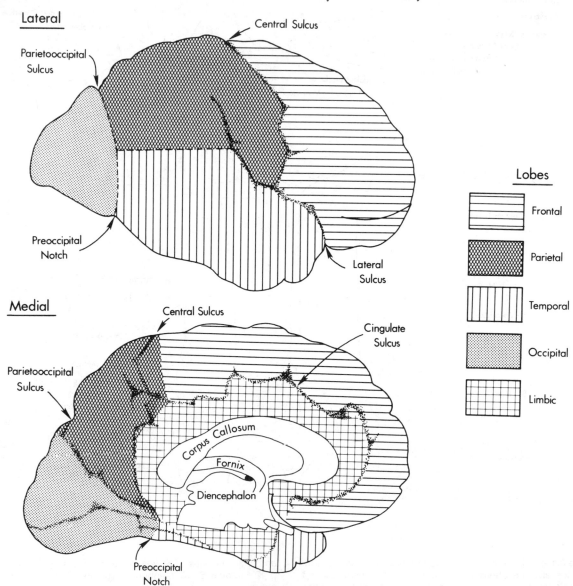

**Figure 3.1–6.** Lateral (upper) and medial (lower) views of the cerebral hemisphere, showing the landmarks used to divide the cortex into its main lobes. On the lateral aspect the central sulcus (of Rolando) separates the frontal and parietal lobes. The lateral sulcus (of Sylvius) forms the border between the frontal lobes and the temporal lobe. The occipital lobe is located caudal to an arbitrary line drawn between the terminus of the parieto-occipital sulcus and the preoccipital notch. A horizontal line drawn from the upper two thirds of the lateral fissure to the rostral edge of the occipital lobe represents the border between the parietal and temporal lobes. On the medial aspect the cingulate sulcus separates the medial portions of the frontal and parietal lobes from the limbic lobe. An imaginary continuation of the central sulcus intersects with the cingulate sulcus and forms the border between the frontal and parietal lobes. The parieto-occipital sulcus and an arbitrary continuation of that line to the preoccipital notch separates the parietal, limbic, and temporal lobes from the occipital lobe. (Figure from D E Haines: *Neuroanatomy: An Atlas of Structures, Sections, and Systems,* ed 2, p 13. Urban & Schwarzenberg, Baltimore, 1987. Used with permission.)

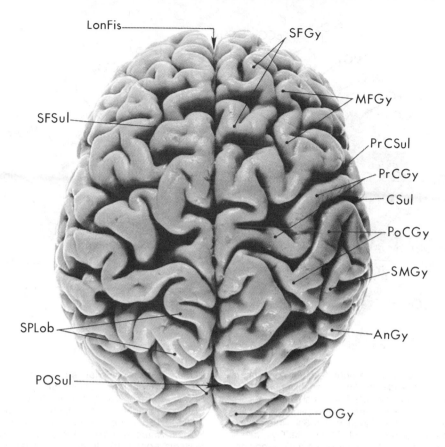

**Figure 3.1–7.** Dorsal view of the cerebral hemispheres, showing the principal gyri and sulci. **AnGy**—angular gyrus, **CSul**—central sulcus (of Rolando), **LonFis**—longitudinal fissure, **MFGy**—middle frontal gyrus, **OGy**—occipital gyri, **PoCGy**—postcentral gyrus, **POSul**—parieto-occipital sulcus, **PrCGy**—precentral gyrus, **PrCSul**—precentral sulcus, **SFGy**—superior frontal gyrus, **SFSul**—superior frontal sulcus, **SMGy**—supramarginal gyrus, **SPLob**—superior parietal lobule. (Figure from D E Haines: *Neuroanatomy: An Atlas of Structures, Sections, and Systems,* ed 2, p 14. Urban & Schwarzenberg, Baltimore, 1987. Used with permission.)

Many neuroanatomists have developed classification systems for specific cortical areas based on differential arrangements of the cortical areas. The neuroanatomists include Iain Campbell, who described 20 cortical areas; Korbinian Brodmann, 47 areas; Constantin von Economo, 109 areas; and Cecile Vogt and Oskar Vogt, more than 200 areas. Of those systems, the cortical mapping system devised by Brodmann in 1909 is the one most commonly used (Figure 3.1–12). Whereas Brodmann's system was based on differences among the cortical regions, another system of classifying gray matter areas is based on similarities among gray matter regions (Table 3.1–2).

## Modality

The four major categories of cortex divided by modality are the primary motor, the primary sensory, the motor association, and the sensory association (Table 3.1–3). There are both unimodal and heteromodal association areas. *Unimodal motor association* areas are involved in the planning of motor activity and project to the primary motor cortex; *unimodal sensory association* areas are involved in the interpretation of primary sensory input and receive afferent pathways from a single primary sensory cortical area. *Heteromodal as-*

**Table 3.1–2**
**Classification of Gray Matter Areas**

| Gray Matter Areas | Anatomical Areas | Functions |
|---|---|---|
| Corticoid | Hypothalamus ⎫ | Regulation of person's internal state, e.g., memory, learning, modulation of drives, affective coloring of experience, hormonal regulation, autonomic functioning |
| Allocortical | Hypothalamus ⎭ | |
| Paralimbic | Limbic areas | Functional bridge between less complex and more complex cortical areas |
| Homotypic association cortex | Association cortices | Interpreting external environment |
| Idiotypic | Primary motor and sensory cortices | Receiving primary sensory information |

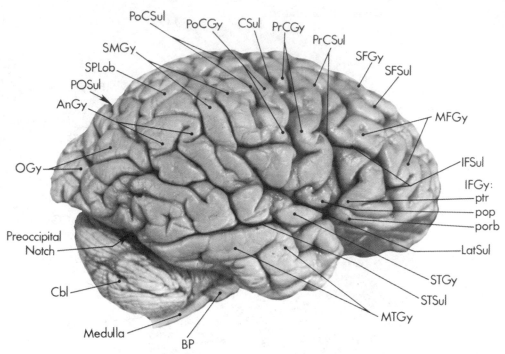

**Figure 3.1–8.** Lateral view of the right cerebral hemisphere, showing the principal gyri and sulci. **AnGy**—angular gyrus, **BP**—basilar pons, **Cbl**—cerebellum, **CSul**—central sulcus (of Rolando), **IFGy**—inferior frontal gyrus (**pop**—pars opercularis, **porb**—pars orbitalis, **ptr**—pars triangularis), **IFSul**—inferior frontal sulcus, **LatSul**—lateral sulcus (of Sylvius), **MFGy**—middle frontal gyrus, **MTGy**—middle temporal gyrus, **OGy**—occipital gyri, **PoCGy**—postcentral gyrus, **PoCSul**—postcentral sulcus, **POSul**—parieto-occipital sulcus, **PrCGy**—precentral gyrus, **PrCSul**—precentral sulcus, **SFGy**—superior frontal gyrus, **SFSul**—superior frontal sulcus, **SMGy**—supramarginal gyrus, **SPLob**—superior parietal lobule, **STGy**—superior temporal gyrus, **STSul**—superior temporal sulcus. (Figure from D E Haines: *Neuroanatomy: An Atlas of Structures, Sections, and Systems*, ed 2, p 16. Urban & Schwarzenberg, Baltimore, 1987. Used with permission.)

**Table 3.1–3**
**Classification of Cerebral Cortex by Modality**

| Cortical Functions | Brodmann's Areas | Location |
|---|---|---|
| Primary motor | 4 | Anterior to the central sulcus in the precentral gyrus |
| Primary sensory: | | |
|   Visual | 17 | Occipital poles and along the calcarine fissure in the occipital lobes |
|   Auditory | 41, 42 | Heschl's gyrus in the temporal lobes |
|   Somatosensory | 1, 2, 3 | Postcentral gyrus of the parietal lobes |
| Unimodal association: | | |
|   Motor association | 6 | Anterior to primary motor cortex |
|   Visual association | 18–21, 37 | Occipital and temporal lobes |
|   Auditory association | 22 | Wernicke's area |
|   Somatosensory association | 5 | Parietal cortex |
| Heteromodal association (probable functions): | | |
|   Sensory evaluation, language | Many | Parietal, temporal, and occipital lobes |
|   Cognitive planning and motor activity | Many | Prefrontal cortex |
|   Memory and emotions | Many | Limbic areas |

*sociation* areas receive afferent inputs from unimodal association areas and are involved in organizing the totality of the sensory and motor information that the brain receives.

## Interhemispheric Connectivity and Laterality

The two cerebral hemispheres are connected by the myelinated axons that run through the corpus callosum, which is the major commissural tract, and through the anterior commissure, the hippocampal commissure, the posterior commissure, and the habenular commissure. In most humans, one of the two hemispheres is definable as the dominant hemisphere and is characterized as the hemisphere organized to express language. The left hemisphere is dominant in 97 percent of the population, including 99 percent of right-handed persons and 60 to 70 percent of

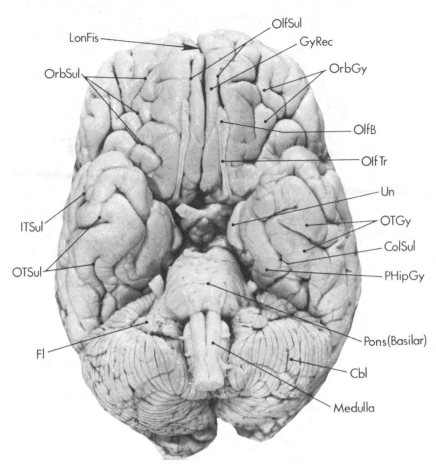

**Figure 3.1–9.** Ventral view of the cerebral hemispheres, the diencephalon, the brainstem, and the cerebellum. **Cbl**—cerebellum, **ColSul**—collateral sulcus, **Fl**—flocculus, **GyRec**—gyrus rectus (straight gyrus), **ITSul**—inferior temporal sulcus, **LonFis**—longitudinal fissure, **OlfB**—olfactory bulb, **OlfSul**—olfactory sulcus, **OlfTr**—olfactory tract, **OrbGy**—orbital gyri, **OrbSul**—orbital sulcus, **OTGy**—occipitotemporal gyri, **OTSul**—occipitotemporal sulcus, **PHipGy**—parahippocampal gyrus, **Un**—uncus. (Figure from D E Haines: *Neuroanatomy: An Atlas of Structures, Sections, and Systems,* ed 2, p 20. Urban & Schwarzenberg, Baltimore, 1987. Used with permission.)

left-handed persons. Language dominance is not completely synonymous with hand dominance, and a few persons have mixed dominance for language. With patients, typical questions to define handedness are the following: "With which hand do you write? With which hand do you throw a ball?" A comprehensive determination of handedness may involve a dozen questions or tasks and results in a numerical scale of handedness ranging from fully right-handed to fully left-handed.

Two commonly used tests for perceptual laterality are the dichotic listening test and the tachistoscopic viewing test. Those tests have also been used to study sensory laterality in psychiatric patients. In the dichotic listening test the two ears are presented with similar but different stimuli. One example of such a test is the simultaneous input of two different numbers to the different ears, so that the left ear may hear "1" and the right ear may hear "7." The person is then asked what number was heard. Persons who have a dominant left hemisphere have a right ear advantage; the number presented to the right ear is identified more often than is the number presented to the left ear. That is the expected result, since about 65 percent of the pathways from each ear go to the contralateral hemisphere; the majority of the information from the left ear goes first to the right hemisphere and then to the left

hemisphere through the corpus callosum. The extra distance the information must traverse before getting to the left-sided language centers is why the information is heard less often than is information presented to the right ear. The converse ear advantage is present for nonverbal material; musical sounds presented to the left ear of right-handed persons have an advantage over musical sounds presented to the right ear. The second common sensory laterality test is tachistoscopic viewing, in which different visual information is presented to the left and right visual fields. For left hemisphere-dominant persons the right visual field has an advantage for verbal input, and the left visual field has an advantage for spatial input.

Psychological studies of persons with unilateral brain trauma or epileptic lesions have led to many theories about hemispheric function. In addition to regulating language ability, the left hemisphere has been described as being the rational half of the brain, the one concerned with analytical, sequencing, abstracting, and logistical abilities. The right hemisphere is more involved with perceptual, visual-spatial, artistic, musical, and synthetic cortical activity; it is also involved with both the perception and the expression of affective content, including the perception of social cues. Although those differentiations of right-hemispheric and left-hemispheric functions are generally

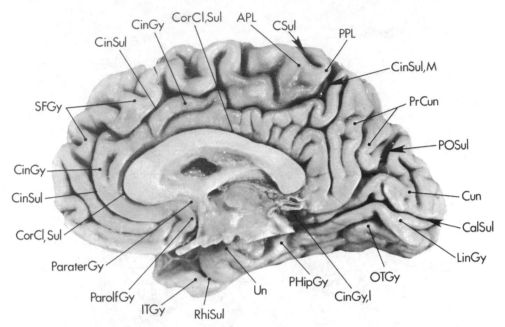

**Figure 3.1–10.** Midsagittal view of the right cerebral hemisphere and the diencephalon, with the brainstem removed, showing the principal gyri and sulci. **APL**—anterior paracentral lobule, **CalSul**—calcarine sulcus, **CinGy**—cingulate gyrus, **CinGy, I**—cingulate gyrus, isthmus, **CinSul**—cingulate sulcus, **CinSul, M**—cingulate sulcus, marginal branch, **CorCl, Sul**—corpus callosum, sulcus, **CSul**—central sulcus (of Rolando), **Cun**—cuneus, **ITGy**—inferior temporal gyrus, **LinGy**—lingual gyrus, **OTGy**—occipitotemporal gyri, **ParaterGy**—paraterminal gyri, **ParolfGy**—parolfactory gyri, **PHipGy**—parahippocampal gyrus, **POSul**—parieto-occipital sulcus, **PPL**—posterior paracentral lobule, **PrCun**—precuneus, **RhiSul**—rhinal sulcus, **SFGy**—superior frontal gyrus, **Un**—uncus. (Figure from D E Haines: *Neuroanatomy: An Atlas of Structures, Sections, and Systems,* ed 2, p 24. Urban & Schwarzenberg, Baltimore, 1987. Used with permission.)

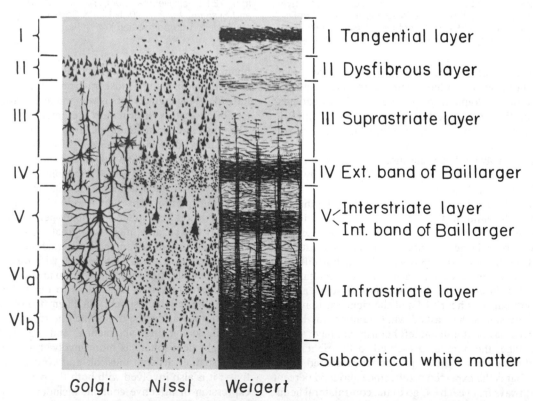

**Figure 3.1–11.** The cell layers and fiber arrangement of the human cerebral cortex (semischematic) (after Brodmann). (Figure from M B Carpenter, J Sutin: *Human Neuroanatomy,* p 644. Williams & Wilkins, Baltimore, 1983. Used with permission.)

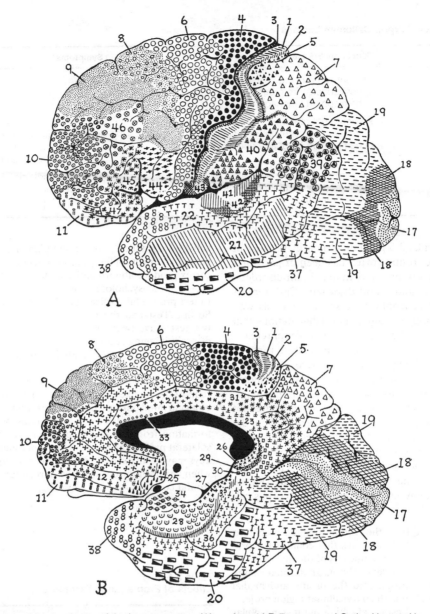

**Figure 3.1–12.** Cytoarchitectural map of the human cortex. (A) Convex surface; (B) medial surface (after Brodmann). (Figure from M B Carpenter, J Sutin: *Human Neuroanatomy*, p 652. Williams & Wilkins, Baltimore, 1983. Used with permission.)

true, an increasing number of studies report many exceptions to those generalizations. For example, although verbal ability is thought to be firmly localized to the dominant hemisphere, some case reports indicate that the ability to create and understand metaphors, humor, and proverbs may be located in the nondominant hemisphere.

The psychiatric disorder in which laterality has been the major subject of research is schizophrenia. Unfortunately for the student of psychiatry, psychiatric researchers and theorists have postulated ideas and presented data consistent with lesions in both hemispheres in schizophrenic patients. The original theory postulated that left-hemisphere dysfunction is more common in schizophrenia than is right-hemisphere dysfunction, although recent theories have postulated right-hemisphere dysfunction. The apathy and indifference seen in patients with right-sided lesions is suggestive of the negative symptoms seen in many schizophrenic patients. Studies of affective symptoms in patients

with cerebrovascular diseases have indicated that left-sided lesions more often cause depression than do right-sided lesions. In addition to lesions of the cerebral hemispheres themselves, a variety of syndromes are seen with lesions of their major commissural tract, the corpus callosum (Table 3.1–4). Recent brain imaging studies have shown that the size of the corpus callosum decreases with age, and MRI studies indicate that the quality of the tissue itself (perhaps of the myelin) may also change with age. Such changes could hypothetically be linked to the appearance of certain geriatric psychiatric symptoms.

### Frontal Cortex

The frontal cortex, particularly the prefrontal area, is uniquely enlarged in humans, compared with other species. The prefrontal cortex in humans constitutes 29 percent of the cortical area; in chimpanzees, 17 percent; in

**Table 3.1–4**
**Symptoms of Selected Corpus Callosum Lesions**

| Site of Lesion | Functional Effects | Symptoms |
| --- | --- | --- |
| Posterior | Prevent written language (seen by right hemisphere) from getting to the left hemisphere language center | Alexia |
| Anterior | Prevent right motor and sensory cortices from communicating with the left hemisphere language and praxis center | Agraphia with left hand<br>Inability to name unseen objects placed in left hand<br>Generalized apraxia of left hand |
| Complete transection | Two independent hemispheres, with retained sense of themselves as belonging to a unitary being | Multiple symptoms of two independent hemispheres |

dogs, 7 percent; in cats, 3.5 percent. Primarily because of that observation, the frontal cortex has been of particular interest to researchers of uniquely human brain disorders, such as schizophrenia and mood disorders. Case reports in the literature tell of frontal lobe seizure patients who describe intrusive thoughts and visual hallucinations that are strikingly similar to the symptoms of schizophrenia.

Anatomically, the superior, middle, and inferior frontal gyri (Figure 3.1–8) make up the lateral aspects of the frontal lobes. Functionally, the motor cortex, the premotor cortex, and the prefrontal association cortex are the major division. The *motor cortex* is involved in the movement of specific muscles; the *premotor cortex* is involved in the coordinated movement of multiple muscles; and the *association cortex* is involved in the integration of sensory information that is processed by the primary sensory cortices. On the medial aspect of the frontal cortex (Figure 3.1–10), the cingulate gyrus wraps around the corpus callosum.

The pathways to and from the frontal lobe are numerous and complex, but one set of pathways that connect the prefrontal area with the mediodorsal nucleus of the thalamus has relevance to psychiatric disorders. The magnocellular region of the thalamic nucleus projects to the orbital and medial aspects of the prefrontal area; the parvicellular region projects to the dorsolateral area. Lesions affecting the magnocellular pathway lead to hyperkinesis, euphoria, and inappropriate behavior, sometimes referred to as a pseudopsychopathic syndrome. Lesions affecting the parvicellular pathway lead to hypokinesis, apathy, and impaired cognition, sometimes referred to as a pseudodepression syndrome. Additional symptoms can include poor grooming, psychomotor retardation, decreased attention, motor perseveration, difficulty in changing mental sets, and poor ability to abstract. Many of those symptoms are similar to those seen in negative-symptom schizophrenia. Frontal lobe dysfunction often produces *witzelsucht*, which is the tendency to make puns and jokes and then to laugh aloud at them.

The most common neurological disorders involving the frontal lobes are tumors, trauma, cerebrovascular diseases, and multiple sclerosis. About 90 percent of brain tumor patients who present initially with psychiatric symptoms have frontal lobe tumors. Those patients can easily be misclassified as having a psychiatric disorder because of the absence of most classic neurological signs, although a careful neurological examination may reveal abnormal frontal lobe reflexes (for example, snout reflex).

The major functions of the frontal cortex involve motor

activation, intellect, conceptual planning, aspects of personality, and aspects of language production; lesions of the frontal cortex produce abnormalities in those functional areas (Table 3.1–5). Two psychological procedures that are commonly used to test prefrontal cortical functioning are the Wisconsin Card Sorting Test and the Continuous Performance Test. Those two tests have been used as challenge tests in various types of brain imaging studies.

One series of experiments in monkeys involved lesioning the dorsal lateral prefrontal cortex. The lesions consistently impaired the ability of the monkeys to perform tasks that require the monkey to maintain a spatial representation of an object in mind during a delayed performance task. It is thought that the lesion interferes with the relay of somatosensory information from parietal lobe association regions to the dorsolateral prefrontal cortex. That experimental model in monkeys may be an example of the type of dysfunction that occurs when lesions interfere with the normal functioning of the prefrontal cortex.

**Table 3.1–5**
**Effects of Frontal Lobe Disorders**

Alterations of motor activities
  Lack of spontaneity
  Reduced rate and amount of mental and physical activity
  Akinetic mutism
Intellectual impairments
  Poor concentration
  Inability to carry out plans
  Attention deficit
  Trouble sequencing tasks
  Slowed mental processing
Personality changes
  Placidity
  Lack of concern over consequences of action
  Social indifference, especially with bathing, dressing, bowel and bladder control
  Childish excitement (moria)
  Inappropriate joking, punning (*witzelsucht*)
  Instability and superficiality of emotions
Language dysfunctions
  Broca's aphasia
  Mutism

Table from D Z Skuster, K B Digre, J J Corbett: Neurologic conditions presenting as psychiatric disorders. Psychiatr Clin North Am *15*: 311, 1992. Used with permission.

## Temporal Cortex

The superior, middle, and inferior gyri form the lateral aspect of the temporal lobe (Figure 3.1–8). Language, memory, and emotion are the primary functions of the temporal cortex. Lesions of the temporal cortex result in related symptoms (Table 3.1–6). Because lesions of the temporal cortex and related limbic nuclei located within the temporal lobe can lead to symptoms resembling those of psychiatric conditions (for example, hallucinations), the area has received particular attention in psychiatric research.

Patients who have seizure foci in their temporal lobes can be misclassified as having psychiatric disorders. According to one hypothesis, some patients with psychiatric disorders actually have a *forme fruste* of temporal lobe epilepsy. Common symptoms of temporal lobe epilepsy include olfactory and gustatory hallucinations, *déjà vu*, derealization, depersonalization, and repetitive motor acts. With time, the patients can have depressive and schizophrenialike symptoms and changes in their personalities.

## Parietal Cortex

The superior parietal lobule and the inferior parietal lobule form the parietal lobe (Figure 3.1–8). The inferior parietal lobule includes the supramarginal gyrus and the angular gyrus. The association cortices for visual, tactile, and auditory input are contained within the parietal lobes. The left parietal lobe has a preferential role in verbal processing; the right parietal lobe has a greater role in visual-spatial processing.

Symptoms of dominant and nondominant parietal lobe lesions are listed in Table 3.1–7. One symptom involving parietal lobe lesions is denial or neglect; patients deny or neglect aspects of their own bodies or personal space. For example, a

**Table 3.1–6**
**Psychiatric Manifestations of Temporal Lobe Disease**

Unilateral temporal lobe lesions—dominant temporal lobe
  Wernicke's aphasia: frequently mistaken for a psychotic break
    with neologisms
  Dysfunctions in memory
  Amusia: defect in ability to appreciate music
Nondominant temporal lobe
  Agnosia for sounds
  Dysprosody: disturbed tonal lilt to spoken speech
Bilateral temporal lobe lesion
  Korsakoff's amnesia
  Klüver-Bucy syndrome with
    visual agnosia
    apathy and placidity
    disturbed sexual function
    dementia, aphasia, amnesia
Ictal phenomenon
  Psychosensory
    hallucinations (visual, auditory, olfactory)
    illusions (visual, auditory)
  Affective symptoms
  Cognitive symptoms (*déjà vu, jamais vu*, forced thinking)
  Impaired consciousness
  Automatism

**Table 3.1–7**
**Effects of Parietal Lobe Diseases**

Dominant (usually left) parietal lobe disease
  Alexia with agraphia, with or without anomia
  Constructional difficulty
  Gerstmann syndrome (right-left disorientations, inability to
    localize fingers, agraphia, acalculia)
  Astereognosis (inability to recognize objects in the hand)
  Pain asymbolia
  Ideomotor apraxia
  Fluent aphasias
Nondominant (usually right) parietal lobe disease
  Constructional apraxia
  Dressing apraxia
  Geographic disorientation
  Astereognosis of the left side
  Calculation or writing difficulties
  Denial or neglect of contralateral space (anosognosia)

patient with a right-sided lesion may deny that the left arm exists and may even fail to put clothes on the left side of the body. Denial and neglect can result from lesions of either hemisphere, but they are seen with right-side lesions about seven times more often than with left-side lesions. Denial and neglect can also be caused, though much less often, by lesions in the frontal lobes, the thalamus, the cingulate, and the basal ganglia. *Gerstmann syndrome* has been attributed to lesions of the dominant parietal lobe; the syndrome includes agraphia, calculation difficulties (acalculia), right-left disorientation, and finger agnosia.

## Occipital Cortex

The occipital lobe includes the superior and inferior occipital gyri and the cuneus and lingual gyri (Figures 3.1–7 and 3.1–8). The occipital lobe is the primary sensory cortex for visual input, and lesions of the lobe result in various visual symptoms (Table 3.1–8). *Anton's syndrome* is associated with bilateral occlusion of the posterior cerebral arteries, resulting in cortical blindness and the denial of blindness. The most common causes are hypoxic injury, encephalitis, leukodystrophy, and trauma. *Balint's syndrome* is caused by bilateral occipital lesions and is characterized by optic ataxia (abnormal visual guidance of limb movements), loss of panoramic vision, and supranuclear gaze paralysis. Those unusual visual complaints in the absence of other neurological symptoms may lead a clinician to an inaccurate diagnosis of a psychotic disorder. The

**Table 3.1–8**
**Effects of Occipital Lobe Disorder**

Anton's syndrome: denial of blindness
Balint's syndrome
Visual agnosias: a normal percept stripped of meaning
Prosopagnosia: inability to recognize faces
Color agnosia: inability to distinguish color
Alexia: inability to read
Hallucinations

hallucinations that are caused by lesions of the occipital lobe are often geometric, colored, and nonformed, which may help a clinician differentiate those hallucinations from the more fully formed hallucinations of psychotic patients. Another related symptom of occipital lobe lesions is *palinopsia*, which is the persistence of a visual image after the object is gone.

## Aphasias

*Aphasia* is an acquired disorder of language (comprehension, word choice, expression, syntax) that is not due to dysarthria—that is, a dysfunction of the muscles necessary for speech production (Table 3.1–9). Aphasias are of interest for classic neurological reasons vis-à-vis the localization of cortical functioning. Aphasias are also of interest to the field of psychiatry because many patients have symptoms that affect their language—for example, the disordered speech of a schizophrenic patient. Although the dominant (usually left) hemisphere is the focus of most language capabilities, the nondominant hemisphere is also involved in some aspects of language.

Positron emission tomographic (PET) studies of aphasic patients have shown decreased metabolism in the left angular gyrus (97 percent of patients), supramarginal gyrus (89 percent), and the lateral and transverse superior temporal gyri (87 percent). Those findings were not completely dependent on the location of the structural lesion as determined by computed tomography (CT) and magnetic resonance imaging (MRI). That dissociation implies that structural lesions in various specific regions of the language areas can result in distant functional deficiencies. That observation should suggest to psychiatric researchers that a functional abnormality in a particular brain region may result from a lesion in a different neuroanatomical area.

When assessing a patient's speech, the clinician must study the fluency of speech production (including grammar and syntax), the presence of paraphasias, auditory comprehension, the ability or lack of ability (anomia) to name things, and the ability to repeat phrases. A patient's ability to read, comprehend, and write should also be tested. When testing the patient's ability to name things, the examiner can ask the patient to name colors, people, body parts, and parts of objects (for example, the teeth of a comb). A patient may not be able to find nature-related words (for example, horse) but can find manufacture-related words (for example, car). Another example of dis-

sociation is the inability to find nouns but the retained ability to find verbs. In addition, cuing an anomic patient with the first sound of the word can often help the patient find the word. That finding suggests that the lesion is not in word finding but in word completion. *Paraphasia* is the unintentional inclusion of a syllable, a phrase, or a word. *Phonemic paraphasia* is an error in the order of syllables, the addition of a syllable, or a distortion of the sound of a word. An example is "pucomtertat" for "computer." Semantic paraphasia is a substitution of related words— for example, "head" for "hat."

**Broca's aphasia.** Broca's area (Brodmann's area 44 in the frontal lobe) is involved in the motor production of speech. Broca's aphasia is also called anterior aphasia, motor aphasia, and expressive aphasia. Comprehension is unimpaired, but the patient's speech is telegraphic and agrammatical. Depressive symptoms are common in patients with Broca's aphasia; however, some patients experience inappropriate elation and irritability. Some severely depressed patients and schizophrenic patients may evidence a paucity of speech that is reminiscent of Broca's aphasia, but the speech of such patients usually remains grammatically correct, in contrast to the ungrammatical speech of patients with Broca's aphasia.

**Wernicke's aphasia.** Wernicke's area (Brodmann's area 22 in the superior temporal gyrus) is involved in the comprehension of speech. Wernicke's aphasia is also called posterior aphasia, fluent aphasia, and receptive aphasia. The speech of patients with Wernicke's aphasia is characterized by a fluent but incoherent speech because the patients are unable to comprehend their own language or that of others. Because Wernicke's aphasia can present without other major neurological symptoms, a clinician may misclassify a patient with Wernicke's aphasia as having a thought disorder associated with a psychotic disorder. Although the examination may not always reveal it, a psychotic patient almost always retains normal comprehension of spoken and written language and the ability to repeat phrases. Those abilities are lost in a patient with Wernicke's aphasia, who may use neologisms frequently in a random, changeable manner. In contrast, a schizophrenic patient tends to use neologisms infrequently but consistently, because the neologisms have a systemized and delusional significance. Psychiatric symptoms that can be seen in patients with Wernicke's aphasia include delusions, paranoia, agitation, and occasional euphoria and indifference.

**Table 3.1–9**
**Aphasias and Their Impairments**

| Type | Fluency | Comprehension | Repetition | Naming |
|---|---|---|---|---|
| Broca's | No* | Yes† | No | No |
| Wernicke's | Yes | No | No | No |
| Conduction | Yes | Yes | No | No |
| Motor transcortical | No | Yes | Yes | No |
| Sensory transcortical | Yes | No | Yes | No |
| Mixed transcortical | No | No | Yes | No |
| Global | No | No | No | No |
| Anomic | Yes | Yes | Yes | No |
| Thalamic | Yes | Variable | Yes | No |

˄ No = Impaired.
† Yes = Relatively spared.

**Other aphasias.** Broca's area and Wernicke's area are connected by the arcuate fasciculus; a lesion in the arcuate fasciculus leads to *conduction aphasia,* with symptoms resulting from the disconnection of the center of language production from the center of language comprehension. Comprehension and speech production are not severely impaired. An inability to repeat phrases is the most profound symptom of conduction aphasia. Broca's, Wernicke's, and conduction aphasias affect regions surrounding the fissure of Sylvius.

*Transcortical aphasias* can be caused by lesions in the medial aspect of the frontal lobe, the basal ganglia, or the pulvinar thalamus. Patients with transcortical aphasias are able to repeat phrases normally; in fact, echolalia can be seen in some patients with severe transcortical aphasias. Transcortical aphasias can result in impaired comprehension or impaired speech production or both.

*Global aphasia* usually results from an infarction of the entire region of the left hemisphere that receives its blood supply from the middle cerebral artery. Patients with global aphasia almost invariably have a right hemiparesis and hemisensory defect. All language functions are lost, although some patients still spontaneously say such overlearned words as "good-bye" and "no."

Although anomia is present in all aphasias, patients with *anomic aphasia* have an isolated defect in naming. Their speech is characterized by frequent pauses while the person searches for words and by the frequent use of such vague words as "it" and "thing." Anomic aphasia is caused by a lesion localized to the dominant angular gyrus.

The previously discussed aphasias all involve the cerebral cortex; however, a lesion of the dominant thalamus may produce *thalamic aphasia,* with symptoms similar to those of sensory transcortical aphasia. *Basal ganglia aphasias* are characterized by long word strings, dysarthria, and comprehension deficits in the presence of hemiparesis.

PROGRESSIVE APHASIA. A rare aphasia is progressive aphasia, which is characterized by the progressive deterioration of language abilities in the absence of other signs of cognitive decline. The major symptom of progressive aphasia is usually anomia, although phonemic paraphasias are also common. A general cognitive decline eventually appears in most patients. The most common underlying causes are Pick's disease and focal spongiform degeneration of the left perisylvian fissure.

**Aprosody.** Although most attention has been focused on the dominant hemisphere in speech production, regional cerebral blood flow studies have shown increased blood flow to the nondominant hemisphere during speech. The nondominant hemisphere has a parallel role in the *prosody* of language, the emotional inflections in speech as it is produced and received. Patients with frontal nondominant lesions are not able to inflect their speech with affect, and patients with posterior nondominant lesions are not able to comprehend the prosody of another person's speech.

### Apraxias

*Apraxia* is loss of the ability to carry out small tasks and specific movements in response to stimuli that usually elicit the tasks and movements. The loss of ability is not due to weakness, incoordination, loss of sensation, poor comprehension, or inattention.

*Ideomotor apraxia* is loss of the ability to perform a simple task (for example, hitting a nail with a hammer) on request by the examiner. The patient may, however, be able to perform the identical task within its usual context (for example, hanging a picture on a wall). Lesions are most often either in the dominant hemisphere or bilateral in the supramarginal gyrus or the motor association cortex or in the conduction fibers between those two areas. Essentially, the receptive language areas are disconnected from the motor execution areas.

Ideational apraxia is a more severe apraxia than ideomotor apraxia, and most patients with ideational apraxia also have ideomotor apraxia. *Ideational apraxia* is loss of the ability to perform a short sequence of movements. For example, afflicted patients are unable, on request, to fold a letter, insert it into an envelope, close the envelope, and put a stamp on the envelope. Such patients often have difficulty in folding the letter or putting it in the envelope in the correct position. Such patients may put the stamp on the letter, instead of on the envelope. Lesions are usually in the dominant parietal lobe or the corpus callosum. Ideation apraxias are commonly seen in combination with aphasia and dementia.

*Constructional apraxia* is loss of the ability to draw or copy a geometric design or to arrange toy building blocks in a particular way. Patients with constructional apraxia have impaired spatial recognition and tend to simplify, rotate, or overlap parts of the design. Lesions are most often in the posterior right hemisphere but can also appear in the left parietal lobe; in those cases the lesions are associated with aphasia and ideomotor and ideational apraxias.

*Dressing apraxia* is loss of the ability to dress correctly. Patients with dressing apraxia may attempt to put a shirt on as if it were a pair of pants, for example. The lesions are most often right-sided. Dressing apraxia is commonly associated with neglect when the lesion is unilateral and with constructional apraxia when the lesion is bilateral.

### Agnosias

The word "gnosis" means knowledge. In order to know something, a person has to compare present sensory information with past sensory information. The key symptom of agnosia is failure to recognize sensory stimuli in the absence of an intellectual or primary sensory mechanism impairment.

*Visual agnosia* is loss of the ability to identify a previously recognizable object by visual inspection alone. Patients with visual agnosia may, however, be able to identify the object when they handle it. Visual agnosia must be distinguished from anomia, the inability to name objects. A patient with anomia may not be able to name a comb but is able to describe its use. A patient with visual agnosia can neither name nor describe the use of such an object. Lesions, either unilateral or bilateral, affect the posterior portions of the hemispheres, classically Brodmann's areas 18 and 19. Left-sided lesions tend to result in agnosias for objects and colors; right-sided lesions tend to result in agnosias for spatial relations. Bilateral lesions can result in agnosia for faces, a condition known as *prosopagnosia*. Agnosia for colors is indicated by an inability to name colors or to select or match colors on command. Spatial agnosia is indicated by an inability to locate unmarked places on a map. Patients with spatial agnosia may also have trouble in orienting themselves within a space—for example, they do not know how to stand in front of a mirror. Visual agnosias are further classified as being either associative or apperceptive. A person with associative visual agnosia can describe the physical features of an object but cannot find the name for it. A person with apperceptive visual agnosia can neither describe nor name an object.

*Tactile agnosia* is inability to recognize objects that are touched, although a person with tactile agnosia may instantly recognize the object once it is seen. Lesions are most often contralateral to the affected hand and are located in Brodmann's areas 1, 2, 3, and 5 and in the supramarginal gyrus of the parietal lobe.

*Auditory agnosia* is inability to recognize nonverbal sounds (for example, paper rustling and car horns) and music (*amusia*). Auditory agnosia is commonly associated with word deafness, which is the inability to understand spoken words, although the ability to read, write, and speak is unimpaired. Word deafness usually involves a lesion of the left superior temporal gyrus. Amusia usually includes the inability to recognize tones, melodies, and rhythms. Lesions are usually located bilaterally in the superior temporal convolution (Brodmann's area 22).

## Alexia

*Alexia* is loss of the ability to read. Reading comprehension and reading out loud can be independently impaired. Alexia should be distinguished from dyslexia, which is a developmental problem in reading. Alexia is commonly seen in association with aphasia. Alexia is sometimes accompanied by agraphia (described below). The left occipital cortex and the posterior corpus callosum are the usual lesion sites for alexia without agraphia. Right homonymous hemianopsia (the inability to see the right visual field) also results from an occipital lesion. The inability to transfer the intact visual image from the left visual field (received by the right occipital cortex) to the left posterior hemisphere language-comprehension centers results from a corpus callosal lesion. As a result, the patient cannot see in one visual field and cannot decode the written information seen in the other visual field. Alexia with agraphia can be a symptom in patients with Gerstmann syndrome, Wernicke's aphasia, and Broca's aphasia.

## Agraphia

*Agraphia* is loss of the ability to write. Agraphia always accompanies aphasia. In Broca's aphasia, the patient's writing is sparse and agrammatical; in Wernicke's aphasia, the patient's writing appears to be grossly normal but contains nonsense words and neologisms. Agraphia should be distinguished from illiteracy, which is lack of knowledge and training about how to read and write.

## THALAMUS

The thalamus arises in tandem with the cortex and the limbic system. The thalamus itself is a complex anatomical area with many distinct parts. Moreover, the increasing appreciation of the interconnections between the thalamus and the cortical structures has caused many neuroanatomists interested in psychiatric disorders to consider the thalamus as a potential area for pathology in neuropsychiatric disorders.

### Anatomy

The thalamus is a deep brain structure located above the hypothalamus. The many nuclei of the thalamus (Figure 3.1–13) can be subdivided into six groups: anterior, medial, lateral, reticular, intralaminar, and midline nuclei. The large groups are separated by a Y-shaped group of myelinated fibers, the internal medullary lamina. A central feature of the thalamus is that most nuclei within it receive afferent projections from specific anatomical areas and, in turn, project reciprocal efferent processes. Moreover, the arrangement of neuronal fibers within each of the projection pathways remains relatively constant; fibers from one part of a distant neuroanatomical region project to a specific part of a particular thalamic nucleus.

In a general sense, the thalamic nuclei can be separated into specific relay nuclei, association relay nuclei, diffuse projection nuclei, and the reticular nucleus. *Specific relay nuclei* receive input and send output regarding a single incoming sensory input or outgoing motor output. *Association relay nuclei* receive input from multiple association areas, which have already processed the information, and then relay the input to a wide range of anatomical locations. *Diffuse projection nuclei* receive from and send to an even more diverse range of neuroanatomical areas. The *reticular nucleus* receives input from the axon collaterals of thalamic neurons and from the cortex; then it projects back to the specific thalamic nuclei.

**Pathways.** The three major pathways through the thalamus are the thalamocortical sensory, motor, and association systems. The *sensory pathways* receive input from the peripheral sensory systems; then they relay the information to the cortex. The *motor pathways* go in the opposite direction and relay cortical motor information to the brainstem and the spinal cord. The *association pathways* relay information both dorsally and ventrally and, thus, are involved in the processing of association information. The essential point is that information relay in the thalamus has the potential to be modulated by the thalamus itself and by input into the thalamus from the cortex.

## LIMBIC SYSTEM

The limbic system was originally proposed as an anatomical substrate for the emotions. Subsequently, it has become clear that memory is a major function of the limbic system. The limbic system includes a diverse group of deep brain structures (for example, the amygdala), selected areas of the cerebral cortex (for example, the cingulate), and segments of other structures (for example, specific nuclei within the hypothalamus). Although the limbic circuit was originally described in 1939 as a restricted group of structures, modern anatomical techniques and other

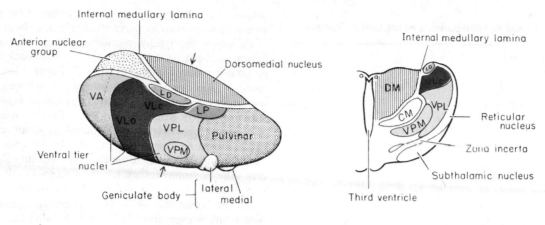

A.

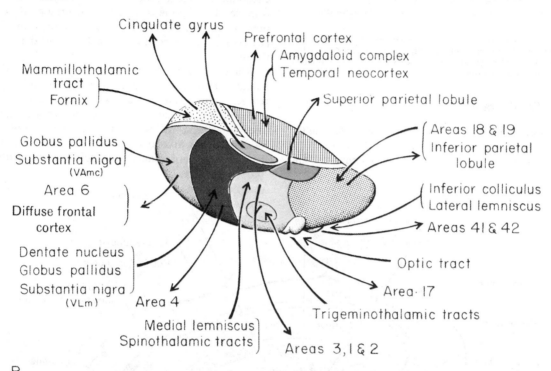

B.

**Figure 3.1–13.** Schematic diagrams of the major thalamic nuclei. An oblique dorsolateral view of the thalamus and its major subdivisions is shown in A. A transverse section of the thalamus at the level of the arrows, shown on the right in A, indicates (1) the relations between the ventral posterior medial (VPM) and the ventral posterior lateral (VPL) and (2) the location of the central medial (CM) with respect to the internal medullary lamina of the thalamus. In B, the principal afferent and efferent projections of particular thalamic subdivisions are indicated. Most cortical areas project fibers back to the thalamic nuclei from which fibers are received, but not all are shown. (Figure from M D Carpenter, J Sutin: *Human Neuroanatomy,* p 508. Williams & Wilkins, Baltimore, 1983. Used with permission.)

types of neuroscientific research have expanded the number of structures thought to be part of the limbic system (Table 3.1–10 and Figure 3.1–14).

## Anatomy

The reverberating limbic circuit proposed by James Papez originally included the hippocampus, which transmits information through the fornices to the mammillary bodies (of the hypothalamus), which, in turn, transmit information through the mammillothalamic tracts to the anterior nucleus of the thalamus. The anterior nucleus of the thalamus then transmits

information through the internal capsule back to the hippocampus.

Two neuroanatomists, Paul MacLean and Walle Nauta, have also theorized about the architecture of the limbic system. MacLean developed the concept of the triune brain, which includes a neomammalian brain (the neocortex), a paleomammalian brain (the limbic system), and a reptilian brain (the brainstem). MacLean coined the term "limbic system" to unite the original limbic circuit described by Papez with the basolateral limbic circuit, which includes the orbitofrontal cortex, the temporal pole, and the insula. The work of Walle Nauta helped expand the boundaries of the limbic system to include the hypothalamus.

**Table 3.1–10**
**Components and Subcomponents of the Limbic System**

Regions of the limbic cortex:
  Cingulate
  Parahippocampal gyrus
    Entorhinal cortex
Hippocampal formation
  Dentate gyrus
  Subicular complex (also part of the temporal cortex)
  Hippocampus
Amygdala
  Basolateral complex
  Centromedial complex
  "Extended amygdala" (bed nucleus of the stria terminalis
    and parts of the hypothalamus)
Nucleus accumbens
Hypothalamus (mammillary bodies)*
Thalamus (anterior nucleus, dorsomedial nucleus)*
Other cerebral cortical regions (orbitofrontal, temporal pole,
  insula)*

---

*Only selected nuclei and areas of those regions are currently thought to
be involved in the limbic system, but specifically which nuclei and areas
are involved remains controversial.

## Clinical Considerations

The most common neurological disorders affecting the
limbic system are tumors, cerebrovascular diseases,
trauma, multiple sclerosis, encephalitis, meningitis, and
amyotrophic lateral sclerosis (ALS). Some of the psychiatric symptoms seen in those conditions are disinhibition
of the emotions, apathy, placidity, changes in sexual behavior, and personality changes. The emotional disinhibition can result in unprovoked rage or aggression, spontaneous laughing or crying, and smiling or frowning for no
reason. A rare but important clinical diagnosis is *paraneoplastic limbic encephalitis*. The disorder is a remote effect
of a primary tumor, which is commonly small-cell lung
cancer or breast cancer but can also be associated with
stomach, uterine, renal, testicular, thyroid, and colon cancers. The pathophysiology for the encephalitis is poorly
understood. The symptoms include a change in mental
status, problems with memory, depression, anxiety, and
personality changes and can also include hallucinations and
catatonia. The incorrect diagnosis of a psychiatric disorder
is made likely by the fact that the neurological examination, a CT or MRI scan, and an electroencephalogram
(EEG) may all be read as normal early in the course of
the disorder.

**Klüver-Bucy syndrome.** The original signs after bilateral anterior lobectomies in monkeys described by Hein-
rich Klüver and Paul C. Bucy were visual agnosia, the use
of the mouth to examine objects, an increased tendency
to explore the world by touching, the absence of fear responses, and increased sexual activity. The symptoms of
the same lesion in humans include placidity, apathy, bu-

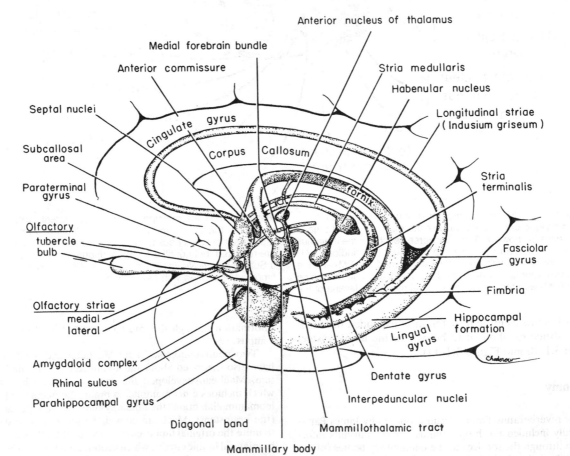

**Figure 3.1–14.** Semischematic drawing showing the anatomical relations of the amygdala, the hippocampus, other components of the limbic system, and part of the olfactory pathway.

(Figure from M B Carpenter, J Sutin: *Core Text of Neuroanatomy*,
ed 33, p 329. Williams & Wilkins, Baltimore, 1985. Used with
permission.)

limia, hypersexuality, and visual and auditory agnosias. Amnesia, aphasia, dementia, and seizures are also seen in humans with that type of lesion. The syndrome can be caused by tumors, trauma, herpes, encephalitis, Alzheimer's disease, and bilateral temporal lobe surgery.

**Korsakoff's syndrome.** Korsakoff's syndrome is an amnestic syndrome caused by chronic thiamine deficiency and associated with alcohol dependence. Korsakoff's syndrome can be associated with Wernicke's encephalopathy, which has neurological signs and symptoms of ataxia, confusion, and oculomotor abnormalities. Patients with Korsakoff's syndrome have difficulty in learning new information (*anterograde amnesia*) and are often amnestic for past events (*retrograde amnesia*). Patients attempt to hide their amnesia by talking around questions and by confabulation. Associated psychiatric symptoms are apathy and passivity. The amnesia is the result of neuronal damage in the mammillary bodies and the thalamus, although other brain regions are commonly affected. Once the neurons are damaged, treatment with thiamine is not effective in restoring memory abilities. Other causes of thiamine deficiency include intestinal malabsorption, gastric carcinoma, and prolonged intravenous hyperalimentation. Damage to other parts of the limbic system, especially the hippocampus, also results in various amnestic syndromes.

**Memory.** The hippocampus and the amygdala play critical roles in learning and memory. The function of memory is as crucial to the understanding of psychiatric disorders as it is to the understanding of neurological disorders. For example, hallucinations and delusions can be conceptualized as the abnormal and unwanted recall of memories. If hallucinations and delusions did not draw on memory systems, they would be completely unformed assortments of sounds and sights. Psychotherapy also engages the memory system, since a major goal of some types of psychotherapy is to change the emotional loading associated with past memories.

One of the earliest clinical observations regarding memory was in a patient who had undergone a bilateral anterior temporal lobectomy in an attempt to control his intractable epilepsy. The operation left the patient with a profound anterograde amnesia. Since that early observation, many research reports have identified the amygdala and the hippocampus as critical to the process of memory formation. The amygdala is also thought to be involved in the integration of memories and facial recognition and in social behavior. Two types of memory have been conceptualized by researchers. *Working memory* is short-term memory, what may be held in mind for a matter of minutes (for example, a telephone number). The physiological basis for working memory is supposedly a neurochemical change at specific synapses. *Consolidated memory* is long-term memory, what can be held for years and decades. The physiological basis for long-term memory is thought to involve permanent changes in the synaptic architecture and possibly the synthesis of new protein molecules.

**Violence.** An association between violence and the limbic system is suggested by the docility of animals with lesions of the amygdala and by animal experiments that have shown rage reactions to amygdala stimulation. Lesions of the amygdala and the anterior temporal lobes have been clinically correlated with a variety of behaviors in humans, including symptoms similar to schizophrenia, depression, and mania. A history of brain trauma and the presence of abnormal findings on electroencephalograms (EEGs) are common in populations of violent children and prisoners. Lesions of the posterior hypothalamus, not usually considered part of the limbic system, can result in sham rage, a syndrome of excessive rage in reaction to trivial stimuli.

## HYPOTHALAMUS AND PITUITARY

The hypothalamus and the pituitary are intimately linked and related to the limbic system; the hypothalamus and the pituitary constitute a major effector mechanism, principally through hormonal release, for the output of the limbic system. The relation between the hypothalamus and the pituitary is one of reciprocal regulation. The hypothalamus delivers releasing factors and release-inhibiting factors to the pituitary, which releases hormones (Table 3.1–11) that usually affect peripheral endocrine glands. The hypothalamus and the pituitary are involved in the regulation of sleep, appetite, and sexual activity; in addition to being the major endocrine regulators in the body, the hypothalamus and the pituitary have significant influence over the immune system and the autonomic nervous system.

### Anatomy

The hypothalamus is located beneath the thalamus and on either side of the third ventricle. The four hypothalamic nuclei of particular relevance to mental functioning are the mammillary bodies of the middle hypothalamic nuclei and the suprachiasmatic, supraoptic, and paraventricular nuclei of the anterior hypothalamic nuclei. The mammillary bodies are part of the limbic system; the suprachiasmatic nuclei are involved in maintaining many of the diurnal rhythms; and the supraoptic and paraventricular nuclei produce and release vasopressin

**Table 3.1–11**
**Pituitary Hormones**

Anterior lobe:
 Thyroid-stimulating hormone (TSH), also called thyrotropin
 Adrenocorticotropic hormone (ACTH), also called corticotropin
 Growth hormone (GH), also called somatotropin
 Follicle-stimulating hormone (FSH)
 Luteinizing hormone (LH), also called lutropin
 β-Lipotropic hormone (β-LPH), also called β-lipotropin
 γ-Melanocyte-stimulating hormone (γ-MSH)
Posterior lobe:
 Antidiuretic hormone (ADH), also called vasopressin
 Oxytocin
Additional hormones, less well characterized regarding release site:
 α- and β-Melanocyte stimulating hormone
 γ-Lipotropic hormone (γ-LPH), also called γ-lipotropin
 Corticotropinlike intermediate lobe peptide (CLIP)
 Fragments of pro-opiomelanocortin
 Cholecystokinin
 Gastrins
 Renin
 Angiotensin II
 Calcitonin-gene-related peptide (CGRP)

and oxytocin. For psychiatry, the most important pathways are the fornix, connecting the hippocampal formation with the mammillary bodies, and the stria terminalis and ventral amygdalofugal pathway, connecting the amygdala with the hypothalamus. The mammillothalamic tract connects the mammillary bodies to the anterior thalamus. The mesolimbic dopamine pathway and the ascending noradrenergic, serotonergic, and cholinergic pathways from the brainstem (the medial forebrain bundle) have terminations in the hypothalamus. Thus, the activity of the hypothalamus is affected by most of the psychotherapeutic drugs that are commonly used.

The pituitary (hypophysis) consists of the anterior pituitary (adenohypophysis) and the posterior pituitary (neurohypophysis) (Figure 3.1–15). The supraopticohypophyseal tract contains axons from the supraoptic and paraventricular nuclei that project to the posterior pituitary, where they release vasopressin and oxytocin into the venous drainage of the posterior pituitary. The ventromedial and infundibular nuclei of the medial hypothalamic nuclei and other basomedial hypothalamic nuclei project their axons into the pituitary stalk, where they terminate on the capillaries of the hypophyseal portal veins. The nuclei release inhibiting and releasing hormones that control the emission of trophic hormones from the anterior pituitary.

## Clinical Considerations

The hypothalamus and the pituitary are involved in the regulation of the endocrine and autonomic nervous sys-

tems and the control of eating behavior, sexual activity, body temperature, and the sleep-wake cycle. Various nuclei of the hypothalamus project sympathetic and parasympathetic nuclei to the brainstem and regulate and coordinate the autonomic nervous system. The involvement in the autonomic nervous system implicates the hypothalamus in psychosomatic disorders. The hypothalamic regulation of temperature may be the anatomical focus of pathology in neuroleptic malignant syndrome, a life-threatening complication of antipsychotics involving autonomic dysregulation and hyperthermia. The hypothalamic regulation of temperature ia also affected by drugs of abuse, such as ecstacy (3,4-methylenedioxymethamphetamine [MDMA]), which is associated with hyperthermia.

**Control of eating behavior.** Many studies of animals have shown that destruction of the ventromedial hypothalamus results in hyperphagia and obesity and that destruction of the lateral hypothalamus results in anorexia and starvation. Those areas of the hypothalamus have been called the satiety center and the appetitive center, respectively. The limbic system and the prefrontal cortex are also involved in regulating eating behavior.

**Homosexuality.** One recent study has reported that a particular nucleus of the hypothalamus differs in size between homosexual men and heterosexual men. The third interstitial nucleus of the anterior hypothalamus was found in a postmortem study to be twice as large in heterosexual

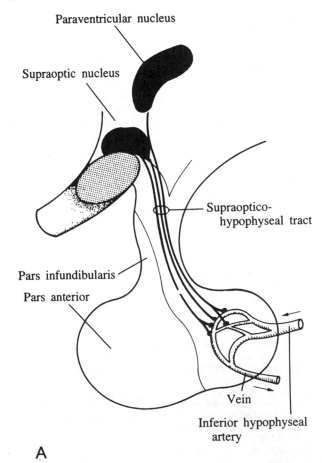

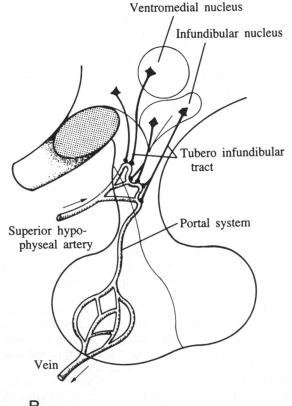

**Figure 3.1–15.** Hypothalamohypophyseal pathways. A. Supraopticohypophyseal tract. B. Tuberoinfundibular tract and the hypophyseal portal system. (Figure from L Heimer: *The Human*

*Brain and Spinal Cord, p 62.* Springer, New York, 1983. Used with permission.)

men as in either women or homosexual men. Preliminary animal data are consistent with the hypothesis that the nucleus may play an important biological role in the determination of sexual orientation. However, that finding remains controversial, and the results need to be replicated in additional studies before final conclusions can be made.

## BASAL GANGLIA

The basal ganglia (Figure 3.1–16) are a group of deep nuclei within the cerebral hemispheres. They have been of classic neurological interest regarding both normal movement and abnormal movement. Specifically, the basal ganglia are involved in the *feedback regulation* of movement—that is, the basal ganglia evaluate and correct movements as they are happening. That is in contrast to the *feed-forward regulation* of movements by the cerebellum. Feed-forward regulation involves the planning of movements before they are initiated.

Three sets of observations have prompted neuropsychiatrists to pay attention to the basal ganglia with regard to psychiatric disorders. First, many disorders of the basal ganglia (for example, Parkinson's disease and Huntington's disease) are associated with psychiatric symptoms. Second, several psychiatric disorders are associated with symptoms that can be interpreted as reflecting movement disorders. Two examples of such movement disorders are the paucity of movements seen in depression and the abnormal movements seen in schizophrenic patients. Untreated schizophrenic patients may show many subtle movement disorders—such as extreme opening and closing of the eyes, flaring of the nares, grimacing and pouting with the mouth, protrusion of the tongue, and shaking of the head—that imply an involvement of the basal ganglia. Third, the basal ganglia contain the highest concentration of dopamine type 2 ($D_2$) receptors in the brain. The $D_2$ receptors are of interest to psychiatry because they are believed to be the primary site of action for the typical antipsychotic agents, such as haloperidol (Haldol).

### Anatomy

The basal ganglia are deep brain structures (Figure 3.1–17). There are reciprocal connections between the striatum and the sensory association areas and to the limbic system. The pars compacta of the substantia nigra, which contains the dopaminergic cells that project to the striatum, is actually continuous with the globus pallidus. Although not considered part of the basal ganglia, the ventral tegmental area is medial to the substantia nigra and contains the dopaminergic neurons that project to the cortex and the limbic system. Blockade of the receptors for those neurons is hypothesized to be critical for the therapeutic effects of conventional antipsychotic drugs. The substantia innominata is a poorly defined group of cells related to the amygdala, the lateral hypothalamus, and the globus pallidus. The basal nucleus of Meynert is sometimes considered part of the substantia innominata. The nucleus contains a group of cholinergic neurons that project to the cortex. Those neurons may degenerate in some forms of dementia (for example, Alzheimer's disease, Parkinson's disease, Down's syndrome). The subthalamic nucleus is caudal to the substantia nigra, and lesions to that nucleus result in hemiballismus.

### Clinical Considerations

The key conceptual point regarding disorders of the basal ganglia is that the psychiatric symptoms are as much a result of the organic lesions as are the neurological symptoms. The most common psychiatric symptoms of basal ganglia disorders are depression, cognitive deficits, and psychosis. A feature of almost all the movement disorders associated with basal ganglia disorders is that the movement disorders themselves are aggravated by stress and are alleviated by rest and sleep.

**Parkinson's disease.** Parkinson's disease is a progressive disease of late adult life with characteristic symptoms of bradykinesia, rigidity, and a tremor at rest. Associated symptoms are decreased postural reflexes, masklike face, stooped posture, shuffling gait, and dysarthria. Often, the first characteristic sign is a loss of associated movements; the patient shows a peculiar immobility. Tremor may become apparent later. The tremor is a characteristic pill-rolling tremor that is most prominent at rest and when the patient assumes a posture. As in most extrapyramidal disorders, the tremor becomes prominent with tension and disappears with sleep. In some patients the tremor never becomes an important part of the illness; in others, it may be the most prominent symptom. Parkinson's syndrome is differentiated from Parkinson's disease by the syndrome's relative prominence of rigidity and bradykinesia and lack

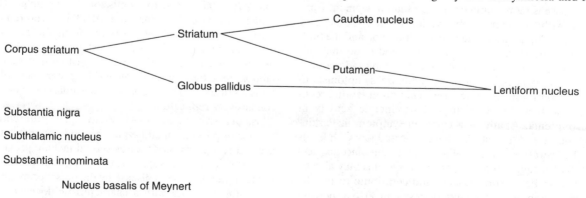

**Figure 3.1–16.** Components of the basal ganglia. *Also considered part of the limbic system.

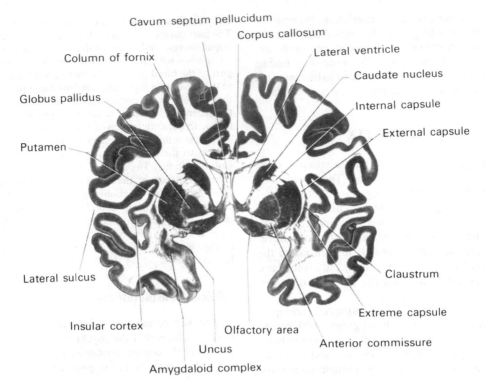

Cavum septum pellucidum
Corpus callosum
Column of fornix
Lateral ventricle
Caudate nucleus
Globus pallidus
Internal capsule
External capsule
Putamen
Lateral sulcus
Claustrum
Insular cortex
Extreme capsule
Olfactory area
Uncus
Anterior commissure
Amygdaloid complex

**Figure 3.1–17.** Photograph of a frontal section of the brain passing through the columns of the fornix and the anterior commissure. (Figure from M B Carpenter, J Sutin: *Human Neuro-* *anatomy*, p 580. Williams & Wilkins, Baltimore, 1983. Used with permission.)

of response to levodopa (Larodopa, Dopar), which is the standard treatment of Parkinson's disease.

The annual incidence in the Western hemisphere has been reported to be about 200 per 100,000 persons. In most cases the cause is unknown. The patient experiences a loss of cells in the substantia nigra, a decrease in the concentration of dopamine, and a degeneration of dopaminergic tracts. Physical examination reveals an impairment of fine movements and a peculiar cogwheel kind of rigidity that is most apparent in the neck and the arms. Sucking reflexes, positive Babinski's signs, and other evidence of pyramidal tract involvement are also present.

Depression and dementia are more common in Parkinson's disease patients than is expected by chance or is explainable by the psychosocial factors of the disorder. The prevalence of depression in Parkinson's disease has been reported to be between 40 and 60 percent; depression in the disease is more common in men than in women. Consistent with that clinical observation is the hypothesis of decreased dopaminergic activity in depression and the finding that L-dopa (levodopa) elevates mood in normal volunteers. Up to 60 percent of patients taking L-dopa on a long-term basis have serious psychiatric symptoms, including confusion and psychoses. That observation is consistent with a theory of hyperdopaminergic activity in schizophrenia. Apathy is a common symptom in Parkinson's disease. A few studies have reported low CSF levels of the serotonin metabolite 5-hydroxindolacetic acid (5-HIAA), suggesting that serotonin systems may also be affected in Parkinson's disease and contribute to the depressive symptoms. Dementia is present in 30 to 60 percent of Parkinson's disease patients. The dementia may be similar to that seen in Alzheimer's disease, a correlation that

is supported by the common presence of basal ganglia-related movement disorders in many patients with Alzheimer's disease. Cognitive testing of patients with Parkinson's disease often shows decreases in verbal memory and decreased performance in time-dependent tasks.

The cause of Parkinson's disease can be idiopathic (most common), encephalitic, toxic (carbon monoxide), or traumatic. Parkinson's disease can also be caused by ingesting a contaminant of an illicitly made synthetic heroin, N-methyl-4-phenyl-1,2,3,6 tetrahydropyridine (MPTP). One hypothetical mechanism for the neurotoxic effect is as follows: MPTP is converted into 1-methyl-4-phenylpyridinium (MPP$^+$) by the enzyme monoamine oxidase (MAO) and then is taken up by the dopaminergic neurons. Because MPP$^+$ binds to melanin in substantia nigra neurons, MPP$^+$ is concentrated in those neurons and causes them to die by inhibition of the mitochondrial respiratory chain. Positron emission tomographic (PET) studies of persons who ingested MPTP but who remained asymptomatic have shown a decrease in the number of dopamine-binding sites in the substantia nigra. Although two studies have reported data suggesting that MAO inhibitors may be useful in slowing the progression of Parkinson's disease, the results of those studies have not been conclusively replicated.

PROGRESSIVE SUPRANUCLEAR PALSY. The differential diagnosis of parkinsonianlike patients and patients with depressed and psychotic features should include progressive supranuclear palsy. Supranuclear palsy can be differentiated from Parkinson's disease by the presence in the palsy of ophthalmoplegia with a characteristic downward gaze of the eyes and a paresis of upward gaze. Other symptoms of the palsy are rigidity of the neck, mild dementia, impaired balance, and frequent falls. Patients with supranuclear palsy do not respond to levodopa, because the neurons with the dopamine receptors, not the neurons that release the dopamine, have been affected in the palsy.

**Huntington's disease.** Huntington's disease is characterized by choreiform movements and dementia that begin in adult life. Huntington's disease was described in 1872 by George Huntington, who recognized the disease as an autosomal-dominant disorder with complete penetrance. Huntington's disease is rare—only an estimated 6 cases per 100,000 persons in the Western hemisphere. The neuropathology involves atrophy of the caudate nuclei and the putamen, which can be visualized by computed tomography (CT) and magnetic resonance imaging (MRI) in many patients. One MRI study found that atrophy of the putamen is better correlated with the duration of illness than is atrophy of the caudate nucleus.

The onset is usually insidious; it is often heralded by a personality change that interferes with the patient's ability to adapt to the environment. The disease may begin at any age but is most common in late middle life. Juvenile-onset Huntington's disease is characterized by relatively mild chorea but with more marked rigidity, extrapyramidal symptoms, and seizures than in the adult-onset form of the disease. The juvenile-onset form also has a greater likelihood of psychosis, which is an interesting observation, given the characteristic early age of onset of the schizophrenic psychoses. The two sexes are affected by Huntington's disease in equal numbers.

When choreiform movements are first noted, they are frequently misinterpreted as inconsequential habit spasms or tics. As a result, the disease is usually not recognized for several years, especially if the family history is not known. One study found that as many as 75 percent of patients with Huntington's disease were initially misclassified as having a primary psychiatric disorder. The diagnosis depends on recognition of the progressive choreiform movements and dementia in a patient with a family history of the disorder. Eventually, the choreiform movements and dementia make long-term hospitalization necessary. The clinical course is one of gradual progression, with death occurring 15 to 20 years after the onset of the disease. The only satisfactory treatment at present is the prevention of the transmission of the responsible gene. Some symptomatic relief of the movement disorder and the psychotic symptoms may be achieved by an antipsychotic, such as haloperidol.

Dementia is the presenting symptom in about 10 percent of cases, and at least 90 percent of patients experience dementia during the illness. Depression is the major psychiatric symptom in Huntington's disease (approximately 40 percent of patients), and suicide is a major complication of the disorder; about 7 percent of nonhospitalized patients with Huntington's disease commit suicide. Psychosis is reported in about 20 percent of cases, but many other psychiatric disorders have been reported.

The application of restriction fragment length polymorphism (RFLP) studies to Huntington's disease has identified the short arm of human chromosome 4 as the site of genetic abnormalities in the disease. The studies used large affected pedigrees from Venezuela and North America. The specific gene or gene product involved in Huntington's disease is yet to be determined. However, identification of a specific genetic marker for Huntington's disease greatly facilitates accurate genetic counseling.

**Wilson's disease.** Wilson's disease, hepatolenticular degeneration, is an autosomal-recessive disorder resulting in diminished levels of ceruloplasmin, a copper-binding enzyme, and the subsequent deposition of copper in the liver, the brain (lenticular nuclei), the corneas, and the kidneys. The hepatic deposition of copper results in hepatomegaly, acute or chronic hepatitis, and cirrhosis. Clinically, the CNS signs include irritability, depression, psychosis, and dementia. More than half of the patients have the onset in the second or third decade of life, and those patients are likely to be misclassified as having a primary psychiatric disorder. The patients are particularly likely to have their illness complicated by alcohol dependence. Other clinical signs include jaundice, Kayser-Fleischer rings in the corneas, blue moons on the fingernails, and a wide flapping tremor of the arms. In addition, the patients often experience rigidity, dysarthria, and dysphagia. Since almost 100 percent of the patients with Wilson's disease and psychiatric symptoms have Kayser-Fleischer rings, a referral to an ophthalmologist who can evaluate their corneas is indicated if the disorder is suspected. The correct diagnosis of Wilson's disease can have remarkable benefits to the patient, since the copper deposition can be stopped and perhaps reversed by treatment with penicillamine (Cuprimine), although antidepressant and antipsychotic medications should also be used when indicated.

**Fahr's disease.** Fahr's disease is a rare hereditary disorder that presents with a parkinsonian movement disorder, neuropsychiatric symptoms, and calcification of the basal ganglia on CT. Fahr's disease is also called idiopathic calcification of the basal ganglia. There is a bimodal curve for age of onset: patients about age 30 present with psychosis that progresses to dementia, and patients about age 50 present with dementia. The disease has a close clinical resemblance to negative-symptom schizophrenia and is important in both differential diagnosis and theoretical formulations.

**Subcortical dementia.** The common association of dementia with disease processes of the basal ganglia was first noted in progressive supranuclear palsy. Patients with the condition were noted to have forgetfulness, slowness of thought processes, abnormal mood states, changes in personality, and an impairment in the ability to manipulate newly acquired information. Subsequently, patients with Huntington's disease were noted to be impaired in problem-solving abilities, insight, judgment, attention, concentration, and motivation. Those findings led several theorists to differentiate cortical dementias from subcortical dementias. Dementias caused by cortical disease characteristically present with aphasia, amnesia, agnosia, acalculia, and apraxias. Those cortical signs are usually absent in the subcortical dementias, which are characterized by slowness in thinking (bradyphrenia) and impairments in motivation, attention, and arousal. Subcortical dementias are also commonly associated with depressive and psychotic symptoms. Several researchers have hypothesized that aspects of a subcortical dementialike syndrome can be seen in depressed patients and in schizophrenic patients with prominent negative symptoms.

## PINEAL BODY

The pineal body develops from the epithalamus, which, with the hypothalamus and the thalamus, constitutes the diencephalon. The major function of the pineal gland is the excretion of melatonin. The pineal body is a single midline structure located on the roof of the third ventricle. The secretion of melatonin by the pineal body is involved in the maintenance of circadian rhythms and the sleep-wake cycle.

## CEREBELLUM

The cerebellar cortex, the midline cerebellar vermis, and the deep cerebellar nuclei (dentate, emboliform, globose, and fastigial) are the components of the cerebellum. The cerebellum is involved in the control of movements and postural adjustment. The cerebellum projects reciprocally to the cerebral cortex, the limbic system, the brainstem, and the spinal cord. Therefore, it is possible that the cerebellum is involved in higher mental functions as well. Animal studies have shown that parts of the cerebellum are necessary for the acquisition of particular conditioned responses. And in some case reports, cerebellar tumors and vascular events present as psychiatric disorders.

## BRAINSTEM

The brainstem is composed of the mesencephalon, the pons, and the medulla oblongata. The most basic functions of the brainstem concern respiration, cardiovascular activity, sleep, and consciousness. However, the brainstem is also the site of the neuronal cell bodies for the ascending biogenic amine (dopamine, norepinephrine, serotonin) pathways to higher brain areas. Those ascending biogenic amine pathways have been called the medial forebrain bundle.

## RETICULAR ACTIVATING SYSTEM

The reticular activating system is a loosely organized network of neurons coursing up the midline of the brainstem. The neurons receive input from ascending sensory neurons, the cerebellum, the basal ganglia, the hypothalamus, and the cerebral cortex; they send projections to the hypothalamus, the thalamus, and the spinal cord. Stimulation of the reticular activating system activates the cortex into a state of alert wakefulness. Psychiatric disorders in which motivation and level of arousal are impaired may involve pathology in the reticular activating system.

### References

Aggleton J P: The contribution of the amygdala to normal and abnormal emotional states. Trends Neurosci 16: 328, 1993.
Baxter L R, Mazziotta J C, Grafton S T, St. George-Hyslop P, Haines J L, Gusella J F, Szuba M P, Selin C E, Guze B H, Phelps M E: Psychiatric, genetic, and positron emission tomographic evaluation of persons at risk for Huntington's disease. Arch Gen Psychiatry 49: 148, 1992.
Biller J, Kathol R G, editors: The interface of psychiatry and neurology. Psychiatr Clin North Am 15: 1, 1992.
Calne D B: Treatment of Parkinson's disease. N Engl J Med 329: 1021, 1933.
Convit A, Czobor P, Volavka J: Lateralized abnormality in the EEG of persistently violent psychiatric inpatients. Biol Psychiatry 30: 363, 1991.
Cummings J L: Clinical Neuropsychiatry. Grune & Stratton, Orlando, 1985.
Cummings J L: Depression and Parkinson's disease: A review. Am J Psychiatry 149: 443, 1992.
Davis M: The role of the amygdala in fear-potentiated startle: Implications for animal models of anxiety. Trends Pharmacol Sci 13: 35, 1992.
Fornazzari L, Farcnik K, Smith I, Heasman G A, Ichise M: Violent visual hallucinations and aggression in frontal lobe dysfunction: Clinical manifestations of deep orbitofrontal foci. J Neuropsychiatry Clin Neurosci 4: 42, 1992.
He X, Rosenfeld M G: Mechanisms of complex transcriptional regulation: Implications for brain development. Neuron 7: 183, 1991.
Heimer L, de Olmos J, Alheid G F, Zaborszky L: "Perestroika" in the basal forebrain: Opening the border between neurology and psychiatry. In Progress in Brain Research, vol 87, G Holsteger, editor, p 109. Elsevier, New York, 1991.
Hoover J E, Strick P L: Multiple output channels in the basal ganglia. Science 259: 819, 1993.
Komuro H, Rakic P: Modulation of neuronal migration by NMDA receptors. Science 260: 95, 1993.
Lauder J M: Neurotransmitters as growth regulatory signals: Role of receptors and second messengers. Trends Neurosci 16: 233, 1993.
Markham C H, editor: Parkinson's disease. Clin Neurosci 1: 2, 1993.
McKay R D G: The origins of cellular diversity in the mammalian central nervous system. Cell 58: 815, 1989.
Mesulam M M: Principles of Behavioral Neurology. Davis, Philadelphia, 1985.
Roberts J K A: Differential Diagnosis in Neuropsychiatry. Wiley, New York, 1984.
Strub R L, Black F W: Neurobehavioral Disorders: A Clinical Approach. Davis, Philadelphia, 1988.
Tonkonogy J M, Geller J L: Hypothalamic lesions and intermittent explosive disorder. J Neuropsychiatry Clin Neurosci 4: 45, 1992.
Walsk C, Cepko C L: Widespread dispersion of neuronal clones across functional regions of the cerebral cortex. Science 255: 434, 1992.

# 3.2 / Brain Imaging

The field of brain imaging includes a number of techniques that have two common features. First, brain imaging techniques measure or assay some aspect or characteristic of the brain. Second, brain imaging techniques translate that information into a visual image or sometimes a numerical printout for the clinician or research investigator to study. As powerful as are other techniques, such as molecular genetics and protein biochemistry, only the brain imaging techniques permit the investigator to study the intact, whole, living human brain.

## STRUCTURAL AND FUNCTIONAL TECHNIQUES

The conventional division of the various brain imaging techniques has been into structural and functional types of techniques. An example of a purely structural brain imaging technique is computed tomography (CT), with which an investigator is able to obtain an X-ray picture of the brain. A CT image of a living human being's brain is virtually identical to a CT image of that same person's brain two hours after death. An example of a purely functional brain imaging technique is primitive cerebral blood flow measurements that tell the investigator the total amount of blood flowing to the brain, without identifying which areas of the brain receive how much blood.

CT is the only strictly structural brain imaging technique (other than a skull X-ray) that is used in contemporary psychiatric practice and research. Every other brain imaging technique detects some degree of both brain structure and brain function. Moreover, as the development of the so-called functional brain imaging techniques continues to advance, the ability of those techniques to resolve brain structure will probably equal that of the so-called structural techniques. Nevertheless, the convention has been to divide brain imaging techniques into structural and functional categories.

The two classically defined structural brain imaging techniques are CT and magnetic resonance imaging (MRI). The three classically defined functional brain imaging techniques are positron emission tomography (PET), single photon emission computed tomography (SPECT), and magnetic resonance spectroscopy (MRS). An array of electrophysiological techniques constitute a third type of brain imaging technique. Those techniques include electroencephalography (EEG), polysomnography, evoked potentials (EPs), and the computer-analyzed versions of those techniques—computed topographic EEGs and computed topographic EPs. A fourth and final brain imaging technique is magnetoencephalography.

The brain imaging techniques discussed in this section are listed in Table 3.2–1. In the following discussion of each of the techniques, other than CT, the description of the technique reveals how the techniques are not easily classified as being purely structural (in the case of MRI) or purely functional (for the remainder of the techniques).

## COMPUTED TOMOGRAPHY

Computed tomography (CT) is based on the same physical principles as a skull X-ray—that is, the measurement of the attenuation of X-ray photons that have been passed through the brain (Figure 3.2–1). X-ray photons are attenuated less by low-density tissues, such as cerebrospinal fluid (CSF), than by high-density tissues, such as bone. Thus, the image of low-density tissues appears black, and the image of high-density tissues appears white. The major differences between CT and a skull X-ray are CT's application of X-ray photon detectors and computers in lieu of X-ray film. The X-ray tube and detector are rotated around the head and are also moved in parallel in a rostral-caudal direction (Figure 3.2–2). The detector feeds the information into a computer, which is able to reconstruct images of planes or slices in the brain (Figure 3.2–3). The CT image can be enhanced by the use of iodinated contrast materials that are injected into the blood circulation and that cause a high attenuation of the X-ray photons and thus appear white in the image. The use of contrast materials can help the radiologist detect certain types of tumors, infections, and cerebrovascular diseases. The major disadvantages of the use of contrast material are its associated adverse effects, ranging from relatively common adverse effects, such as a metal taste in the mouth, to the rare complication of an anaphylactic reaction to the contrast material. Some evidence

**Table 3.2–1**
**Brain Imaging Techniques**

Computed tomography (CT)—structural
Magnetic resonance (MR) techniques
  MR imaging (MRI)—primarily structural, with some functional information
  MR spectroscopy (MRS)—primarily functional, with some structural information
Single photon emission computed tomography (SPECT)—primarily functional with significant structural information (The technique includes the xenon-133 regional cerebral blood flow [rCBF] technique.)
Positron emission tomography (PET)—primarily functional with significant structural information
Electrophysiological techniques—primarily functional with varying degrees of structural information
  Electroencephalography (EEG)
  Polysomnography
  Evoked potentials (EPs)
  Computed topographic EEG
  Computed topographic EPs
Magnetoencephalography (MEG)—primarily functional with some structural information

indicates that patients with other allergies and asthma are at greater than usual risk of an anaphylactic reaction.

### Use of CT in Psychiatry

CT scans of psychiatric patients are performed for two reasons. First, CT scans are commonly used in the workup of psychiatric patients to rule out organic brain disorders, such as tumors and cerebrovascular diseases; various clinical researchers have suggested an array of indications for ordering a CT scan in a psychiatric patient (Table 3.2–2). Second, CT scans have commonly been used in psychiatric research; CT studies of schizophrenic patients were among the first research reports that conclusively demonstrated organic brain pathology in schizophrenia.

### CT versus MRI

Whether to order a CT scan or a more expensive MRI scan is one of the common clinical questions in psychiatric practice. The resolution of both techniques is under 1 mm, but MRI does have superior resolution, can distinguish between white matter and gray matter, and has the capability of taking thinner slices through the brain (Table 3.2–3). There are, nonetheless, reasons to order a CT scan, rather than an MRI scan (Table 3.2–4). One reason to order a CT scan in preference to an MRI scan is CTs superiority in detecting calcified brain lesions, such as those seen in Fahr's disease (Figure 3.2–4). There are other reasons to order an MRI scan, rather than a CT scan (Table 3.2–5) or in addition to a CT scan (Table 3.2–6)

### MAGNETIC RESONANCE TECHNIQUES

The principles of magnetic resonance (MR) have been applied to brain imaging to produce two types of brain images. Magnetic resonance imaging (MRI) produces images of the brain that look much like CT scans but that

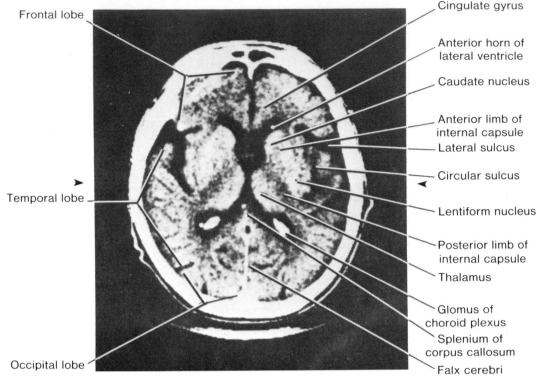

**Figure 3.2–1.** Computed tomogram taken parallel to the zero-degree plane through the thalamus, the internal capsule, and the corpus striatum. (Figure from J Hanaway, W R Scott, C W Strother: *Atlas of the Human Brain and the Orbit for Computed Tomography*. Green, St. Louis, 1980. Used with permission.)

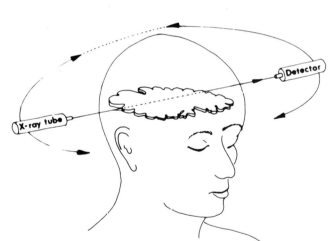

**Figure 3.2–2.** Principles of computed tomography. (Figure from G Sedvall: Brain imaging. In *Comprehensive Textbook of Psychiatry,* ed 5, H I Kaplan, B J Sadock, editors, p 92. Williams & Wilkins, Baltimore, 1989.)

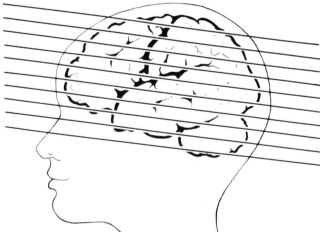

**Figure 3.2–3.** Cross-section through the head illustrating the planes of 10 CT scans parallel with the canto-meatal line. (Figure from G Sedvall: Brain imaging. In *Comprehensive Textbook of Psychiatry,* ed 5, H I Kaplan, B J Sadock, editors, p 92. Williams & Wilkins, Baltimore, 1989.)

have an increased in-focus appearance and that are able to discriminate white matter and gray matter. The ability to discriminate gray matter and white matter and other subtle differences within the brain tissue makes MRI good for such lesions as those seen in multiple sclerosis (Figure 3.2–5). Thus, MR images can look almost like anatomical preparations of the brain itself. However, the specific manner in which an MR image is obtained can be adjusted to obtain information about the quality of the tissue itself.

Thus, an MR image is not strictly a structural image, since it can provide additional information about the functional state of the tissues.

The second type of MR image is obtained through the use of magnetic resonance spectroscopy (MRS). Whereas MRI uses the magnetic resonance of the hydrogen nucleus (primarily found in the water in the brain), MRS uses the magnetic resonance of other nuclei and, thus, is able to assess a variety of metabolic functions.

**Table 3.2–2**
**Clinical Indications for a Computed Tomography (CT) Scan in a Psychiatric Patient**

Catatonia
Change in personality after age 50
Cognitive deficits seen on mental status examination
Dementia or delirium
Eating disorder
Electroencephalographic abnormalities
First affective episode after age 50
First episode of psychosis
Focal neurological findings
History of alcohol abuse
History of head trauma
History of seizures
Movement disorder

**Table 3.2–4**
**Computed Tomography (CT) instead of Magnetic Resonance Imaging (MRI)**

No localizing abnormalities present
No specific disease suspected that would be better evaluated with MRI
Suspected pathology well studied in CT
  Meningeal tumor (primary or metastatic)
  Pituitary lesions
  Calcified lesions
  Acute subarachnoid or parenchymal hemorrhage
  Acute parenchymal infarction
MRI contraindicated because of
  Pacemaker
  Aneurysm clip
  Ferromagnetic foreign body
  Pregnancy

Table from H J Garber, J B Weinberg, F S Buonanno: Use of magnetic resonance imaging in psychiatry. Am J Psychiatry *145*: 164, 1988. Copyright 1988, American Psychiatric Association. Used with permission.

## Magnetic Resonance Imaging

MRI was introduced into clinical practice in 1983 and has become a widely used technique. MRI is performed by placing the patient in a long tubelike structure that contains powerful magnets. In fact, the MRI device itself causes such feelings of claustrophobia in some patients that they are unable to undergo the procedure. The most common magnets are in the range of 1.5 to 2 tesla (T), but magnets are available up to 4.7 T, although the use of such strong magnetic fields for human studies is still being evaluated for safety. Once the patient is in the magnetic field, all the patient's hydrogen-containing molecules (especially water) line up in parallel and antiparallel arrays and move in a symmetrical fashion around their axes, in a movement called *precession*. That orderly arrangement and movement are interrupted by radiofrequency pulses from the MR device. The radiofrequency pulses cause the molecules to flip 90 degrees or 180 degrees from their axes; then the return of the molecules to their original positions in the magnetic field results in the release of electromagnetic energy that is detected by the MR equipment. Those data, which are essentially measurements of hydrogen nuclei densities, are then relayed into the computer, which can process the information into images of the brain. The clinical indications for MRI are identical to those for CT scans (Table 3.2–2), and the reasons to choose MRI over CT are enumerated in Table 3.2–5.

**MRI terminology.** The magnetic field itself is referred to as $B_0$. Two major components of MRI are $T_1$ and $T_2$. $T_1$ is the time required after excitation for the longitudinal magnetization of the hydrogen nuclei to return to pre-excitation values. $T_2$ is the time required after excitation for the transverse magnetization of the hydrogen nuclei to return to pre-excitation values. The terms $T_1$, spin-lattice, and longitudinal refer to related components of MRI and are often used interchangeably, as are the terms $T_2$, spin-spin, and transverse. The $T_1$ and $T_2$ aspects of MRI can be differentially weighted in the image by varying the radiofrequency pulse frequencies used to perturb the hydrogen nuclei in the magnetic field. $T_1$-weighted images, also called inversion-recovery images, are particularly good for distinguishing anatomical details, includ-

**Table 3.2–5**
**Magnetic Resonance Imaging (MRI) Instead of Computed Tomography (CT)**

Anatomical regions suspected:
  Temporal lobes
  Cerebellum
  Subcortical structures
  Brainstem
  Spinal cord
Particular disease suspected:
  White matter of demyelinating disorders
  Seizure focus
  Dementia
  Infarction
  Neoplasm (other than meningeal)
  Vascular malformation (including angiographically occult)
  Huntington's disease (and other degenerative diseases)
Children (posterior fossa, temporal lobe, midline)
CT contraindicated to avoid:
  Radiation
  Iodine-based contrast material
  Intravenous procedure

Table from H J Garber, J B Weinberg, F S Buonanno: Use of magnetic resonance imaging in psychiatry. Am J Psychiatry *145*: 164, 1988. Copyright 1988, American Psychiatric Association. Used with permission.

**Table 3.2–3**
**Comparison of Computed Tomography (CT) and Magnetic Resonance Imaging (MRI)**

| | CT | MRI |
|---|---|---|
| Physical principle | X-ray attenuation | Hydrogen nucleus magnetic resonance |
| Tissue property measured | Tissue density | Proton density |
| Resolution (in slice) | < 1 mm | < 1 mm |
| Slice thickness | 2–5 mm | 1–3 mm |
| Cost per scan | About $500 | About $1,000 |

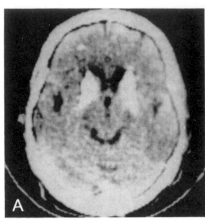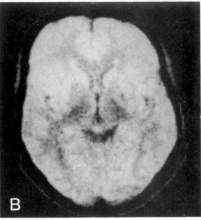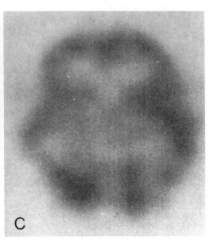

**Figure 3.2–4.** (A) A CT scan showing calcification of basal ganglia in Fahr's disease. (B) MRI is able to show only minimal change in basal ganglia. (C) A SPECT scan using radiolabeled HMPAO shows normal blood flow in the basal ganglia. (Figure from J A O Besson: Magnetic resonance imaging and its applications in neuropsychiatry. Br J Psychiatry *157*: 25, 1990. Used with permission.)

ing the differentiation of white matter from gray matter. $T_2$-weighted images, also called spin-echo images, are particularly sensitive to the amount of water present in the tissue and are good for distinguishing areas of anatomical pathology. As in CT scans, contrast material can be used in MR studies to highlight the blood vessels. The most commonly used contrast material is gadolinium-diethylenetriamine pentaacetic acid (DPTA).

## Magnetic Resonance Spectroscopy

Of all the techniques discussed in this section, magnetic resonance spectroscopy (MRS) may yet lead to the most revolutionary advances in brain imaging. Unlike MRI, which detects the hydrogen nucleus to determine brain structure, MRS is designed to detect a number of different nuclei (Table 3.2–7). The ability of MRS to detect biologically important nuclei permits the use of the technique to study a wide range of metabolic processes. Although the resolution of current MRS machines is poor compared with currently available PET and SPECT devices (Table 3.2–8), the use of stronger magnetic fields will improve that feature in the future. As stated above, MRS is an example of a brain imaging technique that is usually classified as functional, even though it localizes functions within the brain and, thus, is also structural.

**MRS technology.** MRS is able to image nuclei that have an odd number of protons and neutrons (Table 3.2–7). The unpaired protons and neutrons (nucleons) appear naturally and are nonradioactive. As in MRI, in the strong magnetic field produced by an MRS device, the nuclei line up in parallel and antiparallel fashion and precess around their axes. For a given nucleus and a given magnetic field, there is a *Lamour frequency* at which a radiofrequency pulse can be emitted. The radiofrequency pulse causes the nuclei of interest to absorb and then emit energy. The readout of an MRS device is usually in the form of a spectrum, such as those presented for phosphorus-31 (Figure 3.2–6) and hydrogen-1 (Figure 3.2–7) nuclei, although the spectrum can also be converted into a pictorial image of the brain. The multiple peaks for each nucleus reflect the fact that the same nucleus is exposed to different electron environments (electron clouds) in different molecules. The hydrogen-1 nuclei in a molecule of creatine, therefore, have a different *chemical shift* (position in the spec-

**Table 3.2–6**
**Magnetic Resonance Imaging (MRI) after Computed Tomography (CT)**

CT findings abnormal but not diagnostic
Equivocal or normal CT findings but high index of suspicion for disease likely to be seen better with MRI
Normal CT findings but atypical symptoms or course
Normal CT findings but strong clinical or emotional need for reassurance with MRI

Table from H J Garber, J B Weinberg, F S Buonanno: Use of magnetic resonance imaging in psychiatry. Am J. Psychiatry *145*: 164, 1988. Copyright 1988, American Psychiatric Association. Used with permission.

tra) than the hydrogen-1 nuclei in a choline molecule, for example (Figure 3.2–7). Thus, the position in the spectrum (the chemical shift) indicates the identity of the molecule in which the nuclei are present. The height of the peak, when compared with the height of a reference standard of the molecule, indicates the amount of the molecule present.

MRS of the hydrogen-1 nuclei is best at measuring N-acetyl-aspartate (NAA), creatine, and choline-containing molecules; however, MRS can also detect glutamate, glutamine, lactate, and *myo*-inositol. Although glutamate and γ-aminobutyric acid (GABA), the major inhibitory amino acid neurotransmitters, can be detected by MRS, the biogenic amine neurotransmitters (for example, dopamine) are present in concentrations too low to be detected with the technique. MRS of phosphorus-31 can be used to determine the pH of brain regions and the concentrations of phosphorus-containing compounds (for example, phosphocreatine and nucleoside triphosphate), which are important in the energy metabolism of the brain.

Additional current and potential applications of MRS are listed in Table 3.2–7. The additional indications include the use of MRS to measure the concentrations of psychotherapeutic drugs in the brain. One study used MRS to measure lithium (Eskalith) concentrations in the brains of bipolar I disorder patients and found that the brain lithium concentrations were half those in the plasma during depressed and euthymic periods but rose to greater than those in the plasma during manic episodes. Some compounds, such as fluoxetine (Prozac) and trifluoperazine (Stelazine) contain fluorine-19

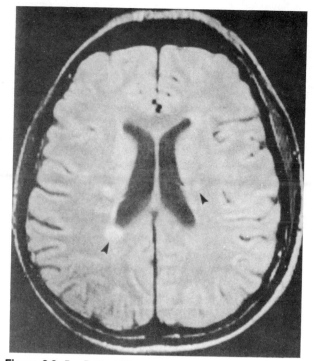

**Figure 3.2–5.** Brain MRI proton-density-weighted axial scan that shows several multiple sclerosis plaques located bilaterally in the white matter and adjacent to the lateral ventricles (arrows). (Figure from G Mattingly, K Baker, C F Zorumski, G S Figiel: Multiple sclerosis and ECT: Possible value of gadolinium-enhanced magnetic resonance scans for identifying high-risk patients. J Neuropsychiatry 4: 145, 1992. Used with permission.)

and thus can also be detected in the brain and measured by using the MRS technique.

## SINGLE PHOTON EMISSION COMPUTED TOMOGRAPHY

Whereas MRS uses naturally occurring, nonradioactive nuclei, single photon emission computed tomography (SPECT) and positron emission tomography (PET) require the introduction of manufactured radioactive compounds. The major advantage of SPECT over PET is the longer half-lives of SPECT's isotopes, which do not require an on-site cyclotron. A major disadvantage is that SPECT has a poorer image resolution than does PET.

### SPECT Technology

SPECT uses compounds that have been labeled with single photon-emitting isotopes: iodine-123, technetium-99m, and xenon-133. Technetium-99m ($Tc^{99m}$) is a metastable isotope with a molecular weight of 99. Those isotopes are attached to molecules that cross the blood-brain barrier. The two most commonly used commercially available products are d,l,hexamethylpropyleneamide-oxime (HMPAO [Ceretec]) and iodoamphetamine (Spectamine). Xenon-133 ($Xe^{133}$) is a noble gas that can be inhaled directly. The xenon quickly enters the blood and is distributed to areas of the brain as a function of regional blood flow. The particular subtype of SPECT that uses $Xe^{133}$ and measures blood flow is sometimes referred to as the regional cerebral blood flow (rCBF) technique, although that term incorrectly distinguishes $Xe^{133}$ from other isotopes that can also be used in SPECT and PET for measuring the regional distribution of blood flow in the brain. In addition to those compounds used for measuring blood flow, iodine-123 ($I^{123}$)-labeled ligands for the muscarinic, do-

**Table 3.2–7**
**Nuclei Available for in Vivo Magnetic Resonance Spectroscopy (MRS)**

| Nucleus | Natural Abundance | Relative Sensitivity | Potential Clinical Uses |
|---|---|---|---|
| $H^1$ | 99.99 | 1.00 | MR imaging |
| | | | Analysis of metabolism |
| | | | Identification of unusual metabolites |
| $F^{19}$ | 100.00 | 0.83 | Characterization of hypoxia |
| | | | Measurement of $pO_2$ |
| | | | Analysis of glucose metabolism |
| | | | Measurement of pH |
| $Li^7$ | 92.58 | 0.27 | Noninvasive pharmacokinetics |
| $Na^{23}$ | 100.00 | 0.09 | Pharmacokinetics |
| $P^{31}$ | 100.00 | 0.07 | MR imaging |
| | | | Analysis of bioenergetics |
| | | | Identification of unusual metabolites |
| | | | Characterization of hypoxia |
| $N^{14}$ | 93.08 | 0.001 | Measurement of pH |
| $K^{39}$ | 93.08 | 0.0005 | Measure glutamate, urea, ammonia |
| $O^{13}$ | 1.11 | 0.0002 | ? |
| | | | Analysis of metabolite turnover rate |
| $O^{17}$ | 0.04 | 0.00001 | Pharmacokinetics of labeled drugs |
| $H^2$ | 0.02 | 0.000002 | Measurement of metabolic rate |
| | | | Measurement of perfusion |

Natural abundance is given as percent abundance of the isotope of interest. Nuclei are tabulated in order of decreasing relative sensitivity; relative sensitivity is calculated by multiplying the relative sensitivity for equal numbers of nuclei (at a given field strength) by the natural abundance of that nucleus. A considerable gain in relative sensitivity can be obtained by isotopic enrichment of the nucleus of choice or by the use of novel pulse sequences. (Table adapted from Fisk and Becker, 1987.)
Table from S R Dager, R G Steen: Applications of magnetic resonance spectroscopy to the investigation of neuropsychiatric disorders. Neuropsychopharmacology 6: 249, 1992. Used with permission.

**Table 3.2–8**
**Comparison of Magnetic Resonance Spectroscopy (MRS), Photon Emission Tomography (PET), and Single Photon Emission Computed Tomography (SPECT)**

| | MRS | PET | SPECT |
|---|---|---|---|
| Minimal molarity of substances to be detected | $10^{-6}$ mol/L | $10^{-12}$ mol/L | $10^{-11}$ mol/L |
| Resolution | 7 mm($H^1$) >10 mm (other nuclei) | 5–6 mm | 7–8 mm |
| Isotopes | See Table 3.2–7 | $O^{15}$ $N^{13}$ $C^{11}$ $F^{18}$ | $I^{123}$ $Tc^{99m}$ $Xe^{133}$ |
| Half-life of isotopes | Nondecaying | 2–110 min | 6–130 hrs |

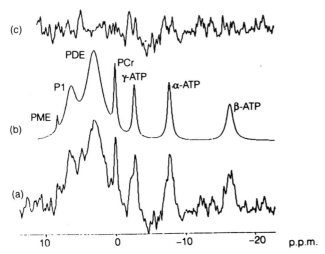

**Figure 3.2–6.** An in vivo $P^{31}$ spectrum of brain tissue: (a) original processed spectrum, (b) the spectrum after a computerized curve-fitting routine, and (c) original spectrum with the fitted spectrum subtracted. The spectrum represents in vivo phosphorus metabolism in cortical gray and white matter. The broad hump underlying the PME, Pi, PDE, and PCr resonances is derived from tissue phospholipids and mineral phosphates in bone. The phosphorus metabolites are not in solution and are, therefore, unable to resonate freely. ATP—adenosine triphosphate (γ, α, and β positions of $P^{31}$ nucleus), PC—phosphocreatine, PDE—phosphodiester, Pi—inorganic phosphate, PME—phosphomonoester. (Figure from T Lock, M T Abou-Saleh, R H T Edwards: Psychiatry and the new magnetic resonance era. In Br J Psychiatry *157* (9, Suppl): 41, 1990. Used with permission.)

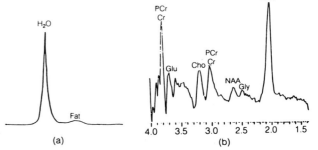

**Figure 3.2–7.** The $H^1$ spectrum of brain tissue. (a) Without solvent suppression, the only $H^1$ metabolites detectable in the spectrum are water and fat. (b) With solvent suppression, several metabolites are seen. Other metabolites are better visualized by changing the acquisition parameters. The scale of the two spectra differ. Were they drawn to the same scale, the $H_2O$ peak in (a) would be several feet high. NAA—n-acetyl aspartate, PCr—phosphocreatine, PDE—phosphodiester. (Figure from T Lock, M T Abou-Saleh, R H T Edwards: Psychiatry and the new magnetic resonance era. In Br J Psychiatry *157* (9, Suppl): 41, 1990. Used with permission.)

paminergic, and serotonergic receptors can be used to study those receptors by using SPECT technology.

Once the photon-emitting compounds reach the brain, their γ-emitting property can be detected by detectors that surround the patient's head. That information is relayed to a computer, which constructs a two-dimensional image of the distribution of the isotope within a slice of the brain. A key point of differentiation between SPECT and PET is that in SPECT a single particle is emitted, whereas in PET two particles are emitted, giving a more precise location of the event and better resolution of the image. For both SPECT and PET studies, investigators are increasingly performing prestudy MRI or CT studies, then superimposing the SPECT or PET image on the MRI or CT image to obtain a more accurate anatomical location of the functional information (Figure 3.2–8).

## POSITRON EMISSION TOMOGRAPHY

Positron emission tomography (PET) is perhaps the most powerful currently available brain imaging technique. A wide range of compounds can be used in PET studies (Table 3.2–9), and the resolution of PET continues to be refined closer to its theoretical minimum of 3 mm (Table 3.2–8). The main disadvantage of PET continues to be the expense of needing an on-site cyclotron with which to make the isotopes.

### PET Technology

The most commonly used isotopes in PET are fluorine-18, nitrogen-13, and oxygen-15. Those isotopes are usually linked to another molecule, except in the case of oxygen-15 ($O^{15}$), and administered to the patient. In the brain the radioactive isotopes emit positrons that move up to 3 mm before colliding with an electron. The collision between matter and antimatter results in the annihilation of the particles and the production of a pair of protons that theoretically move away from the site of collision at a 180-degree angle to each other. The head of the patient is in the PET camera, which has a ring of detection crystals designed to detect the simultaneous arrival of protons at 180 degrees from each other. That information is relayed to a computer that can generate the two-dimensional images commonly reported in the literature.

The most commonly reported ligand has been fluorine-18 ($F^{18}$)-deoxyglucose (FDG), which is an analogue of glucose that the brain cannot metabolize. Thus, the brain regions with the highest metabolic rate and the highest blood flow take up the most FDG but are unable to metabolize and excrete the usual metabolic products. The concentration of $F^{18}$ builds up in those neurons and is detected by the PET camera. Water$^{15}$ ($H_2O^{15}$) and nitrogen-13 ($N^{13}$) are used to measure blood flow, and oxygen-15 ($O^{15}$) can be used to determine metabolic rate.

### Types of PET Studies

PET has been increasingly used to study normal brain development and function as well as to study neuropsychiatric disorders. With regard to brain development (Figure 3.2–9), PET studies have found that glucose use is greatest in the sensorimotor cortex, the thalamus, the brainstem, and the cerebellar vermis when the infant is aged 5 weeks or younger. By 3 months of age, most areas of the cortex have increased use except for the frontal and association cortices, which do not begin to increase until the infant is 8 months old. An adult pattern of glucose metabolism is achieved by the age of 1 year, but the cortex continues to rise to above adult levels until the child is about age 9 years, when the cortex begins to decrease, reaching its final adult level in the late teen years. In view of the common onset of schizophrenia during that same period, one may speculate what the development of glucose use in a schizophrenic patient is. FDG studies have also been used to study pathology in neurological disorders (Figure 3.2–10) and psychiatric disorders (Figure 3.2–11).

Two other types of studies use precursor molecules and receptor ligands. With the dopamine precursor dopa, pathology has been visualized in Parkinson's disease patients. Radiolabeled ligands for receptors have been useful in determining the occupancy of receptors by specific psychotherapeutic drugs (Figure 3.2–12).

### ISSUES COMMON TO PET AND SPECT

### Image Resolution

Four major factors affect the resolution level of both PET and SPECT techniques: Compton scattering, signal attenuation, anatomical resolution, and partial volume effects.

**Compton scattering.** The emitted photons in both PET and SPECT are deviated from a straight path by the tissues through which they pass. That effect of the tissue is called Compton scattering; it limits the anatomical resolution of both PET and SPECT.

**Signal attenuation.** Not only are the photons deviated from their straight path by the tissue, but also the energy of the photons is dissipated by bone, air, fluid, and brain tissue. In fact, the most carefully done PET and SPECT studies use prestudy CT examinations to correct for variable attenuations or the signal caused by differences in patients' head sizes.

**Anatomical resolution.** A common term used in describing the resolution for both PET and SPECT is "full width at half maximum" (FWHM), which refers to the width of the curve of distribution for the signal at 50 percent of the maximal signal. For PET studies, FWHM is about 5 to 6 mm; for SPECT studies, FWHM is about 8 to 9 mm, thus reflecting the better resolution of the PET technique compared with the SPECT technique.

**Partial volume effects.** For both PET and SPECT, areas of interest within the slice are selected. However, the signal from each area of interest also has an effect on the neighboring areas of interest. In some studies of SPECT and PET, the investigators use various computer modeling programs to subtract the energy contribution of neighboring areas from the areas of interest.

### Pharmacological and Neuropsychological Probes

With both PET and SPECT and eventually with MRS, more studies and possibly diagnostic procedures will use pharmacological and neuropsychological probes. The purpose of such probes is to stimulate particular regions of brain activity, so that, when compared with a baseline, conclusions can be reached about the functional correspondence to particular brain regions. One example of the approach is the use of PET to detect regions of the brain involved in the processing of shape, color, and velocity in the visual system. Another example is the use of cognitive activation tasks (for example, the Wisconsin Card Sorting Test) to study frontal blood flow in schizophrenic patients.

A key consideration in the evaluation of those reports is the establishment of a true baseline value in the study design. Typically, the reports use an awake, resting state, but there is variability in whether the patients have their eyes closed or their ears blocked; both conditions can affect brain function. There is also variability in such baseline brain function factors as gender, age, anxiety regarding the test, nonpsychiatric drug treatment, and time of day.

## ELECTROPHYSIOLOGICAL TECHNIQUES

### Electroencephalography

The electroencephalogram (EEG), the most classic of the currently used brain imaging techniques, was developed in 1929 by Hans Berger. The major determinant in EEG is the electrical activity of the neurons in the uppermost neuronal layers of the cortex. Electrodes placed on the patient's scalp measure the electrical activity in those cortical neurons. The graphic recordings from each electrode are usually drawn by recording pens and placed in various arrangements, called montages, on the recording paper.

The frequencies of the waves seen on EEG recordings are classically divided into the following groups: delta activity (<4 cycles per second or hertz [Hz]), theta activity (4 to 8 Hz), alpha activity (8 to 13 Hz), and beta activity (>13 Hz). Normal awake adults whose eyes are closed have predominantly alpha activity. When the persons are stimulated or open their eyes, alpha activity is replaced by beta activity. Sleep is characterized by the presence of delta activity and theta activity.

The interpretation of an EEG begins with an overall visual inspection of the montage. The key characteristics to be assessed are the frequency, the amplitude, and the distribution of the wave forms. The evaluation of an EEG

**Figure 3.2–8.** Stages of the superimposition of a SPECT cerebral blood-flow image (A), which has been redefined (B), and an MRI $T_1$-weighted image (C), to produce a combination (D). (Figure from J A O Besson: Magnetic resonance imaging and its applications in neuropsychiatry. Br J Psychiatry *157* (9, Suppl): 25, 1990. Used with permission.)

**Figure 3.2–9.** $F^{18}$-deoxyglucose (FDG) PET images illustrating developmental changes in local cerebral metabolism in the normal human infant and with increasing age. Sections are at the level of the cingulate gyrus (level 1), the striatum and the thalamus (level 2), and the cerebellum (level 3). (Figure from H T Chugani, M E Phelps, J C Mazziotta: Positron emission tomography study of human brain functional development. Ann Neurol *22*: 487, 1987. Used with permission.)

**Figure 3.2–10.** PET scans with $F^{18}$ fluorodeoxyglucose in a control (top) and six patients with neurological disorders. The three images from the control show transverse sections of the brain at a high level through the parietal lobes (left), an intermediate level through the basal ganglia and the thalamus (center), and a low level through the base of the frontal lobes, the temporal lobes, and the cerebellum (right). The level of each image corresponds approximately to the level of the scans below. The bar indicates the level of glucose metabolic activity in the images, with colors on the left indicating low levels of metabolism and colors on the right high levels. The middle and bottom scans are from patients with multi-infarct dementia (MID) (also known as vascular dementia), Alzheimer's disease (AD), temporal lobe epilepsy, brain tumor (primitive neuroectodermal tumor), Huntington's disease (HD), and olivopontocerebellar atrophy (OPCA). A small region of absent glucose metabolism is seen in the patient with multi-infarct dementia (arrow); PET scans at other levels in the patient revealed a number of similar areas, which represent small focal infarctions. The scan in the patient with Alzheimer's disease shows hypometabolism in both parietal lobes (arrows).

The image in the patient with epilepsy shows hypometabolism in the right temporal lobe (arrow), which is the site of origin of the seizure disorder. The scan in the patient with a tumor shows a region of hypermetabolism in the thalamus, which is the location of the tumor (arrow). The image in the patient with Huntington's disease shows hypometabolism in the caudate nuclei bilaterally (arrows). The scan in the patient with olivopontocerebellar atrophy shows hypometabolism in the cerebellum (arrows) and the brainstem. (Figure from S Gilman: Advances in neurology. N Engl J Med *326*: 1610, 1992. Used with permission.)

**Figure 3.2–11.** Positron emission tomographic scans illustrating extreme cases of low glucose metabolic rates in the left dorsal anteriolateral prefrontal cortex (arrows), divided by the rate for the hemisphere as a whole in a patient with severe obsessive-compulsive disorder with secondary major depressive disorder. Horizontal and rectilinear lateral views are shown. Scan A is of the disease state, and scan B is of the same patient six weeks later, after effective treatment with antidepressant medication. (Figure from L R Baxter, J M Schwartz, M E Phelps, J C Mazziotta, B H Guze, C E Selin, R H Gerner, R M Sumida: Reduction of prefrontal cortex glucose metabolism common to three types of depression. Arch Gen Psychiatry *46*: 247, 1989. Used with permission.)

**Figure 3.2–12.** PET images showing radioactivity in a horizontal brain section through the striatal level after an intravenous injection of $C^{11}$ raclopride into a healthy volunteer. (A) PET image before medication. Corresponding PET images at different time points after the administration of 4 mg haloperidol are shown after 3 hours (B), and after 6 hours (C), and after 27 hours (D). (Figure from A-L Nordström, L Farde, C Halldin: Time course of $D_2$-dopamine receptor occupancy examined by PET after single oral doses of haloperidol. Psychopharmacology *106*: 436, 1992. Used with permission.)

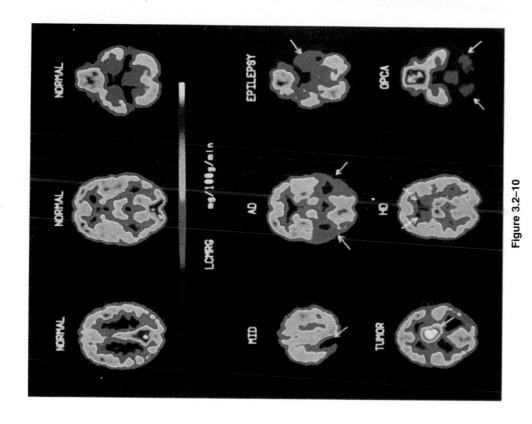

Figure 3.2-10

Figure 3.2-8

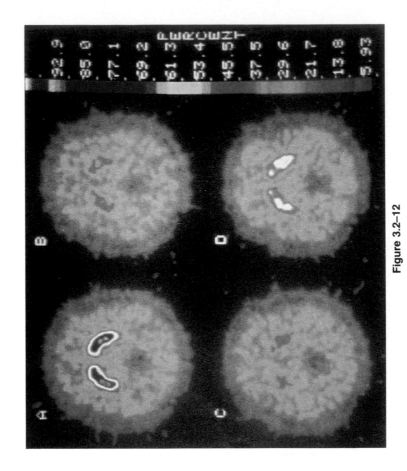

Figure 3.2–12

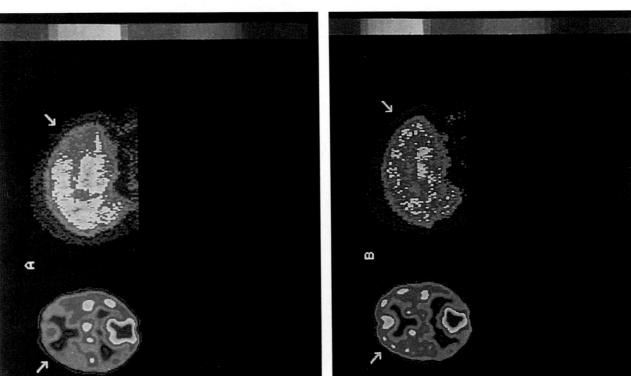

Figure 3.2–11

**Table 3.2–9**
**PET Approaches to Cerebral Function**

| Process or Parameter | Tracer |
|---|---|
| Blood flow | $H_2O^{15}$, $CO_2^{15}$, $Kr^{85m}$, $C^{11}H_3$, $F^{18}$, $C^{11}$-labeled alcohols |
| Blood volume | $CO^{15}$-labeled and $CO^{11}$-labeled red blood cells, $Ga^{68}$-labeled EDTA |
| Tissue pH | $[C^{11}]DMO$, $C^{11}O_2$ |
| Transport and metabolism | |
|   Oxygen | $O^{15}_2$ |
|   Glucose, glucose analogues, carbohydrates | 2-Deoxy-[2-$F^{18}$]fluoro-D-glucose, [2-$C^{11}$]deoxy-D-glucose, [$C^{11}$]D-glucose,3-O-[methyl-$C^{11}$]D-glucose, and $C^{11}$-labeled lactate, pyruvate, acetate, and succinate |
|   Amino acids: $N^{13}$ | $N^{13}$-labeled L-glutamate, -glutamine, -alanine, -leucine, -aspartate, -valine, -isoleucine, and -methionine |
|   Amino acids: $C^{11}$ | $C^{11}$-labeled L-aspartate, -glutamate, -valine, -leucine, -phenylalanine, and -methionine; $C^{11}$-labeled D,L-1-aminocyclopentane and carboxylic acid |
| Protein synthesis | 1-$C^{11}$-labeled-L-leucine, -methionine, and -phenylalanine; L-[methyl-$C^{11}$]methionine |
| Receptor systems | |
|   Dopaminergic | $F^{18}$-spiperone, [$C^{11}$]spiperone, [$C^{11}$]raclopride, [$Br^{75}$]- and [$Br^{76}$]-bromospiperone, $F^{18}$-haloperidol, [$C^{11}$]pimozide, [methyl-$C^{11}$]ethylspiperone, L-[$C^{11}$]dopa, [6-$F^{18}$]fluoro-L-dopa, $F^{18}$-ethylspiperone |
|   Cholinergic | [$C^{11}$]imipramine, [$C^{11}$]quinuclidinyl benzilate |
|   Benzodiazepam | $C^{11}$-labeled flunitrazepam, diazepam, RO-15-1788, and PK-11195; [$F^{18}$]fluorovalium |
|   Opiate | $C^{11}$-labeled etorphine, N-methylmorphine, heroin, and carfentanil |
|   Adrenergic | [$C^{11}$]norepinephrine, [$C^{11}$]propranolol |
| Anticonvulsants | [$C^{11}$]valproate, [$C^{11}$]diphenylhydantoin |

Table from S T Grafton, J C Mazziotta: Cerebral pathophysiology evaluated with positron emission tomography. In *Diseases of the Nervous System: Clinical Neurobiology*, ed 2, A K Asbury, G M McKhann, W I McDonald, editors, p 421. Saunders, Philadelphia, 1992. Used with permission.

recording also requires an inspection for any paroxysmal events, such as spike and wave bursts, which may indicate epileptic activity. The presence of abnormal slow-wave activity, the suppression of EEG amplitude, and abnormal asymmetries are other EEG abnormalities that should be noted.

One of the most challenging aspects of EEG interpretation is the recognition of EEG artifacts. The two most common sources of artifacts in an EEG recording are scalp muscle activity, which may be confused with fast beta activity, and eye movements, which may be confused with slow delta activity over the frontal poles.

**Clinical indications.** The evaluation of suspected epilepsy in a patient is the major clinical indication for an EEG, although an EEG is also obtained in the evaluation of dementia and delirium. Other possible indications for an EEG are altered levels of consciousness, automatisms, head injury, hallucinations, and dissociative phenomena.

The EEG is not a sensitive test. Patients with epileptic activity are often not detected on a routine EEG. Four common approaches are used to stimulate the appearance of abnormal activity in an EEG: (1) Photic stimulation involves showing the patient a flashing strobe light during the EEG. An abnormal result is the appearance of paroxysmal activity not in phase with the flashing light. (2) Having a patient hyperventilate for about three minutes can also cause the appearance of spikes, sharp waves, or paroxysms of slow-wave activity. (3) Sleep deprivation involves keeping a patient awake the night before the EEG, thus causing the patient to be drowsy and in and out of sleep during the EEG procedure itself. The EEG during sleep and the EEG during changes between sleep and wakefulness often reveal pathology. (4) Special nasopharyngeal leads can be used to get physically closer to the limbic areas of the brain that may be involved in epileptic activity involving the temporal lobes.

### Polysomnography

The technique of recording an EEG when the person is sleeping is called polysomnography. Polysomnography is often performed along with an electrocardiogram (ECG), an electromyogram (EMG), and sometimes a recording of penile tumescence. Recordings of blood oxygen saturation, body movement, body temperature, galvanic skin response, and gastric acid secretion are additional measurements that can be used with polysomnography in research settings. Polysomnography is most often used in the evaluation of sleep-related disorders, such as insomnia, nocturnal myoclonus, sleep apnea, enuresis, and somnambulism. In a research-oriented application of polysomnography, the technique has been used extensively to study the sleep architecture of psychiatric patients. Such research has been directed toward describing abnormalities in sleep architecture, which may serve as markers of specific psychiatric disorders, particularly depressive disorders. The most common variables that are assessed in polysomnographic studies of psychiatric patients are the amount of time spent in rapid eye movement (REM) sleep, how soon after falling asleep the first REM episode appears (REM latency), and the number of REM episodes in a night.

REM sleep and non-REM sleep are the two major divisions within sleep architecture. There are four stages of non-REM sleep. Stage 4 represents the deepest sleep and stage 1 the lightest. As described above, alpha activity is present when adults lie down in bed and close their eyes. The alpha activity gradually disappears during stage 1 sleep. Slow delta activity increases in sleep stages 2 through 4. High-amplitude slow delta waves are replaced by beta-like activity that resembles the EEG of an awake, alert person during REM sleep.

### Evoked Potentials

The recording of evoked potentials (EPs) uses the same electrode and recording arrangements as in EEG recording.

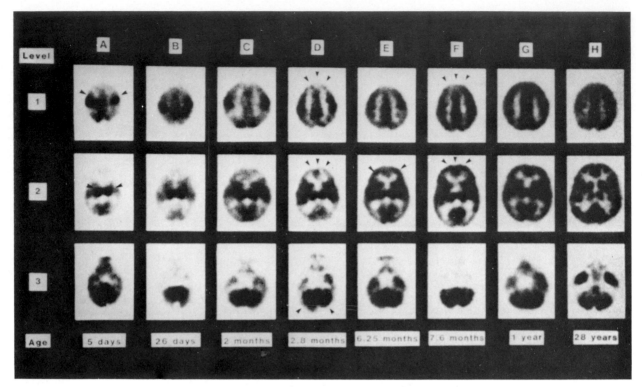

**Figure 3.2–9.** F[18]-deoxyglucose (FDG) PET images illustrating developmental changes in local cerebral metabolism in the normal human infant and with increasing age. Sections are at the level of the cingulate gyrus (level 1), the striatum and the thalamus (level 2), and the cerebellum (level 3). (Figure from H T Chugani, M E Phelps, J C Mazziotta: Positron emission tomography study of human brain functional development. Ann Neurol 22: 487, 1987. Used with permission.)

Evoked potentials provide a measure of how the cortex responds to particular sensory stimuli. The following types of EPs are the most commonly tested: somatosensory evoked potentials (SEPs), auditory evoked potentials (AEPs), and visual evoked potentials (VEPs). In EP testing, a stimulus from one sensory modality (for example, a mild electric shock, a click, or a light flash) is presented multiple times while the EEG recording is made. The EEG tracing that follows each repeated stimulus is then averaged by a computer to reduce nonstimulus-related activity. The result is a smooth curve (the EP) that includes peaks and valleys (Figure 3.2–13). *Positive waves* are the downward deflections, and *negative waves* are the upward deflections. Particular waves are further identified by the number of milliseconds that occur after the stimulus. The P300 wave, therefore, is a downward (positive) deflection that occurs approximately 300 ms after the stimulus. The magnitude and the timing of EP waves constitute the basis of the clinical and research evaluation of an EP recording.

The EP waves have been classified into early (<50 ms after the stimulus), middle (50 to 250 ms), and late (>250 ms) components. The relay of sensory information as it passes from a sensory organ (for example, the eyes) to the primary sensory cortex and to the association cortex is reflected in the early EP components. Increasingly complex cognitive and psychological processing of sensory information is reflected in the late EP components.

**Clinical indications.** The assessment of a demyelinating disorder, such as multiple sclerosis, is the most common reason for conducting an EP evaluation of a patient. An EP is probably not indicated in the routine workup of a psychiatric patient unless a demyelinating disorder is suspected. However, psychiatric researchers have used EP recordings extensively to study groups of psychiatric patients. Many of the studies found that specific groups of psychiatric patients have larger or smaller waves that occur either earlier or later than in nonpsychiatrically ill persons. EP recordings are especially subject to contamination by various artifacts in addition to those affecting EEG recordings. Attention, compliance, fatigue, coffee and cigarette consumption, the age of the person, and diurnal variations have all been reported to affect the data from EP recordings.

### Computed Topographic EEGs and EPs

Although the visual inspection of EEGs and EPs by trained electroencephalographers is the standard and accepted method of EEG evaluation, much useful information is likely missed by relying solely on the human eye. Various computer programs have been designed to translate EEG and EP recordings into graphic and understandable images of the brain. Those computer programs quantitate the amount of voltage present in each of the basic frequency ranges—alpha, beta, theta, and delta—for each electrode. The results of those calculations are then represented on topographic maps of the brain and use either a gray scale or a color scale to indicate which parts of the brain have more or less activity in a specific frequency range. Although some researchers have reported that computed topographic EEGs and EPs already have clinical relevance in psychiatry, most psychiatrists believe that the technique should still be limited to research applications.

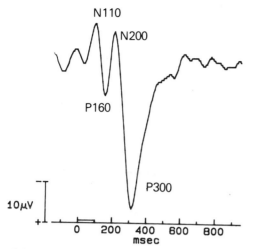

**Figure 3.2–13.** An auditory evoked potential elicited by a 50-dB SL tone pip. (Figure courtesy of Connie C Duncan, Ph.D., Unit on Psychophysiology, Laboratory of Psychology and Psychopathology, National Institute of Mental Health, Bethesda, Maryland.)

## MAGNETOENCEPHALOGRAPHY

The brain imaging technique that is the earliest in terms of its development and applications is magnetoencephalography (MEG). The application of MEG is almost entirely limited to research settings, although some clinicians are using the technique in the evaluation of epileptic patients. Minute magnetic fields are produced as a result of the electrical activity of neurons. Those minute magnetic fields are detected and computer-analyzed by MEG. Like the EEG and EPs, MEG does not expose the patient to any radiation or chemical substances; in contrast to EEG and EPs, MEG is able to provide information about both cortical and subcortical brain structures.

Although several studies have attempted to demonstrate that MEG is superior to EEG for the assessment of epileptic activity, those attempts have generally been unsuccessful. Moreover, MEG is an expensive technology because of the superconducting technology needed to amplify the small signal to achieve an acceptable signal-to-noise ratio. Ongoing research on the simultaneous use of EEG and MEG may be of benefit in the study of neuropsychiatric patients.

### References

Abou-Saleh M T, editor: Brain imaging in psychiatry. Br J Psychiatry *157* (9, Suppl): 1, 1990.
Andreasen N C, Cohen G, Harris G, Cizadlo T, Parkkinen J, Rezai K, Swayze V W: Image processing for the study of brain structure and function: Problems and programs. J Neuropsychiatry Clin Neurosci *4*: 125, 1992.
Corbetta M, Miezin F M, Dobmeyer S, Shulman G L, Petersen S E: Attentional modulation of neural processing of shape, color, and velocity in humans. Science *248*: 1556, 1990.
Dager S R, Steen R G: Applications of magnetic resonance spectroscopy to the investigation of neuropsychiatric disorders. Neuropsychopharmacology *6*: 249, 1992.
Garber H J, Weilburg J B, Duffy F H, Manschreck T L: Clinical use of topographic brain electrical activity mapping in psychiatry. J Clin Psychiatry *50*: 205, 1989.
Gilman S: Advances in neurology. N Engl J Med *326*: 1608, 1992.
Gur R C, Erwin R J, Gur R E: Neurobehavioral probes for physiologic neuroimaging studies. Arch Gen Psychiatry *49*: 409, 1992.

Holman L B, Tumeh S S: Single-photon emission computed tomography (SPECT): Applications and potential. JAMA *263*: 561, 1990.
Kato T, Takahashi S, Inubushi T: Brain lithium concentration by $^7$Li- and $^1$H-magnetic resonance spectroscopy in bipolar disorder. Psychiatry Res Neuroimaging *45*: 53, 1992.
Keshavan M S, Kapur S, Pettegrew J W: Magnetic resonance spectroscopy in psychiatry: Potential, pitfalls, and promise. Am J Psychiatry *148*: 967, 1991.
Lock T, Abou-Saleh M T, Edwards R H T: Psychiatry and the new magnetic resonance area. Br J Psychiatry *157*: 38, 1990.
Moonen C T W, Van Zijl P C M, Frank J A, Le Bihan D, Becker E D: Functional magnetic resonance imaging in medicine and physiology. Science *250*: 53, 1990.
Reeve A, Rose D F, Weinberger D R: Magnetoencephalography: Applications in psychiatry. Arch Gen Psychiatry *46*: 573, 1989.
Therapeutics and Technology Assessment Subcommittee of the American Academy of Neurology: Assessment: Magnetoencephalography (MEG). Neurology *42*: 1, 1992.
Warner M D, Boutros N N, Peabody C A: Usefulness of screening EEGs in psychiatric inpatient population. J Clin Psychiatry *51*: 363, 1990.

# 3.3 / Neurophysiology and Neurochemistry

A student of behavior can approach the brain on many conceptual levels. Section 3.1, "Neuroanatomy and Neuropsychiatry," approaches the brain at the level of the whole brain and individual brain areas (for example, the amygdala and the hypothalamus). This section approaches the brain at the level of the neuron. Just as the whole brain or a single brain area can be seen as performing an integrating function, so can an individual neuron be seen as performing an integrating function. An individual neuron receives diverse incoming information, integrates that information, and responds by modulating how often it generates an action potential and how much of which neurotransmitter molecules it releases from its axon terminals. Most neurons receive synaptic input from hundreds or thousands of neurons. In addition to that synaptic input, an individual neuron can be affected by hormones, the immune system, and the chronobiological rhythms of the organism. The study of those three effects are called, respectively, psychoneuroendocrinology, psychoneuroimmunology, and chronobiology and are discussed at the end of this section.

Although it is tempting to stop at the level of the neuron as the smallest integrating mechanism in the brain, there are significant integrating mechanisms within the neurons themselves. Those integrating mechanisms include the regulation of protein function and the regulation of gene expression. Many important molecules within the neuron are proteins, including neurotransmitter receptors, enzymes, and cytoskeletal elements. Inasmuch as the function of a protein is a function of its shape and electric charge, biochemical processes, such as protein phosphorylation, that can affect the shape and charge of a protein can affect its function. Specifically, an individual protein molecule may have its function regulated by several reversible, posttranslational modifications, each having been initiated by a different source—for example, synaptic input, hormonal effects, and chronobiological rhythms. The concept of integration at the level of proteins is discussed in this section, and the concept of the regulation of gene expression is discussed in Section 3.4, "Behavioral Genetics."

## BASIC ELECTROPHYSIOLOGY

In the resting state the intracellular compartment of a neuron is negatively charged in comparison with the extracellular compartment. The difference in electrical potential is produced and maintained by the neuronal membrane itself and by the ion pumps and ion channels contained in the membrane. The principal ion pump is the energy-requiring sodium-potassium exchange pump; the principal ion channels are the sodium, potassium, calcium, and chloride ion channels. The membrane is said to be semipermeable because it is selective regarding which ions can pass through it. The semipermeable property of the membrane is the basis for its functional role, which is similar to the role of a capacitor. The electrical potential of the membrane follows the equation of *Ohm's law*, $E = IR$. In that equation, E is the transmembrane potential, I is the current, and R is the resistance.

### Neuronal Membrane

Phospholipids, organized as a bilayer with the hydrophobic ends of the molecules pointing toward each other, make up the neuronal membrane. Cholesterol and protein molecules can be found within the sea of phospholipids. The cholesterol is believed to regulate membrane rigidity (that is, stiffness). The major types of proteins found in the membranes are neurotransmitter receptors, their related proteins (for example, adenylyl cyclase), and ion channels.

### Action Potentials

In the resting state the intracellular compartment of the neuron is negatively charged, but during an action potential the neuron is positively charged. For an action potential to be generated by a neuron, the inside of the neuron has to become less negatively charged than the outside. The point at which the interior of the neuron is sufficiently less negatively charged is called the *spike threshold* and is characteristically approximately $-55$ mV. Regulation of the neuronal electrical potential is one of the principal effects of some neurotransmitter actions. Specific neurotransmitters have been classified as either inhibitory or excitatory. For example, γ-aminobutyric acid (GABA) is an inhibitory amino acid neurotransmitter, and glutamate is an excitatory amino acid neurotransmitter. The effect of an *inhibitory neurotransmitter* is to make the intracellular compartment of a neuron more negatively charged and, thus, less likely to reach the spike threshold and generate an action potential. The effect of an *excitatory neurotrans-*

*mitter* is to make the intracellular compartment of a neuron less negatively charged and, thus, move the neuronal electrical potential to the spike threshold and more likely to generate an action potential. Inhibitory and excitatory neurotransmitters act through the control or *gating* of ion channels that are selective for either positively charged ions—particularly sodium ($Na^+$), potassium ($K^+$), and calcium ($Ca^{2+}$)—and negatively charged ions, particularly chlorine ($Cl^-$).

The action potential itself is a brief (0.1 to 2 msec) wave of reversal of membrane potential that moves along an axon away from the cell body (Figure 3.3–1). During an action potential the interior of the neuron is positively charged in comparison with the outside of the neuron. The initial ion channel involved in the action potential is the $Na^+$ channel, which, when opened, allows positively charged sodium ions to enter the neuron. The $Ca^{2+}$ channels are next to open, thus allowing the positively charged calcium ions to enter the neuron and further contribute to the spike of the action potential. Not only does the entry of calcium ions affect the membrane potential, but the calcium ion is also an important second-messenger molecule that is involved in initiating additional neuronal processes. Entry of the calcium ion into the synaptic terminal is also critical for the release of neurotransmitter molecules. And calcium ion entry activates ion channels that carry an outgoing flow of potassium ions that are involved in arresting the action potential. The activation of those $K^+$ channels results in the afterhyperpolarization of the neuron after an action potential. During the afterhyperpolarization the inside of the neuron is even more negatively charged than it was at baseline. The afterhyperpolarization contributes to the refractory period of a neuron after an action potential; during that period, another action potential cannot be generated.

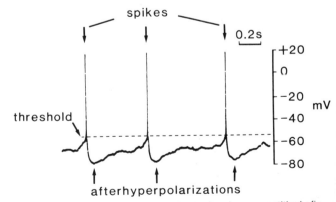

**Figure 3.3–1.** An oscilloscope trace showing a repetitively firing neuron recorded intracellularly in vivo. This example was taken from a serotonergic neuron in the dorsal raphe nucleus of the rat midbrain. As can be seen from the trace, when membrane potential, in millivolts, reaches threshold ($-55$ mV), an all-or-none spike occurs. After each spike an afterhyperpolarization moves the cell away from the threshold into a more negative zone (near $-80$ mV). As the afterhyperpolarization decays, the cell again approaches spike threshold. (Figure from G K Aghajanian, K Rasmussen: Basic electrophysiology. In *Comprehensive Textbook of Psychiatry,* ed 5, H I Kaplan, B J Sadock, editors, p 68. Williams & Wilkins, Baltimore, 1989. Used with permission.)

## Ion Channels

One way to classify ion channels is as ligand-gated or voltage-gated. *Ligand-gated* ion channels are activated by the binding of a neurotransmitter to the ion channel itself or to a physiologically connected molecule. *Voltage-gated* ion channels, also called voltage-sensitive and electrically activated ion channels, are activated by changes in the electrical potential of the neuron. For example, the ion channels described in the generation and the cessation of the action potential are voltage-gated ion channels.

The ion channels themselves are glycoproteins (proteins with sugar moieties) that span the neuronal membrane and contain a pore that can be opened and closed and through which specific ions can flow. The ligand-gated channels are particularly relevant in the study of psychiatry, since many psychotherapeutic and psychoactive drugs affect those channels directly (Table 3.3–1). There are three general types of ligand-gated channels: direct-coupled, G protein-coupled, and second messenger-coupled (Figure 3.3–2). The neurotransmitter acts directly on direct-coupled ligand-gated ion channels. With G protein-coupled ion channels the neurotransmitter acts on its receptor protein, which then activates a G protein, which activates the ion channel. The second messenger-coupled ion channel is activated by a second-messenger product of some physically removed neurotransmitter receptor.

## SYNAPSES

The components of the synapse are the axon terminal of the presynaptic neuron, the synaptic cleft, and the dendrite of the postsynaptic neuron (Figures 3.3–3 and 3.3–4). When an action potential develops in the presynaptic neuron, the action potential moves down the axon to the axon terminal or to other functionally similar regions of the axons called axonal varicosities. The action potential causes calcium ions to enter the axon terminal. The entry of the calcium ions triggers synaptic vesicles that contain neurotransmitter molecules to fuse with the presynaptic membrane, thus releasing their contents of neurotransmitter molecules into the *synaptic cleft*, the small space between the presynaptic neuron and the postsynaptic neuron. The neurotransmitter molecules diffuse across the synaptic cleft and then bind to their specific receptors on the external membrane of the dendrite of the postsynaptic neuron.

The most common type of synapse involves the termination of the presynaptic neuronal axon on the postsynaptic neuronal cell body, an axon, or a dendrite. Those synapses are called axosomatic, axoaxonic, and axodendritic, respectively. Two additional types of synapses are the dendrodendritic and the dendroaxonic. In those synapses the dendrites release the neurotransmitter, and the receptors are either on the dendrites or on the axons. Available basic science data support the hypothesis that those synapses are involved in the local modulation of the synapse, and their existence should not be allowed to cloud the key role of the classic axodendritic and axosomatic synapses.

In addition to the chemical synapses, *electrical synapses,* also called gap junctions, allow the direct transfer of ions between two neurons as a form of intraneuronal neurochemical communication. To complicate matters further, *conjoint synapses* are synapses that have both electrical and chemical characteristics.

## RECEPTORS

Neurotransmitter receptors are the sites of action for virtually all the psychotherapeutic and psychoactive drugs used today. The techniques of molecular biology have led to the identification of many new subtypes of receptors and have allowed investigators to know the specific protein sequences of all the receptors. The importance of those advances lies in the long-standing hypothesis that the ability to subtype receptors would refine both the hunt for

**Table 3.3–1**
**Some Ligand-Gated Ion Channels**

| Neurotransmitter | Receptor Subtype | G Protein or Direct[1] | Ion Channel Activated | Physiological Response[2] |
|---|---|---|---|---|
| Acetylcholine | Nicotinic | D | $Na^+/K^+$ | E |
| | Muscarinic | G | $K^+$ | E |
| Dopamine | $D_2$ | G | $K^+$ | E |
| Norepinephrine | $\alpha_1$ | G | $K^+$ | I |
| | $\alpha_2$ | G | $K^+$ | E |
| | $\beta$ | G | $K^+$ | I |
| Serotonin | $5\text{-}HT_{1}$ | G | $K^+$ | I |
| | $5\text{-}HT_{1C/2}$ | G | $K^+$ | E |
| | $5\text{-}HT_3$ | D | $Na^+/K^+$ | E |
| GABA | $GABA_A$ | D | $Cl^-$ | I |
| Glutamate | AMPA | D | $Na^+/K^+$ | E |
| | Kainate | D | $Na^+/K^+$ | E |
| | NMDA | D | $Ca^{2+}$ | E |
| Opiate | $\mu, \delta$ | G | $K^+$ | I |
| Substance P | - | G | $K^+$ | E |

[1]D—direct-coupled; G—G protein-coupled.
[2]E—excitatory; I—inhibitory.

## A. Direct-coupled

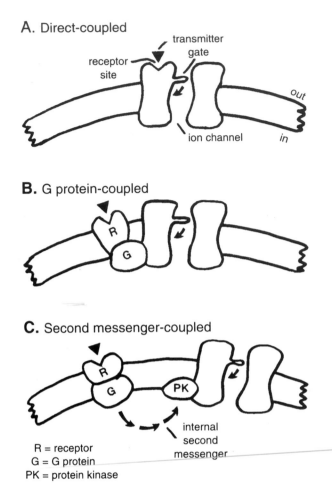

## B. G protein-coupled

## C. Second messenger-coupled

R = receptor
G = G protein
PK = protein kinase

**Figure 3.3–2.** Schematic representation of three forms of coupling that can occur between receptors and ion channel. **A.** Direct coupling, in which the receptor site is located on the protein complex of the ion channel itself. **B.** G protein coupling, in which an intervening G protein (the transducer) links the receptor to the ion channel. **C.** Second-messenger coupling, in which a receptor is linked by a G protein to a second-messenger system (e.g., adenylate cyclase); the second messenger may then interact with the ion channel through a phosphorylation reaction catalyzed by a protein kinase. B and C are not mutually exclusive mechanisms and may occur simultaneously to give rise to a dual form of coupling that can link a receptor to more than one type of channel. (Figure from G K Aghajanian, K Rasmussen: Basic electrophysiology. In *Comprehensive Textbook of Psychiatry*, ed 5, H I Kaplan, B J Sadock, editors, p 70. Williams & Wilkins, Baltimore, 1989. Used with permission.)

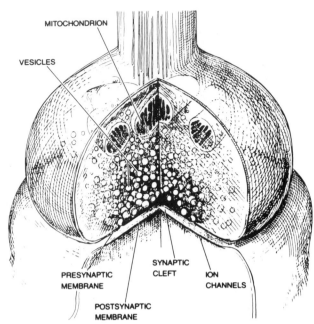

**Figure 3.3–3.** Synapse consists of two parts: the knoblike tip of an axon terminal and the receptor region on the surface of another neuron. The membranes are separated by a synaptic cleft some 20 to 30 nanometers across. Molecules of chemical transmitter, stored in vesicles in the axon terminal, are released into the cleft by arriving nerve impulses and change the electrical state of the receiving neuron, making it either more likely or less likely to fire an impulse. (Figure from C F Stevens: The neuron. In *The Biology of the Brain from Neurons to Networks*, R L Llinás, editor, p 3. Freedman, New York, 1988. Used with permission.)

pathology in disease states and the design of specifically acting drugs.

In a synapse, receptors can be on both the presynaptic neuron and the postsynaptic neuron. The classic function of a presynaptic receptor is to act as a negative feedback loop to the presynaptic neuron. For example, many norepinephrine-releasing neurons have presynaptic $\alpha_2$ receptors, which, when occupied by the released norepinephrine, cause the releasing neuron to decrease or stop the release of norepinephrine. When a presynaptic receptor binds the neurotransmitter of the parent neuron, it is called a *presynaptic homoreceptor*; when a presynaptic receptor binds a different neurotransmitter than that released by the parent neuron, it is called a *presynaptic heteroreceptor*.

Two terms often used in conjunction with receptors are

"supersensitivity" and "subsensitivity." Those terms refer to, respectively, a greater than usual response of the receptor to a constant amount of neurotransmitter and a less than usual response. The sensitivity of a receptor may be due to the number of receptors present, the affinity of the receptor for the neurotransmitter, and the efficiency with which the binding of the neurotransmitter to the receptor is translated into an intraneuronal message. All those steps in receptor function are variable and subject to regulation.

Fundamentally, there are two types of receptors: receptors linked to G proteins and receptors located directly on ion channels. Many of the receptors located directly on ion channels are discussed above and are listed in Table 3.3–1. The biogenic amine receptors, regardless of whether they are associated with G proteins or directly with ion channels, are listed in Table 3.3–2. The receptors that are linked to G proteins all have a characteristic structure, consisting of seven transmembrane domains with the NH₂-terminal end of the protein located extracellularly and the COOH-terminal end of the protein located intracellularly. Moreover, the third intracytoplasmic loop of the receptor tends to be the largest loop. Occasionally, the second intracytoplasmic loop is also fairly large. The first intracytoplasmic loop seems invariably to be the smallest. The length of the COOH-terminal intracytoplasmic tail is variable. The large intracytoplasmic loops and the COOH-tail contain identified or potential sites of phosphorylation, a feature that is involved in the regulation of receptor function.

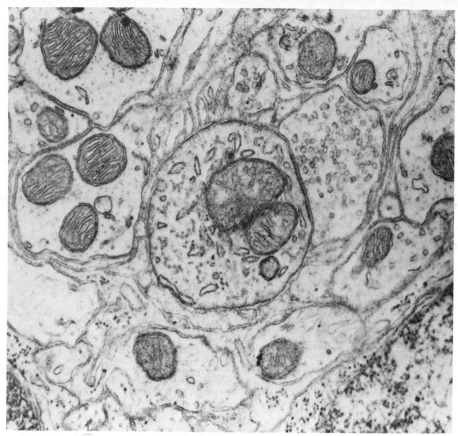

**Figure 3.3–4.** Axoaxonal synapse subverts the classic concept that axons always transmit signals to dendrites or to cell bodies. The large, more or less circular region bounded by cell membrane at the center of the field of view is an axon cut in cross section. In particular, it is the initial segment of the axon of a Purkinje's cell from the cerebellum of a rat. It includes an assortment of intracellular structures, ranging from mitochondria to neurofilaments and occasional ribosomes. Its microtubules are in groups, a characteristic of the initial axon segment. At the right the axon is abutted by an axon terminal: that of a cerebellar basket cell, which is filled with synaptic vesicles. The vesicles are flattened, betokening an inhibitory synapse. (Figure from W J H Nauta, M Feirtag: *Fundamental Neuroanatomy*, p 22. Freeman, New York, 1986. Used with permission.)

## G Proteins

G proteins are a family of guanosine triphosphate (GTP)-binding proteins with similar structures. GTP is interconvertible with guanosine diphosphate (GDP). The G proteins themselves consist of three smaller proteins, called the $\alpha$, $\beta$, and $\gamma$ subunits. When an intact G protein (all three subunits with GDP bound to the $\alpha$ subunit) binds to a receptor, the receptor is converted into a state with a high affinity for the neurotransmitter molecule (Figure 3.3–5). When the neurotransmitter binds to that complex, it triggers the replacement of GDP with GTP on the $\alpha$ subunit, thereby destabilizing the associations among the neurotransmitter, the receptor, and the G protein. The G protein further dissociates into the GTP-binding $\alpha$ subunit and the $\beta\gamma$ subunit, which contains both of those subunits. The GTP-associated $\alpha$ subunit is the active fragment involved in activating or inhibiting a particular effector molecule (for example, adenylyl cyclase, an ion channel). Because the $\alpha$ subunit itself contains the ability to convert GTP to GDP, the activity of the GTP-associated $\alpha$ subunit is stopped when the GTP is converted to GDP. The conversion of GTP to GDP permits the reassociation of the $\alpha$ unit with a $\beta\gamma$ unit.

The family of G proteins is created by the diversity of subunit types that have been identified (Table 3.3–3). The greatest diversity has been found for the $\alpha$ subunit, although an increasing number of reports describe diversity of the $\beta$ and $\gamma$ subunits. The classically described $\alpha$ subunits have been $\alpha_s$, $\alpha_i$, and $\alpha_o$. The $\alpha_s$ subunit has been associated with the stimulation of adenylyl cyclase activity; the $\alpha_i$ subunit has been associated with the inhibition of adenylyl cyclase activity; the $\alpha_o$ subunit has been associated with the stimulation of the phosphoinositol second-messenger system.

## NEUROTRANSMITTERS

For a molecule to be classified as a neurotransmitter, it must meet a number of criteria (Table 3.3–4). Those criteria must usually be met through a variety of basic science and clinical research studies. Some substances, which have been shown to meet a few of the criteria, are referred to as *putative neurotransmitters*, meaning that all the criteria have not been demonstrated as yet.

**Table 3.3–2**
**Receptor Subtypes for Biogenic Amine Neurotransmitters**

| Neurotransmitter | Receptor Subtype | G/I[1] | Effector Mechanism[2] |
|---|---|---|---|
| Acetylcholine | $M_1$ | G | $IP_3$/DG, increase cGMP |
| | $M_2$ | G | Decrease cAMP, increase $K^+$ conductance |
| | $M_3$ | G | $IP_3$/DG, increase cGMP |
| | $M_4$ | G | Decrease cAMP |
| | Nicotinic | I | $Na^+$/$K^+$ |
| Dopamine | $D_1$ | G | Increase cAMP |
| | $D_2$ | G | Decrease cAMP, increase $K^+$ conductance |
| | $D_3$ | G | ?Decrease cAMP |
| | $D_4$ | G | ?Decrease cAMP |
| | $D_5$ | G | Increase cAMP |
| Epinephrine and Norepinephrine | $\alpha_{1a, b, and c}$ | G | $IP_3$/DG |
| | $\alpha_{2a, b, and c}$ | G | Decrease cAMP, increase $K^+$ conductance |
| | $\beta_{1, 2, and 3}$ | G | Increase cAMP |
| Histamine | $H_1$ | G | $IP_3$/DG |
| | $H_2$ | G | Increase cAMP |
| | $H_3$ | ? | ? |
| Serotonin | $5-HT_{1A}$ | G | Decrease cAMP, increase $K^+$ conductance |
| | $5-HT_{1B}$ | G | Decrease cAMP |
| | $5-HT_{1C}$ | G | $IP_3$/DG |
| | $5-HT_{1D}$ | G | Increase cAMP |
| | $5-HT_2$ | G | $IP_3$/DG |
| | $5-HT_3$ | I | $Na^+$/$K^+$ |
| | $5-HT_4$ | G | Increase cAMP |

[1]G—G protein-linked; I—direct linkage to an ion channel.
[2]$IP_3$—stimulation of phosphoinositol turnover, resulting in an increase in the concentrations of inositol triphosphate and diacylglycerol.

## Chemical Neurotransmission

Chemical neurotransmission is the process involving the release of a neurotransmitter by one neuron and the binding of that neurotransmitter molecule to a receptor on another neuron. The process of chemical neurotransmission is affected by most drugs used in psychiatry. All antipsychotics, with the exception of clozapine (Clozaril), are believed to have their effects by blocking dopamine type 2 ($D_2$) receptors; virtually all antidepressants are believed to have their effects by increasing the amount of serotonin or norepinephrine or both in the synaptic cleft; and almost all anxiolytics are believed to have their effects on the $GABA_A$ receptors that are linked to chloride ion channels.

**Neuromodulators and neurohormones.** The most common word used to denote the chemical signals that flow between neurons is "neurotransmitter," although the words "neuromodulators" and "neurohormones" are also used in some cases to emphasize specific characteristics. In contrast to the characteristically immediate and short-lived effects of a neurotransmitter, a neuromodulator substance, as the name implies, modulates the response of a neuron to a neurotransmitter. The modulatory effect may be present for a longer time than it is usual for a neurotransmitter molecule to be present. Thus, a neuromodulating substance may have an effect on a neuron over a long period of time, and that effect may be more involved with tuning than with activating or directly inhibiting the neuron. A neurohormone is distinguished by the fact that it is released into the bloodstream, rather than into the extraneuronal space in the brain. Once in the bloodstream, the neurohormone can then reenter the extraneuronal space and have its effects on neurons.

**Dale-Feldberg law.** As originally stated, the Dale-Feldberg law held that the same neurotransmitter substance is released by all the processes of a single neuron. A recent observation is that neurotransmitters coexist within a single neuron. The most common pairing is a biogenic amine neurotransmitter (for example, dopamine) and a peptide neurotransmitter (for example, cholecystokinin). Some neurons have even more than two neurotransmitters coexisting within their axon terminals. Currently available data suggest that the Dale-Feldberg law still holds and that, in neurons with multiple neurotransmitters, the same neurotransmitters are released from all the processes of a single neuron. What is still poorly understood is whether the amount released of one neurotransmitter or the other is regulated and, if so, what the mechanism of that differential regulation is.

**Classification.** The three major types of neurotransmitters in the brain are the biogenic amines, the amino acids, and the peptides (Figure 3.3–6). The biogenic amines are the best known and most understood neurotransmitters because they were the first to be discovered. However, they constitute the neurotransmitter substance in only a few percentage of neurons. The amino acid neurotransmitters were late in being discovered, principally because of the difficulty in differentiating amino acids present in most proteins from the same amino acids acting separately as neurotransmitters. The amino acid neurotransmitters are present in upward of 70 percent of neurons. The peptide neurotransmitters are intermediate in terms of the percentage of neurons that contain a peptide neurotransmitter but far surpass the other two categories in the sheer number (about 200 to 300) of peptide neurotransmitters that have been putatively identified. The

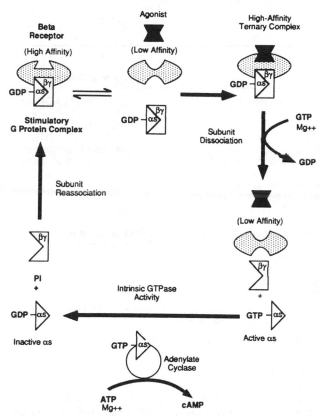

**Figure 3.3–5.** Mechanisms of G protein activation-deactivation. At rest an equilibrium exists between the receptor in the high-affinity state (coupled to the G protein) and the receptor in the low-affinity state. Activation of receptors by an agonist induces a conformational change in the receptor, allowing it to interact with the G protein, and forms a short-lived high-affinity ternary complex consisting of those components. The receptor-G protein interaction facilitates the replacement of GDP by GTP on the guanine nucleotide site (on the α subunit of the G protein). Binding of guanine nucleotides to the G protein causes a destabilization of the high-affinity complex and a dissociation of the G protein into α-GTP and βγ subunits. For most effector systems, the α-GTP complex activates the enzyme or ion channel. The continued activation is terminated by the action of a GTPase enzyme intrinsic to the α subunit, which hydrolyzes GTP to GDP; the reassociation of GDP-α with βγ completes the cycle with the formation of the inactive G protein. (Figure from H K Manji: G proteins: Implications for psychiatry. Am J Psychiatry *149:* 749, 1992. Used with permission.)

full neurotransmitter criteria have been met for only a few of those peptides at this time. Nevertheless, the evidence indicating that the putative peptide neurotransmitters are, in fact, neurotransmitters is generally robust.

BIOGENIC AMINE NEUROTRANSMITTERS. The six biogenic amine neurotransmitters are dopamine, norepinephrine, epinephrine, serotonin, acetylcholine, and histamine (Figure 3.3–6). Dopamine, epinephrine, and norepinephrine are all synthesized from the same amino acid precursor, tyrosine, and are classified as a group as the catecholamines. Serotonin is synthesized from the amino acid precursor tryptophan and is the only indolamine in the group. Serotonin is also known as 5-hydroxytryptamine (5-HT). Therefore, the abbreviation for serotonin is often written as 5-HT. A common feature of all the biogenic amine neurotransmitters is that they are synthesized in the axon terminal. The enzymes necessary for their

synthesis are synthesized in the cell body but are transported down the axon, so that the actual production of the neurotransmitter occurs at the site of its release. As a result of that design, the supply of the biogenic amines is readily replenished on release, in contrast to the peptide neurotransmitters, which must be made in the cell body and transported down to the axon terminals.

AMINO ACID NEUROTRANSMITTERS. Amino acids are best known as the building blocks of proteins. However, some amino acids also serve as neurotransmitters. The two major amino acid neurotransmitters are γ-aminobutyric acid (GABA) and glutamate. GABA is an inhibitory amino acid, and glutamate is an excitatory amino acid. It is occasionally suggested that a simplified way to look at the brain is as a balance between just those two neurotransmitters, with all the biogenic amine and peptide neurotransmitters simply involved in modulating that balance. Recent discoveries have further increased the importance of the study of amino acid neurotransmitters. Those discoveries include the observations that the benzodiazepines act primarily through GABAergic mechanisms and that an important substance of abuse, phencyclidine (PCP), acts at glutamate receptors. Those observations have led to an intensive study of those receptors with regard to major psychiatric disorders, such as anxiety disorders and schizophrenia.

PEPTIDE NEUROTRANSMITTERS. Peptides are made of short chains of amino acids; thus, peptides are short proteins. Arbitrarily, chains of fewer than 100 amino acids are usually considered peptides, and longer chains are considered proteins. Peptides differ from the other two major types of neurotransmitters in that peptides must be made in the cell body, where the genetic information for making them resides. Peptide neurotransmitters are usually first synthesized as longer forms called preprohormones and are further processed during their transport to the axon terminals. First, the preprohormones are cleaved to make prohormones; then the prohormones are cleaved to make the final hormones. Unlike the biogenic amine neurotransmitters, replenishing released neuroactive peptides takes a comparably long time. Peptide neurotransmitters may have a longer duration of action than either biogenic amine neurotransmitters or amino acid neurotransmitters. In that sense, peptide neurotransmitters may serve a neuromodulatory role at some synapses. In addition to cleavage of the long forms to make the final forms of the peptides, other posttranslational modifications can modify the structure and the function of the peptides. Those posttranslational modifications include such biochemical reactions as phosphorylation, glycosylation, sulfation, disulfide bond formation, and COOH-terminal amidation.

**Other types.** The many advances in basic science research have led to the identification of substances that seem to act as neurotransmitters but that do not fit into one of the above standard categories. Three of the molecules about which a fair amount is known are nitric oxide, adenosine, and adenosine triphosphate (ATP). A fourth area of interest is in the identification of the sigma receptors, for which an endogenous ligand is assumed, although such a ligand has not yet been found.

SIGMA RECEPTORS. Only recently has the site now known as the sigma receptor been distinguished from the phencyclidine (PCP) receptor. For many years, there was a confusion among scientists because the benzomorphan opioids (for example, pentazocine [Talwin]) and PCP seemed to share the same receptor site. It is now clear that the principal site of

**Table 3.3–3**
**Key Features of G Protein Subunits**

| Subunit | Toxin Targeting Subunit (Cholera or Pertussis) | Effectors[1] | Examples of Receptors |
|---|---|---|---|
| $G\alpha_s$ (four types) | Cholera | AC($^+$); L-type $Ca^{+2}$ channels ($^+$) | $\beta_1$, $\beta_2$, $D_1$, $A_2$, $H_2$, ACTH, CRH, $V_2$, $PGE_1$ |
| $G_{s,olf}$ | Cholera | AC (+) | Olfactory signals |
| $G\alpha$ (three types) | Pertussis | AC (−); $K^+$ channels (+) | $\alpha_2$, $D_2$, $A_1$, $\mu$, $M_2$, 5-$HT_{1A}$ |
| $G\alpha_{t,r}$ | Both | Cyclic GMP phosphodiesterase ($^+$) | Retinal rods (rhodopsins) |
| $G\alpha_{t,c}$ | Both | Cyclic GMP phosphodiesterase (+) | Retinal cones (rhodopsins) |
| $G\alpha_o$ (two types) | Pertussis | $K^+$ channels (+); $Ca^{+2}$ channels (−); PLC (+) (sensitive to pertussis toxin) | $\alpha_2$, $\mu$, $GABA_B$ |
| $G\alpha_z$ | Neither | PLC (+)[2] (insensitive to pertussis toxin) | Unknown |
| $G_q$, $G_{11}$, $G_{14}$ | Neither | PLC (+) (insensitive to pertussis toxin) | Thromboxane $A_2$, vasopressin |
| $\beta$ (four types) | Neither | Direct interaction with AC (−)[c]; inactivates $\alpha_s$ | |
| $\gamma$ (three types) | Neither | $\beta\gamma$ required for interaction of $\alpha$ subunit with receptor | |

[1]AC—adenylyl cyclase, PLC—phospholipase C, +—stimulatory effects of subunit on effector,—inhibitory effect.
[2]Finding uncertain.
Table from H K Manji: G proteins: Implications for psychiatry. Am J Psychiatry *149*: 748, 1992. Used with permission.

**Table 3.3–4**
**Criteria for a Neurotransmitter**

1. The molecule is synthesized in the neuron.
2. The molecule is present in the presynaptic neuron and is released on depolarization in physiologically significant amounts.
3. When administered exogenously as a drug, the exogenous molecule mimics the effects of the endogenous neurotransmitter.
4. A mechanism exists in the neurons or the synaptic cleft for the removal or the deactivation of the neurotransmitter.

action for PCP is the N-methyl-D-aspartate (NMDA) glutamate receptor, where PCP binding results in an indirect inhibition of calcium ion influx. It is also now clear that there is a distinct set of sigma receptors. Although drugs that bind to the sigma receptors have been identified, the endogenous ligand for the receptors has not been identified.

Among the drugs that bind with high affinity to the sigma receptors are haloperidol (Haldol) and remoxipride. Remoxipride is being developed as an antipsychotic drug and appears to be associated with less extrapyramidal adverse effects than are currently available antipsychotics, other than clozapine. Recently, at least two subtypes of sigma receptors have been suggested, and basic researchers are actively synthesizing and testing novel sigma antagonists as potential antipsychotic agents.

NITRIC OXIDE. The recent discovery that the gas nitric oxide (NO) apparently serves both as an intraneuronal second messenger and as a neurotransmitter has been one of the most interesting discoveries in neuroscience. NO is formed from the amino acid arginine by the actions of NO synthase (NOS). One of the first observations regarding the effects of NO was its role as an endothelial-derived relaxing factor. When acetylcholine acts on receptors on the endothelium, NO is formed in the endothelial cells and then diffuses to the adjacent smooth muscle, in which it causes an increase in the concentration of cyclic guanosine monophosphate (cGMP) and the relaxation of the muscle.

NO and NOS have been described in the brain. NOS can be found in specific, discrete regions of the brain, particularly in the striatum, the hypothalamus, the basal forebrain, and the cerebellum. The best understood pathway resulting in the generation of NO starts at the NMDA receptor subtype of glutamate. Activation of that receptor allows calcium to enter the neuron, thereby activating a variety of calcium-mediated events. One of the calcium-mediated events is the activation of NOS and the generation of NO. NO then acts on the iron molecule contained in guanylyl cyclase and results in the formation of cGMP, a potent second-messenger molecule. Data suggest that NO can diffuse to adjacent neurons, in which it can then result in cGMP formation in neighboring neurons.

NO is an unusual putative neurotransmitter. It is not stored in synaptic vesicles. It is not necessarily released only on depolarization. Its receptors are the iron molecule and perhaps other reactive metals. Nevertheless, inhibitors of NOS may be useful in reducing ischemic damage after a cerebrovascular disease. Other experimental data suggest that NO is involved in learning and memory.

ADENOSINE AND ADENOSINE TRIPHOSPHATE. Adenosine is a purine, and adenosine triphosphate (ATP) is synthesized from adenosine. Receptors for purines have been found in the brain. $P_1$ receptors have a high affinity for adenosine, and $P_2$ receptors have a high affinity for ATP. Subtypes of $P_1$ and $P_2$ receptors may also exist. The $P_1$ receptors are blocked by xanthines, such as caffeine and theophylline. Two subtypes of the $P_1$ receptor are the adenosine $A_1$ and $A_2$ receptors, both of which are G protein-linked receptors. Adenosine is concentrated in discrete regions of the brain and appears to have the general effect of inhibiting the release of most other neurotransmitters. That characteristic has led to various research efforts to study adenosine analogues for use as anticonvulsants or sedatives. ATP itself may also serve as a neurotransmitter. It is stored in synaptic vesicles along with catecholamines and is released when the catecholamines are released. It prefer-

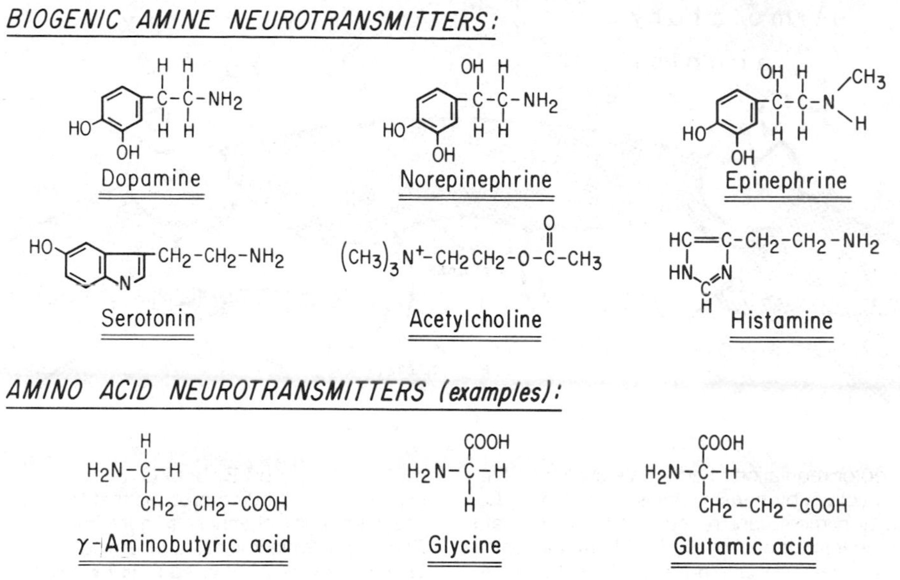


*PEPTIDE NEUROTRANSMITTERS (examples):*

*NEUROTENSIN:*

Glu-Leu-Tyr-Glu-Asn-Lys-Pro-Arg-Arg-Pro-Tyr-Ile-Leu

*THYROTROPIN-RELEASING HORMONE (TRH):*

Glu-His-Pro

*CHOLECYSTOKININ OCTAPEPTIDE (CCK-8):*

Asp-Tyr-Met-Gly-Trp-Met-Asp-Phe

**Figure 3.3–6.** The three classes of neurotransmitters.

entially acts on $P_2$ receptors, and data show that at least one function of ATP is the excitatory activation of $Na^+$-$K^+$ and $Ca^{2+}$ ion channels.

## Signal Transduction

Whereas chemical neurotransmission refers more or less strictly to the steps occurring within the synaptic cleft, the term "signal transduction" refers to those steps preceding neurotransmitter release in the presynaptic neuron and to those steps after neurotransmitter binding to receptors in the postsynaptic neuron. The principal overall processes of signal transduction are (1) the conversion of an electrical signal (that is, the action potential) in the presynaptic neuron into a chemical signal (that is, neurotransmitter release) and (2) the conversion of a chemical signal (that is, the neurotransmitter-receptor interaction) into an electrical signal. The fundamental steps of signal transduction involve the production of so-called second-messenger molecules and their subsequent activation of a class of enzymes known as the protein kinases.

**Second messengers.** The neurotransmitters themselves are conceptualized as the first messengers that bring a signal to a neuron. For the neuron to act on the signal, the first-messenger signal must be translated into an intraneuronal signal. That process is achieved by a cascade of messenger steps. The first of the steps is the formation of a second-messenger molecule. The most classic second messengers are the cyclic nucleotides (cyclic adenosine monophosphate [cAMP] and cGMP), the calcium ion ($Ca^{2+}$), and the phosphoinositol metabolites (inositol triphosphate [$IP_3$] and diacylglycerol [DAG]). Another increasingly appreciated class of second messengers are the eicosanoid metabolites. Novel molecules, such as NO, may serve as intraneuronal second-messenger molecules.

CYCLIC NUCLEOTIDES. Cyclic AMP is produced from ATP by the enzyme adenylyl cyclase (Figure 3.3–7). Adenylyl cyclase is linked to receptors by G proteins. The G protein $G_s$ stimulates the activity of adenylyl cyclase, and the G protein $G_i$ inhibits the activity of adenylyl cyclase. Once formed, cAMP has its biological effects; then the cAMP activity is terminated by its conversion into $5^1$-AMP by phosphodiesterase. An exactly analogous pathway is involved in the formation of cGMP, only the involved enzyme is guanylyl cyclase.

CALCIUM. Calcium, as a second messenger, can come from two sources. First, calcium can enter the cell through either voltage-gated or ligand-gated ion channels. Second, calcium can be released from intraneuronal stores by the action of a phosphoinositol metabolite, $IP_3$. Calcium can act either alone as a second messenger or in tandem with a variety of calcium-binding proteins (for example, calmodulin). The intraneuronal calcium ion concentration is very low ($10^{-7}$M), compared with its extraneuronal concentrations ($10^{-3}$M), and very small increases in the intraneuronal calcium concentration can have profound biological effects.

PHOSPHOINOSITOL METABOLITES. In a manner analogous to adenylyl cyclase, another receptor-activated enzyme, phospholipase C, converts a membrane lipid, phosphatidylinositol 4,5-bisphosphate, into two active metabolites, $IP_3$ and DAG (Figure 3.3–8). As mentioned above, the major effect of $IP_3$ is to cause the release of calcium from intraneuronal stores of calcium in the endoplasmic reticulum. The major activity of DAG is to activate a specific protein kinase.

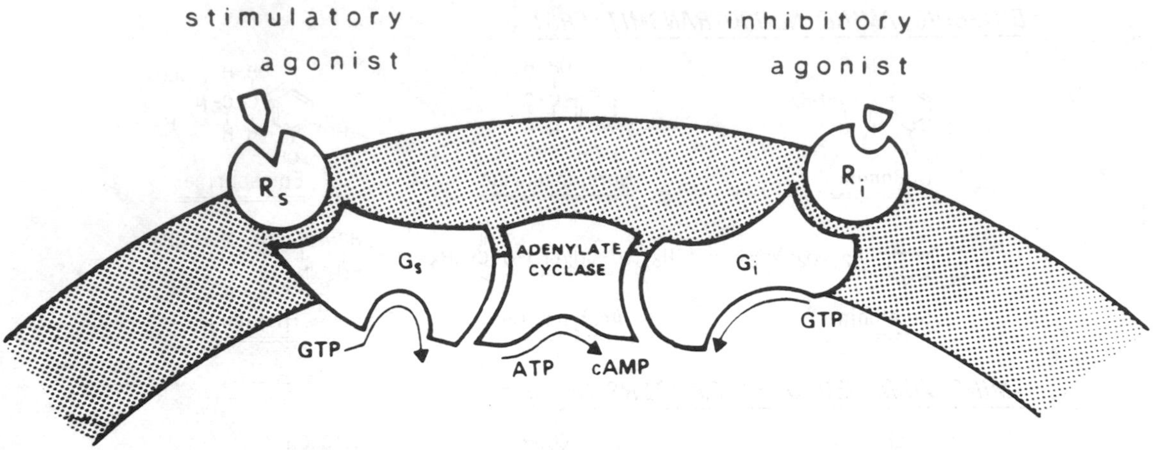

stimulatory          inhibitory

agonist              agonist

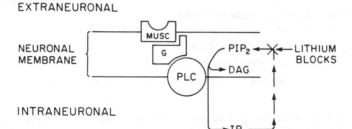

**Figure 3.3–7.** Receptor regulation of adenylate cyclase. Stimulation of adenylate cyclase by transmitters is mediated by $G_s$, which couples stimulatory membrane receptors ($R_s$) to adenylate cyclase, enhancing the formation of cyclic AMP from adenosine triphosphate (ATP). Activation of another set of membrane receptors ($R_i$), such as $\alpha_2$-adrenergic receptors by clonidine (Catapres) or $\mu$ opiate receptors by morphine, inhibits adenylate cyclase activity by $G_i$. Both $G_s$ and $G_i$ are members of a larger group of GTP-binding proteins that link membrane receptors to enzymes or ion channels. (Figure from J M Baraban, J T Coyle: Receptors, monamines, and amino acids. In *Comprehensive Textbook of Psychiatry,* ed 5, H I Kaplan, B J Sadock, editors, p 47. Williams & Wilkins, Baltimore, 1989. Used with permission.)

EXTRANEURONAL

NEURONAL
MEMBRANE

INTRANEURONAL

**Figure 3.3–8.** Schematic representation of the phosphatidylinositol second-messenger system. The muscarinic acetylcholine receptor provides one example of how a neurotransmitter can regulate the production of inositol triphosphate ($IP_3$) and diacylglycerol (DAG). When the muscarinic receptor (MUSC) is stimulated by acetylcholine, phospholipase C (PLC) is activated by the activity of an as-yet-unidentified G protein (G). Phospholipase C catalyzes the conversion of membrane-bound $PIP_2$ into $IP_3$ and DAG. $IP_3$ causes the release of calcium ions from endoplasmic reticulum. DAG is involved in the activation of protein kinase C. DAG is inactivated by DAG kinase. $IP_3$ is recycled back into $PIP_2$ by a series of enzymatic steps, the last of which is catalyzed by inositol-1-phosphatase. Lithium blocks the activity of inositol-1-phosphatase, and that effect may be the basis for the therapeutic effects of lithium in mood disorders. (Figure from J A Grebb, M D Browning: Intraneuronal biochemical signals. In *Comprehensive Textbook of Psychiatry,* ed 5, H I Kaplan, B J Sadock, editors, p 62. Williams & Wilkins, Baltimore, 1989. Used with permission.)

EICOSANOIDS. In a manner analogous to phospholipase C, another receptor-activated enzyme, phospholipase $A_2$, converts membrane phospholipids into free arachidonic acid. Arachidonic acid can then be cleaved by cyclo-oxygenase and other enzymes to produce a wide array of second-messenger molecules, including several types of prostaglandins, cyclic endoperoxides (for example, prostacyclins and thromboxanes), and leukotrienes. Those three classes of molecules have a variety of second-messenger activities that are the subject of many ongoing basic science investigations.

**Protein phosphorylation.** One of the primary activities of the second-messenger molecules is to activate a class of molecules known as the protein kinases. *Protein kinases* catalyze the transfer of the terminal phosphate group of ATP onto protein molecules (Figure 3.3–9). Each of the second-messenger molecules is associated with the activation of a specific protein kinase (Table 3.3–5). Four protein kinases (cAMP-dependent protein kinase [PKA],

cGMP-dependent protein kinase [PKG], calcium/calmodulin-dependent protein kinase [CaMK], and calcium/phosphatidylserine-dependent protein kinase, also known as protein kinase C [PKC]) phosphorylate proteins on serine and threonine residues. Another class of protein kinases, the tyrosine-specific protein kinases, phosphorylate proteins on tyrosine residues. Little is known about how tyrosine kinases are activated.

Protein phosphorylation is the best-studied example of how a reversible, posttranslational modification of a protein can change the function of the protein. Protein phosphorylation is reversible by the activities of another class of enzymes, the protein phosphatases, that remove the phosphate group from the protein (Figure 3.3–9). The addition or the deletion of the negatively charged phosphate group changes the charge and can change the shape of the protein molecule. That change in charge and shape can affect the function of the protein and essentially serves

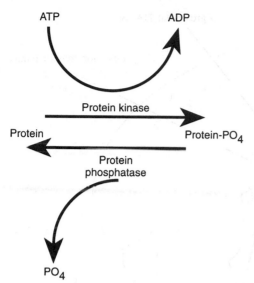

**Figure 3.3–9.** General model of protein phosphorylation. A protein kinase catalyzes the transfer of the terminal phosphate group (PO₄) of adenosine triphosphate (ATP) onto a substrate protein. A protein phosphatase catalyzes the removal of the phosphate group from the protein. (Courtesy of Jack A Grebb, M.D.)

as a molecular on-off switch for the function of the protein. Moreover, proteins are usually phosphorylated on multiple sites by different protein kinases; therefore, fine adjustment of the function of the protein is possible, in addition to simply turning the protein on or off. An example of regulation by phosphorylation is the β-adrenergic receptor. The sensitivity of that receptor to its ligand is regulated by the state of the receptor's phosphorylation.

## BIOGENIC AMINES

### Dopamine

**CNS dopaminergic tracts.** The three most important dopaminergic tracts for psychiatry are the nigrostriatal tract, the mesolimbic-mesocortical tract, and the tuberoinfundibular tract (Figure 3.3–10). The *nigrostriatal tract* projects from its cell bodies in the substantia nigra to the corpus striatum. When the dopamine receptors at the end of that tract are blocked by classic antipsychotic drugs, the parkinsonian side effects of those drugs are the result. In Parkinson's disease the nigrostriatal tract degenerates, resulting in the motor symptoms of the disease. Because of

the significant association between Parkinson's disease and depression, the nigrostriatal tract may somehow be involved with the control of mood, in addition to its classic role in motor control.

The *mesolimbic-mesocortical tract* projects from its cell bodies in the ventral tegmental area (VTA), which lies adjacent to the substantia nigra, to most areas of the cerebral cortex and the limbic system. Because the tract projects to the limbic system and the neocortex, the tract may be involved in mediating the antipsychotic effects of antipsychotic drugs.

The cell bodies of the *tuberoinfundibular tract* are in the arcuate nucleus and the periventricular area of the hypothalamus and project to the infundibulum and the anterior pituitary. Dopamine acts as a release-inhibiting factor in the tract by inhibiting the release of prolactin from the anterior pituitary. Patients who take antipsychotic drugs have elevated prolactin levels because the blockade of dopamine receptors in the tract eliminates the inhibitory effect of dopamine.

**Dopaminergic synapse.** The dopaminergic axon terminal is the site of synthesis for dopamine. Dopamine is one of the three catecholamine neurotransmitters that is synthesized by starting with the amino acid tyrosine. The other two catecholamine neurotransmitters are norepinephrine and epinephrine (Figure 3.3–11). The rate-limiting enzymatic step in the synthesis of any of the catecholamines is tyrosine hydroxylase. Tyrosine hydroxylase is a phosphoprotein—that is, subject to regulation by a range of protein kinases and protein phosphatases. Once dopamine is produced, it is taken up by synaptic vesicles and then released into the synaptic cleft on depolarization of the axon terminal.

The actions of dopamine are terminated by two general routes: First, dopamine can be taken back up into the presynaptic neuron and recycled as a neurotransmitter; that pathway is generally referred to as the *uptake* mechanism, although it is also referred to as the somewhat misleading *reuptake* mechanism. Second, dopamine can be metabolized (Figure 3.3–12). The two major enzymes involved in the metabolism of dopamine are monoamine oxidase (MAO) and catechol-*O*-methyltransferase (COMT). MAO is an intraneuronal enzyme, and COMT is an extraneuronal enzyme. When dopamine is metabolized extraneuronally by COMT, the resulting metabolites are then taken back into the neuron and further metabolized by MAO. The two types of MAO are MAO_A and MAO_B, and MAO_B selectively metabolizes dopamine. The primary metabolite of dopamine is homovanillic acid (HVA), and many research studies of cerebrospinal fluid, urine, and

**Table 3.3–5**
**Second-Messenger Activation of Protein Kinases**

| Second Messenger | Associated Activators | Protein Kinase |
|---|---|---|
| cAMP | None | cAMP-dependent protein kinase |
| cGMP | None | cGMP-dependent protein kinase |
| Calcium | Calmodulin | Calcium/calmodulin-dependent protein kinase |
| Diacylglycerol | Calcium Phosphatidylserine | Calcium/phosphatidylserine-dependent protein kinase (also known as protein kinase C) |
| Unknown | Unknown | Tyrosine-specific protein kinases |

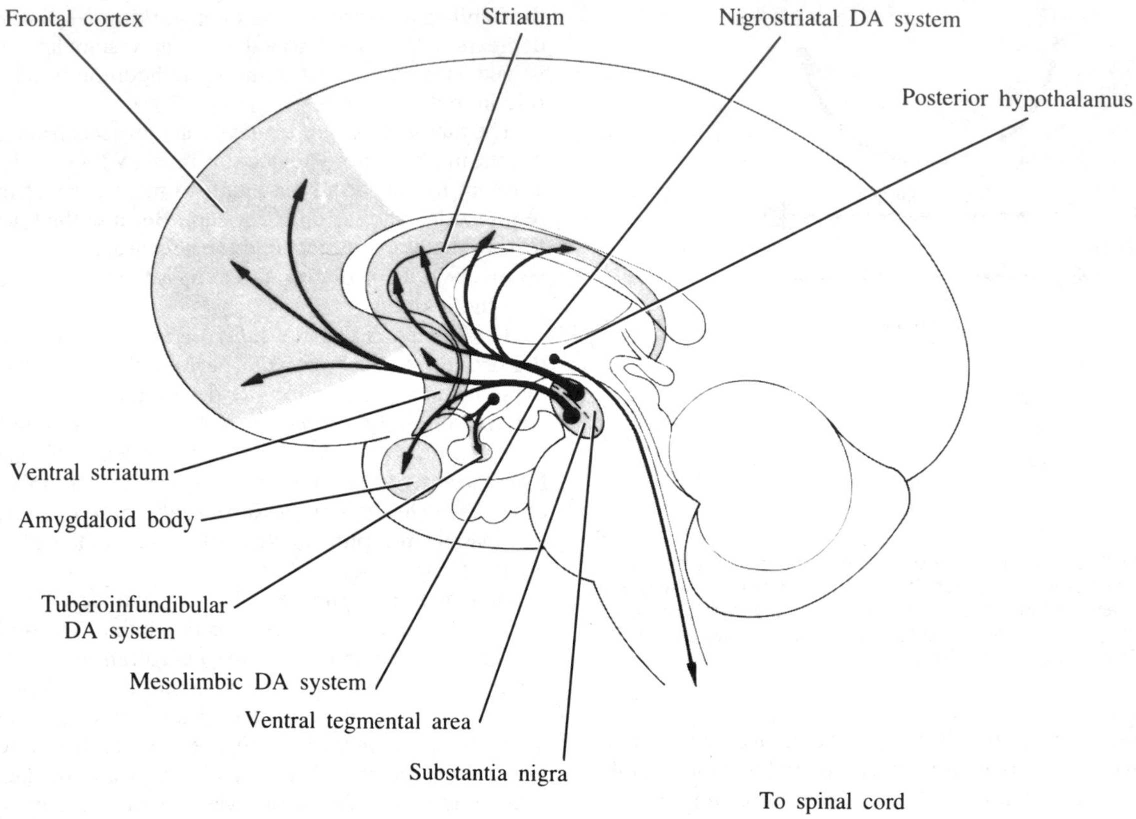

**Figure 3.3–10.** Dopaminergic (DA) pathways. The nigrostriatal DA system originates in the substantia nigra and terminates in the main dorsal part of the striatum. The ventral tegmental area gives rise to the mesolimbic DA system, which terminates in the ventral striatum, the amygdaloid body, the frontal lobe, and some other basal forebrain areas. The tuberoinfundibular system innervates the median eminence and the posterior and intermediate lobes of the pituitary, and dopamine neurons in the posterior hypothalamus project to the spinal cord. (Figure from L Heimer: *The Human Brain and Spinal Cord*. Springer, New York, 1983. Used with permission.)

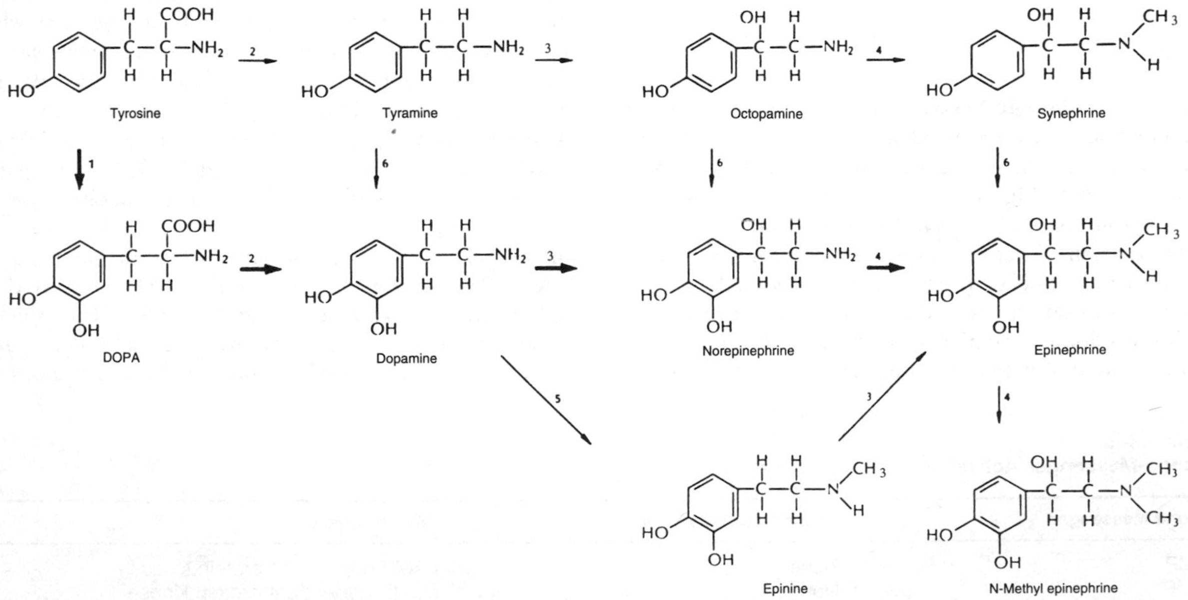

**Figure 3.3–11.** Primary and alternative pathways in the formation of catecholamine: (I) tyrosine hydroxylase; (2) aromatic amino acid decarboxylase; (3) dopamine-β-hydroxylase; (4) phenylethanolamine-*N*-methyltransferase; (5) nonspecific *N*-methyltransferase in lung and folate-dependent *N*-methyltransferase in brain; (6) catechol-forming enzyme. (Figure from J R Cooper, F E Bloom, R H Roth: *The Biochemical Basis of Neuropharmacology*, ed 6, p 225. Oxford University Press, New York, 1991. Used with permission.)

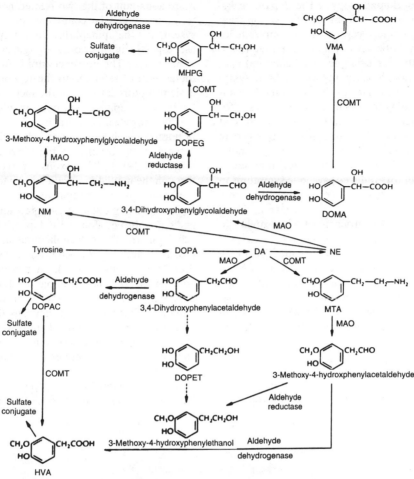

**Figure 3.3–12.** Dopamine and norepinephrine metabolism. DOPA—dihydroxyphenylalanine; DA—dopamine; NE—norepinephrine; DOMA—3,4-dihydroxymandelic acid; DOPAC—3,4-dihydroxyphenylacetic acid; DOPEG—3,4-dihydroxyphenylglycol; DOPET—3,4-dihydroxyphenylethanol; MOPET—3-methoxy-4-hydroxyphenylethanol; MHPG—3-methoxy-4-hydroxyphenylglycol; HVA—homovanillic acid; VMA—3-methoxy-4-hydroxy-mandelic acid; NM—normetanephrine; MTA—3-methoxytyramine; MAO—monoamine oxidase; COMT—catechol-O-methyltransferase. Dashed arrows indicate steps that have not been firmly established. (Figure from J R Cooper, F E Bloom, R H Roth: *The Biological Basis of Neuropharmacology*, ed 6, p 245. Oxford University Press, New York, 1991. Used with permission.)

serum attempt to assess central nervous system (CNS) dopamine activity by measuring concentrations of HVA.

**Dopamine receptors.** The five subtypes of dopamine receptors are listed in Table 3.3–2. The five subtypes can be put into two groups. In the first group the $D_1$ and $D_5$ receptors stimulate the formulation of cAMP by activating the stimulatory G protein, $G_s$. The $D_5$ receptor has only recently been discovered, and less is known about it than about the $D_1$ receptor. One difference between those two receptors is that the $D_5$ receptor has a much higher affinity for dopamine than does the $D_1$ receptor. The second group of dopamine receptors is made up of the $D_2$, $D_3$, and $D_4$ receptors. The $D_2$ receptor inhibits the formation of cAMP by activating the inhibitory G protein, $G_i$, and some data indicate that the $D_3$ and $D_4$ receptors act similarly. One of the differences among the $D_2$, $D_3$, and $D_4$ receptors is their differential distribution. The $D_3$ receptor is especially concentrated in the nucleus accumbens, in addition to other regions, and the $D_4$ receptor is especially concentrated in the frontal cortex, in addition to other regions. In the past the potency of antipsychotic compounds has been corre-

lated with their affinity for the $D_2$ receptor. It is now possible to study whether specific antagonists of the $D_3$ or $D_4$ receptors would be more effective antipsychotics with fewer adverse effects than are the antagonists of the $D_2$ receptor.

**Dopamine and drugs.** Since blockade of dopamine receptors, particularly the $D_2$ receptor, has been associated with the efficacy of antipsychotic drugs, long-term administration of dopamine receptor antagonists results in an up-regulation in the number of dopamine receptors present. That up-regulation may be involved in the development of tardive dyskinesia. Other substances that affect the dopamine system are amphetamine and cocaine. Amphetamine causes the release of dopamine, and cocaine blocks the uptake of dopamine. Thus, both substances increase the amount of dopamine present in the synapse. Cocaine and especially the related substance of abuse, crack, are perhaps the most addicting substances. The dopaminergic systems may be particularly involved in the brain's so-called reward system, and that involvement may explain the high addiction potential of cocaine.

**Dopamine and psychopathology.** The *dopamine hypothesis of schizophrenia* grew from the observations that drugs that block dopamine receptors (for example, haloperidol) have antipsychotic activity and drugs that stimulate dopamine activity (for example, amphetamine) can, when given in high enough doses, induce psychotic symptoms in nonschizophrenic persons. The dopamine hypothesis remains the leading neurochemical hypothesis for schizophrenia. A recent series of studies showed that plasma concentrations of HVA are, in fact, reduced in many schizophrenic patients who respond to antipsychotic drugs. A major problem with the hypothesis is that blockade of dopamine receptors reduces psychotic symptoms in virtually any disorder, such as psychosis associated with a brain tumor and psychosis associated with mania. Thus, some as yet unrecognized neurochemical abnormality in schizophrenia may be unique to the condition.

Dopamine may also be involved in the pathophysiology of mood disorders. Dopamine activity may be low in depression and high in mania. The observation that L-dopa can cause mania and psychosis in some parkinsonian patients supports the hypothesis. Some studies have found low levels of dopamine metabolites in depressed patients.

### Norepinephrine and Epinephrine

Although norepinephrine and epinephrine are discussed together, norepinephrine is the more important and more abundant of the two related neurotransmitters. The terminology can be confusing, since the norepinephrine system and the epinephrine system are usually referred to as, respectively, the noradrenergic system and the adrenergic system. The nomenclature is further confounded by the custom of referring to the receptors simply as adrenergic receptors, in spite of the fact that they are receptors for both epinephrine and norepinephrine.

**CNS noradrenergic tracts.** The major concentration of noradrenergic (and adrenergic) cell bodies that project upward in the brain is in the locus ceruleus in the pons (Figure 3.3–13). The axons of those neurons project through the medial forebrain bundle to the cerebral cortex, the limbic system, the thalamus, and the hypothalamus.

**Noradrenergic and adrenergic synapse.** Norepinephrine and epinephrine, along with dopamine, constitute the catecholamines. The catecholamines are synthesized from tyrosine, and the rate-limiting enzyme is tyrosine hydroxylase (Figure 3.3–11). In neurons that release norepinephrine, the enzyme dopamine β-carboxylase converts dopamine to norepinephrine; neurons that release dopamine lack that enzyme. In neurons that release epinephrine, the enzyme phenylethanolamine-*N*-methyltransferase (PNMT) converts norepinephrine into epinephrine. Neurons that release either dopamine or norepinephrine do not have PNMT.

Once norepinephrine or epinephrine is formed, it is taken into synaptic vesicles, from which it is released on

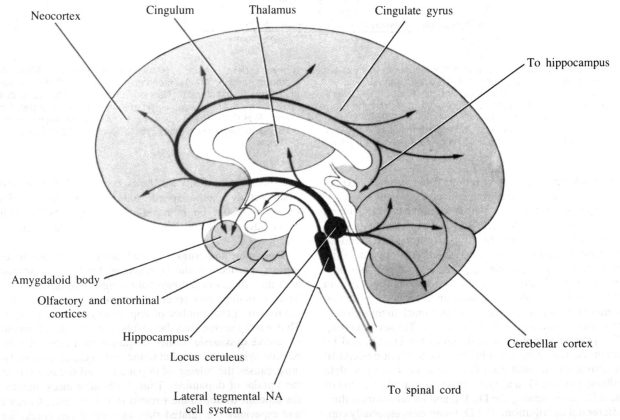

**Figure 3.3–13.** Noradrenergic pathways. The locus ceruleus, which is located immediately underneath the floor of the fourth ventricle in the rostrolateral part of the pons, is the most important noradrenergic nucleus in the brain. Its projections reach many areas in the forebrain, the cerebellum, and the spinal cord. Nor-

adrenergic neurons in the lateral brainstem tegmentum innervate several structures in the basal forebrain, including the hypothalamus and the amygdaloid body. (Figure from L Heimer: *The Human Brain and Spinal Cord.* Springer, New York, 1983. Used with permission.)

depolarization of the axonal terminal. As with dopamine, the two major routes of deactivation are uptake back into the presynaptic neuron and metabolism by MAO and COMT (Figure 3.3–12). The $MAO_A$ subtype preferentially metabolizes norepinephrine and epinephrine, as well as serotonin.

**Noradrenergic and adrenergic receptors.** The two broad groups of adrenergic and noradrenergic receptors, often just referred to as adrenergic receptors, are the α-adrenergic receptors and the β-adrenergic receptors (Table 3.3–2). The advances of molecular biology have now subtyped those receptors into three types of $α_1$ receptors ($α_{1a}$, $α_{1b}$, and $α_{1c}$), three types of $α_2$ receptors ($α_{2a}$, $α_{2b}$, and $α_{2c}$), and three types of β receptors ($β_1$, $β_2$, and $β_3$). Although the field is changing rapidly, all $α_1$ receptors seem to be linked to the phosphoinositol turnover system, $α_2$ receptors seem to inhibit the formation of cAMP, and β receptors seem to stimulate the formation of cAMP.

**Norepinephrine and drugs.** The drugs that are most associated with norepinephrine are the classic antidepressant drugs, the tricyclic drugs and the MAO inhibitors (MAOIs). The tricyclic drugs block the uptake of norepinephrine (and serotonin) back into the presynaptic neuron, and the MAOIs block the metabolism of norepinephrine (and serotonin). Thus, the immediate effect of tricyclic drugs and MAOIs is to increase the concentrations of norepinephrine (and serotonin) in the synaptic cleft. Since antidepressants take two to four weeks to exert their therapeutic effects, it is obviously not the immediate effect that results in their beneficial effects. However, the immediate effects may eventually lead to a down-regulation of the number of postsynaptic β-adrenergic receptors, and that down-regulation of postsynaptic β-adrenergic receptors may be correlated with clinical improvement.

The α-adrenergic system is also involved in the production of some of the adverse events that can be seen with many psychotherapeutic drugs. Blockade of the $α_1$-adrenergic receptors is commonly associated with sedation and postural hypotension. Another drug that affects the α-adrenergic system is clonidine (Catapres), which is an $α_2$ receptor agonist. Adrenergic $α_2$ receptors are generally located on the presynaptic neuron, and activation of those receptors down-regulates the production and the release of norepinephrine. Clonidine has been used for a variety of psychiatric disorders, including opioid withdrawal.

The β-adrenergic antagonists, such as propranolol (Inderal), have also been used in psychiatry. In general, β-adrenergic receptors are located postsynaptically, and inhibition of their activity results in a decrease in cAMP formation in the postsynaptic neuron. The β-adrenergic antagonists have been used to treat social phobia (for example, anxiety in performing musicians), akathisia (a movement disorder associated with antipsychotic compounds), and lithium (Eskalith)-induced tremor.

**Norepinephrine and psychopathology.** The *biogenic amine hypothesis of mood disorders* was based on the observation that the tricyclic drugs and the MAOIs are effective in alleviating the symptoms of depression. What the relative roles of serotonin and norepinephrine are in the pathophysiology of depression is still unclear. Drugs

that affect both neurotransmitters are effective, and drugs that affect primarily norepinephrine—for example, desipramine (Norpramin)—and drugs that affect primarily serotonin—for example fluoxetine (Prozac)—are also effective. However, when noradrenergic neurons are destroyed in experimental animal models, drugs that affect serotonin do not have their usual effects; and when serotonergic neurons are destroyed, drugs that affect norepinephrine do not have their usual effects. Those experimental results indicate that the interrelationships between serotonin and norepinephrine are incompletely understood.

## Serotonin

**CNS serotonergic tracts.** The major site of serotonergic cell bodies is in the upper pons and the midbrain—specifically, the median and dorsal raphe nuclei, the caudal locus ceruleus, the area postrema, and the interpeduncular area (Figure 3.3–14). Those neurons project to the basal ganglia, the limbic system, and the cerebral cortex.

**Serotonergic synapse.** As with the catecholamines, serotonin is synthesized in the axonal terminal (Figure 3.3–15). The precursor amino acid is tryptophan. In contrast to the catecholamines, the availability of tryptophan is the rate-limiting function, and the enzyme tryptophan hydroxylase is not rate-limiting. The key enzyme involved in the metabolism of serotonin is MAO, preferentially $MAO_A$, and the primary metabolite is 5-hydroxyindoleacetic acid (5-HIAA) (Figure 3.3–15).

**Serotonergic receptors.** Four types of serotonin receptors are now recognized—$5\text{-}HT_1$, $5\text{-}HT_2$, $5\text{-}HT_3$, and $5\text{-}HT_4$—with four subtypes of $5\text{-}HT_1$ ($5\text{-}HT_{1A}$, $5\text{-}HT_{1B}$, $5\text{-}HT_{1C}$, and $5\text{-}HT_{1D}$). The various functional effector mechanisms of those receptors are listed in Table 3.3–2. The diversity of serotonin receptors has initiated a significant effort to study the distribution of serotonin receptor subtypes in pathological states and to design subtype-specific drugs that may be of particular therapeutic benefit in specific conditions. For example, buspirone (BuSpar), a clinically effective antidepressant, is a potent $5\text{-}HT_{1A}$ agonist, and other $5\text{-}HT_{1A}$ agonists are being developed for the treatment of anxiety and depression. Clozapine, the atypical antipsychotic agent, has significant activity as an antagonist of $5\text{-}HT_2$ receptors, and that observation has initiated a major effort to study the role of that serotonin receptor subtype and to develop drugs that are $5\text{-}HT_2$ antagonists for the treatment of schizophrenia. Antagonists of the $5\text{-}HT_3$ receptor are also under study as potential antianxiety and antipsychotic compounds.

**Serotonin and drugs.** Some of the new relations between serotonin and drugs under development are discussed above; however, the classic association of serotonin and psychotropic drugs is with the tricyclic drugs and the MAOIs, as described for norepinephrine and epinephrine. The tricyclic drugs and the MAOIs, respectively, block the uptake and the metabolism of serotonin, thus increasing the concentration of serotonin in the synaptic cleft. Fluoxetine is the first of a class of serotonin-specific uptake inhibitors that are effective in the treatment of depression. Other drugs in that class include paroxetine (Paxil) and sertraline (Zoloft), and all those drugs are associated with

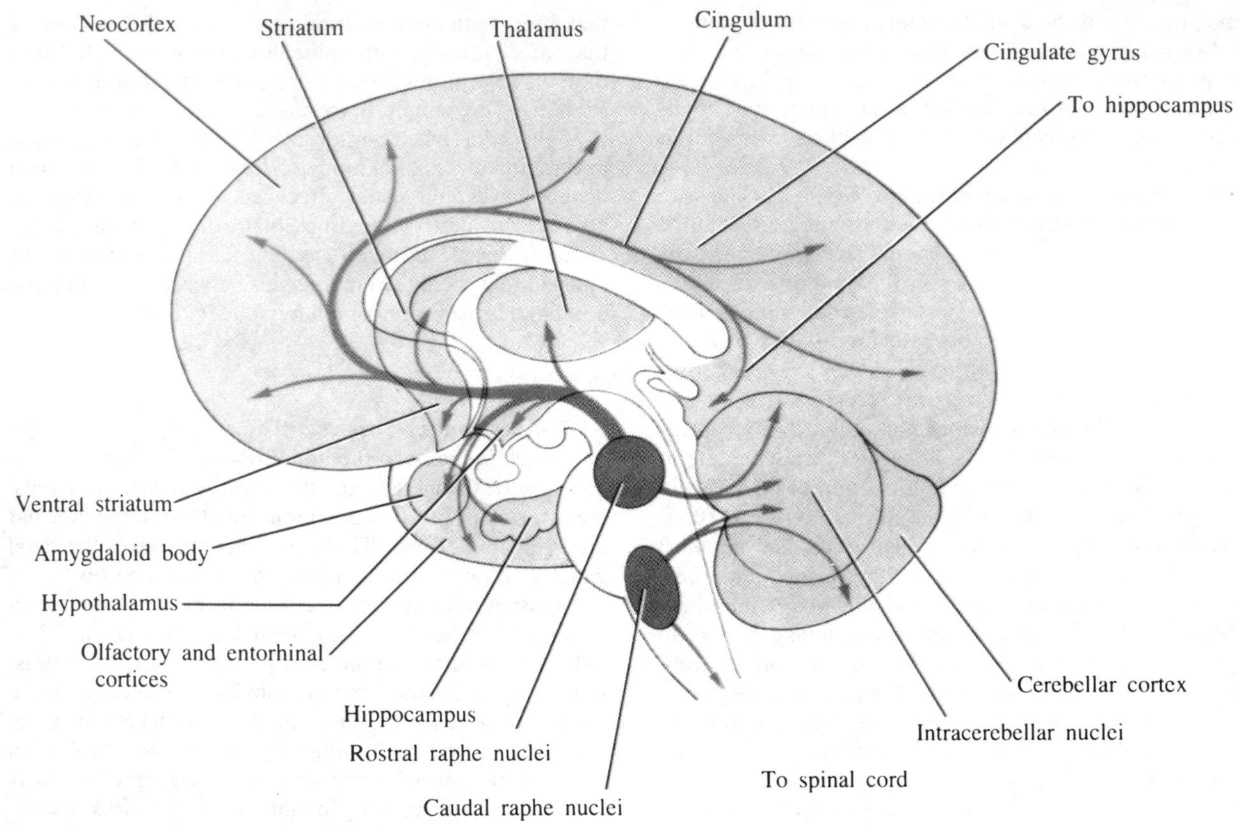

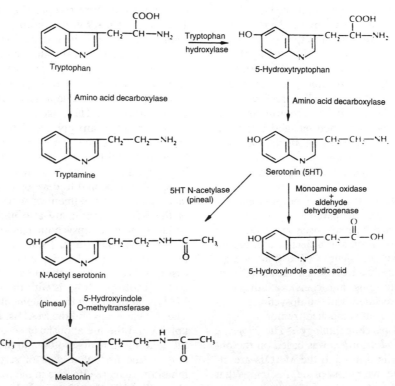

**Figure 3.3–14.** Serotonergic pathways. The raphe nuclei form a more or less continuous collection of cell groups close to the midline throughout the brainstem, but, for the sake of simplicity, they have been subdivided into a rostral group and a caudal group in the drawing. The rostral raphe nuclei project to a large number of forebrain structures. The fibers that project laterally through the internal and external capsules to widespread areas of the neocortex are not indicated in this highly schematic drawing. (Figure from L Heimer: *The Human Brain and Spinal Cord.* Springer, New York, 1983. Used with permission.)

**Figure 3.3–15.** The metabolic pathways available for the synthesis and the metabolism of serotonin. (Figure from J R Cooper, F E Bloom, R H Roth: *The Biochemical Basis of Neuropharmacology,* ed 6, p 341. Oxford University Press, New York, 1991. Used with permission.)

minimal adverse effects, especially in comparison with the tricyclic drugs and the MAOIs.

Another serotonergic drug that has been used in psychiatry is L-tryptophan. Because the concentration of L-tryptophan is the rate-limiting function in the synthesis of serotonin, ingestion of L-tryptophan can increase the concentration of serotonin in the CNS. L-Tryptophan was withdrawn from the market in 1990 in the United States by the Food and Drug Administration (FDA) because a contaminant from the production process at one particular manufacturing site caused an eosinophilia-myalgia syndrome in some patients taking the drug.

Serotonin is also involved in the mechanism of at least two major substances of abuse, lysergic acid diethylamide (LSD) and 3,4-methylenedioxymethamphetamine (MDMA), also known as ecstacy. The serotonin system is the major site of action for LSD, but exactly how LSD exerts its effects remains unclear. MDMA has dual effects as an uptake blocker to serotonin and as an inducer of the massive release of the serotonin contents of serotonergic neurons.

**Serotonin and psychopathology.** The principal association for serotonin with a psychopathological condition is with depression, as suggested in the biogenic amine hypothesis of mood disorders. That hypothesis is simply that depression is associated with too little serotonin and that mania is associated with too much serotonin. As explained above for norepinephrine, that simplified view is undoubtedly not entirely accurate. The *permissive hypothesis* postulates that low levels of serotonin permit abnormal levels of norepinephrine to cause depression or mania. With the introduction of a variety of new drugs, serotonin is one of the most exciting areas for research in the anxiety disorders and schizophrenia, in addition to its role in depression.

## Acetylcholine

**CNS cholinergic tracts.** A group of cholinergic neurons in the nucleus basalis of Meynert project to the cerebral cortex and the limbic system. Additional cholinergic neurons in the reticular system project to the cerebral cortex, the limbic system, the hypothalamus, and the thalamus. Some patients with dementia of the Alzheimer's type or Down's syndrome appear to have a specific degeneration of the neurons in the nucleus basalis of Meynert.

**Cholinergic synapse.** Acetylcholine is synthesized in the cholinergic axon terminal from acetylcoenzyme A (acetyl-CoA) and choline by the enzyme choline acetyltransferase. Acetylcholine is metabolized in the synaptic cleft by acetylcholinesterase, and the resulting choline is taken back up into the presynaptic neuron and is recycled to make new acetylcholine molecules.

**Cholinergic receptors.** The two major subtypes of cholinergic receptors are muscarinic and nicotinic (Table 3.3–2). There are four recognized types of muscarinic receptors with various effects on phosphoinositol turnover, cAMP and cGMP production, and potassium ion channel activity. Muscarinic receptors are antagonized by atropine. The nicotinic receptors are ligand-gated ion channels that have the receptor site directly on the ion channel itself. The nicotinic receptor is actually made up of four subunits ($\alpha$, $\beta$, $\gamma$, and $\delta$). Nicotinic receptors can vary in the number of each of those subunits; thus, there are a multitude of subtypes of nicotinic receptors, based on the specific configuration of the subunits.

**Acetylcholine and drugs.** The most common use of anticholinergic drugs in psychiatry is as a treatment of the motor abnormalities caused by the use of classic antipsychotic drugs (for example, haloperidol). The efficacy of the drugs for that indication is determined by the balance between acetylcholine activity and dopamine activity in the basal ganglia. Blockade of muscarinic cholinergic receptors is a common pharmacodynamic effect of many psychotropic drugs. Blockade of those receptors leads to the commonly seen side effects of blurred vision, dry mouth, constipation, and difficulty in initiating urination. Excessive blockade of CNS cholinergic receptors causes confusion and delirium. Drugs that increase cholinergic activity (for example, tacrine [Cognex]) have been reported to be effective in the treatment of dementia.

**Acetylcholine and psychopathology.** The most common association with acetylcholine is dementia of the Alzheimer's type and other dementias. With the recent identification of the protein structures of the various muscarinic and nicotinic receptors, many researchers are working on specific muscarinic and nicotinic agonists that may prove to be of some benefit in the treatment of dementia of the Alzheimer's type. Acetylcholine may also be involved in mood and sleep disorders.

## Histamine

Neurons that release histamine as their neurotransmitter are located in the hypothalamus and project to the cerebral cortex, the limbic system, and the thalamus. There are three types of histamine receptors: $H_1$ receptor stimulation increases the production of $IP_3$ and DAG; $H_2$ stimulation increases the production of cAMP; and the function of the $H_3$ receptor remains uncertain. Blockade of $H_1$ receptors is the mechanism of action for allergy medications and is partly the mechanism for commonly observed side effects—such as sedation, weight gain, and hypotension—seen with some psychotropic drugs.

## AMINO ACIDS

Amino acid neurotransmitters are the most abundant neurotransmitters in the brain. The major excitatory amino acid (EAA) is glutamate, although aspartate and homocysteate may also be EAAs. The major inhibitory amino acid (IAA) is GABA, although glycine is also an inhibitory amino acid of increasing interest to researchers. All EAAs are dicarboxylic amino acids, and all IAAs are monocarboxylic amino acids. That structural difference is thought to be a major contributor to the differential activities of the two classes of amino acids.

## Glutamate

**Synthesis, metabolism, and pathways.** Glutamate is synthesized from several precursors in presynaptic neuron terminals. Once released into the synaptic cleft, the glutamate is taken up into the presynaptic neuron and into adjacent glia. One report found that a defect in the uptake of glutamate is associated with amyotrophic lateral sclerosis (ALS). Glutamate is the primary neurotransmitter in thalamocortical, pyramidal cell, and corticostriatal projections. It is also a major neurotransmitter within the hippocampus.

**Glutamate receptors and drugs.** There are five major types of glutamate receptors (Table 3.3–1). The N-methyl-D-aspartate (NMDA) receptor is the best understood of the receptors. Two other receptors are the α-amino-3-hydroxy-5-methyl-4-isoxazole proprionic acid (AMPA) and the kainate receptors, which share depolarization as their principal effect with the NMDA receptor. The NMDA receptor requires two molecules of glutamate and a molecule of glycine for activation (Figure 3.3–16). The excitatory amino acid binding site for glycine is referred to as the nonstrychnine-sensitive glycine receptor, and it contrasts with the strychnine-sensitive glycine receptor, which is an inhibitory receptor. The NMDA receptor is also blocked by physiological concentrations of magnesium, phencyclidine (PCP), and PCP-related substances (for example, MK-801). The two remaining types of glutamate receptors are the AP4 (1-2-amino-4-phosphonobutyrate) and ACPD (trans-1-aminocyclopentane-1-3-dicarboxylic acid) receptors. The AP4 receptor is thought to be an inhibitory autoreceptor. The ACPD receptor (also called the metabotropic receptor) has its effects through the phosphoinositol second-messenger system.

**Glutamate and psychopathology.** The major pathophysiological conditions currently associated with the glutamate system are excitotoxicity and schizophrenia. *Excitotoxicity* is the hypothesis that excessive stimulation of glutamate receptors leads to prolonged and excessive intraneuronal concentrations of calcium. Such conditions activate many enzymes, especially proteases, that are destructive to neuronal integrity. The association with schizophrenia is partly due to the psychotomimetic effects observed with PCP. Some basic science studies find that dopamine and glutamate have opposing effects. Because of that association, glutamate may be involved in the pathophysiology of Parkinson's disease. Many types of experiments suggest that glutamate in the hippocampus is involved in the neurochemical basis of learning and memory.

## GABA

**Synthesis, metabolism, and pathways.** GABA is synthesized from glutamate by the rate-limiting enzyme glutamic acid decarboxylase (GAD), which requires pyridoxine (vitamin $B_6$) as a cofactor. Once released into the synaptic cleft, GABA is taken up into the presynaptic neuron and adjacent glia, where it is metabolized by mitochondrial-associated GABA transaminase (GABA-T). GABA is the primary neurotransmitter in intrinsic neurons that function as local mediators for the inhibitory feedback loops. GABA commonly coexists with peptide neurotransmitters, including somatostatin, neuropeptide Y (NPY), and vasoactive intestinal peptide (VIP).

**Receptors and drugs.** There are two types of GABA receptors, $GABA_A$ and $GABA_B$. The $GABA_B$ receptor is a G protein-associated receptor; $GABA_A$ is a directly acting, ligand-gated chloride ion channel (Figure 3.3–17). The $GABA_A$ receptor has binding sites for GABA and the benzodiazepines. The benzodiazepines increase the affinity of the GABA receptor for GABA. The benzodiazepine receptors are sometimes referred to as the omega receptors. The β-carbolines are a class of drugs that are inverse agonists of the benzodiazepine receptors; thus, their activity results in anxiety and convulsions. Flumazemil (Mazicon) is a benzodiazepine antagonist that is currently being used in hospital emergency rooms as a treatment for benzodiazepine overdoses.

**Psychopathology.** Because of the association with benzodiazepines, clinical research on the GABAergic sys-

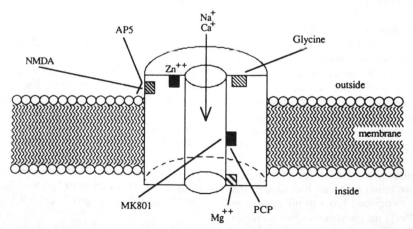

**Figure 3.3–16.** Schematic illustration of the N-methyl-D-aspartate (NMDA) receptor and the sites of action of different agents on the receptor. The NMDA receptor gates a cation channel that is permeable to $Ca^{2+}$ and $Na^+$ and is gated by $Mg^{2+}$ in a voltage-dependent fashion; $K^+$ is the counterion. The NMDA receptor channel is blocked by PCP and MK-8OI, and the complex is regulated at two modulatory sites by glycine and $Zn^{2+}$; AP5 and CPP are competitive antagonists at the NMDA site. (Figure from J R Cooper, F E Bloom, R H Roth: *The Biochemical Basis of Neuropharmacology,* ed 6, p 182. Oxford University Press, New York, 1991. Used with permission.)

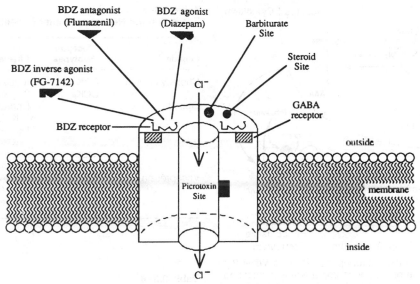

**Figure 3.3–17.** Schematic illustration of the GABA$_A$ receptor complex and the sites of action of different agents on the receptor. (Figure from J R Cooper, F E Bloom, R H Roth: *The*

*Biochemical Basis of Neuropharmacology,* ed 6, p 147. Oxford University Press, New York, 1991. Used with permission.)

tem has focused on its potential role in the pathophysiology of anxiety disorders. Many of the standard anticonvulsants also have their effects on the GABA system; therefore, researchers in epilepsy also are actively studying the GABA system.

## Glycine

Glycine is synthesized primarily from serine by the actions of serine transhydroxymethylase and β-glycerate dehydrogenase, both of which are rate-limiting. Glycine does double duty as a mandatory adjunctive neurotransmitter for glutamate activity and as an independent inhibitory neurotransmitter at its own receptors. The glycine receptor is a chloride ion channel similar in general structure and function to the nicotinic or GABA receptors.

## PEPTIDES

As many as 300 peptide neurotransmitters may be in the human brain (Table 3.3–6). A *peptide* is a short protein consisting of fewer than 100 amino acids. Peptides are made in the neuronal cell body by the transcription and translation of a genetic message (Figure 3.3–18). Peptides are stored in synaptic vesicles and are released from the axon terminals. The activity of peptides is terminated by the action of enzymes, peptidases, that cleave the peptides between specific amino acid residues. In addition to the regulatory mechanisms shared with other neurotransmitters, neuroactive peptides are subject to additional refinements in regulation. Differential ribonucleic acid (RNA) processing of the RNA first transcribed from the deoxyribonucleic acid (DNA) (heterogeneous nuclear RNA [hnRNA]) can result in different messenger RNAs (mRNAs). Most of those initial mRNAs for peptide neurotransmitters actually code for much longer peptides, called preprohormones, which are cleaved in the cell body before they are packaged as prohormones into vesicles for

**Table 3.3–6**
**Selected CNS Neuroactive Peptides**

Adrenocorticotropic hormone
Androgens
Angiotensin I, II, and III
Bombesin
Bradykinin
Calcitonin
Cardioexcitatory peptide
Carnosine
Cholecystokinin
Corticotropin-releasing hormone
Cortisol
Endogenous opioids
Estrogens
Follicle-stimulating hormone
Gastrin
Gastrin-inhibiting peptide
Glucagon
Gonadotropin-releasing hormone
Growth hormone
Growth hormone-releasing factor
Insulin
Luteinizing hormone
Melanocyte-inhibiting factor
Melanocyte-stimulating hormone
Melatonin
Motilin
Neural growth factor
Neuronal polypeptide
Neuropeptide Y
Neurotensin
Oxytocin
Progesterone
Prolactin
Secretin
Sleep-inducing peptide
Somatostatin
Substance K
Substance P
Thyroid hormones
Thyroid-stimulating hormone
Thyrotropin-releasing hormone
Vasoactive intestinal peptide
Vasopressin

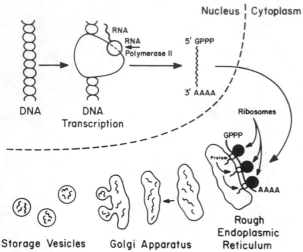

**Figure 3.3–18.** Sequence of neuropeptide synthesis. Within the nucleus, the gene for the precursor neuropeptide is transcribed into messenger ribonucleic acid (mRNA). The mRNA is transported from the nucleus into the cytoplasm, where it binds to ribosomes. The mRNA is then translated by protein synthesis on the ribosomes in the rough endoplasmic reticulum. Within the Golgi apparatus, the precursor peptide is enzymatically modified to yield the neuropeptide, which is packaged in storage vesicles for axoplasmic transport to the nerve terminal. (Figure from J T Coyle: Neuroscience and psychiatry. In *The American Psychiatric Press Textbook of Psychiatry*, J A Talbott, R E Hales, S C Yudofsky, editors, p 9. American Psychiatric Press, Washington, 1988. Used with permission).

**Table 3.3–7**
**Some Peptide Neurotransmitter Receptor Subtypes**

| Peptide | Receptor Subtypes | Effector Mechanism |
| --- | --- | --- |
| Cholecystokinin | $CCK_A$ | $IP_3$/DAG |
|  | $CCK_B$ | ? |
| Opioid | μ | Decrease cAMP, increase $K^+$ conductance |
|  | δ | Decrease cAMP, increase $K^+$ conductance |
|  | kappa | Decrease $Ca^{2+}$ conductance |
| Vasopressin | $V_{1A}$ | $IP_3$/DAG |
|  | $V_{1B}$ | $IP_3$/DAG |
|  | $V_2$ | Increase cAMP |

**Table 3.3–8**
**Examples of Biogenic Amine and Peptide Coexistence in Neurons**

| | |
| --- | --- |
| Acetylcholine | Vasoactive intestinal peptide |
|  | Substance P |
| Dopamine | Cholecystokinin |
|  | Neurotensin |
| GABA | Somatostatin |
|  | Cholecystokinin |
| Norepinephrine | Somatostatin |
|  | Enkephalin |
|  | Neuropeptide Y |
|  | Neurostensin |
| Serotonin | Substance P |
|  | Enkephalin |

transport to the axon terminals. During the transport phase, the prohormone is usually further cleaved to form the final form of the peptide, which can then be subject to additional posttranslational modifications.

Peptide receptors are similar to biogenic amine G protein-linked receptors. The effector mechanisms of some subtypes of peptide transmitters are listed in Table 3.3–7. In addition, most if not all peptide neurotransmitters coexist with other neurotransmitters. Examples of such coexistence are listed in Table 3.3–8.

### Selected Peptide Neurotransmitters

**Endogenous opioids.** The three subgroups of opioid peptides are derived from three precursors: proopiomelanocortin, proenkephalin, and prodynorphin. Processing of proopiomelanocortin (POMC) results in adrenocorticotrophic hormone (ACTH), melanocyte-stimulating hormones, and β-endorphin. Processing of proenkephalin produces metenkephalin and leuenkephalin, and processing of prodynorphin produces β-neoendorphin and dynorphin. The endogenous opioids act on three major receptors (Table 3.3–7) and are believed to be involved in the regulation of stress, pain, and mood.

**Substance P.** Substance P is the primary neurotransmitter in most primary afferent sensory neurons and in the striatonigral pathway. Abnormalities affecting substance P have been hypothesized for Huntington's disease, dementia of the Alzheimer's type, and mood disorders.

**Neurotensin.** Neurotensin has been hypothesized to be involved in the pathophysiology of schizophrenia, mostly because of its coexistence with dopamine in some axon terminals. Some preliminary reports suggest that neurotensin-related peptides or drugs have beneficial effects for some psychotic symptoms.

**Cholecystokinin.** Like neurotensin and for the same reasons, cholecystokinin (CCK) has been hypothesized to be involved in the pathophysiology of schizophrenia. CCK has also been implicated in the pathophysiologies of eating disorders and movement disorders.

**Somatostatin.** Somatostatin is also known as growth-hormone-inhibiting factor. Somatostatin has been implicated by postmortem studies in Huntington's disease and dementia of the Alzheimer's type.

**Vasopressin and oxytocin.** Vasopressin and oxytocin, two related peptides, have been postulated to be involved in the regulation of mood. They are both synthesized in the hypothalamus and are released in the posterior pituitary.

### PSYCHONEUROENDOCRINOLOGY

Three related areas involving peptides and psychiatry need to be differentiated. First, neuroactive peptide neurotransmitters are a class of peptides that function like classic neurotransmitters. Second, the hormones of the classic neuroendocrine axes (for example, the limbic-hypothalamic-pituitary-adrenal axis) can feed back to the brain through the bloodstream to affect neuronal function. Third, specific psychiatric syndromes are associated with hyperactivity and hypoactivity of those same classic neuroendocrine axes. The first and second areas are discussed here. The third area is covered in Chapter 10.

## Hormone Receptors

There are a variety of hormone receptors; however, it is instructive to describe the steroid receptor. *Steroid hormones* are produced by the ovaries (estrogen and progestins), the testes (androgens), and the adrenal cortex (glucocorticoids). After secretion, steroid hormones are tightly bound to steroid-binding proteins in the blood, with which the steroid hormones can diffuse into the cytoplasm of cells, including neurons. Once inside the cell, the steroid hormones can bind to receptor proteins that are specific to each type of cell. Therefore, although the steroid hormones can diffuse into any cell, only those cells with the appropriate receptors will respond. Once bound to its appropriate receptor, the steroid receptor complex can diffuse through the nuclear membrane. Once inside the nucleus, the steroid can interact with DNA and regulate RNA synthesis. Steroids are an example of hormones with nuclear receptors; other hormones have conventional surface receptors; and still other hormones have both types of receptors.

## Selected Hormonal Axes

**Adrenal axis.** The components of the adrenal axis are corticotropin-releasing hormone (CRH) from the hypothalamus, ACTH from the anterior pituitary, and cortisol from the adrenal gland. The plasma concentrations of cortisol are at their highest in the early morning (around 6 AM) and at their lowest values in the late afternoon and evening. The adrenal axis reacts to stress by increasing the secretion of cortisol. The released cortisol performs many peripheral functions, as well as feeding back to the brain itself to induce new protein synthesis, presumably adaptive to handling stressful situations.

**Thyroid axis.** The components of the thyroid axis are thyrotropin-releasing hormone (TRH) from the hypothalamus, thyroid-stimulating hormone (TSH) from the anterior pituitary, and thyroid hormone from the thyroid gland. The active forms of thyroid hormone, $T_4$ and $T_3$, are deactivated when they are converted into reverse $T_3$ ($rT_3$). There are both surface and nuclear receptors for thyroid hormones. The absence of thyroid hormone in early infancy results in a severe form of mental retardation called *cretinism*. The administration of TRH has brief mood-elevating effects in depressed patients, and some antidepressant-nonresponsive patients are converted into antidepressant-responsive patients with the addition of $T_3$ to their antidepressant regimen. Experimental data indicate that the additional $T_3$ acts by modulating the function of the β-adrenergic receptor.

**Growth hormone.** The components of the growth hormone axis are growth-hormone-releasing hormone (GHRH) and growth-hormone-release-inhibiting factor (GHRIH), also known as somatostatin, from the hypothalamus and growth hormone itself from the anterior pituitary. Growth hormone is released in pulses throughout the day, but the pulses are closer together during the first hours of sleep than at other times. Growth hormone regulation has been studied particularly in schizophrenia and mood disorders, in which some data suggest a disordered regulation of the growth hormone axis.

**Prolactin.** The release of prolactin from the anterior pituitary is regulated by prolactin-releasing factors (PRFs) and prolactin-inhibiting factor (PIF), which is the neurotransmitter dopamine. Especially with the novel antipsychotic drugs under development, interest is increasing in correlating the effects of antipsychotic drugs on the release of prolactin with therapeutic effects.

**Melatonin.** Melatonin is released by the pineal body, which also contains many other peptides and hormones. Melatonin is secreted when the eyes perceive darkness, and its release is inhibited when the eyes perceive light. Melatonin is synthesized from serotonin by the action of two enzymes: serotonin-N-acetylase and 5-hydroxyindole-O-methyltransferase. Melatonin is involved in the regulation of circadian rhythms and has been implicated in the pathophysiology of depression.

## Endocrine Dysregulation in Psychiatric Disorders

Some patients with psychiatric disorders, particularly depressive disorders and schizophrenia, have abnormal regulation of some of their neuroendocrine axes. The unresolved question is whether the abnormal regulation is involved in the pathophysiology and the cause of the disorder or is merely reflective of abnormal brain function. The latter case is likely for two reasons: First, the biogenic amine neurotransmitters, which are affected by most psychotherapeutic drugs, are also key regulators of the neuroendocrine axes. Second, most neuroendocrine abnormalities return to normal baseline values once the psychotic or depressive episode has past, suggesting that the abnormality is a state marker (reflective of the condition), rather than a trait marker (reflective of an underlying predisposition to the illness).

## Endocrine Assessment

Neuroendocrine function can be studied by assessing baseline measures and by measuring the response of the axis to some neurochemical or hormonal challenge. The first method has two approaches: One approach is to measure a single time point—for example, morning levels of growth hormone; that approach is subject to significant error because of the pulsatile nature of the release of most hormones. The second approach is to collect blood samples at multiple points or to collect 24-hour urine samples; those measurements are less prone to major errors. The best approach, however, is to do a neuroendocrine challenge test, in which the person is given a drug or a hormone that perturbs the endocrine axis in some standard way. Nondiseased persons show much less variation in their responses to such challenge studies than they do in their baseline measurements.

## PSYCHONEUROIMMUNOLOGY

The immune system is interactive with both the CNS and the endocrine system. Although psychiatric conditions can be associated with abnormalities in the immune system, it is not known whether that association represents a primary defect or a secondary effect of a nervous system disorder. It is known, however, that the immune system can be involved in the pathophysiology of psychiatric conditions either by allowing a pathogen to damage nervous tissue, as happens in acquired immune deficiency syndrome (AIDS), or by damaging nervous tissue itself, as in autoimmune disorders. The role of the immune system is to remove foreign pathogens from the body without damaging the body itself. When a patient has erythema, swelling, and pain around a site of infection, those signs and symptoms are evidence that the immune system is working, although it is on the verge of damaging the body itself.

### Neural Regulation of Immunity

Norepinephrine, β-endorphin, metenkephalin, and cortisol are thought to be the principal chemical and hormonal mediators of the immune system. The hypothalamus, the hippocampus, and the pituitary are the major sites for that regulation. The immune system can communicate back to the CNS by the release of chemical messengers, including ACTH, β-endorphin, and unique chemicals secreted by the lymphocytes.

**Stress.** The principal experimental approach to the effects of stress on the immune system has been with animals who have been stressed. The studies have shown a decrease in lymphocyte number, a decreased proliferation in response to stimulation, and a reduction in the production of antibodies. Those effects on the immune system are most marked in experimental paradigms in which the animal does not have a way to escape the stressful situation. Parallel changes in immune responses have been reported in humans in stressful situations.

**Conditioning.** Some experiments have shown that immune responses can be conditioned to occur in the presence of nonbiologically relevant stimuli (for example, a bell ringing). That finding is consistent with data showing that the CNS can influence the immune system.

**Immunological abnormalities in psychiatric patients.** Two studies have reported a decreased T-cell proliferation in bereaved spouses, even two months after the death of the spouse. Natural killer cell activity is affected by levels of stress in college students. Students with poor coping skills or who complain of loneliness are most likely to have abnormal immune system function. Patients with major depressive disorder have decreased T-cell proliferation and an overall decrease in the number of lymphocytes.

Schizophrenia may also be associated with immunological abnormalities. Abnormal immune function in some schizophrenic patients has suggested to some investigators

that the patients may have been susceptible to infection with a neurotoxic virus that led to the degeneration of selective neuronal populations.

## CHRONOBIOLOGY

The study of the regular biological rhythms in biological organisms is called *chronobiology*. Some sort of rhythm is found in virtually all biological functions, including endocrine secretion, neurotransmitter synthesis, receptor sensitivity, and enzyme concentrations. The lengths of the rhythms vary: less than a day (ultradian), approximately 24 hours (circadian), more than a day (infradian), approximately one week (circaseptan), approximately one month, and approximately one year (circannual).

The sleep-wake cycle, hormonal levels, the body temperature, and the menstrual cycle are all examples of biological rhythms in the human body that can be measured. When a person is in a healthy state, all the rhythms have a natural relation, and they are said to be *in phase*. When the system is perturbed (by staying up all night, for example), certain biological rhythms are thrown off (for example, those for growth hormone and cortisol), and the rhythms are then considered to be *out of phase*. The state of having one's biological rhythms out of phase contributes to the ill effects experienced by the person. Some disorders have phase perturbations as part of their symptoms. When rhythms are disordered, a particular rhythm may have an abnormal *phase advance*, in which it begins earlier than usual, or a *phase delay*, in which it begins later than usual. Under experimental conditions a *phase responsive curve* for a biological rhythm may show that a particular stimulation (for example, light) causes either a phase advance or a phase delay when it is delivered at different times in a cycle (for example, the sleep-wake cycle).

Biological rhythms are set by both internal and external forces, generally called *zeitgebers* (time givers, time clues, synchronizers). The suprachiasmatic nuclei of the hypothalamus is the principal endogenous zeitgeber. The light-dark cycle, patterned mealtimes, and the nine-to-five workday are examples of exogenous zeitgebers. In the absence of exogenous clues, the period of human circadian rhythms is a bit longer than a day—24.5 hours.

### Chronobiology and Psychiatry

Jet lag is perhaps the most common example of a perturbation of chronobiological rhythms. When people travel from east to west, they experience a phase delay, which is not a large problem, because the body actually wants a slightly longer (24.5-hour) day. Traveling west to east, however, presents a phase advance that opposes the natural tendency and that disrupts biological rhythms. Shift work, including the difficult hours of interns and residents, also disrupts biological rhythms in an analogous manner.

Depression is the psychiatric symptom that has been most associated with disruptions in biological rhythms. Early morning awakening, decreased latency of rapid eye movement (REM) sleep, and neuroendocrine perturbations that are seen in depression can all be conceptualized as reflecting a disorder of coordination in biological rhythms. One hypothesis is that depression occurs in some persons when the sleep-sensitive phase of the circadian system advances from the first hours of awakening to the last hours of sleep. Research indicates that alterations in the light-dark cycle—by exposing the patient to artificial light or by changing the patient's sleep-wake cycle—can relieve the symptoms. Lithium and many of the tricyclic drugs and MAOIs delay rhythms in experimental animal models, supporting the hypothesis that at least some forms of depression represent phase-advance disorders.

### References

Apud J A: The 5-HT$_3$ receptor in mammalian brain: A new target for the development of psychotropic drugs? Neuropsychopharmacology 8: 117, 1993.

Bean B P: Pharmacology and electrophysiology of ATP-activated channels. Trends Pharmacol Sci 13: 87, 1992.

Bowery N G: GABA$_A$ receptors as targets for drug action. Arzneimittelforschung Drug Res 42: 15, 1992.

Bowery N G: GABA$_B$ receptor pharmacology. Annu Rev Pharmacol Toxicol 33: 109, 1993.

Costa E: The allosteric modulation of GABA$_A$ receptors. Neuropsychopharmacology 4: 225, 1991.

Deneris E S, Connolly J, Rogers S W, Duvoisin R: Pharmacological and functional diversity of neuronal nicotinic acetylcholine receptors. Trends Pharmacol Sci 12: 34, 1991.

Dubovsky S L, Murphy J, Christiano J, Lee C: The calcium second messenger system in bipolar disorders: Data supporting new research directions. J Neuropsychiatry Clin Neurosci 4: 3, 1992.

Göthert M: 5-Hydroxytryptamine receptors. Arzneimittelforschung Drug Res 42: 238, 1992.

Huganir R L, Greengard P: Regulation of neurotransmitter receptor desensitization by protein phosphorylation. Neuron 5: 555, 1990.

Jessell T M, Kandel E R: Synaptic transmission: A bidirectional and self-modifiable form of cell-cell communication. Cell 72/Neuron 10 (2, Suppl):1, 1993.

Krogsgaard-Larsen P: GABA and glutamate receptors as therapeutic targets in neurodegenerative disorders. Pharmacol Toxicol 70: 95, 1992.

Kruger B K: Toward an understanding of structure and function of ion channels. FASEB J 3: 1906, 1989.

Linden J: Structure and function of A$_1$ adenosine receptors. FASEB J 5: 2668, 1991.

Manji H K: G proteins: Implications for psychiatry. Am J Psychiatry 149: 746, 1992.

McCall T, Vallance P: Nitric oxide takes centre-stage with newly defined roles. Trends Pharmacol Sci 13: 1, 1992.

McEwen B S, Angulo J, Cameron H, Chao H M, Daniels D, Gannon M N, Gould E, Mendelson S, Sakai R, Spencer R, Woolley C: Paradoxical effects of adrenal steroids on the brain: Protection versus degeneration. Biol Psychiatry 31: 177, 1992.

Middlemiss D N, Tricklebank M D: Centrally active 5-HT receptor agonists and antagonists. Neurosci Biobehav Rev 16: 75, 1992.

Milligan G: Mechanisms of multifunctional signalling by G protein-linked receptors. Trends Pharmacol Sci 14: 239, 1993.

Newman M E, Lerer B, Shapira B: 5-HT-1A receptor-mediated effects of antidepressants. Prog Neuropsychopharmacol Biol Psychiatry 17: 1, 1993.

Peroutka S J: 5-Hydroxytryptamine receptors. J Neurochem 60: 408, 1993.

Peroutka S J, Sleight A J, McCarthy B G, Pierce P A, Schmidt A W, Hekmatpanah C R: The clinical utility of pharmacological agents that act on serotonin receptors. J Neuropsychiatry 1: 253, 1989.

Quirion R, Bowen W D, Itzhak Y, Junien J L, Musacchio J M, Rothman R B, Tu T-P, Tam S W, Taylor D P: A proposal for the classification of sigma binding sites. Trends Pharmacol Sci 13: 85, 1992.

Raymond L A, Blackstone C D, Huganir R L: Phosphorylation of amino acid neurotransmitter receptors in synaptic plasticity. Trends Neurosci 16: 117, 1993.

Riederer P, Lange K W, Kornhuber J, Danielczyk W: Glutamatergic-dopaminergic balance in the brain. Arzneimittelforschung Drug Res 42: 265, 1992.

Robash M, Hall J C: The molecular biology of circadian rhythms. Neuron 3: 387, 1989.

Rothstein J D, Martin L J, Kuncl R W: Decreased glutamate transport by the brain and spinal cord in amyotrophic lateral sclerosis. N Engl J Med 326: 1464, 1992.

Schwartz J-C, Levesque D, Martres M-P, Sokoloff P: Dopamine D$_3$ receptor: Basic and clinical aspects. Clin Neuropharmacol 16: 295, 1993.

Seeburg P H: The TiPS/TINS lecture: The molecular biology of mammalian glutamate receptor channels. Trends Pharmacol Sci 14: 297, 1993.

Seeman P, Van Tol H H M: Dopamine receptor pharmacology. Curr Opin Neurol Neurosurg 6: 602, 1993.

Sibley D R, Monsma F J Jr: Molecular biology of dopamine receptors. Trends Pharmacol Sci 13: 61, 1992.

Simon M I, Strathmann M P, Gautam N: Diversity of G proteins in signal transduction. Science 252: 802, 1991.

---

# 3.4 / Behavioral Genetics

Although at least the major mental disorders (for example, schizophrenia, bipolar I disorder, and panic disorder) have a genetic component in their causes, little is known about what constitutes the genetic component and how the genetic component interacts with environmental factors to result in the development of a mental disorder in a particular person. The advances in molecular biology in the last five years, however, make it likely that the current state of relative ignorance on those topics will yield to discoveries that will elucidate specific and fundamental roles for identified genes in the development of psychiatric disorders. Table 3.4–1 is a glossary of genetic terms.

## GENETIC AND ENVIRONMENTAL INTERACTIONS

A trait that is purely *hereditary* depends solely on the particular genes that a person inherits. An example of such a trait is eye color. A trait that is purely *acquired* depends solely on nongenetic factors. An example of such a trait is a person's choice of hairstyle. Probably all mental disorders will eventually be shown to be the result of interactions between genetic and environmental influences, rather than being solely hereditary or acquired. That is, the environment, through both psychological mechanisms (for example, stress) and biological mechanisms (for example, infections), can affect gene expression, and the expression of abnormal genes or the failure of expression of normal genes is a major common pathway in the development of disease states.

Confusion often exists between, on the one hand, the concepts of genetic and environmental influences and, on the other hand, the concepts of biological and psychological causes of mental illness. Strictly speaking, a genetic influence is independent of environmental influence. Although the initiation of an environmental influence—for example, infection with human immunodeficiency virus (HIV)—may be independent of a person's genetic makeup, the effects of the environmental influence are likely to involve the regulation of gene expression in the organism. The concept of a biological cause of mental illness is usually taken to be synonymous with a genetic basis; the concept of environmental influence is often mis-

**Table 3.4–1**
**Glossary of Genetic Terms**

**Age-correction procedure**: A statistical procedure used in genetic studies of families that takes into account the fact that different psychiatric diagnoses have different ages of onset.

**Allele (allelomorph)**: Alternative form of a gene. There may be many alleles for a given gene, but each person possesses only two alleles for each gene, receiving one of each pair of alleles from each parent. A person with a pair of similar alleles is a homozygote; one with a dissimilar pair is a heterozygote.

**Amniography**: Opacification of amniotic fluid by injecting radiopaque material to visualize the fetal skeleton and soft tissues clearly.

**Aneuploidy**: An irregular number of chromosomes (e.g., 45, 47, or 48 chromosomes in a human being), caused by the loss or the addition of one or more chromosomes or parts of chromosomes.

**Autoradiography**: The process by which a radioactive label is used to identify a specific biological process or material by overlaying with X-ray film and observing exposed areas that usually appear as dots or bands.

**Autosomal**: Located on or transmitted by an autosome.

**Autosome**: A chromosome that is not a sex chromosome. A human being has 22 pairs of autosomes.

**Barr body**: The **sex chromatin** mass in somatic cells of the female.

**Carrier**: One who carries a recessive gene, either autosomal or sex-linked, together with its normal allele, but who does not show any clinically detectable effect of the gene (i.e., a heterozygote for a recessive gene).

**Centimorgan**: The genetic distance in which the probability of a recombination occurring is 1 percent.

**Centromere**: The constricted portion of the chromosome, which is the point of attachment to the equatorial plane of the mitotic or meiotic spindle.

**Chromatid**: A chromosome at prophase and metaphase consists of two strands attached to the centromere. Each strand is a chromatid (see Mitosis).

**Chromatin**: The substance in cell nuclei and chromosomes that stains intensely with basic dyes and that is composed of DNA combined with proteins. In the fixed intermitotic nucleus, chromatin usually takes the form of an irregular network of long coiled threads, which are gradually condensed into individual chromosomes as the cell undergoes division.

**Chromatin-negative**: Nuclei that lack the sex chromatin mass or Barr body. It is characteristic of the normal human male.

**Chromatin-positive**: Nuclei containing the distinctive sex chromatin mass. It is characteristic of the normal human female.

**Chromosomal aberration (or abnormality)**: A deviation from the normal morphology of chromosomes.

**Chromosome**: One of a number of small bodies, occurring in pairs, into which the chromatin material of a cell nucleus resolves itself before cell division. Chromosomes are visible only during cell division. Homologous chromosomes are the two members of one pair, one of maternal origin and one of paternal origin. Chromosomes bear the vehicles of hereditary traits, the genes. The morphological characteristics of the individual chromosomes and their total number are constant for all the somatic cells of a given species. Major chemical components are DNA, RNA, histones, and nonhistone proteins.

**Chromosome number**: The number of chromosomes found in the somatic cells of an individual or of a species: normally, 46 in a human being.

**Clone**: A colony of cells that originated from a single cell.

**Concordance rate**: A measure of the similarity of the presence or the absence of a disease or a specific trait in pairs of twins.

**Congenital**: Present at birth; not necessarily genetic.

**Consanguinity**: Relationship by descent from a common ancestor.

**Crossing-over**: The exchange of corresponding segments between maternal and paternal homologous chromsomes, occurring when maternal and paternal homologous chromosomes are paired during prophase of the first meiotic division.

**Cytogenetics:** The branch of genetics dealing with the cytological basis of heredity (i.e., with the study of the chromosomes).

**Deoxyribonucleic acid (DNA)**: The primary storage molecule for genetic information. DNA consists of a long chain of nucleotides, each of which is made up of a deoxyribose (a five-carbon sugar) molecule, a phosphate group, and one of four organic bases—adenine (A), guanine (G), thymine (T), or cytosine (C). The genetic code is contained in the linear array of those organic bases. Each arrangement of three bases (e.g., ACA, GCG) specifies the incorporation of a specific amino acid into a protein molecule.

**Diploid**: The normal complement of chromosomes (in humans, 22 pairs of homologous chromosomes and the sex chromosomes).

**Dizygotic (or dizygous) twins**: Twins resulting from the simultaneous fertilization of two ova by two spermatozoa. Recurrence in families is common. (*Synonym:* Fraternal twins.)

**Dominant gene**: A gene that expresses its effect even when it is present on only one chromosome.

**Empiric risk**: The prediction of the probability that a genetic or congenital abnormality will occur in a family.

**Exon**: A segment of a gene that is represented in the mature messenger RNA and that codes for a portion of the structure of a protein.

**Expressivity**: The extent to which a trait is manifested. The kind or the degree of phenotypic expression may be slight or pronounced.

**Family-risk study**: Study of the occurrence of a specific disorder in the family members of an identified person, the proband, who has the specific disorder.

**Gamete**: A male or female reproductive cell; a spermatozoon or an ovum.

**Gene**: A segment of DNA that contains the coding information for a single protein molecule or a limited set of protein molecules.

**Gene frequency**: The relative proportion of each of two or more alleles of a particular gene in a given population. The gene frequency may be expressed as a percentage (0 to 100 percent) or as a probability (0 to 1).

**Gene marker**: Identified chromosomal locus for which the genomic position is known. Gene markers are used in RFLP studies.

**Genetic code**: The sequential order of the bases of DNA, which carry the genetic information.

**Genocopy**: One who shares a trait with another because they have the same gene or genes.

**Genome**: All the genes found in a diploid set of chromosomes.

**Genotype**: The full set of genes carried by a person. The term is sometimes used in a limited way to refer to the alleles present at one or more loci.

**Haploid**: The number of chromosomes in a normal gamete, which contains only one member of each chromosome pair; in a human being, the haploid number is 23.

**Hemizygous**: Having unpaired genes. Since males have only one X chromosome, they are said to be hemizygous with respect to X-linked genes.

**Heritability**: A measure of the relative importance of genetic information in the determination of a particular observable feature.

**Hermaphrodite**: One with both male and female gonadal tissue (not necessarily functional).

**Table 3.4–1**
*Continued*

**Heterologous**: Having chromosomes or chromosomal segments that are nonhomologous (see Homologous) or nonidentical.

**Heterozygote**: One possessing differing alleles at a given locus on a pair of homologous chromosomes. (*Adjective*: Heterozygous.)

**Homologous**: Having chromosomes or chromosomal segments that are identical with respect to genetic loci and visible structure; e.g., two normal chromosome 15s. (*Noun*: Homologue.)

**Homozygote**: One possessing a pair of identical alleles at a given locus on a pair of homologous chromosomes. (*Adjective*: Homozygous.)

**Inborn error of metabolism**: A genetically determined biochemical disorder in which a specific enzyme defect produces a metabolic block that may have pathological consequences.

**Incidence**: The rate of new cases; e.g., the number of infants born with a condition divided by the number of live births in a given population in a period of time. (Compare with Prevalence.)

**Intron**: A segment of a gene that is initially transcribed but then spliced out of the messenger RNA. It is an intervening segment of DNA between two exons.

**Isochromosome**: A chromosome in which the arms on either side of the centromere are identical.

**Karyotype**: The full complement of chromosomes; the term covers the number, relative sizes, and morphology of the chromosomes.

**Linkage**: Genes that have their loci on the same chromosome are said to be linked. Also used to describe traits transmitted by a gene of known locus on a specific chromosome (e.g., see X-linkage).

**Locus**: The precise location of a gene on a chromosome. Different forms of the gene (alleles) are always found at the same locus on the chromosome.

**LOD score**: A measure of the probability of genetic linkage between a genetic trait and a polymorphism within a particular pedigree or series of pedigrees. The LOD score ranges from 0.0 to 0.5, with 0.5 representing no linkage.

**Meiosis**: Nucluear division that occurs during the formation of gametes. Two consecutive cell divisions (the first and second meiotic divisions) occur, but only one division of the chromosomes occurs. Thus, the number of chromosomes is reduced from the diploid (46) to the haploid (23) number. During meiosis, pairing of homologous chromosomes takes place, followed by chromosomal breakage and crossing-over. The end result of meiosis is four cells, each with half the number of chromosomes possessed by the original cell.

**Mendelian**: According to the genetic principles of Gregor Mendel, which included the descriptions of the heritability of dominant and recessive traits.

**Metaphase**: That stage of cell division (mitosis or meiosis) during which the chromosomes line up on the spindle equatorial plate.

**Mitosis**: A form of nuclear division in which each chromosome splits lengthwise (replicates itself); one chromatid of each chromosome passes to one daughter cell and the other chromatid to the second daughter cell. Thus, each daughter cell receives the full complement of 46 chromosomes. This type of cell division is characteristic of somatic cells and of germ cells before the onset of meiosis.

**Mode of inheritance**: The pattern of inheritance (e.g., dominant or recessive) of a particular allele.

**Monozygotic (or monozygous) twins**: Twins resulting from the division of a single zygote into two embryos after fertilization of a single ovum by a single spermatozoon. Recurrence within families is rare. (*Synonum*: Identical or one-egg twins.)

**Mosaic**: One with two or more cell lines differing in genotype.

**Multifactorial inheritance**: Inheritance of a trait governed by many genes or multiple factors. Each gene may act independently with cumulative total effect. Height, weight, and other body dimensions are determined by multifactorial inheritance.

**Mutation**: A permanent heritable change in the genetic material. Mutations are an important source of hereditary diversity.

**Mutation rate**: The frequency of detectable mutations for a genetic locus in a generation.

**Northern hybridization**: A research technique involving the hybridization (i.e., annealing) of complementary DNA probes to messenger RNA molecules that have been separated by gel electrophoresis and then transferred onto specialized materials (e.g., nitrocellulose membranes).

**Oncogene**: A gene that encodes a protein that is involved in tumor formation.

**Pedigree study**: A study of a family that usually includes multiple members of multiple generations. The heritability or lack of heritability of a particular trait can then be studied from one generation to the next and among members of the same generation.

**Penetrance**: The frequency of phenotypic expression of a dominant gene or a homozygous recessive gene. When a dominant gene produces no detectable phenotypic expression, it shows lack of penetrance.

**Phenocopy**: One with all the hallmarks of a particular genetic disorder but with no hereditary cause apparent in the pedigree or genome.

**Phenotype**: The total of all observable features of a person (including anatomical, physiological, biochemical, and psychological makeup and disease reactions, potential or actual). The phenotype is the result of interaction between the genotype and the environment. The term may also apply to the trait produced by a single gene or several genes.

**Population genetics**: The study of mutant genes in populations, rather than in individuals.

**Prediction study**: A type of family genetic study based on the prospective study of persons who are at high risk (e.g., the child of two affected parents) for the development of a specific disorder.

**Prevalence**: The number with a specific condition in a given population at a particular time. (Compare with Incidence.)

**Proband:** The person with an abnormality whose relatives are studied to determine the hereditary or genetic aspects of the trait. (*Synonyms*: Propositus [male]; proposita [female]; index case.)

**Probe**: A radioactive DNA or RNA sequence used to detect the presence of a complementary sequence by molecular hybridization.

**Prophase**: The first stage of cell division, during which the chromosomes become visible as discrete structures.

**Recessive**: Denoting a trait or gene expressed only in those who are homozygous (or hemizygous) for the gene concerned.

**Recombination**: The process by which a pair of homologous chromosomes physically exchange sections, yielding a new combination of genes.

**Restriction endonucleases**: A family of bacterial enzymes, each of which breaks DNA or RNA at specific base sequences. In bacteria, the enzymes restrict the entry of foreign genetic material (e.g., viruses) that would be harmful.

**Restriction fragment length polymorphism (RFLP)**: Different-length fragments of DNA containing the same site or locus in a chromosome, as revealed by exposure of the DNA to restriction endonucleases.

**Ribonucleic acid (RNA)**: A long chain of nucleotides that differ in two ways from the nucleotides of DNA; ribose is the sugar, instead of deoxyribose, and uracil is substituted for thymine. Several subtypes of RNA molecules are involved in the process by which the genetic information in DNA is transformed into a specific protein molecule.

**Ring chromosome**: A circular chromosome, resulting from

*Continued*

**Table 3.4–1**
*Continued*

breakage in both arms of a chromatid followed by fusion of the broken ends to form a ring. Varying amounts of chromosomal material are lost or deleted from both arms.

**Segregation**: The separation of the two alleles of a pair of allelic genes during meiosis, so that they pass to different gametes.

**Sex chromatin**: A chromatin mass in the nucleus of interphase cells of females. It represents a single X chromosome, which is inactive in the metabolism of the cell. Normal females have sex chromatin and, thus, are **chromatin-positive**; normal males lack it and, hence, are **chromatin-negative**. (*Synonym:* Barr body.)

**Sex chromosomes**: Chromosomes responsible for sex determination (XX in females; XY in males).

**Sex-limited**: Affecting one sex only.

**Sex-linkage**: Inheritance by genes on the sex chromosomes, especially on the X chromosomes.

**Somatic cell**: A nonreproductive cell. Somatic cells are diploid; germ cells are haploid.

**Southern blot**: A technique for transferring DNA fragments separated by gel electrophoresis onto nitrocellulose paper for molecular hybridization to labeled probes.

**State-dependent**: Denoting measures that vary with the person's particular clinical status. For example, intoxicated behavior is state-dependent on a person's being intoxicated.

**Teratogen**: Any agent that causes a physical defect or defects in a developing embryo or fetus.

**Trait-dependent**: Denoting measures that do not vary with the person's particular clinical status. For example, the genetic marker for Huntington's disease is present in an affected person both before and after the person has the symptoms of Huntington's disease.

**Transcription**: The molecular process by which the genetic code contained in a DNA molecule is used as a template to make a corresponding molecule of RNA.

**Translation**: The molecular process by which the genetic code contained in an RNA molecule is used as a template to construct a specific protein molecule.

**Translocation**: A change in location of genetic material, either within a chromosome or from one chromosome to another.

**Trisomy**: The presence of three, rather than two, chromosomes in a particular set; humans with three sex chromosomes—XXX, XXY, or XYY—are trisomic for the sex chromosomes.

**X-chromosome**: A sex chromosome that occurs singly in the normal male and in duplicate in the normal female.

**X-linkage**: Transmission of a trait by a gene on the X chromosome.

**Y chromosome**: A sex chromosome that occurs singly in the normal male and is absent in the normal female.

Table adapted from R Berkow, editor: *Merck Manual*, ed 15, p 2161. Merck Sharp & Dohme Research Laboratories, Rahway, N J, 1987. Used with permission.

takenly taken to be synonymous with psychological factors. In fact, environmental factors can be either psychological or nonpsychological. Examples of psychological environmental factors that may be involved in the causes of mental disorders include a wide range of life experiences that may induce significant stress, anxiety, sense of loss, or guilt feelings. Examples of nonpsychological environmental factors that may be involved in the causes of mental disorders include perinatal insults, infections, trauma, poor nutrition, and drugs. A further complication in the conceptualization of the relations is that the mere demonstration that some abnormal behavioral or psychological symptom (for example, depression) is more common in certain families than in the general population is not proof of a genetic basis for the observed symptom. Such symptoms can be spread through families by the same processes that other behaviors (for example, table manners) are acquired. The other processes include simple learning of behaviors, role modeling of significant caretakers, and acquisition and incorporation of behaviors observed in social settings.

## GENETIC MODELS

Although genetic models have myriad variations, the two basic models are the single major gene or single major locus model and the multifactorial-polygenic model. The *single major gene model* hypothesizes that a single gene is involved in transmitting the trait and that environmental factors are minimal or nonexistent. The *multifactorial-polygenic model* supposes that two or more genes are involved and that environmental factors (both psychological and nonpsychological) are involved in the development of the final phenotype.

## GENETIC SUSCEPTIBILITY

Not many psychiatric disorders are likely to be caused by single genes. Rather, multiple genes probably contribute to the development of a mental illness in a person. One theoretical formulation is the concept of genetic susceptibility genes. A *susceptibility gene* is one that increases the risk that a person with the gene will have a particular disorder. The presence of additional susceptibility genes or the action of environmental variables may be necessary for the development of the disorder.

## GENES AND TREATMENT

### Psychoactive Drugs

Although students of behavior often think of genes as the causes of mental disorders, they rarely think of gene regulation with regard to commonly used psychoactive drugs. Neurotransmitters and hormones, acting through second messengers and intracellular receptors, can regulate gene expression. Currently used antidepressant, antipsychotic, and antimanic agents can take weeks to have their therapeutic effects and can be associated with continuing clinical improvement for months. Those effects are in contrast to their immediate biochemical effects, such as blocking neurotransmitter uptake and blocking receptor binding. The most likely biological mechanism to explain the delayed therapeutic effects of the drugs is the regulation of gene expression. Although gene expression can be stimulated or inhibited within minutes of an appropriate stimulus, the regulation of genetic expression is a likely explanation for delayed or sustained changes in cellular function.

## Gene Therapy

Current clinical trials are using gene therapy in humans for an increasing number of medical illnesses. The trials include the use of gene transfer techniques in patients who lack specific enzymes (for example, adenosine deaminase) and in patients with various types of cancers that may be controllable by the introduction of another gene and its resultant protein product. Although gene therapy for psychiatric disorders is not likely to evolve for some time, safe viruses carrying DNA for a particular dopamine receptor may someday be targeted to transfect specific populations of limbic neurons in the brains of schizophrenic patients.

## COMPLEXITIES

### Diagnosis

If researchers want to study the genetic contribution to a mental disorder, they have to be able to identify who has the disorder and who does not have the disorder. Although diagnostic systems such as the fourth edition of *Diagnostic and Statistical Manual of Mental Disorders* (DSM-IV) have codified diagnostic practices and are reliable and valid, two unresolved issues regarding diagnosis remain. First, it is necessary to decide whether to study a narrowly defined population (for example, just schizophrenic patients) or to study a broadly defined population that may include patients with disorders related to the primary disorder. For example, in a study of the genetics of schizophrenia, an investigator may want to include families and relatives affected with schizoaffective disorder, schizotypal personality disorder, and brief reactive psychosis. Second, because a mental illness can have its onset at various times during a person's life, it is possible to mistakenly classify a particular person in a study as being mentally healthy when, in fact, in some years' time, that person will have the psychiatric disease under study. Various mathematical models, all falling under the rubric of *age-correction procedures*, have been developed to deal with the variability in the age of onset of psychiatric disorders.

### Heterogeneity

Each disorder classified in DSM-IV probably has many causes. Thus, when an investigator gathers a group of depressed patients together to study the genetic factors leading to depressive disorders, the investigator is likely to be examining several disease processes. Different susceptibility genes may be contributing to the development of the depression in different patients, and different environmental influences may have affected the patients. A cynical view of the situation is to compare such a study to a study of people with stomachaches. Stomachache is a symptom that can be caused by food poisoning, overeating, gastric ulcers, gastric cancer, anxiety, stress, and a legion of other factors. The argument against that cynical view is simply that science has to start

somewhere in its exploration of mental disorders. Furthermore, some investigators are beginning to limit their studies to types of affected persons who share some common, objective, biological marker—for example, specific findings on a computerized topographic electroencephalographic (EEG) study.

### Family History

In studies of the genetics of psychiatric disorders, investigators must usually assess the psychiatric status of as many family members as possible. It is often difficult enough to feel completely comfortable with the psychiatric assessment of a single psychiatric patient, and it is even more difficult to obtain complete psychiatric information on all relatives of a patient. Even when all living relatives are willing to be interviewed, a researcher is left with the psychiatric assessment of deceased and missing relatives.

### Assortative Mating

One of the first tenets of theoretical genetics assumed nonselective mating practices as part of the mathematical considerations in the equations regarding gene frequencies. However, in psychiatric disorders, mating is not nonselective; mentally ill persons are more likely to mate with other mentally ill persons than would be expected by chance. The increased likelihood for affected persons to mate with other affected persons is called *assortative mating*.

## BASIC GENETICS

### DNA and RNA

Each of the two strands in the double helix of deoxyribonucleic acid (DNA) consists of a linear arrangement of four basic nucleotide units. The nucleotides are the two purines—adenine (A) and guanine (G)—and the two somewhat smaller pyrimidines—cytosine (C) and thymine (T). Adenine in one DNA strand is always paired with thymine in the complementary strand; guanine is always paired with cytosine in the complementary strand. Ribonucleic acid (RNA) is similar to DNA but contains ribose, instead of deoxyribose, as its sugar and contains uracil, instead of thymine. There are several types of RNA, including heterogeneous nuclear RNA (hnRNA), messenger RNA (mRNA), transfer RNA (tRNA), and ribosomal RNA (rRNA).

### Genes and Chromosomes

A gene has been classically defined as the segment of DNA that encodes the information regarding the amino acid sequence for a single protein or a limited set of proteins. The old concept of one gene, one protein is no longer considered completely valid. An estimated 100,000 genes are in the human genome. Because all people receive half of their genetic material from one parent and half from the other parent, each person is considered to have two alleles for each gene. If the alleles for a particular gene are the same, the person is *homozygous* for that gene; if the alleles for a particular gene are different, the person is *heterozygous* for that gene. A dominant allele is expressed even when a recessive allele is present. A recessive allele is expressed only in the absence of a dominant allele.

Human genes are contained within the 46 chromosomes, which are located in the nucleus of every cell. The chromosomes contain DNA and structural and regulatory proteins. The 46 chromosomes comprise 22 pairs of somatic chromosomes and one pair of sex chromosomes (XX for females, XY for males).

## Transcription and Translation

The sole products of genes are proteins. The genetic message in DNA is first transcribed into a complementary RNA genetic message by the actions of an enzyme, RNA polymerase II. The resultant RNA is sometimes referred to as heterogeneous nuclear RNA (hnRNA) and is an exact, albeit complementary, copy of the DNA. That original transcript, the hnRNA, is further processed in the nucleus to form mature mRNA, which encodes the final sequence for the first protein product. The mRNA is transported out of the nucleus into the cytoplasm, where the mRNA template is translated into a protein, by a mechanism involving ribosomes (made up of rRNA) and tRNAs, which transport the appropriate amino acids to the elongating polypeptide chain of the emerging protein.

A *protein* consists of a long chain made up of a variable linear arrangement of the 20 available amino acids. The order of amino acids in a protein is determined by the DNA message and is called the *primary structure* of the protein. On the basis of the primary structure of a protein and the resultant placement of charges and sizes of amino acids, the protein folds into a unique shape, which constitutes the *secondary and tertiary structures* of the protein. Often, several proteins form complexes of proteins, and such complexes are referred to as the *quaternary structures* of the proteins.

## Introns and Exons

The 100,000 human genes account for only about 1 percent of the human DNA. The function of the DNA that does not code protein information is poorly understood but is thought to involve regulatory mechanisms and structural integrity for the DNA. The surplus DNA is found both outside the genes and within the genes. Thus, within the genes, *exons* are segments of the gene that are *ex*ported to the cytoplasm in the form of mRNA, whereas *introns* are segments of the gene that remain *in*side the nucleus. The process of removing the introns from the hnRNA and splicing the exons into mature mRNA is performed by a recently discovered nuclear organelle, the *spliceosome*, and the overall process of splicing a single hnRNA transcript into a finite number of mRNAs is referred to as *alternative or differential splicing*.

## Gene Expression Regulation

Although the details of gene regulation may, at first, seem far removed from clinical psychiatry, it is likely that, before the next edition of this textbook is published, articles will appear in the major psychiatric journals about transcription factors and immediate early genes and their potential associations with psychiatric disorders. That possibility is made likely by the obvious, yet not explicated,

association between gene regulation, on the one hand, and the cause, onset, course, and treatment of brain disorders, on the other hand.

A major clue to the complexity of gene regulation is the fact that every cell (except the germ cells) contains the same genetic information in its DNA, yet there are countless varieties of cell types and cell functions. The differentiation of cell types occurs because genes are differentially expressed in each cell type. In a particular cell, some genes are expressed, and some genes are not expressed. Also, the amount of gene expression can vary among cells. For example, some cells produce lots of a particular enzyme, and other cells produce limited amounts of the same enzyme. The process of transcription of RNA from DNA begins with the initiation step of transcription, and the initiation of RNA transcription has been the focus of most of the research on the regulation of gene expression.

Many regulatory elements are involved in the initiation of the transcription of RNA from a gene. Specific segments of DNA within a gene, called *cisregulatory elements*, modulate the positioning of the RNA polymerase and the efficiency of the transcriptional process. Cisregulatory elements include promotor and enhancer regions. The *promotor regions* have been characterized as being closer to the start site of transcription, and the *enhancer regions* have been characterized as being further removed; however, that differentiation may not be of substantive importance in their effects on gene regulation. Cisregulatory elements serve as binding sites for a wide variety of *transcription factors* (also called *transacting factors*), which are proteins that can act as either activators or repressors at the cisregulatory sites.

## Gene Regulation by Hormones and Neurotransmitters

Various hormones, most notably the steroid and thyroid hormones, and neurotransmitters can regulate the process of transcription of the DNA message into an RNA molecule. The common element in the process, regardless of the initiating molecule, is the production or the activation of a transcriptional factor. Steroid hormones bind to their intracellular receptors; then that hormonal-receptor complex binds to a particular cisregulatory element, the glucocorticoid response element (GRE), and either activates or suppresses the transcription of a protein, depending on the particular hormone, receptor, and GRE involved. Neurotransmitters act in an analogous fashion, primarily by activating protein kinases, which then phosphorylate and thereby activate transcription factors, which then interact with cisregulatory elements and either activate or suppress transcription of a particular gene. Another transacting factor is the second messenger, cyclic adenosine monophosphate (cAMP); it is involved, for example, in the regulation of the number of β-adrenergic receptors (Figure 3.4–1). The molecule, cAMP, binds to cisacting regulatory elements, called cAMP response elements (CREs), that are located in specific genes. Another mechanism of regulation of protein synthesis is by regulation of the life span of mature mRNA in the cytoplasm, which, for example, is part of the regulatory pathway for the β-adrenergic receptors (Figure 3.4–1).

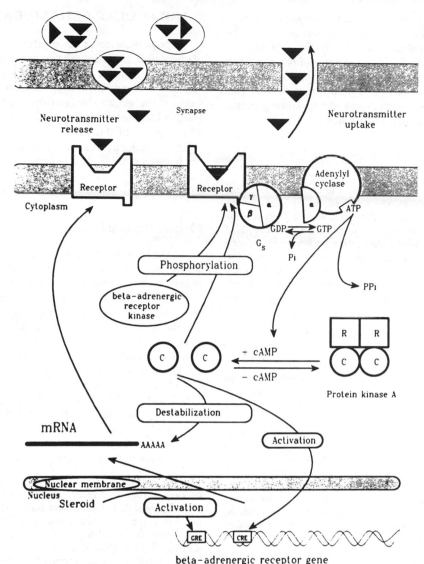

**Figure 3.4–1.** Agonist regulation of G-protein-linked receptor messenger ribonucleic acid (mRNA): transcriptional, posttranscriptional, and posttranslational controls. Agonist regulation of β-adrenergic receptors is divided into two distinct phases. In the early phase (up to four hours of stimulation), uptake of the neurotransmitter and phosphorylation of the receptor play central roles in attenuating the response to catecholamines. An early, transient, agonist-induced increase in the transcription rate (after one hour of stimulation) of the β₂-adrenergic receptor gene increases receptor mRNA levels. In the late phase of agonist regulation (more than four hours of stimulation), the rate of transcription of the receptor gene is unaffected by the agonist. Agonist-induced down-regulation of a receptor reflects down-regulation of receptor mRNA levels by the destabilization of the mRNA. CRE—cAMP-responsive element; GRE—glucocorticoid-responsive element; $G_s$ the stimulatory G protein coupled to adenylyl cyclase; PPi and Pi—inorganic phosphate; R and C—regulatory and catalytic subunits of cAMP-dependent protein kinase, respectively. (Figure from J R Hadcock, C C Malbon: Regulation of receptor expression by agonists: Transcriptional and post-transcriptional controls. Trends Neurosci *14*: 245, 1991. Used with permission.)

## Immediate Early Genes

Recent research has shown that one particular class of genes, the immediate early genes (IEGs), are activated within minutes of synaptic activity. One function of IEGs is to act as transcription factors for other genes. Two of the better understood IEGs are c-Fos and Jun. The transcription of the c-Fos gene is stimulated by selected synaptic activation; the c-Fos mRNA is transported into the cytoplasm, where c-Fos protein is made. The c-Fos protein then forms a dimer with the Jun protein, and the combination of the two proteins acts as a potent transcriptional activator for other genes. The study of c-Fos, Jun, and other IEGs is now an active field of investigation in psychopharmacology; investigators are attempting to distinguish drug-stimulated and brain region-specific areas of c-Fos and Jun production.

## POPULATION GENETICS

*Population genetics* is the study of genetic transmission in families and populations. The key aspects of population genetics in psychiatry are identifying persons affected with a particular set of psychiatric signs or symptoms (that is, possessing a particular phenotype) and inferring the genetic makeup of those persons (their genotype). The fundamental equation of population genetics is the *Hardy-Weinberg law*, which states that, if two alleles ($a_1$ and $a_2$) of a gene have frequencies in two parents of $p_1$ and $p_2$, the progeny of those parents will have genotypes of $a_1a_1$, $a_1a_2$, and $a_2a_2$ at frequencies of $p_1^2$, $2p_1p_2$, $p_2^2$, respectively. The three major approaches to the study of population genetics are family, twin, and adoption studies.

## Family Studies

Family studies usually begin with the unbiased identification of an affected person, the *proband*, and the subsequent study of that person's family. An example of a probably unbiased identification strategy is the selection of every third schizophrenic patient who comes into a particular emergency room. If an illness has a significant genetic component, the *first-degree relatives* (mother, father, siblings, children) are more likely to be affected with the illness than are second-degree relatives, who are more likely to be affected than third-degree relatives.

## Twin Studies

The two types of twins are monozygotic (MZ) twins, who develop from a single ovum, and dizygotic (DZ) twins, who develop from two ova. MZ twins share 100 percent of their genetic material, whereas DZ twins share no more of their genetic material than do any two siblings with the same parents. Studies of twin pairs in which at least one twin is affected with a mental disorder have been used as an additional way to determine the extent to which a psychiatric disorder is genetically determined. If a disorder has genetic determinants, both MZ twins should be affected (that is, be *concordant*) much more often than both DZ twins are affected. That is, the DZ twins should be discordant for the disorder more often than are the MZ twins.

## Adoption Studies

A major research strategy for the assessment of the effects of the environment on the expression of genes is the adoption study approach. In studies using the *adoptees' family method*, the biological and adoptive parents of affected adopted probands are compared with the biological and adoptive parents of unaffected adopted controls. If the adoptive parents of affected probands have a higher rate of the disorder under study than do the adoptive parents of unaffected controls, the family environment is implicated in the development of the disorder. If the biological parents of affected probands have a higher rate of the disorder under study than do the biological parents of unaffected controls, genetic factors are implicated in the development of the disorder. In the *adoptees' study method*, adopted children who had affected parents are studied for the development of the disorder under investigation. If the adopted children have the disorder more often than do a control group, a genetic factor from the biological parents is implicated. The most powerful version of the study involves MZ twins who are reared apart in different environments—for example, one twin with adoptive parents and the other twin with the biological parents. In the *cross-fostering method*, adopted children of affected biological parents and unaffected adoptive parents are compared with the children of unaffected biological parents and affected adoptive parents.

## MOLECULAR BEHAVIORAL GENETICS

The combination of the carefully worked out methods of population genetics with the powerful tools of molecular biology has fostered the field of molecular behavioral genetics. The commitment of the scientific community to the study of the genetic basis of disease is evidenced by the Human Genome Project, which plans to identify and map all the genes of the human genome in the next decade. Since the majority of genes are expressed only in the central nervous system, the Human Genome Project will particularly benefit neuroscientists and clinical neuropsychiatrists.

## Meiotic Recombination

At the heart of all molecular genetic methods is the fact that genes can exchange their chromosomal locations between alleles during meiosis. At meiosis, the maternally derived chromosomes and the paternally derived chromosomes are in close proximity and may undergo meiotic recombination. Genes that are close together are less likely to be separated by meiotic recombination than are genes that are far apart. Genes that are close together and, thus, usually inherited together by the daughter cells after meiosis are said to be *genetically linked*. Two hypothetical genes that are inherited together 99 percent of the time and that recombine 1 percent of the time are said to be separated on the chromosome by a distance of 1 centimorgan (1 cM). The physical distance of 1 cM is estimated to be 1 million base pairs of DNA (1 megabase of DNA).

**LOD scores.** The *recombinant fraction* (theta) is the percentage of time that recombination occurs between two particular genes. If the genes are far apart and inherited independently, the recombinant fraction is 50 percent; if two genes are always inherited together because there is no recombination, the recombinant fraction is 0 percent. The *odds ratio* is the ratio of (1) the likelihood of the observed data occurring if the experimentally determined theta value is correct to (2) the likelihood of the observed data occurring if the theta value were 0.5 (the theta value if the genes were not linked). The *LOD score* is defined as the $\log_{10}$ of the odds ratio. The LOD score values from different families can simply be added together to determine a cumulative LOD score. In single-gene Mendelian models, a LOD score of more than 3 is considered evidence for linkage, and a LOD score of less than $-2$ is evidence against linkage.

## Restriction Fragment Length Polymorphisms

Since more than 99 percent of the DNA is not gene-related DNA, most recombinations occur outside the genes themselves, in areas in which the recombination may be silent—that is, without observable physiological effects. The major technique to explore those recombination events is restriction fragment length polymorphisms (RFLPs). The RFLP approach could be developed only after the identification of *restriction endonucleases*, a class of enzymes that are able to cleave DNA at selected sites defined by the presence of specific base sequences. When a person's DNA is exposed to a restriction endonuclease, the DNA is cut into many small fragments (Figure 3.4–2). The pattern of resulting pieces into which a particular restriction endonuclease cuts a person's DNA is constant; however, the pattern differs among persons. The specific pattern of resultant DNA pieces can be identified by the technique of Southern blotting, in combination with the use of radiolabeled molecular probes (Figure 3.4–2).

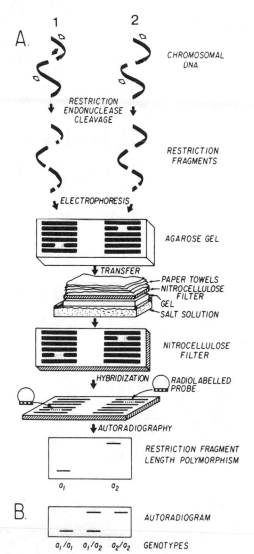

**Figure 3.4–2.** Restriction fragment length polymorphisms (RFLPs). (A) Two homologous chromosomes, 1 and 2, that differ in the presence or the absence of a polymorphic restriction endonuclease cleavage site (closed arrowhead) in the vicinity of a unique marker locus (hatched region). Endonuclease cleavage (arrowheads) results, on average, in tens of thousands of restriction fragments. The variable sites result in different-sized fragments from each chromosome. Restriction fragments are separated by size, using agarose gel electrophoresis, and are transferred by capillary action to a nitrocellulose filter (Southern blotting). The filter is then hybridized to a radiolabeled probe containing the complementary base sequence to the marker locus. After autoradiography, individual bands corresponding to restriction fragments from each chromosome are visualized. The combination of restriction endonuclease and probe permits the detection of allelic variations ($a_1$ and $a_2$) in DNA sequence around the marker locus. (B) Autoradiographic patterns for each of three possible genotypes (pairs of alleles) are shown. (Figure from R O Reider, C A Kaufmann: Genetics. In *The American Psychiatric Press Textbook of Psychiatry*, J A Talbott, R E Hales, S C Yudofsky, editors, p 44. American Psychiatric Press, Washington, 1988. Used with permission.)

## RFLP Strategies

The overall strategy of RFLP studies is to find an association between an RFLP and a particular disease. Large families, preferably with multiple affected members and generations, are used in RFLP studies. The DNA from each family member can be obtained by collecting a blood sample and immortalizing the lymphocytes, thus providing a constant source of DNA for subsequent experiments. Two general approaches are the candidate gene approach and the reverse genetics approach. In the *candidate gene approach* a probe for a gene that is hypothetically related to the disease under study (for example, the β-adrenergic receptor in the study of depression) is used as the radiolabeled probe in the Southern blotting technique. With that approach the experimenter is looking for an RFLP that is detected with the candidate gene and is associated with the presence of the disease. The *reverse genetics approach* uses a wide array of genetic probes, which are not in any way theoretically related to the disease under question, in the hope of finding a probe that detects an RFLP associated with the disease state. If such an association is found, the investigator may hypothesize, from the known location of the probe on the chromosome, that the disease gene is located on the particular fragment of DNA that was cut by the specific restriction endonuclease and labeled with the specific molecular probe. That segment of DNA can theoretically be analyzed to determine its entire base pair sequence, thus revealing the involved gene. The reverse genetics approach was used successfully to locate the gene for Huntington's disease to the short arm of chromosome 4; however, the identification of the specific gene involved has proved to be much more difficult.

**Variable number of tandem repeats.** Within the genome are regions in which particular segments of DNA are repeated a variable number of times. Those repeating segments are referred to as regions of a variable number of tandem repeats (VNTRs). On both sides of a VNTR region, specific segments of DNA can be cleaved with a restriction endonuclease. VNTR regions are not distributed evenly throughout the genome and are not abundant, but they do offer some advantages over the RFLP technique, so their use in the study of psychiatric disorders is increasing. As with RFLPs, the experiments are designed to determine if there is an association between a particular VNTR region and a psychiatric disorder.

## References

Alper J S, Natowicz M R: On establishing the genetic basis of mental disease. Trends Neurosci *16*: 387, 1993.
Anderson W F: Human gene therapy. Science *256*: 808, 1992.
Baron M, Endicott J, Ott J: Genetic linkage in mental illness: Limitations and prospects. Br J Psychiatry *157*: 645, 1990.
Ehrlich H A, Gelfand D, Sninsky J J: Recent advances in the polymerase chain reaction. Science *252*: 1643, 1991.
Emson P C: In situ hybridization as a methodological tool for the neuroscientist. Trends Neurosci *16*: 9, 1993.
Hadcock J R, Malbon C C: Regulation of receptor expression by agonists: Transcriptional and post-transcriptional controls. Trends Neurosci *14*: 242, 1991.
Kelsoe J R: The search for genes for psychiatric illness. Neuropsychopharmacology *6*: 215, 1992.
Miller A D: Human gene therapy comes of age. Nature *357*: 455, 1992.
Mullan M J, Murray R M: The impact of molecular genetics on our understanding of the psychoses. Br J Psychiatry *154*: 591, 1989.

Plomin R: The role of inheritance in behavior. Science *248*: 183, 1990.

Reiss D, Plomin R, Hetherington E M: Genetics and psychiatry: An unheralded window on the environment. Am J Psychiatry *148*: 283, 1991.

Ross C A, McInnis M G, Margolis R L, Li S-H: Genes with triplet repeats: Candidate mediators of neuropsychiatric disorders. Trends Neurosci *16*: 254, 1993.

Stephens J C, Cavanaugh M L, Gradie M I, Mador M L, Kidd K K: Mapping the human genome: Current status. Science *250*: 237, 1990.

# 4

# Contributions of the Psychosocial Sciences to Human Behavior

## 4.1 / Jean Piaget

Jean Piaget (1896–1980) was born in Neuchatel, Switzerland (Figure 4.1–1). He was trained in psychology and studied at various centers, including the Burgholzi Psychiatric Hospital with Eugen Bleuler. He developed a broad theoretical system of intellectual and perceptual development and in that respect resembled Sigmund Freud; however, Piaget's focus was on how children and adolescents think and acquire knowledge.

Piaget referred to his theory as *genetic epistemology*, which is defined as the study of the acquisition, modification, and growth of abstract ideas and abilities on the basis of an inherited or biological substrate. What is innate is an intelligent functioning that makes the growth of abstract thought possible. Piaget derived his theories from direct observations of children (including his own) and by questioning children about their thinking. He was less interested in whether children answered correctly than in how they arrived at their answers. Piaget viewed intelligence as an extension of biological adaptation and as having a logical structure. Central to Piaget's theory is the concept of *epigenesis*, which holds that growth and development occur in a series of stages, each of which is built on the successful mastery of the preceding stage. Every stage occurs at a certain age, and the child shows a higher level of thought organization during each successive stage of development.

### COGNITIVE ORGANIZATION

Cognitive organization is the process of learning and knowing that occurs in a predictable manner. The major process involved in cognitive organization is *adaptation*, which is the ability of the person to adjust to the environment and interact with it. Adaptation occurs as a result of two complementary processes: assimilation and accommodation. *Assimilation* is the taking in of new experiences through one's own system of knowledge. It has been compared to the taking in and digestion of food, which then becomes part of the substance of the organism. *Accommodation* is the adjustment of one's system of knowledge to the reality demands of the environment. Together, the two processes, which are in dynamic equilibrium, create schemata. A *schema* can be defined as a specific cognitive structure that has a behavioral pattern. Piaget spoke of a schema of sucking, grasping, and seeing. Those early schemata become more complex as the person grows. Later schemata, which Piaget referred to as *operations*, include imitation, abstraction, and higher intelligence. As the infant or the child grows, it continues to adapt to the outside world and continues to react with increasingly complex patterns of cognitive organization.

Organization is both biological and psychological, and all species inherit the ability to organize, which is different for different species. Birds organize flying, and human babies organize crawling. Organization varies among individual members of a species, but its function is constant. For instance, every baby crawls in its own way, but crawling is constant.

Organization occurs in stages, each of which represents a stage of cognitive development, described below with the approximate ages at which they first occur.

## STAGES OF COGNITIVE DEVELOPMENT

Piaget described four major stages leading to the capacity for adult thought. Each stage is a prerequisite for the one that follows. However, the rate at which different children move through different stages varies with their native endowment and environmental circumstances. The four stages are (1) the sensorimotor stage, (2) the stage of preoperational thought, (3) the stage of concrete operations, and (4) the stage of formal operations.

### Sensorimotor Stage (Birth to 2 Years)

Piaget used the term "sensorimotor" to describe this stage because infants first begin to learn through sensory observation, and they gain control of their motor functions through activity, exploration, and manipulation of the environment. Piaget divided this stage into six substages, listed in Table 4.1–1.

From the outset, biology and experience blend to produce learned behavior. For example, infants are born with a sucking reflex. A type of learning occurs when an infant alters the shape of its mouth and discovers the location of the nipple. A stimulus is received, and a response results, accompanied by a sense of awareness that is the first schema or elementary concept. As the infant becomes more mobile, one schema is built on another, and new and more complex schemata are developed. The infant's spatial, visual, and tactile world expands during this period, and the child actively interacts with the environment, using previously learned behavior patterns. For example, having learned to use a rattle, infants shake a new toy like the rattle they have already learned to use. Infants also use the rattle in new ways.

The critical achievement of this period is the development of *object permanence* or the *schema of the permanent object*. That term relates to the child's ability to understand that objects have an existence independent of the child's involvement with them. Infants learn to differentiate themselves from the world and are able to maintain a mental image of an object, even though it is not present and visible.

If an object is dropped in front of infants, they look down to the ground to search for the object; that is, they behave for the first time as though the object has a reality outside themselves.

At about 18 months, infants begin to develop mental symbols and to use words, a process known as *symbolization*. Infants are able to create a visual image of a ball or a mental symbol of the word "ball" to stand for or signify the real object. Such mental representations allow children to operate on new conceptual levels. The attainment of object permanence marks the transition from the sensorimotor stage to the preoperational stage of development.

**Table 4.1–1**
**Piaget's Sensorimotor Period of Cognitive Development**

| Age | Characteristics |
| --- | --- |
| Birth–2 months | Uses inborn motor and sensory reflexes (sucking, grasping, looking) to interact and accommodate to the external world |
| 2–5 months | Primary circular reaction—coordinates activities of own body and five senses (e.g., sucking thumb); reality remains subjective—does not seek stimuli outside of its visual field; displays curiosity |
| 5–9 months | Secondary circular reaction—seeks out new stimuli in the environment; starts both to anticipate consequences of own behavior and to act purposefully to change the environment; beginning of intentional behavior |
| 9 months–1 year | Shows preliminary signs of object permanence; has a vague concept that objects exist apart from itself; plays peekaboo; imitates novel behaviors |
| 1 year–18 months | Tertiary circular reaction—seeks out new experiences; produces novel behaviors |
| 18 months–2 years | Symbolic thought—uses symbolic representations of events and objects; shows signs of reasoning (e.g., uses one toy to reach for and get another); attains object permanence |

Table adapted from H P Ginsburg: Jean Piaget. In *Comprehensive Textbook of Psychiatry*, ed 4, H I Kaplan, B J Sadock, editors, p 179. Williams & Wilkins, Baltimore, 1985.

### Stage of Preoperational Thought (2 to 7 Years)

During the stage of preoperational thought, the child uses symbols and language more extensively than in the sensorimotor stage. Thinking and reasoning are on an intuitive level in that the child learns without the use of reasoning. Children are unable to think logically or deductively, and their concepts are primitive; they can name objects but not classes of objects. Preoperational thought is midway between socialized adult thought and the completely autistic Freudian unconscious. Events are not linked by logic. Early in this stage, if children drop a glass and it breaks, they have no sense of cause and effect. The children believe that the glass was ready to break, not that they broke the glass. Also, children in this stage are unable to grasp the sameness of an object in different circumstances; the same doll in a carriage, a crib, or a chair is perceived to be three different objects. During this time, things are represented in terms of their function. For example, a child defines a bike as "to ride" and a hole as "to dig."

In this stage, children begin to use language and drawings in more elaborate ways. From one-word utterances, two-word phrases develop, made up of either a noun and a verb or a noun and an objective. A child may say, "Bobby eat" or "Bobby up."

Children in the preoperational stage are unable to deal with moral dilemmas, although they have a sense of what is good and what is bad. For example, when asked, "Who is more guilty: the person who breaks one dish on purpose or the person who breaks 10 dishes by accident?" the young child usually answers that the person who breaks 10 dishes by accident is more guilty because more dishes are broken.

Children in this stage have a sense of *immanent justice*, the belief that punishment for bad deeds is inevitable.

During this stage, children are described as *egocentric*. They see themselves as the center of the universe, they have a limited point of view, and they are unable to take the role of the other person. Children are unable to modify their behavior for someone else. For example, children are not being negativistic when they do not listen to commands to be quiet because their brother has to study. Instead, egocentric thinking prevents an understanding of their brother's point of view.

During this stage, children also use a type of magical thinking, called *phenomenalistic causality*, in which events that occur together are thought to cause one another (for example, thunder causes lightning, and bad thoughts cause accidents). In addition, children use *animistic thinking*, which is the tendency to endow physical events and objects with lifelike psychological attributes, such as feelings and intentions.

**Semiotic function.** The semiotic function occurs during the preoperational period. With this new ability, a child can represent something—such as an object, an event, or a conceptual scheme—with a signifier, which serves a representative function (for example, language, mental image, symbolic gesture). During this stage, the child is able to use a symbol or a sign to stand for something else. Drawing is a semiotic function that is initially done as a playful exercise but that eventually signifies something else in the real world.

## Stage of Concrete Operations (7 to 11 Years)

The stage of concrete operations is so named because in this period the child operates and acts on the concrete, real, and perceivable world of objects and events. Egocentric thought is replaced by *operational thought*, which involves attending to and dealing with a wide array of information outside the child. Therefore, a child can now see things from someone else's perspective.

Children in this stage begin to use limited logical thought processes and are able to serialize, order, and group things in classes on the basis of common characteristics. *Syllogistic reasoning*, in which a logical conclusion is formed from two premises, occurs during this stage; for example, all horses are mammals (premise); all mammals are warm blooded (premise); therefore, all horses are warm-blooded (conclusion). Children are able to reason and follow rules and regulations. They are able to regulate themselves and begin to develop a moral sense and a code of values.

Children who become overly invested in rules may show obsessive-compulsive behavior; children who resist a code of values often seem willful and inactive. The most desirable developmental outcome in this stage is for the child to attain a healthy respect for rules and to understand that there are legitimate exceptions to rules.

*Conservation* is the ability to recognize that, even though the shape and the form of objects may change, the objects still maintain or conserve other characteristics that enable them to be recognized as the same. For example, if a ball of clay is rolled into a long and thin sausage shape, the child recognizes that the same amount of clay is in the two forms. An inability to conserve (which is characteristic of the preoperational stage) is observed when the child declares that more clay is in the sausage-shaped form because it is longer. *Reversibility* is the capacity to understand the relation between things, to understand that one thing can turn into another and back again—for example, ice and water.

The most important sign that children are still in the preoperational stage is that they have not achieved conservation or reversibility. The ability of children to understand concepts of quantity is one of Piaget's most important cognitive developmental theories. Measures of quantity include measures of substance, length, number, liquids, and area (Figure 4.1–2).

The task of the 7-to-11-year-old is to organize and order occurrences in the real world. Dealing with the future and its possibilities occurs in the formal operational stage.

## Stage of Formal Operations (11 Years Through the End of Adolescence)

The stage of formal operations is characterized by the young person's ability to think abstractly, to reason deductively, and to define concepts. This stage is so named because the person's thinking operates in a formal, highly logical, systematic, and symbolic manner. This stage is also characterized by skills in dealing with permutations and combinations; the young person can grasp the concept of probabilities. The adolescent attempts to deal with all possible relations and hypotheses to explain data and events. During this stage, language use is complex, follows formal rules of logic, and is grammatically correct. Abstract thinking is shown by the adolescent's interest in a variety of issues: philosophy, religion, ethics, and politics.

**Hypothetico-deductive thinking.** This type of thinking is the highest organization of cognition; it enables the person to make a hypothesis or a proposition and to test it against reality. *Deductive reasoning* is characterized by going from the general to the particular; it is a more complicated process than *inductive reasoning*, which is the opposite—going from the particular to the general.

Because young people can reflect on their own and other people's thinking, they are prone to self-conscious behavior. As adolescents attempt to master new cognitive tasks, they may return to egocentric thought but on a higher level than in the past. For example, adolescents may think that they can accomplish everything or can change events by thought alone.

Not all adolescents enter the stage of formal operations at the same time or to the same degree. Depending on individual capacity and intervening experience, some may not reach the stage of formal operational thought at all and may remain in the concrete operational mode throughout life.

## APPLICATIONS TO PSYCHIATRY AND EDUCATION

### Psychiatry

Piaget's theories have psychiatric implications. Hospitalized children who are in the sensorimotor stage have

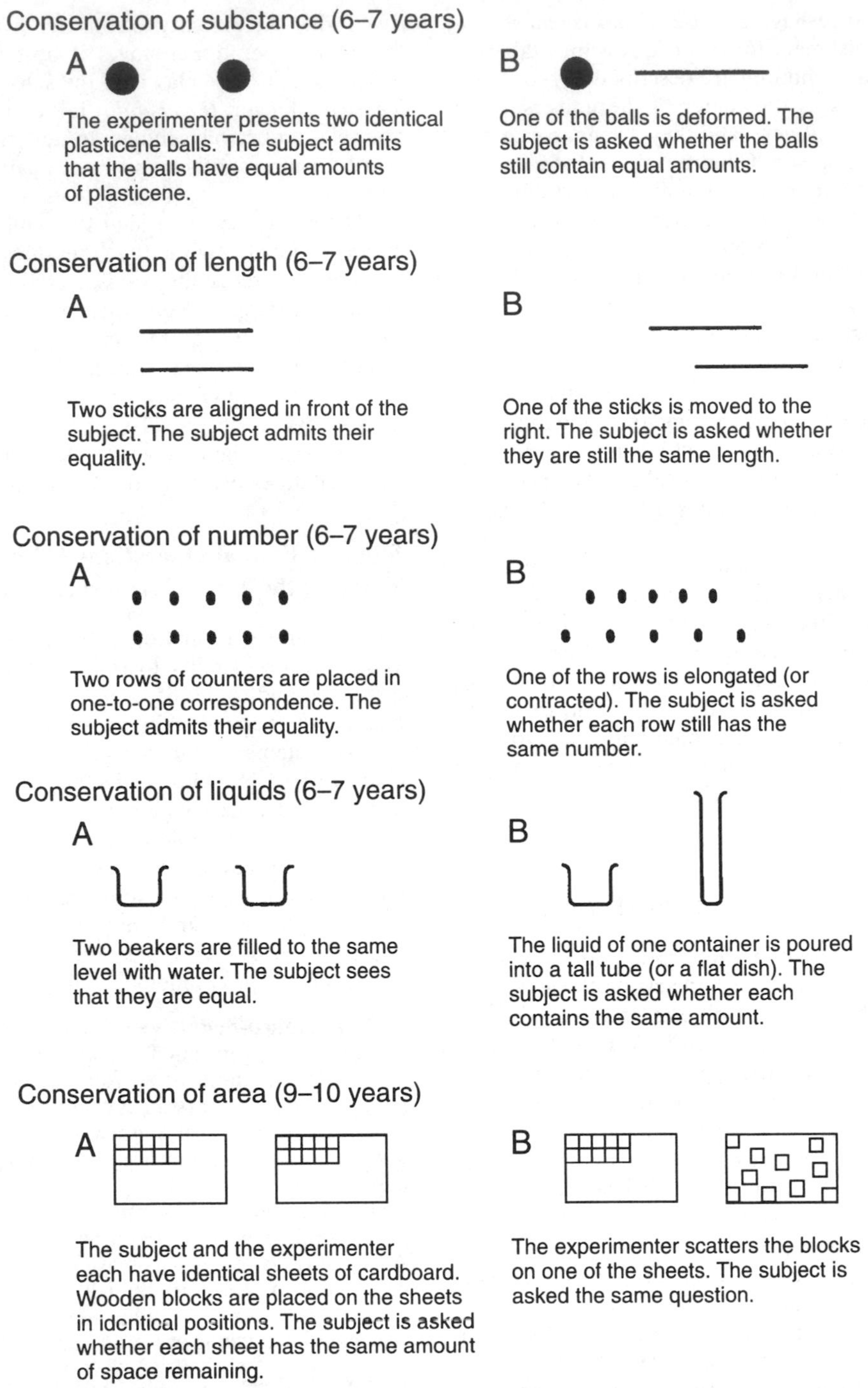

### Conservation of substance (6–7 years)

A

The experimenter presents two identical plasticene balls. The subject admits that the balls have equal amounts of plasticene.

B

One of the balls is deformed. The subject is asked whether the balls still contain equal amounts.

### Conservation of length (6–7 years)

A

Two sticks are aligned in front of the subject. The subject admits their equality.

B

One of the sticks is moved to the right. The subject is asked whether they are still the same length.

### Conservation of number (6–7 years)

A

Two rows of counters are placed in one-to-one correspondence. The subject admits their equality.

B

One of the rows is elongated (or contracted). The subject is asked whether each row still has the same number.

### Conservation of liquids (6–7 years)

A

Two beakers are filled to the same level with water. The subject sees that they are equal.

B

The liquid of one container is poured into a tall tube (or a flat dish). The subject is asked whether each contains the same amount.

### Conservation of area (9–10 years)

A

The subject and the experimenter each have identical sheets of cardboard. Wooden blocks are placed on the sheets in identical positions. The subject is asked whether each sheet has the same amount of space remaining.

B

The experimenter scatters the blocks on one of the sheets. The subject is asked the same question.

**Figure 4.1–2.** Some simple tests for conservation, with approximate ages of attainment. When the sense of conservation is achieved, the child answers that Figure B contains the same quantity as that in Figure A. (Figure from G R Lefrancois: *Of Children: An Introduction to Child Development*, p 305. Wadsworth, Belmont, Calif., 1973. Used with permission.)

not achieved object permanence and, therefore, suffer from separation anxiety. Such children are best off if their mothers are allowed to stay in the room with them overnight. Preoperational children, who are unable to deal with concepts and abstractions, benefit more from role-playing proposed medical procedures and situations than by having them described verbally in detail. For example, if the child is to receive intravenous therapy, it may be useful to act out the procedure, using a toy intravenous set and dolls. Also, since preoperational children do not understand

cause and effect, physical illness may be interpreted as punishment for bad thoughts or deeds. Because the children have not yet mastered the capacity to conserve and do not understand the concept of reversibility (which normally occurs during the concrete operational stage), they cannot understand that a broken bone can mend or that blood lost in an accident can be replaced.

The thinking of an adolescent during the stage of formal operations may appear to be overly abstract when it is, in fact, a normal developmental stage. Adolescent turmoil may not herald a psychotic process; it may well be the result of a normal adolescent's coming to grips with newly acquired abilities to deal with the unlimited possibilities of the surrounding world.

Adults under stress can regress cognitively, as well as emotionally. Their thinking can become preoperational, egocentric, and sometimes animistic.

## Education

Piaget's theories have been applied more in the area of education than in psychiatry. Educational problems—such as assessing intellectual development, scholastic aptitude, grade placement, and reading readiness—have been aided by Piaget's concepts. Such innovative early school programs as Head Start, which provide an enriched environment for children raised in poor families, can be traced to Piaget's belief that experience plays a major role in the maturation of cognitive functioning. Throughout his writings, Piaget emphasized that the greater the richness, complexity, and diversity in the environment, the greater is the likelihood that high levels of mental functioning will be achieved.

### References

Chapman M: *Constructive Evolution: Origins and Development of Piaget's Thought.* Cambridge University Press, Cambridge, 1988.
Chapman M: Piaget, attentional capacity, and the functional implications of formal structure. Adv Child Dev Behav 20: 289, 1987.
Elkind D: Egocentrism in adolescence. Child Dev 38: 1025, 1967.
Elkind D: Piagetian psychology and the practice of child psychiatry. J Am Acad Child Psychiatry 21: 435, 1982.
Flavell J: Concept development. In *Carmichael's Manual of Child Psychology,* P Mussen, editor, p 983. Wiley, New York, 1970.
Flavell J: *The Developmental Psychology of Jean Piaget.* Van Nostrand, New York, 1963.
Ginsburg H, Brant S O: *Piaget's Theory of Intellectual Development,* ed 3. Prentice-Hall, Englewood Cliffs, N J, 1988.
Greenspan S I, Curry J F: Piaget's approach to intellectual functioning. In *Comprehensive Textbook of Psychiatry,* ed 5, H I Kaplan, B J Sadock, editors, p 256. Williams & Wilkins, Baltimore, 1989.
Inhelder B, Piaget J: *The Growth of Logical Thinking from Childhood to Adolescence.* Basic Books, New York, 1958.
Kitchener R F: *Piaget's Theory of Knowledge: Genetic Epistemology and Scientific Reason.* Yale University Press, New Haven, 1986.
Lane R O, Schwartz G E: Levels of emotional awareness: A cognitive developmental theory and its application to psychopathology. Am J Psychol 144: 133, 1987.
Moses N, Klein H B, Altman E: An approach to assessing and facilitating causal language in adults with learning disabilities based on Piagetian theory. J Learn Disabil 23: 220, 1990.
Parkins E J: Piaget's genetic epistemology. Genet Soc Gen Psychol Monogr 114: 77, 1988.
Piaget J: *Genetic Epistemology.* Columbia University Press, New York, 1973.
Piaget J: *The Grasp of Consciousness.* Harvard University Press, Cambridge, 1976.
Piaget J: *Judgement and Reasoning in the Child.* Harcourt, New York, 1926.
Piaget J: *The Language and Thought of the Child.* Routledge and Kegnan Paul, London, 1926.
Piaget J: *Logic and Psychology.* Basic Books, New York, 1957.
Piaget J: *The Moral Judgement of the Child.* Harcourt, New York, 1932.
Piaget J: *The Origins of Intelligence in Children.* International Universities Press, New York, 1952.
Piaget J: *Play, Dreams, and Imitation in Childhood.* Norton, New York, 1951.
Piaget J, Inhelder B: *Memory and Intelligence.* Basic Books, New York, 1973.
Piaget J, Inhelder B: *The Origin of the Idea of Chance in Children.* Norton, New York, 1975.
Piaget J, Inhelder B: *The Psychology of the Child.* Basic Books, New York, 1969.
Soffer J: Jean Piaget and George Kelly: Toward a stronger constructivism. Int J Pers Construct Psychol 6: 59, 1993.

# 4.2 / Attachment Theory

*Attachment* is the emotional tone that exists between the developing child and the provider or caretaker. It is characterized by the infant's seeking out, clinging to, and wanting to be near that person. By the first month, with some individual variations, infants begin to show attachment behavior that is designed to promote proximity to the person to whom they are attached.

Proper attachments in infancy play an important part in a person's ability to form relationships later in life. The process of attachment occurs in every human social group, subhuman primates, and many other animals.

## NORMAL ATTACHMENT

The British psychoanalyst John Bowlby (1907–1990) formulated a theory that normal attachment is crucial to healthy development. According to Bowlby, attachment occurs when there is a "warm, intimate and continuous relationship with the mother in which both find satisfaction and enjoyment." Infants tend to attach to one person—they are monotropic—but multiple attachments may also occur, and attachment may be directed toward the father or a surrogate. Attachment is a gradually developing phenomenon; it results in one person's wanting to be with a preferred person, who is perceived as stronger, wiser, and able to reduce anxiety or distress. Attachment produces a feeling of security in the infant. It is a process that is facilitated by interaction between the mother and the infant. The amount of time together is less important than the amount of activity between the two.

The term "bonding" is sometimes used synonymously with attachment, but they are different phenomena. *Bonding* concerns the mother's feelings for her infant and differs from attachment because a mother does not normally rely on her infant as a source of security, a requirement of attachment behavior. A great deal of research on the bonding of mother to infant reveals that it occurs when there is skin-to-skin contact between the two or when other types of contact are made, such as voice and eye contact. Some workers have concluded that a mother who has skin-to-skin contact with her baby immediately after birth shows a stronger bonding pattern and may provide more attentive care than does a mother who does not have that experience. Some researchers have even proposed a critical period immediately after birth, during which such skin-to-skin contact must occur if bonding is to take place. That is a much-disputed concept, because many mothers are clearly bonded to their infants and display excellent maternal care even though they did not have skin-to-skin contact immediately postpartum. Human beings are also able to develop representational models of their babies in utero and even before conception. That representational thinking may be as important to the bonding process as is skin, voice, or eye contact.

## Signal Indicators

Signal indicators are signs of distress in the infant that prompt or elicit a behavioral response in the mother. The primary signal is crying. There are three types of crying: hunger (the most common), anger, and pain. Some mothers are able to distinguish between them, but most mothers generalize the hunger cry to represent distress from pain, frustration, or anger. Other signal indicators that reinforce attachment are smiling, cooing, and looking. The sound of an adult human voice can prompt those indicators.

## Ethological Studies

Bowlby suggested a Darwinian evolutionary basis for attachment behavior; the behavior ensures that adults protect their young. Ethological studies show that subhuman primates and other animals show attachment behavior patterns that are presumed to be instinctual and governed by inborn tendencies. An instinctual attachment system is seen in *imprinting*, in which certain stimuli are capable of eliciting innate behavior patterns during the first few hours of the animal's behavioral development; thus, the animal offspring becomes attached to its mother at a critical period early in its development. A similar sensitive or critical period during which attachment occurs has been postulated for human infants. The presence of imprinting behavior in humans is highly controversial, but bonding and attachment behavior during the first year of life closely approximate that critical period; however, in humans it occurs over a span of years, rather than hours.

**Harry Harlow.** Harry Harlow's work with monkeys is relevant to attachment theory. Harlow demonstrated the emotional and behavioral effects in monkeys who were isolated from birth and were thereby kept from forming attachments. The isolates were withdrawn, unable to relate to peers, unable to mate, and incapable of caring for their offspring. Harlow's work is discussed further in Section 4.5.

## ATTACHMENT PHASES

In the first phase, sometimes called the *preattachment stage* (birth to 8 or 12 weeks), the baby orients to its mother, follows her with its eyes over a 180-degree range, and turns toward and moves rhythmically with her voice. In the second phase, sometimes called *attachment-in-the-making* (8 or 12 weeks to 6 months), the infant becomes attached to one or more persons in the environment. In the third phase, sometimes called *clear-cut attachment* (6 months through 24 months), the infant cries and shows other signs of distress when separated from the caretaker or mother; it may occur as early as 3 months in some infants. On being returned to its mother, the infant stops crying and clings, as if to gain further assurance of its mother's return. Sometimes, seeing its mother after a separation is sufficient for crying to stop. In the fourth phase (25 months and beyond), the mother figure is seen as independent, and a more complex relationship between the mother and the child develops.

Table 4.2–1 summarizes the development of normal attachment from birth through 3 years.

## Separation

Separation from the attachment person may or may not produce intense anxiety, depending on the child's developmental level and the current phase of attachment.

*Separation anxiety* is an anxiety response, expressed as tearfulness or irritability, in a child who is isolated or separated from its mother or caretaker. It is most common at 10 to 18 months of age, and it disappears generally by the end of the third year. Somewhat earlier (at about 8 months) *stranger anxiety* appears. It is an anxiety response to someone other than the caretaker.

## ATTACHMENT AND ANXIETY

Bowlby's theory of anxiety holds that the child's sense of distress during separation is perceived and experienced as anxiety. It is the prototype of anxiety. Any stimuli that alarm the child and cause fear (such as loud noises, falling, and cold blasts of air) mobilize signal indicators (for example, crying) that cause the mother to respond in a caring way by cuddling and reassuring the child. The ability of the mother to relieve the infant's anxiety or fear is fundamental to the increasing attachment in the infant. The child has a sense of *security*, the opposite of anxiety, when the mother is close to the child and the child experiences no fear.

When the mother is unavailable to the infant because of physical absence (for example, the mother is in prison) or because of psychological impairment (for example, severe depression), anxiety develops in the infant.

## Mary Ainsworth

Mary Ainsworth expanded on Bowlby's observations and found that the interaction between the mother and her baby during the attachment period significantly influences the baby's current and future behavior. Patterns of attachment also vary among babies; for example, some babies signal or cry less than others. Sensitive responsiveness to infant signals, such as cuddling the baby when it cries, causes infants to cry less in later months, rather than reinforcing crying behavior. Close bodily contact with the mother when the baby signals for her is also associated with the growth of self-reliance, rather than a clinging dependence, as the baby grows older. Unresponsive mothers produce anxious babies, and those mothers are characterized as having lower intelligence quotients (I.Q.s) and as being emotionally immature and younger than responsive mothers.

Ainsworth also confirmed that attachment serves the purpose of reducing anxiety. What she called the *secure base effect* enables a child to move away from the attachment figure and to explore the environment. Inanimate objects, such as a teddy bear and a blanket (called the *transitional object* by Donald Winnicott), also serve as a secure base, one that often accompanies children as they investigate the world.

**Strange situation.** Ainsworth developed a research protocol called *strange situation* for assessing the quality and the security of an infant's attachment. In that procedure the infant

**Table 4.2–1**
**Normal Attachment**

**Birth to 30 Days**
  Reflexes at birth
    Rooting
    Head turning
    Sucking
    Swallowing
    Hand-mouth
    Grasp
    Digital extension
    Crying—signal for particular kind of distress
    Responsiveness and orientation to mother's face, eyes,
      and voice
  4 days—anticipatory approach behavior at feeding
  3 to 4 weeks—infant smiles preferentially to mother's voice
**Age 30 Days Through 3 Months**
  Vocalization and gaze reciprocity further elaborated from 1
    to 3 months; babbling at 2 months, more with the mother
    than with a stranger
  Social smile
  In strange situation, increased clinging response to mother
**Age 4 Through 6 Months**
  Briefly soothed and comforted by sound of mother's voice
  Spontaneous, voluntary reaching for mother
  Anticipatory posturing to be picked up
  Differential preference for mother intensifies
  Subtle integration of responses to mother
**Age 7 Through 9 Months**
  Attachment behaviors further differentiated and focused
    specifically on mother
  Separation distress, stranger distress, strange-place distress
**Age 10 Through 15 Months**
  Crawls or walks toward mother
  Subtle facial expressions (coyness, attentiveness)
  Responsive dialogue with mother clearly established
  Early imitation of mother (vocal inflections, facial expression)
  More fully developed separation distress and mother
    preference
  Pointing gesture
  Walking to and from mother
  Affectively positive reunion responses to mother after
    separation or, paradoxically, short-lived, active avoidance
    or delayed protest
**Age 16 Months Through 2 Years**
  Involvement in imitative jargon with mother (12 to 14
    months)
  Head-shaking "no" (15 to 16 months)
  Transitional object used during the absence of mother
  Separation anxiety diminishes
  Mastery of strange situations and persons when mother is
    near
  Evidence of delayed imitation
  Object permanence
  Microcosmic symbolic play
**Age 25 Months Through 3 Years**
  Able to tolerate separations from mother without distress
    when familiar with surroundings and given reassurances
    about mother's return
  Two- and three-word speech
  Stranger anxiety much reduced
  Object consistency achieved—maintains composure and
    psychosocial functioning without regression in absence of
    mother
  Microcosmic play and social play; cooperation with others
    begins

Table based on material by Justin Call, M.D.

is exposed to escalating amounts of stress—for example, the infant and the parent enter an unfamiliar room, an unfamiliar adult then enters the room, and the parent then leaves the room. The protocol has seven steps (Table 4.2–2). According to Ainsworth's studies, about 65 percent of infants are securely attached by age 24 months.

## ATTACHMENTS THROUGHOUT LIFE

Attachment behavior persists throughout life, from the cradle to the grave, as Bowlby hypothesized. Clinical studies have found attachment behavior in middle childhood, adolescence, and adulthood. College students away from home for the first time make good social adjustments if their early attachments to caretakers were secure. Low self-esteem, poor social relatedness, and emotional vulnerability to stress are associated with insecure attachments during the first year of life.

Human beings continue to be attached to their parents, regardless of whether their early attachments were optimal. At various stages in life, attachments are made to various other persons—such as teachers, relatives, coaches, and older siblings—especially when attachments to the parent are poor or inadequate. Those attachment figures are cast in the parental role and may be mentors or even therapists. By inspiring trust, those figures provide a secure base from which persons gain confidence in themselves and in their ability to deal with the outside world. Thus, the new attachment figures promote corrective emotional experiences. In addition, George Vaillant's finding that early close sibling relationships are related to adult mental health points to the importance of developing and maintaining attachments.

Affectional bonds that later develop between persons other than parents and children have attachment components in them. The sharing of experiences is important in a variety of attachment bonds, such as those between siblings, friends, relatives, and marital pairs. What makes the adult attachment bond unique is that it provides a sense of being able to give.

**Table 4.2–2**
**The Strange Situation[1]**

| Episode[2] | Persons Present | Change |
|---|---|---|
| 1 | Parent, infant | Enter room |
| 2 | Parent, infant, stranger | Unfamiliar adult joins the dyad |
| 3 | Infant, stranger | Parent leaves |
| 4 | Parent, infant | Parent returns, stranger leaves |
| 5 | Infant | Parent leaves |
| 6 | Infant, stranger | Stranger returns |
| 7 | Parent, infant | Parent returns, stranger leaves |

[1]Adapted from M D Ainsworth, B A Witlig: Attachment and the exploratory behavior of 1-year-olds in a strange situation. In *Determinants of Infant Behavior*. B M Foss, editor, vol 4, p 113. Methuen, London, 1969.
[2]All episodes are usually three minutes long, but episodes 3, 5, and 6 can be curtailed if the infant becomes too distressed, and episodes 4 and 7 are sometimes extended.
Table from M E Lamb, A Nash, D M Teti, M H Bornstein: Infancy. In *Child and Adolescent Psychiatry: A Comprehensive Textbook*, M. Lewis, editor, p 241. Williams & Wilkins, Baltimore, 1991. Used with permission.

The absence of the attachment figure makes the person feel lonely or anxious. Love relationships are a major factor in maintaining emotional stability throughout life.

## Infant Day Care and Attachment

The effect of day-care experiences on the infant's attachment process is controversial. Some studies have shown that day care of more than 20 hours a week during the first year results in insecure attachments; however, no consistent findings have emerged. In view of the fact that the majority of infants in day care are securely attached to their mothers, there seem to be no adverse effects of such programs, provided they are of high quality and have competent, nurturing caretakers.

## Severing Attachments

Reactions to the death of a parent or a spouse can be traced to the nature of the person's past and present attachment to the lost figure. When demonstrable grief is lacking, it may be due to real experiences of rejection and to the lack of closeness in the relationship. The person may even consciously offer an idealized picture of the deceased. Such persons usually try to present themselves as independent types for whom closeness and attachment mean little.

The severing of attachments, however, can be traumatic. The death of a parent or a spouse can precipitate a depressive disorder and even suicide in some persons. Similarly, the death of a spouse increases the chance that the surviving spouse will experience a physical or mental disorder during the next year. The onset of depression and other dysphoric states often involves having been rejected by a significant person in one's life.

## ATTACHMENT DISORDERS

Attachment disorders are characterized by biopsychosocial pathology that results from maternal deprivation, a lack of care by and interaction with the mother or caretaker. Failure-to-thrive syndromes, psychosocial dwarfism, separation anxiety disorder, avoidant personality disorder, depressive disorders, delinquency, academic problems, and borderline intelligence have been traced to negative attachment experiences. When maternal care is deficient because the mother is mentally ill, because the child is institutionalized for a long period of time, or because the primary object of attachment dies, the child suffers emotional damage. Bowlby originally thought that the damage is permanent and invariable; but he revised his theories to take into account the time at which the separation took place, the type and the degree of separation, and the level of security that the child experienced before the separation.

Bowlby described a predictable set and sequence of behavior patterns in children who are separated from their mothers for long periods of time (more than three months): (1) *protest*, in which the child protests against the separation by crying, calling out, and searching for the lost person; (2) *de-*

*spair*, in which the child appears to lose hope that the mother will ever return; and (3) *detachment*, in which the child emotionally separates itself from its mother. Bowlby believed that sequence involves ambivalent feelings toward the mother; the child both wants her and is angry at her for her desertion.

The child in the detachment stage responds in an indifferent manner when the mother returns; the mother has not been forgotten, but the child is angry at her for having gone away in the first place and fears that she will go away again. Some children have affectionless personalities characterized by emotional withdrawal, little or no feeling, and a limited ability to form affectionate relationships.

## Anaclitic Depression

Anaclitic depression, also known as hospitalism, was first described by René Spitz in infants who had made normal attachments and were then suddenly separated from their mothers for varying lengths of time and placed in institutions or hospitals. They became depressed, withdrawn, nonresponsive, and vulnerable to physical illness. They recovered when their mothers returned or when surrogate mothering was available.

## CHILD ABUSE

Abused children often maintain their attachments to abusive parents. Animal studies in dogs have shown that severe punishment and maltreatment increase attachment behavior. If children are hungry, sick, or in pain, they show clinging attachment behavior. Similarly, if children are rejected by their parents or are afraid of their parents, their attachment may increase. Therefore, some children want to remain with an abusive parent. Nevertheless, if a choice must be made between a punishing figure and a nonpunishing figure, the nonpunishing person is chosen, especially if that person is sensitive to the needs of the child. Child abuse is discussed in depth in Chapter 29.

## APPLICATION OF THEORY

Attachment theory has applications in psychotherapy. If a patient is able to attach to a therapist, a secure base effect is seen. The patient may then be able to take risks, mask anxiety, and practice new patterns of behavior that otherwise might not have been attempted. Those patients whose impairments can be traced to never having made a specific attachment in early life may do so for the first time in therapy, with salutary effects.

Patients whose pathology stems from exaggerated attachments early in life may attempt to replicate those attachments in therapy. The therapist must enable such patients to recognize how those early experiences have interfered with the patients' ability to achieve independence.

For the child patient, whose difficulties in attachment may be more apparent than such difficulties in adults, the therapist becomes a consistent and trusted figure who is able to engender a sense of warmth and self-esteem in the child, often for the first time.

## References

Ainsworth M S: Attachments across the life span. Bull N Y Acad Med *61*: 792, 1985.

Ainsworth M S: John Bowlby (1907–1990): Obituary. Am Psychol *47*: 668, 1992.

Bowlby J: *Attachment and Loss*, vols 1, 2, 3. Basic Books, New York, 1969, 1973, 1980.

Bowlby J: *Maternal Care and Mental Health*. World Health Organization, Geneva, 1951.

Bowlby J: The nature of the child's tie to his mother. Int J Psychoanal *39*: 350, 1958.

Crittenden P M: Children's strategies for coping with adverse home environments: An interpretation using attachment theory. Child Abuse Negl *16*: 329, 1992.

DeFrain J D, Jakub D K, Mendoza B L: The psychological effects of sudden infant death on grandmothers and grandfathers. Omega J Death Dying *24*: 165, 1992.

High H: Impediments to the development of attachment. Psychoanal Psychother *6*: 107, 1992.

Klaus M H, Kennell J H: *Bonding: The Beginnings of Parent-Infant Attachment*. Mosby, St. Louis, 1983.

Klaus M H, Kennell J H: *Parent-Infant Bonding*, ed 2. Mosby, St. Louis, 1982.

Osofsky J D, editor: *Handbook of Infant Development*. Wiley, New York, 1979.

Papovsek K H, Papovsek M: The evolution of parent-infant attachment: New psychobiological perspectives. In *Frontiers of Infant Psychiatry*, J D Can, editor, vol 2, p 276. Saunders, Philadelphia, 1984.

Sroufe L A: Bowlby's contribution to psychoanalytic theory and developmental psychology: Attachment, separation, loss. J Child Psychol Psychiatry *27*: 841, 1986.

Tavecchio L W C, Van Ijzendoorn M H, editors: *Attachment in Social Networks: Contributions to the Bowlby-Ainsworth Attachment Theory*. Elsevier, New York, 1987.

# 4.3 / Learning Theory

*Learning* is defined as the change in a person's behavior in a given situation brought about by repeated experiences in that situation, provided that the behavior cannot be explained on the basis of the person's native response tendencies, maturation, or temporary state.

To assess learning, one must measure some aspect of performance, such as the accuracy of a motor skill or the ability to recognize and repeat words. Learning and performance are related; but it is important not to confuse the two concepts. Performance can be adversely affected by insufficient motivation or anxiety, so that learning may have occurred but is not demonstrable. *State-dependent learning*—that is, the facilitated recall of information when one is in the same internal state or external environment in which the information was first acquired—is another case in which performance may be impaired. If a behavior is acquired under the influence of a pharmacological agent and tests for learning are carried out in the absence of the drug, there may be little or no evidence of acquisition. However, if the learning test is carried out under the influence of the drug, performance may change, and learning may then be demonstrated.

Among the building blocks of learning theory are classical and operant conditioning. In *classical conditioning*, learning is thought to take place as a result of the contiguity of environmental events. When events occur closely together in time, persons will probably come to associate the two. In the case of *operant conditioning*, learning is thought to occur as a result of the consequences of one's actions and the resultant effect on the environment. As B.F. Skinner put it, "A person does not act upon the world, the world acts upon him." Skinner, in his definition of the sphere of interest of psychology, specifically eschewed the role of intervening variables, such as thoughts. *Social learning theory* incorporates both the classical and the operant models of learning but considers a reciprocal interaction between the person and the environment. Cognitive processes are viewed as important factors in modulating the person's responses to environmental events.

Psychoanalytic theory and practice developed concurrently with learning theory. A number of attempts have been made over the past half century to integrate the two theoretical approaches. For example, in 1950 John Dollard and Neal Miller reformulated many psychoanalytic concepts in terms of learning theory. But such attempts have not had a lasting influence on psychoanalytic thought or therapy.

Recently, much interest has been shown in the neurophysiological and biochemical components of learning. For example, research with simple organisms, such as the aplysia, a sea mollusk, has revealed that the learning of avoidance behavior alters the chemical structure of cells in the nervous system and that, when the avoidance is unlearned, those chemical changes are reversed. Thus, the foundation for understanding the neurochemistry of learning has been laid, and it is now clear that there is a reciprocal interaction between ongoing biological processes in the central nervous system and behavior changes resulting from environmental influences.

## CONDITIONING

Two types of conditioning have been described: classical and operant.

### Classical Conditioning

*Classical conditioning* (also known as *respondent conditioning*) results from the repeated pairing of a neutral (conditioned) stimulus with one that evokes a response (unconditioned stimulus) such that the neutral stimulus eventually comes to evoke the response. The time relation between the presentation of the conditioned and unconditioned stimuli is important, varying for optimal learning from a fraction of a second to several seconds.

Ivan Petrovich Pavlov (1849–1936), the Russian physiologist and Nobel prize winner, observed in his work on gastric secretion that a dog salivated not only when food was placed in its mouth but also at the sound of the footsteps of the person coming to feed the dog, even though the dog could not see or smell the food. Pavlov analyzed those events and called the flow of saliva that occurred with the sound of footsteps a *conditioned response* (CR)—that is, a response that could be elicited under certain conditions by a particular stimulus. In a typical Pavlovian experiment, a *stimulus* (S) that had no capacity to evoke a particular type of response before training does so after consistent association with another stimulus. For example, under normal circumstances, a dog does not salivate when a bell is sounded. However, if bell sounds are always followed by the presentation of food, the dog ultimately pairs the bell and food. Eventually, the bell sound alone elicits salivation (CR). Because the food naturally produces salivation, it is referred to as an *unconditioned stimulus* (UCS). Salivation, a response that is reliably elicited by food (UCS), is referred to as an *unconditioned response* (UCR). The bell, which was originally unable to evoke salivation but came to do so when paired with food, is referred to as a *conditioned stimulus* (CS). Classical conditioning is most often applied to responses mediated by the autonomic nervous system.

Classical conditioning is diagramed as follows:

*Before Conditioning*

Food (UCS) ———————————→ Salivation (UCR)
Bell (CS) paired with food (UCS) ——→Salivation (UCR)

*After Conditioning*

Bell (CS) ———————————→ Salivation (CR)

**Extinction.** Extinction occurs when the conditioned stimulus is constantly repeated without the unconditioned stimulus until the response evoked by the conditioned stimulus gradually weakens and eventually disappears. In the above example, extinction occurs if the bell (CS) is presented repeatedly without being paired with food (UCS). Eventually, salivation (CR) will not occur when the bell sounds, and extinction will take place. However, extinction is not a complete destruction of the conditioned response. If an animal is rested after extinction, the conditioned response returns but is less strong than before; that phenomenon is known as *partial recovery*.

The American psychologist John B. Watson (1878–1958) used Pavlov's theory of classical conditioning to explain certain aspects of human behavior. In 1920 Watson described how he produced a phobia in an 11-month-old boy called Little Albert. At the same time that the boy was shown a white rat that he initially did not fear, a loud frightening noise was sounded. After several such pairings, Albert became fearful of the white rat, even though no loud noise was present. Watson and his colleagues obtained the same results using a white rabbit, and, eventually, the response was generalized to any furry object. Many theorists believe that the process accounts for the development of childhood phobias in general; that is, they are learned responses based on classical conditioning.

**Stimulus generalization.** Stimulus generalization is the process whereby a conditioned response is transferred from one stimulus to another. Animals respond to stimuli that are similar to the original conditioned stimulus. A dog conditioned to respond to a bell also responds to the sound of a tuning fork. Stimulus generalization is one theory used to explain higher learning because it enables one to learn similarities. For example, a street sign is recognized whether or not it is on a pole, a building, or a curb because there is sufficient stimulus similarity for generalization to occur.

**Discrimination.** Discrimination is the process of recognizing and responding to the differences between similar stimuli. If the two stimuli are sufficiently different, the animal can be taught to respond to one and not to the other; for example, an animal can learn to respond differentially to similar bells. A child learns to discriminate four-legged animals (the common stimulus) into dogs, cats, cows, and other quadrupeds.

Learning can be viewed as a balance of generalization and discrimination. Some disorders of thinking may stem from difficulties with those two processes. For example, a person may have had a traumatic experience as a child involving a person with a moustache. The transfer of those negative feelings to all men with moustaches is an example of both faulty discrimination and stimulus generalization.

## Operant Conditioning

B. F. Skinner (1904–1990) proposed a theory of learning and behavior known as operant or instrumental conditioning. In classical conditioning, the animal is passive or restrained. In operant conditioning, however, the animal is active and behaves in a way that produces a reward—that is, learning occurs as a consequence of action. For example, a rat receives the reinforcing stimulus (food) only if it gives the response of pressing a lever. In addition to food, approval, praise, good grades, or any other response that satisfies a need in the animal or the person can serve as a reward. In operant conditioning, in contrast, behavior is reinforced by the experimenter.

Operant conditioning is related to trial-and-error learning, as described by the American psychologist Edward L. Thorndike (1874–1949). In trial-and-error learning, one attempts to solve a problem by trying out a variety of actions until one proves successful; a freely moving organism behaves in a way that is instrumental in producing a reward. For example, a cat in a Thorndike puzzle box must learn to lift a latch to escape from the box. Operant conditioning is sometimes called instrumental conditioning for that reason. Thorndike's law of effect states that certain responses are reinforced by reward, and the organism learns from those experiences.

Four kinds of instrumental or operant conditioning are described in Table 4.3-1: primary reward conditioning, es-

**Table 4.3–1**
**Four Kinds of Operant or Instrumental Conditioning**

| | |
|---|---|
| Primary reward conditioning | The simplest kind of conditioning. The learned response is instrumental in obtaining a biologically significant reward, such as a pellet of food or a drink of water. |
| Escape conditioning | The organism learns a response that is instrumental in getting out of some place it prefers not to be. |
| Avoidance conditioning | The kind of learning in which a response to a cue is instrumental in avoiding a painful experience. A rat on a grid, for example, may avoid a shock if it quickly pushes a lever when a light signal goes on. |
| Secondary reward conditioning | The kind of learning in which instrumental behavior to get at a stimulus has no biological usefulness itself but has in the past been associated with a biologically significant stimulus. For example, chimpanzees learn to press a lever to obtain poker chips, which they insert into a slot to secure grapes. Later they work to accumulate poker chips even when they are not interested in grapes. |

cape conditioning, avoidance conditioning, and secondary reward conditioning.

**Respondent and operant behavior.**   Skinner described two types of behavior: (1) *respondent behavior*, behavior that results from known stimuli (for example, the knee jerk reflex to patellar stimulation or the pupillary constriction to light), and (2) *operant behavior*, which is independent of a stimulus (for example, the random movements of an infant or the aimless movements of a laboratory rat in a cage). Skinner took advantage of operant behavior by placing one of those rats in a Skinner box (named after him, its developer). The rat was deprived of food and randomly pressed a bar. At some point in the experiment, food was released by the experimenter when the bar was pressed. The food reinforced the bar pressing, which increased or decreased in rate depending on the level of reinforcement given by the experimenter. A *reinforcer* is anything that maintains a response or increases its strength. It is used synonymously with the term *reward*; however, some workers make this distinction: responses are reinforced; subjects are rewarded.

**Reinforcement schedule (programming).**   Reinforcers are described as *primary* when they are independent of previous learning (for example, the need for food or water) or *secondary* when based on previous learning that has led to rewards (for example, money and grades). In operant conditioning, it is possible to vary the schedule of reward or reinforcement given to a behavioral pattern—a process known as programming. The intervals between reinforcements may be *fixed* (for example, every third response is rewarded) or *variable* (for example, sometimes the third response is rewarded; at other times, the sixth response is rewarded). A *continuous reinforcement* (also known as contingency reinforcement or management) schedule, in which every response is reinforced, leads to the most rapid acquisition of a behavior. When the response is reinforced only a fraction of the times the behavior occurs, it is called *partial reinforcement*. Partial or intermittent reinforcement is effective in maintaining behavior and is resistant to extinction. For example, a person's use of a gambling slot machine is most frequent when the reward is partially reinforced—that is, when money is won at variable times. That procedure keeps the gambler guessing or trying to anticipate when a payoff will occur. The strength of operant learning is reflected in how often an animal responds. A high response frequency indicates strong operant learning.

A decrease in frequency indicates that extinction is occurring. Table 4.3-2 lists the effects of various reinforcement schedules on behavior.

In operant conditioning, *positive reinforcement* is the process by which certain consequences of a response increase the probability that the response will occur again. Food, water, praise, and money are positive reinforcers. However, events viewed as aversive by some may be reinforcing for others. For example, the behavior of some children is reinforced by scolding, which, after all, is a form of attention. Many substances also appear to be positive reinforcers, including opium, cocaine, nicotine, and barbiturates.

*Negative reinforcement* is the process by which a response that leads to the removal of an aversive event increases that response. For example, a teenager mows the lawn to avoid parental complaints, or an animal jumps off a grid to escape a painful shock. Any behavior that enables one to avoid or escape a punishing consequence is strengthened.

Negative reinforcement is not punishment. *Punishment* is an aversive stimulus (for example, a slap) that is presented specifically to weaken or suppress an undesired response. Punishment reduces the probability that a response will recur. The usual use of the term "punishment" must be distinguished from the technical use of the term. In learning theory, the punishing event delivered is always contingent on performance and demonstrably reduces the frequency of the behavior being punished. That is different from the use of the term to denote imprisonment, for example, because the prison sentence follows long after the crime has been committed and may not affect future criminal behavior.

**Aversive control.**   In aversive control or conditioning, the organism changes its behavior to avoid a painful, noxious, or aversive stimulus. Electric shocks are common aversive stimuli used in laboratory experiments. Any behavior that avoids an aversive stimulus is reinforced as a result.

**Escape learning and avoidance learning.**   Negative reinforcement is related to two types of learning, escape learning and avoidance learning. In *escape learning*, the animal learns a response to get out of some place where it does not want to be (for example, an animal jumps off an electric grid whenever the grid is charged). *Avoidance learning* requires an additional response. The same rat on the grid learns to avoid a shock if it quickly pushes a lever when a light signal goes on. To move from escape learning to avoidance learning, the animal must make an *anticipatory response* to prevent the pun-

**Table 4.3–2**
**Reinforcement Schedules in Operant Conditioning**

| Reinforcement Schedule | Example | Behavioral Effect |
|---|---|---|
| Fixed-ratio (FR) schedule | Reinforcement occurs after every 10 responses (10:1 ratio); 10 bar presses release a food pellet; workers are paid for every 10 items they make. | Rapid rate of response to obtain the greatest number of rewards. Animal knows that the next reinforcement depends on a certain number of responses being made. |
| Variable-ratio (VR) schedule | Variable reinforcement occurs (e.g., after the third, sixth, then second response, and so on). | Generates a fairly constant rate of response because the probability of reinforcement at any given time remains relatively stable. |
| Fixed-interval (FI) schedule | Reinforcement occurs at regular intervals (e.g., every 10 minutes or every third hour). | Animal keeps track of time. Rate of responding drops to near 0 after reinforcement and then increases at about the expected time of reward. |
| Variable-interval (VI) schedule | Reinforcement occurs after variable intervals (e.g., every 3, 6, and then 2 hours), similar to VR schedule. | Response rate does not change between reinforcements. Animal responds at a steady rate to get the reward when it is available; common in trout fisherman, use of slot machines, checking mailbox. |

ishment. Escape learning and avoidance learning are two forms of aversive control. Behavior that terminates the source of aversive stimuli is strengthened and maintained.

**Shaping behavior.** Shaping involves changing behavior in a deliberate and predetermined way. By reinforcing those responses that are in the desired direction, the experimenter shapes the animal's behavior. If the experimenter wants to train a seal to ring a bell with its nose, the experimenter can give a food reinforcement as the animal's random behavior brings its nose near the bell. To teach a mute schizophrenic patient to talk, the therapist may first reward the patient for simply looking at the therapist. That is followed by the reinforcement of any vocalizations and then by the reinforcement of simple speech. The closer the time of the reinforcement to the operant behavior, the better is the learning. Shaping is also called successive approximation.

**Adventitious reinforcement.** Responses that are reinforced accidentally by coincidental pairing of response and reinforcement are adventitious. Such events may have clinical implications in the development of phobias and other behavior.

**Premack's principle.** The concept developed by David Premack states that a behavior engaged in at a high frequency can be used to reinforce a low-frequency behavior. In one experiment, Premack observed that children spent more time playing with a pinball machine than eating candy when both were freely available. When he made playing with the pinball machine contingent on eating a certain amount of candy, the children increased the amount of candy they ate. In a therapeutic application of that principle, schizophrenic patients were observed to spend more time sitting down doing nothing than working at a simple task in a rehabilitation center. When five minutes of sitting down was made contingent on a certain amount of work, the work output was considerably increased, as was skill acquisition. That principle is also known as Grandma's rule (for example, "If you eat your spinach, you can have dessert").

## Applications of Conditioning Theory

In 1950 Joseph Wolpe defined anxious behavior as persistent habits of learned or conditioned responses acquired in anxiety-generating situations. If a response inhibitory to anxiety can occur in the presence of anxiety-evoking stimuli, it weakens the connection between the stimuli and the anxiety response. Wolpe referred to that process as *reciprocal inhibition*. Relaxation, for example, is considered incompatible with anxiety and, therefore, inhibits it.

**Anxiety hierarchy.** In Wolpe's method of therapy, known as systematic desensitization, the goal is to eliminate maladaptive anxiety and behavior. To accomplish that goal, Wolpe asked his patient to imagine the least disturbing item on a list of potentially anxiety-evoking stimuli and then to proceed step by step up the list to the most disturbing stimulus. For example, a patient with a fear of heights ranked the sight of a tall building lower in the anxiety hierarchy than standing on a high ledge; being on the 10th floor of a building fell somewhere in between. In a relaxed state (usually induced by hypnosis but sometimes induced by drugs), the patient was instructed to visualize the least anxiety-producing situation; if that visualization did not produce anxiety, the person moved up the hierarchy. Eventually, the patient was desensitized to the source of anxiety.

**Tension-reduction theory.** John Dollard and Neal Miller attempted to reconcile behavioral theory and Freudian

psychodynamics by stressing the commonalities between the two. Subscribing to the tension-reduction theory of behavior, they saw behavior as motivated by the organism's attempt to reduce tension produced by unsatisfied or unconscious drives. Sigmund Freud's pleasure principle is a tension-reducing force and, consequently, is a strong motivator. If repressed, fear is learned and is transformed into anxiety. In either case, it acts as an acquired drive; thus, a person's behavior may be motivated by an attempt to reduce fear. Early childhood events may be traumatic—that is, may cause anxiety. If such events are repressed, the adult may avoid situations that are likely to stimulate anxiety but may be completely unaware of those avoidance patterns. Therapy, in part, is an unlearning process. The patient learns that certain behaviors can reduce anxiety, and avoidance patterns are replaced by approach patterns.

Table 4.3–3 gives a comparison of the behavioral and psychoanalytic models.

**Learned helplessness model of depression.** A laboratory animal may be classically conditioned to accept a painful stimulus when restrained. Such restraint eventually teaches the animal that it has no way to avoid the aversive stimulus. A condition known as learned helplessness de-

**Table 4.3–3**
**Behavioral and Psychoanalytic Models**

| Behavioral Model | Psychoanalytic Model |
|---|---|
| Behavior is determined by current contingencies, reinforcement history, and genetic endowment. | Behavior is determined by intrapsychic processes. |
| Problem behavior is the focus of study and treatment. | Behavior is but a symbol of intrapsychic processes and a symptom of unconscious conflict. The underlying conflict is the focus of treatment. |
| Contemporary variables, such as contingencies of reinforcement, are the focus of the analysis. | Historical variables, such as childhood experiences, are the focus of the analysis. |
| Treatment entails the application of the principles of operant or classical conditioning. | Treatment consists of bringing unconscious conflicts into consciousness. |
| Objective observation, measurement, and experimentation are the methods used. The focus is on observable behavior and environmental events (antecedents and consequences). | Subjective methods of interpretation of behavior and inference regarding unobservable events (e.g., intrapsychic processes) are used. |
| Theory is based on experimentation. | Theory is predominantly based on case histories. |
| Tenets can be formulated into testable hypotheses and evaluated through experimentation. | Many tenets cannot be formulated into testable hypotheses to be evaluated through experimentation. |

Table from P G Dorsett: Behavioral and social learning psychology. In *Human Behavior: An Introduction for Medical Students,* A Stoudemire, editor, p 105. Lippincott, Philadelphia, 1990. Used with permission.

velops when an organism learns that no behavioral pattern can influence the environment. The learned helplessness paradigm has been used to explain depression in humans who feel helpless, without options, and unable to control events.

**Brain stimulation and reinforcement.** When certain areas of the hypothalamus are electrically stimulated, intense pleasure is experienced by both animals and humans. Nonhuman primates were provided with a method by which they could stimulate pleasure centers in their brains. The animals preferred stimulating themselves to eating or drinking. In human beings, similar phenomena occur; in one case, a patient stimulated his brain 1,000 times in a six-hour period until he was forced to stop.

## COGNITIVE LEARNING THEORY

*Cognition* is defined as the process of obtaining, organizing, and using intellectual knowledge. Cognitive learning theories focus on the role of understanding. The person performs mental operations and stores bits of information in memory to be retrieved at some later time. Cognition implies an understanding of the connection between cause and effect, between action and the consequences of that action. *Cognitive strategies* are mental plans used by a person to understand self and the environment.

Depressed patients have a cognitive strategy that focuses on what is wrong, rather than what is right. A form of cognitive therapy developed by Aaron Beck for the treatment of depression teaches patients to recognize and value their assets and alerts them to the cognitive pattern that causes their depression. Beck described the cognitive triad that exists in depression as consisting of a person's (1) negative view of self, (2) negative interpretation of experience, and (3) negative expectation of the future.

Many theorists, such as Jean Piaget, define a series of stages in cognitive growth. Another approach toward cognition is termed *information processing*, a sequence of mental operations involving input, storage, and output of information. Cognition involves calling up and processing relevant information from stored memory.

Behavior can change through techniques in which persons learn by listening to or reading instructions. Therapeutic instructions modify both outcome and efficacy expectations of patients. For example, patients told that their blood pressure readings would drop if they followed certain relaxation procedures did show a decline in blood pressure. To learn new patterns of behavior, patients can monitor their behavior by charting events, such as when they eat or smoke. Self-monitoring also reduces the rate of relapse. If the therapist helps patients define and set realistic and well-specified goals, they have a greater likelihood of achieving them than if goals are poorly defined or unrealistic. Goal attainment enhances self-efficacy, which in turn positively affects future performance.

## ATTRIBUTION THEORY

*Attribution theory* is a cognitive approach; it is concerned with how people perceive the causes of behavior.

According to attribution theory, (1) persons are likely to attribute their own behavior to situational causes but are likely to attribute others' behavior to stable internal dispositions (personality traits), and (2) the particular cause that a person attributes to a given event influences subsequent feelings and behavior. In psychiatry, attribution theory may help explain why some persons attribute a change in behavior to an external event (situation) or to a change in one's internal state (disposition or ability). Similarly, behavioral change may be attributed to the results of a drug or to the results of interpersonal events. Research on drug effects by attribution theorists have shown that it may be unwise to describe a drug as very strong or as very effective because, if it does have the desired effect, patients may believe that is the only reason they got better.

## SOCIAL LEARNING THEORY

*Social learning theory* relies on role modeling, identification, and human interactions. A person can learn by imitating the behavior of another person, but personal factors are involved. If the role model is not someone the person likes, imitative behavior is not likely to occur. Social learning theorists combine operant and classical conditioning theories. For example, although the observation of models may be a major factor in the learning process, imitation of the model must be reinforced or rewarded if the behaviors are to become part of the person's repertoire.

Albert Bandura is a major proponent of the social learning school. Behavior occurs as a result of the interplay between cognitive and environmental factors, a concept known as *reciprocal determinism*. Persons learn by observing others, intentionally or accidentally; that process is known as *modeling* or learning through imitation. The person's choice of a model is influenced by a variety of factors, such as age, sex, status, and similarity to oneself. If the chosen model reflects healthy norms and values, the person develops *self-efficacy*, the capacity to adapt to normal everyday life and to threatening situations. It is possible to eliminate negative behavior patterns by having a person learn alternative techniques from other role models. For example, fearful children become less fearful when they watch other children acting fearlessly in the same situation. Similarly, demonstrating a fearless approach to a phobic situation may be useful to motivate a patient's approach to the feared object or situation.

Modeling has also been used in weight reduction and smoking cessation programs. It is an important component of group treatment plans in which members of the group learn from one another.

## NEUROPHYSIOLOGY OF LEARNING

One of the first theorists to approach the neurophysiological aspects of learning was Clark L. Hull (1884–1952), who developed a drive-reduction theory of learning. Hull postulated that neurophysiological connections are established in the central nervous system that reduce the level of a drive (for example, obtaining food reduces hunger).

An external stimulus stimulates an efferent system and elicits a motor impulse. The critical connection is between the stimulus and the motor response, which is a neurophysiological reaction that leads to what Hull called a habit. Habits are strengthened when a response leads to a further reduction in the drive associated with the aroused need.

By exploring the human brain, researchers such as Pierre Broca and Karl Wernicke identified specific areas of the brain involved in the development and the retention of speech and language. Electrical stimulation of certain brain sites evoked vivid mental imagery in patients. Also, lesions of the amygdaloid nucleus in animals interfered with learning. Learning produces changes in the structure and the function of nerve cells. In one study, monkeys that were trained to use a particular finger to obtain food showed hypertrophy of the area of the brain responsible for finger control.

## Habituation and Sensitization

In the study of the snail aplysia, Eric Kandel showed how simple forms of learning—habituation and sensitization—can occur. The specific behavior studied is a defensive reflex involving the withdrawal of the snail's siphon when the animal is tactually stimulated. If the snail is touched repeatedly, it is subject to habituation and learns not to withdraw its syphon and gill. Habituation causes the organism to stop responding reflexively as a result of the repeated stimulus.

Aplysia can also be sensitized; that is, a reflex response can be made more sensitive, so that a subthreshold stimulus elicits a response. Thus, if the snail receives a strong stimulus (for example, an electric shock), it becomes sensitized; then even a previously subthreshold stimulation causes the animal to withdraw its gill and siphon. Experimental work with aplysia has also shown that the processes of habituation and sensitization develop at different times, habituation before sensitization.

## Memory Formation and Storage

The neurobiological basis of learning is located in the structures of the brain involved in forming and storing information. Those structures include the hippocampus, the cortex, and the cerebellum. One hundred billion neurons in the brain are involved in forming memories, including a layer of 4.6 million cells in the hippocampus.

Learning begins with the senses taking in an environmental stimulus that is eventually transformed into a memory trace or memory link. An electrical or chemical impulse passes through the neuron when the brain receives information, which triggers the formation of connections between synapses. Animal experiments have shown an increase in synaptic connections when learning occurs.

Long-term memories are retained longer than short-term memories because of the increased time such memories have had to link up with a number of locations in the cortex. The more connections, the better is the chance of contacting a neural pathway leading to the memory. Repeated reliving of a memory enhances its permanence.

Storage is the key to a good memory. Relating material to something that is already known creates more pathways and increases the storage power. Processing information at a semantic level involves more of the mind than does rote memorization. That information decays at a slower rate than does information memorized on a superficial level, without meaning and comprehension.

Memory is divided into short-term and long-term memory. Long-term memory is also known as recent memory, recent past memory, remote memory, and secondary memory. Short-term memory—also called immediate memory, working memory, primary memory, and buffer memory—is adversely affected by chronic emotional stress and lack of effort caused by psychological exhaustion or too much input. Short-term memory and long-term memory differ in the amount of information that can be stored. The capacity of short-term memory is limited (five to nine bits of information).

Smell and emotion may underlie long-term memories. Scent conveys information through the olfactory nerve to the hippocampus, which plays a role in the control of emotions. Learning and memory are affected by stress. The increase in adrenaline resulting from stress can enhance learning, but, if stress is too great, learning is inhibited. A person's mood affects the learning and the recall of material; that is, learning material while in a happy mood enhances memory, and the person recalls material better while in a happy mood. Some childhood memories survive. They are usually those memories associated with the period when the child learned to speak, between the ages of 3 and 5 years. Before that time, only memories associated with traumatic events or with smell are likely to be remembered.

# MOTIVATION

Motivation is a state of being that produces a tendency toward some type of action. That state may be a state of deprivation (for example, hunger), a value system, or a strongly held belief (for example, religion). In the mediation of learning and perception, biological mechanisms play an important role in motivating behavior. The organism tries to maintain homeostasis or internal balance against any disturbance of equilibrium (for example, the thirsty animal is motivated to find water and drink). Social motives, such as the need for recognition and achievement, also account for behavioral patterns (for example, studying hard to get good grades). However, the intensity of motivation to achieve at any task in any particular situation is determined by at least two factors: the achievement motive (desire to achieve) and the likelihood of success.

There are marked individual differences in the values placed on objects and goals. Some students strive for A's; others depreciate the importance of grades, placing higher value on intellectual satisfactions or on extracurricular activities. The expectancy factor refers to the subjective probability that, with the expenditure of sufficient effort, the object may be acquired or the goal reached.

## Cognitive Dissonance

Cognitive dissonance means incongruity or disharmony among one's beliefs, knowledge, and behavior. When dissonance becomes too great, the person changes ways of thinking or behaving so that there is less disharmony. An example of cognitive dissonance is the unwillingness of persons to believe that a car for which they paid a great deal of money or that is considered a status symbol could have anything wrong with it or be defective in any way; another example is believing most strongly in a decision after it has been made. In general, dissonance occurs when there is a palpable disparity between two experimental or behavioral elements. It is postulated that cognitive dissonance produces an uncomfortable tension state (like hunger) that one is motivated to change.

## References

Agras W S: Learning theory. In *Comprehensive Textbook of Psychiatry*, ed 5, H I Kaplan, B J Sadock, editors, p 262. Williams & Wilkins, Baltimore, 1989.

Bandura A, Walters R H: *Social Learning and Personality Development.* Holt, Rinehart and Winston, New York, 1963.

Byrnes J P: Categorizing and combining theories of cognitive development and learning. Educ Psychol Rev *4*: 309, 1992.

Cattell R B: *Psychotherapy by Structured Learning Theory.* Springer, New York, 1987.

Dollard J, Miller N E: *Personality and Psychotherapy.* McGraw-Hill, New York, 1950.

Dunn A J: Neurochemistry of learning and memory: An evaluation of recent data. Annu Rev Psychol *33*: 343, 1982.

Ettenberg A : Dopamine, neuroleptics, and reinforced behavior. Neurosci Biobehav Rev *13*: 105, 1989.

Hilgard E R, Bower G H: *Theories of Learning*, ed 3. Appleton-Century-Crofts, New York, 1966.

Hull C L: *Principles of Behavior: An Introduction to Behavior Therapy.* Appleton-Century-Crofts, New York, 1943.

Lovibond P F: Animal learning theory and the future of human Pavlovian conditioning. Biol Psychol *27*: 199, 1988.

Mowrer O H: *Learning Theory and Behavior.* Wiley, New York, 1960.

Pavlov I P: *Conditioned Reflexes.* Oxford University Press, London, 1927.

Rescorla R A, Holland P C: Behavioral studies of associative learning in animals. Annu Rev Psychol *33*: 265, 1982.

Skinner B F: *Science and Human Behavior.* Macmillan, New York, 1953.

Slangen J L, Earley B, Jaffard R, Richelle M, Olton D S: Behavioral models of memory and amnesia. Pharmacopsychiatry *23*: 81, 1990.

Walker S: *Learning Theory and Behavior Modification.* Methuen, London, 1984.

Watson J B, Rayner R: Conditioned emotional reactions. J Exp Psychol *3*: 1, 1920.

Windholz G: Pavlov's conceptualization of learning. Am J Psychol *105*: 459, 1992.

Wolpe J: The genesis of neurosis. S Afr Med J *24*: 613, 1950.

Zolten A J: Constructive integration of learning theory and phenomenological approaches to biofeedback training. Biofeedback Self Regul *14*: 89, 1989.

# 4.4 / Aggression, Accidents, and Injuries

## AGGRESSION

Aggression is any form of behavior directed toward the goal of harming or injuring another person who is motivated to avoid such treatment. Aggression also implies the intent to do harm, which must be inferred from events that precede or follow acts of aggression.

Aggression and violence may be seen in many clinical situations, ranging from alcohol and other substance intoxication to cognitive disorders to child abuse to chronic antisocial acts. Violence has been described as occurring when the balance breaks down between impulses and internal control (Figure 4.4–1).

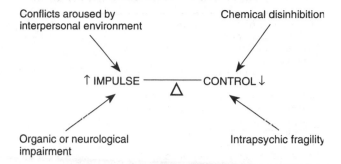

**External states necessary**

**Internal states sufficient**

**Figure 4.4–1.** Mechanisms of violence.

A person may have violent thoughts or fantasies, but, unless the person loses control, the thoughts do not become acts. Any set of conditions that produce increased aggressive impulses in the context of diminished control may produce violent acts. Situations in which the combination of factors may be observed include toxic and organic states, developmental disabilities, florid psychosis, conduct disorder, and overwhelming psychological and environmental stress. Table 4.4–1 outlines some of the disorders listed in the fourth edition of *Diagnostic and Statistical Manual of Mental Disorders* (DSM-IV) that have been associated with violent and aggressive behavior.

A number of investigators have attempted to use their understanding of the forces shaping violent acts to predict who will become violent. Tables 4.4–2 and 4.4–3 summarize some of the best-known conceptualizations of violence predictors. Many investigators summarize all the findings into the simple conceptualization that the best predictor of violent acts is previous violent acts. However, any predictor is merely a guideline for the possibility of an increased risk for violence, and many potentially violent people do not fit any of the predictors.

**Table 4.4–1**
**Some DSM-IV Disorders Associated with Aggression**

Mental retardation
Attention-deficit/hyperactivity disorder
Conduct disorder
Cognitive disorders
   Deliria
   Dementias
Psychotic disorders
   Schizophrenia
   Psychotic disorder not otherwise specified
Mood disorders
   Mood disorder due to a general medical condition
   Substance-induced mood disorder
Intermittent explosive disorder
Adjustment disorder with disturbance of conduct
Personality disorders
   Paranoid personality disorder
   Antisocial personality disorder
   Borderline personality disorder
   Narcissistic personality disorder
Axis V codes
   Childhood, adolescent, or adult antisocial behavior

**Table 4.4–2**
**Commonly Cited Predictors of Dangerousness to Others**

High degree of intent to harm
Presence of a victim
Frequent and open threats
Concrete plan
Access to instruments of violence
History of loss of control
Chronic anger, hostility, or resentment
Enjoyment in watching or inflicting harm
Lack of compassion
Self-view as victim
Resentful of authority
Childhood brutality or deprivation
Decreased warmth and affection in home
Early loss of parent
Fire setting, bed-wetting, and cruelty to animals
Prior violent acts
Reckless driving

## Incidence

According to the Federal Bureau of Investigation (FBI) Uniform Crime Reports, 1,932,274 violent crimes (murder, rape, forcible robbery, and aggravated assault) were committed in the United States in 1992. Of that number, 109,062 crimes were rape, and 23,760 crimes were homicide. Violent crime rates are highest in large metropolitan areas and lowest in rural areas.

Homicides are most prevalent among people who know each other, and more than 50 percent are committed with handguns. In the United States, homicide is the second leading cause of death among those 15 to 24 years of age. Furthermore, a young black male is eight times more likely to be murdered than is a white male of the same age. Much lower rates of homicide have been reported in such countries as England, Sweden, Japan, and Canada; all have strict handgun-control laws. Homicide is most prevalent in the low socioeconomic groups and is more commonly committed by men than by women.

One national survey of high school students reported that 28 percent of the boys and 7 percent of the girls had been in a physical fight in the previous month. Nearly 35 percent of those surveyed reported having been in at least one physical fight that resulted in an injury requiring medical attention.

## Characteristics

The majority of adults with and without mental disorders who commit aggressive acts are likely to do so against persons they know, usually family members. That fact indicates that aggression is not indiscriminately directed. A possible exception to the familiar-person generalization is reported among male adolescents, who often aggress against casual acquaintances or persons who are unknown to them.

Generally, the probability of aggressive behavior increases as persons become more psychologically decompensated and perhaps also if the onset of a mental disorder is rapid. Otherwise, little is known about the relation between the course of illness and aggression. Episodic decompensation may occur in persons who ingest large quantities of alcohol; more than 50 percent of persons who commit criminal homicides and who engage in assaultive behavior are reported to have imbibed significant amounts of alcohol immediately before aggressing.

Recently, interest has increased in sex differences in the predisposition to and frequency of aggression. For aggression classified as homicide, battery, assault with a weapon, or rape, the frequency among males clearly exceeds that among females. For domestic violence, in which one marital partner acts to hurt another, the frequency among males and females is about equal. Studies of persons who are hospitalized in psychiatric facilities over long pe-

**Table 4.4–3**
**Assessing the Risk of Committing a Homicide**

| Clinical Characteristics | Low Risk | Medium Risk | High Risk |
|---|---|---|---|
| Hostility indicators (history) | | | |
| Family life | Wanted child, good loving family | Some family disruption, loss of a parent or one-parent family | Early violence, battered child, poor parent model |
| Significant others | Several reliable family members or friends available | Few or one available | None available |
| Daily functioning | Good in most activities | Moderately good in some activities | Not good in any activities |
| Life-style | Stable | Moderately stable | Unstable |
| Socioeconomic | Upper | Middle | Lower |
| Employment | Employed | Employment history fairly stable | Unemployed |
| Education | High school graduate or more (university or technical training) | High school dropout, can read and write | School dropout, semiliterate to illiterate |

**Table 4.4–3**
*Continued*

| Clinical Characteristics | Low Risk | Medium Risk | High Risk |
|---|---|---|---|
| Housing | Lives in adequate housing, clean environment and space | Fair housing, some overcrowding | Poor housing, crowded, slums |
| Isolation or withdrawal | Able to relate well to others, outgoing | Mild, some withdrawal and feelings of hopelessness | Long history of being a loner, antisocial, withdrawn, hopeless and helpless feelings |
| Alcohol or other substance use | Nondrinker, occasional social use | Social drinker or user to occasional abuse | Chronic abuse |
| Psychological help | No history of need for or use of psychiatric hospitalization | Some outpatient psychiatric help, moderately satisfied with self | History of psychiatric hospitalization, negative view of help |
| Personal history | No history of violence or impulsive behavior | Occasional history of violence or impulsive behavior | Frequent history of violence or impulsive behavior |
| Perturbation (negative emotional states) | | | |
| Anxiety | Low, good emotional control | Occasional feelings of anxiety | Easily aroused to anxiety, high or panic state |
| Depression | Low | Occasional depression | Severe, chronically moody |
| Self-esteem | Good, has reinforcements from others | Usually good | Chronically poor self-image |
| Hostility | Low | Some | Marked, aggressive |
| Impulse control | Controlled | Some impulsive acting out not physically violent | Feels need for violence |
| Constriction (narrowing of vision) | | | |
| Coping strategies and devices being used | Able to cope with stress and outside irritating influences; well-developed defense mechanisms | Usually can cope under most pressures; sometimes becomes constrictive in thinking and acts out | Becomes constrictive under most stress; acts out in destructive, socially unacceptable ways |
| Disorientation and disorganization | None, is in good contact with what is happening | Little to moderate | Marked, losing contact with reality |
| Resources | Able to make good use of resources available | Some use of resources, aware of most resources | Unable either to use resources available or to recognize that help is available |
| Cessation (stop the person causing the problem) | | | |
| Previous arrests | None | Has been arrested, has not served time | Multiple arrest history, served time in prison, would murder to avoid going back to prison |
| Previous homicide | None | Has exhibited aggressive behavior; been in fights but no attempt to kill another | Yes, looks at the killing of another as a feasible act |
| Homicide plan | None | Has held fleeting thoughts of killing another, no definite plan | Frequent or constant thoughts with a specific plan |
| Weapon available | None that person thinks of | Yes, person aware of weapons in immediate environment but not seriously considering use | Yes, and planning on use (a loaded gun should be considered highly lethal) |

No one clinical characteristic predicts homicide. However, the greater the number of clinical characteristics in the medium-risk and high-risk categories, the greater is the risk.
Table adapted from N Allen: *Homicide: Perspectives on Prevention.* Human Sciences, New York, 1979. Used with permission.

riods of time indicate that the prevalence of male and female aggression is about equal.

## Theoretical Perspectives

### Aggression as instinctive behavior

FREUD'S VIEW.    In his early writings Sigmund Freud held that all human behavior stems either directly or indirectly from Eros—the life instinct—whose energy, or libido, is directed toward the enhancement or the reproduction of life. In that framework, aggression was viewed simply as a reaction to the blocking or the thwarting of libidinal impulses. As such, it was neither an automatic part nor an inevitable part of life.

After the tragic events of World War I, Freud gradually came to adopt a gloomier position regarding the nature of human aggression. He proposed the existence of a second major instinct—Thanatos, the death force—the energy of which is directed toward the destruction or the termination of life. According to Freud, all human behavior stems from the complex interplay of Thanatos and Eros and the constant tension between them.

Because the death instinct, if unrestrained, soon results in self-destruction, Freud hypothesized that through other mechanisms, such as displacement, the energy of Thanatos is redirected outward, so that it serves as the basis for aggression against others. In Freud's view, aggression stems primarily from the redirection of the self-destructive death instinct away from the self and toward others.

LORENZ'S VIEW.    According to Konrad Lorenz, aggression that causes physical harm to others springs from a fighting instinct that humans share with other organisms. The energy associated with that instinct is spontaneously produced in organisms at a more or less constant rate. The probability of aggression increases as a function of the amount of stored energy and the presence and the strength of aggression-releasing stimuli. Aggression is inevitable, and, at times, spontaneous eruptions occur.

### Aggression as learned social behavior.    Another perspective regards aggression primarily as a learned form of social behavior—one that is acquired and maintained in much the same manner as other forms of activity. According to Albert Bandura, neither innate urges toward violence nor aggressive drives aroused by frustration are the roots of human aggression. Rather, persons engage in assaults against others because (1) they acquired aggressive responses through past experience, (2) they receive or anticipate various forms of reward for performing such ac-

tions, or (3) they are directly instigated to aggression by specific social or environmental conditions. In contrast to instinct and drive theories (the psychological representation of a need that impels an organism to seek a goal), the social learning perspective does not attribute aggression to one or a few potential causes. It suggests that the roots of such behavior are varied, involving aggressors' past experiences and learning and a wide range of external, situational factors. For example, soldiers receive medals for killing enemy troops during times of war, and professional athletes attain widespread admiration and large financial rewards by competing aggressively (Table 4.4–4).

### Aggression as neuroanatomical damage.    Increasingly, a number of investigators are hypothesizing that, for a certain group of chronically aggressive persons, the root of the aggressive behavior is organic brain damage. That perspective is an elaboration of the theory that aggression is a learned social behavior, in that persons who have been the victims of severe physical abuse themselves may suffer neurological sequelae secondary to the abuse, and the sequelae predispose them biologically to violent behavior. In 1986 Dorothy Lewis reported that every death-row inmate studied by her team of researchers had a history of head injury, often inflicted by abusive parents. That study concluded that death-row inmates constitute an especially neuropsychiatrically impaired prison population. Researchers investigating the association between head injury and violent behavior have been careful to point out that the linkage of physical abuse, head injury, and violence is uncertain, although most studies do show an association between early physical abuse and later aggressive behavior. Some researchers speculate that the combination of brain injury and a history of undergoing and observing chronic severe abuse is particularly lethal.

## Determinants

### Social determinants

FRUSTRATION.    The single most potent means of inciting human beings to aggress is frustration. Widespread acceptance of that view stems mainly from John Dollard's frustration-aggression hypothesis. In its original form the hypothesis indicated that (1) frustration always leads to some form of aggression and (2) aggression always stems from frustration.

Frustrated persons, however, do not always respond with

**Table 4.4–4**
**Theoretical Perspectives on Aggression**

| Theory | Assumed Source of Aggression | Possibility of Preventing or Controlling Aggression |
|---|---|---|
| Instinct theory | Innate tendencies or instincts | Low: aggressive impulses are constantly generated and impossible to avoid |
| Drive theory | Externally elicited aggressive drive | Low: external sources of aggressive drive are common (e.g., frustration) and impossible to eliminate |
| Social learning theory | Present social or environmental conditions plus past social learning | Moderate to high: appropriate changes in current social and environmental conditions or in reinforcement contingencies can reduce or prevent overt aggressive actions |

Table from R A Baron: Aggression. In *Comprehensive Textbook of Psychiatry*, ed 4, H I Kaplan, B J Sadock, editors, p 216. Williams & Wilkins, Baltimore, 1985.

aggressive thoughts, words, or deeds. They may show a wide variety of reactions, ranging from resignation, depression, and despair to attempts to overcome the sources of their frustration. And not all aggression results from frustration. People (for example, boxers and football players) act aggressively for many reasons and in response to many stimuli.

An examination of the evidence indicates that whether frustration increases or fails to enhance overt aggression depends largely on two factors: First, frustration appears to increase aggression only when the frustration is intense. When the frustration is mild or moderate, aggression may not be enhanced. Second, frustration is likely to facilitate aggression when it is perceived as arbitrary or illegitimate, rather than when it is viewed as deserved or legitimate.

DIRECT PROVOCATION BY OTHERS.   Evidence indicates that physical abuse and verbal taunts from others often elicit aggressive actions. Once aggression begins, it often shows an unsettling pattern of escalation; as a result, even mild verbal slurs or glancing blows may initiate a process in which stronger and stronger provocations are exchanged.

EXPOSURE TO AGGRESSIVE MODELS.   A link between aggression and exposure to televised violence has been noted. The more televised violence children watch, the greater is their level of aggression against others. The strength of the relation appears to increase over time, pointing to the cumulative effects of media violence. The processes that account for the effects of filmed and televised violence on the behavior of viewers are outlined in Table 4.4–5.

## Environmental determinants

AIR POLLUTION.   Exposure to noxious odors, such as the ones produced by chemical plants and other industries, may increase personal irritability and, therefore, aggression. That effect appears to be true only up to a point. If the odors in question are truly foul, aggression appears to decrease—perhaps because escaping from the unpleasant environment becomes a dominant goal for the persons involved.

NOISE.   Several studies have reported that persons who are exposed to loud and irritating noise direct stronger assaults against others than do persons who are not exposed to such environmental conditions.

CROWDING.   Some studies indicate that overcrowding may produce elevated levels of aggression; other investigations

**Table 4.4–5**
**Mechanisms Underlying the Effects of Televised and Filmed Violence on the Behavior of Viewers**

| Mechanism | Effects |
|---|---|
| Observational learning | Viewers acquire new means of harming others not previously present in their behavior repertoires. |
| Disinhibition | Viewers' restraints or inhibitions against performing aggressive actions are weakened as a result of observing others engaging in such behavior. |
| Densensitization | Viewers' emotional responsivity to aggressive actions and their consequences—signs of suffering on the part of victims—is reduced. As a result, they show little, if any, emotional arousal in response to such stimuli. |

Table from R A Baron: Aggression. In *Comprehensive Textbook of Psychiatry*, ed 4, H I Kaplan, B J Sadock, editors, p 219. Williams & Wilkins, Baltimore, 1985.

have failed to obtain evidence of such a link. Crowding may enhance the likelihood of aggressive outbursts when typical reactions are negative (for example, annoyance, irritation, and frustration).

## Situational determinants

HEIGHTENED PHYSIOLOGICAL AROUSAL.   Some research indicates that heightened arousal stemming from such diverse sources as participation in competitive activities, vigorous exercise, and exposure to provocative films enhances overt aggression.

SEXUAL AROUSAL.   Recent investigations indicate that the effects of sexual arousal on aggression strongly depend on the type of erotic materials used to induce such reactions and on the precise nature of the reactions themselves. When the erotica viewed are mild, such as photos of attractive nudes, aggression is reduced. When they are explicit, such as films of couples engaged in various acts of lovemaking, aggression is enhanced.

PAIN.   Physical pain may arouse an aggressive drive— the motive to harm or injure others. That drive, in turn, may find expression against any available target, including ones not in any way responsible for the aggressor's discomfort. That hypothesis may explain, in part, why persons exposed to aggression act aggressively toward others.

**Hormones, drugs, and other substances.**   Aggression has been linked in animals with testosterone, progesterone, luteinizing hormone, renin, beta endorphin, prolactin, melatonin, norepinephrine, dopamine, epinephrine, acetylcholine, serotonin, 5-hydroxyindoleacetic acid (5-HIAA), and phenylacetic acid, among others.

Some studies have related the level of aggression to androgen levels. Those studies point to the androgen insensitivity syndrome (in which there is defective binding of androgens to proteins, resulting in male offspring who have a feminine appearance and a decreased propensity for rough-and-tumble play) and to the adrenogenital syndrome (in which the mother's adrenal cortex exposes the fetus to elevated adrenal androgens, resulting in masculinization, as evidenced in part by an increase in rough-and-tumble play in masculinized girls).

In regard to drugs and substances of abuse, the following generalizations appear to hold: small doses of alcohol inhibit aggression and large doses facilitate it; barbiturate effects are similar to the effects of alcohol; aerosol and commercial solvent effects also resemble alcohol's effects; anxiolytics generally inhibit aggression, although paradoxical aggression is sometimes observed; opioid dependence (but not opioid intoxication) is associated with increased aggression, as is the use of stimulants, cocaine, hallucinogens, and, in some cases, variable doses of marijuana.

**Neurotransmitters.**   Generally, cholinergic and catecholaminergic mechanisms seem to be involved in the induction and the enhancement of predatory aggression, whereas serotonergic systems and γ-aminobutyric acid (GABA) seem to inhibit that type of behavior. Affective aggression is evidently modulated by both the catecholaminergic and serotonergic systems. Dopamine seems to facilitate aggression, whereas norepinephrine and serotonin appear to inhibit it. Recently, serotonin has again gained attention as a potentially important mediating factor in aggression. Rapid declines in serotonin levels or function are associated with increased irritability and, in nonhuman primates, with increased aggression. Some human studies have indicated that 5-HIAA levels in cerebrospinal fluid inversely correlate with the frequency of aggression, particularly among persons who commit suicide.

### Genetic determinants

TWIN STUDIES. Research involving monozygotic twins indicates a hereditary component to aggressive behavior. Thus far, most studies have focused on nonpsychiatric populations. In those studies, the concordance rates for monozygotic twins exceed the rates for dizygotic twins.

PEDIGREE STUDIES. A number of studies show that persons from families with histories of mental disorders are more prone to mental disorders and engage in more aggressive behavior than do persons without such histories. Persons with low intelligence quotient (I.Q.) scores appear to have a higher frequency of delinquency and aggression than do persons with normal I.Q. scores. Observed correlations between aggressive behavior and other atypical behaviors indicate that genetic predispositions to atypical behavior, including behaviors associated with mental disorders, are associated with atypical physiological functions, one consequence of which is an increase in the probability of aggression.

CHROMOSOME INFLUENCES. Behavior research involving the influence of chromosomes has concentrated primarily on abnormalities in X and Y chromosomes, particularly the 47-chromosome XYY syndrome. Early studies indicated that persons with the syndrome could be characterized as tall, of below-average intelligence, and likely to be apprehended and in prison for engaging in criminal behavior. Subsequent studies indicated that, at most, the XYY syndrome contributes to aggressive behavior in only a small percentage of the cases. Studies of the androgen and gonadotropin characteristics of XYY syndrome persons have been inconclusive and have not established that such persons are biochemically atypical.

Certain inborn metabolic disorders, genetic in origin, that diffusely involve the nervous system have been reported to be associated with aggressive personalities. Examples include Sanfilippo's syndrome (increased mucopolysaccharide storage), Vogt syndrome (a diffuse neuronal storage disorder with increased ganglioside storage), and phenylketonuria.

### Prevention and Control

The prevention of death and disability resulting from aggressive, violent, or homicidal behavior begins for the physician at the individual level. For instance, violence within a family (for example, sexual and physical abuse of children, wife beating, and self-destructive behavior) is often revealed through sensitive questioning and a high index of suspicion on the part of the physician. Preventive interventions include psychiatric referral, notification of the proper legal or other authorities (mandatory in such cases as child abuse and specific threats of harm to persons), and skilled counseling by appropriately trained people.

**Punishment.** Punishment is sometimes effective as a deterrent to overt aggression. Research findings indicate that the frequency or the intensity of such behavior can be reduced by even mild forms of punishment, such as social disapproval; but punishment may not always or even usually produce such effects.

The recipients of punishment often interpret it as an attack against them. To the extent that it is so, the aggressors may respond even more aggressively. Strong punishment is more likely to provoke desires for revenge or retribution than to instill lasting restraints against violence. Persons who administer punishment may serve as aggressive models for those on the receiving end of such discipline, and, as noted earlier, exposure to such models may potentiate violent acts. Punishment, because of the conditions under which it is usually administered (a long time after the aggression is committed), may only temporarily reduce the strength or the frequency of the aggressive behavior. Once the punishment is discontinued, the aggressive acts quickly reappear. For those reasons, certain types of punishment may backfire and actually enhance, rather than inhibit, the dangerous actions they are designed to prevent.

**Catharsis.** For many years it has been widely believed that providing angry persons with an opportunity to engage in expressive but noninjurious behaviors reduces their tension or arousal and weakens their tendency to engage in overt and potentially dangerous acts of aggression. Those effects embody the catharsis hypothesis. Although Sigmund Freud accepted the existence of such catharsis, he was relatively pessimistic about its usefulness in preventing overt aggression. At present, the benefits of catharsis are thought to be mixed. It may help some people discharge aggression; other people may become more aggressive as a result of the expressive behaviors.

**Training in social skills.** A major reason why many persons become involved in repeated aggressive encounters is that they lack basic social skills. They do not know how to communicate effectively; therefore, they adopt an abrasive style of self-expression. Their ineptness in performing such basic tasks as making requests, engaging in negotiations, and lodging complaints often irritates friends, acquaintances, and strangers. Their severe social deficits seem to ensure that they will experience repeated frustration and that they will frequently anger those with whom they have direct contact. One technique for reducing the frequency of such behavior involves providing such persons with the social skills that they sorely lack. Social skills training has been applied to diverse groups, including highly aggressive teenagers, police, and even child-abusing parents. In many cases, dramatic changes in the targeted behaviors have been produced (for example, enhanced interpersonal communication and improved ability to handle rejection and stress), and reductions in aggressive behavior related to those shifts have frequently been observed. The results are encouraging and indicate that training in appropriate social skills can offer a promising approach to the reduction of human violence.

### Induction of incompatible responses

EMPATHY. When aggressors attack other persons in face-to-face confrontations, the aggressors may block out, ignore, or deny signs of pain and suffering on the part of their victims. If the aggressor is exposed to such feedback, one reaction may be the arousal of empathy and a subsequent reduction in further aggression. In several experiments, exposure to signs of pain or discomfort on the part of the victim has inhibited further aggression.

HUMOR.    Informal observation indicates that anger can often be reduced through exposure to humorous material, and some laboratory studies support that hypothesis. Several types of humor, presented in several formats, may induce reactions or emotions incompatible with aggression among the persons who observe the humor.

OTHER INCOMPATIBLE RESPONSES.    Many other reactions may also be incompatible with anger or overt aggression. As noted above, mild sexual arousal sometimes operates in that fashion. Similarly, feelings of guilt concerning the performance of aggressive actions often reduce such behavior. Participation in absorbing cognitive tasks, such as solving mathematics problems, may induce reactions incompatible with anger and aggressive actions.

**Drug treatment.**    Several types of drugs and clinical monitoring—for example, blood pressure and electroencephalogram (EEG)—are essential for the optimal treatment of specific aggressive persons. Lithium (Eskalith) appears to be a drug of major promise for some violent patients, especially delinquent adolescent boys. Anticonvulsants occasionally reduce seizure-induced forms of aggression, and they may have the same effect on persons who do not have epilepsy. Antipsychotic medications appear to reduce aggression in both psychotic and nonpsychotic violent patients. Antidepressants may be effective in reducing violence in some depressed patients. Antianxiety agents appear to have a limited role in reducing aggression. Antiandrogen agents may be effective in the treatment of aggressive sex offenders. β-Blockers and stimulants may be effective in aggressive children. And electroconvulsive therapy may be effective in a small group of selected patients.

Table 4.4–6 outlines some of the possible psychopharmacological interventions for aggression.

### Victims

An estimated 18 million Americans have suffered psychiatric disturbance at some point as a result of crime. At any given moment, up to 5 million Americans may suffer from crime-related symptoms. The National Institute of Justice estimates that a 12-year-old American has an 80 percent chance of being the victim of a serious crime at some point in his or her life. Recent research indicates that many victims of violent crimes are at increased risk for major psychiatric problems. Long-term depressive disorders and phobias are two of the mental disorders reported to occur more frequently in the victims of crime than in the general population. Many researchers believe that distinct and characteristic emotional effects are associated with being the victim of a crime and that those effects are related to the fact that victims are the targets of another person's intentional aggression. Table 4.4–7 lists the main emotional aftereffects of crime.

## ACCIDENTS AND INJURIES

An accident is an event that occurs by chance or unexpectedly, without any conscious planning. Studies of accidents show that causes can sometimes be determined and possibly corrected. However, causes are often multiple and require a many-faceted approach to the problem. For instance, both behavioral and psychological characteristics can be related to the occurrence of accidents. Those characteristics include anxiety, boredom, fatigue, and the ingestion of substances that alter concentration and motor coordination. In 1992, according to the National Safety Council, a total of 83,000 deaths and 17.1 million disabling injuries resulted from accidents.

Accidents are the most common cause of death in the United States for persons 15 to 24 years of age. Accidents are the fifth most common cause of death overall in the United States. The most recent national data on the cost of injuries reported that for the noninstitutionalized population intentional and unintentional injuries were the second leading cause of direct medical costs (second only to heart disease and exceeding cancer) and also accounted for major indirect costs, such as work loss and disability.

Vehicular accidents, industrial accidents, and home accidents were the most frequent types of injury. One third of all injury deaths are secondary to automobile accidents, and one third are secondary to other accidents. The remaining third is evenly divided between suicide and homicide. After motor vehicle accidents, the most common causes of accidental death are falls, followed by fire, drowning, and poisoning.

### Psychophysiological Considerations

The victim's psychophysiological state must be considered in all injuries and accidents. A physical condition, such as fatigue, may lead either to distraction or to an inability to respond quickly enough to avoid an accident. Such toxic factors as barbiturates, antihistamines, marijuana, and particularly alcohol are important. About half of the automobile accidents reported occur in conjunction with alcohol intake. Persons with diabetes, epilepsy, cardiovascular disease, and mental disorders are involved in more than twice the number of accidents per 1,000 miles of driving as are persons who do not have those illnesses.

Age-related impairments, both motor and cerebral function deficits, may lead to potentially impaired judgment, which contributes to fatal accidents among persons 65 and older.

### Motivations

From a motivational point of view, the first writings dealing with the subject of an accident-prone personality date back to *The Psychopathology of Everyday Life* (1904), in which Freud wrote:

Many apparently accidental injuries that happen to such patients are really instances of self-injury. What happens is an impulse to self-punishment, which is constantly on the watch and which normally finds expression in self-reproach or contributes to the formation of a symptom, takes ingenious advantage of an external situation that chance happens to offer, or lends *assistance* [italics added] to that situation until the desired injurious effect is brought about.

**Table 4.4–6**
**Schematic Differential Diagnosis and the Pharmacological Treatment of Violence**

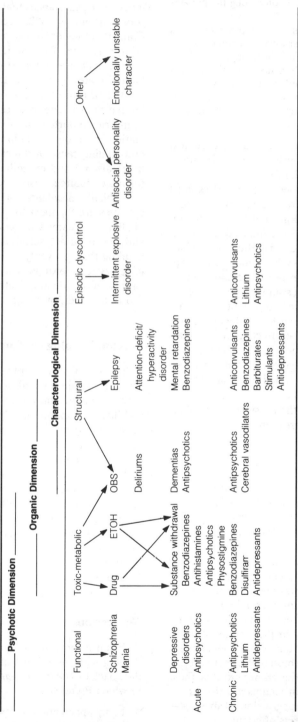

ETOH—ethanol
OBS—organic brain syndrome
Table adapted from A Skodol: Emergency management of potentially violent patients. In *Emergency Psychiatry: Concepts, methods and practice,* E Bassuk, A Birk, Plenum, New York, 1984.

**Table 4.4–7**
**Aftermath of Crime: Main Emotional Effects**

Sense of helplessness: The world seems unsafe; victims lack confidence in their judgment and competence to deal with the world.

Rage at being a victim: Intense anger is usually expressed toward family members and those who try to help; conversely, sometimes the victim is unable to express any anger at anything.

Sense of being permanently damaged: Rape victims, for example, may feel that they will never be attractive again.

Inability to trust or to be intimate with others: The effect can include a loss of faith in institutions like the police and the courts.

Persistent preoccupation with the crime: Excessive concern with the crime and its details may reach the point of obsession.

Loss of belief that the world is just: The effect may include self-blame and a sense of having done something to deserve being a victim.

Table courtesy of Stuart Kleinman, M.D.

A number of retrospective studies have looked at the personality characteristics of people who have had severe or frequent accidents. Those studies have speculated that persons repeatedly involved in accidents may have an underlying self-destructive tendency suggestive of the existence of depression, poor control of hostility, a tendency to be more action-oriented and less reflective than the general population, and a propensity for intrapsychic or interpersonal difficulties at least partially resolved by the occurrence of the accident. The concept of an unconscious sense of guilt and a need to atone or to be punished for such guilt feelings may provide the motivation of many unintended accidents. Motivations other than an unconscious sense of guilt may be found by examining the life situations of people involved in accidents. An unconscious wish to escape or to avoid something is often apparent. The desire to escape may be related to external situations in which an accident provides a convenient way of avoiding a possibly humiliating experience. One such example is the man who has an accident on his way to a job interview, thereby avoiding the possible humiliation of not obtaining the position he was seeking. Accidents help a person to avoid new responsibilities by providing a convenient and acceptable rationale for not entering into the new situation without losing self-esteem or the esteem of others.

**References**

Alessi N E, Wittekindt J: Childhood aggressive behavior. Pediatr Ann *18*: 94, 1989.
Archer J, Browne K, editors: *Human Aggression: Neutralistic Approaches.* Routledge, London, 1989.
Bandura A: *Aggression: A Social Learning Analysis.* Prentice-Hall, Englewood Cliffs, N J, 1973.
Baron R A: *Human Aggression.* Plenum, New York, 1977.
Berkowitz L: On the formation and regulation of anger and aggression: A cognitive-neoassociationistic analysis. Am Psychol *45*: 494, 1990.
Berkowitz L, Cochran S T, Embree M C: Physical pain and the goal of adversively stimulated aggression. J Pers Soc Psychol *40*: 687, 1981.
Callahan C M, Rivara F P: Urban high school youth and handguns: A school-based survey. JAMA *267*: 3038, 1992.
Coccaro E F: Central serotonin and impulsive aggression. Br J Psychiatry Suppl *8*: 52, 1989.
Council on Scientific Affairs: Assault weapons as a public health hazard in the United States. JAMA *267*: 3067, 1992.
Danforth J S, Drabman R S: Aggressive and disruptive behavior. Monogr Am Assoc Ment Retard *12*: 111, 1989.
Dollard J, Doob L, Miller N, Mowrer O H, Sears R R: *Frustration and Aggression.* Yale University Press, New Haven, Conn, 1939.
Eichelman B: Toward a rational pharmacotherapy for aggressive and violent behavior. Hosp Community Psychiatry *39*: 31, 1988.
Eichelman B S: Neurochemical and psychopharmacologic aspects of aggressive behavior. Annu Rev Med *41*: 149, 1990.
Elliott F A: Violence: The neurologic contribution: An overview. Arch Neurol *49*: 595, 1992.
Else L, Wonderlich S A, Beatty W W, Christie, D W, et al: Personality characteristics of men who physically abuse women. Hosp Community Psychiatry *44*: 54, 1993.
Federal Bureau of Investigation: *Uniform Crime Reports.* U S Government Printing Office, Washington, 1991.
Fonberg E: Dominance and aggression. Int J Neurosci *41*: 201, 1988.
Gentry J, Eron L D: American Psychological Association Commission on Violence and Youth. Am Psychol *48*: 89, 1993.
Ghaziuddin M, Ghaziuddin N: Violence against staff by mentally retarded inpatients. Hosp Community Psychiatry *43*: 503, 1992.
Goldstein A P, Carr E G, Davidson W S, Wehr P: *In Response to Aggression.* Pergamon, New York, 1981.
Kinzie J D, Boehnlein J K: Psychotherapy of the victims of massive violence: Countertransference and ethical issues. Am Psychother *47*: 90, 1993.
Liebert R M: *The Early Window: Effects of Television on Children and Youth,* ed 3. Allyn & Bacon, Needham Heights, Mass, 1992.
Lorenz K: *On Aggression.* Bantam, New York, 1966.
McGuire M T, Troisi A: Aggression. In *Comprehensive Textbook of Psychiatry,* ed 5, H I Kaplan, B J Sadock, editors, p 271. Williams & Wilkins, Baltimore, 1989.
Miczek K A, Mos J, Oliver B: Brain 5-HT and inhibition of aggressive behavior in animals: 5-HIAA and receptor subtypes. Psychopharmacol Bull *25*: 399, 1989.
National Center for Environmental Health and Injury Control: Physical fighting among high school students: United States, 1990. MMWR Morb Mortal Wkly Rep *41*: 91, 1992.
Neuman G G, editor: *Origins of Human Aggression: Dynamics and Etiology.* Human Sciences, New York, 1987.
Parkes C M: Psychiatric problems following bereavement by murder or manslaughter. Br J Psychiatry *162*: 49, 1993.
Toch H: *Violent Men.* Schenkman, Cambridge, Mass, 1980.
Weiger W A, Bear D M: An approach to the neurology of aggression. J Psychiatr Res *22*: 85, 1988.
Weil D S, Hemenway D: Loaded guns in the home: Analysis of a national random survey of gun owners. JAMA *267*: 3033, 1992.

## 4.5 / Ethology, Experimental Disorders, and Sociobiology

Ethology, experimental disorders, and sociobiology are important contributors of knowledge to human psychological behavior and should be studied to understand human physiological functioning. Therefore, they are relevant to psychiatry.

Ethologists are concerned with the study of animal behavior and the origins of such behavior. The direct observation of animals in their natural environments has been the basic technique of behavioral measurement. However, ethologists have increasingly used other techniques, from introducing experimental factors into a natural environment to conducting laboratory investigations. In 1973 the Nobel prize in medicine was awarded to three ethologists: Konrad Lorenz, Nikolaas Tinbergen, and Karl von Frisch, whose work is described below.

## KONRAD LORENZ

Born in Austria, Konrad Lorenz (1903–1988) is best known for his studies of imprinting. *Imprinting* implies that, during a certain short period of development, a young animal is highly sensitive to a certain type of stimulus that then, but not at other times, provokes a specific behavior pattern. Lorenz described how newly hatched goslings are programmed to follow a moving object, whereupon they rapidly become imprinted to follow that and possibly similar objects. Typically, the mother is the first moving object the young sees, but should it see something else first, the gosling will follow it. For instance, a gosling imprinted by Lorenz followed him and refused to follow a goose (Figure 4.5–1). Imprinting is an important concept for psychiatrists to understand in their effort to link early developmental experiences with later behaviors.

Lorenz also studied the forms of behavior that function as sign stimuli—that is, as social releasers—in communications between individual animals of the same species. Many of the signals have the character of fixed motor patterns in that they appear automatically and the reaction of other members of the species is equally automatic.

Lorenz is also well-known for his study of aggression. He wrote about the practical function of aggression, such as the defense of their territory by fish and birds. Aggression among members of the same species is common, but Lorenz pointed out that, in normal conditions, it seldom leads to killing or even to serious injury. Although the animals attack one an-

other, a certain balance appears between tendencies to fight and flight, with the tendency to fight being strongest in the center of the territory and the tendency to flight strongest at a distance from the center.

In many of his works, Lorenz tried to draw conclusions from his ethological studies of animals that can also be applied to human problems. The postulation of a primary need for aggression in humans, cultivated by the pressure of selection, is a primary example. The need may have served a practical purpose at an early time, when human beings lived in small groups that had to defend themselves from other groups. Competition with neighboring groups became the most important factor of selection. However, Lorenz pointed out how that need has survived the advent of weapons that can be used not merely to kill individuals but to wipe out all human beings.

## NIKOLAAS TINBERGEN

Born in the Netherlands, Nikolaas Tinbergen, (1907–1988), a British zoologist, conducted a series of experiments to analyze various aspects of animal behavior. He was also successful in quantifying behavior and in obtaining measures of the power or strength of various stimuli in eliciting specific behavior. Tinbergen described displacement activities, which have been studied mainly in birds. For example, in a conflict situation, when the need for fight and the need for flight are of roughly equal strength, birds sometimes do neither. Rather, they display behavior that appears to be irrelevant to the situation (for example, a herring gull defending its territory can start to pick grass). Displacement activities of that kind vary according to the situation and the species concerned. Human beings can engage in displacement activities when under stress.

Lorenz and Tinbergen described *innate releasing mechanisms*, animal responses triggered by releasers, which are specific environmental stimuli. Releasers (including shapes, colors, and sounds) evoke sexual, aggressive, or other responses. For example, big eyes in human infants evoke more caretaking behavior than small eyes do.

In his later work Tinbergen, along with his wife, studied early childhood autistic disorder. They began by observing the behavior of autistic and normal children when they meet strangers, which is analogous to the techniques used in observing animal behavior. In particular, they observed in animals the conflict that arises between fear and the need for contact and noted that it can lead to behavior that is similar to that of autistic children. They hypothesized that, in certain predisposed children, fear can greatly predominate and can also be provoked by stimuli that normally have a positive social value for most children. That innovative approach to studying infantile autistic disorder opened up new avenues of inquiry. Although their conclusions regarding preventive measures and treatment must be considered tentative, the method shows another way in which ethology and clinical psychiatry can relate to each other.

## KARL VON FRISCH

Born in Austria, Karl von Frisch (1886–1982) conducted studies on changes of color in fish and demonstrated that fish could learn to distinguish among several colors and that their sense of color was fairly congruent with that of human beings. He later went on to study the color vision

**Figure 4.5–1.** In a famous experiment, Konrad Lorenz demonstrated that goslings responded to him as if he were the natural mother. (From E H Hess: Imprinting: An effect of early experience. *Science 130:* 133, 1959. Used with permission.)

and behavior of bees and is most widely known for his analysis of how bees communicate with one another—that is, their language or what is known as their dances. His description of the exceedingly complex behavior of bees prompted an investigation of information systems in other animal species.

# ANIMAL MODELS OF PSYCHOPATHOLOGY

## Pharmacological Experimentation

With the emergence of biological psychiatry, many researchers have used pharmacological means to produce syndrome analogues in animal subjects. Two classic examples are the reserpine (Serpasil) model of depression and the amphetamine psychosis model of paranoid schizophrenia. In the depression studies, animals given the norepinephrine-depleting drug reserpine exhibited behavioral abnormalities analogous to those of major depressive disorder in humans. The behavioral abnormalities produced were generally reversed by antidepressant drugs. Those studies tended to corroborate the theory that depression in humans is, in part, the result of diminished levels of norepinephrine. Similarly, animals given amphetamines acted in a stereotyped, inappropriately aggressive, and apparently frightened manner that was similar to paranoid psychotic symptoms in humans. Both of those models are thought to be too simplistic in their concepts of cause, but they remain as early paradigms for that type of research.

Studies were done on the effects of catecholamine-depleting drugs on monkeys during separation and reunion periods. Those studies showed that catecholamine depletion and social separation can interact in a highly synergistic fashion, yielding depressive symptoms in subjects for whom mere separation or low-dosage treatment by itself is not sufficient to produce depression.

## Environmental Experimentation

A number of researchers, including Ivan Petrovich Pavlov in Russia and W. Horsley Gantt and Howard Scott Liddell in America, studied the effects of stressful environments on animals, such as dogs and sheep. Pavlov produced a phenomenon in dogs, which he labeled experimental neurosis, by the use of a conditioning technique that led to symptoms of extreme and persistent agitation. The technique involved teaching dogs to discriminate between a circle and an ellipse and then progressively diminishing the difference between the two. Gantt used the term "behavior disorders" to describe the reactions he elicited from dogs forced into similar conflictual learning situations. Liddell described the stress response he obtained in sheep, goats, and dogs as experimental neurasthenia, which was obtained in some cases by merely doubling the number of daily test trials in an unscheduled manner.

**Learned helplessness.** The learned helplessness model of depression, developed by Martin Seligman, is a good example of an experimental disorder. Dogs were exposed to electric shocks from which they could not escape. The dogs eventually gave up, making no attempt to escape new shocks. The apparent giving up generalized to other situations, and eventually the dogs always appeared to be helpless and apathetic. Because the cognitive, motivational, and affective deficits displayed by the dogs resembled symptoms common to human depressive disorders, learned helplessness, although controversial, was proposed as an animal model of human depression. Research on subjects with learned helplessness and the expectation of inescapable punishment has found brain release of endogenous opiates, destructive effects on the immune system, and elevation of the pain threshold.

A social application of that concept involves school children who have learned that they fail in school no matter what they do; they view themselves as helpless losers, and that self-concept causes them to stop trying. Teaching them to persist may reverse the process, with excellent results in self-respect and school performance.

**Chronic stress.** Rats subjected to chronic unpredictable stress (crowding, shocks, irregular feeding, and interrupted sleep time) show decreased movement and exploratory behavior, which illustrates the role that unpredictability and not having any control over the environment has in producing stress. Those behavioral changes can be reversed by antidepressant medication. Animals under experimental stress (Figure 4.5–2) become tense, restless, hyperirritable, or inhibited in certain conflict situations.

**Dominance hierarchy.** Animals in a dominant position in a hierarchy have certain advantages (for example, mating and feeding). Being more dominant than one's peers is associated with elation, and a fall in one's position in the hierarchy is associated with depression. When persons lose jobs, are replaced in organizations, or otherwise have their dominance or hierarchical status changed, they can experience depression.

**Genetics and temperament.** Temperament mediated by genetics plays a role in behavior. For example, one group of pointer dogs were bred for fearfulness and a lack of friendliness toward people, and another group were bred for the opposite characteristics. The phobic dogs were extremely timid and fearful and showed decreased exploratory capacity, increased startle response, and cardiac arrhythmias. Benzodiazepines diminished those fearful, anxious responses. Amphetamines and cocaine aggravated the responses of genetically nervous dogs to a greater extent than the responses of the stable dogs.

**Intracranial stimulation.** Pleasurable sensations have been produced in both humans and animals through self-stimulation of certain brain areas, such as the medial forebrain bundle, the septal area, and the lateral hypothalamus. Rats have engaged in repeated self-stimulation (2,000 stimulations per hour) to gain rewards. Catecholamine production increases with self-stimulation of the brain areas, and drugs that decrease catecholamines decrease the process.

# DEVELOPMENTAL PROCESSES IN NONHUMAN PRIMATES

An area of animal research that has important relevance to human behavior and psychopathology is the longitudinal

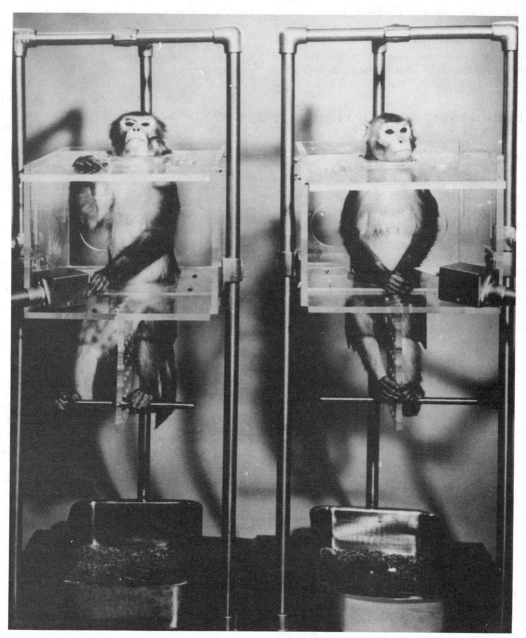

**Figure 4.5–2.** The monkey on the left, known as the executive monkey, controls whether or not both will receive an electric shock. The decision-making task produces a state of chronic tension. Note the more relaxed attitude of the monkey on the right. (From United States Army photographs.)

study of nonhuman primates. Monkeys have been observed from birth to maturity, not only in their natural habitats and laboratory facsimiles but also in laboratory settings that involve various degrees of social deprivation early in life. Social deprivation has been produced through two predominant conditions: social isolation and separation. Socially isolated monkeys are raised in varying degrees of isolation and are not permitted to develop normal attachment bonds. Monkeys that are separated are taken from their primary caretakers and thereby experience a disruption in an already developed bond. Social isolation techniques illustrate the effects of an infant's early social environment on subsequent development (Figure 4.5–3), and separation techniques illustrate the effects of loss

of a significant attachment figure. The name most associated with isolation and separation studies is Harry Harlow. A summary of Harlow's work is presented in Table 4.5–1.

In a series of experiments, Harlow separated rhesus monkeys from their mothers during their first weeks of life. During that time, the monkey infant depends on its mother for nourishment and protection, as well as for physical warmth and emotional security—contact comfort, as Harlow first termed it in 1958. Harlow substituted a surrogate mother made from wire or cloth for the real mother. The infants preferred the cloth-covered surrogate mother, which provided contact comfort, to the wire-covered surrogate, which provided food but no contact comfort.

**Figure 4.5–3.** Social isolate after removal of isolation screen.

## Rehabilitation of Abnormal Behavior

In 1972 Stephen Suomi demonstrated that isolates can be rehabilitated if they are exposed to monkeys that promote physical contact without threatening the isolates with aggression or overly complex play interactions. Those monkeys were called therapist monkeys. To fill such a therapeutic role, young normal monkeys were chosen that would play gently with the isolates and approach and cling to them. Within two weeks, the isolates were reciprocating the social contact, and their incidence of abnormal self-directed behaviors began to decline significantly. By the end of the six-month therapy period, the isolates were

**Table 4.5–1**
**Social Deprivation in Nonhuman Primates***

| Type of Social Deprivation | Effect |
|---|---|
| Total isolation (not allowed to develop caretaker or peer bond) | Self-orality, self-clasping, very fearful when placed with peers, unable to copulate (Figure 4.5–3). If impregnated, female is unable to nurture young (motherless mothers). If isolation goes beyond six months, no recovery is possible. |
| Mother-only-reared | Fails to leave mother and explore. Terrified when finally exposed to peers. Unable to play or to copulate. |
| Peer-only-reared | Engages in self-orality, grasps others in clinging manner, easily frightened, reluctant to explore, timid as adult, play is minimal (Figure 4.5–4). |
| Partial isolation (can see, hear, and smell other monkeys) | Stares vacantly into space, engages in self-mutilation, stereotyped behavior patterns. |
| Separation (taken from caretaker after bond has developed) | Initial protest stage changing to despair 48 hours after separation; refuses to play. Rapid reattachment when returned to mother. |

*Table adaped from work of Harry Harlow, M.D.

actively initiating play bouts with both the therapists and each other, and most of their self-directed behaviors had disappeared. The isolates were observed closely for the next two years, and their improved behavioral repertoires

**Figure 4.5–4.** Choo-choo phenomenon in peer-only-reared infant rhesus monkeys.

did not regress over time. The results of that and subsequent monkey-therapist studies underscored the potential reversibility of early cognitive and social deficits at the human level. The studies also served as a model for developing therapeutic treatments for socially retarded and withdrawn children.

Several investigators have argued that social separation manipulations with nonhuman primates provide a compelling basis for animal models of depression and anxiety. Some monkeys react to separations with behavioral and physiological symptoms similar to those seen in depressed human patients; both electroconvulsive therapy (ECT) and tricyclic drugs are effective in reversing the symptoms in monkeys. Not all separations produce depressive reactions in monkeys, just as separation does not always precipitate depression in humans, young or old.

### Individual Differences

Recent research has revealed that some rhesus monkey infants consistently display fearfulness and anxiety in situations in which similarly reared peers show normal exploratory behavior and play. Those situations generally involve exposure to some kind of novel object or situation. Once the object or situation has become familiar, any behavioral differences between the anxiety-prone or timid infants and their outgoing peers disappear. However, the individual differences appear to be stable during development. Infant monkeys at 3 to 6 months of age that are at high risk for fearful or anxious reactions tend to remain at high risk for such reactions, at least until adolescence.

Long-term follow-up study of the above monkey subjects has revealed some behavioral differences between fearful and nonfearful females when they become adults and have their first infants. Fearful female monkeys who grow up in socially benign and stable environments typically become fine mothers; however, fearful females who have reacted to frequent social separations during childhood with depression are at high risk for maternal dysfunction; more than 80 percent of those mothers either neglect or abuse their first offspring. Yet nonfearful females who encounter the same number of social separations but do not react to any of those separations with depression subsequently turn out to be good mothers.

### SENSORY DEPRIVATION

The history of sensory deprivation and its potentially deleterious effects evolved from instances of aberrant mental behavior in explorers, shipwrecked sailors, and prisoners in solitary confinement. Toward the end of World War II, startling confessions, induced by brainwashing prisoners of war, caused a rise of interest in that psychological phenomenon brought about by the deliberate diminution of sensory input.

To test the hypothesis that an important element in brainwashing is prolonged exposure to sensory isolation, D. O. Hebb and his coworkers brought solitary confinement into the laboratory and demonstrated that volunteer subjects—under conditions of visual, auditory, and tactile deprivation for periods of up to seven days—reacted with increased suggestibility. Some of the subjects also showed characteristic symptoms of the sensory deprivation state: anxiety, tension, inability to concentrate or organize one's thoughts, increased suggestibility, body illusions, somatic complaints, intense subjective emotional distress, and vivid sensory imagery—usually visual and sometimes reaching the proportions of hallucinations with a delusionary quality.

### Psychological Theories

Anticipating psychological explanations, Sigmund Freud wrote: "It is interesting to speculate what could happen to ego function if the excitations or stimuli from the external world were either drastically diminished or repetitive. Would there be an alteration in the unconscious mental processes and an effect upon the conceptualization of time?"

Indeed, under conditions of sensory deprivation, the abrogation of such ego functions as perceptual contact with reality and logical thinking brings about confusion, irrationality, fantasy formation, hallucinatory activity, and wish-dominated mental reactions. In the sensory deprivation situation the subject becomes dependent on the experimenter and must trust the experimenter for the satisfaction of such basic needs as feeding, toileting, and physical safety. A patient undergoing psychoanalysis may be in a kind of sensory deprivation room (for example, sound-proofed, dim lights, couch) in which primary process mental activity is encouraged through free association.

### Physiological Theories

The maintenance of optimal conscious awareness and accurate reality testing depends on a necessary state of alertness. That alert state, in turn, depends on a constant stream of changing stimuli from the external world, mediated through the ascending reticular activating system in the brainstem. In the absence or the impairment of such a stream, as occurs in sensory deprivation, alertness falls away, direct contact with the outside world diminishes, and impulses from the inner body and the central nervous system may gain prominence. For example, idioretinal phenomena, inner ear noise, and somatic illusions may take on a hallucinatory character.

### Other Theories

**Personality.** Personality theories attempt to explain not the phenomena of sensory deprivation but, rather, the variation in those phenomena from subject to subject. For example, why do some volunteers in experiments quit sooner than others? Various approaches are offered by various investigators—introversion-extroversion, body-field orientation, and optimal stimulation level.

**Expectation.** Expectation hypotheses involve social influences, including the important role played by the experimenter. Modern researchers place great emphasis on anticipation, instructional set, and the demand characteristics of the experimental situation (tacit and overt suggestion).

**Cognitive.** Cognitive theories stress the fact that the organism is an information-processing machine, the purpose of which is optimal adaptation to the perceived environment. Lacking sufficient information, the machine is unable to form a cognitive map, against which current experience is matched. Disorganization and maladaptation are the result. To monitor one's own behavior and attain optimal responsiveness, the organism must receive continuous feedback. Without that feedback, the person is forced to project outward idiosyncratic themes that have little relation to reality. That situation is similar to that of many psychotic patients.

# SOCIOBIOLOGY

Sociobiology is the study of the biological basis of social behavior. It is a relatively new discipline that integrates principles of evolution, genetics, ecology, and ethology. Sociobiologists see many similarities in animal and human behavior, such as competition, territoriality, aggression, reproduction, mate selection, male-female differences, parenting, and altruism. A sociobiological postulate is that human behavior has evolved to achieve maximum fitness and adaptation. *Fitness* is defined as the highest measure of evolutionary success in that the best genes are passed on from one generation to the next. *Inclusive fitness* is the sum of a person's personal fitness and that of the person's relatives compared with the rest of the population.

## Role of Evolution

Evolution is any change in the genetic makeup of a population. It occurs through natural (Darwinian) selection, which is the reproduction of those genes produced by mutation that account for the most successful offspring. Lamarckian evolution occurs through the inheritance of acquired characteristics and explains the evolution of culture.

## Competition

Animals vie with one another for resources or territory. Territory is an area that is defended for the exclusive use of the animal and that ensures access to food and reproduction. The ability of one animal to defend a disputed territory or resource is called *resource holding potential*, and the greater that potential, the more successful is the animal.

## Aggression

Aggression serves both to increase territory and to eliminate competitors. Defeated animals can emigrate, disperse, or remain in the social group as subordinate animals. A dominance hierarchy in which animals are associated with one another in subtle but well-defined ways is part of every social pattern.

## Reproductive Strategies

Because behavior is influenced by heredity, those behaviors that promote reproduction and survival of the species are among the most important. The usual pattern is for males to compete with other males for the females and to produce the most fit offspring. Male-male competition can take various forms. For example, sperm can be thought of as competing for access to the ovum. Females compete with females but in more subtle ways, primarily in terms of dominance, nest-building ability, and breeding potential. Different behavioral patterns between males and females, called *sexual dimorphism*, evolve to ensure the maintenance of resources and reproduction.

## Altruism

Altruistic behavior benefits another and appears to enhance the other's success, with no benefit derived to the altruist. Altruism is explained by sociobiology as a way of maintaining the gene pool at its highest level. It is a selfish act but selfishness at the level of the gene, rather than the individual animal. The classic case of altruism is in the female worker classes of certain wasps, bees, and ants. Those insects are sterile and do not reproduce; rather, they labor altruistically for the reproductive success of the queen.

Another possible mechanism for the evolution of altruism is group selection. If groups containing altruists are more successful than those composed entirely of selfish members, the altruistic groups succeed at the expense of the selfish ones, and altruism evolves. But, within each group, altruists are at a severe disadvantage relative to selfish members, however well the group as a whole is able to do.

## References

Ainsworth M S, Bowlby J: An ethological approach to personality development. Am Psychol 46: 333, 1991.

Alcock J: *Animal Behavior: An Evolutionary Approach*. Sinauer, Sunderland, Mass, 1989.

Barabasz A F: Restricted environmental stimulation and the enhancement of hypnotizability: Pain, EEG alpha, skin conductance and temperature responses. Int Clin Exp Hypn 30: 147, 1982.

Barash D P: *Sociobiology and Behavior*, ed 2. Elsevier, New York, 1982.

Borrie R A, Suedfeld P: Restricted environmental stimulation therapy in a weight reduction program. J Behav Med 3: 147, 1980.

Dixon A K, Fisch H U, Huber C, Walser A: Ethological studies in animals and man: Their use in psychiatry. Pharmacopsychiatry 22: 44, 1989.

Fine T H, Turner J W Jr: The effect of brief restricted environmental stimulation therapy in the treatment of essential hypertension. Behav Res Ther 20: 567, 1982.

Harlow H F: The nature of love. Am Psychol 13: 673, 1958.

Lerner R M, von Eye A: Sociobiology and human development: Arguments and evidence. Hum Dev 35: 12, 1992.

Lieberman L, Reynolds L T, Friedrich D: The fitness of human sociobiology: The future utility of four concepts in four subdisciplines. Soc Biol 39: 158, 1992.

Lister R G. Ethologically based animal models of anxiety disorders. Pharmacol Ther 46: 321, 1990.

Lorenz K Z: *The Foundations of Ethology*. Springer, New York, 1981.

McKinney W T: Interdisciplinary animal research and its relevance to psychiatry. In *Comprehensive Textbook of Psychiatry*, ed 5, H I Kaplan, B J Sadock, editors, p 326. Williams & Wilkins, Baltimore, 1989.

Pavlov I P: *Conditioned Reflexes*. Oxford University Press, London, 1927.

Pitman R K, Kolb B, Orv S P, Singh M: Ethological study of facial behavior in non-paranoid and paranoid schizophrenic patients. Am J Psychiatry 144: 99, 1987.

Schwartz A: Not art but science: Applications of neurobiology, experimental psychology, and ethology to psychoanalytic technique: I. Neuroscientifically guided approaches to interpretive "what's" and "when's." Psychoanal Inq 12: 445, 1992.

Spear N E, Miller J S, Jagielo J A: Animal memory and learning. Annu Rev Psychol 41: 169, 1990.

Suedfeld P, Ballard E J, Murphy M: Water immersion and flotation: From stress experiment to stress treatment. J Environ Psychol 3: 147, 1983.

Suomi S J: Social development in rhesus monkeys: Consideration of individual difference. In *The Behaviour of Human Infants*, A Oilverio, M Zappella, editors, p 52. Plenum, New York, 1983.

Suomi S J, Harlow H F: Social rehabilitation of isolate-reared monkeys. Dev Psychol 6: 487, 1972.

Tinbergen N: *The Study of Instinct*. Clarendon, Oxford, 1989.

## 4.6 / Anthropology and Psychiatry

Anthropology and psychiatry are both concerned with the understanding of human behavior. Anthropology is the study of culture, which is the external expression of individual mental life as represented by manners, customs, skills, language, parent-child interactions, beliefs, and social life. Cultures differ in their definitions of health, illness, and healing and also vary greatly in child-rearing patterns, social models and expectations, role opportunities, and other variables. Anthropology also includes cross-cultural studies, which are used in the field of comparative psychiatry to describe and analyze cross-cultural variations in the incidence and the prevalence of syndromes and symptoms. Disorders are compared from one culture to another to see if universal characteristics transcend cultural differences.

Culture is traditional in that social practices are passed from generation to generation. Culture also encompasses the notion of a group of persons sharing a system of action and beliefs capable of persisting longer than the life span of any one person, a group whose adherents come from the sexual reproduction of the group members. In that sense, every culture is historical and genetic. A culture also possesses a value system of good, bad, desirable, and undesirable behavioral patterns and can be examined from both a psychological viewpoint and a normative viewpoint in terms of how the majority adapt to stresses unique to a particular culture.

### PSYCHOANALYTICAL ANTHROPOLOGY

Beginning with Sigmund Freud, psychoanalysts have applied their insights to cultural data. In 1913 in *Totem and Taboo*, Freud described earliest humans as a group of brothers who killed and devoured their violent primal father. That criminal act and the so-called totem meal made the brothers feel guilty. Consequently, they set up rules formulated so that similar acts would never occur again; those rules were the beginning of social organization. Carl Gustav Jung's writings include many anthropological references, especially to archeology and mythology. In *Symbols and Transformations*, written in 1912, Jung traced patients' fantasies back to earliest human artifacts. Neither Freud nor Jung had field experience, but Erik Erikson, for one example, did. Erikson is best known for his psychocultural biographies of Mohandas Gandhi and Martin Luther and for the 1950 book *Childhood and Society*, in which he attempted to integrate individual psychosexual development with cultural influences. Many of his conclusions were based on his experiences with the Pine Ridge Indians in the Dakotas and the Yurok Indians in Oregon.

George Devereux studied American Plains Indians and provided insights into the problems that arise in dealing with patients from diverse ethnic backgrounds. In the 1930s and the 1940s Abraham Kardiner worked with the concept of national character and suggested that each culture is associated with a common (or at least widely shared) personality structure. Kardiner believed that the adult Russian personality, for example, is characterized by depressive and manic traits. Other such generalities about national character were set forth by various workers, but those descriptions were often used to foster political, ideological, or discriminatory attitudes and, so, have fallen out of favor. The current consensus is that a clinically meaningful prediction about one's personality cannot be made on the basis of nationality alone. But as Ruth Benedict wrote in *Patterns of Culture*, personality types may reflect a culture's configuration because people are malleable and they assume a society's expected behavior pattern.

Bronislaw Malinowski and Margaret Mead were among the anthropologists who examined the psychoanalytic concept that adult personality and mental functioning are largely determined during childhood. Malinowski examined childhood and adult sexuality in the Trobriand Islanders and claimed that he found no evidence of the Oedipus complex, which at the time was believed to be universal. Margaret Mead examined gender and sex-role behavior. She observed three tribes in New Guinea and found different patterns of sex-role behavior for men and women in each tribe. According to Mead, behavior is relative, and a society can create deviance by either condoning or condemning certain behavior patterns. Mead believed the Oedipus complex to be a useful concept in its widest meaning, which is that in all societies adults are involved in the growing child's sexual attitudes, especially toward the parent of the opposite sex.

### Child-Rearing Practices

The effects of early life experiences on adult mental health and what accounts for deviance or maladaptive behavior are still controversial issues. Psychodynamic psychiatrists and theorists rely on historical data about adverse experiences to explain later behavior; but new work shows that few experiences are irreversible. Some affection-deprived children described by John Bowlby were able to grow up capable of forming attachments if other experiences later in life were favorable. Similarly, many successful adults come from deprived or otherwise toxic homes and appear to be or are invulnerable to those stressors. Nevertheless, studies of child-rearing practices among various cultures have included the following conclusions: (1) Indulgence and care in early infancy are important determinants of adult mental health; (2) the nurture of the child by various caretakers, in addition to the mother, is not harmful; (3) a wide variety of child-rearing practices are found in cultures; and (4) the major influences on personality development revolve around love-hate and dependence-independence issues, rather than the control of sexual behavior. However, the basic relation between child-rearing patterns and subsequent adult personality in complex societies, such as the United States, has not yet been elucidated. In this country there are cycles of permissiveness and constraint, reward and punishment, and a general tendency to focus on bowel and bladder training as important child-rearing practices.

Some universals observed among children of various cultures are the following: (1) Smiling is a social greeting exhibited by all normal members of every known society; (2) there is a taboo against incest and homicide; (3) there are gender differences in roles that go beyond reproduction; (4) males are more aggressive than females; and (5) strong attachments and fear of separation and of strangers appear in the second half of the first year of life.

Anthropologists place humans in the same group as other Old-World higher primates, which include monkeys and apes. Those primates share the following characteristics: (1) single birth, (2) frequent nursing, (3) late weaning, (4) high mother-infant proximity, (5) gradual transition to peer play in groups, and (6) variable but low direct involvement by adult males in child rearing.

## CROSS-CULTURAL STUDIES

Cross-cultural studies examine and compare various cultures along a number of parameters: attitudes, beliefs, expectations, memories, opinions, roles, stereotypes, prejudices, and values. Usually, the cultures studied use different languages and have different political organizations. Cross-cultural studies are subject to extreme bias because of problems in translation. Questions have to be asked in ways that are clearly understood by the group under study. One of the best known cross-cultural studies, *Psychiatric Disorder among the Yoruba* by Alexander Leighton, was his attempt to replicate in Nigeria the Stirling County study he had conducted in Canada. The study was criticized because not only did it fail to distinguish psychophysiological symptoms from those associated with infections, parasites, and nutritional diseases but it assumed that the same indicators for sociocultural disintegration in Stirling County could be used among the Yoruba. Other studies have confirmed that psycholinguistics—the study of language and its communicative functions—must be taken into account if cross-cultural approaches are to be valid. All cultures are relative; that is, each must be examined within the context of its own language, customs, and beliefs. Various cultures assign different roles depending on status. Research has shown a high incidence of depression among adult women in Kikuyu society, where women are subject to heavy role demands. There is also a high prevalence of schizophrenia among last-born sons in rural Ireland because of the stresses linked to that role.

Diagnoses of mental disorders have been conducted among various cultures by the World Health Organization. The International Pilot Study of Schizophrenia confirmed that schizophrenia exists among all groups and is constant across cultures. Outcome studies of patients with schizophrenia, however, are not reliable because some societies (in contrast to the United States) do not stigmatize persons with mental illness, who are quickly reintegrated into the society. A major difficulty in cross-cultural diagnosis is the bias arising from the researcher's cultural background. That bias can be reduced if careful attention is given to translation and to the attitude of the examiner. Nevertheless, some generalizations can be made about cross-cultural or comparative psychiatry. Certain symptoms exist in all societies: anxiety, mania, depression, suicidal ideation, somatization, paranoia (persecutory delusions), and thought disorder. Although various labels may be applied in various cultures, recognition of deviant behavior and agreement that conditions are treatable (whether by the psychiatrist in one culture or the shaman in another) are universal.

## ETHNOGRAPHY

Ethnography (from the Greek *ethnos*, meaning race or people) is an inductive method of describing cultural forms through the examination of a series of cases. Ethnographers document phenomena by various methods, such as the examination of written records, folk tales, and myths; linguistic analysis; interviews with key informants; collections of life histories; questionnaire surveys; psychological tests; and, most important, participant observation.

### United States Culture

The United States is a multiethnic country, but the values of the white middle class predominate. The numerous subgroups that represent waves of immigration over the years have influenced the culture but not to such an extent that those groups have lost their identity. They have been partially *acculturated*; that is, they have assumed characteristics of the larger or more advanced society. But they have not been *assimilated*; that is, their unique cultural traits have not been absorbed totally. Recognized minority subcultures in this country include Hispanics (Mexican Americans, Puerto Ricans, Cuban Americans), Asian Americans (Chinese, Japanese, Korean, Pacific Islanders), African Americans, and Native Americans (American Indians, Eskimos).

According to the 1980 census, the resident population in the United States by race and national origin was as follows: white, 188 million; African American, 26 million; American Indian (including Eskimo), 1.4 million; Chinese, 806,000; Filipino, 775,000; Japanese, 701,000; Asian Indian, 361,000; Korean, 354,000; Vietnamese, 262,000; Americans of Hispanic origin, 14.5 million. The 1990 census shows that the Asian population grew by 65 percent between 1980 and 1990, and the number of Hispanics grew by 44 percent. There are now 22.3 million Hispanic Americans. Asians, however, are still a small part of the population—just 3 percent in 1990. Hispanics are now 8 percent of Americans, up from 6 percent in 1980. African Americans hold a steady 12 percent share of the population, and the white share has fallen slightly, to 84 percent from 86 percent.

Attempting to describe the ethnic characteristics of a culture is hazardous. The risk of stereotyping is great, and, as mentioned above, the concept of national character is controversial among contemporary anthropologists. Nevertheless, United States society has been described as having certain characteristics against which the ethnic groups in this country are compared. Table 4.6-1 lists the characteristics attributed to the national character of the United States.

Some subcultures approximate the United States national character more than do others, and some charac-

**Table 4.6–1**
**American Cultural Characteristics\***

1. Nuclear family unit valued highly with few children; financially independent by age 18
2. Bowel and bladder training important in child rearing
3. Personal hygiene emphasized, neatness valued
4. Self-reliance and rugged individualism valued
5. Avoidance of dependent role, especially after age 65; unwillingness to be cared for by children
6. Ambivalence about overt expressions of sexuality
7. Ownership of own home desirable
8. Belief that hard work will be rewarded
9. Collective approach to solving common problems
10. Upward social mobility desirable

\*The concept of national character is controversial among contemporary anthropologists, many of whom do not agree with this list.

**Table 4.6–2**
**Family Systems**

| Types | Characteristics |
|---|---|
| Monandry | Woman has one husband. |
| Polyandry | Woman has multiple husbands at once; the biological father is generally unknown, all males in family take paternal responsibility. |
| Polygamy | Husband has multiple wives at once; woman's status is inferior to man's; pecking order among wives exists in some form, one claiming more rights than others. |
| Patrimony | Property is inherited from the father. |
| Patronymic | Bride takes the groom's name; son takes the name of the father. |
| Patrilocal | Fathers arrange marriages of sons and daughters by making contracts with other fathers; wife resides with the family or the tribe of her husband. |
| Patrilineal | Kinship or descent is through the father. |
| Matrilineal | Kinship or descent is through the mother. |
| Bigamy | The crime of marrying while one has a wife or husband still living from whom one is not divorced. |
| Monogamy | Marriage with only one person at a time. |
| Matrilocal | Married couple lives in the home of the bride. |
| Neolocal | Married couple sets up new home independent of mother and father. |
| Bilineal | Both male and female parents are considered equal in regard to descent. |

teristics are more highly valued and prevalent within a particular ethnic group than in the culture as a whole. Hispanics, for example, value the nuclear family and place great emphasis on having many, rather than few, children. Asian Americans place an extremely high value on education; although they make up about 3 percent of the general population, they make up about 15 to 20 percent of all college students. Another example is that of filial piety, a strong value among Chinese Americans; Chinese-American parents expect their children to care for them in their old age.

The nuclear family of mother, father, and children is a universal unit in all cultures. The extended family—in which grandparents, parents, children, and other relatives all live under the same roof—is no longer common in the United States, but it is still prevalent in less industrialized cultures. Functions of the extended family, such as caring for the sick and the elderly, have been taken over by institutions.

In the United States, more than 85 percent of the men and women between the ages 35 and 45 are husband or wife in a nuclear family. Even though close to one out of two marriages ends in divorce, a majority of persons remarry and create new nuclear units. In fact, serial monogamy, in which persons remarry after divorce but remain faithful to the spouse during the course of the marriage, is a noticeable trend. Other family configurations are outlined in Table 4.6-2.

**Urbanization.** Urbanization is a major social, cultural, and ecological process in 20th-century America. By the year 2000, more than 90 percent of the population will live in urban areas. City life has altered the factors that cause illness and has affected the incidence and the prevalence of many diseases. Accordingly, urbanization has influenced many approaches used in the diagnosis and treatment of somatic illness and the methods used in the delivery of health services.

The U.S. Bureau of the Census uses operational definitions that recognize degrees of urbanization. The basic urban unit, according to the Census Bureau, is the standard metropolitan statistical area. That unit represents an integrated economic and social region with a recognized urban population nucleus of substantial size. In formulating the boundaries of an urban unit, the Census Bureau also takes into account such features as population density,

nonagricultural employment, and community ties. The population living outside metropolitan areas is subdivided into farm population and nonfarm population.

The trend of people's migrating and populating urban areas continues. The country's top 25 metropolitan areas are home to one in three Americans. Of those metropolitan areas, six are in the Northeast, five are in the Midwest, seven are in the South, and seven are in the West.

The major metropolitan areas in the South and the West are rapidly growing. Riverside-San Bernadino, California, grew faster than any other large metropolitan area in the 1980s, up by 45 percent. It jumped to 17th place, up from 24th place in 1980. In contrast, Pittsburgh lost 6 percent of its population and now ranks 20th among large metropolitan areas. In 1980 it was 11th.

Nearly 1 in 10 Americans lives alone, accounting for 24 percent of all households. Since 1980 single-person households have grown by almost 5 million. Most people who live alone are women, primarily old widows. But an increasing number of Americans live alone at all ages, as people postpone marriage into their late 20s and divorce in middle age.

**Redefining the family.** The number of family units in this country has declined slightly over the past 15 years. Of the country's 94 million households (minimum of three people), 71 percent are families, down from 74 percent in 1980. The definition of a *family* is two or more related people living together. The number of *traditional or nu-*

*clear families*, defined as married couples with children under age 18 in the home, fell by 5 percent between 1980 and 1990. Married couples with children in the home are now 26 percent of households, down from 31 percent in 1980. By contrast, the number of couples without dependent children at home grew by 17 percent during the 1980s.

The number of people living with nonrelatives has been growing faster than any other household type, up by 46 percent in the 1980s. Those households include unmarried male-female couples, homosexual couples, and nonromantic partners—for example, friends sharing an apartment. People living with nonrelatives, however, are not a large segment of households, accounting for just 5 percent of the total, up from 4 percent in 1980.

A modern ethnographic approach in Western subcultures is demonstrated by the 1971 study of a predominantly African-American ghetto in a large northern United States city. The researchers studied the community by living in it and by experiencing ghetto life directly. They progressed from being observer-participants to active participants in community life, becoming partisans who openly identified with the population under study. The scientific motivation for their study was to examine the patterns usually ascribed to persons living in a culture of poverty. They found that 83 percent of African-American families were conventional male-headed households and that the social structure beyond the family level consisted of a multiplicity of local institutions, such as churches, social clubs, and political organizations. Since then, a radical change has occurred: In 1983 only 42 percent of African-American families were made up of two parents with a male head of household, and that figure has continued to decline.

## Culture Change

Persons respond to culture change either by moving into a different culture or by staying put while the culture changes around them. When change is sudden and sweeping, the adaptive mechanisms of individuals and of their social support may be overwhelmed. *Culture shock* is characterized by anxiety or depression, a sense of isolation, derealization, and depersonalization. Culture shock is minimized if persons are part of an intact family unit and if they are prepared for the new culture in advance. It is minimal if refugees, for example, are clustered in a few central locations, rather than dispersed throughout the nation.

Studies have found a higher rate of psychiatric hospitalization in the United States for immigrants, especially young men, than for the native-born. There also appears to be a high incidence of paranoid symptoms among immigrant groups, which may be related to their differences (color, language, habit) from the larger society. Acute psychotic episodes that occur among third-world immigrants in this country usually have clear-cut precipitating factors, are recurrent, and have a good prognosis.

## MEDICAL ANTHROPOLOGY

Medical anthropology focuses on the practice of medicine and the cultural aspects of providing and receiving health care. It is considered a subfield of anthropology. The study of culture, attitudes, and beliefs has a special importance for psychiatry and medicine. For example, an effective prevention program for alcohol dependence involves changing attitudes and values about drinking. Similarly, the success of antismoking campaigns depends on altering attitudes about tobacco. Cultural aspects of health care are best understood within the context of the particular culture under study.

## Culture of the Mental Hospital

The physical and sociocultural environment of mental hospitals was studied in terms of its effects on patients. When disagreements concerning a patient's management occurred among staff members, patients did not do as well as when staff consensus existed. The environment of the hospital is as much a therapeutic agent as the medication a patient receives. A psychiatric hospital, as described by Alfred Staunton, is a small society with established hierarchical categories. Dissension or confusion about staff roles or expectations may be transmitted to patients, whose symptoms may be exacerbated as a result. The English psychiatrist Maxwell Jones attempted to organize the psychiatric hospital as a therapeutic community. Jones's primary goal was the elimination of the divisions between various mental health professions, for he believed divisions to be artificial and harmful to the patient.

## Cultural Aspects of Disease

Class status and ethnic identity influence the experience of illness. However, generalizations must be avoided. Patients must be understood in terms of the specific cultures or ethnic groups to which they belong. Mexican Americans and Puerto Rican Americans, for example, share as many group cultural differences as they do commonalities. Different cultures—Haitians, West Indians, Puerto Ricans, and Christian faith healers—incorporate shamans, persons who follow a divine call to healing. The clinician must find out how acculturated the patient is to the cultural mainstream of life. The influence of culture on the reporting and the presentation of symptoms must be considered. A reluctance to discuss certain topics may stem from the patient's individual psychology or from adherence to the customs and etiquette of the social group.

**Hispanic Americans.**  Mexican Americans make up the largest group (10 million) of Americans of Hispanic origin and are referred to as Chicanos, particularly in the southwestern United States, where most Mexican Americans live. They frequently receive health care from folk healers (*curanderos*), who prescribe herbs or dietary change or use magic.

Puerto Rican Americans are the second largest Hispanic group (2 million). Most live in the northeastern states. In a study of Puerto Rican households in New York City, a significant number of adults visited folk healers or spiritists (*espiritismos*) during times of emotional crisis. Spiritism is practiced in small neighborhood centers (*centros*) where a medium performs magical procedures, such as drawing off evil spirits that may have entered into the patient, a therapeutic process known as *trabajando la causa* (working the cause).

**Asian Americans.**  In the United States the Asian-American population more than doubled during the 1980s. The two largest groups of Asian Americans, Chinese and Japanese, have shown different degrees of acculturation in the United States. During World War II, internment of second-generation

**Table 4.6–3**
**Culture-Bound Syndromes**

| Diagnosis | Country or Culture | Characteristics |
|---|---|---|
| Amok | Southeast Asia, Malaysia | Sudden rampage, usually including homicide and suicide; occurs in males; ends in exhaustion and amnesia |
| Bouffée délirante | France | Transient psychosis with elements of trance or dream states |
| Brain fog | Sub-Saharan Africa | Headache, agnosia, chronic fatigue, visual difficulties, anxiety; seen in male students |
| Bulimia nervosa | North America | Food binges, self-induced vomiting; may occur with depression, anorexia nervosa, or substance abuse |
| Colera | Mayan Indians (Guatemala) | Temper tantrums, violent outbursts, gasping, stuporousness, hallucinations, delusions |
| Empacho | Mexican and Cuban American | Inability to digest and excrete recently ingested food |
| Grisi siknis | Miskito of Nicaragua | Headache, anxiety, anger, aimless running |
| Hi-Wa itck | Mohave American Indian | Anorexia nervosa, insomnia, depression, suicide associated with unwanted separation from loved one |
| Involutional paraphrenia | Spain, Germany | Paranoid disorder occurring in midlife; distinct from schizophrenia but may have elements of both schizophrenia and paranoia |
| Koro | Asia | Fear that the penis will withdraw into the abdomen, causing death |
| Latah | Southeast Asia, Malaysia, Bantu of Africa, Ainu of Japan | Automatic obedience reaction with echopraxia and echolalia precipitated by a sudden minimal stimulus; occurs in females; also called a startle reaction. |
| Mal de ojo | Mediterranean | Vomiting, fever, restless sleep; caused by evil eye |
| Nervios | Costa Rica and Latin America | Headache, insomnia, anorexia, fears, anger, diarrhea, despair |
| Piblokto (Arctic hysteria, pibloktoq) | Eskimos of northern Greenland | Mixed anxiety and depression, confusion, depersonalization, derealization; occurs mainly in females; ends in stuporous sleep and amnesia |
| Reactive psychosis | Scandinavia | Psychosis precipitated by psychosocial stress; sudden onset with good prognosis, premorbid personality intact; in DSM-IV known as schizophreniform disorder |
| Shinkeishitsu | Japan | Syndrome marked by obsessions, perfectionism, ambivalence, social withdrawal, neurasthenia, and hypochondriais |
| Susto | Latin America | Severe anxiety, restlessness, fear of black magic and of evil eye |
| Tabanka | Trinidad | Depression in men abandoned by their wives; high risk of suicide |
| Taijin-kyofusho | Japan | Anxiety, fear of rejection, easy blushing, fear of eye contact, concern about body odor |
| Windigo | Native American Indians (Algonkian) | Fear of being turned into a cannibal through possession by supernatural monster, the windigo |

West Coast Japanese (Nisei) in concentration camps was imposed by the United States government. More than 100,000 people were forcibly detained; when they regained their freedom in 1945, they were filled with fear and resentment. Chinese immigration preceded that of the Japanese, and they, too, were subject to discriminatory legislation. Prejudice tends to reinforce ethnic identity and retard assimilation. Since the 1960s civil rights movement, increased assimilation of Asian Americans has occurred. Nevertheless, the clinician must be aware of unique cultural behavior patterns. For example, a Japanese patient may say yes (*hai*) as a sign of polite participation in a conversation, rather than as a sign of agreement; Hawaiian patients may avoid eye contact if they were taught that eye contact is a sign of aggression; Chinese patients may smile or laugh when they are embarrassed or sad; and Pacific Islanders may miss medical sessions because it is socially acceptable to be casual about fixed dates and appointments.

**Native Americans.** Native Americans are among the most widely studied groups and have the best known ethnographies. They are the only ethnic group in America to have a separate medical care program administered by the federal government, the Indian Health Service. There is a long tradition of healing rituals among Native Americans, who make no distinction between mental illness and physical illness. Illness is thought to result from a disharmony among a person's natural, supernatural, and human environments caused by culturally unacceptable behavior or by witchcraft. High rates of alcohol dependence and suicide are found in Native Americans and Eskimos.

**African Americans.** The 30.5 million African Americans constitute a heterogeneous group; however, most belong to the lower and lower-middle socioeconomic classes. Only 20 percent hold white-collar jobs, compared with 40 percent of white workers, and the median income of African-American families is only about 55 percent that of white families.

Unique to certain African-American subgroups, such as those from Haiti, is root work or voodoo. Rites, hexes, prayers, curses, and other practices are used by shamans and witch doctors to influence health or illness. Persons undergoing healing experiences often enter trance states, during which they are vulnerable to shamanistic suggestions. Shamans give objective reality to popular and emotionally accepted beliefs of the cultural group.

Certain generalizations about the health of African Americans can be made. They have a shorter life expectancy than whites, a higher incidence of hypertensive disease, and a higher homicide rate. Some of those differences are related to the low socioeconomic level of most African Americans; in general, the poor do not use health care facilities as readily as the more affluent do.

**Christian beliefs.** The past two decades have seen a growing interest in Christian faith healing directed toward what is called sickness of the spirit, the emotions, and the body. According to certain fundamentalist groups, any form of sickness may have a demonic origin, and some cases call for prayer and exorcism for recovery to occur. The role of the physician is to heal through divine intervention. Some faith healers are willing to work with physicians. Others, however, believe that participation in a close-knit Christian community, participation in a bible-study group, and prayer are sufficient.

## Culture-Bound Syndromes

Some disorders are found only in certain cultures or among certain groups. The disorders often occur with little warning, their course is usually short, and their prognosis is generally favorable.

The notion of culture-bound syndromes is conceptually simple but operationally complex. Because culture is the matrix in which all biological, psychological, and social functioning operates, it follows that all psychiatric syndromes are, to some extent, culture-bound. Western psychiatrists, for example, tend to view mental disorders in Western societies as culture-free; but bulimia nervosa is as shaped by Western culture as koro is by Oriental culture. If African healers with limited Western contact were transplanted briefly to this country, they would be equally surprised by the odd symptoms of the patients here.

Conversion disorder is seen much less frequently in America today than in 19th-century European society. The symptoms of anorexia nervosa are related to the cultural expectations of weight and body image in modern Western industrial society. Table 4.6-3 briefly outlines some culture-bound syndromes. Culture-bound syndromes are discussed further in Section 14.1.

## References

Andreasen N C: The American concept of schizophrenia. Schizophr Bull *15*: 519, 1989.
Andrews G R: Cross cultural studies: An important development in aging research. J Am Geriatr Soc *37*: 483, 1989.
Armelagos G J, Leatherman T, Ryan M, Sibley L: Biocultural synthesis in medical anthropology. Med Anthropol *14*: 35, 1992.
Benedict R: *Patterns of Culture.* Houghton Mifflin, Boston, 1934.
Bracken P J: Post-empiricism and psychiatry: Meaning and methodology in cross-cultural research. Soc Sci Med *36*: 265, 1993.
Cole M: *Comparative Studies of How People Think: An Introduction.* Harvard University Press, Cambridge, 1981.
Erikson E: *Childhood and Society.* Norton, New York, 1950.
Fabrega H Jr: Culture and the psychosomatic tradition. Psychosom Med *54*: 561, 1992.
Fabrega H Jr: An ethnomedical perspective of Anglo-American psychiatry. Am J Psychiatry *146*: 588, 1989.
Fabrega H Jr: On the significance of an anthropological approach to schizophrenia. Psychiatry *52*: 45, 1989.
Favazza A, Faheem A: *Themes in Cultural Psychiatry.* University of Missouri Press, Columbia, 1982.
Freud S: Totem and taboo. In *Standard Edition of the Complete Psychological Works of Sigmund Freud*, vol 13, p 1. Hogarth Press, London, 1955.
Jung C: *Symbols and Transformations*, ed 2. Princeton University Press, Princeton, 1967.
Kardiner A, Linton R, DuBois C: *The Psychological Frontiers of Society.* Columbia University Press, New York, 1945.
Kirmayer L J: Cultural variations in the response to psychiatric disorders and emotional distress. Soc Sci Med *29*: 327, 1989.
Kleinman A, Eisenberg L, Good B: Culture, illness, and care. Ann Intern Med *88*: 251, 1978.
Koegel P: Through a different lens: An anthropological perspective on the homeless mentally ill. Cult Med Psychiatry *16*: 1, 1992.
Konner M: Anthropology and psychiatry. In *Comprehensive Textbook of Psychiatry*, ed 5, H I Kaplan, B J Sadock, editors, p 283. Williams & Wilkins, Baltimore, 1989.
Landrine H, Klonoff E A: Culture and health-related schemas: A review and proposal for interdisciplinary integration. Health Psychol *11*: 267, 1992.
Leff J: *Psychiatry around the Globe: A Transcultural View.* Dekker, New York, 1981.
Malinowski B: *Sex and Repression in Savage Society.* Harcourt, New York, 1927.
Mezzich J E: International diagnostic systems and Latin-American contributions and issues. Br J Psychiatry Suppl *4*: 84, 1989.
Mollica R, Wyshak G, de Marneffe D, Khwon F, Lavelle J: Indochinese versions of the Hopkins symptom checklist-25: A screening instrument for the psychiatric care of refugees. Am J Psychiatry *144*: 497, 1987.
Westermeyer J: Psychiatric diagnosis across cultural boundaries. Am J Psychiatry *142*: 7, 1985.
Wohl J: Integration of cultural awareness into psychotherapy. Am J Psychother *43*: 343, 1989.

# 4.7 / Epidemiology, Biostatistics, and Social Psychiatry

Epidemiology, biostatistics, and social psychiatry rely on methods that observe, describe, and record events. That process, called the *scientific method*, is based on strict adherence to honesty, accuracy, and controlled experimentation. An *experiment* is a test designed to validate a hypothesis or to determine the probability of a theory. It relies on two types of reasoning—inductive and deductive. *Inductive reasoning* is the process of reasoning from the particular to the general or making a hypothesis from observing events. It is the complement to *deductive reasoning*, which is reasoning from the general to the particular or making a new hypothesis from already known principles.

The scientific method stems from several philosophical schools. The first system relevant to psychology and psychiatry is that of *empiricism*, which is the doctrine that all knowledge is derived from experience. Most empiricists recognize that the mind and inner experience affect one's perceptions of the outer world. That position is contrary to the school of *rationalism*, which holds that by reason alone, unaided by experience, one can arrive at basic truths regarding the world.

The school of *determinism* is also relevant to psychiatry because of its tenet that the individual is a product of and controlled by his or her history and personal experience. The scientific method as applied to the behavioral sciences relies on the theory of *parsimony*, which holds that there should be one explanation, rather than many. In medicine the theory of parsimony is expressed in the adage that two diagnoses should not be made when one diagnosis can account for all the signs and symptoms. In view of the complexities of human behavior and experience, however, a parsimonious approach is often not possible.

## EPIDEMIOLOGY

*Epidemiology* is the study of the distribution, incidence, prevalence, and duration of disease. In psychiatry, epidemiological methods contribute to an understanding of the causes, treatment, and prevention of mental disorders. Such methods also help define and evaluate strategies to prevent and control disease and disability. In addition, epidemiological studies help in the overall planning and evaluating of mental health programs on both a local level and a national level.

Epidemiological surveys reveal that about one third of all Americans have had or will have a mental disorder at some time in their lives. The most common mental disorders are anxiety disorders, and the next most common are depressive disorders and alcohol or other substance abuse. In addition, surveys have found that about 15 percent of all patients seen for a medical or surgical problem by nonpsychiatric physicians have an associated emotional disorder, most often depression or alcohol abuse or both.

Epidemiology advances psychiatric research by correlating clinical findings with such sociodemographic variables as age, gender, and socioeconomic status. For example, higher rates of almost every mental disorder are found in persons under age 45 than in those over 45. In general, women have significantly higher rates than do men for all disorders, particularly depressive and anxiety disorders. Men, however, have significantly higher rates of substance-related disorders and antisocial personality disorder. Schizophrenia, which affects about 1 percent of the population, shows similar rates for men and women.

Epidemiological studies are also used to compare the incidence and the prevalence of diseases internationally and cross-culturally. In general, the prevalence of mental disorders appears to be fairly constant, regardless of nationality or cultural background; however, schizophrenia has a better prognosis and outcome in less-developed third-world countries than it does in better-developed societies, such as the United States and the United Kingdom.

## Types of Clinical and Epidemiological Studies

Clinical and epidemiological studies in psychiatry attempt to answer questions relating to the causes, treatment, course, prognosis, and prevention of various disorders. There are two main types: (1) *observational*, in which the natural course of an illness is followed without any intervention, and (2) *experimental*, in which some or all factors under study are controlled by the investigator. Most studies are experimental in design; however, because of the many variables involved in mental disorders, it is difficult to design well-controlled experimental studies. The most common types of experimental designs used in psychiatry are described below.

**Cohort study.** A cohort is a group chosen from a well-defined population that is studied over a long period of time. Cohort studies are also known as longitudinal studies. An example is the study by Stella Chess and Alexander Thomas of temperamental characteristics of the same group of infants at ages 3 months, 2 years, 5 years, and 20 years. The researchers were able to discern a relation between the initial characteristics of the infant and a subgroup of children who eventually had clinical psychiatric problems. In that study the cohort was the group born and studied in the year the study began.

Cohort studies provide direct estimates of risk associated with a suspected causal factor. They are more time-consuming and expensive to perform than case-history studies, which are usually quick and inexpensive. Cohort studies are usually conducted when ample evidence from case-history studies indicates that a relation exists between a risk factor and a disorder. For example, in the relation between lung cancer and smoking, many case-history studies had been published before the first cohort study was published.

**Retrospective and prospective studies.** Prospective studies, also called longitudinal studies, are based on observing events as they occur. A major problem in psychiatric longitudinal studies is that some persons are lost to follow-up over time. Retrospective studies are based on past data or past events.

**Cross-sectional study.** Cross-sectional studies provide information about the prevalence of disease in a representative study population at a particular point in time. For that reason, they are also known as prevalence studies.

**Case-history study.** A case-history study is a retrospective study that examines persons with a particular disease.

**Case-control study.** A case-control study is a retrospective study that examines persons without a particular disease.

**Clinical trial.** Specially selected patients receive a course of treatment, and another group does not in a clinical trial. Eligible patients are assigned to the treatment group or to the control group on a random basis, and the goal of the study is to determine the effects of a given treatment.

**Double-blind study.** A double-blind study helps eliminate bias because neither the patient nor the persons involved in the study know which, if any, treatment is being given to the patient. In drug studies, a control group of patients may receive a *placebo*, an inert substance prepared to resemble the active drug being tested in the experiment. A response to the placebo may represent the psychological effect of taking a pill, a response not due to any psychopharmacological property (so-called *placebo effect*). In addition, the investigators do not know the treatment given because drugs are identified by special codes unknown to them. The assessment of the outcome may be made by persons other than those administering the treatment— the so-called blind evaluators. Control subjects may receive an alternative comparison treatment, rather than just a placebo.

**Crossover study.** A crossover study is a variation of the double-blind study. The treatment group and the control or placebo group change at some point, so that the placebo group gets the treatment and the first treatment group gets the placebo. That procedure eliminates bias because, if the treatment group improves in each instance and the placebo group does not, one can conclude that the makeup of both groups was truly random. Each group serves as the control for the other.

**Psychiatric case register.** A case register maintains a longitudinal record of psychiatric contacts for each person receiving care in a geographically defined community. Not all areas lend themselves to a register because persons may leave the area for treatment or the population may be highly mobile. A well-maintained register is of great value in reporting accurate treated-incidence rates, lifetime- or period-treated-prevalence rates, comparative rates for different time periods for the same population, information regarding the use of services over time, and identification of high-risk groups for further study.

## Major Epidemiological Studies

Major psychiatric epidemiological research studies have been conducted over the years. The goal of each study was to determine the prevalence of psychopathology in a defined community. Persons in a particular community were interviewed directly (usually using a structured interview protocol) to determine the presence or the absence of psychological symptoms. The major studies are described below.

**Chicago study.** A team under the direction of Robert E. L. Faris and Henry Warren Dunham examined about 35,000 admissions to mental hospitals in Chicago between 1922 and 1934. The survey found that first hospital admissions for schizophrenia were highest among persons from the central sections of Chicago, members of the city's lowest socioeconomic group. Rates of admission decreased as one moved away from the central areas and into more affluent communities. Faris and Dunham postulated a *drift hypothesis*, which holds that impaired persons slide down the social scale because of their illness. By contrast, a *segregation hypothesis* holds that, instead of helplessly drifting downward, schizophrenic persons actively seek city areas where anonymity and isolation protect them from the demands that more organized societies make on them. That study helped conceptualize two additional hypotheses about mental illness: (1) the *social causation theory,* which holds that being a member of a low socioeconomic group is significant in causing illness, and (2) the *social selection theory,* which holds that having a mental disorder leads one to become a member of the low socioeconomic group as a secondary phenomenon. In other words, the disorder is caused by genetic or psychological factors, and the drift downward occurs as a result.

**Monroe County study.** The Monroe County, New York, psychiatric case register is an epidemiological data file maintained by the University of Rochester School of Medicine since 1960. The case register contains information on all county residents who use psychiatric services. In 1970 the data found that 3 percent of the county received care in mental health care facilities in the region, including the offices of private practitioners. The so-called newly treated incidence rate was less than 1 percent.

**Midtown Manhattan study.** In 1954 a team directed by Thomas Rennie and Leo Srole designed and conducted a survey involving 1,660 adults sampled from a specific section of New York City. The objectives of the study were to determine the effects of demographic, social, and personal factors on mental health and illness, using a structured interview conducted by nonpsychiatrists. Mental disorder was rated not present, mild, moderate, or marked. The main objective was to test the association between life stress and psychological symptoms. Some of the findings follow: Mental disorders rose as age increased; 81 percent of persons from 20 to 59 years of age had symptoms that were mild to severely incapacitating, and 23.4 percent of persons in that age group were substantially impaired. Socioeconomic status was the single most significant variable affecting mental illness, persons in the low socioeconomic group having six times as many symptoms as those in the high groups.

**New Haven study.** In 1950 August De Belmont Hollingshead and Fredrick Carl Redlich studied the relation of social class to the prevalence of treated mental disorders in New Haven, Connecticut. Their studies included a census of psychiatric patients, a survey of the population at large, a study of psychiatrists, and a controlled case study. Analysis of the data revealed a definite relation between social class and mental disorders. Neurosis was most prevalent among persons in the high socioeconomic groups; psychosis was most prevalent among persons in the low socioeconomic groups. The poor were more often seen in mental health clinics than by private psychiatrists. In addition, low socioeconomic status, occupational instability, and downward mobility were associated with the highest frequency of psychiatric disability. Hollingshead and Redlich devised a subgrouping of class structure in the county based on education, occupation, and income. Their class distinctions, described in Table 4.7-1, are used widely by sociologists and epidemiologists. Another New Haven study used a structured diagnostic interview to make specific diag-

**Table 4.7–1**
**Class Status and Cultural Characteristics of Subjects in the New Haven Study**

| Class | Class Status and Cultural Characteristics |
|---|---|
| I | Class I, containing the community's business and professional leaders, has two segments: a long-established core group of interrelated families and a smaller upwardly mobile group of new people. Members of the core group usually inherit money, along with group values that stress tradition, stability, and social responsibility. Those in the new group are highly educated, self-made, able, and aggressive. Their family relationships often are not cohesive or stable. Socially, they are rejected by the core group, to whom they are, however, a threat by the vigor of their leadership in community affairs. |
| II | Class II is marked by at least some education beyond high school and occupations as managers or in the lower-ranking professions. Four of five are upwardly mobile. They are joiners at all ages and tend to have stable families, but they have usually gone apart from parental families and often from their home communities. Tensions arise generally from striving for educational, economic, and social success. |
| III | Class III men for the most part are in salaried administrative and clerical jobs (51 percent) or own small businesses (24 percent); many of the women also have jobs. Typically, they are high school graduates. They usually have economic security but little opportunity for advancement. Families tend to be less stable than in class II. Family members of all ages tend to join organizations and to be active in them. There is less satisfaction with present living conditions and less optimism than in class II. |
| IV | In class IV, 53 percent say they belong to the working class. Seven of 10 show no generational mobility. Most are content and make no sacrifices to get ahead. Most of the men are semiskilled (53 percent) or skilled (35 percent) manual employees. Practically all the women who are able to hold jobs do so. Education usually stops shortly after graduation from grammar school for both parents and children. Families are much different from those in class III. Families are larger, and they are more likely to include three generations. Households are more likely to include boarders and roomers. Homes are more likely to be broken. |
| V | Class V adults usually have not completed elementary school. Most are semiskilled factory workers or unskilled laborers. They are concentrated in tenement and cold-water-flat areas of New Haven or in suburban slums. There are generally brittle family ties. Very few participate in organized community institutions. Leisure activities in the household and on the street are informal and spontaneous. Adolescent boys frequently have contact with the law in their search for adventure. There is a struggle for existence. There is much resentment, expressed freely in primary groups, about how they are treated by those in authority. There is much acting out of hostility. |

noses. A major finding of that study was that 15.1 percent of the adult population over age 26 showed evidence of a mental disorder, and a probable mental disorder was present in an additional 2.7 percent.

**Stirling County study.** In 1952 Alexander H. Leighton conducted a psychiatric epidemiological study of Stirling County, a Nova Scotian county of 20,000 persons. Information was recorded by using structured interviews by nonclinician interviewers. The information was later rated by a psychiatrist. Unlike the New Haven and Midtown Manhattan surveys, the subjects of the Stirling County study lived in rural areas—small villages, one small town, and many isolated farms. Male and female household heads were interviewed. The major findings were that 57 percent of the persons interviewed could be identified as having a lifetime prevalence of some mental disorder, 24 percent had a notable impairment, and 20 percent were in need of psychiatric attention. Women showed considerably more psychiatric disorders than did men, and mental disorders were found to increase with age and degree of poverty.

**NIMH Epidemiologic Catchment Area (NIMH-ECA) survey.** The NIMH-ECA project evolved from the report of the 1977 President's Commission on Mental Health, which highlighted the need to identify the mentally ill and indicate how they are treated and by whom. Darrel Regier and his associates at the Division of Biometry and Epidemiology of the National Institute of Mental Health (NIMH) sought to identify the percentage of the population with mental disorders. The objective was to determine what percentage of the population with mental disorders were receiving treatment in mental health settings (such as psychiatric clinics), private psychiatrists' offices, and such nonpsychiatric settings as general medical treatment centers and internists' offices. In 1978 provisional estimates indicated that at least 15 percent of the population of the United States were affected by mental disorders in one year, and only one fifth of those persons received care from mental health specialists. Three fifths of the persons with identified mental disorders were treated by primary care physicians.

A major goal of the NIMH-ECA study is to determine specifically the prevalence of mental disorders as defined by the third edition of *Diagnostic and Statistical Manual of Mental Disorders* (DSM-III), its revision (DSM-III-R), and eventually the fourth edition (DSM-IV) and to establish longitudinal data on the course of various mental disorders.

Various sites around the country are being studied to assess mental disorder prevalence, incidence, and service use in geographically defined community populations of at least 200,000 residents. Random samples are drawn to obtain completed interviews on at least 20,000 community and institutional residents. The *Diagnostic Interview Schedule* (DIS)—which assesses the presence, duration, and severity of symptoms—is the major instrument that the trained lay interviewer uses to interview each subject.

Compared with all previous studies, the NIMH-ECA study uses better diagnostic tools and more specific critieria to make a reliable diagnosis, including careful clinical descriptions and follow-up studies. Much larger samples are used than in the previously described studies.

In general, early findings of the ECA survey show the

following: Rates of depression are twice as high for females as for males; males are more likely than females to have alcohol dependence; and substance abuse is more common in persons under age 30 than in older persons.

The epidemiological findings of prevalence rates for specific mental disorders in the five ECA sites are listed in Table 4.7-2. More specific data about each disorder are found in the chapter that discusses the disorder in depth.

**Table 4.7–2**
**Comparison of Standardized One-Month, Six-Month, and Lifetime Prevalence Rates of DIS/*DSM-III* Disorders per 100 Persons 18 Years and Older: All Sites Combined\***

| Disorders | Rate, % (Standard Error) | | |
| --- | --- | --- | --- |
| | 1 mo | 6 mo | Lifetime |
| Any DIS disorder covered | 15.4 (0.4) | 19.1 (0.4) | 32.2 (0.5) |
| Any DIS disorder except cognitive impairment, substance use disorder, and antisocial personality | 11.2 (0.3) | 13.1 (0.4) | 19.6 (0.4) |
| Any DIS disorder except phobia | 11.2 (0.3) | 14.0 (0.4) | 25.2 (0.5) |
| Any DIS disorder except substance use disorders | 12.6 (0.3) | 14.8 (0.4) | 22.1 (0.4) |
| Any DIS disorder except substance use or phobia | 8.3 (0.3) | 9.4 (0.3) | 13.8 (0.4) |
| Substance use disorders | 3.8 (0.2) | 6.0 (0.3) | 16.4 (0.4) |
| Alcohol abuse and dependence | 2.8 (0.2) | 4.7 (0.2) | 13.3 (0.4) |
| Drug abuse and dependence | 1.3 (0.1) | 2.0 (0.1) | 5.9 (0.2) |
| Schizophrenic/ schizophreniform disorders | 0.7 (0.1) | 0.9 (0.1) | 1.5 (0.1) |
| Schizophrenia | 0.6 (0.1) | 0.8 (0.1) | 1.3 (0.1) |
| Schizophreniform disorder | 0.1 (0.0) | 0.1 (0.0) | 0.1 (0.0) |
| Affective [mood] disorders | 5.1 (0.2) | 5.8 (0.3) | 8.3 (0.3) |
| Manic episode | 0.4 (0.1) | 0.5 (0.1) | 0.8 (0.1) |
| Major depressive episode | 2.2 (0.2) | 3.0 (0.2) | 5.8 (0.3) |
| Dysthymia† | 3.3 (0.2) | 3.3 (0.2) | 3.3 (0.2) |
| Anxiety disorders | 7.3 (0.3) | 8.9 (0.3) | 14.6 (0.4) |
| Phobia | 6.2 (0.2) | 7.7 (0.3) | 12.5 (0.3) |
| Panic | 0.5 (0.1) | 0.8 (0.1) | 1.6 (0.1) |
| Obsessive-compulsive | 1.3 (0.1) | 1.5 (0.1) | 2.5 (0.2) |
| Somatization disorder | 0.1 (0.0) | 0.1 (0.0) | 0.1 (0.0) |
| Personality disorder, antisocial personality | 0.5 (0.1) | 0.8 (0.1) | 2.5 (0.2) |
| Cognitive impairment (severe)† | 1.3 (0.1) | 1.3 (0.1) | 1.3 (0.1) |

\*The rates are standardized to the age, sex, and race distribution of the 1980 noninstitutionalized population of the United States age 18 years and older. DIS indicates Diagnostic Interview Schedule.
†Dysthymia and cognitive impairment have no recency information; thus, the rates are the same for all three time periods.
Data from D A Regier, J H Boyd, J D Burke Jr, D S Rae, J K Myers, M Kramer, L N Robins, L K George, M Karno, B Z Locke: One-month prevalence of mental disorders in the United States. Arch Gen Psychiatry 45: 981, 1988. Used with permission.

## Assessment Instruments

The major obstacle to the identification of cases has been the lack of an explicit set of criteria for diagnostic classification. Over the years a variety of diagnostic procedures and assessment instruments have been developed.

Information about a subject can be collected in several ways. Medical records are often used for patients in clinical settings. Records in central data banks called *case registers* can be used. In Scandinavian countries, particularly Sweden, control data banks are extensive. An important source of information about a subject is the *direct interview*, which is a person-to-person interaction. *Indirect surveys* using a structured self-report form may be used, but they lack the clinical judgment of an experienced practitioner that are necessary in some instances.

The most common assessment approach is an interview format, which may be *structured* (the same questions asked of all subjects) or *unstructured* (interviewers choose their questions based on their own clinical judgment). Several structured instruments with acceptable interrater reliability are outlined in Table 4.7-3.

An effective assessment instrument must be reliable, valid, and free of bias. *Reliability* concerns whether or not the findings of the assessment instrument or diagnostic procedure are reproducible and can be replicated when the instrument is used by different examiners (*interrater reliability*) or on different occasions (*test-retest reliability*). For example, are various clinicians referring to the same thing when they diagnose schizophrenia?

*Validity* concerns whether the test measures what it is supposed to measure. Does the assessment instrument identify cases that it is designed to identify? Validity can be broken down further into the following categories: *criterion validity*, in which results from one test instrument are compared with the results of another test whose validity has already been established; *face validity*, which concerns the test's making sense to the investigator using it; *content validity*, which concerns the test's covering specific types of information that can be interpreted or scored at a later date; *concurrent validity*, which concerns the results' corresponding to the results of another test with the same variable; and *construct validity*, which concerns the test instrument's being constructed so that it measures what it is designed to measure. The two properties of validity and reliability are extremely important in psychiatric epidemiology, especially if one is attempting to identify a specific disorder or syndrome.

Analytic studies can also be flawed by *bias*, an error in construction that favors one outcome over another. Bias can occur if examiners know something about the status of the case that influences their judgment (for example, they know that one group is receiving medication). Those potential flaws can affect the validity of a study's findings. To eliminate that kind of bias, researchers developed the double-blind method. Bias is also diminished by *randomization* of the sample, in which each member of the total group studied has an equal chance of being selected; for example, each person may be assigned a number from a table of random numbers.

Assessment instruments must be *sensitive*; that is, they must be able to detect the thing being evaluated (for ex-

**Table 4.7–3**
**Commonly Used Assessment Instruments**

| Instrument | Condition | Interviewer | Comments |
|---|---|---|---|
| Present State Examination (PSE) | Psychotic disorders, schizophrenia | Psychiatrists | Limited to 1-month period before interview; can be used with computer program CATEGO |
| Schedule for Affective Disorders and Schizophrenia (SADS) | Schizophrenia and mood disorders | Psychiatrists or specially trained interviewer | Variations: SADS-C measures current disorder, and SADS-L measures lifetime disorders |
| General Health Questionnaire (GHQ) | Medical patients with psychiatric symptoms of anxiety or depression | Self-report | Does not identify specific mental disorders |
| Diagnostic Interview Schedule (DIS) | Covers more than 30 mental disorders, including schizophrenia, mood disorders, anxiety disorders, substance abuse, cognitive disorders | Self-report combined with specially trained interviewers | Correlates with range of DSM-III diagnostic classification; assesses symptoms over lifetime; used in the NIMH-ECA program |
| Iowa Structured Psychiatric Interview (ISPI) | Major mental disorders | Trained interviewer | Provides detailed psychosocial and family history; covers lifetime prevalence |

ample, to diagnose a disorder when it is present). If an instrument detects a disorder in a person who does not have the disorder, the result is called a false positive, rather than a true positive. Tests must also be *specific*; that is, they must not detect things not being evaluated. For example, tests must be able to detect the absence of a disorder in a person who does not have the disorder, which is called true negative. If a disorder is reported to be absent in a person when it is present, that is called a false-negative result. Assessment instruments should also have good *predictive value*, which is the proportion of true-positive or true-negative results. Predictive values indicate what percentage of test outcomes are expected to coincide with assigned diagnoses. Table 4.7-4 summarizes the interpre-

tation of the concepts of sensitivity, specificity, and predictive value.

# BIOSTATISTICS

*Biostatistics* is the mathematical science of describing, organizing, and interpreting data related to medicine. Epidemiology relies on statistics to enable investigators to examine possible causes of disease and to determine which causes, if any, are relevant. Similarly, treatment strategies can be tested for specific disorders with analytical epidemiological studies using statistics.

The principles of statistics are beyond the scope of this

**Table 4.7–4**
**Definitions and Calculations for Interpreting Performance of Diagnostic Tests**

| Term | Definition | Calculation |
|---|---|---|
| True positive (TP) | Diseased person with abnormal test results | |
| True negative (TN) | Nondiseased person with normal test results | |
| False positive (FP) | Nondiseased person with abnormal test results | |
| False negative (FN) | Diseased person with normal test results | |
| Referent value | A value to which laboratory results can be referred and from which the probability of disease or predictive value can be calculated | |
| Sensitivity | True positive rate | $\dfrac{TP}{TP + FN} \times 100$ |
| Specificity | True negative rate | $\dfrac{TN}{TN + FP} \times 100$ |
| Predictive value of abnormal test results (PV +) | Proportion of abnormal test results that are true positive | $\dfrac{TP}{TP + FP} \times 100$ |
| Predictive value of normal test results (PV −) | Proportion of normal test results that are true negative | $\dfrac{TN}{TN + FN} \times 100$ |
| Efficiency | Percentage of all results that are true results, whether positive or negative | $\dfrac{TP + TN}{\text{Grand Total}} \times 100$ |

Table by John F. Greden, M.D.

book; however, a glossary of statistical terms that can be found in most elementary textbooks of statistics is presented below. A knowledge of such terms is necessary not only for understanding epidemiological concepts but also for accurately assessing statistical methods that appear in scientific publications.

## Statistical Overview

The two major types of statistics are descriptive and inferential. *Descriptive statistics* are numerical values for summarizing, organizing, and describing observations (for example, the average number of symptoms associated with an anxiety disorder). Examples include the mean, standard deviation, and variance. *Inferential statistics* are numerical values used to draw general conclusions about probabilities on the basis of a sample (for example, the influences of drug A versus drug B in the treatment of a group of depressed patients). Examples include the *t*-test, chi-square, and analysis of variance.

*Data* are factual information derived from a population or a sample. A *population* is the entire collection of a set of objects, people, or events in a particular context (for example, all schizophrenic patients in a particular hospital). A *sample* is a subset selected from that population (for example, one half of the schizophrenic patients in a particular hospital). Data can be nominal (organized into categories), ordinal (ranked in order), or organized into interval ratios (measured on a scale, a graph, or a table).

## Glossary of Statistical Terms

**Analysis of variance (ANOVA).** A set of statistical procedures designed to compare two or more groups of observations. It determines whether the differences between groups are due to experimental influence or to chance alone.

**Canonical correlation.** A multivariate technique for simultaneously finding the relation of linear combinations of two or more predictors and two or more outcomes.

**Chi-square.** A nonparametric statistic used to evaluate the relative frequency or proportion of events in a population that fall into well-defined categories.

**Coefficient of correlation.** The relation between two sets of paired measurements. Correlation coefficients—which may be positive, negative, or curvilinear, depending on whether the variations are in the same direction, the opposite direction, or both directions—can be computed in a variety of ways (see Scatter diagram). The most common is the product moment correlation referred to as Pearson's *r* or simply *r*. Correlation coefficients are intended to show the degree of relation and not that one variable causes the other. The maximum value of a correlation coefficient is 1; the minimum value of 0 indicates that no relation exists between two variables.

**Confidence interval.** An interval that is likely to capture the population mean with a specified level of confidence. For the 95 percent confidence interval, the changes are estimated to be 95 in 100 that the true mean falls within that interval.

**Control group.** A group that does not receive treatment and is used as a standard of comparison.

**Critical ratio.** In a statistical study involving 30 or more subjects, the system used to determine whether differences found between two items are larger than could be expected from chance. The term "T-ratio" is used in studies involving fewer than 30 subjects to determine whether differences are related to chance.

**Discriminant analysis.** A multivariate method for finding the relation between a single discrete outcome and a linear combination of two or more predictors.

**Distribution.** A series or range of values that can be organized according to their frequency of occurrence (*frequency distribution*). A symmetrical, bell-shaped frequency distribution of scores is called a *normal distribution* (the bell curve).

**Factor analysis.** A data reduction technique used to reduce a large number of variables to a smaller number of linear combinations of variables.

**Incidence.** The number of new cases occurring over a specified period of time. The most common time period used is one year, producing an annual incidence calculated as follows:

$$\text{Incidence} = \frac{\begin{array}{c}\text{Number of new persons}\\\text{with a disease}\\\text{(over a one-year period)}\end{array}}{\begin{array}{c}\text{Total number of persons at risk}\\\text{(over a one-year period)}\end{array}}$$

A study of incidence is more difficult to do than a study of prevalence cases because one has to exclude from the incidence numerator those persons who already have the disease; they cannot be considered new cases. Since persons who have had the disease are no longer at risk for it, they must also be excluded from the denominator. A broader concept of total incidence includes those persons with a new episode of illness, regardless of whether they had previous episodes.

*Lifetime expectancy* is the total probability of a person's having a disorder during a lifetime. Prevalence and incidence vary for sex and age; thus, sex-specific rates and age-specific rates are used to express the relative frequency of cases in each category.

**McCall's T.** A specialized standard score with a mean of 50 and a standard deviation of 10.

**Mean deviation.** A measure of variation determined by dividing the sum of deviations in a set of variables by the number of cases involved.

**Measure of central tendency.** A central value in a distribution around which other values are distributed. Three measures of central tendency are the mean, the median, and the mode.

MEAN. A statistical measurement derived from adding a set of scores and then dividing by the number of scores. The mean is the average score.

MEDIAN. The value in the middle of a set of measurements. For example, in the series 2, 3, 5, 11, 21, the number "5" is the median value.

MODE. The value that appears most frequently in a set of measurements.

**Multiple regression.** A form of multivariate analysis in which a scaled variable is correlated with a linear combination of independent or predictor variables.

**Multivariate analysis.** Method for considering the relation of three or more variables. Multivariate methods include multiple regression, discriminant analysis, canonical correlation, and factor analysis.

**Multivariate analysis of variance (MANOVA).** A multivariate technique that uses an ANOVA design but includes multiple dependent variables.

**Nonparametric.** Not requiring restrictive assumptions about population distributions.

**Null hypothesis.** The assumption that there is no significant difference between two random samples of population. When the null hypothesis is rejected, observed differences between groups are deemed to be improbable by chance alone.

**Percentile rank.** The percentage of scores in a distribution exceeded by any particular score. For example, a percentile rank of 80 means that 20 percent of the scores exceed a score of 80.

**Population.** The entire collection of a set having the same definition.

**Power.** The probability of rejecting the null hypothesis when, in the real world, it should have been rejected. Power is the probability of identifying a true difference.

**Predictive value.** Ability of a test to predict a condition. *Positive predictive value* is the number of true positives divided by the sum of the number of true positives and false positives; it is the probability that a patient with a positive test result does, in fact, have the condition in question. *Negative predictive value* is the number of true negatives divided by the sum of the number of true negatives and false negatives; it is the probability that a patient with a negative test result is, in fact, free of the condition in question.

**Prevalence.** The number of cases of a disorder that exist. There are several types of prevalence.

POINT PREVALENCE. The number of persons who have a disorder at a specified point in time. The point can be a certain calendar day (for example, April 1, 1993) or any day during a particular study (for example, the fourth day of the study), regardless of the calendar day. It is calculated as follows:

$$\text{Point prevalence} = \frac{\text{Number of persons with a disorder at a specified point in time}}{\text{Total population at specified point in time}}$$

PERIOD PREVALENCE. The number of people who have a disorder at any time during a specified time period (longer than a calendar day or point in time). It is calculated as follows:

$$\text{Period prevalence} = \frac{\text{Number of persons with a disorder during a time period}}{\text{Total population during time period}}$$

The numerator includes any existing cases at the start of the time period and any new cases that develop during the period. Period prevalence may be used to determine the number of persons with a disorder, the number of persons in treatment, and the duration of an illness.

LIFETIME PREVALENCE. A measure at a point in time of the number of persons who had the disorder at some time during their lives. A potential problem with lifetime prevalence is that it is almost always based on subject recall, which can be inaccurate.

TREATED PREVALENCE. The number of persons being treated for a disorder, arrived at by counting all the persons in a defined geographic area who are receiving treatment. One may measure treated point prevalence (for example, the number of patients being treated for a disorder in a clinic on a certain day) or treated period prevalence (for example, the number of patients being treated for a disorder at a clinic over the past year).

CROSS-SECTIONAL PREVALENCE. A single assessment of prevalence at a particular point in time. It differs from a longitudinal study, in which a population is studied over a long period of time.

**Probability.** A quantitative statement of the likelihood that an event will occur. A probability of 0 means that the event is certain not to occur; a probability of 1 means that the event will occur with certainty.

**P value.** The probability of obtaining a result by chance alone. A *p* value of .01 means that the probability of obtaining a result by chance alone is 1 in 100; a value of .05 means that the result will occur more than 5 times out of every 100 times by chance alone.

**Random assignment.** The nonsystematic selection of subjects into a group to ensure that there are differences in group composition.

**Randomization.** The process that allows each patient in a clinical trial to have an equal chance to be assigned to a control or experimental treatment group. It protects against selection bias and guarantees the validity of statistical tests of significance.

**Random variable.** A variable for which the variation is determined by chance.

**Regression analysis.** A method for obtaining a prediction from observed data in order to predict the value of one variable ($x$) in relation to the value of another variable ($y$).

**Relative frequency.** The number of persons in a specific group (for example, sex or age) who have a disorder. Measures of disease frequency involve two major concepts, prevalence and incidence.

**Risk factor.** Something associated with a disorder that may support a causal connection. A risk may be *factor-specific* (for example, it occurs in only one sex) or *factor-related* (for example, it is likely to occur in a certain environment). A causal connection between a risk factor and a disorder is shown by (1) temporality, a factor precedes the disorder being studied; (2) the repeated appearance of the same risk factor in multiple studies; (3) specificity, a risk factor is associated with one disorder only; and (4) finding that the experimental intervention that eliminates the risk factor also eliminates the disorder. Determining what factor or factors account for the increased risk of a disorder is one of the challenges of psychiatric epidemiology.

RELATIVE RISK. The ratio of the incidence of the disease among persons exposed to the risk factor to the incidence among those not exposed. For example, the relative risk of lung cancer is much greater for heavy smokers than for nonsmokers.

ATTRIBUTABLE RISK. The absolute incidence of the disease in exposed persons that can be attributed to the exposure. The measure is derived by subtracting the incidence of the disease in question among unexposed persons from its total incidence among exposed persons. For example, the lung cancer death rate for nonsmokers may be subtracted from the total community lung cancer death rate. The results are the attributable community risk for lung cancer. Attributable risk is a useful concept because it tells what may be expected if the risk is removed. For example, on the basis of available data, the attributable risk for deaths from lung cancer could be avoided if smoking were eliminated.

**Sample.** A subset of observations selected from a population.

**Scatter diagram.** A visual means of determining the relation between two variables. It may be linear (positive relation), curvilinear (negative relation), or nonlinear (no relation).

**Sensitivity.** The number of true positives divided by the sum of the number of true positives and false negatives. It is the proportion of patients with the condition in question that the test is able to detect.

**Specificity.** The number of true negatives divided by the sum of the number of true negatives and false positives. It is the proportion of patients who do not have the condition that the test calls negative.

**Standard deviation (SD).** A measure of variation derived by squaring each deviation in a set of scores, taking the average of those squares, and then taking the square root of the result. The standard deviation is represented by the Greek letter sigma ($\Sigma$). In a normal distribution, $\pm$ 1 SD includes 68 percent of the population; $\pm$ 2 SD includes 95 percent of the population; and $\pm$ 3 SD includes 99 percent of the population.

**Standard error (SE).** A measure of how much variation in test results is due to chance and error and how much is due to experimental influences.

**Standardized or Z-score.** The deviation of a score from its group mean expressed in standard deviation units.

**Time-series design.** The type of experiment in which there are repeated observations of the same subject over a specific time period.

**T-test.** A statistical procedure designed to compare two sets of observations. *T*-tests can be compared by using an advanced statistical concept called the Bonferroni procedure that reduces errors between experiments.

**Type I error.** The error that occurs when the null hypothesis is rejected when it should have been retained or the false claim of a true difference because the observed difference is due entirely to chance.

**Type II error.** The error that occurs when the null hypothesis is retained when it should have been rejected or the false acceptance of the null hypothesis when, in fact, there is a true difference but the difference is so small that it falls within the acceptance region of the null hypothesis.

**Variable.** A characteristic that can assume different values in different experimental situations. In research, *independent variables* are those qualities that the experimenter systematically varies (for example, time, age, sex, type of drug) in the experiment. *Dependent variables* are those qualities that measure the influence of the independent variable or the outcome of the experiment (for example, the measurement of a person's specific physiological reactions to a drug).

**Variance.** A measure arrived at by squaring all the deviations in a set of measures, summing them, and then dividing them by the number of measures. Variance is helpful in analyzing how much variation is due to experimental influence and how much is due to chance or error influence.

**Variation.** A term referring to different results obtained in measuring the same phenomenon. Variation may be associated with known variables within the data or with variables that result from error or chance.

**Z-score.** The difference between the score and the mean, divided by the standard deviation. It is a transformation into standardized units that are easier to interpret.

## SOCIAL PSYCHIATRY

*Social psychiatry* is the behavioral science concerned with the social and cultural determinants of behavior, both normal and abnormal. It deals with the distribution of disorders and in that sense relates to the field of epidemiology. It also addresses the social and cultural responses to health and illness and to that extent relates to cross-cultural psychiatry. In addition, the field is concerned with the prevention and the maintenance of physical and mental health (salutogenesis) and with the role of the environment and life-style factors as contributory determinants of illness.

Social psychiatry is part of the broader field of medical sociology, which has been by described by David Mechanic as covering the following areas: social groups and organizations and their role in health delivery services; demographics of illness; cultural and social attitudes about illness; mortality and morbidity and the accommodation of medical institutions to changing patterns of disease and health; and the sociology of medical practice, community health care, and hospital practice.

### Sociocultural Determinants of Mental Disorders

The concept of social class has been variously formulated in terms of economic power, social prestige, political identification, and patterns of association. In American society, class position is most frequently characterized by occupation and education. White-collar occupations, which are usually coupled with a college education, tend to place one in the middle class; blue-collar occupations, which are coupled with a high-school education at most, tend to place one in the working class. Studies by social psychologists have shown that life-styles, aspirations, and, to a degree, cognition and modes of personality, coping, and defense tend to differ by class. However, a major problem with social class studies is the tendency toward broad generalization that may promote stereotypical thinking. For example, statements that characterize working-class persons as impulsive and unable to delay gratification have little validity. Many studies that compare traits among class groups are related, on careful examination, more to income than to other factors. Similarly, feelings of personal efficacy—of being in control of one's destiny and not subject to external controls—are more characteristic of the middle class than of the working class. But a sense of autonomy and one's level of income are related. Nevertheless, behavioral science research has established that chronic life stresses occur more often in the working class than in the middle class. Moreover, working-class members are more vulnerable to stressors than are members of the middle class. The preponderance of evidence indicates that both treated mental disorders and the symptoms of psychological discomfort are found most frequently (1) in the lowest socioeconomic class, (2) among persons without meaningful social ties, (3) among those who do not have useful social roles, and (4) among those who have suffered the traumatic loss of significant social ties.

### Social Network and Social Support

The term "social network" refers to the network of persons to whom someone relates, and the term "social support" refers to the mechanism by which interpersonal relationships protect people from the deleterious effects of stress. In general, when someone has a strong social support system, the vulnerability to mental illness is low, and the chance for recovery, should a disorder develop, is high. Research comparing the social networks of psychiatric patients and normal persons has shown that schizophrenic patients have a much smaller social network than do controls and that neurotic patients have a loose or sparse network. Similarly, a stable support system can ameliorate the effects of physical illness on the person. For example, patients with low social support are more likely to die after myocardial infarcts than are patients with a large and supportive social network. A similar correlation is found in obstetrical and asthmatic patients: those with low social support have an increased incidence of complications.

**Expressed emotion (EE).** The sociologist George Brown and his colleagues in London isolated a pattern of EE characterized by hostile feelings and intrusiveness on the part of the families of schizophrenic patients. EE is strongly associated with poor prognosis after discharge. If EE can be diminished through family therapy, the relapse of first-episode schizophrenia is reduced.

## Life Events and Illness

A number of studies of life events and life crises suggest a correlation between physical illness and mental illness. Studies of schizophrenic patients, for example, indicate that specific life changes in the weeks immediately preceding a breakdown frequently serve as precipitants of the onset of schizophrenia. One study found that in the three weeks before the onset of a schizophrenic episode, 60 percent of schizophrenic patients experienced objectively confirmable events that impinged directly on themselves or on close relatives. The comparable figure for a control group was only 19 percent. Other investigators have shown that life changes are associated with psychiatric symptoms and with a number of physical ailments.

In the Midtown Manhattan study mentioned above, life stress was taken into account in the following categories: economic deprivation, single-parent homes, medical illness, social isolation, and concern about work. A correlation between psychiatric symptoms and life stresses was found.

In a well-known study by Thomas H. Holmes and Richard Rahe, point values were assigned to various life changes that required the person to change or adapt. That is known as the social readjustment rating scale. If a critical number of events happened to a person during a one-year period, he or she was at risk for some type of medical or psychiatric illness. Of those people who accumulated 300 points in one year, 80 percent were at risk for illness in the near future.

However, recent work indicates that external events may not, in and of themselves, be sufficient to cause mental disorders. Rather, a combination of genetic and experiential factors have to exist for illness to occur. That *vulnerability theory* presumes that the occurrence of a mental disorder depends on such factors as child-rearing practices, physical disorders, psychological stressors, genetics, and adverse social stressors. Each person has a personal threshold of vulnerability and an innate ability to tolerate stress. It had been thought that any response could be conditioned

to any stimulus. It is now known that conditioning associations occur on the basis of the *principle of preparedness*—that is, organisms are biologically prepared to make some associations more easily than others. That factor is important in conditioned states of sickness, such as reactions to radiation therapy—that is, some patients are more likely than others to become ill from the treatment.

Hans Selye, who developed the major theories of stress and illness, did not view stress as always being a negative factor in a person's life. Only when stress overwhelms the person and produces distress did he consider it to be damaging. Similarly, Holmes and Rahe's work has been reviewed in terms of whether the life change is viewed as pleasant or unpleasant, wanted or unwanted, and expected or unexpected. The quality of the stress and the effect of change on the person's life are as important as the nature of the life event itself.

The effects of stress and psychosomatic disorders are discussed further in Chapter 27.

**Effects of crises.** Studies of specific life crises have focused on how people react to crises and how those reactions change over time.

Comparative studies have found that people who experience a crisis such as bereavement, rape, or a life-threatening illness have higher rates of psychopathology than do people who have not been subjected to such an event. Furthermore, evidence indicates that between 20 and 40 percent of the people who experience a major life crisis do not recover emotionally with the passage of time. Among the bereaved, for example, one study found that 30 percent had a bad outcome on a combined assessment of psychological distress, social functioning, and physical health measured two to four years after the loss.

## Psychiatric Help Seeking

Needs-assessment surveys show that most people with serious emotional problems do not seek professional help. That practice is changing, however, as people increasingly accept the view that emotional problems should be treated by a mental health professional. Nonetheless, informal helpers are still sought most often in times of emotional turmoil. Furthermore, a person seeking professional help is more likely to turn to a primary care physician than to a psychiatrist. That choice is partly a result of the lack of psychiatrists in some areas of the country, but other variables are also involved.

Sociologists have been particularly interested in structural determinants, the strongest and most consistent of which is social class. A positive correlation between social class and help seeking has persisted, even though community mental health centers and other inexpensive treatment facilities have reduced the financial barriers to care. Education has emerged as a stronger predictor of help seeking than income, which suggests that some cultural facilitating factors are more important than financial resources in accounting for the influence of social class.

Women are much more likely than are men to seek mental health care, even given the higher prevalence of disorder among women. Sociological research over the past few years has made considerable progress in understanding the sex difference by showing that women are more likely to recognize their problems than are men and that the recognition of a problem is the main point in the decision-making process that distinguishes men and women. Once either men or women recognize that they have a problem, they do not differ in the likelihood that they will obtain professional help.

## Community Responses to the Mentally Ill

Attitudes about the mentally ill have been charted in public opinion surveys since the 1950s. Dislike and fear have remained high among the attitudes surveyed. Negative attitudes are particularly pronounced among poorly educated and elderly people. Men consistently report more negative attitudes than do women.

The core concerns about persons who are mentally ill revolve around their presumed unpredictability and dangerousness. Those concerns have some basis in reality, as patients released from state psychiatric hospitals have comparatively high arrest rates. However, most crimes committed by released patients are property crimes that do not involve violence.

Fortunately, most people have feelings that can be modified on the basis of experience, and, as they become increasingly knowledgeable, they can learn to make fine distinctions about kinds of mental illness and treatment. Visits to a psychotherapist, for example, have much less stigma attached than does hospitalization for a mental disorder. Private hospitalization seems to be less stigmatizing than public hospitalization.

## References

Bland R C: Psychiatric epidemiology. Can J Psychiatry 33: 618, 1988.
Breslau M, Davis G C: Chronic stress and major depression. Arch Gen Psychiatry 43: 309, 1986.
Cooper B: Epidemiology and prevention in the mental health field. Soc Psychiatry Psychiatr Epidemiol 25: 9, 1990.
Costello E J: Developments in child psychiatric epidemiology. J Am Acad Child Adolesc Psychiatry 28: 836, 1989.
Duncan R, Knapp R, Miller M C: Introductory Biostatistics for the Health Sciences, ed 2. Wiley, New York, 1983.
Fenton W S, Robinowitz C B, Leaf P J: Male and female psychiatrists and their patients. Am J Psychiatry 144: 358, 1987.
Friedman G D: Primer of Epidemiology. McGraw-Hill, New York, 1987.
Grant I, Kaplan R M: Statistics and experimental design. In Comprehensive Textbook of Psychiatry, ed 5, H I Kaplan, B J Sadock, editors, p 340. Williams & Wilkins, Baltimore, 1989.
Johnson E H: Psychiatric morbidity and health problems among black Americans: A national survey. J Natl Med Assoc 81: 1217, 1989.
Kessler R C: Sociology and psychiatry. In Comprehensive Textbook of Psychiatry, ed 5, H I Kaplan, B J Sadock, editors, p 299. Williams & Wilkins, Baltimore, 1989.
Klerman G L: Paradigm shifts in USA psychiatric epidemiology since World War II. Soc Psychiatry Psychiatr Epidemiol 25: 27, 1990.
Regier D A, Burke J D: Epidemiology. In Comprehensive Textbook of Psychiatry, ed 5, H I Kaplan, B J Sadock, editors, p 308. Williams & Wilkins, Baltimore, 1989.
Regier D A, Goldberg I D, Taube C A: The de facto U.S. mental health services system: A public health perspective. Arch Gen Psychiatry 35: 685, 1978.
Robins L N: Epidemiology: Reflection on testing the validity of psychiatric interviews. Arch Gen Psychiatry 42: 918, 1985.
Robins L N, Helzer J E, Croughan J, Ratcliff K S: National Institute of Mental Health diagnostic interview schedule: Its history, characteristics, and validity. Arch Gen Psychiatry 38: 381, 1981.
Rogers J L, Howard K I, Vessey J T: Using significance tests to evaluate equivalence between two experimental groups. Psychol Bull 113: 553, 1993.
Srole L, Langner T S, Michael S T, Opler M K, Rennie T A C: Mental Health in the Metropolis: The Midtown Manhattan Study. McGraw-Hill, New York, 1962.
Visotsky H M: Courage, creativity, and cost-effectiveness: The challenge for a psychiatric program administration. New Dir Ment Health Serv 49: 51, 1991.
Weissman M M, Klerman G L: Epidemiology of mental disorders: Emerging trends in the United States. Arch Gen Psychiatry 35: 705, 1978.
Westermeyer J: National differences in psychiatric morbidity: Methodological issues, scientific interpretations, and social implications. Acta Psychiatr Scand Suppl 344: 23, 1988.

# 4.8 / Community (Public) Psychiatry

Community psychiatry is responsible for the comprehensive treatment of the severely mentally ill in the community at large. All aspects of care—from hospitalization, case management, and crisis intervention to day treatment and supportive living arrangements—are included under the umbrella of community psychiatry. The field is also known as public psychiatry, reflecting the fact that community-based services are only part of a system that also includes hospitalization as a crucial aspect of the provision of total care for public-sector patients. Community psychiatry has been called the third psychiatry revolution. The first was the age of enlightenment (after the Middle Ages), when it was decided that mental illness was not the result of witchcraft, and the second was the development of psychoanalysis by Sigmund Freud.

Deinstitutionalization has shifted the emphasis in community psychiatry from long-term hospitalization to outpatient treatment modalities. As the 21st century approaches, community psychiatry continues to grapple with the tragedy of the homeless mentally ill and the challenge of providing continuity of care and comprehensive integrated services in an era when fragmentation and financial limitations have left the sickest patients in a neglected state—homeless, imprisoned, or rotating through a revolving door of grossly inadequate and disparate services. With a knowledge of the fate and the needs of those patients, community psychiatry can address the problems produced by deinstitutionalization.

## HISTORY

In 1963, under the leadership of President John F. Kennedy, Congress passed the Community Mental Health Centers Act, which provided funds for the construction of community mental health centers with specified catchment areas (geographic regions with a population of 75,000 to 200,000). Each community mental health center must provide five basic psychiatric services: inpatient care, emergency services (on a 24-hour basis), community consultation, day care (including partial hospitalization programs, halfway houses, aftercare services, and a broad range of outpatient services), and research and education. In 1975 Congress required the addition of services for children and the aged, screening before hospitalization, follow-up services for those who had been hospitalized, transitional housing, and alcoholism and drug-abuse services. By the early 1980s the community mental health center movement had strongly influenced mental health services, the practice of psychiatry, and the other mental health professions. At that time, about 800 centers were in operation, with more than half of them in urban areas. Currently, because of severe financial constraints, the community mental health centers are severely limited and are considered by many to be an ineffective program.

In 1981 a block grant program was created to provide federal funds to states for drug abuse, alcohol abuse, and other mental health programs. Several states established community support systems to help furnish needed mental health services; those programs are currently available nationwide. In spite of those efforts, state mental hospitals still use the majority of state-allocated mental health dollars. Financial limitations have interfered with the block grant programs and state programs.

## CHARACTERISTICS

### Commitment

Commitment to a population implies a responsibility for planning. Commitment suggests (1) that the plan should identify all the mental health needs of the population, inventory the resources available to meet those needs, and organize a system of care; (2) that citizens and political figures should be involved in the planning process; (3) that prevention is at least as important as direct treatment; and (4) that the responsibility is to all persons in the population, including children, the aged, minorities, the chronically ill, the acutely ill, and those who live in geographically remote areas.

The requirement that mental health services be located close to the patient's residence or place of work makes it easy for people to get to a treatment site. Furthermore, with proximity, illness can be identified early, making it likely that hospitalization, when required, will be brief.

### Services

Community mental health is a total system, not a single service. To be effective, services must be integrated and balanced, so that appropriate treatment modalities are available to fit patients' needs. A lack of services in one area (such as community placements) can delay other services (such as hospital discharges) and can lead to a lack of services for some patients (for example, those who cannot gain admission to overcrowded hospitals). A central authority must provide the needed integration.

The community mental health team includes psychiatrists (including child psychiatrists), clinical psychologists, psychiatric social workers, psychiatric nurses, necessary administrative and clerical staff members, and occupational and recreational therapists for inpatient and partial hospitalization programs. Links to welfare workers, the clergy, family agencies, schools, and other human services groups are also maintained.

### Long-Term Care

Because of concerns about the fragmentation of care and the tendency to keep patients hospitalized or unnecessarily restricted to one type of service, community mental health programs encourage continuity of care. Continuity of care enables a single clinician to follow a patient through emergency services, hospitalization, partial hospitalization as a transition to the community, and outpatient treatment as follow-up. Continuity also provides an exchange of information and team responsibility for the patient when various therapists, for reasons of convenience or economy, treat the patient in several settings. A free exchange of clinical information between centers and a liaison between agencies are also part of the total system of care.

### Case Management

Intensive case managers are clinicians who can provide continuity of care by following patients through all the phases of treatment while helping patients negotiate a system that is complex and fragmented. Intensive case managers provide support, advocacy, and systems management. They engage patients in treatment through outreach in single-room-occupancy residences and shelters, they ensure continuing treatment by initiating contact during hospitalization and continuing support through aftercare, and they serve as liaisons between patients and other mental health providers and between the providers themselves. Ideally, intensive care managers should have small caseloads that allow for intensive contact with their patients.

### Community Participation

The community should participate in decisions about its mental health care needs and programs, instead of having them defined solely by professionals. Mental health services are sensitive to the needs of those served if the public is actively involved. The National Mental Health Association (NMHA) and the National Alliance for the Mentally Ill (NAMI) are two lay advocacy groups working at local, state, and national levels to improve care for the mentally ill. Liaisons with those groups can provide links to the general public, facilitating outreach and educational efforts.

### Consultation

Consultation ranges from attention to or even treatment of the emotional problems of an individual patient to using knowledge about human behavior to help organizations achieve their professional goals with the program and their patients. The consultant offers assistance to the mental health professional who works in an outpatient center or agency. The consultant may also provide direct educational activities, liaison with consumer and advocacy groups, and administrative services.

## Evaluation and Research

Evaluation is the process of obtaining information about the total community mental health program and its effect on persons, institutions, and communities. Program evaluation should also provide feedback to the planners and decision makers, so that the operating programs can be modified and new ones planned. It is a required activity on which federally funded centers have to spend at least 2 percent of their budgets.

Research may focus specifically on key issues, rather than on the total program. The problem addressed may be a particular disorder or a treatment method.

## PREVENTION

Preventive psychiatry is part of community psychiatry. The goal of prevention is to decrease the onset (incidence), duration (prevalence), and residual disability of mental disorders. The prevention of mental disorders is based on public health principles and is divided into primary, secondary, and tertiary prevention.

### Primary Prevention

The goal of primary prevention is to prevent the onset of a disease or disorder, thereby reducing its incidence (the ratio of new cases to the population in a specific period of time). That goal is reached by eliminating causative agents, reducing risk factors, enhancing host resistance, and interfering with disease transmission. For some physical disorders the identification and the modification of one or more of those factors revolutionized health care. Those successes are best exemplified by the virtual elimination of many infectious diseases and vitamin deficiency states and by the reduction of some forms of cancer, heart disease, and lung disease.

Examples of primary prevention to help people cope include mental health education programs (for example, parent training in child development and alcohol and drug education programs); efforts at competence building (for example, Outward Bound and Head Start and other enriched day-care programs for disadvantaged children); the development and use of social support systems to reduce the effects of stress on persons at high risk (for example, widow-to-widow programs); anticipatory guidance programs to assist people in preparing for expected stressful situations (for example, counseling of Peace Corps volunteers); and crisis intervention after stressful life events, such as bereavement, marital separation, divorce, traumas, and group disasters. The hostage-release program, in which American hostages released from captivity are prepared for reentry into their culture, is another example of primary prevention.

Primary prevention programs also aim at eradicating stressful agents and reducing stress. Such programs include prenatal and perinatal care to decrease the incidence of mental retardation and cognitive disorders in children (for example, improved nutrition and abstinence from alcohol and other substances during pregnancy, improved obstetrical services, specific dietary modification for neonates vulnerable to phenylketonuria); strict lead-elimination laws to reduce the incidence of lead encephalopathy; modification of divorce,

adoption, and child abuse laws to provide a healthy environment for child development; enrichment or replacement of institutional settings for infants, children, and the elderly; modification of certain risk factors for mental disorders that appear to be associated with low socioeconomic status; and genetic counseling for parents at high risk for chromosomal abnormalities to prevent the unwitting conception of compromised infants; and efforts to reduce the spread of certain sexually transmitted diseases (for example, acquired immune deficiency syndrome [AIDS] and syphilis), which can lead to mental disorders.

### Secondary Prevention

Secondary prevention is defined as the early identification and prompt treatment of an illness or disorder, with the goal of reducing the prevalence (the proportion of existing cases in the population at risk at a specified time) of the condition by shortening its duration. Crisis intervention and public education are components of secondary prevention. In psychiatry, secondary prevention targets emotionally ill children for early intervention. The National Institute of Mental Health's (NIMH's) Child and Adolescent Services System identifies and treats those children to support their family structures and prevent or reduce later disability.

### Tertiary Prevention

The goal of tertiary prevention is to reduce the prevalence of residual defects and disabilities caused by an illness or a disorder. In the case of mental disorders, tertiary prevention enables those with chronic mental illnesses to reach the highest level of functioning that is feasible.

The disabilities associated with chronic mental illness are major social, economic, and public health problems. In the United States those disabilities afflict more than 3 million people, are costly, and create suffering for the affected persons, their families, and society. Although the term "chronic mental illness" has traditionally been associated with elderly patients who have a long history of mental hospitalization, it has recently been broadened to include young adults with a variety of mental disorders who have grown up in the era of deinstitutionalization. Many of them have never been hospitalized, but their ability to lead productive lives in the community is severely impaired. Psychiatric rehabilitation addresses the medical, psychiatric, and social needs of persistently mentally ill persons.

## DEINSTITUTIONALIZATION

Deinstitutionalization is the process by which large numbers of patients are discharged from public psychiatric hospitals back into the community to receive outpatient care.

The policy, which began in the late 1950s, resulted in a decrease in the state psychiatric hospital population from more than 560,000 beds at that time to roughly 100,000 beds today. Many patients were released into various aftercare clinics, where they continued to receive psychiatric treatment and rehabilitative services. Others were placed in new types of institutions, such as halfway houses, board-and-care facilities, and public housing units. Many had to be rehospitalized, and a revolving-door policy emerged, with up to 80 percent of patients being readmitted within two years of discharge.

Transinstitutionalization is the transfer of state hospital patients to other facilities. Many believe that one set of problems has been exchanged for another without solving the problem of the chronically mentally ill. As the number of state hospital beds has been reduced, the number of general hospital psychiatric beds has increased to 48,000, private psychiatric beds to 67,000, and Veterans Affairs beds to 25,000.

A significant percentage of the mentally ill receive psychiatric services as prison inmates. Incarceration remains a significant component of transinstitutionalization. One study estimated that 31 percent of the mentally ill in an urban jail were homeless before arrest. Severe mental illness is two to three times more prevalent in prison populations than in the general public. Many of the incarcerated homeless mentally ill are arrested for minor crimes that are survival strategies (for example, trespassing in buildings or cars as a means of obtaining shelter) or for behavior directly produced by psychosis.

Several studies have found that—without an active, multifaceted treatment system that is willing to assume ongoing responsibility for all facets of the patient's care—mentally ill patients regress in the community as they did in the state hospital. One of the major problems faced by chronically ill patients is that their illnesses interfere with their coping skills, rendering them particularly likely to drift downward into even more stressful, impoverished environments. The end result is an increase in homeless persons in urban areas.

The deinstitutionalized patient needs extensive social support, such as vocational and recreational counseling, comprehensive psychiatric treatment, a paying job, and affordable housing. That support has not been given to the extent that the planners and the supporters of deinstitutionalization would like, primarily because of the lack of adequate funding on the federal, state, and local levels. It is scandalous that funding for aftercare community services for the mentally ill continues to decline; unless that trend is reversed, deinstitutionalization will remain a failed public policy. Some have suggested that the limited funds available be channeled into improving existing state hospitals, so that chronically mentally ill patients and the homeless mentally ill can be referred to the system and receive appropriate care.

## HOMELESS MENTALLY ILL

The homeless mentally ill population continues to grow; one major survey found a 7 percent rise in the urban homeless mentally ill over a 19-month period, with a concurrent decline in the number of shelter beds.

A 1991 study estimated that an average of 33 percent of the homeless are mentally ill. The percentage ranges from 15 percent of the homeless in Kansas City, Missouri, to 70 percent of the homeless single adults in Boston. On average, 45 percent of the homeless mentally ill are also dependent on alcohol or other substances. The estimated percentage of those dual-diagnosis patients ranges from 23 percent in Philadelphia to more than 60 percent in several major United States cities. There was a 9 percent rise in the dually diagnosed homeless during a recent 19-month period, with a concurrent increase in the average length of time of homelessness for the homeless mentally ill.

### Characteristics

Like the chronically mentally ill, the homeless mentally ill are a heterogeneous population, with no uniformity in diagnosis, demographics, functional performance, or residential history. One categorization divides them into street people, the episodic homeless, and the situationally homeless. Street people usually have schizophrenia or substance dependence or both, a history of psychiatric hospitalization, and a variety of health problems. The episodic homeless are usually younger than street people and are likely to be regarded as difficult patients, with personality disorders, substance abuse, and mood disorders; they sporadically use a wide variety of mental health services. The situationally homeless have problems in regard to situational stress more than to their psychopathology.

The homeless mentally ill are not simply undomiciled. They are often totally disaffiliated and have few, if any, links to the community. They are unemployed, socially isolated, and out of contact with their families. Homeless women may be more likely than are men to have intact social skills and social networks. In general, the homeless mentally ill are difficult to treat because of their high levels of withdrawal and suspicion, psychopathology, homeless life-style, or negative past experiences with the mental health system.

In one group of homeless mentally ill patients studied, the majority suffered from schizophrenia and schizoaffective disorder. A large number of patients had histories of alcohol and other substance abuse. Close to one third of the patients had concomitant physical illnesses that were secondary to alcohol dependence. The patients also suffered from significant medical problems, including anemia, lice infestation, nutritional deficiencies ($B_{12}$, folate, and iron deficiencies), cellulitis, and evidence of exposure to and an increased incidence of tuberculosis.

A 35-year-old man with a 10-year history of paranoid schizophrenia complicated by alcohol abuse resided in a city-run shelter, where he was identified as psychotic on the basis of his bizarre behavior related to hallucinations. He was enrolled in an intensive case management program. Through repeated outreach efforts, his intensive case manager helped the patient obtain benefits and begin treatment with fluphenazine (Prolixin), as prescribed by a visiting psychiatrist.

After the patient stabilized, his intensive case manager placed him in a supportive residence with on-site social workers and psychiatric staff members. The residence acted as the representative payee of the patient's entitlement check. At the same time, the patient attended an intensive program for mentally ill substance abusers at a nearby city hospital. He remained in the program and continued taking his medication for two years before leaving the program because of his desire for more control over his finances.

One year later, an outreach team found him bizarrely posturing and talking to himself in a city train terminal. He accepted a sandwich and voluntary transport to a specialized ward for the treatment of the homeless mentally ill. After stabilization, he was transferred to a state hospital for intermediate care. As his insight into the interplay of his psychiatric illness and his alcohol abuse improved, community placement was sought.

## Treatment

Some homeless mentally ill persons remain within geographic limits; others travel from one part of the country to another. Because demography, epidemiology, history, and treatment needs vary, no single treatment method is recommended. In addition to the full range of traditional services—evaluation, crisis intervention, medication review, psychosocial skills training, and housing—homeless mentally ill patients may require less traditional services, such as a mailbox where welfare checks can be delivered, bathing facilities, and delousing services.

Traditional mental health service systems may present barriers to access by homeless mentally ill persons. Sometimes the barriers are simply the result of a lack of services to meet the patient's special needs or the result of geographic or functional limitations. Housing programs for chronically mentally ill persons are often limited to high-functioning patients, thereby screening out poorly functioning street people. Effective service programs include provisions for shelter and food, drop-in centers, outreach contact, and a cooperative endeavor between mental health agencies and other agencies in the community (for example, the Salvation Army and church-affiliated organizations).

The homeless mentally ill can be treated through outreach programs and treatment geared to their specific needs. Effective treatment can be achieved with appropriate community placements and mentally ill substance abuser programs. Many of the patients cannot function in the community, even with significant support. For them, long-term state hospitalization may be the only way to safeguard their well-being. The government needs to accept that reality if the patients' needs are to be met.

## Outreach Programs

Street outreach programs are crucial components in addressing the problems of the homeless mentally ill, since many of the patients do not use shelters. Those who do use shelters require shelter-based outreach programs, since they do not seek treatment by traditional routes.

Street outreach programs have succeeded by using a multidisciplinary team consisting of psychiatrists, social workers, and nurses. The approach to the homeless mentally ill involves making repeated brief contacts while offering food and concrete services as a means of engagement. The patients do not tolerate a standard psychiatric interview; therefore, assessment must be made by observation, with particular attention to self-care, bizarre behavior, possible physical problems, and changing trends in appearance or behavior over time. Collateral histories from the police and workers in the community are often valuable.

## Hospitalization

Patients who are suicidal, homicidal, or unable to care for themselves to the point of constituting a danger to themselves require hospitalization. Involuntary hospitalization under those circumstances is controversial because of the infringement of patients' rights. However, for many of those patients, involuntary hospitalization is lifesaving. Outreach teams must have strong links with local law enforcement officials. Some outreach physicians may be legally empowered to involuntarily transport patients to designated hospitals. Once the patients are hospitalized, comprehensive assessment is needed, with particular attention to concomitant medical problems, substance abuse, and cognitive disorders. Psychotropic medication and a therapeutic milieu that emphasizes nursing observation, activity therapy, and psychoeducation are needed.

Many homeless mentally ill patients are nonverbal and profoundly regressed. As a result, many require more than short-term hospitalization; they need transfers to state facilities. Many patients improve so much that they can be placed in the community. The most appropriate placements are community residences with on-site social work and psychiatric services combined with some degree of structure. Discharging patients to a shelter or an unsupervised apartment is inadequate. Such a practice is reprehensible and unfair to the sick patient who requires help, and it is disastrous to urban communities where homeless people are found on every corner. Assigning patients to intensive case managers before discharge can ease the transition, providing needed support and continuity of care. Attention to the patients' individual needs is essential if a long-term plan is to be effective. It is tragic that funding such long-term planning is an unresolved political issue.

## PSYCHOGERIATRIC LONG-TERM CARE

The elderly population will increase an estimated 125 percent by the year 2030 and will need three times the nursing home care now available. The cost of such care will grow from $44 billion in 1990 to an estimated $187 billion in 2030. The need for professional care will increase because an increasing proportion of the elderly will lack family supports. As a result, long-term care financing is a major problem.

Some have suggested private-sector solutions that include making long-term care insurance affordable through tax incentives, insurance regulations, and an increased emphasis on the provision of home care as a substitute for nursing home care to decrease insurance payments and premiums. Others have called for a national long-term care program as part of a national health plan. At present, much of the burden of elderly long-term care falls on the family. More than 70 percent of the people receiving long-term care rely on unpaid caretakers. It is clear that sweeping changes in the financing and delivery of long-term care will be needed to meet the increasing needs of this growing portion of the population.

**References**

Avison W R, Nixon Speechley K: The discharged psychiatric patient: A review of social, social-psychological and psychiatric correlates of outcome. Am J Psychiatry *144*: 10, 1987.

Bachrach L L: What we know about homelessness among mentally ill persons: An analytical review and commentary. Hosp Community Psychiatry *43*: 453, 1992.

Bachrach L L, Lamb H R: Public psychiatry in an era of deinstitutionalization. New Dir Ment Health Serv *42*: 9, 1989.

Barrett J, Rose R M: *Mental Disorders in the Community*. Guilford, New York, 1986.

Borus J F: Strangers bearing gifts: A retrospective look at the early years of community mental health center consultation. Am J Psychiatry *141*: 868, 1984.

Burns B J, Taube J E, Permutt T, Rudin S C, Mulcare M E, Harbin H T, Goldman H H: Evaluation of a Maryland fiscal incentive plan for placing state hospital patients in nursing homes. Hosp Community Psychiatry *42*: 1228, 1991.

Caplan G: *Population-Oriented Psychiatry*. Human Sciences, New York, 1989.

Caplan G: *Principles of Preventive Psychiatry*. Basic Books, New York, 1964.

Chacko R C, editor: *The Chronic Mental Patient in a Community Context*. American Psychiatric Press, Washington, 1985.

Dencker K, Gottfries C-G: The closure of a major psychiatric hospital: Can psychiatric patients in long-term care be integrated into existing nursing homes? J Geriatr Psychiatry Neurol *4*: 149, 1991.

Friedman M J, West A N: Current need versus treatment history: Predictors of use of outpatient psychiatric care. Am J Psychiatry *144*: 355, 1987.

Goering P, Wasylenki D, St. Onge M, Paduchak D, Lancee W: Gender differences among clients of a case management program for the homeless. Hosp Community Psychiatry *43*: 160, 1992.

Hess R, Morgan J, editors: *Prevention in Community Mental Health Centers*. Haworth, New York, 1990.

Jones M: *The Therapeutic Community*. Basic Books, New York, 1953.

Katz S E: Hospitalization and the mental health service system. In *Comprehensive Textbook of Psychiatry*, ed 5, H I Kaplan, B J Sadock, editors, p 2083. Williams & Wilkins, Baltimore, 1989.

Katz S E, Nardacci D, Sabatini A, editors: *Intensive Treatment of the Homeless Mentally Ill*. American Psychiatric Press, Washington, 1993.

Marmor T R, Gill K C: The political and economic context of mental health care in the United States. J Health Polit Policy Law *14*: 459, 1989.

Marshall E J, Reed J L: Psychiatric morbidity in homeless women. Br J Psychiatry *160*: 761, 1992.

Menninger W W: The chronically mentally ill. In *Comprehensive Textbook of Psychiatry*, ed 5, H I Kaplan, B J Sadock, editors, p 2090. Williams & Wilkins, Baltimore, 1989.

Moak G S, Fisher W H: Geriatric patients and services in state hospitals: Data from a national survey. Hosp Community Psychiatry *42*: 273, 1991.

Okin R L, Borus J F: Primary, secondary, and tertiary prevention of mental disorders. In *Comprehensive Textbook of Psychiatry*, ed 5, H I Kaplan, B J Sadock, editors, p 2067. Williams & Wilkins, Baltimore, 1989.

Saathoff G B, Cortina J A, Jacobson R, Aldrich C K: Mortality among elderly patients discharged from a state hospital. Hosp Community Psychiatry *43*: 280, 1992.

Shore J H: Community psychiatry. In *Comprehensive Textbook of Psychiatry*, ed 5, H I Kaplan, B J Sadock, editors, p 2063. Williams & Wilkins, Baltimore, 1989.

Solomon P L, Draine J N, Marcenko M O, Meyerson A T: Homelessness in a mentally ill urban jail population. Hosp Community Psychiatry *43*: 169, 1992.

Zedlewski S R, McBride T D: The changing profile of the elderly: Effects on future long-term care needs and financing. Milbank Q *70*: 247, 1992.

# 4.9 / Socioeconomic Aspects of Health Care

Social and economic factors significantly affect the nation's health status and the delivery of health services. Knowing the qualities of a population that influence its health, illness, and death is valuable when assessing current health care requirements, designing future facilities and programs, and allocating dollars to optimize the provision of adequate services.

The World Health Organization (WHO) defines health as the state of complete physical, mental, and social well-being and not merely the absence of disease. In its effort to promote health, the American health care delivery system attempts to provide and maintain high-quality medical care for all its citizens while advancing medical research and technology. The current emphasis in health care is on prevention and health promotion, as well as the treatment and diagnosis of medical disorders. Increasing health care costs have become significant obstacles in fulfilling those objectives. The focus on efforts to control those costs affects the distribution of health care funds, the delivery of health care services, and the reimbursement mechanisms for those services.

The major socioeconomic issue in health care is the American Health Security Bill proposed by President Bill Clinton in 1993. The provisions of the bill and its implications are discussed in detail at the end of this section.

## SOCIAL FACTORS

### Life-Style

Life-style and personal habits are major factors in the causes of illness and death in the United States, accounting for about 70 percent of all illness, both mental and physical. Obesity, for example, is related to heart disease and diabetes, and a person's weight bears a direct relation to habit patterns of eating and exercise.

Many cancer deaths have been related to both poor dietary habits and chewing and smoking of tobacco. Over the past five years cigarette smoking has continued to decline steadily. The age-adjusted percentage of men 18 years of age and over who smoke cigarettes declined, from 31 percent in 1987 to 28 percent in 1991; smoking among women decreased from 26 percent in 1987 to 24 percent in 1991. For women 55 to 70 years of age, lung cancer is the primary cause of cancer deaths.

Regular physical activity has a positive effect on stress reduction. It is also useful in treating and preventing such mental problems as anxiety disorders and depressive disorders and such physical problems as obesity, heart disease, diabetes, and high blood pressure. A trend in this country over the past two decades indicates that, although the number of adults involved in a daily exercise regimen is rising, less than half of all school-age children are exercising on a daily basis.

Accident prevention would also avoid many premature deaths. Education about safe driving habits, especially the need to abstain from alcohol when driving, would save more than 100,000 lives each year, especially among young adults.

Table 4.9–1 lists personal health practices related to life-style.

### Age

The incidence of illness is affected by age. Eighty-six percent of persons more than 65 years of age have one or more chronic conditions. The three leading chronic conditions of old age are arthritis, hypertension, and heart disease. Hearing impairments, diabetes, cataracts, and varicose veins are also

**Table 4.9–1**
**Personal Health Practices**
**[For persons 18 years of age and over. Based on National Health Interview Survey.]**

| Characteristic | Sleeps 6 Hours or Less (%) | Never Eats Breakfast (%) | Snacks Every Day (%) | Less Physically Active Than Contemporaries (%) | Had 5 or More Drinks on Any One Day (%) | Current Smoker (%) | 30% or More above Desirable Weight† (%) |
|---|---|---|---|---|---|---|---|
| All persons‡ | 22.0 | 24.3 | 39.0 | 16.4 | 37.5 | 30.1 | 13.0 |
| Age | | | | | | | |
| 18–29 years old | 19.8 | 30.4 | 42.2 | 17.1 | 54.4 | 31.9 | 7.5 |
| 30–44 years old | 24.3 | 30.1 | 41.4 | 18.3 | 39.0 | 34.5 | 13.6 |
| 45–64 years old | 22.7 | 21.4 | 37.9 | 15.3 | 24.6 | 31.6 | 18.1 |
| 65 years old and over | 20.4 | 7.5 | 30.7 | 13.5 | 12.2 | 16.0 | 13.2 |
| 65–74 years old | 19.7 | 9.0 | 32.4 | 15.8 | NA | 19.7 | 14.9 |
| 75 years old and over | 21.5 | 5.1 | 27.8 | 9.8 | NA | 10.0 | 10.3 |
| Sex | | | | | | | |
| Male | 22.7 | 25.2 | 40.7 | 16.5 | 49.3 | 32.6 | 12.1 |
| Female | 21.4 | 23.6 | 37.5 | 16.3 | 23.3 | 27.8 | 13.7 |
| Race | | | | | | | |
| White | 21.3 | 24.5 | 39.4 | 16.7 | 38.3 | 29.6 | 12.4 |
| All other | 26.6 | 23.2 | 36.3 | 14.3 | 29.9 | 33.1 | 16.4 |
| Black | 27.8 | 23.6 | 37.2 | 13.9 | 29.3 | 34.9 | 18.7 |
| Other | 21.4 | 21.5 | 32.6 | 16.5 | 33.3 | 24.8 | 6.7 |
| Education level | | | | | | | |
| Less than 12 years | 23.3 | 22.6 | 37.8 | 12.3 | 35.9 | 35.4 | 17.5 |
| 12 years | 21.9 | 26.5 | 39.6 | 16.5 | 38.9 | 33.4 | 13.4 |
| More than 12 years | 21.2 | 23.3 | 39.2 | 19.1 | 36.8 | 23.1 | 9.4 |
| Family income | | | | | | | |
| Less than $7,000 | 24.4 | 22.4 | 37.0 | 13.5 | NA | 31.1 | 16.1 |
| $7,000 to $14,999 | 21.6 | 22.9 | 37.4 | 14.7 | NA | 33.4 | 15.3 |
| $15,000 to $24,999 | 21.2 | 24.9 | 40.3 | 16.8 | NA | 32.2 | 13.4 |
| $25,000 to $39,999 | 22.4 | 26.1 | 41.2 | 17.2 | NA | 30.0 | 12.1 |
| $40,000 or more | 21.8 | 25.4 | 39.9 | 19.4 | NA | 25.2 | 9.4 |

NA = not available.
†Based on 1960 Metropolitan Life Insurance Company standards. Data are self-reported.
‡Excludes persons whose health practices are unknown.
Table from U.S. National Center for Health Statistics: *Health Promotion and Disease Prevention, United States 1985*, series 10, No 163 and unpublished data.

common chronic problems. Mental health problems increase with age as well. Although chronicity is a factor among the elderly, young persons are more predisposed than are the elderly to acute illnesses. The three most common acute medical problems, across age groups, are upper respiratory conditions, influenza, and injuries.

Age influences the use of all health care services. Both young persons (ages 20 to 30) and persons more than 65 tend to have more illnesses and health care needs than do persons in middle adulthood. Young children's health care habits are often modeled after those of their parents. Prior experiences with health care influence future attitudes and behavior.

Education about accidents in the home would save about 28,000 lives each year, especially among the elderly, who account for two thirds of all accidents that occur at home.

### Socioeconomic Status

A person's socioeconomic status (SES) is not based solely on income but includes such factors as education, occupation, and life-style. The incidence of physical illness is affected by SES. Persons in low SES groups are likely to be afflicted with hypertension, arthritis, upper respiratory illness, speech difficulties, and eye diseases. Low SES persons have a reduced life expectancy, as longevity is positively correlated to SES level.

A positive correlation exists between SES and mental health; consequently, high SES persons have better mental

health than do persons of low SES. With regard to the incidence of psychopathology, some studies have found a slightly higher than usual percentage of bipolar I disorder among high SES persons and a greater number than usual of schizophrenic persons in low SES groups.

### Poverty

Poverty is associated with many long-term problems, such as poor health and increased mortality, mental disorders, school failure, crime, and substance abuse. In 1992 about 14.5 percent of all Americans fell below the poverty level, which is set by the federal government at $11,186 a year for a three-person household of two adults and one child. Women are more likely to be poor than are men, and children are the poorest age group, with one child in five living below the poverty line. Poverty is also associated with ethnicity, with about 85 percent of the poor being black or Hispanic.

### Sex

Regardless of age, women seek health care and are hospitalized more often than men. Women are most frequently hospitalized for childbirth, heart disease, and cancer, whereas men are hospitalized for heart disease, cancer, and fractures. The three leading chronic conditions that can limit activity for men are heart conditions, arthritis, and impairment of the back or the spine; for women, the leading chronic conditions are arthritis, heart conditions, and hypertension.

## Race

Race affects the use of health care facilities. In 1990 the average number of physician contacts was 10 percent higher for white persons than for black persons (5.6 compared with 5.1 contacts). Ambulatory care for black persons was twice as likely to occur in hospital outpatient and clinic settings as was care for white persons (24 percent compared with 12 percent of physician contacts in 1990). The rates of such chronic conditions as obesity, diabetes, heart disease, hypertension, and arthritis are higher among blacks than among whites.

## Environment

The environment contributes to about one quarter of today's health problems. The exposure to such environmental risks as toxic waste, natural disasters, lead, asbestos, and dioxins is a major source of disease and death in humans. Waterborne diseases, especially those that occur in shellfish from polluted waters, are a major cause of morbidity and mortality.

About 75 percent of all carcinogens come from the environment. One of the highest incidences of bladder cancer is in certain industrial sites in New Jersey, where 25 percent of all workers are employed in the chemical industry. Nearly 67 percent of the men who die from coal workers' pneumoconiosis live in Pennsylvania.

Between 1985 and 1986, lead emissions declined by almost 60 percent, from 21,000 to 9,000 metric tons a year, in large part because of Environmental Protection Agency (EPA) rules requiring petroleum refineries to lower the lead content of gasoline.

With regard to mental health, mental disorders generally rise among people as their environments change from the suburban community to the inner city.

## MORTALITY AND MORBIDITY TRENDS

The health status and the health needs of a population can be assessed by examining general health trends, including death rates, causes of death, and longevity. The existence of certain medical disorders influences the need for particular health care delivery systems, programs, and personnel. A population's general health status determines the overall need for services and dollars.

In 1991 the death rate across all age groups in the United States was 860.3 per 100,000, according to the National Center for Health Statistics. The death rate fell about 10.5 percent in the 1980s, and the rate continues to decline.

In 1991 the three leading causes of death were heart disease, cancer, and stroke, in decreasing order. Chronic obstructive pulmonary diseases (including bronchitis, asthma, and emphysema) overtook accidents as the fourth leading cause of death, partly because of a drop in motor vehicle fatalities. In 1991 the human immunodeficiency virus (HIV) became the ninth leading cause of death (up from the 15th leading cause of death in 1988). Currently, HIV is the leading cause of death among men aged 25 to 44. Although mental disorders do not play a major role in the mortality rate, they are probably the major factor in

the morbidity rate and are also a major cause of days lost from work.

Mortality rates differ considerably by race and sex. Females have lower mortality rates than do males in all age groups, but the difference has been decreasing in recent years. Racial minorities within a given population have higher death rates than does the majority population.

The primary cause of death for each of the sex and race groups is heart disease. The mortality rate for heart disease, cancer, and stroke is greatest among black males and is higher for males than for females.

The most common cause of death among adolescents and young adults (ages 15 to 24) is accidents; three fourths of those fatalities occur in automobiles. Homicide and suicide are the second and third leading causes of death, respectively, in that age group. For children under age 14, the leading causes of death are accidents, cancer, and congenital anomalies in that order.

Men are more likely than women to die of myocardial infarction, but women have a higher rate of cerebrovascular diseases. Cancer accounts for about 22 percent of all deaths. Cancer deaths increased among women while dropping for men, pointing to increased smoking by women beginning in the 1960s as a likely factor in that change. Cigarette smoking poses a higher risk for women than for men: a 55-year-old woman who smokes has a higher risk for hypertension, high cholesterol, and myocardial infarction than does a 55-year-old man who smokes.

## Infant Mortality

Infant mortality in the United States is high compared with other countries. The rate is 8.9 deaths per 1,000 live births as of 1989, which ranks this country behind 11 other nations. The mortality rate for black infants (17.6) is twice as high as for white infants (7.3). Good prenatal care contributes to a low infant mortality rate; although about 80 percent of white women receive prenatal care, only about 65 percent of black women, 60 percent of Native Americans, and 75 percent of Asian Americans receive such care. In addition, a disproportionately high number of black women have acquired immune deficiency syndrome (AIDS), which contributes to neonatal mortality. As of 1993, blacks made up 55 percent of all AIDS cases among children under 13 years of age, and Hispanic Americans accounted for 24 percent.

The three leading causes of infant death are congenital anomalies, respiratory distress syndrome, and sudden infant death syndrome, in descending order of frequency.

## Life Expectancy

According to the U.S. National Center for Health Statistics, in the United States life expectancy of all age, sex, and race groups has been steadily increasing since the turn of the century. The increase in Americans' longevity in the past 25 years is due in part to the dramatic decline in deaths from heart disease and cerebrovascular diseases, down 33 percent. In 1992 the average life expectancy from birth was 75.5 years. Black males have the shortest life expectancy from birth (64.6 years). White males (72.9 years), black females (73.8 years), and white females (79.6 years) all live longer than black males. Although the life expectancy of females is greater than that of males (78.9 years versus 72 years), that difference has been diminishing in recent years.

## HEALTH CARE PROVIDERS

Health care providers include a broad array of persons from a variety of professions who care for the sick. In addition to physicians, health care personnel include nurses, dentists, psychologists, social workers, podiatrists, speech therapists, and vocational therapists. More than 3 million people are employed in health-related occupations.

### Physician Supply

In 1992 there were about 635,000 physicians, 151,000 dentists, and 1.9 million nurses practicing in the United States. About 21 percent of M.D.s were educated outside the United States or Canada, a figure that has remained fairly constant since 1980. Psychiatrists number about 35,000. Although the number of physicians is adequate, their distribution is a problem. High physician-patient ratios exist in the Northeast and in California; but low concentrations are the norm in the South and in the mountain states. Psychiatrists tend to be concentrated in urban areas.

Primary care physicians number about 35 percent of all physicians and are usually defined as general practitioners, family practitioners, internists, and pediatricians. Primary care has been defined as a type of medical care delivery that emphasizes first-contact care and assumes ongoing responsibility for the patient in both health maintenance and therapy. Many believe that psychiatry should also be classified as a primary care specialty. That is not currently the case.

Projections through the 1990s show shortages, balances, and surpluses in the overall distribution of physicians in various specialties. By the year 2000, there will be more than 650,000 physicians in the United States. There will be an oversupply of physicians in certain specialties, such as surgery, ophthalmology, internal medicine, obstetrics and gynecology, and neurosurgery. Fields in which the supply will equal the demand are dermatology, family practice, otolaryngology, and pediatrics. The only fields in which a shortage is expected are psychiatry, emergency medicine, and preventive medicine.

There is a trend toward increasing primary care physicians to 50 percent of all physicians and decreasing the number of specialists.

### Physician Earnings

In 1990 the average physician had gross earnings of about $200,000 a year; neurosurgery, orthopedic surgery, and plastic surgery are the highest-paid specialties (more than $350,000 a year); family practice, pediatrics, and psychiatry are the lowest paid (less than $150,000 a year). The average net income after expenses for all physicians was $164,300 in 1990; however, half of all physicians earned less than $130,000 (Table 4.9–2 and Figure 4.9–1).

**Table 4.9–2**
**Average Physician Net Income by Specialty***

| Specialty | Yearly Income |
|---|---|
| General/family practice | $102,700 |
| Pediatrics | 106,500 |
| Psychiatry | 116,500 |
| Internal medicine | 152,500 |
| Pathology | 172,500 |
| Obsterics/gynecology | 207,300 |
| Anesthesiology | 207,400 |
| Radiology | 219,400 |
| Surgery | 236,400 |

*After expenses and before taxes.

**Physician earnings in context.** In 1993 the American Medical Association made the following observations:

Physician income is high in comparison with those of many other occupations. There is no single explanation for why this is the case. Following are a few factors that should be considered.

Physicians work long hours, often under stress, and must continually keep up with new medical developments. The average number of hours worked per week was 59.1 in 1990, about 48% in excess of the typical 40-hour week.

Part of the reason for the rising trend in the statistics reported here is that the physician population is aging slightly and most are still on the rising section of the career earnings path. Income statistics will rise over time as more physicians enter their peak earnings years.

Physicians do not begin their careers until later in life. In 1989, the average age of a medical school graduate was 28. Counting residency training, many physicians are in their early thirties before beginning to practice.

Many physicians incur a high educational debt by the time they begin to practice. According to the Association of American Medical Colleges, about 79% of 1990 graduates reported some level of educational debt, with the average for those with indebtedness amounting to $46,224. For the same graduating class, 31.6% had debt greater than $50,000, while 12.8% had debt of over $75,000.

### Private Practice

Most physicians in America are in traditional autonomous office-based practices, and the majority of patients receive health care in physicians' private offices. Physicians use their own facilities and equipment to provide a variety of health care services.

Private practices are organized in one of three ways: independent, partnership, and group. Independent or solo practitioners constitute a significant part of the health care delivery system today. Physicians in independent private practices work for themselves and provide personalized service to patients.

In a partnership the overhead (office, personnel, and equipment expenses) is shared by two or more physicians. The patients, in contrast, may or may not be shared by the doctors; the practice may remain independent in that respect.

Group practice is gaining popularity in the United States. The American Medical Association defines group practice as the delivery of medical services by three or

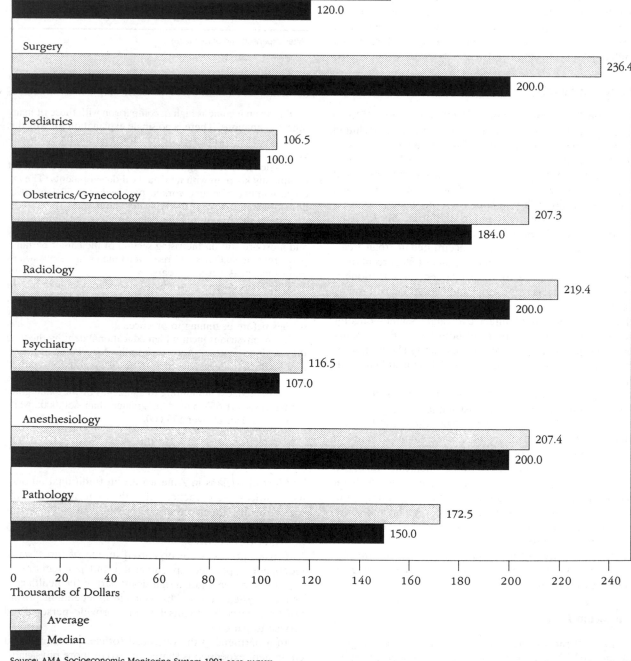

Source: AMA Socioeconomic Monitoring System 1991 core survey.

**Figure 4.9–1.** Average and median physician net income (in thousands of dollars) after expenses before taxes, by specialty, 1990. (Figure from M L Gonzalez, editor: *Socioeconomic Char-* *acteristics of Medical Practice 1992.* American Medical Association, Chicago, 1992. Used with permission.)

more physicians who are formally organized to provide care, consultation, diagnosis, and treatment. The group shares the use of equipment and personnel, and income from the medical practice is distributed among the members of the group.

Group practices may concentrate on a single specialty or may be multidisciplinary, delivering a variety of services to patients. As with the partnership, the group practice offers the physician economic benefits and fewer working hours than in a solo practice. The group practice also enables the physician to maintain a regular work schedule. The ability to form ongoing doctor-patient relationships diminishes, however, as the number of patients increases. Recently, private practitioners have been inclined to move away from independent practice and to participate in group practices and, to a smaller extent, partnerships.

In private practice, patients pay for services directly or through third-party payers—that is, insurance companies or government agencies. As economic conditions change, however, office-based physicians are joining, at an increasing rate, prospective (prepayment) reimbursement systems.

There is a major concern that the private practice of psychiatry may be constrained or even eliminated if plans to cap fee-for-service medicine are instituted. Psychiatrists have been instructed by Medicare to limit their fees, which represents a form of price control on the medical profession in general. Should that occur, it will be difficult for many physicians (regardless of specialty) to cover their costs of maintaining an independent fee-for-service private practice.

### Liability Insurance

One of the most expensive components of physician practices is liability insurance. From 1982 to 1990 average premiums increased at an annual rate of 12.1 percent, from $5,800 to $14,500. The high premiums result from the increased incidence of malpractice claims and high jury awards. More then one third of all physicians have been sued at least once during their medical careers. The average award is about $500,000 in liability cases. In 1990, for the first time in a decade, liability insurance rates began to level off because of increased diligence and quality assurance by physicians and because of tort reform, limiting monetary awards in various states. However, in 1993 premiums started to rise once again.

### Patient Visits

Physician services tend to be underused. Twenty-two percent of the population do not see a physician at all in a given year. Of the 78 percent who do, most are very young or old or are women, and they average about five visits a year. Physician visits may take place in the doctor's office (60 percent); hospital outpatient departments, including the emergency room (14 percent); over the telephone (13 percent); and at home (2 percent). As family income rises, the rates of office and phone consultations increase, and the rate of hospital outpatient visits decreases. The five leading reasons for office visits are a general examination, a prenatal examination, throat problems, hypertension, and postoperative visits, in descending order of frequency.

Americans do not use physician services as much as persons in other countries do. The average number of visits a year to their doctors by Germans is 14, by French 7, and by Americans 5. Americans give as their reason for not seeking care the cost of an office visit. Both Germany and France have national health systems that cover the bulk of medical care.

Women visit their doctors more often than do men and whites more often than do blacks. Most visits are to family physicians, followed by pediatricians. The average American visits a dentist twice a year.

## HEALTH CARE COSTS

The provision of adequate cost-effective services to the American public is a critical concern. Spending for all types of health care, including the care of the mentally ill, continues to escalate. The growth rate of health care expenditures continues to outdistance the pace of growth of the economy. Health care has become increasingly expensive as a result of inflation, population growth, and advanced technology.

In 1992 about $900 billion, 13 percent of the gross national product (GNP), was spent for health care. By 2000 it will reach $1.5 trillion, 15 percent of the GNP. The 1992 GNP percentage compares with 9 percent in Canada and Sweden, 8.5 percent in France, 8 percent in Germany, 7 percent in Japan, and 6 percent in the United Kingdom. The health share of the GNP remains fairly stable in most industrialized countries but increases by about one fifth each year in the United States, thereby widening the gap between the health care expenditures of the United States and those of other countries.

Mental disorders account for a large proportion of health care expenditures. The cost of mental disorders is about $2.5 billion a year.

Government spending for health care is on the rise. In part because of Medicare and Medicaid, the federal government's monetary contribution to health care has grown from about 8 percent in 1965 to about 30 percent in 1990. Overall, the government pays about 41 percent (30 percent federal, 11 percent state) of personal health care expenditures. Private funds account for the other 59 percent through direct payments (24 percent), private health insurance (32 percent), and industry and philanthropy (3 percent).

Representing about 41 percent of expenditures, hospitals use the largest proportion of health care dollars. Physicians' fees are about 20 percent of costs, followed by nursing homes, drugs, and dental services. In general, hospital costs and general medical care services have risen at a far greater rate than have physicians' fees.

As many as 85 percent of Americans have some form of health insurance, which covers about 80 percent of hospital costs and 60 percent of physicians' services, except in the case of psychiatry. Twenty-five percent of hospital costs to the patient represent laboratory tests and imaging, and the remaining costs are for drugs, administration, nursing, and other support services.

## HEALTH CARE DELIVERY

### Hospitals

The hospital is the institutional provider of general medical and surgical services in the United States health care system. There are currently more than 6,000 hospitals of all types in the United States, with about 1 million beds. About 66 percent of all beds are occupied at any one time. According to the WHO, hospitals must have physician staff, offer continuous medical and nursing care to patients, and maintain inpatient facilities. Because hospitals consume the biggest percentage of health dollars, their use is the focus of current cost-containment strategies.

In the past decade 75 percent of all adults have been in a hospital at least once, women more often than men. Rates of hospitalization for all illnesses increase with age. The average general hospital stay across specialties is 6.3 days, a reduction from 7.1 days in 1980. However, a slight increase in hospital use has been reported for children and elderly persons. At present, there is a 10 percent oversupply of hospital beds in this country, particularly in urban areas; the expense of maintaining the beds continues even if they are empty. The health care staff is the largest component of hospital costs.

The classification of hospitals may be based on ownership, length of stay, or the nature of the service offered. Table 4.9–3 presents an overview of important aspects of hospital organization.

### Nursing Homes

In 1991 there were about 25,000 nursing homes in the United States, with about 1,500,000 beds. Nursing homes are classified by the intensity of the care they offer: (1) *nursing care homes,* which employ one or more full-time registered or licensed practical nurses and provide nursing care to at least

**Table 4.9–3**
**Aspects of Hospital Organization**

| Criteria | Voluntary Hospital | Investor-Owned Hospital | State Mental Hospital System | Municipal Hospital System | Federal Hospital System | Special Hospital |
|---|---|---|---|---|---|---|
| Patient population | All illnesses | All illnesses, although hospital may specialize | Mental illness | All illnesses | All illnesses | 70 percent of facility must be for single diagnosis |
| Number of hospitals | 5,843 | 834 | 285 (119,000 beds nationally) | Variable by city | 342 | 150 |
| Profit orientation | Nonprofit | For profit | Nonprofit | Nonprofit | Nonprofit | For profit or nonprofit |
| Ownership | Private management board | Private corporation; may be owned by MDs | State | City government | Federal government | Private or public |
| Affiliation | 1,200 church-affiliated; remainder are privately owned or univorsity sponsored | May be owned by large chains such as Humana Corporation | Free-standing or affiliated with various medical schools | Voluntary teaching hospitals and medical schools | Department of Defense (190); Public Health Service, Coast Guard, Prison, Merchant Marine, Indian Health Service; Veterans Affairs (139) | Optional affiliation with medical schools |
| Other | Provide bulk of care in U.S. | Increasing in importance nationally | Deinstitutionalization—number of patients has been reduced | Most physicians at municipal hospitals are employed by their affiliated medical school | V.A. hospitals usually have affiliations with medical schools | Less regulated than other types of hospitals (see note 5) |

Notes: (1) To be designated a teaching hospital, a hospital must offer at least four types of approved residencies, clinical experiences for medical students, and an affiliation with a medical school. (2) As of 1982, there were 364 state-operated facilities and approximately 14,600 private facilities for the mentally retarded. (3) In 1989 there were 751 investor-owned for-profit hospitals for psychiatric patients in the United States. (4) Short-term hospitals have an average patient stay of less than 30 days; long-term, an average of longer duration. (5) Special hospitals include obstetrics and gynecology; eye, ear, nose, and throat. They do not include psychiatric hospitals or substance abuse hospitals.

half the residents; (2) *personal care homes with nursing,* which employ one or more registered or licensed practical nurses and provide medications and treatments in accordance with physicians' orders; (3) *personal care homes without nursing;* (4) *domiciliary care homes,* which primarily provide supervisory care but also provide one or two personal services; (5) *skilled nursing facilities,* which provide the most intensive nursing care available outside a hospital, such as the application of dressings or bandages, bowel and bladder care, catheterization, enemas, intramuscular and intravenous injections, irrigation, nasal feeding, and oxygen therapy; and (6) *intermediate care facilities,* which are certified by the Medicaid program to provide health-related services on a regular basis to Medicaid-eligible persons who do not require hospital or skilled nursing facility care but who do require institutional care above the level of room and board.

## Psychiatric Care Delivery

Psychiatric care is provided by a variety of mental health organizations in addition to the private practitioner. The organizations include the following: (1) psychiatric hospitals, including Veterans Affairs psychiatric hospitals, state and county mental hospitals, and private mental hospitals; (2) psychiatric units of general hospitals; (3) residential treatment centers for emotionally disturbed children; (4) federally funded community mental health centers; and (5) free-standing psychiatric outpatient clinics, where a psychiatrist has medical responsibility for all patients in the program.

Most patients are seen in one of those organizations; fewer than 5 percent of all psychiatric patients are seen by psychiatrists in private practice.

## Health Maintenance Organizations

A health maintenance organization (HMO) is an organized system providing comprehensive (both inpatient and outpatient) health care in all specialties, including psychiatry. Members voluntarily enroll in the plan and pay a prepayment or capitation fee to cover all health care services for a fixed period of time (a month or a year). There are currently 553 HMOs in the United States, down from 647 in 1987, despite an increase in enrollment to about 34 million people.

By using a capitation or prospective payment method, the HMO is assuming a dominant role in United States health care. The primary reason for the popularity of the HMO is that it decreases health care costs by limiting the number of new hospitalizations and by discharging patients from the hospital earlier than usual. The emphasis on prevention and health promotion and on performing as much diagnosis and therapy as possible on an outpatient basis also helps control expenses.

There are three types of HMOs: (1) In the staff model, physicians receive a salary to provide services in the HMO's own facility. (2) In the group model, health care is furnished by one or more groups of doctors; payment is received on a contractual basis at a predetermined rate. Physicians in staff and group models often own stock in their HMO. (3) The individual practice association (IPA) is also referred to as the network model. The HMO negotiates with individual physicians to receive a capitation fee for providing services to each IPA member seen in their private offices. Physicians retain their office-based private practices when they join an IPA. The percentage of IPAs in HMOs increased from 7 percent in 1976 to 63 percent in 1992 (Table 4.9–4).

In a 1993 nationwide study of 17,000 patients enrolled in HMOs, the patients voiced widespread dissatisfaction regarding the care they received. Independent doctors, the patients said, were easier to reach by telephone, were more apt to schedule office appointments on short notice, and spent more time with the patient than did doctors who worked in large medical groups and HMOs. Managed-care organizations typically restrict payments to specialists unless care is approved in advance by a designated primary care doctor. That practice also contributed to patient dissatisfaction, because they are prevented from seeking a specialist of their own choosing.

**Table 4.9–4**
**HMO Model Types and Enrollment Patterns**

| Top 5 HMO Market Penetrations (by percentage of population) | | Percent of Plans and Enrollees by HMO Model | | | |
|---|---|---|---|---|---|
| Area | Rate | Primary Model Type | Percentage of Plans | Number of Enrollees (in millions) | Percentage of Enrollees |
| Rochester, N.Y. | 54 | | | | |
| Worcester, Mass. | 51 | Staff | 11.2 | 5.6 | 13.5 |
| San Francisco Bay Area, Calif. | 49 | Group | 10.1 | 10.1 | 24.4 |
| Minneapolis-St. Paul, Minn. | 46 | Network | 16.1 | 6.6 | 16.0 |
| Albuquerque, N.M. | 40 | IPA | 62.6 | 19.1 | 46.1 |

| 5 Largest HMO Companies, Year-End 1992 Organization | Model Type | Enrollment | National Enrollment (%) |
|---|---|---|---|
| Kaiser Foundation Health Plans | Group | 6,614,830 | 16.0 |
| CIGNA Employee Benefits Co. | All | 1,965,535 | 4.7 |
| United HealthCare Corp. | Staff-network | 1,648,659 | 4.0 |
| U.S. Healthcare Inc. | IPA | 1,406,756 | 3.4 |
| Humana Inc. | All | 1,303,973 | 3.2 |

Source: Group Health Association of America, Inc.
Table from Am Med News, p 7, July 9, 1993.

## Preferred Provider Organizations

Like the HMO, the preferred provider organization (PPO) uses a prospective payment system. In the PPO, however, a corporation or an insurance company makes an agreement with a particular group of community hospitals and doctors to supply health services to PPO members at a previously determined rate lower than their usual rates. Patients who enroll in a PPO select their physicians from among the list of participating doctors, which includes both specialists and primary care physicians. Inpatient care is provided at the designated hospital that the patient chooses. There are about 1,000 PPOs in the United States at this time.

## BASIC CONCEPTS OF HEALTH CARE ORGANIZATION

### Regulation of Hospital Standards and Performance

A group of agencies, such as the Joint Commission on Accreditation of Healthcare Organizations (JCAHO) (previously called the Joint Commission on Accreditation of Hospitals [JCAH]) and the Liaison Committee on Medical Education (LCME), influence the standards of hospital care and performance. In addition, hospitals must comply with governmental regulations (city and state health rules). The JCAHO inspects hospitals every two years. The JCAHO is also responsible for determining the requirements for hospital accreditation. Hospital reimbursements from Medicare and Medicaid are contingent on meeting those standards. The accreditation, however, is done on a voluntary basis. The LCME and the Liaison Committee on Graduate Education are charged with accrediting medical schools and residency training programs, respectively. The two accrediting committees review education and training programs every four years; the procedure is voluntary.

The current trend is toward monitoring all the hospitals in a community as a single health entity and community resource. That means that each unit does not have the prerogative to develop new facilities without concern for the services offered by the other hospitals in the area.

**Utilization review.** This in-house evaluation process was created to make sure that institutions provide efficient, quality health care that meets patients' needs. The members of the utilization review committee consist of hospital administrators, physicians, and nurses. The committee reviews each patient's chart within a specified number of days of admission. The appropriateness of the admission, treatment strategies, and the length of the hospital stay are reviewed to facilitate the patient's discharge. Through that process the utilization review committee determines whether a particular admission was really indicated and whether the hospital stay was longer than necessary. A hospital must conduct utilization reviews to be eligible for JCAHO accreditation.

**Professional Standards Review Organization.** The Professional Standards Review Organization (PSRO) was set up by the federal government to review and to monitor care received by patients whose care is paid for with government funds. PSROs have been established by local medical associations and serve several functions: they attempt to ensure high-quality care, control costs, determine maximum lengths

of stay by patients in hospitals, conduct utilization reviews, and censure physicians who do not adhere to established guidelines. The PSRO may conduct a medical audit to evaluate the quality of care retrospectively by carefully examining charts. The PSRO is made up of physicians elected by local medical societies.

**Peer Review Organization.** In the early 1980s, the Peer Review Organization (PRO) replaced the PSRO as the federal review organization for hospitals receiving Medicare funds. To promote compliance with federal guidelines for health and hospital care, the PRO conducts independent utilization reviews and quality-of-care studies, validates Diagnosis-Related Group (DRG) assignments, and reviews hospital admissions and readmissions.

Federally mandated and funded, the PROs have greater authority than the PSROs. PROs can impose sanctions on hospitals for inadequate care. They can even recommend the termination of federal funding to hospitals that consistently violate federal standards. In addition, PROs can adjust or refuse payment for health services that they consider unnecessary.

The PRO operates on a statewide level and can be either for profit or nonprofit in nature. To reduce costs, a PRO is chosen through a competitive bidding process from among qualified physician-sponsored organizations.

**Health systems agency.** Health systems agencies (HSAs) are nonprofit organizations mandated by the federal government and set up on a statewide basis. HSAs promote or limit the development of health services and facilities, depending on the needs of a particular locality or state. They are made up of consumers and have considerable power in medicine. For example, before one can build a new hospital or conduct extensive renovations on an existing one, the HSA must approve a certificate of need (CON). Before a CON is issued, the necessity for a new facility in a specified locale must be established. HSAs control capital expenditures and, therefore, the availability of health resources. In each state, HSAs develop both long-term and short-term goals and plans, approve health care proposals requesting federal funding, review existing facilities and services, and suggest future construction and renovation projects on the basis of their findings.

### Reimbursement Programs

**Medicare (Title 18).** Set up by the Federal Social Security Act of 1965, Medicare is a federally funded health insurance program. It provides both hospital and medical insurance for persons 65 years of age and older and for persons with certain disabilities (for example, blindness and renal disease). Medicare consists of two parts. Part A covers inpatient hospital care, home health services, dialysis, and nursing home care after hospitalization. Funding is derived from a federal trust fund, which, in turn, receives its funds from Social Security contributions. Part B is optional medical insurance that can be purchased to cover such services as physicians' fees, medical supplies, home health care, outpatient hospital care, and therapy services. Benefits and eligibility standards of Medicare are uniform throughout the United States. More than 34 million persons are covered by Medicare.

**Medicaid (Title 19).** Mandated by the federal government in 1965, Medicaid is an assistance program for certain needy and low-income persons. It is financed by both federal and state governments, but each state defines its requirements for eligibility and is responsible for its administration. Although benefits vary from state to state, federal provisions require that Medicaid cover inpatient and outpatient hospital care (including psychiatric care), physician's services, laboratory tests, diagnostic imaging, home health care services, and nursing home care. Additional services may be provided at the state's option. Increasingly tight eligibility requirements have left many low-income people without coverage and unable to pay. Currently, about 25 million people are covered by Medicaid.

**Blue Cross Association.** The Blue Cross Association (BCA) of more than 80 independent insurance plans around the country pays primarily for inpatient hospital service. Blue Shield pays for physician services during the patient's hospital stay. In contrast to commercial insurance carriers, BCA is a nonprofit organization. Its premiums cover administrative expenses and benefits and provide a reserve to cover financial losses. It is regulated by state insurance departments. Benefits for psychiatric services are severely limited, compared with those for other medical illnesses, though inpatient psychiatric care is less limited than is outpatient care.

**Self-pay.** Persons contract with commercial insurance companies to cover both inpatient and outpatient costs, including physicians' fees, diagnostic procedures, and laboratory tests. For that type of insurance, self-pay patients pay a premium that may be based on (1) an experience rating determined by one's risk or prior record for reimbursement on insurance claims or (2) a community rating system in which each participant pays the same premium because the plan's cost is divided equally among group members.

As a result of increased claim costs of private insurance companies, cost control strategies are being used to reduce financial risk and increase profits. By using such procedures as benefit maximums for a given year, deductibles, and co-payments, health insurance companies can limit increases in premium rates while still covering most of the costs incurred by the patient.

## Cost Containment

As protection against soaring health care expenditures, government and commercial insurance programs have enacted measures to limit spending. Most physicians acknowledge the need for accountability but view the procedures as cumbersome and inequitable. A doctor may have to deal with 10 to 20 review organizations, each of which has its own criteria as to what constitutes a necessary medical procedure for which it is willing to allow payment. A troubling aspect is that denial of payment occurs for some treatments that are called experimental but that are considered accepted treatment by medical experts. Payment denials of that sort are on the increase and threaten to interfere with both innovative medical treatment and traditional medical care. Another particularly troubling issue resulting from the overseeing activities has been the breaching of confidentiality in the doctor-patient relationship. Moreover, denials of payment, demands to justify clinical decisions, and requirements for prior approval of procedures undermine professional decision making and contribute to a growing sense of frustration among physicians in all specialties.

**Managed care.** Managed care is a system by which the health care insurer and the provider work together to ensure cost containment. Its goal is to eliminate unnecessary medical procedures and to obtain discounted services from physicians and hospitals. Business and insurance companies have advocated managed care in an effort to cut their medical costs for employees and insurance beneficiaries.

Classic examples of managed care are health maintenance organizations (HMOs) and similar networks of health care providers (for example, IPAs) who have agreed to certain fees and certain guidelines before a service is rendered. In some cases a second opinion is mandatory before benefits are paid. If the patient objects to obtaining a second opinion, the insurance company can withhold payment. Half of all Blue Cross enrollees are now part of a managed care system that requires (1) that mandatory second opinions be obtained for surgical procedures and (2) that precertification of need be obtained before a patient is admitted to a hospital.

**Diagnosis-related group.** A diagnosis-related group (DRG) is a classification system consisting of 470 disease categories. In the 1970s DRGs were developed at Yale University as a way to help health care personnel determine the appropriate length of hospitalization for any given patient. The assignment of a patient to a DRG category is based on principal diagnosis, treatment procedures, personal attributes (for example, age and sex), complications, and discharge status.

In 1983 the federal Health Care Financing Administration adopted DRGs as the method for repaying hospitals for Medicare services. Most states now use this prospective payment system, whereby a hospital is reimbursed for patient care on the basis of a predetermined rate for each diagnostic category. An advantage of a prospective price system is that hospitals and physicians must deliver health services with greater than usual efficiency to conserve resources and funds. The hospital knows in advance the dollar amount it will be reimbursed for each DRG, and it will make money if the actual cost of treatment is less than that designated amount. The institution assumes a monetary loss, however, if the costs of hospitalization exceed that amount.

Criticisms of the DRG system include the concern that necessary but cost-ineffective medical services and programs will be eliminated. It is also feared that, if the service provider anticipates that adequate treatment will cost more than the assigned rate, patients will be either prematurely released or refused care.

**Resource-based relative value scale.** The resource-based relative value scale (RBRVS) is a method by which reimbursement to physicians by third-party payers can be determined. Developed at Harvard University, the RBRVS is based on several factors, including the number of years and the cost of training to become a specialist, the cost of running an office, other overhead costs, and the amount of time spent with the patient either in discussion (cognitive skills) or in performing a procedure. Some specialists, such as surgeons, are reimbursed a smaller than usual amount, and some, such as family physicians, are reimbursed a greater than usual amount.

**Claims review.** This method of peer review consists of the examination of claims for the payment of fees after treatment has been rendered. It has the disadvantage of being a decision to pay or not to pay after the treatment has been given. Insurance companies and governments have been doing claims reviews for many years. Traditionally, such a review has consisted of the examination of a claim by a clerk, with the determination of eligibility made by nonprofessionals. For example, when a claim for psychiatric treatment payment is turned down and appealed or when a claim is for a large amount, in the past the claim was reviewed by a single psychiatric consultant, who was an employee of the insurance company concerned. That system resulted in idiosyncratic decisions that may or may not have reflected local practice quality. In many instances, guidelines for insurance companies were developed without any input from practicing psychiatrists.

The first level of claims review generally consists of a clerical examination to determine whether the bill shows the necessary administrative information and whether the claimant is, indeed, insured. There is no determination of the appropriateness of the care given. The second level of claims review is generally done by trained personnel, often nurses. Here the claims reviewer compares the treatment rendered with previously established criteria for treatment that have been established as appropriate for the condition. The second-level reviewer may approve payment for the claim. If the second-level reviewer has questions or if the treatment is considered inappropriate according to the criteria, the claim is reviewed by a third-level group or a true peer review committee. Here a professional determination is made as to the appropriateness of the care rendered. The peer review committee—one or more psychiatrists, for example, review each claim—may approve or disapprove. There are levels of appeal for the practitioner who is dissatisfied with the committee determination. The appeals process often goes to a special committee of the county or state medical society.

**Benefit-consulting services.** Many large insurance companies and other groups have developed benefit-consulting services, which evaluate all medical claims in an effort to cut medical costs. Some of the companies receive a percentage of the amount of money saved as payment for their services, a practice that has led to charges of conflict of interest.

## AMERICAN HEALTH SECURITY BILL

The American Health Security Bill was proposed by President Bill Clinton in 1993 to guarantee comprehensive health coverage for all Americans, regardless of health or employment status. Under the bill, health coverage continues without interruption if a person loses or changes a job, moves from one area to another, becomes ill, or confronts a family crisis. A system of regional and corporate health alliances or purchasing groups would be established to purchase health care services for consumers. Regional health alliances would be the responsibility of the state, and corporate health alliances could be established by any large employer (more than 5,000 workers). Networks of doctors, hospitals, and insurers would provide coverage through contracts negotiated with regional or corporate health alliances. Table 4.9–5 outlines the provisions of the bill.

### National Health Board

A seven-member federal panel, appointed by the President, would oversee the states' creation of regional health alliances. It would have broad powers to set the guaranteed benefits package, enforce the national health care budget, and monitor the quality of medical services. It would also investigate the pricing of new drugs introduced by pharmaceutical companies if it suspected that prices were artificially inflated.

### Covered Health Services

Each health plan would provide coverage for the following categories of services: hospital care, emergency services, fees of doctors and other health professionals, pregnancy-related services, hospice and home health care, ambulances, outpatient laboratory tests, and prescription drugs. Free preventive care—including periodic medical examinations, immunizations, and mammograms—would be provided in accordance with a schedule set by the government. For example, periodic physical examinations would be given every three years for persons aged 20 to 39, every two years for those aged 40 to 65, and annually for those over age 65.

Persons enrolled in Medicare would continue in that program but could later join the regional alliances. Medicaid recipients would be enrolled in regional alliances and receive the standard package of benefits.

**Mental health and substance abuse.** Mental health services would be subject to significant limitations. There would be a limit of 30 inpatient days for each spell of illness, with a 60-day limit each year. A maximum of 30 outpatient psychotherapy sessions would be allowed each year, with the patient paying 50 percent of the cost.

**Exclusions.** The benefit package would not cover services that are decided to be not medically necessary or appropriate, private duty nursing, cosmetic orthodontic and other cosmetic surgery, hearing aids, adult eyeglasses, in vitro fertilization services, sex change surgery and related services (for example, hormone replacement therapy), or private room accommodations. Extended care services in a skilled nursing or rehabilitative facility would be provided only after an acute illness or injury.

**Payment.** The employer would pay 80 percent of the cost of the workers' package, with the workers paying the remaining 20 percent. The government would offer financial assistance to low-income and unemployed people and to small low-wage businesses. Families and individuals could pay their share of the premium directly or through withholding; alliances could require salary withholding to avoid bad debts. The self-employed and the unemployed would be responsible for the entire amount of the premium, unless they were eligible for assistance based on income. Retired workers under 65 would be responsible for 20 percent of the premium. Employers would pay for part-time workers on a prorated basis. Out-of-pocket costs would depend on the kind of service chosen. Alliances would be required to offer high-cost, low-cost, and combination plans. Those terms refer respectively to traditional fee-for-service coverage, HMOs, and preferred provider networks.

### Controlling Costs

The National Health Board would oversee the system and set a national health budget, with the goal of limiting

**Table 4.9–5**
**Provisions of American Health Security Bill**

## Funding

Employers: Employers would pay the bulk of the cost. The plan requires them to pay at least 80 percent of the average cost of the premiums in their region and to support family coverage for married workers.

Employees: Employees would contribute an average of 20 percent toward their own insurance premiums, plus any required deductibles and co-payments.

Self-employed workers and nonworkers: They would be required to buy insurance, paying the full cost of the premiums, unless they qualify for government subsidies. The cost would be fully tax-deductible for them.

Government: The federal government would subsidize the costs for many small and low-wage businesses and for those persons (such as part-time workers and unemployed persons) who have incomes less than 150 percent of the poverty-line income. Medicare payments would continue for elderly and disabled patients.

Medicaid: Medicaid would continue to pay for health care for the poor but through health alliances.

Large corporations: They would have the option to negotiate directly with insurers for their employees' coverage but would still be required to pay at least 80 percent of their employees' premiums.

Cost: The Clinton Administration initially estimates that the average plan cost would be $1,800 a year from an individual and $4,200 for a family, but the cost would vary by region of the country. Plans of any type would vary in price; people choosing costly plans would pay a higher share of the premiums. Plans could offer supplemental policies, covering such items as extra dental and mental health benefits; employers could choose to pay for those supplemental policies, or consumers could buy them with their own after-tax funds.

## Health Alliances

Access: All citizens and legal residents would be covered.

Cost: A health alliance would determine a target range for the average premiums charged by plans in its area. Plans would not be eligible if their charges were higher than that range.

Eligible plans: Health alliances would write a contract with any plan that met state requirements.

Options: Health alliances would offer a range of medical plans of three types: an HMO, a fee-for-service plan, and a combination of those two types. Patients could not be turned away unless a plan is oversubscribed.

Quality: Health alliances would publish information to help consumers compare the services and the medical performances of the various plans.

Size: Health alliance size would be based on population: therefore, the number of alliances in each state would vary. A large city would have one alliance.

Structure: Health alliance structure in each state would be determined by the state. A health alliance could function as a nonprofit corporation or as a state agency, but consumers and employers would have to be equally represented in the management of the alliance.

Corporate alliances: If employers decided to negotiate directly with insurers and form their own alliances, they would still have to offer the guaranteed benefits package and a choice of plans, although their employers might have fewer providers to choose from.

## Plans

HMO: A health maintenance organization (HMO) would be the least-expensive option. Patients would sign up with a health maintenance organization and consult only physicians affiliated with that organization. Subscribers would typically pay only $10 for an office visit. If they visited a physician who was not part of the HMO, the subscribers would pay 40 percent of that physician's bill.

Fee-for-service plan: A fee-for-service plan would be the most expensive option, offering the widest choice of doctors. Patients could see any physician they chose, but they would pay the deductibles ($200 for an individual and $400 for a family) and 20 percent of the cost of office visits and hospitalization, up to a limit of $1,500 for an individual and $3,000 for a family.

Combination plan: In a combination plan, the middle option, patients would sign up with a group for most of their care but would reserve the right to consult physicians outside the plan. Subscribers would pay 20 percent of the fee for those visits to outside physicians.

## Covered Benefits

Dental: Preventive dental care for children would be provided. Adult benefits would be phased in by the year 2000.

Medication: Prescription drugs would be covered.

Eye and ear care: Routine vision and hearing examinations would be covered. Eyeglasses would be covered only for children.

Extended care: Nursing homes and rehabilitation centers (as alternatives to hospital stays) would be covered for a maximum of 100 days each year.

Home care: As an alternative to hospitalization, home care would be covered. Home care for a patient would be reevaluated every 60 days.

Hospice care: Hospice care for terminally ill people would be covered.

Hospital stays: Semiprivate rooms would be covered. Private rooms would be covered only when medically necessary.

Mental health: Only 30 sessions of limited psychotherapy would be covered. Limited inpatient services and psychiatric hospital stays would be covered.

Office visits: Professional services, emergency care, and other outpatient hospital services would be covered. Laboratory tests and ambulance service would be covered.

Outpatient therapy: Physical, occupational, and speech therapy to restore skills lost because of illness or injury would be covered. The need for the therapy would be reevaluated every 60 days.

Preventive care: Immunizations, mammograms, Pap smears, prenatal care, and cholesterol screening would be covered.

Substance abuse: Limited outpatient and inpatient services for the treatment of substance abuse patients would be covered.

Exclusions: The plan would exclude services that are not medically necessary or appropriate, such as cosmetic orthodontia, hearing aids, contact lenses, sex-change surgery, and in vitro fertilization.

## Glossary of Health Care Terms

Employer mandate: The requirement that employers pay at least 80 percent of the cost of health coverage for their workers.

*Continued*

**Table 4.9–5**
*Continued*

Guaranteed national benefit package: The standard comprehensive coverage that all Americans would receive.

Health alliance: A purchasing group that would buy health care services for thousands of consumers. The alliances would be of two types: regional health alliances, whose creation would be the states' responsibility, and corporate health alliances. A corporate alliance could be established by any large employer (in general, one with more than 5,000 workers). Large employers would have the option of joining a regional alliance, instead of setting up a corporate alliance.

Health plan: A network of doctors, hospitals, and insurers that would provide coverage through contracts negotiated with regional and corporate alliances.

Managed competition: A policy that combines free-market forces with government regulation. Large groups of consumers would buy health care from networks of providers. The aim is to create business competition, thereby restraining prices and encouraging a high quality of care.

Medicaid: The existing federal-state program of health coverage for the poor would be folded into the health alliance system.

Medicare: The existing federal program of health coverage for elderly and disabled persons would continue. Under the Clinton plan, a state could apply to the federal government for permission to include Medicare beneficiaries in the alliance system, and a person who was already included in an alliance could remain in the alliance after turning 64.

National Health Board: A seven-member federal panel would be appointed by the President to oversee the states' regional heatlh alliances, interpret the guaranteed benefits package, enforce a national health care budget, monitor the quality of care, and investigate pharmaceutical companies' prices for new drugs if evidence indicated that the prices were unreasonably high.

National Health Security Card: An identification card would serve as proof of a person's eligibility for the government-guaranteed package of benefits. All citizens and legal aliens would be eligible for the card and the care.

Single-payer option: In the Clinton plan, a state would be allowed to enact a single-payer plan as an alternative to the system of regional health alliances. Under that alternative, the state would make direct payments to health care providers, with no intermediaries.

the rate of increase of health care spending to that of the general rate of inflation by 1999. If the competitive process did not reduce growth to that level, the board would impose mandatory limits on the growth of annual premiums, forcing health plans to spend less. When introducing the plan, the President would urge all sectors of the health care industry to limit price and spending increases to a specific amount not yet disclosed. Prices and spending would be monitored by the Secretary of Health and Human Services. The National Health Board would make public declarations about the costs of existing drugs it considers overpriced. It would have no authority to set drug prices. The rate of increase of Medicare and Medicaid payments would be reduced.

## Special Issues

**Underserved areas.** Rural and inner-city residents would get expanded services through various incentives, such as giving physicians who locate in such underserved

areas extra money (for example, $1,000 a month) during the first five years of practice.

**Medical schools.** The government would direct funding to medical schools that train 50 percent of their students to enter primary care, instead of specialties.

**Hospitals.** Hospitals would be forced to improve efficiency by cutting administrative costs. Most hospitals are dependent on federal programs, such as Medicare, for their revenue; if that spending were cut, hospital income would decrease.

**Timetable.** The states would have to establish alliances no later than January 1, 1998. All health plans would adopt a single standard claim form by January 1995.

## Implications

Physicians would be affected by the plan in various ways: (1) they would face increased monitoring of their work by outsiders—not necessarily other physicians—who would oversee their use of services (for example, labora-

**Table 4.9–6**
**Health Plan's Devilish Details: An article by Elisabeth McCaughey from *The Wall Street Journal***

The news from the White House wasn't adding up. An estimated 38 million uninsured Americans would be given health coverage, yet the only new tax would be on cigarettes. The nation would limit health care spending, but no one would sacrifice choice or quality. I felt uneasy about the missing pieces.

So I called the office of Sen. Harris Wofford (D., Pa) and asked for a copy of the Clinton health plan. I read it and reread it—all 239 pages plus charts—poring over the details, consulting doctors and health care experts, and shaking my head at how different the plan is from what we are hearing.

Here are the facts that surprised me, and that will probably trouble most people. . . .

•*Under the Clinton plan, most Americans will not be able to hold onto their personal physician or buy the kind of insurance that 77% of Americans now choose.* Such fee-for-service insurance allows them to pick a doctor, go to a specialist when they feel they need one, get a second opinion if they have doubts, and select the hospital they think is best.

The Clinton plan will make almost all Americans buy basic health coverage through the "regional alliance" where they live. Regional alliances are huge, government monopolies that will purchase basic health care for everyone in the area.

Alliance officials will negotiate benefit packages and prices with insurers and health maintenance organizations (HMOs)—groups of physicians and hospitals that provide total health

**Table 4.9–6**
*Continued*

care through cost-conscious methods to each consumer for a prepaid premium. Unless you now receive health care through Medicare, military or veterans benefits, or unless you or your spouse works for a large company, the law will require you to buy basic health coverage from the limited choices offered by your alliance. It will be illegal to buy it elsewhere. . . .

Under the plan, the federal government will set ceilings on how much each regional alliance can spend on payments to insurers and HMOs annually. The goal is to limit private health care spending. Alliances can reject any health insurance option that would push spending through the ceiling. Fee-for-service insurance, which tends to be more costly than HMO coverage, will be the first to go. . . .

In addition, an alliance cannot offer any plan that costs 20% more than the average price of all plans it offers. . . . Plans with added benefits (such as Pap smears every year instead of every third year) and many fee-for-service plans will be excluded by the 20% rule. A primary goal of the Clinton plan is to eliminate a two-tier health care system, where people who can pay more for medical care will receive more. The plan mandates "care based only on differences of need.". . .

Annual ceilings and the 20% rule will make it virtually impossible for some alliances to offer choose-your-own-doctor health insurance. Americans have been told that they will always have the option to buy fee-for-service insurance. But the plan says that, with a waiver from the National Health Board, alliances can exclude all fee-for-service plans, effectively forcing million of citizens to join an HMO. . . .

Where a fee-for-service plan is offered, an alliance can impose a costly surcharge that will discourage consumers from choosing it. . . . Another rule, "community rating," requires insurers to offer the same basic package to everyone in the region for the same price. . . . Smokers and nonsmokers, drug abusers and nonusers pay the same. Community rating means that the sick are not thrown overboard, but it also makes those who adopt healthy behavior subsidize those who do not, and it pushes fee-for-service insurance out of reach of many Americans who now can afford it.

•*It will be hard to buy additional insurance.* The basic benefit package is skimpy in some areas. But because of the community rating rule, insurers must offer supplemental policies to every person in a region at the same price. . . . High risk individuals will line up, but insurers will not. Cara Walinsky of the Health Care Advisory Board and Governance Committee, which advises 800 hospitals world-wide, explains that the plan "will make it as difficult as possible for you to buy more" than the standard package.

•*Seeing a specialist and paying for it out-of-pocket will be almost impossible.* Few doctors will be practicing outside HMOs. The Clinton proposal is designed to drive doctors out of private practice. The plan has "very strong incentives built in that work against fee-for-service, not only on the consumer side, but also on the provider side," explains Ms. Walinsky. Even Drs. David Himmelstein and Steffe Woolhandler, leading proponents of a Canadian-style single-payer system, warn that the plan will "obliterate private practice."

•*Price controls will make private practice unfeasible.* Americans have been told that there are no price controls. But the plan empowers alliances to set fees for doctors seeing patients on a fee-for-service basis. The plan states: "A provider may not charge or collect from a patient a fee in excess of the fee schedule adopted by an alliance.". . .

•*Americans have been told that the quality of health care will not decline. Many experts believe it will.* In HMOs, gatekeepers, or primary care physicians, tightly limit patient use of specialists. Physician-subscriber ratios at HMOs average 1 to 800, half the ratio of physicians to the nation's population. Under the plan, pressure on gatekeepers to curb

access to specialists will increase. Ms. Walinsky predicts that above a threshold level of "reasonable quality," alliances will choose HMOs based on lowest cost, not highest quality, in order to meet federal spending limits.

A parent lying awake, worried about a child's illness and whether the gatekeeper will OK a specialist, might think about bribes or even going outside the system. The Clinton Plan anticipates the problem, with new criminal penalties for "payment of bribes or gratuities to influence the delivery of health service.". . . Doctors, meanwhile, joke about "offshore" practices, hospital ships outside the three-mile limit, and other ways for families to escape controls and buy the health care they want.

•*The plan also takes away from HMO users the legal protection many state lawmakers believe they should have.* Some states have passed "any willing provider" laws to prevent HMOs from arbitrarily excluding hospitals, pharmacies, or physicians from their networks. HMOs have protested that these laws hobble cost containment. The Clinton administration apparently agrees. The plan preempts state laws protecting consumer choice. . . .

•*The plan's biggest surprise is who bears the cost of universal health coverage.* The plan requires states to create health alliance regions—similar to election districts. How those alliance lines are drawn will determine which areas of the state are hit with the highest health care premiums, because they are shouldering the costs of health coverage for the inner city poor. The system promises to pit black against white, poor against rich, city against suburb.

The average treatment cost of a baby born addicted to drugs is $63,000. Because of community rating, anyone who lives in an urban alliance is going to pay high premiums, regardless of his health or behavior. Part of the premium covers his own care; part is a hidden tax to provide universal health coverage within the alliance. Some alliances will bear especially heavy social burdens, others will not. Everyone will figure out that you get more health care for your dollar or pay lower premiums in an alliance without inner city problems. The plan will be an incentive for employers to abandon cities and relocate.

Considering the number of court battles when states draw election districts, lawsuits over "medical gerrymandering" are inevitable. The plan sets out rules that will be dissected in courtrooms across the nation: States may not "concentrate racial or ethnic minority groups, socio-economic groups, or Medicaid beneficiaries," and may not "subdivide a primary metropolitan statistical area." An alliance drawn to include a city and its surrounding suburbs will be considered in compliance. . . . Home prices and litigation fees will rise and fall depending on which suburbs are sucked into a metropolitan alliance and which escape.

Suppose a state fails to establish its regional alliances on time, or to meet all federal requirements? The plan empowers the secretary of the Treasury to "impose a payroll tax on all employers in the state. The payroll tax shall be sufficient to allow the federal government to provide health coverage to all individuals . . . and to reimburse the federal government for the costs of monitoring and operating the state system.". . . The plan does not set any limits on this tax.

The Clinton plan is coercive. It takes personal health choices away from patients and families, and it also imposes a system of financing health care based on regional alliances that will make racial tensions fester and produce mean-spirited political struggles and lawsuits to shift the cost of medical care for the urban poor.

Members of Congress should read the 239-page draft, rather than relying on what they hear, and then turn their attention to alternative proposals that aim to provide universal coverage while avoiding the devastating consequences of the Clinton health plan.

Table from Elisabeth McCaughey: Health plan's devilish details, Wall Street J, October 20, 1993. Used with permission.

tory tests). Most physicians would join HMOs or other groups of physicians and enter into formal arrangements with hospitals or health networks. Doctors have prized autonomy in decision making, and the plan would affect that process. *The Wall Street Journal* (September 15, 1993) criticized the Clinton plan, which it described as a huge new bureaucracy that is overpriced and underfinanced. The newspaper reflected the position held by many physicians that not enough input was obtained from specialists who expressed disagreement. In particular, few physicians in practice were consulted.

As Edward F. X. Hughes, a physician and the director of the Center for Health Services and Policy Research at Northwestern University, Evanston, Illinois, was reported to have said (*The Wall Street Journal,* September 13, 1993), "it has to translate in a very short time into a problem of physician morale. There's nothing in the organizational literature that says a successful enterprise runs well with unhappy workers." Further criticisms of the plan are discussed in Table 4.9–6.

The American Health Security Bill was presented to Congress in October 1993. It must be approved by Congress before becoming law. Such approval is subject to substantial negotiation, change, and compromise. The full effects of the plan may not be implemented for many years.

## References

Bennett M J: The greening of the HMO: Implications for prepaid psychiatry. Am J Psychiatry *145:* 1544, 1988.

Bureau of the Census: *National Data Book and Guide to Sources: Statistical Abstracts of the United States,* ed 106. U S Department of Commerce, Washington, 1986.

Center for Health Policy Research (American Medical Association): *Socioeconomic Characteristics of Medical Practice, 1987.* Center for Health Policy Research, Chicago, 1987.

Chang R S, editor: *Preventive Health Care.* Hall, Boston, 1981.

Chollet D: *Uninsured in the United States: The Nonelderly Population Without Health Insurance.* Employee Benefit Research Institute, Washington, 1987.

Dallek G, Hurwit C, Golde M: *Insuring the Uninsured: Options for State Action.* Americans for Health and Citizen Action, Washington, 1987.

Enthoven A, Kronick R: A consumer-choice health plan for the 1990s: Universal health insurance in a system designed to promote quality and economy. N Engl J Med *320:* 29, 1989.

Flaskerud J H, Hu L: Racial-ethnic identity and amount and type of psychiatric treatment. Am J Psychiatry *149:* 379, 1992.

Freiman M P, Mitchell J B, Rosenbach M L: An analysis of DRG-based reimbursement for psychiatric admissions to general hospitals. Am J Psychiatry *144:* 603, 1987.

Freis J R: Aging, natural death, and the compression of morbidity. N Engl J Med *303:* 130, 1980.

Gonzalez M L, editor: *Socioeconomic Characteristics of Medical Practice 1992.* American Medical Association, Chicago, 1992.

Haddon W, Barker S P: Injury control. In *Preventive and Community Medicare,* D Clark, B MacMahon, editors, p 188. Little, Brown, Boston, 1981.

Health Insurance Institute: *Source Book of Health Insurance Data.* Health Insurance Institute, New York, 1989.

Himmelstein D U, Woolhandler S: A national health program for the United States: A physicians' proposal. N Engl J Med *320:* 102, 1989.

Iglehart J K: The new era of prospective payment for hospitals. N Engl J Med *307:* 1288, 1982.

Mitchell J B, Dickey B, Liptzin B, Sederer L I: Bringing psychiatric patients into the Medicare prospective payment system: Alternative to DRGs. Am J Psychiatry *144:* 610, 1987.

National Center for Health Statistics: *Health, United States, 1991.* Public Health Service, Hyattsville, Md, 1992.

Steven R S, Epstein A M: Institutional responses to prospective payment based on diagnostic-related groups. N Engl J Med *312:* 621, 1985.

Wennberg J E, McPherson K, Caper P: Will payment based on diagnostic-related groups control hospital costs? N Engl J Med *311:* 295, 1984.

# Psychology and Psychiatry: Psychometric and Neuropsychological Testing

## 5.1 / Psychological Testing of Intelligence and Personality

Formal psychological testing of intelligence and personality plays an integral role in clinical practice. Personality assessment provides information on patients' strengths and weaknesses, on how and why they are in their current situations, and on their prognoses. Valuable information regarding diagnosis may result from a thorough personality evaluation. It may also help in assessing the progress that patients make over the course of psychotherapy or other treatment programs.

Most of the commonly used assessment instruments are standardized against normal controls, who are required to respond to the same stimuli or set of questions. The responses are tabulated into a normal distribution pattern against which new subjects are compared. When responses are limited—that is, when the subject is required to answer in some fixed response pattern (for example, yes or no, true or false)—standardization is used to make sure that any variability that occurs is in the subject and not in the test.

With standardization, test administration and scoring are invariant across time and examiners. Related to the standardization of any test are the available data that presumably show whether the test is valid and reliable. Reliability assesses the reproducibility of results; validity assesses whether the test measures what it purports to measure.

### CLASSIFICATION OF TESTS

#### Objective Tests

Objective tests are typically pencil-and-paper tests based on specific items and questions. They yield numerical scores and profiles easily subjected to mathematical or statistical analysis. An example is the Minnesota Multiphasic Personality Inventory (MMPI).

#### Projective Tests

Projective tests present stimuli whose meanings are not immediately obvious; that is, some degree of ambiguity forces persons to project their own needs into the test situation. The projective tests presumably have no right or wrong answers. The persons being tested must give meaning to the stimulus in accordance with their inner needs, drives, abilities, and defenses. Examples include the Thematic Apperception Test (TAT), the Draw-a-Person test, the Rorschach test, and the Sentence Completion Test.

#### Individual or Group Tests

Tests may be administered individually or given simultaneously to a group. Individual testing has the advantage of providing an opportunity for the examiner to evaluate rapport and motivational factors and to observe and record the person's behavior during testing. Careful timing of responses is also possible. Group tests, however, are usually easily administered and scored.

#### Battery Tests

A number of individual tests used together make up a psychological or neuropsychological battery. The test battery can give more information about various areas of function than can an individual test and can increase the level of confidence if there is a positive correlation between them. The Halstead-Reitan is an example of a test battery.

### INTELLIGENCE TESTING

*Intelligence* can be defined as a person's ability to assimilate factual knowledge, to recall either recent or remote events, to reason logically, to manipulate concepts (either numbers or words), to translate the abstract to the literal and the literal to the abstract, to analyze and synthesize forms, and to deal meaningfully and accurately with problems and priorities deemed important in a particular setting. There are tremendous individual differences in intelligence.

In 1905 Alfred Binet introduced the concept of the mental age (M.A.), which is the average intellectual level of a particular age. The intelligence quotient (I.Q.) is the ratio of M.A. over C.A. (chronological age) multiplied by

100 to do away with the decimal point; it is represented by the following equation:

$$I.Q. = \frac{M.A.}{C.A.} \times 100$$

When chronological and mental ages are equal, the I.Q. is 100—that is, average. Since it is impossible to measure increments of intellectual power past the age of 15 by available intelligence tests, the highest divisor in the I.Q. formula is 15. One way of expressing the relative standing of a person within a group is by percentile. The higher the percentile, the higher one's rank within a group. An I.Q. of 100 corresponds to the 50th percentile in intellectual ability for the general population.

As measured by most intelligence tests, I.Q. is an interpretation or a classification of a total test score in relation to norms established by a group. I.Q. is a measure of present functioning ability, not necessarily of future potential. Although under ordinary circumstances the I.Q. is stable throughout life, there is no absolute certainty about its predictive properties. A person's I.Q. must be examined in the light of past experiences and future opportunities.

The I.Q. itself is no indicator of the origins of its reflected capacities, genetic (innate) or environmental. The most useful intelligence test must measure a variety of skills and abilities, including verbal and performance, early learned and recently learned, timed and untimed, culture-free and culture-bound. No intelligence test is totally culture-free, although tests do differ significantly in degree.

## Wechsler Adult Intelligence Scale (WAIS)

The Wechsler Adult Intelligence Scale (WAIS) is the best standardized and most widely used intelligence test in clinical practice today. It was constructed by David Wechsler at New York University Medical Center and Bellevue Psychiatric Hospital.

Designed in 1939, the original WAIS has gone through several revisions. A scale for children ages 5 through 15 years has been devised (WISC—Wechsler Intelligence Scale for Children) and a scale for children ages 4 to 6½ years (WPPSI—Wechsler Preschool and Primary Scale of Intelligence). In practice, the WAIS, WISC, or WPPSI is used as part of a battery of psychological tests. A revised version of the WAIS (WAIS-R) was constructed in 1981, and it has been translated for use with Spanish-speaking persons. A revised version of the WISC (WISC-R) has also been constructed.

The WAIS comprises 11 subtests made up of six verbal subtests and five performance subtests, yielding a verbal I.Q., a performance I.Q., and a combined or full-scale I.Q.. Intelligence levels are based on the assumption that intellectual abilities are normally distributed (in a bell-shaped curve) throughout the population (Figure 5.1–1). Verbal and performance I.Q.s and the full-scale I.Q. are determined by the use of separate tables for each of the seven age groups (from 16 to 64 years) on which the test was standardized. Variability in functioning is revealed through discrepancies between verbal and performance I.Q.s and by the scatter pattern between subtests.

**Construction of the test.** The following subtests are described in the order in which they are presented to the subject.

VERBAL

*Information.* This subtest covers general information and general knowledge and is subject to cultural variables. Persons from low socioeconomic groups with little schooling do not perform as well as those from high socioeconomic groups with more schooling.

*Comprehension.* This subtest measures the subject's ability to adhere to social conventions and to understand social judgment by asking about proverbs and how one ought to behave under certain circumstances.

*Arithmetic.* The ability to do arithmetic and other simple calculations is reflected on this subtest, which is adversely influenced by anxiety and poor attention and concentration.

*Similarities.* This subtest covers the ability to abstract by asking subjects to explain the similarity between two things. It is a sensitive indicator of intelligence.

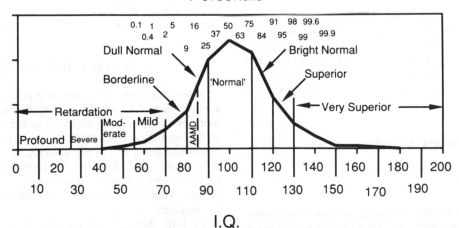

**Figure 5.1–1.** The distribution of Wechsler Adult Intelligence Scale I.Q. categories. (Figure adapted from J D Matarazzo: *Wechsler's Measurement and Appraisal of Adult Intelligence,* ed 5, p 124. Oxford University Press, New York, 1972. Used with permission.)

*Digit span.* Immediate retention is measured in this subtest. The subject is asked to learn a series of two to nine digits, which are immediately recalled both forward and backward. Anxiety, poor attention span, and brain dysfunction interfere with recall.

*Vocabulary.* The subject is asked to define 35 vocabulary words of increasing difficulty. Intelligence has a high correlation with vocabulary, which is related to level of education. Idiosyncratic definitions of words may give clues to personality structure.

PERFORMANCE

*Picture completion.* This subtest initiates the performance part of the WAIS and consists of completing a picture that is missing a part. Visuoperceptive defects become evident when mistakes are made.

*Block design.* This subtest requires the subject to match colored blocks and visual designs. Brain dysfunction involving impairment of left-right dominance interferes with performance.

*Picture arrangement.* The subject is required to arrange a series of pictures in a sequence that tells a story (for example, a person committing a crime). In addition to testing performance, this subtest provides data about the subject's cognitive style.

*Object assembly.* The subject has to assemble objects, such as the figure of a woman or an animal, in their proper order and organization. Visuoperception, somatoperception, and manual dexterity are tested.

*Digit symbol.* In this final subtest of the WAIS, the subject is given a code that pairs symbols with digits. The test consists of matching a series of digits to their corresponding symbols in as little time as possible.

**Distribution of I.Q. scores.** The average or normal range of I.Q. is 90 to 110; I.Q. scores of at least 120 are considered superior (Table 5.1–1). According to the American Association of Mental Deficiency (AAMD) and the fourth edition of *Diagnostic and Statistical Manual of Mental Disorders* (DSM-IV), mental retardation is defined as an I.Q. of less than 70, which corresponds to the lowest 2.2 percent of the population. Consequently, 2 out of every 100 persons have I.Q. scores consistent with mental deficiency, which can range from mild to profound.

**Interpretation of I.Q. scores.** The reliability of the WAIS is very high. Retesting of persons 18 years and older rarely reveals changes in I.Q. scores.

The verbal scale of the I.Q. measures the retention of previously acquired factual information, and the performance scale measures visuospatial capacity and visuomotor speed in problem-solving tasks. The performance scale is more sensitive to normal aging than is the verbal scale, which is more sensitive to education. Arithmetic and memory for digits are adversely affected by anxiety. A disparity between the verbal test and the performance test (usually greater than 15 points) may indicate psychopathology and requires further testing.

### Stanford-Binet Test

Lewis Terman at Stanford University devised the Stanford-Binet Test in 1916. It is a comprehensive intelligence test that is used in psychiatry and education. The WAIS, however, is more widely used that the Stanford-Binet.

## ADULT PERSONALITY ASSESSMENT

### Objective Personality Assessment

The objective approach to personality assessment is characterized by the reliance on structured, standardized measurement devices, which are typically of a self-report nature. "Structured" reflects the tendency to use straightforward test stimuli, such as direct questions regarding the persons' opinions of themselves, and unambiguous instructions regarding the completion of the test.

*Response sets* are attitudes or styles in responding to personality questionnaires. For the most part, the sets appear to be problematic with objective inventories; however, they are also potential error sources with projective and behavioral assessments. A socially desirable response set is indicative of persons who attempt to present themselves in a favorable light. Conversely, "faking bad" indicates an opposite response set; that is, persons attempt to present a more dismal outlook than is the case. Some of the well-constructed objective personality measures, such as the Minnesota Multiphasic Personality Inventory (MMPI) and the California Personality Inventory (CPI), have built-in scales designed to detect the presence of those types of response sets.

Table 5.1–2 lists some popular objective tests of personality.

**Minnesota Multiphasic Personality Inventory (MMPI).** The Minnesota Multiphasic Personality Inventory (MMPI) is a self-report inventory that is the most widely used and most thoroughly researched of the objective personality assessment instruments. It was developed in 1937 by Starke Hathaway, a psychologist, and J. Charnley McKinley, a psychiatrist. The test was recently updated and is called the MMPI-2. The test consists of over 500 statements—such as, "I worry about sex matters," "I sometimes tease animals," "I believe I am being plotted against"—to which the subject must respond with "true," "false," or "cannot say." The test may be used in card or booklet form, and several programs exist to process the responses by computer.

The MMPI gives scores on 10 standard clinical scales, each of which was derived empirically (that is, homogeneous criterion groups of psychiatric patients were used in developing the scales). The items for each scale were selected for their ability to separate medical and psychiatric patients from normal controls.

**Table 5.1–1**
**Classification of Intelligence by I.Q. Range**

| Classification | I.Q. Range |
|---|---|
| Profound mental retardation (MR)^ | Below 20 or 25 |
| Severe MR^ | 20–25 to 35–40 |
| Moderate MR* | 35–40 to 50–55 |
| Mild MR^ | 50–55 to about 70 |
| Borderline | 70–79 |
| Dull normal | 80 to 90 |
| Normal | 90 to 110 |
| Bright normal | 110 to 120 |
| Superior | 120 to 130 |
| Very superior | 130 and above |

^According to the fourth edition of *Diagnostic and Statistical Manual of Mental Disorders* (DSM-IV).

**Table 5.1–2**
**Objective Measures of Personality**

| Name | Description | Strengths | Weaknesses |
|---|---|---|---|
| Minnesota Multiphasic Personality Inventory (MMPI) | Over 500 items, true-false; self-report format; 17 scales (numerous special scales) | Provides wide range of data on numerous personality variables; strong research base | Tends to emphasize major psychopathology |
| Millon Clinical Multiaxial Inventory (MCMI) | 175 items, true-false; self-report format; 20 scales | Brief administration time; corresponds well with DMS-III-R diagnostic classifications | In need of more validation research; no information on disorder severity |
| 16 Personality Factor Questionnaire (16 PF) | True-false; self-report format; 16 personality dimensions | Sophisticated psychometric instrument with considerable research conducted on nonclinical population | Limited usefulness with clinical populations |
| California Personality Inventory (CPI) | True-false; self-report format; 17 scales | Well-accepted method of assessing patients who do not present with major psychopathology | Limited usefulness with clinical populations |
| Jackson Personality Inventory (JPI) | True-false; self-report format; 15 personality scales | Constructed in accord with sophisticated psychometric techniques; controls for response sets | Unproved usefulness in clinical settings |
| Edwards Personal Preference Schedule (EPPS) | Forced choice; self-report format | Follows Murray's theory of personology; accounts for social desirability | Not widely used clinically because of restricted nature of information obtained |
| Beck Depression Inventory (BDI) | Self-report on Likert-type format; measures depression | Follows Beck's theory of depression; widely used | Assesses mood and thought well but inadequate on neurovegetative symptoms |
| State-Trait Anxiety Inventory (STAI) | Self-report on Likert-type format; measures anxiety | Allows for differentiation of state and trait anxiety; well researched | STAI items are transparent |
| Psychological Screening Inventory (PSI) | 130 items, true-false; self-report format | Produces 4 scores, which can be used as screening measures on the possiblity of a need for psychological help | The scales are short and have correspondingly low reliability |
| Eysenck Personality Questionnaire (EPQ) or Inventory (EPI) | True-false; self-report format | Useful as a screening device; test has a theoretical basis with research support | Scales are short, and items are transparent as to purpose; not recommended for other than a screening device |
| Adjective Checklist (ACL) | True-false; self-report or informant report | Can be used for self or other rating | Scores rarely correlate highly with conventional personality inventories |
| Comrey Personality Scales (CPS) | True-false; self-report format; 8 scales | Factor analytic techniques used with a high degree of sophistication in test construction | Not widely used; factor analytic interpretation problems |
| Tennessee Self-Concept Scale (TSCS) | 100 items; true-false; self-report format; 14 scales | Brief administration time yields considerable information | Brevity is also a disadvantage, lowering reliability and validity; useful as a screening device only |

Table by Robert W. Butler, Ph.D., and Paul Satz, Ph.D.

CLINICAL SCALES. The clinical scales are numbered and are often referred to by number, rather than by name, particularly in coding deviantly high scores. A high score on a particular scale does not mean that the person has that illness. For example, an elevated 8 (Sc) score does not indicate that the patient is necessarily schizophrenic.

The scales are listed in Table 5.1–3.

INTERPRETATION. An accurate interpretation requires great experience with the test and some understanding of the social, educational, and socioeconomic background from which the patient comes. Recent evidence indicates that religion and race are both potential variables in MMPI responses.

Although the MMPI was initially viewed as a diagnostic aid (that is, a patient with major depressive disorder would show an elevation on the depression scale), the advantages of a configural approach to interpretation quickly became apparent. The configural approach, which involves interpretations based on the patterning of the entire profile, has become the preferred method and has increased the effectiveness of the MMPI as a personality measurement device. Various researchers have identified numerous personality correlates of

various MMPI scale configurations, frequently using the two highest scales as the basis for core interpretive statements. Actuarial research of that nature has also served as the basis for computerized interpretative services. Those services, although not a substitute for a comprehensive personality evaluation, can assist the clinician in hypothesis formulation. Computerized services are especially useful when the MMPI is to be interpreted by a person knowledgeable in all aspects of the MMPI and the nature of the development of the computerized program. The blind use of those services by professionals not trained in the use of the MMPI is clearly inappropriate and, perhaps, even unethical.

The fact that the MMPI is the most widely used and researched psychological personality measurement device is undoubtedly one of its major strengths. Several hundred research papers on the MMPI appear in the literature each year, and it has been used extensively in cross-cultural clinical and research applications. The huge body of literature generated has resulted in a catalog of MMPI correlates on a wide variety of clinical cases, providing descriptive, predictive, diagnostic, and prognostic information. Another strength of the MMPI is its atheoretical nature, a characteristic that probably in-

**Table 5.1–3**
**MMPI Validity and Clinical Scales**

**Validity**

**L: Lie Scale** A nonempirically derived social desirability scale. Items tend to reflect behaviors that are considered socially desirable but rarely practiced. The score can suggest defensiveness, illiteracy, psychosis, or personality processes, depending on various factors.

**F: Infrequency Scale** Measures a tendency to endorse selected items that are statistically rare responses (less than 10 percent of the original normal sample). Useful in identifying illiteracy, malingering, panic, confusion, psychosis, and personality processes.

**K: Suppressor Scale** Used to adjust mathematically certain clinical scales to decrease false positives and false negatives. The scale is also useful in determining overall test-taking attitude and is an indication of personality variables.

**Clinical**

**1: Hypochondriasis** Reflects somatic concerns and preoccupation with bodily functioning. Interpretation needs to take into account such factors as age and actual health status. As with all MMPI scales, interpretation is furthered by looking at its relation to other scales.

**2: Depression** Tends to reflect depression as a mood disorder. The fact that the scale is sensitive to situational variables suggests that it may be a good index of state personality status.

**3: Hysteria** Involves the identification of classic histrionic symptoms, including the presence of physical symptoms coupled with indifference, denial, repression, and inhibition. The scale does not necessarily measure other popularly conceived traits, such as lability and melodramatic attitude.

**4: Psychopathic Deviance** Developed to assess the amorality and asociality aspects of psychopathy, rather than the criminal or antisocial. Its meaning depends on other scale configurations. The scale provides good information on the quality of interpersonal relationships.

**5: Masculinity-Femininity** Originally developed to identify homosexuality but rarely used for that purpose, although it does provide information on gender identity. The scale reflects a variety of personality and interest areas, such as dependence, sensitivity, intellectuality, and tendencies toward introspection.

**6: Paranoia** Developed by the empirical identification of classic paranoiacs, assesses vigilance, sensitivity, delusional thought, distrust, and suspicion. Except for the paranoid areas, the members of the original criterion group were considered functional in their lives.

**7: Psychasthenia** A diverse scale designed to measure anxiety and obsessive-compulsive traits. Endorsed items can reflect fear, obsessive-compulsive symptoms, interpersonal hostility, tension, specific phobias, and impaired concentration.

**8: Schizophrenia** Reflects the acute positive symptoms of psychotic breaks with reality, rather than the chronic negative symptoms. The scale also assesses alienation, impaired self-identity, and isolation.

**9: Hypomania** Measures the classic symptoms of mania, including elated and unstable mood, psychomotor excitement, and flight of ideas. It also appears to reflect narcissistic personality traits. In general, the scale provides information on the degree of drivenness of the person's personality characteristics. It has a strong age component.

**10: Social Introversion** Provides information on social withdrawal, shyness, leadership, talkativeness, levels of gregariousness, and, to a small degree, self-concept and neurotic tendencies. It is more two-dimensional and bipolar (introversion versus extroversion) than the other scales.

**Special**

**A: Anxiety** The first general factor extracted from factor analytic studies on the MMPI. It is thought to reflect generalized endorsement of psychopathology.

**R: Repression** The second factor that is found on factor analytic studies of the MMPI. It can be conceptualized as measuring the tendency to engage in denial.

**ES: Ego Strength** Provides an index of how functional the patient may be in terms of work and other social areas, regardless of level of psychopathology.

**MAC: MacAndrews Alcoholism Scale** Estimates the person's degree of addiction proneness, especially with alcohol, opiates, and opioids. It is especially sensitive to daily substance abuse, rather than episodic abuse.

Table produced by Robert W. Butler, Ph.D., and Paul Satz, Ph.D., with the assistance of Alex Caldwell, Ph.D.

creases its usefulness over a broad spectrum. The presence of validity scales designed to assess test-taking attitude, in addition to clinical and personality information, is a distinct advantage that the MMPI maintains over many personality assessment tools.

The MMPI has been restandardized on the basis of a contemporary sample of normal people. Questions and language have been updated to reflect current cultural views.

**Millon Clinical Multiaxial Inventory (MCMI).** The Millon Clinical Multiaxial Inventory (MCMI) is a 175-item, true-false, paper-and-pencil personality inventory that was developed by Theodore Millon and his co-workers in the late 1970s. The original test allowed for scoring and interpretation on 11 scales, which represented personality disorders from the third edition of the American Psychiatric Association's *Diagnostic and Statistical Manual of Mental Disorders* (DSM-III). The test also contained a brief validity scale and nine scales designed to assess reactive symptom disorders, which the test authors claimed were of a less enduring nature than the personality scales. The scales are described in detail in Table 5.1–4.

The MCMI was revised in 1987; the new version is the MCMI-II. Item content was reevaluated for the MCMI-II, and new validity scales were added. Normative data were enhanced by the addition of clinical samples, and the MCMI-II is compatible with the revised third edition of DSM (DSM-III-R) but not necessarily with the fourth edition (DSM-IV).

**Type A-type B behavior.** Two cardiologists, Meyer Friedman and Ray Rosenman, developed the concept that a specific behavior pattern, type A, sets into motion the pathophysiology necessary for the production of coronary artery disease. They further hypothesized that the type A behavior pattern is a major risk factor (along with cholesterol, hypertension, smoking, and a positive family history) for the disease.

According to Friedman, the most important aspects of the type A behavior pattern are excesses of time urgency and competitive hostility (Table 5.1–5). Persons designated as type B display obverse qualities of behavior. They are relaxed, less aggressive, unhurried, and less apt to strive vigorously to achieve a goal than are type A persons. Although one might expect type A persons to be more successful than type B persons, that is not the case. In fact, some data indicate that type A persons are less successful than type B persons, despite the ardent desire of type A persons to achieve.

**Eysenck Personality Inventory.** Developed by Hans Eysenck, this self-assessment personality scale measures emotionality versus stability, extroversion versus introversion, tough-mindedness, sociability, and a tendency by some subjects to fake good answers (comparably to the Lie Scale on the MMPI). Eysenck introduced the concept of psychotocism, which is an underlying personality trait present in varying degrees in all persons. If present to a marked degree, it predisposes a person to the development of a psychiatric disorder.

**Table 5.1–4**
**MCMI Clinical Scales**

**Personality Disorders (Axis II)**
**Scale 1: Schizoid** Assesses the probability (as do the other scales of the MCMI) that a person meets DSM-III diagnostic criteria for schizoid personality disorder. The symptoms include indifference, insensitivity, affect deficit, and apathy.
**Scale 2: Avoidant** Includes the measurement of characteristics of dysphoria, alienation, aversion to interpersonal behavior, and hypersensitivity.
**Scale 3: Dependent** Assesses trait characteristics of docility, submissiveness, initiation difficulties, poor self-image, and naivete.
**Scale 4: Histrionic** Assesses lability of affect, sociability, seductiveness, immaturity, inability to delay immediate need gratification, and a dissociative cognitive style.
**Scale 5: Narcissistic** Measures the presence of inflated self-image, exploitiveness, expansive thinking, imperturbability, and deficits in social conscience.
**Scale 6: Antisocial (Aggressive)** Assesses hostile affect, vindictiveness, power-oriented life-style, malevolence, poor impulse control, and an inability to benefit from punishment.
**Scale 7: Compulsive** Assesses restrained affect, conscientiousness, adherence to social conventions, conforming, cognitive constriction, and behavioral rigidity.
**Scale 8: Passive-Aggressive** Assesses labile affect, contrariness, disillusionment, interpersonal ambivalence, and a discontented self-image.
**Scale S: Schizotypal** Assesses the presence of social detachment, eccentricity, nondelusional autistic thinking, depersonalization, emptiness, emotional flatness, and anxious wariness.
**Scale C: Borderline** Assesses intense moodiness, dysregulated activation, self-destructive behavior, dependence anxiety, and ambivalence between thought-affect and action.

**Scale P: Paranoid** Measures the enduring traits of vigilant mistrust, distorted thought, criticalness, and provocative interpersonal behavior.
**Clinical Syndromes (Axis I)**
**Scale A: Anxiety** Assesses apprehension, phobias, tension, indecision, and psychophysiological symptoms.
**Scale H: Somatoform** Assesses the degree to which psychological conflict is likely to be channeled physically and overall preoccupation with health.
**Scale N: Hypomanic** Measures the presence of unstable mood, restlessness, overactivity, pressured speech, impulsiveness, irritability, and other manic-type behavior.
**Scale D: Dysthymia** Assesses despondence, guilt, discouragement, futility, and other symptoms of depression. The scale does not necessarily reflect extreme severity and, instead, implies preserved ego strength.
**Scale B: Alcohol Abuse** Provides a probability index for the presence of history of alcohol abuse.
**Scale T: Drug Abuse** Extends Scale B to include substance abuse in general and also implies poor impulse control and unconventionality.
**Scale SS: Psychotic Thinking** Assesses disorganized-regressed behavior, hallucinatory experiences, delusions, and inappropriate affect.
**Scale CC: Psychotic Depression** Assesses the presence of severe depression that is usually of incapacitating proportions.
**Scale PP: Psychotic Delusions** Assesses delusions, usually persecutory or grandiose in nature. Accompanying belligerency is common.

Table produced by Robert W. Butler, Ph.D., and Paul Satz, Ph.D., with the assistance and permission of Theodore Millon, Ph.D.

**Table 5.1–5**
**Diagnostic Indicators of Type A Behavior**

| Time Urgency | Excessive Competitiveness and Hostility |
|---|---|
| Psychomotor manifestations<br>  Characteristic facial tautness expressing tension<br>  Rapid horizontal eyeball movements during ordinary conversation<br>  Rapid eye blinking (more than 40 blinks a minute)<br>  Knee jiggling or rapid vigorous tapping of fingers<br>  Rapid, frequently dysrhythmic speech involving elimination of terminal words of sentences<br>  Lip clicking during ordinary speaking<br>  Rapid ticlike eyebrow lifting<br>  Head nodding when speaking<br>  Sucking in of air during speech<br>  Humming (tuneless)<br>  Speech hurrying<br>  Tense posture<br>  Motorization accompanying responses<br>  Expiratory sighing<br>  Rapid body movements<br>Direct behavior tests<br>  The interviewer, in posing a question whose answer is already clear from its content, hesitates, becomes laboriously tedious or repetitive, and then stammers. The subject interrupts the stammering with the answer.<br>Physiological indicators<br>  Periorbital pigmentation<br>  Excessive forehead and upper lip perspiration<br>Significant biographical content<br>  Self-awareness of presence of type A behavior<br>  Polyphasic activities, e.g. reads while driving, reads while using electric shaver, and thinks of other matters during conversation with others<br>  Walks fast, eats fast, and does not dawdle at table<br>  Person makes fetish of always being on time under all circumstances | Has been told by spouse to slow down in working and living habits<br>Difficulty in sitting and doing nothing<br>Person habitually substitutes numerals for metaphors in speech<br>Psychomotor manifestations<br>  Characteristic facial set exhibiting aggression and hostility (eye and jaw muscles)<br>  Characteristic ticlike drawing back of corners of lips, almost exposing teeth<br>  Hostile, jarring laugh<br>  Use of clenched fist and table pounding or excessively forceful use of hands and fingers<br>  Explosive, staccato, frequently unpleasant voice<br>  Frequent use of obscenity<br>  Person exhibits irritation and rage when asked about some past event in which he or she became angered<br>Direct behavior tests<br>  The interviewer directly challenges the validity of some comment or behavior that the person has reported. The person reacts in a hostile or unpleasant manner.<br>  The interviewer questions the person about his or her views on politics, races, women or men, or competitors. The person responds with absolute, almost angry generalizations.<br>Significant biographical content<br>  The person reports that he or she is irritated if kept waiting for any reason or if driving behind a car moving too slowly in his or her view.<br>  The person expresses general distrust of other people's motives, e.g. distrust of altruism.<br>  The person reports that he or she almost always plays any type of game to win (even with young children). |

Table from M Friedman, C E Thoresen, J J Gill, D Ulmer, L Thompson, L Powell, V Price, S R Elek, D D Rabin, W S Breall, G Piaget, T Dixon, E Bourge, R A Levy, D L Tasto: Feasibility of altering type A behavior pattern after myocardial infarction: Recurrent Coronary Prevention Project Study: Methods, baseline results, and preliminary findings. Circulation 66: 83, 1982. Used with permission.

**Structured Clinical Interview for DSM-IV Dissociative Disorders.** The development of such diagnostic instruments as the Structured Clinical Interview for DSM-IV Dissociative Disorders (SCID-D) has made possible the assessment of specific dissociative disorder symptoms. The SCID-D is a semistructured diagnostic interview for the systematic assessment of five dissociative disorder symptoms: amnesia, depersonalization, derealization, identity confusion, and identity alteration. It allows for the diagnosis of dissociative disorders on the basis of DSM-III-R criteria and DSM-IV criteria. Severity rating definitions were developed to operationalize the assessment of the five symptom areas.

## Projective Personality Assessment

The projective approach to personality assessment is defined by the use of unstructured, often ambiguous test stimuli. A basic assumption is that, when confronted with a vague stimulus and required to respond to it in some manner, persons cannot help but reveal information about themselves—not only in the way in which or the process by which the ambiguity is confronted but also in the content of their responses.

The projective approach is essentially idiographic in nature, and most commonly the tests are not interpreted by comparing a person's responses with a set of criterion-referenced normative data. Typically, interpretation is based on a theory of human behavior and personality, and it is assumed that persons bring certain needs, characteristics, defenses, and other qualities that become apparent through the testing process.

A number of semistructured situations and projective-type stimuli have been developed, including perceiving inkblots, drawing pictures, and telling stories on the basis of presented pictures.

**Rorschach test.** With the possible exception of the WAIS, the Rorschach test is the most frequently used individual test in clinical settings throughout the United States. The Rorschach test was devised by Hermann Rorschach, a Swiss psychiatrist, who began around 1910 to experiment with ambiguous inkblots. A standard set of 10 inkblots serves as stimuli for associations, one of which is shown in Figure 5.1–2. In the standard series, the blots are reproduced on cards 7 by 9½ inches and are numbered from I to X. Five of the blots are in black and white; the other five include colors. The cards are shown to the patient in a particular order. A record is kept of the patient's verbatim responses, along with initial reaction times and total time spent on each card. After completion of what is called the free-association phase, an inquiry phase is conducted by the examiner to determine important

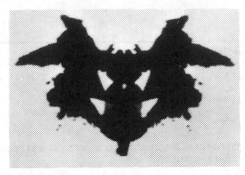

**Figure 5.1–2.** Plate I of the Rorschach test. (Figure from Hans Huber Medical Publisher, Berne. Used with permission.)

aspects of each response that will be crucial to its scoring. Table 5.1–6 contains examples of responses to Rorschach stimuli.

SCORING. The scoring of responses converts the important aspects of each response into a symbol system related to location areas, determinants, content areas, and popularity.

*Location.* Location is scored in terms of which portion of the blot was used as the basis for a response (for example, the whole blot, a common detail of the blot, an unusual detail of the blot, or an area of white space). Attention to the whole blot with accurate form perception reflects good organiza-

tional ability and high intelligence. Overattention to detail is common in obsessive and paranoid subjects.

*Determinants.* The determinants of each response reflect the features of the blot that made it look the way the patient thought it looked (for example, form, shading, color, movement of either humans or animals, inanimate movements, or combinations of those determinants with varying emphasis). Overemphasis on form suggests rigidity and constriction of the personality. Color responses relate to the emotional reactions of the person to the environment and to the control of affect.

*Content.* Responses are scored in terms of the content they reflect—human, animal, anatomy, sex, food, nature, and so on. In general, content areas reflect the subject's breadth and range of interests.

*Popularity.* Certain responses to the cards are more popular than others.

INTERPRETATION. The Rorschach test is particularly useful as an aid in diagnosis. The subject's thinking and association patterns are brought clearly into focus because the ambiguity of the stimulus provides relatively few cues about what are conventional, standard, or normal responses. Proper interpretation, however, requires a great deal of experience. There is a high reliability among experienced clinicians who administer the test. In proper hands, the test is extremely useful, especially in eliciting psychodynamic formulations, defense mechanisms, and subtle disorders of thinking.

The Rorschach test elicits data that can aid in differential diagnosis, particularly in evaluating whether or not a thought

**Table 5.1–6**
**Responses to Rorschach Card I by Five Male Patients**

| Free Association | Inquiry |
|---|---|
| Patient A: A bug with two witches attached to it. | This whole thing in the middle, just the way it looks. [Points] Just the wings here. Looks like a witch. |
| Also a halloween mask. About all I can see. | That—the whole thing. The eyes, the mouth [White space][?] Nothing else about it. |
| Patient B: A bat, a bug. | Bat. [Whole] The blackness and the wings. Bug—that was just a pure reference to the color. I just see it as unpleasant. |
| One of the furies. A headless woman with black wings, grasping hands, claws, whatever. Bottom part of her torso is compressed, held in, like she's reaching forward. | Furies. [Whole] The central portion could represent legs pressed together. She represents a figure of death launching forward, and the head gets lost. Sort of snakelike, and the outer parts are reaching forth at the shadow of the earth. |
| Patient C: It looks like a monster bat. It has pincers. And an ass over here. | The whole thing. It has wings. It's kind of ragged, that's all. [Top center] Arches. Just shaped that way. Feel uptight, knowing I'm taking a test[?] Shape, two mounds. |
| And a butterfly. | Whole object. The wings, the shape. I just feel I want to get out of here. |
| Patient D: Two dancers and two children in between them like they're dancing around them. | [Whole] Head, cape, clothing, legs. Matching heads. A pair of children or a pair of dancers, since it's symmetrical, one on one side and one on the other. |
| Patient E: Looks like a bat? That's all I can make of it. | Whole blot. The middle makes it look like a body. And it looks like he has a tail and two short feet. |

This table gives the Rorschach responses, both free associations and inquiries, given to Card I by five male patients. The extracted test responses are reported primarily to illustrate the range given by various patients to the same stimulus. As such, the responses may not themselves always delineate the varying DSM-IV diagnoses represented.
*Patient A*: 26 years old, multiple psychiatric hospitalizations within past four years. Unable to care for himself, believing himself controlled by a force that makes him act inappropriately. Suffers from chronic delusions, obsessional thinking, and social withdrawal. Schizophrenia.
*Patient B*: 23 years old, long history of social isolation, repetitive self-destructive behavior, depression, and inability to function academically. Has shown depersonalization and derealization phenomena but no admitted delusions or hallucinations. Schizotypal personality disorder.

*Patient C*: 28 years old, complaints of chronic and overwhelming anxiety, feelings of loneliness, and ambivalence about homosexual identification. History of excessive use of psychotropic medication. Borderline personality disorder.
*Patient D*: 20 years old, presently hospitalized for manic episode, with history of two clear-cut manic and depressive episodes, followed by remissions. Bipolar I disorder.
*Patient E*: 33 years old, hospitalized on neurology service for cognitive disorder assumed to be related to occupational hazard: mercury poisoning. Prior history of behavior difficulties.
Table by Arthur C. Carr, Ph.D.

disorder exists. For example, patients with schizotypal and borderline personality disorders are characterized by idiosyncratic thoughts, peculiarities of language, and unconventional thinking.

**Thematic Apperception Test (TAT).** The Thematic Apperception Test (TAT) was designed by Henry Murray and Christiana Morgan as part of the normal personality study conducted at the Harvard Psychological Clinic in 1943. It consists of a series of 30 pictures and one blank card. Not all the pictures are used. The choice depends on what conflict area one wishes to clarify with a patient. Examples of TAT pictures are a young woman seated on a couch looking up at an older man, a man standing beside a nude woman in a bed, and a gray-haired man looking at a younger man.

Although most of the pictures depict people and all are representational (making the test stimuli more structured than the inkblots of the Rorschach test), there is ambiguity in each picture. Unlike the Rorschach blots, to which the patient is asked to associate, the TAT requires that the patient construct or create a story.

As the test was originally conceived, an important aspect of each story was the figure (the hero) with whom subjects seemed to identify and to whom they were presumably attributing their own wishes, strivings, and conflicts. The characteristics of people other than the hero were considered to represent the subject's views of other people in his or her environment. It is now assumed that all the figures in a TAT story are equally representative of the subject, with the more accepted and conscious traits and motives attributed to figures closest to the subject in age, sex, and appearance and the more unacceptable and unconscious traits and motives attributed to figures most unlike the subject.

The stories must be considered from the standpoint of unusualness of theme or plot. Whether the subjects are dealing with a common or uncommon theme, their stories reflect their own idiosyncratic approaches to organization, sequence, vocabulary, style, preconceptions, assumptions, and outcome. TAT cards have varying stimulus values and can be assumed to elicit data pertaining to various areas of functioning. Generally, the TAT is more useful as a technique for inferring motivational aspects of behavior than as a basis for making a diagnosis.

**Sentence Completion Test (SCT).** The Sentence Completion Test (SCT) is designed to tap the patient's conscious associations to areas of functioning in which the clinician may be interested. It is composed of a series (usually 75 to 100) of sentence stems—such as, "I like. . ." "Sometimes I wish. . ."—that the patient is asked to complete in his or her own words.

Most frequently, some time pressure is applied, and the patient is instructed to write down the first thing that comes to mind. In other instances, the test is administered orally by the examiner, as in the word-association technique. Sentence stems vary in their ambiguity; hence, some items serve as projective test stimuli ("Sometimes I . . . "). Others closely resemble direct-response questionnaires ("My greatest fear is. . . ").

With the individual protocol, most clinicians use an inspection technique, noting particularly those responses that are expressive of strong affects, that tend to be given repetitively, or that are unusual or particularly informative in any way. Areas in which denial operates are often revealed through omissions, bland expressions, or factual reports ("My mother is a woman"). Humor may also reflect an attempt to deny anxiety about a particular issue, person, or event. Important historical material is sometimes revealed directly ("I feel guilty about the way my sister was drowned").

**Word-association technique.** The word-association technique was devised by Carl Gustav Jung, who presented stimulus words to patients and had them respond with the first word that came to mind. After the initial administration of the list, some clinicians repeat the list, asking the patient to respond with the same words that he or she used previously; discrepancies between the two administrations may reveal associational difficulties. Complex indicators include long reaction times, blocking difficulties in making responses, unusual responses, repetition of the stimulus word, apparent misunderstanding of the word, clang associations, perseveration of earlier responses, and ideas or unusual mannerisms or movements accompanying the response. Because it is easily quantified, the test has continued to be used as a research instrument, although its popularity has diminished greatly over the years.

**Draw-a-Person test.** The Draw-a-Person test was first used as a measure of intelligence in children. Detail was correlated with intelligence and developmental level. It has since become useful as an adult test. The test is easily administered, usually with the instructions, "I'd like you to draw a picture of a person; draw the best person you can." After the completion of the first drawing, the patient is asked to draw a picture of a person of the sex opposite to that of the first drawing. Some clinicians use an interrogation procedure in which the patient is questioned about his or her drawings. ("What is he doing?" "What are her best qualities?") Modifications include asking for a drawing of a house and a tree (House-Tree-Person test), of one's family, and of an animal.

A general assumption is that the drawing of a person represents the expression of the self or of the body in the environment. Interpretive principles rest largely on the assumed functional significance of each body part. Most clinicians use drawings primarily as a screening technique, particularly for the detection of brain damage.

## INTEGRATION OF TEST FINDINGS

The integration of test findings into a comprehensive, meaningful report is probably the most difficult aspect of psychological evaluation. Inferences from various tests must be related to one another in terms of the confidence the clinician holds about them and the presumed level of the patient's awareness or consciousness being tapped.

Most clinicians follow some general outline in preparing a psychological report, such as test behavior, intellectual functioning, personality functioning (reality-testing ability, impulse control, manifest depression and guilt, manifestations of major dysfunction, major defenses, overt symptoms, interpersonal conflicts, self-concept, affects), inferred diagnosis, degree of present overt disturbance, prognosis for social recovery, motivation for personality change, primary assets and weaknesses, recommendations, and summary.

### References

American Psychological Association: *Standards for Educational and Psychological Tests and Manuals.* American Psychological Association, Washington, 1974.

Anastasi A: *Psychological Testing,* ed 5. Macmillan, New York, 1968.

Barlow D, editor: *Behavioral Assessment of Adult Disorders.* Guilford, New York, 1981.

Bremner J, Steinberg M, Southwick S M, Johnson D R, Charney D S: Use of the Structured Clinical Interview for DSM-IV Dissociative Disorders for systematic assessment of dissociative symptoms in posttraumatic stress disorder. Am J Psychiatry *150*: 1011, 1993.

Butcher J N, Keller L S: Objective personality assessment. In *Handbook of Psychological Assessment*, G Goldstein, M Hersen, editors, p 307. Pergamon, New York, 1984.

Butler R W, Satz P: Psychological assessment of personality of adults and children. In *Comprehensive Textbook of Psychiatry*, ed 5, H I Kaplan, B J Sadock, editors, p 475. Williams & Wilkins, Baltimore, 1989.

Caligan R C, Offord K P: Revitalizing the MMPI: The development of contemporary norms. Psychiatr Ann *15*: 558, 1985.

Cronbach L: *Essentials of Psychological Testing*. Harper & Row, New York, 1960.

Dahlstrom W G, Welsh G, Dahlstrom L: *An MMPI Handbook*: vol 1, *Clinical Interpretation*. University of Minnesota Press, Minneapolis, 1972.

Exner J E: *The Rorschach: A Comprehensive System,* vols 1, 2, 3. Wiley, New York, 1982.

Hackett T P, Rosenbaum J F, Cassem N H: Cardiovascular disorders. In *Comprehensive Textbook of Psychiatry*, ed 5, H I Kaplan, B J Sadock, editors, p 1186. Williams & Wilkins, Baltimore, 1989.

Halstead W: *Brain and Intelligence: A Quantitative Study of the Frontal Lobes*. University of Chicago Press, Chicago, 1947.

Holt R R: *Assessing Personality*. Harcourt Brace Jovanovich, Orlando, 1971.

Kleinmuntz B: *Personality and Psychological Assessment*. St. Martin's Press, New York, 1982.

Lezak M D: *Neuropsychological Assessment,* ed 2. Oxford University Press, New York, 1983.

Matarazzo J D: *Wechsler's Measurement and Appraisal of Adult Intelligence,* ed 5. Oxford University Press, New York, 1972.

Millon T: *Millon Clinical Multiaxial Inventory Manuals,* ed 5. Interpretive Scoring Systems, Minneapolis, 1983.

Rorschach H: *Psychodiagnostik*. Bircher, Bern, 1921.

Schnurr P P, Friedman M J, Rosenberg S D: Preliminary MMPI scores as predictors of combat-related PTSD symptoms. Am J Psychiatry *150*: 479, 1993.

Steinberg M: *The Structured Clinical Interview for DSM-IV Dissociative Disorders*. American Psychiatric Press, Washington, 1993.

Terman L M, Merrill M A: *Stanford-Binet: Manual for the Third Revision*. Houghton Mifflin, Boston, 1960.

Wechsler D: *WAIS-R Manual*. Psychological Corporation, New York, 1981.

Wolman B, editor: *Handbook of Clinical Diagnosis of Mental Disorders*. Plenum, New York, 1978.

Zimmerman I, Woo-Sam J: *Clinical Interpretation of the Wechsler Adult Scale*. Grune & Stratton, New York, 1973.

Zubin J, Eron L, Schumer B J, editors: *An Experimental Approach to Projective Techniques*. Wiley, New York, 1965.

# 5.2 / Neuropsychological Assessment of Adults

Neuropsychological tests are standardized techniques that yield quantifiable and reproducible results that are referable to the scores of normal persons of an age and demographic background similar to those of the person being tested.

Neuropsychological assessment applies the methods of experimental and clinical psychology to the analysis of the cognitive and behavioral disturbances produced by injury, disease, or abnormal development of the brain. The procedures, which are used both in clinical evaluation and in research, may be viewed as constituting a refinement and an extension of certain aspects of the neurological examination. The same behavioral and mental capacities (for example, orientation, memory, language functions) that are evaluated in the neurological examination are also eval-uated in a precise and objective manner by neuro-psychological assessment.

## PURPOSES AND GOALS

The purposes and the indications for assessment are (1) to identify cognitive defects, (2) to differentiate incipient depression from dementia, (3) to determine the course of the illness, (4) to assess the neurotoxic effects (for example, memory impairment by substance abuse), (5) to evaluate the effects of treatment (for example, surgery for epilepsy, pharmacotherapy), and (6) to evaluate learning disorders.

## GENERAL INTELLIGENCE AND DEMENTIA

Patients with cerebral disease may show an overall be-havioral inefficiency and be unable to meet the diverse intellectual demands associated with the responsibilities of daily life. Dementia implies an overall impairment in men-tal capacity, with a consequent decline in social and eco-nomic competence. There are clinically distinguishable types of dementia—for example, an aphasic type, an amnestic type, a type showing prominent visuoperceptual and somatoperceptual defects, and a relatively pure type manifesting impairment in abstract reasoning and problem solving within a setting of fairly intact linguistic and per-ceptual capacity.

In this country the Wechsler Adult Intelligence Scale (WAIS) is by far the most widely used test battery to assess general intelligence in adults. In its clinical application a number of procedures have been used to evaluate the pos-sibility of a decline in general intelligence that may be attributable to the presence of cerebral disease. The most direct approach is to compare the patient's obtained age-corrected intelligence quotient (I.Q.) score with the age-corrected I.Q. score that might be expected in view of the patient's educational background, cultural level, and oc-cupational history. An obtained I.Q. below the expected I.Q. may raise the question of the presence of cerebral disease. However, many patients with unquestionable ce-rebral disease do not show an overall decline in general intelligence of sufficient severity to be reflected in a sig-nificant lowering of their WAIS I.Q. scores. Conse-quently, the procedure may yield a fair proportion of false-negative results.

## REASONING, CONCEPT FORMATION, AND PROBLEM SOLVING

The patient with cerebral disease is likely to show cog-nitive impairment of a general nature, which Kurt Gold-stein designated the "loss of the abstract attitude." He characterized the deficit as a loss of the capacity to reason abstractly and a lack of flexibility in problem solving or in adapting to changed situations. Frontal lobe disease is often associated with impaired abstract reasoning, al-though other areas of the brain may also be involved.

A number of tests are used to assess the capacity for concept formation.

## Wisconsin Card-Sorting Test (WCST)

Stimulus cards differing in color, form, and number are presented to the patient for sorting into groups according to a principle established by the examiner. The number of trials required to achieve 10 consecutive correct responses is recorded. The procedure is repeated a number of times, and measures of the capacity for abstract thinking (that is, the number of trials required to achieve a solution) and of flexibility in problem solving (that is, perseverative errors on successive sorting trials) are derived from the patient's performance.

Patients who have undergone frontal lobe excisions for amelioration of epilepsy exhibit a greater deficit on the WCST than do patients with posterior surgical lesions. Long-term schizophrenic patients also show impaired performance on the WCST in relation to reduced cerebral blood flow in their frontal lobes.

## Shipley Abstraction Test

The Shipley Abstraction Test requires the patient to complete logical sequences; it assesses the capacity to abstract. Because performance on a test of this type is related to educational background, an accompanying vocabulary test is also given to the patient, and a comparison is made between performances on the two tests. A low abstraction score in relation to vocabulary level is interpreted as reflecting an impairment in conceptual thinking.

## MEMORY

Impairment of various types of memory, most notably short-term and recent memory, is a prominent behavioral deficit in brain-damaged patients, and it is often the first sign of cerebral disease and of aging. Memory is a comprehensive term that covers the retention of all types of material over various periods of time and involves diverse forms of response. Consequently, the neuropsychological examiner is more inclined to give specific memory tests and evaluate them separately than to use an omnibus battery that provides a brief assessment of a large variety of performances and yields a single score.

## Types of Memory

*Immediate* (or *short-term*) *memory* may be defined as the reproduction, recognition, or recall of perceived material within a period of up to 30 seconds after presentation. It is most often assessed by digit repetition and reversal (auditory) and memory-for-designs (visual) tests. Both an auditory-verbal task, such as digit span or memory for words or sentences, and a nonverbal visual task, such as memory for designs or for objects or faces, should be given to assess the patient's immediate memory. Patients can also be asked to listen to a standardized story and to repeat the story as closely as possible to what they heard. Patients with lesions of the right hemisphere are likely to show more severe defects on visual nonverbal tasks than on auditory verbal tasks. Conversely, patients with left hemisphere dis-

ease, including those who are not aphasic, are likely to show severe deficits on the auditory verbal tests, with variable performance on the visual nonverbal tasks.

*Recent memory* concerns events over the past few hours or days and can be tested by asking patients what they had for breakfast and who visited with them in the hospital.

*Recent past memory* concerns the retention of information over the past few months. The patient can be asked questions about current events.

*Remote memory* is the ability to remember events in the distant past. It is commonly believed that remote memory is well-preserved in patients who show pronounced defects in recent memory. However, the remote memory of senile and amnestic patients is usually significantly inferior to that of normal persons of comparable age and education. Even patients who appear to be able to recount their past fairly accurately show, on close examination, gaps and inconsistencies in their recitals.

Memory theorists have described three other types of memory: (1) episodic, for specific events (for example, a telephone message); (2) semantic, for knowledge and facts (for example, the first President of the United States); and (3) implicit, for automatic skills (for example, speaking grammatically or driving a car). Semantic and implicit memory do not decline with age, and persons continue to accumulate information over a lifetime. There is a minimal decline in episodic memory with aging that may relate to impaired frontal lobe functioning.

## Testing Memory

**Wechsler Memory Scale.** The Wechsler Memory Scale (WMS) is the most widely used memory test battery for adults. It is a composite of verbal paired associate and paragraph retention, visual memory for designs, orientation, digit span, rote recall of the alphabet, and counting backward. The scale yields a memory quotient (M.Q.), which is corrected for age and generally approximates the Wechsler Adult Intelligence Scale intelligence quotient (WAIS I.Q.); amnestic conditions, such as amenstic Korsakoff's syndrome, are characterized by a disproportionately low M.Q. but a relatively preserved I.Q.

**Benton Visual Retention Test.** The Benton Visual Retention Test is sensitive to short-term memory loss (Figure 5.2–1).

**Figure 5.2–1.** Test item from the Benton Visual Retention Test. The most frequently used testing condition involves the presentation of each geometric figure for 10 seconds, after which the patient attempts to draw the figure from memory. (Figure from A L Benton: *The Revised Visual Retention Test: Clinical and Experimental Applications*, ed 4, p 32. Psychological Corporation, New York, 1974. Used with permission.)

## ORIENTATION

Orientation for person or place is rarely disturbed in the brain-damaged patient who is not psychotic or severely demented; but defects in temporal orientation, which can reflect the integrity of recent memory, are common. Those defects are often missed by the clinical examiner because of the tendency to regard as inconsequential slight inaccuracy in giving the day of the week or the date of the month. However, about 25 percent of nonpsychotic patients with hemispheric cerebral disease are likely to show significant decreased performance with respect to the precision of the temporal orientation. A simple test for orientation is outlined in Table 5.2–1.

## PERCEPTUAL AND PERCEPTUOMOTOR PERFORMANCE

Many patients with brain disease show an impaired ability to analyze complex stimulus constellations or an inability to translate their perception into appropriate motor action. Unless the impairment is of a gross nature, as in visual object agnosia or dressing apraxia, or interferes with a specific occupation skill, those deficits are not likely to be the subject of spontaneous complaint. However, appropriate testing discloses a remarkably high incidence of impaired performance on visuoanalytic, visuospatial, and visuoconstructive tasks in brain-damaged patients, particularly in those persons with disease involving the right

**Table 5.2–1**
**Temporal Orientation Schedule**

**Administration**

What is today's date? (The patient is required to give month, day, and year.)

What day of the week is it?

What time is it now? (Examiner makes sure that the patient cannot look at a watch or clock.)

**Scoring**

Day of week: 1 error point for each day removed from the correct day to a maximum of 3 points

Day of month: 1 error point for each day removed from the correct day to a maximum of 15 points

Month: 5 error points for each month removed from the correct month with the qualification that, if the stated date is within 15 days of the correct date, no points are scored for the incorrect month (for example, May 29 for June 2 = 4 points off)

Year: 10 error points for each year removed from the correct year to a maximum of 60 points with the qualification that, if the stated date is within 15 days of the correct date, no points are scored for the incorrect year (for example, December 26, 1982, for January 2, 1983 = 7 points off)

Time of day: 1 error point for each 30 minutes removed from the correct time to a maximum of 5 points

hemisphere. That type of impairment also extends to tactile and auditory perceptual task performances.

Visuoperceptive and visuoconstructive capacity and somatoperceptual defects can be assessed by tests. Double simultaneous stimulation is tested by lightly touching one of the patient's cheeks with one hand and simultaneously touching the back of one of the patient's hands with the other. A patient with brain dysfunction is unable to recognize one or both of the stimuli. The double simultaneous stimulation is a general test of defective capacity for perceptual integration.

Perceptuomotor tests often help localize the cerebral lesion. A significant portion of patients with lesions of the right hemisphere who do not show obvious impairment in language functions perform poorly on perceptual tests.

### Bender Visual Motor Gestalt Test

The Bender gestalt test is a test of visuomotor coordination that is useful for both children and adults. It was designed in 1938 by Lauretta Bender of New York University Medical Center and Bellevue Psychiatric Hospital, who used it to evaluate maturational levels in children. Developmentally, a child under 3 years of age is generally unable to reproduce any of the test's designs meaningfully. Around 4 years of age, the child may be able to copy several designs but poorly. At about age 6, the child should produce some recognizable, though still uneven, representations of all the designs. By age 10 and certainly by age 12, the child's copies should be reasonably accurate and well organized. Bender also presented studies of adults with cognitive disorders, mental retardation, aphasias, psychoses, neuroses, and malingering.

The test material consists of nine separate designs, adapted from those used by Max Wertheimer in his studies in Gestalt psychology. Each design is printed against a white background on a separate card (Figure 5.2–2). Presented with unlined paper, patients are asked to copy each design with the card in front of them. There is no time limit. That phase of the test is highly structured and does not investigate memory function, because the cards remain in front of patients while they copy them. Many clinicians include a subsequent recall phase, in which (after an interval of 45 to 60 seconds) patients are asked to reproduce as many of the designs as they can from memory. That phase not only investigates visual memory but also presents a less structured situation, since patients must rely essentially on their own resources. It is often particularly helpful to compare the patient's functioning under the two conditions.

Probably, the Bender gestalt test is used most frequently with adults as a screening device for signs of organic dysfunction. Evaluation of the protocol depends on the form of the reproduced figures and on their relation to one another and to the whole spatial background (Figures 5.2–3 and 5.2–4).

### Complex Visual Discrimination

Although the inability to recognize familiar faces (prosopagnosia) is an uncommon disorder, defective discrimination of unfamiliar faces is a common finding in patients with right-hemisphere or bilateral lesions. The Facial Recognition Test, in which the patient is required to identify a photograph of a face presented in a front view when it is included in various displays (for example, side view and a front view with shadows) produces a high frequency of failure in patients with

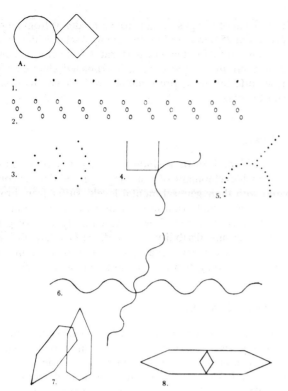

**Figure 5.2–2.** Test figures from the Bender Visual Motor Gestalt Test, adopted from Max Wertheimer (Figure from L Bender: *A Visual Motor Gestalt Test and Its Clinical Use*, p 33. American Orthopsychiatric Association, New York, 1938.)

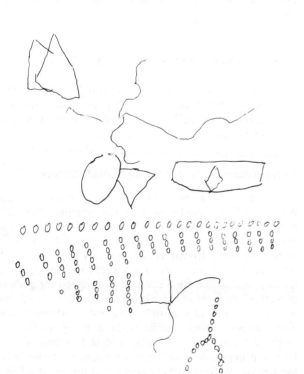

**Figure 5.2–3.** Bender-Gestalt drawing of a 57-year-old brain-damaged female patient.

posterior right-hemisphere lesions. Performance is generally intact in patients with left-hemisphere lesions (provided that receptive language is not seriously limited) and patients with schizophrenia.

**Visual Matrices**

Raven's Progressive Matrices requires the patient to select from a multiple-choice pictorial display the stimulus that completes a design in which a part is omitted. The difficulty of the discrimination increases over trials in the lengthy test. A briefer, less difficult version (Color Matrices) is especially useful for patients who are unable to complete the standard test, which can require 30 to 45 minutes. Impaired performance is associated with poor visuoconstructive ability and with posterior lesions of either hemisphere, but receptive language deficit may be contributory in patients with dominant-hemisphere damage.

## LANGUAGE

Relatively minor defects in the use of language may be valid indicators of the presence of brain disease. The dominant hemisphere controls language function. The affective part of speech that conveys mood is called prosody and is controlled by the nondominant hemisphere. Fluency is tested by asking patients to give all the words they can think of beginning with a given letter of the alphabet. Aphasic patients with left-hemisphere disease fail that task. Variables influencing language tests are educational background, sex, and age. Reading and writing are also associated with the dominant hemisphere and are tested by asking patients to read aloud from prepared material and to write their names or a brief passage. Dyslexia and dysgraphia are suspected if difficulties in performing those tasks are found.

The Boston Diagnostic Aphasia Examination includes a speech rating scale that is useful for comparing with test scores and a brief schedule of items for assessing ideomotor praxis—that is, symbolic buccofacial and limb movements to exhibit gestures and to demonstrate the use of imagined or real objects.

## ATTENTION AND CONCENTRATION

The capacity to sustain a maximal level of attention over a period of time is sometimes impaired in brain-damaged patients, and that impairment is reflected in an oscillation in performance level on a continuous or repeated activity. Some evidence indicates that the instability in

**Figure 5.2.–4.** Bender-Gestalt recall of the 57-year-old brain-damaged female patient in Figure 5.2–3.

performance is related to an electroencephalographic abnormality and that an inexplicable decline in performance is related temporally to the occurrence of certain types of abnormal electrical activity. Simple reaction time provides a convenient measure of the variability and speed of simple responses.

The reaction time needed to respond to a stimulus is impaired in 40 to 45 percent of brain-damaged patients and is a sensitive indicator of overall cerebral integrity. Comparison of the reaction times of the right and left hands often provides an indication of the site of the lesion in a patient and of unilateral cerebral disease.

Behavioral flexibility is also reduced in brain-damaged patients who are unable to modify the approach to a problem in accordance with changing requirements. That inability was described by Kurt Goldstein as part of the catastrophic reaction first noted in brain-injured soldiers.

Attention and information processing can be evaluated by a number of widely used clinical procedures—for example, the arithmetic, digit school (coding), and digit span subtests to the WAIS, the Wechsler Intelligence Scale for Children (WISC), the mental control section of the Wechsler Memory Scale, the Reitan Trail Making Test, and cancellation tests in which the patient marks only designated letters (targets) interspersed with other letters (nontarget or distractor items) in lengthy sequences.

The Continuous Performance Test, an experimental task that involves the rapid identification of a target and the withholding of responses to distractor stimuli, permits the analysis of both the accuracy and the latency of response. The test, which is one of the few tests designed to assess attention, has been widely used in psychopharmacological research and in studies of attentional deficit in schizophrenic patients. In an adjustive version of the test, a microcomputer changes the rate of presentation according to the patient's performance. The shortest interstimulus interval at which responding is still accurate is the primary performance measure.

## BEHAVIORAL INDEXES OF BRAIN DAMAGE IN CHILDREN

If present, the behavioral consequences of early brain damage may take many forms, of which attention-deficit/hyperactivity disorder is only one. Early brain damage may result in little or no behavioral deficit; when such a deficit does appear, it is usually less severe than that caused by a comparable lesion in adults. Thus, many brain-damaged children may not be identified by current methods of behavioral assessment.

### General Intelligence

The most frequently used batteries are the WISC, the Stanford-Binet, and the Wechsler Preschool and Primary Scale of Intelligence (WPPSI). A relatively low level of general intelligence is probably the most constant behavioral result of brain damage in children.

### Perceptual and Perceptuomotor Performances

Many brain-damaged children with adequate verbal skills show strikingly defective visuoperceptive and visuomotor performance. The test most frequently used is the copying of designs, either from a model or from memory. About 25 percent of brain-damaged schoolchildren of adequate verbal intelligence perform defectively. The task helps discriminate between brain-damaged children and those suffering from presumably psychogenic emotional disturbances.

### Language

Considerable evidence indicates that children who show gross maldevelopment of oral language abilities, as compared with their general mental levels, suffer from brain damage. Perinatal brain injury may be a causative factor in at least some cases of developmental dyslexia or generalized learning disability. The finding of a relatively high incidence of electroencephalographic abnormalities in children with learning disorders points to the same conclusion.

### Motor Performances

Motor awkwardness and inability to carry out movement sequences on command or by imitation are commonly seen in brain-damaged children. A variety of tests are available for the assessment of manual dexterity (for example, manipulations with tweezers, paper cutting, and peg placing).

Motor impersistence—as inability to sustain an action initiated on command, such as keeping the eyes closed—is seen in a relatively small proportion of adult patients with cerebral disease. However, it is seen with high frequency in nondefective brain-damaged children. Many children with mental defects also show excessive motor impersistence, particularly those children with brain damage.

## COMPREHENSIVE TESTING

A number of test batteries have been developed to help in the neuropsychological and neuropsychiatric evaluation. Among them are the Luria-Nebraska and the Halstead-Reitan neuropsychological test batteries.

### Luria-Nebraska Neuropsychological Battery

Based on the work of the Russian neuropsychologist Alexander Luria, the Luria-Nebraska Neuropsychological Battery was developed at the University of Nebraska. The test assesses a wide range of cognitive functions: memory; motor functions; rhythm; tactile, auditory, and visual functions; receptive and expressive speech; writing; spelling; reading; and arithmetic. The test is designed for persons at least 15 years of age, and there is a children's version for use with 8-to-12-year-olds. The test is extremely sensitive for identifying specific types of problems (for example, dyslexia and dyscalculia), rather than being limited to global impressions of brain dysfunction. It also helps localize the various cortical zones that are involved in a particular function and is useful in establishing left or right cerebral dominance.

**Table 5.2–2**
**Mental Status Cognitive Tests**

| Task | Dysfunction | Abnormal Response | Suggested Localization |
|---|---|---|---|
| Spell "earth" backward | Concentration | Any improper letter sequence | Frontal lobes |
| Serial sevens | Concentration | One or more errors or longer than 90 seconds | Frontal lobes |
| Name the day of the week, month, year, location | Global disorientation | Any error | Frontal lobes (if memory intact) |
| Repeat: "No ifs, ands, or buts," "The President lives in Washington," "Methodist Episcopal," "Massachusetts" | Expressive language | Missed words or syllables; repetition of internal syllables; dropping of word endings | Dominant frontal lobe |
| Name common objects (e.g., key, watch, button) | Anomia | Cannot name; word approximations; describes functions, rather than word | Dominant temporal lobe, angular gyrus |
| Conversation during examination | Receptive language | Word approximations, neologisms, word salad, stock words, tangential speech | Dominant temporal lobe |
| Repeat four words or items (e.g., blue, chair, swim, glove) | Immediate recall | One or more errors | Temporal lobes and frontal lobes (hippocampus) |
| Remember them after 10 minutes with interposed tasks | Recent memory | One or more errors | Temporal lobes (hippocampus, thalamus, fornix, mamillothalamic tract) |
| Provide accurate detail and sequence of past events | Long-term memory | Significant loss of detail; confused sequence | Temporal lobes (hippocampus) |
| Copy examiner's hand and arm movements (each hand and arm) | Dyspraxia | Any error, mirror movements | Contralateral parietal lobe |
| Demonstrate use of key, hammer, flipping a coin | Ideomotor apraxia | Use of hand as object; failure to use fine hand and wrist movements; verbal overflow | Dominant parietal lobe, disconnected dominant from nondominant frontal lobe |
| Left hand only plus some expressive language difficulty | | | Dominant frontal lobe or anterior corpus callosum |
| Both hands | | | Dominant parietal lobe, arcuate fasciculus |
| Name fingers | Finger agnosia | Two or more errors; cannot identify after examiner numbers each | Dominant parietal lobe |
| Calculations | Dyscalculia | Errors in borrowing or carrying over when concentration is intact | Dominant parietal lobe |
| Write a sentence | Dysgraphia | No longer able to write cursive; loss of word structure; abnormally formed letters | Dominant parietal lobe |
| In individual steps, copy sentence, read it, and do what it says ("Put the paper in your pocket") | Dysgraphia, dyslexia, comprehension | No longer able to write cursively; loss of sentence structure; loss of word structure; abnormally formed letters | Dominant temporoparietal lobe |
| Place left hand to right ear, right elbow, right knee; same for right hand | Right-left disorientation | Two or more errors or two or more seven-second delays in carrying out tasks | Dominant parietal lobe |
| Copy the outline of simple objects (e.g., Greek cross, key) | Construction apraxia | Loss of gestalt, loss of symmetry, distortion of figures | Nondominant parietal lobe |
| Camouflaged object(s) | Visual-perception deficit | Cannot name when camouflaged, can name when clear | Occipital lobes |

Table from M A Taylor, R Abrams, R Faber, G Almy: Cognitive tasks in the mental status examination. J Nerv Ment Dis *168*: 168, 1980. Used with permission.

## Halstead-Reitan Battery of Neuropsychological Tests

In the early 1940s, Ward Halstead at Chicago and his student Ralph Reitan developed a battery of tests that were used to determine the location and the effects of specific brain lesions. The battery is composed of the following 10 tests:

1. Category test.   The patient must discover the common element in a set of pictures; the test measures concept function, abstraction, and visual acuity.

2. Tactual performance test.   The patient places shapes in a form board while blindfolded and then must recall the arrangement of the board; it tests dexterity, spatial memory, and tactual discrimination.

3. Rhythm test.   The patient identifies 30 pairs of rhythmic beats as either the same or different; it tests auditory perception, attention, and concentration.

4. Finger-oscillation test.   The patient taps the index finger of each hand in a measured 10-second period; the test measures dexterity and motor speed.

5. Speech-sounds perception test.   The patient matches 60 nonsense syllables that he or she hears with several printed alternatives; the test measures auditory discrimination and phonetic skills.

6. Trail-making test.   The patient first connects 25 numbered circles in order and then connects 25 lettered and numbered circles in order, alternating between numbered and alphabetical circles; it tests visuomotor perception and motor speed.

7. Critical flicker frequency.   The patient notes when a flickering light becomes steady; it tests visual perception.

8. Time sense test.   The patient judges, without looking, the time it takes for the second hand of a watch to make several revolutions; it tests memory and spatial perception.

9. Aphasia screening test.   The patient must name objects, read, write, calculate, draw shapes, identify body parts, perform acts, differentiate between left and right; it tests a wide range of verbal and nonverbal brain functions.

10. Sensory-perceptual tests.   The patient performs a number of tasks with eyes closed—such as identifying where he or she is touched when touched on the hand and the face simultaneously (simultaneous sensory stimulation test), which finger is touched (finger localization), what coins are placed in the hand (stereognosis), and what numbers are written on the skin (tactile perception).

The Halstead-Reitan Battery has the advantage of providing a uniform profile of scores that must be weighed against the considerable time required for administration. The test is able to differentiate brain-damaged persons from neurologically intact persons. Schizophrenic patients tend to perform above the level of subacutely brain-damaged patients but not differently from chronically brain-damaged patients. Moreover, the pattern of deficits on the Halstead-Reitan Battery is similar in brain-damaged and schizophrenic patients.

## INTERPRETATION

In any neuropsychiatric examination the clinician must be careful that a deviation from normal is not due to factors unrelated to neuropathology. Anxiety and depression are two major causes of cognitive dysfunction, and a careful assessment of the patient's mental state should be carried out to rule out those conditions as sources of poor performance. Other sources of error result from the patient's not understanding the directions given by the examiner, problems with language, and general uncooperativeness. A summary of the many mental status cognitive tasks discussed in this section and other tasks that can be used to test and localize various dysfunctions is presented in Table 5.2–2.

**References**

Axelrod B N, Goldman R S, Henry R R: Sensitivity of the Mini-Mental State Examination to frontal lobe dysfunction in normal aging. J Clin Psychol *48*: 68, 1992.
Bender L: *A Visual Motor Gestalt Test and Its Clinical Use.* American Orthopsychiatric Association, New York, 1938.
Benton A L, Hamsher K deS, Varney N R: *Contributions to Neuropsychological Assessments.* Oxford University Press, New York, 1983.
Benton A L, Hamsher K deS, Varney N R, Spreen O: *Contributions to Neuropsychological Assessment: A Clinical Manual.* Oxford University Press, New York, 1983.
Christensen A-L: *Luria's Neuropsychological Investigation,* ed 2. Ejnar Munksgaards, Copenhagen, 1979.
Filskov S B, Boll T J: *Handbook of Clinical Neuropsychology.* Wiley, New York, 1981.
Gazzaniga M S: Right hemisphere language following brain bisection: A 20-year perspective. Am Psychol *38*: 525, 1983.
Gilandas A, Touyz S, Bermont P J V, Greenberg H P: *Handbook of Neuropsychological Assessment.* Grune & Stratton, Orlando, 1984.
Grant I, Adams K M: *Neuropsychological Assessment of Neuropsychiatric Disorders.* Oxford University Press, New York, 1986.
Heaton R K, Baade L E, Johnson K L: Neuropsychological test results associated with psychiatric disorders in adults. Psychol Bull *85*: 141, 1978.
Heilman K M, Bowers D, Valenstein E, Watson R T: The right hemisphere: Neuropsychological functions. J Neurosurg *64*: 693, 1986.
Incagnoli T, Goldstein G, Golden C J: *Clinical Application of Neuropsychological Test Batteries,* Plenum, New York, 1986.
Levin H S, Benton A L, Fletcher J M, Satz P: Neuropsychological and intellectual assessment of adults. In *Comprehensive Textbook of Psychiatry,* ed 5, H I Kaplan, B J Sadock, editors, p 496. Williams & Wilkins, Baltimore, 1989.
Lezak, M D: *Neuropsychological Assessment,* ed 2. Oxford University Press, New York, 1983.
Matarazzo J D: Computerized clinical psychological test interpretations. Am Psychol *41*: 14, 1986.
Milner B: Effects of different brain lesions on card sorting. Arch Neurol *9*: 90, 1963.
Mittenberg W, Azrin R, Millsaps C, Heilbronner R: Identification of malingered head injury on the Weschsler Memory Scale-Revised. Psychol Assess *5*: 34, 1993.
Moses J A: Relationship of the profile evaluation and impairment scales of the Luria-Nebraska Neuropsychological Battery to neuropsychological examination outcome. Int J Clin Neuropsychol *7*: 4, 1985.
Reitan R M: Theoretical and methodological bases of the Halstead-Reitan Neuropsychological Test Battery. In *Neuropsychological Assessment of Neuropsychiatric Disorders,* I Grant, K M Adams, editors, p 3. Oxford University Press, New York, 1986.
Reitan R M, Davison L A: *Clinical Neuropsychology: Current Status and Applications.* Wiley, New York, 1974.
Reitan R M, Wolfson D: Conventional intelligence measurements and neuropsychological concepts of adaptive abilities. J Clin Psychol *48*: 521, 1992.
Sperry R W: Lateral specialization in the surgically separated hemispheres. In *Hemispheric Specialization and Interaction,* B Milner, editor, p 481. MIT Press, Cambrige, 1975.
Wexler B E: Cerebral laterality and psychiatry: A review of the literature. Am J Psychiatry *137*: 3, 1980.
Wishaw I Q, Kolb B: *Fundamentals of Human Neuropsychology.* Freeman, New York, 1985.

# Theories of Personality and Psychopathology

## 6.1 / Sigmund Freud: Founder of Classic Psychoanalysis

When it comes to unraveling the mysteries of the human mind, no body of knowledge approaches that of psychoanalytic theory. Although the basic contributions of Sigmund Freud, the founder of psychoanalysis, have undergone considerable revision since their development 100 years ago, several of Freud's fundamental hypotheses regarding the workings of the mind remain central to psychiatric practice today. Included among the basic tenets are psychic determinism, the dynamic unconscious, and the crucial role of childhood development in the shaping of the adult.

Freud discerned that such diverse aspects of human experience as symptoms of psychiatric disorders, vocational choice, dreams, the selection of romantic partners, and slips of the tongue all have meaning. Behavior, thoughts, feelings, and symptoms are the final common pathways of unsciousness processes. Psychic determinism is best represented in Freud's concept of overdetermination—the idea that several intrapsychic factors operate simultaneously to create a specific symptom, thought, or behavior. Even when biological factors are influential in producing symptoms such as hallucinations, the meanings given to those phenomena are still physically determined on the basis of the person's psychological makeup.

As implied by the principle of psychic determinism, the construct of the unconscious mind is also a central feature of psychoanalytic thinking. In his clinical work with hysterical patients, Freud noted that long-forgotten memories reemerged in the process of the treatment. That discovery led him to conclude that the human mind has a form of censorship that deems certain memories, thoughts, and feelings unacceptable. The material is *repressed*—that is, buried in the unconscious, and the person is no longer consciously aware of the phenomena that have undergone repression. Freud observed that *parapraxes*, slips of the tongue, provided concrete evidence of the role of the unconscious in everyday life. The eruption of a repressed thought or feeling when one word is substituted for another often reveals an unacceptable unconscious wish.

The idea that past is prologue was also fundamental to Freud's model of the mind. Indeed, all major psychoanalytic schools of thought view developmental successes and failures as central to the evolution of adult character and as highly influential in the pathogenesis of adult psychiatric disorders. Pathogenetic factors may include both actual traumas and subtle and repetitive forms of interaction that occur between children and their parents and between children and their siblings.

Psychoanalysis today is considered to have three aspects: it is a method of investigation, a therapeutic technique, and a body of scientific and theoretical knowledge. Although this section is devoted to psychoanalysis proper as both a theory and a treatment, the basic tenets enumerated here are useful in a variety of nonanalytic settings in clinical psychiatry.

### LIFE OF FREUD

Sigmund Freud was born on May 6, 1856, of Jewish parents, in Freiburg, a small town in Moravia, which later became a part of Czechoslovakia. When Freud was 4 years old, his father, a wool merchant, moved the family to Vienna, where Freud spent most of his life. After graduating from medical school, he specialized in neurology and studied in Paris with Jean-Martin Charcot for a year. He was also influenced by Ambroise-August Leibault and Hippolyte-Marie Bernheim, both of whom taught him hypnosis while he was in France. After his education in France, he returned to Vienna and began clinical work with hysterical patients. Between 1887 and 1897, his work with those patients led him to develop psychoanalysis. Figures 6.1–1 through 6.1–9 show the highlights of Freud's life.

### BEGINNINGS OF PSYCHOANALYSIS

#### Case of Anna O.

The body of theory, knowledge, and technique that is now referred to as psychoanalysis had its origins in one typical case treated by Josef Breuer, a prominent Viennese physician who was a close friend of Freud. The patient, Bertha Pappenheim, consulted Breuer in December 1880 and continued in treatment with him until June 1882. Referred to by Breuer as

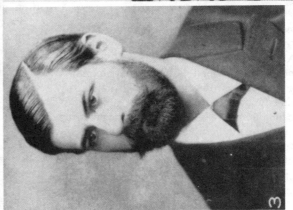

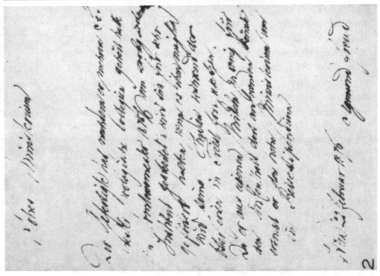

**Figure 6.1–1.** Sigmund Freud with several of his early collaborators: top, left to right, A. A. Brill, Ernest Jones, Sandor Ferenczi; bottom, left to right, Freud, G. Stanley Hall, and Carl Gustav Jung. (Figure from Culver Pictures, New York, N. Y.)

**Figure 6.1–2.** Sigmund Freud's handwriting. (Figure from Austrian Information Service, New York N. Y.)

**Figure 6.1–3.** Sigmund Freud as a young man. (Figure from Austrian Information Service, New York, N. Y.)

**Figure 6.1–4.** Berggasse 19, the building in which Freud had his offices and that now houses the Freud Museum. (Figure from Austrian Information Service, New York, N. Y.)

**Figure 6.1–5.** Sigmund Freud and his father. (Figure from Austrian Information Service, New York, N. Y.)

**Figure 6.1–6.** Sigmund Freud and his mother in 1872. (Figure from Austrian Information Service, New York, N. Y.)

**Figure 6.1–7.** Sigmund Freud's office in Vienna. (Figure from Austrian Information Service, New York, N. Y.)

**Figure 6.1–8.** Sigmund Freud at his desk in his Vienna office. (Figure from Austrian Information Service, New York, N. Y.)

**Figure 6.1–9.** Mrs. Paula Fichtl, Freud's last maid, with some personal items: hat, cane. (Figure from Austrian Information Service, New York, N. Y.)

"Anna O.," she was an intelligent and attractive woman of 21 years who presented a plethora of hysterical symptoms in association with her father's fatal illness. The symptoms included serious disturbances of sight and speech, inability to ingest food, paralysis of three extremities with contractures and anesthesias, and a nervous cough. She also manifested two distinct states of consciousness: one, a relatively normal young woman; the other, a troublesome and naughty child. Breuer observed that the shift between the two discrete personalities seemed to be induced by some form of autohypnosis, and he was able to bring about the transition from one personality to the other by placing Anna O. in a hypnotic state.

Breuer knew that Anna had been very attached to her father and had nursed him alongside her mother while he was on his deathbed. During her altered states of consciousness (called hypnoid states), Anna could recall vivid fantasies and powerful feelings she had experienced as her father lay dying. Breuer was astonished to note that his patient's recollection of the affect-laden circumstances during which her symptoms first appeared led those same symptoms to disappear. Anna O. dubbed the process the "talking cure." She was so taken by it that she continued to discuss one symptom after another. For example, she remembered sitting at her father's side while her mother was absent and having a fantasy or daydream about a snake. In her vision the snake was about to bite her father. She tried to ward off the snake, but her arm had gone to sleep as a result of having been draped over the back of her chair. The paralysis remained until she was able to recall the scene under hypnosis, whereupon she regained use of her arm.

Breuer became enchanted with his extraordinary patient. He spent so much time with her that his wife grew jealous and resentful. Frightened by the sexual connotations of his wife's complaints, he abruptly terminated the treatment of Anna O. Several hours after that termination, he was called to Anna's bedside in the midst of a crisis. He found her agitated and in the throes of hysterical childbirth. Although he had been unaware of any sexual feelings toward him, the phantom pregnancy (pseudocyesis) reflected Anna O.'s intense erotic longings for Breuer. He calmed his patient down by inducing a hypnotic trance, and, in a state of extreme agitation, he arranged for an immediate departure to Venice with his wife for a second honeymoon.

### Freud's Use of Hypnosis

In the latter part of 1887, Freud began to use hypnosis as a routine part of his clinical practice. He was fascinated by Breuer's treatment of Anna O., and he was determined to investigate what lay behind the symptoms of hysterical patients. In 1889 Freud turned to the cathartic method. Used in conjunction with hypnosis, the approach attempted to remove symptoms through a process of recovering and verbalizing suppressed feelings with which they were associated, a method that came to be known as *abreaction*.

Through his experiments with abreaction and catharsis, Freud learned that his patients were often unable or unwilling to recount memories that subsequently proved to be of great significance. He referred to that reluctance as *resistance*. He later determined that resistance is caused by largely unconscious but active forces in the patient's mind. Freud described the active process of excluding distressing material from conscious awareness as *repression*. Freud came to regard repression as essential to symptom formation. Because of the forces of repression and resistance, Freud abandoned his cathartic method and switched to *free association*—inviting his patients

to say whatever came into their minds without censoring their thoughts.

### THE INTERPRETATION OF DREAMS

Freud became aware of the significance of dreams when he noted that patients frequently reported their dreams in the process of free association. Through their further associations to the dream content, he learned that the dreams were definitely meaningful, even though that meaning was often hidden or disguised. Most of all, Freud was struck by the intimate connection between dream content and unconscious memories or fantasies that were long repressed. That observation led Freud to declare that the interpretation of dreams was the royal road to the understanding of the unconscious.

*The Interpretation of Dreams*, one of Freud's greatest works, appeared in 1900. In it he asserted that a dream is a wish fulfillment—the disguised fulfillment of an unconscious childhood wish that is not readily accessible to conscious awareness in waking life. In attempting to characterize the psychology of dreaming, Freud laid the foundations for ego psychology. He wrote that unconscious childhood wishes can be transformed into disguised conscious manifestations only if a censor exists in the mind. The censor, acting in the service of the ego, functions to preserve sleep. By disguising disturbing thoughts and feelings, the censor makes sure that the dreamer's sleep will not be disturbed. Moreover, early forms of defense mechanisms in the ego were delineated by Freud's investigation of the various methods of disguise used by the ego—for example, displacement, condensation, and symbolic representation. Freud drew beginning parallels between the dream mechanisms and the pathological thoughts of psychotic patients in the waking state.

The analysis of dreams elicits material that has been repressed. Unconscious mental activity that occurs during sleep threatens to interfere with sleep itself. Those unconscious thoughts and wishes include nocturnal sensory stimuli (sensory impressions such as pain, hunger, thirst, and urinary urgency), the day residue (thoughts and ideas that are connected with the activities and the preoccupations of the dreamer's current waking life), and repressed unacceptable impulses. Those nocturnal forms of mental activity must be associated with one or more repressed wishes to give rise to a dream, which then allows the dreamer to continue sleeping, instead of waking. Because motility is blocked by the sleep state, the dream enables partial but limited gratification of the repressed impulse that gives rise to the dream.

Freud distinguished between two layers of dream content. The *manifest* content is what is recalled by the dreamer; the *latent* content involves the unconscious thoughts and wishes that threaten to awaken the dreamer. Freud described the unconscious mental operations by which the latent dream content is transformed into the manifest dream as the *dream work*. Repressed wishes and impulses must attach themselves to innocent or neutral images to pass the scrutiny of the dream censor. That process involves the selection of apparently meaningless or trivial images from the dreamer's current experience, images that are associated dynamically with the latent images that they resemble in some respect.

## Condensation

In condensation several unconscious impulses, wishes, or feelings can be combined and attached to one manifest dream image. For example, a composite character may appear in the dream that has the name of one person in the dreamer's life, a beard like another person, and a musical instrument that indicates a third person.

## Displacement

In displacement the energy or intensity associated with one object is diverted to a substitute object that is associatively related but acceptable to the dreamer's ego. Murderous wishes toward one's mother, for example, may be redirected toward a neutral or insignificant person in one's life. In that manner the dream censor has displaced affective energy in such a way that the dreamer's sleep can continue undisturbed. A special instance of displacement, projection, involves the attribution of the dreamer's own unacceptable impulses or wishes to another character in the dream.

## Symbolic Representation

Freud noted that the dreamer often represents ideas or objects that are highly charged by using innocent images that are in some way connected with the idea or object being represented. In that manner an abstract concept or a complex set of feelings toward a person can be symbolized by a simple, concrete, or sensory image. Freud noted that symbols have unconscious meanings that can be discerned through the patient's associations to the symbol. However, he also believed that certain symbols have universal meanings.

## Secondary Revision

The mechanisms of condensation, displacement, and symbolic representation are characteristic of a type of thinking that Freud referred to as *primary process*. That primitive mode of cognitive activity is characterized by illogical, bizarre, and absurd images that seem incoherent. Freud believed that a mature and reasonable aspect of the ego is at work during the dream to organize some of those primitive aspects of the dream into a coherent form. He called that process *secondary revision*, in which mature intellectual processes make the dream somewhat rational. The processes are related to the mature activity characteristic of waking life, which Freud termed *secondary process*.

## Affects in Dreams

Repressed emotions may not appear in the dream at all, or they may be experienced in somewhat altered form. For example, repressed rage toward one's father may take the form of mild annoyance. Feelings may also appear as their opposites.

## Anxiety Dreams

Freud's dream theory preceded his development of a comprehensive theory of the ego. Hence, his understanding of dreams stressed the importance of discharging drives or wishes through the hallucinatory contents of the dream. He viewed such mechanisms as condensation, displacement, symbolic representation, projection, and secondary revision primarily as facilitating the discharge of latent impulses, rather than as protecting the dreamer from anxiety and pain. Freud understood anxiety dreams as reflecting a failure in the protective function of the dreamwork mechanisms. In other words, the repressed impulses succeed in working their way into the manifest content in a more or less recognizable manner.

## Punishment Dreams

Dreams in which the dreamer experiences punishment were a special challenge for Freud because they appear to be an exception to his wish-fulfillment theory of dreams. He came to understand such dreams as compromises between the repressed wish and the repressing agency or conscience. In the punishment dream the ego anticipates condemnation by the dreamer's conscience if the latent unacceptable impulses are allowed direct expression in the manifest dream content. Hence, the wish for punishment by the patient's conscience is satisfied by giving expression to punishment fantasies.

## TOPOGRAPHICAL MODEL OF THE MIND

The publication of *The Interpretation of Dreams* in 1900 heralded the arrival of Freud's topographical model of the mind. That model divides the mind into three regions: the conscious system, the preconscious system, and the unconscious system, each of which has its own unique characteristics.

## Conscious System

The conscious system in the topographical model is characterized as the part of the mind in which the perceptions coming from the outside world or from within the body or the mind are brought into awareness. Within the organism, however, only elements in the preconscious enter consciousness; the rest of the mind is outside the awareness. Consciousness is viewed as a subjective phenomenon whose content can be communicated only by means of language or behavior. *Cathexis* is a term used to describe psychic energy invested in an object. Freud assumed that consciousness uses a form of neutralized psychic energy that he referred to as *attention cathexis*. In other words, one is aware of a particular idea or feeling as a result of the investment of a discrete amount of psychic energy in that particular idea or feeling.

## Preconscious System

The preconscious system comprises those mental events, processes, and contents that are capable of being brought into conscious awareness by the act of focusing attention. Although most people are not consciously aware of the appearances of their first-grade teachers, they can ordinarily bring those images to mind by the deliberate focusing of attention on their memories. Conceptually, the preconscious interfaces with both the unconscious region and the conscious region of the mind. To reach conscious awareness, the contents of the unconscious must become linked with words and thus become preconscious. The preconscious also maintains the repressive barrier and censors unacceptable wishes and desires.

The type of mental activity associated with the preconscious is called *secondary process thinking*. Such thinking is aimed at avoiding unpleasure, delaying instinctual discharge, and binding mental energy in accordance with the demands of external reality and the person's moral precepts or values. It respects logical connections and tolerates inconsistencies less well than does the primary process. Thus, the secondary process is closely allied with the reality principle, which governs its activities for the most part.

## Unconscious System

The unconscious system is the dynamic one. In other words, the mental contents and processes of the unconscious are kept out of conscious awareness through the force of censorship or repression. The essence of the unconscious can be captured in five key features:

1. The unconscious is closely related to instinctual drives. In Freud's theory of development, instincts were then thought to consist of sexual and self-preservative drives, and the unconscious was thought to contain primarily the mental representations and derivatives of the sexual instinct.

2. The content of the unconscious is limited to wishes that are seeking fulfillment. Those wishes provide the motivation for dream and neurotic symptom formation. That view is now considered reductionistic.

3. The unconscious system is characterized by *primary process thinking*, which has as its principal aim the facilitation of wish fulfillment and instinctual discharge. Primary process thinking is governed by the pleasure principle and, therefore, disregards logical connections, has no conception of time, represents wishes as fulfillments, permits contradictory ideas to exist simultaneously, and denies the existence of negatives. It is characteristic of very young children, who are dedicated to the immediate gratification of their desires. Primary process thinking is also characterized by extreme mobility of drive cathexis, meaning that the investment of psychic energy can shift from object to object without opposition.

4. Memories in the unconscious have been divorced from their connections with verbal symbols. Hence, when words are reapplied to forgotten memory traits, as in psychoanalytic treatment, the verbal recathexis allows the memories to reach consciousness again.

5. The contents of the unconscious can become conscious only by passing through the preconscious, where censors are overpowered, allowing the elements to enter into consciousness.

## Limitations of the Topographical Theory

Freud soon realized that two main deficiencies in the topographical theory limited its usefulness. First, many of the defense mechanisms that patients use to avoid distressing wishes, feelings, or thoughts are themselves not initially accessible to consciousness. Repression, then, cannot be identical with the preconscious, since by definition that region of the mind is not accessible to consciousness. The second major deficiency was that Freud's patients frequently showed an unconscious need for punishment. That clinical observation made it unlikely that the moral agency making the demand for punishment was allied with anti-instinctual forces that were available to conscious awareness in the preconscious.

Those difficulties led Freud to discard the topographical theory. However, certain concepts derived from the theory continue to be useful, particularly primary and secondary thought processes, the fundamental importance of wish fulfillment, the existence of a dynamic unconscious, and a tendency toward regression under frustrating conditions.

## INSTINCT OR DRIVE THEORY

After the development of the topographical model, Freud turned his attention to the complexities of instinct theory. Freud was determined to anchor his psychological theory in biology. That choice led to terminological and conceptual difficulties when Freud used terms derived from biology to denote psychological constructs. Instinct, for example, is a pattern of species-specific behavior that is genetically derived and, therefore, more or less independent of learning. However, modern research demonstrating that instinctual patterns are modified through experiential learning has made Freud's instinctual theory problematic. Further confusion stems from the ambiguity inherent in a concept on the border between the biological and the psychological. Should the mental representation aspect of the term and the physiological component be integrated or separated? Although "drive" may have been closer than "instinct" to Freud's meaning, in contemporary usage the two terms are often used interchangeably.

In Freud's view an instinct has four principal characteristics: source, impetus, aim, and object. The *source* is the part of the body from which the instinct arises. The *impetus* is the amount of force or intensity associated with the instinct. The *aim* refers to any action directed toward tension discharge or satisfaction. The *object* is the target (often a person) for that action.

## Instincts

**Libido.** Freud defined *libido* as "the force by which the sexual instinct is represented in the mind." The association of libido with sexuality is somewhat misleading in that Freud's intent was to encompass not only sexuality but also the general notion of pleasure, including the physiological underpinnings and the mental representations. The linkage of genital sexuality with libido was viewed as the end result of a course of development in which libidinal expression takes a variety of forms.

**Ego instincts.** From 1905 on, Freud maintained a dual-instinct theory subsuming sexual instincts and ego instincts connected with self-preservation. Until 1914, with the publication of "On Narcissism," Freud had paid little attention to ego instincts. In that paper Freud invested ego instinct with libido for the first time. He postulated an ego libido and an object libido. Freud thus viewed narcissistic investment as an essentially libidinal instinct and called the remaining nonsexual components the ego instincts.

**Aggression.** When psychoanalysts today discuss the dual-instinct theory, they are generally referring to libido and aggression. However, Freud originally conceptualized aggression as a component of the sexual instincts in the form of sadism. As he became aware that sadism has nonsexual aspects to it, he made finer gradations, enabling him to categorize aggression and hate as part of the ego instincts and to categorize the libidinal aspects of sadism as components of the sexual instincts. Finally, to account for the clinical data he was observing, in 1923 he conceived of aggression as a separate instinct in its own right. The source of that instinct, according to Freud, is largely in skeletal muscles, and the aim of the aggressive instinct is destruction.

**Life and death instincts.** In 1920, before the designation of aggression as a separate instinct, Freud subsumed the ego instincts under a broad category of life instincts. That classification of the instincts is more abstract and has broader applications than his previous concept of libidinal and aggressive drives. Life instincts were juxtaposed with death instincts, and the two were referred to as Eros and Thanatos, respectively, in *Beyond the Pleasure Principle*. The life and death instincts were regarded as forces underlying the sexual and aggressive instincts. Although Freud could not provide clinical data that directly verified the death instinct, he thought it could be inferred by observing the *repetition compulsion*, the tendency of persons to repeat past traumatic behavior. Freud felt that a dominant force in biological organisms had to be the death instinct. He viewed it as a tendency of all organisms and their component selves to return to an inanimate state. In contrast to the death instinct, Eros (the life instinct) is the tendency of particles to reunite or bind to one another, as in sexual reproduction. The prevalent view today is that the dual instincts of sexuality and aggression are sufficient to explain most clinical phenomena without recourse to a death instinct.

### Pleasure and Reality Principles

In 1911 Freud described two basic tenets of mental functioning, the pleasure principle and the reality principle. He essentially recast the primary process and secondary process dichotomy into the pleasure and reality principles, thus taking an important step toward solidifying the concept of the ego. Both principles, in Freud's view, are aspects of ego functioning. The *pleasure principle* is defined as an inborn tendency of the organism to avoid pain and to seek pleasure through the discharge of tension. The *reality principle* is considered a learned function, closely related to the maturation of the ego, that modifies the pleasure principle and requires the delay or the postponement of immediate gratification.

### Infantile Sexuality

Freud set forth the three major tenets of psychoanalytic theory when he published *Three Essays on the Theory of Sexuality*. First of all, he broadened the definition of sexuality to include forms of pleasure that transcend genital sexuality. Second, Freud established a developmental theory of childhood sexuality that delineated the vicissitudes of erotic activity from birth through puberty. Third, he forged a conceptual linkage between neuroses and perversions. The idea that children are influenced by sexual drives has made some people reluctant to accept psychoanalysis throughout its 100-year history.

Freud noted that infants are capable of erotic activity from birth, but the earliest manifestations of infantile sexuality are basically nonsexual. The manifestations are associated with such bodily functions as feeding and bowel and bladder control. As the libidinal energy shifts from the oral zone to the anal zone to the phallic zone, each stage of development is thought to build on and to subsume the accomplishments of the preceding stage. The *oral stage* occupies approximately the first 18 months of life, centers on the mouth and the lips, and is manifested in chewing, biting, and sucking. The dominant erotic activity of the *anal stage*, which extends from 1 to 3 years of age, involves bowel function and control. The *phallic stage*, from 3 to 5 years of life, initially focuses on urination as the source of erotic activity. Freud suggested that phallic erotic activity in boys is a preliminary stage leading to adult genital activity. Whereas the penis remains the principal sexual organ throughout male psychosexual development, Freud postulated that the female has two principal erotogenic zones, the vagina and the clitoris. He thought that the clitoris is the chief erotogenic focus during the infantile genital period but that erotic primacy shifts to the vagina after puberty. Studies on human sexuality have subsequently questioned the validity of that distinction.

Freud described the erotic impulses that arise from the pregenital zones as component or part instincts. Ordinarily, in the course of development, those component instincts undergo repression or retain a restricted role in sexual foreplay. The failure to achieve genital primacy may result in various forms of pathology. The persistent attachment of the sexual instinct at a particular phase of pregenital development was termed a *fixation*.

Freud discovered that, in the psychoneuroses, only a limited number of the sexual impulses that had undergone repression and were responsible for creating and maintaining the neurotic symptoms were normal. For the most part, they were the same impulses that were given overt expression in the perversions. The neuroses, then, were the negative of perversions.

## Object Relationships in Instinct Theory

Freud suggested that the choice of a love object in adult life, the love relationship itself, and the nature of all other object relationships depend primarily on the nature and the quality of the child's relationships during the early years of life. In describing the libidinal phases of psychosexual development, Freud repeatedly referred to the significance of the child's relationships with parents and other significant persons in the environment

The awareness of the external world of objects develops gradually in infants. Soon after birth, infants are primarily aware of physical sensations—such as hunger, cold, and pain—that give rise to tension, and caretakers are primarily regarded as persons who relieve their tension or remove painful stimuli. Recent infant research, however, suggests that awareness of others begins much sooner than Freud originally thought. Table 6.1–1 provides a summary of the stages of psychosexual development and the object relationships associated with each stage. Although the table goes only as far as young adulthood, development is now recognized as continuing throughout adult life.

## Concept of Narcissism

According to the Greek myth, Narcissus was a young man who fell in love with his own reflection in the water of a pool and drowned in his attempt to embrace the beloved image. Freud used the term *"narcissism"* for situations in which a person's libido is invested in the ego itself, rather than in other people. That conceptualization of narcissism presented Freud with vexing problems for his instinct theory. It essentially violated his distinction between libidinal instinct and ego or self-preservative instincts.

Freud's understanding of narcissism led him to use the term for a wide array of psychiatric disorders, very much in contrast to the contemporary usage of the term to describe a specific kind of personality disorder. Freud lumped the disorders together as the narcissistic neuroses, in which the person's libido is withdrawn from objects and is turned inward. In 1908 Freud observed that, in cases of dementia precox (schizophrenia), libido appeared to have been withdrawn from other persons or objects, and he concluded that the withdrawal may account for the loss of contact with reality that was typical of such patients. He believed that the withdrawal of libidinal attachments accounted for the loss of reality testing in other psychotic patients as well. Grandiosity and omnipotence in such patients reflect excessive libidinal investment in the ego.

Freud did not limit his use of "narcissism" to psychoses. In states of physical illness and hypochondriasis, libidinal investment, he observed, is frequently withdrawn from external objects and from outside activities and interests. Similarly, he believed that, in normal sleep, libido is withdrawn from external objects and reinvested in the sleeper's own body. Freud regarded homosexuality as a perversion and understood it as an instance of a narcissistic form of object choice, one in which persons fall in love with an idealized version of themselves projected onto another person. He also found narcissistic manifestations in the beliefs and myths of primitive people, especially those beliefs involving the ability to influence external events through the magical omnipotence of people's own thought processes. In the course of normal development, children also exhibit a belief in their own omnipotence.

Freud postulated a state of primary narcissism at birth in which the libido is stored in the ego. He viewed the neonate as completely narcissistic, with the entire libidinal investment in physiological needs and their satisfaction. He referred to that self-investment as *ego libido*. The infantile state of self-absorption changes only gradually, according to Freud, with the dawning awareness that a separate person—the mothering figure—is responsible for the gratification of the infant's needs. That realization leads to the gradual withdrawal of the libido from the self and its redirection toward the external object. Hence, the development of object relations in the infant parallels the shift from primary narcissism to object attachment. The libidinal investment in the object is referred to as *object libido*. If the developing child suffers rebuffs or traumas from the caretaking figure, object libido may be withdrawn and reinvested in the ego. Freud called that regressive posture *secondary narcissism*.

Freud used the term "narcissism" for a variety of dimensions of human experience. At times he used it for a perversion in which persons use their own bodies or body parts as objects of sexual arousal. Narcissism differs from autoeroticism in that autoeroticism refers to eroticism in relation to the person's own body or its parts; narcissism refers to the love of something more abstract, either the self or the person's ego.

At other times Freud used the term "narcissism" for a developmental phase, as in the state of primary narcissism. In still other instances, he used the term for a particular type of object choice. Freud distinguished love objects who are chosen "according to the narcissistic type" (in which case the object resembles the subject's idealized or fantasied self-image) from objects chosen according to the "anaclitic type" (in which the love object resembles a caretaker from early in life). Persons who have an intense degree of self-love, especially certain beautiful women, have, according to Freud, an appeal over and above their esthetic attraction. Such women supply for their lovers the lost narcissism that was painfully renounced in the process of turning toward object love. Freud also used the word "narcissism" interchangeably and synonymously with "self-esteem."

## EGO PSYCHOLOGY

Although Freud had used the construct of the ego throughout the evolution of psychoanalytic theory, ego psychology as it is known today really began with the publication of *The Ego and the Id* in 1923. That landmark publication represented a transition in Freud's thinking from the topographical model of the mind to the tripartite structural model of ego, id, and superego. He had repeatedly observed that not all unconscious processes can be relegated to the person's instinctual life. Elements of the conscience, as well as the functions of the ego, are clearly unconscious as well.

**Table 6.1–1**
**Stages of Psychosexual Development**

| | Oral Stage | | |
| --- | --- | --- | --- |
| Definition | The earliest stage of development, in which the infant's needs, perceptions, and modes of expression are primarily centered in the mouth, lips, tongue, and other organs related to the oral zone. | Objectives | To establish a trusting dependence on nursing and sustaining objects, to establish comfortable expression and gratification of oral libidinal needs without excessive conflict or ambivalence from oral sadistic wishes. |
| Description | The oral zone maintains its dominant role in the organization of the psyche through approximately the first 18 months of life. Oral sensations include thirst, hunger, pleasurable tactile stimulations evoked by the nipple or its substitute, sensations related to swallowing and satiation. Oral drives consist of two separate components: libidinal and aggressive. States of oral tension lead to a seeking for oral gratification, typified by quiescence at the end of nursing. The oral triad consists of the wish to eat, to sleep, and to reach the relaxation that occurs at the end of sucking just before the onset of sleep. Libidinal needs (oral erotism) are thought to predominate in the early parts of the oral phase, whereas they are mixed with more aggressive components later (oral sadism). Oral aggression may express itself in biting, chewing, spitting, or crying. Oral aggression is connected with primitive wishes and fantasies of biting, devouring, and destroying. | Pathological traits | Excessive oral gratifications or deprivation can result in libidinal fixations that contribute to pathological traits. Such traits can include excessive optimism, narcissism, pessimism (often seen in depressive states), and demandingness. Oral characters are often excessively dependent and require others to give to them and to look after them. Such persons want to be fed but may be exceptionally giving to elicit a return of being given to. Oral characters are often extremely dependent on objects for the maintenance of their self-esteem. Envy and jealousy are often associated with oral traits. |
| | | Character traits | Successful resolution of the oral phase provides a basis in character structure for capacities to give to and receive from others without excessive dependence or envy and a capacity to rely on others with a sense of trust, as well as with a sense of self-reliance and self-trust. |

| | Anal Stage | | |
| --- | --- | --- | --- |
| Definition | The stage of psychosexual development that is prompted by maturation of neuromuscular control over sphincters, particularly the anal sphincters, thus permitting more voluntary control over retention or expulsion of feces. | | pendence on and control of the parent. The objectives of sphincter control without overcontrol (fecal retention) or loss of control (messing) are matched by the child's attempts to achieve autonomy and independence without excessive shame or self-doubt from loss of control. |
| Description | This period, which extends roughly from 1 to 3 years of age, is marked by a recognizable intensification of aggressive drives mixed with libidinal components and in sadistic impulses. Acquisition of voluntary sphincter control is associated with an increasing shift from passivity to activity. The conflicts over anal control and the struggle with the parent over retaining or expelling feces in toilet training give rise to increased ambivalence, together with a struggle over separation, individuation, and independence. Anal erotism refers to the sexual pleasure in anal functioning, both in retaining the precious feces and in presenting them as a precious gift to the parent. Anal sadism refers to the expression of aggressive wishes connected with discharging feces as powerful and destructive weapons. Those wishes are often displayed in such children's fantasies as bombing and explosions. | Pathological traits | Maladaptive character traits, often apparently inconsistent, are derived from anal erotism and the defenses against it. Orderliness, obstinancy, stubbornness, willfulness, frugality, and parsimony are features of the anal character derived from a fixation on anal functions. When defenses against anal traits are less effective, the anal character reveals traits of heightened ambivalence, lack of tidiness, messiness, defiance, rage, and sadomasochistic tendencies. Anal characteristics and defenses are most typically seen in obsessive-compulsive neuroses. |
| Objectives | The anal period is essentially a period of striving for independence and separation from the de- | Character traits | Successful resolution of the anal phase provides the basis for the development of personal autonomy, a capacity for independence and personal initiative without guilt, a capacity for self-determining behavior without a sense of shame or self-doubt, a lack of ambivalence, and a capacity for willing cooperation without either excessive willfulness or sense of self-diminution or defeat. |

| | Urethral Stage | | |
| --- | --- | --- | --- |
| Definition | This stage was not explicitly treated by Freud but was envisioned as a transitional stage between the anal and the phallic stages of development. It shares some of the characteristics of the preceding anal stage and some from the subsequent phallic stage. | | often subsumed under those of the phallic stage. Urethral erotism, however, is used to refer to the pleasure in urination, as well as the pleasure in urethral retention analogous to anal retention. Similar issues of performance and control are related to urethral functioning. Urethral functioning may also be invested with a sadistic quality, often reflecting the persistence of anal sadistic urges. Loss of urethral control, |
| Description | The characteristics of the urethral stage are | | |

*Continued*

**Table 6.1–1**
*Continued*

| | Urethral Stage | | |
|---|---|---|---|
| | as in enuresis, may frequently have regressive significance that reactivates anal conflicts. | | feminine sense of shame and inadequacy in being unable to match the male urethral performance. It is also related to issues of control and shaming. |
| Objectives | Issues of control and urethral performance and loss of control. It is not clear whether or to what extent the objectives of urethral functioning differ from those of the anal period. | Character traits | Besides the healthy effects analogous to those from the anal period, urethral competence provides a sense of pride and self-competence derived from performance. Urethral performance is an area in which the small boy can imitate and match his father's more adult performance. The resolution of urethral conflicts sets the stage for budding gender identity and subsequent identifications. |
| Pathological traits | The predominant urethral trait is that of competitiveness and ambition, probably related to the compensation for shame caused by loss of urethral control. In control it may be the start for the development of penis envy, related to the | | |

| | Phallic Stage | | |
|---|---|---|---|
| Definition | The phallic stage of sexual development begins sometime during the third year of life and continues until approximately the end of the fifth year. | Pathological traits | The derivation of pathological traits from the phallic-oedipal involvement are sufficiently complex and subject to such a variety of modifications that it encompasses nearly the whole of neurotic development. The issues, however, focus on castration in males and on penis envy in females. The other important focus of developmental distortions in this period derives from the patterns of identification that are developed out of the resolution of the oedipal complex. The influence of castration anxiety and penis envy, the defenses against both, and the patterns of identification that emerge from the phallic stage are the primary determinants of the development of human character. They also subsume and integrate the residues of previous psychosexual stages, so that fixations or conflicts that derive from any of the preceding stages can contaminate and modify the oedipal resolution. |
| Description | The phallic stage is characterized by a primary focus of sexual interests, stimulation, and excitement in the genital area. The penis becomes the organ of principal interest to children of both sexes, with the lack of a penis in the female being considered evidence of castration. The phallic stage is associated with an increase in genital masturbation, accompanied by predominantly unconscious fantasies of sexual involvement with the opposite-sex parent. The threat of castration and its related castration anxiety arise in connection with guilt over masturbation and oedipal wishes. During this phase the oedipal involvement and conflict are established and consolidated. | | |
| Objectives | The objective of this stage is to focus erotic interest in the genital area and genital functions. This focusing lays the foundation for gender identity and serves to integrate the residues of previous stages of psychosexual development into a predominantly genital-sexual orientation. The establishing of the oedipal situation is essential for the furtherance of subsequent identifications that will serve as the basis for important and perduring dimensions of character organization. | Character traits | The phallic stage provides the foundations for an emerging sense of sexual identity, a sense of curiosity without embarrassment, initiative without guilt, as well as a sense of mastery not only over objects and persons in the environment but also over internal processes and impulses. The resolution of the oedipal conflict at the end of the phallic period gives rise to powerful internal resources for the regulation of drive impulses and their direction to constructive ends. The internal source of regulation is the superego, and it is based on identifications derived primarily from parental figures. |

| | Latency Stage | | |
|---|---|---|---|
| Definition | The stage of relative quiescence or inactivity of the sexual drive during the period from the resolution of the Oedipus complex until pubescence (from about 5–6 years until about 11–13 years). | | a period for the development of important skills. The relative strength of regulatory elements often gives rise to patterns of behavior that are somewhat obsessive and hypercontrolling. |
| Description | The institution of the superego at the close of the oedipal period and the further maturation of ego functions allow for a considerably greater degree of control of instinctual impulses. Sexual interests during this period are generally thought to be quiescent. This is a period of primarily homosexual affiliations for both boys and girls, as well as a sublimation of libidinal and aggressive energies into energetic learning and play activities, exploring the environment, and becoming more proficient in dealing with the world of things and persons around them. It is | Objectives | The primary objective in this period is the further integration of oedipal identifications and a consolidation of sex-role identity and sex roles. The relative quiescence and control of instinctual impulses allow for the development of ego apparatuses and mastery skills. Further identificatory components may be added to the oedipal ones on the basis of broadening contacts with other significant figures outside the family, such as teachers, coaches, and other adults. |
| | | Pathological traits | The danger in the latency period can arise either from a lack of development of inner controls or an excess of them. The lack of control can lead |

| Latency Stage | | | |
|---|---|---|---|
| | to a failure of the child to sufficiently sublimate energies in the interests of learning and development of skills; an excess of inner control, however, can lead to premature closure of personality development and the precocious elaboration of obsessive character traits. | | made to the basic postoedipal identifications. It is a period of integrating and consolidating previous attainments in psychosexual development and establishing decisive patterns of adaptive functioning. The child can develop a sense of industry and a capacity for mastery of objects and concepts that allows autonomous function and with a sense of initiative without running the risk of failure or defeat or a sense of inferiority. These important attainments need to be further integrated, ultimately as the essential basis for a mature adult life of satisfaction in work and love. |
| Character traits | The latency period has frequently been regarded as a period of relatively unimportant inactivity in the developmental schema. Recently, great respect has been gained for the developmental processes that take place in this period. Important consolidations and additions are | | |

| Genital Stage | | | |
|---|---|---|---|
| Definition | The genital or adolescent stage of psychosexual development extends from the onset of puberty from ages 11 to 13 until the person reaches young adulthood. In current thinking, there is a tendency to subdivide this stage into preadolescent period, early adolescent, middle adolescent, late adolescent, and even postadolescent periods. | Pathological traits | The pathological deviations due to a failure to achieve successful resolution of this stage of development are multiple and complex. Defects can arise from the whole spectrum of psychosexual residues, since the developmental task of the adolescent period is in a sense a partial reopening and reworking and reintegrating of all those aspects of development. Previous unsuccessful resolutions and fixations in various phases or aspects of psychosexual development will produce pathological defects in the emerging adult personality. A more specific defect from a failure to resolve adolescent issues has been described by Erikson as identity diffusion. |
| Description | The physiological maturation of systems of genital (sexual) functioning and attendant hormonal systems leads to an intensification of drives, particularly libidinal drives. This produces a regression in personality organization, which reopens conflicts of previous stages of psychosexual development and provides the opportunity for a reresolution of these conflicts in the context of achieving a mature sexual and adult identity. | | |
| | | Character traits | The successful resolution and reintegration of previous psychosexual stages in the adolescent, fully genital phase sets the stage normally for a fully mature personality with a capacity for full and satisfying genital potency and a self-integrated and consistent sense of identity. Such a person has reached a satisfying capacity for self-realization and meaningful participation in the areas of work and love and in the creative and productive application to satisfying and meaningful goals and values. Only in the last few years has the presumed relation between psychosexual genitality and maturity of personality functioning been put in question. |
| Objectives | The primary objectives of this period are the ultimate separation from dependence on and attachment to the parents and the establishment of mature, nonincestuous object relations. Related to this are the achievement of a mature sense of personal identity and acceptance and the integration of a set of adult roles and functions that permit new adaptive integrations with social expectations and cultural values. | | |

Table adapted from W. W. Meissner, M.D., by Glen O. Gabbard, M.D.

## Structural Theory of the Mind

The structural model of the psychic apparatus is the cornerstone of ego psychology. The three provinces—id, ego, and superego—are distinguished by their different functions.

**Id.** Freud used the term "id" to refer to a reservoir of the unorganized instinctual drives. Operating under the domination of the primary process, the id lacks the capacity to delay or modify the instinctual drives with which the infant is born. The id should not, however, be viewed as synonymous with the unconscious, because both the ego and the superego have unconscious components.

**Ego.** The ego spans all three topographical dimensions of conscious, preconscious, and unconscious. Logical and abstract thinking and verbal expression are associated with conscious and preconscious functions of the ego. Defense mechanisms reside in the unconscious domain of the ego. It is the executive organ of the psyche and controls motility, perception, contact with reality, and, through the mechanisms of defense available to it, the delay and modulation of drive expression.

Freud believed that the modification of the id occurs as a result of the effects of the external world on the drives. The pressures of external reality enable the ego to appropriate the energies of the id to do the work of the ego. As the ego brings influences from the external world to bear on the id, it simultaneously substitutes the reality principle for the pleasure principle. Freud emphasized the role of conflict within the structural model and observed that conflict is initially between the id and the outside world, only to be transformed later to conflict between the id and the ego.

**Superego.** The third component of the tripartite structural model is the superego. The superego establishes and maintains the person's moral conscience on the basis of a complex system of ideals and values internalized from one's parents. Freud viewed the superego as the heir to the Oedipus complex. In other words, the child internalizes the parental values and standards around the age of 5 or 6 years. The superego then serves as an agency that provides ongoing scrutiny of the person's behavior, thoughts, and feelings. It makes comparisons with expected standards of behavior and offers approval or disapproval. Those activities occur unconsciously to a large extent.

The ego-ideal is often regarded as a component of the superego. It is an agency that prescribes what one should do according to internalized standards and values. The superego, by contrast, is an agency of moral conscience that *proscribes*—that is, dictates what one should *not* do. Throughout the latency period and thereafter, persons continue to build on early identifications through their contact with other admired persons who contribute to the formation of moral standards, aspirations, and ideals.

## Functions of the Ego

Modern ego psychologists have identified a set of basic ego functions that characterize the operations of the ego. The following descriptions reflect the ego activities that are generally regarded as fundamental.

**Control and regulation of instinctual drives.** The development of the capacity to delay or postpone drive discharge is closely related to the progression in early childhood from the pleasure principle to the reality principle. That capacity is also an essential aspect of the ego's role as mediator between the id and the outside world. Part of the infant's socialization to the external world is the acquisition of language and secondary process or logical thinking.

**Judgment.** A closely related ego function is judgment, which involves the ability to anticipate the consequences of one's actions. As with the control and regulation of instinctual drives, judgment develops in parallel with the growth of secondary process thinking. The ability to think logically allows for an assessment of how one's contemplated behavior may affect others.

**Relation to reality.** The mediation between the internal world and external reality is a crucial function of the ego. The relation with the outside world can be divided into three aspects: the sense of reality, reality testing, and adaptation to reality. The *sense of reality* develops in concert with the infant's dawning awareness of bodily sensations. The ability to distinguish what is outside the body from what is inside is an essential aspect of the sense of reality, and disturbances of body boundaries, such as depersonalization, reflect impairments in that ego function. *Reality testing*, an ego function of paramount importance, refers to the capacity to distinguish internal fantasy from external reality. That function differentiates psychotic persons from nonpsychotic persons. *Adaptation to reality* involves the ability to use one's resources to develop effective responses to changing circumstances on the basis of previous experiences with reality.

**Object relationships.** The capacity to form mutually satisfying relationships is, in part, related to patterns of internalization stemming from early interactions with parents and other significant persons. The term "object" refers to the relationship of the infant with another person. That ability is also a fundamental function of the ego, in that satisfying relatedness depends on the ability to integrate positive and negative aspects of others and oneself and to maintain an internal sense of others, even in their absence. Similarly, mastery of drive derivatives is crucial to the achievement of satisfying relationships. Although Freud did not develop an extensive object relations theory, British psychoanalysts, such as Ronald Fairbairn (1889–1964) and Michael Balint (1886–1970), elaborated in great detail on the early stages in the relationship of the infant with need-satisfying objects and on the gradual development of a sense of separateness from the mother. Another of their British colleagues, Donald W. Winnicott (1897–1971), described the *transitional object* (for example, a blanket, a teddy bear, a pacifier) as the link between developing children and their mothers. The child is able to separate from the mother because the transitional object provides feelings of security in her absence.

The stages of human development and object relations theory are summarized in Figure 6.1–10.

**Synthetic function of the ego.** First described by Herman Nunberg in 1931, the synthetic function is the ego's capacity to integrate diverse elements into an overall unity. Various aspects of oneself and others, for example, are synthesized into a consistent representation that endures over time. The function also involves organizing, coordinating, and generalizing or simplifying large amounts of data.

**Primary autonomous ego functions.** A direct outgrowth of the work of Heinz Hartmann, the primary autonomous functions are the rudimentary apparatuses that are present at birth and that develop independently of intrapsychic conflicts between drives and defenses, provided that what Hartmann referred to as an *average expectable environment* is available to the infant. Those functions include perception, learning, intelligence, intuition, language, thinking, comprehension, and motility. In the course of development, some of those conflict-free aspects of the ego may eventually become involved in conflicts if they encounter opposing forces.

**Secondary autonomous ego functions.** Hartmann originally used the concept of the conflict-free sphere of ego functioning to identify areas of primary autonomy. However, that area may be enlarged by functions that originally arise in the service of defense against drives but subsequently become independent of them. Those functions are referred to as secondary autonomous ego functions. For example, a child may develop caretaking functions as a reaction formation against murderous wishes during the first few years of life. Later, the defensive functions of that style may be neutralized or deinstinctualized when the child grows up to be a social worker and cares for the homeless.

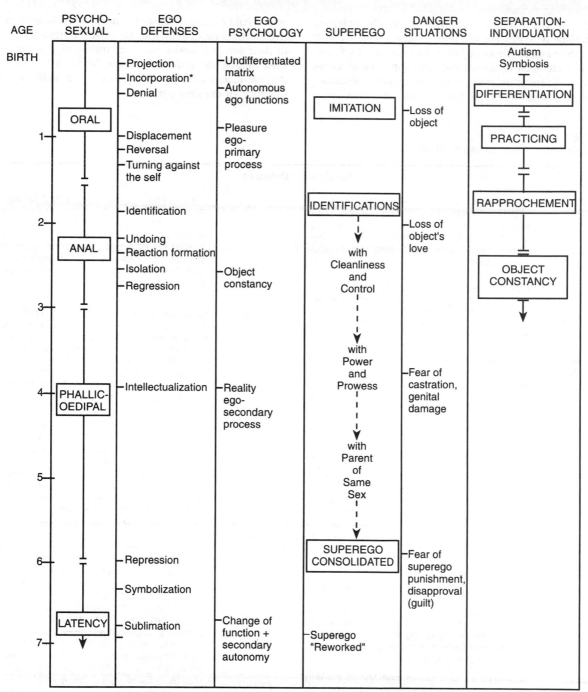

**Figure 6.1–10.** Parallel lines of human development. *Also introjection. (Figure from L B Inderbitzin, C M Luke, M E James: Psychoanalytic psychotherapy. In *Human Behavior: An Intro-* *duction for Medical Students*, A Stoudemire, editor, p 74. Lippincott, Philadelphia, 1990. Used with permission.)

## Defense Mechanisms

Freud acknowledged the existence of several defense mechanisms, but his writings focused predominantly on repression, which he regarded as the major, most significant, and most often used defense. The first comprehensive study of defense mechanisms was written by his daughter Anna Freud in her landmark book *The Ego and the Mechanisms of Defense*, in which she maintained that everyone, normal or neurotic, uses a characteristic repertoire of defense mechanisms. She also insisted that the ego should

be the focus of psychoanalytic treatment, in addition to the uncovering of repressed drive derivatives. Her observation that "there is depth in the surface" reflected her appreciation of the complexity of the defensive aspects of the ego.

At each phase of libidinal development, specific drive components evoke characteristic ego defenses. The anal phase, for example, is associated with reaction formation, as manifested by the development of shame and disgust in relation to anal impulses and pleasures.

Defenses can be grouped hierarchically according to the

relative degree of maturity associated with the defenses. Narcissistic defenses are the most primitive and are used by children and psychotically disturbed persons. Immature defenses are seen in adolescents and some nonpsychotic patients. Neurotic defenses are encountered in obsessive-compulsive and hysterical patients and in adults under stress. And mature defenses are normal and healthy adaptive mechanisms of adult life. Those groupings are not rigid in their borders, and some overlapping of defenses may exist among the different groups. Table 6.1–2 lists the defense mechanisms according to George Vaillant's classification of the four types.

**Table 6.1–2**
**Classification of Defense Mechanisms**

### Narcissistic Defenses

| | |
|---|---|
| Denial | The avoidance of the awareness of some painful aspect of reality by negating sensory data. Repression defends against affects and drive derivatives, but denial abolishes external reality. Denial may be used in both normal and pathological states. |
| Distortion | External reality is grossly reshaped to suit inner needs—including unrealistic megalomanic beliefs, hallucinations, wish-fulfilling delusions—and is used to sustain feelings of delusional superiority or entitlement. |
| Primitive idealization | External objects that are viewed as either "all good" or "all bad" are unrealistically endowed with great power. Most commonly, the "all-good" object is seen as omnipotent or ideal, and the badness in the "all-bad" object is greatly inflated. |
| Projection | Unacceptable inner impulses and their derivatives are perceived and reacted to as though they were outside the self. On a psychotic level, it takes the form of frank delusions about external reality, usually persecutory, and includes both perception of one's own feelings in another and subsequent acting on the perception (psychotic paranoid delusions). The impulses may derive from the id or the superego (hallucinated recriminations) but may undergo transformation in the process. Thus, according to Freud's analysis of paranoid projections, homosexual libidinal impulses are transformed into hatred and then projected onto the object of the unacceptable homosexual impulse. |
| Projective identification | Unwanted aspects of the self are deposited into another person so that the person projecting feels at one with the object of the projection. The extruded aspects are modified by and recovered from the recipient. The defense allows one to distance and make oneself understood by exerting pressure on another person to experience feelings similar to one's own. |
| Splitting | External objects are divided into "all good" and "all bad," accompanied by the abrupt shifting of an object from one extreme category to the other. Sudden and complete reversal of feelings and conceptualizations about a person may occur. The extreme repetitive oscillation between contradictory self-concepts is another manifestation of the mechanism. |

### Immature Defenses

| | |
|---|---|
| Acting out | The person expresses an unconscious wish or impulse through action to avoid being conscious of an accompanying affect. The unconscious fantasy is lived out impulsively in behavior, thereby gratifying the impulse, rather than the prohibition against it. Acting out involves chronically giving in to an impulse to avoid the tension that would result from the postponement of expression. |
| Blocking | A temporary or transient inhibition of thinking occurs in blocking. Affects and impulses may also be involved. Blocking closely resembles repression but differs in that tension arises when the impulse, affect, or thought is inhibited. |
| Hypochondriasis | Reproach arising from bereavement, loneliness, or unacceptable aggressive impulses toward others is transformed into self-reproach and complaints of pain, somatic illness, and neurasthenia. An illness may also be exaggerated or overemphasized for the purpose of evasion and regression. In hypochondriasis, responsibility can be avoided, guilt may be circumvented, and instinctual impulses are warded off. Because hypochondriacal introjects are ego-alien, the afflicted person experiences dysphoria and a sense of affliction. |
| Identification | Identification, which plays a crucial role in ego development, may also be used as a defense mechanism under certain circumstances. Identification with the loved object may serve as a defense against the anxiety or pain that accompanies separation from or loss of the object, whether real or threatened. If identification occurs out of guilt, the person identifies for self-punitive purposes with a quality or symptom of the person who is the source of the guilt feelings. The mechanism of identification with the aggressor, first described by Anna Freud, may also be enlisted as a defense mechanism. |
| Introjection | Although vital to the person's developmental stages, introjection also serves specific defensive functions. The process of introjection involves the internalization of the qualities of an object; when used as a defense, it can obliterate the distinction between the subject and the object. Through introjection of a loved object, the painful awareness of separateness or the threat of loss may be avoided. Introjection of a feared object serves to avoid anxiety when the aggressive characteristics of the object are internalized, thus placing the aggression under one's own control. A classic example is identification with the aggressor. An identification with the victim may also take place, whereby the self-punitive qualities of the object are taken over and established within one's self as a symptom or character trait. |

## Immature Defenses

| | | | |
|---|---|---|---|
| Passive-aggressive behavior | Aggression toward others is expressed indirectly through passivity, masochism, and turning against the self. Manifestations of passive-aggressive behavior include failures, procrastination, and illnesses that affect others more than oneself. | | basic tendency to gain instinctual gratification at a less-developed period. Regression is also a normal phenomenon, as a certain amount of regression is essential for relaxation, sleep, and orgasm in sexual intercourse. Regression is considered an essential concomitant of the creative process. |
| Projection | A person attributes his or her own feelings and wishes to another person because of intolerable inner feelings or painful affects. Characteristically present in psychotic states, especially paranoid syndromes, projection is also widely used under normal conditions. In psychoses, projection takes the form of frank delusions about external reality, usually persecutory in nature, and includes the perception of one's own feelings toward another and subsequent acting on the perception. | Schizoid fantasy | Through fantasy, a person indulges in autistic retreat to resolve conflicts and to obtain gratification. Interpersonal intimacy is avoided, and eccentricity serves to repel others. The person does not fully believe in the fantasies or insist on acting them out. |
| Regression | Through regression, the person attempts to return to an earlier libidinal phase of functioning to avoid the tension and conflict evoked at the present level of development. It reflects the | Somatization | Psychic derivatives are converted into bodily symptoms, and the person tends to react with somatic manifestations, rather than psychic manifestations. In desomatization, infantile somatic responses are replaced by thought and affect; in resomatization, the person regresses to earlier somatic forms in the face of resolved conflicts. |

## Neurotic Defenses

| | | | |
|---|---|---|---|
| Controlling | An excessive attempt exists to manage or regulate events or objects in the environment to minimize anxiety and to resolve inner conflicts. | | cessively placed on irrelevant details to avoid perceiving the whole. |
| Displacement | An emotion or drive cathexis from one idea or object is shifted to another that resembles the original in some aspect or quality. Displacement permits the symbolic representation of the original idea or object in a way that is less highly cathected or that evokes less distress than the original. | Isolation | Isolation is the splitting or separation of an idea from the affect that accompanies it but is repressed. Social isolation is the absence of object relationships. |
| Dissociation | A temporary but drastic modification of a person's character or of one's sense of personal identity takes place to avoid emotional distress. Fugue states and hysterical conversion reactions are common manifestations of dissociation. Dissociation may also be found with counterphobic behavior, dissociative identity disorder, the use of pharmacological highs, and religious joy. | Rationalization | Rational explanations are offered by a person in an attempt to justify attitudes, beliefs, or behavior that may otherwise be unacceptable. Such underlying motives are usually instinctually determined. |
| Externalization | A more general term than projection, externalization refers to the tendency to perceive in the external world and in external objects elements of one's own personality, including instinctual impulses, conflicts, moods, attitudes, and styles of thinking. | Reaction formation | An unacceptable impulse is transformed into its opposite. Reaction formation is characteristic of obsessional neurosis, but it may occur in other forms of neurosis as well. If the mechanism is frequently used at an early stage of ego development, it can become a character trait on a permanent basis, as in an obsessional character. |
| Inhibition | In inhibition, limitations or renunciations of ego functions occur consciously, alone or in combination, to evade anxiety arising out of conflicts with instinctual impulses, the superego, or environmental forces or figures. | Repression | An idea or feeling may be expelled or withheld from consciousness in repression. Primary repression is the curbing of ideas and feelings before they have attained consciousness; secondary repression excludes from awareness what was once experienced at a conscious level. The repressed is not really forgotten, in that symbolic behavior may be present. Repression differs from suppression by effecting the conscious inhibition of impulses to the point of losing and not just postponing cherished goals. The conscious perception of instincts and feelings is blocked. |
| Intellectualization | Closely allied to rationalization, intellectualization is the excessive use of intellectual processes to avoid affective expressions or experiences. Undue emphasis is focused on the inanimate in order to avoid intimacy with people, attention is paid to external reality to avoid the expression of inner feelings, and stress is ex- | Sexualization | An object or function is endowed with sexual significance that it did not previously have or that it possessed to a smaller degree in order to ward off anxieties associated with prohibited impulses or their derivatives. |

*Continued*

**Table 6.1–2**
*Continued*

| Mature Defenses | | | |
|---|---|---|---|
| Altruism | The person undergoes a vicarious experience by means of constructive and instinctually gratifying service to others. Altruism includes benign and constructive reaction formation. Altruism is distinguished from altruistic surrender, in which a surrender of direct gratification or of instinctual needs takes place in favor of fulfilling the needs of others to the detriment of the self and in which the satisfaction can be enjoyed only vicariously through introjection. | Humor | Humor permits the overt expression of feelings and thoughts without personal discomfort or immobilization and does not produce an unpleasant effect on others. It allows the person to tolerate and yet focus on what is too terrible to be borne; it is different from wit, a form of displacement that involves distraction from the affective issue. |
| Anticipation | Realistic anticipation of or planning for future inner discomfort that is goal-directed implies careful planning or worrying and premature but realistic affective anticipation of dire and potentially dreadful outcomes. | Sublimation | Impulse gratification and the retention of goals are achieved, but the aim or the object is altered from one that may have been socially objectionable to a socially acceptable one. Sublimation allows instincts to be channeled, rather than blocked or diverted. Feelings are acknowledged, modified, and directed toward a significant object or goal, and modest instinctual satisfaction occurs. |
| Asceticism | The pleasurable effects of experiences are eliminated. There is a moral element in assigning values to specific pleasures. Gratification is derived from renunciation, and asceticism is directed against all base pleasures perceived consciously. | Suppression | A conscious or semiconscious decision to postpone attention to a conscious impulse or conflict takes place. Issues may be deliberately cut off, but they are not avoided. Discomfort is acknowledged but minimized. |

Table adapted from G E Vaillant: *Adaptation to Life*, Little, Brown, Boston, 1977; E Semrad: The operation of ego defenses in object loss. In *The Loss of Loved Ones*, D M Moriarity, editor, p 36. Thomas, Springfield, Ill, 1967; and G L Bibring, T F Dwyer, D S Huntington, A·A Valenstein: A study of the psychological process in pregnancy and of the earliest mother-child relationship: II. Methodological considerations. Psychoanal Study Child *16*: 25, 1961.

## Theory of Anxiety

Sigmund Freud initially conceptualized anxiety as "dammed-up libido." In other words, a physiological increase in sexual tension leads to a corresponding increase in libido, the mental representation of that physiological event. He referred to the conditions caused by that buildup as the *actual neuroses*.

Later, with the development of the structural model, he developed a new theory of a second type of anxiety that he referred to as *signal anxiety*. In that model, anxiety operates at an unconscious level and serves to mobilize the ego's resources to avert danger. Either external or internal sources of danger may produce a signal that leads the ego to marshal specific defense mechanisms to guard against instinctual excitation or to reduce its degree.

Freud's new theory of anxiety explains neurotic symptoms as a partial failure of the ego to cope with distressing stimuli. The drive derivatives associated with danger may not have been adequately contained by the defense mechanisms used by the ego. In phobias, for example, Freud explained that fear of an external threat (such as dogs or snakes) is an externalization of an internal danger.

## Character

In 1913 Freud distinguished between neurotic symptoms and personality or character traits. *Neurotic symp-* *toms* develop as a result of the failure of repression; *character traits* owe their existence to the success of repression—that is, to the defense system that achieves its aim through a persistent pattern of reaction formation and sublimation. In 1923 Freud also observed that the ego can give up important objects only by identifying with them or introjecting them. The accumulated pattern of identifications and introjections also contributes to character formation. Freud specifically emphasized the importance of superego formation in the construction of character.

Contemporary psychoanalysts regard character as the pattern of adaptation to drive forces from within and external environmental forces that are habitual or typical for a particular person. "Character" and "personality" are used interchangeably and are distinguished from the ego in that they largely refer to styles of defense and directly observable behavior, rather than to feeling and thinking.

Character is also influenced by constitutional temperament, the interaction of drive forces with early ego defenses and with environmental influences, and various identifications and internalizations of other people throughout one's life. The extent to which the ego has developed a capacity to tolerate the delay of impulse discharge and to neutralize instinctual energy determines the degree to which such character traits emerge in later life. The exaggerated development of certain character traits at the expense of others may lead to personality disorders or produce a vulnerability or predisposition to the psychoses.

# CLASSIC PSYCHOANALYTIC THEORY OF NEUROSIS

The classic view of neurotogenesis regards conflict as essential. The conflict may be between instinctual drives and external reality, or it may be between internal agencies, such as the id and the superego or the id and the ego. Moreover, because the conflict has not been worked through to a realistic solution, the drives or wishes that seek discharge have been expelled from consciousness through repression or another defense mechanism. Their expulsion from conscious awareness, however, does not make the drives any less powerful or influential. As a result, the unconscious tendencies (that is, the disguised neurotic symptoms) have fought their way back into consciousness. That theory of the development of neurosis assumes that a rudimentary neurosis based on the same type of conflict existed in early childhood.

Deprivation during the first few months of life because of absent or impaired caretaking figures may adversely affect ego development. That impairment, in turn, may result in the failure to make appropriate identifications. The resulting ego difficulties create problems mediating between the drives and the environment. Lack of capacity for the constructive expression of drives, especially aggression, may lead some children to turn their aggression on themselves and become overtly self-destructive. Parents who are inconsistent, excessively harsh, or overly indulgent may induce disordered superego functioning in their children. Severe conflict that cannot be managed through symptom formation may lead to extreme restrictions in ego functioning and to a fundamental impairment of the capacity to learn and develop new skills.

Traumatic events that seem to threaten survival may break through defenses when the ego has been weakened. Great amounts of libidinal energy are then required to master the excitation that results. The libido thus mobilized, however, is withdrawn from the supply that is normally applied to external objects. That withdrawal further diminishes the strength of the ego and produces a sense of inadequacy. Frustrations or disappointments in adults may revive infantile longings that are then dealt with through symptom formation or further regression.

## Secondary Gains of Neurosis

The reduction of conflict and tension through neurosis is the primary purpose or gain of the disorder. However, the ego may try to gain advantages from the external world by provoking attention and sympathy from others, by manipulating others, or even by receiving financial compensation. All those factors are called *secondary gains*.

Each neurosis has its characteristic form of secondary gain. In phobias, persons regress to childhood, when they were still protected. Gaining attention through dramatic acting out and, at times, deriving material advantages are characteristic of conversion disorder.

## TREATMENT AND TECHNIQUE

Psychoanalysis as a treatment method devised by Freud depends on the patient's capacity to think psychologically about subjective experiences and external events and to develop and retain insight. Repressed material must be brought into conscious awareness, and, on the basis of an understanding of unconscious wishes and motives, realistic solutions to current conflicts are developed. That type of psychoanalysis is known as Freudian, classic, traditional, or orthodox psychoanalysis.

The cornerstone of psychoanalytic technique is *free association*, in which the patient says whatever comes to mind. Free association does more than provide content for the analysis. It also induces the necessary regression and dependence connected with establishing and working through the transference neurosis. When that development has occurred, all the original wishes, drives, and defenses associated with the infantile neurosis have been transferred to the person of the analyst.

As patients attempt to free-associate, they soon learn that they have difficulty in saying whatever comes to mind without censoring certain thoughts. Conflicts develop about their wishes and feelings toward the analyst that reflect childhood conflicts. The displacement onto the analyst of early wishes and feelings toward other persons is called *transference*. Associated with transference is the development of *resistance*, an inhibition of free association and an opposition to the goals of the analysis. Although it remains the basic technique that guides the patient's participation in the analysis, the use of free association in the analytical process is a relative matter. The *fundamental rule* of psychoanalysis is that the patient agrees to be completely honest with the analyst. The systematic analysis of transference and resistance is the essence of psychoanalysis. By understanding the intense feelings that occur in the analytic relationship, the patient has a broadened understanding of past relationships and current relationships outside the analysis. Also, the development of insight into neurotic conflicts expands the ego and provides an increased sense of mastery. Psychoanalysis and other techniques devised from it are discussed in detail in Section 32.1.

**References**

Brenner C: *The Mind in Conflict*. International Universities Press, New York, 1982.
Compton A: The psychoanalytic view of phobias: I. Freud's theories of phobias and anxiety. Psychoanal Q *61*: 206, 1992.
Fenichel O: *The Psychoanalytic Theory of Neurosis*. Norton, New York, 1945.
Freud A: *The Ego and the Mechanisms of Defense*. International Universities Press, New York, 1946.
Freud S: *The Standard Edition of the Complete Psychological Works of Sigmund Freud*, vols 1–24. Hogarth Press, London, 1953–1966.
Gabbard G O: *Psychodynamic Psychiatry in Clinical Practice: The DSM-IV Edition*. American Psychiatric Press, Washington, 1994.
Ginsburg L M, Ginsburg S A: Paradise in the life of Sigmund Freud: An understanding of its imagery and paradoxes. Int Rev Psychoanal *19*: 285, 1992.
Holt R R: *Freud Reappraised: A Fresh Look at Psychoanalytic Theory*. Guilford, New York, 1989.
McLeod M N: The evolution of Freud's theory about dreaming. Psychoanal Q *61*: 37, 1992.
Thompson J M, Baxter L R, Schwartz J M: Freud, obsessive-compulsive disorder and neurobiology. Psychoanal Contemp Thought *15*: 483, 1992.
Winnicott D W: *Playing and Reality*. Basic Books, New York, 1971.

# 6.2 / Schools Derived from Psychoanalysis and Psychology

## KARL ABRAHAM (1877–1925)

Karl Abraham was the first psychoanalyst in Germany and was one of Sigmund Freud's earliest disciples. He is best known for his explication of depression from a psychoanalytic perspective and for his elaboration of Freud's stages of psychosexual development. He divided the oral stage into a biting phase and a sucking phase, the anal stage into a destructive-expulsive (anal-sadistic) phase and a mastering-retentive (anal-erotic) phase, and the phallic stage into an early phase of partial genital love (true phallic phase) and a later mature genital phase. Abraham also linked the psychosexual stages to specific syndromes. For example, he postulated that obsessional neurosis is the result of fixation at the anal-sadistic phase and that depression is the result of fixation at the oral stage.

## ALFRED ADLER (1870–1937)

Alfred Adler was one of Freud's prize pupils, but theoretical differences led to their eventual estrangement. Adler felt that Freud overemphasized the sexual theory of neurosis. In Adler's view, aggression is of far more importance, specifically in its manifestation as a striving for power, which he believed to be a masculine trait. He introduced the term "*masculine protest*" to depict the tendency to move from a feminine and passive role to a masculine and active role. Adler's theories are collectively known as individual psychology.

Adler coined the term "*inferiority complex*" to refer to a sense of inadequacy and weakness that is universal and inborn. The developing child's self-esteem is compromised by any physical defect, and Adler referred to that phenomenon as *organ inferiority*. He also thought that a basic inferiority is tied to the child's oedipal longings, which can never be gratified.

Adler was one of the first developmental theorists to recognize the importance of children's birth order in their families of origin. The firstborn child reacts with anger to the birth of siblings and struggles with giving up the powerful position of being the only child. The second-born child must constantly strive to compete with the firstborn. Adler felt that one's sibling position results in lifelong influences on one's character and life-style.

The primary therapeutic approach in Adlerian therapy is encouragement, through which Adler believed that his patients could overcome feelings of inferiority. Consistent human relatedness, in his view, leads to hope, decreased isolation, and increased affiliation with society. He thought that patients need to develop a sense of their own dignity and worth and a renewed appreciation for their abilities and strengths.

## FRANZ ALEXANDER (1891–1964)

Franz Alexander emigrated from his native Germany to the United States, where he settled in Chicago and founded the Chicago Institute for Psychoanalysis. He wrote extensively on the association between specific personality traits and certain psychosomatic ailments, a point of view that came to be known as the *specificity hypothesis*. He fell out of favor with classic analysts for advocating the *corrective emotional experience* as part of analytic technique. In that approach Alexander suggested that the analyst deliberately adopt a particular mode of relatedness with the patient to counteract noxious influences in childhood from the patient's parents. He believed that the trusting, supportive relationship between patient and analyst enables the patient to master childhood traumas and to grow from the experience.

## GORDON ALLPORT (1897–1967)

Gordon Allport is known as the founder of the *humanistic school* of psychology, which holds that each person has an inherent potential for autonomous function and growth. At Harvard he taught the first course in the psychology of personality at an American college.

Allport believed that a person's only real guarantee of personal existence is a sense of self. Selfhood develops through a series of stages, from awareness of the body to self-identity. Allport used the term "*propriem*" for strivings related to the maintenance of self-identity and self-esteem. He used the term "*traits*" for the chief units of personality structure. *Personal dispositions* are individual traits that are the essence of one's unique personality. *Maturity* is characterized by a capacity to relate to others with warmth, intimacy, and an expanded sense of self. In Allport's view, mature persons have security, humor, insight, enthusiasm, and zest. Psychotherapy is geared to helping the patient realize those characteristics.

## ERIC BERNE (1910–1970)

Eric Berne began his professional life with training in classic psychoanalytic theory and technique but ultimately developed his own school, known as transactional analysis. A *transaction* is a stimulus from one person that evokes a corresponding response in someone else. Berne defined psychological *games* as stereotyped and predictable transactions that people learn in childhood and continue to play throughout their lives. *Strokes* are the basic motivating factors of human behavior and consist of specific kinds of rewards, such as approval and love. Each person has three ego states: (1) the *Child*, the primitive elements that become fixed in early childhood; (2) the *Adult*, the part of the personality capable of objective appraisals of reality; and (3) the *Parent*, an introject of the person's actual parents' values. The therapeutic process is geared to helping patients understand whether they are functioning in the Child, Adult, or Parent mode in their interactions with others. The patient learns to recognize characteristic games played again and again throughout life. With that understanding, the patient is ultimately able to function in the Adult mode as much as possible in interpersonal relationships.

## WILFRED BION (1897–1979)

Wilfred Bion expanded the Kleinian concept of *projective identification* to include an interpersonal process in which the therapist feels coerced by the patient into playing a particular role in the patient's internal world. Bion also developed the idea that the therapist must contain what has been projected by the patient, so that it is processed and returned to the patient in modified form. Bion thought that a similar process goes on between mother and infant. He also observed that "psychotic" and "nonpsychotic" aspects of the mind function simultaneously as suborganizations. Bion is probably best known for his application of psychoanalytic ideas to groups. Whenever a group gets derailed from its task, it deteriorates into one of three *basic assumptions*: dependency, pairing, or fight-flight.

## RAYMOND CATTELL (b. 1905)

Raymond Cattell obtained his Ph.D. in England before moving to the United States. He introduced the use of *multivariate analysis* and *factor analysis*—statistical procedures that simultaneously examine the relations among multiple variables and factors—to the study of personality. By objectively examining the person's life record, using personal interviewing and questionnaire data, Cattell described a variety of traits that represent the building blocks of personality.

Traits are both biologically based and environmentally determined or learned. Biological traits include sex, gregariousness, aggression, and parental protectiveness. Environmentally learned traits include cultural ideas, such as work, religion, intimacy, romance, and identity. An important concept is the *law of coercion to the biosocial mean*, which holds that society exerts pressure on genetically different persons to conform to social norms. For example, a person with a strong genetic tendency toward dominance is likely to receive social encouragement for restraint, whereas the naturally submissive person will be encouraged toward self-assertion.

## RONALD FAIRBAIRN (1889–1964)

Ronald Fairbairn, a Scottish analyst who worked most of his life in relative isolation, was one of the major psychoanalytic theorists in the British school of object relations. He wrote that infants are primarily motivated not by the drives of libido and aggression but by an object-seeking instinct. Fairbairn replaced the Freudian ideas of energy, ego, and Id with the idea of *dynamic structures*: when the infant encounters frustration, a portion of the ego is defensively split off in the course of development and functions as an entity in relation to internal objects and in relation to other subdivisions of the ego. Fairbairn also stressed that not only an object but an object relationship is internalized during development, so that a self is always in relationship to an object, and the two are connected with an affect.

## SANDOR FERENCZI (1873–1933)

Sandor Ferenczi was analyzed by Freud and influenced by him but later discarded Freud's techniques and replaced them with his own method of analysis. Ferenczi understood the symptoms of his patients as related to sexual and physical abuse in childhood. He proposed that analysts love their patients in a way that compensates for the love the patients did not receive as children. He developed a procedure known as *active therapy*, in which he encouraged the patient to develop an awareness of reality through active confrontation by the therapist. Ferenczi also experimented with *mutual analysis*, in which he analyzed his patient for a session and then allowed the patient to analyze him for a session.

## ERICH FROMM (1900–1980)

Erich Fromm came to the United States in 1933 from Germany, where he had received his Ph.D. He was instrumental in the founding of the William Alanson White Institute for Psychiatry in New York. Fromm identified five character types that are common to and determined by Western culture; each person may possess qualities from one or more types. The types are (1) the *receptive personality*, who is passive; (2) the *exploitative personality*, who is manipulative; (3) the *marketing personality*, who is opportunistic and changeable; (4) the *hoarding personality*, who saves and stores; and (5) the *productive personality*, who is mature and enjoys love and work. The therapeutic process involves strengthening the person's sense of ethical behavior toward others and developing *productive love*, which is characterized by care, responsibility, and respect for other persons.

## KURT GOLDSTEIN (1878–1965)

Kurt Goldstein was born in Germany and received his M.D. from the University of Breslau; he was influenced by existentialism and Gestalt psychology. Every organism has dynamic properties, which are energy supplies that are relatively constant and evenly distributed. When states of tension-disequilibrium occur, the organism automatically attempts to return to its normal state. What happens in one part of the organism affects every other part, a phenomenon known as *holocoenosis*.

*Self-actualization* is a concept used by Goldstein for the creative powers in each person that lead one to fulfill one's potentialities. Because each person has a different set of innate potentialities, people strive for self-actualization along different paths.

Sickness severely disrupts self-actualization. Responses to the disruption of the organism's integrity may be rigid and compulsive. Regression to primitive modes of behavior are characteristic. One of Goldstein's major contributions was his identification of the *catastrophic reaction* to brain damage, in which a person becomes fearful and agitated and refuses to perform simple tasks because of the fear of possible failure.

## KAREN HORNEY (1885–1952)

Karen Horney was an American psychiatrist who believed that a person's current personality attributes are the result of the interaction between the person and the environment and are not based on infantile libidinal strivings carried over from childhood. Her theory, known as *holistic psychology*, maintains that a person needs to be seen as a unitary whole who influences the environment and is influenced by it. She believed that the Oedipus complex is overvalued in terms of its contribution to adult psychopathology. She believed that rigid parental attitudes regarding sexuality lead to excessive concern with the genitals.

She proposed three concepts of the self: (1) the *actual self* consists of the sum total of experience; (2) the *real self* is the harmonious healthy person; and (3) the *idealized self* is the neurotic expectation or glorified image of what the person feels he or she should be. The *pride system* alienates the person from the real self because it overemphasizes prestige, intellect, power, strength, appearance, and sexual prowess. It can lead to self-effacement and self-hatred. Horney also established the concepts of basic anxiety and basic trust. The thrust of the therapeutic process is toward *self-realization*, which removes distorting influences on the personality that prevent growth.

## EDITH JACOBSON (1897–1978)

Edith Jacobson believed that the structural model and the emphasis on object relations are not fundamentally incompatible. She thought that the ego and self-images and object images exert reciprocal influences on one another's development. She also stressed that the infant's disappointment with the maternal object is not necessarily related to the mother's actual failure. In Jacobson's view, disappointment is related to a specific, drive-determined demand, rather than to a global striving for contact or engagement. She viewed the infant's experience of pleasure or unpleasure as the core of the early mother-infant relationship. Satisfactory experiences lead to the formation of good or gratifying images, whereas unsatisfactory experiences create bad or frustrating images. Normal and pathological development are based on the evolution of those self-images and object images. Jacobson believed that the concept of *fixation* refers to modes of object relatedness, rather than to modes of gratification.

## CARL GUSTAV JUNG (1875–1961)

Carl Gustav Jung's psychoanalytic school, known as analytical psychology, includes basic ideas related to Freud's theories but going beyond them. Jung parted ways with Freud, after initially being his disciple, because he disagreed with Freud's emphasis on infantile sexuality. He expanded on Freud's concept of the unconscious by describing the *collective unconscious* as consisting of all humankind's common and shared mythological and symbolic past. The collective unconscious includes *archetypes*—representational images and configurations that have universal symbolic meanings. Archetypal figures exist for the mother, the father, the child, and the hero, among others. Archetypes contribute to *complexes*, which are feeling-toned ideas that develop as a result of personal experience interacting with archetypal imagery. Thus, a mother complex is determined not only by the mother-child interaction but also by the conflict between archetypal expectation and actual experience with the real woman who functions in a motherly role.

Jung noted that there are two types of personality organizations: introversion and extroversion. *Introverts* focus more on their inner world of thoughts, intuitions, emotions, and sensations; *extroverts* are more oriented toward the outer world, other people, and material goods. Each person has a mixture of both components. The *persona* is the mask covering the personality that the person presents to the outside world. The persona may become fixed, so that the real person is hidden from himself or herself. Anima and animus are unconscious traits possessed by men and women, respectively,

and are contrasted with the persona. *Anima* is a man's undeveloped femininity, whereas *animus* is a woman's undeveloped masculinity.

The aim of Jungian treatment is to bring about an adequate adaptation to reality, which involves fulfilling one's creative potentialities. The ultimate goal is to achieve *individuation*, a process that continues throughout life in which a person develops a unique sense of his or her own identity. That developmental process may lead persons down new paths that may differ from their previous directions in life.

## OTTO KERNBERG (b. 1928)

Otto Kernberg is perhaps the most influential of the American object relations theorists. Influenced by both Melanie Klein and Edith Jacobson, his theory is largely derived from his clinical work with patients suffering from borderline personality disorder. Kernberg has placed great emphasis on the splitting of the ego and on the elaboration of good and bad self-configurations and object configurations. Although he has continued to use the structural model, he views the id as composed of self-images, object images, and their associated affects. Drives appear only to manifest themselves in the context of the internalization of interpersonal experience. Good and bad self-relationships and object relationships become associated, respectively, with libido and aggression. Not only do object relations constitute the building blocks of structure, but they are also the building blocks of drives. Goodness and badness in relational experiences precede drive cathexis. In other words, the dual instincts of libido and aggression arise from object-directed affective states of love and hate.

Kernberg proposed the term "*borderline personality organization*" for a lack of an integrated sense of identity; ego weakness; absence of superego integration; reliance on primitive defense mechanisms, such as splitting and projective identification; and a tendency to shift into primary process thinking. He suggested a specific type of psychoanalytic psychotherapy for borderline patients in which transference issues are interpreted early in the process.

## SØREN KIERKEGAARD (1813–1855)

Søren Kierkegaard was one of the major philosophers associated with existentialism. His major preoccupation was the meaning of existence, and he had major concerns about methods that view persons as objects and theories that are based on stimulus-response patterns. The controversy of nature versus nurture was of no concern to Kierkegaard, who thought that existential anxiety is the primary source of psychological distress. The awareness of one's ultimate death can be dealt with only by striving for *authenticity*, the ability to live one's life with dignity and self-respect. Despite its popularity as a philosophy, existentialism has not evolved into a systematic therapeutic technique. However, many therapists have been influenced by extentialism insofar as they explore what is experienced by patients and in what manner mental phenomena present themselves to the patient's consciousness—a school known as *phenomenology*.

## MELANIE KLEIN (1882–1960)

Melanie Klein evolved a theory of internal object relations that is intimately linked to drives. Her unique perspective grew largely out of her psychoanalytic work with children, in which she became impressed with the role of unconscious intrapsychic fantasy. She postulated that the ego undergoes a splitting process to deal with the terror of annihilation. She also thought that Freud's concept of the death instinct is central to understanding aggression, hatred, sadism, and other forms of "badness," all of which she viewed as derivatives of the death instinct.

Klein viewed projection and introjection as the primary defensive operations in the first months of life. The infant projects derivatives of the death instinct into the mother and then fears attack from the "bad mother," a phenomenon that Klein referred to as *persecutory anxiety*. That anxiety is intimately associated with the *paranoid-schizoid position*, the infant's mode of organizing experience in which all aspects of the infant and the mother are split into good and bad elements. *Splitting*, a major defense mechanism used in development, occurs when good and bad objects exist with a splitting of love and aggression between them. As the disparate views are integrated, the infant becomes concerned that it may have harmed or destroyed its mother through its hostile and sadistic fantasies directed toward her. At that developmental point the child has arrived at the *depressive position*, in which it views the mother ambivalently as having both positive and negative aspects and as being the target of a mixture of loving and hateful feelings.

Klein was also instrumental in the development of child analysis, which evolved from an analytic play technique in which children use toys and play in a symbolic fashion that allows the analyst to make interpretations of the play.

## HEINZ KOHUT (1913–1981)

Heinz Kohut is best known for his writings on narcissism and the development of self psychology. He viewed the development and the maintenance of self-esteem and self-cohesion as more important than sexuality or aggression. He viewed Freud's concept of narcissism as judgmental in that development was supposed to proceed toward object relatedness and away from narcissism. Kohut thought that there are two lines of development, one moving in the direction of object relatedness and the other in the direction of enhancement of the self.

In infancy the child fears losing the early mother-infant bliss and resorts to one of three pathways to save the lost perfection: (1) the grandiose self, (2) the alter ego or twinship, and (3) the idealized parental imago. Those three poles of the self manifest themselves in psychoanalytic treatment in terms of characteristic transferences, known as *selfobject transferences*. The *grandiose self* leads to a *mirror transference*, in which the patient attempts to capture the gleam in the analyst's eye through exhibitionistic self-display. The *alter ego* leads to the *twinship transference*, in which the patient perceives the analyst as a twin. The *idealized parental imago* leads to an *idealizing transference*, in which the patient feels enhanced self-esteem by being in the presence of the exalted figure of the analyst.

Kohut wrote that empathic failures in the mother lead to a developmental arrest at a particular stage, when the child needs to use others to perform selfobject functions. Although Kohut originally applied that formulation to narcissistic personality disorder, he later expanded it to apply to all psychopathology.

## JACQUES LACAN (1901–1981)

Born in Paris and trained as a psychiatrist, Jacques Lacan founded his own institute, the Freudian School of Paris. He attempted to integrate the intrapsychic concepts of Freud with concepts related to linguistics and semiotics, the latter being the study of language and symbols. Whereas Freud saw the unconscious as a seething cauldron of needs, wishes, and instincts, Lacan saw it as a sort of language that helps to structure the world. Two of his principal concepts are that the unconscious is structured like a language and that the unconscious is a discourse. Primary process thoughts are actually uncontrolled free-flowing sequences of meaning. Symptoms are signs or symbols of underlying processes. The role of the therapist is to interpret the semiotic text of the personality structure. Lacan's most basic phase is the mirror stage; it is here that infants learn to recognize themselves by taking the perspective of others. In that sense the ego is not a part of the self but something outside of and viewed by the self. The ego comes to represent parents and society, more than it represents the actual self of the person.

Lacan's therapeutic approach involves the need to become less alienated from the self and more involved with others. Relationships are often fantasized, which distorts reality and which must be corrected. Among his most controversial beliefs was that the resistance to understanding the real relationship can be reduced by shortening the length of the therapy session and that psychoanalytic sessions need to be standardized not to time but, rather, to content and process.

## KURT LEWIN (1890–1947)

Kurt Lewin received his Ph.D. in Berlin. He came to the United States in the 1930s and taught at Cornell, Harvard, and the Massachusetts Institute of Technology. He adapted the field approach from physics into a concept called field theory. A *field* is the totality of coexisting parts that are mutually interdependent. Behavior becomes a function of people and their environment, which together make up the *life space*. The life space is a field in constant flux that has *valences* or needs that require satisfaction. A hungry person is more aware of restaurants than is someone who has just eaten, and a person who wants to mail a letter is aware of mailboxes.

Lewin applied field theory to groups. *Group dynamics* is the interaction among members of a group, each of whom is dependent on the others. The group is capable of exerting pressure on a person to change behavior, but the person also influences the group when change occurs.

## ABRAHAM MASLOW (1908–1970)

Abraham Maslow was born in Brooklyn, New York, and completed his undergraduate and graduate work at the University of Wisconsin. Along with Kurt Goldstein, Maslow believed in the *self-actualization theory*—the need to understand the totality of a person. A leader in humanistic psychology, Maslow described a hierarchical organization of needs present in everyone. As the primitive needs, such as hunger and thirst, are satisfied, the advanced psychological needs, such as affection and self-esteem, become the primary motivators. Self-actualization is the highest need.

A *peak experience*, which frequently occurs in self-actualizers, is an episodic, brief occurrence in which a person suddenly experiences a powerful transcendental state of consciousness. During that state, a person experiences a sense of heightened understanding, an intense euphoria, an integrated nature, unity with the universe, and an altered perception of time and space. The powerful experience tends to occur most often in the psychologically healthy, and it may produce long-lasting beneficial effects.

## ADOLF MEYER (1866–1950)

Adolf Meyer came to the United States from Switzerland in 1892 and eventually became director of the psychiatric Henry Phipps Clinic of Johns Hopkins Medical School. Although he did not entirely reject Freud's theoretical emphasis on mental functioning, Meyer preferred to examine the verifiable and objective aspects of a person's life. His theory of *psychobiology* explains disordered behavior as reactions to genetic, physical, psychological, environmental, and social stresses. Meyer introduced the concept of *common sense psychiatry*, which focuses on ways in which the patient's current life situation can be realistically improved. He coined the concept of *ergasia*, which stands for the action of the total organism. The goal of therapy is to aid patients' adjustment by helping them modify unhealthy adaptations. One of Meyer's tools was an autobiographical life chart constructed by the patient during therapy.

## GARDNER MURPHY (1895–1979)

Gardner Murphy was born in Ohio and received his Ph.D. at Columbia University. He was among the first to publish a comprehensive history of psychology, and he made major contributions to social, general, and educational psychology.

According to Murphy, three essential stages of personality development are (1) undifferentiated wholeness, (2) differentiation, and (3) integration. The development is frequently uneven, with both regression and progression occurring along the way.

There are four inborn human needs: visceral, motor, sensory, and emergency-related. Those needs become increasingly specific in time as they are molded by a person's experiences in various social and environmental contexts. *Canalization* brings about those changes by establishing a connection between a need and a specific way of satisfying that need.

Murphy was interested in parapsychology. States such as sleep, drowsiness, certain drug and toxic conditions, hypnosis, and delirium tend to be favorable to paranormal experiences. Impediments to paranormal awareness include various intrapsychic barriers, conditions in the general social environment, and a heavy investment in the ordinary types of sensory experience.

## HENRY MURRAY (1893–1988)

Henry Murray was born in New York City, attended medical school there, and was a founder of the Boston Psychoanalytic Institute. He proposed the term "personology" to describe the study of human behavior. He focused on *motivation*, which is a need that is aroused by internal or external stimulation; once aroused, motivation produces continued activity until the need is reduced or satisfied. Murray developed the

*Thematic Apperception Test (TAT)*, a projective technique used to reveal both unconscious and conscious mental processes and problem areas.

## FREDERICK S. PERLS (1893–1970)

Gestalt theory developed in Germany under the influence of several men: Max Westheimer (1880–1943), Wolfgang Kohler (1887–1967), and Kurt Lewin (1890–1947).

Frederick "Fritz" Perls applied Gestalt theory to a type of therapy that emphasizes the current experiences of the patient in the here and now, as contrasted to the there and then of the psychoanalytic schools. In terms of motivation, patients learn to recognize what their needs are at any given time and how the drive to satisfy those needs may influence their current behavior. According to the Gestalt point of view, behavior represents more than the sum of its parts. A *gestalt*, a whole, both includes and goes beyond the sum of smaller, independent events; it deals with essential characteristics of actual experience, such as value, meaning, and form.

## SANDOR RADO (1890–1972)

Sandor Rado came to the United States from Hungary in 1945 and founded the Columbia Psychoanalytic Institute in New York. His theories of *adaptational dynamics* hold that the organism is a biological system operating under hedonic control, which is somewhat similar to Freud's pleasure principle. Cultural factors often cause excessive hedonic control and disordered behavior by interfering with the organism's ability for *self-regulation*. In therapy, the patient needs to relearn how to experience pleasurable feelings.

## OTTO RANK (1884–1939)

In his 1924 book, *The Trauma of the Birth*, Otto Rank broke with Freud and developed a new theory, which he called birth trauma. Anxiety is correlated with separation from the mother—specifically, with separation from the womb, the source of effortless gratification. That painful separation results in *birth anxiety*. Sleep and dreams symbolize the return to the womb.

The personality is divided into impulses, emotions, and will. The child's impulses seek immediate discharge and gratification. As impulses are mastered, as in toilet training, the child begins the process of will development. If will is carried too far, pathological traits—such as stubbornness, disobedience, and inhibitions—may develop.

The therapeutic process—called *will therapy*—emphasizes the relationship between patient and therapist; the goal of treatment is to help patients accept their separateness. A definite termination date for therapy is used to protect against excessive dependence on the therapist.

## WILHELM REICH (1897–1957)

Wilhelm Reich made major contributions to psychoanalysis in the area of character formation and character types. *Character armor* consists of the defenses built up by the personality that serve as a resistance to self-understanding and change. There are four major character types: (1) The *hysterical character* is sexually seductive, anxious, and fixated at the phallic phase of libido development. (2) The *compulsive character* is controlled, distrustful, indecisive, and fixated at the anal phase. (3) The *narcissistic character* is fixated at the phallic stage of development; such a man has a contempt for women. (4) The *masochistic character* is long-suffering, complaining, and self-deprecatory, with an excessive demand for love.

## CARL ROGERS (1902–1987)

Carl Rogers received a Ph.D. in psychology at Columbia University. While attending Union Theological Seminary in New York, Rogers studied for the ministry. His name is most clearly associated with the *person-centered theory* of personality and psychotherapy, in which the major concepts are self-actualization and self-direction. Specifically, people are born with a capacity to direct themselves in the healthiest way, toward a level of completeness called *self-actualization*. From his person-centered approach, Rogers viewed personality not as a static entity composed of traits and patterns but as a dynamic phenomenon involving ever-changing communications, relationships, and self-concepts.

Rogers developed a treatment program called *client-centered psychotherapy*. In it, the therapist attempts to produce an atmosphere in which clients can reconstruct their strivings for self-actualization. The therapist holds the client in *unconditional positive regard*, which is the total nonjudgmental acceptance of clients as they are. Other therapeutic practices include attention to the present, focus on the feelings of the client, emphasis on process, trust in the client's potential and self-responsibility, and a philosophy grounded in a positive attitude toward the client, rather than a preconceived structure of treatment.

## B. F. SKINNER (1904–1990)

B. F. Skinner received his Ph.D. in psychology from Harvard University, where he taught for many years. Skinner's work in operant learning laid much of the groundwork for many of the current methods of behavior modification, programmed instruction, and general education. His global beliefs about the nature of behavior have been applied more widely, it can be argued, than those of any other theorist except, perhaps, Freud. His influence has been impressive in scope and magnitude.

Skinner's approach to personality was derived more from his basic beliefs about behavior than from a specific theory of personality. To Skinner, personality is not different from other behaviors or sets of behaviors; it is acquired, maintained, and strengthened or weakened according to the same rules of reward and punishment that alter any other form of behavior. *Behaviorism*, as Skinner's basic theory is most commonly known, is concerned only with observable, measurable, and operationalizable behavior. Many of the abstract and mentalistic hallmarks of other dominant personality theories have little place in Skinner's framework. Concepts such as self, ideas, and ego are considered unnecessary for the understanding of behavior and are shunned. Through the process of operant conditioning and the application of basic principles of learning, sets of behavior develop that characterize people's responses to the world of stimuli that they face in their lives. That set of responses is called *personality*.

## HARRY STACK SULLIVAN (1892–1949)

Harry Stack Sullivan received his training in psychiatry in the 1930s, during the early years of Freud's profound influence on American psychiatry; but, like Adolf Meyer, under whom he studied, Sullivan insisted on formulating his concepts on observable data.

There are three modes of experiencing and thinking about the world: (1) The *prototaxic mode* is undifferentiated thought that is unable to separate the whole into parts or to use symbols. It occurs normally in infancy and is also seen in patients with schizophrenia. (2) The *parataxic mode* sees events as causally related because of temporal or serial connections. Logical relationships, however, are not perceived. (3) The *syntaxic mode* is the logical, rational, and most mature type of cognitive functioning of which a person is capable. Those three types of thinking and experiencing occur side by side in all persons; it is the rare person who functions in the syntaxic mode exclusively.

The total configuration of personality traits is known as the *self-system*, which develops in various stages and is the outgrowth of interpersonal experiences, rather than the unfolding of intrapsychic forces. During infancy, anxiety occurs for the first time when the infant's primary needs are not satisfied. During childhood, from age 2 to 5 years, the child's main tasks are to become educated about the requirements of the culture and to learn how to deal with powerful adults. As a juvenile, ranging from 5 to 8 years, the child has a need for peers and must learn how to deal with them. In preadolescence, ranging from 8 to 12 years, the development of the capacity for love and collaboration with another person of the same sex develops. That so-called chum period is the prototype for a sense of intimacy; in the history of schizophrenic patients, that experience of chums is often missing. During adolescence, major tasks include the separation from one's family, the development of standards and values, and the transition to heterosexuality.

The therapy process requires the active participation of the therapist, who is known as a *participant observer*. Modes of experience, particularly the parataxic, need to be clarified, and new patterns of behavior need to be implemented. Ultimately, persons need to see themselves as they really are, instead of what they think they are or what they want others to think they are.

Sullivan is best known for his creative psychotherapeutic work with severely disturbed patients. He thought even the most psychotic patients suffering from schizophrenia can be reached through the human relationship of psychotherapy.

## DONALD W. WINNICOTT (1897–1971)

Donald W. Winnicott was one of the central figures in the British school of object relations theory. His theory of *multiple self-organizations* included a *true self*, which develops in the context of a responsive *holding environment* provided by a *good-enough mother*. However, when infants experience a traumatic disruption of their developing sense of self, a false self emerges that monitors and adapts to the conscious and unconscious needs of the mother and, in so doing, provides a protected exterior behind which the true self is afforded a privacy that it requires to maintain its integrity.

Winnicott also developed the concept of the transitional object. Ordinarily a pacifier, a blanket, or a teddy bear, the *transitional object* serves as a substitute for the mother during the infant's efforts to separate and become independent. It provides a soothing sense of security in the absence of the mother. Winnicott viewed the *transitional space*, in which the transitional object functions, as the source of art, creativity, and religion.

### References

Adler A: *The Individual Psychology of Alfred Adler: A Systematic Presentation in Selections from His Writings*, H L Ansbacher, R R Ansbacher, editors. Basic Books, New York, 1956.

Baker H S, Baker M N: Heinz Kohut's self psychology: An overview. Am J Psychiatry *144*: 1, 1987.

Davis D M: Review of the psychoanalytic literature on countertransference. Int J Short-Term Psychother *6*: 131, 1991.

Dervin D: Feminizing Freud: A psychohistorical perspective on four pioneering women analysts. J Psychohistory *19*: 479, 1992.

Gabbard G O: *Psychodynamic Psychiatry in Clinical Practice: The DSM-IV Edition*. American Psychiatric Press, Washington, 1994.

Grosskurth P: *Melanie Klein: Her World and Her Work*. Knopf, New York, 1986.

Horney K: *The Neurotic Personality of Our Time*. Norton, New York, 1937.

Jung C G: *Memories, Dreams, Reflections*. Random House, New York, 1961.

Levine H B: Freudian and Kleinian theory: A dialogue of comparative perspectives. J Am Psychoanal Assoc *40*: 801, 1992.

Millon T: *Theories of Psychopathology* (part 2). Saunders, Philadelphia, 1967.

Ogden T H: The concept of internal object relations. Int J Psychoanal *64*: 227, 1983.

Padel J: The psychoanalytic theories of Melanie Klein and Donald Winnicott and their interaction in the British Society of Psychoanalysis. Psychoanal Rev *78*: 325, 1991.

Perry H S: *Psychiatrist of America: The Life of Harry Stack Sullivan*. Belknap Press, Harvard University Press, Cambridge, 1982.

Rayner E: *The Independent Mind in British Psychoanalysis*. Aronson, Northvale, N J, 1991.

Rubin T I: Horney, here and now: 1991. Am J Psychoanal *51*: 313, 1991.

Segal H: *Melanie Klein*. Viking, New York, 1980.

Smith S: *Ideas of the Great Psychologists*. Harper & Row, New York, 1983.

---

# 6.3 / Erik Erikson

---

Erik Homburger Erikson (Figure 6.3–1) was born in 1902 in Germany. His father, a Danish Protestant, and his mother, a Danish Jew, separated before he was born, and he grew up in the home of his mother and German-Jewish stepfather, Theodore Homburger, a pediatrician. Erikson trained as a lay psychoanalyst in Europe and was schooled in the Montessori method of education.

Erikson emigrated to the United States in 1933. He worked at the Austen Riggs Center in Stockbridge, Massachusetts, and conducted research at Harvard, Yale, and the University of California at Berkeley. As a result of his studies of psychological development in the 1930s and the 1940s, including anthropological work with the Sioux Indians in South Dakota and the Yurok Indians in northern California, his book *Childhood and Society* was published in 1950. In that book he presented a psychosocial theory of development that describes crucial steps in the person's relation with the social world, based on the interplay between biology and society.

**Figure 6.3.–1.** Erik Erikson.

Erikson recognized much of Freudian psychology but added to Sigmund Freud's theory of infantile sexuality by concentrating on the child's development beyond puberty. Erikson believes that the human personality is determined not only by childhood experience but also by adult experience. Erikson stated: "If everything goes back into childhood, then everything is somebody else's fault and taking responsibility for oneself is undermined." Most important, Erikson formulated a theory of human development that covers the entire span of the life cycle, from infancy and childhood through old age and senescence.

## EPIGENETIC PRINCIPLE

Erikson's formulations were based on the concept of epigenesis, a term borrowed from embryology. The *epigenetic principle* holds that development occurs in sequential, clearly defined stages and that each stage must be satisfactorily resolved for development to proceed smoothly. According to the epigenetic model, if successful resolution of a particular stage does not occur, all subsequent stages reflect that failure in the form of physical, cognitive, social, or emotional maladjustment.

### Relation to Freudian Theory

Erikson accepted Freud's concepts of instinctual development and infantile sexuality. For each of Freud's psychosexual stages (for example, oral, anal, phallic), Erikson described a corresponding zone. Each zone has a specific pattern or mode of behavior. Thus, the oral zone is associated with sucking or taking-in behavior, and the anal zone is associated with holding on and letting go. Erikson brought into focus the fact that the development of the ego is more than the result of intrapsychic wants or inner psychic energies. It is also a matter of mutual regulation between the growing child and the society's culture and traditions.

## Stages of the Life Cycle

Erikson described eight stages of the life cycle (Table 6.3–1). The stages are marked by one or more internal crises, which are defined as turning points—periods when the person is in a state of increased vulnerability. Ideally, a crisis is mastered successfully, and the person gains strength and is able to move on to the next stage.

Erikson's stages are not fixed in time. Development is continuous; even though a particular stage may dominate at a certain time, the person may have residual problems carried over from one stage to the next or may be under severe stress and regress to an earlier stage in whole or in part. The time boundaries listed below represent approximations agreed on by most workers in the field.

**Stage 1. Basic trust versus basic mistrust** (birth to about 1 year). Trust versus mistrust is the first crisis the infant must face. Erikson wrote in *Growth and Crisis of the Healthy Personality:*

For the first component of a healthy personality I nominate a sense of basic trust which I think is an attitude toward oneself and the world derived from the experience of the first year of life. Trust is the expectation that one's needs will be taken care of and that the world or outer providers can be relied upon.

This period coincides with Freud's oral stage of development, in which the mouth is the most sensitive zone of the body. Finding the nipple, sucking, and taking in nutrients fill the infant's primary needs. The trust-inducing mother attends to those needs assiduously, thus laying the groundwork for the infant's future positive expectations of the world. Erikson added the term "sensory" to Freud's oral stage (calling it oral-sensory) because the parent also attends to the infant's senses—sight, taste, smell, touch, and hearing. Through that interaction, either infants develop the feeling of trust that their wants will be satisfied,

**Table 6.3–1**
**Erik Erikson's Stages of the Life Cycle**

**Stage 1. Basic Trust versus Basic Mistrust**
(birth to about 1 year)
  Corresponds to the oral psychosexual stage
  Trust shown by ease of feeding, depth of sleep, bowel relaxation
  Depends on consistency and sameness of experiences provided by caretaker or outerprovider
  Second six months: teething and biting move infant from getting to taking
  Weaning leads to nostalgia for lost paradise
  If basic trust is strong, child maintains hopeful attitude, develops self-confidence
  Oral zone associated with mode of being satisfied

**Stage 2. Autonomy versus Shame and Doubt**
(about 1 to 3 years)
  Corresponds to the muscular-anal stage
  Biologically includes learning to walk, feed self, talk
  Need for outer control, firmness of caretaker before development of autonomy
  Shame occurs when child is overtly self-conscious through negative exposure and punishment
  Self-doubt can evolve if parents overly shame child, e.g., about elimination
  Anal zone associated with mode of holding on and letting go

**Stage 3. Initiative versus Guilt**
(3 to 5 years)
  Corresponds to the phallic psychosexual stage
  Initiative arises in relation to tasks for the sake of activity, both motor and intellectual
  Guilt may arise over goals contemplated (especially aggressive goals)
  Desire to mimic adult world; involvement in oedipal struggle leads to resolution through social role identification
  Sibling rivalry frequent
  Phallic zone associated with mode of competition and aggression

**Stage 4. Industry versus Inferiority**
(6 to 11 years)
  Corresponds to the latency psychosexual stage
  Child is busy building, creating, accomplishing
  Receives systematic instruction and fundamentals of technology

  Danger of sense of inadequacy and inferiority if child despairs of tools, skills, and status among peers
  Socially decisive age
  No dominant zone or mode

**Stage 5. Identity versus Role Diffusion**
(11 years through end of adolescence)
  Struggle to develop ego identity (sense of inner sameness and continuity)
  Preoccupation with appearance, hero worship, ideology
  Group identity (with peers) develops
  Danger of role confusion, doubts about sexual and vocational identity
  Psychosexual moratorium, stage between morality learned by the child and the ethics developed by the adult
  No dominant zone or mode

**Stage 6. Intimacy versus Isolation**
(21 to 40 years)
  Tasks are to love and to work
  Intimacy is characterized by self-abandonment, mutuality of sexual orgasm, intense friendship, attachments that are life-long
  Isolation is marked by separation from others and view that others are dangerous
  General sense of productivity in this stage
  No dominant zone or mode

**Stage 7. Generativity versus Stagnation**
(40 to 65 years)
  Generativity includes raising children, guiding new generation, creativity, altruism
  Stagnation not prevented by having a child; parent must provide nurturance and love
  Self-concern, isolation, and absence of intimacy are characteristic of stagnation
  No dominant zone or mode

**Stage 8. Integrity versus Despair**
(over 65 years)
  Integrity is a sense of satisfaction that life has been productive and worthwhile
  Despair is a loss of hope that produces misanthropy and disgust
  Persons in the state of despair are fearful of death
  An acceptance of one's place in the life cycle is characteristic of integrity

or, if the mother is not attentive, infants develop the mistrustful sense that they are not going to get what they want.

ORAL CRISIS. Toward the second half of the first year, the oral crisis occurs. At that point the infant's teeth develop, and a drive to bite occurs. The infant progresses from simply being passive to becoming active. If the infant bites too aggressively, however, the nipple is taken away. The mother's responses are influenced in part by the child's behavior, and the infant learns that it must control the urge to bite. As a result, infants learn that they can influence the environment, and they begin to develop a sense of themselves as individuals separate from the environment. In today's culture, weaning from the breast or the bottle begins toward the end of this phase. Erikson believed that the separation is the basis of a sense of sorrow, nostalgia, or homesickness. However, if basic trust is strong, the child develops a sense of hope, optimism, and confidence.

An affectionate, loving mother or surrogate mother who gives consistent, high-quality care provides the basis for the development of trust. According to Erikson, the infant's first social achievement is the willingness to let the mother out of sight without undue anxiety or rage. That happens because she becomes an inner certainty in the infant's mental representation. The parallel is to Jean Piaget's concept of object permanence—which is the child's ability to maintain a mental image of a person or object, even though it is not present and not visible—and to Margaret Mahler's concept of object constancy, in which the child has a mental representation of the mother as reliable and stable. (That developmental phase occurs at 24 to 36 months, according to Mahler.)

**Stage 2. Autonomy versus shame and doubt** (about 1 to 3 years).   Autonomy concerns children's sense of mastery over themselves and over their drives and impulses. Toddlers gain a sense of their separateness from others. "I," "you," "me," and "mine" are common words used by children during this period. Children have a choice of holding on or letting go, of being cooperative or stubborn. This period coincides with Freud's anal stage of development. For Erikson, it is the time for the child either to retain feces (holding in) or to eliminate feces (letting go); both behaviors have an effect on the mother.

Children in the second and third years of life learn to walk alone, to feed themselves, to control the anal sphincter, and to talk. That muscular maturation sets the tone for this stage of development. If parents permit the child to function with some autonomy and are supportive without being overprotective, toddlers gain self-confidence and feel that they can control themselves and their world. But if toddlers either are punished for being autonomous or are overcontrolled, they feel angry and ashamed. If parents show approval when the child shows self-control, the child's self-esteem is enhanced, and a sense of pride develops. Parental overcontrol or the child's loss of self-control, also called muscular and anal impotence by Erikson, produces a sense of doubt and shame. Shame implies that one is looked down on by the outside world. It exploits the child's sense of being small as one stands upright for the first time. Feeling small, the child is easily shamed by poor parenting experiences.

**Stage 3. Initiative versus guilt** (3 to 5 years).   This stage

corresponds to Freud's phallic-oedipal phase. During this period, the child's growing sense of sexual curiosity is manifested by engaging in group sex play or touching one's own genitalia or those of a peer. If parents do not make an issue of those childhood impulses (Erikson gives this example: "If you touch it, the doctor will cut it off"), the impulses are eventually repressed and reappear during adolescence as part of puberty. If the parents make too much of the impulses, the child may become sexually inhibited.

As children approach the end of the third year, they are able to initiate both motor and intellectual activities. Whether initiative is reinforced depends on how much physical freedom children are given and on how well their intellectual curiosity is satisfied. If toddlers are made to feel inadequate about their behavior or interests, they may emerge from this period with a sense of guilt about self-initiated activity. Conflicts over initiative can prevent developing children from experiencing their full potential and can interfere with their sense of ambition, which develops during this stage.

The child is able to move independently and vigorously by the end of this stage. By playing with peers, the child learns how to interact with others. If aggressive fantasies have been managed properly (neither punished nor encouraged), the child develops a sense of initiative and ambition.

At the end of the stage of initiative versus guilt, the child's conscience (Freud's superego) is established. The child learns not only that there are limits to one's behavioral repertoire (for example, that a boy cannot sleep with his mother or murder his father) but also that aggressive impulses can be expressed in constructive ways, such as healthy competition, playing games, and using toys. The development of a conscience sets the tone for the moral sense of right and wrong. Excessive punishment, however, can restrict the child's imagination and initiative. Children who develop too strong a superego, one with an all-or-nothing quality, may insist as adults that other persons adhere to their moral code and, therefore, may become dangers to themselves and others. If the crisis of initiative is successfully resolved, a sense of responsibility, dependability, and self-discipline develops.

**Stage 4. Industry versus inferiority** (6 to 11 years).   This stage is the school age period, during which the child begins to participate in an organized program of learning. It is equivalent to Freud's latency period, when biological drives are dormant and peer interaction prevails. In all cultures, children receive formal instruction at about the age of 6; in Western culture, children learn to be literate and technical. In other societies, learning may involve becoming familiar with tools and weapons.

Industry, the ability to work and acquire adult skills, is the keynote of the stage. Children learn that they are able to make things and, most important, able to master and complete a task. If too great an emphasis is placed on rules, regulations, shoulds, or oughts, the child develops a sense of duty at the expense of a natural desire to work. The productive child learns the pleasure of work completion and the pride of doing something well.

A sense of inadequacy and inferiority, the potential negative outcome of this stage, results from several sources: children may be discriminated against at school; children may be told that they are inferior; children may be overprotected at home or excessively dependent on the emotional support of their families; children may compare themselves unfavorably with the same-sex parent. Good teachers and good parents who encourage children to value diligence and productivity and to persevere in difficult enterprises are bulwarks against a sense of inferiority. Whereas Freud placed most of the blame or credit for a child's development squarely on the shoulders of the parents, Erikson emphasized that sensitive social situations may counteract nonsupportive parents. Conversely, a school environment that denigrates or discourages children can diminish their self-esteem, even if their parents reward their industriousness at home.

**Stage 5. Identity versus role diffusion** (11 years through end of adolescence). Developing a sense of identity is the main task of this period, which coincides with puberty and adolescence. Identity is defined as the characteristics that establish who persons are and where they are going. Healthy identity is built on their success in passing through the earlier stages. How successful they have been in attaining trust, autonomy, initiative, and industry has much to do with developing a sense of identity. Identifying with either healthy parents or parent surrogates facilitates the process.

Identity implies a sense of inner solidarity with the ideas and the values of a social group. The adolescent is in a psychosocial moratorium between childhood and adulthood; during that moratorium, various roles are tested. The adolescent may make several false starts before deciding on an occupation or may drop out of school, to return at a later date to complete a course of study. Moral values may change, but eventually an ethical system is consolidated into a coherent organizational framework.

IDENTITY CRISIS. An identity crisis occurs at the end of adolescence. Erikson calls it a normative crisis, because it is a normal event. Failure to negotiate this stage leaves the adolescent without a solid identity; the person suffers from identify diffusion or role confusion, characterized by not having a sense of self and by confusion about one's place in the world. Role confusion may manifest itself in such behavioral abnormalities as running away, criminality, and overt psychosis. Problems in gender identity and sexual role may become manifest at this time. The adolescent may defend against role diffusion by joining cliques or cults or by identifying with folk heroes.

**Stage 6. Intimacy versus self-absorption or isolation** (21 to 40 years). This period extends from late adolescence through early middle age. Erikson pointed out that an important psychosocial conflict can arise during this stage and that, as in previous stages, success or failure depends on how well the groundwork has been laid in earlier periods and on how the young adult interacts with the environment. The intimacy of sexual relations, friendships, and all deep associations are not frightening to the person with a resolved identity crisis. In contrast, the person who reaches the adult years in a state of continued role confusion is unable to become involved in intense and long-term relationships. Without a friend or a partner in marriage, a person may become self-absorbed and self-indul-

gent; as a result, a sense of isolation may grow to dangerous proportions.

In true intimacy there is mutuality. That word is reminiscent of the first stage of life. If a child achieves initiative in genitality, the sensual pleasure of childhood merges with the idea of genital orgasm, and the young adult is able to make and share love with another person. Through the crisis of intimacy versus isolation, a person transcends the exclusivity of earlier dependencies and establishes a mutuality with an extended and diverse social group.

Erikson quoted Freud's view that a normal person must be able to love and work (*lieben und arbeiten*). Similarly, Erikson believes that meaningful work, procreation, and recreation within a loving relationship represent utopia.

**Stage 7. Generativity versus stagnation** (40 to 65 years). During the decades that span the middle years of life, the adult chooses between generativity and stagnation. Generativity not only concerns a person's having or raising children but also includes a vital interest outside the home in establishing and guiding the oncoming generation or in improving society. Childless people can be generative if they develop a sense of altruism and creativity. But most persons, if able, want to continue their personalities and energies in the production and care of offspring. Wanting or having children, however, does not ensure generativity. Parents need to have achieved successful identities themselves to be truly generative.

The adult who has no interest in guiding or establishing the oncoming generation is likely to look obsessively for intimacy that is not truly intimate. Such people may marry and even produce children but all within a cocoon of self-concern and isolation. Those persons pamper themselves as if they were the children and become preoccupied with themselves. Indeed, parents who do not truly believe that life in a given society is worthwhile may find that their children absorb that message only too well, the result being a lack of grandchildren.

Stagnation is a barren state. The inability to transcend the lack of creativity is dangerous because the person is not able to accept the eventuality of not being and the idea that death is inescapably a part of life.

**Stage 8. Integrity versus despair and isolation** (over 65 years). Old age is Erik Erikson's eighth stage of the life cycle. The stage is described as the conflict between integrity (the sense of satisfaction that one feels in reflecting on a life productively lived) and despair (the sense that life has had little purpose or meaning). Late adulthood can be a period of contentment—a time to enjoy grandchildren, to contemplate one's major efforts, and perhaps to see the fruits of one's labor being put to good use by younger generations. Integrity allows for an acceptance of one's place in the life cycle and of the knowledge that one's life is one's own responsibility. There is an acceptance of who one's parents are or were and an understanding of how they lived their lives.

Without the conviction that one's life has been meaningful and that one has made a contribution, either by producing happy children or by giving to the next generation, the elderly person fears death and has a sense of despair or disgust. Misanthropes and others who are contemptuous of people are in a state of despair.

Recently, Erikson wrote about the problem of those over age 85 who have to balance autonomy with the real need for help (for example, physical and economic assistance). Everyone must recognize that growing old requires active preparation, which must begin at an earlier stage of life. Because society is not yet prepared to meet the demands of the very old, a great responsibility remains with the individual.

In a concluding remark about this stage in *Childhood and Society*, Erikson wrote the following: "Healthy children will not fear life if their parents have integrity enough not to fear death."

# PSYCHOPATHOLOGY

Each stage of the life cycle has its own psychopathological outcome if it is not mastered successfully.

## Basic Trust

An impairment of basic trust leads to basic mistrust. Social trust in the infant is characterized by ease of feeding, depth of sleep, smiling, and general physiological homeostasis. Prolonged separation during infancy can lead to hospitalism or anaclitic depression (Section 4.2). In later life that lack of trust can be manifested by dysthymic disorder, a depressive disorder, or a sense of hoplessness. Persons who develop and rely on the defense of projection—in which, according to Erikson, "we endow significant people with the evil which actually is in us"—experienced a sense of social mistrust in the first years of life and are likely to develop paranoid or delusional disorders. Basic mistrust is a major contribution to the development of schizoid personality disorder and, in most severe cases, to the development of schizophrenia. Substance-related disorders can also be traced to social mistrust; substance-dependent personalities have strong oral-dependency needs and use chemical substances to satisfy themselves because of their belief that human beings are unreliable and, at worst, dangerous. If not nurtured properly, infants may feel empty, starved not just for food but also for sensual and visual stimulation. They may become, as adults, seekers after stimulating thrills that do not involve intimacy and that help ward off feelings of depression.

## Autonomy

As children attempt to develop into autonomous beings, the stage is often called "the terrible 2s," referring to the toddlers' willfulness at that stage of development. If shame and doubt dominate over autonomy, compulsive doubting may occur. The inflexibility of the obsessive personality also results from an overabundance of doubt.

Too rigorous toilet training—which is commonplace in today's society, which requires a clean, punctual, and deodorized body—can produce an overly compulsive personality that is stingy, meticulous, and selfish. Known as anal personalities, such persons are parsimonious, punctual, and perfectionistic.

Too much shaming causes the child to feel evil or dirty and may pave the way for delinquent behavior. In effect, the child is saying, "If that's what they think of me, that's the way I'll behave." Paranoid personalities feel that others are trying to control them, a feeling that may have its origin during the stage of autonomy versus shame and doubt. If coupled with mistrust, the seeds are planted for persecutory delusions. Impulsive disorders may be explained as the person's refusing to be inhibited or controlled.

## Initiative

Erikson stated: "In pathology, the conflict over initiative is expressed either in hysterical denial, which causes the repression of the wish or the abrogation of its executive organ by paralysis or impotence; or in overcompensatory showing off, in which the scared individual, so eager to 'duck,' instead 'sticks his neck out.' " In the past, hysteria was the usual form of pathological regression in this area, but a plunge into psychosomatic disease is now common.

Excessive guilt may lead to a variety of conditions, such as generalized anxiety disorder and phobias. Patients feel guilty because of normal impulses, and they repress those impulses, with resulting symptom formation. Sexual inhibitions can occur if punishments or severe prohibitions occur during the stage of initiative versus guilt. Conversion disorder or specific phobia may result if the oedipal conflict is not resolved. As sexual fantasies are accepted as unrealizable, children may punish themselves for those fantasies by fearing harm to their genitals. Under the brutal assault of the developing superego, they may repress their wishes and begin to deny them. If that pattern is carried forward, paralysis, inhibition, or impotence can result. Or, in fear of not being able to live up to what others expect, the children may turn to psychosomatic disease.

## Industry

Erikson described industry as a "sense of being able to make things and make them well and even perfectly." When children's efforts are thwarted, they are made to feel that personal goals cannot be accomplished or are not worthwhile, and a sense of inferiority develops. In the adult, that sense of inferiority can result in severe work inhibitions and a character structure marked by feelings of inadequacy. In some persons the feelings may result in a compensatory drive for money, power, and prestige. Work can become the main focus of life, at the expense of intimacy.

## Identity

Many of the disorders of adolescence can be traced to identity confusion. The danger is role diffusion. Erikson stated:

Where this is based on a strong previous doubt as to one's sexual identity, delinquent and outright psychotic incidents are not uncommon. If diagnosed and treated correctly, those incidents do not have the same fatal significance that they have at other ages. It is primarily the inability to settle on an occupational identity that disturbs young people. To keep themselves together, they temporarily overidentify, to the point of apparent complete loss of identity, with the heroes of cliques and crowds.

Other disorders during the stage of identity versus role diffusion include conduct disorder, disruptive behavior disorder, gender identity disorder, schizophreniform disorder, and other psychotic disorders. The ability to leave home and live independently is an important task during this period. An inability to separate from the parent and prolonged dependence may occur.

## Intimacy

The successful formation of a stable marriage and family depends on the capacity to become intimate. The years of early adulthood are crucial for deciding whether to get married and to whom. Gender identity determines object choice, either heterosexual or homosexual, but making an intimate connection with another person is a major task. The person with schizoid personality disorder remains isolated from others because of fear, suspicion, the inability to take risks, or the lack of a capacity to love.

## Generativity

From about 40 to 65 years, the period of middle adulthood, the specific disorders are less clearly defined than in the other stages described by Erikson. The middle-aged show a higher incidence of depression than do younger adults, which may be related to middle-aged persons' disappointments and failed expectations as they review the past, consider how their lives have gone, and contemplate the future. The increased use of alcohol and other psychoactive substances also occurs during this time.

## Integrity

Anxiety disorders often develop in the elderly. In Erikson's formulation, that development may be related to the persons' looking back on their lives with a sense of panic. Time has run out, and chances are used up. The decline in physical functions can contribute to psychosomatic illness, hypochondriasis, and depression. The suicide rate is highest over the age of 65. Persons facing dying and death may find it intolerable if they have not been generative or able to make significant attachments in life. Integrity for Erikson is characterized by an acceptance of one's life. If that acceptance is absent, the person enters into a state of despair and hopelessness that can result in severe depressive disorders.

## TREATMENT

Although no independent Eriksonian psychoanalytic school exists in the same way as Freudian and Jungian schools exist, Erikson made many important contributions to the therapeutic process. Among the most important contributions is his belief that the establishment of a state of trust between doctor and patient is the basic requirement for successful therapy. When psychopathology stems from basic mistrust (for example, depression), the patient must reestablish trust with the therapist, whose task, like that of the good mother, is to be sensitive to the patient's needs. The therapist must have a sense of personal trustworthiness that can be transmitted to the patient.

## Techniques

For Erikson the psychoanalyst is not a passive tabula rasa or blank slate in the therapeutic process, as is commonly practiced in Freudian psychoanalysis. To the contrary, effective therapy requires that the therapist actively convey to patients the belief that they are understood. That is done not only through empathetic listening but also by verbal assurances, which enable a positive transference, built on mutual trust, to develop.

Beginning as an analyst for children, Erikson tried to provide that mutuality and trust while he observed children re-creating their own worlds by structuring dolls, blocks, vehicles, and miniature furniture into the dramatic situations that were bothering them. Then Erikson correlated his observations with statements by the children and their family members. He began the treatment of a child only after eating an evening meal with the entire family. His therapy was usually conducted with much cooperation from the family. After each regressive episode in the treatment of a schizophrenic child, for instance, Erikson discussed with every member of the family what had been going on with them before the episode. Only when he was thoroughly satisfied that he had identified the problem did treatment begin. Erikson sometimes provided corrective information to the child—for instance, telling a boy who could not release his feces and has made himself ill from constipation that food is not an unborn infant.

Erikson often turned to play, which, along with specific recommendations to the parents, proved fruitful as a treatment modality. Play, for Erikson, is diagnostically revealing and thus helpful for the therapist who seeks to promote a cure, but it is also curative in its own right. Play is a function of the ego and gives the child a chance to synchronize social and bodily processes with the self. The child playing with blocks or the adult playing out an imagined dramatic situation can manipulate the environment and develop the sense of control that the ego needs. However, play therapy is not the same for children and adults. Children create models in an effort to gain control of reality; they look ahead to new areas of mastery. Adults use play to correct the past and to redeem their failures.

Mutuality, which is important in Erikson's system of health, is also vital to the cure. Erikson applauded Freud for the moral choice of abandoning hypnosis, since hypnosis heightens the demarcation between the healer and the sick and heightens the inequality that Erikson compares to the inequality of child and adult. Erikson urged that the relationship of the healer to the sick person be one of equals "in which the observer who has learned to observe himself teaches the observed to become self-observant."

. **Goals**

Erikson discussed four dimensions of the psychoanalyst's job: (1) The patient's desire to be cured and the analyst's desire to cure is the first dimension. There is mutuality in that the patient and the therapist are motivated by cure, and there is a division of labor. The goal is always to help the patient's ego get stronger and cure itself. (2) The second dimension Erikson called objectivity-participation. Therapists must keep their minds open. "Neuroses change," wrote Erikson. New generalizations must be made and arranged in new configurations. (3) The third dimension runs along the axis of knowledge-participation. The therapist "applies selected insights to more strictly experimental approaches." (4) The fourth dimension is tolerance-indignation. Erikson stated: "Identities based on Talmudic argument, on messianic zeal, on punitive orthodoxy, on faddist sensationalism, on professional and social ambition" are harmful and tend to control the patient. Control widens the gap of inequality between the doctor and the patient and makes the realization of that recurrent idea in Erikson's thought—mutuality—difficult.

According to Erikson, the therapist has the opportunity to work through past unresolved conflicts in the therapeutic relationship. Erikson encouraged the therapist not to shy away from guiding the patient; Erikson believes that it is necessary for the therapist to offer the patient both prohibitions and permissions. Nor should the therapist be so engrossed in the patient's past life experiences that current conflicts in the patient's ways of relating to the external world are overlooked.

The goal of therapy is to recognize how the patient has passed through the various stages of the life cycle and how the various crises in each stage have or have not been mastered. Equally important, future stages and crises must be anticipated, so that they can be negotiated and mastered appropriately. Unlike Freud, Erikson does not believe that the personality is so inflexible that change cannot occur in middle and late adulthood. For Erikson, psychological growth and development occur throughout the entire span of the life cycle.

**References**

Coles R: *Erik Erikson: The Growth of His Work*. Little, Brown, Boston, 1970.
Erikson E: *Childhood and Society*. Norton, New York, 1950.
Erikson E: The dream specimen of psychoanalysis. J Am Psychoanal Assoc 2: 5, 1954.
Erikson E: The first psychoanalyst. Yale Rev 46: 40, 1956.
Erikson E: Freud's "The Origins of Psychoanalysis." Int J Psychoanal 36: 1, 1955.
Erikson E: *Gandhi's Truth*. Norton, New York, 1969.
Erikson E: Hitler's imagery and German youth. Psychiatry 5: 475, 1942.
Erikson E: *Identity and the Life Cycle*. Norton, New York, 1980.
Erikson E: *Identity: Youth and Crisis*. Norton, New York, 1968.
Erikson E: *Insight and Responsibility*. Norton, New York, 1964.
Erikson E: *Life History and the Historical Moment*. Norton, New York, 1975.
Erikson E: Observations on Sioux education, J Psychol 7: 101, 1939.
Erikson E: The problem of ego identity. Psychol Issues 1: 22, 1959.
Erikson E: *Young Man Luther*. Norton, New York, 1962.
Erikson E, Erikson J, Kivnik H: *Vital Involvement in Old Age*. Norton, New York, 1986.
Evans R: *Dialogue with Erik Erikson*. Harper & Row, New York, 1967.
Ginsburg H J: Childhood injuries and Erikson's psychosocial stages. Soc Behav Pers 20: 95, 1992.
Schein S, editor: *Erik Erikson: A Way of Looking at Things*. Norton, New York, 1987.

# Clinical Examination
# of the Psychiatric Patient

## 7.1 / Psychiatric Interview, History, and Mental Status Examination

### PSYCHIATRIC INTERVIEW

To treat a psychiatric patient effectively—whether with medications, environmental manipulations, or psychodynamic psychotherapy—the psychiatrist must make a reliable and accurate diagnosis. To formulate such a diagnosis, the psychiatrist must learn as much as possible about who the patient is in terms of genetic, temperamental, biological, developmental, social, and psychological influences. The psychiatrist must be able to convey concern, empathy, respect, and competence to the patient in order to create a rapport and trust that allow the patient to speak honestly and intimately. The psychiatrist must develop interviewing skills and techniques that most effectively allow the patient to describe the signs and the symptoms that, gathered together, constitute the various syndromes that are potentially definable and treatable. Patients range from those who are clear, articulate, and easy to engage to those who are thought-disordered, paranoid, responding to internal stimuli, and severely disorganized. The interview itself may vary, depending on the specific challenges presented by each patient. Some techniques are universal to all situations; other techniques are especially applicable to certain types of interviews. Nancy Andreasen and Donald Black have listed 11 techniques common to most psychiatric interview situations (Table 7.1–1).

### Management of Time

The initial consultation lasts for 30 minutes to one hour, depending on the circumstances. Interviews with psychotic or medically ill patients are brief because the patient may find the interview stressful. Long interviews may be required in the emergency room. Second visits and ongoing therapeutic interviews also vary in length. The American Board of Psychiatry and Neurology in its clinical oral examination in psychiatry allows 30 minutes for a psychiatric examination.

Patients' management of appointment times reveals im-

### Table 7.1–1
### Common Interview Techniques

1. Establish rapport as early in the interview as possible.
2. Determine the patient's chief complaint.
3. Use the chief complaint to develop a provisional differential diagnosis.
4. Rule the various diagnostic possibilities out or in by using focused and detailed questions.
5. Follow up on vague or obscure replies with enough persistence to accurately determine the answer to the question.
6. Let the patient talk freely enough to observe how tightly the thoughts are connected.
7. Use a mixture of open-ended and closed-ended questions.
8. Don't be afraid to ask about topics that you or the patient may find difficult or embarrassing.
9. Ask about suicidal thoughts.
10. Give the patient a chance to ask questions at the end of the interview.
11. Conclude the initial interview by conveying a sense of confidence and, if possible, of hope.

Table adapted from N C Andreasen, D W Black: *Introductory Textbook of Psychiatry*. American Psychiatric Association Press, Washington, 1991. Used with permission.

portant aspects of personality and coping. Most often, patients arrive a few minutes before their appointments. An anxious patient may arrive as much as a half hour early. If the patient arrives very early, the clinician may want to explore the reasons. The patient who arrives significantly late for an appointment poses another set of potential questions. The first time it occurs, the clinician may listen to the explanation offered and respond sympathetically if the lateness is due to circumstances beyond the patient's control. If the patient states, "I forgot all about the appointment," that is a clue that something about going to the doctor is making the patient anxious or uncomfortable, and that needs to be explored further. The psychiatrist may ask directly, "Did you feel reluctant to come in today?" If the answer is, "Yes," the psychiatrist can begin to explore the possible reasons for the patient's reluctance. If the answer is, "No," it is probably best to drop the direct questioning about the lateness and just listen to the patient. By listening carefully, the psychiatrist can usually detect themes that the patient may not be aware of. Those themes can then be explored by both the patient and the psychiatrist in an attempt to understand better what the patient is experiencing.

The psychiatrist's handling of time is also an important factor in the interview. Carelessness regarding time indi-

267

cates a lack of concern for the patient. If the psychiatrist is unavoidably detained for an interview, it is appropriate to express regret at having kept the patient waiting.

## Seating Arrangements

The way chairs are arranged in the psychiatrist's office affects the interview. Both chairs should be of approximately equal heights, so that neither person looks down on the other. Most psychiatrists think that it is desirable to place the chairs without any furniture between the clinician and the patient. If the room contains several chairs, the psychiatrist indicates his or her own chair and then allows the patient to choose the chair in which he or she will feel most comfortable.

If the patient being interviewed is one who is potentially dangerous, the door to the interview room should be left open, the psychiatrist should sit closest to the open door, with nothing obstructing the space from the clinician to the door, and, if necessary, a third person should be asked to stand outside or even inside the room, to be available if there is trouble.

## Psychiatrist's Office

A psychiatrist can never remain entirely unknown to the patient. The physician's office can tell the patient a good deal about the personality of the psychiatrist. The color of the office, paintings and diplomas on the wall, furniture, plants, books, and personal photographs—all describe the psychiatrist in ways that are not directly verbalized. Patients often have reactions to their doctors' offices that may or may not be distortions, and carefully listening to any comments can help the psychiatrist understand patients. Studies have shown that patients respond more positively to male physicians who wear jackets and ties than to those who do not. No studies have been done on the dress of female physicians, but, by extrapolation, a positive response would probably be elicited by professional attire.

## Note Taking

For legal and medical reasons an adequate written record of each patient's treatment must be maintained. The patient's record also aids the psychiatrist's memory. Each clinician must establish a system of record keeping and decide which information to record. Many psychiatrists make complete notes during the first few sessions while eliciting historical data. After that time most psychiatrists record only new historical information, important events in the patient's life, medications prescribed, dreams, and general comments about the patient's progress. Some psychiatrists maintain detailed process notes (verbatim record of a session) on specific patients, writing out immediately after a session as much of the session as they can remember. Process notes make it much easier to determine trends in the treatment (with regard to transference and countertransference issues) and to go back over the session to pick up ideas that may have been

missed. Process notes are also helpful if the psychiatrist is working with a supervisor or a consultant who needs an accurate presentation of a particular session.

Most psychiatrists do not recommend taking extensive notes during a session, as writing can cut down on the ability to listen. Some patients, however, may express resentment if the psychiatrist does not write notes during an interview; they may fear that their comments were not important enough to record or that the psychiatrist was not interested in them. Since, presumably, not taking notes during a session has no relation to the psychiatrist's listening, that type of feeling on a patient's part can be further explored in order to understand the fear of not being taken seriously.

## Subsequent Interviews

Interviews subsequent to the initial one allow the patient to correct any misinformation provided in the first meeting. It is often helpful to start the second interview by asking the patient whether he or she has thought about the first interview and for any reactions to that experience. Another variation of that technique is to say: "Frequently, people think of additional things they wanted to discuss after they leave. What thoughts have you had?"

Psychiatrists often learn something of value when they ask patients if they have discussed the interview with anyone else. If the patient has done so, the details of that conversation and with whom the patient spoke are enlightening. There are no set rules concerning which topics are best deferred until the second interview. In general, as patients' comfort and familiarity with the psychiatrist increase, they become increasingly able to reveal the intimate details of their lives.

## Interviewing Situations

The manner in which an interview is conducted—the specific techniques and structure—vary depending on the setting in which the interview takes place, the interview's purpose, and the particular patient's strengths, weaknesses, and diagnosis. Psychiatrists are trained to be flexible in modifying their interview style to fit the existing situation. Patients who carry varying psychiatric diagnoses differ in their capacities to participate in an interview and differ in the challenges they present to the interviewing psychiatrist. Certain consistent themes are often observed in interviews with patients who have the same diagnosis, although, even with the same diagnosis, patients may require subtly different interview strategies.

**Depressed and potentially suicidal patient.** Depressed patients are often unable to provide spontaneously an adequate account of their illness because of such factors as psychomotor retardation and hopelessness. The psychiatrist must be prepared to ask a depressed person specifically about history and symptoms related to depression, including questions about suicidal ideation, which the patient may not initially volunteer. Another reason for being specific in questioning a depressed patient is that the patient may not realize that such symptoms as waking during the night or increased somatic complaints are related to depressive disorders.

One of the most difficult aspects of dealing with depressed patients is experiencing their hopelessness. Many severely depressed patients believe that their current feeling will continue indefinitely and that there is no hope. The psychiatrist must be careful not to reassure such patients prematurely that everything is going to be fine, as the patients most likely will experience that reassurance as an indication that the psychiatrist does not understand the degree of pain that they are feeling. A reasonable approach is for the psychiatrist to indicate that he or she is aware how bad patients are feeling, that help is certainly possible, and that it is understandable at that point for patients not to believe that they can be helped. Furthermore, the psychiatrist must make it clear that he or she is committed to helping patients feel better, that all specific and effective pharmacological and psychological tools will be used, and that patients will not be abandoned during what may be a lengthy period of recovery. Up to that point, everything patients have done to relieve their distress has not worked, and, by the time the psychiatrist interviews them, they may be desperate. It can be a relief to depressed patients when the psychiatrist truthfully tells them that their depression can be treated but that it may take a little work and time for the psychiatrist to find the method that will most effectively treat their specific depressive disorder. That message conveys not a false sense of reassurance, which could make depressed patients feel even more depressed than before, but a sense that the psychiatrist is committed to understanding who the patient is and what treatment will work most quickly and most effectively for him or her. Every depressed person hopes, consciously or unconsciously, that the psychiatrist will magically and immediately produce a cure, but most people are willing to proceed along a therapeutic path, even when a part of them believes there is no hope. The interviewing psychiatrist must be careful not to make promises about specific treatments' being the answer. If those treatments turn out not to work for the patient, the disappointment may eliminate the patient's last hope.

SUICIDE. Of special concern when interviewing depressed patients is the potential for suicide. Being mindful of the possibility of suicide is imperative when interviewing any depressed patient, even if there is no apparent suicidal risk. The psychiatrist must inquire in some detail about the presence of suicidal thoughts. The psychiatrist should ask specifically, "Are you suicidal now, or do you have plans to take your own life?" A suicide note, a family history of suicide, or previous suicidal behavior on the part of the patient increases the risk for suicide. Evidence of impulsivity or of pervasive pessimism about the future also places patients at risk. If the psychiatrist decides that the patient is in imminent risk for suicidal behavior, the patient must be hospitalized or otherwise protected. A difficult situation arises when there does not seem to be an immediate risk but the potential for suicide is present as long as the patient remains depressed. If the decision is made not to hospitalize the patient immediately, the psychiatrist should insist that the patient promise to call at any time suicidal pressure mounts. In such situations the patient commonly has a crisis after midnight and calls the psychiatrist, who should assure the patient that he or she is reach-able at all times. Having determined that the psychiatrist is, in fact, available, the patient is often reassured and can control the impulses and use regularly scheduled sessions for exploration of the suicidal feelings.

**Violent patient.** Potentially violent patients should be approached with some of the same attitudes and techniques used with suicidal patients. For example, indicating that one is capable of dealing with the patient's capacity for violence is important. It conveys that one is accustomed to the unpleasant, as well as the pleasant, in life and that part of one's job is to help the patient stay in control and to make sure that neither the patient nor anyone else is going to get hurt.

Frequently, the psychiatrist encounters a violent patient in the hospital setting. For example, when the police bring a patient into the emergency room, the patient is often in some type of physical restraint (for example, handcuffs). The psychiatrist must establish whether effective verbal contact can be made with the patient or whether the patient's sense of reality is so impaired that effective interviewing is impossible. If impaired reality testing is an issue, the psychiatrist may have to medicate the patient before any attempts at interviewing can begin. If reality testing is not severely impaired, however, one of the first questions to be addressed is whether it is safe to remove the physical restraints from the patient. That question can be addressed in a straightforward manner, expressing concern for the safety of the patient and other persons in the surrounding area. Many psychiatrists opt to leave restraints on the patient until at least some history has been obtained and some rapport established. Should a decision be made to undo the restraints, the psychiatrist must carefully monitor what is happening to the patient as the restraints are loosened. If the patient remains calm and seems to be relieved, the process of removing the restraints can continue. If the patient does or says anything that indicates that the removal of the restraints is leading to increased agitation, the decision to remove them should be reassessed immediately.

With or without restraints, a violent patient should not be interviewed alone; at least one other person should always be present, and in some situations that other person should be a security guard or a police officer. Other precautions include leaving the interview room's door open and sitting between the patient and the door, so that the interviewer has unrestricted access to an exit should it become necessary. The psychiatrist must make it clear, in a firm but nonangry manner, that the patient may say or feel anything but is not free to act in a violent way. That statement must be backed up by a unified, calm, consistent staff presence that the patient understands is there to lend support in efforts to maintain control, including the ability to subdue the patient physically if necessary.

Confrontation with a violent patient is to be assiduously avoided, as is any behavior that could be construed as demeaning or disrespectful of the patient. Within the limits of safety, the interviewer should respect as much as possible the patient's need for space.

Specific questions that need to be asked of violent patients include those pertaining to their previous acts of violence and to violence experienced as a child. The psychiatrist should determine under what specific conditions the patient resorts to violence, and corroboration as to critical aspects of the patient's history must be obtained from friends and family members. Table 7.1–2 summarizes the dos and don'ts of treating the violent patient.

**Delusional patient.** A patient's delusion should never be directly challenged. Delusions may be thought of as a patient's defensive and self-protective, albeit maladaptive, strategy against overwhelming anxiety, lowered self-esteem, and confusion. Challenging a delusion by insisting that it is not true or possible only increases the patient's anxiety and often leads the threatened patient to defend the belief ever more desperately. It is inadvisable, however, to pretend that one believes the patient's delusion. Often, the helpful approach is to indicate that one understands that the patient believes the delusion to be true but that one does not hold the same belief. It is probably most productive to focus on the feelings, fears, and hopes that underlie the delusional belief to understand what particular function the delusion holds for the patient. The more that patients feel that the psychiatrist respects, understands, and listens to them, the more likely they are to talk about themselves, not about the delusion.

Delusions may be excessively fixed, immutable, and chronic, or they may be subject to question and doubt by the patient and may last only a relatively brief time. The patient may or may not be influenced by the delusional beliefs and may be able to recognize their effects.

Delusions, as with most psychiatric symptoms, occur on a spectrum from severe to mild and must be evaluated for the degree of severity, fixedness, elaborateness, power to influence the patient's actions, and deviation from normal beliefs. Andreasen and Black have suggested some helpful methods for eliciting delusional beliefs from patients (Table 7.1–3).

**Interviewing relatives.** Interviews with family members of a patient can be both valuable and fraught with difficulties. For example, a spouse may be so closely identified with the patient that anxiety overwhelms the spouse's ability to provide coherent information. Family members may not realize that certain kinds of information are best provided by an observer and that other kinds of information may be obtained only from the patient; for example, family members may be able to describe the patient's social activity, but only the patient can describe what he or she is thinking and feeling. The psychiatrist must be highly sensitive to discussions with family members; if those discussions are not properly handled by the psychiatrist, the relationship between the patient and the clinician may break down.

Interviews with family members can be viewed from a variety of perspectives. If one's goal is to diagnose a disorder, then the more facts at one's disposal, the easier it will be to formulate a diagnosis, prognosis, and treatment. From the dynamic or analytical viewpoint, however, if one sees patients' problems as largely influenced by interac-

**Table 7.1–2**
**Dos and Don'ts of Treating Violent Patients**

| Do | Don't |
|---|---|
| Anticipate possible violence from hostile, threatening, agitated, restless, abusive patients or from those who lack control for any reason. | Don't ignore your gut feeling that a patient may be dangerous. |
| Heed your gut feeling. If you feel frightened or uneasy, discontinue the interview and get help. | Don't see angry, threatening, restless persons right away. |
| Summon as many security guards or orderlies as possible at the first sign of violence. Patients who see that you take them seriously often will not act out further. If they do, you will be prepared. | Don't compromise your ability to escape a dangerous situation. Don't sit behind a desk. |
| Ask if the patient is carrying a weapon. Weapons must be surrendered to security personnel. Never see an armed patient. | Don't antagonize the patient by responding angrily or being patronizing. |
| Offer help, food, medication. Bolster the patient by commenting on his or her strength and self-control. | Don't touch or startle the patient or approach quickly without warning. |
| If restraint becomes necessary, assign one team member each to the patient's head and to each extremity. Be humane but firm, and do not bargain. Search the patient for psychoactive substances and weapons. | Don't try to restrain a patient without sufficient backup. Don't neglect looking for organic causes of violence. Don't bargain with a violent person about the need for restraints, medication, or psychiatric admission. |
| If the patient refuses oral medication, offer an injection after a few moments. Be prepared to administer it if the patient continues to refuse. | Don't forget medicolegal concerns, such as full documentation of all interventions and the duty to warn and protect. If the patient is transferred, tell the admitting physician about any specific threats and victims. |
| Keep a close eye on patients who are sedated or restrained. Restrained patients should never be left alone. | Don't overlook family and friends as important sources of information. |
| Hospitalize patients who state their intention to harm anyone, refuse to answer questions about their intent to harm, are abusing alcohol or other substances, are psychotic, have a cognitive disorder, or refuse to cooperate with treatment. | |
| Warn potential victims of threatened violence, and notify the appropriate protection agencies. | |
| Follow up on any violent person, and document it in the chart. | |

Table adapted from B Dwyer, M Weissberg: Treating violent patients. Psychiatric Times p 11, December 1988. Used with permission.

**Table 7.1–3**
**Methods for Eliciting Delusional Beliefs**

| Delusions | Questions |
|---|---|
| Persecutory delusions (e.g., one is being followed, one's mail is being opened, one's home is bugged, one is being monitored by the government) | Have you had trouble getting along with people? Have you felt that people were against you? Has anyone been trying to harm you or plot against you? |
| Delusions of jealousy (e.g., one's mate is having an affair) | Have you worried that your partner may be unfaithful? What evidence do you have? |
| Delusions of sin or guilt (e.g., one has committed a terrible sin, one is responsible for an unpardonable act, one deserves to be punished) | Have you felt that you have done some terrible thing? Is anything bothering your conscience? What is it? Do you feel you deserve to be punished for it? |
| Grandiose delusions (e.g., one is possessed of special powers, abilities, identities) | Do you have any special powers, talents, or abilities? Do you feel that you are going to achieve great things? |
| Somatic delusions (e.g., one believes one's body is diseased, abnormal, or changed) | Is anything wrong with the way your body is working? Have you noticed any change in your appearance? What has caused it? |
| Ideas and delusions of reference (e.g., one believes that insignificant remarks, statements, or events refer back to one or have some special meaning) | Have you walked into a room and thought people were talking about you or laughing at you? Have you seen things in magazines or on TV that refer to you or contain special meaning for you? Have you received special messages in other ways? |
| Thought broadcasting, thought insertion, and thought withdrawal | Have you heard your thoughts out loud, as if there were a voice outside your head? Have you felt that your thoughts were being broadcast so that others could hear them? Have you felt that thoughts were being put into your head by some outside source or person? Have you felt that your thoughts were being taken away by some outside source or person? |

Table adapted from N C Andreasen, D Black: *Introductory Textbook of Psychiatry*, American Psychiatric Association Press, Washington, 1991. Used with permission.

tions with the important figures in their lives, the external reality is less important than the patients' own perceptions. In general, the more serious a patient's presenting situation (for example, major depressive disorder, suicidal ideation, or psychotic disorder), the more likely and perhaps the more appropriate it is for the psychiatrist to deal with family members.

One of the most important aspects related to talking with family members has to do with confidentiality. Ultimately, the physician must learn to elicit information and to offer hope to family members without revealing information concerning the patient that the patient does not want revealed. Betraying a confidence can make treatment of the patient impossible. If the issues concern suicidal or homicidal ideation, however, the patient must understand that the information cannot remain entirely confidential, for the protection of the patient and others.

## PSYCHIATRIC HISTORY

The psychiatric history is the record of the patient's life that allows the psychiatrist to understand who the patient is, where the patient has come from, and where the patient is likely to go in the future. The history is the patient's life story told to the psychiatrist in the patient's own words from his or her own point of view. Many times the history also includes information about the patient obtained from other sources, such as a parent or a spouse. Obtaining a comprehensive history from a patient and, if necessary, from informed sources is essential to making a correct diagnosis and formulating a specific and effective treatment plan. The psychiatric history differs slightly from histories taken in medicine or surgery. In addition to gathering the concrete and factual data related to the chronology of symptom formation and to psychiatric and medical history, the psychiatrist strives to derive from the history the elusive picture of patients' individual personality characteristics, including both their strengths and their weaknesses. The psychiatric history provides insight into the nature of relationships with those closest to the patients and includes all the important people in their past and present lives. A reasonably comprehensive picture of the patients' development, from the earliest formative years until the present, can usually be elicited.

The most important technique in obtaining the psychiatric history is to allow patients to tell their own stories in their own words in the order that they feel is most important. Skillful interviewers recognize the points, as patients relate their stories, at which they can introduce relevant questions concerning the areas described in the outline of the history and mental status examination.

The structure presented in this section is not intended as a rigid plan for interviewing a patient; it is intended as a guide to organizing the patient's history when it is written up. A number of acceptable and standard formats for the psychiatric history are available. One such format is presented in Table 7.1–4.

## Identifying Data

The identifying data provide a succinct demographic summary of the patient by name, age, marital status, sex, occupation, language if other than English, ethnic background and religion insofar as they are pertinent, and current circumstances of living. The information can also include in what place or situation the current interview took place, the sources of the information, the reliability of the source, and whether the current disorder is the first episode of that type for the patient. The psychiatrist should indicate whether the patient came in on his or her own, was referred by someone else, or was brought in by someone else. The identifying data are meant to provide a thumbnail sketch of potentially important patient characteristics that may affect diagnosis, prognosis, treatment, and compliance.

An example of the written report of the identifying data is as follows:

John Jones is a 25-year-old white single Catholic man, currently unemployed and homeless, living in public shelters and on the street. The current interview occurred in the emergency room (ER) with the patient in four-point restraints in the presence of two clinical staff members and one police officer. It was the 10th such visit to the ER for Mr. Jones in the past year. The sources of information on Mr. Jones included the patient himself and the police officer who brought the patient to the ER. The police officer had witnessed the patient on the street and knew him from previous episodes.

## Chief Complaint

The chief complaint, in the patient's own words, states why he or she has come or been brought in for help. It

**Table 7.1–4**
**Outline of Psychiatric History**

I.  Identifying data
II.  Chief complaint
III.  History of present illness
    1. Onset
    2. Precipitating factors
IV.  Previous illnesses
    A. Psychiatric
    B. Medical
    C. Alcohol and other substance history
V.  Personal history (anamnesis)
    A. Prenatal and perinatal
    B. Early childhood (through age 3)
    C. Middle childhood (ages 3–11)
    D. Late childhood (puberty through adolescence)
    E. Adulthood
        1. Occupational history
        2. Marital and relationship history
        3. Military history
        4. Educational history
        5. Religion
        6. Social activity
        7. Current living situation
        8. Legal history
    F. Psychosexual history
    G. Family history
    H. Dreams, fantasies, and values

should be recorded even if the patient is unable to speak, and a description of the person who provided the information should be included. The patient's explanation, regardless of how bizarre or irrelevant it is, should be recorded verbatim in the section on the chief complaint. The others present as sources of information can then give their versions of the presenting events in the section on the history of the present illness.

Examples of chief complaints follow:

"I was feeling very depressed and thinking about killing myself." "Every car outside my house has a license plate number that is sending me hidden messages concerning a plot to kill the President." "There's nothing wrong with me; it's her that's crazy." The patient was mute.

## History of Present Illness

This part of the psychiatric history provides a comprehensive and chronological picture of the events leading up to the current moment in the patient's life. It is the part of the history that will probably be most helpful in making a diagnosis: what was the onset of the current episode, and what were the immediate precipitating events or triggers? An understanding of the history of the present illness helps answer the question, "Why now?" Why did the patient come to the doctor at this time? What were the patient's life circumstances at the onset of the symptoms or behavioral changes, and how did they affect the patient so that the presenting disorder became manifest? Knowing what the personality was of the previously well patient also helps give perspective on the currently ill patient.

The evolution of the patient's symptoms should be determined and summarized in an organized and systematic way. Symptoms not present should also be delineated. The more detailed the history of the present illness, the more likely the clinician is to make an accurate diagnosis. What past precipitating events were part of the chain leading up to the immediate events? In what ways has the patient's illness affected his or her life activities (for example, work, important relationships)? What is the nature of the dysfunction (for example, details about changes in such factors as personality, memory, speech)? Are there psychophysiological symptoms? If so, they should be described in terms of location, intensity, and fluctuation. If there is a relation between physical and psychological symptoms, it should be noted. Evidence of secondary gain—the extent to which illness serves some additional purpose—should also be noted. A description of the patient's current anxieties, whether they are generalized and nonspecific (free-floating) or are specifically related to particular situations, is helpful. How does the patient handle those anxieties? Frequently, a relatively open-ended question—such as, "How did this all begin?"—leads to an adequate unfolding of the history of the present illness. A well-organized patient is generally able to present a chronological account of the history. However, a disorganized patient is difficult to interview, as the chronology of events is confused. In that case, contacting other informants, such as family members and friends, can be a valuable aid in clarifying the patient's story.

## Previous Illnesses

This section of the psychiatric history is a transition between the story of the present illness and the patient's personal history (anamnesis). Past episodes of both psychiatric and medical illnesses are described. Ideally, at this point a detailed account of the patient's preexisting and underlying psychological and biological substrates is given, and important clues and evidence of vulnerable areas in the patient's functioning are provided. The patient's symptoms, extent of incapacity, type of treatment received, names of hospitals, length of each illness, effects of prior treatments, and degree of compliance should all be explored and recorded chronologically. Particular attention should be paid to the first episode that signaled the onset of illness, as first episodes can often provide crucial data about precipitating events, diagnostic possibilities, and coping capabilities.

With regard to medical history, the psychiatrist should obtain a medical review of symptoms and note any major medical or surgical illnesses and major traumas, particularly those requiring hospitalization, experienced by the patient. Episodes of craniocerebral trauma, neurological illness, tumors, and seizure disorders are especially relevant to psychiatric histories and so is a history of having tested positive for the human immunodeficiency virus (HIV) or of having acquired immune deficiency syndrome (AIDS). Specific questions need to be asked about the presence of a seizure disorder, episodes of loss of consciousness, changes in usual headache patterns, changes in vision, and episodes of confusion and disorientation. A history of infection with syphilis is critical and relevant.

Causes, complications, and treatment of any illness and the effects of the illness on the patient should be noted. Specific questions about psychosomatic disorders should be asked and noted. Included in that category are hay fever, rheumatoid arthritis, ulcerative colitis, asthma, hyperthyroidism, gastrointestinal upsets, recurrent colds, and skin conditions. All patients must be asked about alcohol and other substance use, including details about the quantity and the frequency of use. It is often advisable to frame one's questions in the form of an assumption of use, such as, "How much alcohol would you say you drink in a day?" rather than "Do you drink?" The latter question may put the patient on the defensive, concerned about what the physician will think if the answer is yes. If the physician assumes that drinking is a fact, the patient is likely to feel comfortable admitting use.

## Personal History (Anamnesis)

In addition to studying the patient's present illness and current life situation, the psychiatrist needs a thorough understanding of the patient's past life and its relationship to the present emotional problem. The anamnesis or personal history is usually divided into the major developmental periods of prenatal and perinatal, early childhood, middle childhood, late childhood, and adulthood. The predominant emotions associated with the different life periods (for example, painful, stressful, conflictual) should be noted. Depending on time and situation, the psychiatrist may go into detail with regard to each of those areas.

**Prenatal and perinatal history.** The psychiatrist considers the nature of the home situation into which the patient was born and whether the patient was planned and wanted. Were there any problems with the mother's pregnancy and delivery? Was there any evidence of defect or injury at birth? What was the mother's emotional and physical state at the time of the patient's birth? Were there any maternal health problems during pregnancy? Was the mother abusing alcohol or other substances during her pregnancy?

**Early childhood (birth through age 3 years).** The early childhood period consists of the first three years of the patient's life. The quality of the mother-child interaction during feeding and toilet training is important. It is frequently possible to learn whether the child presented problems in those areas. Early disturbances in sleep patterns and signs of unmet needs, such as head banging and body rocking, provide clues about possible maternal deprivation or developmental disability. In addition, the psychiatrist should obtain a history of human constancy during the first three years. Was there psychiatric or medical illness present in the parents that may have interfered with parent-child interactions? Did persons other than the mother care for the patient? Did the patient exhibit excessive problems at an early period with stranger anxiety or separation anxiety? The patient's siblings and the details of his or her relationship to them should be explored. The emerging personality of the child is also a topic of crucial importance. Was the child shy, restless, overactive, withdrawn, studious, outgoing, timid, athletic, friendly? The clinician should seek data concerning the child's increasing ability to concentrate, to tolerate frustration, and to postpone gratification. The child's preference for active or passive roles in physical play should also be noted. What were the child's favorite games or toys? Did the child prefer to play alone, with others, or not at all? What is the patient's earliest memory? Were there any recurrent dreams or fantasies during that period? A summary of the important areas to be covered follows:

FEEDING HABITS. Breast-fed or bottle-fed, eating problems

EARLY DEVELOPMENT. Walking, talking, teething, language development, motor development, signs of unmet needs, sleep pattern, object constancy, stranger anxiety, maternal deprivation, separation anxiety, other caretakers in the home

TOILET TRAINING. Age, attitude of parents, feelings about it

SYMPTOMS OF BEHAVIOR PROBLEMS. Thumb sucking, temper tantrums, tics, head bumping, rocking, night terrors, fears, bed wetting or bed soiling, nail biting, excessive masturbation

PERSONALITY AS A CHILD. Shy, restless, overactive, withdrawn, persistent, outgoing, timid, athletic, friendly; patterns of play

EARLY OR RECURRENT DREAMS OR FANTASIES.

**Middle childhood (ages 3 to 11 years).** In this section the psychiatrist can address such important subjects as gender identification, punishments used in the home, and who provided the discipline and influenced early conscience formation. The psychiatrist must inquire about the patient's early school experiences, especially how the patient first tolerated being separated from his or her mother. Data about the patient's earliest friendships and personal relationships are valuable. The psychiatrist should identify and define the number and the closeness of the patient's friends, describe whether the patient took the role of a leader or a follower, and describe the patient's social popularity and participation in group or gang activities. Was the child able to cooperate with peers, to be fair, to understand and comply with rules, and to develop an early conscience? Early patterns of assertion, impulsiveness, aggression, passivity, anxiety, or antisocial behavior emerge in the context of school relationships. A history of the patient's learning to read and the development of other intellectual and motor skills are important. A history of learning disabilities, their management, and their effects on the child are of particular significance. The presence of nightmares, phobias, bed wetting, fire setting, cruelty to animals, and excessive masturbation should also be explored.

**Late childhood (puberty through adolescence).** During late childhood, people begin to develop independence from their parents through relationships with peers and in group activities. The psychiatrist should attempt to define the values of the patient's social groups and determine who were the patient's idealized figures. That information provides useful clues concerning the patient's emerging idealized self-image.

Further exploration is indicated of the patient's school history, relationships with teachers, and favorite studies and interests, both in school and in the extracurricular area. The psychiatrist should ask about the patient's participation in sports and hobbies and inquire about any emotional or physical problems that may have first appeared during this phase. Examples of the types of questions that are commonly asked include the following: What was the patient's sense of personal identity? How extensive was the use of alcohol and other substances? Was the patient sexually active, and what was the quality of the sexual relationships? Was the patient interactive and involved with school and peers, or was he or she isolated, withdrawn, perceived as odd by others? Did the patient have a generally intact self-esteem, or was there evidence of excessive self-loathing? What was the patient's body image? Were there suicidal episodes? Were there problems in school, including excessive truancy? How did the patient use private time? What was the relationship with the parents? What were the feelings about the development of secondary sex characteristics? What was the response to menarche? What were the attitudes about dating, petting, crushes, parties, and sex games? One way to organize the diverse and large amount of information is to break late childhood into subsets of behavior (for example, social relationships, school history, cognitive and motor development, emotional and physical problems, and sexuality), as described below.

SOCIAL RELATIONSHIPS. Attitudes toward sibling(s) and playmates, number and closeness of friends, leader or follower, social popularity, participation in group or gang activities, idealized figures, patterns of aggression, passivity, anxiety, antisocial behavior

SCHOOL HISTORY. How far the patient progressed, adjustment to school, relationships with teachers—teacher's pet versus rebel—favorite studies or interests, particular abilities or assets, extracurricular activities, sports, hobbies, relations of problems or symptoms to any social period

COGNITIVE AND MOTOR DEVELOPMENT. Learning to read and other intellectual and motor skills, minimal cerebral dysfunctions, learning disabilities—their management and effects on the child

EMOTIONAL AND PHYSICAL PROBLEMS. Nightmares, phobias, masturbation, bed wetting, running away, delinquency, smoking, alcohol or other substance use, anorexia, bulimia, weight problems, feelings of inferiority, depression, suicidal ideas and acts

SEXUALITY
a. Early curiosity, infantile masturbation, sex play
b. Acquisition of sexual knowledge, attitude of parents toward sex, sexual abuse
c. Onset of puberty, feelings about it, kind of preparation, feelings about menstruation, development of secondary sex characteristics

d. Adolescent sexual activity: crushes, parties, dating, petting, masturbation, nocturnal emissions and attitudes toward them
e. Attitudes toward opposite sex: timid, shy, aggressive, need to impress, seductive, sexual conquests, anxiety
f. Sexual practices: sexual problems, paraphilias, promiscuity
g. Sexual orientation: homosexual experiences in both heterosexual and homosexual adolescents, gender identity issues, self-esteem

**Adulthood**

OCCUPATIONAL HISTORY. The psychiatrist should describe the patient's choice of occupation, the requisite training and preparation, any work-related conflicts, and the long-term ambitions and goals. The interviewer should also explore the patient's feelings about his or her current job and relationships at work (with authorities, peers, and, if applicable, subordinates) and describe the job history (for example, number and duration of jobs, reasons for job changes, and changes in job status). What would the patient do for work if he or she could freely choose?

MARITAL AND RELATIONSHIP HISTORY. In this section the psychiatrist describes the history of each marriage, legal or common law. Significant relationships with persons with whom the patient has lived for a protracted period of time are also included. The story of the marriage or long-term relationship should give a description of the evolution of the relationship, including the age of the patient at the beginning of the marriage or the long-term relationship. The areas of agreement and disagreement—including the management of money, housing difficulties, the roles of the in-laws, and attitudes toward raising children—should be described. Other questions include: Is the patient currently in a long-term relationship? How long is the longest relationship that the patient has had? What is the quality of the patient's sexual relationship (for example, is the patient's sexual life experienced as satisfactory or inadequate)? What does the patient look for in a partner? Is the patient able to initiate a relationship or to approach someone he or she feels attracted to or compatible with? How does the patient describe the current relationship in terms of its positive and negative qualities? How does the patient perceive failures of past relationships in terms of understanding what went wrong and who was or was not to blame?

MILITARY HISTORY. The psychiatrist should inquire about patients' general adjustment to the military, whether they saw combat or sustained an injury, and the nature of their discharges. Were they ever referred for psychiatric consultation, and did they suffer any disciplinary action during their periods of service?

EDUCATIONAL HISTORY. The psychiatrist needs to have a clear picture of the patient's educational background. That information can provide clues as to the patient's social and cultural background, intelligence, motivation, and any obstacles to achievement. For instance, a patient from an economically deprived background who never had the opportunity to attend the best schools and whose parents never graduated from high school shows strength of character, intelligence, and tremendous motivation by graduating from college. A patient who dropped out of high school because of violence and substance use displays creativity and determination by going to school at night to obtain a high school diploma while working during the day as a drug counselor. How far did the patient go in school? What was the highest grade or graduate level attained? What did the patient like to study, and what was the level of academic performance? How far did the other members of the patient's family go in school, and how does that compare with the patient's progress? What is the patient's attitude toward academic achievement?

RELIGION. The psychiatrist should describe the religious background of both parents and the details of the patient's religious instruction. Was the family's attitude toward religion strict or permissive, and were there any conflicts between the parents over the child's religious education? The psychiatrist should trace the evolution of the patient's adolescent religious practices to present beliefs and activities. Does the patient have a strong religious affiliation, and, if so, how does that affiliation affect the patient's life? What does the patient's religion say about the treatment of psychiatric or medical illness? What is the religious attitude toward suicide?

SOCIAL ACTIVITY. The psychiatrist should describe the patient's social life and the nature of friendships, with an emphasis on the depth, the duration, and the quality of human relationships. What type of social, intellectual, and physical interests does the patient share with friends? What types of relationships does the patient have with people of the same sex and the opposite sex? Is the patient essentially isolated and asocial? Does the patient prefer isolation, or is the patient isolated because of anxieties and fears about other people? Who visits the patient in the hospital and how frequently?

CURRENT LIVING SITUATION. The psychiatrist should ask the patient to describe where he or she lives in terms of the neighborhood and the residence. He or she should include the number of rooms, the number of family members living in the home, and the sleeping arrangements. The psychiatrist should inquire as to how issues of privacy are handled, with particular emphasis on parental and sibling nudity and bathroom arrangements. He or she should ask about the sources of family income and any financial hardships. If applicable, the psychiatrist may inquire about public assistance and the patient's feelings about it. If the patient has been hospitalized, have provisions been made so that he or she will not lose a job or an apartment? The psychiatrist should ask who is caring for the children at home, who visits the patient in the hospital, and how frequently.

LEGAL HISTORY. Has the patient ever been arrested and, if so, for what? How many times? Was the patient ever in jail? For how long? Is the patient on probation, or are charges pending? Is the patient mandated to be in treatment as part of a stipulation of probation? Does the patient have a history of assault or violence? Against whom? Using what? What is the patient's attitude toward the arrests or prison terms? An extensive legal history, as well as the patient's attitude toward it, may indicate an antisocial personality disorder. An extensive history of violence may alert the psychiatrist to the potential for violence in the future.

**Psychosexual history.** Much of the history of infantile sexuality is not recoverable, although many patients are able to recall curiosities and sexual games played from the ages of 3 to 6 years. The psychiatrist should ask how patients learned about sex and what they felt their parents' attitudes were about their sexual development. The interviewer can also inquire if the patient was sexually abused during childhood. Some of the material discussed in this section may also be covered in the section on adolescent sexuality. It is not important where in the history it is covered, as long as it is included.

The onset of puberty and the patient's feelings about that milestone are important. The adolescent masturbatory history, including the nature of the patient's fantasies and feelings about them, is of significance. Attitudes toward sex should be described in detail. Is the patient shy, timid, aggressive? Or does the patient need to impress others and boast of sexual conquests? Did the patient experience anxiety in the sexual setting? Was there promiscuity? What is the patient's sexual orientation?

The sexual history should include any sexual symptoms, such as anorgasmia, vaginismus, impotence, premature or retarded ejaculation, lack of sexual desire, and paraphilias (for example, sexual sadism, fetishism, voyeurism). Attitudes toward fellatio, cunnilingus, and coital techniques may be discussed. The topic of sexual adjustment should include a description of how sexual activity is usually initiated, the frequency of sexual relations, and sexual preferences, variations, and techniques. It is usually appropriate to inquire if the patient has engaged in extramarital relationships and, if so, under what circumstances and whether the spouse knew of the affair. If the spouse did learn of the affair, the psychiatrist should ask the patient to describe what happened. The reasons underlying an extramarital affair are just as important as an understanding of its effect on the marriage. Attitudes toward contraception and family planning are important. What form of contraception does the patient use? However, the psychiatrist should not assume that the patient uses birth control. A lesbian patient asked by an interviewer to describe what type of birth control she uses (on the assumption that she is heterosexual) may surmise that the interviewer will not be understanding or accepting of her sexual orientation. A better question is "Do you need to use birth control?" or "Is contraception something that is part of your sexuality?"

The psychiatrist should ask whether the patient wants to mention other areas of sexual functioning and sexuality. Is the patient aware of the issues involved in safe sex? Does the patient have a sexually transmitted disease, such as herpes or AIDS? Does the patient worry about being HIV-positive?

**Family history.** A brief statement about any psychiatric illnesses, hospitalizations, and treatments of the patient's immediate family members should be placed in this part of the report. Is there a family history of alcohol and other substance abuse or of antisocial behavior? In addition, the family history should provide a description of the personalities and the intelligence of the various people living in the patient's home from childhood to the present and descriptions of the various households lived in. The psychiatrist should also define the role each person has played in the patient's upbringing and the current relationship with the patient. What have been the family's ethnic, national, and religious traditions? Informants other than the patient may be available to contribute to the family history, and the source should be cited in the written record. Often, various members of the family give different descriptions of the same people and events. The psychiatrist should determine the family's attitude toward and insight into the patient's illness. Does the patient feel that the family members are supportive, indifferent, or destructive? What is the role of illness in the family?

Other questions that provide useful information in this section include the following: What are the patient's attitudes toward his or her parents and siblings? The psychiatrist should ask the patient to describe each family member. Whom does the patient mention first? Whom does the patient leave out? What does each of the parents do for a living? What do the siblings do? How does that compare with what the patient is currently doing, and how does the patient feel about it? Whom does the patient feel he or she is most like in the family and why?

**Dreams, fantasies, and values.** Sigmund Freud stated that the dream is the royal road to the unconscious. Repetitive dreams are of particular value. If the patient has nightmares, what are their repetitive themes? Some of the most common dream themes are food, examinations, sex, helplessness, and impotence. Can the patient describe a recent dream and discuss its possible meanings? Fantasies and daydreams are another valuable source of unconscious material. As with dreams, the psychiatrist can explore and record all manifest details and attendant feelings.

What are the patient's fantasies about the future? If the patient could make any change in his or her life, what would it be? What are the patient's most common or favorite current fantasies? Does the patient experience daydreams? Are the patient's fantasies grounded in reality, or is the patient unable to tell the difference between fantasy and reality?

The psychiatrist may inquire about the patient's system of values—both social and moral—including values that concern work, money, play, children, parents, friends, sex, community concerns, and cultural issues. For instance, are children seen as a burden or a joy? Is work experienced as a necessary evil, an avoidable chore, or an opportunity? What is the patient's concept of right and wrong?

## MENTAL STATUS EXAMINATION

The mental status examination is the part of the clinical assessment that describes the sum total of the examiner's observations and impressions of the psychiatric patient at the time of the interview. Whereas the patient's history remains stable, the patient's mental status can change from day to day or hour to hour. The mental status examination is the description of the patient's appearance, speech, actions, and thoughts during the interview. Even when a patient is mute or incoherent or refuses to answer questions, one can obtain a wealth of information through careful observation. Although practitioners' organizational formats for writing up the mental status examination vary slightly, the format must contain certain categories of information. One such format is outlined in Table 7.1–5.

### General Description

**Appearance.**  This is a description of the patient's appearance and overall physical impression conveyed to the

**Table 7.1–5**
**Outline of the Mental Status Examination**

---

  I. General description
    A. Appearance
    B. Behavior and psychomotor activity
    C. Attitude toward examiner
  II. Mood and affect
    A. Mood
    B. Affect
    C. Appropriateness
  III. Speech
  IV. Perceptual disturbances
  V. Thought
    A. Process or form of thought
    B. Content of thought
  VI. Sensorium and cognition
    A. Alertness and level of consciousness
    B. Orientation
    C. Memory
    D. Concentration and attention
    E. Capacity to read and write
    F. Visuospatial ability
    G. Abstract thinking
    H. Fund of information and intelligence
  VII. Impulse control
  VIII. Judgment and insight
  IX. Reliability

---

psychiatrist, as reflected by posture, poise, clothing, and grooming. If the patient appears particularly bizarre, one may ask, "Has anyone ever commented on how you look?" "How would you describe how you look?" "Can you help me understand some of the choices you make in how you look?"

Examples of items in the appearance category include body type, posture, poise, clothes, grooming, hair, and nails. Common terms used to describe appearance are healthy, sickly, ill at ease, poised, old-looking, young-looking, disheveled, childlike, and bizarre. Signs of anxiety are noted: moist hands, perspiring forehead, tense posture, wide eyes.

**Behavior and psychomotor activity.**  This category refers to both the quantitative and the qualitative aspects of the patient's motor behavior. Included are mannerisms, tics, gestures, twitches, stereotyped behavior, echopraxia, hyperactivity, agitation, combativeness, flexibility, rigidity, gait, and agility. Restlessness, wringing of hands, pacing, and other physical manifestations are described. Psychomotor retardation or generalized slowing down of body movements should be noted. Any aimless, purposeless activity should be described.

**Attitude toward examiner.**  The patient's attitude toward the examiner can be described as cooperative, friendly, attentive, interested, frank, seductive, defensive, contemptuous, perplexed, apathetic, hostile, playful, ingratiating, evasive, or guarded; any number of other adjectives can be used. The level of rapport established should be recorded.

### Mood and Affect

**Mood.**  *Mood* is defined as a pervasive and sustained emotion that colors the person's perception of the world. The psychiatrist is interested in whether the patient remarks voluntarily about feelings or whether it is necessary to ask the patient how he or she feels. Statements about the patient's mood should include depth, intensity, duration, and fluctuations. Common adjectives used to describe mood include depressed, despairing, irritable, anxious, angry, expansive, euphoric, empty, guilty, awed, futile, self-contemptuous, frightened, and perplexed. Mood may be labile, meaning that it fluctuates or alternates rapidly between extremes (for example, laughing loudly and expansive one moment, tearful and despairing the next).

**Affect.**  *Affect* may be defined as the patient's present emotional responsiveness. Affect is what the examiner infers from the patient's facial expression, including the amount and the range of expressive behavior. Affect may or may not be congruent with mood. Affect is described as being within normal range, constricted, blunted, or flat. In the normal range of affect, there is a variation in facial expression, tone of voice, use of hands, and body movements. When affect is *constricted*, there is a clear reduction in the range and the intensity of expression. Similarly, in *blunted* affect, emotional expression is further reduced. To diagnose *flat* affect, one should find virtually no signs of affective expression, the patient's voice should be monotonous, and the face should be immobile. "Blunted," "flat," and "constricted" are terms used to refer to the apparent depth of emotion; depressed, proud, angry, fearful, anxious, guilty, euphoric, and expansive are terms used to refer to particular moods. The psychiatrist should note the patient's difficulty in initiating, sustaining, or terminating an emotional response.

**Appropriateness.** The appropriateness of the patient's emotional responses can be considered in the context of the subject matter the patient is discussing. Delusional patients who are describing a delusion of persecution should be angry or frightened about the experiences they believe are happening to them. Anger or fear in that context is an appropriate expression. Some psychiatrists have reserved the term "inappropriateness of affect" for a quality of response found in some schizophrenic patients, in which the patient's affect is incongruent with what the patient is saying (for example, flattened affect when speaking about murderous impulses).

## Speech

This part of the report describes the physical characteristics of speech. Speech can be described in terms of its quantity, rate of production, and quality. The patient may be described as talkative, garrulous, voluble, taciturn, unspontaneous, or normally responsive to cues from the interviewer. Speech may be rapid or slow, pressured, hesitant, emotional, dramatic, monotonous, loud, whispered, slurred, staccato, or mumbled. Impairments of speech, such as stuttering, are included in this section. Unusual rhythms (termed dysprosody) and any accent that may be present should be noted. Is the patient's speech spontaneous or not?

## Perceptual Disturbances

Perceptual disturbances, such as hallucinations and illusions, may be experienced in reference to the self or the environment. The sensory system involved (for example, auditory, visual, olfactory, or tactile) and the content of the illusion or the hallucinatory experience should be described. The circumstances of the occurrence of any hallucinatory experience are important, because hypnagogic hallucinations (occurring as a person falls asleep) and hypnopompic hallucinations (occurring as a person awakens) are of much less serious significance than other types of hallucinations. Hallucinations may also occur in particular times of stress for individual patients. Feelings of depersonalization and derealization (extreme feelings of detachment from one's self or the environment) are other examples of perceptual disturbance. Formication, the feeling of bugs crawling on or under the skin, is seen in cocainism.

Examples of questions used to elicit the experience of hallucinations include the following: Have you ever heard voices or other sounds that no one else could hear or when no one else was around? Have you experienced any strange sensations in your body that others do not seem to experience? Have you ever had visions or seen things that other people do not seem to see?

## Thought

Thought is divided into process (or form) and content. Process refers to the way in which a person puts together ideas and associations, the form in which a person thinks. Process or form of thought may be logical and coherent or completely illogical and even incomprehensible. Content refers to what a person is actually thinking about: ideas, beliefs, preoccupations, obsessions. Table 7.1–6 lists common disorders of thought, divided into process and content.

**Thought process (form of thinking).** The patient may have either an overabundance or a poverty of ideas. There may be rapid thinking, which, if carried to the extreme, is called a *flight of ideas*. A patient may exhibit slow or hesitant thinking. Thought may be vague or empty. Do the patient's replies really answer the questions asked, and does the patient have the capacity for goal-directed thinking? Are the responses relevant or irrelevant? Is there a clear cause-and-effect relation in the patient's explanations? Does the patient have *loose associations* (for example, do the ideas expressed appear to be unrelated and idiosyncratically connected)? Disturbances of the continuity of thought include statements that are tangential, circumstantial, rambling, evasive, and perseverative. *Blocking* is an interruption of the train of thought before an idea has been completed; the patient may indicate an inability to recall what was being said or intended to be said. *Circumstantiality* indicates the loss of capacity for goal-directed thinking; in the process of explaining an idea, the patient brings in many irrelevant details and parenthetical comments but eventually does get back to the original point. *Tangentiality* is a disturbance in which the patient loses the thread of the conversation and pursues tangential thoughts stimulated by various external or internal irrelevant stimuli and never returns to the original point. Thought process impairments may be reflected by

**Table 7.1–6**
**Examples of Disorders of Thought**

**Process (or Form) of Thought**

Loosening of associations or derailment
Flight of ideas
Racing thoughts
Tangentiality
Circumstantiality
Word salad or incoherence
Neologisms
Clang associations
Punning
Thought blocking
Vague thought

**Content of Thought**

Delusions
Paranoia
Preoccupations
Obsessions and compulsions
Phobias
Suicidal or homicidal ideas
Ideas of reference and influence
Poverty of content

incoherent or incomprehensible connections of thoughts (*word salad*), *clang associations* (association by rhyming), *punning* (association by double meaning), and *neologisms* (new words created by the patient through the combination or the condensation of other words).

**Content of thought.** Disturbances in content of thought include delusions, preoccupations (which may involve the patient's illness), obsessions ("Are there ideas that you have that are intrusive and repetitive?"), compulsions ("Are there things you do over and over, in a repetitive manner?" "Are there things you must do in a particular way or order, and, if not done that way, must you repeat them?" "Do you know why you do things that way?"), phobias, plans, intentions, recurrent ideas about suicide or homicide, hypochondriacal symptoms, and specific antisocial urges. Does the patient have thoughts of doing harm to himself or herself? Is there a plan? A major category of disturbances of thought content involves delusions. Delusions may be *mood-congruent* (in keeping with a depressed or elated mood) or mood-incongruent. *Delusions* are fixed, false beliefs out of keeping with the patient's cultural background. The content of any delusional system should be described, and the psychiatrist should attempt to evaluate its organization and the patient's conviction as to its validity. The manner in which it affects the patient's life is appropriately described in the history of the present illness. Delusions may be bizarre and may involve beliefs about external control. Delusions may have themes that are persecutory or paranoid, grandiose, jealous, somatic, guilty, nihilistic, or erotic. Ideas of reference and ideas of influence should also be described. Examples of *ideas of reference* include beliefs that one's television or radio is speaking to or about one. Examples of *ideas of influence* are beliefs involving another person or force controlling some aspect of one's behavior.

### Sensorium and Cognition

This portion of the mental status examination seeks to assess organic brain function and the patient's intelligence, capacity for abstract thought, and level of insight and judgment.

The Mini-Mental State Examination (MMSE) is a brief instrument designed to grossly assess cognitive functioning. It assesses orientation, memory, calculations, reading and writing capacity, visuospatial ability, and language. The patient is quantitatively measured on those functions; a perfect score is 30 points. The MMSE is widely used as a simple, quick assessment of possible cognitive deficits. Table 10.1–2 gives an example of the MMSE.

**Alertness and level of consciousness.** Disturbances of consciousness usually indicate organic brain impairment. *Clouding of consciousness* is an overall reduced awareness of the environment. A patient may be unable to sustain attention to environmental stimuli or to sustain goal-directed thinking or behavior. Clouding or obtunding of consciousness is frequently not a fixed mental state. The typical patient manifests fluctuations in the level of awareness of the surrounding environment. The patient who has an altered state of consciousness often shows some impairment of orientation as well, although the reverse is not necessarily true. Some terms used to describe the patient's level of consciousness are clouding, somnolence, stupor, coma, lethargy, alertness, and fugue state.

**Orientation.** Disorders of orientation are traditionally separated according to time, place, and person. Any impairment usually appears in that order (that is, sense of time is impaired before sense of place); similarly, as the patient improves, the impairment clears in the reverse order. The psychiatrist must determine whether patients can give the approximate date and time of day. In addition, if patients are in a hospital, do they know how long they have been there? Do the patients behave as though they are oriented to the present? In questions about the patients' orientation to place, it is not sufficient that they be able to *state* the name and the location of the hospital correctly; they should also *behave* as though they know where they are. In assessing orientation for person, the psychiatrist asks patients whether they know the names of the people around them and whether they understand their roles in relationship to them. Do they know who the examiner is? It is only in the most severe instances that patients do not know who they themselves are.

**Memory.** Memory functions have traditionally been divided into four areas: remote memory, recent past memory, recent memory, and immediate retention and recall. Recent memory may be checked by asking patients about their appetite and then inquiring what they had for breakfast or for dinner the previous evening. Patients may be asked at that point if they recall the interviewer's name. Asking patients to repeat six digits forward and then backward is a test for immediate retention. Remote memory can be tested by asking patients for information about their childhoods that can be later verified. Asking patients to recall important news events from the past few months checks recent past memory. Often in cognitive disorders, recent or short-term memory is impaired first, and remote or long-term memory is impaired later. If there is impairment, what are the efforts made to cope with it or to conceal impairment? Is denial, confabulation, catastrophic reaction, or circumstantiality used to conceal a deficit? Reactions to the loss of memory can give important clues to underlying disorders and coping mechanisms. For instance, a patient who appears to have memory impairment but, in fact, is depressed is more likely to be concerned about memory loss than is someone with memory loss secondary to dementia. *Confabulation* (unconsciously making up false answers when memory is impaired) is most closely associated with cognitive disorders. Table 7.1–7 gives a summary of memory tests.

**Concentration and attention.** A patient's concentration may be impaired for a variety of reasons. For instance, a cognitive disorder, anxiety, depression, and internal stimuli, such as auditory hallucinations—all may contribute to impaired concentration. Subtracting serial 7s from 100 is a simple task that requires that both concentration and cognitive capacities be intact. Was the patient able to subtract 7 from 100 and keep subtracting 7s? If the patient could not subtract 7s, could 3s be subtracted? Were easier tasks accomplished—4 × 9, 5 × 4? The examiner must always assess whether anxiety, some disturbance of mood or consciousness, or a learning deficit is responsible for the difficulty.

**Table 7.1–7**
**Summary of Memory Tests**

Try to assess whether the process of registration, retention, or recollection of material is involved.

*Remote memory:* childhood data, important events known to have occurred when the patient was younger or free of illness, personal matters, neutral material

*Recent past memory:* the past few months

*Recent memory:* the past few days, what the patient did yesterday, the day before; what the patient had for breakfast, lunch, dinner

*Immediate retention and recall:* digit-span measures; ability to repeat six figures after examiner dictates them—first forward, then backward (patients with unimpaired memory can usually repeat six digits backward); ability to repeat three words immediately and three to five minutes later

---

Attention is assessed by calculations or by asking the patient to spell the word "world" (or others) backward. The patient can also be asked to name five things that start with a particular letter.

**Capacity to read and write.** The patient should be asked to read a sentence (for example, "Close your eyes") and then to do what the sentence says. The patient should also be asked to write a simple but complete sentence.

**Visuospatial ability.** The patient should be asked to copy a figure, such as a clock face or interlocking pentagons.

**Abstract thinking.** Abstract thinking is the ability of patients to deal with concepts. Patients present with disturbances in the manner in which they conceptualize or handle ideas. Can patients explain similarities, such as those between an apple and a pear or those between truth and beauty? Are the meanings of simple proverbs, such as "A rolling stone gathers no moss," understood? Answers may be concrete (giving specific examples to illustrate the meaning) or overly abstract (giving too generalized an explanation). Appropriateness of answers and the manner in which answers are given should be noted. In a catastrophic reaction, brain-damaged patients become extremely emotional and cannot think abstractly.

**Fund of information and intelligence.** If a possible cognitive impairment is suspected, does the patient have trouble with mental tasks, such as counting the change from $10 after a purchase of $6.37. If that task is too difficult, are easy problems (such as how many nickels are in $1.35) solved? The patient's intelligence is related to vocabulary and general fund of knowledge (for example, the distance from New York to Paris, Presidents of the United States). The patient's educational level (both formal and self-education) and socioeconomic status must be taken into account. A patient's handling of difficult or sophisticated concepts can be reflective of intelligence, even in the absence of formal education or an extensive fund of information. Ultimately, the psychiatrist estimates the patient's intellectual capability and whether the patient is capable of functioning at the level of basic endowment.

## Impulse Control

Is the patient capable of controlling sexual, aggressive, and other impulses? An assessment of impulse control is critical in ascertaining the patient's awareness of socially appropriate behavior and is a measure of the patient's potential danger to self and others. Some patients may be unable to control impulses secondary to cognitive disorders, others secondary to psychotic disorders, and others as the result of chronic characterological defects, as observed in the personality disorders. Impulse control can be estimated from information in the patient's recent history and from behavior observed during the interview.

## Judgment and Insight

**Judgment.** During the course of the history taking, the psychiatrist should be able to assess many aspects of the patient's capability for social judgment. Does the patient understand the likely outcome of his or her behavior, and is he or she influenced by that understanding? Can the patient predict what he or she would do in imaginary situations? For instance, what would the patient do if he or she smelled smoke in a crowded movie theater?

**Insight.** Insight is the patients' degree of awareness and understanding that they are ill. Patients may exhibit a complete denial of their illness or may show some awareness that they are ill but place the blame on others, on external factors, or even on organic factors. They may acknowledge that they have an illness but ascribe it to something unknown or mysterious in themselves.

Intellectual insight is present when patients can admit that they are ill and acknowledge that their failures to adapt are, in part, due to their own irrational feelings. However, the major limitation to intellectual insight is that patients are unable to apply the knowledge to alter future experiences. True emotional insight is present when patients' awareness of their own motives and deep feelings leads to a change in their personality or behavior patterns.

A summary of levels of insight follows:

1. Complete denial of illness
2. Slight awareness of being sick and needing help but denying it at the same time
3. Awareness of being sick but blaming it on others, on external factors, or on organic factors
4. Awareness that illness is due to something unknown in the patient
5. *Intellectual insight:* admission that the patient is ill and that symptoms or failures in social adjustment are due to the patient's own particular irrational feelings or disturbances without applying that knowledge to future experiences
6. *True emotional insight:* emotional awareness of the motives and feelings within the patient and the important people in his or her life, which can lead to basic changes in behavior

## Reliability

The mental status part of the report concludes with the psychiatrist's impressions of the patient's reliability and capacity to report his or her situation accurately. It includes an estimate of the psychiatrist's impression of the patient's truthfulness or veracity. For instance, if the patient is open about significant active substance abuse or about circumstances that the patient knows may reflect badly (for example, trouble with the law), the psychiatrist may estimate the patient's reliability to be good.

## PSYCHIATRIC REPORT

When the psychiatrist has completed a comprehensive psychiatric history and mental status examination, the information obtained is written up and organized into the psychiatric report. The report follows the outline of the standard psychiatric history and mental status examination. In the psychiatric report the examiner (1) addresses the critical questions of further diagnostic studies that must be performed, (2) adds a summary of both positive and negative findings, (3) makes a tentative multiaxial diagnosis, (4) gives a prognosis, (5) gives a psychodynamic formulation, and (6) gives a set of management recommendations.

### Further Diagnostic Studies

A. General physical examination
B. Neurological examination
C. Additional psychiatric diagnostic interviews
D. Interviews with family members, friends, or neighbors by a social worker
E. Psychological, neurological, or laboratory tests as indicated: electroencephalogram, computed tomography scan, magnetic resonance imaging, tests of other medical conditions, reading comprehension and writing tests, tests for aphasia, projective psychological tests, dexamethasone-suppression test, 24-hour urine test for heavy-metal intoxication

### Summary of Positive and Negative Findings

Mental symptoms, historical data (for example, family history), medical and laboratory findings, and psychological and neurological test results, if available, are summarized.

### Diagnosis

Diagnostic classification is made according to the fourth edition of the American Psychiatric Association's *Diagnostic and Statistical Manual of Mental Disorders* (DSM-IV). DSM-IV uses a multiaxial classification scheme consisting of five axes, each of which should be covered in the diagnosis.

Axis I consists of all clinical syndromes (for example, mood disorders, schizophrenia, generalized anxiety disorder) and other conditions that may be a focus of clinical attention.

Axis II consists of personality disorders and mental retardation.

Axis III consists of any general medical conditions (for example, epilepsy, cardiovascular disease, endocrine disorders).

Axis IV refers to psychosocial and environmental problems (for example, divorce, injury, death of a loved one) relevant to the illness.

Axis V relates to the global assessment of functioning exhibited by the patient during the interview (for example, social, occupational, and psychological functioning); a rating scale with a continuum from 100 (superior functioning) to 1 (grossly impaired functioning) is used.

The DSM-IV multiaxial classification scheme is discussed in detail in Chapter 9.

### Prognosis

The prognosis is an opinion about the probable immediate and future course, extent, and outcome of the disorder. The good and bad prognostic factors, as known, are listed.

### Psychodynamic Formulation

The psychodynamic formulation is a summary of proposed psychological influences on or causes of the patient's disturbance; influences in the patient's life that contributed to the present disorder; environmental and personality factors relevant to determining the patient's symptoms and how those influences have interacted with the patient's genetic, temperamental, and biological makeup; primary and secondary gains. An outline of the major defense mechanisms used by the patient should be listed.

### Recommendations

In formulating the treatment plan, the clinician should note whether the patient requires psychiatric treatment at the time and, if so, at which problems and target symptoms the treatment is aimed, what kind of treatment or combination of treatments the patient should receive, and what treatment setting seems most appropriate. For instance, the examiner evaluates the role of medication, inpatient or outpatient treatment, frequency of sessions, probable duration of therapy, and type of psychotherapy (individual, group, or family therapy). Specific goals of therapy are noted. If hospitalization is recommended, the clinician should specify the reasons for hospitalization, the type of hospitalization indicated, the urgency with which the patient has to be hospitalized, and the anticipated duration of inpatient care. The clinician should also estimate the length of treatment.

If either the patient or family members are unwilling to accept the recommendations for treatment and the clinician thinks that the refusal of the recommendations may have serious consequences, the patient (or the parent or guardian) should sign a statement that the recommended treatment was refused.

### References

American Psychiatric Association: *Diagnostic and Statistical Manual of Mental Disorders,* ed 4. American Psychiatric Association, Washington, 1994.
Baker N J, Berry S L, Adler L E: Family diagnoses missed on a clinical inpatient service. Am J Psychiatry *144*: 630, 1987.

Corty E, Lehman A F, Myers C P: Influence of psychoactive substance use on the reliability of psychiatric diagnosis. J Consult Clin Psychol 61: 165, 1993.

Keller M B, Manschreck T C: The bedside mental status examination: Reliability and validity. Compr Psychiatry 22: 500, 1981.

Kerns L L: Falsifications in the psychiatric history: A differential diagnosis. Psychiatry 49: 13, 1986.

Kosten T A, Rounsaville B J: Sensitivity of psychiatric diagnosis based on the best estimate procedure. Am J Psychiatry 149: 1225, 1992.

Leon R L, Bowden C L, Faber R A: The psychiatric interview, history, and mental status examination. In Comprehensive Textbook of Psychiatry, ed 5, H I Kaplan, B J Sadock, editors, p 449. Williams & Wilkins, Baltimore, 1989.

Lewis N D C: Outlines for Psychiatric Examinations, ed 3. New York State Department of Mental Hygiene, Albany, 1943.

MacKinnon R A, Michels R: The Psychiatric Interview in Clinical Practice. Saunders, New York, 1971.

Ryback R: The Problem-Oriented Record in Psychiatry and Mental Health Care. Grune & Stratton, New York, 1974.

Shea S C, Mezzich J E: Contemporary psychiatric interviewing: New directions for training. Psychiatry 51: 385, 1988.

Stevenson I: The Psychiatric Examination. Little, Brown, Boston, 1969.

Strub R L, Black F W: The Mental Status Examination in Neurology, ed 2. Davis, Philadelphia, 1985.

Westermeyer J, Wahmenholm K: Assessing the victimized psychiatric patient. Hosp Community Psychiatry 40: 245, 1989.

Wittchen H U, Burke J D, Semler G, Pfister H, VonCranach M, Zaudig M: Recall and dating of psychiatric symptoms: Test-retest reliability of time-related symptom questions in a standardized psychiatric interview. Arch Gen Psychiatry 46: 437, 1989.

Zarin D A, Earls F: Diagnostic decision making in psychiatry. Am J Psychiatry 150: 197, 1993.

# 7.2 / Laboratory Tests in Psychiatry

Psychiatrists are more dependent than are other medical specialists on the clinical examination and on the patient's signs and symptoms. No laboratory tests in psychiatry can confirm or rule out such diagnoses as schizophrenia, bipolar I disorder, and major depressive disorder. However, with the continuing advances in biological psychiatry and neuropsychiatry, laboratory tests have become increasingly valuable, both to the clinical psychiatrist and to the biological researcher.

In clinical psychiatry, laboratory tests can help rule out potential underlying organic causes of psychiatric symptoms—for example, impaired copper metabolism in Wilson's disease and a positive result on an antinuclear antibody (ANA) test in systemic lupus erythematosus (SLE). Laboratory work is then used to monitor treatment, such as measuring the blood levels of antidepressant medications and assessing the effects of lithium (Eskalith) on electrolytes, thyroid metabolism, and renal function. However, laboratory data can serve only as an underlying support for the essential skill of clinical assessment.

## BASIC SCREENING TESTS

Before initiating psychiatric treatment, a clinician should undertake a routine medical evaluation for the purposes of screening for concurrent disease, ruling out or-

ganicity, and establishing baseline values of functions to be monitored. Such an evaluation includes a medical history and routine medical laboratory tests, such as a complete blood count (CBC); hematocrit and hemoglobin; renal, liver, and thyroid function; electrolytes; and blood sugar.

Thyroid disease and other endocrinopathies may present as a mood disorder or a psychotic disorder; cancer or infectious disease may present as depression; infection and connective tissue diseases may present as short-term changes in mental status. In addition, a range of organic mental and neurological conditions may present initially to the psychiatrist. Those conditions include multiple sclerosis, Parkinson's disease, dementia of the Alzheimer's type, Huntington's disease, dementia due to human immunodeficiency virus (HIV) disease, and temporal lobe epilepsy. Any suspected medical or neurological condition should be thoroughly evaluated with appropriate laboratory tests and consultation.

## NEUROENDOCRINE TESTS

### Thyroid Function Tests

A number of thyroid function tests are available, including tests for thyroxine ($T_4$) by competitive protein binding ($T_4D$) and by radioimmunoassay ($T_4RIA$) involving a specific antigen-antibody reaction. Table 7.2–1 lists some of the common thyroid function tests. More than 90 percent of $T_4$ is bound to serum protein and is responsible for thyroid-stimulating hormone (TSH) secretion and cellular metabolism. Other thyroid measures include the free $T_4$ index ($FT_4I$), triiodothyronine uptake, and total serum triiodothyronine measured by radioimmunoassay ($T_3RIA$). Those tests are used to rule out hypothyroidism, which can present with symptoms of depression. In some studies, up to 10 percent of patients complaining of depression and associated fatigue had incipient hypothyroid disease. Other associated signs and symptoms common to both depression and hypothyroidism include weakness, stiffness, poor appetite, constipation, menstrual irregularities, slowed speech, apathy, impaired memory, and even hallucinations and delusions. Lithium can cause hypothyroidism and, more rarely, hyperthyroidism. Table 7.2–2 outlines the suggested monitoring of thyroid function for patients taking lithium. Neonatal hypothyroidism results in mental retardation and is preventable if the diagnosis is made at birth. Table 7.2–3 lists the thyroid function test changes associated with hypothyroidism.

**Thyrotropin-releasing hormone stimulation test.** The thyrotropin-releasing hormone (TRH) stimulation test is indicated in patients who have marginally abnormal thyroid test results with suspected subclinical hypothyroidism, which may account for clinical depression. It is also used in patients with possible lithium-induced hypothyroidism. The procedure entails an intravenous (IV) injection of 500 mg of TRH, which produces a sharp rise in serum TSH when measured at 15, 30, 60, and 90 minutes. Table 7.2–4 summarizes one suggested TRH test protocol. An increase in serum TSH of from 5 to 25 μIU/mL above the baseline is normal. An increase of less than 7μIU/mL is considered a blunted response, which may correlate with a diagnosis of a depressive disorder. Eight percent of all patients with depressive disorders have some thyroid illness.

**Table 7.2–1**
**Common Thyroid Function Tests***

| Type of Test | Normal Values | Cost ($) | Interference |
|---|---|---|---|
| **In vitro (serum tests)** | | | |
| $T_4$ | 4.5–13 µg/100 mL<br>58–167 nmol/L | 7–22 | Changes in TBG, drugs, etc. |
| Resin $T_3$ uptake | 25–35% | 3–10 | Changes in TBG, drugs, etc. |
| $T_7$ and ETR | Combinations of values for $T_4$ and resin<br>$T_3$ uptake | | |
| TSH | 0–10 µIU/mL<br>2–7 µIU/mL | 39 | Pituitary disease |
| $T_3$RIA | 80–200 ng/100 mL<br>1.2–3.1 nmol/L | 41 | Changes in TBG, drugs, etc. |
| Autoantibodies | Absent | 30–60 | |
| **In vivo tests** | | | |
| Radioiodine uptake ($I^{131}$, $I^{123}$) | 10–25%/24 hours | 60–95 | Never use in pregnancy: iodides $T_3$<br>and $T_4$ therapy, antithyroid<br>drugs, thyroiditis |
| Thyroid scan radioiodine | Both lobes homogeneous | 80 | Iodides $T_3$, $T_4$: never use in<br>pregnancy |
| TRH injection | TSH increase to 2× control | 115 | |
| TSH stimulation | No effect or increased uptake | 115 | |
| $T_4$ suppression | Uptake reduced to half of original value | 115 | Heart disease or other<br>contraindication of $T_4$ therapy |
| **Histology (biopsy)** | | | |
| Fine needle aspiration biopsy | Normal cytology | 28 | Inadequate sample |
| Cutting needle biopsy | Normal cytology | † | Significant danger of hemorrhage |

*Tests are listed in order of decreasing frequency of practical application. Adapted from J A Halsted, C H Halsted, editors: *The Laboratory in Clinical Medicine: Interpretation and Application*, ed 2. Saunders, Philadelphia, 1981.
†Cost data vary from laboratory to laboratory.
Table from A MacKinnon, S C Yudofsky: *Principles of the Psychiatric Evaluation*, p 96. Lippincott, Philadelphia, 1991. Used with permission.

**Table 7.2–2**
**Thyroid Monitoring for Patients Taking Lithium**

| Evaluation | Before<br>Treatment | Repeat at<br>6 months | Repeat<br>Yearly |
|---|---|---|---|
| **Medical** | | | |
| 1. Careful medical and family history to detect family history of thyroid disease | X | | |
| 2. Review of symptoms of hyperthyroidism and hypothyroidism | X | X | X |
| 3. Physical examination, including palpation of thyroid | X | | X |
| **Laboratory** | | | |
| $T_3$RU | X | | X |
| $T_4$RIA | X | | X |
| $T_2$I (free thyroxine index) | X | | X |
| TSH | X | X | X |
| Antithyroid antibodies | X | | X |

Table adapted from J M Silver, S C Yudofsky: Psychopharmacology and electroconvulsive therapy. In *The American Psychiatric Press Textbook of Psychiatry*, J A Talbott, R E Hales, S C Yudofsky, editors, p 822. American Psychiatric Press, Washington, 1987. Used with permission. Table from A MacKinnon, S C Yudofsky: *Principles of the Psychiatric Evaluation*, p 104. Lippincott, Philadelphia, 1991. Used with permission.

**Table 7.2–3**
**Thyroid Function Test Changes in Patients with Hypothyroidism**

1. Serum $T_4$ concentration is decreased.
2. Serum-free thyroxine is decreased.
3. Serum $T_3$ concentration is decreased.
4. Serum $T_3$ uptake is decreased.
5. Serum PBI is decreased.
6. Serum thyroxine-binding globulin is normal.
7. Serum $T_3$-$T_4$ ratio is increased.
8. Serum thyroid-stimulating hormone is increased.

Table from A MacKinnon, S C Yudofsky: *Principles of the Psychiatric Evaluation*, p 97. Lippincott, Philadelphia, 1991. Used with permission.

### Dexamethasone-Suppression Test

Dexamethasone is a long-acting synthetic glucocorticoid with a long half-life. About 1 mg of dexamethasone is equivalent to 25 mg of cortisol. The dexamethasone-suppression test (DST) is used to help confirm a diagnostic impression of major depressive disorder (fourth edition of *Diagnostic and Statistical Manual of Mental Disorders* [DSM-IV] classification) or endogenous depression (Research Diagnostic Criteria [RDC] classification).

**Procedure.** The patient is given 1 mg of dexamethasone by mouth at 11 PM, and plasma cortisol is measured at 8 AM, 4 PM, and 11 PM. Plasma cortisol above 5 µg/dL (known as nonsuppression) is considered abnormal (that is, positive).

**Table 7.2–4**
**TRH Test Protocol**

1. Patient takes nothing by mouth after midnight and is at rest in bed at 8:30 AM.
2. Indwelling venous catheter is placed, and a normal saline drip is started to keep the line open.
3. At 8:59 AM blood is taken through a three-way stopcock for determination of $T_3RU$, $T_3RIA$, $T_4$, and TSH levels (reverse $T_3$ is optional).
4. At 9 AM intravenous TRH (protirelin) 500 μg is given slowly over 30 seconds. Side effects from the infusions may include a transient sensation of warmth, desire to urinate, nausea, metallic taste, headache, dry mouth, chest tightness, or a pleasant genital sensation. Those effects are generally short-lived and mild.
5. Blood samples are taken through the stopcock before the TRH is administered and at 15, 30, 60, and 90 minutes after infusion to measure changes in TSH.

Table from A MacKinnon, S C Yudofsky: *Principles of the Psychiatric Evaluation*, p 94. Lippincott, Philadelphia, 1991. Used with permission.

Suppression of cortisol indicates that the hypothalamic-adrenal-pituitary axis is functioning properly. Since the 1930s, dysfunction of that axis has been known to be associated with stress.

The DST can be used to follow the response of a depressed person to treatment. Normalization of the DST, however, is not an indication to stop antidepressant treatment, because the DST may normalize before the depression resolves.

Some evidence indicates that patients with a positive DST result (especially 10 μg/dL) will have a good response to somatic treatment, such as electroconvulsive therapy (ECT) or cyclic antidepressant therapy. The problems associated with the DST include varying reports of sensitivity and specificity. False-positive and false-negative results are common and are listed in Table 7.2–5. The sensitivity of the DST is considered to be 45 percent in major depressive disorder and 70 percent in major depressive episode with psychotic features. The specificity is 90 percent compared with controls and 77 percent compared with other psychiatric diagnoses. Figure 7.2–1 illustrates the suppression of plasma cortisol in a patient with major depressive disorder before and six weeks after the initiation of treatment with a tricyclic drug.

## Other Endocrine Tests

A variety of other hormones affect behavior. Exogenous hormonal administration has been shown to affect behavior, and known endocrine diseases have associated mental disorders.

In addition to thyroid hormones, those hormones include the anterior pituitary hormone prolactin, growth hormone, somastatin, gonadotrophin-releasing hormone (GnRH), and the sex steroids—luteinizing hormone (LH), follicle-stimulating hormone (FSH), testosterone, and estrogen. Melatonin from the pineal gland has been implicated in seasonal affective disorder (called mood disorder with seasonal pattern in DSM-IV).

Symptoms of anxiety or depression may be explained in some patients on the basis of unspecified changes in endocrine function or homeostasis.

## Catecholamines

The serotonin metabolite 5-hydroxyindoleacetic acid (5-HIAA) is elevated in the urine of patients with carcinoid tu-

**Table 7.2–5**
**Medical Conditions and Pharmacological Agents That May Interfere with Results of the Dexamethasone-Suppression Test**

False-positive results are associated with
  Phenytoin
  Barbiturates
  Meprobamate
  Glutethimide
  Carbamazepine
  Cardiac failure
  Hypertension
  Renal failure
  Disseminated cancer and serious infections
  Recent major trauma or surgery
  Fever
  Nausea
  Dehydration
  Temporal lobe disease
  High-dosage estrogen treatment
  Pregnancy
  Cushing's disease
  Unstable diabetes mellitus
  Extreme weight loss (malnutrition, anorexia nervosa)
  Alcohol abuse
  Benzodiazepine withdrawal
  Tricyclic drug withdrawal
  Dementia
  Bulimia nervosa
  Acute psychotic disorder
  Advanced age
False-negative results are associated with
  Hypopituitarism
  Addison's disease
  Long-term synthetic steroid therapy
  Indomethacin
  High-dosage cyproheptadine treatment
  High-dosage benzodiazepine treatment

Table from M Young, J Stanford: The dexamethasone suppression test for the detection, diagnosis, and management of depression. Arch Intern Med *100:* 309, 1984. Used with permission.

mors and at times in patients who take phenothiazine medication and in persons who eat foods high in serotonin (for example, walnuts, bananas, avocados). The amount of 5-HIAA in cerebrospinal fluid is low in some persons who are in a suicidal depression and in those who have committed suicide in particularly violent ways. Low cerebrospinal fluid 5-HIAA is associated with violence in general. Norepinephrine and its metabolic products—metanephrine, normetanephrine, and vanillylmandelic acid (VMA)—can be measured in the urine, the blood, and the plasma. Plasma catecholamines are markedly elevated in pheochromocytoma, which is associated with anxiety, agitation, and hypertension. Some cases of chronic anxiety may share elevated blood norepinephrine and epinephrine levels. Some depressed patients have a low urinary norepinephrine to epinephrine ratio (NE:E).

High levels of urinary norepinephrine and epinephrine have been found in some patients with posttraumatic stress disorder. The norepinephrine metabolite 3-methoxy-4-hydroxyphenylglycol (MHPG) level is decreased in patients with severe depressive disorders, especially in those patients who attempt suicide.

## Renal Function Tests

Creatinine clearance detects early kidney damage and can be serially monitored to follow the course of renal disease.

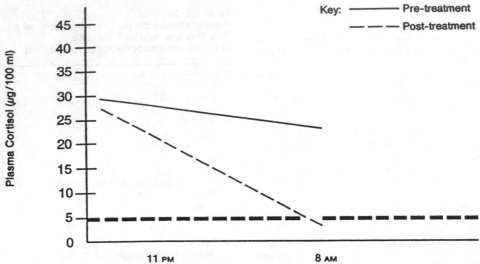

**Figure 7.2–1.** Dexamethasone-suppression test results for a patient with major depressive disorder. (Figure from A Mac-Kinnon, S C Yudofsky: *Principles of the Psychiatric Evaluation.* Lippincott, Philadelphia, 1991. Used with permission.)

Blood urea nitrogen (BUN) is also elevated in renal disease and is excreted by way of the kidneys, and the serum BUN and the creatinine are monitored in patients taking lithium. If the serum BUN or the creatinine is abnormal, the patient's two-hour creatinine clearance and ultimately the 24-hour creatinine clearance are tested. Table 7.2–6 outlines a suggested protocol for the monitoring of renal function in patients taking lithium. Table 7.2–7 summarizes other laboratory testing for patients taking lithium.

### Liver Function Tests

Total bilirubin and direct bilirubin are elevated in hepatocellular injury and intrahepatic bile stasis that can occur with phenothiazine or tricyclic medication and with alcohol and other substance abuse. Certain drugs—for example, phenobarbital (Luminal)—may decrease serum bilirubin. Liver damage or disease, which is reflected by abnormal findings in liver function tests (LFTs), may present with signs and symptoms of a cognitive disorder, including disorientation and delirium. Impaired hepatic function may increase the elimination

half-lives of certain drugs, including some of the benzodiazepines, so that the drug may stay in the patient's system longer than it would under normal circumstances. LFTs need to be routinely monitored when using certain drugs, such as carbamazepine (Tegretol) and valproate (Depakene).

### BLOOD TESTS FOR SEXUALLY TRANSMITTED DISEASES

The Veneral Disease Research Laboratory (VDRL) test is used as a screening test for syphilis. If positive, the result is confirmed by using the specific fluorescent treponemal antibody-absorption test (FTA-ABS test), which uses the spirochete *Treponema pallidum* as the antigen. Central nervous system VDRL is measured in patients with suspected neurosyphilis. A positive HIV test result indicates that the person has been exposed to infection with the virus that causes acquired immune deficiency syndrome (AIDS).

**Table 7.2–6**
**Renal Monitoring for Patients Taking Lithium**

| Evaluation | Before Treatment | Repeat at 6 months | Repeat Yearly |
|---|---|---|---|
| Medical | | | |
| 1. Careful medical and family history to detect presence of familial kidney disease or predisposition to kidney disease (diabetes, hypertension) | x | | |
| 2. Specific comprehensive review of genitourinary system symptoms | x | x | x |
| 3. Physical examination | x | | x |
| Laboratory | | | |
| BUN | x | | x |
| Creatinine | x | x | x |
| Creatinine clearance (24-hour urine) urinalysis | x | | x |
| 24-hour urine volume | x | | x |
| 12-hour fluid deprivation test | x | | |

Table adapted from J M Silver, S C Yudofsky: Psychopharmacology and electroconvulsive therapy. In *The American Psychiatric Press Textbook of Psychiatry*, J A Talbott, R E Hales, S C Yudofsky, editors: p 822. American Psychiatric Press, Washington, 1987. Used with permission. Table from A MacKinnon, S C Yudofsky: *Principles of the Psychiatric Evaluation*, p 103. Lippincott, Philadelphia, 1991. Used with permission.

**Table 7.2–7**
**Other Laboratory Testing for Patients Taking Lithium**

| Test | Frequency |
|---|---|
| 1. Complete blood count | Before treatment and yearly |
| 2. Serum electrolytes | Before treatment and yearly |
| 3. Fasting blood glucose | Before treatment and yearly |
| 4. Electrocardiogram | Before treatment and yearly |
| 5. Pregnancy testing for women of childbearing age* | Before treatment |

*Take more frequently when compliance with treatment plan is uncertain.
Table from A MacKinnon, S C Yudofsky: *Principles of the Psychiatric Evaluation*, p 106. Lippincott, Philadelphia, 1991. Used with permission.

# TESTS RELATED TO PSYCHOTROPIC DRUGS

There is a trend in caring for patients receiving psychotropic medication to have regular measurements taken of their plasma levels of the prescribed drug. For some types of drugs, such as lithium, the monitoring is essential; but for other types of drugs, such as antipsychotics, it is mainly of academic or research interest. The clinician need not practice defensive medicine by insisting that all patients receiving psychotropic drugs have blood levels taken for medicolegal purposes. In the discussion that follows, the major classes of drugs and the suggested guidelines are outlined. The current status of psychopharmacological treatment is such that the psychiatrist's clinical judgment and experience, except in rare instances, is a better indication of a drug's therapeutic efficacy than is a plasma-level determination. Moreover, the reliance on plasma levels cannot replace clinical skills and the need to maintain the humanitarian aspects of patient care.

## Benzodiazepines

No special tests are needed for patients taking benzodiazepines. Among those metabolized in the liver by oxidation, impaired hepatic function increases the half-life. Baseline LFTs are indicated in patients with suspected liver damage. Urine testing for benzodiazepines is used routinely in cases of substance abuse.

## Antipsychotics

Antipsychotics can cause leukocytosis, leukopenia, mild anemia, and, in rare cases, agranulocytosis. A baseline may be desirable; but, because bone marrow side effects can occur abruptly, even when the dosage of a drug has remained constant, a baseline normal CBC is not conclusive. Antipsychotics are metabolized in the liver, so LFTs may be useful. Antipsychotic plasma levels do not correlate with clinical response; however, there is a possible correlation between high plasma levels and toxic side effects, especially with chlorpromazine (Thorazine) and haloperidol (Haldol). There is no known relation between antipsychotic levels and tardive dyskinesia. Plasma levels are currently of clinical use only to detect noncompliance and nonabsorption and, thus, may be useful in identifying the nonresponder.

**Clozapine.** Because of the risk of agranulocytosis (1 to 2 percent), patients who are being treated with clozapine (Clozaril) must have a baseline white blood cell (WBC) and differential count before the initiation of treatment, a WBC count every week throughout treatment, and a WBC count for four weeks after the discontinuation of clozapine. Physicians and pharmacists who provide clozapine are required to be registered through the Clozaril National Registry (1-800-448-5938). Table 7.2–8 summarizes the clinical management of reduced WBC, leukopenia, and agranulocytosis for patients treated with clozapine.

## Cyclic Drugs

An electrocardiogram (ECG) should be given before starting cyclic drugs to assess for conduction delays, which may lead to heart block at therapeutic levels. Some clinicians believe that all patients receiving prolonged cyclic drug therapy should have an annual ECG. At therapeutic levels, the drugs suppress arrhythmias through a quinidinelike effect. Trazodone (Desyrel), an antidepressant unrelated to cyclic drugs, has been reported to cause ventricular arrhythmias and priapism, mild leukopenia, and neutropenia.

Blood levels should be tested routinely when using imipramine (Tofranil), desipramine (Norpramin), or nortriptyline (Pamelor) in the treatment of depressive disorders. Taking blood levels may also be of use in patients with a poor response at normal dosage ranges and in high-risk patients for whom there is an urgent need to know whether a therapeutic or toxic plasma level of the drug has been reached. Blood level tests should also include the measurement of active metabolites (for example, imipramine is converted to desipramine, amitryptiline [Elavil] to nortriptyline). Some characteristics of tricyclic drug plasma levels are as follows:

1. *Imipramine.* The percentage of favorable responses correlates with plasma levels in a linear manner between 200 and 250 ng/mL, but some patients may respond at a lower level. At levels over 250 ng/mL, there is no improved favorable response, and side effects increase.
2. *Nortriptyline.* The *therapeutic window* (the range within which a drug is most effective) is between 50 and 150 ng/mL. There is a decreased response rate at levels over 150 ng/mL.
3. *Desipramine.* Levels greater than 125 ng/mL correlate with a higher percentage of favorable responses.
4. *Amitryptyline.* Different studies have produced conflicting results with regard to blood levels.

**Procedure.** The procedure for taking blood levels is as follows: The blood specimen should be drawn 10 to 14 hours after the last dose, usually in the morning after a bedtime dose. Patients must be on a stable daily dosage for at least five days for the test to be valid. Some patients are unusually poor metabolizers of cyclic drugs and may have levels as high as 2,000 ng/mL while taking normal dosages and before showing a favorable clinical response. Such patients must be monitored closely for cardiac side effects.

**Table 7.2–8**
**Clinical Management of Reduced White Blood Cell Count, Leukopenia, and Agranulocytosis**

| Problem Phase | WBC Findings | Clinical Findings | Treatment Plan |
|---|---|---|---|
| Reduced WBC | WBC count reveals a significant drop (even if WBC count is still in normal range). "Significant drop" = (1) drop of more than 3,000 cells from prior test or (2) three or more consecutive drops in WBC counts | No symptoms of infection | 1. Monitor patient closely<br>2. Institute twice-weekly CBC tests with differentials if deemed appropriate by attending physician<br>3. Clozapine therapy may continue |
| Mild leukopenia | WBC = 3,000–3,500 | Patient may or may not show clinical symptoms, such as lethargy, fever, sore throat, weakness | 1. Monitor patient closely<br>2. Institute a minimum of twice-weekly CBC tests with differentials<br>3. Clozapine therapy may continue |
| Leukopenia or granulocytopenia | WBC = 2,000–3,000 or granulocytes = 1,000–1,500 | Patient may or may not show clinical symptoms, such as fever, sore throat, lethargy, weakness | 1. Interrupt clozapine at once<br>2. Institute daily CBC tests with differentials<br>3. Increase surveillance, consider hospitalization<br>4. Clozapine therapy may be reinstituted after normalization of WBC |
| Agranulocytosis (uncomplicated) | WBC count less than 2,000 or granulocytes less than 1,000 | The patient may or may not show clinical symptoms, such as fever, sore throat, lethargy, weakness | 1. Discontinue clozapine at once<br>2. Place patient in protective isolation in a medical unit with modern facilities<br>3. Consider a bone marrow specimen to determine if progenitor cells are being suppressed<br>4. Monitor patient every 2 days until WBC and differential counts return to normal (about 2 weeks)<br>5. Avoid use of concomitant medications with bone marrow-suppressing potential |
| Agranulocytosis (with complications) | WBC count less than 2,000 or granulocytes less than 1,000 | Definite evidence of infection, such as fever, sore throat, lethargy, weakness, malaise, skin ulcerations, etc. | 6. Consult with hematologist or other specialist to determine appropriate antibiotic regimen<br>7. Start appropriate therapy; monitor closely |
| Recovery | WBC count more than 4,000 and granulocytes more than 2,000 | No symptoms of infection | 1. Once-weekly CBC with differential counts for 4 consecutive normal values<br>2. Clozapine must not be restarted |

Table reprinted with permission of Sandoz Pharmaceuticals Corporation. Table from A MacKinnon, S C Yudofsky: *Principles of the Psychiatric Evaluation*, p 118. Lippincott, Philadelphia, 1991. Used with permission.

Patients with levels greater than 1,000 ng/mL are generally at risk for cardiotoxicity.

## Monoamine Oxidase Inhibitors

Patients taking monoamine oxidase inhibitors (MAOIs) are instructed to avoid tyramine-containing foods because of the danger of a potential hypertensive crisis. A baseline normal blood pressure (BP) must be recorded, and the BP must be monitored during treatment. MAOIs may also cause orthostatic hypotension as a direct drug side effect unrelated to diet. Other than their potential for causing elevated BP when taken with certain foods, MAOIs are relatively free of other side effects. A test used both in research and in current clinical practice involves correlating the therapeutic response with the degree of platelet monoamine oxidase inhibition.

## Lithium

Patients receiving lithium should have baseline thyroid function tests, electrolyte monitoring, a white blood cell count (WBC), renal function tests (specific gravity, BUN, and creatinine), and a baseline ECG. The rationale for those tests is that lithium can cause renal concentrating defects, hypothyroidism, and leukocytosis; sodium depletion can cause toxic lithium levels; and about 95 percent of lithium is excreted in the urine. Lithium has also been shown to cause ECG changes, including various conduction defects.

Lithium is most clearly indicated in the prophylactic treatment of manic episodes (its direct antimanic effect may take up to two weeks) and is commonly coupled with antipsychotics for the treatment of acute manic episodes. Lithium itself may also have antipsychotic activity. The maintenance level is 0.6 to 1.2 mEq per L, although acutely manic patients can tolerate up to 1.5 to 1.8 mEq per L. Some patients may respond at lower levels, whereas others may require higher levels. A response below 0.4 mEq per L is probably a placebo. Toxic reactions may occur with levels over 2.0 mEq per L. Regular lithium monitoring is essential, since there is a narrow therapeutic range beyond which cardiac problems and central nervous system (CNS) effects can occur.

Lithium levels are drawn 8 to 12 hours after the last dose, usually in the morning after the bedtime dose. The level should be measured at least twice a week while stabilizing the patient and may be drawn monthly thereafter.

## Carbamazepine

A pretreatment CBC including platelet count should be done. Reticulocyte count and serum iron tests are also desirable. Those tests should be repeated weekly during the first three months of treatment and monthly thereafter. Carbamazepine can cause aplastic anemia, agranulocytosis, thrombocytopenia, and leukopenia. Because of the minor risk of hepatotoxicity, LFTs should be done every three to six months. The medication should be discontinued if the patient shows any signs of bone marrow suppression as measured with periodic CBCs. The therapeutic level of cabamazepine is 8 to 12 ng/mL, with toxicity most often reached at levels of 15 ng/mL. Most clinicians report that levels as high as 12 ng/mL are hard to achieve. Table 7.2–9 summarizes one suggested protocol for the laboratory monitoring of patients taking carbamazepine.

## PROVOCATION OF PANIC ATTACKS WITH SODIUM LACTATE

Up to 72 percent of patients with panic disorder have a panic attack when administered an IV injection of sodium lactate. Therefore, lactate provocation is used to confirm a diagnosis of panic disorder. Lactate provocation has also been used to trigger flashbacks in patients with posttraumatic stress disorder. Hyperventilation, another known trigger of panic attacks in predisposed persons, is not as sensitive as lactate provocation in inducing panic attacks. Carbon dioxide ($CO_2$) inhalation also precipitates panic attacks in those so predisposed. Panic attacks triggered by sodium lactate are not inhibited by peripherally acting β-blockers but are inhibited by alprazolam (Xanax) and tricyclic drugs.

**Table 7.2–9**
**Laboratory Monitoring of Patients Taking Carbamazepine**

| Test | Frequency |
|---|---|
| 1. Complete blood count | Before treatment and every two weeks for the first two months of treatment; thereafter, once every three months |
| 2. Platelet count and reticulocyte count | Before treatment and yearly |
| 3. Serum electrolytes | Before treatment and yearly |
| 4. Electrocardiogram | Before treatment and yearly |
| 5. SGOT, SGPT, LDH alkaline phosphatase | Before treatment and every month for the first two months of treatment; thereafter, every three months |
| 6. Pregnancy test for women of childbearing age | Before treatment and as frequently as monthly in noncompliant patients |

Table from A MacKinnon, S C Yudofsky: *Principles of the Psychiatric Evaluation*, p 108. Lippincott, Philadelphia, 1991. Used with permission.

## AMOBARBITAL INTERVIEW

Amobarbital (Amytal) interviews have both diagnostic and therapeutic indications. Diagnostically, the interviews are helpful in differentiating nonorganic and organic conditions, particularly in patients who present with symptoms of catatonia, stupor, and muteness. Organic conditions tend to worsen with infusions of amobarbital, but nonorganic or psychogenic conditions tend to get better because of disinhibition, decreased anxiety, or increased relaxation. Therapeutically, amobarbital interviews are useful in disorders of repression and dissociation—for example, in

**Table 7.2–10**
**Substances of Abuse That Can Be Tested in Urine**

| Substance | Length of Time Detected in Urine |
|---|---|
| Alcohol | 7–12 hours |
| Amphetamine | 48 hours |
| Barbiturate | 24 hours (short-acting) 3 weeks (long-acting) |
| Benzodiazepine | 3 days |
| Cannabis | 3 days to 4 weeks (depending on use) |
| Cocaine | 6–8 hours (metabolites 2–4 days) |
| Codeine | 48 hours |
| Heroin | 36–72 hours |
| Methadone | 3 days |
| Methaqualone | 7 days |
| Morphine | 48–72 hours |
| Phencyclidine (PCP) | 8 days |
| Propoxyphene | 6–48 hours |

Table 7.2–11
**Blood Level Data for Clinical Assessment**

| Substance | Therapeutic or Normal (%) | Toxic (%) | Lethal (%) |
|---|---|---|---|
| Acetaminophen (Tylenol) | 1.0–2.0 mg | 15.0 mg | 150.0 mg |
| Acetylsalicylic acid (salicylate) | 10–30.0 mg | >39.0 mg | 50.0 mg |
| Aminophylline (theophylline) | 1.0–2.0 mg | 3.0–4.0 mg | 21.0–25.0 mg |
| Amitriptyline (Elavil) | 5.0–20.0 μg | >50.0 μg | 1.0–2.0 mg |
| Amphetamines | 2.0–3.0 μg | 50.0 μg | 200.0 μg |
| Arsenic | 0.0–2.0 μg | 0.10 mg | 1.5 mg |
| Barbiturates | | | |
|   Short-acting | 0.1 mg | 0.7 mg | 1.0 mg |
|   Intermediate-acting | 0.1–0.5 mg | 1.0–3.0 mg | >3.0 mg |
|   Phenobarbital | 1.5–3.9 mg | 4.0–6.0 mg | 8.0–>15 mg |
|   Barbital | 1.0 mg | 6.0–8.0 mg | >10.0 mg |
| Bromide | 5.0–30 mg | 50–150 mg | 200 mg |
| Carbamazepine (Tegretol) | 0.8–1.2 mg | >1.5 mg | |
| Chloral hydrate (Noctec) | 0.2–1.0 mg | 10.0 mg | 25.0 mg |
| Chlordiazepoxide (Librium) | 0.1–0.3 mg | 0.55 mg | 2.0 mg |
| Chlorpromazine (Thorazine) | 0.05 mg | 0.1–0.2 mg | 0.3–1.2 mg |
| Cocaine | 5.0–15.0 μg | 90.0 μg | 0.1–2.0 mg |
| Codeine | 2.5–12.0 μg | | 20.0–60.0 μg |
| Desipramine (Norpramin) | 15.0–30.0 μg | >50.0 μg | 1.0–2.0 mg |
| Diazepam (Valium) | 0.05–0.25 mg | 0.5–2.0 mg | >2.0 mg |
| Digoxin | 0.06–0.20 μg | 0.21–0.90 μg | 1.5 μg |
| Diphenhydramine (Benadryl) | 1.0–10.0 μg | 0.5 mg | >1.0 mg |
| Doxepin (Sinequan) | 10.0–25.0 μg | 50.0–200.0 μg | >1.0 mg |
| Ethanol | | 100.0 mg (legal intoxication) | 350.0 mg |
| Glutethimide (Doriden) | 0.02–0.08 mg | 1.0–8.0 mg | 3.0–10.0 mg |
| Haloperidol (Haldol) | 0.05–0.9 μg | 1.0–4.0 mg | |
| Imipramine (Tofranil) | 15.0–25.0 μg | 50.0–150.0 μg | 0.2 mg |
| Lead | 0.0–30.0 μg | 130 μg | 110.0–350.0 μg |
| Lithium | 0.42–0.83 mg (0.6–1.2 mEq/L) | 1.39 mg (2.0 mEq/L) | >3.47 mg (>4.0 mEq/L) |
| LSD | | 0.1–0.4 μg | |
| Meperidine (Demerol) | 0.03–0.10 mg | 0.5 mg | 3.0 mg |
| Meprobamate | 0.8–2.4 mg | 6.0–10.0 mg | 14.0–35.0 mg |
| Mercury | 0.0–8 μg | 100 μg | 600.0 μg |
| Methadone (Dolophine) | 30.0–110.0 μg | 0.2 mg | >0.4 mg |
| Methamphetamine | 0.02–0.06 mg | 0.06–0.5 mg | 1.0–4.0 mg |
| Methanol | | 20.0 mg | >89.0 mg |
| Methaqualone (Quaalude) | 0.3–0.6 mg | 1.0–3.0 mg | >3.0 mg |
| Methylphenidate (Ritalin) | 1.0–6.0 μg | 80.0 μg | 230.0 μg |
| Morphine | 10.0 μg | | 5.0–400 μg (free morphine from heroin) |
| Nortriptyline (Aventyl) | 12.0–16.0 μg | 0.05 mg | 1.3 mg |
| Oxycodone (Percodan) | 1.7–3.6 μg | 20.0–500.0 μg | |
| Paraldehyde | 2.0–11.0 mg | 20.0–40.0 mg | >50.0 mg |
| Pentazocine (Talwin) | 0.01–0.06 mg | 0.2–0.5 mg | 1.0–2.0 mg |
| Perphenazine (Trilafon) | 0.5 μg | 100.0 μg | |
| Phencyclidine (PCP) | | 0.7–24.0 μg | 100.0–500.0 μg |
| Phenytoin (Dilantin) | 1.0–2.0 mg | 2.0–5.0 mg | >10 mg |
| Primidone (Mysoline) | 0.5–1.2 mg | 5.0–8.0 mg | 10.0 mg |
| Propoxyphene (Darvon) | 5.0–20.0 μg | 30.0–60.0 μg | 80.0–200.0 μg |
| Propranolol (Inderal) | 2.5–20.0 μg | | 0.8–1.2 mg |
| Quinidine | 0.03–0.6 mg | 1.0 mg | 3.0–5.0 mg |
| Quinine | 0.18 mg | | 1.2 mg |
| Thioridazine (Mellaril) | 0.10–0.15 mg | 1.0 mg | 2.0–8.0 mg |
| Trifluoperazine (Stelazine) | 0.08 mg | 0.12–0.3 mg | 0.3–0.8 mg |

Table from L Winek: *Drug and Chemical Blood-Level Data*. Fisher Scientific, Pittsburgh, 1985. Used with permission.

**Table 7.2–12**
**Other Laboratory Tests**

| Test | Major Psychiatric Indications | Comments |
|---|---|---|
| Acid phosphatase | Organic workup for cognitive disorders | Increased in prostate cancer, benign prostatic hypertrophy, excessive platelet destruction, bone disease |
| Adrenocorticotropic hormone (ACTH) | Organic workup | Increased in steroid abuse; may be increased in seizures, psychotic disorders, Cushing's disease, and in response to stress<br>Decreased in Addison's disease |
| Alanine aminotransferase (ALT) (formerly called serum glutamic-pyruvic transaminase [SGPT]) | Organic workup | Increased in hepatitis, cirrhosis, liver metastases<br>Decreased in pyridoxine (vitamin $B_6$) deficiency |
| Albumin | Organic workup | Increased in dehydration<br>Decreased in malnutrition, hepatic failure, burns, multiple myeloma, carcinomas |
| Aldolase | Eating disorders<br>Schizophrenia | Increased in patients who abuse ipecac (e.g., bulimic patients), schizophrenia (60–80%) |
| Alkaline phosphatase | Organic workup<br>Use of psychotropic medications | Increased in Paget's disease, hyperparathyroidism, hepatic disease, hepatic metastases, heart failure, phenothiazine use<br>Decreased in pernicious anemia (Vitamin $B_{12}$ deficiency) |
| Ammonia, serum | Organic workup | Increased in hepatic encephalopathy |
| Amylase, serum | Eating disorders | May be increased in bulimia nervosa |
| Antinuclear antibodies | Organic workup | Found in systemic lupus erythematosus (SLE) and drug-induced lupus (e.g., secondary to phenothiazines, anticonvulsants); SLE can be associated with delirium, psychotic disorders, mood disorders |
| Aspartate aminotransferase (AST) (formerly SGOT) | Organic workup | Increased in heart failure, hepatic disease, pancreatitis, eclampsia, cerebral damage, alcohol dependence<br>Decreased in pyridoxine (vitamin $B_6$) deficiency, terminal stages of liver disease |
| Bicarbonate, serum | Panic disorder<br>Eating disorders | Decreased in hyperventilation syndrome, panic disorder, anabolic steroid abuse<br>May be elevated in patients with bulimia nervosa, in laxative abuse, in psychogenic vomiting |
| Bilirubin | Organic workup | Increased in hepatic disease |
| Blood urea nitrogen (BUN) | Delirium<br>Use of psychotropic medications | Elevated in renal disease, dehydration<br>Elevations associated with lethargy, delirium<br>If elevated, can increase toxic potential of psychiatric medications, especially lithium and amantadine (Symmetrel) |
| Bromide, serum | Dementia<br>Psychosis | Bromide intoxication can cause psychosis, hallucinations, delirium<br>Part of dementia workup, especially when serum chloride is elevated |
| Caffeine level, serum | Anxiety | Evaluation of patients with suspected caffeinism |
| Calcium (Ca), serum | Organic workup<br>Mood disorders<br>Psychosis<br>Eating disorders | Increased in hyperparathyroidism, bone metastases<br>Increase associated with delirium, depression, psychosis<br>Decreased in hypoparathyroidism, renal failure<br>Decrease associated with depression, irritability, delirium, long-term laxative abuse |
| Carotid ultrasound | Dementia | Occasionally included in dementia workup, especially to rule out multi-infarct dementia<br>Primary value is in search for possible infarct causes |
| Catecholamines, urinary and plasma | Panic attacks<br>Anxiety disorders | Elevated in pheochromocytoma |
| Cerebrospinal fluid (CSF) | Organic workup | Increased protein and cells in infection, positive VDRL in neurosyphilis, bloody CSF in hemorrhagic conditions |
| Ceruloplasmin, serum; copper, serum | Organic workup | Low in Wilson's disease (hepatolenticular disease) |
| Chloride (Cl), serum | Eating disorders<br>Panic disorder | Decreased in patients with bulimia nervosa and psychogenic vomiting<br>Mild elevation in hyperventilation syndrome, panic disorder |

*Continued*

**Table 7.2–12**
*Continued*

| Test | Major Psychiatric Indications | Comments |
|---|---|---|
| Cholecystokinin (CCK) | Eating disorders | Compared with controls, blunted in bulimic patients after eating meal (may normalize after treatment with antidepressants) |
| $CO_2$ inhalation; sodium bicarbonate infusion | Anxiety | Panic attacks produced in subgroup of patients |
| Coombs' test, direct and indirect | Hemolytic anemias secondary to psychotropic medications | Evaluation of drug-induced hemolytic anemias, such as those secondary to chlorpromazine, phenytoin, levodopa, and methyldopa |
| Copper, urine | Organic workup | Elevated in Wilson's disease |
| Cortisol (hydrocortisone) | Organic workup<br>Mood disorders | Excessive level may indicate Cushing's disease associated with anxiety, depression, and a variety of other conditions |
| Creatine phosphokinase (CPK) | Use of antipsychotics<br>Use of restraints<br>Substance abuse | Increased in neuroleptic malignant syndrome, intramuscular injection, rhabdomyolysis (secondary to substance abuse), patients in restraints, patients experiencing dystonic reactions; asymptomatic elevations seen with use of antipsychotics |
| Creatinine, serum | Organic workup | Elevated in renal disease |
| Dopamine (DA) (L-dopa stimulation of dopamine) | Depression | Inhibits prolactin<br>Test used to assess functional integrity of dopaminergic system, which is impaired in Parkinson's disease, depression |
| Doppler ultrasound | Impotence<br>Organic workup | Carotid occlusion, transient ischemic attack (TIA), reduced penile blood flow in impotence |
| Echocardiogram | Panic disorder | 10–40% of patients with panic disorder show mitral valve prolapse |
| Electroencephalogram (EEG) | Organic workup | Seizures, brain death, lesions; shortened REM latency in depression<br>High-voltage activity in stupor; low-voltage fast activity in excitement; in functional nonorganic cases (e.g., dissociative disorders), alpha activity is present in the background, which responds to auditory and visual stimuli<br>Biphasic or triphasic slow bursts seen in dementia of Creutzfeldt-Jakob disease |
| Epstein-Barr virus (EBV); cytomegalovirus (CMV) | Organic workup<br>Chronic fatigue<br>Mood disorders | Part of herpes virus group<br>EBV is causative agent for infectious mononucleosis, which can present with depression and personality change<br>CMV can produce anxiety, confusion, mood disorders<br>EBV associated with chronic mononucleosislike syndrome associated with chronic depression and fatigue; may be association between EBV and major depressive disorder |
| Erythrocyte sedimentation rate (ESR) | Organic workup | An increase in ESR represents a nonspecific test of infectious, inflammatory, autoimmune, or malignant disease; sometimes recommended in the evaluation of anorexia nervosa |
| Estrogen | Mood disorder | Decreased in menopausal depression and premenstrual syndrome; variable changes in anxiety |
| Ferritin, serum | Organic workup | Most sensitive test for iron deficiency |
| Folate (folic acid), serum | Alcohol abuse<br>Use of specific medications | Usually measured with vitamin $B_{12}$ deficiencies associated with psychotic disorders, paranoia, fatigue, agitation, dementia, delirium<br>Associated with alcohol dependence, use of phenytoin, oral contraceptives, estrogen |
| Follicle-stimulating hormone (FSH) | Depression | High normal in anorexia nervosa, higher values in postmenopausal women; low levels in patients with panhypopituitarism |
| Glucose, fasting blood (FBS) | Panic attacks<br>Anxiety<br>Delirium<br>Depression | Very high FBS associated with delirium<br>Very low FBS associated with delirium, agitation, panic attacks, anxiety, depression |
| Glutamyl transaminase, serum | Alcohol abuse<br>Organic workup | Increase in alcohol abuse, cirrhosis, liver disease |

| Test | Major Psychiatric Indications | Comments |
|---|---|---|
| Gonadotropin-releasing hormone (GnRH) | Depression<br>Anxiety<br>Schizophrenia | Decrease in schizophrenia; increase in anorexia nervosa; variable in depression, anxiety |
| Growth hormone (GH) | Depression<br>Schizophrenia | Blunted GH responses to insulin-induced hypoglycemia in depressed patients; increased GH responses to dopamine agonist challenge in schizophrenic patients; increased in some cases of anorexia nervosa |
| Hematocrit (Hct); hemoglobin (Hb) | Organic workup | Assessment of anemia (anemia may be associated with depressive and psychotic disorders) |
| Hepatitis A viral antigen (HAAg) | Mood disorders<br>Organic workup | Less severe, better prognosis than hepatitis B; may present with anorexia nervosa, depression |
| Hepatitis B surface antigen (HBsAg); hepatitis Bc antigen (HBcAg) | Mood disorders<br>Organic workup | Active hepatitis B infection indicates greater degree of infectivity and of progression to chronic liver disease<br>May present with depression |
| Holter monitor | Panic disorder | Evaluation of panic-disordered patients with palpitations and other cardiac symptoms |
| Human immunodeficiency virus (HIV) | Organic workup | CNS involvement: AIDS dementia, personality change due to a general medical condition, mood disorder due to a general medical condition, acute psychotic disorders |
| 17-Hydroxycorticosteroid | Depression | Deviations detect hyperadrenocorticalism, which can be associated with major depressive disorder<br>Increased in steroid abuse |
| 5-Hydroxyindoleacetic acid (5-HIAA) | Depression<br>Suicide<br>Violence | Decrease in CSF in aggressive or violent patients with suicidal or homicidal impulses<br>May be indicator of decreased impulse control and predictor of suicide |
| Iron, serum | Organic workup | Iron-deficiency anemia |
| Lactate dehydrogenase (LDH) | Organic workup | Increased in myocardial infarction, pulmonary infarction, hepatic disease, renal infarction, seizures, cerebral damage, megaloblastic (pernicious) anemia, factitious elevations secondary to rough handling of blood specimen tube |
| Lupus anticoagulant (LA) | Use of phenothiazines | An antiphospholipid antibody, which has been described in some patients using phenothiazines, especially chlorpromazine |
| Lupus erythematosus (LE) test | Depression<br>Psychosis<br>Delirium<br>Dementia | Positive test associated with systemic LE, which may present with various psychiatric disturbances, such as psychotic disorders, depressive disorders, delirium, dementia; also tested for with antinuclear antibody (ANA) and anti-DNA antibody tests |
| Luteinizing hormone (LH) | Depression | Low in patients with panhypopituitarism; decrease associated with depression |
| Magnesium, serum | Alcohol abuse<br>Organic workup | Decreased in alcohol dependence; low levels associated with agitation, delirium, seizures |
| MAO, platelet | Depression | Low in depression |
| MCV (mean corpuscular volume) (average volume of a red blood cell) | Alcohol abuse | Elevated in alcohol dependence, vitamin $B_{12}$, folate deficiency |
| Melatonin | Mood disorder with seasonal pattern | Produced by light and pineal gland and decreased in mood disorder with seasonal pattern |
| Metal (heavy) intoxication (serum or urinary) | Organic workup | Lead—apathy, irritability, anorexia nervosa, confusion<br>Mercury—psychosis, fatigue, apathy, decreased memory, emotional lability, "mad hatter"<br>Manganese—manganese madness, Parkinson-like syndrome<br>Aluminum—dementia<br>Arsenic—fatigue, blackouts, hair loss |

*Continued*

**Table 7.2–12**
*Continued*

| Test | Major Psychiatric Indications | Comments |
|---|---|---|
| 3-Methoxy-4-hydroxyphenyglycol (MHPG) | Depression<br>Anxiety | Most useful in research; decreases in urine may indicate decreases centrally |
| Myoglobin, urine | Phenothiazine use<br>Substance abuse<br>Use of restraints | Increased in neuroleptic malignant syndrome; in PCP, cocaine, or lysergic acid diethylamide (LSD) intoxication; in patients in restraints |
| Nicotine | Anxiety<br>Nicotine addiction | Anxiety, smoking |
| Nocturnal penile tumescence | Impotence | Quantification of penile circumference changes, penile rigidity, frequency of penile tumescence<br>Evaluation of erectile function during sleep<br>Erections associated with rapid eye movement (REM) sleep<br>Helpful in differentiation between organic and functional causes of impotence |
| Parathyroid (parathormone) hormone | Anxiety<br>Organic workup | Low level causes hypocalcemia and anxiety<br>Dysregulation associated with wide variety of cognitive disorders |
| Phosphorus, serum | Organic workup<br>Panic disorder | Increased in renal failure, diabetic acidosis, hypoparathyroidism, hypervitamin D<br>Decreased in cirrhosis, hypokalemia, hyperparathyroidism, panic attack, hyperventilation syndrome |
| Platelet count | Use of psychotropic medications | Decreased by certain psychotropic medications (carbamazepine, clozapine, phenothiazines) |
| Porphobilinogen (PBG) | Organic workup | Increased in acute porphyria |
| Porphyria synthesizing enzyme | Psychosis<br>Organic workup | Acute panic attack or a cognitive disorder can occur in acute porphyria attack, which may be precipitated by barbiturates, imipramine |
| Potassium (K), serum | Organic workup<br>Eating disorders | Increased in hyperkalemic acidosis; increase is associated with anxiety in cardiac arrhythmia<br>Decreased in cirrhosis, metabolic alkalosis, laxative abuse, diuretic abuse; decrease is common in bulimic patients and in psychogenic vomiting, anabolic steroid abuse |
| Prolactin, serum | Use of antipsychotic medications<br>Cocaine use<br>Pseudoseizures | Antipsychotics, by decreasing dopamine, increase prolactin synthesis and release, especially in women<br>Elevated prolactin levels may be seen secondary to cocaine withdrawal<br>Lack of prolactin rise after seizure suggests pseudoseizure |
| Protein, total serum | Organic workup<br>Use of psychotropic medications | Increased in multiple myeloma, myxedema, lupus<br>Decreased in cirrhosis, malnutrition, overhydration<br>Low serum protein can result in greater sensitivity to conventional doses of protein-bound medications (lithium is not protein-bound) |
| Prothrombin time (PT) | Organic workup | Elevated in significant liver damage (cirrhosis), patients with lupus coagulant, which can be found in certain patients receiving antipsychotic medications, especially chlorpromazine |
| Reticulocyte count (estimate of red blood cell production in bone marrow) | Organic workup<br>Use of carbamazepine | Low in megaloblastic or iron deficiency anemia and anemia of chronic disease<br>Must be monitored in patient taking carbamazepine |
| Salicylate, serum | Psychotic disorder due to a general medical condition with hallucinations<br>Suicide attempts | Toxic levels may be seen in suicide attempts and may cause psychotic disorder due to a general medical condition with hallucinations |
| Sodium (NA), serum | Organic workup | Decreased with water intoxication; SIADH<br>Increased with excessive salt intake; diabetes<br>Decreased in hypoadrenalism, myxedema, congestive heart failure, diarrhea, polydipsia, use of carbamazepine, anabolic steroids<br>Low levels associated with greater sensitivity to conventional dose of lithium |

| Test | Major Psychiatric Indications | Comments |
|---|---|---|
| Testosterone, serum | Impotence<br>Hypoactive sexual desire disorder | Increase in anabolic steroid abuse<br>Follow-up of sex offenders treated with medroxyprogesterone<br>May be decreased in organic workup of impotence<br>Decrease may be seen in hypoactive sexual desire disorder<br>Decreased with medroxyprogesterone treatment |
| Thyroid function tests | Organic workup<br>Depression | Detection of hypothyroidism or hyperthyroidism<br>Abnormalities can be associated with depression, anxiety, psychosis, dementia, delirium |
| Urinalysis | Organic workup<br>Pretreatment workup of lithium<br>Drug screening | Provides clues to cause of various cognitive disorders (assessing general appearance, pH, specific gravity, bilirubin, glucose, blood, ketones, protein, etc.); specific gravity may be affected by lithium |
| Urinary creatinine | Organic workup<br>Substance abuse<br>Lithium use | Increased in renal failure, dehydration<br>Part of pretreatment workup for lithium |
| Venereal Disease Research Laboratory (VDRL) | Syphilis | Positive (high titers) in secondary syphilis (may be positive or negative in primary syphilis)<br>Low titers (or negative) in tertiary syphilis |
| Vitamin A, serum | Depression<br>Delirium | Hypervitaminosis A is associated with a variety of mental status changes |
| Vitamin $B_{12}$, serum | Organic workup<br>Dementia | Part of workup of megaloblastic anemia and dementia<br>$B_{12}$ deficiency associated with psychosis, paranoia, fatigue, agitation, dementia, delirium<br>Often associated with chronic alcohol abuse |
| White blood cell (WBC) | Use of psychotropic medications | Leukopenia and agranulocytosis associated with certain psychotropic medications, such as phenothiazines, carbamazepine, clozapine<br>Leukocytosis associated with lithium and neuroleptic malignant syndrome |

the recovery of memory in psychogenic amnestic disorders and fugue, in the recovery of function in conversion disorder, and in the facilitation of emotional expression in posttraumatic stress disorder.

## URINE TESTING FOR SUBSTANCE ABUSE

A number of substances may be detected in a patient's urine if the urine is tested within a specific (and variable) period of time after ingestion. Knowledge of urine substance testing is becoming crucial for practicing physicians in view of the controversial issue of mandatory or random substance testing. Table 7.2–10 provides a summary of substances of abuse that can be tested in urine.

Laboratory tests are also used in the detection of substances that may be contributing to cognitive disorders. Table 7.2–11 is an outline of therapeutic, toxic, and lethal levels of substances most commonly implicated in cognitive disorders.

## OTHER LABORATORY TESTS

Laboratory tests not discussed above are covered in Table 7.2–12 in terms of their indications and significance in medical conditions that affect behavior.

References

Anfinson T J, Kathol R G: Screening laboratory evaluation in psychiatric patients: A review. Gen Hosp Psychiatry 14 (4, Suppl): 248, 1992.
Arana G W, Baldessarini R J, Ornsteen M: The dexamethasone suppression test for diagnosis and prognosis in psychiatry. Arch Gen Psychiatry 42: 1193, 1985.
Belkin B, Miller N S: Agreement among laboratory tests, self-reports, and collateral reports of alcohol and drug use. Ann Clin Psychiatry 4: 33, 1992.
Brower K J, Catlin D H, Blow F C, Eliopulos G A, Beresford T P: Clinical assessment and urine testing for anabolic-androgenic steroid abuse and dependence. Am J Drug Alcohol Abuse 17: 161, 1991.
Carroll B J: Dexamethasone suppression test: A review of contemporary confusion. J Clin Psychiatry 46: 13, 1985.
Davidson M, Kahn R S, Knott P, Kaminsky R, Cooper M, DuMont K, Apter S, Davis K L: Effects of neuroleptic treatment on symptoms of schizophrenia and plasma homovanillic acid concentrations. Arch Gen Psychiatry 48: 910, 1991.
Evans L: Some biological aspects of panic disorder. Int J Clin Pharmacol Res 9: 139, 1989.
Galen R S, Gambino S R: Beyond Normality: The Predictive Value and Efficiency of Medical Diagnoses. Wiley, New York, 1975.
Garattini S, Tognoni G, editors: Biological markers in mental disorders (symposium). J Psychiatr Res 18: 327, 1984.
Gold M S, Pottash A L C: Diagnostic and Laboratory Testing in Psychiatry. Plenum, New York, 1986.
Griner P F, Glaser R J: Misuse of laboratory tests and diagnostic procedures. N Engl J Med 307: 1336, 1982.
Hall R C W, Beresford T P, editors: Handbook of Psychiatric Diagnostic Procedures, vols 1, 2. SP Medical and Scientific, New York, 1984, 1985.
Kirch D G: Medical assessment and laboratory testing in psychiatry. In Comprehensive Textbook of Psychiatry, ed 5, H I Kaplan, B J Sadock, editors, p 525. Williams & Wilkins, Baltimore, 1989.
Koranyi E K: Morbidity and rate of undiagnosed physical illnesses in a psychiatric clinic population. Arch Gen Psychiatry 36: 414, 1979.
Lake C R, Ziegler M G, editors: The Catecholamines in Psychiatric and Neurologic Disorders, Butterworth, Boston, 1985.

Martin R L, Preskorn S H: Use of the laboratory in psychiatry. In *The Medical Basis of Psychiatry*, G Winokur, P Clayton, editors, p 522. Saunders, Philadelphia, 1986.

Norman T R, Burrows G D, Judd F K, McIntyre I M: Serotonin and panic disorders: A review of clinical studies. Int J Clin Pharmacol Res 9: 151, 1989.

Perry J C, Jacobs, D: Overview: Clinical applications of the Amytal interview in psychiatric emergency settings. Am J Psychiatry *139*: 552, 1982.

Rapp M S, Bibr J, Campbell K: The use of laboratory tests in a psychiatric hospital. Can J Psychiatry *37*: 137, 1992.

Usdin E, Hanin I, editors: *Biological Markers in Psychiatry and Neurology*. Pergamon, New York, 1982.

Weinberger D R: Brain disease and psychiatric illness: When should a psychiatrist order a CAT scan? Am J Psychiatry *141*: 1521, 1984.

# 7.3 / Medical Assessment in Psychiatry

The medical assessment of a psychiatric patient consists of a thorough medical history, a review of systems, general observation, physical examination, and diagnostic laboratory studies. Psychiatrists do not perform routine physical examinations of their patients. The complex interplay between somatic illness and psychiatric illness may require the psychiatrist to differentiate physical diseases that mimic psychiatric illnesses and vice versa. Also, the presenting symptoms of some physical illnesses may be psychiatric signs or symptoms. For example, a chief complaint of anxiety may be associated with mitral valve prolapse, which is revealed by cardiac auscultation. Some psychiatrists contend that a complete medical workup is essential for every patient; others maintain the opposite. In any case, the patient's medical status should always be considered at the outset; the psychiatrist is often called on to decide whether a medical evaluation is needed and, if so, what it should include.

## MEDICAL HISTORY

In the course of conducting a psychiatric evaluation, information should be gathered about (1) known bodily diseases or dysfunctions, (2) hospitalizations and operative procedures, (3) medications taken recently or at present, (4) personal habits and occupational history, (5) family history of illnesses, and (6) specific physical complaints. Information about medical illnesses should be gathered from both the patient and the referring physician.

Information about previous episodes of illness may provide valuable clues about the nature of the present disorder. For example, if the present disorder is distinctly delusional, the patient has a history of several similar episodes, and each responded promptly to diverse forms of treatment, the possibility of substance-induced psychotic disorder is strongly suggested. To pursue that lead, the psychiatrist should order a drug screen. The history of a surgical procedure may also be useful; for example, a thy-roidectomy suggests hypothyroidism as the cause of depression.

A side effect of several medications prescribed for hypertension is depression. Medication taken in a therapeutic dosage occasionally reaches high blood levels. Digitalis intoxication, for example, may occur under such circumstances and result in impaired mental functioning. Proprietary drugs may cause or contribute to an anticholinergic delirium. Therefore, the psychiatrist must inquire about over-the-counter remedies, as well as prescribed medications.

An occupational history may provide essential information. Exposure to mercury may result in complaints suggesting a psychosis, and exposure to lead, as in smelting, may produce a cognitive disorder. The latter clinical picture can also result from imbibing moonshine with a high lead content.

In eliciting information concerning specific symptoms, the psychiatrist brings medical and psychological knowledge into full play. For example, the psychiatrist should elicit sufficient information from the patient complaining of headache to predict, with considerable certainty, whether the pain is or is not the result of intracranial disease. Also, the psychiatrist should be able to recognize that the pain in the right shoulder of a hypochondriacal patient with abdominal discomfort may be the classic referred pain of gallbladder disease.

## REVIEW OF SYSTEMS

An inventory by systems should follow the open-ended inquiry. The review may be organized according to organ systems (for example, liver, pancreas), functional systems (for example, gastrointestinal), or a combination of the two, as in the outline below; but the review should be comprehensive and thorough.

### Head

Many patients give a history of headache; its duration, frequency, character, location, and severity should be ascertained. Headaches often result from substance abuse, including alcohol, nicotine, and caffeine. Vascular (migraine) headaches are precipitated by stress. Temporal arteritis causes unilateral throbbing headaches and may lead to blindness. Brain tumors are associated with headaches as a result of increases in intracranial pressure. A history of head injury may result in subdural hematoma and in boxers can cause progressive dementia with extrapyramidal symptoms. The headache of subarachnoid hemorrhage is sudden, severe, and associated with changes in the sensorium. Normal pressure hydrocephalus may follow a head injury or encephalitis and may be associated with dementia and a shuffling gait.

### Eye, Ear, Nose, and Throat

Visual acuity, diplopia, hearing problems, tinnitus, glossitis, and bad taste are covered in this area. A patient taking antipsychotics who gives a history of twitching about the mouth or disturbing movements of the tongue may be in the early and potentially reversible stage of tardive dyskinesia. Impaired vision may occur with thioridazine (Mellaril) in high dosages. A history of glaucoma contraindicates drugs with anticholinergic side effects. Aphonia may be hysterical in nature. The late stage of cocaine abuse can result in perforations of the nasal septum and difficulty in breathing. A transitory episode of diplopia may herald multiple sclerosis. Delusional disorder is more common in hearing-impaired persons than in those with normal hearing.

## Respiratory System

Cough, asthma, pleurisy, hemoptysis, dyspnea, and orthopnea are considered in this section. Hyperventilation is suggested if the patient's symptoms include all or a few of the following: onset at rest, sighing respirations, apprehension, anxiety, depersonalization, palpitations, inability to swallow, numbness of the feet and hands, and carpopedal spasm. Dyspnea and breathlessness may occur in depression. In pulmonary or obstructive airway disease the onset of symptoms is usually insidious, whereas in depression it is sudden. In depression, breathlessness is experienced at rest, shows little change with exertion, and may fluctuate within a matter of minutes; the onset of breathlessness coincides with the onset of a mood disorder and is often accompanied by attacks of dizziness, sweating, palpitations, and paresthesias. In obstructive airway disease, only the patients with the most advanced respiratory incapacity experience breathlessness at rest. Most striking and of greatest assistance in making a differential diagnosis is the emphasis placed on the difficulty in inspiration experienced by patients with depression and on the difficulty in expiration experienced by patients with pulmonary disease. Bronchial asthma has sometimes been associated with childhood histories of extreme dependence on the mother. Patients with bronchospasm should not receive propranolol (Inderal) because it may block catecholamine-induced bronchodilation; propranolol is specifically contraindicated for patients with bronchial asthma because epinephrine given to such patients in an emergency will not be effective.

## Cardiovascular System

Tachycardia, palpitations, and cardiac arrhythmia are among the most common signs of anxiety about which the patient may complain. Pheochromocytoma usually produces symptoms that mimic anxiety disorders, such as rapid heart beat, tremors, and pallor. Increased urinary catecholamines are diagnostic of pheochromocytoma. Patients taking guanethidine (Micronase) for hypertension should not receive tricyclic drugs, which reduce or eliminate the antihypertensive effect of guanethidine. A history of hypertension may preclude the use of monoamine oxidase inhibitors (MAOIs) because of the risk of a hypertensive crisis if such hypertensive patients inadvertently take foods high in tyramine. Patients with a suspected cardiac disease should have an electrocardiogram before tricyclics or lithium (Eskalith) is prescribed. A history of substernal pain should be evaluated, keeping in mind that psychological stress can precipitate anginal-type chest pain in the presence of normal coronary arteries.

## Gastrointestinal System

This area covers such topics as appetite, distress before or after meals, food preferences, diarrhea, vomiting, constipation, laxative use, and abdominal pain. A history of weight loss is common in depressive disorders; but depression may accompany the weight loss caused by ulcerative colitis, regional enteritis, and cancer. Anorexia nervosa is accompanied by severe weight loss in the presence of normal appetite. Avoidance of certain foods may be a phobic phenomenon or part of an obsessive ritual. Laxative abuse and induced vomiting is common in bulimia nervosa. Constipation is caused by opioid dependence and by psychotropic drugs with anticholinergic side effects. Cocaine abuse and amphetamine abuse cause a loss of appetite and weight loss. Weight gain occurs under stress. Polyphagia, polyuria, and polydipsia are the triad of diabetes mellitus. Polyuria, polydipsia, and diarrhea are signs of lithium toxicity.

## Genitourinary System

Urinary frequency, nocturia, pain or burning on urination, and changes in the size and the force of the stream are some of the signs and symptoms in this area. Anticholinergic side effects associated with antipsychotics and tricyclic drugs may cause urinary retention in men with prostate hypertrophy. Erectile difficulty and retarded ejaculation are also common side effects of those drugs, and retrograde ejaculation occurs with thioridazine. A baseline level of sexual responsivity before using pharmacological agents should be obtained. A history of venereal diseases—for example, gonorrheal discharge, chancre, herpes, and pubic lice—may indicate sexual promiscuity. In some cases the first symptom of acquired immune deficiency syndrome (AIDS) is the gradual onset of mental confusion leading to dementia. If a psychotic patient remains incontinent after treatment for several days with a psychotropic medication, some cause other than a mental disorder should be suspected.

## Menstrual System

A menstrual history should include the age of the onset of menarche and menopause; the periods' interval, regularity, duration, and amount of flow; irregular bleeding; dysmenorrhea; and abortions. Amenorrhea is characteristic of anorexia nervosa and also occurs in women who are psychologically stressed. Women who are afraid of becoming pregnant or who have a wish to be pregnant may have delayed periods. Pseudocyesis is false pregnancy with complete cessation of the menses. Perimenstrual mood changes (for example, irritability, depression, and dysphoria) should be noted. Painful menstruation can result from uterine disease (for example, myomata), from psychological conflicts about the menses, or from a combination of the two. Many women report an increase in sexual desire premenstrually. The emotional distress that some women experience after an abortion is usually mild and self-limited.

## GENERAL OBSERVATION

An important part of the medical examination is subsumed under the broad head of general observation—visual, auditory, and olfactory. Such nonverbal clues as posture, facial expression, and mannerisms should also be noted.

## Visual Evaluation

The scrutiny of the patient begins at the first encounter. When the patient goes from the waiting room to the interview room, the psychiatrist should observe the patient's gait. Is the patient unsteady? Ataxia suggests diffuse brain disease, alcohol or other substance intoxication, chorea, spinocerebellar degeneration, weakness based on a debilitating process, and an underlying disorder, such as myotonic dystrophy. Does the patient walk without the usual associated arm movements and turn in a rigid fashion, like a toy soldier, as is seen in early Parkinson's disease? Does the patient have an asymmetry of gait, such as turning one foot outward, dragging a leg, or not swinging one arm, suggesting a focal brain lesion?

As soon as the patient is seated, the psychiatrist should direct attention to grooming. Is the patient's hair combed, are the nails clean, and are the teeth brushed? Has clothing been chosen with care, and is it appropriate? Although inattention to dress and hygiene is common in mental disorders—in particular, depressive disorders—it is also a hallmark of cognitive disorders. Lapses—such as mismatching socks, stockings, or shoes—may suggest a cognitive disorder.

The patient's posture and automatic movements or the lack of them should be noted. A stooped, flexed posture with a paucity of automatic movements may be due to Parkinson's disease, diffuse cerebral hemispheric disease, or the side effects of antipsychotics. An unusual tilt of the head may be adopted to avoid eye contact, but it can also result from diplopia, a visual field defect, or focal cerebellar dysfunction. Frequent quick, purposeless movements are characteristic of anxiety disorders, but they are equally characteristic of chorea and hyperthyroidism. Tremors, although commonly seen in anxiety disorders, may point to Parkinson's disease, essential tremor, or side effects of psychotropic medication. Patients with essential tremor sometimes seek psychiatric treatment because they believe the tremor must be due to unrecognized fear or anxiety, as others often suggest. Unilateral paucity or excess of movement suggests focal brain disease.

The patient's appearance is then scrutinized to assess general health. Does the patient appear to be robust, or is there a sense of ill health? Does looseness of clothing indicate recent weight loss? Is the patient short of breath or coughing? Does the patient's general physiognomy suggest a specific disease? Men with Klinefelter's syndrome have a feminine fat distribution and lack the development of secondary male sex characteristics. Acromegaly is usually immediately recognizable.

What is the patient's nutritional status? Recent weight loss, although often seen in depressive disorders and schizophrenia, may be due to gastrointestinal disease, diffuse carcinomatosis, Addison's disease, hyperthyroidism, and many other somatic disorders. Obesity may result from either emotional distress or organic disease. Moon facies, truncal obesity, and buffalo hump are striking findings in Cushing's syndrome. The puffy, bloated appearance seen in hypothyroidism and the massive obesity and periodic respiration seen in Pickwickian syndrome are easily recognized in patients referred for psychiatric help.

The skin frequently provides valuable information. The yellow discoloration of hepatic dysfunction and the pallor of anemia are reasonably distinctive. Intense reddening may be due to carbon monoxide poisoning or to photosensitivity resulting from porphyria or phenothiazines. Eruptions may be manifestations of such disorders as systemic lupus erythematosus, tuberous sclerosis with adenoma sebaceum, and sensitivity to drugs. A dusky purplish cast to the face, plus telangiectasia, is almost pathognomonic of alcohol abuse.

A young woman, complaining of depression and listlessness, mentioned in an offhand manner that she had a skin rash. An on-the-spot examination of her skin revealed petechial hemorrhages on both arms and both legs. Further inquiry disclosed information about bleeding from several sites. Her blood platelet count was 4,000. The diagnosis was thrombocytopenia.

Careful observation may reveal clues that lead to the correct diagnosis in patients who create their own skin lesions. For example, the location and the shape of the lesions and the time of their appearance may be characteristic of dermatitis factitia.

The patient's face and head should be scanned for evidence of disease. Premature whitening of the hair occurs in pernicious anemia, and thinning and coarseness of the hair occurs in myxedema. Pupillary changes are produced by various drugs—constriction by opioids and dilation by anticholinergic agents and hallucinogens. The combination of dilated and fixed pupils and dry skin and mucous membranes should immediately suggest the likelihood of atropine use or atropinelike toxicity. Diffusion of the conjunctiva suggests alcohol abuse, cannabis abuse, or obstruction of the superior vena cava. Flattening of the nasolabial fold on one side or weakness of one side of the face—as manifested in speaking, smiling, and grimacing—may be the result of focal dysfunction of the contralateral cerebral hemisphere.

The patient's state of alertness and responsiveness should be carefully evaluated. Drowsiness and inattentiveness may be due to a psychological problem, but they are more likely to result from an organic brain dysfunction, whether secondary to an intrinsic brain disease or to an exogenous factor, such as substance intoxication.

## Auditory Evaluation

Listening intently is just as important as looking intently for evidence of somatic disorders.

Slowed speech is characteristic not only of depression but also of diffuse brain dysfunction and subcortical dysfunction; unusually rapid speech is characteristic not only of manic episodes and anxiety disorders but also of hyperthyroidism. A weak voice with monotony of tone may be clues to Parkinson's disease in patients who complain mainly of depression. A slow, low-pitched, hoarse voice should suggest the possibility of hypothyroidism; that voice quality has been described as sounding like a bad record of a drowsy, slightly intoxicated person with a bad cold and a plum in the mouth.

Difficulty in initiating speech may be due to anxiety or stuttering, or it may be indicative of Parkinson's disease or aphasia. Easy fatigability of speech may sometimes be a manifestation of an emotional problem, but it is also characteristic of myasthenia gravis. Patients with those complaints are likely to be seen by a psychiatrist before the correct diagnosis is made.

Word production, as well as the quality of speech, is important. When words are mispronounced or incorrect words are used, the possibility of aphasia caused by a lesion of the dominant hemisphere should be entertained. The same possibility exists when the patient perseverates, has trouble finding a name or a word, or describes an object or an event in an indirect fashion (*paraphasia*). When not consonant with the patient's socioeconomic and educational level, coarseness, profanity, or inappropriate disclosures may indicate loss of inhibition caused by dementia.

## Olfactory Evaluation

Much less is learned through the sense of smell than through the senses of sight and hearing, but occasionally smell provides useful information. The unpleasant odor of a patient who fails to bathe suggests an organic brain dysfunction and a depressive disorder. The odor of alcohol or of substances used to hide it is revealing in a patient who attempts to conceal a drinking problem. Occasionally, a uriniferous odor calls attention to bladder dysfunction secondary to a nervous system disease. Characteristic odors are also noted in patients with diabetic acidosis, uremia, and hepatic coma.

# PHYSICAL EXAMINATION

## Selection of Patients

The nature of the patient's complaints is critical in determining if a complete physical examination is required. Complaints fall into three categories involving (1) the body, (2) the mind, and (3) social interactions.

Bodily symptoms—such as headaches, erectile disorder, and palpitations—call for a thorough medical examination to determine what part, if any, somatic processes play in causing the distress. The same can be said for mental symptoms—such as depression, anxiety, hallucinations, and persecutory delusions—because they can be expressions of somatic processes. If the problem is clearly limited to the social sphere—as in long-standing difficulties in interactions with teachers, employers, parents, or a spouse—there may be no special indication for a physical examination.

## Psychological Considerations

Even a routine physical examination may evoke adverse reactions; instruments, procedures, and the examining room may be frightening. A simple running account of what is being done can prevent much needless anxiety. Moreover, if the patient is consistently forewarned of what will be done, the dread of being suddenly and painfully surprised recedes. Comments such as, "There's nothing to this" and "You don't have to be afraid because this won't hurt" leave the patient in the dark and are much less reassuring than a few words about what actually will be done. Although the physical examination is likely to engender

or intensify a reaction of anxiety, it can also stir up sexual feelings. Some women with fantasies of being seduced may misinterpret an ordinary movement in the physical examination as a sexual advance. Similarly, a delusional man with homosexual fears may perceive a rectal examination as a sexual attack.

Lingering over the examination of a particular organ because an unusual but normal variation has aroused the physician's scientific curiosity is likely to raise concern in the patient that a serious pathological process has been discovered. Such a reaction in an anxious or hypochondriacal patient may be profound.

The physical examination occasionally serves a psychotherapeutic function. An anxious patient may be relieved to learn that, in spite of troublesome symptoms, there is no evidence of the serious illness that is feared. The young person who complains of chest pain and is certain that the pain heralds a heart attack can usually be reassured by the report of normal findings after a physical examination and electrocardiogram. However, the reassurance relieves only the worry occasioned by the immediate episode. Unless psychiatric treatment succeeds in dealing with the determinants of the reaction, recurrent episodes are likely.

Sending a patient who has a deeply rooted fear of malignancy for still another test that is intended to be reassuring is usually unrewarding.

In spite of repeated examinations, a patient (a physician) was convinced that he had carcinoma of the pharynx. A colleague, in an effort to produce positive proof, biopsied the area of complaint. When the patient was shown a microscopic section of normal tissue, he immediately declared that the normal section had been substituted for one showing malignant cells.

During the performance of the physical examination, an observant physician may note indications of emotional distress. For instance, during genital examinations, patients' behavior may reveal information about their sexual attitudes and problems, and their reactions may be used later to open that area for exploration.

## Deferring the Physical Examination

Occasionally, circumstances make it desirable or necessary to defer a complete medical assessment. For example, a delusional or manic patient may be combative or resistive or both. In that instance a medical history should be elicited from a family member if possible, but, unless there is a pressing reason to proceed with the examination, it should be deferred until the patient is tractable.

For psychological reasons it may be ill-advised to recommend a medical assessment at the time of an initial office visit. For example, with today's increased sensitivity and openness about sexual matters and a proneness to turn quickly to psychiatric help, young men may complain about their failure in an initial attempt to consummate a sexual relationship. After taking a detailed history, the psychiatrist may conclude that the failure has been prematurely defined as a problem requiring attention. If that is the case, neither a physical examination nor psychotherapy should be recommended, because they would have the undesirable effect of reinforcing the notion of pathology.

## Neurological Examination

If the psychiatrist suspects that the patient has an underlying somatic disorder, such as diabetes mellitus or Cushing's syndrome, referral is usually made to a medical physician for diagnosis and treatment. The situation is different if a cognitive disorder is suspected. The psychiatrist often chooses to assume responsibility in those cases, even though neurological evaluation may be especially difficult when the brain disease is in an early stage.

During the history-taking process in such cases, the patient's level of awareness, attentiveness to the details of the examination, understanding, facial expression, speech, posture, and gait are noted. It is also assumed that a thorough mental status examination will be performed. The neurological examination should then be performed with two objectives in mind: (1) to elicit signs pointing to focal, circumscribed cerebral dysfunction and (2) to elicit signs suggesting diffuse, bilateral cerebral disease. The first objective is met by the routine neurological examination, which is designed primarily to reveal asymmetries in the motor, perceptual, and reflex functions of the two sides of the body caused by focal hemispheric disease. The second objective is met by seeking to elicit signs that have been attributed to diffuse brain dysfunction and to frontal lobe disease. Those signs include the suckling, snout, palmomental, and grasp reflexes and the persistence of the glabella tap response. Regrettably, with the exception of the grasp reflex, such signs do not correlate strongly with the presence of underlying brain pathology.

## Incidental Findings

Psychiatrists should be able to evaluate the significance of findings uncovered by consultants. With a patient who complains of a lump in the throat (globus hystericus) and who is found on examination to have hypertrophied lymphoid tissue, it is tempting to wonder about a cause-and-effect relation. How can one be sure that the finding is not incidental? Has the patient been known to have hypertrophied lymphoid tissue at a time when no complaint was made? Are there many persons with hypertrophied lymphoid tissue who never experience the sensation of a lump in the throat?

With a patient with multiple sclerosis who complains of an inability to walk but, on neurological examination, has only mild spasticity and a unilateral Babinski's sign, it is tempting to ascribe the symptom to the neurological disorder. However, in that instance the evidence of a neurological abnormality is out of keeping with the manifest dysfunction. The same holds true for a patient with profound dementia in whom a small frontal meningioma is seen on a computed tomography (CT) scan. The knowledgeable psychiatrist should recognize that profound dementia may not result from such a small lesion so situated.

Often, a lesion is found that may account for a symptom, but the psychiatrist should make every effort to separate an incidental finding from a causative one, to separate a lesion merely found in the area of the symptom from a lesion producing the symptom.

## PATIENT IN PSYCHIATRIC TREATMENT

While patients are being treated for psychiatric disorders, the psychiatrist should be alert to the possibility of intercurrent illnesses that call for diagnostic studies. Patients in psychotherapy, particularly those in psychoanalysis, may be all too willing to ascribe their new symptoms to emotional causes. Attention should be given to the possible use of denial, especially if the symptoms seem to be unrelated to the conflicts currently in focus.

At a time of increased psychological stress, a patient had urinary frequency, which she ascribed to the pressure that she was under. Only after much urging did she agree to see a urologist, who diagnosed and treated her cystitis.

Not only may patients in psychotherapy be prone to attribute new symptoms to emotional causes, but sometimes their therapists do so as well. There is an ever-present danger of providing psychodynamic explanations for physical symptoms.

A disturbed young women in a psychiatric unit, who would curl up in a clothes basket and remain there for long periods of time, was described as regressing and assuming the fetal position. Later, when the diagnosis of meningoencephalitis was confirmed, it seemed that a better explanation for her behavior was the need to relieve pressure on nerve roots.

Symptoms such as drowsiness and dizziness and signs such as a skin eruption and a gait disturbance, common side effects of psychotropic medication, call for a medical reevaluation if the patient fails to respond in a reasonable time to changes in the dosage or the kind of medication prescribed. If patients who are receiving tricyclic drugs or antipsychotic drugs complain of blurred vision, usually an anticholinergic side effect, and if the condition does not recede with a reduction in dosage or a change in medication, they should be evaluated to rule out other causes. In one case the diagnosis proved to be Toxoplasmia chorioretinitis. The absence of other anticholinergic side effects, such as a dry mouth and constipation, is an additional clue alerting the psychiatrist to the possibility of a concomitant medical illness.

Early in an illness, few, if any, positive physical or laboratory results may be found. In such instances, especially if the evidence of psychic trauma or emotional conflicts is glaring, all symptoms are likely to be regarded as psychosocial in origin and new symptoms also seen in that light. Indications for repeating portions of the medical workup may be missed unless the psychiatrist is alert to clues suggesting that some symptoms do not fit the original diagnosis and point, instead, to a medical illness. Occasionally, a patient with an acute illness, such as encephalitis, is hospitalized with the diagnosis of schizophrenia; or a patient with a subacute illness, such as carcinoma of the pancreas, is treated in a private office or clinic with the diagnosis of a depressive disorder. Although it may not be possible to make the correct diagnosis at the time of the initial psychiatric evaluation, continued surveillance and attention to clinical details usually provide clues leading to the recognition of the cause.

The likelihood of intercurrent illness is greater with some psychiatric disorders than with others. Substance abusers, for example, because of their life patterns, are susceptible to infection and are likely to suffer from the adverse effects of trauma, dietary deficiencies, and poor hygiene.

When somatic and psychological dysfunctions are known to coexist, the psychiatrist should be thoroughly conversant with the patient's medical status. In cases of cardiac decompensation, peripheral neuropathy, and other disabling disorders, the nature and the degree of the impairment that can be attributed to the physical disorder should be assessed. It is important to answer the question: Does the patient exploit a disability, or is it ignored or denied with resultant overexertion? To answer that question, the psychiatrist must assess the patient's capabilities and limitations, rather than make sweeping judgments based on a diagnostic label.

Special vigilence regarding medical status is required for some patients in treatment for somatoform and eating disorders. Such is the case for patients with ulcerative colitis who are bleeding profusely and for patients with anorexia nervosa who are losing appreciable weight. Those disorders may become life-threatening.

## Importance of Medical Illness

Numerous articles have called attention to the need for thorough medical screening of patients seen in psychiatric inpatient services and clinics. (A similar need has been shown to exist for the psychiatric evaluation of patients seen in medical inpatient services and clinics.)

Among identified psychiatric patients, anywhere from 24 percent to 60 percent have been shown to suffer from associated physical disorders. In a survey of 2,090 psychiatric clinic patients, 43 percent were found to have associated physical disorders; of those, almost half the physical disorders had not been diagnosed by the referring sources.

(In that study, 69 patients were found to have diabetes mellitus, but only 12 of the cases of diabetes had been diagnosed before referral.)

Expecting all psychiatrists to be experts in internal medicine is unrealistic, but expecting them to recognize physical disorders when present is realistic. Moreover, they should make appropriate referrals and collaborate in treating patients who have both physical and mental disorders.

Psychiatric symptoms are nonspecific; they can herald medical illness, as well as psychiatric illness. Moreover, psychiatric symptoms often precede the appearance of definitive medical symptoms. Some psychiatric symptoms—such as visual hallucinations, distortions, and illusions—should call forth a high level of suspicion.

The medical literature abounds with case reports of patients whose disorders were initially considered emotional but ultimately proved to be organic in origin. The data in most of the reports revealed features pointing toward organicity. Diagnostic errors arose because such features were accorded too little weight.

### References

DeGowin R L: *DeGowin and DeGowin's Bedside Diagnostic Examination*, ed 5. Macmillian, New York, 1987.
D'Ercole A, Skodol A E, Struening E, Curtis J, Millman J: Diagnosis of physical illness in psychiatric patients using Axis III and a standardized medical history. Hosp Community Psychiatry *42*: 395, 1991.
Dolan J G, Mushlin A I: Routine laboratory testing for medical disorders in psychiatric inpatients. Arch Intern Med *145*: 2085, 1985.
Ellenhorn M J, Barceloux D G: *Medical Toxicology: Diagnosis and Treatment of Human Poisoning*. Elsevier, New York, 1988.
Hoffman R S, Koran L M: Detecting physical illness in patients with mental disorders. Psychosomatics *25*: 654, 1984.
Kaaya S, Goldberg D, Gask L: Management of somatic presentations of psychiatric illness in general medical settings: Evaluation of a new training course for general practitioners. Med Educ *26*: 138, 1992.
Kirch D G: Medical assessment and laboratory testing in psychiatry. In *Comprehensive Textbook of Psychiatry*, ed 5, H I Kaplan, B J Sadock, editors, p 525. Williams & Wilkins, Baltimore, 1989.
Osterloh J D, Becker C E: Chemical dependency and drug testing in the workplace. West J Med *152*: 506, 1990.
Rosse R B, Giese A A, Deutsch S I, Morihisa J M: *A Concise Guide to Laboratory and Diagnostic Testing in Psychiatry*. American Psychiatric Press, Washington, 1989.
Weinberger D R: Brain disease and psychiatric illness: When should a psychiatrist order a CT scan? Am J Psychiatry *141*: 1521, 1984.

# Typical Signs and Symptoms of Psychiatric Illness Defined

Psychiatry is concerned with phenomenology and the study of mental phenomena. Psychiatrists must learn to be masters of precise observation and evocative description, and the learning of those skills involves the learning of a new language. Part of the language in psychiatry involves the recognition and the definition of behavioral and emotional signs and symptoms. *Signs* are objective findings observed by the clinician (for example, constricted affect and psychomotor retardation); *symptoms* are subjective experiences described by the patient (for example, depressed mood and decreased energy). A *syndrome* is a group of signs and symptoms that occur together as a recognizable condition that may be less than specific than a clear-cut disorder or disease. Most psychiatric conditions are, in fact, syndromes. Becoming an expert in recognizing specific signs and symptoms allows the clinician to understandably communicate with other clinicians, accurately make a diagnosis, effectively manage treatment, reliably predict a prognosis, and thoroughly explore pathophysiology, causes, and psychodynamic issues.

The outline that follows gives a comprehensive list of signs and symptoms, each with a precise definition or description. Most psychiatric signs and symptoms have their roots in essentially normal behavior and represent various points on the spectrum of behavior from normal to pathological.

Table 8–1 lists in alphabetical order the mental phenomena and the signs and symptoms of psychiatric illness discussed in this chapter. The numbers and letters in the right-hand column refer to the place in the chapter where each term is defined.

## I. Consciousness: state of awareness

Apperception: perception modified by one's own emotions and thoughts. Sensorium: state of cognitive functioning of the special senses (sometimes used as a synonym for consciousness). Disturbances of consciousness are most often associated with brain pathology.

### A. Disturbances of consciousness

1. Disorientation: disturbance of orientation in time, place, or person
2. Clouding of consciousness: incomplete clear-mindedness with disturbances in perception and attitudes
3. Stupor: lack of reaction to and unawareness of surroundings
4. Delirium: bewildered, restless, confused, disoriented reaction associated with fear and hallucinations
5. Coma: profound degree of unconsciousness
6. Coma vigil: coma in which the patient appears to be asleep but ready to be aroused (also known as akinetic mutism)
7. Twilight state: disturbed consciousness with hallucinations
8. Dreamlike state: often used as a synonym for complex partial seizure or psychomotor epilepsy
9. Somnolence: abnormal drowsiness

**B. Disturbances of attention:** attention is the amount of effort exerted in focusing on certain portions of an experience; ability to sustain a focus on one activity; ability to concentrate

1. Distractibility: inability to concentrate attention; attention drawn to unimportant or irrelevant external stimuli
2. Selective inattention: blocking out only those things that generate anxiety
3. Hypervigilance: excessive attention and focus on all internal and external stimuli, usually secondary to delusional or paranoid states
4. Trance: focused attention and altered consciousness, usually seen in hypnosis, dissociative disorders, and ecstatic religious experiences

**C. Disturbances in suggestibility:** compliant and uncritical response to an idea or influence

1. *Folie à deux* (or *folie à trois*): communicated emotional illness between two (or three) persons
2. Hypnosis: artificially induced modification of consciousness characterized by a heightened suggestibility

**II. Emotion:** a complex feeling state with psychic, somatic, and behavioral components that is related to affect and mood

**A. Affect:** observed expression of emotion; may be inconsistent with patient's description of emotion

1. Appropriate affect: condition in which the emotional tone is in harmony with the accompanying idea, thought, or speech; also further described as broad or full affect, in which a full range of emotions is appropriately expressed
2. Inappropriate affect: disharmony between the emotional feeling tone and the idea, thought, or speech accompanying it
3. Blunted affect: a disturbance in affect manifested by a severe reduction in the intensity of externalized feeling tone

**Table 8-1**
**Index to Signs and Symptoms of Psychiatric Illness. (This table lists in alphabetical order the mental phenomena and the signs and symptoms of psychiatric illness discussed in this chapter. The numbers and letters in the right-hand column refer to the place in the chapter where each item is defined.)**

*Continued*

**Table 8–1**
*Continued*

| | | | |
|---|---|---|---|
| *Folie à deux (folie à trois)* | I, C, 1 | Mourning | II, B, 11 |
| Formal thought disorder | IV, A, 4 | Multiple personality | VI, C, 7 |
| Formication | VI, A, 1g | Munchausen syndrome | IV, C, 3m |
| Free-floating anxiety | II, C, 2 | Mutism | III, 9 |
| Freudian slip | IV | | |
| Fugue | VI, C, 6 | Negativism | III, 3 |
| | | Neologism | IV, B, 1 |
| Global aphasia | V, B, 6 | Neurosis | IV, A, 2 |
| Glossolalia | IV, B, 16 | Nihilistic delusion | IV, C, 3e |
| Grief | II, B, 11 | Noesis | IV, C, 12 |
| Guilt | II, C, 11 | Nominal aphasia | V, B, 3 |
| Gustatory hallucination | VI, A, 1f | Nonfluent aphasia | V, B, 1 |
| | | Nymphomania | III, 10f, iii |
| Hallucination | VI, A, 1 | | |
| Hallucinosis | VI, A, 1l | Obsession | IV, C, 8 |
| Haptic hallucination | VI, A, 1g | Olfactory hallucination | VI, A, 1e |
| Hyperactivity (hyperkinesis) | III, 10b | Overactivity | III, 10 |
| Hypermnesia | VII, A, 3 | Overvalued idea | IV, C, 2 |
| Hyperphagia | II, D, 2 | | |
| Hypersomnia | II, D, 4 | Panic | II, C, 6 |
| Hypervigilance | I, B, 3 | Panphobia | IV, C, 11h |
| Hypnagogic hallucination | VI, A, 1a | Paramnesia | VII, A, 2 |
| Hypnopompic hallucination | VI, A, 1b | Paranoid delusions | IV, C, 3h |
| Hypnosis | I, C, 2 | Paranoid ideation | IV, C, 3h |
| Hypoactivity (hypokinesis) | III, 11 | Parapraxis | IV |
| Hypochondria | IV, C, 7 | Pathological jealousy | IV, C, 3k |
| Hysterical anesthesia | VI, C, 1 | Perception | VI |
| | | Persecutory delusion | IV, C, 3h, i |
| Idea of reference | IV, C, 3h, iii | Perseveration | IV, B, 6 |
| Illogical thinking | IV, A, 5 | Phantom limb | VI, A, 1g |
| Illusion | VI, A, 2 | Phobia | IV, C, 11 |
| Immediate memory | VII, B, 1 | Physiological disturbances associated | |
| Impaired insight | IX, C | with mood | II, D |
| Impaired judgment | X, C | Polyphagia | III, 10h |
| Inappropriate affect | II, A, 2 | Posturing | III, 2e |
| Incoherence | IV, B, 5 | Poverty of content of speech | V, A, 5 |
| Increased libido | II, D, 6 | Poverty of speech | V, A, 3 |
| Initial insomnia | II, D, 3a | Preoccupation of thought | IV, C, 4 |
| Insight | IX | Pressure of speech | V, A, 1 |
| Insomnia | II, D, 3 | Primary process thinking | IV, A, 9 |
| Intellectual insight | IX, A | Prosopagnosia | VI, B, 5 |
| Intelligence | VIII | Pseudodementia | VIII, C |
| Irrelevant answer | IV, B, 10 | Pseudologia phantastica | IV, C, 3m |
| Irritable mood | II, B, 4 | Psychomotor agitation | III, 10a |
| | | Psychosis | IV, A, 2 |
| *Jamais vu* | VII, A, 2g | | |
| Jargon aphasia | V, B, 5 | Reality testing | IV, A, 3 |
| | | Recent memory | VII, B, 2 |
| Kleptomania | III, 10f, ii | Recent past memory | VII, B, 3 |
| | | Receptive aphasia | V, B, 2 |
| Labile affect | II, A, 6 | Remote memory | VII, B, 4 |
| Labile mood | II, B, 5 | Repression | VII, A, 6 |
| Lethologica | VII, A, 7 | Restricted affect | II, A, 4 |
| Lilliputian hallucination | VI, A, 1i | Retrograde amnesia | VII, A, 1b |
| Logorrhea | V, A, 2 | Retrospective falsification | VII, A, 2b |
| Loosening of associations | IV, B, 11 | Rigidity | III, 2d |
| | | Ritual | III, 10f, vi |
| Macropsia | VI, C, 2 | Rumination | IV, C, 8 |
| Magical thinking | IV, A, 8 | | |
| Mannerism | III, 6 | Satyriasis | III, 10f, iv |
| Memory | VII | Screen memory | VII, A, 5 |
| Mental disorder | IV, A, 1 | Selective inattention | I, B, 2 |
| Mental retardation | VIII, A | Sensorium | I |
| Micropsia | VI, C, 3 | Sensory aphasia | V, B, 2 |
| Middle insomnia | II, D, 3b | Shame | II, C, 10 |
| Mimicry | III, 12 | Simultagnosia | VI, B, 7 |
| Monomania | IV, C, 6 | Sleepwalking | III, 10d |
| Mood | II, B | Social phobia | IV, C, 11b |
| Mood-congruent delusion | IV, C, 3c | Somatic delusion | IV, C, 3g |
| Mood-congruent hallucination | VI, A, 1j | Somatic hallucination | VI, A, 1h |
| Mood-incongruent delusion | IV, C, 3d | Somatopagnosia | VI, B, 2 |
| Mood-incongruent hallucination | VI, A, 1k | Somnambulism | III, 10d |
| Mood swings | II, B, 5 | Somnolence | I, A, 9 |
| Motor aphasia | V, B, 1 | Speaking in tongues | IV, B, 16 |
| Motor behavior (conation) | III | | |

4. Restricted or constricted affect: reduction in intensity of feeling tone less severe than blunted affect but clearly reduced
5. Flat affect: absence or near absence of any signs of affective expression; voice monotonous, face immobile
6. Labile affect: rapid and abrupt changes in emotional feeling tone, unrelated to external stimuli

**B. Mood:** a pervasive and sustained emotion, subjectively experienced and reported by the patient and observed by others; examples include depression, elation, anger

1. Dysphoric mood: an unpleasant mood
2. Euthymic mood: normal range of mood, implying absence of depressed or elevated mood
3. Expansive mood: expression of one's feelings without restraint, frequently with an overestimation of one's significance or importance
4. Irritable mood: easily annoyed and provoked to anger
5. Mood swings (labile mood): oscillations between euphoria and depression or anxiety
6. Elevated mood: air of confidence and enjoyment; a mood more cheerful than usual
7. Euphoria: intense elation with feelings of grandeur
8. Ecstasy: feeling of intense rapture
9. Depression: psychopathological feeling of sadness
10. Anhedonia: loss of interest in and withdrawal from all regular and pleasurable activities, often associated with depression
11. Grief or mourning: sadness appropriate to a real loss
12. Alexithymia: inability or difficulty in describing or being aware of one's emotions or moods

**C. Other emotions**

1. Anxiety: feeling of apprehension caused by anticipation of danger, which may be internal or external
2. Free-floating anxiety: pervasive, unfocused fear not attached to any idea

3. Fear: anxiety caused by consciously recognized and realistic danger
4. Agitation: severe anxiety associated with motor restlessness
5. Tension: increased motor and psychological activity that is unpleasant
6. Panic: acute, episodic, intense attack of anxiety associated with overwhelming feelings of dread and autonomic discharge
7. Apathy: dulled emotional tone associated with detachment or indifference
8. Ambivalence: coexistence of two opposing impulses toward the same thing in the same person at the same time
9. Abreaction: emotional release or discharge after recalling a painful experience
10. Shame: failure to live up to self-expectations
11. Guilt: emotion secondary to doing what is perceived as wrong

**D. Physiological disturbances associated with mood:** signs of somatic (usually autonomic) dysfunction of the person, most often associated with depression (also called vegetative signs)

1. Anorexia: loss of or decrease in appetite
2. Hyperphagia: increase in appetite and intake of food
3. Insomnia: lack of or diminished ability to sleep
   a. Initial: difficulty in falling asleep
   b. Middle: difficulty in sleeping through the night without waking up and difficulty in going back to sleep
   c. Terminal: early morning awakening
4. Hypersomnia: excessive sleeping
5. Diurnal variation: mood is regularly worst in the morning, immediately after awakening, and improves as the day progresses
6. Diminished libido: decreased sexual interest, drive,

and performance (increased libido is often associated with manic states)

7. Constipation: inability or difficulty in defecating

**III. Motor behavior (conation):** the aspect of the psyche that includes impulses, motivations, wishes, drives, instincts, and cravings, as expressed by a person's behavior or motor activity

1. Echopraxia: pathological imitation of movements of one person by another
2. Catatonia: motor anomalies in nonorganic disorders (as opposed to disturbances of consciousness and motor activity secondary to organic pathology)
   a. Catalepsy: general term for an immobile position that is constantly maintained
   b. Catatonic excitement: agitated, purposeless motor activity, uninfluenced by external stimuli
   c. Catatonic stupor: markedly slowed motor activity, often to a point of immobility and seeming unawareness of surroundings
   d. Catatonic rigidity: voluntary assumption of a rigid posture, held against all efforts to be moved
   e. Catatonic posturing: voluntary assumption of an inappropriate or bizarre posture, generally maintained for long periods of time
   f. *Cerea flexibilitas* (waxy flexibility): the person can be molded into a position that is then maintained; when the examiner moves the person's limb, the limb feels as if it were made of wax
3. Negativism: motiveless resistance to all attempts to be moved or to all instructions
4. Cataplexy: temporary loss of muscle tone and weakness precipitated by a variety of emotional states
5. Stereotypy: repetitive fixed pattern of physical action or speech
6. Mannerism: ingrained, habitual involuntary movement
7. Automatism: automatic performance of an act or acts generally representative of unconscious symbolic activity
8. Command automatism: automatic following of suggestions (also called automatic obedience)
9. Mutism: voicelessness without structural abnormalities
10. Overactivity
    a. Psychomotor agitation: excessive motor and cognitive overactivity, usually nonproductive and in response to inner tension
    b. Hyperactivity (hyperkinesis): restless, aggressive, destructive activity, often associated with some underlying brain pathology
    c. Tic: involuntary, spasmodic motor movement
    d. Sleepwalking (somnambulism): motor activity during sleep
    e. Akathisia: subjective feeling of muscular tension secondary to antipsychotic or other medication, which can cause restlessness, pacing, repeated sitting and standing; can be mistaken for psychotic agitation
    f. Compulsion: uncontrollable impulse to perform an act repetitively
       i. Dipsomania: compulsion to drink alcohol
       ii. Kleptomania: compulsion to steal
       iii. Nymphomania: excessive and compulsive need for coitus in a woman
       iv. Satyriasis: excessive and compulsive need for coitus in a man
       v. Trichotillomania: compulsion to pull out one's hair
       vi. Ritual: automatic activity, compulsive in nature, anxiety-reducing in origin
    g. Ataxia: failure of muscle coordination; irregularity of muscle action
    h. Polyphagia: pathological overeating
11. Hypoactivity (hypokinesis): decreased motor and cognitive activity, as in psychomotor retardation; visible slowing of thought, speech, and movements
12. Mimicry: simple, imitative motor activity of childhood
13. Aggression: forceful goal-directed action that may be verbal or physical; the motor counterpart of the affect of rage, anger, or hostility
14. Acting out: direct expression of an unconscious wish or impulse in action; unconscious fantasy is lived out impulsively in behavior
15. Abulia: reduced impulse to act and think, associated with indifference about consequences of action; association with neurological deficit

**IV. Thinking:** goal-directed flow of ideas, symbols, and associations initiated by a problem or a task and leading toward a reality-oriented conclusion; when a logical sequence occurs, thinking is normal; parapraxis (unconsciously motivated lapse from logic is also called Freudian slip) considered part of normal thinking

**A. General disturbances in form or process of thinking**

1. Mental disorder: clinically significant behavioral or psychological syndrome, associated with distress or disability, not just an expected response to a particular event or limited to relations between the person and society
2. Psychosis: inability to distinguish reality from fantasy; impaired reality testing, with the creation of a new reality (as opposed to neurosis: mental disorder in which reality testing is intact, behavior may not violate gross social norms, relatively enduring or recurrent without treatment)
3. Reality testing: the objective evaluation and judgment of the world outside the self
4. Formal thought disorder: disturbance in the form of thought, instead of the content of thought; thinking characterized by loosened associations, neologisms, and illogical constructs; thought process is disordered, and the person is defined as psychotic
5. Illogical thinking: thinking containing erroneous conclusions or internal contradictions; it is psychopathological only when it is marked and when not caused by cultural values or intellectual deficit
6. Dereism: mental activity not concordant with logic or experience
7. Autistic thinking: preoccupation with inner, private world; term used somewhat synonymously with dereism

8. Magical thinking: a form of dereistic thought; thinking that is similar to that of the preoperational phase in children (Jean Piaget), in which thoughts, words, or actions assume power (for example, they can cause or prevent events)
9. Primary process thinking: general term for thinking that is dereistic, illogical, magical; normally found in dreams, abnormally in psychosis

## B. Specific disturbances in form of thought

1. Neologism: new word created by the patient, often by combining syllables of other words, for idiosyncratic psychological reasons
2. Word salad: incoherent mixture of words and phrases
3. Circumstantiality: indirect speech that is delayed in reaching the point but eventually gets from original point to desired goal; characterized by an overinclusion of details and parenthetical remarks
4. Tangentiality: inability to have goal-directed associations of thought; patient never gets from desired point to desired goal
5. Incoherence: thought that, generally, is not understandable; running together of thoughts or words with no logical or grammatical connection, resulting in disorganization
6. Perseveration: persisting response to a prior stimulus after a new stimulus has been presented, often associated with cognitive disorders
7. Verbigeration: meaningless repetition of specific words or phrases
8. Echolalia: psychopathological repeating of words or phrases of one person by another; tends to be repetitive and persistent, may be spoken with mocking or staccato intonation
9. Condensation: fusion of various concepts into one
10. Irrelevant answer: answer that is not in harmony with question asked (patient appears to ignore or not attend to question)
11. Loosening of associations: flow of thought in which ideas shift from one subject to another in a completely unrelated way; when severe, speech may be incoherent
12. Derailment: gradual or sudden deviation in train of thought without blocking; sometimes used synonymously with loosening of associations
13. Flight of ideas: rapid, continuous verbalizations or plays on words produce constant shifting from one idea to another; the ideas tend to be connected, and in the less severe form a listener may be able to follow them
14. Clang association: association of words similar in sound but not in meaning; words have no logical connection, may include rhyming and punning
15. Blocking: abrupt interruption in train of thinking before a thought or idea is finished; after a brief pause, the person indicates no recall of what was being said or was going to be said (also known as thought deprivation)
16. Glossolalia: the expression of a revelatory message through unintelligible words (also known as speaking in tongues); not considered a disturbance in thought if associated with practices of specific Pentecostal religions

## C. Specific disturbances in content of thought

1. Poverty of content: thought that gives little information because of vagueness, empty repetitions, or obscure phrases
2. Overvalued idea: unreasonable, sustained false belief maintained less firmly than a delusion
3. Delusion: false belief, based on incorrect inference about external reality, not consistent with patient's intelligence and cultural background, that cannot be corrected by reasoning
   a. Bizarre delusion: an absurd, totally implausible, strange false belief (for example, invaders from space have implanted electrodes in the patient's brain)
   b. Systematized delusion: false belief or beliefs united by a single event or theme (for example, patient is being persecuted by the CIA, the FBI, the Mafia, or the boss)
   c. Mood-congruent delusion: delusion with mood-appropriate content (for example, a depressed patient believes that he or she is responsible for the destruction of the world)
   d. Mood-incongruent delusion: delusion with content that has no association to mood or is mood-neutral (for example, a depressed patient has delusions of thought control or thought broadcasting)
   e. Nihilistic delusion: false feeling that self, others, or the world is nonexistent or ending
   f. Delusion of poverty: false belief that one is bereft or will be deprived of all material possessions
   g. Somatic delusion: false belief involving functioning of one's body (for example, belief that one's brain is rotting or melting)
   h. Paranoid delusions: includes persecutory delusions and delusions of reference, control, and grandeur (distinguished from paranoid ideation, which is suspiciousness of less than delusional proportions)
      i. Delusion of persecution: false belief that one is being harassed, cheated, or persecuted; often found in litigious patients who have a pathological tendency to take legal action because of imagined mistreatment
      ii. Delusion of grandeur: exaggerated conception of one's importance, power, or identity
      iii. Delusion of reference: false belief that the behavior of others refers to oneself; that events, objects, or other people have a particular and unusual significance, usually of a negative nature; derived from idea of reference, in which one falsely feels that one is being talked about by others (for example, belief that people on television or radio are talking to or about the patient)
   i. Delusion of self-accusation: false feeling of remorse and guilt
   j. Delusion of control: false feeling that one's will, thoughts, or feelings are being controlled by external forces
      i. Thought withdrawal: delusion that one's thoughts are being removed from one's mind by other people or forces

ii. Thought insertion: delusion that thoughts are being implanted in one's mind by other people or forces

iii. Thought broadcasting: delusion that one's thoughts can be heard by others, as though they were being broadcast into the air

iv. Thought control: delusion that one's thoughts are being controlled by other people or forces

k. Delusion of infidelity (delusional jealousy): false belief derived from pathological jealousy that one's lover is unfaithful

l. Erotomania: delusional belief, more common in women than in men, that someone is deeply in love with them (also known as Clérambault-Kandinsky complex)

m. Pseudologia phantastica: a type of lying, in which the person appears to believe in the reality of his or her fantasies and acts on them; associated with Munchausen syndrome, repeated feigning of illness

4. Trend or preoccupation of thought: centering of thought content on a particular idea, associated with a strong affective tone, such as a paranoid trend or a suicidal or homicidal preoccupation

5. Egomania: pathological self-preoccupation

6. Monomania: preoccupation with a single object

7. Hypochondria: exaggerated concern about one's health that is based not on real organic pathology but, rather, on unrealistic interpretations of physical signs or sensations as abnormal

8. Obsession: pathological persistence of an irresistible thought or feeling that cannot be eliminated from consciousness by logical effort, which is associated with anxiety (also termed rumination)

9. Compulsion: pathological need to act on an impulse that, if resisted, produces anxiety; repetitive behavior in response to an obsession or performed according to certain rules, with no true end in itself other than to prevent something from occurring in the future

10. Coprolalia: compulsive utterance of obscene words

11. Phobia: persistent, irrational, exaggerated, and invariably pathological dread of some specific type of stimulus or situation; results in a compelling desire to avoid the feared stimulus

a. Specific phobia: circumscribed dread of a discrete object or situation (for example, dread of spiders or snakes)

b. Social phobia: dread of public humiliation, as in fear of public speaking, performing, or eating in public

c. Acrophobia: dread of high places

d. Agoraphobia: dread of open places

e. Algophobia: dread of pain

f. Ailurophobia: dread of cats

g. Erythrophobia: dread of red (refers to a fear of blushing)

h. Panphobia: dread of everything

i. Claustrophobia: dread of closed places

j. Xenophobia: dread of strangers

k. Zoophobia: dread of animals

12. Noesis: a revelation in which immense illumination occurs in association with a sense that one has been chosen to lead and command

13. *Unio mystica*: an oceanic feeling, one of mystic unity with an infinite power; not considered a disturbance in thought content if congruent with patient's religious or cultural milieu

**V. Speech:** ideas, thoughts, feelings as expressed through language; communication through the use of words and language

**A. Disturbances in speech**

1. Pressure of speech: rapid speech that is increased in amount and difficult to interrupt

2. Volubility (logorrhea): copious, coherent, logical speech

3. Poverty of speech: restriction in the amount of speech used; replies may be monosyllabic

4. Nonspontaneous speech: verbal responses given only when asked or spoken to directly; no self-initiation of speech

5. Poverty of content of speech: speech that is adequate in amount but conveys little information because of vagueness, emptiness, or stereotyped phrases

6. Dysprosody: loss of normal speech melody (called prosody)

7. Dysarthria: difficulty in articulation, not in word finding or in grammar

8. Excessively loud or soft speech: loss of modulation of normal speech volume; may reflect a variety of pathological conditions ranging from psychosis to depression to deafness

9. Stuttering: frequent repetition or prolongation of a sound or syllable, leading to markedly impaired speech fluency

10. Cluttering: erratic and dysrhythmic speech, consisting of rapid and jerky spurts

**B. Aphasic disturbances:** disturbances in language output

1. Motor aphasia: disturbance of speech caused by a cognitive disorder in which understanding remains but ability to speak is grossly impaired; speech is halting, laborious, and inaccurate (also known as Broca's, nonfluent, and expressive aphasia)

2. Sensory aphasia: organic loss of ability to comprehend the meaning of words; speech is fluid and spontaneous but incoherent and nonsensical (also known as Wernicke's, fluent, and receptive aphasia)

3. Nominal aphasia: difficulty in finding correct name for an object (also termed anomia and amnestic aphasia)

4. Syntactical aphasia: inability to arrange words in proper sequence

5. Jargon aphasia: words produced are totally neologistic; nonsense words repeated with various intonations and inflections

6. Global aphasia: combination of a grossly nonfluent aphasia and a severe fluent aphasia

**VI. Perception:** process of transferring physical stimulation into psychological information; mental process by which sensory stimuli are brought to awareness

**A. Disturbances of perception**

1. Hallucination: false sensory perception not associated with real external stimuli; there may or may not be a

delusional interpretation of the hallucinatory experience

  a. Hypnagogic hallucination: false sensory perception occurring while falling asleep; generally considered nonpathological phenomenon
  b. Hypnopompic hallucination: false perception occurring while awakening from sleep; generally considered nonpathological
  c. Auditory hallucination: false perception of sound, usually voices but also other noises, such as music; most common hallucination in psychiatric disorders
  d. Visual hallucination: false perception involving sight consisting of both formed images (for example, people) and unformed images (for example, flashes of light); most common in medically determined disorders
  e. Olfactory hallucination: false perception of smell; most common in medical disorders
  f. Gustatory hallucination: false perception of taste, such as unpleasant taste caused by an uncinate seizure; most common in medical disorders
  g. Tactile (haptic) hallucination: false perception of touch or surface sensation, as from an amputated limb (phantom limb), crawling sensation on or under the skin (formication)
  h. Somatic hallucination: false sensation of things occurring in or to the body, most often visceral in origin (also known as cenesthesic hallucination)
  i. Lilliputian hallucination: false perception in which objects are seen as reduced in size (also termed micropsia)
  j. Mood-congruent hallucination: hallucination in which the content is consistent with either a depressed or a manic mood (for example, a depressed patient hears voices saying that the patient is a bad person; a manic patient hears voices saying that the patient is of inflated worth, power, and knowledge)
  k. Mood-incongruent hallucination: hallucination in which the content is not consistent with either depressed or manic mood (for example, in depression, hallucinations not involving such themes as guilt, deserved punishment, or inadequacy; in mania, hallucinations not involving such themes as inflated worth or power)
  l. Hallucinosis: hallucinations, most often auditory, that are associated with chronic alcohol abuse and that occur within a clear sensorium, as opposed to delirium tremens (DTs), hallucinations that occur in the context of a clouded sensorium
  m. Synesthesia: sensation or hallucination caused by another sensation (for example, an auditory sensation is accompanied by or triggers a visual sensation; a sound is experienced as being seen, or a visual experience is heard)
  n. Trailing phenomenon: perceptual abnormality associated with hallucinogenic drugs in which moving objects are seen as a series of discrete and discontinuous images
 2. Illusion: misperception or misinterpretation of real external sensory stimuli

**B. Disturbances associated with cognitive disorder:** agnosia—an inability to recognize and interpret the significance of sensory impressions

  1. Anosognosia (ignorance of illness): inability to recognize a neurological deficit as occurring to oneself
  2. Somatopagnosia (ignorance of the body): inability to recognize a body part as one's own (also called autopagnosia)
  3. Visual agnosia: inability to recognize objects or persons
  4. Astereognosis: inability to recognize objects by touch
  5. Prosopagnosia: inability to recognize faces
  6. Apraxia: inability to carry out specific tasks
  7. Simultagnosia: inability to comprehend more than one element of a visual scene at a time or to integrate the parts into a whole
  8. Adiadochokinesia: inability to perform rapid alternating movements.

**C. Disturbances associated with conversion and dissociative phenomena:** somatization of repressed material or the development of physical symptoms and distortions involving the voluntary muscles or special sense organs; not under voluntary control and not explained by any physical disorder

  1. Hysterical anesthesia: loss of sensory modalities resulting from emotional conflicts
  2. Macropsia: state in which objects seem larger than they are
  3. Micropsia: state in which objects seem smaller than they are (both macropsia and micropsia can also be associated with clear organic conditions, such as complex partial seizures)
  4. Depersonalization: a subjective sense of being unreal, strange, or unfamiliar to oneself
  5. Derealization: a subjective sense that the environment is strange or unreal; a feeling of changed reality
  6. Fugue: taking on a new identity with amnesia for the old identity; often involves travel or wandering to new environments
  7. Multiple personality: one person who appears at different times to be two or more entirely different personalities and characters (called dissociative identity disorder in the fourth edition of *Diagnostic and Statistical Manual of Mental Disorders* (DSM-IV)

**VII. Memory:** function by which information stored in the brain is later recalled to consciousness

**A. Disturbances of memory**

  1. Amnesia: partial or total inability to recall past experiences; may be organic or emotional in origin
    a. Anterograde: amnesia for events occurring after a point in time
    b. Retrograde: amnesia prior to a point in time
  2. Paramnesia: falsification of memory by distortion of recall
    a. *Fausse reconnaissance:* false recognition
    b. Retrospective falsification: memory becomes unintentionally (unconsciously) distorted by being filtered through patient's present emotional, cognitive, and experiential state

c. Confabulation: unconscious filling of gaps in memory by imagined or untrue experiences that patient believes but that have no basis in fact; most often associated with organic pathology

d. *Déjà vu:* illusion of visual recognition in which a new situation is incorrectly regarded as a repetition of a previous memory

e. *Déjà entendu:* illusion of auditory recognition

f. *Déjà pensé:* illusion that a new thought is recognized as a thought previously felt or expressed

g. *Jamais vu:* false feeling of unfamiliarity with a real situation one has experienced

3. Hypermnesia: exaggerated degree of retention and recall

4. Eidetic image: visual memory of almost hallucinatory vividness

5. Screen memory: a consciously tolerable memory covering for a painful memory

6. Repression: a defense mechanism characterized by unconscious forgetting of unacceptable ideas or impulses

7. Lethologica: temporary inability to remember a name or a proper noun

**B. Levels of memory**

1. Immediate: reproduction or recall of perceived material within seconds to minutes

2. Recent: recall of events over past few days

3. Recent past: recall of events over past few months

4. Remote: recall of events in distant past

**VIII. Intelligence:** the ability to understand, recall, mobilize, and constructively integrate previous learning in meeting new situations

**A. Mental retardation:** lack of intelligence to a degree in which there is interference with social and vocational performance: mild (I.Q. of 50 or 55 to approximately 70), moderate (I.Q. of 35 or 40 to 50 or 55), severe (I.Q. of 20 or 25 to 35 or 40), or profound (I.Q. below 20 or 25); obsolete terms are idiot (mental age less than 3 years), imbecile (mental age of 3 to 7 years), and moron (mental age of about 8)

**B. Dementia:** organic and global deterioration of intellectual functioning without clouding of consciousness

1. Dyscalculia (acalculia): loss of ability to do calculations not caused by anxiety or impairment in concentration

2. Dysgraphia (agraphia): loss of ability to write in cursive style; loss of word structure

3. Alexia: loss of a previously possessed reading facility; not explained by defective visual acuity

**C. Pseudodementia:** clinical features resembling a dementia not caused by an organic condition; most often caused by depression (dementia syndrome of depression)

**D. Concrete thinking:** literal thinking; limited use of metaphor without understanding of nuances of meaning; one-dimensional thought

**E. Abstract thinking:** ability to appreciate nuances of meaning; multidimensional thinking with ability to use metaphors and hypotheses appropriately

**IX. Insight:** ability of the patient to understand the true cause and meaning of a situation (such as a set of symptoms)

**A. Intellectual insight:** understanding of the objective reality of a set of circumstances without the ability to apply the understanding in any useful way to master the situation

**B. True insight:** understanding of the objective reality of a situation, coupled with the motivation and the emotional impetus to master the situation

**C. Impaired insight:** diminished ability to understand the objective reality of a situation

**X. Judgment:** ability to assess a situation correctly and to act appropriately within that situation

**A. Critical judgment:** ability to assess, discern, and choose among various options in a situation

**B. Automatic judgment:** reflex performance of an action

**C. Impaired judgment:** diminished ability to understand a situation correctly and to act appropriately

**References**

Andreasen N C: The clinical assessment of thought, language, and communication disorders: I. The definition of terms and evaluation of their reliability. Arch Gen Psychiatry *36*: 1315, 1979.
Bender M D: *Disorders of Perception.* Thomas, Springfield, Ill, 1952.
Bensen D F, Blumer D, editors: *Psychiatric Aspects of Neurological Disease,* vol 2. Grune & Stratton, Orlando, 1982.
Bleuler E: *Dementia Praecox: The Group of Schizophrenias.* International Universities Press, New York, 1950.
Campbell R J: *Psychiatric Dictionary,* ed 6. Oxford University Press, New York, 1989.
Cassano G B, Perugi G, Musetti L, Akiskal H S: The nature of depression presenting concomitantly with panic disorder. Compr Psychiatry *30*: 473, 1989.
Cavenar J O, Brodie H K M: *Signs and Symptoms in Psychiatry.* Lippincott, Philadelphia, 1983.
Fenichel O: *Psychoanalytic Theory of Neuroses,* Norton, New York, 1945.
Frances A J, Hales R E: *Annual Review,* vol 5. American Psychiatric Press, Washington, 1986.
Geschwind N: Aphasia. N Engl J Med *284*: 654, 1971.
Hellerstein D, Frosch W, Koenigsberg H W: The clinical significance of command hallucinations. Am J Psychiatry *144*: 219, 1987.
Kaplan H I, Sadock B J: Typical signs and symptoms of psychiatric illness. In *Comprehensive Textbook of Psychiatry,* ed 5, H I Kaplan, B J Sadock, editors, p 468. Williams & Wilkins, Baltimore, 1989.
Sadler J Z, Hulgus Y F: Clinical problem solving and the biopsychosocial model. Am J Psychiatry *149*: 1315, 1992.
Spitzer R L, Skodol A E, Williams J B W: *Case Book: Diagnostic and Statistical Manual of Mental Disorders.* American Psychiatric Association, Washington, 1988.

# Classification in Psychiatry and Psychiatric Rating Scales

## INTERNATIONAL CLASSIFICATION OF DISEASES

The 10th revision of the International Classification of Diseases and Related Health Problems (ICD-10) is the official classification system used in Europe (Table 9–1). All the categories used in the fourth edition of *Diagnostic and Statistical Manual of Mental Disorders* (DSM-IV) are found in ICD-10, but not all ICD-10 categories are in DSM-IV. According to DSM-IV:

The tenth revision of the *International Statistical Classification of Diseases and Related Health Problems* (ICD-10), developed by WHO, was published in 1992, but will probably not come into official use in the United States until the late 1990s. Those preparing ICD-10 and DSM-IV have worked closely to coordinate their efforts, resulting in much mutual influence. ICD-10 consists of an official coding system and other related clinical and research documents and instruments. The codes and terms provided in DSM-IV are fully compatible with both ICD-9-CM and ICD-10. . . . The clinical and research drafts of ICD-10 were thoroughly reviewed by the DSM-IV Work Groups and suggested important topics for DSM-IV literature reviews and data reanalyses. Draft versions of the ICD-10 Diagnostic Criteria for Research were included as alternatives to be compared with DSM-III, DSM-III-R and suggested DSM-IV criteria sets in the DSM-IV field trials. The many consultations between the developers of DSM-IV and ICD-10 (which were facilitated by NIMH, NIDA, and NIAAA) were enormously useful in increasing the congruence and reducing meaningless differences in wording between the two systems.

Until ICD-10 becomes official in the United States, the clinical modification of the ninth revision (ICD-9-CM) is used here. The terms and codes in DSM-IV are fully compatible with both ICD-9-CM and ICD-10.

## DSM-IV

The fourth edition of *Diagnostic and Statistical Manual of Mental Disorders* (DSM-IV), published in 1994, is the latest and most up-to-date classification of mental disorders. DSM-IV is used by mental health professionals of all disciplines and is cited for insurance reimbursement, disability deliberations, and forensic matters.

The fourth edition correlates with the 10th revision of the World Health Organization's International Classifi-

cation of Diseases and Related Health Problems (ICD-10), developed in 1992. Diagnostic systems used in the United States must be compatible with ICD to ensure uniform reporting of national and international health statistics. In addition, Medicare requires that billing codes for reimbursement follow ICD.

Although many psychiatrists have been critical of the many versions of DSM that have appeared since the first edition (DSM-I) appeared in 1952, DSM-IV is the official nomenclature. All terminology used in this textbook conforms to DSM-IV nomenclature.

### History

The various classification systems used in psychiatry date back to Hippocrates, who introduced the terms "mania" and "hysteria" as forms of mental illness in the fifth century B.C. Since then, each era has introduced its own psychiatric classification. The first American classification was introduced in 1869 at the annual meeting of the American Medico-Psychological Association, which was then the name of the American Psychiatric Association.

In 1952 the American Psychiatric Association's Committee on Nomenclature and Statistics published the first edition of *Diagnostic and Statistical Manual of Mental Disorders* (DSM-I). Four editions have been published since then: DSM-II (1968); DSM-III (1980); a revised DSM-III, DSM-III-R (1987); and DSM-IV (1994).

The DSM-IV revision process consisted of three stages: (1) extensive scientific literature reviews to use as a data base, (2) data reanalysis to provide additional information, and (3) 12 field trials to compare sets of criteria. A 27-member task force—assisted by more than 1,000 psychiatrists, mental health professionals, and other health care experts—prepared the manual.

### Basic Features

**Descriptive approach.** The approach to DSM-IV, as it was in DSM-III-R, is atheoretical with regard to causes. Thus, DSM-IV attempts to describe what the manifestations of the mental disorders are; only rarely does it attempt to account for how the disturbances come about. The definitions of the disorders usually consist of descriptions of the clinical features.

**Diagnostic criteria.** Specified diagnostic criteria are provided for each specific mental disorder. Those criteria include a list of features that must be present for the di-

**Table 9–1**
**ICD-10 Classification of Mental Disorders**

F00–F09
Organic, including symptomatic, mental disorders

**F00 Dementia in Alzheimer's disease**
   F00.0 Dementia in Alzheimer's disease with early
       onset
   F00.1 Dementia in Alzheimer's disease with late onset
   F00.2 Dementia in Alzheimer's disease, atypical or
       mixed type
   F00.9 Dementia in Alzheimer's disease, unspecified

**F01 Vascular dementia**
   F01.0 Vascular dementia of acute onset
   F01.1 Multi-infarct dementia
   F01.2 Subcortical vascular dementia
   F01.3 Mixed cortical and subcortical vascular
       dementia
   F01.8 Other vascular dementia
   F01.9 Vascular dementia, unspecified

**F02 Dementia in other diseases classified elsewhere**
   F02.0 Dementia in Pick's disease
   F02.1 Dementia in Creutzfeldt-Jakob disease
   F02.2 Dementia in Huntington's disease
   F02.3 Dementia in Parkinson's disease
   F02.4 Dementia in human immunodeficiency virus
       [HIV] disease
   F02.8 Dementia in other specified diseases classified
       elsewhere

**F03 Unspecified dementia**

A fifth character may be added to specify dementia in
   F00–F03, as follows:

   .x 0 Without additional symptoms
   .x 1 Other symptoms, predominantly delusional
   .x 2 Other symptoms, predominantly hallucinatory
   .x 3 Other symptoms, predominantly depressive
   .x 4 Other mixed symptoms

**F04 Organic amnesic syndrome, not induced by
alcohol and other psychoactive substances**

**F05 Delirium, not induced by alcohol and other
psychoactive substances**
   F05.0 Delirium, not superimposed on dementia, so
       described
   F05.1 Delirium, superimposed on dementia
   F05.8 Other delirium
   F05.9 Delirium, unspecified

**F06 Other mental disorders due to brain damage and
dysfunction and to physical disease**
   F06.0 Organic hallucinosis
   F06.1 Organic catatonic disorder
   F06.2 Organic delusional [schizophrenia-like] disorder
   F06.3 Organic mood [affective] disorders
       .30 Organic manic disorder
       .31 Organic bipolar disorder
       .32 Organic depressive disorder
       .33 Organic mixed affective disorder
   F06.4 Organic anxiety disorder
   F06.5 Organic dissociative disorder
   F06.6 Organic emotionally labile [asthenic] disorder
   F06.7 Mild cognitive disorder
   F06.8 Other specified mental disorders due to brain
       damage and dysfunction and to physical
       disease

   F06.9 Unspecified mental disorder due to brain
       damage and dysfunction and to physical
       disease
**F07 Personality and behavioural disorders due to brain
disease, damage and dysfunction**
   F07.0 Organic personality disorder
   F07.1 Postencephalitic syndrome
   F07.2 Postconcussional syndrome
   F07.8 Other organic personality and behavioural
       disorders due to brain disease, damage and
       dysfunction
   F07.9 Unspecified organic personality and behavioural
       disorder due to brain disease, damage and
       dysfunction

**F09 Unspecified organic or symptomatic mental
disorder**

F10–F19
**Mental and behavioural disorders due to psychoactive
substance use**

**F10.—Mental and behavioural disorders due to use of
   alcohol**

**F11.—Mental and behavioural disorders due to use of
   opioids**

**F12.—Mental and behavioural disorders due to use of
   cannabinoids**

**F13.—Mental and behavioural disorders due to use of
   sedatives or hypnotics**

**F14.—Mental and behavioural disorders due to use of
   cocaine**

**F15.—Mental and behavioural disorders due to use of
   other stimulants, including caffeine**

**F16.—Mental and behavioural disorders due to use of
   hallucinogens**

**F17.—Mental and behavioural disorders due to use of
   tobacco**

**F18.—Mental and behavioural disorders due to use of
   volatile solvents**

**F19.—Mental and behavioural disorders due to multiple
   drug use and use of other psychoactive
   substances**

Four- and five-character categories may be used to
specify the clinical conditions, as follows:
   F1x.0 Acute intoxication
       .00 Uncomplicated
       .01 With trauma or other bodily injury
       .02 With other medical complications
       .03 With delirium
       .04 With perceptual distortions
       .05 With coma
       .06 With convulsions
       .07 Pathological intoxication

   F1x.1 Harmful use

   F1x.2 Dependence syndrome
       .20 Currently abstinent
       .21 Currently abstinent, but in a protected
           environment

.22 Currently on a clinically supervised maintenance or replacement regime [controlled dependence]
.23 Currently abstinent, but receiving treatment with aversive or blocking drugs
.24 Currently using the substance [active dependence]
.25 Continuous use
.26 Episodic use [dipsomania]

F1x.3 Withdrawal state
.30 Uncomplicated
.31 Convulsions

F1x.4 Withdrawal state with delirium
.40 Without convulsions
.41 With convulsions

F1x.5 Psychotic disorder
.50 Schizophrenia-like
.51 Predominantly delusional
.52 Predominantly hallucinatory
.53 Predominantly polymorphic
.54 Predominantly depressive symptoms
.55 Predominantly manic symptoms
.56 Mixed

F1x.6 Amnesic syndrome

F1x.7 Residual and late-onset psychotic disorder
.70 Flashbacks
.71 Personality or behaviour disorder
.72 Residual affective disorder
.73 Dementia
.74 Other persisting cognitive impairment
.75 Late-onset psychotic disorder

F1x.8 Other mental and behavioural disorders

F1x.9 Unspecified mental and behavioural disorder

## F20–F29
## Schizophrenia, schizotypal and delusional disorders

### F20 Schizophrenia
F20.0 Paranoid schizophrenia
F20.1 Hebephrenic schizophrenia
F20.2 Catatonic schizophrenia
F20.3 Undifferentiated schizophrenia
F20.4 Post-schizophrenic depression
F20.5 Residual schizophrenia
F20.6 Simple schizophrenia
F20.8 Other schizophrenia
F20.9 Schizophrenia, unspecified

A fifth character may be used to classify course:
.x 0 Continuous
.x 1 Episodic with progressive deficit
.x 2 Episodic with stable deficit
.x 3 Episodic remittent
.x 4 Incomplete remission
.x 5 Complete remission
.x 8 Other
.x 9 Period of observation less than one year

### F21 Schizotypal disorder

### F22 Persistent delusional disorders
F22.0 Delusional disorder
F22.8 Other persistent delusional disorders
F22.9 Persistent delusional disorder, unspecified

### F23 Acute and transient psychotic disorders
F23.0 Acute polymorphic psychotic disorder without symptoms of schizophrenia

F23.1 Acute polymorphic psychotic disorder with symptoms of schizophrenia
F23.2 Acute schizophrenia-like psychotic disorder
F23.3 Other acute predominantly delusional psychotic disorders
F23.8 Other acute transient psychotic disorders
F23.9 Acute and transient psychotic disorders unspecified

A fifth character may be used to identify the presence or absence of associated acute stress:
.x 0 Without associated acute stress
x 1 With associated acute stress

### F24 Induced delusional disorder

### F25 Schizoaffective disorders
F25.0 Schizoaffective disorder, manic type
F25.1 Schizoaffective disorder, depressive type
F25.2 Schizoaffective disorder, mixed type
F25.8 Other schizoaffective disorders
F25.9 Schizoaffective disorder, unspecified

### F28 Other nonorganic psychotic disorders

### F29 Unspecified nonorganic psychosis

### F30–F39
### Mood [affective] disorders

### F30 Manic episode
F30.0 Hypomania
F30.1 Mania without psychotic symptoms
F30.2 Mania with psychotic symptoms
F30.8 Other manic episodes
F30.9 Manic episode, unspecified

### F31 Bipolar affective disorder
F31.0 Bipolar affective disorder, current episode hypomanic
F31.1 Bipolar affective disorder, current episode manic without psychotic symptoms
F31.2 Bipolar affective disorder, current episode manic with psychotic symptoms
F31.3 Bipolar affective disorder, current episode mild or moderate depression
.30 Without somatic symptoms
.31 With somatic symptoms
F31.4 Bipolar affective disorder, current episode severe depression without psychotic symptoms
F31.5 Bipolar affective disorder, current episode severe depression with psychotic symptoms
F31.6 Bipolar affective disorder, current episode mixed
F31.7 Bipolar affective disorder, currently in remission
F31.8 Other bipolar affective disorders
F31.9 Bipolar affective disorder, unspecified

### F32 Depressive episode
F32.0 Mild depressive episode
.00 Without somatic symptoms
.01 With somatic symptoms
F32.1 Moderate depressive episode
.10 Without somatic symptoms
.11 With somatic symptoms
F32.2 Severe depressive episode without psychotic symptoms
F32.3 Severe depressive episode with psychotic symptoms
F32.8 Other depressive episodes
F32.9 Depressive episode, unspecified

*Continued*

**Table 9–1**
*Continued*

**F33 Recurrent depressive disorder**
    F33.0 Recurrent depressive disorder, current episode mild
        .00 Without somatic symptoms
        .00 With somatic symptoms
    F33.1 Recurrent depressive disorder, current episode moderate
        .10 Without somatic symptoms
        .11 With somatic symptoms
    F33.2 Recurrent depressive disorder, current episode severe without psychotic symptoms
    F33.3 Recurrent depressive disorder, current episode severe with psychotic symptoms
    F33.4 Recurrent depressive disorder, currently in remission
    F33.8 Other recurrent depressive disorders
    F33.9 Recurrent depressive disorder, unspecified

**F34 Persistent mood [affective] disorders**
    F34.0 Cyclothymia
    F34.1 Dysthymia
    F34.8 Other persistent mood [affective] disorders
    F34.9 Persistent mood [affective] disorder, unspecified

**F38 Other mood [affective] disorders**
    F38.0 Other single mood [affective] disorders
        .00 Mixed affective episode
    F38.1 Other recurrent mood [affective] disorders
        .10 Recurrent brief depressive disorder
    F38.8 Other specified mood [affective] disorders

**F39 Unspecified mood [affective] disorder**

**F40–F48**
**Neurotic stress-related and somatoform disorders**

**F40 Phobic anxiety disorders**
    F40.0 Agoraphobia
        .00 Without panic disorder
        .01 With panic disorder
    F40.1 Social phobias
    F40.2 Specific (isolated) phobias
    F40.8 Other phobic anxiety disorders
    F40.9 Phobic anxiety disorder, unspecified

**F41 Other anxiety disorders**
    F41.0 Panic disorder [episodic paroxysmal anxiety]
    F41.1 Generalized anxiety disorder
    F41.2 Mixed anxiety and depressive disorder
    F41.3 Other mixed anxiety disorders
    F41.8 Other specified anxiety disorders
    F41.9 Anxiety disorder, unspecified

**F242 Obsessive-compulsive disorder**
    F42.0 Predominantly obsessional thoughts or ruminations
    F42.1 Predominantly compulsive acts [obsessional rituals]
    F42.2 Mixed obsessional thoughts and acts
    F42.8 Other obsessive-compulsive disorders
    F42.9 Obsessive-compulsive disorder, unspecified

**F43 Reaction to severe stress, and adjustment disorders**
    F43.0 Acute stress reaction
    F43.1 Post-traumatic stress disorder
    F43.2 Adjustment disorders
        .20 Brief depressive reaction
        .21 Prolonged depressive reaction

        .22 Mixed anxiety and depressive reaction
        .23 With predominant disturbance of other emotions
        .24 With predominant disturbance of conduct
        .25 With mixed distubance of emotions and conduct
        .28 With other specified predominant symptoms
    F43.8 Other reactions to severe stress
    F43.9 Reaction to severe stress, unspecified

**F44 Dissociative [conversion] disorders**
    F44.0 Dissociative amnesia
    F44.1 Dissociative fugue
    F44.2 Dissociative stupor
    F44.3 Trance and possession disorders
    F44.4 Dissociative motor disorders
    F44.5 Dissociative convulsions
    F44.6 Dissociative anaesthesia and sensory loss
    F44.7 Mixed dissociative [conversion] disorders
    F44.8 Other dissociative [conversoin] disorders
        .80 Ganser's syndrome
        .81 Multiple personality disorder
        .82 Transient dissociative [conversion] disorders occurring in childhood and adolescence
        .88 Other specified dissociative [conversion] disorders
    F44.9 Dissociative [conversion] disorder, unspecified

**F45 Somatoform disorders**
    F45.0 Somatization disorder
    F45.1 Undifferentiated somatoform disorder
    F45.2 Hypochondriacal disorder
    F45.3 Somataform autonomic dysfunction
        .30 Heart and cardiovascular system
        .31 Upper gastrointestinal tract
        .32 Lower gastrointestinal tract
        .33 Respiratory system
        .34 Genitourinary system
        .38 Other organ or system
    F45.4 Persistent somatoform pain disorder
    F45.8 Other somatoform disorders
    F45.9 Somatoform disorder, unspecified

**F48 Other neurotic disorders**
    F48.0 Neurasthenia
    F48.1 Depersonalization-derealization syndrome
    F48.8 Other specified neurotic disorders
    F48.9 Neurotic disorder, unspecified

**F50–F59**
**Behavioural syndromes associated with physiological disturbances and physical factors**

**F50 Eating disorders**
    F50.0 Anorexia nervosa
    F50.1 Atypical anorexia nervosa
    F50.2 Bulimia nervosa
    F50.3 Atypical bulimia nervosa
    F50.4 Overeating associated with other psychological disturbances
    F50.5 Vomiting associated with other psychological disturbances
    F50.8 Other eating disorders
    F50.9 Eating disorder, unspecified

**F51 Nonorganic sleep disorders**
    F51.0 Nonorganic insomnia
    F51.1 Nonorganic hypersomnia

F51.2 Nonorganic disorder of the sleep-wake schedule
F51.3 Sleepwalking [somnambulism]
F51.4 Sleep terrors [night terrors]
F51.5 Nightmares
F51.8 Other nonorganic sleep disorders
F51.9 Nonorganic sleep disorder, unspecified

**F52 Sexual dysfunction, not caused by organic disorder or disease**
F52.0 Lack or loss of sexual desire
F52.1 Sexual aversion and lack of sexual enjoyment
　.10 Sexual aversion
　.11 Lack of sexual enjoyment
F52.2 Failure of genital response
F52.3 Orgasmic dysfunction
F52.4 Premature ejaculation
F52.5 Nonorganic vaginismus
F52.6 Nonorganic dyspareunia
F52.7 Excessive sexual drive
F52.8 Other sexual dysfunction, not caused by organic disorders or disease
F52.9 Unspecified sexual dysfunction, not caused by organic disorder or disease

**F53 Mental and behavioural disorders associated with the puerperium, not elsewhere classified**
F53.0 Mild mental and behavioural disorders associated with the puerperium, not elsewhere classified
F53.1 Severe mental and behavioural disorders associated with the puerperium, not elsewhere classified
F53.8 Other mental and behavioural disorders associated with the puerperium, not elsewhere classified
F53.9 Puerperal mental disorder, unspecified

**F54 Psychological and behavioural factors associated with disorders or diseases classified elsewhere**

**F55 Abuse of non-dependence-producing substances**
F55.0 Antidepressants
F55.1 Laxatives
F55.2 Analgesics
F55.3 Antacids
F55.4 Vitamins
F55.5 Steroids or hormones
F55.6 Specific herbal or folk remedies
F55.8 Other substances that do not produce dependence
F55.9 Unspecified

**F59 Unspecified behavioural syndromes associated with physiological disturbances and physical factors**

**F60–F69**
**Disorders of adult personality and behaviour**

**F60 Specific personality disorders**
F60.0 Paranoid personality disorder
F60.1 Schizoid personality disorder
F60.2 Dissocial personality disorder
F60.3 Emotionally unstable personality disorder
　.30 Impulsive type
　.31 Borderline type
F60.4 Histrionic personality disorder
F60.5 Anankastic personality disorder
F60.6 Anxious [avoidant] personality disorder
F60.7 Dependent personality disorder
F60.8 Other specific personality disorders

F60.9 Personality disorder, unspecified

**F61 Mixed and other personality disorders**
F61.0 Mixed personality disorders
F61.1 Troublesome personality changes

**F62 Enduring personality changes, not attributable to brain damage and disease**
F62.0 Enduring personality change after catastrophic experience
F62.1 Enduring personality change after psychiatric illness
F62.8 Other enduring personality changes
F62.9 Enduring personality change, unspecified

**F63 Habit and impulse disorders**
F63.0 Pathological gambling
F63.1 Pathological fire-setting [pyromania]
F63.2 Pathological stealing [kleptomania]
F63.3 Trichotillomania
F63.8 Other habit and impulse disorders
F63.9 Habit and impulse disorder, unspecified

**F64 Gender identity disorders**
F64.0 Transsexualism
F64.1 Dual-role transvestism
F64.2 Gender identity disorder of childhood
F64.8 Other gender identity disorders
F64.9 Gender identity disorder, unspecified

**F65 Disorders of sexual preference**
F65.0 Fetishism
F65.1 Fetishistic transvestism
F65.2 Exhibitionism
F65.3 Voyeurism
F65.4 Paedophilia
F65.5 Sadomasochism
F65.6 Multiple disorders of sexual preference
F65.8 Other disorders of sexual preference
F65.9 Disorder of sexual preference, unspecified

**F66 Psychological and behavioural disorders associated with sexual development and orientation**
F66.0 Sexual maturation disorder
F66.1 Egodystonic sexual orientation
F66.2 Sexual relationship disorder
F66.8 Other psychosexual development disorders
F66.9 Psychosexual development disorder, unspecified

A fifth character may be used to indicate association with:
　.x 0 Heterosexuality
　.x 1 Homosexuality
　.x 2 Bisexuality
　.x 8 Other, including prepubertal

**F68 Other disorders of adult personality and behaviour**
F68.0 Elaboration of physical symptoms for psychological reasons
F68.1 Intentional production or feigning of symptoms or disabilities, either physical or psychological [factitious disorder]
F68.8 Other specified disorders of adult personality and behaviour

**F69 Unspecified disorder of adult personality and behaviour**

**F70–F79**
**Mental retardation**

**F70 Mild mental retardation**

**F71 Moderate mental retardation**

*Continued*

**Table 9–1**
*Continued*

**F72 Severe mental retardation**

**F73 Profound mental retardation**

**F78 Other mental retardation**

**F79 Unspecified mental retardation**

A fourth character may be used to specify the extent of associated behavioral impairment:

F7x.0 No, or minimal, impairment of behaviour
F7x.1 Significant impairment of behaviour requiring attention or treatment
F7x.8 Other impairments of behaviour
F7x.9 Without mention of impairment of behaviour

**F80–F89**
**Disorders of psychological development**

**F80 Specific developmental disorders of speech and language**

F80.0 Specific speech articulation disorder
F80.1 Expressive language disorder
F80.2 Receptive language disorder
F80.3 Acquired aphasia with epilepsy [Landau-Kleffner syndrome]
F80.8 Other developmental disorders of speech and language
F80.9 Developmental disorder of speech and language, unspecified

**F81 Specific developmental disorders of scholastic skills**

F81.0 Specific reading disorder
F81.1 Specific spelling disorder
F81.2 Specific disorder of arithmetical skills
F81.3 Mixed disorder of scholastic skills
F81.8 Other developmental disorders of scholastic skills
F81.9 Developmental disorder of scholastic skills, unspecified

**F82 Specific developmental disorder of motor function**

**F83 Mixed specific developmental disorders**

**F84 Pervasive developmental disorders**

F84.0 Childhood autism
F84.1 Atypical autism
F84.2 Rett's syndrome
F84.3 Other childhood disintegrative disorder
F84.4 Overactive disorder associated with mental retardation and stereotyped movements
F84.5 Asperger's syndrome
F84.8 Other pervasive developmental disorders
F84.9 Pervasive developmental disorder, unspecified

**F88 Other disorders of psychological development**

**F89 Unspecified disorder of psychological development**

**F90–F98**
**Behavioural and emotional disorders with onset usually occurring in childhood and adolescence**

**F90 Hyperkinetic disorders**

F90.0 Disturbance of activity and attention
F90.1 Hyperkinetic conduct disorder

F90.8 Other hyperkinetic disorders
F90.9 Hyperkinetic disorder, unspecified

**F91 Conduct disorders**

F91.0 Conduct disorder confined to the family context
F91.1 Unsocialized conduct disorder
F91.2 Socialized conduct disorder
F91.3 Oppositional defiant disorder
F91.8 Other conduct disorders
F91.9 Conduct disorder, unspecified

**F92 Mixed disorders of conduct and emotions**

F92.0 Depressive conduct disorder
F92.8 Other mixed disorders of conduct and emotions
F92.9 Mixed disorder of conduct and emotions, unspecified

**F93 Emotional disorders with onset specific to childhood**

F93.0 Separation anxiety disorder of childhood
F93.1 Phobic anxiety disorder of childhood
F93.2 Social anxiety disorder of childhood
F93.3 Sibling rivalry disorder
F93.8 Other childhood emotional disorders
F93.9 Childhood emotional disorder, unspecified

**F94 Disorders of social functioning with onset specific to childhood and adolescence**

F94.0 Elective mutism
F94.1 Reactive attachment disorder of childhood
F94.2 Disinhibited attachment disorder of childhood
F94.8 Other childhood disorders of social functioning
F94.9 Childhood disorders of social functioning, unspecified

**F95 Tic disorders**

F95.0 Transient tic disorder
F95.1 Chronic motor or vocal tic disorder
F95.2 Combined vocal and multiple motor tic disorder [de la Tourette's syndrome]
F95.8 Other tic disorders
F95.9 Tic disorder, unspecified

**F98 Other behavioural and emotional disorders with onset usually occurring in childhood and adolescence**

F98.0 Nonorganic enuresis
F98.1 Nonorganic encopresis
F98.2 Feeding disorder of infancy and childhood
F98.3 Pica of infancy and childhood
F98.4 Stereotyped movement disorders
F98.5 Stuttering [stammering]
F98.6 Cluttering
F98.8 Other specified behavioural and emotional disorders with onset usually occurring in childhood and adolescence
F98.9 Unspecified behavioural and emotional disorders with onset usually occurring in childhood and adolescence

**F99**
**Unspecified mental disorder**

**F99 Mental disorder, not otherwise specified**

Table from World Health Organization: *The ICD-10 Classification of Mental and Behavioural Disorders: Clinical Descriptions and Diagnostic Guidelines.* World Health Organization, Geneva, 1992. Used with permission.

agnosis to be made. Such criteria increase the reliability of the diagnostic process among clinicians.

**Systematic description.** DSM-IV also systematically describes each disorder in terms of its associated features: specific age, cultural, and gender-related features; prevalence, incidence, and risk; course; complications; predisposing factors; familial pattern; and differential diagnosis. In some instances, when many of the specific disorders share common features, that information is included in the introduction to the entire section. Laboratory findings and associated physical examination signs and symptoms are described when relevant. DSM-IV does not purport to be a textbook. No mention is made of theories of causes, management, or treatment, nor are the controversial issues surrounding a particular diagnostic category discussed.

**Diagnostic uncertainties.** DSM-IV provides explicit rules to be used when the information is insufficient (diagnosis to be deferred or provisional) or the patient's clinical presentation and history do not meet the full criteria of a prototypical category (an atypical, residual, or not otherwise specified [NOS] type within the general category).

## Multiaxial Evaluation

DSM-IV is a multiaxial system that evaluates the patient along several variables and contains five axes. Axis I and Axis II comprise the entire classification of mental disorders, 17 major classifications and more than 300 specific disorders (Table 9–2). In many instances the patient has a disorder on both axes. For example, a patient may have major depressive disorder noted on Axis I and obsessive-compulsive personality disorder on Axis II.

**Axis I.** Axis I consists of clinical disorders and other conditions that may be a focus of clinical attention (Table 9–3).

**Axis II.** Axis II consists of personality disorders and mental retardation (Table 9–4). The habitual use of a particular defense mechanism can be indicated on Axis II.

**Axis III.** Axis III lists any physical disorder or general medical condition that is present in addition to the mental

**Table 9–2**
**Classes or Groups of Conditions in DSM-IV**

Disorders usually first diagnosed in infancy, childhood, or adolescence
Delirium, dementia, and amnestic and other cognitive disorders
Mental disorders due to a general medical condition not elsewhere classified
Substance-related disorders
Schizophrenia and other psychotic disorders
Mood disorders
Anxiety disorders
Somatoform disorders
Factitious disorders
Dissociative disorders
Sexual and gender identity disorders
Eating disorders
Sleep disorders
Impulse-control disorders not elsewhere classified
Adjustment disorders
Personality disorders
Other conditions that may be a focus of clinical attention

**Table 9–3**
**Axis I: Clinical Disorders and Other Conditions That May Be a Focus of Clinical Attention**

Disorders usually first diagnosed in infancy, childhood, or adolescence (excluding mental retardation, which is diagnosed on Axis II)
Delirium, dementia, and amnestic, and other cognitive disorders
Mental disorders due to a general medical condition
Substance-related disorders
Schizophrenia and other psychotic disorders
Mood disorders
Anxiety disorders
Somatoform disorders
Factitious disorders
Dissociative disorders
Sexual and gender identity disorders
Eating disorders
Sleep disorders
Impulse-control disorders not elsewhere classified
Adjustment disorders
Other conditions that may be a focus of clinical attention

**Table 9–4**
**Axis II: Personality Disorders and Mental Retardation**

Paranoid personality disorder
Schizoid personality disorder
Schizotypal personality disorder
Antisocial personality disorder
Borderline personality disorder
Histrionic personality disorder
Narcissistic personality disorder
Avoidant personality disorder
Dependent personality disorder
Obsessive-compulsive personality disorder
Personality disorder not otherwise specified
Mental retardation

disorder. The physical condition may be causative (for example, kidney failure causing delirium), the result of a mental disorder (for example, alcohol gastritis secondary to alcohol dependence), or unrelated to the mental disorder. When a medical condition is causative or causally related to a mental disorder, a mental disorder due to a general condition is listed on Axis I and the general medical condition is listed on both Axis I and Axis III. In DSM-IV's example—a case in which hypothyroidism is a direct cause of major depressive disorder—the designation on Axis I is mood disorder due to hypothyroidism with depressive features, and hypothyroidism is listed again on Axis III (Table 9–5).

**Axis IV.** Axis IV is used to code the psychosocial and environmental problems that significantly contribute to the development or the exacerbation of the current disorder (Table 9–6).

The evaluation of stressors is based on the clinician's assessment of the stress that an average person with similar sociocultural values and circumstances would experience from the psychosocial stressors. That judgment considers the amount of change in the person's life caused by the

**Table 9–5**
**Axis III: ICD-9-CM General Medical Conditions**

Infectious and parasitic diseases (001–139)
Neoplasms (140–239)
Endocrine, nutritional, and metabolic diseases and immunity disorders (240–279)
Diseases of the blood and blood-forming organs (280–289)
Diseases of the nervous system and sense organs (320–389)
Diseases of the circulatory system (390–459)
Diseases of the respiratory system (460–519)
Diseases of the digestive system (520–579)
Diseases of the genitourinary system (580–629)
Complications of pregnancy, childbirth, and the puerperium (630–676)
Diseases of the skin and subcutaneous tissue (680–709)
Diseases of the musculoskeletal system and connective tissue (710–739)
Congenital anomalies (740–759)
Certain conditions originating in the perinatal period (760–779)
Symptoms, signs, and ill-defined conditions (780–799)
Injury and poisoning (800–999)

Table from DSM-IV, *Diagnostic and Statistical Manual of Mental Disorders*, ed 4. Copyright American Psychiatric Association, Washington, 1994. Used with permission.

**Table 9–6**
**Axis IV: Psychosocial and Environmental Problems**

Problems with primary support group
Problems related to the social environment
Educational problems
Occupational problems
Housing problems
Economic problems
Problems with access to health care services
Problems related to interaction with the legal system/crime
Other psychosocial and environmental problems

Table from DSM-IV, *Diagnostic and Statistical Manual of Mental Disorders*, ed 4. Copyright American Psychiatric Association, Washington, 1994. Used with permission.

stressor, the degree to which the event is desired and under the person's control, and the number of stressors. Stressors may be positive (for example, a job promotion) or negative (for example, the loss of a loved one). Information about stressors may be important in formulating a treatment plan that includes attempts to remove the psychosocial stressors or to help the patient cope with them.

**Axis V.** Axis V is a global assessment of functioning (GAF) scale in which the clinician judges the patient's overall level of functioning during a particular time period (for example, the patient's level of functioning at the time of the evaluation or the patient's highest level of functioning for at least a few months during the past year). Functioning is conceptualized as a composite of three major areas: social functioning, occupational functioning, and psychological functioning. The GAF scale, based on a continuum of mental health and mental illness, is a 100-point scale, 100 representing the highest level of functioning in all areas (Table 9–7).

Patients who had a high level of functioning before an episode of illness generally have a better prognosis than do those who had a low level of functioning.

**Multiaxial evaluation report form.** Table 9–8 shows the DSM-IV multiaxial evaluation report form. Examples of how to record the results of a DSM-IV multiaxial evaluation are given in Table 9–9.

**Nonaxial Format**

DSM-IV also allows clinicians who do not wish to use the multiaxial format to list the diagnoses serially, with the principal diagnosis listed first (Table 9–10).

**Severity of Disorder**

Depending on the clinical picture, the presence or the absence of signs and symptoms, and their intensity, the severity of a disorder may be mild, moderate, or severe, and the disorder may be in partial remission or in full remission. The following guidelines are used by DSM-IV.

**Mild.** Few, if any, symptoms in excess of those required to make the diagnosis are present, and symptoms result in no more than minor impairment in social or occupational functioning.

**Moderate.** Symptoms or functional impairment between "mild" and "severe" are present.

**Severe.** Many symptoms in excess of those required to make the diagnosis, or several symptoms that are particularly severe, are present, or the symptoms result in marked impairment in social or occupational functioning.

**In partial remission.** The full criteria for the disorder were previously met, but currently only some of the symptoms or signs of the disorder remain.

**In full remission.** There are no longer any symptoms or signs of the disorder but it is still clinically relevant to note the disorder . . . . The differentiation of in full remission from recovered requires consideration of many factors, including the characteristic course of the disorder, the length of time since the last period of disturbance, the total duration of the disturbance, and the need for continued evaluation or prophylactic treatment.

**Multiple Diagnoses**

When a patient has more than one Axis I disorder, the principal diagnosis is indicated by listing it first. According to DSM-IV:

The remaining disorders are listed in order of focus of attention and treatment. When a person has both an Axis I and an Axis II diagnosis, the principal diagnosis or the reason for visit will be assumed to be on Axis I unless the Axis II diagnosis is followed by the qualifying phrase "(Principal diagnosis)" or "(Reason for visit)."

DSM-IV also states:

When more than one diagnosis for an individual is given in an inpatient setting, the *principal diagnosis* is the condition established after study to be chiefly responsible for occasioning the admission of the individual. When more than one diagnosis is given for an individual in an outpatient setting, the *reason for visit* is the condition that is chiefly responsible for the ambulatory care medical services received during the visit. In most cases, the principal diagnosis or the reason for visit is also the main focus of attention or treatment. It is often difficult (and somewhat arbitrary) to determine which diagnosis is the principal diagnosis or the reason for visit, especially in situations of "dual diagnosis" (a substance-related diagnosis

**Table 9–7**
**Global Assessment of Functioning (GAF) Scale[1]**

Consider psychological, social, and occupational functioning on a hypothetical continuum of mental health-illness. Do not include impairment in functioning due to physical (or environmental) limitations.

| Code | (Note: Use intermediate codes when appropriate, e.g., 45, 68, 72.) |
|---|---|
| 100 | Superior functioning in a wide range of activities, life's problems never seem to get out of hand, is sought out by others because of his or her many |
| 91 | positive qualities. No symptoms. |
| 90 | Absent or minimal symptoms (e.g., mild anxiety before an exam), good functioning in all areas, interested and involved in a wide range of activities, socially effective, generally satisfied with life, no more than everyday problems or concerns (e.g., an occasional argument with |
| 81 | family members). |
| 80 | If symptoms are present, they are transient and expectable reactions to psychosocial stressors (e.g., difficulty concentrating after family argument); no more than slight impairment in social, occupational, or school functioning (e.g., |
| 71 | temporarily falling behind in schoolwork). |
| 70 | Some mild symptoms (e.g., depressed mood and mild insomnia) OR some difficulty in social, occupational, or school functioning (e.g., occasional truancy, or theft within the household), but generally functioning pretty well, has some |
| 61 | meaningful interpersonal relationships. |
| 60 | Moderate symptoms (e.g., flat affect and circumstantial speech, occasional panic attacks) OR moderate difficulty in social, occupational, or school functioning (e.g., few friends, conflicts |
| 51 | with peers or co-workers). |
| 50 | Serious symptoms (e.g., suicidal ideation, severe obsessional rituals, frequent shoplifting) OR any serious impairment in social, occupational, or school functioning (e.g., no friends, unable to |
| 41 | keep a job). |
| 40 | Some impairment in reality testing or communication (e.g., speech is at times illogical, obscure, or irrelevant) OR major impairment in several areas, such as work or school, family relations, judgment, thinking, or mood (e.g., depressed man avoids friends, neglects family, and is unable to work; child frequently beats up younger children, is defiant at home, and is |
| 31 | failing at school). |
| 30 | Behavior is considerably influenced by delusions or hallucinations OR serious impairment in communication or judgment (e.g., sometimes incoherent, acts grossly inappropriately, suicidal preoccupation) OR inability to function in almost all areas (e.g., stays in bed all day; no job, |
| 21 | home, or friends). |
| 20 | Some danger of hurting self or others (e.g., suicide attempts without clear expectation of death, frequently violent, manic excitement) OR occasionally fails to maintain minimal personal hygiene (e.g., smears feces) OR gross impairment in communication (e.g., largely |
| 11 | incoherent or mute). |
| 10 | Persistent danger of severely hurting self or others (e.g., recurrent violence) OR persistent inability to maintain minimal personal hygiene OR serious suicidal act with clear expectation of |
| 1 | death. |
| 0 | Inadequate information. |

[1]The GAF Scale is a revision of the GAS (J Endicott, R L Spitzer, J L Fleiss, J Cohen: The Global Assesment Scale: A procedure for measuring overall severity of psychiatric disturbance. Arch Gen Psychiatry 33: 766, 1976) and CGAS (D Shaffer, M S Gould, J Brasic, P Ambrosini, P Fisher, H Bird, S Aluwahlia: Children's Global Assessment Scale (CGAS). Arch Gen Psychiatry 40: 1228, 1983). They are revisions of the Global Scale of the Health-Sickness Rating Scale (L Luborsky: Clinicians' judgments of mental health. Arch Gen Psychiatry 7: 407, 1962).
Table from DSM-IV, *Diagnostic and Statistical Manual of Mental Disorders,* ed 4. Copyright American Psychiatric Association, Washington, 1994. Used with permission.

**Table 9–8**
**Multiaxial Evaluation Report Form**

The following form is offered as one possibility for reporting multiaxial evaluations. In some settings, this form may be used exactly as is; in other settings, the form may be adapted to satisfy special needs.

AXIS I: Clinical Disorders
      Other Conditions that May Be a Focus of
         Clinical Attention

Diagnostic code      DSM-IV name

___ ___ ___ ___   _____
___ ___ ___ ___   _____
___ ___ ___ ___   _____

AXIS II: Personality Disorders
        Mental Retardation

Diagnostic code      DSM-IV name

___ ___ ___ ___   _____
___ ___ ___ ___   _____

AXIS III: General Medical Conditions

ICD-9-CM code      ICD-9-CM name

___ ___ ___ ___   _____
___ ___ ___ ___   _____
___ ___ ___ ___   _____

AXIS IV: Psychosocial and Environmental Problems
Check:
☐ Problems with primary support group
    *Specify*: _____
☐ Problems related to the social environment
    *Specify*: _____
☐ Educational problems *Specify*: _____
☐ Occupational problems *Specify*: _____
☐ Housing problems *Specify*: _____
☐ Economic problems *Specify*: _____
☐ Problems with access to health care services
    *Specify*: _____
☐ Problems related to interaction with the legal system/crime
    *Specify*: _____
☐ Other psychosocial and environmental problems
    *Specify*: _____

AXIS V: Global Assessment of Functioning Scale
               Score: ___ ___ ___
               Time frame: _____

Table from DSM-IV, *Diagnostic and Statistical Manual of Mental Disorders,* ed 4. Copyright American Psychiatric Association, Washington, 1994. Used with permission.

**Table 9–9**
**Examples of How to Record the Results of a DSM-IV Multiaxial Evaluation**

*Example 1:*

| | | |
|---|---|---|
| Axis I | 296.23 | Major depressive disorder, single episode, severe without psychotic features |
| | 305.00 | Alcohol abuse |
| Axis II | 301.6 | Dependent personality disorder Frequent use of denial |
| Axis III | | None |
| Axis IV | | Threat of job loss |
| Axis V | GAF = 35 | (current) |

*Example 2:*

| | | |
|---|---|---|
| Axis I | 300.4 | Dysthymic disorder |
| | 315.00 | Reading disorder |
| Axis II | V71.09 | No diagnosis |
| Axis III | 382.9 | Otitis media, recurrent |
| Axis IV | | Victim of child neglect |
| Axis V | GAF = 53 | (current) |

*Example 3:*

| | | |
|---|---|---|
| Axis I | 293.83 | Mood disorder due to hypothyroidism, with depressive features |
| Axis II | V71.09 | No diagnosis, histrionic personality features |
| Axis III | 244.9 | Hypothyroidism |
| | 365.23 | Chronic angle-closure glaucoma |
| Axis IV | | None |
| Axis V | GAF = 45 | (on admission) |
| | GAF = 65 | (at discharge) |

*Example 4:*

| | | |
|---|---|---|
| Axis I | V61.1 | Partner relational problem |
| Axis II | V71.09 | No diagnosis |
| Axis III | | None |
| Axis IV | | Unemployment |
| Axis V | GAF = 83 | (highest level past year) |

Table from DSM-IV, *Diagnostic and Statistical Manual of Mental Disorders,* ed 4. Copyright American Psychiatric Association, Washington, 1994. Used with permission.

like Amphetamine Dependence accompanied by a non-substance-related diagnosis like Schizophrenia). For example, it may be unclear which diagnosis should be considered "principal" for an individual hospitalized with both Schizophrenia and Amphetamine Intoxication, because each condition may have contributed equally to the need for admission and treatment.

## Provisional Diagnosis

According to DSM-IV:

The modifier *provisional* can be used when there is a strong presumption that the full criteria will ultimately be met for a disorder, but not enough information is available to make a firm diagnosis. The clinician can indicate the diagnostic uncertainty by writing "(Provisional)" following the diagnosis. For example, the individual appears to have a Major Depressive Disorder, but is unable to give an adequate history to establish that the full criteria are met. Another use of the term *provisional* is for those situations in which differential diagnosis depends exclusively on the duration of illness. For example, a diagnosis of Schizophreniform Disorder requires a duration of less than 6 months and can only be given provisionally if assigned before remission has occurred.

**Table 9–10**
**Nonaxial Format**

Clinicians who do not wish to use the multiaxial format may simply list the appropriate diagnoses. Those choosing this option should follow the general rule of recording as many coexisting mental disorders, general medical conditions, and other factors that are relevant to the care and treatment of the individual. The principal diagnosis or the reason for visit should be listed first.

The examples below illustrate the reporting of diagnoses in a format that does not use the multiaxial system.

*Example 1:*

| | |
|---|---|
| 296.23 | Major depressive disorder, single episode, severe without psychotic features |
| 305.00 | Alcohol abuse |
| 301.6 | Dependent personality disorder Frequent use of denial |

*Example 2:*

| | |
|---|---|
| 300.4 | Dysthymic disorder |
| 315.00 | Reading disorder |
| 382.9 | Otitis media, recurrent |

*Example 3:*

| | |
|---|---|
| 293.83 | Mood disorder due to hypothyroidism, with depressive features |
| 244.9 | Hypothyroidism |
| 365.23 | Chronic angle-closure glaucoma |
| | Histrionic personality features |

*Example 4:*

| | |
|---|---|
| V61.1 | Partner relational problem |

Table from DSM-IV, *Diagnostic and Statistical Manual of Mental Disorders,* ed 4. Copyright American Psychiatric Association, Washington, 1994. Used with permission.

## Prior History

According to DSM-IV:

For some purposes, it may be useful to note a history of the criteria having been met for a disorder even when the individual is considered to be recovered from it. Such past diagnoses of mental disorder would be indicated by using the specifier Prior History (e.g., Separation Anxiety Disorder, Prior History, for an individual with a history of Separation Anxiety Disorder who has no current disorder or who currently meets criteria for Panic Disorder).

## Not Otherwise Specified Categories

According to DSM-IV, "not otherwise specified" (NOS) categories are used as follows:

Because of the diversity of clinical presentations, it is impossible for the diagnostic nomenclature to cover every possible situation. For this reason, each diagnostic class has at least one Not Otherwise Specified (NOS) category and some classes have several NOS categories. There are four situations in which an NOS diagnosis may be appropriate:

- The presentation conforms to the general guidelines for a mental disorder in the diagnostic class, but the symptomatic picture does not meet the criteria for any of the specific disorders. This would occur either when the symptoms are below the diagnostic threshold for one of the specific disorders or when there is an atypical or mixed presentation.

- The presentation conforms to a symptom pattern that has not been included in the DSM-IV classification but that causes clinically significant distress or impairment. Research criteria for some of these symptom patterns have been included in Appendix B ("Criteria Sets and Axes Provided for Further Study"), in which case a page reference to the suggested research criteria set in Appendix B is provided.
- There is uncertainty about etiology (i.e., whether the disorder is due to a general medical condition, is substance induced, or is primary).
- The presentation conforms to the general guidelines for a mental disorder in the diagnostic class, but the symptomatic picture does not meet the criteria for any of the specific disorders. This would occur either when the symptoms are below the diagnostic threshold for one of the specific disorders or when there is an atypical or mixed presentation.

## Frequently Used Criteria

**Criteria used to exclude other diagnoses and to suggest differential diagnoses.** Most of the criteria sets used in DSM-IV include exclusion criteria to establish boundaries between disorders and to clarify differential diagnoses. The wordings of the exclusion criteria reflect the various types of relations between disorders:

- **"Criteria have never been met for . . ."** This exclusion criterion is used to define a lifetime hierarchy between disorders. For example, a diagnosis of Major Depressive Disorder can no longer be given once a Manic Episode has occurred and must be changed to a diagnosis of Bipolar I Disorder.
- **"Criteria are not met for . . ."** This exclusion criterion is used to establish a hierarchy between disorders (or subtypes) defined cross-sectionally. For example, the specifier With Melancholic Features takes precedence over With Atypical Features for describing the current Major Depressive Episode.
- **"does not occur exclusively during the course of . . ."** This exclusion criterion prevents a disorder from being diagnosed when its symptom presentation occurs only during the course of another disorder. For example, dementia is not diagnosed separately if it occurs only during delirium; Conversion Disorder is not diagnosed separately if it occurs only during Somatization Disorder; Bulimia Nervosa is not diagnosed separately if it occurs only during Anorexia Nervosa. This exclusion criterion is typically used in situations in which the symptoms of one disorder are associated features or a subset of the symptoms of the preempting disorder. The clinician should consider periods of partial remission as part of the "course of another disorder." It should be noted that the excluded diagnosis can be given at times when it occurs independently (e.g., when the excluding disorder is in full remission).
- **"not due to the direct physiological effects of a substance (e.g., a drug of abuse, a medication) or a general medical condition."** This exclusion criterion is used to indicate that a substance induced and general medical etiology must be considered and ruled out before the disorder can be diagnosed (e.g., Major Depressive Disorder can be diagnosed only after etiologies based on substance use and a general medical condition have been ruled out).
- **"not better accounted for by . . ."** This exclusion criterion is used to indicate that the disorders mentioned in the criterion must be considered in the differential di-

agnosis of the presenting psychopathology and that, in boundary cases, clinical judgment will be necessary to determine which disorder provides the most appropriate diagnosis. In such cases, the "Differential Diagnosis" section of the text for the disorders should be consulted for guidance.

The general convention in DSM-IV is to allow multiple diagnoses to be assigned for those presentations that meet criteria for more than one DSM-IV disorder. There are three situations in which the above-mentioned exclusion criteria help to establish a diagnostic hierarchy (and thus prevent multiple diagnoses) or to highlight differential diagnostic considerations (and thus discourage multiple diagnoses):

- When a Mental Disorder Due to a General Medical Condition or a Substance-Induced Disorder is responsible for the symptoms, it preempts the diagnosis of the corresponding primary disorder with the same symptoms (e.g., Cocaine-Induced Mood Disorder preempts Major Depressive Disorder). In such cases, an exclusion criterion containing the phrase "not due to the direct effects of . . ." is included in the criteria set for the primary disorder.
- When a more pervasive disorder (e.g., Schizophrenia) has among its defining symptoms (or associated symptoms) what are the defining symptoms of a less pervasive disorder (e.g., Dysthymic Disorder), one of the following three exclusion criteria appears in the criteria set for the less pervasive disorder, indicating that only the more pervasive disorder is diagnosed: "Criteria have never been met for . . .", "Criteria are not met for . . .", "does not occur exclusively during the course of . . . ."
- When there are particularly difficult differential diagnostic boundaries, the phrase "not better accounted for by . . ." is included to indicate that clinical judgment is necessary to determine which diagnosis is most appropriate. For example, Panic Disorder With Agoraphobia includes the criterion "not better accounted for by Social Phobia" and Social Phobia includes the criterion "not better accounted for by Panic Disorder With Agoraphobia" in recognition of the fact that this is a particularly difficult boundary to draw. In some cases, both diagnoses might be appropriate.

**Criteria for substance-induced disorders.** It is often difficult to determine whether presenting symptomatology is substance induced, that is, the direct physiological consequence of Substance Intoxication or Withdrawal, medication use, or toxin exposure. In an effort to provide some assistance in making this determination, the two criteria listed below have been added to each of the Substance-Induced Disorders. These criteria are intended to provide general guidelines, but at the same time allow for clinical judgment in determining whether or not the presenting symptoms are best accounted for by the direct physiological effects of the substance.

- There is evidence from the history, physical examination, or laboratory findings of either (1) or (2):
  (1) the symptoms developed during, or within a month of, Substance Intoxication or Withdrawal.
  (2) medication use is etiologically related to the disturbance.
- The disturbance is not better accounted for by a disorder that is not substance induced. Evidence that the symptoms are better accounted for by a disorder that is not substance induced might include the following: the symptoms precede the onset of the substance use (or medication use); the symptoms persist for a substantial period of time (e.g., about a month) after the cessation of acute

withdrawal or severe intoxication, or are substantially in excess of what would be expected given the type, duration, or amount of the substance used; or there is other evidence that suggests the existence of an independent non-substance-induced disorder (e.g., a history of recurrent non-substance-related episodes).

**Criteria for a mental disorder due to a general medical condition.** The criterion listed below is necessary to establish the etiological requirement for each of the Mental Disorders Due to a General Medical Condition (e.g., Mood Disorder Due to Hypothyroidism). . . .

There is evidence from the history, physical examination, or laboratory findings that the disturbance is the direct physiological consequence of a general medical condition.

## DSM-IV Classification of Mental Disorders

Table 9–11 presents the DSM-IV classification of mental disorders (Axis I and Axis II).

**Table 9–11**
**DSM-IV Classification of Mental Disorders**

### DISORDERS USUALLY FIRST DIAGNOSED IN INFANCY, CHILDHOOD, OR ADOLESCENCE

Mental Retardation
*Note: These are coded on Axis II.*
| | |
|---|---|
| 317 | Mild mental retardation |
| 318.0 | Moderate mental retardation |
| 318.1 | Severe mental retardation |
| 318.2 | Profound mental retardation |
| 319 | Mental retardation, severity unspecified |

Learning Disorders
| | |
|---|---|
| 315.00 | Reading disorder |
| 315.1 | Mathematics disorder |
| 315.2 | Disorder of written expression |
| 315.9 | Learning disorder NOS |

Motor Skills Disorder
| | |
|---|---|
| 315.4 | Developmental coordination disorder |

Communication Disorders
| | |
|---|---|
| 315.31 | Expressive language disorder |
| 315.31 | Mixed receptive-expressive language disorder |
| 315.39 | Phonological disorder |
| 307.0 | Stuttering |
| 307.9 | Communication disorder NOS |

Pervasive Developmental Disorders
| | |
|---|---|
| 299.00 | Autistic disorder |
| 299.80 | Rett's disorder |
| 299.10 | Childhood disintegrative disorder |
| 299.80 | Asperger's disorder |
| 299.80 | Pervasive developmental disorder NOS |

Attention-Deficit and Disruptive Behavior Disorders
| | |
|---|---|
| 314.xx | Attention-deficit/hyperactivity disorder |
| .01 | combined type |
| .00 | predominantly inattentive type |
| .01 | predominantly hyperactive-impulsive type |
| 314.9 | Attention-deficit/hyperactivity disorder NOS |
| 312.8 | Conduct disorder |
| 313.81 | Oppositional defiant disorder |
| 312.9 | Disruptive behavior disorder NOS |

Feeding and Eating Disorders of Infancy or Early Childhood
| | |
|---|---|
| 307.52 | Pica |
| 307.53 | Rumination disorder |
| 307.59 | Feeding disorder of infancy or early childhood |

Tic Disorders
| | |
|---|---|
| 307.23 | Tourette's disorder |
| 307.22 | Chronic motor or vocal tic disorder |
| 307.21 | Transient tic disorder |
| 307.20 | Tic disorder NOS |

Elimination Disorders
| | |
|---|---|
| ——.— | Encopresis |
| 787.6 | With constipation and overflow incontinence |
| 307.7 | Without constipation and overflow incontinence |
| 307.6 | Enuresis (not due to a general medical condition) |

Other Disorders of Infancy, Childhood, or Adolescence
| | |
|---|---|
| 309.21 | Separation anxiety disorder |

| | |
|---|---|
| 313.23 | Selective mutism |
| 313.89 | Reactive attachment disorder of infancy or early childhood |
| 307.3 | Stereotypic movement disorder |
| 313.9 | Disorder of infancy, childhood, or adolescence NOS |

### DELIRIUM, DEMENTIA, AND AMNESTIC AND OTHER COGNITIVE DISORDERS

Delirium
| | |
|---|---|
| 293.0 | Delirium due to a general medical condition |
| ——.— | Substance intoxication delirium (*refer to substance-related disorders for substance-specific codes*) |
| ——.— | Substance withdrawal delirium (*refer to substance-related disorders for substance-specific codes*) |
| ——.— | Delirium due to multiple etiologies (*code each of the specific etiologies*) |
| 780.09 | Delirium NOS |

Dementia
| | |
|---|---|
| 290.xx | Dementia of the Alzheimer's type, with early onset (*also code 331.0 Alzheimer's disease on Axis III*) |
| | .10 uncomplicated |
| | .11 with delirium |
| | .12 with delusions |
| | .13 with depressed mood |
| 290.xx | Dementia of the Alzheimer's type, with late onset (*also code 331.0 Alzheimer's disease on Axis III*) |
| | .0 uncomplicated |
| | .3 with delirium |
| | .20 with delusions |
| | .21 with depressed mood |
| 290.xx | Vascular dementia |
| | .40 uncomplicated |
| | .41 with delirium |
| | .42 with delusions |
| | .43 with depressed mood |

Dementia Due to Other General Medical Conditions
| | |
|---|---|
| 294.9 | Dementia due to HIV disease (*also code 043.1 HIV infection affecting central nervous system on Axis III*) |
| 294.1 | Dementia due to head trauma (*also code 854.00 head injury on Axis III*) |
| 294.1 | Dementia due to Parkinson's disease (*also code 332.0 Parkinson's disease Axis III*) |
| 294.1 | Dementia due to Huntington's disease (*also code 333.4 Huntington's disease on Axis III*) |
| 290.10 | Dementia due to Pick's disease (*also code 331.1 Pick's disease on Axis III*) |
| 290.10 | Dementia due to Creutzfeldt-Jakob disease (*also code 046.1 Creutzfeldt-Jakob disease on Axis III*) |
| 294.1 | Dementia due to other general medical condition |

(*also code the general medical condition on Axis III*)

——.— Substance-induced persisting dementia (*refer to substance-related disorders for substance-specific codes*)

——.— Dementia due to multiple etiologies (*code each of the specific etiologies*)

294.8 Dementia NOS

Amnestic Disorders

294.0 Amnestic disorder due to a general medical condition

——.— Substance-induced persisting amnestic disorder (*refer to substance-related disorders for substance-specific codes*)

294.8 Amnestic disorder NOS

Other Cognitive Disorders

294.9 Cognitive disorder NOS

## MENTAL DISORDERS DUE TO A GENERAL MEDICAL CONDITION NOT ELSEWHERE CLASSIFIED

293.89 Catatonic disorder due to a general medical condition

310.1 Personality change due to a general medical condition

293.9 Mental disorder NOS due to a general medical condition

## SUBSTANCE-RELATED DISORDERS
Alcohol-Related Disorders

Alcohol Use Disorders

303.90 Alcohol dependence
305.00 Alcohol abuse

Alcohol-Induced Disorders

303.00 Alcohol intoxication
291.8 Alcohol withdrawal
291.0 Alcohol intoxication delirium
291.0 Alcohol withdrawal delirium
291.2 Alcohol-induced persisting dementia
291.1 Alcohol-induced persisting amnestic disorder
291.x Alcohol-induced psychotic disorder
.5 with delusions
.3 with hallucinations
291.8 Alcohol-induced mood disorder
291.8 Alcohol-induced anxiety disorder
291.8 Alcohol-induced sexual dysfunction
291.8 Alcohol-induced sleep disorder

291.9 Alcohol-related disorder NOS

Amphetamine (or Amphetamine-like)-Related Disorders

Amphetamine Use Disorders

304.40 Amphetamine dependence
305.70 Amphetamine abuse

Amphetamine-Induced Disorders

292.89 Amphetamine intoxication
292.0 Amphetamine withdrawal
292.81 Amphetamine intoxication delirium
292.xx Amphetamine-induced psychotic disorder
.11 with delusions
.12 with hallucinations
292.84 Amphetamine-induced mood disorder
292.89 Amphetamine-induced anxiety disorder
292.89 Amphetamine-induced sexual dysfunction
292.89 Amphetamine-induced sleep disorder

292.9 Amphetamine-Related disorder NOS

Caffeine-Related Disorders

Caffeine-Induced Disorders

305.90 Caffeine intoxication
292.89 Caffeine-induced anxiety disorder
292.89 Caffeine-induced sleep disorder
292.9 Caffeine-related disorder NOS

Cannabis-Related Disorders

Cannabis Use Disorders

304.30 Cannabis dependence
305.20 Cannabis abuse

Cannabis-Induced Disorders

292.89 Cannabis intoxication
292.81 Cannabis intoxication delirium
292.xx Cannabis-induced psychotic disorder
.11 with delusions
.12 with hallucinations
292.89 Cannabis-induced anxiety disorder
292.9 Cannabis-related disorder NOS

Cocaine-Related Disorders
Cocaine Use Disorders

304.20 Cocaine dependence
305.60 Cocaine abuse

Cocaine-Induced Disorders

292.89 Cocaine intoxication
292.0 Cocaine withdrawal
292.81 Cocaine intoxication delirium
292.xx Cocaine-induced psychotic disorder
.11 with delusions
.12 with hallucinations
292.84 Cocaine-induced mood disorder
292.89 Cocaine-induced anxiety disorder
292.89 Cocaine-induced sexual dysfunction
292.89 Cocaine-induced sleep disorder

292.9 Cocaine-related disorder NOS

Hallucinogen-Related Disorders

Hallucinogen Use Disorders

304.50 Hallucinogen dependence
305.30 Hallucinogen abuse

Hallucinogen-Induced Disorders

292.89 Hallucinogen intoxication
292.89 Hallucinogen persisting perception disorder (flashbacks)
292.81 Hallucinogen intoxication delirium
292.xx Hallucinogen-induced psychotic disorder
.11 with delusions
.12 with hallucinations
292.84 Hallucinogen-induced mood disorder
292.89 Hallucinogen-induced anxiety disorder

292.9 Hallucinogen-related disorder NOS

Inhalant-Related Disorders

Inhalant Use Disorders

304.60 Inhalant dependence
305.90 Inhalant abuse

Inhalant-Induced Disorders

292.89 Inhalant intoxication
292.81 Inhalant intoxication delirium
292.82 Inhalant-induced persisting dementia
292.xx Inhalant-induced psychotic disorder
.11 with delusions
.12 with hallucinations
292.84 Inhalant-induced mood disorder
292.89 Inhalant-induced anxiety disorder

292.9 Inhalant-related disorder NOS

Nicotine-Related Disorder

Nicotine Use Disorder

305.10 Nicotine dependence

Nicotine-Induced Disorder

292.0 Nicotine withdrawal

292.9 Nicotine-related disorder NOS

Opioid-Related Disorders

Opioid Use Disorders

304.00 Opioid dependence
305.50 Opioid abuse

*Continued*

**Table 9–11**
*Continued*

Opioid-Induced Disorders
292.89 Opioid intoxication
292.0 Opioid withdrawal
292.81 Opioid-intoxication delirium
292.xx Opioid-induced psychotic disorder
.11 with delusions
.12 with hallucinations
292.84 Opioid-induced mood disorder
292.89 Opioid-induced sexual dysfunction
292.89 Opioid-induced sleep disorder

292.9 Opioid-related disorder NOS

Phencyclidine (or Phencyclidine-like) Related Disorders

Phencyclidine Use Disorders
304.90 Phencyclidine dependence
305.90 Phencyclidine abuse

Phencyclidine-induced Disorders
292.89 Phencyclidine intoxication
292.81 Phencyclidine intoxication delirium
292.xx Phencyclidine-induced psychotic disorder
.11 with delusions
.12 with hallucinations
292.84 Phencyclidine-induced mood disorder
292.89 Phencyclidine-induced anxiety disorder

292.9 Phencyclidine-related disorder NOS

Sedative-, Hypnotic-, or Anxiolytic-Related Disorders

Sedative, Hypnotic, or Anxiolytic Use Disorders
304.10 Sedative, hypnotic, or anxiolytic dependence
305.40 Sedative, hypnotic, or anxiolytic abuse

Sedative-, Hypnotic-, or Anxiolytic-Induced Disorders
292.89 Sedative, hypnotic, or anxiolytic intoxication
292.0 Sedative, hypnotic, or anxiolytic withdrawal
292.81 Sedative, hypnotic, or anxiolytic intoxication delirium
292.81 Sedative, hypnotic, or anxiolytic withdrawal delirium
292.82 Sedative-, hypnotic-, or anxiolytic-induced persisting dementia
292.83 Sedative-, hypnotic-, or anxiolytic-induced persisting amnestic disorder
292.xx Sedative-, hypnotic-, or anxiolytic-induced psychotic disorder
.11 with delusions
.12 with hallucinations
292.84 Sedative-, hypnotic-, or anxiolytic-induced mood disorder
292.89 Sedative-, hypnotic-, or anxiolytic-induced anxiety disorder
292.89 Sedative-, hypnotic-, or anxiolytic-induced sexual dysfunction
292.89 Sedative-, hypnotic-, or anxiolytic-induced sleep disorder

292.9 Sedative-, hypnotic-, or anxiolytic-related disorder NOS

Polysubstance-Related Disorder
304.80 Polysubstance dependence

Other (or Unknown) Substance-Related Disorders

Other (or Unknown) Substance Use Disorders
304.90 Other (or unknown) substance dependence
305.90 Other (or unknown) substance abuse

Other (or Unknown) Substance-Induced Disorders
292.89 Other (or unknown) substance intoxication
292.0 Other (or unknown) substance withdrawal
292.81 Other (or unknown) substance-induced delirium
292.82 Other (or unknown) substance-induced persisting dementia

292.83 Other (or unknown) substance-induced persisting amnestic disorder
292.xx Other (or unknown) substance-induced psychotic disorder
.11 with delusions
.12 with hallucinations
292.84 Other (or unknown) substance-induced mood disorder
292.89 Other (or unknown) substance-induced anxiety disorder
292.89 Other (or unknown) substance-induced sexual dysfunction
292.89 Other (or unknown) substance-induced sleep disorder

292.9 Other (or unknown) substance-related disorder NOS

**SCHIZOPHRENIA AND OTHER PSYCHOTIC DISORDERS**
295.xx Schizophrenia
.30 paranoid type
.10 disorganized type
.20 catatonic type
.90 undifferentiated type
.60 residual type
295.40 Schizophreniform disorder
295.70 Schizoaffective disorder
297.1 Delusional disorder
298.8 Brief psychotic disorder
297.3 Shared psychotic disorder

293.xx Psychotic disorder due to a general medical condition
.81 with delusions
.82 with hallucinations
——.— Substance-induced psychotic disorder
(*refer to substance-related disorders for substance-specific codes*)
298.9 Psychotic disorder NOS

**MOOD DISORDERS**

*Code current state of major depressive disorder or bipolar I disorder in fifth digit:*

1 mild
2 moderate
3 severe, without psychotic features
4 severe with psychotic features
5 in partial remission
6 in full remission
0 unspecified

Depressive Disorders
296.xx Major depressive disorder
.2x single episode
.3x recurrent
300.4 Dysthymic disorder
311 Depressive disorder NOS

Bipolar Disorders
296.xx Bipolar I disorder
.0x single manic episode
.40 most recent episode hypomanic
.4x most recent episode manic
.6x most recent episode mixed
.5x most recent episode depressed
.7 most recent episode unspecified
296.89 Bipolar II disorder
301.13 Cyclothymic disorder
296.80 Bipolar disorder NOS

293.83 Mood disorder due to a general medical condition
——.— Substance-induced mood disorder
(*refer to substance-related disorders for substance-specific codes*)

296.90    Mood disorder NOS

## ANXIETY DISORDERS

| | |
|---|---|
| 300.01 | Panic disorder without agoraphobia |
| 300.21 | Panic disorder with agoraphobia |
| 300.22 | Agoraphobia without history of panic disorder |
| 300.29 | Specific phobia |
| 300.23 | Social phobia |
| 308.3 | Obsessive-compulsive disorder |
| 309.81 | Posttraumatic stress disorder |
| 300.3 | Acute stress disorder |
| 300.02 | Generalized anxiety disorder |
| 293.89 | Anxiety disorder due to a general medical condition |
| ——.— | Substance-induced anxiety disorder (*refer to substance-related disorders for substance-specific codes*) |
| 300.00 | Anxiety disorder NOS |

## SOMATOFORM DISORDERS

| | |
|---|---|
| 300.81 | Somatization disorder |
| 300.81 | Undifferentiated somatoform disorder |
| 300.11 | Conversion disorder |
| 307.xx | Pain disorder |
| .80 | Associated with psychological factors |
| .89 | Associated with both psychological factors and a general medical condition |
| 300.7 | Hypochondriasis |
| 300.7 | Body dysmorphic disorder |
| 300.81 | Somatoform disorder NOS |

## FACTITIOUS DISORDERS

| | |
|---|---|
| 300.xx | Factitious disorder |
| .16 | with predominantly psychological signs and symptoms |
| .19 | with predominantly physical signs and symptoms |
| .19 | with combined psychological and physical signs and symptoms |
| 300.19 | Factitious disorder NOS |

## DISSOCIATIVE DISORDERS

| | |
|---|---|
| 300.12 | Dissociative amnesia |
| 300.13 | Dissociative fugue |
| 300.14 | Dissociative identity disorder |
| 300.6 | Depersonalization disorder |
| 300.15 | Dissociative disorder NOS |

## SEXUAL AND GENDER IDENTITY DISORDERS

Sexual Dysfunctions
Sexual Desire Disorders

| | |
|---|---|
| 302.71 | Hypoactive sexual desire disorder |
| 302.79 | Sexual aversion disorder |

Sexual Arousal Disorders

| | |
|---|---|
| 302.72 | Female sexual arousal disorder |
| 302.72 | Male erectile disorder |

Orgasmic Disorders

| | |
|---|---|
| 302.73 | Female orgasmic disorder |
| 302.74 | Male orgasmic disorder |
| 302.75 | Premature ejaculation |

Sexual Pain Disorders

| | |
|---|---|
| 302.76 | Dyspareunia (not due to a general medical condition) |
| 306.51 | Vaginismus (not due to a general medical condition) |

Sexual Dysfunction Due to a General Medical Condition

| | |
|---|---|
| 625.8 | Female hypoactive sexual desire disorder due to a general medical condition |
| 608.89 | Male hypoactive sexual desire disorder due to a general medical condition |
| 607.84 | Male erectile disorder due to a general medical condition |
| 625.0 | Female dyspareunia due to a general medical condition |
| 608.89 | Male dyspareunia due to a general medical condition |
| 625.8 | Other female sexual dysfunction due to a general medical condition |
| 608.89 | Other male sexual dysfunction due to a general medical condition |
| ——.— | Substance-induced sexual dysfunction (*refer to substance-related disorders for substance-specific codes*) |
| 302.70 | Sexual dysfunction NOS |

Paraphilias

| | |
|---|---|
| 302.4 | Exhibitionism |
| 302.81 | Fetishism |
| 302.89 | Frotteurism |
| 302.2 | Pedophilia |
| 302.83 | Sexual masochism |
| 302.84 | Sexual sadism |
| 302.3 | Transvestic fetishism |
| 302.82 | Voyeurism |
| 302.9 | Paraphilia NOS |

Gender Identity Disorders

| | |
|---|---|
| 302.xx | Gender identity disorder |
| .6 | In children |
| .85 | In adolescents or adults |
| 302.6 | Gender identity disorder NOS |
| 302.9 | Sexual disorder NOS |

## EATING DISORDERS

| | |
|---|---|
| 307.1 | Anorexia nervosa |
| 307.51 | Bulimia nervosa |
| 307.50 | Eating disorder NOS |

## SLEEP DISORDERS

Primary Sleep Disorders
Dyssomnias

| | |
|---|---|
| 307.42 | Primary insomnia |
| 307.44 | Primary hypersomnia |
| 347 | Narcolepsy |
| 780.59 | Breathing-related sleep disorder |
| 307.45 | Circadian rhythm sleep disorder |
| 307.47 | Dyssomnia NOS |

Parasomnias

| | |
|---|---|
| 307.47 | Nightmare disorder |
| 307.46 | Sleep terror disorder |
| 307.46 | Sleepwalking disorder |
| 307.47 | Parasomnia NOS |

Sleep Disorders Related to Another Mental Disorder

| | |
|---|---|
| 307.42 | Insomnia related to another mental disorder |
| 307.44 | Hypersomnia related to another mental disorder |

Other Sleep Disorders

| | |
|---|---|
| 780.xx | Sleep disorder due to a general medical condition |
| .52 | insomnia type |
| .54 | hypersomnia type |
| .59 | parasomnia type |
| .59 | mixed type |
| ——.— | Substance-induced sleep disorder (*refer to substance-related disorders for substance-specific codes*) |

## IMPULSE-CONTROL DISORDERS NOT ELSEWHERE CLASSIFIED

| | |
|---|---|
| 312.34 | Intermittent explosive disorder |
| 010.00 | Kleptomania |
| 312.33 | Pyromania |
| 312.31 | Pathological gambling |
| 312.39 | Trichotillomania |
| 312.30 | Impulse-control disorder NOS |

## ADJUSTMENT DISORDERS

| | |
|---|---|
| 309.xx | Adjustment disorder |
| .0 | with depressed mood |

*Continued*

**Table 9–11**
*Continued*

| | |
|---|---|
| .24 | with anxiety |
| .28 | with mixed anxiety and depressed mood |
| .3 | with disturbance of conduct |
| .4 | with mixed disturbance of emotions and conduct |
| .9 | Unspecified |

### PERSONALITY DISORDERS
*Note: These are coded on Axis II.*

| | |
|---|---|
| 301.0 | Paranoid personality disorder |
| 301.20 | Schizoid personality disorder |
| 301.22 | Schizotypal personality disorder |
| 301.7 | Antisocial personality disorder |
| 301.83 | Borderline personality disorder |
| 301.50 | Histrionic personality disorder |
| 301.81 | Narcissistic personality disorder |
| 301.82 | Avoidant personality disorder |
| 301.6 | Dependent personality disorder |
| 301.4 | Obsessive-compulsive personality disorder |
| 301.9 | Personality disorder NOS |

### OTHER CONDITIONS THAT MAY BE A FOCUS OF CLINICAL ATTENTION

| | |
|---|---|
| 316 | Psychological factors affecting medical condition<br>*Choose name based on nature of factors:*<br>Mental disorder affecting medical condition<br>Psychological symptoms affecting medical condition<br>Personality traits or coping style affecting medical condition<br>Maladaptive health behaviors affecting medical condition<br>Stress-related physiological response affecting medical conditions<br>Other or unspecified psychological factors affecting medical condition |

Medication-Induced Movement Disorders

| | |
|---|---|
| 332.1 | Neuroleptic-induced parkinsonism |
| 333.92 | Neuroleptic malignant syndrome |
| 333.7 | Neuroleptic-induced acute dystonia |
| 333.99 | Neuroleptic-induced acute akathisia |
| 333.82 | Neuroleptic-induced tardive dyskinesia |
| 333.1 | Medication-induced postural tremor |
| 333.90 | Medication-induced movement disorder NOS |

Other Medication-Induced Disorder

| | |
|---|---|
| 995.2 | Adverse effects of medication NOS |

Relational Problems

| | |
|---|---|
| V61.9 | Relational problem related to a mental disorder or general medical condition |
| V61.20 | Parent-child relational problem |
| V61.1 | Partner relational problem |
| V61.8 | Sibling relational problem |
| V62.81 | Relational problem NOS |

Problems Related to Abuse or Neglect

| | |
|---|---|
| V61.21 | Physical abuse of child (*code 995.5 if focus of attention is on victim*) |
| V61.21 | Sexual abuse of child (*code 995.5 if focus of attention is on victim*) |
| V61.21 | Neglect of child (*code 995.5 if focus of attention is on victim*) |
| V61.1 | Physical abuse of adult (*code 995.81 if focus of attention is on victim*) |
| V61.1 | Sexual abuse of adult (*code 995.81 if focus of attention is on victim*) |

Additional Conditions That May Be a Focus of Clinical Attention

| | |
|---|---|
| V15.81 | Noncompliance with treatment |
| V65.2 | Malingering |
| V71.01 | Adult antisocial behavior |
| V71.02 | Childhood or adolescent antisocial behavior |
| V62.89 | Borderline intellectual functioning |
| 780.9 | Age-related cognitive decline |
| V62.82 | Bereavement |
| V62.3 | Academic problem |
| V62.2 | Occupational problem |
| 313.82 | Identity problem |
| V62.89 | Religious or spiritual problem |
| V62.4 | Acculturation problem |
| V62.89 | Phase of life problem |

### ADDITIONAL CODES

| | |
|---|---|
| 300.9 | Unspecified mental disorder (nonpsychotic) |
| V71.09 | No diagnosis or condition on Axis I |
| 799.9 | Diagnosis or condition deferred on Axis I |
| V71.09 | No diagnosis on Axis II |
| 799.9 | Diagnosis deferred on Axis II |

Table based on DSM-IV, *Diagnostic and Statistical Manual of Mental Disorders,* ed 4. Copyright American Psychiatric Association, Washington, 1994. Used with permission.

**Definition of mental disorder.** According to DSM-IV:

[E]ach of the mental disorders is conceptualized as a clinically significant behavioral or psychological syndrome or pattern that occurs in an individual and that is associated with present distress (e.g., a painful symptom) or disability (i.e., impairment in one or more important areas of functioning) or with a significantly increased risk of suffering death, pain, disability, or an important loss of freedom. In addition, this syndrome or pattern must not be merely an expectable and culturally sanctioned response to a particular event, for example, the death of a loved one. Whatever its original cause, it must currently be considered a manifestation of a behavioral, psychological, or biological dysfunction in the individual. Neither deviant behavior (e.g., political, religious, or sexual), nor conflicts that are primarily between the individual and society are mental disorders unless the deviance or conflict is a symptom of a dysfunction in the individual, as described above . . . .

*Distinction Between* Mental Disorder *and* General Medical Condition. The terms *mental disorder* and *general medical condition* are used throughout this manual. The term *mental disorder* is explained above. The term *general medical condition* is used merely as a convenient shorthand to refer to conditions and disorders that are listed outside the "Mental and Behavioural Disorders" chapter of ICD. It should be recognized that these are merely terms of convenience and should not be taken to imply that there is any fundamental distinction between mental disorders and general medical conditions, that mental disorders are unrelated to physical or biological factors or processes, or that general medical conditions are unrelated to behavioral or psychosocial factors or processes.

**Organization.** The DSM-IV organizational plan is described as follows:

The first section is devoted to "Disorders Usually First Diagnosed in Infancy, Childhood, or Adolescence." This division of the Classification according to age at presentation is for convenience only and is not absolute. Although disorders in this section are usually first evident in childhood and adolescence, some individuals diagnosed with disorders located in this section (e.g., Attention-Deficit/Hyperactivity Disorder) may not present for clinical attention until adulthood. In addition, it is not uncommon for the age at onset for many disorders placed in other sections to be during childhood or adolescence (e.g., Major Depressive Disorder, Schizophrenia, Generalized Anxiety Disorder). Clinicians who work primarily with children and adolescents should therefore be familiar with the entire manual, and those who work primarily with adults should also be familiar with this section.

The next three sections—"Delirium, Dementia, and Amnestic and Other Cognitive Disorders"; "Mental Disorders Due to a General Medical Condition"; and "Substance-Related Disorders"—were grouped together in DSM-III-R under the single heading of "Organic Mental Syndromes and Disorders.". . . As in DSM-III-R, these sections are placed before the remaining disorders in the manual because of their priority in differential diagnosis (e.g., substance-related causes of depressed mood must be ruled out before making a diagnosis of Major Depressive Disorder). To facilitate differential diagnosis, complete lists of Mental Disorders Due to a General Medical Condition and Substance-Related Disorders appear in these sections, whereas the text and criteria for these disorders are placed in the diagnostic sections with disorders with which they share phenomenology. For example, the text and criteria for Substance-Induced Mood Disorder and Mood Disorder Due to a General Medical Condition are included in the Mood Disorders section.

The organizing principle for all the remaining sections (except for Adjustment Disorders) is to group disorders based on their shared phenomenological features in order to facilitate differential diagnosis. The "Adjustment Disorders" section is organized differently in that these disorders are grouped based on their common etiology (e.g., maladaptive reaction to a stressor). Therefore, the Adjustment Disorders include a variety of heterogeneous clinical presentations (e.g., Adjustment Disorder With Depressed Mood, Adjustment Disorder With Anxiety, Adjustment Disorder With Disturbance of Conduct).

Finally, DSM-IV includes a section for Other Conditions That May be a Focus of Clinical Attention.

## Psychosis and Neurosis

**Psychosis.** Although the traditional meaning of the term "psychotic" emphasized loss of reality testing and impairment of mental functioning—manifested by delusions, hallucinations, confusion, and impaired memory—two other meanings have evolved during the past 50 years. In the most common psychiatric use of the term, "psychotic" became synonymous with severe impairment of social and personal functioning characterized by social withdrawal and inability to perform the usual household and occupational roles. The other use of the term specifies the degree of ego regression as the criterion for psychotic illness. As a consequence of those multiple meanings, the term has lost its precision in current clinical and research practice.

According to the glossary of the American Psychiatric Association, the term "psychotic" means grossly impaired in reality testing. The term may be used to describe the behavior of a person at a given time or a mental disorder in which at some time during its course all persons with the disorder have grossly impaired reality testing. With

gross impairment in reality testing, persons incorrectly evaluate the accuracy of their perceptions and thoughts and make incorrect inferences about external reality, even in the face of contrary evidence. The term "psychotic" does not apply to minor distortions of reality that involve matters of relative judgment. For example, depressed persons who underestimate their achievements are not described as psychotic, whereas those who believe that they have caused natural catastrophes are so described.

Direct evidence of psychotic behavior is the presence of either delusions or hallucinations without insight into their pathological nature. The term "psychotic" is sometimes appropriate when behavior is so grossly disorganized that a reasonable inference can be made that reality testing is disturbed. Examples include markedly incoherent speech without apparent awareness by the person that the speech is not understandable and the agitated, inattentive, and disoriented behavior seen in alcohol intoxication delirium. A person with a nonpsychotic mental disorder may exhibit psychotic behavior, although rarely. For example, a person with obsessive-compulsive disorder may at times come to believe in the reality of the danger of being contaminated by shaking hands with strangers. In DSM-IV the psychotic disorders include pervasive developmental disorders, schizophrenia, schizophreniform disorder, schizoaffective disorder, delusional disorder, brief psychotic disorder, shared psychotic disorder, psychotic disorder due to a general medical condition, substance-induced psychotic disorder, and psychotic disorder not otherwise specified. In addition, some severe mood disorders have psychotic features.

**Neurosis.** A neurosis is a chronic or recurrent nonpsychotic disorder characterized mainly by anxiety, which is experienced or expressed directly or is altered through defense mechanisms; it appears as a symptom, such as an obsession, a compulsion, a phobia, or a sexual dysfunction. Although not used in DSM-IV, the term "neurosis" is still found in the literature and in ICD-10. In the third edition of DSM (DSM-III), a neurotic disorder was defined as follows:

A mental disorder in which the predominant disturbance is a symptom or group of symptoms that is distressing to the individual and is recognized by him or her as unacceptable and alien (ego-dystonic); reality testing is grossly intact. Behavior does not actively violate gross social norms (though it may be quite disabling). The disturbance is relatively enduring or recurrent without treatment, and is not limited to a transitory reaction to stressors. There is no demonstrable organic etiology or factor.

In DSM-IV no overall diagnostic class is called "neuroses"; however, many clinicians consider the following diagnostic categories neuroses: anxiety disorders, somatoform disorders, dissociative disorders, sexual disorders, and dysthymic disorder. The term "neuroses" encompasses a broad range of disorders of various signs and symptoms. As such, it has lost any degree of precision except to signify that the person's gross reality testing and personality organization are intact. However, a neurosis can be and usually is sufficient to impair the person's functioning in a number of areas. The authors believe that the term is useful in contemporary psychiatry and should be retained.

**ICD-10.** In ICD-10 a class called neurotic, stress-related, and somatoform disorders encompasses the following: phobic anxiety disorders, other anxiety disorders (including panic disorder, generalized anxiety disorder, and mixed anxiety and depressive disorder), obsessive-compulsive disorder, adjustment disorders, dissociative (conversion) disorders, and somatoform disorders. In addition, ICD-10 includes neurasthenia as a neurotic disorder characterized by mental and physical fatigability, a sense of general instability, irritability, anhedonia, and sleep disturbances. Many of the cases so diagnosed outside the United States fit the descriptions of anxiety disorders and depressive disorders and are diagnosed as such by American psychiatrists.

## Changes from DSM-III-R

The term "organic mental disorders" was eliminated from DSM-IV, because it incorrectly implied that other mental disorders do not have a biological component.

An appendix was added to DSM-IV to reflect the influence of culture and ethnicity on psychiatric assessment and diagnosis. That appendix describes culturally specific symptom patterns, preferred idioms for describing distress, and prevalence when such information is available. It also provides the clinician with guidance on how the clinical presentation may be influenced by the patient's cultural setting.

Multiple personality disorder was renamed "dissociative identity disorder" to highlight the failure of integration that is its central feature.

In DSM-III-R, self-defeating personality disorder was a proposed diagnostic category needing further study; after extensive debate the category was removed from DSM-IV's appendix.

A diagnostic criterion for panic disorder without agoraphobia and panic disorder with agoraphobia now emphasizes worry about the implications of the panic attack or the behavior changes, rather than the frequency of the attacks.

Appendix H lists the corresponding ICD-10 codes for DSM-IV disorders.

## New and Controversial Categories

Proposed new categories that were considered controversial or for which there was insufficient information to warrant inclusion in DSM-IV were placed in Appendix B, "Criteria Sets and Axes Provided for Further Study." Not all psychiatrists agree that those categories are discrete psychological disorders. Moreover, psychiatrists do not agree on the essential diagnostic features. Each category requires systematic research to determine whether it will eventually be included in the official nomenclature. Nevertheless, clinicians should be familiar with the conditions, some of which are already included in ICD-10.

In addition to the categories listed below, DSM-IV includes a list of defense mechanisms that can be added to the principal diagnosis if the clinician chooses.

**Postconcussional disorder.** This disorder is discussed in Section 10.5. In ICD-10 it is referred to as postconcussional

syndrome, which occurs after a head trauma that is usually sufficiently severe to result in loss of consciousness. The symptoms include headache, dizziness (usually lacking the features of true vertigo), fatigue, irritability, difficulty in concentrating and performing mental tasks, memory impairment, insomnia, and reduced tolerance for stress, emotional excitement, and alcohol.

**Mild neurocognitive disorder.** This condition is discussed in Section 10.1.

**Caffeine withdrawal.** This disorder is covered in Section 12.4.

**Postpsychotic depressive disorder of schizophrenia.** This disorder is discussed in Section 14.1. In ICD-10, postschizophrenic depression is described as follows:

"A depressive episode, which may be prolonged, arising in the aftermath of a schizophrenic illness. Some schizophrenic symptoms must still be present but no longer dominate the clinical picture. These persisting schizophrenic symptoms may be "positive" or "negative," though the latter are more common. It is uncertain, and immaterial to the diagnosis, to what extent the depressive symptoms have merely been uncovered by the resolution of earlier psychotic symptoms (rather than being a new development) or are an intrinsic part of schizophrenia rather than a psychological reaction to it. They are rarely sufficiently severe or extensive to meet criteria for a severe depressive episode, and it is often difficult to decide which of the patient's symptoms are due to depression and which to neuroleptic medication or to the impaired volition and affective flattening of schizophrenia itself. This depressive disorder is associated with an increased risk of suicide."

**Simple deteriorative disorder.** This disorder is covered in Section 14.1. In ICD-10 it is described as an uncommon disorder characterized by oddities of conduct, an inability to meet the demands of society, blunting of affect, loss of volition, and social impoverishment. Delusions and hallucinations are not evident.

**Minor depressive disorder, recurrent brief depressive disorder, and premenstrual dysphoric disorder.** These disorders are covered in Section 15.3. Minor depressive disorder is associated with comparatively mild symptoms, such as worry and overconcern with minor autonomic symptoms (for example, tremor and palpitations). Most cases never come to medical or psychiatric attention. In ICD-10, recurrent brief depressive disorder is characterized by recurrent episodes of depression, each of which lasts less than two weeks (typically two to three days) and each of which ends with complete recovery.

**Mixed anxiety-depressive disorder.** This disorder is covered in Section 16.1. Mixed anxiety and depressive disorder is listed in ICD-10, where it is described as encompassing symptoms of both anxiety and depression, neither of which predominates.

**Factitious disorder by proxy.** This disorder is discussed in Chapter 18. It is also known as Munchausen syndrome by proxy. In the disorder, parents feign illness in their children.

**Dissociative trance disorder.** The dissociative disorders are discussed in Chapter 19. ICD-10 lists trance and possession disorders, in which the patient experiences a temporary loss of both the sense of personal identity and full awareness of the surroundings. The disorders are involuntary or unwanted. In some cases the patient acts as if taken over by another personality, spirit, or force.

**Binge-eating disorder.** This disorder is a variant of bulimia nervosa, which is discussed in Section 22.2. It consists of recurrent episodes of binge eating without the compensatory behavior, such as self-induced vomiting and laxative abuse.

**Depressive personality disorder and passive-aggressive personality disorder.** These personality disorders are classified in the not otherwise specified (NOS) category of personality disorders. Chapter 26 describes each disorder.

**Medication-induced movement disorders.** These disorders are caused by the adverse effects of medication. They include (1) parkinsonism, (2) neuroleptic malignant syndrome, (3) acute dystonia, (4) acute akathisia, (5) tardive dyskinesia, (6) postural tremor, and (7) movement disorder NOS. They are discussed in Section 33.2.

### Culture-Bound Syndromes

An appendix of culturally related syndromes includes the name for each condition, the culture in which it was first described, a brief description of its psychopathology, and a list of possibly related DSM-IV categories. Sections 4.6 and 14.1 discuss culture-bound syndromes.

The implication of culture and its relation to diagnosis is set forth in DSM-IV as follows:

Diagnostic assessment can be especially challenging when a clinician from one ethnic or cultural group uses the DSM-IV Classification to evaluate an individual from a different ethnic or cultural group. A clinician who is unfamiliar with the nuances of an individual's cultural frame of reference may incorrectly judge as psychopathology those normal variations in behavior, belief, or experience that are particular to the individual's culture. For example, certain religious practices or beliefs (e.g., hearing or seeing a deceased relative during bereavement) may be misdiagnosed as manifestations of a Psychotic Disorder. Applying Personality Disorder criteria across cultural settings may be especially difficult because of the wide cultural variation in concepts of self, styles of communication, and coping mechanisms.

### Guidelines

**Cautionary statement.** The American Psychiatric Association has issued a cautionary statement concerning the proper use and interpretation of the diagnostic categories in DSM-IV. It reads as follows:

The specified diagnostic criteria for each mental disorder are offered as guidelines for making diagnoses, because it has been demonstrated that the use of such criteria enhances agreement among clinicians and investigators. The proper use of these criteria requires specialized clinical training that provides both a body of knowledge and clinical skills.

These diagnostic criteria and the DSM-IV Classification of mental disorders reflect a consensus of current formulations of evolving knowledge in our field. They do not encompass, however, all the conditions for which people may be treated or appropriate topics for research efforts.

The purpose of DSM-IV is to provide clear descriptions of diagnostic categories in order to enable clinicians and investigators to diagnose, communicate about, study, and treat people with various mental disorders. It is to be understood that inclusion here, for clinical and research purposes, of a diagnostic category such as Pathological Gambling or Pedophilia does not imply that the condition meets legal or other nonmedical criteria for what constitutes mental disease, mental disorder, or mental disability. The clinical and scientific considerations involved in categorization of these conditions as

mental disorders may not be wholly relevant to legal judgments, for example, that take into account such issues as individual responsibility, disability determination, and competency.

**Caveats.** DSM-IV describes specific caveats regarding its use:

LIMITATIONS OF THE CATEGORICAL APPROACH. DSM-IV is a categorical classification that divides mental disorders into types based on criteria sets with defining features. This naming of categories is the traditional method of organizing and transmitting information in everyday life and has been the fundamental approach used in all systems of medical diagnosis. A categorical approach to classification works best when all members of a diagnostic class are homogeneous, when there are clear boundaries between classes, and when the different classes are mutually exclusive. Nonetheless, the limitations of the categorical classification system must be recognized.

In DSM-IV, there is no assumption that each category of mental disorder is a completely discrete entity with absolute boundaries dividing it from other mental disorders or from no mental disorder. There is also no assumption that all individuals described as having the same mental disorder are alike in all important ways. The clinician using DSM-IV should therefore consider that individuals sharing a diagnosis are likely to be heterogeneous even in regard to the defining features of the diagnosis and that boundary cases will be difficult to diagnose in any but a probabilistic fashion. This outlook allows greater flexibility in the use of the system, encourages more specific attention to boundary cases, and emphasizes the need to capture additional clinical information that goes beyond diagnosis. In recognition of the heterogeneity of clinical presentations, DSM-IV often includes polythetic criteria sets, in which the individual need only present with a subset of items from a longer list (e.g., the diagnosis of Borderline Personality Disorder requires only five out of nine items).

It was suggested that the DSM-IV Classification be organized following a dimensional model rather than the categorical model used in DSM-III-R. A dimensional system classifies clinical presentations based on quantification of attributes rather than the assignment to categories and works best in describing phenomena that are distributed continuously and that do not have clear boundaries. Although dimensional systems increase reliability and communicate more clinical information (because they report clinical attributes that might be subthreshold in a categorical system), they also have serious limitations and thus far have been less useful than categorical systems in clinical practice and in stimulating research. Numerical dimensional descriptions are much less familiar and vivid than are the categorical names for mental disorders. Moreover, there is as yet no agreement on the choice of the optimal dimensions to be used for classification purposes. Nonetheless, it is possible that the increasing research on, and familiarity with, dimensional systems may eventually result in their greater acceptance both as a method of conveying clinical information and as a research tool.

USE OF CLINICAL JUDGMENT. DSM-IV is a classification of mental disorders that was developed for use in clinical, educational, and research settings. The diagnostic categories, criteria, and textual descriptions are meant to be employed by individuals with appropriate clinical training and experience in diagnosis. It is important that DSM-IV not be applied mechanically by untrained individuals. The specific diagnostic criteria included in DSM-IV are meant to serve as guidelines to be informed by clinical judgment and are not meant to be used in a cookbook fashion. For example, the exercise of clinical judgment may justify giving a certain diagnosis to an individual even though the clinical presentation falls just short of meeting the full criteria for the diagnosis as long as the symptoms that are present are persistent and severe. On the other hand, lack of familiarity with DSM-IV or excessively flexible and idiosyncratic application of DSM-IV criteria or conventions substantially reduces its utility as a common language for communication.

USE OF DSM-IV IN FORENSIC SETTINGS.    When the DSM-IV categories, criteria, and textual descriptions are employed for forensic purposes, there are significant risks that diagnostic information will be misused or misunderstood. These dangers arise because of the imperfect fit between the questions of ultimate concern to the law and the information contained in a clinical diagnosis. In most situations, the clinical diagnosis of a DSM-IV mental disorder is not sufficient to establish the existence for legal purposes of a "mental disorder," "mental disability," "mental disease," or "mental defect." In determining whether an individual meets a specified legal standard (e.g., for competence, criminal responsibility, or disability), additional information is usually required beyond that contained in the DSM-IV diagnosis. This might include information about the individual's functional impairments and how these impairments affect the particular abilities in question. It is precisely because impairments, abilities, and disabilities vary widely within each diagnostic category that assignment of a particular diagnosis does not imply a specific level of impairment or disability.

Nonclinical decision makers should also be cautioned that a diagnosis does not carry any necessary implications regarding the causes of the individual's mental disorder or its associated impairments. Inclusion of a disorder in the Classification (as in medicine generally) does not require that there be knowledge about its etiology. Moreover, the fact that an individual's presentation meets the criteria for a DSM-IV diagnosis does not carry any necessary implication regarding the individual's degree of control over the behaviors that may be associated with the disorder. Even when diminished control over one's behavior is a feature of the disorder, having the diagnosis in itself does not demonstrate that a particular individual is (or was) unable to control his or her behavior at a particular time.

It must be noted that DSM-IV reflects a consensus about the classification and diagnosis of mental disorders derived at the time of its initial publication. New knowledge generated by research or clinical experience will undoubtedly lead to an increased understanding of the disorders included in DSM-IV, to the identification of new disorders, and to the removal of some disorders in future classifications. The text and criteria sets included in DSM-IV will require reconsideration in light of evolving new information.

The use of DSM-IV in forensic settings should be informed by an awareness of the risks discussed above. When used appropriately, diagnoses and diagnostic information can assist decision makers in their determinations. For example, when the presence of a mental disorder is the predicate for a subsequent legal determination (e.g., involuntary civil commitment), the use of an established system of diagnosis enhances the value and reliability of the determination. By providing a compendium based upon a review of the pertinent clinical and research literature, DSM-IV may facilitate the legal decision-makers' understanding of the relevant characteristics of mental disorders. The literature related to diagnoses also serves as a check on ungrounded speculation about mental disorders and about the functioning of a particular individual. Finally, diagnostic information regarding longitudinal course may improve decision-making when the legal issue concerns an individual's mental functioning at a past or future point in time.

## Decision Trees

Decision trees, also known as algorithms, are diagrammatic tracks that organize the clinician's thinking so that all differential diagnoses are considered and ruled in or out, resulting in a presumptive diagnosis. Beginning with specific signs or symptoms, the psychiatrist follows the positive or negative track down the tree (by answering "yes" or "no") until a point in the tree with no outgoing branches (known as a leaf) is found. That point is the final diagnosis. Figure 9–1 is an example of a decision tree for psychotic disorders. DSM-IV includes an appendix of diagnostic decision trees.

## PSYCHIATRIC RATING SCALES

Psychiatric rating scales, also called rating instruments, provide a way to quantify aspects of a patient's psyche, behavior, and relationships with individuals and society. The measurement of pathology in those areas of a person's life may initially seem to be much less straightforward than the measurement of pathology—hypertension, for example—seen by other medical specialists. Nevertheless, many psychiatric rating scales are able to measure carefully chosen features of well-formulated concepts. Moreover, psychiatrists who do not use those rating scales are left with only their clinical impressions, which are difficult to record in a manner that allows for reliable comparison and communication in the future. Without psychiatric rating scales, quantitative data in psychiatry are crude (for example, length of hospitalization or other treatment, discharge and readmission to hospital, length of relationships or employment, and the presence of legal troubles).

Some commonly used instruments are found in Tables 9–12 through 9–14. Table 9–15 lists a variety of rating scales and the initial reference source for each.

### Characteristics of Rating Scales

Rating scales can be specific or comprehensive, and they can measure both internally experienced variables (for example, mood) and externally observable variables (for example, behavior). Specific scales measure discrete thoughts, moods, or behaviors, such as obsessive thoughts and temper tantrums; comprehensive scales measure broad abstractions, such as depression and anxiety.

**Signs and symptoms.**    Classic items from the mental status examination are the most frequently assessed items on rating scales. Those items include thought disorders, mood disturbances, and gross behaviors. Another type of information covered by rating scales is the assessment of adverse effects from psychotherapeutic drugs. Social adjustments (for example, occupational success and quality of relationships) and psychoanalytic concepts (for example, ego strength and defense mechanisms) are also measured by some rating scales, although the reliability and the validity of such scales are lowered by the absence of agreed-on norms, the high level of inference required on some items, and the lack of independence between measures.

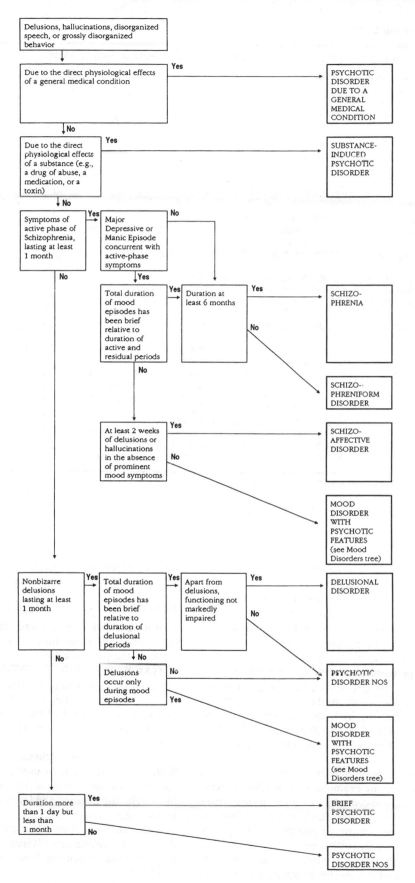

**Figure 9–1.** Differential diagnosis of psychotic disorders. (Figure from DSM-IV, *Diagnostic and Statistical Manual of Mental Disorders*, ed 4. Copyright American Psychiatric Association, Washington, 1994. Used with permission.)

**Table 9–12**
**Brief Psychiatric Rating Scale**

DIRECTIONS: Place an X in the appropriate box to represent level of severity of each symptom.

PATIENT _____
RATER _____
NO. _____
DATE _____

| | Not Present = 0 | Very Mild = 1 | Mild = 2 | Moderate = 3 | Mod. Severe = 4 | Severe = 5 | Extremely Severe = 6 |
|---|---|---|---|---|---|---|---|
| | 0 | 1 | 2 | 3 | 4 | 5 | 6 |
| 1. Somatic concern—preoccupation with physical health, fear of physical illness, hypochondriases | ☐ | ☐ | ☐ | ☐ | ☐ | ☐ | ☐ |
| 2. Anxiety—worry, fear, overconcern for present or future | ☐ | ☐ | ☐ | ☐ | ☐ | ☐ | ☐ |
| 3. Emotional withdrawal—lack of spontaneous interaction, isolation, deficiency in relating to others | ☐ | ☐ | ☐ | ☐ | ☐ | ☐ | ☐ |
| 4. Conceptual disorganization—thought processes confused, disconnected, disorganized, disrupted | ☐ | ☐ | ☐ | ☐ | ☐ | ☐ | ☐ |
| 5. Guilt feelings—self-blame, shame, remorse for past behavior | ☐ | ☐ | ☐ | ☐ | ☐ | ☐ | ☐ |
| 6. Tension—physical and motor manifestations or nervousness, overactivation, tension | ☐ | ☐ | ☐ | ☐ | ☐ | ☐ | ☐ |
| 7. Mannerisms and posturing—peculiar, bizarre unnatural motor behavior (not including tic) | ☐ | ☐ | ☐ | ☐ | ☐ | ☐ | ☐ |
| 8. Grandiosity—exaggerated self-opinion, arrogance, conviction of unusual power or abilities | ☐ | ☐ | ☐ | ☐ | ☐ | ☐ | ☐ |
| 9. Depressive mood—sorrow, sadness, despondency, pessimism | ☐ | ☐ | ☐ | ☐ | ☐ | ☐ | ☐ |
| 10. Hostility—animosity, contempt, belligerence, disdain for others | ☐ | ☐ | ☐ | ☐ | ☐ | ☐ | ☐ |
| 11. Suspiciousness—mistrust, belief that others harbor malicious or discriminatory intent | ☐ | ☐ | ☐ | ☐ | ☐ | ☐ | ☐ |
| 12. Hallucinatory behavior—perceptions without normal external stimulus correspondence | ☐ | ☐ | ☐ | ☐ | ☐ | ☐ | ☐ |
| 13. Motor retardation—slowed, weakened movements or speech, reduced body tone | ☐ | ☐ | ☐ | ☐ | ☐ | ☐ | ☐ |
| 14. Uncooperativeness—resistance, guardedness, rejection of authority | ☐ | ☐ | ☐ | ☐ | ☐ | ☐ | ☐ |
| 15. Unusual thought content—unusual, odd, strange, bizarre thought content | ☐ | ☐ | ☐ | ☐ | ☐ | ☐ | ☐ |
| 16. Blunted affect—reduced emotional tone, reduction in normal intensity of feelings, flatness | ☐ | ☐ | ☐ | ☐ | ☐ | ☐ | ☐ |
| 17. Excitement—heightened emotional tone, agitation, increased reactivity | ☐ | ☐ | ☐ | ☐ | ☐ | ☐ | ☐ |
| 18. Disorientation—confusion or lack of proper association for person, place, or time | ☐ | ☐ | ☐ | ☐ | ☐ | ☐ | ☐ |

Table reproduced with permission of John E. Overall, Ph.D.

**Other characteristics.** Other characteristics of rating scales include the time period covered, the level of judgment required, and the method of recording the answers. The time period covered by a rating scale must be specified, and the rater must adhere to that time period. For example, a particular rating scale may rate a five-minute observation period, a week-long period of time, or the entire life of the patient.

The most reliable rating scales require a limited amount of judgment or inference on the part of the rater. Whatever the level of judgment required, clear definitions of the answer scale, preferably with clinical examples, should be provided by the developer of the scale and should be read by the rater.

The actual answer given may be recorded as either a dichotomous variable (for example, true or false, present or absent) or a continuous variable. Continuous items may ask the rater to choose a term to describe severity (absent, slight, mild, moderate, severe, or extreme) or frequency (never, rarely, occasionally, often, very often, or always). Although many psychiatric symptoms are thought of as existing in dichotomous states—for example, the presence

or the absence of delusions—most experienced clinicians know that the world is not that simple.

### Rating Scales Used in DSM-IV

Rating scales form an integral part of DSM-IV. The rating scales used are broad and measure the overall severity of the patient's illness.

**GAF Scale.** Axis V in DSM-IV uses the Global Assessment of Functioning (GAF) Scale (Table 9–7). That axis is used for reporting the clinician's judgment of the patient's overall level of functioning. The information is used to decide on a treatment plan and later to measure the plan's effect.

**Social and Occupational Functioning Assessment Scale.** This scale can be used to track the patient's progress in social and occupational areas. It is independent of the psychiatric diagnosis and of the severity of the patient's psychological symptoms.

**Other scales.** Two other scales that may be useful are the Global Assessment of Relational Functioning (GARF) Scale and the Defensive Functioning Scale (Tables 9–16 and 9–17).

**Table 9–13**
**Hamilton Anxiety Rating Scale**

*Instructions:* This checklist is to assist the physician or psychiatrist in evaluating each patient as to his degree of anxiety and pathological condition. Please fill in the appropriate rating:

NONE = 0    MILD = 1    MODERATE = 2    SEVERE = 3    SEVERE, GROSSLY DISABLING = 4

| Item | | Rating | Item | | Rating |
|---|---|---|---|---|---|
| Anxious | Worries, anticipation of the worst, fearful anticipation, irritability | | Somatic (sensory) | Tinnitus, blurring of vision, hot and cold flushes, feelings of weakness, picking sensation | |
| Tension | Feelings of tension, fatigability, startle response, moved to tears easily, trembling, feelings of restlessness, inability to relax | | Cardiovascular symptoms | Tachycardia, palpitations, pain in chest, throbbing of vessels, fainting feelings, missing beat | |
| Fears | Of dark, of strangers, of being left alone, of animals, of traffic, of crowds | | Respiratory symptoms | Pressure or constriction in chest, choking feelings, sighing, dyspnea | |
| Insomnia | Difficulty in falling asleep, broken sleep, unsatisfying sleep and fatigue on waking, dreams, nightmares, night-terrors | | Gastrointestinal symptoms | Difficulty in swallowing, wind, abdominal pain, burning sensations, abdominal fullness, nausea, vomiting, borborygmi, looseness of bowels, loss of weight, constipation | |
| Intellectual (cognitive) | Difficulty in concentration, poor memory | | Genitourinary symptoms | Frequency of micturition, urgency of micturition, amenorrhea, menorrhagia, development of frigidity, premature ejaculation, loss of libido, impotence | |
| Depressed mood | Loss of interest, lack of pleasure in hobbies, depression, early waking, diurnal swing | | Autonomic symptoms | Dry mouth, flushing, pallor, tendency to sweat, giddiness, tension headache, raising of hair | |
| Somatic (muscular) | Pains and aches, twitching, stiffness, myoclonic jerks, grinding of teeth, unsteady voice, increased muscular tone | | Behavior at interview | Fidgeting, restlessness or pacing, tremor of hands, furrowed brow, strained face, sighing or rapid respiration, facial pallor, swallowing, belching, brisk tendon jerks, dilated pupils, exophthalmos | |

ADDITIONAL COMMENTS _____

Investigator's signature: _____

Table from M Hamilton: The assessment of anxiety states by rating. Br J Psychiatry *32:* 50, 1959. Used with permission.

**Table 9–14**
**Hamilton Depression Rating Scale**

Clinic No. _____ Date _____ Rating No. _____ Code Number _____

Sex _____ Age _____ Patient's Name _____

Patient's Address _____ Tel. _____

| Item | Range | Score |
|---|---|---|
| 1. Depressed mood | 0–4 | |
| 2. Guilt | 0–4 | |
| 3. Suicide | 0–4 | |
| 4. Insomnia initial | 0–2 | |
| 5. Insomnia middle | 0–2 | |
| 6. Insomnia delayed | 0–2 | |
| 7. Work and interest | 0–4 | |
| 8. Retardation | | |
| 9. Agitation | 0–4 | |
| 10. Anxiety (psychic) | 0–4 | |
| 11. Anxiety (somatic) | 0–4 | |
| 12. Somatic gastrointestinal | 0–2 | |
| 13. Somatic general | 0–2 | |
| 14. Genital | 0–2 | |
| 15. Hypochondriasis | 0–2 | |
| 16. Insight | 0–4 | |
| 17. Loss of weight | 0–2 | |
| | | Total Score |
| Diurnal variation (morning, afternoon, evening) | 0–2 | |
| Depersonalization | 0–4 | |
| Paranoid symptoms | 0–4 | |
| Obsessional symptoms | 0–4 | |

The scale is designed to measure the severity of illness of patients already classified as suffering from depressive illness. It is obviously not a diagnostic instrument because that requires much more information (e.g., previous history, family history, precipitating factors).

As far as possible, the scale should be used in the manner of a clinical interview. The first time, the interview should be conducted in a relaxed, free, and easy manner, giving the patients time to unburden themselves and giving them the opportunity to speak of their problems and ask whatever questions they wish. It may then be necessary to obtain further information by asking them questions. At subsequent assessments, the interview can be briefer and more to the point.

An observer rating scale is not a checklist in which each item is strictly defined. The raters must have sufficient clinical experience and judgment to be able to interpret the patients' statements and reticences about some symptoms and to compare them with other patients. The raters should use all sources of information (e.g., from relatives and nurses).

The scale consists of 17 items, the scores on which are summed to give a total score. There are four other items, one of which (diurnal variation) is excluded on the grounds that it is not an additional burden on the patient. The last three are excluded from the total score because they occur infrequently, although information on them may be useful for other purposes. The method of assessment is simple. For some symptoms it is difficult to elicit such information as will permit of full quantification. If present, score 2; if absent, score 0; and if doubtful or trivial, score 1. For those symptoms for which more detailed information can be obtained, the score of 2 is expanded into 2 for mild, 3 for moderate, and 4 for severe. In case of difficulty, the raters should use their judgment as clinicians.

Table from Maxwell Hamilton: Personal communication to the authors, February 1988.

**Table 9–15**
**Psychiatric Rating Scales**

| Scale | Source |
|---|---|
| **Rating Scales Used for Schizophrenia and Psychosis** | |
| Brief Psychiatric Rating Scale | Psychological Reports *10:* 799, 1962 |
| Schedule for Affective Disorders and Schizophrenia (SADS) | Archives of General Psychiatry *35:* 837, 1978 |
| Scale for the Assessment of Negative Symptoms (SANS) | University of Iowa Press, 1983 |
| Scale for the Assessment of Thought, Language, and Communication (TLC) | University of Iowa Press, 1978 |
| Thought Disorder Index (TDI) | Archives of General Psychiatry *40:* 1281, 1983 |
| Quality of Life Scale (QLS) | Schizophrenia Bulletin *10:* 383, 1984 |
| Chestnut Lodge Prognostic Scale for Chronic Schizophrenia | Schizophrenia Bulletin *13:* 277, 1987 |
| **Rating Scales Used for Mood Disorders** | |
| Beck Depression Inventory | Archives of General Psychiatry *4:* 561, 1961 |
| Standard Assessment of Depressive Disorders (SADD) | Psychological Medicine *10:* 743, 1979 |
| Zung Self-Rating Scale for Depression | Archives of General Psychiatry *12:* 63, 1965 |
| Carroll Rating Scale for Depression | British Journal of Psychiatry *138:* 194, 1981 |
| Montgomery-Asberg Scale | British Journal of Psychiatry *134:* 382, 1979 |
| Raskin Depression Rating Scale | Journal of Nervous and Mental Disease *148:* 87, 1969 |
| Inventory to Diagnose Depression | Archives of General Psychiatry *43:* 1976, 1986 |
| Mania Rating Scale | Journal of Clinical Psychiatry *44:* 98, 1983 |
| Manic State Rating Scale | Archives of General Psychiatry *25:* 256, 1971 |
| **Rating Scales Used for Anxiety Disorders** | |
| Brief Outpatient Psychopathology Scale | Journal of Clinical Pharmacology *9:* 187, 1969 |
| Physicians Questionnaire | Psychopharmacologia *17:* 338, 1970 |
| Covi Anxiety Scale | Psychopharmacology Bulletin *18:* 69, 1982 |
| Anxiety States Inventory | Psychosomatics *12:* 371, 1971 |
| Fear Questionnaire | Behavioral Research and Therapeutics *17:* 263, 1979 |
| Mobility Inventory for Agoraphobia | Behavioral Research and Therapeutics *23:* 35, 1985 |
| Social Avoidance and Distress Scale | Journal of Consulting and Clinical Psychology *33:* 448, 1969 |
| Acute Panic Inventory | Archives of General Psychiatry *41:* 764, 1984 |
| Leyton Obsessional Inventory | Psychological Medicine *1:* 48, 1970 |
| Maudsley Obsessional-Compulsive Inventory | Behavioral Research and Therapeutics *15:* 389, 1977 |
| Fear Thermometer | Journal of Consulting and Clinical Psychiatry *15:* 488, 1983 |
| Impact of Events Scale | Psychosomatic Medicine *41:* 209, 1979 |
| **Other Rating Scales** | |
| *Child and adolescent patients* | |
| General reference for adult scales that have been modified for children | Psychopharmacology Bulletin *21*(4): 737, 1985 |
| *Adverse effects of drugs* | |
| Systematic Assessment for Treatment of Emergent Events (SAFTEE): General Inquiry (GI) Systematic Inquiry (SI) | Psychopharmacology Bulletin *22:* 343, 1986 |
| *Quality of Life* | |
| Patterns of Individual Change Scale (PICS) | Archives of General Psychiatry *42:* 703, 1985 |
| *Dissociative disorders* | |
| Structured Clinical Interview for DSM-IV Dissociative Disorders (SCID-IV) | American Journal of Psychiatry *150*: 1011, 1993. |

**Table 9–16**
**Global Assessment of Relational Functioning (GARF)**

*INSTRUCTIONS:* The GARF Scale can be used to indicate an overall judgment of the functioning of a family or other ongoing relationship on a hypothetical continuum ranging from competent, optimal relational functioning to a disrupted, dysfunctional relationship. It is analogous to Axis V (Global Assessment of Functioning Scale) provided for individuals in DSM-IV. The GARF Scale permits the clinician to rate the degree to which a family or other ongoing relational unit meets the affective and/or instrumental needs of its members in the following areas:

A. *Problem solving*—skills in negotiating goals, rules, and routines; adaptability to stress; communication skills; ability to resolve conflict

B. *Organization*—maintenance of interpersonal roles and subsystem boundaries; hierarchical functioning, coalitions and distribution of power, control and responsibility

C. *Emotional climate*—tone and range of feelings; quality of caring, empathy, involvement and attachment/commitment; sharing of values; mutual affective responsiveness, respect, and regard; quality of sexual functioning.

In most instances, the GARF Scale should be used to rate functioning during the current period (i.e., the level of relational functioning at the time of the evaluation). In some settings, the GARF Scale may also be used to rate functioning for other time periods (i.e., the highest level of relational functioning for at least a few months during the past year). **Note:** Use specific, intermediate codes when possible, for example, 45, 68, 72. If detailed information is not adequate to make specific ratings, use midpoints of the five ranges, that is, 90, 70, 50, 30, or 10.

**(81–100) Overall**: Relational unit is functioning satisfactorily from self-report of participants and from perspectives of observers.

Agreed-on patterns or routines exist that help meet the usual needs of each family/couple member; there is flexibility for change in response to unusual demands or events; occasional conflicts and stressful transitions are resolved through problem-solving communication and negotiation.

There is a shared understanding and agreement about roles and appropriate tasks; decision making is established for each functional area, and there is recognition of the unique characteristics and merit of each subsystem (e.g., parents/spouses, siblings, and individuals).

There is a situationally appropriate, optimistic atmosphere in the family; a wide range of feelings is freely expressed and managed within the family; there is a general atmosphere of warmth, caring, and sharing of values among all family members. Sexual relations of adult members are satisfactory.

**(61–80) Overall**: Functioning of relational unit is somewhat unsatisfactory. Over a period of time, many but not all difficulties are resolved without complaints.

Daily routines are present but there is some pain and difficulty in responding to the unusual. Some conflicts remain unresolved, but do not disrupt family functioning.

Decision making is usually competent, but efforts at control of one another quite often are greater than necessary or are ineffective. Individuals and relationships are clearly demarcated but sometimes a specific subsystem is depreciated or scapegoated.

A range of feeling is expressed, but instances of emotional blocking or tension are evident. Warmth and caring are present but are marred by a family member's irritability and frustrations. Sexual activity of adult members may be reduced or problematic.

**(41–60) Overall**: Relational unit has occasional times of satisfying and competent functioning together, but clearly dysfunctional, unsatisfying relationships tend to predominate.

Communication is frequently inhibited by unresolved conflicts that often interfere with daily routines; there is significant difficulty in adapting to family stress and transitional change.

Decision making is only intermittently competent and effective; either excessive rigidity or significant lack of structure is evident at these times. Individual needs are quite often submerged by a partner or coalition.

Pain or ineffective anger or emotional deadness interfere with family enjoyment. Although there is some warmth and support for members, it is usually unequally distributed. Troublesome sexual difficulties between adults are often present.

**(21–40) Overall:** Relational unit is obviously and seriously dysfunctional; forms and time periods of satisfactory relating are rare.

Family/couple routines do not meet the needs of members; they are grimly adhered to or blithely ignored. Life cycle changes, such as departures or entries into the relational unit, generate painful conflict and obviously frustrating failures of problem solving.

Decision making is tyrannical or quite ineffective. The unique characteristics of individuals are unappreciated or ignored by either rigid or confusingly fluid coalitions.

There are infrequent periods of enjoyment of life together; frequent distancing or open hostility reflect significant conflicts that remain unresolved and quite painful. Sexual dysfunction among adult members is commonplace.

**(1–20) Overall:** Relational unit has become too dysfunctional to retain continuity of contact and attachment.

Family/couple routines are negligible (e.g., no mealtime, sleeping, or waking schedule); family members often do not know where others are or when they will be in or out; there is little effective communication among family members.

Family/couple members are not organized in such a way that personal or generational responsibilities are recognized. Boundaries of relational unit as a whole and subsystems cannot be identified or agreed upon. Family members are physically endangered or injured or sexually attacked.

Despair and cynicism are pervasive; there is little attention to the emotional needs of others; there is almost no sense of attachment, commitment, or concern about one another's welfare.

**0** Inadequate information.

**Table 9–17**
**Defensive Functioning Scale**

**High adaptive level.** This level of defensive functioning results in optimal adaptation in the handling of stressors. These defenses usually maximize gratification and allow the conscious awareness of feelings, ideas, and their consequences. They also promote an optimum balance among conflicting motives. Examples of defenses characteristically at this level are
- anticipation
- affiliation
- altruism
- humor
- self-assertion
- self-observation
- sublimation
- suppression

**Mental inhibitions (compromise formation) level.** Defensive functioning at this level keeps potentially threatening ideas, feelings, memories, wishes, or fears out of awareness. Examples are
- displacement
- dissociation
- intellectualization
- isolation of affect
- reaction formation
- repression
- undoing

**Minor image-distorting level.** This level is characterized by distortions in the image of the self, body, or others that may be employed to regulate self-esteem. Examples are
- devaluation
- idealization
- omnipotence

**Disavowal level.** This level is characterized by keeping unpleasant or unacceptable stressors, impulses, ideas, affect, or responsibility out of awareness with or without a misattribution of these to external causes. Examples are
- denial
- projection
- rationalization

**Major image-distorting level.** This level is characterized by gross distortion or misattribution of the image of self or others. Examples are
- autistic fantasy
- projective identification
- splitting of self-image or image of others

**Action level.** This level is characterized by defensive functioning that deals with internal or external stressors by action or withdrawal. Examples are
- acting out
- apathetic withdrawal
- help-rejecting complaining
- passive aggression

**Level of defensive dysregulation.** This level is characterized by failure of defensive regulation to contain the individual's reaction to stressors, leading to a pronounced break with objective reality. Examples are
- delusional projection
- psychotic denial
- psychotic distortion

Table from DSM-IV, *Diagnostic and Statistical Manual of Mental Disorders*, ed 4. Copyright American Psychiatric Association, Washington, 1994. Used with permission.

## References

Akiskal H S: The classification of mental disorders. In *Comprehensive Textbook of Psychiatry*, ed. 5, H I Kaplan, B J Sadock, editors, p 583. Williams & Wilkins, Baltimore, 1989.

American Psychiatric Association: *Diagnostic and Statistical Manual of Mental Disorders*, ed 4. American Psychiatric Association, Washington, 1994.

Berrios G E, Hauser R: The early development of Kraepelin's ideas on classification: A conceptual history. Psychol Med *18:* 813, 1988.

Bryant K J, Rounsaville B, Spitzer R L, Williams J B: Reliability of dual diagnosis: Substance dependence and psychiatric disorders. J Nerv Ment Dis *180:* 251, 1992.

Buros O K, editor: *Personality Tests and Reviews*. Gryphon, Highland Park, N J, 1970.

Frances A: An introduction to DSM-IV. Hosp Community Psychiatry *41:* 49, 1990.

Fyer A J, Mannuzza S, Endicott J: Differential diagnosis and assessment of anxiety: Recent developments. In *Psychopharmacology: The Third Generation of Progress*, H Y Meltzer, editor, p 326. Raven, New York, 1987.

Goldberg L R: Objective diagnostic tests and measures. Annu Rev Psychol *25:* 102, 1974.

Hughes J R, O'Hara M W, Rehm L P: Measurement of depression in clinical trials: An overview. J Clin Psychiatry *43:* 85, 1982.

Kearns N P, Cruikshank C A, McGuigan K J, Riley S A, Shaw S P, Snaith R P: A comparison of depression rating scales. Br J Psychiatry *141:* 45, 1982.

Kendell R E: *The Role of Diagnosis in Psychiatry*. Blackwell, Oxford, 1975.

Levine J, Ban T A: Assessment methods in clinical trials. In *Psychophar-*macology: The Third Generation of Progress, H Y Meltzer, editor, p 118. Raven, New York, 1987.

Lyerly S B: *Handbook of Psychiatric Rating Scales*, ed 2. National Institute of Mental Health, Bethesda, Md, 1973.

Mezzich J E: International experience with DSM-III. J Nerv Ment Dis *173:* 12, 1985.

Raskin A, Jarvik L S: *Psychiatric Symptoms and Cognitive Loss in the Elderly*. Wiley, New York, 1979.

Riskind J H, Beck A T, Brown G, Steer R A: Taking measure of anxiety and depression. J Nerv Ment Dis *175:* 474, 1987.

Spitzer R L, Williams J B W: *Instruction Manual for the Structured Clinical Interview for DSM-III (SCID) New York*. Biometrics Research Department, State Psychiatric Institute, New York, 1985.

Strauss J S: A comprehensive approach to psychiatric diagnosis. Am J Psychiatry *132:* 1193, 1975.

Waskow I G, Parloff M B: *Psychotherapy Change Measures: Report on the Clinical Research and Branch-NIMH Outcome Measures Project*. National Institute of Mental Health, Bethesda, Md, 1975.

Wilson M: DSM-III and the transformation of American psychiatry: A history. Am J Psychiatry *150:* 399, 1993.

World Health Organization: *The ICD-10 Classification of Mental and Behavioural Disorders: Clinical Descriptions and Diagnostic Guidelines*. World Health Organization, Geneva, 1992.

Zarin D A, Earls F: Diagnostic decision making in psychiatry. Am J Psychiatry *150:* 197, 1993.

Zimmerman M: Is DSM-IV needed at all? Am J Psychiatry *147:* 974, 1990.

Zimmerman M, Coryell W, Black D: Variability in the application of contemporary diagnostic criteria: Endogenous depression as an example. Am J Psychiatry *147:* 1173, 1990.

# Delirium, Dementia, and Amnestic and Other Cognitive Disorders and Mental Disorders Due to a General Medical Condition

## 10.1 / Overview

In its classification of the cognitive disorders, the fourth edition of *Diagnostic and Statistical Manual of Mental Disorders* (DSM-IV) follows in the tradition of the third edition (DSM-III) and the revised third edition (DSM-III-R) by choosing diagnostic nomenclature that is consistent with current clinical experience and reflective of advances in the understanding of those syndromes and disorders. Specifically, just as DSM-III removed references to unsupported theoretical models from its diagnostic criteria, DSM-IV has removed the classic but unsupported distinction between organic and functional psychiatric disorders.

### ORGANIC VERSUS FUNCTIONAL

Traditionally, *organic brain disorders* have been defined as disorders for which there is an identifiable pathology (for example, brain tumor, cerebrovascular disease, drug intoxication). Those brain disorders for which there is no generally accepted organic basis (for example, schizophrenia, depression) have been called *functional disorders*. Historically, the field of neurology has been associated with the treatment of the so-called organic disorders, and psychiatry has been associated with the treatment of the so-called functional disorders.

The authors of DSM-IV have decided that the century-old distinction between organic disorders and functional disorders is outdated enough to be dropped from the nomenclature. The medical, neurological, and psychiatric journals, as well as this and other textbooks, are filled with reports and data about the organic basis of the major psychiatric disorders. No unbiased evaluation of the available data could reach any other conclusion than that every psychiatric disorder has an organic (that is, biological) component. Because of that assessment of the data, the concept of functional disorders has been determined to be misleading, and both the term "functional" and its historical opposite, "organic," are dropped from DSM-IV. Thus, the section called organic mental disorders in DSM-III-R is called delirium, dementia, and amnestic and other cognitive disorders in DSM-IV. Some diagnoses from the former DSM-III-R category of organic mental disorders are found in a new DSM-IV section, mental disorders due to a general medical condition not elsewhere classified.

### STRUCTURAL VERSUS FUNCTIONAL

The other context in which the term "functional" is used is in basic science, in which functional abnormalities are contrasted with structural abnormalities. That distinction is also antiquated, since basic neuroscience can now identify structural correlates of functional abnormalities at the level of genes and other molecules. The division between structural and functional rests solely on which biological level is arbitrarily chosen as the cutoff point. An accurate approach is to accept the ideas that each biological disorder, including mental illness, has a structural pathology at some level or assortment of levels and that the structural abnormality is reflected as a disorder of function or regulation.

### COGNITIVE DISORDERS

DSM-IV classifies three groups of disorders—delirium, dementia, and the amnestic disorders—into a broad category that acknowledges the primary symptoms common to all the disorders—that is, an impairment in cognition (for example, memory, language, or attention). Although DSM-IV acknowledges that other psychiatric disorders can include a degree of cognitive impairment as a symptom, cognitive impairment is the cardinal symptom in delirium, dementia, and the amnestic disorders. Within each of those diagnostic categories, DSM-IV delimits specific types (Table 10.1–1).

For each of the three major categories (delirium, dementia, and amnestic disorders), there are subcategories for disorders caused by (1) general medical conditions, (2) substance use, and (3) causes not otherwise specified (NOS). For delirium and dementia, DSM-IV includes a diagnostic category for multiple causes, which is a commonly encountered clinical situation. For dementia, DSM-IV includes seven general medical conditions as diagnostic possibilities.

**Table 10.1–1**
**DSM-IV Cognitive Disorders**

Delirium
   Delirium due to a general medical condition
   Substance-induced delirium
   Delirium due to multiple etiologies
   Delirium not otherwise specified (NOS)
Dementia
   Dementia of the Alzheimer's type
   Vascular dementia
   Dementia due to other general medical conditions
      Dementia due to HIV disease
      Dementia due to head trauma
      Dementia due to Parkinson's disease
      Dementia due to Huntington's disease
      Dementia due to Pick's disease
      Dementia due to Creutzfeldt-Jakob disease
      Dementia due to other general medical conditions
   Substance-induced persisting dementia
   Dementia due to multiple etiologies
   Dementia not otherwise specified (NOS)
Amnestic disorders
   Amnestic disorder due to a general medical condition
   Substance-induced persisting amnestic disorder
   Amnestic disorder not otherwise specified (NOS)
Cognitive disorder not otherwise specified (NOS)

### Evaluation of Cognitive Impairment

Although formal evaluation of cognitive impairment requires time-consuming consultation with an expert in psychological testing, one practical and clinically useful test for the practitioner is the Mini-Mental State Examination (MMSE) (Table 10.1–2). The MMSE is a screening test that can be used during the clinical examination of a patient. It is also a practical test to track how a patient's cognitive state changes with time. Out of a possible 30 points, a score of less than 25 suggests impairment, and a score of less than 20 indicates definite impairment.

### Cognitive Disorder Not Otherwise Specified

DSM-IV allows for the diagnosis of cognitive disorders that do not fit into the other categories available. Those disorders fit into the not otherwise specified (NOS) category (Table 10.1–3). Patients with syndromes of cognitive impairment that do not meet the criteria for delirium, dementia, or amnestic disorders are classified within the NOS category. The causes of those syndromes are presumed to involve either a specific general medical condition or a pharmacologically active agent or possibly both.

## MENTAL DISORDERS DUE TO A GENERAL MEDICAL CONDITION

Whereas DSM-III and DSM-III-R included such diagnoses as organic mood disorder and organic hallucinosis, DSM-IV introduces two major changes to the nomenclature. First, DSM-IV drops the term "organic" and substitutes the phrase "due to a general medical condition." Second, the psychiatric disorders due to a general medical condition are now included within the DSM-IV diagnostic categories that contain other disorders with the same pri-

**Table 10.1–2**
**Mini-Mental State Examination (MMSE) Questionnaire**

Orientation (score 1 if correct)
   Name this hospital or building. _____
   What city are you in now? _____
   What year is it? _____
   What month is it? _____
   What is the date today? _____
   What state are you in? _____
   What county is this? _____
   What floor of the building are you on? _____
   What day of the week is it? _____
   What season of the year is it? _____

Registration
   Name three objects and have the patient repeat
   them. Score number repeated by the patient.
   Name the three objects several more times if
   needed for the patient to repeat correctly
   (record trials ___). _____

Attention and calculation
   Subtract 7 from 100 in serial fashion to 65. _____
      Maximum score = 5

Recall
   Do you recall the three objects named before? _____

Language tests
   Confrontation naming: watch, pen = 2 _____
   Repetition: "No ifs, ands, or buts" = 1 _____
   Comprehension: Pick up the paper in your right
      hand, fold it in half, and set it on the
      floor = 3 _____
   Read and perform the command "close your
      eyes" = 1 _____
   Write any sentence (subject, verb, object) = 1 _____

Construction
   Copy the design below = 1 _____

Total MMSE questionnaire score (maximum = 30) _____

Table adapted from M F Folstein, S Folstein, P R McHugh: Mini-mental state: A practical method for grading the cognitive state of patients for the clinician. *J Psychiatr Res 12*: 189, 1975. Used with permission.

**Table 10.1–3**
**Diagnostic Criteria for Cognitive Disorder**
**Not Otherwise Specified**

This category is for disorders that are characterized by cognitive dysfunction presumed to be due to the direct physiological effects of a general medical condition that do not meet criteria for any of the specific deliriums, dementias, or amnestic disorders listed in this section and that are not better classified as delirium not otherwise specified, dementia not otherwise specified, or amnestic disorder not otherwise specified. For cognitive dysfunction due to a specific or unknown substance, the specific substance-related disorder not otherwise specified category should be used.
   Examples include
1. Mild neurocognitive disorder: impairment in cognitive functioning as evidenced by neuropsychological testing or quantified clinical assessment, accompanied by objective evidence of a systemic general medical condition or central nervous system dysfunction.
2. Postconcussional disorder: following a head trauma, impairment in memory or attention with associated symptoms.

Table from DSM-IV, *Diagnostic and Statistical Manual of Mental Disorders*, ed 4. Copyright American Psychiatric Association, Washington, 1994. Used with permission.

mary symptom. For example, anxiety disorder due to a general medical condition is now included within the anxiety disorders section of DSM-IV. The inclusion of the secondary psychiatric disorder within the general anxiety disorders section is meant to facilitate a clinician's formulation regarding the differential diagnosis of patients who present with a particular symptom. Delirium, dementia, or amnesia due to a general medical condition is contained in the diagnostic section on delirium, dementia, and amnestic and other cognitive disorders.

The use of the phrase "due to a general medical condition" requires some clarification. The term is meant to convey the clinician's opinion that a particular psychiatric symptom (for example, depression) is probably primarily related to a specific nonpsychiatric disorder (for example, pancreatic cancer) and that the DSM-IV-defined disorder (for example, depression due to pancreatic cancer) is a distinct diagnosis that requires its own treatment plan. The phrase "due to a general medical condition" does not imply a specific temporal relation to the associated nonpsychiatric condition. In the above example, depression associated with pancreatic cancer may be the presenting complaint and, thus, may be identified before the pancreatic cancer is diagnosed. The use of the phrase "due to a general medical condition" can perhaps be criticized as being overly simplistic, since it disregards the other variables that may affect the appearance of a psychiatric symptom in association with a general medical condition. Such other variables may include other biological factors (for example, a genetic diathesis to depression), psychosocial problems, prescribed or illicit drug use, and psychological stressors. Realistically, any diagnostic nosological system must reduce the available information somewhat, and the intent of DSM-IV is to highlight the principal causative factor involved.

Within DSM-IV, most mental disorders due to a general medical condition are listed with other diagnoses for the major symptom, including psychotic disorder due to a general medical condition, mood disorder due to a general medical condition, anxiety disorder due to a general medical condition, sexual dysfunction due to a general medical condition, and sleep disorder due to a general medical condition. The three disorders listed in the DSM-IV section called mental disorders due to a general medical condition not elsewhere classified are catatonic disorder due to a general medical condition, personality change due to a general medical condition, and mental disorder not otherwise specified due to a general medical condition.

### References

Caine E D: Should age-associated cognitive decline be included in DSM-IV? J Neuropsychiatry Clin Neurosci 5: 1, 1993.
Frances A, Pincus H A, Widiger T A, Davis W W, First M B: DSM-IV: Work in progress. Am J Psychiatry 147: 1439, 1990.
Lipowski Z J: Is "organic" obsolete? Psychosomatics 31: 342, 1990.
Reynolds E H: Structure and function in neurology and psychiatry. Br J Psychiatry 157: 481, 1990.
Spitzer R L, First M B, Williams J B W, Kendler K, Pincus H A, Tucker G: Now is the time to retire the term "organic mental disorders." Am J Psychiatry 149: 240, 1992.
Spitzer R L, Williams J B W, First M B, Kendler K S: A proposal for DSM-IV: Solving the "organic/nonorganic problem." J Neuropsychiatry 147: 947, 1990.
Sullivan M D: Organic or functional? Why psychiatry needs a philosophy of mind. Psychiatr Ann 20: 271, 1990.

## 10.2 / Delirium

The hallmark symptom of delirium is an impairment of consciousness, usually seen in association with global impairments of cognitive functions. Abnormalities of mood, perception, and behavior are common psychiatric symptoms; tremor, asterixis, nystagmus, incoordination, and urinary incontinence are common neurological symptoms. Classically, delirium has a sudden onset (hours or days), a brief and fluctuating course, and a rapid improvement when the causative factor is identified and eliminated. However, each of those characteristic features can be variable in individual patients.

Delirium is a syndrome, not a disease. Delirium is acknowledged to have many causes, all of which result in a similar pattern of symptoms relating to the patient's level of consciousness and cognitive impairment. Most of the causes of delirium lie outside the central nervous system—for example, renal or hepatic failure.

Delirium remains an underrecognized and underdiagnosed clinical disorder. Part of the problem is that the syndrome is called a wide variety of other names—for example, acute confusional state, acute brain syndrome, metabolic encephalopathy, toxic psychosis, and acute brain failure. The intent of *Diagnostic and Statistical Manual of Mental Disorders* in its third edition (DSM-III), revised third edition (DSM-III-R), and fourth edition (DSM-IV) has been to help consolidate the myriad terms into a single diagnostic label.

The importance of recognizing delirium involves (1) the clinical need to identify and treat the underlying cause and (2) the need to avert the development of delirium-related complications. Such complications include accidental injury because of the patient's clouded consciousness or impaired coordination or the unnecessary use of restraints. The disruption of ward routine is an especially troubling problem on nonpsychiatric units, such as intensive care units and general medical and surgical wards.

### EPIDEMIOLOGY

Delirium is a common disorder. About 10 to 15 percent of patients on general surgical wards and 15 to 25 percent of patients on general medical wards experience delirium during their hospital stays. About 30 percent of patients in surgical intensive care units and cardiac intensive care units and 40 to 50 percent of patients who are recovering from surgery for hip fractures have an episode of delirium. An estimated 20 percent of patients with severe burns and 30 percent of patients with acquired immune deficiency syndrome (AIDS) have episodes of delirium while hospitalized. The causes of *postoperative delirium* include the stress of surgery, postoperative pain, insomnia, pain medication, electrolyte imbalances, infection, fever, and blood loss.

Advanced age is a major risk factor for the development of delirium. About 30 to 40 percent of hospitalized patients more than 65 years old have an episode of delirium. Other predisposing factors for the development of delirium are young age (that is, children), preexisting brain damage (for example, dementia, cerebrovascular disease, tumor), a history of delirium, alcohol dependence, diabetes, cancer, sensory impairment (for example, blindness), and malnutrition.

The presence of delirium is a bad prognostic sign. The three-month mortality rate of patients who have an episode of delirium is estimated to be 23 to 33 percent. The one-year mortality rate for patients who have an episode of delirium may be as high as 50 percent.

## ETIOLOGY

The major causes of delirium are central nervous system disease (for example, epilepsy), systemic disease (for example, cardiac failure), and either intoxication or withdrawal from pharmacological or toxic agents (Table 10.2–1). When evaluating a delirious patient, the clinician should assume that any drug the patient has taken may be causatively relevant to the delirium.

The major neurotransmitter hypothesized to be involved in delirium is acetylcholine, and the major neuroanatomical area is the reticular formation. Several types of studies have reported that a variety of delirium-inducing factors result in decreased acetylcholine activity in the brain. Also, one of the most common causes of delirium is toxicity from too many prescribed medications that have anticholinergic activity. In addition to the anticholinergic drugs themselves, amitriptyline (Elavil), doxepin (Sinequan), nortriptyline (Aventyl), imipramine (Tofranil), thioridazine (Mellaril), and chlorpromazine (Thorazine) are among the most anticholinergic drugs used in psychiatry. The reticular formation of the brainstem is the principal area regulating attention and arousal, and the major pathway implicated in delirium is the dorsal tegmental pathway, which projects from the mesencephalic reticular formation to the tectum and the thalamus.

Other pathophysiological mechanisms have been suggested for delirium. In particular, the delirium associated with alcohol withdrawal has been associated with hyperactivity of the locus ceruleus and its noradrenergic neurons. Other neurotransmitters that have been implicated are serotonin and glutamate.

### Lithium-Induced Delirium

Patients with lithium serum concentrations greater than 1.5 mEq/L are at risk for delirium. The onset of delirium in those patients may be heralded by general lethary, stammering, stuttering, and muscle fasciculations that develop over the course of several days to a week. Lithium-induced delirium may take up to two weeks to resolve even after lithium administration has been stopped. The appearance of seizures and episodes of stupor during recovery is common. The primary treatments, in addition to stopping lithium administration, are supportive treatment, maintenance of the patient's electrolyte balance, and fa-

**Table 10.2–1**
**Causes of Delirium**

Intracranial causes
  Epilepsy and postictal states
  Brain trauma (especially concussion)
  Infections
    Meningitis
    Encephalitis
  Neoplasms
  Vascular disorders

Extracranial causes
  Drugs (ingestion or withdrawal) and poisons
    Anticholinergic agents
    Anticonvulsants
    Antihypertensive agents
    Antiparkinsonian agents
    Antipsychotic drugs
    Cardiac glycosides
    Cimetidine
    Clonidine
    Disulfiram
    Insulin
    Opiates
    Phencyclidine
    Phenytoin
    Ranitidine
    Salicylates
    Sedatives (including alcohol) and hypnotics
    Steroids
  Poisons
    Carbon monoxide
    Heavy metals and other industrial poisons
  Endocrine dysfunction (hypofunction or hyperfunction)
    Pituitary
    Pancreas
    Adrenal
    Parathyroid
    Thyroid
  Diseases of nonendocrine organs
    Liver
      Hepatic encephalopathy
    Kidney and urinary tract
      Uremic encephalopathy
    Lung
      Carbon dioxide narcosis
      Hypoxia
    Cardiovascular system
      Cardiac failure
      Arrhythmias
      Hypotension
  Deficiency diseases
    Thiamine, nicotinic acid, $B_{12}$, or folic acid deficiencies
  Systemic infections with fever and sepsis
  Electrolyte imbalance of any cause
  Postoperative states
  Trauma (head or general body)

Table adapted from Charles E. Wells, M.D.

cilitation of lithium excretion. The use of proximal segment-acting drugs (for example, aminophylline, acetazolamide [Diamox]) is more effective than the use of distal tubule-acting drugs. The most effective way to eliminate lithium from the patient's body is by hemodialysis, especially if the hemodialysis is done early in the course of the disorder.

## DIAGNOSIS

DSM-IV strives to group all the causes of delirium under one section. Thus, delirium due to a general medical condition (Table 10.2–2), substance intoxication delirium (Table 10.2–3), substance withdrawal delirium (Table 10.2–4), and delirium due to multiple etiologies (Table 10.2–5) are included in the section on delirium. A diagnostic category of delirium not otherwise specified (NOS) (Table 10.2–6) is included for states of delirium due to causes not included in the other categories. DSM-IV gives

### Table 10.2–2
### Diagnostic Criteria for Delirium Due to a General Medical Condition

A. Disturbance of consciousness (i.e., reduced clarity of awareness of the environment) with reduced ability to focus, sustain, or shift attention.
B. A change in cognition (such as memory deficit, disorientation, language disturbance) or the development of a perceptual disturbance that is not better accounted for by a preexisting, established, or evolving dementia.
C. The disturbance develops over a short period of time (usually hours to days) and tends to fluctuate during the course of the day.
D. There is evidence from the history, physical examination, or laboratory findings that the disturbance is caused by the direct physiological consequences of a general medical condition.

**Coding note**: Include the name of the general medical condition on Axis I, e.g., delirium due to hepatic encephalopathy; also code the general medical condition on Axis III.

Table from DSM-IV, *Diagnostic and Statistical Manual of Mental Disorders*, ed 4. Copyright American Psychiatric Association, Washington, 1994. Used with permission.

### Table 10.2–3
### Diagnostic Criteria for Substance Intoxication Delirium

A. Disturbance of consciousness (i.e., reduced clarity of awareness of the environment) with reduced ability to focus, sustain, or shift attention.
B. A change in cognition (such as memory deficit, disorientation, language disturbance) or the development of a perceptual disturbance that is not better accounted for by a preexisting, established, or evolving dementia.
C. The disturbance develops over a short period of time (usually hours to days) and tends to fluctuate during the course of the day.
D. There is evidence from the history, physical examination, or laboratory findings of either (1) or (2):
   (1) the symptoms in criteria A and B developed during substance intoxication
   (2) medication use is etiologically related to the disturbance

**Note:** This diagnosis should be made instead of a diagnosis of substance intoxication only when the cognitive symptoms are in excess of those usually associated with the intoxication syndrome and when the symptoms are sufficiently severe to warrant independent clinical attention.
**Note:** The diagnosis should be recorded as substance-induced delirium if related to medication use.

*Code* [Specific substance] intoxication delirium (Alcohol; amphetamine [or amphetamine-like substance]; cannabis; cocaine; hallucinogen; inhalant; opioid; phencyclidine [or phencyclidine-like substance]; sedative, hypnotic, or anxiolytic; other [or unknown] substance [e.g., cimetidine, digitalis, benztropine])

Table from DSM-IV, *Diagnostic and Statistical Manual of Mental Disorders*, ed 4. Copyright American Psychiatric Association, Washington, 1994. Used with permission.

delirium related to sensory deprivation as an example of such a situation.

### Changes from DSM-III-R

The diagnostic criteria for delirium in DSM-IV have been changed from those in DSM-III-R and are probably less restrictive. DSM-IV has moved closer to the 10th revision of the International Classification of Disease (ICD-10) by making impairment of consciousness the cardinal feature of delirium. DSM-IV is also less specific than DSM-III-R regarding which impairments of cognition are present; DSM-IV merely requires a change in cognition that is "not better accounted for by a preexisting, established, or evolving dementia" (Table 10.2–2).

Substance intoxication delirium and substance withdrawal dementia are included in the section on delirium in DSM-IV (Tables 10.2–3 and 10.2–4), although the clinician is referred to the specific drug involved within the substance-related disorders section. When the diagnosis of substance-related delirium is used, the specific substance should be noted.

### Physical and Laboratory Examination

Delirium is usually diagnosed at the bedside and is characterized by the sudden onset of symptoms. The use of a bedside mental status examination—such as the Mini-Mental State Examination (MMSE) (Table 10.1–2), the Mental Status Examination, or the Face-Hand Test—can be useful in documenting the cognitive impairment and providing a baseline from which to measure the patient's clinical course. The physical examination often reveals clues to the cause of the delirium (Table 10.2–7). The presence of a known physical illness or a history of head trauma or alcohol or other substance dependence increases the likelihood of the diagnosis.

The laboratory workup of a patient with delirium should include standard tests and additional studies indicated by the clinical situation (Table 10.2–8). The electroenceph-

### Table 10.2–4
### Diagnostic Criteria for Substance Withdrawal Delirium

A. Disturbance of consciousness (i.e., reduced clarity of awareness of the environment) with reduced ability to focus, sustain, or shift attention.
B. A change in cognition (such as memory deficit, disorientation, language disturbance) or the development of a perceptual disturbance that is not better accounted for by a preexisting, established, or evolving dementia.
C. The disturbance develops over a short period of time (usually hours to days) and tends to fluctuate during the course of the day.
D. There is evidence from the history, physical examination, or laboratory findings that the symptoms in criteria A and B developed during, or shortly after, a withdrawal syndrome.

**Note:** This diagnosis should be made instead of a diagnosis of substance withdrawal only when the cognitive symptoms are in excess of those usually associated with the withdrawal syndrome and when the symptoms are sufficiently severe to warrant independent clinical attention.

*Code* [Specific substance] withdrawal delirium: (Alcohol; sedative, hypnotic, or anxiolytic; other [or unknown] substance)

Table from DSM-IV, *Diagnostic and Statistical Manual of Mental Disorders*, ed 4. Copyright American Psychiatric Association, Washington, 1994. Used with permission.

**Table 10.2–5**
**Diagnostic Criteria for Delirium Due to Multiple Etiologies**

A. Disturbance of consciousness (i.e., reduced clarity of awareness of the environment) with reduced ability to focus, sustain, or shift attention.
B. A change in cognition (such as memory deficit, disorientation, language disturbance) or the development of a perceptual disturbance that is not better accounted for by a preexisting, established, or evolving dementia.
C. The disturbance develops over a short period of time (usually hours to days) and tends to fluctuate during the course of the day.
D. There is evidence from the history, physical examination, or laboratory findings that the delirium has more than one etiology (e.g., more than one etiological general medical condition, a general medical condition plus substance intoxication or medication side effect).

**Coding note**: Use multiple codes reflecting specific delirium and specific etiologies, e.g., delirium due to viral encephalitis, alcohol withdrawal delirium.

Table from DSM-IV, *Diagnostic and Statistical Manual of Mental Disorders*, ed 4. Copyright American Psychiatric Association, Washington, 1994. Used with permission.

**Table 10.2–6**
**Diagnostic Criteria for Delirium Not Otherwise Specified**

This category should be used to diagnose a delirium that does not meet criteria for any of the specific types of delirium described in this section.
  Examples include
  1) A clinical presentation of delirium that is suspected to be due to a general medical condition or substance use but for which there is insufficient evidence to establish a specific etiology.
  2) Delirium due to causes not listed in this section (e.g., sensory deprivation).

Table from DSM-IV, *Diagnostic and Statistical Manual of Mental Disorders*, ed 4. Copyright American Psychiatric Association, Washington, 1994. Used with permission.

alogram (EEG) in delirium characteristically shows a generalized slowing of activity and may be useful in differentiating delirium from depression or psychosis. The EEG of a delirious patient sometimes shows focal areas of hyperactivity. In rare cases, it may be difficult to differentiate delirium related to epilepsy from delirium related to other causes.

## CLINICAL FEATURES

The key feature of delirium is an impairment of consciousness, which DSM-IV describes as being a "reduced clarity of awareness of the environment," with reduced ability to focus, sustain, or shift attention. Indeed, some investigators have suggested that the inability of delirious patients to maintain attention is the central feature of delirium. Most commonly, the impairment of consciousness and the inability to attend fluctuate over the course of a day, such that relatively lucid periods alternate with symptomatic periods. The delirious state may be preceded over a few days by the development of anxiety, drowsiness, insomnia, transient hallucinations, nightmares, and restlessness. The appearance of those symptoms in a patient who is at risk for delirium should prompt the clinician to monitor the patient carefully. Moreover, patients who

have had a prior episode of delirium are likely to have a recurrent episode under the same conditions.

### Arousal

Two general patterns of abnormal arousal have been noted in patients with delirium. One pattern is characterized by hyperactivity associated with increased alertness. The other pattern is characterized by hypoactivity associated with decreased alertness. Patients with delirium related to substance withdrawal often have the hyperactive delirium, which can also be associated with autonomic signs, such as a flushing, pallor, sweating, tachycardia, dilated pupils, nausea, vomiting, and hyperthermia. Patients with the hypoactive symptoms are occasionally classified as being depressed, catatonic, or demented. Patients with a mixed symptom pattern of hypoactivity and hyperactivity are also seen in clinical settings.

### Orientation

Orientation to time, place, and person should be tested in a patient with delirium. Orientation to time is commonly lost, even in mild cases of delirium. Orientation to place and the ability to recognize other persons (for example, the doctor, family members) may also be impaired in severe cases. A delirious patient rarely loses orientation to self.

### Language and Cognition

Patients with delirium often have abnormalities in language. The abnormalities may include rambling, irrelevant, or incoherent speech, and an impaired ability to comprehend speech. However, DSM-IV no longer requires the presence of an abnormality of language for diagnosis, since such an abnormality may be impossible to diagnosis in a mute patient.

Other cognitive functions that may be impaired in a delirious patient include memory and generalized cognitive functions. The ability to register, retain, and recall memories may be impaired, although the recall of remote memories may be preserved. In addition to decreased attention, patients may have a dramatically decreased cognitive output as a characteristic of the hypoactive symptoms of delirium. Delirious patients also have impaired problem-solving abilities and may also have unsystematized, often paranoid, delusions.

### Perception

Patients with delirium often have a generalized inability to discriminate sensory stimuli and to integrate present perceptions with their past experiences. Therefore, patients are often distracted by irrelevant stimuli or become agitated when presented with new information. Hallucinations are also relatively common in delirious patients. The hallucinations are most often visual or auditory, although they can also be tactile or olfactory. The visual hallucinations can range from simple geometric figures or colored patterns to fully formed people and scenes. Visual and auditory illusions are often common in delirium.

**Table 10.2–7**
**Physical Examination of the Delirious Patient**

| Parameter | Finding | Clinical Implication |
|---|---|---|
| 1. Pulse | Bradycardia | Hypothyroidism<br>Stokes-Adams syndrome<br>Increased intracranial pressure |
| | Tachycardia | Hyperthyroidism<br>Infection<br>Heart failure |
| 2. Temperature | Fever | Sepsis<br>Thyroid storm<br>Vasculitis |
| 3. Blood pressure | Hypotension | Shock<br>Hypothyroidism<br>Addison's disease |
| | Hypertension | Encephalopathy<br>Intracranial mass |
| 4. Respiration | Tachypnea | Diabetes<br>Pneumonia<br>Cardiac failure<br>Fever<br>Acidosis (metabolic) |
| | Shallow | Alcohol or other substance intoxication |
| 5. Carotid vessels | Bruits or decreased pulse | Transient cerebral ischemia |
| 6. Scalp and face | Evidence of trauma | |
| 7. Neck | Evidence of nuchal rigidity | Meningitis<br>Subarachnoid hemorrhage |
| 8. Eyes | Papilledema | Tumor<br>Hypertensive encephalopathy |
| | Pupillary dilatation | Anxiety<br>Autonomic overactivity (e.g., delirium tremens) |
| 9. Mouth | Tongue or cheek lacerations | Evidence of generalized tonic-clonic seizures |
| 10. Thyroid | Enlarged | Hyperthyroidism |
| 11. Heart | Arrhythmia<br>Cardiomegaly | Inadequate cardiac output, possibility of emboli<br>Heart failure<br>Hypertensive disease |
| 12. Lungs | Congestion | Primary pulmonary failure<br>Pulmonary edema<br>Pneumonia |
| 13. Breath | Alcohol<br>Ketones | <br>Diabetes |
| 14. Liver | Enlargement | Cirrhosis<br>Liver failure |
| 15. Nervous system<br>  a. Reflexes—<br>     muscle<br>     stretch | Asymmetry with Babinski's signs<br><br><br>Snout | Mass lesion<br>Cerebrovasclar disease<br>Preexisting dementia<br>Frontal mass<br>Bilateral posterior cerebral artery occlusion |
|   b. Abducent nerve<br>     (sixth cranial<br>     nerve) | Weakness in lateral gaze | Increased intracranial pressure |
|   c. Limb strength | Asymmetrical | Mass lesion<br>Cerebrovascular disease |
|   d. Autonomic | Hyperactivity | Anxiety<br>Delirium |

Table from R L Strub, F W Black: *Neurobehavioral Disorders: A Clinical Approach*, p 120. Davis, Philadelphia, 1981. Used with permission.

**Table 10.2–8**
**Laboratory Workup of Patient with Delirium**

**Standard Studies**
Blood chemistries (including electrolytes, renal and hepatic
    indexes, and glucose)
Complete blood count (CBC) with white cell differential
Thyroid function tests
Serologic tests for syphilis
Human immunodeficiency virus (HIV) antibody test
Urinalysis
Electrocardiogram (ECG)
Electroencephalogram (EEG)
Chest X-ray
Blood and urine drug screens
**Additional Tests When Indicated**
Blood, urine, and cerebrospinal fluid (CSF) cultures
$B_{12}$, folic acid concentrations
Computed tomography (CT) or magnetic resonance imaging
    (MRI) brain scan
Lumbar puncture and CSF examination

## Mood

Patients with delirium often have abnormalities in the
regulation of mood. The most common symptoms are
anger, rage, and unwarranted fear. Other abnormalities
of mood seen in delirious patients are apathy, depression,
and euphoria. Some patients rapidly alternate among those
emotions within the course of a day.

## Associated Symptoms

**Sleep-wake disturbances.** The sleep of delirious patients is characteristically disturbed. Patients are often
drowsy during the day and can be found napping in their
beds or in the dayrooms. The sleep of delirious patients,
however, is almost always short and fragmented. Sometimes the entire sleep-wake cycle of patients with delirium
is simply reversed. Patients sometimes have an exacerbation of delirious symptoms just about bedtime, a clinical
situation widely known as *sundowning*. Occasionally, the
nightmares and the disturbing dreams of delirious patients
continue into wakefulness as hallucinatory experiences.

**Neurological symptoms.** Patients with delirium commonly have associated neurological symptoms, including
dysphasia, tremor, asterixis, incoordination, and urinary
incontinence. Focal neurological signs can also be seen as
part of the symptom pattern of patients with delirium.

An internist requested a psychiatric consultation on a 59-
year-old antique dealer admitted to the hospital for a workup
of severe hypertension. On the third hospital day the patient
appeared to be depressed. The consultant found him dozing
in bed; it was apparent that the patient had spilled some of
his lunch on the bed sheets. The patient was difficult to arouse;
he responded to his name and looked at the consultant but
did not appear to understand simple questions, such as where
he was or what the date was. He mumbled incoherently and,
when tested, had obvious weakness in his right arm and right
leg. A neurological consultation confirmed the diagnosis of a
cerebrovascular disease.

*Discussion.* Reduced ability to maintain attention (the
patient did not appear to understand simple questions), disorganized thinking (incoherent speech), reduced level of consciousness (he dozed in bed and was difficult to arouse), and
disorganized thinking (his speech was incoherent) in the pres-

ence of evidence of an organic cause (right-sided weakness)
indicated delirium. Although in the past the term "delirium"
had the connotation of an agitated or excited confusional state,
recently the essence of the syndrome is thought to be a disturbance in attention and goal-directed thinking. Other common symptoms of delirium, which the patient did not display,
include perceptual disturbances (misinterpretations, illusions,
or hallucinations), increased psychomotor activity, and memory impairment.

Although neurologists generally agree that, technically, the
patient had a delirium when he was seen by the psychiatric
consultant, they would probably not note it in their own diagnostic formulation, as they would focus diagnostically on
the causative process, the cerebrovascular disease.

## DIFFERENTIAL DIAGNOSIS

### Delirium versus Dementia

It is necessary to distinguish delirium from dementia,
and a number of clinical features help in the differentiation
(Table 10.2–9). In contrast to the sudden onset of delirium,
the onset of dementia is usually insidious. Although both
conditions include cognitive impairment, the changes in
dementia are more stable over time and do not fluctuate
over the course of a day, for example. A patient with
dementia is usually alert; a patient with delirium has episodes of decreased consciousness. Occasionally, delirium
occurs in a patient suffering from dementia, a condition
known as *beclouded dementia*. A diagnosis of delirium can
be made when there is a definite history of preexisting
dementia.

**Table 10.2–9**
**Frequency of Clinical Features of Delirium**
**Contrasted with Dementia**

| Feature | Delirium | Dementia |
|---|---|---|
| Impaired memory | + + + | + + + |
| Impaired thinking | + + + | + + + |
| Impaired judgment | + + + | + + + |
| Clouding of consciousness | + + + | − |
| Major attention deficits | + + + | +* |
| Fluctuation over course of a day | + + + | + |
| Disorientation | + + + | + +* |
| Vivid perceptual disturbances | + + | + |
| Incoherent speech | + + | +* |
| Disrupted sleep-wake cycle | + + | +* |
| Nocturnal exacerbation | + + | +* |
| Insight | + +† | +† |
| Acute or subacute onset | + + | −‡ |

+ + + Always present.
+ + Usually present.
+ Occasionally present.
− Usually absent.
*More frequent in advanced stages of dementia.
†Present during lucid intervals or on recovery from delirium; present during
early stages of dementia.
‡Onset may be acute or subacute in some dementias, e.g., multi-infarction,
hypoxemia, certain reversible dementias.
Table from E H Liston: Diagnosis and management of delirium in the elderly
patient. Psychiatr Ann *14*: 117, 1984. Used with permission.

## Delirium versus Psychosis or Depression

Delirium must also be differentiated from schizophrenia and depressive disorders. Patients with factitious disorders may attempt to simulate the symptoms of delirium; however, they usually reveal the factitious nature of their symptoms by inconsistencies on their mental status examinations, and an EEG can easily separate the two diagnoses. Some patients with psychotic disorders, usually schizophrenia, or manic episodes may have episodes of extremely disorganized behavior that may be difficult to distinguish from delirium. In general, however, the hallucinations and the delusions of schizophrenic patients are more constant and better organized than are those of delirious patients. Also, schizophrenic patients usually experience no change in their level of consciousness or orientation. Patients with hypoactive symptoms of delirium may appear somewhat similar to severely depressed patients but can be distinguished on the basis of an EEG. Other psychiatric diagnoses to consider in the differential diagnosis of delirium are brief psychotic disorder, schizophreniform disorder, and dissociative disorders.

## COURSE AND PROGNOSIS

Although the onset of delirium is usually sudden, prodromal symptoms (for example, restlessness and fearfulness) may occur in the days preceding the onset of florid symptoms. The symptoms of delirium usually last as long as the causally relevant factors are present, although delirium generally lasts less than a week. After the identification and the removal of the causative factors, the symptoms of delirium usually recede over a three-to-seven-day period, although some symptoms may take up to two weeks to resolve completely. The older a patient is and the longer the patient has been delirious, the longer it takes for the delirium to resolve. Recall of what transpired during a delirium, once it is over, is characteristically spotty, and the patient may refer to it as a bad dream or a nightmare that is remembered only vaguely. As mentioned in the discussion on epidemiology, the occurrence of delirium is associated with a high mortality rate in the next year, primarily because of the serious nature of the associated medical conditions that lead to delirium.

Whether delirium progresses to dementia has not been demonstrated in carefully controlled studies, although many clinicians believe they have seen such a progression. A clinical observation that has been validated by some studies, however, is that periods of delirium are sometimes followed by depression or posttraumatic stress disorder.

## TREATMENT

The primary goal is to treat the underlying condition that is causing the delirium. When the condition is anticholinergic toxicity, the use of physostigmine salicylate (Antilirium) 1 to 2 mg intravenously (IV) or intramuscularly (IM), with repeated doses in 15 to 30 minutes, may be indicated. The other important goal of treatment is the provision of physical, sensory, and environmental support. Physical support is necessary so that delirious patients do not get into situations in which they may have accidents.

Patients with delirium should be neither sensory-deprived nor overly stimulated by the environment. Usually, delirious patients are helped by having a friend or a relative in the room or by the presence of a regular sitter. Familiar pictures and decorations, the presence of a clock or a calendar, and regular orientations to person, place, and time help delirious patients be comfortable. Delirium can sometimes occur in elderly patients with eye patches after cataract surgery (black-patch delirium). Such patients can be helped by placing pin holes in the patches to let in some stimuli or by occasionally removing one patch at a time during recovery.

## Pharmacological Treatment

The two major symptoms of delirium that may require pharmacological treatment are psychosis and insomnia. The drug of choice for psychosis is haloperidol (Haldol), a butyrophenone antipsychotic drug. Depending on the patient's age, weight, and physical condition, the initial dose may range from 2 to 10 mg intramuscularly, repeated in an hour if the patient remains agitated. As soon as the patient is calm, oral medication in liquid concentrate or tablet form should begin. Two daily oral doses should suffice, with two thirds of the dose being given at bedtime. To achieve the same therapeutic effect, the oral dose should be about 1.5 times higher than the parenteral dose. The effective total daily dosage of haloperidol may range from 5 to 50 mg for the majority of delirious patients.

Droperidol (Inapsine) is a butyrophenone that is available as an alternative IV formulation, although careful monitoring of the electrocardiogram may be prudent with that treatment. Phenothiazines should be avoided in delirious patients, because those drugs are associated with significant anticholinergic activity.

Insomnia is best treated with either benzodiazepines with short half-lives or with hydroxyzine (Vistaril), 25 to 100 mg. Benzodiazepines with long half-lives and barbiturates should be avoided unless they are being used as part of the treatment for the underlying disorder (for example, alcohol withdrawal).

## References

Beresin E: Delirium in the elderly. J Geriatr Psychiatry Neurol *1*: 127, 1988.

Francis J, Kapoor W N: Delirium in hospitalized elderly. J Gen Intern Med *5*: 65, 1990.

Francis J, Martin D, Kapoor W N: A prospective study of delirium in hospitalized elderly. JAMA *263*: 1097, 1990.

Lipowski Z J: Update on delirium. Psychiatr Clin North Am *15*: 335, 1992.

Liptzin B, Levkoff S E, Cleary P D, Pilgrim D M, Reilly C H, Albert M, Wetle T T: An empirical study of diagnostic criteria for delirium. Am J Psychiatry *148*: 454, 1991.

Liston E H: Diagnosis and management of delirium in the elderly patient. Psychiatr Ann *14*: 112, 1984.

Metzger E, Friedman R: Prolongation of the corrected QT and torsades de pointes cardiac arrhythmia associated with intravenous haloperidol in the medically ill. J Clin Psychopharmacol *13*: 128, 1993.

Pompei P: Delirium in hospitalized elderly patients. Hosp Pract (Off Ed) *28*: 69, 1993.

Shapira J, Roper J, Schulzinger J: Managing delirious patients. Nursing *23*: 78, 1993.

Smith L W, Dimsdale J E: Postcardiotomy delirium: Conclusions after 25 years? Am J Psychiatry *146*: 452, 1989.

Taylor D, Lewis S: Delirium. J Neurol Neurosurg Psychiatry *56*: 742, 1993.

Thomas R I, Cameron D J, Fahs M C: A prospective study of delirium and prolonged hospital stay. Arch Gen Psychiatry *45*: 937, 1988.

# 10.3 / Dementia

Dementia is a syndrome characterized by multiple impairments in cognitive functions without impairment in consciousness. The cognitive functions that can be affected in dementia include general intelligence, learning and memory, language, problem solving, orientation, perception, attention and concentration, judgment, and social abilities. The patient's personality is also affected. If the patient has an impairment of consciousness, then the patient probably fits the diagnostic criteria for delirium. In addition, a diagnosis of dementia, according to the fourth edition of *Diagnostic and Statistical Manual of Mental Disorders* (DSM-IV), requires that the symptoms result in a significant impairment in social or occupational functioning and represent a significant decline from a previous level of functioning.

The critical clinical points of dementia are the identification of the syndrome and the clinical workup of its cause. The disorder may be progressive or static, permanent or reversible. An underlying cause is always assumed, although in rare cases it is impossible to determine a specific cause. The potential reversibility of dementia is related to the underlying pathology and to the availability and the application of effective treatment. An estimated 15 percent of persons with dementia have illnesses that are reversible if the physician initiates timely treatment, before irreversible damage has taken place.

## EPIDEMIOLOGY

Dementia is essentially a disease of the aged. Of Americans over the age of 65, about 5 percent have severe dementia, and 15 percent have mild dementia. Of Americans over the age of 80, about 20 percent have severe dementia. Of all patients with dementia, 50 to 60 percent have dementia of the Alzheimer's type, the most common type of dementia. About 5 percent of all persons who reach age 65 have dementia of the Alzheimer's type, compared with 15 to 25 percent of all persons age 85 or older. Patients with dementia of the Alzheimer's type occupy more than 50 percent of nursing home beds. The risk factors for the development of dementia of the Alzheimer's type include being female, having a first-degree relative with the disorder, and having a history of head injury. Down's syndrome is also characteristically associated with the development of dementia of the Alzheimer's type.

The second most common type of dementia is vascular dementia—that is, dementia causally related to cerebrovascular diseases. Vascular dementias account for 15 to 30 percent of all dementia cases. Vascular dementia is most common in persons between the ages of 60 and 70 and is more common in men than in women. Hypertension predisposes a person to the disease. About 10 to 15 percent of patients have coexisting vascular dementia and dementia of the Alzheimer's type.

Other common causes of dementia, each representing 1 to 5 percent of all cases, include head trauma, alcohol-related dementias, and various movement disorder-related dementias—for example, Huntington's disease and Parkinson's disease (Table 10.3–1). Because dementia is a fairly general syndrome, it has many causes, and clinicians must embark on a careful clinical workup of a demented patient to establish the cause of the dementia in that particular patient.

The cost of dementia to society is staggering. By the year 2030 an estimated 20 percent of the population will be more than 65 years old. Thus, the current annual cost of $15 billion for caring for dementia patients is likely to increase even further.

## ETIOLOGY

Dementia has many causes (Table 10.3–1); however, dementia of the Alzheimer's type and vascular dementia together represent as much as 75 percent of all cases. Other causes of dementia that are specified in DSM-IV are Pick's disease, Creutzfeldt-Jakob disease, Huntington's disease, Parkinson's disease, human immunodeficiency virus (HIV), and head trauma.

### Dementia of the Alzheimer's Type

Alois Alzheimer first described the condition that later assumed his name in 1907, when he described a 51-year-old woman with a 4½-year course of progressive dementia. The final diagnosis of Alzheimer's disease is based on a neuropathological examination of the brain; nevertheless, dementia of the Alzheimer's type is commonly diagnosed in the clinical setting after other causes of dementia have been excluded from diagnostic consideration.

Although the cause of dementia of the Alzheimer's type remains unknown, progress has been made in understanding the molecular basis of the amyloid deposits that are a hallmark of the disorder's neuropathology. Some studies have indicated that as many as 40 percent of patients have a family history of dementia of the Alzheimer's type; thus, genetic factors are presumed to play a part in the disorder's development in at least some cases. Additional support for a genetic influence is that the concordance rate for monozygotic twins is higher than the rate for dizygotic twins. And in several well-documented cases the disorder has been transmitted in families through an autosomal dominant gene, although such transmission is rare.

**Neuropathology.** The classic gross neuroanatomical observation of a brain from a patient with Alzheimer's disease is diffuse atrophy (Figure 10.3–1) with flattened cortical sulci and enlarged cerebral ventricles. The classic and pathognomonic microscopic findings are senile plaques, neurofibrillary tangles, neuronal loss (particularly in the cortex and the hippocampus), synaptic loss (perhaps as much as 50 percent in the cortex), and granulovascular degeneration of the neurons. Neurofibrillary tangles are

**Table 10.3–1**
**Disorders That May Produce Dementia**

Alzheimer's disease*

Vascular dementia†
  Varieties: Multiple infarcts (called multi-infarct dementia)
            Lacunae
            Binswanger's disease
            Cortical microinfarction

Drugs and toxins (including chronic alcoholic dementia)‡

Intracranial masses: tumors, subdural masses, brain
  abscesses‡

Anoxia

Trauma
  Head injury‡
  Dementia pugilistica (punch-drunk syndrome)

Normal-pressure hydrocephalus‡

Neurodegenerative disorders
  Parkinson's disease§
  Huntington's disease§
  Progressive supranuclear palsy§
  Pick's disease§
  Amyotrophic lateral sclerosis
  Spinocerebellar degenerations
  Olivopontocerebellar degeneration
  Ophthalmoplegia plus
  Metachromatic leukodystrophy (adult form)
  Hallervorden-Spatz disease
  Wilson's disease

Infections
  Creutzfeldt-Jakob disease
  AIDS§
  Viral encephalitis
  Progressive multifocal leukoencephalopathy
  Behçet's syndrome
  Neurosyphilis
  Chronic bacterial meningitis
  Cryptococcal meningitis
  Other fungal meningitides

Nutritional disorders
  Wernicke-Korsakoff syndrome (thiamine deficiency)‡
  Vitamin $B_{12}$ deficiency
  Folate deficiency
  Pellagra
  Marchiafava-Bignami disease
  ?Zinc deficiency

Metabolic disorders
  Metachromatic leukodystrophy
  Adrenal leukodystrophy
  Dialysis dementia
  Hypothyroidism and hyperthyroidism
  Renal insufficiency, severe
  Cushing's syndrome
  Hepatic insufficiency
  Parathyroid disease

Chronic inflammatory disorders§
  Lupus and other collagen-vascular§ disorders with
    intracerebral vasculitis
  Multiple sclerosis
  Whipple's disease

*Accounts for 50 to 60 percent of cases.
†Accounts for 10 to 20 percent of cases.
‡Accounts for 1 to 5 percent of cases.
§Accounts for about 1 percent of cases.
No symbol: less than 1 percent of cases.
Table from M Rosser: Dementia. In *Diseases of the Nervous System: Clinical Neurobiology*, ed 2, A K Asbury, G M McKhann, W I McDonald, editors, p. 789. Saunders, Philadelphia, 1992. Used with permission.

composed of cytoskeletal elements, primarily phosphorylated tau protein, although other cytoskeletal proteins are also present. Neurofibrillary tangles are not unique to Alzheimer's disease, since they are also found in Down's syndrome, dementia pugilistica (punch-drunk syndrome), Parkinson-dementia complex of Guam, Hallervorden-Spatz disease, and the brains of normal aging persons. Neurofibrillary tangles are commonly found in the cortex, the hippocampus, the substantia nigra, and the locus ceruleus.

Senile plaques, also referred to as amyloid plaques, are much more indicative of Alzheimer's disease, although they are also present in Down's syndrome and, to some extent, in normal aging. Senile plaques are composed of a particular protein, β/A4 and astrocytes, dystrophic neuronal processes, and microglia. The number and the density of senile plaques present in postmortem brains have been correlated with the severity of the disease that affected the person.

**Amyloid precursor protein.** The gene for amyloid precursor protein is on the long arm of chromosome 21. Through the process of differential splicing, there are actually four forms of amyloid precursor protein. The β/A4 protein, which is the major constituent of senile plaques, is a 42-amino acid peptide that is a breakdown product of amyloid precursor protein. In Down's syndrome (trisomy 21), there are three copies of the amyloid precursor protein gene, and in a disease in which there is a mutation at codon 717 in the amyloid precursor protein gene, a pathological process results in the excessive deposition of β/A4 protein. The question of whether abnormal amyloid precursor protein processing is of primary causative significance in Alzheimer's disease remains unanswered; however, many research groups are actively studying both the normal metabolic processing of amyloid precursor protein and its processing in patients with dementia of the Alzheimer's type in an attempt to answer that question.

**Neurotransmitter abnormalities.** The neurotransmitters that are most implicated in the pathophysiology are acetylcholine and norepinephrine, both of which are hypothesized to be hypoactive in Alzheimer's disease. Several studies have reported data consistent with the hypothesis that a specific degeneration of cholinergic neurons is present in the nucleus basalis of Meynert in patients with Alzheimer's disease. Other data in support of a cholinergic deficit in Alzheimer's disease are decreases in acetylcholine and choline acetyltransferase concentrations in the brains. Choline acetyltransferase is the key enzyme for the synthesis of acetylcholine, and a reduction in choline acetyltransferase concentrations suggests a decrease in the number of cholinergic neurons present. Additional support for the cholinergic deficit hypothesis comes from the observation that cholinergic antagonists, such as scopolamine and atropine, impair cognitive abilities, whereas cholinergic agonists, such as physostigmine and arecholine, have been reported to enhance cognitive abilities. The decrease in norepinephrine activity in Alzheimer's disease is suggested by the decrease in norepinephrine-containing neurons in the locus ceruleus that has been found in some pathological examinations of brains from patients with Alzheimer's disease. Two other neurotransmitters that have been implicated in the pathophysiology of Alzheimer's dis-

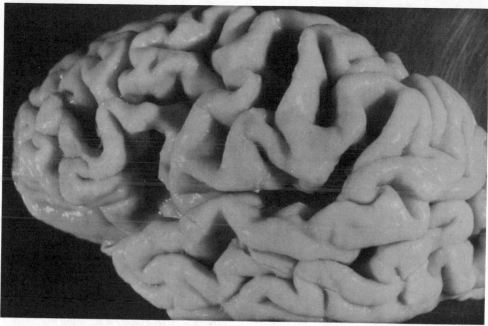

**Figure 10.3–1.**   Gross external appearance of the brain of a patient who had dementia of the Alzheimer's type, with late onset. The leptomeninges have been removed so that the generalized atrophy may be fully appreciated. (Courtesy of Daniel P. Perl, M.D.)

ease are two neuroactive peptides, somatostatin and corticotropin, both of which have been reported to be decreased in Alzheimer's disease.

**Other potential causes.**   Other causative theories have been proposed to explain the development of Alzheimer's disease. One theory is that an abnormality in the regulation of membrane phospholipid metabolism results in membranes that are less fluid—that is, more rigid—than normal. Several investigators are using molecular resonance spectroscopic (MRS) imaging to assess that hypothesis directly in patients with dementia of the Alzheimer's type. Aluminum toxicity has also been hypothesized to be a causative factor, since high levels of aluminum have been found in the brains of some patients with Alzheimer's disease.

A gene (E4) has been implicated in the etiology of Alzheimer's disease. Persons with one copy of the gene had Alzheimer's disease three times more frequently than those with no E4 gene. Persons with two E4 genes had the disease eight times more frequently than persons with no E4 gene.

## Vascular Dementia

The primary cause of vascular dementia is presumed to be multiple cerebral vascular disease, resulting in a symptom pattern of dementia. The disorder was formerly referred to as multi-infarct dementia in the revised third edition of *Diagnostic and Statistical Manual of Mental Disorders* (DSM-III-R). Vascular dementia is most common in men, especially those with preexisting hypertension or other cardiovascular risk factors. The disorder primarily affects small and medium-size cerebral vessels, which undergo infarction and produce multiple parenchymal le-

sions spread over wide areas of the brain (Figure 10.3–2). The cause of the infarctions may include occlusion of the vessels by arteriosclerotic plaques or thromboemboli from distant origins (for example, heart valves). An examination of the patient may reveal carotid bruits, funduscopic abnormalities, or enlarged cardiac chambers.

**Binswanger's disease.**   Binswanger's disease is also known as subcortical arteriosclerotic encephalopathy. It is characterized by the presence of many small infarctions of the white matter, thus sparing the cortical regions. Although Binswanger's disease was previously considered a rare condition, the advent of sophisticated and powerful imaging techniques, such as magnetic resonance imaging (MRI), has revealed that the condition is more common than was previously thought.

## Pick's Disease

In contrast to the parietal-temporal distribution of pathology in Alzheimer's disease, Pick's disease is characterized by a preponderance of atrophy in the frontotemporal regions. Those regions also have neuronal loss, gliosis, and the presence of neuronal Pick's bodies, which are masses of cytoskeletal elements. Pick's bodies are seen in some postmortem specimens but are not necessary for the diagnosis. The cause of Pick's disease is not known. Pick's disease constitutes about 5 percent of all irreversible dementias. It is most common in men, especially those who have a first-degree relative with the condition. Pick's disease is difficult to distinguish from dementia of the Alzheimer's type, although the early stages of Pick's disease are more often characterized by personality and behavioral changes, with a relative preservation of other cognitive functions. Features of Klüver-Bucy syndrome (for exam-

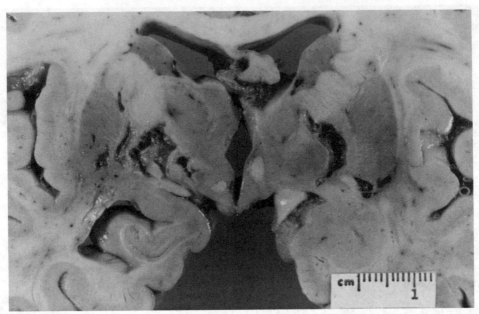

**Figure 10.3–2.** Gross appearance of the cerebral cortex on coronal section from a case of vascular dementia. The multiple bilateral lacunar infarcts involve the thalamus, the internal capsule, and the globus pallidus. (Courtesy of Daniel P. Perl, M.D.)

ple, hypersexuality, placidity, and hyperorality) are much more common in Pick's disease than in Alzheimer's disease.

## Creutzfeldt-Jakob Disease

Creutzfeldt-Jakob disease is a rare degenerative brain disease caused by a slowly progressive, transmissible (that is, infective) agent, most probably a prion, which is a proteinaceous agent that does not contain DNA or RNA. Other prion-related diseases are scrapie (a disease of sheep), kuru (a fatal central nervous system degenerative disorder of New Guinea highland tribes in which the prion is transmitted through ritualistic cannibalism), and Gerstman-Straussler syndrome (a rare, familial progressive dementia). All of the prion-related disorders result in a spongiform degeneration of the brain, characterized by the absence of an inflammatory immune response.

Evidence exists that in humans Creutzfeldt-Jakob disease can be transmitted iatrogenically, through infected, transplanted corneas or surgical instruments. Most cases of the disease, however, appear to be sporadic, affecting persons in their 50s. There is evidence that the incubation period may be relatively short (one to two years) or relatively long (8 to 16 years). The onset of the illness is characterized by the development of tremor, ataxia of gait, myoclonus, and dementia. The disease is usually rapidly progressive, leading to severe dementia and death in 6 to 12 months. The examination of the cerebrospinal fluid usually reveals no abnormalities, and the computed tomographic (CT) or MRI scan may be normal until late in the course of the disorder. The disease is characterized by the presence of an unusual pattern on the electroencephalogram (EEG), consisting of bursts of high-voltage slow waves.

## Huntington's Disease

Huntington's disease is classically associated with the development of dementia. The dementia seen in Huntington's disease is the *subcortical type of dementia*, which is characterized by more motor abnormalities and fewer language abnormalities than the cortical type of dementia (Table 10.3–2). The dementia of Huntington's disease is characterized by psychomotor slowing and difficulty with complex tasks, but memory, language, and insight remain relatively intact in the early and middle stages of the illness. As the disease progresses, however, the dementia becomes complete, and the features distinguishing it from dementia of the Alzheimer's type are the high incidence of depression and psychosis, in addition to the classic choreoathetoid movement disorder.

## Parkinson's Disease

Like Huntington's disease, parkinsonism is a disease of the basal ganglia that is commonly associated with dementia and depression. An estimated 20 to 30 percent of patients with Parkinson's disease have dementia, and an additional 30 to 40 percent have a measurable impairment in cognitive abilities. The slow movements of a patient with Parkinson's disease are paralleled in the slow thinking of some affected patients, a feature that some clinicians refer to as *bradyphenia*.

## HIV-Related Dementia

Infection with human immunodeficiency virus (HIV) commonly leads to dementia and other psychiatric symptoms. Patients infected with HIV experience dementia at an annual rate of about 14 percent. An estimated 75 per-

**Table 10.3–2**
**Distinguishing Features of Subcortical and Cortical Dementias**

| Characteristic | Subcortical Dementia | Cortical Dementia | Recommended Tests |
|---|---|---|---|
| Language | No aphasia (anomia, impercipience if severe) | Aphasia early | FAS test Boston Naming test WAIS-R vocabulary test |
| Memory | Impaired recall (retrieval) > recognition (encoding) | Recall and recognition impaired | Wechsler memory scale; Symbol Digit Paired Associate Learning (Brandt) WAIS-R digit span |
| Attention and immediate recall | | | |
| Visuospatial skills | Impaired | Impaired | Picture arrangement, object assembly and block design; WAIS subtests |
| Calculation | Preserved until late | Involved early | Mini-Mental State |
| Frontal systems abilities (executive function) | Disproportionately affected | Degree of impairment consistent with other involvement | Wisconsin Card Sorting Task; Odd Man Out test; Picture Absurdities |
| Speed of cognitive processing | Slowed early | Normal until late in disease | Trail making A and B; Paced Auditory Serial Addition Test (PASAT) |
| Personality | Apathetic, inert | Unconcerned | MMPI |
| Mood | Depressed | Euthymic | Beck and Hamilton depression scales |
| Speech | Dysarthric | Articulate until late | Verbal fluency Rosen, 1980 |
| Posture | Bowed or extended | Upright | |
| Coordination | Impaired | Normal until late | |
| Motor speed and control | Slowed | Normal | Finger-tap; grooved pegboard |
| Adventitious movements | Chorea, tremor tics, dystonia | Absent (Alzheimer's dementia—some myoclonus) | |
| Abstraction | | | Category test (Halstead Battery) |

Table adapted from J L. Cummings, *Subcortical Dementia*, Oxford University Press, New York, 1990. Used with permission.
Table from A K Pajeau, G C Román: HIV encephalopathy and dementia. In *The Psychiatric Clinics of North America: The Interface of Psychiatry and Neurology*, vol 15, J Biller, R G Kathol, editors, p 457. Saunders, Philadelphia, 1992. Used with permission.

cent of patients with acquired immune deficiency syndrome (AIDS) have involvement of the central nervous system (CNS) at the time of autopsy. The development of dementia in HIV-infected patients is often paralleled by the appearance of parenchymal abnormalities in MRI scans.

### Head Trauma-Related Dementia

Dementia can be a sequela of head trauma, as can a wide range of neuropsychiatric syndromes.

## DIAGNOSIS

### DSM-IV

DSM-IV has eliminated the general syndrome of dementia that was included in DSM-III-R. The dementia diagnoses in DSM-IV are dementia of the Alzheimer's type (DAT) (Table 10.3–3), vascular dementia (Table 10.3–4), dementia due to other general medical conditions (Table 10.3–5), substance-induced persisting dementia (Table 10.3–6), dementia due to multiple etiologies (Table 10.3–

7), and dementia not otherwise specified (NOS) (Table 10.3–8).

**Dementia of the Alzheimer's type.** The DSM-IV diagnostic criteria for dementia of the Alzheimer's type emphasize the presence of memory impairment and the associated presence of at least one other symptom of cognitive decline (aphasia, apraxia, agnosia, or abnormal executive functioning). The diagnostic criteria also require a continuing and gradual decline in functioning, impairment in social or occupational functioning, and the exclusion of other causes of dementia. DSM-IV suggests that the age of onset be characterized as early (at age 65 or below) or late (after age 65) and that a predominant behavioral symptom be coded with the diagnosis, if appropriate.

**Vascular dementia.** The general symptoms of vascular dementia are the same as those for dementia of the Alzheimer's type, but the diagnosis of vascular dementia requires the presence of either clinical or laboratory evidence supportive of a vascular cause of the dementia.

**Dementia due to other general medical conditions.** DSM-IV lists six specific causes of dementia that

**Table 10.3–3**
**Diagnostic Criteria for Dementia of the Alzheimer's Type**

A. The development of multiple cognitive deficits manifested by both
   (1) memory impairment (impaired ability to learn new information and to recall previously learned information)
   (2) one (or more) of the following cognitive disturbances:
       (a) aphasia (language disturbance)
       (b) apraxia (impaired ability to carry out motor activities despite intact motor function)
       (c) agnosia (failure to recognize or identify objects despite intact sensory function)
       (d) disturbance in executive functioning (i.e., planning, organizing, sequencing, abstracting)

B. The cognitive deficits in criteria A1 and A2 each cause significant impairment in social or occupational functioning and represent a significant decline from a previous level of functioning.

C. The course is characterized by gradual onset and continuing cognitive decline.

D. The cognitive deficits in criteria A1 and A2 are not due to any of the following:
   (1) other central nervous system conditions that cause progressive deficits in memory and cognition (e.g., cerebrovascular disease, Parkinson's disease, Huntington's disease, subdural hematoma, normal-pressure hydrocephalus, brain tumor)
   (2) systemic conditions that are known to cause dementia (e.g., hypothyroidism, vitamin $B_{12}$ or folic acid deficiency, niacin deficiency, hypercalcemia, neurosyphilis, HIV infection)
   (3) substance-induced conditions

E. The deficits do not occur exclusively during the course of a delirium.

F. The disturbance is not better accounted for by another Axis I disorder (e.g., major depressive disorder, schizophrenia).

*Code* based on type of onset and predominant features:
   **With early onset:** if onset is at age 65 years or below
   **With delirium**: if delirium is superimposed on the dementia
   **With delusions**: if delusions are the predominant feature
   **With depressed mood:** if depressed mood (including presentations that meet full symptom criteria for a major depressive episode) is the predominant feature. A separate diagnosis of mood disorder due to a general medical condition is not given.
   **Uncomplicated:** if none of the above predominates in the current clinical presentation

   **With late onset:** if onset is after age 65 years
   **With delirium:** if delirium is superimposed on the dementia
   **With delusions:** if delusions are the predominant feature
   **With depressed mood:** if depressed mood (including presentations that meet full symptom criteria for a major depressive episode) is the predominant feature. A separate diagnosis of mood disorder due to a general medical condition is not given.
   **Uncomplicated:** if none of the above predominates in the current clinical presentation

*Specify* if:
   **With behavioral disturbance**
   **Coding note:** Also code Alzheimer's disease on Axis III.

Table from DSM-IV, *Diagnostic and Statistical Manual of Mental Disorders*, ed 4. Copyright American Psychiatric Association, Washington, 1994. Used with permission.

can be coded directly: HIV disease, head trauma, Parkinson's disease, Huntington's disease, Pick's disease, and Creutzfeldt-Jakob disease. A seventh category allows the clinician to specify other nonpsychiatric medical conditions associated with dementia.

**Table 10.3–4**
**Diagnostic Criteria for Vascular Dementia**

A. The development of multiple cognitive deficits manifested by both
   (1) memory impairment (impaired ability to learn new information or to recall previously learned information)
   (2) one (or more) of the following cognitive disturbances:
       (a) aphasia (language disturbance)
       (b) apraxia (impaired ability to carry out motor activities despite intact motor function)
       (c) agnosia (failure to recognize or identify objects despite intact sensory function)
       (d) disturbance in executive functioning (i.e., planning, organizing, sequencing, abstracting)

B. The cognitive deficits in criteria A1 and A2 each cause significant impairment in social or occupational functioning and represent a significant decline from a previous level of functioning.

C. Focal neurological signs and symptoms (e.g., exaggeration of deep tendon reflexes, extensor plantar response, pseudobulbar palsy, gait abnormalities, weakness of an extremity) or laboratory evidence indicative of cerebrovascular disease (e.g., multiple infarctions involving cortex and underlying white matter) that are judged to be etiologically related to the disturbance.

D. The deficits do not occur exclusively during the course of a delirium.

*Code* based on predominant features:
   **With delirium:** if delirium is superimposed on the dementia
   **With delusions:** if delusions are the predominant feature
   **With depressed mood:** if depressed mood (including presentations that meet full symptom criteria for a major depressive episode) is the predominant feature. A separate diagnosis of mood disorder due to a general medical condition is not given.
   **Uncomplicated:** if none of the above predominates in the current clinical presentation

*Specify* if:
   **With behavioral disturbance**
   **Coding note:** Also code cerebrovascular condition on Axis III.

Table from DSM-IV, *Diagnostic and Statistical Manual of Mental Disorders*, ed 4. Copyright American Psychiatric Association, Washington, 1994. Used with permission.

**Substance-induced persisting dementia.** The primary reason that this DSM-IV category is listed with both the dementias and the substance-related disorders is to facilitate the clinician's thinking regarding differential diagnosis. The specific substances that DSM-IV cross-references are alcohol; inhalant; sedative, hypnotic, or anxiolytic; and other or unknown substances.

### Clinical Diagnosis

The diagnosis of dementia is based on a clinical examination of the patient, including a mental status examination, and on information from the patient's family, friends, and employers. Complaints of a personality change in a patient more than 40 years old suggest that a diagnosis of dementia should be carefully considered.

Complaints by the patient about intellectual impairment and forgetfulness should be noted, as should any evidence of evasion, denial, or rationalization aimed at concealing cognitive deficits. Excessive orderliness, social withdrawal, or a tendency to relate events in minute detail can be characteristic. Sudden outbursts of anger or sarcasm may

**Table 10.3–5**
**Diagnostic Criteria for Dementia Due to Other General Medical Conditions**

A. The development of multiple cognitive deficits manifested by both
(1) memory impairment (impaired ability to learn new information and to recall previously learned information)
(2) one (or more) of the following cognitive disturbances:
(a) aphasia (language disturbance)
(b) apraxia (impaired ability to carry out motor activities despite intact motor function)
(c) agnosia (failure to recognize or identify objects despite intact sensory function)
(d) disturbance in executive functioning (i.e., planning, organizing, sequencing, abstracting)

B. The cognitive deficits in criteria A1 and A2 each cause significant impairment in social or occupational functioning and represent a significant decline from a previous level of functioning.

C. There is evidence from the history, physical examination, or laboratory findings that the disturbance is the direct physiological consequence of one of the general medical conditions listed below.

D. The deficits do not occur exclusively during the course of a delirium.

**Dementia due to HIV disease**
**Coding note**: Also code HIV infection affecting central nervous system on Axis III.
**Dementia due to head trauma**
**Coding note**: Also code head injury on Axis III.
**Dementia due to Parkinson's disease**
**Coding note:** Also code Parkinson's disease on Axis III.
**Dementia due to Huntington's disease**
**Coding note:** Also code Huntington's disease on Axis III.
**Dementia due to Pick's disease**
**Coding note:** Also code Pick's disease on Axis III.
**Dementia due to Creutzfeldt-Jakob disease**
**Coding note:** Also code Creutzfeldt-Jakob disease on Axis III.
**Dementia due to . . . [indicate the general medical condition not listed above]**
For example, normal pressure hydrocephalus, hypothyroidism, brain tumor, vitamin $B_{12}$ deficiency, intracranial radiation)
**Coding note:** Also code the general medical condition on Axis III.

Table from DSM-IV, *Diagnostic and Statistical Manual of Mental Disorders*, ed 4. Copyright American Psychiatric Association, Washington, 1994. Used with permission.

occur. The patient's appearance and behavior should be noted. Lability of emotions, sloppy grooming, uninhibited remarks, silly jokes, or a dull, apathetic, or vacuous facial expression and manner suggest the presence of dementia, especially when coupled with memory impairment.

## CLINICAL FEATURES

At the initial stages of dementia, the patient shows difficulty in sustaining mental performance, fatigue, and a tendency to fail when a task is novel or complex or requires a shift in problem-solving strategy. The inability to perform tasks becomes increasingly severe and spreads to everyday tasks, such as grocery shopping, as the dementia progresses. Eventually, the demented patient may require constant supervision and help in order to perform even the most basic tasks of daily living. The major defects in dementia involve orientation, memory, perception, intellectual functioning, and reasoning, and all those functions

**Table 10.3–6**
**Diagnostic Criteria for Substance-Induced Persisting Dementia**

A. The development of multiple cognitive deficits manifested by both
(1) memory impairment (inability to learn new information and to recall previously learned information)
(2) one (or more) of the following cognitive disturbances:
(a) aphasia (language disturbance)
(b) apraxia (impaired ability to carry out motor activities despite intact motor function)
(c) agnosia (failure to recognize or identify objects despite intact sensory function)
(d) disturbance in executive functioning (i.e., planning, organizing, sequencing, abstracting)

B. The cognitive deficits in criteria A1 and A2 each cause significant impairment in social or occupational functioning and represent a significant decline from a previous level of functioning.

C. The deficits do not occur exclusively during the course of a delirium and persist beyond the usual duration of substance intoxication or withdrawal.

D. There is evidence from the history, physical examination, or laboratory findings that the deficits are etiologically related to the persisting effects of substance use (e.g., a drug of abuse, a medication).

*Code:* (Specific substance)-induced persisting dementia: (Alcohol; inhalant; sedative, hypnotic, or anxiolytic; other [or unknown] substance)

Table from DSM-IV, *Diagnostic and Statistical Manual of Mental Disorders*, ed 4. Copyright American Psychiatric Association, Washington, 1994. Used with permission.

**Table 10.3–7**
**Diagnostic Criteria for Dementia Due to Multiple Etiologies**

A. The development of multiple cognitive deficits manifested by both
(1) memory impairment (inability to learn new information and to recall previously learned information)
(2) one (or more) of the following cognitive disturbances:
(a) aphasia (language disturbance)
(b) apraxia (impaired ability to carry out motor activities despite intact motor function)
(c) agnosia (failure to recognize or identify objects despite intact sensory function)
(d) disturbance in executive functioning (i.e., planning, organizing, sequencing, abstracting)

B. The cognitive deficits in criteria A1 and A2 each cause significant impairment in social or occupational functioning and represent a significant decline from a previous level of functioning.

C. There is evidence from the history, physical examination, or laboratory findings that the disturbance has more than one etiology (e.g., head trauma plus chronic alcohol use, dementia of the Alzheimer's type with the subsequent development of vascular dementia).

D. The deficits do not occur exclusively during the course of delirium.

**Coding note:** Use multiple codes based on specific dementias and specific etiologies, e.g., dementia of the Alzheimer's type, with late onset uncomplicated; vascular dementia, uncomplicated.

Table from DSM-IV, *Diagnostic and Statistical Manual of Mental Disorders*, ed 4. Copyright American Psychiatric Association, Washington, 1994. Used with permission.

**Table 10.3–8**
**Diagnostic Criteria for Dementia Not Otherwise Specified**

This category should be used to diagnose a dementia that does not meet criteria for any of the specific types described in this section.

An example is a clinical presentation of dementia for which there is insufficient evidence to establish a specific etiology.

Table from DSM-IV, *Diagnostic and Statistical Manual of Mental Disorders*, ed 4. Copyright American Psychiatric Association, Washington, 1994. Used with permission.

become progressively affected as the disease process advances. Affective and behavioral changes, such as defective control of impulses and lability of mood, are frequent, as are accentuations and alterations of premorbid personality traits.

## Memory Impairment

Memory impairment is typically an early and prominent feature in dementia, especially in dementias involving the cortex, such as dementia of the Alzheimer's type. Early in the course of dementia, memory impairment is mild and is usually most marked for recent events, such as forgetting telephone numbers, conversations, and events of the day. As the course of dementia progresses, memory impairment becomes severe, and only the most highly learned information (for example, place of birth) is retained.

## Orientation

Inasmuch as memory is important for orientation to person, place, and time, orientation can be progressively affected during the course of a dementing illness. For example, patients with dementia may forget how to get back to their rooms after going to the bathroom. No matter how severe the disorientation seems, however, the patient shows no impairment in the level of consciousness.

## Language Impairment

Dementing processes that affect the cortex, primarily dementia of the Alzheimer's type and vascular dementia, can affect the patient's language abilities. In fact, DSM-IV includes aphasia as one of the diagnostic criteria. The language difficulty may be characterized by a vague, stereotyped, imprecise, or circumstantial locution. The patient may also have difficulty in naming objects.

## Personality Changes

Changes in a demented person's personality are among the most disturbing features for the families of affected patients. Preexisting personality traits may be accentuated during the development of a dementia. Patients with dementia may also become introverted and may seem to be less concerned about the effects of their behavior on others. Demented patients who have paranoid delusions are generally hostile to family members and caretakers. Patients with frontal and temporal involvement are likely to have marked personality changes and may be irritable and explosive.

## Psychosis

An estimated 20 to 30 percent of demented patients, primarily patients with dementia of the Alzheimer's type, have hallucinations, and 30 to 40 percent have delusions, primarily of a paranoid or persecutory and unsystematized nature, although complex, sustained, and well-systematized delusions are also reported by demented patients. Physical aggression and other forms of violence are common in demented patients who also have psychotic symptoms.

## Other Impairments

**Psychiatric.** In addition to psychosis and personality changes, depression and anxiety are major symptoms in an estimated 40 to 50 percent of demented patients, although the full syndrome of depressive disorder may be present in only 10 to 20 percent of demented patients. Patients with dementia may also exhibit pathological laughter or crying—that is, extremes of emotions with no apparent provocation.

**Neurological.** In addition to the aphasias in demented patients, apraxias and agnosias are common, and their presence is included as potential diagnostic criteria in DSM-IV. Other neurological signs that can be associated with dementia are seizures, seen in about 10 percent of patients with dementia of the Alzheimer's type and 20 percent of patients with vascular dementia, and atypical neurological presentations, such as nondominant parietal lobe syndromes. Primitive reflexes—such as the grasp, snout, suck, tonic-foot, and palmomental reflexes—may be present on neurological examination, and myoclonic jerks are present in 5 to 10 percent of patients.

Patients with vascular dementia may have additional neurological symptoms—such as headaches, dizziness, faintness, weakness, focal neurological signs, and sleep disturbances—that may be attributable to the location of the cerebrovascular disease. Pseudobulbar palsy, dysarthria, and dysphagia are also more common in vascular dementia than in other dementing conditions.

**Catastrophic reaction.** The dementia patient also exhibits a reduced ability to apply what Kurt Goldstein called the abstract attitude. The patient has difficulty in generalizing from a single instance, in forming concepts, and in grasping similarities and differences among concepts. Further, the ability to solve problems, to reason logically, and to make sound judgments is compromised. Goldstein also described a *catastrophic reaction*, which is marked by agitation secondary to the subjective awareness of one's intellectual deficits under stressful circumstances. Patients usually attempt to compensate for defects by using strategies to avoid demonstrating failures in intellectual performance, such as changing the subject, making jokes, or otherwise diverting the interviewer. Lack of judgment and poor impulse control are commonly found, particularly in dementias that primarily affect the frontal lobes. Examples of those impairments include coarse language, inappropriate jokes, the neglect of personal appearance and hygiene, and a general disregard for the conventional rules of social conduct.

**Sundowner syndrome.** Sundowner syndrome is characterized by drowsiness, confusion, ataxia, and accidental falls. It occurs in the aged who are overly sedated and in demented patients who react adversely to even a small dose of a psychoactive drug. The syndrome also occurs in demented patients when external stimuli, such as light and interpersonal orienting cues, are diminished.

A 65-year-old architectural draftsman began to have difficulty in remembering details necessary for performing his job. At home he was having problems keeping accurate financial records and, on several occasions, forgot to pay bills. It became increasingly difficult for him to function properly at work, and eventually he was forced to retire. Intellectual deterioration continued, and behavioral problems appeared. He became extremely stubborn and, when thwarted, was verbally and physically abusive.

When seen by a neurological consultant five years after the problem began, the patient was fully alert and cooperative but obviously anxious and fidgety. He thought that he was at his place of employment and that the year was "1960 or something" (it was actually 1982). He could not remember any one of six objects after an interval of 10 minutes, even when prompted by multiple-choice answers. He knew his birthplace and high school but not the names of his parents or siblings. He said he had two children, whereas in fact he had only one. Although he insisted he was still working, he could not describe his job. He did not know the current President and could not explain the resignation of President Nixon or remember the assassination of President Kennedy. His speech was well articulated but vague and circuitous, with many empty, meaningless phrases. He had difficulty in naming common objects and in repeating sentences. He could not do the simplest arithmetic calculations. He could not write a proper sentence, copy a two- or three-dimensional figure, or draw a house. He interpreted proverbs concretely and had difficulty in finding similarities between related objects.

An elementary neurological examination revealed nothing abnormal. The results of all laboratory studies were normal, including $B_{12}$, folate, $T_4$ levels, and serology; but a computed tomography (CT) scan showed marked cortical atrophy.

*Discussion.* The difficulties with short-term and long-term memory, abstract thinking (difficulty in finding similarities between related objects), and other higher cortical functions (for example, inability to name common objects, to do arithmetic calculations, and to copy a figure)—all severe enough to interfere with social and occupational functioning, occurring in a clear state of consciousness, and not accounted for by a mental disorder such as major depressive disorder—indicate a dementia.

The insidious onset with a generally progressive deteriorating course, the absence of focal neurological signs, the absence of a history of trauma or a cerebrovascular disease, the normal results on blood tests, and the cortical atrophy evident from the CT scan add up to the diagnosis of dementia of the Alzheimer's type. Because there were no psychotic features or mood disturbances, the diagnosis was noted to be uncomplicated. The severity of the dementia was noted to be moderate because the patient required some supervision.

## DIFFERENTIAL DIAGNOSIS

A comprehensive laboratory workup must be performed when evaluating a patient with dementia (Table 10.3–9). The purposes of the workup are to detect re-

**Table 10.3–9**
**Comprehensive Workup of Dementia**

Physical examination including thorough neurological
    examination
Vital signs
Mental status examination
Mini-Mental State Examination (MMSE)
Review of medications and drug levels
Blood and urine screens for alcohol, drugs, and heavy metals*
Physiological workup
    Serum electrolytes/glucose/$Ca^{++}$, $Mg^+$
    Liver, renal function tests
    SMA-12 or equivalent serum chemistry profile
    Urinalysis
    Complete blood cell count with differential cell type count
    Thyroid function tests (including TSH level)
    RPR (serum screen)
    FTA-ABS (if CNS disease is suspected)
    Serum $B_{12}$
    Folate levels
    Urine corticosteroids*
    Erythrocyte sedimentation rate (Westergren)
    Antinuclear antibody* (ANA), $C_3C_4$, Anti-DS DNA*
    Arterial blood gases*
    HIV screen*†
    Urine porphobilinogens*
Chest X-ray
Electrocardiogram
Neurological workup
    CT or MRI scan of head*
    SPECT**
    Lumbar puncture*
    EEG*
Neuropsychological testing§

---

*If indicated by history and physical examination.
†Requires special consent and counseling.
**May detect cerebral blood flow perfusion deficits.
§May be useful in differentiating dementia from other neuropsychiatric syndromes if it cannot be done clinically.
Table adapted from A Stoudemire, T L Thompson: Recognizing and treating dementia. *Geriatrics* 36: 112, 1981. Used with permission.

versible causes of dementia and to provide the patient and the family with a definitive diagnosis.

The continued improvements in brain imaging techniques, particularly MRI, have made the differentiation between dementia of the Alzheimer's type and vascular dementia somewhat more straightforward than in the past in some cases. An active area of research is the use of single photon emission computed tomography (SPECT) to detect patterns of brain metabolism in various types of dementia; within the near future, the use of SPECT images may help in the clinical differential diagnosis of dementing illnesses.

## Dementia of the Alzheimer's Type versus Vascular Dementia

Classically, vascular dementia has been distinguished from dementia of the Alzheimer's type by the decremental deterioration that may accompany cerebrovascular disease over a period of time. Although the discrete, stepwise deterioration may not be apparent in all cases, focal neurological symptoms are more common in vascular dementia than in dementia of the Alzheimer's type, as are the standard risk factors for cerebrovascular disease.

## Vascular Dementia versus Transient Ischemic Attacks

Transient ischemic attacks are brief episodes of focal neurological dysfunction lasting less than 24 hours (usually 5 to 15 minutes). Although a variety of mechanisms may be responsible, the episodes are frequently the result of microembolization from a proximal intracranial arterial lesion that produces transient brain ischemia, and the episodes usually resolve without significant pathological alteration of the parenchymal tissue. About a third of untreated patients with transient ischemic attacks later experience a brain infarction; therefore, recognition of transient ischemic attacks is an important clinical strategy to prevent brain infarction.

The clinician should distinguish episodes involving the vertebrobasilar system from those involving the carotid arterial system. In general, symptoms of vertebrobasilar disease reflect a transient functional disturbance in either the brainstem or the occipital lobe; carotid distribution symptoms reflect unilateral retinal or hemispheric abnormality. Anticoagulant therapy, antiplatelet agglutinating drugs such as acetylsalicylic acid (aspirin), and extracranial and intracranial reconstructive vascular surgery have been reported to be effective in reducing the risk of infarction in patients with transient ischemic attacks.

## Delirium

The differentiation between delirium and dementia can be more difficult than the DSM-IV classification indicates. In general, however, delirium is distinguished by rapid onset, brief duration, fluctuation of cognitive impairment during the course of the day, nocturnal exacerbation of symptoms, marked disturbance of the sleep-wake cycle, and prominent disturbances in attention and perception.

## Depression

Some patients with depression have symptoms of cognitive impairment that can be difficult to distinguish from symptoms of dementia. The clinical picture is sometimes referred to as *pseudodementia*, although the term *depression-related cognitive dysfunction* is a preferable and more descriptive term (Table 10.3–10). In general, patients with depression-related cognitive dysfunction have prominent depressive symptoms, have more insight into their symp-

**Table 10.3–10**
**Major Clinical Features Differentiating Pseudodementia from Dementia**

| Pseudodementia | Dementia |
|---|---|
| Clinical course and history | |
| Family always aware of dysfunction and its severity | Family often unaware of dysfunction and its severity |
| Onset can be dated with some precision | Onset can be dated only within broad limits |
| Symptoms of short duration before medical help is sought | Symptoms usually of long duration before medical help is sought |
| Rapid progression of symptoms after onset | Slow progression of symptoms throughout course |
| History of previous psychiatric dysfunction common | History of previous psychiatric dysfunction unusual |
| Complaints and clinical behavior | |
| Patients usually complain much of cognitive loss | Patients usually complain little of cognitive loss |
| Patients' complaints of cognitive dysfunction usually detailed | Patients' complaints of cognitive dysfunction usually vague |
| Patients emphasize disability | Patients conceal disability |
| Patients highlight failures | Patients delight in accomplishments, however trivial |
| Patients make little effort to perform even simple tasks | Patients struggle to perform tasks |
| | Patients rely on notes, calendars, etc., to keep up |
| Patients usually communicate strong sense of distress | Patients often appear unconcerned |
| Affective change often pervasive | Affect labile and shallow |
| Loss of social skills often early and prominent | Social skills often retained |
| Behavior often incongruent with severity of cognitive dysfunction | Behavior usually compatible with severity of cognitive dysfunction |
| Nocturnal accentuation of dysfunction uncommon | Nocturnal accentuation of dysfunction common |
| Clinical features related to memory, cognitive, and intellectual dysfunctions | |
| Attention and concentration often well preserved | Attention and concentration usually faulty |
| "Don't know" answers typical | Near-miss answers frequent |
| On tests of orientation, patients often give "don't know" answers | On tests of orientation, patients often mistake unusual for usual |
| Memory loss for recent and remote events usually severe | Memory loss for recent events usually more severe than for remote events |
| Memory gaps for specific periods or events common | Memory gaps for specific periods unusual* |
| Marked variability in performance on tasks of similar difficulty | Consistently poor performance on tasks of similar difficulty |

*Except when caused by delirium, trauma, seizures, etc.
Table from C. E. Wells: Pseudodementia. Am J Psychiatry *136*: 898, 1979. Used with permission.

toms than do demented patients, and often have a past history of depressive episodes.

## Factitious Disorder

Persons who attempt to simulate memory loss, as in factitious disorder, do so in an erratic and inconsistent manner. In true dementia, memory for time and place is lost before memory for person, and recent memory is lost before remote memory.

## Schizophrenia

Although schizophrenia may be associated with some degree of acquired intellectual impairment, its symptoms are much less severe than are the related symptoms of psychosis and thought disorder seen in dementia.

## Normal Aging

Aging is not necessarily associated with any significant cognitive decline, but a minor degree of memory problems can occur as a normal part of aging. Those normal occurrences are sometimes referred to as *benign senescent forgetfulness* or *age-associated memory impairment*. They are distinguished from dementia by their minor severity and by the fact that they do not significantly interfere with the patient's social or occupational life.

## COURSE AND PROGNOSIS

The classic course of dementia is an onset in the patient's 50s or 60s, with gradual deterioration over 5 to 10 years, leading eventually to death. The age of onset and the rapidity of deterioration vary among different types of dementia and within individual diagnostic categories. For example, the mean survival for patients with dementia of the Alzheimer's type is about 8 years, with a range of 1 to 20 years. Data suggest that the patients with an early onset of dementia or with a family history of dementia are likely to have a rapid course. Once dementia is diagnosed, the patient must undergo a complete medical and neurological workup, since 10 to 15 percent of all patients with dementia have a potentially reversible condition if treatment is initiated before permanent brain damage occurs.

The most common course of dementia begins with a number of subtle signs that may, at first, be ignored by both the patient and the people closest to the patient. A gradual onset of symptoms is most commonly associated with dementia of the Alzheimer's type, vascular dementia, endocrinopathies, brain tumors, and metabolic disorders. Conversely, the onset of dementia resulting from head trauma, cardiac arrest with cerebral hypoxia, or encephalitis may be sudden. Although the symptoms of the early phase of dementia are subtle, the symptoms become conspicuous as the dementia progresses, and family members may then bring the patient to a physician's attention. Demented patients may be sensitive to the use of benzodi-

azepines or alcohol, which may precipitate agitated, aggressive, or psychotic behavior. In the terminal stages of dementia, patients become empty shells of their former selves—profoundly disoriented, incoherent, amnestic, and incontinent of urine and feces.

With psychosocial and pharmacological treatment and possibly because of self-healing properties of the brain, the symptoms of dementia may progress only slowly for a time or even recede a bit. That regression of symptoms is certainly a possibility of reversible dementias (for example, dementias caused by hypothyroidism, normal pressure hydrocephalus, and brain tumors) once treatment is initiated. The course of the dementia varies from a steady progression (commonly seen with dementia of the Alzheimer's type) to an incrementally worsening dementia (commonly seen with vascular dementia) to a stable dementia (as may be seen in dementia related to head trauma).

## Psychosocial Factors

The severity and the course of dementia can be affected by psychosocial factors. For example, the greater the patient's premorbid intelligence and education, the better is the patient's ability to compensate for intellectual deficits. Patients who have a rapid onset of dementia use fewer defenses than do patients who experience an insidious onset. Anxiety and depression may intensify and aggravate the symptoms. *Pseudodementia* occurs in depressed patients who complain of impaired memory but are, in fact, suffering from a depressive disorder. When the depression is treated, the cognitive defects disappear.

## Dementia of the Alzheimer's Type

Dementia of the Alzheimer's type may begin at any age. DSM-IV suggests that the age of onset be specified and classified as early onset (at age 65 or below) or as late onset (after age 65). About half of all patients with dementia of the Alzheimer's type experience their first symptoms between the ages of 65 and 70. The course of the disorder is characteristically one of gradual decline over 8 to 10 years, although the course may be much more rapid or much more gradual that that. Once the symptoms of dementia have become severe, death often follows in a short time.

## Vascular Dementia

In contrast to the onset of dementia of the Alzheimer's type, the onset of vascular dementia is likely to be sudden. Also in contrast to dementia of the Alzheimer's type, there is a greater preservation of personality in patients with vascular dementia. The course of vascular dementia has previously been described as stepwise and patchy; however, the refinements in brain imaging techniques have revealed that patients with vascular dementia can have clinical courses that are as gradual and smooth as the clinical course characteristically associated with dementia of the Alzheimer's type.

## TREATMENT

Some cases of dementia are regarded as treatable because the dysfunctional brain tissue may retain the capacity for recovery if treatment is timely. A complete medical history, physical examination, and laboratory tests, including appropriate brain imaging, should be undertaken as soon as the diagnosis is suspected (Table 10.3–9). If the patient is suffering from a treatable cause of dementia, therapy is directed toward treating the underlying disorder.

The general treatment approach to demented patients is to provide supportive medical care, emotional support for the patients and their families, and pharmacological treatment for specific symptoms, including disruptive behavior. The maintenance of the patient's physical health, a supportive environment, and symptomatic psychopharmacological treatment are indicated in the treatment of most types of dementia. Symptomatic treatment includes the maintenance of a nutritious diet, proper exercise, recreational and activity therapies, attention to visual and auditory problems, and the treatment of associated medical problems, such as urinary tract infections, decubitus ulcers, and cardiopulmonary dysfunction. Particular attention must be provided to caretakers and family members who deal with frustration, grief, and psychological burnout as they care for the patient over a long period.

When the diagnosis of vascular dementia is made, risk factors contributing to cerebrovascular disease should be identified and therapeutically addressed. Those factors include hypertension, hyperlipidemia, obesity, cardiac disease, diabetes, and alcohol dependence. Patients who smoke should be encouraged to stop, since smoking cessation is associated with improved cerebral perfusion and cognitive functioning.

### Pharmacological Treatments

**Currently available treatments.** The clinician may prescribe benzodiazepines for insomnia and anxiety, antidepressants for depression, and antipsychotic drugs for delusions and hallucinations; however, the clinician should be aware of possible idiosyncratic drug effects in the elderly (such as paradoxical excitement, confusion, and increased sedation). In general, drugs with high anticholinergic activity should be avoided, although some data indicate that thioridazine (Mellaril), which does have high anticholinergic activity, may be an especially effective drug in controlling behavior in demented patients when given in low dosages. Short-acting benzodiazepines in small dosages are the preferred anxiolytic and sedative medication for demented patients. In addition, zolpidem (Ambien) may also be used for sedative purposes.

Tetrahydroaminoacridine (Tacrine) has been approved by the Food and Drug Administration (FDA) as a treatment for Alzheimer's disease. The drug is a moderately long-acting inhibitor of cholinesterase activity, and well-controlled trials have shown a clinically significant improvement in 20 to 25 percent of patients who take it. Because of the cholinomimetic activity of the drug, some patients are not able to tolerate it because of side effects. Some patients also have to discontinue the drug because of elevations in liver enzymes.

**Experimental treatment approaches.** A wide variety of experimental pharmacological treatments for the cognitive decline of depression are currently being developed by pharmaceutical companies. Many of the compounds are designed to enhance the functioning of the cholinergic neurotransmitter system. Some drugs that are being tested for cognitive-enhancing activity include general cerebral metabolic enhancers, calcium channel blockers, and serotonergic agents.

### Psychodynamic Factors

The deterioration of mental faculties has significant psychological meaning for patients with dementia. The experience of oneself as having continuity over time depends on memory. Since recent memory is lost before remote memory in most cases of dementia, many patients are highly distressed because they can clearly recall how they used to function while observing their obvious deterioration. At the most fundamental level, the self is a product of brain functioning. Hence, the patients' identities begin to fade as the illness progresses, and they can recall less and less of their past. Emotional reactions ranging from depression to severe anxiety to catastrophic terror can stem from the realization that the sense of self is disappearing before one's eyes.

From a psychodynamic standpoint, there is no such thing as an untreatable dementia. Patients often benefit from a supportive and educational psychotherapy in which the nature and the course of their illness are clearly explained to them. They may also benefit from assistance in grieving and accepting the extent of their disability. At the same time, they can benefit from attention to self-esteem issues. Any areas of intact functioning should be maximized by helping the patient identify activities in which successful functioning is possible. A psychodynamic assessment of defective ego functions and cognitive limitations can also be useful. The clinician can assist patients in finding ways to deal with the defective ego functions, such as keeping calendars for orientation problems, making schedules to help structure activities, and taking notes for memory problems.

Psychodynamic interventions with family members of dementia patients may be of enormous assistance. Loved ones who take care of the patient struggle with feelings of guilt, grief, anger, and exhaustion as they watch the family member gradually deteriorate. A common problem that develops among caretakers is that they sacrifice themselves in the service of caring for the patient. The gradually developing resentment from that self-sacrifice is often suppressed because of the guilt feelings it produces. Clinicians can help caretakers understand the complex mixture of feelings associated with seeing a loved one decline and can provide understanding and permission to express those feelings. Attention must also be given to tendencies to blame oneself or others for the patient's illness and for an appreciation of the role that the dementia patient plays in the lives of family members.

### References

Almkvist O, Bäckman L: Detection and staging of early clinical dementia. Acta Neurol Scand 88: 10, 1993.

Bondareff W, Raval J, Woo B, Hauser D L, Colletti P M: Magnetic resonance imaging and the severity of dementia in older adults. Arch Gen Psychiatry *47*: 47, 1990.

Burns A, Jacoby R, Levy R: Psychiatric phenomena in Alzheimer's disease: I–IV. Br J Psychiatry *157*: 72, 1990.

Chatterjee A, Strauss M E, Smyth K A, Whitehouse P J: Personality changes in Alzheimer's disease. Arch Neurol *49*: 486, 1992.

Corder E H, Saunders A M, Strittmatter W J, Schmechel D E, Gaskell P C, Small G W, Roses A D, Haines J L, Pericak-Vance M A: Gene dose of apolipoprotein E type 4 allele and the risk of Alzheimer's disease in late onset families. Science *261*: 921, 1993.

Davidson M, editor: Alzheimer's disease. Psychiatr Clin North Am *14* (2, Suppl): 1, 1991.

Davis R E, Emmerling M R, Jaen J C, Moos W H, Spiegel K: Therapeutic intervention in dementia. Crit Rev Neurobiol *7*: 41, 1993.

Day J J, Grant I, Atkinson J H, Brysk L T, McCutchan J A, Hesselink J R, Heaton R K, Weinrich J D, Spector S A, Richman D D: Incidence of AIDS dementia in a two-year follow-up of AIDS and ARC patients on an initial phase II AZT placebo-controlled study: San Diego cohort. J. Neuropsychiatry Clin Neurosci *4*: 16, 1992.

Deutsch L H, Bylsma F W, Rovner B W, Steele C, Folstein M F: Psychosis and physical aggression in probable Alzheimer's disease. Am J Psychiatry *148*: 1159, 1991.

Flint A J: Delusions in dementia: A review. J Neuropsychiatry Clin Neurosci *3*: 121, 1991.

Gabbard G O: *Psychodynamic Psychiatry in Clinical Practice: The DSM-IV Edition.* American Psychiatric Press, Washington, 1994.

Gandy S, Greengard P: Amyloidogenesis in Alzheimer's disease: Some possible therapeutic opportunities. Trends Pharmacol Sci *13*: 108, 1992.

Greenamyre J T, Maragos W F: Neurotransmitter receptors in Alzheimer disease. Cerebrovasc Brain Metab Rev *5*: 61, 1993.

Harper R G, Chacko R C, Kotik-Harper D, Kirby H B: Comparison of two cognitive screening measures for efficacy in differentiating dementia from depression in a geriatric inpatient population. J Neuropsychiatry Clin Neurosci *4*: 179, 1992.

Hyman B T, Tanzi R E: Amyloid dementia and Alzheimer's disease. Curr Opin Neurol Neurosurg *5*: 88, 1992.

Luchins D J, Cohen D, Hanrahan P, Eisdorfer C, Pavaza G, Ashford J W, Gorelich P, Hirschman R, Freels S, Levy P, Semla T, Shaw H: Are there clinical differences between familial and nonfamilial Alzheimer's disease? Am J Psychiatry *149*: 1023, 1992.

O'Connor D W, Pollitt P A, Roth M, Brook P B, Reiss B B: Memory complaints and impairments in normal, depressed, and demented elderly persons identified in a community survey. Arch Gen Psychiatry *47*: 224, 1990.

Pajeau A K, Roman G C: HIV encephalopathy and dementia. Psychiatr Clin North Am *15*: 455, 1992.

Reed K R, Rogers R L, Meyer J S: Cerebral magnetic resonance imaging compared in Alzheimer's and multi-infarct dementia. J Neuropsychiatry Clin Neurosci *3*: 51, 1991.

Stern G M: New drug interventions in Alzheimer's disease. Curr Opin Neurol Neurosurg *5*: 100, 1992.

Yesauage J: Differential diagnosis between depression and dementia. Am J Med *94* (Suppl, 5): 235, 1993.

# 10.4 / Amnestic Disorders

The amnestic disorders are characterized primarily by the single symptom of a memory disorder that causes significant impairment in social or occupational functioning. The diagnosis of amnestic disorder cannot be made when the patient has other signs of cognitive impairment, such as those seen in dementia, or when the patient has impaired attention or consciousness, such as that seen in delirium. The amnestic disorders are differentiated from the dissociative disorders (for example, dissociative amnesia, dissociative fugue, and dissociative identity disorder) by the identified or presumed presence of a causally related general medical condition (for example, a history of head trauma or carbon monoxide poisoning).

## EPIDEMIOLOGY

No adequate studies have been reported on the incidence or the prevalence of the amnestic disorders. However, some studies report the incidence or the prevalence of memory impairments in specific disorders (for example, multiple sclerosis). Amnesia is most commonly found in alcohol use disorders and head injury. In general practice and hospital settings, a decrease has been seen in the frequency of amnesia related to chronic alcohol abuse and an increase in the frequency of amnesia related to head trauma.

## ETIOLOGY

The major neuroanatomical structures involved in memory and the development of an amnestic disorder are particular diencephalic structures (for example, dorsomedial and midline nuclei of the thalamus) and midtemporal lobe structures (for example, the hippocampus, the mammillary bodies, and the amygdala). Although amnesia is usually the result of bilateral damage to those structures, some cases of unilateral damage result in an amnestic disorder, and evidence indicates that the left hemisphere may be more critical than the right hemisphere in the development of memory disorders. Many studies of memory and amnesia in animals have suggested that other brain areas may also be involved in the symptoms that accompany amnesia. For example, frontal lobe involvement may result in such symptoms as confabulation and apathy, which can be seen in patients with amnestic disorders.

Amnestic disorders have many potential causes (Table 10.4–1). Thiamine deficiency, hypoglycemia, hypoxia (including carbon monoxide poisoning), and herpes simplex encephalitis all have a predilection to damage the temporal

**Table 10.4–1**
**Major Causes of Amnestic Disorders**

Systemic medical conditions
   Thiamine deficiency (Korsakoff's syndrome)
   Hypoglycemia
Primary brain conditions
   Seizures
   Head trauma (closed and penetrating)
   Cerebral tumors (especially thalamic and temporal lobe)
   Cerebrovascular diseases (especially thalamic and temporal lobe)
   Surgical procedures on the brain
   Encephalitis due to herpes simplex
   Hypoxia (including nonfatal hanging attempts and carbon monoxide poisoning)
   Transient global amnesia
   Electroconvulsive therapy
   Multiple sclerosis
Substance-related causes
   Alcohol use disorders
   Neurotoxins
   Benzodiazepines (and other sedative-hypnotics)
   Many over-the-counter preparations

lobes, particularly the hippocampi. Thus, those conditions can be associated with the development of amnestic disorders. Similarly, when tumors, cerebrovascular diseases, surgical procedures, or multiple sclerosis plaques involve the diencephalic or temporal regions of the brain, the symptoms of an amnestic disorder may develop in a patient. General insults to the brain—for example, seizures, electroconvulsive therapy (ECT), and head trauma—may also result in memory impairments. Transient global amnesia is presumed to be a cerebrovascular disorder involving transient impairment in blood flow through the vertebrobasilar arteries.

Many drugs have been associated with the development of amnesia, and a review of all drugs that a patient has taken, including nonprescription drugs, should be considered in the diagnostic workup of an amnestic patient. The benzodiazepines are the most commonly used prescription drugs associated with amnesia. One benzodiazepine in particular, the short-acting hypnotic triazolam (Halcion), has been inaccurately singled out by the popular press as being associated with anterograde amnesia. A review of the scientific data has concluded that all benzodiazepines can be associated with amnesia and that the association is related to dosage. When triazolam is used in doses equivalent to (generally less than or equal to 0.25 mg) standard doses of other benzodiazepines, amnesia is no more often associated with triazolam than with other benzodiazepines.

## DIAGNOSIS

In the fourth edition of *Diagnostic and Statistical Manual of Mental Disorders* (DSM-IV), the differentiation between amnestic syndrome and amnestic disorder used in the revised third edition (DSM-III-R) has been eliminated. For the diagnosis of amnestic disorder, DSM-IV requires the "development of memory impairment as manifested by impairment in the ability to learn new information or the inability to recall previously learned information," and the "memory disturbance causes significant impairment in social or occupational functioning." A diagnosis of amnestic disorder due to a general medical condition (Table 10.4–2) is made when there is evidence of a causatively relevant specific medical condition (including physical trauma). DSM-IV further categorizes the diagnosis as being transient or chronic. A diagnosis of substance-induced persisting amnestic disorder is made when there is evidence that the symptoms are causatively related to the use of a substance (Table 10.4–3). DSM-IV refers the clinician to specific diagnoses within substance-related disorders: alcohol-induced persisting amnestic disorder; sedative, hypnotic, or anxiolytic-induced persisting amnestic disorder; and other (or unknown) substance-induced persisting amnestic disorder. DSM-IV also provides for the diagnosis of amnestic disorder not otherwise specified (NOS) (Table 10.4–4).

## CLINICAL FEATURES AND SUBTYPES

The central symptom of amnestic disorders is the development of a memory disorder characterized by impair-

**Table 10.4–2**
**Diagnostic Criteria for Amnestic Disorder Due to a General Medical Condition**

A. The development of memory impairment as manifested by impairment in the ability to learn new information or the inability to recall previously learned information.

B. The memory disturbance causes significant impairment in social or occupational functioning and represents a significant decline from a previous level of functioning.

C. The memory disturbance does not occur exclusively during the course of a delirium or a dementia.

D. There is evidence from the history, physical examination, or laboratory findings that the disturbance is the direct physiological consequence of a general medical condition (including physical trauma).

*Specify* if:
    **Transient:** if memory impairment lasts for 1 month or less
    **Chronic:** if memory impairment lasts for more than 1 month

**Coding note:** Include the name of the general medical condition on Axis I, e.g., amnestic disorder due to head trauma; also code the general medical condition on Axis III.

Table from DSM-IV, *Diagnostic and Statistical Manual of Mental Disorders*, ed 4. Copyright American Psychiatric Association, Washington, 1994. Used with permission.

**Table 10.4–3**
**Diagnostic Criteria for Substance-Induced Persisting Amnestic Disorder**

A. The development of memory impairment as manifested by impairment in the ability to learn new information or the inability to recall previously learned information.

B. The memory disturbance causes significant impairment in social or occupational functioning and represents a significant decline from a previous level of functioning.

C. The memory disturbance does not occur exclusively during the course of a delirium or a dementia and persists beyond the usual duration of substance intoxication or withdrawal.

D. There is evidence from the history, physical examination, or laboratory findings that the memory disturbance is etiologically related to the persisting effects of substance use (e.g., a drug of abuse, a medication).

*Code:* (Specific substance)-induced persisting amnestic disorder: (Alcohol; sedative, hypnotic, or anxiolytic; other [or unknown] substance)

Table from DSM-IV, *Diagnostic and Statistical Manual of Mental Disorders*, ed 4. Copyright American Psychiatric Association, Washington, 1994. Used with permission.

**Table 10.4–4**
**Diagnostic Criteria for Amnestic Disorder Not Otherwise Specified**

This category should be used to diagnose an amnestic disorder that does not meet criteria for any of the specific types described in this section.

An example is a clinical presentation of amnesia for which there is insufficient evidence to establish a specific etiology (i.e., dissociative, substance induced, or due to a general medical condition).

Table from DSM-IV, *Diagnostic and Statistical Manual of Mental Disorders*, ed 4. Copyright American Psychiatric Association, Washington, 1994. Used with permission.

ment in the ability to learn new information (*anterograde amnesia*) and the inability to recall previously remembered knowledge (*retrograde amnesia*). The symptom must result in significant problems for patients in their social or occupational functioning. The period of time for which a patient is amnestic may begin directly at the point of trauma or may include a period before the trauma. Memory for the time during the physical insult (for example, during a cerebrovascular event) may also be lost.

Short-term memory and recent memory are usually impaired. Patients cannot remember what they had for breakfast or lunch, the name of the hospital, or their doctor. In some patients the amnesia is so profound that the patients cannot orient themselves to city and time, although orientation to person is seldom lost in amnestic disorders. Memory for overlearned information or events from the remote past, such as childhood experiences, is good; but memory for events from the less remote past (over the past decade) is impaired. Immediate memory (tested, for example, by asking the patient to repeat six numbers) remains intact. With improvement, the patient may experience a gradual shrinking of the time period for which memory has been lost, although some patients experience a gradual improvement in their memory for the entire period.

The onset of symptoms may be sudden—as in trauma, cerebrovascular events, and neurotoxic chemical assaults—or gradual, as in nutritional deficiency and cerebral tumors. The amnesia can be of short duration (specified as transient by DSM-IV if lasting a month or less) or of long duration (specified as persistent by DSM-IV if lasting more than one month).

A variety of other symptoms can be associated with amnestic disorders. However, if the patient has other cognitive impairments, a diagnosis of dementia or delirium is more appropriate than a diagnosis of an amnestic disorder. Both subtle and gross changes in personality can accompany the symptoms of memory impairment in amnestic disorders. Patients with amnestic disorders may be apathetic, lack initiative, have unprovoked episodes of agitation, or appear to be overly friendly or agreeable. Patients with amnestic disorders may also appear bewildered and confused and may attempt to cover their confusion with confabulatory answers to questions. Characteristically, patients with amnestic disorders do not have good insight about their neuropsychiatric conditions.

## Cerebrovascular Diseases

Cerebrovascular diseases affecting the hippocampus involve the posterior cerebral and basilar arteries and their branches. Infarctions are rarely limited to the hippocampus; they often involve the occipital or parietal lobes. Thus, common accompanying symptoms of cerebrovascular diseases in that region are focal neurological signs involving vision or sensory modalities. Cerebrovascular diseases affecting the bilateral medial thalamus, particularly the anterior portions, are often associated with symptoms of amnestic disorders. A few case studies report amnestic disorders from ruptures of an aneurysm of the anterior communicating artery, resulting in an infarction of the basal forebrain region.

## Multiple Sclerosis

The pathophysiological process of multiple sclerosis involves the seemingly random formation of plaques within the brain parenchyma. When the plaques occur in the temporal lobe and the diencephalic regions, symptoms of memory impairment can occur. In fact, the most common cognitive complaints in patients with multiple sclerosis involve impaired memory, which occurs in 40 to 60 percent of patients. Characteristically, digit span memory is normal, but immediate recall and delayed recall of information are impaired. The memory impairment can affect both verbal and nonverbal material.

## Korsakoff's Syndrome

Korsakoff's syndrome is the amnestic syndrome caused by thiamine deficiency, which is most commonly associated with the poor nutritional habits of persons with chronic alcohol abuse. Other causes of poor nutrition (for example, starvation), gastric carcinoma, hemodialysis, hyperemesis gravidarum, prolonged intravenous hyperalimentation, and gastric plication may also result in thiamine deficiency. Korsakoff's syndrome is often associated with *Wernicke's encephalopathy*, which is the associated syndrome of confusion, ataxia, and ophthalmoplegia. In patients with those thiamine deficiency-related symptoms, the neuropathological findings include hyperplasia of the small blood vessels with occasional hemorrhages, hypertrophy of astrocytes, and subtle changes in neuronal axons. Although the delirium clears up within a month or so, the amnestic syndrome either accompanies or follows untreated Wernicke's encephalopathy in about 85 percent of all cases.

The onset of Korsakoff's syndrome may be gradual. Recent memory tends to be affected more than remote memory; however, that feature is variable. Confabulation, apathy, and passivity are often prominent symptoms in the syndrome. With treatment, patients may remain amnestic for up to three months and then gradually improve over the next year. The administration of thiamine may prevent the development of additional amnestic symptoms, but rarely is the treatment able to reverse severe amnestic symptoms, once they are present. About a third to a quarter of all patients recover completely, and about a quarter of all patients have no improvement of their symptoms.

## Alcoholic Blackouts

In some persons with severe alcohol abuse, the syndrome commonly referred to as an alcoholic blackout may occur. Characteristically, the alcoholic person awakens in the morning with a conscious awareness of being unable to remember a period of time the night before, while intoxicated. Sometimes specific behaviors (hiding money in a secret place and provoking fights) are associated with a person's blackouts.

## Electroconvulsive Therapy

Electroconvulsive therapy (ECT) treatments are usually associated with a retrograde amnesia for a period of several minutes before the treatment and an anterograde amnesia after the treatment, although the anterograde amnesia usually resolves within five hours of the treatment. Mild memory deficits may remain for one to two months after a course of ECT treatments, but the symptoms are completely resolved six to nine months after treatment.

## Head Injury

Head injuries (both closed and penetrating) can result in a wide range of neuropsychiatric symptoms, including dementia, depression, personality changes, and amnestic disorders. Amnestic disorders caused by head injuries are commonly associated with a period of retrograde amnesia leading up to the traumatic incident and amnesia for the traumatic incident itself. The severity of the brain injury is somewhat correlated with the duration and the severity of the amnestic syndrome, but the best correlate of eventual improvement is the degree of clinical improvement of the amnesia during the first week after the patient has regained consciousness.

## Transient Global Amnesia

Transient global amnesia is characterized by the abrupt loss of the ability to recall recent events or to remember new information. The syndrome is often characterized by a lack of insight regarding the problem, a clear sensorium, some mild degree of confusion, and, occasionally, the abil-

ity to perform some well-learned complex tasks. Episodes last from 6 to 24 hours. Studies suggest that transient global amnesia occurs in 5 to 10 cases per 100,000 people per year, although, for patients more than 50 years old, the rate may be as high as 30 cases per 100,000 people per year. The pathophysiology is unknown, but it is likely to involve ischemia of the temporal lobe and the diencephalic brain regions. Several studies of patients with single photon emission computed tomography (SPECT) have found decreased blood flow in the temporal and parietal-temporal regions, particularly in the left hemisphere (Figure 10.4–1). Patients with transient global amnesia almost universally experience complete improvement, although one study found that about 20 percent of patients may have a recurrence of the episode, and another study found that about 7 percent of patients may have epilepsy. Patients with transient global amnesia have been differentiated from patients with transient ischemic attacks as having less diabetes, hypercholesterolemia, and hypertriglyceridemia but more hypertension and migrainous episodes.

## DIFFERENTIAL DIAGNOSIS

Table 10.4–1 lists the major causes of amnestic disorders. To make the diagnosis, the clinician must obtain the patient's history, conduct a complete physical examination, and order all appropriate laboratory tests. However, other diagnoses can be confused with the amnestic disorders.

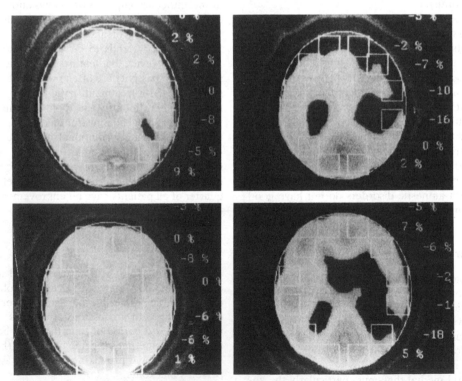

**Figure 10.4–1.** Technetium-99m HM-PAO single photon emission computed tomographic scans. Left-sided temporal hypoperfusion is seen in patients 2 (top left), 3 (top right), 4 (bottom left), and 5 (bottom right), 18 months, 4 days, 1 day, and 4 days, respectively, after the transient global amnestic attack. The right side of the patient is at the left side of the figure. (Figure from P Laloux, C Brichant, F Cauwe, P Decoster: Technetium-99m HM-PAO single photon emission computed tomography imaging in transient global amnesia. Arch Neurol *49*: 545, 1992. Used with permission.)

## Dementia and Delirium

The clinician must differentiate amnestic disorders from dementia and delirium. Memory impairment is commonly present in dementia but is accompanied by other cognitive deficits. Memory impairment is also commonly present in delirium but occurs in the setting of an impairment in attention and consciousness.

## Normal Aging

Some minor impairment in memory may accompany normal aging; however, the DSM-IV requirement that the memory impairment cause significant impairment in social or occupational functioning should exclude normal aging patients from the diagnosis.

## Dissociative Disorders

The dissociative disorders can sometimes be difficult to differentiate from the amnestic disorders. However, patients with dissociative disorders are more likely to have lost their orientation to self and may have more selective memory deficits than do patients with amnestic disorders. For example, patients with dissociative disorders may not know their names or home addresses but may still be able to learn new information and to remember selected past memories. Dissociative disorders are also often associated with emotionally stressful life events involving money, the legal system, or troubled relationships.

## Factitious Disorders

Patients with factitious disorders who are mimicking an amnestic disorder often have inconsistent results on memory tests and have no evidence of an identifiable cause. Those findings, coupled with evidence of primary or secondary gain by the patient, should suggest a factitious disorder.

## COURSE AND PROGNOSIS

The specific cause of the amnestic disorder determines the course and the prognosis for a patient. The onset may be sudden or gradual; the symptoms may be transient or persistent; and the outcome can range from no improvement to complete recovery. Transient amnestic disorder with full recovery is common in temporal lobe epilepsy, ECT, the intake of such drugs as benzodiazepines and barbiturates, and resuscitation from cardiac arrest. Permanent amnestic syndromes may follow a head trauma, carbon monoxide poisoning, a cerebral infarction, subarachnoid hemorrhage, and herpes simplex encephalitis.

## TREATMENT

The primary approach is to treat the underlying cause of the amnestic disorder. While the patient is amnestic, supportive prompts regarding the date, the time, and the patient's location can be helpful and can reduce the pa-

tient's anxiety. After the resolution of the amnestic episode, psychotherapy of some type (for example, cognitive, psychodynamic, or supportive) may help patients incorporate the amnestic experience into their lives.

## Psychodynamic Factors

Psychodynamic interventions may be of considerable value for patients suffering from amnestic disorders that result from insults to the brain. Understanding the course of recovery in such patients helps the clinician be sensitive to the narcissistic injury inherent in damage to the central nervous system.

The first phase of recovery, in which the patient is incapable of processing what happened because the ego defenses are overwhelmed, requires that the clinician serve as a supportive auxiliary ego who explains to the patient what is happening and provides missing ego functions. In the second phase of recovery, as the realization of the injury sets in, the patient may become angry and feel victimized by the malevolent hand of fate. The patient may view others, including the clinician, as bad or destructive, and the clinician must contain those projections without becoming punitive or retaliatory. The clinician can build a therapeutic alliance with the patient by explaining slowly and clearly what happened and by offering an explanation for the patient's internal experience. The third phase of recovery is an integrative one. As the patient accepts what happened, the clinician can help the patient form a new identity by connecting current experiences of the self with past experiences of the self. Grieving over one's lost faculties may be an important feature of the third phase.

Most patients who are amnestic from a brain injury engage in denial. The clinician must respect and empathize with patients' need to deny the reality of what has happened. Insensitive and blunt confrontations will destroy any developing therapeutic alliance and may cause patients to feel attacked. A sensitive approach is to help the patients accept their cognitive limitations by exposing them to those deficits bit by bit over time. When the patients fully accept what has happened, they may need assistance in forgiving themselves and any others involved, so that they can get on with their lives. Clinicians must also be wary of being seduced into thinking that all the patient's symptoms are directly related to the brain insult. An evaluation of preexisting personality disorders—such as borderline, antisocial, and narcissistic personality disorders—must be part of the overall assessment, because many patients with personality disorders place themselves in situations that predispose them to injuries. Those personality features may become a crucial part of the psychodynamic psychotherapy.

## References

Caine E D: Amnesic disorders. J Neuropsychiatry Clin Neurosci 5: 6, 1993.
Erickson K R: Amnestic disorders: Pathophysiology and patterns of memory dysfunction. West J Med 152: 159, 1990.
Gabbard G O: *Psychodynamic Psychiatry in Clinical Practice: The DSM-IV Edition.* American Psychiatric Press, Washington, 1994.
Gandolofo C, Caponnetto C, Conti M, Dagino N, Del Sette M, Primavera A: Prognosis of transient global amnesia: A long-term follow-up study. Eur Neurol 32: 52, 1992.

Gasquonine P G: Learning in post-traumatic amnesia following extremely severe closed head injury. Brain Inj *5*: 169, 1991.

Hodges J R, Warlow C P: The aetiology of transient global amnesia: A case-control study of 114 cases with prospective follow-up. Brain *113*: 639, 1990.

Hodges J R, Warlow C P: Syndromes of transient amnesia: Towards a classification: A study of 153 cases. J Neurol Neurosurg Psychiatry *53*: 834, 1990.

Jonides J, Smith E E, Koeppe R A, Awh E, Minoshima S, Mintun M A: Spatial working memory in humans as revealed by PET. Nature *363*: 623, 1993.

Kim J J, Fanselow M S: Modality-specific retrograde amnesia of fear. Science *256*: 675, 1992.

Kirk T, Roache J D, Griffiths R R: Dose-response evaluation of the amnestic effects of triazolam and pentobarbital in normal subjects. J Clin Psychopharmacol *10*: 161, 1990.

Krupa D J, Thompson J K, Thompson R F: Localization of a memory trace in the mammalian brain. Science *260*: 989, 1993.

Laloux P, Brichant C, Cauwe F, Decoster P: Technetium-99m HM-PAO single photon emission computed tomography imaging in transient global amnesia. Arch Neurol *49*: 543, 1992.

Melo T P, Ferro J M, Ferro H: Transient global amnesia: A case control study. Brain *115*: 261, 1992.

Saneda D L, Corrigan J D: Predicting clearing of post-traumatic amnesia following closed-head injury. Brain Inj *6*: 167, 1992.

Squire L R, Amaral D G, Press G A: Magnetic resonance imaging of the hippocampal formation and mammillary nuclei distinguish medial temporal lobe and diencephalic amnesia. J Neurosci *10*: 3106, 1990.

Squire L R, Zola-Morgan S: The medical temporal lobe memory system. Science *253*: 1380, 1991.

# 10.5 / Mental Disorders Due to a General Medical Condition

The fourth edition of *Diagnostic and Statistical Manual of Mental Disorders* (DSM-IV) has introduced the phrase "due to a general medical condition" as part of its resolve to eliminate the long-standing but misleading distinction between organic disorders and functional disorders. An assessment that a mental disorder is due to a general medical condition indicates that the clinician, on the weight of the available data, thinks that the psychiatric symptoms are part of a syndrome caused by a nonpsychiatric medical condition. An example is the depression associated with Cushing's disease. The diagnosis of a mental disorder due to a general medical condition also implies that the clinician thinks that the psychiatric symptom is severe enough to warrant treatment as an identified problem.

DSM-IV has taken a different approach to categorizing the mental disorders due to a general medical condition than did the revised third edition (DSM-III-R). In DSM-III-R the disorders were classified under the broader category of organic mental disorders. In DSM-IV each mental disorder due to a general medical condition is classified within the category that most resembles its symptoms (Table 10.5–1). For example, the diagnosis psychotic disorder due to a general medical condition is found in the DSM-IV section on schizophrenia and other psychotic disorders. The symptom-based organization of DSM-IV is meant to facilitate clinical decision making regarding the differential diagnosis of symptoms. For example, the clinician who is evaluating a patient with depression can refer to the DSM-IV section on mood disorders and find "mood disorder due to a general medical condition" as one of the diagnoses. That diagnosis should help clarify the importance of considering the possibility of a mental disorder due to a general medical condition for almost all psychiatric presentations.

DSM-IV has three additional diagnostic categories for clinical presentations of mental disorders due to a general medical condition that do not meet the diagnostic criteria for specific diagnoses. The first of the diagnoses is catatonic disorder due to a general medical condition (Table 10.5–

**Table 10.5–1**
**Mental Disorders Due to a General Medical Condition**

| DSM-IV Category | Mental Disorders Due to a General Medical Condition | Section |
|---|---|---|
| Delirium, dementia, amnestic, and other cognitive disorders | Delirium due to a general medical condition | 10.2 |
| | Dementia due to other general medical conditions | 10.3 |
| | Amnestic disorder due to a general medical condition | 10.4 |
| Schizophrenia and other psychotic disorders | Psychotic disorder due to a general medical condition | 14.1 |
| Mood disorders | Mood disorder due to a general medical condition | 15.3 |
| Anxiety disorders | Anxiety disorder due to a general medical condition | 16.1 |
| Sexual disorders | Sexual dysfunction due to a general medical condition | 20.2 |
| Sleep disorders | Sleep disorder due to a general medical condition | 23.2 |
| Mental disorders due to a general medical condition not elsewhere classified | Catatonic disorder due to a general medical condition | 10.5 |
| | Personality change due to a general medical condition | 10.5 |
| | Mental disorder NOS due to a general medical condition | 10.5 |

2). The second diagnosis is personality change due to a general medical condition (Table 10.5–3). The third diagnosis is mental disorder not otherwise specified due to a general medical condition (Table 10.5–4).

In addition to the mental disorders due to a general medical condition within the DSM-IV symptom categories, diagnoses for substance-induced psychiatric disorders appear. Specifically, DSM-IV allows for the diagnosis of intoxication-related or withdrawal-related substance-induced disorders with features of psychotic, mood, anxiety, and sleep disorders.

As a general rule, the differential diagnosis for a mental syndrome in a patient should always include consideration of any general medical disease or disorder a patient may have and consideration of any prescription, nonprescription, or illegal substances a patient may be taking. Although some general medical conditions have classically been associated with mental syndromes, a much larger number of general medical conditions have been associated with mental syndromes in case reports and small studies.

## DEGENERATIVE DISORDERS

Degenerative disorders affecting the basal ganglia are commonly associated not only with movement disorders but also with depression, dementia, and psychosis. The most widely known examples of the degenerative disorders are Parkinson's disease, Huntington's disease, Wilson's disease, and Fahr's disease. Parkinson's disease involves a degeneration primarily of the substantia nigra, and it usually has an unknown cause. Huntington's disease involves a degeneration primarily of the caudate nucleus, and it is an autosomal dominant disease. Wilson's disease is an autosomal recessive disease that results in the destructive deposition of copper in the lenticular nuclei. Fahr's disease is a rare hereditary disorder that involves the calcification and destruction of the basal ganglia.

**Table 10.5–2**
**Diagnostic Criteria for Catatonic Disorder Due to a General Medical Condition**

A. The presence of catatonia as manifested by motoric immobility, excessive motor activity (that is apparently purposeless and not influenced by external stimuli), extreme negativism or mutism, peculiarities of voluntary movement, or echolalia or echopraxia.

B. There is evidence from the history, physical examination, or laboratory findings that the disturbance is the direct physiological consequence of a general medical condition.

C. The disturbance is not better accounted for by another mental disorder (e.g., a manic episode).

D. The disturbance does not occur exclusively during the course of a delirium.

**Coding note:** Include the name of the general medical condition on Axis I, e.g., catatonic disorder due to hepatic encephalopathy; also code the general medical condition on Axis III.

Table from DSM-IV, *Diagnostic and Statistical Manual of Mental Disorders*, ed 4. Copyright American Psychiatric Association, Washington, 1994. Used with permission.

**Table 10.5–3**
**Diagnostic Criteria for Personality Change Due to a General Medical Condition**

A. A persistent personality disturbance that represents a change from the individual's previous characteristic personality pattern. (In children, the disturbance involves a marked deviation from normal development or a significant change in the child's usual behavior patterns lasting at least one year.)

B. There is evidence from the history, physical examination, or laboratory findings that the disturbance is the direct physiological consequence of a general medical condition.

C. The disturbance is not better accounted for by another mental disorder (including other mental disorders due to a general medical condition).

D. The disturbance does not occur exclusively during the course of a delirium and does not meet criteria for a dementia.

E. The disturbance causes clinically significant distress or impairment in social, occupational, or other important areas of functioning.

*Specify* **type:**
**Labile type**: if the predominant feature is affective lability
**Disinhibited type**: if the predominant feature is poor impulse control as evidenced by sexual indiscretions, etc.
**Aggressive type**: if the predominant feature is aggressive behavior
**Apathetic type**: if the predominant feature is marked apathy and indifference
**Paranoid type**: if the predominant feature is suspiciousness or paranoid ideation
**Other type**: if the predominant feature is not one of the above, e.g., personality change associated with a seizure disorder
**Combined type**: if more than one feature predominates in the clinical picture
**Unspecified type**

**Coding note:** Include the name of the general medical condition on Axis I, e.g., personality change due to temporal lobe epilepsy, also code the general medical condition on Axis III.

Table from DSM-IV, *Diagnostic and Statistical Manual of Mental Disorders*, ed 4. Copyright American Psychiatric Association, Washington, 1994. Used with permission.

**Table 10.5–4**
**Diagnostic Criteria for Mental Disorder Not Otherwise Specified Due to a General Medical Condition**

This residual category should be used for situations in which it has been established that the disturbance is caused by the direct physiological effects of a general medical condition, but the criteria are not met for a specific mental disorder due to a general medical condition (e.g., dissociative symptoms due to a complex partial seizures).

**Coding note:** Include the name of the general medical condition on Axis I, e.g., mental disorder not otherwise specified due to HIV disease; also code the general medical condition on Axis III.

Table from DSM-IV, *Diagnostic and Statistical Manual of Mental Disorders*, ed 4. Copyright American Psychiatric Association, Washington, 1994. Used with permission.

# EPILEPSY

Epilepsy is the most common chronic neurological disease in the general population, affecting about 1 percent of the population in the United States. For psychiatrists the major concerns regarding epilepsy are consideration of an epileptic diagnosis in psychiatric patients, the psychosocial ramifications of a diagnosis of epilepsy for a patient, and the psychological and cognitive effects of commonly used antiepileptic drugs. With regard to the first of those concerns, 30 to 50 percent of all epileptic persons have psychiatric difficulties sometime during the course of their illness. The most common behavioral symptom of epilepsy is a change in personality; psychosis, violence, and depression are much less common symptoms of an epileptic disorder.

## Definitions

A *seizure* is a transient paroxysmal pathophysiological disturbance of cerebral function that is caused by a spontaneous, excessive discharge of neurons. Patients are said to have *epilepsy* if they have a chronic condition characterized by recurrent seizures. The *ictus* or *ictal event* of a seizure is the seizure itself. The nonictal time periods can be categorized as preictal, postictal, and interictal. The symptoms present during the ictal event are primarily determined by the site of origin in the brain for the seizure and by the pattern of the spread of the seizure activity

through the brain. Interictal symptoms are influenced by the ictal event and other neuropsychiatric and psychosocial factors, such as coexisting psychiatric or neurological disorders, the presence of psychosocial stressors, and premorbid personality traits.

## Classification

The two major categories of seizures are partial and generalized. *Partial seizures* involve epileptiform activity in localized brain regions; *generalized seizures* involve the entire brain (Figure 10.5–1). A classification system for seizures is outlined in Table 10.5–5.

**Generalized seizures.** Generalized tonic-clonic seizures have the classic symptoms of loss of consciousness, generalized tonic-clonic movements of the limbs, tongue biting, and incontinence. Although the diagnosis of the ictal events of the seizure is relatively straightforward, the postictal state—which is characterized by a slow, gradual recovery of consciousness and cognition—occasionally presents a diagnostic dilemma for a psychiatrist in an emergency room. The period of recovery from a generalized tonic-clonic seizure ranges from a few minutes to many hours. The clinical picture is that of a gradually clearing delirium. The most common psychiatric problems associated with generalized seizures involve helping the patient adjust to a chronic neurological disorder and assessing the cognitive or behavioral effects of antiepileptic drugs.

ABSENCES (PETIT MAL). A difficult type of generalized

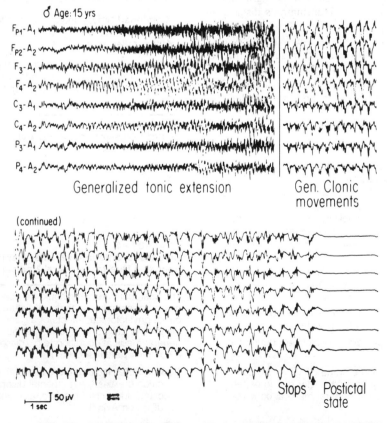

**Figure 10.5–1.** EEG recording during generalized tonic-clonic seizure, showing rhythmic sharp waves and muscle artifact during tonic phase, spike-and-wave discharges during clonic phase, and attenuation of activity during postictal state. (Figure courtesy of Barbara F. Westmoreland, M.D.)

**Table 10.5–5**
**International Classification of Epileptic Seizures**

I. Partial seizures (seizures beginning locally)
  A. Partial seizures with elementary symptoms generally without impairment of consciousness)
    1. With motor symptoms
    2. With sensory symptoms
    3. With autonomic symptoms
    4. Compound forms
  B. Partial seizures with complex symptoms (generally with impairment of consciousness; temporal lobe or psychomotor seizures)
    1. With impairment of consciousness only
    2. With cognitive symptoms
    3. With affective symptoms
    4. With psychosensory symptoms
    5. With psychosensory symptoms (automatisms)
    6. Compound forms
  C. Partial seizures secondarily generalized
II. Generalized seizures (bilaterally symmetrical and without local onset)
  A. Absences (petit mal)
  B. Myoclonus
  C. Infantile spasms
  D. Clonic seizures
  E. Tonic seizures
  F. Tonic-clonic seizures (grand mal)
  G. Atonic seizures
  H. Akinetic seizures
III. Unilateral seizures
IV. Unclassified seizures (because of incomplete data)

Table adapted from H Gastaut: Clinical and electroencephalographical classification of epileptic seizures. Epilepsia *11*: 102, 1970.

seizure for a psychiatrist to diagnose is an absence or petit mal seizure. The epileptic nature of the episodes may go unrecognized, because the characteristic motor or sensory manifestations of epilepsy may be absent or so slight that they do not arouse the physician's suspicion. Petit mal epilepsy usually begins in childhood between the ages of 5 and 7 years and ceases by puberty. Brief disruptions of consciousness, during which the patient suddenly loses contact with the environment, are characteristic of petit mal epilepsy; however, the patient has no true loss of consciousness or convulsive movements during the episodes. The electroencephalogram (EEG) produces a characteristic pattern of three-per-second spike-and-wave activity (Figure 10.5–2). In rare instances, petit mal epilepsy has its onset during adulthood. Adult-onset petit mal epilepsy can be characterized by sudden, recurrent psychotic episodes or deliriums that appear and disappear abruptly. The symptoms may be accompanied by a history of falling or fainting spells.

**Partial seizures.** Partial seizures are classified as either simple (without alterations in consciousness) or complex (with an alteration in consciousness). Somewhat more than half of all patients with partial seizures have complex partial seizures. Other terms used for complex partial seizures are temporal lobe epilepsy, psychomotor seizures, and limbic epilepsy; however, those terms are not accurate descriptions of the clinical situation. Complex partial epilepsy is the most common form of epilepsy in adults, affecting about 3 in 1,000 persons.

## Symptoms

**Preictal symptoms.** Preictal events (auras) in complex partial epilepsy include autonomic sensations (for example, fullness in the stomach, blushing, and changes in respiration), cognitive sensations (for example, *déjà vu, jamais vu,* forced thinking, and dreamy states), affective states (for example, fear, panic, depression, and elation), and, classically, automatisms (for example, lip smacking, rubbing, and chewing).

**Ictal symptoms.** Brief, disorganized, and uninhibited behavior characterizes the ictal event. Although some de-

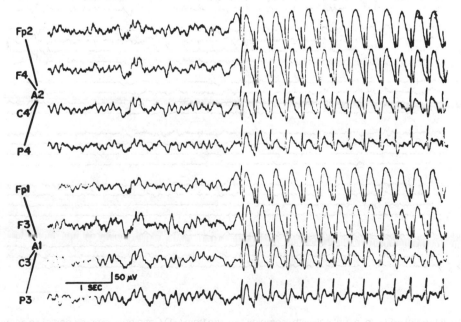

**Figure 10.5–2.** Petit mal epilepsy characterized by bilaterally synchronous, 3-Hz spike-and-slow-wave activity.

fense attorneys may claim otherwise, rarely does a person exhibit organized, directed violent behavior during an epileptic episode. The cognitive symptoms include amnesia for the time during the seizure and a period of resolving delirium after the seizure. In patients with complex partial epilepsy, a seizure focus can be found on an EEG in 25 to 50 percent of all patients (Figure 10.5–3). The use of sphenoidal or anterior temporal electrodes and of sleep-deprived EEGs may increase the likelihood of finding an EEG abnormality. Multiple normal EEGs are often obtained from a patient with complex partial epilepsy; therefore, normal EEGs cannot be used to exclude a diagnosis of complex partial epilepsy. The use of long-term EEG recordings (usually 24 to 72 hours) can help the clinician detect a seizure focus in some patients. Most studies show that the use of nasopharyngeal leads does not add much to the sensitivity of an EEG, and they certainly do add to the discomfort of the procedure for the patient.

### Interictal symptoms

PERSONALITY DISTURBANCES.   The most frequent psychiatric abnormalities reported in epileptic patients are personality disorders, and they are especially likely to occur in patients with epilepsy of temporal lobe origin. The most common features are changes in sexual behavior, a quality usually called viscosity of personality, religiosity, and a heightened experience of emotions. The syndrome in its complete form is relatively rare, even in those with complex partial seizures of temporal lobe origin. Many patients are not affected by personality disturbances; others suffer from a variety of disturbances that differ strikingly from the classic syndrome.

Changes in sexual behavior may be manifested by hypersexuality; deviations in sexual interest, such as fetishism and

transvestism; and, most commonly, hyposexuality. The hyposexuality is characterized both by a lack of interest in sexual matters and by reduced sexual arousal. Some patients with the onset of complex partial epilepsy before puberty may fail to reach a normal level of sexual interest after puberty, although that characteristic may not disturb the patient. For patients with the onset of complex partial epilepsy after puberty, the change in sexual interest may be bothersome and worrisome.

The symptom of viscosity of personality is usually most noticeable in a patient's conversation, which is likely to be slow, serious, ponderous, pedantic, overly replete with nonessential details, and often circumstantial. The listener may grow bored but be unable to find a courteous and successful way to disengage from the conversation. The speech tendencies are often mirrored in the patient's writing, resulting in a symptom known as hypergraphia, which some clinicians consider virtually pathognomonic for complex partial epilepsy.

Religiosity may be striking and may be manifested not only by increased participation in overtly religious activities but also by unusual concern for moral and ethical issues, preoccupation with right and wrong, and heightened interest in global and philosophical concerns. The hyperreligious features can sometimes seem like the prodromal symptoms of schizophrenia and can result in a diagnostic problem in an adolescent or a young adult.

PSYCHOTIC SYMPTOMS.   Interictal psychotic states are more common than ictal psychoses. Schizophrenialike interictal episodes can occur in patients with epilepsy, particularly those with temporal lobe origins. An estimated 10 to 30 percent of all patients with complex partial epilepsy have psychotic symptoms. Risk factors for the symptoms include female gender, left-handedness, the onset of seizures during puberty, and a left-sided lesion.

The onset of psychotic symptoms in epilepsy is variable.

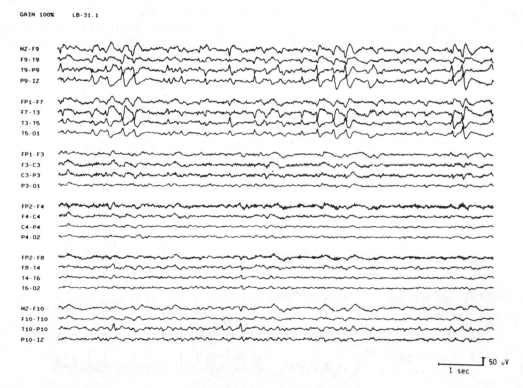

GAIN 100%    LB-31.1

1 sec    50 µV

**Figure 10.5–3.**   An interictal EEG in a patient with complex partial seizures reveals frequent left temporal spike discharges and rare, independent right temporal, sharp wave activity. (Figure from G D Cascino: Complex partial seizures: Clinical features and differential diagnosis. Psychiatr Clin North Am *15*: 377, 1992. Used with permission.)

Classically, psychotic symptoms appear in patients who have had epilepsy for a long time, and the onset of psychotic symptoms is preceded by the development of personality changes related to the epileptic brain activity.

The most characteristic symptoms of the psychoses are hallucinations and paranoid delusions. Usually, patients remain warm and appropriate in affect, in contrast to the abnormalities of affect that are commonly seen in schizophrenic patients. The thought disorder symptoms in psychotic epilepsy patients are most commonly those involving conceptualization and circumstantiality, rather than the classic schizophrenic symptoms of blocking and looseness.

VIOLENCE. Episodic violence has been a problem in some patients with epilepsy, especially epilepsy of temporal and frontal lobe origin. Whether the violence is a manifestation of the seizure itself or is of interictal psychopathology is uncertain. To date, most of the evidence points to the extreme rarity of violence as an ictal phenomenon. Only in rare cases should an epileptic patient's violence be attributed to the seizure itself.

MOOD DISORDER SYMPTOMS. Mood disorder symptoms, such as depression and mania, are seen less often in epilepsy than are schizophreniclike symptoms. The mood disorder symptoms that do occur tend to be episodic and to occur most often when the epileptic foci affect the temporal lobe of the nondominant cerebral hemisphere. The importance of the mood disorder symptoms in epilepsy may be attested to by the increased incidence of attempted suicide in persons with epilepsy.

## Diagnosis

A correct diagnosis of epilepsy can be particularly difficult when the ictal and interictal symptoms of epilepsy are severe manifestations of psychiatric symptoms in the absence of significant changes in consciousness and cognitive abilities. Therefore, psychiatrists must maintain a high level of suspicion during the evaluation of a new patient and must consider the possibility of an epileptic disorder, even in the absence of the classic signs and symptoms. Another differential diagnosis to consider is that of *pseudoseizure*, in which a patient has some conscious control over mimicking the symptoms of a seizure (Table 10.5–6).

In patients who have previously received a diagnosis of epilepsy, the appearance of new psychiatric symptoms should be considered as possibly representing an evolution in their epileptic symptoms. The appearance of psychotic symptoms, mood disorder symptoms, personality changes, or symptoms of anxiety (for example, panic attacks) should cause the clinician to evaluate the control of the patient's epilepsy and to assess the patient for the presence of an independent mental disorder. In such circumstances the clinician should evaluate the patient's compliance with the antiepileptic drug regimen and should consider whether the psychiatric symptoms could be toxic effects from the antiepileptic drugs themselves. When psychiatric symptoms appear in a patient who has had epilepsy diagnosed or considered as a diagnosis in the past, the clinician should obtain one or more EEG examinations.

In patients who have not previously received a diagnosis of epilepsy, four characteristics should cause the clinician to be suspicious of the possibility: the abrupt onset of psychosis in a person previously regarded as psychologically healthy, the abrupt onset of delirium without a recognized cause, a history of similar episodes with abrupt onset and spontaneous recovery, and a history of previous unexplained falling or fainting spells.

## Treatment

The drugs of choice for various types of seizures are listed in Table 10.5–7. Carbamazepine (Tegretol) and valproic acid (Depakene) may be helpful in controlling the symptoms of irritability and outbursts of aggression, as are the typical antipsychotic drugs. Psychotherapy, family counseling, and group therapy may be useful in addressing the psychosocial issues that may be associated with epilepsy. In addition, the clinician should be aware that many antiepileptic drugs have a mild to moderate degree of cognitive impairment, and an adjustment of the dosage or a change in medications should be considered if symptoms of cognitive impairment are a problem in a particular patient.

## BRAIN TUMORS

Brain tumors and cerebrovascular diseases can cause virtually any psychiatric symptom or syndrome. However, cerebrovascular diseases, by the nature of their onset and symptom pattern, are rarely misdiagnosed as mental disorders. In general, tumors are associated with much less

**Table 10.5–6**
**Differentiating Features of Pseudoseizures and Epileptic Seizures**

| Feature | Epileptic Seizure | Pseudoseizure |
|---|---|---|
| Clinical features | | |
| Nocturnal seizure | Common | Uncommon |
| Stereotyped aura | Usually | None |
| Cyanotic skin changes during seizures | Common | None |
| Self-injury | Common | Rare |
| Incontinence | Common | Rare |
| Postictal confusion | Present | None |
| Body movements | Tonic or clonic or both | Nonstereotyped and asynchronous |
| Affected by suggestion | No | Yes |
| EEG features | | |
| Spike and waveforms | Present | Absent |
| Postictal slowing | Present | Absent |
| Interictal abnormalities | Variable | Variable |

Table from J M Stevenson, J H King: Neuropsychiatric aspects of epilepsy and epileptic seizures. In *American Psychiatric Press Textbook of Neuropsychiatry,* R E Hales, S C Yodofsky, editors, p 220. American Psychiatric Press, Washington, 1987. Used with permission.

**Table 10.5–7**
**Drugs of Choice for Various Types of Seizures**

Generalized tonic-clonic (grand mal) seizures
    Phenobarbital (Luminal)
    Phenytoin (Dilantin)
    Carbamazepine (Tegretol)
    Valproic acid (Depakene)
Absence (petit mal) seizures
    Ethosuximide (Zarontin)
    Valproic acid (Depakene)
    Trimethadione (Tridione)
Simple partial (focal) seizures
    Phenobarbital (Luminal)
    Phenytoin (Dilantin)
Complex partial (temporal lobe) seizures
    Phenytoin (Dilantin)
    Carbamazepine (Tegretol)
Myoclonic, atonic, akinetic, and atypical absence seizures
    Clonazepam (Klonopin)
    Diazepam (Valium)
Infantile spasms
    Adrenocorticotropic hormone
    Corticosteroids
Satus epilepticus
    Diazepam (Valium)
    Phenobarbital (Luminal)
    Amobarbital (Amytal)
    Phenytoin (Dilantin)
    Paraldehyde
    Anesthetic agent

psychopathology than are cerebrovascular diseases affecting a similar volume of brain tissue. The two key approaches to the diagnosis of either condition are a comprehensive clinical history and a complete neurological examination. The choice of the appropriate brain imaging technology is usually the final diagnostic procedure; the imaging should usually confirm the clinical diagnosis, rather than discover an unsuspected cause.

## Clinical Features, Course, and Prognosis

At some time during the course of their illnesses, about 50 percent of patients with brain tumors experience mental symptoms. About 80 percent of brain tumor patients with mental symptoms have their tumors in frontal or limbic brain regions, rather than in parietal or temporal regions. Another general guideline is that meningiomas are likely to cause focal symptoms, since they compress a limited region of the cortex, whereas gliomas are likely to cause diffuse symptoms. Delirium is most often a component of rapidly growing, large, or metastic tumors. If the patient's history and a physical examination reveal bowel or bladder incontinence, a frontal lobe tumor should be suspected; if the history and the examination reveal abnormalities in memory and speech, a temporal lobe tumor should be suspected.

**Cognition.** Impaired intellectual functioning often accompanies the presence of a brain tumor, regardless of its type or location.

**Language skills.** Disorders of language function may be severe, particularly if the tumor growth is rapid. In fact, defects of language function often obscure all other mental symptoms.

**Memory.** Loss of memory is a frequent symptom of brain tumors. Patients with brain tumors may present with Korsakoff's syndrome, retaining no memory of events that occurred since the illness began. Events of the immediate past, even painful ones, are lost. Old memories, however, are retained, and patients are unaware of their loss of recent memory.

**Perception.** Prominent perceptual defects are often associated with behavioral disorders, especially when the patient needs to integrate tactile, auditory, and visual perceptions.

**Awareness.** Alterations of consciousness are common late symptoms of increased intracranial pressure caused by a brain tumor. Tumors arising in the upper part of the brainstem may produce a unique symptom called akinetic mutism or vigilant coma. The patient is immobile and mute, yet alert.

## Colloid Cysts

Although not, strictly speaking, brain tumors, colloid cysts located in the third ventricle can exert physical pressure on structures within the diencephalon, resulting in such mental symptoms as depression, emotional lability, psychotic symptoms, and personality changes. The classic associated neurological symptoms are position-dependent intermittent headaches.

## HEAD TRAUMA

Head trauma can result in an array of mental symptoms. Head trauma can lead to a diagnosis of dementia due to head trauma or to mental disorder not otherwise specified due to a general medical condition (for example, postconcussional disorder). The postconcussive syndrome remains controversial, since it focuses on the wide range of psychiatric symptoms, some quite serious, that can follow what seem to be minor head traumas. DSM-IV includes a set of research criteria for postconcussional disorder in an appendix (Table 10.5–8).

### Pathophysiology

Head trauma is a common clinical situation; an estimated 2 million incidents involve head trauma each year. Head trauma most commonly occurs in persons 15 to 25 years of age, and it has a male-to-female predominance of about 3 to 1. Gross estimates based on the severity of the head trauma suggest that virtually all patients with serious head trauma, more than half of the patients with moderate head trauma, and about 10 percent of the patients with mild head trauma have ongoing neuropsychiatric sequelae resulting from the head trauma.

Head trauma can be grossly divided into penetrating head trauma (for example, a bullet) and blunt trauma, in which there is no physical penetration of the skull. Blunt trauma is far more common than penetrating head trauma, and motor vehicle accidents account for more than half of all the incidents of blunt central nervous system (CNS) trauma. Falls, violence, and sports-related head trauma account for most of the remaining cases of blunt head trauma.

Whereas brain injury from penetrating wounds is usu-

## Table 10.5–8
**Diagnostic Criteria for Postconcussional Disorder**

A. A history of head trauma that has caused significant cerebral concussion.

   **Note:** The manifestations of concussion include loss of consciousness, posttraumatic amnesia, and less commonly, posttraumatic onset of seizures. The specific method of defining this criterion needs to be established by further research.

B. Evidence from neuropsychological testing or quantified cognitive assessment of difficulty in attention (concentrating, shifting focus of attention, performing simultaneous cognitive tasks) or memory (learning or recalling information).

C. Three (or more) of the following occur shortly after the trauma and last at least 3 months.

   (1) becoming fatigued easily
   (2) disordered sleep
   (3) headache
   (4) vertigo or dizziness
   (5) irritability or aggression on little or no provocation
   (6) anxiety, depression, or affective lability
   (7) changes in personality (e.g., social or sexual inappropriateness)
   (8) apathy or lack of spontantiety

D. The symptoms in criteria B and C have their onset following head trauma or else represent a substantial worsening of preexisting symptoms.

E. The disturbance causes significant impairment in social or occupational functioning and represents a significant decline from a previous level of functioning. In school-age children, the impairment may be manifested by a significant worsening in school or academic performance dating from the trauma.

F. The symptoms do not meet criteria for dementia due to head trauma and are not better accounted for by another mental disorder (e.g., amnestic disorder due to head trauma, personality change due to head trauma).

Table from DSM-IV, *Diagnostic and Statistical Manual of Mental Disorders*, ed 4. Copyright American Psychiatric Association, Washington, 1994. Used with permission.

---

ally localized to the areas directly affected by the missile, brain injury from blunt trauma involves several mechanisms. During the actual head trauma, the head usually moves back and forth violently, thus causing the brain to crash repeatedly against the skull as it and the skull are mismatched in their rapid deceleration and acceleration. That crashing results in focal contusions. The stretching of the brain parenchyma results in diffuse axonal injury. Later-developing processes, such as edema and hemorrhaging, may result in further damage to the brain.

### Symptoms

The two major clusters of symptoms related to head trauma are those of cognitive impairment and those of behavioral sequelae. After a period of posttraumatic amnesia, there is usually a 6-to-12-month period of recovery, after which the remaining symptoms are likely to be permanent. The most common cognitive problems are a decreased speed in information processing, decreased attention, increased distractibility, deficits in problem solving and in the ability to sustain effort, and problems with memory and learning new information. A variety of language disabilities may also be present.

Behaviorally, the major symptoms involve changes in personality, depression, increased impulsivity, and increased aggression. Those symptoms may be further exacerbated by the use of alcohol, which was often involved in the head trauma event itself. A debate has ensued about how preexisting character and personality traits affect the development of behavioral symptoms after a head trauma. The critical studies needed to answer the question definitively have not been done yet, but the weight of opinion is leaning toward a biologically and neuroanatomically based association between the head trauma and the behavioral sequelae.

### Treatment

The treatment of the cognitive and behavioral disorders in head trauma patients is basically similar to the treatment approaches used in other patients with those symptoms. One difference is that head trauma patients may be particularly susceptible to the side effects associated with psychotropic drugs; therefore, those agents should be initiated in lower dosages than usual and should be titrated upward more slowly than usual. Standard antidepressants can be used to treat depression, and either anticonvulsants or antipsychotics can be used to treat aggression and impulsivity. Other approaches to the symptoms include lithium (Eskalith), calcium channel blockers, and β-adrenergic antagonists.

The clinician must support the patient through individual and group psychotherapy and should support the major caretakers through couples and family therapy. Especially with minor and moderate head traumas, the patients will rejoin their families and restart their jobs, so all involved parties need help to adjust to any changes in the affected patient's personality and mental abilities.

## DEMYELINATING DISORDERS

The major demyelinating disorder is multiple sclerosis (MS). Other demyelinating disorders include amyotrophic lateral sclerosis, metachromatic leukodystrophy, adrenoleukodystrophy, gangliosidoses, subacute sclerosing panencephalitis, and Kufs disease. All those disorders can be associated with neurological, cognitive, and behavioral symptoms.

### Multiple Sclerosis

MS is characterized by multiple episodes of symptoms, pathophysiologically related to multifocal lesions in the white matter of the CNS. The cause remains unknown, but studies have focused on slow viral infections and disturbances in the immune system.

The estimated prevalence of multiple sclerosis in the Western hemisphere is 50 patients per 100,000 people. The disease is much more frequent in cold and temperate climates than in the tropics and subtropics. It is more common in women than in men and is predominantly a disease of young adults. The onset in the vast majority of patients is between the ages of 20 and 40 years.

The neuropsychiatric symptoms of MS can be divided into the cognitive symptoms and the behavioral symptoms. Research reports have found that 30 to 50 percent of patients with MS have some cognitive impairment and that 20 to 30 percent of MS patients have serious cognitive impairments. Although evidence indicates that MS patients experience a decline in their general intelligence, memory is the most commonly affected cognitive function. The severity of the memory impairment does not seem to be correlated with the severity of the neurological symptoms or the duration of the illness. Other cognitive impairments can be seen in MS, as is expected for a disease in which any part of the brain can be affected by the white matter lesions.

The behavioral symptoms associated with MS are euphoria, depression, and personality changes. Psychosis is a rare complication of MS. About 25 percent of patients with MS have a euphoric mood that is not hypomanic in severity but, rather, somewhat more cheerful than their situation warrants and not necessarily in character with their disposition before the onset of MS. Only 10 percent of MS patients have a sustained and elevated mood, although it is still not truly hypomanic in severity. Depression, however, is common, affecting 25 to 50 percent of patients with MS and resulting in a higher rate of suicide than is seen in the general population. Risk factors for suicide in MS patients are male sex, the onset of MS before age 30, and a relatively recent diagnosis of the disorder. Personality changes are also common in MS patients, affecting 20 to 40 percent of patients and often characterized by increased irritability or apathy.

## Amyotrophic Lateral Sclerosis

Amyotrophic lateral sclerosis (ALS) is a progressive, noninherited disease of asymmetrical muscle atrophy. It begins in adult life and progresses over months or years to involve all the striated muscles except the cardiac and ocular muscles. In addition to muscle atrophy, patients have signs of pyramidal tract involvement. The illness is rare, occurring in about 1.6 persons per 100,000 a year. A few of the patients have concomitant dementia. The disease progresses rapidly, and death generally occurs within four years of onset.

## INFECTIOUS DISEASES

### Herpes Simplex Encephalitis

Herpes simplex encephalitis is the most common type of focal encephalitis; it most commonly affects the frontal and temporal lobes. The symptoms often involve anosomia, olfactory and gustatory hallucinations, and personality changes and can also involve bizarre or psychotic behaviors. Complex partial epilepsy may also develop in patients with herpes simplex encephalitis. Although the mortality for the infection has decreased, a high morbidity involves personality changes, symptoms of memory loss, and psychotic symptoms.

### Rabies Encephalitis

The inoculation period for rabies ranges from 10 days to one year, after which symptoms of restlessness, overactivity, and agitation can develop. *Hydrophobia,* present in up to 50 percent of patients, is characterized by an intense fear of drink-

ing water. The fear develops from the severe laryngeal and diaphragmatic spasms that the patients experience from drinking water. Once rabies encephalitis develops, the disease is fatal within days or weeks.

## Neurosyphilis

Neurosyphilis (also known as general paresis) appears 10 to 15 years after the primary *Treponema* infection. Since the advent of penicillin, neurosyphilis has become a rare disorder, although acquired immune deficiency syndrome (AIDS) has reintroduced neurosyphilis into medical practice in some urban settings. Neurosyphilis generally affects the frontal lobes, resulting in personality changes, the development of poor judgment, irritability, and decreased care for self. Delusions of grandeur develop in 10 to 20 percent of affected patients. The disease progresses with the development of dementia and tremor, resulting eventually in bedridden patients with paretic neurosyphilis. The neurological symptoms include Argyll-Robertson pupils, which are small, irregular, and unequal and have light-near reflex dissociation; tremor; dysarthria; and hyperreflexia. A cerebrospinal fluid (CSF) examination of the patients shows a lymphocytosis, increased protein, and a positive result on a Venereal Disease Research Laboratory (VDRL) test.

## Chronic Meningitis

Chronic meningitis is also seen more often today than in the recent past because of the immunocompromised condition of AIDS patients. The most usual causative agents are *Mycobacterium tuberculosis, Cryptococcus,* and *Coccidioides.* The usual symptoms are headache, memory impairment, confusion, and fever.

## Subacute Sclerosing Panencephalitis

Subacute sclerosing panencephalitis is a disease of childhood and early adolescence, with a 3 to 1 male-to-female ratio. The onset usually follows either an infection with measles or a vaccination for measles. The initial symptoms may be a change in behavior, temper tantrums, sleepiness, and hallucinations, but the classic symptoms of myoclonus, ataxia, seizures, and intellectual deterioration eventually develop. The disease relentlessly progresses to coma and death in one to two years.

## Creutzfeldt-Jakob Disease

Creutzfeldt-Jakob disease is a rare degenerative brain disease caused by a slow virus infection. A progressive dementia occurs, accompanied by ataxia, extrapyramidal signs, choreoathetosis, and dysarthria. The disease is most common in adults in their 50s, and death occurs usually within one year after the diagnosis is made. Men and women are affected equally. No treatment is known. Computed tomography (CT) scans show cerebellar and cortical atrophy, and specific EEG changes occur in the late stages.

## Kuru

Kuru is a progressive dementia accompanied by extrapyramidal signs. It is found among the natives of New Guinea who practice cannibalistic rites. By eating the brains of infected persons, the natives take in the slow virus that produces the fatal disease.

## IMMUNE DISORDERS

The major immune disorder affecting contemporary society is AIDS. However, other immune disorders can also present diagnostic and treatment challenges to mental health clinicians.

### Systemic Lupus Erythematosus

Systemic lupus erythematosus (SLE) is an autoimmune disease that involves a sterile inflammation of multiple organ systems. The officially accepted diagnosis of SLE requires that the patient have 4 of 11 criteria that have been defined by the American Rheumatism Association. Between 5 and 50 percent of SLE patients have mental symptoms at the initial presentation, and about 50 percent of patients eventually show neuropsychiatric manifestations. The major symptoms are depression, insomnia, emotional lability, nervousness, and confusion. Treatment with steroids commonly induces further psychiatric complications, including mania and psychosis.

## ENDOCRINE DISORDERS

### Thyroid Disorders

Hyperthyroidism is characterized by confusion, anxiety, and an agitated depressive syndrome. Patients may also complain of easy fatigability and generalized weakness. Insomnia, weight loss in spite of increased appetite, tremulousness, palpitations, and increased perspiration are also common symptoms. Serious psychiatric symptoms include impairments in memory, orientation, and judgment; manic excitement; delusions; and hallucinations.

Hypothyroidism was called "myxedema madness" in 1949 by Irvin Asher. In its most severe form, it is characterized by paranoia, depression, hypomania, and hallucinations. Slowed thinking and delirium can also be part of the symptom picture. The physical symptoms include weight gain, a deep voice, thin and dry hair, loss of the lateral eyebrow, facial puffiness, cold intolerance, and impaired hearing. About 10 percent of all patients have residual neuropsychiatric symptoms after hormone replacement therapy.

### Parathyroid Disorders

Dysfunction of the parathyroid gland results in the abnormal regulation of calcium metabolism. Excessive secretion of the parathyroid hormone causes hypercalcemia, which can result in delirium, personality changes, and apathy in 50 to 60 percent of patients and in cognitive impairments in about 25 percent of patients. Neuromuscular excitability, which depends on proper calcium ion concentration, is reduced, and muscle weakness may appear.

Hypocalcemia can occur with hypoparathyroid disorders and can result in neuropsychiatric symptoms of delirium and personality changes. If the calcium level drops gradually, the clinician may see the psychiatric symptoms without the characteristic tetany seen with hypocalcemia. Other symptoms of hypocalcemia are cataract formation, seizures, extrapyramidal symptoms, and increased intracranial pressure.

### Adrenal Disorders

Adrenal disorders cause changes in the normal secretion of hormones from the adrenal cortex and produce significant neurological and psychological changes. Patients with chronic adrenocortical insufficiency (Addison's disease), which is most frequently the result of adrenocortical atrophy or granulomatous invasion caused by tuberculous or fungal infection, exhibit mild mental symptoms, such as apathy, easy fatigability, irritability, and depression. Occasionally, psychotic reactions or confusion develop. Cortisone or one of its synthetic derivatives is effective in correcting such abnormalities.

Excessive quantities of cortisol produced endogenously by an adrenocortical tumor or hyperplasia (Cushing's syndrome) lead to a secondary mood disorder, a syndrome of agitated depression, and, often, suicide. Decreased concentration and memory deficits may also be present. Psychotic reactions, with schizophrenialike symptoms, are seen in a small number of patients. The administration of high dosages of exogenous corticosteroids typically leads to a secondary mood disorder similar to mania. Severe depression may follow the termination of steroid therapy.

### Pituitary Disorders

Total pituitary failure can present with psychiatric symptoms, particularly in a postpartum woman who has hemorrhaged into her pituitary, a condition known as *Sheehan's syndrome*. Patients have a combination of symptoms, especially of thyroid and adrenal disorders, and can present with virtually any psychiatric symptom.

## METABOLIC DISORDERS

Metabolic encephalopathy is a common cause of organic brain dysfunction and is capable of producing alterations in mental processes, behavior, and neurological functions. The diagnosis should be considered whenever recent and rapid changes in behavior, thinking, and consciousness have occurred. The earliest signals are likely to be an impairment of memory, particularly recent memory, and an impairment of orientation. Some patients become agitated, anxious, and hyperactive; others become quiet, withdrawn, and inactive. As metabolic encephalopathies progress, confusion or delirium gives way to decreased responsiveness, to stupor, and, eventually, to death.

### Hepatic Encephalopathy

Severe hepatic failure can result in hepatic encephalopathy, characterized by alterations in consciousness, asterixis, hyperventilation, and EEG abnormalities. The alterations in consciousness can range from apathy to drowsiness to coma. Associated psychiatric symptoms are changes in memory, in general intellectual skills, and in personality.

### Uremic Encephalopathy

Renal failure is associated with alterations in memory, orientation, and consciousness. Restlessness, crawling sensations on the limbs, muscle twitching, and persistent hiccups are also associated symptoms. In young people with brief episodes of uremia, the neuropsychiatric symptoms tend to be reversible; in elderly people with long episodes of uremia, the neuropsychiatric symptoms can be irreversible.

## Hypoglycemic Encephalopathy

Hypoglycemic encephalopathy can be caused either by the excessive endogenous production of insulin or by excessive exogenous insulin administration. The premonitory symptoms, which do not occur in every patient, include nausea, sweating, tachycardia, and feelings of hunger, apprehension, and restlessness. With the progression of the disorder, disorientation, confusion, and hallucinations can develop, as well as other neurological and medical symptoms. Stupor and coma can develop, and a residual and persistent dementia can sometimes be a serious neuropsychiatric sequela of the disorder.

## Diabetic Ketoacidosis

Diabetic ketoacidosis begins with feelings of weakness, easy fatigability, and listlessness and with increasing polyuria and polydipsia. Headache and sometimes nausea and vomiting appear. Patients with diabetes mellitus have an increased likelihood of a chronic dementia with general arteriosclerosis.

## Acute Intermittent Porphyria

The porphyrias are disorders of heme biosynthesis, resulting in the excessive accumulation of porphyrins. The triad of symptoms are (1) acute, colicky abdominal pain; (2) motor polyneuropathy; and (3) psychosis. Acute intermittent porphyria is an autosomal dominant disorder that affects more women than men and that has its onset between ages 20 and 50. The psychiatric symptoms include anxiety, insomnia, lability of mood, depression, and psychosis. Some studies have found that between 0.2 and 0.5 percent of chronic psychiatric patients may have undiagnosed porphyrias. Barbiturates precipitate or aggravate the attacks of acute porphyria. The use of barbiturates for any reason is absolutely contraindicated in a person with acute intermittent porphyria and in anyone who has a relative with the disease.

## NUTRITIONAL DISORDERS

## Niacin Deficiency

Dietary insufficiency of niacin (nicotinic acid) and its precursor, tryptophan, is associated with *pellagra,* a nutritional deficiency disease of global importance. Pellagra is seen in association with alcohol abuse, vegetarian diets, and extreme poverty and starvation. The neuropsychiatric symptoms include apathy, irritability, insomnia, depression, and delirium. The medical symptoms include dermatitis, peripheral neuropathies, and diarrhea. Traditionally, pellagra was described with five Ds: dermatitis, diarrhea, delirium, dementia, and death. The response to treatment with nicotinic acid is rapid; however, dementia from prolonged illness may improve only slowly and incompletely.

## Thiamine Deficiency

Thiamine (vitamin B₁) deficiency leads to *beriberi,* characterized chiefly by cardiovascular and neurological changes, and to Wernicke-Korsakoff syndrome, which is most often associated with chronic alcohol abuse. Beriberi occurs primarily in Asia and in areas of famine and poverty. The psychiatric symptoms include apathy, depression, irritability, nervousness, and poor concentration; severe memory disorders can develop with severe and prolonged deficiencies.

## Cobalamin Deficiency

Deficiencies in cobalamin (vitamin B₁₂) arise because of the failure of the gastric mucosal cells to secrete a specific substance, intrinsic factor, which is required for the normal absorption of vitamin B₁₂ from the ileum. The deficiency state is characterized by the development of a chronic macrocytic megaloblastic anemia (pernicious anemia) and by neurological manifestations resulting from degenerative changes in the peripheral nerves, the spinal cord, and the brain. Neurological changes are seen in about 80 percent of all patients. Those changes are commonly associated with megaloblastic anemia, but they occasionally precede the onset of hematological abnormalities.

Mental changes such as apathy, depression, irritability, and moodiness are common. In a few patients, encephalopathy and its associated delirium, delusions, hallucinations, dementia, and sometimes paranoid features are prominent and are sometimes called megaloblastic madness. The neurological manifestations of vitamin B₁₂ deficiency can be completely and rapidly arrested by the early and continued administration of parenteral vitamin therapy.

## TOXINS

Environmental toxins are becoming an increasingly serious threat to physical and mental health in contemporary society. Although the delirium and the dementia associated with arsenic is of historical interest, mercury poisoning is an increasingly important differential diagnosis.

## Mercury

Mercury poisoning can be from either inorganic mercury or organic mercury. Inorganic mercury poisoning results in the Mad Hatter syndrome (mercury is used in the hat industry), with depression, irritability, and psychosis. Associated neurological symptoms are headache, tremor, and weakness. Organic mercury poisoning can come from contaminated fish or grain and can result in depression, irritability, and cognitive impairments. Associated symptoms are sensory neuropathies, cerebellar ataxia, dysarthria, paresthesias, and visual field defects.

### References

Biller J, Kathol R H: The interface of psychiatry and neurology. Psychiatr Clin North Am *15* (2): 283, 1992.

Currier M B, Murray G B, Elch C C: Electroconvulsive therapy for poststroke depressed geriatric patients. J Neuropsychiatry Clin Neurosci *4:* 140, 1992.

Dunlop T W, Udvarhelyi G B, Stedem A F A, O'Connor J M C, Isaacs M L, Puig J G, Mather J H: Comparison of patients with and without emotional/behavioral deterioration during first year after traumatic brain injury. J Neuropsychiatry Clin Neurosci *3*: 150, 1991.

Fedoroff J P, Starkstein S E, Forrester A W, Giesler F H, Jorge R E, Arndt S V, Robinson R G: Depression in patients with acute traumatic brain injury. Am J Psychiatry *149*: 918, 1992.

Fornazzari L, Farcnik K, Smith I, Heasman G A, Ichise M: Violent visual hallucinations and aggression in frontal lobe dysfunction: Clinical manifestations of deep orbitofrontal foci. J Neuropsychiatry Clin Neurosci *4*: 42, 1992.

Herman B P, Seidenberg M, Haltiner A, Wyler A R: Mood state in unilateral temporal lobe epilepsy. Biol Psychiatry *30*: 1205, 1991.

Iverson G L: Psychopathology associated with systemic lupus erythema-

tosus: A methodological review. Semin Arthritis Rheum *22*: 242, 1993.

Jorge R E, Robinson R G, Starkstein S E, Arndt S V: Depression and anxiety following traumatic brain injury. J Neuropsychiatry *5*: 369, 1993.

Lishman W A: *Organic Psychiatry: The Psychological Consequences of Cerebral Disorder,* ed 2. Blackwell Scientific, Oxford, 1987.

Masand P, Murray G B, Pickett P: Psychostimulants in post-stroke depression. J Neuropsychiatry Clin Neurosci *3*: 23, 1991.

Stenager E N, Stenager E, Koch-Henriksen N, Bronnum-Hansen H, Hyllested K, Jensen K, Bille-Brahe U: Suicide and multiple sclerosis: An epidemiological investigation. J Neurol Neurosurg Psychiatry *55*: 542, 1992.

# 11 |||||

# Neuropsychiatric Aspects of Human Immunodeficiency Virus (HIV) Infection and Acquired Immune Deficiency Syndrome (AIDS)

Acquired immune deficiency syndrome (AIDS) results from infection by the human immunodeficiency virus (HIV), which is causally related to a broad array of other medical conditions and neuropsychiatric syndromes. HIV is a ribonucleic acid (RNA)-containing retrovirus that was isolated and identified in 1983. HIV infects cells of the immune system and the nervous system. Infection of T4 (helper) lymphocytes eventually results in impaired cell-mediated immunity, dramatically limiting the ability of the body to protect itself from other infectious agents and to prevent the development of specific neoplastic disorders. Infection of cells (primarily astrocytes) within the central nervous system (CNS) results directly in the development of neuropsychiatric syndromes, which are commonly further complicated in patients with AIDS by the neuropsychiatric effects of opportunistic CNS infections, CNS neoplasms, antiviral treatment-related adverse effects, independent psychiatric syndromes, and myriad psychosocial stresses related to having an HIV-related disorder.

HIV-related disorders (including AIDS) have profoundly changed the face of health care worldwide. Mental health clinicians have had a major role in the health care system in the efforts to cope with HIV-related disorders. Mental health clinicians are involved in three major areas of care for HIV-infected patients: First, pathological involvement of the brain has been reported to be present in 75 to 90 percent of autopsies performed on persons who had had AIDS. Clinically, neuropsychiatric complications (for example, HIV encephalopathy) occur in at least 50 percent of HIV-infected patients and may be the first signs of the disease in about 10 percent of patients. Mental health clinicians are, therefore, involved in the assessment and the treatment of those neuropsychiatric syndromes. Second, classic psychiatric syndromes (for example, anxiety disorders, depressive disorders, and psychotic disorders) are commonly associated with HIV-related disorders. Mental health clinicians are essential to the assessment and the treatment of those syndromes with both pharmacological and psychotherapeutic modalities. Third, the entire field of mental health has been involved in helping society cope with the effects of this modern plague. Mental health professionals and mental health organizations (for example, the National Institute of Mental Health) have used their influence to educate people about the societal effects of HIV-related disorders and about the need for change in behaviors that are generally held to be private, such as sexual and substance-using behaviors.

## HIV AND ITS TRANSMISSION

At least two types of HIV have been identified, HIV-1 and HIV-2. HIV-1 is the causative agent for the vast majority of HIV-related diseases; however, there seems to be an increasing occurrence of infection by HIV-2 in Africa. HIV is a retrovirus related to the human T-cell leukemia viruses (HTLV) and to a variety of retroviruses that infect animals, including nonhuman primates.

HIV is present in the blood, the semen, cervical and vaginal secretions, and, to a smaller extent, the saliva, tears, breast milk, and cerebrospinal fluid of infected persons. Transmission of HIV most often occurs through sexual intercourse or the transfer of contaminated blood between persons. Unprotected anal, vaginal, and oral sex are the sexual activities most likely to transmit the virus. Health providers should be aware of the guidelines for safe sexual practices and should advise their patients to practice safe sex (Table 11–1).

Although male-to-male transmission has been the most common route of sexual transmission, male-to-female transmission and female-to-male transmission have been documented and represent an increasingly large percentage of the transmission routes. Some studies have found that about 50 percent of the regular sex partners of HIV-infected persons have become infected themselves, suggesting that some persons have an as yet not understood immunity or resistance to HIV infection.

Transmission by contaminated blood most often occurs when intravenous (IV) substance-dependent persons share hypodermic needles without proper sterilization techniques. Transmission of HIV through blood transfusions, organ transplantation, and artificial insemination is no longer a problem because of the testing of donors for HIV infection. Tragically, the transfusions of blood products did infect many hemophiliacs before HIV was identified as the causative agent.

Children can be infected in utero or through breast feeding when their mothers are infected with HIV.

Health workers are theoretically at risk because of potential contact with bodily fluids from HIV-infected patients. In practice, however, the incidence of such transmission is very low, and almost all reported cases have been traced back to accidental needle punctures with contaminated hypodermic needles.

No evidence has been found that HIV can be contracted through casual contact, such as sharing a living space or a

**Table 11–1**
**AIDS Safe-Sex Guidelines**

Remember: Any activity that allows for the exchange of body fluids of one person through the mouth, anus, vagina, bloodstream, cuts, or sores of another person is considered unsafe at this time.

**Safe-Sex Practices**
Massage, hugging, body-to-body rubbing
Dry social kissing
Masturbation
Acting out sexual fantasies (that do not include any unsafe-sex practices)
Using vibrators or other instruments (provided they are not shared)

**Low-Risk Sex Practices**
These activities are not considered completely safe:
French (wet) kissing (without mouth sores)
Mutual masturbation
Vaginal and anal intercourse while using a condom
Oral sex, male (fellatio), while using a condom
Oral sex, female (cunnilingus), while using a barrier
External contact with semen or urine, provided there are no breaks in the skin

**Unsafe-Sex Practices**
Vaginal or anal intercourse without a condom
Semen, urine, or feces in the mouth or the vagina
Unprotected oral sex (fellatio or cunnilingus)
Blood contact of any kind
Sharing sex instruments or needles

Table from B Moffatt, J Spiegel, S Parrish, M Helquist: *AIDS: A Self-Care Manual,* p 125. IBS Press, Santa Monica, Calif, 1987. Used with permission.

**Table 11–2**
**CDC Guidelines for the Prevention of HIV Transmission from Infected to Uninfected Persons**

Infected persons should be counseled to prevent the further transmission of HIV by:

1. Informing prospective sex partners of their infection with HIV, so they can take appropriate precautions. Abstention from sexual activity with another person is one option that would eliminate any risk of sexually transmitted HIV infection.

2. Protecting a partner during any sexual activity by taking appropriate precautions to prevent that person's coming into contact with the infected person's blood, semen, urine, feces, saliva, cervical secretions, or vaginal secretions. Although the efficacy of using condoms to prevent infections with HIV is still under study, the consistent use of condoms should reduce the transmission of HIV by preventing exposure to semen and infected lymphocytes.

3. Informing previous sex partners and any persons with whom needles were shared of their potential exposure to HIV and encouraging them to seek counseling and testing.

4. For IV drug abusers, enrolling or continuing in programs to eliminate the abuse of IV substances. Needles, other apparatus, and drugs must never be shared.

5. Never sharing toothbrushes, razors, or other items that could become contaminated with blood.

6. Refraining from donating blood, plasma, body organs, other tissue, or semen.

7. Avoiding pregnancy until more is known about the risks of transmitting HIV from the mother to the fetus or newborn.

8. Cleaning and disinfecting surfaces on which blood or other body fluids have spilled, in accordance with previous recommendations.

9. Informing physicians, dentists, and other appropriate health professionals of antibody status when seeking medical care, so that the patient can be appropriately evaluated.

Table from Morbidity and Morality Weekly Report *35*: 152, 1986. Used with permission.

classroom with an HIV-infected person, although direct and indirect contact with an infected person's body fluids (for example, blood and semen) should be avoided (Table 11–2).

The estimated length of time to the development of AIDS after infection with HIV is 8 to 11 years, although that time is gradually increasing because of early implementation of treatment. Once a person is infected by HIV, the virus has the T4 (helper) lymphocyte, also called the CD4+ lymphocyte, as a primary target, to which the virus binds because a glycoprotein (gp-120) on the viral surface has a high and selective affinity for the CD4 receptor on T4 lymphocytes. After binding, the virus is able to inject its RNA into the infected lymphocyte; there the RNA is transcribed into deoxyribonucleic acid (DNA) by the action of reverse transcriptase. The resultant DNA can then be incorporated into the host's cell genome and translated and eventually transcribed, once the lymphocyte is stimulated to divide. When the viral proteins have been produced by lymphocytes, the various components of the virus can assemble, and new, mature viruses can then bud off from the host cell. Although the process of budding may cause lysis of the lymphocyte, a variety of other pathophysiological mechanisms by HIV can gradually disable a patient's entire complement of T4 lymphocytes.

## AIDS

The definition of AIDS has changed over time as researchers have learned more about the disease. The Centers for Disease Control and Prevention (CDC) originally described AIDS as the presence of "a disease, at least moderately predictive of a defect in cell-mediated immunity, occurring in a person with no known cause for diminished resistance to that disease. Such diseases include Kaposi's sarcoma (KS), *Pneumocystis carinii* pneumonia (PCP), and other serious opportunistic infections." Other conditions considered indicative of AIDS are HIV encephalopathy, HIV wasting syndrome, recurrent salmonella septicemia, lymphoid interstitial pneumonia, extrapulmonary tuberculosis, and multiple and recurrent pyogenic infections in children.

The 1987 CDC AIDS criteria, which are still commonly used, classified AIDS into four groups: group I, acute infection, often with seroconversion illness; group II, asymptomatic infection; group III, asymptomatic infection, with the exception of the presence of persistent, generalized lymphadenopathy; and group IV, the presence of AIDS-defining diseases, such as constitutional and neurological syndromes, and secondary infections and cancers. That 1987 classification system is being replaced by a two-dimensional classification system for persons who are known to be infected by HIV. One dimension is the degree of immunosuppression, as indicated by the T4 cell count; the second dimension records the presence of complications (for example, infections, cancers, and encephalopathies).

## Epidemiology

The first patient with AIDS was reported in 1981; however, analysis of specimens retained from people who had died previously has shown that cases of HIV infection were present as early as 1959, suggesting that, in the 1960s and the 1970s, HIV-related disorders and AIDS were increasingly common but unrecognized, particularly in Africa and North America. At the end of 1993, more than 340,000 cases of AIDS were reported (including more than 185,000 deaths), and an estimated 1 million people were infected in the United States. The ratio of men to women who are infected is estimated to be 8 to 1, but the number of infected women is growing four times faster than the number of infected men. At the end of 1993, the World Health Organization (WHO) estimated that, worldwide, 2.5 million adults and 1 million children had AIDS, and about 10 million people were infected with HIV. Although estimates of future cases have varied widely, it appears likely that by 1995 there will be more than 500,000 cases of AIDS in the United Sates and more than 5 million worldwide.

In the United States the major groups at risk have been homosexual and bisexual men and IV substance abusers; they account for about 60 percent and 20 percent, respectively, of the first 100,000 cases of AIDS. Because of changes in sexual behaviors by homosexual and bisexual men and because of the continued spread of the virus through heterosexual sex, the percentage of total cases for homosexual and bisexual men has gradually declined, but the percentage of total cases for other groups has increased—specifically, IV substance abusers, women, heterosexual men, children, and minority groups (particularly blacks and Hispanics). More women are now being infected through heterosexual intercourse than through IV substance use. Some reports have linked the use of crack cocaine with HIV infection in women. Although the geographic distribution is heavily skewed toward large urban centers—with the cities of New York, Los Angeles, San Francisco, and Miami accounting for more than 50 percent of all cases—cases of AIDS have been reported in every state.

## Diagnosis

**Serum testing.** Two assay techniques are now widely available to detect the presence of anti-HIV antibodies in human serum. Both health care workers and their patients must understand that the presence of HIV antibodies is indicative of infection, not of immunity to infection. Persons with a positive finding on an HIV test have been exposed to the virus, have the virus within their bodies, have the potential to transmit the virus to another person,

and will almost certainly have AIDS eventually. Persons with a negative HIV test result either have not been exposed to the HIV virus and are not infected or were exposed to the HIV virus but do not yet have antibodies, a possibility if the exposure was less than a year before the testing.

The two assay techniques are the enzyme-linked immunosorbent assay (ELISA) and the Western blot assay. The ELISA is used as an initial screening test because it is less expensive than the Western blot assay and more easily used to screen a large number of samples. The ELISA is sensitive and reasonably specific; although it is unlikely to report a false-negative result, it may indicate a false-positive result. For that reason, positive results from an ELISA are confirmed by using the more expensive and cumbersome Western blot assay, which is sensitive and specific.

*Seroconversion* is the change, after infection with HIV, from a negative HIV antibody test result to a positive HIV antibody test result. Seroconversion most commonly occurs between 6 and 12 weeks after infection, although in rare cases seroconversion can take 6 to 12 months.

**Counseling.** The major issues regarding the counseling of persons about HIV serum testing are (1) who, in general, should be tested, (2) why a particular person should be (or should not be) tested, (3) what the test results signify, and (4) what the implications are. Although it is increasingly an arguable point to have the entire world population tested for HIV, specific groups of people are at high risk for contracting HIV and should probably be tested (Table 11–3). However, any person who wants to be tested should probably be tested, although the reasons for requesting a test should be ascertained to detect unspoken concerns and motivations that may merit psychotherapeutic intervention. Counseling both before and after testing should be done in person, not over the telephone, and should cover both the significance of the test results

---

**Table 11–3**
**Possible indications for Human Immunodeficiency Virus (HIV) Testing**

1. Patients who belong to a high-risk group: (1) men who have had sex with another man since 1977; (2) intravenous drug abusers since 1977; (3) hemophiliacs and other patients who have received since 1977 blood or blood product transfusions not screened for HIV; (4) sexual partners of people from any of those groups; (5) sexual partners of people with known HIV exposure—people with cuts, wounds, sores, or needlesticks whose lesions have had direct contact with HIV-infected blood.

2. Patients who request testing. Not all patients admit to the presence of risk factors (e.g., because of shame, fear).

3. Patients with symptoms of AIDS or ARC (AIDS-related complex).

4. Women belonging to a high-risk group who are planning pregnancy or who are pregnant.

5. Blood, semen, or organ donors.

6. Patients with dementia in a high-risk group.

---

Table from R B Rosse, A A Giese, S I Deutsch, J M Morihisa: *Laboratory and Diagnostic Testing in Psychiatry,* p 54. American Psychiatric Press, Washington, 1989. Used with permission.

and their implications for behavioral changes. It is good practice to repeat the meaning of the test results and their implications several times at both pretest and posttest interviews because many people are so anxious at those sessions that they may miss anything that is said only once.

Pretest counseling should review past practices that may have put the testee at risk for HIV infection and should include education about safe sexual practices (Table 11–4). During posttest counseling (Table 11–5) a negative test finding should suggest to the person that safe sexual behavior and the avoidance of shared hypodermic needles are recommended to remain free of HIV infection. A positive test result indicates that the person is infected with HIV and is capable of spreading the disease. Persons with positive results must receive counseling regarding safe practices and potential treatment options. They may need additional psychotherapeutic interventions if anxiety or depressive disorders develop after they discover that they are infected. Common issues and concerns are fear of disclosure, relationships with friends and family, employment and financial security, their medical condition, and such psychological issues as self-esteem and self-blame. A person may react to a positive HIV test finding with a syndrome similar to that of posttraumatic stress disorder. Concern about minor physical symptoms, insomnia, and

## Table 11–4
### Pretest HIV Counseling

1. Discuss meaning of a positive result and clarify distortions (e.g., the test detects exposure to the AIDS virus; it is not a test for AIDS).

2. Discuss the meaning of a negative result (e.g., seroconversion requires time, recent high-risk behavior may require follow-up testing).

3. Be available to discuss the patient's fears and concerns (unrealistic fears may require appropriate psychological intervention).

4. Discuss why the test is necessary. (Not all patients will admit to high-risk behaviors.)

5. Explore the patient's potential reactions to a positive result (e.g., "I'll kill myself if I'm positive"). Take appropriate necessary steps to intervene in a potentially catastrophic reaction.

6. Explore past reactions to severe stresses.

7. Discuss the confidentiality issues relevant to the testing situation (e.g., is it an anonymous or nonanonymous setting?). Inform the patient of other possible testing options where the counseling and testing can be done completely anonymously (e.g., where the result is not made a permanent part of a hospital chart). Discuss who has access to the test results.

8. Discuss with the patient how being seropositive can potentially affect social status (e.g., health and life insurance coverage, employment, housing).

9. Explore high-risk behaviors and recommend risk-reducing interventions.

10. Document discussions in chart.

11. Allow the patient time to ask questions.

Table from R B Rosse, A A Giese, S I Deutsch, J M Morihisa: *Laboratory and Diagnostic Testing in Psychiatry*, p 55. American Psychiatric Press, Washington, 1989. Used with permission.

## Table 11–5
### Posttest HIV Counseling

1. Interpretation of test result:
   Clarify distortion (e.g., "a negative test still means you could contract the virus at a future time; it does not mean you are immune from AIDS").
   Ask questions about the patient's understanding and emotional reaction to the test result.

2. Recommendations for prevention of transmission (careful discussion of high-risk behaviors and guidelines for prevention of transmission).

3. Recommendations on the follow-up of sexual partners and needle contacts.

4. If test result is positive, recommendations against donating blood, sperm, or organs and against sharing razors, toothbrushes, and anything else that may have blood on it.

5. Referral for appropriate psychological support: HIV-positive patients often need access to a mental health team (assess need for inpatient versus outpatient care; consider individual or group supportive therapy). Common themes include the shock of the diagnosis, the fear of death, and social consequences, grief over potential losses, and dashed hopes for good news. Also look for depression, hopelessness, anger, frustration, guilt, and obsessional themes. Activate supports available to patient (e.g., family, friends, community services).

Table from R B Rosse, A A Giese, S I Deutsch, J M Morihisa: *Laboratory and Diagnostic Testing in Psychiatry*, p 58. American Psychiatric Press, Washington, 1989. Used with permission.

dependence on health care workers are commonly seen. Adjustment disorder with anxiety or depressed mood may develop in as many as 25 percent of persons informed of a positive HIV test result. The clinical interactions with the patient should emphasize the meaning of a positive test result and should encourage the reestablishment of emotional and functional stability.

Couples who are considering taking the HIV antibody test need to decide who will be tested and whether to go alone or together. The therapist should ask why they are considering taking the test, because often the partners first discuss issues of commitment, honesty, and trust, such as sexual contacts outside the relationship. They need to be prepared for the possibility that one or both are infected and what effect it will have on their relationship.

L and M met six months ago, started dating, and had a few safe-sex encounters (mutual masturbation). Both men had been tested for HIV more than a year ago, and both tested HIV-negative. They convinced each other to be tested again to allow more open and relaxed sexual interaction and to herald the possible start of a committed relationship. The testing results, however, did not follow their expectations: L tested HIV-negative, but M tested positive. The men sought couples help to deal with the crisis. The evaluation explored their fears, anger, hurt, and sense of betrayal, deception, and lack of trust. They decided, however, to remain together and take care of each other, no matter what, and they terminated therapy prematurely.

**Confidentiality.** Confidentiality is a key issue in serum testing. No persons should be given HIV tests without their prior knowledge and consent, although various jurisdictions and organizations (for example, the military) now require HIV testing for all its inhabitants or members. The results of an HIV test can be shared with other members of a medical treatment team, although that information should be provided to no one else except in the special circumstances discussed below. The patient should be advised against too readily disclosing the results of HIV testing to employers, friends, and family members, since the information may result in discrimination in employment, housing, and insurance.

The major exception to an approach of restricted disclosure is the need to notify potential and past sexual or IV substance partners. The majority of HIV-positive patients act responsibly. If, however, the treating physician knows that an HIV-infected patient is putting another person at risk of becoming infected, the physician may try either to hospitalize the infected person involuntarily to prevent danger to others or to notify the potential victim. The clinician should be aware of the laws concerning such issues, which vary among the states. Those guidelines also apply to inpatient psychiatric wards when an HIV-infected patient is believed to be sexually active with other patients.

## CLINICAL FEATURES

### Nonneurological

About 30 percent of HIV-infected persons experience a flulike syndrome three to six weeks after becoming infected; the majority of persons never notice any symptoms immediately or shortly after their infection. When symptoms do appear, the flulike syndrome includes fever, myalgia, headaches, fatigue, gastrointestinal symptoms, and sometimes a rash. The syndrome may be accompanied by splenomegaly and lymphadenopathy. Rarely, an acute aseptic meningitis develops shortly after infection, as does an encephalopathy or Guillain-Barré syndrome.

In the United States the median duration of the asymptomatic stage is 10 years, although nonspecific symptoms—such as lymphadenopathy, chronic diarrhea, weight loss, malaise, fatigue, fevers, and night sweats—may make variable appearances. During the asymptomatic period, however, the T4 cell count almost always declines from normal values ($>1,000/mm^3$) to grossly abnormal values ($<200/mm^3$).

The most common infection affecting HIV-infected persons who have AIDS is *Pneumocystis carinii* pneumonia, which is characterized by a chronic, nonproductive cough and dyspnea that are sometimes severe enough to result in hypoxemia and resultant cognitive effects. Diagnosis is made with fiberoptic bronchoscopy and alveolar lavage. The pneumonia is usually treatable with trimethoprim and sulfamethoxazole (Bactrim, Septra) or pentamidine isethionate (Pentam), which can also be used for prophylaxis against the pneumonia. The other disease that was initially associated with the development of AIDS is Kaposi's sarcoma, a previously rare, blue-purple-tinted skin lesion. For unknown reasons, Kaposi's sarcoma is less commonly associated with AIDS recently diagnosed.

Although *Pneumocystis carnii* pneumonia and Kaposi's sarcoma are the two classic AIDS-related infectious and neoplastic disorders, the severely disabled cellular immune system of HIV-infected patients permits the development of a staggering array of infections and neoplasms. The most common infections are from protozoa (for example, *Toxoplasma gondii*), fungi (for example, *Cryptococcus neoformans* and *Candida albicans*), bacteria (for example, *Mycobacterium avium-intracellulare*), and viruses (for example, cytomegalovirus and herpes simplex virus).

For the psychiatrist, the importance of those nonneurological, nonpsychiatric complications lies in their biological effects on the patient's brain function (for example, hypoxia with *Pneumocystis carinii* pneumonia) and their psychological effects on the patient's mood and state of anxiety. In addition, since each of the conditions is usually treated by an additional drug, the psychiatrist needs to be aware of the adverse CNS effects of the large armamentarium of drugs.

### Neurological

An extensive array of disease processes can affect the brain of an HIV-infected patient (Table 11–6). The most important disease for mental health workers is HIV encephalopathy, which is associated with the development of a subcortical type of dementia and which may affect 50

**Table 11–6**
**Diseases Affecting CNS in Patients with AIDS**

Primary viral diseases
  HIV encephalopathy
  Atypical aseptic meningitis
  Vacuolar myelopathy
Secondary viruses (encephalitis, myelitis, retinitis, vasculitis)
  Cytomegalovirus
  Herpes simplex virus types 1 and 2
  Herpes varicella-zoster virus
  Papovavirus (PML)
Nonviral infections (encephalitis, meningitis, abscess)
  *Toxoplasma gondii*
  *Cryptococcus neoformans*
  *Candida albicans*
  *Histoplasma capsulatum*
  *Aspergillus fumigatus*
  *Coccidiodes immitis*
  *Acremonium albamensis*
  *Rhizopus* species
  *Mycobacterium avium-intracellulare*
  *Mycobacterium tuberculosis hominis*
  *Mycobacterium kansasii*
  *Listeria monocytogenes*
  *Nocardia asteroides*
Neoplasms
  Primary CNS lymphoma
  Metastatic systemic lymphoma
  Metastatic Kaposi's sarcoma
Cerebrovascular diseases
  Infarction
  Hemorrhage
  Vasculitis
Complications of systemic therapy

Table from A Beckett: The neurobiology of human immunodeficiency virus infection. In *American Psychiatric Press Review of Psychiatry,* vol 9, A Tasman, S M Goldfinger, C A Kaufman, editors, p 595. American Psychiatric Press, Washington, 1990. Used with permission.

percent of HIV-infected patients to some degree. The other diseases and complications of treatment must also be considered in the differential diagnosis of an HIV-infected patient with neuropsychiatric symptoms. Symptoms such as photophobia, headache, stiff neck, motor weakness, sensory loss, and changes in level of consciousness should alert a mental health worker that the patient should be examined for the possible development of a CNS opportunistic infection or a CNS neoplasm. HIV infection can also result in a variety of peripheral neuropathies that should prompt the mental health clinician to reconsider the extent of CNS involvement.

**HIV encephalopathy.** Although the means by which HIV enters the CNS remains controversial, it is known that HIV does enter the CNS, where it infects primarily glial cells, particularly astrocytes. The virus is also harbored within immune cells in the CNS. The neuropathological picture includes multinucleated giant cells, microglial nodules, diffuse astrocytosis, perivascular lymphocyte cuffing, cortical atrophy, and white matter vacuolation and demyelination (Figure 11–1). HIV encephalopathy was previously referred to as "AIDS dementia complex"; however, the fact that HIV-related encephalopathy and dementia can develop in a patient who does not meet the diagnostic criteria for AIDS makes "HIV encephalopathy" a preferable term.

CLINICAL SYMPTOMS. HIV encephalopathy is a subacute encephalitis that results in a progressive subcortical dementia without focal neurological signs. The differentiation between cortical dementia and subcortical dementia is presented in Table 10.3–2. The major differentiating feature between the two types of dementia is the absence of classic cortical symptoms (for example, aphasia) until late in the illness. Patients with HIV encephalitis or their friends usually notice subtle mood and personality changes, problems with memory and concentration, and some psychomotor slowing. Additional symptoms include apathy, distractibility, confusion, malaise, anhedonia, and social withdrawal. Some of those symptoms are virtually indistinguishable from those of depressive disorders, although careful cognitive testing may help suggest the correct diagnosis. In addition to an overlap with the symptoms of depressive disorders, HIV encephalopathy can result in a delirium that may present symptoms suggesting manic episodes or schizophrenia. The presence of motor symptoms may also suggest a diagnosis of HIV encephalopathy. Motor symptoms associated with subcortical dementia include hyperreflexia, spastic or ataxic gait, paraparesis, and increased muscle tone.

Children infected in utero with HIV have a variety of symptoms, including microcephaly, severe cognitive defects, weakness, failure to reach developmental milestones, pseudobulbar palsy, extrapyramidal rigidity, and seizures.

DIFFERENTIAL DIAGNOSIS. The differential diagnosis for HIV encephalopathy includes aseptic meningitis and all the other CNS-related conditions listed in Table 11–6. Aseptic meningitis occurs shortly after HIV infection and is characterized by a flulike illness in the presence of fluctuating levels of consciousness, meningeal signs, and facial palsies. Diagnostic testing should include detailed psychometric testing (Table 10.3–2), cerebrospinal fluid (CSF) examination, and brain imaging studies. The CSF examination may show slight elevations in protein concentrations and, in about one quarter of all HIV-infected patients, a mononuclear pleocytosis. Magnetic resonance imaging (MRI) and computed tomography (CT) studies of the patients often show cortical atrophy, ventricular enlargement, and areas of demyelination within the white matter (Figure 11–2). Positron emission tomography (PET) and single photon emission computed tomography (SPECT) studies have reported hypermetabolism of the basal

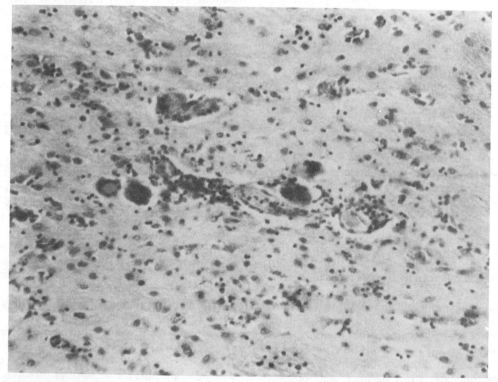

**Figure 11–1.** Typical multinucleated giant cells formed by macrophage-derived cells. (Figure from A K Pajeau, G C Román: HIV encephalopathy and dementia. Psychiatr Clin North Am *15*: 461, 1992. Used with permission.)

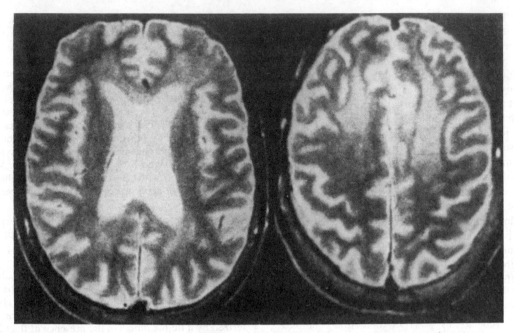

**Figure 11–2.** T$_2$-weighted (3000/80) spin echo axial magnetic resonance (MR) images at the level of the lateral ventricles and centrum semiovale. Bilateral, relatively symmetrical, supratentorial white matter disease is visible. Those areas of increased signal intensity often show a frontal lobe predilection. The cortical sulci and ventricles are prominent for the patient's age (34-year-old HIV-positive man). (Figure from A K Pajeau, G C Román: HIV encephalopathy and dementia. Psychiatr Clin North Am *15*: 458, 1992. Used with permission.)

ganglia early in the course of HIV encephalopathy, progressing to subcortical and cortical hypometabolism later in the course of the illness. Electroencephalographic (EEG) studies usually show generalized slowing, and evoked potential (EP) studies may show a delay in the P300 wave.

## Psychiatric Syndromes

**Dementia.** The fourth edition of *Diagnostic and Statistical Manual of Mental Disorders* (DSM-IV) allows for the diagnosis of dementia due to HIV disease (Section 10.3). Although HIV encephalopathy is found in a large proportion of HIV-infected patients, other causes of dementia in HIV-infected patients need to be considered. Those causes include CNS infections, CNS neoplasms, CNS abnormalities caused by systemic disorders and endocrinopathies, and adverse CNS responses to drugs. The development of dementia is generally a poor prognostic sign, and 50 to 75 percent of patients with dementia die within six months.

**Delirium.** Delirium can result from the same variety of causes that lead to dementia in HIV-infected patients (Table 11–6). Delirious states characterized by both increased activity and decreased activity have been described. Delirium in HIV-infected patients is probably underdiagnosed; however, delirium should always precipitate a medical workup of an HIV-infected patient to determine whether a new CNS-related process has begun.

**Anxiety disorders.** Patients with HIV infection may have any of the anxiety disorders, but generalized anxiety disorder, posttraumatic stress disorder, and obsessive-compulsive disorder are particularly common.

**Adjustment disorder.** Adjustment disorder with anxiety or depressed mood has been reported to occur in 5 to 20 percent of HIV-infected patients. The incidence of adjustment disorder is higher than usual in some special populations, such as military recruits and prison inmates.

**Depressive disorders.** A range of 4 to 40 percent of HIV-infected patients have been reported to meet the diagnostic criteria for depressive disorders. The pre-HIV infection prevalence of depressive disorders may be higher than usual in some groups who are at risk for contracting HIV. Another reason for the variation in prevalence rates is the variable application of the diagnostic criteria, since some of the criteria for depressive disorders (poor sleep and weight loss) can also be caused by the HIV infection itself.

**Substance abuse.** Substance abuse is a problem not only for IV substance abusers who contract HIV-related diseases but also for all other HIV patients, who may have used illegal substances only occasionally in the past but who may be tempted to use them regularly in an attempt to deal with depression or anxiety.

**Suicide.** Suicidal ideation and suicide attempts may be increased in patients with HIV infection and AIDS. The risk factors for suicide in the HIV-infected population are having friends who died from AIDS, recent notification of HIV seropositivity, relapses, difficult social issues relating to homosexuality, inadequate social and financial support, and the presence of dementia or delirium.

**Worried well.** The worried well are persons in high-risk groups who, although they are seronegative and disease-free, are anxious or have an obsession about contracting the virus. Some of those persons are reassured by repeated negative serum test results. Others, however, obsess about the possible long incubation period and cannot be reassured. Their symptoms can include generalized anxiety, panic attacks, obsessive-compulsive disorder, and hypochondriasis.

## TREATMENT

The primary approach to HIV infection should be prevention. All persons at any risk for HIV infection should be informed about safe-sex practices and the need to avoid sharing contaminated hypodermic needles. Preventive strategies are complicated by the complex societal values surrounding sexual acts, sexual orientation, birth control, and substance abuse. Many public health officials have advocated condom distribution in schools and the distribution of clean needles to drug addicts, but those issues remain controversial. Condoms have been shown to be a fairly (although not completely) safe and effective preventive strategy against HIV infection. Some conservative and religious persons argue that sexual abstinence should be the educational message. Many university laboratories and pharmaceutical companies are attempting to develop a vaccine that will protect people from infection by HIV. However, the development of such a vaccine is probably at least a decade away.

### Medical Treatment

Primary prevention involves protecting people from getting the disease; secondary prevention involves modification of the course of the disease. Azidothymidine (AZT) is an inhibitor of reverse transcriptase and has been shown to slow the course of the disease in many patients and to prolong the survival of some patients. The use of AZT is often limited by associated severe adverse effects, although other antiretroviral drugs are being used clinically—for example, dideoxyinosine (ddI)—and other pharmacological approaches are also in development. The prophylactic use of aerosolized pentamidine and of trimethoprim and sulfamethoxazole against the development of *Pneumocystis carnii* pneumonia is also in common practice now. In addition, most physicians advise patients to get adequate nutrition, rest, and exercise and to minimize their use of alcohol and other psychoactive substances.

A number of studies have reported that treatment with antiretroviral agents, such as AZT, prevents or reverses the neuropsychiatric symptoms associated with HIV encephalopathy. Although dopamine antagonists, such as haloperidol (Haldol), may be required for the control of agitation, they should be used in as low a dosage as possible because of the patients' increased sensitivity for extrapyramidal effects and the development of neuroleptic malignant syndrome.

Because of HIV-infected patients' susceptibility to delirium, the use of psychoactive medications with significant anticholinergic activity should be avoided.

An attempt to treat some aspects of anxiety disorders in HIV-infected patients with an appropriate psychotherapeutic technique can be made; however, the use of anx-

iolytic drugs—benzodiazepine or nonbenzodiazepine (for example, buspirone [BuSpar]) sedatives—or the use of antidepressant drugs may become necessary. When using a benzodiazepine, most clinicians prefer to use one with either a short or medium half-life.

Many clinicians believe that depressive disorders in HIV-infected patients should be aggressively treated with antidepressant medications. The starting dose of antidepressants should be about one quarter of that normally used in adults, and the dosage should be raised in small increments every two to three days until a therapeutic effect is reached. Tricyclic drugs and serotonin-specific reuptake inhibitors have both been used effectively by HIV-infected patients. The use of sympathomimetic drugs (for example, amphetamine) is also a reasonable treatment approach, as is electroconvulsive therapy (ECT) if a neurological examination confirms the absence of increased intracranial pressure or space-occupying CNS lesions.

Manic and psychotic symptoms may require the use of typical antipsychotic drugs to control grossly disorganized behavior or to reduce delusions or hallucinations. HIV-infected patients are sensitive to the adverse effects of those drugs; therefore, both initial and maintenance dosages should be lower than usual. HIV-infected patients who had previously been treated with lithium for the control of bipolar I disorder can continue to take lithium; however, the lithium concentrations must be monitored closely, especially if the patient has significant gastrointestinal disturbances (for example, vomiting and diarrhea) that may affect lithium absorption and excretion. The use of anticonvulsants—for example, carbamazepine (Tegretol) and valproic acid (Depakene)—may also be effective for controlling episodic behavioral dyscontrol.

### Psychotherapy

Major psychodynamic themes for HIV-infected patients involve self-blame, self-esteem, and issues regarding death. The psychiatrist can help patients deal with feelings of guilt regarding behaviors that contributed to the development of AIDS. Some AIDS patients feel that they are being punished for a deviant life-style. Difficult health care decisions, such as whether to participate in an experimental drug trial, and terminal care and life-support systems should be explored. Major practical themes for the patients involve employment, medical benefits, life insurance, career plans, and relationships with families and friends. The entire range of psychotherapeutic approaches may be appropriate for patients with HIV-related disorders. Both individual therapy and group therapy can be effective. Individual therapy may be either short-term or long-term and may be supportive, cognitive, behavioral, or psychodynamic. Group therapy techniques can range from psychodynamic to completely supportive in nature.

The homosexual community has provided a significant support system for HIV-infected people, particularly homosexual and bisexual persons. Public education campaigns within that community have resulted in significant (more than 50 percent) reductions in the highest-risk sexual practices, although some homosexual men still practice high-risk sex. Homosexual men are likely to practice safe sex if they know the safe-sex guidelines, have access to a support group, are in a steady relationship, and have a close relationship with a person with AIDS. Unfortunately, IV substance abusers with AIDS have received little support, partly because of the many biases about them. It is particularly unfortunate that there has been little progress in educating IV substance abusers, since they are a major reservoir from which the virus is spreading to women, heterosexual men, and children.

The assessment of HIV-infected patients should include a complete sexual and substance-abuse history, a psychiatric history, and an evaluation of the support systems available to the patient. The clinician must understand the patient's history with regard to sexual orientation and substance abuse, and the patient must feel that the therapist is not judging past or present behaviors. A sense of trust and empathy can often be encouraged by the therapist's asking specific, well-informed, and straightforward questions about the homosexual or substance-using culture. The therapist must also determine what the patient's knowledge about HIV and AIDS is.

Countertransference issues and the burnout of therapists who treat many HIV-infected patients are two key issues to evaluate on a regular basis. Therapists must acknowledge to themselves their predetermined attitudes toward sexual orientation and substance abuse so that those attitudes do not interfere with the treatment of the patient. Issues regarding the therapist's own sexual identity, past behaviors, and eventual death may also give rise to countertransference issues. For some psychotherapists who have practices with many HIV-infected patients, professional burnout can begin to affect their effectiveness. Some studies have found that seeing many HIV-infected patients in a short period of time seems to be more stressful to therapists than seeing a smaller number of HIV-infected patients over a long period of time.

The treatment approach to adjustment disorder in HIV-infected patients usually involves either individual or group psychotherapy, sometimes supplemented with short-term (two to three weeks) use of anxiolytic drugs.

Direct counseling regarding substance abuse and its potential adverse effects on the HIV-infected patient's health is indicated. Specific treatments for particular substance abuse disorders should be initiated if necessary for the total well-being of the patient.

Some concern among healthy members of high-risk groups is warranted, but, when the concern evolves into psychological symptoms that impair functioning, psychiatric attention is warranted. Supportive or insight-oriented psychotherapy is indicated in those cases.

Afflicted children may require special schooling. Children with AIDS who come from single-parent homes or who have parents who are unable to provide care may require foster care placement. HIV-infected children who are not severely neurologically impaired can attend regular schools without putting fellow classmates at risk for infection as long as reasonable guidelines are followed.

**Involvement of significant others.** The patient's family, lover, and close friends are often important allies in treatment. The patient's spouse or lover may have guilt feelings about possibly having infected the patient or may experience anger at the patient for possibly infecting him or her. The involvement of members of the patient's support group can help the therapist assess the patient's cognitive function and can also aid in planning financial and living arrangements. The patient's significant others may themselves benefit from the attention of the therapist in helping them cope with the illness and the impending loss of a friend or family member.

**Legal issues.** Mental health care workers are often enlisted to help the patient deal with legal matters, such as making a will and taking care of hospital and other medical expenses. The resolution of such matters is of such practical importance that it is often well worth the time of the mental health workers to make sure that those matters are addressed satisfactorily.

## References

Angrist B, d'Hollosy M, Sanfilipo M, Satriano J, Diamond G, Simberkoff M, Weinreb H: Central nervous system stimulants as symptomatic treatments for AIDS-related neuropsychiatric impairment. J Clin Psychopharmacol *12*: 268, 1992.

Batki S L: Buspirone in drug users with AIDS or AIDS-related complex. J Clin Psychopharmacol *10*: 111S, 1990.

Day J J, Grant I, Atkinson J H, Brysk L T, McCutchan J A, Hesselink J R, Heaton R K, Weinrich J D, Spector S A, Richman D D: Incidence of AIDS dementia in a two-year follow-up of AIDS and ARC patients on an initial phase II AZT placebo-controlled study: San Diego cohort. J Neuropsychiatry Clin Neurosci *4*: 15, 1992.

Empfield M, Cournos F, Meyer I, McKinnon K, Horwarth E, Silver M, Schrage H, Herman R: HIV seroprevalence among homeless patients admitted to a psychiatric inpatient unit. Am J Psychiatry *150*: 47, 1993.

Goldfinger S M, Robinowitz C B, editors, AIDS and HIV infections. In *American Psychiatric Press Review of Psychiatry*, A Tasman, S M Goldfinger, C A Kaufmann, editors, vol 9, p 571. American Psychiatric Press, Washington, 1990.

Graham N M H, Zeger S L, Park L P, Vermund S H, Detels R, Rinaldo C R, Phair J P: The effects on survival of early treatment of human immunodeficiency virus infection. N Engl J Med *326*: 1037, 1992.

Handelsman L, Aronson M, Maurer G, Wiener J, Jacobson J, Bernstein D, Ness R, Herman S, Losonczy M, Song I S, Holloway K, Horvath T, Donnelley N, Hirschowitz J, Rowan A J: Neuropsychological and neurological manifestations of HIV-1 dementia in drug users. J Neuropsychiatry Clin Neurosci *4*: 21, 1992.

Harris M J, Jeste D V, Gleghorn A, Sewell D D: New-onset psychosis in HIV-infected patients. J Clin Psychiatry *52*: 369, 1991.

Hirsch M S, D'Aquila R T: Therapy for human immunodeficiency virus infection. N Engl J Med *328*: 1686, 1993.

Janssen R S, St Louis M E, Satten G A, Critchley S E, Petersen L R, Stafford R S, Ward J W, Hanson D L, Olivo N, Schable C A, Dondero T J, Hospital HIV Surveillance Group: HIV infection among patients in U S acute care hospitals. N Engl J Med *327*: 445, 1992.

Kieburtz K, Zettelmaier A E, Ketonen L, Tuite M, Caine E D: Manic syndrome in AIDS. Am J Psychiatry *148*: 1068, 1991.

Mapou R L, Law W A, Martin A, Kampen D, Salazar A M, Rundell J R: Neuropsychological performance, mood, and complaints of cognitive and motor difficulties in individuals infected with the human immunodeficiency virus. J Neuropsychiatry Clin Neurosci *5*: 86, 1993.

McKegny F P, O'Dowd M A: Suicidality and HIV status. Am J Psychiatry *149*: 396, 1992.

Pajeau A K, Román G C: HIV encephalopathy and dementia. Psychiatr Clin North Am *15*: 455, 1992.

Perry S, Fishman B, Jacobsberg L, Frances A: Relationships over 1 year between lymphocyte subsets and psychosocial variables among adults with infection by human immunodeficiency virus. Arch Gen Psychiatry *49*: 396, 1992.

Sacks M, Dermatis H, Looser-Ott S, Burton W, Perry S: Undetected HIV infection among acutely ill psychiatric inpatients. Am J Psychiatry *149*: 544, 1992.

Silverman D C: Psychosocial impact of HIV-related caregiving on health providers: A review and recommendations for the role of psychiatry. Am J Psychiatry *150*: 705, 1993.

van Gorp W G, Mandlekern M A, Gee M, Hinkin C H, Stern C F, Paz D K, Dizon W, Evans G, Flynn F, Frederick C J, Ropchan J R, Blahd W H: Cerebral metabolic dysfunction in AIDS: Findings in a sample with and without dementia. J Neuropsychiatry Clin Neurosci *4*: 280, 1992.

# 12 ||||

# Substance-Related Disorders

## 12.1 / Overview

The widespread illegal use of brain-altering substances has caused such a degree of havoc in contemporary Western society that one United States presidential candidate in the early 1990s referred to the situation as domestic chemical warfare. Calculating the effect of illegal substance use on society is difficult because many of the effects take decades to reveal themselves. Such late-appearing effects include the effects on development in persons whose parents took illicit substances and the effects on the structure of society itself, as measured by employment, education, and poverty. The scope of the problem is enormous. More than 15 percent of the United States population over 18 years of age have serious substance use problems, with about two thirds of them abusing alcohol primarily and the other one third abusing substances other than alcohol primarily. The annual total cost to society in the mid-1990s has been estimated to be almost $200 billion.

The phenomenon of substance abuse has many implications for brain research, clinical psychiatry, and society in general. Simply stated, some substances can affect both internally perceived mental states (for example, mood) and externally observable activities (that is, behavior). The ramifications of that simple statement, however, are staggering. One of the ramifications is that the substances can cause neuropsychiatric symptoms that are indistinguishable from those of common psychiatric disorders with no known causes (for example, schizophrenia and mood disorders). That observation can then be taken to suggest that psychiatric disorders and disorders involving the use of brain-altering substances are related. If the depressive symptoms seen in some persons who have not taken a brain-altering substance are indistinguishable from the depressive symptoms in a person who has taken a brain-altering substance, there may be some brain-based commonality between substance-taking behavior and depression. The fact that brain-altering substances exist is a fundamental clue regarding how the brain works in both normal and abnormal states.

The nation's Surgeon General, Joycelyn Elders, M.D. recommended that the government study the idea of le-

galizing drugs of abuse, suggesting that doing so might reduce the incidence of violent crimes. But she stopped short of endorsing such a radical reversal of the nation's drug policy.

According to *The New York Times* (December 7, 1993) Dr. Elders stated:

I do feel that we would markedly reduce our crime rate if drugs were legalized . . . . But I don't know all of the ramifications of this. I do feel that we need to do some studies. And in some of the countries that have legalized drugs and made it legal, they certainly have shown that there has been a reduction in their crime rate and there has been no increase in their drug use rate.

Dr. Elder's comments revived a perennial debate about the most effective way to handle the nation's drug problems. In the past few years a small but growing number of former and present government officials, commentators, and academics have argued that the present policy of aggressively prosecuting drug sellers and users should be reconsidered. They have compared the current state of drug policy to the prohibition of alcohol earlier this century and have said that the abolition of drug laws would eliminate the profit motive, the gangs, and the drug dealers.

### TERMINOLOGY

#### Substance-Related Disorders

The complexity engendered by illicit substance use is reflected in its associated terminology, which seems to change on a regular basis as various professional and governmental committees convene to discuss the problem. One example concerns what to call the brain-altering substances. For example, the revised third edition of *Diagnostic and Statistical Manual of Mental Disorders* (DSM-III-R) referred to them as "psychoactive substances," but the fourth edition (DSM-IV) refers to them simply as "substances" and to the related disorders as "substance-related disorders." One reason the word "psychoactive" was dropped was that it risked limiting attention to those substances that have brain-altering activity as a primary effect (for example, cocaine). That concept of psychoactive substance does not include chemicals with brain-altering properties (for example, organic solvents) that may be ingested either on purpose or by accident. It is also not possible to separate illegal substances from legal substances, since many legal substances (for example, morphine) are often obtained by illegal means and used for nonprescribed purposes. And the word "substance" is generally preferable to the word "drug," since "drug" implies a manufactured chemical, whereas many of the substances associated with abuse patterns are naturally occurring (for example, opium) or not meant for human consumption (for example, airplane glue). Thus, in DSM-IV the topic is best described by the general heading of substance-related disorders (Table 12.1–1).

In addition to the change from "psychoactive substance use disorders" to "substance-related disorders," DSM-IV has eliminated the DSM-III-R diagnostic category of "psychoactive substance-induced organic mental disorders." The concept of organic mental disorders has been dropped entirely from DSM-IV. Thus, what were previously labeled "psychoactive substance-induced organic mental disorders" are now labeled "substance-related disorders." Moreover, substance-related disorders are now cross-referenced in the DSM-IV categories that cover those particular symptoms or syndromes (Table 12.1–2). For example, a patient with depression related to cocaine withdrawal receives a diagnosis of cocaine-induced mood disorder with depressive features, with onset during withdrawal, which is also cross-referenced within the DSM-IV section on mood disorders. The cross-referencing emphasizes the differential diagnosis of mood disorder symptoms while maintaining the point that a single substance of abuse can result in many neuropsychiatric symptoms and syndromes.

Although all substances considered by DSM-IV in the substance-related disorders category are associated with a pathological intoxication state, the substances vary as to whether or not a pathological state is associated with withdrawal or persists after the elimination of the substance from the body (Table 12.1–3). Within the DSM-IV system, patients who are experiencing substance intoxication or withdrawal accompanied by psychiatric symptoms but who do not meet the criteria for a specific syndromal pattern of symptoms (for example, depression) receive the diagnosis of substance intoxication (Table 12.1–4) or substance withdrawal (Table 12.1–5), possibly along with dependence or abuse.

## Substance Dependence

In 1964 the World Health Organization concluded that the term "addiction" is no longer a scientific term and recommended substituting the term "drug dependence." The concept of substance dependence has had many officially recognized meanings and many commonly used meanings over the decades. Basically, two concepts have been invoked regarding the definition of dependence—behavioral dependence and physical dependence. Behavioral dependence has emphasized the substance-seeking activities and related evidence of pathological use patterns, and physical dependence has emphasized the physical (that is, physiological) effects of multiple episodes of substance use. Specifically, definitions of dependence that have emphasized physical dependence have used the presence of tolerance or withdrawal in their classification criteria.

Somewhat related to "dependence" is the word "addiction" and the related word "addict." The word "addict" has acquired a distinctive, unseemly, and pejorative connotation that does not reflect the concept of substance abuse as a medical disorder. "Addiction" has also been trivialized in popular

**Table 12.1–1**
**Substances Associated with Substance-Related Disorders**

| Substance | Behavioral Effects | Physical Effects | Laboratory Findings | Treatment |
|---|---|---|---|---|
| Opiates and opioids: opium, morphine, heroin, meperidine (Demerol), methadone, pentazocine (Talwin) | Euphoria, drowsiness, anorexia, decreased sex drive, hypoactivity, change in personality | Miosis; pruritus; nausea; bradycardia; constipation; needle tracks in arms, legs, groin | Detected in blood up to 24 hours after last dose | For gradual withdrawal: methadone 5–10 mg every 6 hours for 24 hours, then decrease dose for 10 days; for overdose: naloxone (Narcan) 0.4 mg IM every 20 minutes for 3 doses, keep airway open; give $O_2$ |
| Amphetamine and other sympathomimetics, including cocaine | Alertness, loquaciousness, euphoria, hyperactivity, irritability, aggressiveness, agitation, paranoid trends, impotence, visual and tactile hallucinations | Mydriasis, tremor, halitosis, dry mouth, tachycardia, hypertension, weight loss, arrhythmias, fever, convulsions, perforated nasal septum (with cocaine) | Detected in blood and urine | For agitation: diazepam (Valium) IM or by mouth 5–10 mg every 3 hours; for tachyarrhythmias: propranolol (Inderal) 10–20 mg by mouth every 4 hours; vitamin C 0.5 g four times a day by mouth may increase urinary excretion by acidifying urine |
| Central nervous system depressants: barbiturates, methaqualone (illegal to make in U.S.), meprobamate (Equanil), benzodiazepines, glutethimide (Doriden) | Drowsiness, confusion, inattentiveness | Diaphoresis, ataxia, hypotension, seizures, delirium, miosis | Detected in blood | For barbiturates: substitute 30 mg liquid phenobarbital for every 100 mg barbiturates abused and give in divided doses every 6 hours and then decrease by 20% every other day; may also substitute diazepam (Valium) for barbiturate abused; give 10 mg every 2–4 hours for 24 hours and then reduce dose; for benzodiazepines: gradual reduction of diazepam every other day over 10-day period |

| Substance | Behavioral Effects | Physical Effects | Laboratory Findings | Treatment |
|---|---|---|---|---|
| Other inhalants: nitrous oxide | Euphoria, drowsiness, confusion | Ataxia, analgesia, respiratory depression, hypotension | None | Hypoxia is treated with $O_2$ inhalation |
| Alcohol | Poor judgment, loquaciousness, mood change, aggression, impaired attention, amnesia | Nystagmus, flushed face, ataxia, slurred speech | Blood level between 100 and 200 mg/dL | For delirium: diazepam (Valium) 5–10 mg IM or by mouth every 3 hours, IM vitamin B complex, hydration; for hallucinosis: haloperiodol (Haldol) 1–4 mg every 6 hours IM or by mouth |
| Hallucinogens: LSD (lysergic acid diethylamide), psilocybin (mushrooms), mescaline (peyote), DET (diethyltryptalmine), DMT (dimethyltryptamine), DOM or STP (dimethoxymethyl-amphetamine), MDA (methylene dioxyamphetamine) | 8–12-hour duration with flashback after abstinence, visual hallucinations, paranoid ideation, false sense of achievement and strength, suicidal or homicidal tendencies, depersonalization, derealization | Mydriasis, ataxia, hyperemic conjunctiva, tachycardia, hypertension | None | Emotional support (talking down); for mild agitation: diazepam (Valium) 10 mg IM or by mouth every 2 hours for 4 doses; for severe agitation: haloperidol (Haldol) 1–5 mg IM and repeat every 6 hours as needed; may have to continue haloperidol 1–2 mg a day by mouth for weeks to prevent flashback syndrome; phenothiazines may be used only with LSD Caution: phenothiazines can produce fatal results if used with other hallucinogens (DET, DMT, etc.), especially if they are adulterated with strychnine or belladonna alkaloids |
| Phencyclidine (PCP) | 8–12-hour duration, hallucinations, paranoid ideation, labile mood, loose associations (may mimic schizophrenia), catatonia, violent behavior, convulsions | Nystagmus, mydriasis, ataxia, tachycardia, hypertension | Detected in urine up to 5 days after ingestion | Phenothiazines contraindicated for first week after ingestion; for violent delusions: haloperidol (Haldol) 1–4 mg IM or by mouth every 2–4 hours until patient is calm |
| Volatile hydrocarbons and petroleum derivatives: glue, benzene, gasoline, varnish thinner, lighter fluid, aerosols | Euphoria, clouded sensorium, slurred speech, hallucinations in 50% of cases, psychoses | Ataxia; odor on breath; tachycardia with possible ventricular fibrillation; possible damage of brain, liver, kidneys, myocardium; permanent brain damage if used daily over 6 months | Relevant to determine tissue damage (SGOT) | For agitation: haloperidol (Haldol) 1–5 mg every 6 hours until calm; avoid epinephrine because of myocardial sensitization |
| Belladonna alkaloids (found in over-the-counter medications and morning glory seeds); stramonium, homatropine, atropine, scopolamine, hyoscyamine | Confusion, excitement, delirium, stupor, coma (antioholinorgic delirium) | Hot skin, erythema, weakness, thirst, blurred vision, dry mouth and throat, mydriasis, twitching, dysphagia, light sensitivity, pyrexia, hypertension followed by shock, urinary retention | None | Antidote is physostigmine (Antilirium) 2 mg IV every 20 minutes; IV should be controlled at no more than 1 mg a minute; watch for copious salivary secretion because of anticholinesterase activity; propranolol (Inderal) for tachyarrhythmias |

Table modified from *Desk Reference on Drug Misuse and Abuse,* New York State Medical Society, New York, 1984. Used with permission.

**Table 12.1–2**
**DSM-IV Substance-Induced Disorders Outside of Substance-Related Disorders Category**

| Diagnosis | DSM-IV Category | Synopsis Section |
|---|---|---|
| Substance intoxication delirium | Delirium, dementia, and amnestic and other cognitive disorders | 10.2 |
| Substance withdrawal delirium | Delirium, dementia, and amnestic and other cognitive disorders | 10.2 |
| Substance-induced persisting dementia | Delirium, dementia, and amnestic and other cognitive disorders | 10.3 |
| Substance-induced persisting amnestic disorder | Delirium, dementia, and amnestic and other cognitive disorders | 10.4 |
| Substance-induced psychotic disorder | Schizophrenia and other psychotic disorders | 14 |
| Substance-induced mood disorder | Mood disorders | 15.3 |
| Substance-induced anxiety disorder | Anxiety disorders | 16.1 |
| Substance-induced sexual dysfunction | Sexual and gender identity disorders | 20.2 |
| Substance-induced sleep disorder | Sleep disorders | 23.2 |

**Table 12.1–3**
**Substance-Induced Disorders Distributed in Other DSM-IV Sections with Phenomenologically Similar Disorders**

| | Dependence | Abuse | Intoxication | Withdrawal | Intoxication Delirium | Withdrawal Delirium | Dementia | Amnestic Disorder | Psychotic Disorders | Mood Disorders | Anxiety Disorders | Sexual Dysfunctions | Sleep Disorders |
|---|---|---|---|---|---|---|---|---|---|---|---|---|---|
| Alcohol | X | X | X | X | I | W | P | P | I/W | I/W | I/W | I | I/W |
| Amphetamines | X | X | X | X | I | | | | I | I/W | I | I | I/W |
| Caffeine | | | X | | | | | | | | I | | I |
| Cannabis | X | X | X | | I | | | | I | | I | | |
| Cocaine | X | X | X | X | I | | | | I | I/W | I/W | I | I/W |
| Hallucinogens | X | X | X | | I | | | | I* | I | I | | |
| Inhalants | X | X | X | | I | | P | | I | I | I | | |
| Nicotine | X | | | X | | | | | | | | | |
| Opioids | X | X | X | X | I | | | | I | I | | I | I/W |
| Phencyclidine | X | X | X | | I | | | | I | I | I | | |
| Sedatives, hypnotics, or anxiolytics | X | X | X | X | I | W | P | P | I/W | I/W | W | I | I/W |
| Polysubstance | X | | | | | | | | | | | | |
| Other | X | X | X | X | I | W | P | P | I/W | I/W | I/W | I | I/W |

*Also hallucinogen persisting perception disorder (flashbacks)
Note: X, I, W, I/W, and P indicate that the category is recognized in DSM-IV. In addition, *I* indicates the specifier "with onset during intoxication" may be noted for the category (except for intoxication delirium); *W* indicates that the specifier "with onset during withdrawal" may be noted for the category (except for withdrawal delirium); and *I/W* indicates that either "with onset during intoxication" or "with onset during withdrawal" may be noted for the category; *P* indicates that the disorder is "persisting."
Table from DSM-IV, *Diagnostic and Statistical Manual of Mental Disorders*, ed 4. Copyright American Psychiatric Association, Washington, 1994. Used with permission.

**Table 12.1–4**
**Diagnostic Criteria for Substance Intoxication**

A. The development of a reversible substance-specific syndrome due to recent ingestion of (or exposure to) a substance. **Note:** Different substances may produce similar or identical syndromes.

B. Clinically significant maladaptive behavioral or psychological changes that are due to the effect of the substance on the central nervous system (e.g., belligerence, mood lability, cognitive impairment, impaired judgment, impaired social or occupational functioning) and develop during or shortly after use of the substance.

C. The symptoms are not due to a general medical condition and are not better accounted for by another mental disorder.

Table from DSM-IV, *Diagnostic and Statistical Manual of Mental Disorders*, ed 4. Copyright American Psychiatric Association, Washington, 1994. Used with permission.

**Table 12.1–5**
**Diagnostic Criteria for Substance Withdrawal**

A. The development of a substance-specific syndrome due to the cessation of (or reduction in) substance use that has been heavy and prolonged.

B. The substance-specific syndrome causes clinically significant distress or impairment in social, occupational, or other important areas of functioning.

C. The symptoms are not due to a general medical condition and are not better accounted for by another mental disorder.

Table from DSM-IV, *Diagnostic and Statistical Manual of Mental Disorders*, ed 4. Copyright American Psychiatric Association, Washington, 1994. Used with permission.

usage, as in "TV addiction" and "money addiction." Although those reasons have helped lead to the avoidance of the word "addiction" in officially sanctioned nomenclature, there may be some neurochemical and neuroanatomical substrates in common among all the addictions, whether they be substance addictions or other addictions (for example, gambling, stealing, and eating). Those various addictions may have similar effects on the activities of specific reward areas of the brain,

such as the ventral tegmental area, the locus ceruleus, and the nucleus accumbens.

The third edition of DSM (DSM-III) in 1980 included evidence of physical dependence in its diagnostic criteria for dependence; DSM-III-R in 1987 dropped the evidence of physical dependence from its diagnostic criteria for dependence; and DSM-IV allows the clinician to specify whether or not symptoms of physiological dependence are present (Table

12.1–6). One should not oversimplify the presence or the absence of physiological dependence with, respectively, physical or psychological dependence. That distinction is close to the flawed organic-functional distinction, since psychological or behavioral dependence undoubtedly reflects physiological changes in the behavioral centers of the brain. DSM-IV also allows the clinician to assess the current state of the substance dependence by providing a list of course modifiers (Table 12.1–7). *Psychological dependence*, also referred to as habituation, is characterized by a continuous or intermittent craving for the substance in order to avoid a dysphoric state.

### Substance Abuse

DSM-IV defines substance abuse as being characterized by the presence of at least one specific symptom that indicates that substance use has interfered with the person's life (Table 12.1–8). Persons cannot meet the diagnosis of substance abuse for a particular substance if they have ever met the criteria for dependence on the same substance.

## EPIDEMIOLOGY

One large recent survey found that the lifetime prevalence of a diagnosis of substance abuse or dependence among the United States population over the age of 18 was 16.7 percent. The lifetime prevalence for alcohol abuse or dependence was 13.8 percent, and for nonalcohol substances it was 6.2 percent. The lifetime prevalence and current use of substances in 1991 is presented in Table 12.1–9 and Figure 12.1–1. Alcohol and nicotine (cigarettes) are the most commonly used substances, but marijuana, hashish, and cocaine are also commonly used. In general, however, for all four of those substances—alcohol, marijuana, cigarettes, and cocaine—there has been a gradual but consistent decrease in use from a high around 1980 to the early 1990s. However, some evidence indicates that substance abuse is again increasing among children and adolescents under age 18.

Abuse and dependence on substances is more common in men than in women, with the difference more marked for nonalcohol substances than for alcohol. Substance abuse is also higher among the unemployed and among some minority groups than among working people and majority groups. Substance use is not limited to adults. As shown by a recent survey of high school seniors, about 30 percent of them had tried a nonalcohol substance at least once, and about 16 percent of them had tried a nonalcohol, nonmarijuana substance (for example, amphetamine, inhalant, hallucinogen, sedative, or cocaine) at least once.

Substance use is more common among medical professionals than among nonmedical professionals of equal levels of training (for example, lawyers). One possible explanation for the difference is simply the relative ease of access that medical professionals have to some classes of substances (for example, sedatives and stimulants).

The following epidemiological data for 1991 come from the National Institute on Drug Abuse (NIDA):

### Prevalence of Use

In 1991 some 37 percent (75.1 million) of the population reported that they had used one or more illicit substances in

**Table 12.1–6**
**Diagnostic Criteria for Substance Dependence**

A maladaptive pattern of substance use, leading to clinically significant impairment or distress, as manifested by three (or more) of the following, occurring at any time in the same 12-month period:

(1) tolerance, as defined by either of the following:

    (a) a need for markedly increased amounts of the substance to achieve intoxication or desired effect
    (b) markedly diminished effect with continued use of the same amount of the substance

(2) withdrawal, as manifested by either of the following:

    (a) the characteristic withdrawal syndrome for the substance (refer to criteria A and B of the criteria sets for withdrawal from the specific substances)
    (b) the same (or closely related) substance is taken to relieve or avoid withdrawal symptoms

(3) the substance is often taken in larger amounts or over a longer period than was intended

(4) there is a persistent desire or unsuccessful efforts to cut down or control substance use

(5) a great deal of time is spent in activities necessary to obtain the substance (e.g., visiting multiple doctors or driving long distances), use the substance (e.g., chain-smoking), or recover from its effects

(6) important social, occupational, or recreational activities are given up or reduced because of substance use

(7) the substance use is continued despite knowledge of having a persistent or recurrent physical or psychological problem that is likely to have been caused or exacerbated by the substance (e.g., current cocaine use despite recognition of cocaine-induced depression, or continued drinking despite recognition that an ulcer was made worse by alcohol consumption)

*Specify* If:
  **with physiological dependence:** evidence of tolerance or withdrawal (i.e., either item 1 or 2 is present)
  **without physiological dependence:** no evidence of tolerance or withdrawal (i.e., neither item 1 nor 2 is present)

*Course specifiers:*
  **Early full remission**
  **Early partial emission**
  **Sustained full remission**
  **Sustained partial remission**
  **On agonist therapy**
  **In a controlled environment**

Table from DSM-IV, *Diagnostic and Statistical Manual of Mental Disorders,* ed 4. Copyright American Psychiatric Association, Washington, 1994. Used with permission.

their lifetimes, 13 percent (25.8 million) had used illicit substances in the past year, and 6 percent (12.8 million) had used them in the month before the survey.

Approximately 85 percent (171.9 million) of the population had ever used alcohol, 68 percent (138 million) had used it in the past year, and 51 percent (103.2 million) had used it in the past month.

Approximately 73 percent (147.5 million) of the population had ever smoked cigarettes, 32 percent (65.1 million) had smoked in the past year, and 27 percent (54.8 million) had smoked in the past month.

Marijuana was the most commonly used illicit substance in 1991. Of the total population aged 12 and older, approximately 33 percent (67.7 million) had ever used marijuana, and 5 percent (9.7 million) were current users.

**Table 12.1–7**
**Diagnostic Criteria for Course Modifiers for Substance Dependence**

Six course specifiers are available for substance dependence. The four remission specifiers can be applied only after none of the criteria for substance dependence or substance abuse have been present for at least 1 month. The definition of these four types of remission is based on the interval of time that has elapsed since the cessation of dependence (early versus sustained remission) and whether there is continued presence of one or more of the items included in the criteria sets for dependence or abuse (partial versus full remission). Because the first 12 months following dependence is a time of particularly high risk for relapse, this period is designated early remission. After 12 months of early remission have passed without relapse to dependence, the person enters into sustained remission. For both early remission and sustained remission, a further designation of full is given if no criteria for dependence or abuse have been met during the period of remission; a designation of partial is given if at least one of the criteria for dependence or abuse has been met, intermittently or continuously, during the period of remission. The differentiation of sustained full remission from recovered (no current substance use disorder) requires consideration of the length of time since the last period of disturbance, the total duration of the disturbance, and the need for continued evaluation. If, after a period of remission or recovery, the individual again becomes dependent, the application of the early remission specifier requires that there again be at least 1 month in which no criteria for dependence or abuse are met. Two additional specifiers have been provided: on agonist therapy and in a controlled environment. For an individual to qualify for early remission after cessation of agonist therapy or release from a controlled environment, there must be a 1-month period in which none of the criteria for dependence or abuse are met.

The following remission specifiers can be applied only after no criteria for dependence or abuse have been met for at least 1 month. Note that these specifiers do not apply if the individual is on agonist therapy or in a controlled environment (see below).

**Early full remission.** This specifier is used if, for at least 1 month, but for less than 12 months, no criteria for dependence or abuse have been met.

← Dependence → 1 → 0–11 months →
month

**Early partial remission.** This specifier is used if, for at least 1 month, but less than 12 months, one or more criteria for dependence or abuse have been met (but the full criteria for dependence have not been met).

← Dependence → 1 → 0–11 months →
month

**Sustained full remission.** This specifier is used if none of the criteria for dependence or abuse have been met at any time during a period of 12 months or longer.

← Dependence → 1 → 11+ months →
month

**Sustained partial remission.** This specifier is used if full criteria for dependence have not been met for a period of 12 months or longer; however, one or more criteria for dependence or abuse have been met.

← Dependence → 1 → 11+ months →
month

The following specifiers apply if the individual is on agonist therapy or in a controlled environment:

**On agonist therapy.** This specifier is used if the individual is on a prescribed agonist medication, and no criteria for dependence or abuse have been met for the class of medication for at least the past month (except tolerance to, or withdrawal from, the agonist). This category also applies to those being treated for dependence using a partial agonist or an agonist/antagonist.

**In a controlled environment.** This specifier is used if the individual is in an environment where access to alcohol and controlled substances is restricted, and no criteria for dependence or abuse have been met for at least the past month. Examples of these environments are closely supervised and substance-free jails, therapeutic communities, or locked hosptial units.

**Table 12.1–8**
**Diagnostic Criteria for Substance Abuse**

A. A maladaptive pattern of substance use leading to clinically significant impairment or distress, as manifested by one (or more) of the following, occurring within a 12-month period:

(1) recurrent substance use resulting in a failure to fulfill major role obligations at work, school, or home (e.g., repeated absences or poor work performance related to substance use; substance-related absences, suspensions, or expulsions from school; neglect of children or household)
(2) recurrent substance use in situations in which it is physically hazardous (e.g., driving an automobile or operating a machine when impaired by substance use)
(3) recurrent substance-related legal problems (e.g., arrests for substance-related disorderly conduct)
(4) continued substance use despite having persistent or recurrent social or interpersonal problems caused or exacerbated by the effects of the substance (e.g., arguments with spouse about consequences of intoxication, physical fights)

B. The symptoms above never met the criteria for substance dependence for this class of substance.

The next most commonly used types of illicit substances in 1991 were prescription-type psychotherapeutic substances and cocaine. The prevalence of lifetime use was 12.5 percent (25.4 million) for psychotherapeutic substances and 11.5 percent (23.7 million) for cocaine. The prevalence of past-month use for the same two substances was 1.6 percent (3.3 million) and 0.9 percent (1.9 million) respectively.

Other illicit substances (hallucinogens, inhalants, and heroin) were used by fewer than 9 percent of the population in their lifetimes and fewer than 1 percent in the past month.

**Table 12.1–9**
**Population Estimates of Lifetime and Current Substance Use, 1991**

The following figures are estimates of the percentage of people, by age category, who reported that they have used substances nonmedically. Substances used under a physician's care are not included. The estimates were developed from the 1991 National Household Survey on Drug Abuse.

| | 12–17 Years (pop. 20,145,033) | | 18–25 Years (pop. 28,496,148) | | 26 + Years (pop. 154,217,972) | | Total (pop. 202,859,153) | |
|---|---|---|---|---|---|---|---|---|
| | % Ever Used | % Current Users | % Ever Used | % Current Users | % Ever Used | % Current Users | % Ever Used | % Current Users |
| Marijuana and hashish | 13 | 4 | 51 | 13 | 33 | 3 | 33 | 5 |
| Cocaine | 2 | * | 18 | 2 | 12 | 1 | 12 | 1 |
| Crack | 1 | * | 4 | * | 2 | * | 2 | * |
| Heroin | * | * | 1 | * | 2 | * | 2 | * |
| Hallucinogens | 3 | 1 | 13 | 1 | 6 | * | 8 | * |
| Inhalants | 7 | 2 | 11 | 2 | 4 | * | 6 | 1 |
| Stimulants | 3 | 1 | 9 | 1 | 7 | * | 7 | * |
| Sedatives | 2 | 1 | 4 | 1 | 5 | * | 4 | * |
| Tranquilizers | 2 | * | 8 | 1 | 6 | * | 6 | * |
| Analgesics | 4 | 1 | 10 | 2 | 6 | 1 | 6 | 1 |
| Alcohol | 46 | 20 | 90 | 64 | 89 | 53 | 85 | 51 |
| Cigarettes | 36 | 11 | 71 | 32 | 78 | 28 | 73 | 27 |
| Smokeless tobacco | 12 | 3 | 22 | 6 | 13 | 3 | 14 | 3 |

*Low precision, no estimate shown.
All figures are rounded to the nearest whole number.
Ever used: Used at least once in a person's lifetime.
Current users: Used at least once in the 30 days before the survey.
Table by Jerome H. Jaffe, M.D.

## Demographic Correlates

**Age group.** The prevalence of the use of illicit substances in the past month was highest among those aged 18 to 25, significantly higher than among youths aged 12 to 17 and the two older age groups. Some 1.3 million youths aged 12 to 17, 4.4 million young adults aged 18 to 25, and 7 million older adults had used one or more illicit substances in the past month.

**Sex.** Males were significantly more likely than females to have used illicit substances in the past month. A total of 7.4 million males were current users, compared with 5.4 million females.

**Race and ethnicity.** Blacks were significantly more likely than whites and Hispanics to have used illicit substances in the past month, but Hispanics did not differ significantly from whites. Even though the prevalence of use of illicit substances in the past month was higher among blacks than among whites, about three fourths (72.4 percent) of illicit substance users in 1991 were white. A total of 9.2 million whites used illicit substances in the past month, compared with 2.2 million blacks and 1 million Hispanics.

**Population density.** Residents of large metropolitan areas were the most likely to have used illicit substances in the past month, and residents of nonmetropolitan areas were the least likely to have done so. Almost half (47.7 percent) of those who had used illicit substances in the past month lived in large metropolitan areas. A total of 6.1 million residents of large metropolitan areas, 4.2 million residents of small metropolitan areas, and 2.5 million residents of nonmetropolitan areas had used illicit substances in the past month.

**Region.** The prevalence of illicit substance use in the past month was significantly higher in the West than in the Northeast, South, and North Central regions. No differences among the other three regions were statistically significant.

## COMORBIDITY (DUAL DIAGNOSIS)

Comorbidity (also known as dual diagnosis) is the diagnosis of two or more psychiatric disorders in a single patient. A recent large community survey found that 76 percent of men and 65 percent of women with a diagnosis of substance abuse or dependence had an additional psychiatric diagnosis. The most common comorbidity involves two substances of abuse, usually alcohol abuse and the abuse of some other substance. Other psychiatric diagnoses that are commonly associated with substance abuse are antisocial personality disorder, phobias (and other anxiety disorders), major depressive disorder, and dysthymic disorder. In general, the most potent and dangerous substances have the highest comorbidity rates. For example, comorbidity of psychiatric disorders is more common for opioid and cocaine use than for marijuana use.

### Antisocial Personality Disorder

In various studies a range of 35 to 60 percent of patients with substance abuse or substance dependence also meet the diagnostic criteria for antisocial personality disorder. The range is even higher if investigators include patients who meet all the antisocial personality disorder diagnostic criteria except the requirement that the symptoms started at an early age. That is, a high percentage of patients who have substance abuse or substance dependence diagnoses have a pattern of antisocial behavior, whether it was present before the substance use started or developed during the course of the substance use. Patients with substance abuse or substance dependence diagnoses who have an-

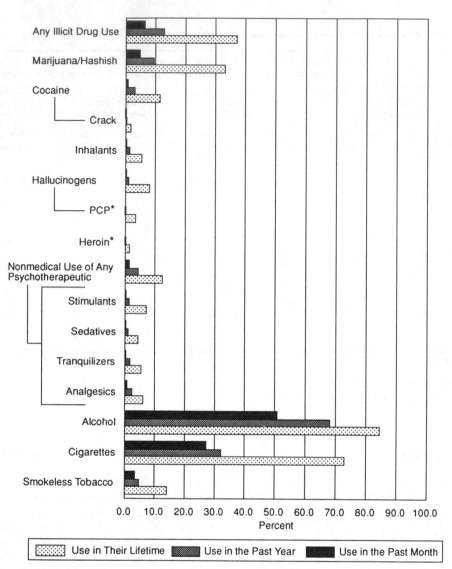

**Figure 12.1–1.** Percentage of U.S. civilian, noninstitutionalized population aged 12 and older reporting use of illicit drugs, alcohol, and tobacco in their lifetimes, the past year, and the past month, 1991. *Low precision: No estimate reported for past month. (Figure from Office of Applied Studies, SAMHSA: *National Household Survey on Drug Abuse, 1991.*)

tisocial personality disorder are likely to be using more illegal substances, to have more psychopathology, to be less satisfied with their lives, and to be more impulsive, isolated, and depressed than other patients with antisocial personality disorders alone.

### Depression and Suicide

Depressive symptoms are common among persons with substance abuse or substance dependence. About one third to one half of all persons who have opioid abuse or opioid dependence and about 40 percent of persons who have alcohol abuse or alcohol dependence meet the criteria for major depressive disorder sometime during their lives. Substance use is also a major precipitating factor for suicide. Persons who abuse substances are about 20 times more likely to die by suicide than are the general population. About 15 percent of persons with alcohol abuse or alcohol dependence have been reported to commit suicide. That frequency of suicide is second only to the frequency seen in patients with major depressive disorder.

### ETIOLOGY

At one level, substance abuse and substance dependence are caused by a person's taking a particular substance in an abusive pattern. Such a simplification fails to answer questions regarding why only some people and not others have substance abuse or substance dependence. As with all psychiatric disorders, the initial causative theories grew from psychodynamic models; subsequent models invoked behavioral, genetic, or neurochemical explanations. Most recent causative models for substance abuse invoke the entire range of those theories (Figure 12.1–2).

### Psychosocial and Psychodynamic Theories

The range of psychodynamic theories regarding substance abuse reflects the various psychodynamic theories that have had their periods of popularity during the past 100 years. Classic theories suggest that substance abuse is a masturbatory equivalent, a defense against homosexual impulses, or a manifestation of oral regression. Recent

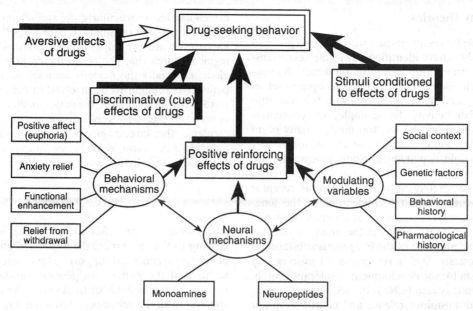

**Figure 12.1–2.** A psychopharmacological model of dependence as substance-seeking behavior controlled by four main processes: positive reinforcing and discriminative effects of substances and of stimuli associated with them (which facilitate substance-seeking) and aversive effects of substances (which weaken the behavior). The four processes are common to substances of many classes. A detailed framework for analyzing positive reinforcing effects is shown (similar analyses could be made for discriminative and aversive effects); at this level, the relative importance of the factors shown in the diagram varies considerably between classes of substances. (Figure from I Stolerman: Drugs of abuse: Behavioural principles, methods, and terms. Trends Pharmacol Sci *13*: 171, 1992. Used with permission.)

psychodynamic formulations involve a relation between substance use and depression or involve substance use as a reflection of disturbed ego functions.

Psychodynamic approaches to persons with substance abuse are more widely valued and accepted than they are in the treatment of alcoholic patients. In contrast to alcoholic patients, those with polysubstance abuse are more likely to have had unstable childhoods, more likely to self-medicate with substances, and more likely to benefit from psychotherapy. Considerable research links personality disorders with the development of substance dependence.

Other psychosocial theories invoke relationships with the family and with society in general. There are many reasons to suspect a societal role in the development of patterns of substance abuse and substance dependence. Urban newspapers are filled with gripping stories about how a drug culture has permeated areas of urban poverty. Such articles often describe how children are brought into the drug world at early ages. Yet, even under those social pressures, not every child receives a diagnosis of substance abuse or substance dependence, thus suggesting the possible involvement of other causal factors.

**Coaddiction.** The concept of coaddiction or codependence has become popularized in recent years, although some experts in the addiction field reject the concept of coaddiction as invalid. Coaddiction occurs when more than one person, usually a couple, have a relationship that is primarily responsible for the maintenance of addictive behavior in at least one of the persons. Each person may have enabling behaviors that help perpetuate the situation, and denial of the situation is a prerequisite for such a dyadic relationship to develop. The treatment of such a coaddictive situation involves directly addressing the elements of the enabling behavior and the denial.

**Behavioral theories.** Some behavioral models of sub-

stance abuse have focused on substance-seeking behavior, rather than the symptoms of physical dependence (Figure 12.1–2). For a behavioral model to have relevance to all substances, the model must not be dependent on the presence of withdrawal symptoms or tolerance, since many substances of abuse are not associated with the development of physiological dependence. Some researchers hypothesize that four major behavioral principles are at work in inducing substance-seeking behavior. The first and second principles are the positive reinforcing qualities and the adverse effects of some substances. Most substances of abuse are associated with a positive experience after taking them the first time; thus, the substance acts as a positive reinforcer for substance-seeking behavior. Many substances are also associated with adverse effects, which act to reduce substance-seeking behavior. Third, the person must be able to discriminate the substance of abuse from other substances. Fourth, almost all substance-seeking behavior is associated with other cues that become associated with the substance-taking experience.

### Genetic Theories

Strong evidence from studies of twins, adoptees, and siblings raised apart indicates that alcohol abuse has a genetic component in its cause. There are many less conclusive data that other types of substance abuse or substance dependence have a genetic pattern in their development. Some studies, however, have found a genetic basis for nonalcohol substance dependence and abuse. Recently, researchers have used the technology of restriction fragment length polymorphism (RFLP) in the study of substance abuse and substance dependence, and a few reports of RFLP associations have been published.

## Neurochemical Theories

For most substances of abuse, with the exception of alcohol, researchers have identified particular neurotransmitters or neurotransmitter receptors on which the substances have their effects. For example, the opiates act on the opiate receptors. Thus, a person who has too little endogenous opiate activity (for example, low concentrations of endorphins) or who has too much activity of an endogenous opiate antagonist may be at risk for the development of opioid dependence. Some researchers are following that type of hypothesis in their studies. Even in a person with completely normal endogenous receptor function and neurotransmitter concentration, the long-term use of a particular substance of abuse may eventually modulate those receptor systems in the brain, so that the brain requires the presence of the exogenous substance to maintain homeostasis. Such a receptor-level process may be the mechanism for the development of tolerance within the central nervous system (CNS). In fact, however, modulation of neurotransmitter release and neurotransmitter receptor function has proved to be difficult to demonstrate, and recent research focuses on the effects of substances on the second-messenger system and on gene regulation.

**Pathways and neurotransmitters.** The major neurotransmitters that may be involved in the development of substance abuse and substance dependence are the opiate, catecholamine (particularly dopamine), and γ-aminobutyric acid (GABA) systems (Figure 12.1–3). Of particular importance are the dopaminergic neurons in the ventral tegmental area that project to the cortical and limbic regions, especially the nucleus accumbens. That particular pathway is thought to be involved in the sensation of reward and is thought to be the major mediator of the effects of such substances as amphetamine and cocaine. The locus ceruleus, the largest group of adrenergic neurons, is thought to be involved in the mediation of the effects of the opiates and the opioids.

## TREATMENT

Treatment approaches for substance abuse vary according to the substance, the pattern of abuse, the availability of psychosocial support systems, and the individual features of the patient. In general, substance abuse involves two major goals of treatment. The first goal is abstinence from the substance. Although some persons have been able to change from an abusive pattern of use to a moderate pattern of use, they are exceptions to the majority of abusers, in whom complete abstinence is the only way to control the problem. The second goal is the physical, psychiatric, and psychosocial well-being of the patient. Significant damage has often been done to the pa-

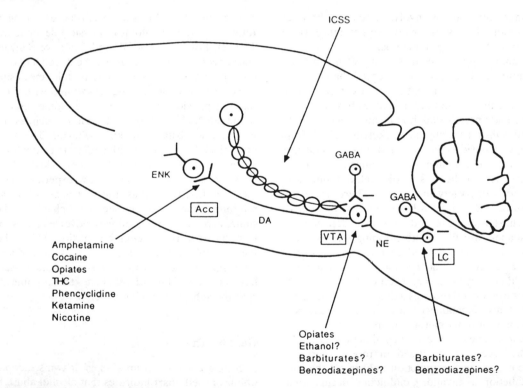

**Figure 12.1–3.** Schematic diagram of the brain-reward circuitry of the mammalian (laboratory rat) brain, with sites at which various abusable substances appear to act to enhance brain reward and thus to induce substance-using behavior and possibly craving. ICSS indicates the descending, myelinated, moderately fast-conducting component of the brain-reward circuitry that is preferentially activated by electrical intracranial self-stimulation. DA indicates the subcomponent of the ascending mesolimbic dopaminergic system that appears to be preferentially activated by abusable substances. LC indicates the locus ceruleus, VTA indicates the ventral tegmental area, and Acc indicates the nucleus accumbens. NE indicates the nonadrenergic fibers, which originate in the locus ceruleus and synapse into the general vicinity of the ventral mesencephalic DA cell fields. GABA indicates the GABAergic inhibitory fiber systems synapsing on both the locus ceruleus nonadrenergic fibers and the ventral mesencephalic DA cell fields. (From E Gardner: Brain reward mechanism. In *Substance Abuse: A Comprehensive Textbook,* ed 2, J H Lowinson, P Ruiz, R B Millman, editors, p 87. Williams & Wilkins, Baltimore, 1992. Used with permission.)

tient's support systems during a prolonged period of substance abuse. If a patient is going to stop a pattern of substance abuse successfully, adequate psychosocial supports must be in place to foster that difficult change in behavior.

Initial treatment approaches to substance abuse may be conducted in either an inpatient setting or an outpatient setting. Although an outpatient setting is more naturalistic than an inpatient setting, the temptations available to an outpatient may present too high a hurdle for the initiation of treatment. Inpatient treatment is also indicated in the presence of severe medical or psychiatric symptoms, a history of failed outpatient treatments, a lack of psychosocial supports, or a particularly severe or long-term history of substance abuse. After an initial period of detoxification, the patient needs a sustained period of rehabilitation. Throughout the treatment period, individual, family, and group therapies can be effective. Education about substance abuse and support for the patient's efforts are essential factors in treatment. In some cases the use of a psychotherapeutic drug—for example, disulfiram (Antabuse)—may be indicated to discourage the patient from using the abused substance, to reduce the effects of withdrawal (for example, methadone), or to treat a presumptive underlying psychiatric disorder (for example, antidepressants).

## Psychotherapy

The role of psychotherapy in alcohol dependence is highly controversial, but some patients who cannot or will not make use of Alcoholics Anonymous (AA) may require psychotherapeutic intervention. Alcohol dependence is a highly heterogeneous disorder, and the person with the disorder must always be taken into account in treatment planning. Although no specific personality traits are connected with alcohol dependence, clinicians have observed that alcohol may serve the function of replacing missing psychological structures and, therefore, serve to restore a sense of self-esteem in the patient. For some patients, psychotherapy and Alcoholics Anonymous work synergistically—AA helps them achieve abstinence, and psychotherapy deals with psychological and interpersonal factors that caused distress in their lives.

The early psychoanalytic interpretation of substance abuse as a regression to the oral stage of psychosexual development has recently been replaced by a view of most substance abuse as adaptive and defensive, rather than regressive. Regressive states may actually be reversed by using substances because the substance reinforces weakened defenses against intense affects, such as shame and rage. Moreover, those with substance dependence tend to have significant deficits in self-care, resulting from early developmental disturbances that contribute to the impaired internalization of parents. As a consequence, those with substance dependence find it difficult to soothe themselves and to regulate impulse control and self-esteem.

Methodologically rigorous research has shown that the addition of psychotherapy to the overall treatment plan of those with opioid dependence produces far greater benefit than do treatment plans without psychotherapy. Those patients with significant psychiatric symptoms make little or no progress with counseling alone but are the best candidates for psychotherapy and benefit the most from it. However, abstinence from the abused substance is a requirement for psychotherapy to be effective in dealing with the underlying psychiatric disturbances.

## RESIDUAL DIAGNOSTIC CATEGORIES

### Other Substance Use Disorders

DSM-IV includes a diagnostic category for substances that are not listed in the specific sections. DSM-IV also allows for a complete range of substance-induced syndromes caused by other or unknown substances (Table 12.1–10). And DSM-IV allows for the diagnosis of other (or unknown) substance use disorder not otherwise specified to cover any syndrome that is assessed to be causally related to any substance.

**Anabolic (androgenic) steroids.** The naturally occurring anabolic-androgenic steroid in men is testosterone; many synthetic anabolic steroids are now available—for example, Dianabol, Anavar, and Winstrol-V. Those preparations are available in both oral and intramuscular formulations. Anabolic steroids are schedule III drugs and, therefore, are subject to the same regulatory requirements for dispensing as are narcotics. Although anabolic steroids have legitimate medical uses, they are illegally used primarily by men to enhance their physical performance and appearance as measured by muscle bulk, muscle definition, and athletic prowess. An estimated $400 million a year is

**Table 12.1–10**
**Diagnostic Criteria for Other (or Unknown) Substance-Related Disorders**

The other (or unknown) substance-related disorders category is for classifying substance-related disorders associated with substances not listed above. Examples of these substances, which are described in more detail below, include anabolic steroids, nitrite inhalants ("poppers"), nitrous oxide, over-the-counter and prescription medications not otherwise covered by the 11 categories (e.g., cortisol, antihistamines, benztropine), and other substances that have psychoactive effects. In addition, this category may be used when the specific substance is unknown (e.g., an intoxication after taking a bottle of unlabeled pills).

**Anabolic steroids** sometimes produce an initial sense of enhanced well-being (or even euphoria), which is replaced after repeated use by lack of energy, irritability, and other forms of dysphoria. Continued use of these substances may lead to more severe symptoms (e.g., depressive symptomatology) and general medical conditions (liver disease).
**Nitrite inhalants** ("poppers"—forms of amyl, butyl, and isobutyl nitrite) produce an intoxication that is characterized by a feeling of fullness in the head, mild euphoria, a change in the perception of time, relaxation of smooth muscles, and a possible increase in sexual feelings. In addition to possible compulsive use, these substances carry dangers of potential impairment of immune functioning, irritation of the respiratory system, a decrease in the oxygen-carrying capacity of the blood, and a toxic reaction that can include vomiting, severe headache, hypotension, and dizziness.
**Nitrous oxide** ("laughing gas") causes rapid onset of an intoxication that is characterized by light-headedness and a floating sensation that clears in a matter of minutes after administration is stopped. There are reports of temporary but clinically relevant confusion and reversible paranoid states when nitrous oxide is used regularly.

*Continued*

**Table 12.1–10**
*Continued*

Other substances that are capable of producing mild intoxication include **catnip**, which can produce states similar to those observed with marijuana and which in high doses is reported to result in LSD-type perceptions; **betel nut**, which is chewed in many cultures to produce a mild euphoria and floating sensation; and **kava** (a substance derived from the South Pacific pepper plant), which produces sedation, incoordination, weight loss, mild forms of hepatitis, and lung abnormalities. In addition, individuals can develop dependence and impairment through repeated self-administration of **over-the-counter** and **prescription drugs**, including **cortisol, antiparkinsonian agents** that have anticholinergic properties, and **antihistamines.**

Texts and criteria sets have already been provided to define the generic aspects of substance dependence, substance abuse, substance intoxication, and substance withdrawal that are applicable across classes of substances. The other (or unknown) substance-induced disorders are described in the sections of the manual with disorders with which they share phenomenology (e.g., other (or unknown) substance-induced mood disorder is included in the mood disorders section). Listed below are the other (or unknown) substance use disorders and the other (or unknown) substance-induced disorders.

*Other (or unknown) substance use disorders*

**Other (or unknown) substance dependence**
**Other (or unknown) substance abuse**

*Other (or unknown) substance-induced disorders*

**Other (or unknown) substance intoxication**
*Specify if:*
    with perceptual disturbances
**Other (or unknown) substance withdrawal**
*Specify if:*
    with perceptual disturbances
**Other (or unknown) substance-induced delirium**
**Other (or unknown) substance-induced persisting dementia**
**Other (or unknown) substance-induced persisting amnestic disorder**
**Other (or unknown) substance psychotic disorder, with delusions**
*Specify if:*
    with onset during intoxication
    with onset during withdrawal
**Other (or unknown) substance-induced psychotic disorder, with hallucinations**
*Specify if:*
    with onset during intoxication
    with onset during withdrawal
**Other (or unknown) substance-induced mood disorder**
*Specify if:*
    with onset during intoxication
    with onset during withdrawal
**Other (or unknown) substance-induced anxiety disorder**
*Specify if:*
    with onset during intoxication
    with onset during withdrawal
**Other (or unknown) substance-induced sexual dysfunction**
*Specify if:*
    with onset during intoxication
**Other (or unknown) substance-induced sleep disorder**
*Specify if:*
    with onset during intoxication

**Other (or unknown) substance-related disorder not otherwise specified**

Table from DSM-IV, *Diagnostic and Statistical Manual of Mental Disorders*, ed 4. Copyright American Psychiatric Association, Washington, 1994. Used with permission.

spent in illegal sales of anabolic steroids in the United States, although many young athletes, some as young at 10 years of age, spend a lot of money on *blanks*—that is, useless and sometimes harmful nonsteroid formulations. Although virtually every athletic regulatory agency has officially forbidden the use of anabolic steroids, sophisticated athletes and less-than-honest trainers have developed the use of the steroids to a fine art and are able to adjust the amount and the timing of doses to remain undetected by currently used screening tests.

An estimated 1 million people in the United States have used illegal steroids at least once. Male users of anabolic steroids greatly outnumber female users, approximately 50 to 1. About half of the users start before the age of 16. The users are primarily middle-class and white. Although the steroids are used to enhance muscle mass and athletic performance, perhaps one third to one half of all users are not currently engaged in serious competitive sports activities. Many young users report that they have been influenced by muscle magazines and by reports of steroid use by successful sports stars. The users tend to use the steroids in cycles of 6 to 12 months. The users also tend to stack their use—that is, they take small amounts of two or more types of anabolic steroids at the same time, believing that doing so maximizes the desired effects while minimizing the risks.

Anabolic steroid use has obvious physical effects. The most obvious effect is that their use causes rapid development and enhancement of muscle bulk, definition, and power. Males who abuse the steroids also have acne, premature balding, yellowing of the skin and the eyes, gynecomastia, and decreased size of the testicles and the prostate. Young boys abusing the steroids can have a painful enlargement of the genitalia. The use of the steroids in young adolescents can also lead to stunted growth, because the use causes premature closure of the bone plates. In females who abuse the steroids, the voice may deepen, the breasts shrink, the clitoris enlarge, and the menstrual cycle become irregular.

Laboratory values may also be changed, including elevated liver function, decreased high-density lipoproteins, and increased low-density lipoproteins. Decreased spermatogenesis has been reported, as has an association between anabolic steroid abuse and myocardial infarction and cerebrovascular diseases.

Anabolic steroids have come to the attention of psychiatrists because of the steroids' psychiatric effects. Initially, the steroids may induce euphoria and hyperactivity, but after relatively short periods their use can become associated with increased anger, arousal, irritability, hostility, anxiety, somatization, and depression (especially during periods off the steroids). A number of studies have found that from 2 to 15 percent of anabolic steroid abusers experience hypomanic or manic episodes, and a smaller percentage may have clear psychotic symptoms. Also disturbing is an association between abuse of the steroids and violence, termed "roid rage" in the parlance of users. A number of murders and other violent crimes have been reported in steroid abusers who had no prior record of sociopathy or violence.

The steroids are apparently addictive substances. When abusers stop taking the steroids, they can become depressed, anxious, and concerned about the physical state of their bodies. Some similarities are noted between those athletes' views of their muscles and the views of patients with anorexia nervosa regarding their own bodies. Both groups seem to distort the realistic assessment of their bodies. Treatment for anabolic steroid abuse involves the same basic principles as for any other substance abuse problem—abstinence in an environment that provides the necessary psychosocial support.

**Nitrite inhalants.** The nitrite inhalants include amyl, butyl, and isobutyl nitrites, all of which are referred to as "poppers" in popular jargon. Nitrite inhalant use is specifically excluded from the inhalant use disorders, as is anesthetic gas use, because the intoxication syndromes seen with nitrites can be markedly different from the syndromes seen with the standard inhalant substances (for example, lighter fluid and airplane glue). Nitrite inhalants are used by persons who seek the associated mild euphoria, altered sense of time, feeling of fullness in the head, and possibly increased sexual feelings. The nitrite compounds are used by some homosexual men to reduce sexual inhibitions, to delay orgasm, and to relax the anal sphincter for penile penetration. Under such circumstances a person may inhale the substance from a small bottle from a few times to dozens of times within several hours. Adverse reactions include a toxic syndrome characterized by nausea, vomiting, headache, hypotension, drowsiness, and irritation of the respiratory tract. Some evidence indicates that nitrite inhalants may adversely affect the immune function.

**Nitrous oxide.** Nitrous oxide is a widely available anesthetic agent that is commonly known as laughing gas. It is subject to abuse because its use is associated with a feeling of light-headedness and of floating, which some persons can experience as pleasurable. With long-term abuse patterns, nitrous oxide use has been associated with delirium and paranoia. Female dental assistants who have been exposed to high levels of nitrous oxide have been reported to have reduced fertility.

**Other substances.** Nutmeg, the spice, can be ingested in a number of preparations; if taken in high-enough doses, it can induce some depersonalization, derealization, and a feeling of heaviness in the limbs. Morning glory seeds, in high-enough doses, can produce a syndrome similar to that seen with lysergic acid diethylamide (LSD), characterized by altered sensory perceptions and mild visual hallucinations. Catnip can produce a marijuanalike intoxication in low doses and LSD-like intoxication in high doses. The betel nut, when chewed, can produce a mild euphoria and a feeling of floating in space. Kava, which is derived from a pepper plant in the South Pacific, can produce sedation and incoordination and is associated with hepatitis, lung abnormalities, and weight loss. DSM-IV also notes that over-the-counter and prescription medications—such as cortisol, antiparkinsonian agents, and antihistamines—can be subject to abuse by some persons.

## Polysubstance-Related Disorder

Substance users often abuse more than one substance. DSM-IV allows for a diagnosis of polysubstance dependence if, for a period of at least 12 months, the person has

**Table 12.1–11**
**Diagnostic Criteria for Polysubstance Dependence**

This diagnosis is reserved for behavior during the same 12-month period in which the person was repeatedly using at least three groups of substances (not including caffeine and nicotine), but no single substance has predominated. Further, during this period, the dependence criteria were met for substances as a group but not for any specific substance.

Table from DSM-IV, *Diagnostic and Statistical Manual of Mental Disorders*, ed 4. Copyright American Psychiatric Association, Washington, 1994. Used with permission.

repeatedly used substances from at least three categories of substances (not including nicotine and caffeine), even if the diagnostic criteria for a substance-related disorder are not met for any single substance, as long as, during that period, the criteria for substance dependence have been met for the substances considered as a group. (Table 12.1–11).

## References

Brooner R K, Schmidt C W, Felch L J, Bigelow F E: Antisocial behavior of intravenous drug abusers: Implications for diagnosis of antisocial personality disorder. Am J Psychiatry *149*: 482, 1992.

Brower K J, editor: Anabolic steroids: A mind-body problem. Psychiatry Ann *22*: 2, 1992.

Clancy G P, Yates W R: Anabolic steroid use among substance abusers in treatment. J Clin Psychiatry *53*: 97, 1992.

DuRant R H, Rickert V I, Ashworth C S, Newman C, Slavens G: Use of multiple drugs among adolescents who use anabolic steroids. N Engl J Med *328*: 922, 1993.

Gabbard G O: *Psychodynamic Psychiatry in Clinical Practice: The DSM-IV Edition.* American Psychiatric Press, Washington, 1994.

Gerstley L J, Alterman A I, McLellan A T, Woody G E: Antisocial personality disorder in patients with substance abuse disorders: A problematic diagnosis? Am J Psychiatry *147*: 173, 1990.

Goldstein A, Kalant H: Drug policy: Striking the right balance. Science *249*: 1513, 1990.

Group for the Advancement of Psychiatry Committee on Alcoholism and the Addictions: Substance abuse disorders: A psychiatric priority. Am J Psychiatry *148*: 1291, 1991.

Grove W M, Eckert E D, Heston L, Bouchard T J Jr, Segal N, Lykken D T: Heritability of substance abuse and antisocial behavior: A study of monozygotic twins reared apart. Biol Psychiatry *27*: 1293, 1990.

Hughes P H, Baldwin D C, Sheehan D V, Conrad S, Storr C L: Resident physician substance use, by specialty. Am J Psychiatry *149*: 1348, 1992.

Israelstam S, Lambert S, Oko G: Poppers: A new recreational drug craze. Can Psychiatr Assoc J *23*: 493, 1978.

Kolb L C: The 100 years war. Psychiatr Ann *21*: 499, 1991.

Koob G F: Drugs of abuse. Anatomy, pharmacology and function of reward pathways. Trends Pharmacol Sci *13*: 177, 1992.

Kranzler K R, Liebowitz N R: Anxiety and depression in substance abuse: Clinical implications. Med Clin North Am *72*: 867, 1988.

Nace E P, Davis C W, Gaspari J P: Axis II comorbidity in substance abusers. Am J Psychiatry *148*: 118, 1991.

National Institute on Drug Abuse: *National Household Survey on Drug Abuse: Highlights, 1991.* U S Government Printing Office, Washington, 1991.

Nestler E J: Molecular mechanisms of drug addiction. J Neurosci *12*: 2439, 1992.

Rowland A S, Baird D D, Weinberg C R, Shore D L, Shy C M, Wilcox A J: Reduced fertility among women employed as dental assistants exposed to high levels of nitrous oxide. N Engl J Med *327*: 993, 1992.

Satel S L, Kosten T R, Schuckit M A, Fischman M W: Should protracted withdrawal from drugs be introduced in DSM-IV? Am J Psychiatry *150*: 695, 1993.

Smith S S, O'Hara B F, Persico A M, Gorelick D A, Newlin D B, Vlahov D, Soloman L, Pickens R, Uhl G R: Genetic vulnerability to drug abuse. Arch Gen Psychiatry *49*: 723, 1992.

Stolerman I: Drugs of abuse: Behavioral principles, methods and terms. Trends Pharmacol Sci *13*: 170, 1992.

Uhl G, Blum K, Noble E, Smith S: Substance abuse vulnerability and $D_2$ receptor genes. Trends Neurosci *16*: 83, 1993.

# 12.2 / Alcohol-Related Disorders

Alcohol abuse and dependence are, by far, the most common substance-related disorders. The direct and indirect costs to society in the United States for alcohol-related disorders is estimated to be more than $150 billion, about $600 per capita. Alcohol abuse and dependence are commonly referred to as alcoholism; however, because "alcoholism" lacks a precise definition, it is not used in the fourth edition of *Diagnostic and Statistical Manual of Mental Disorders* (DSM-IV) or in most other officially recognized diagnostic systems.

## EPIDEMIOLOGY

About 85 percent of all United States residents have had an alcohol-containing drink at least once in their lives, and about 51 percent of all United States adults are current users of alcohol. Those figures merely support the observation that the drinking of alcohol-containing beverages is generally considered an acceptable and common habit. After heart disease and cancer, alcohol-related disorders constitute the third largest health problem in the United States today. In the United States, beer accounts for about half of all alcohol consumption, liquor for about a third, and wine for about a sixth. About 30 to 45 percent of all adults in the United States have had at least one transient episode of alcohol-related problems, usually involving an alcohol-induced amnestic episode (for example, a blackout), driving a motor vehicle while intoxicated, or having missed school or work because of excessive drinking. By the criteria in the revised third edition of DSM (DSM-III-R), 10 percent of women and 20 percent of men have met the diagnostic criteria for alcohol abuse during their lifetimes, and 3 to 5 percent of women and 10 percent of men have met the diagnostic criteria for the more serious diagnosis of alcohol dependence during their lifetimes. About 200,000 deaths each year are directly related to alcohol abuse. The common causes of death among persons with alcohol-related disorders are suicide, cancer, heart disease, and hepatic disease. Although not always involving persons who meet the diagnostic criteria for an alcohol-related disorder, about half of all automotive fatalities involve a drunken driver, and that percentage increases to about 75 percent if only accidents occurring in the late evening are considered. Alcohol use and alcohol-related disorders are also associated with about 50 percent of all homicides and 25 percent of all suicides. Alcohol abuse reduces life expectancy by about 10 years. Alcohol leads all other substances in substance-related deaths.

The following epidemiological data for 1991 come from the National Institute on Drug Abuse (NIDA):

## Prevalence

Nearly 85 percent of the members of the United States civilian, noninstitutionalized population aged 12 and older had used alcohol one or more times in their lifetimes, 68 percent had used alcohol in the past year, and 51 percent had used it in the past month.

Those percentages translate to 171.7 million people who had used alcohol in their lifetimes, 138.0 million who had used it in the past year, and 103.2 million who had used it in the past month.

About 90 percent of young adults aged 18 to 25, 92 percent of adults aged 26 to 34, and 87 percent of adults aged 35 and older had used alcohol in their lifetimes, compared with about 46 percent of youths aged 12 to 17.

About 64 percent of young adults and 62 percent of adults aged 26 to 34 had used alcohol in the past month, a significantly greater percentage than the 20 percent of youth and 50 percent of adults aged 35 and older.

## Trends

Lifetime, past-year, and past-month alcohol use was highest in 1979 and decreased thereafter for most age groups, although for adults aged 26 and older the rate of alcohol use in their lifetimes remained relatively stable after 1979.

The rates for alcohol use have been more stable than the rates for other substances, although the percentage of youths who reported that they had ever used alcohol decreased dramatically from 1979 to 1991.

Between 1990 and 1991 slight increases occurred in the percentages of adults aged 18 to 25 and those 26 and older who reported alcohol use in their lifetimes, the past year, and the past month. None of those changes, however, was statistically significant. In contrast, alcohol use in their lifetimes, the past year, and the past month among youths aged 12 to 17 decreased, but only the decrease in the past-month use was statistically significant.

## Demographic Correlates of Past-Month Use

**Sex.** Males were significantly more likely than females to have used alcohol in the past month, approximately 58 percent compared with 44 percent. Those differences were greater for adults 26 and older than for younger age groups.

**Race and ethnicity.** Whites were significantly more likely than blacks and Hispanics to have used alcohol in the past month, and Hispanics were more likely than blacks to have used alcohol during that time period.

**Population density.** Residents of large metropolitan areas and small metropolitan areas were significantly more likely than residents of nonmetropolitan areas to have used alcohol in the past month. Residents of large metropolitan areas were somewhat more likely than those living in small metropolitan areas to have used alcohol during that time period.

**Region.** Residents of the Northeast, North Central, and West were significantly more likely than residents of the South to have used alcohol in the past month.

## Age and Sex

The age group with the highest percentage of active alcohol users, which is also the age group that consumes the most alcohol, is the group in the ages from 20 to 35. That fact, however, risks overshadowing the fact that about 50 percent of adolescents aged 12 to 17 have tried alcohol-containing beverages at least once, and about 25 percent of that age group describe themselves as current users of alcohol. Most persons who drink had their first drinks during their early to middle teens. Although the peak ages of alcohol use extend to age 35, persons in their subsequent decades—their 40s, 50s, 60s, and 70s—have a gradually declining pattern of alcohol use. Among persons 65 years and older, abstainers exceed drinkers in both sexes, and only 7 percent of men and 2 percent of women in that age group are considered heavy drinkers (defined as those who drink almost every day and become intoxicated several times a month).

More men than women use alcohol, and the ratio of men to women for alcohol-related disorder diagnoses is about 2 to 1 or 3 to 1. The course of alcohol abuse also differs between the sexes. Although the symptoms of an alcohol-related disorder may be present in a man while he is in his 20s, the presence of the condition is often not recognized until the man is in his 30s, perhaps because of the relative lack of obligations a man in his 20s has compared with a man in his 30s, who may by then have a family and a responsible job. It is rare for the symptoms of an alcohol-related disorder to appear in a man after age 45, and the appearance of such symptoms should prompt the physician to evaluate the patient for the presence of a mood disorder or secondary psychiatric syndrome. In contrast to the predictable course of alcohol-related disorders among men, the course of the disorders among women is variable. The onset of alcohol abuse is generally later in women than in men.

## Race and Locale

Although the rate of alcohol-related disorders has traditionally been highest among young white men, evidence now indicates that young black men and young Hispanic men may have surpassed young white men in their rates of alcohol-related disorders. Native American and Eskimo men and women also have a high prevalence of alcohol-related disorders. Asian Americans have a low prevalence of alcohol-related disorders, although some data suggest that the prevalence is rising among young Asian Americans.

The consumption of alcohol varies markedly in geographic areas. Drinking is more common in urban areas than in rural areas. Alcohol consumption is greatest in the Northeast of the United States and is lowest in the South. Expectancy rates for alcohol-related disorders are about the same in the United States as in Germany, Sweden, Denmark, and England. Expectancy rates are higher in Portugal, Spain, Italy, France, and the former Soviet Union than in the United States.

## Psychosocial Factors

Alcohol-related disorders are present in persons from all socioeconomic classes. In fact, stereotyped skid-row alcoholic persons constitute less than 5 percent of persons with alcohol-related disorders in the United States. Moreover, alcohol-related disorders are particularly high in persons who have attained advanced degrees and are in high socioeconomic classes.

In high school, alcohol-related problems are correlated with a history of school difficulties. High school dropouts and persons with a record of frequent truancy and delinquency appear to be at a particularly high risk for alcohol abuse. Those epidemiological data are consistent with the high comorbidity seen between alcohol-related disorders and antisocial personality disorder.

## Comorbidity (Dual Diagnosis) with Other Mental Disorders

Comorbidity usually means the presence of additional psychiatric diagnoses in a person who has a diagnosis of an alcohol-related disorder. The most common associated psychiatric diagnoses with the alcohol-related disorders are other substance-related disorders, antisocial personality disorder, mood disorders, and anxiety disorders. Although the data are somewhat controversial, most data suggest that persons with alcohol-related disorders have a markedly higher suicide rate than do the general population.

**Antisocial personality disorder.** A relation between antisocial personality disorder and alcohol-related disorders has frequently been reported. Some studies have suggested that antisocial personality disorder is particularly common in men with an alcohol-related disorder and can precede the development of the alcohol-related disorder. Other studies have suggested that antisocial personality disorder and alcohol-related disorders are completely distinct entities that are not causally related.

**Mood disorders.** About 30 to 40 percent of persons with an alcohol-related disorder meet the diagnostic criteria for major depressive disorder sometime during their lifetimes. Depression is more common in alcoholic women than in alcoholic men. Several studies found that depression is likely to occur in alcohol-related disorder patients who have a high daily consumption of alcohol and who have a family history of alcohol abuse. Persons with an alcohol-related disorder and major depressive disorder are at great risk for attempting suicide and are likely to have other substance-related disorder diagnoses. Some clinicians recommend that depressive symptoms that remain after two to three weeks of sobriety be treated with antidepressant drugs. Bipolar I disorder patients are thought to be at risk for the development of an alcohol-related disorder because they may use alcohol to self-medicate their manic episodes. Some studies have shown that persons with both alcohol-related disorder and depressive disorder diagnoses have low cerebrospinal fluid (CSF) concentrations of dopamine metabolites (homovanillic acid) and $\gamma$-aminobutyric acid (GABA).

**Anxiety disorders.** Alcohol is effective in alleviating anxiety, and many persons use alcohol for that reason. Although the comorbidity between alcohol-related disorders and mood disorders is fairly widely recognized, it is less well known that perhaps 25 to 50 percent of all persons with alcohol-related disorders also meet the diagnostic criteria for an anxiety disorder (Table 12.2–1). Phobias and panic disorder are particularly frequent comorbid diagnoses in those patients. Some data indicate that alcohol may be used in an attempt to self-medicate symptoms of agoraphobia or social phobia, but an alcohol-related dis-

**Table 12.2–1**
**Anxiety Disorders Found in Inpatient Alcoholic Samples**

| Study | N | Sex | Diagnostic Method, Criteria, and Time Frame | Anxiety Disorder | Patients with Disorder (%) |
|---|---|---|---|---|---|
| Mullaney and Trippett | 102 | M and F | Self-report; criteria and time frame not specified | Agoraphobia | 42.2 |
| | | | | Social phobia | 56.8 |
| | | | | Agoraphobia or social phobia | 68.7 |
| Powell et al. | 565 | M | Psychiatric diagnostic interview; criteria not specified; lifetime history | Phobic disorder | 10.0 |
| | | | | Panic attacks | 13.0 |
| | | | | Obsessive-compulsive disorder | 12.0 |
| Bowen et al. | 48 | M and F | SADS; RDC; lifetime history | Agoraphobia | 12.5 |
| | | | | Social phobia | 8.3 |
| | | | | Simple phobia | 6.2 |
| | | | | Panic disorder | 8.3 |
| | | | | Generalized anxiety disorder | 22.9 |
| | | | | Any anxiety disorder | 44.0 |
| Hesselbrock et al. | 321 | M and F | DIS; DSM-III; lifetime history | Simple phobia | 17.0 |
| | | | | Panic disorder | 6.0 |
| | | | | Obsessive-compulsive disorder | 5.0 |
| | | | | Agoraphobia | 15.0 |
| Smail et al. | 60 | M and F | Self-report; criteria and time frame not specified | Social phobia | 39.0 |
| | | | | Agoraphobia | 41.0 |
| | | | | Social phobia or agoraphobia | 53.0 |
| Weiss and Rosenberg | 84 | M and F | Structured clinical interview; DSM-III; lifetime history | Simple phobia | 7.1 |
| | | | | Generalized anxiety disorder | 8.3 |
| | | | | Panic disorder | 2.4 |
| | | | | Agoraphobia | 2.4 |
| | | | | Social phobia | 2.4 |
| | | | | Any anxiety disorder | 22.6 |
| Stravynski et al. | 173 | —[a] | Structured clinical interview; DSM-III; lifetime history | Agoraphobia | 8.5 |
| | | | | Social phobia | 7.5 |
| Chambless et al. | 75 | —[a] | SADS; RDC; lifetime history | Agoraphobia | 8.0 |
| | | | | Simple phobia | 9.3 |
| | | | | Panic disorder | 9.3 |
| | | | | Obsessive-compulsive disorder | 2.7 |
| | | | | Social phobia | 18.7 |
| | | | | Any anxiety disorder | 37.3 |
| Ross et al. | 370[b] | M and F | DIS; criteria not specified; lifetime history | Panic disorder | 10.8 |
| | | | | Phobias[c] | 36.5 |
| | | | | Generalized anxiety disorder | 56.2 |
| | | | | Obsessive-compulsive disorder | 10.8 |

[a]Data not given.
[b]Of the 501 patients described by Ross et al., this table represents only the findings for a subsample of 370 patients who reported an alcohol or alcohol and drug problem. Also, this study sample was an unspecified mix of inpatients and outpatients.
[c]Agoraphobia with and without panic attacks, simple phobia, and social phobia.
Table from M G Kushner, K J Sher, B D Beitman: The reaction between alcohol problems and the anxiety disorders. Am J Psychiatry *147*: 687, 1990. Used with permission.

order is likely to precede the development of panic disorder or generalized anxiety disorder.

**Suicide.** Most estimates of the prevalence of suicide among alcohol-related disorder patients range from 10 to 15 percent, although alcohol use itself may be involved in a much higher percentage of suicides. Some investigators have questioned whether the suicide rate among alcohol-related disorder persons is as high as those numbers suggest. Factors that have been associated with suicide among alcohol-related disorder persons include the presence of a major depressive episode, weak psychosocial support systems, a serious coexisting medical condition, unemployment, and living alone.

## ETIOLOGY

Alcohol-related disorders, like virtually all other psychiatric conditions, probably represent a heterogeneous group of disease processes. In any individual case, psychosocial, genetic, or behavioral factors may be more important than other factors. Within any single set of factors—biological factors, for example—one element (such as a neurotransmitter receptor gene) may be more critically involved than another element (such as a neurotransmitter uptake pump). Except for research purposes, it is not necessary to identify the single causative factor, since the treatment approach to the alcohol-related disorder should be to do whatever is effective, regardless of theory.

### Childhood History

Several factors have been identified in the childhood histories of persons who later have an alcohol-related disorder and in the children who are at high risk for having an alcohol-related disorder because one or both of their parents are affected. Children at high risk for alcohol-related disorders have been found in experimental studies to have, on average, a range of deficits on neurocognitive testing, a decreased amplitude of the P300 wave on evoked potential testing, and a variety of abnormalities on electroencephalogram (EEG) recordings. Studies of high-risk offspring in their 20s have also shown a generally blunted effect of alcohol compared with the effect seen in persons who do not have parents with alcohol-related disorder diagnoses. Those findings suggest that some biological heritable brain function may predispose a person to an alcohol-related disorder.

A childhood history of attention-deficit/hyperactivity disorder or conduct disorder or both increases a child's risk for an alcohol-related disorder as an adult. Personality disorders, especially antisocial personality disorder, as noted above, also predispose a person to an alcohol-related disorder.

### Psychoanalytic Factors

Psychoanalytic theories regarding alcohol-related disorders have centered on hypotheses regarding overly punitive superegos and fixation at the oral stage of psychosexual development. According to psychoanalytic theory, persons with harsh superegos who are self-punitive turn to alcohol as a way of diminishing their unconscious stress. Anxiety in persons fixated at the oral stage may be reduced by taking substances, such as alcohol, by mouth. Some psychodynamic psychiatrists describe the general personality of a person with an alcohol-related disorder as shy, isolated, impatient, irritable, anxious, hypersensitive, and sexually repressed. A common psychoanalytic aphorism is that the superego is soluble in alcohol. On a less theoretical level, alcohol may be abused by some persons as a way of reducing tension, anxiety, and various types of psychic pain. Alcohol consumption in some persons also leads to a sense of power and increased self-worth.

### Social and Cultural Factors

Some social settings commonly lead to excessive drinking. College dormitories and military bases are two examples of settings where excessive drinking and frequent drinking are often seen as completely normal and socially expected behaviors. Recently, colleges and universities have tried to educate students about the health risks of drinking large quantities of alcohol. Some cultural and ethnic groups are more restrained than others about alcohol consumption. For example, Asian and conservative Protestant persons use alcohol less frequently than do liberal Protestant and Catholic persons.

### Behavioral and Learning Factors

Just as cultural factors can affect drinking habits, so can the habits within the family itself, specifically the parental drinking habits. However, some evidence indicates that, although familial drinking habits do affect the children's drinking habits, familial drinking habits are less directly linked to the development of alcohol-related disorders than was previously thought, although they do play an important role. From a behavioral point of view, the emphasis is on the positive reinforcing aspects of alcohol, which can induce feelings of well-being and euphoria in a person. Furthermore, alcohol consumption can reduce fear and anxiety, which may further encourage drinking.

### Genetic and Other Biological Factors

The data strongly indicate a genetic component in at least some forms of alcohol-related disorders. The data for the heritability of alcohol-related disorders in males are stronger than the data for the heritability of alcohol-related disorders in females. Both the design of the studies and the interpretation of their results are complicated, however, by the likely heterogeneity of the disorders and by the likely polygenic causes. Many studies have shown that persons with first-degree relatives affected with an alcohol-related disorder are three to four times more likely to have an alcohol-related disorder than are persons without affected first-degree relatives. And alcohol-related disorder patients with family histories of alcohol abuse are likely to have severe forms of the disorder and to have higher rates of alcohol intake and more alcohol-related problems than do patients without such family histories. That finding is supported by studies of monozygotic and dizygotic twins, which consistently show a much higher concordance rate among monozygotic twins than among dizygotic twins, who are no more likely to be concordant for alcohol-related disorders than are siblings who are not twins.

The effects of shared environmental factors have been approached through adoptee studies. Those studies show that the children of parents with alcohol-related disorders are still at risk for an alcohol-related disorder, even if the children are raised by families in which the parental figures do not have alcohol-related disorders. Moreover, children whose biological parents do not have an alcohol-related disorder are not put at increased risk for the disorder if they are raised in households in which the paternal figures do have alcohol-related disorders.

Recently, genetic studies of families affected with alcohol-related disorders have used the technique of restriction fragment length polymorphism (RFLP). Some studies report an association between alcohol-related disorders and the dopamine type 2 ($D_2$) receptors, although that finding has not been consistently replicated. The finding is attractive from a theoretical point of view, since it implicates pathology in the reward mechanisms involving the ventral tegmental area and the nucleus accumbens in the pathophysiology of the alcohol-related disorders. The association with the $D_2$ receptors may be correct for a subset of affected persons, and subsequent studies may find additional associations between particular RFLP markers and alcohol-related disorders.

The biological consequences of genetic inheritance are not known. As discussed above, some evidence indicates that the brains of children of parents with alcohol-related disorders have different qualities in terms of electrophysiological measures—for example, evoked potentials and electroencephalograms (EEGs)—and response to alcohol infusions. The neurotransmitter receptors, such as the $D_2$ receptors, may be factors in the inheritance of alcohol-related disorders. Some studies have found abnormal concentrations of neurotransmitters and neurotransmitter metabolites in the CSF of alcohol-related disorder patients. Many of those studies have reported decreased concentrations of serotonin, dopamine, and GABA or their metabolites.

## PHYSIOLOGICAL EFFECTS OF ALCOHOL

The term "alcohol" refers to a large group of organic molecules that have a hydroxyl group (-OH) attached to a saturated carbon atom. Ethyl alcohol, also called ethanol, is the common form of alcohol; sometimes referred to as beverage alcohol, ethyl alcohol is used for drinking. The chemical formula for ethanol is $CH_3$-$CH_2$-OH.

The characteristic tastes and flavors of various alcohol-containing beverages are the results of their methods of production, which result in various congeners in the final product. The congeners include methanol, butanol, aldehydes, phenols, tannins, and trace amounts of various metals. Although the congeners may confer some differential psychoactive effects on the various alcohol-containing beverages, those differences in effects are minimal compared with the effects of ethanol itself. A single drink is usually considered to contain about 12 grams of ethanol, which is the content of 12 ounces of beer (7.2-proof, 3.6 percent ethanol in the United States), one 4-ounce glass of nonfortified wine, or 1 ounce to 1.5 ounces of an 80-proof (40 percent ethanol) liquor (for example, whiskey or gin). In calculating a patient's intake of alcohol, however, the clinician should be aware that beers vary in their content of alcohol, that beers come in small and big cans and mugs, that glasses of wine range from two to six ounces, and that mixed drinks at some bars and in most homes contain two to three ounces of liquor. Nonetheless, using the moderate sizes of drinks, a clinician can estimate that a single drink increases the blood alcohol level of a 150-pound man 15 to 20 mg/dL, which is about the concentration of alcohol that an average person can metabolize in one hour.

Increasing publicity is being given, especially by the makers and the distributors of alcohol, to the possible beneficial effects of alcohol intake. Most of the attention is on some epidemiological data that suggest that one or two glasses of red wine each day lower the incidence of cardiovascular disease; however, those findings are highly controversial.

## Absorption

About 10 percent of consumed alcohol is absorbed from the stomach, with the remainder absorbed from the small intestine. Peak blood concentration of alcohol is reached in 30 to 90 minutes, usually in 45 to 60 minutes, depending on whether the alcohol was taken on an empty stomach, which enhances absorption, or with food, which delays absorption. The time to peak blood concentration is also a factor of the time during which the alcohol was consumed; a short time reduces the time to peak concentration, and a long time increases the time to peak concentration. Absorption is most rapid with 15 to 30 percent (30- to 60-proof) alcohol-containing beverages. There is some dispute about whether carbonation (for example, in champagne and mixed drinks with seltzer) enhances the absorption of alcohol.

The body has protective devices against inundation by alcohol. For example, if the concentration of alcohol becomes too high in the stomach, mucus is secreted, and the pyloric valve closes. Those actions slow the absorption and keep the alcohol from passing into the small intestine, where no significant restraints to absorption exist. Thus, a large amount of alcohol can remain unabsorbed in the stomach for hours. Furthermore, the pylorospasm often results in nausea and vomiting.

Once alcohol is absorbed into the bloodstream, it is distributed to all the tissues of the body. Because alcohol is uniformly dissolved in the water of the body, tissues containing a high proportion of water receive a high concentration of alcohol. The intoxicating effects are greater when the blood alcohol concentration is rising than when it is falling (the *Mellanby effects*). For that reason the rate of absorption has a direct bearing on the intoxication response.

## Metabolism

About 90 percent of absorbed alcohol is metabolized through oxidation in the liver; the remaining 10 percent is excreted unchanged by the kidneys and the lungs. The rate of oxidation by the liver is constant and is independent of the body's energy requirements. The body is capable of metabolizing about 15 mg/dL an hour, with a range of 10 to 34 mg/dL an hour. Stated another way, the average person oxidizes three fourths of an ounce of 40 percent (80-proof) alcohol in an hour. In persons who have a history of alcohol consumption, there is an up-regulation of the necessary enzymes, resulting in fast metabolism of the alcohol.

Alcohol is metabolized by two enzymes: alcohol dehydrogenase (ADH) and aldehyde dehydrogenase. ADH catalyzes the conversion of alcohol into acetaldehyde, which is a toxic compound. Aldehyde dehydrogenase catalyzes the conversion of acetaldehyde into acetic acid. Aldehyde dehydrogenase is inhibited by disulfiram (Antabuse), which is often used in the treatment of alcohol-related disorders. Some studies have shown that women have a lower ADH content than do men, which may account for women's tendency to become more intoxicated than men after drinking the same amount of alcohol. The decreased function of alcohol-metabolizing enzymes in some Asian persons can also lead to easy intoxication and toxic symptoms.

### Effects on the Brain

**Biochemistry.** In contrast to most other substances of abuse that have identified receptor targets—for example, the N-methyl-D-aspartate (NMDA) receptor of phencyclidine—no single molecular target has been identified as the mediator for the effects of alcohol. The long-standing theory regarding the biochemical effects of alcohol involves its effects on the membranes of neurons. Data support the hypothesis that alcohol has its effects by intercalating itself into membranes, resulting in increased fluidity of the membranes with short-term use. With long-term use, however, the theory hypothesizes that the membranes become rigid or stiff. The fluidity of the membranes is critical to the normal functioning of receptors, ion channels, and other membrane-bound functional proteins. Recent studies attempt to identify specific molecular targets for the effects of alcohol. Most of the attention has been focused on the effects of alcohol at ion channels. Specifically, studies have found that alcohol ion channel activities associated with the nicotinic acetylcholine, serotonin (5-hydroxytryptamine) type 3 (5-HT$_3$), and GABA type A (GABA$_A$) receptors are enhanced by alcohol, whereas ion channel activities associated with glutamate receptors and voltage-gated calcium channels are inhibited.

**Behavioral effects.** The net result of the molecular activities is that alcohol functions as a depressant, much like the barbiturates and the benzodiazepines, with which there is some degree of cross-tolerance and cross-dependence. At a level of 0.05 percent alcohol in the blood, thought, judgment, and restraint are loosened and sometimes disrupted. At a concentration of 0.1 percent, voluntary motor actions usually become perceptibly clumsy. In most states, legal intoxication ranges from 0.1 to 0.15 percent blood alcohol level. At 0.2 percent the function of the entire motor area of the brain is measurably depressed; the parts of the brain that control emotional behavior are also affected. At 0.3 percent a person is commonly confused or may become stuporous. At 0.4 to 0.5 percent a person is in a coma. At higher levels the primitive centers of the brain, which control breathing and heart rate, are affected, and death ensues. Death is secondary to direct respiratory depression or to the aspiration of vomitus. Persons with long-term histories of alcohol abuse, however, are able to tolerate much higher concentrations of alcohol than do alcohol-naive persons and may falsely appear to be less intoxicated than they really are because of their tolerance.

**Sleep effects.** Although alcohol intake in the evening usually results in an increased ease of falling asleep (that is, decreased sleep latency), alcohol also has adverse effects on sleep architecture. Specifically, alcohol use is associated with decreased rapid eye movement sleep (REM or dream sleep), decreased deep sleep (stage 4), and increased sleep fragmentation, including more and longer episodes of awakening. Therefore, it is a myth that drinking alcohol aids sleeping.

## Other Physiological Effects

**Liver.** The major adverse effects associated with alcohol use are related to liver damage. Alcohol use, even short (week-long) episodes of increased drinking, can result in an accumulation of fats and proteins, resulting in the appearance of a fatty liver, which is sometimes found on physical examination as an enlarged liver. The association between fatty infiltration of the liver and serious liver damage remains unclear. However, alcohol use is associated with the development of alcoholic hepatitis and hepatic cirrhosis.

**Gastrointestinal system.** Long-term heavy drinking is associated with the development of esophagitis, gastritis, achlorhydria, and gastric ulcers. The development of esophageal varices can accompany particularly heavy alcohol abuse, and the rupture of the varices is a medical emergency that often results in death due to exsanguination. Occasionally, disorders of the small intestine also occur. Pancreatitis, pancreatic insufficiency, and pancreatic cancer are also associated with heavy alcohol use. Heavy alcohol intake may interfere with the normal processes of food digestion and absorption. As a result, the food that is consumed is inadequately digested. Alcohol abuse also appears to inhibit the capacity of the intestine to absorb various nutrients, including vitamins and amino acids. That effect, coupled with the often poor dietary habits of persons with alcohol-related disorders, can result in serious vitamin deficiencies, particularly of the B vitamins.

**Other bodily systems.** A significant intake of alcohol has been associated with increased blood pressure, dysregulation of lipoproteins and triglycerides, and increased risk for myocardial infarctions and cerebrovascular diseases. Alcohol has been shown to affect the hearts of even nonalcoholic persons, increasing the resting cardiac output, heart rate, and myocardial oxygen consumption. Evidence indicates that alcohol intake can adversely affect the hematopoietic system and can increase the incidence of cancer, particularly head, neck, esophageal, stomach, hepatic, colonic, and lung cancer. Acute intoxication may also be associated with hypoglycemia, which, when unrecognized, may be responsible for some of the sudden deaths of intoxicated people. Muscle weakness is a side effect of alcoholism.

**Laboratory tests.** The adverse effects of alcohol are reflected in common laboratory tests, which can be useful diagnostic aids in identifying persons with alcohol-related disorders. The γ-glutamyltranspeptidase levels are elevated in about 80 percent of all persons with alcohol-related disorders, and the mean corpuscular volume (MCV) is elevated in about 60 percent, more so in women than in men. Other laboratory test results that may be elevated in association with alcohol abuse are uric acid, triglycerides, serum glutamic-oxaloacetic transaminase (SGOT), also called aspartate aminotransferase (AST), and serum glutamic-pyruvic transaminase (SGPT), also called alanine aminotransferase (ALT) results.

## Drug Interactions

The interaction between alcohol and other substances can be dangerous, even fatal. Certain substances, such as alcohol and phenobarbital (Luminal) are metabolized by the liver, their prolonged use may lead to an acceleration of their metabolism. When alcoholic persons are sober, that accelerated metabolism makes them unusually tolerant to many drugs, such as sedatives and hypnotics; but, when alcoholic persons are intoxicated, those drugs compete with the alcohol for the same detoxification mechanisms, and potentially toxic blood levels of all involved substances can accumulate.

The effects of alcohol and other central nervous system (CNS) depressants are usually synergistic. Sedatives, hypnotics, and drugs that relieve pain, motion sickness, head colds, and allergy symptoms must be used with caution by alcoholic persons. Narcotics depress the sensory areas of the cerebral cortex, resulting in pain relief, sedation, apathy, drowsiness, and sleep. High doses can result in respiratory failure and death. Increasing the dosages of sedative-hypnotic drugs, such as chloral hydrate (Noctec) and benzodiazepines, especially when they are combined with alcohol, produces a range of effects from sedation to motor and intellectual impairment and progressing to stupor, coma, and death. Since sedatives and other psychotropics can potentiate the effects of alcohol, patients should be instructed about the dangers of combining CNS depressants and alcohol, particularly when they are driving or operating machinery.

## DISORDERS

DSM-IV lists the alcohol-related disorders (Table 12.2–2) and specifies the diagnostic criteria for alcohol intoxi-

**Table 12.2–2**
**Alcohol-Related Disorders**

*Alcohol use disorders*
**Alcohol dependence**
**Alcohol abuse**

*Alcohol-induced disorders*
**Alcohol intoxication**
**Alcohol withdrawal**
*Specify if:*
  with perceptual disturbances
**Alcohol intoxication delirium**
**Alcohol withdrawal delirium**
**Alcohol-induced persisting dementia**
**Alcohol-induced persisting amnestic disorder**
**Alcohol-induced psychotic disorder, with delusions**
*Specify if:*
  with onset during intoxication
  with onset during withdrawal
**Alcohol-induced psychotic disorder, with hallucinations**
*Specify if:*
  with onset during intoxication
  with onset during withdrawal
**Alcohol-induced mood disorder**
*Specify if:*
  with onset during intoxication
  with onset during withdrawal
**Alcohol-induced anxiety disorder**
*Specify if:*
  with onset during intoxication
  with onset during withdrawal
**Alcohol-induced sexual dysfunction**
*Specify if:*
  with onset during intoxication
**Alcohol-induced sleep disorder**
*Specify if:*
  with onset during intoxication
  with onset during withdrawal

**Alcohol-related disorder not otherwise specified**

**Table 12.2–3**
**Diagnostic Criteria for Alcohol Intoxication**

A. Recent ingestion of alcohol.

B. Clinically significant maladaptive behavior or psychological changes (e.g., inappropriate sexual or aggressive behavior, mood lability, impaired judgment, impaired social or occupational functioning) that developed during, or shortly after, alcohol ingestion.

C. One (or more) of the following signs, developing during, or shortly after, alcohol use:

  (1) slurred speech
  (2) incoordination
  (3) unsteady gait
  (4) nystagmus
  (5) impairment in attention or memory
  (6) stupor or coma

D. The symptoms are not due to a general medical condition and are not better accounted for by another mental disorder.

cation (Table 12.2–3) and alcohol withdrawal (Table 12.2–4). The diagnostic criteria for the other alcohol-related disorders are listed in DSM-IV under the major symptom. For example, the diagnostic criteria for alcohol-induced anxiety disorder are found in the anxiety disorders category, under the heading "substance-induced anxiety disorder."

## Alcohol Dependence and Alcohol Abuse

**Diagnosis and clinical features.**   In DSM-IV all substance-related disorders use the same criteria for depen-

**Table 12.2–4**
**Diagnostic Criteria for Alcohol Withdrawal**

A. Cessation of (or reduction in) alcohol use that has been heavy and prolonged.

B. Two (or more) of the following, developing within several hours to a few days after criterion A:

  (1) autonomic hyperactivity (e.g., sweating or pulse rate greater than 100)
  (2) increased hand tremor
  (3) insomnia
  (4) nausea or vomiting
  (5) transient visual, tactile, or auditory hallucinations or illusions
  (6) psychomotor agitation
  (7) anxiety
  (8) grand mal seizures

C. The symptoms in criterion B cause clinically significant distress or impairment in social, occupational, or other important areas of functioning.

D. The symptoms are not due to a general medical condition and not better accounted for by another mental disorder.

*Specify* if:
  **with perceptual disturbances**

dence and abuse (Tables 12.1–6, 12.1–7, and 12.1–8). With regard to alcohol dependence and alcohol abuse, the need for the daily use of large amounts of alcohol for adequate functioning, a regular pattern of heavy drinking limited to weekends, and long periods of sobriety interspersed with binges of heavy alcohol intake lasting for weeks or months are strongly suggestive of those alcohol use disorders. The patterns are often associated with such behaviors as (1) the inability to cut down or stop drinking, (2) repeated efforts to control or reduce excessive drinking by going on the wagon (periods of temporary abstinence) or restricting drinking to certain times of the day, (3) binges (remaining intoxicated throughout the day for at least two days), (4) the occasional consumption of a fifth of spirits (or its equivalent in wine or beer), (5) amnestic periods for events occurring while intoxicated (blackouts), (6) the continuation of drinking despite a serious physical disorder that the person knows is exacerbated by alcohol use, and (7) the drinking of nonbeverage alcohol, such as fuel and commercial products containing alcohol. In addition, people with alcohol dependence and alcohol abuse show impaired social or occupational functioning because of alcohol use, such as violence while intoxicated, absence from work, loss of job, legal difficulties (for example, arrest for intoxicated behavior and traffic accidents while intoxicated), and arguments or difficulties with family members or friends because of excessive alcohol use.

**Subtypes of alcohol dependence.** Various researchers have attempted to divide alcohol dependence into subtypes, based primarily on phenomenological characteristics. One recent classification notes that persons with *type A* alcohol dependence have a late onset, few childhood risk factors, relatively mild dependence, few alcohol-related problems, and little psychopathology. Persons with *type B* alcohol dependence have many childhood risk factors, severe dependence, an early onset of alcohol-related problems, much psychopathology, a strong family history of alcohol abuse, frequent polysubstance abuse, a long history of alcohol treatment, and a high number of severe life stresses. Some researchers have found that type A alcohol-dependent persons may respond to interactional psychotherapies, whereas type B alcohol-dependent persons may respond best to the training of coping skills.

A number of other subtyping schemes of alcohol dependence have received fairly wide recognition in the literature. One group of investigators proposed three subtypes: (1) *early-stage problem drinkers,* who do not yet have complete alcohol dependence syndromes; (2) *affiliative drinkers,* who tend to drink daily in moderate amounts in social settings; and (3) *schizoid-isolated drinkers,* who have severe dependence and tend to drink in binges and often alone.

Another investigator's *gamma* alcohol dependence, which is thought to be common in the United States and is representative of the alcohol dependence seen in persons who are active in Alcoholics Anonymous (AA), concerns control problems. Such persons are unable to stop drinking once they start. If the drinking ends as a result of ill health or lack of money, they are capable of abstaining for varying periods of time. In *delta* alcohol dependence, which is perhaps more common in Europe than in the United States, the alcohol-dependent person must drink a certain amount each day but is unaware of a lack of control. The alcohol use disorder may not be discovered until the person must stop drinking for some reason and then feels the symptoms of withdrawal.

Still another investigator suggested the *type I, male-limited* subtype of alcohol dependence; it is characterized by a late onset, more evidence of psychological dependence than of physical dependence, and the presence of guilt feelings concerning the use of alcohol. *Type II, male-limited* alcohol dependence is characterized by an onset at an early age, the spontaneous seeking of alcohol for consumption, and a socially disruptive set of behaviors when the person is intoxicated.

Yet another investigator postulated four subtypes of alcoholism. First, *antisocial alcoholism* is characterized by a male predominance, a poor prognosis, an early onset of alcohol-related problems, and a close association with antisocial personality disorder. Second, *developmentally cumulative alcoholism* involves a primary tendency to abuse alcohol that is exacerbated with time as cultural expectations foster increased opportunities to drink. Third, *negative-affect alcoholism* is more common in women than in men; according to the hypothesis, women are likely to use alcohol for mood regulation and to help with social relationships. Fourth, *developmentally limited alcoholism* is characterized by frequent bouts of the consumption of large amounts of alcohol; the bouts become less frequent as the persons age and respond to the increased expectations of society regarding their jobs and families.

## Alcohol Intoxication

**Diagnosis and clinical features.** DSM-IV has formal criteria regarding the diagnosis of alcohol intoxication (Table 12.2–3). The criteria emphasize a sufficient amount of alcohol consumption, specific maladaptive behavioral changes, signs of neurological impairment, and the absence of other confounding diagnoses or conditions. Alcohol intoxication is not a trivial condition. Extreme alcohol intoxication can lead to coma, respiratory depression, and death, either because of respiratory arrest or because of the aspiration of vomitus. Treatment for severe alcohol intoxication involves mechanical ventilatory support in an intensive care unit, with attention to the patient's acid-base balance, electrolytes, and temperature. Some studies of cerebral blood flow (CBF) during alcohol intoxication have found a modest increase in CBF after the ingestion of small amounts of alcohol, but CBF decreases with continued drinking.

The severity of the symptoms of alcohol intoxication correlates roughly with the blood concentration of alcohol, which reflects the alcohol concentration in the brain. At the onset of intoxication, some persons become talkative and gregarious; some become withdrawn and sullen; others become belligerent. Some patients show a lability of mood, with intermittent episodes of laughing and crying. A short-term tolerance to alcohol may occur, such that the person seems to be less intoxicated after many hours of drinking than after only a few hours.

The medical complications of intoxication include those that result from falls, such as subdural hematomas and fractures. Telltale signs of frequent bouts of intoxication are facial hematomas, particularly about the eyes, which are the result of falls or fights while drunk. In cold climates, hypothermia and death may occur because the intoxicated person is exposed to the elements. A person with alcohol intoxication may also be predisposed to infections, secondary to a suppression of the immune system.

**Idiosyncratic alcohol intoxication.** A significant debate concerns whether the diagnostic entity of idiosyncratic alcohol intoxication really exists; it is not recognized as an official diagnosis in DSM-IV. Several well-controlled studies of persons who supposedly have the disorder have raised questions regarding its validity. The condition has been variously called pathologic, complicated, atypical, and paranoid alcohol intoxication; all those terms indicate that a severe behavioral syndrome develops rapidly after the person consumes a small amount of alcohol that, in most people, has minimal behavioral effects. The importance of the diagnosis lies in the forensic arena. Alcohol intoxication is generally not accepted as grounds for not being held responsible for one's activities. Idiosyncratic alcohol intoxication, however, can be used in a person's defense if a defense lawyer can successfully argue that the defendant has an unexpected, idiosyncratic, and pathological reaction to a minimal amount of alcohol.

Anecdotal reports of persons with idiosyncratic alcohol intoxication have described confusion, disorientation, illusions, transitory delusions, and visual hallucinations. The persons also have greatly increased psychomotor activity. They may display impulsive, aggressive behavior and be dangerous to others. They may also exhibit suicidal ideation and make suicide attempts. The disorder, which is usually described as lasting for a few hours, terminates in a prolonged period of sleep. The affected persons are unable to recall the episodes on awakening. The cause of the condition is unknown but is reported to be most common in persons with high levels of anxiety. One hypothesis is that the alcohol causes sufficient disorganization and loss of control to release aggressive impulses. Another suggestion is that brain damage, particularly encephalitic or traumatic damage, predisposes some people to an intolerance for alcohol, which may lead to abnormal behavior after they ingest only small amounts of alcohol. Other predisposing factors may include advancing age, the taking of sedative-hypnotic drugs, and feeling fatigued. The person's behavior while intoxicated tends to be atypical of the person when not under the influence of alcohol; for example, a quiet, shy person after one weak drink becomes belligerent and aggressive.

The treatment of idiosyncratic alcohol intoxication involves protecting patients from harming themselves and others. Physical restraint may be necessary but is difficult because of the abrupt onset of the condition. Once the patient has been restrained, an injection of an antipsychotic drug, such as haloperidol (Haldol), is useful for controlling assaultiveness.

The condition must be differentiated from other causes of abrupt behavioral change, such as complex partial epilepsy. Several persons with the disorder have been reported to show temporal lobe spiking on an electroencephalogram (EEG) after ingesting small amounts of alcohol.

**Alcohol Withdrawal**

**Diagnosis and clinical features.** The diagnosis of alcohol withdrawal was called uncomplicated alcohol withdrawal in DSM-III-R to distinguish it from alcohol withdrawal delirium. The word "uncomplicated" was dropped from DSM-IV because alcohol withdrawal, even without delirium, can be serious and can include seizures and autonomic hyperactivity. Conditions that may predispose to or aggravate withdrawal symptoms include fatigue, malnutrition, physical illness, and depression. The DSM-IV criteria for alcohol withdrawal (Table 12.2–4) require the cessation or reduction of alcohol use that was heavy and prolonged, as well as the presence of specific physical or neuropsychiatric symptoms. The DSM-IV diagnosis also allows for the specification of "with perceptual disturbances." One recent positron emission tomographic (PET) study of blood flow during alcohol withdrawal in otherwise healthy persons with alcohol dependence found a globally low rate of metabolic activity (Figure 12.2–1), although, with further inspection of the data, the authors concluded that activity was especially decreased in the left parietal and right frontal areas.

The classic sign of alcohol withdrawal is tremulousness, although the spectrum of symptoms can expand to include psychotic and perceptual symptoms (for example, delusions and hallucinations), seizures, and the symptoms of delirium tremens (DTs), now called alcohol withdrawal delirium in DSM-IV. Tremulousness (commonly called the shakes or jitters) develops six to eight hours after the cessation of drinking, the psychotic and perceptual symptoms start in 8 to 12 hours, seizures in 12 to 24 hours, and DTs within 72 hours, although physicians should watch for the development of DTs for the first week of withdrawal. The syndrome of withdrawal sometimes skips the usual progression and, for example, goes directly to DTs.

The tremor of alcohol withdrawal can be similar either to physiological tremor, with a continuous tremor of great amplitude and of more than 8 Hz, or to familial tremor, with bursts of tremor activity slower than 8 Hz. Other symptoms of withdrawal include general irritability, gastrointestinal symptoms (for example, nausea and vomiting), and sympathetic autonomic hyperactivity, including anxiety, arousal, sweating, facial flushing, mydriasis, tachycardia, and mild hypertension. Patients experiencing alcohol withdrawal are generally alert but may startle easily.

**Withdrawal seizures.** Seizures associated with alcohol withdrawal are stereotyped, generalized, and tonic-clonic in character. Patients often have more than one seizure in the three to six hours after the first seizure. Status epilepticus is relatively rare in alcohol withdrawal patients, occurring in less than 3 percent of all patients. Although anticonvulsant medications are not required in the management of alcohol withdrawal seizures, the cause of the seizures is difficult to establish when a patient is first assessed in the emergency room; thus, many patients with withdrawal seizures receive anticonvulsant medications, which are then discontinued once the cause of the seizures is recognized. Seizure activity in patients with known alcohol abuse histories should still prompt the clinician to consider other possible causative factors, including head

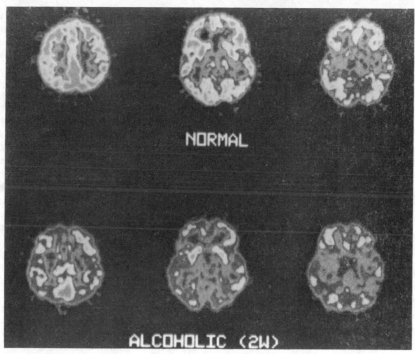

**Figure 12.2–1.** Brain PET metabolic images in a normal control subject and an alcoholic subject tested two weeks after the last use of alcohol. Notice the decreased cortical metabolic activity in the alcoholic person. (Figure from N D Volkow, R Hitzemann, G-J Wang, J S Fowler, G Burr, K Pascani, S L Dewey, A Wolf: Decreased brain metabolism in neurologically intact healthy alcoholics. Am J Psychiatry *149*: 1019, 1992. Used with permission.)

injuries, CNS infections, CNS neoplasms, and other cerebrovascular diseases; long-term severe alcohol abuse can result in hypoglycemia, hyponatremia, and hypomagnesemia—all of which can also be associated with seizures.

**Treatment.** The primary medications for the control of alcohol withdrawal symptoms are the benzodiazepines (Table 12.2–5). Many studies have found that benzodiazepines help control seizure activity, delirium, anxiety, tachycardia, hypertension, diaphoresis, and tremor associated with alcohol withdrawal. Benzodiazepines can be given either orally or parenterally; however, neither diazepam (Valium) nor chlordiazepoxide (Librium) should be given intramuscularly (IM) because of their erratic absorption by that route. The clinician must titrate the dosage of the benzodiazepine, starting with a high dosage and lowering the dosage as the patient recovers. Sufficient ben-

**Table 12.2–5**
**Drug Therapy for Alcohol Intoxication and Withdrawal**

| Clinical Problem | Drug | Route | Dosage | Comment |
|---|---|---|---|---|
| Tremulousness and mild to moderate agitation | Chlordiazepoxide | Oral | 25–100 mg every 4–6 hrs | Initial dose can be repeated every 2 hours until patient is calm; subsequent doses must be individualized and titrated |
| | Diazepam | Oral | 5–20 mg every 4–6 hrs | |
| Hallucinosis | Lorazepam | Oral | 2–10 mg every 4–6 hrs | |
| Extreme agitation | Chlordiazepoxide | Intravenous | 0.5 mg/kg at 12.5 mg/min | Give until patient is calm; subsequent doses must be individualized and titrated |
| Withdrawal seizures | Diazepam | Intravenous | 0.15 mg/kg at 2.5 mg/min | |
| Delirium tremens | Lorazepam | Intravenous | 0.1 mg/kg at 2.0 mg/min | |

Table adapted from J K Weser, E M Sellers, H Kalant: Drug therapy: Alcohol intoxication and withdrawal. N Engl J Med *294*: 757, 1976. Used with permission.
Table from F A Rubino: Neurologic complications of alcoholism. Psychiatr Clin North Am *15*: 364, 1992. Used with permission.

zodiazepines should be used to keep patients calm and sedated but not so sedated that they cannot be aroused for the clinician to perform appropriate procedures, including neurological examinations.

Although benzodiazepines are the standard treatment for alcohol withdrawal, a number of studies have shown that carbamazepine (Tegretol) in dosages of 800 mg a day is as effective as benzodiazepines and has the added benefit of minimal abuse liability. That use of carbamzepine is gradually becoming common in the United States and Europe. The β-adrenergic receptor antagonists and clonidine (Catapres) have also been used to block the symptoms of sympathetic hyperactivity; however, neither of those drugs is an effective treatment for seizures or delirium.

## Delirium

**Diagnosis and clinical features.** DSM-IV contains the diagnostic criteria for alcohol intoxication delirium in the category of substance intoxication delirium and the diagnostic criteria for alcohol withdrawal delirium in the category of substance withdrawal delirium (Section 10.2). Patients with recognized alcohol withdrawal symptoms should be carefully monitored to prevent progression to alcohol withdrawal delirium, the most severe form of the withdrawal syndrome, also known as *delirium tremens* (the DTs). Alcohol withdrawal delirium is a medical emergency that can result in significant morbidity and mortality. Delirious patients are a danger to themselves and to others because of the unpredictability of their behavior. The patients may be assaultive or suicidal or may be acting on hallucinations or delusional thoughts as if they were genuine dangers. Untreated, DTs has a mortality rate of 20 percent, usually as a result of an intercurrent medical illness, such as pneumonia, renal disease, hepatic insufficiency, or heart failure. Although withdrawal seizures commonly precede the development of alcohol withdrawal delirium, the delirium can also appear unheralded. The essential feature of the syndrome is delirium that occurs within one week after the person stops drinking or reduces his or her intake of alcohol. In addition to the symptoms of delirium, the features include (1) autonomic hyperactivity, such as tachycardia, diaphoresis, fever, anxiety, insomnia, and hypertension; (2) perceptual distortions, which are most frequently visual or tactile hallucinations; and (3) fluctuating levels of psychomotor activity, ranging from hyperexcitability to lethargy.

About 5 percent of all alcoholic persons who are hospitalized have DTs. Since the syndrome usually develops on the third hospital day, a patient admitted for an unrelated condition may unexpectedly go into an episode of delirium, which is the first sign of a previously undiagnosed alcohol-related disorder. Episodes of DTs usually begin in the patient's 30s or 40s after 5 to 15 years of heavy drinking, typically of the binge type. Physical illness (for example, hepatitis or pancreatitis) predisposes to the syndrome; a person in good physical health rarely has DTs during alcohol withdrawal.

A 43-year-old divorced carpenter was examined in a hospital emergency observation ward. The patient's sister was available to provide some information. She reported that the patient had consumed large quantities of cheap wine daily for more than five years. He had had a reasonably stable home life and job record until his wife left him for another man five years before. The sister indicated that the patient had been consuming more than a fifth of wine a day since his divorce. He often had blackouts from drinking and had missed days from work; consequently, he had been fired from several jobs. Fortunately for him, carpenters are in great demand, and he had been able to provide marginally for himself during those years. However, three days before hospitalization, he had run out of money and wine and had to beg on the street to buy a meal. The patient had been poorly nourished, eating perhaps one meal a day and evidently relying on wine for nourishment.

The morning after his last day of drinking (three days earlier), he felt increasingly tremulous, his hands shaking so grossly that he could hardly light a cigarette. He also had an increasing sense of inner panic, which had made him virtually unable to sleep. A neighbor became concerned about the patient when he seemed not to be making sense and was clearly unable to take care of himself. The neighbor called the sister, who brought him to the hospital.

On examination, the patient alternated between apprehension and chatty, superficial warmth. He was keyed up and talked almost constantly in a rambling and unfocused manner. At times he recognized the doctor, but at other times he got confused and thought the doctor was his older brother. Twice during the examination he called the doctor by his older brother's name and asked when he had arrived, evidently having lost track entirely of the interview up to that point. He had a gross hand tremor at rest, and sometimes he picked at "bugs" he saw on the bed sheets. He was disoriented and thought that he was in a supermarket parking lot, rather than in a hospital. He indicated that he felt he was fighting against a terrifying sense that the world was ending in a holocaust. He was startled every few minutes by sounds and scenes of fiery car crashes (evidently provoked by the sound of rolling carts in the hall). Efforts to test his memory and his calculation ability failed because his attention shifted rapidly. An electroencephalogram indicated a pattern of diffuse encephalopathy.

**Treatment.** The best treatment for DTs is its prevention. Patients who are withdrawing from alcohol who exhibit any withdrawal phenomena should receive a benzodiazepine, such as 25 to 50 mg of chlordiazepoxide (Librium) every two to four hours until they seem to be out of danger. Once the delirium appears, however, 50 to 100 mg of chlordiazepoxide should be given every four hours orally, or intravenous lorazepam (Ativan) should be used if oral medication is not possible (Table 12.2–5). A high-calorie, high-carbohydrate diet supplemented by multivitamins is also important. Physically restraining patients with the DTs is risky, since they may fight against the restraints to a dangerous level of exhaustion. When patients are disorderly and uncontrollable, a seclusion room can be used. Dehydration, often contributed to by diaphoresis and fever, can be corrected with fluids by mouth or intravenously. Anorexia, vomiting, and diarrhea often occur during withdrawal. Antipsychotic medications should be avoided because they may reduce the seizure threshold in the patient.

The need for warm, supportive psychotherapy in the treatment of DTs is essential. Patients are often bewildered, frightened, and anxious because of their tumultuous symptoms. Skillful verbal support is imperative.

The emergence of focal neurological symptoms, lateralizing seizures, increased intracranial pressure, evidence of skull fractures, or other indications of CNS pathology should prompt the clinician to examine the patient for additional neurological diseases. Nonbenzodiazepine anticonvulsant medication is not useful in preventing or treating alcohol withdrawal convulsions, although benzodiazepines are generally effective.

## Alcohol-Induced Persisting Dementia

The legitimacy of the concept of alcohol-induced persisting dementia remains controversial, inasmuch as some clinicians and researchers believe that it is difficult to separate the toxic effects of alcohol abuse from the CNS damage done by poor nutrition, multiple trauma, and the CNS damage that follows the malfunctioning of other bodily organs (for example, the liver, the pancreas, and the kidneys). Although several studies have found enlarged ventricles and cortical atrophy in persons with dementia and a history of alcohol dependence, the studies do not help clarify the cause of the dementia. Nonetheless, the diagnosis of alcohol-induced persisting dementia is contained in DSM-IV (Section 10.3). The controversy regarding the diagnosis should encourage the clinician to complete a diagnostic assessment of the dementia before concluding that the dementia was caused by alcohol.

## Alcohol-Induced Persisting Amnestic Disorder

**Diagnosis and clinical features.** The diagnostic criteria of alcohol-induced persisting amnestic disorder are contained in the DSM-IV category of substance-induced persisting amnestic disorder (Section 10.4). The essential feature of alcohol-induced persisting amnestic disorder is a disturbance in short-term memory caused by the prolonged heavy use of alcohol. Since the disorder usually occurs in persons who have been drinking heavily for many years, the disorder is rare in persons under the age of 35.

**Wernicke's and Korsakoff's syndromes.** The classic names for alcohol-induced persisting amnestic disorder are Wernicke's syndrome (a set of acute symptoms) and Korsakoff's syndrome (a chronic condition). Whereas Wernicke's syndrome is completely reversible with treatment, only about 20 percent of Korsakoff's syndrome patients recover. The pathophysiological connection between the two syndromes is thiamine deficiency, caused either by poor nutritional habits or by malabsorption problems. Thiamine is a cofactor for several important enzymes, and it may also be involved in the conduction of the axon potential along the axon and in synaptic transmission. The neuropathological lesions are symmetrical and paraventricular, involving the mammillary bodies, the thalamus, the hypothalamus, the midbrain, the pons, the medulla, the fornix, and the cerebellum.

Wernicke's syndrome, also called alcoholic encephalopathy, is an acute neurological disorder characterized by ataxia (affecting primarily the gait), vestibular dysfunction, confusion, and a variety of ocular motility abnormalities, including horizontal nystagmus, lateral rectal palsy, and gaze palsy. Usually, those eye signs are bilateral, although not necessarily symmetrical. Other eye signs may include a sluggish reaction to light and anisocoria. Wernicke's syndrome may clear spontaneously in a few days or weeks, or it may progress into Korsakoff's syndrome.

**Treatment.** The early stages of Wernicke's syndrome respond rapidly to large doses of parenteral thiamine, which is believed to be effective in preventing the progression into Korsakoff's syndrome. The dosage of thiamine is usually initiated at 100 mg by mouth two to three times daily and is continued for one to two weeks. In patients with alcohol-related disorders who are being given intravenous (IV) administrations of glucose solution, it is good practice to include 100 mg of thiamine in each liter of the glucose solution.

Korsakoff's syndrome is the chronic amnestic syndrome that can follow Wernicke's syndrome, and the two syndromes are believed to be pathophysiologically related. The cardinal features of Korsakoff's syndrome are impaired mental syndrome (especially recent memory) and anterograde amnesia in an alert and responsive patient. The patient may or may not have the symptom of confabulation. Treatment of Korsakoff's syndrome is also thiamine given 100 mg by mouth two to three times daily; the treatment should be continued for 3 to 12 months. Few patients who progress to Korsakoff's syndrome ever fully recover, although a substantial proportion have some improvement in their cognitive abilities with thiamine and nutritional support.

A clinical case example of Wernicke-Korsakoff syndrome follows:

A 46-year-old house painter was admitted to a hospital with a history of 30 years of heavy drinking. He had had two previous admissions for detoxification, but his family stated that he had not had a drink in several weeks, and he showed no signs of alcohol withdrawal. He looked malnourished, however, and on examination was found to be ataxic and to have a bilateral sixth-cranial-nerve palsy. He appeared to be confused and mistook one of his physicians for a dead uncle.

Within a week the patient walked normally, and he no longer showed any sign of a sixth-nerve palsy. He seemed to be less confused than at admission and could find his way to the bathroom without direction. He remembered the names and the birthdays of his siblings but had difficulty naming the past five United States Presidents. He had great difficulty in retaining information for longer than a few minutes. He could repeat a list of numbers immediately after he had heard them but a few minutes later did not recall being asked to perform the task. Shown three objects (keys, comb, ring), he could not recall them three minutes later. He did not seem to be worried about his memory failure. Asked if he could recall the name of his doctor, he replied, "Certainly," and proceeded to call him "Dr. Masters" (not his name), whom he claimed he had first met during the Korean War. He told a long untrue story about how he and "Dr. Masters" had served as fellow soldiers.

The patient was calm, alert, and friendly. Because of his intact immediate memory and spotty but sometimes adequate remote memory, one could be with him for a short period and not realize that he had a severe memory impairment. His amnesia, in short, was largely anterograde. Although treated with high doses of thiamine, the short-term memory deficit persisted and appeared to be irreversible.

**Blackouts.** Alcohol-related blackouts are not included in DSM-IV's diagnostic classification, although the symptom of alcohol intoxication does exist and is common. Blackouts are similar to episodes of transient global amnesia (Section 10.4) in that they are discrete episodes of anterograde amnesia, although blackouts occur in association with alcohol intoxication. The periods of amnesia can be particularly distressing because people may fear that they have unknowingly harmed someone or behaved imprudently while intoxicated. During a blackout, people have relatively intact remote memory; however, they experience a specific short-term memory deficit in which they are unable to recall events that happened in the previous 5 or 10 minutes. Because their other intellectual faculties are well preserved, they can perform complicated tasks and appear to be normal to the casual observer. Although the neurobiological mechanisms for alcoholic blackouts are now known at the molecular level, alcohol in the patients blocks the consolidation of new memories into old memories, a process that is thought to involve the hippocampus and related temporal lobe structures.

### Alcohol-Induced Psychotic Disorder

**Diagnosis and clinical features.** The diagnostic criteria for alcohol-induced psychotic disorder (for example, delusions, hallucinations) are found in the DSM-IV category of substance-induced psychotic disorder (Section 14.1). DSM-IV further allows the specification of onset (during intoxication or withdrawal) and whether hallucinations or delusions are present (Table 12.2–2). The term for hallucinations occurring during alcohol withdrawal that was used in DSM-III-R but that is not used in DSM-IV is *alcohol hallucinosis*. The most common hallucinations are auditory, usually voices, but they are often unstructured. The voices are characteristically maligning, reproachful, or threatening, although some patients report that the voices are pleasant and nondisruptive. The hallucinations usually last less than a week, although during that week impaired reality testing is common. After the episode, most patients realize the hallucinatory nature of the symptoms.

Hallucinations after alcohol withdrawal are considered rare symptoms, and the syndrome is distinct from that of alcohol withdrawal delirium. The hallucinations can occur at any age, but they are usually associated with persons who have been abusing alcohol for a long time. Although the hallucinations usually resolve within a week, some may linger; in those cases, the clinician must begin to consider other psychotic disorders in the differential diagnosis. Alcohol withdrawal-related hallucinations are differentiated from the hallucinations of schizophrenia by the temporal association with alcohol withdrawal, the absence of a classic history of schizophrenia, and the usually short-lived duration of the hallucinations. Alcohol withdrawal-related hallucinations are differentiated from the DTs by the presence of a clear sensorium in the patients.

**Treatment.** The treatment of alcohol withdrawal-related hallucinations is much like the treatment of DTs—benzodiazepines, adequate nutrition, and fluids if necessary. If that regimen fails and in long-term cases, antipsychotics may be used.

A 44-year-old unemployed man who lived alone in a single-room-occupancy hotel was brought to an emergency room by the police, to whom he had gone for help, complaining that he was frightened by hearing voices of men in the street below his window talking about him and threatening him with harm. When he looked out the window, the men had always "disappeared."

The patient had a 20-year history of almost daily alcohol use, was commonly drunk each day, and often experienced the shakes on awakening. On the previous day he had reduced his intake to one pint of vodka because of gastrointestinal distress. He was fully alert and oriented on the mental status examination.

### Other Alcohol-Related Disorders

**Alcohol-induced mood disorder.** DSM-IV allows for the diagnosis of alcohol-induced mood disorder with manic, depressive, or mixed features (Section 15.3) and also for the specification of onset during either intoxication or withdrawal. As with all the secondary and substance-induced disorders, the clinician must consider whether the abused substance and the symptoms have a causal relation.

**Alcohol-induced anxiety disorder.** DSM-IV allows for the diagnosis of alcohol-induced anxiety disorder (Section 16.1). DSM-IV further suggests that the diagnosis specify whether the symptoms are those of generalized anxiety, panic attacks, obsessive-compulsive symptoms, or phobic symptoms and whether the onset was during intoxication or during withdrawal. The association between alcohol use and anxiety symptoms has been discussed above; deciding whether the anxiety symptoms are primary or secondary can be difficult.

**Alcohol-induced sexual dysfunction.** DSM-IV allows for the diagnosis of symptoms of sexual dysfunction associated with alcohol intoxication. The formal diagnosis is alcohol-induced sexual dysfunction (Section 20.2).

**Alcohol-induced sleep disorder.** DSM-IV allows for the diagnosis of sleep disorders that have their onset during either alcohol intoxication or alcohol withdrawal. The diagnostic criteria for alcohol-induced sleep disorder are found in the sleep disorders section (Section 23.2).

**Alcohol-related use disorder not otherwise specified.** DSM-IV allows for the diagnosis of alcohol-related disorder not otherwise specified (NOS) for alcohol-related disorders that do not meet the diagnostic criteria for any of the other diagnoses (Table 12.2–6).

### Other Alcohol-Related Neurological Disorders

Only the most major neuropsychiatric syndromes associated with alcohol use are discussed above. The complete list of neurological syndromes is lengthy (Table 12.2–7).

**Alcoholic pellagra encephalopathy.** From the long list in Table 12.2–7, one diagnosis is of potential interest to

**Table 12.2–6**
**Diagnostic Criteria for Alcohol-Related Disorder Not Otherwise Specified**

The alcohol-related disorder not otherwise specified category is for disorders associated with the use of alcohol that are not classifiable as alcohol dependence, alcohol abuse, alcohol intoxication, alcohol withdrawal, alcohol intoxication delirium, alcohol withdrawal delirium, alcohol-induced persisting dementia, alcohol-induced persisting amnestic disorder, alcohol-induced psychotic disorder, alcohol-induced mood disorder, alcohol-induced anxiety disorder, alcohol-induced sexual dysfunction, or alcohol-induced sleep disorder.

Table from DSM-IV, *Diagnostic and Statistical Manual of Mental Disorders*, ed 4. Copyright American Psychiatric Association, Washington, 1994. Used with permission.

**Table 12.2–7**
**Neurological and Medical Complications of Alcohol Use**

Alcohol intoxication
  Acute intoxication
  Pathological intoxication (atypical, complicated, unusual)
  Blackouts

Alcohol withdrawal syndromes
  Tremulousness (the shakes or the jitters)
  Alcoholic hallucinosis (horrors)
  Withdrawal seizures (rum fits)
  Delirium tremens (shakes)

Nutritional diseases of the nervous system secondary to
    alcohol abuse
  Wernicke-Korsakoff syndrome
  Cerebellar degeneration
  Peripheral neuropathy
  Optic neuropathy (tobacco-alcohol amblyopia)
  Pellagra

Alcoholic diseases of uncertain pathogenesis
  Central pontine myelinolysis
  Marchiafava-Bignami disease
  Fetal alcohol syndrome
  Myopathy
  Alcoholic dementia (?)
  Alcoholic cerebral atrophy

Systemic diseases due to alcohol with secondary neurological
    complications
  Liver disease
    Hepatic encephalopathy
    Acquired (non-Wilsonian) chronic hepatocerebral
      degeneration
  Gastrointestinal diseases
    Malabsorption syndromes
    Postgastrectomy syndromes
    Possible pancreatic encephalopathy
  Cardiovascular diseases
    Cardiomyopathy with potential cardiogenic emboli and
      cerebrovascular disease
    Arrhythmias and abnormal blood pressure leading to
      cerebrovascular disease
  Hematological disorders
    Anemia, leukopenia, thrombocytopenia (could possibly
      lead to hemorrhagic cerebrovascular disease)
  Infectious disease, especially meningitis (especially
    pneumococcal and meningococcal)
  Hypothermia and hyperthermia
  Hypotension and hypertension
  Respiratory depression and associated hypoxia
  Toxic encephalopathies, including alcohol and other
    substances
  Electrolyte imbalances leading to acute confusional states
    and rarely focal neurological signs and symptoms
    Hypoglycemia
    Hyperglycemia
    Hyponatremia
    Hypercalcemia
    Hypomagnesemia
    Hypophosphatemia
Increased incidence of trauma
  Epidural, subdural, and intracerebral hematoma
  Spinal cord injury
  Posttraumatic seizure disorders
  Compressive neuropathies and brachial plexus injuries
    (Saturday night palsies)
  Posttraumatic symptomatic hydrocephalus (normal pressure
    hydrocephalus)
  Muscle crush injuries and compartmental syndromes

Table adapted from M Victor: Neurological disorders due to alcoholism
and malnutrition. In *Clinical Neurology*, vol 4, R J Joint, editor, p 8. Lippincott, Philadelphia, 1990. Used with permission.
Table from F A Rubino: Neurologic complications of alcoholism. Psychiatr
Clin North Am *15*: 361, 1992. Used with permission.

psychiatrists who may be presented with a patient who
appears to be afflicted with Wernicke's syndrome or Korsakoff's syndrome but who has no response to thiamine
treatment. The symptoms of alcoholic pellagra encephalopathy include confusion, clouding of consciousness, myoclonus, oppositional hypertonias, fatigue, apathy, irritability, anorexia, insomnia, and sometimes delirium. The
patients suffer from a deficiency of niacin (nicotinic acid),
and the specific treatment is 50 mg of niacin by mouth four
times daily or 25 mg parenterally two to three times daily.

### Fetal Alcohol Syndrome

The data clearly indicate that women who are pregnant
or who are breast-feeding should not drink alcohol. Fetal
alcohol syndrome is the result of exposing fetuses to alcohol in utero when their mothers drink alcohol. Fetal
alcohol syndrome is the leading cause of mental retardation
in the United States. The presence of the alcohol inhibits
intrauterine growth and postnatal development. Microcephaly, craniofacial malformations, and limb and heart
defects are common in affected infants. Short stature as
adults and the development of a range of adult maladaptive
behaviors have also been associated with fetal alcohol syndrome.

The risk of an alcoholic woman's having a defective
child is as high as 35 percent. Although the precise mechanism of the damage to the fetus is unknown, the damage
seems to be the result of exposure in utero to ethanol or
its metabolites. Alcohol may also cause hormone imbalances that increase the risk of abnormalities.

## TREATMENT

Although some clinicians and groups are proponents of
the concept of controlled drinking, most clinicians and the
majority of well-controlled research studies indicate that
complete abstinence from alcohol has to be the centerpiece
of a successful treatment strategy for alcohol abuse. Most
people with alcohol-related disorders come to treatment
as a result of pressure from a spouse or an employer or
fear that continued drinking will have a fatal outcome. The
patients who are persuaded, encouraged, or even coerced
into treatment by persons who are meaningful to them are
more apt to remain in treatment and have a better prognosis than are those who are not so pressured. The best
prognosis, however, is for the affected persons who come
to a mental health worker voluntarily because they conclude that they are alcoholics and that they need help.

### Psychotherapy

When psychotherapy focuses on the reasons that the
person drinks, it is more successful than when it focuses
on vague psychodynamic issues. The specific focus is on
the situations in which the patient drinks, the motivating
forces behind the drinking, the expected results from
drinking, and alternate ways of dealing with those situations. Involving an interested and cooperative spouse in
conjoint therapy for at least some of the sessions is highly
effective.

The initial contact with a person with an alcohol-related

disorder is crucial to successful treatment. In the early encounter the therapist needs to be active and supportive, because patients with alcohol problems often anticipate rejection and may misinterpret a passive therapeutic role as rejecting. The patients often have an ambivalent relation to therapy, and they may miss appointments or have relapses with regard to drinking. Many therapists attempt to view alcohol abuse less in terms of an individual patient and more in terms of how that patient interacts with family members, work or school colleagues, and society in general.

The therapist must also deal with alcohol as a psychological defense; the removal of the emotional and intellectual barriers between the patient and the therapist should be an early goal. The therapist must be prepared to have the therapeutic bond tested again and again and cannot hide behind the screen of the patient's lack of motivation when relapses become threatening to the therapist. Depressions can be countered by the active, supportive role of the therapist and at times by the addition of antidepressant drug medication.

## Medication

**Disulfiram.** Disulfiram (Antabuse) competitively inhibits the enzyme aldehyde dehydrogenase, so that even a single drink usually causes a toxic reaction because of acetaldehyde accumulation in the blood. Administration of the drug should not begin until 24 hours have elapsed since the patient's last drink. The patient must be in good health, highly motivated, and cooperative. The physician must warn the patient about the consequences of ingesting alcohol while taking the drug and for as long as two weeks thereafter. Those who drink while taking the 250 mg daily dose of disulfiram experience flushing and feelings of heat in the face, the sclera, the upper limbs, and the chest. They may become pale, hypotensive, and nauseated and experience serious malaise. They may also experience dizziness, blurred vision, palpitations, air hunger, and numbness of the extremities. The most serious potential consequence is severe hypotension. Patients may also have a response to alcohol ingested in such substances as sauces and vinegars and even to inhaled alcohol vapors from after-shave lotions. The syndrome, once elicited, typically lasts some 30 to 60 minutes but can persist longer. With dosages of more than 250 mg, toxic psychoses can occur, with memory impairment and confusion. The drug can also exacerbate psychotic symptoms in some schizophrenic patients in the absence of alcohol intake.

**Psychotropics.** Both antianxiety agents and antidepressants may be useful in the treatment of anxiety and depressive symptoms in patients with alcohol-related disorders. However, increasing attention is being given to the possibility of using psychoactive drugs in the control of the sensation of craving for alcohol. Several trials of lithium (Eskalith) in patients who have both an alcohol-related disorder and a mood disorder of any type have shown a reduction in both the desire to drink and the mood cycles. Other studies with lithium have not consistently confirmed those results. Nonetheless, in particularly difficult or complex cases a trial of lithium may be warranted.

There is also increasing interest in the use of serotonergic drugs in the control of drinking and alcohol craving.

Some evidence indicates that the serotonin-specific reuptake inhibitors or trazodone (Desyrel) may be effective. Recent research focuses on specific serotonin receptor agonists and serotonin type 3 (5-HT$_3$) receptor antagonists. Some data indicate that dopaminergic agonists, such as low dosages of apomorphine or bromocriptine (Parlodel), may also be effective in reducing the patient's craving. For the most part, however, the treatment strategies directed at reducing the craving are still in early stages of research and require further validation.

## Behavior Therapy

Behavior therapy teaches the person with an alcohol-related disorder other ways to reduce anxiety. Relaxation training, assertiveness training, self-control skills, and new strategies to master the environment are emphasized. A number of operant conditioning programs condition people with alcohol-related disorders to modify their drinking behavior or to stop drinking. The reinforcements have included monetary rewards, an opportunity to live in an enriched inpatient environment, and access to pleasurable social interactions.

## Alcoholics Anonymous

Alcoholics Anonymous (AA) is a voluntary supportive fellowship of hundreds of thousands of persons with alcohol-related disorders that was founded in 1935 by two alcohol-dependent men, a stockbroker and a surgeon. Physicians should refer alcoholic patients to AA as part of a multiple-treatment approach. Frequently, patients who object when AA is initially suggested later derive much benefit from the organization and become enthusiastic participants. Its members make a public admission of their alcohol-related disorder, and abstinence is the rule.

**Al-Anon.** Al-Anon is an organization for the spouses of persons with alcohol-related disorders; it is structured along the same lines as AA. The aims of Al-Anon are, through group support, to assist the efforts of the spouses to regain self-esteem, to refrain from feeling responsible for the spouse's drinking, and to develop a rewarding life for themselves and their families. Alateen is directed toward the children of alcohol-dependent persons—to help them understand their parents' alcohol dependence.

## Halfway Houses

The discharge of an alcoholic patient from a hospital often poses serious placement problems. Home or other familiar environments may be counterproductive, unsupportive, or too unstructured. A halfway house is an important treatment resource that provides emotional support, counseling, and progressive entry back into society.

### References

Babor T F, Hofman M, DelBoca F K, Hesselbrock V, Meyer R E, Dolinsky Z S, Rounsaville B: Types of alcoholics: I. Evidence for an empirically derived typology based on indicators of vulnerability and severity. Arch Gen Psychiatry 49: 599, 1992.
Chick J, Gough K, Falkowski W, Kershaw P, Hore B, Mehta B, Ritson B, Ropner R, Torley D: Disulfiram treatment of alcoholism. Br J Psychiatry 161: 84, 1992.
Limson R, Goldman D, Roy A, Lamparski D, Ravitz B, Adinoff B, Lin-

noila M: Personality and cerebrospinal fluid monoamine metabolites in alcoholics and controls. Arch Gen Psychiatry 48: 437, 1991.

Litt M D, Babor T F, DelBoca F K, Kadden R M, Cooney N L: Types of alcoholics: II. Application of an empirically derived typology to treatment matching. Arch Gen Psychiatry 49: 609, 1992.

Litten R Z, Allen J P: Pharmacotherapies for alcoholism: Promising agents and clinical issues. Alcohol Clin Exp Res 15: 620, 1991.

Murphy G E, Wetzel R D, Robins E, McEvoy L: Multiple risk factors predict suicide in alcoholism. Arch Gen Psychiatry 49: 459, 1992.

National Institute on Drug Abuse: *National Household Survey on Drug Abuse: Highlights, 1991.* U S Government Printing Office, Washington, 1991.

Noble E P: The D₂ dopamine receptor gene: A review of association studies in alcoholism. Behav Genet 23: 119, 1993.

Pickens R W, Svikis D S, McGue M, Lykken D T, Heston L L, Clayton P J: Heterogeneity in the inheritance of alcoholism: A study of male and female twins. Arch Gen Psychiatry 48: 19, 1991.

Roy A, DeJong J, Lamparski D, George T, Linnoila M: Depression among alcoholics: Relationship to clinical and cerebrospinal fluid variables. Arch Gen Psychiatry 48: 428, 1991.

Rubino F A: Neurologic complications of alcoholism. Psychiatr Clin North Am 15: 359, 1992.

Schuckit M A, Smith T L, Anthenelli R, Irwin M: Clinical course of alcoholism in 636 male inpatients. Am J Psychiatry 150: 786, 1993.

Sellers E M, Higgins G A, Sobell M B: 5-HT and alcohol abuse. Trends Pharmacol Sci 13: 69, 1992.

Uhl G R, Persico A M, Smith S S: Current excitement with D₂ dopamine receptor gene alleles in substance abuse. Arch Gen Psychiatry 49: 157, 1992.

Volkow N D, Hitzemann R, Wang G-J, Fowler J S, Burr G, Pascani K, Dewey S L, Wolf A: Decreased brain metabolism in neurologically intact healthy alcoholics. Am J Psychiatry 149: 1016, 1992.

# 12.3 / Amphetamine (or Amphetaminelike)-Related Disorders

The racemate amphetamine sulfate (Benzedrine) was first synthesized in 1887 and was introduced to clinical practice in 1932 as an over-the-counter inhaler for the treatment of nasal congestion and asthma. In 1937 amphetamine sulfate tablets were introduced for the treatment of narcolepsy, postencephalitic parkinsonism, depression, and lethargy. The production, the legal use, and the illicit use of amphetamines increased until the 1970s, when a variety of social and regulatory factors began to curb their widespread use. The currently approved indications for amphetamine are limited to attention-deficit/hyperactivity disorder, narcolepsy, and depressive disorders. Amphetamines are also used in the treatment of obesity, although their efficacy and safety for that indication are controversial.

## FORMS

Currently, the major amphetamines available in the United States are dextroamphetamine (Dexedrine), methamphetamine, and methylphenidate (Ritalin). Those drugs go by such street names as crack, crystal, crystal meth, and speed. As a general class, the amphetamines are also referred to as sympathomimetics, stimulants, and psychostimulants.

The typical amphetamines are used to increase performance and to induce a euphoric feeling. Students studying for examinations, long-distance truck drivers on long hauls, business people with important deadlines, and ath-

letes in competition are some examples of the people and situations for which amphetamines are used. Amphetamines are addictive drugs, although not as addictive as cocaine.

Other amphetamine-related substances are ephedrine and propranolamine, which are available over the counter in the United States as nasal decongestants. Phenylpropranolamine (PPA) is also available as an appetite suppressant. Although less potent than the classic amphetamines, ephedrine and propranolamine are subject to abuse, partly because of their easy availability and low price. Both drugs, propranolamine in particular, can dangerously exacerbate hypertension, precipitate a toxic psychosis, or result in death. The safety margin for propranolamine is particularly narrow, and three to four times the normal dose can result in life-threatening hypertension.

### Ice

Ice is a pure form of methamphetamine that can be inhaled, smoked, or injected intravenously by abusers of the substance. Ice has been used most heavily on the West Coast of the United States and in Hawaii. The psychological effects of ice last for hours and are described as being particularly powerful. Unlike crack cocaine, which has to be imported, ice is a synthetic drug that can be manufactured in domestic illicit laboratories. Some law enforcement agencies and urban emergency room physicians think that ice may become a widespread drug of abuse over the next five years.

### Amphetamine-Related Substances

The classic amphetamine drugs (dextroamphetamine, methamphetamine, and methylphenidate) have their major effects through the dopaminergic system. A number of so-called designer amphetamines have been synthesized and have neurochemical effects on both the serotonergic and the dopaminergic systems and behavioral effects that reflect a combination of amphetaminelike and hallucinogenlike activities. Some psychopharmacologists classify the designer amphetamines as hallucinogens; however, this textbook classifies them with the amphetamines because they are closely related structurally. Examples of the designer amphetamines include 3,4-methylenedioxymethamphetamine (MDMA), also referred to as ecstasy, XTC, and Adam; N-ethyl-3,4-methylenedioxyamphetamine (MDEA), also referred to as Eve; 5-methoxy-3,4-methylenedioxyamphetamine (MMDA), and 2,5-dimethoxy-4-methylamphetamine (DOM), also referred to as STP. Of those drugs, MDMA has been studied most closely and is perhaps the most widely available.

## EPIDEMIOLOGY

In 1991 about 7 percent of the United States population had used stimulants at least once, although fewer than 1 percent were current users. The 18 to 25 year-old age group had the highest level of use, with 9 percent reporting use at least once and 1 percent describing themselves as current users. Use among the 12-to-17-year-old age group is alarmingly high, with 3 percent reporting use at least once and 1 percent reporting current use. Amphetamine use is present in all socioeconomic groups, and the general trend is for amphetamine use to be high among white professionals. Since amphetamines are available by prescription for specific indications, the prescribing physician must be aware of the risk of abuse of the amphetamine by others, including friends and family members of the patient receiving the amphetamine. No reliable data are available on the epidemiology of designer amphetamine use.

## NEUROPHARMACOLOGY

All the amphetamines are rapidly absorbed orally and are associated with a rapid onset of action, usually within one hour when taken orally. The classic amphetamines are also taken intravenously; by that route they have an almost immediate effect. Nonprescribed amphetamines and designer amphetamines are also ingested by inhaling (snorting). Tolerance does develop with both the classic amphetamines and the designer amphetamines, although amphetamine users often overcome the tolerance by taking more of the drug. Amphetamine is less addictive than cocaine, as evidenced by the animal experiments in which not all the rats spontaneously self-administered low doses of amphetamine. The further study of such animal models may help clinicians understand the susceptibility of some patients to amphetamine dependence.

The classic amphetamines (dextroamphetamine, methamphetamine, and methylphenidate) have their primary effects by causing the release of catecholamines, particularly dopamine, from presynaptic terminals. The effects are particularly potent for the dopaminergic neurons that project from the ventral tegmental area to the cerebral cortex and the limbic areas. That pathway has been termed the reward pathway, and its activation is probably the major addicting mechanism for the amphetamines.

The designer amphetamines (for example, MDMA, MDEA, MMDA, and DOM) cause the release of catecholamines (that is, dopamine and norepinephrine) and the release of serotonin. Serotonin is the neurotransmitter that is implicated as the major neurochemical pathway involved in the effects of the hallucinogens. Therefore, the clinical effects of the designer amphetamines is a cross between the effects of the classic amphetamines and the effects of the hallucinogens. The pharmacology of MDMA is the best understood of the group. MDMA is taken up in serotonergic neurons by the serotonin transporter responsible for serotonin reuptake. Once in the neuron, MDMA causes a rapid release of a bolus of serotonin and inhibits the activity of the serotonin-producing enzymes. As a result, patients who are taking a serotonin-specific reuptake inhibitor—for example, fluoxetine (Prozac)—cannot get high when they take MDMA because the serotonin-specific reuptake inhibitor prevents the MDMA from being taken up into the serotonergic neurons.

## DIAGNOSIS

The fourth edition of *Diagnostic and Statistical Manual of Mental Disorders* (DSM-IV) lists many amphetamine (or amphetaminelike)-related disorders (Table 12.3–1) but specifies the diagnostic criteria only for amphetamine intoxication (Table 12.3–2) amphetamine withdrawal (Table 12.3–3), and amphetamine-related disorder not otherwise specified (Table 12.3–4) in the section on amphetamine

**Table 12.3–1**
**Amphetamine (or Amphetaminelike)-Related Disorders**

*Amphetamine use disorders*

**Amphetamine dependence**
**Amphetamine abuse**

*Amphetamine-induced disorders*

**Amphetamine intoxication**
*Specify if:*
  with perceptual disturbances
**Amphetamine withdrawal**
**Amphetamine intoxication delirium**
**Amphetamine-induced psychotic disorder, with delusions**
*Specify if:*
  with onset during intoxication
**Amphetamine-induced psychotic disorder, with hallucinations**
*Specify if:*
  with onset during intoxication
**Amphetamine-induced mood disorder**
*Specify if:*
  with onset during intoxication
  with onset during withdrawal
**Amphetamine-induced anxiety disorder**
*Specify if:*
  with onset during intoxication
**Amphetamine-induced sexual dysfunction**
*Specify if:*
  with onset during intoxication
**Amphetamine-induced sleep disorder**
*Specify if:*
  with onset during intoxication
  with onset during withdrawal

**Amphetamine-related disorder not otherwise specified**

Table based on DSM-IV, *Diagnostic and Statistical Manual of Mental Disorders*, ed 4. Copyright American Psychiatric Association, Washington, 1994. Used with permission.

(or amphetaminelike)-related disorders. The diagnostic criteria for the other amphetamine (or amphetaminelike)-related disorders are contained in the DSM-IV sections that deal with the primary phenomenological symptom (for example, psychosis).

### Dependence and Abuse

The DSM-IV criteria for dependence and abuse are applied to amphetamine and its related substances (Tables 12.1–6, 12.1–7, and 12.1–8). Amphetamine dependence can result in a rapid down spiral of a person's abilities to cope with work-related and family-related obligations and stresses. An amphetamine-abusing person requires increasingly high doses of amphetamine to obtain the usual high, and physical signs of amphetamine abuse (for example, decreased weight and paranoid ideas) almost always develop with continued abuse.

### Intoxication

The intoxication syndromes from cocaine (which blocks dopamine reuptake) and amphetamines (which cause the release of dopamine) are similar. Because more rigorous and in-depth research has been done on cocaine abuse and intoxication than on amphetamines, the clinical literature on amphetamines has been strongly influenced by the clinical findings of cocaine abuse. For example, in the third edition of DSM (DSM-III), the diagnostic criteria for cocaine and amphetamine intoxication were identical, although listed separately in two places. The revised third edition (DSM-III-R) noted small diagnostic differences between amphetamine intoxication and cocaine intoxication; however, the validity of those differences has been questioned. In DSM-IV, the diagnostic criteria for amphetamine intoxication (Table 12.3–2) and cocaine intoxication (Table 12.6–2) are separated but are virtually the same. DSM-IV allows for the specification of the presence of perceptual disturbances. If intact reality testing is not present, a diagnosis of amphetamine-induced psychotic disorder with onset during intoxication is indicated. The symptoms of amphetamine intoxication are mostly resolved after 24 hours and are generally completely resolved after 48 hours.

## Withdrawal

The crash after amphetamine intoxication can be associated with anxiety, tremulousness, dysphoric mood, lethargy, fatigue, nightmares (accompanied by rebound rapid eye movement [REM] sleep), headache, profuse sweating, muscle cramps, stomach cramps, and insatiable hunger. The withdrawal symptoms generally peak in two to four days and are resolved in a week. The most serious withdrawal symptom is depression, which can be particularly severe after the sustained use of high doses of amphetamine and which can be associated with suicidal ideation or behavior. The DSM-IV diagnostic criteria for amphetamine withdrawal (Table 12.3–3) specify that a dys-

**Table 12.3–2**
**Diagnostic Criteria for Amphetamine Intoxication**

A. Recent use of amphetamine or a related substance (e.g., methylphenidate).

B. Clinically significant maladaptive behavioral or psychological changes (e.g., euphoria or affective blunting; changes in sociability; hypervigilance; interpersonal sensitivity; anxiety, tension, or anger; stereotyped behaviors; impaired judgment; or impaired social or occupational functioning) that developed during, or shortly after, use of amphetamine or a related substance.

C. Two (or more) of the following, developing during, or shortly after, use of amphetamine or related substance:

(1) tachycardia or bradycardia
(2) pupillary dilation
(3) elevated or lowered blood pressure
(4) perspiration or chills
(5) nausea or vomiting
(6) evidence of weight loss
(7) psychomotor agitation or retardation
(8) muscular weakness, respiratory depression, chest pain or cardiac arrhythmias
(9) confusion, seizures, dyskinesias, dystonias, or coma

D. The symptoms are not due to a general medical condition and not better accounted for by another mental disorder.

*Specify* if:
  **with perceptual disturbances**

Table from DSM-IV, *Diagnostic and Statistical Manual of Mental Disorders*, ed 4. Copyright American Psychiatric Association, Washington, 1994. Used with permission.

**Table 12.3–3**
**Diagnostic Criteria for Amphetamine Withdrawal**

A. Cessation of (or reduction in) of amphetamine (or related substance) use which has been heavy and prolonged.

B. Dysphoric mood and two (or more) of the following physiological changes, developing within a few hours to several days after criterion A:

(1) fatigue
(2) vivid, unpleasant dreams
(3) insomnia or hypersomnia
(4) increased appetite
(5) psychomotor retardation or agitation

C. The symptoms in criterion B cause clinically significant distress or impairment in social, occupational, or other important areas of functioning.

D. The symptoms are not due to a general medical condition and not better accounted for by another mental disorder.

Table from DSM-IV, *Diagnostic and Statistical Manual of Mental Disorders*, ed 4. Copyright American Psychiatric Association, Washington, 1994. Used with permission.

phoric mood and a number of physiological changes are necessary for the diagnosis.

## Delirium

Amphetamine intoxication delirium is a DSM-IV diagnosis (Section 10.2). Delirium associated with amphetamine is usually the result of high doses of amphetamine or the sustained use of amphetamine, such that sleep deprivation affects the clinical presentation. The combination of amphetamines with other substances and the use of amphetamines by a person with preexisting brain damage can also result in the development of delirium.

## Psychotic Disorder

Amphetamine-induced psychosis has been extensively studied in psychiatry because of its close resemblance to paranoid schizophrenia. The clinical similarity has prompted researchers to attempt to understand the pathophysiology of paranoid schizophrenia by studying the neurochemistry of amphetamine-induced psychosis. The hallmark of amphetamine-induced psychotic disorder is the presence of paranoia. Paranoid schizophrenia can be distinguished from amphetamine-induced psychotic disorder by a number of differentiating characteristics associated with amphetamine-induced psychotic disorder, including a predominance of visual hallucinations, generally appropriate affects, hyperactivity, hypersexuality, confusion and incoherence, and little evidence of disordered thinking (for example, looseness of associations). Several studies have also found that, although the positive symptoms of schizophrenia and amphetamine induced psychotic disorder are similar, the affective flattening and alogia of schizophrenia are generally absent in amphetamine-induced psychotic disorder. Clinically, however, acute amphetamine-induced psychotic disorder can be completely indistinguishable from schizophrenia, and only the resolution of the symptoms in a few days or a positive finding in a urine drug screen test eventually reveals the correct diagnosis. Some evidence indicates that the long-term use of amphetamines is associated with an increased vulnerability to the development of psychosis under a number of circumstances, including alcohol intoxication and stress. The treatment of choice for amphetamine-induced psychotic disorder is the short-term use of dopamine receptor antagonists—for example, haloperidol (Haldol). DSM-IV lists the diagnostic criteria for amphetamine-induced psychotic disorder with the other psychotic disorders (Section 14.1). DSM-IV allows the clinician to specify whether delusions or hallucinations are the predominant symptoms.

## Mood Disorder

DSM-IV allows the clinician to diagnose amphetamine-induced mood disorder with onset during intoxication or withdrawal (Section 15.3). In general, intoxication is associated with manic or mixed mood features, whereas withdrawal is associated with depressive mood features.

## Anxiety Disorder

DSM-IV allows for the possibility of amphetamine-induced anxiety disorder with onset during intoxication or withdrawal (Section 16.1). Amphetamine, like cocaine, can induce symptoms similar to those seen in obsessive-compulsive disorder, panic disorder, and phobic disorders, in particular.

## Sexual Dysfunction

Although amphetamine is often used to enhance sexual experiences, high doses and long-term use are associated with impotence and other sexual dysfunctions. Those sexual dysfunctions are classified in DSM-IV as amphetamine-induced sexual dysfunction with onset during intoxication (Section 20.2).

## Sleep Disorder

The diagnostic criteria for amphetamine-induced sleep disorder with onset during intoxication or withdrawal are found in the DSM-IV section on sleep disorders (Section 23.2). Amphetamine intoxication is associated with insomnia and sleep deprivation, whereas amphetamine withdrawal can be associated with hypersomnolence and nightmares.

## Disorder Not Otherwise Specified

If an amphetamine (or amphetaminelike)-related disorder does not meet the criteria of one or more of the above categories, it can be diagnosed as an amphetamine-related disorder not otherwise specified (NOS) (Table 12.3–4). With the increasing illicit use of the designer amphetamines, syndromes may arise that do not meet the criteria outlined in DSM-IV, necessitating the frequent use of the NOS category for those designer amphetamines.

**Table 12.3–4**
**Amphetamine-Related Disorder Not Otherwise Specified**

The amphetamine-related disorder not otherwise specified category is for disorders associated with the use of amphetamine (or a related substance) that are not classifiable as amphetamine dependence, amphetamine abuse, amphetamine intoxication, amphetamine withdrawal, amphetamine intoxication delirium, amphetamine-induced psychotic disorder, amphetamine-induced mood disorder, amphetamine-induced anxiety disorder, amphetamine-induced sexual dysfunction, or amphetamine-induced sleep disorder.

Table from DSM-IV, *Diagnostic and Statistical Manual of Mental Disorders*, ed 4. Copyright American Psychiatric Association, Washington, 1994. Used with permission.

# CLINICAL FEATURES

## Classic Amphetamines

In persons who have not previously used amphetamines, a single 5 mg dose increases their sense of well-being and induces elation, euphoria, and friendliness. Small doses generally improve their attention and increase their performance on written, oral, and performance tasks. There is also an associated decrease in fatigue, an induction of anorexia, and a heightening of the pain threshold. Undesirable effects accompany the use of high doses for long periods of time.

## Designer Amphetamines

Because of their effects on the dopaminergic system, the designer amphetamines are activating and energizing. Their effects on the serotonergic system, however, color the experience of those drugs with a hallucinogenic character. The designer amphetamines are associated with much less disorientation and perceptual distortion than are the classic hallucinogens—for example, lysergic acid diethylamide (LSD). A sense of closeness with other people and of comfort with oneself and an increased luminescence of objects are commonly reported effects of MDMA (Table 12.3–5). Some psychotherapists have used and advocated further research into the use of designer amphetamines as adjuvants to psychotherapy. That suggestion is controversial; other clinicians emphasize the potential dangers of the use of such drugs.

## Adverse Effects

### Classic amphetamines

PHYSICAL. Cerebrovascular, cardiac, and gastrointestinal effects are among the most serious adverse effects associated with amphetamine abuse. The specific life-threatening conditions include myocardial infarction, severe hypertension, cerebrovascular disease, and ischemic colitis. A continuum of neurological symptoms, from twitching to tetany to seizures to coma and death, is associated with increasingly high amphetamine doses. The intravenous use of amphetamines is associated with the transmission of human immunodeficiency virus (HIV) and hepatitis and with the development of lung abscesses, endocarditis, and necrotizing angiitis. Several studies have found that information about safe-sex practices and the use of condoms is not well-known by abusers of amphetamines. The less than life-threatening adverse effects include flushing, pallor, cyanosis, fever, headache, tachycardia, palpitations, nausea, vomiting, bruxism (teeth grinding), shortness of breath, tremor, and ataxia. The use of amphetamines by pregnant women has been associated with low birth weight, small head circumference, early gestational age, and growth retardation.

PSYCHOLOGICAL. The adverse psychological effects associated with amphetamine use include restlessness, dysphoria, insomnia, irritability, hostility, and confusion. Symptoms of anxiety disorders, such as generalized anxiety disorder and panic disorder, can be induced by amphetamine use. Ideas of reference, paranoid delusions, and hallucinations can be caused by amphetamine use.

**Designer amphetamines.** The designer amphetamines carry many of the same adverse effects as do the classic amphetamines. However, a variety of other adverse effects have also been associated with the designer drugs (Tables 12.3–5 and 12.3–6). Clinically, a severe adverse effect associated with MDMA is hyperthermia caused by the drug and then exacerbated by excessive activity (for example, dancing wildly in a crowded, hot dance club [known as "raves"] ). There have been a number of clinical reports of deaths associated with MDMA use under such circumstances. Basic researchers are divided in their opinions about whether MDMA causes neurotoxicity in the doses that are used by humans.

## TREATMENT

The treatment of amphetamine (or amphetaminelike)-related disorders shares with the cocaine-related disorders

**Table 12.3–5**
**Short-Term Effects of MDMA**

| Subjective Sensation | Subjects Affected* |
|---|---|
| Sense of "closeness" with other people | 90 |
| Trismus | 75 |
| Tachycardia | 72 |
| Bruxism | 65 |
| Dry mouth | 61 |
| Increased alertness | 50 |
| Luminescence of objects | 42 |
| Tremor | 42 |
| Palpitations | 41 |
| Diaphoresis | 38 |
| Difficulty in concentrating | 38 |
| Paresthesias | 35 |
| Insomnia | 33 |
| Hot or cold flashes | 31 |
| Increased sensitivity to cold | 27 |
| Dizziness or vertigo | 24 |
| Visual hallucinations | 20 |
| Blurred vision | 20 |

*Total number tested: 100.
Table from S J Peroutka, H Newman, H Harris: Subjective effects of 3, 4-methylenedioxymethamphetamine in recreational users. Neuropsychopharmacology 1: 275, 1988. Used with permission.

**Table 12.3–6**
**Moderate-Term Effects of MDMA**

| Subjective Sensation | Subjects Affected* |
|---|---|
| Drowsiness | 36 |
| Muscle aches or fatigability | 32 |
| Sense of "closeness" with other people | 22 |
| Depression | 21 |
| Tight jaw muscles | 21 |
| Difficulty in concentrating | 21 |
| Headache | 17 |
| Dry mouth | 14 |
| Anxiety, worry, or fear | 12 |
| Irritability | 12 |

*Total number tested: 100.
Table from S J Peroutka, H Newman, H Harris: Subjective effects of 3, 4-methylenedioxymethamphetamine in recreational users. Neuropsychopharmacology 1: 275, 1988. Used with permission.

the difficulty in helping the patient remain abstinent from the drug, which has powerfully reinforcing qualities and which induces craving. An inpatient setting and the use of multiple therapeutic modalities (individual, family, and group psychotherapy) are usually necessary to achieve a lasting abstinence from the substance. The treatment of specific amphetamine-induced disorders (for example, amphetamine-induced psychotic disorder and amphetamine-induced anxiety disorder) with specific drugs (for example, antipsychotics and anxiolytics) may be necessary on a short-term basis. Antipsychotics, either a phenothiazine or haloperidol, may be prescribed for the first few days. In the absence of psychosis, diazepam (Valium) is useful to treat the patient's agitation and hyperactivity.

The physician should establish a therapeutic alliance with the patient to deal with the underlying depression or personality disorder or both; however, because many patients are heavily dependent on the drug, psychotherapy may be especially difficult.

### References

Cho A K: Ice: A new dosage form of an old drug. Science 249: 631, 1990.
Cox D E: "Rave" to the grave. Forensic Sci Int 60: 5, 1993.
Dackis C A, Gold M S: Addictiveness of central stimulants. Adv Alcohol Subst Abuse 9: 9, 1990.
Derlet R W, Heischober B: Methamphetamine: Stimulant of the 1990s? West J Med 153: 625, 1990.
Fulton A I, Yates W R: Family abuse of methylphenidate. Am Fam Physician 38: 143, 1988.
Gillogley K M, Evans A T, Hansen R L, Samuels S J, Batra K K: The perinatal impact of cocaine, amphetamine, and opiate use detected by universal intrapartum screening. Am J Obstet Gynecol 163: 1535, 1990.
Grob C S, Bravo G L, Walsh R N, Liester M B: The MDMA-neurotoxicity controversy: Implications for clinical research with novel psychoactive drugs. J Nerv Ment Dis 180: 355, 1992.
Hall W, Darke S, Ross M, Wodak A: Patterns of drug use and risk-taking among injecting amphetamine and opioid drug users in Sydney, Australia. Addiction 88: 509, 1993.
Heishman S J, Henningfield J E: Discriminative stimulus effects of d-amphetamine, methylphenidate, and diazepam in humans. Psychopharmacology 103: 436, 1991.
Kall K I: Effects of amphetamine on sexual behavior of male IV drug users in Stockholm: A pilot study. AIDS Educ Prev 4: 7, 1992.
Klee H: A new target for behavioral research: Amphetamine misuse. Br J Addict 87: 439, 1992.
Koelega H S: Stimulant drugs and vigilance performance: A review. Psychopharmacology 111: 1, 1993.
Liester M B, Grob C S, Bravo G L, Walsh R N: Phenomenology and sequelae of 3,4-methylenedioxymethamphetamine use. J Nerv Ment Dis 180: 345, 1992.

Lynch J, House M A: Cardiovascular effects of methamphetamine. J Cardiovasc Nurs *6:* 12, 1992.

McCann U D, Ricaurte G E: Lasting neuropsychiatric sequelae of (±) methylenedioxymethamphetamine ("ecstasy") in recreational users. J Clin Psychopharmacol *11:* 302, 1991.

McKenna D J, Peroutka S J: Neurochemistry and neurotoxicity of 3,4-methylenedioxymethamphetamine (MDMA, "ecstasy"). J Neurochem *54:* 14, 1990.

Miller N S, Millman R B, Gold M S: Amphetamines: Pharmacology, abuse and addiction. Adv Alcohol Subst Abuse *8:* 53, 1989.

Parran T V, Jasinski D R: Intravenous methylphenidate abuse: Prototype for prescription drug abuse. Arch Intern Med *151:* 171, 1991.

Peroutka S J, Newman H, Harris H: Subjective effects of 3,4-methylenedioxymethamphetamine in recreational users. Neuropsychopharmacology *1:* 273, 1988.

Piazza P V, Deminiere J-M, Le Moal M, Simo H: Factors that predict individual vulnerability to amphetamine self-administration. Science *245:* 1511, 1989.

Ragland A S Ismail Y, Arsura E L: Myocardial infarction after amphetamine use. Am Heart J *125:* 247, 1993.

Rudnick G, Wall S C: The molecular mechanism of "ecstasy" (3,4-methylenedioxymethamphetamine [MDMA]): Serotonin transporters are targets for MDMA-induced serotonin release. Proc Natl Acad Sci U S A *89:* 1817, 1992.

Sato M: A lasting vulnerability to psychosis in patients with previous methamphetamine psychosis. Ann N Y Acad Sci *654:* 160, 1992.

Sato M, Numachi Y, Hamamura T: Relapse of paranoid psychotic state in methamphetamine model of schizophrenia. Schizophr Bull *18:* 115, 1992.

Tomiyama G: Chronic schizophrenia-like states in methamphetamine psychosis. Jpn J Psychiatry Neurol *44:* 531, 1990.

Zacny J P, Bodker B K, de Wit H: Effects of setting on the subjective and behavioral effects of *d*-amphetamine in humans. Addict Behav *17:* 27, 1992.

# 12.4 / Caffeine-Related Disorders

Caffeine, most often in the form of coffee or tea, is the most widely used psychoactive substance in Western countries. About 80 percent of North American adults regularly drink caffeine-containing beverages. The fourth edition of *Diagnostic and Statistical Manual of Mental Disorders* (DSM-IV) has provisions for the diagnosis of caffeine intoxication, caffeine-induced anxiety disorder, and caffeine-induced sleep disorder. DSM-IV does not have diagnostic categories for caffeine abuse, caffeine dependence, or caffeine withdrawal, in spite of the fact that a number of studies have reported data consistent with the presence of caffeine-related physical dependence and withdrawal phenomena. However, research criteria for caffeine withdrawal are included in an appendix.

## EPIDEMIOLOGY

Caffeine is contained in a variety of drinks, foods, prescription medicines, and over-the-counter medicines (Table 12.4–1). The average adult in the United States consumes about 200 mg of caffeine a day, although 20 to 30 percent of all adults consume more than 500 mg a day. The per capita use of coffee in the United States is 10.2 pounds a year. A cup of coffee generally contains 100 to 150 mg of caffeine; tea contains about one third as much. Many over-the-counter medications contain one third to one half as much caffeine as that in a cup of coffee, although some migraine medications and over-the-counter

**Table 12.4–1**
**Common Sources of Caffeine and Representative Decaffeinated Products**

| Source | Caffeine per Unit |
|---|---|
| Beverages and foods (5–6 oz) | |
|   Fresh drip coffee, brewed coffee | 90–140 mg |
|   Instant coffee | 66–100 mg |
|   Tea (leaf or bagged) | 30–100 mg |
|   Cocoa | 5–50 mg |
|   Decaffeinated coffee | 2–4 mg |
|   Chocolate bar or ounce of baking chocolate | 25–35 mg |
|   Soft drinks (8–12 oz) | |
|     Pepsi, Coke, Tab, Royal Crown, Dr. Pepper, Mountain Dew | 25–50 mg |
|     Canada Dry Ginger Ale, Caffeine Free Coke, Caffeine Free Pepsi, 7-Up, Sprite, Squirt, Caffeine Free Tab | 0 mg |
| Prescription medications (1 tablet or capsule) | |
|   Cafergot, Migralam | 100 mg |
|   Anoquan, Aspir-code, BAC, Darvon, Fiorinal | 32–50 mg |
| Over-the-counter analgesics and cold preparations (1 tablet or capsule) | |
|   Excedrin | 60 mg |
|   Aspirin compound, Anacin, B-C powder, Capron, Cope, Dolor, Midol, Nilain, Norgesic, PAC, Trigesic, Vanquish | ~30 mg |
|   Advil, aspirin, Empirin, Midol 200, Nuprin, Pamprin | 0 mg |
| Over-the-counter stimulants and appetite suppressants (1 tablet or capsule) | |
|   Caffin-TD, Caffedrine | 250 mg |
|   Vivarin, Ver | 200 mg |
|   Quick-Pep | 140–150 mg |
|   Amostat, Anorexin, Appedrine, Nodoz, Wakoz | 100 mg |

Table adapted from table by Jerome H Jaffe, M.D.

stimulants contain more caffeine than does a cup of coffee. Significant amounts of caffeine are contained in cocoa, chocolate, and soft drinks. The amount of caffeine contained in those products can be enough to cause some symptoms of caffeine intoxication in small children when they ingest a candy bar and a 12-ounce cola drink.

## NEUROPHARMACOLOGY

Caffeine, a methylxanthine, is more potent than another commonly used methylxanthine, theophylline (Primatene). The half-life of caffeine in the human body is 3 to 10 hours, and the time to peak concentration is 30 to 60 minutes. Caffeine readily crosses the blood-brain barrier. The primary mechanism of action for caffeine is as an antagonist of the adenosine receptors. Activation of adenosine receptors activates an inhibitory G protein ($G_i$), thus inhibiting the formation of the second-messenger cyclic adenosine monophosphate (cAMP). Caffeine intake, therefore, results in an increase in intraneuronal cAMP concentrations in neurons that have adenosine receptors. It has been estimated that three cups of coffee results in so much caffeine in the brain that about 50 percent of the adenosine receptors are occupied by caffeine. Several experiments indicate that caffeine, especially at high doses or concentrations, can affect dopamine and noradrenergic neurons. Specifically, dopamine activity may be enhanced by caffeine, which may explain clinical reports associating caffeine intake with an exacerbation of psychotic symptoms in patients with schizophrenia. Activation of noradrenergic neurons has been hypothesized to be involved in the mediation of some of the symptoms associated with caffeine withdrawal.

## Caffeine as a Substance of Abuse

Caffeine evidences all the traits that are associated with commonly accepted substances of abuse. First, caffeine can act as a positive reinforcer, particularly at low doses. Caffeine doses of about 100 mg induce a mild euphoria in humans and behavioral effects in other animals that are associated with repeated substance-seeking behavior. Caffeine doses of 300 mg, however, are associated with increased anxiety and mild dysphoria in humans and do not act as positive reinforcers. Second, studies in animals and humans have found that caffeine can be discriminated from a placebo in blinded experimental conditions. Third, both animal and human studies have found that physical tolerance to some effects of caffeine does develop and that withdrawal symptoms do occur.

## Effects on Cerebral Blood Flow

Most studies have found that caffeine results in global cerebral vasoconstriction, with a resultant decrease in cerebral blood flow (CBF), although that effect may not occur in persons more than 65 years of age. One recent study found that tolerance does not develop to those vasoconstrictive effects and that the CBF shows a rebound increase after withdrawal from caffeine.

## DIAGNOSIS

The diagnosis of caffeine intoxication or other caffeine-related disorders depends primarily on the clinician's taking a comprehensive history of the patient's intake of caffeine-containing products. The history should cover whether or not the patient has experienced any symptoms of caffeine withdrawal during periods when caffeine consumption was either stopped or severely reduced. The differential diagnosis for caffeine-related disorders should include the following psychiatric diagnoses: generalized anxiety disorder, panic disorder with or without agoraphobia, bipolar II disorder, attention-deficit/hyperactivity disorder, and sleep disorders. The differential diagnosis should also include the abuse of caffeine-containing over-the-counter medications, anabolic steroids, and other stimulants, such as amphetamines and cocaine. A urine sample may be needed to screen for those substances. The differential diagnosis should also include hyperthyroidism and pheochromocytoma.

DSM-IV lists the caffeine-related disorders (Table 12.4-2) and provides diagnostic criteria for caffeine intoxication (Table 12.4-3) but does not formally recognize a diagnosis of caffeine withdrawal, which is classified as a caffeine-related disorder not otherwise specified (NOS). The diagnostic criteria for other caffeine-related disorders

**Table 12.4–2**
**Caffeine-Related Disorders**

*Caffeine-Induced Disorders*

**Caffeine intoxication**
**Caffeine-induced anxiety disorder**
  *Specify if*: with onset during intoxication
**Caffeine-induced sleep disorder**
  *Specify if*: with onset during intoxication
**Caffeine-related disorder not otherwise specified**

Table based on DSM-IV, *Diagnostic and Statistical Manual of Mental Disorders*, ed 4. Copyright American Psychiatric Association, Washington, 1994. Used with permission.

**Table 12.4–3**
**Diagnostic Criteria for Caffeine Intoxication**

A. Recent consumption of caffeine, usually in excess of 250 mg (e.g., more than 2–3 cups of brewed coffee).

B. Five (or more) of the following signs, developing during, or shortly after, caffeine use:

    (1) restlessness
    (2) nervousness
    (3) excitement
    (4) insomnia
    (5) flushed face
    (6) diuresis
    (7) gastrointestinal disturbance
    (8) muscle twitching
    (9) rambling flow of thought and speech
    (10) tachycardia or cardiac arrhythmia
    (11) periods of inexhaustibility
    (12) psychomotor agitation

C. The symptoms in criterion B cause clinically significant distress or impairment in social, occupational, or other important areas of functioning.

D. The symptoms are not due to a general medical condition and are not better accounted for by another mental disorder (e.g., an anxiety disorder).

Table from DSM-IV, *Diagnostic and Statistical Manual of Mental Disorders*, ed 4. Copyright American Psychiatric Association, Washington, 1994. Used with permission.

are contained in those sections specific for the principal symptom (for example, as a substance-induced anxiety disorder for caffeine-induced anxiety disorder).

## Caffeine Intoxication

DSM-IV specifies the diagnostic criteria for caffeine intoxication (Table 12.4–3), which include the recent consumption of caffeine, usually in excess of 250 mg. The annual incidence of caffeine intoxication is an estimated 10 percent, although some clinicians and investigators suspect that the actual incidence is much higher than that figure. The common symptoms associated with caffeine intoxication include anxiety, psychomotor agitation, restlessness, irritability, and psychophysiological complaints, such as muscle twitching, flushed face, nausea, diuresis, gastrointestinal distress, excessive perspiration, tingling in the fingers and toes, and insomnia. The consumption of more than 1 gram of caffeine can be associated with rambling speech, confused thinking, cardiac arrhythmias, inexhaustability, marked agitation, tinnitus, and mild visual hallucinations (light flashes). The consumption of more than 10 grams of caffeine can cause generalized tonic-clonic seizures, respiratory failure, and death.

## Caffeine Withdrawal

In spite of the fact that DSM-IV does not include a diagnosis of caffeine withdrawal, a number of well-controlled studies indicate that caffeine withdrawal does exist, and DSM-IV does give research criteria for caffeine withdrawal (Table 12.4–4). The appearance of withdrawal symptoms is a reflection of the tolerance and the physiological dependence that develops with continued caffeine use. Several epidemiological studies have reported symptoms of caffeine withdrawal in 50 to 75 percent of all caffeine users studied. The most common symptoms of caffeine withdrawal are headache and fatigue; other symptoms include anxiety, irritability, mild depressive symptoms, impaired psychomotor performance, nausea, vomiting, craving for caffeine, and muscle pain and stiffness. The number and the severity of the withdrawal symptoms is correlated with the amount of caffeine that had been taken and the abruptness of the withdrawal. Caffeine withdrawal symptoms have their onset 12 to 24 hours after the last dose; the symptoms peak in 24 to 48 hours and resolve within one week.

The induction of caffeine withdrawal can sometimes be iatrogenic. Physicians often ask their patients to discontinue caffeine intake before certain medical procedures, such as endoscopy, colonoscopy, and cardiac catheterization. Physicians also often recommend stopping caffeine intake by patients who have anxiety symptoms, cardiac arrhythmias, esophagitis, hiatal hernias, fibrocystic disease of the breast, and insomnia. Some persons simply decide that it would be good for them to stop using caffeine-containing products. In all those situations the caffeine user should taper the use of caffeine-containing products over a 7-to-14-day period, rather than stop abruptly.

## Other Caffeine-Related Disorders

**Caffeine-induced anxiety disorder.** Caffeine-induced anxiety disorder, which can occur during caffeine intoxication, is a DSM-IV diagnosis (Section 16.1). The anxiety related to caffeine use can appear to be similar to the anxiety symptoms associated with generalized anxiety disorder. Patients with the disorder may be perceived as wired, overly talkative, and irritable, and they may complain of not sleeping well and of having energy to burn. Although caffeine induces and exacerbates panic attacks in persons with a panic disorder, a causative association between caffeine and a panic disorder has not yet been demonstrated.

**Caffeine-induced sleep disorder.** Caffeine-induced sleep disorder, which can occur during caffeine intoxication, is a DSM-IV diagnosis (Section 23.2). Caffeine is associated with a delay in falling asleep, an inability to remain asleep, and early morning awakening.

**Caffeine-related disorder not otherwise specified.** DSM-IV contains a residual category for caffeine-related disorders, caffeine-related disorder not otherwise specified (Table 12.4–5). The category is for caffeine-related diagnoses that do not meet the criteria for caffeine intoxication, caffeine-induced anxiety disorder, or caffeine-induced sleep disorder.

## Other Substance-Related Disorders

Persons with caffeine-related disorders are more likely to have additional substance-related disorders than are persons without diagnoses of caffeine-related disorders. About two thirds of the persons who consume large amounts of caffeine every day also use sedative and hypnotic drugs.

## CLINICAL FEATURES

After the ingestion of 50 to 100 mg of caffeine, common symptoms include increased alertness, a mild sense of well-being, and a sense of improved verbal and motor performance. Caffeine ingestion is also associated with diureses, cardiac muscle stimulation, increased intestinal peristalsis, increased gastric acid secretion, and a usually mild increase in blood pressure.

## Adverse Effects

Although caffeine is not associated with cardiac-related risks in healthy persons, those with preexisting cardiac disease are often advised to limit their caffeine intake because of a possible association between cardiac arrhythmias and caffeine. Caffeine is clearly associated with increased gastric acid secretion, so clinicians usually advise patients with gastric ulcers not to ingest any caffeine-containing products. Limited data suggest that caffeine is as-

---

**Table 12.4–4**
**Research Criteria for Caffeine Withdrawal**

A. Prolonged daily use of caffeine.

B. Abrupt cessation of caffeine use, or reduction in the amount of caffeine used, closely followed by headache and one (or more) of the following symptoms:

   (1) marked fatigue or drowsiness
   (2) marked anxiety or depression
   (3) nausea or vomiting

C. The symptoms in criterion B cause clinically significant distress or impairment in social, occupational, or other important areas of functioning.

D. The symptoms are not due to the direct physiological effects of a general medical condition (e.g., migraine, viral illness) and are not better accounted for by another mental disorder.

---

**Table 12.4–5**
**Caffeine-Related Disorder Not Otherwise Specified**

The caffeine-related disorder not otherwise specified category is for disorders associated with the use of caffeine that are not classifiable as caffeine intoxication, caffeine-induced anxiety disorder, or caffeine-induced sleep disorder. An example is caffeine withdrawal.

sociated with fibrocystic disease of the breasts in women. Although the question of whether caffeine is associated with birth defects remains controversial, women who are pregnant or breast-feeding should probably avoid caffeine-containing products. No solid data link caffeine intake with cancer.

## TREATMENT

The primary treatment of caffeine-related disorders is either the elimination or the severe reduction of caffeine-containing products from the person's diet or habits. Education of patients regarding the wide range of products that contain caffeine is essential for therapeutic success. Clinicians can advise patients to substitute other beverages—for example, water and decaffeinated soft drinks and coffee—to help deal with the habit of frequent drinks during the day. Spouses or significant others can often help the patients stop their caffeine use. Usually, the spouses or significant others agree to eliminate caffeine from their own diets.

Analgesics, such as aspirin, are almost always sufficient for the control of the headaches and muscle aches that may accompany caffeine withdrawal. Rarely do patients require benzodiazepines for the relief of their withdrawal symptoms. If benzodiazepines are used for that indication, they should be used in small dosages for a brief period of time, about 7 to 10 days at the longest.

### References

Ammon H P: Biochemical mechanism of caffeine tolerance. Arch Pharm *324*: 261, 1991.
Battig K: Acute and chronic cardiovascular and behavioural effects of caffeine, aspirin and ephedrine. Int J Obes *17* (2, Suppl): 61, 1993.
Battig K: Coffee, cardiovascular and behavioral effects: Current research trends. Rev Environ Health *9*: 53, 1992.
Bradley J R, Petree A: Caffeine consumption, expectancies of caffeine-enhanced performance, and caffeinism symptoms among university students. J Drug Educ *20*: 319, 1990.
Holtzman S G: Caffeine as a model drug of abuse. Trends Pharmacol Sci *11*: 355, 1990.
Hughes J R, Higgins S T, Bickel W K, Hunt W K, Fenwick J W, Gulliver S B, Mireault G C: Caffeine self-administration, withdrawal, and adverse effects among coffee drinkers. Arch Gen Psychiatry *48*: 611, 1991.
Hughes J R, Oliveto A H, Bickel W K, Higgins S T, Badger G J: Caffeine self-administration and withdrawal: Incidence, individual differences and interrelationships. Drug Alcohol Depend *32*. 239, 1993.
Hughes J R, Oliveto A H, Helzer J E, Higgins S T, Bickel W K: Should caffeine abuse, dependence, or withdrawal be added to DSM-IV and ICD-10? Am J Psychiatry *149*: 33, 1992.
Jacobson B H, Thurman-Lacey S R: Effects of caffeine on motor performance by caffeine-naive and -familiar subjects. Mot Skills *74*: 151, 1992.
Kozlowski L T, Henningfield J E, Keenan R M, Lei H, Leight G, Jelinek L C, Pope M A, Haertzen C A: Patterns of alcohol, cigarette, and caffeine and other drug use in two drug abusing populations. J Subst Abuse Treat *10*: 171, 1993.
Lucas P B, Pickar D, Kelsoe J, Rapaport M, Pato C. Hommer D: Effects of the acute administration of caffeine in patients with schizophrenia. Biol Psychiatry *28*: 35, 1990.
Mathew R J, Wilson W H: Behavioral and cerebrovascular effects of caffeine in patients with anxiety disorders. Acta Psychiatr Scand *82*: 17, 1990.
Silverman K, Evans S M, Strain E C, Griffiths R R: Withdrawal syndrome after the double-blind cessation of caffeine consumption. N Engl J Med *327*: 1109, 1992.
Silverman K, Griffiths R R: Low-dose caffeine discrimination and self-reported mood effects in normal volunteers. J Exp Anal Behav *57*: 91, 1992.
Yu G, Maskray V, Jackson S H, Swift C G, Tiplady B: A comparison of the central nervous system effects of caffeine and theophylline in elderly subjects. Br J Clin Pharmacol *32*: 341, 1991.

# 12.5 / Cannabis-Related Disorders

Cannabis is the abbreviated name for the hemp plant *Cannabis sativa*. All parts of the plant contain psychoactive cannabinoids, of which $(-)$-$\Delta^9$-tetrahydrocannabinol ($\Delta^9$-THC) is most abundant. The cannabis plant is usually cut, dried, chopped, and then rolled into cigarettes (commonly called joints), which are then smoked. The common names for cannabis are marijuana, grass, pot, weed, tea, and Mary Jane. Other names for cannabis, which describe cannabis types of various strengths, are hemp, chasra, bhang, ganja, dagga, and sinsemilla. The most potent forms of cannabis come from the flowering tops of the plants or from the dried, black-brown, resinous exudate from the leaves, which is referred to as hashish or hash.

The euphoriant effects of cannabis have been known for thousands of years. The potential medicinal effects of cannabis as an analgesic, anticonvulsant, and hypnotic were recognized in the 19th and early 20th centuries. Recently, cannabis and its primary active component, $\Delta^9$-THC, have been used successfully to treat nausea secondary to cancer treatment drugs and to stimulate appetite in patients with acquired immune deficiency syndrome (AIDS). Some less convincing reports concern the use of $\Delta^9$-THC in the treatment of glaucoma.

## EPIDEMIOLOGY

Cannabis is the most commonly used illicit substance in the United States. In 1991 about one third of the total population had used cannabis at least once, and about 5 percent were current users. Within the 18-to-25-year-old age group, about 50 percent had used cannabis at least once, and 13 percent were current users. Within the 12-to-17-year-old age group, about 13 percent had used cannabis at least once, and 4 percent were current users. In general, however, cannabis use has decreased from its high levels in the late 1970s.

The following epidemiological data for 1991 come from the National Institute on Drug Abuse (NIDA).

### Prevalence

About one third (33.2 percent) of the population reported that they had used marijuana one or more times in their lifetimes, 9.5 percent had used it in the past year, and 4.8 percent had used it in the past month.

Those percentages translate to 67.4 million members of the population who had used marijuana in their lifetimes, 19.2 million in the past year, and 9.7 million in the past month.

Adults aged 26 to 34 were the most likely age group to have ever used marijuana, but those aged 18 to 25 were the most likely to have used marijuana in the past year or the past month. About 60 percent of adults aged 26 to 34 had ever used marijuana, compared with about 51 percent of adults 18 to 25, 24 percent of adults over 34, and 13 percent of youths.

An estimated 13 percent of the adults 18 to 25 had used marijuana in the past month, compared with 7 percent of those aged 26 to 34 and smaller percentages of those in other age groups.

Youths aged 12 to 17 were the least likely of the age groups to have used marijuana in their lifetimes, and adults aged 35 and older were the least likely to have used marijuana in the past year and the past month.

## Demographic Correlates

**Sex.** The rate of past-month marijuana use by males was almost twice the rate for females. A total of 6.1 million males in the population had used marijuana in the past month, as had 3.6 million females.

**Race and ethnicity.** Blacks were about 1.6 times more likely than whites or Hispanics to have used marijuana in the past month. Even though blacks were proportionately more likely to have used marijuana in the past month, almost three fourths (73.4 percent) of the current users were white. A total of 7.1 million whites had used marijuana in the past month, compared with 1.7 million blacks, 0.7 million Hispanics, and 0.2 million others.

**Population density.** Residents of large and small metropolitan areas were significantly more likely than were residents of nonmetropolitan areas to have used marijuana in the past month. Although 42.9 percent of the United States population live in large metropolitan areas, 48.2 percent of those who had used marijuana in the past month were from large metropolitan areas. A total of 4.7 million residents of large metropolitan areas, 3.3 million from small metropolitan areas, and 1.7 million from nonmetropolitan areas had used marijuana in the past month.

**Region.** Residents of the West were significantly more likely than were residents of the South or North Central regions to have used marijuana in the past month. The other regions did not differ significantly. More than 2 million residents of each region had used marijuana in the past month.

## NEUROPHARMACOLOGY

As previously stated, the principal component of cannabis is $\Delta^9$-THC; however, the cannabis plant contains more than 400 chemicals, of which about 60 are chemically related to $\Delta^9$-THC. In the human, $\Delta^9$-THC is rapidly converted into 11-hydroxy-$\Delta^9$-THC, the metabolite that is active in the central nervous system (CNS).

A specific receptor for the cannabinols has been identified, cloned, and characterized. The receptor is a member of the G protein-linked family of receptors. The cannabinoid receptor is linked to the inhibitory G protein ($G_i$), which is linked to adenylyl cyclase in an inhibitory fashion. The cannabinoid receptor is found in highest concentrations in the basal ganglia, the hippocampus, and the cerebellum, with lower concentrations in the cerebral cortex (Figure 12.5–1). The receptor is not found in the brainstem, a fact that is consistent with the minimal effects cannabis has on respiratory and cardiac functions. Studies in animals have found that the cannabinoids affect the monoamine and $\gamma$-aminobutyric acid (GABA) neurons.

Most studies have shown that animals do not self-administer cannabinoids, as they do most other substances of abuse. Moreover, some debate concerns whether the cannabinoids stimulate the so-called reward centers of the brain, such as the dopaminergic neurons of the ventral tegmental area. However, tolerance to cannabis does develop, and psychological dependence has been found, but the evidence for physiological dependence is not strong. Withdrawal symptoms in humans are limited to modest increases in irritability, restlessness, insomnia, anorexia, and mild nausea; all those symptoms are seen only when a person abruptly stops taking high doses of cannabis.

When cannabis is smoked, the euphoric effects appear within minutes, peak in about 30 minutes, and last two to

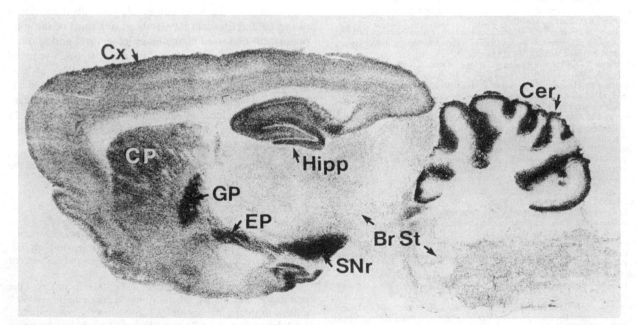

**Figure 12.5–1.** Autoradiography of cannabinoid receptor distribution in a sagittal section of rat brain. Binding of tritiated ligand is dense in the hippocampus (Hipp), the globus pallidus (GP), the entopenduncular nucleus (EP), the substantia nigra pars reticulata (SNr), and the cerebellum (Cer). Binding is moderate in the cerebral cortex (Cx) and the caudate putamen (CP) and sparse in the brainstem (Br St) and the spinal cord. (Figure from A C Howlett, M Bidaut-Russell, W A DeVane, L S Melvin, M R Johnson, M Herkenham: The cannabinoid receptor: Biochemical, anatomical, and behavioral characterization. Trends Neurosci *13*: 422, 1990. Used with permission.)

four hours. Some of the motor and cognitive effects last 5 to 12 hours. Cannabis can also be taken orally when it is prepared in food, such as brownies and cakes. About two to three times as much cannabis must be taken orally to be as potent as cannabis taken by the inhalation of its smoke. Many variables affect the psychoactive properties of cannabis, including the potency of the cannabis used, the route of administration, the smoking technique, the effects of pyrolysis on the cannabinoid content, the dose, the setting, the user's past experience, the user's expectations, and the user's unique biological vulnerability to the effects of cannabinoids.

## DIAGNOSIS AND CLINICAL FEATURES

The most common physical effects of cannabis are dilation of the conjunctival blood vessels (that is, red eye) and a mild tachycardia. At high doses, orthostatic hypotension may appear. Increased appetite—often referred to as the munchies—and dry mouth are other common effects of cannabis intoxication. There has never been a clearly documented case of death caused by cannabis intoxication alone, which reflects the substance's lack of effect on the respiratory rate. The most serious potential adverse effects of cannabis use come from the inhalation of the same carcinogenic hydrocarbons that are present in conventional tobacco, and some data indicate that heavy cannabis users are at risk for chronic respiratory disease and lung cancer. The practice of smoking cannabis-containing cigarettes to their very ends, so-called roaches, further increases the intake of tar (that is, particulate matter). Many reports indicate that long-term cannabis use is associated with cerebral atrophy, seizure susceptibility, chromosomal damage, birth defects, impaired immune reactivity, alterations in testosterone concentrations, and dysregulation of menstrual cycles; however, those reports have not been conclusively replicated, and the association between those effects and cannabis use is uncertain.

The fourth edition of *Diagnostic and Statistical Manual of Mental Disorders* (DSM-IV) lists the cannabis-related disorders (Table 12.5–1) but has specific criteria within the cannabis-related disorders section only for cannabis intoxication (Table 12.5–2). The diagnostic criteria for the other cannabis-related disorders are contained in those DSM-IV sections that focus on the major phenomenological symptom—for example, cannabis-induced psychotic disorder, with delusions, in the DSM-IV section on substance-induced psychotic disorder (Section 14.1).

### Cannabis Dependence and Cannabis Abuse

DMS-IV includes the diagnoses of cannabis dependence and cannabis abuse (Tables 12.1–6, 12.1–7, and 12.1–8). The experimental data clearly show tolerance to many of the effects of cannabis; however, the data are less supportive of the presence of physical dependence. Psychological dependence on cannabis use does develop in long-term users.

### Cannabis Intoxication

DSM-IV formalizes the diagnostic criteria for cannabis intoxication (Table 12.5–2). The diagnostic criteria specify

**Table 12.5–1**
**Cannabis-Related Disorders**

*Cannabis use disorders*

**Cannabis dependence**
**Cannabis abuse**

*Cannabis-induced disorders*

**Cannabis intoxication**
    *Specify if:*
      with perceptual disturbances
**Cannabis intoxication delirium**
**Cannabis-induced psychotic disorder, with delusions**
    *Specify if:*
      with onset during intoxication
**Cannabis-induced psychotic disorder, with hallucinations**
    *Specify if:*
      with onset during intoxication
**Cannabis-induced anxiety disorder**
    *Specify if:*
      with onset during intoxication

**Cannabis-related disorder not otherwise specified**

Table based on DSM-IV, *Diagnostic and Statistical Manual of Mental Disorders*, ed 4. Copyright American Psychiatric Association, Washington, 1994. Used with permission.

**Table 12.5–2**
**Diagnostic Criteria for Cannabis Intoxication**

A. Recent use of cannabis.

B. Clinically significant maladaptive behavioral or psychological changes (e.g., impaired motor coordination, euphoria, anxiety, sensation of slowed time, impaired judgment, social withdrawal) that develop during, or shortly after, cannabis use.

C. Two (or more) of the following signs, developing within 2 hours of cannabis use:

    (1) conjunctival injection
    (2) increased appetite
    (3) dry mouth
    (4) tachycardia

D. The symptoms are not due to a general medical condition and are not better accounted for by another mental disorder.

*Specify* if:
  **with perceptual disturbances**

Table from DSM-IV, *Diagnostic and Statistical Manual of Mental Disorders*, ed 4. Copyright American Psychiatric Association, Washington, 1994. Used with permission.

that the diagnosis can be augmented with the phrase "with perceptual disturbances." If intact reality testing is not present, the diagnosis is cannabis-induced psychotic disorder.

Cannabis intoxication commonly heightens the user's sensitivity to external stimuli, reveals new details, makes colors seem brighter and richer than in the past, and subjectively slows down the appreciation of time. In high doses, the user may also experience depersonalization and derealization.

Motor skills are impaired by cannabis use, and the impairment in motor skills remains after the subjective, euphoriant effects have resolved. For 8 to 12 hours after using cannabis, the user has an impairment of motor skills that interferes with the operation of motor vehicles and other heavy machinery. Moreover, those effects are additive to those of alcohol, which is commonly used in combination with cannabis.

### Cannabis Intoxication Delirium

Cannabis intoxication delirium is a DSM-IV diagnosis (Section 10.2). The delirium associated with cannabis intoxication is characterized by marked impairment on cognition and performance tasks. Even modest doses of cannabis result in impairment in memory, reaction time, perception, motor coordination, and attention. High doses that also impair the user's level of consciousness have marked effects on those cognitive measures.

### Cannabis-Induced Psychotic Disorder

Cannabis-induced psychotic disorder (Section 14.1) is diagnosed in the presence of a cannabis-induced psychosis. Cannabis-induced psychotic disorder is rare, but transient paranoid ideation is more common. Florid psychosis is somewhat common in countries in which some persons have long-term access to cannabis of a particularly high potency. The psychotic episodes are sometimes referred to as hemp insanity. Cannabis use is rarely associated with a bad-trip experience, which is often associated with hallucinogen intoxication. When cannabis-induced psychotic disorder does occur, it may be associated with a preexisting personality disorder in the affected person.

### Cannabis-Induced Anxiety Disorder

Cannabis-induced anxiety disorder (Section 16.1) is a common diagnosis for acute cannabis intoxication, which in many persons induces short-lived anxiety states that are often provoked by paranoid thoughts. In such circumstances, panic attacks may be induced, based on ill-defined and disorganized fears. The appearance of anxiety symptoms is correlated with the dose and is the most frequent adverse reaction to the moderate use of smoked cannabis. Inexperienced users are much more likely to experience anxiety symptoms than are experienced users.

### Cannabis-Related Disorder Not Otherwise Specified

DSM-IV does not formally recognize cannabis-induced mood disorders; therefore, such disorders are classified as cannabis-related disorders not otherwise specified (Table 12.5–3). Cannabis intoxication can be associated with depressive symptoms, although such symptoms may suggest

**Table 12.5–3**
**Cannabis-Related Disorder Not Otherwise Specified**

The cannabis-related disorder not otherwise specified category is for disorders associated with the use of cannabis that are not classifiable as cannabis dependence, cannabis abuse, cannabis intoxication, cannabis intoxication delirium, cannabis-induced psychotic disorder, or cannabis-induced anxiety disorder.

Table from DSM-IV, *Diagnostic and Statistical Manual of Mental Disorders,* ed 4. Copyright American Psychiatric Association, Washington, 1994. Used with permission.

long-term cannabis use. Hypomania, however, is a common symptom in cannabis intoxication.

DSM-IV also does not formally recognize cannabis-induced sleep disorders or cannabis-induced sexual dysfunction; therefore, both are classified as cannabis-related disorders not otherwise specified (NOS). When either sleep disorder symptoms or sexual dysfunction symptoms are present and related to cannabis use, they almost always resolve within days or a week after the cessation of cannabis use.

**Flashbacks.** Persisting perceptual abnormalities after cannabis use are not formally classified in DSM-IV, although there are case reports of persons who have experienced sensations related to cannabis intoxication—at times significantly—after the short-term effects of the substance have disappeared. Continued debate concerns whether flashbacks are related to cannabis use alone or whether they are related to the concomitant use of hallucinogens or of cannabis tainted with phencyclidine (PCP).

**Amotivational syndrome.** Another controversial cannabis-related syndrome is amotivational syndrome. The debate involves whether the syndrome is related to cannabis use or whether it reflects characterological traits in a subgroup of persons, regardless of cannabis use. Traditionally, the amotivational syndrome has been associated with long-term heavy use and has been characterized by a person's unwillingness to persist in a task—be it at school, at work, or in any setting that requires prolonged attention or tenacity. The person is described as becoming apathetic and anergic, usually gaining weight, and appearing slothful.

## TREATMENT

Treatment of cannabis use rests on the same principles as does treatment of other substances of abuse—abstinence and support. Abstinence can be achieved through direct interventions, such as hospitalization, or through careful monitoring on an outpatient basis by the use of urine drug screens, which can detect cannabis for three days to four weeks after use. Support can be achieved through the use of individual, family, and group psychotherapies. Education should be a cornerstone for both abstinence and support programs, since a patient who does not understand the intellectual reasons for addressing the substance-abuse problem shows little motivation to stop. For some patients an antianxiety drug may be useful for the short-term relief of withdrawal symptoms. For other patients the cannabis use may be related to an underlying depressive disorder that may respond to specific antidepressant treatment.

**References**

Abood M E, Martin B R: Neurobiology of marijuana abuse. Trends Pharmacol Sci *13*: 201, 1992.
Bailey S L, Flewelling R L, Rachal J V: Predicting continued use of marijuana among adolescents: The relative influence of drug-specific and social context factors. J Health Soc Behav *33*: 51, 1992.
Chait L D, Zacny J P: Reinforcing and subjective effects of oral delta 9-THC and smoked marijuana in humans. Psychopharmacology *107*: 255, 1992.
Chaudry H R, Moss H B, Bashir A, Suliman T: Cannabis psychosis following bhang ingestion. Br J Addict *86*: 1075, 1991.
Gardner E L, Lowinson J H: Marijuana's interaction with brain reward systems: Update 1991. Pharmacol Biochem Behav *40*: 571, 1991.

Hammer T, Vaglum P: Users and nonusers within a high risk milieu of cannabis use: A general population study. Int J Addict 26: 595, 1991.

Heishman S J, Huestis M A, Henningfield J E, Cone E J: Acute and residual effects of marijuana: Profiles of plasma THC levels: Physiological, subjective, and performance measures. Pharmacol Biochem Behav 37: 561, 1990.

Howlett A C, Bidaut-Russell M, DeVane W A, Melvin L S, Johnson M R, Herkenham M: The cannabinoid receptor: Biochemical, anatomical, and behavioral characterization. Trends Neurosci 13: 420, 1990.

Imade A G, Ebie J C: A retrospective study of symptom patterns of cannabis-induced psychosis. Acta Psychiatr Scand 83: 134, 1991.

Munro S, Thomas K L, Abu-Shaar M. Molecular characterization of a peripheral receptor for cannabinoids. Nature 365: 61, 1993.

Nahas G, Latour C: The human toxicity of marijuana. Med J Aust 156: 495, 1992.

National Institute on Drug Abuse: *National Household Survey on Drug Abuse: Highlights, 1991*. U S Government Printing Office, Washington, 1991.

Perez-Reyes M, White W R, McDonald S A, Hicks R E, Jeffcoat A R, Cook C E: The pharmacologic effects of daily marijuana smoking in humans. Pharmacol Biochem Behav 40: 691, 1991.

Schwartz R H, Lewis D C, Hoffman N G, Kyriazi N: Cocaine and marijuana use by medical students before and during medical school. Arch Intern Med 150: 883, 1990.

Stacy A W, Newcomb M D, Bentler P M: Cognitive motivation and drug use: A 9-year longitudinal study. J Abnorm Psychol 100: 502, 1991.

Stenbacka M, Allebeck P, Romelsjo A: Do cannabis drug abusers differ from intravenous drug abusers? The role of social and behavioral risk factors. Br J Addict 87: 259, 1992.

Tashkin D P, Gliederer F, Rose J, Chang P, Hui K K, Yu J L, Wu T C: Tar, CO and delta 9 THS delivery from the 1st to 2nd halves of a marijuana cigarette. Pharmacol Biochem Behav 40: 657, 1991.

Vulcano B A, Barnes G E, Langstaff P: Predicting marijuana use among adolescents. Int J Addict 25: 531, 1990.

# 12.6 / Cocaine-Related Disorders

Cocaine is one of the most addictive, commonly abused substances and one of the most dangerous. Cocaine—variously referred to as snow, coke, girl, and lady—is also abused in its most potent forms, freebase and crack (crack cocaine). Cocaine is an alkaloid that is derived from the shrub *Erythroxylon coca,* which is indigenous to South America, where the leaves of the shrub are chewed by the local inhabitants to obtain the stimulating effects. The cocaine alkaloid was first isolated in 1860 and was first used as a local anesthetic in 1880. Cocaine is still used as a local anesthetic, especially for eye, nose, and throat surgery, for which its vasoconstrictive effects are also helpful. In 1884 Sigmund Freud made a study of its general pharmacological effects. In the 1880s and 1890s, cocaine was widely touted as a cure for many ills. In 1914, however, cocaine was classified as a narcotic, along with morphine and heroin, because its addictive and adverse effects had by then been recognized.

## EPIDEMIOLOGY

About 1.9 million Americans, including 1.9 percent of high school seniors, have used cocaine within the past month; however, current cocaine use is on the decline. The decrease in the use of cocaine in the United States is primarily due to increased awareness of the risks involved with cocaine use; that awareness has likely been affected by a comprehensive public campaign about cocaine and its effects. The societal effects of the decrease in the use of cocaine, however, have been somewhat offset by the emergence over the past decade of the frequent use of crack, a highly potent form of cocaine. Crack use is most common in persons aged 18 to 25, who are particularly susceptible to the low street price of a single 50 to 100 mg dose of crack, usually around $10. Cocaine usually sells for around $100 to $150 for each one-gram vial.

In 1991 about 12 percent of the United States population had used cocaine at least once, and 1.9 percent had used crack at least once. The highest use was in the 18-to-25-year-old age group; 18 percent of them had used cocaine at least once, and 2 percent were current users. In that age group, 3.8 percent had used crack at least once. Although cocaine use is highest among the unemployed, cocaine is also used by highly educated persons in high socioeconomic groups. Cocaine use among males is twice as frequent as cocaine use among females. Although cocaine use among blacks and whites has declined since the mid-1980s, its use among Hispanics has increased. Cocaine is a dangerous drug, associated not only with gross behavioral disorders but also with medical morbidity. There were about 80,000 cocaine-related emergency room visits in the United States in 1990.

The following epidemiological data for 1991 come from the National Institute on Drug Abuse (NIDA):

### Prevalence of Cocaine Use

Approximately 12 percent of the United States population in 1991 reported that they had used cocaine (including crack) one or more times in their lifetimes, an estimated 3 percent reported using it in the past year, and fewer than 1 percent reported using it in the past month.

Those percentages mean that 23.4 million people had ever used cocaine, 6.1 million had used it in the past year, and 1.9 million had used it in the past month.

In 1991, 18 percent of young adults (aged 18 to 25) and 26 percent of adults aged 26 to 34 reported that they had ever used cocaine. Those age groups were the most likely to report ever using cocaine and using it in the past year (7.7 percent and 5.1 percent) and past month (2 percent and 1.8 percent). The differences between lifetime and past-year rates of use for those two age groups were statistically significant.

Prevalence rates in each period for those aged 12 to 17 and those aged 35 and older were much lower than those for other adults. Past-year and past-month rates for those aged 12 to 17 were almost the same as the rates for those 35 and older (1.5 percent and 1.4 percent; 0.4 percent and 0.5 percent), and each was significantly lower than the comparable rate for other adults.

### Trends in Cocaine Use

The rates of use of cocaine by the population in their lifetimes, the past year and the past month were for most age groups highest between 1979 and 1983. Lifetime use among adults aged 26 and older is an exception, having increased steadily since 1974 to a peak of 11.6 percent in 1991. That increase most likely reflects the many who used cocaine as adolescents and young adults during the 1970s and a small number of new users.

In 1991 all rates of cocaine use for most age groups were similar to those of the early 1970s. However, lifetime use among young adults aged 18 to 25 was higher than in the 1970s and has risen steadily since 1972 for adults aged 26 and older. Past-year use among adults aged 26 and older steadily increased to a peak in 1985 and has since been declining.

Between 1990 and 1991 the percentages of each age group reporting cocaine use in their lifetimes, the past year, or the past month were relatively stable, and none of the differences between the two years was statistically significant.

## Demographic Correlates of Cocaine Use

**Sex.** Males were about twice as likely as females to have used cocaine in the past month (1.3 percent versus 0.6 percent), and the difference was statistically significant. An estimated 1.3 million males and 0.6 million females in the population had used cocaine in the past month.

**Race and ethnicity.** Blacks and Hispanics had similar past-month rates of cocaine use. Both rates were significantly higher than the rate for whites. Although Hispanics represented only 8 percent of the United States population in 1991, they were 13.6 percent of past-month cocaine users. Blacks represented 11.4 percent of the population and 21.8 percent of past-month cocaine users. A total of 1.1 million whites, 0.4 million blacks, and 0.2 million Hispanics reported that they had used cocaine in the past month.

**Population density.** The rates of past-month cocaine use were significantly higher in large metropolitan areas than in nonmetropolitan areas. Other comparisons did not yield statistically significant differences. Almost half of all past-month cocaine users (0.9 million) lived in large metropolitan areas. Fewer past-month users lived in small metropolitan areas (0.7 million users), and the smallest number lived in nonmetropolitan areas (0.3 million users).

**Region.** Although the West had a slightly higher prevalence of past-month cocaine use than did the other regions, none of the differences across regions was statistically significant.

## Prevalence of Crack Use

Of the United States population, 1.9 percent reported that they had ever used crack cocaine, 0.5 percent had used it in the past year, and 0.2 percent had used it in the past month.

About 3.9 million members of the population aged 12 and older in 1991 reported that they had used crack cocaine in their lifetimes, 1 million in the past year, and 0.5 million in the past month.

Adults 18 to 25 and adults 26 to 34 were the most likely to have ever used crack cocaine (3.8 percent and 3.7 percent, respectively) and to have used crack cocaine in the past month (0.4 percent for both groups). The rates of use among those adults were significantly higher than the rates of youths aged 12 to 17 and adults aged 35 and older for most comparisons of lifetime, past-year, and past-month use.

## NEUROPHARMACOLOGY

The primary pharmacodynamic effect of cocaine that is related to its behavioral effects is competitive blockade of dopamine reuptake by the dopamine transporter. Blockade of that reuptake mechanism increases the concentration of dopamine in the synaptic cleft and results in increased activation of both dopamine type 1 ($D_1$) and dopamine type 2 ($D_2$) receptors. The effects of cocaine on the activity mediated by $D_3$, $D_4$, and $D_5$ receptors is not well understood at this time, but at least one preclinical study has implicated the $D_3$ receptor. Although the behavioral effects are thought to be mediated primarily by the blockade of dopamine reuptake, cocaine also blocks the reuptake of the other major catecholamine, norepinephrine, and the reuptake of serotonin. The behavioral effects related to those activities are receiving increased attention in the scientific literature. The effects of cocaine on cerebral blood flow and cerebral glucose use have also been studied. In general, most studies have found that cocaine is associated with decreased cerebral blood flow and possibly with the development of patchy areas of decreased glucose use.

The behavioral effects of cocaine are felt almost immediately and last for a relatively brief time (30 to 60 minutes), thus necessitating repeated administration to maintain the effects of intoxication. Although the behavioral effects are short-lived, metabolites of cocaine may be present in the blood and the urine for up to 10 days.

Cocaine has potent addictive qualities. A psychological dependence on cocaine can develop after a single use because of its potency as a positive reinforcer of behavior. With repeated administration, both tolerance and sensitivity to various effects of cocaine can develop, although the development of tolerance or sensitivity is apparently due to many factors and is not easily predicted. Physiological dependence on cocaine does develop, although cocaine withdrawal is mild compared with the effects of withdrawal from opiates and opioids.

## METHODS OF USE

The cocaine that is available on the street varies greatly in purity, since drug dealers often dilute the cocaine powder with sugar or procaine (Figure 12.6–1). Cocaine is sometimes cut with amphetamine. The most common method of using cocaine is by inhaling the finely chopped powder into the nose, a practice referred to as snorting or tooting. Other methods of ingesting cocaine are subcutaneous or intravenous (IV) injection and smoking (free-basing). Free-basing involves mixing street cocaine with chemically extracted pure cocaine alkaloid (the freebase) to get an increased effect. Smoking is also the method used for ingesting crack cocaine. Inhaling is the least dangerous

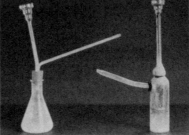

**Figure 12.6–1.** Pure cocaine (left) and typical free-basing pipes (middle) used to synthesize crack (right). (Figure from W L Woolverton, K M Johnson: Neurobiology of cocaine abuse. Trends Pharmacol Sci *13*: 194, 1992. Used with permission.)

method of cocaine use; IV injection and smoking are the most dangerous methods. The most direct methods of ingestion are often associated with cerebrovascular diseases, cardiac abnormalities, and death. Although cocaine can be taken orally, that route is rarely used because it is the least effective route.

### Crack

Crack is an extremely potent, freebase form of cocaine. Crack is sold in small, ready-to-smoke amounts, often called rocks (Figure 12.6–1). Crack cocaine is highly addictive; even one or two experiences with the drug can cause intense craving for more. Users have been known to resort to extremes of behavior to obtain the money to buy more crack. Anecdotal reports from urban emergency rooms have also associated extremes of violence with crack abuse.

## DIAGNOSIS AND CLINICAL FEATURES

The fourth edition of *Diagnostic and Statistical Manual of Mental Disorders* (DSM-IV) lists many cocaine use disorders (Table 12.6–1) but specifies the diagnostic criteria for only cocaine intoxication (Table 12.6–2) and cocaine withdrawal (Table 12.6–3) within the cocaine-related disorders section. The diagnostic criteria for the other cocaine-related disorders are in the DSM-IV sections that

**Table 12.6–1**
**Cocaine Use Disorders**

*Cocaine use disorders*
**Cocaine dependence**
**Cocaine abuse**

*Cocaine-induced disorders*
**Cocaine intoxication**
  *Specify if:*
    with perceptual disturbances
**Cocaine withdrawal**
**Cocaine intoxication delirium**
**Cocaine-induced psychotic disorder, with delusions**
  *Specify if:*
    with onset during intoxication
**Cocaine-induced psychotic disorder, with hallucinations**
  *Specify if:*
    with onset during intoxication
**Cocaine-induced mood disorder**
  *Specify if:*
    with onset during intoxication
    with onset during withdrawal
**Cocaine-induced anxiety disorder**
  *Specify if:*
    with onset during intoxication
    with onset during withdrawal
**Cocaine-induced sexual dysfunction**
  *Specify if:*
    with onset during intoxication
**Cocaine-induced sleep disorder**
  *Specify if:*
    with onset during intoxication
    with onset during withdrawal

**Cocaine-related disorder not otherwise specified**

Table based on DSM-IV, *Diagnostic and Statistical Manual of Mental Disorders,* ed 4. Copyright American Psychiatric Association, Washington, 1994. Used with permission.

**Table 12.6–2**
**Diagnostic Criteria for Cocaine Intoxication**

A. Recent use of cocaine.

B. Clinically significant maladaptive behavioral or psychological changes (e.g., euphoria or affective blunting; changes in sociability; hypervigilance; interpersonal sensitivity; anxiety, tension, or anger; stereotyped behaviors; impaired judgment; or impaired social or occupational functioning) that developed during, or shortly after, use of cocaine.

C. Two (or more) of the following, developing during, or shortly after, cocaine use:

  (1) tachycardia or bradycardia
  (2) pupillary dilation
  (3) elevated or lowered blood pressure
  (4) perspiration or chills
  (5) nausea or vomiting
  (6) evidence of weight loss
  (7) psychomotor agitation or retardation
  (8) muscular weakness, respiratory depression, chest pain, or cardiac arrhythmias
  (9) confusion, seizures, dyskinesias, dystonias, or coma

D. The symptoms are not due to a general medical condition and not better accounted for by another mental disorder.

*Specify if:*
  **with perceptual disturbances**

Table from DSM-IV, *Diagnostic and Statistical Manual of Mental Disorders,* ed 4. Copyright American Psychiatric Association, Washington, 1994. Used with permission.

**Table 12.6–3**
**Diagnostic Criteria for Cocaine Withdrawal**

A. Cessation of (or reduction in) cocaine use that has been heavy and prolonged.

B. Dysphoric mood and two (or more) of the following physiological changes, developing within a few hours to several days after criterion A:

  (1) fatigue
  (2) vivid, unpleasant dreams
  (3) insomnia or hypersomnia
  (4) increased appetite
  (5) psychomotor retardation or agitation

C. The symptoms in criterion B cause clinically significant distress or impairment in social, occupational, or other important areas of functioning.

D. The symptoms are not due to a general medical condition and are not better accounted for by another mental disorder.

Table from DSM-IV, *Diagnostic and Statistical Manual of Mental Disorders,* ed 4. Copyright American Psychiatric Association, Washington, 1994. Used with permission.

focus on the principal symptom—for example, cocaine-induced mood disorder in the mood disorders section (Section 13.3).

DSM-IV uses the general guidelines for substance dependence and substance abuse to diagnose cocaine dependence and cocaine abuse (Tables 12.1–6, 12.1–7, and 12.1–8). Clinically and practically, cocaine dependence or cocaine abuse can be suspected in patients who evidence unexplained changes in their personalities. Common changes associated with cocaine use are irritability, impaired ability to concentrate, compulsive behavior, severe insomnia, and weight loss. Colleagues at work and family members may notice a general and increasing inability to perform the expected tasks associated with work and family life. The patient may show new evidence of increased debt or inability to pay bills on time because of the large sums used to buy cocaine. Cocaine abusers often excuse themselves from work or social situations every 30 to 60 minutes to find a secluded place in which they can inhale some more cocaine. Because of the vasoconstricting effects of cocaine, its users almost always develop nasal congestion, which many attempt to self-medicate with decongestant sprays.

## Comorbidity (Dual Diagnosis)

As with other substance-related disorders, cocaine-related disorders are often accompanied by other psychiatric disorders. In general, the development of mood disorders and alcohol-related disorders follows the onset of cocaine-related disorders, whereas anxiety disorders, antisocial personality disorder, and attention-deficit/hyperactivity disorder are thought to precede the development of cocaine-related disorders. Most studies of comorbidity in patients with cocaine-related disorders have shown that major depressive disorder, bipolar II disorder, cyclothymic disorder, anxiety disorders, and antisocial personality disorder are the most commonly associated psychiatric diagnoses. The percentages of cormorbidity in one study of 298 cocaine users who sought treatment are presented in Table 12.6–4.

## Adverse Effects

A common adverse effect associated with cocaine use is nasal congestion, although serious inflammation, swelling, bleeding, and ulceration of the nasal mucosa can also occur. Long-term use of cocaine can also lead to the perforation of the nasal septa. Free-basing and smoking crack can cause damage to the bronchial passages and the lungs. The IV use of cocaine is associated with infection, embolisms, and the transmission of acquired immune deficiency syndrome (AIDS). Minor neurological complications with cocaine use include the development of acute dystonia, tics, and migrainelike headaches. The major complications of cocaine use, however, are its cerebrovascular, epileptic, and cardiac effects. About two thirds of those acute toxic effects occur within one hour of intoxication; about one fifth occur in one to three hours; the remainder occur up to several days later.

**Cerebrovascular effects.** The most common cerebrovascular diseases associated with cocaine use are nonhemorrhagic cerebral infarctions. When hemorrhagic infarctions do occur, they can include subarachnoid hemorrhages, intraparenchymal hemorrhages, and interventricular hemorrhages. Transient ischemic attacks have also been associated with cocaine use. Although those vascular disorders usually affect the brain, spinal cord hemorrhages have also been reported. The obvious pathophysiological mechanism for those vascular disorders is through vasoconstriction, but other pathophysiological mechanisms have also been proposed.

**Seizures.** Seizures have been reported to account for 3 to 8 percent of cocaine-related emergency room visits.

**Table 12.6–4**
**Current and Lifetime Rates of Psychiatric Disorders (Research Diagnostic Criteria) in Treatment-Seeking Cocaine Abusers**

| Characteristic | Number (%) | |
|---|---|---|
| | Current | Lifetime |
| Total | 298 (100.0) | 298 (100.0) |
| Any psychiatric disorder (excluding drug disorders, alcoholism, or childhood disorders) | 166 (55.7) | 221 (73.5) |
| Affective disorders | | |
| Major depression | 14 (4.7) | 91 (30.5) |
| Minor depression | 2 (0.7) | 35 (11.7) |
| Intermittent depressive personality | 33 (11.1) | 33 (11.1) |
| Chronic depressive personality | 22 (7.4) | 22 (7.4) |
| Intermittent hyperthymic personality | 27 (9.1) | 21 (9.1) |
| Chronic hyperthymic personality | 21 (7.1) | 21 (7.1) |
| intermittent cyclothymic personality | 8 (2.7) | 8 (2.7) |
| Chronic cyclothymic personality | 3 (1.0) | 3 (1.0) |
| Mania | 0 (0.0) | 11 (3.7) |
| Hypomania | 6 (2.0) | 22 (7.4) |
| Any affective disorder | 132 (44.3) | 181 (60.7) |
| Anxiety disorders | | |
| Panic | 1 (0.3) | 5 (1.7) |
| Generalized anxiety | 11 (3.7) | 21 (7.0) |
| Generalized anxiety with depression | 3 (1.0) | 4 (1.3) |
| Obsessive-compulsive disorder | 1 (0.3) | 1 (0.3) |
| Phobia | 35 (11.7) | 40 (13.4) |
| Any anxiety disorder | 47 (15.8) | 62 (20.8) |
| Schizophrenic disorders | | |
| Schizophrenia | 0 (0.0) | 1 (0.3) |
| Schizoaffective, depressed | 1 (0.3) | 2 (0.7) |
| Schizoaffective, manic | 0 (0.0) | 1 (0.3) |
| Alcoholism (Research Diagnostic Criteria) | 86 (28.9) | 184 (61.7) |
| Personality disorders | | |
| Antisocial personality | 23 (7.7) | 23 (7.7) |
| Briquet's syndrome | 0 (0.0) | 0 (0.0) |
| Childhood disorders | | |
| Attention-deficit disorder | 0 (0.0) | 104 (34.9) |
| Gambling disorder | 7 (2.3) | 44 (14.8) |
| Suicide gestures or attempts | — | 67 (22.5) |

Table from B J Rounsaville, S F Anton, K Carroll, D Budde,, B A Prusoff, F Gawin: Psychiatric diagnoses of treatment-seeking cocaine abusers. Arch Gen Psychiatry *48*: 45, 1991. Used with permission.

Cocaine is the substance of abuse that is most commonly associated with seizures; the second most common substance is amphetamine. Usually, cocaine-induced seizures are single events, although multiple seizures and status epilepticus are also possible. A rare and easy-to-misdiagnose complication of cocaine use is partial complex status epilepticus, which should be considered as a diagnosis in a patient who seems to have cocaine-induced psychotic disorder with an unusually fluctuating course. The risk of having cocaine-induced seizures is highest in patients who have a history of epilepsy, who use high doses of cocaine, and who use crack.

**Cardiac effects.** Myocardial infarctions and arrhythmias are perhaps the most common cocaine-induced cardiac abnormalities. Cardiomyopathies can develop with the long-term use of cocaine. Cardioembolic cerebral infarctions can be a further complication arising from cocaine-induced myocardial dysfunction.

**Death.** High doses of cocaine are associated with seizures, respiratory depression, cerebrovascular diseases, and myocardial infarctions—all of which can lead to death in cocaine users. The users may experience warning signs of syncope or chest pain but may ignore those signs because of the irrepressible desire to take more cocaine. Deaths have also been reported with the ingestion of speedballs, combinations of opioids and cocaine.

## Cocaine Intoxication

DSM-IV specifies the diagnostic criteria for cocaine intoxication (Table 12.6–2), emphasizing the behavioral and physical signs and symptoms of cocaine use. The DSM-IV diagnostic criteria allow for the specification of the presence of perceptual disturbances. If hallucinations are present in the absence of intact reality testing, the appropriate diagnosis is cocaine-induced psychotic disorder, with hallucinations.

Cocaine is used because it characteristically causes elation, euphoria, heightened self-esteem, and perceived improvement on mental and physical tasks. Actually, some studies have indicated that low doses of cocaine can be associated with improved performance on some cognitive tasks. With high doses of cocaine, however, the symptoms of intoxication include agitation, irritability, impaired judgment, impulsive and potentially dangerous sexual behavior, aggression, a generalized increase in psychomotor activity, and, potentially, symptoms of mania. The major associated physical symptoms are tachycardia, hypertension, and mydriasis.

## Cocaine Withdrawal

After the cessation of cocaine use or after acute intoxication, a postintoxication depression (crash) is characterized by dysphoria, anhedonia, anxiety, irritability, fatigue, hypersomnolence, and sometimes agitation. With mild to moderate cocaine use, those withdrawal symptoms are over within 18 hours. With heavy use, such as that seen with cocaine dependence, the withdrawal symptoms can last up to a week (Figure 12.6–2), usually peaking in two to four days. Some patients and anecdotal reports have described cocaine withdrawal syndromes that have lasted for weeks or months. The withdrawal symptoms can also be associated with suicidal ideation in the affected person. In the state of withdrawal, the craving for cocaine can be powerful and intense, since the person knows that taking cocaine can eliminate the uncomfortable symptoms of cocaine withdrawal. Persons experiencing cocaine withdrawal often attempt to self-medicate the symptoms with alcohol, sedatives, hypnotics, or antianxiety agents, such as diazepam (Valium). DSM-IV has formalized the diagnostic criteria for cocaine withdrawal (Table 12.6–3).

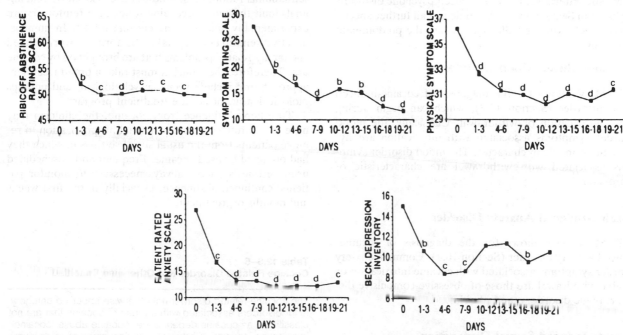

**Figure 12.6–2.** Mean symptom scores of 22 cocaine-dependent patients during the initial three weeks of abstinence. The ranges of possible scores were as follows: Ribicoff Abstinence Rating Scale, 41–205; Symptom Rating Scale, 0–72; Physical Symptom Scale, 27–108; Patient-Rated Anxiety Scale, 0–144; Beck Depression Inventory, 0–63. The p values are based on paired t tests, time point versus baseline: b—p < 0.05, c—p < 0.005, d—p < 0.001. (Figure from S L Satel, L H Price, J M Palumbo, C J McDougle, J H Krystal, F Gawin, D S Charney, G R Heninger, H D Kleber: Clinical phenomenology and neurobiology of cocaine abstinence: A prospective inpatient study. Am J Psychiatry *148*: 1714, 1991. Used with permission.)

## Cocaine Intoxication Delirium

DSM-IV has specified a diagnosis for cocaine intoxication delirium (Section 10.2). Cocaine intoxication delirium is most common when high doses of cocaine are used; when the cocaine has been used over a short period of time, thereby resulting in a rapid increase in cocaine blood concentrations; or when the cocaine is mixed with other psychoactive substances (for example, amphetamine, opiates, opioids, and alcohol). Persons with preexisting brain damage (often resulting from previous episodes of cocaine intoxication) are also at increased risk for cocaine intoxication delirium.

## Cocaine-Induced Psychotic Disorders

Paranoid delusions and hallucinations may occur in as many as 50 percent of all cocaine users. The occurrence of those psychotic symptoms depends on the dose, the duration of use, and the user's individual sensitivity to the substance. Cocaine-induced psychotic disorders are most common with IV users and crack users. Males are much more likely to have psychotic symptoms than are females. Of the psychotic symptoms, paranoid delusions are the most frequent, although auditory hallucinations are also common. Visual and tactile hallucinations may be less common than paranoid delusions. The sensation of bugs crawling just beneath the skin (formication) has been reported to be associated with cocaine use. The development of psychotic disorders can be associated with grossly inappropriate sexual behavior, generally bizarre behavior, and homicidal or other violent behavior related to the content of the paranoid delusions or hallucinations. The DSM-IV diagnostic criteria for cocaine-induced psychotic disorders are listed in Section 14.1. The clinician can further specify whether delusions or hallucinations are the predominant symptoms.

## Cocaine-Induced Mood Disorder

DSM-IV allows for the diagnosis of cocaine-induced mood disorder (Section 15.3), which can begin during either intoxication or withdrawal. Classically, the mood disorder symptoms associated with intoxication are hypomanic or manic in character. The mood disorder symptoms associated with withdrawal are characteristic of depression.

## Cocaine-Induced Anxiety Disorder

DSM-IV also allows for the diagnosis of cocaine-induced anxiety disorder (Section 16.1). Common anxiety disorder symptoms associated with cocaine intoxication or cocaine withdrawal are those of obsessive-compulsive disorder, panic disorders, and phobias.

## Cocaine-Induced Sexual Dysfunction

DSM-IV allows for the diagnosis of cocaine-induced sexual dysfunction (Section 20.2), which can begin when a person is intoxicated with cocaine. Although cocaine is used as an aphrodisiac and as a way to delay orgasm, its repeated use can result in impotence.

## Cocaine-Induced Sleep Disorder

Cocaine-induced sleep disorder, which can begin during either intoxication or withdrawal, is described under the heading of substance-induced sleep disorder (Section 23.2). Cocaine intoxication is associated with the inability to sleep; cocaine withdrawal is associated with disrupted sleep or hypersomnolence.

## Cocaine-Related Disorder Not Otherwise Specified

DSM-IV provides a diagnosis of cocaine-related disorder not otherwise specified (NOS) for cocaine-related disorders that cannot be classified into one of the above diagnoses (Table 12.6–5).

## TREATMENT

Many cocaine users do not come to treatment voluntarily. Their experience with the substance is too positive and the negative effects perceived as too minimal to warrant seeking treatment. One study of cocaine users who sought treatment compared with those who did not seek treatment found that those who did not seek treatment more often had polysubstance-related disorder, fewer negative consequences associated with cocaine use, fewer work-related or family-related obligations, and increased contact with the legal system and with illegal activities.

The major hurdle to overcome in the treatment of cocaine-related disorders is the intense craving that the cocaine user has for the drug. Although animal studies have shown that cocaine is a powerful inducer of cocaine self-administration, those studies have also shown that animals limit their use of cocaine if negative reinforcers are experimentally linked to the cocaine intake. In humans, negative reinforcers may take the form of work-related and family-related problems that are brought on by cocaine use. Therefore, the clinician must take a broad treatment approach and include social, psychological, and perhaps biological strategies in the treatment program.

To attain abstinence from cocaine, the clinician may have to institute complete or partial hospitalization to remove patients from the usual social settings in which they had obtained or used cocaine. Frequent and unscheduled urine testing is almost always necessary to monitor patients' continued abstinence, especially in the first weeks and months of treatment.

**Table 12.6–5**
**Cocaine-Related Disorder Not Otherwise Specified**

The cocaine-related disorder not otherwise specified category is for disorders associated with the use of cocaine that are not classifiable as cocaine dependence, cocaine abuse, cocaine intoxication, cocaine withdrawal, cocaine intoxication delirium, cocaine-induced psychotic disorder, cocaine-induced mood disorder, cocaine-induced anxiety disorder, cocaine-induced sexual dysfunction, or cocaine-induced sleep disorder.

Table from DSM-IV, *Diagnostic and Statistical Manual of Mental Disorders*, ed 4. Copyright American Psychiatric Association, Washington, 1994. Used with permission.

Psychological intervention usually involves individual, group, and family modalities. Individual therapy is most effectively focused on the dynamics that led to the cocaine use, the perceived positive effects of the cocaine, and how those aims may be met in a different manner. Group therapy and support groups (such as Narcotics Anonymous) often involve discussions with other cocaine abusers and the sharing of past experiences and effective coping methods. Family therapy is often an essential component of the treatment strategy. Common issues in family therapy are discussing how past behavior has harmed the family and allowing other family members to voice their responses to those behaviors. However, the therapy should maintain a focus on the future and on how changes in the family's activities may help the cocaine abuser stay off the drug and direct energies in different directions.

A variety of pharmacological strategies have been used to help cocaine abusers resist the urge to take cocaine. The two most successful classes of drugs are the dopaminergic agonists and some of the tricyclic drugs. The two most commonly used dopaminergic agonists are amantadine (Symmetrel), 100 mg twice daily, and bromocriptine (Parlodel), 2.5 mg twice daily; both have been reported to reduce the patient's craving, increase energy, and normalize sleep. Carbamazepine (Tegretol) has also been used as a pharmacological approach to cocaine detoxification. Carbamazepine has been found to be effective in reducing craving, except in patients with coexisting antisocial personality disorder.

### References

Brady K T, Lydiard R B, Malcolm R, Ballenger J C: Cocaine-induced psychosis. J Clin Psychiatry 52: 509, 1991.

Burke W M, Ravi N V, Dhopesh V, Vandegrift B, Maany I: Prolonged presence of metabolite in urine after compulsive cocaine use. J Clin Psychiatry 51: 145, 1990.

Caine S B, Koob G F: Modulation of cocaine self-administration in the rat through D-3 dopamine receptors. Science 260: 1814, 1993.

Carroll K M, Rounsaville B J: Contrast of treatment-seeking and untreated cocaine abusers. Arch Gen Psychiatry 49: 464, 1992.

Gallanter M, Egelko S, De Leon G, Rohrs C, Franco H: Crack-cocaine abusers in the general hospital: Assessment and initiation of care. Am J Psychiatry 149: 810, 1992.

Gawin F H: Cocaine addiction: Psychology and neurophysiology. Science 251: 1580, 1991.

Griffin M L, Weiss R D, Mirin S M, Lange U: A comparison of male and female cocaine abusers. Arch Gen Psychiatry 46: 122, 1989.

Higgins S T, Budney A J, Bickel W K, Hughes J R, Foerg F, Badger G: Achieving cocaine abstinence with a behavioral approach. Am J Psychiatry 150: 763, 1993.

Kang S-Y, Kleinman P H, Woody G E, Millman R B, Todd T C, Kemp J, Lipton D S: Outcomes for cocaine abusers after once-a-week psychosocial therapy. Am J Psychiatry 148: 630, 1991.

McKelway R, Vieweg V, Westerman P: Sudden death from acute cocaine intoxication in Virginia in 1988. Am J Psychiatry 147: 1667, 1990.

National Institute on Drug Abuse: National Household Survey, Highlights, 1991. U S Government Printing Office, Washington, 1991.

Rounsaville B J, Anton S F, Carroll K, Budde D, Prusoff B A, Gawin F: Psychiatric diagnoses of treatment-seeking cocaine abusers. Arch Gen Psychiatry 48: 43, 1991.

Satel S L, Price L H, Palumbo J M, McDougle C J, Krystal J H, Gawin F, Charney D S, Heninger G R, Kleber H D: Clinical phenomenology and neurobiology of cocaine abstinence: A prospective inpatient study. Am J Psychiatry 148: 1712, 1991.

Satel S L, Southwick S M, Gawin F H: Clinical features of cocaine-induced paranoia. Am J Psychiatry 148: 495, 1991.

Strang J, Johns A, Caan W: Cocaine in the UK—1991. Br J Psychiatry 162: 1, 1993.

Volkow N D, Fowler J S, Wolf A P, Hitzeman R, Dewey S, Bendriem B, Alpert R, Hoff A: Changes in brain glucose metabolism in cocaine dependence and withdrawal. Am J Psychiatry 148: 621, 1991.

Woolverton W L, Johnson K M: Neurobiology of cocaine abuse. Trends

## 12.7 / Hallucinogen-Related Disorders

The hallucinogens are variously called psychedelics or psychotomimetics because, besides inducing hallucinations, they cause loss of contact with reality and an expanding and heightening of consciousness. The hallucinogens are classified as schedule I drugs; the Food and Drug Administration (FDA) has decreed that they have no medical use and a high abuse potential. More than 100 natural and synthetic hallucinogens are used by humans. The classic naturally occurring hallucinogens are psilocybin (from some mushrooms) and mescaline (from peyote cactus). Other naturally occurring hallucinogens are harmine, harmaline, ibogaine, and dimethyltryptamine (DMT). The classic synthetic hallucinogen is lysergic acid diethylamide (LSD), which was synthesized in 1938 by Albert Hoffman, who later accidentally ingested some of the drug and experienced the first LSD-induced hallucinogenic episode.

### EPIDEMIOLOGY

In 1991 an estimated 8.1 percent of the inhabitants of the United States had used a hallucinogen at least once, 1.2 percent had used a hallucinogen in the preceding year, and 0.3 percent had used a hallucinogen in the preceding month. Hallucinogen use is most common among young (15 to 35 years of age) white males. The ratio of whites to blacks who have used a hallucinogen is 2 to 1, and the white to Hispanic ratio is around 1.5 to 1. Males represent 62 percent of those who have ever used a hallucinogen and 75 percent of those who have used a hallucinogen in the preceding month, thus reflecting a pattern of more frequent use than by females. Those 26 to 34 years of age have the highest use of hallucinogens, with 15.5 percent having used a hallucinogen at least once. Those 18 to 25 years of age have the highest recent use of a hallucinogen— 1.2 percent of the age group. Cultural factors influence the use of hallucinogens; their use in the western United States is significantly higher than in the southern United States. Hallucinogen use is associated with less morbidity and less mortality than are some other substances. For example, one study found that only 1 percent of substance-related emergency room visits were related to hallucinogens, in comparison with 40 percent for cocaine-related problems. However, of those visiting the emergency room, more than 50 percent were under 20 years of age. There is a reported resurgence in the popularity of hallucinogens.

The following epidemiological data come from the National Institute on Drug Abuse (NIDA):

Young adults (aged 18 to 25) were much more likely than were youths (aged 12 to 17) or older adults to report that they had ever used hallucinogens. In 1991 an estimated 13.1 percent of young adults, 7.8 percent of older adults, and 3.3 percent of youths (aged 12 to 17) reported that they had ever used hallucinogens. For past-month use the prevalence rates among youths and young adults were significantly higher than those of the older age groups. However, the rates of use in the past month were low in all age groups.

The rates of use among members of the population in their lifetimes were highest in 1979 for young adults and youths and decreased thereafter. The rates of lifetime use steadily increased among older adults from 1974 to 1991. That increase in lifetime rates among adults over 25 is expected, because the rates reflect the experience of that group in previous years, when rates of substance abuse were high.

Between 1990 and 1991 the percentages of each age group using hallucinogens in their lifetimes and in the past month were relatively stable. Although the percentage of past-month users rose slightly among young adults aged 18 to 25 (from 0.8 percent to 1.2 percent), there were no significant changes for any age group.

## NEUROPHARMACOLOGY

Although the myriad hallucinogenic substances vary in their pharmacological effects, LSD can be discussed as a general prototype of a hallucinogen. The fundamental pharmacodynamic effect of LSD remains controversial, although it is generally well accepted that the principal effects are on the serotonergic system. The controversy regards whether LSD acts as an antagonist or as an agonist; the data at this time suggest that LSD acts as a partial agonist at postsynaptic serotonin receptors.

Most hallucinogens are well absorbed after oral ingestion, although some types of hallucinogens are ingested by inhalation, smoking, or intravenous injection. Tolerance for LSD and other hallucinogens develops rapidly and is virtually complete after three or four days of continuous use. Tolerance also reverses quickly, usually in four to seven days. There is no physical dependence on hallucinogens, and there are no withdrawal symptoms. However, a psychological dependence can develop to the insight-inducing experiences that a user may associate with episodes of hallucinogen use.

## DIAGNOSIS

The fourth edition of *Diagnostic and Statistical Manual of Mental Disorders* (DSM-IV) lists a number of hallucinogen-related disorders (Table 12.7–1) but contains specific diagnostic criteria only for hallucinogen intoxication (Table 12.7–2) and hallucinogen persisting perception disorder (flashbacks) (Table 12.7–3). The diagnostic criteria for the other hallucinogen use disorders are contained in the DSM-IV sections that are specific to each symptom—for example, hallucinogen-induced mood disorder (Section 15.3).

### Hallucinogen Dependence and Hallucinogen Abuse

Long-term hallucinogen use is not common. There is no physical addiction; although psychological dependence occurs, it is rare, partly because each LSD experience is

**Table 12.7–1**
**Hallucinogen-Related Disorders**

*Hallucinogen use disorders*

**Hallucinogen dependence**
**Hallucinogen abuse**

*Hallucinogen-induced disorders*

**Hallucinogen intoxication**
**Hallucinogen persisting perception disorder (flashbacks)**
**Hallucinogen intoxication delirium**
**Hallucinogen-induced psychotic disorder, with delusions**
  *Specify if:*
    with onset during intoxication
**Hallucinogen-induced psychotic disorder, with hallucinations**
  *Specify if:*
    with onset during intoxication
**Hallucinogen-induced mood disorder**
  *Specify if:*
    with onset during intoxication
**Hallucinogen-induced anxiety disorder**
  *Specify if:*
    with onset during intoxication
**Hallucinogen-related disorder not otherwise specified**

Table based on DSM-IV, *Diagnostic and Statistical Manual of Mental Disorders*, ed 4. Copyright American Psychiatric Association, Washington, 1994. Used with permission.

different and partly because there is no reliable euphoria. Nonetheless, hallucinogen dependence and hallucinogen abuse do exist, and both syndromes are defined by DSM-IV criteria (Tables 12.1–6, 12.1–7, and 12.1–8).

### Hallucinogen Intoxication

Intoxication with hallucinogens is defined in DSM-IV as being characterized by maladaptive behavioral and perceptual changes and by certain physiological signs (Table 12.7–2). The differential diagnosis for hallucinogen intoxication includes anticholinergic and amphetamine intoxication and alcohol withdrawal. The preferred treatment for hallucinogen intoxication is *talking down* the patient; during that process, guides can reassure patients that the symptoms are drug-induced, that they are not going crazy, and that the symptoms will resolve shortly. In the most severe cases, dopaminergic antagonists—for example, haloperidol (Haldol)—or benzodiazepines—for example, diazepam (Valium)—can be used for a limited time. In general, no withdrawal syndrome is associated with hallucinogen intoxication.

### Hallucinogen Persisting Perception Disorder

At times distant to the ingestion of a hallucinogen, a person can experience a flashback involving hallucinogenic symptoms. The syndrome is diagnosed as hallucinogen persisting perception disorder (Table 12.7–3) in DSM-IV. It was called posthallucinogen perception disorder in the revised third edition of DSM (DSM-III-R). Various studies have reported that a range from 15 to 80 percent of hallucinogen users report having experienced flashbacks. The differential diagnosis for flashbacks includes migraine, seizures, visual system abnormalities, and posttraumatic

**Table 12.7–2**
**Diagnostic Criteria for Hallucinogen Intoxication**

A. Recent use of a hallucinogen.

B. Clinically significant maladaptive behavioral or psychological changes (e.g., marked anxiety or depression, ideas of reference, fear of losing one's mind, paranoid ideation, impaired judgment, or impaired social or occupational functioning) that developed during, or shortly after, hallucinogen use.

C. Perceptual changes occurring in a state of full wakefulness and alertness (e.g., subjective intensification of perceptions, depersonalization, derealization, illusions, hallucinations, synesthesias) that developed during, or shortly after, hallucinogen use.

D. Two (or more) of the following signs, developing during, or shortly after, hallucinogen use:

   (1) pupillary dilation
   (2) tachycardia
   (3) sweating
   (4) palpitations
   (5) blurring of vision
   (6) tremors
   (7) incoordination

E. The symptoms are not due to a general medical condition and are not better accounted for by another mental disorder.

Table from DSM-IV, *Diagnostic and Statistical Manual of Mental Disorders*, ed 4. Copyright American Psychiatric Association, Washington, 1994. Used with permission.

**Table 12.7–3**
**Diagnostic Criteria for Hallucinogen Persisting Perception Disorder (Flashbacks)**

A. The reexperiencing, following cessation of use of a hallucinogen, of one or more of the perceptual symptoms that were experienced while intoxicated with the hallucinogen (e.g., geometric hallucinations, false perceptions of movement in the peripheral visual fields, flashes of color, intensified colors, trails of images of moving objects, positive afterimages, halos around objects, macropsia, and micropsia).

B. The symptoms in criterion A cause clinically significant distress or impairment in social, occupational, or other important areas of functioning.

C. The symptoms are not due to a general medical condition (e.g., anatomical lesions and infections of the brain, visual epilepsies) and are not better accounted for by another mental disorder (e.g., delirium, dementia, schizophrenia) or hypnopompic hallucinations.

Table from DSM-IV, *Diagnostic and Statistical Manual of Mental Disorders*, ed 4. Copyright American Psychiatric Association, Washington, 1994. Used with permission.

stress disorder. A flashback experience can be triggered by emotional stress, sensory deprivation (for example, monotonous driving), or the use of another psychoactive substance (for example, alcohol or marijuana).

The flashback is a spontaneous, transitory recurrence of the substance-induced experience. Most flashbacks are episodes of visual distortion, geometric hallucinations, hallucinations of sounds or voices, false perceptions of movement in peripheral fields, flashes of color, trails of images from moving objects, positive afterimages and halos, ma-

cropsia, micropsia, time expansion, physical symptoms, or relived intense emotion. The episodes usually last a few seconds to a few minutes, but sometimes they last longer than that.

Most often, even in the presence of distinct perceptual disturbances, the person has insight into the pathological nature of the disturbance. Suicidal behavior, major depressive disorder, and panic disorders are potential complications.

## Hallucinogen Intoxication Delirium

DSM-IV allows for the diagnosis of hallucinogen delirium (Section 10.2). The disorder is thought to be relatively rare. It begins during intoxication in persons who have ingested pure hallucinogens. However, hallucinogens are often mixed with other substances, and the other components or their interactions with the hallucinogens can result in a clinical delirium.

## Hallucinogen-Induced Psychotic Disorders

If psychotic symptoms are present in the absence of retained reality testing, a diagnosis of hallucinogen-induced psychotic disorder may be warranted (Section 14.1). DSM-IV also allows the clinician to specify whether hallucinations or delusions are the prominent symptoms. The most common adverse effect of LSD and related substances is a bad trip, which resembles the acute panic reaction to cannabis but which can be more severe; a bad trip occasionally produces true psychotic symptoms. The bad trip generally ends when the immediate effects of the hallucinogen wear off. However, the course of a bad trip is variable, and occasionally a protracted psychotic episode is difficult to distinguish from a nonorganic psychotic disorder. Whether a chronic psychosis after a drug ingestion is the result of the drug ingestion or is unrelated to the drug ingestion or is a combination of both the drug ingestion and predisposing factors is currently an unanswerable question.

Occasionally, the psychotic disorder is prolonged; prolonged reactions are thought to be most common in persons with preexisting schizoid personality disorder and prepsychotic personalities, an unstable ego balance, or a great deal of anxiety. Such persons cannot cope with the perceptual changes, body-image distortions, and symbolic unconscious material stimulated by the hallucinogen. The rate of previous mental instability in persons hospitalized for LSD reactions is high. In the late 1960s a number of adverse reactions occurred because LSD was being promoted as a self-prescribed psychotherapy for emotional crises in the lives of seriously disturbed people. Because that is happening less today, prolonged adverse reactions are much less commonly seen now than in the past.

## Hallucinogen-Induced Mood Disorder

DSM-IV provides a diagnostic category for hallucinogen-induced mood disorder (Section 15.3). Unlike cocaine-induced mood disorder and amphetamine-induced mood disorder, in which the symptoms are somewhat predictable, mood disorder symptoms accompanying hallucinogen abuse can be variable. Abusers may experience maniclike symptoms involving grandiose delusions or depressionlike feelings and ideas or mixed symptoms. As with the hallucinogen-induced psychotic disorder symptoms, the symptoms of hallucinogen-induced mood disorder almost invariably resolve once the drug has been eliminated from the patient's body.

### Hallucinogen-Induced Anxiety Disorder

Hallucinogen-induced anxiety disorder (Section 16.1) is also variable in its symptom pattern, and few data regarding symptom patterns are available. Anecdotally, physicians who treat patients who come into emergency rooms with hallucinogen-related disorders have frequently reported panic disorder with agorophobia.

### Hallucinogen-Related Disorder Not Otherwise Specified

If a patient with a hallucinogen-related disorder does not meet the diagnostic criteria for any of the standard hallucinogen-related disorders, the patient may be classified as having hallucinogen-related disorder not otherwise specified (NOS) (Table 12.7–4). DSM-IV does not have a diagnostic category of hallucinogen withdrawal, but some clinicians anecdotally report a syndrome with depression and anxiety that follows the cessation of frequent hallucinogen use. Such a syndrome may best fit the diagnosis of hallucinogen-related disorder NOS.

## CLINICAL FEATURES

The onset of action of LSD occurs within one hour, peaks in two to four hours, and lasts 8 to 12 hours. The sympathomimetic effects of LSD include tremors, tachycardia, hypertension, hyperthermia, sweating, blurring of vision, and mydriasis. Death can be caused by hallucinogenic use. The cause of death can be related to cardiac or cerebrovascular pathology related to hypertension or hyperthermia. A syndrome similar to neuroleptic malignant syndrome has been reported to be associated with LSD use. The cause of death can also be related to a physical injury after the use of impaired judgment—for example, regarding traffic or the person's ability to fly. The psychological effects are usually well tolerated; however, if persons are unable to recall experiences or unable to appreciate that the experiences are substance-induced, they may fear the onset of insanity.

**Table 12.7–4**
**Hallucinogen-Related Disorder Not Otherwise Specified**

The hallucinogen-related disorder not otherwise specified category is for disorders associated with the use of hallucinogens that are not classifiable as hallucinogen dependence, hallucinogen abuse, hallucinogen intoxication, hallucinogen persisting perception disorder, hallucinogen intoxication delirium, hallucinogen-induced psychotic disorder, hallucinogen-induced mood disorder, or hallucinogen-induced anxiety disorder.

With hallucinogen use, perceptions become unusually brilliant and intense. Colors and textures seem to be richer than in the past, contours sharpened, music more emotionally profound, and smells and tastes heightened. Synesthesia is common; colors may be heard or sounds seen. Changes in body image and alterations of time and space perception also occur. Hallucinations are usually visual, often of geometric forms and figures, but auditory and tactile hallucinations are sometimes experienced. Emotions become unusually intense and may change abruptly and often; two seemingly incompatible feelings may be experienced at the same time. Suggestibility is greatly heightened, and sensitivity or detachment from other people may arise. Other features that often appear are a seeming awareness of internal organs, the recovery of lost early memories, the release of unconscious material in symbolic form, and regression and the apparent reliving of past events, including birth. Introspective reflection and feelings of religious and philosophical insight are common. The sense of self is greatly changed, sometimes to the point of depersonalization, merging with the external world, separation of self from body, or total dissolution of the ego in mystical ecstasy.

There is no clear evidence of drastic personality change or chronic psychosis produced by long-term LSD use in moderate users not otherwise predisposed to those conditions. However, some heavy users of hallucinogens may suffer from chronic anxiety or depression and may benefit from a psychological or pharmacological approach that addresses the underlying problem.

Many persons maintain that a single experience with LSD has given them increased creative capacity, new psychological insight, relief from neurotic or psychosomatic symptoms, or a desirable change in personality. Psychiatrists in the 1950s and 1960s showed great interest in LSD and related substances, both as a potential model for functional psychosis and as possible pharmacotherapeutic agents. The availability of those compounds to researchers in the basic neurosciences has led to many scientific advances.

## TREATMENT

The treatment of choice for acute psychiatric symptoms associated with hallucinogen intoxication is supportive counseling, talking down. The best treatment for a person who is having a severely unpleasant experience under the influence of LSD is protection, companionship, and reassurance. Occasionally, a short course of psychotherapeutic drugs may be necessary, usually with dopamine receptor antagonists for psychotic symptoms or with benzodiazepines for anxiety symptoms. When a hallucinogen-induced drug experience is temporally related to the onset of a persisting psychiatric condition (for example, a depressive disorder, manic episodes, or schizophrenia), the treatment of the persisting psychiatric condition should generally follow the usual guidelines for that diagnosis.

### References

Behan W M, Bakheit A M, Behan P O, More I A: The muscle findings in the neuroleptic malignant syndrome associated with lysergic acid diethylamide. J Neurol Neurosurg Psychiatry *54*: 741, 1991.
Cousineau D, Savard M, Allard D: Illicit drug use among adolescent stu-

dents. A peer phenomenon? Can Fam Physician Med Fam Can *39*: 523, 1993.

Dinges M M, Oetting E R: Similarity in drug use patterns between adolescents and their friends. Adolescence *28*: 253, 1993.

Glennon R A: Do classical hallucinogens act as 5-HT$_2$ agonists or antagonists? Neuropsychopharmacology *3*: 509, 1990.

Johnston L D, O'Malley P M, Bachman J G: Drug abuse among American high school seniors, college students, and young adults, 1975–1990. Department of Health and Human Services, Washington, 1991.

Kulig K: LSD. Emerg Med Clin North Am *8*: 551, 1990.

National Institute on Drug Abuse: *National Household Survey, Highlights, 1991*. U S Government Printing Office, Washington, 1991.

Pierce P A, Peroutka S J: Antagonist properties of d-LSD at 5-hydroxytryptamine$_2$ receptors. Neuropsychopharmacology *3*: 503, 1990.

Rainey J M, Aleem A, Ortiz A, Yeragani V, Pohl R, Berchou R: A laboratory procedure for the induction of flashbacks. Am J Psychiatry *144*: 1317, 1987.

Spoerke D G, Hall A H: Plants and mushrooms of abuse. Emerg Med Clin North Am *8*: 579, 1990.

Strassman R J: Adverse reactions to psychedelic drugs: A review of the literature. J Nerv Ment Dis *172*: 577, 1984.

Ulrich R F, Patten B M: The rise, decline, and fall of LSD. Perspect Biol Med *34*: 561, 1991.

# 12.8 / Inhalant-Related Disorders

In the fourth edition of *Diagnostic and Statistical Manual of Mental Disorders* (DSM-IV), the category of inhalant-related disorders includes the psychiatric syndromes resulting from the use of solvents, glues, adhesives, aerosol propellants, paint thinners, and fuels. Specific examples of those substances include gasoline, varnish remover, lighter fluid, airplane glue, rubber cement, cleaning fluid, spray paint, shoe conditioner, and typewriter correction fluid. A resurgence of inhalants' popularity among the young has been reported. The active compounds in those inhalants include toluene, acetone, benzene, trichloroethane, perchloroethylene, trichloroethylene, 1,2-dichloropropane, and halogenated hydrocarbons. DSM-IV specifically excludes anesthetic gases (for example, nitrous oxide and ether) and short-acting vasodilators (for example, amylnitrite) from the inhalant-related disorders; DSM-IV classifies those as other (or unknown) substance-related disorders.

## EPIDEMIOLOGY

Inhalant substances are available legally, inexpensively, and easily. Those three factors contribute to the high use of inhalants among the poor and the young. In 1991 about 5 percent of the total United States population had used inhalants at least once, and about 1 percent were current users. Among young adults 18 to 25 years old, 11 percent had used inhalants at least once, and 2 percent were current users. Among youths 12 to 17 years old, 7 percent had used inhalants at least once, and 2 percent were current users. In one study of high school seniors, 18 percent reported having used inhalants at least once, and 2.7 percent reported having used inhalants within the preceding month. White users of inhalants are more common than either black or Hispanic users. Some data suggest that, in the United States, inhalant use may be more common in suburban communities than in urban communities.

Inhalant use accounts for 1 percent of all substance-related deaths and fewer than 0.5 percent of all substance-related emergency room visits. About 20 percent of the emergency room visits for inhalant use involve persons less than 18 years old. Inhalant use among adolescents may be most common in those who have parents or older siblings who use illegal substances. Inhalant use among adolescents is also associated with an increased likelihood of being classified as having conduct disorder or antisocial personality disorder.

The following epidemiological data for 1991 come from the National Institute on Drug Abuse (NIDA):

About 5 percent of the population aged 12 and older reported that they had ever used inhalants, and fewer than 1 percent had used inhalants in the past month.

The highest prevalence of inhalant use in the past month was 3.4 percent for youths in 1985. That rate decreased thereafter and has been lower than that in other age groups.

Between 1990 and 1991 the prevalence of inhalant use by members of the population in their lifetimes and in the past month was relatively stable. The only significant change was an increase from 7.2 percent to 9.2 percent in the prevalence of lifetime use for adults aged 26 to 34.

In 1991 young adults aged 18 to 25 were significantly more likely than youths or older adults to have used inhalants in their lifetimes. Youths were significantly more likely than were adults aged 35 and older to have used inhalants in their lifetimes.

In 1991 an estimated 10.9 percent of young adults aged 18 to 25 years, 9.2 percent of adults aged 26 to 34 years, 7.0 percent of youths 12 to 17 years, and 2.5 percent of adults aged 35 and older reported that they had ever used inhalants. Use in the past month was less than 2 percent for all age groups combined.

## NEUROPHARMACOLOGY

The inhalants are usually delivered to the lungs by using a tube, a can, a plastic bag, or an inhalant-soaked rag, through or from which the user can sniff the inhalant through the nose or huff the inhalant through the mouth. The general action of inhalants is as a central nervous system (CNS) depressant. Tolerance for inhalants does develop, although the withdrawal symptoms are usually fairly mild and are not classified in DSM-IV as a disorder.

The inhalants are rapidly absorbed through the lungs and are rapidly delivered to the brain. The effects appear within five minutes and may last for 30 minutes to several hours, depending on the inhalant substance and the dose. For example, 15 to 20 breaths of a 1 percent solution of gasoline may result in a high that lasts several hours. The blood concentrations of many inhalant substances are increased when used in combination with alcohol, perhaps because of competition for hepatic enzymes. Although about one fifth of an inhalant substance is excreted unchanged by the lungs, the remainder is metabolized by the liver. Inhalants are detectable in the blood for 4 to 10 hours after use, and blood samples should be taken in the emergency room if inhalant use is suspected.

Much like alcohol, inhalants have specific pharmacodynamic effects that are not well understood. Because their effects are generally similar to and additive to the effects of other CNS depressants (for example, ethanol, barbiturates, and benzodiazepines), some investigators have suggested that the inhalants operate through an enhancement of the γ-aminobutyric acid (GABA) system. Other investigators have suggested that inhalants have their effects through membrane fluidization, which has also been hypothesized to be a pharmacodynamic effect of ethanol.

## DIAGNOSIS

DSM-IV lists a number of inhalant-related disorders (Table 12.8–1) but contains specific diagnostic criteria only for inhalant intoxication (Table 12.8–2) within the inhalant-related disorders section. The other inhalant-related disorders have their diagnostic criteria specified in the DSM-IV sections that specifically address the major symptoms—for example, inhalant-induced psychotic disorders (Section 14.1).

### Inhalant Dependence and Inhalant Abuse

Most persons probably use inhalants for a short time and do not develop a pattern of long-term use that results in dependence and abuse. Nonetheless, dependence and abuse of inhalants do occur and are diagnosed according to the standard DSM-IV criteria for those syndromes (Tables 12.1–6, 12.1–7, and 12.1–8).

### Inhalant Intoxication

The DSM-IV diagnostic criteria for inhalant intoxication (Table 12.8–2) specify the presence of maladaptive behavioral changes and at least two physical symptoms.

**Table 12.8–1**
**Inhalant-Related Disorders**

***Inhalant use disorders***

**Inhalant dependence**
**Inhalant abuse**

***Inhalant-induced disorders***

**Inhalant intoxication**
**Inhalant intoxication delirium**
**Inhalant-induced persisting dementia**
**Inhalant-induced psychotic disorder, with delusions**
*Specify if:*
  with onset during intoxication
**Inhalant-induced psychotic disorder, with hallucinations**
*Specify if:*
  with onset during intoxication
**Inhalant-induced mood disorder**
*Specify if:*
  with onset during intoxication
**inhalant-induced anxiety disorder**
*Specify if:*
  with onset during intoxication

**Inhalant-related disorder not otherwise specified**

The intoxicated state is often characterized by apathy, diminished social and occupational functioning, impaired judgment, and impulsive or aggressive behavior. The person may later be amnestic for the period of intoxication. Intoxication is often accompanied by nausea, anorexia, nystagmus, depressed reflexes, and diplopia. The user's neurological status can progress to stupor and unconsciousness with high doses and long exposures. Clinicians can sometimes identify a recent user of inhalants by rashes around the patient's nose and mouth; unusual breath odors; the residue of the inhalant substances on the patient's face, hands, or clothing; and irritation of the patient's eyes, throat, lungs, and nose.

### Inhalant Intoxication Delirium

DSM-IV provides a diagnostic category for inhalant intoxication delirium (Section 10.2). Delirium can be induced by the effects of the inhalants themselves, by pharmacodynamic interactions with other substances, and by the hypoxia that may be associated with either the inhalant or its method of inhalation. If the delirium results in severe behavioral disturbances, short-term treatment with a dopamine receptor antagonist—for example, haloperidol (Haldol)—may be necessary. Benzodiazepines should be avoided because of the possibility of adding to the patient's respiratory depression.

### Inhalant-Induced Persisting Dementia

Inhalant-induced persisting dementia (Section 10.3), like delirium, may be due to the neurotoxic effects of the

**Table 12.8–2**
**Diagnostic Criteria for Inhalant Intoxication**

A. Recent intentional use or short-term, high-dose exposure to volatile inhalants (excluding anesthetic gases and short-acting vasodilators).

B. Clinically significant maladaptive behavioral or psychological changes (e.g., belligerence, assaultiveness, apathy, impaired judgment, impaired social or occupational functioning) that developed during, or shortly after, use of or exposure to volatile inhalants.

C. Two (or more) of the following signs, developing during, or shortly after, inhalant use or exposure:
  (1) dizziness
  (2) nystagmus
  (3) incoordination
  (4) slurred speech
  (5) unsteady gait
  (6) lethargy
  (7) depressed reflexes
  (8) psychomotor retardation
  (9) tremor
  (10) generalized muscle weakness
  (11) blurred vision or diplopia
  (12) stupor or coma
  (13) euphoria

D. The symptoms are not due to a general medical condition and are not better accounted for by another mental disorder.

inhalants themselves, the neurotoxic effects of the metals commonly used in inhalants (for example, lead), or the effects of frequent and prolonged periods of hypoxia. The dementia caused by inhalants is likely to be irreversible in all but the mildest cases.

### Inhalant-Induced Psychotic Disorder

Inhalant-induced psychotic disorder is a DSM-IV diagnosis (Section 14.1). The clinician can specify whether hallucinations or delusions are the predominant symptoms. Paranoid states are probably the most common psychotic syndromes during inhalant intoxication.

### Inhalant-Induced Mood Disorder and Inhalant-Induced Anxiety Disorder

Inhalant-induced mood disorder (Section 15.3) and inhalant-induced anxiety disorder (Section 16.1) are DSM-IV diagnoses that allow the classification of inhalant-related disorders that are characterized by prominent mood and anxiety symptoms. Depressive disorders are the most common mood disorders associated with inhalant use, and panic disorders and generalized anxiety disorder are the most common anxiety disorders.

### Inhalant-Related Disorder Not Otherwise Specified

The diagnosis of inhalant-related disorder not otherwise specified (NOS) is the recommended DSM-IV diagnosis for inhalant-related disorders that do not fit into one of the above diagnostic categories (Table 12.8–3).

## CLINICAL FEATURES

In small initial doses the inhalants may be disinhibiting and may result in feelings of euphoria, excitement, and pleasant floating sensations; the drugs are presumably used for those effects. Other psychological symptoms of high doses of the substance can include fearfulness, sensory illusions, auditory and visual hallucinations, and distortions of body size. The neurological symptoms can include slurred speech, decreased speed of talking, and ataxia. Use over a long period can be associated with irritability, emotional lability, and impaired memory.

Tolerance for the inhalants does develop; although not recognized by DSM-IV, a withdrawal syndrome can accompany the cessation of inhalant use. The withdrawal

**Table 12.8–3**
**Inhalant-Related Disorder Not Otherwise Specified**

The inhalant-related disorder not otherwise specified category is for disorders associated with the use of inhalants that are not classifiable as inhalant dependence, inhalant abuse, inhalant intoxication, inhalant intoxication delirium, inhalant-induced persisting dementia, inhalant-induced psychotic disorder, inhalant-induced mood disorder, or inhalant-induced anxiety disorder.

Table from DSM-IV, *Diagnostic and Statistical Manual of Mental Disorders*, ed 4. Copyright American Psychiatric Association, Washington, 1994. Used with permission.

syndrome does not occur frequently; when it does, it can be characterized by sleep disturbances, irritability, jitteriness, sweating, nausea, vomiting, tachycardia, and sometimes delusions and hallucinations.

### Adverse Effects

The inhalants are associated with many potentially serious adverse effects. The most serious adverse effect is death, which can result from respiratory depression, cardiac arrhythmias, asphyxiation, the aspiration of vomitus, or accident or injury (for example, by driving while intoxicated with inhalants). Other serious adverse effects associated with long-term inhalant use include irreversible hepatic or renal damage and permanent muscle damage associated with rhabdomyolysis. The combination of organic solvents and high concentrations of copper, zinc, and heavy metals has been associated with the development of brain atrophy, temporal lobe epilepsy, decreased intelligence quotient (I.Q.), and a variety of electroencephalographic (EEG) changes. Several studies of house painters and factory workers who have been exposed to solvents for long periods have found evidence of brain atrophy on computed tomography (CT) scans and decreases in cerebral blood flow. Additional adverse effects include cardiovascular and pulmonary symptoms (for example, chest pain and bronchospasm), gastrointestinal symptoms (for example, pain, nausea, vomiting, and hematemesis), and other neurological signs and symptoms (for example, peripheral neuritis, headache, paresthesia, cerebellar signs, and lead encephalopathy). There are reports of brain atrophy, renal tubular acidosis, and long-term motor impairment in toluene users. A number of reports concern serious adverse effects on fetal development when the pregnant mother uses or is exposed to inhalant substances.

## TREATMENT

Usually, the use of inhalants is a relatively short-lived period in a person's life. The person either ceases substance-taking activity or moves on to other substances of abuse. The identification of inhalant use in an adolescent is an indication that the teenager should receive counseling and education about the general topic of substance use. The presence of an associated diagnosis of conduct disorder or antisocial pesonality disorder should prompt the clinician to address the situation in depth because of the increased likelihood that the adolescent will become further inolved in substance use. For the most part, however, persons with inhalant abuse or inhalant dependence are older, debilitated persons who need substantial social interventions as part of the treatment approach.

**References**

Byrne A, Kirby B, Zibin T, Ensminger S: Psychiatric and neurological effects of chronic solvent abuse. Can J Psychiatry 36: 735, 1991.
Dinwiddie S H, Reich T, Cloninger C R: The relationship of solvent use to other substance use. Am J Drug Alcohol Abuse 17: 173, 1991.
Dinwiddie S H, Reich T, Cloninger C R: Solvent use and psychiatric comorbidity. Br J Addict 85: 1647, 1990.
Donnelly N, Oldenburg B, Quine S, Macaskill P, Flaherty B, Spooner C, Lyle D: Changes in reported drug prevalence among New South Wales secondary school students, 1983–1989. Aust J Public Health 16: 50, 1992.
Espeland K: Inhalant abuse: Assessment guidelines. J Psychosoc Nurs Ment Health Serv 31: 11, 1993.

Evans E B, Balster R L: CNS depressant effects of volatile organic solvents. Neurosci Biobehav Rev *15*: 233, 1991.

Farrow J A, Schwartz R H: Adolescent drug and alcohol usage: A comparison of urban and suburban pediatric practices. J Natl Med Assoc *84*: 409, 1992.

Flanagan R J, Ruprah M, Meredith T J, Ramsey J D: An introduction to the clinical toxicology of volatile substances. Drug Saf *5*: 359, 1990.

Griesel R D, Jansen P, Richter L M: Electro-encephalographic disturbances due to chronic toxin abuse in young people, with special reference to glue-sniffing. S Afr Med J *78*: 544, 1990.

Johns A: Volatile substance abuse and 963 deaths. Br J Addict *86*: 1053, 1991.

Lindren C H: Volatile substances of abuse. Emerg Med Clin North Am *8*: 559, 1990.

Miller N S, Gold M S: Organic solvent and aerosol abuse. Am Fam Physician *44*: 183, 1991.

National Institute on Drug Abuse: *National Household Survey, Highlights, 1991*. U S Government Printing Office, Washington, 1991.

Pollard T G: Relative addiction potential of major centrally-active drugs and drug classes: Inhalants and anesthetics. Adv Alcohol Subst Abuse *9*: 149, 1990.

Prasher V P, Corbett J A: Aerosol addiction. Br J Psychiatry *157*: 922, 1990.

Tenenbein M, Pillay N: Sensory evoked potentials in inhalant (volatile solvent) abuse. J Paediatr Child Health *29*: 206, 1993.

Wheeler M G, Rozycki A A, Smith R P: Recreational propane inhalation in an adolescent male. J Toxicol Clin Toxicol *30*: 135, 1992.

# 12.9 / Nicotine-Related Disorders

In 1988 *The Surgeon General's Report on the Health Consequences of Smoking: Nicotine Addiction* was published. It clearly stated that nicotine is an addicting drug, just as cocaine and heroin are addicting drugs. As a result of that report and other public health information campaigns, the percentage of persons who smoke in the United States has decreased from 44 percent in 1964 to approximately 27 percent in 1991. The fact that 27 percent of all persons in the United States continue to smoke in spite of the mountain of data showing how dangerous the habit is to their health is testament to the powerfully addictive properties of nicotine. The ill effects of cigarette smoking are reflected in the estimate that 60 percent of the direct health care costs in the United States go to treat tobacco-related illnesses and come to an estimated $1 billion a day.

## EPIDEMIOLOGY

As noted above, the number of Americans who smoke is decreasing, but it is still estimated that 22 percent of all Americans will still be smoking in the year 2000. The rate of quitting smoking has been fastest among well-educated, white men and less fast among women, blacks, teenagers, and persons with low levels of education.

The most common form of nicotine is tobacco, which is smoked in cigarettes, cigars, and pipes. Tobacco can also be used as snuff and chewing tobacco (also called smokeless tobacco); both forms are increasingly popular in the United States. About 3 percent of all persons in the United States are current users of snuff or chewing tobacco; however, about 6 percent of young adults aged 18 to 25 use those forms of tobacco.

The following epidemiological data for 1991 come from the National Institute on Drug Abuse (NIDA):

## Prevalence

About 73 percent of the United States population aged 12 and older had smoked cigarettes in their lifetimes, 32 percent had smoked cigarettes in the past year, and 27 percent had smoked cigarettes in the past month.

Those percentages translate to 147.6 million members of the population who had ever smoked cigarettes, 65.1 million who had smoked in the past year, and 54.8 million who had smoked in the past month.

About 71 percent of young adults (aged 18 to 25 years), 76 percent of adults aged 26 to 34 years, and 78 percent of adults aged 35 and older had smoked cigarettes in their lifetimes, compared with about 38 percent of youths aged 12 to 17.

Although adults 18 to 25 and adults 26 to 34 did not differ significantly from each other in their prevalence of cigarette use in the past month, both groups had a significantly higher rate of past-month use than did youths and older adults. Older adults (35 and older) were also significantly more likely than were youths to have smoked cigarettes in the past month.

In 1991 about 11 percent of youths, 32 percent of adults 18 to 25 years, 33 percent of adults 26 to 34 years, and 27 percent of older adults reported that they had smoked cigarettes in the past month.

## Trends

The percentages of youths and adults 18 to 25 years reporting cigarette use in their lifetimes were highest in 1979 and generally decreased after then. The rates for older adults have been relatively stable since 1979.

Current cigarette use was higher during the 1970s than in the 1980s for all age groups. During the 1980s, current cigarette use decreased steadily for all adults, but no consistent trend was apparent for youths.

Between 1990 and 1991 the prevalence of cigarette use among members of the population in their lifetimes, the past year, and the past month did not change significantly for any of the age groups. However, when adults aged 26 to 34 were distinguished from older adults, significant decreases between 1990 and 1991 in lifetime, past-year, and past-month use of cigarettes were observed for them.

## Demographic Correlates

**Sex.** Males were significantly more likely than females to have smoked cigarettes in the past month.

**Race and ethnicity.** Whites and blacks were significantly more likely than Hispanics to have smoked cigarettes in the past month.

**Population density.** Residents of nonmetropolitan areas were more likely than were residents of small metropolitan and large metropolitan areas to be cigarette smokers. The difference between residents of nonmetropolitan areas and large metropolitan areas was statistically significant.

**Region.** There were no statistically significant differences in the rates of current cigarette smoking among the four regions of the country.

## Current Cigarette Smoking

**Age group.** Adults 26 to 34 and older adults were the most likely to have smoked a pack or more of cigarettes a day in the past month (that is, about 17 percent of those adults compared with about 13 percent of young adults 18 to 25 and almost 2 percent of youths).

Differences between age groups in the prevalence of heavy smoking (smoking a pack or more a day) were statistically significant for all comparisons except for adults 26 to 34 versus older adults.

The proportion of smokers who smoked a pack a day or more of cigarettes steadily increased with age group.

About 16 percent of youths who smoked cigarettes in the past month smoked a pack or more a day, compared with about 65 percent of adult smokers aged 35 and older.

**Other demographic characteristics.** About 17 percent of males, compared with 13 percent of females, reported smoking a pack of cigarettes a day or more in the past month. Among those who smoked cigarettes, about 61 percent of males reported heavy use, compared with 51 percent of females.

Although blacks and whites smoked cigarettes at about the same rate in the preceding month (both about 27 percent), whites were significantly more likely than blacks to have smoked heavily (17 percent and 10 percent, respectively). The rate of heavy smoking among Hispanics was about 7 percent, which was significantly lower than the rate of heavy smoking for both whites and blacks.

The rate of heavy smoking in small metropolitan areas was significantly higher than in large metropolitan areas. The highest prevalence of heavy smoking was in nonmetropolitan areas, and it was significantly higher than the rates for both small metropolitan areas and large metropolitan areas.

Rates of heavy smoking did not vary substantially across regions of the country. However, the prevalence of heavy smoking was significantly higher in the North Central region than in either the Northeast or the West.

## Smokeless Tobacco Use

In 1991 an estimated 14.1 percent of the population aged 12 and older reported that they had used smokeless tobacco in their lifetimes, 4.7 percent had used it in the past year, and 3.4 percent had used it in the past month.

Those percentages translate to 28.6 million who had ever used smokeless tobacco, 9.6 million who had used it in the past year, and about 6.9 million who had used it in the past month.

In 1991 an estimated 5.8 percent of those aged 18 to 25 were current users of smokeless tobacco, a rate that was significantly higher than the rates for other age groups.

Smokeless tobacco use in the past month was most common among males (6.5 percent), whites (3.9 percent), residents of nonmetropolitan areas (6.5 percent), and Southerners (5.4 percent).

## Psychiatric Patients

Psychiatrists must be particularly concerned and knowledgeable about nicotine dependence because of the very high proportion of psychiatric patients who smoke. Approximately 50 percent of all psychiatric outpatients, 70 percent of bipolar I disorder outpatients, and almost 90 percent of schizophrenic outpatients smoke. Moreover, data indicate that patients with depressive disorders or anxiety disorders are much less successful in their attempt to quit smoking than are other people, thus suggesting that part of a holistic health approach to such persons includes helping the patients address their smoking habits, in addition to the primary mental disorder.

## Death

The primary adverse effect of cigarette smoking is death. Tobacco use is associated with approximately 400,000 premature deaths each year in the United States, representing 25 percent of all deaths. The causes of death include chronic bronchitis and emphysema (51,000 deaths), bronchogenic cancer (106,000 deaths), 35 percent of fatal myocardial infarctions (115,000 deaths), cerebrovascular disease, cardiovascular disease, and almost all cases of chronic obstructive pulmonary disease and lung cancer. Lung cancer is now the leading cause of cancer-related deaths in women, having recently surpassed breast cancer. The increased use of chewing tobacco and snuff has been associated with the development of oropharyngeal cancer.

## NEUROPHARMACOLOGY

The psychoactive component of tobacco is nicotine, which has its central nervous system (CNS) effects by acting as an agonist at the nicotinic subtype of acetylcholine receptors. About 25 percent of the nicotine inhaled when smoking a cigarette reaches the blood, through which the nicotine reaches the brain within 15 seconds. The half-life of nicotine is about two hours. Nicotine is believed to have its positive reinforcing and addictive properties because it activates the dopaminergic pathway projecting from the ventral tegmental area to the cerebral cortex and the limbic system. In addition to activating that reward dopamine system, nicotine causes an increase in the concentrations of circulating norepinephrine and epinephrine and an increase in the release of vasopressin, β-endorphin, adrenocorticotropic hormone (ACTH), and cortisol. Those hormones are thought to contribute to the basic stimulatory effects of nicotine on the CNS.

## DIAGNOSIS

The fourth edition of *Diagnosis and Statistical Manual of Mental Disorders* (DSM-IV) lists three nicotine-related disorders (Table 12.9–1) but contains specific diagnostic criteria for only nicotine withdrawal (Table 12.9–2) in the nicotine-related disorders section. The other nicotine-related disorders recognized by DSM-IV are nicotine dependence and nicotine-related disorder not otherwise specified.

## Nicotine Dependence

DSM-IV allows for the diagnosis of nicotine dependence (Tables 12.1–6 and 12.1–7) but not nicotine abuse. Dependence on nicotine develops quickly, probably because of the activation by nicotine of the ventral tegmental area dopaminergic system, the same system affected by cocaine and amphetamine. The development of dependence is enhanced by strong social factors that encourage smoking in some settings and by the powerful effects of tobacco company advertising. Persons are likely to smoke if they have parents or siblings who smoke and who serve as role models. Several recent studies have also suggested a genetic diathesis toward nicotine dependence. Most per-

**Table 12.9–1**
**Nicotine-Related Disorders**

*Nicotine use disorder*
**Nicotine dependence**

*Nicotine-induced disorder*
**Nicotine withdrawal**
**Nicotine-related disorder not otherwise specified**

Table based on DSM-IV, *Diagnostic and Statistical Manual of Mental Disorders*, ed 4. Copyright American Psychiatric Association, Washington, 1994. Used with permission.

**Table 12.9–2**
**Diagnostic Criteria for Nicotine Withdrawal**

A. Daily use of nicotine for at least several weeks.

B. Abrupt cessation of nicotine use, or reduction in the amount of nicotine used, followed within 24 hours by at least four of the following signs:
  (1) dysphoric or depressed mood
  (2) insomnia
  (3) irritability, frustration, or anger
  (4) anxiety
  (5) difficulty concentrating
  (6) restlessness
  (7) decreased heart rate
  (8) increased appetite or weight gain

C. The symptoms in criterion B cause clinically significant distress or impairment in social, occupational, or other important areas of functioning.

D. The symptoms are not due to a general medical condition and are not better accounted for by another mental disorder.

Table from DSM-IV, *Diagnostic and Statistical Manual of Mental Disorders*, ed 4. Copyright American Psychiatric Association, Washington, 1994. Used with permission.

sons who smoke want to quit and have tried many times to quit but have been unsuccessful in their efforts.

## Nicotine Withdrawal

DSM-IV does not have a diagnostic category for nicotine intoxication; however, DSM-IV does have a diagnostic category for nicotine withdrawal (Table 12.9–2). Withdrawal symptoms from nicotine can develop within two hours of smoking the last cigarette, generally peak in the first 24 to 48 hours, and can last for weeks or months. The common symptoms include an intense craving for nicotine, tension, irritability, difficulty in concentrating, drowsiness and paradoxical trouble in sleeping, decreased heart rate and blood presure, increased appetite and weight gain, decreased motor performance, and increased muscle tension. A mild syndrome of nicotine withdrawal can appear when a smoker switches from regular cigarettes to low-nicotine cigarettes.

## Nicotine-Related Disorder Not Otherwise Specified

Nicotine-related disorder not otherwise specified (NOS) is a diagnostic category for nicotine-related disor-

ders that do not fit into one of the categories discussed above (Table 12.9–3). Such diagnoses may include nicotine intoxication, nicotine abuse, and mood disorders and anxiety disorders associated with nicotine use.

## CLINICAL FEATURES

Behaviorally, the stimulatory effects of nicotine result in improved attention, learning, reaction time, and problem-solving ability. The users of tobacco also report that cigarette smoking lifts their mood, decreases tension, and lessens depressive feelings. The effects of nicotine on the cerebral blood flow (CBF) have been studied, and the results suggest that short-term nicotine exposure increases the CBF without changing cerebral oxygen metabolism but that long-term nicotine exposure is associated with decreases in the CBF. In contrast to its stimulatory CNS effects, nicotine acts as a skeletal muscle relaxant.

### Adverse Effects

Nicotine is a highly toxic chemical. Doses of 60 mg in an adult are fatal secondary to respiratory paralysis; doses of 0.5 mg are delivered by smoking the average cigarette. In low doses the signs and symptoms of nicotine toxicity include nausea, vomiting, salivation, pallor (caused by peripheral vasoconstriction), weakness, abdominal pain (caused by increased peristalsis), diarrhea, dizziness, headache, increased blood pressure, tachycardia, tremor, and cold sweats. Toxicity is also associated with an inability to concentrate, confusion, and sensory disturbances. Nicotine is further associated with a decrease in the user's amount of rapid eye movement (REM) sleep. Tobacco use during pregnancy has been associated with an increased incidence of low-birth-weight babies.

### Health Benefits of Smoking Cessation

In a report by the Surgeon General in 1990 on the health benefits of smoking cessation, the following five major conclusions were reached: (1) Smoking cessation has major and immediate health benefits for persons of all ages and provides benefits for persons with and without smoking-related diseases. (2) Former smokers live longer than do those who continue to smoke. (3) Smoking cessation decreases the risk for lung cancer and other cancers, myocardial infarction, cerebrovascular diseases, and chronic lung diseases. (4) Women who stop smoking before pregnancy or during the first three to four months of pregnancy reduce their risk for having low-birth-weight infants to that of women who never smoked. (5) The health benefits of smoking cessation substantially exceed any risks from the

**Table 12.9–3**
**Nicotine-Related Disorder Not Otherwise Specified**

The nicotine-related disorder not otherwise specified category is for disorders associated with the use of nicotine that are not classifiable as nicotine dependence or nicotine withdrawal.

Table from DSM-IV, *Diagnostic and Statistical Manual of Mental Disorders*, ed 4. Copyright American Psychiatric Association, Washington, 1994. Used with permission.

average five-pound (2.3-kilogram) weight gain or any adverse psychological effects after quitting.

## TREATMENT

The combined use of transdermal nicotine administration (nicotine patches) and behavioral counseling has resulted in sustained abstinence rates of 60 percent in well-controlled clinical trials. That figure is significantly greater than the estimated 10 percent success rate for persons who quit cigarette smoking without specific support treatment. The most effective behavioral support programs address such issues as how to perform common daily activities (for example, eating, driving, and socializing) without smoking and how to cope with the dysphoric mood and the weight gain that can accompany smoking cessation. A further advantage of transdermal nicotine use is that doses of the nicotine can be individually titrated to patients' needs and their experiences of nicotine withdrawal symptoms. A variety of other psychopharmacological agents have also been used with some success in maintaining abstinence from nicotine. Those other preparations and drugs include nicotine-containing chewing gum, lobeline (a congener of nicotine), clonidine (Catapres), antidepressants—particularly fluoxetine (Prozac)—and buspirone (BuSpar). In addition, people who successfully discontinue smoking are likely to have been encouraged by someone close to them (such as a spouse or children), to have been fearful of the ill effects of smoking, and to have joined a support group of some type for ex-smokers. Encouragement from a non-smoking physician is also highly correlated with abstinence.

## References

Breslau N, Kilbey M M, Andreski P: Nicotine withdrawal symptoms and psychiatric disorders: Findings from an epidemiologic study of young adults. Am J Psychiatry 149: 464, 1992.

Carmell D, Swan G E, Robinette D, Fabsitz R: Genetic influence on smoking: A study of male twins. N Engl J Med 327: 829, 1992.

DeGrandpre R J, Bickel W K, Rizvi S A, Hughes J R: Effects of income on drug choice in humans. J Exp Anal Behav 59: 483, 1993.

Fiore M C: Trends in cigarette smoking in the United States: The epidemiology of tobacco use. Med Clin North Am 76: 289, 1992.

Ginsberg D, Hall S M, Rosinski M: Partner support, psychological treatment, and nicotine gum in smoking treatment: An incremental study. Int J Addict 27: 503, 1992.

Hall S M, Tunstall C D, Vila K L, Duffy J: Weight gain prevention and smoking cessation: Cautionary findings. Am J Public Health 82: 799, 1992.

Hatsukami D K, Skoog K, Huber M, Hughes J: Signs and symptoms from nicotine gum abstinence. Psychopharmacology 104: 496, 1991.

Hughes J R, Gust S W, Skoog K, Keenan R M, Fenwick J W: Symptoms of tobacco withdrawal: A replication and extension. Arch Gen Psychiatry 48: 52, 1991.

Le Houezec J, Benowitz N L: Basic and clinical psychopharmacology of nicotine. Clin Chest Med 12: 681, 1991.

Miller G H, Golish J A, Cox C E: A physician's guide to smoking cessation. J Fam Pract 34: 759, 1992.

National Institute on Drug Abuse: National Household Survey, Highlights 1991. U S Government Printing Office, Washington, 1991.

Newhouse P A, Hughes J R: The role of nicotine and nicotinic mechanisms in neuropsychiatric disease. Br J Addict 86: 521, 1991.

Perkins K A, Grobe J E, Epstein L H, Caggiula A, Stiller R L, Jacob R G: Chronic and acute tolerance to subjective effects of nicotine. Pharmacol Biochem Behav 45: 375, 1993.

Pomerleau D F: Nicotine and the central nervous system: Biobehavioral effects of cigarette smoking. Am J Med 93(1A): 2S, 1992.

Russell M A, Stapleton J A, Feyerabend C, Wiseman S M, Gustavsson G, Sawe U, Connor P: Targeting heavy smokers in general practice: Randomised controlled trial of transdermal nicotine patches. BMJ 306: 1308, 1993.

Schelling T C: Addictive drugs: The cigarette experience. Science 255: 430, 1992.

Schwartz J L: Methods of smoking cessation. Med Clin North Am 76: 451, 1992.

Srivastava E D, Russell M A, Feyerabend C, Masterson J G, Rhodes J: Sensitivity and tolerance to nicotine in smokers and nonsmokers. Psychopharmacology 105: 63, 1991.

Stolerman I P, Shoaib M: The neurobiology of tobacco addiction. Trends Pharmacol Sci 12: 467, 1991.

Vaughan D A: Frontiers in pharmacologic treatment of alcohol, cocaine, and nicotine dependence. Psychiatr Ann 20: 695, 1990.

Warburton D M: Nicotine as a cognitive enhancer. Prog Neuropsychopharmacol Biol Psychiatry 16: 181, 1992.

# 12.10 / Opioid-Related Disorders

In addition to the morbidity and the mortality associated directly with the opioid-related disorders, the association between the transmission of the human immunodeficiency virus (HIV) and intravenous opioid and opiate use is now recognized as a leading national health concern. Although the focus on acquired immune deficiency syndrome (AIDS) and intravenous substance use has emphasized the use of those drugs by disenfranchised groups in society, the following case report illustrates an opioid-related disorder in a patient who may be considered mainstream.

A 42-year-old executive in a public relations firm was referred for psychiatric consultation by his surgeon, who discovered him sneaking large quantities of a codeine-containing cough medicine into the hospital. The patient had been a heavy cigarette smoker for 20 years and had a chronic hacking cough. He had come to the hospital for a hernia repair and found the pain from the incision unbearable when he coughed.

An operation on his back five years ago had led his doctor to prescribe codeine to help relieve the incisional pain. Over the intervening five years, however, the patient had continued to use codeine-containing tablets and had increased his intake to 60 to 90 tablets (5 mg) daily. He stated that he often "just took them by the handful—not to feel good, you understand, just to get by." He had spent considerable time and effort developing a circle of physicians and pharmacists to whom he would make the rounds at least three times a week to obtain new supplies of pills. He had tried several times to stop using codeine but had failed. He had lost two jobs because of lax work habits, and he was divorced by his wife of 11 years.

The words "opiate" and "opioid" come from the word "opium," the juice of the opium poppy, Papaver somniferum, which contains approximately 20 opium alkaloids, including morphine. (The fourth edition of Diagnostic and Statistical Manual of Mental Disorders [DSM-IV] uses the word "opioid" to encompass "opiate," any preparation or derivative of opium, as well as "opioid," a synthetic narcotic that resembles an opiate in action but that is not derived from opium.) The naturally occurring opiates are smuggled into the United States from the Middle East and the Far East, where the opium poppy is a major revenue-producing crop. Other naturally occurring opiates or opiates that are synthesized from naturally occurring opiates

**440** ☐ *Chapter 12. SUBSTANCE-RELATED DISORDERS*

are heroin (diacetylmorphine), codeine (3-methoxymorphine), and hydromorphone (Dilaudid). Heroin is about twice as potent as morphine and is the most commonly used opiate in persons with opioid-related disorders.

Heroin, which is pharmacologically similar to morphine, induces analgesia, drowsiness, and changes in mood. Although the manufacture, the sale, and the possession of heroin are illegal in the United States, attempts have been made to make heroin available to pain-ridden terminal cancer patients because of its excellent analgesic and euphoric effects. Many people, including some legislators, favor a change in the law, but such legislation has been repeatedly voted down by the U.S. Congress.

A large number of synthetic narcotics (opioids) have been manufactured, including meperidine (Demerol), methadone (Dolophine), pentazocine (Talwin), and propoxyphene (Darvon). Methadone is the current gold standard in the treatment of opioid dependence. Opioid antagonists have been synthesized to treat opioid overdose and opioid dependence, and that class of drugs includes naloxone (Narcan), naltrexone (Trexan), nalorphine, levallorphan, and apomorphine. A number of compounds with mixed agonist and antagonist activity at opiate receptors have been synthesized, and they include pentazocine, butorphanol (Stadol), and buprenorphine (Buprenex). A number of studies have found buprenorphine to be an effective treatment for opioid dependence.

## EPIDEMIOLOGY

Heroin is the most widely used opiate in persons with opioid dependence. In 1991 an estimated 1.3 percent of the United States population had used heroin at least once. About 500,000 persons with opioid dependence are in the United States, about half of them in New York City. The male-to-female ratio of persons with opioid dependence is about 3 to 1. Typically, users of opiates and opioids started to use substances in their teens and early 20s; currently, most persons with opioid dependence are in their 30s and 40s. In the United States, persons tend to experience their first opioid-induced experience in their early teens or even as young as 10 years old. Such early induction into the drug culture is likely to happen in communities in which substance abuse is rampant and in families in which the parents are substance abusers. Heroin habits can cost a person hundreds of dollars a day; thus, the person with opioid dependence needs to obtain money through criminal activities and prostitution. The involvement of persons with opioid dependence in prostitution accounts for much of the spread of HIV.

The following epidemiological data come from the National Institute on Drug Abuse (NIDA):
In 1991 an estimated 1.3 percent of the population reported that they had ever used heroin. Use in the past month was so low that reliable estimates could not be developed.

The rates of use of heroin in their lifetimes were significantly higher among adults aged 26 to 34 (1.8 percent) than among adults aged 18 to 25 (0.8 percent) or youths aged 12 to 17 (0.3 percent).

Between 1990 and 1991 the prevalence of lifetime heroin use among adults aged 35 and older increased significantly, from 0.7 percent to 1.5 percent. No other changes for specific age groups were statistically significant.

## NEUROPHARMACOLOGY

The primary effects of the opiates and the opioids are mediated through the opiate receptors, which were discovered in the second half of the 1970s. The μ-opiate receptors are involved in the regulation and the mediation of analgesia, respiratory depression, constipation, and dependence; the κ-opiate receptors with analgesia, diuresis, and sedation; and the Δ-opiate receptors possibly with analgesia.

In 1974 enkephalin, an endogenous pentapeptide with opiatelike actions, was identified. That discovery led to the identification of three classes of endogenous opiates within the brain, including the endorphins and the enkephalins. Endorphins are involved in neural transmission and serve to suppress pain. They are released naturally in the body when a person is physically hurt and account in part for the absence of pain during acute injuries.

The opiates and the opioids also have significant effects on the dopaminergic and noradrenergic neurotransmitter systems. Several types of data indicate that the addictive, rewarding properties of opiates and opioids are mediated through the activation of the ventral tegmental area dopaminergic neurons that project to the cerebral cortex and the limbic system.

Heroin is the most commonly abused opiate and is more potent and lipid-soluble than morphine. Because of those properties, heroin crosses the blood-brain barrier in less time and has a more rapid onset than does morphine. Heroin was first introduced as a treatment of morphine addiction, but it is, in fact, more dependence-producing than is morphine. Codeine, which occurs naturally as about 0.5 percent of the opiate alkaloids in opium, is absorbed easily through the gastrointestinal tract and is subsequently transformed into morphine in the body. At least one positron emission tomographic (PET) study has suggested that one effect of all opiates and opioids is a decrease in cerebral blood flow in selected brain regions in persons with opioid dependence (Figure 12.10–1).

### Tolerance and Dependence

Tolerance to opiates and opioids develops rapidly and can, for example, be so profound that terminally ill cancer patients may need 200 to 300 mg a day of morphine, whereas a dose of 60 mg can easily be fatal to an opiate-naive person. The symptoms of opioid withdrawal, however, do not occur unless a person has been using opiates or opioids for a long time or when the cessation is particularly abrupt, as functionally occurs when an opiate antagonist is given. The long-term use of opiates or opioids results in changes in the number and the sensitivity of opiate receptors, which are mediators for at least some of the effects of tolerance and withdrawal. Although long-term use is associated with increased sensitivity of the dopaminergic, cholinergic, and serotonergic neurons, the effect of opiates and opioids on the noradrenergic neurons is probably the primary mediator of the symptoms of opioid withdrawal (Figure 12.1–2). Short-term use of opiates or opioids decreases the activity of the noradrenergic neurons in the locus ceruleus; long-term use activates a compensatory homeostatic mechanism within the neurons; and opioid withdrawal results in a rebound hyperactivity. That hypothesis also provides a basis for why clonidine (Catapres), an α$_2$-adrenergic receptor agonist that decreases the release of norepinephrine, is useful in the treatment of opioid withdrawal symptoms.

## ACUTE OPIATE ACTION IN THE LC

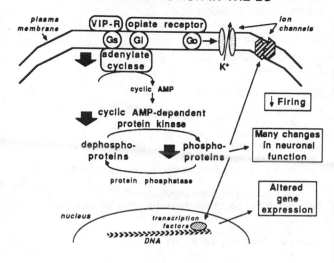

## CHRONIC OPIATE ACTION IN THE LC

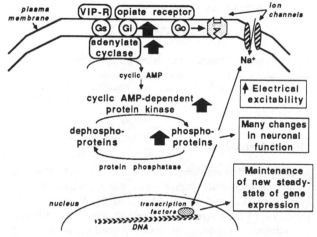

**Figure 12.10–1.** Schematic illustration of the mechanisms of short-term and long-term opiate action in the locus ceruleus (LC). (*Top*) Opiates inhibit LC neurons by increasing the conductance of a K$^+$ channel (*stippled*) by coupling with a pertussis toxin-inhibitable G protein (perhaps G$_o$) and by decreasing the conductance of a nonspecific cation channel (*hatched*) through coupling with the inhibitory G protein (G$_i$) and the consequent inhibition of the adenosine 3$^1$, 5$^1$-cyclic phosphate (cAMP) pathway (*large downward arrows*) and reduced phosphorylation of the channel or a closely associated protein. Inhibition of the cAMP pathway, through decreased phosphorylation of numerous other proteins, affects many processes in the neuron; in addition to reducing the firing rates, for example, it initiates alterations in gene expression through regulation of transcription factors. (*Bottom*) Long-term administration of opiates leads to a compensatory up-regulation of the cAMP pathway (*large upward arrows*); that contributes to opiate dependence in the neurons by increasing their intrinsic excitability through increased activation of the nonspecific cation channel. In addition, up-regulation of the cAMP pathway is presumably associated with persistent changes in transcription factors that maintain the long-term morphine-treated state. Long-term opiate administration also leads to a relative decrease in the degree of activation of the K$^+$ channel because of tolerance, the mechanism of which is unknown. Also shown in the figure are *VIP-R*, vasoactive intestinal polypeptide receptor (VIP is a major activator of the cAMP pathway in the LC), and G$_s$, the stimulatory G protein that activates adenylate cyclase. (Figure from E J Nestler: Molecular mechanisms of drug addiction. J Neurosci *12*: 2441, 1992. Used with permission.)

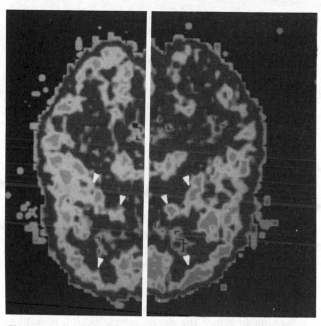

**Figure 12.10–2.** Glucose utilization, as revealed by positron emission tomography, in the brain of a heroin addict. High rates are pictured as light areas. On the left, the addict was given a placebo. On the right, the addict was given 30 mg of morphine intramuscularly. (Figure courtesy of E. D. London, Ph.D.)

## ETIOLOGY

### Societal and Cultural Factors

Opioid dependence is not limited to the low socioeconomic classes, although the incidence of opioid dependence is higher in those groups than in higher socioeconomic classes. A variety of social factors associated with urban poverty probably contribute to opioid dependence. About 50 percent of urban heroin users are children of single parents or divorced parents and are from families in which at least one other member has a substance-related disorder. Children from such settings are at high risk for opioid dependence, especially if they also evidence behavioral problems in school or other signs of conduct disorder.

Some consistent behavior patterns seem to be especially pronounced in adolescents with opioid dependence. Those patterns have been called the *heroin behavior syndrome*: underlying depression, often of an agitated type and frequently accompanied by anxiety symptoms; impulsiveness expressed by a passive-aggressive orientation; fear of failure; use of heroin as an antianxiety agent to mask feelings of low self-esteem, hopelessness, and aggression; limited coping strategies and low frustration tolerance, accompanied by the need for immediate gratification; sensitivity to drug contingencies, with a keen awareness of the relation between good feelings and the act of drug taking; feelings of behavioral impotence counteracted by momentary control over the life situation by means of substances; disturbances in social and interpersonal relationships with peers maintained by mutual substance experiences.

### Comorbidity (Dual Diagnosis)

About 90 percent of persons with opioid dependence have an additional psychiatric diagnosis. The most common comorbid psychiatric diagnoses are major depressive disorder, alcohol-related disorders, antisocial personality disorder, and anxiety disorders. About 15 percent of persons with opioid dependence attempt to commit suicide at least once. The high prevalence of comorbidity with other psychiatric diagnoses highlights the need to develop a broad-based treatment program that also addresses the associated psychiatric disorders in the patient.

## Biological and Genetic Factors

A person with an opioid-related disorder may have had a genetically determined hypoactivity of the opiate system. Such hypoactivity may be caused by opiate receptors that were too few or were less sensitive than possible, by having too little release of endogenous opiates, or by having too high concentrations of a hypothesized endogenous opiate antagonist. A number of researchers are investigating those possibilities. A biological predisposition to an opioid-related disorder may also be associated with abnormal functioning in either the dopaminergic neurotransmitter system or the noradrenergic neurotransmitter system. Because of the difficulties inherent in the study of substance-related disorders, the data are still limited; however, some data do support the idea that there are genetic determinants for the development of opioid-related disorders.

## Psychoanalytic Theory

In the psychoanalytic literature the behavior of narcotic addicts was described in terms of libidinal fixation, with regression to pregenital, oral, or even more archaic levels of psychosexual development. The need to explain the relation of drug abuse, defense mechanisms, impulse control, affective disturbances, and adaptive mechanisms led to the shift from psychosexual formulations to formulations emphasizing ego psychology. Serious ego pathology is often thought to be associated with substance abuse and is considered to be indicative of profound developmental disturbances. Problems of the relation between the ego and affects emerge as a key area of difficulty.

## DIAGNOSIS

DSM-IV lists a number of opioid-related disorders (Table 12.10–1) but contains specific diagnostic criteria only for opioid intoxication (Table 12.10–2) and opioid withdrawal (Table 12.10–3) within the section on opioid-related disorders. The diagnostic criteria for the other opioid-related disorders are contained within the DSM-IV sections that deal specifically with the predominant symptom—for example, opioid-induced mood disorder (Section 15.3).

## Opioid Dependence and Opioid Abuse

Opioid dependence and opioid abuse are defined in DSM-IV according to the general criteria for those disorders (Tables 12.1–6, 12.1–7, and 12.1–8).

**Table 12.10–1**
**Opioid-Related Disorders**

*Opioid use disorders*
**Opioid dependence**
**Opioid abuse**

*Opioid-induced disorders*
**Opioid intoxication**
  *Specify if:*
    with perceptual disturbances
**Opioid withdrawal**
**Opioid intoxication delirium**
**Opioid-induced psychotic disorder, with delusions**
  *Specify if:*
    with onset during intoxication
**Opioid-induced psychotic disorder, with hallucinations**
  *Specify if:*
    with onset during intoxication
**Opioid-induced mood disorder**
  *Specify if:*
    with onset during intoxication
**Opioid-induced sexual dysfunction**
  *Specify if:*
    with onset during intoxication
**Opioid-induced sleep disorder**
  *Specify if:*
    with onset during intoxication
    with onset during withdrawal

**Opioid-related disorder not otherwise specified**

Table based on DSM-IV, *Diagnostic and Statistical Manual of Mental Disorders*, ed 4. Copyright American Psychiatric Association, Washington, 1994. Used with permission.

## Opioid Intoxication

DSM-IV defines opioid intoxication as including maladaptive behavioral changes and some specific physical symptoms of opioid use (Table 12.10–2). In general, the presence of an altered mood, psychomotor retardation, drowsiness, slurred speech, and impaired memory and attention in the presence of other indicators of recent opioid use strongly suggests a diagnosis of opioid intoxication. DSM-IV allows for the specification of "with perceptual disturbances."

## Opioid Withdrawal

The general rule regarding the onset and the duration of withdrawal symptoms is that substances with short durations of action tend to produce short, intense withdrawal syndromes and that substances with long durations of action produce prolonged but mild withdrawal syndromes. An exception to the rule is that narcotic antagonist-precipitated withdrawal after long-acting opiate or opioid dependence can be severe.

An abstinence syndrome can be precipitated by the administration of an opiate antagonist. The symptoms may begin within seconds of such an intravenous injection and may peak in about one hour. Opiate craving rarely occurs in the context of analgesic administration for pain from physical disorders or surgery. The full withdrawal syndrome, including intense craving for opiates or opioids, usually occurs only secondary to an abrupt cessation of use in persons with opioid dependence.

**Morphine and heroin.** The morphine and heroin with-

**Table 12.10–2**
**Diagnostic Criteria for Opioid Intoxication**

A. Recent use of an opioid.

B. Clinically significant maladaptive behavioral or psychological changes (e.g., initial euphoria followed by apathy, dysphoria, psychomotor agitation or retardation, impaired judgment, or impaired social or occupational functioning) that developed during, or shortly after, opioid use.

C. Pupillary constriction (or pupillary dilation due to anoxia from severe overdose) and one (or more) of the following signs, developing during, or shortly after, opioid use:

   (1) drowsiness or coma
   (2) slurred speech
   (3) impairment in attention or memory

D. The symptoms are not due to a general medical condition and are not better accounted for by another mental disorder.

Specify if:
**with perceptual disturbances**

Table from DSM-IV, *Diagnostic and Statistical Manual of Mental Disorders*, ed 4. Copyright American Psychiatric Association, Washington, 1994. Used with permission.

**Table 12.10–3**
**Diagnostic Criteria for Opioid Withdrawal**

A. Either of the following:

  (1) cessation of (or reduction in) opioid use that has been heavy and prolonged (several weeks or longer).
  (2) administration of an opioid antagonist after a period of opioid use

B. Three (or more) of the following, developing within minutes to several days after criterion A:

   (1) dysphoric mood
   (2) nausea or vomiting
   (3) muscle aches
   (4) lacrimation or rhinorrhea
   (5) pupillary dilation, piloerection, or sweating
   (6) diarrhea
   (7) yawning
   (8) fever
   (9) insomnia

C. The symptoms in criterion B cause clinically significant distress or impairment in social, occupational, or other important areas of functioning.

D. The symptoms are not due to a general medical condition and are not better accounted for by another mental disorder.

Table from DSM-IV, *Diagnostic and Statistical Manual of Mental Disorders*, ed 4. Copyright American Psychiatric Association, Washington, 1994. Used with permission.

drawal syndrome begins in six to eight hours after the last dose, usually after a one-to-two-week period of continuous use or the administration of a narcotic antagonist. The withdrawal syndrome reaches its peak intensity during the second or third day and subsides during the next 7 to 10 days. However, some symptoms may persist for six months or longer.

**Meperidine.** The withdrawal syndrome from meperidine begins quickly, reaches a peak in 8 to 12 hours, and is complete in four to five days.

**Methadone.** Methadone withdrawal usually begins one to three days after the last dose and is complete in 10 to 14 days.

**Symptoms.** Opioid withdrawal is officially defined in DSM-IV (Table 12.10–3). The disorder consists of severe muscle cramps and bone aches, profuse diarrhea, abdominal cramps, rhinorrhea, lacrimation, piloerection or gooseflesh (from which comes the term "cold turkey" for the abstinence syndrome), yawning, fever, pupillary dilation, hypertension, tachycardia, and temperature dysregulation, including hypothermia and hyperthermia. A person with opioid dependence seldom dies from opioid withdrawal, unless the person has a severe preexisting physical illness, such as cardiac disease. Residual symptoms—such as insomnia, bradycardia, temperature dysregulation, and a craving for opiates or opioids—may persist for months after withdrawal. At any time during the abstinence syndrome, a single injection of morphine or heroin eliminates all the symptoms. Associated features of opioid withdrawal include restlessness, irritability, depression, tremor, weakness, nausea, and vomiting.

**Opioid Intoxication Delirium**

Opioid intoxication delirium is a diagnostic category within DSM-IV (Section 10.2). Opioid intoxication delir-

ium is most likely to happen when opiates or opioids are used in high doses, are mixed with other psychoactive compounds, or are used by a person with preexisting brain damage or a central nervous system (CNS) disorder (for example, epilepsy).

**Opioid-Induced Psychotic Disorder**

Opioid-induced psychotic disorder can begin during opioid intoxication. The DSM-IV diagnostic criteria are contained in the section on schizophrenia and other psychotic disorders (Section 14.1). The clinician can specify whether the predominant symptoms are hallucinations or delusions.

**Opioid-Induced Mood Disorder**

Opioid-induced mood disorder, which can begin during opioid intoxication, is a diagnostic category in DSM-IV (Section 15.3). Opioid-induced mood disorder symptoms may be of a manic, depressed, or mixed nature, depending on the person's response to the opiates or opioids. A person coming to psychiatric attention with opioid-induced mood disorder usually has mixed symptoms, combining irritability, expansiveness, and depression.

**Opioid-Induced Sleep Disorder and Opioid-Induced Sexual Dysfunction**

Opioid-induced sleep disorder (Section 23.2) and opioid-induced sexual dysfunction (Section 20.2) are diagnostic categories in DSM-IV. Hypersomnia is likely to be a more common sleep disorder with opiates or opioids than is insomnia. The most common sexual dysfunction is likely to be impotence.

## Opioid-Related Disorder Not Otherwise Specified

DSM-IV includes diagnoses for opioid-related disorders with symptoms of delirium, abnormal mood, psychosis, abnormal sleep, and sexual dysfunction. Clinical situations that do not fit into those categories are examples of appropriate cases for the use of the DSM-IV diagnosis of opioid-related disorder not otherwise specified (NOS) (Table 12.10–4).

## CLINICAL FEATURES

Opiates and opioids can be taken orally, snorted intranasally, injected intravenously (Figure 12.10–3), or injected subcutaneously (Figure 12.10–4). Opiates and opioids are subjectively addictive because of the euphoric high (the *rush*) experienced by opiate and opioid users, especially those who take the substances intravenously. The associated symptoms include a feeling of warmth, heaviness of the extremities, dry mouth, itchy face (especially the nose), and facial flushing. The initial euphoria is followed by a period of sedation, known in street parlance as *nodding off*. For opioid-naive persons, the use of opiates or opioids can induce dysphoria, nausea, and vomiting.

The physical effects of opiates and opioids include respiratory depression, pupillary constriction, smooth-muscle contraction (including the ureters and the bile ducts), constipation, and changes in blood pressure, heart rate, and body temperature. The respiratory depressant effects are mediated at the level of the brainstem and are additive to the effects of the phenothiazines and the monoamine oxidase inhibitors.

## Adverse Effects

The most common and most serious adverse effect associated with the opioid-related disorders is the potential transmission of hepatitis and HIV through the use of contaminated needles by more than one person. Another serious adverse effect is an idiosyncratic drug interaction between meperidine and monoamine oxidase inhibitors

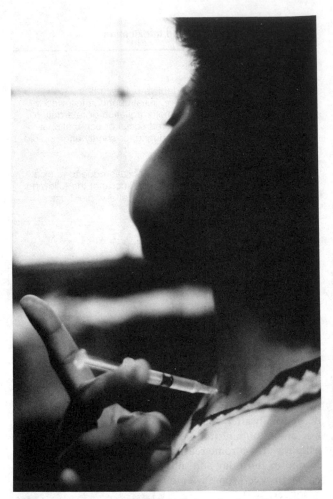

**Figure 12.10–3.** A heroin user puffs her cheeks to force blood into the jugular vein. (Figure courtesy of Steve Raymer, Copyright National Geographic Society, 1985.)

(MAOIs) that can result in gross autonomic instability, severe behavioral agitation, coma, seizures, and death. Idiosyncratic allergic reactions to opiates and opioids can also occur, resulting in anaphylactic shock, pulmonary edema, and death if the person does not receive prompt and adequate treatment.

## Opioid Overdose

Death from an overdose of an opiate or an opioid is almost always due to respiratory arrest from the respiratory depressant effect of the drug. The symptoms of overdose include marked unresponsiveness, coma, slow respiration, hypothermia, hypotension, and bradycardia. When presented with the clinical triad of coma, pinpoint pupils, and respiratory depression, the clinician should consider opiate or opioid overdose as a primary diagnosis. The clinician can also inspect the patient's body for needle tracks in the arms, legs, ankles, groin, and even the dorsal vein of the penis.

**Overdose treatment.** Opiate or opioid overdose is a medical emergency. The patient's respiration is severely

**Table 12.10–4**
**Opioid-Related Disorder Not Otherwise Specified**

---

The opioid-related disorder not otherwise specified category is for disorders associated with the use of opioids that are not classified as opioid dependence, opioid abuse, opioid intoxication, opioid withdrawal, opioid intoxication delirium, opioid-induced psychotic disorder, opioid-induced mood disorder, opioid-induced sexual dysfunction, or opioid-induced sleep disorder.

---

Table from DSM-IV, *Diagnostic and Statistical Manual of Mental Disorders*, ed 4. Copyright American Psychiatric Association, Washington, 1994. Used with permission.

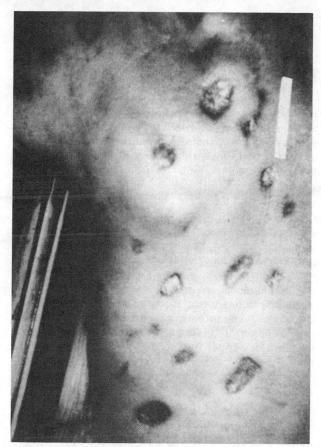

**Figure 12.10–4.** Skin-popper; circular depressed scars, often with underlying chronic abscesses, on the back of a subcutaneous narcotic user. Thighs are also commonly used skin-popping areas. (Figure courtesy of Michael Baden, M.D.)

depressed, and the patient may be semicomatose, comatose, or in shock. The first task is to make sure that the patient has an open airway and that vital signs are maintained. An opiate antagonist, naloxone, can be administered, 0.4 mg intravenously; that dose can be repeated four to five times within the first 30 to 45 minutes. The patient generally becomes responsive, but, because naloxone has a short duration of action, the patient may relapse into a semicomatose state in four or five hours; therefore, careful observation is imperative. Grand mal seizures occur with meperidine overdose and can be prevented by naloxone. Antagonists must be used carefully because they can precipitate a severe withdrawal reaction. Other narcotic antagonists useful in the treatment of overdose include nalorphine and levallorphan.

## MPTP-Induced Parkinsonism

In 1976, after ingesting an opioid contaminated with N-methyl-4-phenyl-1,2,3,6 tetrahydropyridine (MPTP), a number of persons had a syndrome of irreversible parkinsonism. The mechanism for the neurotoxic effect is as follows: MPTP is converted into 1-methyl-4-phenylpyridinium ($MPP^+$) by the enzyme monoamine oxidase and is then taken up by dopaminergic neurons. Because $MPP^+$ binds to melanin in substantia nigra neurons, $MPP^+$ is concentrated in those neurons and eventually kills the cells. Positron emission tomographic (PET) studies of persons who ingested MPTP but who remained asymptomatic have shown a decrease in the number of dopamine-binding sites in the substantia nigra, thus reflecting a loss in the number of dopaminergic neurons in that region.

## TREATMENT

### Education and Needle Exchange

Although the core treatment of opioid use disorders is the encouragement of abstinence from opiates and opioids, education about the transmission of HIV must receive equal priority. Persons with opioid dependence who use intravenous or subcutaneous routes of administration must be educated about safe-sex practices available to them. Although subject to intense political and societal pressures, free needle-exchange programs, where allowed, should be made available to persons with opioid dependence. Several studies have indicated that unsafe needle sharing is common when it is difficult to obtain a sufficient supply of clean needles and is common in persons with legal difficulties, severe substance problems, and psychiatric symptoms. Those are just the persons who may be most likely to be involved in the continued transmission of HIV.

### Methadone

Methadone is a synthetic narcotic (an opioid) that substitutes for heroin and can be taken orally. It is given to addicts in place of their usual substance of abuse, and it suppresses withdrawal symptoms. The action of methadone is such that 20 to 80 mg a day is sufficient to stabilize a patient, although dosages of up to 120 mg a day have been used. Methadone has a duration of action exceeding 24 hours, thus once-daily dosing is adequate. Methadone maintenance is continued until the patient can be withdrawn from methadone, which itself causes dependence. Patients are detoxified from methadone more easily than from heroin, although a similar abstinence syndrome occurs with methadone withdrawal. Usually, clonidine (Catapres) (0.1 to 0.3 mg three to four times a day) is given during the detoxification period.

Methadone maintenance has several advantages. First, it frees the person with opioid dependence from dependence on injectable heroin, thus reducing the chance of spreading HIV through the use of contaminated needles. Second, methadone causes minimal euphoria and rarely causes drowsiness or depression when taken for a long time. Third, methadone allows the patient to engage in gainful employment, instead of criminal activity. The major disadvantage is that the patient remains dependent on a narcotic.

### Other Opioid Substitutes

Levo-α-acetylmethadol (LAMM), a longer-acting opioid than methadone, is also used for the treatment of persons with opioid dependence. In contrast to the daily methadone treatment, LAMM can be administered in dosages of 30 to 80 mg three times a week. Buprenorphine is a mixed agonist-antagonist at the opiate receptor, and a number of studies have reported promising data regarding its use as an opioid substitute in treatment strategies.

## Opiate Antagonists

Opiate antagonists block or antagonize the effects of opiates and opioids. Unlike methadone, they do not in themselves exert narcotic effects and do not cause dependence. The antagonists include the following drugs: naloxone, which is used in the treatment of opiate and opioid overdose because it reverses the effects of narcotics, and naltrexone, which is the longest-acting (72 hours) antagonist. The theory behind the use of an antagonist for opioid-related disorders is that the blocking of opiate agonist effects, particularly euphoria, discourages persons with opioid dependence from substance-seeking behavior and thus deconditions their substance-seeking behaviors. The major weakness of the antagonist treatment model is the lack of any mechanism that compels the person to continue to take the antagonist.

## Pregnant Women with Opioid Dependence

Neonatal addiction is a significant problem; about three fourths of all infants born to addicted mothers experience the withdrawal syndrome.

Although opioid withdrawal is almost never fatal for the otherwise healthy adult, opioid withdrawal is hazardous to the fetus and can lead to miscarriage or fetal death. Maintaining the pregnant woman with opioid dependence on a low dosage of methadone (10 to 40 mg a day) may be the least hazardous course to follow. At that dosage, neonatal withdrawal is usually mild and can be managed with low doses of paregoric. If the pregnancy begins while the woman is taking high doses of methadone, the dosage should be reduced slowly (for example, 1 mg every three days), and fetal movements should be monitored. If withdrawal is necessary or desired, it is accomplished with least hazard during the second trimester.

**Fetal AIDS transmission.** The other major risk for the fetus of a woman with opioid dependence is AIDS. Pregnant women can pass HIV, the causative agent of AIDS, to the fetus through the placental circulation. The HIV-infected mother can also pass HIV to the infant through breast feeding.

## Psychotherapies

The entire range of psychotherapeutic modalities is appropriate for the treatment of opioid-related disorders in individual cases. Individual psychotherapy, behavioral therapy, cognitive-behavioral therapy, family therapy, support groups (such as Narcotics Anonymous), and social skills training may all prove to be effective treatments for specific patients. Social skills training should be particularly emphasized for patients who have few social skills with which to operate in the community. Family therapy

is almost always indicated when family members are still living with the patient.

## Therapeutic Communities

The therapeutic community is a residence composed of members who all have the same problem of substance abuse. Abstinence is the rule; in order to be admitted to such a community, the person must show a high level of motivation. The goals are to effect a complete change of life-style, including abstinence from substances; the development of personal honesty, responsibility, and useful social skills; and the elimination of antisocial attitudes and criminal behavior.

The staff members of most therapeutic communities are former substance-dependent persons, who often put the prospective candidate through a rigorous screening process to test the person's motivation. Self-help through the use of confrontational groups and isolation from the outside world and from friends associated with the drug life are emphasized. The prototypical community for substance-dependent persons is Phoenix House, where the residents live for long periods (usually 12 to 18 months) while receiving treatment. They are allowed to return to their old environments only when they have demonstrated their ability to handle increased responsibility within the therapeutic community. Therapeutic communities are effective, but they require large staffs and extensive facilities. Moreover, dropout rates are high; as many as 75 percent of those who enter therapeutic communities leave within the first month.

### References

Darke S, Wodak A, Hall W, Heather N, Ward J: Prevalence and predictors of psychopathology among opioid users. Br J Addict *87*: 771, 1992.
Di Chiara G, North R A: Neurobiology of opiate abuse. Trends Pharmacol Sci *13*: 185, 1992.
Goldstein A: Heroin addiction: Neurobiology, pharmacology, and policy. J Psychoactive Drugs *23*: 123, 1991.
Kane S: HIV, heroin and heterosexual relations. Soc Sci Med *32*: 1037, 1991.
Koob G F, Maldonado R, Stinus L: Neural substrates of opiate withdrawal. Trends Neurosci *15*: 186, 1992.
Kosten T A, Bianchi M S, Kosten T R: The predictive validity of the dependence syndrome in opiate abusers. Am J Drug Alcohol Abuse *18*: 145, 1992.
Kosten T R, Rosen M I, Schottenfeld R, Ziedonis D: Buprenorphine for cocaine and opiate dependence. Psychopharmacol Bull *28*: 15, 1992.
Kreek M J: Rationale for maintenance pharmacotherapy of opiate dependence. Res Publ Assoc Res Nerv Ment Dis *70*: 2, 1992.
Ling W, Wesson D R: Drugs of abuse: Opiates. West J Med *152*: 565, 1990.
London E D, Broussolle E P M, Links J M, Wong D F, Cascella N G, Dannals R F, Sano M, Herning R, Snyder F R, Rippetoe L R, Toung T J K, Jaffe J H: Morphine-induced metabolic changes in human brain: Studies with positron emission tomography and [fluorine 18] fluorodeoxyglucose. Arch Gen Psychiatry *47*: 73, 1990.
Luthar S S, Anton S F, Merikangas K R, Rounsaville B J: Vulnerability to substance abuse and psychopathology among siblings of opioid abusers. J Nerv Ment Dis *180*: 153, 1992.
Metzger D, Woody G, De Philippis D, McLellan A T, O'Brien C P, Platt J J: Risk factors for needle sharing among methadone-treated patients. Am J Psychiatry *148*: 636, 1991.
National Institute on Drug Abuse: *National Household Survey, Highlights, 1991.* U S Government Printing Office, Washington, 1991.
Neslter E J: Molecular mechanisms of drug addiction. J Neurosci *12*: 2439, 1992.
Novick D M, Joseph H: Medical maintenance: The treatment of chronic opiate dependence in general medical practice. J Subst Abuse Treat *8*: 233, 1991.

Platt J J, Husband S D, Taube D: Major psychotherapeutic modalities for heroin addiction: A brief overview. Int J Addict 25: 1453, 1990.

Resnick R B, Galanter M, Pycha C, Cohen A, Grandison P, Flood N: Buprenorphine: An alternative to methadone for heroin dependence treatment. Psychopharmacol Bull 28: 109, 1992.

Rounsaville B J, Hosten T R, Weissman M M, Prusoff B, Pauls D, Anton S F, Merikangas K: Psychiatric disorders in relatives of probands with opiate addiction. Arch Gen Psychiatry 48: 33, 1991.

Trujillo K A, Akil H: Opiate tolerance and dependence: Recent findings and synthesis. New Biol 3: 915, 1991.

# 12.11 / Phencyclidine (or Phencyclidinelike)-Related Disorders

Phencyclidine [1-(1-phenylcyclohexy-1)piperidine] is the most commonly abused arylcyclohexylamine. Phencyclidine is most commonly known as PCP, but it is also referred to as angel dust, crystal, peace, supergrass (when sprinkled on a cannabis cigarette), hog, rocket fuel, and horse tranq's. PCP was developed and is classified as a dissociative anesthetic; however, its use as an anesthetic in humans was associated with disorientation, agitation, delirium, and unpleasant hallucinations on awakening. For those reasons, PCP is no longer used as an anesthetic in humans, although it is used in some countries in veterinary medicine as an anesthetic. A related compound, ketamine, is still used as a human anesthetic in the United States; it has not been associated with the same adverse effects, although ketamine is also subject to abuse by humans.

PCP was first used illicitly in San Francisco in the late 1960s. Since then, about 30 chemical analogues have been produced and are intermittently available on the streets of major United States cities.

The effects of PCP are similar to those of such hallucinogens as lysergic acid diethylamide (LSD); however, because of differing pharmacology and some difference in clinical effects, DSM-IV classifies the arylcyclohexylamines as a separate category. PCP has also been of interest to schizphrenia researchers, who have used PCP-induced chemical and behavioral changes in animals as a possible model of schizophrenia.

## EPIDEMIOLOGY

PCP and some of the related substances are relatively easy to synthesize in illegal laboratories and are relatively inexpensive to buy on the streets. The variable quality of the laboratories, however, results in a range of potency and purity. PCP use varies most markedly as a factor of geography. Some areas of some cities have a 10-fold higher usage rate of PCP than do other areas. The highest PCP use in the United States is in Washington, D.C., where PCP accounts for 18 percent of all substance-related deaths. In Los Angeles, Chicago, and Baltimore the com-parable figure is 6 percent. The national average is 3 percent. In general, PCP is used by men, aged 20 to 40, who are members of a minority group. Most users of PCP also use other substances, particularly alcohol but also opiates, opioids, marijuana, amphetamines, and cocaine.

## NEUROPHARMACOLOGY

PCP and its related compounds are variously sold as a crystalline powder, paste, liquid, or drug-soaked paper (blotter). PCP is most commonly used as an additive to a cannabis- or parsley-containing cigarette. Experienced users report that the effects of 2 to 3 mg of smoked PCP occur in about five minutes and plateau in 30 minutes. PCP has a bioavailability of about 75 percent when taken by intravenous administration and a bioavailability of about 30 percent when smoked. The half-life of PCP in humans is about 20 hours.

The primary pharmacodynamic effect of PCP is as an antagonist at the N-methyl-D-aspartate (NMDA) subtype of glutamate receptors. PCP binds to a site within the NMDA-associated calcium channel and prevents the influx of calcium ions. Another effect of PCP is the activation of the dopaminergic neurons of the ventral tegmental area, which project to the cerebral cortex and the limbic system. The activation of those neurons is usually involved in mediating the reinforcing qualities of PCP.

Tolerance for the effects of PCP does occur in humans, although physical dependence generally does not occur. However, in animals that are administered more PCP per pound for longer periods of time than in virtually any humans, PCP does induce physical dependence, such that marked withdrawal symptoms consisting of lethargy, depression, and craving do occur. Physical symptoms of withdrawal in humans are rare, probably as a function of dose and duration of use. Although physical dependence is rare in humans, psychological dependence is common, as some users become psychologically dependent on the PCP-induced psychological state.

The fact that PCP is made in illicit laboratories contributes to the increased likelihood of impurities in the final product. One such contaminant is 1-piperidenocyclohexane carbonitrite, which releases hydrogen cyanide in small quantities when ingested. Another contaminant is piperidine, which can be recognized by its strong fishy odor.

## DIAGNOSIS

The fourth edition of *Diagnostic and Statistical Manual of Mental Disorders* (DSM-IV) lists a number of phencyclidine (or phencyclidinelike)-related disorders (Table 12.11–1) but outlines the specific diagnostic criteria for only phencyclidine intoxication (Table 12.11–2) within the phencyclidine (or phencyclidinelike)-related disorders section. Other phencyclidine (or phencyclidinelike)-related disorders have their diagnostic criteria listed in the sections that deal with specific symptoms—for example, phencyclidine-induced anxiety disorder in the anxiety disorders section of DSM-IV (Section 16.1).

Table 12.11–1
**Phencyclidine-Related Disorders**

*Phencyclidine use disorders*

**Phencyclidine dependence**
**Phencyclidine abuse**

*Phencyclidine-induced disorders*

**Phencyclidine intoxication**
*Specify if:*
  with perceptual disturbances
**Phencyclidine intoxication delirium**
**Phencyclidine-induced psychotic disorder, with delusions**
*Specify if:*
  with onset during intoxication
**Phencyclidine-induced psychotic disorder, with hallucinations**
*Specify if:*
  with onset during intoxication
**Phencyclidine-induced mood disorder**
*Specify if:*
  with onset during intoxication
**Phencyclidine-induced anxiety disorder**
*Specify if:*
  with onset during intoxication

**Phencyclidine-related disorder not otherwise specified**

Table based on DSM-IV, *Diagnostic and Statistical Manual of Mental Disorders*, ed 4. Copyright American Psychiatric Association, Washington, 1994. Used with permission.

Table 12.11–2
**Diagnostic Criteria for Phencyclidine Intoxication**

A. Recent use of phencyclidine (or a related substance).

B. Clinically significant maladaptive behavioral changes (e.g., belligerence, assaultiveness, impulsiveness, unpredictability, psychomotor agitation, impaired judgment, or impaired social or occupational functioning) that developed during, or shortly after, use of phencyclidine.

C. Within an hour (less when smoked, "snorted," or used intravenously), two (or more) of the following signs:

  (1) vertical or horizontal nystagmus
  (2) hypertension or tachycardia
  (3) numbness or diminished responsiveness to pain
  (4) ataxia
  (5) dysarthria
  (6) muscle rigidity
  (7) seizures or coma
  (8) hyperacusis

D. The symptoms are not due to a general medical condition and are not better accounted for by another mental disorder.

*Specify* if:
  **with perceptual disturbances**

Table from DSM-IV, *Diagnostic and Statistical Manual of Mental Disorders*, ed 4. Copyright American Psychiatric Association, Washington, 1994. Used with permission.

## Dependence and Abuse

DSM-IV uses the general criteria for phencyclidine dependence and phencyclidine abuse (Tables 12.1–6, 12.1–7, and 12.1–8). Some long-term users of PCP are said to be crystallized, a syndrome characterized by dulled thinking, decreased reflexes, loss of memory, loss of impulse control, depression, lethargy, and impaired concentration.

## Intoxication

Short-term phencyclidine intoxication can have potentially severe complications and often must be considered a psychiatric emergency. Phencyclidine intoxication is defined by specific criteria in DSM-IV (Table 12.11–2). The clinician can specify the presence of perceptual disturbances.

Some patients may be brought to psychiatric attention within hours of ingesting PCP, but often two to three days elapse before psychiatric help is sought. The long interval between drug ingestion and the appearance of the patient in a clinic usually reflects the attempts of friends to deal with the psychosis by talking down; persons who lose consciousness are brought for help earlier than are those who remain conscious. Most patients recover completely within a day or two, but some remain psychotic for as long as two weeks. Patients who are first seen in a coma often manifest disorientation, hallucinations, confusion, and difficulty in communication on regaining consciousness. Those symptoms may also be seen in noncomatose patients, but their symptoms appear to be less severe than the comatose patients' symptoms. Sometimes the behavioral disturbances are severe; they may include public masturbation, stripping off clothes, violence, urinary incontinence, crying, and inappropriate laughing. Frequently, the patient has amnesia for the entire period of the psychosis.

## Intoxication Delirium

Phencyclidine intoxication delirium is included as a diagnostic category in DSM-IV (Section 10.2). An estimated 25 percent of all PCP-related emergency room patients may meet the criteria for the disorder, which can be characterized by agitated, violent, and bizarre behavior.

## Psychotic Disorder

Phencyclidine-induced psychotic disorder is included as a diagnostic category in DSM-IV (Section 14.1). The clinician can further specify whether delusions or hallucinations are the predominant symptoms. An estimated 6 percent of PCP-related emergency room patients may meet the criteria for the disorder. About 40 percent of those patients have physical signs of hypertension and nystagmus, and 10 percent have been injured accidentally during the psychosis. The psychosis can last from 1 to 30 days, with an average of four to five days.

## Mood Disorder

Phencyclidine-induced mood disorder is included as a diagnostic category in DSM-IV (Section 15.3). An estimated 3 percent of PCP-related emergency room patients meet the criteria for the disorder, with most fitting the criteria for a maniclike episode. About 40 to 50 percent of those persons have been accidentally injured during the course of their manic symptoms.

## Anxiety Disorder

Phencyclidine-induced anxiety disorder is included as a diagnostic category in DSM-IV (Section 16.1). Anxiety is probably the most common symptom that brings a PCP-intoxicated person to the emergency room seeking help.

## Phencyclidine-Related Disorder Not Otherwise Specified

The diagnosis of phencyclidine-related disorder not otherwise specified (NOS) is the appropriate diagnosis for a patient who does not fit into any of the above diagnoses (Table 12.11–3).

## CLINICAL FEATURES

The amount of PCP varies greatly from PCP-laced cigarette to cigarette; 1 gram may be used to make as few as four or as many as several dozen cigarettes. Less than 5 mg of PCP is considered a low dose, and doses above 10 mg are considered high. The variability of dose makes it difficult to predict the effect, although smoking PCP is the easiest and most reliable way users can titrate the dose.

People who have just taken PCP are frequently uncommunicative, appear to be oblivious, and report active fantasy production. They experience speedy feelings, euphoria, bodily warmth, tingling, peaceful floating sensations, and occasionally feelings of depersonalization, isolation, and estrangement. Sometimes they have auditory and visual hallucinations. They often have striking alterations of body image, distortions of space and time perception, and delusions. They may experience an intensification of dependence feelings, confusion, and disorganization of thought. Users may be sympathetic, sociable, and talkative at one moment but hostile and negative at another. Anxiety is sometimes reported; it is often the most prominent presenting symptom during an adverse reaction. Nystagmus, hypertension, and hyperthermia are common effects of PCP. Head-rolling movements, stroking, grimacing, muscle rigidity on stimulation, repeated episodes of vomiting, and repetitive chanting speech are sometimes observed.

The short-term effects last three to six hours and sometimes give way to a mild depression in which the user becomes irritable, somewhat paranoid, and occasionally belligerent, irrationally assaultive, suicidal, or homicidal.

**Table 12.11–3**
**Phencyclidine-Related Disorder Not Otherwise Specified**

The phencyclidine-related disorder not otherwise specified category is for disorders associated with the use of phencyclidine that are not classifiable as phencyclidine dependence, phencyclidine abuse, phencyclidine intoxication, phencyclidine intoxication delirium, phencyclidine-induced psychotic disorder, phencyclidine-induced mood disorder, or phencyclidine-induced anxiety disorder.

Table from DSM-IV, *Diagnostic and Statistical Manual of Mental Disorders*, ed 4. Copyright American Psychiatric Association, Washington, 1994. Used with permission.

The effects can last for several days. Users sometimes find that it takes one to two days to recover completely; laboratory tests show that PCP may remain in the patient's blood and urine for more than a week.

## Adverse Effects

As with the other effects of PCP, neurological and physiological symptoms are dose-related. PCP doses of more than 20 mg are likely to cause convulsions, coma, and death. Death can also be caused by hyperthermia and autonomic instability, for which benzodiazepine treatment may be useful. Another serious adverse effect associated with PCP use is rhabdomyolysis with associated renal failure, which may occur in 2 percent of all PCP users. A mild increase in muscle-derived creatinine phosphokinase occurs in about 70 percent of all PCP users. Among the common symptoms seen in emergency rooms are hypertension, increased pulse rate, and nystagmus (horizontal or vertical or both). At low doses, the patient may experience dysarthria, gross ataxia, and muscle rigidity, particularly of the face and the neck. Increased deep tendon reflexes and diminished response to pain are commonly observed. High doses may lead to massive heat production and fatal hyperthermia, agitated and repetitive movements, athetosis or clonic jerking of the extremities, and occasionally opisthotonic posturing. With even higher doses, patients may be drowsy, stuporous with their eyes open, comatose, and, in some instances, responsive only to noxious stimuli. Clonic movements and muscle rigidity may sometimes precede generalized seizure activity, and status epilepticus has been reported. Cheyne-Stokes breathing has also been observed; respiratory arrest can occur and be fatal. Vomiting, probably of central origin, may occur; hypersalivation and diaphoresis are occasional symptoms, and ptosis, usually bilateral, has been observed.

## DIFFERENTIAL DIAGNOSIS

Depending on the patient's status at the time of admission, the differential diagnosis may include sedative or narcotic overdose, psychotic disorder as a consequence of the use of psychedelic drugs, and brief psychotic disorder. Laboratory analysis may be helpful in establishing the diagnosis, particularly in the many cases in which the substance history is unreliable or unattainable.

## TREATMENT

The treatment for each of the phencyclidine (or phencyclidinelike)-related disorders is symptomatic. Talking down, which may work after hallucinogen use, is generally not useful for phencyclidine intoxication. Benzodiazepines and dopamine receptor antagonists are the drugs of choice for controlling behavior pharmacologically. The physician must monitor the patient's level of consciousness, blood pressure, temperature, and muscle activity and must be ready to treat severe medical abnormalities as necessary.

The clinician must carefully monitor unconscious patients, particularly those who have toxic reactions to PCP, because excessive secretions may interfere with already-compromised respiration. In an alert patient who has recently taken PCP, gastric lavage presents a risk of inducing laryngeal spasm and aspiration of emesis. Muscle spasms and seizures are best treated with diazepam (Valium). The environment should afford minimal sensory stimulation. Ideally, one person stays with the patient in a quiet, dark room. Four-point restraint is dangerous, because it may lead to rhabdomyolysis; total body immobilization may occasionally be necessary. A benzodiazepine is often effective in reducing agitation, but a patient with severe behavioral disturbances may require short-term treatment with a dopamine receptor antagonist—for example, haloperidol (Haldol). For patients with severe hypertension, a hypotensive-inducing drug such as phentolamine (Regitine) may be needed. Ammonium chloride in the early stage and ascorbic acid or cranberry juice later on are used to acidify the patient's urine and promote the elimination of the substance, although the efficacy of the procedure is controversial.

If the symptoms are not severe and if one can be certain that enough time has elapsed so that all the PCP has been absorbed, the patient may be monitored in the outpatient department and, if the symptoms improve, released to family or friends. Even at low doses, however, symptoms may worsen, requiring that the person be hospitalized to prevent violence and suicide.

### References

Baldridge E B, Bessen H A: Phencyclidine. Emerg Med Clin North Am 8: 541, 1990.
Carroll M E: PCP and hallucinogens. Adv Alcohol Subst Abuse 9: 167, 1990.
Gorelick D A, Wilkins J N: Inpatient treatment of PCP abusers and users. Am J Drug Alcohol Abuse 15: 1, 1989.
Gorelick D A, Wilkins J N, Wong C: Outpatient treatment of PCP abusers. Am J Drug Alcohol Abuse 15: 367, 1989.
Jansen K L: Ketamine: Can chronic use impair memory? Int J Addict 25: 133, 1990.
Javitt D C, Zukin S R: Recent advances in the phencyclidine model of schizophrenia. Am J Psychiatry 148: 1301, 1991.
National Institute on Drug Abuse: National Household Survey on Drug Abuse: Highlights, 1991. U S Government Printing Office, Washington, 1991.
Polkis A, Graham M, Maginn D, Branch C A, Gantner G E: Phencyclidine and violent deaths in St. Louis, Missouri: A survey of medical examiners' cases from 1977 through 1986. Am J Drug Alcohol Abuse 16: 265, 1990.
Rahbar F, Fomufod A, White D, Westney L S: Impact of intrauterine exposure to phencyclidine (PCP) and cocaine on neonates. J Natl Med Assoc 85: 349, 1993.
Tabor B L, Smith-Wallace T, Yonekura M L: Perinatal outcome associated with PCP versus cocaine use. Am J Drug Alcohol Abuse 16: 337, 1990.

# 12.12 / Sedative-, Hypnotic-, or Anxiolytic-Related Disorders

*Sedatives* are drugs that reduce subjective tension and induce mental calmness. The term "sedative" is virtually synonymous with the term "*anxiolytic*," which is a drug that reduces anxiety. *Hypnotics* are drugs that are used to induce sleep. The differentiation between anxiolytics and sedatives as daytime drugs and hypnotics as nighttime drugs is not accurate. When sedatives and anxiolytics are given in high doses, they can induce sleep, just as the hypnotics do. Conversely, when hypnotics are given in low doses, they can induce daytime sedation, just as the sedatives and anxiolytics do. In some literature, especially old literature, the sedatives, anxiolytics, and hypnotics are grouped together as the *minor tranquilizers*. That term is poorly defined and subject to ambiguous meanings and, therefore, is best avoided.

The drugs contained within this class of substance-related disorders are the benzodiazepines (for example, diazepam [Valium]), barbiturates (for example, secobarbital [Seconal]), and the barbituratelike substances, which include methaqualone (Quaalude), meprobamate (Equanil), and glutethimide (Doriden). The major nonpsychiatric indications for those drugs are as antiepileptics, muscle relaxants, anesthetics, and anesthetic adjuvants. All drugs of this class and alcohol are cross-tolerant, and their effects are additive. Physical and psychological dependence develop to all the drugs, and all are associated with withdrawal symptoms.

## SUBSTANCES

### Benzodiazepines

A wide variety of benzodiazepines, differing primarily in their half-lives, are available in the United States. Examples of benzodiazepines are diazepam, flurazepam (Dalmane), oxazepam (Serax), and chlordiazepoxide (Librium). Benzodiazepines are used primarily as anxiolytics, hypnotics, antiepileptics, and anesthetics and for alcohol withdrawal. After their introduction in the United States in the 1960s, the benzodiazepines rapidly became the most prescribed drugs; about 15 percent of all persons in this country have had a benzodiazepine prescribed by a physician. However, increasing awareness of the risks for dependence on benzodiazepines and increased regulatory requirements have caused a decrease in the number of benzodiazepine prescriptions. All benzodiazepines are classified as schedule IV controlled substances by the Drug Enforcement Agency (DEA).

### Barbiturates

Before the introduction of the benzodiazepines, the barbiturates were frequently prescribed; however, because of their high abuse potential, their use is much rarer today than in the past. Secobarbital (popularly known as reds, red devils, seggies, and downers), pentobarbital (Nembutal) (known as yellow jackets, yellows, and nembies), and a combination of secobarbital and amobarbital (Amytal) (known as reds and blues, rainbows, double-trouble, and tooies) are easily available on the street from drug dealers. Pentobarbital, secobarbital, and amobarbital are now under the same federal legal controls as morphine.

The first barbiturate, barbital (Veronal), was introduced in the United States in 1903. Barbital and phenobarbital (Luminal), which was introduced shortly thereafter, are long-acting drugs with half-lives of 12 to 24 hours. Amobarbital is an intermediate-acting barbiturate with a half-life of 6 to 12 hours. Pentobarbital and secobarbital are short-acting barbiturates with half-lives of three to six hours.

## Barbituratelike Substances

The most commonly abused barbituratelike substance is methaqualone, which is no longer manufactured in the United States. Methaqualone is often used by young people who believe that the substance heightens the pleasure of sexual activity. Abusers of methaqualone commonly take one or two standard tablets (usually 300 mg a tablet) to obtain the desired effects. The street names for methaqualone include mandrakes (from the United Kingdom preparation Mandrax) and soapers (from the brand name Sopor). Luding out (from the brand name Quaalude) means getting high on methaqualone, which is often combined with excessive alcohol intake.

## EPIDEMIOLOGY

About one quarter to one third of all substance-related emergency room visits involve substances from this class. The patients have a female-to-male ratio of 3 to 1 and a white-to-black ratio of 2 to 1. Benzodiazepines are abused alone, but cocaine abusers often use them to reduce withdrawal symptoms, and opiate and opioid abusers use them to enhance the euphoric effects of opiates and opioids. Benzodiazepines, because they are easily obtained, are also used by abusers of stimulants, hallucinogens, and phencyclidine (PCP) to help reduce the anxiety effects that can be caused by those substances.

Whereas barbiturate abuse is common among mature adults who have long histories of abuse of those substances, benzodiazepines are abused by a younger age group, usually under 40 years of age. That group of benzodiazepine abusers may have a slight male predominance, and a white-to-black ratio of about 2 to 1. Benzodiazepines are probably not abused as frequently as are other substances for the purpose of getting high, in the sense of inducing a euphoric feeling. Rather, benzodiazepines are used when the person wishes to experience a relaxed evening.

## NEUROPHARMACOLOGY

The benzodiazepines, barbiturates, and barbituratelike substances all have their primary effects on the $\gamma$-aminobutyric acid (GABA) type A ($GABA_A$) receptor complex, which contains a chloride ion channel, a binding site for GABA, and a well-defined binding site for benzodiazepines. The barbiturates and barbituratelike substances are also believed to bind somewhere on the $GABA_A$ receptor complex. When a benzodiazepine, barbiturate, or barbituratelike substance does bind to the complex, the effect is to increase the affinity of the receptor for its endogenous neurotransmitter, GABA, and to increase the flow of chloride ions through the channel into the neuron. The effect of the influx of negatively charged chloride ions into the neuron is inhibitory, since it hyperpolarizes the neuron relative to the extracellular space.

Although all the substances in this class induce tolerance and physical dependence, the mechanisms behind

those effects are best understood for the benzodiazepines. After long-term benzodiazepine use there is an attenuation of the receptor effects caused by the agonist. Specifically, after the long-term use of benzodiazepines, GABA stimulation of the $GABA_A$ receptors results in less influx of chloride than was caused by GABA stimulation before the benzodiazepine administration. That down-regulation of receptor response is not due to a decrease in receptor number or to a decrease in the affinity of the receptor for GABA. The basis for the down-regulation seems to be in the coupling between the GABA binding site and the activation of the chloride ion channel. That decreased efficiency in coupling may be regulated within the $GABA_A$ receptor complex itself or by other neuronal mechanisms.

## DIAGNOSIS

The fourth edition of *Diagnostic and Statistical Manual of Mental Disorders* (DSM-IV) lists a number of sedative-, hypnotic-, or anxiolytic-related disorders (Table 12.12–1) but contains specific diagnostic criteria only for sedative, hypnotic, or anxiolytic intoxication (Table 12.12–2) and sedative, hypnotic, or anxiolytic withdrawal (Table 12.12–3). Other sedative-, hypnotic-, or anxiolytic-related disorders have their diagnostic criteria outlined in those DSM-IV sections that are specific for the major symptom—for example, sedative-, hypnotic-, or anxiolytic-induced psychotic disorder (Section 14.1).

### Dependence and Abuse

Sedative, hypnotic, or anxiolytic dependence and sedative, hypnotic, or anxiolytic abuse are diagnosed according to the general criteria in DSM-IV for substance dependence and substance abuse (Tables 12.1–6, 12.1–7, and 12.1–8).

### Intoxication

DSM-IV contains a single set of diagnostic criteria for intoxication by any sedative, hypnotic, or anxiolytic substance (Table 12.12–2). Although the intoxication syndromes induced by all those drugs are similar, subtle clinical differences are observable, especially with intoxications that involve low doses. The diagnosis of intoxication by one of this class of substances is best confirmed by obtaining a blood sample for substance screening.

**Benzodiazepines.** Benzodiazepine intoxication can be associated with behavioral disinhibition, potentially resulting in hostile or aggressive behavior in some persons. The effect is perhaps most common when benzodiazepines are taken in combination with alcohol. Benzodiazepine intoxication is associated with less euphoria than is intoxication by other drugs in this class. That characteristic is the basis for the lower abuse and dependence potential of benzodiazepines when compared with the barbiturates.

**Barbiturates and barbituratelike substances.** When barbiturates and barbituratelike substances are taken in relatively low doses, the clinical syndrome of intoxication is indistinguishable from that associated with alcohol intoxication. The symptoms include sluggishness, incoordination, difficulty in thinking, poor memory, slowness of

**Table 12.12–1**
**Sedative-, Hypnotic-, or Anxiolytic-Related Disorders**

*Sedative, hypnotic, or anxiolytic use disorders*

**Sedative, hypnotic, or anxiolytic dependence**
**Sedative, hypnotic, or anxiolytic abuse**

*Sedative-, hypnotic-, or anxiolytic-induced disorders*

**Sedative, hypnotic, or anxiolytic intoxication**
**Sedative, hypnotic, or anxiolytic withdrawal**
*Specify if:*
    with perceptual disturbances
**Sedative, hypnotic, or anxiolytic intoxication delirium**
**Sedative, hypnotic, or anxiolytic withdrawal delirium**
**Sedative-, hypnotic-, or anxiolytic-induced persisting dementia**
**Sedative-, hypnotic-, or anxiolytic-induced psychotic disorder, with delusions**
*Specify if:*
    with onset during intoxication
    with onset during withdrawal
**Sedative-, hypnotic-, or anxiolytic-induced psychotic disorder, with hallucinations**
*Specify if:*
    with onset during intoxication
    with onset during withdrawal
**Sedative-, hypnotic-, or anxiolytic-induced mood disorder**
*Specify if:*
    with onset during intoxication
    with onset during withdrawal
**Sedative-, hypnotic-, or anxiolytic-induced anxiety disorder**
*Specify if:*
    with onset during withdrawal
**Sedative-, hypnotic-, or anxiolytic-induced sexual dysfunction**
*Specify if:*
    with onset during intoxication
**Sedative-, hypnotic-, or anxiolytic-induced sleep disorder**
*Specify if:*
    with onset during intoxication
    with onset during withdrawal

**Sedative-, hypnotic-, or anxiolytic-related disorder not otherwise specified**

Table based on DSM-IV, *Diagnostic and Statistical Manual of Mental Disorders,* ed 4. Copyright American Psychiatric Association, Washington, 1994. Used with permission.

**Table 12.12–2**
**Diagnostic Criteria for Sedative, Hypnotic, or Anxiolytic Intoxication**

A. Recent use of a sedative, hypnotic, or anxiolytic.

B. Clinically significant maladaptive behavioral or psychological changes (e.g., inappropriate sexual or aggressive behavior, mood lability, impaired judgment, impaired social or occupational functioning) that developed during, or shortly after, sedative, hypnotic, or anxiolytic use.

C. One (or more) of the following signs, developing during, or shortly after, sedative, hypnotic, or anxiolytic use:

    (1) slurred speech
    (2) incoordination
    (3) unsteady gait
    (4) nystagmus
    (5) impairment in attention or memory
    (6) stupor or coma

D. The symptoms are not due to a general medical condition and are not better accounted for by another mental disorder.

Table from DSM-IV, *Diagnostic and Statistical Manual of Mental Disorders,* ed 4. Copyright American Psychiatric Association, Washington, 1994. Used with permission.

**Table 12.12–3**
**Diagnostic Criteria for Sedative, Hypnotic, or Anxiolytic Withdrawal**

A. Cessation of (or reduction in) sedative, hypnotic, or anxiolytic use that has been heavy and prolonged.

B. Two (or more) of the following, developing within several hours to a few days after criterion A:

    (1) autonomic hyperactivity (e.g., sweating or pulse rate greater than 100)
    (2) increased hand tremor
    (3) insomnia
    (4) nausea or vomiting
    (5) transient visual, tactile, or auditory hallucinations or illusions
    (6) psychomotor agitation
    (7) anxiety
    (8) grand mal seizures

C. The symptoms in criterion B cause clinically significant distress or impairment in social, occupational, or other important areas of functioning.

D. The symptoms are not due to a general medical condition and are not better accounted for by another mental disorder.

*Specify if:*
**with perceptual disturbances**

Table from DSM-IV, *Diagnostic and Statistical Manual of Mental Disorders,* ed 4. Copyright American Psychiatric Association, Washington, 1994. Used with permission.

speech and comprehension, faulty judgment, disinhibition of sexual and aggressive impulses, a narrowed range of attention, emotional lability, and an exaggeration of basic personality traits. The sluggishness usually resolves after a few hours, but the impaired judgment, distorted mood, and impaired motor skills may remain for 12 to 24 hours, depending primarily on the half-life of the abused substance. Other potential symptoms are hostility, argumentativeness, moroseness, and, occasionally, paranoid and suicidal ideation. The neurological effects include nystagmus, diplopia, strabismus, ataxic gait, positive Romberg's sign, hypotonia, and decreased superficial reflexes.

### Withdrawal

DSM-IV contains a single set of diagnostic criteria for withdrawal from any sedative, hypnotic, or anxiolytic substance (Table 12.12–3). The clinician can specify "with perceptual disturbances" if illusions, altered perceptions, or hallucinations are present but are accompanied by intact reality testing. Two important issues to remember about withdrawal are that benzodiazepines are associated with a withdrawal syndrome and that withdrawal from barbiturates can be life-threatening. Withdrawal from benzodiazepines can also result in serious medical complications, such as seizures.

**Benzodiazepines.**   The severity of the withdrawal syndromes associated with the benzodiazepines varies significantly according to the average dose and the duration of use. However, a mild withdrawal syndrome can follow even short-term use of relatively low doses of benzodiazepines. A significant withdrawal syndrome is likely to occur at the cessation of dosages in the 40 mg a day range for diazepam, for example, although 10 to 20 mg a day, taken for a month, can also result in a withdrawal syndrome when the drug is stopped. The onset of withdrawal symptoms usually occurs two to three days after the cessation of use, but with long-acting drugs, such as diazepam, the latency before onset may be five or six days. The symptoms include anxiety, dysphoria, intolerance for bright lights and loud noises, nausea, sweating, muscle twitching, and sometimes seizures (generally at dosages of 50 mg a day or more of diazepam).

**Barbiturates and barbituratelike substances.** The barbiturate and barbituratelike substances withdrawal syndrome ranges from mild symptoms (for example, anxiety, weakness, sweating, and insomnia) to severe symptoms (for example, seizures, delirium, cardiovascular collapse, and death). Persons who have been abusing pentobarbital in the range of 400 mg a day may experience mild withdrawal symptoms; persons who have been abusing the substance in the range of 800 mg a day experience orthostatic hypotension, weakness, tremor, and severe anxiety. About 75 percent of those persons have withdrawal-related seizures. Users of dosages even higher than 800 mg a day may experience anorexia, delirium, hallucinations, and repeated seizures.

Most of the symptoms appear in the first three days of abstinence, and seizures generally occur on the second or third day, when the symptoms are worst. If seizures do occur, they always precede the development of delirium. The syndrome rarely occurs more than a week after stopping the substance. A psychotic disorder, if it develops, starts on the third to eighth day. The various symptoms generally run their course within two to three days but may last as long as two weeks. The first episode of the syndrome usually occurs after 5 to 15 years of heavy substance use.

### Delirium

DSM-IV allows for the diagnosis of sedative, hypnotic, or anxiolytic intoxication delirium and sedative, hypnotic, or anxiolytic withdrawal delirium (Section 10.2). Delirium that is indistinguishable from delirium tremens associated with alcohol withdrawal is more commonly seen with barbiturate withdrawal than with benzodiazepine withdrawal. Delirium associated with intoxication can be seen with either barbiturates or benzodiazepines if the dosages are high enough.

### Persisting Dementia

DSM-IV allows for the diagnosis of sedative-, hypnotic-, or anxiolytic-induced persisting dementia (Section 10.3). The existence of the disorder is controversial, inasmuch as there is uncertainty whether a persisting dementia is due to the substance use itself or to associated features of the substance use. It will be necessary to evaluate the diagnosis further, using DSM-IV criteria to ascertain its validity.

### Persisting Amnestic Disorder

DSM-IV allows for the diagnosis of sedative-, hypnotic-, or anxiolytic-induced persisting amnestic disorder (Section 10.4). Amnestic disorders associated with sedatives, hypnotics, and anxiolytics may have been underdiagnosed. One exception has been the increased number of reports associated with amnestic episodes associated with the short-term use of benzodiazepines with short half-lives (such as triazolam [Halcion]).

### Psychotic Disorders

The psychotic symptoms of barbiturate withdrawal can be indistinguishable from those of alcohol-associated delirium tremens. Agitation, delusions, and hallucinations are usually visual, but sometimes tactile or auditory features develop after about one week of abstinence. Psychotic symptoms associated with intoxication or withdrawal are much more common with barbiturates than with benzodiazepines and are diagnosed as sedative-, hypnotic-, or anxiolytic-induced psychotic disorders (Section 14.1). The clinician can further specify whether delusions or hallucinations are the predominent symptoms.

### Other Disorders

Sedative, hypnotic, and anxiolytic use has also been associated with mood disorders (Section 15.3), anxiety disorders (Section 16.1), sleep disorders (Section 23.2), and sexual dysfunctions (Section 20.2). When none of the above diagnostic categories is appropriate for a person with a sedative, hypnotic, or anxiolytic use disorder, the appropriate diagnosis is sedative-, hypnotic-, or anxiolytic-related disorder not otherwise specified (NOS) (Table 12.12–4).

## CLINICAL FEATURES

### Patterns of Abuse

**Oral use.** The sedatives, hypnotics, and anxiolytics can all be taken orally, either occasionally to achieve a time-limited specific effect or regularly to obtain a constant, usually mild, intoxication state. The occasional-use pattern is associated with young persons who take the substance to achieve specific effects—relaxation for an evening, intensification of sexual activities, and a short-lived period of mild euphoria. The user's personality and expectations about the substance's effects and the setting in which the substance is taken also affect the substance-induced experience. The regular-use pattern is associated

**Table 12.12–4**
**Sedative-, Hypnotic-, or Anxiolytic-Related Disorder Not Otherwise Specified**

The sedative-, hypnotic-, or anxiolytic-related disorder not otherwise specified category is for disorders associated with the use of sedatives, hypnotics, or anxiolytics that are not classifiable as sedative, hypnotic, or anxiolytic dependence; sedative, hypnotic, or anxiolytic abuse; sedative, hypnotic, or anxiolytic intoxication; sedative, hypnotic, or anxiolytic withdrawal; sedative, hypnotic, or anxiolytic intoxication delirium; sedative, hypnotic, or anxiolytic withdrawal delirium; sedative-, hypnotic-, or anxiolytic-induced persisting dementia; sedative-, hypnotic-, or anxiolytic-induced persisting amnestic disorder; sedative-, hypnotic-, or anxiolytic-induced psychotic disorder; sedative-, hypnotic-, or anxiolytic-induced mood disorder; sedative-, hypnotic-, or anxiolytic-induced anxiety disorder; sedative-, hypnotic-, or anxiolytic-induced sexual dysfunction; or sedative-, hypnotic-, or anxiolytic-induced sleep disorder.

Table from DSM-IV, *Diagnostic and Statistical Manual of Mental Disorders*, ed 4. Copyright American Psychiatric Association, Washington, 1994. Used with permission.

with middle-aged, middle-class people who usually obtain the substance from the family physician as a prescription for insomnia or anxiety. Abusers of that type may have prescriptions from several physicians, and the pattern of abuse may go undetected until obvious signs of abuse or dependence are noticed by the person's family, coworkers, or physicians.

**Intravenous use.** A severe form of abuse involves the intravenous use of this class of substances. The users are mainly young adults intimately involved with illegal substances. Intravenous barbiturate use is associated with a pleasant, warm, drowsy feeling, and users may be inclined to use barbiturates more than opiates or opioids because of the low cost of barbiturates. The physical dangers of injection include the transmission of the human immunodeficiency virus (HIV), cellulitis, vascular complications from accidental injection into an artery, infections, and allergic reactions to contaminants. Intravenous use is associated with a rapid and profound degree of tolerance and dependence and with a severe withdrawal syndrome.

## Overdose

**Benzodiazepines.** The benzodiazepines, in contrast to the barbiturates and the barbituratelike substances, have a large margin of safety when taken in overdoses, a feature that contributed significantly to their rapid acceptance. The ratio of lethal-to-effective dose is about 200 to 1 or higher because of the minimal degree of respiratory depression associated with the benzodiazepines. Even when grossly excessive amounts (more than 2 grams) are taken in suicide attempts, the symptoms include only drowsiness, lethargy, ataxia, some confusion, and mild depression of the user's vital signs. A much more serious condition prevails when benzodiazepines are taken in overdose in combination with other sedative-hypnotic substances, such as alcohol. In such cases, small doses of benzodiazepines can cause death. The availability of flumazenil (Mazicon), a specific benzodiazepine antagonist, has reduced the lethality of the benzodiazepines, since flumazenil can be used in emergency rooms to reverse the effects of the benzodiazepines.

**Barbiturates.** Barbiturates are lethal when taken in overdose because of their induction of respiratory depression. In addition to intentional suicide attempts, accidental or unintentional overdoses are common. Barbiturates in home medicine cabinets are a common cause of fatal drug overdoses in children. As with benzodiazepines, the lethal effects of the barbiturates are additive to those of other sedative-hypnotics, including alcohol and benzodiazepines. Barbiturate overdose is characterized by the induction of coma, respiratory arrest, cardiovascular failure, and death.

The lethal dose varies with the route of administration and the degree of tolerance for the substance after a history of long-term abuse. For the most commonly abused barbiturates, the ratio of lethal-to-effective dose ranges between 3 to 1 and 30 to 1. Dependent users often take an average daily dose of 1.5 grams of a short-acting barbiturate, and some have been reported to take as much as 2.5 grams a day for months. The lethal dose is not much

greater for the long-term abuser than it is for the neophyte. Tolerance develops quickly to the point at which withdrawal in a hospital becomes necessary to prevent accidental death from overdose.

**Barbituratelike substances.** The barbituratelike substances vary in their lethality and are usually intermediate between the relative safety of the benzodiazepines and the high lethality of the barbiturates. An overdose of methaqualone, for example, may result in restlessness, delirium, hypertonia, muscle spasms, convulsions, and, in very high doses, death. Unlike barbiturates, methaqualone rarely causes severe cardiovascular or respiratory depression, and most fatalities result from combining methaqualone with alcohol.

## TREATMENT

### Withdrawal

**Benzodiazepines.** Because some benzodiazepines are eliminated from the body slowly, the symptoms of withdrawal may continue to develop for several weeks. To prevent seizures and other withdrawal symptoms, the clinician should reduce the dosage gradually. Several reports indicate that carbamazepine (Tegretol) may be useful in the treatment of benzodiazepine withdrawal.

**Barbiturates.** To avoid sudden death during barbiturate withdrawal, the clinician must follow conservative clinical guidelines. The clinician should not give barbiturates to a patient who is comatose or grossly intoxicated. The clinician should attempt to determine the patient's usual daily dose of barbiturates and then verify that dosage clinically. For example, the clinician can give a test dose of 200 mg of pentobarbital every hour until a mild intoxication is present but withdrawal symptoms are absent. The clinician can then taper the total daily dose at a rate of about 10 percent of the total daily dose. Once the correct dosage is determined, a long-acting barbiturate can be used for the detoxification period. During that process the patient may begin to experience withdrawal symptoms, in which case, the clinician should halve the daily decrement.

Phenobarbital may be substituted in the withdrawal procedure for the more commonly abused short-acting barbiturates. The effects of phenobarbital last longer, and, because there is less fluctuation of barbiturate blood levels, phenobarbital does not produce observable toxic signs or a serious overdose. An adequate dose is 30 mg of phenobarbital for every 100 mg of the short-acting substance. The user should be maintained for at least two days at that level before the dosage is reduced further. The regimen is analogous to the substitution of methadone for heroin.

After withdrawal is complete, the patient must overcome the desire to start taking the substance again. Although it has been suggested that nonbarbiturate sedative-hypnotics be substituted for barbiturates as a preventive therapeutic measure, doing so often results in replacing one substance dependence with another. If a user is to remain substance-free, follow-up treatment, usually with psychiatric help and community support, is vital. Otherwise, the patient will almost certainly return to barbiturates or to a substance with similar hazards.

## Overdose

The treatment of overdose of this general class of substances involves gastric lavage, activated charcoal, and careful monitoring of vital signs and central nervous system (CNS) activity. Overdose patients who come to medical attention while awake should be kept from slipping into unconsciousness. Vomiting should be induced, and activated charcoal should be administered to delay gastric absorption. If the patient is comatose, the clinician must establish an intravenous fluid line, monitor the patient's vital signs, insert an endotracheal tube to maintain a patent airway, and provide mechanical ventilation, if necessary. Hospitalization of a comatose patient in an intensive care unit is usually required during the early stages of recovery from such overdoses.

## LEGAL ISSUES

State and federal agencies have attempted to restrict the distribution of benzodiazepines by requiring special reporting forms. For example, through the use of New York State triplicate prescription forms, the names of doctors and patients are kept on file in a data bank. Such measures have been taken to stem the tide of abuse. But most abuse is the result of the illicit manufacture, sale, and diversion of substances, particularly to cocaine and opioid addicts, and not from physicians' prescriptions or legitimate pharmaceutical companies. To attempt to curtail the use of the substances, which have unquestionable and invaluable therapeutic benefits, is an example of increasing governmental interference in the practice of medicine and in the confidential relationship between doctor and patient. Such restrictions will do little to curb cocaine, opioid, or benzodiazepine abuse.

The number of benzodiazepine prescriptions has decreased in New York State (Figure 12.12–1), but whether that decrease is due to improved medical prescribing standards of practice or to the intimidation of physicians is open to question.

New York is now among 10 states that regulate schedule II controlled substances with multiple-copy prescriptions (triplicates). California has the oldest triplicate program

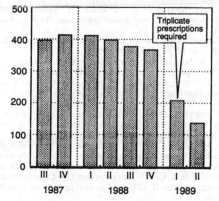

**Figure 12.12–1.** Number (in thousands) of prescriptions paid for by New York State Medicaid for benzodiazepines, including diazepam (Valium) and alprazolam (Xanax). (Source: New York State Department of Health. Courtesy of *The Wall Street Journal*, Jan. 30, 1990.)

**Table 12.12–5**
**Physicians' Reactions to Triplicate Prescriptions**

New York State's triplicate prescription program has not only failed to reduce prescription drug abuse but has also hampered prescribing of clinically indicated medications, according to data presented at a recent symposium sponsored by the Medical Society of the State of New York.

According to their proponents, triplicate prescription programs in New York and other states have caused a significant decline in the prescribing of regulated drugs. They attribute this reduction largely to decreases in inappropriate prescribing and in diversion of these drugs to street use. But the preponderance of evidence supports the opposite view, according to the data presented at the symposium. These data show that triplicate prescription programs do not reduce prescription drug abuse. In addition, these programs have several important unintended negative consequences.

**Triplicate prescription programs inhibit physicians from prescribing drugs for patients whose medical conditions warrant them**

- According to a Gallup poll, since 1989, when New York State extended its triplicate prescription program to cover benzodiazepines, 49% of responding physicians have reduced their prescribing of these agents—even though 56% of the physicians were concerned about patients being denied access to appropriate medication. Some physicians said that they felt pressured to prescribe alternative medications that were less safe (42%) or more expensive (31%).
- Prescription data show that in New York, use of outmoded or ineffective alternative medications to benzodiazepines, such as meprobamate, chloral hydrate, butabarbital, and fluoxetine, has increased markedly. In one study, 25% of nursing home residents taking benzodiazepines were switched to antipsychotic medications, which have more severe long-term adverse effects.
- Some physicians say that they are afraid to prescribe scheduled drugs because the criteria for government-agency review of their prescribing patterns are arbitrary and because of concerns about record-keeping and security requirements. Many physicians—particularly those in high-crime neighborhoods—do not even have triplicate prescription pads, because they fear their offices will be burglarized for the forms.
- Many cancer patients require multiple controlled drugs, often in high doses, to control severe pain. Fear of sanctions may prevent some physicians from treating cancer pain as aggressively as these patients deserve.
- In Texas, during 1982, the year following the adoption of a triplicate prescription program, there was a 60% decrease in the prescribing of Schedule II analgesics and a corresponding increase in the prescribing of less effective Schedule III analgesics and a potent nonsteroidal anti-inflammatory drug (NSAID).

**Triplicate prescription programs threaten the confidentiality of the physician-patient relationship**

- According to a Gallup survey, 63% of physicians felt that triplicate prescriptions violate patient confidentiality.
- Patients with epilepsy, anxiety disorders, depression, and other medical conditions requiring controlled medications express concern that triplicate prescriptions are an invasion of their privacy and may worsen the stigmatization they experience because of their illness.

**Triplicate prescription programs are costly to operate and provide no useful information on prescribing that is not available elsewhere, at lower cost**

- Triplicate prescription programs have financial costs that often go unrecognized by proponents—not only the programs' administrative costs, estimated at $1 per prescription, but also the "hidden" costs of alternative drugs,

*Continued*

**Table 12.12–5**
*Continued*

out-of-pocket expenses to patients for nonreimbursed drugs and additional visits, and untreated illnesses that may eventually require more intensive medical care.
• Several alternative prescription-monitoring programs already exist that can accomplish the same goals as triplicate prescription—at far lower cost. These include systems available from the American Medical Association, the Drug Enforcement Administration, and the U.S. Department of Health and Human Services.

**Triplicate prescription programs do not reduce prescription drug diversion and abuse**

• California has had a triplicate prescription program for more than 50 years. Recent analysis of data from the Epidemiologic Catchment Area study, sponsored by the National Institute of Mental Health, suggests that Los Angeles does not have a lower rate of illicit use of Schedule II prescription drugs than four other cities in states that do not have triplicate prescription. Furthermore, nearly 100% of abused prescription drugs in all cities surveyed were illicitly obtained, not prescribed by physicians.
• New York's triplicate prescription program has not affected the ability of drug abusers to obtain controlled agents from street dealers, who can easily find alternative sources for drugs, including overseas manufacturers, diversion from other states, and illicit laboratories.
• Adding benzodiazepines to the triplicate prescription program did not reduce the number of emergency room admissions for tranquilizer overdoses reported to the New York City Poison Control Center.

**The Conclusion: Triplicate Prescription Jeopardizes Patient Care**

Measures to adopt or discard triplicate prescription programs are before state and federal legislators this year. Lawmakers who hear only the testimony of regulatory and drug enforcement agencies may not be aware of the drawbacks of triplicate prescription. Legislators should also know of physicians' serious reservations about triplicate prescription, the harm these regulations do to patients, and the evidence that these programs are not the most effective way to control prescription drug abuse.

Table from highlights of the symposium, "Triplicate Prescription: Issues and Answers," sponsored by the Medical Society of the State of New York, February 28, 1991. Used with permission.

**Table 12.12–6**
**Advantages of New York's Triplicate Prescription Program**

| | |
|---|---|
| Reduces inappropriate prescribing of benzodiazepines | 77%* |
| Targets patients who abuse benzodiazepines | 43 |
| Represents a cost benefit to New York State | 15 |
| Other advantages | 19 |
| Reduces abuse of other controlled substances | |
| Allows more active control of medicine by the state | |
| Provides accurate record of prescriptions written | |
| Subjects MDs to peer review | |
| Provides reason for not prescribing benzodiazepines to patients | |

*Percentages reflect proportion of those (N = 328) who thought that the triplicate prescription program had any advantages.
Table from highlights of the symposium, "Triplicate Prescription: Issues and Answers," sponsored by the Medical Society of the State of New York, February 28, 1991. Used with permission.

**Table 12.12–7**
**Disadvantages of New York's Triplicate Prescription Program**

| | |
|---|---|
| Inappropriately allows legislators to dictate practice of medicine | 75%* |
| Consumes too much physician time | 74 |
| Violates physician-patient confidentiality | 64 |
| Imposes unnecessary physician monitoring | 56 |
| Increases cost burden to patients | 49 |
| Poses benzodiazepine withdrawal concerns | 29 |
| Other disadvantages | 20 |
| Increases possibility of robbery and assault | |
| Requires physician to practice defensive or reactive medicine | |
| Increases expense to physician | |
| Has not been proven to eliminate drug abuse | |
| Increases possibility of malpractice liability | |
| Forces prescribing of less efficacious, more hazardous medications | |
| Sets precedent for further government controls | |
| Coerces patient to seek alternative sources of drugs | |

*Percentages reflect proportion of those (N = 1,185) who thought that the triplicate prescription program had any disadvantages.
Table from highlights of the symposium, "Triplicate Prescription: Issues and Answers," sponsored by the Medical Society of the State of New York, February 28, 1991. Used with permission.

(established in 1939), but in 1989 New York, with its reported high prescription abuse rate, became the first state to extend triplicate regulation to benzodiazepines, against the recommendation of most physicians in New York. In 1991, a symposium sponsored by the Medical Society of the State of New York concluded that triplicate prescriptions jeopardize patient care (Table 12.12–5). The advantages and the disadvantages of New York's triplicate prescription program were summarized from a survey of 1,513 physicians (Tables 12.12–6 and 12.12–7).

**References**

American Psychiatric Association: *Benzodiazepine Dependence, Toxicity, and Abuse.* American Psychiatric Association, Washington, 1990.
Cole J O, Chaiarello R J: The benzodiazepines as drugs of abuse. J Psychiatr Res *24* (3, Suppl 2): 135, 1990.
Juergens S M: Benzodiazepines and addiction. Psychiatr Clin North Am *16*: 75, 1993.
Lader M, Farr I, Morton S: A comparison of alpidem and placebo in relieving benzodiazepine withdrawal symptoms. Int Clin Psychopharmacol *8*: 31, 1993.
Nutt D J: Pharmacological mechanisms of benzodiazepine withdrawal. J Psychiatr Res *24* (3, Suppl 2): 105, 1990.
Patterson J F: Withdrawal from alprazolam dependency using clonazepam: Clinical observations. J Clin Psychiatry *51* (9, Suppl): 47, 1990.
Rickels K, Schweizer E, Case W G, Greenblatt D J: Long-term therapeutic use of benzodiazepines: I. Effects of abrupt discontinuation. Arch Gen Psychiatry *47*: 899, 1990.
Rickels K, Warren G C, Schweizer E, Garcia-España F, Fridman R: Long-term benzodiazepine users 3 years after participation in a discontinuation program. Am J Psychiatry *148*: 757, 1991.
Schweizer E, Rickels K, Case W G, Greenblatt D J: Carbamazepine treatment in patients discontinuing long-term benzodiazepine therapy: Effects on withdrawal severity and outcome. Arch Gen Psychiatry *48*: 448, 1991.
Schweizer E, Rickels K, Case W G, Greenblatt D J: Long-term therapeutic use of benzodiazepines: II. Effects of gradual taper. Arch Gen Psychiatry *47*: 908, 1990.
Seivewright N, Dougal W: Withdrawal symptoms from high dose benzodiazepines in poly drug users. Drug Alcohol Depend *32*: 15, 1993.

# 13 |||||

# Schizophrenia

The past five years have brought major advances in the understanding of schizophrenia in three major areas. First, advances in brain imaging techniques, especially magnetic resonance imaging (MRI), and refinements in neuropathological techniques have focused much interest on the limbic system as central to the pathophysiology of schizophrenia. The particular brain areas of interest are the amygdala, the hippocampus, and the parahippocampal gyrus. The focus on those brain regions does not negate interest in other brain areas but does increasingly generate hypotheses that can be tested as the knowledge base regarding schizophrenia expands. Second, after the introduction of clozapine (Clozaril), an atypical antipsychotic with minimal neurological side effects, there has been a significant amount of research regarding other atypical antipsychotic drugs, particularly risperidone and remoxipride. Those and other atypical drugs that will be introduced in the second half of the 1990s could be more effective in reducing the negative symptoms of schizophrenia and could be associated with a low incidence of neurological adverse effects. Third, as drug treatments improve and as a solid biological basis for schizophrenia is broadly recognized, there is an increase in interest in the psychosocial factors affecting schizophrenia, including those that may affect onset, relapse, and treatment outcome.

## HISTORY

The history of psychiatrists and neurologists who have written and theorized about schizophrenia parallels the history of psychiatry itself. The magnitude of the clinical problem has consistently attracted the attention of major figures throughout the history of the discipline. Emil Kraepelin (1856–1926) and Eugen Bleuler (1857–1939) are the two key figures in the history of schizophrenia. Benedict A. Morel (1809–1873), a French psychiatrist, used the term *démense précoce* for deteriorated patients whose illnesses had begun in adolescence; Karl Ludwig Kahlbaum (1828–1899) described the symptoms of catatonia; and Ewold Hecker (1843–1909) wrote about the bizarre behavior of hebephrenia.

### Emil Kraepelin

Emil Kraepelin (Figure 13–1) latinized Morel's term to *dementia precox,* a term that emphasized a distinct cognitive process (dementia) and the early onset (precox) that is characteristic of the disorder. Kraepelin further distinguished patients with dementia precox from those he classified as being afflicted with manic-depressive psychosis or paranoia. Patients with dementia precox were characterized as having a long-term deteriorating course and common clinical symptoms of hallucinations and delusions. Kraepelin's views regarding the course of schizophrenia are sometimes misrepresented in terms of the certainty of a deteriorating course, since he did acknowledge that about 4 percent of his patients had complete recoveries and 13 percent had significant remissions. Patients with manic-depressive psychosis were differentiated from patients with dementia precox by the presence of distinct episodes of illness that were separated by periods of normal functioning. Patients with paranoia had persistent persecutory delusions as their major symptom but did not have the deteriorating course of dementia precox or the intermittent symptoms of manic-depressive psychosis.

### Eugen Bleuler

Eugen Bleuler (Figure 13–2) coined the term "schizophrenia," and the term replaced "dementia precox" in the literature. Bleuler conceptualized the term to signify the presence of a schism between thought, emotion, and behavior in affected patients. However, the term is widely misunderstood, especially by the lay public, as signifying a split personality. Split personality (now called dissociative identity disorder is an entirely different disorder that is categorized in the fourth edition of *Diagnostic and Statistical Manual of Mental Disorders* (DSM-IV) with the other dissociative disorders. A major distinction that Bleuler drew between his concept of schizophrenia and Kraepelin's concept of dementia precox was that a deteriorating course is not necessary in the concept of schizophrenia, as it was in dementia precox. One effect of Bleuler's conceptualization was to increase the number of patients who meet the conceptual criteria for a diagnosis of schizophrenia. That widening of the diagnosis may have led to as much as a twofold difference in the incidence of schizophrenia before the introduction of the third edition of DSM (DSM-III) when comparing European countries (which tended to follow Kraepelin's principles) with the United States (which tended to follow Bleuler's principles). Since the introduction of DSM-III, the United States diagnostic system has clearly moved toward Kraepelin's ideas, although Bleuler's term, "schizophrenia," has become the internationally accepted label for the disorder.

**The four As.** To explain further his theory regarding the internal mental schisms of affected patients, Bleuler described specific *fundamental (or primary) symptoms* of schizophrenia, including a thought disorder characterized by associational disturbances, particularly looseness. Other fundamental symptoms were affective disturbances, autism, and ambivalence. Thus, Bleuler's four As consist of associations, affect, autism, and ambivalence. Bleuler also described *accessory (secondary) symptoms,* which included hallucinations and de-

**Figure 13–1.** Emil Kraepelin. (Figure from G C Davison, J M Neale: *Abnormal Psychology: An Experimental Clinical Approach.* Wiley, New York, 1974. Used with permission.)

**Figure 13–2.** Eugen Bleuler. (Figure from G C Davison, J M Neale: *Abnormal Psychology: An Experimental Clinical Approach.* Wiley, New York, 1974. Used with permission.)

lusions, symptoms that had been a prominent part of Kraepelin's conceptualization of the disorder.

## Other Theorists

Adolf Meyer, Harry Stack Sullivan, Gabriel Langfeldt, and Kurt Schneider also made major contributions to the understanding of the many facets of schizophrenia. Meyer, the founder of psychobiology, believed that schizophrenia and

other mental disorders are reactions to a variety of life stresses, so he called the syndrome a schizophrenic reaction. Sullivan, the founder of the interpersonal psychoanalytic school, emphasized social isolation as both a cause and a symptom of schizophrenia.

Ernst Kretschmer's data supported the idea that schizophrenia is more common in patients with asthenic, athletic, and dysplastic body types than in patients with pyknic body types, who are more likely to have bipolar disorders. Although that observation seems unusual, it is not inconsistent with a superficial impression regarding the body types of many homeless persons.

**Gabriel Langfeldt.** Langfeldt divided the patients with major psychotic symptoms into two groups, those with true schizophrenia and those with schizophreniform psychosis. Langfeldt emphasized the importance of depersonalization, autism, emotional blunting, an insidious onset, and feelings of derealization in his description of *true schizophrenia*. True schizophrenia also came to be known as nuclear schizophrenia, process schizophrenia, and nonremitting schizophrenia in the literature that followed Langfeldt's papers.

**Kurt Schneider.** Kurt Schneider described a number of first-rank symptoms that he considered in no way specific for schizophrenia but of pragmatic value in making a diagnosis (Table 13–1). Schizophrenia, Schneider pointed out, can also be diagnosed exclusively on the basis of second-rank symptoms and an otherwise typical clinical appearance. Schneider did not mean those symptoms to be applied rigidly. He warned the clinician that the diagnosis of schizophrenia should be made in certain patients who failed to show first-rank symptoms. Unfortunately, that warning is frequently ignored, and the absence of such symptoms in a single interview is sometimes taken as evidence that the person does not have schizophrenia.

**Karl Jaspers.** Karl Jaspers was a psychiatrist and a philosopher, and he was a major contributor to existential psychoanalysis. Jaspers approached psychopathology with the idea that there are no firm conceptual frameworks or fundamental principles. In his theories regarding schizophrenia, therefore, Jaspers attempted to remain unencumbered by traditional concepts, such as subject and object, cause and effect, and reality and fantasy. One specific development of that philosophy was his interest in the content of psychiatric patients' delusions.

## EPIDEMIOLOGY

In the United States the lifetime prevalence of schizophrenia has been variously reported as ranging from 1 to 1.5 percent; consistent with that range, the National Institute of Mental Health (NIMH)-sponsored Epidemiologic Catchment Area (ECA) study reported a lifetime prevalence of 1.3 percent. About 0.025 to 0.05 percent of the total population are treated for schizophrenia in any one year. Although two thirds of those treated patients require hospitalization, only about half of all schizophrenic patients obtain treatment, in spite of the severity of the disorder.

### Age and Sex

Schizophrenia is equally prevalent in men and women. However, the two sexes show several differences in the onset and the course of illness. Men have an earlier onset

**Table 13–1**
**Essential Features of Various Diagnostic Criteria for Schizophrenia**

## KURT SCHNEIDER CRITERIA

1. First-rank symptoms
   a. Audible thoughts
   b. Voices arguing or discussing or both
   c. Voices commenting
   d. Somatic passivity experiences
   e. Thought withdrawal and other experiences of influenced thought
   f. Thought broadcasting
   g. Delusional perceptions
   h. All other experiences involving volition, made affects, and made impulses

2. Second-rank symptoms
   a. Other disorders of perception
   b. Sudden delusional ideas
   c. Perplexity
   d. Depressive and euphoric mood changes
   e. Feelings of emotional impoverishment
   f. ". . . and several others as well"

## GABRIEL LANGFELDT CRITERIA

1. Symptom criteria
   Significant clues to a diagnosis of schizophrenia are (if no sign of cognitive impairment, infection, or intoxication can be demonstrated):
   a. Changes in personality, which manifest themselves as a special type of emotional blunting followed by lack of initiative, and altered, frequently peculiar behavior. (In hebephrenia, especially, the changes are characteristic and are a principal clue to the diagnosis.)
   b. In catatonic types, the history and the typical signs in periods of restlessness and stupor (with negativism, oily facies, catalepsy, special vegetative symptoms, etc.)
   c. In paranoid psychoses, essential symptoms of split personality (or depersonalization symptoms) and a loss of reality feeling (derealization symptoms) or primary delusions
   d. Chronic hallucinations
2. Course criterion
   A final decision about diagnosis cannot be made before a follow-up period of at least five years has shown a long-term course of disease

## NEW HAVEN SCHIZOPHRENIA INDEX

1. a. Delusions: not specified or other-than-depressive — 2 points
   b. Auditory hallucinations
   c. Visual hallucinations — any one: 2 points
   d. Other hallucinations
2. a. Bizarre thoughts
   b. Autism or grossly unrealistic private thoughts — any one: 2 points
   c. Looseness of associations, illogical thinking, overinclusion
   d. Blocking
   e. Concreteness — either: 2 points
   f. Derealization
   g. Depersonalization — each: 1 point
3. Inappropriate affect — 1 point
4. Confusion — 1 point
5. Paranoid ideation (self-referential thinking, suspiciousness) — 1 point
6. Catatonic behavior
   a. Excitement
   b. Stupor
   c. Waxy flexibility
   d. Negativism — any one: 1 point
   e. Mutism
   f. Echolalia
   g. Stereotyped motor activity

Scoring: To be considered part of the schizophrenic group, the patient must score on Item 1 or Item 2a, 2b, or 2c and must receive a total score of at least 4 points.

## FLEXIBLE SYSTEM

Minimum number of symptoms required can be four to eight, depending on investigator's choice:
1. Restricted affect
2. Poor insight
3. Thoughts aloud
4. Poor rapport
5. Widespread delusions

**Table 13–1**
*Continued*

## FLEXIBLE SYSTEM

6. Incoherent speech
7. Unreliable information
8. Bizarre delusions
9. Nihilistic delusions
10. Absence of early awakening (one to three hours)
11. Absence of depressed facies
12. Absence of elation

## RESEARCH DIAGNOSTIC CRITERIA

Criteria 1 through 3 required for diagnosis:
1. At least two of the following for definite illness and one for probable (not counting those occurring during period of drug or alcohol abuse or withdrawal):
   a. Thought broadcasting, insertion, or withdrawal
   b. Delusions of being controlled or influenced, other bizarre delusions, or multiple delusions
   c. Delusions other than persecution or jealousy lasting at least one month
   d. Delusions of any type if accompanied by hallucinations of any type for at least one week
   e. Auditory hallucinations in which either a voice keeps up a running commentary on subject's behaviors or thoughts as they occur or two or more voices converse with each other
   f. Nonaffective verbal hallucinations spoken to subject
   g. Hallucinations of any type throughout day for several days or intermittently for at least one month
   h. Definite instances of marked formal thought disorders accompanied by blunted or inappropriate affect, delusions, or hallucinations of any type or grossly disorganized behavior
2. One of the following:
   a. Current period of illness lasted at least two weeks from onset of noticeable change in subject's usual condition
   b. Subject has had previous period of illness lasting at least two weeks, during which he or she met criteria, and residual signs of illness have remained (e.g., extreme social withdrawal, blunted or inappropriate affect, formal thought disorder, or unusual thoughts or perceptual experiences)
3. At no time during active period of illness being considered did subject meet criteria for probable or definite manic or depressive syndrome to the degree that it was a prominent part of illness

## ST. LOUIS CRITERIA

1. Both necessary:
   a. Chronic illness with at least six months of symptoms before index evaluation without return to premorbid level of psychosocial adjustment
   b. Absence of period of depressive or manic symptoms sufficient to qualify for mood disorder or probable mood disorder
2. At least one of the following:
   a. Delusions or hallucinations without significant perplexity or disorientation
   b. Verbal production that makes communication difficult owing to lack of logical or understandable organization (in presence of muteness, diagnostic decision must be deferred)
3. At least three for definite, two for probable, illness:
   a. Never married
   b. Poor premorbid social adjustment or work history
   c. Family history of schizophrenia
   d. Absence of alcohol or other substance abuse within one year of onset
   e. Onset before age 40

## TAYLOR AND ABRAMS CRITERIA

All criteria must be met for diagnosis:
1. Duration of episode greater than six months
2. Clear consciousness
3. Presence of delusions, hallucinations, or formal thought disorder (verbigeration, non sequiturs, word approximations, neologisms, blocking, and derailment)
4. Absence of broad affect
5. Absence of signs and symptoms sufficient to make diagnosis of mood disorder
6. No alcohol or other substance abuse within one year of index episode
7. Absence of focal signs and symptoms of coarse brain disease or major medical illness known to produce significant behavioral changes

## PRESENT STATE EXAMINATION

The following 12 items from the Present State Examination correspond to a 12-point diagnostic system for schizophrenia, with varying levels of certainty of diagnosis based on the cut-off score determined by the examiner. Nine of the symptoms are scored 1 point each when present ( + ), and three are scored 1 point each when absent ( − ).
1. Restricted affect ( + )
2. Poor insight ( + )
3. Thoughts aloud ( + )
4. Awaking early ( − )

5. Poor rapport (+)
6. Depressed facies (−)
7. Elation (−)
8. Widespread delusions (+)
9. Incoherent speech (+)
10. Unreliable information (+)
11. Bizarre delusions (+)
12. Nihilistic delusions (+)

## TSUANG AND WINOKUR CRITERIA

I.  Hebephrenic (A through D must be present):
   A. Age of onset and sociofamilial data (one of the following):
      1. Age of onset before 25 years
      2. Unmarried or unemployed
      3. Family history of schizophrenia
   B. Disorganized thought
   C. Affect changes (either 1 or 2):
      1. Inappropriate affect
      2. Flat affect
   D. Behavioral symptoms (either 1 or 2):
      1. Bizarre behavior
      2. Motor symptoms (either a or b):
         a. Hebephrenic traits
         b. Catatonic traits (if present, subtype may be modified to hebephrenia with catatonic traits)
II. Paranoid (A through C must be present):
   A. Age of onset and sociofamilial data (one of the following):
      1. Age of onset after 25 years
      2. Married or employed
      3. Absence of family history of schizophrenia
   B. Exclusion criteria:
      1. Disorganized thoughts must be absent or of mild degree, such that speech is intelligible
      2. Affective and behavioral symptoms, as described in hebephrenia, must be absent or of mild degree
   C. Preoccupation with extensive, well-organized delusions or hallucinations

The criteria of Schneider and Langfeldt from World Psychiatric Association: *Diagnostic Criteria for Schizophrenic and Affective Psychoses.* American Psychiatric Press, Washington, 1983. Used with permission. The criteria of St. Louis, RDC, NHSI, Flexible, and Taylor and Abrams from J Endicott, J Nee, L Fleiss, J Cohen, J B W Williams, R Simon: Diagnostic criteria for schizophrenia. Arch Gen Psychiatry 39: 884, 1982. Used with permission. The criteria for Tsuang and Winokur from M T Tsuang, G Winokur: Criteria for hebephrenic and paranoid schizophrenia. Arch Gen Psychiatry 31: 43, 1974. Used with permission.

of schizophrenia than do women. More than half of all male schizophrenic patients but only a third of all female schizophrenic patients have their first psychiatric hospital admission before age 25. The peak ages of onset for men are 15 to 25; for women the peak ages are 25 to 35. The onset of schizophrenia before age 10 or after age 50 is extremely rare. About 90 percent of the patients in treatment of schizophrenia are between 15 and 55 years old. Some studies have indicated that men are more likely than are women to be impaired by negative symptoms and that women are more likely to have better social functioning than men. In general, the outcome for female schizophrenic patients is better than the outcome for male schizophrenic patients.

### Seasonality of Birth

A robust finding in schizophrenia research is that persons who later have schizophrenia are more likely to have been born in the winter and early spring and less likely to have been born in late spring and summer. Specifically, in the northern hemisphere, including the United States, schizophrenic persons were more often born in the months from January to April. In the southern hemisphere, schizophrenic persons were more often born in the months from July to September. Various hypotheses to explain that observation have been put forward. They include the hypothesis that some season-specific risk factor is operative, such as a virus or a seasonal change in diet. Another hypothesis is that persons who have the genetic predisposition for schizophrenia have an increased biological advantage to survive season-specific insults.

### Geographical Distribution

Schizophrenia is not evenly distributed geographically throughout the United States or throughout the world. Historically, the prevalence of schizophrenia in the Northeast and the West in the United States was higher than in other areas, although that unequal distribution has eroded. However, some geographical regions in the world have an unusually high prevalence of schizophrenia. Some have interpreted those geographical pockets of schizophrenia as supportive of an infective (for example, viral) cause of schizophrenia.

## Reproduction Rates

The use of psychotherapeutic drugs, the open-door policies in hospitals, the deinstitutionalization in state hospitals, the emphasis on rehabilitation, and the community-based care for patients with schizophrenia have all led to a general increase in the marriage and fertility rates among schizophrenic persons. Because of those factors, the number of children born to schizophrenic parents doubled from 1935 to 1955. The fertility rate for schizophrenic persons is now close to the rate of the general population.

## Medical Illness

Schizophrenic persons have a higher mortality rate from accidents and natural causes than do the general population. That increase in mortality is not explained by institution-related or treatment-related variables. The higher rate may be related to the fact that the diagnosis and the treatment of medical and surgical conditions in schizophrenic patients can be a clinical challenge. Several studies have found that up to 80 percent of all schizophrenic patients have significant concurrent medical illnesses and that up to 50 percent of those conditions may be undiagnosed.

## Suicide

Suicide is a common cause of death among schizophrenic patients, partly because clinicians still tend to associate suicide more with mood disorders than with the psychotic disorders. About 50 percent of all patients with schizophrenia attempt suicide at least once in their lifetimes, and 10 to 15 percent of schizophrenic patients die by suicide during a 20-year follow-up period. Male and female schizophrenic patients are equally likely to commit suicide. The major risk factors for suicide among schizophrenic persons include the presence of depressive symptoms, young age, and high levels of premorbid functioning (especially a college education). That group may realize the devastating significance of their illness more than do other groups of schizophrenic patients and may see suicide as a reasonable alternative. Treatment approaches to such patients may include pharmacological treatment of the depression, addressing issues of loss in psychotherapy, and the use of support groups to help direct the patient's ambitions toward some obtainable goal.

## Associated Substance Use and Abuse

**Cigarette smoking.** Most surveys have reported that more than three fourths of all schizophrenic patients smoke cigarettes, compared with less than half of psychiatric patients as a whole. In addition to the well-known health risks associated with smoking, cigarette smoking affects other aspects of a schizophrenic patient's care. Several studies have reported that cigarette smoking is associated with the use of high dosages of antipsychotic drugs, possibly because cigarette smoking increases the metabolism rate of those drugs. However, cigarette smoking is associated with a decrease in antipsychotic drug-related par-

kinsonism, possibly because of nicotine-dependent activation of dopamine neurons.

**Substance abuse.** Comorbidity of schizophrenia and substance-related disorders is common, although the implications of substance abuse in schizophrenic patients are unclear. About 30 to 50 percent of schizophrenic patients may meet the diagnostic criteria for alcohol abuse or alcohol dependence; and the two most commonly used other substances are cannabis (about 15 to 25 percent) and cocaine (about 5 to 10 percent). Patients tend to report that they use those substances to obtain pleasure and to reduce their depression and anxiety. In general, most studies have associated the comorbidity of substance-related disorders with schizophrenia as an indicator of poor prognosis.

## Population Density

The prevalence of schizophrenia has been correlated with local population density in cities with populations of more than 1 million people. That correlation is weaker in cities of 100,000 to 500,000 people and is not present in cities with fewer than 10,000 people. The effect of population density is consistent with the observation that the incidence of schizophrenia in children of either one or two schizophrenic parents is twice as high in cities as in rural communities. Those observations suggest that social stressors in urban settings may affect the development of schizophrenia in persons at risk.

## Cultural and Socioeconomic Considerations

Schizophrenia has been described in all cultures and socioeconomic status groups studied. In industrialized nations a disproportionate number of schizophrenic patients are in the low socioeconomic groups. That observation has been explained by the *downward drift hypothesis,* which suggests that affected persons either move into a lower socioeconomic group or fail to rise out of a low socioeconomic group because of the illness. An alternative explanation is the *social causation hypothesis,* which proposes that stresses experienced by members of low socioeconomic groups contribute to the development of schizophrenia.

In addition to hypothesizing that the stress of industrialization causes schizophrenia, some investigators have presented data indicating that the stress of immigration can lead to a schizophrenialike condition. Some studies report a high prevalence of schizophrenia among recent immigrants, and that finding has implicated abrupt cultural change as a stressor involved in the cause of schizophrenia. Perhaps consistent with both hypotheses is the observation that the prevalence of schizophrenia appears to rise among third-world populations as contact with technologically advanced cultures increases.

Advocates of a social cause for schizophrenia argue that cultures may be more or less schizophrenogenic, depending on how mental illness is perceived in the culture, the nature of the patient role, the available system of social and family supports, and the complexity of social communication. Schizophrenia has been reported to be prognostically more benign in less developed nations where patients are reintegrated into their communities and families more completely than they are in highly civilized Western societies.

**Homelessness.** The problem of the homeless in large cities may be related to the deinstitutionalization of schizophrenic patients who were not adequately followed up. Although the exact percentage of homeless persons who are schizophrenic is difficult to obtain, an estimated one third to two thirds of the homeless are probably afflicted with schizophrenia.

**Financial cost to society.** The estimation of an illness's cost to society is a complex task; nevertheless, the financial cost of schizophrenia to the United States is widely acknowledged to be enormous. About 1 percent of the United States national income goes toward the treatment of mental illness (excluding substance-related disorders); that percentage came to about $40 billion in 1985. When the indirect costs to society (for example, lost production and mortality) are added, the figure tops $100 billion annually. The majority of that amount is related to covering the direct and indirect costs of schizophrenia.

## Mental Hospital Beds

Both the development of effective antipsychotic drugs and changes in political and popular attitudes toward the treatment and the rights of mentally ill people have resulted in a dramatic change in the patterns of hospitalization for schizophrenic patients over the past four decades. The probability of readmission within two years after discharge from the first hospitalization is about 40 to 60 percent. Schizophrenic patients occupy about 50 percent of all mental hospital beds and account for about 16 percent of all psychiatric patients who receive any type of treatment.

## ETIOLOGY

Although schizophrenia is discussed as if it were a single disease, the diagnostic category can include a variety of disorders that present with somewhat similar behavioral symptoms. Schizophrenia probably comprises a group of disorders with heterogeneous causes and definitely includes patients whose clinical presentations, treatment responses, and courses of illness are varied.

## Stress-Diathesis Model

One model for the integration of biological factors and psychosocial and environmental factors is the stress-diathesis model. That model postulates that a person may have a specific vulnerability (diathesis) that, when acted on by some stressful environmental influence, allows the symptoms of schizophrenia to develop. In the most general stress-diathesis model the diathesis or the stress can be biological or environmental or both. The environmental component can be either biological (for example, an infection) or psychological (for example, a stressful family situation or the death of a close relative). The biological

basis of a diathesis can be further shaped by epigenetic influences, such as substance abuse, psychosocial stress, and trauma.

## Biological Factors

The cause of schizophrenia is not known. In the past decade, however, an increasing amount of research has implicated a pathophysiological role for certain areas of the brain, including the limbic system, the frontal cortex, and the basal ganglia. Those three areas are, of course, interconnected, so that dysfunction in one area may involve primary pathology in another area. Two types of research have implicated the limbic system as a potential site for the primary pathology in at least some proportion, perhaps even the majority, of schizophrenic patients. Those two types of research are brain imaging of living persons and neuropathological examination of postmortem brain tissue.

The time a neuropathological lesion appears in the brain and the interaction of the lesion with environmental and social stressors remain areas of active research. The basis for the appearance of the abnormality may lie in abnormal development (for example, abnormal migration of neurons along the radial glial cells during development) or in degeneration of neurons after development (for example, abnormally early preprogrammed cell death, as appears to occur in Huntington's disease). However, theorists are still left with the fact that monozygotic twins have a 50 percent discordance rate, thus implying that there is some poorly understood interaction between the environment and the development of schizophrenia. An alternative explanation is that, although monozygotic twins have the same genetic information, the regulation of gene expression as they go through their separate lives may be different. The factors regulating gene expression are just beginning to be understood; possibly through differential gene regulation, one monozygotic twin has schizophrenia, whereas the other does not.

**General research principles.** A basic design in biological research in schizophrenia is to measure some biological variable in a group of schizophrenic patients and in a group of nonpsychiatrically ill persons or nonschizophrenic psychiatric patients. The means of those measures are then compared to determine whether the schizophrenic group is different from the comparator group. That approach involves several caveats. First, it is difficult to find a control group that is truly matched to the schizophrenic group, since the schizophrenic group has been affected by drug treatments and psychosocial situations that most control populations have not experienced. Second, when a difference is determined by using that approach, it is difficult to know the significance of the difference. The demonstration of such a between-group difference does not indicate that the measure is causally related to schizophrenia. A difference in such a biological measure could be secondary to the disease process or to the treatment.

Clinical neurology has many examples of a single type of lesion that results in an entire range of psychological states, ranging from normal to every diagnosis in DSM-

IV. For example, many people have cerebrovascular diseases, but some of them have no psychological symptoms, some have depressive disorders, and others have mania or psychosis. Another example is Huntington's disease, which can be limited to a strictly neurological disorder or can be associated with every diagnosis in DSM-IV. Conversely, a single specific abnormality in the brain can have many different causes. Parkinson's disease, for example, has idiopathic, infectious, traumatic, and toxic causes.

**Integration of biological theories.** The major brain areas implicated in schizophrenia are the limbic structures, the frontal lobes, and the basal ganglia. The thalamus and the brainstem have also been implicated because of the role of the thalamus as an integrating mechanism and the fact that the brainstem and the midbrain are the primary locations for the ascending aminergic neurons. However, the limbic system is increasingly the focus of much of the theory-building exercises. For example, one study of twins who were discordant for schizophrenia used both magnetic resonance imaging and the measurement of regional cerebral blood flow. The investigators had previously determined that the hippocampal area of almost every affected twin was smaller than that of the unaffected twin and that the affected twin also had a smaller increase in blood flow to the dorsolateral prefrontal cortex while performing a psychological-activation procedure. The study found a correlation between those two abnormalities, suggesting that the two findings were related, although some third factor may have affected both variables.

**Dopamine hypothesis.** The simplest formulation of the *dopamine hypothesis of schizophrenia* posits that schizophrenia results from too much dopaminergic activity. The theory evolved out of two observations. First, except for clozapine, the efficacy and the potency of antipsychotics is correlated with their abilities to act as antagonists of the dopamine type 2 ($D_2$) receptor. Second, drugs that increase dopaminergic activity, most notably amphetamine, are psychotomimetic. The basic theory does not elaborate on whether the dopaminergic hyperactivity is due to too much release of dopamine, too many dopamine receptors, hypersensitivity of the dopamine receptors to dopamine, or some combination of those mechanisms. Nor does the basic theory specify which dopamine tracts in the brain may be involved, although the mesocortical and mesolimbic tracts are most often implicated. The dopaminergic neurons in those tracts project from their cell bodies in the midbrain to dopaminoceptive neurons in the limbic system and the cerebral cortex.

The dopamine hypothesis of schizophrenia continues to be refined and expanded. One area of speculation is that the dopamine type 1 ($D_1$) receptor may play a role in negative symptoms, and some researchers are interested in using $D_1$ agonists as a treatment approach for those symptoms. The recently discovered dopamine type 5 ($D_5$) receptor is related to the $D_1$ receptor and may merit research. In a parallel fashion the dopamine type 3 ($D_3$) and dopamine type 4 ($D_4$) receptors are related to the $D_2$ receptor and will be the subject of increasing research as specific agonists and antagonists are developed for those receptors. At least one study has reported an increase in $D_4$ receptors in postmortem brain samples from schizophrenic patients.

Although the dopamine hypothesis of schizophrenia has stimulated schizophrenia research for more than two decades and remains the leading neurochemical hypothesis, the hypothesis has two major problems. First, dopamine antagonists are effective in treating virtually all psychotic and severely agitated patients, regardless of diagnosis. It is not possible, therefore, to conclude that dopaminergic hyperactivity is unique to schizophrenia. For example, dopamine antagonists are also used in the treatment of acute mania. Second, some electrophysiological data suggest that dopaminergic neurons may increase their firing rate in response to long-term exposure to antipsychotic drugs. The data imply that the initial abnormality in schizophrenia may involve a hypodopaminergic state.

A significant role for dopamine in the pathophysiology of schizophrenia is consistent with studies that have measured plasma concentrations of the major dopamine metabolite, homovanillic acid. Several preliminary studies have indicated that, under carefully controlled experimental conditions, plasma homovanillic acid concentrations can reflect central nervous system (CNS) concentrations of homovanillic acid. Those studies have reported a positive correlation between high pretreatment concentrations of homovanillic acid and two factors: the severity of the psychotic symptoms and the treatment response to antipsychotic drugs. Studies of plasma homovanillic acid have also reported that, after a transient increase in plasma homovanillic acid concentrations, the concentrations decline steadily. That decline is correlated with symptom improvement in at least some patients.

**Other neurotransmitters.** Although dopamine is the neurotransmitter that has received the most attention in schizophrenia research, increasing attention is being paid to other neurotransmitters. The consideration of other neurotransmitters is warranted for at least two reasons. First, since schizophrenia is likely to be a heterogeneous disorder, it is possible that abnormalities in different neurotransmitters lead to the same behavioral syndrome. For instance, hallucinogenic substances that affect serotonin—for example, lysergic acid diethylamide (LSD)—and high doses of substances that affect dopamine—for example, amphetamine—can cause psychotic symptoms that are difficult to distinguish from intoxication. Second, basic neuroscience research has clearly shown that a single neuron may contain more than one neurotransmitter and may have neurotransmitter receptors for a half dozen more neurotransmitters. Thus, the various neurotransmitters in the brain are involved in complex interactional relations, and abnormal functioning may result from changes in any single neurotransmitter substance.

SEROTONIN. Serotonin has become of much interest in schizophrenia research since the observation that many of the so-called atypical antipsychotics have potent serotonin-related activities (for example, clozapine, risperidone, ritanserin). Specifically, antagonism at the serotonin (5-hydroxytryptamine) type 2 ($5\text{-}HT_2$) receptor has been emphasized as important in reducing psychotic symptoms and in mitigating against the development of $D_2$-antagonism-related movement disorders. As has also been suggested in the research on mood disorders, serotonin activity has been implicated in suicidal and impulsive behavior that can also be seen in schizophrenic patients.

NOREPINEPHRINE. Several investigators have reported that long-term antipsychotic administration decreases the activity of noradrenergic neurons in the locus ceruleus and that the therapeutic effects of some antipsychotics may involve their activities at $\alpha_1$-adrenergic and $\alpha_2$-adrenergic receptors. Although the relation between dopaminergic and noradrenergic activity remains unclear, an increasing body of data suggests that the noradrenergic system modulates the dopaminergic system in such a way that abnormalities of the noradrenergic system predispose a patient to relapse frequently.

AMINO ACIDS. The inhibitory amino acid neurotransmitter γ-aminobutyric acid (GABA) has also been implicated in the pathophysiology of schizophrenia. The available data are consistent with the hypothesis that some patients with schizophrenia have a loss of GABA-ergic neurons in the hippocampus. The loss of inhibitory GABA-ergic neurons could theoretically lead to the hyperactivity of dopaminergic and noradrenergic neurons.

The excitatory amino acid neurotransmitter glutamate has also been reported to be involved in the biological basis of schizophrenia. A range of hypotheses have been put forth regarding glutamate, including hyperactivity, hypoactivity, and glutamate-induced neurotoxicity hypotheses.

**Neuropathology.** Although the failure of neuropathologists in the 19th century to find a neuropathological basis for schizophrenia led to the classification of schizophrenia as a functional disorder, the past decade of neuropathological research has seen significant strides made in revealing a potential neuropathological basis for schizophrenia. The two brain areas that have received the most attention are the limbic system and the basal ganglia, although several controversial reports concern neuropathological or neurochemical abnormalities in the cerebral cortex, the thalamus, and the brainstem.

LIMBIC SYSTEM. The limbic system, because of its role in the control of emotions, has been hypothesized to be involved in the pathophysiological basis of schizophrenia. In fact, the limbic system has proved to be the most fertile area for neuropathological studies of schizophrenia. More than a half-dozen well-controlled studies of postmortem schizophrenic brain samples have found a decrease in the size of the region including the amygdala, the hippocampus, and the parahippocampal gyrus. That neuropathological finding supports a similar observation made by using magnetic resonance imaging (MRI) of living schizophrenic patients. A disorganization of the neurons within the hippocampus of schizophrenic patients has also been reported (Figure 13–3).

BASAL GANGLIA. The basal ganglia have been of theoretical interest in schizophrenia for at least two reasons. First, many schizophrenic patients have odd movements, even in the absence of medication-induced movement disorders (for example, tardive dyskinesia). The odd movements can include an awkward gait, facial grimacing, and stereotypies. Inasmuch as the basal ganglia are involved in the control of movement, pathology in the basal ganglia is thereby implicated in the pathophysiology of schizophrenia. Second, of all the neurological disorders that can have psychosis as an associated symptom, the movement disorders involving the basal ganglia (for example, Huntington's disease) are the ones most commonly associated with psychosis in affected patients. Another factor implicating the basal ganglia in the pathophysiology of schizophrenia is the fact that the basal ganglia are reciprocally connected to the frontal lobes, thus raising the possibility that the abnormalities in frontal lobe function seen in some brain imaging studies may be due to pathology within the basal ganglia, rather than in the frontal lobes themselves.

Neuropathological studies of the basal ganglia have produced variable and inconclusive reports concerning cell loss or the reduction of volume of the globus pallidus and the substantia nigra. In contrast, many studies have shown an increase in the number of D₂ receptors in the caudate, the putamen, and the nucleus accumbens; however, the question remains whether the increase is secondary to the patients' having received antipsychotic medications. Some investigators have begun to study the serotonergic system in the basal ganglia, since a role for serotonin in psychotic disorders is suggested by the clinical usefulness of antipsychotic drugs with serotonergic activity (for example, clozapine, risperidone).

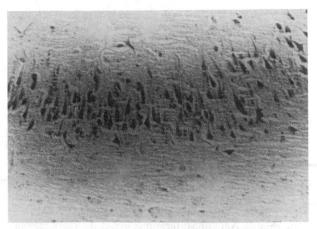
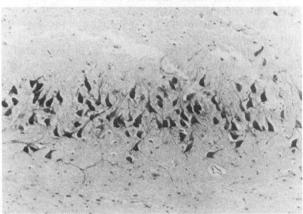

**Figure 13–3.** Comparison of cell orientation patterns of hippocampal pyramids at the CA1 to CA2 interface between nonschizophrenic control subjects (top) and schizophrenic subjects (bottom) (cresylecht violet stain, original magnification x 250). Positives were overexposed to enhance contrast. (Figure from A J Conrad, T Abebe, R Austin, S Forsythe, A B Scheibel: Hippocampal pyramidal cell disarray in schizophrenia as a bilateral phenomenon. Arch Gen Psychiatry *48*: 415, 1991. Used with permission.)

**Brain imaging.** Before the advent of brain imaging technologies, the study of schizophrenia depended on the distant measurement of brain activity—for example, the measurement of neurotransmitters in cerebrospinal fluid (CSF), plasma, or urine—in living patients or the direct measurement of the brain in deceased persons. Brain imaging techniques now allow researchers to make specific measurements of neurochemicals or brain function in living patients. However, the technology of those methods can be seductive. The reader of the research literature must be aware that many assumptions are used to develop models regarding the calculation of the data derived from the brain imaging machines. Differences in those mathematical models between two research groups can potentially lead to different conclusions from the same data. To protect against that possibility, researchers in those fields are constantly exchanging their ideas regarding the appropriate mathematical models to use.

COMPUTED TOMOGRAPHY. The initial studies using computed tomography (CT) in schizophrenic populations may have produced the earliest and most convincing data that schizophrenia is a bona fide brain disease. Those studies have consistently shown that the brains of schizophrenic patients have lateral and third ventricular enlargement and some degree of reduction in cortical volume. Those findings can be interpreted as consistent with the presence of less than usual brain tissue in affected patients; whether that decrease in the amount of brain tissue is due to abnormal development or to degeneration remains unresolved.

Other CT studies have reported abnormal cerebral asymmetry, reduced cerebellar volume, and brain density changes in schizophrenic patients. Many of the CT studies have correlated the presence of CT scan abnormalities with the presence of negative or deficit symptoms, neuropsychiatric impairment, increased neurological signs, frequent extrapyramidal symptoms from antipsychotics, and poor premorbid adjustment. Although not all CT studies have confirmed those associations, it makes intuitive sense that the more evidence of neuropathology is present, the more serious the symptoms are. However, the abnormalities reported in CT studies of schizophrenic patients have also been reported in other neuropsychiatric conditions, including mood disorders, alcohol-related disorders, and dementias. Thus, those changes are not likely to be specific for the pathophysiological processes underlying schizophrenia.

A number of studies have attempted to determine whether the abnormalities detected by CT are progressive or static. Some of the studies have concluded that the lesions observed on CT are present at the onset of the illness and do not progress. Other studies, however, have concluded that the pathology visualized on CT continues to progress during the illness. Thus, whether an active pathological process is continuing to evolve in schizophrenic patients is still uncertain.

Although the enlarged ventricles in schizophrenic patients can be shown when groups of patients and controls are used, the difference between affected and unaffected persons is variable and usually small. Therefore, the use of CT in the diagnosis of schizophrenia is limited. However, some data indicate that ventricles are more enlarged in patients with tardive dyskinesia than in patients who do not have tardive dyskinesia. Also, some data indicate that the enlargement of ventricles is seen more often in male patients than in female patients.

MAGNETIC RESONANCE IMAGING.   Magnetic resonance imaging (MRI) was initially used to verify the findings of the CT studies but has subsequently been used to expand the knowledge about the pathophysiology of schizophrenia. One of the most important MRI studies examined monozygotic twins who were discordant for schizophrenia (Figure 13–4). The study found that virtually all the affected twins had larger cerebral ventricles than did the nonaffected twins, although most of the affected twins had cerebral ventricles within a normal range.

Investigators using MRI in schizophrenia research have used its properties of superior resolution, compared with CT, and the qualitative information obtainable by using various signal sequences to get $T_1$- or $T_2$-weighted images, for example. MRI's superior resolution has resulted in several reports that the volumes of the hippocampal-amygdala complex and the parahippocampal gyrus are reduced in schizophrenic patients. One recent study found a specific reduction of those

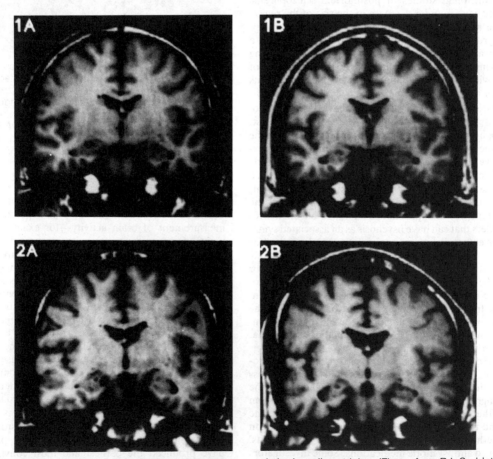

**Figure 13–4.**   Magnetic resonance images (MRI). MRI coronal views from two sets of monozygotic twins discordant for schizophrenia showing subtle enlargement of the lateral ventricles in the affected twins (panels 1B and 2B) as compared with the unaffected twins (panels 1A and 2A), even when the affected twin had small ventricles. (Figure from R L Suddath, G W Christison, E F Torrey, M F Casanova, D R Weinberger: Anatomical abnormalities in the brains of monozygotic twins discordant for schizophrenia. N Engl J Med *322*: 789, 1990. Used with permission.)

brain areas in the left hemisphere (Figure 13–5) and not in the right, although other studies have found bilateral reductions in volume. Some of the studies have correlated the reduction in limbic system volume with the degree of psychopathology or other measures of severity of illness. There have

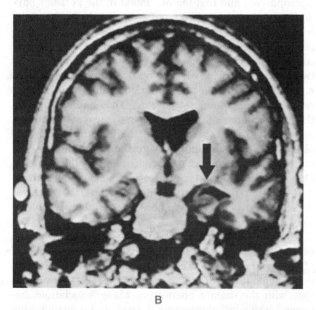

**Figure 13–5.** Coronal slice (1.5 mm) of the temporal lobe of a control (panel A) and a patient with schizophrenia (panel B). In panel A the regions of interest used to evaluate the temporal lobe have been outlined; the neocortical gray matter of the superior temporal gyrus is on the subject's left (the viewer's right); more medially, the amygdala-hippocampal complex is shown as an almondlike shape, with the parahippocampal gyrus underneath. The temporal lobe is outlined on the subject's right. In panel B the amount of cerebrospinal fluid (black area) surrounding the left superior temporal gyrus (sylvian fissure) is increased, as compared with the amount in the control. Tissue is lost in the parahippocampal gyrus, and the size of the temporal horn surrounding the amygdala-hippocampal complex (arrow) is increased. (Figure from M E Shenton, R Kikinis, F A Jolesz, S D Pollak, M LeMay, C G Wible, H Hokama, J Martin, D Metcalf, M Coleman, R W McCarley: Abnormalities of the left temporal lobe and thought disorder in schizophrenia. N Engl J Med *327*: 606, 1992.)

also been reports of differential $T_1$ and $T_2$ relaxation times in schizophrenic patients, particularly as measured in the frontal and temporal regions.

MAGNETIC RESONANCE SPECTROSCOPY. Magnetic resonance spectroscopy (MRS) is a technique that allows the measurement of the concentrations of specific molecules—for example, adenosine triphosphate (ATP)—in the brain. Although the technique is still early in its development, several preliminary reports of using MRS to study schizophrenia have appeared in the literature. One study that used MRS imaging of the dorsolateral prefrontal cortex found that, compared with a control group, schizophrenic patients had lower levels of phosphomonoesters and inorganic phosphate and higher levels of phosphodiesters and adenosine triphosphate. Those data concerning the metabolism of phosphate-containing compounds were consistent with hypoactivity of that brain region, thus supporting the findings of other brain imaging studies—for example, positron emission tomography (PET).

POSITRON EMISSION TOMOGRAPHY. Although many studies using positron emission tomography (PET) to study schizophrenia have been reported, few clear conclusions can be drawn at this time. Most PET studies have measured either glucose utilization or cerebral blood flow, and the positive findings have included hypoactivity of the frontal lobes, impaired activation of certain brain areas after psychological test stimulation, and hyperactivity of the basal ganglia relative to the cerebral cortex. A number of studies, however, have failed to replicate those findings, although the abnormal-activation results seem to be a robust finding. In those studies the person's blood flow is assayed by using PET, single photon emission computed tomography (SPECT), or regional cerebral blood flow (rCBF) brain imaging systems. While the cerebral blood flow is being measured, the person is asked to perform a psychological task that presumably activates a particular part of the cerebral cortex in normal control subjects. One of the best-controlled studies of that design found that schizophrenic patients, in contrast to the control group, failed to increase blood flow to the dorsolateral prefrontal cortex while performing the Wisconsin Card-Sorting Test.

A second type of PET study has used radioactive ligands to estimate the quantity of $D_2$ receptors present. The two most discussed studies disagree; one group reported an increased number of $D_2$ receptors in the basal ganglia, and the other group reported no change in the number of $D_2$ receptors in the basal ganglia. The difference between the two studies may involve the use of different ligands, different types of schizophrenic patients, or other differences in method or data analysis. The controversy remains unresolved at this time. However, the technique will continue to be used in the study of schizophrenia, and subsequent research reports will use ligands for other neurotransmitter systems, such as the noradrenergic and glutamate systems.

**Electrophysiology.** Electroencephalographic (EEG) studies of schizophrenic patients indicate that a high number of patients have abnormal records, increased sensitivity to activation procedures (for example, frequent spike activity after sleep deprivation), decreased alpha activity, increased theta and delta activity, possibly more than usual epileptiform activity, and possibly more than usual left-sided abnormalities.

COMPLEX PARTIAL EPILEPSY. Schizophrenialike psychoses have been reported to occur more frequently than expected in patients with complex partial seizures, especially seizures involving the temporal lobes. Factors associated with the development of psychosis in those patients include a left-sided seizure focus, medial temporal location of the lesion, and early onset of seizures. The first-rank symptoms described by Schneider may be similar to symptoms seen in patients with complex partial epilepsy and may reflect the presence of temporal lobe pathology when seen in patients with schizophrenia.

EVOKED POTENTIALS. A large number of abnormalities in evoked potentials in schizophrenic patients have been described in the research literature. The P300 has been most studied and is defined as a large, positive evoked-potential wave that occurs about 300 milliseconds after a sensory stimulus is detected. The major source of the P300 wave may be located in the limbic system structures of the medial temporal lobes. In schizophrenic patients the P300 has been reported to be statistically smaller and later than in comparison groups. Abnormalities in the P300 wave have also been reported to be more common in children who are at high risk for schizophrenia because of having affected parents. Whether the characteristics of the P300 represent a state phenomenon or a trait phenomenon remains controversial. Other evoked potentials that have been reported to be abnormal in schizophrenic patients are the N100 and the contingent negative variation. The N100 is a negative wave that occurs about 100 milliseconds after the stimulus, and the contingent negative variation is a slowly developing, negative-voltage shift that follows the presentation of a sensory stimulus that is a warning for an upcoming stimulus. The evoked-potential data have been interpreted as indicating that, although schizophrenic patients are unusually sensitive to sensory stimulus (larger early evoked potentials), they compensate for the increased sensitivity by blunting the processing of information at higher cortical levels (indicated by smaller late evoked potentials).

**Eye movement dysfunction.** The inability of a person to accurately follow a moving visual target is the defining basis for the disorders of smooth visual pursuit and the disinhibition of saccadic eye movements seen in schizophrenic patients. Eye movement dysfunction may be a trait marker for schizophrenia, since it is independent of drug treatment and clinical state, and it is also seen in first-degree relatives of schizophrenic probands. Various studies have reported abnormal eye movements in 50 to 85 percent of schizophrenic patients, in comparison with about 25 percent in nonschizophrenic psychiatric patients and less than 10 percent in nonpsychiatrically ill control subjects. Since eye movement is partly controlled by centers in the frontal lobes, a disorder in eye movement is consistent with theories that implicate frontal lobe pathology in schizophrenia.

**Psychoneuroimmunology.** A number of immunological abnormalities have been associated with schizophrenic patients. The abnormalities include decreased T cell interleukin-2 production, reduced number and responsiveness of peripheral lymphocytes, abnormal cellular and humoral reactivity to neurons, and the presence of brain-directed (antibrain) antibodies. The data can be interpreted variously as representing the effects of a neurotoxic virus or of an endogenous autoimmune disorder. Most carefully conducted investigations that have searched for evidence of neurotoxic viral infections in schizophrenia have had negative results, although epidemiological data show a high incidence of schizophrenia after prenatal exposure to influenza during several epidemics of the disease. Other data that support a viral hypothesis are an increased number of physical anomalies at birth, an increased rate of pregnancy and birth complications, seasonality of birth consistent with viral infection, geographical clusters of adult cases, and seasonality of hospitalizations. Nonetheless, the inability to detect genetic evidence of viral infection reduces the significance of all the circumstantial data. The possibility of autoimmune brain antibodies has some data to support it; however, the pathophysiological process, if it exists, probably explains only a subset of the schizophrenic populations.

**Psychoneuroendocrinology.** Many reports describe neuroendocrine differences between groups of schizophrenic patients and groups of normal control subjects. For example, the dexamethasone-suppression test has been reported to be abnormal in various subgroups of schizophrenic patients, although the practical or predictive value of the test in schizophrenia has been questioned. However, one carefully done report has correlated persistent nonsuppression on the dexamethasone-suppression test in schizophrenia with a poor long-term outcome.

Some data suggest decreased concentrations of luteinizing hormone-follicle stimulating hormone (LH/FSH), perhaps correlated with age of onset and length of illness. Two additional reported abnormalities are a blunted release of prolactin and growth hormone to gonadotropin-releasing hormone (GnRH) or thyrotropin-releasing hormone (TRH) stimulation and a blunted release of growth hormone to apomorphine stimulation that may be correlated with the presence of negative symptoms.

## Genetics

A wide range of genetic studies strongly suggested a genetic component to the inheritance of schizophrenia. The early, classic studies of the genetics of schizophrenia, done in the 1930s, found that a person is likely to have schizophrenia if other members of the family also have schizophrenia and that the likelihood of the person's having schizophrenia is correlated with the closeness of the relationship (for example, first-degree or second-degree relative) (Table 13–2). Monozygotic twins have the highest concordance rate. The studies of adopted monozygotic twins show that twins who are reared by adoptive parents have schizophrenia at the same rate as their twin siblings raised by their biological parents. That finding suggests that the genetic influence outweighs the environmental influence. In further support of the genetic basis is the observation that the more severe the schizophrenia, the more likely the twins are to be concordant for the disorder. One study that supports the stress-diathesis model showed that adopted monozygotic twins who later had schizophrenia were likely to have been adopted by psychologically disordered families.

**Chromosomal markers.** Current approaches in genetics are directed toward identifying large pedigrees of affected persons and investigating the families for restriction fragment length polymorphisms (RFLPs) that segregate with the disease phenotype. Many associations between particular chromosomal sites and schizophrenia have been reported in the literature since the widespread application of the techniques of molecular biology. More

**Table 13–2**
**Prevalence of Schizophrenia in Specific Populations**

| Population | Prevalence (%) |
|---|---|
| General population | 1.0 |
| Nontwin sibling of a schizophrenic patient | 8.0 |
| Child with one schizophrenic parent | 12.0 |
| Dzygotic twin of a schizophrenic patient | 12.0 |
| Child of two schizophrenic parents | 40.0 |
| Monozygotic twin of a schizophrenic patient | 47.0 |

than half of the chromosomes have been associated with schizophrenia in those various reports, but the long arms of chromosomes 5, 11, and 18; the short arm of chromosome 19; and the X chromosome have been the most commonly reported. At this time, the literature is best summarized as indicating a potentially heterogeneous genetic basis for schizophrenia.

### Psychosocial Factors

The rapidly evolving understanding regarding the biology of schizophrenia and the introduction of effective and safe pharmacological treatments have further emphasized the important need for an understanding of individual, family, and social issues that affect the patient with schizophrenia. If schizophrenia is a disease of the brain, it is likely to parallel diseases of other organs (for example, myocardial infarctions and diabetes) whose courses are affected by psychosocial stress. Also in parallel with other chronic diseases (for example, chronic congestive pulmonary disease), drug therapy alone is rarely sufficient to obtain maximal clinical improvement. Thus, the clinician should consider the psychosocial factors that affect schizophrenia. Although, historically, it has been argued that some of the psychosocial factors are directly and causally linked to the development of schizophrenia, that prior view should not prevent the contemporary clinician from using the relevant theories and guidelines from those past observations and hypotheses.

**Theories regarding the individual patient.** Regardless of the controversies regarding the cause or causes of schizophrenia, it remains irrefutable that schizophrenia affects individual patients, each of whom has a unique psychological makeup. Although many psychodynamic theories regarding the pathogenesis of schizophrenia seem out of date to contemporary readers, their perceptive clinical observations can help the contemporary clinician understand how the disease may affect the patient's psyche.

PSYCHOANALYTIC THEORIES. Sigmund Freud postulated that schizophrenia results from fixations in development that occurred earlier than those that result in the development of neuroses. Freud also postulated the presence of an ego defect that also contributes to the symptoms of schizophrenia. Ego disintegration is a return to the time when the ego was not yet established or had just begun to be established. Thus, intrapsychic conflict resulting from the early fixations and the ego defect, which may have resulted from poor early object relations, fuel the psychotic symptoms. Central to Freud's theories regarding schizophrenia were a decathexis of objects and a regression in response to frustration and conflict with others. Many of Freud's ideas regarding schizophrenia were colored by his lack of intensive involvement with schizophrenic patients. In contrast, Harry Stack Sullivan engaged schizophrenic patients in intensive psychoanalysis and concluded that the illness results from early interpersonal difficulties, particularly those related to what he considered faulty, overly anxious mothering.

The general psychoanalytic view of schizophrenia hypothesizes that the ego defect affects the interpretation of reality and the control of inner drives, such as sex and aggression. The disturbances occur as a consequence of distortions in the reciprocal relationship between the infant and the mother. As described by Margaret Mahler, the child is unable to separate and progress beyond the closeness and complete dependence that characterizes the mother-child relationship in the oral phase of development. The schizophrenic person never achieves object constancy, which is characterized by a sense of secure identity and which results from a close attachment to the mother during infancy. Paul Federn concluded that the fundamental disturbance in schizophrenia is the patient's early inability to achieve self-object differentiation. Some psychoanalysts hypothesize that the defect in rudimentary ego functions permits intense hostility and aggression to distort the mother-infant relationship, leading to a personality organization that is vulnerable to stress. The onset of symptoms during adolescence occurs at a time when the person requires a strong ego to deal with the need to function independently, to separate from the parents, to identify tasks, to control increased internal drives, and to cope with intense external simulation.

Psychoanalytic theory also postulates that the various symptoms of schizophrenia have symbolic meaning for the individual patient. For example, fantasies of the world coming to an end may indicate a perception that the person's internal world has broken down. Feelings of grandeur may reflect reactivated narcissism, in which persons believe that they are omnipotent. Hallucinations may be substitutes for the patients' inability to deal with objective reality and may represent their inner wishes or fears. Delusions, similar to hallucinations, are regressive, restitutive attempts to create a new reality or to express hidden fears or impulses.

PSYCHODYNAMIC THEORIES. Genetic studies clearly suggest that schizophrenia is an illness with a biological substrate. Nevertheless, studies of monozygotic twins repeatedly show that environmental and psychological factors have some importance in the development of schizophrenia, since many twins are discordant for the illness. Freud regarded schizophrenia as a regressive response to overwhelming frustration and conflict with persons in the environment. That regression involves a withdrawal of emotional investment or *cathexis* from both internal object representations and actual persons in the environment, leading to a return to an autoerotic stage of development. The patient's cathexis is reinvested in the self, thus giving the appearance of autistic withdrawal. Freud later added that, although neurosis involves a conflict between the ego and the id, psychosis can be viewed as a conflict between the ego and the external world in which reality is disavowed and subsequently remodeled.

Later psychodynamic views of schizophrenia have differed from Freud's complex model. They tend to regard the constitutionally based hypersensitivity to perceptual stimuli as a deficit. Indeed, a good deal of research suggests that patients with schizophrenia find it difficult to screen out various stimuli and to focus on one piece of data at a time. That defective stimulus barrier creates difficulty throughout every phase of development during childhood and places particular stress on interpersonal relatedness. Psychodynamic views of schizophrenia are often mistakenly regarded as parent-blaming, when actually they focus on psychological and neurophysiological difficulties that create problems for most people in close relationships with the schizophrenic patient.

Regardless of which theoretical model is preferred, all psychodynamic approaches operate from the premise that psychotic symptoms have meaning in schizophrenia. For example, patients may become grandiose after an injury to their self-esteem. Similarly, all theories recognize that human relatedness may be terrifying for persons suffering from schizophrenia. Although the research on the efficacy of psychotherapy with schizophrenia shows mixed results, concerned persons who offer human compassion and a sanctuary from a confusing world must be a cornerstone of any overall treatment plan. Long-term follow-up studies find that some patients who seal over psychotic episodes probably do not benefit from exploratory psychotherapy, but those who are able to integrate the psychotic experience into their lives may benefit from some insight-oriented approaches.

LEARNING THEORIES. According to learning theorists, children who later have schizophrenia learn irrational reactions and ways of thinking by imitating parents who may have their own significant emotional problems. The poor interpersonal relationships of schizophrenic persons, according to learning theory, also develop because of poor models from which to learn during childhood.

**Theories regarding the family.** No well-controlled evidence indicates that any specific family pattern plays a causative role in the development of schizophrenia. That is an important point for clinicians to understand, since many parents of schizophrenic children still harbor anger against the psychiatric community, which for a long time was fairly outspoken regarding a correlation between dysfunctional families and the development of schizophrenia. Some schizophrenic patients do come from dysfunctional families, just as many nonpsychiatrically ill persons come from dysfunctional families. It is of clinical relevance, however, to recognize pathological family behavior, since such behavior can significantly increase the emotional stress that a vulnerable schizophrenic patient must cope with.

DOUBLE BIND. The double bind concept was formulated by Gregory Bateson to describe a hypothetical family in which children receive conflicting parental messages regarding their behavior, attitudes, and feelings. Within that hypothesis, children withdraw into their own psychotic state to escape the unsolvable confusion of the double bind. Unfortunately, the family studies that were conducted to prove the theory were seriously flawed methodologically and cannot be taken to show the validity of the theory.

SCHISMS AND SKEWED FAMILIES. Theodore Lidz described two abnormal patterns of family behavior. In one type of family, there is a prominent schism between the parents, and one parent gets overly close to a child of the opposite sex. In the other type of family, a skewed relationship with one parent involves a power struggle between the parents and the resulting dominance of one parent.

PSEUDOMUTUAL AND PSEUDOHOSTILE FAMILIES. Lyman Wynne described families in which emotional expression is suppressed by the consistent use of a pseudomutual or pseudohostile verbal communication. That suppression results in the development of a verbal communication that is unique to that family and not necessarily comprehensible to anyone outside the family; problems arise when the child leaves home and has to relate to other people.

EXPRESSED EMOTION. Expressed emotion (often abbreviated EE) is usually defined as including the criticism, hostility, and overinvolvement that can characterize the behavior of parents or other caretakers toward a schizophrenic person. Many studies have indicated that, in families with high levels of expressed emotion, the relapse rate for schizophrenia is high. The assessment of expressed emotion involves analyzing both what is said and the manner in which it is said.

**Social theories.** Some theorists have suggested that industrialization and urbanization are involved in the causes of schizophrenia. Although some data support such theories, the stresses are now thought to have their major effects on the timing of the onset and the severity of the illness.

# DIAGNOSIS

DSM-IV contains the American Psychiatric Association's official diagnostic criteria for schizophrenia (Table 13–3). The criteria in other diagnostic systems are given in Table 13–1. Of particular note are the diagnostic criteria of Ming T. Tsuang, and George Winokur, who in 1974 made a distinction between paranoid and nonparanoid schizophrenic patients.

The DSM-IV diagnostic criteria are largely unchanged from those in the revised third edition of DSM (DSM-III-R), although the DSM-IV course specifiers offer more options to the clinician and are more descriptive of actual clinical situations (Table 13–3). As in DSM-III-R, neither hallucinations nor delusions are required for the diagnosis of schizophrenia, since patients can meet the diagnosis if they have two of the symptoms listed as symptoms 3 to 5 in criterion A (Table 13–3). Criterion B eliminates the word "deterioration" in acknowledgment of the variable course of schizophrenia among patients. Nevertheless, criterion B still requires impaired functioning during the active phase of the illness. DSM-IV still requires symptoms for a minimum of six months and the absence of a diagnosis of schizoaffective disorder or a mood disorder.

## DSM-IV Subtypes

DSM-IV uses the same subtypes of schizophrenia that were used in DSM-III-R: paranoid, disorganized, catatonic, undifferentiated, and residual types (Table 13–4). The DSM-IV subtyping scheme is based predominantly on clinical presentation. The DSM-IV subtypes are not closely correlated with differentiations of prognosis; such differentiation can best be done by looking at specific predictors of prognosis (Table 13–5).

**Paranoid type.** DSM-IV specifies that the paranoid type is characterized by preoccupation with one or more delusions or frequent auditory hallucinations and that other specific behaviors suggestive of the disorganized or

**Table 13–3**
**Diagnostic Criteria for Schizophrenia**

A. *Characteristic symptoms:* Two (or more) of the following, each present for a significant portion of time during a 1-month period (or less if successfully treated):
   (1) delusions
   (2) hallucinations
   (3) disorganized speech (e.g., frequent derailment or incoherence)
   (4) grossly disorganized or catatonic behavior
   (5) negative symptoms, i.e., affective flattening, alogia, or avolition
   **Note:** Only one criterion A symptom is required if delusions are bizarre or hallucinations consist of a voice keeping up a running commentary on the person's behavior or thoughts, or two or more voices conversing with each other.

B. *Social/occupational dysfunction:* For a significant portion of the time since the onset of the disturbance, one or more major areas of functioning, such as work, interpersonal relations, or self-care, are markedly below the level achieved prior to the onset (or when the onset is in childhood or adolescence, failure to achieve expected level of interpersonal, academic, or occupational achievement).

C. *Duration:* Continuous signs of the disturbance persist for at least 6 months. This 6-month period must include at least 1 month of symptoms (or less if successfully treated) that meet criterion A (i.e., active-phase symptoms) and may include periods of prodromal or residual symptoms. During these prodromal or residual periods, the signs of the disturbance may be manifested by only negative symptoms or two or more symptoms listed in criterion A present in an attenuated form (e.g., odd beliefs, unusual perceptual experiences).

D. *Schizoaffective and mood disorder exclusion:* Schizoaffective disorder and mood disorder with psychotic features have been ruled out because either: (1) no major depressive, manic, or mixed episodes have occurred concurrently with the active-phase symptoms; or (2) if mood episodes have occurred during active-phase symptoms, their total duration has been brief relative to the duration of the active and residual periods.

E. *Substance/general medical condition exclusion:* The disturbance is not due to the direct physiological effects of a substance (e.g., a drug of abuse, a medication) or a general medical condition.

F. *Relationship to a pervasive developmental disorder:* If there is a history of autistic disorder or another pervasive developmental disorder, the additional diagnosis of schizophrenia is made only if prominent delusions or hallucinations are also present for at least a month (or less if successfully treated).

*Classification of longitudinal course* (can be applied only after at least 1 year has elapsed since the initial onset of active-phase symptoms):
**Episodic with interepisode residual symptoms** (episodes are defined by the reemergence of prominent psychotic symptoms); *also specify if:* **with prominent negative symptoms**
**Episodic with no interepisode residual symptoms**
**Continuous** (prominent psychotic symptoms are present throughout the period of observation); *also specify if:* **with prominent negative symptoms**
**Single episode in partial remission;** *also specify if:* **with prominent negative symptoms**
**Single episode in full remission**
**Other or unspecified pattern**

**Table 13–4**
**Diagnostic Criteria for Schizophrenia Subtypes**

**Paranoid Type**
A type of schizophrenia in which the following criteria are met:

A. Preoccupation with one or more delusions or frequent auditory hallucinations

B. None of the following is prominent: disorganized speech, disorganized or catatonic behavior, or flat or inappropriate affect.

**Disorganized Type**
A type of schizophrenia in which the following criteria are met:

A. All of the following are prominent:
   (1) disorganized speech
   (2) disorganized behavior
   (3) flat or inappropriate affect

B. The criteria are not met for catatonic type.

**Catatonic Type**
A type of schizophrenia in which the clinical picture is dominated by at least two of the following:
   (1) motoric immobility as evidenced by catalepsy (including waxy flexibility) or stupor
   (2) excessive motor activity (that is apparently purposeless and not influenced by external stimuli)
   (3) extreme negativism (an apparently motiveless resistance to all instructions or maintenance of a rigid posture against attempts to be moved) or mutism
   (4) peculiarities of voluntary movement as evidenced by posturing (voluntary assumption of inappropriate or bizarre postures), stereotyped movements, prominent mannerisms, or prominent grimacing
   (5) echolalia or echopraxia

**Undifferentiated Type**
A type of schizophrenia in which symptoms that meet criterion A are present, but the criteria are not met for the paranoid, disorganized, or catatonic type.

**Residual Type**
A type of schizophrenia in which the following criteria are met:

A. Absence of prominent delusions, hallucinations, disorganized speech, and grossly disorganized or catatonic behavior.

B. There is continuing evidence of the disturbance, as indicated by the presence of negative symptoms or two or more symptoms listed in criterion A for schizophrenia, present in an attenuated form (e.g., odd beliefs, unusual perceptual experiences).

catatonic type are absent. Classically, the paranoid type of schizophrenia is characterized mainly by the presence of delusions of persecution or grandeur. Paranoid schizophrenic patients are usually older than catatonic or disorganized schizophrenic patients when they have the first episode of illness. Patients who have been well up to their late 20s or 30s have usually established a social life that may help them through their illness. Also, the ego resources of paranoid patients tend to be greater than those of catatonic and disorganized patients. Paranoid schizophrenic patients show less regression of their mental faculties, emotional response, and behavior than do the other types of schizophrenic patients.

**Table 13–5**
**Features Weighting toward Good to Poor Prognosis in Schizophrenia**

| Good Prognosis | Poor Prognosis |
| --- | --- |
| Late onset | Young onset |
| Obvious precipitating factors | No precipitating factors |
| Acute onset | Insidious onset |
| Good premorbid social, sexual, and work histories | Poor premorbid social, sexual, and work histories |
| Mood disorder symptoms (especially depressive disorders) | Withdrawn, autistic behavior |
| Married | Single, divorced, or widowed |
| Family history of mood disorders | Family history of schizophrenia |
| Good support systems | Poor support systems |
| Positive symptoms | Negative symptoms |
| | Neurological signs and symptoms |
| | History of perinatal trauma |
| | No remissions in three years |
| | Many relapses |
| | History of assaultiveness |

Typical paranoid schizophrenic patients are tense, suspicious, guarded, and reserved. They can also be hostile or aggressive. Paranoid schizophrenic patients can occasionally conduct themselves adequately in social situations. Their intelligence in areas not invaded by their psychosis tends to remain intact.

A 44-year-old single unemployed man was brought into an emergency room by the police for striking an elderly woman in his apartment building. He complained that the woman he struck was a bitch and that she and "the others" deserved more than that for what they put him through.

The patient had been continuously ill since the age of 22. During his first year of law school, he gradually became more and more convinced that his classmates were making fun of him. He noticed that they would snort and sneeze whenever he entered the classroom. When a girl he was dating broke off the relationship with him, he believed that she had been replaced by a look-alike. He called the police and asked for their help in solving the "kidnapping." His academic performance in school declined dramatically, and he was asked to leave and seek psychiatric care.

The patient got a job as an investment counselor at a bank, which he held for seven months. However, he was getting an increasing number of distracting "signals" from coworkers, and he became more and more suspicious and withdrawn. At that time he first reported hearing voices. He was eventually fired and soon thereafter was hospitalized for the first time, at age 24. He had not worked since.

The patient had been hospitalized 12 times; the longest stay was for eight months. However, in the past five years he had been hospitalized only once, for three weeks. During the hospitalizations he had received various antipsychotic drugs. Although outpatient medication had been prescribed, he usually stopped taking it shortly after leaving the hospital. Aside from twice-yearly lunch meetings with his uncle and his contacts with mental health workers, he was totally isolated socially. He lived on his own and managed his own financial affairs, including a modest inheritance. He read *The Wall Street Journal* daily. He cooked and cleaned for himself.

The patient maintained that his apartment was the center of a large communication system that involved all three major television networks, his neighbors, and apparently hundreds of "actors" in his neighborhood. There were secret cameras in his apartment that carefully monitored all his activities. When he was watching television, many of his minor actions (for example, getting up to go to the bathroom) were soon directly commented on by the announcer. Whenever he went outside, the "actors" had all been warned to keep him under surveillance; everyone on the street watched him. His neighbors operated two "machines"; one was responsible for all his voices, except the "joker." He was not certain who controlled that voice, which visited him only occasionally and was very funny. The other voices, which he heard many times each day, were generated by that machine, which he sometimes thought was directly run by the neighbor whom he attacked. For example, when he was going over his investments, those "harassing" voices constantly told him which stocks to buy. The other machine he called "the dream machine." That machine put erotic dreams into his head, usually of black women.

The patient described other unusual experiences. For example, he recently went to a shoe store 30 miles from his home in the hope of getting some shoes that would not be "altered." However, he soon found out that, like the rest of the shoes he bought, special nails had been put into the bottoms of the shoes to annoy him. He was amazed that his decision about which shoe store to go to must have been known to his "harassers" before he himself knew it, so that they had time to get the altered shoes made up especially for him. He realized that great effort and "millions of dollars" were involved in keeping him under surveillance. He sometimes thought that was all part of a large experiment to discover the secret of his superior intelligence.

At the interview, the patient was well-groomed, and his speech was coherent and goal-directed. His affect was, at most, only mildly blunted. He was initially angry at being brought in by the police. After several weeks of treatment with an antipsychotic drug failed to control his psychotic symptoms, he was transferred to a long-stay facility with the plan to arrange a structured living situation for him.

*Discussion.* The patient's long illness apparently began with delusions of reference (his classmates making fun of him by snorting and sneezing when he entered the classroom). Over the years his delusions had become increasingly complex and bizarre (his neighbors were actually actors; his thoughts were monitored; a machine put erotic dreams into his head). In addition, he had prominent hallucinations of voices that harassed him.

Bizarre delusions and prominent hallucinations are the characteristic psychotic symptoms of schizophrenia. The diagnosis was confirmed by the marked disturbance in his work and social functioning and the absence of a sustained mood disturbance and of any known organic factor that could account for the disturbance.

All the patient's delusions and hallucinations seemed to involve the single theme of a conspiracy to harass him. That systematized persecutory delusion—in the absence of incoherence, marked loosening of associations, flat or grossly inappropriate affect, or catatonic or grossly disorganized behavior—indicates the paranoid type. Schizophrenia, paranoid type, is further specified as continuous if, as in this case, all past and present active phases of the illness have been the paranoid type. The prognosis for the continuous paranoid type is better than the prognosis for the disorganized and undifferentiated types. The patient did, in fact, do remarkably well in spite of a chronic psychotic illness; over the past five years he had been able to take care of himself.

**Disorganized type.** The disorganized (formerly called hebephrenic) type is characterized by a marked regression to primitive, disinhibited, and unorganized behavior and by the absence of symptoms that meet the criteria for the catatonic type. The onset is usually early, before age 25. Disorganized patients are usually active but in an aimless, nonconstructive manner. Their thought disorder is pronounced, and their contact with reality is poor. Their personal appearance and their social behavior are dilapidated. Their emotional responses are inappropriate, and they often burst out laughing without any apparent reason. Incongruous grinning and grimacing are common in this type of patient, whose behavior is best described as silly or fatuous.

The patient was a 40-year-old man who looked 30. He was brought in for this 12th hospitalization by his mother because she was afraid of him. He was dressed in a ragged overcoat, bedroom slippers, and a baseball cap and wore several medals around his neck. His affect ranged from anger at his mother—"She feeds me shit . . . what comes out of other people's rectums"—to a giggling, obsequious seductiveness toward the interviewer. His speech and manner had a childlike quality, and he walked with a mincing step and exaggerated hip movements. His mother reported that he had stopped taking his medication about a month before and had since begun to hear voices and to act bizarrely. When asked what he had been doing, he said, "Eating wires and lighting fires." His spontaneous speech was often incoherent and marked by frequent rhyming and clang associations.

The patient's first hospitalization occurred after he dropped out of school at age 16. Since that time he had never been able to attend school or hold a job. He lived with his elderly mother but sometimes disappeared for several months at a time and was eventually picked up by the police as he wandered the streets. He had no known history of alcohol or other substance abuse.

*Discussion.* The combination of a chronic illness with marked incoherence, inappropriate affect, auditory hallucinations, and bizarre behavior leaves little doubt that the diagnosis is schizophrenia. The presence of marked loosening of associations and grossly inappropriate affect and the absence of prominent catatonic symptoms indicate the disorganized type.

**Catatonic type.** Although the catatonic type was common several decades ago, it is now rare in Europe and North America. The classic feature of the catatonic type is a marked disturbance in motor function, which may involve stupor, negativism, rigidity, excitement, or posturing. Sometimes the patient shows a rapid alteration between extremes of excitement and stupor. Associated fea-

tures include stereotypies, mannerisms, and waxy flexibility. Mutism is particularly common. During catatonic stupor or excitement, schizophrenic patients need careful supervision to avoid hurting themselves or others. Medical care may be needed because of malnutrition, exhaustion, hyperpyrexia, or self-inflicted injury.

**Undifferentiated type.** Frequently, patients who are clearly schizophrenic cannot be easily fitted into one of the other types. DSM-IV classifies those patients as the undifferentiated type.

A 15-year-old girl was seen at the request of her school district authorities for advice on placement. She had recently moved into the area with her family and, after a brief period in a regular class, was placed in a class for the emotionally disturbed. She proved difficult, had a poor understanding of schoolwork, and functioned at about the fifth-grade level despite an apparently good vocabulary. She disturbed the class by making animal noises and telling fantastic stories, causing other students to laugh at her.

At home the patient was aggressive, biting or hitting her parents or brother when frustrated. She was often bored, had no friends, and found it difficult to occupy herself. She spent a lot of time drawing pictures of robots, spaceships, and fantastic or futuristic inventions. Sometimes she said she would like to die, but she never made any attempt at suicide and apparently had not thought of killing herself. Her mother said that from birth she had been different and that the onset of her current behavior had been so gradual that no definite date could be assigned to it.

The patient's prenatal and parental histories were unremarkable. Her milestones were delayed, and she did not use single words until 4 or 5 years of age. Ever since she entered school, there had been concern about her ability. Repeated evaluations had suggested an intelligence quotient (I.Q.) in the low 70s, but her achievement was somewhat behind what was expected at that level of ability. Because her father was in the military service, the family had moved many times, and the results of her earlier evaluations were not available.

The parents reported that the patient had always been difficult and restless. Several doctors had said that she was not just mentally retarded but that she also suffered from a serious mental disorder. The results of an evaluation done at the age of 12, because of difficulties in school, showed evidence of bizarre thought processes and a fragmented ego structure. At that time she was sleeping well at night and was not getting up with nightmares or bizarre requests, although that had apparently been a feature of her earlier behavior. At that time she was reported to sleep poorly, disturbing the household nightly by getting up and wandering around. Her mother emphasized the patient's unpredictability, the funny stories that she told, and the way in which she talked to herself in "funny voices." Her mother regarded the stories the patient told as childish make-believe and preoccupation and paid little attention to them. She said that, since the patient went to see the movie *Star Wars,* she was obsessed with ideas about space, spaceships, and the future.

Her parents were in their early 40s. Her father, having retired from military service, worked as an engineer. The patient's mother had many unusual beliefs about herself. She was loquacious and circumstantial in her history giving. She dwelled a great deal on her strange childhood experiences. She claimed to have grown up in India and to have had a bizarre early childhood, full of dramatic and violent episodes. Many of those episodes sounded improbable. Her husband, in contrast, refused to let her talk about her past in his presence and tried to play down that material and the patient's problems. The parents appeared to have a restricted relationship. The father played the role of a taciturn, masterful head of household, and the mother bore the brunt of everyday family duties.

In the interview the patient presented as a tall, overweight, pasty-looking child, dressed untidily and with a somewhat disheveled appearance. She complained vociferously of her insomnia, although it was difficult to elicit details of the sleep disturbance. She talked at length about her interests and occupations. She said she had made a robot in the basement that ran amok and was about to cause a great deal of damage when she was finally able to stop it by remote control. She claimed to have built the robot from spare computer parts, which she acquired from the local museum.

When pressed for details of how the robot worked, the patient became increasingly vague. When asked to draw a picture of one of her inventions, she drew a picture of an overhead railway and went into what appeared to be complex mathematical calculations to substantiate the structural details, which, in fact, consisted of meaningless repetitions of symbols (for example, plus, minus, divide, multiply). When the interviewer expressed some gentle incredulity, she blandly replied that many people did not believe that she was a supergenius. She also talked about her unusual ability to hear things other people cannot hear and said she was in communication with some sort of creature. She thought she might be haunted, or perhaps the creature was a being from another planet. She could hear his voice talking to her and asking her questions, but he did not attempt to tell her what to do. The voice was outside her head and was inaudible to others. She did not regard the questions being asked as upsetting; they did not make her angry or frightened.

Her teacher commented that, although the patient's reading was apparently at the fifth-grade level, her comprehension was much lower. She read what was not there and sometimes changed the meaning of the paragraph. Her spelling was at about the third-grade level, and her mathematics was a little below that. She worked hard at school, although slowly. If pressure was placed on her, she became upset, and her work deteriorated.

*Discussion.* At that time the patient exhibited several psychotic symptoms. She was apparently delusional in that she believed she had made a complicated invention and that she was in communication with "some sort of creature." She had auditory hallucinations of voices talking to her and asking her questions. The presence of delusions and hallucinations, in the absence of a specific organic factor that initiated and maintained the disturbance or of a full mood disorder, raised the question of schizophrenia.

The DSM-IV diagnostic criteria for schizophrenia require that "For a significant portion of the time since the onset of the disturbance, one or more major areas of functioning such as work, interpersonal relations, or self-care are markedly below the level achieved prior to the onset (or when the onset is in childhood or adolescence, failure to achieve expected level of interpersonal, academic, or occupational achievement)." Certainly, the onset of the patient's illness was in childhood, and she had failed to achieve the expected level of social development for someone her age. Therefore, the diagnosis of the patient's condition was schizophrenia. Because her delusions had many different themes, they were not systematized, ruling out the paranoid type; the absence of prominent catatonic features ruled out the catatonic type; and the absence of flat or grossly inappropriate affect ruled out the disorganized type. That left the undifferentiated type.

The patient's I.Q. level above 70 spared her from the additional diagnosis of mild mental retardation. One could argue for a diagnosis of borderline intellectual functioning. However, it was not the patient's limited intellectual capacity but, rather, her bizarre behavior that was creating difficulties at school.

**Residual type.** According to DSM-IV, the residual type is characterized by the presence of continuing evidence of the schizophrenic disturbance, in the absence of a complete set of active symptoms or sufficient symptoms to meet another type of schizophrenia (Table 13–4). Emotional blunting, social withdrawal, eccentric behavior, illogical thinking, and mild loosening of associations are common in the residual type. If delusions or hallucinations are present, they are not prominent and are not accompanied by strong affect.

## Type I and Type II

While DSM-IV was being written, a major discussion in the literature concerned whether to use a subtyping scheme based on the presence or the absence of positive (or productive) and negative (or deficit) symptoms (Table 13–6). In 1980 T. J. Crow proposed a classification of schizophrenic patients into type I and type II. Although that system was not accepted as part of the DSM-IV classification, the clinical distinction of those two types has significantly influenced psychiatric research. The *negative symptoms* include affective flattening or blunting, poverty of speech or speech content, blocking, poor grooming, lack of motivation, anhedonia, social withdrawal, cognitive defects, and attention deficits. The *positive symptoms* include loose associations, hallucinations, bizarre behavior, and increased speech. Type I patients tend to have mostly positive symptoms, normal brain structures on CT, and relatively good responses to treatment; type II patients tend to have mostly negative symptoms, structural brain abnormalities on CT scans, and poor responses to treatment.

## Other Subtypes

The subtyping of schizophrenia has had a long history, and other subtyping schemes can be found in the literature, especially from countries other than the United States.

The names of some of those subtypes are self-explanatory—for example, late-onset, childhood, and process. *Late-onset schizophrenia* is usually defined as schizophrenia that has an onset after age 45. Schizophrenia with a *childhood onset* is simply called schizophrenia in DSM-IV, although even the literature in the United States tends to refer to childhood schizophrenia. *Process schizophrenia* means schizophrenia with a particularly debilitating and deteriorating course.

***Bouffée délirante* (acute delusional psychosis).** This French diagnostic concept is differentiated from schizophrenia primarily on the basis of a symptom duration of less than three months. The diagnosis is similar to the DSM-IV diagnosis of schizophreniform disorder. French clinicians report that about 40 percent of patients with a diagnosis of *bouffée délirante* progress in their illness and are eventually classified as having schizophrenia.

**Latent.** The concept of latent schizophrenia developed during a time when there was a broad diagnostic conceptualization of schizophrenia. Currently, patients must be very mentally ill to warrant a diagnosis of schizo-

**Table 13–6**
**Percentage of Patients with Negative and Positive Symptoms (111 Consecutively Admitted Schizophrenic Patients)**

| Symptoms | Mild or Moderate | Severe or Extreme |
|---|---|---|
| **Negative symptoms** | | |
| Affective flattening | | |
| Unchanging facial expression | 54 | 33 |
| Decreased spontaneous movements | 37 | 14 |
| Paucity of expressive gestures | 34 | 24 |
| Poor eye contact | 39 | 16 |
| Affective nonresponsivity | 18 | 18 |
| Inappropriate affect | 29 | 22 |
| Lack of vocal inflections | 40 | 9 |
| Alogia | | |
| Poverty of speech | 20 | 20 |
| Poverty of content of speech | 33 | 6 |
| Blocking | 12 | 3 |
| Increased response latency | 17 | 6 |
| Avolition-apathy | | |
| Grooming and hygiene | 33 | 41 |
| Impersistence at work or school | 13 | 74 |
| Physical anergia | 36 | 31 |
| Anhedonia-asociality | | |
| Recreational interests, activities | 38 | 41 |
| Sexual interest, activity | 11 | 23 |
| Intimacy, closeness | 24 | 35 |
| Relationship with friends, peers | 25 | 63 |
| Attention | | |
| Social inattentiveness | 25 | 32 |
| Inattentiveness during testing | 33 | 19 |
| **Positive symptoms** | | |
| Hallucinations | | |
| Auditory | 19 | 51 |
| Voices commenting | 22 | 12 |
| Voices conversing | 27 | 12 |
| Somatic-tactile | 10 | 6 |
| Olfactory | 5 | 1 |
| Visual | 16 | 15 |
| Delusions | | |
| Persecutory | 19 | 47 |
| Jealousy | 2 | 1 |
| Guilt, sin | 16 | 2 |
| Grandiose | 15 | 15 |
| Religious | 12 | 11 |
| Somatic | 11 | 11 |
| Delusions of reference | 13 | 21 |
| Delusions of being controlled | 25 | 12 |
| Delusions of mind reading | 19 | 14 |
| Thought broadcasting | 11 | 2 |
| Thought insertion | 15 | 4 |
| Thought withdrawal | 11 | 6 |
| Bizarre behavior | | |
| Clothing, appearance | 8 | 4 |
| Social, sexual behavior | 17 | 7 |
| Aggressive-agitated behavior | 14 | 6 |
| Repetitive-stereotyped behavior | 7 | 4 |
| Positive formal thought disorder | | |
| Derailment | 30 | 4 |
| Tangentiality | 28 | 4 |
| Incoherence | 9 | 1 |
| Illogicality | 10 | 1 |
| Circumstantiality | 14 | 0 |
| Pressure of speech | 14 | 0 |
| Distractible speech | 12 | 1 |
| Clanging | 1 | 0 |

Table adapted from N C Andreasen: The diagnosis of schizophrenia. Schizophr Bull *13*: 9, 1987. Used with permission.

phrenia; however, with a broad diagnostic conceptualization of schizophrenia, patients who would not today be seen as severely ill can receive a diagnosis of schizophrenia. Latent schizophrenia, for example, was often the diagnosis used for patients with what now may be called schizoid and schizotypal personality disorders. Those patients may occasionally present peculiar behaviors or thought disorders but do not consistently manifest psychotic symptoms. The syndrome was also termed borderline schizophrenia in the past.

**Oneiroid.** The oneiroid state is a dreamlike state in which the patient may be deeply perplexed and not fully oriented in time and place. The term "oneiroid schizophrenic" has been used for schizophrenic patients who are particularly engaged in their hallucinatory experiences to the exclusion of involvement in the real world. When an oneiroid state is present, the clinician should be particularly careful to examine the patient for a medical or neurological cause of the symptoms.

**Paraphrenia.** This term is sometimes used as a synonym for "paranoid schizophrenia." In other usages the term is used for either a progressively deteriorating course of illness or the presence of a well-systemized delusional system. The multiple meanings of the term render it not very useful in communicating information.

**Pseudoneurotic.** Occasionally, patients who initially present such symptoms as anxiety, phobias, obsessions, and compulsions later reveal symptoms of thought disorder and psychosis. Those patients are characterized by symptoms of pananxiety, panphobia, panambivalence, and sometimes a chaotic sexuality. Unlike patients suffering from anxiety disorders, they have anxiety that is free-floating and that hardly ever subsides. In clinical descriptions of the patients, they rarely become overtly and severely psychotic.

**Simple schizophrenia.** As with "latent schizophrenia," the term "simple schizophrenia" was used during a period when schizophrenia had a broad diagnostic conceptualization. Simple schizophrenia was characterized by a gradual, insidious loss of drive and ambition. Patients with the disorder were usually not overtly psychotic and did not experience persistent hallucinations or delusions. The primary symptom is the withdrawal of the patient from social and work-related situations. The syndrome may reflect depression, a phobia, a dementia, or an exacerbation of personality traits. The clinician should be sure that the patient truly meets the diagnostic criteria for schizophrenia before making that diagnosis. In spite of those reservations, simple deteriorative disorder (simple schizophrenia) appears as a diagnostic category in an appendix of DSM-IV (Table 14.1–4).

## CLINICAL FEATURES

The clinical signs and symptoms of schizophrenia raise three key issues. First, no clinical sign or symptom is pathognomonic for schizophrenia; every sign or symptom seen in schizophrenia can be seen in other psychiatric and neurological disorders. That observation is contrary to the often-heard clinical opinion that certain signs and symptoms are diagnostic of schizophrenia. Therefore, a clinician cannot diagnose schizophrenia simply by a mental status examination. The patient's history is essential for the diagnosis of schizophrenia. Second, a patient's symptoms change with time. For example, a patient may have intermittent hallucinations and a varying ability to perform adequately in social situations. Or, for another example, significant symptoms of a mood disorder may also come and go during the course of schizophrenia. Third, the clinician must take into account the patient's educational level, intellectual ability, and cultural and subcultural membership. An impaired ability to understand abstract concepts, for example, may reflect the patient's education or intelligence. Various religious organizations and cults may have customs that seem strange to those outside that organization but that are considered perfectly normal to those within the cultural setting.

## Premorbid Signs and Symptoms

In theoretical formulations of the course of schizophrenia, premorbid signs and symptoms appear before the prodromal phase of the illness. That differentiation implies that premorbid signs and symptoms exist before the disease process evidences itself and that the prodromal signs and symptoms are parts of the evolving disorder. The typical but not invariable premorbid history of schizophrenic patients is that they had schizoid or schizotypal personalities. Such a personality may be characterized as quiet, passive, and introverted; as a result, the child had few friends. A preschizophrenic adolescent may have had no close friends and no dates and may have avoided team sports. Such an adolescent may enjoy watching movies and television or listening to music to the exclusion of social activities.

The prodromal signs and symptoms are almost invariably recognized retrospectively after the diagnosis of schizophrenia has been made. Therefore, their validity is uncertain; once schizophrenia is diagnosed, the retrospective remembrance of early signs and symptoms is affected. Nevertheless, although the first hospitalization is often considered the beginning of the disorder, signs and symptoms have often been present for months or even years. They may have started with complaints about somatic symptoms, such as headache, back and muscle pain, weakness, and digestive problems. The initial diagnosis may be malingering or somatization disorder. Family and friends may eventually notice that the person has changed and is no longer functioning well in occupational, social, and personal activities. During that stage the patient may begin to develop a new interest in abstract ideas, philosophy, the occult, or religious matters. Additional prodromal signs and symptoms may include markedly peculiar behavior, abnormal affects, unusual speech, bizarre ideas, and strange perceptual experiences.

## Mental Status Examination

**General description.** The general appearance of a schizophrenic patient can cover a broad range—from that of a completely disheveled, screaming, agitated person to an obsessively groomed, completely silent, and immobile

person. Between those two poles, the patient may be talkative and may exhibit bizarre postures. The behavior may become agitated or violent, apparently in an unprovoked manner but usually in response to hallucinations. That behavior contrasts dramatically with catatonic stupor, often referred to merely as catatonia, in which the patient seems completely lifeless and may exhibit such signs as muteness, negativism, and automatic obedience. Waxy flexibility used to be a common sign in catatonia, but it is now rare (Figure 13–6). A less extreme presentation of that type may include marked social withdrawal and egocentricity, lack of spontaneous speech or movement, and an absence of goal-directed behavior. Catatonic patients may sit immobile and speechless in their chairs, respond only with short answers to questions, and move only when directed to. Other obvious behaviors may include an odd clumsiness or stiffness in body movements, signs that are now seen as possibly indicating pathology in the basal ganglia. Schizophrenic patients often have poor grooming, fail to bathe, and dress much too warmly for the prevailing temperatures. Other odd behaviors include tics, stereotypies, mannerisms, and, occasionally, *echopraxia*, in which the patient imitates the posture or the behaviors of the examiner.

PRECOX FEELING.   Some clinicians report a precox feeling, an intuitive experience of their inability to establish an emotional rapport with the patient. Although the experience is common, no data indicate that it is a valid or reliable criterion in the diagnosis of schizophrenia.

**Mood, feelings, and affect.**   Depression can be a feature of acute psychosis and an aftermath of a psychotic

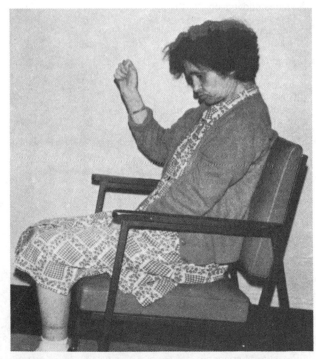

**Figure 13–6.**   Long-term catatonic patient. This patient is immobile, demonstrating waxy flexibility. Her arm is in an uncomfortable position, elevated without support, and her stony facial expression has a *Schnauzkrampf* or frozen pout. (Figure courtesy of Heinz E Lehmann.)

episode. The depressive symptoms are sometimes referred to as secondary depression in schizophrenia or as postpsychotic depressive disorder of schizophrenia. Some studies indicate that about 25 percent of all schizophrenic patients meet carefully defined criteria for postpsychotic depressive disorder of schizophrenia. Some data indicate that depression correlates with the presence of antipsychotic-induced extrapyramidal symptoms. Those data could suggest that schizophrenic patients with depressive features are sensitive to the extrapyramidal side effects of antipsychotics. Other feeling tones include perplexity, terror, a sense of isolation, and overwhelming ambivalence. Postpsychotic depressive disorder of schizophrenia is further discussed in Section 14.1.

OTHER AFFECTIVE SYMPTOMS. Two other common affective symptoms in schizophrenia are reduced emotional responsiveness, which is sometimes severe enough to warrant the label of anhedonia, and overly active and inappropriate emotions, such as extremes of rage, happiness, and anxiety. A flat or blunted affect can be a symptom of the illness itself, the parkinsonian side effects of antipsychotic medications, or depression. The differentiation of those symptoms can be a clinical challenge. Overly emotional patients may describe exultant feelings of omnipotence, religious ecstacy, terror at the disintegration of their souls, or paralyzing anxiety about the destruction of the universe.

**Perceptual disturbances.** Any of the five senses may be affected by hallucinatory experiences in schizophrenic patients. However, the most common hallucinations are auditory. The voices are often threatening, obscene, accusatory, or insulting. Two or more voices may converse among themselves, or a voice may comment on the patient's life or behavior. Visual hallucinations are common, but tactile, olfactory, and gustatory hallucinations are unusual; their presence should prompt the clinician to consider the possibility of an underlying medical or neurological disorder that is causing the entire syndrome.

CENESTHETIC HALLUCINATIONS. Cenesthetic hallucinations are unfounded sensations of altered states in bodily organs. Examples of cenesthetic hallucinations include a burning sensation in the brain, a pushing sensation in the blood vessels, and a cutting sensation in the bone marrow.

ILLUSIONS. *Illusions*, as differentiated from hallucinations, are distortions of real images or sensations, whereas *hallucinations* are not based on real images or sensations. Illusions can occur in schizophrenic patients during active phases of the disorder, but they also occur during the prodromal phases of the disorder and during periods of remission. Whenever illusions or hallucinations occur, the clinician should still consider the possibility of a substance-related cause for the symptoms, even in a patient who has already received a diagnosis of schizophrenia.

**Thought.** Disorders of thought are the most difficult symptoms to understand for many clinicians and students. Disorders of thought may, in fact, be the core symptoms of schizophrenia. One way to clarify the disorders of thought is to divide them into disorders of thought content, form of thought, and thought process.

THOUGHT CONTENT. Disorders of thought content reflect the patient's ideas, beliefs, and interpretations of stim-

uli. Delusions are the most obvious examples of a disorder of thought content. Delusions can be varied in schizophrenia—persecutory, grandiose, religious, or somatic. Patients may believe that some outside entity is controlling their thoughts or behavior or, conversely, that they are controlling outside events in some extraordinary fashion (for example, causing the sun to rise and set and preventing earthquakes). Patients may have an intense and consuming preoccupation with esoteric, abstract, symbolic, psychological, or philosophical ideas (Figure 13–7). Patients may also be concerned about allegedly life-threatening but completely bizarre and implausible somatic conditions—for example, the presence of aliens inside the patient's testicles and affecting his ability to have children.

The phrase "loss of ego boundaries" describes the lack of a clear sense of where the patient's own body, mind, and influence end and where those of other animate and inanimate objects begin. For example, patients may think that other people, the television, or the newspapers are making reference to them (*ideas of reference*). Other symptoms of the loss of ego boundaries include the sense that the patient has physically fused with an outside object (for example, a tree or another person) or that the patient has disintegrated and fused with the entire universe. Given that state of mind, some schizophrenic patients have doubts as to what sex they are or what their sexual orientation is. Those symptoms should not be confused with transvestism, transsexuality, or homosexuality.

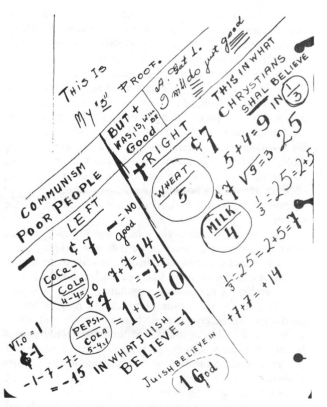

**Figure 13–7.** Schizophrenic patient's schema. It illustrates his fragmented, abstract, and overly inclusive thinking and preoccupation with religious ideologies and mathematical proofs. (Figure courtesy of Heinz E Lehmann.)

FORM OF THOUGHT. Disorders of the form of thought are objectively observable in patients' spoken and written language. The disorders include looseness of associations, derailment, incoherence, tangentiality, circumstantiality, neologisms, echolalia, verbigeration, word salad, and mutism. Although looseness of associations was once described as pathognomonic for schizophrenia, the symptom is frequently seen in mania. Distinguishing between looseness of associations and tangentiality can be difficult for even the most experienced clinician.

THOUGHT PROCESS. Disorders in thought process concern the way ideas and language are formulated. The examiner infers a disorder from what and how the patient speaks, writes, or draws. The examiner may also assess the patient's thought process by observing the patient's behavior, especially in carrying out discrete tasks in occupational therapy, for example. Disorders of thought process include flight of ideas, thought blocking, impaired attention, poverty of thought content, poor abstraction abilities, perseveration, idiosyncratic associations (for example, identical predicates and clang associations), overinclusion, and circumstantiality.

**Impulsiveness, suicide, and homicide.** Patients with schizophrenia may be agitated and have little impulse control when ill. They may also have decreased social sensitivity, appearing to be impulsive when, for example, they grab another patient's cigarettes, change television channels abruptly, or throw food on the floor. Some apparently impulsive behavior, including suicide and homicide attempts, may be in response to hallucinations commanding the patient to act.

SUICIDE. About 50 percent of all schizophrenic patients attempt suicide, and 10 to 15 percent of schizophrenic patients die by suicide. Perhaps the most underappreciated factor involved in the suicide of schizophrenic patients is depression that has been misdiagnosed as flat affect or a medication side effect. Other precipitants of suicide include feelings of absolute emptiness, a need to escape from the mental torture, or auditory hallucinations that command patients to kill themselves. The risk factors for suicide are the patient's awareness of the illness, being male, a college education, young age, a change in the course of the disease, an improvement after a relapse, dependence on the hospital, overly high ambitions, prior suicide attempts early in the course of the illness, and living alone.

HOMICIDE. In spite of the sensational attention that the news media provide when a patient with schizophrenia murders someone, the available data indicate that a schizophrenic patient is no more likely to commit homicide than is a member of the general population. When a schizophrenic patient does commit homicide, it may be for unpredictable or bizarre reasons based on hallucinations or delusions. Possible predictors of homicidal activity are a history of prior violence, dangerous behavior while hospitalized, and hallucinations or delusions involving such violence.

**Sensorium and cognition**

ORIENTATION. Schizophrenic patients are usually oriented to person, time, and place. The lack of such orientation should prompt the clinician to investigate the possibility of a medical or neurological brain disorder. Some schizophrenic patients may give incorrect or bizarre answers to questions regarding orientation—for example, "I am Christ; this is heaven; and it is 35 A.D."

MEMORY. Memory, as tested in the mental status examination, is usually intact. It may be impossible, however, to get a patient to attend closely enough to the memory tests for the ability to be assessed adequately.

**Judgment and insight.** Classically, schizophrenic patients are described as having poor insight into the nature and the severity of their disorder. The so-called lack of insight is associated with poor compliance with treatment. When examining a schizophrenic patient, the clinician should carefully define various aspects of insight, such as awareness of symptoms, trouble in getting along with people, and the reasons for those problems. Such information can be clinically useful in tailoring a treatment strategy and theoretically useful in postulating what areas of the brain contribute to the observed lack of insight (for example, the parietal lobes).

**Reliability.** A schizophrenic patient is no less reliable than is any other psychiatric or nonpsychiatric patient. However, the nature of the disorder requires that the examiner verify important information through additional sources.

## Neurological Findings

Localizing and nonlocalizing neurological signs (also known as hard and soft signs, respectively) have been reported to be present more commonly in patients with schizophrenia than in other psychiatric patients. Nonlocalizing signs include dysdiadochokinesia, astereognosis, mirror sign, primitive reflexes, and diminished dexterity. The presence of neurological signs and symptoms correlates with increased severity of illness, affective blunting, and a poor prognosis. Other abnormal neurological signs include tics, stereotypies, grimacing, impaired fine motor skills, abnormal motor tone, and abnormal movements. One study has found that only about 25 percent of schizophrenic patients are aware of their own abnormal involuntary movements and that the lack of awareness is correlated with lack of insight regarding the primary psychiatric disorder and the duration of illness.

**Eye examination.** In addition to the disorder of smooth ocular pursuit, schizophrenic patients have an elevated blink rate. The elevated blink rate is thought to reflect hyperdopaminergic activity. In primates, blinking can be increased by dopamine agonists and reduced by dopamine antagonists.

**Speech.** Although the disorders of speech in schizophrenia (for example, looseness of associations) are classically thought of as indicating a thought disorder, the disorders of speech may also indicate a *forme fruste* of an aphasia, perhaps implicating the dominant parietal lobe. The inability of schizophrenic patients to perceive the prosody of speech or to inflect their own speech can be seen as a neurological symptom of a disorder in the nondominant parietal lobe. Other parietal lobelike symptoms in schizophrenia include the inability to carry out tasks (that is, *apraxia*), right-left disorientation, and lack of concern about the disorder.

## Other Physical Findings

An increased incidence of minor physical anomalies is associated with the diagnosis of schizophrenia. Such anomalies are most likely associated with early stages of embryonic and fetal growth, usually during the first trimester. Such physical anomalies have been reported to be present in 30 to 75 percent of schizophrenic patients, compared with 0 to 13 percent of normal persons. Some studies now suggest that the presence of the anomalies is more common in males than in females and are probably associated with genetic factors, although obstetric complications cannot be ruled out as a causative factor.

## Psychological Tests

In general, schizophrenic patients perform similarly to patients with mental disorders with organic causes. The data are consistent with the idea that schizophrenia is a brain disease that disrupts the normal functioning of many cognitive abilities. Schizophrenic patients generally perform poorly on a wide range of neuropsychological tests. One recent study, however, compared the neuropsychological performances of schizophrenic twins with their nonaffected monozygotic twins. The study found that vigilance, memory, and concept formation were most affected and suggested that the pattern was most consistent with pathology in the frontotemporal cortex. Moreover, the study found that those impairments were most related to the disease process itself and were not attributable to genetic trait markers or environmental factors.

**Neuropsychological testing.** Formal neuropsychological assessment of cognitive functions in schizophrenic patients can often provide data that may be used clinically. Objective measures of neuropsychological performance, such as the Halstead-Reitan battery and the Luria-Nebraska battery, often give abnormal findings, but the results may suggest practical approaches to take with patients that take into account their cognitive weaknesses. In general, the test results are consistent with bilateral frontal and temporal lobe dysfunction, including impairments in attention, retention time, and problem-solving ability.

**Intelligence tests.** When groups of schizophrenic patients are compared with groups of nonschizophrenic psychiatric patients or with the general population, the schizophrenic patients tend to have lower scores on intelligence tests. Statistically, the evidence suggests that low intelligence is often present at the onset, and intelligence may continue to deteriorate with the progression of the disorder.

**Projective and personality tests.** Projective tests—for example, the Rorschach test and the Thematic Apperception Test (TAT)—may indicate bizarre ideation. Personality inventories—for example, the Minnesota Multiphasic Personality Inventory (MMPI)—often give abnormal results in schizophrenia, but the contribution to diagnosis and treatment planning is minimal.

## DIFFERENTIAL DIAGNOSIS

### Secondary and Substance-Induced Psychotic Disorders

Symptoms of psychosis and catatonia can be caused by a wide range of nonpsychiatric medical conditions and can be induced by a wide range of substances (Table 13–7). When psychosis or catatonia is caused by a nonpsychiatric medical condition or induced by a substance, the most appropriate diagnosis is *psychotic disorder due to a general medical condition, catatonic disorder due to a general medical condition,* or *substance-induced psychotic disorder.* The psychiatric manifestations of many of the nonpsychiatric medical conditions can come early in the course

**Table 13–7**
**Differential Diagnosis of Schizophrenialike Symptoms**

**Medical and Neurological:**
Substance-induced—amphetamine, hallucinogens, belladonna alkaloids, alcohol hallucinosis, barbiturate withdrawal, cocaine, phencyclidine (PCP)
Epilepsy—especially temporal lobe epilepsy
Neoplasm, cerebrovascular disease, or trauma—especially frontal or limbic
Other conditions—Acquired immune deficiency syndrome (AIDS)
    Acute intermittent porphyria
    $B_{12}$ deficiency
    Carbon monoxide poisoning
    Cerebral lipoidosis
    Creutzfeldt-Jakob disease
    Fabry's disease
    Fahr's disease
    Hallervorden-Spatz disease
    Heavy metal poisoning
    Herpes encephalitis
    Homocystinuria
    Huntington's disease
    Metachromatic leukodystrophy
    Neurosyphilis
    Normal pressure hydrocephalus
    Pellagra
    Systemic lupus erythematosus
    Wernicke-Korsakoff syndrome
    Wilson's disease

**Psychiatric**
Atypical psychosis
Autistic disorder
Brief psychotic disorder
Delusional disorder
Factitious disorder with predominantly psychological signs and symptoms
Malingering
Mood disorders
Normal adolescence
Obsessive-compulsive disorder
Personality disorders—schizotypal, schizoid, borderline, paranoid
Schizoaffective disorder
Schizophrenia
Schizophreniform disorder

of the illness, often before the development of other symptoms. Therefore, the clinician must consider a wide range of nonpsychiatric medical conditions in the differential diagnosis of psychosis, even in the absence of obvious physical symptoms. Generally, patients with neurological disorders have more insight into their illnesses and more distress from their psychiatric symptoms than do schizophrenic patients, a fact that can help the clinician differentiate the two groups of patients.

When evaluating a psychotic patient, the clinician should follow three general guidelines regarding the assessment of nonpsychiatric conditions. First, the clinician should be especially aggressive in pursuing an undiagnosed nonpsychiatric medical condition if the patient exhibits any unusual or rare symptoms or any variation in the level of consciousness. Second, the clinician should attempt to obtain a complete family history, including a history of medical, neurological, and psychiatric disorders. Third, the clinician should consider the possibility of a nonpsychiatric medical condition, even in patients with previous diagnoses of schizophrenia. A schizophrenic patient is just as likely to have a brain tumor resulting in psychotic symptoms as is a nonschizophrenic patient.

## Malingering and Factitious Disorders

Either malingering or a factitious disorder may be an appropriate diagnosis in a patient who is imitating the symptoms of schizophrenia but does not actually have schizophrenia. People have faked schizophrenic symptoms and been admitted into and treated at psychiatric hospitals. Patients who are completely in control of their symptom production may qualify for a diagnosis of malingering; such patients usually have some obvious financial or legal reason to be considered insane. Patients who are less in control of their falsification of psychotic symptoms may qualify for a diagnosis of a factitious disorder. However, some patients with schizophrenia sometimes falsely complain of an exacerbation of psychotic symptoms to obtain increased assistance benefits or to gain admission to a hospital.

## Other Psychotic Disorders

The psychotic symptoms seen in schizophrenia can be identical to those seen in schizophreniform disorder, brief psychotic disorder, and schizoaffective disorder. *Schizophreniform disorder* differs from schizophrenia in having a duration of symptoms that is at least one month but less than six months. Brief psychotic disorder is the appropriate diagnosis if the symptoms have lasted at least one day but less than one month and if the patient has not returned to the premorbid level of functioning. *Schizoaffective disorder* is the appropriate diagnosis when a manic or depressive syndrome develops concurrently with the major symptoms of schizophrenia.

A diagnosis of *delusional disorder* is warranted if nonbizarre delusions have been present for at least one month in the absence of the other symptoms of schizophrenia or a mood disorder.

## Mood Disorders

The differential diagnosis of schizophrenia and mood disorders can be difficult, but it is important because of the availability of specific and effective treatments for mania and depression. Affective or mood symptoms in schizophrenia should be brief relative to the duration of the primary symptoms. In the absence of information other than a single mental status examination, the clinician should delay a final diagnosis or should assume the presence of a mood disorder, rather than make a diagnosis of schizophrenia prematurely.

## Personality Disorders

A variety of personality disorders may present with some features of schizophrenia; schizotypal, schizoid, and borderline personality disorders are the personality disorders with the most similar symptoms. Personality disorders, unlike schizophrenia, have mild symptoms, a history of being present throughout the patient's life, and the absence of an identifiable date of onset.

## COURSE AND PROGNOSIS

### Course

A premorbid pattern of symptoms may be the first evidence of illness, although the import of the symptoms is usually recognized only retrospectively. Characteristically, the symptoms begin in adolescence, followed by the development of prodromal symptoms in days to a few months. The onset of the disturbing symptoms may seem to have been precipitated by a social or environmental change, such as moving away to college, an experience with substances, or the death of a relative. The prodromal syndrome may last a year or more before the onset of overt psychotic symptoms.

After the first psychotic episode, the patient has a gradual period of recovery, which can be followed by a lengthy period of relatively normal functioning. However, a relapse usually occurs, and the general pattern of illness that is evidenced in the first five years after the diagnosis is usually predictive of the course that the patient follows. Each relapse of the psychosis is followed by a further deterioration in the patient's baseline functioning. The classic course of schizophrenia is one of exacerbations and remissions. The major distinction between schizophrenia and the mood disorders is the schizophrenic patient's failure to return to baseline functioning after each relapse. Sometimes a clinically observable postpsychotic depression follows a psychotic episode, and the schizophrenic patient's vulnerability to stress is usually lifelong. Positive symptoms tend to become less severe with time, but the socially debilitating negative or deficit symptoms may increase in severity. Although about one third of all schizophrenic patients have some marginal or integrated social existence, the majority have lives characterized by aimlessness, inactivity, frequent hospitalizations, and, in urban settings, homelessness and poverty.

## Prognosis

Several studies have found that over the 5-to-10-year period after the first psychiatric hospitalization for schizophrenia, only about 10 to 20 percent of the patients can be described as having a good outcome. More than 50 percent of the patients can be described as having a poor outcome, with repeated hospitalizations, exacerbations of symptoms, episodes of major mood disorders, and suicide attempts. In spite of those glum figures, schizophrenia does not always run a deteriorating course, and a number of factors have been associated with a good prognosis (Table 10–5).

The range of recovery rates reported in the literature is from 10 to 60 percent, and a reasonable estimate is that 20 to 30 percent of all schizophrenic patients are able to lead somewhat normal lives. About 20 to 30 percent of patients continue to experience moderate symptoms, and 40 to 60 percent of patients remain significantly impaired by their disorder for their entire lives. Schizophrenic patients do much less well than do patients with mood disorders, although 20 to 25 percent of mood disorder patients are also severely disturbed at long-term follow-up.

## TREATMENT

Three fundamental observations about schizophrenia warrant attention when considering the treatment of the disorder. First, regardless of cause, schizophrenia occurs in a person who has a unique individual, familial, and social psychological profile. The treatment approach must be tailored to how the particular patient has been affected by the disorder and how the particular patient will be helped by the treatment. Second, the fact that the concordance rate for schizophrenia among monozygotic twins is 50 percent has been taken by many investigators to suggest that unknown but probably specific environmental and psychological factors have contributed to the development of the disorder. Thus, just as pharmacological agents are used to address presumed chemical imbalances, nonpharmacological strategies must address nonbiological issues. Third, schizophrenia is a complex disorder, and any single therapeutic approach is rarely sufficient to address the multifaceted disorder satisfactorily.

Although antipsychotic medications are the mainstay of the treatment of schizophrenia, research has found that psychosocial interventions can augment the clinical improvement. Psychosocial modalities should be carefully integrated into the drug treatment regimen and should support it. Most schizophrenic patients benefit from the combined use of antipsychotics and psychosocial treatment.

## Hospitalization

The primary indications for hospitalization are for diagnostic purposes, stabilization on medications, patient safety because of suicidal or homicidal ideation, and grossly disorganized or inappropriate behavior, including the inability to take care of basic needs, such as food, clothing, and shelter. A primary goal of hospitalization should be to establish an effective link between the patient and community support systems.

Introduced in the early 1950s, antipsychotic medications have revolutionized the treatment of schizophrenia. About two to four times as many patients relapse when treated with a placebo than when treated with antipsychotics. However, antipsychotics treat the symptoms of the disorder and are not a cure for schizophrenia.

Other aspects of clinical management flow logically from a medical model of the disorder. Rehabilitation and adjustment imply that the patient's specific handicaps are taken into account when treatment strategies are planned. The physician must also educate the patient and the patient's caretakers and family about schizophrenia.

Hospitalization decreases stress on patients and helps them structure their daily activities. The length of hospitalization depends on the severity of the patient's illness and the availability of outpatient treatment facilities. Research has shown that short hospitalizations (four to six weeks) are just as effective as long-term hospitalizations and that hospitals with active behavioral approaches are more effective than custodial institutions and insight-oriented therapeutic communities.

The hospital treatment plan should have a practical orientation toward issues of living, self-care, quality of life, employment, and social relationships. Hospitalization should be directed toward aligning patients with aftercare facilities, including their family homes, foster families, board-and-care homes, and halfway houses. Day care centers and home visits can sometimes help patients remain out of the hospital for long periods and can improve the quality of the patients' daily lives.

## Somatic Treatments

**Antipsychotics.** The antipsychotic drugs are sometimes referred to as "neuroleptics," which is an acceptable term. The term "major tranquilizers," however, should be avoided, since it has been used to indicate various types of drugs and inaccurately implies that the antipsychotics have a sedative or tranquilizing effect as a major mode of action. The antipsychotics include three major classes of drugs: dopamine receptor antagonists, risperidone (Risperdal), and clozapine (Clozaril).

CHOICE OF DRUG. The *dopamine receptor antagonists* are the classic antipsychotic drugs and are effective in the treatment of schizophrenia. The drugs have two major shortcomings. First, only a small percentage of patients (perhaps 25 percent) are helped sufficiently to recover a reasonable amount of normal mental functioning. As noted above, even with treatment, about 50 percent of schizophrenic patients lead severely debilitated lives. Second, the dopamine receptor antagonists are associated with both annoying and serious adverse effects. The most common annoying effects are akathisia and parkinsonianlike symptoms of rigidity and tremor. The potential serious effects include tardive dyskinesia and neuroleptic malignant syndrome.

*Remoxipride* is a dopamine receptor antagonist of a different class than the currently available dopamine receptor antagonists. In Europe, remoxipride has been shown to be an effective antipsychotic, and early data indicate that it is associated with significantly fewer neurological adverse effects than are other dopamine receptor antagonists. Very recent data, however, suggest that remoxipride may be associated with aplastic anemia, thus limiting its clinical value

*Risperidone* is an antipsychotic drug with significant antagonist activity at the serotonin type 2 (5-HT$_2$) receptor and at the dopamine type 2 (D$_2$) receptor. Research data indicate that it may be more effective than currently available dopamine receptor antagonists at treating both the positive symptoms and the negative symptoms of schizophrenia. The available research data also indicate that risperidone is associated with significantly fewer and less severe neurological adverse effects than are typical dopaminergic antagonist drugs. However, the data about superior efficacy and safety are derived from the still limited research conducted on the compound; understanding of the efficacy and the safety of the new compound will probably increase rapidly as clinical experience is gained in its use. Risperidone may become a first-line drug in the treatment of schizophrenia because of the possibility that it is both more effective and safer than the typical dopaminergic receptor antagonists.

*Clozapine* is an effective antipsychotic drug. Its mechanism of action is not well understood, although it is known that clozapine is a weak antagonist of the D$_2$ receptor but appears to be a potent antagonist of the D$_4$ receptor and has antagonistic activity at the serotonergic receptors. Clozapine, unfortunately, is associated with a 1 to 2 percent incidence of agranulocytosis, an adverse effect that necessitates the weekly monitoring of the blood indexes. In addition, clozapine is expensive, which is a limiting factor in its use. Nonetheless, clozapine is a clear second-line drug for those patients who either do not respond to other currently available drugs or have severe tardive dyskinesia. Clozapine is indicated in patients with tardive dyskinesia because the available data indicate that clozapine is not associated with the development or the exacerbation of that disorder.

THERAPEUTIC PRINCIPLES. The use of antipsychotic medications in schizophrenia should follow five major principles. (1) The clinician should carefully define the target symptoms to be treated. (2) An antipsychotic that has worked well in the past for the patient should be used again. In the absence of such information, the choice of an antipsychotic is usually based on the side-effect profile. Currently available data indicate that risperidone, remoxipride, and drugs similar to them that may be introduced in the next few years may offer a superior side-effect profile and the possibility of superior efficacy. Within the standard dopaminergic antagonists, all members of that class are equally efficacious. (3) The minimum length of an antipsychotic trial is four to six weeks at adequate dosages. If the trial is unsuccessful, a different antipsychotic, usually from a different class, can be tried. However, an unpleasant experience by the patient to the first dose of an antipsychotic drug correlates highly with future poor response and noncompliance. Negative experiences can include a peculiar subjective negative feeling, oversedation, or an acute dystonic reaction. If a severe and negative initial reaction is observed, the clinician may consider switching to a different antipsychotic drug in less than four weeks. (4) In general, the use of more than one antipsychotic medication at a time is rarely, if ever, indicated, although some psychiatrists use thioridazine (Mellaril) for treating insomnia in a patient who is receiving another antipsychotic for the treatment of schizophrenic symptoms. In particularly treatment-resistant patients, combinations of antipsychotics with other drugs—for example, carbamazepine (Tegretol)—may be indicated. (5) Patients should be maintained on the lowest possible effective dosage of medication. The dosage is often lower than the dosage that was needed to achieve symptom control during the psychotic episode.

INITIAL WORKUP. In spite of the annoyance of the neurological effects and the looming possibility of tardive dyskinesia, antipsychotic drugs are remarkably safe, especially when given over a relatively short period. Thus, in emergency situations, a clinician can administer the drugs, with the exception of clozapine, without conducting a physical or laboratory examination of the patient. In the usual assessment, however, the clinician should obtain a complete blood count (CBC) with white blood cell indexes, liver function tests, and an electrocardiogram (ECG), especially in women over 40 and men over 30. The major contraindications to antipsychotics are (1) a history of a serious allergic response; (2) the possibility that the patient has ingested a substance that will interact with the antipsychotic to induce central nervous system (CNS) depression—for example, alcohol, opioids, opiates, barbiturates, benzodiazepines—or anticholinergic delirium—for example, scopolamine (Donnagel) and possibly phencyclidine (PCP); (3) the presence of a severe cardiac abnormality; (4) a high risk for seizures from organic or idiopathic causes; and (5) the presence of narrow-angle glaucoma if an antipsychotic with significant anticholinergic activity is to be used.

FAILURE OF A DRUG TRIAL. In the acute state, virtually all patients respond eventually to repeated doses of an antipsychotic—every one to two hours with intramuscular (IM) administration or every two to three hours by mouth. A benzodiazepine is sometimes needed to sedate the patient further. The failure of a patient to respond in the acute state should cause the clinician to consider the possibility of an organic lesion.

Noncompliance with antipsychotics is a major reason for relapse and for failure of a drug trial. Another major reason for a failed drug trial is insufficient time for the trial. It is generally a mistake to increase the dosage or to change antipsychotic medications in the first two weeks of treatment. If a patient is improving on the current regimen at the end of two weeks, continued treatment with the same regimen will probably result in steady clinical improvement. If, however, a patient has shown little or no improvement in two weeks, the possible reasons for a drug failure, including noncompliance, should be considered. In a noncompliant patient the use of a liquid preparation or depot forms of fluphenazine (Prolixin) or haloperidol (Haldol) may be indicated. Because of the diversity in the metabolism of the drugs, the clinician should obtain plasma levels if the laboratory capability is available. Plasma levels of antipsychotics provide only a gross measure of compliance, absorption, and metabolism. There are no clearly defined therapeutic blood level ranges for antipsychotics similar to those for some antidepressants.

Having eliminated other possible reasons for an antipsychotic's therapeutic failure, the clinician may try a second antipsychotic with a chemical structure different from that of the first one. Additional strategies include supplementing the antipsychotic with lithium (Eskalith), an anticonvulsant such as carbamazepine or valproate (Depakene), or a benzodiazepine. The use of so-called megadose antipsychotic therapy (for example, 100 to 200 mg of haloperidol) is rarely indicated, since almost no data support the practice.

**Other drugs.** If adequate trials with at least one dopaminergic receptor antagonist have all been unsuccessful, combination therapy with one of those drugs and an adjuvant medication may be indicated. The adjuvant medications with the most supportive data are lithium, two anticonvulsants (carbamazepine and valproate), and the benzodiazepines.

LITHIUM. Lithium may be effective in further reducing psychotic symptoms in up to 50 percent of patients with schizophrenia. Lithium may also be a reasonable drug to try in patients who are unable to take any of the antipsychotic medications.

ANTICONVULSANTS. Carbamazepine or valproate may be used alone or in combination with lithium or an antipsychotic. Although neither of the anticonvulsants has been shown to be effective in reducing psychotic symptoms in schizophrenia when used alone, data suggest that the anticonvulsants may be effective in reducing episodes of violence in some schizophrenic patients.

BENZODIAZEPINES. Data support the practice of coadministering alprazolam (Xanax) with antipsychotics to patients who have not responded to antipsychotic administration alone. There are also reports of schizophrenic patients' responding to high dosages of diazepam (Valium) alone. However, the severity of the psychosis may be exacerbated after the withdrawal of a benzodiazepine.

**Other somatic treatments.** Although much less effective than antipsychotics, electroconvulsive therapy (ECT) may be indicated for catatonic patients and for patients who for some reason cannot take antipsychotics. Patients who have been ill for less than one year are the ones most likely to respond.

In the past, schizophrenia was treated with insulin-induced coma and barbiturate-induced coma. Those treatments are no longer used because of the associated hazards. Psychosurgery, particularly frontal lobotomies, were used from 1935 to 1955 for the treatment of schizophrenia. Although sophisticated approaches to psychosurgery for schizophrenia may eventually be developed, psychosurgery is no longer considered an appropriate treatment of schizophrenia, but it is being used on a limited experimental basis.

## Psychosocial Treatments

**Behavior therapy.** Treatment planning for schizophrenia should address both the abilities and the deficits of the patient. Behavioral techniques use token economies and social skills training to increase social abilities, self-sufficiency, practical skills, and interpersonal communication. Adaptive behaviors are reinforced by praise or tokens that can be redeemed for desired items, such as hospital privileges and passes. Consequently, the frequency of maladaptive or deviant behavior—such as talking loudly, talking to oneself in public, and bizarre posturing—can be reduced.

BEHAVIORAL SKILLS TRAINING. Behavioral skills training is sometimes referred to as social skills therapy; regardless of the name, the therapy can be directly supportive and useful to the patient and is naturally additive to pharmacological therapy (Table 13–8). In addition to the personal symptoms of schizophrenia, some of the most noticeable symptoms of schizophrenia involve the patients'

**Table 13–8**
**Goals and Targeted Behaviors for Social Skills Therapy**

| Phase | Goals | Targeted Behaviors |
|---|---|---|
| Stabilization and assessment | Establish therapeutic alliance<br>Assess social performance and perception skills<br>Assess behaviors that provoke expressed emotion | Empathy and rapport<br>Verbal and nonverbal communication |
| Social performance within family | Express positive feelings within family<br>Teach effective strategies for coping with conflict | Compliments, appreciation, interest in others<br>Avoidance response to criticism, stating preferences and refusals |
| Social perception in the family | Correctly identify content, context, and meaning of messages | Reading a message<br>Labeling an idea<br>Summarizing other's intent |
| Extrafamilial relationships | Enhance socialization skills<br>Enhance prevocational and vocational skills | Conversational skills<br>Dating<br>Recreational activities<br>Job interviewing, work habits |
| Maintenance | Generalize skills to new situations | |

Table adapted from G E Hogarty, C M Anderson, D J Reiss, S J Komblith, D P Greenwald, C D Javna, M J Madonia: Family psychoeducation, social skills training and maintenance chemotherapy: I. One-year effects of a controlled study on relapse and expressed emotion. Arch Gen Psychiatry 43: 633, 1986. Used with permission.

relationships with others, including poor eye contact, unusual delays in response, odd facial expressions, lack of
spontaneity in social situations, and inaccurate perceptions
or lack of perception of emotions in other people. Those
behaviors are specifically addressed in behavioral skills
training. Behavioral skills training involves the use of videotapes of others and of the patient, role playing in therapy, and homework assignments regarding the specific
skills being practiced.

**Family-oriented therapies.** A variety of family-oriented therapies are useful in the treatment of schizophrenia. Because schizophrenic patients are often discharged
in an only partially remitted state, a family to which a
schizophrenic patient is returning can often benefit from
a brief but intensive (as often as daily) course of family
therapy. The focus of the therapy should be on the immediate situation and should include identifying and avoiding potentially troublesome situations. When problems do
emerge with the patient in the family, the focus of the
therapy should be on the rapid resolution of the problem.

Subsequent to the immediate postdischarge period, an
important topic to cover in family therapy is the recovery
process, particularly its length and its rate. Too often,
family members, in a well-meaning fashion, encourage a
schizophrenic relative to resume regular activities too
quickly. That overly optimistic plan stems both from ignorance about the nature of schizophrenia and from denial
regarding its severity. The therapist must help the family
and the patient understand schizophrenia without being
overly discouraging. The therapist may discuss the psychotic episode itself and the events leading up to it. The
common practice of ignoring the psychotic episode often
adds to the shame associated with the event and does not
take advantage of the recency of the event as a source of
discussion, education, and understanding. Family members are often frightened by the psychotic symptoms, and
open discussion with the psychiatrist and the schizophrenic
relative can often be helpful for all parties. Subsequent
family therapy can be directed toward the long-range implementation of stress-reducing and coping strategies and
toward gradual reinvolvement of the patient in activities.

In any family session with schizophrenic patients, the
therapist must control the emotional intensity of the session. The excessive expression of emotion during a session
can be damaging to the recovery process of a schizophrenic
patient and can undermine the potential success of subsequent family therapy sessions. A number of studies have
found family therapy to be especially effective in reducing
relapse. However, each of those studies used a different
type of family therapy, and the commonality among the
therapies remains unclear. In controlled studies the reduction in relapse rate was dramatic—25 to 50 percent
annual relapse rate without family therapy and 5 to 10
percent with family therapy.

NAMI. The National Alliance for the Mentally Ill
(NAMI) and similar groups are support groups for the
family members and the friends of mentally ill patients and
for the patients themselves. Such organizations give emotional and practical advice about obtaining care in a sometimes overly complex health care delivery system. NAMI
is often a supportive group to which to refer family mem-

bers. NAMI has also waged a campaign to destigmatize
mental illness and to increase awareness in government
regarding the needs and the rights of the mentally ill and
their families.

**Group therapy.** Group therapy for schizophrenia generally focuses on real-life plans, problems, and relationships. Groups may be behaviorally oriented, psychodynamically or insight-oriented, or supportive. Some doubt
exists about whether dynamic interpretation and insight
therapy are valuable for the typical schizophrenic patient.
But group therapy is effective in reducing social isolation,
increasing the sense of cohesiveness, and improving reality
testing for patients with schizophrenia. Groups led in a
supportive manner, rather than in an interpretative way,
appear to be most helpful for schizophrenic patients.

**Individual psychotherapy.** The best conducted studies
of the effects of individual psychotherapy in the treatment
of schizophrenia have provided data that the therapy is
helpful and is additive to the effects of pharmacological
treatment. The types of therapies studied include supportive psychotherapy and insight-oriented psychotherapy. A critical concept in the psychotherapy for a schizophrenic patient is the development of a therapeutic
relationship that the patient experiences as safe. That experience is affected by the reliability of the therapist, the
emotional distance between the therapist and the patient,
and the genuineness of the therapist as interpreted by the
patient. Inexperienced psychotherapists often provide
interpretations too quickly to schizophrenic patients. The
psychotherapy for a schizophrenic patient should be conceptualized in terms of decades, rather than sessions,
months, or even years. That reality makes it unfortunate
that residency training programs permit only a few years,
at most, for residents to spend with schizophrenic patients.

Some clinicians and researchers have emphasized that
the ability of a schizophrenic patient to form a therapeutic
alliance with a therapist can predict the outcome. At least
one study found that schizophrenic patients who were able
to form a good therapeutic alliance were likely to remain
in psychotherapy, to remain compliant with their medications, and to have good outcomes at a two-year follow-
up evaluation.

The relationship between the clinician and the patient
is different from that encountered in the treatment of
nonpsychotic patients. Establishing a relationship is often
a difficult matter; the schizophrenic patient is desperately
lonely yet defends against closeness and trust and is likely
to become suspicious, anxious, hostile, or regressed when
someone attempts to draw close. The scrupulous obser-
vance of distance and privacy, simple directness, patience,
sincerity, and sensitivity to social conventions are preferable to premature informality and the condescending use
of first names. Exaggerated warmth or professions of
friendship are out of place and are likely to be perceived
as attempts at bribery, manipulation, or exploitation.

However, in the context of a professional relationship,
flexibility may be essential in establishing a working alliance with the patient. The therapist may have meals with
the patient, sit on the floor, go for a walk, eat at a restaurant, accept and give gifts, play table tennis, remember
the patient's birthday, or just sit silently with the patient.

The major aim is to convey the idea that the therapist can be trusted, wants to understand the patient and will try to do so, and has faith in the patient's potential as a human being, no matter how disturbed, hostile, or bizarre the patient may be at the moment. Mandred Bleuler stated that the correct therapeutic attitude toward schizophrenic patients is to accept them, rather than watch them as persons who have become unintelligible and different from the therapist.

## References

Abi-Dargham A, Laruelle M, Lipska B, Jaskiw G E, Wong D T, Robertson D W, Weinberger D R, Kleinman J E: Serotonin 5-HT₃ receptors in schizophrenia: A postmortem study in the amygdala. Brain Res *616*: 53, 1993.

Addington D E, Addington J M: Attempted suicide and depression in schizophrenia. Acta Psychiatr Scand *85*: 288, 1992.

Adler L E, Griffith J M: Concurrent medical illness in the schizophrenic patient: Epidemiology, diagnosis, and management. Schizophr Res *4*: 91, 1991.

Amador X F, Strauss D H, Yale S A, Gorman J A: Awareness of illness in schizophrenia. Schizophr Bull *17*: 113, 1991.

Andreasen N C, Flaum M: Schizophrenia: The characteristic symptoms. Schizophr Bull *17*: 27, 1991.

Basset A S: Chromosomal aberrations and schizophrenia: Autosomes. Br J Psychiatry *161*: 323, 1992.

Bogerst B, Lieberman J A, Ashtari M, Bilder R M, Degreef G, Lerner G, Johns C, Masiar S: Hippocampus-amygdala volumes and psychopathology in chronic schizophrenia. Biol Psychiatry *33*: 236, 1993.

Böker W, Brenner H D, editors: Onset and course of schizophrenic disorders: Dynamic interactions between relevant factors. Br J Psychiatry *161* (Suppl, 18): 2, 1992.

Breier A, Schreiber J L, Dyer J, Pickar D: National Institute of Mental Health longitudinal study of chronic schizophrenia: Prognosis and predictors of outcome. Arch Gen Psychiatry *48*: 239, 1991.

Buchsbaum M S: The frontal lobes, basal ganglia, and temporal lobes as sites for schizophrenia. Schizophr Bull *16*: 379, 1990.

Carone B J, Harrow M, Westermeyer J F: Posthospital course and outcome in schizophrenia. Arch Gen Psychiatry *48*: 247, 1991.

Deutch A Y, Moghaddam B, Innis R B, Krystal J H, Aghajanian G K, Bunney B S, Charney D S: Mechanisms of action of atypical antipsychotic drugs: Implications for novel therapeutic strategies for schizophrenia. Schizophr Res *4*: 121, 1991.

Fenton W S, McGlashan T H: Natural history of schizophrenia subtypes: I. Longitudinal study of paranoid, hebephrenic, and undifferentiated schizophrenia. Arch Gen Psychiatry *48*: 969, 1991.

Fenton W S, McGlashan T H: Natural history of schizophrenia subtypes: II. Positive and negative symptoms and long-term course. Arch Gen Psychiatry *48*: 978, 1991.

Frank A F, Gunderson J G: The role of the therapeutic alliance in the treatment of schizophrenia. Arch Gen Psychiatry *47*: 228, 1990.

Gabbard G O: *Psychodynamic Psychiatry in Clinical Practice: The DSM-IV Edition.* American Psychiatric Press, Washington, 1994.

Goff D C, Henderson D C, Amico E: Cigarette smoking in schizophrenia: Relationship to psychopathology and medication side effects. Am J. Psychiatry *149*: 1189, 1992.

Goldberg T E, Gold J M, Greenberg R, Griffin S, Schulz S C, Pickar D, Kleinman J E, Weinberger D R: Contrasts between patients with affective disorders and patients with schizophrenia on a neuropsychological test battery. Am J Psychiatry *150*: 1355, 1993.

Goldstein J M, Tsuang M T: Gender and schizophrenia: An introduction and synthesis of findings. Schizophr Bull *16*: 179, 1990.

Gur R E, Pearlson G D: Neuroimaging in schizophrenia research. Schizophr Bull *19*: 337, 1993.

Heinrichs R W, Awad G: Neurocognitive subtypes of chronic schizophrenia. Schizophr Res *9*: 49, 1993.

Holland D, Watanabe M D, Sharma R: Atypical antipsychotics. Psychiatr Med *9*: 5, 1991.

Kavanagh D J: Recent developments in expressed emotion and schizophrenia. Br J Psychiatry *160*: 601, 1992.

Kendler K S, Diehl S R: The genetics of schizophrenia: A current, genetic-epidemiologic perspective. Schizophr Bull *19*: 261, 1993.

Knight J, Knight A, Ungvari G: Can autoimmune mechanisms account for the genetic predisposition to schizophrenia? Br J Psychiatry *160*: 533, 1992.

Levinson D F: Pharmacologic treatment of schizophrenia. Clin Ther *13*: 326, 1991.

Lewis S: Sex and schizophrenia: Vive la difference. Br J Psychiatry *161*: 445, 1992.

Lieberman J A, Koreen A R: Neurochemistry and neuroendocrinology of schizophrenia: A selective review. Schizophr Bull *19*: 371, 1993.

Maas J W, Contreras S A, Miller A L, Berman N, Bowden C L, Javors M A, Seleshi E, Weintraub S: Studies of catecholamine metabolism in schizophrenia/psychosis: I. Neuropsychopharmacology *8*: 97, 1993.

Marder S R, Wirshing W C, Van Putten T: Drug treatment of schizophrenia: Overview of recent research. Schizophr Res *4*: 81, 1991.

McCarley R W, Faux S F, Shenton M E, Nestor P G, Adams J: Event-related potentials in schizophrenia: Their biological and clinical correlates and a new model of schizophrenic pathophysiology. Schizophr Res *4*: 209, 1991.

McGuire T G: Measuring the economic costs of schizophrenia. Schizophr Bull *17*: 375, 1991.

Meltzer H Y, Nash J F: Effects of antipsychotic drugs on serotonin receptors. Pharmacol Rev *43*: 587, 1991.

Moller H-J: Neuroleptic treatment of negative symptoms in schizophrenic patients: Efficacy problems and methodological difficulties. Eur Neuropsychopharmacol *3*: 1, 1993.

Nordstrom A-L, Farde L, Wiesel F-A, Forslund K, Paulie S, Halldin C, Uppfeldt G: Central D2-dopamine receptor occupancy in relation to antipsychotic drug effects: A double-blind PET study of schizophrenic patients. Biol Psychiatry *33*: 227, 1993.

O'Callaghan E, Larkin C, Kinsella A, Waddington J L: Familial, obstetric, and other clinical correlates of minor physical anomalies in schizophrenia. Am J Psychiatry *148*: 479, 1991.

Pantelis C, Barnes T R E, Nelson H E: Is the concept of frontal-subcortical dementia relevant to schizophrenia? Br J Psychiatry *160*: 442, 1992.

Pettegrew J W, Keshavan M S, Panchanlingam K, Strychor S, Kaplan D B, Tretta M G, Allen M: Alterations in brain high-energy phosphate and membrane phospholipid metabolism in first-episode, drug-naive schizophrenics. Arch Gen Psychiatry *48*: 563, 1991.

Pulver A E, Liang K-Y, Brown C H, Wolyniec P, McGrath J, Adler L, Tam D, Carpenter D, Childs B: Risk factors in schizophrenia: Season of birth, gender, and familial risk. Br J Psychiatry *161*: 65, 1992.

Roberts G W, Done D J, Bruton C, Crow T J: A "mock up" of schizophrenia: Temporal lobe epilepsy and schizophrenia-like psychosis. Biol Psychiatry *28*: 127, 1990.

Schröder J, Niethammer R, Geider F-J, Reitz C, Binkert M, Jauss M, Sauer H: Neurological soft signs in schizophrenia. Schizophr Res *6*: 25, 1992.

Scottish Schizophrenia Research Group: The Scottish First Episode Schizophrenia Study: VIII. Five-year follow-up: Clinical and psychosocial findings. Br J Psychiatry *161*: 496, 1992.

Sedvall G: The current status of PET scanning with respect to schizophrenia. Neuropsychopharmacology *7*: 41, 1992.

Seeman P, Guan H-C, Van Tol H H M: Dopamine D4 receptors elevated in schizophrenia. Science *365*: 441, 1993.

Shalev A, Hermesh H, Rothberg J, Munitz H: Poor neuroleptic response in acutely exacerbated schizophrenic patients. Acta Psychiatr Scand *87*: 86, 1993.

Sham P C, O'Callaghan E, Takei N, Murray G K, Hare E H, Murray R M: Schizophrenia following pre-natal exposure to influenza epidemics between 1939 and 1960. Br J Psychiatry *160*: 461, 1992.

Sharma R P, Javaid J I, Pandey G N, Janicak P G, Davis J M: Behavioral and biochemical effects of methylphenidate in schizophrenic and non-schizophrenic patients. Biol Psychiatry *30*: 459, 1991.

Shenton M E, Kikinis R, Jolesz F A, Pollak S D, LeMay M, Wible C G, Hokama H, Martin J, Metcalf D, Coleman M, McCarley R W: Abnormalities of the left temporal lobe and thought disorder in schizophrenia: A quantitative magnetic resonance imaging study. N Engl J Med *327*: 604, 1992.

Siegel B V, Buchsbaum M S, Bunney W E, Gottschalk L A, Haier R J, Lohr J B, Lottenberg S, Najafi A, Nuechterlein K H, Potkin S G, Wu J C: Cortical-striatal-thalamic circuits and brain glucose metabolic activity in 70 unmedicated male schizophrenic patients. Am J Psychiatry *150*: 1325, 1993.

Siris S G: Diagnosis of secondary depression in schizophrenia: Implications for DSM-IV. Schizophr Bull *17*: 65, 1991.

Stoll A L, Tohen M, Baldessarini R J, Goodwin D C, Stein S, Katz S, Geenens D, Swinson R P, Goethe J W, McGlashan T: Shifts in diagnostic frequencies of schizophrenia and major affective disorders at six North American psychiatric hospitals, 1972–1988. Am J Psychiatry *150*: 1668, 1993.

Szymanski S, Kane J M, Lieberman J A: A selective review of biological markers in schizophrenia. Schizophr Bull *17*: 99, 1991.

Tandon R, Mazzara C, DeQuardo J, Craig K A, Meador-Woodruff J H, Goldman R, Greden J F: Dexamethasone suppression test in schizophrenia: Relationship to symptomatology, ventricular enlargement, and outcome. Biol Psychiatry *29*: 953, 1991.

Tarrier N, Turpin G: Psychosocial factors, arousal and schizophrenic relapse: The psychophysiological data. Br J Psychiatry *161*: 3, 1992.

Tsuang M T, Gilbertson M W, Faraone S V: The genetics of schizophrenia: Current knowledge and future directions. Schizophr Res *4*: 157, 1991.

Turner W M, Tsuang M T: Impact of substance abuse on the course and outcome of schizophrenia. Schizophr Bull *16*: 87, 1990.

van Horn, J D, McManus I C: Ventricular enlargement of schizophrenia: A meta-analysis of studies of the ventricle:brain ratio (VBR). Br J Psychiatry *160*: 687, 1992.

van Kammen D P, Kelley M: Dopamine and norepinephrine activity in schizophrenia: An integrative perspective. Schizophr Res *4*: 173, 1991.

Weinberger D R, editor: Schizophrenia. In *American Psychiatric Press Review of Psychiatry,* vol 10, A Tasman, S M Goldfinger, editors, p 5. American Psychiatric Press, Washington, 1991.

Weinberger D R, Berman K F, Suddath R, Torrey E F: Evidence of dysfunction of a prefrontal-limbic network in schizophrenia: A magnetic resonance imaging and regional cerebral blood flow study of discordant monozygotic twins. Am J Psychiatry *149*: 890, 1992.

Zipursky R B, Lim K O, Sullivan E V, Brown B W, Pfefferbaum A: Widespread cerebral gray matter volume deficits in schizophrenia. Arch Gen Psychiatry *49*: 195, 1992.

# 14 ||||||

# Other Psychotic Disorders

## 14.1 / Overview

Schizophrenia is both the classic and the most common psychotic disorder. There are, however, many other psychotic syndromes that do not meet the diagnostic criteria for schizophrenia. The other major psychotic syndromes are schizophreniform disorder, schizoaffective disorder, delusional disorder, and brief psychotic disorder. Briefly, the symptoms of *schizophreniform disorder* are identical to those of schizophrenia except that the symptoms have been present for at least one month but less than six months. *Schizoaffective disorder* is characterized by the presence of a complete syndrome of symptoms for both schizophrenia and a mood disorder. *Delusional disorder*, like schizophrenia, is a chronic disorder but is characterized by the presence of delusions as the predominant symptom. And *brief psychotic disorder* is characterized primarily by the brief duration (at least one day but less than one month) of schizophrenic symptoms.

In the evaluation of any psychotic patient, the possibility that the psychosis is caused by a general medical condition or is induced by a substance must be considered. Those two situations are classified in the fourth edition of *Diagnostic and Statistical Manual of Mental Disorders* (DSM-IV) as *psychotic disorder due to a general medical condition* and *substance induced psychotic disorder*, respectively. DSM-IV also includes a diagnosis of *catatonic disorder due to a general medical condition* to emphasize the special considerations regarding the differential diagnosis of catatonic symptoms (Section 10.5).

DSM-IV introduces into an appendix two new psychotic disorder diagnoses, postpsychotic depressive disorder of schizophrenia and simple deteriorative disorder (simple schizophrenia). *Postpsychotic depressive disorder of schizophrenia* is characterized by the presence of all the symptoms of a major depressive episode during the residual phase of schizophrenia. *Simple deteriorative disorder (simple schizophrenia)*, a still controversial diagnostic category, is characterized as the progressive development of symptoms of social withdrawal and other symptoms similar to the deficit symptoms of schizophrenia.

In addition to the common psychotic disorders and the newly introduced DSM-IV diagnoses, a variety of rare or atypical psychotic disorders have been either officially or clinically recognized. DSM-IV includes diagnostic criteria for *shared psychotic disorder*, which is the classification for persons with psychotic symptoms that develop because of their association with another psychotic person. *Postpartum psychosis* occurs in some women after the delivery of a child. In addition to those and other atypical psychoses, there are a variety of culture-bound psychotic syndromes, such as amok and koro.

The main thrust of treatment for this group of psychotic disorders is a comprehensive treatment plan that attends to the biological, psychological, and environmental factors in the disorders. Medication is a major part of the treatment plan with all the disorders. However, anywhere from a fourth to a half of all patients do not comply with the medication as prescribed. Psychodynamic approaches may be helpful in uncovering the reasons for noncompliance. In some cases, states of ego-syntonic grandiosity are so pleasurable that the patient prefers psychosis to stabilization on medication. In instances in which there has been only one psychotic episode, patients may refuse to comply with medication regimens because they are using denial to deal with the reality of a serious psychotic disorder. In their minds, taking a medication may translate into the stigma of mental illness.

Other psychodynamic factors that must be assessed in this group of psychotic disorders include the precipitating stressors and the interpersonal environment. In the course of taking a history and examining the patient, clinicians should pay attention to any changes or stresses in the patient's interpersonal environment. Patients prone to psychosis need to maintain a certain interpersonal distance; frequently, the encroachment on the patient by others may create overwhelming stress that leads to decompensation. Similarly, any recent successes or losses may be important stressors in particular cases. Often, a relatively minor event has profound psychological meaning, and dynamic exploration of the meaning of events is, therefore, crucial in assessing triggers of psychotic episodes.

### PSYCHOTIC DISORDER DUE TO A GENERAL MEDICAL CONDITION AND SUBSTANCE-INDUCED PSYCHOTIC DISORDER

The evaluation of a psychotic patient requires the consideration of the possibility that the psychotic symptoms are the result of a general medical condition (for example, a brain tumor) or the ingestion of a substance (for example, phencyclidine).

## Epidemiology

Relevant epidemiological data about psychotic disorder due to a general medical condition and substance-induced psychotic disorder are lacking. The disorders are most often encountered in patients who abuse alcohol or other substances on a long-term basis. The delusional syndrome that may accompany complex partial seizures is more common in women than in men.

## Etiology

Physical conditions—such as cerebral neoplasms, particularly of the occipital or temporal areas—can cause hallucinations. Sensory deprivation, as occurs in blind and deaf persons, can also result in hallucinatory or delusional experiences. Lesions involving the temporal lobe and other cerebral regions, especially the right hemisphere and the parietal lobe, are associated with delusions.

Psychoactive substances are common causes of psychotic syndromes. The most commonly involved substances are alcohol, indole hallucinogens—for example, lysergic acid diethylamide (LSD)—amphetamine, cocaine, mescaline, phencyclidine (PCP), and ketamine. Many other substances, including steroids and thyroxine, can be associated with substance-induced hallucinations.

A list of general medical conditions and substances that can be associated with psychotic symptoms is found in Table 13–7.

## Diagnosis

**Psychotic disorder due to a general medical condition.** The DSM-IV diagnosis of psychotic disorder due to a general medical condition (Table 14.1–1) combines into one diagnosis the two similar diagnostic categories in the revised third edition of DSM (DSM-III-R), organic delusional disorder and organic hallucinosis. The phenomena of the psychotic disorder are defined in DSM-IV by further specifying the predominant symptoms. When the diagnosis is used, the medical condition, along with the predominant symptom pattern, should be included in the diagnosis—for example, psychotic disorder due to a brain tumor, with delusions. The DSM-IV criteria further specify that the disorder does not occur exclusively while the patient is delirious or demented and that the symptoms are not better accounted for by another mental disorder.

**Catatonic disorder due to a general medical condition.** DSM-IV has a separate diagnostic category for catatonic symptoms when they are secondary to a general medical condition (Section 10.5).

**Substance-induced psychotic disorder.** DSM-IV has combined the various DSM-III-R diagnostic categories that relate to psychoactive substance-induced psychotic disorders into a single diagnostic category, substance-induced psychotic disorder (Table 14.1–2). The diagnosis is reserved for persons who have substance-induced psychotic symptoms and impaired reality testing. Persons

**Table 14.1–1**
**Diagnostic Criteria for Psychotic Disorder Due to a General Medical Condition**

A. Prominent hallucinations or delusions.

B. There is evidence from the history, physical examination, or laboratory findings that the disturbance is the direct physiological consequence of a general medical condition.

C. The disturbance is not better accounted for by another mental disorder.

D. The disturbance does not occur exclusively during the course of a delirium.

*Code* based on predominant symptom:
　**with delusions:** if delusions are the predominant symptom
　**with hallucinations:** if hallucinations are the predominant symptom

**Coding note:** Include the name of the general medical condition on Axis I, e.g., psychotic disorder due to malignant lung neoplasm, with delusions; also code the general medical condition on Axis III.

**Coding note:** If delusions are part of a preexisting dementia, indicate the delusions by coding the appropriate subtype of the dementia of one is available, e.g., dementia of the Alzheimer's type, with late onset, with delusions.

Table from DSM-IV, *Diagnostic and Statistical Manual of Mental Disorders*, ed 4. Copyright American Psychiatric Association, Washington, 1994. Used with permission.

who have substance-induced psychotic symptoms (for example, hallucinations) but who have retained reality testing should be classified as having a substance-related disorder—for example, phencyclidine intoxication with perceptual disturbances. The intent of including the diagnosis of substance-induced psychotic disorder with the other psychotic disorder diagnoses is to prompt the clinician to consider the possibility that a substance is causally involved in the production of the psychotic symptoms. The full diagnosis of substance-induced psychotic disorder should include the type of substance involved, the stage of substance use when the disorder began (for example, during intoxication or withdrawal), and the clinical phenomena (for example, hallucinations or delusions).

## Clinical Features

**Hallucinations.** Hallucinations may occur in one or more sensory modalities. Tactile hallucinations (such as the sensation of bugs crawling on the skin) are characteristic of cocaine use. Auditory hallucinations are usually associated with psychoactive substance abuse; auditory hallucinations may also occur in deaf people. Olfactory hallucinations can occur in temporal lobe epilepsy. Visual hallucinations may occur in people who are blind from cataracts. Hallucinations are either recurrent or persistent. They are experienced in a state of full wakefulness and alertness, and the patient shows no significant changes in cognitive functions. Visual hallucinations often take the form of scenes involving diminutive (lilliputian) human figures or various small animals. Rare muscial hallucinations typically feature religious songs. Patients with psychotic disorder due to a general medical condition and substance-induced psychotic disorder may act on their hallucinations. In alcohol-related hallucinations, threatening,

**Table 14.1–2**
**Diagnostic Criteria for Substance-Induced Psychotic Disorder**

A. Prominent hallucinations or delusions. **Note:** Do not include hallucinations if the person has insight that they are substance-induced.

B. There is evidence from the history, physical examination, or laboratory findings of either (1) or (2):

    (1) the symptoms in criteria A developed during, or within a month of, substance intoxication or withdrawal
    (2) medication use is etiologically related to the disturbance

C. The disturbance is not better accounted for by a psychotic disorder that is not substance induced. Evidence that the symptoms are better accounted for by a psychotic disorder that is not substance induced might include the following: the symptoms precede the onset of the use (or medication use); the symptoms persist for a substantial period of time (e.g., about a month) after the cessation of acute withdrawal or severe intoxication, or are substantially in excess of what would be expected given the type or amount of the substance used or the duration of use; or there is other evidence that suggests the existence of an independent non-substance-induced psychotic disorder (e.g., a history of recurrent non-substance-related episodes).

D. The disturbance does not occur exclusively during the course of a delirium.

**Note:** This diagnosis should be made instead of a diagnosis of substance intoxication or substance withdrawal only when the symptoms are in excess of those usually associated with the intoxication or withdrawal syndrome and when the symptoms are sufficiently severe to warrant independent clinical attention.

*Code:* [Specific substance]-induced psychotic disorder (Alcohol, with delusions; alcohol, with hallucinations; amphetamine [or amphetaminelike substance], with delusions; amphetamine [or amphetaminelike substance], with hallucinations; cannabis, with delusions; cannabis, with hallucinations; cocaine, with delusions; cocaine, with hallucinations; hallucinogen, with delusions; hallucinogen, with hallucinations; inhalant, with delusions; inhalant, with hallucinations; opioid, with delusions; opioid, with hallucinations; phencyclidine [or phencyclidinelike substance], with delusions; phencyclidine [or phencyclidinelike substance], with hallucinations; sedative, hypnotic or anxiolytic, with delusions; sedative, hypnotic or anxiolytic, with hallucinations; other [or unknown] substance, with delusions; other [or unknown] substance, with hallucinations)

*Specify* if:
    **with onset during intoxication:** if criteria are met for intoxication with the substance and the symptoms develop during the intoxication syndrome
    **with onset during withdrawal:** if criteria are met for withdrawal from the substance and the symptoms develop during, or shortly after, a withdrawal syndrome

Table from DSM-IV, *Diagnostic and Statistical Manual of Mental Disorders*, ed 4. Copyright American Psychiatric Association, Washington, 1994. Used with permission.

critical, or insulting voices speak about the patients in the third person. They may tell the patients to harm either themselves or others; such patients are dangerous and are at significant risk for suicide or homicide. The patient may or may not believe that the hallucinations are real.

**Delusions.** Secondary and substance-induced delusions are usually present in a state of full wakefulness. The

patient experiences no change in the level of consciousness, although mild cognitive impairment may be observed. The delusions may be systematized or fragmentary, and their content may vary. Persecutory delusions are the most common. The person may appear confused, disheveled, or eccentric. Speech may be tangential or even incoherent. Hyperactivity and apathy may be observed. An associated dysphoric mood is thought to be common.

### Differential Diagnosis

Psychotic disorder due to a general medical condition and substance-induced psychotic disorder need to be distinguished from delirium, in which the patient has a clouded sensorium; from dementia, in which the patient has major intellectual deficits; and from schizophrenia, in which the patient has other symptoms of thought disorder and impaired functioning. Psychotic disorder due to a general medical condition and substance-induced psychotic disorder must also be differentiated from psychotic mood disorders, in which other affective symptoms are pronounced.

### Treatment

Treatment involves the identification of the general medical condition or the particular substance involved. At that point, treatment is directed toward the underlying condition and the immediate behavioral control of the patient. Hospitalization may be necessary to evaluate the patient completely and to ensure the patient's safety. Antipsychotic agents may be necessary for the immediate and short-term control of psychotic or aggressive behavior, although benzodiazepines may also be useful for the control of agitation and anxiety.

## PSYCHOTIC DISORDERS IN DSM-IV APPENDIX

### Postpsychotic Depressive Disorder of Schizophrenia

Depressive symptoms after a psychotic episode in a schizophrenic patient were categorized as an example of depressive disorder not otherwise specified in DSM-III-R. In DSM-IV the syndrome has been given its own diagnostic classification in an appendix (Table 14.1–3).

**Epidemiology.** In the absence of specific diagnostic criteria, the reported incidence of postpsychotic depression of schizophrenia varied widely from less than 10 to more than 70 percent. A reasonable estimate from the large studies is about 25 percent, although a definitive incidence figure will have to wait for controlled studies using the DSM-IV criteria.

**Prognostic significance.** The prognostic significance of the DSM-IV diagnosis is uncertain at this point, since studies using the official diagnostic category have not yet been conducted. Nonetheless, data from other studies indicate that patients with postpsychotic depressive disorder of schizophrenia are likely to have had poor premorbid adjustment, marked schizoid personality disorder traits,

**Table 14.1–3**
**Research Criteria for Postpsychotic Depressive Disorder of Schizophrenia**

A. Criteria are met for a major depressive episode.

   **Note:** The major depressive episode must include criterion A1: depressed mood. Do not include symptoms that are better accounted for as medication side effects or negative symptoms of schizophrenia.

B. The major depressive episode is superimposed on and occurs only during the residual phase of schizophrenia.

C. The major depressive episode is not due to the direct physiological effects of a substance or a general medical condition.

Table from DSM-IV, *Diagnostic and Statistical Manual of Mental Disorders*, ed 4. Copyright American Psychiatric Association, Washington, 1994. Used with permission.

and an insidious onset of their psychotic symptoms. Patients with postpsychotic depressive disorder of schizophrenia are also likely to have first-degree relatives with mood disorders. Although not a consistent finding in the literature, postpsychotic depressive disorder of schizophrenia has been associated with a less favorable prognosis, a higher likelihood of relapse, and an increased incidence of suicide than is seen in schizophrenic patients without postpsychotic depressive disorder. Although some data indicate that schizophrenic patients with and without postpsychotic depressive disorder may differ in a number of biological variables—for example, in dexamethasone-suppression test (DST) and thyrotropin-releasing hormone (TRH) test results and in monoamine oxidase (MAO) activity—the validity and the usefulness of those tests in the diagnosis are still uncertain.

**Diagnosis and differential diagnosis.** The clinical boundaries of the diagnosis are hard to define operationally. The symptoms of postpsychotic depressive disorder of schizophrenia can closely resemble the symptoms of the residual phase of schizophrenia and the side effects of commonly used antipsychotic medications. It can also be difficult to distinguish the diagnosis from schizoaffective disorder, depressive type. The DSM-IV criteria specify that the criteria for a major depressive episode be met and that the symptoms occur only during the residual phase of schizophrenia. The symptoms cannot be substance-induced or part of a mood disorder due to a general medical condition.

A major criticism of the disorder is that it may be almost entirely due to the effects of antipsychotic medications. But several types of data indicate that antipsychotic medications cannot explain the entire extent of the symptoms. First, depressive symptoms are often present during the psychotic episode itself and, generally, decrease in severity, along with the psychotic symptoms, with successful antipsychotic treatment. Second, the severity of depressive symptoms in postpsychotic schizophrenic patients has not been correlated with the dosage of antipsychotic medication. Third, depressive symptoms have been frequently reported in nonmedicated schizophrenic patients who are recovering from psychotic episodes. Nonetheless, the clinician should not confuse the antipsychotic-induced side effects of akathisia and akinesia as symptoms of postpsychotic depressive disorder of schizophrenia.

**Treatment.** The use of antidepressants in the treatment of postpsychotic depressive disorder of schizophrenia has been reported in a number of studies. About half of the studies have reported positive effects, and the other half have reported no effects in the relief of the depressive symptoms. Antidepressant medications probably relieve depressive symptoms in some of the patients, but the mixed results of the studies reflect the current inability to distinguish those patients who will respond from those who will not.

## Simple Deteriorative Disorder (Simple Schizophrenia)

Simple deteriorative disorder (simple schizophrenia) (Table 14.1–4) is a controversial diagnostic category. The use of the DSM-IV research criteria in subsequent studies will help either refute or support the reliability and the validity of the diagnostic category. The research criteria outline the gradual and progressive onset of symptoms that are similar to the deficit symptoms and the cognitive decline that can be seen in schizophrenia. Hallucinations and delusions are not part of the proposed symptom pattern.

Although few clinicians would say that they have not seen patients who meet the research criteria of simple schizophrenia, many researchers and clinicians have raised serious concerns about the diagnosis. (1) The term "simple schizophrenia" may incorrectly imply a close relation to schizophrenia and may unfairly stigmatize patients given the diagnosis. (2) The criteria may define an overinclusive group of patients, who may be better classified as having major depressive disorder, dysthymic disorder, substance abuse, or a personality disorder. In fact, the overlap with those other diagnostic categories is obviously present and necessitates the use of variable and unpredictable clinical judgment in deciding among the diagnostic alternatives. (3) The lack of a scientific literature regarding the criteria limits their usefulness in terms of predicting prognosis or suggesting treatment.

The diagnostic category may eventually be shown to have prognostic and treatment implications. While clini-

**Table 14.1–4**
**Research Criteria for Simple Deteriorative Disorder (Simple Schizophrenia)**

A. Progressive development over a period of at least a year of all of the following:

   (1) marked decline in occupational or academic functioning
   (2) gradual appearance and deepening of negative symptoms such as affective flattening, alogia, and avolition
   (3) poor interpersonal rapport, social isolation, or social withdrawal

B. Criterion A for schizophrenia has never been met.

C. The symptoms are not better accounted for by schizotypal or schizoid personality disorder, a psychotic disorder, a mood disorder, an anxiety disorder, a dementia, or mental retardation and are not due to the direct physiological effects of a substance or a general medical condition.

Table from DSM-IV, *Diagnostic and Statistical Manual of Mental Disorders*, ed 4. Copyright American Psychiatric Association, Washington, 1994. Used with permission.

cans are waiting for the appropriate studies to be completed, they should use the diagnosis with caution and forethought.

# ATYPICAL PSYCHOTIC DISORDERS

## Shared Psychotic Disorder (Folie à Deaux)

Shared psychotic disorder is a rare disorder and is perhaps better known as *folie à deux*. A patient is classified as having shared psychotic disorder when the patient's psychotic symptoms developed during a long-term relationship with another person who had a similar psychotic syndrome before the onset of symptoms in the patient with shared psychotic disorder. The disorder most commonly involves two people—a dominant person (the inducer, the principal, or the primary patient) and a submissive person, who is the patient with shared psychotic disorder. Occasionally, cases involving more than two persons have been reported, and those have been called *folie à trois*, *folie à quatre*, *folie à cinq*, and so on. One case involving an entire family (*folie à famille*) involved 12 persons (*folie à douze*).

Jules Baillarger first described the syndrome, calling it *folie à communiquée*, in 1860, although the first description is commonly attributed to Ernest Charles Lasègue and Jules Falret, who described the condition in 1877 and gave it the name of *folie à deux*. The syndrome has also been called communicated insanity, contagious insanity, infectious insanity, psychosis of association, and double insanity. Marandon de Montyel divided *folie à deux* into three groups (*folie imposée*, *folie simultanée*, and *folie communiquée*), and Heinz Lehmann added a fourth group, *folie induite*.

*Folie imposée* is the most common and classic form of the disorder; the dominant person develops a delusional system and then progressively imposes that delusional system onto the usually younger and more passive person. In *folie simultanée* similar delusional systems develop independently in two persons who are closely associated. In contrast to *folie imposée*, in which separation often causes an improvement of the symptoms in the submissive person, separation of the two persons in *folie simultanée* does not lead to improvement in either person. In *folie communiquée* the dominant person is involved in the induction of a similar delusional system in the submissive person, but the submissive person develops his or her own delusional system, which does not remit after the separation of the two parties. In *folie induite* one delusional person has his or her delusions extended by taking on the delusions of a second person. The various types of *folie* are difficult to differentiate in practice and are of historical interest more than clinical interest.

**Epidemiology.** More than 95 percent of all cases of shared psychotic disorder involve two members of the same family. About a third of the cases involve two sisters; another third involve a husband and a wife or a mother and her child. Two brothers, a brother and a sister, and a father and his child have been reported less frequently. The dominant person is usually affected by schizophrenia or a similar psychotic disorder. In about 25 percent of all cases, the submissive person is affected with physical disabilities, including deafness, cerebrovascular diseases, or other disabilities that increase the submissive person's dependence on the dominant person. Shared psychotic disorder may

be more common in low socioeconomic groups than in high socioeconomic groups. Shared psychotic disorder is more common in women than in men.

**Etiology.** The disorder has a psychosocial basis. Although the primary theory regarding the disorder is psychosocial, the fact that the affected persons are in the same family more than 95 percent of the time has also been interpreted to suggest a significant genetic component to the disorder. A modest amount of data indicate that affected persons often have a family history of schizophrenia.

The dominant member of the dyad has a preexisting psychotic disorder, almost always schizophrenia or a related psychotic disorder and rarely an affective or dementia-related psychosis. The dominant person is usually older, more intelligent, and better educated and possesses stronger personality traits than the submissive person, who is usually dependent on the dominant person. The two (or more) persons inevitably live together or have an extremely close personal relationship. The closeness is associated with a background of shared life experiences, common needs and hopes, and, often, a deep emotional rapport with each other. The relationship between the involved persons is usually somewhat or completely isolated from external societal and cultural inputs.

The submissive person may be predisposed to a mental disorder and may have a history of a personality disorder with dependent or suggestible qualities. The submissive person may also have a history of depression, suspiciousness, and social isolation. The relationship between the two persons, although one of dependence, may also be characterized by ambivalence, with deeply held feelings of both love and hate. The dominant person may be moved to induce the delusional system in the submissive person as a mechanism for maintaining contact with another person in spite of the dominant person's psychosis. The dominant person's psychotic symptoms may develop in the submissive person through the process of identification. By adopting the psychotic symptoms of the dominant person, the submissive person gains the acceptance of the dominant person. However, the admiration the submissive person has for the dominant person may evolve into hatred, which the submissive person considers unacceptable, and so the hatred is directed inward, often resulting in depression and sometimes suicide.

**Diagnosis.** The DSM-IV criteria for shared psychotic disorder (Table 14.1–5) include the development of de-

---

**Table 14.1–5**
**Diagnostic Criteria for Shared Psychotic Disorder**

A. A delusion develops in an individual in the context of a close relationship with another person(s), who has an already-established delusion.

B. The delusion is similar in content to that of the person who already has the established delusion.

C. The disturbance is not better accounted for by another psychotic disorder (e.g., schizophrenia) or a mood disorder with psychotic features and is not due to the direct physiological effects of a substance (e.g., a drug of abuse, a medication) or a general medical condition.

---

lusions in a person who has a close relationship with a person who already has a similar delusional system. The person with shared psychotic disorder does not have a preexisting psychotic disorder.

**Clinical features.** The key symptom is the unquestioning acceptance of the delusions of another person. The delusions themselves are often in the realm of possibility and usually not as bizarre as those seen in many patients with schizophrenia. The content of the delusions is often persecutory or hypochondriacal. Symptoms of a coexisting personality disorder may be present, but signs and symptoms that meet the diagnostic criteria for schizophrenia, mood disorders, and delusional disorder are absent. The patient may have ideation about suicide or pacts regarding homicide; that information must be elicited during the clinical interview.

A 43-year-old married woman entered the hospital with a chief complaint of being concerned about her sex problem; she stated that she needed hypnotism to find out what was wrong with her sexual drive. Her husband supplied the history: he complained that she had had many extramarital affairs, with many different men, all through their married life. He insisted that in one two-week period she had had as many as a hundred sexual experiences with men outside the marriage. The patient herself agreed with that assessment of her behavior but would not speak of the experiences, saying that she blocked the memories out. She denied any particular interest in sexuality but said that apparently she felt a compulsive drive to go out and seek sexual activity, despite her lack of interest.

The patient had been married to her husband for more than 20 years. He was clearly the dominant partner in the marriage. The patient feared his frequent jealous rages, and apparently it was he who suggested that she enter the hospital to receive hypnosis. The patient maintained that she could not explain why she sought out other men, that she really did not want to do that. Her husband stated that on occasion he had tracked her down, and, when he found her, she acted as if she did not know him. She confirmed that statement and believed it was because the episodes of her sexual promiscuity were blotted out by amnesia.

When the physician indicated that he questioned the reality of the wife's sexual adventures, the husband became furious and accused the doctor and a ward attendant of having sexual relations with her.

Neither an amobarbital (Amytal) interview nor considerable psychotherapy with the woman was able to clear the blocked-out memory of periods of sexual activity. The patient did admit to a memory of having had two extramarital relationships in the past: one, 20 years before the time of the hospital admission, and the other just a year before the admission. She stated that the last one had actually been planned by her husband and that he was in the same house at the time. She continued to believe that she had actually had countless extramarital sexual experiences, although she remembered only two of them.

*Discussion.* The first impression was that an amnestic syndrome, either psychogenic or organic, should be considered. However, evidence accumulated that the husband, the chief informant, had delusional jealousy, believing that his wife was repeatedly unfaithful to him. Apparently, under his influence, his wife had accepted that delusional belief, explaining her lack of memory of the events by believing that she had amnesia. It seemed that she had adopted his delusional system and did not have any kind of amnesia. Before the onset of her delusion, there was no indication that she had a preexisting psychotic disorder or that she had any of the prodromal

symptoms of schizophrenia. Because her delusional system developed as a result of a close relationship with another person who had an already established delusion (that is, her husband) and because her delusions were similar in content to his delusions, the diagnosis was shared psychotic disorder, formerly called *folie à deux*. A twist to the case was that it was the patient who, by virtue of her alleged extramarital activity, was the source of the husband's distress. It is more common in shared psychotic disorder for the person who has adopted the other's delusional system to believe that he or she is also being harmed.

**Differential diagnosis.** Malingering, factitious disorder with predominantly psychological signs and symptoms, psychotic disorder due to a general medical condition, and substance-induced psychotic disorder need to be considered in the differential diagnosis of the condition. The boundary between shared psychotic disorder and generic group madness, such as the Jonestown massacre in Guyana, is unclear.

**Course and prognosis.** The nature of the disorder suggests that separation of the submissive person, the person who has shared psychotic disorder, from the dominant person should result in the resolution and the disappearance of the submissive person's psychotic symptoms. In fact, that probably happens in less than 40 percent of all cases and perhaps in only 10 percent of all cases. Often, the submissive person requires treatment with antipsychotic drugs, just as the dominant person needs antipsychotic drugs for his or her psychotic disorder. Because the persons almost always come from the same family, they usually move back together after release from a hospital.

**Treatment.** The initial step in treatment is the separation of the affected person from the source of the delusions, the dominant partner. The patient may need significant support to compensate for the loss of that person. The patient with shared psychotic disorder should be observed for the remission of the delusional symptoms. Antipsychotic drugs can be used if the delusional symptoms have not abated in one or two weeks.

Psychotherapy with nondelusional members of the patient's family should be undertaken, and psychotherapy with both the patient with shared psychotic disorder and the dominant partner may be indicated later in the course of treatment. In addition, the mental disorder of the dominant partner should be treated.

To prevent the recurrence of the syndrome, the clinician must use family therapy and social support to modify the family dynamics and to prevent the redevelopment of the syndrome. It is often useful to make sure that the family unit is exposed to input from outside sources to decrease the family's isolation.

## Other Atypical Psychotic Disorders

**Autoscopic psychosis.** The characteristic symptom of autoscopic psychosis is a visual hallucination of all or part of the person's own body. The hallucinatory perception, which is called a phantom, is usually colorless and transparent and is perceived as though appearing in a mirror, since the phantom imitates the person's movements. The phantom tends to appear suddenly and without warning.

EPIDEMIOLOGY. Autoscopy is a rare phenomenon. Some persons have an autoscopic experience only once or a few times; other persons have the experience more often. Although the data are limited, sex, age, heredity, and intelligence do not seem to be related to the occurrence of the syndrome.

ETIOLOGY.   The cause of the autoscopic phenomenon is unknown. A biological hypothesis is that abnormal, episodic activity in areas of the temporoparietal lobes is involved with one's sense of self, perhaps combined with abnormal activity in parts of the visual cortex. Psychological theories have associated the syndrome with personalities characterized by imagination, visual sensitivity, and, possibly, narcissistic personality disorder traits. Such persons may be likely to experience autoscopic phenomena during periods of stress.

COURSE AND PROGNOSIS.   The classic descriptions of the phenomenon indicate that in most cases the syndrome is neither progressive nor incapacitating. The affected persons usually maintain some emotional distance from the phenomenon, possibly suggesting a specific neuroanatomical lesion. Rarely do the symptoms reflect the onset of schizophrenia or other psychotic disorders.

**Capgras's syndrome.**   The characteristic symptom of Capgras's syndrome is the delusion that other persons, usually persons closely related to the affected person, have been replaced by exact doubles, who are imposters. Those imposters assume the roles of the persons they impersonate and behave identically. The syndrome was originally described in 1923 by the French psychiatrist Jean Marie Joseph Capgras, who called it *l'illusion des sosies*, which means the illusion of doubles.

EPIDEMIOLOGY.   The rare syndrome occurs more frequently in women than in men. The condition is sometimes classified as a delusional disorder, although it may also be a symptom of schizophrenia in some patients.

ETIOLOGY.   Capgras explained the nature of the delusion as a result of feelings of strangeness, combined with a paranoid tendency to distrust. A biological hypothesis is that it is a neurobiological dysfunction in the brain areas that usually relate perceptions to the recognition of persons. A psychoanalytic hypothesis posits that what the patients feel about the persons with whom they are confronted (for example, anger or fear) is displaced to the doubles, who are imposters and, therefore, may be safely and righteously rejected.

PROGNOSIS AND TREATMENT.   The symptoms of Capgras's syndrome respond to antipsychotic treatment. However, when patients have Capgras's syndrome as the sole symptom of their psychotic disorder, the clinician should do an extensive neuropsychological workup to identify any organic lesions that may be causing the syndrome.

**Cotard's syndrome.**   In the 19th century the French psychiatrist Jules Cotard described several patients who suffered from a syndrome referred to as *délire de négation*. The syndrome is sometimes referred to as nihilistic delusional disorder. Patients with the syndrome complain of having lost not only possessions, status, and strength but also their heart, blood, and intestines. The world beyond them is reduced to nothingness.

EPIDEMIOLOGY.   The syndrome is usually seen as a precursor to a schizophrenic or depressive episode. It is relatively rare; with the common use today of antipsychotic drugs, the syndrome is seen even less frequently than in the past.

ETIOLOGY.   In its pure form the syndrome is seen in patients suffering from depression, schizophrenia, and psychotic disorder due to a general medical condition, often associated with dementia.

PROGNOSIS AND TREATMENT.   The syndrome usually lasts only a few days or weeks and responds to treatment that is directed at the underlying disorder. Long-term forms of the

syndrome are usually associated with dementing syndromes, such as dementia of the Alzheimer's type.

**Atypical schizophrenia.**   A particular form of schizophrenia was described by R. Gjessing and called periodic catatonia. Patients affected with the disorder have periodic bouts of stuporous or excited catatonia, which Gjessing believed were related to metabolic shifts in nitrogen balance. The syndrome is rarely seen, responds well to standard antipsychotic agents, and is prevented by maintenance medication.

## CULTURE-BOUND PSYCHOTIC SYNDROMES

A variety of culture-bound psychotic syndromes have been described in the literature. In general, the culture-bound psychotic syndromes can be fit into one or another DSM-IV diagnosis, including psychotic disorder not otherwise specified. However, the existence of the syndromes raises two possibilities. First, if the syndromes are unique and limited to specific cultures, they raise the possibility that specific cultural or biological factors are contributing to the psychosis. Second, if the syndromes are forms of standard diagnoses—schizophrenia, for example—their existence suggests that the content of their delusions and hallucinations can be strongly influenced by the society and the culture. Other syndromes in addition to those discussed below are listed in Table 4.6–3.

### Amok

The Malayan word "amok" means to engage furiously in battle. The amok syndrome consists of a sudden, unprovoked outburst of wild rage that causes affected persons to run about madly, indiscriminately attacking and maiming any persons and animals in their way. The savage homicidal attack is generally preceded by a period of preoccupation, brooding, and mild depression. After the attack, the person feels exhausted, has no memory of the attack, and often commits suicide. The Malayan natives also refer to the attack as *mata elap* (darkened eye). Examples of persons with a syndrome similar to amok in the United States are commonly reported in the newspapers. Often, those persons are found to be suffering from schizophrenia, a bipolar disorder, or a depressive disorder. In other cases, the cause may be a general medical condition, such as epilepsy or another brain lesion. A cultural explanation of the syndrome involves the theory that a culture that imposes strict restrictions on adolescents and adults but allows children free rein to express their aggression may be especially prone to psychopathological reactions of the amok type. The belief in magical possession by demons and evil spirits, as is the case in some primitive cultures, may be another cultural factor that contributes to the development of the amok syndrome.

The only immediate treatment consists of overpowering amok persons and gaining complete physical control over them. The attack is usually over within a few hours. Afterward, the patient may require treatment for a chronic psychotic disorder, which may have been the underlying cause.

## Koro

Koro is characterized by the patient's delusion that his penis is shrinking and may disappear into his abdomen and that he may die. The koro syndrome occurs among the people of Southeast Asia and in some areas of China, where it is known as *suk-yeong*. A corresponding disorder in women involves complaints of the shrinkage of the vulva, the labia, and the breasts. Occasional cases of koro syndrome among people belonging to a Western culture have been reported. Koro has usually been thought of as a psychogenic disorder resulting from the interaction of cultural, social, and psychodynamic factors in especially predisposed persons. Culturally elaborated fears about nocturnal emission, masturbation, and sexual overindulgence seem to give rise to the condition. Alternatively, the disorder may be seen as a delusional disorder or as a symptom of another psychotic disorder.

Patients have been treated with psychotherapy, antipsychotic drugs, and, in a few cases, electroconvulsive therapy. As with other psychiatric disorders, the prognosis is related to the patient's premorbid personality adjustment and to any associated pathology. Some cultures prescribe fellatio as a cure.

## Piblokto

Occurring among Eskimos and sometimes referred to as Arctic hysteria, piblokto is characterized by attacks lasting from one to two hours, during which patients (usually women) begin to scream and to tear off and destroy their clothing. While imitating the cry of some animal or bird, the patients may throw themselves on the snow or run wildly about on the ice, although the temperature may be well below zero. After the attack, the persons appear to be normal and usually have no memory of the episode. The Eskimos are reluctant to touch afflicted persons during the attacks because they believe that the attacks involve evil spirits. Piblokto is almost certainly a hysterical state of a dissociative disorder. It has become much less frequent than it used to be among Eskimos.

## Wihtigo

Wihtigo or windigo psychosis is a psychiatric disorder confined to the Cree, Ojibwa, and Salteaux Indians of North America. Affected persons believe that they may be transformed into a wihtigo, a giant monster that eats human flesh. During times of starvation, affected persons may have the delusion that they have been transformed into a wihtigo, and they may feel and express a craving for human flesh. Because of the patient's belief in witchcraft and in the possibility of such a transformation, symptoms concerning the alimentary tract, such as loss of appetite and nausea from trivial causes, may sometimes cause the patient to become greatly excited for fear of being transformed into a wihtigo.

# PSYCHOTIC DISORDER NOT OTHERWISE SPECIFIED

This DSM-IV category is used for patients who have psychotic symptoms (for example, delusions, hallucinations, and disorganized speech and behavior) but who do not meet the diagnostic criteria for other specifically defined psychotic disorders. In some cases the diagnosis of psychotic disorder not otherwise specified may be used when not enough information is available to make a specific diagnosis. DSM-IV has listed some examples of the diagnosis to help guide clinicians (Table 14.1–6).

## Postpartum Psychosis

Postpartum psychosis, one of the examples of psychotic disorder not otherwise specified, is a syndrome most often characterized by depression, delusions, and thoughts by the mother of harming either the infant or herself. Such ideation of suicide or infanticide must be carefully monitored, since some mothers have acted on those ideas. Most of the available data suggest a close relation between postpartum psychosis and the mood disorders, particularly bipolar disorders and major depressive disorder.

**Epidemiology.** The incidence of postpartum psychosis is about 1 per 1,000 childbirths, although some reports have indicated that the incidence may be as high as 2 per 1,000 childbirths. About 50 to 60 percent of the affected women have just had their first child, and about 50 percent

**Table 14.1–6**
**Diagnostic Criteria for Psychotic Disorder Not Otherwise Specified**

This category includes psychotic symptomatology (i.e., delusions, hallucinations, disorganized speech, grossly disorganized or catatonic behavior) about which there is inadequate information to make a specific diagnosis or about which there is contradictory information, or disorders with psychotic symptoms that do not meet the criteria for any specific psychotic disorder.

Examples include:

1. Postpartum psychosis that does not meet criteria for mood disorder with psychotic features, brief psychotic disorder, psychotic disorder due to a general medical condition, or substance-induced psychotic disorder
2. Psychotic symptoms that have lasted for less than 1 month but that have not yet remitted, so that the criteria for brief psychotic disorder are not met
3. Persistent auditory hallucinations in the absence of any other features
4. Persistent nonbizarre delusions with periods of overlapping mood episodes that have been present for a substantial portion of the delusional disturbance
5. Situations in which the clinician has concluded that a psychotic disorder is present, but is unable to determine whether it is primary, due to a general medical condition, or substance induced

Table from DSM-IV, *Diagnostic and Statistical Manual of Mental Disorders*, ed 4. Copyright American Psychiatric Association, Washington, 1994. Used with permission.

of the cases involved deliveries associated with nonpsychiatric perinatal complications. About 50 percent of the affected women have a family history of mood disorders. Although postpartum psychosis is fundamentally a disorder of women, some rare cases affect fathers. In those rare instances the husband may feel displaced by the child and may be competitive for the mother's love and attention. However, the father probably has a coexisting major mental disorder that has been exacerbated by the stress of fatherhood.

**Etiology.** The most robust data indicate that an episode of postpartum psychosis is essentially an episode of a mood disorder, usually a bipolar disorder but possibly a depressive disorder. Relatives of persons with postpartum psychosis have an incidence of mood disorders that is similar to the incidence in relatives of persons with mood disorders. Schizoaffective disorder and delusional disorder are rarely appropriate diagnoses. The validity of those diagnoses is usually verified in the year after the birth, when as many as two thirds of the patients may have a second episode of the underlying disorder. The delivery process may best be seen as a nonspecific stress, perhaps through a major hormonal mechanism, that causes the development of an episode of a major mood disorder.

A few instances of postpartum psychosis result from a general medical condition associated with perinatal events, such as infection, drug intoxication—for example, scopolamine (Donnagel) and meperidine (Demerol)—toxemia, and blood loss. The sudden fall in estrogen and progesterone concentrations immediately after delivery may also contribute to the disorder. However, treatment with those hormones has not been effective.

Some investigators have written that a purely psychosocial causal mechanism is suggested by the preponderance of primiparous mothers and an association between postpartum psychosis and recent stressful events. Psychodynamic studies of postpartum mental illness have suggested the presence of conflicted feelings in the mother about her mothering experience. Some women may not have wanted to become pregnant; others may feel trapped in unhappy marriages by motherhood. Marital discord during pregnancy has been associated with an increased incidence of illness, although the discord may be related to the slow development of mood disorder symptoms in the mother.

**Diagnosis.** Specific diagnostic criteria are not included in DSM-IV. The diagnosis can be made when psychosis occurs in close temporal association with childbirth, although a DSM-IV diagnosis of a mood disorder should be considered in the differential diagnosis. Characteristic symptoms include delusions, cognitive deficits, motility disturbances, mood abnormalities, and occasionally hallucinations. The content of the psychotic material revolves around mothering and pregnancy.

DSM-IV also allows for the diagnosis of brief psychotic disorder with postpartum onset. Brief psychotic disorder is discussed in Section 14.5.

**Clinical features.** The symptoms of postpartum psychosis can often begin within days of the delivery, although the mean time to onset is two to three weeks and almost always within eight weeks of delivery. Characteristically, the patient begins to complain of fatigue, insomnia, and restlessness and may have episodes of tearfulness and emotional lability. Later, suspiciousness, confusion, incoherence, irrational statements, and obsessive concerns about the baby's health and welfare may be present. Delusions may be present in 50 percent of all patients and hallucinations in about 25 percent. Complaints regarding the inability to move, stand, or walk are also common.

The patient may have feelings of not wanting to care for the baby, of not loving the baby, and, in some cases, of wanting to do harm to the baby or to self or to both. Delusional material may involve the idea that the baby is dead or defective. The patient may deny the birth and may express thoughts of being unmarried, virginal, persecuted, influenced, or perverse. Hallucinations may occur with similar content and may involve voices telling the patient to kill the baby.

**Differential diagnosis.** As with any psychotic disorder, the clinician should consider the possibility of either a psychotic disorder due to a general medical condition or a substance-induced psychotic disorder. Potential general medical conditions include hypothyroidism and Cushing's syndrome. Substance-induced psychotic disorder may be associated with the use of pain medications—for example, pentazocine (Talwin)—or antihypertensive drugs during the pregnancy. Other potential medical causes include infections, toxemia, and neoplasms.

Women with a history of a mood disorder should be classified as having recurrences of that disorder. Postpartum psychosis should not be confused with the so-called postpartum blues, a normal condition that occurs in up to 50 percent of women after childbirth. Postpartum blues is self-limited, lasts only a few days, and is characterized by tearfulness, fatigue, anxiety, and irritability that begin shortly after childbirth and lessen in severity over the course of a week.

**Course and prognosis.** The onset of florid psychotic symptoms is usually preceded by prodromal signs, such as insomnia, restlessness, agitation, lability of mood, and mild cognitive deficits. Once the psychosis occurs, the patient may be a danger to herself or to her newborn, depending on the content of her delusional system and her degree of agitation. In one study, 5 percent of the patients committed suicide, and 4 percent committed infanticide. A favorable outcome is associated with a good premorbid adjustment and a supportive family network.

Since an episode of postpartum psychosis is most likely an episode of a mood disorder, the course of the syndrome is similar to that seen in patients with mood disorders. Specifically, mood disorders are usually episodic disorders, and patients with postpartum psychosis often experience another episode of symptoms within a year or two of the birth. Subsequent pregnancies are associated with an increased risk of having another episode.

**Treatment.** Postpartum psychosis is a psychiatric emergency. Antidepressants and lithium (Eskalith), sometimes in combination with an antidepressant, are the treatments of choice. No pharmacological agents should be prescribed to a woman who is breast-feeding. Suicidal patients may require transfer to a psychiatric unit to help prevent a suicide attempt.

It is usually advantageous for the mother to have contact with her baby if she so desires. But the visits must be closely supervised, especially if the mother is preoccupied with doing harm to the infant. Psychotherapy is indicated after the period of acute psychosis is past. Therapy is usually directed at the conflictual areas that have become evident during the evaluation. Therapy may involve helping the patient accept and be comfortable with the mothering role. Changes in environmental factors may also be indicated. Increased support from the husband and other persons in the environment may help reduce the woman's stress. Most studies report high rates of recovery from the acute illness.

### References

Anis-ur-Rehman, St Clair D, Platz C: Puerperal insanity in the 19th and 20th centuries. Br J Psychiatry *156*: 861, 1990.

Bandelow B, Müller P, Frick U, Gaebel W, Linden M, Müller-Spahn F, Pietzcker A, Tegeler J: Depressive syndromes in schizophrenic patients under neuroleptic therapy. Eur Arch Psychiatry Clin Neurosci *241*: 291, 1992.

Benvenuti P, Cabras P L, Servi P, Rosseti S, Marchetti G, Pazzagli: Puerperal psychoses: A clinical case study with follow-up. J Affect Disord *26*: 25, 1992.

Bernstein R L, Gaw A C: Koro: Proposed classification for DSM-IV. Am J Psychiatry *147*: 1670, 1990.

Dippel B, Kemper J, Berger M: Folie à six: A case report on induced psychotic disorder. Acta Psychiatr Scand *83*: 137, 1991.

Enoch M D, Trethowan W: *Uncommon Psychiatric Syndromes*, ed 3. Butterworth-Heinemann, Oxford, 1991.

Harding J J: Postpartum psychotic disorders: A review. Compr Psychiatry *30*: 109, 1989.

McClellan J M, Werry J S, Ham M: A follow-up study of early onset psychosis: Comparison between outcome diagnoses of schizophrenia, mood disorders, and personality disorders. J Autism Dev Disord *23*: 243, 1993.

Popkin M K, Tucker G J: "Secondary" and drug-induced mood, anxiety, psychotic, catatonic, and personality disorders: A review of the literature. J Neuropsychiatry Clin Neurosci *4*: 369, 1992.

Siris S G: Diagnosis of secondary depression in schizophrenia: Implications for DSM-IV. Schizophr Bull *17*: 75, 1991.

Tsuang D, Coryell W: An 8-year follow-up of patients with DSM-III-R psychotic depression, schizoaffective disorder, and schizophrenia. Am J Psychiatry *150*: 1182, 1993.

# 14.2 / Schizophreniform Disorder

Schizophreniform disorder is identical in every respect to schizophrenia except that its symptoms last at least one month but less than six months. Patients with schizophreniform disorder return to their baseline level of functioning once the schizophreniform disorder has resolved. In contrast, for a patient to meet the diagnostic criteria for schizophrenia, the symptoms must have been present for at least six months.

## HISTORY

The term "schizophreniform" was coined by Gabriel Langfeldt, working at the University Psychiatric Clinic in Oslo, in 1939. Langfeldt emphasized that schizophreniform psychosis defined a heterogeneous group of patients characterized only by (1) the similarity of their symptoms to those of schizophrenia and (2) the presence of a good clinical outcome. Before Langfeldt's arrival at the clinic, patients with schizophrenia had been classified as having either typical schizophrenia or schizophrenia (??. . . ), in which the number of question marks was a semiofficial method of denoting the questionableness of the diagnosis. Using sound scientific methods, Langfeldt studied a group of typical schizophrenic patients and a group of schizophrenic (?) patients and concluded that a group of patients with schizophrenic symptoms had a good outcome. He classified that group as having schizophreniform disorder. Langfeldt noted that those patients often had good premorbid adjustment, an abrupt onset of symptoms, the frequent presence of a psychosocial stressor, and a good prognosis.

## EPIDEMIOLOGY

The incidence, the prevalence, and the sex ratio of schizophreniform disorder have not yet been reported in the literature. Some clinicians have the impression that the disorder is most common in adolescents and young adults, and most investigators believe that the disorder is less than half as common as schizophrenia.

### Family History

Several studies have shown that the relatives of patients with schizophreniform disorder are at high risk of having psychiatric disorders but that the distribution of the disorders differs from the distribution seen in the relatives of patients with schizophrenia and bipolar disorders. Specifically, the relatives of patients with schizophreniform disorder are more likely to have mood disorders than are the relatives of patients with schizophrenia. In addition, the relatives of patients with schizophreniform disorder are more likely to have a diagnosis of a psychotic mood disorder than are the relatives of patients with bipolar disorders.

## ETIOLOGY

As in all the classic psychotic disorders, the cause of schizophreniform disorder is not known. As Langfeldt noted in 1939, the group of patients with the diagnostic label are likely to be heterogeneous. In general, some patients have a disorder similar to schizophrenia, whereas others have a disorder similar to a mood disorder. Because of their generally good outcome, the disorder probably has similarities to the episodic nature of mood disorders. However, some data indicate a close relation to schizophrenia.

In support of the relation to mood disorders, several studies have shown that schizophreniform disorder patients, as a group, have more affective symptoms (especially mania) and a better outcome than do schizophrenic patients. Also, the increased presence of mood disorders in the relatives of patients with schizophreniform disorder indicates a relation to mood disorders. Thus, the biological and epidemiological data are most consistent with the hypothesis that the current diagnostic category defines a group of patients, some of whom have a disorder similar to schizophrenia and others of whom have a disorder similar to a mood disorder.

## Brain Imaging

As has been reported for schizophrenia, a relative activation deficit in the inferior prefrontal region of the brain while the patient is performing a region-specific psychological task (the Wisconsin Card-Sorting Test) has been reported in schizophreniform disorder patients (Figure 14.2–1). In one study the deficit was limited to the left hemisphere. That study also found impaired striatal activity suppression, also limited to the left hemisphere, during the activation procedure. The data can be interpreted to indicate a physiological similarity between the psychosis of schizophrenia and the psychosis of schizophreniform disorder. Additional central nervous system (CNS) factors, as yet unidentified, may lead to either the long-term course of schizophrenia or the foreshortened course of schizophreniform disorder.

Although some data indicate that patients with schizophreniform disorder may have enlarged cerebral ventricles, as determined by computed tomography (CT) and magnetic resonance imaging (MRI), other data indicate that, unlike the enlargement seen in schizophrenia, the ventricular enlargement in schizophreniform disorder is not correlated with outcome measures or other biological measures.

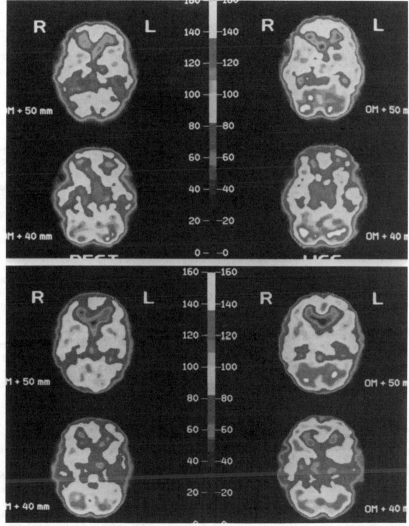

**Figure 14.2–1.** Regional cerebral blood flow distribution at rest (left) and during cerebral activation with the Wisconsin Card-Sorting Test (right) in a patient with schizophreniform disorder (top) and a healthy volunteer (bottom). OM indicates orbitomeatal line. (Figure from P Rubin, S Holm, L Friberg, P Videbech, H S Andersen, B B Bendsen, N Strømsø, J K Larsen, N A Lassen, R Hemmingsen: Altered modulation of prefrontal and subcortical brain activity in newly diagnosed schizophrenia and schizophreniform disorder. Arch Gen Psychiatry 48: 992, 1991. Used with permission.)

## Other Biological Measures

Although brain imaging studies point to a similarity between schizophreniform disorder and schizophrenia, at least one study of electrodermal activity has indicated a difference. Schizophrenic patients born during the winter and spring months (a period of high risk for the birth of schizophrenic patients) had hyporesponsive skin conductances, but that association was absent in patients with schizophreniform disorder. The significance and the meaning of that single study are difficult to interpret; however, the results do suggest caution in assuming similarity between schizophrenic patients and schizophreniform disorder patients. Data from at least one study of eye tracking in schizophreniform disorder patients and schizophrenic patients also indicate that the two groups may differ in some biological measures.

## DIAGNOSIS

The diagnostic criteria for schizophreniform disorder in the fourth edition of *Diagnostic and Statistical Manual of Mental Disorders* (DSM-IV) (Table 14.2–1) include three criteria identical to those for schizophrenia. The first criterion is the presence of active-phase symptoms (for example, delusions, hallucinations, and flat affect) for one month. The next two criteria are exclusion criteria for schizoaffective disorder, mood disorder with psychotic features, substance-related disorders, and mental disorders due to a general medical condition. The other criteria for schizophreniform disorder specify that the entire episode, including the prodromal and residual phases, last at least one month but less than six months.

The diagnosis of provisional schizophreniform disorder is made while waiting to see if the symptoms resolve. A diagnosis of schizophreniform disorder is more accurate than a diagnosis of schizophrenia when the clinician is

**Table 14.2–1**
**Diagnostic Criteria for Schizophreniform Disorder**

A. Criteria A, D, and E of schizophrenia are met.

B. An episode of the disorder (including prodromal, active, and residual phases) lasts at least one month but less than six months. (When the diagnosis must be made without waiting for recovery, it should be qualified as "provisional.")

*Specify if:*
**Without good prognostic features**
**With good prognostic features** as evidenced by two (or more) of the following:

  (1) onset of prominent psychotic symptoms within four weeks of the first noticeable change in usual behavior or functioning
  (2) confusion or perplexity at the height of the psychotic episode
  (3) good premorbid social and occupational functioning
  (4) absence of blunted or flat affect

unable to obtain a reliable history from psychotic patients regarding the duration of their symptoms. However, a patient's personal history of prodromal symptoms may mislead the physician away from a correct diagnosis of schizophrenia, and a patient's personal history of affective symptoms may cause the physician to miss a diagnosis of a mood disorder or schizoaffective disorder.

## Prognostic Subtypes

DSM-IV allows for the specification of the presence or the absence of good prognostic features (Table 14.2–1). The good prognostic features include a rapid onset, a degree of cognitive impairment, good premorbid adjustment, and the absence of deficit affective symptoms. One study found that schizophreniform disorder patients with poor prognoses exhibit affective flattening, alogia (inability to speak), and poor eye contact with examiners.

## CLINICAL FEATURES

The clinical signs and symptoms and the mental status examination for a patient with schizophreniform disorder are identical to those for a patient with schizophrenia. However, the presence of affective symptoms may predict a favorable course. Alternatively, a flat or blunted affect may predict an unfavorable course.

The patient was a 19-year-old man who, until admission to a hospital, was working in a mail room while waiting to apply to college. The onset of his illness was not clear. According to the patient, he had not been the same since his mother died of a cerebral hemorrhage nine months before his hospital admission. According to his father, however, the patient exhibited a normal mourning response to his mother's death, and the change took place six months after his mother died.

At that time, shortly after his girlfriend had rejected him for another man, the patient began to think that male coworkers were making homosexual advances toward him. He began to fear that he was homosexual and that his friends believed he was homosexual. He finally had the conviction that he had a disorder of the reproductive system—that he had one normal testicle that produced sperm and one testicle that was actually an ovary and produced eggs. He thought that was evidence that a "woman's body resides inside my man's body." He began to gamble and was convinced that he had won $400,000 and was not paid by his bookie and that he was sought after by talk-show hosts to be a guest on their shows and to tell his unusual story (all not true). He claimed that he had a heightened awareness, an "extra sense," and that sounds were unusually loud. He had difficulty sleeping at night but no appetite disturbance.

On admission, the patient's speech was somewhat rapid, and he jumped from topic to topic. His affect was not irritable, euphoric, or expansive. He said that he was seeking treatment because "there is a war between my testicles, and I prefer to be male."

When the patient was 10 years old, his pediatrician became concerned that he had an undersized penis. That concern led to a complete endocrine workup and examinations of his genitals every four months for the next four years. The physician concluded that the patient had no significant abnormalities.

During high school the patient was a poor student with poor attendance. He claimed to have had many friends throughout his life. He had never received psychiatric treatment. He admitted to occasional marijuana and phencyclidine use in the past but denied any use of hallucinogens.

The patient was the oldest child in a family of six children. His parents met when they were both patients in a psychiatric hospital.

*Discussion.* The significant features of the patient's illness include bizarre somatic delusions, grandiose delusions, and disorganization in his speech (he jumped from topic to topic). Although the grandiose delusions and pressured speech suggested the possibility of a manic episode, that disorder was ruled out by the absence of an elevated, expansive, or irritable mood.

When did his illness begin? Although he said he had not been the same since his mother died nine months ago, he did not describe any change in himself that was out of keeping with normal bereavement. Furthermore, his father claimed that his abnormal behavior began only three months ago. The interviewer dated the onset of the illness three months before admission. The presence of the characteristic symptoms of schizophrenia in a disorder with a duration of less than six months indicated schizophreniform disorder. The patient's affect was not blunted or flat. However, because it was unclear whether the onset of the disorder was rapid (he and his father gave different accounts), the disorder could not be specified either with or without good prognostic features.

## DIFFERENTIAL DIAGNOSIS

The differential diagnosis for schizophreniform disorder is identical to that for schizophrenia. Factitious disorder with predominantly psychological signs and symptoms, psychotic disorder due to a general medical condition, and substance-induced psychotic disorder must be ruled out. One of the general medical conditions that should be considered is infection with human immunodeficiency virus (HIV). Temporal lobe epilepsy, CNS tumors, and cerebrovascular diseases can also be associated with relatively short-lived psychotic episodes. There has also been an increasing frequency of reports of psychosis associated with the use of anabolic steroids by young men who are attempting to build up their musculature to perform better in athletic endeavors.

## COURSE AND PROGNOSIS

The prognosis of schizophreniform disorder varies, a fact that is addressed in DSM-IV by distinguishing patients with and without good prognostic features. The good prognostic features noted in DSM-IV were gathered from the literature. However, the validity of those features has been questioned. Confusion or perplexity at the height of the psychotic episode is the feature best correlated with a good outcome. The validity of the other features remains uncertain.

In addition to the predictors of a good prognosis in DSM-IV, the shorter the period of illness, the better the prognosis is likely to be. There is a significant risk of suicide in patients with schizophreniform disorder. They are likely to have a period of depression after the psychotic period, and psychotherapy addressed to helping the patient understand the psychotic episode is likely to improve the prognosis and speed the patient's recovery.

By definition, schizophreniform disorder resolves within six months with a return to baseline mental functioning. Studies have indicated that the requirement for at least six months of symptoms in schizophrenia weighs heavily toward a poor prognosis; therefore, schizophreniform disorder patients have a better prognosis than do most schizophrenic patients.

## TREATMENT

Hospitalization is often necessary in the treatment of patients with schizophreniform disorder. Hospitalization allows for an effective assessment, treatment, and supervision of the patient's behavior. The psychotic symptoms can usually be treated by a three-to-six-month course of antipsychotic drugs. Several studies have shown that patients with schizophreniform disorder respond much more rapidly to antipsychotic treatment than do patients with schizophrenia. One study found that about three fourths of the schizophreniform disorder patients, in comparison with only one fifth of the schizophrenic patients, responded to antipsychotic medications within eight days. Electroconvulsive therapy (ECT) may be indicated for some patients, especially those with marked catatonic or depressed features. A trial of lithium (Eskalith), carbamazepine (Tegretol), or valproate (Depakene) may be warranted for treatment and prophylaxis if a patient has a recurrent episode. Psychotherapy is usually necessary to help patients integrate the psychotic experience into their understanding of their minds, brains, and lives.

**References**

Bergem A L M, Dahl A A, Guldberg C, Hansen H: Langfeldt's schizophreniform psychoses fifty years later. Br J Psychiatry *157*: 351, 1990.

Coryell W H, Tsuang M T: DSM-III schizophreniform disorder: Comparisons with schizophrenia and affective disorder. Arch Gen Psychiatry *39*: 66, 1982.

Coryell W H, Tsuang M T: Outcome after 40 years in DSM-III schizophreniform disorder. Arch Gen Psychiatry *43*: 324, 1986.

Cuesta M J, Peralta V: Does formal thought disorder differ among patients with schizophrenic, schizophreniform and manic schizoaffective disorders? Schizophr Res *10*: 151, 1993.

Guldberg C A, Dahl A A, Hansen H, Bergem M: Predictive value of the four prognostic features in DSM-III-R schizophreniform disorder. Acta Psychiatr Scand *82*: 23, 1990.

Iacono W G, Moreau M, Beiser M, Fleming J A, Lin T Y: Smooth-pursuit eye tracking in first-episode psychotic patients and their relatives. J Abnorm Psychol *101*: 104, 1992.

Katsanis J, Ficken J, Iacono W G, Beiser M: Season of birth and electrodermal activity in functional psychoses. Biol Psychiatry *31*: 841, 1992.

Katsanis J, Iacono W G, Beiser M: Relationship of lateral ventricular size to psychophysiological measures and short-term outcome. Psychiatry Res *37*: 115, 1991.

Marengo J T, Harrow M, Westermeyer J F: Early longitudinal course of acute-chronic and paranoid-undifferentiated schizophrenia subtypes and schizophreniform disorder. J Abnorm Psychol *100*: 600, 1991.

McDermott B E, Sautter F J, Garver D L: Heterogeneity of schizophrenia: Relationship to latency of neuroleptic response. Psychiatry Res *37*: 97, 1991.

Pulver A E, Brown C H, Wolyniec P S, McGrath J A, Tam D: Psychiatric morbidity in the relatives of patients with DSM-III schizophreniform disorder: Comparisons with the relatives of schizophrenic and bipolar disorder patients. J Psychiatr Res *25*: 19, 1991.

Rao M L, Gross G, Halaris A, Huber G, Marler M, Strebel B, Braunig P: Hyperdopaminergia in schizophreniform psychosis: A chronobiological study. Psychiatry Res *47*: 187, 1993.

Rubin P, Holm S, Friberg L, Videbech P, Andersen H S, Bendsen B B, Strømsø N, Larsen J K, Lassen N A, Hemmingsen R: Altered modulation of prefrontal and subcortical brain activity in newly diagnosed schizophrenia and schizophreniform disorder: A regional cerebral blood flow study. Arch Gen Psychiatry *48*: 987, 1991.

Sautter F, McDermott B, Garver D: The course of DSM-III-R schizophreniform disorder. J Clin Psychol *49*: 339, 1993.

Taylor M A, Abrams R: Mania and DSM-III schizophreniform disorder. J Affect Disord *170*: 19, 1984.

Troisi A, Pasini A, Bersani G, Mauro M, Ciani N: Negative symptoms and visual behavior in DSM-III-R prognostic subtypes of schizophreniform disorder. Acta Psychiatr Scand *83*: 391, 1991.

# 14.3 / Schizoaffective Disorder

As the term implies, schizoaffective disorder has features of both schizophrenia and affective disorders (now called mood disorders). The diagnostic criteria for schizoaffective disorder have changed over time, mostly as a reflection of changes in the diagnostic criteria for schizophrenia and the mood disorders. Regardless of the mutable nature of the diagnosis, it remains the best diagnosis for patients whose clinical syndrome would be distorted if it were considered as only schizophrenia or only a mood disorder.

## HISTORY

In 1913 George H. Kirby and in 1921 August Hoch both described patients with mixed features of schizophrenia and affective (mood) disorders. Because their patients did not have the deteriorating course of dementia precox, Kirby and Hoch classified them in Emil Kraepelin's manic-depressive psychosis group.

In 1933 Jacob Kasanin introduced the term "schizoaffective disorder" for a disorder with schizophrenic symptoms and significant mood disorder symptoms. Patients with the disorder were also characterized by a sudden onset of symptoms, often in their adolescence. The patients tended to have a good premorbid level of functioning, and often a specific stressor preceded the onset of the symptoms. The family histories of the patients often included a mood disorder. Because Eugen Bleuler's broad concept of schizophrenia had eclipsed Emil Kraepelin's narrow concept, Kasanin believed that the patients had a type of schizophrenia. From 1933 to about 1970, patients whose symptoms were similar to those of Kasanin's patients were variously classified as having schizoaffective disorder, atypical schizophrenia, good prognosis schizophrenia, remitting schizophrenia, and cycloid psychosis—terms that emphasized a relation to schizophrenia.

Around 1970 two sets of data caused a shift from viewing schizoaffective disorder as a schizophrenic illness to viewing it as a mood disorder. First, lithium carbonate (Eskalith) was shown to be an effective and specific treatment for both bipolar disorders and some cases of schizoaffective disorder. Second, the United States-United Kingdom study published in 1968 by John Cooper and his colleagues showed that the variation in the number of patients classified as schizophrenic in the United States and in the United Kingdom was the result of an overemphasis in the United States on the presence of psychotic symptoms as a diagnostic criterion for schizophrenia.

## EPIDEMIOLOGY

The lifetime prevalence of schizoaffective disorder is less than 1 percent, possibly in the range of 0.5 to 0.8 percent. However, those figures are estimates, since the various studies of schizoaffective disorder have used varying diagnostic criteria. In clinical practice a preliminary diagnosis of schizoaffective disorder is frequently used when the clinician is uncertain of the diagnosis.

### Gender Differences

The literature describing gender differences among patients with schizoaffective disorder is limited. However, some preliminary observations may eventually be replicated in subsequent studies. The prevalence of the disorder has been reported to be lower in men than in women, particularly married women; the age of onset for women is later than the age for men, as in schizophrenia. Men with schizoaffective disorder are likely to exhibit antisocial behavior and to have marked flatness or inappropriateness of affect.

## ETIOLOGY

The cause of schizoaffective disorder is unknown, but four conceptual models have been advanced. (1) Schizoaffective disorder may be either a type of schizophrenia or a type of mood disorder. (2) Schizoaffective disorder may be the simultaneous expression of schizophrenia and a mood disorder. (3) Schizoaffective disorder may be a distinct third type of psychosis, one that is not related to either schizophrenia or a mood disorder. (4) The most likely possibility is that schizoaffective disorder is a heterogeneous group of disorders encompassing all the first three possibilities.

Studies designed to explore those possibilities have examined family histories, biological markers, short-term treatment responses, and long-term outcomes. Most of the studies have considered patients with schizoaffective disorder as a homogeneous group. Recent studies have examined the bipolar and depressive types of schizoaffective disorder separately.

Although much of the family and genetic work done to study schizoaffective disorder is based on the premise that schizophrenia and the mood disorders are completely separate entities, some data indicate that schizophrenia and the mood disorders may be related genetically. Some of the confusion that arises in the family studies of schizoaffective disorder patients may reflect the nonabsolute distinction between the two primary disorders. Not surprisingly, therefore, studies of the relatives of patients with schizoaffective disorder have reported inconsistent results. An increased prevalence of schizophrenia is not found among the relatives of probands with schizoaffective disorder, bipolar type; however, the relatives of patients with schizoaffective disorder, depressive type, may be at higher risk for schizophrenia than for a mood disorder.

Depending on the type of schizoaffective disorder studied, an increased prevalence of schizophrenia or mood disorders may be found in the relatives of schizoaffective disorder probands. The possibility that schizoaffective disorder is distinct from schizophrenia and mood disorders is not supported by the observation that only a small percentage of the relatives of schizoaffective disorder probands have schizoaffective disorder.

As a group, schizoaffective disorder patients have a better prognosis than do patients with schizophrenia and a worse prognosis than do patients with mood disorders. As a group, schizoaffective disorder patients respond to lithium and tend to have a nondeteriorating course.

### Consolidation of Data

One reasonable conclusion from the available data is that patients with schizoaffective disorder are a heterogeneous group: some have schizophrenia with prominent affective symptoms, others have a mood disorder with prominent schizophrenic symptoms, and a third group have a distinct clinical syndrome. The hypothesis that schizoaffective disorder patients have both schizophrenia and a mood disorder is untenable, because the calculated co-occurrence of the two disorders is much lower than the incidence of schizoaffective disorder.

## CLINICAL FEATURES

The clinical signs and symptoms of schizoaffective disorder include all the signs and symptoms of schizophrenia, manic episodes, and depressive disorders. The schizophrenic and mood disorder symptoms can present together or in an alternating fashion. The course can vary from one of exacerbations and remissions to one of a long-term deteriorating course.

Many researchers and clinicians have speculated about the mood-incongruent psychotic features; the psychotic content (that is, hallucinations or delusions) is not consistent with the prevailing mood. In general, the presence of mood-incongruent psychotic features in a mood disorder is likely to be an indicator of a poor prognosis. That association is likely to be true for schizoaffective disorder as well, although the data are limited.

A 44-year-old mother of three teenagers was hospitalized for treatment of depression. She gave the following history: One year previously, after breaking up with her lover, she became acutely psychotic. She was frightened that people were going to kill her, and she heard voices of friends and strangers, sometimes talking to one another, talking about killing her. She heard her own thoughts broadcast aloud and was afraid that others could also hear what she was thinking. Over a three-week period she stayed in her apartment, had new locks put on the doors, kept the shades down, and avoided everyone but her immediate family. She was unable to sleep at night because the voices kept her awake, and she was unable to eat because of a constant "lump" in her throat. In retrospect, she could not say whether she was depressed. She denied being elated or overactive and remembered only that she was terrified of what would happen to her. Her family persuaded her to enter a hospital, where, after six weeks of treatment with chlorpromazine (Thorazine), the voices stopped. She remembered feeling "back to normal" for a week or two, but then she seemed to lose her energy and motivation to do anything.

She became increasingly depressed, lost her appetite, and woke at 4 or 5 every morning and was unable to get back to sleep. She could no longer read a newspaper or watch TV because she could not concentrate.

The patient's condition had persisted for nine months. She had done little except sit in her apartment and stare at the walls. Her children had managed most of the cooking, shopping, and bill paying. She had continued in outpatient treatment and was maintained on chlorpromazine until four months before admission to the hospital. She had no recurrence of the psychotic symptoms after the medication was discontinued; but her depression, with all the accompanying symptoms, had persisted.

The patient was guarded when discussing her history. There was, however, no evidence of a diagnosable disorder before the previous year. She was apparently a shy, emotionally constricted person who "had never broken any rules." She had been separated from her husband for 10 years but in that time had had two enduring relationships with boyfriends. In addition to rearing three apparently healthy and likable children, she had cared for a succession of foster children full-time in the four years before her illness. She enjoyed that work and was highly valued by the agency she worked for. She had maintained close relationships with a few girlfriends and with her extended family.

*Discussion.* During her initial period of illness, the patient showed such characteristic schizophrenic symptoms as bizarre delusions (people could hear what she was thinking) and auditory hallucinations (voices of friends and strangers talking to each other). There was a deterioration in functioning to the point that she was unable to take care of her house. With treatment, after about nine weeks the psychotic symptoms remitted, but she remembered being "back to normal" for only about a week. She then had the characteristic symptoms of a major depressive episode, with depressed mood, poor appetite, insomnia, lack of energy, loss of interest, and poor concentration. The depressive period lasted about nine months.

The case seemed to be an instance in which it is impossible to make a differential diagnosis with any degree of certainty between a mood disorder and schizophrenia or schizophreniform disorder; hence, a diagnosis of schizoaffective disorder seemed appropriate. The diagnosis conveyed the lack of certainty and the prominence of both affective and schizophrenic-like features.

## DIAGNOSIS

Since the concept of schizoaffective disorder involves the diagnostic concepts of both schizophrenia and the mood disorders, some of the evolution in the diagnostic criteria for schizoaffective disorder reflects the changes that have occurred in the diagnostic criteria for the other two conditions. The diagnostic criteria for schizoaffective disorder have changed significantly from the third edition of *Diagnostic and Statistical Manual of Mental Disorders* (DSM-III) to the revised third edition (DSM-III-R) and now to the fourth edition (DSM-IV).

The primary diagnostic criteria for schizoaffective disorder (Table 14.3–1) are that the patient has met the diagnostic criteria for a major depressive episode or a manic episode concurrently with meeting the diagnostic criteria for the active phase of schizophrenia. In addition, the patient must have had delusions or hallucinations for at least two weeks in the absence of prominent mood disorder symptoms. The mood disorder symptoms must also be

**Table 14.3–1**
**Diagnostic Criteria for Schizoaffective Disorder**

A. An uninterrupted period of illness during which, at some time, there is either a major depressive episode, a manic episode, or a mixed episode concurrent with symptoms that meet criterion A for schizophrenia.

   **Note:** The major depressive episode must include criterion A1: depressed mood.

B. During the same period of illness, there have been delusions or hallucinations for at least 2 weeks in the absence of prominent mood symptoms.

C. Symptoms that meet criteria for a mood episode are present for a substantial portion of the total duration of the active and residual periods of the illness.

D. The disturbance is not due to the direct physiological effects of a substance (e.g., a drug of abuse, a medication) or a general medical condition.

*Specify* type:
   **Bipolar type:** if the disturbance includes a manic or a mixed episode (or a manic or a mixed episode and major depressive episodes)
   **Depressive type:** if the disturbance only includes major depressive episodes

Table from DSM-IV, *Diagnostic and Statistical Manual of Mental Disorders*, ed 4. Copyright American Psychiatric Association, Washington, 1994. Used with permission.

present for a substantial part of the active and residual psychotic periods. Essentially, the criteria are written to help the clinician avoid diagnosing a mood disorder with psychotic features as schizoaffective disorder.

DSM-IV also allows the clinician to specify whether the patient has schizoaffective disorder, bipolar type, or schizoaffective disorder, depressive type. A patient is classified as having the bipolar type if the present episode is of the manic type or a mixed episode or a manic or a mixed episode and major depressive episodes. Otherwise, the patient is classified as having the depressive type.

## DIFFERENTIAL DIAGNOSIS

All the conditions listed in the differential diagnoses of schizophrenia and mood disorders need to be considered in the differential diagnosis of schizoaffective disorder. Patients treated with steroids, abusers of amphetamine and phencyclidine (PCP), and some patients with temporal lobe epilepsy are particularly likely to present with concurrent schizophrenic and mood disorder symptoms.

The psychiatric differential diagnosis also includes all the possibilities usually considered for schizophrenia and mood disorders. In clinical practice, psychosis at the time of the presentation may hinder the detection of current or past mood disorder symptoms. Therefore, the clinician may delay making a final psychiatric diagnosis until the most acute symptoms of psychosis have been controlled.

## COURSE AND PROGNOSIS

As a group, patients with schizoaffective disorder have prognoses intermediate between the prognoses of patients with schizophrenia and the prognoses of patients with mood disorders. As a group, patients with schizoaffective disorder have much worse prognoses than do patients with depressive disorders, have worse prognoses than do patients with bipolar disorders, and better prognoses than do patients with schizophrenia. Those generalities have been supported by several studies that followed patients for two to five years after the index episode and that assessed social and occupational functioning, as well as the course of the disorder itself. The results of one such study are shown in Tables 14.3–2 and 14.3–3.

Data indicate that patients with schizoaffective disorder, bipolar type, have prognoses similar to those for patients with bipolar I disorder and that patients with schizoaffective disorder, depressive type, have prognoses similar to those for patients with schizophrenia. Regardless of the type, the following variables weigh toward a poor prognosis: a poor premorbid history; an insidious onset; no precipitating factor; a predominance of psychotic symptoms, especially deficit or negative symptoms; an early onset; an unremitting course; and a family history of schizophrenia. The opposite of each of those characteristics weighs toward a good outcome. The presence or the absence of Schneiderian first-rank symptoms does not seem to predict the course.

**Table 14.3–2**
**Overall Outcome for Patients with Schizoaffective Disorder and Patients in Other Major Diagnostic Groups at Two Follow-Up Times**

| | First Follow-Up (2 years after hospitalization) | | | | Second Follow-Up (4–5 years after hospital discharge) | | | |
|---|---|---|---|---|---|---|---|---|
| | Overall Score on Strauss-Carpenter Scale* | | Patients with Very Poor Outcome‡ | | Overall Score on Strauss-Carpenter Scale* | | Patients with Very Poor Outcome‡ | |
| Diagnostic Group | Mean | SD | N | % | Mean | SD | N | % |
| Schizoaffective disorder (N = 41) | 9.68 | 4.0 | 17/40 | 43 | 9.73 | 3.3 | 17/40 | 43 |
| Schizophrenia (N = 20) | 9.40 | 4.7 | 11/20 | 55 | 8.60 | 3.9 | 11/20 | 55 |
| Bipolar disorder (N = 20) | 10.40 | 4.0 | 7.20 | 35 | 10.08 | 3.5 | 4/14 | 29 |
| Major depressive disorder (N = 20) | 10.60 | 3.4 | 2/20 | 10 | 10.20 | 3.5 | 2/15 | 13 |

*On this 16-point scale, higher scores reflect better functioning.
‡LKP Scale score of 7 or higher.
Table from L S Grossman, M Harrow, J F Goldberg, C G Fichtner: Outcome of schizoaffective disorder at two long-term follow-ups: Comparisons with outcome of schizophrenia and affective disorders. Am J Psychiatry *148*: 1361, 1991. Used with permission.

Table 14.3–3
**Rehospitalization of Patients with Schizoaffective Disorder and Patients in Other Major Diagnostic Groups at Two Follow-Up Times**

| Diagnostic Group | First Follow-Up (2 years after hospitalization) | | | | Second Follow-Up (4–5 years after hospital discharge) | | | |
| | Rehospitalization Score on Strauss-Carpenter Scale* | | Patients Rehospitalized | | Rehospitalization on Strauss-Carpenter Scale* | | Patients Rehospitalized | |
| | Mean | SD | N | % | Mean | SD | N | % |
|---|---|---|---|---|---|---|---|---|
| Schizoaffective disorder (N = 41) | 3.24 | 1.2 | 16 | 39 | 3.46 | 0.9 | 15 | 37 |
| Schizophrenia (N = 20) | 3.10 | 0.8 | 9 | 45 | 3.55 | 0.5 | 8 | 40 |
| Bipolar disorder (N = 20) | 3.45 | 0.8 | 9 | 45 | 3.60 | 0.6 | 7 | 35 |
| Major depressive disorder (N = 20) | 3.65 | 0.7 | 5 | 25 | 3.75 | 0.6 | 4 | 20 |

*On this 5-point subscale, higher scores reflect better functioning.
Table from L S Grossman, M Harrow, J F Goldberg, C G Fichtner: Outcome of schizoaffective disorder at two long-term follow-ups: Comparisons with outcome of schizophrenia and affective disorders. Am J Psychiatry *148*: 1363, 1991. Used with permission.

Although there do not appear to be gender-related differences in outcome for schizoaffective disorder, some data indicate that suicidal behavior may be more common in women with schizoaffective disorder than in men with the disorder. The incidence of suicide among patients with schizoaffective disorder is thought to be at least 10 percent.

## TREATMENT

The major treatment modalities for schizoaffective disorder are hospitalization, medication, and psychosocial interventions. The basic principles underlying pharmacotherapy for schizoaffective disorder are that anitdepressant and antimanic protocols be followed if at all indicated and that antipsychotics be used only as needed for short-term control. If thymoleptic protocols are not effective in controlling the symptoms on an ongoing basis, antipsychotic medications may be indicated. Patients with schizoaffective disorder, bipolar type, should receive trials of lithium, carbamazepine (Tegretol), valproate (Depakene), or some combination of those drugs if one drug alone is not effective. Patients with schizoaffective disorder, depressive type, should be given trials of antidepressants and electroconvulsive therapy (ECT) before they are determined to be unresponsive to antidepressant treatment.

## References

Bardenstein K K, McGlashan T H: Gender differences in affective, schizo-affective, and schizophrenic disorders: A review. Schizophr Res *3*: 159, 1990.
Beatty W W, Jocic Z, Monson N, Staton R D: Memory and frontal lobe dysfunction in schizophrenia and schizoaffective disorder. J Nerv Ment Dis *181*: 448, 1993.
del Rio Vega J M, Ayuso-Gutierrez J L: Course of schizoaffective psychosis: Further data from a retrospective study. Acta Psychiatr Scand *85*: 328, 1992.
Grossman L S, Harrow M, Goldberg J F, Fichtner C G: Outcome of schizoaffective disorder at two long-term follow-ups: Comparisons with outcome of schizophrenia and affective disorders. Am J Psychiatry *148*: 1359, 1991.
Kendler K S: Mood-incongruent psychotic affective illness: A historical and empirical review. Arch Gen Psychiatry *48*: 362, 1991.
Lapensée M A: A review of schizoaffective disorder: I. Current concepts. Can J Psychiatry *37*: 335, 1992.
Lapensée M A: A review of schizoaffective disorder: II. Somatic treatment. Can J Psychiatry *37*: 347, 1992.
Maier W, Lichtermann D, Minges J, Heun R, Hallmayer J, Benkert O: Schizoaffective disorder and affective disorders with mood-incongruent psychotic features: Keep separate or combine? Evidence from a family study. Am J Psychiatry *149*: 1666, 1992.
Maj M, Perris C: Patterns of course in patients with a cross-sectional diagnosis of schizoaffective disorder. J Affect Disord *20*: 71, 1990.
Maj M, Starace F, Pirossi R: A family study of DSM-III-R schizoaffective disorder, depressive type, compared with schizophrenia and psychotic and nonpsychotic major depression. Am J Psychiatry *148*: 612, 1991.
Marneros A, Deister A, Rohde A: Stability of diagnoses in affective, schizoaffective and schizophrenic disorders: Cross-sectional versus longitudinal diagnosis. Eur Arch Psychiatry Clin Neurosci *241*: 187, 1991.
McGlashan T H, Williams P V: Predicting outcome in schizoaffective psychosis. J Nerv Ment Dis *178*: 518, 1990.
Retzer A, Simon F B, Weber G, Stierlin H, Schmidt G: A follow-up study of manic-depressive and schizoaffective psychoses after systemic family therapy. Fam Process *30*: 139, 1991.
Simhandl C, Meszaros K: The use of carbamazepine in the treatment of schizophrenic and schizoaffective psychoses: A review. J Psychiatry Neurosci *17*: 1, 1992.
Smith T E, Deutsch A, Schwartz F, Terkelsen K G: The role of personality in the treatment of schizophrenic and schizoaffective disorder inpatients: A pilot study. Bull Menninger Clin *57*: 88, 1993.
Taylor M A: Are schizophrenia and affective disorder related? A selective literature review. Am J Psychiatry *149*: 22, 1992.
Tsuang D, Coryell W: An 8-year follow-up of patients with DSM-III-R psychotic depression, schizoaffective disorder, and schizophrenia. Am J Psychiatry *150*: 1182, 1993.
Tsuang M T: Morbidity risks of schizophrenia and affective disorders among first-degree relatives of patients with schizoaffective disorders. Br J Psychiatry *158*: 165, 1991.
Zaudig M: Cycloid psychoses and schizoaffective psychoses: A comparison of different diagnostic classification systems and criteria. Psychopathology *23*: 233, 1990.

# 14.4 / Delusional Disorder

Delusional disorder is defined as a psychiatric disorder in which the predominant symptoms are delusions. Delusional disorder was formerly called "paranoia" or "paranoid disorder." Those terms, however, incorrectly imply that the delusions are always persecutory in content, and that is not the case. The delusions in delusional disorder can also be grandiose, erotic, jealous, somatic, and mixed in primary content.

Delusional disorder must be differentiated from both mood disorders and schizophrenia. Although patients with delusional disorder may have a mood that is consistent with the content of their delusions, they do not evidence the pervasiveness of the affective symptoms seen in the mood disorders. Similarly, patients with delusional disorder differ from schizophrenic patients in the nonbizarre nature of their delusions (for example, "being followed by the FBI," which is unlikely but possible, versus "being controlled by Martians," which is not possible). Patients with delusional disorder also lack other symptoms seen in schizophrenia, such as prominent hallucinations, affective flattening, and additional symptoms of thought disorder.

## HISTORY

The former term for delusional disorder, "paranoia," was derived from the Greek words meaning "beside" and "mind." In that sense, "paranoia" was historically used to describe a variety of mental states, including dementia and delirium. In modern usage, "paranoia" is taken to mean extreme suspiciousness, usually not based on a realistic assessment of the situation. Often, however, the term "paranoia" is used in a casual way by both laypersons and mental health professionals to mean any type of suspiciousness. In mental health settings, it is preferable to limit the use of the word "paranoid" to those clinical situations in which the degree of paranoia is delusional.

In 1818 Johann Christian Heinroth introduced the basic concept of paranoia into psychiatry when he described disorders of the intellect under the term *"Verrücktheit."* In 1838 the French psychiatrist Jean Etienne Dominique Esquirol coined the term "monomania" to characterize delusions with no associated defect in logical reasoning or general behavior.

### Karl Ludwig Kahlbaum

Karl Ludwig Kahlbaum in 1863 used the term "paranoia" and characterized the disorder as uncommon but distinct. Kahlbaum referred to the condition as a partial insanity that affects the intellect but not other areas of mental functioning. Patients with paranoia, according to Kahlbaum, are characterized by a persistent delusional system that remains relatively static throughout the disorder.

### Emil Kraepelin

Emil Kraepelin also recognized a condition that he called "paranoia" that is characterized by a persistent delusional system in the absence of hallucinations and personality deterioration. However, Kraepelin considered the disorder to be rare. Two other paranoid disorders that Kraepelin identified were paraphrenia and dementia paranoides. Paraphrenia was differentiated from paranoia by the presence in paraphrenia of hallucinations and a later onset but was similar to paranoia in the absence of a deteriorating course. Dementia paranoides was characterized by an early onset of symptoms that resembled those of paranoia but then progressed to a disorder with a deteriorating course, perhaps akin to paranoid schizophrenia.

### Eugen Bleuler

Eugen Bleuler, who coined the term "schizophrenia," was responsible for broadening the range of persons who can receive the diagnosis of schizophrenia. Bleuler thought that paranoia, as distinct from schizophrenia, was such a rare condition that it did not warrant a separate diagnostic category.

### Sigmund Freud

Sigmund Freud's formulation regarding the development of paranoid symptoms was an important milestone in the development of the concept. Freud used the autobiographical writings of a noted judge, Daniel Paul Schreber, as a source of material to prove his hypothesis that paranoid delusions develop out of repressed homosexual impulses. Freud did not define any types of paranoia and suggested that the term "paraphrenia" be used solely to describe schizophrenia.

## EPIDEMIOLOGY

An accurate assessment of the epidemiology of delusional disorder is hampered by the relative uncommonness of the disorder, as well as by the changing definitions of the disorder over recent history. Moreover, delusional disorder may be underreported because delusional patients rarely seek psychiatric help unless forced to do so by their families or by the courts. Even in the face of those limitations, however, the literature does support the contention that delusional disorder, although an uncommon disorder, has been present in the population at a relatively steady rate.

The prevalence of delusional disorder in the United States is currently estimated to be 0.025 to 0.03 percent. Thus, delusional disorder is much rarer than schizophrenia, which has a prevalence of about 1 percent, and the mood disorders, which have a prevalence of about 5 percent. The annual incidence of delusional disorder is one to three new cases per 100,000 population, about 4 percent of all first admissions to psychiatric hospitals for psychoses not due to a general medical condition or a substance.

The mean age of onset is about 40 years, but the range for the age of onset runs from 18 to the 90s. There is a slight preponderance of female patients. Many patients are married and employed, but there may be some association with recent immigration and low socioeconomic status.

## ETIOLOGY

As with all the major psychiatric disorders, the cause of delusional disorder is not known. Moreover, the patients currently classified as having delusional disorder probably have a heterogeneous group of conditions with delusions as the predominant symptom. The central concept regarding the cause of delusional disorder is its distinctness from schizophrenia and the mood disorders. Delusional disorder is much rarer than either schizophrenia or mood disorders, thus suggesting that it is a separate disorder. In addition, delusional disorder has a later onset than does schizophrenia and has a much less pronounced female predominance than that seen in the mood disorders. The most convincing data come from family studies that report an increased prevalence of delusional disorder and related personality traits (for example, suspiciousness, jealousy, and secretiveness) in the relatives of delusional disorder probands. Family studies have reported neither an increased incidence of schizophrenia and mood disorders in the families of delusional disorder probands nor an increased incidence of delusional disorder in the families of schizophrenic probands. Long-term follow-up of delusional disorder patients indicates that the diagnosis of delusional disorder is relatively stable, with less than one quarter of the patients eventually reclassified as having schizophrenia and less than 10 percent of patients eventually reclassified as having a mood disorder. Those data indicate that delusional disorder is not simply an early stage in the development of one or both of those two more common disorders.

## Biological Factors

A wide range of nonpsychiatric medical conditions and substances can cause delusions, thus indicating that clear-cut biological factors can cause delusions. However, not everyone with a brain tumor, for example, has delusions. Unique and as yet not understood factors in a patient's brain and personality are likely to be relevant to the specific pathophysiology of delusional disorder.

The neurological conditions most commonly associated with delusions are conditions that affect the limbic system and the basal ganglia. Patients who have delusions caused by neurological diseases in the absence of intellectual impairment tend to have complex delusions that are similar to those seen in patients with delusional disorder. Conversely, neurological disorder patients with intellectual impairments often have simple delusions that are unlike those seen in patients with delusional disorder. Thus, delusional disorder may involve pathology of the limbic system or basal ganglia in patients who have intact cerebral cortical functioning.

Delusional disorder may arise as a normal response to abnormal experiences in the environment, the peripheral nervous system, or the central nervous system. Thus, if patients have erroneous sensory experiences of being followed (for example, people staring, hearing footsteps), they may come to believe that they are actually being followed. That hypothesis hinges on the presence of hallucinatorylike experiences that need to be explained. The presence of such hallucinatory experiences in delusional disorder has not been proved.

## Psychodynamic Factors

Practitioners have a strong clinical impression that many patients with delusional disorder are socially isolated and have attained less than expected levels of achievement. Specific psychodynamic theories regarding the cause and the evolution of delusional symptoms involve suppositions regarding hypersensitive persons and specific ego mechanisms: reaction formation, projection, and denial.

**Freud's contributions.** Freud believed that delusions, rather than being symptoms of the disorder, are part of a healing process. In 1896 he described projection as the main defense mechanism in paranoia. Later, Freud read *Memories of My Nervous Illness*, an autobiographical account by Daniel Paul Schreber. Although he never personally met Schreber, Freud theorized from his review of the autobiography that unconscious homosexual tendencies are defended against by denial and projection. According to classic psychodynamic theory, the dynamics underlying the formation of delusions for a female patient are the same as for a male patient.

Freud theorized that, because homosexuality is consciously inadmissible to some paranoid patients, male patients' feeling of "I love him" is denied and changed by reaction formation into "I do not love him; I hate him." That feeling is further transformed through projection into "It is not I who hate him; it is he who hates me." In a full-blown paranoid state the feeling is elaborated into "I am persecuted by him." Patients are then able to rationalize their anger by consciously hating those they perceive to hate them. Instead of being aware of the passive homosexual impulses, the patients reject the love of anyone except themselves. In erotomanic delusions the male patient changes "I love him" to "I love her," and that feeling, through projection, becomes "She loves me." In delusional grandiosity "I do not love him" becomes "I love myself."

Freud also believed that unconscious homosexuality is the cause of delusions of jealousy. In an attempt to ward off threatening impulses, the patient becomes preoccupied by jealous thoughts; thus, the male patient asserts, "I do not love him; she [a wife, for example] loves him." Freud believed that the man the paranoid patient suspects his wife of loving is a man to whom the patient feels sexually attracted.

Clinical evidence has not supported Freud's thesis. A significant number of delusional patients do not have demonstrable homosexual inclinations, and the majority of homosexual men do not have symptoms of paranoia or delusions.

**Paranoid pseudocommunity.** Norman Cameron described seven situations that favor the development of delusional disorders: (1) an increased expectation of receiving sadistic treatment, (2) situations that increase distrust and suspicion, (3) social isolation, (4) situations that increase envy and jealousy, (5) situations that lower self-esteem, (6) situations that cause persons to see their own defects in others, and (7) situations that increase the potential for rumination over probable meanings and motivations. When frustration from any combination of those conditions exceeds the limits that the persons can tolerate, they become withdrawn and anxious; they realize that something is wrong and seek an explanation for the problem. The crystallization of a delusional system offers a solution. Elaboration of the delusion to include imagined persons and the attribution of malevolent motivations to both real and imagined people results in the organization of the *pseudocommunity*—that is, a perceived community of plotters. That delusional entity hypothetically binds together projected fears and wishes to justify the patient's aggression and to provide a tangible target for the patient's hostilities.

**Other psychodynamic factors.** Clinical observations indicate that some paranoid patients experience a lack of trust in relationships. That distrust has been hypothesized to be related to a consistently hostile family environment, often with an overcontrolling mother and a distant or sadistic father.

Patients with delusional disorder primarily use the defense mechanisms of reaction formation, denial, and projection. *Reaction formation* is used as a defense against aggression, dependence needs, and feelings of affection. The need for dependence is transformed into staunch independence. *Denial* is used to avoid awareness of painful reality. Consumed with anger and hostility and unable to face responsibility for the rage, the patients project their resentment and anger onto others. *Projection* is used to protect patients from recognizing unacceptable impulses in themselves.

Hypersensitivity and feelings of inferiority have been hypothesized to lead, through reaction formation and projection, to delusions of superiority and grandiosity. Delusions of erotic ideas have been suggested as replacements for feelings of rejection. Some clinicians have noted that children who are expected to perform impeccably and are undeservedly punished when they fail to do so may develop elaborate fantasies as a way of enhancing their injured self-esteem. Their secret thoughts may eventually evolve into delusions. Critical and frightening delusions are often described as projections of superego criticism.

The delusions of female paranoid patients often involve accusations of prostitution. As a child, the female paranoiac turned to her father for the maternal love that she was unable to receive from her mother. Incestuous desires developed. Later heterosexual encounters are an unconscious reminder of the incestuous desires of childhood; those desires are defended against by superego projections accusing the female paranoiac of prostitution.

Somatic delusions can be psychodynamically explained as a regression to the infantile narcissistic state, in which patients withdraw emotional involvement from other people and fixate on their physical selves. In erotic delusions the love can be conceptualized as projected narcissistic love used as a defense against low self-esteem and severe narcissistic injury. Delusions of grandeur may be a regression to the omnipotent feelings of childhood, in which feelings of undenied and undiminished powers predominated.

## DIAGNOSIS

The conceptual challenge in the diagnosis of delusional disorder rests in the necessity to differentiate the disorder from schizophrenia. The revised third edition of *Diagnostic and Statistical Manual of Mental Disorders* (DSM-III-R) attempted to make the differentiation on two criteria. First, the delusions of delusional disorder were defined as nonbizarre—that is, the content of the delusion is at least possible (for example, being followed), even if unlikely. Second, the delusions had to occur in the absence of other symptoms of schizophrenia, including bizarre behavior,

catatonia, and flat affect. Practically, the clinical distinction between bizarre and nonbizarre delusions can be difficult. Furthermore, both clinicians and researchers noted that the emphasis in the distinction between delusional disorder and schizophrenia should rest on the mild functional impairment seen in delusional disorder when compared with that seen in schizophrenia. The fourth edition of DSM (DSM-IV) addresses both of those areas in its diagnostic criteria for delusional disorder (Table 14.4–1).

DSM-IV has two criteria for describing the clinical symptoms of delusional disorder. Criterion A requires the presence of delusions for at least one month and describes the delusions as nonbizarre in an attempt to assist the clinician in discriminating those delusions from the bizarre delusions seen in schizophrenic patients. Criterion B requires the absence of other symptoms of schizophrenia at any time during the course of the disorder. One exception to that exclusion is the presence of tactile or olfactory hallucinations if they are consistent with the delusional system. DSM-IV also specifies that the effects of the disorder on the patient's functioning are limited to the effects that the delusions themselves have on the patient's life. That criterion is meant to exclude patients who have func-

**Table 14.4–1**
**Diagnostic Criteria for Delusional Disorder**

A. Nonbizarre delusions (i.e., involving situations that occur in real life, such as being followed, poisoned, infected, loved at a distance, or deceived by spouse or lover, or having a disease) of at least 1 month's duration.

B. Criterion A for schizophrenia has never been met. **Note:** Tactile and olfactory hallucinations may be present in delusional disorder if they are related to the delusional theme.

C. Apart from the impact of the delusion(s) or its ramifications, functioning is not markedly impaired and behavior is not obviously odd or bizarre.

D. If mood episodes have occurred concurrently with delusions, their total duration has been brief relative to the duration of the delusional periods.

E. The disturbance is not due to the direct physiological effects of a substance (e.g., a drug of abuse, a medication) or a general medical condition.

*Specify* type (the following types are assigned based on the predominant delusional theme):

**Erotomanic type:** delusions that another person, usually of higher status, is in love with the individual
**Grandiose type:** delusions of inflated worth, power, knowledge, identity, or special relationship to a deity or famous person
**Jealous type:** delusions that the individual's sexual partner is unfaithful
**Persecutory type:** delusions that the person (or someone to whom the person is close) is being malevolently treated in some way
**Somatic type:** delusions that the person has some physical defect or general medical condition
**Mixed type:** delusions characteristic of more than one of the above types but no one theme predominates
**Unspecified type**

Table from DSM-IV, *Diagnostic and Statistical Manual of Mental Disorders*, ed 4. Copyright American Psychiatric Association, Washington, 1994. Used with permission.

tional impairment because of characteristic schizophrenic symptoms, such as ambivalence.

## Types

DSM-IV allows the clinician to specify one of seven types of delusional disorder, based on the predominant content of the delusions (Table 14.4–1). The types include erotomanic type, grandiose type, jealous type, persecutory type, and somatic type. Two additional types are mixed type, for patients with delusions containing more than one theme, and unspecified type, for patients with delusions that do not fit into any of the above categories. Persecutory and jealous types are the most common; grandiose type is not as common; erotomanic and somatic types are the most unusual.

## Other Delusions

Other delusions have been given specific names in the literature. In the absence of an organic explanation, patients with those delusions may be classified according to DSM-IV either as having delusional disorder (unspecified type) or as having a psychotic disorder not otherwise specified. *Capgras's syndrome* is the delusion that familiar people have been replaced by identical impostors. *Fregoli's phenomenon* is the delusion that a persecutor is taking on a variety of faces, like an actor. *Lycanthropy* is the delusion of being a werewolf, and *heutoscopy* is the false belief that one has a double. *Cotard's syndrome* was originally called *délire de négation*; persons with the syndrome may believe that they have lost everything—possessions, strength, and even bodily organs, such as the heart.

## CLINICAL FEATURES

### Mental Status

**General description.** The patient is usually well-groomed and well-dressed, without evidence of gross disintegration of personality or daily activities. However, the patient may seem to be eccentric, odd, suspicious, or hostile. The patient is sometimes litigious and may make that inclination clear to the examiner. If the patient attempts to engage the clinician as an ally in a delusion, the clinician should not pretend to accept the delusion, since doing so further confounds reality and sets the stage for eventual distrust between the patient and the therapist. What is usually most remarkable about patients with delusional disorder is that the mental status examination shows them to be remarkably normal except for the presence of a markedly abnormal delusional system.

**Mood, feelings, and affect.** The patient's mood is consistent with the content of the delusion. A patient with grandiose delusions is euphoric; a patient with persecutory delusions is suspicious. Whatever the nature of the delusional system, the examiner may sense some mild depressive qualities.

**Perceptual disturbances.** By definition, patients with delusional disorder do not have prominent or sustained hallucinations. According to DSM-IV, tactile or olfactory delusions may be present if they are consistent with the delusion (for example, somatic delusion of body odor). A few delusional patients have other hallucinatory experiences—virtually always auditory, rather than visual.

**Thought.** Disorder of thought content, in the form of delusions, is the key symptom of the disorder. The delusions are usually systematized and are characterized as being possible—for example, delusions of being persecuted, having an unfaithful spouse, being infected with a virus, and being loved by a famous person. Those examples of delusional content are contrasted with the bizarre and impossible delusional content seen in some schizophrenic patients. The delusional system itself may be complex or simple. The patient lacks other signs of thought disorder, although some patients may be verbose, circumstantial, or idiosyncratic in their speech when they talk about their delusions. The clinician should not assume that all unlikely scenarios are delusional. The veracity of an identified patient's beliefs should be checked before automatically considering their content to be delusional.

#### Sensorium and cognition

ORIENTATION. Patients with delusional disorder usually have no abnormality in orientation unless they have a specific delusion concerning person, place, or time.

MEMORY. Memory and other cognitive processes are intact in patients with delusional disorder.

**Impulse control.** The clinician must evaluate patients with delusional disorder for ideation or plans to act on their delusional material by suicide, homicide, or other violence. The incidence of those behaviors in delusional disorder patients is not known. The therapist should not hesitate to ask patients about their suicidal, homicidal, or sexual plans. Destructive aggression is most common in patients with a history of violence. If aggressive feelings existed in the past, the therapist should ask patients how they managed those feelings. If the patients are unable to control their impulses, hospitalization is probably necessary. The therapist can sometimes help foster a therapeutic alliance by openly discussing how hospitalization can help patients gain additional control of their impulses.

**Judgment and insight.** Patients with delusional disorder have virtually no insight into their condition and are almost always brought to the hospital by the police, family members, or employers. Judgment can best be assessed by evaluating the patient's past, present, and planned behavior.

**Reliability.** Patients with delusional disorder are usually reliable in their information, except when it impinges on their delusional system.

### Types

**Erotomanic type.** In the erotomanic type the central delusion is that the affected patient is loved intensely by another person—usually a famous person, such as a movie star, or a superior at work. Patients with erotic delusions are significant sources of harassment to public figures. The erotomanic type of delusional disorder has also been referred to as erotomania, *psychose passionelle*, and de Clerambault syndrome. The onset of the symptom can be sudden and often becomes the central focus of the affected person's life. Efforts to contact the object of the delusion—through telephone calls, letters, gifts, visits, and even surveillance and stalking—are common, although occasionally the person attempts to keep the delusion secret. The symptom of *paradoxical conduct* consists of interpreting all verbal and physical denials of love as cryptic proof of love.

Whereas in clinical samples most patients with the erotomanic type are women, in forensic samples most are men. Some people with the disorder, particularly men, come into conflict with the law in their efforts to pursue the objects of their delusions or in misguided efforts to rescue them from some imagined dangers. For example, a man with delusional disorder may attempt to murder the husband of a woman whom he believes is really in love with him.

Affected persons are often found to have lived isolated and withdrawn lives. They are usually single and have had limited sexual contacts. Affected persons are often employed in modest occupations.

**Grandiose type.** The grandiose type of delusion disorder has also been referred to as megalomania. The most common form of grandiose delusion is the belief that one has some great but unrecognized talent or insight or has made some important discovery, which the patient may take to various governmental agencies, such as the Federal Bureau of Investigation (FBI) and the U.S. Patent Office. Less common is the delusion that one has a special relationship with a prominent person, such as the President of the United States. Grandiose delusions may have a religious content, and persons with the delusions can become leaders of religious cults.

**Jealous type.** The jealous type of delusional disorder is also known, when the delusion concerns the fidelity of the spouse, as conjugal paranoia and Othello syndrome. Men are more commonly affected than women. The disorder is rare, affecting probably less than 0.2 percent of all psychiatric patients. The onset is often sudden, and the symptoms may resolve only after separation or the death of the spouse. The jealous delusion can lead to significant verbal and physical abuse against the spouse and can even result in the murder of the spouse. In 1891 Richard von Krafft-Ebing emphasized the frequent association between alcoholism and jealous delusions.

When a person is affected with the jealous type of delusional disorder, bits of "evidence," such as disarrayed clothing and spots on the sheets, may be collected and used to justify the delusion. Almost invariably, persons with the delusion confront their spouses or lovers and may take extraordinary steps to intervene in the imagined infidelity. Those attempts may include restricting autonomy by insisting that the spouse or lover never leave the house unaccompanied, secretly following the spouse or lover, and investigating the other "lover."

A beautiful, successful 34-year-old interior designer was brought to a clinic by her 37-year-old husband, a prominent attorney. The husband lamented that for the past three years his wife had made increasingly shrill accusations that he was unfaithful to her. He declared that he had done everything in his power to convince her of his innocence, but there was no

shaking her conviction. A careful examination of the facts revealed no evidence that the man had been unfaithful. When his wife was asked what her evidence was, she became vague and mysterious, declaring that she could tell such things by a faraway look in his eyes.

She was absolutely sure that she was right and felt highly insulted by the suggestion that she was imagining the disloyalty. Her husband reported that for the past year she had been increasingly bitter, creating a cold-war atmosphere in the household. Militantly entrenched against her husband, she refused to show him any affection except at social gatherings. She seemed intent on giving the impression socially that they had a good relationship; but when they were alone, the coldness reentered the picture. She had physically assaulted her husband on occasion, but her account obscured the fact that she initiated the assaults; her description of the tussles began at the point at which the husband attempted to interrupt her assault by holding her arms. She declared that she would never forgive him for holding her down and squeezing her arms, and her account made it appear that she was unfairly restrained.

The patient experienced no hallucinations; her speech was well organized; she interpreted proverbs with no difficulty; she seemed to have a good command of current events and generally displayed no difficulty in thinking, aside from her conviction of the infidelity. She described herself as having a generally full life, with a few close friends and no problems except those centering on her experiences of unhappiness in the marriage. The husband reported that his wife was respected for her skills but that she had had difficulties for most of her life in close relationships with friends. She had lost a number of friends because of her apparent intolerance of differences in opinion. The patient reported that she did not want to leave the marriage, nor did she want her husband to leave her; instead, she was furious about the "injustice" and demanded that it be confessed and redeemed.

*Discussion.* Not all complaints of infidelity are unfounded, but in this case the evidence supported the idea that the wife's jealousy was delusional. Delusional jealousy may be seen in schizophrenia; but in the absence of the characteristic psychotic symptoms of schizophrenia—such as bizarre delusions, hallucinations, and disorganized speech—it is a symptom of delusional disorder. As is commonly the case in delusional disorder, the woman's impairment because of her delusion did not involve her daily functioning apart from her relationship with her husband.

**Persecutory type.** This is the most common type of delusional disorder. The persecutory delusion may be simple or elaborate, and it usually involves a single theme or a series of connected themes, such as being conspired against, cheated, spied on, followed, poisoned or drugged, maliciously maligned, harassed, or obstructed in the pursuit of long-term goals. Small slights may be exaggerated and become the focus of a delusional system. In certain cases the focus of the delusion is some injustice that must be remedied by legal action (*querulous paranoia*), and the affected person often engages in repeated attempts to obtain satisfaction by appeals to the courts and other government agencies. Persons with persecutory delusions are often resentful and angry, and they may resort to violence against those they believe to be hurting them.

A 42-year-old married black postal worker, the father of two, was brought to the emergency room by his wife because he had been insisting, "There is a contract out on my life."

According to the patient, his problems began four months before, when his supervisor at work accused him of tampering with a package. The patient denied that he had and, because his job was in jeopardy, filed a protest. At a formal hearing he was exonerated and, according to him, "This made my boss furious. He felt he had been publicly humiliated."

About two weeks later the patient noticed that his co-workers were avoiding him. "When I'd walk toward them, they'd just turn away like they didn't want to see me." Shortly thereafter, he began to feel that they were talking about him at work. He never could make out clearly what they were saying, but he gradually became convinced that they were avoiding him because his boss had taken out a contract on his life.

That state of affairs was stable for about two months, until the patient began noticing several "large white cars," new to his neighborhood, driving up and down the street on which he lived. He became increasingly frightened and was convinced that the "hit men" were in those cars. He refused to go out of his apartment without an escort. Several times, when he saw the white cars, he would panic and run home. After one such incident, his wife finally insisted that he accompany her to the emergency room.

The patient was described by his wife and his brother as a basically well-adjusted, outgoing man who enjoyed being with his family. He had served with distinction in Vietnam. He saw little combat there but was pulled from a burning truck by a buddy seconds before the truck blew up.

When interviewed, the patient was obviously frightened. Aside from his belief that he was in danger of being killed, his speech, behavior, and demeanor were in no way odd or strange. His predominant mood was anxious. He denied having hallucinations and all other psychotic symptoms except those noted above. He claimed not to be depressed; although he noted that he had recently had some difficulty in falling asleep, he said there had been no change in his appetite, sex drive, energy level, or concentration.

*Discussion.* The patient's anxiety stemmed from his belief that his boss had a contract out on his life. There was no reason to believe that; thus, psychiatrists concluded that he had a delusion. Since contract killers *are* sometimes hired in real life, the delusion was nonbizarre. The patient had no auditory or visual hallucinations, no manic or depressive syndrome, and no evidence of an organic factor that initiated and maintained the disturbance. His behavior, apart from the delusion and its ramifications, was not odd or bizarre. Those are the characteristics of delusional disorder. Since the content of his delusion involved the theme of being malevolently treated in some way, the disorder is specified as persecutory type.

Often, people with the persecutory type of delusional disorder are reluctant to seek help. The patient, however, was apparently frightened enough to be persuaded to seek help.

**Somatic type.** The somatic type of delusional disorder is also known as monosymptomatic hypochondriacal psychosis. The differentiation between hypochondriasis and the somatic type of delusional disorder rests on the degree of conviction that patients with delusional disorder have about their presumed illness. The most common delusional afflictions are infection (for example, bacteria, viruses, parasites); infestation of insects on or in the skin; dysmorphophobia (for example, misshapen nose or breasts); delusions regarding body odors coming from the skin, mouth, or vagina; and delusions that certain parts of the body, such as the large intestine, are not functioning. The somatic type affects both sexes equally and is thought to be rare, although most patients probably go to nonpsychiatric physicians. Histories of substance abuse or head injury may be common in patients with the disorder. The

frustration caused by the symptom may lead some patients to suicide.

A fit-looking man of 70 consulted a dermatologist, complaining of being infested with fleas for about a year. The dermatologist found no evidence of infestation and referred him for a psychiatric consultation. Although angry about the referral, the patient followed through and gave the following history.

About a year previously, he had bought a canary and soon noticed that it had fleas. He applied an insecticide, but the fleas "attacked" him and "invaded" his house. He washed his clothes repeatedly, applied many lotions, and saw a number of physicians, but nothing helped. He insisted he could see the fleas. He was distressed and too ashamed to see his friends, so he had become almost completely isolated.

The patient had enjoyed good health until two years before, when he had had a severe myocardial infarction. He had made a good recovery and kept himself active. He had given up heavy pipe smoking at that time. He had always been a moderate drinker. There was no personal or family history of emotional problems. He had married as a young man, but his wife had deserted him, and he had lived alone for many years.

When interviewed, the patient looked considerably younger than his stated age and was alert and friendly, although he became angry when talking about the "incompetent" doctors who had failed to cure him, and he bristled when asked if the infestation could possibly be due to his imagination. His sensorium and cognitive functions were normal; his mood was essentially normal except for some anxiety and, at times, anger. His basic personality appeared to be stable. His conviction about the infestation was unshakable, but there was no evidence of other false beliefs.

*Discussion.* It was unclear whether the insects the patient "saw" were the result of delusional misinterpretations of normal visual stimuli or visual hallucinations with a delusional explanation. In any case, his primary symptom was a somatic delusion. Since it is possible to be infested with fleas, the delusion was not bizarre. The persistence of nonbizarre somatic delusions in the absence of other psychotic symptoms—such as prominent hallucinations and incoherence, a mood syndrome, or a known organic cause—indicates delusional disorder, somatic type.

## DIFFERENTIAL DIAGNOSIS

Many medical and neurological illnesses can present with delusions (Table 14.4–2). The most common sites for lesions are the basal ganglia and the limbic system. The medical evaluation should include toxicology screening and routine admission laboratory work. Neuropsychological testing (such as the Bender Gestalt test and the Wechsler memory scale) and an electroencephalogram (EEG) or a computed tomography (CT) scan may be indicated at the time of the initial presentation, especially if other signs or symptoms suggest cognitive impairment or electrophysiological or structural lesions.

### Delirium, Dementia, and Substance-Related Disorders

Delirium and dementia need to be considered in the differential diagnosis of a patient with delusions. Delirium can be differentiated by the presence of a fluctuating level of consciousness or impaired cognitive abilities. Delusions

**Table 14.4–2**
**Neurological and Medical Conditions That Can Present with Delusions**

Basal ganglia disorders—Parkinson's disease, Huntington's disease

Deficiency states—$B_{12}$ folate, thiamine, niacin

Delirium

Dementia—Alzheimer's disease, Pick's disease

Drug-induced—amphetamines, anticholinergics, antidepressants, antihypertensives, antituberculosis drugs, antiparkinson agents, cimetidine, cocaine, disulfiram (Antabuse), hallucinogens

Endocrinopathies—adrenal, thyroid, parathyroid

Limbic system pathology—epilepsy, cerebrovascular diseases, tumors

Systemic—hepatic encephalopathy, hypercalcemia, hypoglycemia, porphyria, uremia

---

early in the course of a dementing illness, as in dementia of the Alzheimer's type, may give the appearance of a delusional disorder; however, neuropsychological testing usually detects cognitive impairment. Although alcohol abuse is an associated feature for patients with delusional disorder, delusional disorder should be distinguished from alcohol-induced psychotic disorder with hallucinations. Intoxication with sympathomimetics (including amphetamine), marijuana, or L-dopa is likely to result in delusional symptoms.

## Other Disorders

The psychiatric differential diagnosis for delusional disorder includes malingering and factitious disorder with predominantly psychological signs and symptoms. The nonfactitious disorders in the differential diagnosis are schizophrenia, mood disorders, obsessive-compulsive disorder, somatoform disorders, and paranoid personality disorder. Delusional disorder is distinguished from schizophrenia by the absence of other schizophrenic symptoms and by the nonbizarre quality of the delusions. Also, patients with delusional disorder lack the impairment of functioning that is seen in schizophrenia. The somatic type of delusional disorder may resemble a depressive disorder or a somatoform disorder. The somatic type of delusional disorder is differentiated from depressive disorders by the absence of other signs of depression and by the lack of a pervasive quality to the depression. Delusional disorder can be differentiated from somatoform disorders by the degree to which the somatic belief is held by the patient. Patients with somatoform disorders allow for the possibility that their disorder does not exist, whereas patients with delusional disorder have no doubt. Separating paranoid personality disorder from delusional disorder requires the sometimes difficult clinical distinction between extreme suspiciousness and a frank delusion. In general, if the clinician doubts that the symptom is a delusion, the diagnosis of delusional disorder should not be made.

## COURSE AND PROGNOSIS

Some clinicians and some research data indicate that an identifiable psychosocial stressor is often present at the onset of the disorder. The nature of the stressor may be such that some degree of suspicion or concern on the part of the patient is warranted. Examples of such stressors are recent immigration, social conflict with family members or friends, and social isolation. In general, a sudden onset is thought to be more common than an insidious onset. Some clinicians believe that the premorbid personality of a patient with delusional disorder is likely to be extroverted, dominant, and hypersensitive. Some clinicians also believe that a patient with delusional disorder is likely to be below average in intelligence. The patient's initial suspicions or concerns gradually become elaborate, consuming much of the patient's attention, and finally become delusional. Patients may begin quarreling with coworkers, may seek protection from the FBI or the police, or may begin visiting many medical or surgical doctors to seek consultations. Thus, the initial contact with the patient may be not with a psychiatrist but, rather, with lawyers regarding suits, primary care physicians regarding medical complaints, or the police regarding delusional suspicions.

Delusional disorder is thought to be a fairly stable diagnosis. Less than 25 percent of all patients with delusional disorder go on to schizophrenia; less than 10 percent of patients with delusional disorder go on to a mood disorder. About 50 percent of patients are recovered at long-term follow-up; another 20 percent have a decrease in their symptoms; and 30 percent have no change in their symptoms. The following factors correlate with a good prognosis: high levels of occupational, social, and functional adjustment; female sex; onset before age 30; sudden onset; short duration of illness; and the presence of precipitating factors. Although reliable data are limited, patients with persecutory, somatic, and erotic delusions are thought to have a better prognosis than do patients with grandiose and jealous delusions.

## TREATMENT

### Hospitalization

In general, patients with delusional disorder can be treated on an outpatient basis. However, a clinician should consider hospitalization for a number of specific reasons. First, a complete medical and neurological evaluation of the patient may be needed to determine whether a nonpsychiatric medical condition is causing the delusional symptoms. Second, patients need to be assessed regarding their ability to control violent impulses, such as suicide and homicide, that may be related to the delusional material. Third, patients' behavior regarding the delusions may have significantly affected their ability to function within their families or occupational settings, thereby requiring professional intervention to stabilize the social or occupational relationships.

If the physician is convinced that the patient would be best treated in a hospital, an attempt should be made to persuade the patient to accept hospitalization; failing that, legal commitment may be indicated. Often, if the physician convinces the patient that hospitalization is inevitable, the patient voluntarily enters a hospital to avoid legal commitment.

## Pharmacotherapy

In an emergency, severely agitated patients should be given an antipsychotic drug intramuscularly. Although adequately conducted clinical trials with large numbers of patients have not been conducted, most clinicians think that antipsychotic drugs are the treatment of choice for delusional disorder. Delusional disorder patients are likely to refuse medication because they can easily incorporate the administration of drugs into their delusional system. The physician should not insist on medication immediately after hospitalization but, rather, should spend a few days establishing rapport with the patient. The physician should explain potential side effects to the patient, so that the patient does not later suspect that the physician lied.

The patient's history of medication response is the best guide in choosing a drug. Often, the physician should start with low doses—for example, 2 mg of haloperidol (Haldol)—and increase the dosage slowly. If a patient fails to respond to a drug at a reasonable dosage in a six-week trial, antipsychotics from other classes should be given clinical trials. Some investigators have indicated that pimozide (Orap) may be particularly effective in delusional disorder, especially in patients with somatic delusions. A common cause of drug failure is noncompliance, and that possibility should be evaluated.

If the patient receives no benefit from antipsychotic medication, the drug should be discontinued. In patients who do respond to antipsychotics, some data indicate that maintenance dosages can be low. Although essentially no data evaluate the use of antidepressants, lithium (Eskalith), or anticonvulsants—for example, carbamazepine (Tegretol) and valproate (Depakene)—in the treatment of delusional disorder, trials with those drugs may be warranted in patients who are unresponsive to antipsychotic drugs. Trials of those drugs should be considered when a patient has either the features of a mood disorder or a family history of mood disorders.

## Psychotherapy

The essential element in effective psychotherapy is establishing a relationship in which the patient begins to trust the therapist. Individual therapy seems to be more effective than group therapy. Insight-oriented supportive, cognitive, and behavioral therapies are often effective. Initially, the therapist should neither agree with nor challenge the patient's delusions. Although the therapist must ask about the delusion to establish its extent, persistent questioning about the delusion should probably be avoided. The physician may stimulate the motivation to receive help by emphasizing a willingness to help patients with their anxiety or irritability, without suggesting that the delusions be treated. However, the therapist should not actively support the notion that the delusions represent reality.

The therapist's unwavering reliability is essential. The therapist should be on time and make appointments as regularly as possible, the goal being to develop a solid and trusting relationship with the patient. Overgratification may actually increase the patient's hostility and suspiciousness because of the core realization that not all demands can be met. The therapist can avoid overgratification by not extending the designated appointment period, by not giving extra appointments unless absolutely necessary, and by not being lenient about the fee.

The therapist should not make disparaging remarks about patients' delusions or ideas but can sympathetically indicate to patients that their preoccupation with their delusions both distresses themselves and interferes with a constructive life. When patients begin to waver in their delusional beliefs, the therapist may increase reality testing by asking the patients to clarify their concerns.

**Psychodynamic factors.** The internal experience of delusional patients is that they are victims of a world that persecutes them. Projection is the principal defense mechanism, and all malevolence is projected into persons or institutions in the environment. By substituting an external threat for an internal one, delusional patients feel a sense of control. The need to control everyone around them reflects the low self-esteem at the core of paranoia. Paranoid patients compensate for feelings of weakness and inferiority by assuming that they are so special that governmental agencies, famous people, and a host of other significant persons in the environment are all deeply concerned about them and trying to persecute them.

Clinicians who attempt to treat patients with delusional disorder must respect the patient's need for the defense of projection. Psychotherapists must be willing to serve as a container for all the negative feelings projected by the patient; any efforts to turn such feelings prematurely will result in the patient's feeling attacked and blamed. One corollary of that principle is that delusions should not be challenged when working psychotherapeutically with delusional patients. Instead, the therapist should simply ask for further elaborations of the patient's perceptions and feelings.

Another approach that is useful in building a therapeutic alliance is to empathize with the patient's internal experience of being overwhelmed by persecution. It may be helpful to make such comments as, "You must be exhausted, considering what you've been through." Without agreeing with every delusional misperception, the therapist can acknowledge that, from the patient's perspective, such perceptions create a good deal of distress. The ultimate goal is to help the patient entertain the possibility of a doubt about the perceptions. As the patient becomes less rigid, feelings of weakness and inferiority that are associated with some depression may surface. When the patient allows feelings of vulnerability to enter into the therapy, a positive therapeutic alliance has been established, and constructive therapeutic work becomes a possibility.

**Family therapy.** When family members are available, the clinician may decide to involve them in the treatment plan. Without being delusionally seen as siding with the enemy, the clinician should attempt to enlist the family as allies in the treatment process. Consequently, both the patient and the family members need to understand that physician-patient confidentiality will be maintained by the therapist and that communications from relatives will be discussed at some point with the patient. The family may benefit from the support of the therapist and may thus be supportive of the patient.

A good therapeutic outcome depends on the psychiatrist's ability to respond to the patient's mistrust of others and the resulting interpersonal conflicts, frustrations, and failures. The mark of successful treatment may be a satisfactory social adjustment, rather than an abatement of the patient's delusions.

### References

Albus M, Strauss A, Stieglitz R D: Schizophrenia, schizotypal and delusional disorders (section F2): Results of the ICD-10 field trial. Pharmacopsychiatry *23* ( Suppl, 4): 155, 1990.

Bentall R P, Kaney S, Dewey M E: Paranoia and social reasoning: An attribution theory analysis. Br J Clin Psychol *30*: 12, 1991.

Block B, Pristach C A: Diagnosis and management of the paranoid patient. Am Fam Physician *45*: 2634, 1992.

Candido C L, Romney D M: Attributional style in paranoid vs. depressed patients. Br J Med Psychol *63*: 355, 1990.

Gabbard G O: *Psychodynamic Psychiatry in General Practice: The DSM-IV Edition*. American Psychiatric Press, Washington, 1994.

Gabriel E, Schanda H: Why do the results of follow-up studies in delusional disorders differ? Psychopathology *24*: 304, 1991.

Gambini O, Colombo C, Cavallaro R, Scarone S: Smooth pursuit eye movements and saccadic eye movements in patients with delusional disorder. Am J Psychiatry *150*: 1411, 1993.

Garety P A, Hemsley D R, Wessely S: Reasoning in deluded schizophrenic and paranoid patients: Biases in performance on a probabilistic inference task. J Nerv Ment Dis *179*: 194, 1991.

Garfield D, Havens L: Paranoid phenomena and pathological narcissism. Am J Psychother *45*: 160, 1991.

Hart J J: Paranoid states: Classification and management. Br J Hosp Med *44*: 34, 1990.

Houseman C: The paranoid person: A biopsychosocial perspective. Arch Psychiatr Nurs *4*: 176, 1990.

Kennedy H G, Kemp L I, Dyer D E: Fear and anger in delusional (paranoid) disorder: The association with violence. Br J Psychiatry *160*: 488, 1992.

Marino C, Nobile M, Bellodi L, Smeraldi E: Delusional disorder and mood disorder: Can they coexist? Psychopathology *26*: 53, 1993.

Newhill C E: The role of culture in the development of paranoid symptomatology. Am J Orthopsychiatry *60*: 176, 1990.

Opjordsmoen S, Retterstol N: Delusional disorder: The predictive validity of the concept. Acta Psychiatr Scand *84*: 250, 1991.

Opjordsmoen S, Retterstol N: Outcome in delusional disorder in different periods of time: Possible implications for treatment with neuroleptics. Psychopathology *26*: 90, 1993.

Retterstol N, Opjordsmoen S: Fatherhood, impending or newly established, precipitating delusional disorders: Long-term course and outcome. Psychopathology *24*: 232, 1991.

Rippon G: Paranoid-nonparanoid differences: Psychophysiological parallels. Int J Psychophysiol *13*: 79, 1992.

Rudden M, Sweeney J, Frances A: Diagnosis and clinical course of erotomanic and other delusional patients. Am J Psychiatry *147*: 625, 1990.

Statel S L, Southwick S M, Gawin F H: Clinical features of cocaine-induced paranoia. Am J Psychiatry *148*: 495, 1991.

# 14.5 / Brief Psychotic Disorder

The fourth edition of *Diagnostic and Statistical Manual of Mental Disorders* (DSM-IV) combines two diagnostic concepts into the diagnosis of brief psychotic disorder. First, the disorder has lasted a short time, defined in DSM-IV as less than one month but at least one day; the symptoms may or may not meet the diagnostic criteria for schizophrenia. Second, the disorder may have developed in response to a severe psychosocial stressor or group of stressors. The grouping of those two concepts together in DSM-IV as brief psychotic disorder acknowledges the practical difficulty of differentiating those concepts in routine clinical practice.

## HISTORY

In general, brief psychotic disorder has been poorly studied in American psychiatry. At least part of the problem in the United States is the frequent changes in diagnostic criteria that have occurred over the past 15 years. The diagnosis has been better appreciated and more completely studied in Scandinavia and in the other Western European countries than in the United States. Patients with disorders similar to brief psychotic disorder have previously been classified as having reactive, hysterical, stress, and psychogenic psychoses.

Reactive psychosis was often used as a synonym for good-prognosis schizophrenia; the DSM-IV diagnosis of brief psychotic disorder is not meant to imply a relation with schizophrenia. In 1913 Karl Jaspers described a number of essential features for the diagnosis of reactive psychosis, including the presence of an identifiable and extremely traumatic stressor, a close temporal relation between the stressor and the development of the psychosis, and a generally benign course for the psychotic episode. In addition, the content of the psychosis often reflected the nature of the traumatic experience, and the development of the psychosis was hypothesized to serve the patient some purpose, often a type of escape from a traumatic condition.

## EPIDEMIOLOGY

Few studies were conducted on the epidemiology of the revised third edition of DSM (DSM-III-R) diagnosis of brief reactive psychosis, and none has been conducted using the DSM-IV criteria. Therefore, reliable estimates of the incidence, the prevalence, the sex ratio, and the average age of onset for the disorder are not available. In general, the disorder is considered uncommon, as indicated by one study of military recruits in which the incidence of DSM-III-R brief reactive psychosis was estimated to be 1.4 per 100,000 recruits. With the inclusion of brief psychotic episodes not associated with a clear precipitating factor in DSM-IV, the incidence for the DSM-IV diagnosis may be higher than that figure. Another widely held clinical impression is that the disorder is more common among young patients than among older patients, although some case reports present case histories that do involve older people.

Some clinicians indicate that the disorder may be seen most frequently in patients from low socioeconomic classes and in patients with preexisting personality disorders (most commonly, histrionic, narcissistic, paranoid, schizotypal, and borderline personality disorders). Persons who have experienced disasters or who have gone through major cultural changes (for example, immigrants) may also be at risk for the disorder after subsequent psychosocial stressors. Those clinical impressions, however, have not been shown to be true in well-controlled clinical studies.

## ETIOLOGY

In DSM-III-R a significant psychosocial factor was considered to be causally involved in brief reactive psychosis, but that diagnostic criterion has been eliminated from DSM-IV. That change in DSM-IV places the diagnosis of brief psychotic disorder in the same category as the many other major psychiatric diagnoses in which the cause is not known and the diagnosis is likely to include a heterogeneous group of disorders.

Patients with brief psychotic disorder who have had a personality disorder may have a biological or psychological vulnerability toward the development of psychotic symptoms. Although patients with brief psychotic disorder as a group may not have an increased incidence of schizophrenia in their families, some data indicate an increased incidence of mood disorders. Psychodynamic formulations have emphasized the presence of inadequate coping mechanisms and the possibility of secondary gain for those patients with psychotic symptoms. As with the biological theories for the disorder, the psychological theories have not been validated by carefully controlled clinical studies. Additional psychodynamic theories suggest that the psychotic symptoms are a defense against a prohibited fantasy, the fulfillment of an unattained wish, or an escape from a specific psychosocial situation.

## DIAGNOSIS

DSM-IV has a continuum of diagnoses for psychotic disorders, based primarily on the duration of the symptoms. For psychotic symptoms that last at least one day but less than one month and that are not associated with a mood disorder, a substance-related disorder, or a psychotic disorder due to a general medical condition, a diagnosis of brief psychotic disorder is likely to be the appropriate diagnosis. For psychotic symptoms that last more than one month, the appropriate diagnoses to consider are delusional disorder (if delusions are the primary psychotic symptoms), schizophreniform disorder (if the symptoms have lasted less than six months), and schizophrenia (if the symptoms have lasted more than six months).

Thus, brief psychotic disorder is classified in DSM-IV as being a psychotic disorder of short duration (Table 14.5–1). The diagnostic criteria specify the presence of at least one clearly psychotic symptom lasting from one day to one month. DSM-IV further allows the specification of two features: (1) the presence or the absence of one or more marked stressors and (2) a postpartum onset.

As with any acutely ill psychiatric patient, the history necessary to make the diagnosis may not be obtainable solely from the patient. Although the presence of psychotic symptoms may be obvious, information about prodromal symptoms, previous episodes of a mood disorder, and the recent history of the ingestion of a psychotomimetic substance may not be available from the clinical interview

---

**Table 14.5–1**
**Diagnostic Criteria for Brief Psychotic Disorder**

A. Presence of one (or more) of the following symptoms:

   (1) delusions
   (2) hallucinations
   (3) disorganized speech (e.g., frequent derailment or incoherence)
   (4) grossly disorganized or catatonic behavior

  **Note:** Do not include a symptom if it is a culturally sanctioned response pattern.

B. Duration of an episode of the disturbance is at least 1 day but less than 1 month, with eventual full return to premorbid level of functioning.

C. The disturbance is not better accounted for by a mood disorder with psychotic features, schizoaffective disorder, or schizophrenia and is not due to the direct physiological effects of a substance (e.g., a drug of abuse, a medication) or a general medical condition.

*Specify* if:
  **With marked stressor(s)** (brief reactive psychosis): if symptoms occur shortly after and apparently in response to events that, singly or together, would be markedly stressful to almost anyone in similar circumstances in the person's culture
  **Without marked stressor(s):** if psychotic symptoms do *not* occur shortly after, or are not apparently in response to events that, singly or together, would be markedly stressful to almost anyone in similar circumstances in the person's culture
  **With postpartum onset:** if onset within 4 weeks postpartum

Table from DSM-IV, *Diagnostic and Statistical Manual of Mental Disorders*, ed 4. Copyright American Psychiatric Association, Washington, 1994. Used with permission.

---

alone. In addition, the clinician may not be able to obtain accurate information regarding the presence or the absence of precipitating stressors. Such information is usually best and most accurately obtained from a relative or a friend.

## CLINICAL FEATURES

The symptoms of brief psychotic disorder always include at least one major symptom of psychosis, usually with an abrupt onset, but do not always include the entire symptom pattern seen in schizophrenia. Some clinicians have observed that affective symptoms, confusion, and impaired attention may be more common in brief psychotic disorder than in the chronic psychotic disorders. Characteristic symptoms in brief psychotic disorder include emotional volatility, outlandish dress or behavior, screaming or muteness, and impaired memory for recent events. Some of the symptoms seen in the disorder suggest a diagnosis of delirium and certainly warrant a complete organic workup, although the results may be negative.

The Scandinavian and other European literature differentiate several characteristic symptom patterns seen in brief psychotic disorder, although the symptom patterns may not hold exactly for this side of the Atlantic Ocean. The symptom patterns include acute paranoid reactions, reactive confusions, reactive excitations, and reactive depressions. Some data suggest that, in the United States, paranoia is often the predominant symptom in the disorder. In French psychiatry, *bouffée délirante* is similar to brief psychotic disorder.

## Precipitating Stressors

The clearest examples of precipitating stressors are major life events that would cause any person significant emotional upset. Such events include the loss of a close family member and a severe auto accident. Some clinicians argue that the severity of the event must be considered in relation to the patient's life. Although that view is reasonable, it may broaden the definition of precipitating stressor to include events that were not related to the psychotic episode. Others have argued that the stressor may be a series of modestly stressful events, rather than a single markedly stressful event. But the summation of the degree of stress caused by a sequence of events calls for an almost impossible degree of clinical judgment.

A 17-year-old high school junior was brought to the emergency room by her distraught mother, who was at a loss to understand her daughter's behavior. Two days earlier the patient's father had been buried; he had died of a sudden myocardial infarction earlier in the week. The patient had become wildly agitated at the cemetery, screaming uncontrollably and needing to be restrained by relatives. She was inconsolable at home, sat rocking in a corner, and talked about a devil that had come to claim her soul. Before her father's death, she had been a "typical teenager, popular, and a very good student but sometimes prone to overreacting." There was no previous psychiatric history.

*Discussion.* Grief is an expected reaction to the loss of a loved one. The young woman's reaction, however, not only was more severe than would be expected (wildly agitated, screaming uncontrollably) but also involved psychotic symptoms (the belief that a devil had come to claim her soul). The sudden onset of a florid psychotic episode immediately after a marked psychosocial stressor, in the absence of prodromal signs of schizophrenia or a schizotypal personality disorder preceding the onset of the disturbance, indicated the Axis I diagnosis of brief psychotic disorder, with marked stressor. Typically, the psychotic symptoms last for at least one day but less than one month. The diagnosis can be made before the one-month period—the maximum duration of symptoms consistent with the diagnosis—has elapsed, but it should be qualified as provisional. In this case it was anticipated that the symptoms would subside and that the patient would return to her usual level of good functioning. If the symptoms persist beyond one month, the diagnosis is changed to another psychotic disorder, such as schizophreniform disorder.

## DIFFERENTIAL DIAGNOSIS

The clinician must not assume that the correct diagnosis for a briefly psychotic patient is brief psychotic disorder, even when a clear precipitating psychosocial factor is identified. Such a factor may be merely coincidental. Other diagnoses to consider in the differential diagnosis include factitious disorder with predominantly psychological signs and symptoms, malingering, psychotic disorder due to a general medical condition, and substance-induced psychotic disorder. A patient may be unwilling to admit the use of illicit substances, thereby making the assessment of substance intoxication or substance withdrawal difficult without the use of laboratory testing. Patients with epilepsy or delirium can also present with psychotic symptoms that resemble those seen in brief psychotic disorder. Additional psychiatric disorders to be considered in the differential diagnosis include dissociative identity disorder and psychotic episodes associated with borderline and schizotypal personality disorders.

## COURSE AND PROGNOSIS

By definition, the course of brief psychotic disorder is less than one month. Nonetheless, the development of such a significant psychiatric disorder may signify a mental vulnerability in the patient. An unknown percentage of patients who are first clasified as having brief psychotic disorder later display chronic psychiatric syndromes, such as schizophrenia and mood disorders. In general, however, patients with brief psychotic disorder have good prognoses, and European studies have indicated that 50 to 80 percent of all patients have no further major psychiatric problems.

The length of the acute and residual symptoms is often just a few days. Occasionally, depressive symptoms follow the resolution of the psychotic symptoms. Suicide is a concern during both the psychotic phase and the postpsychotic depressive phase. A number of indicators have been associated with a good prognosis (Table 14.5–2). Patients with those features are not likely to have subsequent episodes and are not likely to later have schizophrenia or a mood disorder.

## TREATMENT

### Hospitalization

When a patient is acutely psychotic, a brief hospitalization may be necessary for both the evaluation and the protection of the patient. The evaluation of the patient requires close monitoring of the symptoms and an assessment of the patient's level of danger to self and others. In addition, the quiet and structured setting of a hospital may help patients regain their sense of reality. While the clinician is waiting for the setting or drugs to have their effects, seclusion, physical restraints, or one-to-one monitoring of the patient may be necessary.

**Table 14.5–2**
**Good Prognostic Features for Brief Psychotic Disorder**

Good premorbid adjustment
Few premorbid schizoid traits
Severe precipitating stressor
Sudden onset of symptoms
Affective symptoms
Confusion and perplexity during psychosis
Little affective blunting
Short duration of symptoms
Absence of schizophrenic relatives

## Pharmacotherapy

The two major classes of drugs to be considered in the treatment of brief psychotic disorder are the dopamine receptor antagonist antipsychotic drugs and the benzodiazepines. When an antipsychotic is chosen, a high-potency antipsychotic—for example, haloperidol (Haldol)—is usually used. Especially in patients who are at high risk for the development of extrapyramidal side effects (for example, young men), an anticholinergic drug should probably be coadministered with the antipsychotic as prophylaxis against medication-induced movement disorder symptoms. Alternatively, benzodiazepines can be used in the short-term treatment of psychosis. Although benzodiazepines have limited or no usefulness in the long-term treatment of psychotic disorders, they can be effective for a short time and are associated with fewer side effects than are the antipsychotics. In rare cases the benzodiazepines are associated with increased agitation and, more rarely still, withdrawal seizures, which usually occur only with the sustained use of high dosages. The use of other drugs in the treatment of brief psychotic disorder, although reported in case reports, has not been supported in any large-scale studies. However, hypnotic medications are often useful during the first two to three weeks after the resolution of the psychotic episode. The long-term use of any medication should be avoided in the treatment of the disorder. If maintenance medication is necessary, the clinician may have to reconsider the diagnosis.

## Psychotherapy

Although hospitalization and pharmacotherapy are likely to control short-term situations, the difficult part of treatment is the psychological integration of the experience (and possibly the precipitating trauma, if one was present) into the lives of the patients and their families. Individual, family, and group psychotherapies may be indicated. Discussion of the stressors, the psychotic episode, and the development of coping strategies are the major topics for such therapies. Associated issues include helping the patient cope with the loss of self-esteem and confidence.

## References

Beighley P S, Brown G R, Thompson J W: DSM-III-R brief reactive psychosis among Air Force recruits. J Clin Psychiatry 53: 283, 1992.
Chaven B, Kulhara P: Outcome of reactive psychosis: A prospective study from India. Acta Psychiatr Scand 77: 477, 1988.
Jauch D A, Carpenter W T: Reactive psychosis: I. Does the pre-DSM-III concept define a third psychosis? J Nerv Ment Dis 176: 72, 1988.
Jorgensen P: Long-term course of acute reactive paranoid psychosis: A follow-up study. Acta Psychiatr Scand 71: 30, 1985.
Jorgensen P, Mortensen P: Reactive psychosis and mortality. Acta Psychiatr Scand 81: 277, 1990.
Munoz R A, Amado H, Hyatt S: Brief reactive psychosis. J Clin Psychiatry 48: 324, 1987.
Okasha A, el Dawla A S, Khalil A H, Saad A: Presentation of acute psychosis in an Egyptian sample: A transcultural comparison. Compr Psychiatry 34: 4, 1993.
Stephens J H, Shaffer J W, Carpenter W T: "Reactive psychoses." J Nerv Ment Dis 170: 657, 1982.
Vanderhart O, Witztum E, Friedman B: From hysterical psychosis to reactive dissociative psychosis. J Traumatic Stress 6: 43, 1993.

# Mood Disorders

## 15.1 / Major Depressive Disorder and Bipolar I Disorder

As clinical and biological researchers have studied the mood disorders, previously recognized clinical distinctions among patients have become appreciated and are now officially recognized by the fourth edition of *Diagnostic and Statistical Manual of Mental Disorders* (DSM-IV). The two major mood disorders are major depressive disorder and bipolar I disorder, called simply bipolar disorder in the revised third edition of DSM (DSM-III-R). Major depressive disorder and bipolar I disorder are often referred to as affective disorders; however, the critical pathology in those disorders is one of *mood,* the sustained internal emotional state of a person, and not one of *affect,* the external expression of present emotional content. Patients who are afflicted with only depressive episodes are said to have major depressive disorder, sometimes called unipolar depression (not a DSM-IV term). Patients with both manic and depressive episodes and patients with manic episodes alone are said to have bipolar I disorder. The terms "unipolar mania" and "pure mania" (not DSM-IV terms) are sometimes used for bipolar I disorder patients who do not have depressive episodes.

Two additional mood disorders, dysthymic disorder and cyclothymic disorder, have also been appreciated clinically for some time. Dysthymic disorder and cyclothymic disorder are characterized by the presence of symptoms that are less severe than the symptoms of major depressive disorder and of bipolar I disorder, respectively. DSM-IV has codified additional mood disorders, both in the main body of the text and in the appendixes. Those disorders include syndromes related to depression (minor depressive disorder, recurrent brief depressive disorder, and premenstrual dysphoric disorder) and disorders related to bipolar I disorder (bipolar II disorder). In minor depressive disorder the symptom severity does not reach the severity necessary for a diagnosis of major depressive disorder; in recurrent brief depressive disorder the depressive episodes do reach the severity of symptoms required for a diagnosis

of major depressive disorder but do so for only a brief period of time, insufficient in length to meet the diagnostic criteria for major depressive disorder. Bipolar II disorder is characterized by the presence of major depressive episodes alternating with episodes of hypomania—that is, episodes of manic symptoms that do not meet the full criteria for the manic episodes seen in bipolar I disorder. Additional mood disorder diagnoses include mood disorder due to a general medical condition, substance-induced mood disorder, and mood disorder not otherwise specified (NOS).

Mood may be normal, elevated, or depressed. Normal persons experience a wide range of moods and have an equally large repertoire of affective expressions; they feel in control, more or less, of their moods and affects. Mood disorders are a group of clinical conditions characterized by a loss of that sense of control and a subjective experience of great distress. Patients with an elevated mood (that is, mania) show expansiveness, flight of ideas, decreased sleep, heightened self-esteem, and grandiose ideas. Patients with depressed mood (that is, depression) have a loss of energy and interest, feelings of guilt, difficulty in concentrating, loss of appetite, and thoughts of death or suicide. Other signs and symptoms of mood disorders include changes in activity level, cognitive abilities, speech, and vegetative functions (such as sleep, appetite, sexual activity, and other biological rhythms). Those changes almost always result in impaired interpersonal, social, and occupational functioning.

Patients with mood disorders often report an ineffable but distinct quality to their pathological state. The concept of a continuum with normal variations in mood may reflect the clinician's overidentification with the pathology, thus possibly distorting the approach to patients with mood disorders.

At least three major theories consider the relation between major depressive disorder and bipolar I disorder. The most accepted hypothesis, which is supported by several types of genetic and biochemical studies, is that major depressive disorder and bipolar I disorder are two different disorders. Recently, some investigators have suggested that bipolar I disorder is a more severe expression of the same pathophysiological process seen in major depressive disorder. The third hypothesis is that depression and mania are two extremes of a continuum of emotional experience; that conceptualization is not supported by the common clinical observation that many patients have mixed states with both depressed and manic features.

## HISTORY

Depression has been recorded since antiquity, and descriptions of what are now called mood disorders can be found in many ancient documents. The Old Testament story of King Saul describes a depressive syndrome, as does the story of Ajax's suicide in Homer's *Iliad*. About 400 B.C. Hippocrates used the terms "mania" and "melancholia" for mental disturbances. About A.D. 30 Aulus Cornelius Celsus described melancholia in his work *De re medicina* as a depression caused by black bile. The term continued to be used by other medical authors, including Arateus (120–180), Galen (129–199), and Alexander of Tralles in the sixth century. The 12th-century Jewish physician Moses Maimonides considered melancholia a discrete disease entity. In 1686 Bonet described a mental illness that he called *maniaco-melancholicus*.

In 1854 Jules Falret described a condition called *folie circulaire,* in which the patient experiences alternating moods of depression and mania. About the same time, another French psychiatrist, Jules Baillarger, described the condition *folie à double forme,* in which patients become deeply depressed and fall into a stuporous state from which they eventually recover. In 1882 the German psychiatrist Karl Kahlbaum, using the term "cyclothymia," described mania and depression as stages of the same illness.

### Emil Kraepelin

In 1899 Emil Kraepelin, building on the knowledge of previous French and German psychiatrists, described a manic-depressive psychosis that contained most of the criteria that psychiatrists now use to establish the diagnosis for bipolar I disorder. The absence of a dementing and deteriorating course in manic-depressive psychosis differentiated it from dementia precox (that is, schizophrenia). Kraepelin also described a type of depression that began after menopause in women and during late adulthood in men that came to be known as involutional melancholia and has since come to be viewed as a form of mood disorder with a late onset.

## EPIDEMIOLOGY

Major depressive disorder is a common disorder, with a lifetime prevalence of about 15 percent, perhaps as high as 25 percent for women. The incidence of major depressive disorder is also higher than usual in primary care patients, in whom it approaches 10 percent, and in medical inpatients, in whom it approaches 15 percent. Bipolar I disorder is less common than major depressive disorder, with a lifetime prevalence of about 1 percent, similar to the figure for schizophrenia. Since it is increasingly appreciated that the course of bipolar I disorder is not as favorable as the course for major depressive disorder, the cost of bipolar I disorder to patients, their families, and society is significant. Another difference between bipolar I disorder and major depressive disorder is that, whereas most persons with bipolar I disorder eventually come to the attention of a physician and receive treatment, only about half of all persons with major depressive disorder ever receive specific treatment. Although the National Institute of Mental Health (NIMH) has begun a program to increase the awareness of depression in the general population and among physicians, the symptoms of depression are often inappropriately dismissed as understandable reactions to stress, evidence of a weakness of will, or simply a conscious attempt to achieve some secondary gain.

### Sex

An almost universal observation, independent of country or culture, is the twofold greater prevalence of major depressive disorder in women than in men. Although the reasons for the difference are unknown, research has clearly shown that the difference in Western countries is not solely because of socially biased diagnostic practices. The reasons for the difference have been hypothesized to involve hormonal differences, the effects of childbirth, differing psychosocial stressors for women and for men, and behavioral models of learned helplessness. In contrast to major depressive disorder, bipolar I disorder has a prevalence that is equal for men and women.

### Age

In general, the onset of bipolar I disorder is earlier than that for major depressive disorder. The age of onset for bipolar I disorder ranges from childhood (as early as age 5 or 6) to 50 years or even older in rare cases, with a mean age of 30. The mean age of onset for major depressive disorder is about 40 years; 50 percent of all patients have an onset between the ages of 20 and 50. Major depressive disorder can also have its onset in childhood or in the elderly, although that is uncommon. Some recent epidemiological data suggest that the incidence of major depressive disorder may be increasing among persons less than 20 years old. If that observation is true, it may be related to the increased use of alcohol and other substances in that age group.

### Race

The prevalence of mood disorders does not differ from race to race. However, clinicians tend to underdiagnose mood disorders and to overdiagnose schizophrenia in patients who have racial or cultural backgrounds different from their own. White psychiatrists, for example, tend to underdiagnose mood disorders in blacks and Hispanics.

### Marital Status

In general, major depressive disorder occurs most often in persons who have no close interpersonal relationships or who are divorced or separated. Bipolar I disorder may be more common in divorced and single persons than among married persons, but that difference may reflect the early onset and the resulting marital discord that are characteristic of the disorder.

### Socioeconomic and Cultural Considerations

No correlation has been found between socioeconomic status and major depressive disorder; a higher than average incidence of bipolar I disorder does appear among the upper socioeconomic groups, possibly because of biased diagnostic practices. Depression may be more common in rural areas than in urban areas. Bipolar I disorder is more common in persons who did not graduate from college than in college graduates, probably reflecting the relatively early age of onset for the disorder.

## ETIOLOGY

The causal basis for mood disorders is not known. The many attempts to identify a biological or psychosocial cause of mood disorders may have been hampered by the heterogeneity of the patient population that is defined by any of the available, clinically based diagnostic systems, including DSM-IV. The causative factors can artificially be divided into biological factors, genetic factors, and psychosocial factors. That division is artificial because of the likelihood that the three realms interact among themselves. For example, psychosocial factors and genetic factors can affect biological factors (for example, concentrations of a certain neurotransmitter). Biological and psychosocial factors can also affect gene expression. And biological and genetic factors can affect the response of a person to psychosocial factors.

### Biological Factors

A large number of studies have reported various abnormalities in biogenic amine metabolites—such as 5-hydroxyindoleacetic acid (5-HIAA), homovanillic acid (HVA), and 3-methoxy-4-hydroxyphenylglycol (MHPG)—in blood, urine, and cerebrospinal fluid (CSF) from patients with mood disorders (Table 15.1–1). The data reported are most consistent with the hypothesis that mood disorders are associated with heterogeneous dysregulations of the biogenic amines.

**Biogenic amines.** Of the biogenic amines, norepinephrine and serotonin are the two neurotransmitters most implicated in the pathophysiology of mood disorders. In animal models, virtually all effective somatic antidepressant treatments that have been tested are associated with a decrease in the sensitivity of postsynaptic β-adrenergic and 5-hydroxytryptamine type 2 ($5-HT_2$) receptors after long-term treatment, although other changes resulting from long-term treatment with those drugs have also been reported (Table 15.1–2). The temporal response of those receptor changes in animal models correlates with the one-week to three-week delay in clinical improvement usually seen in patients. In addition to norepinephrine, serotonin, and dopamine, evidence points to dysregulation of acetylcholine in mood disorders.

NOREPINEPHRINE. The correlation suggested by basic science studies between the down-regulation of β-adrenergic receptors and clinical antidepressant responses is probably the single most compelling piece of data indicating a direct role for the noradrenergic system in depression. Other types of evidence have also implicated the presynaptic $\alpha_2$-adrenergic receptors in depression, since activation of those receptors results in a decrease in the amount of norepinephrine released. Presynaptic $\alpha_2$-adrenergic receptors are also located on serotonergic neurons and regulate the amount of serotonin released. The existence of almost purely noradrenergic, clinically effective antidepressant drugs—for example, desipramine (Norpramin)—is further support of a role for norepinephrine in the pathophysiology of at least the symptoms of depression.

SEROTONIN. With the huge effect that the serotonin-specific reuptake inhibitors (SSRIs)—for example, fluoxetine (Prozac)—have made on the treatment of depression, serotonin has become the biogenic amine neurotransmitter that is most commonly associated with depression. The identification of multiple serotonin receptor subtypes has also increased the excitement within the research community regarding the development of even more specific treatments for depression. Besides the fact that SSRIs and other serotonergic antidepressants are effective in the treatment of depression, other types of data indicate that serotonin is involved in the pathophysiology of depression. Depletion of serotonin may precipitate depression, and some suicidal patients have low CSF concentrations of serotonin metabolites and low concentrations of serotonin uptake sites on platelets, as measured by imipramine (Tofranil) binding on platelets. Some depressed patients also have abnormal neuroendocrine responses—for example, growth hormone, prolactin, and adrenocorticotropic hormone (ACTH)—to challenges with serotonergic agents. Although current serotonin-active antidepressants act pri-

**Table 15.1–1**
**Frequently Reported Neurotransmitter and Metabolite Changes in Some Depressed Patients (Compared with Normal Controls)[1]**

| | NE | MHPG | NM | VMA | Epi | MET | DA | HVA | 5-HT | 5-HIAA | GABA | GAD | CRH | Endorphins |
|---|---|---|---|---|---|---|---|---|---|---|---|---|---|---|
| CSF | nd | ↓ ↑ ↔ | nd | nd | nd | nd | nd | ↓ ↑ psychotic dep. ↔ | nd | ↓ | ↓ | nd | ↑ | ↑ mania ↔ dep. |
| Plasma | nd | nd | nd | nd | nd | nd | nd | nd | ↓ | nd | ↓ | nd | nd | ↑ ↔ |
| Uptake into platelets | nd | nd | nd | nd | nd | nd | nd | nd | ↓ | nd | nd | nd | nd | nd |
| Urine | ↑ ↔ | ↓ | ↑ ↔ | ↑ ↔ | ↑ ↔ | ↑ ↔ | ↑ mania | nd | nd | nd | nd | nd | nd | nd |
| Brain tissue | nd | nd | nd | nd | nd | nd | nd | nd | ↓ | ↓ | nd | ↓ ↔ | nd | nd |

[1]nd, no data in this review; ↑, increased levels as compared with controls; ↓, decreased levels as compared with controls; ↔, no change as compared with controls. NE, norepinephrine; MHPG, 3-methoxy-4-hydroxyphenethyleneglycol; NM, normetanephrine; VMA, 3-methoxy-4-hydroxymandelic acid; Epi, epinephrine; MET, metanephrine; DA, dopamine; HVA, homovanillic acid; 5-HT, serotonin; 5-HIAA, 5-hydroxyindoleacetic acid; GABA, γ-aminobutyric acid; GAD, glutamatic acid decarboxylase; CRH, corticotropin-releasing hormone.
Table from S Caldecott-Hazard, D G Morgan, F DeLeon-Jones, D H Overstreet, D Janowsky: Clinical and biochemical aspects of depressive disorders: II. Transmitter/receptor theories. Synapse 9 : 253, 1991. Used with permission.

**Table 15.1–2**
**Antidepressant-Induced Changes in Neurotransmitters, Metabolites, and Their Receptors in Humans and Animals[1]**

| What Was Measured | Drugs | | | | | |
|---|---|---|---|---|---|---|
| | Tricyclics | MAOIs | SUBs | Iprindole | Li | ECT |
| **Concentrations in brain tissue** | | | | | | |
| MHPG | ↑ | nd | nd | nd | nd | nd |
| Enkephalins | ↑ | nd | nd | ↑ | nd | ↑ |
| **Concentrations in CSF** | | | | | | |
| MHPG | ↓ | ↓ | ↓ | nd | nd | nd |
| HVA | nd | ↓ | nd | nd | nd | nd |
| 5-HIAA | ↓ | ↓ | ↓ | nd | nd | nd |
| β-Endorphin | nd | nd | nd | nd | nd | ↑ |
| **Concentrations in urine** | | | | | | |
| MHPG | ↓ ↑ ↔ | nd | nd | nd | nd | nd |
| **Effects on uptake of** | | | | | | |
| NE | ↓ | nd | ↔ | ↔ | nd | nd |
| 5-HT | ↓ | nd | ↓ | ↔ | nd | nd |
| GABA | ↓ | nd | nd | nd | nd | nd |
| **Number of receptors** | | | | | | |
| Brain α-2 | ↓ ↑ ↔ | nd | nd | nd | nd | nd |
| Platelet α-2 | nd | nd | nd | nd | ↓ | nd |
| Brain α-1 | ↑ ↔ | nd | nd | nd | ↑ | nd |
| Brain β | ↓ | ↓ | ↓ ↔ | ↓ | nd | ↓ |
| Brain 5-HT-2 | ↓ | ↓ | ↓ | ↓ | nd | ↑ |
| Brain 5-HT-1 | ↓ ↑ ↔ | ↓ | ↓ ↔ | nd | nd | nd |
| Brain mACh | ↑ | nd | nd | nd | ↑ ↔ | nd |
| Brain dopamine-1 | nd | nd | nd | nd | nd | ↓ |
| Brain GABA$_B$ | ↑ ↔ | ↑ | ↑ | nd | nd | ↑ |
| Brain μ and Δ opioid | nd | nd | nd | nd | nd | ↑ ↓ |
| Sensitivity of somatodendritic DA receptors | ↓ ↔ | ↓ | nd | nd | nd | ↓ |
| Effect on stimulation of cAMP by NE | ↓ | ↓ | ↓ | ↓ | nd | ↓ |
| Effect on stimulation of PI by muscarinic agonists | nd | nd | nd | nd | ↓ ↔ | nd |
| Amount of glucocorticoid mRNA on receptor sites in brain | ↑ ↓ | nd | nd | nd | nd | nd |

[1]nd, no data in this review; ↑ increased; ↓ decreased; ↔, no change. Arrows represent the most frequently observed (not necessarily all) effects of the drugs in each group. MAOI, monoamine oxidase inhibitor; SUB, serotonin uptake blocker; Li, lithium; ECT, electroconvulsive therapy; CSF, cerebrospinal fluid; MHPG, 3-methoxy-4-hydroxyphenethyleneglycol; HVA, homovanillic acid; 5-HIAA, 5-hydroxyindoleacetic acid; 5-HT, serotonin; NE, norepinephrine; DA, dopamine, GABA, γ-aminobutyric acid; mACh. muscarinic cholinergic; cAMP, cyclic adenosine monophosphate; PI, phosphoinositide; mRNA, messenger ribonucleic acid.
Table from S Caldecott-Hazard, D G Morgan, F DeLeon-Jones, D H Overstreet, D Janowsky: Clinical and biochemical aspects of depressive disorders: II. Transmitter/receptor theories. Synapse 9: 254, 1991. Used with permission.

marily through the blockade of serotonin reuptake, future generations of antidepressants may have other effects on the serotonin system, including antagonism of the serotonin type 2 (5-HT$_2$) receptor (for example, netazodone) and agonism of the serotonin type 1$_A$ (5-HT$_{1A}$) receptor (for example, ipsapirone).

It is perhaps consistent with the decrease in serotonin receptors after long-term exposure to antidepressants that a decrease in the number of serotonin reuptake sites (assessed by measuring the binding of H$^3$-imipramine) and an increased concentration of serotonin have been found at postmortem in the brains of suicide victims. Decreased tritiated-imipramine binding to blood platelets from some depressed persons has also been found.

DOPAMINE. Although norepinephrine and serotonin are the biogenic amines most often associated with the pathophysiology of depression, dopamine has also been theorized to play a role in depression. The data suggest that dopamine activity may be reduced in depression and increased in mania. The discovery of new subtypes of the dopamine receptors and in-

creasing understanding of the presynaptic and postsynaptic regulation of dopamine function have further enriched the research into the relation between dopamine and mood disorders. Drugs that reduce dopamine concentrations—for example, reserpine (Serpasil)—and diseases that reduce dopamine concentrations (for example, Parkinson's disease) are associated with depressive symptoms. Also, drugs that increase dopamine concentrations—for example, tyrosine, amphetamine, and bupropion (Wellbutrin)—reduce the symptoms of depression. Two recent theories regarding dopamine and depression are that the mesolimbic dopamine pathway may be dysfunctional in depression and that the dopamine type 1 (D$_1$) receptor may be hypoactive in depression.

**Other neurochemical factors.** Although the data are not conclusive at this time, amino acid neurotransmitters—particularly γ-aminobutyric acid (GABA)—and neuroactive peptides (particularly vasopressin and the endogenous opiates) have been implicated in the pathophysiology of mood disorders. Some investigators have suggested that second-messenger systems—such as adenylate cyclase, phosphotidylinositol, and calcium regulation—may also be of causal relevance.

**Neuroendocrine regulation.** The hypothalamus is central to the regulation of the neuroendocrine axes and itself receives many neuronal inputs that use biogenic amine neurotransmitters. A variety of neuroendocrine dysregulations have been reported in patients with mood disorders. Therefore, the abnormal regulation of neuroendocrine axes may be a result of abnormal functioning of biogenic amine-containing neurons. Although it is theoretically possible for a particular dysregulation of a neuroendocrine axis (for example, thyroid axis, adrenal axis) to be involved in the cause of a mood disorder, the dysregulations are more likely reflections of a fundamental underlying brain disorder. The major neuroendocrine axes of interest in mood disorders are the adrenal, thyroid, and growth hormone axes. Other neuroendocrine abnormalities that have been described in patients with mood disorders include decreased nocturnal secretion of melatonin, decreased prolactin release to tryptophan administration, decreased basal levels of follicle-stimulating hormone (FSH) and luteinizing hormone (LH), and decreased testosterone levels in men.

ADRENAL AXIS. A correlation between the hypersecretion of cortisol and depression is one of the oldest observations in biological psychiatry. Basic and clinical research regarding the relation has resulted in an understanding of how cortisol release is regulated in both normal and depressed persons. Neurons in the paraventricular nucleus (PVN) release corticotropin-releasing hormone (CRH), which stimulates the release of adrenocorticotropic hormone (ACTH) from the anterior pituitary. (ACTH is coreleased with β-endorphin and β-lipotropin, two peptides that are synthesized from the same precursor protein from which ACTH is synthesized.) ACTH, in turn, stimulates the release of cortisol from the adrenal cortex. The cortisol feedback on the loop works through at least two mechanisms: a fast feedback mechanism, sensitive to the rate of cortisol concentration increase, operates through cortisol receptors on the hippocampus and results in a decreased release of ACTH; a slow feedback mechanism, sensitive to the steady-state cortisol concentration, is thought to operate through pituitary and adrenal receptors.

*Dexamethasone-suppression test.* Dexamethasone is a synthetic analogue of cortisol. Many researchers have noted that a significant proportion, perhaps 50 percent, of depressed patients fail to have the normal cortisol suppression response to a single dose of dexamethasone. Although the test, the dexamethasone-suppression test (DST), was initially thought to be of diagnostic usefulness, that is not the case, because of the many patients with other psychiatric disorders who also show a positive result (that is, nonsuppression of cortisol) on the DST. New data, however, indicate that the DST may correlate with the likelihood of a relapse. Depressed patients whose DSTs do not normalize with clinical responses to treatment are more likely to relapse than are depressed patients whose DSTs do normalize with clinical responses. Recent research has shown at least two problems with the DST. First, considerable variation in the results of the DST is due to variability in how the dexamethasone is metabolized. Second, since dexamethasone seems to have its major effects at only pituitary receptors, the DST does not effectively assess the functional state of cortisol receptors located elsewhere in the limbic-hypothalamic-pituitary-adrenal (LHPA) axis.

The most recent advance in the assessment of the LHPA axis in depression used infusions of cortisol in depressed and normal persons. Cortisol, the naturally occurring hormone, is a better test substance than is dexamethasone, which does not reach or activate all the relevant receptors. One study found that depressed patients had impaired function of their fast-feedback loop, indicating that at least some depressed persons may have abnormal functioning of cortisol receptors in the hippocampus. Since other researchers have found that hypercortisolemia can damage hippocampal neurons, a cycle involving stress, stimulation of cortisol release, and inability to stop cortisol release may result in increasing damage to an already impaired hippocampus.

THYROID AXIS. Thyroid disorders are often associated with affective symptoms, and researchers have described abnormal regulation of the thyroid axis in patients with mood disorders. One direct clinical implication of the association is the critical importance of testing all affectively ill patients to determine their thyroid status. A consistent finding in studies has been that about one third of all patients with major depressive disorder who have an otherwise normal thyroid axis have a blunted release of thyrotropin—that is, thyroid-stimulating hormone (TSH)—to an infusion of thyrotropin-releasing hormone (TRH) (protirelin). However, that same abnormality has been reported in a wide range of other psychiatric diagnoses, thus limiting the diagnostic usefulness of the test. Moreover, attempts to subtype depressed patients on the basis of their TRH test results have been contradictory.

Recent research has focused on the possibility that a subset of depressed persons suffer from an unrecognized autoimmune disorder that affects their thyroid glands. Several studies have reported that about 10 percent of patients with mood disorders, perhaps particularly bipolar I disorder patients, have detectable concentrations of antithyroid antibodies. Whether the antibodies are, in fact, associated pathophysiologically with depression has not yet been determined. Another potential association is between hypothyroidism and the development of a rapidly cycling course in bipolar I disorder patients. The available research data at this time indicate that the association is independent of the effects of lithium treatment.

GROWTH HORMONE. Several studies have found a statistical difference between depressed patients and normal persons in the regulation of growth hormone release. Depressed patients have a blunted sleep-induced stimulation of growth hormone release. Inasmuch as sleep abnormalities are common symptoms of depression, a neuroendocrine marker related to sleep is an avenue for research. Studies have also found that depressed patients have a blunted response to clonidine (Catapres)-induced increases in growth hormone secretion.

**Sleep abnormalities.** Problems with sleeping—initial and terminal insomnia, multiple awakenings, hypersomnia—are common and classic symptoms of depression, and perceived decreased need for sleep is a classic symptom of mania. Researchers have long recognized that the sleep electroencephalograms (EEGs) of many depressed persons show abnormalities. Common abnormalities are delayed sleep onset, shortened rapid eye movement (REM) latency (the time between falling asleep and the first REM period), an increased length of the first REM period, and abnormal delta sleep. Some investigators have attempted to use the sleep EEG in the diagnostic assessment of patients with mood disorders.

**Kindling.** Kindling is the electrophysiological process in which repeated subthreshold stimulation of a neuron eventually generates an action potential. At the organ level, repeated subthreshold stimulation of an area of the brain results in a seizure. The clinical observation that anticonvulsants—for example, carbamazepine (Tegretol) and valproic acid (Depakene)—are useful in the treatment of mood disorders, particularly bipolar I disorder, has given rise to the theory that the pathophysiology of mood disorders may involve kindling in the temporal lobes.

**Circadian rhythms.** The abnormalities of sleep architecture in depression and the transient clinical improvement in depression that is associated with sleep deprivation have led to theories that depression reflects an abnormal regulation of circadian rhythms. Some experimental studies with animals indicate that many of the standard antidepressant treatments are effective in changing the setting of internal biological clocks (that is, endogenous *zeitgebers*).

**Neuroimmune regulation.** Researchers have reported immunological abnormalities in depressed persons and in persons who are grieving the loss of a relative, spouse, or close friend. The dysregulation of the cortisol axis may affect the immune status; there may be abnormal hypothalamic regulation of the immune system. A less likely possibility is that in some patients a primary pathophysiological process involving the immune system leads to the psychiatric symptoms of mood disorders.

**Brain imaging.** Brain imaging studies of patients with mood disorders have provided a number of inconclusive clues regarding abnormal brain function in those disorders. No brain imaging data regarding the mood disorders have been replicated as consistently as has the finding of increased ventricular size in schizophrenic patients. Nevertheless, structural brain imaging studies with computed tomography (CT) and magnetic resonance imaging (MRI) have produced interesting data. Although the studies have not reported consistent findings (Figure 15.1–1), the data do indicate the following: (1) a significant set of bipolar I disorder patients, predominantly male patients, have enlarged cerebral ventricles; (2) ventricular enlargement is much less common in patients with major depressive disorder than in patients with bipolar I disorder. One caveat to that second point is that patients with major depressive disorder with psychotic features do tend to have enlarged cerebral ventricles. MRI studies have also indicated that patients with major depressive disorder have smaller caudate nuclei and smaller frontal lobes than do control subjects; the depressed patients also have abnormal hippocampal T1 relaxation times, compared with control subjects. At least one MRI study reported that patients with bipolar I disorder have a significantly increased number of deep white matter lesions, when compared with control subjects.

Many reports in the literature concern cerebral blood flow in mood disorders, usually measured by using single photon emission computed tomography (SPECT) or positron emission tomography (PET). A slight majority of the studies have reported decreased blood flow affecting the cerebral cortex in general and the frontal cortical areas in particular. In contrast, one study found increases in cerebral blood flow in patients with major depressive disorder. That study found state-dependent increases in the cortex, the basal ganglia, and the medial thalamus, with

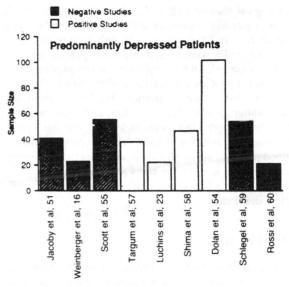

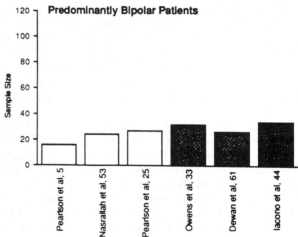

**Figure 15.1–1.** Sample sizes in studies of VBR in mood disorder. (Figure from N C Andreasen, V Swayze II, M Flaum, R Alliger, G Cohen: Ventricular abnormalities in affective disorder: Clinical and demographic correlates. Am J Psychiatry *147*: 894, 1990. Used with permission.)

the suggestion of a trait-dependent increase in the amygdala.

One additional brain imaging technique that has begun to be applied to a broad range of mental disorders is magnetic resonance spectroscopy (MRS). MRS studies of patients with bipolar I disorder have produced data consistent with the hypothesis that the pathophysiology of the disorder may involve an abnormal regulation of membrane phospholipid metabolism. MRS studies of animals that have been treated with lithium have shown the effects of lithium on phospholipids. Another application of MRS to bipolar I disorder is the use of Li[1] MRS to study brain and plasma concentrations of lithium in patients. Those studies have found that the brain concentrations of lithium are about 40 percent of the plasma concentrations after about one week of treatment.

**Neuroanatomical considerations.** Both the symptoms of mood disorders and biological research findings support the hypothesis that mood disorders involve pathology of the limbic system, the basal ganglia, and the hypothalamus.

Neurological disorders of the basal ganglia and the limbic system (especially excitatory lesions of the nondominant hemisphere) are likely to present with depressive symptoms. The limbic system and the basal ganglia are intimately connected, and a major role in the production of emotions is hypothesized for the limbic system. Dysfunction of the hypothalamus is suggested by the depressed patient's alterations in sleep, appetite, and sexual behavior and by the biological changes in endocrine, immunological, and chronobiological measures. The depressed patient's stooped posture, motor slowness, and minor cognitive impairment are similar to the signs seen in disorders of the basal ganglia, such as Parkinson's disease and other subcortical dementias.

## Genetic Factors

The genetic data strongly indicate that a significant factor in the development of a mood disorder is genetics. However, the pattern of genetic inheritance is clearly through complex mechanisms; not only is it impossible to exclude psychosocial effects, but nongenetic factors probably play causative roles in the development of mood disorders in at least some people. In addition, there is a stronger genetic component for the transmission of bipolar I disorder than for the transmission of major depressive disorder.

**Family studies.** Family studies have repeatedly found that the first-degree relatives of bipolar I disorder probands are 8 to 18 times more likely than are the first-degree relatives of control subjects to have bipolar I disorder and 2 to 10 times more likely to have major depressive disorder. Family studies have also found that the first-degree relatives of major depressive disorder probands are 1.5 to 2.5 times more likely to have bipolar I disorder than are the first-degree relatives of normal control subjects and two to three times more likely to have major depressive disorder. Family studies have found that the likelihood of having a mood disorder decreases as the degree of relationship widens. For example, a second-degree relative (for example, a cousin) is less likely to be affected than is a first-degree relative (for example, a brother). The inheritability of bipolar I disorder is also shown by the fact that about 50 percent of all bipolar I disorder patients have at least one parent with a mood disorder, most often major depressive disorder. If one parent has bipolar I disorder, there is a 25 percent chance that any child has a mood disorder; if both parents have bipolar I disorder, there is a 50 to 75 percent chance that a child has a mood disorder.

**Adoption studies.** Adoption studies have also produced data that support the genetic basis for the inheritance of mood disorders. Two of three adoption studies have found a strong genetic component for the inheritance of major depressive disorder; the only adoption study for bipolar I disorder also indicated a genetic basis. Essentially, those adoption studies have found that the biological children of affected parents remain at increased risk of a mood disorder, even if they are reared in nonaffected, adoptive families. Adoption studies have also shown that the biological parents of adopted mood-disordered children have a prevalence of mood disorder similar to that of the parents of nonadopted mood-disordered children. The prevalence of mood disorders in the adoptive parents is similar to the baseline prevalence in the general population.

**Twin studies.** Twin studies have shown that the concordance rate for bipolar I disorder in monozygotic twins is 33 to 90 percent, depending on the particular study; for major depressive disorder the concordance rate in monozygotic twins is about 50 percent. By contrast, the concordance rates in dizygotic twins are about 5 to 25 percent for bipolar I disorder and 10 to 25 percent for major depressive disorder.

**Linkage studies.** The availability of modern techniques of molecular biology, including restriction fragment length polymorphisms (RFLPs), has led to many studies that have reported, replicated, or failed to replicate various associations between specific genes or gene markers and one of the mood disorders. At this time, no genetic association has been consistently replicated. The most reasonable interpretation of the studies is that the particular genes identified in the positive studies may be involved with the genetic inheritance of the mood disorder in the families studied but may not be involved in the genetic inheritance of the mood disorder in other families. Associations between the mood disorders, particular bipolar I disorder, and genetic markers have been reported for chromosomes 5, 11, and X. The $D_1$ receptor gene is located on chromosome 5. The gene for tyrosine hydroxylase, the rate-limiting enzyme for catecholamine synthesis, is located on chromosome 11.

CHROMOSOME 11 AND BIPOLAR I DISORDER. A study reported in 1987 an association between bipolar I disorder among members of an Old Order Amish family and genetic markers on the short arm of chromosome 11. With subsequent extension of that pedigree and the development of bipolar I disorder in previously unaffected family members, the statistical association ceased to apply. That turn of events effectively suggested the degree of caution that must be used in carrying out and interpreting genetic linkage studies in mental disorders.

X CHROMOSOME AND BIPOLAR I DISORDER. Linkage has long been suggested between bipolar I disorder and a region on the X chromosome that contains genes for color blindness and glucose-6-phosphate dehydrogenase deficiency. As with most linkage studies in psychiatry, the application of molecular genetic techniques has produced contradictory results; some studies find a linkage and others do not. The most conservative interpretation remains the possibility that an X-linked gene is a factor in the development of bipolar I disorder in some patients and families.

## Psychosocial Factors

**Life events and environmental stress.** One long-standing clinical observation that has been replicated is that stressful life events more often precede the first episodes of mood disorders than subsequent episodes. That association has been reported for both major depressive disorder and bipolar I disorder patients. One theory proposed to explain the observation is that the stress that accompanies the first episode results in long-lasting changes in the biology of the brain. Those long-lasting changes may result in changes in the functional states of various neurotransmitter and intraneuronal signaling systems. The changes may even include the loss of neurons and an excessive reduction in synaptic contacts. The net result of the changes is to cause the person to be at a higher risk of suffering from subsequent episodes of a mood disorder, even in the absence of an external stressor.

Some clinicians strongly believe that life events play the primary or principal role in depression; other clinicians suggest that life events have only a limited role in the onset and the timing of depression. The most compelling data indicate that the life event most associated with the later development of depression is the loss of a parent before age 11. The environmental stressor most associated with the onset of an episode of depression is the loss of a spouse.

FAMILY. Several theoretical articles and many anecdotal reports concern the relation between family functioning and the onset and the course of mood disorders, particularly major depressive disorder. Several reports have indicated that the psychopathology observed in the family during the time the identified patient is being treated tends to remain, even after the patient has recovered. Moreover, the degree of psychopathology in the family may affect the rate of recovery, the return of symptoms, and the patient's postrecovery adjustment. The clinical and anecdotal data support the clinical importance of evaluating the family life of a patient and of addressing any identified family-related stresses.

**Premorbid personality factors.** No single personality trait or type uniquely predisposes one to depression. All humans, of whatever personality pattern, can and do become depressed under appropriate circumstances; however, certain personality types—oral-dependent, obsessive-compulsive, hysterical—may be at greater risk for depression than are antisocial, paranoid, and other personality types who use projection and other externalizing defense mechanisms. No evidence indicates that any particular personality disorder is associated with the later development of bipolar I disorder. However, dysthymic disorder and cyclothymic disorder are associated with the later development of bipolar I disorder.

**Psychoanalytic and psychodynamic factors.** In attempting to understand depression, Sigmund Freud postulated a relation between object loss and melancholia. He suggested that the depressed patient's rage is internally directed because of identification with the lost object. Freud believed that introjection may be the only way for the ego to relinquish an object. He differentiated melancholia or depression from grief on the basis that the depressed patient feels profound self-depreciation in association with guilt and self-reproach, while the mourner does not.

Melanie Klein later linked depression to the depressive position. She understood manic-depressive cycles as a reflection of a failure in childhood to establish loving introjects. In her view, depressed patients suffer from the concern that they may have destroyed loving objects through their own destructiveness and greed. As a result of that fantasied destruction, they experience persecution by the remaining hated objects. The worthless feeling that is characteristic of depressed patients grows out of a sense that their good internal parents have been transformed into persecutors because of the patient's destructive fantasies

and impulses. Klein regarded mania as a set of defensive operations designed to idealize others, deny any aggression or destructiveness toward others, and restore the lost love objects.

E. Bibring regarded depression as a primary affective state that has little to do with aggression turned inward. Instead, he regarded depression as an affect arising from tension within the ego between one's aspirations and one's reality. When depressed patients realize that they have not lived up to their ideals, they feel helpless and powerless as a result. In essence, depression can be summarized as a partial or complete collapse of the self-esteem within the ego.

Recently, Heinz Kohut redefined depression in terms of self psychology. When self object needs for mirroring, twinship, or idealization are not forthcoming from significant people, the depressed person feels a sense of incompleteness and despair at not receiving the longed-for response. Within that conceptualization, certain responses in the environment are necessary to sustain self-esteem and a feeling of wholeness.

**Learned helplessness.** In experiments in which animals were repeatedly exposed to electric shocks from which they could not escape, the animals eventually gave up and made no attempt at all to escape future shocks. They learned that they were helpless. In humans who are depressed, one can find a similar state of helplessness. According to learned-helplessness theory, depression can improve if the clinician instills in the depressed patient a sense of control and mastery of the environment. The clinician uses behavioral techniques of reward and positive reinforcement in such efforts.

**Cognitive theory.** According to cognitive theory, common cognitive misinterpretations involve negative distortions of life experience, negative self-evaluation, pessimism, and hopelessness. Those learned negative views then lead to the feeling of depression. A cognitive therapist attempts to identify negative cognitions by using behavioral tasks, such as recording and consciously modifying the patient's thoughts.

## DIAGNOSIS

In addition to the diagnostic criteria for major depressive disorder and bipolar disorders, DSM-IV includes specific diagnostic criteria for cross-sectional symptom features, course specifiers, and longitudinal course specifiers. Each of those sets of diagnostic criteria can be used to qualify the diagnosis of major depressive disorder or bipolar I disorder.

### Major Depressive Disorder

Like DSM-III-R, DSM-IV lists the criteria for a major depressive episode separately from the diagnostic criteria for depression-related diagnoses (Table 15.1–3) and also lists severity descriptors for a major depressive episode (Table 15.1–4). One obvious change has been made from DSM-III-R to DSM-IV. The name of the disorder has been changed from major depression to major depressive disorder. An additional change in DSM-IV is the addition of a criterion that the disorder has caused social or occupa-

**Table 15.1–3**
**Criteria for Major Depressive Episode**

A. Five (or more) of the following symptoms have been present during the same 2-week period and represent a change from previous functioning; at least one of the symptoms is either (1) depressed mood or (2) loss of interest or pleasure.

**Note:** Do not include symptoms that are clearly due to a general medical condition, or mood-incongruent delusions or hallucinations.

(1) depressed mood most of the day, nearly every day, as indicated by either subjective report (e.g., feels sad or empty) or observation made by others (e.g., appears tearful). **Note:** in children and adolescents, can be irritable mood.

(2) markedly diminished interest or pleasure in all, or almost all, activities most of the day, nearly every day (as indicated either by subjective account or observation made by others)

(3) significant weight loss when not dieting or weight gain (e.g., a change of more than 5% of body weight in a month), or decrease or increase in appetite nearly every day. **Note:** in children, consider failure to make expected weight gains.

(4) insomnia or hypersomnia nearly every day

(5) psychomotor agitation or retardation nearly every day (observable by others, not merely subjective feelings of restlessness or being slowed down)

(6) fatigue or loss of energy nearly every day

(7) feelings of worthlessness or excessive or inappropriate guilt (which may be delusional) nearly every day (not merely self-reproach or guilt about being sick)

(8) diminished ability to think or concentrate, or indecisiveness, nearly every day (either by subjective account or as observed by others)

(9) recurrent thoughts of death (not just fear of dying), recurrent suicidal ideation without a specific plan, or a suicide attempt or a specific plan for committing suicide

B. The symptoms do not meet criteria for a mixed episode.

C. The symptoms cause clinically significant distress or impairment in social, occupational, or other important areas of functioning.

D. The symptoms are not due to the direct physiological effects of a substance (e.g., a drug of abuse, a medication) or a general medical condition (e.g., hypothyroidism).

E. The symptoms are not better accounted for by Bereavement, i.e., after the loss of a loved one, the symptoms persist for longer than 2 months or are characterized by marked functional impairment, morbid preoccupation with worthlessness, suicidal ideation, psychotic symptoms, or psychomotor retardation.

Table from DSM-IV, *Diagnostic and Statistical Manual of Mental Disorders*, ed 4. Copyright American Psychiatric Association, Washington, 1994. Used with permission.

**Table 15.1–4**
**Criteria for Severity/Psychotic/Remission Specifiers for Current (or Most Recent) Major Depressive Episode**

**Note:** Code in fifth digit. Can be applied to the most recent major depressive episode in major depressive disorder and to a major depressive episode in bipolar I or II disorder only if it is the most recent type of mood episode.

**Mild:** Few, if any, symptoms in excess of those required to make the diagnosis and symptoms result in only minor impairment in occupational functioning or in usual social activities or relationships with others.

**Moderate**: Symptoms or functional impairment between "mild" and "severe"

**Severe without psychotic features**: Several symptoms in excess of those required to make the diagnosis, **and** symptoms markedly interfere with occupational functioning or with usual social activities or relationships with others.

**With psychotic features**: Delusions or hallucinations. If possible, specify whether the psychotic features are mood-congruent or mood-incongruent:

**Mood-congruent psychotic features**: Delusions or hallucinations whose content is entirely consistent with the typical depressive themes of personal inadequacy, guilt, disease, death, nihilism, or deserved punishment.

**Mood-incongruent psychotic features**: Delusions or hallucinations whose content does not involve typical depressive themes of personal inadequacy, guilt, disease, death, nihilism, or deserved punishment. Included here are such symptoms as persecutory delusions (not directly related to depressive themes), thought insertion, thought broadcasting, and delusions of control.

**In partial remission:** Symptoms of a major depressive episode are present but full criteria are not met, or there is a period without any significant symptoms of a major depressive episode lasting less than 2 months following the end of the major depressive episode. (If the major depressive episode was superimposed on dysthymic disorder, the diagnosis of dysthymic disorder alone is given once the full criteria for a major depressive episode are no longer met.)

**In full remission:** During the past 2 months, no significant signs or symptoms of the disturbance.

**Unspecified**

Table from DSM-IV, *Diagnostic and Statistical Manual of Mental Disorders*, ed. 4. Copyright American Psychiatric Association, Washington, 1994. Used with permission.

Clinicians and researchers had dichotomized depressive illness along a psychotic-neurotic continuum. A review of the literature comparing psychotic with nonpsychotic major depressive disorder indicates that the two conditions may be distinct in their pathogenesis. One difference is that bipolar I disorder is more common in the families of probands with psychotic depression than in the families of probands with nonpsychotic depression.

The psychotic symptoms themselves are often categorized as either *mood-congruent*—that is, in harmony with the mood disorder ("I deserve to be punished because I am so bad")—or *mood-incongruent*—that is, not in harmony with the mood disorder. Although mood disorder patients with mood-congruent psychoses have a psychotic type of mood disorder, mood disorder patients with mood-incongruent psychotic symptoms have been variously typed as having schizoaffective disorder or a subtype of schizophrenia or some completely distinct diagnostic entity. Although the classification of those mood-incongruent patients remains controversial, the weight of the research

tional impairment or has caused marked distress to the patient. DSM-III-R did not include such a criterion because it was thought that the presence of the symptoms alone would guarantee that such an impairment or distress is present. Research has indicated that that is not necessarily the case; therefore, the criterion has now been formally included.

**With psychotic features.** The presence of psychotic features (Table 15.1–4) in major depressive disorder reflects severe disease and is a poor prognostic indicator.

data and the guidelines in DSM-IV indicate that one should classify such patients as having a psychotic mood disorder.

Psychotic features are generally a sign of a poor prognosis for patients with mood disorders. The following factors have been associated with a poor prognosis: long duration of episodes, temporal dissociation between the mood disorder and the psychotic symptoms, and a poor premorbid history of social adjustment. The presence of psychotic features also has significant treatment implications; patients with psychotic features almost invariably require antipsychotic drugs in addition to antidepressants or may require electroconvulsive therapy (ECT) to obtain clinical improvement.

**Major depressive disorder, single episode.** DSM-IV specifies the diagnostic criteria for the first episode of major depressive disorder (Table 15.1–5). The differentiation between patients who have a single episode of major depressive disorder and patients who have two or more episodes of major depressive disorder is justified because of the uncertain course of the patients who have just one episode. Several studies have reported data consistent with the formulation that the DSM-III-R diagnostic criteria for major depression define a heterogeneous population of disorders. One type of study assessed the stability of a diagnosis of major depression in a patient over time. The studies found that 25 to 50 percent of the patients were later reclassified as having a different psychiatric condition or a nonpsychiatric medical condition with psychiatric symptoms. A second type studied first-degree relatives of affectively ill patients to determine the presence and the type of psychiatric diagnoses present in those relatives over time. Both types of study found that depressed patients with more depressive symptoms are more likely to have stable diagnoses over time and are more likely to have affectively ill relatives than are depressed patients with fewer depressive symptoms. Also, patients with bipolar I disorder and with bipolar II disorder (recurrent major depressive episodes with hypomania) are likely to have stable diagnoses over time.

**Major depressive disorder, recurrent.** Patients who are experiencing at least their second episode of depression are classified in DSM-IV as having major depressive disorder, recurrent (Table 15.1–6). The major problem with diagnosing recurrent episodes of major depressive disorder is deciding what criteria to use to designate the resolution of each period. The two variables are the degree of resolution of the symptoms and the length of the resolution. Like DSM-III-R, DSM-IV requires that distinct episodes of depression be separated by at least a two-month period, during which the patient has no significant symptoms of depression.

## Bipolar I Disorder

Like DSM-III-R, DSM-IV contains a separate list of criteria for a manic episode (Table 15.1–7) and also lists severity descriptors for a manic episode (Table 15.1–8). One change from DSM-III-R is that DSM-IV requires the presence of a distinct period of abnormal mood lasting at least a week, whereas DSM-III-R did not specify the length of time. Another change is the inclusion in DSM-IV of separate bipolar I disorder diagnoses for a single manic episode and specific types of recurrent episodes, based on the symptoms of the most recent episode.

The designation bipolar I disorder is synonymous with what was known as bipolar disorder—that is, a syndrome with a complete set of symptoms for mania during the

---

**Table 15.1–5**
**Diagnostic Criteria for Major Depressive Disorder, Single Episode**

A. Presence of a single major depressive episode.

B. The major depressive episode is not better accounted for by schizoaffective disorder, and is not superimposed on schizophrenia, schizophreniform disorder, delusional disorder, or psychotic disorder NOS.

C. There has never been a manic episode, a mixed episode, or a hypomanic episode. **Note:** This exclusion does not apply if all of the manic-like, mixed-like, or hypomanic-like episodes are substance or treatment induced or are due to the direct physiological effects of a general medical condition.

*Specify* (for current or most recent episode):
**Severity/psychotic/remission specifiers**
**Chronic**
**with catatonic features**
**with melancholic features**
**with atypical features**
**with postpartum onset**

---

**Table 15.1–6**
**Diagnostic Criteria for Major Depressive Disorder, Recurrent**

A. Presence of two or more major depressive episodes.

   **Note:** To be considered separate episodes, there must be an interval of at least 2 consecutive months in which criteria are not met for a major depressive episode.

B. The major depressive episodes are not better accounted for by schizoaffective disorder and are not superimposed on schizophrenia, schizophreniform disorder, delusional disorder, or psychotic disorder not otherwise specified.

C. There has never been a manic episode, a mixed episode, or a hypomanic episode. **Note:** This exclusion does not apply if all of the manic-like, mixed-like, or hypomanic-like episodes are substance or treatment induced or are due to the direct physiological effects of a general medical condition.

*Specify* (for current or most recent episode):
**Severity/psychotic/remission specifiers**
**Chronic**
**with catatonic features**
**with melancholic features**
**with atypical features**
**with postpartum onset**

*Specify:*
**Longitudinal course specifiers (with and without interepisode recovery)**
**with seasonal pattern**

**Table 15.1–7**
**Criteria for Manic Episode**

A. A distinct period of abnormally and persistently elevated, expansive, or irritable mood, lasting at least 1 week (or any duration if hospitalization is necessary).

B. During the period of mood disturbance, three (or more) of the following symptoms have persisted (four if the mood is only irritable) and have been present to a significant degree:

   (1) inflated self-esteem or grandiosity
   (2) decreased need for sleep (e.g., feels rested after only 3 hours of sleep)
   (3) more talkative than usual or pressure to keep talking
   (4) flight of ideas or subjective experience that thoughts are racing
   (5) distractibility (i.e., attention too easily drawn to unimportant or irrelevant external stimuli)
   (6) increase in goal-directed activity (either socially, at work or school, or sexually) or psychomotor agitation
   (7) excessive involvement in pleasurable activities that have a high potential for painful consequences (e.g., engaging in unrestrained buying sprees, sexual indiscretions, or foolish business investments)

C. The symptoms do not meet criteria for a mixed episode.

D. The mood disturbance is sufficiently severe to cause marked impairment in occupational functioning or in usual social activities or relationships with others, or to necessitate hospitalization to prevent harm to self or others, or there are psychotic features.

E. The symptoms are not due to the direct physiological effects of a substance (e.g., a drug of abuse, a medication, or other treatment) or a general medical condition (e.g., hyperthyroidism).

**Note:** Manic-like episodes that are clearly caused by somatic antidepressant treatment (e.g., medication, electroconvulsive therapy, light therapy) should not count toward a diagnosis of bipolar I disorder.

Table from DSM-IV, *Diagnostic and Statistical Manual of Mental Disorders,* ed 4. Copyright American Psychiatric Association, Washington, 1994. Used with permission.

**Table 15.1–8**
**Criteria for Severity/Psychotic/Permission Specifiers for Current (or Most Recent) Manic Episode**

**Note:** Code in fifth digit. Can be applied to a manic episode in bipolar I disorder only if it is the most recent type of mood episode.

**Mild**: Minimum symptom criteria are met for a manic episode.

**Moderate**: Extreme increase in activity or impairment in judgment.

**Severe, without psychotic features**: Almost continual supervision required to prevent physical harm to others.

**Severe, with psychotic features**: Delusions or hallucinations. If possible, specify whether the psychotic features are mood-congruent or mood-incongruent:

   **Mood-congruent psychotic features**: Delusions or hallucinations whose content is entirely consistent with the typical manic themes of inflated worth, power, knowledge, identity, or special relationship to a deity or famous person.

   **Mood-incongruent psychotic features**: Delusions or hallucinations whose content does not involve typical manic themes of inflated worth, power, knowledge, identity, or special relationship to a deity or famous person. Included are such symptoms as persecutory delusions (not directly related to grandiose ideas or themes), thought insertion, and delusions of being controlled.

**In partial remission**: Symptoms of a manic episode are present but full criteria are not met, or there is a period without any significant symptoms of a manic episode lasting less than 2 months following the end of the manic episode.

**In full remission**: During the past 2 months no significant signs or symptoms of the disturbance were present.

**Unspecified**.

Table from DSM-IV, *Diagnostic and Statistical Manual of Mental Disorders,* ed 4. Copyright American Psychiatric Association, Washington, 1994. Used with permission.

course of the disorder. DSM-IV has now formalized the diagnostic criteria for a disorder known as bipolar II disorder; it is characterized by the presence during the course of the disorder of depressive episodes and hypomanic episodes—that is, episodes of manic symptoms that do not quite meet the diagnostic criteria for a full manic syndrome (Table 15.1–9). Bipolar II disorder is discussed in Section 15.3.

DSM-IV specifically states (Table 15.1–7) that manic episodes that are clearly precipitated by antidepressant treatment (for example, pharmacotherapy, electroconvulsive therapy) are not indicative of bipolar I disorder.

**Bipolar I disorder, single manic episode.** According to DSM-IV, patients must be experiencing their first manic episode to meet the diagnostic criteria for bipolar I disorder, single manic episode (Table 15.1–10). The logic rests on the fact that patients who are having their first episode of bipolar I disorder depression cannot be distinguished from patients with major depressive disorder.

**Bipolar I disorder, recurrent.** The issues regarding the definition of the end of an episode of depression also apply to the definition of the end on an episode of mania. In DSM-IV, episodes are considered distinct if they are sep-

arated by at least two months without significant symptoms of mania or hypomania. DSM-IV specifies diagnostic criteria for recurrent bipolar I disorder based on the symptoms of the most recent episode: bipolar I disorder, most recent episode hypomanic (Table 15.1–11); bipolar I disorder, most recent episode manic (Table 15.1–12); bipolar I disorder, most recent episode mixed (Table 15.1–13); bipolar I disorder, most recent episode depressed (Table 15.1–14); and bipolar I disorder, most recent episode unspecified (Table 15.1–15).

MIXED EPISODES. DSM-III-R defined the mixed type of bipolar disorder as characterized by rapidly alternative depressive and manic states or by the concurrent presence of depressive and manic symptoms. DSM-IV reclassifies the rapidly alternating condition as a course specifier, thereby leaving the classification of mixed state for those bipolar I disorder patients in whom the full criteria for a major depressive episode and the full criteria for a manic episode are met concurrently (Table 15.1–13).

### Cross-Sectional Symptom Features

DSM-IV defines three additional symptom features that can be used to describe patients with various mood disorders. Two of the cross-sectional symptom features (melancholic features and atypical features) are limited to the description of depressive episodes. The third cross-sec-

## Table 15.1–9
### Diagnostic Criteria for Hypomanic Episode

A. A distinct period of persistently elevated, expansive, or irritable mood, lasting throughout four days, that is clearly different from the usual nondepressed mood

B. During the period of mood disturbance, three (or more) of the following symptoms have persisted (four if the mood is only irritable) and have been present to a significant degree:

   (1) inflated self-esteem or grandiosity
   (2) decreased need for sleep (e.g., feels rested after only 3 hours of sleep)
   (3) more talkative than usual or pressure to keep talking
   (4) flight of ideas or subjective experience that thoughts are racing
   (5) distractibility (i.e., attention too easily drawn to unimportant or irrelevant external stimuli)
   (6) increase in goal-directed activity (either socially, at work or school, or sexually) or psychomotor agitation
   (7) excessive involvement in pleasurable activities that have a high potential for painful consequences (e.g., the person engages in unrestrained buying sprees, sexual indiscretions, or foolish business investments)

C. The episode is associated with an unequivocal change in functioning that is uncharacteristic of the person when not symptomatic

D. The disturbance in mood and the change in functioning are observable by others

E. The episode is not severe enough to cause marked impairment in social or occupational functioning, or to necessitate hospitalization, and there are no psychotic features

F. The symptoms are not due to the direct physiological effects of a substance (e.g., a drug of abuse, a medication, or other treatment) or a general medical condition (e.g., hyperthyroidism).

**Note:** Hypomanic-like episodes that are clearly precipitated by somatic antidepressant treatment (e.g., medication, electroconvulsive therapy, light therapy) should not count toward a diagnosis of bipolar II disorder.

Table from DSM-IV, *Diagnostic and Statistical Manual of Mental Disorders,* ed 4. Copyright American Psychiatric Association, Washington, 1994. Used with permission.

## Table 15.1–10
### Diagnostic Criteria for Bipolar I Disorder, Single Manic Episode

A. Presence of only one manic episode and no past major depressive episodes.

**Note:** Recurrence is defined as either a change in polarity from depression or an interval of at least 2 months without manic symptoms.

B. The manic episode is not better accounted for by schizoaffective disorder, and is not superimposed on schizophrenia, schizophreniform disorder, delusional disorder, or psychotic disorder not otherwise specified.

*Specify* if:
  **Mixed.** If symptoms meet criteria for a mixed episode

*Specify* (for current or most recent episode):
  **Severity/psychotic/remission specifiers**
  **with catatonic features**
  **with postpartum onset**

Table from DSM-IV, *Diagnostic and Statistical Manual of Mental Disorders,* ed 4. Copyright American Psychiatric Association, Washington, 1994. Used with permission.

## Table 15.1–11
### Diagnostic Criteria for Bipolar I Disorder, Most Recent Episode Hypomanic

A. Currently (or most recently) in a hypomanic episode.

B. There has previously been at least one manic episode or mixed episode.

C. The mood symptoms cause clinically significant distress or impairment in social, occupational, or other important areas of functioning.

D. The mood episodes in criteria A and B are not better accounted for by schizoaffective disorder and are not superimposed on schizophrenia, schizophreniform disorder, delusional disorder, or psychotic disorder not otherwise specified.

*Specify:*
  **Longitudinal course specifiers (with and without interepisode recovery)**
  **with seasonal pattern** (applies only to the pattern of major depressive episodes)
  **with rapid cycling**

Table from DSM-IV, *Diagnostic and Statistical Manual of Mental Disorders,* ed 4. Copyright American psychiatric Association, Washington, 1994. Used with permission.

## Table 15.1–12
### Diagnostic Criteria for Bipolar I Disorder, Most Recent Episode Manic

A. Currently (or most recently) in a manic episode.

B. There has previously been at least one major depressive episode, manic episode, or mixed episode.

C. The mood episodes in criteria A and B are not better accounted for by schizoaffective disorder and are not superimposed on schizophrenia, schizophreniform disorder, delusional disorder, or psychotic disorder not otherwise specified.

*Specify* (for current or most recent episode):
  **Severity/psychotic remission specifiers**
  **with catatonic features**
  **with postpartum onset**

*Specify:*
  **Longitudinal course specifiers (with and without interepisode recovery)**
  **with seasonal pattern** (applies only to the pattern of major depressive episodes)
  **with rapid cycling**

Table from DSM-IV, *Diagnostic and Statistical Manual of Mental Disorders,* ed 4. Copyright American Psychiatric Association, Washington, 1994. Used with permission.

tional symptom feature (catatonic features) can be applied to the description of either depressive or manic episodes.

**With melancholic features.** In the literature on the melancholic features of depression, about 10 systems have been suggested, with almost three times as many specific criteria for symptoms and course specifiers. In view of the absence of sufficient data on any one of those systems and the absence of adequate comparative studies of those systems, any decision regarding the specific criteria is essentially arbitrary. Moreover, the arbitrary nature of the decisions has not succeeded in discouraging frequent changes in the officially accepted definition of melancholia. The potential importance of identifying the melancholic fea-

**Table 15.1–13**
**Diagnostic Criteria for Bipolar I Disorder,**
**Most Recent Episode Mixed**

A. Currently (or most recently) in a mixed episode.

B. There has previously been at least one major depressive episode, manic episode, or mixed episode.

C. The mood episodes in criteria A and B are not better accounted for by schizoaffective disorder and are not superimposed on schizophrenia, schizophreniform disorder, delusional disorder, or psychotic disorder not otherwise specified.

*Specify* (for current or most recent episode):
  **Severity/psychotic remission specifiers**
  **with catatonic features**
  **with postpartum onset**

*Specify:*
  **Longitudinal course specifiers (with and without**
    **interepisode recovery)**
  **with seasonal pattern** (applies only to the pattern of major depressive episodes)
  **with rapid cycling**

Table from DSM-IV, *Diagnostic and Statistical Manual of Mental Disorders,* ed. 4. Copyright American Psychiatric Association, Washington, 1994. Used with permission.

**Table 15.1–14**
**Diagnostic Criteria for Bipolar I Disorder,**
**Most Recent Episode Depressed**

A. Currently (or most recently) in a major depressive episode.

B. There has previously been at least one manic episode or mixed episode.

C. The mood episodes in criteria A and B are not better accounted for by schizoaffective disorder and are not superimposed on schizophrenia, schizophreniform disorder, delusional disorder, or psychotic disorder not otherwise specified.

Table from DSM-IV, *Diagnostic and Statistical Manual of Mental Disorders,* ed 4. Copyright American Psychiatric Association, Washington, 1994. Used with permission.

**Table 15.1–15**
**Diagnostic Criteria for Bipolar I Disorder,**
**Most Recent Episode Unspecified**

A. Criteria, excerpt for duration, are currently (or most recently) met for a manic, a hypomanic, a mixed, or a major depressive episode.

B. There has previously been at least one manic episode or mixed episode.

C. The mood symptoms cause clinically significant distress or impairment in social, occupational, or other important areas of functioning.

D. The mood symptoms in criteria A and B are not better accounted for by schizoaffective disorder and are not superimposed on schizophrenia, schizophreniform disorder, delusional disorder, or psychotic disorder not otherwise specified.

E. The mood symptoms in criteria A and B are not due to the direct physiological effects of a substance (e.g., a drug of abuse, a medication, or other treatment) or a general medical condition (e.g., hyperthyroidism).

*Specify:*
  **Longitudinal course specifiers (with and without**
    **interepisode recovery)**
  **with seasonal pattern** (applies only to the pattern of major depressive episodes)
  **with rapid cycling**

Table from DSM-IV, *Diagnostic and Statistical Manual of Mental Disorders,* ed 4. Copyright American Psychiatric Association, Washington, 1994. Used with permission.

**Table 15.1–16**
**Criteria for Melancholic Features Specifier**

*Specify* if:
  **with melancholic features** (can be applied to major depressive episodes occurring in major depressive disorder, bipolar I disorder or bipolar II disorder only if it is the most recent type of mood episode)

A. Either of the following, occurring during the most severe period of the current episode:

  (1) loss of pleasure in all, or almost all, activities.
  (2) lack of reactivity to usually pleasurable stimuli (does not feel much better, even temporarily, when something good happens).

B. Three (or more) of the following:

  (1) distinct quality of depressed mood (i.e., the depressed mood is perceived as distinctly different from the kind of feeling experienced after the death of a loved one)
  (2) the depression is regularly worse in the morning
  (3) early morning awakening (at least 2 hours before usual time of awakening)
  (4) marked psychomotor retardation or agitation
  (5) significant anorexia or weight loss
  (6) excessive or inappropriate guilt

Table from DSM-IV, *Diagnostic and Statistical Manual of Mental Disorders,* ed 4. Copyright American Psychiatric Association, Washington, 1994. Used with permission.

tures of major depressive episodes is to identify a group of patients whom some data indicate are more responsive to pharmacotherapeutic treatment than are nonmelancholic depressed patients.

The DSM-IV melancholic features can be applied to major depressive episodes in major depressive disorder, bipolar I disorder, or bipolar II disorder (Table 15.1–16).

**With atypical features.** The introduction of a formally defined type of depression with atypical features is in response to research and clinical data indicating that patients with atypical features have specific, predictable characteristics. The classic atypical features are overeating and oversleeping. Those symptoms have sometimes been referred to as reversed vegetative symptoms, and the symptom pattern has sometimes been referred to as hysteroid dysphoria. When major depressive disorder patients with the features are compared with major depressive disorder patients without the features, the patients with the atypical features are found to have a younger age of onset, a more severe degree of psychomotor slowing, and more frequent coexisting diagnoses of panic disorder, substance abuse or

dependence, and somatization disorder. The high incidence and the severity of anxiety symptoms in patients with atypical features has been correlated in some research with the likelihood of their being misclassified as having an anxiety disorder, rather than a mood disorder. Patients with atypical features may also be likely to have a long-term course, a diagnosis of bipolar I disorder, or a seasonal pattern to their disorder. The major treatment implication of atypical features is that the patients are more likely to respond to monoamine oxidase inhibitors than to tricyclic drugs. However, the significance of atypical features remains controversial, as does the preferential treatment response to monoamine oxidase inhibitors. Moreover, the absence of specific diagnostic criteria have limited the ability to assess their validity and prevalence and to ascertain the existence of any other biological or psychosocial factors that may differentiate it from other symptom patterns.

The DSM-IV atypical features can be applied to the most recent major depressive episode in major depressive disorder, bipolar I disorder, bipolar II disorder, or dysthymic disorder (Table 15.1–17).

**With catatonic features.** The decision to include a specific classification for catatonic features (Table 15.1–18) in the mood disorders category was motivated by two factors. First, since one of the intents of DSM-IV is to be helpful in the differential diagnosis of mental disorders, the inclusion of a specific catatonic type of mood disorders helps balance the presence of a catatonic type of schizophrenia. Catatonia is a symptom that can be present in a number of mental disorders, most commonly schizophrenia and the mood disorders. Second, although as yet incompletely studied, the presence of catatonic features in patients with mood disorders will probably be shown to have prognostic and treatment significance.

The hallmark symptoms of catatonia—stuporousness, blunted affect, extreme withdrawal, negativism, and marked psychomotor retardation—can be seen in both catatonic and noncatatonic schizophrenia, major depressive disorder (often with psychotic features), and medical and neurological disorders. However, catatonic symptoms are probably most commonly associated with bipolar I disorder. That association is often not made in the clinician's

**Table 15.1–17**
**Criteria for Atypical Features Specifier**

*Specify* if:
  **with atypical features** (can be applied when these features predominate during the most recent 2 weeks of a major depressive episode in major depressive disorder or in bipolar I or bipolar II disorder when the major depressive episode is the most recent type of mood episode, or when these features predominate during the most recent 2 years of dysthymic disorder)

  A. Mood reactivity (i.e., mood brightens in response to actual or potential positive events).

  B. Two (or more) of the following features, present for most of the time, for at least two weeks:

    (1) significant weight gain or increase in appetite
    (2) hypersomnia
    (3) leaden paralysis (i.e., heavy, leaden feelings in arms or legs)
    (4) long-standing pattern of interpersonal rejection sensitivity (not limited to episodes of mood disturbance) resulting in significant social or occupational impairment

  C. Criteria are not met with melancholic features or with catatonic features during the same episode.

Table from DSM-IV, *Diagnostic and Statistical Manual of Mental Disorders*, ed 4. Copyright American Psychiatric Association, Washington, 1994. Used with permission.

**Table 15.1–18**
**Criteria for Catatonic Features Specifier**

*Specify* if:
  **with catatonic features** (can be applied to the current or most recent major depressive episode, manic episode, or mixed episode in major depressive disorder, bipolar I disorder, or bipolar II disorder)

  The clinical picture is dominated by at least two of the following:

    (1) motoric immobility as evidenced by catalepsy (including waxy flexibility) or stupor
    (2) excessive motor activity (that is apparently purposeless and not influenced by external stimuli)
    (3) extreme negativism (an apparently motiveless resistance to all instructions or maintenance of a rigid posture against attempts to be moved) or mutism
    (4) pecularities of voluntary movement as evidenced by posturing (voluntary assumption of inappropriate or bizarre postures), stereotyped movements, prominent mannerisms, or prominent grimacing
    (5) echolalia or echopraxia

Table from DSM-IV, *Diagnostic and Statistical Manual of Mental Disorders*, ed 4. Copyright American Psychiatric Association, Washington, 1994. Used with permission.

mind, because of the marked contrast between the symptoms of stuporous catatonia and the classic symptoms of mania. The most important clinical point is that catatonic symptoms are a behavioral syndrome that can be seen in a number of medical and psychiatric conditions; catatonic symptoms do not imply a single diagnosis.

In DSM-IV catatonic features can be applied to the most recent manic episode or major depressive episode in major depressive disorder, bipolar I disorder, or bipolar II disorder.

**Non-DSM-IV types.** Other systems also identify types of patients with mood disorders; those systems usually separate patients with good and poor prognoses or patients who may respond to one particular treatment or another. The differentiations include endogenous-reactive and primary-secondary schemes.

The endogenous-reactive continuum is a controversial division because it implies that endogenous depressions are biological and that reactive depressions are psychological; the division is based primarily on the presence or the absence of an identifiable precipitating stress. Other symptoms of endogenous depression have been described as diurnal variation, delusions, psychomotor retardation, early morning awakening, and feelings of guilt; thus, endogenous depression is similar to the DSM-IV diagnosis of major depressive disorder with psychotic features or melancholic features or both. Symptoms of reactive depression have been described as including initial insomnia, anxiety, emotional lability, and multiple somatic complaints.

Primary depressions are what DSM-IV refers to as mood disorders except for the diagnoses of mood disorder due to a general medical condition and substance-induced mood disorder, which are considered secondary depressions. *Double depression* is the condition in which major depressive disorder is superimposed on dysthymic disorder. A *depressive equivalent* is a symptom or syndrome that may be a *forme fruste* of a depressive episode. For example, a triad of truancy, alcohol abuse, and sexual promiscuity in a formerly well-behaved adolescent may constitute a depressive equivalent.

## Course Specifiers

DSM-IV includes criteria for three distinct course specifiers for mood disorders (Table 15.1–19). One of the course specifiers, with rapid cycling, is restricted to bipolar I disorder and bipolar II disorder. Another course specifier, with seasonal pattern, can be applied to bipolar I disorder, bipolar II disorder, and major depressive disorder, recurrent. The third course specifier, with postpartum onset, can be applied to major depressive or manic episodes in bipolar I disorder, bipolar II disorder, major depressive disorder, and brief psychotic disorder.

**Rapid cycling.** Rapid cycling bipolar I disorder patients are likely to be female and to have had depressive and hypomanic episodes. No data indicate that rapid cy-

**Table 15.1–19**
**Diagnostic Criteria for Course Specifiers**

*Specify* if:
  **with rapid cycling** (can be applied to bipolar I disorder or bipolar II disorder)

  At least four episodes of a mood disturbance in the previous 12 months that meet criteria for a major depressive, manic, mixed, or hypomanic episode.

  Note: Episodes are demarcated either by partial or full remission for at least 2 months or a switch to an episode of opposite polarity (e.g., major depressive episode to manic episode).

*Specify* if:
  **with seasonal pattern** (can be applied to the pattern of major depressive episodes in bipolar I disorder, bipolar II disorder, or major depressive disorder, recurrent)

  A. There has been a regular temporal relationship between the onset of major depressive episodes in bipolar I or bipolar II disorder or major depressive disorder, recurrent, and a particular time of the year (e.g., regular appearance of the major depressive episode in the fall or winter).

    **Note:** Do not include cases in which there is an obvious effect of seasonal-related psychosocial stressors (e.g., regularly being unemployed every winter).

  B. Full remissions (or a change from depression to mania or hypomania) also occur at a characteristic time of the year (e.g., depression disappears in the spring).

  C. In the last 2 years, two major depressive episodes have occurred that demonstrate the temporal seasonal relationships defined in criteria A and B, and no nonseasonal major depressive episodes have occurred during that same period.

  D. Seasonal major depressive episodes (as described above) substantially outnumber any nonseasonal major depressive episodes that may have occurred over the individual's lifetime.

*Specify* if:
  **with postpartum onset** (can be applied to the current or most recent major depressive, manic, or mixed episode in major depressive disorder, bipolar I disorder, or bipolar II disorder; or to brief psychotic disorder)

  Onset of episode within 4 weeks postpartum.

Table from DSM-IV, *Diagnostic and Statistical Manual of Mental Disorders*, ed 4. Copyright American Psychiatric Association, Washington, 1993. Used with permission.

cling has a familial pattern of inheritance, thus suggesting that some external factor (for example, stress or drug treatment) is involved in the pathogenesis of rapid cycling. The DSM-IV criteria specify that the patient must have at least four episodes within a 12-month period (Table 15.1–19).

**Seasonal pattern.** Patients with a seasonal pattern to their mood disorders tend to experience depressive episodes during a particular time of the year, most commonly winter. The pattern has become known as seasonal affective disorder (SAD), although that term is not used in DSM-IV (Table 15.1–19). Two types of evidence indicate that the seasonal pattern may represent a separate diagnostic entity. First, the patients are likely to respond to treatment with light therapy, although adequate studies to evaluate light therapy in nonseasonally depressed patients have not been conducted. Second, at least one PET study has found that the patients have decreased metabolic activity in the orbital frontal cortex and in the left inferior parietal lobule. Although that study has yet to be replicated, future studies will probably attempt to differentiate depressed persons with seasonal pattern from other depressed persons.

**Postpartum onset.** DSM-IV allows for the specification of a postpartum mood disturbance if the onset of symptoms is within four weeks postpartum (Table 15.1–19). Postpartum mental disorders commonly include psychotic symptoms. Postpartum psychotic disorders are discussed in Section 14.1.

**Longitudinal course specifiers.** Beyond the specification of single and recurrent episodes, partial and full remission, and time of onset, DSM-III-R basically ignored the description and the prognostic implication of the longitudinal course. That oversight has been corrected in DSM-IV by the inclusion of specific descriptions of longitudinal courses for both major depressive disorder (Table 15.1–20) and bipolar I disorder (Table 15.1–21). The purpose of the inclusion of the longitudinal course specifiers in DSM-IV is to allow clinicians and researchers to use the criteria to identify prospectively any treatment or prognostic significance in various longitudinal courses. Although preliminary studies of the DSM-IV longitudinal course specifiers indicate that clinicians can assess the longitudinal course, more and larger studies are needed to develop a solid appreciation of the assessment and the implications of variations in the longitudinal course. The cyclothymic and dysthymic features in the longitudinal course specifiers are described in Section 15.2.

## CLINICAL FEATURES

There are two basic symptom patterns in mood disorders, one for depression and one for mania. Depressive episodes can occur in both major depressive disorder and bipolar I disorder. Although many studies have attempted to find reliable differences between bipolar I disorder depressive episodes and episodes of major depressive disorder, the differences are difficult to find. In the clinical situation, only the patient's history, family history, and future course can help differentiate the two conditions. Some patients with bipolar I disorder have mixed states with both manic and depressive features. Also, some bipolar I disorder patients seem to experience brief—min-

**Table 15.1–20**
**Longitudinal Course Specifiers for Major Depressive Disorder**

*Specify*: **With full interepisode recovery,** if full remission attained between two most recent major depressive episodes.
**Without full interepisode recovery,** if full remission not attained between two most recent major depressive episodes.

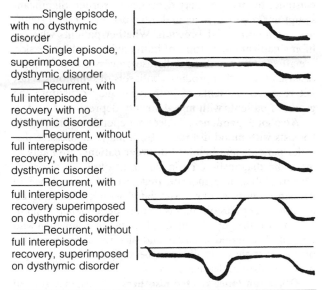

_____Single episode, with no dysthymic disorder

_____Single episode, superimposed on dysthymic disorder

_____Recurrent, with full interepisode recovery with no dysthymic disorder

_____Recurrent, without full interepisode recovery, with no dysthymic disorder

_____Recurrent, with full interepisode recovery superimposed on dysthymic disorder

_____Recurrent, without full interepisode recovery, superimposed on dysthymic disorder

Table adapted from DSM-IV, *Diagnostic and Statistical Manual of Mental Disorders,* (Draft Criteria). Copyright American Psychiatric Association, Washington, 1993. Used with permission.

**Table 15.1–21**
**Longitudinal Course Specifiers for Bipolar I Disorder**

**Specify: With full interepisode recovery,** if full remission attained between two most recent manic or major depressive episodes.
**Without full interepisode recovery,** if full remission attained between two most recent manic or major depressive episodes.

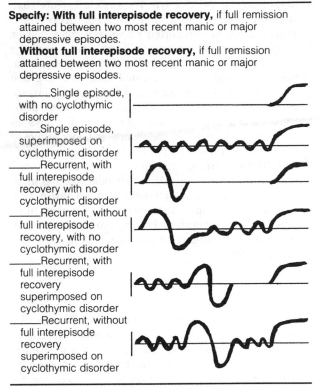

_____Single episode, with no cyclothymic disorder

_____Single episode, superimposed on cyclothymic disorder

_____Recurrent, with full interepisode recovery with no cyclothymic disorder

_____Recurrent, without full interepisode recovery, with no cyclothymic disorder

_____Recurrent, with full interepisode recovery superimposed on cyclothymic disorder

_____Recurrent, without full interepisode recovery superimposed on cyclothymic disorder

Table adapted from DSM-IV, *Diagnostic and Statistical Manual of Mental Disorders,* (Draft Criteria). Copyright American Psychiatric Association, Washington, 1993. Used with permission.

utes to a few hours—episodes of depression during manic episodes.

## Depressive Episodes

A depressed mood and a loss of interest or pleasure are the key symptoms of depression. Patients may say that they feel blue, hopeless, in the dumps, or worthless. For the patient the depressed mood often has a distinct quality that differentiates it from the normal emotion of sadness or grief. Patients often describe the symptom of depression as one of agonizing emotional pain. Depressed patients sometimes complain about being unable to cry, a symptom that resolves as they improve.

About two thirds of all depressed patients contemplate suicide, and 10 to 15 percent commit suicide. However, depressed patients sometimes appear to be unaware of their depression and do not complain of a mood disturbance, even though they exhibit withdrawal from family, friends, and activities that previously interested them.

Almost all depressed patients (97 percent) complain about reduced energy that results in difficulty in finishing tasks, school and work impairment, and decreased motivation to undertake new projects. About 80 percent of patients complain of trouble in sleeping, especially early morning awakening (that is, terminal insomnia) and multiple awakenings at night, during which they ruminate about their problems.

Many patients have decreased appetite and weight loss. Some patients, however, have increased appetite, weight gain, and increased sleep. Those patients are classified in DSM-IV as having atypical features and are also known as having hysteroid dysphoria. Anxiety, in fact, is a common symptom of depression, affecting as many as 90 percent of all depressed patients. The various changes in food intake and rest can aggravate coexisting medical illnesses, such as diabetes, hypertension, chronic obstructive lung disease, and heart disease. Other vegetative symptoms include abnormal menses and decreased interest and performance in sexual activities. Sexual problems can sometimes lead to inappropriate referrals, such as to marital counseling and sex therapy, if the clinician fails to recognize the underlying depressive disorder.

Anxiety (including panic attacks), alcohol abuse, and somatic complaints (such as constipation and headaches) often complicate the treatment of depression. About 50 percent of all patients describe a diurnal variation in their symptoms, with an increased severity in the morning and a lessening of symptoms by evening. Cognitive symptoms include subjective reports of an inability to concentrate (84 percent of patients in one study) and impairments in thinking (67 percent of patients in another study).

**Depression in children and adolescents.** School phobia and excessive clinging to parents may be symptoms of depression in children. Poor academic performance, substance abuse, antisocial behavior, sexual promiscuity, truancy, and running away may be symptoms of depression in adolescents. Chapter 46 discusses this area further.

**Depression in the elderly.** Depression is more common in the elderly than it is in the general population. Various studies have reported prevalence rates ranging from 25 to almost 50 percent, although what percentage of those cases are major depressive disorder is uncertain. A number of studies have reported data indicating that depression in the elderly may be correlated with low socioeconomic status, the loss of a spouse, a concurrent physical illness, and social isolation. Several studies have indicated that depression in the elderly is underdiagnosed and undertreated, perhaps particularly by general practitioners. The underrecognition of depression in the elderly may be due to the observation that depression is more often present with somatic complaints in the elderly than in younger age groups. Also, more than an element of ageism may be found in physicians, who may unconsciously accept more depressive symptoms in elderly patients than in younger patients.

## Manic Episodes

An elevated, expansive, or irritable mood is the hallmark of a manic episode. The elevated mood is euphoric and often infectious, sometimes causing a countertransferential denial of illness by an inexperienced clinician. Although uninvolved people may not recognize the unusual nature of the patient's mood, those who know the patient recognize it as abnormal. Alternatively, the mood may be irritable, especially when the patient's overtly ambitious plans are thwarted. Often, a patient exhibits a change of predominant mood from euphoria early in the course of the illness to irritability later in the disorder.

The treatment of manic patients on an inpatient ward can be complicated by their testing of the limits of ward rules, a tendency to shift responsibility for their acts onto others, exploitation of the weaknesses of others, and a tendency to divide staffs. Outside the hospital, manic patients often drink alcohol excessively, perhaps in an attempt to self-medicate. Their disinhibited nature is reflected in their excessive use of the telephone, especially the making of long-distance calls during the early hours of the morning. Pathological gambling, a tendency to disrobe in public places, clothing and jewelry of bright colors in unusual combinations, and an inattention to small details (such as forgetting to hang up the telephone) are also symptomatic of the disorder. The impulsive nature of many of the patient's acts is coupled with a sense of conviction and purpose. The patient is often preoccupied by religious, political, financial, sexual, or persecutory ideas that can evolve into complex delusional systems. Occasionally, manic patients become regressed and play with their urine and feces.

**Mania in adolescents.** Mania in adolescents is often misdiagnosed as antisocial personality disorder or schizophrenia. Symptoms of mania in adolescents may include psychosis, alcohol or other substance abuse, suicide attempts, academic problems, philosophical brooding, obsessive-compulsive disorder symptoms, multiple somatic complaints, marked irritability resulting in fights, and other antisocial behaviors. Although many of those symptoms are seen in normal adolescence, severe or persistent symptoms should cause the clinician to consider bipolar I disorder in the differential diagnosis.

## Coexisting Disorders

**Anxiety.** In the anxiety disorders, DSM-IV notes the existence of mixed anxiety-depressive disorder. Significant symptoms of anxiety can and often do coexist with significant symptoms of depression. Whether patients who exhibit significant symptoms of both anxiety and depression are affected by two distinct disease processes or by a single disease process that produces both sets of symptoms is not yet resolved. Patients of both types may constitute the group of patients with mixed anxiety-depressive disorder.

**Alcohol dependence.** Alcohol dependence frequently coexists with mood disorders. Both major depressive disorder patients and bipolar I disorder patients are likely to meet the diagnostic criteria for an alcohol use disorder. The available data indicate that alcohol dependence in women is more strongly associated with a coexisting diagnosis of depression than is alcohol dependence in men. In contrast, the genetic and family data regarding men who have both a mood disorder and alcohol dependence indicates that they are likely to be suffering from two genetically distinct disease processes.

**Other substance-related disorders.** Substance-related disorders other than alcohol dependence are also commonly associated with mood disorders. In any individual patient the abuse of substances may be involved in the precipitation of an episode of illness, or, conversely, the abuse of substances may be patients' attempts to treat their own illnesses. Although manic patients seldom use sedatives to dampen their euphoria, depressed patients often use stimulants, such as cocaine and amphetamines, to relieve their depression.

**Medical conditions.** Depression commonly coexists with medical conditions, especially in the elderly. When depression and medical conditions coexist, the clinician must try to determine whether the underlying medical condition is pathophysiologically related to the depression or whether any drugs that the patient is taking for the medical condition are causing the depression. Many studies indicate that treatment of a coexisting major depressive disorder can improve the course of the underlying medical disorder, including cancer.

## MENTAL STATUS EXAMINATION

### Depressive Episodes

**General description.** Generalized psychomotor retardation is the most common symptom, although psychomotor agitation is also seen, especially in elderly patients. Hand wringing and hair pulling are the most common symptoms of agitation. Classically, a depressed patient has a stooped posture, no spontaneous movements, and a downcast, averted gaze (Figures 15.1–2 and 15.1–3). On clinical examination, depressed patients exhibiting gross

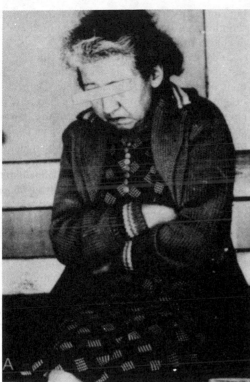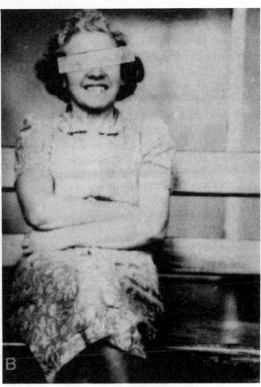

**Figure 15.1–2.** A 38-year-old woman during a state of deep retarded depression (A) and two months later, after recovery (B). The turned-down corners of her mouth, her stooped posture, her drab clothing, and her hairdo during the depressed episode are noteworthy. (Courtesy of Heinz E Lehmann, M.D.)

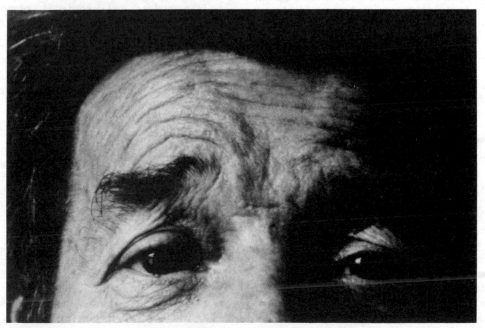

**Figure 15.1–3.** The Swiss neuropsychiatrist Otto Veraguth described a peculiar triangle-shaped fold in the nasal corner of the upper eyelid. The fold is often associated with depression and referred to as Veraguth's fold. The photograph illustrates this physiognomic feature in a 50-year-old man during a major depressive episode. Veraguth's fold may also be seen in persons who are not clinically depressed, usually while they are harboring a mild depressive affect. Distinct changes in the tone of the corrugator and zygomatic facial muscles accompany depression, as shown on electromyograms. (Courtesy of Heinz E Lehmann, M.D.)

symptoms of psychomotor retardation may appear identical to patients with catatonic schizophrenia. That fact is recognized in DSM-IV by the inclusion of the symptom qualifier "with catatonic features" for some mood disorders.

**Mood, affect, and feelings.** Depression is the key symptom, although about half of the patients deny depressive feelings and do not appear to be particularly depressed. Those patients are often brought in by family members or employers because of social withdrawal and generally decreased activity.

**Speech.** Many depressed patients evidence a decreased rate and volume of speech, responding to questions with single words and exhibiting delayed responses to questions. The examiner may literally have to wait two or three minutes for a response to a question.

**Perceptual disturbances.** Depressed patients with delusions or hallucinations are said to have a major depressive episode with psychotic features. Some clinicians also use the term "psychotic depression" for grossly regressed depressed patients—mute, not bathing, soiling—even in the absence of delusions or hallucinations. Such patients are probably better described as having catatonic features.

Delusions and hallucinations that are consistent with a depressed mood are said to be mood-congruent. Mood-congruent delusions in a depressed person include those of guilt, sinfulness, worthlessness, poverty, failure, persecution, and terminal somatic illnesses (for example, cancer and "rotting" brain). The content of the mood-incongruent delusions or hallucinations is not consistent with the depressed mood. Mood-incongruent delusions in a depressed person involve grandiose themes of exaggerated power, knowledge, and worth—for example, the belief that one is being persecuted because one is the Messiah. Hallucinations also occur in major depressive episodes with psychotic features but are relatively rare.

**Thought.** Depressed patients customarily have a negative view of the world and of themselves. Their thought content often involves nondelusional ruminations about loss, guilt, suicide, and death. About 10 percent of all depressed patients have marked symptoms of a thought disorder, usually thought blocking and profound poverty of content.

**Sensorium and cognition**

ORIENTATION. Most depressed patients are oriented to person, place, and time, although some may not have enough energy or interest to answer questions about those subjects during an interview.

MEMORY. About 50 to 75 percent of all depressed patients have a cognitive impairment sometimes referred to as depressive pseudodementia. Such patients commonly complain of impaired concentration and forgetfulness.

**Impulse control.** About 10 to 15 percent of all depressed patients complete suicide, and about two thirds have suicidal ideation. Depressed patients with psychotic features occasionally consider killing a person involved with their delusional systems. However, the most severely depressed patients often lack the motivation or the energy to act in an impulsive or violent way. Patients with depressive disorders are at increased risk of suicide as they begin to improve and to regain the energy needed to plan and carry out a suicide (paradoxical suicide). It is usually not clinically wise to give a depressed patient a large prescription for antidepressants, especially tricyclic drugs, on discharge from the hospital.

**Judgment and insight.** Patients' judgment is best assessed by reviewing their actions in the recent past and their behavior during the interview. Depressed patients' insight into their disorder is often excessive; they overemphasize their symptoms, their disorder, and their life problems. It is difficult to convince such patients that improvement is possible.

**Reliability.** All information obtained from a depressed patient overemphasizes the bad and minimizes the good. A common clinical mistake is to unquestioningly believe a depressed patient who states that a previous trial of antidepressant medications did not work. Such statements may be false, and they require confirmation from another source. The psychiatrist should not view the patients' misinformation as an intentional fabrication, since the admission of any hopeful information may be impossible for a person in a depressed state of mind.

**Objective rating scales for depression.** Objective rating scales for depression can be useful in clinical practice for the documentation of the depressed patient's clinical state.

ZUNG. The Zung Self-Rating Depression Scale is a 20-item report scale. A normal score is 34 or less; a depressed score is 50 or more. The scale provides a global index of the intensity of the patient's depressive symptoms, including the affective expression of depression.

RASKIN. The Raskin Depression Scale is a clinician-rated scale that measures the severity of the patient's depression, as reported by the patient and as observed by the physician, on a five-point scale of three dimensions: verbal report, behavior displayed, and secondary symptoms. It has a range of 3 to 13: normal is 3, and depressed is 7 or more.

HAMILTON. The Hamilton Rating Scale for Depression (HAM-D) is a widely used depression scale with up to 24 items, each of which is rated 0 to 4 or 0 to 2, with a total score of 0 to 76. The ratings are derived from a clinical interview with the patient. The clinician evaluates the patient's answers to questions about feelings of guilt, suicide, sleep habits, and other symptoms of depression.

## Manic Episodes

**General description.** Manic patients are excited, talkative, sometimes amusing, and frequently hyperactive. At times they are grossly psychotic and disorganized, requiring physical restraints and the intramuscular injection of sedating drugs.

**Mood, affect, and feelings.** Manic patients are classically euphoric but can also be irritable, especially when the mania has been present for some time. They also have a low frustration tolerance, which may lead to feelings of anger and hostility. Manic patients may be emotionally labile, switching from laughter to irritability to depression in minutes or hours.

**Speech.** Manic patients cannot be interrupted while they are speaking, and they are often intrusive nuisances to those around them. Speech is often disturbed. As the mania gets more intense, speech becomes louder, more rapid, and difficult to interpret. As the activated state increases, speech becomes full of puns, jokes, rhymes, plays on words, and irrelevancies. As the activity level increases still more, associations become loosened. The ability to concentrate fades, leading to flight of ideas, word salad, and neologisms. In acute manic excitement, speech may be totally incoherent and indistinguishable from that of a schizophrenic person.

**Perceptual disturbances.** Delusions are present in 75 percent of all manic patients. Mood-congruent manic delusions often involve great wealth, abilities, or power. Delusions and hallucinations that are bizarre and mood-incongruent are also seen in mania.

**Thought.** Manic patients' thought content includes themes of self-confidence and self-aggrandizement. Manic patients are often easily distracted. The cognitive functioning of the manic state is characterized by an unrestrained and accelerated flow of ideas.

**Sensorium and cognition.** Although much has been written about the cognitive deficits seen in schizophrenic patients, much less has been written about similar deficits in bipolar I disorder patients, who may have similar minor cognitive deficits. The cognitive deficits reported can be interpreted as reflecting diffuse cortical dysfunction, although subsequent work may be able to localize the abnormal areas. Grossly, orientation and memory are intact, although some manic patients may be so euphoric that they answer incorrectly. The symptom was called "delirious mania" by Emil Kraepelin.

**Impulse control.** About 75 percent of all manic patients are assaultive or threatening. Manic patients do attempt suicide and homicide, but the incidence of those behaviors is not known. Patients who threaten particularly important people (such as the President of the United States) more often have bipolar I disorder than schizophrenia.

**Judgment and insight.** Impaired judgment is a hallmark of manic patients. They may break laws regarding credit cards, sexual activities, and finances, sometimes involving their families in financial ruin. Manic patients also have little insight into their disorder.

**Reliability.** Manic patients are notoriously unreliable in their information. Lying and deceit are common in mania, often causing inexperienced clinicians to treat manic patients with inappropriate disdain.

## DIFFERENTIAL DIAGNOSIS

### Major Depressive Disorder

**Medical disorders.** When a nonpsychiatric medical condition causes a mood disorder, the DSM-IV diagnosis is mood disorder due to a general medical condition. When a substance causes a mood disorder, the DSM-IV diagnosis is substance-induced mood disorder. Both of those diagnostic categories are discussed in Section 15.3.

Failure to obtain a good clinical history or to consider the context of the patient's current life situation may lead to diagnostic errors. Depressed adolescents should be tested for mononucleosis. Patients who are markedly overweight or underweight should be tested for adrenal and thyroid dysfunctions. Homosexuals, bisexual men, and intravenous substance abusers should be tested for acquired immune deficiency syndrome (AIDS). Elderly patients should be evaluated for viral pneumonia and other medical conditions.

Many neurological and medical disorders and pharmacological agents can produce symptoms of depression (Table 15.1–22). Many patients with depressive disorders first go to their general practitioners with somatic complaints. Most organic causes of depressive disorders can be detected with a comprehensive medical history, a complete physical and neurological examination, and routine blood and urine tests. The workup should include tests for thyroid and adrenal functions, because disorders of both of those endocrine systems can present as depressive disorders. In substance-induced mood disorder, a reasonable rule of thumb is that any drug a depressed patient is taking should be considered a potential factor in the mood disorder. Cardiac drugs, antihypertensives, sedatives, hypnotics, antipsychotics, antiepileptics, antiparkinsonian drugs, analgesics, antibacterials, and antineoplastics are all commonly associated with depressive symptoms.

NEUROLOGICAL CONDITIONS. The most common neurological problems that manifest depressive symptoms are Parkinson's disease, dementing illnesses (including dementia of the Alzheimer's type), epilepsy, cerebrovascular diseases, and tumors. About 50 to 75 percent of all patients with Parkinson's disease have marked symptoms of depressive disorder that are not correlated with the patient's degree of physical disability, age, or duration of illness but are correlated with the presence of abnormalities found on neuropsychological tests. The symptoms of depressive disorder may be masked by the almost identical motor symptoms of Parkinson's disease. Depressive symptoms often respond to antidepressant drugs or electroconvulsive therapy (ECT).

The interictal changes associated with temporal lobe epilepsy can mimic a depressive disorder, especially if the epileptic focus is on the right side. Depression is a common complicating feature of cerebrovascular diseases, particularly in the two years after the episode. Depression is more common after anterior events than after posterior events. The depression often responds to antidepressant medications. Tumors of the diencephalic and temporal regions are particularly likely to be associated with depressive disorder symptoms.

PSEUDODEMENTIA. The clinician can usually differentiate the pseudodementia of major depressive disorder from the dementia of a disease, such as dementia of the Alzheimer's type, on clinical grounds. The cognitive symptoms in major depressive disorder have a sudden onset, and other symptoms of major depressive disorder, such as self-reproach, are present. A diurnal variation to the cognitive problems that is not seen in primary dementias may be present. Depressed patients with cognitive difficulties often do not try to answer questions ("I don't know"), whereas demented patients may confabulate. In depressed patients, recent memory is more affected than is remote memory. And depressed patients can sometimes be coached and encouraged during an interview into remembering, an ability that demented patients lack.

**Mental disorders.** Depression can be a feature of vir-

**Table 15.1–22**
**Neurological, Medical, and Pharmacological Causes of Depressive Symptoms**

*Neurological*
Cerebrovascular diseases
Dementias (including dementia of the Alzheimer's type)
Epilepsy*
Fahr's disease*
Huntington's disease*
Hydrocephalus
Infections (including HIV and neurosyphilis)*
Migraines*
Multiple sclerosis*
Narcolepsy
Neoplasms*
Parkinson's disease
Progressive supranuclear palsy
Sleep apnea
Trauma*
Wilson's disease*

*Endocrine*
Adrenal (Cushing's*, Addison's diseases)
Hyperaldosteronism
Menses-related*
Parathyroid disorders (hyper- and hypo-)
Postpartum*
Thyroid disorders (hypothyroidism and apathetic hyperthyroidism)*

*Infectious and Inflammatory*
Acquired immune deficiency syndrome (AIDS)*
Chronic fatigue syndrome
Mononucleosis
Pneumonia—viral and bacterial
Rheumatoid arthritis
Sjögren's arteritis
Systemic lupus erythematosus*
Temporal arteritis
Tuberculosis

*Miscellaneous Medical*
Cancer (especially pancreatic and other GI)
Cardiopulmonary disease
Porphyria
Uremia (and other renal diseases)*
Vitamin deficiencies (B$_{12}$, C, folate, niacin, thiamine)*

*Pharmacological* (representative drugs)
Analgesics and anti-inflammatory
  Ibuprofen
  Indomethacin
  Opiates
  Phenacetin
Antibacterials and antifungals
  Ampicillin
  Cycloserine
  Ethionamide
  Griseofulvin
  Metronidazole
  Nalidixic acid

*Pharmacological* (continued)
  Nitrofurantoin
  Streptomycin
  Sulfamethoxazole
  Sulfonamides
  Tetracycline
Antihypertensives and cardiac drugs
  Alphamethyldopa
  Bethanidine
  β-Blockers (propranolol)
  Clonidine
  Digitalis
  Guanethidine
  Hydralazine
  Lidocaine
  Prazosin
  Procainamide
  Quanabenzacetate
  Rescinnamine
  Reserpine
  Veratrum
Antineoplastics
  C-Asparaginase
  Azathioprine (AZT)
  6-Azauridine
  Bleomycin
  Trimethoprim
  Vincristine
Neurological and psychiatric
  Amantadine
  Antipsychotics (butyrophenones, phenothiazines, oxyindoles)
  Baclofen
  Bromocriptine
  Carbamazepine
  Levodopa
  Phenytoin
  Sedatives and hypnotics (barbiturates, benzodiazepines, chloral hydrate)
  Tetrabenazine
Steroids and hormones
  Corticosteroids (including ACTH)
  Danazol
  Oral contraceptives
  Prednisone
  Triamcinolone
Miscellaneous
  Acetazolamide
  Choline
  Cimetidine
  Cyproheptadine
  Diphenoxylate
  Disulfiram
  Methysergide
  Stimulants (amphetamines, fenfluramine)

*These conditions are associated with manic symptoms.

tually any mental disorder listed in DSM-IV, but the mental disorders listed in Table 15.1–23 should be particularly considered in the differential diagnosis.

OTHER MOOD DISORDERS. DSM-IV has added a number of mood disorders that were not contained in DSM-III-R. Therefore, the clinician must consider the range of DSM-IV diagnostic categories available before arriving at a final diagnosis. First, the clinician must rule out mood disorder due to a general medical condition and substance-induced mood disorder. Next, the clinician must determine whether

the patient has had episodes of maniclike symptoms, indicating bipolar I disorder (complete manic and depressive syndromes), bipolar II disorder (recurrent major depressive episodes with hypomania), or cyclothymic disorder (incomplete depressive and manic syndromes). If the patient's symptoms are limited to those of depression, the clinician must assess the severity and the duration of the symptoms to differentiate among major depressive disorder (complete depressive syndrome for two weeks), minor depressive disorder (incomplete but episodic depressive

**Table 15.1–23**
**Mental Disorders That Commonly Have Depressive Features**

Adjustment disorder with depressed mood

Alcohol use disorders

Anxiety disorders
    Generalized anxiety disorder
    Mixed anxiety-depressive disorder
    Panic disorder
    Posttraumatic stress disorder
    Obsessive-compulsive disorder

Eating disorders
    Anorexia nervosa
    Bulimia nervosa

Mood disorders
    Bipolar I disorder
    Bipolar II disorder
    Cyclothymic disorder
    Dysthymic disorder
    Major depressive disorder
    Minor depressive disorder
    Mood disorder due to a general medical condition
    Recurrent brief depressive disorder
    Substance-induced mood disorder

Schizophrenia

Schizophreniform disorder

Somatoform disorders (especially somatization disorder)

syndrome), recurrent brief depressive disorder (complete depressive syndrome but for less than two weeks per episode), and dysthymic disorder (incomplete depressive syndrome without clear episodes).

OTHER MENTAL DISORDERS. Substance-related disorders, psychotic disorders, eating disorders, adjustment disorders, somatoform disorders, and anxiety disorders are all commonly associated with depressive symptoms and must be considered in the differential diagnosis of a patient with depressive symptoms. Perhaps the most difficult differential is between anxiety disorders with depression and depressive disorders with marked anxiety. The difficulty of making the differentiation is reflected in the inclusion of the diagnosis of mixed anxiety-depressive disorder in DSM-IV. An abnormal result on the dexamethasone-suppression test, the presence of shortened REM latency on a sleep EEG, and a negative lactate infusion test result support a diagnosis of major depressive disorder in particularly troublesome cases.

UNCOMPLICATED BEREAVEMENT. Uncomplicated bereavement is not considered a mental disorder, even though about one third of all bereaved spouses meet the diagnostic criteria for major depressive disorder for a time. Some patients with uncomplicated bereavement do go on to major depressive disorder. However, the diagnosis is not made unless a resolution of the grief does not occur; the differentiation is based on the symptoms' severity and length. The symptoms commonly seen in major depressive disorder that evolve from unresolved bereavement are a morbid preoccupation with worthlessness, suicidal ideation, feelings that one has committed an act (not just an omission) that caused the death, mummification (keeping the deceased's belongings exactly as they were), and a particularly severe anniversary reaction, which sometimes includes a suicide attempt.

## Bipolar I Disorder

**Medical disorders.** In contrast to depressive symptoms, which are present in almost all psychiatric disorders, manic symptoms are more distinctive, although they can be caused by a wide range of medical and neurological conditions (Table 15.1–22) and substances (Table 15.1–24). Antidepressant treatment can also be associated with the precipitation of mania in some patients.

**Mental disorders.** When a bipolar I disorder patient presents with a depressive episode, the differential diagnosis is the same as that for a patient who is being considered for a diagnosis of major depressive disorder. When a patient is manic, however, the differential diagnosis includes bipolar I disorder, bipolar II disorder, cyclothymic disorder, mood disorder due to a general medical condition, and substance-induced mood disorder. Of special consideration with manic symptoms are borderline, narcissistic, histrionic, and antisocial personality disorders.

SCHIZOPHRENIA. A great deal has been published about the clinical difficulty of separating a manic episode from schizophrenia. Although difficult, a differential diagnosis is possible with a few clinical guidelines. Merriment, elation, an infectiousness of mood are much more common in manic episodes than in schizophrenia. The combination of a manic mood, rapid or pressured speech, and hyperactivity weights heavily toward a diagnosis of manic episode. The onset in a manic episode is often rapid and is perceived as a marked change from the patient's previous behavior. Half of all bipolar I disorder patients have a family history of a mood disorder. Catatonic features may be a depressive phase in bipolar I disorder. When evaluating catatonic patients, the clinician should carefully look for a past history of manic or depressive episodes and for a family history of mood disorders. Manic symptoms in minorities (particularly blacks and Hispanics) are often misdiagnosed as schizophrenic symptoms.

**Table 15.1–24**
**Drugs Associated with Manic Symptoms**

Amphetamines
Baclofen
Bromide
Bromocriptine
Captopril
Cimetidine
Cocaine
Corticosteroids (including ACTH)
Cyclosporine
Disulfiram
Hallucinogens (intoxication and flashbacks)
Hydralazine
Isoniazid
Levodopa
Methylphenidate
Metrizamide (following myelography)
Opiates and opioids
Procarbazine
Procyclidine

## COURSE AND PROGNOSIS

The many studies of the course and the prognosis of mood disorders have reached the general conclusion that mood disorders tend to have long courses and that patients tend to have relapses. Although mood disorders are often considered benign in contrast to schizophrenia, that is not entirely the case; mood disorders exact a profound toll on affected patients. Another common conclusion from studies is that life stressors more frequently precede the first episode of mood disorders than subsequent episodes (Table 15.1–25). That finding has been interpreted to indicate that psychosocial stress may play a role in the initial cause of mood disorders and that, even though the initial episode may resolve, a long-lasting change in the biology of the brain puts the patient at great risk for subsequent episodes.

## Major Depressive Disorder

### Course

ONSET. About 50 percent of patients in the first episode of major depressive disorder had significant depressive symptoms before the first identified episode. One implication of that observation is that early identification and treatment of early symptoms may prevent the development of a full depressive episode. Although symptoms may have been present, patients with major depressive disorder usually have not had a premorbid personality disorder. The first depressive episode occurs before age 40 in about 50 percent of patients. A later onset is associated with the absence of a family history of mood disorders, antisocial personality disorder, and alcohol abuse.

DURATION. An untreated depressive episode lasts 6 to 13 months; most treated episodes last about three months.

**Table 15.1–25**
**Studies of Association Between Life Events and First Versus Subsequent Episodes of Mood Disorders**

| Author | Disorder | Number of Episodes | N | Percentage of Patients for Whom Major Life Event Preceded Episode | | p | Assessment |
|---|---|---|---|---|---|---|---|
| | | | | First Episode | Later Episode | | |
| Matussek et al. | Depression | 1 | 242 | 44 | | — | Stressors (138 psychological; 58 somatic) had to clearly precede onset of episode |
| | | 2 | 135 | | 34 | — | |
| | | 3 | 82 | | 24 | — | |
| | | 4 | 119 | | 19 | — | |
| Angst | Depression | 1 | 103 | 60 | | — | No inventory |
| | | ≥4 | | | 38 | — | |
| Okuma and Shimoyama | Bipolar | 1 | 134 | 45 | | — | Any event (3 months prior) |
| | | 2 | 134 | | 26 | — | |
| | | 3 | 134 | | 13 | — | |
| Glassner et al. | Bipolar | 1 | 25 | 75 | | — | Event rated stressful by patient and on Holmes and Rahe Scale (1 year prior; usually 2–24 days); role loss critical in patients and comparison subjects |
| | | >1[a] | | | 56 | | |
| Ambelas[b] | Mania | 1 | 14 | 50 | | <0.01 | Paykel Life Events Scale (4 weeks prior); one third of cases followed bereavement |
| | | ≥2 | 67 | | 28 | | |
| Gutierrez et al. | Depression | 1 | 43 | 55.8 | | <0.05 | Social and somatic stressors; patients with late onset had more events than did those with early onset |
| | | 2 | 35 | | 40.0 | | |
| | | 3 | 18 | | 38.8 | | |
| | | ≥4 | 47 | | 29.7 | | |
| Perris | Depression | 1 | 37 | 62 | 50[c] | <0.02 | Semistructured interview; 56-item inventory (3 months prior) |
| | | ≥2 | 112 | 43 | 19[d] | <0.001 | |
| Dolan et al. | Depression | 1 | 21 | 62 | | <0.05 | Bedford College-Life Events and Difficulties Schedule (6 months prior)(Brown, Harris, 1978) |
| | | ≥2 | 57 | | 29 | | |
| Ezquiaga et al. | Depression | <3 | 52 | 50 | | <0.01 | Semistructured interview (Brown, Harris); no effect of chronic stress |
| | | ≥3 | 45 | | 16 | | |
| Ambelas | Mania | 1 | 50 | 66 | | <0.001 | Paykel Life Events Scale (4 weeks prior) |
| | | ≥2 | 40 | | 20 | | |
| Ghaziuddin et al. | Depression | 1 | 33 | 91 | | <0.05 | Paykel Life Events Scale (6 months prior) |
| | | ≥2 | 40 | | 50 | | |
| Cassano et al. | Depression | 1 | 94 | 66.0 | | <0.05 | Paykel Life Events Scale |
| | | ≥2 | 173 | | 49.4 | | |

[a] For this group, the most recent hospitalization was preceded by a life event resulting in role loss.
[b] Of surgical comparison subjects, 6.6% had experienced recent major life events.
[c] Percentage for negative or undesirable events.
[d] Percentage for events involving psychological conflict.
Table from R M Post: Transduction of psychosocial stress into the neurobiology of recurrent affective disorder. Am J Psychiatry *149*: 1000, 1992. Used with permission.

The withdrawal of antidepressants before three months has elapsed almost always results in the return of the symptoms. As the course of the disorder progresses, patients tend to have more frequent episodes that last longer. Over a 20-year period the mean number of episodes is five or six.

DEVELOPMENT OF MANIC EPISODES. About 5 to 10 percent of patients with an initial diagnosis of major depressive disorder have a manic episode 6 to 10 years after the first depressive episode. The mean age for that switch is 32 years, and it often occurs after two to four depressive episodes. Although the data are inconsistent and controversial, some clinicians report that the depression of patients who are later classified as bipolar I disorder patients is often characterized by hypersomnia, psychomotor retardation, psychotic symptoms, a history of postpartum episodes, a family history of bipolar I disorder, and a history of antidepressant-induced hypomania.

**Prognosis.** Major depressive disorder is not a benign disorder. It tends to be a chronic disorder, and patients tend to relapse. Patients who have been hospitalized for a first episode of major depressive disorder have about a 50 percent chance of recovering in the first year. The percentage of patients recovering after hospitalization decreases with passing time, and at five years posthospitalization, 10 to 15 percent of patients have not recovered. Many of the unrecovered patients remain affected with dysthymic disorder. Recurrences of major depressive episodes are also common. About 25 percent of patients experience a recurrence in the first six months after release from a hospital, about 30 to 50 percent in the first two years, and about 50 to 75 percent in five years. The incidence of relapse is much lower than those figures in patients who continue prophylactic psychopharmacological treatment and in patients who have had only one or two depressive episodes. Generally, as a patient experiences more and more depressive episodes, the time between the episodes decreases, and the severity of each episode increases.

PROGNOSTIC INDICATORS. Many studies have attempted to identify both good and bad prognostic indicators in the course of major depressive disorder. Mild episodes, the absence of psychotic symptoms, and a short hospital stay are good prognostic indicators. Psychosocial indicators of a good course include a history of solid friendships during adolescence, stable family functioning, and a generally solid social functioning for the five years preceding the illness. Additional good prognostic signs are the absence of a comorbid psychiatric disorder, the absence of a personality disorder, no more than one previous hospitalization for major depressive disorder, and an advanced age of onset. The possibility of a poor prognosis is increased by coexisting dysthymic disorder, abuse of alcohol and other substances, anxiety disorder symptoms, and a history of more than one previous depressive episode. Men are more likely than women to experience a chronically impaired course.

## Bipolar I Disorder

**Course.** The natural history of bipolar I disorder is such that it is often useful to make a graph of the patient's disorder and to keep the graph up-to-date as treatment progresses (Figure 15.1–4). Although cyclothymic disorder is sometimes diagnosed retrospectively in bipolar I disorder patients, no identified personality traits are specifically associated with bipolar I disorder. Bipolar I disorder most often starts with depression (75 percent of the time in women, 67 percent in men) and is a recurring disorder. Most patients experience both depressive and manic episodes, although 10 to 20 percent experience only manic episodes. The manic episodes typically have a rapid onset (hours or days), but they may evolve over a few weeks. An untreated manic episode lasts about three months; therefore, the clinician should not discontinue drugs before that time. As the disorder progresses, the time between episodes often decreases. After about five episodes, however, the interepisode interval often stabilizes at six to nine months. Some bipolar I disorder patients have rapidly cycling episodes.

BIPOLAR I DISORDER IN CHILDREN AND THE ELDERLY. Bipolar I disorder can affect both the very young and the elderly. The incidence of bipolar I disorder in children and adolescents is about 1 percent, and the onset can be as early as age 8. Common misdiagnoses are schizophrenia and oppositional defiant disorder. Bipolar I disorder with such an early onset is associated with a poor prognosis. Manic symptoms are common in the elderly, although the range of causes is broad, including nonpsychiatric medical conditions, dementia, delirium, and bipolar I disorder. Currently available data indicate that the onset of true bipolar I disorder in the elderly is relatively uncommon.

**Prognosis.** Patients with bipolar I disorder have a poorer prognosis than do patients with major depressive disorder. About 40 to 50 percent of bipolar I disorder patients may have a second manic episode within two years of the first episode. Although lithium (Eskalith) prophylaxis improves the course and the prognosis of bipolar I disorder, probably only 50 to 60 percent of patients achieve significant control of their symptoms with lithium. One four-year follow-up study of patients with bipolar I disorder found that a premorbid poor occupational status, alcohol dependence, psychotic features, depressive features, interepisode depressive features, and male gender were all factors that weighted toward a poor prognosis. Short duration of manic episodes, advanced age of onset, few suicidal thoughts, and few coexisting psychiatric or medical problems weight toward a good prognosis.

About 7 percent of all bipolar I disorder patients do not have a recurrence of symptoms, 45 percent have more than one episode, and 40 percent have a chronic disorder. Patients may have from 2 to 30 manic episodes, although the mean number is about nine. About 40 percent of all patients have more than 10 episodes. On long-term follow-up, 15 percent of all bipolar I disorder patients are well, 45 percent are well but have multiple relapses, 30 percent are in partial remission, and 10 percent are chronically ill. One third of all bipolar I disorder patients have chronic symptoms and evidence of significant social decline.

## TREATMENT

The treatment of patients with mood disorders must be

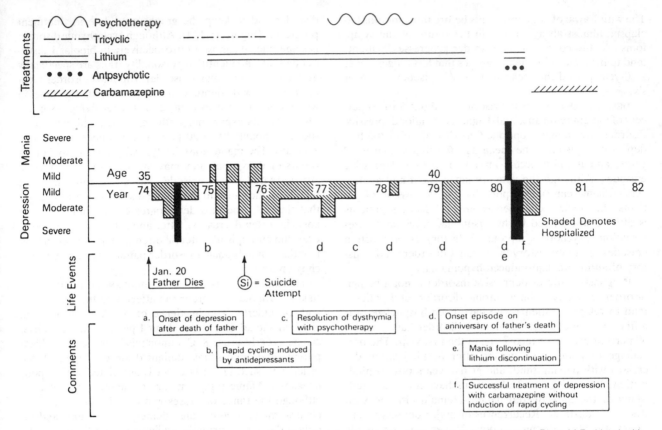

**Figure 15.1–4.** Graphing the course of a mood disorder. Prototype of a life chart. (Figure by Robert M. Post, M.D. Used with permission.)

directed toward a number of goals. First, the safety of the patient must be guaranteed. Second, a complete diagnostic evaluation of the patient must be carried out. Third, a treatment plan must be initiated that addresses not only the immediate symptoms but also the patient's prospective well-being. Although the current emphasis is on pharmacotherapy and psychotherapy addressed to the individual patient, stressful life events are also associated with increases in relapse rates among patients with mood disorders. Thus, treatment must reduce the number and the severity of the stressors in patients' lives.

Overall, the treatment of mood disorders is rewarding for the psychiatrist. Specific treatments are now available for both manic and depressive episodes, and the data indicate that prophylactic treatment is also effective. Because the prognosis for each episode is good, optimism is always warranted and welcomed by both the patient and the patient's family, even if initial treatment results are not promising. However, mood disorders are chronic, and the patient and the family must be advised about future treatment strategies.

### Hospitalization

The first and most critical decision the physician must make is whether to hospitalize the patient or to attempt outpatient treatment. Clear indications for hospitalization are the need for diagnostic procedures, the risk of suicide or homicide, and the patient's grossly reduced ability to get food and shelter. A history of rapidly progressing symp-

toms and the rupture of the patient's usual support systems are also indications for hospitalization.

Mild depression or hypomania may be safely treated in the office if the physician evaluates the patient frequently. Clinical signs of impaired judgment, weight loss, or insomnia should be minimal. The patient's support system should be strong, neither overinvolved nor withdrawing from the patient. Any adverse changes in the patient's symptoms or behavior or the attitude of the patient's support system may be sufficient to warrant hospitalization.

Patients with mood disorders are often unwilling to enter a hospital voluntarily, so they may have to be involuntarily committed. Patients with major depressive disorder are often incapable of making decisions because of their slowed thinking, negative *Weltanschauung* (world view), and hopelessness. Manic patients often have such a complete lack of insight into their disorder that hospitalization seems absolutely absurd to them.

### Psychosocial Therapies

Although most studies indicate—and most clinicians and researchers believe—that combined psychotherapy and pharmacotherapy is the most effective treatment for major depressive disorder, some data indicate a different view. Specifically, some data indicate that either pharmacotherapy or psychotherapy alone is effective, at least in patients with mild major depressive episodes, and that the regular use of combined therapy adds to the cost of treatment and exposes patients to unnecessary side effects.

Three types of short-term psychotherapies—cognitive therapy, interpersonal therapy, and behavior therapy—have been studied regarding their efficacy in the treatment of major depressive disorder. Psychoanalytically oriented psychotherapy, although not as well researched regarding its efficacy in major depressive disorder, has long been used for depressive disorders, and many clinicians use the technique as their primary method. What differentiates the three short-term psychotherapy modalities from the psychoanalytically oriented approach are the active and directive roles of the therapist, the directly recognizable goals, and the endpoints for short-term therapy.

Table 15.1–26 summarizes the features of the psychodynamic, cognitive, and interpersonal approaches, Table 15.1–27 summarizes some nonselective and selective patient variables for psychotherapy, Table 15.1–28 summarizes the advantages and the limitations of the three approaches, and Tables 15.1–29 and 15.1–30 summarize features that may affect the choice of pharmacotherapy or psychotherapy or combined therapy. The NIMH Treatment of Depression Collaborative Research Program found the following predictors of response to various treatments: (1) low social dysfunction suggested a good response to interpersonal therapy, (2) low cognitive dysfunction suggested a good response to cognitive-behavior therapy and pharmacotherapy, (3) high work dysfunction suggested a good response to pharmacotherapy, and (4) high depression severity suggested a good response to interpersonal therapy and pharmacotherapy.

**Cognitive therapy.** Cognitive therapy, developed originally by Aaron Beck, focuses on the cognitive distortions postulated to be present in major depressive disorder. Such distortions include selective attention to the negative aspects of circumstances and unrealistically morbid inferences about consequences. For example, apathy and low energy are results of the patient's expectation of failure in all areas. The goal of cognitive therapy is to alleviate depressive episodes and to prevent their recurrence by helping patients identify and test negative cognitions; develop alternative, flexible, and positive ways of thinking; and rehearse new cognitive and behavioral responses.

About a dozen studies have found that cognitive therapy is effective in the treatment of major depressive disorder; most of the studies found that cognitive therapy is equal in efficacy to pharmacotherapy, associated with fewer side effects than is pharmacotherapy, and associated with better follow-up than is pharmacotherapy. However, most of the studies can be criticized for using antidepressant dosages that were too low and for using the antidepressant medications for too short a period. Some of the best controlled studies have indicated that the combination of cognitive therapy and pharmacotherapy is more efficacious than either therapy alone, although other studies have not found that additive effect. At least one study,

**Table 15.1–26**
**Major Features of Three Psychotherapeutic Approaches to Depression**

| Feature | Psychodynamic Approach | Cognitive Approach | Interpersonal Approach |
|---|---|---|---|
| Major theorists | Freud, Abraham, Jacobson, Kohut | Plato, Adler, Beck, Rush | Meyer, Sullivan, Klerman, Weissman |
| Concepts of pathology and cause | Ego regression: damaged self-esteem and unresolved conflict due to childhood object loss and disappointment | Distorted thinking: dysphoria due to learned negative views of self, others, and the world | Impaired interpersonal relations: absent or unsatisfactory significant social bonds |
| Major goals and mechanisms of change | To promote personality change through understanding of past conflicts; to achieve insight into defenses, ego distortions, and superego defects; to provide a role model; to permit cathartic release of aggression | To provide symptomatic relief through alteration of target thoughts; to identify self-destructive cognitions; to modify specific erroneous assumptions; to promote self-control over thinking patterns | To provide symptomatic relief through solution of current interpersonal problems; to reduce stress involving family or work; to improve interpersonal communication skills |
| Primary techniques and practices | Expressive-empathic: fully or partially analyzing transference and resistance; confronting defenses; clarifying ego and superego distortions | Behavioral-cognitive: recording and monitoring cognitions; correcting distorted themes with logic and experimental testing; providing alternative thought content; homework | Communicative-environmental: clarifying and managing maladaptive relationships and learning new ones through communication and social skills training; providing information on illness |
| Therapist role-therapeutic relationship | Interpreter-reflector: establishment and exploration of transference; therapeutic alliance for benign dependence and empathic understanding | Educator-shaper: positive relationship instead of transference; collaborative empiricism as basis for joint scientific (logical) task | Explorer-prescriber: positive relationship-transference without interpretation; active therapist role for influence and advocacy |
| Marital-family role | Full individual confidentiality; exclusion of significant others except in life-threatening situations | Use of spouse as objective reporter; couples therapy for disturbed cognitions sustained in marital relationship | Integral role of spouse in treatment; examination of spouse's role in patient's predisposition to depression and effects of illness on marriage |

Table from T B Karasu: Toward a clinical model of psychotherapy for depression: I. Systematic comparison of three psychotherapies. Am J Psychiatry *147*: 141, 1990. Used with permission.

**Table 15.1–27**
**Nonselective and Selective Patient Variables for Psychotherapy for Depression**

| Nonselective Patient Variables | Selective Patient Variables | | |
| --- | --- | --- | --- |
| | Psychodynamic Therapy | Cognitive Therapy | Interpersonal Therapy |
| Feelings of hopelessness and helplessness<br>Apathy, decreased enjoyment, diminished desire or gratification<br>Too high ego ideals and expectations<br>Oversleeping, morbid dreams or nightmares<br>Feelings of restlessness or being slowed down<br>Lack of motivation or will<br>Low self-esteem, inappropriate or excessive guilt and self-reproach<br>Distractibility, sluggish thinking or decision making<br>Wish or intention to be dead<br>Social withdrawal, fear of rejection or failure<br>Psychosomatic complaints, hypochondriasis | Long-term sense of emptiness and underestimation of self-worth<br>Loss or long separation in childhood<br>Conflicts in past relationships (e.g., with parent, sexual partner)<br>Capacity for insight<br>Ability to modulate regression<br>Access to dreams and fantasy<br>Little need for direction and guidance<br>Stable environment | Obvious distorted thoughts about self, world, and future<br>Pragmatic (logical) thinking<br>Real inadequacies (including poor response to other psychotherapies)<br>Moderate to high need for direction and guidance<br>Responsiveness to behavioral training and self-help (high degree of self-control) | Recent, focused dispute with spouse or significant other<br>Social or communication problems<br>Recent role transition or life change<br>Abnormal grief reaction<br>Modest to moderate need for direction and guidance<br>Responsiveness to environmental manipulation (available support network) |

Table from T B Karasu: Toward a clinical model of psychotherapy for depression: II. An integrative and selective treatment approach. Am J Psychiatry *147*: 275, 1990. Used with permission.

**Table 15.1–28**
**Advantages and Limitations of Three Psychotherapeutic Approaches to Depression**

| Feature | Psychodynamic Approach | Cognitive Approach | Interpersonal Approach |
| --- | --- | --- | --- |
| Theory<br>  Advantages | Individual depth approach encourages patient to look inward for solutions, rather than depending on external sources | Cognitive-behavioral orientation is tangible and objective | Interpersonal orientation addresses broader (e.g., social, family) context, useful in focusing on man-woman relations |
|   Limitations | Focus on intrapsychic phenomena may obscure other (e.g., interpersonal, environmental) factors; aggression-depression theory can be overgeneralized and lead to overreliance on catharsis | Cognitive-behavioral emphasis may neglect whole person, especially affective component; symptom-oriented perspective overlooks past history, complex problem areas, and hidden conflicts | Emphasis on four designated interpersonal problems can bias toward preconceived themes; interpersonal orientation may stress marital/family factors while underplaying intrapsychic forces |
| Goals<br>  Advantages | Enduring structural change transcends symptomatic relief; strengthened adaptive capacities can be useful beyond specific depressive pathology | Primary goal of symptom relief is expedient in itself and is first stage in changing cognitive style | Improvement of interpersonal relations is expedient in itself and may also result in relief of symptoms |
|   Limitations | Personality alteration can be too ambitious and may be unnecessary or excessive for most depression diagnoses | Symptom reduction may be insufficient, superficial, or temporary; focus on current problems can preclude enduring modification of personality or prophylactic function of treatment | Symptom relief may be fragile and temporary if it is highly dependent on external factors |
| Structure<br>  Advantages | Indefinite duration allows long-term or flexible goals[a] | Brief or fixed duration is cost-effective and can foster results in short period, may heighten expectation of rapid change and encourage optimism | Predetermined duration is cost-effective; approach reengages family and may have preventive effect |
|   Limitations | Long-term or open-ended treatment is uneconomical and difficult to evaluate[a] | Short or predetermined duration may be insufficient or inflexible | Time limitation predetermines the extent of personal growth and independence |
| Therapist role<br>  Advantages | Neutral, accepting stance ensures nonjudgmental attitude and | Active therapist can directly intervene to interrupt | Therapist position between activity and reactivity can reassure |

| Feature | Psychodynamic Approach | Cognitive Approach | Interpersonal Approach |
|---|---|---|---|
| Limitations | objectivity; receptive listening encourages transference formation and ensuing analytic process<br><br>Transference regression can produce overidealization of therapist and underestimation of patient self-worth; therapist silence may be misconstrued as rejection, which can perpetuate depression and cause premature termination | depressive schemata and suggest alternatives to faulty thinking<br><br>Active suggestion and direction can undermine patient responsibility and self-esteem by imposing therapist point of view or values | patient and provide supportive person for patient to relate to<br><br>Supportive interpersonal role may encourage dependence and rage at withdrawal of therapist |
| Techniques<br>Advantages | Free association provides verbal catharsis; interpretations provide new understanding of depressogenic conflicts and historical events | Specific approach is directly tailored to depressed population and aims at particular target symptoms; identification of depressogenic assumptions and homework to test new thinking foster cognitive modification | Specific approach is directly tailored to depressed population and can address particular current interpersonal maladaptions |
| Limitations | No specific techniques developed; focus on past events and spontaneous associations may encourage repetitive litany of depressive complaints at the expense of present therapeutic tasks | Emphasis on specific cognitive schemata may bias toward certain preconceived themes; overt simplicity of techniques may lead to underestimation of technical skill required | Identification of specific interpersonal problem areas may be overly restrictive, yet techniques are relatively nonspecific; legitimation of patient sick role may encourage passivity |
| Research status<br>Advantages | Longitudinal case study approach useful for detailed examination and follow-up of individual patients | Operational manual allows for replication of treatment and training and empirical establishment of efficacy | Same as for cognitive approach |
| Limitations | Idiographic approach or anecdotal case history is not amenable to controlled or comparative research | Research-oriented operationalized approach may become oversimplified formula for complex clinical phenomena | Same as for cognitive approach |
| Relation to other modalities<br>Advantages | Integrity of transference is maintained through elimination of outside influences | Competition with pharmacotherapy encourages research on relative efficacy, especially instances when cognitive therapy alone is most effective | Approach designed to be used alone or with drugs; it is especially amenable to combination with marital therapy |
| Limitations | Need for neutrality may limit use of other helpful treatment approaches (e.g., family therapy, drug treatment) | Competition with pharmacotherapy fosters polarization of approaches and partisan resistance to integration with drug treatment | Amenability to additive or eclectic modalities requires integrative theoretical model, clinical expertise in more than one modality, and ability to collaborate with other disciplines, which may lead to role diffusion and insufficient knowledge or training |
| Patient population<br>Advantages | Special patient requisites (e.g., verbal orientation, psychological-mindedness) ensure maximal insight | Logical thinking ensures maximal potential to deal with and change depressogenic assumptions and thought patterns | Orientation toward interpersonal relations, especially marital interaction, can address gender issues in marriage, especially important given high prevalence of women among depressed patients |
| Limitations | Special patient requisites may limit usefulness to verbal, psychological-minded population | Cognitively impaired population may not benefit; sophisticated, introspective patients may find approach too simple-minded or superficial | Interpersonal orientation may overemphasize marriage; primarily female population may bias toward women; conjoint focus may bias against unmarried population |

*a* Advantages and limitations of short-term psychodynamic therapy are similar to those for the cognitive and interpersonal approaches.
Table from T B Karasu: Toward a clinical model of psychotherapy for depression: I. Systematic comparison of three psychotherapies. Am J Psychiatry 147: 142, 1990. Used with permission.

Table 15.1–29
**Indications for Psychotherapy and Pharmacotherapy in the Treatment of Depression**

| Variable | Indication for Treatment[a] | |
| --- | --- | --- |
| | Pharmacotherapy | Psychotherapy |
| Symptom criteria for major depressive episode | | |
| Depressed mood | Marked vegetative signs; extreme or uncontrolled mood | Mild to moderate situational or characterological depressed mood |
| Diminished interest or pleasure | Anhedonia; loss of libido; impaired sexual function or performance | Apathy, decreased enjoyment; diminished sexual desire or gratification |
| Weight loss or gain | Significant weight loss | Insignificant weight gain |
| Insomnia or hypersomnia | Early morning wakening | Oversleeping, morbid dreams or nightmares |
| Psychomotor agitation | Hyperactivity or motor retardation | Restlessness or feelings of being slowed down |
| Fatigue or loss of energy (anergia) | Depressive stupor | Lack of motivation or will |
| Feelings of worthlessness or excessive guilt | Nihilistic or self-deprecatory delusions, self-berating auditory hallucinations | Low self-esteem, inappropriate guilt feelings, self-reproach |
| Diminished ability to think or concentrate, indecisiveness | Loss of control over thinking, obsessive rumination, inability to focus or act | Distractibility, sluggish thinking or decision making; negative cognitions |
| Recurrent thoughts of death or suicide | Acute, episodic, and uncontrolled suicidal acts or plans[b] | Chronic feelings of hopelessness or helplessness[c] |
| Associated features | Panic (anxiety) attacks or phobias; persecutory delusions; pseudodementia; physical symptoms or somatic delusions | Social withdrawal or fears of rejection or failure; psychosomatic complaints or hypochondriasis |
| Family history | Genetic loading (bipolar disorder or depressive disorder) | No genetic loading (dysthymic disorder) |
| Predisposing factors | Other mental disorders, e.g., schizophrenia, alcohol dependence, anorexia nervosa | Psychosocial stressors, e.g., loss of significant other, change in status or role |
| Personality disorders | Borderline, histrionic, obsessive-compulsive | Dependent, inadequate, masochistic |

[a] These are not mutually exclusive categories.
[b] Hospitalization may be required.
[c] Medication may also be useful.
Table from T B Karasu: Toward a clinical model of psychotherapy for depression: II. An integrative and selective treatment approach. Am J Psychiatry *147*: 274, 1990. Used with permission.

Table 15.1–30
**Approach to Pharmacotherapy of Three Psychotherapies for Depression**

| Feature of Combined Treatment | Psychodynamic Therapy | Cognitive Therapy | Interpersonal Therapy |
| --- | --- | --- | --- |
| Basic stance | Medication is avoided except in life-threatening situation, used judiciously for severe vegetative signs | Pharmacotherapy and cognitive therapy alone are in ongoing competition, but drugs are used in case of poor response to cognitive therapy and for breaking psychotherapeutic impasses in severe depression when symptomatic relief is required | Interpersonal therapy and pharmacotherapy are considered having different effects and response timetables (early drug effects on vegetative symptoms, later psychotherapy effects on suicidal ideation, work, and interests) |
| Techniques | Personal (unconscious and conscious) meanings are explored and interpreted within therapy session | Information and rationale for use is provided; special tasks are assigned to increase adherence, e.g., postsession homework (lists of side effects); phone contact with therapist is encouraged | Information and rationale for use is provided, in line with medical model; time is set aside in each session to discuss pharmacological issues |

Table from T B Karasu: Toward a clinical model of psychotherapy for depression: II. An integrative and selective treatment approach. Am J Psychiatry *147*: 272, 1990. Used with permission.

the NIMH Treatment of Depression Collaborative Research Program, found that pharmacotherapy, either alone or with psychotherapy, may be the treatment of choice for patients with severe major depressive episodes.

**Interpersonal therapy.** Interpersonal therapy, developed by Gerald Klerman, focuses on one or two of the patient's current interpersonal problems, using two assumptions: First, current interpersonal problems are likely to have their roots in early dysfunctional relationships. Second, current interpersonal problems are likely to be involved in precipitating or perpetuating the current depressive symptoms. Several controlled trials have compared interpersonal therapy, cognitive therapy, pharmacotherapy, and the combination of pharmacotherapy with psychotherapy. Those trials indicated that interpersonal therapy is effective in the treatment of major depressive disorder and may, not surprisingly, be specifically helpful in addressing interpersonal problems. The data are less solid regarding the efficacy of interpersonal therapy in the treatment of severe major depressive episodes, although some data indicate that interpersonal therapy may be the most effective modality for severe major depressive episodes when the treatment choice is psychotherapy alone.

The interpersonal therapy program usually consists of 12 to 16 weekly sessions. The therapy is characterized by an active, therapeutic approach. Intrapsychic phenomena, such as defense mechanisms and internal conflicts, are not addressed in the therapy. Discrete behaviors—such as lack of assertiveness, impaired social skills, and distorted thinking—may be addressed but only in the context of their meaning or their effect on interpersonal relationships.

**Behavior therapy.** Behavior therapy is based on the hypothesis that maladaptive behavioral patterns result in a person's receiving little positive feedback from society and perhaps outright rejection. By addressing maladaptive behaviors in therapy, patients learn to function in the world in such a way that they receive positive reinforcement. Behavior therapy for major depressive disorder has not been the subject of many controlled studies as yet, although individual and group therapies have been studied. The data to date indicate that behavior therapy is an effective treatment modality for major depressive disorder.

**Psychoanalytically oriented therapy.** The psychoanalytic approach to mood disorders is based on the psychoanalytic theories about depression and mania. In general, the goal of psychoanalytic psychotherapy is to effect a change in the patient's personality structure or character, not simply to alleviate symptoms. Improvements in interpersonal trust, intimacy, coping mechanisms, the capacity to grieve, and the ability to experience a wide range of emotions are some of the aims of psychoanalytic therapy. Treatment often requires the patient to experience heightened anxiety and distress during the course of therapy, which may continue for several years.

**Family therapy.** Family therapy is not generally viewed as a primary therapy for the treatment of major depressive disorder, but increasing evidence indicates that helping a patient with a mood disorder reduce stress and cope with stress can reduce the chance of a relapse. Family therapy is indicated if the disorder jeopardizes the patient's marriage or family functioning or if the mood disorder is promoted or maintained by the family situation. Family therapy examines the role of the mood-disordered member in the overall psychological well-being of the whole family; it also examines the role of the entire family in the maintenance of the patient's symptoms. Patients with mood disorders have a high rate of divorce, and about 50 percent of all spouses report that they would not have married the patient or had children if they had known that the patient was going to have a mood disorder.

## Pharmacotherapy

Although the specific, short-term psychotherapies (for example, interpersonal therapy and cognitive therapy) have influenced the treatment approaches to major depressive disorder, the pharmacotherapeutic approach to mood disorders has revolutionized their treatment and has dramatically affected the courses of mood disorders and reduced their inherent costs to society.

The physician must integrate pharmacotherapy with psychotherapeutic interventions. If physicians view mood disorders as fundamentally evolving from psychodynamic issues, their ambivalence about the use of drugs may result in a poor response, noncompliance, and probably inadequate dosages for too short a treatment period. Alternatively, if physicians ignore the psychosocial needs of the patient, the outcome of pharmacotherapy may be compromised.

**Major depressive disorder.** Effective and specific treatments (for example, tricyclic drugs) have been available for the treatment of major depressive disorder for 40 years. The use of specific pharmacotherapy approximately doubles the chance that a depressed patient will recover in one month. Several problems remain in the treatment of major depressive disorder: some patients do not respond to the first treatment; all currently available antidepressants take three to four weeks to exert significant therapeutic effects, although they may begin to show their effects earlier; and, until relatively recently, all available antidepressants have been toxic in overdoses and have had adverse effects. Now, however, the introduction of bupropion (Wellbutrin) and the serotonin-specific reuptake inhibitors (SSRIs)—for example, fluoxetine, paroxetine (Paxil), and sertraline (Zoloft)—gives clinicians drugs that are much safer and much better tolerated than previous drugs but that are equally effective. Recent indications (for example, eating disorders and anxiety disorders) for antidepressant medications make the grouping of those drugs under the single label of antidepressants somewhat confusing.

The principal indication for antidepressants is a major depressive episode. The first symptoms to improve are often poor sleep and appetite patterns, although that may be less true when SSRIs are used than when tricyclic drugs are used. Agitation, anxiety, depressive episodes, and hopelessness are the next symptoms to improve. Other target symptoms include low energy, poor concentration, helplessness, and decreased libido.

PATIENT EDUCATION. Adequate patient education regarding the use of antidepressants is as critical to treatment success as is choosing the most appropriate drug and dosage. When introducing the topic of a drug trial to the patient, the physician should emphasize that major depressive disorder is a combination of biological and psychological factors, and all benefit from drug therapy. The physician should also stress that the patient will not become addicted to antidepressants, because those drugs do not give immediate gratification. The physician should tell the patient that it will probably take three to four weeks for the effects of the antidepressant to be felt and that, even if the patient shows no improvement at that time, other medications are available. The physician should explain the expected side effects in detail; some clinicians say that the appearance of side effects shows that the drug is working. With tricyclic drugs and monoamine oxidase inhibitors, the physician may find it useful to tell the patient that sleep and appetite will improve first, followed by a sense of returned energy, and that the feeling of depression, unfortunately, will be the last symptom to change.

The physician must always consider the risk of suicide in mood disorder patients. Most antidepressants are lethal if taken in large amounts. It is unwise to give most mood disorder patients large prescriptions when they are discharged from the hospital unless another person will monitor the drug's administration.

ALTERNATIVES TO DRUG TREATMENT. Two organic therapies that are alternatives to pharmacotherapy are electroconvulsive therapy and phototherapy. Electroconvulsive therapy (ECT) is generally used when (1) the patient is unresponsive to pharmacotherapy, (2) the patient cannot tolerate pharmacotherapy, or (3) the clinical situation is so severe that the rapid improvement seen with ECT is needed. Although the use of ECT is often limited to those three situations, it is an effective antidepressant treatment and can be reasonably considered as the treatment of choice in some patients, such as elderly depressed persons. Phototherapy is a novel treatment that has been used with patients with a seasonal pattern to their mood disorder. Phototherapy can be used alone for patients with mild cases of mood disorder with a seasonal pattern, and it can be used in combination with pharmacotherapy for severely affected patients, although studies of the efficacy of that combination have not yet produced definitive results.

AVAILABLE DRUGS. The tricyclic drugs, the closely related tetracyclic drugs, and the monoamine oxidase inhibitors (MAOIs) are the classic antidepressant drugs. Although those drugs are usually used, the antidepressant armamentarium has been significantly augmented by the addition of the serotonin-specific reuptake inhibitors (SSRIs) and bupropion. Both the SSRIs and bupropion are generally much safer (particularly the SSRIs) than either tricyclic drugs or MAOIs, and they have been shown to be equally effective in studies of depressed outpatients. Other atypical antidepressants include trazodone (Desyrel) and alprazolam (Xanax). The sympathomimetics (for example, amphetamine) are also indicated for the treatment of major depressive disorder in special therapeutic situations.

CYCLIC NOMENCLATURE. The use of "cyclic" nomenclature, as in "tricyclic" and "tetracyclic," can lead to confusion because of the lack of common agreement regarding the terms. Various antidepressant drugs have been developed that are monocyclics (or unicyclics), dicyclics (or bicyclics), tricyclics, and tetracyclics. Sometimes the drugs are grouped together as the heterocyclics, although doing so leads to the improper grouping of unrelated compounds.

PHARMACOLOGICAL ACTIONS. The currently available antidepressants vary in their pharmacological effects. The variation is the basis for the observation that individual patients may respond to one antidepressant but not another. The variation is also the basis for the differing side effects seen with antidepressants. The most basic differentiation among the available antidepressants is whether they have their major short-term pharmacodynamic effects at reuptake sites or at the level of enzyme inhibition of monoamine oxidase. Among the drugs that effect neurotransmitter reuptake, the currently available drugs variously effect the reuptake of norepinephrine or serotonin or both. Table 15.1–31 lists the norepinephrine, serotonin, and dopamine reuptake potencies of a range of currently available drugs. Dopamine reuptake is considered in the table because of its possible relation to the therapeutic effects of bupropion. Table 15.1–32 lists the affinities of a range of currently available drugs for specific neurotransmitter receptors. The table lists the short-term effects; some of the effects of long-term administration on neurotransmitter receptors are listed in Table 15.1–2. The primary effects of specific receptor blockade are the production of adverse effects; the associations between specific receptor blockade and adverse effects are listed in Table 15.1–33.

CHOICE OF DRUG. Because of the many antidepressant drugs now available on the commercial market, the physician faces many clinical considerations in the choice of a first-line drug (Table 15.1–34). In the treatment of all mental disorders, the best reason for choosing a particular drug is a history of a good response to that agent by the patient or a family member. If such information is not available, the choice of a drug is based principally on the adverse effects of the drug (Table 15.1–35). The clinician must consider both the severity and the frequency of potential adverse effects when using side effects as the basis for choosing among available antidepressants.

Most clinicians choose either one of the tricyclic or tetracyclic drugs or one of the SSRIs as the first-line drug in the treatment of major depressive disorder. Tricyclic and tetracyclic drugs are often chosen because of the level of the clinician's comfort with those old drugs. They are also less expensive than the new drugs, because most of the tricyclic and tetracyclic drugs are available in generic formulations. SSRIs are frequently chosen by clinicians whose experience supports the research data that SSRIs are as efficacious as the tricyclic and tetracyclic drugs and are much better tolerated. The tricyclic and tetracyclic drugs also differ in their side-effect profiles, with nortriptyline (Aventyl), desipramine, and protriptyline (Vivactil)—that is, the secondary amine tricyclic and tetracyclic drugs—generally having a more benign side-effect profile than the tertiary tricyclic and tetracyclic drugs (for example, imipramine).

As first-line drugs, the MAOIs, the sympathomimetics, and other atypical drugs (for example, alprazolam, trazodone, and bupropion) are chosen less often than the tricyclic and tetracyclic drugs and the SSRIs. The MAOIs are usually not chosen as first-line drugs because of their association with tyramine-induced hypertensive crises, which are caused when a patient taking conventional MAOIs ingests certain drugs or foods with a high tyramine

**Table 15.1–31**
**Antidepressant Potencies* for Blockade of Norepinephrine Uptake Into Rat Brain Synaptosome**

| Variable | Norepinephrine (NE) Uptake Potency | Serotonin (5-HT) Uptake Potency | NE/5-HT Selectivity | Dopamine Uptake Potency |
|---|---|---|---|---|
| Drug | | | | |
| Amitriptyline | 4.2 | 1.5 | 2.8 | 0.043 |
| Amoxapine | 23 | 0.21 | 110 | 0.053 |
| Bupropion | 0.043 | 0.0064 | 6.8 | 0.16 |
| Clomipramine | 3.6 | 18 | 0.19 | 0.057 |
| Desipramine | 110 | 0.29 | 3.8 | 0.019 |
| Doxepin | 5.3 | 0.36 | 15 | 0.018 |
| Fluoxetine | 0.36 | 8.3 | 0.043 | 0.063 |
| Imipramine | 7.7 | 2.4 | 3.2 | 0.020 |
| Maprotiline | 14 | 0.030 | 470 | 0.034 |
| Nortriptyline | 25 | 0.38 | 65 | 0.059 |
| Protriptyline | 100 | 0.36 | 29 | 0.054 |
| Trazodone | 0.020 | 0.53 | 0.038 | 0.0070 |
| Trimipramine | 0.20 | 0.040 | 4.9 | 0.029 |
| Reference compounds | | | | |
| d-Amphetamine | 2.00 | | | 1.2 |
| Cocaine | 0.65 | | | 0.37 |

*$10^{-7} \times 1/K$ = inhibitor constant in molarity. The larger the number, the more potent is the drug. Data can be compared both vertically and horizontally to find the most potent drug for a specific property and to find the most potent property of a specific drug.
Table from E Richelson: Biological basis of depression and therapeutic relevance. J Clin Psychiatry 52: 6, 1991. Used with permission.

**Table 15.1–32**
**Antidepressant Affinities for Neurotransmitter Receptors of Human Brain***

| Variable | Histamine $H_1$ Affinity | Muscarinic Affinity | $\alpha_1$-Adrenoceptor Affinity | $\alpha_2$-Adrenoceptor Affinity | Dopamine $D_2$ Affinity | 5-HT$_{1a}$ Affinity | 5-HT$_2$ Affinity |
|---|---|---|---|---|---|---|---|
| Drug | | | | | | | |
| Amitriptyline | 91 | 5.6 | 3.70 | 0.106 | 0.10 | 0.526 | 3.4 |
| Amoxapine | 4.0 | 0.10 | 2.00 | 0.038 | 0.62 | 0.455 | 170 |
| Bupropion | 0.015 | 0.0021 | 0.0217 | 0.0012 | 0.00048 | 0.00059 | 0.0011 |
| Clomipramine | 3.2 | 2.70 | 2.63 | 0.031 | 0.53 | 0.014 | 3.7 |
| Desipramine | 0.91 | 0.50 | 0.77 | 0.014 | 0.030 | 0.010 | 0.36 |
| Doxepin | 420 | 1.2 | 4.17 | 0.091 | 0.042 | 0.345 | 4.0 |
| Fluoxetine | 0.016 | 0.050 | 0.0169 | 0.0077 | 0.015 | 0.0042 | 0.48 |
| Imipramine | 9.1 | 1.1 | 1.11 | 0.031 | 0.050 | 0.011 | 1.2 |
| Maprotiline | 50 | 0.18 | 1.11 | 0.011 | 0.29 | 0.0083 | 0.83 |
| Nortriptyline | 10 | 0.67 | 1.67 | 0.040 | 0.083 | 0.323 | 2.3 |
| Proptriptyline | 4.0 | 4.0 | 0.77 | 0.015 | 0.043 | 0.026 | 1.5 |
| Trazodone | 0.29 | 0.00031 | 2.78 | 0.204 | 0.026 | 1.695 | 13 |
| Trimipramine | 370 | 1.7 | 4.17 | 0.147 | 0.56 | 0.012 | 3.1 |
| Reference compounds | | | | | | | |
| Diphenhydramine | 7.1 | | | | | | |
| Atropine | | 42 | | | | | |
| Phentolamine | | | 6.7 | 2.3 | | | |
| Yohimbine | | | | 62 | | | |
| Haloperidol | | | | | 26 | | |
| Busipirone | | | | | | 26 | |
| Methysergide | | | | | | | 15 |

*Antidepressant affinities: $10^{-7} \times 1/K_d$, where $K_d$ = equilibrium dissociation constant in molarity. The larger the number, the more potent is the drug. Data can be computed both vertically and horizontally to find the most potent drug for a specific property and to find the most potent property of a specific drug.
Table from E Richelson: Biological basis of depression and therapeutic relevance. J Clin Psychiatry 52 (6, Suppl): 7, 1991. Used with permission.

content Although that adverse interaction can be avoided by the patient's following simple dietary guidelines, the potentially life-threatening nature of a hypertensive crisis and the need for dietary restrictions limit the acceptability of MAOIs. The sympathomimetics are rarely used as first-line drugs because of their high potential for abuse. Alprazolam, a benzodiazepine, is not a common first-line drug because of its potential for sedation, motor impair-

ment, and abuse. Trazodone as a first-line drug is limited by its significant sedative properties and its association with priapism in men. Although bupropion is basically a safe and effective antidepressant drug, its association with seizures when used incorrectly may have inappropriately limited its choice as a first-line drug.

ADVERSE EFFECTS. One of the most serious concerns regarding antidepressants is their lethality when taken in

**Table 15.1–33**
**Possible Clinical Consequences of Some Pharmacological Properties of Antidepressants**

| Property | Possible Clinical Consequences |
| --- | --- |
| Blockade of norepinephrine uptake at nerve endings | Tremors<br>Tachycardia<br>Insomnia<br>Erectile and ejaculatory dysfunction<br>Blockade of the antihypertensive effects of guanethidine (Ismelin and Esimil) and guanadrel (Hylorel)<br>Augmentation of pressor effects of sympathomimetic amines |
| Blockade of serotonin uptake at nerve endings | Gastrointestinal disturbances<br>Increase or decrease in anxiety (dose-dependent)<br>Sexual dysfunction<br>Extrapyramidal side effects<br>Interactions with L-tryptophan, monoamine oxidase inhibitors, fenfluramine |
| Blockade of dopamine uptake at nerve endings | Improvement of parkinsonism<br>Aggravation of psychosis |
| Blockade of histamine $II_1$ receptors | Potentiation of central depressant drugs<br>Sedation drowsiness<br>Weight gain<br>Hypotension |
| Blockade of muscarinic receptors | Blurred vision<br>Dry mouth<br>Sinus tachycardia<br>Constipation<br>Urinary retention<br>Memory dysfunction |
| Blockade of $\alpha_1$-adrenoceptors | Potentiation of the antihypertensive effect of prazosin (Minipress) and terazosin (Hytrin)<br>Postural hypotension, dizziness<br>Reflex tachycardia |
| Blockade of $\alpha_1$-adrenoceptors | Blockade of the antihypertensive effects of clonidine (Catapres), guanabenz (Wytensin), $\alpha$-methyldopa (Aldomet), and guanfacine (Tenex)<br>Priapism |
| Blockade of dopamine $D_2$ receptors | Extrapyramidal movement disorders<br>Endocrine changes<br>Sexual dysfunction (males) |
| Blockade of serotonin 5-$HT_1$ receptors | Ejaculatory disturbances |
| Blockade of serotonin 5-$HT_2$ | Hypotension<br>Prevention of migraine headaches |

Table from E Richelson: Biological basis of depression and therapeutic relevance. J Clin Psychiatry 52: (6, Suppl): 8, 1991. Used with permission.

overdoses. Tricyclic and tetracyclic drugs are, by far, the most lethal of the antidepressants; the SSRIs, bupropion, trazodone, and the MAOIs are much safer, although even those drugs can be lethal when taken in overdose in combination with alcohol or other drugs. Another concern is the cardiac safety of antidepressants. Again, tricyclic and tetracyclic drugs are generally the least safe; the SSRIs, bupropion, trazodone, and the MAOIs are significantly safer than tricyclic and tetracyclic drugs. Hypotension is a potentially serious adverse effect of many antidepressants, particularly in the elderly; among the conventional antidepressants, amoxapine (Asendin), maprotiline (Ludiomil), nortriptyline, and trazodone are associated with little hypotension, and bupropion and the SSRIs are associated with the least hypotension. One set of adverse effects that many clinicians inappropriately ignore are the sexual adverse effects of antidepressants. Almost all the antidepressants, except bupropion, have been associated with decreased libido, erectile dysfunction, or anorgasmia.

The serotonergic drugs are probably more closely associated with sexual adverse effects than are the noradrenergic compounds.

TYPE-SPECIFIC TREATMENTS. Some clinical types of major depressive episodes may have varying responses to particular antidepressants. For example, major depressive disorder patients with atypical features (sometimes called hysteroid dysphoria) may preferentially respond to treatment with MAOIs. Two other specific groups are depressed bipolar I disorder patients and patients with major depressive episodes with psychotic features.

Lithium is a potential first-line pharmacological agent in treating depression in bipolar I disorder patients and in some major depressive disorder patients with a marked periodicity to their disorder. Bipolar I disorder patients who are being treated with conventional antidepressants must be observed carefully for the emergence of manic symptoms.

Antidepressants alone are not likely to be effective in

**Table 15.1–34**
**Considerations When Selecting an Antidepressant: Comparison of Classes**

| Consideration | Tricyclic and Tetracyclic Drugs (e.g., nortriptyline) | SSRIs (e.g., sertraline) | Triazolopyridines (i.e., trazodone) | Aminoketones (i.e., bupropion) | MAOIs (e.g., tranylcypromine) |
|---|---|---|---|---|---|
| Likelihood of response | High | Equivalent to tricyclic in outpatients | Possibly less than tricyclics | Less than tricyclics | Less than tricyclics |
| Unique spectrum of activity | Can work in SSRI failures | Can work in tricyclic failures | None shown | Can work in tricyclic failures | Can work in tricyclic failures |
| Maintenance of response | Evidence from controlled studies | Evidence from controlled studies | None shown | None shown | None shown |
| Safety | Serious systemic toxicity can result from overdose (either heavy ingestion or gradual accumulation because of slow clearance) | No serious systemic toxicity shown | Minimal serious systemic toxicity because of acute overdose | Seizures as primary acute systemic toxicity because of acute overdose; easily managed in medical setting | Serious systemic toxicity can result from heavy ingestion |
| Tolerability | Generally good with secondary amine tricyclics, much superior to tertiary amine tricyclics | Generally good, especially if dosage is kept to effective minimum dosage | Sedation and cognitive slowing are frequently problems, even at effective minimum dosage | Generally good, especially if dosage is kept to effective minimum dosage | Generally good except for the occurrence of hypotension and the need for dietary restrictions |
| Pharmacokinetic interactions | Can be affected by other drugs (e.g., SSRIs) to a clinically significant extent but do not affect other drugs | Can inhibit oxidative metabolism of a variety of drugs but considerable differences among class in terms of magnitude and duration of effect; no known clinically significant effect of other drugs on SSRIs | Neither affected by other drugs nor affect other drugs in a clinically significant way | Can be affected by some SSRIs (e.g., fluoxetine) and possibly others in a clinically significant way; no known effect on the metabolism of other drugs | Neither affected by other drugs nor affect other drugs in a clinically significant way |
| Pharmacodynamic interactions | Multiple because of large number of effects of tricyclics; can be agonistic (additive or potentiating) or antagonistic; such interactions are more likely and more significant with tertiary as opposed to secondary amines | See MAOI interaction; may occur with other serotonin agonists; fluoxetine can have agonistic interaction with dopamine agonists in terms of extrapyramidal effects; minimal experience with sertraline in this regard | Can have interactions with other agents that decrease arousal or impair cognitive performance; can interact with adrenergic agents affecting blood pressure regulation; complex interactions with other serotonin-active agents | Can have interactions with dopamine agonists and antagonists | Clinically significant interactions with: Tyramine and sympathomimetic agents on blood pressure Serotonin-active agents inducing the central serotonin syndrome |
| Physician confidence | Excellent because of extensive data base in terms of human exposure (e.g., patient-years of exposure, total number of patients exposed, variety of patients exposed) | Excellent primarily because of efficacy and safety profile; less extensive data base in terms of human exposure compared with tricyclics but rapidly expanding | Satisfactory because of substantial data base in terms of human exposure; concerns are with spectrum of activity and tolerability | Reserved because of less extensive data base concerning human exposure coupled with concerns about safety caused by seizure risk | Caution because of safety concerns primarily about patient compliance with dietary restrictions |

*Continued*

**Table 15.1–34**
*Continued*

| Consideration | Tricyclic and Tetracyclic Drugs (e.g., nortriptyline) | SSRIs (e.g., sertraline) | Triazolopyridines (i.e., trazodone) | Aminoketones (i.e., bupropion) | MAOIs (e.g., tranylcypromine) |
|---|---|---|---|---|---|
| Ease of administration | Excellent, generally can be administered once a day | Excellent for sertraline because of once-a-day administration; good for fluoxetine typically administered once a day, but long half-life of parent compound and active metabolite makes dosage difficult and has a long carryover effect | Satisfactory but require multiple dosing for antidepressant effect | Satisfactory but require multiple dosing for antidepressant effect | Satisfactory but clinical practice generally is to give in divided doses |

Table from S H Preskorn, M Burke: Somatic therapy for major depressive disorder: Selection of an antidepressant. J Clin Psychiatry 53: (9, Suppl): 8, 1992. Used with permission.

**Table 15.1–35**
**Adverse Drug Reaction Profiles**

| Drug and Risk | Nuisance | Moderate Discomfort | Intolerable or Unacceptable |
|---|---|---|---|
| *Fluoxetine* | | | |
| Frequent | Nausea | Anxiety<br>Insomnia | |
| Occasional | | Sedation<br>Decreased libido<br>Headaches | |
| Rare | Anorexia | Rash<br>Flatulence<br>Anorgasmia<br>Weight gain<br>Impotence | Vomiting |
| *Bupropion* | | | |
| Frequent | | | |
| Occasional | Nausea<br>Jitteriness<br>Insomnia | Anxiety | |
| Rare | | Sexual dysfunction<br>Cognitive difficulties | Seizure |
| *Tertiary Amines: Imipramine, Amitriptyline, Doxepine, and Trimipramine* | | | |
| Frequent | Sedation<br>Dry mouth | Constipation | |
| Occasional | Light-headedness<br>Dizziness<br>Urinary hesitancy | Severe constipation<br>Sweating<br>Weight gain of 10 lbs<br>Tachycardia<br>Urinary hesitancy<br>Skin rash<br>Blurry vision | Fainting, falling |
| Rare | | Pain on ejaculation<br>Memory problems<br>Severe blurry vision<br>Tremor<br>Agitation, akithisia | Seizures<br>Urinary blockade<br>Paralytic ilcus<br>Delirium<br>Mania |

| Drug and Risk | Severity | | |
|---|---|---|---|
| | Nuisance | Moderate Discomfort | Intolerable or Unacceptable |
| *Secondary Amines: Nortriptyline, Desipramine, and Protriptyline* | | | |
| Frequent | Mild dry mouth | Tremor Tachycardia | |
| Occasional | Dry mouth Dizziness | Jitteriness Anxiety Constipation Sweating | |
| Rare | | Sedation Rash Urinary hesitancy | Seizures Memory problems Mania |
| *Monoamine Oxidase Inhibitors: Phenelzine, Tranylcypromine, and Isocarboxozid* | | | |
| Frequent | Insomnia | Weight gain | |
| Occasional | Daytime sedation | Light-headedness Anorgasmia Decreased blood pressure | Hypertension episode |
| Rare | | Profuse sweating Dry mouth Urinary hesitancy | Fainting Liver toxicity Hypertensive crisis Cerebrovascular disease Mania |
| *Trazodone* | | | |
| Frequent | | Sedation | |
| Occasional | Dry mouth Constipation Light-headedness | Nausea Headache Flulike malaise | Vomiting |
| Rare | | Weight gain | Fainting Priapism Mania |

Table from A A Nierenberg, J O Cole: Antidepressant adverse drug reactions. J Clin Psychiatry *52*: 45, 1991. Used with permission.

the treatment of major depressive episodes with psychotic features. One exception may be amoxapine, an antidepressant closely related to loxapine (Loxitane), an antipsychotic. The usual practice, however, is to use a combination of an antidepressant and an antipsychotic. Several studies have also shown that electroconvulsive therapy (ECT) is effective for that indication—perhaps more effective than pharmacotherapy.

GENERAL CLINICAL GUIDELINES. The most common clinical mistake leading to an unsuccessful trial of an antidepressant drug is the use of too low a dosage for too short a time. Table 15.1–36 lists the guidelines for determining the quality of trials as definite or probable in terms of the certainty with which one can conclude that the trial was adequate. Unless adverse events prevent it, the dosage of an antidepressant should be raised to the maximum recommended level and maintained at that level for at least four weeks before a drug trial can be considered unsuccessful. Alternatively, if a patient is improving clinically on a low dosage of the drug, that dosage should not be raised unless clinical improvement stops before the maximal benefit is obtained. If a patient does not begin to respond to appropriate dosages of a drug after two or three weeks, the clinician may decide to obtain a plasma concentration of the drug if the test is available for the particular drug being used. The test may indicate either noncompliance or particularly unusual pharmacokinetic

disposition of the drug, thereby suggesting an alternative dosage.

DURATION AND PROPHYLAXIS. Antidepressant treatment should be maintained for at least six months or the length of a previous episode, whichever is greater. Several studies show that prophylactic treatment with antidepressants is effective in reducing the number and the severity of recurrences (Figure 15.1–5). One study concluded that, if episodes are less than 2½ years apart, prophylactic treatment for five years is probably indicated. Another factor suggesting prophylactic treatment is the seriousness of previous depressive episodes. Episodes that have involved significant suicidal ideation or impairment of psychosocial functioning may indicate that the clinician should consider prophylactic treatment. When antidepressants are stopped, they should be tapered gradually over one to two weeks, depending on the half-life of the particular compound.

FAILURE OF DRUG TRIAL. If the first antidepressant drug has been used for an adequate trial and, if appropriate, the clinician is sure that adequate plasma concentrations were obtained, two options face the clinician—augmenting the drug with lithium, liothyronine (T₃ or L-triiodothyronine) (Cytomel), or L-tryptophan or switching to an alternative primary agent (Figure 15.1–6). A now rarely used strategy is the combination of a tricyclic or tetracyclic drug with an MAOI. When switching agents, the clinician should switch a patient who has been taking a tricyclic or

**Table 15.1–36**
**Criteria for Adequacy of Antidepressant Trials**

| | Criteria | |
|---|---|---|
| | **Definite Trials with Durations ≥6 wk** | **Probable Trials with Duration ≥4 and <6 wk** |
| **Antidepressant** | **Daily Dose** | **Daily Dose** |
| Tricyclics | | |
|   Imipramine, desipramine | ≥250 mg or plasma levels of desipramine ≥125 mg/mL and of imipramine ≥200 ng/mL | 200–249 mg |
|   Nortriptyline | ≥100 mg or plasma levels between 50 and 150 ng/mL | 75–99 mg |
|   Amitriptyline, doxepin | ≥250 mg | 200–249 mg |
|   Maprotiline | ≥200 mg | 150–199 mg |
|   Protriptyline | >60 mg | 40–59 mg |
| Monoamine oxidase inhibitors | | |
|   Phenelzine | ≥60 mg | 45–59 mg |
|   Isocarboxazid or tranylcypromine | >40 mg | 30–39 mg |
| Fluoxetine | ≥20 mg | 5–19 mg |
| Other agents | | |
|   Bupropion | >400 mg | 300–399 mg |
|   Trazodone | ≥300 mg | 200–299 mg |
|   Amoxapine | >300 mg | 200–299 mg |
|   Lithium | plasma levels, 0.7–1.1 mEq/L | plasma levels, 0.4–0.69 mEq/L |
| Electroconvulsive therapy | ≥12 total, with at least six bilateral | ≥9–11 unilateral |

Table from A A Nierenberg: A systematic approach to treatment-resistant depression. J Clin Psychiatry Monogr *10*: 7, 1992. Used with permission.

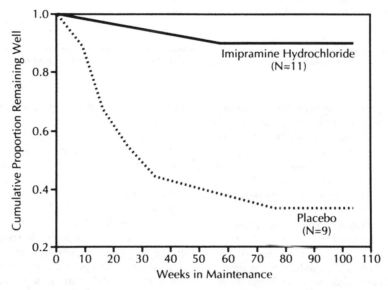

**Figure 15.1–5.** Survival analysis for maintenance therapies in recurrent depression. Difference between the two groups, P = 0.006 by the Mantel-Cox test. (Figure from D J Kupfer, E Frank, J M Perel, C Cornes, A G Mallinger, M E Thase, A B McEachran, V J Grochocinski: Five-year outcome for maintenance therapies in recurrent depression. Arch Gen Psychiatry *49*: 771, 1992. Used with permission.)

tetracyclic drug to an SSRI (or possibly an MAOI) and should switch a patient who has been taking an SSRI to a tricyclic or tetracyclic drug (or possibly an MAOI). At least two weeks should elapse between the use of an SSRI and the use of an MAOI, and the two drugs should never be used concurrently. The clinician can also consider switching a first-line drug nonresponder to trazodone or bupropion.

*Lithium.* Lithium (900 to 1,200 mg a day, serum level between 0.6 and 0.8 mEq per liter) can be added to the antidepressant dosage for 7 to 14 days. That approach converts a significant number of antidepressant nonresponders to responders. The mechanism of action is not known, although the lithium may potentiate the serotonergic neuronal system. Some data indicate that pretreatment with the antidepressant alone is necessary for that

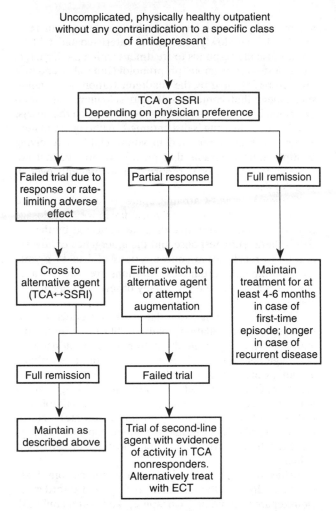

**Figure 15.1-6.** Algorithm for treating patient with major depressive disorder. (Figure from S H Preskorn, M Burke: Somatic therapy for major depressive disorder: Selection of an antidepressant. *J Clin Psychiatry 53* (9, Suppl): 10, 1992. Used with permission.)

effect and that starting the treatment with the two drugs simultaneously is not as effective as starting with an antidepressant and then adding lithium.

*Liothyronine.* The addition of 25 to 50 μg a day of T₃ to an antidepressant regimen for 7 to 14 days may convert antidepressant nonresponders to responders. The adverse effects of T₃ are minor but may include headaches and feeling warm. The mechanism of action for T₃ augmentation is not known, although the modulation of β-adrenergic receptors and the presence of undetectable thyroid axis abnormalities in major depressive disorder have been suggested. If T₃ augmentation is successful, the T₃ should be continued for two months and then tapered at the rate of 12.5 μg a day every three to seven days.

*L-Tryptophan.* L-Tryptophan, the amino acid precursor to serotonin, has been used as an adjuvant both to antidepressant drugs in major depressive disorder and to lithium in bipolar I disorder. L-Tryptophan has also been used alone as an antidepressant and a hypnotic. L-Tryptophan-containing products have been recalled in the United States because of an outbreak of eosinophilia-myalgia syndrome associated with the use of L-tryptophan. The symptoms of

the syndrome include fatigue, myalgia, shortness of breath, rashes, and swelling of the extremities. Congestive heart failure and death can also occur. Although several studies have shown that L-tryptophan is an effective adjuvant in the treatment of mood disorders, the drug should not be used for any purpose until the problem with the syndrome is completely resolved. The syndrome is probably related to a contaminant in a single manufacturing plant, but that has yet to be proved.

*Tricyclic or tetracyclic drug and MAOI combinations.* The combination of a tricyclic or tetracyclic drug and an MAOI is sometimes used for patients who have not responded to several other pharmacological treatments. However, with the availability of a broad range of antidepressants, that combination therapy is rarely used. It is not a treatment of first, second, or even third choice, because of the high incidence of adverse effects. When the combination is used, the clinician should initiate treatment with the two drugs simultaneously at low dosages for each and should then raise the dosages slowly. Imipramine or trimipramine (Surmontil) and an MAOI should not be used in combination because of their high incidence of toxic effects, including restlessness, dizziness, tremulousness, muscle twitching, sweating, convulsions, hyperpyrexia, and sometimes death.

If a patient has been taking a tricyclic or tetracyclic drug, the physician should quarter the dosage of the drug for five to seven days and then slowly add the MAOI to the regimen. If the patient has been taking an MAOI, the physician should stop the drug for two weeks and then start the two drugs simultaneously. The reasons for that strategy are that MAOIs irreversibly inhibit monoamine oxidase and it takes about two weeks for normal MAO activity levels to be achieved.

**Bipolar I disorder.** Whereas the treatment of major depressive disorder has been changed by the introduction of the SSRIs, the treatment of bipolar I disorder has been changed by the many studies that have demonstrated the efficacy of two anticonvulsants—carbamazepine and valproate (Depakene)—in the treatment of manic episodes and probably in the prophylaxis of manic and depressive episodes in bipolar I disorder. Although the data in support of the efficacy of lithium are numerous, sufficient data have accumulated to warrant consideration of the two anticonvulsants as first-line treatments of bipolar I disorder. Such a decision should be based primarily on the compatibility between the patient and the relevant side effects of the drugs. The long-term treatment of bipolar I disorder is an indication for those anticonvulsants, but the initial stages of manic episodes often require the addition of drugs with potent sedative effects. Drugs commonly used at the initiation of therapy for bipolar I disorder include clonazepam (Klonopin) (1 mg every four to six hours), lorazepam (Ativan) (2 mg every four to six hours), and haloperidol (Haldol) (5 mg every two to four hours). The physician should taper those medications and discontinue them as soon as the initial phase of the manic episode has subsided and the effects of the lithium, carbamazepine, or valproate are beginning to be seen clinically.

Whereas lithium and possibly carbamazepine and valproate are the first-line drugs for the treatment of bipolar I disorder, the second-line drugs now include another anticonvulsant (clonazepam), a calcium channel inhibitor (verapamil [Calan]), an $\alpha_2$-adrenergic receptor agonist (clonidine), and antipsychotics (especially clozapine [Clozaril]); electroconvulsive therapy (ECT) is another second-line treatment.

LITHIUM.  Lithium is still the standard treatment of bipolar I disorder. The adverse effects that may limit the use of lithium and cause the clinician to consider using either carbamazepine or valproate include renal effects (thirst, polyuria), nervous system effects (tremor, memory loss), metabolic effects (weight gain), gastrointestinal effects (diarrhea), dermatological effects (acne, psoriasis), and thyroid effects (goiter, myxedema). Of potentially serious concern with lithium treatment are its effects on the kidneys, which can include moderate and occasionally severe impairment of tubular function; uncommon, moderate, and unspecific morphological changes; and, rarely, a nephrotic syndrome. Those many adverse effects require careful monitoring of the patient's renal and thyroid status.

Compliance with lithium treatment is increased with the early initiation of treatment, adequate treatment of concomitant illnesses, treatment of coexisting substance abuse, the early detection and prevention of side effects, and the inclusion of the patient in individual and group psychotherapy. Responsiveness to lithium treatment is improved when adequate lithium levels are maintained, adjunctive medication is used as indicated, and laboratory and clinical monitoring is carried out. Nonresponsiveness to lithium treatment is most likely with severe illness, the presence of schizoaffective disorder symptoms, mixed manic and depressive symptoms, somatic symptoms, alcohol abuse and other substance abuse, rapid cycling, and the absence of a family history of bipolar I disorder.

ANTICONVULSANTS.  As stated above, the efficacy data for carbamazepine and valproate are now sufficient to warrant their consideration as first-line drugs and to warrant their use either as adjuvants to lithium or as alternatives to lithium for patients who are not responsive to lithium alone or who are intolerant of lithium-induced adverse effects. The decision to use carbamazepine or valproate is based on the presence of adverse effects and possibly the price of the prescriptions. Carbamazepine is associated with sedation, nausea, blurred vision, rash, blood dyscrasias, and hyponatremia. Valproate has a relatively benign safety profile, but it is associated with gastrointestinal symptoms, tremor, hair loss, weight gain, and blood dyscrasias. Both valproate and carbamazepine require routine blood monitoring for hepatic and hematological indexes of function.

*Valproate.* A significant number of patients seem to tolerate valproate better than they tolerate lithium and carbamazepine. The initial dosage of valproate in manic patients is usually 20 mg per kg a day, which usually achieves therapeutic blood concentrations of 50 to 150 $\mu$g/mL. Patients who respond usually have significant improvements in their symptoms a week after reaching those blood concentrations. Outpatients usually tolerate a starting dosage of 500 to 1,000 mg a day, depending on the size of the patient. The dosage can then be adjusted upward until therapeutic plasma concentrations are obtained.

The common gastrointestinal problems can usually be minimized by initiating therapy with low dosages, increasing the dosage slowly, and using enteric-coated tablets. Tremor usually responds to treatment with a $\beta$-adrenergic antagonist—for example, propranolol (Inderal)—and hair loss can be lessened by the coadministration of a vitamin supplement that contains zinc and selenium. Thrombocytopenia is usually mild and is reversible when the dosage is reduced or the drug is discontinued. Although fatal hepatoxicity has been reported in young children receiving multiple anticonvulsants that include valproate, that adverse effect has not been reported in any patients over 10 years of age.

*Carbamazepine.* Carbamazepine is usually initiated with dosages in the 200 to 600 mg a day range. The dosage can be increased every five days, as indicated by the patient's therapeutic response and the emergence of adverse effects, to reach serum concentrations of 4 to 15 $\mu$g/mL. Once therapeutic serum concentrations are reached, a favorable clinical response is usually observed in one to two weeks.

The most common dose-related adverse effects of carbamazepine are sedation, nausea, blurred vision, and ataxia. Rash develops in about 10 percent of all patients. Although rash is not an indication to discontinue carbamazepine, other signs of an allergic reaction (for example, bleeding, fever, and joint pain) are important signs that it may be necessary to discontinue the drug. Exfoliative rashes (for example, Stevens-Johnson syndrome), aplastic anemia, agranulocytosis, and thrombocytopenia, although rare, can be potentially fatal complications of carbamazepine.

OTHER AGENTS.  Other drugs that should be considered third-line drugs in the treatment of bipolar I disorder are clonazepam, clonidine, clozapine, and verapamil. Although some studies have found those four compounds effective, the data base to support their routine use in the treatment of bipolar I disorder is not yet as solid as that for lithium, carbamazepine, and valproate. Electroconvulsive therapy is another alternative treatment of bipolar I disorder that may be considered in particularly severe or drug-resistant cases.

RAPID CYCLING.  The development of rapid cycling in bipolar I disorder patients has been associated with the use of conventional antidepressants, especially tricyclic drugs, and with the presence of hypothyroidism. In addition to the use of thyroid treatments—that is, levothyroxine ($T_4$) (Levothroid) 0.3 to 0.5 mg a day—some researchers and clinicians have reported preliminary positive results with the use of other psychopharmacological agents, including bupropion and nimodipine (Nimotop).

MAINTENANCE.  The decision to maintain a patient on lithium (or other drug) prophylaxis is based on the severity of the patient's disorder, the risk of adverse effects from the particular drug, and the quality of the patient's support systems. In general, maintenance treatment is indicated for the prophylaxis of bipolar I disorder in any patient who has had more than one episode. The rationale for that practice is the relative safety of the available drugs, their demonstrated efficacy, and the significant potential for psychosocial problems if another bipolar I disorder episode occurs.

## References

Andreasen N C, Swayze V, Flaum M, Alliger R, Cohen G: Ventricular abnormalities in affective disorder: Clinical and demographic correlates. Am J Psychiatry 147: 893, 1990.

Bauer M S, Whybrow P S: Rapid cycling bipolar affective disorder: II. Treatment of refractory rapid cycling with high-dose levothyroxine: A preliminary study. Arch Gen Psychiatry 47: 435, 1990.

Bauer M S, Whybrow P C: Validity of rapid cycling as a modifier for bipolar disorder in DSM-IV. Depression 1: 11, 1993.

Caldecott-Hazard S, Morgan D G, DeLeon-Jones F, Overstreet D H, Janowsky D: Clinical and biochemical aspects of depressive disorders: II. Transmitter/receptor theories. Synapse 9: 251, 1991.

Cassano G B, Akiskal H S, Savino M, Musetti L, Perugi G: Proposed subtypes of bipolar II and related disorders: With hypomanic episodes (or cyclothymia) and with hyperthymic temperament. J Affect Disord 26: 127, 1992.

Clayton P J, Guse S B, Cloninger C R, Martin R L: Unipolar depression: Diagnostic inconsistency and its implications. J Affect Disord 26: 111, 1992.

Coffey C E, Wilkinson W E, Weiner R D, Parashos I A, Djang W T, Webb W C, Figiel G S, Spritzer C F: Quantitative cerebral anatomy in depression: A controlled magnetic resonance imaging study. Arch Gen Psychiatry 50: 7, 1993.

Coryell W, Endicott J, Keller M: Major depression in a nonclinical sample: Demographic and clinical risk factors for first onset. Arch Gen Psychiatry 49: 117, 1992.

Coryell W, Endicott J, Keller M: Rapid cycling affective disorder: Demographics, diagnosis, family history, and course. Arch Gen Psychiatry 49: 126, 1992.

Deakin J F W: Depression and 5HT. Int Clin Psychopharmacol 6: 23, 1991.

Drevets W C, Videen T O, Price J L, Preskorn S H, Carmichael S T, Raichle M E: A functional anatomical study of unipolar depression. J Neurosci 12: 3628, 1992.

Emery V O, Oxman T E: Update on the dementia spectrum of depression. Am J Psychiatry 149: 305, 1992.

Gabbard G O: *Psychodynamic Psychiatry in Clinical Practice: The DSM-IV Edition.* American Psychiatric Press, Washington, 1994.

Gastpar M, Gilsdorf U, Abou-Aleh M T, Ngo-Khac T: Clinical correlates of response to CST: The dexamethasone suppression test in depression: A World Health Organization collaborative study. J Affect Disord 26: 17, 1992.

Guscott R, Grof P: The clinical meaning of refractory depression: A review for the clinician. Am J Psychiatry 148: 695, 1991.

Harrow M, Goldberg J F, Grossman L S, Meltzer H Y: Outcome in manic disorders: A naturalistic follow-up study. Arch Gen Psychiatry 47: 665, 1990.

Horwath E, Johnson J, Weissman M M, Hornig C D: The validity of major depression with atypical features based on a community study. J Affect Disord 26: 117, 1992.

Hunt N, Bruce-Jones W, Silverstone T: Life events and relapse in bipolar affective disorder. J Affect Disord 25: 13, 1992.

Jorge R E, Robinson R G, Starkstein S E, Arndt S V, Forrester A W, Geisler F M: Secondary mania following traumatic brain injury. Am J Psychiatry 150: 916, 1993.

Kapjur S, Mann J J: Role of the dopaminergic system in depression. Biol Psychiatry 32: 1, 1992.

Karasu T B: Toward a clinical model of psychotherapy for depression: I. Systematic comparison of three psychotherapies. Am J Psychiatry 147: 133, 1990.

Karasu T B: Toward a clinical model of psychotherapy for depression: II. An integrative and selective treatment approach. Am J Psychiatry 147: 269, 1990.

Kato T, Takahashi S, Shioiri T, Inubushi T: Alterations in brain phosphorous metabolism in bipolar disorder detected by in vivo $^{31}$P and $^{7}$Li magnetic resonance spectroscopy. J Affect Disord 27: 53, 1993.

Katon W, Schulberg H: Epidemiology of depression in primary care. Gen Hosp Psychiatry 14: 237, 1992.

Keck P E, McElroy S L, Nemeroff C B: Anticonvulsants in the treatment of bipolar disorder. J Neuropsychiatry Clin Neurosci 4: 395, 1992.

Keitner G I, Ryan C E, Miller I W, Norman W H: Recovery and major depression: Factors associated with twelve-month outcome. Am J Psychiatry 149: 93, 1992.

Keller M B, Lavori P W, Mueller T I, Endicott J, Coryell W, Hirschfield R M A, Shea T: Time to recovery, chronicity, and levels of psychopathology in major depression: A 5-year prospective follow-up of 431 subjects. Arch Gen Psychiatry 49: 809, 1992.

Kendler K S: Mood-incongruent psychotic affective illness: A historical and empirical review. Arch Gen Psychiatry 48: 362, 1991.

Kohut H: *The Analysis of the Self.* International Univaersities Press, New York, 1971.

Krishnan K R R, McDonald W M, Escalona P R, Doraiswamy P M, Na C, Husain M M, Figiel G S, Boyko O B, Ellinwood E H, Nemeroff C B: Magnetic resonance imaging of the caudate nuclei in depression. Arch Gen Psychiatry 49: 553, 1992.

Kupfer D J, Ehlers C L, Frank E, Grochocinski V J, McEachran A B: EEG sleep profiles and recurrent depression. Biol Psychiatry 30: 641, 1991.

Kupfer D J, Frank E, Perel J M, Cornes C, Mallinger A G, Thase M E, McEachran A B, Grochocinski V J: Five-year outcome for maintenance therapies in recurrent depression. Arch Gen Psychiatry 49: 769, 1992.

Miller A H, Spencer R L, Pulera M, Kang S, McEwen B S, Stein M: Adrenal steroid receptor activation in rat brain and pituitary following dexamethasone: Implications for the dexamethasone suppression test. Biol Psychiatry 32: 850, 1992.

Mitchell P, Parker G, Jamieson K, Wilhelm K, Hickie I, Brodaty B, Boyce P, Hadzi-Pavlovic D, Roy K: Are there any differences between bipolar and unipolar melancholia? J Affect Disord 25: 97, 1992.

Parker G, Roy K, Hadzi-Pavlovic D, Pedic F: Psychotic (delusional) depression: A meta-analysis of physical treatments. J Affect Disord 24: 17, 1992.

Post R M: Transduction of psychosocial stress into the neurobiology of recurrent affective disorder. Am J Psychiatry 149: 999, 1992.

Power A C, Cowen P J: Neuroendocrine challenge tests: Assessment of 5-HT function in anxiety and depression. Mol Aspects Med 13: 205, 1992.

Rice J P, Rochberg N, Endicott J, Lavori P W, Miller C: Stability of psychiatric diagnoses: An application to the affective disorders. Arch Gen Psychiatry 49: 824, 1992.

Roy A: Features associated with suicide attempts in depression: A partial replication. J Affect Disord 27: 35, 1993.

Schatzberg A F, Rothschild A J: Psychotic (delusional) major depression: Should it be included as a distinct syndrome in DSM-IV? Am J Psychiatry 149: 733, 1992.

Shamoian C A, editor: Depression in the elderly. Psychiatr Ann 20 (2, Suppl): 2, 1990.

Shelton R C, Winn S, Ekhatore N, Loosen P T: The effects of antidepressants on the thyroid axis in depression. Biol Psychiatry 33: 120, 1993.

Sotsky S M, Glass D R, Shea M T, Pilkonis P A, Collins J F, Elkin I, Watkins J T, Imber S D, Leber W R, Moyer J, Oliveri M E: Patient predictors of response to psychotherapy and pharmacotherapy: Findings in the NIMH treatment of depression collaborative research program. Am J Psychiatry 148: 997, 1991.

Stephens J H, McHugh P R: Characteristics and long-term follow-up of patients hospitalized for mood disorders in the Phipps Clinic, 1913–1940. J Nerv Ment Dis 179: 64, 1991.

Stravynski A, Greenberg D: The psychological management of depression. Acta Psychiatr Scand 85: 407, 1992.

Thomsen P H, Moller L L, Dehlholm B, Brask B H: Manic-depressive psychosis in children younger than 15 years: A register-based investigation of 39 cases in Denmark. Acta Psychiatr Scand 85: 401, 1992.

Toben M, Waternaux C M, Tsuang M T: Outcome in mania: A 4-year prospective follow-up of 75 patients utilizing survival analysis. Arch Gen Psychiatry 47: 1106, 1990.

Vestergaard P: Treatment and prevention of mania: A Scandinavian perspective. Neuropsychopharmacology 7: 249, 1992.

Wexler B E, Cicchetti D V: The outpatient treatment of depression: Implications of outcome research for clinical practice. J Nerv Ment Dis 180: 277, 1992.

Workman E A, Short D D: Atypical antidepressants versus imipramine in the treatment of major depression: A meta-analysis. J Clin Psychiatry 54: 5, 1993.

Young E A, Haskett R F, Murphy-Weinberg V, Watson S J, Akil H: Loss of glucocorticold fast feedback in depression. Arch Gen Psychiatry 48: 693, 1991.

Young R C, Klerman G L: Mania in late life: Focus on age at onset. Am J Psychiatry 149: 867, 1992.

# 15.2 / Dysthymic Disorder and Cyclothymic Disorder

Dysthymic disorder and cyclothymic disorder were referred to in the revised third edition of *Diagnostic and*

*Statistical Manual of Mental Disorders* (DSM-III-R) as dysthymia and cyclothymia, respectively, and are sometimes known in unofficial parlance as the subaffective disorders. That latter term suggests that dysthymic disorder and cyclothymic disorder are mild forms of major depressive disorder and bipolar I disorder, respectively. However, some research data indicate that, although the disorders may be related, they probably have fundamental biological and psychosocial differences. One major difference is that, whereas major depressive disorder is characterized by discrete episodes of symptoms, dysthymic disorder is characterized by chronic, nonepisodic symptoms.

The conceptualization of dysthymic disorder and cyclothymic disorder as subaffective disorders must also be considered with respect to other mood disorders, besides major depressive disorder and bipolar I disorder. The other disorders are bipolar II disorder, minor depressive disorder, and recurrent brief depressive disorder.

The inclusion of the so-called subaffective disorders, such as dysthymic disorder and cyclothymic disorder, with the mood disorders is controversial in the field of psychiatry. Their inclusion with the major mood disorders implies similarities in cause, genetic bases, prognoses, and treatment responses. In disagreement with that view, some psychodynamically oriented psychiatrists believe that dysthymic disorder and cyclothymic disorder are conceptualized as primarily the results of incompletely resolved issues in a person's psychodynamic development.

## DYSTHYMIC DISORDER

Dysthymic disorder is a chronic disorder characterized by the presence of a depressed (or irritable in children and adolescents) mood that lasts most of the day and is present on most days. The term "dysthymia," which means ill-humored, was introduced in 1980 and changed to "dysthymic disorder" in DSM-IV. Before 1980, most patients now classified as having dysthymic disorder were classified as having depressive neurosis (also called neurotic depression), although some patients were classified as having cyclothymic personality. The diagnosis of depressive neurosis was the most common psychiatric diagnosis in the 1970s. In fact, its patently obvious heterogeneity and the lack of clinical agreement about the diagnosis may have helped increase the appreciation of the need for a diagnostic manual such as the third edition of DSM (DSM-III).

The theoretical biases of various diagnostic systems are reflected in the various DSM-IV and non-DSM-IV names for the disorder. "Dysthymia" implies a temperamental dysphoria—that is, an inborn tendency to experience a depressed mood. In contrast, "depressive neurosis" implies a maladaptive, repetitive pattern of thinking and behavior that results in depression. Patients described as having depressive neurosis are often anxious, obsessive, and prone to somatization. "Characterological depression" implies a dysphoric mood that is integral to a patient's character. "Hypochondriacal depression" implies a condition characterized by multiple somatic complaints; in DSM-IV, patients with such complaints may more appropriately be classified as having somatization disorder.

## Epidemiology

Dysthymic disorder is a common disorder among the general population, affecting 3 to 5 percent of all persons, and it is common among patients in general psychiatric clinics, affecting between one half and one third of all clinic patients. At least one study reported prevalences of dysthymic disorder among young adolescents of about 8 percent in boys and 5 percent in girls. Dysthymic disorder is more common in women less than 64 years old than in men of any age. Dysthymic disorder is also more common among unmarried and young persons and in persons with low incomes. Moreover, dysthymic disorder frequently coexists with other mental disorders, especially major depressive disorder, anxiety disorders (especially panic disorder), substance abuse, and, probably, borderline personality disorder. Such patients with dysthymic disorder are likely to be taking a wide range of psychiatric medications, including antidepressants, antimanic agents—for example, lithium (Eskalith) and carbamazepine (Tegretol)—and sedative-hypnotics.

## Etiology

A major theme regarding the cause of dysthymic disorder is whether it is related to other psychiatric diagnoses, including major depressive disorder and borderline personality disorder. At this point, one cannot come to a final conclusion; however, as with most psychiatric diagnoses, the patients defined by the DSM-IV criteria have a heterogeneous assortment of disease processes—for example, decreased rapid eye movement (REM) sleep and a family history of mood disorders.

**Biological factors.** Some studies of biological measures in dysthymic disorder support the classification of dysthymic disorder with the mood disorders; other studies question that association. One hypothesis drawn from the data is that the biological basis for the symptoms of dysthymic disorder and major depressive disorder are similar; however, the biological bases for the underlying pathophysiology in the two disorders are different.

SLEEP STUDIES. Decreased rapid eye movement (REM) latency and increased REM density are two state markers of depression in major depressive disorder that are also found in a significant proportion of patients with dysthymic disorder. Some investigators have reported preliminary data indicating that the presence of those sleep abnormalities in patients with dysthymic disorder predict a response to antidepressant drugs.

NEUROENDOCRINE STUDIES. The two most studied neuroendocrine axes in major depressive disorder and dysthymic disorder are the adrenal axis and the thyroid axis, which have been tested by using the dexamethasone-suppression test (DST) and the thyrotropin-releasing hormone (TRH)-stimulation test, respectively. Although the studies are not absolutely consistent, the majority of the studies indicate that patients with dysthymic disorder are much less likely to have abnormal results on a DST than are patients with major depressive disorder. The studies of the TRH-stimulation test have been fewer in number but have produced preliminary data indicating that abnormalities in the thyroid axis may be a trait variable that is associated with chronic illness. That hypothesis is supported by a generally increased percentage of patients with dysthymic disorder who have thyroid axis abnormalities when compared with normal controls.

**Psychosocial factors.** Psychodynamic theories regarding the development of dysthymic disorder posit that the disorder results from faulty personality and ego development, culminating in difficulty in adapting to adolescence and young adulthood. Karl Abraham, for example, thought that the conflicts of depression center on oral and anal-sadistic traits. Anal traits include excessive orderliness, guilt, and concern for others; anal traits are postulated to be a defense against preoccupation with anal matters and with disorganization, hostility, and self-preoccupation. A major defense mechanism used is reaction formation. Low self-esteem, anhedonia, and introversion are often associated with the depressive character.

FREUD. In "Mourning and Melancholia" Sigmund Freud asserted that a vulnerability to depression can be caused by an interpersonal disappointment early in life that leads to ambivalent love relationships as an adult; real or threatened losses in adult life then trigger depression. Persons prone to depression are orally dependent and require constant narcissistic gratification. If deprived of love, affection, and care, they become clinically depressed. When those persons experience a real loss, they internalize or introject the lost object and turn their anger on it and, thus, on themselves.

COGNITIVE THEORY. The cognitive theory of depression also applies to dysthymic disorder; it holds that a disparity between actual and fantasized situations leads to diminished self-esteem and a sense of helplessness. The success of cognitive therapy in the treatment of some patients with dysthymic disorder may provide some support for that theoretical model.

## Diagnosis

The DSM-IV diagnostic criteria for dysthymic disorder (Table 15.2–1) are similar to those for dysthymia in DSM-III-R, except for the addition in DSM-IV of some characteristic symptoms in criterion B. The diagnostic criteria require the presence of a depressed mood most of the time for at least two years (or one year for children and adolescents). To meet the diagnostic criteria, the patient should not have symptoms that are better accounted for as major depressive disorder. The patient should never have had a manic or hypomanic episode. DSM-IV allows the clinician to specify whether the onset was early (before age 21) or late (age 21 or older). DSM-IV also allows for the specification of atypical features in dysthymic disorder (Table 15.1–17).

## Clinical Features

Dysthymic disorder is a chronic disorder that is characterized not by episodes of illness but, rather, by the steady presence of symptoms. Nevertheless, dysthymic disorder patients can have some temporal variations in the severity of their symptoms. The symptoms themselves are similar to those for major depressive disorder, and the presence of a depressed mood—characterized by feeling sad, blue, down in the dumps, or low and by a lack of interest in the patient's usual activities—is central to the

**Table 15.2–1**
**Diagnostic Criteria for Dysthymic Disorder**

A. Depressed mood for most of the day, for more days than not, as indicated either by subjective account or observation by others, for at least 2 years. **Note:** In children and adolescents, mood can be irritable and duration must be at least 1 year.

B. Presence, while depressed, of two (or more) of the following:

    (1) poor appetite or overeating
    (2) insomnia or hypersomnia
    (3) low energy or fatigue
    (4) low self-esteem
    (5) poor concentration or difficulty making decisions
    (6) feelings of hopelessness

C. During the 2-year period (1 year for children or adolescents) of the disturbance, the person has never been without the symptoms in criteria A and B for more than 2 months at a time.

D. No major depressive episode has been present during the first 2 years of the disturbance (1 year for children and adolescents); i.e., the disturbance is not better accounted for by chronic major depressive disorder, or major depressive disorder, in partial remission.

**Note:** There may have been a previous major depressive episode provided there was a full remission (no significant signs or symptoms for 2 months) before development of the dysthymic disorder. In addition, after the initial 2 years (1 year in children or adolescents) of dysthymic disorder, there may be superimposed episodes of major depressive disorder, in which case both diagnoses may be given when the criteria are met for a major depressive episode.

E. There has never been a manic episode, a mixed episode, or a hypomanic episode, and criteria have never been met for cyclothymic disorder.

F. The disturbance does not occur exclusively during the course of a chronic psychotic disorder, such as schizophrenia or delusional disorder.

G. The symptoms are not due to the direct physiological effects of a substance (e.g., a drug of abuse, a medication) or a general medical condition (e.g., hypothyroidism).

H. The symptoms cause clinically significant distress or impairment in social, occupational, or other important areas of functioning.

    *Specify* if:
    **Early onset:** if onset before age 21 years
    **Late onset:** if onset is age 21 years or older

    *Specify* (for most recent 2 years of dysthymic disorder):
    **with atypical features**

Table from DSM-IV, *Diagnostic and Statistical Manual of Mental Disorders*, ed 4. Copyright American Psychiatric Association, Washington, 1994. Used with permission.

disorder. The severity of the depressive symptoms in dysthymic disorder is generally less than in major depressive disorder, but it is the lack of discrete episodes that most weights toward the diagnosis of dysthymic disorder.

Patients with dysthymic disorder can often be sarcastic, nihilistic, brooding, demanding, and complaining. They can be tense and rigid and resistant to therapeutic interventions, even though they come regularly to appointments. As a result, the clinician may feel angry toward the patient and may even disregard the patient's complaints. By definition, dysthymic disorder patients do not have any psychotic symptoms.

**Associated symptoms.** Associated symptoms include changes in appetite and sleep patterns, low self-esteem, loss of energy, psychomotor retardation, decreased sexual drive, and obsessive preoccupation with health matters. Pessimism, hopelessness, and helplessness may cause dysthymic disorder patients to be seen as masochistic. However, if the pessimism is directed outward, the patients may rant against the world and complain that they have been poorly treated by relatives, children, parents, colleagues, and the system.

**Social impairment.** Impairment in social functioning is sometimes the reason why patients with dysthymic disorder seek treatment. In fact, divorce, unemployment, and social problems are common problems for those patients. They may complain that they have difficulty in concentrating and may report that their school or work performance is suffering. Because of complaints of physical illness, patients may miss workdays and social occasions. Dysthymic disorder patients may have marital problems resulting from sexual dysfunction (for example, impotence) or from an inability to sustain emotional intimacy.

**Coexisting diagnoses.** As mentioned previously, the diagnosis of dysthymic disorder is frequently made for persons who are also suffering from other mental disorders. Data indicate that the comorbidity of dysthymic disorder with other mental disorders is a significant negative predictor of a good prognosis. That is, the presence of a chronic, untreated depressive disorder appears to limit the rate and the extent of improvement a patient can obtain in other mental disorders. Frequently found comorbid disorders are major depressive disorder and substance-related disorders.

DOUBLE DEPRESSION. An estimated 40 percent of patients with major depressive disorder also meet the criteria for dysthymic disorder. That combination of disorders is often referred to as double depression. Available data support the conclusion that patients with double depression have a poorer prognosis than do patients with only major depressive disorder. The treatment of patients with double depression should be directed toward both disorders, since the resolution of the symptoms of a major depressive episode in those patients still leaves them with significant psychiatric impairment.

ALCOHOL AND OTHER SUBSTANCE ABUSE. Patients with dysthymic disorder commonly meet the diagnostic criteria for a substance-related disorder. That comorbidity may be seen as logical, given the propensity of dysthymic disorder patients to develop coping methods for their chronically depressed state. Therefore, patients with dysthymic disorder are likely to use alcohol, stimulants (for example, cocaine), or marijuana, the choice perhaps depending primarily on the patient's social context. The presence of a comorbid diagnosis of substance abuse presents a diagnostic dilemma for the clinician, since the long-term use of many substances can result in a symptom picture indistinguishable from that of dysthymic disorder.

## Differential Diagnosis

The differential diagnosis for dysthymic disorder is essentially identical to that for major depressive disorder. Many substances and medical illnesses can cause chronic depressive symptoms. Two disorders are particularly important to consider in the differential diagnosis of dysthymic disorder—minor depressive disorder and recurrent brief depressive disorder.

**Minor depressive disorder.** Minor depressive disorder, discussed in Section 15.3, is characterized by episodes of depressive symptoms that are less severe than those seen in major depressive disorder. The difference between dysthymic disorder and minor depressive disorder is primarily the episodic nature of the symptoms in minor depressive disorder. Between episodes, patients with minor depressive disorder have a euthymic mood, whereas patients with dysthymic disorder have virtually no euthymic periods.

**Recurrent brief depressive disorder.** Recurrent brief depressive disorder, discussed in Section 15.3, is characterized by brief (less than two weeks) periods during which depressive episodes are present. Patients with the disorder would meet the diagnostic criteria for major depressive disorder if their episodes lasted longer. Patients with recurrent brief depressive disorder differ from dysthymic disorder patients on two counts: first, they have an episodic disorder, and, second, the severity of their symptoms is greater.

## Course and Prognosis

About 50 percent of dysthymic disorder patients experience an insidious onset of the symptoms before age 25. Despite the early onset, patients often suffer with the symptoms for a decade before seeking psychiatric help. Those affected may consider early-onset dysthymic disorder simply as part of life. Patients who have an early onset of symptoms are at risk for either major depressive disorder or bipolar I disorder in the course of their disorder. Studies of patients with the diagnosis of depressive neurosis indicated that about 20 percent of them progressed to major depressive disorder, 15 percent to bipolar II disorder, and less than 5 percent to bipolar I disorder.

The prognosis for patients with dysthymic disorder is variable. Future studies may indicate that the use of new antidepressive agents—for example, fluoxetine (Prozac) and bupropion (Wellbutrin)—or specific types of psychotherapy (for example, cognitive and behavior therapies) have positive effects on the course and the prognosis of dysthymic disorder. The available data regarding previously available treatments indicate that only 10 to 15 percent of dysthymic disorder patients are in remission one year after the initial diagnosis. About 25 percent of all dysthymic disorder patients never attain a complete recovery.

## Treatment

Historically, patients with dysthymic disorder received no treatment or were seen as candidates for long-term, insight-oriented psychotherapy. Contemporary data offer objective support for only cognitive therapy, behavior therapy, and pharmacotherapy. The combination of pharmacotherapy and either cognitive or behavior therapy may be the most effective treatment for the disorder. Other therapies may be beneficial; however, the benefit has yet to be proved in well-controlled studies.

**Cognitive therapy.** Cognitive therapy is a technique in which patients are taught new ways of thinking and behaving to replace faulty negative attitudes about themselves, the world, and the future. It is a short-term therapy program oriented toward current problems and their resolution.

**Behavior therapy.** Behavior therapy for depressive disorders is based on the theory that depression is caused by a loss of positive reinforcement as a result of separation, death, or sudden environmental change. The various treatment methods focus on specific goals to increase activity, to provide pleasant experiences, and to teach patients how to relax. Altering personal behavior in depressed patients is believed to be the most effective way to change the associated depressed thoughts and feelings. Behavior therapy is often used to treat the learned helplessness of some patients who seem to meet every life challenge with a sense of impotence.

**Insight-oriented (psychoanalytic) psychotherapy.** Individual insight-oriented psychotherapy is the most common treatment modality for dysthymic disorder, and many clinicians believe it to be the treatment of choice. The psychotherapeutic approach attempts to relate the development and the maintenance of depressive symptoms and maladaptive personality features to unresolved conflicts from early childhood. Insight into depressive equivalents (such as substance abuse) or into childhood disappointments as antecedents to adult depression can be gained through treatment. Ambivalent current relationships with parents, friends, and others in the patient's current life are examined. Patients' understanding of how they try to gratify an excessive need for outside approval to counter low self-esteem and a harsh superego is an important goal in the therapy.

Dysthymic disorder involves a chronic state of depression that becomes a way of life for certain persons. They consciously experience themselves to be at the mercy of a tormenting internal object that is unrelenting in its persecution of them. Usually conceptualized as a harsh superego, the internal agency criticizes them, punishes them for not measuring up to expectations, and generally contributes to their feelings of misery and unhappiness. The pattern may be associated with self-defeating tendencies, because they do not feel that they deserve to be successful. They may also have a long-standing sense of despair about ever getting their emotional needs met by important people in their lives. The patients' bleak outlook on life and their pessimism about relationships result in a self-fulfilling prophecy: many people avoid them because their company is unpleasant.

**Interpersonal therapy.** In interpersonal therapy for depressive disorders, the patient's current interpersonal experiences and ways of coping with stress are examined in order to reduce depressive symptoms and improve self-esteem. Interpersonal therapy consists of about 12 to 16 weekly sessions and can be combined with antidepressant medication.

**Family and group therapies.** Family therapy may help both the patient and the patient's family deal with the symptoms of the disorder, especially when a biologically based subaffective syndrome seems to be present. Group therapy may help withdrawn patients learn new ways to overcome their interpersonal problems in social situations.

**Pharmacotherapy.** Because of long-standing and commonly held theoretical beliefs that dysthymic disorder is primarily a psychologically determined disorder, many clinicians avoid the use of antidepressants in patients with the disorder. Many studies have had therapeutic success with antidepressants in the disorder. In general, however, the data indicate that monoamine oxidase inhibitors (MAOIs) may be more beneficial than tricyclic drugs. The relatively recent introduction of the well-tolerated serotonin-specific reuptake inhibitors (SSRIs) has led to their frequent use by patients with dysthymic disorder; preliminary reports indicate that the SSRIs may be the drugs of choice for the disorder. Similarly, initial reports indicate that bupropion may be an effective treatment for patients with dysthymic disorder. Sympathomimetics, such as amphetamine, have also been of use in selected patients.

FAILURE OF THERAPEUTIC TRIAL. A therapeutic trial of an antidepressant in the treatment of dysthymic disorder should use maximal tolerated dosages for a minimum of eight weeks before the clinician concludes that the trial was not effective. If a drug trial is unsuccessful, the clinician should reconsider the diagnosis, especially regarding the possibility of an underlying medical disorder (especially a thyroid disorder) or adult attention-deficit disorder. If a reconsideration of the differential diagnosis still leaves dysthymic disorder as the most likely diagnosis, the clinician may follow the same therapeutic strategy one would follow in major depressive disorder. Specifically, the clinician may attempt to augment the first antidepressant by adding lithium (Eskalith) or triiodothyronine (Cytomel), although augmentation strategies have not been studied for dysthymic disorder. Or the clinician may decide to switch to an antidepressant from a completely different class of drugs. For example, if a trial with an SSRI is unsuccessful, the clinician may switch to bupropion or an MAOI.

**Hospitalization.** Hospitalization is usually not indicated for dysthymic disorder patients; however, the presence of particularly severe symptoms, marked social or professional incapacitation, the need for extensive diagnostic procedures, and suicidal ideation are all indications for hospitalization.

## CYCLOTHYMIC DISORDER

Cyclothymic disorder, previously called cyclothymia in DSM-III-R, is symptomatically a mild form of bipolar II disorder; it is characterized by episodes of hypomania and episodes of mild depression. In DSM-IV, cyclothymic disorder is differentiated from bipolar II disorder, which is characterized by the presence of major depressive episodes and hypomanic episodes. As with dysthymic disorder, the categorization of cyclothymic disorder with the mood disorders implies a relation, probably biological, to bipolar I disorder. However, some psychiatrists conceptualize cyclothymic disorder as being distinct from bipolar I disorder and as resulting from chaotic object relations early in life.

The history of cyclothymic disorder is based to some extent on the observations of Emil Kraepelin and Kurt

Schneider that one third to two thirds of patients with mood disorders exhibit personality disorders. Kraepelin described four types of personality disorders: depressive (gloomy), manic (cheerful and uninhibited), irritable (labile and explosive), and cyclothymic. Kraepelin described the irritable personality as the simultaneous presence of the depressive and manic personalities, and he described the cyclothymic personality as the alternation of the depressive and manic personalities.

## Epidemiology

Patients with cyclothymic disorder may constitute from 3 to 10 percent of all psychiatric outpatients, perhaps particularly those with significant complaints regarding marital and interpersonal difficulties. In the general population the lifetime prevalence of cyclothymic disorder is estimated to be about 1 percent. That figure is probably lower than the actual prevalence, since, as with bipolar I disorder patients, the patients may not be aware that they have a psychiatric problem. Cyclothymic disorder, like dysthymic disorder, frequently coexists with borderline personality disorder. An estimated 10 percent of outpatients and 20 percent of inpatients with borderline personality disorder have a coexisting diagnosis of cyclothymic disorder. The female-to-male ratio in cyclothymic disorder is about 3 to 2, and 50 to 75 percent of all patients have an onset between ages 15 and 25.

## Etiology

As with dysthymic disorder, controversy concerns whether cyclothymic disorder is related to the mood disorders, either biologically or psychologically. Some researchers have postulated that cyclothymic disorder has a closer relation to borderline personality disorder than to the mood disorders. In spite of those controversies, the preponderance of the biological and genetic data favors the conceptualization of cyclothymic disorder as a bona fide mood disorder.

**Biological factors.** The genetic data are the strongest supports for the hypothesis that cyclothymic disorder is a mood disorder. About 30 percent of all cyclothymic disorder patients have positive family histories for bipolar I disorder; that rate is similar to the rate for patients with bipolar I disorder. Moreover, the pedigrees of families with bipolar I disorder often contain generations of bipolar I disorder patients linked by a generation with cyclothymic disorder. Conversely, the prevalence of cyclothymic disorder in the relatives of bipolar I disorder patients is much higher than is the prevalence of cyclothymic disorder either in the relatives of patients with other mental disorders or in mentally healthy persons. The observations that about one third of patients with cyclothymic disorder subsequently have major mood disorders, that they are particularly sensitive to antidepressant-induced hypomania, and that about 60 percent respond to lithium add further support to the conceptualization of cyclothymic disorder as a mild or attenuated form of bipolar I disorder.

**Psychosocial factors.** Most psychodynamic theories postulate that the development of cyclothymic disorder lies in traumas and fixations during the oral stage of infant development. Freud hypothesized that the cyclothymic state is the ego's attempt to overcome a harsh and punitive superego. Hypomania is explained psychodynamically as occurring when a depressed person throws off the burden of an overly harsh superego, resulting in a lack of self-criticism and an absence of inhibitions. The major defense mechanism in hypomania is denial, by which the patient avoids external problems and internal feelings of depression.

Patients with cyclothymic disorder are characterized by periods of depression alternating with periods of hypomania. Psychoanalytic exploration of such patients reveals that underlying depressive themes are defended against by euphoric or hypomanic periods. Hypomania is frequently triggered by a profound interpersonal loss. The false euphoria generated in such instances is a way the patient denies dependence on love objects while simultaneously disavowing any aggression or destructiveness that may have contributed to the loss of the loved person. Hypomania may also be associated with an unconscious fantasy that the lost object has been restored. That denial is generally short-lived, and the patient soon resumes the preoccupation with suffering and misery characteristic of dysthymic disorder.

## Diagnosis

Although many patients seek psychiatric help for depression, their problems are often related to the chaos that their manic episodes have caused. The clinician must consider a diagnosis of cyclothymic disorder when a patient presents with what may seem to be sociopathic behavioral problems. Marital difficulties and instability in relationships are common complaints because cyclothymic disorder patients are often promiscuous and irritable while in manic and mixed states. Although there are anecdotal reports of increased productivity and creativity while patients are hypomanic, most clinicians report that their patients become disorganized and ineffective in work and school during those periods.

The DSM-IV diagnostic criteria for cyclothymic disorder (Table 15.2–2) require that the patient has never met the criteria for a major depressive episode and did not meet the criteria for a manic episode during the first two years of the disturbance. The criteria also require the more or less constant presence of symptoms for two years (or one year for children and adolescents).

## Clinical Features

The symptoms of cyclothymic disorder are identical to the symptoms seen in bipolar I disorder, except that they are generally less severe. On occasion, however, the symptoms may be equal in severity but be of shorter duration than those seen in bipolar I disorder. About half of all cyclothymic disorder patients have depression as their major symptom, and those patients are most likely to seek psychiatric help while depressed. Some cyclothymic disorder patients have primarily hypomanic symptoms and are less likely to consult a psychiatrist than are primarily depressed patients. Almost all cyclothymic disorder pa-

**Table 15.2–2**
**Diagnostic Criteria for Cyclothymic Disorder**

A. For at least 2 years, the presence of numerous periods with hypomanic symptoms and numerous periods with depressive symptoms that do not meet criteria for a major depressive episode. **Note:** In children and adolescents, the duration must be at least 1 year.

B. During the above 2-year period (1 year in children and adolescents), the person has not been without the symptoms in criterion A for more than 2 months at a time.

C. No major depressive episode, manic episode, or mixed episode has been present during the first 2 years of the disturbance.

**Note:** After the initial 2 years (1 year in children and adolescents) of cyclothymic disorder, there may be superimposed manic or mixed episodes (in which case both bipolar I disorder and cyclothymic disorder may be diagnosed) or major depressive episodes (in which case both bipolar II disorder and cyclothymic disorder may be diagnosed).

D. The symptoms in criterion A are not better accounted for by schizoaffective disorder and are not superimposed on schizophrenia, schizophreniform disorder, delusional disorder, or psychotic disorder not otherwise specified.

E. The symptoms are not due to the direct physiological effects of a substance (e.g., a drug of abuse, a medication) or a general medical condition (e.g., hyperthyroidism).

F. The symptoms cause clinically significant distress or impairment in social, occupational, or other important areas of functioning.

Table from DSM-IV, *Diagnostic and Statistical Manual of Mental Disorders*, ed 4. Copyright American Psychiatric Association, Washington, 1994. Used with permission.

tients have periods of mixed symptoms with marked irritability.

Most cyclothymic disorder patients seen by psychiatrists have not succeeded in their professional and social lives as a result of their disorder. However, a few cyclothymic disorder patients have become high achievers who have worked especially long hours and have required little sleep. The ability of some persons to successfully control the symptoms of the disorder depends on multiple individual, social, and cultural attributes.

The lives of most cyclothymic disorder patients are difficult. The cycles of cyclothymic disorder tend to be much shorter than those in bipolar I disorder. In cyclothymic disorder the changes in mood are irregular and abrupt, sometimes occurring within hours. Occasional periods of normal mood and the unpredictable nature of the mood changes cause the patients a great deal of stress. Patients often feel that their moods are out of control. In irritable, mixed periods the patients may become involved in unprovoked disagreements with friends, family, and coworkers.

**Substance abuse.** Alcohol abuse and other substance abuse are common in cyclothymic disorder patients, who use substances either to self medicate (with alcohol, benzodiazepines, and marijuana) or to achieve even further stimulation (with cocaine, amphetamines, and hallucinogens) when they are manic. About 5 to 10 percent of all cyclothymic disorder patients have substance dependence.

Cyclothymic disorder persons often have a history of multiple geographical moves, involvements in religious cults, and dilettantism.

A 29-year-old car salesman was referred by his current girlfriend, a psychiatric nurse, who suspected that he had a mood disorder, even though the patient was reluctant to admit that he was a moody person. According to him, since the age of 14 he had experienced repeated alternating cycles that he termed "good times and bad times." During a "bad" period, usually lasting four to seven days, he slept 10 to 14 hours daily and lacked energy, confidence, and motivation—"just vegetating," as he put it. Often, he abruptly shifted, characteristically on waking up in the morning, to a three-to-four-day stretch of overconfidence, heightened social awareness, promiscuity, and sharpened thinking—"things would flash in my mind." At such times he indulged in alcohol to enhance the experience but also to help him sleep. Occasionally the "good" periods lasted 7 to 10 days but culminated in irritable and hostile outbursts, which often heralded the transition back to another period of bad days. He admitted to the frequent use of marijuana, which he claimed helped him "adjust" to daily routines.

In school, As and Bs had alternated with Cs and Ds, with the result that the patient was considered a bright student whose performance was mediocre overall because of unstable motivation. As a car salesman, he had shown uneven performance, with good days canceling out the bad days; yet even during his good days he was sometimes perilously argumentative with customers and lost sales that appeared sure. Although considered a charming man in many social circles, he alienated friends when he was hostile and irritable. He typically accumulated social obligations during the bad days and took care of them all at once on the first day of a good period.

*Discussion.* The patient had had numerous periods during the preceding two years in which he had had some symptoms characteristic of both depressive and manic episodes. Characteristic of the good days were overconfidence, heightened social awareness, promiscuity, and sharpened thinking. Although those periods came close to meeting the criteria for a manic episode, they were not sufficiently severe to justify a diagnosis of bipolar I disorder. Similarly, the bad days—characterized by oversleeping and lack of energy, confidence, and motivation—were not of sufficient severity and duration to meet the criteria for a major depressive episode. Moreover, the brief cycles followed each other with intermittent irregularity on a repeated basis. Therefore, the appropriate diagnosis was cyclothymic disorder.

**Differential Diagnosis**

When a diagnosis of cyclothymic disorder is under consideration, all the possible medical and substance-related causes of depression and mania must be considered. Seizures and particular substances (cocaine, amphetamine, and steroids) need to be considered in the differential diagnosis. Borderline, antisocial, histrionic, and narcissistic personality disorders should also be considered in the differential diagnosis. Attention-deficit/hyperactivity disorder can be difficult to differentiate from cyclothymic disorder in children and adolescents. A trial of stimulants helps most patients with attention-deficit/hyperactivity disorder and exacerbates the symptoms of most patients with cyclothymic disorder. The diagnostic category of bipolar II disorder, discussed in Section 15.3, is characterized by the combination of major depressive episodes and hypomanic episodes.

## Course and Prognosis

Some patients with cyclothymic disorder are characterized as having been sensitive, hyperactive, or moody as young children. The onset of frank symptoms of cyclothymic disorder often occurs insidiously in the person's teens and early 20s. The emergence of symptoms at that time may hinder the person's performance in school and ability to establish friendships with peers. The reactions of patients to such a disorder vary; patients with adaptive coping strategies or ego defenses have better outcomes than do patients with poor coping strategies. About one third of all cyclothymic disorder patients go on to have a major mood disorder, most often bipolar II disorder.

## Treatment

**Biological treatment.** The antimanic drugs are the first line of treatment of patients with cyclothymic disorder. Although the experimental data are limited to studies with lithium, other antimanic agents—for example, carbamazepine and valproate (Depakene)—are also effective, and such results have been reported. Dosages and plasma concentrations of those agents should be the same as in bipolar I disorder. The treatment of depressed cyclothymic disorder patients with antidepressants should be done with caution, because of their increased susceptibility to antidepressant-induced hypomanic or manic episodes. About 40 to 50 percent of all cyclothymic disorder patients treated with antidepressants experience such episodes.

**Psychosocial treatment.** The psychotherapy for cyclothymic disorder patients is best directed toward increasing the patients' awareness of their condition and helping them develop coping mechanisms for their mood swings. Therapists usually need to help patients repair any damage done during episodes of hypomania. Such damage may include both work-related and family-related problems.

Because of the long-term nature of cyclothymic disorder, patients often require lifelong treatment. Family and group therapies may be supportive, educational, and therapeutic for the patients and those involved in their lives.

## References

Akiskal H S: Depression in cyclothymic and related temperaments: Clinical and pharmacologic considerations. J Clin Psychiatry Monogr *10*: 37, 1992.

Bloch A L, Shear M K, Markowitz J C, Leon A C, Perry J C: An empirical study of defense mechanisms in dysthymia. Am J Psychiatry *150*: 1194, 1993.

Gabbard G O: *Psychodynamic Psychiatry in Clinical Practice: The DSM-IV Edition.* American Psychiatric Press, Washington, 1994.

Garrison C Z, Addy C L, Jackson K L, McKeown R E, Waller J L: Major depressive disorder and dysthymia in young adolescence. Am J Epidemiol *135*: 792, 1992.

Hellerstein D J, Yanowitch P, Rosenthal J, Samstag L W, Maurer M, Kasch K, Burrows L, Poster M, Cantillon M, Winston A: A randomized double-blind study of fluoxetine versus placebo in the treatment of dysthymic. Am J Psychiatry *150*: 1169, 1993.

Howland R H: Pharmacotherapy of dysthymia: A review. J Clin Psychopharmacol *11*: 83, 1991.

Howland R H, Thase M E: Biological studies of dysthymia. Biol Psychiatry *30*: 283, 1991.

Howland R H, Thase M E: A comprehensive review of cylothymic disorder. J Nerv Ment Dis *181*: 485, 1993.

Levitt A J, Joffe R T, Ennis J, MacDonald C, Kutcher S P: The prevalence of cyclothymia in borderline personality disorder. J Clin Psychiatry *51*: 335, 1990.

Markowitz J C, Moran M E, Kocsis J H, Francis A J: Prevalence and comorbidity of dysthymic disorder among psychiatric outpatients. J Affect Disord *24*: 63, 1992.

Osser D N: A systematic approach to the classification and pharmacotherapy of nonpsychotic major depression and dysthymia. J Clin Psychopharmacol *13*: 133, 1993.

Rosenthal J, Hemlock C, Hallerstein D J, Yanowitch P, Kasch K, Shupak C, Samstag L, Winston A: A preliminary study of serotonergic antidepressants in treatment of dysthymia. Prog Neuropsychopharmacol Biol Psychiatry *16*: 933, 1992.

Stewart J W, McGrath P J, Quitkin F M: Can mildly depressed outpatients with atypical depression benefit from antidepressants? Am J Psychiatry *149*: 615, 1992.

Wells K B, Burnam M A, Rogers W, Hays R, Camp P: The course of depression in adult outpatients: Results from the medical outcomes study. Arch Gen Psychiatry *49*: 788, 1992.

Zisook S: Treatment of dysthymia and atypical depression. J Clin Psychiatry Monogr *10*: 15, 1992.

# 15.3 / Other Mood Disorders

The fourth edition of *Diagnostic and Statistical Manual of Mental Disorders* (DSM-IV) introduces one new mood disorder diagnostic category (bipolar II disorder) in the body of the text and three new mood disorder diagnostic categories (minor depressive disorder, recurrent brief depressive disorder, and premenstrual dysphoric disorder) in the appendixes. Additional new DSM-IV mood disorder diagnoses are mood disorder due to a general medical condition and substance-induced mood disorder. Those changes are designed to broaden the recognition of mood disorder diagnoses, to describe mood disorder symptoms more specifically than in the past, and to facilitate the differential diagnosis of mood disorders.

## DEPRESSIVE DISORDERS

The diagnostic criteria for major depressive disorder specify a certain level of severity and a certain duration of symptoms as minimum requirements to meet the diagnosis. Although the criteria reflect a great deal of research and discussion, they are, by necessity, arbitrary. Many clinicians, especially primary care physicians, report that they have seen many patients who have depressive symptoms and suffer psychosocial impairment from them but who do not meet the diagnostic criteria for major depressive disorder. Usually, such patients fall short of the criteria either because their symptoms are not severe enough or because their symptoms have not lasted long enough. DSM-IV addresses the diagnostic problem posed by those patients by including two additional diagnostic categories.

The diagnostic criteria for minor depressive disorder are derived from the Research Diagnostic Criteria. The criteria apply to patients who have depressive symptoms that fail to meet the criteria for major depressive disorder in terms of severity but that do meet the criteria for duration. The diagnostic criteria for recurrent brief depressive disorder are derived from the 10th revision of the International Classification of Diseases (ICD-10). The criteria apply to patients who have depressive symptoms that fail to meet the criteria for major depressive disorder in terms of duration but that do meet the criteria for severity.

Minor depressive disorder and recurrent brief depressive disorder differ from dysthymic disorder, discussed in Section 15.2. Dysthymic disorder is a chronic depressive disorder that is not characterized by discrete episodes. In contrast, both minor depressive disorder and recurrent brief depressive disorder are characterized by discrete episodes.

## Depressive Disorder Not Otherwise Specified

If a patient exhibits depressive symptoms as the major feature and does not meet the diagnostic criteria for any other mood disorder or other DSM-IV mental disorder, the most appropriate diagnosis is depressive disorder not otherwise specified (NOS) (Table 15.3–1). Listed as examples here and also discussed in the appendixes are minor

### Table 15.3–1
### Diagnostic Criteria for Depressive Disorder Not Otherwise Specified

The depressive disorder not otherwise specified category includes disorders with depressive features that do not meet the criteria for major depressive disorder, dysthymic disorder, adjustment disorder with depressed mood, or adjustment disorder with mixed anxiety and depressed mood. Sometimes depressive symptoms can present as part of an anxiety disorder not otherwise specified. Examples of depressive disorder not otherwise specified include:

1. Premenstrual dysphoric disorder: in most menstrual cycles during the past year, symptoms (e.g., markedly depressed mood, marked anxiety, marked affective lability, decreased interest in activities) regularly occurred during the last week of the luteal phase (and remitted within a few days of the onset of menses). These symptoms must be severe enough to markedly interfere with work, school, or usual activities and be entirely absent for at least 1 week postmenses.

2. Minor depressive disorder: episodes of at least two weeks of depressive symptoms but with fewer than the five items required for major depressive disorder.

3. Recurrent brief depressive disorder: depressive episodes lasting from 2 days up to two weeks, occurring at least once a month for 12 months (not associated with the menstrual cycle).

4. Postpsychotic depressive disorder of schizophrenia: a major depressive episode that occurs during the residual phase of schizophrenia.

5. A major depressive episode superimposed on delusional disorder, psychotic disorder not otherwise specified, or the active phase of schizophrenia.

6. Situations in which the clinician has concluded that a depressive disorder is present but is unable to determine whether it is primary, due to a general medical condition, or substance induced.

Table from DSM-IV, *Diagnostic and Statistical Manual of Mental Disorders*, ed 4. Copyright American Psychiatric Association, Washington, 1994. Used with permission.

depressive disorder, recurrent brief depressive disorder, and premenstrual dysphoric disorder.

**Minor depressive disorder.** The literature in the United States on minor depressive disorder is limited, partly by the fact that the term "minor depression" is used to describe a wide range of disorders, including what is called dysthymic disorder in DSM-IV. The European literature on minor depressive disorder, although limited, is more extensive than the United States literature. The information about minor depressive disorder is helped considerably by the introduction in the appendix of DSM-IV of specific diagnostic guidelines that allow researchers to use a single definition of the disorder.

EPIDEMIOLOGY. The epidemiology of minor depressive disorder is not known, but preliminary data indicate that it may be as common as major depressive disorder—that is, about 5 percent prevalence in the general population. Preliminary data also indicate that the disorder is more common in women than in men. Minor depressive disorder probably affects persons of virtually any age, from childhood to old age.

ETIOLOGY. The cause of minor depressive disorder is not known. The same causative considerations given major depressive disorder should be considered. Specifically, the biological theories involve the activities of noradrenergic and serotonergic biogenic amine systems and the thyroid and adrenal neuroendocrine axes. The psychological theories center on issues of loss, guilt, and punitive superegos.

DIAGNOSIS. The DSM-IV diagnostic criteria for minor depressive disorder list symptoms equal in duration to those of major depressive disorder but of less severity (Table 15.3–2). The availability of the diagnostic category allows for the specific diagnosis of patients whose lives are affected by depressive symptoms but whose symptoms do not meet the severity required for a diagnosis of major depressive disorder.

CLINICAL FEATURES. The clinical features of minor depressive disorder are virtually identical to the clinical features of major depressive disorder, except that they are of less severity. The central symptoms of both disorders is the same—that is, a depressed mood.

DIFFERENTIAL DIAGNOSIS. The differential diagnosis for minor depressive disorder is the same as that for major depressive disorder. Of special importance for the differential diagnosis of minor depressive disorder are dysthymic disorder and recurrent brief depressive disorder. Dysthymic disorder is characterized by the presence of chronic depressive symptoms, whereas recurrent brief depressive disorder is characterized by multiple brief episodes of severe depressive symptoms.

COURSE AND PROGNOSIS. No definitive data on the course and the prognosis of minor depressive disorder are available. However, minor depressive disorder is probably similar to major depressive disorder: a long-term course that may require long-term treatment. A significant proportion of patients with minor depressive disorder are probably at risk for other mood disorders, including dysthymic disorder, bipolar I disorder, bipolar II disorder, and major depressive disorder.

TREATMENT. The treatment of minor depressive disorder can include psychotherapy or pharmacotherapy or

**Table 15.3–2**
**Research Criteria for Minor Depressive Disorder**

A. A mood disturbance, defined as follows:

(1) At least two (but less than five) of the following symptoms have been present during the same 2-week period and represent a change from previous functioning; at least one of the symptoms is either (a) or (b):

  (a) depressed mood most of the day, nearly every day, as indicated by either subjective report (e.g., feels sad or empty) or observation made by others (e.g., appears tearful). **Note:** In children and adolescents, can be irritable mood.

  (b) markedly diminished interest or pleasure in all, or almost all, activities most of the day, nearly every day (as indicated by either subjective account or observation made by others)

  (c) significant weight loss when not dieting or weight gain (e.g., a change of more than 5% of body weight in a month), or decrease or increase in appetite nearly every day. **Note:** In chidren, consider failure to make expected weight gains.

  (d) insomnia or hypersomnia nearly every day

  (e) psychomotor agitation or retardation nearly every day (observable by others, not merely subjective feelings of restlessness or being slowed down)

  (f) fatigue or loss of energy nearly every day

  (g) feelings of worthlessness or excessive or inappropriate guilt (which may be delusional) nearly every day (not merely self-reproach or guilt about being sick)

  (h) diminished ability to think or concentrate, or indecisiveness, nearly every day (either by subjective account or as observed by others)

  (i) recurrent thoughts of death (not just fear of dying), recurrent suicidal ideation without a specific plan, or a suicide attempt or a specific plan for committing suicide

(2) the symptoms cause clinically significant distress or impairment in social, occupational, or other important areas of functioning

(3) the symptoms are not due to the direct physiological effects of a substance (e.g., a drug of abuse, a medication) or a general medical condition (e.g., hypothyroidism)

(4) the symptoms are not better accounted for by Bereavement (i.e., a normal reaction to the death of a loved one)

B. There has never been a major depressive episode, and criteria are not met for dythymic disorder.

C. There has never been a manic episode, a mixed episode, or a hypomanic episode, and criteria are not met for cyclothymic disorder. **Note:** This exclusion does not apply if all of the manic-, mixed-, or hypomanic-like episodes are substance or treatment induced.

D. The mood disturbance does not occur exclusively during schizophrenia, schizophreniform disorder, schizoaffective disorder, delusional disorder, or psychotic disorder not otherwise specified.

Table from DSM-IV, *Diagnostic and Statistical Manual of Mental Disorders*, ed 4. Copyright American Psychiatric Association, Washington, 1994. Used with permission.

both. Some psychotherapists advocate the use of multiple psychotherapeutic approaches, but using the psychotherapy data for major depressive disorder is a more conservative approach. Insight-oriented psychotherapy, cognitive therapy, interpersonal therapy, and behavior therapy are the psychotherapeutic treatments for major depressive disorder and, by implication, for minor depressive disorder. Although the experimental data are limited, patients with minor depressive disorder are probably responsive to pharmacotherapy, particularly serotonin-specific reuptake inhibitors (SSRIs) and bupropion (Wellbutrin).

**Recurrent brief depressive disorder.** Recurrent brief depressive disorder is characterized by multiple, relatively brief (less than two weeks) episodes of depressive symptoms that, except for their brief duration, meet the diagnostic criteria for major depressive disorder. Recurrent brief depressive disorder has been written about mostly in the European literature; however, with its introduction as a diagnostic category in the appendix of DSM-IV, the disorder is likely to gain rapid acceptance in the United States. Its acceptance in the United States will likely be further facilitated by clinicians' increasing awareness that recurrent brief depressive disorder is a relatively common disorder associated with significant morbidity.

EPIDEMIOLOGY. Extensive studies on the epidemiology of recurrent brief depressive disorder have not been conducted in the United States. Available data indicate that the 10-year prevalence rate for the disorder is estimated to be 10 percent for persons in their 20s; the one-year prevalence rate for the general population is estimated to be 5 percent. Those figures indicate that recurrent brief depressive disorder is most common among young adults, but many more studies must be conducted to refine the data.

ETIOLOGY. One study found that patients with recurrent brief depressive disorder share several biological abnormalities with patients with major depressive disorder when compared with mentally healthy control subjects. The variables include nonsuppression on the dexamethasone-suppression test (DST), a blunted response to thyrotropin-releasing hormone (TRH), and a shortening of rapid eye movement (REM) sleep latency. The data are consistent with the idea that recurrent brief depressive disorder is closely related to major depressive disorder in its cause and pathophysiology. The available data also indicate that family histories of mood disorders are similar for recurrent brief depressive disorder and major depressive disorder, suggesting a close relation between the two disorders.

DIAGNOSIS. The DSM-IV diagnostic criteria for recurrent brief depressive disorder specify that the symptom duration for each episode is less than two weeks (Table 15.3–3). Otherwise, the diagnostic criteria for recurrent brief depressive disorder and major depressive disorder are essentially identical.

CLINICAL FEATURES. The clinical features of recurrent brief depressive disorder are almost identical to those of major depressive disorder. One subtle difference is that the lives of patients with recurrent brief depressive disorder may seem more disrupted or chaotic because of the frequent changes in their moods when compared with the lives of patients with major depressive disorder, whose depressive episodes occur at a measured pace. One study calculated the mean length of time between depressive episodes in recurrent brief depressive disorder to be 18 days. Another study reported that episodes of sleep dis-

**Table 15.3–3**
**Research Criteria for Recurrent Brief Depressive Disorder**

A. Criteria, except for duration, are met for a major depressive episode.

B. The depressive periods in criterion A last at least 2 days but less than 2 weeks.

C. The depressive periods occur at least once a month for 12 consecutive months and are not associated with the menstrual cycle.

D. The periods of depressed mood cause clinically significant distress or impairment in social, occupational, or other important areas of functioning.

E. The symptoms are not due to the direct physiological effects of a substance (e.g., a drug of abuse, a medication) or a general medical condition (e.g., hypothyroidism).

F. There has never been a major depressive episode, and criteria are not met for dysthymic disorder.

G. There has never been a manic episode, a mixed episode, or a hypomanic episode, and criteria are not met for cyclothymic disorder. **Note:** This exclusion does not apply if all of the manic-, mixed-, or hypomanic-like episodes are substance or treatment induced.

H. The mood disturbance does not occur exclusively during schizophrenia, schizophreniform disorder, schizoaffective disorder, delusional disorder, or psychotic disorder not otherwise specified.

Table from DSM-IV, *Diagnostic and Statistical Manual of Mental Disorders*, ed 4. Copyright American Psychiatric Association, Washington, 1994. Used with permission.

turbance closely coincide with the episodes of depression, thus helping the clinician establish the periodicity of the depressive episodes.

DIFFERENTIAL DIAGNOSIS. The differential diagnosis for recurrent brief depressive disorder is the same as that for major depressive disorder. The clinician should consider bipolar disorders and major depressive disorder with seasonal pattern in the differential diagnosis. Research into recurrent brief depressive disorder may find an association with the rapid cycling type of bipolar disorders. The clinician should also assess whether there is a seasonal pattern to the recurrence of depressive episodes in a patient being evaluated for a diagnosis of recurrent brief depressive disorder. At least one researcher has proposed that patients with recurrent brief depressive disorder be subtyped according to the relative frequencies of their depressive episodes. That differentiation is not included in DSM-IV, although the differentiation may yet prove to have prognostic or treatment implications.

COURSE AND PROGNOSIS. The course and the prognosis for patients with recurrent brief depressive disorder are not well known. Based on the available data, their course, including age of onset, and their prognosis are similar to those of patients with major depressive disorder.

TREATMENT. The treatment of patients with recurrent brief depressive disorder should be similar to the treatment of patients with major depressive disorder. The main treatments should be psychotherapy (insight-oriented psychotherapy, cognitive therapy, interpersonal therapy, or be-

havior therapy) and pharmacotherapy with the standard antidepressant drugs. Some of the treatments for bipolar I disorder—lithium (Eskalith) and anticonvulsants—may be of therapeutic value, but those agents have not yet been studied in patients with recurrent brief depressive disorder.

**Premenstrual dysphoric disorder.** DSM-IV includes suggested diagnostic criteria for premenstrual dysphoric disorder in its appendixes to help researchers and clinicians in the evaluation of the validity of the diagnosis. Premenstrual dysphoric disorder has also been referred to as late luteal phase dysphoric disorder, premenstrual syndrome, and simply PMS. Whether the syndrome warrants an official diagnosis remains controversial. Nevertheless, the generally recognized syndrome is one involving mood symptoms (for example, lability), behavior symptoms (for example, changes in eating patterns), and physical symptoms (for example, breast tenderness, edema, and headaches). That pattern of symptoms occurs at a specific time during the menstrual cycle, and the symptoms resolve for some period of time between menstrual cycles.

EPIDEMIOLOGY. Because of the absence of generally agreed on diagnostic criteria, the epidemiology of premenstrual dysphoric disorder is not known with certainty. One study reported that about 40 percent of women have at least mild symptoms of the disorder and that from 2 to 10 percent meet the full diagnostic criteria for the disorder.

ETIOLOGY. On the one hand, the cause of premenstrual dysphoric disorder is not known. On the other hand, because of the timing of the symptoms with the menstrual cycle, the hormonal changes occuring during the menstrual cycle are probably involved in the production of symptoms. Among the theories that have been put forth for the disorder, one of the most commonly stated is that the disorder is characterized by an abnormally high estrogen-to-progesterone ratio in affected women. Other hypotheses are that affected women have biogenic amine neurons that are abnormally affected by changes in the hormones, that the disorder is an example of a chronobiological phase disorder, and that the disorder is the result of abnormal prostaglandin activity. In addition to the biological theories, societal and personal issues regarding menstruation and womanhood may affect the symptoms of individual patients.

DIAGNOSIS. The appendix of DSM-IV contains suggested diagnostic criteria for premenstrual dysphoric disorder (Table 15.3–4). The criteria include symptoms regarding abnormal mood, abnormal behavior, and somatic complaints.

CLINICAL FEATURES. The most common mood and cognitive symptoms are lability of mood, irritability, anxiety, decreased interest in activities, increased fatigability, and difficulty in concentrating. Behavioral symptoms often include changes in appetite and sleep patterns. The most common somatic complaints are headache, breast tenderness, and edema. In affected women the symptoms appear during most (if not all) menstrual cycles, although the symptoms usually remit before the end of the blood flow. Affected women are symptom-free for at least a week during each menstrual cycle.

DIFFERENTIAL DIAGNOSIS. If symptoms are present throughout the menstrual cycle, with no intercycle symp-

**Table 15.3–4**
**Research Criteria for Premenstrual Dysphoric Disorder**

A. In most menstrual cycles during the past year, five (or more) of the following symptoms were present for most of the time during the last week of the luteal phase, began to remit within a few days after the onset of the follicular phase, and were absent in the week postmenses, with at least one of the symptoms being either (1), (2), (3), or (4):

   (1) markedly depressed mood, feelings of hopelessness, or self-deprecating thoughts
   (2) marked anxiety, tension, feelings of being "keyed up" or "on edge"
   (3) marked affective liability (e.g., feeling suddenly sad or tearful or increased sensitivity to rejection)
   (4) persistent and marked anger or irritability or increased interpersonal conflicts
   (5) decreased interest in usual activities (e.g., work, school, friends, hobbies)
   (6) subjective sense of difficulty in concentrating
   (7) lethargy, easy fatigability, or marked lack of energy
   (8) marked change in appetite, overeating, or specific food cravings
   (9) hypersomnia or insomnia
  (10) a subjective sense of being overwhelmed or out of control
  (11) other physical symptoms, such as breast tenderness or swelling, headaches, joint or muscle pain, a sensation of "bloating," weight gain.

**Note:** In menstruating females, the luteal phase corresponds to the period between ovulation and the onset of menses, and the follicular phase begins with menses. In nonmenstruating females (e.g., those who have had a hysterectomy), the timing of luteal and follicular phases may require measurement of circulating reproductive hormones.

B. The disturbance markedly interferes with work or school or with usual social activities and relationships with others (e.g., avoidance of social activities, decreased productivity and efficiency at work or school).

C. The disturbance is not merely an exacerbation of the symptoms of another disorder, such as major depressive disorder, panic disorder, dysthymic disorder, or a personality disorder (although it may be superimposed on any of these disorders).

D. Criteria A, B, and C must be confirmed by prospective daily ratings during at least two consecutive symptomatic cycles. (The diagnosis may be made provisionally prior to this confirmation.)

Table from DSM-IV, *Diagnostic and Statistical Manual of Mental Disorders*, ed 4. Copyright American Psychiatric Association, Washington, 1994. Used with permission.

tom relief, the clinician should consider one of the non-menstrual-cycle-related mood disorders and anxiety disorders. Even if the symptoms have a cyclical nature, the presence of especially severe symptoms should prompt the clinician to consider other mood disorders and anxiety disorders.

COURSE AND PROGNOSIS. The course and the prognosis of premenstrual dysphoric disorder have not been adequately studied to reach any reasonable conclusions. Anecdotally, the symptoms tend to be chronic unless effective treatment is initiated.

TREATMENT. Treatment of premenstrual dysphoric disorder includes support for the patient regarding the pres-

ence and the recognition of the symptoms. In preliminary studies, progesterone supplementation, fluoxetine (Prozac), and alprazolam (Xanax) have all been reported to be effective, although no treatment has been conclusively demonstrated to be effective in multiple well-controlled trials.

# BIPOLAR DISORDERS

Clinicians have long reported that in some patients the primary symptom seems to be depressive episodes, but the course of the disorder is interspersed with episodes of mild manic symptoms (that is, hypomanic episodes). Such disorders have been called bipolar II disorder (by those researchers who think that the disorder belongs in the bipolar disorders spectrum) and major depressive disorder with hypomanic episodes (by those researchers who think that the disorder belongs in the depressive disorders spectrum). The revised third edition of DSM (DSM-III-R) used the diagnosis bipolar disorder not otherwise specified, but in DSM-IV the diagnosis is bipolar II disorder. The distinction between bipolar II disorder and recurrent major depressive episodes with hypomania has important implications for prognostic and treatment assessments and decisions.

## Bipolar II Disorder

Bipolar II disorder, alternatively called recurrent major depressive episodes with hypomania, is a new diagnostic category in DSM-IV. Patients with the disorder were formerly classified as having bipolar disorder not otherwise specified (NOS).

**Epidemiology.** The epidemiology of bipolar II disorder is not known accurately at this time because of the relatively recent recognition of the disorder.

**Etiology.** Although the classification of bipolar II disorder with the mood disorders implies a close association with the mood disorders, some investigators have hypothesized that bipolar II disorder is related to borderline personality disorder. However, some data indicate that bipolar II disorder tends to be inherited as bipolar II disorder, thus suggesting that it has its own unique genetic predisposition.

**Diagnosis.** The diagnostic criteria for bipolar II disorder specify a particular severity, frequency, and duration of the hypomanic symptoms. The diagnostic criteria for a hypomanic episode (Table 15.1–9) are listed separately from the criteria for bipolar II disorder (Table 15.3–5). The criteria have been established to decrease the over-diagnosis of hypomanic episodes and the incorrect classification of patients with major depressive disorder as patients with bipolar II disorder. Clinically, the psychiatrist may find it difficult to distinguish euthymia from hypomania in a patient who has been chronically depressed for many months or years. As with bipolar I disorder, antidepressant-induced hypomanic episodes are not diagnostic of bipolar II disorder.

DIAGNOSTIC QUALIFIERS. DSM-IV allows the qualification of the diagnosis of bipolar II disorder with specific

## Table 15.3–5
### Diagnostic Criteria for Bipolar II Disorder

A. Presence (or history) of one or more major depressive episodes.

B. Presence (or history) of at least one hypomanic episode.

C. There has never been a manic episode.

D. The mood symptoms in criteria A and B are not better accounted for by schizoaffective disorder, and are not superimposed on schizophrenia, schizophreniform disorder, delusional disorder, or psychotic disorder NOS.

E. The symptoms cause clinically significant distress or impairment in social, occupational, or other important areas of functioning.

*Specify* current or most recent episode:
   **Hypomanic:** if currently (or most recently) in a hypomanic episode
   **Depressed:** if currently (or most recently) in a major depressive episode

*Specify* (for current or most recent major depressive episode only if it is the most recent type of mood episode):
   **Severity/psychotic/remission specifiers. Note:** Fifth-digit codes cannot be used here because the code for bipolar II disorder already uses the fifth digit.
   **Chronic**
   **With catatonic features**
   **With melancholic features**
   **With atypical features**
   **With postpartum onset**

*Specify*:
   **Longitudinal course specifiers (with or without interepisode recovery)**
   **With seasonal pattern** (applies only to the pattern of major depressive episodes)
   **With rapid cycling**

Table from DSM-IV, *Diagnostic and Statistical Manual of Mental Disorders*, ed 4. Copyright American Psychiatric Association, Washington, 1994. Used with permission.

terms, including the specification of the symptom picture as being with melancholic, atypical, or catatonic features (Tables 15.1–16, and 15.1–18). DSM-IV also allows the following course specifiers: with rapid cycling, with seasonal pattern, and with postpartum onset (Table 15.1–19).

**Clinical features.** The clinical features of bipolar II disorder are those of major depressive disorder combined with those of hypomanic episode. Although the data are limited, a few studies indicate that bipolar II disorder is associated with more marital disruption and onset at an earlier age than is bipolar I disorder. Evidence also indicates that bipolar II disorder patients are at greater risk of both attempting and completing suicide than are bipolar I disorder and major depressive disorder patients.

**Differential diagnosis.** The differential diagnosis of patients being evaluated for a diagnosis of bipolar II disorder should include bipolar I disorder, major depressive disorder, and borderline personality disorder. The differentiation between bipolar II disorder on the one hand and major depressive disorder and bipolar I disorder on the other hand rests on the clinical evaluation of the maniclike episodes. The clinician should not mistake euthymia in a chronically depressed patient as a hypomanic or manic episode. Patients with borderline personality disorder often have the same type of severely disrupted life that

patients with bipolar II disorder have, because of the multiple episodes of significant mood disorder symptoms.

**Course and prognosis.** The course and the prognosis of bipolar II disorder have just begun to be studied; however, preliminary data indicate that it is a stable diagnosis, as shown by the high likelihood that patients with bipolar II disorder will have the same diagnosis up to five years later. The data indicate that bipolar II disorder is a chronic disease that warrants long-term treatment strategies.

**Treatment.** The treatment of bipolar II disorder must be approached cautiously, since the treatment of depressive episodes with antidepressants can frequently precipitate a manic episode. Whether or not typical bipolar I disorder medication strategies (for example, lithium and anticonvulsants) are effective in the treatment of bipolar II disorder patients is still under investigation. A trial of such agents seems warranted, especially when treatment with antidepressants alone has not been successful.

## Bipolar Disorder Not Otherwise Specified

If patients exhibit depressive and manic symptoms as the major features of their disorder and do not meet the diagnostic criteria for any other mood disorder or other DSM-IV mental disorder, the most appropriate diagnosis is bipolar disorder not otherwise specified (NOS) (Table 15.3–6). DSM-IV allows for the further specification of with rapid cycling, with seasonal pattern, or with postpartum onset (Table 15.1–19).

**Atypical cycloid psychoses.** This group of disorders shows some features of bipolar I disorder but generally do not meet the complete diagnostic criteria for that category. Some patients with atypical cycloid psychoses may be classified as having bipolar disorder not otherwise specified.

MOTILITY PSYCHOSIS. The two forms of motility psychosis are akinetic and hyperkinetic. The akinetic form of motility psychosis has a clinical presentation similar to that of catatonic stupor. In contrast to the catatonic type of schizophrenia, however, akinetic motility psychosis has a rapidly resolving and favorable course that does not lead to personality dete-

## Table 15.3–6
### Diagnostic Criteria for Bipolar Disorder Not Otherwise Specified

The bipolar disorder not otherwise specified category includes disorders with bipolar features that do not meet criteria for any specific bipolar disorder. Examples include:

1. Very rapid alternation (over days) between manic symptoms and depressive symptoms that do not meet minimal duration criteria for a manic episode or major depressive episode

2. Recurrent hypomanic episodes without intercurrent depressive symptoms

3. A manic or mixed episode superimposed on delusional disorder, residual schizophrenia, or psychotic disorder not otherwise specified

4. Situations in which the clinician has concluded that a bipolar disorder is present but is unable to determine whether it is primary, due to a general medical condition, or substance induced

Table from DSM-IV, *Diagnostic and Statistical Manual of Mental Disorders*, ed 4. Copyright American Psychiatric Association, Washington, 1994. Used with permission.

rioration. In its hyperkinetic form, motility psychosis may resemble manic or catatonic excitement. As with the akinetic form, the hyperkinetic form has a rapidly resolving and favorable course.

CONFUSIONAL PSYCHOSIS. Excited confusional psychosis, as originally described, was differentiated from mania by several characteristics: in excited confusional psychosis, more anxiety, less distractibility, and a degree of speech incoherence out of proportion to the severity of the flight of ideas. Confusional psychosis is probably a clinical variation of the mania seen in bipolar I disorder.

ANXIETY-BLISSFULNESS PSYCHOSIS. Anxiety-blissfulness psychosis may resemble agitated depression, but it may also be characterized by so much inhibition that the patient can hardly move. Periodic states of overwhelming anxiety and paranoid ideas of reference are characteristic of the condition, but self-accusation, hypochondriacal preoccupation, other depressive symptoms, and hallucinations may also accompany it. The blissful phase manifests itself most frequently in expansive behavior and grandiose ideas, which are concerned less with self-aggrandizement than with the mission of making others happy and saving the world.

## OTHER MOOD DISORDERS

Two mood disorder diagnoses to be considered in the differential diagnosis of any patient with mood disorder symptoms are mood disorder due to a general medical condition and substance-induced mood disorder. DSM-IV includes those diagnostic categories within the mood disorders to encourage and facilitate the process of differential diagnosis.

In DSM-III-R those diagnoses were labeled organic mood disorders and were listed in two separate places—with psychoactive substance-induced organic mental disorders and with organic mental disorders associated with Axis III physical disorders or conditions or whose etiology is unknown. That somewhat cumbersome organization has been changed in DSM-IV by (1) eliminating the term "organic" from DSM-IV and (2) moving both diagnostic categories into the mood disorders section.

It can be difficult to determine whether mood disorder symptoms in a patient with a general medical condition are (1) secondary to the effects on the brain of the general medical condition (classified as a mood disorder due to a general medical condition), (2) secondary to the effects on the brain of drugs used to treat the general medical condition (classified as a substance-induced mood disorder), (3) reflective of an adjustment disorder caused by the general medical condition (classified as an adjustment disorder), or (4) reflective of a primary mood disorder (for example, major depressive disorder). The difficulty of the clinical differentiation is recognized in DSM-IV by the grouping of the disorders (except for adjustment disorder) in the mood disorders section.

## Mood Disorder Due to a General Medical Condition

When depressive or manic symptoms are present in a patient with a general medical condition, attributing the

depressive symptoms to either the general medical condition or a mood disorder can be difficult. Many general medical conditions present depressive symptoms, such as poor sleep, decreased appetite, and fatigue.

**Epidemiology.** The epidemiology of mood disorder due to a general medical condition is not known. However, the disorder is probably common and often undiagnosed.

**Etiology.** A wide array of somatic disorders have been implicated as causes of mood disorder symptoms, including endocrine disorders, especially Cushing's syndrome, and neurological disorders, such as brain tumors, encephalitis, and epilepsy. Structural damage to the brain, similar to

**Table 15.3–7**
**Principal Neurological and Systemic Disorders Producing Depression**

Neurological disorders
  Extrapyramidal diseases
    Parkinson's disease
    Huntington's disease
    Progressive supranuclear palsy
  Cerebrovascular disease (especially anterior hemispheric lesions)
  Cerebral neoplasms
  Cerebral trauma
  CNS infections
  Multiple sclerosis
  Epilepsy
  Narcolepsy
  Hydrocephalus

Systemic disorders
  Infections
    Viral
    Bacterial

Endocrine disorders
  Hyperthyroidism
  Hypothyroidism
  Hyperparathyroidism
  Hypoparathyroidism
  Cushing's syndrome (steroid excess)
  Addison's disease (steroid insufficiency)
  Hyperaldosteronism
  Premenstrual depression

Inflammatory disorders
  Systemic lupus erythematosus
  Rheumatoid arthritis
  Temporal arteritis
  Sjögren's syndrome

Vitamin deficiencies
  Folate
  Vitamin $B_{12}$
  Niacin
  Vitamin C

Miscellaneous systemic disorders
  Cardiopulmonary disease
  Renal disease and uremia
  Systemic neoplasms
  Porphyria
  Klinefelter's syndrome
  Acquired immune deficiency syndrome (AIDS)
  Postpartum mood disorders
  Postoperative mood disorders

Table from J L Cummings: *Clinical Neuropsychiatry*, p 187. Grune & Stratton, Orlando, 1985. Used with permission.

**Table 15.3–8**
**Causes of Secondary Mania**

Neurological disorders
  Extrapyramidal disease
    Huntington's disease
    Postencephalitic Parkinson's disease
    Wilson's disease

  CNS infections
    General paresis
    Viral encephalitis

  Miscellaneous conditions
    Cerebral neoplasms
    Cerebral trauma
    Thalamotomy
    Cerebrovascular accidents
    Multiple sclerosis
    Temporal lobe epilepsy
    Pick's disease
    Kleine-Levin syndrome
    Klinefelter's syndrome

Systemic disorders
  Uremia and hemodialysis
  Dialysis dementia
  Hyperthyroidism
  Pellagra
  Carcinoid syndrome
  Vitamin $B_{12}$ deficiency
  Postpartum mania

Drugs
  Levodopa
  Bromocriptine
  Sympathomimetics
  Isoniazid
  Procarbazine
  Bromide
  Cocaine
  Amphetamines
  Procyclidine
  Hydralazine
  Cyclobenzaprine
  Phencyclidine (PCP)
  Cimetidine
  Yohimbine
  Baclofen
  Metrizamide (following myelography)

Table from J L Cummings: *Clinical Neuropsychiatry*, p 187. Grune & Stratton, Orlando, 1985. Used with permission.

**Table 15.3–9**
**Diagnostic Criteria for Mood Disorder Due to a General Medical Condition**

A. A prominent and persistent disturbance in mood predominates in the clinical picture and is characterized by either (or both) of the following:

  (1) Depressed mood or markedly diminished interest or pleasure in all, or almost all, activities
  (2) elevated, expansive, or irritable mood

B. There is evidence from the history, physical examination, or laboratory findings that the disturbance is the direct physiological consequence of a general medical condition.

C. The disturbance is not better accounted for by another mental disorder (e.g., adjustment disorder with depressed mood, in response to the stress of having a general medical condition).

D. The disturbance does not occur exclusively during the course of delirium or dementia.

E. The symptoms cause clinically significant distress or impairment in social, occupational, or other important areas of functioning.

*Specify* type:
  **with depressive features:** if the predominant mood is depressed but the full criteria are not met for a major depressive episode
  **with major depressive-like episode:** if the full criteria are met (except criterion D) for a major depressive episode
  **with manic features:** if the predominant mood is elevated, euphoric, or irritable
  **with mixed features:** if symptoms of both mania and depression are present and neither predominates

Table from DSM-IV, *Diagnostic and Statistical Manual of Mental Disorders*, ed 4. Copyright American Psychiatric Association, Washington, 1994. Used with permission.

what occurs in hemispheric cerebrovascular diseases, is a common cause of mood disorder due to a general medical condition. Some of the common medical conditions associated with depression are listed in Table 15.3–7, and those associated with mania are listed in Table 15.3–8.

**Diagnosis.** The DSM-IV diagnostic criteria for mood disorder due to a general medical condition (Table 15.3–9) allow the clinician to specify whether the symptoms are manic (full or partial symptoms), depressive (full or partial symptoms), or mixed.

**Clinical features.** Disturbances of mood resembling those observed in depressive and manic states are the predominant and essential clinical features. To make the diagnosis, the physician must find a general medical condition that antedates the onset of the mood disorder symptoms. The disorder varies in severity from mild to severe or psychotic and may be indistinguishable from the symptoms seen in major depressive disorder and bipolar I disorder. Delusions and hallucinations may be present, as well as mild to moderate cognitive impairment.

**Differential diagnosis.** The differential diagnosis should include substance-induced mood disorder (involving substances used to treat the medical condition), the primary mood disorders, and adjustment disorders. In some health delivery systems, malingering must also be considered in the differential diagnosis.

**Course and prognosis.** The onset of the symptoms may be sudden or insidious, and the course varies, depending on the underlying cause. The removal of the cause does not necessarily result in the patient's prompt recovery from the mood disorder. The disorder may persist for weeks or months after the successful treatment of the underlying physical condition. As with the other mood disorders, suicide is a risk for patients with mood disorder due to a general medical condition.

**Treatment.** Management of the disorder involves determining the cause and treating the underlying disorder. Psychopharmacological treatment may be indicated and should follow the guidelines applicable to the treatment of depression or mania, with due regard for the coexisting physical condition. Psychotherapy may be useful as an adjunct to other treatments.

## Substance-Induced Mood Disorder

Substance-induced mood disorder must always be considered in the differential diagnosis of mood disorder symptoms. In general, the clinician should consider three possibilities: First, the patient may be taking drugs for the treatment of nonpsychiatric medical problems. Second, the patient may have been accidentally and perhaps unknowingly exposed to neurotoxic chemicals. Third, the patient may have taken a substance for recreational purposes or may be dependent on such a substance.

**Epidemiology.** The epidemiology of substance-induced mood disorder is not known. However, the prevalence is probably high, given the number of prescription drugs that can cause depression and mania, the number of toxic chemicals in the environment and the workplace, and the widespread use of so-called recreational drugs.

**Table 15.3–10**
**Drugs Implicated in Producing Depression Syndromes**

| | |
|---|---|
| **Cardiac and antihypertensive drugs** | |
| Bethanidine | Digitalis |
| Clonidine | Prazosin |
| Guanethidine | Procainamide |
| Hydralazine | Veratrum |
| Methyldopa | Lidocaine |
| Propranolol | Oxprenolol |
| Reserpine | Methoserpidine |
| **Sedatives and hypnotics** | |
| Barbiturates | Benzodiazepines |
| Chloral hydrate | Chlormethiazole |
| Ethanol | Chlorazepate |
| **Steroids and hormones** | |
| Corticosteroids | Triamcinalone |
| Oral contraceptives | Norethisterone |
| Prednisone | Danazol |
| **Stimulants and appetite suppressants** | |
| Amphetamine | Diethylpropion |
| Fenfluramine | Phenmetrazine |
| **Psychotropic drugs** | |
| Butyrophenones | Phenothiazines |
| **Neurological agents** | |
| Amantadine | Baclofen |
| Bromocriptine | Carbamazepine |
| Levodopa | Methosuximide |
| Tetrabenazine | Phenytoin |
| **Analgesics and anti-inflammatory drugs** | |
| Fenoprofen | Phenacetin |
| Ibuprofen | Phenylbutazone |
| Indomethacin | Pentazocine |
| Opiates | Benzydamine |
| **Antibacterial and antifungal drugs** | |
| Ampicillin | Griseofulvin |
| Sulfamethoxazole | Metronidazole |
| Clotrimazole | Nitrofurantoin |
| Cycloserine | Nalidixic acid |
| Dapsone | Sulfonamides |
| Ethionamide | Streptomycin |
| Tetracycline | Thiocarbanilide |
| **Antineoplastic drugs** | |
| Azathioprine | 6-Azauridine |
| C-Asparaginase | Bleomycin |
| Mithramycin | Trimethoprim |
| Vincristine | |
| **Miscellaneous drugs** | |
| Acetazolamide | Anticholinesterases |
| Choline | Cimetidine |
| Cyproheptadine | Diphenoxylate |
| Disulfiram | Lysergide |
| Methysergide | Mebeverine |
| Meclizine | Metaclopramide |
| Pizotifen | Salbutamol |

Table from J L Cummings: *Clinical Neuropsychiatry*, p 187. Grune & Stratton, Orlando, 1985. Used with permission.

**Table 15.3–11**
**Diagnostic Criteria for Substance-Induced Mood Disorder**

A. A prominent and persistent disturbance in mood predominates in the clinical picture and is characterized by either (or both) of the following:

    (1) depressed mood or markedly diminished interest or pleasure in all, or almost all, activities
    (2) elevated, expansive, or irritable mood

B. There is evidence from the history, physical examination, or laboratory findings of substance intoxication or withdrawal, and the symptoms in A developed during, or within a month of, significant substance intoxication or withdrawal.

C. The disturbance is not better accounted for by a mood disorder that is not substance-induced. Evidence that the symptoms are better accounted for by a mood disorder that is not substance-induced might include: the symptoms precede the onset of the substance abuse or dependence; persist for a substantial period of time (e.g., about a month) after the cessation of acute withdrawal or severe intoxication; are substantially in excess of what would be expected given the character, duration, or amount of the substance used; or there is other evidence suggesting the existence of an independent non-substance-induced mood disorder (e.g., a history of recurrent non-substance-related major depressive episodes).

D. The disturbance does not occur exclusively during the course of delirium.

E. The symptoms cause clinically significant distress or impairment in social, occupational, or other important areas of functioning.

**Note:** This diagnosis should be made instead of a diagnosis of substance intoxication or substance withdrawal only when the mood symptoms are in excess of those usually associated with the intoxication or withdrawal syndrome and when the symptoms are sufficiently severe to warrant independent clinical attention.

*Code:* [specific substance] mood disorder:
(alcohol; amphetamine [or amphetamine-like substance]; cocaine; hallucinogen; inhalant; opioid; phencyclidine [or phencyclidine-like substance]; sedative, hypnotic, or anxiolytic, other [or unknown] substance)

*Specify* type:
    **with depressive features:** if the predominant mood is depressed.
    **with manic features:** if the predominant mood is elevated, euphoric, or irritable.
    **with mixed features:** if symptoms of both mania and depression are present and neither predominates.

*Specify* if:
    **with onset during intoxication:** if the criteria are met for intoxication with the substance and the symptoms develop during the intoxication syndrome
    **with onset during withdrawal:** if criteria are met for withdrawal from the substance and the symptoms develop during, or shortly after, a withdrawal syndrome

Table from DSM-IV, *Diagnostic and Statistical Manual of Mental Disorders*, ed 4. Copyright American Psychiatric Association, Washington, 1994. Used with permission.

**Etiology.** Medications, especially antihypertensives, are probably the most frequent cause of substance-induced mood disorder, although a wide range of drugs can cause depression (Table 15.3–10) and mania (Table 15.3–8). Drugs such as reserpine (Serpasil) and methyldopa (Aldomet), both antihypertensive agents, can precipitate a depressive disorder, presumably by depleting serotonin, as happens in more than 10 percent of all persons who take the drugs.

**Diagnosis.** The DSM-IV diagnostic criteria for substance-induced mood disorder allow the specification of (1) the substance involved, (2) whether the onset was during intoxication or withdrawal, and (3) the nature of the symptoms (for example, manic or depressed) (Table 15.3–11). A maximum of a month between the use of the substance and the appearance of the symptoms is allowed in DSM-IV, although the usual time frame is probably shorter than a month. However, the diagnosis may sometimes be warranted after more than a month.

**Clinical features.** The substance-induced manic and depressive features can be identical to those of bipolar I disorder and major depressive disorder. However, substance-induced mood disorder may present more waxing and waning of the symptoms and a fluctuation in the patient's level of consciousness.

**Differential diagnosis.** The presence of a history of mood disorders in the patient or the patient's family weights toward the diagnosis of a primary mood disorder, although such a history does not rule out the possibility of substance-induced mood disorder. Substances may also trigger an underlying mood disorder in a patient who is biologically vulnerable to mood disorders.

**Course and prognosis.** The course and the prognosis of substance-induced mood disorder are variable; in general, shortly after the substance has been cleared from the body, a normal mood returns. Sometimes, however, the substance exposure seems to precipitate a long-lasting mood disorder that may take weeks or months to resolve completely.

**Treatment.** The primary treatment of substance-induced mood disorder is the identification of the causally involved substance. Usually, stopping the intake of the substance is sufficient to cause the mood disorder symptoms to abate. If the symptoms linger, treatment with appropriate psychiatric drugs may be necessary.

## Table 15.3–12
### Diagnostic Criteria for Mood Disorder Not Otherwise Specified

This category includes disorders with mood symptoms that do not meet the criteria for any specific mood disorder and in which it is difficult to choose between depressive disorder not otherwise specified and bipolar disorder not otherwise specified (e.g., acute agitation).

Table from DSM-IV, *Diagnostic and Statistical Manual of Mental Disorders*, ed 4. Copyright American Psychiatric Association, Washington, 1994. Used with permission.

## Mood Disorder Not Otherwise Specified

If patients exhibit depressive or manic symptoms or both as the major features of their disorder and do not meet the diagnostic criteria for any other mood disorder or other DSM-IV mental disorder, including depressive disorder not otherwise specified (NOS) and bipolar disorder NOS, the most appropriate diagnosis is mood disorder not otherwise specified (Table 15.3–12).

### References

Angst J: Recurrent brief depression: A new concept of depression. Pharmacopsychiatry 23: 63, 1990.

Angst J, Dobler-Mikola A: The Zurich study: A prospective epidemiological study of depressive, neurotic and psychosomatic syndromes: IV. Recurrent and nonrecurrent brief depression. Eur Arch Psychiatry Neurol Sci 234: 408, 1985.

Caplan L R, Ahmed I: Depression and neurological disease: Their distinction and association. Gen Hosp Psychiatry 14: 177, 1992.

Cassano G B, Akiskal H S, Musetti L, Perugi G, Soriani A, Mignani V: Psychopathology, temperament, and past course in primary major depressions: 2. Toward a redefinition of bipolarity with a new semistructured interview for depression. Psychopathology 5: 278, 1989.

Coryell W, Endicott J, Andreasen N, Keller M: Bipolar I, bipolar II, and nonbipolar major depression among relatives of affectively ill probands. Am J Psychiatry 142: 817, 1985.

Coryell W, Endicott J, Keller M, Andreasen N, Grove W, Hirschfeld R M, Scheftner W: Bipolar affective disorder and high achievement: A familial association. Am J Psychiatry 146: 983, 1989.

Coryell W, Keller M, Endicott J, Andreasen N, Clayton P, Hirschfeld R: Bipolar II illness: Course and outcome over a five-year period. Psychol Med 19: 129, 1989.

Depue R A, Arbisi P, Krauss S, Iacono W G, Leon A, Muir R, Allen J: Seasonal independence of low prolactin concentration and high spontaneous eye blink rates in unipolar and bipolar II seasonal affective disorder. Arch Gen Psychiatry 47: 356, 1990.

Fogel B S: Major depression versus organic mood disorder: A questionable distinction. J Clin Psychiatry 51: 53, 1990.

Freeman E W, Rickels K, Sondheimer S J: Course of premenstrual syndrome symptom severity after treatment. Am J Psychiatry 149: 531, 1992.

Gitlin M J, Pasnau R O: Psychiatric syndromes linked to reproductive function in women: A review of current knowledge. Am J Psychiatry 146: 1413, 1989.

Harrison W M, Endicott J, Nee J: Treatment of premenstrual dysphoria with alprazolam: A controlled study. Arch Gen Psychiatry 47: 270, 1990.

Heun R, Maier W: The distinction of bipolar II disorder from bipolar I and recurrent unipolar depression: results of a controlled family study. Acta Psychiatr Scand 87: 279, 1993.

Hurt S W, Schnurr P P, Severino S K, Freeman E W, Gise L H, Rivera-Tovar A, Steege J F: Late luteal phase dysphoric disorder in 670 women evaluated for premenstrual complaints. Am J Psychiatry 149: 525, 1992.

Kasper S, Ruhrmann S, Hasse T, Moller H J: Recurrent brief depression and its relationship to seasonal affective disorder. Eur Arch Psychiatry Clin Neurosci 242: 20, 1992.

Kupfer D J, Carpenter L L, Frank E E: Is bipolar II a unique disorder? Compr Psychiatry 29: 228, 1988.

Lazarus A A: The multimodal approach to the treatment of minor depression. Am J Psychother 46: 50, 1992.

Moline M L: Pharmacologic strategies for managing premenstrual syndrome. Clin Pharm 12: 181, 1993.

Montgomery S A, Montgomery D, Baldwin D, Green M: The duration, nature and recurrence rate of brief depressions. Prog Neuropsychopharmacol Biol Psychiatry 14: 729, 1990.

Parry B L, Berga S L, Kripke D F, Klauber M R, Laughlin G A, Yen S S C, Gillin C: Altered waveform of plasma nocturnal melatonin secretion in premenstrual dysphoria. Arch Gen Psychiatry 47: 1139, 1990.

Paykel E, moderator: Workshop IV: Depression in medical illness. Int Clin Psychopharmacol 7: 205, 1993.

Phillipp M, Delmo C D, Buller R, Schwarze H, Winter P, Maier W, Benkert O: Differentiation between major and minor depression. Psychopharmacology 106 (2, Suppl): S75, 1992.

Rice J P, McDonald-Scott P, Endicott J, Coryell W, Grove W M, Keller M B, Altis D: The stability of diagnosis with an application to bipolar II disorder. Psychiatry Res 19: 285, 1986.

Rihmer Z, Barsi J, Arato M, Demeter E: Suicide in subtypes of primary major depression. J Affect Disord 18: 221, 1990.

Simpson S G, Folstein S E, Meyers D A, McMahon F J, Brusco D M, DePaulo J R Jr: Bipolar II: the most common bipolar phenotype? Am J Psychiatry *150*: 901, 1993.

Staner L, De La Fuente J M, Kerkhofs M, Linkowski P, Mendlewicz J: Biological and clinical features of recurrent brief depression: A comparison with major depressed and healthy subjects. J Affect Disord *26*: 241, 1992.

Starkstein S E, Fedoroff P, Berthier M L, Robinson R G: Manic-depressive and pure manic states after brain lesions. Biol Psychiatry *29*: 149, 1991.

Stuart J W, Quitkin F M, Klein D F: The pharmacotherapy of minor depression. Am J Psychother *46*: 23, 1992.

Sunblad C, Hedberg M A, Eriksson E: Clomipramine administered during the luteal-phase reduces the symptoms of premenstrual-syndrome–A placebo-controlled trial. Neuropsychopharmacology *9*: 133, 1993.

# 16 ||||
# Anxiety Disorders

## 16.1 / Anxiety Disorders: Overview

The anxiety disorders are the disorders most affected by the diagnostic criteria in the third edition of *Diagnostic and Statistical Manual of Mental Disorders* (DSM-III), the revised third edition (DSM-III-R), and the fourth edition (DSM-IV) and by the growing knowledge of the biology of anxiety. Over the past 15 years, American psychiatry has seen the anxiety disorders move away from a conceptualization based on psychodynamic formulations of neuroses (Table 16.1–1). The result has been that the word "neurosis" has been dropped from the official nomenclature, and the divisions among the various anxiety disorders have been made on the basis of valid and reliably recognizable clinical criteria.

When evaluating a patient with anxiety, the clinician must still distinguish between normal and pathological types of anxiety. On a practical level, pathological anxiety is differentiated from normal anxiety by the assessments by patients, their families, their friends, and the clinician that pathological anxiety is, in fact, present. Such assessments are based on the patients' reported internal states, their behaviors, and their abilities to function. A patient with pathological anxiety requires a complete neuropsychiatric evaluation and an individually tailored treatment plan. The clinician must be aware that anxiety can be a component of many medical conditions and other mental disorders, especially depressive disorders.

Because it is clearly to one's advantage to respond with anxiety in certain threatening situations, one can speak of normal anxiety in contrast to abnormal or pathological anxiety. For example, anxiety is normal for the infant who is threatened by separation from parents or by loss of love, for children on their first day in school, for adolescents on their first date, for adults when they contemplate old age and death, and for anyone who is faced with illness. Anxiety is a normal accompaniment of growth, of change, of experiencing something new and untried, and of finding one's own identity and meaning in life. Pathological anxiety, by contrast, is an inappropriate response to a given stimulus by virtue of either its intensity or its duration.

## HISTORY

Nearly a century ago, Sigmund Freud coined the term "anxiety neurosis" and identified two forms of anxiety. One type of anxiety results from dammed-up libido. In other words, a physiological increase in sexual tension leads to a corresponding increase in libido, the mental representation of that physiological event. The normal outlet for such tension is, in Freud's view, sexual intercourse. However, other sexual practices, such as abstinence and coitus interruptus, prevent tension release and result in actual neuroses. The conditions of heightened anxiety related to libidinal blockage include neurasthenia, hypochondriasis, and anxiety neuroses, all of which Freud regarded as having a biological basis.

The other form of anxiety is best characterized as a diffuse sense of worry or dread that originates in a repressed thought or wish. That form of anxiety is responsible for the psychoneuroses—hysteria, phobias, and obsessional neuroses. Freud understood those conditions and the anxiety associated with them to be primarily related to psychological factors, rather than physiological factors. Intrapsychic conflict is responsible for anxiety and psychoneuroses, and Freud observed that the resulting anxiety is less intense and less dramatic than what he observed in actual neuroses.

With the publication of *Inhibitions, Symptoms, and Anxiety* in 1926, Freud created a new theory of anxiety that accounted for both real external anxiety and neurotic internal anxiety as a response to a dangerous situation. Freud identified two types of anxiety-provoking situations. One situation involves overwhelming instinctual stimulation, the prototype of which is the experience of birth. In situations of that variety, the excessive amount of drive pressure penetrates the protective barriers of the ego, producing a state of helplessness and trauma. The second and more common situation involves anxiety that develops in anticipation of danger, rather than as the result of danger. That warning to the organism, known as signal anxiety, operates at an unconscious level and serves to mobilize the ego's resources to avert the danger. Either external or internal sources of danger may produce such a signal that leads the ego to marshal specific defense mechanisms to guard against or to reduce the degree of instinctual excitation.

## NORMAL ANXIETY

The sensation of anxiety is commonly experienced by virtually all humans. The feeling is characterized by a diffuse, unpleasant, vague sense of apprehension, often accompanied by autonomic symptoms (Table 16.1–2), such as headache, perspiration, palpitations, tightness in the chest, and mild stomach discomfort. An anxious person

**Table 16.1–1**
**Psychoanalytic Neuroses and Disorders in DSM-IV**

| Classic Neuroses | DSM-IV Classification |
| --- | --- |
| Anxiety | Generalized anxiety disorder |
| Phobic | Agoraphobia, specific and social phobias |
| Obsessive-compulsive | Obsessive-compulsive disorder |
| Depressive | Dysthymic disorder |
| Hysterical (conversion) | Conversion disorder |
| Hysterical (dissociative) | Depersonalization disorder |
| Hypochondriacal | Hypochondriasis |
| Paraphilic | Sexual disorders |

**Table 16.1–2**
**Peripheral Manifestations of Anxiety**

Diarrhea
Dizziness, light-headedness
Hyperhidrosis
Hyperreflexia
Hypertension
Palpitations
Pupillary mydriasis
Restlessness (e.g., pacing)
Syncope
Tachycardia
Tingling in the extremities
Tremors
Upset stomach ("butterflies")
Urinary frequency, hesitancy, urgency

may also feel restless, as indicated by an inability to sit or stand still for long. The particular constellation of symptoms present during anxiety tends to vary among people.

## Fear and Anxiety

Anxiety is an alerting signal; it warns of impending danger and enables the person to take measures to deal with a threat. Fear, a similar alerting signal, should be differentiated from anxiety. Fear is in response to a threat that is known, external, definite, or nonconflictual in origin; anxiety is in response to a threat that is unknown, internal, vague, or conflictual in origin.

The distinction between fear and anxiety arose by accident. Freud's early translator mistranslated "*angst*," the German word for fear, as anxiety. Freud himself generally ignored the distinction that associates anxiety with a repressed, unconscious object and fear with a known, external object. The distinction may be difficult to make because fear may also be due to an unconscious, repressed, internal object displaced to another object in the external world. For example, a boy may be afraid of barking dogs because he is actually afraid of his father and unconsciously associates his father with barking dogs.

According to post-Freudian psychoanalytic formulations, the separation of fear and anxiety is psychologically justifiable. The emotion caused by a rapidly approaching car as one crosses the street differs from the vague dis-

comfort one may experience when one meets new people in a strange setting. The main psychological difference between the two emotional responses is the acuteness of fear and the chronicity of anxiety.

Charles Darwin pointed out that the word "fear" is derived from words meaning what is sudden and dangerous. Duration also seems to be vital in the neurophysiological phenomena of anxiety and fear. In 1896 Darwin gave the following psychophysiological description of acute fear merging into terror:

Fear is often preceded by astonishment, and is so far akin to it, that both lead to the senses of sight and learning being instantly aroused. In both cases the eyes and mouth are widely opened, and the eyebrows raised. The frightened man at the first stands like a statue motionless and breathless, or crouches down as if instinctively to escape observation. The heart beats quickly and violently, so that it palpitates or knocks against the ribs; but it is very doubtful whether it then works more efficiently than usual, so as to send a greater supply of blood to all parts of the body; for the skin instantly becomes pale, as during incipient faintness. This paleness of the surface, however, is probably in large part, or exclusively, due to the vasomotor centre being affected in such a manner as to cause the contraction of the small arteries of the skin. That the skin is much affected under the sense of great fear, we see in the marvelous and inexplicable manner in which perspiration immediately exudes from it. This exudation is all the more remarkable, as the surface is then cold, and hence the term a cold sweat; whereas, the sudorific glands are properly excited into action when the surface is heated. The hairs also on the skin stand erect; and the superficial muscles shiver. In connection with the disturbed action of the heart, the breathing is hurried. The salivary glands act imperfectly; the mouth becomes dry, and is often opened and shut. I have also noticed that under slight fear there is a strong tendency to yawn. One of the best-marked symptoms is the trembling of all the muscles of the body; and this is often first seen in the lips. From this cause, and from the dryness of the mouth, the voice becomes husky or indistinct, or may altogether fail. . . .

As fear increases into an agony of terror, we behold, as under all violent emotions, diversified results. The heart beats wildly or may fail to act and faintness ensues; there is a death-like pallor; the breathing is labored; the wings of the nostrils are widely dilated; there is a gasping and convulsive motion of the lips, a tremor on the hollow cheek, a gulping and catching of the throat; the uncovered and protruding eyeballs are fixed on the object of terror; or they may roll restlessly from side to side. The pupils are said to be enormously dilated. All the muscles of the body may become rigid, or may be thrown into convulsive movements. The hands are alternately clenched and opened, often with a twitching movement. The arms may be protruded, as if to avert some dreadful danger, or may be thrown wildly over the head. . . . In other cases there is a sudden and uncontrollable tendency to headlong flight; and so strong is this, that the boldest soldiers may be seized with a sudden panic.

## Adaptive Functions of Anxiety

When considered simply as an alerting signal, anxiety can be considered basically the same emotion as fear. Anxiety warns of an external or internal threat; it has lifesaving qualities. At a lower level, anxiety warns of threats of bodily damage, pain, helplessness, possible punishment, or the frustration of social or bodily needs; of separation from loved ones; of a menace to one's success or status; and ultimately of threats to one's unity or wholeness. It prompts the person to take the necessary steps to prevent the threat or to lessen its consequences. Examples of warding off threats in daily life include getting down to the hard work of preparing for an examination, dodging a ball thrown at one's head, sneaking into the dormitory after curfew to prevent punishment, and running to catch the last commuter train. Thus, anxiety prevents damage by alerting the person to carry out certain acts that forestall the danger.

## Stress, Conflict, and Anxiety

Whether an event is perceived as stressful depends on the nature of the event and on the person's resources, psychological defenses, and coping mechanisms. All involve the ego, a collective abstraction for the process by which a person perceives, thinks, and acts on external events or internal drives. A person whose ego is functioning properly is in adaptive balance with both external and internal worlds; if the ego is not functioning properly and the resulting imbalance continues long enough, the person experiences chronic anxiety.

Whether the imbalance is external, between the pressures of the outside world and the person's ego, or internal, between the patient's impulses (for example, aggressive, sexual, and dependent impulses) and conscience, the imbalance produces a conflict. Conflicts caused by external events are usually interpersonal, whereas those caused by internal events are intrapsychic or intrapersonal. A combination of the two is possible, as in the case of employees who have an excessively demanding or critical boss and who must control their impulses to hit the boss for fear of losing their jobs. Interpersonal and intrapsychic conflicts are, in fact, usually combined, because human beings are social and their main conflicts are usually with other people.

## Psychological and Cognitive Symptoms

The experience of anxiety has two components: (1) the awareness of the physiological sensations (such as palpitations and sweating) and (2) the awareness of being nervous or frightened. The anxiety may be increased by a feeling of shame—"Others will recognize that I am frightened." Many persons are astonished to find out that others are not cognizant of their anxiety or, if others are cognizant, do not appreciate the intensity of the anxiety.

In addition to its motor and visceral effects, anxiety affects thinking, perception, and learning. Anxiety tends to produce confusion and distortions of perception, not only of time and space but of people and the meaning of events. Those distortions can interfere with learning by lowering concentration, reducing recall, and impairing the ability to relate one item to another—that is, to make associations.

An important aspect of emotions is their effects on the selectivity of attention. Anxious persons are apt to select certain things in their environment and overlook others in their effort to prove that they are justified in considering the situation frightening and in responding accordingly. If they falsely justify their fear, their anxieties are augmented by the selective response, setting up a vicious circle of anxiety, distorted perception, and increased anxiety. If, alternatively, they falsely reassure themselves by selective thinking, appropriate anxiety may be reduced, and they may fail to take the necessary precautions.

# PATHOLOGICAL ANXIETY

## Psychological Theories

Three major schools of psychological theory—psychoanalytic, behavioral, and existential—have contributed theories regarding the causes of anxiety. Each of those theories has both conceptual and practical usefulness in the treatment of patients with anxiety disorders.

**Psychoanalytic theories.** The evolution of Freud's theories regarding anxiety can be traced from his 1895 paper "Obsessions and Phobias" to the 1895 book *Studies in Hysteria* and finally to his 1926 book *Inhibitions, Symptoms, and Anxiety*. In that 1926 book Freud proposed that anxiety is a signal to the ego that an unacceptable drive is pressing for conscious representation and discharge. As a signal, anxiety arouses the ego to take defensive action against the pressures from within. If anxiety rises above the low level of intensity characteristic of its function as a signal, it may emerge with all the fury of a panic attack. Ideally, the use of repression alone results in a restoration of psychological equilibrium without symptom formation, because effective repression completely contains the drives and their associated affects and fantasies, rendering them unconscious. If repression is unsuccessful as a defense, other defense mechanisms (such as conversion, displacement, and regression) may result in symptom formation, thus producing the picture of a classic neurotic disorder (such as hysteria, phobia, and obsessive-compulsive neurosis).

Within psychoanalytic theory, anxiety is seen as falling into four major categories, depending on the nature of the feared consequences: id or impulse anxiety, separation anxiety, castration anxiety, and superego anxiety. Those varieties of anxiety are hypothesized to develop at various stages of growth and development. Id or impulse anxiety is related to the primitive, diffuse discomforts of infants when they feel overwhelmed with needs and stimuli over which their helpless state provides no control. Separation anxiety occurs in somewhat older but still preoedipal children, who fear the loss of love or even abandonment by their parents if they fail to control and direct their impulses in conformity with their parents' standards and demands. The fantasies of castration that characterize the oedipal child, particularly in relation to the child's developing sexual impulses, are reflected in the castration anxiety of the adult. Superego anxiety is the direct result of the final development of the superego that marks the passing of the Oedipus complex and the advent of the prepubertal period of latency.

Psychoanalysts differ about the sources and the nature of anxiety. Otto Rank, for example, traced the genesis of all anxiety back to the trauma of birth. Harry Stack Sullivan emphasized the early relationship between the mother and the child and the transmission of the mother's anxiety to her infant. Regardless of the school of psychoanalysis, however, treatment of anxiety disorders usually involves long-term, insight-oriented psychotherapy or psychoanalysis directed toward the formation of a transference, which allows the reworking of the development problem and the resolution of the neurotic symptoms.

**Behavioral theories.** The behavioral or learning theories of anxiety have spawned some of the most effective treatments for anxiety disorders. Behavioral theories state that anxiety is a conditioned response to specific environmental stimuli. In a model of classic conditioning, a person who does not have any food allergies may become sick after eating contaminated shellfish in a restaurant. Subsequent exposures to shellfish may cause that person to feel sick. Through generalization, such a person may come to distrust all food prepared by others. As an alternative causal possibility, persons may learn to have an internal response of anxiety by imitating the anxiety responses of their parents (social learning theory). In either case, treatment is usually with some form of desensitization by repeated exposure to the anxiogenic stimulus, coupled with cognitive psychotherapeutic approaches.

In recent years, proponents of behavioral theories have shown increasing interest in cognitive approaches to conceptualizing and treating anxiety disorders, and cognitive theorists have proposed alternatives to traditional learning theory causal models of anxiety. Cognitive conceptualization of nonphobic anxiety states state that faulty, distorted, or counterproductive thinking patterns accompany or precede maladaptive behaviors and emotional disorders. According to one model, patients suffering from anxiety disorders tend to overestimate the degree of danger and the probability of harm in a given situation and tend to underestimate their abilities to cope with perceived threats to their physical or psychological well-being. That model asserts that patients with panic disorder often have thoughts of loss of control and fears of dying that follow inexplicable physiological sensations (such as palpitations, tachycardia, and light-headedness) but precede and then accompany panic attacks.

**Existential theories.** Existenial theories of anxiety provide models for generalized anxiety disorder, in which there is no specifically identifiable stimulus for a chronically anxious feeling. The central concept of existential theory is that persons become aware of a profound nothingness in their lives, feelings that may be even more profoundly discomforting than an acceptance of their inevitable death. Anxiety is the person's response to that vast void of existence and meaning. Existential concerns may have increased since the development of nuclear weapons.

## Biological Theories

Biological theories regarding anxiety have developed out of preclinical studies with animal models of anxiety, the study of patients in whom biological factors were ascertained, the growing knowledge regarding basic neuroscience, and the actions of psychotherapeutic drugs. One pole of thought posits that measurable biological changes in patients with anxiety disorders reflect the results of psychological conflicts; the opposite pole posits that the biological events precede the psychological conflicts. Both situations may exist in specific persons, and a range of biologically based sensitivities may exist among persons with the symptoms of anxiety disorders.

**Autonomic nervous system.** Stimulation of the autonomic nervous system causes certain symptoms—cardiovascular (for example, tachycardia), muscular (for example, headache), gastrointestinal (for example, diarrhea), and respiratory (for example, tachypnea). Those peripheral manifestations of anxiety are neither peculiar to anxiety disorders nor necessarily correlated with the subjective experience of anxiety. In the first third of the 20th century, Walter Cannon demonstrated that cats exposed to barking dogs exhibit behavioral and physiological signs of fear that are associated with the adrenal release of epinephrine. The James-Lange theory states that subjective anxiety is a response to peripheral phenomena. It is now generally thought that central nervous system (CNS) anxiety precedes the peripheral manifestations of anxiety, except when a specific peripheral cause is present, such as when a patient has a pheochromocytoma. Some anxiety disorder patients, especially those with panic disorder, have autonomic nervous systems that exhibit increased sympathetic tone, adapt slowly to repeated stimuli, and respond excessively to moderate stimuli.

**Neurotransmitters.** The three major neurotransmitters associated with anxiety on the basis of animal studies and responses to drug treatment are norepinephrine, serotonin, and γ-aminobutyric acid (GABA). Much of the basic neuroscience information about anxiety comes from animal experiments involving behavioral paradigms and psychoactive agents. One such animal model of anxiety is the conflict test, in which the animal is simultaneously presented with stimuli that are positive (for example, food) and negative (for example, electric shock). Anxiolytic drugs (for example, benzodiazepines) tend to facilitate the adaptation of the animal to that situation, whereas other drugs (for example, amphetamines) further disrupt the behavioral responses of the animal.

NOREPINEPHRINE. The general theory regarding the role of norepinephrine in anxiety disorders is that affected patients may have a poorly regulated noradrenergic system that has occasional bursts of activity. The cell bodies of the noradrenergic system are primarily localized to the locus ceruleus in the rostral pons, and they project their axons to the cerebral cortex, the limbic system, the brainstem, and the spinal cord. Experiments in primates have demonstrated that stimulation of the locus ceruleus produces a fear response in the animals and that ablation of the same area inhibits or completely blocks the ability of the animals to form a fear response.

Human studies have found that, in patients with panic disorder, β-adrenergic agonists—for example, isoproterenol (Isuprel)—and α2-adrenergic antagonists—for example, yohimbine (Yocon)—can provoke frequent and severe panic attacks. Conversely, clonidine (Catapres), an α2-adrenergic agonist, reduces anxiety symptoms in some experimental and therapeutic situations. A less consistent finding is that patients with anxiety disorders, particularly panic disorder, have elevated cerebrospinal fluid (CSF) or urinary levels of the noradrenergic metabolite 3-methoxy-4-hydroxyphenylglycol (MHPG).

SEROTONIN. The identification of many serotonin receptor types has stimulated the search for a role for serotonin in the pathogenesis of anxiety disorders. The interest in that relation was initially motivated by the observation that serotonergic antidepressants have therapeutic effects in some anxiety disorders—for example, clomipramine (Anafranil) in obsessive-compuslive disorder. The effectiveness of buspirone (BuSpar), a serotonergic type 1A (5-HT$_{1A}$) receptor agonist, in the treatment of anxiety disorders also suggests the possibility of an association between serotonin and anxiety. The cell bodies of most of the serotonergic neurons are located in the raphe nuclei in the rostral brainstem and project to the cerebral cortex, the limbic system (especially the amygdala and the hippocampus), and the hypothalamus. Although the administration of serotonergic agents to animals results in behavior suggestive of anxiety, the data on similar effects in humans are less robust. Several reports indicate that *m*-chlorophenylpiperazine (mCPP), a drug with multiple serotonergic and nonserotonergic effects, and fenfluramine (Pondimin), which causes the release of serotonin, do cause increased anxiety in patients with anxiety disorders; and many anecdotal reports indicate that serotonergic hallucinogens and stimulants—for example, lysergic acid diethylamide (LSD) and 3,4-methylenedioxymethamphetamine (MDMA) are associated with the development of both acute and chronic anxiety disorders in persons who use those drugs.

GABA. A role of γ-aminobutyric acid (GABA) in anxiety disorders is most strongly supported by the undisputed efficacy of benzodiazepines, which enhance the activity of GABA at the GABA$_A$ receptor, in the treatment of some types of anxiety disorders. Although low-potency benzodiazepines are most effective for the symptoms of generalized anxiety disorder, high-potency benzodiazepines, such as alprazolam (Xanax), are effective in the treatment of panic disorder. Studies in primates have found that autonomic nervous system symptoms of anxiety disorders are induced when a benzodiazepine inverse agonist, β-carboline-3-carboxylic acid (BCCE), is administered. BCCE also causes anxiety in normal control volunteers. A benzodiazepine antagonist, flumazenil, causes frequent severe panic attacks in patients with panic disorder. Those data have led researchers to hypothesize that some patients with anxiety disorders have abnormal functioning of their GABA$_A$ receptors, although that connection has not been proved directly.

APLYSIA. A neurotransmitter model for anxiety disorders is based on the study of *Aplysia californica*, a sea snail that reacts to danger by moving away, withdrawing into its shell, and decreasing its feeding behavior. Those behaviors can be classically conditioned, so that the snail responds to a neutral stimulus as if it were a dangerous stimulus. The snail can also be sensitized by random shocks, so that it exhibits a flight response in the absence of real danger. Parallels have previously been drawn between classical conditioning and human phobic anxiety. The classically conditioned aplysia shows measurable changes in presynaptic facilitation, resulting in the release of increased amounts of neurotransmitter. Although the sea snail is a simple animal, that work shows an experimental approach to complex neurochemical processes potentially involved in anxiety disorders in humans.

**Brain-imaging studies.** A range of brain-imaging studies, almost always conducted with a specific anxiety disorder, have found several possible leads in the understanding of anxiety disorders. Structural studies—for example, computed tomography (CT) and magnetic resonance imaging (MRI)—have occasionally found some increase in the size of cerebral ventricles. In one study the increase was correlated with the length of time patients had been taking bnezodiazepines. In one MRI study a specific defect in the right temporal lobe was noted in patients with panic disorder. Several other brain-imaging studies have reported abnormal findings in the right hemisphere but not the left hemisphere, suggesting that some type of cerebral asymmetry may be important in the development of anxiety disorder symptoms in specific patients. Functional brain-imaging studies—for example, positron emission tomography (PET), single photon emission tomography (SPECT), and electroencephalography (EEG)—of anxiety disorder patients have variously reported abnormalities in the frontal cortex, the occipital and temporal areas, and, in one study, the parahippocampal gyrus in a study of panic disorder. A conservative interpretation of those data is that some patients with anxiety disorders have demonstrable functional cerebral pathology and that the pathology may be causally relevant to their anxiety disorder symptoms.

**Genetic studies.** Genetic studies have produced solid data that at least some genetic component contributes to the development of anxiety disorders. Almost half of all patients with panic disorder have at least one affected relative. The figures for other anxiety disorders, although not as high, also indicate a higher frequency of the illness in first-degree relatives of affected patients than in the relatives of nonaffected persons. Although adoption studies with anxiety disorders have not been reported, data from twin registers also support the hypothesis that anxiety disorders are at least partially genetically determined.

**Neuroanatomical considerations.** The locus ceruleus and the raphe nuclei project primarily to the limbic system and the cerebral cortex. In combination with the data from brain-imaging studies, those areas have become the focus of much hypothesis-building regarding the neuroanatomical substrates of anxiety disorders.

LIMBIC SYSTEM. In addition to receiving noradrenergic and serotonergic innervation, the limbic system also contains a high concentration of GABA$_A$ receptors. Ablation and stimulation studies in nonhuman primates have also implicated the limbic system in the generation of anxiety and fear responses. Two areas of the limbic system have received special attention in the literature: increased activity in the septohippocampal pathway may lead to anxiety, and the cingulate gyrus has been implicated, particularly in the pathophysiology of obsessive-compulsive disorder.

CEREBRAL CORTEX. The frontal cerebral cortex is connected with the parahippocampal region, the cingulate gyrus, and the hypothalamus; therefore, it may be involved in the production of anxiety disorders. The temporal cortex has also been implicated as a pathophysiological site in anxiety disorders. That association is based in part on the similarity in clinical presentation and electrophysiology between some patients with temporal lobe epilepsy and patients with obsessive-compulsive disorder.

## DSM-IV ANXIETY DISORDERS

DSM-IV lists the following anxiety disorders: panic disorder with and without agoraphobia, agoraphobia without a history of panic disorder, specific and social phobias, obsessive-compulsive disorder, posttraumatic stress disorder, acute stress disorder, generalized anxiety disorder (all discussed in other sections in this chapter), anxiety disorder due to a general medical condition, substance-induced anxiety disorder, and anxiety disorder not otherwise specified, including mixed anxiety-depressive disorder (all discussed below).

Virtually everyone who drinks alcohol has on at least a few occasions used alcohol to reduce anxiety, most often social anxiety. In contrast, carefully controlled studies have found that the effects of alcohol on anxiety are variable and can be significantly affected by gender, the amount of alcohol ingested, and cultural attitudes. Nevertheless, alcohol use disorders and other substance-related disorders are commonly associated with anxiety disorders. Alcohol use disorders are about four times more common among patients with panic disorder than among the general population, about 3.5 times more common among patients with obsessive-compulsive disorder, and about 2.5 times more common among patients with phobias. Several studies have reported data indicating that genetic diatheses for both anxiety disorders and alcohol use disorders may cosegregate in some families.

### Anxiety Disorder Due to a General Medical Condition

Anxiety disorder due to a general medical condition was listed in DSM-III-R as organic anxiety syndrome, one of the organic mental disorders associated with Axis III physical disorders or conditions. As with other major syndromes (for example, psychosis and mood disorder symptoms), anxiety disorder due to a general medical condition has been included within the relevant section to encourage the formulation and the consideration of a complete differential diagnosis.

**Epidemiology.** The occurrence of anxiety symptoms related to general medical conditions is common, although the incidence of the disorder varies for each specific general medical condition.

**Etiology.** A wide range of medical conditions can cause symptoms similar to those seen in anxiety disorders (Table 16.1–3). Hyperthyroidism, hypothyroidism, hypoparathyroidism, and vitamin $B_{12}$ deficiency are frequently associated with anxiety symptoms. A pheochromocytoma produces epinephrine, which can cause paroxysmal episodes of anxiety symptoms. Certain lesions of the brain and postencephalitic states reportedly produce symptoms identical to those seen in obsessive-compulsive disorder. Some other medical conditions, such as cardiac arrhythmia, can produce physiological symptoms of panic disorder. Hypoglycemia can also mimic the symptoms of an anxiety disorder. The diverse list of medical conditions that can cause symptoms of anxiety disorder may do so through a common mechanism, the noradrenergic system, although the effects on the serotonergic system are also being studied.

**Table 16.1–3**
**Disorders Associated with Anxiety**

| | |
|---|---|
| **Neurological disorders** | **Miscellaneous conditions** |
| Cerebral neoplasms | Hypoglycemia |
| Cerebral trauma and | Carcinoid syndrome |
| postconcussive | Systemic malignancies |
| syndromes | Premenstrual syndrome |
| Cerebrovascular disease | Febrile illnesses and |
| Subarachnoid | chronic infections |
| hemorrhage | Porphyria |
| Migraine | Infectious mononucleosis |
| Encephalitis | Posthepatitis syndrome |
| Cerebral syphilis | Uremia |
| Multiple sclerosis | |
| Wilson's disease | **Toxic conditions** |
| Huntington's disease | Alcohol and drug |
| Epilepsy | withdrawal |
| | Amphetamines |
| **Systemic conditions** | Sympathomimetic agents |
| Hypoxia | Vasopressor agents |
| Cardiovascular disease | Caffeine and caffeine |
| Cardiac arrhythmias | withdrawal |
| Pulmonary insufficiency | Penicillin |
| Anemia | Sulfonamides |
| | Cannabis |
| **Endocrine disturbances** | Mercury |
| Pituitary dysfunction | Arsenic |
| Thyroid dysfunction | Phosphorus |
| Parathyroid dysfunction | Organophosphates |
| Adrenal dysfunction | Carbon disulfide |
| Pheochromocytoma | Benzene |
| Virilization disorders of | Aspirin intolerance |
| females | |
| | **Idiopathic psychiatric** |
| **Inflammatory disorders** | **disorders** |
| Lupus erythematosus | Depression |
| Rheumatoid arthritis | Mania |
| Polyarteritis nodosa | Schizophrenia |
| Temporal arteritis | Anxiety disorders |
| | Generalized anxiety |
| **Deficiency states** | Panic attacks |
| Vitamin $B_{12}$ deficiency | Phobic disorders |
| Pellagra | Posttraumatic stress |
| | disorder |

Table from J L Cummings: *Clinical Neuropsychiatry*, p 214. Grune & Stratton, Orlando, 1985. Used with permission.

**Diagnosis.** The DSM-IV diagnosis of anxiety disorder due to a general medical condition (Table 16.1–4) requires the presence of symptoms of an anxiety disorder. DSM-IV allows clinicians to specify if the disorder is characterized by symptoms of generalized anxiety, panic attacks, or obsessive-compulsive symptoms.

The clinician should have an increased level of suspicion for the diagnosis when chronic or paroxysmal anxiety is associated with a physical disease that is known to cause such symptoms in some patients. Paroxysmal bouts of hypertension in an anxious patient may indicate that a workup for a pheochromocytoma is appropriate. A general medical workup may reveal diabetes, an adrenal tumor, thyroid disease, or a neurological condition. For example, some patients with complex partial epilepsy have extreme episodes of anxiety or fear as their only manifestation of the epileptic activity.

**Clinical features.** The symptoms of anxiety disorder due to a general medical condition can be identical to those of the primary anxiety disorders. A syndrome similar to panic disorder is the most common clinical picture, and a syndrome similar to a phobia is the least common.

**Table 16.1–4**
**Diagnostic Criteria for Anxiety Disorder Due to a General Medical Condition**

A. Prominent anxiety, panic attacks, or obsessions or compulsions predominate the clinical picture.

B. There is evidence from the history, physical examination, or laboratory findings that the disturbance is the direct physiological consequence of a general medical condition.

C. The disturbance is not better accounted for by another mental disorder (e.g., adjustment disorder with anxiety, in which the stressor is a serious general medical condition).

D. The disturbance does not occur exclusively during the course of a delirium.

E. The disturbance causes clinically significant distress or impairment in social, occupational, or other important areas of functioning.

*Specify* if:
   **with generalized anxiety:** if excessive anxiety or worry about a number of events or activities predominates in the clinical presentation
   **with panic attacks:** if panic attacks predominate in the clinical presentation
   **with obsessive-compulsive symptoms:** if obsessions or compulsions predominate in the clinical presentation

Table from DSM-IV, *Diagnostic and Statistical Manual of Mental Disorders*, ed 4. Copyright American Psychiatric Association, Washington, 1994. Used with permission.

PANIC ATTACKS. Patients who have cardiomyopathy may have the highest incidence of panic disorder secondary to a general medical condition. One study reported that 83 percent of cardiomyopathy patients awaiting cardiac transplantation had panic disorder symptoms. Increased noradrenergic tone in those patients may be the provoking stimulus for the panic attacks. In some studies, about 25 percent of patients with Parkinson's disease and chronic obstructive pulmonary disease have symptoms of panic disorder. Other medical disorders associated with panic disorder include chronic pain, primary biliary cirrhosis, and epilepsy, particularly when the focus is in the right parahippocampal gyrus.

GENERALIZED ANXIETY. A high prevalence of generalized anxiety disorder symptoms in patients with Sjögren's syndrome has been reported, and that may be related to the effects of Sjögren's syndrome on cortical and subcortical functions and on thyroid function. The highest prevalence of generalized anxiety disorder symptoms in a medical disorder seems to be Graves' disease, in which as many as two thirds of all patients meet the criteria for generalized anxiety disorder.

OBSESSIVE-COMPULSIVE SYMPTOMS. Reports in the literature have associated the development of obsessive-compulsive disorder symptoms with Sydenham's chorea and multiple sclerosis.

PHOBIAS. Symptoms of phobias appear to be uncommon, although one study reported a 17 percent prevalence of symptoms of social phobia in patients with Parkinson's disease.

**Differential diagnosis.** Anxiety as a symptom can be associated with many psychiatric disorders, in addition to the anxiety disorders themselves. A mental status examination is necessary to determine the presence of mood symptoms or psychotic symptoms that may suggest another

psychiatric diagnosis. For the clinician to conclude that a patient has an anxiety disorder due to a general medical condition, the patient should clearly have anxiety as the predominant symptom and should have a specific causative nonpsychiatric medical disorder. To ascertain the degree to which a general medical condition is causative for the anxiety, the clinician should know how closely related the medical condition and the anxiety symptoms have been related in the literature, the age of onset (primary anxiety disorders usually have their onset before age 35), and the patient's family history of both anxiety disorders and relevant general medical conditions (for example, hyperthyroidism). A diagnosis of adjustment disorder with anxiety must also be considered in the differential diagnosis.

**Course and prognosis.** The unremitting experience of anxiety can be disabling, interfering with every aspect of life, including social, occupational, and psychological functioning. A sudden change in the level of anxiety may prompt the affected person to seek medical or psychiatric help more quickly than when the onset is insidious. The treatment or the removal of the primary medical cause of the anxiety usually initiates a clear course of improvement in the anxiety disorder symptoms. In some cases, however, the anxiety disorder symptoms continue even after the primary medical condition is treated—for example, in continuing anxiety after an episode of encephalitis. Also, some symptoms, particularly obsessive-compulsive disorder symptoms, linger for a longer time than do other anxiety disorder symptoms. When anxiety disorder symptoms are present for a significant period after the medical disorder has been treated, the remaining symptoms should probably be treated as if they were primary—that is, with psychotherapy or pharmacotherapy or both.

**Treatment.** The primary treatment for anxiety disorder due to a general medical condition is the treatment of the underlying medical condition. If the patient also has an alcohol or other substance use disorder, that disorder must also be therapeutically addressed to gain control of the anxiety disorder symptoms. If the removal of the primary medical condition does not reverse the anxiety disorder symptoms, treatment of those symptoms should follow the treatment guidelines for the specific mental disorder. In general, behavioral modification techniques, anxiolytic agents, and serotonergic antidepressants have been the most effective treatment modalities.

### Substance-Induced Anxiety Disorder

DSM-IV includes the substance-induced mental disorders in the categories for the relevant mental disorder syndromes. Substance-induced anxiety disorder, therefore, is contained in the category of anxiety disorders. In DSM-III-R, patients with the disorder were classified as having a psychoactive substance-induced organic mental disorder.

**Epidemiology.** Substance-induced anxiety disorder is common, both as the result of the ingestion of so-called recreational drugs and as the result of prescription drug use.

**Etiology.** A wide range of substances can cause symptoms of anxiety that can mimic any of the DSM-IV anxiety disorders. Although sympathomimetics (for example, amphetamine, cocaine, and caffeine) have been most associated with the production of anxiety disorder symptoms, many serotonergic drugs (for example, LSD and MDMA) can also cause both acute and chronic anxiety syndromes in users of those drugs. A wide range of prescription medications are also associated with the production of anxiety disorder symptoms in susceptible persons.

**Diagnosis.** The DSM-IV diagnostic criteria for substance-induced anxiety disorder require the presence of prominent anxiety, panic attacks, obsessions, or compulsions (Table 16.1–5). The DSM-IV guidelines state that the symptoms should have developed during the use of the substance or within a month of the cessation of substance use. However, DSM-IV encourages the clinician to use appropriate clinical judgment to assess the relation between substance exposure and anxiety symptoms. The structure of the diagnosis includes specification of the substance (for example, cocaine), specification of the appropriate state during the onset (for example, intoxication), and mention of the specific symptom pattern (for example, panic attacks).

**Clinical features.** The associated clinical features vary with the particular substance involved. Even infrequent use of psychostimulants can result in anxiety disorder symptoms in some persons. Associated with the anxiety disorder symptoms may also be cognitive impairments in comprehension, calculation, and memory. Those cognitive deficits are usually reversible if the substance use is stopped.

**Differential diagnosis.** The differential diagnosis includes the primary anxiety disorders, anxiety disorder due to a general medical condition (for which the patient may be receiving an implicated drug), and mood disorders, which are frequently accompanied by symptoms of anxiety disorders. Personality disorders and malingering must be considered in the differential diagnosis, particularly in some urban emergency rooms.

**Course and prognosis.** The course and the prognosis generally depend on the removal of the causally involves substance and the long-term ability of the affected patient to limit the use of the substance. The anxiogenic effects of most drugs are reversible. When the anxiety does not reverse with the cessation of the drug, the clinician should reconsider the diagnosis of substance-induced anxiety disorder or consider the possibility that the substance causes irreversible brain damage.

**Treatment.** The primary treatment for substance-induced anxiety disorder is the removal of the causally involved substance. Treatment then must focus on finding an alternative treatment if the substance was a medically indicated drug, on limiting the patient's exposure if the substance was introduced through environmental exposure, or on treating the underlying substance-related disorder. If anxiety disorder symptoms continue even though the substance use has stopped, treatment of the anxiety disorder symptoms with appropriate psychotherapeutic or pharmacotherapeutic modalities may be appropriate.

## Anxiety Disorder Not Otherwise Specified

Some patients have symptoms of anxiety disorders that do not meet the criteria for any specific DSM-IV anxiety disorder or adjustment disorder with anxiety or mixed anx-

**Table 16.1–5**
**Diagnostic Criteria for Substance-Induced Anxiety Disorder**

A. Prominent anxiety, panic attacks, obsessions or compulsions predominate in the clinical picture.

B. There is evidence from the history, physical examination, or laboratory findings of either (1) or (2):

   (1) the symptoms in criterion A developed during, or within 1 month of, substance intoxication or withdrawal

   (2) medication use is etiologically related to the disturbance

C. The disturbance is not better accounted for by an anxiety disorder that is not substance induced. Evidence that the symptoms are better accounted for by an anxiety disorder that is not substance induced might include the following: the symptoms precede the onset of the substance use (or medication use); the symptoms persist for a substantial period of time (e.g., about a month) after the cessation of acute withdrawal or severe intoxication or are substantially in excess of what would be expected given the type or amount of the substance used or the duration of use; or there is other evidence suggesting the existence of an independent non-substance-induced anxiety disorder (e.g., a history of recurrent non-substance-related episodes).

D. The disturbance does not occur exclusively during the course of a delirium.

E. The disturbance causes clinically significant distress or impairment in social, occupational, or other important areas of functioning.

**Note:** This diagnosis should be made instead of a diagnosis of substance intoxication or substance withdrawal only when the anxiety symptoms are in excess of those usually associated with the intoxication or withdrawal syndrome and when the anxiety symptoms are sufficiently severe to warrant independent clinical attention.

*Code* [Specific substance-induced anxiety disorder (alcohol; amphetamine (or amphetamine-like substance); caffeine; cannabis; cocaine; hallucinogen; inhalant; phencyclidine (or phencyclidine-like substance); sedative, hypnotic, or anxiolytic; other [or unknown] substance)

*Specify* if:
**With generalized anxiety:** if excessive anxiety or worry about a number of events or activities predominates in the clinical presentation
**With panic attacks:** if panic attacks predominate in the clinical presentation
**With obsessive-compulsive symptoms:** if obsessions or compulsions predominate in the clinical presentation
**With phobic symptoms:** if phobic symptoms predominate in the clinical presentation

*Specify* if:
**With onset during intoxication:** if the criteria are met for intoxication with the substance and the symptoms develop during the intoxication syndrome
**With onset during withdrawal:** if criteria are met for withdrawal from the substance and the symptoms develop during, or shortly after, a withdrawal syndrome

Table from DSM-IV, *Diagnostic and Statistical Manual of Mental Disorders*, ed 4. Copyright American Psychiatric Association, Washington, 1994. Used with permission.

iety and depressed mood. Such patients are most appropriately classified as having anxiety disorder not otherwise specified (NOS). DSM-IV includes four examples of conditions that are appropriate for the diagnosis (Table 16.1–6). One of the examples is mixed anxiety-depressive disorder.

**Table 16.1–6**
**Diagnostic Criteria for Anxiety Disorder Not Otherwise Specified**

This category includes disorders with prominent anxiety or phobic avoidance that do not meet criteria for any specific anxiety disorder, adjustment disorder with anxiety, or adjustment disorder with mixed anxiety and depressed mood. Examples include

1. Mixed anxiety-depressive disorder: clinically significant symptoms of anxiety and depression but the criteria are not met for either a specific mood disorder or a specific anxiety disorder.

2. Clinically significant social phobic symptoms that are related to the social impact of having a general medical condition or mental disorder (e.g., Parkinson's disease, dermatological conditions, stuttering, anorexia nervosa body dysmorphic disorder).

3. Situations in which the clinician has concluded that an anxiety disorder is present but is unable to determine whether it is primary, due to a general medical condition, or substance induced.

Table from DSM-IV, *Diagnostic and Statistical Manual of Mental Disorders*, ed 4. Copyright American Psychiatric Association, Washington, 1994. Used with permission.

**Mixed anxiety-depressive disorder.** DSM-IV follows the lead of the 10th revision of the International Classification of Diseases (ICD-10) by including, in the DSM-IV appendix and as an example of anxiety disorder NOS, mixed anxiety-depressive disorder. That disorder covers patients who have both anxiety and depressive symptoms but who do not meet the diagnostic criteria for either an anxiety disorder or a mood disorder. The combination of depressive and anxiety symptoms results in a significant functional impairment for the affected person. The condition may be particularly prevalent in primary care practices and outpatient mental health clinics. However, opponents have argued that the condition borders on the edge of normality and does not warrant classification as a mental disorder. Opponents have further argued that the mere availability of the diagnosis discourages clinicians from taking the necessary time to obtain a complete psychiatric history to differentiate true depressive disorders from true anxiety disorders.

EPIDEMIOLOGY. The coexistence of major depressive disorder and panic disorder is common. As many as two thirds of all patients with depressive symptoms have prominent anxiety symptoms, and one third may meet the diagnostic criteria for panic disorder. Researchers have reported that from 20 to 90 percent of all patients with panic disorder have episodes of major depressive disorder. Those data suggest that the coexistence of depressive and anxiety symptoms, neither of which meet the diagnostic criteria for other depressive or anxiety disorders, may be common. At this time, however, formal epidemiological data on mixed anxiety-depressive disorder are not available. Nevertheless, some clinicians and researchers have estimated that the prevalence of the disorder in the general population is as high as 10 percent and in primary care clinics as high as 50 percent, although conservative estimates suggest a prevalence of about 1 percent in the general population.

ETIOLOGY. Four principal lines of evidence suggest that anxiety symptoms and depressive symptoms are causally linked in some affected patients. First, a number of investigators have reported similar neuroendocrine findings in depressive disorders and anxiety disorders, particularly panic disorder, including blunted cortisol response to adrenocorticotropic hormone (ACTH), blunted growth hormone response to clonidine, and blunted thyroid-stimulating hormone (TSH) and prolactin responses to thyrotropin-releasing hormone (TRH). Second, several investigators have reported data indicating that hyperactivity of the noradrenergic system is causally relevant to some patients with depressive disorders and to some patients with panic disorder. Specifically, those studies have found elevated concentrations of the norepinephrine metabolite 3-methoxy-4-hydroxyphenylethyleneglycol (MHPG) in the urine, the plasma, or the CSF of depressed patients and panic disorder patients who were actively experiencing a panic attack. As with other anxiety and depressive disorders, serotonin and γ-aminobutyric acid (GABA) may also be causally involved in mixed anxiety-depressive disorder. Third, many studies have found that serotonergic drugs, such as fluoxetine (Prozac) and clomipramine (Anafranil), are useful in treating both depressive and anxiety disorders. Fourth, a number of family studies have reported data indicating that anxiety and depressive symptoms are genetically linked in at least some families.

DIAGNOSIS. The DSM-IV diagnostic criteria are similar to the ICD-10 criteria for mixed anxiety and depressive disorder, which require the presence of subsyndromal symptoms of both anxiety and depression and the presence of some autonomic symptoms, such as tremor, palpitations, dry mouth, and the sensation of a churning stomach. Some preliminary studies have indicated that the sensitivity of general practitioners to a syndrome of mixed anxiety-depressive disorder is low, although that lack of recognition may reflect the lack of an appropriate diagnostic label for the patients.

CLINICAL FEATURES. The clinical features of mixed anxiety-depressive disorder are a combination of some of the symptoms of anxiety disorders and some of the symptoms of depressive disorders. In addition, symptoms of autonomic nervous system hyperactivity, such as gastrointestinal complaints, are common and contribute to the high frequency with which the patients are seen in outpatient medical clinics.

DIFFERENTIAL DIAGNOSIS. The differential diagnosis includes other anxiety and depressive disorders and personality disorders. Among the anxiety disorders, generalized anxiety disorder is the one most likely to overlap with mixed anxiety-depressive disorder. Among the mood disorders, dysthymic disorder and minor depressive disorder are the ones most likely to overlap with mixed anxiety-depressive disorder. Among the personality disorders, avoidant, dependent, and obsessive-compulsive personality disorders may have symptoms that resemble those seen in mixed anxiety-depressive disorder. A diagnosis of a somatoform disorder should also be considered. Only a psychiatric history, a mental stauts examination, and a working knowledge of the specific DSM-IV criteria can help the clinician differentiate among those conditions.

COURSE AND PROGNOSIS.   On the basis of clinical data to date, patients seem to be equally likely to begin with prominent anxiety symptoms, prominent depressive symptoms, or an equal mixture of the two symptoms. During the course of the illness, anxiety or depressive symptoms may alternate in their predominance. The prognosis is not known at this time.

TREATMENT.   Since adequate studies comparing treatment modalities for mixed anxiety-depressive disorder are not currently available, the clinician is probably most likely to treat the patient on the basis of the symptoms present, their severity, and the clinician's own level of comfort and experience with various treatment modalities. Psychotherapeutic approaches may involve time-limited approaches, such as cognitive therapy or behavior modification, although some clinicians use a less structured psychotherapeutic approach, such as insight-oriented psychotherapy. Pharmacotherapy for mixed anxiety-depressive disorder may include antianxiety drugs or antidepressive drugs or both. Among the anxiolytic drugs, some data indicate that the use of triazolobenzodiazepines (for example, alprazolam) may be indicated because of their effectiveness in treating depression associated with anxiety. A drug that affects the serotonin type-1A ($5\text{-HT}_{1A}$) receptor, such as buspirone, may also be indicated. Among the antidepressants, in spite of the noradrenergic theories linking the anxiety disorders and the depressive disorders, the serotongeric antidepressants (for example, fluoxetine) may be most effective in treating mixed anxiety-depressive disorder, although the data to support that assumption are lacking.

### References

Cassem E H: Depression and anxiety secondary to medical illness. Psychiatr Clin North Am *13*: 597, 1990.
Coryell W, Endicott J, Winokur G: Anxiety syndromes as epiphenomena of primary major depression: Outcome and familial psychopathology. Am J Psychiatry *149*: 100, 1992.
Davis M: The role of the amygdala in fear-potentiated startle: Implications for animal models of anxiety. Trends Pharmacol Sci *13*: 35, 1992.
Dubovsky S L: Approaches to developing new anxiolytics and antidepressants. J Clin Psychiatry *54* (5, suppl): 75–83, 1993.
Fawcett J: Targeting treatment in patients with mixed symptoms of anxiety and depression. J Clin Psychiatry *51* (11, Suppl): 40, 1990.
Fick S N, Roy-Byrne P P, Cowley D S, Shores M M, Dunner D L: DSM-III-R personality disorders in a mood and anxiety disorders clinic: prevalence, comorbidity, and clinical correlates. J Aff Disorders *27*: 71–79, 1993.
Gabbard G O: Psychodynamic psychiatry in the "decade of the brain." Am J Psychiatry *149*: 991, 1992.
Gorman J M, Papp L A, editors: Anxiety disorders. In *Review of Psychiatry*, vol 11, A Tasman, M B Riba, editors, p 243. American Psychiatric Press, Washington, 1992.
Hecht H, von Zerssen D, Wittchen H U: Anxiety and depression in a community sample: The influence of comorbidity on social functioning. J Affect Disord *18*: 137, 1990.
Johnson E O, Kamilaris T C, Chrousos G P, Gold P W: Mechanisms of stress: A dynamic overview of hormonal and behavioral homeostases. Neurosci Biobehav Rev *16*: 115, 1992.
Journal of Clinical Psychiatry: Mixed anxiety and depression: A nosologic reality? J Clin Psychiatry *54* (1, Suppl): 2, 1993.
Katon W, Roy-Byrne P P: Mixed anxiety and depression. J Abnorm Psychol *100*: 337, 1991.
Lydiard R B: Coexisting depression and anxiety: Special diagnostic and treatment issues. J Clin Psychiatry *52* (6, Suppl): 48, 1991.
Mathew R J, Wilson W H: Anxiety and cerebral blood flow. Am J Psychiatry *147*: 838, 1990.
Wesner R B: Alcohol use and abuse secondary to anxiety. Psychiatr Clin North Am *13*: 699, 1990.

# 16.2 / Panic Disorder and Agoraphobia

Since panic disorder was codified in 1980 as a diagnosis in the third edition of *Diagnostic and Statistical Manual of Mental Disorders* (DSM-III), a wealth of research data about the disorder and clinical experiences with affected patients have accumulated. The ability of health care providers to recognize the symptoms of panic disorder has increased since 1980, and, most important, effective and specific treatments have been developed and have been proved to be effective. All health care providers must be able to recognize the symptoms of panic disorder, so that affected patients can receive the appropriate therapy, including pharmacotherapeutic agents and psychotherapy.

Panic disorder is characterized by the spontaneous, unexpected occurrence of panic attacks. *Panic attacks* are relatively short-lived (usually less than one hour) periods of intense anxiety or fear, which are accompanied by such somatic symptoms as palpitations and tachypnea. Because patients with panic attacks often present to medical clinics, the symptoms may be misdiagnosed as either a serious medical condition (for example, myocardial infarction) or a so-called hysterical symptom. The frequency with which patients with panic disorder experience panic attacks varies from multiple attacks during a single day to only a few attacks during the course of a year. Panic disorder is often accompanied by *agoraphobia*, the fear of being alone in public places (for example, supermarkets), especially places from which a rapid exit would be difficult if the person experienced a panic attack. Agoraphobia can be the most disabling of the phobias, since its presence may significantly interfere with a person's ability to function in social and work situations outside the home.

In the United States, most researchers in the field of panic disorder believe that agoraphobia almost always develops as a complication in patients who have panic disorder. In other words, agoraphobia is hypothesized to be caused by the development of the fear that the person will experience a panic attack in a public place from which egress would be difficult. Researchers in other countries, as well as some United States researchers and clinicians, do not accept that theory. However, the fourth edition of DSM (DSM-IV) does make panic disorder the predominant disorder in the dyad and contains diagnoses for panic disorder with agoraphobia and panic disorder without agoraphobia. DSM-IV also contains diagnostic criteria for agoraphobia without history of panic disorder. Panic attacks themselves can occur in a variety of mental disorders (for example, depressive disorders) and medical conditions (for example, substance withdrawal or intoxication); the occurrence of a panic attack does not in itself merit the diagnosis of panic disorder.

## HISTORY

The conceptualization of panic disorder may have its roots in the concept of irritable heart syndrome, which was noted in soldiers in the American Civil War by Jacob Mendes Da Costa. *DaCosta's syndrome* included many of the psychic and somatic symptoms now included in the diagnostic criteria for panic disorder. In 1895 Sigmund Freud introduced the concept of *anxiety neurosis*, consisting of acute and chronic psychic and somatic symptoms. Freud's acute anxiety neurosis was similar to DSM-IV panic disorder. It was Freud who first noted the relation between panic attacks and agoraphobia. The term "agoraphobia" had been coined in 1871 for the condition in which patients seem afraid to venture into public places unaccompanied by friends or relatives. The word is derived from the Greek *agora* and *phobos* and means fear of the marketplace. In 1980 DSM-III formally dropped the diagnosis of anxiety neurosis and introduced the diagnosis of panic disorder. The validity of the classification has been well justified since 1980 by the development of specific treatments for panic disorder.

## EPIDEMIOLOGY

Epidemiological studies have reported lifetime prevalence rates of 1.5 to 3 percent for panic disorder and 3 to 4 percent for panic attacks. The studies have used DSM-III criteria, which are more restrictive than the criteria in the revised third edition (DSM-III-R) and DSM-IV; therefore, the true lifetime prevalence is likely to be higher than those figures indicate. For example, one recent study of more than 1,600 randomly selected adults in Texas found a lifetime prevalence rate of 3.8 percent for panic disorder, 5.6 percent for panic attacks, and 2.2 percent for panic attacks with limited symptoms that did not meet the full diagnostic criteria.

Women are two to three times more likely to be affected than are men, although underdiagnosis of panic disorder in men may contribute to that skewed distribution. The differences among Hispanics, non-Hispanic whites, and blacks are small. The only social factor identified as contributing to the development of panic disorder is a recent history of divorce or separation. Panic disorder most commonly develops in young adulthood—the mean age of presentation is about 25—but both panic disorder and agoraphobia can develop at any age. For example, panic disorder has been reported to occur in children and adolescents, and it is probably underdiagnosed in them.

The lifetime prevalence of agoraphobia has been reported as ranging from as low as 0.6 percent to as high as 6 percent. The major factor leading to that wide range of estimates is the use of varying diagnostic criteria and assessment methods. Although studies of agoraphobia in psychiatric settings have reported that at least three fourths of the affected patients have panic disorder as well, studies of agoraphobia in community samples have found that as many as half of the patients have agoraphobia without panic disorder. The reasons for those divergent findings are not known but probably involve differences in ascertainment techniques. In many cases the onset of agoraphobia follows a traumatic event.

## ETIOLOGY

### Biological Factors

Research regarding the biological basis of panic disorder has produced a range of findings; one interpretation is that the symptoms of panic disorder can result in a range of biological abnormalities in brain structure and brain function. The greatest amount of work has been done in the area of using biological stimulants to induce panic attacks in patients with panic disorder. Those and other studies have resulted in hypotheses implicating both peripheral and central nervous system dysregulation in the pathophysiology of panic disorder. The autonomic nervous systems of some panic disorder patients have been reported to exhibit increased sympathetic tone, to adapt slowly to repeated stimuli, and to respond excessively to moderate stimuli. Studies of the neuroendocrine status of panic disorder patients have reported several abnormalities, although the studies have been inconsistent in their findings.

The major neurotransmitter systems that have been implicated are those for norepinephrine, serotonin, and γ-aminobutyric acid (GABA). The totality of the biological data has led to a focus on the brainstem (particularly the noradrenergic neurons of the locus ceruleus and the serotonergic neurons of the median raphe nucleus), the limbic system (possibly responsible for the generation of anticipatory anxiety), and the prefrontal cortex (possibly responsible for the generation of phobic avoidance).

**Panic-inducing substances.** Panic-inducing substances (sometimes called panicogens) are substances that induce panic attacks in a majority of patients with panic disorder and in a much smaller proportion of persons without panic disorder or a history of panic attacks. The use of panic-inducing substances is strictly limited to the research setting; there are no clinically indicated reasons to stimulate panic attacks in patients. So-called respiratory panic-inducing substances cause respiratory stimulation and a shift in the acid-base balance. Those substances include carbon dioxide (5 to 35 percent mixtures), sodium lactate, and bicarbonate. Neurochemical panic-inducing substances, which act through specific neurotransmitter systems, include yohimbine (Yocon), an $\alpha_2$-adrenergic receptor antagonist; fenfluramine (Pondimin), a serotonin-releasing agent; *m*-chlorophenylpiperazine (mCPP), an agent with multiple serotonergic effects; β-carboline drugs; $GABA_B$ receptor inverse agonists; flumazenil, a $GABA_B$ receptor antagonist; cholecystokinin; and caffeine. Isoproterenol (Isuprel) is also a panic-inducing substance, although its mechanism of action in inducing panic attacks is poorly understood. The respiratory panic-inducing substances may act initially at the peripheral cardiovascular baroreceptors and relay their signal by vagal afferents to the nucleus tractus solitarii and then on to the nucleus paragigantocellularis of the medulla. The neurochemical panic-inducing substances are presumed to have their primary effects directly on the noradrenergic, serotonergic, and GABA receptors of the central nervous system.

**Brain imaging.** Structural brain-imaging studies—for example, magnetic resonance imaging (MRI)—in panic disorder patients have implicated pathology in the temporal lobes, particularly the hippocampus. For example, one MRI study reported abnormalities, particularly cortical atrophy, in the right temporal lobe of panic disorder patients. Functional brain-imaging studies—for example, positron emission tomography (PET)—have implicated a dysregulation of cerebral blood flow. Specifically, anxiety disorders and panic attacks are associated with cerebral vasoconstriction, which may result in central nervous system symptoms, such as dizziness, and in peripheral nervous system symptoms that may be induced by hyperventilation and hypocapnia. Most functional brain-imaging studies have used a specific panic-inducing substance (for example, lactate, caffeine, or yohimbine) in combination with PET or single photon emission tomography (SPECT) to assess the effects of the panic-inducing substance and the induced panic attack on cerebral blood flow.

**Mitral valve prolapse.** Although great interest was formerly expressed in an association between mitral valve prolapse and panic disorder, research has almost completely removed any clinical significance or relevance to the association. Mitral valve prolapse is a heterogeneous syndrome consisting of the prolapse of one of the mitral valve leaflets, resulting in a midsystolic click on cardiac auscultation. Research studies have found that the prevalence of panic disorder in patients with mitral valve prolapse is no different from the prevalence of panic disorder in patients without mitral valve prolapse.

## Genetic Factors

Although the number of well-controlled studies of the genetic basis of panic disorder and agoraphobia is small, the data to date support the conclusion that the disorders have a distinct genetic component. In addition, some data indicate that panic disorder with agoraphobia is a severe form of panic disorder without agoraphobia and is, thus, more likely to be inherited. Various studies have found a fourfold to eightfold increase in the risk for panic disorder among first-degree relatives of panic disorder patients compared with first-degree relatives of other psychiatric patients. The twin studies conducted to date have generally reported that monozygotic twins are more likely to be concordant for panic disorder than are dizygotic twins.

## Psychosocial Factors

Both cognitive-behavioral and psychoanalytic theories have been developed to explain the pathogenesis of panic disorder and agoraphobia. The success of cognitive-behavioral approaches to the treatment of those disorders may add credence to the cognitive-behavioral theories.

**Cognitive behavioral theories.** Behavioral theories posit that anxiety is a learned response either from modeling parental behavior or through the process of classic conditioning. In a classic conditioning approach to panic disorder and agoraphobia, a noxious stimulus (for example, a panic attack) that occurs with a neutral stimulus (for example, a bus ride) can result in the avoidance of the neutral stimulus. Other behavioral theories posit a linkage between the sensation of minor somatic symptoms (for example, palpitations) and the generation of a complete panic attack. Although cognitive-behavioral theories can help explain the development of agoraphobia or an increase in the number or the severity of panic attacks, they do not explain the occurrence of the first unprovoked and unexpected panic attack that an affected patient experiences.

**Psychoanalytic theories.** Psychoanalytic theories conceptualize panic attacks as resulting from an unsuccessful defense against anxiety-provoking impulses. What was previously a mild signal anxiety becomes an overwhelming feeling of apprehension, complete with somatic symptoms. In agoraphobia, psychoanalytic theories emphasize the loss of a parent in childhood and a history of separation anxiety. Being alone in public places revives the childhood anxiety about being abandoned. The defense mechanisms used include repression, displacement, avoidance, and symbolization. Traumatic separations during childhood may affect the child's developing nervous system in such a manner that the child becomes susceptible to anxieties in adulthood.

Many patients describe panic attacks as coming out of the blue, as though no psychological factors were involved, but psychodynamic exploration frequently reveals a clear psychological trigger for the panic attack. Although panic attacks are correlated neurophysiologically with the locus ceruleus, the onset of panic is generally related to environmental or psychological factors. Patients with panic disorder have a higher incidence of stressful life events, particularly loss, compared with controls in the months before the onset of panic disorder. Moreover, the patients typically experience greater distress about life events than do controls.

The hypothesis that stressful psychological events produce neurophysiological changes in panic disorder finds support from a study of female twins. The research findings revealed that panic disorder was strongly associated with both parental separation and parental death before the age of 17. Separation from the mother early in life was clearly more likely to result in panic disorder than was paternal separation in the cohort of 1,018 pairs of female twins. Further support for psychological mechanisms in panic disorder can be inferred from a study of panic disorder patients who were successfully treated with cognitive therapy. Before the therapy, the patients responded to lactate induction with a panic attack. After successful cognitive therapy, lactate infusion no longer resulted in a panic attack.

The research indicates that the cause of panic attacks is likely to involve the unconscious meaning of stressful events and that the pathogenesis of the panic attacks may be related to neurophysiological factors triggered by the psychological reactions. Psychodynamic clinicians should always do a thorough investigation of possible triggers whenever a diagnostic assessment is being performed on a patient with panic disorder.

# DIAGNOSIS

## Panic Attacks

In DSM-IV, unlike DSM-III-R, the diagnostic criteria for a panic attack are listed as a separate set of criteria (Table 16.2–1). In DSM-III-R the criteria for a panic attack were contained within the diagnostic criteria for panic disorder. The major reason to have a separate set of diagnostic criteria for a panic attack is that panic attacks can occur in mental disorders other than panic disorder, particularly in specific phobia, social phobia, and posttraumatic stress disorder. Furthermore, the inclusion of the criteria for a panic attack within the diagnostic criteria for panic disorder implied that panic attacks had to be unexpected or uncued to meet the diagnostic criteria. Unexpected panic attacks occur out of the blue and are not associated with any identifiable situational stimulus. However, panic attacks do not need to be unexpected, since panic attacks in patients with social and specific phobias are usually expected or cued to a recognized or specific stimulus. Some panic attacks do not fit easily into the distinction between unexpected and expected, and those attacks are referred to as situationally predisposed panic attacks; they may or may not occur when a patient is exposed to a specific trigger, or they may occur either immediately after exposure or after a considerable delay.

## Panic Disorder

DSM-IV contains two diagnostic criteria for panic disorder, one without agoraphobia (Table 16.2–3) and the other with agoraphobia (Table 16.2–4), but both require the presence of panic attacks as described in Table 16.2–1. Some community surveys have indicated that panic attacks are common, and a major issue in the development of the diagnostic criteria for panic disorder was the determination of a threshold number or frequency of panic attacks required to meet the diagnosis. Setting the threshold too low results in the diagnosis of panic disorder in patients who do not have an impairment from an occasional panic attack; setting the threshold too high results in a situation in which patients who are impaired by their panic attacks do not meet the diagnostic criteria. The vagaries of setting the threshold are evidenced by the range of thresholds set in various diagnostic criteria. The Research Diagnostic Criteria (RDC) requires six panic attacks during a six-week period. The 10th revision of the International Classification of Diseases (ICD-10) requires three attacks in three weeks (for moderate disease) or four attacks in four weeks (for severe disease). DSM-III-R required either four attacks in four weeks or one or more attacks that were followed by at least one month of persistent fear about having another attack. DSM-IV does not specify a minimum number of panic attacks or a time frame but does require that at least one attack be followed by at least a month-long period of concern about having another panic attack or about the implications of the attack or a significant change in behavior. DSM-IV also requires that the panic attacks generally be unexpected but allows expected or situation-

**Table 16.2–1**
**Diagnostic Criteria for Panic Attack**

**Note:** A panic attack is not a codable disorder. Code the specific diagnosis in which the panic attack occurs (e.g., panic disorder with agoraphobia).

A discrete period of intense fear or discomfort, in which four (or more) of the following symptoms developed abruptly and reached a peak within 10 minutes:

(1) palpitations, pounding heart, or accelerated heart rate
(2) sweating
(3) trembling or shaking
(4) sensations of shortness of breath or smothering
(5) feeling of choking
(6) chest pain or discomfort
(7) nausea or abdominal distress
(8) feeling dizzy, unsteady, lightheaded, or faint
(9) derealization (feelings of unreality) or depersonalization (being detached from oneself)
(10) fear of losing control or going crazy
(11) fear of dying
(12) paresthesias (numbness or tingling sensations)
(13) chills or hot flushes

Table from DSM-IV, *Diagnostic and Statistical Manual of Mental Disorders*, ed 4. Copyright American Psychiatric Association, Washington, 1994. Used with permission.

**Table 16.2–2**
**Criteria for Agoraphobia**

**Note:** Agoraphobia is not a codable disorder. Code the specific disorder in which the agoraphobia occurs (e.g., panic disorder with agoraphobia or agoraphobia without history of panic disorder).

A. Anxiety about being in places or situations from which escape might be difficult (or embarrassing) or in which help may not be available in the event of having an unexpected or situationally predisposed panic attack or panic-like symptoms. Agoraphobic fears typically involve characteristic clusters of situations that include being outside the home alone; being in a crowd or standing in a line; being on a bridge; and travelling in a bus, train, or automobile.

**Note:** Consider the diagnosis of specific phobia if the avoidance is limited to one or only a few specific situations, or social phobia if the avoidance is limited to social situations.

B. The situations are avoided (e.g., travel is restricted) or else are endured with marked distress or with anxiety about having a panic attack or panic-like symptoms, or require the presence of a companion.

C. The anxiety or phobic avoidance is not better accounted for by another mental disorder, such as social phobia (e.g., avoidance limited to social situations because of fear of embarrassment), specific phobia (e.g., avoidance limited to a single situation like elevators), obsessive-compulsive disorder (e.g., avoidance of dirt in someone with an obsession about contamination), posttraumatic stress disorder (e.g., avoidance of stimuli associated with a severe stressor), or separation anxiety disorder (e.g., avoidance of leaving home or relatives).

Table from DSM-IV, *Diagnostic and Statistical Manual of Mental Disorders*, ed 4. Copyright American Psychiatric Association, Washington, 1994. Used with permission.

**Table 16.2–3**
**Diagnostic Criteria for Panic Disorder**
**Without Agoraphobia**

A. Both (1) and (2):

    (1) recurrent unexpected panic attacks
    (2) at least one of the attacks has been followed by at least
        1 month (or more) of the following:

        (a) persistent concern about having additional attacks
        (b) worry about the implications of the attack or its
            consequences (e.g., losing control, having a heart
            attack, "going crazy")
        (c) a significant change in behavior related to the
            attacks

B. Absence of agoraphobia.

C. The panic attacks are not due to the direct physiological
   effects of a substance (e.g., a drug of abuse, a medication)
   or a general medical condition (e.g., hyperthyroidism).

D. The panic attacks are not better accounted for by another
   mental disorder, such as social phobia (e.g., occurring on
   exposure to feared social situations), specific phobia (e.g.,
   on exposure to a specific phobic situation), obsessive-
   compulsive disorder (e.g., on exposure to dirt in someone
   with an obsession about contamination), posttraumatic
   stress disorder (e.g., in response to stimuli associated with
   a severe stressor), or separation anxiety disorder (e.g., in
   response to being away from home or close relatives).

Table from DSM-IV, *Diagnostic and Statistical Manual of Mental Disorders*, ed 4. Copyright American Psychiatric Association, Washington, 1994. Used with permission.

**Table 16.2–4**
**Diagnostic Criteria for Panic Disorder with Agoraphobia**

A. Both (1) and (2):

    (1) recurrent unexpected panic attacks
    (2) at least one of the attacks has been followed by 1
        month (or more) of the following:

        (a) persistent concern about having additional attacks
        (b) worry about the implications of the attack or its
            consequences (e.g., losing control, having a heart
            attack, "going crazy")
        (c) a significant change in behavior related to the
            attacks

B. The presence of agoraphobia.

C. The panic attacks are not due to the direct physiological
   effects of a substance (e.g., a drug of abuse, a medication)
   or a general medical condition (e.g., hyperthyroidism).

D. The panic attacks are not better accounted for by another
   mental disorder, such as social phobia (e.g., occurring on
   exposure to feared social situations), specific phobia (e.g.,
   on exposure to a specific phobic situation), obsessive-
   compulsive disorder (e.g., on exposure to dirt in someone
   with an obsession about contamination), posttraumatic
   stress disorder (e.g., in response to stimuli associated with
   a severe stressor), or separation anxiety disorder (e.g., in
   response to being away from home or close relatives).

Table from DSM-IV, *Diagnostic and Statistical Manual of Mental Disorders*, ed 4. Copyright American Psychiatric Association, Washington, 1994. Used with permission.

ally predisposed attacks. Table 16.2–2 lists criteria for agoraphobia.

## Agoraphobia Without History of Panic Disorder

The DSM-IV diagnostic criteria for agoraphobia without history of panic disorder (Table 16.2–5) retain the DSM-III-R criteria based on the fear of a sudden incapacitating or embarrassing symptom. In contrast, the ICD-10 criteria require the presence of interrelated or overlapping phobias but do not require that fear of incapacitating or embarrassing symptoms be present.

The DSM-IV criteria also address the avoidance of situation which are based on a concern related to a medical disorder (for example, fear of a myocardial infarction in a patient with severe heart disease).

## CLINICAL FEATURES

### Panic Disorder

The first panic attack is often completely spontaneous, although panic attacks occasionally follow excitement, physical exertion, sexual activity, or moderate emotional trauma. DSM-IV emphasizes that at least the first attacks must be unexpected (uncued) to meet the diagnostic cri-

teria for panic disorder. The clinician should attempt to ascertain any habit or situation that commonly precedes a patient's panic attacks. Such activities may include the use of caffeine, alcohol, nicotine, or other substances; unusual patterns of sleeping or eating; and specific environmental settings, such as harsh lighting at work.

The attack often begins with a 10-minute period of rapidly increasing symptoms. The major mental symptoms are extreme fear and a sense of impending death and doom. Patients are usually not able to name the source of their fear. The patients may feel confused and have trouble in concentrating. The physical signs often include tachycardia, palpitations, dyspnea, and sweating. Patients often try to leave whatever situation they are in to seek help. The attack generally lasts 20 to 30 minutes and rarely more than an hour. A formal mental status examination during a panic attack may reveal rumination, difficulty in speaking (for example, stammering), and an impaired memory. Patients may experience depression or depersonalization during an attack. The symptoms may disappear quickly or gradually. Between attacks, patients may have anticipatory anxiety about having another attack. The differentiation between anticipatory anxiety and generalized anxiety disorder can be difficult, although pain disorder patients with anticipatory anxiety are able to name the focus of their anxiety.

Somatic concerns of death from a cardiac or respiratory problem may be the major focus of patients' attention during panic attacks. Patients may believe that the palpitations and the pain in the chest indicate that they are

**Table 16.2–5**
**Diagnostic Criteria for Agoraphobia Without History of Panic Disorder**

A. The presence of agoraphobia related to fear of developing panic-like symptoms (e.g., dizziness or diarrhea).

B. Criteria have never been met for panic disorder.

C. The disturbance is not due to the direct physiological effects of a substance (e.g., a drug of abuse, a medication) or a general medical condition.

D. If an associated general medical condition is present, the fear described in criterion A is clearly in excess of that usually associated with the condition.

about to die. As many as 20 percent of such patients actually have syncopal episodes during a panic attack. The patients may present to emergency rooms as young (20s), physically healthy persons who nevertheless insist that they are about to die from a heart attack. Rather than immediately diagnosing hypochondriasis, the emergency room physician should consider a diagnosis of panic disorder. Hyperventilation may produce respiratory alkalosis and other symptoms. The age-old treatment of breathing into a paper bag sometimes help.

### Agoraphobia

Agoraphobic patients rigidly avoid situations in which it would be difficult to obtain help. They prefer to be accompanied by a friend or a family member in such places as busy streets, crowded stores, closed-in spaces (such as tunnels, bridges, and elevators), and closed-in vehicles (such as subways, buses, and airplanes). The patients may insist that they be accompanied every time they leave the house. The behavior may result in marital discord, which may be misdiagnosed as the primary problem. Severely affected patients may simply refuse to leave the house. Particularly before a correct diagnosis is made, patients may be terrified that they are going crazy.

### Associated Symptoms

Depressive symptoms are often present in panic disorder and agoraphobia, and in some patients a depressive disorder coexists with the panic disorder. Studies have found that the lifetime risk of suicide in persons with panic disorder is higher than it is in persons with no mental disorder. The clinician should be alert to the risk of suicide. In addition to agoraphobia, other phobias and obsessive-compulsive disorder can coexist with panic disorder. The psychosocial consequences of panic disorder and agoraphobia, in addition to marital discord, can include time lost from work, financial difficulties related to the loss of work, and alcohol and other substance abuse.

A 30-year-old accountant was referred by his internist to a psychiatric consultant because of a six-month history of recurrent bouts of sudden extreme fear, accompanied by sweating, shortness of breath, palpitations, chest pain, dizziness, numbness in his fingers and toes, and the thought that he was going to die. His internist had given him a complete physical examination, an electrocardiogram (ECG), and glucose tolerance and other blood tests and had found no abnormalities.

The patient had been married for five years; he had no children. He went to night school to get a master's degree in business administration. He was successful and well-liked at his firm. He and his wife, a teacher, generally got along well and had several couples with whom they enjoyed going out.

Because of his attacks, which occurred unexpectedly and in a variety of situations several times a week, the patient started to avoid driving his car and going into department stores, lest he have an attack in those places. He began to coax his wife to accompany him on errands; and during the previous month he had felt comfortable only at home with his wife. Finally, he could not face the prospect of leaving home to go to work and took a medical leave of absence. When at home, he experienced only twinges of chest pain and slight numbness in his fingers but no full-blown attacks.

When asked about the circumstances surrounding the onset of his attacks, the patient said that he and his wife had been discussing buying a house and moving from their apartment. He admitted that the responsibilities of home ownership intimidated him and related the significance of the move to similar concerns his mother had had that prevented his parents from ever buying a house.

*Discussion.* Recurrent, unexpected bouts of extreme fear of sudden onset, with sweating, shortness of breath, palpitations, chest pain, dizziness, numbness, and thoughts of being about to die, in the absence of an organic cause, indicate panic disorder.

As is often the case, agoraphobia developed as the patient increasingly constricted his normal activities (he could not face the prospect of leaving home to go to work) because of a fear of being in situations from which escape might be difficult or embarrassing or in which help might not be available in the event of a panic attack (he avoided driving his car or going into department stores).

## DIFFERENTIAL DIAGNOSIS

### Panic Disorder

The differential diagnosis for a patient with panic disorder includes a large number of medical disorders (Table 16.2–6), as well as many mental disorders.

**Medical disorders.** Whenever a patient, regardless of age or risk factors, reports to an emergency room with symptoms of a potentially fatal condition (for example, myocardial infarction), a complete medical history must be obtained and a physical examination performed. Standard laboratory procedures include a complete blood count; studies of electrolytes, fasting glucose, calcium concentrations, liver function, urea, creatinine, and thyroid; a urinalysis; a drug screen; and an electrocardiogram (ECG). Once the presence of an immediately life-threatening condition has been ruled out, the clinical suspicion is that the patient has panic disorder. The possibility that additional medical diagnostic procedures will reveal a medical condition must be weighed against the procedures' potentially adverse effects on helping the patient accept a diagnosis of panic disorder. Nevertheless, the presence of atypical symptoms (for example, vertigo, loss of bladder control, and unconsciousness) or the late onset of the first panic attack (above age 45) should cause the clinician to reconsider the presence of an underlying nonpsychiatric medical condition.

The standard workup described above helps the clinician evaluate the patient for the presence of thyroid, parathyroid, adrenal, and substance-related causes of panic attacks. Symptoms of chest pain, especially in patients with cardiac risk factors (for example, obesity and hypertension) may warrant further cardiac tests, including a 24-hour ECG, a stress test, a chest X-ray, and the measurement of cardiac enzymes. The presence of atypical neurological symptoms may warrant obtaining an electroencephalogram or an MRI to assess the possibility that the patient has temporal lobe epilepsy, multiple sclerosis, or some space-occupying brain lesion. The rare possibility that a patient has carcinoid syndrome or pheochromocytoma can best be checked by measuring a 24-hour urine sample for serotonin metabolites or catecholamines. Although hypoglycemia was once thought to be associated with panic disorder, especially in the lay literature, available data now indicate that hypoglycemia is rarely a cause of panic attacks in the absence of other symptoms that point to hypoglycemia.

**Mental disorders.** The psychiatric differential diagnosis for panic disorder includes malingering, factitious disorders, hypochondriasis, depersonalization disorder, social and specific phobias, posttraumatic stress disorder, depressive disorders, and schizophrenia. In the differential diagnosis, the clinician must determine whether the panic attack was unexpected, situationally bound, or situationally predisposed. Unexpected panic attacks are the hallmark of panic disorder; situationally bound panic attacks generally indicate a different condition, such as social phobia or specific phobia (when exposed to the phobic situation), obsessive-compulsive disorder (when trying to resist a compulsion), or a depressive disorder (when overwhelmed with anxiety). The focus of the anxiety or the fear is also important. Was there no focus (as in panic disorder), or was there a specific focus (for example, fear of becoming tongue-tied in a person with social phobia)? Somatoform disorders should also be considered in the differential diagnosis, although a patient may meet the criteria for both a somatoform disorder and panic disorder.

SPECIFIC AND SOCIAL PHOBIAS. DSM-IV addresses the sometimes difficult diagnostic task of distinguishing between panic disorder with agoraphobia, on the one hand, and specific and social phobias, on the other hand. Some patients who experience a single panic attack in a specific setting (for example, an elevator) may go on to have a long-lasting avoidance of the specific setting, regardless of whether they ever have another panic attack. Those patients meet the diagnostic criteria for a specific phobia, and clinicians must use their judgment about what is the

**Table 16.2–6**
**Organic Differential Diagnosis for Panic Disorder**

Cardiovascular diseases
  Anemia
  Angina
  Congestive heart failure
  Hyperactive β-adrenergic state
  Hypertension
  Mitral valve prolapse
  Myocardial infarction
  Paradoxical atrial tachycardia

Pulmonary diseases
  Asthma
  Hyperventilation
  Pulmonary embolus

Neurological diseases
  Cerebrovascular disease
  Epilepsy
  Huntington's disease
  Infection
  Ménière's disease
  Migraine
  Multiple sclerosis
  Transient ischemic attack
  Tumor
  Wilson's disease

Endocrine diseases
  Addison's disease
  Carcinoid syndrome
  Cushing's syndrome
  Diabetes
  Hyperthryoidism
  Hypoglycemia
  Hypoparathyroidism
  Menopausal disorders
  Pheochromocytoma
  Premenstrual syndrome

Drug intoxications
  Amphetamine
  Amyl nitrite
  Anticholinergics
  Cocaine
  Hallucinogens
  Marijuana
  Nicotine
  Theophylline

Drug withdrawal
  Alcohol
  Antihypertensives
  Opiates and opioids
  Sedative-hypnotics

Other conditions
  Anaphylaxis
  $B_{12}$ deficiency
  Electrolyte disturbances
  Heavy metal poisoning
  Systemic infections
  Systemic lupus erythematosus
  Temporal arteritis
  Uremia

most appropriate diagnosis. In another example, a person who experiences one or more panic attacks may go on to a fear of public speaking for fear of having a panic attack in such a situation. Although the clinical picture is almost identical to the clinical picture in social phobia, a diagnosis of social phobia is excluded because the avoidance of the public situation is based on fear of having a panic attack, rather than fear of the public speaking itself. Because empirical data on the distinctions are limited, DSM-IV advises clinicians to use their clinical judgment to make the diagnosis in difficult cases.

### Agoraphobia Without History of Panic Disorder

The differential diagnosis for agoraphobia without a history of panic disorder includes all the medical disorders that may cause anxiety or depression. The psychiatric differential diagnosis includes major depressive disorder, schizophrenia, paranoid personality disorder, avoidance personality disorder, and dependent personality disorder.

## COURSE AND PROGNOSIS

### Panic Disorder

Panic disorder usually has its onset during late adolescence or early adulthood, although onset during childhood, early adolescence, and midlife does occur. Some data implicate increased psychosocial stressors with the onset of panic disorder, although no psychosocial stressor can be definitely identified in most cases.

Panic disorder, in general, is a chronic disorder, although its course is variable both among patients and within a single patient. The available long-term follow-up studies of panic disorder are difficult to interpret because they have not controlled for the effects of treatment. Nevertheless, about 30 to 40 percent of patients seem to be symptom-free at long-term follow-up; about 50 percent have symptoms that are mild enough not to affect their lives significantly; and about 10 to 20 percent continue to have significant symptoms.

After the first one to two panic attacks, patients may be relatively unconcerned about their condition; however, with repeated attacks, the symptoms may become a major concern. Patients may attempt to keep the panic attacks secret, thereby causing their families and friends concern about unexplained changes in behavior. The frequency and the severity of the panic attacks may fluctuate. Panic attacks may occur several times in a day or less than once a month. The excessive intake of caffeine or nicotine may exacerbate the symptoms.

Depression may complicate the symptom picture in anywhere from 40 to 80 percent of all patients, as estimated by various studies. Although the patients do not tend to talk about suicidal ideation, they are at increased risk for committing suicide. Alcohol and other substance dependence occurs in about 20 to 40 percent of all patients, and obsessive-compulsive disorder may also develop. Perfor-

mance in school and at work and family interactions commonly suffer. Patients with good premorbid functioning and a brief duration of symptoms tend to have good prognoses.

### Agoraphobia

Most cases of agoraphobia are thought to be due to panic disorder. If the panic disorder is treated, the agoraphobia often improves with time. For a rapid and complete reduction of agoraphobia, behavior therapy is sometimes indicated. Agoraphobia without a history of panic disorder is often incapacitating and chronic. Depressive disorders and alcohol dependence often complicate the course of agoraphobia.

## TREATMENT

With treatment, most patients have a dramatic improvement in the symptoms of panic disorder and agoraphobia. The two most effective treatments are pharmacotherapy and cognitive-behavioral therapy. Family and group therapy may help affected patients and their families adjust to the fact that the patients have the disorder and to the psychosocial difficulties the disorder may have precipitated.

### Pharmacotherapy

Tricyclic and tetracyclic drugs, monoamine oxidase inhibitors (MAOIs), serotonin-specific reuptake inhibitors (SSRIs), and benzodiazepines are effective in the treatment of panic disorder. However, β-adrenergic receptor antagonists—for example, propranolol (Inderal)—are not effective for the treatment of panic disorder, and the currently available azaspirones—for example, buspirone (BuSpar)—are probably not effective, although definitive trials have not been conducted. A conservative approach based on currently available data is to use a tricyclic drug—for example, clomipramine (Anafranil) or imipramine (Tofranil)—as the first-line drug, followed by trials of an MAOI, an SSRI, or a benzodiazepine if the tricyclic drug is not effective or is not tolerated. Alternatively, some clinicians choose to use an MAOI, an SSRI, or a benzodiazepine as the first-line drug.

**Tricyclic and tetracyclic drugs.** Among tricyclic drugs, the most robust data show that clomipramine and imipramine are effective in the treatment of panic disorder. However, clinical experience indicates that clomipramine and imipramine should be initiated at low dosages, 10 mg a day, and titrated slowly at first in 10 mg a day intervals every two to three days, then more rapidly, in 25 mg a day intervals every two to three days, if the low dosages are well-tolerated. The most common side effect that causes noncompliance in panic disorder patients treated with clomipramine and imipramine is overstimulation during

Chapter 16. ANXIETY DISORDERS
590 | Chapter 16. ANXIETY DISORDERS

the initiation of treatment. The overstimulation is usually avoided by using the slow dosage titration schedule. Although early studies indicated that panic disorder patients respond more quickly and to lower dosages than do depressive disorder patients, later studies showed that that is not the case. Panic disorder patients need full dosages of clomipramine and imipramine and generally require a long time to respond, usually 8 to 12 weeks, rather than the 6 to 8 weeks for depression.

Some data support the efficacy of desipramine (Norpramin) in the treatment of panic disorder; other data indicate that maprotiline (Ludiomil) and trazodone (Desyrel) are less effective than desipramine. Anecdotal reports and case reports indicate that other tricyclic drugs are effective, including nortriptyline (Aventyl), amitriptyline (Limbitrol), and doxepin (Adapin). Clinical trials with nortriptyline may be indicated because that tricyclic drug is generally associated with fewer adverse effects, especially orthostatic hypotension, than are other tricyclic drugs.

**Monoamine oxidase inhibitors.** Monoamine oxidase inhibitors (MAOIs) are also effective in the treatment of panic disorder. Most studies have used phenelzine (Nardil), although some have used tranylcypromine (Parnate). Some studies have indicated that MAOIs are more effective than tricyclic drugs, and anecdotal reports indicate that patients who do not respond to tricyclic drugs may be likely to respond to MAOIs. When they are treated with MAOIs, panic disorder patients do not seem to have the initial side effect of overstimulation that can occur with tricyclic drugs. The dosages of MAOIs must reach those used for the treatment of depression, and a therapeutic trial should last 8 to 12 weeks.

**Serotonin-specific reuptake inhibitors.** Three SSRIs are available in the United States: fluoxetine (Prozac), sertraline (Zoloft), and paroxetine (Paxil). The data from well-controlled studies of the efficacy of SSRIs in panic disorder are limited, but the efficacy of clomipramine in panic disorder patients suggests that the SSRIs should also be effective. A well-controlled study of fluvoxamine, another SSRI, indicated that the drug is effective in the treatment of panic disorder. Anecdotal reports, however, indicate that panic disorder patients are particularly sensitive to overstimulation caused by SSRIs and that the clinician must titrate the dosages of the drugs slowly. Slow titration for fluoxetine is possible by dissolving a capsule in water or fruit juice or by using the fluoxetine elixir that is now available. Starting dosages can be as low as 2 or 4 mg a day and should be raised in 2 to 4 mg a day intervals every two to four days. The goal should be to reach a full therapeutic dosage of at least 20 mg a day.

**Benzodiazepines.** The use of benzodiazepines in the treatment of panic disorder has been limited because of concerns about dependence, cognitive impairment, and abuse. However, benzodiazepines are effective in the treatment of panic disorder and may have a more rapid onset (onset at one to two weeks, peaking after four to eight weeks) than do other pharmacotherapies. With some patients the clinician may initiate treatment with a benzodiazepine, titrate in another drug (for example, clomipramine), and then taper off (over 4 to 10 weeks) the

benzodiazepine after 8 to 12 weeks. The best data are available for the use of alprazolam (Xanax) in the treatment of panic disorder, although case reports indicate that clonazepam (Klonopin), which is about twice as potent as alprazolam, and lorazepam (Ativan), which is about half as potent as alprazolam, are also effective treatments. Alprazolam treatment can be initiated at 0.5 mg four times daily. Although the Food and Drug Administration (FDA) approves dosages up to 10 mg a day for the treatment of panic disorder, the most commonly effective dosages are usually between 4 and 6 mg a day. The major risks in benzodiazepine treatment are dependence and abuse. Dependence may develop in patients who are treated for several months, thus requiring a gradual tapering of the benzodiazepine, especially alprazolam, when the decision is made to stop the medication. However, solid data indicate that patients do not become tolerant to the antipanic effects of the benzodiazepines, as indicated by the lack of a need to increase the dosage of the benzodiazepine when treatment is long-term.

**Treatment failures.** If a drug from one class (for example, a tricyclic drug) is not effective, a drug from a different class (for example, an MAOI) should be tried. If treatment with a single agent is not effective, combinations can be tried (a benzodiazepine and a tricyclic drug; an SSRI and a tricyclic drug; lithium [Eskalith] and a tricyclic drug). Some reports indicate that anticonvulsants— for example, carbamazepine (Tegretol) and valproate (Depakene)—have been effective, and other reports indicate that calcium channel inhibitors—for example, verapamil (Calan)—have been effective in the treatment of panic disorder. When faced with treatment failure, clinicians should reconsider the diagnosis, assess the patient's compliance with the treatment regimen (possibly with plasma concentrations of the drug), and consider potentially complicating factors (comorbid psychiatric diagnoses—for example, depression—and alcohol, marijuana, and other substance use).

**Duration of pharmacotherapy.** Once effective, pharmacological treatment should generally continue for 8 to 12 months. The available data indicate that panic disorder is a chronic, perhaps lifelong, condition that will recur when treatment is discontinued. Studies have reported that from 30 to 90 percent of successfully treated panic disorder patients relapse when their medication is discontinued. Patients may be likely to relapse if they are treated with benzodiazepines and the benzodiazepine therapy is terminated in such a way as to cause withdrawal symptoms.

## Cognitive and Behavior Therapies

Cognitive and behavior therapies are effective treatments for panic disorder. Various reports have concluded that cognitive and behavior therapies are superior to pharmacotherapy alone; other reports have concluded the opposite. Several studies and reports have found that the combination of cognitive or behavior therapy with pharmacotherapy is more effective than either therapeutic approach alone. Several studies have included long-term follow-up of patients treated with cognitive or behavior therapy and have found that the therapies are effective in producing the long-lasting remission of symptoms.

**Cognitive therapy.** The two major foci of cognitive therapy for panic disorder are instruction regarding the patient's false beliefs and information regarding panic attacks. The instruction regarding false beliefs centers on the patient's tendency to misinterpret mild bodily sensations as indicative of impending panic attacks, doom, or death. The information about panic attacks includes explanations that panic attacks, when they occur, are time-limited and not life-threatening.

**Applied relaxation.** The goal of applied relaxation (for example, Herbert Benson's relaxation training) is to instill a sense of control in patients regarding their levels of anxiety and relaxation. Through the use of standardized techniques for muscle relaxation and the imagining of relaxing situations, patients learn techniques that may help them through a panic attack.

**Respiratory training.** Since the hyperventilation associated with panic attacks is probably related to some symptoms, such as dizziness and faintness, one direct approach to control panic attacks is to train patients how to control the urge to hyperventilate. After that training, patients can use the technique to help control hyperventilation during a panic attack.

**In vivo exposure.** In vivo exposure used to be the primary behavior treatment for panic disorder. The technique involves sequentially greater exposure of the patient to the feared stimulus; over time, the patient becomes desensitized to the experience. Previously, the focus was on external stimuli; recently, the technique has included exposure of the patient to internal feared sensations (for example, tachypnea and fear of having a panic attack).

## Other Psychosocial Therapies

**Family therapy.** The families of patients with panic disorder and agoraphobia may have become disrupted during the course of the disorder. Family therapy directed toward education and support is often beneficial.

**Insight-oriented psychotherapy.** Insight-oriented psychotherapy can be of benefit in the treatment of panic disorder and agoraphobia. Treatment focuses on helping the patient understand the hypothesized unconscious meaning of the anxiety, the symbolism of the avoided situation, the need to repress impulses, and the symptoms' secondary gains. A resolution of early infantile and oedipal conflicts is hypothesized to correlate with the resolution of current stresses.

## Combined Psychotherapy and Pharmacotherapy

Even when pharmacotherapy is effective in eliminating the primary symptoms of panic disorder, psychotherapy may be needed to treat secondary symptoms. Glen O. Gabbard wrote:

Panic-disordered patients frequently require a combination of drug therapy and psychotherapy . . . . Even when patients with panic attacks and agoraphobia have their symptoms pharmacologically controlled, they are often reluctant to venture out into the world again and may require psychotherapeutic interventions to help overcome this fear . . . . Some patients will adamantly refuse any medication because they believe that it stigmatizes them as being mentally ill, so psychotherapeutic intervention is required to help them understand and eliminate their resistance to pharmacotherapy . . . . For a comprehensive and effective treatment plan, these patients require psychotherapeutic approaches in addition to appropriate medications. In all patients with symptoms of panic disorder or agoraphobia, a careful psychodynamic evaluation will help weigh the contributions of biological and dynamic factors.

## References

Ballenger J C: Medication discontinuation in panic disorder. J Clin Psychiatry 53 (3, Suppl): 26, 1992.

Barlow D H: Cognitive-behavioral approaches to panic disorder and social phobia. Bull Menninger Clin 56 (2, Suppl): A14, 1992.

Basoglu M, Marks I M, Sengun S: A prospective study of panic and anxiety in agoraphobia with panic disorder. Br J Psychiatry 160: 57, 1992.

Black D W, Wesner R, Bowers W, Gabel J: A comparison of fluvoxamine, cognitive therapy, and placebo in the treatment of panic disorder. Arch Gen Psychiatry 50: 44, 1993.

Charney D S, Woods S W, Krystal J H, Nagy L M, Heninger G R: Noradrenergic neuronal dysregulation in panic disorder: The effects of intravenous yohimbine and clonidine in panic disorder patients. Acta Psychiatr Scand 86: 273, 1992.

Coplan J D, Gorman J M, Klein D F: Serotonin related functions in panic-anxiety: A critical overview. Neuropsychopharmacology 6: 189, 1992.

Cross-National Collaborative Panic Study, Second Phase Investigators: Drug treatment of panic disorder: Comparative efficacy of alprazolam, imipramine, and placebo. Br J Psychiatry 160: 191, 1992.

de la Fuenta J R, editor: Panic disorder. Psychiatr Ann 20: 2, 1990.

Eaton W W, Keyl P M: Risk factors for the onset of diagnostic interview schedule/DSM-III agoraphobia in a prospective, population-based study. Arch Gen Psychiatry 47: 819, 1990.

Fawcett J: Suicide risk factors in depressive disorders and panic disorder. J Clin Psychiatry 53 (3, Suppl): 9, 1992.

Fontaine R, Breton G, Dery R, Fontaine S, Elie R: Temporal lobe abnormalities in panic disorder: An MRI study. Biol Psychiatry 27: 304, 1990.

Francis G, Last C G, Strauss C C: Avoidant disorder and social phobia in children and adolescents. J Am Acad Child Adolesc Psychiatry 31: 1086, 1992.

Gabbard G O: Psychodynamic Psychiatry in Clinical Practice: The DSM-IV Edition. American Psychiatric Press, Washington, 1994.

Gabbard G O: Psychodynamic psychiatry in the "decade of the brain." Am J Psychiatry 149: 991, 1992.

Gelerntor C S, Uhde T W, Cimbolic P, Arnkoff D B, Vittone B J, Tancer M E, Bartko J J: Cognitive-behavioral and pharmacological treatments of social phobia: A controlled study. Arch Gen Psychiatry 48: 938, 1991.

Heimberg R G, Barlow D H: New developments in cognitive-behavioral therapy for social phobia. J Clin Psychiatry 52 (11, Suppl): 21, 1991.

Himle J A, Crystal D, Curtis G C, Fluent T E: Mode of onset of simple phobia subtypes: Further evidence of heterogeneity. Psychiatry Res 36: 37, 1991.

Horwath E, Herbert J D, Hope D A, Bellack A S: Validity of the distinction between generalized social phobia and avoidant personality disorder. J Abnorm Psychol 101: 332, 1991.

Johnson J, Hornig C D: Epidemiology of panic disorder in African Americans. Am J Psychiatry 150: 465, 1993.

Journal of Clinical Psychiatry: Panic disorder: Strategies for long-term treatment. J Clin Psychiatry 52 (2, Suppl): 2, 1991.

Kahn R S, van Praag H M: Panic disorder: A biological perspective. Eur Neuropsychopharmacol 2: 1, 1992.

Katerndahl D A, Realini J P: Lifetime prevalence of panic states. Am J Psychiatry 150: 246, 1993.

Keller M B, Hanks D L: Course and outcome in panic disorder. Prog Neuro Psychopharmacol Biol Psychiatry 17: 551, 1993.

Kenardy J, Fried L, Kraemer H C, Taylor C B: Psychological precursors of panic attacks. Br J Psychiatry 160: 668, 1992.

Klerman G L: Drug treatment of panic disorder: Reply to comment by Marks and associates. Br J Psychiatry *161*: 465, 1992.

Liebowitz M R, Schneier F, Campeas R, Hollander E, Hatterer J, Fyer A, Gorman J, Papp L, Davies S, Gully R: Phenelzine vs atenolol in social phobia: A placebo-controlled comparison. Arch Gen Psychiatry *49*: 290, 1992.

Lydiard R B, Lesser I M, Ballenger J C, Rubin R T, Laraia M, DuPont R: A fixed-dose study of alprazolam 2 mg, alprazolam 6 mg, and placebo in panic disorder. J Clin Psychopharmacol *12*: 96, 1992.

Margraf J, Barlow D H, Clark D M, Telch M J: Psychological treatment of panic: Work in progress on outcome, active ingredients, and follow-up. Behav Res Ther *31*: 1, 1993.

Modigh K, Westberg P, Eriksson E: Superiority of clomipramine over imipramine in the treatment of panic disorder: A placebo-controlled trial. J Clin Psychopharmacol *12*: 251, 1992.

Moreau D, Weissman M M: Panic disorder in children and adolescents: A review. Am J Psychiatry *149*: 1306, 1992.

Nersch P P, Emmelkamp P M, Lips C: Social phobia: Individual response patterns of the long-term effects of behavioral and cognitive interventions: A follow-up study. Behav Res Ther *20*: 357, 1991.

Noyes R, Reich J, Christiansen J, Suelzer M, Pfohl B, Coryell W A: Outcome of panic disorder: Relationship to diagnostic subtypes and comorbidity. Arch Gen Psychiatry *47*: 809, 1990.

Nutt D, Lawson C: Panic attacks: A neurochemical overview of models and mechanisms. Br J Psychiatry *160*: 165, 1992.

Ost L G: Blood and injection phobia: Background and cognitive, physiological, and behavioral variables. J Abnorm Psychol *101*: 68, 1992.

Rapee R M, Litwin E M, Barlow D H: Impact on life events on subjects with panic disorder and on comparison subjects. Am J Psychiatry *147*: 640, 1990.

Rickels K, Schweizer E, Weiss S, Zavodnick S: Maintenance drug treatment for panic disorder: II. Short- and long-term outcome after drug taper. Arch Gen Psychiatry *50*: 61, 1993.

Ross J: Social phobia: The Anxiety Disorders Association of America helps raise the veil of ignorance. J Clin Psychiatry *52* (11, Suppl): 43, 1991.

Schneier F R, Johnson J, Hornic C D, Liebowitz M R, Weissman M M: Social phobia: Comorbidity and morbidity in an epidemiologic sample. Arch Gen Psychiatry *49*: 282, 1992.

Schweizer E, Rickels K, Weiss S, Zavodnick S: Maintenance drugs treatment of panic disorder: I. Results of a prospective, placebo-controlled comparison of alprazolam and imipramine. Arch Gen Psychiatry *50*: 51, 1993.

Shear M K, Cooper A M, Klerman G L, Busch F N, Shapiro T: A psychodynamic model of panic disorder. Am J Psychiatry *150*: 859, 1993.

# 16.3 / Specific Phobia and Social Phobia

Recent epidemiological studies have found that phobias are the single most common mental disorders in the United States. An estimated 5 to 10 percent of the population are afflicted with those troubling and sometimes disabling disorders. Less conservative estimates have ranged up to 25 percent of the population. The distress associated with phobias, especially when they are not recognized or acknowledged as mental disorders, can lead to further psychiatric complications, including other anxiety disorders, major depressive disorder, and substance-related disorders, especially alcohol use disorders. The underrecognition of phobias is particularly unfortunate, since recent research studies have found that phobias are often responsive to treatment with cognitive and behavioral psychotherapies and to treatment with specific pharmaco-

therapies, including tricyclic drugs, monoamine oxidase inhibitors, and β-adrenergic receptor antagonists.

A *phobia* is an irrational fear resulting in a conscious avoidance of the feared object, activity, or situation. Either the presence or the anticipation of the phobic entity elicits severe distress in the affected person, who recognizes that the reaction is excessive. Nevertheless, the phobic reaction results in a disruption of the person's ability to function in life.

In addition to agoraphobia, the fourth edition of *Diagnostic and Statistical Manual of Mental Disorders* (DSM-IV) lists two other phobias: specific phobia and social phobia. Specific phobia was called simple phobia in the revised third edition of DSM (DSM-III-R). Social phobia, also called social anxiety disorder, is characterized by an excessive fear of humiliation or embarrassment in various social settings, such as public speaking, urinating in a public rest room (also called shy bladder), and speaking to a date. A generalized type of social phobia is often a chronic and disabling condition that is characterized by a phobic avoidance of most social situations. That type of social phobia can be difficult to distinguish from avoidant personality disorder.

## EPIDEMIOLOGY

As mentioned above, phobias are common mental disorders, although a large percentage of phobic persons either do not come to the attention of clinicians for their phobias or are misdiagnosed when they do come to psychiatric or medical attention.

### Specific Phobia

Specific phobia is more common than social phobia. Specific phobia is the most common mental disorder among women and the second most common among men, second only to substance-related disorders. The six-month prevalence of specific phobia is about 5 to 10 per 100 persons. The female-to-male ratio is about 2 to 1, although the ratio is closer to 1 to 1 for the blood, injection, injury type. The peak age of onset for the natural environment type and the blood, injection, injury type is in the range of 5 to 9 years, although onset also occurs at older ages. In contrast, the peak age of onset for the situational type (except fear of heights) is higher, in the mid-20s, which is closer to the age of onset for agoraphobia. The feared objects and situations in specific phobia (listed in descending frequency of appearance) are animals, storms, heights, illness, injury, and death.

### Social Phobia

The six-month prevalence for social phobia is about 2 to 3 per 100 persons. In epidemiological studies, females are affected more often than males, but in clinical samples the reverse is often true. The reasons for those varying observations are not known. The peak age of onset for social phobia is in the person's teens, although onset is common as young as 5 years of age and as old as 35.

## ETIOLOGY

Both specific phobia and social phobia have types, and the precise causes of those types are likely to differ. Even within the types, as in all mental disorders, causative heterogeneity is found. The pathogenesis of the phobias, once it is understood, may prove to be a clear model for interactions between biological and genetic factors, on the one hand, and environmental events, on the other hand. In the blood, injection, injury type of specific phobia, affected persons may have inherited a particularly strong vasovagal reflex, which becomes associated with phobic emotions.

### General Principles

**Behavioral factors.** In 1920 John B. Watson wrote an article called "Conditioned Emotional Reactions," in which he recounted his experiences with Little Albert, an infant with a fear of rats and rabbits. Unlike Sigmund Freud's Little Hans, who had phobic symptoms in the natural course of his maturation, Little Albert's difficulties were the direct result of the scientific experiments of two psychologists who used techniques that had successfully induced conditioned responses in laboratory animals.

Watson's formulation invoked the traditional Pavlovian stimulus-response model of the conditioned reflex to account for the creation of the phobia. That is, anxiety is aroused by a naturally frightening stimulus that occurs in contiguity with a second inherently neutral stimulus. As a result of the contiguity, especially when the two stimuli are paired on several successive occasions, the originally neutral stimulus takes on the capacity to arouse anxiety by itself. The neutral stimulus, therefore, becomes a conditioned stimulus for anxiety production.

In the classic stimulus-response theory the conditioned stimulus gradually loses its potency to arouse a response if it is not reinforced by a periodic repetition of the unconditioned stimulus. In the phobic symptom, the attenuation of the response to the phobic—that is, conditioned—stimulus does not occur; the symptom may last for years without any apparent external reinforcement. Operant conditioning theory provides a model to explain that phenomenon. In operant conditioning theory, anxiety is a drive that motivates the organism to do what it can to obviate the painful affect. In the course of its random behavior, the organism learns that certain actions enable it to avoid the anxiety-provoking stimulus. Those avoidance patterns remain stable for long periods of time as a result of the reinforcement they receive from their capacity to diminish activity. That model is readily applicable to phobias in that avoidance of the anxiety-provoking object or situation plays a central part. Such avoidance behavior becomes fixed as a stable symptom because of its effectiveness in protecting the person from the phobic anxiety.

Learning theory has a particular relevance to phobias and provides simple and intelligible explanations for many aspects of phobic symptoms. Critics contend, however, that it deals mostly with surface mechanisms of symptom formation and is less useful than psychoanalytic theories in providing an understanding of some of the complex underlying psychic processes involved.

**Psychoanalytic factors.** Sigmund Freud presented a formulation of phobic neurosis that has remained the analytic explanation of specific phobia and social phobia. Freud hypothesized that the major function of anxiety is to signal the ego that a forbidden unconscious drive is pushing for conscious expression, thus altering the ego to strengthen and marshal its defenses against the threatening instinctual force. Freud viewed the phobia—anxiety hysteria, as he continued to call it—as a result of conflicts centered on an unresolved childhood oedipal situation. Because the sex drive continues to have a strong incestuous coloring in the adult, sexual arousal tends to kindle an anxiety that is characteristically a fear of castration. When repression fails to be entirely successful, the ego must call on auxiliary defenses. In phobic patients the defense involves primarily the use of displacement; that is, the sexual conflict is displaced from the person who evokes the conflict to a seemingly unimportant, irrelevant object or situation, which then has the power to arouse the constellation of affects, including signal anxiety. The phobic object or situation may have a direct associative connection with the primary source of the conflict and, thus, symbolizes it (the defense mechanism of symbolization). Furthermore, the situation or the object is usually one that the person is able to keep away from; by that additional defense mechanism of avoidance, the person can escape suffering serious anxiety. Freud first discussed the theoretical formulation of phobia formation in his famous case history of Little Hans, a 5-year-old boy who had a fear of horses.

Although theorists originally thought that phobias resulted from castration anxiety, recent psychoanalytic theorists have suggested that other types of anxiety may be involved. In agoraphobia, for example, separation anxiety clearly plays a leading role, and in erythrophobia (a fear of red that can be manifested as a fear of blushing), the element of shame implies the involvement of superego anxiety. Clinical observations lead to the view that anxiety associated with phobias has a variety of sources and colorings.

Phobias illustrate the interaction between a genetic-constitutional diathesis and environmental stressors. Longitudinal studies suggest that certain children are constitutionally predisposed to phobias because they are born with a specific temperament known as behavioral inhibition to the unfamiliar. However, some type of chronic environmental stress must act on that temperamental disposition to create a full-blown phobia. Such stressors as the death of a parent, separation from a parent, criticism or humiliation by an older sibling, and violence in the household may activate the latent diathesis within the child, so that the child becomes symptomatic.

COUNTERPHOBIC ATTITUDE. Otto Fenichel called attention to the fact that phobic anxiety can be hidden attitudes and behavior patterns that represent a denial, either that the dreaded object or situation is dangerous or that one is afraid of it. Basic to that phenomenon is a reversal of the situation in which one is the passive victim of external circumstances to a position of actively attempting to confront and master what one fears. The counterphobic person seeks out situations of danger and rushes enthusiastically toward them. The devotee of potentially dangerous sports, such as parachute jumping and rock climbing, may be exhibiting counterphobic behavior. Such patterns may be secondary to phobic anxiety or may be used as normal means of dealing with a realistically dangerous situation. The play of children may contain counterphobic elements, as when children play doctor and give the doll the shot they received earlier in the day in the pediatrician's office. That pattern of behavior may involve the related defense mechanism of identification with the aggressor.

### Specific Phobia

The development of specific phobia may result from the pairing of a specific object or situation with the emotions of fear and panic. Various mechanisms for the pairing have been postulated. In general, a nonspecific tendency to experience fear or anxiety forms the backgroup; when a specific event (driving, for example) is paired with an emotional experience (an accident, for example), the person is susceptible to a permanent emotional association between driving or cars and fear or anxiety. The emotional experience itself can be either responsive to an external incident, as in a traffic accident, or an internal incident, most commonly a panic attack. Although a person may never experience a panic attack again and may not meet the diagnostic criteria for panic disorder, such a person may have a generalized fear of driving and not an expressed fear of having a panic attack while driving. Other mechanisms of association between the phobic object and the phobic emotions include modeling, in which a person observes the reaction in another (for example, a parent), and information transfer, in which a person is taught or warned about the dangers of specific objects (for example, venomous snakes).

**Genetic factors.** Specific phobia tends to run in families. The blood, injection, injury type has a particularly high familial tendency. Studies have reported that two thirds to three fourths of affected probands have at least one first-degree relative with specific phobia of the same type. However, the necessary twin and adoption studies have not been conducted to rule out a significant contribution by nongenetic transmission of specific phobia.

### Social Phobia

Several studies have reported the possible presence of a trait in some children that is characterized by a consistent pattern of behavioral inhibition. That trait may be particularly common in the children of parents who are affected with panic disorder and may develop into severe shyness as the children grow older. At least some persons with social phobia may have exhibited behavioral inhibition during childhood. Perhaps associated with that trait, which is thought to be biologically based, are the psychologically based data indicating that the parents of persons with social phobia were, as a group, less caring, more rejecting, and more overprotective of their children than were other parents. Some social phobia research has referred to the spectrum from dominance to submission that is observed in the animal kingdom. For example, dominant humans may tend

to walk with their chins in the air and to make eye contact, whereas submissive humans may tend to walk with their chins down and to avoid eye contact.

**Neurochemical factors.** The success of pharmacotherapies in treating social phobia has generated two specific neurochemical hypotheses regarding two types of social phobia. Specifically, the use of β-adrenergic antagonists—for example, propranolol (Inderal)—for performance phobias (for example, public speaking) has led to the development of an adrenergic theory for those phobias. Patients with performance phobias may release more norepinephrine or epinephrine, both centrally and peripherally, than do nonphobic persons, or such patients may be sensitive to a normal level of adrenergic stimulation. The observation that monoamine oxidase inhibitors (MAOIs) may be more effective than tricyclic drugs in the treatment of generalized social phobia, in combination with preclinical data, has led some investigators to hypothesize that dopaminergic activity is related to the pathogenesis of the disorder.

**Genetic factors.** First-degree relatives of persons with social phobia are about three times more likely to be affected with social phobia than are first-degree relatives of persons without mental disorders. And some preliminary data indicate that monozygotic twins are more often concordant than are dizygotic twins, although in social phobia it is particularly important to study twins reared apart to help control for environmental factors.

## DIAGNOSIS

### Specific Phobia

The name for specific phobia in DSM-III-R was simple phobia. The name was changed to make DSM-IV match the nomenclature in the 10th revision of the International Classification of Diseases (ICD-10) and to avoid restricting the scope of the diagnosis. For example, since panic attacks are common in patients with specific phobia, the name "simple phobia" incorrectly implies that panic attacks are not allowed by the diagnostic criteria.

Several additional changes have been made from the DSM-III-R criteria to the DSM-IV criteria for specific phobia (Table 16.3–1). Criteria A and B have been reworded to allow for the possibility that exposure to the phobic stimulus results in a panic attack. In contrast to panic disorder, however, in specific phobia the panic attack is situationally bound to the specific phobic stimulus. Criteria F in DSM-IV includes the words "not better accounted for" to emphasize the need for the clinician's judgment regarding the diagnosis of the symptoms. The specific content of the phobia and the strength of the relation (for example, cued or noncued) between the stimulus and a panic attack also need to be considered.

Because a review of the literature indicated that specific phobia is associated with varying ages of onset, sex ratios, family histories, and physiological responses, DSM-IV includes distinctive types of specific phobia: animal type; natural environment type (for example, storms); blood,

**Table 16.3–1**
**Diagnostic Criteria for Specific Phobia**

A. Marked and persistent fear that is excessive or unreasonable, cued by the presence or anticipation of a specific object or situation (e.g., flying, heights, animals, receiving an injection, seeing blood).

B. Exposure to the phobic stimulus almost invariably provokes an immediate anxiety response, which may take the form of a situationally bound or situationally predisposed panic attack. **Note:** in children, the anxiety may be expressed by crying, tantrums, freezing, or clinging.

C. The person recognizes that the fear is excessive or unreasonable. **Note:** in children, this feature may be absent.

D. The phobic situation(s) is avoided, or else endured with intense anxiety or distress.

E. The avoidance, anxious anticipation, or distress in the feared situation(s) interferes significantly with the person's normal routine, occupational (or academic) functioning, or social activities or relationships with others, or there is marked distress about having the phobia.

F. In individuals under age 18 years, the duration is at least 6 months.

G. The anxiety, panic attacks, or phobic avoidance associated with the specific object or situation are not better accounted for by another mental disorder, such as obsessive-compulsive disorder (e.g., fear of dirt in someone with an obsession about contamination), posttraumatic stress disorder (e.g., avoidance of stimuli associated with a severe stressor), separation anxiety disorder (e.g., avoidance of school), social phobia (e.g., avoidance of social situations because of fear of embarrassment), panic disorder with agoraphobia, or agoraphobia without history of panic disorder.

*Specify* type:
   **Animal type**
   **Natural environment type** (e.g., heights, storms, and water)
   **Blood, injection, injury type**
   **Situational type** (e.g., planes, elevators, enclosed places)
   **Other type** (e.g., phobic avoidance of situations that may lead to choking, vomiting, or contracting an illness; in children, avoidance of loud sounds or costumed characters)

Table from DSM-IV, *Diagnostic and Statistical Manual of Mental Disorders*, ed 4. Copyright American Psychiatric Association, Washington, 1994. Used with permission.

injection, injury type; situational type (for example, cars); and other type (for specific phobias that do not fit into the previous four types). Preliminary data indicate that the natural environment type is most common in children under 10 years old and the situational type in the early 20s. The blood, injection, injury type is differentiated from the others in that bradycardia and hypotension often follow the initial tachycardia that is common in all phobias. The blood, injection, injury type of specific phobia is particularly likely to affect many members and generations of a family. One type of specific phobia that has been reported recently is space phobia, in which patients are afraid of falling when there is no nearby support, such as a wall or a chair. Some data indicate that affected patients may have abnormal function in the right hemisphere, possibly resulting in a visual-spatial impairment.

## Social Phobia

The DSM-IV diagnostic criteria for social phobia (Table 16.3–2) have been modified from those in DSM-III-R. Because social phobia can be associated with panic attacks, DSM-IV criteria B and F have been rewritten to acknowledge that fact (criterion B) and to encourage the use of clinical judgment in making the final diagnosis (criterion F). DSM-IV adds a type of social phobia, generalized type, which may be of use in the prediction of course, prognosis, and treatment response. DSM-IV excludes a diagnosis of social phobia when the symptoms are a result of social avoidance stemming from embarrassment about another psychiatric or nonpsychiatric medical condition.

**Table 16.3–2**
**Diagnostic Criteria for Social Phobia**

A. A marked and persistent fear of one or more social or performance situations in which the person is exposed to unfamiliar people or to possible scrutiny by others. The individual fears that he or she will act in a way (or show anxiety symptoms) that will be humiliating or embarrassing. **Note:** in children, there must be evidence of capacity for age-appropriate social relationships with familiar people and the anxiety must occur in peer settings, not just in interactions with adults.

B. Exposure to the feared social situation almost invariably provokes anxiety, which may take the form of a situationally bound or situationally predisposed panic attack. **Note:** In children, the anxiety may be expressed by crying, tantrums, freezing, or shrinking from social situations with unfamiliar people.

C. The person recognizes that the fear is excessive or unreasonable. **Note:** in children, this feature may be absent.

D. The feared social or performance situations are avoided, or else endured with intense anxiety or distress.

E. The avoidance, anxious anticipation, or distress in the feared social or performance situation(s) interferes significantly with the person's normal routine, occupational (academic) functioning, or social activities or relationships with others, or there is marked distress about having the phobia.

F. In individuals under age 18 years, the duration is at least 6 months.

G. The fear or avoidance is not due to the direct physiological effects of a substance (e.g., a drug of abuse, a medication) or a general medical condition, and is not better accounted for by another mental disorder (e.g., panic disorder with or without agoraphobia, separation anxiety disorder, body dysmorphic disorder, a pervasive developmental disorder, or schizoid personality disorder).

H. If a general medical condition or other mental disorder is present, the fear in criterion A is unrelated to it, e.g., the fear is not of stuttering, trembling in Parkinson's disease, or exhibiting abnormal eating behavior in anorexia nervosa or bulimia nervosa.

*Specify* if:
   **Generalized:** if the fears include most social situations (also consider the additional diagnosis of avoidant personality disorder).

Table from DSM-IV, *Diagnostic and Statistical Manual of Mental Disorders*, ed 4. Copyright American Psychiatric Association, Washington, 1994. Used with permission.

## CLINICAL FEATURES

Phobias are characterized by the arousal of severe anxiety when the patient is exposed to a specific situation or object or when the patient even anticipates exposure to the situation or object. DSM-IV emphasizes the possibility that panic attacks can and frequently do occur in patients with specific and social phobias, but the panic attacks, except perhaps for the first few, are expected. Exposure to the phobic stimulus or anticipation of it almost invariably results in a panic attack in a panic attack-prone person.

Patients with phobias, by definition, try to avoid the phobic stimulus. Some patients go to great trouble to avoid anxiety-provoking situations. For example, a phobic patient may take a bus across the United States, rather than fly, to avoid contact with the object of the patient's phobia, an airplane. Perhaps as another way to avoid the stress of the phobic stimulus, many phobic patients have substance-related disorders, particularly alcohol use disorders. Moreover, an estimated one third of patients with social phobia have major depressive disorder.

The major finding on the mental status examination is the presence of an irrational and ego-dystonic fear of a specific situation, activity, or object; patients are able to describe how they avoid contact with the phobic situation. Depression is commonly found on the mental status examination and may be present in as many as one third of all phobic patients.

The patient was a 33-year-old man who lived in Seattle with his wife. He had been employed as a salesperson since graduating from college, where he had majored in mathematics. He went to a private psychiatrist, recommended by a friend, complaining of "anxiety at work."

The patient described himself as outgoing and popular throughout his adolescence and young adulthood, with no serious problems until his third year of college. He then began to become tense and nervous when studying for tests and writing papers. His heart would pound; his hands would sweat and tremble. Consequently, he often did not write the required papers and, when he did, would submit them after the date due. He could not understand why he was so nervous about doing papers and taking tests when he had always done well in those tasks in the past. As a result of his failure to submit certain papers and his late submission of other papers, his college grades were seriously affected.

Soon after graduation, the patient was employed as a salesperson for an insurance firm. His initial training (attending lectures, completing reading assignments) proceeded smoothly, but as soon as he began to take on clients, his anxiety returned. He became nervous when anticipating phone calls from clients. When his business phone rang, he would begin to tremble and sometimes would not answer. Eventually, he avoided becoming anxious by not scheduling appointments and by not contacting clients whom he was expected to see.

When asked what it was about those situations that made him nervous, he said that he was concerned about what the client would think of him. "The client might sense that I am nervous and might ask me questions that I don't know the answers to, and I would feel foolish." As a result, he would repeatedly rewrite and reword sales scripts for telephone conversations because he was "so concerned about saying the

right thing. I guess I'm just very concerned about being judged."

Although never unemployed, the patient estimated that he had been functioning at only 20 percent of his work capacity, which his employer tolerated because he was paid only on a commission basis. For the previous several years, he had had to borrow large sums of money to make ends meet.

Although financial constraints were a burden, the patient and his wife entertained guests at their home regularly and enjoyed socializing with friends at picnics, parties, and formal affairs. The patient lamented, "It's just when I'm expected to do something. Then, it's like I'm on stage, all alone, with everyone watching me."

## DIFFERENTIAL DIAGNOSIS

Specific phobia and social phobia need to be differentiated from appropriate fear and normal shyness, respectively. DSM-IV aids in the differentiation by requiring that the symptoms impair the patient's ability to function appropriately. Nonpsychiatric medical conditions that can result in the development of a phobia include the use of substances (particularly hallucinogens and sympathomimetics), central nervous system tumors, and cerebrovascular diseases. Phobic symptoms in those instances are unlikely in the absence of additional suggestive findings on physical, neurological, and mental status examinations. Schizophrenia is also in the differential diagnosis of both specific phobia and social phobia, since schizophrenic patients can have phobic symptoms as part of their psychoses. However, unlike schizophrenic patients, phobic patients have insight into the irrationality of their fears and lack the bizarre quality and other psychotic symptoms that accompany schizophrenia.

In the differential diagnosis of both specific phobia and social phobia, the clinician must consider panic disorder, agoraphobia, and avoidant personality disorder. DSM-IV acknowledges that the differentiation among panic disorder, agoraphobia, social phobia, and specific phobia can be difficult in individual cases, and the clinician is advised to use clinical judgment. In general, however, patients with specific phobia or nongeneralized social phobia tend to experience anxiety immediately when presented with the phobic stimulus. Furthermore, their anxiety or panic is limited to the identified situation, and, in general, the patients are not abnormally anxious when they are neither confronted with the phobic stimulus nor caused to anticipate the stimulus.

An agoraphobic patient is often comforted by the presence of another person in an anxiety-provoking situation, whereas the patient with social phobia is made more anxious than before by the presence of other people. Whereas breathlessness, dizziness, a sense of suffocation, and a fear of dying are common in panic disorder and agoraphobia, the symptoms associated with social phobia usually involve blushing, muscle twitching, and anxiety about scrutiny. The differentiation between social phobia and avoidant personality disorder can be difficult and can require extensive interviews and psychiatric histories.

## Specific Phobia

Other diagnoses to consider in the differential diagnosis of specific phobia are hypochondriasis, obsessive-compulsive disorder, and paranoid personality disorder. Hypochondriasis is the fear of having a disease, whereas specific phobia of the illness type is the fear of contracting the disease. Some patients with obsessive-compulsive disorder manifest behavior that is indistinguishable from that of a patient with specific phobia. For example, patients with obsessive-compulsive disorder may avoid knives because they have a compulsive thought about killing their children, whereas patients with specific phobia involving knives may avoid knives for fear of cutting themselves. Paranoid personality disorder can be distinguished from specific phobia by the generalized fear in patients with paranoid personality disorder.

## Social Phobia

Two additional differential diagnostic considerations for social phobia are major depressive disorder and schizoid personality disorder. The avoidance of social situations can often be a symptom in depression; however, a psychiatric interview with the patient is likely to elicit a broad constellation of depressive symptoms. In patients with schizoid personality disorder, the lack of interest in socializing, not fear of socializing, leads to the avoidant social behavior.

## COURSE AND PROGNOSIS

Not a great deal is known about the course and the prognosis of specific phobia and social phobia because of their relatively recent recognition as important mental disorders. The introduction of specific psychotherapies and pharmacotherapies to treat the phobias will also affect the interpretation of data on course and prognosis unless the studies control for the treatment strategies.

Phobic disorders may be associated with more morbidity than was previously recognized. Depending on the degree to which the phobic behavior interferes with the person's ability to function, the affected patient may have financial dependence on others as adults and varying degrees of impairment in their social lives, occupational successes, and, in the case of young people, school performance. The development of associated substance-related disorders can also adversely affect the course and the prognosis of the disorders.

## TREATMENT

### Insight-Oriented Psychotherapy

Early in the development of psychoanalysis and the dynamically oriented psychotherapies, theorists believed that those methods were the treatments of choice for phobic neurosis, which was then thought to stem from oedipalgenital conflicts. Soon, however, therapists recognized

that, in spite of progress in uncovering and analyzing unconscious conflicts, patients frequently failed to lose their phobic symptoms. Moreover, by continuing to avoid the phobic situation, patients excluded a significant degree of anxiety and its related associations from the analytic process. Both Freud and his pupil Sandor Ferenczi recognized that, if progress in analyzing those symptoms was to be made, therapists had to go beyond their analytic roles and actively urge phobic patients to seek out the phobic situation and experience the anxiety and resultant insight. Since then, psychiatrists have generally agreed that a measure of activity on the part of the therapist is often required to treat phobic anxiety successfully. The decision to apply the techniques of psychodynamic insight-oriented therapy should be based not on the presence of the phobic symptom alone but on positive indications from the patient's ego structure and life patterns for the use of that method of treatment. Insight-oriented therapy enables the patient to understand the origin of the phobia, the phenomenon of secondary gain, and the role of resistance and enables the patient to seek healthy ways of dealing with anxiety-provoking stimuli.

### Other Therapies

Hypnosis, supportive therapy, and family therapy may be useful in the treatment of phobias. Hypnosis is used to enhance the therapist's suggestions that the phobic object is not dangerous, and self-hypnosis can be taught to the patient as a method of relaxation when confronted with the phobic object. Supportive psychotherapy and family therapy are often useful in helping the patient actively confront the phobic object during treatment. Not only can family therapy enlist the aid of the family in treating the patient, but it may help the family understand the nature of the patient's problem. An additional therapeutic and supportive activity for patients may be involvement in the Anxiety Disorders Association of America (ADAA).

### Specific Phobia

The most commonly used treatment for specific phobia is exposure therapy, a type of behavior therapy originally pioneered by Joseph Wolpe. The therapist densensitizes the patient, using a series of gradual, self-paced exposures to the phobic stimulus. The therapist teaches the patient various techniques to deal with the anxiety, including relaxation, breathing control, and cognitive approaches to the situation. The cognitive approaches include reinforcing the realization that the situation is, in fact, safe. The key aspects of successful behavior therapy are (1) the patient's commitment to treatment, (2) clearly identified problems and objectives, and (3) available alternative strategies for coping with the patient's feelings. In the special situation of blood, injection, injury phobia, some therapists recommend that patients tense their bodies during the exposure and remain seated during the exposure to help avoid the possibility of fainting from a vasovagal reaction to the phobic stimulation. Some preliminary reports indicate that β-adrenergic antagonists can be useful in the treatment of specific phobia. When specific phobia is associated with panic attacks, pharmacotherapy or psychotherapy directed to the panic attacks may also be of benefit.

## Social Phobia

The treatment of social phobia uses both psychotherapy and pharmacotherapy, and varying approaches are indicated for the generalized type and performance situations. Some studies indicate that the use of both pharmacotherapy and psychotherapy produces better results than either therapy alone, although that finding may not be applicable to all situations and patients.

Several well-controlled studies have found that monoamine oxidase inhibitors, especially phenelzine (Nardil), are effective in the treatment of the generalized type of social phobia. Other drugs that have been reported to be effective, although not in as many well-controlled trials, include alprazolam (Xanax), clonazepam (Klonopin), and possibly the serotonin-specific reuptake inhibitors. Dosages for those drugs parallel those for their use in depressive disorders, and the response can take the usual four to six weeks. Some data indicate that tricyclic drugs and buspirone (BuSpar) may not be effective in social phobia, although the data are limited and not definitive.

The psychotherapy for the generalized type of social phobia usually involves a combination of behavioral and cognitive methods, including cognitive retraining, desensitization, rehearsal during sessions, and a range of homework assignments.

The treatment of social phobia associated with performance situations frequently involves the use of β-adrenergic receptor antagonists shortly before exposure to the phobic stimulus. The two compounds most widely used are atenolol (Tenormin), 50 to 100 mg every morning or one hour before the performance, and propranolol (20 to 40 mg). Cognitive, behavioral, and exposure techniques can also be useful in performance situations.

### References

Chapman T F, Fyer A J, Mannuzza S, Klein D F: A comparison of treated and untreated simple phobia. Am J Psychiatry *150*: 816, 1993.
Clark D B, Agras W S: The assessment and treatment of performance anxiety in musicians. Am J Psychiatry *148*: 598, 1991.
Dilsaver S C, Qamar A B, Del Medico V J: Secondary social phobia in patients with major depression. Psychiatry Res *44*: 33, 1992.
Francis G, Last C G, Strauss C C: Avoidant disorder and social phobia in children and adolescents. J Am Acad Child Adolesc Psychiatry *31*: 1086, 1992.
Fyer A J, Manuzza S, Gallops M S, Martin L Y, Aaronson C, Gorman J M, Liebowitz M R, Klein D F: Familial transmission of simple phobias and fears. Arch Gen Psychiatry *47*: 252, 1990.
Gabbard G O: Psychodynamics of panic disorder and social phobia. Bull Menninger Clin *56* (2, Suppl): A3, 1992.
Journal of Clinical Psychiatry: Social phobia: Advances in understanding and treatment. *52* (11, Suppl): 2, 1991.
Heimberg R G, Dodge C S, Hope D A, et al: Cognitive-behavioral group treatment for social phobia: Comparison with a credible placebo control. Cogn Ther Res *14*: 1, 1990.
Mattick R P, Peters L, Clarke J C: Exposure and cognitive restructuring for social phobia: A controlled study. Behav Ther *20*: 3, 1989.
Parker J D A, Taylor G J, Bagby R M, Acklin M W: Alexithymia in panic disorder and simple phobia: A comparative study. Am J Psychiatry *150*: 1105, 1993.
Potts N L S, Davidson J R T: Social phobia: Biological aspects and pharmacotherapy. Prog Neuropsychopharmacol Biol Psychiatry *16*: 635, 1992.
Schneier F R: Social phobia. Psychiatr Ann *21*: 349, 1991.
Stein M B, Tancer M E, Gelernter C S, Vittone B J, Uhde T W: Major depression in patients with social phobia. Am J Psychiatry *147*: 637, 1990.
Swinson R P, Cox B J, Woszczyna C B: Use of medical services and treatment for panic disorder with agoraphobia and for social phobia. Can Med J *147*: 878, 1992.
Van Ameringen M, Mancini C, Streiner D L: Fluoxetine efficacy in social phobia. J Clin Psychiatry *54*: 27, 1993.
Versiani M, Nardi A E, Mundim F D, Alves A B, Liebowitz M R, Amrein R: Pharmacotherapy of social phobia: A controlled study with moclobemide and phenelzine. Br J Psychiatry *161*: 353, 1992.

# 16.4 / Obsessive-Compulsive Disorder

Obsessive-compulsive disorder is an example of the positive effects that modern research can have on a disorder in a short time. As recently as the 1980s, obsessive-compulsive disorder was considered an uncommon disorder and poorly responsive to treatment. It is now recognized that obsessive-compulsive disorder is common (Figure 16.4–1) and very responsive to treatment.

An *obsession* is a recurrent and intrusive thought, feeling, idea, or sensation. A *compulsion* is a conscious, standardized, recurrent thought or behavior, such as counting, checking, or avoiding. Obsessions increase a person's anxiety, whereas carrying out compulsions reduces a person's anxiety. However, when a person resists carrying out a compulsion, anxiety is increased. A person with obsessive-compulsive disorder generally realizes the irrationality of the obsessions and experiences both the obsession and the compulsion as ego-dystonic. Obsessive-compulsive disorder can be a disabling disorder, because the obsessions can

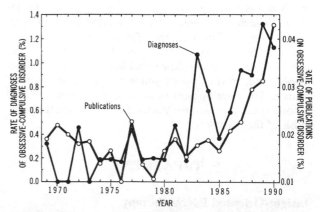

**Figure 16.4–1.** Annual rate of diagnoses of obsessive-compulsive disorder among all diagnoses at a psychiatric hospital and annual rate of publications on the disorder among all published medical research reports, 1969–1990. (Figure from A L Stoll, M Tohen, R J Baldessarini: Increasing frequency of the diagnosis of obsessive-compulsive disorder. Am J Psychiatry *149*: 639, 1992. Used with permission.)

be time-consuming and can interfere significantly with the person's normal routine, occupational functioning, usual social activities, or relationships with friends and family members.

## EPIDEMIOLOGY

The lifetime prevalence of obsessive-compulsive disorder in the general population is an estimated 2 to 3 percent. Some researchers have estimated that obsessive-compulsive disorder is found in as many as 10 percent of the outpatients in psychiatric clinics. Those figures make obsessive-compulsive disorder the fourth most common psychiatric diagnosis after phobias, substance-related disorders, and major depressive disorder. Epidemiological studies in Europe, Asia, and Africa have confirmed those rates across cultural boundaries.

For adults, men and women are equally likely to be affected; however, for adolescents, boys are more commonly affected with obsessive-compulsive disorder than are girls. The mean age of onset is about 20 years, although men have a slightly earlier age of onset (mean around 19 years) than do women (mean around 22 years). Overall, about two thirds of the patients have the onset of symptoms before age 25, and fewer than 15 percent of the patients have the onset of symptoms after age 35. Obsessive-compulsive disorder can have its onset in adolescence or childhood, in some cases as early as age 2 years. Single people are more affected with obsessive-compulsive disorder than are married people, although that finding probably reflects the difficulty that patients with obsessive-compulsive disorder have in maintaining a relationship. Obsessive-compulsive disorder is found less often among blacks than among whites, although access to health care may explain most of that variation, rather than differences in prevalence between the races.

Patients with obsessive-compulsive disorder are commonly affected by other mental disorders. The lifetime prevalence for major depressive disorder in patients with obsessive-compulsive disorder is about 67 percent and for social phobia about 25 percent. Other common comorbid psychiatric diagnoses in patients with obsessive-compulsive disorder include alcohol use disorders, specific phobia, panic disorder, and eating disorders.

## ETIOLOGY

### Biological Factors

**Neurotransmitters.**  The many clinical trials that have been conducted with various drugs support the hypothesis that a dysregulation of serotonin is involved in the symptom formation of obsessions and compulsions in the disorder. Data show that serotonergic drugs are more effective than drugs that affect other neurotransmitter systems. However, whether serotonin is involved in the cause of obsessive-compulsive disorder is not clear at this time. Clinical studies have assayed cerebrospinal fluid (CSF) concentrations of serotonin metabolites—for example, 5-hydroxyindoleacetic acid (5-HIAA)—and affinities and numbers of platelet binding sites of tritiated imipramine (which binds to serotonin reuptake sites) and have re-

ported variable findings of those measures in obsessive-compulsive disorder patients. Some researchers have said that the cholinergic and dopaminergic neurotransmitter systems in obsessive-compulsive disorder patients are two areas for future research studies.

**Brain-imaging studies.**  A variety of functional brain-imaging studies—for example, positron emission tomography (PET)—have found increased activity (for example, metabolism and blood flow) in the frontal lobes, the basal ganglia (especially the caudate), and the cingulum of patients with obsessive-compulsive disorder. Pharmacological and behavioral treatments reportedly reverse those abnormalities (Figure 16.4–2). The data from the functional brain-imaging studies are consistent with the data from structural brain-imaging studies. Both computed tomographic (CT) and magnetic resonance imaging (MRI) studies have found decreased sizes of caudates bilaterally in patients with obsessive-compulsive disorder. Both functional and structural brain-imaging studies are also consistent with the observation that neurological procedures involving the cingulum are sometimes effective in the treatment of obsessive-compulsive disorder patients. One re-

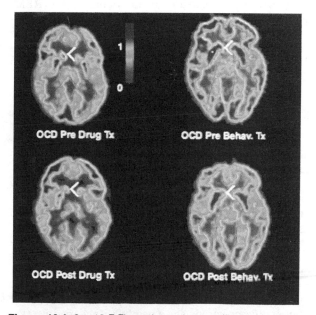

**Figure 16.4–2.**  18-F-Fluorodeoxyglucose (fludeoxygluose F 18) positron emission tomographic scans of representative patients in a horizontal plane at a middle level of the head of the caudate nuclei before and after successful drug treatment or behavior therapy (Behav Tx) for obsessive-compulsive disorder (OCD). Scans were processed to reflect the ratio of glucose metabolic rate registered by each pixel element, divided by that of whole brain. Arrowheads indicate right head of caudate nucleus. (Display follows radiological and anatomical convention of displaying the right side on the viewer's left.) The examples were chosen for illustration because of exactness of scan repositioning and because they show various degrees of visible left-right asymmetry of caudate nucleus change from before to after treatment. (Figure from L R Baxter Jr, J M Schwartz, K S Bergman, M P Szuba, B H Guze, J C Mazziotta, A Alazraki, C E Selin, H-K Ferng, P Munford, M E Phelps: Caudate glucose metabolic rate changes with both drug and behavior therapy for obsessive-compulsive disorder. Arch Gen Psychiatry *49*: 685, 1992. Used with permission.)

cent MRI study reported increased $T_1$ relaxation times in the frontal cortex, a finding that is consistent with the location of abnormalities found in PET studies.

**Genetics.** Available genetic data on obsessive-compulsive disorder are consistent with the hypothesis that the inheritance of obsessive-compulsive disorder has a significant genetic component. The data, however, do not yet distinguish the influence of cultural and behavioral effects on the transmission of the disorder. The studies of concordance in twins for obsessive-compulsive disorder have consistently found a significantly higher concordance rate for monozygotic twins than for dizygotic twins. Family studies of obsessive-compulsive disorder patients have found that 35 percent of the first-degree relatives of obsessive-compulsive disorder patients are also afflicted with the disorder.

**Other biological data.** Electrophysiological studies, sleep electroencephalogram (EEG) studies, and neuroendocrine studies have contributed data that indicate some commonalities between depressive disorders and obsessive-compulsive disorder. A higher than usual incidence of nonspecific EEG abnormalities are found in obsessive-compulsive disorder patients. Sleep EEG studies have found abnormalities similar to those seen in depressive disorders, such as decreased rapid eye movement (REM) latency. Neuroendocrine studies have also found some similarities to depressive disorders, such as nonsuppression on the dexamethasone-suppression test in about one third of the patients and decreased growth hormone secretion with clonidine (Catapres) infusions.

## Behavioral Factors

According to learning theorists, obsessions are conditioned stimuli. A relatively neutral stimulus becomes associated with fear or anxiety through a process of respondent conditioning by being paired with events that are by nature noxious or anxiety-producing. Thus, previously neutral objects and thoughts become conditioned stimuli capable of provoking anxiety or discomfort.

Compulsions are established in a different way. A person discovers that a certain action reduces the anxiety attached to an obsessional thought. Thus, active avoidance strategies in the form of compulsions or ritualistic behaviors are developed to control anxiety. Gradually, because of their efficacy in reducing a painful secondary drive (the anxiety), the avoidance strategies become fixed as learned patterns of compulsive behaviors. Learning theory provides useful concepts for explaining certain aspects of the obsessive-compulsive phenomena—for example, the anxiety-provoking capacity of ideas that are not necessarily frightening in themselves and the establishment of compulsive patterns of behavior.

## Psychosocial Factors

**Personality factors.** Obsessive-compulsive disorder is different from obsessive-compulsive personality disorder. The majority of obsessive-compulsive disorder patients do not have premorbid compulsive symptoms; therefore, such personality traits are neither necessary nor sufficient for the development of obsessive-compulsive disorder. Only about 15 to 35 percent of obsessive-compulsive disorder patients have had premorbid obsessional traits.

**Psychodynamic factors.** Sigmund Freud described three major psychological defense mechanisms that determine the form and the quality of obsessive-compulsive symptoms and character traits: isolation, undoing, and reaction formation.

ISOLATION. Isolation is a defense mechanism that protects a person from anxiety-provoking affects and impulses. Under ordinary circumstances a person experiences in consciousness both the affect and the imagery of an emotion-laden idea, whether it be a fantasy or the memory of an event. When isolation occurs, the affect and the impulse of which it is a derivative are separated from the ideational component and are pushed out of consciousness. If isolation is completely successful, the impulse and its associated affect are totally repressed, and the patient is consciously aware only of the affectless idea that is related to it.

UNDOING. Because of the constant threat that the impulse may escape the primary defense of isolation and break free, secondary defensive operations are required to combat the impulse and to quiet the anxiety that its imminent eruption into consciousness arouses. The compulsive act constitutes the surface manifestation of a defensive operation aimed at reducing anxiety and at controlling the underlying impulse that has not been sufficiently contained by isolation. A particularly important secondary defensive operation is the mechanism of undoing. As the word suggests, undoing is a compulsive act that is performed in an attempt to prevent or undo the consequences that the patient irrationally anticipates from a frightening obsessional thought or impulse.

REACTION FORMATION. Both isolation and undoing are defensive maneuvers that are intimately involved in the production of clinical symptoms. Reaction formation results in the formation of character traits, rather than symptoms. As the term implies, reaction formation involves manifest patterns of behavior and consciously experienced attitudes that are exactly the opposite of the underlying impulses. Often, the patterns seem to an observer to be highly exaggerated and inappropriate.

OTHER PSYCHODYNAMIC FACTORS. In classic psychoanalytic theory, obsessive-compulsive disorder was termed obsessive-compulsive neurosis and was a regression from the oedipal phase to the anal psychosexual phase of development. When patients with obsessive-compulsive disorder feel threatened by anxiety about retaliation or the loss of a significant object's love, they retreat from the oedipal position and regress to an intensely ambivalent emotional stage associated with the anal phase. The ambivalence is connected to the unraveling of the smooth fusion between sexual and aggressive drives characteristic of the oedipal phase. The coexistence of hatred and love toward the same person leaves the patient paralyzed with doubt and indecision.

One of the striking features of patients with obsessive-compulsive disorder is the degree to which they are preoccupied with aggression or cleanliness, either overtly in the content of their symptoms or in the associations that lie behind them. Therefore, the psychogenesis of obsessive-compulsive disorder may lie in disturbances in normal growth and development related to the anal-sadistic phase of development.

*Ambivalence.* Ambivalence is the direct result of a change in the characteristics of the impulse life. It is an important feature of the normal child during the anal-sadistic developmental phase; that is, the child feels both love and murderous hate toward the same object, sometimes simultaneously. The obsessive-compulsive disorder patient often consciously experiences both love and hate toward an object. That conflict of opposing emotions may be seen in the patient's doing-undoing patterns of behavior and paralyzing doubt in the face of choices.

*Magical thinking.* In magical thinking the regression uncovers early modes of thought, rather than impulses; that is, ego functions, as well as id functions, are affected by regression. Inherent in magical thinking is omnipotence of thought. Persons feel that, merely by thinking about an event in the external world, they can cause that event to occur without intermediate physical actions. That feeling makes having an aggressive thought frightening to obsessive-compulsive disorder patients.

## DIAGNOSIS

Although the diagnostic criteria for obsessive-compulsive disorder in the revised third edition of *Diagnostic and Statistical Manual of Mental Disorders* (DSM-III-R) have largely been retained in the fourth edition (DSM-IV) (Table 16.4–1), important modifications have been made in the DSM-IV definitions of obsessions and compulsions. Whereas DSM-III-R defined obsessions as thoughts and compulsions as actions, DSM-IV introduces the clinical observation that thoughts (that is, mental acts) can be either obsessions or compulsions, depending on whether they increase anxiety (obsessions) or reduce anxiety (compulsions). DSM-IV also rewords the definition of obsessions to avoid the word "ego-dystonic" in the third edition (DSM-III) and the DSM-III-R word "senseless," both of which have meanings that are poorly defined and difficult to operationalize. DSM-IV also eliminates the DSM-III-R definition of compulsions as purposeful and intentional, since patients often report that compulsions are neither purposeful nor intentional. DSM-IV allows the clinician to specify that patients have the poor insight type of obsessive-compulsive disorder if they generally do not recognize the excessiveness of their obsessions and compulsions.

## CLINICAL FEATURES

Patients with obsessive-compulsive disorder often go to physicians other than psychiatrists (Table 16.4–2). Patients with both obsessions and compulsions constitute at least 75 percent of the affected patients. Some researchers and clinicians believe that the number may be much closer to 100 percent if patients are carefully assessed for the presence of mental compulsions in addition to behavioral compulsions. For example, an obsession about hurting a child may be followed by a mental compulsion to repeat a specific prayer a specific number of times. However, some researchers and clinicians believe that some patients do have only obsessive thoughts and do not have compulsions.

**Table 16.4–1**
**Diagnostic Criteria for Obsessive-Compulsive Disorder**

A. Either obsessions or compulsions:

*Obsessions as defined by (1), (2), (3), and (4):*
  (1) recurrent and persistent thoughts, impulses, or images that are experienced, at some time during the disturbance, as intrusive and inappropriate and that cause marked anxiety or distress
  (2) the thoughts, impulses, or images are not simply excessive worries about real-life problems
  (3) the person attempts to ignore or suppress such thoughts, impulses, or images, or to neutralize them with some other thought or action
  (4) the person recognizes that the obsessional thoughts, impulses, or images are a product of his or her own mind (not imposed from without as in thought insertion)

*Compulsions as defined by (1) and (2):*
  (1) repetitive behaviors (e.g., handwashing, ordering, checking) or mental acts (e.g., praying, counting, repeating words silently) that the person feels driven to perform in response to an obsession, or according to rules that must be applied rigidly
  (2) the behaviors or mental acts are aimed at preventing or reducing distress or preventing some dreaded event or situation; however, these behaviors or mental acts either are not connected in a realistic way with what they are designed to neutralize or prevent, or are clearly excessive

B. At some point during the course of the disorder, the person has recognized that the obsessions or compulsions are excessive or unreasonable. Note: this does not apply to children.

C. The obsessions or compulsions cause marked distress; are time-consuming (take more than an hour a day); or significantly interfere with the person's normal routine, occupational (or academic) functioning, or usual social activities or relationships.

D. If another Axis I disorder is present, the content of the obsessions or compulsions is not restricted to it (e.g., preoccupation with food in the presence of an eating disorder; hair pulling in the presence of trichotillomania; concern with appearance in the presence of body dysmorphic disorder; preoccupation with drugs in the presence of a substance use disorder; preoccupation with having a serious illness in the presence of hypochondriasis; preoccupation with sexual urges or fantasies in the presence of a paraphilia; or guilty ruminations in the presence of major depressive disorder).

E. The disturbance is not due to the direct effects of a substance (e.g., a drug of abuse, a medication) or a general medical condition.

*Specify* if:
  **with poor insight:** if, for most of the time during the current episode, the person does not recognize that the obsessions and compulsions are excessive or unreasonable

Table from DSM-IV, *Diagnostic and Statistical Manual of Mental Disorders*, ed 4. Copyright American Psychiatric Association, Washington, 1994. Used with permission.

Such patients are likely to have repetitious thoughts of some sexual or aggressive act that is reprehensible to the patient.

Obsessions and compulsions have certain features in common: (1) An idea or an impulse intrudes itself insis-

**Table 16.4-2**
**Nonpsychiatric Clinical Specialists Likely to See Obsessive-Compulsive Disorder Patients**

| Specialist | Presenting Problem |
|---|---|
| Dermatologist | Chapped hands, eczematoid appearance |
| Family practitioner | Family member washing excessively, may mention counting or checking compulsions |
| Oncologist, infectious disease internist | Insistent belief that person has acquired immune deficiency syndrome (AIDS) |
| Neurologist | Obsessive-compulsive disorder associated with Tourette's disorder, head injury, epilepsy, choreas, other basal ganglia lesions or disorders |
| Neurosurgeon | Severe, intractable obsessive-compulsive disorder |
| Obstetrician | Postpartum obsessive-compulsive disorder |
| Pediatrician | Parents' concern about child's behavior, usually excessive washing |
| Pediatric cardiologist | Obsessive-compulsive disorder secondary to Sydenham's chorea |
| Plastic surgeon | Repeated consultations for "abnormal" features |
| Dentist | Gum lesions from excessive teeth cleaning |

Table from J L Rapoport: The neurobiology of obsessive-compulsive disorder. JAMA *260*: 2889, 1988. Used with permission.

**Table 16.4-3**
**Obsessive-Compulsive Symptoms in Adults**

| Variable | Percent |
|---|---|
| Obsessions (N = 200) | |
| Contamination | 45 |
| Pathological doubt | 42 |
| Somatic | 36 |
| Need for symmetry | 31 |
| Aggressive | 28 |
| Sexual | 26 |
| Other | 13 |
| Multiple obsessions | 60 |
| Compulsions (N = 200) | |
| Checking | 63 |
| Washing | 50 |
| Counting | 36 |
| Need to ask or confess | 31 |
| Symmetry and precision | 28 |
| Hoarding | 18 |
| Multiple comparisons | 48 |
| Course of illness (N = 100)* | |
| Type | |
| Continuous | 85 |
| Deteriorative | 10 |
| Episodic | 2 |
| Not present | 71 |
| Present | 29 |

*Age at onset: men, $17.5 \pm 6.8$ years; women, $20.8 \pm 8.5$ years.
Table from S A Rasmussen, J L Eisen: The epidemiology and differential diagnosis of obsessive compulsive disorder. J Clin Psychiatry *53* (4, Suppl): 6, 1992. Used with permission.

tently and persistently into the person's conscious awareness. (2) A feeling of anxious dread accompanies the central manifestation and frequently leads the person to take countermeasures against the initial idea or impulse. (3) The obsession or the compulsion is ego-alien; that is, it is experienced as being foreign to the person's experience of himself or herself as a psychological being. (4) No matter how vivid and compelling the obsession or the compulsion is, the person usually recognizes it as absurd and irrational. (5) The person suffering from obsessions and compulsions usually feels a strong desire to resist them. However, about half of all patients offer little resistance to the compulsion. About 80 percent of all patients believe that the compulsion is irrational. Sometimes obsessions and compulsions become overvalued to the patients—for example, patients may insist that compulsive cleanliness is morally correct, even though they lost their jobs because of time spent cleaning.

The presentation of obsessions and compulsions is heterogeneous in adults (Table 16.4–3) and in children and adolescents (Table 16.4–4). The symptoms of an individual patient may overlap and change with time, but obsessive-compulsive disorder has four major symptom patterns. The most common pattern is an obsession of contamination, followed by washing or accompanied by compulsive avoidance of the presumably contaminated object. The feared object is often hard to avoid (for example, feces, urine, dust, or germs). Patients may literally rub the skin off their hands by excessive hand washing or may be unable to leave their homes because of fear of germs. Although anxiety is the most common emotional response to the feared object, obsessive shame and disgust are also common. Patients with contamination obsessions usually believe that the contamination is spread from object to object or person to person by the slightest contact.

The second most common pattern is an obsession of doubt, followed by a compulsion of checking. The obsession often implies some danger of violence (such as forgetting to turn off the stove or not locking a door). The checking may involve multiple trips back into the house to check the stove, for example. The patients have an obsessional self-doubt, as they always feel guilty for having forgotten or committed something.

The third most common pattern is one with merely intrusive obsessional thoughts without a compulsion. Such obsessions are usually repetitive thoughts of some sexual or aggressive act that is reprehensible to the patient.

The fourth most common pattern is the need for symmetry or precision, which can lead to a compulsion of slowness. Patients can literally take hours to eat a meal or shave their faces. Religious obsessions and compulsive hoarding are common in obsessive-compulsive patients. *Trichotillomania* (compulsive hair pulling) and nail biting may be compulsions related to obsessive-compulsive disorder.

**Table 16.4–4**
**Reported Obsessions and Compulsions**
**for 70 Consecutive Child and Adolescent Patients**

| Major Presenting Symptom | No. (%) Reporting Symptom at Initial Interview* |
|---|---|
| Obsession | |
| Concern or disgust with bodily wastes or secretions (urine, stool, saliva), dirt, germs, environmental toxins, etc. | 30 (43) |
| Fear something terrible may happen (fire, death or illness of loved one, self, or others) | 18 (24) |
| Concern or need for symmetry, order, or exactness | 12 (17) |
| Scrupulosity (excessive praying or religious concerns out of keeping with patient's background) | 9 (13) |
| Lucky and unlucky numbers | 6 (8) |
| Forbidden or perverse sexual thoughts, images, or impulses | 3 (4) |
| Intrusive nonsense sounds, words, or music | 1 (1) |
| Compulsion | |
| Excessive or ritualized hand washing, showering, bathing, toothbrushing, or grooming | 60 (85) |
| Repeating rituals (going in and out of door, up and down from chair, etc) | 36 (51) |
| Checking doors, locks, stove, appliances, car brakes, etc | 32 (46) |
| Cleaning and other rituals to remove contact with contaminants | 16 (23) |
| Touching | 14 (20) |
| Ordering and arranging | 12 (17) |
| Measures to prevent harm to self or others (e.g., hanging clothes a certain way) | 11 (16) |
| Counting | 13 (18) |
| Hoarding and collecting | 8 (11) |
| Miscellaneous rituals (e.g., licking, spitting, special dress pattern) | 18 (26) |

*Multiple symptoms recorded, so total exceeds 70.
Table from J L Rapoport: The neurobiology of obsessive-compulsive disorder. JAMA *260*: 2889, 1988. Used with permission.

## Mental Status Examination

On the mental status examination, obsessive-compulsive disorder patients show symptoms of depressive disorders. Such symptoms are present in about 50 percent of all patients. Some obsessive-compulsive disorder patients have character traits suggestive of obsessive-compulsive personality disorder, but most do not. Obsessive-compulsive disorder patients, especially men, have a higher than average celibacy rate. A greater than usual amount of marital discord is found in the patients.

A 20-year-old junior at a Midwestern college complained to his internist that he was having difficulty in studying because, over the previous six months, he had become increasingly preoccupied with thoughts that he could not dispel. He spent hours each night rehashing the day's events, especially interactions with friends and teachers, endlessly making right in his mind any and all regrets. He likened the process to playing a videotape of each event over and over again in his mind, asking himself if he had behaved properly and telling himself that he had done his best or had said the right thing every step of the way. He would do that while sitting at his desk, supposedly studying; he often looked at the clock after such a period of rumination and noted that, to his surprise, two or three hours had elapsed. His declining grades worried him.

The patient admitted, on further questioning, that he had a two-hour grooming ritual when getting ready to go out with friends. Shaving, showering, combing his hair, and putting on his clothes—all demanded perfection. In addition, for several years he had been bothered by certain superstitions that, it turned out, dominated his daily life. Those superstitions included avoiding certain buildings while walking on campus, always sitting in the third seat in the fifth row in his classrooms, and lining up his books and pencils in a certain configuration on his desk before studying.

*Discussion.* The patient did not experience his rumination about the day's events as under his voluntary control, and he attempted to ignore or suppress them. The ambiguity about whether such thoughts are true obsessions or merely obsessional brooding can be of diagnostic importance in distinguishing obsessive-compulsive disorder from obsessive-compulsive personality disorder and generalized anxiety disorder, in which rumination is often present. In this case, the patient showed clear signs of compulsions—repetitive behavior performed according to certain rules or in a stereotyped fashion that served no useful function and was not pleasurable in itself.

## DIFFERENTIAL DIAGNOSIS

### Medical Conditions

The DSM-IV diagnostic requirement of personal distress and functional impairment differentiates obsessive-compulsive disorder from ordinary or mildly excessive thoughts and habits. The major neurological disorders to consider in the differential diagnosis are Tourette's disorder, other tic disorders, temporal lobe epilepsy, and, occasionally, trauma and postencephalitic complications.

**Tourette's disorder.** The characteristic symptoms of Tourette's disorder are motor and vocal tics that occur frequently and virtually every day. Tourette's disorder and obsessive-compulsive disorder have a similar age of onset and similar symptoms. About 90 percent of Tourette's disorder patients have compulsive symptoms, and as many as two thirds meet the diagnostic criteria for obsessive-compulsive disorder.

### Psychiatric Conditions

The major psychiatric considerations in the differential diagnosis of obsessive-compulsive disorder are schizophrenia, obsessive-compulsive personality disorder, phobias, and depressive disorders. Obsessive-compulsive disorder can usually be distinguished from schizophrenia by the absence of other schizophrenic symptoms, by the less bizarre nature of the symptoms, and by patients' insight into their disorder. Obsessive-compulsive personality disorder does not have the degree of functional impairment associated with obsessive-compulsive disorder. Phobias are distinguished by the absence of a relation between the obsessive thoughts and the compulsions. Major depressive disorder can sometimes be associated with obsessive ideas, but patients with just obsessive-compulsive disorder fail to meet the diagnosic criteria for major depressive disorder.

Other psychiatric conditions that may be closely related to obsessive-compulsive disorder are hypochondriasis, body dysmorphic disorder, and possibly other impulse disorders, such as kleptomania and pathological gambling. In all those disorders the patient has either a repetitious thought (for example, concern about one's body) or a repetitious behavior (for example, stealing). Several research groups are investigating those disorders, their relations to obsessive-compulsive disorder, and their responses to various treatments.

## COURSE AND PROGNOSIS

More than half the patients with obsessive-compulsive disorder have a sudden onset of symptoms. About 50 to 70 percent of the patients have the onset of symptoms after a stressful event, such as a pregnancy, a sexual problem, or the death of a relative. Because many patients manage to keep their symptoms secret, there is often a delay of 5 to 10 years before the patients come to psychiatric attention, although the delay is probably shortening with increased awareness of the disorder among lay and professional people. The course is usually long but variable; some patients experience a fluctuating course, and others experience a constant course.

About 20 to 30 percent of the patients have significant improvement in their symptoms, and 40 to 50 percent have moderate improvement. The remaining 20 to 40 percent of patients either remain ill or have a worsening of their symptoms.

About one third of patients with obsessive-compulsive disorder have major depressive disorder, and suicide is a risk for all patients with obsessive-compulsive disorder. A poor prognosis is indicated by yielding to (rather than resisting) compulsions, childhood onset, bizarre compulsions, the need for hospitalization, a coexisting major depressive disorder, delusional beliefs, the presence of overvalued ideas (that is, some acceptance of obsessions and compulsions), and the presence of a personality disorder (especially schizotypal personality disorder). A good prognosis is indicated by a good social and occupational adjustment, the presence of a precipitating event, and an episodic nature in the symptoms. The obsessional content does not seem to be related to the prognosis.

## TREATMENT

With mounting evidence that obsessive-compulsive disorder is largely determined by biological factors, the classic psychoanalytic theory has fallen out of favor. Moreover, because obsessive-compulsive disorder symptoms appear to be largely refractory to psychodynamic psychotherapy and psychoanalysis, pharmacological and behavioral treatments have become common. However, psychodynamic factors may be of considerable benefit in understanding what precipitates exacerbations of the disorder and in treating various forms of resistance to treatment, such as noncompliance with medication.

Many obsessive-compulsive disorder patients tenaciously resist treatment efforts. They may refuse to take medication and may resist carrying out homework assignments and other prescribed activities given by behavior therapists. The obsessive-compulsive symptoms themselves, no matter how biologically based, may have important psychological meanings that make patients reluctant to give them up. A psychodynamic exploration of the patient's resistance to treatment may result in improved compliance.

Well-controlled studies have found that pharmacotherapy or behavior therapy or the combination are effective in significantly reducing the symptoms of obsessive-compulsive disorder patients. The decision regarding which therapy to use is based on the clinician's judgment and experience and on the patient's acceptance of the various modalities.

### Pharmacotherapy

The efficacy of pharmacotherapy in obsessive-compulsive disorder has been proved in many clinical trials. The efficacy is enhanced by the observation that the studies find a placebo response rate of about 5 percent. That percentage is low, compared with the 30 to 40 percent placebo response rate often seen in studies of antidepressants and anxiolytic drugs.

The available data indicate that the drugs, all of which are used to treat depressive disorders or other mental disorders, can be used in their usual dosage ranges. Initial effects are generally seen after four to six weeks of treatment, although 8 to 16 weeks are usually needed to obtain the maximum therapeutic benefit. Although treatment with antidepressant drugs is still controversial, a significant proportion of patients with obsessive-compulsive disorder who respond to treatment with antidepressant drugs seem to relapse if the drug therapy is discontinued.

The standard approach is to start with a serotonin-specific drug—for example, clomipramine (Anafranil) or a serotonin-specific reuptake inhibitor (SSRI), such as fluoxetine (Prozac)—and then to move to other pharmacological strategies if the serotonin-specific drugs are not effective (Figure 16.4–3).

**Clomipramine.** The standard drug for the treatment of obsessive-compulsive disorder is clomipramine, a serotonin-specific tricyclic drug that is also used for the treatment of depressive disorders. The efficacy of clomipramine in obsessive-compulsive disorder is supported by many

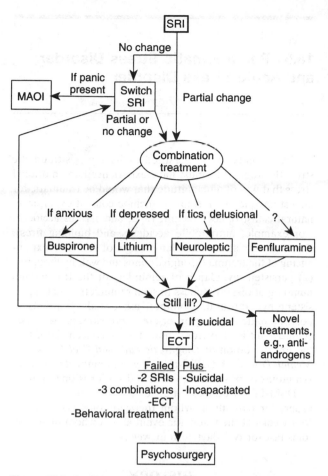

**Figure 16.4–3.** Proposed algorithm for biological treatment of obsessive-compulsive disorder. SRI = potent serotonin reuptake inhibitors (e.g., clomipramine, fluvoxamine, fluoxetine, sertraline, paroxetine). (Figure from W K Goodman, C J McDougle, L H Price: Pharmacotherapy of obsessive compulsive disorder. J Clin Psychiatry 53 (4, Suppl): 34, 1992. Used with permission.)

clinical trials. Clomipramine is usually initiated at dosages of 25 to 50 mg at bedtime and can be increased by increments of 25 mg a day every two to three days, up to a maximum dosage of 250 mg a day or the appearance of dose-limiting side effects. Because clomipramine is a tricyclic drug, it is associated with the usual side effects of those drugs, including sedation, hypotension, sexual dysfunction, and anticholinergic side effects (for example, dry mouth).

**Serotonin-specific reuptake inhibitors.** The SSRIs currently available in the United States include fluoxetine, sertraline (Zoloft), and paroxetine (Paxil). Several clinical trials have shown the efficacy of fluoxetine and sertraline in obsessive-compulsive disorder, and paroxetine may also be effective. Fluvoxamine, another SSRI, is not yet available in the United States but has been shown to be effective in the treatment of obsessive-compulsive disorder. Studies of fluoxetine in obsessive-compulsive disorder have used dosages up to 80 mg a day to achieve therapeutic benefits. Although SSRIs are associated with overstimulation, restlessness, headaches, insomnia, nausea, and gastrointestinal adverse effects, the SSRIs as a group are better tol-

erated than are the tricyclic drugs and, therefore, are sometimes used as the first-line drugs in the treatment of obsessive-compulsive disorder.

**Other drugs.** If treatment with clomipramine or an SSRI is unsuccessful, many therapists augment the first drug by the addition of lithium (Eskalith). Other drugs that can be tried in the treatment of obsessive-compulsive disorder are the monoamine oxidase inhibitors (MAOIs), especially phenelzine (Nardil). Less well studied pharmacological agents for the treatment of unresponsive patients include buspirone (BuSpar), fenfluramine (Pondimin), tryptophan, and clonazepam (Klonopin).

## Behavior Therapy

Although few head-to-head comparisons have been made, behavior therapy is as effective as pharmacotherapies in obsessive-compulsive disorder, and some data indicate that the beneficial effects are longer-lasting with behavior therapy. Therefore, many clinicians consider behavior therapy to be the treatment of choice for obsessive-compulsive disorder. Behavior therapy can be conducted in both outpatient and inpatient settings. The principal behavioral approaches in obsessive-compulsive disorder are exposure and response prevention. Desensitization, thought stopping, flooding, implosion therapy, and aversive conditioning have also been used in obsessive-compulsive disorder patients. In behavior therapy the patient must be truly committed to improvement.

## Psychotherapy

In the absence of adequate studies of insight-oriented psychotherapy for obsessive-compulsive disorder, any valid generalizations about its effectiveness are hard to make, although there are anecdotal reports of successes. Individual analysts have seen striking and lasting changes for the better in patients with obsessive-compulsive personality disorder, especially when they are able to come to terms with the aggressive impulses lying behind the patients' character traits. Likewise, analysts and dynamically oriented psychiatrists have observed marked symptomatic improvement in patients with obsessive-compulsive disorder patients in the course of analysis or prolonged insight psychotherapy.

Supportive psychotherapy undoubtedly has its place, especially for those obsessive-compulsive disorder patients who, despite symptoms of varying degrees of severity, are able to work and make social adjustments. With continuous and regular contact with an interested, sympathetic, and encouraging professional person, patients may be able to function by virtue of that help, without which their symptoms would incapacitate them. Occasionally, when obsessional rituals and anxiety reach an intolerable intensity, it is necessary to hospitalize the patient until the shelter of an institution and the removal from external environmental stresses bring the symptoms down to a tolerable level.

The patient's family members are often driven to the verge of despair by the patient's behavior. Any psychotherapeutic endeavors must include attention to the family members through the provision of emotional support, reassurance, explanation, and advice on how to manage and respond to the patient.

## Other Therapies

Family therapy is often useful in supporting the family, helping reduce marital discord resulting from the disorder, and building a treatment alliance with the family members for the good of the patient.

Group therapy is useful as a support system for some patients.

For severely treatment-resistant patients, electroconvulsive therapy (ECT) and psychosurgery should be considered. ECT is not as effective as psychosurgery but should probably be tried before surgery. The most common psychosurgical procedure for obsessive-compulsive disorder is cingulotomy, which is successful in treating 25 to 30 percent of otherwise treatment-unresponsive patients. The most common complication of psychosurgery is the development of seizures, which are almost always controlled by treatment with phenytoin (Dilantin). Some patients who do not respond to psychosurgery alone and who did not respond to pharmacotherapy or behavior therapy before the operation do respond to pharmacotherapy or behavior therapy after psychosurgery.

### References

Baxter L R, Schwartz J M, Bergman K S, Szuba M P, Guze B H, Mazziotta J C, Alazraki A, Selin C E, Ferng H-K, Munford P, Phelps M E: Caudate glucose metabolic rate changes with both drug and behavior therapy for obsessive-compulsive disorder. Arch Gen Psychiatry 49: 681, 1992.
Black D W, Noyes R, Goldstein R B, Blum N: A family study of obsessive-compulsive disorder. Arch Gen Psychiatry 49: 362, 1992.
Clomipramine Collaborative Study Group: Clomipramine in the treatment of patients with obsessive-compulsive disorder. Arch Gen Psychiatry 48: 730, 1991.
Fineberg N A, Bullock T, Montgomery D B, Montgomery S A: Serotonin reuptake inhibitors are the treatment of choice in obsessive compulsive disorder. Int Clin Psychopharmacol 7 (1, Suppl): 43, 1992.
Gabbard G O: Psychodynamic Psychiatry in Clinical Practice: The DSM-IV Edition. American Psychiatric Press, Washington, 1994.
Gabbard G O: Psychodynamic psychiatry in the "decade of the brain." Am J Psychiatry 149: 991, 1992.
Hewlett W A, Vinogradov A, Agras W S: Clomipramine, clonazepam, and clonidine treatment of obsessive-compulsive disorder. J Clin Psychopharmacol 12: 420, 1992.
Hollander E: Obsessive-compulsive spectrum disorders. Psychiatric Annals. 23: 352, 1993.
Insel T R: Toward a neuroanatomy of obsessive-compulsive disorder. Arch Gen Psychiatry 49: 739, 1992.
Jenike M A: New developments in treatment of obsessive-compulsive disorder. In Review of Psychiatry, vol 11, A Tasman, M B Riba, editors, p 323. American Psychiatric Press, Washington, 1992.
Jenike M A, editor: Obsessional disorders. Psychiatr Clin North Am 15: 743, 1992.
Jenike M A, Baer L, Ballantine T, Martuza R L, Tynes S, Giriunas I, Buttolph M L, Cassem N H: Cingulotomy for refractory obsessive-compulsive disorder. Arch Gen Psychiatry 48: 548, 1991.
Journal of Clinical Psychiatry: Obsessive compulsive disorder: Integrating theory and practice. 53 (4, Suppl): 2, 1992.
Katz R J, DeVeaugh-Geiss J, Landau P: Clomipramine in obsessive-compulsive disorder. Biol Psychiatry 28: 401, 1990.
McDougle C J, Gordman W K, Price L H: The pharmacotherapy of obsessive-compulsive disorder. Pharmacopsychiatry 26 (Suppl):24, 1993.
Stoll A L, Tohen M, Baldessarini R J: Increasing frequency of the diagnosis of obsessive-compulsive disorder. Am J Psychiatry 149: 638, 1992.
Zohar J, Zohar-Kadouch R C, Kindler S: Current concepts in the pharmacological treatment of obsessive-compulsive disorder. Drugs 43: 219, 1992.

# 16.5 / Posttraumatic Stress Disorder and Acute Stress Disorder

For patients to be classified as having posttraumatic stress disorder, they must have experienced an emotional stress that was of a magnitude that would be traumatic for almost anyone. Such traumas include combat experience, natural catastrophes, assault, rape, and serious accidents (for example, automobile accidents and building fires). Posttraumatic stress disorder consists of (1) the reexperiencing of the trauma through dreams and waking thoughts, (2) persistent avoidance of reminders of the trauma and numbing of responsiveness to such reminders, and (3) persistent hyperarousal. Common associated symptoms of posttraumatic stress disorder are depression, anxiety, and cognitive difficulties (for example, poor concentration). In the fourth edition of *Diagnostic and Statistical Manual of Mental Disorders* (DSM-IV), the minimum duration of symptoms of posttraumatic stress disorder is one month.

DSM-IV introduces a new diagnosis, acute stress disorder, for patients in whom the symptoms occur within four weeks of the traumatic event and in whom the symptoms last for two days to four weeks.

## HISTORY

Because of the presence of autonomic cardiac symptoms, soldier's heart was the name given during the American Civil War to a syndrome similar to posttraumatic stress disorder. Jacob DaCosta's 1871 paper, "On Irritable Heart," described such soldiers. In World War I the syndrome was called shell shock and was hypothesized to result from brain trauma caused by the explosion of shells. World War II veterans, survivors of the Nazi concentration camps, and survivors of the atomic bombings in Japan had similar symptoms, sometimes called combat neurosis or operational fatigue. In the 1900s the influence of psychoanalysis was strong, particularly in the United States, and the diagnosis of traumatic neruosis was used for the condition. Traumatic neurosis was hypothesized to involve a reactivation of an early unresolved conflict by the traumatic event. In 1941 the survivors of a fire in a crowded nightclub in Boston, the Coconut Grove, showed increased nervousness, fatigue, and nightmares. The psychiatric morbidity associated with Vietnam War veterans finally brought the concept of posttraumatic stress disorder into full fruition as it is known today. In all those traumatic situations, the appearance of the disorder was roughly correlated with the severity of the stressor; the most severe stresses (for example, concentration camps) resulted in the appearance of the syndrome in more than 75 percent of the victims.

## EPIDEMIOLOGY

The lifetime prevalence of posttraumatic stress disorder is estimated to be from 1 to 3 percent of the general population, although an additional 5 to 15 percent may experience subclinical forms of the disorder. Among high-risk groups whose members experienced traumatic events, the lifetime prevalence rates range from 5 to 75 percent. About 30 percent of Vietnam veterans experienced posttraumatic stress disorder, and an additional 25 percent experienced subclinical forms of the disorder.

Although posttraumatic stress disorder can appear at any age, it is most prevalent in young adults, because of the nature of the precipitating situations. However, children can have posttraumatic stress disorder. The trauma for men is usually combat experience, and the trauma for women is most commonly assault or rape. The disorder is most likely to occur in those who are single, divorced, widowed, economically handicapped, or socially withdrawn.

## ETIOLOGY

### Stressor

By definition, the stressor is the prime causative factor in the development of posttraumatic stress disorder. But not everyone experiences posttraumatic stress disorder after a traumatic event; although the stressor is necessary, it is not sufficient to cause the disorder. The clinician must also consider individual preexisting biological factors, preexisting psychosocial factors, and events that happened after the trauma. For example, being part of a group who live through a disaster sometimes enables a person to deal with the trauma because others shared the experience. However, survivor guilt sometimes complicates the management of posttraumatic stress disorder.

Recent research on posttraumatic stress disorder has placed greater emphasis on a person's subjective response to trauma than on the severity of the stressor itself. Although posttraumatic stress disorder symptoms were once thought to be directly proportional to the severity of the stressor, empirical studies have proved otherwise. As a result, the growing consensus is that the disorder has a great deal to do with the stressor's subjective meaning to the patient.

Even when faced with overwhelming trauma, the majority of people do not experience posttraumatic stress disorder symptoms. Similarly, events that may appear mundane or less than catastrophic to most people may produce posttraumatic stress disorder in some persons because of the subjective meaning of the event. The predisposing vulnerability factors that appear to play primary roles in determining whether the disorder develops include (1) the presence of childhood trauma; (2) borderline, paranoid, dependent, or antisocial personality disorder traits; (3) an inadequate support system; (4) genetic-constitutional vulnerability to psychiatric illness; (5) recent stressful life changes; (6) perception of an external locus of control, rather than an internal one; and (7) recent excessive alcohol intake.

Psychodynamic studies of persons who have survived severe psychic traumas have identified *alexithymia*—the inability to identify or verbalize feeling states—as a common feature. If psychic trauma occurs in childhood, an arrest of emotional development frequently results. If the trauma occurs in adulthood, an emotional regression often occurs. In either case, survivors of trauma usually cannot use internal emotional states as signals and may experience psychosomatic symptoms. They are also incapable of soothing themselves when under stress.

### Psychodynamic Factors

The cognitive model of posttraumatic stress disorder posits that affected persons are unable to process or rationalize the trauma that precipitated the disorder. They continue to experience the stress and attempt to avoid the reexperiencing of the stress by avoidance techniques. Consistent with their partial ability to cope cognitively with the event, the patients experience alternating periods of acknowledging the event and blocking it.

The behavioral model of posttraumatic stress disorder indicates that the disorder has two phases in its development. First, the trauma (the unconditioned stimulus) is paired, through classical conditioning, with a conditioned stimulus (physical or mental reminders of the trauma). Second, through instrumental learning, the patient develops a pattern of avoidance of both the conditioned stimulus and the unconditioned stimulus.

The psychoanalytic model of the disorder hypothesizes that the trauma has reactivated a previously quiescent, yet unresolved psychological conflict. The revival of the childhood trauma results in regression and the use of the defense mechanisms of repression, denial, and undoing. The ego relives and thereby tries to master and reduce the anxiety. The patient also receives secondary gains from the external world, the common gains being monetary compensation, increased attention or sympathy, and the satisfaction of dependence needs. Those gains reinforce the disorder and its presistence. A cognitive view of posttraumatic stress disorder is that the brain is trying to process the massive amount of information that the trauma provoked by alternating periods of acknowledging and blocking the event.

### Biological Factors

The biological theories regarding posttraumatic stress disorder have developed from both preclinical studies of animal models of stress and from measures of biological variables of clinical populations with posttraumatic stress disorder. Many neurotransmitter systems have been implicated by both sets of data. Preclinical models of learned helplessness, kindling, and sensitization in animals have led to theories regarding norepinephrine, dopamine, endogenous opiate, and benzodiazepine receptors and the hypothalamic-pituitary-adrenal axis. In clinical populations, data have supported hypotheses that the noradrenergic and endogenous opiate systems, as well as the hypothalamic-pituitary-adrenal-axis, are hyperactive in at least some patients with posttraumatic stress disorder.

The other major biological findings are increased activity and responsiveness of the autonomic nervous system, as evidenced by elevated heart rates and blood pressure readings, and abnormal sleep architecture (for example, sleep fragmentation and increased sleep latency). Some researchers have suggested a similarity between posttraumatic stress disorder and two other psychiatric disorders, major depressive disorder and panic disorder.

## DIAGNOSIS

The DSM-IV diagnostic criteria for posttraumatic stress disorder (Table 16.5–1) were written to clarify several criteria in the revised third edition of DSM (DSM-III-R). First, DSM-III-R described the stressor as "outside the range of usual human experience." Since that criterion was vague and unreliable, DSM-IV clarifies its meaning (criterion A). In DSM-IV, criterion B specifies, as it did in DSM-III-R, that the patient persistently reexperiences the traumatic event. Criteria C and D remain virtually the same in DSM-IV as in DSM-III-R; they specify persisting avoidance of certain situations and increased arousal in the patients.

DSM-IV specifies that the symptoms of reexperiencing, avoidance, and hyperarousal have lasted more than one month. For patients in whom symptoms have been present less than one month, the appropriate diagnosis may be acute stress disorder (Table 16.5–2). The DSM-IV diagnostic criteria for posttraumatic stress disorder allow the clinician to specify whether the disorder is acute (if the symptoms have lasted less than three months) or chronic (if the symptoms have lasted three months or more). DSM-IV also allows the clinician to specify that the disorder was with delayed onset if the onset of the symptoms was six months or more after the stressful event.

## CLINICAL FEATURES

The principal clinical features of posttraumatic stress disorder are the painful reexperiencing of the event, a pattern of avoidance and emotional numbing, and fairly constant hyperarousal. The disorder may not develop until months or even years after the event. The mental status examination often reveals feelings of guilt, rejection, and

---

**Table 16.5–1**
**Diagnostic Criteria for Posttraumatic Stress Disorder**

A. The person has been exposed to a traumatic event in which both of the following were present:

  (1) the person experienced, witnessed, or was confronted with an event or events that involved actual or threatened death or serious injury, or a threat to the physical integrity of self or others

  (2) the person's response involved intense fear, helplessness, or horror. **Note:** in children, this may be expressed instead by disorganized or agitated behavior

B. The traumatic event is persistently reexperienced in one (or more) of the following ways:

  (1) recurrent and intrusive distressing recollections of the event, including images, thoughts, or perceptions. **Note:** in young children, repetitive play may occur in which themes or aspects of the trauma are expressed

  (2) recurrent distressing dreams of the event. **Note:** in children, there may be frightening dreams without recognizable content

  (3) acting or feeling as if the traumatic event were recurring (includes a sense of reliving the experience, illusions, hallucinations, and dissociative flashback episodes, including those that occur upon awakening or when intoxicated) **Note:** in young children, trauma-specific reenactment may occur.

  (4) intense psychological distress at exposure to internal or external cues that symbolize or resemble an aspect of the traumatic event

  (5) physiologic reactivity on exposure to internal or external cues that symbolize or resemble an aspect of the traumatic event

C. Persistent avoidance of stimuli associated with the trauma and numbing of general responsiveness (not present before the trauma), as indicated by three (or more) of the following:

  (1) efforts to avoid thoughts, feelings, or conversations associated with the trauma

  (2) efforts to avoid activities, places, or people that arouse recollections of the trauma

  (3) inability to recall an important aspect of the trauma

  (4) markedly diminished interest or participation in significant activities

  (5) feeling of detachment or estrangement from others

  (6) restricted range of affect (e.g., unable to have loving feelings)

  (7) sense of a foreshortened future (e.g., does not expect to have a career, marriage, children, or a normal life span)

D. Persistent symptoms of increased arousal (not present before the trauma), as indicated by two (or more) of the following:

  (1) difficulty falling or staying asleep

  (2) irritability or outbursts of anger

  (3) difficulty concentrating

  (4) hypervigilance

  (5) exaggerated startle response

E. Duration of the disturbance (symptoms in criteria B, C, and D) is more than one month.

F. The disturbance causes clinically significant distress or impairment in social, occupational, or other important areas of functioning.

*Specify* if:
  **Acute:** if duration of symptoms is less than 3 months
  **Chronic:** if duration of symptoms is 3 months or more

*Specify* if:
  **with delayed onset:** onset of symptoms at least six months after the

Table from DSM-IV, *Diagnostic and Statistical Manual of Mental Disorders*, ed 4. Copyright American Psychiatric Association, Washington, 1994. Used with permission.

**Table 16.5–2**
**Diagnostic Criteria for Acute Stress Disorder**

A. The person has been exposed to a traumatic event in which both of the following were present:

   (1) the person experienced, witnessed, or was confronted with an event or events that involved actual or threatened death or serious injury, or a threat to the physical integrity of self or others.

   (2) the person's response involved intense fear, helplessness, or horror

B. Either while experiencing or after experiencing the distressing event, the individual has three (or more) of the following dissociative symptoms:

   (1) a subjective sense of numbing, detachment, or absence of emotional responsiveness

   (2) a reduction in awareness of his or her surroundings (e.g., "being in a daze")

   (3) derealization

   (4) depersonalization

   (5) dissociative amnesia (i.e., inability to recall an important aspect of the trauma)

C. The traumatic event is persistently reexperienced in at least one of the following ways: recurrent images, thoughts, dreams, illusions, flashback episodes, or a sense of reliving the experience; or distress on exposure to reminders of the traumatic event.

D. Marked avoidance of stimuli that arouse recollections of the trauma (e.g., thoughts, feelings, conversations, activities, places, people)

E. Marked symptoms of anxiety or increased arousal (e.g., difficulty sleeping, irritability, poor concentration, hypervigilance, exaggerated startle response, and motor restlessness)

F. The disturbance causes clinically significant distress or impairment in social, occupational, or other important areas of functioning, impairs the individual's ability to pursue some necessary task, such as obtaining necessary assistance or mobilizing personal resources by telling family members about the traumatic experience

G. The disturbance lasts for a minimum of 2 days and a maximum of 4 weeks and occurs within 4 weeks of the traumatic event.

H. Not due to the direct physiological effects of a substance (e.g., a drug of abuse, a medication) or a general medical condition, is not better accounted for by brief psychotic disorder, and is not merely an exacerbation of a preexisting Axis I or Axis II disorder.

Table from DSM-IV, *Diagnostic and Statistical Manual of Mental Disorders*, ed 4. Copyright American Psychiatric Association, Washington, 1994. Used with permission.

humiliation. The patient may also describe dissociative states and panic attacks. Illusions and hallucinations may be present. Cognitive testing may reveal that the patient has impairments of memory and attention.

Associated symptoms can include aggression, violence, poor impulse control, depression, and substance-related disorders. The patients have elevated Sc, D, F, and Ps scores on the Minnesota Multiphasic Personality Inventory (MMPI), and the Rorschach test findings often include aggressive and violent material.

A 23-year-old Vietnam veteran was admitted to a hospital one year after the end of the Vietnam War at the request of his wife after he began to experience depression, insomnia, and flashbacks of his wartime experiences. He had been honorably discharged two years previously, having spent nearly a year in combat. He had had only minimal difficulties in returning to civilian life, resuming his college studies, and then marrying within six months of his return. His wife had noticed that he was always reluctant to talk about his military experience, but she wrote it off as a natural reaction to unpleasant memories.

The patient's current symptoms had begun at about the time of the fall of Saigon. He had become preoccupied with watching television news stories about it. He then began to have difficulty in sleeping and at times would awaken at night in the midst of a nightmare in which he was reliving his past experiences. His wife became particularly concerned one day when he had a flashback experience while out in their backyard: As a plane flew overhead, flying somewhat lower than usual, the patient threw himself to the ground, seeking cover, thinking it was an attacking helicopter. The more he watched the news on television, the more agitated and morose he became. Stories began to spill out about atrocities that he had seen and experienced, and he began to feel guilty that he had survived while many of his friends had not. At times he also seemed angry and bitter, feeling that the sacrifices he and others had made were all wasted.

The veteran's wife expressed concern that his preoccupation with Vietnam had become so intense that he seemed uninterested in anything else and was emotionally distant from her. When she suggested that they try to plan their future, including having a family, he responded as if his life consisted completely of the world of events experienced two years earlier, as if he had no future.

## DIFFERENTIAL DIAGNOSIS

A major consideration in the diagnosis of posttraumatic stress disorder is the possibility that the patient also incurred a head injury during the trauma. Other organic considerations that can both cause and exacerbate the symptoms are epilepsy, alcohol use disorders, and other substance-related disorders. Acute intoxication or withdrawal from some substances may also present a clinical picture that is difficult to distinguish from posttraumatic stress disorder until the effects of the substance have worn off.

Posttraumatic stress disorder is commonly misdiagnosed as some other mental disorder, resulting in inappropriate treatment of the condition. The clinician must consider posttraumatic stress disorder in patients who have pain disorder, substance abuse, other anxiety disorders, and mood disorders. In general, posttraumatic stress disorder can be distinguished from other mental disorders by interviewing the patient regarding previous traumatic experiences and by the nature of the current symptoms. Borderline personality disorder, dissociative disorders, factitious disorders, and malingering should also be considered. Borderline personality disorder can be difficult to distinguish from posttraumatic stress disorder. The two disorders may coexist or even may be causally related. Patients with dissociative disorders do not usually have the degree of avoidance behavior, the autonomic hyperarousal, or the history of trauma that patients with posttraumatic stress disorder report. Partly because of the publicity that posttraumatic stress disorder has received in the popular press, clinicians should also consider the possibility of a factitious disorder and malingering.

## COURSE AND PROGNOSIS

Posttraumatic stress disorder usually develops some time after the trauma. The delay can be as short as one week or as long as 30 years. Symptoms can fluctuate over time and may be most intense during periods of stress. About 30 percent of patients recover completely, 40 percent continue to have mild symptoms, 20 percent continue to have moderate symptoms, and 10 percent remain unchanged or become worse. A good prognosis is predicted by a rapid onset of the symptoms, the short duration of the symptoms (less than six months), good premorbid functioning, strong social supports, and the absence of other psychiatric, medical, or substance-related disorders.

In general, the very young and the very old have more difficulty with traumatic events than do those in midlife. For example, about 80 percent of young children who sustain a burn injury show symptoms of posttraumatic stress disorder one or two years after the initial injury; only 30 percent of adults who suffer such an injury have a posttraumatic stress disorder after one year. Presumably, young children do not yet have adequate coping mechanisms to deal with the physical and emotional insults of the trauma. Likewise, elderly people, when compared with younger adults, are likely to have more rigid coping mechanisms and to be less able to muster a flexible approach to dealing with the effects of the trauma. Furthermore, the effects of the trauma may be exacerbated by physical disabilities characteristic of late life, particularly disabilities of the nervous system and the cardiovascular system such as reduced cerebral blood flow, failing vision, palpitations, and arrhythmias. Preexisting psychiatric disability, whether a personality disorder or a more serious condition, also increases the effects of particular stressors. The availability of social supports may also influence the development, the severity, and the duration of posttraumatic stress disorder. In general, patients who have a good network of social support are not likely to have the disorder or to experience it in its severe forms.

## TREATMENT

When a clinician is faced with a patient who has experienced a significant trauma, the major approaches are support, encouragement to discuss the event, and education regarding a variety of coping mechanisms (for example, relaxation). The use of sedatives and hypnotics can also be helpful. When a clinician is faced with a patient who experienced a traumatic event in the past and now has posttraumatic stress disorder, the emphasis should be on education regarding the disorder and its treatment, both pharmacological and psychotherapeutic. Additional support for the patient and the family can be obtained through local and national support groups for patients with posttraumatic stress disorder.

### Pharmacotherapy

The efficacy of imipramine (Tofranil) and amitriptyline (Elavil), two tricyclic drugs, in the treatment of posttraumatic stress disorder are supported by a number of well-controlled clinical trials. Although some trials of the two drugs have had negative findings, most of those trials had serious design flaws, including too short a duration. Dosages of imipramine and amitriptyline should be the same as those used to treat depressive disorders, and the minimum length of an adequate trial should be eight weeks. Patients who respond well should probably continue the pharmacotherapy for at least one year before an attempt is made to withdraw the drug. Some studies indicate that pharmacotherapy is more effective in treating the depression, anxiety, and hyperarousal than in treating the avoidance, denial, and emotional numbing.

Other drugs that may be useful in the treatment of posttraumatic stress disorder include the serotonin-specific reuptake inhibitors (SSRIs), the monoamine oxidase inhibitors (MAOIs), and the anticonvulsant (for example, carbamazepine, valproate). Clonidine (Catapres) and propranolol (Inderal) are suggested by the theories regarding noradrenergic hyperactivity in the disorder. Although some anecdotal reports point to the effectiveness of alprazolam (Xanax) in posttraumatic stress disorder, the use of that drug is complicated by the high association of substance-related disorders in patients with the disorder and by the emergence of withdrawal symptoms on discontinuation of the drug. Almost no positive data concern the use of antipsychotic drugs in the disorder, so the use of those drugs—for example, haloperidol (Haldol)—should be avoided except perhaps for the short-term control of severe aggression and agitation.

### Psychotherapy

Psychodynamic psychotherapy may be useful in the treatment of many patients with posttraumatic stress disorder. In some cases, reconstruction of the traumatic events with associated abreaction and catharsis may be therapeutic. However, psychotherapy must be individualized, because some patients are overwhelmed by reexperiencing the traumas.

Psychotherapeutic interventions for posttraumatic stress disorder include behavior therapy, cognitive therapy, and hypnosis. Many clinicians advocate time-limited psychotherapy for the victims of trauma. Such therapy usually takes a cognitive approach and also provides support and security. The short-term nature of the psychotherapy minimizes the risk of dependence and chronicity. Issues of suspicion, paranoia, and trust often adversely affect compliance. The therapist should overcome patients' denial of the traumatic event, encourage them to relax, and remove them from the source of the stress. The patient should be encouraged to sleep, using medication if necessary. Support from the environment (such as friends and relatives) should be provided. The patient should be encouraged to review and abreact emotional feelings associated with the traumatic event and plan for future recovery.

Psychotherapy after a traumatic event should follow a

model of crisis intervention with support, education, and the development of coping mechanisms and acceptance of the event. When posttraumatic stress disorder has developed, two major psychotherapeutic approaches can be taken. The first is exposure to the traumatic event through imaginal techniques or in vivo exposures. The exposures can be intense, as in implosive therapy, or graded, as in systematic desensitization. The second approach is to teach the patient methods of stress management, including relaxation techniques and cognitive approaches to coping with stress. Some preliminary data indicate that, although stress management techniques are effective more rapidly than are exposure techniques, the results of exposure techniques are more long-lasting.

In addition to individual therapy techniques, group therapy and family therapy have been reported to be effective in cases of posttraumatic stress disorder. The advantages of group therapy include the sharing of multiple traumatic experiences and support from other group members. Group therapy has been particularly successful with Vietnam veterans. Family therapy often helps sustain a marriage through periods of exacerbated symptoms. Hospitalization may be necessary when symptoms are particularly severe or when there is a risk of suicide or other violence.

### References

Blaustein M, editor: Natural disasters: Psychiatric response. Psychiatr Ann *21*: (9):2, 1991.

Bremmer J D, Scott T M, Delaney R C, Southwick S M, Mason J W, Johnson D R, Innis R B, McCarthy G, Charney D S: Deficits in short-term memory in posttraumatic stress disorder. Am J Psychiatry *150*: 1015, 1993.

Bremner J D, Steinberg M, Southwick S M, Johnson D R, Charney D S: Use of the structured clinical interview for DSM-IV dissociative disorders for systematic assessment of dissociative symptoms in posttraumatic stress disorder. Am J Psychiatry *150*: 1011, 1993.

Breslau N, Davis G C, Andreski P, Peterson E: Traumatic events and posttraumatic stress disorder in an urban population of young adults. Arch Gen Psychiatry *48*: 216, 1991.

Davidson J: Drug therapy of post-traumatic stress disorder. Br J Psychiatry *160*: 309, 1992.

Davidson J, Kudler H, Smith R, Mahorney S L, Lipper S, Hammett E, Saunders W B, Cavenar J O: Treatment of posttraumatic stress disorder with amitriptyline and placebo. Arch Gen Psychiatry *47*: 259, 1990.

Davidson J R T, Kudler H S, Saunders W B, Erickson L, Smith R D, Stein R M, Lipper S, Hammett E B, Mahorney S L, Cavenar J O Jr: Predicting response to amitriptyline in posttraumatic stress disorder. Am J Psychiatry *150*: 1024, 1993.

Foa F B, Rothbaum B O, Riggs D S, Murdock T B: Treatment of posttraumatic stress disorder in rape victims: A comparison between cognitive-behavioral procedures and counseling. J Consult Clin Psychol *59*: 715, 1991.

Gabbard G O: *Psychodynamic Psychiatry in Clinical Practice: The DSM-IV Edition.* American Psychiatric Press, Washington, 1994.

Gersons B P R, Carlier I V E: Post-traumatic stress disorder: The history of a recent concept. Br J Psychiatry *161*: 742, 1992.

Gunderson J G, Sabo A N: The phenomenological and conceptual interface between borderline personality disorder and PTSD. Am J Psychiatry *150*: 19, 1993.

Jordan B K, Schlenger W E, Hough R, Kulka R A, Weiss D, Fairbank J A, Marmar C R: Lifetime and current prevalence of specific psychiatric disorders among Vietnam veterans and controls. Arch Gen Psychiatry *48*: 207, 1991.

Koller P, Marmar C R, Kanas N: Psychodynamic group treatment of posttraumatic stress disorder in Vietnam veterans. Int J Group Psychother *42*: 225, 1992.

Mellman T A, Randolph C A, Brawman-Mintzer O, Flores L P, Milanes F J: Phenomenology and course of psychiatric disorders associated with combat-related stress disorder. Am J Psychiatry *149*: 1568, 1992.

Paige S R, Reid G M, Allen M G, Newton J E O: Psychophysiological correlates of posttraumatic stress disorder in Vietnam veterans. Biol Psychiatry *27*: 419, 1990.

Solomon S D, Gerrity E T, Muff A M: Efficacy of treatments for posttraumatic stress disorder: An empirical review. JAMA *268*: 633, 1992.

Southwick S M, Krystal J H, Johnson D R, Charney D S: Neurobiology of posttraumatic stress disorder. In *Review of Psychiatry*, vol 11, A Tasman, M B Riba, editors, p 347. American Psychiatric Press, Washington, 1992.

Yehuda R, Giller E L, Southwick S M, Lowry M T, Mason W T: Hypothalamic-pituitary-adrenal dysfunction in posttraumatic stress disorder. Biol Psychiatry *30*: 1031, 1991.

# 16.6 / Generalized Anxiety Disorder

In 1980 the third edition of *Diagnostic and Statistical Manual of Mental Disorders* (DSM-III) introduced several new diagnostic categories that subgrouped the patients who had previously been classified as having anxiety neurosis. One of the new categories was generalized anxiety disorder (sometimes referred to as GAD), which, in DSM-III, was a residual diagnostic category for those patients who did not meet the criteria for other diagnoses. In the revised third edition of DSM (DSM-III-R) and the fourth edition (DSM-IV), generalized anxiety disorder became a distinct diagnostic entity, no longer conceptualized as a leftover category. Generalized anxiety disorder is defined in DSM-IV as excessive and pervasive worry, accompanied by a variety of somatic symptoms, that causes significant impairment in social or occupational functioning or marked distress in the patient. DSM-IV eliminates the DSM-III-R category of overanxious disorder of childhood and modifies the diagnostic criteria for generalized anxiety disorder to include overanxious children and adolescents.

## EPIDEMIOLOGY

Generalized anxiety disorder is a common condition; however, with the restrictive criteria of DSM-III-R and DSM-IV, generalized anxiety disorder may be found less often now than when the DSM-III criteria were used. Reasonable estimates for the one-year prevalence of generalized anxiety range from 3 to 8 percent. Generalized anxiety disorder is probably the disorder most often found with a coexisting mental disorder, usually another anxiety disorder or a mood disorder. Perhaps 50 percent of patients with generalized anxiety disorder have another mental disorder.

The ratio of women to men is about 2 to 1, but the ratio of women to men who are receiving inpatient treatment for the disorder is about 1 to 1. The age of onset is difficult to specify, since most patients with the disorder report that they have been anxious for as long as they can remember. Patients usually come to a clinician's attention in their 20s, although the first contact with a clinician can occur at virtually any age. Only a third of patients who have generalized anxiety disorder seek psychiatric treatment. Many patients go to general practitioners, internists, cardiologists, pulmonary specialists, or gastroenterologists, seeking treatment for the somatic component of the disorder.

## ETIOLOGY

As with most mental disorders, the cause of generalized anxiety disorder is not known. As currently defined, generalized anxiety disorder probably affects a heterogeneous group of patients. Perhaps because a certain degree of anxiety is normal and adaptive, differentiating normal anxiety from pathological anxiety and differentiating biological causative factors from psychosocial factors is difficult. Biological and psychosocial factors probably work together.

### Biological Factors

The therapeutic efficacies of benzodiazepines and the azapirones—for example, buspirone (BuSpar)—have focused biological research efforts on the γ-aminobutyric acid (GABA) and serotonin (5-hydroxytryptamine [5-HT]) neurotransmitter systems. Benzodiazepines (which are benzodiazepine receptor agonists) are known to reduce anxiety, whereas flumazenil (Mazicon) (a benzodiazepine receptor antagonist) and the β-carbolines (benzodiazepine receptor reverse agonists) are known to induce anxiety. Although no convincing data indicate that the benzodiazepine receptors are abnormal in patients with generalized anxiety disorder, some researchers have focused on the occipital lobe, which has the highest concentrations of benzodiazepine receptors in the brain. Other brain areas that have been hypothesized to be involved in generalized anxiety disorder are the basal ganglia, the limbic system, and the frontal cortex. Because buspirone is an agonist at

the 5-HT$_{1A}$ receptor, several research groups are focusing on the hypothesis that the regulation of the serotonergic system in generalized anxiety disorder is abnormal. Other neurotransmitter systems that have been the subject of research in generalized anxiety disorder include the norepinephrine, glutamate, and cholecystokinin neurotransmitter systems. Some evidence indicates that patients with generalized anxiety disorder may have a subsensitivity of their α$_2$-adrenergic receptors, as indicated by a blunted release of growth hormone after clonidine (Catapres) infusion.

Only a limited number of brain-imaging studies of patients with generalized anxiety disorder have been conducted. One positron emission tomography (PET) study reported a lower metabolic rate in basal ganglia and white matter in generalized anxiety disorder patients than in normal controls (Figure 16.6–1). A few genetic studies have also been conducted in the field. One study found that a genetic relation may exist between generalized anxiety disorder and major depressive disorder in women. Another study found a distinct but difficult-to-quantitate genetic component in generalized anxiety disorder. About 25 percent of first-degree relatives of patients with generalized anxiety disorder are also affected. Male relatives are likely to have an alcohol use disorder. Some twin studies report a concordance rate of 50 percent in monozygotic twins and 15 percent in dizygotic twins.

A variety of electroencephalogram (EEG) abnormalities have been noted in alpha rhythm and evoked potentials. Sleep EEG studies have reported increased sleep discontinuity, decreased delta sleep, decreased stage 1

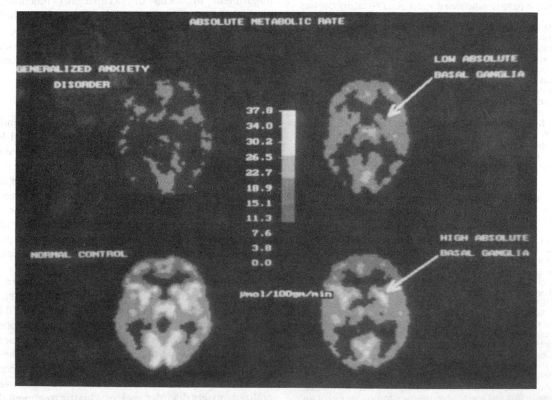

**Figure 16.6–1.** Basal ganglia metabolism. A common glucose scale shows the decrease in absolute glucose metabolic rate in the basal ganglia of two typical subjects with generalized anxiety disorder on top row compared with two normal controls on bottom row. (Figure from J C Wu, M S Buchsbaum, T G Hershey, E Hazlett, N Sicotte, J C Johnson: PET in generalized anxiety disorder. Biol Psychiatry 29: 1188, 1991. Used with permission.)

sleep, and reduced rapid eye movement (REM) sleep. Those changes in sleep architecture are different from the changes seen in depressive disorders.

## Psychosocial Factors

The two major schools of thought regarding the psychosocial factors leading to the development of generalized anxiety disorder are the cognitive-behavioral school and the psychoanalytic school. The cognitive-behavioral school hypothesizes that patients with generalized anxiety disorder are responding to incorrectly and inaccurately perceived dangers. The inaccuracy is generated by selective attention to negative details in the environment, by distortions in information processing, and by an overly negative view of one's own ability to cope. The psychoanalytic school hypothesizes that anxiety is a symptom of unresolved unconscious conflicts. That psychological theory of anxiety was first presented by Sigmund Freud in 1909 with his description of Little Hans; before then, Freud had conceptualized anxiety as having a physiological basis.

A hierarchy of anxieties are related to various developmental levels. At the most primitive level, anxiety may relate to the fear of annihilation or of fusion with another person. At a more mature level of development, anxiety is related to separation from a love object. At a still more mature level, the anxiety is connected to the loss of love from an important object. Castration anxiety is related to the oedipal phase of development and is considered one of the highest levels of anxiety. Superego anxiety, the fear of disappointing one's own ideals and values (derived from internalized parents), is the most mature form of anxiety.

## DIAGNOSIS

The DSM-IV diagnostic criteria (Table 16.6–1) includes some modifications of the DSM-III-R criteria to make them easier to use and to help the clinician differentiate among generalized anxiety disorder, normal anxiety, and other mental disorders. The distinction between generalized anxiety disorder and normal anxiety is emphasized by the use of the words "excessive" and "difficult to control" in the criteria and by the specification that the symptoms cause significant inpairment or distress. The distinction between generalized anxiety disorder and other mental disorders is aided in DSM-IV by examples of distinguishing features in criterion D.

## CLINICAL FEATURES

The primary symptoms of generalized anxiety disorder are anxiety, motor tension, autonomic hyperactivity, and cognitive vigilance. The anxiety is excessive and interferes with other aspects of the patient's life. The motor tension is most commonly manifested as shakiness, restlessness, and headaches. The autonomic hyperactivity is commonly manifested by shortness of breath, excessive sweating, palpitations, and various gastrointestinal symptoms. The cognitive vigilance is evidenced by the patient's irritability and the ease with which the patient is startled.

**Table 16.6–1**
**Diagnostic Criteria for Generalized Anxiety Disorder**

A. Excessive anxiety and worry (apprehensive expectation), occurring more days than not for at least 6 months, about a number of events or activities (such as work or school performance).

B. The person finds it difficult to control the worry.

C. The anxiety and worry are associated with three (or more) of the following six symptoms (with at least some symptoms present for more days than not for the past six months) **Note:** Only one item is required in children.

    (1) restlessness or feeling keyed up or on edge

    (2) being easily fatigued

    (3) difficulty concentrating or mind going blank

    (4) irritability

    (5) muscle tension

    (6) sleep disturbance (difficulty falling or staying asleep, or restless unsatisfying sleep)

D. The focus of the anxiety and worry is not confined to features of an Axis I disorder, e.g., the anxiety or worry is not about having a panic attack (as in panic disorder), being embarrassed in public (as in social phobia), being contaminated (as in obsessive-compulsive disorder), being away from home or close relatives (as in separation anxiety disorder), gaining weight (as in anorexia nervosa), having multiple physical complaints (as in somatization disorder), or having a serious illness (as in hypochondriasis), and the anxiety and worry do not occur exclusively during posttraumatic stress disorder.

E. The anxiety, worry, or physical symptoms cause clinically significant distress or impairment in social, occupational, or other important areas of functioning.

F. The disturbance is not due to the direct physiological effects of a substance (e.g., a drug of abuse, a medication) or a general medical condition (e.g., hyperthyroidism), and does not occur exclusively during a mood disorder, psychotic disorder, or a pervasive developmental disorder.

Table from DSM-IV, *Diagnostic and Statistical Manual of Mental Disorders*, ed 4. Copyright American Psychiatric Association, Washington, 1994. Used with permission.

Most commonly, patients with generalized anxiety disorder seek out a general practitioner or internist for help with some somatic symptom. Alternatively, the patients go to a specialist for a specific symptom—for example, chronic diarrhea. A specific nonpsychiatric medical disorder is rarely found, and patients vary in their doctor-seeking behavior. Some patients accept a diagnosis of generalized anxiety disorder and the appropriate treatment; others seek additional medical consultations for their problems.

A 27-year-old married electrician complained of dizziness, sweating palms, heart palpitations, and ringing in the ears of more than 18 months' duration. He also experienced dry throat, periods of uncontrollable shaking, and a constant edgy and watchful feeling that often interfered with his ability to concentrate. Those feelings had been present most of the time over the previous two years; they had not been limited to discrete periods.

Because of his symptoms, he had seen a family practitioner,

a neurologist, a neurosurgeon, a chiropractor, and an ear, nose, and throat specialist. He had been given a hypoglycemic diet, he received physiotherapy for a pinched nerve, and he was told that he might have an inner ear problem.

For the past two years he had had few social contacts because of his nervous symptoms. Although he sometimes had to leave work when the symptoms became intolerable, he continued to work for the same company for which he had worked since his apprenticeship after high school graduation. He tended to hide his symptoms from his wife and children, to whom he wanted to appear perfect, and he reported few problems with them as a result of his nervousness.

*Discussion.* The symptoms of motor tension (uncontrollable shaking), autonomic hyperactivity (dizziness, sweating palms, heart palpitations), and vigilance and scanning (a constant edgy and watchful feeling) suggested an anxiety disorder. Because the symptoms were not limited to discrete periods, as in panic disorder, and were not focused on a discrete stimulus, as in phobias, the diagnosis was generalized anxiety disorder.

Although the patient had consulted numerous physicians for his symptoms, the absence of a preoccupation with fears of having a specific physical disease precluded a diagnosis of hypochrondriasis.

## DIFFERENTIAL DIAGNOSIS

The differential diagnosis of generalized anxiety disorder includes all the medical disorders that may cause anxiety (Table 16.1–4). The medical workup should include the standard blood chemistry tests, an electrocardiogram, and thyroid function tests. The clinician must rule out caffeine intoxication, stimulant abuse, alcohol withdrawal, and sedative, hypnotic, or anxiolytic withdrawal. The mental status examination and the history should explore the diagnostic possibilities of panic disorder, phobias, and obsessive-compulsive disorder. In general, patients with panic disorder seek treatment earlier, are more disabled by their disorder, have had a sudden onset of symptoms, and are less troubled by their somatic symptoms than are patients with generalized anxiety disorder. Distinguishing generalized anxiety disorder from major depressive disorder and dysthymic disorder can be difficult; in fact, the disorders frequently coexist. Other diagnostic possibilities are adjustment disorder with anxiety, hypochondriasis, adult attention-deficit/hyperactivity disorder, somatization disorder, and personality disorders.

## COURSE AND PROGNOSIS

Because of the high incidence of comorbid mental disorders in patients with generalized anxiety disorder, the clinical course and the prognosis of the disorder is difficult to predict. Nonetheless, some data indicate that life events are associated with the onset of generalized anxiety disorder: the occurrence of several negative life events greatly increases the likelihood that the disorder will develop. By definition, generalized anxiety disorder is a chronic condition that may well be lifelong. As many as 25 percent of the patients eventually experience panic disorder. An additional high percentage of patients are likely to have major depressive disorder.

## TREATMENT

The most effective treatment of patients with generalized anxiety disorder is probably one that combines psychotherapeutic, pharmacotherapeutic, and supportive approaches. The treatment may take a significant amount of time for the involved clinician, regardless of whether the clinician is a psychiatrist, a family practitioner, or another specialist.

### Psychotherapy

The major psychotherapeutic approaches to generalized anxiety disorder are cognitive-behavioral, supportive, and insight-oriented. Data are still limited on the relative merits of those approaches, although the most sophisticated studies have been with the cognitive-behavioral techniques, which seem to have both short-term and long-term efficacy. Cognitive approaches directly address the patient's hypothesized cognitive distortions, and behavioral approaches address the somatic symptoms directly. The major techniques used in the behavioral approaches are relaxation and biofeedback. Some preliminary data indicate that the combination of cognitive and behavioral approaches is more effective than either technique used alone. Supportive therapy offers patients reassurance and comfort, although its long-term efficacy is doubtful. Insight-oriented psychotherapy focuses on uncovering unconscious conflicts and identifying ego strengths. The efficacy of insight-oriented psychotherapy for generalized anxiety disorder is reported in many anecdotal case reports, but large controlled studies are lacking.

Most patients experience a marked lessening of anxiety when given the opportunity to discuss their difficulties with a concerned and sympathetic physician. If the clinician discovers external situations that are anxiety-provoking, the clinician may be able—alone or with the help of the patients or their families—to change the environment and thus reduce the stressful pressures. A reduction in symptoms often allows the patients to function effectively in their daily work and relationships, which provides new rewards and gratifications that are in themselves therapeutic.

The psychoanalytic perspective is that in certain cases anxiety is a signal of unconscious turmoil that deserves investigation. The anxiety can be normal, adaptive, maladaptive, too intense, or too mild, depending on the circumstances. Anxiety appears in numerous situations over the course of the life cycle; in many cases, symptom relief is not the most appropriate course of action.

For patients who are psychologically minded and motivated to understand the sources of their anxiety, psychotherapy may be the treatment of choice. Psychodynamic therapy proceeds with the assumption that anxiety may increase with effective treatment. The goal of the dynamic approach may be to increase the patient's *anxiety tolerance* (defined as a capacity to experience anxiety without having to discharge it), rather than to eliminate anxiety. Empirical research indicates that many patients who have successful psychotherapeutic treatment may continue to experience anxiety after termination of the psychotherapy. However, their increased ego mastery allows them to use the anxiety symptom as a signal to reflect on internal struggles and to expand their insight and understanding. A psychodynamic approach to the patient with generalized anxiety disorder involves a search for the patient's underlying fear.

## Pharmacotherapy

The decision to prescribe an anxiolytic to patients with generalized anxiety disorder should rarely be made on the first visit. Because of the long-term nature of the disorder, a treatment plan must be carefully thought out. The two major drugs to be considered for the treatment of generalized anxiety disorder are buspirone and the benzodiazepines. Other drugs that may be useful are the tricyclic drugs—for example, imipramine (Tofranil)—antihistamines, and the β-adrenergic antagonists—for example, propranolol (Inderal).

Although drug treatment of generalized anxiety disorder is sometimes seen as a 6-to-12-month treatment, some evidence indicates that treatment should be long-term, perhaps lifelong. About 25 percent of patients relapse in the first month after the discontinuation of therapy, and 60 to 80 percent relapse over the course of the next year. Although some patients become dependent on the benzodiazepines, no tolerance develops to the therapeutic effects of either the benzodiazepines or buspirone.

**Benzodiazepines.** Benzodiazepines have been the drugs of choice for generalized anxiety disorder. In the disorder benzodiazepines can be prescribed on an as-needed basis, so that patients take a rapidly acting benzodiazepine when they feel particularly anxious. The alternative approach is to prescribe benzodiazepines for a limited period, during which psychosocial therapeutic approaches are implemented.

Several problems are associated with the use of benzodiazepines in generalized anxiety disorder. About 25 to 30 percent of all patients fail to respond, and tolerance and dependence may occur. Some patients also experience impaired alertness while taking the drugs and are, therefore, at risk for accidents involving automobiles and machinery.

The clinical decision to initiate treatment with a benzodiazepine should be a considered and specific one. The patient's diagnosis, the specific target symptoms, and the duration of treatment—all should be defined, and the information should be shared with the patient. Treatment for most anxiety conditions lasts for two to six weeks, followed by one or two weeks of tapering the drug before it is discontinued. The most common clinical mistake with benzodiazepine treatment is to decide passively to continue treatment indefinitely.

For the treatment of anxiety, it is usual to begin a drug at the low end of its therapeutic range and to increase the dosage to achieve a therapeutic response. The use of a benzodiazepine with an intermediate half-life (8 to 15 hours) is likely to avoid some of the adverse effects associated with the use of benzodiazepines with long half-lives. The use of divided doses prevents the development of adverse effects associated with high peak plasma levels. The improvement produced by benzodiazepines may go beyond a simple antianxiety effect. For example, the drugs may cause the patient to regard various occurrences in a positive light. The drugs may also have a mild disinhibiting action, similar to that observed after modest amounts of alcohol.

**Buspirone.** Buspirone is most likely effective in 60 to 80 percent of patients with generalized anxiety disorder. Data indicate that buspirone is more effective in reducing the cognitive symptoms of generalized anxiety disorder than in reducing the somatic symptoms. Evidence also indicates that patients who have previously been treated with benzodiazepines are not likely to respond to treatment with buspirone. The lack of response may be due to the absence, with buspirone treatment, of some of the nonanxiolytic effects of benzodiazepines (such as muscle relaxation and the additional sense of well-being). Nonetheless, the improved benefit-risk ratio, the lack of cognitive and psychomotor effects, and the absence of withdrawal symptoms may make buspirone the first-line drug in the treatment of generalized anxiety disorder. The major disadvantage of buspirone is that its effects take two to three weeks to become evident, in contrast to the almost immediate anxiolytic effects of the benzodiazepines. Buspirone is not an effective treatment for benzodiazepine withdrawal.

**Other drugs.** If treatment with buspirone or a benzodiazepine is not effective or not completely effective, treatment with a tricyclic drug or a β-adrenergic antagonist can be considered. The tricyclic drugs have been proved to be effective in the treatment of anxiety. The β-adrenergic drugs are limited in their effectiveness to the treatment of the peripheral symptoms of anxiety (for example, palpitations and tremor). Another alternative is to use combinations of drugs, such as benzodiazepines and buspirone or one of those drugs with a tricyclic drug or a β-adrenergic antagonist.

## References

Abelson J L, Glitz D, Cameron O G, Lee M A, Bronzo M, Curtis G C: Blunted growth hormone response to clonidine in patients with generalized anxiety disorder. Arch Gen Psychiatry *48*: 157, 1991.
Butler G: Predicting outcome after treatment for generalised anxiety disorder. Behav Res Ther *31*: 211, 1993.
Butler G, Fennell M, Robson P, Gelder M: Comparison of behavior therapy and cognitive-behavior therapy in the treatment of generalized anxiety disorder. J Consult Clin Psychol *59*: 167, 1991.
Dubovsky S L: Generalized anxiety disorder: New concepts and psychopharmacologic therapies. J Clin Psychiatry *51* (1, Suppl): 3, 1990.
Gabbard G O: Psychodynamic psychiatry in the "decade of the brain." Am J Psychiatry *149*: 991, 1992.
Gammans R E, Stringfellow J C, Hvizdos A J, Seidehamel R J, Cohn J B, Wilcox C S, Fabre L F, Pecknold J C, Smith W T, Rickels K: Use of buspirone in patients with generalized anxiety disorder and coexisting depressive symptoms: A meta-analysis of eight randomized, controlled studies. Neuropsychobiology *25*: 193, 1992.
Gasperini M, Battaglia M, Diaferia G, Bellodi L: Personality features related to generalized anxiety disorder. Compr Psychiatry *31*: 363, 1990.

Gorman J M, Papp L A: Chronic anxiety: Deciding the length of treatment. J Clin Psychiatry *51* (1, Suppl): 11, 1990.

Kendler K S, Neale M C, Kessler R C, Heath A C, Eaves L J: Generalized anxiety disorder in women: A population-based twin study. Arch Gen Psychiatry *49*: 267, 1992.

Kendler K S, Neale M C, Kessler K C, Heath A C, Eaves L J: Major depression and generalized anxiety disorder: Same genes, (partly) different environments? Arch Gen Psychiatry *49*: 716, 1992.

Kollai M, Kollai B: Cardiac vagal tone in generalized anxiety disorder. Br J Psychiatry *161*: 831, 1992.

Massion A O, Warshaw M G, Keller M B: Quality of life and psychiatric morbidity in panic disorder and generalized anxiety disorder. Am J Psychiatry *150*: 600, 1993.

Nisita C, Petracca A, Akiskal H S, Galli L, Gepponi I, Cassano G B: Delimitation of generalized anxiety disorder: Clinical comparisons with panic and major depressive disorders. Compr Psychiatry *31*: 409, 1990.

Noyes R Jr, Woodman C, Garvey M J, Cook B L, Suelzer M, Clancy J, Anderson D J: Generalized anxiety disorder vs panic disorder: Distinguishing characteristics and patterns of comorbidity. J Nerv Ment Dis *180*: 369, 1992.

Rickels K, Schweizer E: The clinical course and long-term management of generalized anxiety disorder. J Clin Psychopharmacol *10*: 101S, 1990.

Rickels K, Schweizer E: The treatment of generalized anxiety disorder in patients with depresion symptomatology. J Clin Psychiatry *54* (1, suppl): 20, 1993.

Sanderson W C, Barlow D H: A description of patients diagnosed with DSM-III-R generalized anxiety disorder. J Nerv Ment Dis *178*: 588, 1990.

Shores M M, Glubin T, Cowley D S, Dager S R, Roy-Byrne P P, Dunner D L: The relationship between anxiety and depression: A clinical comparison of generalized anxiety disorder, dysthymic disorder, panic disorder, and major depressive disorder. Compr Psychiatry *33*: 237, 1992.

Wu J C, Buchsbaum M S, Hershey T G, Hazlet E, Sicotte N, Johnson J C: PET in generalized anxiety disorder. Biol Psychiatry *29*: 1181, 1991.

# 17 ||||||

# Somatoform Disorders

The somatoform disorders are a group of disorders that include physical symptoms (for example, pain, nausea, and dizziness) for which an adequate medical explanation cannot be found. The somatic symptoms and complaints are serious enough to cause the patient significant emotional distress or impairment in the patient's ability to function in social and occupational roles. A diagnosis of a somatoform disorder reflects the clinician's assessment that psychological factors are a large contributor to the symptoms' onset, severity, and duration. Somatoform disorders are not the result of conscious malingering or factitious disorders.

The fourth edition of *Diagnostic and Statistical Manual of Mental Disorders* (DSM-IV) maintains, for the most part, the diagnoses listed in the revised third edition (DSM-III-R). Five specific somatoform disorders are recognized (Table 17–1): (1) *Somatization disorder* is characterized by many physical complaints affecting many organ systems. (2) *Conversion disorder* is characterized by one or two neurological complaints. (3) *Hypochondriasis* is characterized less by a focus on the symptoms than by the patient's belief that he or she has some specific disease. (4) *Body dysmorphic disorder* is characterized by the false belief or exaggerated perception that some body part is defective. (5) *Pain disorder* is characterized by symptoms of pain that are either solely related to psychological factors or significantly exacerbated by psychological factors. DSM-IV also has two residual diagnostic categories for the somatoform disorders: (1) *Undifferentiated somatoform disorder* includes somatoform disorders, not otherwise described, that have been present for six months or longer. (2) *Somatoform disorder not otherwise specified* (NOS) is the category for somatoform symptoms that do not meet any of the previously mentioned somatoform disorder diagnoses.

## SOMATIZATION DISORDER

Somatization disorder is characterized by many somatic symptoms that cannot be explained adequately on the basis of physical and laboratory examinations. Somatization disorder is distinguished from other somatoform disorders because of the multiplicity of the complaints and the multiple organ systems (for example, gastrointestinal and neurological) that are affected. The disorder is chronic (with symptoms present for several years and beginning before age 30) and is associated with significant psychological distress, impairment in social and occupational functioning, and excessive medical help-seeking behavior.

Somatization disorder has been recognized since the time of ancient Egypt. An early name for somatization disorder was *hysteria*, a condition that was incorrectly thought to affect only women. (The word "hysteria" is derived from the Greek word for uterus, *hystera*.) In the 17th century Thomas Sydenham recognized that psychological factors, which he called antecedent sorrows, were involved in the pathogenesis of the symptoms. In 1859 Paul Briquet, a French physician, observed the multiplicity of the symptoms and the affected organ systems and commented on the usually chronic course of the disorder. Because of those astute clinical observations, the disorder was called Briquet's syndrome for a period of time, although the term "somatization disorder" became the standard in the United States when the third edition of DSM (DSM-III) was introduced in 1980.

## Epidemiology

The lifetime prevalence of somatization disorder in the general population is estimated to be 0.1 or 0.2 percent, although several research groups believe that the actual figure may be closer to 0.5 percent. Women with somatization disorder outnumber men 5 to 20 times, although the highest estimates may be due to the early tendency not to diagnose somatization disorder in male patients. Nevertheless, with a 5 to 1 female-to-male ratio, the lifetime prevalence of somatization disorder among women in the general population may be 1 or 2 percent; it is not an uncommon disorder. Among patients in the offices of general practitioners and family practitioners, as many as 5 to 10 percent of patients may meet the diagnostic criteria for somatization disorder. The disorder is inversely related to social position, occurring most often among little-educated and poor patients. Somatization disorder is defined as beginning before age 30; it most often begins during a person's teens.

Several studies have noted that somatization disorder commonly coexists with other mental disorders. About two thirds of all patients with somatization disorder have identifiable psychiatric symptoms, and as many as half of the patients with somatization disorder have other mental disorders. Commonly associated personality traits or personality disorders are those characterized by avoidant, paranoid, self-defeating, and obsessive-compulsive features. Two disorders that are not more commonly seen in patients with somatization disorder than in the general population are bipolar I disorder and substance abuse.

## Etiology

**Psychosocial factors.** The cause of somatization disorder is unknown. Psychosocial formulations of the cause

**Table 17–1**
**Clinical Features of Somatoform Disorders**

| Diagnosis | Clinical Presentation | Demographic and Epidemiological Features | Diagnostic Features | Management Strategy | Prognosis | Associated Disturbances | Primary Differential Presentation | Psychological Processes Contributing to Symptoms | Motivation for Symptom Production |
|---|---|---|---|---|---|---|---|---|---|
| Somatization disorder | Polysymptomatic Recurrent and chronic Sickly by history | Young age Female predominance 20 to 1 Familial pattern 5–10% incidence in primary care populations | Review of systems profusely positive Multiple clinical contacts Polysurgical | Therapeutic alliance Regular appointments Crisis intervention | Poor to fair | Histrionic personality Antisocial personality disorder Alcohol and other substance abuse Many life problems Conversion disorder | Physical disease Depression | Unconscious Cultural and developmental | Unconscious psychological factors |
| Conversion disorder | Monosymptomatic Mostly acute Simulates disease | Highly prevalent Female predominance Young age Rural and low social class Little-educated and psychologically unsophisticated | Simulation incompatible with known physiological mechanisms or anatomy | Suggestion and persuasion Multiple techniques | Excellent except in chronic conversion disorder | Alcohol and other substance dependence Antisocial personality disorder Somatization disorder Histrionic personality disorder | Depression Schizophrenia Neurological disease | Unconscious Psychological stress or conflict may be present | Unconscious psychological factors |
| Hypochondriasis | Disease concern or preoccupation | Previous physical disease Middle or old age Male-female ratio equal | Disease conviction amplifies symptoms Obsessional | Document symptoms Psychosocial review Psychotherapeutic | Fair to good Waxes and wanes | Obsessive-compulsive personality disorder Depressive and anxiety disorders | Depression Physical disease Personality disorder Delusional disorder | Unconscious Stress— bereavement Developmental factors | Unconscious psychological factors |
| Body dysmorphic disorder | Subjective feelings of ugliness or concern with body defect | Adolescence or young adult ? Female predominance Largely unknown | Pervasive bodily concerns | Therapeutic alliance Stress management Psychotherapies Antidepressant medications | Unknown | Anorexia nervosa Psychosocial distress Avoidant or obsessive-compulsive personality disorder | Delusional disorder Depressive disorders Somatization disorder | Unconscious Self-esteem factors | Unconscious psychological factors |
| Pain disorder | Pain syndrome simulated | Female predominance 2 to 1 Older: 4th or 5th decade Familial pattern Up to 40% of pain populations | Simulation or intensity incompatible with known physiological mechanisms or anatomy | Therapeutic alliance Redefine goals of treatment Antidepressant medications | Guarded, variable | Depressive disorders Alcohol and other substance abuse Dependent or histrionic personality disorder | Depression Psychophysiological Physical disease Malingering and disability syndrome | Unconscious Acute stressor and developmental Physical trauma may predispose | Unconscious psychological factors |

involve interpretations of the symptoms as a type of social communication, the result of which is to avoid obligations (for example, going to a job one does not like), to express emotions (for example, anger at one's spouse), or to symbolize a feeling or a belief (for example, a pain in one's guts). Strict psychoanalytic interpretations of symptoms rest on the hypothesis that the symptoms are substitutions for repressed instinctual impulses.

A behavioral perspective on somatization disorder emphasizes that parental teaching, parental example, and ethnic mores may teach some children to somatize more than do others. In addition, some patients with somatization disorder come from unstable homes and have been physically abused. Social, cultural, and ethnic factors may also be involved in the development of symptoms in somatization disorder.

**Biological factors.** Some studies point to a neuropsychological basis for somatization disorder. Those studies propose that the patients have characteristic attention and cognitive impairments that result in the faulty perception and assessment of somatosensory inputs. The reported impairments include excessive distractibility, inability to habituate to repetitive stimuli, the grouping of cognitive constructs on an impressionistic basis, partial and circumstantial associations, and lack of selectivity, as indicated in some studies of evoked potentials. A limited number of brain-imaging studies have reported decreased metabolism in the frontal lobes and in the nondominant hemisphere.

Genetic data indicate that, in at least some families, the transmission of somatization disorder has some genetic components. The data indicate that somatization disorder tends to run in families, occurring in 10 to 20 percent of the first-degree female relatives of somatization disorder patients. Within those families, first-degree male relatives are prone to substance abuse and antisocial personality disorder. One study also reported a concordance rate of 29 percent in monozygotic twins and 10 percent in dizygotic twins, thus indicating a genetic effect.

One new area of basic neuroscience research that may be relevant to somatization disorder and other somatoform disorders concerns the cytokines. Cytokines are messenger molecules that the immune system uses to communicate within itself and to communicate with the nervous system, including the brain. Examples of cytokines are interleukins, tumor necrosis factor, and interferons. Some preliminary experiments indicate that the cytokines may help cause some of the nonspecific symptoms of disease, especially infections, such as hypersomnia, anorexia, fatigue, and depression. Although no data yet support the hypothesis, abnormal regulation of the cytokine system may result in some of the symptoms seen in somatoform disorders.

## Diagnosis

DSM-IV simplifies the diagnostic criteria presented in DSM-III-R. For the diagnosis of somatoform disorder, DSM-IV requires the onset of the symptoms before age 30 (Table 17–2). During the course of the disorder, the patient must have complained of at least four pain symptoms, two gastrointestinal symptoms, one sexual symptom, and one pseudoneurological symptom, none of which is completely explained by physical or laboratory examinations.

## Clinical Features

Patients with somatization disorder have many somatic complaints and long, complicated medical histories. Nausea and vomiting (other than during pregnancy), difficulty in swallowing, pain in the arms and the legs, shortness of breath unrelated to exertion, amnesia, and complications of pregnancy and menstruation are among the most common symptoms. The belief that one has been sickly most of one's life is also common.

Psychological distress and interpersonal problems are prominent; anxiety and depression are the most prevalent psychiatric conditions. Suicide threats are common, but

**Table 17–2**
**Diagnostic Criteria for Somatization Disorder**

A. A history of many physical complaints beginning before age 30 years that occur over a period of several years and result in treatment being sought or significant impairment in social, occupational, or other important areas of functioning.

B. Each of the following criteria must have been met, with individual symptoms occurring at any time during the course of the disturbance:

(1) *four pain symptoms*: a history of pain related to at least four different sites or functions (e.g., head, abdomen, back, joints, extremities, chest, rectum, during menstruation, during sexual intercourse, or during urination)

(2) *two gastrointestinal symptoms*: a history of at least two gastrointestinal symptoms other than pain (e.g., nausea, bloating, vomiting other than during pregnancy, diarrhea, or intolerance of several different foods)

(3) *one sexual symptom*: a history of at least one sexual or reproductive symptom other than pain (e.g., sexual indifference, erectile or ejaculatory dysfunction, irregular menses, excessive menstrual bleeding, vomiting throughout pregnancy)

(4) *one pseudoneurological symptom*: a history of at least one symptom or deficit suggesting a neurological condition not limited to pain (conversion symptoms such as impaired coordination or balance, paralysis or localized weakness, difficulty swallowing or lump in throat, aphonia, urinary retention, hallucinations, loss of touch or pain sensation, double vision, blindness, deafness, seizures; dissociative symptoms such as amnesia; or loss of consciousness other than fainting)

C. Either (1) or (2):

(1) after appropriate investigation, each of the symptoms in criterion B cannot be fully explained by a known general medical condition or the direct effects of a substance (e.g., the effects of injury, medication, drugs, or alcohol)

(2) when there is a related general medical condition, the physical complaints or resulting social or occupational impairment are in excess of what would be expected from the history, physical examination, or laboratory findings

D. The symptoms are not intentionally feigned or produced (as in factitious disorder or malingering).

Table from DSM-IV, *Diagnostic and Statistical Manual of Mental Disorders*, ed 4. Copyright American Psychiatric Association, Washington, 1994. Used with permission.

actual suicide is rare. If suicide does occur, it is often associated with substance abuse. The patients' medical histories are often circumstantial, vague, imprecise, inconsistent, and disorganized. The patients classically but not always describe their complaints in a dramatic, emotional, and exaggerated fashion, with vivid and colorful language. Such patients may confuse temporal sequences and cannot clearly distinguish current symptoms from past symptoms. Female patients with somatization disorder may dress in an exhibitionistic manner. The patients may be perceived as dependent, self-centered, hungry for admiration or praise, and manipulative.

Somatization disorder is commonly associated with other mental disorders, including major depressive disorder, personality disorders, substance-related disorders, generalized anxiety disorder, and phobias. The combination of those disorders and the chronic symptoms result in an increased incidence of marital, occupational, and social problems. A clinical case reported by Arthur J. Barsky, M.D., follows:

A 29-year-old mother of two requested medical clearance for impending surgery for cysts in her breasts. She described the cysts as rapidly enlarging and unbearably painful. While drawing attention to her breasts, she noted, "They are so large and so tender to the touch. And I just can't have relations— forget that."

She also had disabling back pain that spread up and down her spine and made her legs give out on her suddenly, causing her to fall. When discussing that symptom, she winced visibly, adding: "Oh, there it goes; my back keeps clicking. The pain is so severe it affects me with my kids. Pain like that will make anyone into a beast." (She had previously been suspected of child abuse.) She also complained of dyspnea and a dry cough that prevented her walking uphill.

Her medical history began at menarche with dysmenorrhea and menorrhagia. At 18 she had exploratory surgery for a possible ovarian cyst and subsequently underwent another operation for suspected abdominal adhesions. She also had a history of recurrent urinary tract symptoms, although no organisms were ever clearly documented, and she had a normal workup for "an enlarged thyroid". At various times she had received the diagnoses of spastic colon, migraine, and endometriosis.

Two marriages, both to alcoholic and abusive men who refused to pay child support, had ended in divorce. She had lost several clerical jobs because of excessive absences. During the periods when she felt worst, she spent most of the day at home in a bathrobe while her relatives cared for her children. She had a history of narcotic dependence and claimed that she began using analgesics for her back pain and then, "I overdid it."

The physical examination at the time of her visit revealed inconsistencies in the breast tissue but no frank masses, and mammography findings were normal.

## Differential Diagnosis

The clinician must always rule out nonpsychiatric medical conditions that may explain the patient's symptoms. A number of medical disorders often present with nonspecific, transient abnormalities in the same age group. Those medical disorders include multiple sclerosis, myasthenia gravis, systemic lupus erythematosus, acquired immune deficiency syndrome (AIDS), acute intermittent porphyria, hyperparathyroidism, hyperthyroidism, and chronic systemic infections. The onset of multiple somatic symptoms in patients over 40 should be presumed to be caused by a nonpsychiatric medical condition until an exhaustive medical workup has been completed.

Many mental disorders are considered in the differential diagnosis, which is made complicated by the observation that at least 50 percent of patients with somatization disorder have a coexisting mental disorder. Major depressive disorder, generalized anxiety disorder, and schizophrenia may all present with an initial complaint that focuses on somatic symptoms. In all those disorders, however, the symptoms of depression, anxiety, or psychosis eventually predominate over the somatic complaints. Although patients with panic disorder may complain of many somatic symptoms related to their panic attacks, those patients are not bothered by somatic symptoms in between panic attacks.

Among the other somatoform disorders, hypochondriasis, conversion disorder, and pain disorder need to be distinguished from somatization disorder. Hypochondriasis is characterized by the false belief that one has a specific disease, in contrast to somatization disorder, which is characterized by concern with many symptoms. The symptoms of conversion disorder are limited to one or two neurological symptoms, rather than the wide-ranging symptoms of somatization disorder. Pain disorder is limited to one or two complaints of pain symptoms.

## Course and Prognosis

Somatization disorder is a chronic and often debilitating disorder. By definition, the symptoms should have begun before age 30 and been present for several years. Episodes of increased symptom severity and the development of new symptoms are thought to last six to nine months and may be separated by less symptomatic periods lasting 9 to 12 months. Rarely, however, does a patient with somatization disorder go for more than a year without seeking some medical attention. There is often an association between periods of increased or new stress and the exacerbation of somatic symptoms.

## Treatment

Somatization disorder patients are best treated when they have a single identified physician as the primary caretaker. When more than one clinician is involved, the patient has increased opportunities to express somatic complaints. The primary physician should see the patient during regularly scheduled visits, usually at monthly intervals. The visits should be relatively brief; although a partial physical examination should be conducted to respond to each new somatic complaint, additional laboratory and diagnostic procedures should generally be avoided. Once somatization disorder has been diagnosed, the treating physician should listen to the somatic complaints as emotional expressions, rather than as medical complaints. However, patients with somatization disorder can also have bona fide physical illnesses; therefore, physicians must always use their judgment about what symptoms to work up and to what extent. A reasonable long-range strategy for a primary care physician who is treating a patient with somatization disorder is to increase the patient's awareness of the possibility that psychological factors are involved in the symptoms until the patient is willing to see a mental health clinician, probably a psychiatrist, on a regular basis.

Psychotherapy, both individual and group, decreases somatization disorder patients' personal health care expenditures by 50 percent, largely by decreasing their rates of hospitalization. In psychotherapy settings, patients are helped to cope with their symptoms, to express underlying emotions, and to develop alternative strategies for expressing their feelings.

Giving psychotropic medications whenever somatization disorder coexists with a mood or anxiety disorder is always a risk, but psychopharmacological treatment, as well as psychotherapeutic treatment, of the coexisting disorder is indicated. Medication must be monitored, because somatization disorder patients tend to use drugs erratically and unreliably. In patients without coexisting mental disorders, few available data indicate that pharmacological treatment is effective.

## CONVERSION DISORDER

DSM-IV defines conversion disorder as a disorder characterized by the presence of one or more neurological symptoms (for example, paralysis, blindness, and paresthesias) that cannot be explained by a known neurological or medical disorder. In addition, the diagnosis requires that psychological factors be associated with the initiation or the exacerbation of the symptoms.

The syndrome now known as conversion disorder was originally combined with the syndrome now known as somatization disorder and generally referred to as hysteria, conversion reaction, or dissociative reaction. Briquet and Jean-Martin Charcot contributed to the development of the concept of conversion disorder by noting the influence of heredity on the symptom and the common association with a traumatic event. The term "conversion" was introduced by Sigmund Freud, who hypothesized, on the basis of his work with Anna O., that the symptoms of conversion disorder reflect unconscious conflicts. In 1980 DSM-III officially placed polysymptomatic somatic complaints in the category of somatization disorder and symptoms limited to neurological disorders in the category of conversion disorder. Although DSM-III-R introduced nonneurological symptoms to the conversion diagnosis category, DSM-IV returns to the convention of limiting the diagnosis to one involving neurological symptoms.

### Epidemiology

The prevalence of some symptoms of conversion disorder that are not of sufficient severity to warrant the diagnosis may occur in as many as a third of the general population sometime during their lives. One community survey reported that the annual incidence of conversion disorder was 22 per 100,000. Among specific populations, the occurrence of conversion disorder may be higher than that, perhaps making conversion disorder the most common somatoform disorder in some populations. Several studies have reported that 5 to 15 percent of psychiatric consultations in a general hospital and 25 to 30 percent of admissions to a Veterans Affairs hospital involve patients with conversion disorder diagnoses.

The ratio of women to men among adult patients is at least 2 to 1 and as much as 5 to 1; children have an even higher predominance of girls. Men with conversion disorder have often been involved in occupational or military accidents. Conversion disorder can have its onset at any age, from childhood to old age, but it is most common in adolescents and young adults. Data indicate that conversion disorder is most common among rural populations, little-educated persons, those with low intelligence quotients, persons in low socioeconomic groups, and military personnel who have been exposed to combat situations. Conversion disorder is commonly associated with comorbid diagnoses of major depressive disorder, anxiety disorders, and schizophrenia.

### Etiology

**Psychoanalytic factors.** According to psychoanalytic theory, conversion disorder is caused by the repression of unconscious intrapsychic conflict and the conversion of anxiety into a physical symptom. The conflict is between an instinctual impulse (for example, aggressive or sexual) and the prohibitions against its expression. The symptoms allow the partial expression of the forbidden wish or urge but disguise it, so that the patients need not consciously confront their unacceptable impulses; that is, the conversion disorder symptom has a symbolic relation to the unconscious conflict. The conversion disorder symptoms also enable the patients to communicate that they need special consideration and special treatment. Such symptoms may function as a nonverbal means of controlling or manipulating others.

**Biological factors.** Increasing data implicate biological and neuropsychological factors in the development of conversion disorder symptoms. Preliminary brain-imaging studies have found hypometabolism of the dominant hemisphere and hypermetabolism of the nondominant hemisphere and have implicated impaired hemispheric communication in the cause of conversion disorder. The symptoms may be caused by an excessive cortical arousal that sets off negative feedback loops between the cerebral cortex and the brainstem reticular formation. Elevated levels of corticofugal output, in turn, inhibit the patient's awareness of bodily sensation, which in some conversion disorder patients may explain the observed sensory deficits. In some conversion disorder patients, neuropsychological tests reveal subtle cerebral impairments in verbal communication, memory, vigilance, affective incongruity, and attention.

### Diagnosis

DSM-IV narrows one of the diagnostic criteria for conversion disorder (Table 17–3) that were in DSM-III and DSM-III-R back into a diagnostic criterion that is similar to one found in the second edition (DSM-II). Specifically, DSM-IV limits the diagnosis of conversion disorder to those symptoms that affect a voluntary motor or sensory function—that is, neurological symptoms. Patients who met the DSM-III or DSM-III-R diagnostic criteria but who had nonneurological symptoms (for example, pseudo-

**Table 17–3**
**Diagnostic Criteria for Conversion Disorder**

A. One or more symptoms or deficits affecting voluntary motor or sensory function that suggest a neurological or other general medical condition.

B. Psychological factors are judged to be associated with the symptom or deficit because the initiation or exacerbation of the symptom or deficit is preceded by conflicts or other stressors.

C. The symptom or deficit is not intentionally produced or feigned (as in factitious disorder or malingering).

D. The symptom or deficit cannot, after appropriate investigation, be fully explained by a general medical condition, or by the direct effects of a substance, or as a culturally sanctioned behavior or experience.

E. The symptom or deficit causes clinically significant distress or impairment in social, occupational, or other important areas of functioning or warrants medical evaluation.

F. The symptom or deficit is not limited to pain or sexual dysfunction, does not occur exclusively during the course of somatization disorder, and is not better accounted for by another mental disorder.

*Specify* type of symptom or deficit:
 **with motor symptom or deficit**
 **with sensory symptom or deficit**
 **with seizures or convulsions**
 **with mixed presentation**

Table from DSM-IV, *Diagnostic and Statistical Manual of Mental Disorders,* ed 4. Copyright American Psychiatric Association, Washington, 1994. Used with permission.

cyesis) are now classified as having somatoform disorder not otherwise specified. The physician is not able to explain the neurological symptoms solely on the basis of any known neurological condition.

The diagnosis of conversion disorder requires that the clinician find a necessary and critical association between the cause of the neurological symptom and psychological factors, although the symptom cannot be the result of malingering or factitious disorder. The diagnosis of conversion disorder also excludes symptoms of pain and sexual dysfunction and symptoms that occur only in somatization disorder. DSM-IV allows the specification of the type of symptom or deficit seen in conversion disorder (Table 17–3).

## Clinical Features

Paralysis, blindness, and mutism are the most common conversion disorder symptoms. Conversion disorder may be most commonly associated with passive-aggressive, dependent, antisocial, and histrionic personality disorders. Depressive and anxiety disorder symptoms can often accompany the symptoms of conversion disorder, and affected patients are at risk for suicide.

**Sensory symptoms.** In conversion disorder, anesthesia and paresthesia are common, especially of the extremities. All sensory modalities can be involved, and the distribution of the disturbance is usually inconsistent with that of either central or peripheral neurological disease. Thus, one may see the characteristic stocking-and-glove anesthesia of the hands or the feet or the hemianesthesia of the body beginning precisely along the midline.

Conversion disorder symptoms may involve the organs of special sense, producing deafness, blindness, and tunnel vision. Those symptoms may be unilateral or bilateral. However, neurological evaluation reveals intact sensory pathways. In conversion disorder blindness, for example, patients walk around without collisions or self-injury, their pupils react to light, and their cortical evoked potentials are normal.

**Motor symptoms.** The motor symptoms include abnormal movements, gait, disturbance, weakness, and paralysis. Gross rhythmical tremors, choreiform movements, tics, and jerks may be present. The movements generally worsen when attention is called to them. One gait disturbance seen in conversion disorder is astasia-abasia, which is a wildly ataxic, staggering gait accompanied by gross, irregular, jerky truncal movements and thrashing and waving arm movements. Patients with the symptoms rarely fall; if they do, they are generally not injured.

Other common motor disturbances are paralysis and paresis involving one, two, or all four limbs, although the distribution of the involved muscles does not conform to the neural pathways. Reflexes remain normal; the patient has no fasciculations or muscle atrophy (except after long-standing conversion paralysis); electromyography findings are normal.

**Seizure symptoms.** Pseudoseizures are another symptom in conversion disorder. The clinician may find it difficult by clinical observation alone to differentiate a pseudoseizure from an actual seizure. Moreover, about a third of the patients who have pseudoseizures also have a coexisting epileptic disorder. Tongue biting, urinary incontinence, and injuries after falling can occur in pseudoseizures, although those symptoms are generally not present. Pupillary and gag reflexes are retained after pseudoseizure, and the patient has no postseizure increase in prolactin concentrations.

**Other associated features.** Several psychological symptoms have also been associated with conversion disorder.

PRIMARY GAIN. Patients achieve primary gain by keeping internal conflicts outside their awareness. The symptom has symbolic value in that it represents the unconscious psychological conflict.

SECONDARY GAIN. Patients accrue tangible advantages and benefits as a result of their being sick, such as being excused from obligations and difficult life situations, receiving support and assistance that might not otherwise be forthcoming, and controlling other people's behavior.

LA BELLE INDIFFÉRENCE. *La belle indifférence* is the patient's inappropriately cavalier attitude toward a serious symptom; that is, the patient seems to be unconcerned about what appears to be a major impairment. That bland indifference may be lacking in some conversion disorder patients; it is also seen in some seriously ill medical patients who develop a stoic attitude. The presence or the absence of *la belle indifférence* is an inaccurate measure of whether a patient has conversion disorder.

IDENTIFICATION. Conversion disorder patients may unconsciously model their symptoms on those of someone important to them. For example, a parent or a person who has recently died may serve as a model for conversion disorder. It is common during pathological grief reaction for the bereaved person to have the symptoms of the deceased.

A 46-year-old woman was referred by her husband's psychiatrist for consultation. In the course of discussing certain marital conflicts that the husband was having with his wife, he had described attacks of dizziness that his wife experienced and that left her incapacitated.

In consultation the wife described being overcome with feelings of extreme dizziness, accompanied by slight nausea, four or five nights a week. During the attacks the room around her would take on a "shimmering" appearance, and she would have the feeling that she was floating and unable to keep her balance. Inexplicably, the attacks almost always occurred at about 4 PM. She usually had to lie down on a couch and often did not feel better until 7 or 8 PM. After recovering, she generally spent the rest of the evening watching television; more often than not, she fell asleep in the living room, not going to bed in the bedroom until 2 or 3 AM.

The patient had been pronounced physically fit by her internist, a neurologist, and an ear, nose, and throat specialist on more than one occasion. Hypoglycemia had been ruled out by glucose tolerance tests.

When asked about her marriage, the patient described her husband as a tyrant, frequently demanding and verbally abusive of her and their four children. She admitted that she dreaded his arrival home from work each day, knowing that he would comment that the house was a mess and the dinner, if prepared, not to his liking. Since the onset of her attacks, when she was unable to make dinner, he and the four children would go to McDonald's or the local pizza parlor. After that he would settle in to watch a ball game on television in the bedroom, and their conversation was minimal. In spite of their troubles, the patient claimed that she loved and needed her husband very much.

## Differential Diagnosis

One of the major problems in diagnosing conversion disorder is the difficulty in definitively ruling out a medical disorder. Concomitant nonpsychiatric medical disorders are common in hospitalized patients with conversion disorder, and evidence of a current or prior neurological disorder or of a systemic disease affecting the brain has been reported in 18 to 64 percent of such patients. An estimated 25 to 50 percent of patients classified as having conversion disorder eventually receive diagnoses of neurological or nonpsychiatric medical disorders that could have caused their earlier symptoms. Therefore, a thorough medical and neurological workup is essential in all cases. If the symptoms can be resolved by suggestion, hypnosis, or parenteral amobarbital (Amytal) or lorazepam (Ativan), they are probably the result of conversion disorder.

Neurological disorders (such as dementia and other degenerative diseases), brain tumors, and basal ganglia disease must be considered in the differential diagnosis. For example, weakness may be confused with myasthenia gravis, polymyositis, acquired myopathies, or multiple sclerosis. Optic neuritis may be misdiagnosed as conversion disorder blindness. Other diseases that may cause confusing symptoms are Guillain-Barré syndrome, Creutzfeldt-Jakob disease, periodic paralysis, and early neurological manifestations of AIDS. Conversion disorder symptoms occur in schizophrenia, depressive disorders, and anxiety disorders; however, those other disorders are

associated with their own distinct symptoms that eventually make differential diagnosis possible.

Sensorimotor symptoms also occur in somatization disorder. But somatization disorder is a chronic illness that begins early in life and includes symptoms in many other organ systems. In hypochondriasis the patient has no actual loss or distortion of function; the somatic complaints are chronic and are not limited to neurological symptoms, and the characteristic hypochondriacal attitudes and beliefs are present. If the patient's symptoms are limited to pain, pain disorder can be diagnosed. The patient whose complaints are limited to sexual function is classified as having a sexual dysfunction, rather than conversion disorder.

In both malingering and factitious disorder, the symptoms are under conscious, voluntary control. The malingerer's history is usually more inconsistent and contradictory than is the conversion disorder patient's history, and the malingerer's fraudulent behavior is clearly goal-directed.

## Course and Prognosis

The vast majority, perhaps 90 to 100 percent, of patients with conversion disorder have their initial symptoms resolve in a few days or less than a month. A reported 75 percent of patients may not experience another episode, but 25 percent of patients may have additional episodes during periods of stress. Associated with a good prognosis are a sudden onset, an easily identifiable stressor, good premorbid adjustment, no comorbid psychiatric or medical disorders, and no ongoing litigation. The longer the conversion disorder symptoms are present, the worse the prognosis is. As mentioned above, 25 to 50 percent of patients may later have neurological disorders or nonpsychiatric medical conditions affecting the nervous system. Therefore, patients with conversion disorder must have complete medical and neurological evaluations at the time of the diagnosis.

## Treatment

Resolution of the conversion disorder symptom is usually spontaneous, although resolution is probably facilitated by insight-oriented supportive or behavior therapy; the most important feature of the therapy is a caring and authoritative therapeutic relationship. With patients who are resistant to the idea of psychotherapy, the physician can suggest that the psychotherapy will focus on issues of stress and coping. Telling such patients that their symptoms are imaginary often makes the symptoms worse, rather than better. Hypnosis, anxiolytics, and behavioral relaxation exercises are effective in some cases. Parenteral amobarbital or lorazepam may be helpful in obtaining additional historical information, especially if a traumatic event was recently experienced. Psychodynamic approaches include psychoanalysis and insight-oriented psychotherapy, in which patients explore intrapsychic conflicts and the symbolism of the conversion disorder symptom. Brief and direct forms of short-term psychotherapy have also been used to treat conversion disorder. The longer that conversion disorder patients have been in the sick role and the more they have regressed, the more difficult the treatment is.

# HYPOCHONDRIASIS

The term "hypochondriasis" is derived from the old medical term "hypochondrium," which means below the ribs, and reflects the common abdominal complaints that many patients with the disorder have. Hypochondriasis results from patients' unrealistic or inaccurate interpretations of physical symptoms or sensations, leading to preoccupations and fear that they have serious diseases, even though no known medical causes can be found. The patients' preoccupations result in significant distress to the patients and impair their ability to function in their personal, social, and occupational roles.

## Epidemiology

One recent study reported a six-month prevalence of 4 to 6 percent in a general medical clinic population. Men and women are equally affected by hypochondriasis. Although the onset of symptoms can occur at any age, the onset is most common between 20 and 30 years of age. Some evidence indicates that the diagnosis is more common among blacks than among whites, but social position, educational level, and marital status do not appear to affect the diagnosis.

## Etiology

In the diagnostic criteria for hypochondriasis, DSM-IV notes that the symptoms reflect a misinterpretation of bodily symptoms. A reasonable body of data indicates that hypochondriacal persons augment and amplify their somatic sensations; they have lower than usual thresholds for and a lower tolerance of physical discomfort. For example, what a person normally perceives as abdominal pressure, the hypochondriacal person experiences as abdominal pain. The hypochondriacal person may focus on bodily sensations, misinterpret them, and become alarmed by them because of a faulty cognitive scheme.

A second theory is that hypochondriasis is understandable on the basis of a social learning model. The symptoms of hypochondriasis are viewed as a request for admission to the sick role made by a person who is facing seemingly insurmountable and insolvable problems. The sick role offers a way out, because the sick patient is allowed to avoid noxious obligations and to postpone unwelcome challenges and is excused from usually expected duties.

A third theory regarding the cause of hypochondriasis is that it is a variant form of other mental disorders. The disorders most frequently hypothesized to be related to hypochondriasis are depressive disorders and anxiety disorders. An estimated 80 percent of patients with hypochondriasis may have coexisting depressive disorders or anxiety disorders. The patients who meet the diagnostic criteria for hypochondriasis may be a somatizing subtype of those other disorders.

A fourth school of thought regarding hypochondriasis

is the psychodynamic school, which posits that aggressive and hostile wishes toward others are transferred (through repression and displacement) into physical complaints. The anger of hypochondriacal patients originates in past disappointments, rejections, and losses, but the patients express their anger in the present by soliciting the help and concern of other people and then rejecting them as ineffective. Hypochondriasis is also viewed as a defense against guilt, a sense of innate badness, an expression of low self-esteem, and a sign of excessive self-concern. Pain and somatic suffering thus becomes a means of atonement and expiation (undoing) and can be experienced as deserved punishment for past wrongdoing (either real or imaginary) and the sense that one is wicked and sinful.

## Diagnosis

The DSM-IV diagnostic criteria for hypochondriasis require that the patient be preoccupied with the false belief that he or she has a serious disease and that the false belief be based on a misinterpretation of physical signs or sensations (Table 17–4). The criteria require that the belief last at least six months, despite the absence of pathological findings on medical and neurological examinations. The diagnostic criteria also require that the belief not have the intensity of a delusion (more appropriately diagnosed as delusional disorder) and that it not be restricted to distress about appearance (more appropriately diagnosed as body dysmorphic disorder). However, the symptoms of hypochondriasis are required to be of an intensity that causes emotional distress or causes impairment in the patient's ability to function in important areas of life. The clinician may specify the presence of poor insight if the patient does

**Table 17–4**
**Diagnostic Criteria for Hypochondriasis**

A. Preoccupation with fears of having, or the idea that one has, a serious disease based on the person's misinterpretation of bodily symptoms.

B. The preoccupation persists despite appropriate medical evaluation and reassurance.

C. The belief in criterion A is not of delusional intensity (as in delusional disorder, somatic type) and is not restricted to a circumscribed concern about appearance (as in body dysmorphic disorder).

D. The preoccupation causes clinically significant distress or impairment in social, occupational, or other important areas of functioning.

E. The duration of the disturbance is at least 6 months.

F. The preoccupation is not better accounted for by generalized anxiety disorder, obsessive-compulsive disorder, panic disorder, a major depressive episode, separation anxiety, or another somatoform disorder.

*Specify* if:
   **with poor insight:** if, for most of the time during the current episode, the person does not recognize that the concern about having a serious illness is excessive or unreasonable

Table from DSM-IV, *Diagnostic and Statistical Manual of Mental Disorders,* ed 4. Copyright American Psychiatric Association, Washington, 1994. Used with permission.

not consistently recognize that the concerns about disease are excessive.

## Clinical Features

Hypochondriacal patients believe that they have a serious disease that has not yet been detected, and they cannot be persuaded to the contrary. Hypochondriacal patients may maintain a belief that they have one particular disease, or, as time progresses, they may change their belief about the specific disease. The conviction persists despite negative laboratory results, the benign course of the alleged disease over time, and appropriate reassurances from physicians. But the belief is not so fixed that it is a delusion. Hypochondriasis is often accompanied by symptoms of depression and anxiety, and it commonly coexists with a depressive or anxiety disorder.

Although DSM-IV specifies that the symptoms must be present for at least six months, transient hypochondriacal states can occur after major stresses, most commonly the death or serious illness of someone important to the patient or a serious (perhaps life-threatening) illness that has been resolved but that leaves the patient temporarily hypochondriacal in its wake. Such hypochondriacal states that last fewer than six months should be diagnosed as somatoform disorder not otherwise specified. Transient hypochondriacal responses to external stress generally remit when the stress is resolved, but they can become chronic if reinforced by people in the patient's social system or by health professionals.

## Differential Diagnosis

Hypochondriasis must be differentiated from nonpsychiatric medical conditions, especially disorders that can present with symptoms that are not necessarily easily diagnosed. Such diseases include AIDS, endocrinopathies, myasthenia gravis, multiple sclerosis, degenerative diseases of the nervous system, systemic lupus erythematosus, and occult neoplastic disorders.

Hypochondriasis is differentiated from somatization disorder by the emphasis in hypochondriasis on fear of having a disease and emphasis in somatization disorder on concern about many symptoms. A subtle distinction is that patients with hypochondriasis usually complain about fewer symptoms than do patients with somatization disorder. Somatization disorder usually has an onset before age 30, whereas hypochondriasis has a less specific age of onset. The somatization disorder patient is more likely to be a woman than is the patient with hypochondriasis, which has an equal distribution of men to women.

Hypochondriasis must also be differentiated from the other somatoform disorders. Conversion disorder is acute and generally transient and usually involves a symptom, rather than a particular disease. The presence or the absence of *la belle indifférence* is an unreliable feature with which to differentiate the two conditions. Pain disorder is chronic, as is hypochondriasis, but the symptoms are limited to complaints of pain. Body dysmorphic disorder patients wish to appear normal but believe that others notice

that they are not, whereas hypochondriacal patients seek out attention for their presumed diseases.

Hypochondriacal symptoms can also occur in depressive disorders and anxiety disorders. If a patient meets the full diagnostic criteria for both hypochondriasis and another major mental disorder, such as major depressive disorder or generalized anxiety disorder, the patient should receive both diagnoses, unless the hypochondriacal symptoms occur only during episodes of the other mental disorder. Patients with panic disorder may initially complain that they are affected by some disease (for example, heart trouble), but careful questioning during the medical history usually uncovers the classic symptoms of a panic attack. Delusional hypochondriacal beliefs occur in schizophrenia and other psychotic disorders but can be differentiated from hypochondriasis by their delusional intensity and by the presence of other psychotic symptoms. In addition, schizophrenic patients' somatic delusions tend to be bizarre, idiosyncratic, and out of keeping with their cultural milieus.

Hypochondriasis is distinguished from factitious disorder with physical symptoms and from malingering in that hypochondriacal patients actually experience and do not simulate the symptoms they report.

## Course and Prognosis

The course of hypochondriasis is usually episodic; the episodes last from months to years and are separated by equally long quiescent periods. There may be an obvious association between exacerbations of hypochondriacal symptoms and psychosocial stressors. Although well-conducted large outcome studies have not yet been reported, an estimated one third to one half of all hypochondriasis patients eventually improve significantly. A good prognosis is associated with a high socioeconomic status, treatment-responsive anxiety or depression, the sudden onset of symptoms, the absence of a personality disorder, and the absence of a related nonpsychiatric medical condition. Most hypochondriacal children recover by late adolescence or early adulthood.

## Treatment

Hypochondriacal patients are usually resistant to psychiatric treatment. Some hypochondriacal patients accept psychiatric treatment if it takes place in a medical setting and focuses on stress reduction and education in coping with chronic illness. Among such patients, group psychotherapy is the modality of choice, in part because it provides the social support and social interaction that seems to reduce their anxiety. Individual insight-oriented psychotherapy may be useful, but it is generally not successful.

Frequent, regularly scheduled physical examinations are useful to reassure the patients that they are not being abandoned by their doctors and that their complaints are being taken seriously. However, invasive diagnostic and therapeutic procedures should be undertaken only when objective evidence calls for them. When possible, the clinician should refrain from treating equivocal or incidental physical examination findings.

Pharmacotherapy alleviates hypochondriacal symptoms only when the patient has an underlying drug-responsive condition, such as an anxiety disorder or major depressive disorder. When hypochondriasis is secondary to some other primary mental disorder, that disorder must be treated in its own right. When hypochondriasis is a transient situational reaction, the clinician must help patients cope with the stress without reinforcing their illness behavior and their use of the sick role as a solution to the problem.

# BODY DYSMORPHIC DISORDER

Body dysmorphic disorder is a preoccupation with an imagined bodily defect (for example, a misshapen nose) or an exaggerated distortion of a minimal or minor defect. For such as concern to be considered a mental disorder, the concern must cause the patient significant distress or be associated with impairment in the patient's personal, social, or occupational life.

The disorder was recognized and named dysmorphophobia more than 100 years ago. The disorder was recognized by Emil Kraepelin, who considered it a compulsive neurosis, and by Pierre Janet, who called it *obsession de la hontu de corps* (obsession with shame of the body). Freud wrote about the condition in his description of the Wolf-Man, who was excessively concerned about his nose. Although dysmorphophobia was widely recognized and studied in Europe, it was not until the publication of DSM-III in 1980 that dysmorphophobia, as an example of atypical somatoform disorder, was specifically mentioned in the United States diagnostic criteria. In DSM-III-R and DSM-IV, the condition is known as body dysmorphic disorder, because the DSM editors believed that the term "dysmorphophobia" inaccurately implied the presence of a behavioral pattern of phobic avoidance.

## Epidemiology

Body dysmorphic disorder is a poorly studied condition, partly because the patients are more likely to go to dermatologists, internists, or plastic surgeons than to psychiatrists. One study of a group of college students found that more than 50 percent of the students had at least some preoccupation with a particular aspect of their appearance and that, in about 25 percent of the students, the concern had at least some significant effect on their feelings and functioning. Although 25 percent is undoubtedly an overestimate, body dysmorphic disorder or a subsyndromal variant may be common. Another study of patients attending a plastic surgery clinic found that only 2 percent of those patients met the diagnostic criteria, thus indicating that patients with the complete diagnostic criteria may be rare.

Available data indicate that the most common age of onset is between 15 and 20 years and that women are somewhat more often affected than are men. Affected patients are also likely to be unmarried. Body dysmorphic disorder commonly coexists with other mental disorders. One study found that more than 90 percent of the body dysmorphic disorder patients had experienced a major depressive episode in their lifetimes; about 70 percent had had an anxiety disorder; and about 30 percent had had a psychotic disorder.

## Etiology

The cause of body dysmorphic disorder is unknown. The high comorbidity with depressive disorders, a higher-than-expected family history of mood disorders and obsessive-compulsive disorder, and the reported responsiveness of the condition to serotonin-specific drugs indicate that, in at least some patients, the pathophysiology of the disorder may involve serotonin and may be related to other mental disorders. There may be significant cultural or social effects on body dysmorphic disorder patients because of the emphasis on stereotyped concepts of beauty that may be emphasized in certain families and within the culture at large. In psychodynamic models, body dysmorphic disorder is seen as reflecting the displacement of a sexual or emotional conflict onto a nonrelated body part. Such an association occurs through the defense mechanisms of repression, dissociation, distortion, symbolization, and projection.

## Diagnosis

The DSM-IV diagnostic criteria for body dysmorphic disorder require a preoccupation with an imagined defect in appearance or an overemphasis on a slight defect (Table 17–5). The preoccupation causes the patient significant emotional distress or markedly impairs the patient's ability to function in important areas.

## Clinical Features

The most common concerns (Table 17–6) involve facial flaws, particularly those involving specific parts (for example, the nose). Sometimes the concern is vague and difficult to understand, such as extreme concern over a "scrunchy" chin. One study found that, on average, patients had concerns about four body regions during the course of the disorder. The body part of specific concern may change during the time the patient is affected with the disorder. Common associated symptoms include ideas or frank delusions of reference (usually regarding people's noticing the alleged body flaw), either excessive mirror

**Table 17–5**
**Diagnostic Criteria for Body Dysmorphic Disorder**

A. Preoccupation with an imagined defect in appearance. If a slight physical anomaly is present, the person's concern is markedly excessive.

B. The preoccupation causes clinically significant distress or impairment in social, occupational, or other important areas of functioning.

C. The preoccupation is not better accounted for by another mental disorder (e.g., dissatisfaction with body shape and size in anorexia nervosa).

**Table 17–6**
**Location of Imagined Defects in 30 Patients with Body Dysmorphic Disorder[a]**

| Location | N | % |
|---|---|---|
| Hair[b] | 19 | 63 |
| Nose | 15 | 50 |
| Skin[c] | 15 | 50 |
| Eyes | 8 | 27 |
| Head, face[d] | 6 | 20 |
| Overall body build, bone structure | 6 | 20 |
| Lips | 5 | 17 |
| Chin | 5 | 17 |
| Stomach, waist | 5 | 17 |
| Teeth | 4 | 13 |
| Legs, knees | 4 | 13 |
| Breasts, pectoral muscles | 3 | 10 |
| Ugly face (general) | 3 | 10 |
| Ears | 2 | 7 |
| Cheeks | 2 | 7 |
| Buttocks | 2 | 7 |
| Penis | 2 | 7 |
| Arms, wrists | 2 | 7 |
| Neck | 1 | 3 |
| Forehead | 1 | 3 |
| Facial muscles | 1 | 3 |
| Shoulders | 1 | 3 |
| Hips | 1 | 3 |

[a]Total is greater than 100% because most patients had "defects" in more than one location.
[b]Involved head hair in 15 cases, beard growth in two cases, and other body hair in three cases.
[c]Involved acne in seven cases, facial lines in three cases, and other skin concerns in seven cases.
[d]Involved concerns with shape in five cases and size in one case.
Table from K A Phillips, S L McElroy, P E Keck Jr., H G Pope, J I Hudson: Body dysmorphic disorder: 30 cases of imagined ugliness. Am J Psychiatry 150: 303, 1993.

checking or avoidance of reflective surfaces, and attempts to hide the presumed deformity (with makeup or clothing). The effects on a person's life can be significant; almost all affected patients avoid social and occupational exposure. As many as a third of the patients may be housebound by their concern about being ridiculed for their alleged deformities, and as many as a fifth of the affected patients attempt suicide. As previously mentioned, comorbid diagnoses of depressive disorders and anxiety disorders are common, and the patients may also have traits of obsessive-compulsive, schizoid, and narcissistic personality disorders.

The patient was a happily married 23-year-old investment counselor who had reluctantly agreed to see a psychiatrist, an old friend of her husband's. She told the psychiatrist that she did not think she needed to see a psychiatrist, because her problem was "these ugly lines on my forehead." The psychiatrist asked, "What lines?" The patient pointed to the frown lines above her nose, which to the psychiatrist seemed no more pronounced than they are on the foreheads of most people her age.

The patient continued: "It's horrible, isn't it? I mean, I don't have to be the most gorgeous girl on earth, but I also don't want to be disfigured."

The psychiatrist asked, "What makes you think it looks so awful? Everyone has those lines."

"C'mon. I appreciate your trying to make me feel better, but I can see what I look like."

"What *do* you look like?"

"It's horrible. Everybody notices. They make me look so old. I'm sure my husband is turned off. I don't know what I would ever do if he left me. I have started to wear all this heavy makeup to hide them, but try to hide something like this."

"Let me ask you this. Most of us are sensitive about our appearance, and sometimes we exaggerate some minor imperfection. Do you think you may be doing that?"

The patient sighed. "My husband has been saying the same thing. I think about that, and sometimes I can convince myself that I am too concerned about something that is really very minor. But then I go to the mirror, and there it is. Can't you help me convince my husband that I should see if a plastic surgeon can do something about it?"

"Before we get into that, how long have you been bothered by the lines?"

"I'm not sure, but I didn't pay any attention to it until a few months ago. A friend at work mentioned that she had seen a doctor for a bad sunburn and told me I had better be careful because my skin was so fair. I began looking in the mirror and kept noticing the lines."

The psychiatrist asked about other problems in the patient's life and learned that her concern with her appearance was not affecting her ability to work but that she had started to avoid social situations because she did not want people looking at her blemish. The patient acknowledged being upset and unhappy about her problem but denied having a persistently depressed mood or any associated symptoms of depression.

**Differential Diagnosis**

Distortions of body image occur in anorexia nervosa, gender identity disorders, and some specific types of brain damage (for example, neglect syndromes); body dysmorphic disorder should not be diagnosed in those situations. Body dysmorphic disorder also needs to be distinguished from normal concern about one's appearance. The differentiating feature is that in body dysmorphic disorder the person experiences significant emotional distress and functional impairment as a result of the concern. Although making the distinction between a strongly held idea and a delusion is difficult, if the perceived body defect is, in fact, of delusional intensity, the appropriate diagnosis is delusional disorder, somatic type. Other diagnostic considerations are narcissistic personality disorder, depressive disorders, obsessive-compulsive disorder, and schizophrenia. In narcissistic personality disorder, concern about a body part is only a minor feature in the general constellation of personality traits. In depressive disorders, schizophrenia, and obsessive-compulsive disorder, the other symptoms of those disorders usually evidence themselves in short order, even if the initial symptom is excessive concern regarding a body part.

**Course and Prognosis**

The onset of body dysmorphic disorder is usually gradual. An affected person may experience increasing concern over a particular body part until the person notices that functioning is being affected by the concern. At that point the person may seek medical or surgical help to address the presumed problem. The level of concern about the problem may wax and wane over time, although body dysmorphic disorder is generally a chronic disorder if left untreated.

## Treatment

Treatment of patients with body dysmorphic disorder with surgical, dermatological, dental, and other medical procedures to address the alleged defects is almost invariably unsuccessful. Although tricyclic drugs, monoamine oxidase inhibitors, and pimozide (Orap) have been reported to be useful in individual cases, a larger body of data indicate that serotonin-specific drugs—for example, clomipramine (Anafranil) and fluoxetine (Prozac)—are effective in reducing symptoms in at least 50 percent of patients. In any patient with a coexisting mental disorder, such as a depressive disorder or an anxiety disorder, the coexisting disorder should be treated with the appropriate pharmacotherapy and psychotherapy. How long treatment should be continued when the symptoms of body dysmorphic disorder have remitted is unknown.

## PAIN DISORDER

The primary symptom of pain disorder is the presence of pain in one or more sites that is not *fully* accounted for by a nonpsychiatric medical or neurological condition. The symptoms of pain are associated with emotional distress and functional impairment, and the disorder has a plausible causal relation with psychological factors. The disorder was called somatoform pain disorder in DSM-III-R, and it has also been referred to as psychogenic pain disorder, idiopathic pain disorder, and the euphemistic atypical pain disorder.

## Epidemiology

Pain is perhaps the most frequent complaint in medical practice. Intractable pain syndromes are also common. Low back pain has disabled an estimated 7 million Americans and accounts for more than 8 million physician office visits annually. Pain disorder is diagnosed twice as frequently in women as in men. The peak ages of onset are in the fourth and fifth decades, perhaps because the tolerance for pain declines with age. Pain disorder is most common in persons with blue-collar occupations, perhaps because of increased likelihood of job-related injuries. First-degree relatives of pain disorder patients have an increased likelihood for the same disorder, thus indicating the possibility of a genetic inheritance or behavioral mechanisms in the transmission of the disorder. Depressive disorders, anxiety disorders, and substance abuse are also more common in the families of pain disorder patients than in the general population.

## Etiology

**Psychodynamic factors.** Patients who experience aches and pains in their bodies without identifiable adequate physical causes may be symbolically expressing an intrapsychic conflict through the body. Some patients suffer from alexithymia, in which they are unable to articulate their internal feeling states in words, so the body expresses the feelings for them. Other patients may unconsciously regard emotional pain as weak and somehow lacking in legitimacy. By displacing the problem to the body, they may feel that they have a legitimate claim to the fulfillment of their dependence needs. The symbolic meaning of body disturbances may also relate to atonement for perceived sin, expiation of guilt, or suppressed aggression. Many patients have pain that is intractable and unresponsive because they are convinced that they deserve to suffer.

Pain can function as a method of obtaining love, a punishment for wrongdoing, and a way of expiating guilt and of atoning for an innate sense of badness. Among the defense mechanisms used by patients with pain disorder are displacement, substitution, and repression. Identification plays a role when the patient takes on the role of an ambivalent love object who also has pain, such as a parent.

**Behavioral factors.** Pain behaviors are reinforced when rewarded and are inhibited when ignored or punished. For example, moderate pain symptoms may become intense when followed by the solicitous and attentive behavior of others, by monetary gain, or by the successful avoidance of distasteful activities.

**Interpersonal factors.** Intractable pain has been conceptualized as a means for manipulation and gaining advantage in interpersonal relationships—for example, to ensure the devotion of a family member or to stabilize a fragile marriage. Such secondary gain is most important to patients with pain disorder.

**Biological factors.** The cerebral cortex can inhibit the firing of afferent pain fibers. Serotonin is probably the main neurotransmitter in the descending inhibitory pathways, and endorphins also play a role in the central nervous system modulation of pain. Endorphin deficiency seems to correlate with the augmentation of incoming sensory stimuli. Some patients may have pain disorder, rather than another mental disorder, because of sensory and limbic structural or chemical abnormalities that predispose them to experience pain.

## Diagnosis

The DSM-IV diagnostic criteria for pain disorder require the presence of clinically significant complaints of pain (Table 17–7). The complaints of pain must be judged to be significantly affected by psychological factors, and the symptoms must result in significant emotional distress or functional impairment (for example, social or occupational) to the patient. DSM-IV requires that the pain disorder be further defined as being associated primarily with psychological factors or as being associated with both psychological factors and a general medical condition. DSM-IV further specifies that pain disorder associated solely with a general medical condition be diagnosed as an Axis III condition. DSM-IV also allows the clinician to specify whether the pain disorder is acute or chronic, depending on whether the symptoms have lasted six months or longer.

## Clinical Features

Pain disorder patients do not constitute a uniform group but, instead, are a collection of heterogeneous patients with various pains, such as low back pain, headache, atypical facial pain, and chronic pelvic pain. The patients' pain may be posttraumatic, neuropathic, neurological, iatro-

**Table 17–7**
**Diagnostic Criteria for Pain Disorder**

A. Pain in one or more anatomical sites is the predominant focus of the clinical presentation and is of sufficient severity to warrant clinical attention.

B. The pain causes clinically significant distress or impairment in social, occupational, or other important areas of functioning.

C. Psychological factors are judged to have an important role in the onset, severity, exacerbation, or maintenance of the pain.

D. The symptom or deficit is not intentionally produced or feigned (as in factitious disorder or malingering).

E. The pain is not better accounted for by a mood, anxiety, or psychotic disorder and does not meet criteria for dyspareunia.

*Code as follows:*

**Pain disorder associated with psychological factors**: psychological factors are judged to have the major role in the onset, severity, exacerbation, or maintenance of the pain. (If a general medical condition is present, it does not have a major role in the onset, severity, exacerbation, or maintenance of the pain.) This type of pain disorder is not diagnosed if criteria are also met for somatization disorder.

*Specify if:*
  **Acute:** duration of less than 6 months
  **Chronic:** duration of 6 months or longer

**Pain disorder associated with both psychological factors and a general medical condition**: both psychological factors and a general medical condition are judged to have important roles in the onset, severity, exacerbation, or maintenance of the pain. The associated general medical condition or anatomical site of the pain (see below) is coded on Axis III.

*Specify if:*
  **Acute:** duration of less than six months
  **Chronic:** duration of six months or more

  **Note:** the following is not considered to be a mental disorder and is included here to facilitate differential diagnosis.

  **Pain disorder associated with a general medical condition**: a general medical condition has a major role in the onset, severity, exacerbation, or maintenance of the pain. (If psychological factors are present, they are not judged to have a major role in the onset, severity, exacerbation, or maintenance of the pain.) The diagnostic code for the pain is selected based on the associated general medical condition if one has been established or on the anatomical location of the pain if the underlying general medical condition is not yet clearly established—for example, low back, sciatic, pelvic, headache, facial, chest, joint, bone, abdominal, breast, renal, ear, eye, throat, tooth, and urinary.

Table from DSM-IV, *Diagnostic and Statistical Manual of Mental Disorders*, ed 4. Copyright American Psychiatric Association, Washington, 1994. Used with permission.

genic, or musculoskeletal; however, to meet a diagnosis of pain disorder, the disorder must have a psychological factor that is judged to be significantly involved in the pain symptoms and their ramifications.

Pain disorder patients often have long histories of medical and surgical care, visiting many doctors and requesting many medications. They may be especially insistent in their desire for surgery. Indeed, they can be completely preoccupied with their pain, citing it as the source of all their misery. Such patients often deny any other sources of emo-

tional dysphoria and maintain that their lives are blissful except for the pain. Pain disorder patients may have the clinical picture complicated by substance-related disorders, because they attempt to reduce the pain through the use of alcohol and other substances.

At least one study has correlated the number of pain symptoms to the likelihood and the severity of symptoms of somatization disorder, depressive disorders, and anxiety disorders. Major depressive disorder is present in about 25 to 50 percent of all pain disorder patients, and dysthymic disorder or depressive disorder symptoms are reported in 60 to 100 percent of the patients. Some investigators believe that chronic pain is almost always a variant of a depressive disorder, suggesting that it is a masked or somatized form of depression. The most prominent depressive symptoms in pain disorder patients are anergia, anhedonia, decreased libido, insomnia, and irritability; diurnal variation, weight loss, and psychomotor retardation appear to be less common than those symptoms.

## Differential Diagnosis

Purely physical pain can be difficult to distinguish from purely psychogenic pain, especially because they are not mutually exclusive. Physical pain fluctuates in intensity and is highly sensitive to emotional, cognitive, attentional, and situational influences. Pain that does not vary and is insensitive to any of those factors is likely to be psychogenic. If the pain does not wax and wane and is not even temporarily relieved by distraction or analgesics, the clinician can suspect an important psychogenic component.

Pain disorder must be distinguished from other somatoform disorders, although some somatoform disorders can coexist. Hypochondriacal patients may complain of pain, and aspects of the clinical presentation of hypochondriasis, such as bodily preoccupation and disease conviction, can also be present in pain disorder patients. However, hypochondriacal patients tend to have many more symptoms than do pain disorder patients, and their symptoms tend to fluctuate more than do the symptoms of pain disorder patients. Conversion disorder is generally short-lived, whereas pain disorder is chronic. In addition, pain is, by definition, not a symptom in conversion disorder. Malingering patients consciously provide false reports, and their complaints are usually connected to clearly recognizable goals.

The differential diagnosis can be difficult because pain disorder patients often receive disability compensation or a litigation award. They are not, however, pretending to be in pain. For example, muscle contraction (tension) headaches have a pathophysiological mechanism to account for the pain and so are not diagnosed as pain disorder.

## Course and Prognosis

The pain in pain disorder generally begins abruptly and increases in severity over the next few weeks or months. The prognosis for pain disorder patients varies, although pain disorder can often be chronic, distressful, and completely disabling. When psychological factors predominate in pain disorder, the pain may subside with treatment or after the elimination of external reinforcement. The patients with the poorest prognoses, with or without treatment, have preexisting characterological problems, especially pronounced passivity; are involved in litigation or receive financial compensation; use addictive substances; and have long histories of pain.

## Treatment

Since it may not be possible to reduce the pain, the treatment approach must address rehabilitation. The clinician should discuss the issue of psychological factors early in treatment, telling patients frankly that such factors are important in the cause and the consequences of both physical and psychogenic pain. The therapist should also explain how various brain circuits that are involved with emotions (such as the limbic system) may also influence the sensory pain pathways. For example, hitting one's head while happy at a party can seem to hurt less than hitting one's head while angry and at work. However, the therapist must fully understand that the patient's experience of pain is real.

**Pharmacotherapy.** Analgesic medications are not generally helpful for most pain disorder patients. In addition, substance abuse and dependence are often major problems for pain disorder patients who receive long-term analgesic treatment. In addition, sedatives and antianxiety agents are not especially beneficial and often become problems in themselves because of their frequent abuse, misuse, and side effects.

Antidepressants—such as amitriptyline (Elavil), imipramine (Tofranil), and doxepin (Sinequan)—are useful. Whether antidepressants reduce pain through their antidepressant action or exert an independent, direct analgesic effect (possibly by stimulating efferent inhibitory pain pathways) remains controversial. Preliminary data indicate that the serotonergic-antidepressants (for example, clomipramine and fluoxetine) also reduce pain in pain disorder patients. The success of those agents supports the hypothesis that serotonin is important in the pathophysiology of the disorder.

**Behavioral treatment.** Biofeedback can be helpful in the treatment of pain disorder, particularly with migraine pain, myofacial pain, an muscle tension states, such as tension headaches. Hypnosis, transcutaneous nerve stimulation, and dorsal column stimulation also have been used. Nerve blocks and surgical ablative procedures are ineffective for most pain disorder patients; the pain returns after 6 to 18 months.

**Psychotherapy.** Some outcome data indicate that psychodynamic psychotherapy is helpful to patients with pain disorder. The first step in psychotherapy is to develop a solid therapeutic alliance by empathizing with the patient's suffering. Clinicians should not confront somatisizing patients with comments such as, "This is all in your head." For the patient, the pain is real, and clinicians must acknowledge the reality of the pain, even though they suspect that it is largely intrapsychic in origin. A useful entry point into the emotional aspects of the pain is to examine the interpersonal ramifications of the pain in the patient's life. By exploring marital problems, for example, the psychotherapist may soon get to the source of the patient's psy-

chological pain and the function of the physical complaints in significant relationships.

**Pain control programs.** It may sometimes be necessary to remove the patients from their usual settings and place them in a comprehensive inpatient pain control program. Multidisciplinary pain units use many modalities, such as cognitive, behavior, and group therapies. They provide extensive physical conditioning through physical therapy and exercise and offer vocational evaluation and rehabilitation. Concurrent mental disorders are diagnosed and treated, and patients dependent on analgesics and hypnotics are detoxified. Inpatient treatment programs generally report encouraging results.

# UNDIFFERENTIATED SOMATOFORM DISORDER

The DSM-IV diagnosis of undifferentiated somatoform disorder (Table 17–8) is appropriate for patients who present with one or more physical complaints that cannot be explained by a known medical condition or that grossly exceed the expected complaints in a medical condition but who do not meet the diagnostic criteria for a specific somatoform disorder (Table 17–1). The symptoms must have been present at least six months and must cause the patient significant emotional distress or impair the patient's social or occupational functioning.

Two types of symptom patterns may be seen in patients with undifferentiated somatoform disorder: those involving the autonomic nervous system and those involving sensations of fatigue or weakness. In what is sometimes referred to as autonomic arousal disorder, some patients are

**Table 17–8**
**Diagnostic Criteria for Undifferentiated Somatoform Disorder**

A. One or more physical complaints (e.g., fatigue, loss of appetite, gastrointestinal or urinary complaints)

B. Either (1) or (2);

    (1) after appropriate investigation, the symptoms cannot be fully explained by a known general medical condition or by the direct effects of a substance (e.g., the effects of injury, medication, drugs, or alcohol)

    (2) when there is a related general medical condition, the physical complaints or resulting social or occupational impairment is in excess of what would be expected from the history, physical examination, or laboratory findings

C. The symptoms cause clinically significant distress or impairment in social, occupational, or other important areas of functioning.

D. The duration of the disturbance is at least six months

E. The disturbance is not better accounted for by another mental disorder (e.g., another somatoform disorder, sexual dysfunction, mood disorder, anxiety disorder, sleep disorder, or psychotic disorder).

F. The symptom is not intentionally produced or feigned (as in factitious disorder or malingering).

Table from DSM-IV, *Diagnostic and Statistical Manual of Mental Disorders*, ed 4. Copyright American Psychiatric Association, Washington, 1994. Used with permission.

affected with somatoform disorder symptoms that are limited to bodily functions innervated by the autonomic nervous system. Such patients have complaints involving the cardiovascular, respiratory, gastrointestinal, urogenital, and dermatological systems. Other patients have complaints of mental and physical fatigue, physical weakness and exhaustion, and inability to perform many everyday activities because of their symptoms. That syndrome is often referred to as neurasthenia by clinicians and in other diagnostic systems. The syndrome may overlap chronic fatigue syndrome, which various research reports have hypothesized to involve psychiatric, virological, and immunological factors.

## SOMATOFORM DISORDER NOT OTHERWISE SPECIFIED

The DMS-IV diagnostic category of somatoform disorder not otherwise specified (NOS) (Table 17–9) is a residual category for patients who have symptoms suggestive of a somatoform disorder but who do not meet the specific diagnostic criteria for other somatoform disorders (Table 17–1). Such patients may have a symptom not covered in the other somatoform disorders (for example, pseudocyesis) or may not have met the six-month criterion of the other somatoform disorders.

**Table 17–9**
**Diagnostic Criteria for Somatoform Disorder Not Otherwise Specified**

This category includes disorders with somatoform symptoms that do not meet the criteria for any specific somatoform disorder. Examples include:

1. pseudocyesis: a false belief of being pregnant that is associated with objective signs of pregnancy, which may include abdominal enlargement (although the umbilicus does not become everted), reduced menstrual flow, amenorrhea, subjective sensation of fetal movement, nausea, breast engorgement and secretions, and labor pains at the expected date of delivery. Endocrine changes may be present but the syndrome cannot be explained by a general medical condition that causes endocrine changes (e.g., hormone-secreting tumor).

2. a disorder involving nonpsychotic hypochondriacal symptoms of less than six months' duration.

3. a disorder involving unexplained physical complaints (e.g., fatigue or body weakness) of less than 6 months' duration that are not due to another mental disorder.

Table from DSM-IV, *Diagnostic and Statistical Manual of Mental Disorders*, ed 4. Copyright American Psychiatric Association, Washington, 1994. Used with permission.

## References

Barsky A J, Cleary P D, Sarnie M K, Klerman G L: The course of transient hypochondriasis. Psychiatry 150: 484, 1993.

Barsky A J, Coeytaux R R, Sarnie M K, Cleary P D: Hypochondriacal patients' beliefs about good health. Am J Psychiatry 150: 1085, 1993.

Barsky A J, Frank C B, Cleary P D, Wyshak G, Klerman G L: The relation between hypochondriasis and age. Am J Psychiatry 148: 923, 1991.

Barsky A J, Wyshak G, Klerman G L: Psychiatric comorbidity in DSM-III-R hypochondriasis. Arch Gen Psychiatry 49: 101, 1992.

Barsky A J, Wyshak G, Klerman G L: Transient hypochondriasis. Arch Gen Psychiatry 47: 746, 1990.

Barsky A J, Wyshak G, Klerman G L, Latham K S: The prevalence of hypochondriasis in medical outpatients. Soc Psychiatry Psychiatr Epidemiol 25: 89, 1990.

Barsky A J, Wyshak G, Latham K S, Klerman G L: Hypochondriacal patients, their physicians, and their medical care. J Gen Intern Med 6: 413, 1991.

Bass C, Benjamin S: The management of chronic somatisation. Br J Psychiatry 162: 472, 1993.

Bass C, Murphy M: Somatization disorder in a British teaching hospital. Br J Clin Pract 45: 237, 1991.

Botteli T J, Guze G B: The simulation of neurologic disease. Psychiatr Clin North Am 15: 301, 1992.

Brown F W, Golding J M, Smith G R Jr: Psychiatric comorbidity in primary care somatization disorder. Psychosom Med 52: 445, 1990.

Creed F, Guthrie E: Techniques for interviewing the somatising patient. Br J Psychiatry 162: 467, 1993.

Dwoekin S F, Von Korff M, LeResche L: Multiple pains and psychiatric disturbance: An epidemiologic investigation. Arch Gen Psychiatry 47: 239, 1990.

Fink P: Surgery and medical treatment in persistent somatizing patients. J Psychosom Res 36: 439, 1992.

Goldberg R J, Novack D H, Gask L: The recognition and management of somatization: What is needed in primary care training. Psychosomatics 33: 55, 1992.

Golding J M, Smith R Jr, Kashner M: Does somatization disorder occur in men? Clinical characteristics of women and men with multiple unexplained somatic symptoms. Arch Gen Psychiatry 48: 231, 1991.

Hitchcock P B, Mathews A: Interpretation of bodily symptoms in hypochondriasis. Behav Res Ther 30: 223, 1992.

Hollander E, Neville D, Frenkel M, Josephson S, Liebowitz M R: Body dysmorphic disorder: Diagnostic issues and related disorders. Psychosomatics 33: 156, 1992.

Katon W, Lin E, Von Korff M, Russo J, Lipscomb P, Bush T: Somatization: A spectrum of severity. Am J Psychiatry 148: 34, 1991.

Kellner R: Diagnosis and treatments of hypochondriacal syndromes. Psychosomatics 33: 278, 1992.

Kellner R, Hernandez J, Pathak D: Hypochondriacal fears and beliefs, anxiety, and somatization. Br J Psychiatry 160: 525, 1992.

Kent S, Bluthe R-M, Kelley K W, Danzer R: Sickness behavior as a new target for drug development. Trends Pharmacol Sci 13: 24, 1992.

Kirmayer L J, Robbins J M, Dworkin M, Yaffe M J: Somatization and the recognition of depression and anxiety in primary care. Am J Psychiatry 150: 734, 1993.

Krull F, Schifferdecker M: Inpatient treatment of conversion disorder: A clinical investigation outcome. Psychother Psychosom 53: 161, 1990.

Lempert T, Schmidt D: Natural history and outcome of psychogenic seizures: A clinical study in 50 patients. J Neurol 237: 35, 1990.

Mabe P A, Jones R A, Riley W T: Managing somatization phenomenon in primary care. Psychiatr Med 8: 117, 1990.

Mace C J: Hysterical conversion: II. A critique. Br J Psychiatry 161: 378, 1992.

Martin R L: Diagnostic issues for conversion disorder. Hosp Community Psychiatry 43: 771, 1992.

Mayou R: Somatization. Psychother Psychosom 59: 69, 1993.

Phillips K A: Body dysmorphic disorder: The distress of imagined ugliness. Am J Psychiatry 148: 1138, 1991.

Phillips K A, McElroy S L, Keck P E Jr, Pope H G, Judson J I: Body dysmorphic disorder: 30 cases of imagined ugliness. Am J Psychiatry 150: 302, 1993.

Rost K M, Akins R N, Brown F W, Smith G R: The comorbidity of DSM-III-R personality disorders in somatization disorder. Gen Hosp Psychiatry 14: 322, 1992.

Simon G E, VonKorff M: Somatization and psychiatric disorder in the NIMH Epidemiologic Catchment Area study. Am J Psychiatry 148: 1494, 1991.

Smith G R: The epidemiology and treatment of depression when it coexists with somatoform disorders, somatization, or pain. Gen Hosp Psychiatry 14: 265, 1992.

Stern R, Fernandez M: Group cognitive and behavioral treatment for hypochondriasis. Br J Med 303: 1229, 1991.

Tomasson K, Kent D, Coryell W: Somatization and conversion disorders: Comorbidity and demographics at presentation. Act Psychiatr Scand 84: 288, 1991.

Turgay A: Treatment outcome for children and adolescents with conversion disorder. Can J Psychiatry 35: 585, 1990.

Van Kempen G M, Zitman F G, Linssen A C, Edelbroek P M: Biochemical measures in patients with a somatoform pain disorder, before, during, and after treatment with amitriptyline with or without flupentixol. Biol Psychiatry 31: 670, 1992.

# 18 ||||||

# Factitious Disorders

In factitious disorders, patients intentionally produce signs of medical or mental disorders and misrepresent their histories and symptoms. The only apparent objective of the behavior is to assume the role of a patient. For many persons, hospitalization itself is a primary objective and often a way of life. The disorders have a compulsive quality, but the behaviors are considered voluntary in that they are deliberate and purposeful, even if they cannot be controlled.

## EPIDEMIOLOGY

The prevalence of factitious disorders is unknown, although some clinicians believe that they are more common than acknowledged. They appear to occur most frequently in men and among hospital and health care workers. One study reported a 9 percent rate of factitious disorders among all patients admitted to a hospital; another study found factitious fever in 3 percent of all patients. A data bank of persons who feign illness has been established to alert hospitals about such patients, many of whom travel from place to place, seeking admission under different names or simulating different illnesses.

## ETIOLOGY

The psychodynamic underpinnings of factitious disorders are poorly understood because the patients are difficult to engage in an exploratory psychotherapy process. They may insist that their symptoms are physical and, therefore, psychologically oriented treatment is useless. Anecdotal case reports indicate that many of the patients suffered childhood abuse or deprivation, resulting in frequent hospitalizations during early development. In such circumstances an inpatient stay may have been regarded as an escape from a traumatic home situation and the patient may have found a series of caretakers (such as doctors, nurses, and hospital workers) loving and caring. In contrast, the patients' families of origin usually contained a rejecting mother or an absent father. The usual history reveals that the patient perceives one or both parents as rejecting figures who are unable to form close relationships. The facsimile of genuine illness, therefore, is used to re-create the desired positive parent-child bond. The disorders are a form of repetition compulsion—repeating the basic conflict of needing and seeking acceptance and love while expecting that they will not be forth-

coming. Hence, the patient transforms the physician and staff members into rejecting parents.

Patients who seek out painful procedures, such as surgical operations and invasive diagnostic tests, may have a masochistic personality makeup in which pain serves as punishment for past sins, imagined or real. Some patients may attempt to master the past and early trauma of serious medical illness or hospitalization by assuming the role of the patient and reliving the painful and frightening experience over and over again through multiple hospitalizations.

Patients who feign psychiatric illness may have had a relative who was hospitalized with the illness they are simulating. Through identification, the patients hope to reunite with the relative in a magical way.

Many of the patients have the poor identity formation and disturbed self-image that is characteristic of someone with borderline personality disorder. Some patients are as-if personalities who have assumed the identities of those around them. If those patients are health professionals, they are often unable to differentiate themselves from the patients with whom they come in contact.

The cooperation or the encouragement of other persons in simulating a factitious illness occurs in a rare variant of the disorder, suggesting another possible causative factor. Although the majority of the patients act alone, friends or relatives participate in fabricating the illness in some instances.

Significant defense mechanisms are repression, identification, identification with the aggressor, regression, and symbolization.

## DIAGNOSIS AND CLINICAL FEATURES

The diagnostic criteria for factitious disorder in the fourth edition of *Diagnostic and Statistical Manual of Mental Disorders* (DSM-IV) are given in Table 18–1.

The psychiatric examination should emphasize securing information from any available friend, relative, or other informant, because interviews with reliable outside sources often reveal the false nature of the patient's illness. Although time-consuming and tedious, verifying all the facts presented by the patient concerning prior hospitalizations and medical care is essential.

Psychiatric evaluation is requested on a consultation basis in about 50 percent of the cases, usually after the presence of a simulated illness is suspected. The psychiatrist is often asked to confirm the diagnosis of factitious disorder. Under those circumstances it is necessary to avoid pointed or accusatory questioning that may provoke truculence, evasion, or flight from the hospital. There may be a danger of provoking frank psychosis if vigorous confrontation is used, because in some instances the feigned illness serves an adaptive function and is a desperate attempt to ward off further disintegration.

Psychological testing may reveal specific underlying pathology in individual patients. Features that are overrepresented in factitious disorder patients include normal or above-average intelligence quotient (I.Q.); absence of a formal thought disorder; poor sense of identity, including confusion over sexual identity; poor sexual adjustment; poor frustration tolerance; strong dependence needs; and narcissism.

## Factitious Disorder with Predominantly Psychological Signs and Symptoms

Some patients present with psychiatric symptoms that are judged to be feigned. That determination can be difficult and is often made only after a prolonged investigation (Table 18–1). The feigned symptoms often include depression, hallucinations, dissociative and conversion symptoms, and bizarre behavior. Because the patient does not improve after routine therapeutic measures are administered, the patient may receive large doses of psychoactive drugs and may undergo electroconvulsive therapy.

Factitious psychological symptoms resemble the phenomenon of pseudomalingering, conceptualized as satisfying the need to maintain an intact self-image, which would be marred by admitting psychological problems that are beyond the person's capacity to master through conscious effort. In that case, deception is a transient ego-supporting device.

**Table 18–1**
**Diagnostic Criteria for Factitious Disorder**

A. Intentional production or feigning of physical or psychological signs or symptoms.

B. The motivation for the behavior is to assume the sick role.

C. External incentives for the behavior (such as economic gain, avoiding legal responsibility, or improving physical well-being, as in malingering) are absent.

*Code* based on type:

**with predominantly psychological signs and symptoms**: if psychological signs and symptoms predominate in the clinical presentation.

**with predominantly physical signs and symptoms**: if physical signs and symptoms predominate in the clinical presentation.

**with combined psychological and physical signs and symptoms**: if both psychological and physical signs and symptoms are present but neither predominate in the clinical presentation.

Table from DSM-IV, *Diagnostic and Statistical Manual of Mental Disorders*, ed 4. Copyright American Psychiatric Association, Washington, 1994. Used with permission.

Recent findings indicate that factitious psychotic symptoms are more common than was previously suspected. The presence of simulated psychosis as a feature of other disorders, such as mood disorders, indicates a poor overall prognosis.

Psychotic inpatients found to have factitious disorder with predominantly psychological signs and symptoms—that is, exclusively simulated psychotic symptoms—generally have a concurrent diagnosis of borderline personality disorder. In those cases, the outcome appears to be worse than that of bipolar I disorder or schizoaffective disorder.

Patients may present as depressed, offering as the reason a false history of the recent death of a significant friend or relative. Elements of the history that may suggest factitious bereavement include a violent or bloody death, a death under dramatic circumstances, and the dead person's being a child or a young adult. Other patients may present with both recent and remote memory loss or with both auditory and visual hallucinations.

Other symptoms, which also appear in the physical type of factitious disorder, include pseudologia phantastica and impostorship. In pseudologia phantastica, limited factual material is mixed with extensive and colorful fantasies. The listener's interest pleases the patient and, thus, reinforces the symptom. However, the distortion of truth is not limited to the history or an illness's symptoms; the patients often give false and conflicting accounts about other areas of their lives (such as claiming the death of a parent, so as to play on the sympathy of others). Impostorship is commonly related to lying in those cases. Many patients assume the identity of a prestigious person. Men, for example, report being war heroes, attributing their surgical scars to wounds received during battle or other dramatic and dangerous exploits. Similarly, they may say that they have ties to accomplished or renowned figures.

A muscular 24-year-old man presented himself to the admitting office of a state hospital. He told the admitting physician that he had taken thirty 200-mg tablets of chlorpromazine (Thorazine) in the bus on the way over to the hospital. After receiving medical treatment for the "suicide attempt," he was transferred to the inpatient ward.

On mental status examination the patient told a fantastic story about his father, a famous surgeon, who had a woman he was operating on die in surgery and who was then killed by the husband of the woman. The patient then stalked his father's murderer several thousand miles across the United States and, when he found him, was prevented from killing him, at the last moment, by the timely arrival of the man's 94-year-old grandmother. He also related several other intriguing stories involving his $64,000 sports car, which had a 12-cylinder diesel engine, and about his children, two sets of identical triplets. All those stories had a grandiose tinge, and none of them could be confirmed. The patient claimed that he was hearing voices, as on television or in a dream. He answered affirmatively to questions about thought control, thought broadcasting, and other Schneiderian first-rank symptoms; he also claimed depression. He was oriented and alert and had a good range of information except that he kept insisting that it was the Germans (not the Russians) who had invaded Afghanistan. There was no evidence of any associated features of mania or depression, and the patient did not seem elated, depressed, or irritable when he related the stories.

On the ward the patient bullied the other patients and took food and cigarettes from them. He was reluctant to be discharged, and, whenever the subject of his discharge was brought up, he renewed his complaints about "suicidal thoughts" and "hearing voices." It was the opinion of the ward staff members that the patient was not truly psychotic but merely feigned his symptoms whenever the subject of the disposition of his case came up. They thought that he wanted to remain in the hospital primarily so that he could bully the other patients and be a "big man" on the ward.

*Discussion.* Although the patient would have the ward staff members believe that he was psychotic, his story, almost from the start, seemed to conform to no recognizable psychotic syndrome. That his symptoms were not genuine was confirmed by the observation of the ward staff members that he seemed to feign his symptoms whenever the subject of discharge was brought up.

Why did he try so hard to act crazy? His motivation was not to achieve some external incentive, such as avoiding the draft, as would be the case in malingering; his goal of remaining a patient was understandable only with knowledge of his individual psychology (the suggestion that he derived satisfaction from being the "big man" on the ward). The diagnosis was factitious disorder with predominantly psychological signs and symptoms.

## Factitious Disorder with Predominantly Physical Signs and Symptoms

Factitious disorder with predominantly physical signs and symptoms has been designated by a variety of labels, the best known being Munchausen syndrome, named after the German Baron von Münchausen, who lived in the 18th century and wrote many travel and adventure stories. The disorder has also been called hospital addiction, polysurgical addiction, and professional patient syndrome, among other names.

The essential feature of patients with the disorder is their ability to present physical symptoms so well that they are able to gain admission to and stay in a hospital (Table 18–1). To support their history, the patients may feign symptoms suggestive of a disorder that may involve any organ system. They are familiar with the diagnoses of most disorders that usually require hospital admission or medication and can give excellent histories capable of deceiving even the most experienced clinician. Clinical presentations are myriad and include hematoma, hemoptysis, abdominal pain, fever, hypoglycemia, lupuslike syndromes, nausea, vomiting, dizziness, and seizures. Urine is contaminated with blood or feces; anticoagulants are taken to simulate bleeding disorders; insulin is used to produce hypoglycemia; and so on. Such patients often insist on surgery, claiming adhesions from previous surgical procedures. The people may acquire a gridiron abdomen from multiple procedures. Complaints of pain, especially that simulating renal colic, are common, with the patients wanting narcotics. In about half the reported cases, the patients demand treatment with specific medications, usually analgesics. Once in the hospital, they continue to be demanding and difficult. As each test is returned with a negative result, they may accuse the doctor of incompetence, threaten litigation, and become generally abusive. Some may sign out abruptly shortly before they believe they are going to be confronted with their factitious behavior. They then go to another hospital in the same or another city and begin the cycle again. Specific predisposing factors are true physical disorders during childhood leading to extensive medical treatment, a grudge against the medical profession, employment as a medical paraprofessional, and an important relationship with a physician in the past.

A 29-year-old female laboratory technician was admitted to the medical service through the emergency room because of bloody urine. The patient said she was being treated for lupus erythematosus by a physician in a different city. She also mentioned that she had had von Willebrand's disease (a rare hereditary blood disorder) as a child. On the third day of her hospitalization, a medical student mentioned to the resident that she had seen the patient several weeks before at a different hospital in the area, where the patient had been admitted for the same problem. A search of the patient's belongings revealed a cache of anticoagulant medications. When confronted with that information, she refused to discuss the matter and hurriedly signed out of the hospital against medical advice.

*Discussion.* The circumstances (bloody urine, possession of anticoagulants, history of repeated hospitalizations, leaving the hospital when confronted) strongly suggest that the patient's symptoms were intentionally produced and were not genuine symptoms of a physical disorder.

The differential diagnosis of simulated illness was between a factitious disorder and malingering. From what is known of the case, it appeared that the patient had no external incentives for the behavior and that the woman's goal was only to assume the patient role. Therefore, the diagnosis was factitious disorder with predominantly physical signs and symptoms.

If the facts had suggested, for example, that her goal was primarily to get disability payments, that would have indicated malingering, rather than a mental disorder.

## Factitious Disorder with Combined Psychological and Physical Signs and Symptoms

In combined forms of factitious disorder, both psychological and physical signs and symptoms are present. If neither type predominates in the clinical presentation, a diagnosis of factitious disorder with combined psychological and physical signs and symptoms should be made (Table 18–1).

## Factitious Disorder Not Otherwise Specified

Some patients with factitious signs and symptoms do not meet the DSM-IV criteria for a specific factitious disorder and should be classified as having factitious disorder not otherwise specified (Table 18–2). The most notable example of the diagnosis is factitious disorder by proxy, which is also included in a DSM-IV appendix (Table 18–3). In that diagnosis, someone intentionally produces physical signs or symptoms in another person who is under the first person's care. The only apparent purpose of the behavior is for the caretaker to indirectly assume the sick role. The most common case of factitious disorder by proxy involves a mother who deceives medical personnel into believing that her child is ill. The deception may involve a false medical history, the contamination of laboratory samples, the alteration of records, or the induction of injury and illness in the child.

**Table 18–2**
**Diagnostic Criteria for Factitious Disorder Not Otherwise Specified**

This category includes disorders with factitious symptoms that do not meet the criteria for factitious disorder. An example is factitious disorder by proxy: the intentional production or feigning of physical or psychological signs or symptoms in another person who is under the individual's care for the purpose of indirectly assuming the sick role.

Table from DSM-IV, *Diagnostic and Statistical Manual of Mental Disorders*, ed 4. Copyright American Psychiatric Association, Washington, 1994. Used with permission.

**Table 18–3**
**Research Criteria for Factitious Disorder by Proxy**

A. Intentional production or feigning of physical or psychological signs or symptoms in another person who is under the individual's care.

B. The motivation for the perpetrator's behavior is to assume the sick role by proxy.

C. External incentives for the behavior (such as economic gain) are absent.

D. The behavior is not better accounted for by another mental disorder.

Table from DSM-IV, *Diagnostic and Statistical Manual of Mental Disorders*, ed 4. Copyright American Psychiatric Association, Washington, 1994. Used with permission.

# DIFFERENTIAL DIAGNOSIS

Any disorder in which physical signs and symptoms are prominent should be considered in the differential diagnosis, and the possibility of authentic or concomitant physical illness must always be explored.

## Somatoform Disorders

A factitious disorder is differentiated from somatization disorder (Briquet's syndrome) by the voluntary production of factitious symptoms, the extreme course of multiple hospitalizations, and the patient's seeming willingness to undergo an extraordinary number of mutilating procedures. Patients with conversion disorder are not usually conversant with medical terminology and hospital routines, and their symptoms have a direct temporal relation or symbolic reference to specific emotional conflicts.

Hypochondriasis differs from factitious disorder in that the hypochondriacal patient does not voluntarily initiate the production of symptoms, and hypochondriasis typically has a later age of onset. As is the case with somatization disorder, patients with hypochondriasis do not usually submit to potentially mutilating procedures.

## Personality Disorders

Because of their pathological lying, lack of close relationships with others, hostile and manipulative manner, and as-

sociated substance and criminal history, factitious disorder patients are often classified as having antisocial personality disorder; however, antisocial persons do not usually volunteer for invasive procedures or resort to a way of life marked by repeated or long-term hospitalization.

Because of attention seeking and an occasional flair for the dramatic, factitious disorder patients may be classified as having histrionic personality disorder. But not all factitious disorder patients have a dramatic flair; many are withdrawn and bland.

Consideration of the patient's chaotic life-style, past history of disturbed interpersonal relationships, identity crisis, substance abuse, self-damaging acts, and manipulative tactics may lead to the diagnosis of borderline personality disorder.

Factitious disorder persons usually do not have the eccentricities of dress, thought, or communication that characterize schizotypal personality disorder patients.

## Schizophrenia

The diagnosis of schizophrenia is often based on patients' admittedly bizarre life-styles, but factitious disorder patients do not usually meet the diagnostic criteria for schizophrenia unless they have the fixed delusion that they are actually ill and act on that belief by seeking hospitalization. Such a practice seems to be the exception, for few patients with factitious disorder show evidence of a severe thought disorder or bizarre delusions.

## Malingering

Factitious disorders must be distinguished from malingering. Malingerers have an obvious, recognizable environmental goal in producing signs and symptoms. They may seek hospitalization to secure financial compensation, evade the police, avoid work, or merely obtain free bed and board for the night; but they always have some apparent end for their behavior. Moreover, they can usually stop producing their signs and symptoms when they are no longer considered profitable or when the stakes rise too high and the patients risk life and limb.

## Substance Abuse

Although patients with factitious disorders may have a complicating history of substance abuse, they should be considered not merely as substance abusers but as having coexisting diagnoses.

## Ganser's Syndrome

Ganser's syndrome, a controversial condition most typically associated with prison inmates, is characterized by the use of approximate answers. Persons with the syndrome respond to simple questions with astonishingly incorrect answers. For example, when asked about the color of a blue car, the person answers "red." Ganser's syndrome may be a variant of malingering, in that the patients avoid punishment or responsibility for their actions. Ganser's syndrome is classified in DSM-IV as a dissociative disorder not otherwise specified.

## COURSE AND PROGNOSIS

Factitious disorders typically begin in early adult life, although they may appear during childhood or adolescence. The onset of the disorder or of discrete episodes of treatment seeking may follow a real illness, loss, rejection, or abandonment. Usually, the patient or a close relative had a hospitalization in childhood or early adolescence for a genuine physical illness. Thereafter, a long pattern of successive hospitalizations unfolds, beginning insidiously. If that is the case, the onset was earlier than generally reported. As the disorder progresses, the patient becomes knowledgeable about medicine and hospitals.

Factitious disorders are incapacitating to the patient, often producing severe traumas or untoward reactions related to treatment. As may seem obvious, a course of repeated or long-term hospitalization is incompatible with meaningful vocational work and sustained interpersonal relationships. The prognosis in most cases is poor. A few patients occasionally spend time in jail, usually for minor crimes, such as burglary, vagrancy, and disorderly conduct. The patient may also have a history of intermittent psychiatric hospitalization.

Although no adequate data are available about the ultimate outcome for the patients, a few of them probably die as a result of needless medication, instrumentation, or surgery. In view of the patients' often expert simulation and the risks that they take, some may die without the disorder's being suspected. Possible features that indicate a favorable prognosis are (1) the presence of a depressive-masochistic personality; (2) functioning at a borderline, not a continuously psychotic, level; and (3) the presence of minimal psychopathic antisocial personality disorder attributes.

## TREATMENT

No specific psychiatric therapy has been effective in treating factitious disorders. It is a clinical paradox that patients with the disorders simulate serious illness, seeking and submitting to unnecessary treatment, while denying to themselves and others their true illness. Ultimately, the patients elude meaningful therapy by abruptly leaving the hospital or failing to keep follow-up appointments.

Treatment, thus, is best focused on management, rather than on cure. Perhaps the single most important factor in successful management is a physician's early recognition of the disorder. The physician can then forestall the patient's undergoing a multitude of painful and potentially dangerous diagnostic procedures. Good liaison between psychiatrists and the medical or surgical staff is strongly advised.

Legal intervention has been obtained in several instances, particularly with children. An obstacle to successful court action is the senselessness of the disorder and the denial of false action by parents, thereby often making conclusive proof unobtainable. In such cases the child welfare services should be notified and arrangements made for the ongoing monitoring of the children's health.

The personal reactions of physicians and staff members are of great significance in treating and establishing a working alliance with the patients, who invariably evoke feelings of futility, bewilderment, betrayal, hostility, and even contempt. In essence, staff members are forced to abandon a basic element of their relationship with patients: acceptance of the truthfullness of the patient's statements. One appropriate psychiatric intervention is to suggest to the staff ways of maintaining an awareness that, even though the patient's illness is factitious, the patient is ill.

Physicians should try not to feel resentment when patients humiliate their diagnostic prowess, and they should avoid any unmasking ceremony that sets up the patients as adversaries and precipitates their flight from the hospital. Staff anger may also be manifested by performing unnecessary procedures or by discharging patients abruptly.

Clinicians who find themselves involved with patients suffering from factitious disorders often become enraged at the patient for lying and deceiving them. Hence, therapists must be mindful of countertransference whenever they suspect factitious disorder. Often, the diagnosis is unclear because a definitive physical cause cannot be entirely ruled out. Although the use of confrontation is controversial, at some point in the treatment, the patient must be made to face reality. The majority of patients simply leave treatment when their method of gaining attention is identified and brought out into the open. In some cases the clinician should reframe the factitious disorder as a cry for help, so that the patient does not view the clinician's response as a punitive one. A major role for psychiatrists in working with factitious disorder patients is to help other staff members in the hospital deal with their own sense of outrage at having been duped. Education about the disorder and some attempt to understand the patient's motivations may help the staff members maintain their professional conduct in the face of extreme frustration.

Although a few cases of individual psychotherapy have been reported in the literature, no consensus exists regarding the best approach. In general, working in concert with the patient's primary care physician is more effective than working with the patient in isolation.

### References

Asher R: Munchausen's syndrome. Lancet *1*: 339, 1951.
Ballard R S, Stoudemire A: Factitious apraxia. Int J Psychiatry Med *22*: 275, 1992.
Black D: The extended Munchausen syndrome: A family case. Br J Psychiatry *138*: 466, 1981.
Bursten D: On Munchausen's syndrome. Arch Gen Psychiatry *13*: 261, 1965.
Eisendrath S J: Factitious illness: A clarification. Psychosomatics *25*: 100, 1984.
Fairbank J A, McCaffrey R J, Keane T M: Psychometric detection of fabricated symptoms of posttraumatic stress disorder. Am J Psychiatry *142*: 142, 1985.
Heron E A, Kritchevsky M, Delis D C: Neuropsychological presentation of Ganser symptoms. J Clin Exp Neuropsychol *13*: 552, 1991.
Houck C A: Medicolegal aspects of factitious disorder. Psychiatr Med *10*: 105, 1992.
Hyler S E, Sussman N: Chronic factitious disorder with physical symptoms (the Munchausen syndrome). Psychiatr Clin North Am *4*: 365, 1981.
Ireland P, Sapira J D, Templeton B: Munchausen's syndrome. Am J Med *43*: 579, 1967.
Jureidini J: Obstetric factitious disorder and Munchausen syndrome by proxy. J Nerv Ment Dis *181*: 135, 1993.
Lipsit D R: The factitious patient who sues. Am J Psychiatry *143*: 1482, 1986.

London M, Ghaffari K: Munchausen syndrome and drug dependence. Br J Psychiatry *149*: 651, 1986.

Ludviksson B R, Griffin J, Graziano F M: Munchausen's syndrome: The importance of a comprehensive medical history. Wis Med J *92*: 128, 1993.

Meadow R: Management of Munchausen syndrome by proxy. Arch Dis Child *60*: 385, 1985.

Phillips M R, Ward N G, Ries R K: Factitious mourning: Painless parenthood. Am J Psychiatry *140*: 420, 1983.

Raspe R E: *The Singular Travels, Campaigns, and Adventures of Baron Munchausen.* Cresset, London, 1948.

Reich P, Gottfried L A: Factitious disorders in a teaching hospital. Ann Intern Med *99*: 240, 1983.

Schmaling K B, Rosenberg S J, Oppenheimer J, Moran M G: Factitious disorder with respiratory symptoms. Psychosomatics *32*: 457, 1991.

Schreier H A: The perversion of mothering: Munchausen syndrome by proxy. Bull Menninger Clin *56*: 421, 1992.

Sinanan K, Haughton H: Evolution of variants of the Munchausen syndrome. Br J Psychiatry *148*: 465, 1986.

Single T, Henry R L: An unusual case of Munchausen syndrome by proxy. Aust N Z J Psychiatry *25*: 422, 1991.

Sparr L, Pankrantz L D: Factitious posttraumatic stress disorder. Am J Psychiatry *140*: 1016, 1983.

Sussman N: Factitious disorders. In *Comprehensive Textbook of Psychiatry*, ed 5, H I Kaplan, B J Sadock, editors, p 1136. Williams & Wilkins, Baltimore, 1989.

Sussman N, Borod J, Cancelmo J, Braun D: Single case study: Munchausen's syndrome: A reconceptualization of the disorder. J Nerv Ment Dis *175*: 692, 1987.

# 19 ||||

# Dissociative Disorders

In a state of mental health, a person has a unitary sense of self as a single human being with a single basic personality. The key dysfunction in the dissociative disorders is a loss of that unitary state of consciousness; the person feels the lack of such an identity or confusion regarding his or her identity or has multiple identities. The unifying experience of self usually consists of an integration of a person's thoughts, feelings, and actions into a unique personality. Although that unifying experience of personality is abnormal in the dissociative disorders, patients with the disorders exhibit a range of dissociative experiences from normal to pathological.

One may consider the normal range of dissociative phenomena from several perspectives. Many researchers and clinicians think hypnotizability is related to the dissociative disorders. Normal people have a range of hypnotizability. Dissociative disorder patients are not necessarily more hypnotizable than mentally healthy persons, but the phenomenon of hypnosis is an example of a dissociative state in normal people. Researchers have developed several scales to measure dissociative experiences—for example, the Dissociative Experience Scale. That scale asks the interviewee questions about mild and common dissociative phenomena (for example, periods of inattention during conversations) and pathological dissociative phenomena. Studies using such scales have indicated that about 5 percent of the general population have scores that are greater than three times the mean score. Other studies of dissociative phenomena have found that dissociative symptoms decrease with age and that dissociative symptoms are about equally common in women and in men. Many types of studies have indicated an association between traumatic events, especially childhood physical and sexual abuse, and the development of dissociative symptoms and disorders.

Dissociation arises as a defense against trauma. Dissociative defenses perform the dual function of helping victims remove themselves from trauma at the time it occurs while also delaying the necessary working through that places the trauma in perspective with the rest of their lives. In the case of repression, a horizontal split is created by the repression barrier, and the material is transferred to the dynamic unconscious. Dissociation differs by creating a vertical split, so that the mental contents exist in a series of parallel consciousnesses.

In the majority of dissociative states, contradictory representations of the self are maintained in separate mental compartments, because they are in conflict with one another. In the extreme form of dissociative identity disorder (multiple personality), those separate representations of the self take on the metaphoric existence of separate personalities known as alters.

Dissociation and splitting have both similarities and differences. Both involve an active compartmentalization and separation of mental contents. Both are used as defenses to ward off unpleasant affects associated with the integration of contradictory parts of the self. They differ to some extent, however, in the nature of the ego functions that are affected. With splitting, anxiety tolerance and impulse control are specifically impaired. In dissociation, memory and consciousness are affected. Nonetheless, both involve mental cleavages that produce self-representations in connection with internal object representations.

The fourth edition of *Diagnostic and Statistical Manual of Mental Disorders* (DSM-IV) contains specific diagnostic criteria for four dissociative disorders: dissociative amnesia (called psychogenic amnesia in the revised third edition of DSM [DSM-III-R]), dissociative fugue (called psychogenic fugue in DSM-III-R), dissociative identity disorder (called multiple personality disorder in DSM-II-R), and depersonalization disorder. Before DSM-III-R, those disorders were known as hysterical neuroses of the dissociative type. Dissociative amnesia is characterized by an inability to remember information, usually related to a stressful or traumatic event, that cannot be explained by ordinary forgetfulness, the ingestion of substances, or a general medical condition. Dissociative fugue is characterized by sudden and unexpected travel away from home or work, associated with an inability to recall one's past and confusion about one's personal identity or the adoption of a new identity. Dissociative identity disorder is characterized by the presence of two or more distinct personalities within a single person; dissociative identity disorder is generally considered the most severe and chronic of the dissociative disorders. Depersonalization disorder is characterized by recurrent or persistent feelings of detachment from one's body or mind. DSM-IV also has the diagnostic category of dissociative disorder not otherwise specified (NOS) for dissociative disorders that do not meet the diagnostic criteria of the other dissociative disorders. DSM-IV also includes diagnostic guidelines in its appendix for dissociative trance disorder, which is currently categorized as a dissociative disorder NOS.

## DISSOCIATIVE AMNESIA

The symptom of amnesia is common to dissociative amnesia, dissociative fugue, and dissociative identity disorder. Dissociative amnesia is the appropriate diagnosis when the dissociative phenomena are limited to amnesia. The key symptom of dissociative amnesia is the inability to recall information already stored in the patient's memory. The forgotten information is usually about a stressful or traumatic event in the person's life. The inability to remember the information cannot be explained by ordinary forgetfulness, and there is no evidence of an underlying brain disorder. The capacity to learn new information is retained.

A common form of dissociative amnesia involves amnesia for one's personal identity but intact memory of general information. That clinical picture is exactly the reverse of the clinical picture seen in dementia, in which patients may remember their names but forget general information, such as what they had for lunch. Except for their amnesia, patients with dissociative amnesia appear completely intact and function coherently. By contrast, in most amnesias due to a general medical condition (such as postictal and toxic amnesias), the patients may be confused and have disorganized behavior. Other types of amnesias (for example, transient global amnesia and postconcussion amnesia) are associated with an ongoing anterograde amnesia, which does not occur in dissociative amnesia patients.

## Epidemiology

Amnesia is the most common dissociative symptom, since it occurs in almost all the dissociative disorders. Dissociative amnesia is thought to be the most common of the dissociative disorders, although epidemiological data on all the dissociative disorders are limited and uncertain. Nevertheless, dissociative amnesia is thought to occur more often in women than in men and more often in young adults than in older adults. Inasmuch as the disorder is usually associated with stressful and traumatic events, its incidence probably increases during times of war and natural disasters. Cases of dissociative amnesia that are related to domestic settings—for example, spouse abuse and child abuse—are probably constant in number.

## Etiology

The neuroanatomical, neurophysiological, and neurochemical processes of memory storage and retrieval are much better understood today than they were a decade ago. The differentiation between short-term memory and long-term memory, the central role of the hippocampus, and the involvement of neurotransmitter systems have been clarified. The newly appreciated complexity of the formation and the retrieval of memories may make dissociative amnesia intuitively understandable because of the many potential areas for dysfunction. However, the vast majority of patients with dissociative amnesia are unable to retrieve painful memories of stressful and traumatic events. Thus, the emotional content of the memory is clearly related to the pathophysiology and the cause of the disorder.

One particularly relevant observation about normal people is that learning is often state-dependent—that is, dependent on the context in which the learning occurs. Information that is learned or experienced during a particular behavior (for example, while driving a car), a phar-macological state (for example, while drinking alcohol), or a neurochemical state (for example, possibly associated with an emotion such as happiness) or in a particular physical setting (for example, seeing a certain flower) is often recalled only while reexperiencing the original state or is most easily recalled while reexperiencing the original state. Thus, people can remember where the light switch is in their cars more easily while they are driving than when they are watching television. The theory of state-dependent learning applies to dissociative amnesia in that the memory of a traumatic event is laid down during the event, and the emotional state may be so out of the ordinary for the affected person that it is hard for the person to remember information learned during that state.

The psychoanalytic approach to dissociative amnesia is to consider the amnesia primarily as a defense mechanism, in which the person alters consciousness as a way of dealing with an emotional conflict or an external stressor. Secondary defenses involved in dissociative amnesia include repression (disturbing impulses are blocked from consciousness) and denial (some aspect of external reality is ignored by the conscious mind).

## Diagnosis

The diagnostic criteria for dissociative amnesia in DSM-IV (Table 19–1) make three changes from the criteria in DSM-III-R. First, the DSM-III-R name psychogenic amnesia has been changed to dissociative amnesia, which makes the diagnostic category consistent with the name in the 10th revision of the International Classification of Diseases (ICD-10). Second, the DSM-III-R criterion of a sudden onset has been dropped in DSM-IV, since studies of the disorder have indicated that a sudden onset is not necessary for an accurate diagnosis. Third, the diagnostic criteria in DSM-IV emphasize that the forgotten information is usually of a traumatic or stressful nature. Dissociative amnesia can be diagnosed only if the symptoms are not limited to amnesia that occurs in the course of dissociative identity disorder and are not the result of a general medical condition (for example, head trauma) or the ingestion of a substance.

**Table 19–1**
**Diagnostic Criteria for Dissociative Amnesia**

A. The predominant disturbance is one or more episodes of inability to recall important personal information, usually of a traumatic or stressful nature, that is too extensive to be explained by ordinary forgetfulness.

B. The disturbance does not occur exclusively during the course of dissociative identity disorder, dissociative fugue, posttraumatic stress disorder, acute stress disorder, or somatization disorder and is not due to the direct physiological effects of a substance (e.g., a drug of abuse, a medication) or a neurological or other general medical condition (e.g., amnestic disorder due to head trauma).

C. The symptoms cause clinically significant distress or impairment in social, occupational, or other important areas of functioning.

Table from DSM-IV, *Diagnostic and Statistical Manual of Mental Disorders*, ed 4. Copyright American Psychiatric Association, Washington, 1994. Used with permission.

## Clinical Features

Although rare episodes of dissociative amnesia occur spontaneously, the history usually reveals some precipitating emotional trauma charged with painful emotions and psychological conflict—for example, a natural disaster in which patients witnessed severe injuries or feared for their lives. A fantasized or actual expression of an impulse (sexual or aggressive) with which the patient is unable to deal may also act as the precipitant. Amnesia may follow an extramarital affair that the patient finds morally reprehensible.

Although not necessary for diagnosis, the onset is often abrupt, and the patients are usually aware that they have lost their memories. Some patients are upset about the memory loss, but others appear to be unconcerned or indifferent. With patients who are not aware of their memory loss but whom the clinician suspects of having dissociative amnesia, it is often useful to ask specific questions that may reveal the symptoms (Table 19–2). Amnestic patients are usually alert before and after the amnesia occurs. A few patients, however, report a slight clouding of consciousness during the period immediately surrounding the amnestic period. Depression and anxiety are common predisposing factors and are frequently present on the mental status examination of the patient.

The amnesia of dissociative amnesia may take one of several forms: (1) *localized amnesia*, the most common type, is the loss of memory for the events of a short period of time (a few hours to a few days); (2) *generalized amnesia* is the loss of memory for a whole lifetime of experience; (3) *selective* (also known as *systematized*) *amnesia* is the failure to recall some but not all events during a short period of time.

Amnesia may have a primary gain or a secondary gain. The woman who is amnestic for the birth of a dead baby achieves a primary gain by protecting herself from painful emotions. An example of secondary gain is a soldier who has sudden amnesia and is removed from combat as a result.

Psychiatric consultation was requested by an emergency room physician on an 18-year-old man who had been brought into the hospital by the police. The youth appeared exhausted and showed evidence of prolonged exposure to the sun. He identified the current date incorrectly, giving it as September 27, instead of October 1. It was difficult to get him to focus on specific questions, but with encouragement he supplied a number of facts. He recalled sailing with friends on a weekend cruise off the Florida coast, apparently about September 25, when bad weather was encountered. He was unable to recall any subsequent events and did not know what became of his companions. He had to be reminded several times that he was in a hospital, since he expressed uncertainty as to his whereabouts. Each time he was told, he seemed surprised.

He showed no evidence of head injury or dehydration. The results of his electrolytes and cranial nerve examinations were unremarkable. Because of the patient's apparent exhaustion, he was permitted to sleep for six hours. On awakening, he was much more attentive but was still unable to recall events after September 25, including how he came to the hospital. He no longer had any doubt in his mind that he was in the hospital, however, and he was able to recall the contents of the previous interview and the fact that he had fallen asleep.

**Table 19–2**
**Questions to Reveal Dissociative Amnesia**

---

If the answers to the mental status questions (below) are positive, the patient should be asked to describe in detail his or her experience of the symptom, including its relation to the use of psychoactive substances.

Blackouts or time loss
  Mental status questions: "Do you lose time?" "Do you have blackouts?"

Reports by others of disremembered behavior
  Mental status questions: "Are you told of things you say and do for which you have no memory? Out of character behavior? Childlike behavior?"

Appearance of unexplained possessions
  Mental status questions: "Do you find things in your possession that you cannot explain? For example, clothes, tools, weapons, artwork, writings, items in your shopping basket, receipts?"

Perplexing changes in relationships
  Mental status questions: "Do you find that your relationships with people seem influenced by factors that you cannot recall? For example, do you find that people are angry with you or act closer to you apparently based on events for which you have no memory?"

Fuguelike episodes
  Mental status questions: "Do you find yourself in places with no idea how you got there? Do you set out to go somewhere but find yourself somewhere else without knowing how you got there? What is the longest period of time you have lost during such an experience?"

Evidence of unusual fluctuations in abilities, habits, tastes, knowledge
  Mental status questions: "Does your ability to do things—such as athletics, artistic endeavors, mechanical tasks, work tasks, and intellectual tasks—fluctuate markedly in ways you cannot explain? Are you told that you do things you didn't know you could do?"

Fragmentary recall of the life history
  Mental status questions: "Are you aware of gaps in your memory for your life? Are you missing memories for important events in your life, like a wedding or a graduation? For your childhood? For events in wartime? For other important aspects of your adult life?"

Chronic mistaken identity experiences
  Mental status questions: "Do you find that you are approached by people whom you don't know, who insist they know you? Who say they have met you before? Who say they have done things with you? Who even call you by another name?"

Brief (micro) amnesias during personal interactions
  Mental status questions: "Do you find that you do not remember all or part of your interactions or conversations with people? Like this interview? Do you or will you remember all or part of our conversation today?"

---

Table from R J Lowenstein: Psychogenic amnesia and psychogenic fugue: A comprehensive review. In *Review of Psychiatry*, vol 10, A Tasman, S M Goldfinger, editors, p 189. American Psychiatric Press, Washington, 1991. Used with permission.

He was able to remember that he was a student at a Southern college, maintained a B average, had a small group of close friends, and had a good relationship with his family. He denied any previous psychiatric history and said he had never abused drugs or alcohol.

Because of the patient's apparently sound physical condition, a sodium amobarbital (Amytal) interview was conducted. During the interview he related that neither he nor his companions were particularly experienced sailors or capable of coping with the ferocity of the storm they encountered. He had taken the precaution of securing himself to the boat with a life jacket and tie line, but his companions had failed to do that and were washed overboard in the heavy seas. He completely lost control of the boat and felt that he was saved only by virtue of good luck and his lifeline. Over a three-day period he was able to consume a small supply of food that was stowed away in the cabin. He never saw either of his sailing companions again. He was picked up on October 1 by a Coast Guard cutter and brought to shore, and subsequently the police brought him to the hospital.

*Discussion.* The differential diagnosis of acute memory loss begins with a consideration of a delirium, dementia, or amnestic disorder that may be due to head trauma, a cerebrovascular disease, or substance abuse. The normal findings on the physical and neurological examinations and the absence of a history of substance use ruled out those possibilities in this patient. The amobarbital interview made it clear that the amnestic period developed after a particularly traumatic and life-threatening experience. Amnesia that was not due to a cognitive disorder justified the diagnosis of dissociative amnesia. In this case the circumscribed nature of the amnesia and the patient's perplexity and disorientation during the amnestic period, all following a traumatic event, were characteristic of the disorder.

## Differential Diagnosis

The differential diagnosis of dissociative amnesia involves a consideration of both general medical conditions and other mental disorders (Table 19–3). A medical history, a physical examination, a laboratory workup, a psychiatric history, and a mental status examination should be conducted.

Amnesia associated with dementia and delirium is usually associated with many other easily recognized cognitive symptoms. When the patient has amnesia for personal information in those conditions, the dementia or the delirium

**Table 19–3**
**Differential Diagnostic Considerations in Dissociative Amnesia**

Dementia
Delirium
Anoxic amnesia
Cerebral infections (e.g., herpes simplex affecting temporal lobes)
Cerebral neoplasms (especially limbic and frontal)
Substance-induced (e.g., ethanol, sedative hypnotics, anticholinergics, steroids, lithium carbonate, β-adrenergic antagonists, pentazocine, phencyclidine, hypoglycemic agents, marijuana, hallucinogens, methyldopa)
Electroconvulsive therapy (or other strong electric shock)
Epilepsy
Metabolic disorders (e.g., uremia, hypoglycemia, hypertensive encephalopathy, porphyria)
Postconcussion (posttraumatic) amnesia
Sleep-related amnesia (e.g., sleepwalking disorder)
Transient global amnesia
Wernicke-Korsakoff syndrome
Postoperative amnesia
Other dissociative disorders
Posttraumatic stress disorder
Acute stress disorder
Somatoform disorders (somatization disorder, conversion disorder)
Malingering (especially when associated with criminal activity)

is usually advanced and easily differentiated from dissociative amnesia. Especially in a case of delirium, the patient may evidence confabulation during the interview. In general, a prompt return of memory usually indicates dissociative amnesia, rather than amnestic disorder due to a general medical condition.

In postconcussion amnesia the memory disturbance follows a head trauma, is often retrograde (as opposed to the anterograde disturbance of dissociative amnesia), and usually does not extend beyond one week. The clinical evaluation of a patient with postconcussion amnesia may reveal a history of unconsciousness, external evidence of trauma, or other evidence of a brain injury. Some researchers have hypothesized that a history of head trauma may predispose a person to a dissociative disorder. Epilepsy can lead to sudden memory impairment associated with motor and electroencephalogram (EEG) abnormalities. Patients with epilepsy are prone to seizures during periods of stress, and some researchers have hypothesized that an epilepticlike pathology may be involved in the dissociative disorders. A history of an aura, head trauma, or incontinence can help the clinician recognize amnesia related to epilepsy.

**Transient global amnesia.** Transient global amnesia is an acute and transient retrograde amnesia that affects recent memories more than remote memories. Although patients are usually aware of the amnesia, they may still perform highly complex mental and physical acts during the 6 to 24 hours that transient global amnesia episodes usually last. Recovery from the disorder is usually complete. Transient global amnesia is most often caused by transient ischemic attacks (TIAs) that affect limbic midline brain structures. Transient global amnesia can also be associated with migraine headaches, seizures, and intoxication with sedative-hypnotic drugs.

Transient global amnesia can be differentiated from dissociative amnesia in several ways. Transient global amnesia is associated with an anterograde amnesia during the episode; dissociative amnesia is not. Patients with transient global amnesia tend to be more upset and concerned about the symptoms than are patients with dissociative amnesia. The personal identity of the patient with dissociative amnesia is lost; that of the patient with transient global amnesia is retained. The memory loss of a patient with dissociative amnesia may be selective for certain areas and usually does not show a temporal gradient; the memory loss of a patient with transient global amnesia is generalized, and remote events are remembered better than recent events. Because of the association of transient global amnesia with vascular problems, the disorder is most common in patients in their 60s and 70s, whereas dissociative amnesia is most common in patients in their 20s to 40s, a period associated with the common types of psychological stressors seen in those patients.

**Other mental disorders.** Two other dissociative disorders, dissociative fugue and dissociative identity disorder, should be considered in the differential diagnosis. Those disorders are distinguished on the basis of their additional symptoms.

In DSM-IV sleepwalking disorder is classified as a parasomnia, a type of sleep disorder. Patients suffering from sleepwalking disorder behave in a strange manner that resembles the behavior of someone in a dissociative state. In sleepwalking disorder, patients exhibit an altered state of conscious awareness of their surroundings; they often have vivid hallucinatory recollections of an emotionally traumatic event in the past of which there is no memory during the usual waking state. Such patients are out of contact with the environment, appear preoccupied with a private world, and stare into space if their eyes are open. They may appear emotionally upset, speak excitedly in words and sentences that are frequently hard to understand, or engage in a pattern of seemingly meaningful activities that is repeated every time an episode occurs. The patient has amnesia for the sleepwalking episode once it has ended.

Although amnesia for a period of immediate past experience is found in patients with sleepwalking disorder and with localized and general amnesia, the state of consciousness during the period for which they are amnestic differs in character. Patients with sleepwalking disorder seem out of touch with the environment and appear to be dreaming. Amnestic patients, by contrast, usually give no indication to observers that anything is amiss and seem entirely alert both before and after the amnesia occurs.

Posttraumatic stress disorder, acute stress disorder, and the somatoform disorders (especially somatization disorder and conversion disorder) should be considered in the differential diagnosis and may coexist with dissociative amnesia. The somatoform disorders may be associated with the same type of traumatic events that are usually seen in dissociative amnesia. Malingering, in this case a deliberate attempt to mimic amnesia, may be difficult to confirm. Any possible secondary gain, especially in regard to escaping punishment for criminal activity, should increase the clinician's suspicion, although such secondary gain does not rule out the diagnosis of dissociative amnesia.

## Course and Prognosis

The symptoms of dissociative amnesia usually terminate abruptly, and recovery is generally complete with few recurrences. In some cases, especially if there is secondary gain, the condition may last a long time. The clinician should try to restore the patient's lost memories to consciousness as soon as possible; otherwise, the repressed memory may form a nucleus in the unconscious mind around which future amnestic episodes may develop.

## Treatment

Interviewing may give the clinician clues to the psychologically traumatic precipitant. Intermediate and short-acting barbiturates, such as thiopental (Pentothal) and sodium amobarbital given intravenously, and benzodiazepines may be used to help patients recover their forgotten memories. Hypnosis can be used primarily as a means of relaxing the patient enough to recall what has been forgotten. The patient is placed in a somnolent state, at which point mental inhibitions are diminished, and the amnestic material emerges into consciousness and is then recalled. Once the lost memories have been retrieved, psychother-apy is generally recommended to help patients incorporate the memories into their conscious states.

# DISSOCIATIVE FUGUE

The behavior of patients with dissociative fugue is more purposefully integrated with their amnesia than is that of patients with dissociative amnesia. Patients with dissociative fugue have physically traveled away from their customary homes or work situations and fail to remember important aspects of their previous identities (name, family, occupation). Such a patient often, but not necessarily, takes on an entirely new identity and occupation, although the new identity is usually less complete than are the alternate personalities seen in dissociative identity disorder. Also, in dissociative fugue the old and the new identities do not alternate, as they do in dissociative identity disorder.

## Epidemiology

Dissociative fugue is rare and, like dissociative amnesia, occurs most often during wartime, after natural disasters, and as a result of personal crises with intense internal conflicts (for example, extramarital affairs).

## Etiology

Although heavy alcohol abuse may predispose a person to dissociative fugue, the cause of the disorder is thought to be basically psychological. The essential motivating factor appears to be a desire to withdraw from emotionally painful experiences. Patients with mood disorders and certain personality disorders (for example, borderline, histrionic, and schizoid personality disorders) are predisposed to the development of dissociative fugue.

A variety of stressors and personal factors predispose a person to the development of dissociative fugue. The psychosocial factors include marital, financial, occupational, and war-related stressors. Other associated predisposing features include depression, suicide attempts, organic disorders (especially epilepsy), and a history of substance abuse. A history of head trauma also predisposes a person to dissociative fugue.

## Diagnosis

In addition to changing the name of the disorder from the DSM-III-R name of psychogenic fugue to dissociative fugue, DSM-IV makes one of the diagnostic criteria (Table 19–4) less restrictive than in DSM-III-R. Specifically, DSM-IV requires that a person either be confused about his or her identity or assume a new identity; DSM-III-R required the assumption of a new identity. Unlike dissociative amnesia, the diagnosis of dissociative fugue requires that the onset of the symptoms be sudden. The diagnosis is excluded if the symptoms occur only during the course of dissociative identity disorder or are the result of substance ingestion or a general medical condition (for example, temporal lobe epilepsy).

**Table 19–4**
**Diagnostic Criteria for Dissociative Fugue**

A. The predominant disturbance is sudden, unexpected travel away from home or one's customary place of work, with inability to recall one's past.

B. Confusion about personal identity or assumption of a new identity (partial or complete).

C. The disturbance does not occur exclusively during the course of dissociative identity disorder and is not due to the direct physiological effects of a substance (e.g., a drug of abuse, a medication) or a general medical condition (e.g., temporal lobe epilepsy).

D. The symptoms cause clinically significant distress or impairment in social, occupational, or other important areas of functioning.

Table from DSM-IV, *Diagnostic and Statistical Manual of Mental Disorders*, ed 4. Copyright American Psychiatric Association, Washington, 1994. Used with permission.

## Clinical Features

Dissociative fugue has several typical features. Patients wander in a purposeful way, usually far from home and often for days at a time. During that period they have complete amnesia for their past lives and associations, but, unlike patients with dissociative amnesia, they are generally unaware that they have forgotten anything. Only when they suddenly return to their former selves do they recall the time antedating the onset of fugue, but then they remain amnestic for the period of the fugue itself. Patients with dissociative fugue do not seem to others to be behaving in extraordinary ways, nor do they give evidence of acting out any specific memory of a traumatic event. On the contrary, dissociative fugue patients lead quiet, prosaic, reclusive existences; work at simple occupations; live modestly; and, in general, do nothing to draw attention to themselves.

The patient was a 42-year-old man who was brought to the emergency room by the police. He was involved in an argument and fight at the diner where he was employed. When the police arrived and began to question the patient, he gave his name as Burt Tate but had no identification. He had drifted into town several weeks earlier and had begun working as a short-order cook at the diner. He could not recall where he had worked or lived before his arrival in town. There were no charges against him, but the police convinced him to come to the emergency room for an examination.

When questioned in the emergency room, the patient knew what town he was in and the current date. He admitted that it was somewhat unusual that he could not recall the details of his past life, but he did not appear to be upset about that. He showed no evidence of alcohol or other substance abuse, and a physical examination revealed no head trauma or any other physical abnormalities. He was kept overnight for observation.

When the police ran a description check on the patient, they found that he fit the description of a missing person, Gene Saunders, who had disappeared a month before from a city 200 miles away. A visit by Mrs. Saunders confirmed the identity of the patient as Gene Saunders. Mrs. Saunders explained that, for 18 months before his disappearance, her husband, who was a middle-level manager at a large manufacturing company, had been having considerable difficulty at

work. He had been passed over for a promotion, and his supervisor had criticized his work. Several of his staff had left the company for other jobs, and the patient found it impossible to meet his department's production goals. Work stress made him difficult to live with at home. Previously an easygoing, gregarious person, he became withdrawn and critical of his wife and children. Immediately preceding his disappearance, he had had a violent argument with his 18-year-old son. The son had called him a failure and stormed out of the house to live with some friends who had an apartment. Two days after that argument, the patient disappeared.

When brought into the room where his wife was waiting, the patient stated that he did not recognize her. He appeared to be noticeably anxious.

*Discussion.* The police brought the man to the emergency room because of his amnesia concerning where he had previously lived and worked. Although that impairment in memory suggested a general medical disorder affecting brain function, ordinarily in such a disorder the disturbance in memory is more marked for recent events than for remote events. The lack of any disturbance in attention or orientation also weighed against the presence of a general medical disorder affecting brain function.

The critical role of psychological factors in the patient's amnesia became apparent when it was learned that, just before the development of his symptoms, on top of increasing difficulties at work, he had a violent argument with his son. The additional features of sudden, unexpected travel away from his home and the assumption of a new identity justified the diagnosis of dissociative fugue.

## Differential Diagnosis

The differential diagnosis for dissociative fugue is similar to that for dissociative amnesia (Table 19–3). The wandering that is seen in dementia or delirium is usually distinguished from the traveling of a dissociative fugue patient by the aimlessness of the former and the absence of complex and socially adaptive behaviors. Complex partial epilepsy may be associated with episodes of travel, but the patient does not usually assume a new identity, and the episodes are generally not precipitated by psychological stress. Dissociative amnesia presents with a loss of memory as the result of psychological stress, but there are no episodes of purposeful travel or of a new identity. Malingering may be difficult to distinguish from dissociative fugue. Any evidence of a clear secondary gain should raise the clinician's suspicions. Hypnosis and amobarbital interviews may be useful in clarifying the clinical diagnosis.

## Course and Prognosis

The fugue is usually brief—hours to days. Less commonly, a fugue lasts many months and involves extensive travel covering thousands of miles. Generally, recovery is spontaneous and rapid, and recurrences are rare.

## Treatment

Treatment of dissociative fugue is similar to the treatment of dissociative amnesia. Psychiatric interviewing, drug-assisted interviewing, and hypnosis may help reveal to the therapist and to the patient the psychological stressors that precipitated the fugue episode. Psychotherapy is generally indicated to help patients incorporate the precipitating stressors into their psyches in a healthy and integrated manner. The treatment of choice for dissociative fugue is expressive-supportive psychodynamic psychotherapy. The most widely accepted technique requires a mixture of abreaction of the past trauma and integration of the trauma into a cohesive self that no longer requires fragmentation to deal with the trauma.

## DISSOCIATIVE IDENTITY DISORDER (MULTIPLE PERSONALITY DISORDER)

Dissociative identity disorder is the DSM-IV name for what has been commonly known as multiple personality disorder. Dissociative identity disorder is a chronic dissociative disorder, and its cause almost invariably involves a traumatic event, usually childhood physical or sexual abuse. The concept of personality conveys the sense of an integration of the way a person thinks, feels, and behaves and the appreciation of himself or herself as a unitary being. Persons with dissociative identity disorder have two or more distinct personalities, each of which determines behavior and attitudes during any period when it is the dominant personality. Dissociative identity disorder is usually considered the most serious of the dissociative disorders, although some clinicians who are diagnosing a wide range of patients with the disorder have suggested that there may be a wider range of severities than was previously appreciated.

### History

Until about 1800, patients with dissociative identity disorder were mainly seen as suffering from various states of possession. In the early 1800s Benjamin Rush built on the clinical reports of others and provided a clinical description of the phenomenology of dissociative identity disorder. Subsequently, both Jean-Martin Charcot and Pierre Janet described the symptoms of the disorder and recognized the dissociative nature of the symptoms. Both Sigmund Freud and Eugen Bleuler recognized the symptoms, although Freud attributed psychodynamic mechanisms to the symptoms and Bleuler considered the symptoms to be reflective of schizophrenia. Perhaps because of an increased appreciation of the problem of child sexual and physical abuse and perhaps because of the cases described in the popular media (*The Three Faces of Eve, Sybil*), awareness of dissociative identity disorder increased. In 1980, with the inclusion of multiple personality disorder in the third edition of DSM (DSM-III), the stage was set for the development of a solid clinical research base of the disorder.

### Epidemiology

Anecdotal and research reports about dissociative identity disorder have varied in their estimates of the prevalence of the disorder. On one extreme, some investigators believe that dissociative identity disorder is extremely rare; on the other extreme, some investigators believe that dissociative identity disorder is vastly underrecognized. Well-controlled studies have reported that from 0.5 to 2 percent of general psychiatric hospital admissions meet the diagnostic criteria for dissociative identity disorder, as do perhaps as many as 5 percent of all psychiatric patients. Patients who receive the diagnosis of dissociative identity disorder are overwhelmingly women—90 to 100 percent of most samples reported. However, many clinicians and researchers believe that men are underreported in clinical samples because, they believe, most men with the disorder enter the criminal justice system, rather than the mental health system.

The disorder is most common in late adolescence and young adult life, with a mean age of diagnosis of 30 years, although patients have usually had symptoms for 5 to 10 years before the diagnosis. Several studies have found that the disorder is more common in the first-degree biological relatives of people with the disorder than in the general population.

Dissociative identity disorder frequently coexists with other mental disorders, including anxiety disorders, mood disorders, somatoform disorders, sexual dysfunctions, substance-related disorders, eating disorders, sleeping disorders, and posttraumatic stress disorder. The symptoms of dissociative identity disorder are similar to those seen in borderline personality disorder, and the differentiation between the two disorders can be difficult. Suicide attempts are common in patients with dissociative identity disorder, and some studies have reported that as many as two thirds of all patients with dissociative identity disorder do attempt suicide during the course of their illness.

### Etiology

The cause of dissociative identity disorder is unknown, although the histories of the patients invariably (approaching 100 percent) involve a traumatic event, most often in childhood. In general, four types of causative factors have been identified: (1) a traumatic life event, (2) a tendency for the disorder to develop, (3) formulative environmental factors, and (4) the absence of external support.

The traumatic event is usually childhood physical or sexual abuse, commonly incestuous. Other traumatic events may include the death of a close relative or friend during childhood and witnessing a trauma or a death.

The tendency for the disorder to develop may be biologically or psychologically based. The variable ability of persons to be hypnotized may be one example of a risk factor for the development of dissociative identity disorder. Epilepsy has been hypothesized to be involved in the cause of dissociative identity disorder, and a high percentage of abnormal EEG activity has been reported in some studies of affected patients. One study of regional cerebral blood flow revealed temporal hyperperfusion in one of the subpersonalities but not in the main personality. Although several studies have found differences in pain sensitivity and other physiological measures among the personalities, the use of those data as proof of the existence of dissociative identity disorder should be approached with great caution.

The formulative environmental factors involved in the pathogenesis of dissociative identity disorder are nonspecific and are likely to involve such factors as role models and the availability of other mechanisms with which to deal with stress.

In many cases of dissociative identity disorder, a factor in the development of the disorder seems to have been the absence of support from significant others—for example, parents, siblings, other relatives, and nonrelated people, such as teachers.

## Diagnosis

DSM-IV changes the name of the disorder from multiple personality disorder to dissociative identity disorder. In the diagnostic criteria (Table 19–5), DSM-IV also reinstates a criterion that had been included in DSM-III but had been dropped from DSM-III-R. That criterion requires an amnestic component, which research has found to be an essential component of the complete clinical picture. The diagnosis of dissociative identity disorder requires the presence of at least two distinct personality states. The diagnosis of dissociative personality disorder is excluded if the symptoms are the result of a substance (for example, alcohol) or a general medical condition (for example, complex partial seizures).

## Clinical Features

Patients with dissociative identity disorder are often thought to have a personality disorder (commonly borderline personality disorder), schizophrenia, or a rapid-cycling bipolar disorder. Clinicians must be aware of the diagnostic category and must listen for specific suggestive features of dissociative identity disorder in the clinical interview (Table 19–6). The relative frequency of specific symptoms was reported in one study of 102 dissociative identity disorder patients (Table 19–7). In spite of stories in the popular press about patients with more than 20 personalities, the median number of personalities in dissociative identity disorder is in the range of 5 to 10. Often, only two or three of the personalities are evident at di-

**Table 19–5**
**Diagnostic Criteria for Dissociative Identity Disorder**

A. The presence of two or more distinct identities or personality states (each with its own relatively enduring pattern of perceiving, relating to, and thinking about the environment and self).

B. At least two of these identities or personality states recurrently take control of the person's behavior.

C. Inability to recall important personal information that is too extensive to be explained by ordinary forgetfulness.

D. The disturbance is not due to the direct physiological effects of a substance (e.g., blackouts or chaotic behavior during alcohol intoxication) or a general medical condition (e.g., complex partial seizures). **Note:** In children, the symptoms are not attributable to imaginary playmates or other fantasy play.

Table from DSM-IV, *Diagnostic and Statistical Manual of Mental Disorders*, ed 4. Copyright American Psychiatric Association, Washington, 1994. Used with permission.

**Table 19–6**
**Signs of Multiplicity**

1. Reports of time distortions, lapses, and discontinuities
2. Being told of behavioral episodes by others that are not remembered by the patient
3. Being recognized by others or called by another name by people whom the patient does not recognize
4. Notable changes in the patient's behavior reported by a reliable observer; the patient may call himself or herself by a different name or refer to himself or herself in the third person
5. Other personalities are elicited under hypnosis or during amobarbital interviews
6. Use of the word "we" in the course of an interview
7. Discovery of writings, drawings, or other productions or objects (identification cards, clothing, etc.) among the patient's personal belongings that are not recognized or cannot be accounted for
8. Headaches
9. Hearing voices originating from within and not identified as separate
10. History of severe emotional or physical trauma as a child (usually before the age of 5 years)

Table from J L Cummings: Dissociative states, depersonalization, multiple personality, episodic memory lapses. In *Clinical Neuropsychiatry*, J L Cummings, editor, p 122. Grune & Stratton, Orlando, 1985. Used with permission.

**Table 19–7**
**Frequency of 16 Secondary Features of Dissociative Identity Disorder in 102 Patients**

| Item | No. | % |
|---|---|---|
| Another person existing inside | 92 | 90.2 |
| Voices talking | 89 | 87.3 |
| Voices coming from inside | 84 | 82.4 |
| Another person taking control | 83 | 81.4 |
| Amnesia for childhood | 83 | 81.4 |
| Referring to self as "we" or "us" | 75 | 73.5 |
| Person inside has a different name | 72 | 70.6 |
| Blank spells | 69 | 67.7 |
| Flashbacks | 68 | 66.7 |
| Being told by others of unremembered events | 64 | 62.8 |
| Feelings of unreality | 58 | 56.9 |
| Strangers know the patient | 45 | 44.1 |
| Noticing that objects are missing | 43 | 42.2 |
| Coming out of blank spell in a strange place | 37 | 36.3 |
| Objects are present that cannot be accounted for | 32 | 31.4 |
| Different handwriting styles | 28 | 27.5 |

Table from C A Ross, S D Miller, P Reagor, L Bjornson, G A Fraser, G Anderson: Structured interview data from 102 cases of multiple personality disorder from four centers. Am J Psychiatry *147*: 596, 1990. Used with permission.

agnosis; the others are recognized during the course of treatment.

The transition from one personality to another is often sudden and dramatic. The patient generally has amnesia during each personality state for the existence of the others and for the events that took place when another personality was dominant. Sometimes, however, one personality state is not bound by such amnesia and retains complete awareness of the existence, qualities, and activities of the other personalities. At other times, the personalities are aware of all or some of the others to varying degrees and may experience the others as friends, companions, or adversaries. In classic cases, each personality has a fully integrated, highly complex set of associated memories and characteristic attitudes, personal relationships, and behavior patterns. Most often, the personalities have proper names; occasionally, one or more is given the name of its function—for example, the protector. Although some clinicians have emphasized that one of the personalities tends to be the dominant personality, that is not always the case. In fact, sometimes one personality masquerades as one of the others. However, usually a host personality is the one who presents for treatment and carries the patient's legal name. That host personality is likely to be depressed or anxious, may have masochistic personality traits, and may seem overly moral.

The first appearance of the secondary personality or personalities may be spontaneous or may emerge in relation to what seems to be a precipitant (including hypnosis or a drug-assisted interview). The personalities may be of both sexes, of various races and ages, and from families different from the patient's family of origin. The most common subordinate personality is childlike. Often, the personalities are disparate and may even be opposites. In the same person, one of the personalities may be extroverted, even sexually promiscuous, and others may be introverted, withdrawn, and sexually inhibited.

On examination, patients often show nothing unusual in their mental status, other than a possible amnesia for periods of varying durations. Often, only with prolonged interviews or many contacts with a patient with dissociative identity disorder is a clinician able to detect the presence of multiple personalities. Sometimes, by asking a patient to keep a diary, the clinician finds the multiple personalities revealed in the diary entries. An estimated 60 percent of patients switch into alternate personalities only occasionally; another 20 percent of patients not only have rare episodes but also are adept at covering the switches.

## Differential Diagnosis

The differential diagnosis includes two other dissociative disorders, dissociative amnesia and dissociative fugue. However, both of those disorders lack the shifts in identity and the awareness of the original identity that are seen in dissociative identity disorder. Psychotic disorders, notably schizophrenia, may be confused with dissociative identity disorder only because schizophrenic persons may be delusional and believe that they have separate identities or report hearing other personalities' voices. In schizophrenia, a formal thought disorder, chronic social deterioration, and other distinguishing signs are present. Recently, clinicians have increasingly appreciated rapid-cycling bipolar disorders. The symptoms of rapid-cycling bipolar disorders appear to be similar to those of dissociative identity disorder; however, interviewing reveals the presence of discrete personalities in dissociative identity disorder patients. Borderline personality disorder may coexist with dissociative identity disorder, but the alteration of person-

alities in dissociative identity disorder may be mistakenly interpreted as nothing more than the irritability of mood and self-image problems that are characteristic of borderline personality disorder patients. Malingering presents a difficult diagnostic problem. Clear secondary gain raises suspicion, and drug-assisted interviews may be helpful in making the diagnosis. Among the neurological disorders to consider, complex partial epilepsy is the most likely to imitate the symptoms of dissociative identity disorder (Table 19–3).

## Course and Prognosis

Dissociative identity disorder can develop in children as young as 3 years of age. In children the symptoms may appear trancelike and may be accompanied by changes in abilities, depressive disorder symptoms, amnestic periods, hallucinatory voices, disavowal of behaviors, and suicidal or self-injurious behaviors. In spite of the female predominance in the disorder, affected children are more likely to be boys than girls. In adolescence the female predominance develops. Two symptom patterns in affected female adolescents have been observed: One symptom pattern is of a chaotic life with promiscuity, drug use, somatic symptoms, and suicide attempts. Such patients may be classified as having an impulse control disorder, schizophrenia, rapid-cycling bipolar I disorder, or histrionic or borderline personality disorder. A second pattern is characterized by withdrawal and childlike behaviors. Sometimes those patients are misclassified as having a mood disorder, a somatoform disorder, or generalized anxiety disorder. In male adolescents with dissociative identity disorder, the symptoms may get them into trouble with the law or school officials, and they may eventually end up in prison.

The earlier the onset of dissociative identity disorder, the worse the prognosis is. One or more of the personalities may function relatively well, while others function marginally. The level of impairment ranges from moderate to severe, the determining variables being the number, the type, and the chronicity of the various personalities. The disorder is considered the most severe and chronic of the dissociative disorders, and recovery is generally incomplete. In addition, individual personalities may have their own separate mental disorders; mood disorders, personality disorders, and other dissociative disorders are the most common.

## Treatment

The most efficacious approaches to dissociative identity involve insight-oriented psychotherapy, often in association with hypnotherapy or drug-assisted interviewing techniques. Hypnotherapy or drug-assisted interviewing can be useful in obtaining additional history, identifying previously unrecognized personalities, and fostering abreaction. A psychotherapeutic treatment plan should begin by confirming the diagnosis and by identifying and characterizing the various personalities. If any of the personalities are inclined toward self-destructive or otherwise violent behavior, the therapist should engage the patient and the appropriate personalities in treatment contracts regarding those dangerous behaviors. Hospitalization may be necessary in some cases.

Several clinicians and researchers have written about psychotherapy with dissociative identity disorder patients. A summation of the basic principles (Table 19–8) and a description of the stages of therapy (Table 19–9) are useful

**Table 19–8**
**Principles of Successful Therapy for Dissociative Identity Disorder**

1. Condition was created by broken boundaries. Therefore, a successful treatment has a secure treatment frame and firm, consistent boundaries.
2. Condition is one of subjective dyscontrol and passively endured assaults and changes. Therefore, the focus must be on mastery and the patient's active participation in the treatment process.
3. Condition is one of involuntariness. Its sufferers did not elect to be traumatized and find their symptoms are often beyond their control. Therefore, the therapy must be based on a strong therapeutic alliance, and efforts to establish that alliance must be undertaken throughout the process.
4. Condition is one of buried traumata and sequestered affect. Therefore, what has been hidden away must be uncovered, and what feeling has been buried must be abreacted.
5. Condition is one of perceived separateness and conflict among the alters. Therefore, the therapy must emphasize their collaboration, cooperation, empathy, and identification with one another so that their separateness becomes redundant and their conflicts are muted.
6. Condition is one of hypnotic alternate realities. Therefore, the therapist's communications must be clear and straight. There is no room for confusing communication.
7. Condition is related to the inconsistency of important others. Therefore, the therapist must be evenhanded with all the alters, avoiding playing favorites or dramatically altering his or her own behavior toward the various personalities. The therapist's consistency across all the alters is one of the most powerful assaults on the patient's dissociative defenses.
8. Condition is one of shattered security, self-esteem, and future orientation. Therefore, the therapist must make efforts to restore morale and inculcate realistic hope.
9. Condition stems from overwhelming experiences. Therefore, the pacing of the therapy is essential. Most treatment failures occur when the pace of the therapy outstrips the patient's capacity to tolerate the material under discussion. It is wise to adhere to the rule of thirds: if one cannot get into the difficult material one planned to address in the first third of the session, to work on it in the second, and process it and restabilize the patient in the third, not approaching the material, lest the patient leave the session in an overwhelmed state. Abreaction cannot be allowed to become retraumatization.
10. Condition often results from the irresponsibility of others. Therefore, the therapist must be responsible and hold the patient to a high standard of responsibility once the therapist is confident that the patient, across alters, actually grasps what reasonable responsibility entails.
11. Condition often results because people who could have protected a child did nothing. The therapist can anticipate that technical neutrality will be interpreted as uncaring and rejecting and is best served by taking a warm stance that allows for a latitude of affective expression.
12. Patient has many cognitive errors. The therapy must address and correct them on an ongoing basis.

Table adapted from R P Klufe: Multiple personality disorder. In *Review of Psychiatry*, vol 10, A Tasman, S M Goldfinger, editors, p 161. American Psychiatric Press, Washington, 1991. Used with permission.

**Table 19–9**
**Stages of Therapy**
**for Dissociative Identity Disorder**

1. Establishing the psychotherapy involves the creation of an atmosphere of safety in which the diagnosis can be made, the security of the treatment frame can be assured, the patient begins to understand the concept of the treatment alliance in a preliminary way, the nature of the treatment is introduced to the patient, and sufficient hope and confidence are established so that the patient feels prepared to begin what may be a long and difficult process.
2. Preliminary interventions involve gaining access to the most readily reached personalities; establishing agreements or contracts with the alters against terminating treatment abruptly, self-harm, suicide, and as many other dysfunctional behaviors as the patient is able to agree to curtail; fostering communication and cooperation among the alters (a process that is the core of the treatment from here on); expanding the therapeutic alliance by gaining the patient's acceptance of the diagnosis across increasing numbers of the personalities (some deny it to the end); and offering what symptomatic relief is possible. Hypnosis may play a valuable role in facilitating those measures.
3. History gathering and mapping lead to learning more about the personalities, their origins, and their relationships with one another. The patient may be regarded as a system with its own rules of interaction. Here one learns the who, when, why, where, what, and how of the alters; their names (if any); age of onset and self-perceived age; the reasons for their creation and persistence; where they fit in the patient's overall history and in their relationships within the world of the personalities; and their particular problems, functions, and concerns. On that basis, one begins to work with their individual and interactional issues and presses for still more cooperation and collaboration.
4. Metabolism of the trauma refers to the often strenuous efforts needed to access and process the overwhelming events associated with the origins of the disorder. Such work should not be undertaken until one has some idea of the lay of the land in terms of the patient's system of personalities and at least some intellectual insight into what material is likely to be encountered. Negative therapeutic reactions are common. Precipitous or premature entry into this stage before stages 1 through 3 are achieved is a frequent cause of unnecessary crises and interruptions of therapy.
5. Moving toward integration-resolution involves the working through of recovered materials across the alters and facilitating still further cooperation, communication, and mutual awareness with enhanced mutual identification and empathy. Communication is increased, many internal conflicts become muted or resolved, and the alters begin to show some blurring of their once discrete characteristics. Some experience identity diffusion (for example, "for a moment I wasn't sure who I was"; "I guess I am both Sally and Joanie").
6. Integration-resolution consists of the patient's coming to a new and more solid stance toward his or her self and the world. A smooth collaboration among the alters constitutes a resolution; their blending into a unity is an integration.
7. Learning new coping skills is important. The patient may have to face for the first time perspectives on his or her life that were not appreciable before and be helped to negotiate the circumstances that once were handled in a dissociative manner in constructive ways. Many important life decisions and relationships may require renegotiation.
8. Solidification of gains and working through may require as much therapy as reaching integration or resolution. The patient has to relearn how to live in the world. Often working through in the transference what has been learned about the past is valuable. Characterological issues that were inaccessible before or hidden behind a welter of

*Continued*

**Table 19–9**
*Continued*

symptoms must be addressed. Often extensive coaching on the management of relationships and intercurrent traumata is necessary.

9. Follow-up is advisable on several grounds. The stability of the outcome should be assessed, especially for those who opt for resolution rather than integration. Also, layers of personalities that had not entered the prior treatment may be encountered, and some apparent good results are flights into health.

Table adapted from R P Kluft: Multiple personality disorder. In *Review of Psychiatry*, vol 10, A Tasman, S M Goldfinger, editors, p 161. American Psychiatric Press, Washington, 1991. Used with permission.

guides in the difficult therapy for those patients. Usually, the initial therapy stage fosters communication between the personalities to begin reintegration. The relative benefits of reintegration versus resolution continue to be disputed, and the relative benefits of either approach are not known. Communication among the personalities also helps patients control their overall behavior. The clinician must attempt to identify the personalities that remember the traumatic childhood events almost invariably associated with the disorder.

The use of antipsychotic medications in the patients is almost never indicated. Some data indicate that antidepressant and antianxiety medications may be useful as adjuvants to psychotherapy. A few uncontrolled studies report that anticonvulsant medications—for example, carbamazepine (Tegretol)—help selected patients.

# DEPERSONALIZATION DISORDER

DSM-IV characterizes depersonalization disorder as a persistent or recurrent alteration in the perception of the self to the extent that the sense of one's own reality is temporarily lost. Patients with depersonalization disorder may feel that they are mechanical, in a dream, or detached from their bodies. The episodes are ego-dystonic, and the patients realize the unreality of the symptoms.

Some clinicians distinguish between depersonalization and derealization. *Depersonalization* is the feeling that one's body or one's personal self is strange and unreal; *derealization* is the perception of objects in the external world as being strange and unreal. The distinction provides a more accurate description of each phenomenon than is acheived by grouping them together under the rubric of depersonalization.

## Epidemiology

As an occasional isolated experience in the lives of many persons, depersonalization is a common phenomenon and is not necessarily pathological. Studies indicate that transient depersonalization may occur in as much as 70 percent of a given population, with no significant difference between men and women. Depersonalization is a frequent event in children as they develop the capacity for self-awareness, and adults often undergo a temporary sense of unreality when they travel to new and strange places.

Information about the epidemiology of pathological de-

personalization is scanty. In a few recent studies, depersonalization was found to occur in women at least twice as frequently as in men; it is rarely found in persons over 40 years of age.

## Etiology

Depersonalization disorder may be caused by psychological, neurological, or systemic disease. Experiences of depersonalization have been associated with epilepsy, brain tumors, sensory deprivation, and emotional trauma. Depersonalization disorder is associated with an array of substances, including alcohol, barbiturates, benzodiazepines, scopolamine (Donnagel), clioquinol (Vioform), β-adrenergic antagonists, marijuana, and virtually any phencyclidinelike or hallucinogenic substance. Depersonalization phenomena have been caused by electrical stimulation of the cortex of the temporal lobes during neurosurgery. Systemic causes include endocrine disorders of the thyroid and the pancreas. Anxiety and depression are predisposing factors, as is severe stress, such as what one experiences in combat or in an automobile accident. Depersonalization is frequently a symptom seen in association with anxiety disorders, depressive disorders, and schizophrenia.

## Diagnosis

The DSM-IV diagnostic criteria for depersonalization disorder (Table 19–10) are essentially unchanged from those in DSM-III-R. The diagnosis requires persistent or recurrent episodes of depersonalization that result in significant distress to patients or an impairment in their ability to function in social, occupational, or interpersonal relationships. The disorder is largely differentiated from psychotic disorders by the diagnostic requirement that reality testing remains intact in depersonalization disorder. The disorder cannot be diagnosed if the symptoms are better accounted for by another mental disorder, substance ingestion, or a general medical condition.

**Table 19–10**
**Diagnostic Criteria for Depersonalization Disorder**

A. Persistent or recurrent experiences of feeling detached from, and as if one is an outside observer of, one's mental processes or body (e.g., feeling like one is in a dream).

B. During the depersonalization experience, reality testing remains intact.

C. The depersonalization causes clinically significant distress or impairment in social, occupational, or other important areas of functioning.

D. The depersonalization experience does not occur exclusively during the course of another mental disorder, such as schizophrenia, panic disorder, acute stress disorder, or another dissociative disorder, and is not due to the direct physiological effects of a substance (e.g., a drug of abuse, a medication) or a general medical condition (e.g., temporal lobe epilepsy).

Table from DSM-IV, *Diagnostic and Statistical Manual of Mental Disorders*, ed 4. Copyright American Psychiatric Association, Washington, 1994. Used with permission.

## Clinical Features

The central characteristic of depersonalization is the quality of unreality and estrangement. Inner mental processes and external events seem to go on exactly as before, but they feel different and no longer seem to have any relation or significance to the person. Parts of the body or the entire physical being may seem foreign, as may mental operations and accustomed behavior. Particularly common is the sensation of a change in the patient's body; for instance, patients may feel that their extremities are bigger or smaller than usual. Hemidepersonalization, the patient's feeling that half of the body is unreal or does not exist, may be related to contralateral parietal lobe disease. Anxiety often accompanies the disorder, and many patients complain of distortions in their senses of time and space.

An occasional phenomenon is doubling; patients feel that the point of conscious I-ness is outside their bodies, often a few feet overhead; from there they observe themselves, as if they were totally separate persons. Sometimes patients believe that they are in two places at the same time, a condition known as reduplicative paramnesia or double orientation. Most patients are aware of the disturbances in their sense of reality; that awareness is considered one of the salient characteristics of the disorder.

A 20-year-old male college student sought a psychiatric consultation because he was worried that he might be going insane. For the past two years he had experienced increasingly frequent episodes of feeling outside himself. Those episodes were accompanied by a sense of deadness in his body. In addition, during those periods he was uncertain of his balance and frequently stumbled into furniture; the stumbling was most apt to occur in public, especially if he was anxious. During the episodes he felt a lack of easy, natural control of his body; his thoughts seemed foggy, in a way that reminded him of receiving intravenous anesthetic agents for an appendectomy some five years previously.

The patient's subjective sense of lack of control was especially troublesome, and he would fight it by shaking his head and saying "Stop" to himself. Doing so would momentarily clear his mind and restore his sense of autonomy but only temporarily, as the feelings of deadness and of being outside himself would return. Gradually, over a period of several hours, the unpleasant experiences would fade. The patient was anxious, however, about their return, since he found them increasing in both frequency and duration.

At the time the patient came for treatment, he was experiencing the symptoms about twice a week, and each incident lasted from three to four hours. On several occasions the episodes had occurred while he was driving his car and was alone; worried that he might have an accident, he had stopped driving unless someone accompanied him. Increasingly, he had begun to discuss the problem with his girlfriend, and eventually she had become less affectionate toward him, complaining that he had lost his sense of humor and was totally self-preoccupied. She threatened to break off with him unless he changed, and she began to date other men.

The patient's college grades remained unimpaired; they had, in fact, improved over the past six months because the patient was spending more time studying than had previously been the case. Although discouraged by his symptoms, the patient slept well at night, had noted no change in appetite, and had experienced no impairment in concentration. He was neither fatigued nor physically edgy because of his worry.

Because a cousin had been hospitalized for many years with severe mental illness, the patient had begun to wonder if a similar fate would befall him, and he sought direct reassurance on the matter.

*Discussion.* Depersonalization—that is, alteration in the perception or experience of the self, so that the usual sense of one's own reality is lost—can be a symptom of a variety of mental disorders, such as schizophrenia, anxiety disorders, mood disorders, personality disorders, and cognitive disorders. Mild depersonalization, without functional impairment, occurs at some time in a large proportion of young adults and does not by itself warrant diagnosis as a mental disorder. When, as in this case, the symptom of depersonalization occurs in the absence of a pervasive disorder and is sufficiently severe and persistent to cause marked distress, the diagnosis of depersonalization disorder is made.

## Differential Diagnosis

Depersonalization may occur as a symptom in numerous other disorders (Table 19–11). The common occurrence of depersonalization in patients with depressive disorders and schizophrenia should alert the clinician to the possibility that the patient who initially complains of feelings of unreality and estrangement is suffering from one of those more common disorders. A history and the mental status examination should in most cases disclose the characteristic features of depressive disorders and schizophrenia. Because psychotomimetic drugs often induce long-lasting changes in the experience of the reality of the self and the environment, the clinician must inquire about the use of those substances. The presence of other clinical phenomena in patients complaining of a sense of unreality should usually take precedence in determining the diagnosis. In general, the diagnosis of depersonalization dis-

**Table 19–11**
**Causes of Depersonalization**

| | |
|---|---|
| Neurological disorders | Idiopathic mental |
| Epilepsy | disorders |
| Migraine | Schizophrenia |
| Brain tumors | Depressive disorders |
| Cerebrovascular disease | Manic episodes |
| Cerebral trauma | Coversion disorder |
| Encephalitis | Anxiety disorders |
| General paresis | Obsessive-compulsive |
| Dementia of the | disorder |
| Alzheimer's type | Personality disorders |
| Huntington's disease | Phobic-anxiety |
| Spinocerebellar | depersonalization |
| degeneration | syndrome |
| | |
| Toxic and metabolic | In normal persons |
| disorders | Exhaustion |
| Hypoglycemia | Boredom; sensory |
| Hypoparathyroidism | deprivation |
| Carbon monoxide | Emotional shock |
| poisoning | |
| Mescaline intoxication | In hemidepersonalization |
| Botulism | Lateralized (usually right |
| Hyperventilation | parietal) focal brain |
| Hypothyroidism | lesion |

Table adapted from J L Cummings: Dissociative states, depersonalization, multiple personality, episodic memory lapses. In *Clinical Neuropsychiatry*, J L Cummings, editor, p 123. Grune & Stratton, Orlando, 1985. Used with permission.

order is reserved for those conditions in which depersonalization constitutes the predominating symptom.

The fact that depersonalization phenomena may result from gross disturbances in brain function underlies the necessity for a neurological evaluation, especially when the depersonalization is not accompanied by common and obvious psychiatric symptoms. In particular, the possibility of a brain tumor or epilepsy should be considered. The experience of depersonalization may be the earliest presenting symptom of a neurological disorder.

### Course and Prognosis

In the large majority of patients, the symptoms of depersonalization disorder first appear suddenly; only a few patients report a gradual onset. The disorder starts most often between the ages of 15 and 30 years, but it has been seen in patients as young as 10 years of age; it occurs less frequently after age 30 and almost never in the late decades of life. A few follow-up studies indicate that, in more than half of the cases, depersonalization tends to be a long-lasting condition. In many patients the symptoms run a steady course without any significant fluctuation of intensity; but the symptoms may occur episodically, interspersed with symptom-free intervals. Little is known about precipitating factors, although the disorder has been observed to begin during a period of relaxation after a person has experienced fatiguing psychological stress. The disorder is sometimes ushered in by an attack of acute anxiety that is frequently accompanied by hyperventilation.

### Treatment

Little attention has been given to the treatment of patients with depersonalization disorder. At this time there are not sufficient data on which a specific pharmacological treatment may be based. However, the anxiety usually responds to antianxiety agents. An underlying disorder (for example, schizophrenia) can also be treated pharmacologically. Psychotherapeutic approaches are equally untested. As with all patients with neurotic symptoms, the decision to use psychoanalysis or insight-oriented psychotherapy is determined not by the presence of the symptom itself but by a variety of positive indications derived from an assessment of the patient's personality, human relationships, and life situation.

## DISSOCIATIVE DISORDER NOT OTHERWISE SPECIFIED

The diagnosis of dissociative disorder not otherwise specified (NOS) is meant for disorders with dissociative features that do not meet the diagnostic criteria for dissociative amnesia, dissociative fugue, dissociative identity disorder, or depersonalization disorder. The DSM-IV examples of dissociative disorder NOS (Table 19–12) have been modified from those in DSM-III-R to take into account changes in the diagnostic criteria for the other dissociative disorders. Specifically, example 1 (Table 19–12) describes patients who do not meet the diagnostic criteria

**Table 19–12**
**Diagnostic Criteria for Dissociative Disorder Not Otherwise Specified**

This category is included for disorders in which the predominant feature is a dissociative symptom (i.e., a disruption in the usually integrated functions of consciousness, memory, identity, or perception of the environment) that does not meet the criteria for any specific dissociative disorder. Examples include

1. Clinical presentations similar to dissociative identity disorder that fail to meet full criteria for this disorder. Examples include presentations in which (a) there are not two or more distinct personality states, or (b) amnesia for important personal information does not occur

2. Derealization unaccompanied by depersonalization in adults

3. States of dissociation that occur in individuals who have been subjected to periods of prolonged and intense coercive persuasion (e.g., brainwashing, thought reform, or indoctrination while captive)

4. Dissociative trance disorder: single or episodic disturbances in the state of consciousness, identity or memory that are indigenous to particular locations and cultures. Dissociative trance involves narrowing of awareness of immediate surroundings or stereotyped behaviors or movements that are experienced as being beyond one's control. Possession trance involves replacement of the customary sense of personal identity by a new identity, attributed to the influence of a spirit, power, deity, or other person, and associated with stereotyped "involuntary" movements or amnesia. Examples include *amok* (Indonesia), *bebainan* (Indonesia), *latah* (Malaysia), *pibloktoq* (Arctic), *ataque de nervios* (Latin America), and possession (India). The dissociative or trance disorder is not a normal part of a broadly accepted collective cultural or religious practice

5. Loss of consciousness, stupor, or coma not attributable to a general medical condition

6. Ganser syndrome: the giving of approximate answers to questions, (e.g., "2 plus 2 equals 5") when not associated with dissociative amnesia or dissociative fugue

Table from DSM-IV, *Diagnostic and Statistical Manual of Mental Disorders*, ed 4. Copyright American Psychiatric Association, Washington, 1994. Used with permission.

for dissociative identity disorder because the second personality is not sufficiently distinct or because the patient has no amnestic periods. DSM-III-R described a case of dissociative fugue in which the patient did not adopt a new personality. Because in DSM-IV confusion about personal identity is sufficient for the diagnosis of dissociative fugue, that example is no longer necessary. According to DSM-IV, derealization in the absence of depersonalization is an example of dissociative disorder NOS.

### Dissociative Trance Disorder

DSM-IV adds, as an example of dissociative disorder NOS, patients with single or episodic alterations in consciousness that are limited to particular locations or cultures. The example states that the "dissociative or trance disorder is not a normal part of a broadly accepted collective cultural or religious practice." DSM-IV includes in its appendixes a suggested set of diagnostic criteria for dissociative trance disorder (Table 19–13). The disorder is similar to the diagnosis of trance and possession disorder in ICD-10. The DSM-IV diagnostic criteria require that the symptoms cause the patient significant distress or an impairment in the ability to function.

Trance states are altered states of consciousness, and patients exhibit diminished responsivity to environmental stimuli. Children may have repeated amnestic periods or trancelike states after physical abuse or trauma. Possession and trance states are curious and imperfectly understood forms of dissociation. A common example of a trance state is the medium who presides over a spiritual seance. Typically, mediums enter a dissociative state, during which a person from the so-called spirit world takes over much of the mediums' conscious awareness and influences their thoughts and speech.

Automatic writing and crystal gazing are less common manifestations of possession or trance states. In automatic writing the dissociation affects only the arm and the hand that write the message, which often discloses mental contents of which the writer was unaware. Crystal gazing results in a trance state in which visual hallucinations are prominent.

Phenomena related to trance states include highway hypnosis and the similar mental states experienced by airplane pilots. The monotony of moving at high speeds through environments that provide little in the way of distractions to the operator of the vehicle leads to a fixation on a single object—for example, a dial on the instrument panel or the never-ending horizon of a road running straight ahead for miles. A trancelike state of consciousness results in which visual hallucinations may occur and in which the danger of a serious accident is always present. Possibly in the same order of phenomena are the hallucinations and dissociated mental states in patients who have been confined to respirators for long periods without adequate environmental distractions.

The religions of many cultures recognize that the practice of concentration may lead to a variety of dissociative phenomena, such as hallucinations, paralyses, and other sensory disturbances. On occasion, hypnosis may precipitate a self-limited but sometimes prolonged trance state.

## Ganser's Syndrome

Ganser's syndrome is the voluntary production of severe psychiatric symptoms, sometimes described as the giving of approximate answers or talking past the point (for example, when asked to multiply 4 times 5, the patient answers "21"). The syndrome may occur in persons with other mental disorders, such as schizophrenia, depressive disorders, toxic states, paresis, alcohol use disorders, and factitious disorder. The psychological symptoms generally represent the patient's sense of mental illness, rather than any recognized diagnostic category. The syndrome is commonly associated with such dissociative phenomena as amnesia, fugue, perceptual disturbances, and conversion symptoms. Ganser's syndrome is apparently most common in men and in prisoners, although prevalence data and familial patterns are not established. A major predisposing factor is the existence of a severe personality disorder. The differential diagnosis may be extremely difficult. Unless the patient is able to admit the factitious nature of the presenting symptoms or unless conclusive evidence from objective psychological tests indicates that the symptoms are false, the clinician may not be able to determine whether the patient has a true disorder. The syndrome may be recognized by its pansymptomatic nature or by the fact that the symptoms are often worse when patients believe they are being watched. Recovery from the syndrome is sudden; patients claim amnesia for the events. Ganser's syndrome was previously classified as a factitous disorder.

## Dissociated States

Certain degrees of dissociation may occur in persons who have been subjected to periods of prolonged and intensive coercive persuasion (such as brainwashing, thought reform, and indoctrination while being held captive by terrorists or cultists). Whether the states are truly dissociative disorders is open to question, since some evidence, especially in victims of Nazi concentration camps, indicates that the persons are often alexithymic, which results from massive regression, rather than from dissociation.

**Table 19–13**
**Research Criteria for Dissociative Trance Disorder**

A. Either (1) or (2):
   (1) trance, i.e., temporary marked alteration in the state of consciousness or loss of customary sense of personal identity without replacement by an alternate identity, associated with at least one of the following:
      (a) narrowing of awareness of immediate surroundings, or unusually narrow and selective focusing on environmental stimuli
      (b) stereotyped behaviors or movements that are experienced as being beyond one's control
   (2) possession trance, a single or episodic alteration in the state of consciousness characterized by the replacement of customary sense of personal identity by a new identity. This is attributed to the influence of a spirit, power, deity, or other person, as evidenced by one (or more) of the following:
      (a) stereotyped and culturally determined behaviors or movements that are experienced as being controlled by the possessing agent
      (b) full or partial amnesia for the event

B. The trance or possession trance state is not accepted as a normal part of a collective cultural or religious practice.

C. The trance or possession trance state causes clinically significant distress or impairment in social, occupational, or other important areas of functioning.

D. The trance or possession trance state does not occur exclusively during the course of a psychotic disorder (including mood disorder with psychotic features and brief psychotic disorder) or dissociative identity disorder and is not due to the direct physiological effects of a substance or a general medical condition.

## References

Boon S, Draijer N: Multiple personality disorder in The Netherlands: A clinical investigation of 71 patients. Am J Psychatry *150*: 489, 1993.

Brna T G Jr, Wilson C C: Psychogenic amnesia. Am Fam Physician *41*: 229, 1990.

Fahy T A: The diagnosis of multiple personality disorder: A critical review. Br J Psychiatry *153*: 597, 1988.

Fahy T A, Abas M, Brown J C: Multiple personality: A symptom of psychiatric disorder. Br J Psychiatry *154*: 99, 1989.

Gabbard G O: *Psychodyamic Psychiatry in Clinical Practice: The DSM-IV Edition*. American Psychiatric Press, Washington, 1994.

Good M I: Substance-induced dissociative disorders and psychiatric nosology. J Clin Psychopharmacol *9*: 88, 1989.

Hollander E, Liebowitz M R, DeCaria C, Fairbanks J, Fallon B, Klein D F: Treatment of depersonalization with serotonin reuptake blockers. J Clin Psychopharmacol *10*: 200, 1990.

Kapur N: Amnesia in relation to fugue states: Distinguishing a neurological form from a psychogenic basis. Br J Psychiatry *159*: 872, 1991.

Loewenstein R J: Multiple personality disorder. Psychiatr Clin North Am *14* (3): 489, 1991.

Merskey H: The manufacture of personalities: The production of multiple personality disorder. Br J Psychiatry *160*: 327, 1992.

Putnam F W, Loewenstein R J: Treatment of multiple personality disorder: A survey of current practices. Am J Psychiatry *150*: 1048, 1993.

Ross C A, Anderson G, Fleischer W P, Norton G R: The frequency of multiple personality disorder among psychiatric inpatients. Am J Psychiatry *148*: 1717, 1991.

Ross C A, Miller S D, Reagor P, Bjornson L, Fraser G A, Andersen G: Structured interview data on 102 cases of multiple personality disorder from four centers. Am J Psychiatry *147*: 596, 1990.

Rowan A J, Soenbaum D H: Ictal amnesia and fugue states. Adv Neurol *55*: 357, 1991.

Sandberg D A, Lynn S J: Dissociative experiences, psychopathology and adjustment, and child and adolescent maltreatment in female college students. J Abnorm Psychol *101*: 717, 1992.

Saxe G N, van der Kolk B A, Berkowitz R, Chinman G, Hall K, Lieberg G, Schwartz J: Dissociative disorders in psychiatric inpatients. Am J Psychiatry *150*: 1037, 1993.

Simeon D, Hollander E: Depersonalization disorder. Psychiatr Ann *23*: 382, 1993.

Spiegel D, editor: Dissociative disorders. In *Review of Psychiatry*, vol 10, A Tasman, S M Goldfinger, editors, p 141. American Psychiatric Press, Washington, 1991.

Steinberg M, Rounsaville B, Cicchetti D: Detection of dissociative disorder in psychiatric patients by screening instrument and a structured diagnostic interview. Am J Psychiatry *148*: 1050, 1991.

Torch E M: The psychotherapeutic treatment of depersonalization disorder. Hillside J Clin Psychiatry *9*: 133, 1987.

# Human Sexuality

## 20.1 / Normal Sexuality

Sexual behavior is diverse and determined by a complex interaction of factors. It is affected by one's relationships with others, by one's life circumstances, and by the culture in which one lives. A person's sexuality is enmeshed with other personality factors, with biological makeup, and with a general sense of self. It includes the perception of being male or female, and it reflects developmental experiences with sex throughout the life cycle. A rigid definition of normal sexuality is difficult to draw and is clinically impractical. It is easier to define abnormal sexuality—that is, sexual behavior that is destructive to oneself or others, that cannot be directed toward a partner, that excludes stimulation of the primary sex organs, that is inappropriately associated with guilt and anxiety, or that is compulsive. Sex outside of marriage, masturbation, and various forms of sexual stimulation involving other than the primary sexual organs may still fall within normal limits, depending on the total context.

### PSYCHOSEXUALITY

A person's sexuality and total personality are so entwined that it is virtually impossible to speak of sexuality as a separate entity. The term "psychosexual" is, therefore, used to imply personality development and functioning as those are affected by one's sexuality. "Psychosexual" is clearly not limited to sexual feelings and behavior, nor is it synonymous with libido in the broad Freudian sense.

In Sigmund Freud's view, all pleasurable impulses and activities are ultimately sexual and should be so designated from the start. That generalization has led to endless misinterpretations of Freudian sexual concepts by the laity and to confusion of one motivation with another by psychiatrists. For example, some oral activities are directed toward obtaining food, whereas others are directed toward achieving sexual gratification. Just because both are pleasure-seeking behaviors and both use the same organs, they are not, as Freud contended, necessarily sexual. Labeling all pleasure-seeking behaviors "sexual" precludes the clarification of motivation. A person may also use sexual activities for gratification of nonsexual needs, such as dependent, aggressive, and status needs. Although sexual and nonsexual impulses may motivate behavior jointly, the analysis of behavior depends on understanding the underlying individual motivations and their interactions.

### SEXUAL LEARNING IN CHILDHOOD

Not until Freud described the effects of children's experiences on their characters as adults did the world recognize the universality of sexual activity and sexual learning in children. Most sexual learning experiences in childhood occur without the parents' awareness, but consciousness of the child's sex does influence parental behavior. Male infants, for instance, tend to be handled more vigorously and female infants to be cuddled more. Fathers spend more time with their infant sons than with their daughters, and fathers also tend to be more aware of their sons' adolescent concerns than of their daughters' anxieties. Boys are more likely than are girls to be physically disciplined. The child's sex affects parental tolerance for aggression and the reinforcement or the extinction of activity or passivity and of intellectual, aesthetic, and athletic interests.

Direct observation of children in various situations reveals that genital play in infants is part of the normal pattern of development. According to Harry Harlow, interaction with mothers and peers is necessary for the development of effective adult sexual behavior in monkeys, a finding that has relevance to the normal socialization of children. There is a critical period in development beyond which infants may be immune or resistant to certain types of stimulation but during which they are particularly susceptible to such stimuli. The detailed relation of critical periods to psychosexual development has yet to be established; presumably, Freud's stages of psychosexual development—oral, anal, phallic, latent, and genital—provide a broad framework of development.

### PSYCHOSEXUAL FACTORS

A person's sexuality depends on four interrelated factors: sexual identity, gender identity, sexual orientation, and sexual behavior. Those factors affect personality growth, development, and functioning, and their totality is termed "psychosexual factors." Sexuality is something more than physical sex, coital or noncoital, and something less than every aspect of behavior directed toward attaining pleasure.

## Sexual Identity and Gender Identity

*Sexual identity* is a person's biological sexual characteristics: chromosomes, external genitalia, internal genitalia, hormonal composition, gonads, and secondary sex characteristics. In normal development, they form a cohesive pattern, so that a person has no doubt about his or her sex. *Gender identity* is a person's sense of maleness or femaleness.

**Sexual identity.** Modern embryological studies have shown that all mammalian embryos—the genetically male and the genetically female—are anatomically female during the early stages of fetal life. Differentiation of the male from the female results from the action of fetal androgen; the action begins about the sixth week of embryonic life and is completed by the end of the third month. Recent studies have explained the effects of fetal hormones on the masculinization or the feminization of the brain. In animals, prenatal hormonal stimulation of the brain is necessary for male and female reproductive and copulatory behavior. The fetus is also vulnerable to exogenously administered androgen during that period. For instance, if the pregnant mother receives sufficient exogenous androgen, a female fetus possessing ovaries can develop external genitalia resembling those of a male (Table 20.1–1).

**Gender identity.** By the age of 2 or 3 years, almost everyone has a firm conviction that "I am male" or "I am female." Yet even if maleness and femaleness develop normally, the person still has the adaptive task of developing a sense of masculinity or femininity.

Gender identity, according to Robert Stoller, "connotes psychological aspects of behavior related to masculinity and femininity." He considers gender social and sex biological: "Most often the two are relatively congruent, that is, males tend to be manly and females womanly." But sex and gender may develop in conflicting or even opposite ways. Gender identity results from an almost infinite series of cues derived from experiences with family members, teachers, friends, and coworkers and from cultural phenomena. Physical characteristics derived from one's biological sex—such as general physique, body shape, and physical dimensions—interrelate with an intricate system of stimuli, including rewards and punishment and parental gender labels, to establish gender identity.

The formation of gender identity is based on parental and cultural attitudes, the infant's external genitalia, and a genetic influence, which is physiologically active by the sixth week of fetal life. Even though family, cultural, and biological influences may complicate the establishment of a sense of masculinity or femininity, the standard and healthy outcome is a relatively secure sense of identification with one's biological sex—a stable gender identity

GENDER ROLE. Related to and in part derived from gender identity is gender role behavior. John Money described gender role behavior as

all those things that a person says or does to disclose himself

**Table 20.1–1**
**Classification of Intersexual Disorders***

| Syndrome | Description |
| --- | --- |
| Virilizing adrenal hyperplasia (andrenogenital syndrome) | Results from excess androgens in fetus with XX genotype; most common female intersex disorder; associated with enlarged clitoris, fused labia, hirsutism in adolescence |
| Turner's syndrome | Results from absence of second female sex chromosome (XO); associated with web neck, dwarfism, cubitus valgus; no sex hormones produced; infertile; usually assigned as females because of female-looking genitals |
| Klinefelter's syndrome | Genotype is XXY; male habitus present with small penis and rudimentary testes because of low androgen production; weak libido; usually assigned as male |
| Androgen insensitivity syndrome (testicular-feminizing syndrome) | Congenital X-linked recessive disorder that results in inability of tissues to respond to androgens; external genitals look female and cryptorchid testes present; assigned as females, even though they have XY genotype; in extreme form patient has breasts, normal external genitals, short blind vagina, and absence of pubic and axillary hair |
| Enzymatic defects in XY genotype (e.g., 5-α-reductase deficiency, 17-hydroxysteroid deficiency) | Congenital interruption in production of testosterone that produces ambiguous genitals and female habitus; usually assigned as female because of female-looking genitalia |
| Hermaphroditism | True hermaphrodite is rare and characterized by both testes and ovaries in same person (may be 46 XX or 46 XY) |
| Pseudohermaphroditism | Usually the result of endocrine or enzymatic defect (e.g., adrenal hyperplasia) in persons with normal chromosomes; female pseudohermaphrodites have masculine-looking genitals but are XX; male pseudohermaphrodites have rudimentary testes and external genitals and are XY; assigned as males or females, depending on morphology of genitals |

*Intersexual disorders include a variety of syndromes that produce persons with gross anatomical or physiological aspects of the opposite sex.

or herself as having the status of boy or man, girl or woman, respectively. . . . A gender role is not established at birth but is built up cumulatively through experiences encountered and transacted through casual and unplanned learning, through explicit instruction and inculcation, and through spontaneously putting two and two together to make sometimes four and sometimes, erroneously, five.

The standard and healthy outcome is a congruence of

gender identity and gender role. Although biological attributes are significant, the major factor in attaining the role appropriate to one's sex is learning.

Research on sex differences in behavior in children reveals more psychological similarities than differences. However, girls are found to be less prone to tantrums after the age of 18 months than are boys, and boys generally are more aggressive than girls—both physically and verbally—from age 2 onward. Little girls and little boys are similarly active, but the boys are more easily stimulated to sudden bursts of activity when they are in groups. Some researchers speculate that, although aggression is a learned behavior, male hormones may have sensitized boys' neural organizations to absorb those lessons better than girls do.

Gender role can appear to be in opposition to gender identity. Persons may identify with their own sex and yet adopt the dress, hairstyle, or other characteristics of the opposite sex. Or they may identify with the opposite sex yet for expediency adopt much of the behavior characteristics of their own sex.

A further discussion of gender issues appears in Chapter 21.

## Sexual Orientation

*Sexual orientation* describes the object of a person's sexual impulses: heterosexual (opposite sex), homosexual (same sex), or bisexual (both sexes).

## Sexual Behavior

**Physiological responses.** Sexual response is a true psychophysiological experience. Arousal is triggered by both psychological and physical stimuli, levels of tension are experienced both physiologically and emotionally, and, with orgasm, there is normally a subjective perception of a peak of physical reaction and release. Psychosexual development, psychological attitudes toward sexuality, and attitudes toward one's sexual partner are directly involved with and affect the physiology of human sexual response.

Normal men and women experience a sequence of physiological responses to sexual stimulation. In the first detailed description of those responses, William Masters and Virginia Johnson observed that the physiological process involves increasing levels of vasocongestion and myotonia (tumescence) and the subsequent release of the vascular activity and muscle tone as a result of orgasm (detumescence). Tables 20.1–2 and 20.1–3 describe the male and female sexual response cycles. The fourth edition of *Diagnostic and Statistical Manual of Mental Disorders* (DSM-IV) defines a four-phase response cycle: phase 1, desire; phase 2, excitement; phase 3, orgasm; phase 4, resolution.

PHASE 1: DESIRE. The desire (or appetitive) phase is distinct from any phase identified solely through physiology, and it reflects the psychiatrist's fundamental concern with motivations, drives, and personality. The phase is characterized by sexual fantasies and the desire to have sexual activity.

PHASE 2: EXCITEMENT. The excitement phase is brought on by psychological stimulation (fantasy or the presence of a love object) or physiological stimulation (stroking or kissing) or a combination of the two. It consists of a subjective sense of pleasure. The excitement phase is characterized by penile tumescence leading to erection in the man and by vaginal lubrication in the woman. The nipples of both sexes become erect, although nipple erection is more common in women than in men. The woman's clitoris becomes hard and turgid, and her labia minora become thicker as a result of venous engorgement. Initial excitement may last several minutes to several hours. With continued stimulation, the man's testes increase in size 50 percent and elevate. The woman's vaginal barrel shows a characteristic constriction along the outer third, known as the orgasmic platform. The clitoris elevates and retracts behind the symphysis pubis. As a result, the clitoris is not easily accessible. As the area is stimulated, however, traction on the labia minora and the prepuce occurs, and there is intrapreputial movement of the clitoral shaft. Breast size in the woman increases 25 percent. Continued engorgement of the penis and the vagina produces specific color changes, particularly in the labia minora, which become bright or deep red. Voluntary contractions of large muscle groups occur, the rates of heartbeat and respiration increase, and blood pressure rises. Heightened excitement lasts 30 seconds to several minutes.

PHASE 3: ORGASM. The orgasm phase consists of a peaking of sexual pleasure, with the release of sexual tension and the rhythmic contraction of the perineal muscles and the pelvic reproductive organs. A subjective sense of ejaculatory inevitability triggers the man's orgasm. The forceful emission of semen follows. The male orgasm is also associated with four to five rhythmic spasms of the prostate, seminal vesicles, vas, and urethra. In the woman, orgasm is characterized by 3 to 15 involuntary contractions of the lower third of the vagina and by strong sustained contractions of the uterus, flowing from the fundus downward to the cervix. Both men and women have involuntary contractions of the internal and external sphincters. Those and the other contractions during orgasm occur at intervals of 0.8 second. Other manifestations include voluntary and involuntary movements of the large muscle groups, including facial grimacing and carpopedal spasm. Blood pressure rises 20 to 40 mm (both systolic and diastolic), and the heart rate increases up to 160 beats a minute. Orgasm lasts from 3 to 25 seconds and is associated with a slight clouding of consciousness

PHASE 4: RESOLUTION. Resolution consists of the disgorgement of blood from the genitalia (detumescence), and that detumescence brings the body back to its resting state. If orgasm occurs, resolution is rapid; if it does not occur, resolution may take two to six hours and may be associated with irritability and discomfort. Resolution through orgasm is characterized by a subjective sense of well-being, general relaxation, and muscular relaxation.

After orgasm, men have a refractory period that may last from several minutes to many hours; in that period they cannot be stimulated to further orgasm. The refractory period does not exist in women, who are capable of multiple and successive orgasms.

**Differences in erotic stimuli.** Explicit sexual fantasies are common to men and women. The external stimuli for the fantasies frequently differ for the sexes. Men respond

**Table 20.1–2**
**Male Sexual Response Cycle***

| Organ | Excitement Phase | Orgasmic Phase | Resolution Phase |
|---|---|---|---|
| | Lasts several minutes to several hours; heightened excitement before orgasm, 30 seconds to 3 minutes | 3 to 15 seconds | 10 to 15 minutes; if no orgasm, ½ to 1 day |
| Skin | Just before orgasm: sexual flush inconsistently appears; maculopapular rash originates on abdomen and spreads to anterior chest wall, face, and neck and can include shoulders and forearms | Well-developed flush | Flush disappears in reverse order of appearance; inconsistently appearing film of perspiration on soles of feet and palms of hands |
| Penis | Erection in 10 to 30 seconds caused by vasocongestion of erectile bodies of corpus cavernosa of shaft; loss of erection may occur with introduction of asexual stimulus, loud noise; with heightened excitement, size of glans and diameter of penile shaft increase further | Ejaculation; emission phase marked by three to four contractions of 0.8 second of vas, seminal vesicles, prostate; ejaculation proper marked by contractions of 0.8 second of urethra and ejaculatory spurt of 12 to 20 inches at age 18, decreasing with age to seepage at 70 | Erection: partial involution in 5 to 10 seconds with variable refractory period; full detumescence in 5 to 30 minutes |
| Scrotum and testes | Tightening and lifting of scrotal sac and elevation of testes; with heightened excitement, 50% increase in size of testes over unstimulated state and flattening against perineum, signaling impending ejaculation | No change | Decrease to baseline size because of loss of vasocongestion; testicular and scrotal descent within 5 to 30 minutes after orgasm; involution may take several hours if no orgasmic release takes place |
| Cowper's glands | 2 to 3 drops of mucoid fluid that contain viable sperm are secreted during heightened excitement | No change | No change |
| Other | Breasts: inconsistent nipple erection with heightened excitement before orgasm<br>Myotonia: semispastic contractions of facial, abdominal, and intercostal muscles<br>Tachycardia: up to 175 a minute<br>Blood pressure: rise in systolic 20 to 80 mm; in diastolic 10 to 40 mm<br>Respiration: increased | Loss of voluntary muscular control<br><br>Rectum: rhythmical contractions of sphincter<br>Heart rate: up to 180 beats a minute<br>Blood pressure: up to 40 to 100 mm systolic; 20 to 50 mm diastolic<br>Respiration: up to 40 respirations a minute | Return to baseline state in 5 to 10 minutes |

* A desire phase consisting of sex fantasies and desire to have sex precedes excitement phase.
Table by Virginia Sadock, M.D.

to visual stimuli of nude or barely dressed women, who are depicted as lust-driven and interested in only physical satisfaction. Women respond to romantic stories with tender, demonstrative heroes whose passion for the heroine impels him toward a lifetime commitment to her.

**Masturbation.** Masturbation is usually a normal precursor of object-related sexual behavior. It has been said that no other form of sexual activity has been more frequently discussed, more roundly condemned, and more universally practiced than masturbation. Research by Alfred Kinsey into the prevalence of masturbation indicated that nearly all men and three fourths of all women masturbate sometime during their lives.

Longitudinal studies of development show that sexual self-stimulation is common in infancy and childhood. Just as infants learn to explore the functions of their fingers and mouths, they do the same with their genitalia. At about 15 to 19 months of age, both sexes begin genital self-stimulation. Pleasurable sensations result from any gentle touch to the genital region. Those sensations, coupled with the ordinary desire for exploration of one's body, produce a normal interest in masturbatory pleasure at that time. Children also develop an increased interest in the genitalia of others—parents, children, and even animals. As youngsters acquire playmates, the curiosity about their own and others' genitalia motivates episodes of exhibitionism or genital exploration. Such experiences, unless blocked by guilty fear, contribute to continued pleasure from sexual stimulation.

With the approach of puberty, the upsurge of sex hor-

**Table 20.1–3**
**Female Sexual Response Cycle***

| Organ | Excitement Phase | Orgasmic Phase | Resolution Phase |
|---|---|---|---|
| | Lasts several minutes to several hours; heightened excitement before orgasm, 30 seconds to 3 minutes | 3 to 15 seconds | 10 to 15 minutes; if no orgasm, ½ to 1 day |
| Skin | Just before orgasm: sexual flush inconsistently appears; maculopapular rash originates on abdomen and spreads to anterior chest wall, face, and neck; can include shoulders and forearms | Well-developed flush | Flush disappears in reverse order of appearance; inconsistently appearing film of perspiration on soles of feet and palms of hands |
| Breasts | Nipple erection in two thirds of women, venous congestion and areolar enlargement; size increases to one fourth over normal | Breasts may become tremulous | Return to normal in about ½ hour |
| Clitoris | Enlargement in diameter of glans and shaft; just before orgasm, shaft retracts into pupuce | No change | Shaft returns to normal position in 5 to 10 seconds; detumescence in 5 to 30 minutes; if no orgasm, detumescence takes several hours |
| Labia majora | Nullipara: elevate and flatten against perineum <br> Multipara: congestion and edema | No change | Nullipara: increase to normal size in 1 to 2 minutes <br> Multipara: decrease to normal size in 10 to 15 minutes |
| Labia minora | Size increase two to three times over normal; change to pink, red, deep red before orgasm | Contractions of proximal labia minora | Return to normal within 5 minutes |
| Vagina | Color change to dark purple; vaginal transudate appears 10 to 30 seconds after arousal; elongation and ballooning of vagina; lower third of vagina constricts before orgasm | 3 to 15 contractions of lower third of vagina at intervals of 0.8 second | Ejaculate forms seminal pool in upper two thirds of vagina; congestion disappears in seconds or, if no orgasm, in 20 to 30 minutes |
| Uterus | Ascends into false pelvis; laborlike contractions begin in heightened excitement just before orgasm | Contractions throughout orgasm | Contractions cease, and uterus descends to normal position |
| Other | Myotonia <br> A few drops of mucoid secretion from Bartholin's glands during heightened excitement <br> Cervix swells slightly and is passively elevated with uterus | Loss of voluntary muscular control <br> Rectum: rhythmical contractions of sphincter <br> Hyperventilation and tachycardia | Return to baseline status in seconds to minutes <br> Cervix color and size return to normal, and cervix descends into seminal pool |

* A desire phase consisting of sex fantasies and desire to have sex precedes excitement phase. Table by Virginia Sadock, M.D.

mones, and the development of secondary sex characteristics, sexual curiosity is intensified, and masturbation increases. Adolescents are physically capable of coitus and orgasm but are usually inhibited by social restraints. They are under the dual and often conflicting pressures of establishing their sexual identities and controlling their sexual impulses. The result is a great deal of physiological sexual tension that demands release, and masturbation is a normal way of reducing sexual tensions. An important emotional difference between the pubescent child and the youngster of earlier years is the presence of coital fantasies during masturbation in the adolescent. Those fantasies are an important adjunct to the development of sexual identity; in the comparative safety of the imagination, the adolescent learns to perform the adult sex role. That auto-

erotic activity is usually maintained into the young adult years, when it is normally replaced by coitus.

Couples in a sexual relationship do not abandon masturbation entirely. When coitus is unsatisfactory or is unavailable because of illness or the absence of the partner, self-stimulation often serves an adaptive purpose, combining sensual pleasure and tension release.

Kinsey found that, when women masturbate, most prefer clitoral stimulation to any other. Masters and Johnson reported that women prefer the shaft of the clitoris to the glans because the glans is hypersensitive to intense stimulation.

Moral taboos against masturbation have generated myths that masturbation causes mental illness or a decrease in sexual potency. No scientific evidence supports such claims. Masturbation is a psychopathological symptom only when it becomes a compulsion beyond the willful control of the person. It is then a symptom of emotional disturbance—not because it is sexual but because it is compulsive. Masturbation is almost a universal and inevitable aspect of psychosexual development, and in most cases it is adaptive.

## HOMOSEXUALITY

In 1973 homosexuality was eliminated as a diagnostic category by the American Psychiatric Association and was removed from *Diagnostic and Statistical Manual of Mental Disorders*. Doing so was the result of the view that homosexuality is an alternative life-style, rather than a pathological disorder, and that it occurs with some regularity as a variant of human sexuality. As David Hawkins wrote, "The presence of homosexuality does not appear to be a matter of choice; the expression of it is a matter of choice."

### Definitions

The term "*homosexual*" is used most often to describe a person's overt behavior, sexual orientation, and sense of personal or social identity. Hawkins wrote that the terms "*gay*" and "*lesbian*" refer to a combination of self-perceived identity and social identity; the terms reflect the fact that the person has some sense of being part of the social group that is similarly labeled. *Homophobia* is a negative attitude toward or fear of homosexuality or homosexuals. *Heterosexism* is the belief that a heterosexual relationship is preferable to all others; it implies discrimination against and persecution of those practicing other forms of sexuality.

### Prevalence

The first major study of the incidence of homosexuality was conducted by Alfred C. Kinsey in 1948; he found that 10 percent of men are homosexual. For women the figure was 5 percent. Kinsey also found that 37 percent of all persons reported a homosexual experience at some time in their lives, including adolescent sexual activities.

Since 1948, numerous surveys have revised those figures in a downward direction. A 1988 survey by the U. S. Bureau of the Census concluded that the male prevalence rate for homosexuality is 2 to 3 percent. A 1989 University of Chicago study found that less than 1 percent of both sexes are exclusively homosexual. In 1993 the Alan Guttmacher Institute found that the percentage of men reporting exclusively homosexual activity in the previous year was 1 percent and that 2 percent reported a lifetime history of having homosexual experiences.

Since sex surveys are unreliable, no accurate data are available, but government agencies such as the Centers for Disease Control and Prevention no longer use Kinsey's figures for national projections of homosexual behavior. Table 20.1–4 presents the worldwide estimates of homosexual behavior.

Some homosexuals, particularly males, report being aware of same-sex romantic attractions before puberty. According to Kinsey's data, about half of all prepubertal boys have some genital experience with a same-sex partner. However, that experience is often exploratory—particularly if shared with a peer, not an adult—and typically lacks a strong affective component. Most male homosexuals recall the onset of romantic and erotic attractions to same-sex partners during early adolescence. For females the onset of romantic feelings toward same-sex partners may also be in preadolescence. However, the clear recognition of a same-sex partner preference typically occurs in middle to late adolescence or not until young adulthood. More homosexual women than homosexual men appear to have heterosexual experiences during their primary homosexual careers. In one study 56 percent of a lesbian sample had heterosexual intercourse before their first genital homosexual experience, compared with 19 percent of a male homosexual sample who had heterosexual intercourse first. Nearly 40 percent of the lesbians had had heterosexual intercourse during the year preceding the survey.

### Theoretical Issues

**Psychological factors.** The determinants of homosexual behavior are enigmatic. Freud viewed homosexuality as an arrest of psychosexual development. Castration fears

**Table 20.1–4**
**Estimates of Homosexual Behavior**

| Country | Sample | Findings |
|---|---|---|
| Canada | 5,514 first-year college students under age 25 | 98% heterosexual<br>1% bisexual<br>1% homosexual |
| Norway | 6,155 adults, ages 18–26 | 3.5% of males and 3% of females reported past homosexual experience |
| France | 20,055 adults | Lifetime homosexual experience: 4.1% for men and 2.6% for women |
| Denmark | 3,178 adults, ages 18–59 | Less than 1% of men exclusively homosexual |
| Britain | 18,876 adults, ages 16–59 | 6.1% of men reported past homosexual experience |

Data reported by *The Wall Street Journal* (March 31, 1993) and *The New York Times* (April 15, 1993) from research studies on homosexual behavior.

for the male and fears of maternal engulfment in the preoedipal phase of psychosexual development are mentioned. According to psychodynamic theory, early-life situations that can result in male homosexual behavior include a strong fixation on the mother, lack of effective fathering, inhibition of masculine development by the parents, fixation or regression at the narcissistic stage of development, and losing competition with brothers and sisters. Freud's views on the causes of female homosexuality included a lack of resolution of penis envy in association with unresolved oedipal conflicts.

Freud did not consider homosexuality to be a mental illness. In *Three Essays on the Theory of Sexuality,* he wrote that homosexuality "is found in people who exhibit no other serious deviations from normal . . . whose efficiency is unimpaired and who are indeed distinguished by specially high intellectual development and ethical culture." In "Letter to an American Mother," Freud wrote, "homosexuality is assuredly no advantage, but it is nothing to be ashamed of, no vice, no degradation, it cannot be classified as an illness; we consider it to be a variation of the sexual functions produced by a certain arrest of sexual development."

**New psychoanalytic factors.** Some psychoanalysts have advanced new psychodynamic formulations, in contrast to classic psychoanalytic theory. Richard Isay described same-sex fantasies in children aged 3 to 5 years that can be recovered from homosexuals and that occur at about the same ages when heterosexuals have opposite-sex fantasies.

Isay wrote that, in homosexual men, same-sex erotic fantasies center on the father or the father surrogate:

The child's perception of and exposure to these erotic feelings may account for such "atypical" behavior as greater secretiveness than other boys, self-isolation, and excessive emotionality. Some "feminine" traits may also be caused by identification with the mother or a mother surrogate. Such characteristics usually develop as a way of attracting the father's love and attention in a manner similar to the way the heterosexual boy may pattern himself after his father to gain his mother's attention.

The psychodynamics of homosexuality in women may be similar. The little girl does not give up her original fixation on the mother as a love object and continues to seek it in adulthood.

**Biological factors.** Recent studies indicate that genetic and biological components may contribute to homosexual orientation. Homosexual men reportedly exhibit lower levels of circulatory androgen than do heterosexual men. There have also been reports of atypical estrogen feedback patterns among homosexual males. Such males show abnormal rebound increases in luteinizing hormone (LH) levels after estrogen injections. But neither of those results has been replicated in similar studies. Prenatal hormones appear to play a role in the organization of the central nervous system. The effective presence of androgens in prenatal life is purported to contribute to a sexual orientation toward females, and a deficiency of prenatal androgens (or a tissue insensitivity to them) may lead to a sexual orientation toward males. Preadolescent girls exposed to large amounts of androgens before birth are un-

usually aggressive and unfeminine, and boys exposed to excessive female hormones in utero are less athletic, less assertive, and less aggressive than other boys. Women with hyperadrenocorticalism become bisexual or homosexual in greater proportion than is expected in the general population.

Genetic studies have found a higher incidence of homosexual concordance among monozygotic twins than among dizygotic twins, which suggests a genetic predisposition; but chromosome studies have been unable to differentiate homosexuals from heterosexuals. Male homosexuals also show a familial distribution; homosexual men have more brothers who are homosexual than do heterosexual men. One study found that 33 of 40 pairs of homosexual brothers shared a genetic marker on the bottom half of the X chromosome. Another study found a group of cells in the hypothalamus that were smaller in women and in homosexual men than in heterosexual men. Those studies require replication

**Sexual behavior patterns.** The behavioral features of male and female homosexuals are as varied as those of male and female heterosexuals. Sexual practices engaged in by homosexuals are the same as for heterosexuals, with the obvious differences imposed by anatomy.

A variety of ongoing relationship patterns exist among homosexuals, as they do among heterosexuals. Some homosexual dyads live in a common household in either a monogamous or a primary relationship for decades, and other homosexual persons typically have only fleeting sexual contacts. Although more stable male-male relationships exist than were previously thought, male-male relationships appear to be less stable and more fleeting than are female-female relationships. The amount of male homosexual promiscuity is reported to have diminished since the onset of acquired immune deficiency syndrome (AIDS) and its rapid spread in the homosexual community through sexual contact.

Homosexual male couples are subjected to civil and social discrimination and do not have the legal social support system of marriage or the biological capacity for childbearing that bonds some otherwise incompatible heterosexual couples together. Female-female couples experience less social stigmatization and appear to have more enduring monogamous or primary relationships.

**Psychopathology.** The range of psychopathology that may be found among distressed homosexuals parallels that found among heterosexuals. Distress resulting only from conflict between the homosexual and the societal value structure is not classifiable as a disorder. If the distress is sufficiently severe to warrant a diagnosis, adjustment disorder or a depressive disorder is to be considered. Some homosexuals suffering from major depressive disorder may experience guilt and self-hatred that becomes directed toward their sexual orientation; then the desire for sexual reorientation is only a symptom of the depressive disorder.

**Coming out.** According to Richelle Klinger and Robert Cabaj, *coming out* is a "process by which an individual acknowledges his or her sexual orientation in the face of societal stigma and with successful resolution accepts himself or herself." They wrote the following:

Successful coming out involves the individual accepting his

or her sexual orientation and integrating it into all spheres (e.g., social, vocational, and familial). Another milestone that individuals and couples must eventually confront is the degree of disclosure of sexual orientation to the external world. Some degree of disclosure is probably necessary for successful coming out. . . .

Difficulty in negotiating coming out and disclosure is a common cause of relationship difficulties. For each individual, problems in resolving the coming out process may contribute to poor self-esteem caused by internalized homophobia and lead to deleterious effects on the individual's ability to function in the relationship. Conflict can also arise within a relationship when there is disagreement on the degree of disclosure between partners.

**Military policy.** One of the major issues confronting United States society is the role of homosexuals in the military. According to the U.S. Department of Defense:

Applicants for military service will no longer be asked or required to reveal if they are homosexual or bisexual, but applicants will be informed of the conduct that is proscribed for members of the armed forces, including homosexual conduct.

Sexual orientation will not be a bar to service unless manifested by homosexual conduct. The military will discharge members who engage in homosexual conduct, which is defined as a homosexual act, a statement that the member is homosexual or bisexual, or a marriage or attempted marriage to someone of the same gender.

The complete text of the recent policy statement on homosexuals in the military appears in Table 20.1–5.

**Table 20.1–5**
**Text of Pentagon's New Policy Guidelines on Homosexuals in the Military\***

### Accession Policy

Applicants for military service will no longer be asked or required to reveal if they are homosexual or bisexual, but applicants will be informed of the conduct that is proscribed for members of the armed forces, including homosexual conduct.

### Discharge Policy

Sexual orientation will not be a bar to service unless manifested by homosexual conduct. The military will discharge members who engage in homosexual conduct, which is defined as a homosexual act, a statement that the member is homosexual or bisexual, or a marriage or attempted marriage to someone of the same gender.

### Investigations Policy

No investigations or inquiries will be conducted solely to determine a service member's sexual orientation. Commanders will initiate inquiries or investigations when there is credible information that a basis for discharge or disciplinary action exists. Sexual orientation, absent credible information that a crime has been committed, will not be the subject of a criminal investigation. An allegation or statement by another that a service member is a homosexual, alone, is not grounds for either a criminal investigation or a commander's inquiry.

### Activities

Bodily contact between service members of the same sex that a reasonable person would understand to demonstrate a propensity or intent to engage in homosexual acts (e.g. hand-holding or kissing in most circumstances) will be sufficient to initiate separation.

Activities such as association with known homosexuals, presence at a gay bar, possessing or reading homosexual publications or marching in a gay rights rally in civilian clothes will not, in and of themselves, constitute credible information that would provide a basis for initiating an investigation or serve as the basis for an administrative-discharge under this policy. The listing by a service member of someone of the same gender as the person to be contacted in case of an emergency, as an insurance beneficiary, or in a similar context, does not provide a basis for separation or further investigation.

Speech within the context of priest-penitent, husband-wife or attorney-client communications remains privileged.

### Off-Base Conduct

No distinction will be made between off-base and on-base conduct.

From the time a member joins the service until discharge, the service member's duty and commitment to the unit is a 24-hour-a-day, seven-day-a-week obligation. Military members are required to comply with both the Uniform Code of Military Justice, which is Federal law, and military regulations at all times and in all places. Unacceptable conduct, homosexual or heterosexual, is not excused because the service member is not "at work."

### Investigations and Inquiries

Neither investigations nor inquiries will be conducted solely to determine an individual's sexual orientation.

Commanders can initiate investigations into alleged homosexual conduct when there is credible information of homosexual acts, prohibited statements, or homosexual marriage.

Commanders will exercise sound discretion regarding when credible information exists, and will evaluate the information's source and all attendant circumstances to assess whether the information supports a reasonable belief that a service member has engaged in proscribed homosexual conduct. Commanders, not investigators, determine when sufficient credible information exists to justify a detail of investigative resources to look into allegations.

### Credible Information

Credible information of homosexual conduct exists when the information, considered in light of its source and all attendant circumstances, supports a reasonable belief that a service member has engaged in such conduct. It requires a determination based on articulable facts, not just a belief or suspicion.

### Security Clearances

Questions pertaining to an individual's sexual orientation are not asked on personnel security questionnaires. An individual's sexual conduct, whether homosexual or heterosexual, is a legitimate security concern only if it could make an individual susceptible to exploitation or coercion, or indicate a lack of trustworthiness, reliability, or good judgment that is required of anyone with access to classified information.

### The Threat of Extortion

As long as service members continue to be separated from military service for engaging in homosexual conduct, credible information of such behavior can be a basis for extortion. Although the military cannot eliminate the potential for the victimization of homosexuals through blackmail, the policy

**Table 20.1–5**
*Continued*

reduces the risk to homosexuals by making certain categories of information largely immaterial to the military's initiation of investigations.

Only credible information that a service member engaged in homosexual conduct will form the basis for initiating an inquiry or investigation of a service member; suspicion of an individual's sexual orientation is not a basis, by itself, for official inquiry or action.

Extortion is a criminal offense, under both the O.C.M.S. and United States Code, and offenders will be prosecuted. A service member convicted of extortion risks dishonorable discharge and up to three years confinement. Civilians found guilty of blackmail under the U.S. Code may be subject to a $2,000 fine and one year imprisonment. The risk of blackmail will be addressed by educating all service members on the policy and by emphasizing the significant criminal sanctions facing convicted extortionists.

## Outing

A mere allegation or statement by another that a service member is a homosexual is not grounds for official action. Commanders will not take official action against members based on rumor, suspicion or capricious allegations.

However, if a third party provides credible information that a member has committed a crime or act that warrants discharge, e.g. engages in homosexual conduct, the commander may, based on the totality of the circumstances, conduct an investigation or inquiry, and take nonjudicial or administrative action or recommend judicial action, as appropriate.

Commanders are responsible for initiating an investigation when credible information exists that a crime or basis for discharge has been committed. The commander examines the information and decides whether an investigation by the service investigative agency or a commander inquiry is warranted, or if no action should be taken.

## Harassment

Commanders are responsible for maintaining good order and discipline.

All service members will be treated with dignity and respect. Hostile treatment or violence against a service member based on a perception of his or her sexual orientation will not be tolerated.

---

*While a Federal appeals court in November, 1993 would not consider the constitutionality of the policy, the court did say that the equal protection guarantee of the Fifth Amendment did not permit members of the military to be removed merely because they said they were homosexual.
Table from the U S Department of Defense.

## LOVE AND INTIMACY

There are many kinds of love: sexual, parental, filial, fraternal, anaclitic, and narcissistic love, as well as love for group, school, and country. A desire to maintain closeness to the love object typifies being in love. The development of sexuality and the development of the ability to love have reciprocal effects.

A person able to give and receive love with a minimum of fear and conflict has the capacity to develop genuinely intimate relationships with others. When involved in an intimate relationship, the person actively strives for the growth and the happiness of the loved person. Mature heterosexual love is marked by the intimacy that is a special attribute of the relationship between a man and a woman. The quality of intimacy in a mature sexual relationship is what Rollo May called "active receiving," in which a person, while loving, permits himself or herself to be loved. That capability indicates a profound awareness of love for another and for oneself. In such a loving relationship, sex acts as a catalyst. May described the values of sexual love as an expansion of one's self-awareness, the experience of tenderness, an increase of self-affirmation and pride, and sometimes, at the moment of orgasm, even loss of feelings of separateness. In that setting, sex and love are reciprocally enhancing and healthily fused.

A person is attracted to a potential mate for various reasons. One reason may be a purely physical attraction, which ordinarily establishes a transient relationship. Another reason may be a magical desire to find the perfect lover, whose qualities will be reminiscent of the idealized qualities of one's parents or other past sources of love and affection. Expectations of a partner may or may not be realistic. One neurotic motivation for marrying is an inability to separate on one's own from one's parents. Another neurotic motivation is selecting a partner to compensate for unmet childhood needs. Expectations and neurotic themes such as those probably exist in all personalities and in all matings. When they predominate and the couple act mainly to exchange patterns of exploitation or when interlocking complementary needs fail to bring sufficient security or happiness, discomfort and anxiety occur, and a breakdown in the relationship is possible.

## References

Farber M: *Human Sexuality.* Macmillan, New York, 1985.
Freud S: General theory of the neuroses. In *Standard Edition of the Complete Psychological Works of Sigmund Freud,* vol 16, p 241. Hogarth Press, London, 1966.
Freud S: Letter to an American mother. Am J Psychiatry *102:* 786, 1951.
Freud S: Three essays on the theory of sexuality. In *Standard Edition of the Complete Psychological Works of Sigmund Freud,* vol 7, p 135. Hogarth Press, London, 1953.
Harlow H F: The nature of love. Am Psychol *13:* 673, 1958.
Hawkins D M: Group psychotherapy with gay men and lesbians. In *Comprehensive Group Psychotherapy,* ed 3, H I Kaplan, B J Sadock, editors, p 506. Williams & Wilkins, Baltimore, 1993.
Kinsey A C, Pomeroy W B, Martin C E: *Sexual Behavior in the Human Male.* Saunders, Philadelphia, 1948.
Kinsey A C, Pomeroy W B, Martin C E, Gebbard P H: *Sexual Behavior in the Human Female.* Saunders, Philadelphia, 1953.
Kirkpatrick M: *Women's Sexual Development.* Plenum, New York, 1980.
Maccoby E, Jacklen C: *The Psychology of Sex Differences.* Stanford University Press, Palo Alto, 1974.
Masters W H, Johnson V E: *Human Sexual Response.* Little, Brown, Boston, 1966.
May R: *Love and Will.* Norton, New York, 1969.
Money J, Ehrhardt A A: *Man and Woman/Boy and Girl.* Johns Hopkins University Press, Baltimore, 1972.
Sherfey M J: *The Nature and Evolution of Female Sexuality.* Random House, New York, 1972.
Stoller R J: *Sex and Gender.* Science House, New York, 1968.
Tanfer K, Cubbins L A: Coital frequency among single women: Normative constraints and situational opportunities. J Sex Res *29;* 221, 1992.

## 20.2 / Sexual Dysfunctions

Seven major categories of sexual dysfunction are listed in the fourth edition of *Diagnostic and Statistical Manual of Mental Disorders* (DSM-IV): (1) sexual desire disorders, (2) sexual arousal disorders, (3) orgasm disorders, (4) sexual pain disorders, (5) sexual dysfunction due to a general medical condition, (6) substance-induced sexual dysfunction, and (7) sexual dysfunction not otherwise specified.

It is useful to think of the sexual dysfunctions as disorders related to a particular phase of the sexual response cycle. Thus, sexual desire disorders are associated with the first phase of the response cycle, known as the desire phase. Table 20.2–1 lists each of the DSM-IV phases of the sexual response cycle and the sexual dysfunctions usually associated with it.

Sexual dysfunctions can be symptomatic of biological problems (biogenic) or intrapsychic or interpersonal conflicts (psychogenic) or a combination of those factors. Sexual function can be adversely affected by stress of any kind, by emotional disorders, or by ignorance of sexual function and physiology. The dysfunction may be lifelong or acquired—that is, develop after a period of normal functioning. The dysfunction may be generalized or situational—that is, limited to a specific partner or a certain

situation—and it is coded that way in DSM-IV (Table 20.2–2).

In considering each of the disorders, the clinician needs to rule out an acquired medical condition and the use of a pharmacological substance that could account for or contribute to the dysfunction. It the disorder is biogenic, it is coded on Axis III, unless there is substantial evidence of dysfunctional episodes apart from the onset of physiological or pharmacological influences. In some cases a patient suffers from more than one dysfunction—for example, premature ejaculation and male erectile disorder.

### SEXUAL DESIRE DISORDERS

Sexual desire disorders are divided into two classes: hypoactive sexual desire disorder, characterized by a deficiency or the absence of sexual fantasies and desire for sexual activity (Table 20.2–3), and sexual aversion disorder, characterized by an aversion to and avoidance of genital sexual contact with a sexual partner (Table 20.2–4). The former condition is more common than the latter. An estimated 20 percent of the total population have hypoactive sexual desire disorder. The complaint is more common among women than among men.

A variety of causative factors are associated with sexual desire disorders. Patients with desire problems often use inhibition of desire in a defensive way to protect against unconscious fears about sex. Unacceptable homosexual impulses can also suppress libido or cause an aversion to heterosexual contact. Sigmund Freud conceptualized low sexual desire as the result of inhibition during the phallic psychosexual phase and unresolved oedipal conflicts. Some men, fixated at the

**Table 20.2–1**
**DSM-IV Phases of the Sexual Response Cycle and Associated Sexual Dysfunctions\***

| Phases | Characteristics | Dysfunction |
|---|---|---|
| 1. Desire | This phase is distinct from any identified solely through physiology and reflects the patient's motivations, drives, and personality. The phase is characterized by sexual fantasies and the desire to have sex. | Hypoactive sexual desire disorder; sexual aversion disorder; hypoactive sexual desire disorder due to a general medical condition (male or female); substance-induced sexual dysfunction with impaired desire |
| 2. Excitement | This phase consists of a subjective sense of sexual pleasure and accompanying physiological changes. All the physiological responses noted in Masters and Johnson's excitement and plateau phases are combined and occur in this phase. | Female sexual arousal disorder; male erectile disorder (may also occur in stage 3 and in stage 4); male erectile disorder due to a general medical condition; dyspareunia due to a general medical condition (male or female); substance-induced sexual dysfunction with impaired arousal |
| 3. Orgasm | This phase consists of a peaking of sexual pleasure, with release of sexual tension and rhythmic contraction of the perineal muscles and pelvic reproductive organs. | Female orgasmic disorder; male orgasmic disorder; premature ejaculation; other sexual dysfunction due to a general medical condition (male or female); substance-induced sexual dysfunction with impaired orgasm |
| 4. Resolution | This phase entails a sense of general relaxation, well-being, and muscle relaxation. During this phase men are refractory to orgasm for a period of time that increases with age, whereas women are capable of having multiple orgasms without a refractory period. | Postcoital dysphoria; postcoital headache |

\*DSM-IV consolidates the Masters and Johnson excitement and plateau phases into a single excitement phase, which is preceded by the desire (appetitive) phase. The orgasm and resolution phases remain the same as originally described by Masters and Johnson.

**Table 20.2–2**
**Subtypes of Sexual Dysfunctions**

The following types apply to all the sexual dysfunctions:

**Due to psychological factors** or
**Due to combined psychological factors and a general
medical condition**

**Lifelong** (occurring during the person's entire sexual life) or
**acquired**

**Generalized** (occurring in all situations and with all partners)
or **situational**

Table adapted from DSM-IV, *Diagnostic and Statistical Manual of Mental Disorders,* ed 4. Copyright American Psychiatric Association, Washington, 1994. Used with permission.

**Table 20.2–3**
**Diagnostic Criteria for Hypoactive Sexual Desire Disorder**

A. Persistently or recurrently deficient (or absent) sexual
fantasies and desire for sexual activity. The judgment of
deficiency or absence is made by the clinician, taking into
account factors that affect sexual functioning, such as age
and the context of the person's life.

B. The disturbance causes marked distress or interpersonal
difficulty.

C. The sexual dysfunction is not better accounted for by
another Axis I disorder (except another sexual
dysfunction), and is not due exclusively to the direct
physiological effects of a substance (e.g., a drug of abuse,
a medication) or a general medical condition.

Table from DSM-IV, *Diagnostic and Statistical Manual of Mental Disorders,* ed 4. Copyright American Psychiatric Association, Washington, 1994. Used with permission.

**Table 20.2–4**
**Diagnostic Criteria for Sexual Aversion Disorder**

A. Persistent or recurrent extreme aversion to, and avoidance
of, all (or almost all) genital sexual contact with a sexual
partner.

B. The disturbance causes marked distress or interpersonal
difficulty.

C. The sexual dysfunction is not better accounted for by
another Axis I disorder (except another sexual
dysfunction).

Table from DSM-IV, *Diagnostic and Statistical Manual of Mental Disorders,* ed 4. Copyright American Psychiatric Association, Washington, 1994. Used with permission.

phallic stage of development, are fearful of the vagina, believing that they will be castrated if they approach it, a concept Freud called *vagina dentata,* because they believe unconsciously that the vagina has teeth. Hence, they avoid contact with the female genitalia entirely. Lack of desire can also be the result of chronic stress, anxiety, or depression.

Abstinence from sex for a prolonged period sometimes results in suppression of the sexual impulse. Loss of desire may also be an expression of hostility or the sign of a deteriorating relationship.

In one study of young married couples who ceased having sexual relations for a period of two months, marital discord was the reason most frequently given for the cessation or the inhibition of sexual activity.

The presence of desire depends on several factors: biological drive, adequate self-esteem, previous good experiences with sex, the availability of an appropriate partner, and a good relationship in nonsexual areas with one's partner. Damage to any of those factors may result in diminished desire.

In making the diagnosis, the clinician must evaluate the patient's age, general health, and life stresses. The clinician should attempt to establish a baseline of sexual interest before the disorder began. The need for sexual contact and satisfaction varies among persons and over time in any given person. In a group of 100 couples with stable marriages, 8 percent reported having intercourse less than once a month. In another group of couples, one third reported episodic lack of sexual relations for periods averaging eight weeks. The diagnosis should not be made unless the lack of desire is a source of distress to the patient.

## SEXUAL AROUSAL DISORDERS

The sexual arousal disorders are divided by DSM-IV into (1) female sexual arousal disorder, characterized by the persistent or recurrent partial or complete failure to attain or maintain the lubrication-swelling response of sexual excitement until the completion of the sexual act, and (2) male erectile disorder, characterized by the recurrent and persistent partial or complete failure to attain or maintain an erection until the completion of the sex act. The diagnosis takes into account the focus, the intensity, and the duration of the sexual activity in which the patient engages (Tables 20.2–5 and 20.2–6). If sexual stimulation is inadequate in focus, intensity, or duration, the diagnosis should not be made.

### Female Sexual Arousal Disorder

The prevalence of female sexual arousal disorder is generally underestimated. Women who have excitement-phase dysfunction often have orgasm problems as well. In one study of relatively happy married couples, 33 percent of the women described difficulty in maintaining sexual excitement.

Many psychological factors (for example, anxiety, guilt,

**Table 20.2–5**
**Diagnostic Criteria for Female Sexual Arousal Disorder**

A. Persistent or recurrent inability to attain, or to maintain until
completion of the sexual activity, an adequate lubrication-
swelling response of sexual excitement.

B. The disturbance causes marked distress or interpersonal
difficulty.

C. The sexual dysfunction is not better accounted for by
another Axis I disorder (except another sexual dysfunction)
and is not due exclusively to the direct physiological
effects of a substance (e.g., a drug of abuse, a
medication) or a general medical condition.

Table from DSM-IV, *Diagnostic and Statistical Manual of Mental Disorders,* ed 4. Copyright American Psychiatric Association, Washington, 1994. Used with permission.

**Table 20.2–6**
**Diagnostic Criteria for Male Erectile Disorder**

A. Persistent or recurrent inability to attain, or to maintain until completion of the sexual activity, an adequate erection.

B. The disturbance causes marked distress or interpersonal difficulty.

C. The erectile dysfunction is not better accounted for by another Axis I disorder (other than a sexual dysfunction) and is not due exclusively to the direct physiological effects of a substance (e.g., a drug of abuse, a medication) or a general medical condition.

Table from DSM-IV. *Diagnostic and Statistical Manual of Mental Disorders,* ed 4. Copyright American Psychiatric Association, Washington, 1994. Used with permission.

and fear) are associated with female sexual arousal disorder. In some women, excitement-phase disorders are associated with dyspareunia and with lack of desire.

Physiological studies of sexual dysfunctions indicate that a hormonal pattern may contribute to responsiveness in women who have excitement–phase dysfunction. William Masters and Virginia Johnson found women to be particularly desirous of sex before the onset of the menses. However, some women report that they feel the greatest sexual excitement immediately after the menses or at the time of ovulation. Alterations in testosterone, estrogen, prolactin, and thyroxin levels have been implicated in female sexual arousal disorder. Also, medications with antihistaminic or anticholinergic properties cause a decrease in vaginal lubrication. Some evidence indicates that dysfunctional women are less aware of the physiological responses of their bodies, such as vasocongestion, during arousal than are other women.

### Male Erectile Disorder

Male erectile disorder is also called erectile dysfunction and impotence. A man with lifelong male erectile disorder has never been able to obtain an erection sufficient for vaginal insertion. In acquired male erectile disorder the man has successfully achieved vaginal penetration at some time in his sexual life but is later unable to do so. In situational male erectile disorder the man is able to have coitus in certain circumstances but not in others; for example, a man may function effectively with a prostitute but be impotent with his wife.

Acquired male erectile disorder has been reported in 10 to 20 percent of all men. Freud declared it to be a common complaint among his patients. Among all men treated for sexual disorders, more than 50 percent have impotence as the chief complaint. Lifelong male erectile disorder is a rare disorder, occurring in about 1 percent of men under age 35. The incidence of impotence increases with age. Among young adults it has been reported in about 8 percent of the population. Alfred Kinsey reported that 75 percent of all men were impotent at age 80. Masters and Johnson reported a fear of impotence in all men over 40, which the researchers believe reflects the masculine fear of loss of virility with advancing age. However, male erectile disorder is not universal in aging men; having an

available sex partner is closely related to continuing potency, as is a history of consistent sexual activity.

The causes of male erectile disorder may be organic or psychological or a combination of both, but most are psychological. A good history is of primary importance in determining the cause of the dysfunction. If a man reports having spontaneous erections at times when he does not plan to have intercourse, having morning erections, or having good erections with masturbation or with partners other than his usual one, the organic causes of his impotence can be considered negligible, and costly diagnostic procedures can be avoided. Male erectile disorder caused by a general medical condition or a pharmacological substance is discussed below.

Freud described one type of impotence as caused by an inability to reconcile feelings of affection toward a woman with feelings of desire for her. Men with such conflicting feelings can function only with women whom they see as degraded. Other factors that have been cited as contributing to impotence include a punitive superego, an inability to trust, and feelings of inadequacy or a sense of being undesirable as a partner. The man may be unable to express the sexual impulse because of fear, anxiety, anger, or moral prohibition. In an ongoing relationship, impotence may reflect difficulties between the partners, particularly if the man cannot communicate his needs or his anger in a direct and constructive way. In addition, episodes of impotence are reinforcing, with the man becoming increasingly anxious before each sexual encounter.

## ORGASM DISORDERS

### Female Orgasmic Disorder

Female orgasmic disorder, called inhibited female orgasm in the revised third edition of DSM (DSM-III-R) and also called anorgasmia, is defined as the recurrent or persistent inhibition of the female orgasm, as manifested by the recurrent delay in orgasm or the absence of orgasm after a normal sexual excitement phase that the clinician judges to be adequate in focus, intensity, and duration. It is the inability of the woman to achieve orgasm by masturbation or coitus. Women who can achieve orgasm with one of those methods are not necessarily categorized as anorgasmic, although some degree of sexual inhibition may be postulated (Table 20.2–7).

Research on the physiology of the female sexual response has shown that orgasms caused by clitoral stimulation and those caused by vaginal stimulation are physiologically identical. Freud's theory that women must give up clitoral sensitivity for vaginal sensitivity to achieve sexual maturity is now considered misleading; however, some women say that they gain a special sense of satisfaction from an orgasm precipitated by coitus. Some workers attribute that satisfaction to the psychological feeling of closeness engendered by the act of coitus, but others maintain that the coital orgasm is a physiologically different experience. Many women achieve orgasm during coitus by a combination of manual clitoral stimulation and penile vaginal stimulation.

Lifelong female orgasmic disorder exists when the woman has never experienced orgasm by any kind of stimulation.

**Table 20.2–7**
**Diagnostic Criteria for Female Orgasmic Disorder**

A. Persistent or recurrent delay in, or absence of, orgasm following a normal sexual excitement phase. Women exhibit wide variability in the type or intensity of stimulation that triggers orgasm. The diagnosis of female orgasmic disorder should be based on the clinician's judgment that the woman's orgasmic capacity is less than would be reasonable for her age, sexual experience, and the adequacy of sexual stimulation she receives.

B. The disturbance causes marked distress or interpersonal difficulty.

C. The orgasmic dysfunction is not better accounted for by another Axis I disorder (except another sexual dysfunction) and is not due exclusively to the direct physiological effects of a substance (e.g., a drug of abuse, a medication) or a general medical condition.

Table from DSM-IV, *Diagnostic and Statistical Manual of Mental Disorders,* ed 4. Copyright American Psychiatric Association, Washington, 1994. Used with permission.

Acquired orgasmic disorder exists if the woman has previously experienced at least one orgasm, regardless of the circumstances or means of stimulation, whether by masturbation or during sleep while dreaming. Kinsey found that the proportion of married women over 35 years of age who had never achieved orgasm by any means was only 5 percent. The incidence of orgasm increases with age. According to Kinsey, the first orgasm occurs during adolescence in about 50 percent of women; the rest usually experience orgasm as they get older. Lifelong female orgasmic disorder is more common among unmarried women than among married women. Increased orgasmic potential in women over 35 has been explained on the basis of less psychological inhibition or greater sexual experience or both.

Acquired female orgasmic disorder is a common complaint in clinical populations. One clinical treatment facility reported having about four times as many nonorgasmic women in its practice as patients with all other sexual disorders. In another study 46 percent of the women complained of difficulty in reaching orgasm. The true prevalence of problems in maintaining excitement is not known, but inhibition of excitement and orgasmic problems often occur together. The overall prevalence of female orgasmic disorder from all causes is estimated to be 30 percent.

Numerous psychological factors are associated with female orgasmic disorder. They include fears of impregnation, rejection by the sex partner, or damage to the vagina; hostility toward men; and feelings of guilt regarding sexual impulses. For some women, orgasm is equated with loss of control or with aggressive, destructive, or violent behavior; their fear of those impulses may be expressed through inhibition of excitement or orgasm. Cultural expectations and societal restrictions on women are also relevant. Nonorgasmic women may be otherwise symptom-free or may experience frustration in a variety of ways, including such pelvic complaints as lower abdominal pain, itching, and vaginal discharge, as well as increased tension, irritability, and fatigue.

## Male Orgasmic Disorder

In male orgasmic disorder (called inhibited male orgasm in DSM-III-R), the man achieves ejaculation during coitus

with great difficulty, if at all. A man suffers from lifelong orgasmic disorder if he has never been able to ejaculate during coitus. The disorder is diagnosed as acquired if it develops after previous normal functioning (Table 20.2–8).

Some workers think that a differentiation should be made between orgasm and ejaculation. Some men ejaculate but complain of a decreased or absent subjective sense of pleasure during the orgasmic experience (orgasmic anhedonia).

The incidence of male orgasmic disorder is much lower than the incidence of premature ejaculation or impotence. Masters and Johnson reported an incidence of male orgasmic disorder in only 3.8 percent in one group of 447 sexual dysfunction cases. A general prevalence of 5 percent has been reported.

Lifelong male orgasmic disorder is indicative of severe psychopathology. The man often comes from a rigid, puritanical background; he may perceive sex as sinful and the genitals as dirty; and he may have conscious or unconscious incest wishes and guilt. He usually has difficulties with closeness that extend beyond the area of sexual relations.

In an ongoing relationship, acquired male orgasmic disorder frequently reflects interpersonal difficulties. The disorder may be the man's way of coping with real or fantasized changes in the relationship. Those changes may include plans for pregnancy about which the man is ambivalent, the loss of sexual attraction to the partner, or demands by the partner for greater commitment as expressed by sexual performance. In some men the inability to ejaculate reflects unexpressed hostility toward the woman. That problem is more common among men with obsessive-compulsive disorder than among others.

## Premature Ejaculation

In premature ejaculation the man persistently or recurrently achieves orgasm and ejaculation before he wishes to. There is no definite time frame within which to define the dysfunction. The diagnosis is made when the man regularly ejaculates before or immediately after entering the

**Table 20.2–8**
**Diagnostic Criteria for Male Orgasmic Disorder**

A. Persistent or recurrent delay in, or absence of, orgasm following a normal sexual excitement phase during sexual activity that the clinician, taking into account the person's age, judges to be adequate in focus, intensity, and duration.

B. The disturbance causes marked distress or interpersonal difficulty.

C. The orgasmic dysfunction is not better accounted for by another Axis I disorder (except another sexual dysfunction) and is not due exclusively to the direct physiological effects of a substance (e.g., a drug of abuse, a medication) or a general medical condition.

Table from DSM-IV, *Diagnostic and Statistical Manual of Mental Disorders,* ed 4. Copyright American Psychiatric Association, Washington, 1994. Used with permission.

vagina. The clinician needs to consider factors that affect the duration of the excitement phase, such as age, the novelty of the sex partner, and the frequency and the duration of coitus (Table 20.2–9). Masters and Johnson conceptualized the disorder in terms of the couple and considered a man a premature ejaculator if he cannot control ejaculation for a sufficient length of time during intravaginal containment to satisfy his partner in at least half of their episodes of coitus. That definition assumes that the female partner is capable of an orgasmic response. Like the other dysfunctions, premature ejaculation is not caused exclusively by organic factors and is not symptomatic of any other clinical psychiatric syndrome.

Premature ejaculation is more common today among college-educated men than among men with less education. The disorder is thought to be related to their concern for partner satisfaction; however, the true incidence of the disorder has not been determined. About 35 to 40 percent of men treated for sexual disorders have premature ejaculation as the chief complaint. Difficulty in ejaculatory control may be associated with anxiety regarding the sex act or with unconscious fears about the vagina. It may also result from negative cultural conditioning. The man who has most of his early sexual contacts with prostitutes who demand that the sex act proceed quickly or in situations in which discovery would be embarrassing (such as in the back seat of a car or in the parental home) may become conditioned to achieve orgasm rapidly. In ongoing relationships the partner has a great influence on the premature ejaculator. A stressful marriage exacerbates the disorder. The developmental background and the psychodynamics found in premature ejaculation and in impotence are similar.

## Other Orgasm Disorders

Data on female premature orgasm are lacking; no separate category of premature orgasm for women is included in DSM-IV. A case of multiple spontaneous orgasms has been seen in a woman without sexual stimulation that was caused by an epileptogenic focus in the temporal lobe.

## SEXUAL PAIN DISORDERS

### Dyspareunia

Dyspareunia is recurrent or persistent genital pain occurring before, during, or after intercourse in either the

man or the woman. Much more common in women than in men, dyspareunia is related to and often coincides with vaginismus. Repeated episodes of vaginismus may lead to dyspareunia and vice versa; in either case, somatic causes must be ruled out. Dyspareunia should not be diagnosed when an organic basis for the pain is found or when, in a woman, it is caused exclusively by vaginismus or by a lack of lubrication (Table 20.2–10). The incidence of dyspareunia is unknown.

In the majority of cases, dynamic factors are considered causative. Chronic pelvic pain is a common complaint in women with a history of rape or childhood sexual abuse. Painful coitus may result from tension and anxiety about the sex act that cause the woman to involuntarily contract her vaginal muscles. The pain is real and makes intercourse unpleasant or unbearable. The anticipation of further pain may cause the woman to avoid coitus altogether. If the partner proceeds with intercourse regardless of the woman's state of readiness, the condition is aggravated.

### Vaginismus

Vaginismus is an involuntary muscle constriction of the outer third of the vagina that interferes with penile insertion and intercourse. That response may occur during a gynecological examination when involuntary vaginal constriction prevents the introduction of the speculum into the vagina. The diagnosis is not made if the dysfunction is caused exclusively by organic factors or if it is symptomatic of another Axis I mental disorder (Table 20.2–11).

---

**Table 20.2–10**
**Diagnostic Criteria for Dyspareunia**

A. Recurrent or persistent genital pain associated with sexual intercourse in either a male or a female.

B. The disturbance causes marked distress or interpersonal difficulty.

C. The disturbance is not caused exclusively by vaginismus or lack of lubrication, is not better accounted for by another Axis I disorder (except another sexual dysfunction), and is not due exclusively to the direct physiological effects of a substance (e.g., a drug of abuse, a medication) or a general medical condition.

---

Table from DSM-IV, *Diagnostic and Statistical Manual of Mental Disorders*, ed 4. Copyright American Psychiatric Association, Washington, 1994. Used with permission.

---

**Table 20.2–11**
**Diagnostic Criteria for Vaginismus**

A. Recurrent or persistent involuntary spasm of the musculature of the outer third of the vagina that interferes with sexual intercourse.

B. The disturbance causes marked distress or interpersonal difficulty.

C. The disturbance is not better accounted for by another Axis I disorder (e.g., somatization disorder) and is not due exclusively to the direct physiological effects of a general medical condition.

---

Table from DSM-IV, *Diagnostic and Statistical Manual of Mental Disorders*, ed 4. Copyright American Psychiatric Association, Washington, 1994. Used with permission.

---

**Table 20.2–9**
**Diagnostic Criteria for Premature Ejaculation**

---

A. Persistent or recurrent ejaculation with minimal sexual stimulation before, on, or shortly after penetration and before the person wishes it. The clinician must take into account factors that affect duration of the excitement phase, such as age, novelty of the sexual partner or situation, and recent frequency of sexual activity.

B. The disturbance causes marked distress or interpersonal difficulty.

C. The premature ejaculation is not due exclusively to the direct effects of a substance (e.g., withdrawal from opioids).

---

Table from DSM-IV, *Diagnostic and Statistical Manual of Mental Disorders*, ed 4. Copyright American Psychiatric Association, Washington, 1994. Used with permission.

Vaginismus is less prevalent than female orgasmic disorder. It most often afflicts highly educated women and those in the high socioeconomic groups. The woman suffering from vaginismus may consciously wish to have coitus but unconsciously wish to keep the penis from entering her body. A sexual trauma such as rape may result in vaginismus. Women with psychosexual conflicts may perceive the penis as a weapon. In some women, pain or the anticipation of pain at the first coital experience causes vaginismus. A strict religious upbringing that associates sex with sin is frequently noted in those cases. Other women have problems in the dyadic relationship; if the woman feels emotionally abused by her partner, she may protest in that nonverbal fashion.

## SEXUAL DYSFUNCTION DUE TO A GENERAL MEDICAL CONDITION

This category covers sexual dysfunction that results in marked distress and interpersonal difficulty when there is evidence from the history, the physical examination, or the laboratory findings of a general medical condition judged to be causally related to the sexual dysfunction (Table 20.2–12).

**Table 20.2–12**
**Diagnostic Criteria for Sexual Dysfunction Due to a General Medical Condition**

A. Clinically significant sexual dysfunction that results in marked distress or interpersonal difficulty predominates in the clinical picture.

B. There is evidence from the history, physical examination, or laboratory findings that the sexual dysfunction is fully explained by the direct physiological effects of a general medical condition.

C. The disturbance is not better accounted for by another mental disorder (e.g., major depressive disorder)

*Select* code and term based on the predominant sexual dysfunction:
   **Female hypoactive sexual desire disorder due to a general medical condition**: if deficient or absent sexual desire is the predominant feature.
   **Male hypoactive sexual desire disorder due to a general medical condition**: if deficient or absent sexual desire is the predominant feature.
   **Male erectile disorder due to a general medical condition**: if male erectile dysfunction is the predominant feature.
   **Female dyspareunia due to a general medical condition**: if pain associated with intercourse is the predominant feature.
   **Male dyspareunia due to a general medical condition:** if pain associated with intercourse is the predominant feature.
   **Other female sexual dysfunction due to a general medical condition**: if some other feature is predominant (e.g., orgasmic disorder) or no feature predominates.
   **Other male sexual dysfunction due to a general medical condition**: if some other feature is predominant (e.g., orgasmic disorder) or no feature predominates.

**Coding note:** Include the name of the general medical condition on Axis I, e.g., male erectile disorder due to diabetes mellitus; also code the general medical condition on Axis III.

## Male Erectile Disorder Due to a General Medical Condition

The incidence of psychological as opposed to organic male erectile disorder has been the focus of many studies. Statistics indicate that 20 to 50 percent of men with erectile disorder have an organic basis for the disorder. The organic causes of male erectile disorder are listed in Table 20.2–13. Side effects of medication may impair male sexual functioning in a variety of ways (Table 20.2–14). Castration (removal of the testes) does not always lead to sexual dysfunction, depending on the person. Erection may still occur after castration. A reflex arc, fired when the inner thigh is stimulated, passes through the sacral cord erectile center to account for the phenomenon.

A number of procedures, benign and invasive, are used to help differentiate organically caused impotence from functional impotence. The procedures include monitoring nocturnal penile tumescence (erections that occur during sleep), normally associated with rapid eye movement; monitoring tumescence with a strain gauge; measuring blood pressure in the penis with a penile plethysmograph or an ultrasound (Doppler) flow meter, both of which assess blood flow in the internal pudendal artery; and measuring pudendal nerve latency time. Other diagnostic tests that delineate organic bases for impotence include glucose tolerance tests, plasma hormone assays, liver and thyroid function tests, prolactin and follicle-stimulating hormone (FSH) determinations, and cystometric examinations. Invasive diagnostic studies include penile arteriography, infusion cavernosography, and radioactive xenon penography. Invasive procedures require expert interpretation and are used only for patients who are candidates for vascular reconstructive procedures.

### Dyspareunia Due to a General Medical Condition

An estimated 30 percent of all surgical procedures on the female genital area result in temporary dyspareunia. In addition, of women with the complaint who are seen in sex therapy clinics, 30 to 40 percent have pelvic pathology.

Organic abnormalities leading to dyspareunia and vaginismus include irritated or infected hymenal remnants, episiotomy scars, Bartholin's gland infection, various forms of vaginitis and cervicitis, and endometriosis. Postcoital pain has been reported by women with myomata and endometriosis and is attributed to the uterine contractions during orgasm. Postmenopausal women may have dyspareunia resulting from thinning of the vaginal mucosa and reduced lubrication.

Dyspareunia can also occur in men, but it is uncommon and is usually associated with an organic condition, such as Peyronie's disease, which consists of sclerotic plaques on the penis that cause penile curvature.

### Hypoactive Sexual Desire Disorder Due to a General Medical Condition

Desire commonly decreases after major illness or surgery, particularly when the body image is affected after such procedures as mastectomy, ileostomy, hysterectomy, and prostatectomy. Illnesses that deplete a person's energy, chronic conditions that require physical and psychological adaptation, and serious illnesses that may cause the

**Table 20.2–13**
**Diseases and Other Medical Conditions Implicated in Male Erectile Disorder**

| | |
|---|---|
| **Infectious and parasitic diseases**<br>Elephantiasis<br>Mumps<br><br>**Cardiovascular disease***<br>Atherosclerotic disease<br>Aortic aneurysm<br>Leriche's syndrome<br>Cardiac failure<br><br>**Renal and urological disorders**<br>Peyronie's disease<br>Chronic renal failure<br>Hydrocele and varicocele<br><br>**Hepatic disorders**<br>Cirrhosis (usually associated with alcohol dependence)<br><br>**Pulmonary disorders**<br>Respiratory failure<br><br>**Genetics**<br>Klinefelter's syndrome<br>Congenital penile vascular and structural abnormalities<br><br>**Nutritional disorders**<br>Malnutrition<br>Vitamin deficiencies<br><br>**Endocrine disorders***<br>Diabetes mellitus<br>Dysfunction of the pituitary-adrenal-testis axis<br>Acromegaly<br>Addison's disease<br>Chromophobe adenoma<br>Adrenal neoplasia<br>Myxedema<br>Hyperthyroidism | **Neurological disorders**<br>Multiple sclerosis<br>Transverse myelitis<br>Parkinson's disease<br>Temporal lobe epilepsy<br>Traumatic and neoplastic spinal cord diseases*<br>Central nervous system tumor<br>Amyotrophic lateral sclerosis<br>Peripheral neuropathy<br>General paresis<br>Tabes dorsalis<br><br>**Pharmacological contributants**<br>Alcohol and other dependence-inducing substances (heroin, methadone, morphine, cocaine, amphetamines, and barbiturates)<br>Prescribed drugs (psychotropic drugs, antihypertensive drugs, estrogens, and antiandrogens)<br><br>**Poisoning**<br>Lead (plumbism)<br>Herbicides<br><br>**Surgical procedures***<br>Perineal prostatectomy<br>Abdominal-perineal colon resection<br>Sympathectomy (frequently interferes with ejaculation)<br>Aortoiliac surgery<br>Radical cystectomy<br>Retroperitoneal lymphadenectomy<br><br>**Miscellaneous**<br>Radiation therapy<br>Pelvic fracture<br>Any severe systemic disease or debilitating condition |

*In the United States an estimated 2 million men are impotent because they suffer from diabetes mellitus; an additional 300,000 are impotent because of other endocrine diseases; 1.5 million are impotent as a result of vascular disease; 180,000 because of multiple sclerosis; 400,000 because of traumas and fractures leading to pelvic fractures or spinal cord injuries; and another 650,000 are impotent as a result of radical surgery, including prostatectomies, colostomies, and cystectomies.
Table by Virginia A. Sadock, M.D.

person to become depressed can all result in a marked lessening of sexual desire in both men and women.

In some cases, biochemical correlates are associated with hypoactive sexual desire disorder (Table 20.2–15). A recent study found markedly decreased levels of serum testosterone in men complaining of low desire when they were compared with normal controls in a sleep-laboratory situation. Drugs that depress the central nervous system (CNS) or decrease testosterone production can decrease desire.

### Other Male Sexual Dysfunction Due to a General Medical Condition

This category is used when some other dysfunctional feature is predominant (for example, orgasmic disorder) or no feature predominates.

Male orgasmic disorder may have physiological causes and can occur after surgery on the genitourinary tract, such as prostatectomy. It may also be associated with Parkinson's disease and other neurological disorders involving the lumbar or sacral sections of the spinal cord. The antihypertensive drug guanethidine monosulfate (Ismelin), methyldopa (Aldomet), the phenothiazines, the tricyclic drugs, and fluoxetine (Prozac), among others, have been implicated in retarded ejaculation. Male orgasmic disorder

must also be differentiated from retrograde ejaculation, in which ejaculation occurs but the seminal fluid passes backward into the bladder. Retrograde ejaculation always has an organic cause. It can develop after genitourinary surgery and is also associated with medications that have anticholinergic side effects, such as the phenothiazines.

### Other Female Sexual Dysfunction Due to a General Medical Condition

This category is used when some other feature (for example, orgasmic disorder) is predominant or when no feature predominates.

Some medical conditions—specifically, such endocrine diseases as hypothyroidism, diabetes mellitus, and primary hyperprolactinemia—can affect a woman's ability to have orgasms. Also, a number of drugs affect some women's capacity to have orgasms (Table 20.2–16). Antihypertensive medications, CNS stimulants, tricyclic drugs, fluoxetine, and, frequently, monoamine oxidase (MAO) inhibitors have interfered with female orgasmic capacity. However, one study of women taking MAO inhibitors found that, after 16 to 18 weeks of pharmacotherapy, that side effect of the medication disappeared, and the women were able to reexperience orgasms, although they continued taking an undiminished dosage of the drug.

**Table 20.2–14**
**Pharmacological Agents Implicated in Male Sexual Dysfunctions**

| Drug | Impairs Erection | Impairs Ejaculation |
|---|---|---|
| **Psychiatric drugs** | | |
| **Cyclic drugs*** | | |
| Imipramine (Tofranil) | + | + |
| Protriptyline (Vivactil) | + | + |
| Desipramine (Pertofrane) | + | + |
| Clomipramine (Anafranil) | + | + |
| Amitriptyline (Elavil) | + | + |
| Trazodone (Desyrel)† | – | – |
| **Monoamine oxidase inhibitors** | | |
| Tranylcypromine (Parnate) | + | |
| Phenelzine (Nardil) | + | + |
| Pargyline (Eutonyl) | – | + |
| Isocarboxazid (Marplan) | – | + |
| **Other mood-active drugs** | | |
| Lithium (Eskalith) | + | |
| Amphetamines | + | + |
| Fluoxetine (Prozac) | – | + |
| **Antipsychotics‡** | | |
| Fluphenazine (Prolixin) | + | |
| Thioridazine (Mellaril) | + | + |
| Chlorprothiexene (Taractan) | – | + |
| Mesoridazine (Serentil) | – | + |
| Perphenazine (Trilafon) | – | + |
| Trifluoperazine (Stelazine) | – | + |
| Reserpine (Serpasil) | + | + |
| Haloperidol (Haldol) | – | + |
| **Antianxiety agent§** | | |
| Chlordiazepoxide (Librium) | – | + |
| **Antihypertensive drugs** | | |
| Clonidine (Catapres) | + | |
| Methyldopa (Aldomet) | + | + |
| Spironolactone (Aldactone) | + | – |
| Hydrochlorothiazide | + | – |
| Guanethidine (Ismelin) | + | + |
| **Commonly abused substances** | | |
| Alcohol | + | + |
| Barbiturates | + | + |
| Cannabis | + | – |
| Cocaine | + | + |
| Heroin | + | + |
| Methadone | + | – |
| Morphine | + | + |
| **Miscellaneous drugs** | | |
| Antiparkinsonian agents | + | + |
| Clofibrate (Atromid-S) | + | – |
| Digoxin (Lanoxin) | + | – |
| Glutethimide (Doriden) | + | + |
| Indomethacin (Indocin) | + | – |
| Phentolamine (Regitine) | – | + |
| Propranolol (Inderal) | + | – |

*The incidence of male erectile disorder associated with the use of tricyclic drugs is low.
†Trazodone has been causative in some cases of priapism.
‡Impairment of sexual function is not a common complication of the use of antipsychotics. Priapism has occasionally occurred in association with the use of antipsychotics.
˙Benzodiazepines have been reported to decrease libido, but in some patients the diminution of anxiety caused by those drugs enhances sexual function.
Table by Virginia A. Sadock, M.D.

## SUBSTANCE-INDUCED SEXUAL DYSFUNCTION

This diagnosis is used when there is evidence from the history, the physical examination, or the laboratory findings of substance intoxication or withdrawal. Distressing sexual dysfunction occurs within a month of significant substance intoxication or withdrawal (Table 20.2–17). Specified substances include alcohol; amphetamines or related substances; cocaine; opioids; sedatives, hypnotics, or anxiolytics; and other or unknown substances.

Abused recreational substances affect sexual function

**Table 20.2–15**
**Neurophysiology of Sexual Dysfunction**

| | DA | 5-HT | NE | ACh | Clinical Correlation |
|---|---|---|---|---|---|
| Erection | ↑ | O | α, β<br>↓ ↑ | M | Antipsychotics may lead to erectile dysfunction (DA block); DA agonists may lead to enhanced erection and libido; priapism with trazodone (α₁ block); β-blockers may lead to impotence. |
| Ejaculation and orgasm | O | ± ↓ | α₁ ↑ | M | α₁-Blockers (tricyclic drugs, MAOIs, thioridazine) may lead to impaired ejaculation; 5-HT agents may inhibit orgasm. |

↑ —facilitates
↓ —inhibits or decreases
± —some
ACh—acetylcholine
DA—dopamine
5-HT—serotonin
M—modulates
NE—norepinephrine
O—minimal
Table from R Segraves: *Psychiatric Times,* 1990. Used with permission.

**Table 20.2–16**
**Psychiatric Drugs Implicated in Female Orgasmic Disorder***

Amoxapine (Asendin)†
Clomipramine (Anafranil)‡
Fluoxetine (Prozac)ˇ
Imipramine (Tofranil)
Isocarboxazid (Marplan)**
Nortriptyline (Aventyl)ˇ
Phenelzine (Nardil)**
Thioridazine (Mellaril)
Tranylcypromine (Parnate)**
Trifluoperazine (Stelazine)

---

*The interrelation between female sexual dysfunctions and pharmacological agents has been less extensively evaluated than have male reactions. Oral contraceptives are reported to decrease libido in some women, and some drugs with anticholinergic side effects may impair arousal and orgasm. Benzodiazepines have been reported to decrease libido, but in some patients the diminution of anxiety caused by those drugs enhances sexual function.

Both increases and decreases in libido have been reported with psychoactive agents. It is difficult to separate those effects from the underlying condition or from improvement of the condition. Sexual dysfunction associated with the use of a drug disappears when the drug is discontinued.
†Bethanechol (Urecholine) can reverse the effects of amoxapine-induced anorgasmia.
‡Clomipramine is also reported to increase arousal and orgasmic potential.
ˇCyproheptadine (Periactin) reverses fluoxetine- and nortriptyline-induced anorgasmia.
**MAOI-induced anorgasmia may be a temporary reaction to the medication that disappears even though administration of the drug is continued.
Table by Virginia A. Sadock, M.D.

---

in various ways. In small doses, many of the substances enhance sexual performance by decreasing inhibition or anxiety or by causing a temporary elation of mood. However, with continued use, erectile, orgasmic, and ejaculatory capacities become impaired. The abuse of sedatives, anxiolytics, hypnotics, and particularly opiates and opioids nearly always depresses desire. Alcohol may foster the initiation of sexual activity by removing inhibition, but it impairs performance. Cocaine and amphetamines produce similar effects. Although no direct evidence indicates that sexual drive is enhanced, the user initially has a feeling of increased energy and may become sexually active. Ultimately, dysfunction occurs. Men usually go through two stages: the man experiences prolonged erection without ejaculation and then undergoes a gradual loss of erectile capability.

Recovering substance-dependent patients may need therapy to regain sexual function. In part, that is one piece of psychological readjustment to a nondependent state. Many substance abusers have always had difficulty with intimate interactions. Others have missed the experiences that would have enabled them to learn social and sexual skills because they spent their crucial developmental years under the influence of some substance.

## SEXUAL DYSFUNCTION NOT OTHERWISE SPECIFIED

This category is for sexual dysfunctions that cannot be classified under the categories described above (Table 20.2–18). Examples include persons who experience the physiological components of sexual excitement and orgasm but report no erotic sensation or even anesthesia (orgasmic

**Table 20.2–17**
**Diagnostic Criteria for Substance-Induced Sexual Dysfunction**

A. Clinically significant sexual dysfunction that results in marked distress or interpersonal difficulty predominates in the clinical picture.

B. There is evidence from the history, physical examination, or laboratory findings that the sexual dysfunction is fully explained by substance use as manifested by either (1) or (2):

    (1) the symptoms in criterion A developed during, or within a month of, substance intoxication

    (2) medication use is etiologically related to the disturbance

C. The disturbance is not better accounted for by a sexual dysfunction that is not substance induced. Evidence that the symptoms are better accounted for by a sexual dysfunction that is not substance induced might include the following: the symptoms precede the onset of the substance use or dependence (or medication use); the symptoms persist for a substantial period of time (e.g., about a month) after the cessation of intoxication, or are substantially in excess of what would be expected given the type or amount of the substance used or the duration of use; or there is other evidence that suggests the existence of an independent non-substance-induced sexual dysfunction (e.g., a history of recurrent non-substance-related episodes).

**Note:** This diagnosis should be made instead of a diagnosis of substance intoxication only when the sexual dysfunction is in excess of that usually associated with the intoxication syndrome and when the dysfunction is sufficiently severe to warrant independent clinical attention.

*Code:* [Specific substance]-induced sexual dysfunction (Alcohol, Amphetamine [or Amphetamine-Like substance]; Cocaine; Opioid; Sedative, Hypnotic, or Anxiolytic; Other [or unknown] substance)

*Specify* if:
    **with impaired desire**
    **with impaired arousal**
    **with impaired orgasm**
    **with sexual pain**

*Specify* if:
    **with onset during intoxication:** if the criteria are met for Intoxication with the substance and the symptoms develop during the intoxication syndrome

---

Table from DSM-IV, *Diagnostic and Statistical Manual of Mental Disorders,* ed 4. Copyright American Psychiatric Association, Washington, 1994. Used with permission.

**Table 20.2–18**
**Diagnostic Criteria for Sexual Dysfunction Not Otherwise Specified**

---

This category includes sexual dysfunctions that do not meet criteria for any specific sexual dysfunction. Examples include

1. No (or substantially diminished) subjective erotic feelings despite otherwise normal arousal and orgasm.

2. Situations in which the clinician has concluded that a sexual dysfunction is present but is unable to determine whether it is primary, due to a general medical condition, or substance induced.

---

Table from DSM-IV, *Diagnostic and Statistical Manual of Mental Disorders,* ed 4. Copyright American Psychiatric Association, Washington, 1994. Used with permission.

anhedonia). Women with conditions analogous to premature ejaculation in men are classified here. Orgasmic women who desire but have not experienced multiple orgasms can be classified under this heading as well. Also, disorders of excessive rather than inhibited dysfunction, such as compulsive masturbation or coitus (sex addiction), may be classified here, as is genital pain occurring during masturbation. Other unspecified disorders are found in persons who have one or more sexual fantasies about which they feel guilty or otherwise dysphoric. However, the range of common sexual fantasies is broad.

### Postcoital Headache

Postcoital headache is characterized by headache immediately after coitus and may last for several hours. It is usually described as throbbing, and it is localized in the occipital or frontal area. The cause is unknown. There may be vascular, muscle contraction (tension), or psychogenic causes. Coitus may precipitate migraine or cluster headaches in predisposed persons.

### Orgasmic Anhedonia

Orgasmic anhedonia is a condition in which the person has no physical sensation of orgasm, even though the physiological component (for example, ejaculation) remains intact. Organic causes, such as sacral and cephalic lesions that interfere with afferent pathways from the genitalia to the cortex, must be ruled out. Psychic causes usually relate to extreme guilt about experiencing sexual pleasure. Those feelings produce a type of dissociative response that isolates the affective component of the orgasmic experience from consciousness.

### Masturbatory Pain

In some cases, persons may experience pain during masturbation. Organic causes should always be ruled out. A small vaginal tear or early Peyronie's disease may produce a painful sensation. The condition should be differentiated from compulsive masturbation. People may masturbate to the extent that they do physical damage to their genitals and eventually experience pain during subsequent masturbatory acts. Such cases constitute a separate sexual disorder and should be so classified.

Certain masturbatory practices have resulted in what has been called autoerotic asphyxiation. The practices may involve masturbating while hanging oneself by the neck to heighten erotic sensations and the intensity of the orgasm through the mechanism of mild hypoxia. Although the persons intend to release themselves from the noose after orgasm, an estimated 500 to 1,000 persons a year accidentally kill themselves by hanging. Most who indulge in the practice are male, transvestism is often associated with the habit, and the majority of deaths occur among adolescents. Such masochistic practices are usually associated with severe mental disorders, such as schizophrenia and major mood disorders.

## TREATMENT

Before 1970 the most common treatment of sexual dysfunctions was individual psychotherapy. Classic psychodynamic theory holds that sexual inadequacy has its roots in early developmental conflicts, and the sexual disorder is treated as part of a pervasive emotional disturbance. Treatment focuses on the exploration of unconscious conflicts, motivation, fantasy, and various interpersonal difficulties. One of the assumptions of therapy is that the removal of the conflicts will allow the sexual impulse to become structurally acceptable to the patient's ego and thereby find appropriate means of satisfaction in the environment. Unfortunately, the symptoms of sexual dysfunctions frequently become secondarily autonomous and continue to persist, even when other problems evolving from the patient's pathology have been resolved. The addition of behavioral techniques is often necessary to cure the sexual problem.

### Dual-Sex Therapy

The theoretical basis of the dual-sex therapy approach is the concept of the marital unit or dyad as the object of therapy; the approach represents the major advance in the diagnosis and treatment of sexual disorders in this century. The methodology was originated and developed by William Masters and Virginia Johnson. In dual-sex therapy, there is no acceptance of the idea of a sick half of a patient couple. Both are involved in a sexually distressing relationship, and both must, therefore, participate in the therapy program.

The sexual problem often reflects other areas of disharmony or misunderstanding in the marriage. The marital relationship as a whole is treated, with emphasis on sexual functioning as a part of that relationship. The psychological and physiological aspects of sexual functioning are discussed, and an educative attitude is used. Suggestions are made for specific sexual activities, and those suggestions are followed in the privacy of the couple's home. The keystone of the program is the roundtable session in which a male and female therapy team clarifies, discusses, and works through the problems with the couple. The four-way sessions require active participation on the part of the patients. The aim of the therapy is to establish or reestablish communication within the marital unit. Sex is emphasized as a natural function that flourishes in the appropriate domestic climate, and improved communication is encouraged toward that end.

Treatment is short-term and is behaviorally oriented. The therapists attempt to reflect the situation as they see it, rather than interpret underlying dynamics. An undistorted picture of the relationship presented by the therapists often corrects the myopic, narrow view held by each marriage partner. The new perspective can interrupt the couple's vicious circle of relating, and improved, more effective communication can be encouraged.

Specific exercises are prescribed for the couple to help them with their particular problem. Sexual inadequacy often involves lack of information, misinformation, and performance fear. Therefore, the couple are specifically prohibited from any sexual play other than that prescribed by the therapists. Beginning exercises usually focus on heightening sensory awareness to touch, sight, sound, and smell. Initially, intercourse is interdicted, and the couple learn to give and receive bodily pleasure without the pressure of performance. At the same time, they learn how to communicate nonverbally in a mutually satisfactory way and learn that sexual foreplay is as important as intercourse and orgasm.

During the sensate focus exercises, the couple receive

much reinforcement to reduce their anxiety. They are urged to use fantasies to distract them from obsessive concerns about performance (spectatoring). The needs of both the dysfunctional partner and the nondysfunctional partner are considered. If either partner becomes sexually excited by the exercises, the other is encouraged to bring him or her to orgasm by manual or oral means. Open communication between the partners is urged, and the expression of mutual needs is encouraged. Resistances, such as claims of fatigue or not enough time to complete the exercises, are common and must be dealt with by the therapists. Genital stimulation is eventually added to general body stimulation. The couple are instructed sequentially to try various positions for intercourse, without necessarily completing the act, and to use varieties of stimulating techniques before they are instructed to proceed with intercourse.

Psychotherapy sessions follow each new exercise period, and problems and satisfactions, both sexual and in other areas of the couple's lives, are discussed. Specific instructions and the introduction of new exercises geared to the individual couple's progress are reviewed in each session. Gradually, the couple gain confidence and learn to communicate, verbally and sexually. Dual-sex therapy is most effective when the sexual dysfunction exists apart from other psychopathology.

**Specific techniques and exercises.** Various techniques are used to treat the various dysfunctions. In cases of vaginismus, the woman is advised to dilate her vaginal opening with her fingers or with other dilators.

In cases of premature ejaculation, an exercise known as the squeeze technique is used to raise the threshold of penile excitability. In that exercise the man or the woman stimulates the erect penis until the earliest sensations of impending ejaculation are felt. At that point, the woman forcefully squeezes the coronal ridge of the glans, the erection is diminished, and ejaculation is inhibited. The exercise program eventually raises the threshold of the sensation of ejaculatory inevitability and allows the man to become aware of his sexual sensations and confident about his sexual performance. A variant of the exercise is the stop-start technique developed by James H. Semans, in which the woman stops all stimulation of the penis when the man first senses an impending ejaculation. No squeeze is used. Research has shown that the presence or the absence of circumcision has no bearing on a man's ejaculatory control; the glans is equally sensitive in the two states. Sex therapy has been most successful in the treatment of premature ejaculation.

A man with a sexual desire disorder or male erectile disorder is sometimes told to masturbate to prove that full erection and ejaculation are possible. In cases of lifelong female orgasmic disorder, the woman is directed to masturbate, sometimes using a vibrator. The shaft of the clitoris is the masturbatory site most preferred by women, and orgasm depends on adequate clitoral stimulation. An area on the anterior wall of the vagina has been identified in some women as a site of sexual excitation known as the G-spot; however, reports of an ejaculatory phenomenon at orgasm in women have not been satisfactorily verified. Men masturbate by stroking the shaft and the glans of the penis.

Male orgasmic disorder is managed by extravaginal ejaculation initially and gradual vaginal entry after stimulation to the point near ejaculation.

## Hypnotherapy

Hypnotherapists focus specifically on the anxiety-producing symptom—that is, the particular sexual dysfunction. The successful use of hypnosis enables the patient to gain control over the symptom that has been lowering self-esteem and disrupting psychological homeostasis. The cooperation of the patient is first obtained and encouraged during a series of nonhypnotic sessions with the therapist. Those discussions permit the development of a secure doctor-patient relationship, a sense of physical and psychological comfort on the part of the patient, and the establishment of mutually desired treatment goals. During that time the therapist assesses the patient's capacity for the trance experience. The nonhypnotic sessions also permit the clinician to take a psychiatric history and perform a mental status examination before beginning hypnotherapy. The focus of treatment is on symptom removal and attitude alteration. The patient is instructed in developing alternative means of dealing with the anxiety-provoking situation, the sexual encounter.

Patients are also taught relaxation techniques to use on themselves before sexual relations. With those methods to alleviate anxiety, the physiological responses to sexual stimulation can readily result in pleasurable excitation and discharge. Psychological impediments to vaginal lubrication, erection, and orgasm are removed, and normal sexual functioning ensues. Hypnosis may be added to a basic individual psychotherapy program to accelerate the effects of psychotherapeutic intervention.

## Behavior Therapy

Behavior therapists assume that sexual dysfunction is learned maladaptive behavior. Behavioral approaches were initially designed for the treatment of phobias. In cases of sexual dysfunction, the therapist sees the patient as being fearful of sexual interaction. Using traditional techniques, the therapist sets up a hierarchy of anxiety-provoking situations for the patient, ranging from the least threatening to the most threatening situation. Mild anxiety may be experienced at the thought of kissing, and massive anxiety may be felt when imagining penile penetration. The behavior therapist enables the patient to master the anxiety through a standard program of systematic desensitization. The program is designed to inhibit the learned anxious response by encouraging behaviors antithetical to anxiety. The patient first deals with the least anxiety-producing situation in fantasy and progresses by steps to the most anxiety-producing situation. Medication, hypnosis, or special training in deep muscle relaxation is sometimes used to help with the initial mastery of anxiety.

Assertiveness training is helpful in teaching the patient to express sexual needs openly and without fear. Exercises in assertiveness are given in conjunction with sex therapy; the patient is encouraged to make sexual requests and to refuse to comply with requests perceived as unreasonable.

Sexual exercises may be prescribed for the patient to perform at home, and a hierarchy may be established, starting with those activities that have proved most pleasurable and successful in the past.

One treatment variation involves the participation of the patient's sexual partner in the desensitization program. The partner, rather than the therapist, presents items of increasing stimulation value to the patient. In such situations a cooperative partner is necessary to help the patient carry gains made during treatment sessions to sexual activity at home.

## Group Therapy

Group therapy has been used to examine both intrapsychic and interpersonal problems in patients with sexual disorders. The therapy group provides a strong support system for a patient who feels ashamed, anxious, or guilty about a particular sexual problem. It is a useful forum in which to counteract sexual myths, correct misconceptions, and provide accurate information regarding sexual anatomy, physiology, and varieties of behavior.

Groups for the treatment of sexual disorders can be organized in several ways. Members may all share the same problem, such as premature ejaculation; members may all be of the same sex with different sexual problems; or groups may be composed of both men and women who are experiencing a variety of sexual problems. Group therapy may be an adjunct to other forms of therapy or the prime mode of treatment. Groups organized to treat a particular dysfunction are usually behavioral in approach.

Groups composed of sexually dysfunctional married couples have also been effective. The group provides the opportunity to gather accurate information, provides consensual validation of individual preferences, and enhances self-esteem and self-acceptance. Techniques such as role playing and psychodrama may be used in treatment. Such groups are not indicated for couples when one partner is uncooperative, when a patient is suffering from a severe depressive disorder or psychosis, when a patient has a strong repugnance for explicit sexual audiovisual material, or when the patient has a strong fear of groups.

## Analytically Oriented Sex Therapy

One of the most effective treatment modalities is the use of sex therapy integrated with psychodynamic and psychoanalytically oriented psychotherapy. The sex therapy is conducted over a longer than usual time period, and the extended schedule of treatment allows for the learning or the relearning of sexual satisfaction under the realities of the patients' day-to-day lives. The addition of psychodynamic conceptualizations to the behavioral techniques used to treat sexual dysfunctions allows for the treatment of patients with sex disorders associated with other psychopathology.

The themes and the dynamics that emerge in patients in analytically oriented sex therapy are the same as those seen in psychoanalytic therapy, such as relevant dreams, fear of punishment, aggressive feelings, difficulty with trusting the partner, fear of intimacy, oedipal feelings, and fear of genital mutilation.

The combined approach of analytically oriented sex therapy is used by the general psychiatrist, who carefully judges the optimal timing of sex therapy and the ability of patients to tolerate the directive approach that focuses on their sexual difficulties.

## Biological Treatments

Biological forms of treatment have limited application, but more attention than in the past is being given to the approach. Intravenous methohexital sodium (Brevital) has been used in desensitization therapy. Antianxiety agents may have application in tense patients, although the drugs can also interfere with sexual response. Sometimes the side effects of such drugs as thioridazine (Mellaril) and the tricyclic drugs are used to prolong the sexual response in such conditions as premature ejaculation. The use of tricyclics has also been advocated in the treatment of patients who are phobic about sex.

Pharmacological approaches also involve treating any underlying mental disorder that may be contributing to the sexual dysfunction. For example, patients whose sexual functioning is impaired as a result of depression usually show improved performance as their depression responds to antidepressant medication.

Specific medications to deal with the sexual dysfunctions are not generally successful. Testosterone, which affects libido, is beneficial to those patients who have a demonstrated low testosterone level. In women, however, testosterone leads to masculinization—such as deep voice, enlarged clitoris, and hirsutism—which may not be reversible on discontinuing the medication. Testosterone is contraindicated when fertility needs to be maintained. Case reports indicate that cyproheptadine (Periactin) can reverse drug-induced female orgasmic disorder and male orgasmic disorder in men taking fluoxetine. Clomipramine (Anafranil) has been reported to both induce spontaneous orgasms and inhibit orgasms in women. There are no known aphrodisiacs. Although recent studies report improvement in erectile responses in men ingesting yohimbine (Yocon), those findings remain controversial. Also controversial is the use of gonadotropin-releasing hormone as an inhalant. Such substances as powdered rhinoceros horn, used in Asia for their alleged stimulant effects, are of benefit only through the power of suggestion in a particular culture.

Surgical treatment is rarely advocated, but improved penile prosthetic devices are available for men with inadequate erectile responses who are resistant to other treatment methods or who have deficiencies of organic origin. The placement of a penile prosthesis in a man who has lost the ability to ejaculate or have an orgasm because of organic causes will not enable him to recover those functions. Men with prosthetic devices have generally reported satisfaction with their subsequent sexual functioning. Their wives, however, report much less satisfaction than do the men. Presurgical counseling is strongly recommended so that the couple have a realistic expectation of what the prosthesis can do for their sex lives. Some physicians are attempting revascularization of the penis as direct approach to treating erectile dysfunction caused by vascular disorders. In patients with corporal shunts that allow normally entrapped blood to leak from the corporal spaces, leading to inadequate erections (steal phenomenon), such surgical procedures are indicated. There are limited reports of prolonged success with the technique. Endarterectomy can be of benefit if aortoiliac occlusive disease is responsible for erectile dysfunction.

Surgical approaches to female sexual dysfunctions include hymenectomy in the case of dyspareunia in an unconsummated marriage, vaginoplasty in multiparous women who complain of reduced vaginal sensations, and the release of clitoral adhesions in women with sexual arousal disorder. Such surgical treatments have not been carefully studied and should be considered with great caution.

Injections of vasoactive materials into the corporal bodies of the penis produce erections for several hours; usually, a mixture of papaverine (Cerespan), prostaglandin E, and phentolamine (Regitine) is used. Usually, a urologist teaches the patient to inject himself in a series of training sessions. However, fibrosis and prolonged erections (lasting many hours) are occasional side effects of the approach. In addition, some patients become resistant to treating themselves. Vacuum pumps can also be used by patients without vascular disease to obtain erections but they are not very satisfactory.

### References

Dawkins S, Taylor R: Non-consummation of marriage. Lancet 2: 1029, 1961.

Fordney D S: Dyspareunia and vaginismus. Clin Obstet Gynecol 21: 205, 1978.

Frank E: Frequency of sexual dysfunction in "normal" couples. N Engl J Med 299: 111, 1978.

Freud S: Three essays on the theory of sexuality. In *Standard Edition of the Complete Psychological Works of Sigmund Freud*, vol 7, p 125. Hogarth Press, London, 1953.

Furlow W L: Male sexual dysfunction. Urol Clin North Am 8: 1, 1981.

Hawton K, Catalan J, Fagg J: Sex therapy for erectile dysfunction: Characteristics of couples, treatment outcome, and prognostic factors. Arch Sex Behav 21: 161, 1992.

Herman J, Lo Piccolo J: Clinical outcome of sex therapy. Arch Gen Psychiatry 40: 443, 1983.

Marmor J, editor: *Homosexual Behavior*. Basic Books, New York, 1980.

Masters W H, Johnson V E: *Human Sexual Inadequacy*. Little, Brown, Boston, 1970.

Moss H B, Panzak G L, Tarter R E: Sexual functioning of male anabolic steroid abusers. Arch Sex Behav 22: 1, 1993.

Sadock B J, Kaplan H I, Freedman A M, editors: *The Sexual Experience*. Williams & Wilkins, Baltimore, 1976.

Schiavi R C, Karstaedt A, Schreiner-Engel P, Mandeli J: Psychometric characteristics of individuals with sexual dysfunction and their partners. J Sex Marital Ther 18: 219, 1992.

Segraves R T: Effects of psychotropic drugs on human erection and ejaculation. Arch Gen Psychiatry 46: 782, 1989.

Semans J H: Premature ejaculation: A new approach. South Med J 49: 353, 1956.

Zorgniotto A W, Leflueck R S: Autoinjection of corpus cavernosum with vasoactive drug combination with vasculogenic impotence. J Urol 133: 39, 1985.

# 20.3 / Paraphilias and Sexual Disorder NOS

## PARAPHILIAS

Paraphilias are sexual disorders characterized by specialized sexual fantasies and intense sexual urges and practices that are usually repetitive and distressing to the person. The special fantasy, with its unconscious and conscious components, is the pathognomonic element, sexual arousal and orgasm being associated phenomena. The influence of the fantasy and its behavioral manifestations extend beyond the sexual sphere to pervade the person's life. The major functions of sexual behavior for human beings are to assist in bonding, to express and enhance love between two persons, and for procreation. Paraphilias are divergent behaviors in that they are concealed by their participants, appear to exclude or harm others, and disrupt the potential for bonding between persons. Paraphiliac arousal may be transient in some persons who act out their impulses only during periods of stress or conflict.

### Classification

The major categories of paraphilias in the fourth edition of *Diagnostic and Statistical Manual of Mental Disorders* (DSM-IV) are exhibitionism, fetishism, frotteurism, pedophilia, sexual masochism, sexual sadism, voyeurism, transvestic fetishism, and a separate category for other paraphilias not otherwise specified (NOS)—for example, zoophilia. A given person may have multiple paraphiliac disorders.

### Epidemiology

Paraphilias are practiced by a small percentage of the population. However, the insistent, repetitive nature of the disorders results in the high frequency of the commission of paraphiliac acts; thus, a large proportion of the population have been victimized by persons with paraphilias.

Among legally identified cases of paraphilias, pedophilia is far more common than the others. Ten to 20 percent of all children have been molested by age 18. Because a child is the object, the act is taken more seriously, and greater effort is spent tracking down the culprit than in other paraphilias. Persons with exhibitionism, who publicly display themselves to young children, are also commonly apprehended. Those with voyeurism may be apprehended, but their risk is not great. Twenty percent of adult females have been the targets of persons with exhibitionism and voyeurism. Sexual masochism and sexual sadism are underrepresented in any prevalence estimates. Sexual sadism usually comes to attention only in sensational cases of rape, brutality, and lust murder. The excretory paraphilias are scarcely reported, since any activity usually takes place between consenting adults or between prostitute and client. Persons with fetishism ordinarily do not become entangled in the legal system. Those with transvestic fetishism may be arrested occasionally on disturbing-the-peace or other misdemeanor charges if they are obviously men dressed in women's clothes, but arrest is more common among those with the gender identity disorders. Zoophilia as a true paraphilia is rare.

As usually defined, the paraphilias seem to be largely male conditions. Fetishism almost always occurs in men.

More than 50 percent of all paraphilias have their onset before age 18. Paraphilia patients frequently have three to five paraphilias, either concurrently or at different times in their lives. That is especially the case with exhibitionism, fetishism, sexual masochism, sexual sadism, transvestic fetishism, voyeurism, and zoophilia (Table 20.3–1).

The occurrence of paraphiliac behavior peaks between ages 15 and 25 and gradually declines; in men of 50, paraphiliac acts are rare, except for those that occur in isolation or with a cooperative partner.

## Etiology

**Psychosocial factors.** In the classic psychoanalytic model, a person with a paraphilia is someone who has failed to complete the normal developmental process toward heterosexual adjustment; however, that model has been modified by new psychoanalytic approaches. What distinguishes one paraphilia from another is the method chosen by the person (usually male) to cope with the anxiety caused by the threat of (1) castration by the father and (2) separation from the mother. However bizarre its manifestation, the resulting behavior provides an outlet for the sexual and aggressive drives that would otherwise have been channeled into proper sexual behavior.

Failure to resolve the oedipal crisis by identifying with the father-aggressor (for boys) or mother-aggressor (for girls) results either in improper identification with the opposite-sex parent or in an improper choice of object for libido cathexis.

Regardless of the DSM-IV classifications, classic psychoanalytic theory holds that transsexualism and transvestic fetishism are both disorders because each involves identification with the opposite-sex parent, instead of the same-sex parent. For instance, a man dressing in women's clothes is believed to identify with his mother. Exhibitionism and voyeurism are also seen as expressions of feminine identification, since persons with the paraphilias must constantly examine their own or others' genitals to calm their anxiety about castration. Fetishism is an attempt to avoid anxiety by displacing libidinal impulses to inappropriate objects. The person with a shoe fetish unconsciously denies that women have lost their penises through castration by attaching libido to a phallic object, the shoe, that symbolizes the female penis. Persons with pedophilia and sexual sadism have a need to dominate and control their victims, as though to compensate for their feelings of powerlessness during the oedipal crisis. Some theorists believe that the choice of a child as a love object is a narcissistic choice. Persons with sexual masochism overcome their fear of injury and their sense of powerlessness by showing that they are impervious to harm. Although recent developments in psychoanalysis place more emphasis on treating defense mechanisms than on oedipal traumas, the course of psychoanalytic therapy for the patient with a paraphilia remains consistent with Sigmund Freud's theory.

Other theories attribute the development of a paraphilia to early experiences that condition or socialize the child into committing a paraphiliac act. The first shared sexual experience can be important in that regard. Molestation as a child can predispose the person toward being the recipient of continued abuse as an adult or, conversely, toward becoming an abuser of others. The onset of paraphiliac acts can result from modeling one's behavior on the behavior of others who have carried out paraphiliac acts, mimicking sexual behavior depicted in the media, or recalling emotionally laden events from one's past, such as one's own molestation. Learning theory indicates that, because the fantasizing of paraphiliac interests begins at an early age and because personal fantasies and thoughts are not shared with others (who could block or discourage such ideas), the use and the misuse of paraphiliac fantasies and urges continue uninhibited until late in life. Only then does the person begin to realize that such paraphiliac interests and urges are inconsistent with societal norms. Unfortunately, by that time the repetitive use of such fantasies has become ingrained; the person's sexual thoughts and behaviors have become associated with or conditioned to paraphiliac fantasies.

**Organic factors.** A number of studies have identified abnormal organic findings in persons with paraphilias. None has used random samples of such persons; the studies are, instead, extensive investigations of paraphilia patients who have been referred to large medical centers. Of those persons evaluated at referral centers who had positive organic findings, 74 percent had abnormal hormone levels, 27 percent had hard or soft neurological signs, 24 percent had chromosomal abnormalities, 9 percent had seizures, 9 percent had dyslexia, 4 percent had abnormal electroencephalograms (EEGs) without seizures, 4 percent had major mental disorders, and 4 percent were mentally retarded. The remaining question is whether those abnormalities are causatively related to paraphiliac interests or are incidental findings that bear no relevance to the development of paraphiliac interests.

Psychophysiological tests have been developed to measure penile volumetric size in response to paraphiliac and nonparaphiliac stimuli. The procedures may be of use in diagnosis and treatment but are of questionable diagnostic validity because some men are able to suppress their erectile responses.

**Table 20.3–1**
**Frequency of Paraphiliac Acts Committed by Paraphilia Patients Seeking Outpatient Treatment**

| Diagnostic Category | Paraphilia Patients Seeking Outpatient Treatment (%) | Paraphiliac Acts per Paraphilia Patient* |
|---|---|---|
| Pedophilia | 45 | 5 |
| Exhibitionism | 25 | 50 |
| Voyeurism | 12 | 17 |
| Frotteurism | 6 | 30 |
| Sexual masochism | 3 | 36 |
| Transvestic fetishism | 3 | 25 |
| Sexual sadism | 3 | 3 |
| Fetishism | 2 | 3 |
| Zoophilia | 1 | 2 |

*Median number.
Table by Gene G. Abel, M.D.

## Diagnosis and Clinical Features

In DSM-IV the diagnostic criteria for paraphilias include the presence of a pathognomonic fantasy and an intense urge to act out the fantasy, which may distress the patient, or its behavioral elaboration. The fantasy contains unusual sexual material that is relatively fixed and shows only minor variations. Arousal and orgasm depend on the mental elaboration or the behavioral playing out of the fantasy. Sexual activity is ritualized or stereotyped and makes use of degraded, reduced, or dehumanized objects.

**Exhibitionism.** Exhibitionism is the recurrent urge to expose one's genitals to a stranger or an unsuspecting person (Table 20.3–2). Sexual excitement occurs in anticipation of the exposure, and orgasm is brought about by masturbation during or after the event. In almost 100 percent of the cases, those with exhibitionism are males exposing themselves to females.

The dynamic of the man with exhibitionism is to assert his masculinity by showing his penis and by watching the reaction of the victim—fright, surprise, disgust. Unconsciously, the man feels castrated and impotent. Wives of men with exhibitionism often substitute for the mother to whom the men were excessively attached during childhood.

In other related paraphilias the central themes involve derivatives of looking or showing.

**Fetishism.** In fetishism the sexual focus is on objects (such as shoes, gloves, pantyhose, and stockings) that are intimately associated with the human body (Table 20.3–3). The particular fetish is linked to someone closely involved with the patient during childhood and has some quality associated with that loved, needed, or even traumatizing person. Usually, the disorder begins by adolescence, although the fetish may have been established in childhood. Once established, the disorder tends to be chronic.

Sexual activity may be directed toward the fetish itself (for example, masturbation with or into a shoe), or the fetish may be incorporated into sexual intercourse (for example, the demand that high-heeled shoes be worn). The disorder is almost exclusively found in males. According to Freud, the fetish serves as a symbol of the phallus because the person has unconscious castration fears. Learning theorists believe that the object was associated with sexual stimulation at an early age.

**Frotteurism.** Frotteurism is usually characterized by the male's rubbing his penis against the buttocks or other body part of a fully clothed woman to achieve orgasm (Table 20.3–4). At other times, he may use his hands to rub an unsuspecting victim. The acts usually occur in crowded places, particularly subways and buses. The person with frotteurism is extremely passive and isolated, and frottage is often his only source of sexual gratification.

**Pedophilia.** Pedophilia involves, over a period of at least six months, recurrent intense sexual urges toward or arousal by children 13 years of age or younger. The person with pedophilia is at least 16 years of age and at least five years older than the victim (Table 20.3–5). When the perpetrator is a late adolescent involved in an ongoing sexual relationship with a 12- or 13-year-old, the diagnosis is not warranted.

The vast majority of child molestations involve genital fondling or oral sex. Vaginal or anal penetration of the child is an infrequent occurrence except in cases of incest. Although the majority of child victims coming to public attention are girls, that finding appears to be a product of the referral process. Offenders report that, when they touch the child, the majority (60 percent) of the victims are boys. That figure is in sharp contrast to that for nontouching victimization of children, such as window peeping and exhibitionism, which in 99 percent of all cases is perpetrated against girls. Moreover, 95 percent of those with pedophilia are heterosexual, and 50 percent have consumed alcohol to excess at the time of the incident. In addition to their pedophilia, a significant number of the perpetrators are concomitantly or have previously been involved in exhibitionism, voyeurism, or rape.

Incest is related to pedophilia by the frequent selection

---

**Table 20.3–2**
**Diagnostic Criteria for Exhibitionism**

A. Over a period of at least 6 months, recurrent, intense sexually arousing fantasies, sexual urges, or behaviors involving the exposure of one's genitals to an unsuspecting stranger.

B. The fantasies, sexual urges, or behaviors cause clinically significant distress or impairment in social, occupational, or other important areas of functioning.

---

**Table 20.3–3**
**Diagnostic Criteria for Fetishism**

A. Over a period of at least 6 months, recurrent, intense sexually arousing fantasies, sexual urges, or behaviors involving the use of nonliving objects (e.g., female undergarments).

B. The fantasies, sexual urges, or behaviors cause clinically significant distress or impairment in social, occupational, or other important areas of functioning.

C. The fetish objects are not articles of female clothing used in cross-dressing (as in transvestic fetishism) or devices designed for the purpose of tactile genital stimulation (e.g., a vibrator).

---

**Table 20.3–4**
**Diagnostic Criteria for Frotteurism**

A. Over a period of at least 6 months, recurrent, intense sexually arousing fantasies, sexual urges, or behaviors involving touching and rubbing against a nonconsenting person.

B. The fantasies, sexual urges, or behaviors cause clinically significant distress or impairment in social, occupational, or other important areas of functioning.

**Table 20.3–5**
**Diagnostic Criteria for Pedophilia**

A. Over a period of at least 6 months, recurrent, intense sexually arousing fantasies, sexual urges, or behaviors involving sexual activity with a prepubescent child or children (generally age 13 years or younger).

B. The fantasies, sexual urges, or behaviors cause clinically significant distress or impairment in social, occupational, or other important areas of functioning.

C. The person is at least 16 years and at least 5 years older than the child or children in criterion A.

Note: Do not include an individual in late adolescence involved in an ongoing sexual relationship with a 12- or 13-year-old.

*Specify* if:
**Sexually attracted to males**
**Sexually attracted to females**
**Sexually attracted to both**

*Specify* if:
**Limited to incest**

*Specify* type:
**Exclusive type** (attracted only to children)
**Nonexclusive type**

Table from DSM-IV, *Diagnostic and Statistical Manual of Mental Disorders*, ed 4. Copyright American Psychiatric Association, Washington, 1994. Used with permission.

of an immature child as a sex object, the subtle or overt element of coercion, and, occasionally, the preferential nature of the adult-child liaison.

**Sexual masochism.** Masochism takes its name from the activities of Leopold von Sacher-Masoch, a 19th-century Austrian novelist whose characters derived sexual pleasure from being abused and dominated by women. According to DSM-IV, persons with sexual masochism have a recurrent preoccupation with sexual urges and fantasies involving the act of being humiliated, beaten, bound, or otherwise made to suffer (Table 20.3–6). Sexual masochistic practices are more common among men than among women. Freud believed masochism to result from destructive fantasies turned against the self. In some cases, persons can allow themselves to experience sexual feelings only if punishment for them follows. Persons with sexual masochism may have had childhood experiences that convinced them that pain is a prerequisite for sexual pleasure. About 30 percent of those with sexual masochism also have sadistic fantasies. Moral masochism involves a need to suffer but is not accompanied by sexual fantasies.

**Sexual sadism.** The DSM-IV diagnostic criteria for sexual sadism are presented in Table 20.3–7. The onset is

**Table 20.3–6**
**Diagnostic Criteria for Sexual Masochism**

A. Over a period of at least 6 months, recurrent, intense sexually arousing fantasies, sexual urges, or behaviors involving the act (real, not simulated) of being humiliated, beaten, bound, or otherwise made to suffer.

B. The fantasies, sexual urges, or behaviors cause clinically significant distress or impairment in social, occupational, or other important areas of functioning.

Table from DSM-IV, *Diagnostic and Statistical Manual of Mental Disorders*, ed 4. Copyright American Psychiatric Association, Washington, 1994. Used with permission.

**Table 20.3–7**
**Diagnostic Criteria for Sexual Sadism**

A. Over a period of at least 6 months, recurrent, intense sexually arousing fantasies, sexual urges, or behaviors involving acts (real, not simulated) in which the psychological or physical suffering (including humiliation) of the victim is sexually exciting to the person.

B. The fantasies, sexual urges, or behaviors cause clinically significant distress or impairment in social, occupational, or other important areas of functioning.

Table from DSM-IV, *Diagnostic and Statistical Manual of Mental Disorders*, ed 4. Copyright American Psychiatric Association, Washington, 1994. Used with permission.

usually before the age of 18 years, and most persons with sexual sadism are male. According to psychoanalytic theory, sadism is a defense against fears of castration—the persons with sexual sadism do to others what they fear will happen to them. Pleasure is derived from expressing the aggressive instinct. The disorder was named after the Marquis de Sade, an 18th-century French author, who was repeatedly imprisoned for his violent sexual acts against women. Sexual sadism is related to rape, although rape is more aptly considered a form of aggression. Some sadistic rapists, however, kill their victims after having sex (so-called lust murders). In many cases, those persons have underlying schizophrenia. John Money believes that lust murderers have the dissociative disorder of dissociative identity disorder and may have had a history of head trauma. He lists five contributory causes of sexual sadism: hereditary predisposition, hormonal malfunctioning, pathological relationships, a history of sexual abuse, and the presence of other mental disorders.

**Voyeurism.** Voyeurism is the recurrent preoccupation with fantasies and acts that involve observing people who are naked or are engaged in grooming or in sexual activity (Table 20.3–8). It is also known as scopophilia. Masturbation to orgasm usually occurs during or after the event. The first voyeuristic act usually occurs during childhood and is most common in males. When persons with voyeurism are apprehended, it is usually for loitering.

**Transvestic fetishism.** Transvestic fetishism is marked by fantasies and sexual urges by heterosexual men to dress in female clothes for purposes of arousal and as an adjunct to masturbation or coitus (Table 20.3–9). Transvestic fetishism typically begins in childhood or early adolescence.

**Table 20.3–8**
**Diagnostic Criteria for Voyeurism**

A. Over a period of at least 6 months, recurrent, intense sexually arousing fantasies, sexual urges, or behaviors involving the act of observing an unsuspecting person who is naked, in the process of disrobing, or engaging in sexual activity.

B. The fantasies, sexual urges, or behaviors cause clinically significant distress or impairment in social, occupational, or other important areas of functioning.

Table from DSM-IV, *Diagnostic and Statistical Manual of Mental Disorders*, ed 4. Copyright American Psychiatric Association, Washington, 1994. Used with permission.

**Table 20.3–9**
**Diagnostic Criteria for Transvestic Fetishism**

A. Over a period of at least 6 months, in a heterosexual male, recurrent, intense sexually arousing fantasies, sexual urges, or behaviors involving cross-dressing.

B. The fantasies, sexual urges, or behaviors cause clinically significant distress or impairment in social, occupational, or other important areas of functioning.

*Specify* if:
   **With gender dysphoria**: if the person has persistent discomfort with gender role or identity.

Table from DSM-IV, *Diagnostic and Statistical Manual of Mental Disorders*, ed 4. Copyright American Psychiatric Association, Washington, 1994. Used with permission.

As years pass, some men with transvestic fetishism want to dress and live permanently as women. Such persons are classified in DSM-IV as persons with transvestic fetishism with gender dysphoria. Usually, more than one article of clothing is involved; frequently, an entire wardrobe is involved. When a person with transvestic fetishism is cross-dressed, the appearance of femininity may be striking, although usually not to the degree found in transsexualism. When not dressed in women's clothes, men with transvestic fetishism may be hypermasculine in appearance and occupation. Cross-dressing exists on a gradient from solitary, depressed, guilt-ridden dressing to ego-syntonic, social membership in a transvestite subculture.

The overt clinical syndrome of transvestic fetishism may begin in latency, but it is more often seen around pubescence or in adolescence. Frank dressing in women's clothes usually does not begin until mobility and relative independence from parents are well-established.

**Paraphilia not otherwise specified.** The classification of paraphilia not otherwise specified (NOS) includes varied paraphilias that do not meet the criteria for any of the aforementioned categories (Table 20.3–10).

TELEPHONE SCATOLOGIA. In telephone scatologia, characterized by obscene phone calling, tension and arousal begin in anticipation of phoning, an unsuspecting partner is involved, the recipient of the call listens while the telephoner (usually male) verbally exposes his preoccupations or induces her to talk about her sexual activity, and the conversation is accompanied by masturbation, which is often completed after the contact is interrupted.

People also use computer interactive networks to transmit obscene messages by electronic mail. In addition, people use computer networks to transmit sexually explicit messages and video images. Some persons compulsively use those services.

NECROPHILIA. Necrophilia is obsession with obtaining sexual gratification from cadavers. Most persons with necrophilia find corpses for their exploitation from morgues. Some have been known to rob graves. At times, persons murder to satisfy their sexual urges. In the few cases studied, the persons with necrophilia believed that they were inflicting the greatest conceivable humiliation on their lifeless victims. According to Richard Krafft-Ebing, the diagnosis of psychosis is, under all circumstances, justified.

PARTIALISM. In partialism the person focuses on one part of the body to the exclusion of all other parts. Mouth-genital contact—such as cunnilingus (oral contact with the external female genitals), fellatio (oral contact with the penis), and analingus (oral contact with the anus)—is an activity normally associated with foreplay. Freud recognized the mucosal surfaces of the body as being erotogenic and capable of producing pleasurable sensation. But when a person uses those activities as the sole source of sexual gratification and cannot have coitus or refuses to have coitus, a paraphilia exists. It is also known as oralism.

ZOOPHILIA. In zoophilia, animals—which may be trained to participate—are preferentially incorporated into arousal fantasies or sexual activities, including intercourse, masturbation, and oral-genital contact. Zoophilia as an organized paraphilia is rare. For a number of people, animals are the major source of relatedness, so it is not surprising that a broad variety of domestic animals are sensually or sexually used.

Sexual relations with animals may occasionally be an outgrowth of availability or convenience, especially in parts of the world where rigid convention precludes premarital sexuality and in situations of enforced isolation. However, because masturbation is also available in such situations, some predilection for animal contact is probably present in opportunistic zoophilia.

COPROPHILIA AND KLISMAPHILIA. Coprophilia is attraction to sexual pleasure associated with the desire to defecate on a partner, to be defecated on, or to eat feces (coprophagia). A variant is the compulsive utterance of obscene words (coprolalia). Those paraphilias are associated with fixation at the anal stage of psychosexual development. Similarly, the use of enemas as part of sexual stimulation, klismaphilia, is related to anal fixation.

UROPHILIA. Urophilia is interest in sexual pleasure associated with the desire to urinate on a partner or to be urinated on; it is a form of urethral eroticism. It may be associated with masturbatory techniques involving the insertion of foreign objects into the urethra for sexual stimulation in both men and women.

MASTURBATION. Masturbation is a normal activity that is common in all stages of life from infancy to old age. It was not always thought to be so. Freud believed neurasthenia to be caused by excessive masturbation. In the early 1900s, masturbatory insanity was a common diagnosis in hospitals for the criminally insane in the United States. Masturbation can be defined as the achieving of sexual pleasure—usually resulting in orgasm—by oneself (autoeroticism). Alfred Kinsey found it to be more prevalent in males than in females, but that difference may no longer exist. The frequency of masturbation varies from three to four times a week in adolescence to one to two times a week in adulthood. It is common among married people; Kinsey reported that it occurred on the average of once a month among married couples.

The techniques of masturbation vary in both sexes and among persons. The most common technique is direct stimulation of the clitoris or the penis with the hand or the fingers.

**Table 20.3–10**
**Diagnostic Criteria for Paraphilia Not Otherwise Specified**

This category is included for coding paraphilias that do not meet the criteria for any of the specific categories. Examples include, but are not limited to, telephone scatologia (obscene phone calls), necrophilia (corpses), partialism (exclusive focus on part of body), zoophilia (animals), coprophilia (feces), klismaphilia (enemas), and urophilia (urine).

Table from DSM-IV, *Diagnostic and Statistical Manual of Mental Disorders*, ed 4. Copyright American Psychiatric Association, Washington, 1994. Used with permission.

Indirect stimulation may also be used, such as rubbing against a pillow or squeezing the thighs. Kinsey found that 2 percent of women are capable of achieving orgasm through fantasy alone. Men and women have been known to insert objects into the urethra to achieve orgasm. The hand vibrator is now used as a masturbatory device by both sexes.

Masturbation is abnormal when it is the only type of sexual activity performed, when it is done with such frequency as to indicate a compulsion or sexual dysfunction, or when it is consistently preferred to sex with a partner.

HYPOXYPHILIA. Hypoxyphilia is the desire to achieve an altered state of consciousness secondary to hypoxia while experiencing orgasm. In the disorder the persons may use a drug (such as a volatile nitrite or nitrous oxide) that produces hypoxia. Autoerotic asphyxiation is also associated with hypoxic states but should be classified as a form of sexual masochism. A discussion of autoerotic asphyxiation appears in Section 20.2.

## Differential Diagnosis

The clinician needs to differentiate a paraphilia from experimentation in which the act is done for its novel effect and not recurrently or compulsively. Paraphiliac activity is most likely to occur during adolescence. Some paraphilias (especially the bizarre types) are part of another mental disorder, such as schizophrenia. Brain diseases may release perverse impulses.

## Course and Prognosis

A poor prognosis for paraphilias is associated with an early age of onset, a high frequency of the acts, no guilt or shame about the act, and substance abuse. The course and the prognosis are good when the patient has a history of coitus in addition to the paraphilia, when the patient has a high motivation for change, and when the patient is self-referred, rather than referred by a legal agency.

## Treatment

Insight-oriented psychotherapy is the most common approach to treating the paraphilias. Patients have the opportunity to understand their dynamics and the events that caused the paraphilia to develop. In particular, they become aware of the daily events that cause them to act on their impulses (for example, a real or fantasized rejection). Psychotherapy also allows the patients to regain self-esteem and to improve their interpersonal skills and find acceptable methods for sexual gratification. Group therapy is also useful.

Sex therapy is an appropriate adjunct to the treatment of patients who suffer from specific sexual dysfunctions when they attempt nondeviant sexual activities with partners.

Behavior therapy is used to disrupt the learned paraphiliac pattern. Noxious stimuli, such as electric shocks and bad odors, have been paired with the impulse, which then diminishes. The stimuli can be self-administered and used by patients whenever they feel that they will act on the impulse.

Drug therapy, including antipsychotic or antidepressant medication, is indicated for the treatment of schizophrenia or depressive disorders if the paraphilia is associated with those disorders. Antiandrogens, such as cyproterone acetate in Europe and medroxyprogesterone acetate (Depo-Provera) in the United States, have been used experimentally in hypersexual paraphilias. Some cases have reported decreases in the hypersexual behavior. Medroxyprogesterone acetate seems to benefit those patients whose driven hypersexuality (for example, virtually constant masturbation, sexual contact at every opportunity, compulsively assaultive sexuality), is out of control or dangerous. Serotonergic agents such as fluoxetine (Prozac) have been used in some paraphiliac cases with limited success.

# SEXUAL DISORDER NOT OTHERWISE SPECIFIED

Many sexual disorders are not classifiable as sexual dysfunctions or paraphilias. Those unclassified disorders are rare, poorly documented, not easily classified, or not specifically described in DSM-IV (Table 20.3–11).

## Postcoital Dysphoria

Postcoital dysphoria is not listed in DSM-IV. It occurs during the resolution phase of sexual activity, when the person normally experiences a sense of general well-being and muscular and psychological relaxation. Some persons, however, experience postcoital dysphoria. After an otherwise satisfactory sexual experience, they become depressed, tense, anxious, and irritable and show psychomotor agitation. They often want to get away from the partner and may become verbally or even physically abusive. The incidence of the disorder is unknown, but it is more common in men than in women. The causes are several and relate to the attitude of the person toward sex in general and toward the partner in particular. It may occur in adulterous sex and with prostitutes. The fear of acquired immune deficiency syndrome (AIDS) causes some persons to experience postcoital dysphoria. Treatment requires insight-oriented psychotherapy to help patients understand the unconscious antecedents to their behavior and attitudes.

---

**Table 20.3–11**
**Diagnostic Criteria for Sexual Disorder Not Otherwise Specified**

This category is included for coding a sexual disturbance that does not meet the criteria for any specific sexual disorder and is neither a sexual dysfunction nor a paraphilia. Examples include

1. Marked feelings of inadequacy concerning sexual performance or other traits related to self-imposed standards of masculinity or femininity
2. Distress about a pattern of repeated sexual relationships involving a succession of lovers who are experienced by the individual only as things to be used
3. Persistent and marked distress about sexual orientation

Table from DSM-IV, *Diagnostic and Statistical Manual of Mental Disorders*, ed 4. Copyright American Psychiatric Association, Washington, 1994. Used with permission.

## Couple Problems

At times, a complaint must be viewed in terms of the spousal unit or the couple, rather than as an individual dysfunction. An example is a couple in which one prefers morning sex while the other functions more readily at night; another example is a couple with unequal frequencies of desire.

## Unconsummated Marriage

A couple involved in an unconsummated marriage have never had coitus and are typically uninformed and inhibited about sexuality. Their feelings of guilt, shame, or inadequacy are increased by their problem, and they experience conflict between their need to seek help and their need to conceal their difficulty. Couples present with the problem after having been married several months or several years. William Masters and Virginia Johnson reported an unconsummated marriage of 17 years' duration.

Frequently, the couple do not seek help directly, but the woman may reveal the problem to her gynecologist on a visit ostensibly concerned with vague vaginal or other somatic complaints. On examining her, the gynecologist may find an intact hymen. In some cases though, the wife may have undergone a hymenectomy to resolve the problem. That surgical procedure is another stress and often increases the feelings of inadequacy in the couple. The wife may feel put on, abused, or mutilated, and the husband's concern about his manliness may increase. The hymenectomy usually aggravates the situation without solving the basic problem. The inquiry of a physician who is comfortable in dealing with sexual problems may be the first opening to a frank discussion of the couple's distress. Often, the pretext of the medical visit is a discussion of contraceptive methods or—even more ironically—a request for an infertility workup. Once presented, the complaint can often be successfully treated. The duration of the problem does not significantly affect the prognosis or the outcome of the case.

The causes of unconsummated marriage are varied: lack of sex education, sexual prohibitions overly stressed by parents or society, problems of an oedipal nature, immaturity in both partners, overdependence on primary families, and problems in sexual identification. Religious orthodoxy, with severe control of sexual and social development or the equation of sexuality with sin or uncleanliness, has also been cited as a dominant cause. Many women involved in an unconsummated marriage have distorted concepts about their vaginas. They may fear that it is too small or too soft, or they may confuse the vagina with the rectum, leading to feelings of being unclean. The man may share in those distortions about the vagina and, in addition, perceive it as dangerous to himself. Similarly, both partners may have distortions about the man's penis, perceiving it as a weapon, as too large, or as too small. Many patients can be helped by simple education about genital anatomy and physiology, by suggestions for self-exploration, and by correct information from a physician. The problem of the unconsummated marriage is best treated by seeing both members of the couple. Dual-sex therapy involving a male-female cotherapist team has been markedly effective. However, other forms of conjoint therapy, marital counseling, traditional psychotherapy on a one-to-one basis, and counseling from a sensitive family physician, gynecologist, or urologist are all helpful.

## Body Image Problems

Some persons are ashamed of their bodies and experience feelings of inadequacy related to self-imposed standards of masculinity or femininity. They may insist on sex only during total darkness, not allow certain body parts to be seen or touched, or seek unnecessary operative procedures to deal with their imagined inadequacies. Body dysmorphic disorder should be ruled out.

## Don Juanism

Some men who appear to be hypersexual, as manifested by their need to have many sexual encounters or conquests, use their sexual activities to mask deep feelings of inferiority. Some have unconscious homosexual impulses, which they deny by compulsive sexual contacts with women. After having sex, most Don Juans are no longer interested in the woman. The condition is sometimes referred to as satyriasis or sex addiction.

## Nymphomania

Nymphomania signifies excessive or pathological desire for coitus in a woman. There have been few scientific studies of the condition. Those patients who have been studied usually have had one or more sexual disorders, usually including female orgasmic disorder. The woman often has an intense fear of her loss of love. The woman attempts to satisfy her dependence needs, rather than to gratify her sexual impulses through her actions. This is a form of sex addiction.

## Persistent and Marked Distress about Sexual Orientation

Distress about one's sexual orientation is characterized by a dissatisfaction with homosexual arousal patterns, a desire to increase heterosexual arousal, and strong negative feelings about being homosexual. Occasional statements to the effect that life would be easier if the person were not homosexual do not constitute persistent and marked distress about sexual orientation.

Treatment of sexual orientation distress is controversial. One study reported that, with a minimum of 350 hours of psychoanalytic therapy, about a third of about 100 bisexual and homosexual men achieved a heterosexual reorientation at a five-year follow-up; but that study has been challenged. Behavior therapy and avoidance conditioning techniques have also been used, but a basic problem with behavioral techniques is that the behavior may be changed in the laboratory setting but not outside the laboratory. Prognostic factors weighing in favor of heterosexual reorientation for men include being under 35 years of age,

some experience of heterosexual arousal, and a high mo
tivation for reorientation.

Another style of intervention is directed at enabling the
person with persistent and marked distress about sexual
orientation to live comfortably as a homosexual without
shame, guilt, anxiety, or depression. Gay counseling centers are engaged with patients in such treatment programs.
At present, outcome studies of such centers have not been
reported in detail.

As for the treatment of women with persistent and
marked distress about sexual orientation, few data are
available, and those are primarily single-case studies with
variable outcomes. Section 20.1 presents a further discussion on sexual orientation, homosexuality, and coming out.

## References

Abel G G: Paraphilias. In *Comprehensive Textbook of Psychiatry,* ed 5,
H I Kaplan, B J Sadock, editors, p 1069. Williams & Wilkins, Baltimore,
1989.
Abel G G, Blanchard E B: The role of fantasy in the treatment of sexual
deviation. Arch Gen Psychiatry *30*: 467, 1974.
Abel G G, Osborn C: The paraphilias: The extent and nature of sexually
deviant and criminal behavior. Psychiatr Clin North Am *15*: 675, 1992.
Berlin F S, Meinecke C F: Treatment of sex offenders with antiandrogenic
medication: Conceptualization, review of treatment modalities, and pre-
liminary findings. Am J Psychiatry *138*: 237, 1981.
Blair C D, Lanyon R I: Exhibitionism: Etiology and treatment. Psychol
Bull *89*: 439, 1981.
Cook M, Howells K: *Adult Sexual Interest in Children.* Academic, New
York, 1981.
Freud S: Three essays on the theory of sexuality. In *Standard Edition of
the Complete Psychological Works of Sigmund Freud,* vol 7, p 125. Ho-
garth Press, London, 1953.
Gange P: Treatment of sex offenders with medroxyprogesterone acetate.
Am J Psychiatry *138*: 644, 1981.
Kinsey A, Pomeroy W, Martin C E: *Sexual Behavior in the Human Male.*
Saunders, Philadelphia, 1948.
Krafft-Ebing R: *Psychopathia Sexualis.* Stein and Day, New York, 1965.
Langevin R: Biological factors contributing to paraphilic behavior. Psy-
chiatr Ann *22*: 307, 1992.
Leif H, editor: *Sex Problems in Medical Practice.* American Medical As-
sociation, Chicago, 1981.
Levine S M, Stava L: Personality characteristics of sex offenders: A review.
Arch Sex Behav *16*: 57, 1987.
Money J: Forensic sexology: Paraphilic serial rape (biastophilia) and lust
murder (erotophonophilia). Am J Psychother *44*: 26, 1990.
Slag M F: Impotence in medical clinic outpatients. JAMA *249*: 1736, 1983.
Stein D J, Hollander E, Anthony D T, Schneier F R: Serotonergic med-
ications for sexual obsessions, sexual addictions, and paraphilias. J Clin
Psychiatry *53*: 267, 1992.

# Gender Identity Disorders

Gender identity disorders are characterized by the persons' having persistent feelings of discomfort with their own biological sex or the gender role of their own sex. An understanding of the disorder requires that the complex and varied terminology used in discussing this condition be described clearly to avoid confusion.

*Gender identity* is a psychological state that reflects the inner sense of oneself as being male or female. Gender identity is based on culturally determined sets of attitudes, behavior patterns, and other attributes usually associated with masculinity or femininity. The person with a healthy gender identity is able to say with certainty, "I am male" or "I am female." *Gender role* is the external behavioral pattern that reflects the person's inner sense of gender identity. It is a public declaration of gender; the image of maleness versus femaleness is communicated to others.

Under ideal circumstances, gender identity and gender role are congruent; that is, a woman who has a sense of herself as a woman conveys that to the outside world by acting as a woman; similarly, a man who views himself as a man acts as a man. Gender role is everything that one says or does to indicate to others or to oneself the degree to which one is male or female. Gender identity and gender role must be distinguished from *sex* (also known as biological sex), which is strictly limited to the anatomical and physiological characteristics that indicate whether one is male or female (for example, a penis or a vagina).

All those terms must be distinguished from *sexual orientation*, the person's erotic-response tendency (for example, homosexual or heterosexual). Sexual orientation takes into account one's object choice (man or woman) and one's fantasy life—for example, erotic fantasies about men or women or both.

## NOSOLOGY

The nosology of gender identity disorders is simpler in the fourth edition of *Diagnostic and Statistical Manual of Mental Disorders* (DSM-IV) than in earlier editions. The revised third edition (DSM-III-R) listed four gender identity disorder diagnoses: (1) gender identity disorder of childhood; (2) transsexualism; (3) gender identity disorder of adolescence or adulthood, nontranssexual type; and (4) gender identity disorder not otherwise specified. According to DSM-III-R, persons with gender identity disorders felt persistent discomfort that their assigned gender is inappropriate. Those persons with a persistent preoccupation with and a desire to have sex-reassignment surgery or

to use hormones to achieve that end were labeled transsexuals; those without that persistent preoccupation were labeled nontranssexuals. In DSM-IV only three diagnoses are used: (1) gender identity disorder in children; (2) gender identity disorder in adolescents and adults, and (3) gender identity disorder not otherwise specified.

In DSM-III-R, gender identity disorders were classified under the heading of disorders usually first evident in infancy, childhood, or adolescence. Even though most cases begin in childhood, persons who present clinically with gender identity problems may be of any age. Accordingly, in DSM-IV, gender identity disorders are classified under the heading of sexual and gender identity disorders, which may appear at any time in life.

## EPIDEMIOLOGY

Almost no information is available about the prevalence of gender identity disorders among children, teenagers, and adults. Most estimates of prevalence are based on the number of people seeking sex-reassignment surgery, a number that indicates a male preponderance. The ratios of boys to girls reported in three child gender identity clinics were 30 to 1, 17 to 1, and 6 to 1, indicating little experience with girls. That disparity may indicate a greater male vulnerability to gender identity disorders or a greater sensitivity to and worry about cross-gender-identified boys than cross-gender-identified girls in our culture.

Studies of boys referred for outpatient psychiatric treatment revealed that up to about 50 percent had a significant amount of effeminate behavior. The boys were not referred primarily for problems with gender identity. How many met the criteria for gender identity disorders is unclear.

## ETIOLOGY

### Biological Factors

For mammals, the resting state of tissue is initially female; as the fetus develops, a male is produced only if androgen (set off by the Y chromosome, which is responsible for testicular development) is added. Without testes and androgen, female external genitalia develop. Thus, maleness and masculinity depend on fetal and perinatal androgens. Lower animals' sexual behavior is governed by sex steroids; as one ascends the evolutionary scale, that effect diminishes. Sex steroids influence the expression of sexual behavior in the mature man or woman; that is, testosterone can increase libido and aggressiveness in women, and estrogen can decrease libido and aggressiveness in men. But masculinity, femininity, and gender identity are products more of postnatal life events than of prenatal hormonal organization.

The same principle of masculinization or feminization has been applied to the brain. Testosterone affects brain neurons that contribute to the masculinization of the brain in such areas as the hypothalamus. Whether testosterone contributes to so-called masculine or feminine behavioral patterns in gender identity disorders remains a controversial issue.

## Psychosocial Factors

Children develop a gender identity consonant with their sex of rearing (also known as assigned sex). The formation of gender identity is influenced by the interaction of the child's temperament and the parents' qualities and attitudes. There are culturally acceptable gender roles: boys are not expected to be effeminate, and girls are not expected to be tomboys. There are boys' games (for example, cops and robbers) and girls' games (for example, dolls and doll houses). Those roles are learned, although some investigators believe that some boys are temperamentally delicate and sensitive and that some girls are aggressive and energized—traits that stereotypically are known in today's culture as feminine and masculine, respectively.

Sigmund Freud believed that gender identity problems result from conflicts experienced by the child within the oedipal triangle. Those conflicts are fueled by both real family events and the child's fantasies. Whatever interferes with the child's loving the opposite-sex parent and identifying with the same-sex parent interferes with normal gender identity.

The quality of the mother-child relationship in the first years of life is paramount in establishing gender identity. During that period, mothers normally facilitate their children's awareness of and pride in their gender. The child is valued as a little boy or girl. At the same time, the separation-individuation process is unfolding. Devaluing, hostile mothering can result in gender problems. When those problems become associated with separation-individuation problems, the result can be the use of sexuality to remain in relationships characterized by shifts between a desperate infantile closeness and a hostile, devaluing distance.

Some children are given the message that they would be more valued if they adopted the gender identity of the opposite sex. Rejected or abused children may act on the belief that they would be better treated if they were the other sex. Gender identity problems can also be triggered by the mother's death, extended absence, or depression, to which a young boy may react by totally identifying with her—that is, becoming a mother to replace her.

The role of the father is also important in those early years. His presence normally helps the separation-individuation process. The absence of a father figure risks the mother and child's remaining in an overly close bond. For a girl, the father is normally the prototype of future love objects; for a boy, the father is a model for male identification.

## DIAGNOSIS AND CLINICAL FEATURES

According to DSM-IV, the essential feature of gender identity disorders is a persistent and intense distress about one's assigned sex and the desire to be or an insistence that one is of the other sex. In children, both girls and boys show an aversion to normative stereotypical feminine or masculine clothing and repudiate their respective anatomical characteristics. Table 21–1 lists the DSM-IV criteria for the disorder.

At the extreme of gender identity disorder in children are those boys who, by the standards of their cultures, are as feminine as are the most feminine of girls and those girls who are as masculine as are the most masculine of boys. No sharp line can be drawn on the continuum of gender identity disorder between children who should receive a formal diagnosis and those who should not. Girls with the disorder regularly have male companions and an avid interest in sports and rough-and-tumble play; they show no interest in dolls or playing house (unless they play the father or another male role). A girl with the disorder may refuse to urinate in a sitting position, claim that she has or will grow a penis, not want to grow breasts or to menstruate, and assert that she will grow up to become a man (not merely in role). A boy with the disorder is usually preoccupied with female stereotypical activities. He may have a preference for dressing in girls' or women's clothes or may improvise such items from available material when the genuine articles are not available. (The cross-dressing typically does not cause sexual excitement, as in transvestic fetishism.) He often has a compelling desire to participate in the games and pastimes of girls. Female dolls are often his favorite toys, and girls are regularly his preferred playmates. When playing house, he takes the role of a female. His gestures and actions are often judged to be feminine, and he is usually subjected to male peer group teasing and rejection, whereas that rarely occurs in a girl until adolescence. A boy with the disorder may assert that he will grow up to become a woman (not merely in role). A boy with the disorder may claim that his penis or testes are disgusting or will disappear or that it would be better not to have a penis or testes.

Some children refuse to attend school because of teasing or the pressure to dress in attire stereotypical of their assigned sex. Most children with the disorder deny being disturbed by it, except that it brings them into conflict with the expectations of their families or peers.

In adolescents and adults, similar signs and symptoms exist. Adolescents and adults with the disorder manifest a stated desire to be the other sex; they frequently try to pass as a member of the other sex; and they desire to live or to be treated as the other sex. In addition, they desire to acquire the sex characteristics of the opposite sex. They may believe that they were born the wrong sex and may make such characteristic statements as, "I feel that I'm a woman trapped in a male body" or vice versa.

**Table 21–1**
**Diagnostic Criteria for Gender Identity Disorder**

A. A strong and persistent cross-gender identification (not merely a desire for any perceived cultural advantages of being the other sex).

  In children, manifested by four (or more) of the following:

  (1) repeatedly stated desire to be, or insistence that he or she is, the other sex
  (2) in boys, preference for cross-dressing or simulating female attire; in girls, insistence on wearing only stereotypical masculine clothing
  (3) strong and persistent preferences for cross-sex roles in make-believe play or persistent fantasies of being the other sex
  (4) intense desire to participate in the stereotypical games and pastimes of the other sex
  (5) strong preference for playmates of the other sex

  In adolescents and adults, the disturbance is manifested by symptoms such as a stated desire to be the other sex, frequent passing as the other sex, desire to live or be treated as the other sex, or the conviction that he or she has the typical feelings and reactions of the other sex.

B. Persistent discomfort with his or her sex or sense of inappropriateness in the gender role of that sex.

  In children, the disturbance is manifested by any of the following: in boys, assertion that his penis or testes are disgusting or will disappear or assertion that it would be better not to have a penis, or aversion toward rough-and-tumble play and rejection of male stereotypical toys, games, and activities; in girls, rejection of urinating in a sitting position, assertion that she has or will grow a penis, or assertion that she does not want to grow breasts or menstruate, or marked aversion towards normative feminine clothing.

  In adolescents and adults, the disturbance is manifested by symptoms such as preoccupation with getting rid of primary and secondary sex characteristics (e.g., request for hormones, surgery, or other procedures to physically alter sexual characteristics to simulate the other sex) or belief that he or she was born the wrong sex.

C. The disturbance is not concurrent with a physical intersex condition.

D. The disturbance causes clinically significant distress or impairment in social, occupational, or other important areas of functioning.

*Code* based on current age:
  **Gender identity disorder in children**
  **Gender identity disorder in adolescents or adults**

*Specify* if (for sexually mature individuals):
  **Sexually attracted to males**
  **Sexually attracted to females**
  **Sexually attracted to both**
  **Sexually attracted to neither**

Table from DSM-IV, *Diagnostic and Statistical Manual of Mental Disorders,* ed 4. Copyright American Psychiatric Association, Washington, 1994. Used with permission.

Adolescents and adults frequently make requests for medical or surgical procedures to alter their physical appearance. In DSM-III-R such persons were classified as transsexuals; but in DSM-IV that term is not used, and they are categorized simply as having a gender identity disorder. However, many clinicians find the term "transsexual" useful and will probably continue to use it. In addition, transsexualism is included in the 10th revision of the International Classification of Diseases (ICD-10). Also, persons refer to themselves as transsexuals. The transsexual person has a persistent preoccupation with getting rid of his or her primary and secondary sex characteristics and with acquiring the sex characteristics of the other sex. The wish to dress and live as a member of the other sex is always present.

Most retrospective studies of transsexuals report gender identity problems during childhood; however, prospective studies of children with gender identity disorders indicate that few become transsexuals—that is, want to change their sex. The disorder is much more common in men (1 per 30,000 men) than in women (1 per 100,000 women).

Adult transsexuals usually complain that they are uncomfortable wearing the clothes of their assigned sex; therefore, they dress in clothes of the other sex. They engage in activities associated with the other sex. They find their genitals repugnant, a feeling that may lead to persistent requests for surgery. That desire may override all other wishes.

Men take estrogen to create breasts and other feminine contours, have electrolysis to remove their male hair, and have surgery to remove the testes and the penis and to create an artificial vagina. Women bind their breasts or have a double mastectomy, a hysterectomy, and an oophorectomy; take testosterone to build up their muscle mass and deepen the voice; and have surgery in which an artificial phallus is created. Those procedures may make the person indistinguishable from members of the other sex. Some investigators describe behavior in sex-reassigned persons that is almost a caricature of male and female roles.

A 25-year-old patient called Charles requested a sex change operation. Charles had for three years lived socially and been employed as a man. For the past two years, Charles had been the housemate, economic provider, and husband-equivalent of a bisexual woman who had fled from a bad marriage. Her two young children regarded Charles as their stepfather, and they had a strong affectionate bond.

In social appearance the patient passed as a not very virile man whose sexual development in puberty could be conjectured to have been delayed or hormonally deficient. Charles's voice was pitched low but was not baritone. Bulky clothing was worn to camouflage tightly bound, flattened breasts. A strap-on penis produced a masculine-looking bulge in the pants; it was so constructed that, in case of social necessity, it could be used as a urinary conduit in the standing position. Without success the patient had tried to obtain a mastectomy so that in summer only a T-shirt could be worn while working outdoors as a heavy construction machine operator. Charles had also been unsuccessful in trying to get a prescription for testosterone to produce male secondary sex characteristics and to suppress menses. The patient wanted a hysterectomy and an oophorectomy and looked forward to obtaining a successful phalloplasty.

The patient's history was straightforward in its account of progressive recognition in adolescence of being able to fall in love only with a woman, following a tomboyish childhood that had finally consolidated into the transsexual role and identity.

A physical examination revealed normal female anatomy, which the patient found personally repulsive, incongruous, and a source of continual distress. The endocrine laboratory results were within normal limits for a woman.

## Sexual Object Choice

Persons with gender identity disorder may be (1) sexually attracted to males, (2) sexually attracted to females, (3) sexually attracted to both, or (4) sexually attracted to neither males nor females. In almost all cases, such persons do not consider themselves to be homosexual, even if they have undergone a male-to-female change and are attracted to men. Similarly, persons with a female-to-male change who are attracted to women may not consider themselves to be homosexual. Because they believe themselves to be members of the opposite sex, they believe themselves to be heterosexual.

According to DSM-IV, once a diagnosis of gender identity disorder is made, the object of sexual attraction should be specified (for example, male, female, both, or neither).

## Gender Identity Disorder Not Otherwise Specified

This diagnosis is reserved for persons who cannot be classified as having a gender identity disorder with the characteristics described above (Table 21–2). Three examples are listed in DSM-IV: (1) persons with intersex conditions and gender dysphoria; (2) adults with transient, stress-related cross-dressing behavior; and (3) persons who have a persistent preoccupation with castration or penec-

**Table 21–2**
**Diagnostic Criteria for Gender Identity Disorder Not Otherwise Specified**

This category is included for coding disorders in gender identity that are not classifiable as a specific gender identity disorder. Examples include

1. intersex conditions (e.g., androgen insensitivity syndrome or congenital adrenal hyperplasia) and accompanying gender dysphoria

2. transient, stress-related cross-dressing behavior

3. persistent preoccupation with castration or penectomy without a desire to acquire the sex characteristics of the other sex

Table from DSM-IV, *Diagnostic and Statistical Manual of Mental Disorders*, ed 4. Copyright American Psychiatric Association, Washington, 1994. Used with permission.

tomy without a desire to acquire the sex characteristics of the other sex.

**Intersex conditions.** Intersex conditions include a variety of syndromes that produce persons with gross anatomical or physiological aspects of the opposite sex.

TURNER'S SYNDROME. In Turner's syndrome, one sex chromosome is missing (XO). The result is an absence (agenesis) or minimal development (dysgenesis) of the gonads; no significant sex hormones, male or female, are produced in fetal life or postnatally. The sexual tissues remain in a female resting state. Because the second X chromosome, which seems responsible for full femaleness, is missing, the girls have an incomplete sexual anatomy and, lacking adequate estrogens, develop no secondary sex characteristics without treatment. They often suffer other stigmata, such as web neck, low posterior hairline margin, short stature, and cubitus valgus. The infant is born with normal-appearing female external genitals and so is unequivocally assigned to the female sex and is so reared. All the children develop as unremarkably feminine, heterosexually oriented girls; however, later medical management is necessary to assist them with their infertility and absence of secondary sex characteristics.

KLINEFELTER'S SYNDROME. A person (usually XXY) with Klinefelter's syndrome has a male habitus, under the influence of the Y chromosome, but the effect is weakened by the presence of the second X chromosome. Although the patient is born with a penis and testes, the testes are small and infertile, and the penis may also be small. Beginning in adolescence, some patients develop gynecomastia and other feminine-appearing contours. Their sexual desire is usually weak. Sex assignment and rearing should lead to a clear sense of maleness, but the patients often have gender disturbances, ranging from a complete reversal, as in transsexualism, to an intermittent desire to put on women's clothes. As a result of lessened androgen production, the fetal hypogonadal state in some patients seems to have interfered with the completion of the central nervous system organization that should underlie masculine behavior. In fact, many patients have a wide variability of psychopathology, ranging from emotional instability to mental retardation.

CONGENITAL VIRILIZING ADRENAL HYPERPLASIA (ADRENOGENITAL SYNDROME). Congenital virilizing adrenal hyperplasia results from an excess of androgen acting on the fetus. When the condition occurs in females, excessive fetal androgens from the adrenal gland cause androgenization of the external genitals, ranging from mild clitoral enlargement to external genitals that look like a normal scrotal sac, testes, and a penis; but hidden behind those external genitals are a vagina and a uterus. The patients are otherwise normally female. At birth, if the genitals look male, the child is assigned to the male sex and is so reared. The result is a clear sense of maleness and unremarkable masculinity; but, if the child is assigned to the female sex and is so reared, a sense of femaleness and feminity results. If the parents are uncertain to which sex their child belongs, a hermaphroditic identity results. The resultant gender identity reflects the rearing practices, but androgens may help determine behavior; children raised unequivocally as girls have a tomboy quality more intense than that found in a control group. The girls nonetheless do have a heterosexual orientation.

PSEUDOHERMAPHRODITISM.   Infants may be born with ambiguous genitals, which is an obstetrical emergency, because the sex assignment determines gender identity. Male pseudohermaphroditism is incomplete differentiation of the external genitalia, even though a Y chromosome is present. Testes are present but rudimentary. Female pseudohermaphroditism is the presence of virilized genitals in a person who is XX, the most common cause being the adrenogenital syndrome described above.

The genitals' appearance at birth determines the sex assignment, and the core gender identity is male, female, or hermaphroditic, depending on the family's conviction as to the child's sex. Usually, a panel of experts determine the sex of rearing, basing their decision on buccal smears, chromosome studies, and parental wishes. Assignment should usually be made within 24 hours, so that the parents can adapt accordingly. If surgery is necessary to correct the genital deformity, it is generally done before the age of 3 years.

True hermaphroditism is characterized by the presence of both testes and ovaries in the same person; it is a rare condition.

ANDROGEN INSENSITIVITY SYNDROME.   Androgen insensitivity syndrome, a congenital X-linked recessive trait disorder—also known as testicular feminization syndrome—results from an inability of target tissues to respond to androgens. Unable to respond, the fetal tissues remain in their female resting state, and the central nervous system is not organized as masculine. The infant at birth appears to be an unremarkable female, although she is later found to have cryptorchid testes, which produce the testosterone to which the tissues do not respond, and minimal or absent internal sexual organs. Secondary sex characteristics at puberty are female because of the small but sufficient amounts of estrogens typically produced by the testes. The patients invariably sense themselves as females and are feminine.

**Cross-dressing.**   DSM-IV lists cross-dressing—that is, dressing in clothes of the opposite sex—as a gender identity disorder if it is transient and related to stress. If the disorder is not stress-related, persons who cross-dress are classified as having transvestic fetishism, which is classified as a paraphilia in DSM-IV. An essential feature of transvestic fetishism is that it produces sexual excitement. Stress-related cross-dressing may sometimes produce sexual excitement, but it reduces tension and anxiety in the patient. The patient may harbor fantasies of cross-dressing but act them out only under stress. Most male adult cross-dressers have the fantasy that they are female, in whole or in part.

Cross-dressing is commonly known as transvestism and the cross-dresser as a transvestite. Although those terms are no longer used in DSM-IV, they remain in common parlance.

Cross-dressing phenomena range from the occasional solitary wearing of female clothes to extensive feminine identification in men and masculine identification in women and involvement in a transvestic subculture. More than one article of clothing of the other sex is involved, and the person may dress entirely as a member of the opposite sex. The degree to which the cross-dressed person appears as a member of the other sex varies, depending on mannerisms, body habitus, and cross-dressing skill. When not cross-dressed, the persons usually appear as unremarkable members of their assigned sex. Cross-dressing may coexist with paraphilias, such as sexual sadism, sexual masochism, and pedophilia.

Cross-dressing differs from transsexualism in that the patients have no persistent preoccupation with getting rid of their primary and secondary sex characteristics and acquiring the sex characteristics of the other sex.

Some people with the disorder once had transvestic fetishism but no longer become sexually aroused by cross-dressing. Other people with the disorder are homosexuals who cross-dress. The disorder is common among female impersonators.

**Preoccupation with castration.**   This category is reserved for men or women who have a persistent preoccupation with castration or penectomy without a desire to acquire the sex characteristics of the opposite sex. They are clearly uncomfortable with their assigned sex and live a life driven by the fantasy of what it would be like to be a different gender. They are often asexual, having no sexual interest in either men or women.

## COURSE AND PROGNOSIS

The prognosis for gender identity disorder depends on the age of onset and the intensity of the symptoms. Boys begin to have the disorder before the age of 4 years, and peer conflict develops during the early school years, at about the age of 7 or 8 years. Grossly feminine mannerisms may lessen as the boy grows older, especially if attempts are made to discourage such behavior. Cross-dressing may be part of the disorder, and 75 percent of boys who cross-dress begin to do so before age 4. The age of onset is also early for girls, but most give up masculine behavior by adolescence.

In both sexes, homosexuality is likely to develop in one third to two thirds of all cases, although fewer girls than boys have a homosexual orientation, for reasons that are not clear. Steven Levine reported that follow-up studies of gender-disturbed boys consistently indicated that homosexual orientation was the usual adolescent outcome. Transsexualism—that is, the desire for sex-reassignment surgery—occurs in less than 10 percent of cases. Retrospective data on homosexual men indicate a high frequency of cross-gender identifications and feminine gender role behavior during childhood.

Impaired social and occupational functioning as a result of the person's wanting to participate in the desired (and opposite) gender role is common. Depression is also a common problem, especially if the person feels hopeless about obtaining a sex change with surgery or hormones. Men have been known to castrate themselves, not as a suicide attempt but as a way of forcing a surgeon to deal with their problem.

## TREATMENT

Treatment of gender identity disorders is a complex problem and rarely successful if the goal is to reverse the disorder. Most persons with gender identity disorders have fixed ideas and values and are unwilling to change. If and when they enter psychotherapy, it is most often because of depression or anxiety that they attribute to their condition. Countertransference problems must be addressed assiduously by therapists, many of whom are uncomfortable with gender identity disorder patients.

Children with cross-gender behavior patterns are generally brought to a psychiatrist by the parents. Richard Green developed a treatment program designed to inculcate culturally acceptable behavior patterns in boys. Green uses a one-to-one play relationship with the child in which adults or peers role-model masculine behavior. Parental counseling in conjunction with group meetings of parents and their children with the same problem is also used. Parents' encouragement of the child's atypical behavior (such as dressing a boy in girl's clothing or not giving him haircuts) is examined when parents are unaware of how they are fostering cross-gender behavior.

Adolescent patients are difficult to treat because of the coexistence of normal identity crises and gender identity confusion. Acting out is common, and the adolescents rarely have a strong motivation to alter their sterotypical cross-gender roles.

Adult patients generally enter psychotherapy to learn how to deal with their disorder, not to alter it. The therapist generally sets the goal with the patients of helping them become comfortable with the gender identity they desire; the goal is not to create a person with a conventional sexual identity. Therapy also explores sex-reassignment surgery and the indications and contraindications for such procedures, which are often impulsively decided on by severely distressed and anxious patients.

### Sex-Reassignment Surgery

Surgical treatment is definitive, and, because there is no turning back, careful standards preceding the surgery have been developed, which include the following: (1) The patients must go through a trial of cross-gender living for at least three months and sometimes up to one year. For some transsexuals the real-life test may make them change their minds, because they find it uncomfortable to relate to friends, workers, and lovers in that role. (2) The patients must receive hormone treatments, with estradiol and progesterone in male-to-female changes and testosterone in female-to-male changes. Many transsexuals like the changes in their bodies that occur as a result of that treatment, and some stop at that point. About 50 percent of transsexuals who meet the above criteria go on to sex-reassignment surgery. Outcome studies are highly variable

in terms of how success is defined and measured (for example, successful intercourse and body-image satisfaction).

About 70 percent of male-to-female and 80 percent of female-to-male sex-reassignment surgery patients report satisfactory results. Unsatisfactory results correlate with a preexisting mental disorder. Suicide in postoperative sex-reassignment surgery patients has been reported in up to 2 percent of all cases. Sex-reassignment surgery is a highly controversial measure that is undergoing much scrutiny.

### Hormonal Treatment

Both sexes may be treated with hormones in lieu of surgery. Biological males take estrogen, and biological females take testosterone. Patients who take estrogen usually report immediate psychological satisfaction, based on a sense of tranquility, less frequent erections, and fewer sexual drive manifestations than before the hormone treatment. Their new sterility is not of concern to them. After several months, bodily contours become rounded, a limited but pleasing breast enlargement develops, and testicular volume decreases. The quality of the voice does not change. Patients need to be watched for hypertension, hyperglycemia, hepatic dysfunction, and thromboembolic phenomena.

Women who take androgens quickly notice an increased sexual drive, clitoral tingling and enlargement, and, after several months, amenorrhea and hoarseness. If weight lifting is undertaken, a pronounced increase in muscle mass may occur. Depending on the hair distribution already present, the patients may have a moderate increase in the amount and the coarseness of facial and body hair; some develop frontal balding. Thromboembolic phenomena, hepatic dysfunction, and elevations of cholesterol and triglycerides are possible.

### Treatment of Intersex Conditions

Since intersex conditions are present at birth, treatment must be timely, and some physicians believe the conditions to be true medical emergencies. Since the appearance of the genitalia in diverse conditions is often ambiguous, a decision must be made about the assigned sex (boy or girl) and how the child should be reared.

Assignment should be agreed on as early as possible, so that the entire family, can regard the patient in a consistent, relaxed manner. When surgery is necessary to normalize genital appearance, it is generally undertaken well before the age of 3 years. It is easier to assign a child to be female than to assign a child to be male, because male-to-female genital surgical procedures are far more advanced than female-to-male surgical procedures.

Intersex patients may have gender identity problems because of complicated biological influences and familial confusion about their actual sex. When intersex conditions are discovered, a panel of pediatric experts usually determines the sex of rearing on the basis of clinical examination, urological studies, buccal smears, chromosomal analyses, and assessment of the parental wishes.

## Treatment of Cross-Dressing

A combined approach, using psychotherapy and pharmacotherapy, is often useful in the treatment of cross-dressing. The stress factors that precipitate the behavior are identified in therapy. The goal is to help the patient cope with the stressors appropriately and, if possible, eliminate them. Intrapsychic dynamics about attitudes toward the same sex and the opposite sex are examined, and unconscious conflicts are identified. Medication is used to treat the symptoms—for example, antianxiety and antidepressant agents. Because cross-dressing may occur impulsively, medications that reinforce impulse control may be helpful—for example, thioridazine (Mellaril) and fluoxetine (Prozac). Behavior therapy, aversive conditioning, and hypnosis are alternative methods that may be of use in selected cases.

## References

Blanchard R, Steiner B W, editors: *Clinical Management of Gender Identity Disorders in Children and Adults.* American Psychiatric Press, Washington, 1990.

Bleiberg E, Jackson L, Ross J L: Gender identity disorder and object loss. J Am Acad Child Psychiatry *25*: 58, 1986.

Coates S, Person E S: Extreme boyhood femininity: Isolated behavior or pervasive disorder. J Am Acad Child Psychiatry *24*: 702, 1985.

Galenson E, Fields B: Gender disturbance in a 3½-year-old boy. In *The Significance of Infant Observational Research for Clinical Work with Children, Adolescents, and Adults,* S Dowling, A Rothstein, editors, p 194. International Universities Press, Madison, Conn, 1989.

Green R: Gender identity in childhood and later sexual orientation: Followup of 78 males. Am J Psychiatry *142*: 399, 1985.

Hirschfield M: *Transvestites: The Erotic Drive to Cross-Dress.* Prometheus, Buffalo, 1991.

Levine S B: Gender-disturbed males. J Sex Marital Ther *19*: 131, 1993.

Levine S B: Gender identity disorders of childhood, adolescence, and adulthood. In *Comprehensive Textbook of Psychiatry,* ed 5, H I Kaplan, B J Sadock, editors, p 1061. Williams & Wilkins, Baltimore, 1989.

Lothstein L M: *Female to Male Transsexualism: Historical, Clinical, and Theoretical Issues.* Routledge Kegan Paul, Boston, 1982.

Lothstein L M, Levine S B: Expressive psychotherapy with gender dysphoric patients. Arch Gen Psychiatry *38*: 924, 1981.

Marantz S, Coates S: Mothers of boys with gender identity disorder: A comparison of matched controls. J Am Acad Child Adolesc Psychiatry *30*: 310, 1991.

Pauley I B, Edgerton M T: The gender identity movement: A growing surgical-psychiatric liaison. Arch Sex Behav *15*: 315, 1986.

Pleak R R, Meyer-Bahlburg H F L, O'Brien J D, Bowen H A, Morganstein A: Cross-gender behavior and psychopathology in boy psychiatric outpatients. J Am Acad Child Adolesc Psychiatry *28*: 385, 1989.

Sreenivasan V: Effeminate boys in a child psychiatric clinic: Prevalence and associated factors. J Am Acad Child Psychiatry *24*: 689, 1985.

Stoller R J: *Presentations of Gender.* Yale University Press, New Haven, 1986.

Walker P, Berger J, Green R, Laub D, Reynolds C, Wollman L: Standards of care: The hormonal and surgical reassignment of gender dysphoric persons. Arch Sex Behav *14*: 79, 1985.

Zucker K J, Green R: Treatment of the gender identity disorder of childhood. In *APA Task Force on the Treatment of Psychiatric Disorders,* T B Karasu, editor, p 37. American Psychiatric Press, Washington, 1987.

Zucker K J, Wild J, Bradley S J, Lowry C B: Physical attractiveness of boys with gender identity disorder. Arch Sex Behav *22*: 23, 1993.

# Eating Disorders

## 22.1 / Anorexia Nervosa

Anorexia nervosa is characterized by a profound disturbance of body image and the relentless pursuit of thinness, often to the point of starvation. The disorder has been recognized for many decades and has been described in various persons with remarkable uniformity. The disorder is much more prevalent in females than in males and usually has its onset in adolescence. Hypotheses of an underlying psychological disturbance in young women with the disorder include conflicts surrounding the transition from a girl to a woman. Psychological issues related to feelings of helplessness and to difficulty in establishing autonomy have also been suggested as contributing to the development of the disorder.

The diagnostic criteria for anorexia nervosa in the revised third edition and the fourth edition of *Diagnostic and Statistical Manual of Mental Disorders* (DSM-III-R and DSM-IV) are practically the same. In DSM-IV the criteria consist of a persistent refusal to maintain body weight at or above a minimum expected weight (for example, loss of weight leading to a weight of less than 85 percent of expected weight) or a failure to gain the expected weight during a period of growth, leading to a body weight less than 85 percent of the expected weight. The patient has a characteristic pervasive fear of becoming fat, even when drastically underweight. Persons with anorexia nervosa exhibit disturbances of body image; they feel fat or misshapen and often deny their emaciation. To meet the diagnostic criteria for anorexia nervosa, postmenarchal females must have an absence of at least three consecutive menstrual cycles. DSM-IV has added two types of anorexia nervosa that are not part of the DSM-III-R criteria. In the restricting type, during the episode of anorexia nervosa, the person restricts intake but does not regularly engage in binge eating or purging by vomiting or using laxatives or diuretics. In the binge eating/purging type, during the episode of anorexia nervosa, the person regularly engages in binge eating or purging through self-induced vomiting or the use of laxatives or diuretics.

Bulimic symptoms may occur as a separate disorder (bulimia nervosa) or as part of anorexia nervosa. Persons with either anorexia nervosa or bulimia nervosa are excessively preoccupied with weight, food, and body shape.

The outcome of anorexia nervosa is variable and ranges from spontaneous recovery to a waxing and waning course to death.

## EPIDEMIOLOGY

Eating disorders of various kinds have been reported in up to 4 percent of adolescent and young adult students. Anorexia nervosa has been reported more frequently over the past several decades than in the past, with increasing reports of the disorder in prepubertal girls and in males. The most common ages of onset of anorexia nervosa are the mid-teenage years, but up to 5 percent of anorectic patients have the onset of the disorder in their early 20s. Anorexia nervosa is estimated to occur in about 0.5 to 1 percent of adolescent girls. It occurs 10 to 20 times more often in females than in males. The prevalence of young women with some symptoms of anorexia nervosa but who do not meet the diagnostic criteria is estimated to be close to 5 percent. Although the disorder was initially reported most often among the upper classes, recent epidemiological surveys do not show that distribution. It seems to be most frequent in developed countries, and it may be seen with greatest frequency among young women in professions that require thinness, such as modeling and ballet.

## ETIOLOGY

Biological, social, and psychological factors are implicated in the causes of anorexia nervosa. Some evidence points to higher concordance rates in monozygotic twins than in dizygotic twins. Sisters of anorexia nervosa patients are likely to be afflicted, but that association may reflect social influences more than genetic factors. Major mood disorders are more common in family members than in the general population. Neurochemically, diminished norepinephrine turnover and activity are suggested by the reduced 3-methoxy-4-hydroxyphenylglycol (MHPG) in the urine and the cerebrospinal fluid (CSF) of some anorexia nervosa patients. An inverse relation is seen between MHPG and depression in patients with anorexia nervosa:

an increase in MHPG is associated with a decrease in depression.

## Biological Factors

Endogenous opiates may contribute to the denial of hunger in anorexia nervosa patients. Preliminary studies show dramatic weight gains in some patients administered opiate antagonists. Starvation results in many biochemical changes, some of which are also present in depression, such as hypercortisolemia and nonsuppression by dexamethasone. Thyroid function is also suppressed. Those abnormalities are corrected by realimentation. Starvation also results in amenorrhea, which reflects lowered hormonal levels (luteinizing, follicle-stimulating, and gonadotropin-releasing hormones). However, some anorexia nervosa patients become amenorrheic before significant weight loss. Several computed tomographic (CT) studies reveal enlarged CSF spaces (enlarged sulci and ventricles) in anorexia nervosa patients during starvation, a finding that is reversed by weight gain. In one positron emission tomographic (PET) scan study, caudate nucleus metabolism was higher in the anorectic state than after realimentation.

## Social Factors

Anorexia nervosa patients find support for their practices in society's emphasis on thinness and exercise. No family constellations are specific to anorexia nervosa. However, some evidence indicates that anorexia nervosa patients have close but troubled relationships with their parents and, with their illness, tend to draw attention away from strained marital relationships in their homes. Patients with anorexia nervosa are likely to have family histories of depression, alcohol dependence, or an eating disorder.

## Psychological and Psychodynamic Factors

Anorexia nervosa appears to be a reaction to the demands on adolescents for more independence and increased social and sexual functioning. Patients with the disorder substitute their preoccupations with eating and weight gain for other, normal adolescent pursuits. The preoccupations are similar to obsessions.

Patients with anorexia nervosa typically lack a sense of autonomy and selfhood. Many patients with the disorder experience their bodies as somehow under the control of their parents. Self-starvation may be an effort to gain validation as a unique and special person. Only through acts of extraordinary self-discipline can the anorectic patient develop a sense of autonomy and selfhood.

Psychoanalytic clinicians who treat patients with anorexia nervosa generally agree that those young patients have been unable to separate psychologically from their mothers. The body may be perceived as though it were inhabited by an introject of an intrusive and unempathic mother. Starvation may have the unconscious meaning of arresting the growth of that intrusive internal object and thereby destroying it. Often, a projective identification process is involved in the interactions between the patient and the patient's family. Many anorectic patients feel that oral desires are greedy and unacceptable; therefore, those desires are projectively disavowed. Parents respond to the refusal to eat by becoming frantic about whether the patient is actually eating. The patient can then view the parents as the ones who have unacceptable desires and can projectively disavow them. Others are voracious and rule by desire but not the patient.

## DIAGNOSIS AND CLINICAL FEATURES

The onset of anorexia nervosa usually occurs between the ages of 10 and 30 years. Patients outside that age range are not typical, and so their diagnoses should be questioned. After the age of 13 years, the frequency of onset increases rapidly, with the maximum frequency at 17 to 18 years of age. About 85 percent of all anorexia nervosa patients have the onset of the illness between the ages of 13 and 20 years. Some anorexia nervosa patients, before age 10, were picky eaters or had frequent digestive problems. The DSM-IV diagnostic criteria for anorexia nervosa are given in Table 22.1–1.

Most of the aberrant behavior directed toward losing weight occurs in secret. Anorexia nervosa patients usually refuse to eat with their families or in public places. They lose weight by a drastic reduction in their total food intake, with a disproportionate decrease in high-carbohydrate and fatty foods.

**Table 22.1–1**
**Diagnostic Criteria for Anorexia Nervosa**

A. Refusal to maintain body weight at or above a minimally normal weight for age and height (e.g., weight loss leading to maintenance of body weight less than 85% of that expected; or failure to make expected weight gain during period of growth, leading to body weight less than 85% of that expected).

B. Intense fear of gaining weight or becoming fat, even though underweight.

C. Disturbance in the way in which one's body weight or shape is experienced; undue influence of body weight or shape on self-evaluation, or denial of the seriousness of the current low body weight.

D. In post menarchal females, amenorrhea, i.e., the absence of at least three consecutive menstrual cycles. (A woman is considered to have amenorrhea if her periods occur only following hormone, e.g., estrogen, administration.)

*Specify* type:
   **Restricting type:** During the current episode of anorexia nervosa, the person has not regularly engaged in binge eating or purging behavior (i.e., self-induced vomiting or the misuse of laxatives, diuretics, or enemas).
   **Binge eating/purging type:** During the current episode of anorexia nervosa, the person has regularly engaged in binge eating or purging behavior (i.e., self-induced vomiting or the misuse of laxatives, diuretics, or enemas)

Table from DSM-IV, *Diagnostic and Statistical Manual of Mental Disorders*, ed 4. Copyright American Psychiatric Association, Washington, 1994. Used with permission.

Unfortunately, the term "anorexia," meaning loss of appetite, is a misnomer, because the loss of appetite is usually rare until late in the disorder. Evidence that the patients are constantly thinking about food is their passion for collecting recipes and preparing elaborate meals for others. Some patients cannot continuously control their voluntary restriction of food intake, and so they have eating binges. Those binges usually occur secretly and often at night. Self-induced vomiting frequently follows the eating binge. Patients abuse laxatives and even diuretics to lose weight. Ritualistic exercising, extensive cycling, walking, jogging, and running are common activities.

Patients with the disorder exhibit peculiar behavior regarding food. They hide food all over the house and frequently carry large quantities of candies in their pockets and purses. While eating meals, they try to dispose of food in their napkins or hide it in their pockets. They cut their meat into very small pieces and spend a great deal of time rearranging the food pieces on their plates. If the patients are confronted about their peculiar behavior, they often deny that their behavior is unusual or flatly refuse to discuss it.

An intense fear of gaining weight and becoming obese is present in all patients with the disorder and undoubtedly contributes to their lack of interest in therapy and even resistance to it.

Obsessive-compulsive behavior, depression, and anxiety are the other psychiatric symptoms in anorexia nervosa most frequently noted in the literature. Patients tend to be rigid and perfectionistic. Somatic complaints, especially epigastric discomfort, are usual. Compulsive stealing, usually of candies and laxatives but occasionally of clothes and other items, is common.

Poor sexual adjustment is frequently described in patients with the disorder. Many adolescent anorexia nervosa patients have delayed psychosocial sexual development, and adults often have a markedly decreased interest in sex accompanying the onset of the disorder. An unusual minority group of anorexia nervosa patients have a premorbid history of promiscuity or substance abuse or both, and during the disorder they do not show a decreased interest in sex.

Patients usually come to medical attention when their weight loss becomes apparent. As the weight loss becomes profound, physical signs such as hypothermia (as low as 35°C), dependent edema, bradycardia, hypotension, and lanugo (the appearance of neonatallike hair) appear, and the patient presents a variety of metabolic changes (Figure 22.1–1). Some female anorexia nervosa patients come to medical attention because of amenorrhea, which often appears before their weight loss is noticeable.

Some anorexia nervosa patients induce vomiting or abuse purgatives and diuretics, causing concern about hypokalemic alkalosis. Impaired water diuresis may be noted.

Electrocardiographic (ECG) changes—such as flattening or inversion the T waves, ST segment depression, and lengthening of the QT interval—have been noted in the emaciated stage of anorexia nervosa. ECG changes may also occur as a result of potassium loss, which may lead to death. Gastric dilation is a rare complication of anorexia nervosa. In some patients, aortography has shown a superior mesenteric artery syndrome.

Other medical complications of eating disorders are listed in Table 22.1–2.

DSM-IV identifies two types of anorexia nervosa—the restricting type and the binge eating/purging type. Binge eating/purging is common among anorexia nervosa patients; it develops in up to 50 percent of them. Each of the two types appears to have distinct historic and clinical fea-

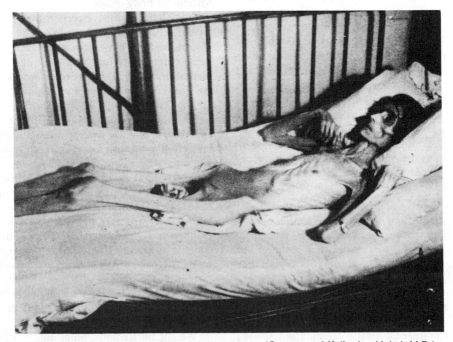

**Figure 22.1–1.** A patient with anorexia nervosa. (Courtesy of Katherine Halmi, M.D.)

**Table 22.1–2.**
**Medical Complications of Eating Disorders**

**Related to weight loss:**
Cachexia: Loss of fat, muscle mass, reduced thyroid
 metabolism (low $T_3$ syndrome), cold intolerance, and
 difficulty in maintaining core body temperature
Cardiac: Loss of cardiac muscle; small heart; cardiac
 arrhythmias, including atrial and ventricular premature
 contractions, prolonged His' bundle transmission (prolonged
 QT interval), bradycardia, ventricular tachycardia; sudden
 death
Digestive-gastrointestinal: Delayed gastric emptying, bloating,
 constipation, abdominal pain
Reproductive: Amenorrhea, low levels of luteinizing hormone
 (LH) and follicle-stimulating hormone (FSH)
Dermatological: Lanugo (fine babylike hair over body), edema
Hematological: Leukopenia
Neuropsychiatric: Abnormal taste sensation (?zinc deficiency),
 apathetic depression, mild cognitive disorder
Skeletal: Osteoporosis

**Related to purging (vomiting and laxative abuse):**
Metabolic: Electrolyte abnormalities, particularly hypokalemic,
 hypochloremic alkalosis; hypomagnesemia
Digestive-gastrointestinal: Salivary gland and pancreatic
 inflammation and enlargement with increase in serum
 amylase, esophageal and gastric erosion, dysfunctional
 bowel with haustral dilation
Dental: Erosion of dental enamel, particularly of front teeth,
 with corresponding decay
Neuropsychiatric: Seizures (related to large fluid shifts and
 electrolyte disturbances), mild neuropathies, fatigue and
 weakness, mild cognitive disorder

Table from J Yager: Eating disorders. In *Clinical Psychiatry for Medical
Students*. A Stoudemire, editor, p 324. Lippincott, Philadelphia, 1990. Used
with permission.

tures. Binge eating/purging anorectic persons share many
features with persons who have bulimia nervosa but not
anorexia nervosa. Binge eating/purging persons tend to
have families in which some members are obese, and they
themselves have histories of heavier body weights than do
restricting persons before the disorder. Binge eating/purg-
ing persons are likely to be associated with substance
abuse, impulse control disorders, and personality disorders. Restricting anorexia nervosa persons limit their food
selection, take in as few calories as possible, and often
have obsessive-compulsive traits with respect to food and
other matters. Both types of persons are preoccupied with
weight and body image, and both may exercise for hours
every day and may exhibit bizarre eating behaviors. Both
types of persons may be socially isolated and have depressive disorder symptoms and diminished sexual interest.
Some anorexia nervosa persons purge but do not binge.

 Anorexia nervosa has high rates of comorbid major
depressive disorders. Major depressive disorder or dysthymic disorder has been reported in up to 50 percent of
anorexia nervosa patients. The suicide rate is higher in the
binge eating/purging type of anorexia nervosa person than
in the restricting type.

 Patients with anorexia nervosa are often secretive, deny
their symptoms, and resist treatment. In almost all cases,
relatives or intimate acquaintances must confirm the patient's history. The mental status examination usually
shows a patient who is alert and knowledgeable on the

subject of nutrition and who is preoccupied with food and
weight.

 The patient must have a thorough general physical and
neurological examination. If the patient is vomiting, a hypokalemic alkalosis may be present. Because most patients
are dehydrated, the clinician must obtain serum electrolytes initially and then again periodically during hospitalization.

## Pathology and Laboratory Examination

 No single laboratory test unconditionally helps with the
diagnosis of anorexia nervosa. A multitude of endocrinological and medical problems can develop secondary to
the starvation that occurs with the disorder; therefore, a
battery of screening laboratory tests are warranted in persons who meet the diagnostic criteria for anorexia nervosa.
The tests include serum electrolytes with renal function
tests; thyroid function tests; glucose, amylase, and hematological tests; an electrocardiogram; cholesterol level;
dexamethasone-suppression test; and carotene level. The
clinician may find decreased thyroid hormone, decreased
serum glucose, nonsuppression of cortisol after dexamethasone, hypokalemia, increased blood urea nitrogen, and
hypercholesterolemia. Cardiovascular complications are
common and include hypotension and bradycardia.

## DIFFERENTIAL DIAGNOSIS

 The differential diagnosis of anorexia nervosa is complicated by the patient's denial of the symptoms, the secrecy surrounding the patient's bizarre eating rituals, and
the patient's resistance to seeking treatment. Thus, it may
be difficult to identify the mechanism of weight loss and
the patient's associated ruminative thoughts regarding distortions of body image.

 The clinician must ascertain that the patient does not
have a medical illness that can account for the weight loss
(for example, a brain tumor or cancer). Weight loss, peculiar eating behaviors, and vomiting can occur in several
mental disorders. Depressive disorders and anorexia nervosa have several features in common, such as depressed
feeling, crying spells, sleep disturbance, obsessive ruminations, and occasional suicidal thoughts. However, the
two disorders have several distinguishing features. Generally, a patient with a depressive disorder has a decreased
appetite, whereas an anorexia nervosa patient claims to
have a normal appetite and to feel hungry. Only in the
severe stages of anorexia nervosa does the patient actually
have a decreased appetite. In contrast to depressive agitation, the hyperactivity seen in anorexia nervosa is
planned and ritualistic. The preoccupation with the caloric
content of food, recipes, and the preparation of gourmet
feasts is typical of the anorexia nervosa patient and is not
present in the patient with a depressive disorder. And in
depressive disorders the patient has no intense fear of obesity or disturbance of body image, as the anorexia nervosa
patient has.

 Weight fluctuations, vomiting, and peculiar food handling may occur in somatization disorder. On rare occa-

sions a patient fulfills the diagnostic criteria for both somatization disorder and anorexia nervosa; in such a case both diagnoses should be made. Generally, the weight loss in somatization disorder is not as severe as that in anorexia nervosa, nor does the patient with somatization disorder express a morbid fear of becoming overweight, as is common in the anorexia nervosa patient. Amenorrhea for three months or longer is unusual in somatization disorder.

Delusions about food in schizophrenia are seldom concerned with the caloric content of food. A patient with schizophrenia is rarely preoccupied with a fear of becoming obese and does not have the hyperactivity that is seen in the anorexia nervosa patient. Schizophrenic patients have bizarre eating habits and not the entire syndrome of anorexia nervosa.

Anorexia nervosa must be differentiated from bulimia nervosa, a disorder in which episodic binge eating—followed by depressive moods, self-deprecating thoughts, and often self-induced vomiting—occurs while patients maintain their weight within a normal range. Furthermore, in bulimia nervosa the patient seldom has a 15 percent weight loss. The two conditions frequently coexist.

## COURSE AND PROGNOSIS

The course of anorexia nervosa varies greatly—spontaneous recovery without treatment, recovery after a variety of treatments, a fluctuating course of weight gains followed by relapses, a gradually deteriorating course resulting in death caused by complications of starvation. In general, the prognosis is not good. In those who have regained sufficient weight, preoccupation with food and body weight often continues, social relationships are often poor, and many patients are depressed. The short-term response of patients to almost all hospital treatment programs is good. Studies have shown a range of mortality rates from 5 to 18 percent.

Indicators of a favorable outcome are the admission of hunger, less denial, less immaturity, and improved self-esteem. Such factors as childhood neuroticism, parental conflict, bulimia nervosa, vomiting, laxative abuse, and various behavioral manifestations (such as obsessive-compulsive, hysterical, depressive, psychosomatic, neurotic, and denial symptoms) have been related to poor outcome in some studies but have not been significant in affecting the outcome in other studies.

Thirty to 50 percent of anorexia nervosa patients have the symptoms of bulimia nervosa, and usually the bulimic symptoms occur within 1½ years after the beginning of anorexia nervosa. Sometimes, the bulimic symptoms precede the onset of anorexia nervosa.

## TREATMENT

Given the complicated psychological and medical implications of anorexia nervosa, a comprehensive treatment plan, including hospitalization when necessary and both individual and family therapy, is recommended. Behavioral, interpersonal, and cognitive approaches and in some cases medication should be considered.

### Hospitalization

The first consideration in the treatment of anorexia nervosa is to restore the patient's nutritional state, since dehydration, starvation, and electrolyte imbalances can lead to serious health compromises and, in some cases, death. The decision to hospitalize the patient is based on the patient's medical condition and the degree of structure needed to ensure patient cooperation. In general, anorexia nervosa patients who are 20 percent below the expected weight for their height are recommended for inpatient programs, and patients who are 30 percent below their expected weight require psychiatric hospitalization that ranges from two to six months.

Inpatient psychiatric programs for anorexia nervosa patients generally use a combination of a behavioral management approach, individual psychotherapy, family education and therapy, and, in some cases, psychotropic medications. Successful treatment is promoted by the ability of the staff members to maintain a firm yet supportive approach to the patient, often through a combination of positive reinforcers (praise) and negative reinforcers (restriction of exercise and purging behavior). However, some flexibility in the program is needed to individualize the treatment to meet the patient's needs and cognitive abilities. Ultimately, the patient must become a willing participant in the treatment for it to succeed in the long run.

Most patients are uninterested in psychiatric treatment and even resistant to it; they are brought to a doctor's office unwillingly by agonizing relatives or friends. The patients rarely accept the recommendation of hospitalization without arguing and criticizing the program being offered. Emphasizing the benefits, such as the relief of insomnia and the patients' depressive signs and symptoms, may help persuade the patients to admit themselves willingly to the hospital. The relatives' support and confidence in the physician and the treatment team are essential when firm recommendations must be carried out. The patients' families should be warned that the patients will resist admission and, for the first several weeks of treatment, will make many dramatic pleas for the family's support to obtain release from the hospital program. Only when the risk of death from the complications of malnutrition is likely should a compulsory admission or commitment be obtained. On rare occasions, patients prove that the doctor's statements about the probable failure of outpatient treatment are wrong. Those patients may gain a specified amount of weight by the time of each outpatient visit; however, that behavior is uncommon, and usually a period of inpatient care is necessary.

The general management of anorexia nervosa patients during a hospitalized treatment program should take into account the following: Each patient should be weighed daily early in the morning after emptying the bladder. The daily fluid intake and urine output should be recorded. If vomiting is occurring, the hospital staff members must obtain serum electrolytes regularly and watch for the development of hypokalemia. Because food is often regurgitated after meals, the staff may be able to control the vomiting by making the bathroom inaccessible for at least two hours after meals or by having an attendant in the bathroom to prevent vomiting. Constipation in anorexia nervosa patients is relieved when they begin to eat normally. Occasionally, stool softeners are given but never laxatives. If diarrhea occurs, it usually means that the patient is surreptitiously taking laxatives. Because of the rare complication of stomach dilation and the possibility of circulatory overload if the patient immediately starts eating an enormous number of calories, the hospital staff should start to give patients about 500 calories over the amount required to maintain their present weight (usually 1,500 to 2,000 calories a day). It is wise to give those calories in six equal feedings throughout the day, so that the patients do not have to eat a large amount of food in one sitting. Starting to give patients a liquid food supplement, such as Sustagen, may be advisable, because they may be less apprehensive about gaining weight slowly with the formula than by eating food.

After patients are discharged from the hospital, the clinician usually finds it necessary to continue some type of outpatient supervision of whatever problems are identified in the patients and their families.

## Psychotherapy

The vast majority of patients with anorexia nervosa require continued interventions after discharge from the hospital. In less severe cases, hospitalization may not even be needed. Since most patients have the onset of the disorder in adolescence, family therapy is part of a comprehensive treatment plan. Although classic psychodynamically oriented therapy has not been useful in the early stages of treatment, especially if the anorexia nervosa patient is in a starvation state, insight-oriented psychotherapies have been helpful in some anorexia nervosa patients when they have been stabilized.

**Dynamic psychotherapy.** Dynamic expressive-supportive psychotherapy is sometimes used in the treatment of anorexia nervosa patients. Patients' resistances, however, may make the process difficult and painstaking. Because the patients view their symptoms as constituting the core of their specialness, therapists must avoid excessive investment in trying to change their eating behaviors. The opening phase of the psychotherapy process must be geared to building a therapeutic alliance. Patients may experience early interpretations as though someone else were telling them what they really feel while their own experiences are minimized and invalidated. However, therapists who empathize with patients' points of view and take an active interest in what the patients think and feel convey to the patients that their autonomy is respected. Above all, psychotherapists must be flexible, persistent, and durable in the face of patients' tendencies to defeat any efforts to help them.

Many clinicians prefer cognitive-behavioral approaches to monitor weight gain and maintenance and to address eating behaviors. Cognitive or interpersonal strategies have also been recommended to explore other issues related to the disorder. Family therapy has been used to examine interactions among family members and the disorder's possible secondary gain for the patient.

## Biological Treatment

Pharmacological studies have not yet identified any medication resulting in definitive improvement of the core symptoms of anorexia nervosa. Some reports support the use of cyproheptadine (Periactin), a drug with antihistaminic and antiserotonergic properties, in the restricting type of anorexia nervosa. Amitriptyline (Elavil) has been reported to have some benefit in patients with anorexia nervosa. Other medications that have been tried by anorexia nervosa patients—including clomipramine (Anafranil), pimozide (Orap), and chlorpromazine (Thorazine)—have not yielded positive responses. Uncontrolled trials of fluoxetine (Prozac) have resulted in some reports of weight gain. In anorexia nervosa patients with coexisting depressive disorders, other antidepressants have been tried with little benefit. Concern exists regarding the use of tricyclic drugs in low-weight, depressed anorexia nervosa patients, since they may be vulnerable to hypotension, cardiac arrhythmia, and dehydration. Once an adequate nutritional status has been attained, the risks of serious side effects from the tricyclics may decrease. However, in some cases the depression improves with weight gain and normalized nutritional status.

Some evidence indicates that electroconvulsive therapy (ECT) is beneficial in certain cases of anorexia nervosa and major depressive disorder.

### References

American Psychiatric Association: Practice guidelines for eating disorders. Am J Psychiatry *150*: 212, 1993.

Artmann H, Grau H, Adelmann M, Scleiffer R: Reversible and nonreversible enlargement of cerebrospinal fluid spaces in anorexia nervosa. Neuroradiology *27*: 304, 1985.

Blinder B J, Chaitin B, Goldstein R, editors: *The Eating Disorders*. Pergamon, New York, 1987.

Brewerton T D, Lydiard R B, Ballenger J C, Herzog D B: Eating disorders and social phobia. Arch Gen Psychiatry *50*: 70, 1993.

Crisp A H, Hsu L K G, Harding B, Hartshorn J: Clinical features of anorexia nervosa: A study of 102 cases. J Psychosom Res *24*: 179, 1980.

Ferguson J M: The use of electroconvulsive therapy in patients with intractable anorexia nervosa. Int J Eating Disord *13*: 171, 1993.

Gabbard G O: *Psychodynamic Psychiatry in Clinical Practice: The DSM-IV Edition*. American Psychiatric Press, Washington, 1994.

Garfinkel P E, Garner D M, Rose J, Darby P L, Brandes O S, O'Hanlon J, Walsh N: A comparison of characteristics in the families of patients with anorexia nervosa and normal controls. Psychol Med *13*: 821, 1983.

Garner D M, Garner M V, Rosen L W: Anorexia nervosa "restricters" who purge: Implications for subtyping anorexia nervosa. Int J Eating Disord *13*: 187, 1993.

Harper-Giuffre H, MacKenzie K R, editors: *Group Psychotherapy for Eating Disorders*. American Psychiatric Press, Washington, 1992.

Herzog D B, Sacks N R, Keller M B, Lavori P W, von Ranson K B, Gray H M: Patterns and predictors of recovery in anorexia nervosa and bulimia nervosa. J Am Acad Child Adolesc Psychiatry *32*: 835, 1993.

Kassett J A, Gwirtsman H E, Kaye H K, Brandt H A, Jimerson D C: Pattern of onset of bulimic symptoms in anorexia nervosa. Am J Psychiatry *145*: 1287, 1988.

Toner B B, Garfinkel P E, Garner D M: Cognitive style of patients with bulimic and diet-restricting anorexia nervosa. Am J Psychiatry *144*: 510, 1987.

Vanderlinden J, Vandereycken W, van Dyck R, Vertommen H: Dissociative experiences and trauma in eating disorders. Int J Eating Disord *13*: 195, 1993.

Waller G: Sexual abuse and eating disorders: Borderline personality disorder as a mediating factor? Br J Psychiatry *162*: 771, 1993.

Wamholdt F S, Kaslow N J, Swift W J, Ritholz M: Short-term course of depressive symptoms in patients with eating disorders. Am J Psychiatry *144*: 362, 1987.

Wilson G T, Fairburn C G: Cognitive treatments for eating disorders. J Consult Clin Psychol *61*: 261, 1993.

Yager J: The treatment of eating disorders. J Clin Psychiatry 49: 137, 1988.

Yates A: Current perspectives on the eating disorders. I. History, psychological and biological aspects. J Am Acad Child Adolesc Psychiatry 28: 813, 1989.

Yates A: Current perspectives on the eating disorders: II. Treatment, outcome, and research directions. J Am Acad Child Adolesc Psychiatry 29: 1, 1990.

# 22.2 / Bulimia Nervosa and Eating Disorder NOS

## BULIMIA NERVOSA

Bulimia nervosa, which is more common than anorexia nervosa, consists of recurrent episodes of eating large amounts of food accompanied by a feeling of being out of control. Social interruption or physical discomfort—that is, abdominal pain or nausea—terminates the binge eating, which is often followed by feelings of guilt, depression, or self-disgust. The person also has recurrent compensatory behaviors—such as purging (self-induced vomiting, repeated laxative use, or diuretic use), fasting, or excessive exercise—to prevent weight gain. Unlike anorexia nervosa patients, those with bulimia nervosa may maintain a normal body weight. According to the diagnostic criteria for bulimia nervosa in the fourth edition of *Diagnostic and Statistical Manual of Mental Disorders* (DSM-IV), the binge eating and compensatory behaviors must both occur an average of at least twice a week for three months. In addition, persons with bulimia nervosa evaluate themselves predominantly on the basis of body shape and weight. In contrast to the revised third edition of DSM (DSM-III-R), DSM-IV adds that bulimia nervosa may not be diagnosed if it occurs exclusively during episodes of anorexia nervosa. In addition, DSM-IV adds several types of bulimia nervosa. In the purging type, the person regularly engages in self-induced vomiting or the misuse of laxatives or diuretics. In the nonpurging type, the person uses other inappropriate compensatory behaviors to prevent weight gain, such as fasting and exercise, but does not purge.

### Epidemiology

Bulimia nervosa is more prevalent than is anorexia nervosa. Estimates of bulimia nervosa range from 1 to 3 percent of young women. Like anorexia nervosa, bulimia nervosa is significantly more common in females than in males, but its onset is often later in adolescence than the onset of anorexia nervosa or in early adulthood. Occasional symptoms of bulimia nervosa, such as isolated episodes of binge eating and purging, have been reported in up to 40 percent of college women. Although bulimia nervosa is often present in normal-weight young women, they sometimes have a history of obesity.

### Etiology

**Biological factors.**   Some investigators have attempted to associate cycles of binging and purging with various neurotransmitters. Because antidepressants often benefit patients with bulimia nervosa, serotonin and norepinephrine have been implicated.

Plasma endorphin levels are raised in some bulimia nervosa patients who vomit, leading to the possibility that the feelings of well-being experienced by some of those patients after vomiting may be mediated by raised endorphin levels.

**Social factors.**   Patients with bulimia nervosa, like those with anorexia nervosa, tend to be high achievers and to respond to societal pressures to be thin. As with anorexia nervosa patients, many bulimia nervosa patients are depressed and have increased familial depression. However, the families of such patients are generally different from those of anorexia nervosa patients. Families of bulimia nervosa patients are less close and more conflictual than the families of anorexia nervosa patients. Bulimia nervosa patients describe their parents as neglectful and rejecting.

**Psychological factors.**   Patients with bulimia nervosa, like those with anorexia nervosa, have difficulties with adolescent demands, but bulimia nervosa patients are more outgoing, angry, and impulsive than are anorexia nervosa patients. Alcohol dependence, shoplifting, and emotional lability (including suicide attempts) are associated with bulimia nervosa. Bulimia nervosa patients generally experience their uncontrolled eating as more egodystonic than do anorexia nervosa patients, so bulimia nervosa patients more readily seek help.

Patients with bulimia nervosa lack the superego control and the ego strength of their counterparts with anorexia nervosa. Bulimia nervosa patients' difficulties in controlling their impulses are often manifested by substance dependence and self-destructive sexual relationships, in addition to the binge eating and the purging that are the hallmarks of the disorder. Many bulimia nervosa patients have histories of difficulties in separating from caretakers, as manifested by the absence of transitional objects during their early childhood years. Some clinicians have observed that bulimia nervosa patients use their own bodies as transitional objects. The struggle for separation from the maternal figure is played out in the ambivalence toward food; eating may represent a wish to fuse with the caretaker, and regurgitating may unconsciously express a wish for separation.

### Diagnosis and Clinical Features

According to DSM-IV, the essential features of bulimia nervosa are recurrent episodes of binge eating; a sense of lack of control over eating during the eating binges; self-induced vomiting, the misuse of laxatives or diuretics, fasting, or excessive exercise to prevent weight gain; and persistent self-evaluation unduly influenced by body shape and weight (Table 22.2–1). Binging usually precedes vomiting by about one year.

Vomiting is common and is usually induced by sticking

**Table 22.2–1**
**Diagnostic Criteria for Bulimia Nervosa**

A. Recurrent episodes of binge eating. An episode of binge eating is characterized by both of the following:

(1) eating, in a discrete period of time (e.g., within any 2 hour period), an amount of food that is definitely larger than most people would eat during a similar period of time and under similar circumstances

(2) a sense of lack of control over eating during the episode (e.g., a feeling that one cannot stop eating or control what or how much one is eating)

B. Recurrent inappropriate compensatory behavior in order to prevent weight gain, such as self-induced vomiting; misuse of laxatives, diuretics, enemas, or other medications; fasting; or excessive exercise.

C. The binge eating and inappropriate compensatory behaviors both occur, on average, at least twice a week for 3 months.

D. Self-evaluation is unduly influenced by body shape and weight.

E. The disturbance does not occur exclusively during episodes of anorexia nervosa.

*Specify* type:
   **Purging type:** during the current episode of bulimia nervosa, the person has regularly engaged in self-induced vomiting or the misuse of laxatives, diuretics, or enemas
   **Nonpurging type:** during the current episode of bulimia nervosa, the person has used other inappropriate compensatory behaviors, such as fasting or excessive exercise, but has not regularly engaged in self-induced vomiting or the misuse of laxatives, diuretics, or enemas

Table from DSM-IV, *Diagnostic and Statistical Manual of Mental Disorders*, ed 4. Copyright American Psychiatric Association, Washington, 1994. Used with permission.

a finger down the throat, although some patients are able to vomit at will. Vomiting decreases the abdominal pain and the feeling of being bloated and allows the patients to continue eating without fear of gaining weight. Depression often follows the episode and has been called postbinge anguish. During their binges the patients eat food that is sweet, high in calories, and generally of smooth texture or soft, such as cakes and pastry. The food is eaten secretly and rapidly and is sometimes not even chewed.

Most bulimia nervosa patients are within their normal weight range, but some may be either underweight or overweight. Bulimia nervosa patients are concerned about their body image and their appearance, worry about how others see them, and are concerned about their sexual attractiveness. Most bulimia nervosa patients are sexually active, compared with anorexia nervosa patients, who are not interested in sex. Pica and struggles during meals are sometimes revealed in the histories of bulimia nervosa patients.

Patients with the purging type of bulimia nervosa may be at risk for certain medical complications, such as hypokalemia from vomiting or laxative abuse, and hypochloremic alkalosis. Those who vomit repeatedly are at risk for gastric and esophageal tears, although those complications are rare. Bulimia nervosa patients who purge may have a different course from the course of those who binge and then diet or exercise.

Bulimia nervosa occurs in persons with high rates of mood disorders and impulse control disorders. Bulimia

nervosa is also reported to occur in persons at risk for substance-related disorders and a variety of personality disorders. Bulimia nervosa patients also have increased rates of anxiety disorders, bipolar I disorder, and dissociative disorders, and histories of sexual abuse.

The patient, a 17-year-old girl who lived with her parents, insisted that she be seen because of binge eating and vomiting. She had achieved her greatest weight of 180 pounds at 16 years of age. Her lowest weight since she had reached her height of 5 feet 9 inches was 150 pounds, and her weight when examined was about 160 pounds.

The patient stated that she had been dieting since age 10 and said that she had always been very tall and slightly chubby. At age 12 she had started binge eating and vomiting. She was a serious competitive swimmer at that time, and it was necessary for her to keep her weight down. She would deprive herself of all food for a few days and then get an urge to eat. She could not control the urge and would raid the refrigerator and cupboards for ice cream, pastries, and other desserts. She would often do so at night, when nobody was looking, and sometimes ate in one sitting a quart of ice cream, an entire pie, and any other desserts she could find. While binging, she would feel that her eating was totally out of control, and she would stop only when she felt physical discomfort. She would then become depressed and fearful of gaining weight, so she would self-induce vomiting by sticking her finger deep into the back of her mouth until she gagged.

The patient had always been concerned about the effect that her behavior was having on her weight and constantly fretted about being overweight, occasionally resorting to dextroamphetamine (Dexedrine) to help her lose weight. When she was 15, she was having eating binges and vomiting four days a week. Since age 13 she had gone through only one period of six weeks without gaining weight or going on eating binges or vomiting. She had quit school at age 17 for five months; during that period she just stayed home, binge eating and vomiting several times a day. She then went back to school and tried to do better in her schoolwork. She obtained average or below-average grades in junior high and high school.

For the preceding two years the patient had been drinking wine and beer on weekends. She drank mostly with girlfriends; she dated infrequently. She stated that she wanted to date but was ashamed of the way she looked. Several months before the psychiatric interview she had been hospitalized for two weeks to control her binge eating. During that time she was depressed and cut her wrists several times while hospitalized.

The patient was neatly dressed and well-oriented and answered inquiries rationally. During the interview she indicated that she realized she had a serious problem with binge eating and vomiting but felt helpless about getting the behavior under control.

*Discussion.* The patient clearly had a gross disturbance in her eating behavior. She had recurrent episodes of binge eating, in which she rapidly consumed a large quantity of food over a discrete period. The food she ate during the binges was typically high in carbohydrates (ice cream, pastries, and other desserts); she ate it in secret (at night when nobody was looking). During the binges she experienced a feeling of lack of control over her eating behavior, so that only the physical discomfort caused by the binge allowed her to stop eating. To keep from gaining weight as a result of her overeating, she regularly engaged in self-induced vomiting and occasionally used dextroamphetamine to help her lose weight. Because of her frequent fluctuations in weight caused by the binges, dieting and the control of her weight were chronic preoccupations. Her eating binges were frequent, sometimes as often as several times a day, warranting the diagnosis of bulimia nervosa.

**Pathology and laboratory examination.** Bulimia nervosa can result in electrolyte abnormalities and various degrees of starvation, although it may not be as obvious as in low-weight patients with anorexia nervosa. Thus, even with normal-weight patients with bulimia nervosa, the clinician should obtain laboratory studies of electrolytes and metabolism. In general, thyroid function remains intact in bulimia nervosa, but the patient may show nonsuppression on the dexamethasone-suppression test. Dehydration and electrolyte disturbances are likely to occur in bulimia nervosa patients who regularly purge. Patients with bulimia nervosa commonly exhibit hypomagnesemia and hyperamylasemia. Although not a core diagnostic feature, many patients with bulimia nervosa have menstrual disturbances. Hypotension and bradycardia occur in some patients.

## Differential Diagnosis

The diagnosis of bulimia nervosa cannot be made if the binge eating and purging behaviors occur exclusively during episodes of anorexia nervosa. In such cases the diagnosis is anorexia nervosa, binge eating/purging type.

The clinician must ascertain that the patient has no neurological disease, such as epileptic-equivalent seizures, central nervous system tumors, Klüver-Bucy syndrome, or Kleine-Levin syndrome. The pathological features manifested by Klüver-Bucy syndrome are visual agnosia, compulsive licking and biting, the examination of objects by the mouth, inability to ignore any stimulus, placidity, altered sexual behavior (hypersexuality), and altered dietary habits, especially hyperphagia. The syndrome is exceedingly rare and is unlikely to cause a problem in differential diagnosis. Kleine-Levin syndrome consists of periodic hypersomnia lasting for two to three weeks and hyperphagia. As in bulimia nervosa, the onset is usually during adolescence; the syndrome is more common in men than in women. Borderline personality disorder patients sometimes binge eat, but the eating is associated with the other signs of the disorder.

## Course and Prognosis

Little is known about the long-range course of bulimia nervosa, and the short-term outcome is variable. Overall, bulimia nervosa seems to have a better prognosis than does anorexia nervosa. In the short run, bulimia nervosa patients who are able to engage in treatment have reported more than 50 percent improvement in binge eating and purging; among outpatients, improvement seems to last more than five years. However, the patients are not symptom-free during periods of improvement; bulimia nervosa is a chronic disorder with a waxing and waning course. Some patients with mild courses have long-term remissions. Other patients are disabled by the disorder and have been hospitalized; less than one third of them are doing well on a three-year follow-up, more than one third have some improvement in their symptoms, and about one third have a poor outcome, with chronic symptoms, within three years.

The prognosis depends on the severity of the purging sequelae—that is, whether the patient has electrolyte imbalances and to what degree the frequent vomiting results

in esophagitis, amylasemia, salivary gland enlargement, and dental caries.

In some cases of untreated bulimia nervosa, spontaneous remission occurs in one to two years.

## Treatment

Treatment of bulimia nervosa consists of various interventions, including individual psychotherapy with a cognitive-behavioral approach, group therapy, family therapy, and pharmacotherapy. Because of the comorbidity of mood disorders, anxiety disorders, and personality disorders with bulimia nervosa, the clinician must factor those additional disorders into the treatment plan.

Most patients with uncomplicated bulimia nervosa do not require hospitalization. In general, patients with bulimia nervosa are not as secretive about their symptoms as are patients with anorexia nervosa; therefore, outpatient treatment is usually not difficult. However, psychotherapy is frequently stormy and may be prolonged. Some obese bulimia nervosa patients who have had prolonged psychotherapy do surprisingly well. In some cases—when eating binges are out of control, outpatient treatment does not work, or the patient exhibits such additional psychiatric symptoms as suicidality and substance abuse—hospitalization may become necessary. In addition, in cases of severe purging, resulting electrolyte and metabolic disturbances may necessitate hospitalization.

**Psychotherapy.** Some reports encourage the use of cognitive-behavioral psychotherapy to address the specific behaviors surrounding and leading up to episodes of eating binges. Some helpful programs include a behavioral contract and desensitization to the thoughts and feelings that bulimia nervosa patients have just before binge eating. However, many bulimia nervosa patients have psychopathology that exceeds the binging behaviors; therefore, additional psychotherapeutic approaches—such as psychodynamic, interpersonal, and family therapies—can be useful.

Psychodynamic treatment of patients with bulimia nervosa has revealed a tendency to concretize introjective and projective defense mechanisms. In a manner analogous to splitting, the patient divides food into two categories: those items that are nutritious and those that are unhealthy. Food that is designated nutritious may be ingested and retained because it unconsciously symbolizes good introjects. But junk food is unconsciously associated with bad introjects and is, therefore, expelled by vomiting, with the unconscious fantasy that all destructiveness, hate, and badness are being evacuated. Patients may temporarily feel good after vomiting because of the fantasized evacuation, but the associated feeling of being all-good is short-lived, because it is based on an unstable combination of splitting and projection.

**Pharmacotherapy.** Antidepressant medications can reduce binge eating and purging independent of the presence of a mood disorder. Thus, for particularly difficult binge-purge cycles that are not responsive to psychotherapy alone, antidepressants have been successfully used. Imipramine (Tofranil), desipramine (Norpramin), trazodone (Desyrel), and monoamine oxidase (MAO) inhibitors have been helpful. Fluoxetine (Prozac) is also promising as an effective treatment. In general, most of the antidepressants have been effective at dosages usually given in the treatment of depressive disorders. However, dosages of fluoxetine that are effective in decreasing binge eating may be higher (60 mg a day) than those used for depressive disorders. In cases of comorbid depressive disorders and bulimia nervosa, medication is helpful. Carbamazepine (Tegretol) and lithium (Eskalith) have not shown impressive results as treatments for binge eating, but they have been used in the treatment of bulimia nervosa patients with comorbid mood disorders, such as bipolar I disorder.

## EATING DISORDER NOT OTHERWISE SPECIFIED

The DSM-IV diagnostic classification of eating disorder not otherwise specified (NOS) is a residual category used for eating disorders that do not meet the criteria for a specific eating disorder (Table 22.2–2). Binge eating disorder—that is, recurrent episodes of binge eating in the absence of the inappropriate compensatory behaviors characteristic of bulimia nervosa (Table 22.2–3)—falls into the category. Such patients are not fixated on body shape and weight.

**Table 22.2–2**
**Diagnostic Criteria for Eating Disorder Not Otherwise Specified**

---

The eating disorder NOS category is for disorders of eating that do not meet the criteria for any specific eating disorder. Examples include:

1. for females, all of the criteria for anorexia nervosa are met except that the individual has regular menses.
2. all of the criteria for anorexia nervosa are met except that, despite significant weight loss, the individual's current weight is in the normal range.
3. all of the criteria for bulimia nervosa are met except that the binge eating and inappropriate compensatory mechanisms occur at a frequency of less than twice a week or for a duration of less than three months.
4. the regular use of inappropriate compensatory behavior by an individual of normal body weight after eating small amounts of food (e.g., self-induced vomiting after the consumption of two cookies).
5. repeatedly chewing and spitting out, but not swallowing, large amounts of food.
6. Binge eating disorder: recurrent episodes of binge eating in the absence of the regular use of inappropriate compensatory behaviors characteristic of bulimia nervosa.

---

Table from DSM-IV, *Diagnostic and Statistical Manual of Mental Disorders*, ed 4. Copyright American Psychiatric Association, Washington, 1994. Used with permission.

**Table 22.2–3**
**Research Criteria for Binge Eating Disorder**

---

A. Recurrent episodes of binge eating. An episode of binge eating is characterized by both of the following:

   (1) eating, in a discrete period of time (e.g., within any two hour period), an amount of food that is definitely larger than most people would eat in a similar period of time under similar circumstances

   (2) a sense of lack of control over eating during the episode (e.g., a feeling that one cannot stop eating or control what or how much one is eating)

B. The binge-eating episodes are associated with three (or more) of the following:

   (1) eating much more rapidly than normal
   (2) eating until feeling uncomfortably full
   (3) eating large amounts of food when not feeling physically hungry
   (4) eating alone because of being embarrassed by how much one is eating
   (5) feeling disgusted with oneself, depressed, or very guilty after overeating

C. Marked distress regarding binge eating is present.

D. The binge eating occurs, on average, at least 2 days a week for 6 months.

   **Note:** The method of determining frequency differs from that used for bulimia nervosa; future research should address whether the preferred method of setting a frequency threshold is counting the number of days on which binges occur or counting the number of episodes of binge eating.

E. The binge eating is not associated with the regular use of inappropriate compensatory behaviors (e.g., purging, fasting, excessive exercise) and does not occur exclusively during the course of anorexia nervosa or bulimia nervosa.

---

Table from DSM-IV, *Diagnostic and Statistical Manual of Mental Disorders*, ed 4. Copyright American Psychiatric Association, Washington, 1994. Used with permission.

Fairburn C G: The current status of the psychological treatments for bulimia nervosa. J Psychosom Res *32*: 635, 1988.

Fairburn C G, Welch S L, Hay P J: The classification of recurrent overeating: The "binge eating disorder" proposal. Int J Eating Disord *13*: 155, 1993.

Fava M, Copeland P M, Schweiger W, Herzog D B: Neurochemical abnormalities of anorexia nervosa and bulimia nervosa. Am J Psychiatry *146*: 963, 1989.

Fichter M M, Quadflieg N, Brandl B: Recurring overeating: An empirical comparison of binge eating disorder, bulimia nervosa, and obesity. Int J Eating Disord *13*: 1, 1993.

Gabbard G O: *Psychodynamic Psychiatry in Clinical Practice: The DSM-IV Edition.* American Psychiatric Press, Washington, 1994.

Garner D M, Rockert W, Davis R, Garner M V: Comparison of cognitive-behavioral and supportive-expressive therapy for bulimia nervosa. Am J Psychiatry *150*: 37, 1993.

Hudson J E, Pope H G Jr, editors: *The Psychobiology of Bulimia.* American Psychiatric Press, Washington, 1987.

Marchi M, Cohen P: Early childhood eating behaviors and adolescent eating disorders. J Am Acad Child Adolesc Psychiatry *29*: 112, 1990.

Pope H G, Keok P E, McElroy S L, Hudson J I: A placebo-controlled study of trazodone in bulimia nervosa. J Clin Psychopharmacol *9*: 254, 1989.

Spitzer R L, Stunkard A, Yanovski S, Marcus M D, Wadden T, Wing R, Mitchell J, Hasin D: Binge eating disorder should be included in DSM-IV: A reply to Fairburn et al.'s "The classification of recurrent overeating: The binge eating disorder proposal." Int J Eating Disord *13*: 161, 1993.

Striegel-Moore R H, Silberstein L R, Rodin J: The social self in bulimia nervosa: Public self-consciousness, social anxiety, and perceived fraudulence. J Abnorm Psychol *102*: 297, 1993.

Walsh B T, Kissileff H R, Cassidy S M, Dantzic S: Eating behavior of women with bulimia. Arch Gen Psychiatry *46*: 54, 1989.

Walters E E, Neale M C, Eaves L J, Health A C, Kessler R C, Kendler K S: Bulimia nervosa: A population-based study of purgers versus nonpurgers. Int J Eating Disord *13*: 265, 1993.

### References

Childress A C, Brewerton T D, Hodges E L, Jarrell M P: The Kids' Eating Disorders Survey (KEDS): A study of middle school students. J Am Acad Child Adolesc Psychiatry *32*: 843, 1993.

Cohen P: Seasonal patterns of bulimia nervosa. Am J Psychiatry *150*: 357, 1993.

Fahy T A, Eisler I, Russell G F M: Personality disorder and treatment response in bulimia nervosa. Br J Psychiatry *162*: 765, 1993.

# Normal Sleep and Sleep Disorders

## 23.1 / Normal Sleep

Sleep is associated with a variety of physiological changes, including respiration, cardiac function, muscle tone, temperature, hormone secretion, and blood pressure. Current interest in sleep research focuses on two main areas: (1) basic sleep mechanisms and sleep physiology and (2) sleep problems in clinical medicine. Research into sleep functions in mental disorders attempts to elucidate the underlying biochemical disturbances in those disorders.

### SLEEP PATTERNS

Sleep is a regular, recurrent, easily reversible state of the organism that is characterized by relative quiescence and by a great increase in the threshold of response to external stimuli relative to the waking state. Close monitoring of sleep is an important part of clinical practice, since sleep disturbance is often an early symptom of impending mental illness. Some mental disorders are associated with characteristic changes in sleep physiology.

As persons fall asleep, their brain waves go through certain characteristic changes (Figure 23.1–1). The waking electroencephalogram (EEG) is characterized by alpha waves of 8 to 12 cycles a second and low-voltage activity of mixed frequency. As the person falls asleep, alpha activity begins to disappear. Stage 1, considered the lightest stage of sleep, is characterized by low-voltage, regular activity at 3 to 7 cycles a second. After a few seconds or minutes, that stage gives way to stage 2, a pattern showing frequent spindle-shaped tracings at 12 to 14 cycles a second (sleep spindles) and slow, triphasic waves known as K complexes. Soon thereafter, delta waves—high-voltage activity at 0.5 to 2.5 cycles a second—make their appearance and occupy less than 50 percent of the tracing (stage 3). Eventually, in stage 4, delta waves occupy more than 50 percent of the record. It is common practice to describe stages 3 and 4 as delta sleep or slow-wave sleep (SWS) because of their characteristic appearance on the EEG record.

## POLYSOMNOGRAM REM FINDINGS

Sleep is made up of two physiological states: nonrapid eye movement (NREM) sleep and rapid eye movement (REM) sleep. NREM sleep is composed of stages 1 through 4. As compared with wakefulness, most physiological functions are markedly reduced during NREM sleep. REM sleep is a qualitatively different kind of sleep characterized by a highly active brain and physiological activity levels similar to those in wakefulness. About 90 minutes after sleep onset, NREM yields to the first REM episode of the night. That REM latency of 90 minutes is a consistent finding in normal adults. A shortening of REM latency frequently occurs with such disorders as depressive disorders and narcolepsy. The EEG records the rapid conjugate eye movements that are the identifying feature of that sleep state (there are no or few rapid eye movements in NREM sleep); the EEG pattern consists of low-voltage, random fast activity with sawtooth waves; the electromyograph (EMG) shows a marked reduction in muscle tone.

In normal persons NREM sleep is a peaceful state relative to waking. The pulse rate is typically slowed 5 or 10 beats a minute below the level of restful waking and is very regular. Respiration behaves in the same way. Blood pressure also tends to be low, with few minute-to-minute variations. The resting muscle potential of the body musculature is lower in REM sleep than in a waking state. Episodic, involuntary body movements are present in NREM sleep. There are few rapid eye movements, if any, and seldom any penile erections. The blood flow through most tissues, including cerebral blood flow, is slightly reduced.

The deepest portions of NREM sleep—stages 3 and 4—are sometimes associated with unusual arousal characteristics. When persons are aroused a half hour to one hour after sleep onset—usually in slow-wave sleep—they are disoriented, and their thinking is disorganized. Brief arousals from slow-wave sleep are also associated with amnesia for events that occur during the arousal. The disorganization during arousal from stage 3 or stage 4 may result in specific problems, including enuresis, somnambulism, and stage 4 nightmares or night terrors.

Polygraphic measures during REM sleep show irregular patterns, sometimes close to aroused waking patterns. Indeed, if one was not aware of the behavioral stage of the person and one happened to be recording a variety of physiological measures (but not muscle tone) during REM periods, one would undoubtedly conclude that the person

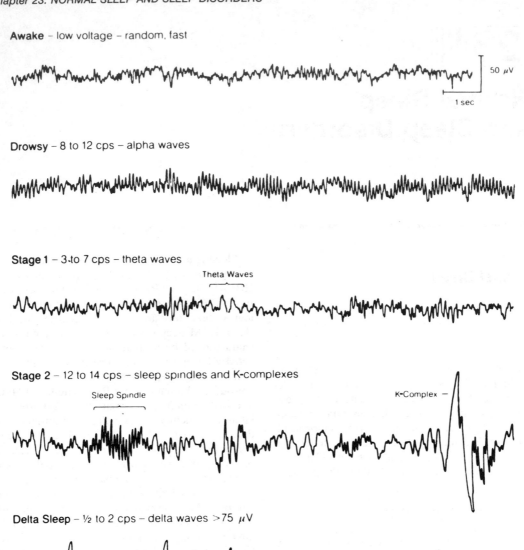

**Awake** – low voltage – random, fast

50 μV

1 sec

**Drowsy** – 8 to 12 cps – alpha waves

**Stage 1** – 3 to 7 cps – theta waves

Theta Waves

**Stage 2** – 12 to 14 cps – sleep spindles and K-complexes

Sleep Spindle

K-Complex —

**Delta Sleep** – ½ to 2 cps – delta waves >75 μV

**REM Sleep** – low voltage – random, fast with sawtooth waves

Sawtooth Waves    Sawtooth Waves

**Figure 23.1–1.** Human sleep stages. (From P Hauri: *The Sleep Disorders,* p 7. Current Concepts, Upjohn, Kalamazoo, Mich, 1982. Used with permission.)

or animal was in an active waking state. Because of that observation, REM sleep has also been termed paradoxical sleep. Pulse, respiration, and blood pressure in humans are all high during REM sleep—much higher than during NREM sleep and often higher than during waking. Even more striking than the level or the rate is the variability from minute to minute. Brain oxygen use increases during REM sleep. The ventilatory response to increased levels

of carbon dioxide ($CO_2$) is depressed during REM sleep, so that there is no increase in tidal volume as partial pressure of carbon dioxide ($pCO_2$) increases. Thermoregulation is altered during REM sleep. In contrast to the homeothermic condition of temperature regulation that is present during wakefulness or NREM sleep, a poikilothermic condition (a state in which animal temperature varies with the changes in the temperature of the surrounding medium) is present during REM sleep. Poiki-lothermia, which is characteristic of reptiles, results in a failure to respond to changes in ambient temperature with shivering or sweating, whichever is appropriate to maintaining body temperature. Almost every REM period is accompanied by a partial or full penile erection. That finding is of significant clinical value in evaluating the cause of impotence. The nocturnal penile tumescence study is one of the most commonly requested sleep laboratory tests. Another physiological change that occurs during REM sleep is the near total paralysis of the skeletal (postural) muscles. Because of that motor inhibition, body movement is absent during REM sleep. Probably the most distinctive feature of REM sleep is dreaming. Persons awakened during REM sleep frequently (60 to 90 percent of the time) report that they had been dreaming. Dreams during REM sleep are typically abstract and surreal. Dreaming does occur during NREM sleep, but it is typically lucid and purposeful.

The cyclical nature of sleep is regular and reliable; a REM period occurs about every 90 to 100 minutes during the night (Figure 23.1–2). The first REM period tends to be the shortest, usually lasting less than 10 minutes; the later REM periods may last 15 to 40 minutes each. Most REM periods occur in the last third of the night, whereas most stage 4 sleep occurs in the first third of the night.

Sleep patterns change over the life span. In the neonatal period, REM sleep represents more than 50 percent of total sleep time. Newborns sleep about 16 hours a day, with brief periods of wakefulness. In the neonatal period, the EEG pattern goes from the alert state directly to the REM state without going through stages 1 through 4. By 4 months of age, the pattern shifts, so that the total percentage of REM sleep drops to less than 40 percent, and entry into sleep occurs with an initial period of NREM

sleep. By young adulthood, the distribution of sleep stages is as follows:

NREM (75 percent)
  Stage 1:  5 percent
  Stage 2: 45 percent
  Stage 3: 12 percent
  Stage 4: 13 percent
REM (25 percent)

That distribution remains relatively constant into old age, although a reduction occurs in both slow-wave sleep and REM sleep in the elderly.

## SLEEP REGULATION

The prevailing view is that there is not a simple sleep control center but a small number of interconnecting systems or centers that are chiefly located in the brainstem and that mutually activate and inhibit one another. Many studies support the role of serotonin in sleep regulation. Prevention of serotonin synthesis or destruction of the dorsal raphe nucleus of the brainstem, which contains nearly all the brain's serotonergic cell bodies, reduces sleep for a considerable time. Synthesis and release of serotonin by serotonergic neurons are influenced by the availability of amino acid precursors of that neurotransmitter, such as L-tryptophan. Ingestion of large amounts of L-tryptophan (1 to 15 g) reduces sleep latency and nocturnal awakenings. Conversely, L-tryptophan deficiency is associated with less time spent in REM sleep.

Norepinephrine-containing neurons with cell bodies located in the locus ceruleus play an important role in controlling normal sleep patterns. Drugs and manipulations that increase the firing of those noradrenergic neurons

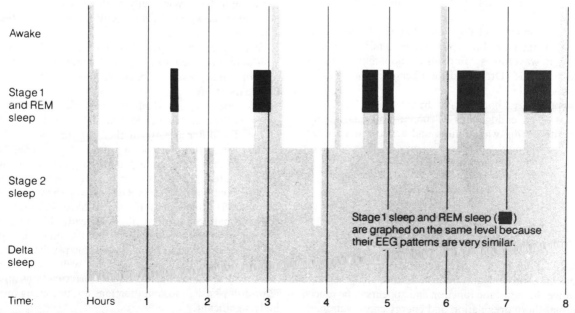

**Figure 23.1–2.** Typical sleep pattern of a young human adult. (From P Hauri: *The Sleep Disorders,* p 8. Current Concepts, Upjohn, Kalamazoo, Mich, 1982. Used with permission.)

produce a marked reduction in REM sleep (REM-off neurons) and an increase in wakefulness. Electrical stimulation of the locus ceruleus in humans with implanted electrodes (for the control of spasticity) profoundly disrupts all sleep parameters.

Brain acetylcholine is also involved in sleep, particularly in the production of REM sleep. In animal studies the injection of cholinergic-muscarinic agonists into pontine reticular formation neurons (REM-on neurons) results in a shift from wakefulness to REM sleep. Disturbances in central cholinergic activity are associated with the sleep changes observed in major depressive disorder. As compared with healthy persons and nondepressed psychiatric controls, depressed patients have marked disruptions of REM sleep patterns. Those disruptions include shortened REM latency (60 minutes or less), an increased percentage of REM sleep, and a shift in REM distribution from the last half to the first half of the night. The administration of a muscarinic agonist, such as arecoline, to depressed patients during the first or second NREM period results in a rapid onset of REM sleep. Depression may be associated with an underlying supersensitivity to acetylcholine.

Drugs that reduce REM sleep, such as antidepressants, produce beneficial effects in depression. Indeed, about half of the patients with major depressive disorder experience temporary improvement when they are deprived of sleep or when sleep is restricted. Conversely, reserpine (Serpasil), which is one of the few drugs that increases REM sleep, also produces depression.

Patients with dementia of the Alzheimer's type have sleep disturbances characterized by reduced REM and slow-wave sleep. The loss of cholinergic neurons in the basal forebrain has been implicated as the cause of those changes. Melatonin secretion from the pineal gland is inhibited by bright light, so the lowest serum melatonin concentrations occur during the day. The suprachiasmatic nucleus of the hypothalamus may act as the anatomical site of a circadian pacemaker that regulates melatonin secretion and the entrainment of the brain to a 24-hour sleep-wake cycle.

Evidence shows that dopamine has an alerting effect. Drugs that increase brain dopamine tend to produce arousal and wakefulness. In contrast, dopamine blockers, such as pimozide (Orap) and the phenothiazines, tend to increase sleep time.

A hypothesized homeostatic drive to sleep, perhaps in the form of an endogenous substance—process S—may accumulate during wakefulness and act to induce sleep. Another compound—process C—may act as a regulator of body temperature and sleep duration.

## FUNCTIONS OF SLEEP

The functions of sleep have been examined in a variety of ways: most investigators conclude that sleep serves a restorative, homeostatic function and appears to be crucial for normal thermoregulation and energy conservation.

## Sleep Deprivation

Prolonged periods of sleep deprivation sometimes lead to ego disorganization, hallucinations, and delusions. Depriving persons of REM sleep by awakening them at the beginning of REM cycles produces an increase in the number of REM periods and in the amount of REM sleep (rebound increase) when they are allowed to sleep without interruption. REM-deprived patients may exhibit irritability and lethargy.

In studies with rats, sleep deprivation produces a syndrome that includes a debilitated appearance, skin lesions, increased food intake, weight loss, increased energy expenditure, decreased body temperature, and death. The neuroendocrine changes include increased plasma norepinephrine and decreased plasma thyroxine.

## Sleep Requirements

Some persons are normally short sleepers who require fewer than six hours of sleep each night and who function adequately. Long sleepers are those who sleep more than nine hours each night in order to function adequately. Long sleepers have more REM periods and more rapid eye movements within each period (known as REM density) than do short sleepers. Those movements are sometimes considered a measure of the intensity of REM sleep and are related to the vividness of dreaming. Short sleepers are generally efficient, ambitious, socially adept, and content. Long sleepers tend to be mildly depressed, anxious, and socially withdrawn. Increased sleep needs occur with physical work, exercise, illness, pregnancy, general mental stress, and increased mental activity. REM periods increase after strong psychological stimuli, such as difficult learning situations and stress, and after the use of chemicals or drugs that decrease brain catecholamines.

## SLEEP-WAKE RHYTHM

Without external clues, the natural body clock follows a 25-hour cycle. The influence of external factors—such as the light-dark cycle, daily routines, meal periods, and other external synchronizers—entrain persons to the 24-hour clock.

Sleep is also influenced by biological rhythms. Within a 24-hour period, adults sleep once, sometimes twice. That rhythm is not present at birth but develops over the first two years of life.

In some women, sleep patterns change during the phases of the menstrual cycle. Naps taken at different times of the day differ greatly in their content of REM and NREM sleep. In a normal nighttime sleeper, a nap taken in the morning or at noon contains a great deal of REM sleep, whereas a nap taken in the afternoon or the early evening contains much less REM sleep. Apparently, a circadian cycle affects the tendency to have REM sleep.

Sleep patterns are not physiologically the same when one sleeps in the daytime or during the time when one's body is accustomed to being awake; the psychological and behavioral effects of sleep differ as well. In a world of industry and communications that often functions on a 24-hour-a-day basis, those interactions are becoming increasingly significant.

Even in persons who do not work at night, interference with the various rhythms can produce problems. The best-known example is jet lag, in which, after flying east to west, one tries to convince one's body to go to sleep at a time that is out of phase with some body cycles. Most bodies adapt within a few days, but some require more time. Conditions in those bodies apparently involve long-term cycle disruption and interference.

### References

Akerstedt T: Sleepiness as a consequence of shift work. Sleep *11*: 17, 1988.

Cespuglio R, Faradji H, Gomez M E, Jouvet M: Single unit recordings in the nuclei raphe dorsalis and magnus during the sleep waking cycle of semichronic prepared cats. Neurosci Lett *24*: 133, 1981.

Czeisler C A, Weitzman E D, Moore-Ede M C, Zimmerman J C, Knaner R S: Human sleep: Its duration and organization depend on its circadian phase. Science *210*: 1264, 1980.

Dement W, Kleitman N: Cyclic variations in EEG during sleep and their relation to eye movements, body motility, and dreaming. Electroencephalogr Clin Neurophysiol *9*: 673, 1975.

Hobson A J: Sleep and dreaming. J Neurosci *10*: 371, 1990.

Koella W P, editor: *Sleep 1982: Sixth European Congress of Sleep Research.* Karger, Basel, 1983.

McGuinty D J, Drucker-Colin R: Sleep mechanisms: Biology and control of REM sleep. Int Rev Neurobiol *23*: 391, 1982.

Monnier M, Gaillard J M: Biochemical regulation of sleep. Experientia *36*: 21, 1980.

Moore C A, Karacan I, Williams R L: Basic science of sleep. In *Comprehensive Textbook of Psychiatry*, ed 5, H I Kaplan, B J Sadock, editors, p 86. Williams & Wilkins, Baltimore, 1989.

O'Hara B F, Young K A, Watson F L, Heller H C, Kilduff T: Immediate early gene expression in brain during sleep deprivation. Sleep *16*: 1, 1993.

Orr W C, Robinson M G, Johnson L F: Acid clearing during sleep in the pathogenesis of reflux esophagitis. Dig Dis Sci *26*: 423, 1981.

Parmeggiani P: Integrative aspects of hypothalamic influences on respiratory brain stem mechanisms during wakefulness and sleep. In *Central Control Mechanisms in Breathing*, C von Euler, H Lagercrantz, editors, p 53. Pergamon, New York, 1979.

Rechtschaffen A, Kales A: *The Manual of Standardized Terminology, Techniques, and Scoring System for Sleep Stages of Human Subjects.* National Institutes of Health, Bethesda, 1968.

Shapiro C M, Flanigan M J: Function of sleep. Br Med J *306*: 383, 1993.

Waterhouse J: Circadian rhythms. Br Med J *306*: 448, 1993.

Wauquier A, Monti J M, Gaillard J M, Radulovacki M R: *Sleep Neurotransmitters and Neuromodulators.* Raven, New York, 1985.

Webb W B, editor: *Biological Rhythms, Sleep, and Performance.* Wiley, New York, 1982.

Williams R L, Karacan I, Hursch C J: *Electroencephalography (EEG) of Human Sleep: Clinical Applications.* Wiley, New York, 1974.

Zales M R, editor: *Eating, Sleeping, and Sexuality: Treatment of Disorders in Basic Life Functions.* Brunner/Mazel, New York, 1982.

# 23.2 / Sleep Disorders

About a third of all American adults experience some type of sleep disorder during their lifetimes. Insomnia is the most common and the most widely recognized sleep disorder, but there are many other kinds of sleep disorders. Careful diagnosis and specific treatment aimed at the cause are essential. Factors associated with the increased prevalence of sleep disorders include female sex, presence of mental and medical disorders, substance abuse, and ad-

vanced age. Table 23.2–1 lists the polysomnographic measures commonly used in diagnosing and describing sleep disorders.

## MAJOR SYMPTOMS

Four major symptoms characterize most sleep disorders: insomnia, hypersomnia, parasomnia, and sleep-wake schedule disturbance. The symptoms often overlap.

### Insomnia

Insomnia is difficulty in initiating or maintaining sleep. It is the most common sleep complaint. Insomnia may be transient or persistent. Common causes of insomnia are given in Table 23.2–2.

A brief period of insomnia is most often associated with anxiety, either as a sequela to an anxious experience or in anticipation of an anxiety-provoking experience (for example, an examination or an impending job interview). In some persons, transient insomnia of that kind may be related to grief, loss, or almost any life change. The condition is not likely to be serious, although a psychotic episode or a severe depression sometimes begins with an acute insomnia. Specific treatment for the condition is usually not required. When treatment with hypnotic medication is indicated, the physician and the patient should both be clear that the treatment is of short duration and that some symptoms, including a brief recurrence of the insomnia, may be expected when the medication is discontinued.

Persistent insomnia is a fairly common type. It consists of a group of conditions in which the problem is most often difficulty in falling asleep, rather than in remaining asleep, and involves two sometimes separable but often intertwined problems: (1) somatized tension and anxiety and (2) a conditioned associative response. The patients often have no clear complaint other than insomnia. They may not experience anxiety per se but discharge the anxiety through physiological channels. They may complain chiefly of apprehensive feelings or ruminative thoughts that appear to keep them from falling asleep. Sometimes but not

**Table 23.2–1**
**Common Polysomnographic Measures**

Sleep latency: Period of time from turning out the lights until the appearance of stage 2 sleep

Early morning awakening: Time of being continuously awake from the last stage of the sleep until the end of the sleep record (usually at 7 AM)

Sleep efficiency: Total sleep time/total time of the sleep record × 100

Apnea index: Number of apneas longer than 10 seconds per hour of sleep

Nocturnal myoclonus index: Number of periodic leg movements per hour

REM latency: Period of time from the onset of sleep until the first REM period of the night

Sleep-onset REM period: REM sleep within the first 10 minutes of sleep.

**Table 23.2–2**
**Common Causes of Insomnia**

| Symptom | Insomnias Secondary to Medical Conditions | Insomnias Secondary to Psychiatric or Environmental Conditions |
|---|---|---|
| Difficulty in falling asleep | Any painful or uncomfortable condition<br>CNS lesions<br>Conditions listed below, at times | Anxiety<br>Tension anxiety, muscular<br>Environmental changes<br>Circadian rhythm sleep disorder |
| Difficulty in remaining asleep | Sleep apnea syndromes<br>Nocturnal myoclonus and restless legs syndrome<br>Dietary factors (probably)<br>Episodic events (parasomnias)<br>Direct substance effects (including alcohol)<br>Substance withdrawal effects (including alcohol)<br>Substance interactions<br>Endocrine or metabolic diseases<br>Infectious, neoplastic, or other diseases<br>Painful or uncomfortable conditions<br>Brainstem or hypothalamic lesions or diseases<br>Aging | Depression, especially primary depression<br>Environmental changes<br>Circadian rhythm sleep disorder<br>Posttraumatic stress disorder<br>Schizophrenia |

Table by Ernest L. Hartmann, M.D.

always, a patient describes how the condition is exacerbated at times of stress at work or at home and remits during vacations.

## Hypersomnia

Hypersomnia manifests as excessive amounts of sleep and excessive daytime sleepiness (somnolence). In some situations both symptoms are present. The term "somnolence" should be reserved for patients who complain of sleepiness and have a clearly demonstrable tendency to fall asleep suddenly in the waking state, who have sleep attacks, and who cannot remain awake; it should not be used for persons who are simply physically tired or weary. The distinction, however, is not always clear. The complaints of hypersomnia are much less frequent than are the complaints of insomnia, but they are by no means rare if the clinician is alert to them. More than 100,000 narcoleptics are estimated to live in the United States. Narcolepsy is just one well-known condition clearly producing hypersomnia. If one includes substance-related conditions, hypersomnia is a common symptom.

Table 23.2–3 lists some common causes of hypersomnia. As with insomnia, hypersomnia is associated with border-

**Table 23.2–3**
**Common Causes of Hypersomnia**

| Symptom | Chiefly Medical | Chiefly Psychiatric or Environmental |
|---|---|---|
| Excessive sleep (hypersomnia) | Kleine-Levin syndrome<br>Menstrual-associated somnolence<br>Metabolic or toxic conditions<br>Encephalitic conditions<br>Alcohol and depressant medications<br>Withdrawal from stimulants | Depression (some)<br>Avoidance reactions |
| Excessive daytime sleepiness | Narcolepsy and narcolepsylike syndromes<br>Sleep apneas<br>Hypoventilation syndrome<br>Hyperthyroidism and other metabolic and toxic conditions<br>Alcohol and depressant medications<br>Withdrawal from stimulants<br>Sleep deprivation or insufficient sleep<br>Any condition producing serious insomnia | Depression (some)<br>Avoidance reactions<br>Circadian rhythm sleep disorder |

Table by Ernest Hartmann, M.D.

line conditions, situations that are hard to classify, and idiopathic cases.

According to a recent survey, the most common conditions responsible for hypersomnia severe enough to be evaluated by all-night recordings at a sleep disorders center were sleep apnea and narcolepsy. Individual sleep requirements vary. Many people are long sleepers and require 9 to 10 hours of sleep a night; but, like short sleepers, they do not have a sleep problem.

Transient and situational hypersomnia consists of a disruption of the normal sleep-wake pattern marked by excessive difficulty in remaining awake and a tendency to remain in bed for unusually long periods or to return to bed frequently during the day to nap. The pattern is experienced suddenly in response to an identifiable recent life change, conflict, or loss. It is much less common than insomnia. It is seldom marked by definite sleep attacks or unavoidable sleep but, rather, is marked by tiredness or falling asleep sooner than usual and by difficulty in arising in the morning.

## Parasomnia

Parasomnia is an unusual or undesirable phenomenon that appears suddenly during sleep or that occurs at the threshold between waking and sleeping. Parasomnia usually occurs in stages 3 and 4 and is thus associated with poor recall of the disturbance.

## Sleep-Wake Schedule Disturbance

Sleep-wake schedule disturbance involves the displacement of sleep from its desired circadian period. The common symptom is that patients cannot sleep when they wish to sleep, although they are able to sleep at other times. Correspondingly, they cannot be fully awake when they want to be fully awake, but they are able to be awake at other times. The disturbance does not produce precisely insomnia or somnolence. In practice the initial complaint is often either insomnia or somnolence only, and the above inabilities are elicited only on careful questioning.

Sleep-wake schedule disturbance can be considered a misalignment between sleep and wake behaviors. A sleep history questionnaire is helpful in diagnosing a patient's sleep disorder (Table 23.2 4).

## CLASSIFICATION

The fourth edition of *Diagnostic and Statistical Manual of Mental Disorders* (DSM-IV) classifies sleep disorders on the basis of clinical diagnostic criteria and presumed etiology. The three major categories of sleep disorders in DSM-IV are primary sleep disorders, sleep disorders related to another mental disorder, and other sleep disorders, most notably those due to a general medical condition or substance-induced. The disorders described in DSM-IV are only a fraction of the known sleep disorders; they provide a framework for a clinical assessment.

## PRIMARY SLEEP DISORDERS

The two main primary sleep disorders are dyssomnias and parasomnias. Dyssomnias are a heterogeneous group of sleep disorders that include primary insomnia, primary hypersomnia, narcolepsy, breathing-related sleep disorder, circadian rhythm sleep disorder (sleep-wake schedule disorder), and dyssomnia not otherwise specified (NOS). Parasomnias include nightmare disorder (dream anxiety disorder), sleep terror disorder, sleepwalking disorder, and parasomnia NOS.

### Dyssomnias

**Primary insomnia.** Primary insomnia is diagnosed when the chief complaint is difficulty in initiating or maintaining sleep or is nonrestorative sleep and the complaint continues for at least a month (Table 23.2–5). The term "primary" indicates that the insomnia occurs independently of any known physical or mental condition. Primary insomnia is often characterized by both difficulty falling asleep and repeated awakenings. Increased nighttime physiological or psychological arousal and negative conditioning for sleep are frequently evident. In general, patients with primary insomnia are preoccupied with getting enough sleep. The more the individual tries to sleep, the greater the sense of frustration and distress and the more difficult it becomes to sleep.

Treatment of primary insomnia is among the most difficult problems in sleep disorders. When the conditioned component is prominent, a deconditioning technique may be useful. The patients are asked to use the bed for sleeping and for nothing else; if they are not asleep after five minutes in bed, they are instructed to simply get up and do something else. Sometimes, changing to another bed or to another room is useful. When somatized tension or muscle tension is prominent, relaxation tapes, transcendental meditation, and practicing the relaxation response and biofeedback are occasionally helpful. Psychotherapy has not been very useful in the treatment of primary insomnia.

Primary insomnia is commonly treated with benzodiazepine hypnotics, chloral hydrate (Noctec), and other sedatives. Hypnotic drugs should be used with care. Various nonspecific measures—so called sleep hygiene—can be helpful in improving sleep (Table 23.2–6). Light therapy is also used.

REPEATED RAPID EYE MOVEMENT (REM) SLEEP INTERRUPTIONS. Repeated REM sleep interruptions are rare but are examples of a primary insomnia. Their cause is unknown. They have been related to psychological difficulties and periods of nightmares or other disturbing dreams. In those cases they may be a conditioned avoidance response in which the patient's central nervous system (CNS) senses the beginning of a dream period (REM period), associates it with an oncoming unpleasant dream or nightmare, and produces an immediate arousal response.

ATYPICAL POLYSOMNOGRAPHIC FEATURES. Another example of a primary insomnia, atypical polysomnographic fea-

**Table 23.2–4**
**Sleep History Questionnaire**

Patient name _____

Date _____

Please check the appropriate box or give short answers for the following:

|  | Yes | No |
|---|---|---|
| 1. Do you feel sleepy or have sleep attacks during the day? | ☐ | ☐ |
| 2. Do you nap during the day? | ☐ | ☐ |
| 3. Do you have trouble concentrating during the day? | ☐ | ☐ |
| 4. Do you have trouble falling asleep when you first go to bed? | ☐ | ☐ |
| 5. Do you awaken during the night? | ☐ | ☐ |
| 6. Do you awaken more than once? | ☐ | ☐ |
| 7. Do you awaken too early in the morning? | ☐ | ☐ |

8. How long have you had trouble sleeping?
What do you think precipitated the problem?

_____

_____

_____

9. How would you describe your usual night's sleep (hours of sleep, quality of sleep, etc.)?

_____

_____

|  | Yes | No |
|---|---|---|
| 10. Does your schedule for sleep and rising on the weekend differ from what it is during the week? | ☐ | ☐ |
| 11. Do others live at home who interrupt your sleep? | ☐ | ☐ |
| 12. Are you regularly awakened at night by pain or the need to use the bathroom? | ☐ | ☐ |
| 13. Does your job require shift changes or travel? | ☐ | ☐ |
| 14. Do you drink caffeinated beverages (coffee, tea, or soft drinks)? | ☐ | ☐ |

15. Apart from difficulty in sleeping, what, if any, other medical problems do you have?

_____

_____

16. What sleep medications, prescription or nonprescription, do you take? (Please include the dosage, how often you take it, and for how many months or years you have taken it.)

_____

_____

_____

17. What other prescription and over-the-counter medications do you regularly use? (Again, please include the dosage, the frequency, and the duration.)

_____

_____

_____

|  | Yes | No |
|---|---|---|
| 18. Have you ever suffered from depression, anxiety, or similar problems? | ☐ | ☐ |
| 19. Do you snore? | ☐ | ☐ |

**Questions for the sleep partner**

|  | Yes | No |
|---|---|---|
| 1. Does your sleep partner snore? | ☐ | ☐ |
| 2. Does your sleep partner seem to stop breathing repeatedly during the night? | ☐ | ☐ |
| 3. Does your sleep partner jerk his or her legs or kick you while he or she is sleeping? | ☐ | ☐ |
| 4. Have you ever experienced trouble sleeping? Please explain. | ☐ | ☐ |

_____

_____

### Table 23.2–5
### Diagnostic Criteria for Primary Insomnia

A. The predominant complaint is difficulty initiating or maintaining sleep, or nonrestorative sleep, for at least one month.

B. The sleep disturbance (or associated daytime fatigue) causes clinically significant distress or impairment in social, occupational, or other important areas of functioning.

C. The sleep disturbance does not occur exclusively during the course of narcolepsy, breathing-related sleep disorder, a circadian rhythm sleep disorder, or a parasomnia.

D. The disturbance does not occur exclusively during the course of another mental disorder (e.g., major depressive disorder, generalized anxiety disorder, a delirium).

E. The disturbance is not due to the direct physiological effects of a substance (e.g., a drug of abuse, a medication) or a general medical condition.

Table from DSM-IV, *Diagnostic and Statistical Manual of Mental Disorders*, ed 4. Copyright American Psychiatric Association, Washington, 1994. Used with permission.

### Table 23.2–6
### Nonspecific Measures to Induce Sleep (Sleep Hygiene)

1. Arise at the same time daily.
2. Limit daily in-bed time to the usual amount present before the sleep disturbance.
3. Discontinue CNS-acting drugs (caffeine, nicotine, alcohol, stimulants).
4. Avoid daytime naps (except when sleep chart shows they induce better night sleep).
5. Establish physical fitness by means of a graded program of vigorous exercise early in the day.
6. Avoid evening stimulation; substitute radio or relaxed reading for television.
7. Try very hot, 20-minute, body temperature-raising bath soaks near bedtime.
8. Eat at regular times daily; avoid large meals near bedtime.
9. Practice evening relaxation routines, such as progressive muscle relaxation or meditation.
10. Maintain comfortable sleeping conditions.

Table from Q R Regestein: Sleep disorders. In *Clinical Psychiatry for Medical Students*, A Stoudemire, editor, p 578. Lippincott, Philadelphia, 1990. Used with permission.

tures, is a condition in which sleep is frequently interrupted and nonrestorative and in which the sleep stage structure is marked by abnormal physiological features. Most commonly, the patient describes the quality of sleep as poor, light, or unrestful.

**Primary hypersomnia.** Primary hypersomnia is diagnosed when no other cause for excessive somnolence occurring for at least one month can be found. Some persons are long sleepers who, like short sleepers, show a normal variation. Their sleep, although long, is normal in architecture and physiology. Sleep efficiency and the sleep-wake schedule are normal. That pattern is without complaints about the quality of sleep, daytime sleepiness, or difficulties with the awake mood, motivation, and performance.

Long sleep may be a lifetime pattern, and it appears to have a familial incidence. Many persons are variable sleepers and may become long sleepers at certain times in their lives.

Some persons have subjective complaints of feeling sleepy without objective findings. They do not have a tendency to fall asleep more often than normal or have any objective signs. One should try to rule out clear-cut causes of excessive somnolence. According to DSM-IV, the disorder should be coded as recurrent if the patient has periods of excessive sleepiness lasting at least three days and occurring several times a year for at least two years (Table 23.2–7).

The treatment of primary hypersomnia consists mainly of stimulant drugs, such as amphetamines, given in the morning or the evening. Nonsedating antidepressant drugs, such as serotonin-specific reuptake inhibitors, may be of value in some cases.

**Narcolepsy.** Narcolepsy consists of excessive daytime sleepiness and abnormal manifestations of REM sleep occurring daily for at least three months (Table 23.2–8). The REM sleep includes hypnagogic and hypnopompic hallucinations, cataplexy, and sleep paralysis. The appearance of REM sleep within 10 minutes of sleep onset (sleep-onset REM periods) is also considered evidence of narcolepsy.

Narcolepsy is not as rare as was once thought. It is estimated to occur in 0.02 to 0.16 percent of adults and shows some familial incidence. Narcolepsy is neither a type of epilepsy nor a psychogenic disturbance. It is an abnormality of the sleep mechanisms—specifically, REM-inhibiting mechanisms—and it has been studied in dogs and humans.

The most common symptom is sleep attacks: the patient cannot avoid falling asleep. Often associated with the problem (close to 50 percent of long-standing cases) is cataplexy—a sudden loss of muscle tone, such as jaw drop, head drop, weakness of the knees, or paralysis of all skeletal muscles with collapse. The patient often remains awake during brief cataplectic episodes; the long episodes usually merge with sleep and show the electroencephalographic (EEG) signs of REM sleep.

### Table 23.2–7
### Diagnostic Criteria for Primary Hypersomnia

A. The predominant complaint is excessive sleepiness for at least 1 month (or less if recurrent) as evidenced by either prolonged sleep episodes or daytime sleep episodes that occur almost daily.

B. The excessive sleepiness causes clinically significant distress or impairment in social, occupational, or other important areas of functioning.

C. The excessive sleepiness is not better accounted for by insomnia and does not occur exclusively during the course of another sleep disorder (e.g., narcolepsy, breathing-related sleep disorder, circadian rhythm sleep disorder, or a parasomnia) and cannot be accounted for by an inadequate amount of sleep.

D. The disturbance does not occur exclusively during the course of another mental disorder.

E. The disturbance is not due to the direct physiological effects of a substance (e.g., a drug of abuse, a medication) or a general medical condition.

*Specify* if:
**Recurrent**: if there are periods of excessive sleepiness that last at least three days occurring several times a year for at least two years.

Table from DSM-IV, *Diagnostic and Statistical Manual of Mental Disorders*, ed 4. Copyright American Psychiatric Association, Washington, 1994. Used with permission.

## Table 23.2–8
**Diagnostic Criteria for Narcolepsy**

A. Irresistible attacks of refreshing sleep that occur daily over at least 3 months.

B. The presence of one or both of the following:

(1) Cataplexy (i.e., brief episodes of sudden bilateral loss of muscle tone, most often in association with intense emotion).

(2) Recurrent intrusions of elements of rapid eye movement (REM) sleep into the transition between sleep and wakefulness, as manifested by either hypnopompic or hypnagogic hallucinations or sleep paralysis at the beginning or end of sleep episodes.

C. The disturbance is not due to the direct physiological effects of a substance (e.g., a drug of abuse, a medication) or another general medical condition.

Other symptoms include hypnagogic or hypnopompic hallucinations: vivid perceptual experiences, either auditory or visual, occurring at sleep onset or on awakening. The patient is often momentarily frightened but within a minute or two returns to an entirely normal frame of mind and is aware that nothing was actually there.

Another uncommon symptom is sleep paralysis, most often occurring on awakening in the morning; during the episode the patient is apparently awake and conscious but unable to move a muscle. If the symptom persists for more than a few seconds, as it often does in narcolepsy, it can become extremely uncomfortable. (Isolated brief episodes of sleep paralysis occur in many nonnarcoleptic persons.) Narcoleptic patients report falling asleep quickly at night but often experience broken sleep.

Narcolepsy can occur at any age, but it most frequently begins in adolescence or young adulthood, in most instances before the age of 30. The disorder either progresses slowly or reaches a plateau that is maintained throughout life. Narcolepsy can be dangerous because it can lead to automobile and industrial accidents.

When the diagnosis is not clear clinically, a nighttime polysomnographic recording reveals a characteristic sleep-onset REM period. A test of daytime multiple sleep latency (several recorded naps at two-hour intervals) shows rapid sleep onset and usually one or more sleep-onset REM periods. A type of human leukocyte antigen called HLA-DR2 is found in more than 90 to 100 percent of narcoleptic patients and only 10 to 35 percent of unaffected persons.

Occasionally, a regimen of forced naps at a regular time of day helps, and in some cases the regimen can almost cure the patient without medication. When medication is required, stimulants—for example, amphetamine and methylphenidate (Ritalin)—are most useful, sometimes combined with antidepressants—for example, protriptyline (Vivactil)—when cataplexy is prominent.

Modafinil, an experimental $\alpha_1$ agonist, has been reported to reduce the number of sleep attacks and to improve psychomotor performance in narcolepsy, suggesting the involvement of noradrenergic mechanisms in the disorder.

**Breathing-related sleep disorder.** Breathing-related sleep disorder is characterized by sleep disruption leading to excessive sleepiness or insomnia that is due to a sleep-related breathing disturbance (Table 23.2–9). Breathing

## Table 23.2–9
**Diagnostic Criteria for Breathing-Related Sleep Disorder**

A. Sleep disruption, leading to excessive sleepiness or insomnia, that is judged to be due to a sleep-related condition (e.g., obstructive or central sleep apnea syndrome or central alveolar hypoventilation syndrome).

B. The disturbance is not better accounted for by another mental disorder and is not due to the direct physiological effects of a substance (e.g., a drug of abuse, a medication) or another general medical condition (other than a breathing-related disorder).

**Coding note:** Also code sleep-related breathing disorder on Axis III.

disturbances that may occur during sleep include apneas, hypopneas, and oxygen desaturations. Those disturbances invariably cause hypersomnia. Two disorders of the respiratory system that can produce hypersomnia are sleep apnea and central alveolar hypoventilation. Both disorders can also cause insomnia; however, hypersomnia is more common than insomnia.

OBSTRUCTIVE SLEEP APNEA SYNDROME. Many persons—elderly persons and obese persons, even those who do not have clinical symptoms—are likely to have apneic periods and, in general, more respiratory problems in sleep than when awake.

Sleep apnea refers to the cessation of air flow at the nose or the mouth. By convention an apneic period is one that lasts 10 seconds or more. Sleep apnea can be of several distinct types. In pure central sleep apnea, both air flow and respiratory effort (abdomen and chest) cease during the apneic episodes and begin again during arousals. In pure obstructive sleep apnea, air flow ceases, but respiratory effort increases during apneic periods, indicating an obstruction in the airway and increasing efforts by the abdominal and thoracic muscles to force air past the obstruction. Again, the episode ceases with an arousal. The mixed types involve elements of both obstructive and central sleep apnea.

Usually, sleep apnea is considered pathological if the patient has at least five apneic episodes an hour or 30 apneic episodes during the night. In severe cases of obstructive sleep apnea, the patients may have as many as 300 apneic episodes, each followed by an arousal, so that almost no normal sleep occurs, even though the patients have been in bed and often assume that they have been sleeping for the entire night.

Sleep apnea can be a dangerous condition. It is thought to account for a number of unexplained deaths and crib deaths of children and infants. It is probably also responsible for a large number of pulmonary and cardiovascular deaths in adults and in the elderly. Episodes of sleep apnea can produce cardiovascular changes, including arrhythmias, and transient alterations in blood pressure for each apneic episode. Long-standing sleep apnea is associated with an increase in pulmonary blood pressure and eventually an increase in systemic blood pressure as well. Those cardiovascular changes in sleep apnea may account for a considerable number of cases in which the diagnosis is essential hypertension.

The prevalence of sleep apnea in the population has not been established, but an increasing number of cases are discovered as growing awareness of its existence develops. In a recent survey of patients with daytime sleepiness whose disorder was serious enough for them to be evaluated polygraphically at a sleep disorders center, 42 percent were found to be suffering from one of the variants of sleep apnea.

A tentative diagnosis of sleep apnea can be made even without polysomnographic recordings. The most characteristic picture is that of middle-aged or elderly men who report tiredness and inability to stay awake in the daytime, sometimes associated with depression, mood changes, and daytime sleep attacks. They may or may not complain of anything unusual during sleep. If a history is obtained from a spouse or bed partner, it includes reports of loud, intermittent snoring, at times accompanied by gasping. Sometimes, observers recall apneic periods when patients appeared to be trying to breathe but were unable to do so. Such patients almost certainly have obstructive sleep apnea. With central or mixed apnea, the complaints are of repeated awakenings during the night, with no difficulty in falling asleep, associated with morning headaches and mood changes. At onset, the patients may have no complaints at all, although bed partners or roommates report heavy snoring and restless sleep. Obese patients with the disorder are said to have Pickwickian syndrome.

Patients suspected of having sleep apnea should undergo laboratory recordings. The usual all-night sleep recordings—including electroencephalogram (EEG), electromyogram (EMG), electrocardiogram (ECG), and respiratory tracings of various kinds—are useful. Recording air flow and respiratory effort is usually necessary to make a diagnosis. The severity of apneic episodes is determined by using oximetry to measure oxygen saturation during the night. Twenty-four-hour ECG monitoring is sometimes useful to monitor cardiac changes.

Nasal continuous positive airway pressure (nCPAP) is the treatment of choice for obstructive sleep apnea. Other procedures include weight loss, nasal surgery, tracheostomy, and uvulopalatoplasty. No medications are consistently effective in normalizing sleep in apneic patients. When sleep apnea is established or suspected, the patient must avoid the use of sedative medication, including alcohol, because it can considerably exacerbate the condition, which may then become life-threatening.

CENTRAL ALVEOLAR HYPOVENTILATION. Central alveolar hypoventilation consists of several conditions marked by impaired ventilation in which the respiratory abnormality appears or greatly worsens only during sleep and in which significant apneic episodes are not present. The ventilatory dysfunction is characterized by inadequate tidal volume or respiratory rate during sleep. Death may occur during sleep (Ondine's curse). Central alveolar hypoventilation is treated with some form of mechanical ventilation (for example, nasal ventilation).

**Circadian rhythm sleep disorder.** Circadian rhythm sleep disorder includes a wide range of conditions involving a misalignment between desired and actual sleep periods. DSM-IV lists four types of circadian rhythm sleep disorder:

(1) delayed sleep phase type, (2) jet lag type, (3) shift work type, and (4) unspecified (Table 23.2–10).

DELAYED SLEEP PHASE TYPE. Delayed sleep phase type of circadian rhythm sleep disorder is marked by sleep and wake times that are intractably later than desired, actual sleep times at virtually the same daily clock hour, no reported difficulty in maintaining sleep once begun, and an inability to advance the sleep phase by enforcing conventional sleep and wake times. The disorder often presents with the major complaint of difficulty in falling asleep at a desired conventional time and may appear to be similar to a sleep-onset insomnia. Daytime sleepiness often occurs secondary to sleep loss.

Delayed sleep phase type can be treated by gradually delaying the hour of sleep over a period of several days until the desired sleep time is achieved. The strategy works when advancing the sleep time does not work. The process of sleep phase adjustment can be assisted by the brief use of short-half-life hypnotic agents, such as triazolam (Halcion), to enforce sleep.

Another approach to treating delayed sleep phase type is the use of light therapy. Evening light therapy tends to delay sleep; regular morning light exposure tends to advance sleep.

JET LAG TYPE. Jet lag type usually disappears spontaneously in two to seven days, depending on the length of the east-to-west trip and individual sensitivity; no specific treatment is required. Some people find that they can prevent the symptoms by altering their mealtimes and sleep times in an appropriate direction before traveling. Others find that what appear to be symptoms of jet lag (tiredness

**Table 23.2–10**
**Diagnostic Criteria for Circadian Rhythm Sleep Disorder**

A. A persistent or recurrent pattern of sleep disruption leading to excessive sleepiness or insomnia that is due to mismatch between the sleep-wake schedule required by a person's environment and his or her circadian sleep-wake pattern.

B. The sleep disturbance causes clinically significant distress or impairment in social, occupational, or other important areas of functioning.

C. The disturbance does not occur exclusively during the course of another sleep disorder or other mental disorder.

D. The disturbance is not due to the direct effects of a substance (e.g., a drug of abuse, a medication) or a general medical condition.

*Specify* type:
   **Delayed sleep phase type:** a persistent pattern of late sleep onset and late awakening times, with an inability to fall asleep and awaken at a desired earlier time.
   **Jet lag type:** sleepiness and alertness that occur at an inappropriate time of day relative to local time, occurring after repeated travel across more than one time zone.
   **Shift work type:** insomnia during major sleep period or excessive sleepiness during major wake period associated with night-shift work or frequently changing shift work.
   **Unspecified type**

and so on) are actually associated with sleep deprivation and that simply obtaining enough sleep helps.

SHIFT WORK TYPE. Shift work type of circadian rhythm sleep disorder occurs in persons who repeatedly and rapidly change their work schedules and occasionally in persons with self-imposed chaotic sleep schedules. The most frequent symptom found is a period of mixed insomnia and somnolence; however, many other symptoms and somatic problems, including peptic ulcer, may be associated with the pattern after some time. Some adolescents and young adults appear to withstand changes of that kind remarkably well with few symptoms, but older persons and persons with sensitivity to change are clearly affected.

The symptoms are generally worst the first few days after shifting to a new schedule, but in some persons the disrupted sleep-wake patterns persist for a long time. Enforcement of new sleep hours and light therapy may help workers adjust to their new schedules. Many persons never adapt completely to unusual shift schedules because they maintain the altered pattern only five days a week, returning to the prevailing pattern of the rest of the population on days off and on vacations.

Shift work schedules are an important area that has not received sufficient study, since a large proportion of the population now work unusual shifts and sometimes in changing shift schedules. People's sensitivities to shifting schedules vary widely, and the bodies of a fair number of persons simply do not adapt to shift work; therefore, those persons should not be assigned to shift work. Temperamentally, some people are "owls," who like to stay up at night and sleep during the day, and others are "larks," who rise early and retire early.

A particular problem occurs in the training of physicians, who are often required to work 36 to 48 hours without sleeping. That condition is dangerous to doctors and their patients. It behooves medical educators to develop more shifts for doctors in training.

UNSPECIFIED

*Advanced sleep phase syndrome.* Advanced sleep phase syndrome is characterized by sleep onsets and wake times that are intractably earlier than desired, actual sleep times at virtually the same daily clock hour, no reported difficulty in maintaining sleep once begun, and an inability to delay the sleep phase by enforcing conventional sleep and wake times. Unlike delayed sleep phase type, the condition does not interfere with the work or school day. The major presenting complaint is the inability to stay awake in the evening and to sleep in the morning until desired conventional times.

*Disorganized sleep-wake pattern.* Disorganized sleep-wake pattern is defined as irregular and variable sleep and waking behavior that disrupts the regular sleep-wake pattern. The condition is associated with frequent daytime naps at irregular times and excessive bed rest. Sleep at night is not of adequate length, and the condition may present as insomnia, although the total amount of sleep in 24 hours is normal for the patient's age.

**Dyssomnia not otherwise specified.** According to DSM-IV, dyssomnia not otherwise specified includes insomnias, hypersomnias, and circadian rhythm disturbances that do not meet the criteria for any specific dyssomnia (Table 23.2–11).

**Table 23.2–11**
**Dyssomnia Not Otherwise Specified**

The dyssomnia not otherwise specified category is for insomnias, hypersomnias, or circadian rhythm disturbances that do not meet criteria for any specific dyssomnia. Examples include

1. Complaints of clinically significant insomnia or hypersomnia that are attributable to environmental factors (e.g., noise, light, frequent interruptions).

2. Excessive sleepiness that is attributable to ongoing sleep deprivation.

3. Idiopathic "restless legs syndrome": uncomfortable sensations (e.g., discomfort, crawling sensations, or restlessness) that lead to an intense urge to move the legs. Typically, the sensations begin in the evening before sleep onset and are temporarily relieved by moving the legs or walking, only to begin again when the legs are immobile. The sensations can delay sleep onset or awaken the individual from sleep.

4. Idiopathic periodic limb movements ("nocturnal myoclonus"): repeated low-amplitude brief limb jerks, particularly in the lower extremities. These movements begin near sleep onset and decrease during stage 3 or 4 non-rapid eye movement (NREM) and rapid eye movement (REM) sleep. Movements usually occur rhythmically every 20–60 seconds, leading to repeated, brief arousals. Individuals are typically unaware of the actual movements, but may complain of insomnia, frequent awakenings, or daytime sleepiness if the number of movements is very large.

5. Situations in which the clinician has concluded that a dyssomnia is present but is unable to determine whether it is primary, due to a general medical condition, or substance induced.

Table from DSM-IV, *Diagnostic and Statistical Manual of Mental Disorders*, ed 4. Copyright American Psychiatric Association, Washington, 1994. Used with permission.

NOCTURNAL MYOCLONUS. Nocturnal myoclonus consists of highly stereotyped abrupt contractions of certain leg muscles during sleep. Patients lack any subjective awareness of the leg jerks. The condition may be present in about 40 percent of people over age 65.

The repetitive leg movements occur every 20 to 60 seconds, with extension of the large toe and flexion of the ankle, the knee, and the hips. Frequent awakenings, unrefreshing sleep, and daytime sleepiness are major symptoms. No treatment for nocturnal myoclonus is universally effective. Treatments that may be useful include benzodiazepines, levodopa (Larodopa), and, in rare cases, opioids.

RESTLESS LEGS SYNDROME. In restless legs syndrome the person feels deep sensations of creeping inside the calves whenever sitting or lying down. The dysesthesias are rarely painful, but they are agonizingly relentless and cause an almost irresistible urge to move the legs, thus interfering with sleep. The syndrome is not limited to sleep but can interfere with falling asleep. It peaks in middle age and occurs in 5 percent of the population.

The syndrome has no established treatment. Symptoms of restless legs syndrome are relieved by movement and leg massage. When pharmacotherapy is required, the benzodiazepines, levodopa, opioids, propranolol (Inderal), and carbamazepine (Tegretol) are of some benefit.

KLEINE-LEVIN SYNDROME. Kleine-Levin syndrome is a relatively rare condition consisting of recurrent periods of prolonged sleep (from which the patient may be aroused) with intervening periods of normal sleep and alert waking. During the hypersomnic episodes, wakeful periods are usually marked by withdrawal from social contacts and a return to bed at the first opportunity; however, the patient may also display apathy, irritability, confusion, voracious eating, loss of sexual inhibitions, delusions, hallucinations, frank disorientation, memory impairment, incoherent speech, excitation or depression, and truculence. Unexplained fevers have occurred in a few patients.

Kleine-Levin syndrome is uncommon. Almost 100 cases with features suggesting the diagnosis have been reported. In most cases, several periods of hypersomnia, each lasting for one or several weeks, are experienced by the patient in a year. With few exceptions the first attack occurs between the ages of 10 and 21 years. Rare instances of onset in the fourth and fifth decades of life have been reported. The syndrome appears to be almost invariably self-limited, enduring remission occurring spontaneously before age 40 in early-onset cases.

MENSTRUAL-ASSOCIATED SYNDROME. Some women experience intermittent marked hypersomnia, altered behavioral patterns, and voracious eating at or shortly before the onset of their menses. Nonspecific EEG abnormalities similar to the ones associated with Kleine-Levin syndrome have been documented in several instances. Endocrine factors are probably involved, but specific abnormalities in laboratory endocrine measures have not been reported. Increased cerebrospinal fluid (CSF) turnover of 5-hydroxy-tryptamine (5-HT) was identified in one case.

INSUFFICIENT SLEEP. Insufficient sleep is defined as an earnest complaint of daytime sleepiness and associated waking symptoms by a person who persistently fails to obtain sufficient daily sleep needed to support alert wakefulness. The person is voluntarily, but often unwittingly, chronically sleep-deprived.

The diagnosis can usually be made on the basis of the history, including a sleep log. Some persons, especially students and shift workers, who want to maintain an active daytime life and perform their nighttime jobs may seriously deprive themselves of sleep, producing somnolence during waking hours.

SLEEP DRUNKENNESS. Sleep drunkenness is an abnormal form of awakening in which the lack of a clear sensorium in the transition from sleep to full wakefulness is prolonged and exaggerated. A confusion state develops that often leads to individual or social inconvenience and sometimes to criminal acts. Essential to the diagnosis is the absence of sleep deprivation. It is a rare condition, and there may be a familial tendency. Before making the diagnosis, the clinician should examine the patient's sleep and rule out such conditions as apnea, nocturnal myoclonus, narcolepsy, and an excessive use of alcohol and other substances.

## Parasomnias

**Nightmare disorder.** A nightmare is characterized by a long, frightening dream from which one awakens fright-

ened (Table 23.2–12). Like other dreams, nightmares almost always occur during REM sleep. They usually occur after a long REM period late in the night. Some persons have frequent nightmares as a lifelong condition; others experience them predominantly at times of stress and illness. About 50 percent of the adult population may report occasional nightmares.

Usually, no specific treatment is required for nightmare disorder. Agents that suppress REM sleep, such as tricyclic drugs, may reduce the frequency of nightmares. Benzodiazepines have also been used.

**Sleep terror disorder.** A sleep terror is an arousal in the first third of the night during deep non-REM (stages 3 and 4) sleep. It is almost invariably inaugurated by a piercing scream or cry and accompanied by behavioral manifestations of intense anxiety bordering on panic (Table 23.2–13).

Typically, patients sit up in bed with a frightened expression, scream loudly, and sometimes awaken immediately with a sense of intense terror. Sometimes patients remain awake in a disoriented state. More often, patients fall asleep, and, as with sleepwalking, they forget the episodes. Frequently, a night terror episode after the original scream develops into a sleepwalking episode. Polygraphic recordings of night terrors are somewhat like those of sleepwalking. In fact, the two conditions appear to be closely related. Night terrors, as isolated episodes, are especially frequent in children. About 1 to 6 percent of children have the disorder, which is more common in boys than in girls and which tends to run in families.

Night terrors may reflect a minor neurological abnormality, perhaps in the temporal lobe or underlying structures, because, when night terrors begin in adolescence and young adulthood, they turn out to be the first symptom of temporal lobe epilepsy. In a typical case of night terrors, however, no signs of temporal lobe epilepsy or other seizure disorders are seen either clinically or on EEG recordings.

### Table 23.2–12
### Diagnostic Criteria for Nightmare Disorder

A. Repeated awakenings from the major sleep period or naps with detailed recall of extended and extremely frightening dreams, usually involving threats to survival, security, or self-esteem. The awakenings generally occur during the second half of the sleep period.

B. On awakening from the frightening dream, the person rapidly becomes oriented and alert (in contrast to the confusion and disorientation seen in sleep terror disorder and some forms of epilepsy).

C. The dream experience, or the sleep disturbance resulting from the awakening, causes clinically significant distress or impairment in social, occupational, or other important areas of functioning.

D. The nightmares do not occur exclusively during the course of another mental disorder (e.g., a delirium, posttraumatic stress disorder) and are not due to the direct physiological effects of a substance (e.g., a drug of abuse, a medication) or a general medical condition.

Table from DSM-IV, *Diagnostic and Statistical Manual of Mental Disorders*, ed 4. Copyright American Psychiatric Association, Washington, 1994. Used with permission.

**Table 23.2–13**
**Diagnostic Criteria for Sleep Terror Disorder**

A. Recurrent episodes of abrupt awakening from sleep, usually occurring during the first third of the major sleep episode and beginning with a panicky scream.

B. Intense fear and signs of autonomic arousal, such as tachycardia, rapid breathing, and sweating, during each episode.

C. Relative unresponsiveness to efforts of others to comfort the person during the episode.

D. No detailed dream is recalled and there is amnesia for the episode.

E. The episodes cause clinically significant distress or impairment in social, occupational, or other important areas of functioning.

F. The disturbance is not due to the direct physiological effects of a substance (e.g., a drug of abuse, a medication) or a general medical condition.

Table from DSM-IV, *Diagnostic and Statistical Manual of Mental Disorders*, ed 4. Copyright American Psychiatric Association, Washington, 1994. Used with permission.

Night terrors are closely related to sleepwalking and are occasionally related to enuresis but are different from nightmares. Night terrors are associated with simply awakening in terror. The patient generally has no dream recall but occasionally recalls a single frightening image.

Specific treatment for night terror disorder is seldom required. Investigation of stressful family situations may be important, and individual or family therapy is sometimes useful. In the rare cases in which medication is required, diazepam (Valium) in small doses at bedtime improves the condition and sometimes completely eliminates the attacks.

**Sleepwalking disorder.** Sleepwalking, also known as somnambulism, consists of a sequence of complex behaviors that are initiated in the first third of the night during deep non-REM (stages 3 and 4) sleep and frequently, although not always, progress—without full consciousness or later memory of the episode—to leaving bed and walking about (Table 23.2–14).

The patient sits up and sometimes performs perseverative motor acts, such as walking, dressing, going to the bathroom, talking, screaming, and even driving. The behavior occasionally terminates in an awakening with several minutes of confusion; more frequently, the person returns to sleep and has no recollection of the sleepwalking event. An artificially induced arousal from stage 4 sleep can sometimes produce the condition. For instance, in children, especially children with a history of sleepwalking, an attack can sometimes be provoked by standing them on their feet and thus producing a partial arousal during stage 4 sleep.

Sleepwalking usually begins between ages 4 and 8. Peak prevalence is at about age 12 years. The disorder is more common in boys than in girls, and about 15 percent of children have an occasional episode. It tends to run in families. A minor neurological abnormality probably underlies the condition; the episodes should not be considered purely psychogenic, although stressful periods are associated with an increase in sleepwalking in affected per-

**Table 23.2–14**
**Diagnostic Criteria for Sleepwalking Disorder**

A. Repeated episodes of rising from bed during sleep and walking about, usually occurring during the first third of the major sleep episode.

B. While sleepwalking, the person has a blank, staring face, is relatively unresponsive to the efforts of others to communicate with him or her, and can be awakened only with great difficulty.

C. On awakening (either from the sleepwalking episode or the next morning), the person has amnesia for the episode.

D. Within several minutes after awakening from the sleepwalking episode, there is no impairment of mental activity or behavior (although there may initially be a short period of confusion or disorientation).

E. The sleepwalking causes clinically significant distress or impairment in social, occupational, or other important areas of functioning.

F. The disturbance is not due to the direct physiological effects of a substance (e.g., a drug of abuse, a medication), or a general medical condition.

Table from DSM-IV, *Diagnostic and Statistical Manual of Mental Disorders*, ed 4. Copyright American Psychiatric Association, Washington, 1994. Used with permission.

sons. Extreme tiredness or prior sleep deprivation exacerbates attacks. The disorder is occasionally dangerous because of the possibility of accidental injury.

Treatment consists of measures to prevent injury and of drugs that suppress stages 3 and 4 sleep.

**Parasomnia not otherwise specified.** The diagnostic criteria for parasomnia not otherwise specified are given in Table 23.2–15.

**Table 23.2–15**
**Diagnostic Criteria for Parasomnia Not Otherwise Specified**

The parasomnia not otherwise specified category is for disturbances that are characterized by abnormal behavioral or physiological events during sleep or sleep-wake transitions, but that do not meet criteria for a more specific parasomnia. Examples include

1. REM sleep behavior disorder: motor activity, often of a violent nature, that arises during rapid eye movement (REM) sleep. Unlike sleepwalking, these episodes tend to occur later in the night and are associated with vivid dream recall.

2. Sleep paralysis: an inability to perform voluntary movement during the transition between wakefulness and sleep. The episodes may occur at sleep onset (hypnagogic) or with awakening (hypnopompic). The episodes are usually associated with extreme anxiety and, in some cases, fear of impending death. Sleep paralysis occurs commonly as an ancillary symptom of narcolepsy and, in such cases, should not be coded separately.

3. Situations in which the clinician has concluded that a parasomnia is present but is unable to determine whether it is primary, due to a general medical condition, or substance induced.

Table from DSM-IV, *Diagnostic and Statistical Manual of Mental Disorders*, ed 4. Copyright American Psychiatric Association, Washington, 1994. Used with permission.

SLEEP-RELATED BRUXISM. Bruxism, tooth grinding, occurs throughout the night, most prominently in stage 2 sleep. According to dentists, 5 to 10 percent of the population suffer from bruxism severe enough to produce noticeable damage to teeth. The condition often goes unnoticed by the sleeper, except for an occasional feeling of jaw ache in the morning; however, bed partners and roommates are consistently awakened by the sound. Treatment consists of a dental bite plate and corrective orthodontic procedures.

REM SLEEP BEHAVIOR DISORDER. REM sleep behavior disorder is a chronic and progressive condition found mainly in men. It is characterized by the loss of atonia during REM sleep and subsequent emergence of violent and complex behaviors. In essence, patients with the disorder are acting out their dreams. Serious injury to the patient or the bed partner is a major risk. The development or the aggravation of the disorder has been reported in narcoleptic patients treated with psychostimulants and tricyclic drugs and in depressed and obsessive-compulsive disorder patients treated with fluoxetine (Prozac). REM sleep behavior disorder is treated with clonazepam (Klonopin), 0.5 to 2.0 mg a day. Carbamazapine, 100 mg three times a day, is also effective in controlling the disorder.

SLEEPTALKING (SOMNILOQUY). Sleeptalking is common in children and adults. It has been studied extensively in the sleep laboratory and is found to occur in all stages of sleep. The talking usually involves a few words that are difficult to distinguish. Long episodes of talking involve the sleeper's life and concerns, but sleeptalkers do not relate their dreams during sleep, nor do they often reveal deep secrets. Episodes of sleeptalking sometimes accompany night terrors and sleepwalking. Sleeptalking alone requires no treatment.

SLEEP-RELATED HEAD BANGING (JACTATIO CAPITIS NOCTURNA). Sleep-related head banging is the term for a sleep behavior consisting chiefly of rhythmic to-and-fro head rocking, less commonly of total body rocking, occurring just before or during sleep. Usually, it is observed in the immediate presleep period and is sustained into light sleep. It uncommonly persists into or occurs in deep non-REM sleep. Treatment consists of measures to prevent injury.

SLEEP PARALYSIS. Familial sleep paralysis is characterized by a sudden inability to execute voluntary movements either just at the onset of sleep or on awakening during the night or in the morning.

## SLEEP DISORDERS RELATED TO ANOTHER MENTAL DISORDER

### Insomnia Related to [Axis I or Axis II Disorder]

Insomnia that occurs for at least one month and that is clearly related to the psychological and behavioral symptoms of the clinically well-known mental disorders are classified here (Table 23.2–16). The category consists of a heterogeneous group of conditions. The sleep problem is usually but not always difficulty in falling asleep and is secondary to anxiety that is part of any of the various

**Table 23.2–16**
**Diagnostic Criteria for Insomnia Related to [Axis I or Axis II Disorder]**

A. The predominant complaint is difficulty initiating or maintaining sleep, or nonrestorative sleep, for at least one month that is associated with daytime fatigue or impaired daytime functioning.

B. The sleep disturbance (or daytime sequelae) causes clinically significant distress or impairment in social, occupational, or other important areas of functioning.

C. The insomnia is judged to be related to another Axis I or Axis II disorder (e.g., major depressive disorder, generalized anxiety disorder, adjustment disorder with anxiety) but is sufficiently severe to warrant independent clinical attention.

D. The disturbance is not better accounted for by another sleep disorder (e.g., narcolepsy, breathing-related sleep disorder, a parasomnia).

E. The disturbance is not due to the direct physiological effects of a substance (e.g., a drug of abuse, a medication) or a general medical condition.

Table from DSM-IV, *Diagnostic and Statistical Manual of Mental Disorders*, ed 4. Copyright American Psychiatric Association, Washington, 1994. Used with permission.

mental disorders listed. The insomnia is more common in females than in males. In clear-cut cases in which the anxiety has psychological roots, psychiatric treatment of the cause of the anxiety (for example, individual psychotherapy, group psychotherapy, or family therapy) often relieves the insomnia.

The insomnia associated with major depressive disorder involves relatively normal sleep onset but repeated awakenings during the second half of the night and premature morning awakening, usually with an uncomfortable mood in the morning. (Morning is the worst time of day for many patients with major depressive disorder.) Polysomnography shows reduced stages 3 and 4 sleep, often a short rapid eye movement (REM) latency, and a long first REM period. The use of partial or total sleep deprivation can accelerate the response to antidepressant medication.

Panic disorder may be associated with paroxysmal awakenings or entering stages 3 and 4 sleep. The emotional and cognitive symptoms of a panic attack are present, as well as tachycardia and increased respiratory rate.

Patients with manic episodes and bipolar II disorder appear to be extreme cases of short sleepers. They sometimes appear to have difficulty in falling asleep but most often do not complain of any sleep problem. They awaken refreshed after two to four hours of sleep and appear to have a true reduction in their need for sleep during the course of the manic or hypomanic episode.

In schizophrenia, total sleep time and slow wave sleep is reduced. REM sleep is often reduced early during an exacerbation.

### Hypersomnia Related to [Axis I or Axis II Disorder]

Hypersomnia that occurs for at least one month and that is associated with a mental disorder is found in a variety of conditions, including mood disorders. Excessive daytime sleepiness may be reported in the initial stages of many mild depressive disorders and characteristically in the depressed phase of bipolar I disorder. It is sometimes associated for a few weeks with uncomplicated grief. Other mental disorders—such as personality disorders, dissociative disorders, somatoform disorders, dissociative fugue, and amnestic disorders—can produce hypersomnia (Table 23.2–17). Treatment of the primary disorder should result in the resolution of the hypersomnia.

# OTHER SLEEP DISORDERS

## Sleep Disorder Due to a General Medical Condition

Any type of sleep disturbance (for example, insomnia, hypersomnia, parasomnia, or a combination) can be caused by a general medical condition (Table 23.2–18).

Almost any medical condition associated with pain and discomfort (for example, arthritis, angina) can produce insomnia. Some conditions are associated with insomnia even when pain and discomfort are not specifically present. Those conditions include neoplasms, vascular lesions, infections, and degenerative and traumatic conditions. Other conditions, especially endocrine and metabolic diseases, frequently involve some sleep disturbance.

Awareness of the possibility of such conditions and obtaining a good medical history usually lead to a correct diagnosis; the treatment, whenever possible, is treatment of the underlying medical condition.

**Sleep-related epileptic seizures.** The relation of sleep and epilepsy is complex. Almost every form of epilepsy either improves or becomes worse at various times in the sleep cycle. When seizures occur almost exclusively during sleep, the condition is called sleep epilepsy.

**Sleep-related cluster headaches and chronic paroxysmal hemicrania.** Sleep-related cluster headaches are agonizingly

**Table 23.2–17**
**Diagnostic Criteria for Hypersomnia Related to [Axis I or Axis II Disorder]**

A. The predominant complaint is excessive sleepiness for at least one month as evidenced by either prolonged sleep episodes or daytime sleep episodes that occur almost daily.

B. The excessive sleepiness causes clinically significant distress or impairment in social, occupational, or other important areas of functioning.

C. The hypersomnia is judged to be related to another Axis I or Axis II disorder (e.g., major depressive disorder, dysthymic disorder), but is sufficiently severe to warrant independent clinical attention.

D. The disturbance is not better accounted for by another sleep disorder (e.g., narcolepsy, breathing-related sleep disorder, a parasomnia) or by an inadequate amount of sleep.

E. The disturbance is not due to the direct physiological effects of a substance (e.g., a drug of abuse, a medication) or a general medical condition.

Table from DSM-IV, *Diagnostic and Statistical Manual of Mental Disorders*, ed 4. Copyright American Psychiatric Association, Washington, 1994. Used with permission.

**Table 23.2–18**
**Diagnostic Criteria for Sleep Disorder Due to a General Medical Condition**

A. A prominent disturbance in sleep that is sufficiently severe to warrant independent clinical attention.

B. There is evidence from the history, physical examination, or laboratory findings that the sleep disturbance is the direct physiological consequence of a general medical condition.

C. The disturbance is not better accounted for by another mental disorder (e.g., an adjustment disorder in which the stressor is a serious medical illness).

D. The disturbance does not occur exclusively during the course of a delirium.

E. The disturbance does not meet criteria for a breathing-related sleep disorder or narcolepsy.

F. The sleep disturbance causes clinically significant distress or impairment in social, occupational, or other important areas of functioning.

*Specify* type:
   **Insomnia type:** if the predominant sleep disturbance is insomnia
   **Hypersomnia type:** if the predominant sleep disturbance is hypersomnia
   **Parasomnia type:** if the prominent sleep disturbance is a parasomnia
   **Mixed type:** if more than one sleep disturbance is present and none predominates

**Coding note:** Include the name of the general medical condition on Axis I, e.g., sleep disorder due to chronic obstructive pulmonary disease, insomnia type; also code the general medical condition on Axis III.

Table from DSM-IV, *Diagnostic and Statistical Manual of Mental Disorders*, ed 4. Copyright American Psychiatric Association, Washington, 1994. Used with permission.

severe unilateral headaches that appear often during sleep and are marked by an on-off pattern of attacks. Chronic paroxysmal hemicrania is a similar unilateral headache that occurs every day with more frequent but short-lived onsets that are without a preponderant sleep distribution. Both types of vascular headache are examples of sleep-exacerbated conditions and appear in association with REM sleep periods, paroxysmal hemicrania being virtually REM sleep-locked.

**Sleep-related abnormal swallowing syndrome.** Abnormal swallowing syndrome is a condition during sleep in which inadequate swallowing results in aspiration of saliva, coughing, and choking. It is intermittently associated with brief arousals or awakenings.

**Sleep-related asthma.** Asthma is exacerbated by sleep in some persons and may result in significant sleep disturbances.

**Sleep-related cardiovascular symptoms.** Sleep-related cardiovascular symptoms derive from disorders of cardiac rhythm, myocardial incompetence, coronary artery insufficiency, and blood pressure variability, which may be induced or exacerbated by sleep-altered or sleep-stage-modified cardiovascular physiology.

**Sleep-related gastroesophageal reflux.** Sleep-related gastroesophageal reflux is a disorder in which the patient awakens from sleep with burning, substernal pain or a feeling of general pain or tightness in the chest or a sour taste in the mouth. Coughing, choking, and vague respiratory discomfort may also occur repeatedly.

**Sleep-related hemolysis (paroxysmal nocturnal hemo-**

**globinuria).** Paroxysmal nocturnal hemoglobinuria is a rare, acquired, chronic hemolytic anemia in which intravascular hemolysis results in hemoglobinemia and hemoglobinuria. The hemolysis and consequent hemoglobinuria are accelerated during sleep, coloring the morning urine a brownish red. Hemolysis is linked to the sleep period, even if the period is shifted.

## Substance-Induced Sleep Disorder

Any type of sleep disturbance (for example, insomnia, hypersomnia, parasomnia, or a combination) can be caused by a substance (Table 23.2–19). According to DSM-IV, the clinician should also specify if the onset of the disorder occurred during intoxication or withdrawal.

Somnolence related to tolerance or withdrawal from a central nervous system (CNS) stimulant is common in persons withdrawing from amphetamines, cocaine, caffeine, and related substances. The somnolence may be associated with severe depression, which occasionally reaches suicidal proportions.

The sustained use of CNS depressants, such as alcohol, can cause somnolence. Heavy alcohol use in the evening produces sleepiness and difficulty in arising the next day. That reaction may present a diagnostic problem if the patient does not admit to alcohol abuse.

Insomnia is associated with tolerance to or withdrawal from sedative-hypnotic drugs, such as benzodiazepines, barbiturates, and chloral hydrate. With the sustained use of such agents—usually undertaken to treat insomnia arising from a different source—tolerance increases, and the drugs lose their sleep-inducing effects; then patients often increase the dosage. On sudden discontinuation of the drug, severe sleeplessness supervenes, often accompanied by the general features of substance withdrawal. Typically the patient experiences a temporary increase in the severity of the insomnia.

Long-term use (more than 30 days) of a hypnotic agent is well tolerated by some patients, but other patients begin to complain of sleep disturbance, most often multiple brief awakenings during the night. Recordings show a disruption of sleep architecture, reduced stages 3 and 4 sleep, increases of stages 1 and 2 sleep, and a fragmentation of sleep throughout the night.

The clinician should be aware of CNS stimulants as a possible cause of insomnia and should remember that various medications for weight reduction, beverages containing caffeine, and occasionally adrenergic drugs taken by asthmatic patients may all produce that sort of insomnia. Alcohol may help induce sleep but frequently results in nocturnal awakening. Alcohol use during the cocktail hour can produce difficulty in falling asleep later in the evening.

For reasons that are not always clear, a wide variety of drugs occasionally produce sleep problems as a side effect. Those drugs include antimetabolites and other cancer chemotherapeutic agents, thyroid preparations, anticonvulsant agents, antidepressant drugs, adrenocorticotropic hormone (ACTH)-like drugs, oral contraceptives, α-methyldopa, and β-blocking drugs.

Another group of agents do not produce sleep disturbance while they are being used but may have that effect after withdrawal. Almost any drug with sedating or tran-

**Table 23.2–19**
**Diagnostic Criteria for Substance-Induced Sleep Disorder**

A. A prominent disturbance in sleep which is sufficiently severe to warrant independent clinical attention.

B. There is evidence from the history, physical examination, or laboratory findings of either (1) or (2):

   (1) the symptoms in criterion A developing during, or within a month of, substance intoxication or withdrawal
   (2) medication use is etiologically related to the sleep disturbance

C. The disturbance is not better accounted for by a sleep disorder that is not substance induced. Evidence that the symptoms are better accounted for by a sleep disorder that is not substance induced might include the following: the symptoms precede the onset of the substance abuse (or medication use); the symptoms persist for a substantial period of time (e.g., about a month) after the cessation of acute withdrawal or severe intoxication, or are substantially in excess of what would be expected given the type or amount of the substance used or the duration of use; or there is other evidence that suggests the existence of an independent non-substance-induced sleep disorder (e.g., a history of recurrent non-substance-related episodes).

D. The disturbance does not occur exclusively during the course of a delirium.

E. The sleep disturbance causes clinically significant distress or impairment in social, occupational, or other important areas of functioning.

**Note:** This diagnosis should be made instead of a diagnosis of substance intoxication or substance withdrawal only when the sleep symptoms are in excess of those usually associated with the intoxication or withdrawal syndrome and when the symptoms are sufficiently severe to warrant independent clinical attention.

*Code:* [Specific substance]-induced sleep disorder (alcohol; amphetamine; caffeine; cocaine; opioid; sedative, hypnotic, or anxiolytic; other [or unknown] substance)

*Specify* type:
   **Insomnia type:** if the predominant sleep disturbance is insomnia
   **Hypersomnia type:** if the predominant sleep disturbance is hypersomnia
   **Parasomnia type:** if the prominent sleep disturbance is a parasomnia
   **Mixed type:** if more than one sleep disturbance is present and none predominates

*Specify* if:
   **with onset during intoxication:** if the criteria are met for intoxication with the substance and the symptoms develop during the intoxication syndrome
   **with onset during withdrawal:** if criteria are met for withdrawal from the substance and the symptoms develop during, or shortly after, a withdrawal syndrome

Table from DSM-IV, *Diagnostic and Statistical Manual of Mental Disorders*, ed 4. Copyright American Psychiatric Association, Washington, 1994. Used with permission.

quilizing agents can have that effect, including at times the benzodiazepines, the phenothiazines, the sedating tricyclic drugs, and various street drugs, including marijuana, opiates, and opioids.

Alcohol is a CNS depressant and produces the serious problems of other CNS depressants, both during administration—perhaps related to the development of tolerance—and after withdrawal. The insomnia after long-term alcohol consumption is sometimes severe and lasts for weeks or longer. The clinician should not give a potentially addicting medication to a patient who has just recovered from an addiction; sleeping medications, if possible, should be avoided.

Among cigarette smokers, the combination of a relaxing ritual and the tendency of low doses of nicotine to cause sedation may actually help sleep. However, high doses of nicotine can interfere with sleep, particularly sleep onset. The typical cigarette smoker sleeps less than a nonsmoker. Nicotine withdrawal may cause drowsiness or arousal.

## References

Bamford C R: Carbamazepine in REM sleep behavior disorder. Sleep *16*: 33, 1992.

Boivin D B, Montplaisir J, Petit D, Lambert C, Lubin S: Effects of modafinil on symptomatology of human narcolepsy. Clin Neuropharmacol *16*: 46, 1993.

Coleman R M, Pollak C P, Weitzman E D: Periodic movements in sleep (nocturnal myoclonus): A case series analysis. Ann Neurol *4*: 416, 1980.

Czeisler C A, Allan J S, Strogatz S H, Ronda J M, Sanchez R, Rios C, Frietag W O, Richardson G S, Kronauer R E: Bright light resets the human circadian pacemaker independent of the timing of the sleep-wake cycle. Science *233*: 667, 1986.

Guilleminault C, editor: *Sleeping and Waking Disorders: Indications and Techniques*. Addison-Wesley, Menlo Park, Calif, 1982.

Guilleminault C, Lugaresi E, editors: *Sleep-Wake Disorders: Natural History, Epidemiology, and Long-Term Evolution*. Raven, New York, 1983.

Karacan I, editor: *Psychophysiological Aspects of Sleep*. Noyes Medical, Park Ridge, N J, 1981.

Karacan I, Williams R L, Moore C A: Sleep disorders. In *Comprehensive Textbook of Psychiatry*, ed 5, H I Kaplan, B J Sadock, editors, p 1105. Williams & Wilkins, Baltimore, 1989.

Kryger M H, Roth T, Dement W C, editors: *Principles and Practice of Sleep Medicine*, ed 2. Saunders, Philadelphia, 1993.

Moran M G, Thompson T L, Nies A S: Sleep disorders in the elderly. Am J Psychiatry *145*: 1369, 1988.

Papadimitriou G N, Christodoulou G N, Katsouyanni K, Stefanis C N: Therapy and prevention of affective illness by total sleep deprivation. J Affect Disord *27*: 107, 1993.

Roffwarg H, Erman M: Evaluation and diagnosis of the sleep disorders: Implications for psychiatry and other clinical specialties. In *Annual Review*, vol 4, R E Hales, A J Frances, editors, p 294. American Psychiatric Association, Washington, 1985.

Schramm E, Hohagen F, Grasshoff U, Riemann D, Hajak G, Weeb H-G, Berger M: Test-retest reliability and validity of the structured interview for sleep disorders according to DSM-III-R. Am J Psychiatry *150*: 867, 1993.

Stradling J R: Recreational drugs and sleep. Br J Med *306*: 573, 1993.

Tyrer P: Withdrawal from hypnotic drugs. Br J Med *306*: 706, 1993.

Williams R L, Karacan I, Moore C, editors: *Sleep Disorders: Diagnosis and Treatment*, ed 2. Wiley, New York, 1988.

Zales M R, editor: *Eating, Sleeping, and Sexuality: Treatment of Disorders of Basic Life Functions*. Brunner/Mazel, New York, 1982.

# Impulse-Control Disorders
# Not Elsewhere Classified

Six categories of impulse-control disorders not elsewhere classified are listed in the fourth edition of *Diagnostic and Statistical Manual of Mental Disorders* (DSM-IV): intermittent explosive disorder, kleptomania, pyromania, pathological gambling, trichotillomania, and impulse-control disorder not otherwise specified.

Patients with disorders of impulse control share the following features: (1) They fail to resist an impulse, drive, or temptation to perform some action that is harmful to themselves or others. They may or may not consciously resist the impulse and may or may not plan the act. (2) Before committing the act, they feel an increasing sense of tension or arousal. (3) While committing the act, they feel pleasure, gratification, or release. The act is ego-syntonic in that it is consonant with the patients' immediate conscious wishes. Immediately after the act, the patients may or may not feel genuine regret, self-reproach, or guilt.

## ETIOLOGY

The causes of impulse disorders are unknown, but psychodynamic, biological, and psychosocial factors seem to interact to cause the disorders. The disorders may have common underlying neurobiological mechanisms.

### Psychodynamic Factors

An *impulse* is a disposition to act in order to decrease the heightened tension caused by the buildup of instinctual drives or by diminished ego defenses against the drives. The impulse disorders have in common an attempt to bypass the experience of disabling symptoms or painful affects by attempting to act on the environment. In his work with delinquent adolescents, August Aichhorn understood impulsive behavior as related to a weak superego and weak ego structures associated with psychic trauma from childhood deprivation.

Otto Fenichel linked impulsive behavior to attempts to master anxiety, guilt, depression, and other painful affects by means of action. He thought that such actions defend against internal danger and that they produce a distorted aggressive or sexual gratification. To an outside observer, impulsive behaviors may appear to be greedy and inquisitive, but they may actually be closely related to relief from pain.

Heinz Kohut understood many forms of impulse control problems—including gambling, kleptomania, and some paraphiliac behaviors—to be related to an incomplete sense of self. He observed that, when patients do not receive the validating and affirming responses that they seek from significant relationships in their lives, the self may fragment. As a way of dealing with that fragmentation and of regaining a sense of wholeness or cohesion in the self, those patients may engage in impulsive behaviors that appear to others to be self-destructive. Kohut's formulation has some similarities to Donald Winnicott's view that impulsive or deviant behavior is a way that a child hopes to recapture a primitive maternal relationship. Winnicott saw such behavior as hopeful in that the child is still searching for affirmation and love from the mother, rather than giving up on ever getting it. Several therapists have stressed the patients' fixation at the oral stage of development. The patients attempt to master anxiety, guilt, depression, and other painful affects by means of action, but such actions aimed at obtaining relief seldom succeed even temporarily.

### Biological Factors

Many investigators have focused on a possible organic involvement in the impulse-control disorders, especially for those patients with overtly violent behavior. Experiments have shown that specific brain regions, such as the limbic system, are associated with impulsive and violent activity and that other brain regions are associated with the inhibition of such behaviors. Certain hormones, especially testosterone, have been associated with violent and aggressive behavior. Some reports have described a relation between temporal lobe epilepsy and certain impulsive violent behaviors, an association of aggressive behavior in patients with histories of head trauma, increased numbers of emergency room visits, and other potential organic antecedents. A high incidence of mixed cerebral dominance may be found in some violent populations.

Impulse-control disorder symptoms may continue into adulthood in persons who are classified as suffering from childhood attention-deficit/hyperactivity disorder. Lifelong or acquired mental deficiency, epilepsy, and even reversible brain syndromes have long been implicated in lapses of impulse control.

Considerable evidence indicates that the serotonin neurotransmitter system mediates symptoms evident in impulse-control disorders. A relation has been found between cerebrospinal fluid (CSF) levels of 5-hydroxyindoleacetic acid (5-HIAA) and impulsive aggression. Brainstem and CSF levels of 5-HIAA are decreased, and 5-hydroxytryptamine

(5-HT) binding sites are increased in suicide victims. Involvement of the dopaminergic and noradrenergic systems has also been implicated in impulsivity.

In some disorders of impulse control, the ego defenses are overwhelmed without actual nervous system pathology. Fatigue, incessant stimulation, and psychic trauma can lower resistance and temporarily suspend the ego's control.

## Psychosocial Factors

Some workers have stressed the disorder's psychosocial aspects, such as early life events, as being important. Improper models for identification and parental figures who themselves have difficulty in controlling impulses have also been implicated. In addition, such parental factors as violence in the home, alcohol abuse, promiscuity, and antisocial tendencies have been thought to be significant.

## INTERMITTENT EXPLOSIVE DISORDER

Intermittent explosive disorder is found in persons who have discrete episodes of losing control of aggressive impulses, resulting in serious assault or the destruction of property. The degree of aggressiveness expressed is grossly out of proportion to any stressors that may have helped elicit the episodes. The symptoms, which the patient may describe as spells or attacks, appear within minutes or hours and, regardless of duration, remit spontaneously and quickly. Each episode is usually followed by genuine regret or self-reproach. Signs of generalized impulsivity or aggressiveness are absent between episodes. The diagnosis of intermittent explosive disorder should not be made if the loss of control can be accounted for by schizophrenia, antisocial or borderline personality disorder, attention-deficit/hyperactivity disorder, conduct disorder, or substance intoxication.

The term "epileptoid personality" has been used to convey the seizurelike quality of the characteristic outbursts, which are not typical of the patient, and to convey the suspicion of an organic disease process. A number of associated features suggest the possibility of an epileptoid state: the patient may experience an aura; postictallike changes in the sensorium, including partial or spotty amnesia; or hypersensitivity to photic, aural, or auditory stimuli. Persons with the disorder have a high incidence of hyperactivity, soft neurological signs, nonspecific electroencephalogram (EEG) findings, and accident-proneness.

## Epidemiology

Intermittent explosive disorder is underreported. It appears to be more common in men than in women. The men are likely to be found in a correctional institution and the women in a psychiatric facility. In one study about 2 percent of all admissions to a university hospital psychiatric service were given diagnoses of intermittent explosive disorder; 80 percent were men.

Evidence indicates that intermittent explosive disorder is more common in first-degree biological relatives of persons with the disorder than in the general population. A variety of factors, other than a simple genetic explanation, may be responsible.

## Etiology

Some investigators suggest that disordered brain physiology, particularly in the limbic system, is involved in most cases of episodic violence. However, an unfavorable environment in childhood is generally believed to be the major determinant. Predisposing factors in childhood are thought to include perinatal trauma, infantile seizures, head trauma, encephalitis, minimal brain dysfunction, and hyperactivity. The patients' childhood environments are often filled with alcohol dependence, beatings, threats to life, and promiscuity.

Those workers who have concentrated on psychogenesis in the cause of episodic explosiveness have stressed identification with assaultive parental figures or the symbolism of the target of the violence. Early frustration, oppression, and hostility have been noted as predisposing factors. Situations that are directly or symbolically reminiscent of those early deprivations (for example, persons who directly or indirectly evoke the image of the frustrating parent) become targets for destructive hostility.

Typical patients have been described as physically large but dependent men whose sense of masculine identity is poor. A sense of being useless and impotent or of being unable to change the environment often precedes the episode of physical violence.

Compelling evidence indicates that serotonergic neurons mediate behavioral inhibition. Decreases in serotonergic transmission—as can be induced by inhibiting serotonin synthesis or antagonizing its effects—result in the decrease of the effect of punishment as a deterrent to behavior. The restoration of serotonin activity—by administering serotonin precursors, such as tryptophan, or drugs that increase synaptic serotonin levels—restores the behavioral effect of punishment. Low levels of CSF 5-HIAA have been correlated with impulsive aggression.

## Diagnosis and Clinical Features

The diagnosis of intermittent explosive disorder should be the result of history taking that reveals several episodes of loss of control associated with aggressive outbursts (Table 24–1). A single discrete episode does not justify the diagnosis. The history is typically of a childhood in the midst of alcohol dependence, violence, and emotional instability. The patients' work histories are poor. The patients report job losses, marital difficulties, and trouble with the law. Most have sought psychiatric help in the past but to no avail. A high level of anxiety, guilt, and depression is usually present after an episode. Neurological examination sometimes reveals soft neurological signs, such as left-right ambivalence and perceptual reversal. EEG findings are frequently normal or show nonspecific changes. Psychological tests for organicity frequently result in normal findings.

**Table 24–1**
**Diagnostic Criteria for Intermittent Explosive Disorder**

A. Several discrete episodes of failure to resist aggressive impulses that result in serious assaultive acts or destruction of property.

B. The degree of aggressiveness expressed during the episodes is grossly out of proportion to any precipitating psychosocial stressors.

C. The aggressive episodes are not better accounted for by another mental disorder (e.g., antisocial personality disorder, borderline personality disorder, a psychotic disorder, a manic episode, conduct disorder, or attention-deficit/hyperactivity disorder) and are not due to the direct physiological effects of a substance (e.g., a drug of abuse, a medication), or a general medical condition (e.g., head trauma, Alzheimer's disease).

Table from DSM-IV, *Diagnostic and Statistical Manual of Mental Disorders*, ed 4. Copyright American Psychiatric Association, Washington, 1994. Used with permission.

### Differential Diagnosis

The diagnosis of intermittent explosive disorder can be made only after disorders associated with the occasional loss of control of aggressive impulses have been ruled out. Those other disorders include psychotic disorders, personality change due to a general medical condition, antisocial or borderline personality disorder, conduct disorder, and intoxication with a psychoactive substance.

One can differentiate intermittent explosive disorder from the antisocial and borderline personality disorders because, in the personality disorders, aggressiveness and impulsivity are part of the patient's character and are present between outbursts. In paranoid and catatonic schizophrenia, the patient may display violent behavior in response to delusions and hallucinations, and the patient has a gross impairment in reality testing. Hostile manic patients may be impulsively aggressive, but the underlying diagnosis is generally clear from their mental status examinations and clinical presentations. Epilepsy, brain tumors, degenerative diseases, and endocrine disorders must be considered and ruled out, as must acute intoxications with such substances as alcohol, barbiturates, hallucinogens, and amphetamines. Conduct disorder is ruled out by its repetitive and resistant pattern of behavior, as opposed to an episodic pattern.

### Course and Prognosis

Intermittent explosive disorder may begin at any stage of life but usually begins in the second or third decade. In most cases the disorder decreases in severity with the onset of middle age. Heightened organic impairment, however, can lead to frequent and severe episodes.

### Treatment

A combined pharmacological and psychotherapeutic approach has the best chance of success. Psychotherapy with the patients is difficult, dangerous, and often unrewarding, as the therapist may have difficulties with countertransference and limit setting. Group psychotherapy may be of some help, as may family therapy, particularly when the explosive patient is an adolescent or a young adult.

Anticonvulsants have long been used in treating explosive patients, with mixed results. Phenothiazines and antidepressants have been effective in some cases, but then one must wonder whether schizophrenia or a mood disorder is the true diagnosis. When there is a likelihood of subcortical seizurelike activity, those medications can aggravate the situation. Benzodiazepines have been reported to produce a paradoxical reaction of dyscontrol in some cases. Lithium (Eskalith) has been reported to be useful in generally lessening aggressive behavior, and carbamazepine (Tegretol) and phenytoin (Dilantin) have also been reported to be helpful. Propranolol (Inderal), buspirone (BuSpar), and trazodone (Desyrel) have also been effective in some cases. Increasing reports indicate that fluoxetine (Prozac) and other serotonin-specific reuptake inhibitors are useful in reducing impulsivity and aggression.

Some neurosurgeons have performed operative treatments for intractable violence and aggression. No evidence indicates that such treatment is effective.

## KLEPTOMANIA

The essential feature of kleptomania is a recurrent failure to resist impulses to steal objects not needed for personal use or their monetary value. The objects taken are often given away, returned surreptitiously, or kept and hidden.

Persons with kleptomania usually have the money to pay for the objects they impulsively steal. Like other impulse control disorders, kleptomania is characterized by mounting tension before the act, followed by gratification and less tension with or without guilt, remorse, or depression during the act. The stealing is not planned and does not involve others. Although the thefts do not occur when immediate arrest is probable, kleptomaniac persons do not always consider the chances of their apprehension, even though repeated arrests lead to pain and humiliation. Kleptomaniac persons may feel guilt and anxiety after the theft, but they do not feel anger or vengeance. Furthermore, when the object stolen is the goal, the diagnosis is not kleptomania, for in kleptomania the act of stealing is itself the goal.

### Epidemiology

The prevalence of kleptomania is not known. The estimated rate of kleptomania ranges from 3.8 to 24 percent of those arrested for shoplifting. The sex ratio is unknown, but kleptomania appears to be more common among females than among males. DSM-IV reports it occurring in fewer than 5 percent of identified shoplifters.

### Etiology

**Psychodynamic factors.** Some psychoanalytic writers have stressed the expression of the aggressive impulses in kleptomania; others have discerned a libidinal aspect.

Those who focus on symbolism see meaning in the act itself, the object stolen, and the victim of the theft.

Kleptomania is often associated with other disturbances, such as mood disorders, obsessive-compulsive disorder, and eating disorders. Kleptomania frequently occurs as part of bulimia nervosa. In some reports, nearly a quarter of the patients with bulimia nervosa meet the diagnostic criteria for kleptomania.

The symptoms of kleptomania tend to appear in times of significant stress—for example, losses, separations, and the ending of important relationships.

Analytic writers have focused on stealing by children and adolescents. Anna Freud pointed out that the first thefts from the mother's purse indicate the degree to which all stealing is rooted in the initial oneness between mother and child. Karl Abraham wrote of the central feeling of being neglected, injured, or unwanted. One theoretician established seven categories of stealing in chronically acting-out children: (1) as a means of restoring the lost mother-child relationship, (20 as an aggressive act, (3) as a defense against fears of being damaged (perhaps a search by females for a penis or a protection against castration anxiety in males), (4) as a means of seeking punishment, (5) as a means of restoring or adding to self-esteem, (6) in connection with and as a reaction to a family secret, and (7) as excitement (*lust Angst*) and a substitute for a sexual act. One or more of those categories can also apply to adult kleptomania.

**Biological factors.** Brain diseases and mental retardation have been associated with kleptomania, as they have with other disorders of impulse control. Focal neurological signs, cortical atrophy, and enlarged lateral ventricles have been found in some patients. Disturbances in monoamine metabolism, particularly of serotonin, have been postulated.

## Diagnosis and Clinical Features

The essential feature of kleptomania consists of recurrent, intrusive, and irresistible urges or impulses to steal unneeded objects (Table 24–2). Kleptomaniac patients may also be distressed about the possibility or the actuality of their being apprehended and so manifest signs of depression and anxiety. Patients feel guilty, ashamed, and embarrassed about their behavior. They often have serious problems with interpersonal relationships and often, but not invariably, show signs of personality disturbance. In one study of kleptomaniac patients, the frequency of stealing ranged from less than one to 120 episodes a month.

Most kleptomaniac patients steal from retail stores, but they may steal from family members in their own households.

## Differential Diagnosis

Because most kleptomaniac patients are referred for examination in connection with legal proceedings after apprehension, the clinical picture may be clouded by subsequent symptoms of depression and anxiety. The major differentiation is between kleptomania and other forms of stealing. For a diagnosis of kleptomania, the stealing must

**Table 24–2**
**Diagnostic Criteria for Kleptomania**

A. Recurrent failure to resist impulses to steal objects that are not needed for personal use or for their monetary value.

B. Increasing sense of tension immediately before committing the theft.

C. Pleasure, gratification, or relief at the same time of committing the theft.

D. The stealing is not committed to express anger or vengeance, and is not in response to a delusion or a hallucination.

E. The stealing is not better accounted for by conduct disorder, a manic episode, or antisocial personality disorder.

Table from DSM-IV, *Diagnostic and Statistical Manual of Mental Disorders*, ed 4. Copyright American Psychiatric Association, Washington, 1994. Used with permission.

always follow a failure to resist the impulse and must be a solitary act, and the stolen articles must be without immediate usefulness or monetary gain. In ordinary stealing the act is usually planned, and the objects are stolen for their use or financial value. Malingerers may try to simulate kleptomania to avoid prosecution. Stealing that occurs in association with conduct disorder, antisocial personality disorder, and manic episodes is clearly related to the pervasive, underlying disorder. Persons with kleptomania do not typically display antisocial behavior other than stealing.

Schizophrenic patients may steal in response to hallucinations and delusions, and patients with cognitive disorders may be accused of stealing because of their forgetting to pay for objects.

## Course and Prognosis

Kleptomania may begin in childhood, although most children and adolescents who steal do not become kleptomaniac adults. The course of the disorder waxes and wanes, but the disorder tends to be chronic. The spontaneous recovery rate is unknown. Serious impairment and complications are usually secondary to being caught, particularly when being arrested. Many persons seem never to have consciously considered the possibility of having to face the consequences of their acts, a feature in line with some descriptions of kleptomaniac patients as people who feel wronged and, therefore, entitled to steal. Some persons have bouts of being unable to resist the impulse to steal, followed by free periods that last for weeks or months. The prognosis with treatment can be good, but few patients come for help of their own accord. Often, the disorder in no way impairs the person's social or work functioning. In quiescent cases, new bouts of the disorder may be precipitated by loss or disappointment.

## Treatment

Because true kleptomania is rare, reports of treatment tend to be individual case descriptions or a short series of cases. Insight-oriented psychotherapy and psychoanalysis have been successful but depend on the patient's motivation. Persons who feel guilt and shame may be helped by insight-oriented psychotherapy, because of their increased motivation to change the behavior.

Behavior therapy—including systematic desensitization, aversive conditioning, and a combination of aversive conditioning and altered social contingencies—has been reported to be successful, even when motivation was lacking. The reports cite follow-up studies of up to two years.

Serotonin-specific reuptake inhibitors, such as fluoxetine, appear to be effective in some kleptomaniac patients.

# PYROMANIA

The essential features of pyromania are deliberate and purposeful fire setting on more than one occasion; tension or affective arousal before setting the fires; fascination with, interest in, curiosity about, or attraction to fire and the activities and equipment associated with fire fighting; and pleasure, gratification, or relief when setting fires or when witnessing or participating in their aftermath. The patient may make considerable advance preparations before starting the fire.

A diagnosis of pyromania should not be made when fires are set to make money, to express a sociopolitical ideology, to conceal criminal activity, to express anger or vengeance, to improve one's living circumstances, or to respond to a delusion or a hallucination.

## Epidemiology

No information is available on the prevalence of pyromania, but only a small percentage of those adults who set fires can be classified as having pyromania. The disorder is found far more often in males than in females, and people who set fires are more likely to be mildly retarded than are the general population. Some studies have noted an increased incidence of alcohol abuse in people who set fires. Fire setters also tend to have a history of antisocial traits, such as truancy, running away from home, and delinquency. Enuresis has been considered a common finding in the history of fire setters, although controlled studies have failed to confirm the findings. However, studies have found an association between cruelty to animals and fire setting.

## Etiology

Sigmund Freud saw fire as a symbol of sexuality. The warmth that is radiated by fire evokes the same sensation that accompanies a state of sexual excitation, and a flame's shape and movements suggest a phallus in activity. Other therapists have associated pyromania with an abnormal craving for power and social prestige. Some pyromaniac patients are volunteer fire fighters who set fires to prove themselves brave, to force other fire fighters into action, or to demonstrate their power to extinguish a blaze. The incendiary act is a way to vent accumulated rage over the frustration caused by a sense of social, physical, or sexual inferiority. A number of studies have noted that the fathers of pyromanic patients were absent from the home. Thus, one explanation of fire setting is that it represents a wish for the absent father to return home as a rescuer, to put out the fire, and to save the child from a difficult existence.

Female fire setters, in addition to being much fewer in number than male fire setters, do not start fires to put fire fighters into action, as men frequently do. Rather, promiscuity without pleasure and petty stealing, often approaching kleptomania, have been frequently noted to be delinquent trends in female fire setters.

Significantly low CSF levels of 5-HIAA and 3-methoxy-4-hydroxyphenylglycol (MHPG) were found in one group of male fire setters.

## Diagnosis and Clinical Features

Persons with pyromania are often regular watchers at fires in their neighborhoods, frequently set off false alarms, and show interest in fire-fighting paraphernalia (Table 24–3). Curiosity is very evident. The persons may be indifferent to the consequences of the fire for life or property, exhibiting a lack of remorse. Fire setters may gain satisfaction from the resulting destruction. Frequently, they leave obvious clues. Common associated features include alcohol intoxication, sexual dysfunctions, lower-than-average intelligence quotient (I.Q.), chronic personal frustrations, and resentment toward authority figures. In some cases, the fire setter becomes sexually aroused by the fire.

## Differential Diagnosis

The clinician should have little trouble distinguishing between pyromania and the fascination of many young children with matches, lighters, and fire as part of the normal investigation of their environments. Pyromania must also be separated from incendiary acts of sabotage carried out by dissident political extremists or paid torches, who are termed arsonists in the legal system.

**Table 24–3**
**Diagnostic Criteria for Pyromania**

A. Deliberate and purposeful fire setting on more than one occasion.

B. Tension or affective arousal before the act.

C. Fascination with, interest in, curiosity about, or attraction to fire and its situational contexts (e.g., paraphernalia, uses, consequences).

D. Pleasure, gratification, or relief when setting fires, or when witnessing or participating in their aftermath.

E. The fire setting is not done for monetary gain, as an expression of sociopolitical ideology, to conceal criminal activity, to express anger or vengeance, to improve one's living circumstances, in response to a delusion or hallucination, or as a result of impaired judgment (e.g., in dementia, mental retardation, substance intoxication).

F. The fire setting is not better accounted for by conduct disorder, a manic episode, or antisocial personality disorder.

Table from DSM-IV, *Diagnostic and Statistical Manual of Mental Disorders*, ed 4. Copyright American Psychiatric Association, Washington, 1994. Used with permission.

When fire setting occurs in conduct disorder and anti-social personality disorder, it is a deliberate act, rather than the failure to resist an impulse. Fires may be set for profit, sabotage, or retaliation. Patients with schizophrenia or mania may set fires in response to delusions or hallucinations. And patients with brain dysfunction may set fires because of a failure to appreciate the consequences of the act.

## Course and Prognosis

Pyromania usually begins in childhood. When the onset is in adolescence or adulthood, the fire setting tends to be deliberately destructive. The prognosis for treated children is good, and complete remission is a realistic goal. The prognosis for adults is guarded, because of their frequent use of denial, their refusal to take responsibility, and their concurrent alcohol dependence and lack of insight.

## Treatment

Little has been written about the treatment of pyromania. The treatment of fire setters has been difficult because of their lack of motivation. Incarceration may be the only method available to prevent a recurrence. Behavior therapy can then be administered in the institution.

Fire setting in children must be treated with the utmost seriousness. Intensive interventions should be undertaken when possible but as therapeutic and preventive measures, rather than as punishment. Because of the recurrent nature of pyromania, any treatment program should include supervision of the patient to prevent a repeated episode of fire setting.

# PATHOLOGICAL GAMBLING

As defined by DSM-IV, the essential feature of pathological gambling is persistent and recurrent maladaptive gambling behavior. Features of the maladaptive behavior include a preoccupation with gambling; the need to gamble with increasing amounts of money to achieve the desired excitement; repeated unsuccessful efforts to control, cut back, or stop gambling; gambling as a way of escaping from problems; gambling to recoup losses; lying to conceal the extent of the involvement with gambling; the commission of illegal acts to finance gambling; the jeopardizing or loss of personal and vocational relationships because of gambling; and a reliance on others for money to pay off debts.

## Epidemiology

Estimates place the number of pathological gamblers at 1 to 3 percent of the adult United States population. The disorder is more common in men than in women. Both the fathers of males and the mothers of females with the disorder are more likely to have the disorder than are the population at large. Women with the disorder are more likely than are those not so affected to be married to al-

coholic men who are usually absent from the home. Alcohol dependence in general is more common among the parents of pathological gamblers than among the overall population.

## Etiology

The following may be predisposing factors for the development of the disorder: loss of a parent by death, separation, divorce, or desertion before the child is 15 years of age; inappropriate parental discipline (absence, inconsistency, or harshness); exposure to and availability of gambling activities for the adolescent; a family emphasis on material and financial symbols; and a lack of family emphasis on saving, planning, and budgeting.

There is an association between pathological gambling and mood disorders, especially major depressive disorder. Other associated disorders include panic disorder, obsessive-compulsive disorder, and agoraphobia. Childhood attention-deficit/hyperactivity disorder may be a predisposing factor for pathological gambling. Disorders of catecholamine metabolism have been suggested, with the gambler seeking to experience the activating effects of norepinephrine that accompany the tension associated with gambling.

## Diagnosis and Clinical Features

In addition to the features described above, pathological gamblers most often appear overconfident, somewhat abrasive, energetic, and free-spending when they have obvious signs of personal stress, anxiety, and depression (Table 24–4). They commonly have the attitude that money is both the cause of and the solution to all their problems. As their gambling increases, they are usually forced to lie to obtain money and to continue gambling while hiding the extent of their gambling behavior. They make no serious attempt to budget or save money. When their borrowing resources are strained, they are likely to engage in antisocial behavior to obtain money for gambling. Their criminal behavior is typically nonviolent, such as forgery, embezzlement, or fraud. The conscious intent is to return or repay the money.

Complications include alienation from family members and acquaintances, the loss of one's life accomplishments, suicide attempts, and association with fringe and illegal groups. Arrest for nonviolent crimes may lead to imprisonment.

A 48-year-old male attorney was interviewed while he was being detained awaiting trial. He had been arrested for taking funds from his firm; he stated that he had fully intended to return the money after he had a big win at gambling. He appeared deeply humiliated and remorseful about his behavior, although he had a history of near arrests for defrauding his company of funds. His father had provided funds to extricate him from those past financial difficulties but refused to assist him this time. The patient had to resign his job under pressure from his firm. That seemed to distress him greatly, since he had worked diligently and effectively at his job, although he had been spending more and more time away from work to pursue gambling.

The patient had gambled on horse racing for many years.

**Table 24-4**
**Diagnostic Criteria for Pathological Gambling**

A. Persistent and recurrent maladaptive gambling behavior as indicated by five (or more) of the following:

    (1) is preoccupied with gambling (e.g., preoccupied with reliving past gambling experiences, handicapping or planning the next venture, or thinking of ways to get money with which to gamble)

    (2) needs to gamble with increasing amounts of money in order to achieve the desired excitement

    (3) has repeated unsuccessful efforts to control, cut back, or stop gambling

    (4) is restless or irritable when attempting to cut down or stop gambling

    (5) gambles as a way of escaping from problems or of relieving a dysphoric mood (e.g., feelings of helplessness, guilt, anxiety, depression)

    (6) after losing money gambling, often returns another day to get even ("chasing" one's losses)

    (7) lies to family members, therapist, or others to conceal the extent of involvement with gambling

    (8) has committed illegal acts such as forgery, fraud, theft, or embezzlement, to finance gambling

    (9) has jeopardized or lost a significant relationship, job, or educational or career opportunity because of gambling

    (10) relies on others to provide money to relieve a desperate financial situation caused by gambling

B. The gambling behavior is not better accounted for by a manic episode.

Table from DSM-IV, *Diagnostic and Statistical Manual of Mental Disorders*, ed 4. Copyright American Psychiatric Association, Washington, 1994. Used with permission.

---

He spent several hours each day studying the results of the previous day's races in the newspaper. Recently, he had been losing heavily and had resorted to illegal borrowing to increase his bets and to win back his losses (called "chasing" in gambling circles). He was being pressured by loan sharks for payment. He stated that he embezzled his firm's money to pay off the illegal debts because the threats of the loan sharks were so frightening to him that he could not concentrate or sleep. He admitted to problems with his friends and his wife since he had borrowed from them. They were now alienated and giving him little emotional support, since they no longer had any faith in his repeated promises to limit his gambling. His wife had decided to leave him and live with her parents.

During the interview the patient was tense and restless, at times having to stand up and pace. He said that he was having a flare-up of a duodenal ulcer. He was tearful throughout the interview and said that, although he realized his problems stemmed from his gambling, he still had a strong urge to gamble.

*Discussion.* The man was preoccupied with gambling, which had led to his being arrested for embezzlement and defaulting on debts and to the disruption of his marriage. His gambling was clearly beyond the bounds of recreational gambling and, in conjunction with the man's inability to limit his gambling behavior, indicated a disturbance in impulse control—pathological gambling. The essential features of the disorder parallel the features of substance dependence. In both cases the person who is addicted has impaired control over the behavior and continues it, despite severe adverse consequences.

Although the patient had engaged in antisocial behavior, a diagnosis of antisocial personality disorder was not appropriate because his antisocial behavior was limited to attempts

to obtain money to pay off gambling debts and he had neither a childhood history of antisocial behavior nor evidence of impaired occupational and interpersonal functioning other than that associated with his gambling.

## Differential Diagnosis

Social gambling is distinguished from pathological gambling in that the former is associated with gambling with friends, on special occasions, and with predetermined acceptable and tolerable losses.

Gambling that is symptomatic of a manic episode can usually be distinguished from pathological gambling by the history of a marked mood change and the loss of judgment preceding the gambling. Maniclike mood changes are common in pathological gambling but always follow winning and are usually followed by depressive episodes because of subsequent losses.

Persons with antisocial personality disorder may have problems with gambling. In cases in which both disorders are present, both should be diagnosed.

## Course and Prognosis

Pathological gambling usually begins in adolescence for males and late in life for females. The disorder waxes and wanes and tends to be chronic. Three phases are seen in pathological gambling: (1) the winning phase, ending with a big win, equal to about a year's salary, which hooks the patient; (2) the progressive-loss phase, in which patients structure their lives around gambling; they move from being excellent gamblers to being stupid ones—taking considerable risks, cashing in securities, borrowing money, missing work, and losing jobs; and (3) the desperate phase, with the patients gambling in a frenzy with large amounts of money, not paying debts, becoming involved with loan sharks, writing bad checks, and possibly embezzling. The disorder may take up to 15 years to reach the third phase, but then, within a year or two, the patients are totally deteriorated.

## Treatment

Gamblers seldom come forward voluntarily for treatment. Legal difficulties, family pressures, or other psychiatric complaints are what bring the gamblers into treatment. Gamblers Anonymous (GA) was founded in Los Angeles in 1957 and modeled on Alcoholics Anonymous (AA); it is accessible—at least in large cities—and is probably the most effective treatment for gambling. It is a method of inspirational group therapy, which involves public confession, peer pressure, and the presence of reformed gamblers available (as are sponsors in AA) to help members resist the impulse to gamble.

In some cases, hospitalizing the patients may help by removing them from their environments. Insight should not be sought until the patients have been away from gambling for three months. At that point, pathological gambling patients may become excellent candidates for insight-oriented psychotherapy.

If gambling is associated with depressive disorders,

mania, anxiety, or other mental disorders, pharmacotherapy with antidepressants, lithium, or antianxiety agents is useful.

## TRICHOTILLOMANIA

According to DSM-IV, the essential feature of trichotillomania is the recurrent pulling out of one's hair, resulting in noticeable hair loss. Other clinical symptoms include an increasing sense of tension before pulling the hair and a sense of pleasure, gratification, or relief when pulling out the hair. The diagnosis should not be made if the hair pulling is the result of another mental disorder (for example, those disorders manifesting delusions or hallucinations) or a general medical disorder (for example, a preexisting lesion of the skin).

### Epidemiology

Trichotillomania is apparently more common in females than in males. No information is available on the familial pattern, but one study reported that 5 of 19 children had family histories of some form of alopecia. Prevalence data are unavailable, but trichotillomania may be more common than is now believed, especially if hair pulling without the sense of tension before the pulling and without the sense of relief afterward is considered trichotillomania. Some experts contend that the DSM-IV criteria are too restrictive. Associated disorders are obsessive-compulsive disorder, obsessive-compulsive personality disorder, borderline personality disorder, and depressive disorders.

### Etiology

Although trichotillomania is regarded as multidetermined, its onset has been linked to stressful situations in more than a quarter of all cases. Disturbances in mother-child relationships, fear of being left alone, and recent object loss are often cited as critical factors contributing to the condition. Substance abuse may encourage the development of the disorder. Depressive dynamics are often cited as predisposing factors; however, no particular personality trait or disorder characterizes the patients. Some see self-stimulation as the primary goal of hair pulling.

Trichotillomania is increasingly being viewed as having a biologically determined substrate that may reflect inappropriately released motor activity or excessive grooming behaviors.

### Diagnosis and Clinical Features

Before engaging in the behavior, trichotillomaniac patients experience an increasing sense of tension and achieve a sense of release or gratification from pulling out their hair (Table 24–5). All areas of the body may be affected. The most common site is the scalp. Other areas involved are the eyebrows, eyelashes, and the beard; less commonly, the trunk, armpits, and the pubic area are involved. Hair loss is often characterized by short, broken strands appearing together with long, normal hairs in the affected

**Table 24–5**
**Diagnostic Criteria for Trichotillomania**

A. Recurrent pulling out of one's hair resulting in noticeable hair loss.

B. An increasing sense of tension immediately before pulling out the hair or when attempting to resist the behavior.

C. Pleasure, gratification, or relief when pulling out the hair.

D. The disturbance is not better accounted for by another mental disorder and not due to a general medical condition (e.g., a dermatologic condition).

E. The disturbance causes clinically significant distress or impairment in social, occupational, or other important areas of functioning.

Table from DSM-IV, *Diagnostic and Statistical Manual of Mental Disorders*, ed 4. Copyright American Psychiatric Association, Washington, 1994. Used with permission.

areas. No abnormalities of the skin or the scalp are present. Hair pulling is not reported to be painful, although pruritus and tingling in the involved area may be present.

Trichophagy, mouthing of the hair, may follow the hair plucking. Complications of trichophagy include trichobezoars, malnutrition, and intestinal obstruction.

Characteristic histopathological changes in the hair follicle, known as trichomalacia, are demonstrated by biopsy and help distinguish trichotillomania from other causes of alopecia. Patients usually deny the behavior and often try to hide the resultant alopecia. Head banging, nail biting, scratching, gnawing, excoriation, and other acts of self-mutilation may be present.

A 25-year-old single woman came to the dermatology clinic of a university hospital with the complaint of increasing baldness of the crown of her scalp. Because no dermatological disease could be identified, she was referred to the psychiatry department. She reported to the psychiatrist that, since childhood, she had pulled out single hairs from the top of her head after twirling the strand of hair on a finger. The behavior was described as usually occurring when she was alone, tired, unoccupied, and ruminating over some unpleasant, stressful interaction. After plucking out the hair, she commonly inspected it and ran it across her lips. That pattern of hair pulling was often repeated for several minutes at a time; she did not find it painful—in fact, it often produced a sense of relief. By wearing her hair up, the patient had always managed to hide the bald area, but that had now become almost impossible. She indicated that seeing a woman with a wig at work had prompted her to seek medical attention; she feared her problem would soon require her to wear a wig.

The patient complained of long-standing problems with her temper, drinking too much, and a series of unsatisfying relationships. She had had no previous psychiatric treatment and had never been hospitalized for any physical reason. She traced the hair pulling to her childhood and associated it with absences of her mother from the home.

Further sessions revealed that the patient had sustained a series of traumatic events in her first decade, foremost among them being the death of her father from a malignancy. In spite of her young age at the time of his death, she had a series of vivid recollections of him, especially memories associated with his illness. Only after many sessions did she mention to the psychiatrist that her father had been a barber.

The patient regarded herself as a clean, orderly person and denied cleaning or compulsive rituals. She smoked a pack of cigarettes a day and had tried speed and marijuana but found that they each made her "paranoid." She had been working long hours in a family business and was considering changing jobs.

*Discussion.* Stroking and fiddling with the hair are common parts of the repertoire of social primates. In the patient's case, however, hair pulling had escalated to the point of marked alopecia. She was unable to control the impulse to pull out her own hair and achieved a sense of release by engaging in the behavior. The behavior met the requirements for the diagnosis of trichotillomania.

The disorder is characterized by specific histopathological changes of the hair follicle, which can be demonstrated by biopsy and distinguished from other causes of alopecia. The disorder usually begins in childhood and is commonly associated with mental retardation and possibly with schizophrenia, although not in this case.

### Differential Diagnosis

Hair pulling may be a wholly benign condition, or it may occur in the context of several mental disorders. The phenomenology of trichotillomania and obsessive-compulsive disorder overlap. Like obsessive-compulsive disorder, trichotillomania is often chronic and recognized by the patient as undesirable. Unlike obsessive-compulsive disorder, patients with trichotillomania do not experience obsessive thoughts, and the compulsive activity is limited to one act—hair pulling.

Patients with factitious disorder with predominantly physical signs and symptoms actively seek medical attention and the patient role and deliberately simulate illness toward those ends. Patients who malinger or have factitious disorder may mutilate themselves to get medical attention, but they do not acknowledge the self-inflicted nature of the lesions.

Patients with stereotypic movement disorder have stereotypical and rhythmic movements, and they usually do not seem distressed by their behavior.

Trichotillomania may be difficult to distinguish from alopecia areata.

### Course and Prognosis

Trichotillomania generally begins in childhood or adolescence, but onsets have been reported much later in life. A late onset may be associated with an increased likelihood of chronicity. The course of the disorder is not well known. Both chronic and remitting forms occur. In some cases the disorder has persisted for more than two decades. About a third of the people presenting for treatment report a duration of one year or less.

### Treatment

No consensus is available on the best treatment modality for trichotillomania. Treatment usually involves psychiatrists and dermatologists in a joint endeavor. Psychopharmacological methods that have been used to treat psychodermatological disorders include topical steroids and hydroxyzine hydrochloride, an anxiolytic with antihistamine properties; antidepressants; serotonergic agents;

and antipsychotics. Whether depression is present or not, antidepressant agents may lead to dermatological improvement. Current evidence strongly points to the efficacy of drugs that alter central serotonin turnover. In patients who respond poorly to serotonin-specific reuptake inhibitors, augmentation with pimozide (Orap), a dopamine blocker, may lead to improvement. A report of successful lithium treatment for trichotillomania cited the possible effect of lithium on aggressivity, impulsivity, and mood instability as an explanation. Lithium also possesses serotonergic activity.

Successful behavioral treatments, such as biofeedback, have been reported; however, most of the reports have been about individual cases or small series of studies with relatively short follow-up periods. Further controlled study of the techniques is warranted. Trichotillomania has been treated successfully with insight-oriented psychotherapy.

Hypnotherapy and behavior therapy have been mentioned as potentially effective modalities in the treatment of dermatological disorders in which psychological factors may be involved. The skin has been shown to be susceptible to hypnotic suggestion. Most of the work has been research-oriented, with little effect yet on clinical management.

## IMPULSE CONTROL DISORDER NOT OTHERWISE SPECIFIED

The DSM-IV diagnostic category of impulse-control disorder not otherwise specified (Table 24–6) is a residual category for disorders of impulse control that do not meet the criteria for a specific impulse control disorder. Included in the not otherwise specified (NOS) disorders are compulsive shopping, addiction to video games, compulsive sexual behavior, and repetitive self-mutilation.

**Table 24–6**
**Diagnostic Criteria for Impulse-Control Disorder Not Otherwise Specified**

This category is for disorders of impulse control that do not meet the criteria for any specific impulse-control disorder or for another mental disorder having features involving impulse control described elsewhere in the manual (e.g., substance dependence, a paraphilia).

Table from DSM-IV, *Diagnostic and Statistical Manual of Mental Disorders*, ed 4. Copyright American Psychiatric Association, Washington, 1994. Used with permission.

### References

Aichhorn A: *Wayward Youth.* Viking, New York, 1906.
Allcock C C: Pathological gambling. Aust N Z J Psychiatry 20: 259, 1986.
Corrigan P W, Yudofsky S C, Silver J M: Pharmacological and behavioral treatments for aggressive psychiatric inpatients. Hosp Community Psychiatry 44: 125, 1993.
Cusack J R, Malaney K R, DePry D L: Insights about pathological gamblers: "Chasing losses" in spite of the consequences. Postgrad Med 93: 169, 1993.
Custer R L: Profile of the pathological gambler. J Clin Psychiatry 45: 35, 1984.
Fenichel O: *The Psychoanalytic Theory of Neurosis.* Norton, New York, 1945.

Frosch J: The relation between acting out and disorders of impulse control. Psychiatry *40*: 295, 1977.

Goldman M J: Kleptomania: Making sense of the nonsensical. Am J Psychiatry *148*: 986, 1991.

Greenberg H R, Sarner C A: Trichotillomania: Symptom and syndrome. Arch Gen Psychiatry *12*: 482, 1965.

Gupta S, Freimer M: Trichotillomania, clomipramine, topical steroids. Am J Psychiatry *150*: 524, 1993.

Jenkins S C, Maruta T: Therapeutic use of propranolol for intermittent explosive disorder. Mayo Clin Proc *62*: 204, 1987.

Kammerer T, Singer L, Michel D: The incendiaries: Criminological, clinical and psychological study of 72 cases. Ann Med Psychol *1*: 687, 1967.

Kohut H: *The Restoration of the Self*. International Universities Press, New York, 1977.

Lion J R: The intermittent explosive disorder. Psychiatr Ann *22*: 64, 1992.

McElroy S L, Pope H G, Hudson J I, Keck P E, White K L: Kleptomania: A report of 20 cases. Am J Psychiatry *148*: 652, 1991.

Popkin M K: Impulse control disorders not elsewhere classified. In *Comprehensive Textbook of Psychiatry,* ed 5, H I Kaplan, B J Sadock, editors, p 1145, Williams & Wilkins, Baltimore, 1989.

Rugle L, Melamed L: Neuropsychological assessment of attention problems in pathological gamblers. J Nerv Ment Dis *181*: 107, 1993.

Stein D J, Hollander E: Impulsive aggression and obsessive-compulsive disorder. Psychiatr Ann *23*: 389, 1993.

Stein D J, Hollander E, Liebowitz M R: Neurobiology of impulsivity and the impulse control disorders. J Neuropsychiatry *5*: 9, 1993.

Swedo S E: Trichotillomania. Psychiatr Ann *23*: 402, 1993.

Vikkunen M, Nuutila A, Goodwin F K, Linnoila M: Cerebrospinal fluid monoamine metabolite levels in male arsonists. Arch Gen Psychiatry *44*: 241, 1987.

Vitulano L A, King R A, Scahill L, Cohen D S: Behavioral treatment of children and adolescents with trichotillomania. J Am Acad Child Adolesc Psychiatry *31*: 109, 1992.

# Adjustment Disorders

Emotional or behavioral symptoms may occur in response to stressful life events. If those symptoms or behaviors appear within three months of the onset of the stressor and are clinically significant—as is evidenced by (1) marked distress that exceeds what is expected from exposure to the stressor or (2) significant impairment in social, vocational, or academic functioning—a diagnosis of adjustment disorder should be made. According to the fourth edition of *Diagnostic and Statistical Manual of Mental Disorders* (DSM-IV), the stress-related disturbance should not meet the criteria for any specific Axis I disorder and should not be merely an exacerbation of a preexisting Axis I or Axis II disorder. Bereavement is not considered an adjustment disorder in DSM-IV.

Adjustment disorder is a short-term maladaptive reaction to what a layperson may call a personal misfortune or to what a psychiatrist calls a psychosocial stressor. Adjustment disorder is expected to remit soon after the stressor ceases or, if the stressor persists, a new level of adaptation is achieved. The response is maladaptive because of an impairment in social or occupational functioning or because of symptoms or behaviors that are beyond the normal, usual, or expected response to such a stressor.

## EPIDEMIOLOGY

Adjustment disorder is one of the most common psychiatric diagnoses among patients hospitalized for medical and surgical problems. In one study 5 percent of hospital admissions over a three-year period were classified as having adjustment disorder. The disorder is most frequently diagnosed in adolescents but may occur at any age.

In one survey of psychiatric patients, 10 percent of the sample population were found to have adjustment disorder. The ratio of females to males was about 2 to 1. Single women are generally overly represented as being most at risk. Among adolescents of either sex, common types of precipitating stresses are school problems, parental rejection, parental divorce, and substance abuse. Among adults, common precipitating stresses are marital problems, divorce, moving to a new environment, and financial problems.

## ETIOLOGY

Adjustment disorder is precipitated by one or more stressors. The severity of the stressor or stressors is not always predictive of the severity of adjustment disorder;

the stressor severity is a complex function of degree, quantity, duration, reversibility, environment, and personal context. For example, the loss of a parent is different for a 10-year-old and a 40-year-old. Personality organization and cultural or group norms and values contribute to the disproportionate responses to stressors.

Stressors may be single, such as a divorce or the loss of a job, or multiple, such as the death of an important person occurring at the same time as one's own physical illness and loss of a job. Stressors may be recurrent, such as seasonal business difficulties, or continuous, such as chronic illness or living in poverty. A discordant intrafamilial relationship may produce adjustment disorder that affects the whole family system. Or the disorder may be limited to the patient, as when the patient is the victim of a crime or has a physical illness. Sometimes adjustment disorder occurs in a group or community setting, and the stressor affects several people, as in a natural disaster or in racial, social, or religious persecution. Specific developmental stages—such as beginning school, leaving home, getting married, becoming a parent, failing to achieve occupational goals, having one's last child leave home, and retiring—are often associated with adjustment disorder.

### Psychoanalytic Factors

Several psychoanalytic researchers have discussed the capacity of the same stress to produce a range of responses in various normal human beings. Throughout his life Sigmund Freud remained interested in why the stresses of ordinary life produce illness in some and not in others, why an illness takes a particular form, and why some experiences and not others predispose a person to psychopathology. He gave considerable weight to constitutional factors and viewed them as interacting with a person's life experiences to produce fixation.

Psychoanalytic research has emphasized the role of the mother and the rearing environment in a person's later capacity to respond to stress. Particularly important was Donald W Winnicott's concept of the good-enough mother, a person who adapts to the infant's needs and provides enough support to enable the growing child to tolerate the frustrations in life.

### Psychodynamic Factors

A concurrent personality disorder or organic impairment may make a person vulnerable to adjustment disorder. Vulnerability is also associated with the loss of a parent during infancy. Actual or perceived support from key relationships may mediate behavioral and emotional responses to stressors.

Pivotal to the understanding of adjustment disorder is an understanding of three factors: (1) the nature of the stressor, (2) the conscious and unconscious meanings of the stressor, and (3) the patient's preexisting vulnerability. The clinician must undertake a detailed exploration of the patient's experience of the stressor. Certain patients commonly place all the blame on a particular event when a less obvious event may have been more significant in terms of the psychological meaning to the patient. Current events may reawaken past traumas or disappointments from childhood, so patients should be encouraged to think about how the current situation relates to similar past events.

Throughout early development, each child develops a unique set of defense mechanisms to deal with stressful events. Because of greater amounts of trauma or greater constitutional vulnerability, some children have less mature defensive constellations than do other children. That disadvantage may cause them as adults to react with substantial impairment in functioning when they are faced with a loss, a divorce, or a financial setback. However, those who have developed mature defense mechanisms are less vulnerable and bounce back more quickly from the stressor. Their resilience is also crucially determined by the nature of the children's early relationships with their parents. Studies of trauma repeatedly indicate that supportive, nurturant relationships prevent traumatic incidents from causing permanent psychological damage.

Psychodynamic clinicians must take into account the relation between a stressor and the human developmental life cycle. When adolescents leave home for college, for example, they are at high developmental risk for reacting with a temporary symptomatic picture. Similarly, if the child who leaves home is the youngest in the family, the parents may be particularly vulnerable to reacting with adjustment disorder. Moreover, middle-aged persons who are confronting their own mortality may be especially sensitive to the effects of loss or death.

## DIAGNOSIS AND CLINICAL FEATURES

Although by definition adjustment disorder follows a stressor, the symptoms do not necessarily begin immediately. According to DSM-IV, up to three months may elapse between the stressor and the development of symptoms. Symptoms do not always subside as soon as the stressor ceases. If the stressor continues, the disorder may be chronic. The disorder may occur at any age. Its symptoms vary considerably, with depressive, anxious, and mixed features the most common in adults.

Physical symptoms are most common in children and the elderly but may occur in any age group. Manifestations may also include assaultive behavior and reckless driving, excessive drinking, defaulting on legal responsibilities, and withdrawal.

The clinical presentations of adjustment disorder can vary widely. DSM-IV lists six types of adjustment disorder, including an unspecified category (Table 25-1).

**Table 25-1**
**Diagnostic Criteria for Adjustment Disorders**

A. The development of emotional or behavioral symptoms in response to an identifiable stressor(s) occurring within 3 months of the onset of the stressor(s).

B. These symptoms or behaviors are clinically significant as evidenced by either of the following:
   (1) marked distress that is in excess of what would be expected from exposure to the stressor
   (2) significant impairment in social or occupational (academic) functioning

C. The stress-related disturbance does not meet the criteria for another specific Axis I disorder and is not merely an exacerbation of a preexisting Axis I or Axis II disorder.

D. The symptoms do not represent bereavement.

E. Once the stressor (or its consequences) has terminated, the symptoms do not persist for more than an additional 6 months.

*Specify* if:
   **Acute:** if the disturbance lasts for less than 6 months
   **Chronic:** if the disturbance lasts for 6 months or longer

Adjustment disorders are coded based on the subtype, which is selected according to the predominant symptoms. The specific stressor(s) can be specified on Axis IV
   **With depressed mood**
   **With anxiety**
   **With mixed anxiety and depressed mood**
   **With disturbance of conduct**
   **With mixed disturbance of emotions and conduct**
   **Unspecified**

Table from DSM-IV, *Diagnostic and Statistical Manual of Mental Disorders*, ed 4. Copyright American Psychiatric Association, Washington, 1994. Used with permission.

## Adjustment Disorder with Anxiety

Symptoms of anxiety—such as palpitations, jitteriness, and agitation—are present in adjustment disorder with anxiety, which must be differentiated from anxiety disorders.

## Adjustment Disorder with Depressed Mood

In adjustment disorder with depressed mood, the predominant manifestations are depressed mood, tearfulness, and hopelessness. This type must be distinguished from major depressive disorder and uncomplicated bereavement.

A 39-year-old divorced woman was referred for psychiatric evaluation after a brief hospitalization for complaints of intermittent numbness in her arms and the right side of her face. Extensive neurological and neurosurgical evaluation revealed stenosis of the outlets of several cervical vertebrae; intermittently compromised nerve roots were thought to account for the physical symptoms. The patient, an artist who composed large structures from various work materials, was advised by her physicians to stop for the next several months all lifting, reaching, raising her arms, and other strenuous activities requisite to her work. She had felt despondent for more than two months, with episodes of tearfulness, anxiety, and increased irritability. She continued to supervise her assistants but was increasingly uninterested in work. She had no sleep or appetite change, but her libido was diminished. She was still able to enjoy music. The patient had no prior personal or familial history of a mood disorder.

The identified stressors in her case were the physical illness and the directive to minimize for an indefinite interval the use of her arms. The net result was to preclude the patient's ability to continue her artistic endeavors, which were crucial to her sense of self. In response, she experienced the emergence of a depressive constellation with less than a full vegetative set of symptoms. The clinician diagnosed adjustment disorder with depressed mood. Intervention was directed to (1) clarification with the neurosurgeon of the likely course and necessary treatment of the outlet problem and (2) several sessions with the patient to explore her responses to and perceptions of the changes in her life imposed by the neurological problem.

## Adjustment Disorder with Disturbance of Conduct

In adjustment disorder with disturbance of conduct, the predominant manifestation involves conduct in which the rights of others are violated or age appropriate societal norms and rules are disregarded. Examples of behavior in this category are truancy, vandalism, reckless driving, and fighting. The category must be differentiated from conduct disorder and antisocial personality disorder.

An 18-year-old male high school senior was referred by his father for evaluation after an episode in which the son was arrested for the second time for shoplifting merchandise worth several hundred dollars from a major department store. In the final three months of his senior year, the patient, a B student without prior legal problems, had displayed a sudden shift in behavior. He was twice ticketed for driving violations, failed several school tests, and became increasingly irritable and uncommunicative. He was given to angry outbursts. Initially uncooperative with his psychiatrist, the patient was forthcoming when his attorney told him that his participation would be viewed favorably by the court. After several sessions with the therapist, the patient admitted that he was overwhelmed by the prospect of moving in the fall from his home to college 2,000 miles away. That stressor had prompted his abuse of alcohol and marijuana and his frequent risk-taking behaviors, each of which was ineptly executed. With several months of weekly psychotherapy, the patient completed his first year of college without incident.

## Adjustment Disorder with Mixed Disturbance of Emotions and Conduct

The combination of disturbances of emotions and conduct sometimes occurs. Clinicians are encouraged to try to make one or the other diagnosis in the interest of parsimony.

## Adjustment Disorder with Mixed Anxiety and Depressed Mood

In adjustment disorder with mixed anxiety and depressed mood, patients exhibit features of both anxiety and depression that do not meet the criteria for an already established anxiety disorder or depressive disorder.

## Adjustment Disorder Unspecified

Adjustment disorder unspecified is a residual category for atypical maladaptive reactions to stress. Examples include inappropriate responses to the diagnosis of physical illness, such as massive denial and severe noncompliance with treatment, and social withdrawal without significant depressed or anxious mood.

## DIFFERENTIAL DIAGNOSIS

Adjustment disorder must be differentiated from other conditions that may be a focus of clinical attention. Patients with other conditions that may be a focus of clinical attention do not have impairment in social or occupational functioning or symptoms beyond the normal and expectable reaction to the stressor. Because no absolute criteria aid in distinguishing between adjustment disorder and a condition that may be a focus of clinical attention, clinical judgment is necessary.

Although uncomplicated bereavement often includes temporarily impaired social and occupational functioning, the person's dysfunctioning remains within the expectable bounds of a reaction to the loss of a loved one and, thus, is not considered adjustment disorder.

Other disorders from which adjustment disorder must be differentiated include major depressive disorder, brief psychotic disorder, generalized anxiety disorder, somatization disorder, various substance-related disorders, conduct disorder, academic problem, occupational problem, identity problem, and posttraumatic stress disorder. Those diagnoses should be given precedence in all cases that meet their criteria, even in the presence of a stressor or group of stressors that served as a precipitant. However, some patients meet the criteria for both adjustment disorder and a personality disorder.

### Posttraumatic Stress Disorder

In posttraumatic stress disorder the symptoms develop after a psychologically traumatizing event or events outside the range of normal human experience. That is, the stressors producing such a syndrome are expected to do so in the average human being. The stressors may be experienced alone, as in rape or assault, or in groups, as in military combat. A variety of mass catastrophes—such as floods, airplane crashes, atomic bombings, and death camps—have also been identified as stressors. The stressor contains a psychological component and frequently a concomitant physical component that may directly damage the nervous system. Clinicians believe that the disorder is more severe and lasts longer when the stressor is of human origin, as in rape, than when it is not, as in floods. In adjustment disorder the precipitating stress need not be severe or unusual.

## COURSE AND PROGNOSIS

The overall prognosis of adjustment disorder is generally favorable with appropriate treatment. Most patients return to their previous level of functioning within three months. Adolescents usually require a longer time to recover than do adults. Some persons (particularly adolescents) who receive a diagnosis of adjustment disorder later have mood disorders or substance-related disorders.

## TREATMENT

### Psychotherapy

Because a stressor can be clearly delineated in adjustment disorder, it is often believed that psychotherapy is not indicated and that the disorder will remit spontaneously. But such thinking fails to consider that many persons exposed to the same stressor do not experience similar symptoms and that the response is pathological. Psychotherapy can help the person adapt to the stressor if it is not reversible or time-limited and can serve as a preventive intervention if the stressor does remit.

Psychotherapy remains the treatment of choice for adjustment disorder. Group therapy can be particularly useful for patients who have undergone similar stresses—for example, a group of retired persons or renal dialysis patients. Individual psychotherapy offers the opportunity to explore the meaning of the stressor to the patient, so that earlier traumas can be worked through. After successful therapy, patients sometimes emerge from adjustment disorder stronger than in the premorbid period, although no pathology was evident during that period.

The psychiatrist treating adjustment disorder must be particularly mindful of problems of secondary gain. The illness role may be rewarding to some normal persons who have had little experience with its capacity to free one from responsibility. Thus, the therapist's attention, empathy, and understanding—which are necessary for success—can become rewarding in their own right, thereby reinforcing the symptoms. Such considerations must be weighed before intensive psychotherapy is begun. When a secondary gain has already been established, therapy is difficult.

Patients in whom adjustment disorder includes a conduct disturbance may have difficulties with the law, authorities, or school. Psychiatrists should not attempt to rescue such patients from the consequences of their actions. Too often, such kindness only reinforces socially unacceptable means of tension reduction and hinders the acquisition of insight and subsequent emotional growth. In those cases family therapy can help.

**Crisis intervention.** A brief type of therapy, crisis intervention is aimed at helping the person with adjustment disorder resolve the situation quickly by supportive techniques, suggestion, reassurance, environmental modification, and even hospitalization, if necessary. The frequency and the length of visits for crisis support vary according to the patient's needs; daily sessions may be necessary, sometimes two or three times each day. Flexibility is essential in the approach.

### Pharmacotherapy

The judicious use of medications can help patients with adjustment disorder, but they should be prescribed for brief periods. A patient may respond to an antianxiety agent or to an antidepressant, depending on the type of adjustment disorder. Patients with severe anxiety bordering on panic or decompensation can benefit from small dosages of antipsychotic medications. Patients in withdrawn or inhibited states may benefit from a short course of psychostimulant medication. Few, if any, cases of adjustment disorder can be adequately treated by medication alone. In most cases, psychotherapy should be added to the treatment regimen.

### References

Andreasen N, Hoenk P: The predictive value of adjustment disorders: A follow-up study. Am J Psychiatry *139*: 584, 1982.

Andreasen N, Wasek P: Adjustment disorders in adolescents and adults. Arch Gen Psychiatry *37*: 1166, 1980.

Bronisch T: Adjustment reactions: A long-term prospective and retrospective follow-up of former patients in a crisis intervention ward. Acta Psychiatr Scand *84*: 86, 1991.

Elliot C, Eisdorfer C: *Stress and Human Health*, Springer, New York, 1982.

Fard F, Hudgens R W, Welner A: Undiagnosed psychiatric illness in adolescents: A prospective and seven-year follow-up. Arch Gen Psychiatry *35*: 279, 1979.

Garmezy N, Rutter M: *Stress, Coping, and Development in Children*. McGraw-Hill, New York, 1983.

Holmes J, Raphe R: The social readjustment rating scale. J Psychosom Res *11*: 213, 1967.

Horowitz M J: *Stress Response Syndromes*. Aronson, New York, 1976.

Lewis D: *Vulnerability to Delinquency*. Spectrum, New York, 1981.

Newcorn J H, Strain J J: Adjustment disorder in children and adolescents. J Am Acad Child Adolesc Psychiatry *31*: 318, 1991.

Pollock D: Structured ambiguity and the definition of psychiatric illness: Adjustment among medical inpatients. Soc Sci Med *35*: 25, 1992.

Popkin M K: Adjustment disorder. In *Comprehensive Textbook of Psychiatry*, ed 5, H I Kaplan, B J Sadock, editors, p 1141. Williams & Wilkins, Baltimore, 1989.

Popkin M K, Mackenzie T B, Callies A L: Psychiatric consultation to geriatric medically ill inpatients in a university hospital. Arch Gen Psychiatry *41*: 703, 1984.

Regier D A, Meyers J K, Kramer M, Robins L N, Blazer D G, Hough R L, Eaton W W, Locke B Z: The NIMH Epidemiologic Catchment Area program. Arch Gen Psychiatry *41*: 934, 1984.

Strain J W, Newcorn J, Wolf D, Fulop G, Davis W: Considering changes in adjustment disorder. Hosp Community Psychiatry *44*: 13, 1993.

Winnicott D W: Translational objects and transitional phenomena. Int J Psychoanal *34*: 89, 1953.

# 26

# Personality Disorders

Personality can be defined as the totality of emotional and behavioral traits that characterize the person in day-to-day living under ordinary conditions; it is relatively stable and predictable. A personality disorder is a variant of those character traits that goes beyond the range found in most people. Only when personality traits are inflexible and maladaptive and cause either significant functional impairment or subjective distress do they constitute a class of personality disorder. Patients with personality disorders show deeply ingrained, inflexible, and maladaptive patterns of relating to and perceiving both the environment and themselves.

Those persons are far more likely to refuse psychiatric help and to deny their problems than are persons with anxiety disorders, depressive disorders, or obsessive-compulsive disorder. The personality disorder symptoms are alloplastic (that is, capable of adapting and altering the external environment) and ego-syntonic (that is, acceptable to the ego); those with a personality disorder do not feel anxiety about their maladaptive behavior. Because such persons do not routinely acknowledge pain from what society perceives as their symptoms, they are often regarded as unmotivated for treatment and impervious to recovery.

## CLASSIFICATION

The personality disorders are grouped into three clusters in the fourth edition of *Diagnostic and Statistical Manual of Mental Disorders* (DSM-IV). Cluster A comprises the paranoid, schizoid, and schizotypal personality disorders; persons with those disorders often appear to be odd and eccentric. Cluster B comprises the antisocial, borderline, histrionic, and narcissistic personality disorders; persons with those disorders often appear to be dramatic, emotional, and erratic. Cluster C comprises the avoidant, dependent, and obsessive-compulsive personality disorders and a category called personality disorder not otherwise specified (examples include passive-aggressive personality disorder and depressive personality disorder); persons with those disorders often appear to be anxious or fearful.

Many people exhibit traits that are not limited to a single personality disorder. If a patient meets the criteria for more than one personality disorder, each one should be diagnosed. Personality disorders are coded on Axis II of DSM-IV.

## ETIOLOGY

### Genetic Factors

The best evidence that genetic factors contribute to the genesis of personality disorders comes from the investigations of psychiatric disorders in 15,000 pairs of twins in the United States. Among monozygotic twins, the concordance for personality disorders was several times higher than that among dizygotic twins. Moreover, according to one study, on multiple measures of personality and temperament, occupational and leisure-time interests, and social attitudes, monozygotic twins reared apart are about as similar as are monozygotic twins reared together.

Cluster A personality disorders (paranoid, schizoid, and schizotypal) are more common in the biological relatives of schizophrenic patients than among control groups. Significantly more relatives with schizotypal personality disorder are found in the family histories of persons with schizophrenia than among control groups. Less correlation is found between paranoid or schizoid personality disorder and schizophrenia.

Cluster B personality disorders (antisocial, borderline, histrionic, and narcissistic) have a genetic base. Antisocial personality disorder is associated with alcohol use disorders. Depression is common in the family backgrounds of borderline personality disorder patients. Borderline personality disorder patients have more relatives with mood disorders than do control groups, and borderline personality disorder and mood disorder often coexist. A strong association is found between histrionic personality disorder and somatization disorder (Briquet's syndrome); patients with each disorder show an overlap of symptoms.

Cluster C personality disorders (avoidant, dependent, obsessive-compulsive, and not otherwise specified) may also have a genetic base. The avoidant personality disorder patient often has a high anxiety level. Obsessive-compulsive traits are more common in monozygotic twins than in dizygotic twins, and obsessive-compulsive personality disorder patients show some signs associated with depression—for example, shortened rapid eye movement (REM) latency period, abnormal dexamethasone-suppression test (DST) results.

### Temperamental Factors

Temperamental factors identified in childhood may be associated with personality disorders in adulthood. For example, children who are temperamentally fearful may go on to have avoidant personality disorder.

Childhood central nervous system dysfunctions associated with soft neurological signs are most common in antisocial and borderline personality disorders. Children with minimal brain damage are at risk for personality disorders, particularly antisocial personality disorder.

Certain personality disorders may arise from poor parental fit—that is, a poor match between temperament and child-rearing practices. For example, an anxious child reared by an equally anxious mother is more vulnerable to a personality disorder than would be the same child raised by a tranquil mother. Stella Chess and Alexander Thomas referred to goodness of fit. Cultures that encourage aggression may unwittingly reinforce and thereby contribute to paranoid and antisocial personality disorders. The physical environment may also play a role. For example, an active young child may appear to be hyperactive if kept in a small closed apartment but may appear to be normal in a large middle-class house with a fenced-in yard.

## Biological Factors

**Hormones.** Persons who show impulsive traits often also show increased levels of testosterone, 17-estradiol, and estrone. In nonhuman primates, androgens increase the likelihood of aggression and sexual behavior; however, the role of testosterone in human aggression is not clear. DST results are abnormal in some borderline personality disorder patients with depressive symptoms.

**Platelet monoamine oxidase.** Low platelet monoamine oxidase (MAO) levels have been associated with activity and sociability in monkeys. College students with low platelet MAO levels report spending more time in social activities than do students with high platelet MAO levels. Low platelet MAO levels have also been noted in some schizotypal patients.

**Smooth pursuit eye movements.** Smooth pursuit eye movements are abnormal in persons with the traits of introversion, low self-esteem, and withdrawal and in patients with schizotypal personality disorder. Movements in those persons are saccadic (that is, jerky). Those findings have no clinical application, but they do indicate the role of inheritance.

**Neurotransmitters.** Endorphins have effects similar to those of exogenous morphine, including analgesia and the suppression of arousal. High endogenous endorphin levels may be associated with a phlegmatic-passive person. Studies of personality traits and the dopaminergic and serotonergic systems indicate an arousal-activating function for those neurotransmitters. Levels of 5-hydroxyindoleacetic acid (5-HIAA), a metabolite of serotonin, are low in persons who attempt suicide and in patients who are impulsive and aggressive.

Raising serotonin levels with such serotonergic agents as fluoxetine (Prozac) may produce dramatic changes in some personality characteristics. Serotonin reduces depression, impulsivity, and rumination in many persons and can produce a sense of general well-being. Increased dopamine in the central nervous system, produced by certain psychostimulants (for example, amphetamines) can induce euphoria. The effects of neurotransmitters on personality traits have generated a great deal of interest and controversy about whether personality traits are inborn or acquired.

In his book *Listening to Prozac* Peter Kramer described dramatic personality changes (for example, decreased sensitivity to rejection, increased assertiveness, improved self-esteem, improved ability to tolerate stress) that can occur when serotonin levels are raised by fluoxetine. Those changes in personality traits occur regardless of diagnosis.

**Electrophysiology.** Changes in electrical conductance on the electroencephalogram (EEG) have been found in some patients with personality disorders, most commonly in the antisocial and borderline types, in which slow-wave activity is seen.

## Psychoanalytic Factors

Sigmund Freud originally suggested that personality traits are related to a fixation at one of the psychosexual stages of development. For example, an oral character is passive and dependent because of being fixated at the oral stage, when the dependence on others for intake of food is prominent. Anal characters are stubborn, parsimonious, and highly conscientious because of struggles around toilet training during the anal period.

Subsequently, Wilhelm Reich coined the term "character armor" to describe characteristic defensive styles that persons use to protect themselves from internal impulses and from interpersonal anxiety in significant relationships. Reich's thinking has had a far-reaching influence on the contemporary conceptualization of personality and personality disorders. The unique stamp of personality on each human being is largely determined by that person's characteristic defense mechanisms. Each personality disorder in Axis II has a cluster of defenses that help a psychodynamic clinician recognize the type of character pathology present. For example, persons with paranoid personality disorder use projection; schizoid personality disorder is associated with withdrawal.

When defenses work effectively, patients with personality disorders are able to master feelings of anxiety, depression, anger, shame, guilt, and other affects. Patients often view their behavior as *ego-syntonic,* meaning that it creates no distress for the patients themselves, even though it may adversely affect others. The patients may also be reluctant to engage in a treatment process because their defenses are important in controlling unpleasant affects and they are not interested in giving up those defenses.

Another central feature of personality disorders is the patient's internal object relations. In the course of development, particular patterns of the self in relation to others are internalized. Through introjection the child internalizes a parent or other significant person as an internal presence that continues to feel like an object, rather than the self. Through identification the patient internalizes parents and other persons in such a way that the traits of the external object are incorporated into the self and the patient "owns" the traits. Those internal self-representations and object representations are crucial in developing the personality. Through externalization and projective identification, aspects of the self-representations and object representations are played out in interpersonal scenarios in which others are coerced into playing a role in the patient's internal life. Hence, patients with personality disorders are also identified by particular patterns of interpersonal relatedness that stem from those internal object relations patterns.

**Defense mechanisms.** To help patients with personality disorders, the psychiatrist needs to appreciate their underlying defenses. Defenses are unconscious mental processes that the ego uses to resolve conflicts among the four lodestars of the inner life—instinct (wish or need), reality, important people, and conscience. When defenses are most effective, especially in personality disorders, they can abolish anxiety and depression. Thus, a major reason that those with personality disorders are reluctant to alter their behavior is that to abandon a defense is to increase conscious anxiety and depression.

Although patients with personality disorders may be characterized by their most dominant or most rigid mechanism, each patient uses several defenses. Therefore, the management of the defense mechanisms used by patients with personality disorders is discussed here as a general topic, rather than under the specific disorders. Many of the formulations presented here in the language of psychoanalytic psychiatry can be translated into principles consistent with cognitive and behavioral approaches.

FANTASY. Many persons—especially eccentric, lonely, frightened persons who are often labeled schizoid—make extensive use of the defense of fantasy. They seek solace and satisfaction within themselves by creating imaginary lives, especially imaginary friends, within their minds. Often, such persons seem to be strikingly aloof. One needs to understand the unsociability of such persons as resting on a fear of intimacy, rather than to criticize them or feel rebuffed by their rejection. The therapist should maintain a quiet, reassuring, and considerate interest in them without insisting on reciprocal responses. Recognition of their fear of closeness and respect for their eccentric ways are useful.

DISSOCIATION. Dissociation or denial consists of a Pollyannalike replacement of unpleasant affects with pleasant ones. Frequent users of dissociation are often seen as dramatizing and as emotionally shallow; they may be labeled histrionic personalities. Their behavior is reminiscent of the stunts of anxious adolescents who, to erase anxiety, carelessly expose themselves to exciting dangers. Accepting such patients as exuberant and seductive is to miss their anxiety; but confronting them with their vulnerabilities and defects is to make them still more defensive. Because they seek appreciation of their attractiveness and courage, the therapist should not be too reserved. While remaining calm and firm, the therapist should realize that those patients are often inadvertent liars. Patients who use dissociation benefit from having a chance to ventilate their own anxieties; in the process they may "remember" what they "forgot." Often, dissociation and denial are best dealt with by the therapist's using displacement. Thus, the clinician may talk with patients about the same affective issue but in a context of a less threatening circumstance. The clinician's empathizing with the denied affect of such patients without directly confronting them with the facts may allow the patients to raise the original topic themselves.

ISOLATION. Isolation is characteristic of the orderly, controlled person, often labeled an obsessive-compulsive personality, who, unlike the histrionic personality, remembers the truth in fine detail but without affect. In a crisis the patient may show an intensification of self-restraint, overformal social behavior, and obstinacy. The patient's quest for control may be annoying or boring to the clinician. Often, such patients respond well to precise, systematic, and rational explanations. They value efficiency, cleanliness, and punctuality as much as they do the clinician's affective responsiveness. Whenever possible, clinicians should allow such patients to control their own care, rather than engage in a battle of wills.

PROJECTION. In projection the patients attribute their own unacknowledged feelings to others. Excessive faultfinding and sensitivity to criticism may seem to be prejudiced, hypervigilant injustice collecting but should not be met by defensiveness and argument. Instead, even minor mistakes on the part of the examiner and the possibility of future difficulties should be frankly acknowledged. Strict honesty, concern for the patient's rights, and maintaining the same formal, concerned distance as with a patient using fantasy are helpful. Confrontation guarantees a lasting enemy and an early termination of the interview. The therapist need not agree with the patient's injustice collecting, though, but should ask if they can agree to disagree.

The technique of counterprojection is especially helpful. In that technique the clinician acknowledges and gives paranoid patients full credit for their feelings and for their perceptions. Further, the clinician neither disputes the patient's complaints nor reinforces them but acknowledges that the world the paranoid patient describes can be imagined. The interviewer can then talk about the real motives and feelings, even though they are misattributed to someone else, and begin to cement an alliance with the patient.

SPLITTING. In splitting the patient divides ambivalently regarded people, both past and present, into good people and bad people. For example, in an inpatient setting, some staff members are idealized, and others are uniformly disparaged. The effect of that defensive behavior on a hospital ward can be highly disruptive; it ultimately provokes the staff to turn against the patient. Splitting is best mastered if the staff members anticipate the process, discuss it at staff meetings, and gently confront the patient with the fact that no one is all-good or all-bad.

PASSIVE AGGRESSION. In passive-aggressive defenses the anger is turned against the self; in psychoanalytic terminology it is most often termed masochism. It includes failure, procrastinations, silly or provocative behavior, self-demeaning clowning, and frankly self-destructive behavior. The hostility in such behavior is never entirely concealed, indeed, the mechanism, as in the case of wrist cutting, engenders such anger in others that they feel that they themselves have been assaulted and view the patient as a sadist, not a masochist. Passive aggression is best dealt with by trying to get the patients to ventilate their anger.

ACTING OUT. In acting out there is direct expression through action of an unconscious wish or conflict to avoid being conscious of either the idea or the affect that accompanies it. Tantrums, apparently motiveless assaults, child abuse, and pleasureless promiscuity are common examples. Because the behavior occurs outside reflective awareness, acting out often appears to the observer to be unaccompanied by guilt. Once acting out is not possible, the conflict behind the defense may be accessible. Faced with acting out, either aggressive or sexual, in an interview situation, the clinician must recognize (1) that the patient has lost control, (2) that anything the interviewer says will probably be misheard, and (3) that getting the patient's attention is of paramount importance. Depending on the circumstances, the clinician's response may be, "How can I help you if you keep screaming?"

Or, if the patient's loss of control seems to be escalating, "If you continue screaming, I'll leave." The interviewer who feels genuinely frightened of the patient can simply leave and ask for help, if necessary, from the police.

PROJECTIVE IDENTIFICATION. The defense mechanism of projective identification is used mainly in borderline personality disorder. It consists of three steps: (1) an aspect of the self is projected onto someone else, (2) the projector tries to coerce the other person to identify with what has been projected, and (3) the recipient of the projection and the projector feel a sense of oneness or union.

## PARANOID PERSONALITY DISORDER

Persons with paranoid personality disorder are characterized by long-standing suspiciousness and mistrust of people in general. They refuse responsibility for their own feelings and assign responsibility to others. They are often hostile, irritable, and angry. The bigot, the injustice collector, the pathologically jealous spouse, and the litigious crank often have paranoid personality disorder.

### Epidemiology

The prevalence of paranoid personality disorder is 0.5 to 2.5 percent. Persons with the disorder rarely seek treatment themselves; when referred to treatment by a spouse or an employer, they can often pull themselves together and not appear to be distressed. Relatives of schizophrenic patients show a higher incidence of paranoid personality disorder than do controls. The disorder is more common in men than in women, and it does not appear to have a familial pattern. The incidence among homosexuals is no higher than usual, as was once thought, but it is believed to be higher among minority groups, immigrants, and the deaf than in the general population.

### Diagnosis

On psychiatric examination, patients with paranoid personality disorder may appear to be formal and baffled at having been required to seek psychiatric help. Muscular tension, an inability to relax, and a need to scan the environment for clues may be evident. The patients' affect is often humorless and serious. Although some of the premises of their arguments may be false, their speech is goal-directed and logical. Their thought content shows evidence of projection, prejudice, and occasional ideas of reference. The DSM-IV diagnostic criteria are listed in Table 26–1.

### Clinical Features

The essential feature of paranoid personality disorder is a pervasive and unwarranted tendency—beginning by early adulthood and present in a variety of contexts—to interpret other people's actions as deliberately demeaning or threatening. Almost invariably, persons with the disorder expect to be exploited or harmed by others in some way. Frequently, they question, without justification, the

**Table 26–1**
**Diagnostic Criteria for Paranoid Personality Disorder**

A. A pervasive distrust and suspiciousness of others such that their motives are interpreted as malevolent, beginning by early adulthood and present in a variety of contexts, as indicated by four (or more) of the following:

   (1) suspects, without sufficient basis, that others are exploiting, harming, or deceiving him or her
   (2) is preoccupied with unjustified doubts about the loyalty or trustworthiness of friends or associates
   (3) is reluctant to confide in others because of unwarranted fear that the information will be used maliciously against him or her
   (4) reads hidden demeaning or threatening meanings into benign remarks or events
   (5) persistently bears grudges, i.e., is unforgiving of insults, injuries, or slights
   (6) perceives attacks on his or her character or reputation that are not apparent to others and is quick to react angrily or to counterattack
   (7) has recurrent suspicions, without justification, regarding fidelity of spouse or sexual partner

B. Does not occur exclusively during the course of schizophrenia, a mood disorder with psychotic features, or another psychotic disorder and is not due to the direct physiological effects of a general medical condition.

   **Note:** if criteria are met prior to the onset of schizophrenia, add "premorbid," e.g., "paranoid personality disorder (premorbid)."

Table from DSM-IV, *Diagnostic and Statistical Manual of Mental Disorders*, ed. 4. Copyright American Psychiatric Association, Washington, 1994. Used with permission.

loyalty or trustworthiness of friends or associates. Often, such persons are pathologically jealous, questioning without justification the fidelity of their spouses or sexual partners.

The patients externalize their own emotions and use the defense of projection—that is, they attribute to others the impulses and thoughts that they are unable to accept in themselves. Ideas of reference and logically defended illusions are common.

Patients with the disorder are affectively restricted and appear to be unemotional. They pride themselves on being rational and objective, but such is not the case. They lack warmth and are impressed with and pay close attention to power and rank, expressing disdain for those who are seen as weak, sickly, impaired, or defective in some way. In social situations, persons with paranoid personality disorder may appear businesslike and efficient, but they often generate fear or conflict in others.

### Differential Diagnosis

Paranoid personality disorder can usually be differentiated from delusional disorder because fixed delusions are absent in paranoid personality disorder. It can be differentiated from paranoid schizophrenia because hallucinations and formal thought disorder are absent in the personality disorders. Paranoid personality disorder can be distinguished from borderline personality disorder because the paranoid patient is rarely as capable as the borderline patient is of overinvolved, tumultuous relationships with others. Paranoid patients lack the antisocial character's long history of antisocial behavior. Persons with schizoid personality disorder are withdrawn and aloof and do not have paranoid ideation.

## Course and Prognosis

No adequate and systematic long-term studies of paranoid personality disorder have been conducted. In some persons the paranoid personality disorder is lifelong. In others it is a harbinger of schizophrenia. In still others, as they mature or as stress diminishes, paranoid traits give way to reaction formation, appropriate concern with morality, and altruistic concerns. In general, however, patients with paranoid personality disorder have lifelong problems working and living with others. Occupational and marital problems are common.

## Treatment

**Psychotherapy.** Psychotherapy is the treatment of choice. Therapists should be straightforward in all their dealings with the patient. If a therapist is accused of some inconsistency or fault, such as lateness for an appointment, honesty and an apology are better than a defensive explanation. Therapists must remember that trust and toleration of intimacy are troubled areas for patients with the disorder. Individual psychotherapy thus requires a professional and not overly warm style from the therapist. Paranoid patients do not do well in group psychotherapy, nor are they likely to tolerate the intrusiveness of behavior therapy. The clinician's too zealous use of interpretation—especially interpretation concerning deep feelings of dependence, sexual concerns, and wishes for intimacy—significantly increases the patient's mistrust.

At times, the behavior of patients with paranoid personality disorder becomes so threatening that the therapist must control it or set limits on it. Delusional accusations must be dealt with realistically but gently and without humiliating the patient. Paranoid patients are profoundly frightened if they feel that those trying to help them are weak and helpless; therefore, therapists should never threaten to take over control unless they are both willing and able to do so.

Behavior therapy has been used to improve social skills and to diminish suspiciousness through role playing.

**Pharmacotherapy.** Pharmacotherapy is useful in dealing with agitation and anxiety. In most cases an antianxiety agent such as diazepam (Valium) is sufficient. But it may be necessary to use an antipsychotic, such as thioridazine (Mellaril) or haloperidol (Haldol), in small dosages and for brief periods to manage severe agitation or quasidelusional thinking.

The antipsychotic drug pimozide (Orap) has been successfully used to reduce paranoid ideation in some patients.

## SCHIZOID PERSONALITY DISORDER

Schizoid personality disorder is diagnosed in patients who display a lifelong pattern of social withdrawal. Their discomfort with human interaction, their introversion, and their bland, constricted affect are noteworthy. Persons with schizoid personality disorder are often seen by others as eccentric, isolated, or lonely.

## Epidemiology

The prevalence of schizoid personality disorder is not clearly established. The disorder may affect 7.5 percent of the general population. The sex ratio of the disorder is unknown, although some studies report a 2-to-1 male-to-female ratio. Persons with the disorder tend to gravitate toward solitary jobs that involve little or no contact with others. Many prefer night work to day work, so that they do not have to deal with many people.

## Diagnosis

On the initial psychiatric examination, patients with schizoid personality disorder may appear to be ill at ease. They rarely tolerate eye contact. The interviewer may surmise that such patients are eager for the interview to end. Their affect may be constricted, aloof, or inappropriately serious. But underneath the aloofness, the sensitive clinician may recognize fear. The patients find it difficult to act lightheartedly. Their efforts at humor may seem adolescent and off the mark. The patients' speech is goal-directed, but they are likely to give short answers to questions and avoid spontaneous conversation. Occasionally, they may use an unusual figure of speech, such as an odd metaphor. Their mental content may reveal an unwarranted sense of intimacy with people they do not know well or whom they have not seen for a long time. They may be fascinated with inanimate objects or metaphysical constructs. The patients' sensorium is intact; their memory functions well; and their proverb interpretations are abstract. The DSM-IV diagnostic criteria are listed in Table 26–2.

## Clinical Features

Persons with schizoid personality disorder give an impression of being cold and aloof, and they display a remote reserve and a lack of involvement with everyday events and the concerns of others. They appear quiet, distant, seclusive, and unsociable. They may pursue their own lives with remarkably little need or longing for emotional ties with others. They are the last to catch on to changes in popular fashion.

The life histories of such persons reflect solitary interests and success at noncompetitive, lonely jobs that others find difficult to tolerate. Their sexual lives may exist exclusively in fantasy, and they may postpone mature sexuality indefinitely. Men may not marry because they are unable to achieve intimacy; women may passively agree to marry an aggressive man who wants the marriage. Usually, persons with schizoid personality disorder reveal a lifelong inability to express anger directly. They are able to invest enormous affective energy in nonhuman interests, such as mathematics and astronomy, and they may be very attached to animals. They are often engrossed in dietary and health fads, philosophical movements, and social improvement schemes, especially those that require no personal involvement.

Although persons with schizoid personality disorder appear to be self-absorbed and engaged in excessive daydreaming, they show no loss of capacity to recognize reality. Because aggressive acts are rarely included in their repertoire of usual responses, most threats, real or imagined, are dealt with by fantasied omnipotence or resignation. They are often seen as aloof; yet, at times, such persons are able to conceive, develop, and give to the world genuinely original, creative ideas.

### Differential Diagnosis

In contrast to patients with schizophrenia and schizotypal personality disorder, patients with schizoid personality disorder do not have schizophrenic relatives, and they may have successful, if isolated, work histories. Schizophrenic patients also differ by exhibiting thought disorder or delusional thinking. Although they share many traits with schizoid personality disorder patients, those with paranoid personality disorder exhibit more social engagement, a history of aggressive verbal behavior, and a greater tendency to project their feelings onto others. If just as emotionally constricted, obsessive-compulsive and avoidant personality disorder patients experience loneliness as dysphoric, possess a richer history of past object relations, and do not engage as much in autistic reverie. Theoretically, the chief distinction between a schizotypal personality disorder patient and a schizoid personality disorder patient is that the schizotypal patient shows a greater sim-

ilarity to the schizophrenic patient in oddities of perception, thought, behavior, and communication. Avoidant personality disorder patients are isolated but strongly wish to participate in activities, a characteristic absent in persons with schizoid personality disorder.

### Course and Prognosis

The onset of schizoid personality disorder is usually in early childhood. Like all personality disorders, schizoid personality disorder is long-lasting but not necessarily lifelong. The proportion of patients who go on to schizophrenia is unknown.

### Treatment

**Psychotherapy.** The treatment of schizoid personality disorder patients is similar to that of those with paranoid personality disorder. However, schizoid patients' tendencies toward introspection are consistent with the psychotherapist's expectations, and schizoid patients may become devoted, if distant, patients. As trust develops, schizoid patients may, with great trepidation, reveal a plethora of fantasies, imaginary friends, and fears of unbearable dependence—even of merging with the therapist.

In group therapy settings, schizoid personality disorder patients may be silent for long periods; nonetheless, they do become involved. The patients should be protected against aggressive attack by group members in regard to their proclivity for silence. With time the group members become important to schizoid patients and may provide the only social contact in their otherwise isolated existence.

**Pharmacotherapy.** Pharmacotherapy with small dosages of antipsychotics, antidepressants, and psychostimulants has been effective in some patients.

## SCHIZOTYPAL PERSONALITY DISORDER

Persons with schizotypal personality disorder are strikingly odd or strange, even to laypersons. Magical thinking, peculiar ideas, ideas of reference, illusions, and derealization are part of the schizotypal person's everyday world.

### Epidemiology

This occurs in about 3 percent of the population. The sex ratio is unknown. There is a greater association of cases among the biological relatives of schizophrenic patients than among controls and a higher incidence among monozygotic twins than among dizygotic twins (33 percent versus 4 percent in one study).

### Diagnosis

Schizotypal personality disorder is diagnosed on the basis of the patients' peculiarities of thinking, behavior, and appearance. History taking may be difficult because of the patients' unusual way of communicating. The DSM-IV diagnostic criteria for schizotypal personality disorder are given in Table 26–3.

## Table 26-3
## Diagnostic Criteria for Schizotypal Personality Disorder

A. A pervasive pattern of social and interpersonal deficits marked by acute discomfort with, and reduced capacity for, close relationships as well as by cognitive or perceptual distortions and eccentricities of behavior, beginning by early adulthood and present in a variety of contexts, as indicated by five (or more) of the following:

(1) ideas of reference (excluding delusions of reference)
(2) odd beliefs or magical thinking that influence behavior and are inconsistent with subcultural norms (e.g., superstitiousness, belief in clairvoyance, telepathy, or "sixth sense;" in children and adolescents, bizarre fantasies or preoccupations)
(3) unusual perceptual experiences, including bodily illusions
(4) odd thinking and speech (e.g., vague, circumstantial, metaphorical, overelaborate, or stereotyped)
(5) suspiciousness or paranoid ideation
(6) inappropriate or constricted affect
(7) behavior or appearance that is odd, eccentric, or peculiar
(8) lack of close friends or confidants other than first-degree relatives
(9) excessive social anxiety that does not diminish with familiarity and tends to be associated with paranoid fears rather than negative judgments about self

B. Does not occur exclusively during the course of schizophrenia, a mood disorder with psychotic features, another psychotic disorder, or a pervasive developmental disorder.

**Note:** if criteria are met prior to the onset of schizophrenia, add "premorbid," e.g., "schizotypal personality disorder (premorbid)."

Table from DSM-IV, *Diagnostic and Statistical Manual of Mental Disorders*, ed. 4. Copyright American Psychiatric Association, Washington, 1994. Used with permission.

## Clinical Features

In schizotypal personality disorder, thinking and communicating are disturbed. Like schizophrenic patients, persons with schizotypal personality disorder may not know their own feelings; yet they are exquisitely sensitive to detecting the feelings of others, especially negative affects like anger. They may be superstitious or claim clairvoyance. Their inner world may be filled with vivid imaginary relationships and childlike fears and fantasies. They may believe that they have special powers of thought and insight. Although frank thought disorder is absent, their speech may often require interpretation. They may admit that they have perceptual illusions or macropsia or that people appear to them as wooden and alike.

The speech of persons with schizotypal personality disorder may be odd or peculiar and have meaning only to them. They show poor interpersonal relationships and may act inappropriately. As a result, they are isolated and have few, if any, friends. The patients may show features of borderline personality disorder, and indeed, both diagnoses can be made. Under stress, schizotypal personality disorder patients may decompensate and have psychotic symptoms, but the symptoms are usually of brief duration. In severe cases, anhedonia and severe depression may be present.

## Differential Diagnosis

Theoretically, those with schizotypal personality disorder can be distinguished from schizoid and avoidant personality disorder patients by the presence of oddities in their behavior, thinking, perception, and communication and perhaps by a clear family history of schizophrenia. Schizotypal personality disorder patients can be distinguished from schizophrenic patients by their absence of psychosis. If psychotic symptoms do appear, they are brief and fragmentary. Some patients meet the criteria for both schizotypal personality disorder and borderline personality disorder. The paranoid personality disorder patient is characterized by suspiciousness but lacks the odd behavior of the schizotypal personality disorder patient.

## Course and Prognosis

A long-term study by Thomas McGlashan reported that 10 percent of persons with schizotypal personality disorder eventually committed suicide. Retrospective studies have shown that many patients thought to have been suffering from schizophrenia actually had schizotypal personality disorder, and the current clinical thinking is that the schizotype is the premorbid personality of the schizophrenic patient. Many patients, however, maintain a stable schizotypal personality throughout their lives and marry and work in spite of their oddities.

## Treatment

**Psychotherapy.** The principles of treatment of schizotypal personality disorder should be no different from those of schizoid personality disorder. However, the odd and peculiar thinking of schizotypal personality disorder patients must be handled carefully. Some patients are involved in cults, strange religious practices, and the occult. Therapists must not ridicule such activities or be judgmental about those beliefs or activities.

**Pharmacotherapy.** Antipsychotic medication may be useful in dealing with ideas of reference, illusions, and other symptoms of the disorder and can be used in conjunction with psychotherapy. Positive results have been reported with haloperidol. Antidepressants are of use when a depressive component of the personality is present.

## ANTISOCIAL PERSONALITY DISORDER

Antisocial personality disorder is characterized by continual antisocial or criminal acts, but it is not synonymous with criminality. Rather, it is an inability to conform to social norms that involves many aspects of the patient's adolescent and adult development. In the 10th revision of the International Classification of Disease (ICD-10), the disorder is called dissocial personality disorder.

## Epidemiology

The prevalence of antisocial personality disorder is 3 percent in men and 1 percent in women. It is most common in poor urban areas and among mobile residents of those areas. Boys with the disorder come from larger families than do girls with the disorder. The onset of the disorder is before the age of 15. Girls usually have symptoms before puberty, and boys even earlier. In prison populations the prevalence of antisocial personality disorder may be as high as 75 percent. A familial pattern is present in that it is five times more common among first-degree relatives of males with the disorder than among controls.

### Diagnosis

The patients may appear composed and credible in the interview. However, beneath the veneer (or, to use Hervey Cleckley's term, the mask of sanity), there is tension, hostility, irritability, and rage. Stress interviews, in which patients are vigorously confronted with inconsistencies in their histories, may be necessary to reveal the pathology. Even the most experienced clinicians have been fooled by such patients.

A diagnostic workup should include a thorough neurological examination. Because the patients often show abnormal EEG results and soft neurological signs suggestive of minimal brain damage in childhood, those findings can be used to confirm the clinical impression. The DSM-IV diagnostic criteria are listed in Table 26–4.

### Clinical Features

Patients with antisocial personality disorder often present a normal and even a charming and ingratiating exterior. Their histories, however, reveal many areas of dis-

**Table 26–4**
**Diagnostic Criteria for Antisocial Personality Disorder**

A. There is a pervasive pattern of disregard for and violation of the rights of others occurring since age 15 years, as indicated by three (or more) of the following:

  (1) failure to conform to social norms with respect to lawful behaviors as indicated by repeatedly performing acts that are grounds for arrest
  (2) deceitfulness, as indicated by repeated lying, use of aliases, or conning others for personal profit or pleasure
  (3) impulsivity or failure to plan ahead
  (4) irritability and aggressiveness, as indicated by repeated physical fights or assaults
  (5) reckless disregard for safety of self or others
  (6) consistent irresponsibility, as indicated by repeated failure to sustain consistent work behavior or honor financial obligations
  (7) lack of remorse, as indicated by being indifferent to or rationalizing having hurt, mistreated, or stolen from another

B. The individual is at least age 18 years.

C. There is evidence of conduct disorder with onset before age 15 years.

D. The occurrence of antisocial behavior is not exclusively during the course of schizophrenia or a manic episode.

*Table from DSM-IV, Diagnostic and Statistical Manual of Mental Disorders, ed 4. Copyright American Psychiatric Association, Washington, 1994. Used with permission.*

ordered life functioning. Lying, truancy, running away from home, thefts, fights, substance abuse, and illegal activities are typical experiences that the patients report as beginning in childhood. Often, antisocial personality disorder patients impress opposite-sex clinicians with the colorful, seductive aspects of their personalities, but same-sex clinicians may regard them as manipulative and demanding. Antisocial personality disorder patients show a lack of anxiety or depression that may seem grossly incongruous with their situations, and their own explanations of their antisocial behavior make it seem mindless. Suicide threats and somatic preoccupations may be common. Nevertheless, the patients' mental content reveals the complete absence of delusions and other signs of irrational thinking. In fact, they frequently have a heightened sense of reality testing. They often impress observers as having good verbal intelligence.

Antisocial personality disorder patients are highly represented by so-called con men. They are highly manipulative and are frequently able to talk others into participating in schemes that involve easy ways to make money or to achieve fame or notoriety, which may eventually lead the unwary to financial ruin or social embarrassment or both. Antisocial personality disorder patients do not tell the truth and cannot be trusted to carry out any task or adhere to any conventional standard of morality. Promiscuity, spouse abuse, child abuse, and drunk driving are common events in the patients' lives. A notable finding is a lack of remorse for those actions; that is, the patients appear to lack a conscience.

### Differential Diagnosis

Antisocial personality disorder can be distinguished from illegal behavior in that antisocial personality disorder involves many areas of the person's life. If antisocial behavior is the only manifestation, the patients are put in the DSM-IV category of additional conditions that may be a focus of clinical attention—specifically, adult antisocial behavior. Dorothy Lewis found that many of those persons have a neurological or mental disorder that has been either overlooked or not diagnosed. More difficult is the differentiation of antisocial personality disorder from substance abuse. When both substance abuse and antisocial behavior begin in childhood and continue into adult life, both disorders should be diagnosed. When, however, the antisocial behavior is clearly secondary to premorbid alcohol abuse or other substance abuse, the diagnosis of antisocial personality disorder is not warranted.

In diagnosing antisocial personality disorder, the clinician must adjust for the distorting effects of socioeconomic status, cultural background, and sex on its manifestations. Furthermore, the diagnosis of antisocial personality disorder is not warranted if mental retardation, schizophrenia, or mania can explain the symptoms.

### Course and Prognosis

Once an antisocial personality disorder develops, it runs an unremitting course, with the height of antisocial behavior usually occurring in late adolescence. The prognosis is variable. Some reports indicate that symptoms decrease as patients grow older. Many patients have somatization disorder and multiple physical complaints. Depressive disorders, alcohol use disorders, and other substance abuse are common.

## Treatment

**Psychotherapy.** If antisocial personality disorder patients are immobilized (for example, placed in hospitals), they often become amenable to psychotherapy. When the patients feel that they are among peers, their lack of motivation for change disappears. Perhaps that is why self-help groups have been more useful than jails in alleviating the disorder.

Before treatment can begin, firm limits are essential. The therapist must find some way of dealing with the patient's self-destructive behavior. And to overcome the antisocial personality disorder patient's fear of intimacy, the therapist must frustrate the patient's wish to run from honest human encounters. In doing so, the therapist faces the challenge of separating control from punishment and of separating help and confrontation from social isolation and retribution.

**Pharmacotherapy.** Pharmacotherapy is used to deal with incapacitating symptoms—such as anxiety, rage, and depression—but, because the patients are often substance abusers, drugs must be used judiciously. If the patient shows evidence of attention-deficit/hyperactivity disorder, psychostimulants, such as methylphenidate (Ritalin), may be of use. Attempts have been made to alter catecholamine metabolism with drugs and to control impulsive behavior with antiepileptic drugs, especially if abnormal wave forms are noted on an EEG.

## BORDERLINE PERSONALITY DISORDER

Borderline personality disorder patients stand on the border between neurosis and psychosis and are characterized by extraordinarily unstable affect, mood, behavior, object relations, and self-image. The disorder has also been called ambulatory schizophrenia, as-if personality (a term coined by Helene Deutsch), pseudoneurotic schizophrenia (described by Paul Hoch and Phillip Politan), and psychotic character (described by John Frosch). In ICD-10 it is called emotionally unstable personality disorder.

## Epidemiology

No definitive prevalence studies are available, but borderline personality disorder is thought to be present in about 1 or 2 percent of the population and is twice as common in women as in men. An increased prevalence of major depressive disorder, alcohol use disorders, and substance abuse is found in first-degree relatives of persons with borderline personality disorder.

## Diagnosis

According to DSM-IV, the diagnosis of borderline personality disorder can be made by early adulthood when the patient shows at least five of the criteria listed in Table 26-5.

Biological studies may aid in the diagnosis, as some borderline personality disorder patients show shortened rapid eye movement (REM) latency and sleep continuity disturbances, abnormal dexamethasone-suppression test results, and abnormal thyrotropin-releasing hormone test results. But those changes are also seen in some cases of depressive disorders.

## Clinical Features

Borderline personality disorder patients almost always appear to be in a state of crisis. Mood swings are common. The patients can be argumentative at one moment and depressed at the next and then complain of having no feelings at another time.

The patients may have short-lived psychotic episodes (so-called micropsychotic episodes), rather than full-blown psychotic breaks, and the psychotic symptoms of borderline personality disorder patients are almost always circumscribed, fleeting, or in doubt. The behavior of borderline personality disorder patients is highly unpredictable; consequently, they rarely achieve up to the level of their abilities. The painful nature of their lives is reflected in repetitive self-destructive acts. Such patients may slash their wrists and perform other self-mutilations to elicit help from others, to express anger, or to numb themselves to overwhelming affect.

---

**Table 26–5**
**Diagnostic Criteria for Borderline Personality Disorder**

---

A pervasive pattern of instability of interpersonal relationships, self-image, and affects, and marked impulsivity by early adulthood and present in a variety of contexts, as indicated by five (or more) of the following:

(1) frantic efforts to avoid real or imagined abandonment. **Note:** do not include suicidal or self-mutilating behavior covered in criterion 5.
(2) a pattern of unstable and intense interpersonal relationships characterized by alternating between extremes of idealization and devaluation
(3) identity disturbance: markedly and persistently unstable self-image or sense of self
(4) impulsivity in at least two areas that are potentially self-damaging (e.g., spending, sex, substance abuse, reckless driving, binge eating). **Note:** do not include suicidal or self-mutilating behavior covered in criterion 5.
(5) recurrent suicidal behavior, gestures, or threats, or self-mutilating behavior
(6) affective instability due to a marked reactivity of mood (e.g., intense episodic dysphoria, irritability, or anxiety usually lasting a few hours and only rarely more than a few days)
(7) chronic feelings of emptiness
(8) inappropriate, intense anger or difficulty controlling anger (e.g., frequent displays of temper, constant anger, recurrent physical fights)
(9) transient, stress-related paranoid ideation or severe dissociative symptoms

---

Table from DSM-IV, *Diagnostic and Statistical Manual of Mental Disorders*, ed 4. Copyright American Psychiatric Association, Washington, 1994. Used with permission.

Because they feel both dependent and hostile, borderline personality disorder patients have tumultuous interpersonal relationships. They can be dependent on those to whom they are close, and they can express enormous anger at their intimate friends when frustrated. However, borderline personality disorder patients cannot tolerate being alone, and they prefer a frantic search for companionship, no matter how unsatisfactory, to sitting by themselves. To assuage loneliness, if only for brief periods, they accept a stranger as a friend or are promiscuous. They often complain about chronic feelings of emptiness and boredom and the lack of a consistent sense of identify (*identity diffusion*); when pressed, they often complain about how depressed they feel most of the time in spite of the flurry of other affects.

Otto Kernberg described the defense mechanism of projective identification used in borderline personality disorder patients. In that primitive defense mechanism, intolerable aspects of the self are projected onto another person. The other person is induced to play the role of what is projected, and the two persons act in unison. Therapists must be aware of the process so that they can act neutrally toward such patients.

Most therapists agree that borderline personality disorder patients show ordinary reasoning abilities on structured tests, such as the Wechsler Adult Intelligence Scale, and show deviant processes only on unstructured projective tests, such as the Rorschach test.

Functionally, borderline personality disorder patients distort their present relationships by putting every person into either an all-good or an all-bad category. They see people as either nurturant and attachment figures or hateful and sadistic persons who deprive them of security needs and threaten them with abandonment whenever they feel dependent. As a result of that splitting, the good person is idealized, and the bad person is devalued. Shifts of allegiance from one person or group to another are frequent.

Some clinicians use the concepts of panphobia, pananxiety, panambivalence, and chaotic sexuality to delineate the borderline personality disorder patient's characteristics.

## Differential Diagnosis

The differentiation from schizophrenia is made on the basis of the borderline patient's having no prolonged psychotic episodes, thought disorder, or other classic schizophrenic signs. Schizotypal personality disorder patients show marked peculiarities of thinking, strange ideation, and recurrent ideas of reference. Paranoid personality disorder patients are marked by extreme suspiciousness. Histrionic and antisocial personality disorder patients are difficult to distinguish from borderline personality disorder patients. In general, the borderline personality disorder patient shows chronic feelings of emptiness, impulsivity, self-mutilation, short-lived psychotic episodes, manipulative suicide attempts, and unusually demanding involvement in close relationships.

## Course and Prognosis

The disorder is fairly stable in that patients change little over time. Longitudinal studies do not show a progression toward schizophrenia, but the patients have a high incidence of major depressive disorder episodes. The diagnosis is usually made before the age of 40, when the patients are attempting to make occupational, marital, and other choices and are unable to deal with the normal stages in the life cycle.

## Treatment

**Psychotherapy.** Psychotherapy for borderline personality disorder patients is an area of intensive investigation and has been the treatment of choice. Recently, pharmacotherapy has been added to the treatment regimen.

Psychotherapy is difficult for patient and therapist alike. Regression occurs easily in borderline personality disorder patients, who act out their impulses and show labile or fixed negative or positive transferences, which are difficult to analyze. Projective identification may also cause countertransference problems if the therapist is unaware that the patient is unconsciously trying to coerce the therapist to act out a particular type of behavior. Splitting as a defense mechanism causes the patient to alternately love and hate the therapist and others in the environment. A reality-oriented approach is more effective than in-depth interpretations of the unconscious.

Behavior therapy has been used with borderline personality disorder patients to control impulses and angry outbursts and to reduce sensitivity to criticism and rejection. Social skills training, especially with videotape playback, is helpful to enable patients to see how their actions affect others and thereby to improve their interpersonal behavior.

Borderline personality disorder patients often do well in a hospital setting in which they receive intensive psychotherapy on both an individual basis and a group basis. They also interact with trained staff members from a variety of disciplines and are provided with occupational, recreational, and vocational therapy. Such programs are especially helpful if the home environment is detrimental to the patient's rehabilitation because of intrafamilial conflicts or other stresses, such as parental abuse. The borderline personality disorder patient who is excessively impulsive, self-destructive, or self-mutilating can be provided with limits and observation within the protected environment of the hospital. Under ideal circumstances, patients remain in the hospital until they show marked improvement, which may take up to one year in some cases. At that time, patients can be discharged to special support systems, such as day hospitals, night hospitals, and halfway houses.

**Pharmacotherapy.** Pharmacotherapy for borderline personality disorder is useful to deal with specific personality features that interfere with the patients' overall functioning. Antipsychotics have been used to control anger, hostility, and brief psychotic episodes. Antidepressants improve the depressed mood that is common in the patients. The monoamine oxidase inhibitors (MAOIs) have been effective in modulating impulsive behavior in some patients. Benzodiazepines, particularly alprazolam (Xanax), help anxiety and depression, but some patients show a disinhibition with that class of drugs. Anticonvulsants, such as carbamazepine (Tegretol), may improve global functioning in some patients. Serotonergic agents, such as fluoxetine, have been helpful in some cases.

# HISTRIONIC PERSONALITY DISORDER

Histrionic personality disorder is characterized by colorful, dramatic, extroverted behavior in excitable, emotional persons. Accompanying their flamboyant presentations, however, is often an inability to maintain deep, long-lasting attachments.

## Epidemiology

According to DSM-IV limited data from general population studies suggest a prevalence of histrionic personality disorder of about 2 to 3 percent. Rates of about 10 to 15 percent have been reported in inpatient and outpatient mental health settings when structured assessment is used. It is diagnosed more frequently in women than in men. Some studies have found an association with somatization disorder and alcohol use disorders.

## Diagnosis

In the interview, histrionic personality disorder patients are generally cooperative and eager to give a detailed history. Gestures and dramatic punctuation in their conversations are common. They may make frequent slips of the tongue, and their language is colorful. Affective display is common, but, when pressed to acknowledge certain feelings (such as anger, sadness, and sexual wishes), they may respond with surprise, indignation, or denial. The results of the cognitive examination are usually normal, although a lack of perseverance may be shown on arithmetic or concentration tasks, and the patients' forgetfulness of affect-laden material may be astonishing. The DSM-IV diagnostic criteria are listed in Table 26–6.

## Clinical Features

Patients with histrionic personality disorder show a high degree of attention-seeking behavior. They tend to exaggerate their thoughts and feelings, making everything sound more important than it really is. They display temper tantrums, tears, and accusations if they are not the center of attention or are not receiving praise or approval.

Seductive behavior is common in both sexes. Sexual fantasies about persons with whom the patients are involved are common, but the patients are inconsistent about verbalizing those fantasies and may be coy or flirtatious, rather than sexually aggressive. In fact, histrionic patients

**Table 26–6**
**Diagnostic Criteria for Histrionic Personality Disorder**

A pervasive pattern of excessive emotionality and attention seeking, beginning by early adulthood and present in a variety of contexts, as indicated by five (or more) of the following:

(1) is uncomfortable in situations in which he or she is not the center of attention
(2) interaction with others is often characterized by inappropriate sexually seductive or provocative behavior
(3) displays rapidly shifting and shallow expression of emotions
(4) consistently uses physical appearance to draw attention to self
(5) has a style of speech that is excessively impressionistic and lacking in detail
(6) shows self-dramatization, theatricality, and exaggerated expression of emotion
(7) is suggestible, i.e., easily influenced by others or circumstances
(8) considers relationships to be more intimate than they actually are

Table from DSM-IV, *Diagnostic and Statistical Manual of Mental Disorders,* ed 4. Copyright American Psychiatric Association, Washington, 1994. Used with permission.

may have a psychosexual dysfunction: the women may be anorgasmic, and the men may be impotent. They may act on their sexual impulses to reassure themselves that they are attractive to the other sex. Their need for reassurance is endless. Their relationships tend to be superficial, however, and the patients can be vain, self-absorbed, and fickle. Their strong dependence needs make them overly trusting and gullible.

The major defenses of histrionic personality disorder patients are repression and dissociation. Accordingly, such patients are unaware of their true feelings and are unable to explain their motivations. Under stress, reality testing easily becomes impaired.

## Differential Diagnosis

The distinction between histrionic personality disorder and borderline personality disorder is difficult. In borderline personality disorder, suicide attempts, identity diffusion, and brief psychotic episodes are more likely. Although both conditions may be diagnosed in the same patient, the clinician should separate the two. Somatization disorder (Briquet's syndrome) may occur in conjunction with histrionic personality disorder. Patients with brief psychotic disorder and dissociative disorders may warrant a coexisting diagnosis of histrionic personality disorder.

## Course and Prognosis

With age, patients with histrionic personality disorder tend to show fewer symptoms, but, because they lack the same energy they had when younger, that difference may be more apparent than real. The patients are sensation seekers and may get into trouble with the law, abuse substances, and act promiscuously.

## Treatment

**Psychotherapy.** Patients with histrionic personality disorder are often unaware of their own real feelings; therefore, clarification of their inner feelings is an important therapeutic process. Psychoanalytically oriented psychotherapy, whether group or individual, is probably the treatment of choice for histrionic personality disorder.

**Pharmacotherapy.** Pharmacotherapy can be adjunctive when symptoms are targeted (such as the use of antidepressants for depression and somatic complaints, antianxiety agents for anxiety, and antipsychotics for derealization and illusions).

## NARCISSISTIC PERSONALITY DISORDER

Persons with narcissistic personality disorder are characterized by a heightened sense of self-importance and grandiose feelings that they are unique in some way.

## Epidemiology

According to DSM-IV, estimates of prevalence of narcissistic personality disorder range from 2 to 16 percent in the clinical population and are less than 1 percent in the general population. There may be a higher than usual risk in the offspring of parents with the disorder who impart to their children an unrealistic sense of omnipotence, grandiosity, beauty, and talent. The number of cases reported is increasing steadily.

## Diagnosis

Table 26–7 gives the DSM-IV diagnostic criteria for narcissistic personality disorder.

## Clinical Features

Persons with narcissistic personality disorder have a grandiose sense of self-importance. They consider themselves special people and expect special treatment. They handle criticism poorly and may become enraged that anyone would dare to criticize them, or they may appear to be completely indifferent to criticism. They want their own way and are frequently ambitious, desiring fame and fortune. Their sense of entitlement is striking. Their relationships are fragile, and they can make others furious because they refuse to obey the conventional rules of behavior. They are unable to show empathy, and they feign sympathy only to achieve their selfish ends. Interpersonal exploitiveness is commonplace. The patients have fragile self-esteem and are prone to depression. Interpersonal difficulties, rejection, loss, and occupational problems are among the stresses that narcissists commonly produce by their behavior—stresses they are least able to handle.

## Differential Diagnosis

Borderline, histrionic, and antisocial personality disorders are often present together with narcissistic person-

**Table 26–7**
**Diagnostic Criteria for Narcissistic Personality Disorder**

A pervasive pattern of grandiosity (in fantasy or behavior), need for admiration, and lack of empathy, beginning by early adulthood and present in a variety of contexts, as indicated by five (or more) of the following:

(1) has a grandiose sense of self-importance (e.g., exaggerates achievements and talents, expects to be recognized as superior without commensurate achievements)
(2) is preoccupied with fantasies of unlimited success, power, brilliance, beauty, or ideal love
(3) believes that he or she is "special" and unique and can only be understood by, or should associate with, other special or high-status people (or institutions)
(4) requires excessive admiration
(5) has a sense of entitlement i.e., unreasonable expectations of especially favorable treatment or automatic compliance with his or her expectations
(6) is interpersonally exploitative i.e., takes advantage of others to achieve his or her own ends
(7) lacks empathy: is unwilling to recognize or identify with the feelings and needs of others
(8) is often envious of others or believes that others are envious of him or her
(9) shows arrogant, haughty behaviors or attitudes

Table from DSM-IV, *Diagnostic and Statistical and Manual of Mental Disorders,* ed 4. Copyright American Psychiatric Association, Washington, 1994. Used with permission.

ality disorder, which means that a differential diagnosis is difficult. Patients with narcissistic personality disorder have less anxiety than do patients with borderline personality disorder, and their lives tend to be less chaotic. Suicidal attempts are also more likely to be associated with borderline personality disorder patients than with narcissistic personality disorder patients. Antisocial personality disorder patients give a history of impulsive behavior, often associated with alcohol or other substance abuse, that frequently gets them into trouble with the law. And histrionic personality disorder patients show features of exhibitionism and interpersonal manipulativeness that are similar to those of narcissistic personality disorder patients.

## Course and Prognosis

Narcissistic personality disorder is chronic and difficult to treat. Patients with the disorder must constantly deal with blows to their narcissism resulting from their own behavior or from life experiences. Aging is handled poorly, as the patients value beauty, strength, and youthful attributes, to which they cling inappropriately. They may be more vulnerable, therefore, to mid-life crises than are other groups.

## Treatment

**Psychotherapy.** The treatment of narcissistic personality disorder is difficult, as the patients must renounce their narcissism if progress is to be made. Psychiatrists such as Otto Kernberg and Heinz Kohut advocate using psychoanalytic approaches to effect change; however, much research is required to validate the diagnosis and to determine the best treatment.

**Pharmacotherapy.** Lithium (Eskalith) has been used with patients who have mood swings as part of the clinical picture. Because narcissistic personality disorder patients tolerate rejection poorly and are prone to depression, antidepressants may also be of use.

# AVOIDANT PERSONALITY DISORDER

Persons with avoidant personality disorder show an extreme sensitivity to rejection, which may lead to a socially withdrawn life. They are not asocial and show a great desire for companionship but are shy; they need unusually strong guarantees of uncritical acceptance. Such persons are commonly referred to as having an inferiority complex. In ICD-10 the patients are classified as having anxious personality disorder.

## Epidemiology

The prevalence of avoidant personality disorder is 1 to 10 percent; as defined, it is common. No information is available on sex ratio or familial pattern. Infants classified as having a timid temperament may be more prone to the disorder than are those high on activity-approach scales.

## Diagnosis

In clinical interviews the most striking aspect is the patients' anxiety about talking with the interviewer. The patients' nervous and tense manner appears to wax and wane with their perception of whether the interviewer likes them. They seem vulnerable to the interviewer's comments and suggestions and may regard a clarification or an interpretation as a criticism. The DSM-IV diagnostic criteria for avoidant personality disorder are listed in Table 26–8.

**Table 26–8**
**Diagnostic Criteria for Avoidant Personality Disorder**

A pervasive pattern of social inhibition, feelings of inadequacy, and hypersensitivity to negative evaluation, beginning by early adulthood and present in a variety of contexts, as indicated by four (or more) of the following:

(1) avoids occupational activities that involve significant interpersonal contact, because of fears of criticism, disapproval, or rejection
(2) is unwilling to get involved with people unless certain of being liked
(3) shows restraint within intimate relationships because of the fear of being shamed or ridiculed
(4) is preoccupied with being criticized or rejected in social situations
(5) is inhibited in new interpersonal situations because of feelings of inadequacy
(6) views self as socially inept, personally unappealing, or inferior to others
(7) is unusually reluctant to take personal risks or to engage in any new activities because they may prove embarrassing

Table from DSM-IV, *Diagnostic and Statistical Manual of Mental Disorders*, ed 4. Copyright American Psychiatric Association, Washington, 1994. Used with permission.

## Clinical Features

Hypersensitivity to rejection by others is the central clinical feature of avoidant personality disorder. Persons with the disorder desire the warmth and security of human companionship but justify their avoidance of forming relationships by their alleged fear of rejection. When talking with someone, they express uncertainty and a lack of self-confidence and may speak in a self-effacing manner. They are afraid to speak up in public or to make requests of others, because they are hypervigilant about rejection. They are apt to misinterpret other people's comments as derogatory or ridiculing. The refusal of any request leads them to withdraw from others and to feel hurt.

In the vocational sphere, avoidant personality disorder patients often take jobs on the sidelines. They rarely attain much personal advancement or exercise much authority. Instead, at work they may seem simply shy and eager to please.

Persons with the disorder are generally unwilling to enter relationships unless they are given an unusually strong guarantee of uncritical acceptance. Consequently, they often have no close friends or confidants. In general, their main personality trait is timidity.

## Differential Diagnosis

Avoidant personality disorder patients desire social interaction, compared with schizoid personality disorder patients, who want to be alone. Avoidant personality disorder patients are not as demanding, irritable, or unpredictable as are borderline and histrionic personality disorder patients. Avoidant personality disorder and dependent personality disorder are similar. The dependent personality disorder patient is presumed to have a greater fear of being abandoned or not loved than does the avoidant personality disorder patient; however, the clinical picture may be indistinguishable.

## Course and Prognosis

Many avoidant personality disorder patients are able to function, provided they are in a protected environment. Some marry, have children, and live their lives surrounded only by family members. Should their support system fail, however, they are subject to depression, anxiety, and anger. Phobic avoidance is common, and avoidant personality disorder patients may give histories of social phobia or go on to social phobia during the course of their illness.

## Treatment

**Psychotherapy.** Psychotherapeutic treatment depends on solidifying an alliance with the patient. As trust develops, the therapist conveys an accepting attitude toward the patient's fears, especially the fear of rejection. The therapist eventually encourages the patient to move out into the world to take what are perceived as great risks of humiliation, rejection, and failure. But the therapist should be cautious when giving assignments to exercise new social skills outside therapy, because failure may reinforce the patient's already poor self-esteem. Group therapy may help patients understand the effects that their sensitivity to rejection has on themselves and others. Assertiveness training is a form of behavior therapy that may teach patients to express their needs openly and to improve their self-esteem.

**Pharmacotherapy.** Pharmacotherapy has been used to manage anxiety and depression when present as associated features. Some patients are helped by β-blockers, such as atenolol (Tenormin), to manage autonomic nervous system hyperactivity, which tends to be high in patients with avoidant personality disorder, especially when they approach feared situations.

## DEPENDENT PERSONALITY DISORDER

Persons with dependent personality disorder subordinate their own needs to those of others, get others to assume responsibility for major areas in their lives, lack self-confidence, and may experience intense discomfort when alone for more than a brief period. In the first edition of *Diagnostic and Statistical Manual of Mental Disorders* (DSM-I), the condition was called passive-dependent personality. Freud described an oral-dependent dimension to personality characterized by dependence, pessimism, fear of sexuality, self-doubt, passivity, suggestibility, and lack of perseverance, which is similar to the DSM-IV categorization of dependent personality disorder.

### Epidemiology

Dependent personality disorder is more common in women than in men. One study diagnosed 2.5 percent of all personality disorders as falling into that category. It is more common in young children than in older children. Persons with chronic physical illness in childhood may be most prone to the disorder.

### Diagnosis

In the interview the patients appear to be compliant. They try to cooperate, welcome specific questions, and look for guidance. The DSM-IV diagnostic criteria for dependent personality disorder are listed in Table 26–9.

### Clinical Features

Dependent personality disorder is characterized by a pervasive pattern of dependent and submissive behavior. Persons with the disorder are unable to make decisions without an excessive amount of advice and reassurance from others.

Dependent personality disorder patients avoid positions of responsibility and become anxious if asked to assume a leadership role. They prefer to be submissive. When on their own, they find it difficult to persevere at tasks but may find it easy to perform those tasks for someone else.

Persons with the disorder do not like to be alone. They seek out others on whom they can depend, and their re-

**Table 26–9**
**Diagnostic Criteria for Dependent Personality Disorder**

A pervasive and excessive need to be taken care of, that leads to submissive and clinging behavior and fears of separation, beginning by early adulthood and present in a variety of contexts, as indicated by five (or more) of the following:

(1) has difficulty making everyday decisions without an excessive amount of advice and reassurance from others
(2) needs others to assume responsibility for most major areas of his or her life
(3) has difficulty expressing disagreement with others because of fear of loss of support or approval. **Note:** do not include realistic fears of retribution.
(4) has difficulty initiating projects or doing things on his or her own (because of a lack of self-confidence in judgment or abilities rather than a lack of motivation or energy)
(5) goes to excessive lengths to obtain nurturance and support from others, to the point of volunteering to do things that are unpleasant
(6) feels uncomfortable or helpless when alone because of exaggerated fears of being unable to care for himself or herself
(7) urgently seeks another relationship as a source of care and support when a close relationship ends
(8) is unrealistically preoccupied with fears of being left to take care of himself or herself

Table from DSM-IV, *Diagnostic and Statistical Manual of Mental Disorders*, ed 4. Copyright American Psychiatric Association, Washington, 1994. Used with permission.

lationships are thus distorted by their need to be attached to that other person. In *folie à deux* (shared psychotic disorder), one member of the pair is usually suffering from dependent personality disorder, and the submissive partner takes on the delusional system of the more aggressive, assertive partner on whom he or she is dependent.

Pessimism, self-doubt, passivity, and fears of expressing sexual and aggressive feelings characterize the behavior of the dependent personality disorder patient. An abusive, unfaithful, or alcoholic spouse may be tolerated for long periods of time in order not to disturb the sense of attachment.

### Differential Diagnosis

The traits of dependence are found in many psychiatric disorders, which makes the differential diagnosis difficult. Dependence is a prominent factor in histrionic and borderline personality disorder patients; however, dependent personality disorder patients usually have a long-standing relationship with one person on whom they are dependent, rather than on a series of persons, and they do not tend to be overtly manipulative. Schizoid and schizotypal personality disorder patients may be indistinguishable from avoidant personality disorder patients.

Dependent behavior may occur in patients with agoraphobia, but agoraphobic patients tend to have a high level of overt anxiety or even panic.

### Course and Prognosis

Little is known about the course of dependent personality disorder. There tends to be impaired occupational functioning, as the patients have an inability to act independently and without close supervision. Social relationships are limited to those on whom the persons can depend, and many suffer physical or mental abuse because they cannot assert themselves. They risk major depressive disorder if they sustain the loss of the person on whom they are dependent. However, the prognosis with treatment is favorable.

## Treatment

**Psychotherapy.** The treatment of dependent personality disorder can often be successful. Insight-oriented therapies enable patients to understand the antecedents of their behavior, and, with the support of a therapist, the patients can become more independent, assertive, and self-reliant than they were before therapy.

A pitfall in the treatment may appear when the therapist encourages the patient to change the dynamics of a pathological relationship (for example, encourages a physically abused wife to seek help from the police). At that point the patient may become anxious, be unable to cooperate in therapy, and feel torn between complying with the therapist and losing a pathological external relationship. The therapist must show great respect for a dependent personality disorder patient's feelings of attachment, no matter how pathological those feelings may seem.

Behavior therapy, assertiveness training, family therapy, and group therapy have all been used, with successful outcomes in many cases.

**Pharmacotherapy.** Pharmacotherapy has been used to deal with such specific symptoms as anxiety and depression, which are common associated features of dependent personality disorder. Those patients who experience panic attacks or who have high levels of separation anxiety may be helped by imipramine (Tofranil). Benzodiazepines and serotonergic agents have also been useful. If the patients' depression or withdrawal symptoms respond to psychostimulants, they may be used.

## OBSESSIVE-COMPULSIVE PERSONALITY DISORDER

Obsessive-compulsive personality disorder is characterized by emotional constriction, orderliness, perseverance, stubbornness, and indecisiveness. The essential feature of the disorder is a pervasive pattern of perfectionism and inflexibility. In ICD-10 the disorder is called anankastic personality disorder.

### Epidemiology

The prevalence of obsessive-compulsive personality disorder is unknown. It is more common in men than in women and is diagnosed most often in oldest children. The disorder also occurs more frequently in first-degree biological relatives of persons with the disorder than in the general population. Patients often have backgrounds characterized by harsh discipline. Freud hypothesized that the disorder is associated with difficulties in the anal stage of

psychosexual development, generally around the age of 2. However, in various studies that theory has not been validated.

### Diagnosis

In the interview, obsessive-compulsive personality disorder patients may have a stiff, formal, and rigid demeanor. Their affect is not blunted or flat but can be described as constricted. They lack spontaneity. Their mood is usually serious. Such patients may be anxious about not being in control of the interview. Their answers to questions are unusually detailed. The defense mechanisms they use are rationalization, isolation, intellectualization, reaction formation, and undoing. The DSM-IV diagnostic criteria for obsessive-compulsive personality disorder are listed in Table 26–10.

### Clinical Features

Persons with obsessive-compulsive personality disorder are preoccupied with rules, regulations, orderliness, neatness, details, and the achievement of perfection. Those traits account for a general constriction of the entire personality. Such persons are formal and serious and often lack a sense of humor. They insist that rules be followed rigidly and are unable to tolerate what they perceive to be infractions. Accordingly, they lack flexibility and are intolerant. They are capable of prolonged work, provided it is routinized and does not require changes to which they cannot adapt.

**Table 26–10**
**Diagnostic Criteria for Obsessive-Compulsive Personality Disorder**

A pervasive pattern of preoccupation with orderliness, perfectionism, and mental and interpersonal control, at the expense of flexibility, openness, and efficiency, beginning by early adulthood and present in a variety of contexts, as indicated by four (or more) of the following:

(1) is preoccupied with details, rules, lists, order, organization, or schedules to the extent that the major point of the activity is lost
(2) shows perfectionism that interferes with task completion (e.g., is unable to complete a project because his or her own overly strict standards are not met)
(3) is excessively devoted to work and productivity to the exclusion of leisure activities and friendships (not accounted for by obvious economic necessity)
(4) is overconscientious, scrupulous, and inflexible about matters of morality, ethics, or values (not accounted for by cultural or religious identification)
(5) is unable to discard worn-out or worthless objects even when they have no sentimental value
(6) is reluctant to delegate tasks or to work with others unless they submit to exactly his or her way of doing things
(7) adopts a miserly spending style toward both self and others; money is viewed as something to be hoarded for future catastrophes
(8) shows rigidity and stubbornness

Table from DSM-IV, *Diagnostic and Statistical Manual of Mental Disorders*, ed 4. Copyright American Psychiatric Association, Washington, 1994. Used with permission.

Obsessive-compulsive personality disorder patients' interpersonal skills are limited. They alienate people, are unable to compromise, and insist that others submit to their needs. They are, however, eager to please those whom they see as more powerful than themselves and carry out their wishes in an authoritarian manner. Because of their fear of making mistakes, they are indecisive and ruminate about making decisions. Although a stable marriage and occupational adequacy are common, obsessive-compulsive personality disorder patients have few friends.

Anything that threatens to upset the routine of the patients' lives or their perceived stability can precipitate a great deal of anxiety that is otherwise bound up in the rituals that they impose on their lives and try to impose on others.

### Differential Diagnosis

When recurrent obsessions or compulsions are present, obsessive-compulsive disorder should be noted on Axis I. Perhaps the most difficult distinction is between the outpatient with some obsessive-compulsive traits and one with obsessive-compulsive personality disorder. The diagnosis of personality disorder is reserved for those patients with significant impairments in their occupational or social effectiveness. In some cases, delusional disorder coexists with personality disorders and should be noted.

### Course and Prognosis

The course of obsessive-compulsive personality disorder is variable and not predictable. From time to time, obsessions or compulsions may develop in the course of the personality disorder. Some adolescents with obsessive-compulsive personality disorder evolve into warm, open, and loving adults; but in others, the disorder can be either the harbinger of schizophrenia or—decades later and exacerbated by the aging process—major depressive disorder.

Persons with obsessive-compulsive personality disorder may do well in positions demanding methodical, deductive, or detailed work, but they are vulnerable to unexpected changes, and their personal lives may remain barren. Depressive disorders, especially those of late onset, are common.

### Treatment

**Psychotherapy.** Unlike patients with the other personality disorders, obsessive-compulsive personality disorder patients often know that they are suffering, and they seek treatment on their own. Free association and nondirective therapy are highly valued by the overtrained, oversocialized obsessive-compulsive personality disorder patient. However, the treatment is often long and complex, and countertransference problems are common.

Group therapy and behavior therapy occasionally offer certain advantages. In both contexts it is easy to interrupt the patients in the midst of their maladaptive interactions or explanations. Having the completion of their habitual behavior prevented raises patients' anxiety and leaves them susceptible to learning new coping strategies. Patients can also receive direct rewards for change in group therapy, something less often possible in individual psychotherapies.

**Pharmacotherapy.** Clonazepam (Klonopin) is a benzodiazepine with anticonvulsant use that has reduced symptoms in patients with severe obsessive-compulsive disorder. Whether it is of use in the personality disorder is not known. Clomipramine (Anafranil) and such serotonergic agents as fluoxetine may be of use if obsessive-compulsive signs and symptoms break through.

## PERSONALITY DISORDER NOT OTHERWISE SPECIFIED

This category in DSM-IV is reserved for disorders that do not fit into any of the previously described personality disorders. Passive-aggressive personality disorder and depressive personality disorder are now listed as examples of personality disorder not otherwise specified (NOS). A narrow spectrum of behavior or a particular trait—such as oppositionalism, sadism, or masochism—can also be classified here. A patient who has features of more than one personality disorder but does not meet the full criteria for any one personality disorder can be classified here.

The DSM-IV diagnostic criteria for personality disorder not otherwise specified are presented in Table 26–11.

### Passive-Aggressive Personality Disorder

The person with passive-aggressive personality disorder is characterized by covert obstructionism, procrastination, stubbornness, and inefficiency. Such behavior is a manifestation of underlying aggression, which is expressed passively. In DSM-IV the disorder is also called negativistic personality disorder.

**Epidemiology.** No data are available about the epidemiology of the disorder. Sex ratio, familial patterns, and prevalence have not been adequately studied.

**Diagnosis.** The diagnostic criteria for passive-aggressive disorder are presented in Table 26–12.

---

**Table 26–11**
**Diagnostic Criteria for Personality Disorder Not Otherwise Specified**

This category is for disorders of personality functioning that do not meet criteria for any specific personality disorder. An example is the presence of features of more than one specific personality disorder that do not meet the full criteria for any one personality disorder ("mixed personality"), but that together cause clinically significant distress or impairment in one or more important areas of functioning (e.g., social or occupational). This category can also be used when the clinician judges that a specific personality disorder that is not included in this classification is appropriate. Examples include passive aggressive personality disorder and depressive personality disorder.

Table from DSM-IV, *Diagnostic and Statistical Manual of Mental Disorders*, ed 4. Copyright American Psychiatric Association, Washington, 1994. Used with permission.

**Table 26–12**
**Research Criteria for Passive-Aggressive Personality Disorder**

A. A pervasive pattern of negativistic attitudes and passive resistance to demands for adequate performance, beginning by early adulthood and present in a variety of contexts, as indicated by four (or more) of the following:

  (1) passively resists fulfilling routine social and occupational tasks
  (2) complains of being misunderstood and unappreciated by others
  (3) is sullen and argumentative
  (4) unreasonably criticizes and scorns authority
  (5) expresses envy and resentment toward those apparently more fortunate
  (6) voices exaggerated and persistent complaints of personal misfortune
  (7) alternates between hostile defiance and contrition

B. Does not occur exclusively during major depressive episodes and is not better accounted for by dysthymic disorder.

Table from DSM-IV, *Diagnostic and Statistical Manual of Mental Disorders*, ed 4. Copyright American Psychiatric Association, Washington, 1994. Used with permission.

**Clinical features.** Passive-aggressive personality disorder patients characteristically procrastinate, resist demands for adequate performance, find excuses for delays, and find fault with those on whom they depend; yet they refuse to extricate themselves from the dependent relationships. They usually lack assertiveness and are not direct about their own needs and wishes. They fail to ask needed questions about what is expected of them and may become anxious when forced to succeed or when their usual defense of turning anger against themselves is removed.

In interpersonal relationships, passive-aggressive personality disorder patients attempt to manipulate themselves into a position of dependence, but their passive, self-detrimental behavior is often experienced by others as punitive and manipulative. Others must do their errands and carry out their routine responsibilities. Friends and clinicians may become enmeshed in trying to assuage the patients' many claims of unjust treatment. The close relationships of passive-aggressive personality disorder patients are rarely tranquil or happy. Because the patients are bound to their resentment more closely than to their satisfaction, they may never even formulate what they want for themselves in regard to enjoyment. People with the disorder lack self-confidence and are typically pessimistic about the future.

**Differential diagnosis.** Passive-aggressive personality disorder needs to be differentiated from histrionic and borderline personality disorders; however, the passive-aggressive personality disorder patient is less flamboyant, dramatic, affective, and openly aggressive than are the histrionic and borderline personality disorder patients.

**Course and prognosis.** In a follow-up study averaging 11 years of 100 passive-aggressive inpatients, Ivor Small found that passive-aggressive personality disorder was the primary diagnosis in 54 of them, 18 were also alcohol abusers, and 30 could be clinically labeled as depressed. Of the 73 former patients located, 58 (79 percent) had per-sistent psychiatric difficulties, and 9 (12 percent) were considered symptom-free. Most seemed irritable, anxious, and depressed; somatic complaints were numerous. Only 32 (44 percent) were employed full-time as workers or homemakers. Although neglect of responsibility and suicide attempts were common, only 1 patient had committed suicide in the interim. Although 28 (38 percent) were readmitted to a hospital, only 3 patients were called schizophrenic.

**Treatment**

PSYCHOTHERAPY. Passive-aggressive personality disorder patients who receive supportive psychotherapy have good outcomes. However, psychotherapy for patients with passive-aggressive personality disorder has many pitfalls: to fulfill their demands is often to support their pathology, but to refuse their demands is to reject them. The therapy session can thus become a battleground in which the patient expresses feelings of resentment against a therapist on whom the patient wishes to become dependent. With passive-aggressive personality disorder patients, the clinician must treat suicide gestures as one would any covert expression of anger and not as one would treat object loss in major depressive disorder. The therapist must point out the probable consequences of passive-aggressive behaviors as they occur. Such confrontations may be more helpful in changing the patient's behavior than is a correct interpretation.

PHARMACOTHERAPY. Antidepressants should be prescribed only when clinical indications of depression and the possibility of suicide exist. Some patients have responded to benzodiazepines and psychostimulants, depending on the clinical features.

## Depressive Personality Disorder

Persons with depressive personality disorder are characterized by lifelong traits that fall along the depressive spectrum. They are pessimistic, anhedonic, duty-bound, self-doubting, and chronically unhappy. The disorder is newly classified in DSM-IV, but melancholic personality was described by early 20th-century European psychiatrists, such as Ernst Kretschmer.

**Epidemiology.** Because depressive personality disorder is a new category, no epidemiological figures are available. However, on the basis of the prevalence of depressive disorders in the overall population, depressive personality disorder seems to be common, to occur equally in men and women, and to occur in families in which depressive disorders are found.

**Etiology.** The cause of depressive personality disorder is unknown, but the factors that are involved in dysthymic disorder and major depressive disorder may be at work. Psychological theories involve early loss, poor parenting, punitive superegos, and extreme feelings of guilt. Biological theories involve the hypothalamic-pituitary-adrenal-thyroid axis, including the noradrenergic and serotonergic amine systems. Genetic predisposition, as indicated by Stella Chess's studies of temperament, may also play a role.

**Diagnosis and clinical features.** A classic description of the depressive personality was provided in 1963 by Arthur Noyes and Laurence Kolb:

They feel but little of the normal joy of living and are inclined to be lonely and solemn, to be gloomy, submissive, pessimistic, and self-depreciatory. They are prone to express regrets and feelings of inadequacy and hopelessness. They are often meticulous, perfectionistic, overconscientious, preoccupied with work, feel responsibility keenly, and are easily discouraged under new conditions. They are fearful of disapproval, tend to suffer in silence and perhaps to cry easily, although usually not in the presence of others. A tendency to hesitation, indecision, and caution betrays an inherent feeling of insecurity.

More recently, H. Akiskal described 7 groups of depressive traits: (1) quiet, introverted, passive, and nonassertive; (2) gloomy, pessimistic, serious, and incapable of fun; (3) self-critical, self-reproaching, and self-derogatory; (4) skeptical, critical of others, and hard to please; (5) conscientious, responsible, and self-disciplined; (6) brooding and given to worry; (7) preoccupied with negative events, feelings of inadequacy, and personal shortcomings.

Patients with depressive personality disorder complain of chronic feelings of unhappiness. They admit to feelings of low self-esteem and find it difficult to find anything in their lives about which they are joyful, hopeful, or optimistic. They are likely to denigrate their work, themselves, and their relationships with others; and they are self-critical and derogatory. Their physiognomy often reflects their mood—poor posture, depressed facies, hoarse voice, and psychomotor retardation.

**Differential diagnosis.** Dysthymic disorder is a mood disorder characterized by greater fluctuation in mood than that found in depressive personality disorder. The personality disorder is chronic and lifelong, whereas dysthymic disorder is episodic, can occur at any time, and usually has a precipitating stressor. The depressive personality can be conceptualized as part of a spectrum of affective conditions in which dysthymic disorder and major depressive disorder are more severe variants.

Avoidant personality disorder patients are introverted and dependent but tend to be more anxious than depressed, compared with persons with depressive personality disorder.

**Course and prognosis.** Persons with depressive personality disorder may be at great risk for dysthymic disorder and major depressive disorder. In a recent study by Donald Klein and Gregory Mills subjects with depressive personality exhibited significantly higher rates of current mood disorder, lifetime mood disorder, major depression, and dysthymia than subjects without depressive personality.

**Treatment.** Psychotherapy is the treatment of choice for depressive personality disorder. Patients respond to insight-oriented psychotherapy, and, because their reality testing is good, they are able to gain insight into the psychodynamics of their illness and to appreciate its effects on their interpersonal relationships. Treatment is likely to be long-term. Cognitive therapy helps the patients understand the cognitive manifestations of their low self-esteem and pessimism. Other types of psychotherapy that are useful include group psychotherapy and interpersonal therapy. Some persons respond to self-help measures.

Psychopharmalogical approaches include the use of antidepressant medications, especially such serotoneric agents as sertraline (Zoloft), 50 mg a day. Some patients respond to small dosages of psychostimulants, such as amphetamine, 5 to 15 mg a day. In all cases, psychopharmacological agents should be combined with psychotherapy to achieve maximum effects.

## Sadomasochistic Personality Disorder

Some personality types are characterized by elements of sadism or masochism or a combination of both. Sadomasochistic personality disorder is listed here because it is of major clinical and historical interest in psychiatry. It is not an official diagnostic category in DSM-IV or its appendix, but it can be diagnosed as personality disorder not otherwise classified.

Sadism (named after the Marquis de Sade, who wrote in the 18th century about persons who experienced sexual pleasure while inflicting pain on others) is the desire to cause others pain by being either sexually abusive or physically or psychologically abusive in general. Freud believed that sadists ward off castration anxiety and are able to achieve sexual pleasure only when they are able to do to others what they fear will be done to them.

Masochism (named after Leopold von Sacher-Masoch, a 19th-century Austrian novelist) is the achievement of sexual gratification by inflicting pain on the self. Generally, the so-called moral masochist seeks humiliation and failure, rather than physical pain. Freud believed that masochists' ability to achieve orgasm is disturbed by anxiety and guilt feelings about sex that are alleviated by their own suffering and punishment.

Clinical observations indicate that elements of both sadistic and masochistic behavior are usually present in the same person. Treatment with insight-oriented psychotherapy, including psychoanalysis, has been effective in some cases. As a result of therapy, the patients become aware of the need for self-punishment secondary to excessive unconscious guilt and also come to recognize their repressed aggressive impulses, which originate in early childhood.

## Sadistic Personality Disorder

Sadistic personality disorder was a controversial addition to an appendix in DSM-III-R, and it is not included in DSM-IV. However, it still appears in the literature and may be of descriptive use. Persons with sadistic personality disorder show a pervasive pattern of cruel, demeaning, and aggressive behavior, beginning in early adulthood, that is directed toward others. Physical cruelty or violence is used to inflict pain on others and not to achieve some other goal, such as mugging someone in order to steal. Persons with the disorder like to humiliate or demean people in front of others and have usually treated or disciplined someone unusually harshly, especially children. In general, sadistic personality disorder persons are fascinated by violence, weapons, injury, or torture. To be included in the category, such persons are not motivated solely by the desire to derive sexual arousal from their behavior; if they are so motivated, the paraphilia of sexual sadism should be diagnosed.

# Personality Change Due to a General Medical Condition

Personality change due to a general medical condition (Section 10.5) deserves some discussion here. ICD-10 lists the diagnosis of personality and behavioral disorders due to brain disease, damage, and dysfunction, which includes organic personality disorder (Table 26–13), postencephalic syndrome, and postconcussional syndrome.

Personality change due to a general medical condition is characterized by a marked change in personality style and traits from a previous level of functioning. The patient must show evidence of a causative organic factor antedating the onset of the personality change.

**Etiology.** Structural damage to the brain is usually the cause of the personality change. Head trauma is probably the most common cause. Cerebral neoplasms and vascular accidents, particularly of the temporal and frontal lobes, are also common causes. The conditions most often associated with personality change are listed in Table 26–14.

**Diagnosis and clinical features.** A change in personality from previous patterns of behavior or an exacerbation of previous personality characteristics is notable. Impaired

**Table 26–13**
**ICD–10 Diagnostic Criteria for Organic Personality Disorder**

This disorder is characterized by a significant alteration of the habitual patterns of premorbid behaviour. The expression of emotions, needs, and impulses is particularly affected. Cognitive functions may be defective mainly or even exclusively in the areas of planning and anticipating the likely personal and social consequences, as in the so-called frontal lobe syndrome. However, it is now known that this syndrome occurs not only with frontal lobe lesions but also with lesions to other circumscribed areas of the brain.

*Diagnostic guidelines*
In addition to an established history or other evidence of brain disease, damage, or dysfunction, a definitive diagnosis requires the presence of two or more of the following features:

(a) consistently reduced ability to persevere with goal-directed activities, especially those involving longer periods of time and postponed gratification;
(b) altered emotional behaviour, characterized by emotional lability, shallow and unwarranted cheerfulness (euphoria, inappropriate jocularity), and easy change to irritability or short-lived outbursts of anger and aggression; in some instances apathy may be a more prominent feature;
(c) expression of needs and impulses without consideration of consequences or social convention (the patient may engage in dissocial acts, such as stealing, inappropriate sexual advances, or voracious eating, or may exhibit disregard for personal hygiene);
(d) cognitive disturbances, in the form of suspiciousness or paranoid ideation, and/or excessive preoccupation with a single, usually abstract, theme (e.g. religion, "right" and "wrong");
(e) marked alteration of the rate and flow of language production, with features such as circumstantiality, over-inclusiveness, viscosity, and hypergraphia;
(f) altered sexual behaviour (hyposexuality or change of sexual preference).

Table from World Health Organization: *The ICD-10 Classification of Mental and Behavioural Disorders: Clinical Descriptions and Diagnostic Guidelines.* World Health Organization, Geneva, 1992. Used with permission.

**Table 26–14**
**Medical Conditions Associated with Personality Change**

Head trauma
Cerebrovascular diseases
Cerebral tumors
Epilepsy (particularly complex partial epilepsy)
Huntington's disease
Multiple sclerosis
Endocrine disorders
Heavy metal poisoning (manganese, mercury)
Neurosyphilis
Acquired immune deficiency syndrome (AIDS)

control of the expression of emotions and impulses is a cardinal feature. Emotions are characteristically labile and shallow, although euphoria or apathy may be prominent. The euphoria may mimic hypomania, but true elation is absent, and the patient may admit to not really feeling happy. There is a hollow and silly ring to the patient's excitement and facile jocularity, particularly if the frontal lobes are involved. Also associated with damage to the frontal lobes, the so-called frontal lobe syndrome, is prominent indifference and apathy, characterized by a lack of concern for events in the immediate environment. Temper outbursts with little or no provocation may occur, especially after alcohol ingestion, and may result in violent behavior. The expression of impulses may be manifested by inappropriate jokes, a coarse manner, improper sexual advances, and antisocial conduct resulting in conflicts with the law, such as assaults on others, sexual misdemeanors, and shoplifting. Foresight and the ability to anticipate the social or legal consequences of one's actions are typically diminished. People with temporal lobe epilepsy characteristically show humorlessness, hypergraphia, hyperreligiosity, and marked aggressiveness during seizures.

Patients with personality change due to a general medical condition have a clear sensorium. Mild disorders of cognitive function often coexist but do not amount to intellectual deterioration. Patients tend to be inattentive, which may account for disorders of recent memory. With some prodding, however, patients are likely to recall what they claim to have forgotten. The diagnosis should be suspected in patients who show marked changes in behavior or personality involving emotional lability and impaired impulse control, who have no history of mental disorder, and whose personality changes occur abruptly or over a relatively brief period of time. The DSM-IV diagnostic criteria appear in Table 10.5–3.

ANABOLIC STEROIDS. An increasing number of high school and college athletes and other persons involved with weight lifting are using anabolic steroids as a shortcut to maximize their physical development. Anabolic steroids include such drugs as oxymetholone (Anadrol), somatropin (Humatrope), stanozolol (Winstrol), and testosterone cypionate (DEPO-Testosterone).

DSM-IV does not include a diagnostic category for substance-induced personality disorder, so it is unclear whether a personality change due to steroid abuse is better diagnosed as personality change due to a general medical condition or as one of the other (or unknown) substance use disorders. It is discussed here because anabolic steroids can cause persistent alterations of personality and behavior.

**Differential diagnosis.** Dementia involves global deterioration in intellectual and behavioral capacities, of which personality change is just one category. A personality change may herald a cognitive disorder that will eventually evolve into dementia. In those cases, as the deterioration begins to encompass significant memory and cognitive deficits, the diagnosis is changed from personality change due to a general medical condition to a dementia. In differentiating the specific syndrome from other disorders in which personality change may occur— such as schizophrenia, delusional disorder, mood disorders, and impulse control disorders—the physician must consider the most important factor, the presence in the personality change disorder of a specific organic causative factor.

**Course and prognosis.** Both the course and the prognosis of personality change due to a general medical condition depend on its cause. If the disorder is the result of structural damage to the brain, the disorder tends to persist. The disorder may follow a period of coma and delirium in cases of head trauma or vascular accident and may be permanent. The personality change may evolve into dementia in cases of brain tumor, multiple sclerosis, and Huntington's disease. Personality changes produced by chronic intoxication, medical illness, or drug therapy (such as levodopa [Larodopa] for parkinsonism) may be reversed if the underlying cause is treated. Some patients require custodial care or, at least, close supervision to meet their basic needs, avoid repeated conflicts with the law, and protect them and their families from the hostility of others and from destitution resulting from impulsive and ill-considered actions.

**Treatment.** Management of the personality change disorder involves treatment of the underlying organic condition if the condition is treatable. Psychopharmacological treatment of specific symptoms may be indicated in some cases, such as imipramine or fluoxetine for depression.

Patients with severe cognitive impairment or weakened behavioral controls may need counseling to help avoid difficulties at work or to prevent social embarrassment. As a rule, the patient's family needs emotional support and concrete advice on how to help minimize the patient's undesirable conduct. Alcohol should be avoided. Social engagements should be curtailed if the patient has a tendency to act in a grossly offensive manner.

## Enduring Personality Changes after Catastrophic Experience and after Psychiatric Illness

ICD-10 has two categories for personality changes that occur after either a catastrophic experience or a psychiatric illness in persons who had no previous personality disorder. According to ICD-10:

These diagnoses should be made only when there is evidence of a definite and enduring change in a person's pattern of perceiving, relating to, or thinking about the environment and the self. The personality change should be significant and associated with inflexible and maladaptive behaviour which was not present before the pathogenic experience. The change should not be a manifestation of another mental disorder, or a residual symptom of any antecedent mental disorder. Such enduring personality change is most often seen following devastating traumatic experience but may also develop in the aftermath of a severe, recurrent, or prolonged mental disor-

der. It may be difficult to differentiate between an acquired personality change and the unmasking or exacerbation of an existing personality disorder following stress, strain, or psychotic experience. Enduring personality change should be diagnosed only when the change represents a permanent and different way of being, which can be etiologically traced back to a profound, existentially extreme experience. The diagnosis should not be made if the personality disorder is secondary to brain damage or disease.

**Enduring personality change after catastrophic experience.** According to ICD-10:

Enduring personality change may follow the experience of catastrophic stress. The stress must be so extreme that it is unnecessary to consider personal vulnerability in order to explain its profound effect on the personality. Examples include concentration camp experiences, torture, disasters, prolonged exposure to life-threatening circumstances (e.g. hostage situations—prolonged captivity with an imminent possibility of being killed). Post-traumatic stress disorder . . . may precede this type of personality change, which may then be seen as a chronic, irreversible sequel of stress disorder. In other instances, however, enduring personality change meeting the description given below may develop without an interim phase of a manifest post-traumatic stress disorder. However, long-term change in personality following short-term exposure to a life-threatening experience such as a car accident should *not* be included in this category, since recent research indicates that such a development depends on a pre-existing psychological vulnerability. . . .

The personality change should be enduring and manifest as inflexible and maladaptive features leading to an impairment in interpersonal, social, and occupational functioning. Usually the personality change has to be confirmed by a key informant. In order to make the diagnosis, it is essential to establish the presence of features not previously seen, such as: (a) a hostile or mistrustful attitude towards the world; (b) social withdrawal; (c) feelings of emptiness or hopelessness; (d) a chronic feeling of being "on edge," as if constantly threatened; (e) estrangement.

This personality change must have been present for at least 2 years, and should not be attributable to a pre-existing personality disorder or to a mental disorder other than post-traumatic stress disorder. . . . The presence of brain damage or disease which may cause similar clinical features should be ruled out.

**Enduring personality change after psychiatric illness.** Personality change after psychiatric illness is described in ICD-10 as follows:

The personality change should be enduring and manifest as an inflexible and maladaptive pattern of experiencing and functioning, leading to long-standing problems in interpersonal, social, or occupational functioning and subjective distress. There should be no evidence of a pre-existing personality disorder that can explain the personality change, and the diagnosis should not be based on any residual symptoms of the antecedent mental disorder. The change in personality develops following clinical recovery from a mental disorder that must have been experienced as emotionally extremely stressful and shattering to the patient's self-image. Other people's attitudes or reactions to the patient following the illness are important in determining and reinforcing his or her perceived level of stress. This type of personality change cannot be fully understood without taking into consideration the subjective emotional experience and the previous personality, its adjustment, and its specific vulnerabilities.

Diagnostic evidence for this type of personality change should include such clinical features as the following: (a) excessive dependence on and a demanding attitude towards others; (b) conviction of being changed or stigmatized by the preceding illness, leading to an inability to form and maintain close and confiding personal relationships and to social isolation; (c) passivity, reduced interests, and diminished involvement in leisure activities; (d) persistent complaints of being ill, which may be associated with hypochondriacal claims and illness behaviour; (e) dysphoric or labile mood, not due to the presence of a current mental disorder or antecedent mental disorder with residual affective symptoms; (f) significant impairment in social and occupational functioning compared with the premorbid situation.

The above manifestations must have been present over a period of 2 or more years. The change is not attributable to gross brain damage or disease. A previous diagnosis of schizophrenia does not preclude the diagnosis.

## References

Akhtar S, Thompson J A: Overview: Narcissistic personality disorder. Am J Psychiatry *139*: 12, 1982.

Akiskal H S: Dysthymic disorder: Psychopathology of proposed chronic depressive subtypes. Am J Psychiatry *140*: 11, 1983.

Baron M, Gruen R, Asnis L, Lord S: Familial transmissions of schizotypal and borderline personality disorders. Am J Psychiatry *142*: 927, 1985.

Bouchard T J Jr, Lykken D T, McGue M, Segal N L, Tellegen A: Sources of human psychological differences: The Minnesota study of twins reared apart. Science *250*: 223, 1990.

Fabrega H, Ulrich R, Pilkonis P, Mezzich J: Personality disorders diagnosed at intake at a public psychiatric facility. Hosp Community Psychiatry *44*: 159, 1993.

Gabbard G O: *Psychodynamic Psychiatry in Clinical Practice: The DSM-IV Edition*. American Psychiatric Press, Washington, 1994.

Gunderson J G: *Borderline Personality Disorder*. American Psychiatric Press, Washington, 1984.

Gunderson J G, Sabo A N: The phenomenological and conceptual interface between borderline personality disorder and PTSD. Am J Psychiatry *150*: 19, 1993.

Kass F, MacKinnon R A, Spitzer R L: Masochistic personality: An empirical study. Am J Psychiatry *143*: 216, 1986.

Kendler K S, Masterson C C, Ungaro R, Davis K L: A family history study of schizophrenia-related personality disorders. Am J Psychiatry *143*: 424, 1984.

Kernberg O F: *Borderline Conditions and Pathological Narcissism*. Aronson, New York, 1975.

Klein D N and Miller G A: Depressive personality. Am J Psychiatry *150*: 11, 1993.

Kohut H, Wolff E S: The disorders of the self and their treatment: An outline. Int J Psychoanal *59*: 413, 1978.

Kramer P D: *Listening to Prozac*. Viking, New York, 1993.

Lazare A, Klerman G, Armor D: Oral, obsessive and hysterical personality patterns: An investigation of psychoanalytic concepts by means of factor analysis. Arch Gen Psychiatry *14*: 624, 1966.

Lion J R, editor: *Personality Disorders: Diagnosis and Management,* ed. 2. Williams & Wilkins, Baltimore, 1981.

Markovitz P J, Schulz S C: Drug treatment of personality disorders. Br J Psychiatry *162*: 122, 1993.

McGlashan T H: Schizotypal personality disorder: Chestnut Lodge follow-up study: VI. Long-term follow-up perspectives. Arch Gen Psychiatry *43*: 329, 1986.

Millon T: *Disorders of Personality: DSM-III Axis II*. Wiley, New York, 1981.

Perkins D O, Davidson E J, Leserman J, Liao D: Personality disorder in patients infected with HIV: A controlled study with implications for clinical care. Am J Psychiatry *150*: 309, 1993.

Perry J C: Depression in borderline personality disorder: Lifetime prevalence at interview and longitudinal course of symptoms. Am J Psychiatry *142*: 15, 1985.

Perry J C, Cooper S H: A preliminary report on defense and conflicts associated with borderline personality disorder. J Am Psychoanal Assoc *34*: 865, 1986.

Perry J C, Cooper S H: Psychodynamics, symptoms and outcome in borderline and antisocial personality disorders and bipolar type II affective disorder. In *The Borderline: Current Empirical Research,* T H McGlashan, editor, p 714. American Psychiatric Press, Washington, 1985.

Perry J C, Vaillant G E: Personality disorders. In *Comprehensive Textbook of Psychiatry,* ed. 5, H I Kaplan, B J Sadock, editors, p 1352. Williams & Wilkins, Baltimore, 1989.

Robins L N: *Deviant Children Grown Up: A Sociological and Psychiatric Study of Sociopathic Personality*. Williams & Wilkins, Baltimore, 1966.

Rost K M, Akins R N, Brown F W, Smith G R: The comorbidity of DSM-III-R personality disorders in somatization disorder. Gen Hosp Psychiatry *14*: 322, 1992.

Rutter M: *Maternal Deprivation Reassessed,* ed 2. Penguin Books, London, 1981.

Silverman J M, Siever L J, Horvath T B, Coccaro E F: Schizophrenia-related and affective personality disorder traits in relatives of probands with schizophrenia and personality disorders. Am J Psychiatry *150*: 435, 1993.

Soloff P H, George A, Nathan S, Schulz P M, Ulrich R F, Perel J M: Progress in pharmacotherapy of borderline disorders: A double-blind study of amitriptyline, haloperidol and placebo. Arch Gen Psychiatry *43*: 691, 1986.

Sternlicht H C: Obsessive-compulsive disorder, fluoxetine, and buspirone. Am J Psychiatry *150*: 526, 1993.

Thomas A, Chess S: *Temperament and Development*. Brunner/Mazel, New York, 1977.

Torgersen S: Genetic and nosologic aspects of schizotypal and borderline personality disorders: A twin study. Arch Gen Psychiatry *41*: 546, 1984.

Vaillant G E: *Adaptation to Life*. Little, Brown, Boston, 1977.

Vaillant G E: Sociopathy as a human process. Arch Gen Psychiatry *32*: 179, 1975.

Woody G E, McLellan A T, Luborsky L, O'Brien C P: Sociopathy and psychotherapy outcome. Arch Gen Psychiatry *42*: 1081, 1985.

# 27 ||||||

# Psychological Factors Affecting Medical Condition (Psychosomatic Disorders)

## 27.1 / Overview

Psychosomatic medicine emphasizes the unity of mind and body and the interaction between them. In general, the conviction is that psychological factors are important in the development of all diseases. Whether that role is in the initiation, the progression, the aggravation, or the exacerbation of a disease or in the predisposition or the reaction to a disease is open to debate and varies from disorder to disorder. The term "psychosomatic" has become part of the concept of behavioral medicine, which was defined in 1978 by the National Academy of Science as "the interdisciplinary field concerned with the development and integration of behavioral and biomedical science knowledge and techniques relevant to health and illness and the application of this knowledge and these techniques to prevention, diagnosis, and rehabilitation." Behavioral medicine, thus, is an inclusive term for the field of psychosomatic medicine.

In the fourth edition of *Diagnostic and Statistical Manual of Mental Disorders* (DSM-IV), the term "psychosomatic" has been replaced with the diagnostic category of psychological factors affecting medical condition. In the revised third edition (DSM-III-R) it was called psychological factors affecting physical condition.

### CLASSIFICATION

The DSM-IV diagnostic criteria for psychological factors affecting medical condition (that is, psychosomatic disorders) specify that psychological factors adversely affect the patient's medical condition in one of a variety of ways. The key is that "the factors have influenced the course of the general medical condition as shown by a close temporal association between the psychological factors and the development or exacerbation of, or delayed recovery from, the general condition." Among the psychological factors are mental disorders (for example, Axis I disorders, such as major depressive disorder), psychological symptoms (for example, depressive symptoms and anxiety), per-

sonality traits or coping style (for example, denial of the need for surgery), and maladaptive health behaviors (for example, overeating). The patient has a general medical condition that is coded on Axis III.

The important change in DSM-IV from DSM-III-R is that DSM-IV allows clinicians to specify the psychological factors that affect the patient's medical condition. In DSM-III-R psychologically meaningful environmental stimuli were temporally related to the physical disorder. The key phrase in DSM-III-R was "environmental stimuli." The DSM-IV emphasis on psychological factors permits a wide range of psychological stimuli to be noted (for example, personality traits, maladaptive health behaviors).

Many believe that the deletion of the nosological term "psychophysiological," a synonym used in the second edition (DSM-II) for "psychosomatic," de-emphasizes the interaction of the mind (psyche) and the body (soma). "Psychosomatic" emphasizes a unitary causative or holistic approach to medicine, since all diseases are influenced by psychological factors, a correlation that has been exploited by various schools of alternative medicine.

The DSM-IV diagnostic criteria for psychological factors affecting medical condition are presented in Table 27.1–1. Excluded are (1) classic mental disorders that present with physical symptoms as part of the disorder (for example, conversion disorder, in which a physical symptom is produced by psychological conflict); (2) somatization disorder, in which the physical symptoms are not based on organic pathology; (3) hypochondriasis, in which patients have an exaggerated concern with their health; (4) physical complaints that are frequently associated with mental disorders (for example, dysthymic disorder, which usually has such somatic accompaniments as muscle weakness, asthenia, fatigue, and exhaustion); and (5) physical complaints associated with substance-related disorders (for example, coughing associated with nicotine dependence).

### HISTORY

The history of psychosomatic medicine parallels the history of humankind. A historical summary of the psyche-soma interaction is presented in Table 27.1–2.

Exactly where and how do the psyche and the soma interact? Representatives from both psychiatry and medicine have agreed for more than 100 years that, in some disorders, emotional and somatic activities overlap. Those disorders were first called psychosomatic by Johann Christian Heinroth in 1818, when he used the term in regard to insomnia. The word

**Table 27.1–1**
**Diagnostic Criteria for Psychological Factors Affecting Medical Condition**

A. A general medical condition (coded on Axis III) is present.

B. Psychological factors adversely affect the general medical condition in one of the following ways:

  (1) the factors have influenced the course of the general medical condition as shown by a close temporal association between the psychological factors and the development or exacerbation of, or delayed recovery from, the general medical condition.

  (2) the factors interfere with the treatment of the general medical condition.

  (3) the factors constitute additional health risks for the individual.

  (4) stress-related physiological responses precipitate or exacerbate symptoms of a general medical condition

Choose name based on the nature of the psychological factors (if more than one factor is present, indicate the most prominent):

**Mental disorder affecting medical condition** (e.g., an Axis I disorder such as major depressive disorder delaying recovery from a myocardial infarction)

**Psychological symptoms affecting medical condition** (e.g., depressive symptoms delaying recovery from surgery; anxiety exacerbating asthma)

**Personality traits or coping style affecting medical condition** (e.g., pathological denial of the need for surgery in a patient with cancer; hostile, pressured behavior contributing to cardiovascular disease)

**Maladaptive health behaviors affecting medical condition** (e.g., lack of exercise, unsafe sex, overeating)

**Stress-related physiological response affecting general medical condition** (e.g., stress-related exacerbations of ulcer, hypertension, arrhythmia, or tension headache)

**Other unspecified psychological factors affecting medical condition** (e.g., interpersonal, cultural, or religious factors)

Table from DSM-IV, *Diagnostic and Statistical Manual of Mental Disorders*, ed 4. Copyright American Psychiatric Association, Washington, 1994. Used with permission.

was later popularized by Maximilian Jacobi, a German psychiatrist. The number of disorders identified as psychosomatic grew to include ulcerative colitis, peptic ulcer, migraine headache, bronchial asthma, and rheumatoid arthritis. Table 27.1–3 lists some psychosomatic disorders.

## ETIOLOGY

Investigators have questioned the validity of the concept of psychophysiological medicine. Some have suggested that it is too vague a term; others say that it is too narrow. But most agree that chronic, severe, and perceived stress plays some causative role in the development of many somatic diseases. The character of the stress, the general underlying psychophysiological factors, the patient's genetic and organ vulnerability, the nature of the patient's emotional conflicts (whether they are specific or nonspecific), and the way they interact to produce disease—all are still controversial.

### General Stress

A stressful life event or situation—internal or external, acute or chronic—generates challenges to which the organism cannot adequately respond. Thomas Holmes and Richard Rahe, in their social readjustment rating scale, listed 43 life events associated with varying amounts of disruption and stress in the average person's life—for example, the death of a spouse, 100 life-change units; divorce, 73 units; marital separation, 65 units; and the death of a close family member, 63 units (Table 27.1–4). The scale was constructed after querying hundreds of persons with varying backgrounds to rank the relative degree of adjustment necessitated by changing life events. An accumulation of 200 or more life-change units in a single year increases the incidence of psychosomatic disorders.

Recent studies have found that persons who face general stresses optimistically, rather than pessimistically, are not apt to experience a psychosomatic disorder; if they do, they are apt to recover from the disorder easily.

### Specific versus Nonspecific Stress

In addition to general stresses, such as a divorce and the death of a spouse, some investigators have suggested that specific personalities and conflicts are associated with specific psychosomatic diseases. Other investigators believe that nonspecific generalized anxiety from any type of conflict may lead to a number of diseases.

*Specific psychic stress* may be defined as a specific personality or unconscious conflict that causes a homeostatic disequilibrium that contributes to the development of a psychosomatic disorder. Specific personality types were first identified in regard to the coronary personality (a hard-driving, aggressive person who tends to experience myocardial occlusion). For example, the so-called type A personality (similar to the coronary personality) was singled out as one that predisposes a person to coronary disease. Type A and type B personalities were first defined by Meyer Friedman and Ray Rosenman. (Section 5.1 discusses type A and type B personalities.)

That specific unconscious conflicts are associated with specific psychosomatic disorders (for example, unconscious dependence conflict predisposes one to peptic ulcer) was hypothesized by Franz Alexander. Alexander's multifactorial theories were later confirmed by Arthur Mirsky and Herbert Weiner. Both the specific personality type and the unconscious conflicts fall under the rubric of specific causative theories of psychosomatic diseases. Table 27.1–5 gives some psychological correlates of psychophysiological disorders.

Alternatively, chronic nonspecific stress, usually with the intervening variable of anxiety, has been suggested as having physiological correlates that, combined with genetic organ vulnerability or debility, predispose certain persons to a psychosomatic disorder. Alexithymic persons are unable to read their own emotions; they have impoverished fantasy lives and are not conscious of their emotional conflicts; psychosomatic disorders may serve as an outlet for their accumulated tensions. Nonspecific causal theories are supported by experimental evidence that, under chronic stress, animals have psychosomatic disorders (such as peptic ulcer); clearly, animals do not have the specific personality or unconscious psychological conflicts that people do.

**Table 27.1–2**
**History of Psychosomatic Medicine**

| Date | Historical Period | Psychosomatic Orientation |
|---|---|---|
| 10,000 B.C. | Primitive society | Disease is caused by spiritual powers and must be fought by spiritual means; the evil spirit that enters and affects the total being must be liberated through exorcism, trepanation, and so on. |
| 2500–500 B.C. | Babylonian-Assyrian civilization | Medicine is dominated by religion, and suggestion is the major tool of treatment. Sigerist: "Mesopotamian medicine was psychosomatic in all its aspects." |
| 400 B.C. | Greek civilization | Socrates: "As it is not proper to cure the eyes without the head, nor the head without the body, so neither is it proper to cure the body without the soul." Hippocrates: "In order to cure the human body, it is necessary to have a knowledge of the whole of things." |
| 100 B.C.–A.D. 400 | Late Greek-early Roman civilization | Galen's humoral theory postulates that disease is caused by disturbances in the fluids of the body. Medicine adopts a holistic approach to disease. |
| 500–1450 | Middle Ages | Mysticism and religion dominate medicine. Sinning is the cause of mental and somatic illnesses. |
| 1500–1700 | Renaissance | Renewed interest in the natural sciences and their application to medicine; advances in anatomy (Vesalius), autopsy (Morgagni), microscopy (Leeuwenhoek). Psychic influences on the soma are rejected as unscientific; the study of the mind is relegated to religion and philosophy. |
| 1800–1900 | 19th century | Modern laboratory-based medicine of Pasteur and Virchow. Virchow: "Disease has its origin in disease of the cell." Psychosomatic approach discarded, as all disease must be associated with structural cell change. The disease is treated, not the patient. |
| 1900–present | 20th century | Freud's psychoanalytic formulations emphasize the role of psychic determinism in somatic conversion reactions (Dora case). Early concepts are limited to major hysterical conversions; subsequently, Alexander differentiates conversion reactions from psychosomatic disorders and studies psychological factors in a series of diseases. |

**Table 27.1–3**
**Some Psychosomatic Disorders**

| | |
|---|---|
| Acne | Migraine |
| Allergic reactions | Mucous colitis |
| Angina pectoris | Nausea |
| Angioneurotic edema | Neurodermatitis |
| Arrhythmia | Obesity |
| Asthmatic wheezing | Painful menstruation |
| Bronchial asthma | Pruritus ani |
| Cardiospasm | Pylorospasm |
| Chronic pain syndromes | Regional enteritis |
| Coronary heart disease | Rheumatoid arthritis |
| Diabetes mellitus | Sacroiliac pain |
| Duodenal ulcer | Skin diseases, such as psoriasis |
| Essential hypertension | |
| Gastric ulcer | Spastic colitis |
| Headache | Tachycardia |
| Herpes | Tension headache |
| Hyperinsulinism | Tuberculosis |
| Hyperthyroidism | Ulcerative colitis |
| Hypoglycemia | Urticaria |
| Immune diseases | Vomiting |
| Irritable colon | Warts |

## Physiological Variables

The mediator between cognitively based stress and disease may be hormonal, as in the general-adaption syndrome of Hans Selye, in which hydrocortisone is the mediator; or the mediator may be changes in the functioning of the anterior pituitary-hypothalamic-adrenal axis, with autonomic effects, adrenal enlargement, and lymphoid shrinkage. In the hormonal linkage, hormones are released from the hypothalamus and travel to the anterior pituitary, where the trophic hormones interact directly or release hormones from other endocrine glands. Alexander pointed to the autonomic nervous system—for example, the parasympathetic nervous system in peptic ulcer and the sympathetic nervous system in hypertension—as the mechanism linking chronic stress and psychosomatic disorders.

Another intervening variable may be the action of the immune system's monocytes. The monocytes interact with brain neuropeptides, which serve as messengers between brain cells. Thus, immunity may influence psychic state and mood. Herbert Benson, in explaining the effects of relaxation therapy on certain psychosomatic disorders, postulated that relaxation decreases the activity of cerebral adrenergic catecholamines and that those substances affect the limbic system—the Papez circuit—which is important in the causes of psychosomatic and mental disorders. A summary of the major theories of psychosomatic medicine is presented in Table 27.1–6.

## TREATMENT

Both psychosomatic medicine and behavioral medicine are concerned with the interaction of the psyche and the

**Table 27.1–4**
**Social Readjustment Rating Scale**

| Life Event | Mean Value |
|---|---|
| 1. Death of spouse | 100 |
| 2. Divorce | 73 |
| 3. Marital separation from mate | 65 |
| 4. Detention in jail or other institution | 63 |
| 5. Death of a close family member | 63 |
| 6. Major personal injury or illness | 53 |
| 7. Marriage | 50 |
| 8. Being fired at work | 47 |
| 9. Marital reconciliation with mate | 45 |
| 10. Retirement from work | 45 |
| 11. Major change in the health or behavior of a family member | 44 |
| 12. Pregnancy | 40 |
| 13. Sexual difficulties | 39 |
| 14. Gaining a new family member (through birth, adoption, oldster moving in, etc.) | 39 |
| 15. Major business readjustment (merger, reorganization, bankruptcy, etc.) | 39 |
| 16. Major change in financial state (a lot worse off or a lot better off than usual) | 38 |
| 17. Death of a close friend | 37 |
| 18. Changing to a different line of work | 36 |
| 19. Major change in the number of arguments with spouse (either a lot more or a lot less than usual regarding child rearing, personal habits, etc.) | 35 |
| 20. Taking on a mortgage greater than $10,000 (purchasing a home, business, etc.)* | 31 |
| 21. Foreclosure on a mortgage or loan | 30 |
| 22. Major change in responsibilities at work (promotion, demotion, lateral transfer) | 29 |
| 23. Son or daughter leaving home (marriage, attending college, etc.) | 29 |
| 24. In-law troubles | 29 |
| 25. Outstanding personal achievement | 28 |
| 26. Wife beginning or ceasing work outside the home | 26 |
| 27. Beginning or ceasing formal schooling | 26 |
| 28. Major change in living conditions (building a new home, remodeling, deterioration of home or neighborhood) | 25 |
| 29. Revision of personal habits (dress, manners, associations, etc.) | 24 |
| 30. Troubles with the boss | 23 |
| 31. Major change in working hours or conditions | 20 |
| 32. Change in residence | 20 |
| 33. Changing to a new school | 20 |
| 34. Major change in usual type or amount of recreation | 19 |
| 35. Major change in church activities (a lot more or a lot less than usual) | 19 |
| 36. Major change in social activities (clubs, dancing, movies, visiting, etc.) | 18 |
| 37. Taking on a mortgage or loan less than $10,000 (purchasing a car, TV, freezer, etc.) | 17 |
| 38. Major change in sleeping habits (a lot more or a lot less sleep or change in part of day when asleep) | 16 |
| 39. Major change in number of family get-togethers (a lot more or a lot less than usual) | 15 |
| 40. Major change in eating habits (a lot more or a lot less food intake or very different meal hours or surroundings) | 15 |
| 41. Vacation | 15 |
| 42. Christmas | 12 |
| 43. Minor violations of the law (traffic tickets, jaywalking, disturbing the peace, etc.) | 11 |

*This figure no longer has any relevance in the light of inflation; what is significant is the total amount of debt from all sources.
Table from T Holmes: Life situations, emotions, and disease. Psychosom Med *19*: 747, 1978. Used with permission.

**Table 27.1–5**
**Some Hypothesized Psychological Correlates of Psychophysiological Disorders**

| Disorder | Psychogenic Causes, Personality Characteristics, and Coping Aims |
|---|---|
| Peptic ulcer | Feels deprived of dependence needs; is resentful; represses anger; cannot vent hostility or actively seek dependence security; characterizes self-sufficient and responsible go-getter types who are compensating for dependence desires; has strong regressive wish to be nurtured and fed; revengeful feelings are repressed and kept unconscious |
| Colitis | Was intimidated in childhood into dependence and conformity; feels conflict over resentment and desire to please; anger restrained for fear of retaliation; is fretful, brooding, and depressive or passive, sweet and bland; seeks to camouflage hostility by symbolic gesture of giving |
| Essential hypertension | Was forced in childhood to restrain resentments; inhibited rage; is threatened by and guilt-ridden over hostile impulses that may erupt; is a controlled, conforming, and "mature" personality; is hard-driving and conscientious; is guarded and tense; needs to control and direct anger into acceptable channels; wishes to gain approval from authority |
| Migraine | Is unable to fulfill excessive self-demands; feels intense resentment and envy toward intellectually or financially more successful competitors; has meticulous, scrupulous, perfectionistic, and ambitious personality; failure to attain perfectionist ambitions results in self-punishment |
| Bronchial asthma | Feels separation anxiety; was given inconsistent maternal affection; has fear and guilt that hostile impulses will be expressed toward loved persons; is demanding, sickly, and cranky or clinging and dependent; symptom expresses suppressed cry for help and protection |
| Neurodermatitis | Has overprotective but ungiving parents; has craving for affection; has conflict regarding hostility and dependence; shows guilt and self-punishment for inadequacies; is a superficially friendly and oversensitive personality with depressive features and low self-image; symptoms are atonement for inadequacy and guilt by self-excoriation; displays oblique expression of hostility and exhibitionism in need for attention and soothing |

Table from T Millon, R Millon: Psychophysiologic disorders. In *Medical Behavioral Science*, T Millon, editor, p 211. Saunders, Philadelphia, 1975. Used with permission.

**Table 27.1–6**
**Modern Concepts of Psychosomatic Medicine**

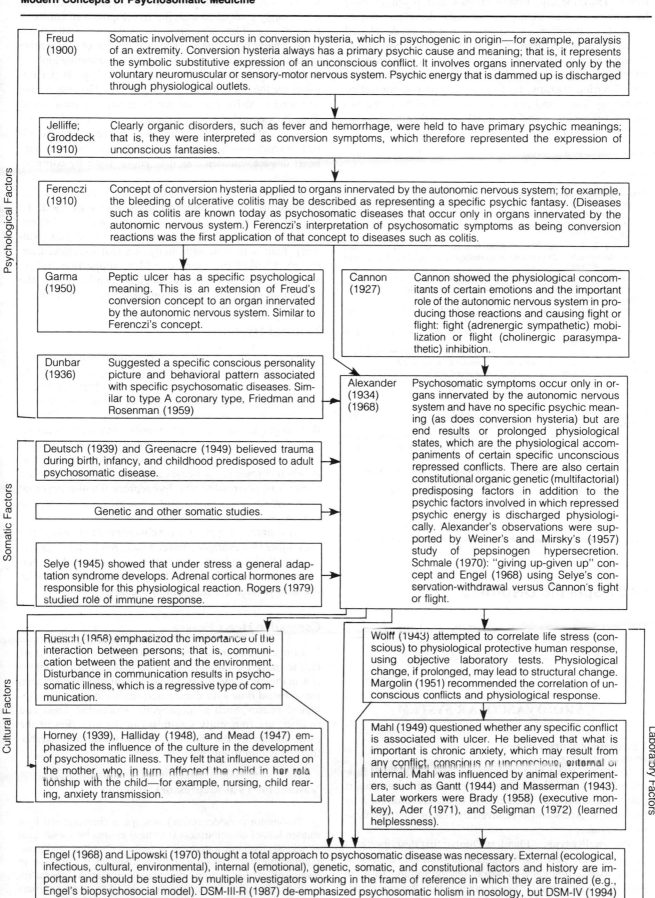

*Psychological Factors*

**Freud (1900)** — Somatic involvement occurs in conversion hysteria, which is psychogenic in origin—for example, paralysis of an extremity. Conversion hysteria always has a primary psychic cause and meaning; that is, it represents the symbolic substitutive expression of an unconscious conflict. It involves organs innervated only by the voluntary neuromuscular or sensory-motor nervous system. Psychic energy that is dammed up is discharged through physiological outlets.

**Jelliffe; Groddeck (1910)** — Clearly organic disorders, such as fever and hemorrhage, were held to have primary psychic meanings; that is, they were interpreted as conversion symptoms, which therefore represented the expression of unconscious fantasies.

**Ferenczi (1910)** — Concept of conversion hysteria applied to organs innervated by the autonomic nervous system; for example, the bleeding of ulcerative colitis may be described as representing a specific psychic fantasy. (Diseases such as colitis are known today as psychosomatic diseases that occur only in organs innervated by the autonomic nervous system.) Ferenczi's interpretation of psychosomatic symptoms as being conversion reactions was the first application of that concept to diseases such as colitis.

**Garma (1950)** — Peptic ulcer has a specific psychological meaning. This is an extension of Freud's conversion concept to an organ innervated by the autonomic nervous system. Similar to Ferenczi's concept.

**Dunbar (1936)** — Suggested a specific conscious personality picture and behavioral pattern associated with specific psychosomatic diseases. Similar to type A coronary type, Friedman and Rosenman (1959)

**Cannon (1927)** — Cannon showed the physiological concomitants of certain emotions and the important role of the autonomic nervous system in producing those reactions and causing fight or flight: fight (adrenergic sympathetic) mobilization or flight (cholinergic parasympathetic) inhibition.

**Alexander (1934) (1968)** — Psychosomatic symptoms occur only in organs innervated by the autonomic nervous system and have no specific psychic meaning (as does conversion hysteria) but are end results or prolonged physiological states, which are the physiological accompaniments of certain specific unconscious repressed conflicts. There are also certain constitutional organic genetic (multifactorial) predisposing factors in addition to the psychic factors involved in which repressed psychic energy is discharged physiologically. Alexander's observations were supported by Weiner's and Mirsky's (1957) study of pepsinogen hypersecretion. Schmale (1970): "giving up-given up" concept and Engel (1968) using Selye's conservation-withdrawal versus Cannon's fight or flight.

*Somatic Factors*

Deutsch (1939) and Greenacre (1949) believed trauma during birth, infancy, and childhood predisposed to adult psychosomatic disease.

Genetic and other somatic studies.

Selye (1945) showed that under stress a general adaptation syndrome develops. Adrenal cortical hormones are responsible for this physiological reaction. Rogers (1979) studied role of immune response.

*Cultural Factors*

Ruesch (1958) emphasized the importance of the interaction between persons; that is, communication between the patient and the environment. Disturbance in communication results in psychosomatic illness, which is a regressive type of communication.

Horney (1939), Halliday (1948), and Mead (1947) emphasized the influence of the culture in the development of psychosomatic illness. They felt that influence acted on the mother, who, in turn, affected the child in her relationship with the child—for example, nursing, child rearing, anxiety transmission.

Wolff (1943) attempted to correlate life stress (conscious) to physiological protective human response, using objective laboratory tests. Physiological change, if prolonged, may lead to structural change. Margolin (1951) recommended the correlation of unconscious conflicts and physiological response.

Mahl (1949) questioned whether any specific conflict is associated with ulcer. He believed that what is important is chronic anxiety, which may result from any conflict, conscious or unconscious, external or internal. Mahl was influenced by animal experimenters, such as Gantt (1944) and Masserman (1943). Later workers were Brady (1958) (executive monkey), Ader (1971), and Seligman (1972) (learned helplessness).

*Laboratory Factors*

Engel (1968) and Lipowski (1970) thought a total approach to psychosomatic disease was necessary. External (ecological, infectious, cultural, environmental), internal (emotional), genetic, somatic, and constitutional factors and history are important and should be studied by multiple investigators working in the frame of reference in which they are trained (e.g., Engel's biopsychosocial model). DSM-III-R (1987) de-emphasized psychosomatic holism in nosology, but DSM-IV (1994) restores a recognition of psychological factors.

soma. Traditionally, psychoanalysis and psychotherapy have been used to treat psychosomatic disorders. Within the past two decades, a great deal of interest has developed in the use of behavior modification (learning theory) techniques to treat those disorders. Among the therapeutic techniques emphasized in behavior modification are muscle relaxation therapy, biofeedback, hypnosis, controlled breathing, yoga, and massage. The goal of both the behavioral techniques and the usual psychotherapeutic modalities is to improve the psychosomatic equation.

### References

Alexander F: *Psychosomatic Medicine*. Norton, New York, 1950.

Alexander F, French T M, Pollack G H: *Psychosomatic Specificity: Experimental Study and Results*. University of Chicago Press, Chicago, 1968.

Angell M: Disease as a reflection of the psyche. N Engl J Med *312*: 1570, 1985.

Barefoot J C, Dahlstrom W G, William R B Jr: Hostility CHD incidence, and total mortality: 25-year follow-up study of 255 physicians. Psychosom Med *45*: 59, 1983.

Benson H: The relaxation response. In *Mind Body Medicine: How to Use Your Mind for Better Health*, D Goleman, J Gurin, editors, p 233. Consumer Reports, Yonkers, N Y, 1993.

Engel G H, Reichsman F, Siegel H L: A study of an infant with a gastric fistula. Psychosom Med *18*: 374, 1956.

Feifel H, Strack S, Nagy V T: Degree of life-threat and differential use of coping modes. J Psychol Res *31*: 91, 1987.

Kiecolt-Glaser J K, Glaser R: Psychoneuroimmunology: Can psychological interventions modulate immunity? J Consult Clin Psychol *60*: 569, 1992.

Mirsky I A: Physiologic, psychologic, and social detriments in the etiology of peptic ulcer. Am J Digestive Dis *3*: 285, 1958.

Rosenman R H: *Type A Behavior and Your Heart*. McGraw-Hill, New York, 1924.

Schwartz G E, Weiss S M: Behavioral medicine revisited: An amended definition. J Behav Med *1*: 249, 1978.

Weiner H: Presidental address: Some comments on the transduction of experience by the brain: Implication for our understanding of mind to body. Psychosom Med *34*: 355, 1972.

Whitehead W E: Behavioral medicine approaches to gastrointestinal disorders. J Consult Clin Psychol *60*: 605, 1992.

Wolf S, Wolff H G: *Human Gastric Function*. Oxford University Press, New York, 1943.

# 27.2 / Specific Disorders

## CARDIOVASCULAR SYSTEM

### Coronary Artery Disease

Coronary artery disease causes a decrease in blood flow to the heart and is characterized by episodic chest and heart pain, discomfort, or pressure. It is usually produced by exertion or stress and is relieved by rest or sublingual nitroglycerine.

**Personality type.** Flanders Dunbar first described coronary disease patients as aggressive-compulsive personalities with a tendency to work long hours and to seize authority. Later, Meyer Friedman and Ray Rosenman de-

fined type A and type B personalities. Type A personalities are strongly associated with the development of coronary heart disease. They are action-oriented persons who struggle to achieve poorly defined goals by means of competitive hostility. They are aggressive, impatient, upwardly mobile, and striving and angry when frustrated. Type B personalities are the opposite: they are relaxed and less aggressive and tend to strive less vigorously to achieve their goals. Type A personalities have increased amounts of low-density lipoprotein, serum cholesterol, triglycerides, and 17-hydroxycorticosteroids, and they tend to have coronary heart disease. Sudden loss may cause death by coronary occlusion.

**Treatment.** When coronary occlusion occurs, various medications for the patient's cardiac status are used. To alleviate the psychic distress associated with the disease, clinicians use psychotropics—for example, diazepam (Valium). Pain is treated with analgesics (for example, morphine). Medical treatment should be supportive and reassuring, with some psychological emphasis on the alleviation of psychic stress, compulsivity, and tension.

### Essential Hypertension

Hypertension is a disease characterized by a blood pressure of 160/95 mm Hg or higher. Twenty percent of the adult population in the United States are hypertensive.

**Personality type.** Hypertensive persons appear to be outwardly congenial, compliant, and compulsive; although their anger is not expressed openly, they have much inhibited rage, which they handle poorly. There appears to be a familial genetic predisposition to hypertension; that is, when chronic stress occurs in a genetically predisposed compulsive personality who has repressed and suppressed rage, hypertension may result. It also tends to occur in type A personalities.

**Treatment.** Supportive psychotherapy and behavioral techniques (for example, biofeedback, meditation, and relaxation therapy) have been reported to be useful in treating hypertension. Medically, the patient must comply with the antihypertensive medication regimen.

### Congestive Heart Failure

Congestive heart failure is a disorder in which the heart fails to move the blood forward normally, causing congestion in the lungs and the systemic circulation and decreased tissue blood flow with diminished cardiac output. Psychological factors, such as nonspecific emotional stress and conflict, are frequently significant in the initiation or the exacerbation of the disorder. Thus, supportive psychotherapy is important in its treatment.

### Vasomotor (Vasodepressor) Syncope

Vasomotor (vasodepressor) syncope is characterized by a sudden loss of consciousness (fainting) caused by a vasovagal attack. Sympathetic autonomic activity is inhibited, and parasympathetic vagal nerve activity is augmented, resulting in decreased cardiac output, decreased vascular peripheral resistance, vasodilation, and bradycardia. According to Franz

Alexander, acute fear or fright inhibits the impulse to fight or flee, thereby pooling the blood in the lower extremities, from the vasodilation of the blood vessels in the extremities. That reaction results in decreased ventricular filling, a drop in the blood supply to the brain, and consequent brain hypoxia and loss of consciousness.

**Treatment.** Because patients with vasomotor syncope normally put themselves or fall into a prone position, the decreased cardiac output is corrected. Raising their legs also helps correct the physiological imbalance. Psychotherapy should be used to determine the cause of the fright or the trauma associated with syncope. When syncope is related to orthostatic hypotension, the patient should be advised to shift slowly from a sitting to a standing position.

## Cardiac Arrhythmias

Potentially life-threatening arrhythmias—such as palpitations, ventricular tachycardia, and ventricular fibrillation—sometimes occur in conjunction with an emotional upset. Also associated with emotional trauma are sinus tachycardia, ST-wave and T-wave changes, ventricular ectopy, increased plasma catecholamines, and free fatty acid concentrations. Emotional stress is nonspecific, as is the personality description associated with the disorders.

**Treatment.** Psychotherapy and β-blocking drugs, such as propranolol (Inderal), help protect against emotionally induced arrhythmias.

## Raynaud's Phenomenon

Idiopathic paroxysmal bilateral cyanosis of the digits due to arteriolar contraction is frequently caused by external stress.

**Treatment.** Raynaud's phenomenon may be treated with supportive psychotherapy, progressive relaxation, or biofeedback and by protecting the body from cold and using a mild sedative. Smoking must cease, because nicotine is a vasoconstrictor. β-Blockers, clonidine (Catapres), and ergot preparations also cause vasoconstriction and are contraindicated.

## Psychogenic Cardiac Nondisease

Some patients are free of heart disease yet complain of symptoms suggestive of cardiac disease. They often exhibit a morbid concern about their hearts and exaggerated fears of heart disease. Their fear may range from an anxious concern, manifested by a severe phobia or hypochondriasis, to a delusional conviction that they have cardiac disease. Many of the patients suffer from an ill-defined syndrome often referred to as neurocirculatory asthenia.

Neurocirculatory asthenia was first described in 1871 by Jacob M. DaCosta, who named it irritable heart. It has some 20 names, including effort syndrome, DaCosta's syndrome, cardiac neurosis, vasoregulatory asthenia, hyperkinetic heart syndrome, and hyperdynamic-adrenergic circulatory state. Psychiatrists tend to view it as a clinical variant of anxiety disorders, although it does not appear in the fourth edition of *Diagnostic and Statistical Manual of Mental Disorders* (DSM-IV).

**Diagnosis.** The diagnostic criteria for neurocirculatory asthenia are (1) respiratory complaints, such as sighing respiration, inability to take a deep breath, smothering and choking, and dyspnea; (2) palpitations, chest pain, or discomfort; (3) nervousness, dizziness, faintness, or discomfort in crowds; (4) undue fatigue or limitation of activities; and (5) excessive sweating, insomnia, and irritability. The symptoms usually start in adolescence or the early 20s but may begin in middle age. Such symptoms are twice as common in women as in men and tend to be chronic, with recurrent acute exacerbations.

**Treatment.** The management of neurocirculatory asthenia may be difficult, and the prognosis is guarded if the condition is chronic. Phobic elements are prominent, and patients often derive primary or secondary gains from the disability. Psychotherapy aimed at uncovering psychodyanmic factors—often relating to hostility, unacceptable sexual impulses, dependence, guilt, and death anxiety—may be effective in some cases, but most patients with the condition tend to shun psychiatric help. Other behavioral techniques may be useful. Physical training programs aimed at correcting faulty breathing habits and gradually increasing the patient's effort tolerance may be helpful, especially if the programs are combined with group psychotherapy. Psychopharmacological treatment focuses on the predominant symptoms. The use of propranolol may interrupt the vicious circle of cardiac symptoms and have a positive reinforcement feedback effect on anxiety, which aggravates the symptoms. Antianxiety agents (for example, diazepam) can be used for major anxiety symptoms. If fatigue, lassitude, and weakness are the major complaints, the judicious use of amphetamines or methylphenidate (Ritalin) may be helpful.

# RESPIRATORY SYSTEM

## Bronchial Asthma

Bronchial asthma is a chronic recurrent obstructive disease of the bronchial airways, which tend to respond to various stimuli by bronchial constriction, edema, and excessive secretion. Genetic factors, allergic factors, infections, and acute and chronic stress—all combine to produce the disease. Whereas the rate and the depth of a healthy person's breathing can be changed voluntarily to correlate with various emotional states, such changes are aggravated and prolonged in a person with asthma.

**Psychological factors.** Although asthmatic patients are characterized as having excessive dependence needs, no specific personality type has been identified. Alexander pointed to psychodynamic conflictual factors, as he found in many asthmatic patients a strong unconscious wish for protection and for envelopment by the mother or surrogate mother. The mother figures tend to be overprotective and oversolicitous, perfectionistic, dominating, and helpful. When protection is sought but is not received, an asthmatic attack occurs.

**Treatment.** Some asthmatic children improve by being separated from the mother (so-called parentectomy). All standard psychotherapies are used: individual, group, behavioral (systematic desensitization), and hypnotic. Asthmatic patients should be treated jointly by internists, allergists, and psychiatrists.

## Hay Fever

Strong psychological factors combine with allergic elements to produce hay fever. One factor may dominate over the others, and they may alternate in importance.

**Treatment.** Psychiatric, medical, and allergic factors must be considered in treating hay fever.

## Hyperventilation Syndrome

Normal persons can voluntarily change the rate, depth, and regularity of their breathing, which can also be correlated with various emotional states. Hyperventilative patients breathe rapidly and deeply for several minutes, feel light-headed, and then faint because of cerebral vasoconstriction and a respiratory alkalosis. Other symptoms, such as paresthesias and carpopedal spasm, may be present. Specific medical differentials for the syndrome are epilepsy, conversion disorder, vasovagal or hypoglycemic attacks, myocardial attacks, bronchial asthma, acute porphyria, Ménière's disease, and pheochromocytoma. Psychiatric differentials include anxiety attacks, panic attacks, schizophrenia, borderline or histrionic personality disorder, and phobic or obsessive complaints.

**Treatment.** Instruction or retraining regarding particular symptoms and how they are evoked by hyperventilation should be provided, so that patients can consciously avoid precipitating symptoms. Breathing into a paper bag can abort the attack. Reassurance and supportive psychotherapy are also indicated.

## Tuberculosis

The onset and the aggravation of tuberculosis are often associated with acute and chronic stress. Psychological factors affect the immune system and may influence the patient's resistance to the disease.

**Treatment.** Treatment in the past was effective with antituberuclosis drugs and antibiotics. In the past five years there has been a significant resurgence in the incidence of tuberculosis and the development of antibiotic-resistant tubercule bacilli. That resurgence has been partially attributed to the increase in the incidence of acquired immune deficiency syndrome (AIDS). Immune-compromised systems readily become hosts to tuberculosis, so many patients with AIDS and human immunodeficiency virus (HIV) also have tuberculosis, particularly the miliary type. The role of stress on the incidence of tuberculosis has not been thoroughly studied, but most AIDS patients have psychiatric and neurological complications and are liable to stress. Supportive psychotherapy is valuable because of the role of stress and the complicated psychosocial situation.

## GASTROINTESTINAL SYSTEM

## Peptic Ulcer

Peptic ulcer is a circumscribed ulceration of the mucous membrane of the stomach or the duodenum, penetrating to the muscularis mucosae and occurring in areas exposed to gastric acid and pepsin.

### Etiology

SPECIFIC THEORY. Alexander hypothesized that chronic frustration of intense dependence needs results in a characteristic unconscious conflict. That unconscious conflict pertains to intense dependent oral-receptive longings to be cared for and loved, which causes a chronic regressive unconscious hunger and anger. That reaction is manifested physiologically by persistent vagal hyperactivity leading to gastric acid hypersecretion, which is particularly ominous in a genetically predisposed hypersecretor of acid. With the aforementioned equation, ulcer formation may result. Genetic factors and preexisting organ damage or disease (for example, gastritis) are causally important. Such gastritis may result from excessive caffeine, nicotine, or alcohol.

NONSPECIFIC THEORIES. Stress and anxiety caused by various nonspecific conflicts may produce gastric hyperacidity and hypersecretion of pepsin, resulting in an ulcer. Because various traumatic occurrences in animals (for example, electric shock in dogs) may produce ulcers, such experimental data support a nonspecific approach. Peptic ulcers have been diagnosed in all personality types.

Recent studies indicate that a bacterium, Helico pylori, has been implicated as an infectious agent that may contribute to the etiology of ulcer.

**Treatment.** Psychotherapy is directed toward the patient's dependence conflicts. Biofeedback and relaxation therapy may be useful. Medical treatment with cimetidine (Tagamet), ranitidine (Zantac), sucralfate (Carafate), or famotidine (Pepcid); antacid medications; and dietary control (for example, no alcohol) are indicated in ulcer management. The treatment of ulcer caused by Helico pylori may include antimicrobial drugs.

## Ulcerative Colitis

Ulcerative colitis is a chronic inflammatory ulcerative disease of the colon and is usually associated with bloody diarrhea. Familial incidence and genetic factors are significant. Related diseases include regional ileitis and irritable bowel syndrome.

**Personality type.** Most studies show a predominance of compulsive personality traits. Patients with ulcerative colitis are neat, orderly, clean, punctual, hyperintellectual, timid, and inhibited in expressing their anger.

### Etiology

SPECIFIC THEORY. Alexander described a typical specific conflictual constellation in ulcerative colitis. The key issue is an inability to fulfill an obligation (usually of accomplishment) to a key dependency figure. Essentially, frustrated dependence stimulates oral-aggressive feelings, producing guilt and anxiety and resulting in restitution through the "gifting" of diarrhea. In regard to colitis, George Engel described a pathological mother-child relationship, resulting in feelings of hopelessness-helplessness and a giving up-given up complex.

NONSPECIFIC THEORY. Nonspecific stress of many types may aggravate ulcerative colitis.

**Treatment.** Nonconfrontive, supportive psychotherapy is indicated during acute ulcerative colitis, with interpretative psychotherapy during the quiescent periods. Medical treatment consists of nonspecific supportive medical measures, such as anticholinergics and antidiarrheal agents. Prednisone therapy is useful in severe cases. Bismuth-containing medications (for example, Pepto-Bismol) are useful in managing diarrhea.

## Obesity

Obesity is a condition characterized by the excessive accumulation of fat (when the body weight exceeds by 20 percent the standard weight listed in the usual height-weight tables).

**Psychosomatic considerations.** There is a familial genetic predisposition to obesity, and early developmental factors are seen in childhood obesity. Those factors indicate that obese children increase the number of their fat cells (hyperplastic obesity), which predisposes them to adult obesity. When obesity occurs first in adult life, it is usually hypertrophic obesity (an increase in the size of fat cells), rather than an increase in the number of fat cells. Obesity also tends to limit physical activity, which further aggravates the condition. Psychological factors are important in hyperphagic obesity (overeating), especially binge eating. Among the psychodynamic factors suggested are oral fixation, oral regression, and the overvaluation of food. Bulimia—usually associated with binge eating—may be present. In addition, the patient often has a history of body-image disparagement and poor early conditioning to food intake.

**Treatment.** Obesity must be controlled through dietary limitation and the reduction of calorie intake. Emotional support and behavior modification are helpful for the anxiety and the depression associated with overeating and dieting. Gastric reduction surgery and similar techniques are of limited value.

## Anorexia Nervosa

Anorexia nervosa is characterized by behavior directed toward losing weight, peculiar patterns of handling food, weight loss, intense fear of gaining weight, disturbance of body image, and, in women, amenorrhea. It is one of the few psychiatric illnesses that may have a course unremitting until death. Anorexia nervosa is discussed further in Section 22.1.

## MUSCULOSKELETAL SYSTEM

### Rheumatoid Arthritis

Rheumatoid arthritis is a disease characterized by chronic musculoskeletal pain caused by inflammatory disease of the joints. The disorder has significant hereditary, allergic, immunological, and psychological causative factors. Psychological stress may predispose patients to rheumatoid arthritis and other autoimmune diseases by immune suppression. The ar-

thritic person feels restrained, tied down, and confined. Because many arthritic persons have a history of physical activity (for example, dancers), they often have repressed rage about the inhibition of their muscle function, which aggravates their stiffness and immobility.

**Treatment.** Treatment should include psychotherapy, which is usually supportive during chronic (sharp) attacks and interpretive between acute attacks. Rest and exercise should be structured, and patients should be encouraged not to become bed-bound and to return to their former activities. The rest and exercise program should be coordinated with the medical treatment of the pain and the inflammation of the joints.

## Low Back Pain

Low back pain is felt in the lower lumbar, lumbosacral, and sacroiliac regions. It is often accompanied by sciatica, with pain radiating down one or both buttocks or following the distribution of the sciatic nerve. Although low back pain may be caused by a ruptured intervertebral disk, a fracture of the back, congenital defects of the lower spine, or a ligamentous muscle strain, many cases are psychosomatic in origin. Some reports indicate that 95 percent of cases are psychological in origin.

The examining physician should be particularly alert to a patient who gives a history of minor back trauma followed by severe disabling pain. Often, the patient with low back pain reports that the pain was initiated at a time of psychological trauma or stress. In addition, the patient's reaction to the pain is disporportionately emotional, with excessive anxiety and depression. Furthermore, the distribution of the pain rarely follows a normal neuroanatomical distribution (for example, of sciatica).

**Treatment.** Treatment should be conservative. Aspirin—up to a total of 4 grams daily—is a useful analgesic. Diazepma, 5 to 10 mg every four to six hours, acts as both a muscle relaxant and an anxiolytic. A careful exercise and physical therapy regimen, supportive psychotherapy regarding the precipitating emotional trauma, relaxation therapy, and biofeedback are helpful. Patients should be encouraged to return to their usual activities as soon as possible. Surgical intervention is rarely indicated.

## HEADACHES

Headaches are the most common neurological symptom and one of the most common medical complaints. Every year about 80 percent of the population are estimated to suffer from at least one headache, and 10 to 20 percent of the population go to physicians with headache as their primary complaint. Headaches are also a major cause of absenteeism from work and avoidance of social and personal activities.

The majority of headaches are not associated with significant organic disease. Many persons are susceptible to headaches at times of emotional stress. Moreover, many psychiatric disorders, including anxiety and depressive disorders, frequently have headaches as a prominent symptom. Patients with headaches are often referred to psychiatrists by primary care physicians and neurologists after extensive biomedical workups, which often include a computed tomography (CT) scan of the head. The overwhelming majority of such workups for common headache complaints have negative findings, and such results may be frustrating for both the patient and the physician. The psychologically unsophisticated physician may attempt to reassure such patients by telling them that there is no disease. But that reassurance may have the opposite effect, increasing the patients' anxiety and even escalating into a disagreement about whether the pain is real or imagined.

Psychological stresses usually exacerbate headaches, whether their primary underlying cause is physical or psychological. Psychosomatic headaches are sometimes differentiated from psychogenic (for example, anxiety, depression, hypochondriacal, delusional) headaches. Headaches may be a conversion symptom of inpatients. In those patients the headache symbolizes unconscious psychological conflicts, and the symptoms are mediated through the voluntary sensorimotor nervous system. In contrast, psychosomatic or unconscious conflicts are not symbolic in nature. That distinction is important for psychiatrists to make so as to reach the proper diagnosis, which then allows the most specific treatment to be recommended.

### Migraine (Vascular) Headaches

Migraine (vascular) headaches are a paroxysmal disorder characterized by recurrent headaches, with or without related visual and gastrointestinal disturbances. They are probably caused by a functional disturbance in the cranial circulation.

**Personality type.** Two thirds of all patients with migraine headaches have family histories of similar disorders. Obsessional personalities who are overly controlled and perfectionistic, who suppress anger, and who are genetically predisposed to migraines may have such headaches under severe nonspecific emotional conflict or stress.

**Treatment.** Migraines are best treated during the prodromal period with ergotamine tartrate (Cafergot) and analgesics. The prophylactic administration of propranolol or phenytoin (Dilantin) is useful if the headaches are frequent. Psychotherapy to diminish the effects of conflict and stress and certain behavioral techniques (for example, biofeedback) have been reported to be useful.

### Tension (Muscle Contraction) Headaches

Emotional stress is often associated with the prolonged contraction of head and neck muscles, which over several hours may constrict the blood vessels and result in ischemia. A dull, aching pain often begins suboccipitally and may spread over the head, sometimes feeling like a tightening band. The scalp may be tender to the touch, and, in contrast to a migraine, the headache is usually bilateral and not associated with prodromata, nausea, and vomiting. The onset is often toward the end of the workday or in the early evening, possibly after the person has been removed from stressful job pressures, has tried to relax, and has focused on somatic sensations. But if family or personal

pressures are equal to or greater than those at work, the headaches may be worse later in the evening, on weekends, or during vacations.

Tension headaches may occur to some degree in about 80 percent of the population during periods of emotional stress. Anxiety and depression are frequently associated with the headaches. Tense, high-strung, competitive, type A personalities are especially prone to the disorder. They may be treated in the initial stage with antianxiety agents, muscle relaxants, and massage or heat application to the head and the neck. If an underlying depression is present, antidepressants may be prescribed. However, psychotherapy is usually the treatment of choice for patients chronically afflicted by tension headaches. Learning to avoid or better cope with tension is the most effective long-term management approach. Electromyogram (EMG) feedback from the frontal or temporal muscles may help some tension-headache patients. Relaxation associated with practice periods, meditation, or other changes in a pressured life-style may provide symptomatic relief for some patients.

## ENDOCRINE SYSTEM

### Hyperthyroidism

Hyperthyroidism (thyrotoxicosis) is a syndrome characterized by biochemical and psychological changes that occur as a result of a chronic endogenous or exogenous excess of thyroid hormone.

**Psychosomatic considerations.** In a genetically predisposed person, stress is often associated with the onset of hyperthyroidism. According to psychoanalytic theory, during childhood, hyperthyroid patients have an unusual attachment to and dependence on a parent, usually the mother, and so they find intolerable any threat to their mother's approval. As children, such patients often have inadequate support because of economic stress, divorce, death, or multiple siblings. That persistent threat to security in early life leads to premature and unsuccessful attempts to identify with an adult object. It also causes early stress and overuse of the endocrine system and further frustration of childhood dependence cravings. The patients continuously strive toward premature self-sufficiency and tend to dominate others with smothering attention and affection. They need to build defenses against a repetition of the unbearable feelings of rejection and isolation that occurred in childhood. Should those mechanisms break down, requiring a premature stimulation of the body's psychophysiological defense in a genetically predisposed patient, thyrotoxicosis may result.

**Treatment.** Antithyroid medication, tranquilizers, and supportive psychotherapy are useful. Crisis intervention may be helpful at the onset of the disease.

### Diabetes Mellitus

Diabetes mellitus is a disorder of metabolism and the vascular system manifested by a disturbance of the body's handling of glucose, lipid, and protein.

**Etiology.** Heredity and family history are important in the onset of diabetes. A sudden onset is often associated with emotional stress, which disturbs the homeostatic balance in a predisposed patient. Psychological factors that seem significant are those provoking feelings of frustration, loneliness, and dejection. Diabetic patients must usually maintain some sort of dietary control of their diabetes. When they are depressed and dejected, they often overeat or overdrink self-destructively, causing their diabetes to get out of control. That reaction is especially common in juvenile diabetic patients. In addition, terms such as oral, dependent, seeking maternal attention, and excessive passivity have been applied to diabetic patients.

**Treatment.** Supportive psychotherapy is necessary to achieve cooperation in the medical management of the complex disease. Therapy should encourage diabetic patients to lead as normal a life as possible, with the recognition that they have a chronic but manageable disease.

## Female Endocrine Disorders

**Premenstrual dysphoric disorder.** Premenstrual dysphoric disorder, also known as premenstrual syndrome (PMS), is characterized by cyclical subjective changes in mood and the general sense of physical and psychological well-being correlated with the menstrual cycle. The symptoms usually begin soon after ovulation, increase gradually, and reach a maximum of intensity about five days before the menstrual period begins. Psychological, social, and biological factors have been implicated in the disorder's pathogenesis. In particular, changes in estrogen, progesterone, androgen, and prolactin levels have been hypothesized to be important to the cause. Excessive exposure to and subsequent abrupt withdrawal from endogenous opiate peptides, which fluctuate under the influence of gonadal steroids, may contribute to premenstrual dysphoric disorder. An increase in prostaglandins secreted by the uterine musculature has been implicated in the pain associated with the disorder. Premenstrual dysphoric disorder also occurs in women past menopause and after hysterectomy, provided the ovaries remain intact. Seventy to 90 percent of all women of childbearing age report at least some symptoms.

**Menopausal distress.** Menopause is a natural physiological event. It is usually dated as having occurred after an absence of menstrual periods for one year. Usually, the menses taper off during a two-to-five-year span, most often between the ages of 48 and 55; the median age is 51.4 years. Menopause also occurs immediately after the surgical removal of the ovaries. The term "involutional period" refers to advancing age, and "climacteric" refers to involution of the ovaries.

CLINICAL FEATURES. Many psychological symptoms have been attributed to the menopause, including anxiety, fatigue, tension, emotional lability, irritability, depression, dizziness, and insomnia. There is no general agreement on the relative contribution of those complaints or of the physiological changes to the psychological and social meanings of menopause and that developmental era in a woman's life.

Physical signs and symptoms include night sweats, flushes, and hot flashes. A hot flash is a sudden perception of heat within or on the body that may be accompanied by sweating and color change. The cause of the hot flash is unknown; it may be linked to pulsatile luteinizing hor-

mone (LH) secretion. Estrogen-dependent functions are sequentially lost, and the woman may have atrophic changes in mucosal surfaces, accompanied by vaginitis, pruritus, dyspareunia, and stenosis. The woman may also have changes in calcium and lipid metabolism, probably as secondary effects of the lowered levels of estrogen, and those changes may be associated with a number of medical problems occurring in the postmenopausal era, such as osteoporosis and coronary artherosclerosis. The physical changes may begin as much as four to eight years before the last menstrual period. During that time, women may have irregular menstrual periods with variations in the menstrual intervals and the quantity of the menstrual flow.

HORMONAL CHANGES. Blood levels of ovarian hormones decline gradually during the climacteric period, usually over a period of several years. For many years, decreasing estrogen levels were thought to be of primary importance in relation to the clinical manifestations of menopause. Both estrogen and progesterone bind directly to brain tissue and were thought to act directly on brain function. Recently, however, it has been thought that other hormones, such as androgens and LH, are also involved. The effects of estrogen on mood may be indirectly moderated through its influence on androgen production. In any case the significance of hormonal changes is evidenced by the severe physical and psychological symptoms that follow abrupt (surgical) depletion of ovarian hormones. One difficulty in those studies that have attempted to assses the relations of changing hormonal levels in normal women is that the date of the last menstrual period is often difficult to establish, as is the menopause, for they merely mark a point on a curve of changing hormonal function. That is, the presence or the absence of menstrual bleeding is not an exact measure of hormonal status.

The severity of the symptoms at the menopause seems to be related to the rate of hormone withdrawal; the amount of hormone depletion; the woman's constitutional ability to withstand the overall aging process, including her overall health and level of activity; and the psychological meaning of aging for her.

PSYCHOLOGICAL AND PSYCHOSOCIAL FACTORS. Clinically significant psychiatric difficulties may develop during the life cycle's involutional phase. Women who have previously experienced psychological difficulties, such as low self-esteem and low life satisfaction, are likely to be vulnerable to difficulties during menopause. A woman's response to menopause has been noted to parallel her response to other crucial developmental events in her life, such as puberty and pregnancy. Attempts to link the severity of menopausal distress with the premenstrual tension syndrome have been inconclusive.

Women who have invested heavily in childbearing and child-rearing activities are most likely to suffer distress during the postmenopausal years. Concerns about aging, loss of childbearing capacity, and changes in appearance—all may be focused on the social and symbolic significance attached to the physical changes of the menopause.

Although in the past it was assumed that the incidence of mental disorders and depression would increase during the menopause, epidemiological evidence casts some doubt on that assumption as an all-inclusive and complete explanation. Epidemiological studies of mental disorders showed no increase in symptoms of mental disorders or in depression during the menopausal years, and studies of psychological complaints found no greater frequency in menopausal women than in younger women.

TREATMENT. Treatment programs must be individualized. Postclimacteric women may be asymptomatic for estrogen deprivation or may manifest estrogen excess (dysfunctional uterine bleeding).

The use of estrogen replacement treatment is still controversial. For women with signs of estrogen depletion, recent studies have been encouraging in regard to the use of long-term combined estrogen and progesterone replacement therapy, both in estrogen depletion syndrome and to prevent osteoporosis. Topical estrogen cream used to treat mucosal atrophy is readily absorbed systemically. The increased risk of cancer, particularly endometrial cancer, has been implicated in the use of exogenous estrogen, but the addition of a progestational agent to the replacement estrogen regimen is thought to reduce that increased risk.

Exercise, diet, and symptomatic treatment are all helpful in reducing physical discomfort. Psychological distress should be evaluated and treated primarily by appropriate psychotherapeutic and sociotherapeutic measures. Psychotherapy should include an exploration of the life stage and the meaning of aging and reproduction to the patient. The patient should be encouraged to accept the menopause as a natural life event and to develop new activities, interests, and gratifications. Psychotherapy should also attend to family dynamics and should enlist family and other social support systems when necessary.

**Idiopathic amenorrhea.** The cessation of normal menstrual cycles in nonpregnant, premenopausal women with no demonstrable structural abnormalities in the brain, the pituitary, or the ovaries is termed idiopathic amenorrhea.

The diagnosis is made first by exclusion and then, if possible, by identifying the primary psychogenic cause. Amenorrhea may occur as one feature of complex clinical psychiatric syndromes, such as anorexia nervosa and pseudocyesis. Other conditions associated with amenorrhea include massive obesity, diseases of the pituitary and the hypothalamus, and, in some cases, excessive amounts of running or jogging. Drugs such as reserpine (Serpasil) and chlorpromazine (Thorazine) can block ovulation and so delay the menses. Drug-induced amenorrhea is almost always accompanied by galactorrhea and elevated levels of prolactin.

The patterns of hormone defect that result in psychogenic amenorrhea are not well understood. Disturbed menstrual function with delayed or precipitate menses is a well-known response by healthy women to stress. The stress can be as minor as going away to college or as catastrophic as being put into a concentration camp.

In most women the menstrual cycling returns without medical intervention, sometimes even in continuing stressful conditions. Psychotherapy should be undertaken for psychological reasons, not just in response to the symptom of amenorrhea and to determine its cause. However, if the amenorrhea has been protracted and refractory, psychotherapy may be helpful in restoring regular menses.

# CHRONIC PAIN

Persistent pain is the most frequent complaint of patients, yet it is one of the most difficult symptoms to treat because of differing causes and individual responses to pain.

Pain is affected by a myriad of subjective, unmeasurable factors, including level of attention, emotional state, personality, and past experiences. Pain may simultaneously serve as a symptom of psychological stress and as a defense against it. Psychological factors may cause a person to become somatically preoccupied and to magnify even normal sensations to chronic pain. Patients may be excessively responsive to pain for personal, social, or financial secondary gain. Chronic pain may be a way of justifying failure in establishing relationships with others. Cultural, ethnic, or religious affiliations may influence the degree and the manner in which persons express pain and the way in which their families react to the symptoms. Therefore, in evaluating and treating persistent pain, the physician should realize that pain is not a simple stimulus-response phenomenon. Rather, the perception of a reaction to pain is multifactorial, combining many biopsychosocial variables.

## Pain Threshold and Perception

Peripheral sensations are transmitted through the pain pathways (for example, lateral spinothalamic tract, posterior thalamus of the diencephalon) to cortical somatosensory regions of the central nervous system (CNS) for conscious perception. The parietal cortex both localizes pain and perceives intensity. However, psychogenic pain may be entirely of central nervous system origin. Complex reactions to pain involve areas of the cortex responsible for memory and conscious and unconscious elements of a person's personality.

The threshold for the perception of pain is the same for most people but may be heightened by about 40 percent by biofeedback, a positive emotional state, relaxation exercises, physical therapy or other physical activity, meditation, guided imagery, suggestion, hypnosis, placebos, and analgesics. The beneficial response to placebos is sometimes falsely thought to differentiate organic from functional causes. In fact, about one third of normal persons, those with organic causes of pain, have at least a transient positive response to a placebo.

Variations in the effectiveness and the responsiveness of persons' endorphin or other neurotransmitter systems may modulate pain perception and tolerance. A proposed gate-control theory suggests that large peripheral afferent nerve fibers modulate sensory input by inhibiting hypothetical sensory transmitting neurons (gateway cells) in the substantia gelatinosa of the spinal cord. Relief of pain by transcutaneous or dorsal column electrical stimulators may result from that system's activation.

## Classification

DSM-IV classifies pain disorder under somatoform disorders. If patients have multiple recurrent pains of at least several years' duration that began before age 30, they are considered to have a somatization disorder. If the patients' pain suggests a physical illness but may be attributed to psychological factors alone, the diagnosis is conversion disorder or pain disorder (if pain is the only symptom). Patients with somatization disorder, major depressive disorder, or schizophrenia complain of various aches and pains, but pain is not the major complaint. In conversion disorder the distribution and the referral of pain are inconsistent.

## Treatment

Psychotherapy with pain patients is summarized in Table 27.2–1.

Patients with pain disorder are often undermedicated with analgesics because of a lack of knowledge of the pharmacology of analgesics, an unrealistic fear of causing addiction (even in terminal patients), and the ethical judgment that only bad physicians prescribe large dosages of narcotics. The clinician must separate patients with chronic benign pain (who tend to do much better with psychotherapy and psychotropic drugs) from those with chronic pain caused by cancer or other chronic medical disorders. The former often respond to the combination of an antidepressant and a phenothiazine. The latter usually respond better to analgesics or nerve blocks. Many cancer patients may be kept relatively active, alert, and comfortable with the judicious use of morphine, avoiding costly and incompletely effective surgical procedures, such as peripheral nerve section, cordotomy, and stereotaxic thalamic ablations.

A behavior modification, deconditioning program may also be useful. Analgesics should be prescribed at regular intervals, rather than only as needed. Otherwise, patients must suffer before receiving relief, which only increases their anxiety and sensitivity to pain. Standing orders dissociate experiencing pain from receiving medication. The deconditioning of needed care from experiencing increased pain should also extend to patients' interpersonal relationships. Patients should receive as much or more attention for displaying active and healthy behavior as they receive for passive, dependent, pain-related behaviors. Their spouses, bosses, friends, physicians, and health care

**Table 27.2–1**
**Psychotherapy with Pain Patients**

Explain the nature of the pain signal.
Explain realistic expectations about the degree and the course of the pain.
Explain realistic expectations of analgesic, and, as much as possible, reframe side effects positively.
Maximize placebo effect by making the initial doses large rather than small, by supporting belief in efficacy, and by using suggestion through the attitude of the physician and the staff administering the analgesic.
Relieve concomitant anxiety, if necessary.
Chronic pain requires special arrangements:
  Eliminate doubts about the availability of medication.
  Do not make medication availability contingent on proof of need, leading to subjective struggles.
  Focus therapeutic encounters on healthy material; do not reinforce obsession with pain.
  Do not make contact with the care system contingent on pain; remove that contingency.

Table by Barry Blackwell, M.D.

or social agencies should not reinforce chronic pain and penalize patients (including threatening to discontinue disability payments) if the patients begin to relinquish the sick role. Patients should be assured of regular and supportive appointments that are not contingent on pain. Hospitalization should be avoided, if possible, to prevent further regression.

Pain clinics with a multispecialty staff evaluate and treat patients with complex pain disorders. The clinics include the early involvement of psychiatrists, rather than only after the organic causes of pain have been ruled out and the patient and the physicians are frustrated. The patients are managed without addictive drugs, although many patients commence treatment already addicted. Exploratory or neurodestructive surgery is not encouraged, especially if the patient has a hysterical personality or a history of multiple surgical procedures. Pain clinics also recognize that most chronic pain patients experience a vicious circle of biological and psychosocial factors, so that the most effective treatment involves a systems approach that addresses each biopsychosocial component relevant to the patient.

## IMMUNE DISORDERS

Considerable evidence points to a relation among psychosocial factors, immune function, and health and illness. Psychosocial processes—including a range of the person's life experiences, stresses, and trait characteristics—seem to influence the CNS, thereby encouraging the suppression of immune activity.

In 1968 George Solomon suggested that emotional stress affects the immune system, especially through a decrease in T lymphocytes; he named the new field psychoimmunology. S. Keller later found a decrease in lymphocytes in rats that were helpless to escape or to stop electric shocks. In 1975 Robert Ader found a conditioned suppression of the immune response in rats and renamed the field psychoneuroimmunology.

Transposing the stress research to humans, other investigators found a decrease in lymphocytic response in bereavement (both conjugal and anticipatory), in the caretakers of patients with dementia of the Alzheimer's type, in nonpsychotic inpatients, in resident physicians, in medical and graduate students during final examinations, in women who were separated or divorced, in the elderly who had a lack of social support, and in the unemployed. A decrease in lymphatic activity parallels a decrease in immunity and an increased incidence of infections and malignancy, which is probably correlated with increased psychic stress. A summary of psychoneuroimmunological factors in health and disease are given in Table 27.2–2.

Most studies have shown the negative effects of psychic stress on psychoimmunity and lymphatic activity and related diseases. A study by David Phillips and Daniel Smith indicates that positive psychological events may have beneficial effects on certain persons in certain areas. The investigators found that important symbolic events have a positive significant short-time effect on mortality and potentially on health in general. Symbolic events that they studied—such as Passover for Jewish men and the Chinese

**Table 27.2–2**
**Summary of Psychoneuroimmunology Factors**
**by Robert Ader**

Nerve endings have been found in the tissues of the immune system. The central nervous system is linked both to the bone marrow and the thymus, where immune system cells are produced and developed, and to the spleen and the lymph nodes, where those cells are stored.

Changes in the central nervous system (the brain and the spinal cord) alter immune responses, and triggering an immune response alters central nervous sytem activity. Animal experiments dating back to the 1960s show that damage to different parts of the brain's hypothalamus can either suppress or enhance the allergic-type response. Recently, researchers have found that inducing an immune response causes nerve cells in the hypothalamus to become more active and that the brain cell anxiety peaks at precisely the same time that levels of antibodies are at their highest. Apparently, the brain monitors immunological changes closely.

Changes in hormone and neurotransmitter levels alter immune responses, and vice versa. The stress hormones generally suppress immune responses. But other hormones, such as growth hormone, also seem to affect immunity. Conversely, when experimental animals are immunized, they show changes in various hormone levels.

Lymphocytes are chemically responsive to hormones and neurotransmitters. Immune system cells have receptors—molecular structures on the surface of their cells—that are responsive to endorphins, stress hormones, and a wide range of other hormones.

Lymphocytes can produce hormones and neurotransmitters. When an animal is infected with a virus, lymphocytes produce minuscule amounts of many of the same substances produced by the pituitary gland.

Activated lymphocytes—cells actively involved in an immune response—produce substances that can be perceived by the central nervous system. The interleukins and interferons—chemicals that immune system cells use to talk to each other—can also trigger receptors on cells in the brain, more evidence that the immune system and the nervous system speak the same chemical language.

Psychosocial factors may alter the susceptibility to or the progression of autoimmune disease, infectious disease, and cancer. Evidence for those connections comes from many researchers.

Immunological reactivity may be influenced by stress. Chronic or intense stress, in particular, generally makes immune system cells less responsive to a challenge.

Immunological reactivity can be influenced by hypnosis. In a typical study, both of a subject's arms are exposed to a chemical that normally causes an allergic reaction. But the subject is told, under hypnosis, that only one arm will show the response—and that, in fact, is often what happens.

Immunological reactivity can be modified by classical conditioning. As Ader's own key experiments showed, the immune system can learn to react in certain ways as a conditioned response.

Psychoactive drugs and substances of abuse influence immune function. A range of substances that affect the nervous system—including alcohol, marijuana, cocaine, heroin, and nicotine—have all been shown to affect the immune response, generally suppressing it. Some psychiatric drugs, such as lithium (prescribed for bipolar I disorder), also modulate the immune system.

Table adapted from D Goleman, J Guerin: *Mind Body Medicine*. Consumer Reports, Yonkers, N Y, 1993. Used with permission.

harvest moon festival for Chinese women—often prolong the lives of patients dying from malignant neoplasms and cerebrovascular diseases. That effect points to an additional parameter, not previously considered, that should be evaluated in the psychosomatic equation.

Recent investigations have revealed that the interaction between neuroendocrines and the CNS is reciprocal (that is, immune responses are affected by the CNS and vice versa). For example, a monokine released by macrophages and monocytes, interleukin-1 (IL-1), activates the hypothalamus-pituitary-adrenal axis (HPA) at the hypothalamus and pituitary level and stimulates the release of the potent adrenocorticotropic hormone (ACTH). Lymphocytes also synthesize peptides, such as ACTH and endorphins, which have numerous behavioral effects. Regulation of the immune system can be learned and conditioned, further indicating the potential effect of the immune system in the brain.

### Infectious Diseases

Clinical studies have indicated that psychological variables influence the rate of recovery from infectious mononucleosis and influenza and the susceptibility to rhinovirus-induced common cold symptoms and tularemia. Recurrent herpes simplex and genital herpes lesions occur most frequently in patients who have a clinical depression or who experience unusual stress. Stressful life events and a poor psychological state decrease resistance to tuberculosis and influence the course of the illness. Social supports play a role in recovery from tuberculosis. Life experiences that induce anger alter the intestine's bacterial composition. College students who respond to upsetting events with maladaptive aggression or affective changes have a high incidence of subsequent upper respiratory infections. Studies indicate that the primary immune response was cell-mediated. In acquired immune deficiency syndrome (AIDS), transmitted by the human immunodeficiency virus (HIV), psychiatric symptoms are common, and many think that the progress of the disease is influenced by the person's psychological state.

### Allergic Disorders

Considerable clinical evidence indicates that psychological factors are related to the precipitation of many allergic disorders. Bronchial asthma is a prime example of a pathological process involving immediate hypersensitivity that is associated with psychosocial processes. Emotional reactions to life experience, personality patterns, and conditioning have been reported to contribute to the onset and the course of asthma.

### Organ Transplantation

Psychosocial factors seem to play a role in organ transplantation. A number of clinical studies have found that stressful life events, anxiety, and depression precede some cases of graft rejection. Psychosocial effects on the immune system may contribute to the mechanisms involved in such rejections.

## Autoimmune Diseases

A prime function of the immune system is to distinguish between self and nonself and to reject foreign antigens (nonself). Occasionally, for reasons that are unclear at the present time, a cell-mediated or humoral immune response develops against a person's own cells. That reaction results in a variety of pathological effects that are known clinically as autoimmune diseases. Disorders in which an autoimmune component has been implicated include Graves' disease, Hashimoto's disease, rheumatoid arthritis, ulcerative colitis, regional ileitis, systemic lupus erythematosus, psoriasis, myasthenia gravis, and pernicious anemia.

## Mental Disorders

Although a number of investigators have found evidence suggesting altered immunity and autoimmunity in patients with schizophrenia, the specific findings have been difficult to replicate. Whether the immune abnormalities are involved in the pathogenesis of some or all types of schizophrenia or whether such abnormalities are related to a wide range of factors, including long-term institutionalization and antipsychotic agents, remains to be determined.

Immune phenomena in mental disorders other than schizophrenia have been less extensively studied. Work indicates that psychiatric patients manifest increased immunoglobulin M (IgM) and immunoglobulin A (IgA) levels. Those findings indicate the need for further study. The notion that patients with depressive disorders have an increased incidence of autoimmune antibodies has sparked some controversy. Marvin Stein concluded that the effect of depression on the modulation of immunity is complex and may involve a range of neurobiological mechanisms.

**Psychosocial and psychotherapeutic implications.** Various research groups have reported positive effects on immunological functioning from biofeedback, relaxation therapy, aerobic exercise training, and group therapy support.

## CANCER

Because improved treatment has changed cancer from an incurable to a frequently chronic and often curable disease, the psychiatric aspects of cancer—the reaction to both the diagnosis and the treatment—are of increasing importance. At least half of the 1 million patients who contracted cancer in the United States in 1987 were alive five years later. Currently, an estimated 3 million cancer survivors have no evidence of the disease.

## Patient Problems

When patients learn that they have cancer, their psychological reactions include fear of death, disfigurement, and disability; fear of abandonment and loss of independence; fear of disruption in relationships, role functioning, and financial standing; and denial, anxiety, anger, and guilt.

About half of all cancer patients have mental disorders. The largest group have adjustment disorder (68 percent),

with major depressive disorder (13 percent) and delirium (8 percent) being the next most common diagnoses. Most of those disorders are thought to be reactive to the knowledge of having cancer. The psychiatric, medical, and environmental factors that should be explored in the cancer patient are listed in Table 27.2–3. Some of the most common causes of mood disorders in cancer patients are listed in Table 27.2–4, and some of the medical conditions associated with delirium in cancer patients are listed in Table 27.2–5.

**Table 27.2–3**
**Areas of Assessment in Cancer Patients**

Psychiatric
  Past history
  Current mental state
  Understanding of the illness
  Meaning of the illness
Medical
  Cancer
  Cancer treatment
  Associated medical conditions and treatments
Environmental
  Interface with the family
  Interface with the medical team
  Other social supports
  Financial issues

Table by Marguerite S. Lederberg, M.D., and Jimmie C. Holland, M.D.

**Table 27.2–4**
**Causes of Mood Disorders Common in Cancer Patients**

Drugs
  Chemotherapeutic agents such as prednisone, dexamethasone, procarbazine, vincristine, vinblastine, L-asparaginase, tamoxifen, interferon
  Additive effect of narcotics and many other drugs known to cause depression, such as antihypertensives, benzodiazepines, antiparkinson agents, and β-blockers
Tumor effects
  Hormone-secreting tumors
  Central nervous system tumors
Associated medical conditions
  Uremia
  Viral encephalopathies
  Electrolyte imbalances

Table by Marguerite S. Lederberg, M.D., and Jimmie C. Holland, M.D.

**Table 27.2–5**
**Medical Conditions Associated with Delirium in Cancer Patients**

Metabolic encephalopathy
Vital organ failure
Electrolyte imbalance (such as hypercalcemia in patients with bony metastases or those receiving tamoxifen, diethylstilbestrol, or chlorotrianisene)
Hypoxia, especially in patients with pulmonary involvement or severe anemia
Nutritional deficiencies, such as thiamine, folic acid, and $B_{12}$
Infections, especially in immunosuppressed hosts
Vascular disorders, especially in patients with coagulopathies
Endocrine and hormonal abnormalities

Table by Marguerite S. Lederberg, M.D., and Jimmie C. Holland, M.D.

**Suicide.** Although suicidal thoughts and wishes are frequent in cancer patients, the incidence of actual suicide is only 1.4 to 1.9 times that found in the general population. Factors that signal a vulnerability to suicide in cancer patients are listed in Table 27.2–6.

## Treatment-Related Problems

The most common medical treatments used with cancer are radiation and drugs (chemotherapy). Drugs are toxic when given in tumoricidal dosages. Patients undergoing long courses of treatment may become much sicker symptomatically from the treatment than from their disease.

**Radiation therapy.** The side effects of radiation therapy include encephalopathy associated with increased intracranial pressure (nausea, vomiting, dizziness), headache, somnolence, personality changes, cognitive disturbances, and reactive psychic symptoms of fear and depression.

**Chemotherapy.** The most common side effects of chemotherapy are nausea and vomiting. In Table 27.2–7 the emetogenic problems with various chemotherapeutic agents are summarized. Antiemetic treatments for those complications are summarized in Table 27.2–8. Other complications of chemotherapy are the neurological complications listed in Table 27.2–9 and the mood and psychotic symptoms listed in Table 27.2–10.

**Pain.** Pain in cancer patients should not be underestimated or undermedicated. (Table 27.2–11). Because cancer patients with pain have a significantly higher incidence of depression and anxiety than those without pain, proper and adequate treatment is essential for their psychological well-being. Cancer patients with acute pain respond well to treatment with antipain medications, such as opiates and opioids, but their tolerance levels rise, and they require more medication if the pain lasts more than a few days.

**Table 27.2–6**
**Suicide Vulnerability Factors in Cancer Patients**

Depression and hopelessness
Poorly controlled pain
Mild delirium (disinhibition)
Feeling of loss of control
Exhaustion
Anxiety
Preexisting psychopathology (substance abuse, character pathology, major psychiatric disorder)
Family problems
Threats and history of prior attempts of suicide
Positive family history of suicide
Other usually described risk factors in psychiatric patients

Table adapted from W Breitbart: Suicide in cancer patients. Oncology *1*: 49, 1987. Used with permission.

**Table 27.2–7**
**Emetogenic Potential of Some Commonly Used Anticancer Agents**

| | |
|---|---|
| Highly emetogenic | Cisplatin |
| | Dacarbazine |
| | Streptozocin |
| | Actinomycin |
| | Nitrogen mustard |
| Moderately emetogenic | Doxorubicin |
| | Daunorubicin |
| | Cyclophosphamide |
| | Nitrosoureas |
| | Mitomycin-C |
| | Procarbazine |
| Minimally emetogenic | Vincristine |
| | Vinblastine |
| | 5-Fluorouracil |
| | Bleomycin |

Table by Marguerite S. Lederberg, M.D., and Jimmie C. Holland, M.D.

**Table 27.2–8**
**Current Chemotherapy Antiemetic Regimens**

| | |
|---|---|
| Neurotransmitter blocking agent | Metoclopramide* 3 mg/kg intravenous piggyback (IVPB) 30 min before therapy, and 1½ hours after therapy<br>or<br>Ondansetron 0.15 mg/kg IVPB 30 min before therapy and 1½ and 3 hours after therapy |
| plus<br>Steroid | Dexamethaseone* 20 mg IVPB 20 min before therapy |
| plus<br>Benzodiazepine<br>or<br>Antihistamine | Lorazepam 1.5 mg/m² (max 3 mg) IVPB before therapy<br>or<br>Diphenhydramine* 50 mg—oral, IV, or IM—every four hours as needed for restlessness or acute dystonic reaction |

*Should also be used in oral form for delayed nausea and vomiting, starting 24 hours after cisplatin therapy.
Table by Marguerite S. Lederberg, M.D., and Jimmie C. Holland, M.D.

**Table 27.2–9**
**Neurological Complications of Chemotherapy**

| | |
|---|---|
| Encephalopathy<br>  Methotrexate with radiotherapy<br>  Hexamethylmelamine<br>  5-Fluorouracil<br>  Procarbazine<br>  Carmustine (BCNU)<br>    (intracarotid)<br>  Cisplatin (intracarotid)<br>  Cyclophosphamide<br>  5-Azacytidine<br>  Spirogermanium<br>  Misonidazole<br>  Cytarabine (high dose)<br>  L-Asparaginase | Myelopathy<br>  Intrathecal methotrexate<br>  Intrathecal cytarabine<br>  Intrathecal thiotepa<br><br>Neuropathy<br>  Vinca alkaloids*<br>  Cisplatin*<br>  Procarbazine<br>  5-Azacytidine<br>  Vasopressin 16<br>  VM-26<br>  Misonidazole<br>  Methyl-G<br>  Cytarabine |
| Acute cerebellar syndrome, ataxia<br>  5-Fluorouracil<br>  Cytarabine<br>  Procarbazine<br>  Hexamethylmelamine | Ototoxicity<br>  Cisplatin<br>  Misonidazole |

*Also involve cranial nerves.
Table by Marguerite S. Lederberg, M.D., and Jimmie C. Holland, M.D.
Table adapted from R A Patchell, J B Posner: Neurologic complications of systemic cancer. In *Symposium on Neuro-oncology Neurologic Clinics*, N A Vick, D D Bigner, editors, vol 3, p 729. Saunders, Philadelphia, 1985. Used with permission.

**Table 27.2–10**
**Chemotherapy Agents with Mood and Psychotic Symptoms**

Dacarbazine: depression and suicide reported, especially when used with hexamethylamine
Vinblastine: frequent reversible depression
Vincristine: 5 percent incidence of hallucinations; depression noted
L-Asparaginase: reversible depression noted
Procarbazine: MAOI; concurrent tricyclics are contraindicated; associated with mania and depression; potentiates alcohol, barbiturates, phenothiazines
Hydroxyurea: hallucinations reported
Interferon: anxiety, depression with suicidal ideation common at doses above 40 million units
Steroids: frequent alterations of mental state ranging from emotional lability through mania or severe, suicidal depression to frank psychosis

Table by Marguerite S. Lederberg, M.D., and Jimmie C. Holland, M.D.

**Table 27.2–11**
**Pain Syndromes in Patients with Cancer**

Pain syndromes associated with direct tumor involvement

  Tumor infiltration of the bone

    Metastases to the cranial vault
      Metastases to the base of the skull
        Jugular foramen syndrome
        Clivus metastases
        Sphenoid sinus metastass
      Vertebral body syndromes
        Fracture of the odontoid vertebra
        C7-T1 metastases
        L1 metastases
        Sacral syndrome

  Tumor infiltration of nerve

    Peripheral nerve
      Peripheral neuropathy
      Intercostal neuropathy
    Plexus
      Brachial plexopathy
      Lumbosacral plexopathy
      Celiac lexopathy
    Root
      Radiculopathy
      Leptomeningeal metastases
    Spinal cord
      Epidural spinal cord compression
      Intramedullary metastases
    Brain
      Intracranial metastases

  Tumor infiltration of viscera

    Infiltration of the pleura
    Small and large bowel obstruction
    Infiltration of the pelvis and the bladder wall

Table by Marguerite S. Lederberg, M.D., and Jimme C. Holland, M.D.

That need is often inappropriately viewed as addiction, for studies have shown that cancer patients easily and voluntarily wean themselves when pain eases. Cancer patients with acute pain require sympathetic and supportive treatment from medical personnel, as do those with chronic pain, whose addictive problems are common and who

nevertheless may require additional medication. As tolerance levels rise, as they always do, patients require increased dosages of narcotics, and there appears to be no ceiling to the dosage required. In cancer patients, however, tolerance to opiates and opioids does not imply addiction. Adjuvants to opiate and opioid medications, which potentiate their effects, are antidepressants, anticonvulsants, phenothiazines, and butyrophenones. One should be cautious about drug-drug interactions, such as meperidine (Demerol) and monoamine oxidase inhibitors (MAOIs), which can be fatal.

**Palliative care.** For the medical staff, palliation should be an active and involved process, with no hint of withdrawal or abandonment. Psychotherapy is useful in pain management (Table 27.2–12).

**Ethical issues.** Included among the ethical issues are questions on informed consent for both traditional and experimental treatments and third-party consent (for example, insurance companies, which may not pay for such treatments in certain cases).

## Staff Problems

The care of cancer patients causes special stresses for caretakers. Table 27.2–13 presents a summary of those stresses.

## Family Problems

Because cancer strikes not only the patient but also the family, caretakers in the family must provide care for the patient and also respond to the increased demands of other family members. Anxiety and depression in family mem-

**Table 27.2–12**
**Cognitive-Behavior Therapy Techniques for Cancer Patients**

Cognitive therapy
  Preparatory information
  Cognitive restructuring
  Focusing
    Controlled mental imagery
  Distraction
    Controlled attention
    Mental, behavioral
  Music therapy
  Hypnosis
  Biofeedback

Behavior therapy
  Self-monitoring
  Systematic desensitization
  Graded task management
  Contingency management
  Modeling
  Behavioral rehearsal
  Relaxation
    Passive, progressive
  Meditation
  Music therapy
  Hypnosis
  Biofeedback

Table from W Breitbart: Psychiatric management of cancer pain. *Cancer* 63: 2336, 1989. Used with permission.

**Table 27.2–13**
**Staff Stresses Common to Special Care Settings**

High morbidity, high mortality
Complex technology used under high pressure
High frequency of life-death decisions
Terminal care issues
Third-party conflicts
Interstaff conflicts
Response to severe debilitation and disfigurement
Response to difficult patients (excessive dependence, anger, uncooperativeness)
Response to suicidal ideation
Issue of inflicting pain as part of treatment

Table by Marguerite S. Lederberg, M.D., and Jimmie C. Holland, M.D.

bers require active intervention. The family problems requiring treatment are preexisting intrafamily conflicts, family abandonment, and family exhaustion.

### Cancer in Children

Fewer children than adults have cancer. Of about 7,000 new cases of cancer in children in the United States in 1986, more than 60 percent had leukemia, lymphoma, and CNS tumors, and they received a combination of chemotherapy and radiation therapy. Five-year survival rates for children with fibrosarcomas, retinoblastomas, Hodgkin's disease, and gonadal and germ cell tumors have passed the 80 percent mark, and the survival rate for most other childhood cancers is between 40 and 60 percent.

## SKIN DISORDERS

Psychosomatic skin disorders include a great variety of abnormal skin sensations. Emotional factors are important in every aspect of skin disorders: manifestations, aggravations, responses, causes, and prognoses.

### Generalized Pruritus

Itch, tickle, and pain are all conveyed by the same afferent fibers and are differentiated only by the frequency of the electrical impulse.

The itching dermatoses include scabies, pediculosis, bites of insects, urticaria, atopic dermatitis, contact dermatitis, lichen ruber planus, and miliaria. Internal disorders that frequently cause itching are diabetes mellitus, nephritis, diseases of the liver, gout, diseases of the thyroid gland, food allergies, Hodgkin's disease, leukemia, and cancer. Itching can also occur during pregnancy and senility.

The term "generalized psychogenic pruritis" denotes that no organic cause for the itching exists or, at least, no longer exists and that, on psychiatric examination, emotional conflicts are seen to account for its occurrence.

The emotions that most frequently lead to generalized psychogenic pruritus are repressed anger and repressed anxiety. Whenever persons consciously or unconsciously experience anger or anxiety, they scratch themselves, often

violently. An inordinate need for affection is a common characteristic of the patients. Frustrations of that need elicit aggressiveness that is inhibited. The rubbing of the skin provides a substitute gratification of the frustrated need, and the scratching represents aggression turned against the self.

### Localized Pruritus

**Pruritus ani.** The investigation of pruritus ani commonly yields a history of local irritation (for example, thread worms, irritant discharge, fungal infection) or general systemic factors (for example, nutritional deficiencies, drug intoxication). However, after running a conventional course, pruritus ani often fails to respond to therapeutic measures and acquires a life of its own, apparently perpetuated by scratching and superimposed inflammation. It is a distressing complaint that often interferes with work and social activity. Investigation of large numbers of patients with the disorder has revealed that personality deviations often precede the condition and that emotional disturbances often precipitate and maintain it.

**Pruritus vulvae.** As in pruritus ani, specific physical causes, either localized or generalized, may be demonstrable in pruritus vulvae, and the presence of glaring psychopathology in no way lessens the need for adequate medical investigation. In some patients, pleasure derived from rubbing and scratching is conscious—they realize that it is a symbolic form of masturbation—but more often than not the pleasure element is repressed. Most of the patients studied gave a long history of sexual frustration, which was frequently intensified at the time of the onset of the pruritus.

### Hyperhidrosis

States of fear, rage, and tension can induce increased sweat secretion. Perspiration in humans has two distinct forms: thermal and emotional. Emotional sweating appears primarily on the palms, the soles, and the axillae; thermal sweating is most evident on the forehead, the neck, the trunk, and the dorsum of the hands and the forearms. The sensitivity of the emotional sweating response serves as the basis for the measurement of sweat by the galvanic skin response (an important tool of psychosomatic research), biofeedback, and the polygraph (lie detector test).

Under conditions of prolonged emotional stress, excessive sweating (hyperhidrosis) may lead to secondary skin changes, rashes, blisters, and infections; therefore, hyperhidrosis may underlie a number of other dermatological conditions that are not primarily related to emotions. Basically, hyperhidrosis may be viewed as an anxiety phenomenon mediated by the autonomic nervous system; it must be differentiated from drug-induced states of hyperhidrosis.

**References**

Ader R, Cohen N, Felten D: Brain, behavior, and immunity. Brain Behav Immun *1*: 1, 1987.
Berman W H, Berman E R, Heymsfield S, Fauci M, et al: The incidence and comorbidity of psychiatric disorders in obesity. J Pers Disord *6*: 168, 1992.
Blackwell B: Chronic pain. In *Comprehensive Textbook of Psychiatry*, ed 5, H I Kaplan, B J Sadock, editors, p 1264. Williams & Wilkins, Baltimore, 1989.
Borbjerg D H: Psychoneuroimmunology implications for oncology. Cancer *67*: 828, 1991.
Breitbart W: Psychiatric management of cancer pain. Cancer *63* (11, Suppl): 2336, 1989.

Byrne D G: Personality, life events and cardiovascular disease. J Psychosom Res *31*: 661, 1987.

Case R B, Heller S S, Case N B: Type A behavior and survival after acute myocardial infarction. N Engl J Med *311*: 737, 1984.

Cassileth B R, Lusk E J, Miller D S, Brown L L, Miller R: Psychosocial correlates of survival in advanced malignant disease. N Engl J Med *312*: 1551, 1985.

Dimsdale J E, Young D, Moore L, Strauss H W: Do plasma norepinephrine levels reflect behavioral stress? Psychosom Med *49*: 375, 1987.

Drossman D A, Powell D W, Sessions J T Jr: The irritable bowel syndrome. Gastroenterology *73*: 811, 1977.

Dunn A J: Nervous system-immune system interactions: An overview. J Recept Res *8*: 589, 1988.

Dworkin R H, Caligor E: Psychiatric diagnosis and chronic pain: DSM-III-R and beyond. J Pain Symp Manag *3*: 87, 1988.

Engel G L: *Psychological Development in Health and Disease*. Saunders, Philadelphia, 1962.

Engel G L: Studies of ulcerative colitis: III. The nature of the psychological processes. Am J Med *19*: 231, 1955.

Fernandez E, Turk D C: The utility of cognitive coping strategies for altering pain perception: A meta-analysis. Pain *38*: 123, 1989.

Goldstein M G, Niaura R: Psychological factors affecting physical condition: Cardiovascular disease literature review. Psychosomatics *33*: 134, 1992.

Kiecolt-Glaser J K, Glaser R: Psychological influences on immunity: Making sense of the relationship between stressful life events and health. Adv Exp Med Biol *245*: 237, 1988.

Kusnecov A, King M G, Husband A J: Immunomodulation by behavioural conditioning. Biol Psychol *28*: 25, 1989.

Lederberg M S, Holland J C: Psycho-oncology. In *Comprehensive Textbook of Psychiatry*, ed 5, H I Kaplan, B J Sadock, editors, p 1249. Williams & Wilkins, Baltimore, 1989.

Massie M J, Holland J C: The cancer patient with pain: Psychiatric complications and their management. J Pain Symp Manag *7*: 99, 1992.

Melnechuck T: Emotions, brain, immunity, and health: A review. In *Emotions and Psychopathology*, M Clynes, J Panksepp, editors, p 13. Plenum, New York, 1988.

Merskey H: Psychiatry and chronic pain. Can J Psychiatry *34*: 329, 1989.

Miller T W: Advances in understanding the impact of stressful life events on health. Hosp Community Psychiatry *39*: 615, 1988.

Niaura R, Goldstein M G: Psychological factors affecting physical condition: Cardiovascular disease literature review: II. Coronary artery disease and sudden death and hypertension. Psychosomatics *33*: 146, 1992.

Norton C S, Clouse R E, Spitznagel E L, Alpers D H: The relation of ulcerative colitis to psychiatric factors: A review of findings and methods. Am J Psychiatry *147*: 974, 1990.

Nunes E V, Frank K A, Kornfeld D S: Psychologic treatment for the type A behavior pattern and for coronary heart disease: A meta-analysis of the literature. Psychosom Med *49*: 159, 1987.

Paykel E S: Methodology of life events research. Adv Psychosom Med *17*: 13, 1987.

Phillips D P, King E W: Death takes a holiday: Mortality surrounding major social occasions. Lancet *2*: 728, 1988.

Phillips D P, Smith D G: Postponement of death until symbolically meaningful occasions. JAMA *263*: 1947, 1990.

Price D D: *Psychological and Neural Mechanisms of Pain*. Raven, New York, 1988.

Shekelle R B, Gale M, Ostfeld A M, Paul O: Hostility, risk of coronary heart disease and mortality: Psychosom Med *45*: 109, 1983.

Siegel L J, Smith K E: Children's strategies for coping with pain. Pediatrician *16*: 110, 1989.

Siegmann A W, Feldstein S, Tomasso C T, Ringel N, Lating B A: Expressive vocal behavior and the severity of coronary artery disease. Psychosom Med *49*: 545, 1987.

Solomon G F: Psychoneuroimmunology: Interactions between central nervous system and immune system. J Neurosci Res *18*: 1, 1987.

Stein M, Miller A H, Restman T: Depression and the immune system, and health and illness. Arch Gen Psychiatry *8*: 171, 1991.

Stoler M H, Eskin T A, Benn R C, Argerer R C, Argerer L M: Human T-cell lymphotropic virus type III infection of the central nervous system: A preliminary in situ analysis. JAMA *256*: 2360, 1986.

Yager J, Kurtzman F, Landsverk J, Wiesmeier E: Behaviors and attitudes related to eating disorders in homosexual male college students. Am J Psychiatry *145*: 4, 1988.

# 27.3 / Consultation-Liaison Psychiatry

In consultation-liaison (C-L) psychiatry, a rapidly growing area of expertise and an expanding field of concentration, the psychiatrist serves as a consultant to a medical colleague (either another psychiatrist or, more commonly, a nonpsychiatric physician) or another mental health professional (psychologist, social worker, or psychiatric nurse). In addition, the C-L psychiatrist consults in regard to patients in medical or surgical settings and provides follow-up psychiatric treatment as needed. In general, C-L psychiatry is associated with all the diagnostic, therapeutic, research, and teaching services that the psychiatrist performs in the general hospital and serves as a bridge between psychiatry and other specialties.

The consultation-liaison psychiatrist must play many roles in the medical wards of the hospital: a skillful and brief interviewer, a good psychiatrist and psychotherapist, a teacher, and a knowledgeable physician who understands the medical aspects of the case. The C-L psychiatrist must be viewed as part of the medical team who makes a unique contribution to the patient's total medical treatment.

## DIAGNOSIS

Knowledge of psychiatric diagnosis is essential to the C-L psychiatrist. Both dementia and delirium frequently complicate organic medical illness, especially among hospital patients. Psychoses and other mental disorders often complicate the treatment of medical illness. And deviant illness behavior, such as suicide, is a common problem in organically ill patients. The C-L psychiatrist must be aware of the many medical illnesses that can present with psychiatric symptoms. (A list of such medical problems is presented in Table 27.3–1). The tools that the C-L psychiatrist has for diagnosis are the interview and serial clinical observations. The purposes of the diagnosis are to identify mental disorders and psychological responses to the physical illness, to identify the patient's personality features, and to identify the patient's characteristic coping techniques in order to recommend the therapeutic intervention that is most appropriate to the patient's needs.

## TREATMENT

The C-L psychiatrist's principal contribution to medical treatment is a comprehensive analysis of the patient's response to illness, psychological and social resources, coping style, and psychiatric illness, if any.

That assessment is the basis of the plan for patient treatment. In discussing that plan, the C-L psychiatrist makes known his or her assessment of the patient to nonpsychiatric health professionals. The psychiatrist's rec-

**Table 27.3–1**
**Medical Conditions That Present with Psychiatric Symptoms**

| Disease | Common Medical Symptoms | Psychiatric Symptoms and Complaints | Impaired Performance and Behavior | Laboratory Tests and Findings | Diagnostic Problems |
|---|---|---|---|---|---|
| Hyperthyroidism (thyrotoxicosis) | Heat intolerance<br>Excessive sweating<br>Diarrhea<br>Weight loss<br>Tachycardia<br>Palpitations<br>Vomiting | Nervousness<br>Excitability<br>Irritability<br>Pressured speech<br>Insomnia<br>May express fear of impending death<br>Psychosis | Fine tremor<br>Impaired cognition<br>Decreased concentration<br>Hyperactivity<br>Intrusiveness | Free $T_4$ increased<br>$T_3$ increased<br>TSH decreased<br>$T_3$ uptake decreased<br>ECG: Tachycardia<br>Atrial fibrillation<br>P and T wave changes | Full range of symptoms may not be present<br>Hyperthyroidism and anxiety states may coexist<br>Rule out occult malignancy, cardiovascular disease, amphetamine intoxication, cocaine intoxication, anxiety states, mania |
| Hypothyroidism (myxedema) | Cold intolerance<br>Dry skin<br>Constipation<br>Weight gain<br>Brittle hair<br>Goiter | Lethargy<br>Depressed affect<br>Personality change<br>Maniclike psychosis<br>Paranoia<br>Hallucinations | Muscle weakness<br>Decreased concentration<br>Psychomotor slowing<br>Apathy<br>Unusual sensitivity to barbiturates | TSH increased<br>TSH low if pituitary disease<br>Free $T_4$<br>ECG: Bradycardia | More common in women<br>Associated with lithium carbonate therapy<br>Rule our pituitary disease, hypothalamic disease, major depressive disorder, bipolar I disorder |
| Hypoglycemia | Sweating<br>Drowsiness<br>Stupor<br>Coma<br>Tachycardia | Anxiety<br>Confusion<br>Agitation | Tremor<br>Restlessness<br>Seizures | Hypoglycemia<br>Tachycardia | Excess insulin often complicated by exercise, alcohol, decreased food intake<br>Rule out insulinoma, postictal states, agitated depression, paranoid psychosis |
| Hyperglycemia | Polyuria<br>Anorexia<br>Nausea<br>Vomiting<br>Dehydration<br>Abdominal complaints | Anxiety<br>Agitation<br>Delirium | Acetone breath<br>Seizures | Hyperglycemia<br>Serum ketones<br>Urine ketones<br>Anion gap acidosis | Almost always associated with brittle diabetes in young juvenile diabetics and elderly non-insulin-dependent diabetics<br>Rule out depressive disorders, anxiety disorders |
| Brain neoplasms | Headache<br>Vomiting<br>Papilledema<br>Focal findings on neurology examination | Personality changes | | Lumbar puncture: increased CSF pressure, skull X-ray, CT scan, EEG | 40–50% gliomas most common in 40–50-year age group<br>Cerebellar tumors most common in children<br>Rule out intracranial abscess, aneurysm, subdural hematoma, seizure disorder, cerebrovascular disease, reactive depression, mania, schizophreniform disorder, dementia |
| Frontal lobe tumor | | Mood changes<br>Irritability<br>Facetiousness<br>Impaired judgment<br>Impaired memory<br>Delirium | Seizures<br>Loss of speech<br>Loss of smell | Angiogram: space-occupying lesion | |
| Parietal lobe tumor | Hyperreflexia<br>Babinski's sign<br>Astereognosis | | Sensory and motor abnormalities<br>Contralateral hemiparesis<br>Focal seizures | | |
| Occipital lobe tumor | Headache<br>Papilledema<br>Homonymous hemianopsia | Aura<br>Visual hallucinations | Visual problems<br>Seizures | | |
| Temporal lobe tumor | Contralateral homonymous field cut | | Psychomotor seizures<br>Aphasia | | |
| Cerebellar tumor | Early evidence of increased intracranial pressure<br>Papilledema | | Disturbed equilibrium<br>Disturbed coordination | | |
| Head trauma | History or evidence of head trauma<br>Headache<br>Dizziness<br>Bleeding from ear<br>Altered level of consciousness<br>Loss of consciousness<br>Focal neurological findings | Confusion<br>Personality changes<br>Memory impairment | Seizures<br>Paralysis | Lumbar puncture, skull X-rays, CT scan show evidence of bleeding or increased intracranial pressure<br>Cerebral angiogram<br>EEG | History of blow to head or bleeding confirms cause of ALS<br>Rule out cerebrovascular disease, seizure disorder, alcohol dependence, diabetes mellitus, hepatic encephalopathy, depression, dementia |
| AIDS | Fever<br>Weight loss<br>Ataxia<br>Incontinence | Progressive dementia<br>Personality changes<br>Depression<br>Loss of libido | Impaired memory<br>Decreased concentration<br>Seizures | HIV testing<br>CT, MRI, lumbar puncture, CSF, and blood cultures | >60% of patients have neuropsychiatric symptoms; always consider in high-risk |

**Table 27.3–1**
*Continued*

| Disease | Common Medical Symptoms | Psychiatric Symptoms and Complaints | Impaired Performance and Behavior | Laboratory Tests and Findings | Diagnostic Problems |
|---|---|---|---|---|---|
| | Focal findings on neurological examination | Psychosis Mutism | | | populations and young patients with signs of dementia<br>Rule out other infections, brain neoplasmas, dementia, depression, schizophreniform disorder |
| Injuries requiring ambulatory surgical evaluation and treatment (for example, wrist slashing) | Alcohol abuse and other substance abuse Recent surgery Chronic pain Chronic illness Terminal illness | >90% have major psychiatric disease History of prior suicide attempts Depressed mood Postpartum psychosis in women | Frequent accidents Repeated emergency room visits Eager to leave emergency room before full evaluation | | Suicidal behavior is a symptom of underlying psychiatric illness<br>Knowledge of risk factors is helpful but not a substitute for good clinical judgment<br>Prediction is best done through assessment of current risk projected into the immediate future |
| Hyponatremia | Excessive thirst Polydipsia Stupor Coma | Confusion Lethargy Personality changes | Seizures Speech abnormalities | Decreased serum $Na^+$<br>Serum $Na^+$ and osmolalities to document syndrome of inappropriate secretion of antidiuretic hormone (SIADH) | Caused by excessive free water for level of total body $Na^+$<br>Often abnormal SIADH<br>May be psychogenic<br>Rule out nephrotic syndrome, liver disease, congestive heart failure, schizophreniform disorder, schizotypal personality disorder |
| Pancreatic carcinoma | Weight loss Abdominal pain | Depression Lethargy Anhedonia | Apathy Decreased energy | Elevated amylase | Always consider in depressed middle-aged patients<br>Rule out other GI illness, major depressive disorder |
| Cushing's syndrome | Central obesity Purple striae Easy bruising Osteoporosis Proximal muscle weakness Hirsutism | Depression Insomnia Emotional lability Suicidality Euphoria Mania Psychosis Delirium | Disturbed sleep Decreased energy Agitation Difficulty in concentrating | Elevated blood pressure Poor glucose tolerance Dexamethasone-suppression test (may be falsely positive) | Must distinguish other causes—for example, cancer from exogenous steroid excess<br>Suicide rate in untreated cases is about 10%<br>Rule out major depressive disorder, bipolar I disorder |
| Adrenocortical insufficiency (Addison's disease) | Nausea Vomiting Anorexia Stupor Coma Hyperpigmentation | Lethargy Depression Psychosis Delirium | Fatigue | Decreased blood pressure Decreased $Na^+$ Increased $K^+$ Eosinophilia | May be primary (Addison's disease) or secondary<br>Rule out eating disorders, mood disorders |
| Seizure disorder | Sensory distortions Aura | Confusion Psychosis Dissociative states Catatoniclike state | Violence Motor automatisms Belligerence Bizarre behavior | EEG, including NP leads | Consider complex partial seizures in all dissociative states<br>Rule out postictal states, catatonic schizophrenia |
| Hyperparathyroidism | Constipation Polydipsia Nausea | Depression Paranoia Confusion | | Increased $Ca^{++}$ PTH variable ECG: shortened QT interval | Causes hypercalcemia<br>Rule out major depressive disorder, schizoaffective disorder |
| Hypoparathyroidism | Headache Paresthesias Tetany Carpopedal spasm Laryngeal spasm Abdominal pain | Anxiety Agitation Depression Confusion | Impaired memory | Low $Ca^{++}$, normal albumin Low blood pressure ECG: QT prolongation, ventricular arrhythmias | Causes hypocalcemia<br>Rule out anxiety disorders, mood disorders |
| Systemic lupus erythematosus | Fever Photosensitivity Butterfly rash Joint pains Headache | Depression Mood disturbances Psychosis Delusions Hallucinations | Fatigue | Positive ANA Positive lupus erythematosus test Anemia Thrombocytopenia Chest X-ray: pleural effusion, pericarditis | Multisystemic autoimmune disease most frequent in women<br>Psychiatric symptoms are present in 50% of cases<br>Steroid treatment can cause psychiatric symptoms<br>Rule out depressive disorders, paranoid psychosis, psychotic mood disorder |

**Table 27.3–1**
**Continued**

| Disease | Common Medical Symptoms | Psychiatric Symptoms and Complaints | Impaired Performance and Behavior | Laboratory Tests and Findings | Diagnostic Problems |
|---|---|---|---|---|---|
| Multiple sclerosis | Sudden transient motor and sensory disturbances Impaired vision Diffuse neurological signs with remissions and exacerbations | Anxiety Euphoria Mania | Slurred speech Incontinence | CSF may show increased gamma globulin CT: degenerative patches in brain and spinal cord | Onset usually in young adults Rule out tertiary syphillis, other degenerative diseases, hysteria, mania (late) |
| Acute intermittent porphyria | Abdominal pain Fever Nausea Vomiting Constipation Peripheral neuropathy Paralysis | Acute depression Agitation Paranoia Visual hallucinations | Restlessness Diaphoresis Weakness | Leukocytosis Elevated δ-aminolevulinic acid Elevated porphobilinogen Tachycardia | Autosomal dominant More common in women in the 20–40 age group May be precipitated by a variety of drugs Rule out acute abdominal disease, acute psychiatric episode, schizophreniform disorder, major depressive disorder |
| Hepatic encephalopathy | Asterixis Hyperreflexia Spider angiomata Palmar erythema Ecchymoses Liver enlargement and atrophy | Euphoria Disinhibition Psychosis Depression | Restlessness Decreased activities of daily living (ADL) Impaired cognition Impaired concentration Ataxia Dysarthria | Abnormal liver function test results Abnormal albumin EEG: diffuse slowing | May be acute or chronic depending on cause Rule out substance intoxication, mania, depressive disorder, dementia |
| Injuries requiring inpatient surgical evaluation and treatment (for example, suicide attempts, self-mutilation) | Alcohol abuse and other substance abuse Serious injury Major blood loss Damage to genitals, eyes, face, etc | 99% have severe psychiatric disease associated with psychosis, psychotic depression Impaired mental status secondary to substance intoxication Bizarre, inappropriate affect | Remain at great risk for suicide | | Must assess and treat the underlying psychiatric condition on a priority basis Maintain a high index of suspicion for suicide risk |
| Pheochromocytoma | Paroxsysmal hypertension Headache | Anxiety Apprehension Feeling of impending doom | Panic Diaphoresis Tremor | Hypertension Elevated VMA in 24-hr. urine Tachycardia | Adrenal medulla secreting catacholamines Rule out anxiety disorders |
| Wilson's disease | Kayser-Fleischer corneal ring Hepatitislike picture | Mood disturbances Delusions Hallucinations | Choreoathetoid movements Gait disturbance Clumsiness Rigidity | Decreased serum ceruloplasm Increased copper in urine | Hepatolenticular degeneration Autosomal recessive disorder of copper metabolism Often presents in adolescence, early adulthood Rule out extrapyramidal reactions, schizophreniform disorder, mood dicorders |
| Huntington's disease | Family history | Depression Euphoria | Rigidity Choreoathetoid movements | | Autosomal dominant Rule out mood disorders, mania, schizophrenia |
| Vitamin deficiencies | | | | | |
| Thiamine | Neuropathy Cardiomyopathy Wernike-Korsakoff syndrome Nystagmus Headache Amnesia | Confusion Confabulation | General malaise Inability to sustain a conversation Poor concentration | Low thiamine level | Most common in alcoholic persons Rule out hypomania, depressive disorder, dementia |
| Nicotinamide | Diarrhea Stocking-glove dermatitis | Confusion Irritability Insomnia Depression Psychosis Dementia | Memory disturbances | | Rule out mood disorders, mania, schizophreniform disorder, dementia |
| Pyridoxine | | Apathy Irritability | Memory disturbance Muscle weakness Seizures | | Often caused by medication: isoniazed Rule out mood disorders, dementia |

**Table 27.3–1**
*Continued*

| Disease | Common Medical Symptoms | Psychiatric Symptoms and Complaints | Impaired Performance and Behavior | Laboratory Tests and Findings | Diagnostic Problems |
|---|---|---|---|---|---|
| Vitamin $B_{12}$ | Pallor<br>Dizziness<br>Peripheral neuropathy<br>Dorsal column signs | Irritability<br>Inattentiveness<br>Psychosis<br>Dementia | Fatigue<br>Ataxia | Low $B_{12}$ level<br>Schilling test<br>Megaloblastic anemia | Often due to pernicious anemia<br>Rule out dementia, mania, mood disorders |
| Tertiary syphilis | Skin lesions<br>Leukoplakia<br>Periostitis<br>Arthritis<br>Respiratory distress<br>Progressive cardiovascular distress | Personality changes<br>Irritability<br>Confusion<br>Psychosis | Irresponsible behavior<br>Decreased attention to activities of daily living (ADL) | VDRL, Treponema antibody test<br>CSF abnormal | General paresis<br>Rule out neoplasias, meningitis, dementia, psychotic mood disorder, schizophrenia |

ommendations should be clear, concrete guidelines for action. The C-L psychiatrist may recommend a specific therapy, suggest areas for further medical inquiry, inform doctors and nurses of their roles in the patient's psychosocial care, recommend a transfer to a psychiatric facility for long-term psychiatric treatment, or suggest or undertake with the patient brief psychotherapy on the medical ward.

The range of problems with which the C-L psychiatrist must deal is broad. Studies show that up to 65 percent of medical inpatients have psychiatric disorders, the most common symptoms being anxiety, depression, and disorientation. Treatment problems account for 50 percent of the consultation requests made of psychiatrists. (Table 27.3-2 covers the most common C-L problems with which the psychiatrist must deal.)

## SPECIAL SETTINGS

### Intensive Care Units

The central psychological aspect of patients in intensive care units (ICUs) is that they are suffering life-threatening illnesses with psychological responses that are predictable and that, if untreated, may threaten life or recovery. Coronary and medical ICU staff members see patients' reactions to acute unexpected illnesses. At first, the patient shows fear and anxiety, followed by the psychological behaviors associated with denial, such as acting out, signing out, hostility, and excessive dependence. Staff members working in burn units encounter patients going through the problems of acute unexpected illness and, later, depression, grief, and dissociation related to pain and disfigurement. Staff members in surgical ICUs see patients recovering from major surgery with the expected disorientation of delirium, depression, and adjustment reactions to surgery.

Treatment of the psychological problems in the ICU requires close attention to diagnostic possibilities and details of the environment, as well as careful team communication. Clinicians are clearly helped by familiarity with the patient's premorbid character, because the reactions to disease and illness are influenced by prior conditioning.

The most common initial reactions to medical disasters include shock, fear, and anxiety. In many patients those reactions respond to treatment by the care team, especially succinct, authoritative, and consistent reassurance. When those measures are insufficient, benzodiazepines—preferably the short-acting forms—should be considered and used cautiously. When fear leads to panic or psychotic loss of control, fast-acting antipsychotics—for example, haloperidol (Haldol)—should be used.

Denial and associated behaviors of acting out, hostility, dependence, and demanding behavior must be dealt with individually on the basis of knowledge of the patient and the reasons for those reactions. Several general points are pertinent. Direct communication with the patient, which allows but does not force a discussion of feelings, often eliminates disruptive behaviors without dealing with them directly. Allowing patients as much mastery as they want and can handle is the most reassuring approach. Permitting patients to make small choices restores some sense of control over the self and the future and calms them far beyond the meaning of the specific choices. They feel a symbolic sense of progress. For example, allowing patients to control pain medications, the lighting level, or where they sit reassures and relaxes them. Whether the disruptive behavior is hostility, dependence, or panic, allowing some behavior to be shown while setting limits on their extremes reassures patients. Thus, the independent patient can be allowed to move around but not too far; the dependent patient can be allowed a limited number of interactions, such as use of the call button; and the hostile patient can be permitted some disagreement and ventilation but be limited in disruptive acts.

All ICUs deal mainly with anxiety, depression, and delirium. ICUs also impose extraordinarily high stress, both on the staff and on the patients related to the intensity of the problems. Patients and staff members alike frequently observe cardiac arrests, deaths, and medical disasters, which leave all autonomically aroused and psychologically defensive. ICU nurses and their patients experience particularly high levels of anxiety, depression, turnover, and burnout.

Attention is often given, especially in the nursing literature, to the problem of stress in the ICU staff. Much

**Table 27.3–2**
**Common Consultation-Liaison Problems**

| Reason for Consultation | Comments |
|---|---|
| Suicide attempt or threat | High-risk factors are men over 45, no social support, alcohol dependence, previous attempt, incapacitating medical illness with pain, and suicidal ideation. If risk is present, transfer to psychiatric unit or start 24-hour nursing care. |
| Depression | Suicidal risks must be assessed in every depressed patient (see above); presence of cognitive defects in depression may cause diagnostic dilemma with dementia; check for history of substance abuse or depressant drugs (e.g., reserpine, propranolol); use antidepressants cautiously in cardiac patients because of conduction side effects, orthostatic hypotension. |
| Agitation | Often related to cognitive disorder, withdrawal from drugs, (e.g., opiods, alcohol, sedative-hypnotics); haloperidol most useful drug for excessive agitation; use physical restraints with great caution; examine for command hallucinations or paranoid ideation to which patient is responding in agitated manner; rule out toxic reaction to medication. |
| Hallucinations | Most common cause in hospital is delirium tremens; onset three to four days after hospitalization. In intensive care units, check for sensory isolation; rule out brief psychotic disorder, schizophrenia, cognitive disorder. Treat with antipsychotic medication. |
| Sleep disorder | Common cause is pain; early morning awakening associated with depression; difficulty in falling asleep associated with anxiety. Use antianxiety or antidepressant agent, depending on cause. Those drugs have no analgesic effect, so prescribe adequate painkillers. Rule out early substance withdrawal. |
| No organic basis for symptoms | Rule out conversion disorder, somatization disorder, factitious disorder, and malingering; glove and stocking anesthesia with autonomic nervous system symptoms seen in conversion disorder; multiple body complaints seen in somatization disorder; wish to be hospitalized seen in factitious disorder; obvious secondary gain in malingering (e.g., compensation case). |
| Disorientation | Delirium versus dementia; review metabolic status, neurological findings, substance history. Prescribe small dose of antipsychotics for major agitation; benzodiazepines may worsen condition and cause sundowner syndrome (ataxia, confusion); modify environment so patient does not experience sensory deprivation. |
| Noncompliance or refusal to consent to procedure | Explore relationship of patient and treating doctor; negative transference is most common cause of noncompliance; fears of medication or of procedure require education and reassurance. Refusal to give consent is issue of judgment; if impaired, patient can be declared incompetent but only by a judge; cognitive disorder is main cause of impaired judgment in hospitalized patients. |

less attention is given to the house staff, especially on the surgical services. All persons in ICUs need to be able to deal directly with their feelings about the extraordinary experiences they are having and the difficult emotional and physical circumstances they are experiencing. Regular support groups in which those persons are able to discuss how they are feeling are important to the ICU staff and the house staff. Such support groups are needed to protect the staff members from the otherwise predictable psychiatric morbidity that some persons experience and also to protect their patients from the loss of concentration, the decreased energy, and the psychomotor-retarded communications that some staff members otherwise exhibit.

## Hemodialysis Units

Hemodialysis units present a paradigm of complex modern medical treatment settings. Patients are coping with lifelong, debilitating, and limiting disease; they are totally dependent on a multiplex group of caretakers for access to a machine controlling their well-being. Dialysis is sched-

uled three times a week and takes four to six hours, thereby disrupting the patients' previous living routines.

In that context, such patients' major struggle is with the disease. Invariably, however, they also have to come to terms with a level of dependence on others, a dependence they probably have not experienced since childhood. Predictably, patients entering dialysis struggle for their independence; regress to childhood states; show denial by acting out against doctor's orders, by breaking their diet, or by missing sessions; show anger directed against staff members; bargain and plead or become infantilized and obsequious; but most often are accepting and courageous. The determinants of the patients' responses to entering dialysis include personality styles and their prior experiences with that or another chronic illness. Patients who have had time to react and adapt to their chronic renal failure face less new psychological work of adaptation than do those to whom renal failure and machine dependence are new.

Although little has been written about social factors, the effect of cultural factors in reaction to dialysis and the management of the dialysis unit are known to be important. Units that are run with a firm hand, are consistent in dealing with patients, have clear contingencies for behavioral failures, and have adequate psychological support for staff members tend to do the best.

Complications of dialysis treatment can include psychiatric problems, such as depression, and suicide is not rare. Sexual problems can be neurogenic, psychogenic, or related to gonadal dysfunction and testicular atrophy.

*Dialysis dementia* is a rare condition that consists of loss of memory, disorientation, dystonias, and seizures. It occurs in patients who have been receiving dialysis treatment for many years. The cause is unknown.

The psychological treatment of dialysis patients falls into two areas. First, careful preparation before dialysis, including the work of adaptation to chronic illness, is important, especially in dealing with denial and unrealistic expectations. All predialysis patients should have a psychosocial evaluation. Second, once in a dialysis program, the patient needs periodic specific inquiries about adaptation, which does not encourage dependence or the sick role. The staff members should be sensitive to the likelihood of depression and sexual problems. Group sessions function well for support, and patient self-help groups restore a useful social network, self-esteem, and self-mastery. When needed, tricyclic drugs or phenothiazines can be used for dialysis patients. Psychiatric care is best if brief and problem-oriented.

The use of home dialysis units has been of great help. The home-treated patients, compared with hospital-treated patients, are better able to integrate the treatment into their daily lives and feel more autonomous and less dependent on others for their care.

## Surgical Units

Some surgeons believe that patients who expect to die during surgery will do so. That belief now seems less superstitious than it did earlier. Chase Patterson Kimball and others have studied the premorbid psychological adjustment of patients headed for surgery and have shown that those who show evident depression or anxiety and deny it have a higher risk for morbidity and mortality than do those who, given similar depression or anxiety, are able to express it. Even better is to have a positive attitude toward impending surgery. The factors that contribute to an improved outcome for surgery are informed consent, the education of patients so that they know what to expect concerning what they will feel, where they will be (for example, it is useful to show patients the recovery room), what loss of function to expect, what tubes and gadgets will be in place, and how to cope with the anticipated pain. In cases in which the patients will not be able to talk or see, it is helpful to explain before the surgery what they can do to compensate for those losses. If postoperative states such as confusion, delirium, and pain can be predicted, they should be discussed with the patients in advance to avoid their experiencing them as unwarranted or as signs of danger. The presence of constructive family support members is helpful both before and after the surgery. Table 27.3–3 lists various surgical conditions with which the C-L psychiatrist must deal.

**Table 27.3–3**
**Transplantation and Surgical Problems**

| Organ | Biological Factors | Psychological Factors |
|---|---|---|
| Kidney | 50 to 90 percent success rate; may not be done if patient is over age 55; increasing use of cadaver kidneys, rather than those from living donors | Living donors must be emotionally stable; parents are best donors, siblings may be ambivalent; donors are subject to depression. Patients who panic before surgery may have poor prognoses; altered body image with fear of organ rejection is common. Group therapy for patients is helpful. |
| Bone marrow | Used in aplastic anemias and immune system disease | Patients are usually very ill and must deal with death and dying; compliance is important. The procedure is commonly done in children who present problems of prolonged dependence; siblings are often donors and may be angry or ambivalent about procedure. |
| Heart | End-stage coronary artery disease and cardiomyopathy | Donor is legally dead; relatives of the deceased may refuse permission or be ambivalent. No fall-back position is available if the organ is rejected; kidney rejection patient can go on hemodialysis. Some patients seek transplantation hoping to die. Postcardiotomy delirium is seen in 25 percent of patients. |
| Breast | Radical mastectomy versus lumpectomy | Reconstruction of breast at time of surgery leads to postoperative adaptation; veteran patients are used to counsel new patients; lumpectomy patients are more open about surgery and sex than are mastectomy patients; group support is helpful. |
| Uterus | Hysterectomy performed on 10 percent of women over 20 | Fear of loss of sexual attractiveness with sexual dysfunction may occur in a small percentage of women; loss of childbearing capacity is upsetting. |

**Table 27.3–3**
*Continued*

| Organ | Biological Factors | Psychological Factors |
|---|---|---|
| Brain | Anatomical location of lesion determines behavioral change | Environmental dependence syndrome in frontal lobe tumors is characterized by inability to show initiative; memory disturbances are involved to periventricular surgery; hallucinations are involved in parieto-occipital area. |
| Prostate | Cancer surgery has more negative psychobiological effects and is more technically difficult than is surgery for benign hypertrophy | Sexual dysfunction is common except in transurethral prostatectomy. Perineal prostatectomy produces the absence of emission, ejaculation, and erection; penile implant may be of use. |
| Colon and rectum | Colostomy and ostomy are common outcomes, especially for cancer | One third of patients with colostomies feel worse about themselves than before bowel surgery; shame and self-consciousness about the stoma can be alleviated by self-help groups that deal with those issues. |
| Limbs | Amputation performed for massive injury, diabetes, or cancer | Phantom-limb phenomenon occurs in 98 percent of cases; the experience may last for years; sometimes the sensation is painful, and neuroma at the stump should be ruled out; the condition has no known cause or treatment; it may stop spontaneously. |

## ALTERNATIVE MEDICINE

Alternative or unconventional medical therapy is being used increasingly today (Table 27.3–4). *The New England Journal of Medicine* found that one in three people uses such therapies at some point for such common ailments as depression, anxiety, chronic pain, and low back pain (Figure 27.3–1). Practitioners of holistic medicine use a total approach to the patient, evaluating psychosocial, environmental, and life-style parameters that have been subsumed under the psychosomatic approach in previous years. The establishment of a National Institute of Health office, the Office of Alternative Medicine, now shows the increasing importance of the area.

Of all the alternative therapies, only hypnosis and biofeedback have entered the mainstream of psychiatry. Each treatment method requires exhaustive evaluation, but most methods appear to work through the power of suggestion. Whether other factors operate in a particular type of therapy remains to be evaluated. Patients should inform their medical doctors that they are using alternative medicine, something that most patients do not do (7 of 10 patients do not tell their physicians of such encounters).

**Table 27.3–4**
**Alternative Therapies**

Some alternative approaches that may be studied by the NIH Office of Alternative Medicine under Joseph J. Jacobs. Some approaches have achieved medical recognition; others have only anecdotal support.

**Manipulation**

Acupuncture: Use of needles to stimulate areas that are supposed to have neural connections with specific organs and body functions.

Acupressure, reflexology: Similar to acupuncture in concept except that finger pressure is used; reflexology involves only the hands and the feet.

Chiropractic: Manipulation or subluxation of the spinal vertebrae to relieve back problems and other ailments.

**Altered mental states**

Relaxation response, visualization, guided imagery: Use of relaxed state—through meditation, for example—to alter body responses.

**Medication**

Antineoplastic therapy: Use of compounds from human urine, now synthesized, that seem to halt the division of some cancer cells.

Bee pollen: Use as a possible treatment for asthma, multiple sclerosis, and allergies.

Herbalism: Use of natural plant substances to treat illnesses, based on folk medicine and modern research.

Homeopathy: Medication based on the premise that with diluted minidoses of various substances, the immune system can fight diseases.

Ozone therapy: Introduction of ozone gas into the bloodstream as a possible way to fight diseases.

Shark cartilage: Use as a possible cancer treatment because of sharks' natural resistance to cancer.

Table from *Medical World News* 34: 54, April 1993. Used with permission.

### References

Burns B S, Scott J, Burke J, Kessler L: Mental health training of primary care residents: A review of recent literature (1974–1984). Gen Hosp Psychiatry 5: 157, 1983.

Cohen-Cole S A, Pincus H A, Stoudemire A, Fiester S, Houpt J L: Recent research developments in consultation-liaison psychiatry. Gen Hosp Psychiatry 8: 316, 1986.

Engle G L: The need for a new medical model: A challenge for biomedical science. Science 196: 129, 1977.

Feifel H, Strack S, Nagy V T: Coping strategies and associated features of medically ill patients. Psychosom Med 49: 545, 1987.

Fulop G, Strain J, Hammer J S, Lyons J S: Psychiatric and medical comorbidity: Length of stay. Am J Psychiatry 144: 878, 1987.

Greenhill M B: The development of liaison programs. In *Psychiatric Medicine*, G Usdin, editor, p 103. Brunner/Mazel, New York, 1977.

Hammer J S, Lyons J, Strain J J: Microcomputers and consultation psychiatry in the general hospital. Gen Hosp Psychiatry 7: 119, 1985.

Houpt J L: Introduction: Psychosomatic medicine, consultation-liaison psychiatry, and behavioral medicine. In *Psychiatry*, R Michael, A M Cooper, S B Guze, L L Judd, G L. Klerman, A J Solnit, A J Stunkard, P J Wilner, editors. Lippincott, Philadelphia, 1991.

Jacobs J, Bernhard M R, Delgado A, Strain J: Screening for organic mental syndrome in the medically ill. Ann Intern Med 86: 40,177.

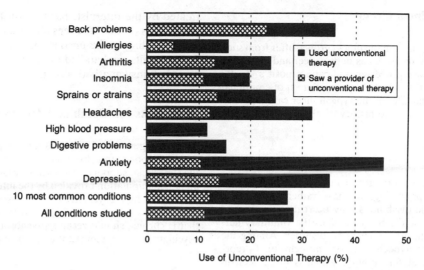

**Figure 27.3–1.** Use of unconventional therapy by respondents who saw a medical doctor for a principal medical condition in 1990. The 10 most commonly reported conditions are shown in descending order of prevalence. (Figure from D M Eisenberg, R C Kessler, C Foster, F E Norlock, D R Calkins, T L Delbanco: Unconventional medicine in the United States. N Engl J Med *328*: 246, 1993. Used with permission.)

Levenson J L, Mishra A, Hamer R, Hastillo A: Denial and medical outcome in unstable angina. Psychosom Med *51*: 27, 1989.

Levitan S, Kornfeld D: Clinical and cost benefits of liaison psychiatry. Am J Psychiatry *138*: 790, 1981.

Lipowski Z J: Consultation-liaison psychiatry at century's end. Psychosomatics *33*: 128, 1992.

Lipowski Z J: Consultation-liaison psychiatry: The first half century. Gen Hosp Psychiatry *8*: 305, 1986.

Lipowski Z J: *Psychosomatic Medicine and Liaison Psychiatry: Selected Papers.* Plenum, New York, 1985.

Mumford E, Schlesinger H J, Glass G V, Patrick C, Cuerdon T: A new look at evidence about reduced cost of medical utilization following mental health treatment. Am J Psychiatry *141*: 1145, 1984.

Olfson M: Depressed patients who do and do not receive psychiatric consultation in general hospitals. Gen Hosp Psychiatry *13*: 39, 1991.

Pincus H A: Linking general health and mental health systems of care: Conceptual models of implementation. Am J Psychiatry *137*: 315, 1980.

Popkin M, MacKenzie T, Callies A: Consultation liaison outcome evaluation system. Arch Gen Psychiatry *40*: 215, 1983.

Regier D A, Myers J K, Kramer M, Robins L N, Blazer D G, Hough R L, Eaton W W, Locke B Z: The NIMH Epidemiologic Catchment Area (ECA) program: Historical context, major objectives, and study population characteristics. Arch Gen Psychiatry *41*: 934, 1984.

Schwab J J: Consultation-liaison psychiatry. A historical overview. Psychosomatics *30*: 245, 1989.

Strain J: Diagnostic considerations in the medical setting. Psychiatr Clin North Am *4*: 287, 1981.

Strain J: *Psychological Interventions in Medical Practice.* Appleton-Century-Crofts, New York, 1978.

Strain J, Hammer J S, Huertas D, Lam H C, et al: The problem of coping as a reason for psychiatric consultation. Gen Hosp Psychiatry *15*: 1, 1993.

Strain J, Pincus H A, Houpt J L, Gise L H, Taintor Z: Models of mental health training for primary care physicians. Psychosom Med *47*: 95, 1985.

Strain J J, Taintor Z: Consultation-liaison psychiatry. In *Comprehensive Textbook of Psychiatry,* ed 5, H I Kaplan, B J Sadock, editors, p 1272. Williams & Wilkins, Baltimore, 1989.

Uhlenhuth E H, Balter M B, Mellinger G D, Cisin I H, Clinthorne J: Symptom checklist syndromes in the general population: Correlations with psychotherapeutic drug use. Arch Gen Psychiatry *40*: 1167, 1983.

Wallen J, Pincus H A, Goldman H A, Marcus S E: Psychiatric consultations in short-term general hospitals. Arch Gen Psychiatry *44*: 163, 1987.

Weiner H: *Psychobiology of Health and Disease.* Elsevier, New York, 1977.

# 27.4 / Treatment

The concept of combined psychotherapeutic and medical treatment—that is, the approach that emphasizes the interrelation of mind and body in the genesis of symptom and disorder—calls for a greatly expanded sharing of responsibility among various professions. If one views disease from a multicausal point of view, every disease can be considered psychosomatic, since every disease is affected in some fashion by emotional factors. The evaluation of all those factors is best done by the primary care physician, who may need the participation of the psychiatrist to explain the psychological factors fully.

Hostility, depression, and anxiety in varying proportions are at the root of most psychosomatic disorders. Psychosomatic medicine is principally concerned with those illnesses that present primarily somatic manifestations. The presenting complaint is usually physical; patients rarely complain of their anxiety or depression or tension but, rather, complain of their vomiting or diarrhea or anorexia.

## TYPES OF PATIENTS

A special evaluation of the psychological and somatic factors of three major groups of medical patients is required.

## Psychosomatic Illness Group

Patients in the psychosomatic illness group suffer from such classic psychosomatic disorders as peptic ulcer and ulcerative colitis. In those disease processes one cannot posit a strictly psychogenic explanation, since the particular set of emotional factors found, for example, in the typical ulcer case may also appear in the patient with no history of ulcer.

## Psychiatric Group

Patients in the psychiatric group suffer from physical disturbances caused by psychological illness, rather than physical illness. Their somatic disabilities may be real (objective) or unreal. When real, the disability involves the voluntary nervous system and is termed conversion disorder. Among the unreal disabilities are hypochondriasis and delusional preoccupation with physical functioning, which is often seen in schizophrenic patients. Patients in this group suffer primarily from a psychological disturbance that requires psychiatric treatment, but auxiliary medical therapy may be necessary.

## Reactive Group

Patients in the reactive group have actual organic disorders, but they also suffer from an associated psychological disturbance. For example, a patient with heart disease or renal disease requiring dialysis may have a reactive anxiety and depression regarding the life-threatening condition. That anxiety, in turn, may produce physical manifestations that complicate the somatic situation.

## COMBINED TREATMENT

The combined treatment approach, in which the psychiatrist handles the psychiatric aspects of the case and the internist or other specialist treats the somatic aspects, requires the closest collaboration between the two physicians. The purpose of the medical therapy is to build up the patient's physical state so that the patient can successfully participate in psychotherapy for total cure.

Disorders such as bronchial asthma, in which psychosocial processes play a distinct role in the development and the course, may respond well to the combined treatment approach. Although the asthmatic attacks themselves may be treated successfully by the internist, psychiatric treatment can be useful in the short run by helping to alleviate the anxiety associated with the attacks and in the long run by helping to uncover the causes of the interdependence involved in the disorder.

In an acute somatic illness, such as an acute attack of ulcerative colitis, medical therapy is the primary form of treatment; psychotherapy, with its long-range goals, consists at that stage of reassurance and support. As the pendulum of disease activity shifts and the illness becomes chronic, psychotherapy assumes the primary role, and medical therapy takes the less active position.

Sometimes reassurance is all that is needed in the treatment of psychosomatic syndromes.

Patients must participate in the process of improving their life situations. The symptoms themselves must be treated by the internist, but the psychiatrist can help patients focus on their feelings about the symptoms and gain understanding of the unconscious processes involved.

If patients are handled insensitively or if their illness is regarded unsympathetically, the results can be grave.

## Indications for Combined Treatment

If during an initial attack of a psychosomatic disorder the patient responds to active medical therapy in association with the superficial support, ventilation, reassurance, and environmental manipulation provided by the internist, additional psychotherapy by a psychiatrist may not be required. Psychosomatic illness that does not respond to medical treatment or that is chronic should receive psychosomatic evaluation by a psychiatrist and combined therapy as indicated.

## Goal of Combined Treatment

It is useful to set up a tentative, flexible spectrum of therapeutic goals in the treatment of psychosomatic disorders. The end desired is cure, which means resolution of the structural impairment and reorganization of the personality, so that needs and tensions no longer produce pathophysiological results. Treatment should aim at a mature general life adjustment, increased capacity for physical and occupational activity, amelioration of the progression of the disease, reversal of the pathology, avoidance of complications of the basic disease process, decreased use of secondary gain associated with the illness, and increased capacity to adjust to the presence of the disease.

## PSYCHIATRIC ASPECTS

Treatment of psychosomatic disorders from the psychiatric viewpoint is a difficult task. The purpose of therapy should be to understand the motivations and the mechanisms of disturbed functioning and to help patients understand the nature of their illness and the implications of their costly adaptive patterns. That insight should result in changed and healthier patterns of behavior.

Psychotherapy based on analytic principles is effective in treating psychosomatic disorders mainly in terms of the patients' experiences in the treatment, particularly regarding their relationships with the therapist. Psychosomatic patients are usually even more reluctant to deal with their emotional problems than are patients with other psychiatric problems. Psychosomatic patients try to avoid responsibility for their illness by isolating the diseased organ and presenting it to the doctor for diagnosis and cure. The patients may be satisfying an infantile need to be cared for passively, at the same time denying that they are adults, with all the attendant stresses and conflicts.

## Resistance to Entering Psychotherapy

When psychosomatic patients first become ill, they are usually convinced that the illness is purely organic in origin. They reject psychotherapy as treatment for their sickness, and, in fact, the very idea of emotional illness may be repugnant because of personal prejudices concerning psychiatry.

In the initial phase, physical treatment and psychotherapeutic procedures must be combined subtly. A good arrangement in the early stage is treatment by a psychologically oriented physician, one who is sensitive to unconscious and transference phenomena and who is perhaps working with a psychotherapist.

## Development of Relationship and Transference

Psychotherapy with the psychosomatic patient must often proceed more slowly and cautiously than with other psychiatric patients. Positive transference should be developed gradually. The psychiatrist must be supportive and reassuring during the acute illness. As the disorder becomes chronic, the psychiatrist may make exploratory interpretations, but a strong patient-physician relationship is essential for any such exploration. The psychosomatic patient is dependent, and that characteristic may be used supportively and interpretatively at crucial periods in the treatment. During therapy, a great deal of hostility appears—first in the form of overt ventilation and then in the framework of the transference. Free and appropriate expression of the patient's hostility is to be encouraged.

## Interpretation

The therapist must pay particular attention to current problems in the patient's immediate life situation and must deal with the patient's reaction to the therapist and to treatment. There should be increased emphasis on evaluation of the patient's characterological difficulties and habitual reactions, particularly reactions to himself or herself (self-esteem, guilt) and reactions to his or her environment (dependence, submission, need for affection). The psychiatrist should also analyze the patient's anxieties and coping mechanisms for stress situations, such as asking for complete care, always having to be right, refraining from self-assertion, and suppressing all forbidden impulses.

Some psychoanalytic investigators have reported dramatic results when unconscious material was interpreted as a drastic measure during an acute illness. Although most Freudian psychoanalysts seem to think that genetic material must eventually be interpreted for a complete cure, new approaches have shown that adequate results can be obtained when psychotherapy is limited to the analysis of characterological and ego defenses associated with disturbed interpersonal relationships.

Psychosomatic patients are often involved in a repetitious pattern involving stress in their interpersonal relationships. Because such patients are usually unaware of the pattern, it is helpful to show them that the pattern is not accidental but is determined by factors of which they are unaware, and it is essential to show them how they may change the disturbing pattern and act in a new and healthier manner.

Psychosomatic patients tend to drive toward psychologically regressed mental and physical behavior. Usually, their regression is to a traumatic or highly conflictual period. By reenacting certain specific attitudes of childhood or infancy, they are attempting to master the anxiety and illness first manifested during those earlier stages.

In the treatment of psychosomatic disorders, the key concept is flexibility in technique. Because of the patient's poor motivation and poor physical condition, it may be necessary to make frequent changes in the psychotherapeutic approach.

## Resistance during Therapy

Since psychosomatic patients frequently have a great deal of resistance to entering psychotherapy, the resistance often continues unabated during therapy. In many patients the motivation for entering treatment is so poor that they frequently drop out of therapy for minor reasons.

## Interruption of Psychotherapy for a Medical Emergency

During a course of psychotherapy, a patient with a psychosomatic disorder may require medical or surgical treatment for the organic disorder. The psychiatrist should cooperate closely with the surgeon or medical personnel and should maintain contact with the patient—in person or by telephone—during the emergency. Such interest offers valuable emotional support in a time of crisis.

If a patient is hospitalized, the psychiatrist should help other hospital personnel recognize and learn to tolerate the frequently difficult and provocative behavior of certain psychosomatic patients. The preparation can be of use to such patients as well; if they see their demands being met considerately, they may be less inclined to view their world as hostile and formidable.

## Danger of Psychosis

There are no simple relations between psychosomatic disorders and psychoses. Some people in whom physiological and psychological processes are poorly integrated manifest both psychosomatic disorders and psychoses. In other people, the ego integration is such that stress produces a breakdown of bodily function, rather than a psychotic maladjustment. Some nonpsychotic psychosomatic patients can become psychotic or exhibit psychotic symptoms as a result of too active an interpretation and the removal of defensive elements in the personality structure.

## MEDICAL ASPECTS

The internist's treatment of psychosomatic disorders should follow the established rules for their medical management. Generally, the internist should spend as much time as possible with the patient and listen sympathetically to the many complaints. The internist must be reassuring and supportive. Before performing a physically manipulative procedure—particularly if it is painful, such as a colonoscopy—the internist should explain to the patient just what will happen. The explanation allays the patient's anxiety, makes the patient more cooperative, and actually facilitates the examination.

The patient's attitude toward taking drugs may also affect the outcome of the psychosomatic treatment. For example, patients suffering from diabetes who do not accept their illness and who have self-destructive impulses of which they are unaware may purposely not control their diet and, as a result, end up in a hyperglycemic coma. In the case of cardiac patients, some refuse to curtail their physical activity after a myocardial infarction because of a reluctance to admit weakness or because of a fear that they will somehow be considered unsuccessful. Others use their illness as a welcome punishment for guilt or as a way of avoiding responsibility. Therapy in such cases must strive to help patients minimize their fears and focus on self-care and the reestablishment of a healthy body image.

## ACCEPTANCE OF PSYCHOMEDICAL TREATMENT

The advantages of the collaborative approach are that the patient receives the benefit of the efforts of specialists trained in various medical disciplines, each working in the area in which he or she is best equipped to function. However, some physicians have resisted the psychiatric approach because of inadequate training in psychiatry in medical school, unfamiliarity with the specialized language of psychiatry, and a general prejudice based on the cost of psychotherapy and the alleged unscientific and subjective aspects of psychiatry.

## OTHER TYPES OF THERAPY

Other types of treatment have been introduced for psychosomatic disorders, some of which are described below. The first category includes psychotherapies based on psychological insight and change, such as group and family psychotherapy; the second category is composed of behavior therapy techniques based on Pavlovian principles of learning new behavior, such as biofeedback and relaxation therapy.

### Group Psychotherapy and Family Therapy

Because of the psychopathological significance of the mother-child relationship in the development of psychosomatic disorders, modification of that relationship has been suggested as a likely focus of emphasis in the psychotherapy of psychosomatic disorders. Toksoz Byram

Karasu wrote that the group approach should also offer greater interpersonal contact, providing increased ego support for the weak egos of psychosomatic patients who fear the threat of isolation and parental separation. Family therapy offers hope of a change in the relationship between the family and the child. Both therapies have had excellent initial clinical results.

The long-term evaluation of the results of the various psychotherapies, individual and group, for psychosomatic disorders remains to be carried out. Karasu concluded after an exhaustive study of psychosomatic psychotherapeutic treatment that

some patients with medical disorders may respond positively to psychological treatment, either physically or psychologically. Some medical disorders appear to be more amenable to psychotherapy than other disorders. Some therapeutic modalities appear to be more effective than others. Some persons appear to be more responsive to psychotherapy than others, especially in relation to the nature of their psychopathology, rather than their physical pathology.

### Behavior Therapy

**Biofeedback.** The application of biofeedback techniques to patients with hypertension, cardiac arrhythmias, epilepsy, and tension headaches has provided encouraging but inconclusive therapeutic results.

**Relaxation techniques.** The treatment of hypertension may include the use of the relaxation techniques. Positive results have been published about the treatment of alcohol and other substance abuse by using transcendental meditation. Workers have also used meditation in the treatment of headaches.

References

Alexander F: *Psychosomatic Medicine*. Norton, New York, 1950.
Book H E: Empathy: Misconceptions and misuses in psychotherapy. Am J Psychiatry *145*: 4, 1988.
Dolinar L J: Obstacles to the care of patients with medical-psychiatric illness on general hospital psychiatry units. Gen Hosp Psychiatry *15*: 14, 1993.
Fink P: Surgery and medical treatment in persistent somatizing patients. J Psychosom Res *36*: 439, 1992.
Gilbert M M: Reactive depression as a model psychosomatic disease. Psychosomatics *11*: 426, 1970.
Karasu T B: Psychotherapy of the medically ill. Am J Psychiatry *136*: 1, 1979.
Karush A, Daniels G E, Flood C, O'Connor J F: *Psychotherapy in Chronic Ulcerative Colitis*. Saunders, Philadelphia. 1977.
Kyle J: *Crohn's Disease*. Heinemann, London, 1972.
Lipowski Z J: Psychosomatic medicine: Past and present. Can J Psychiatry *31*: 2, 1986.
Miller L: The mind and the body. Int J Psychiatry *7*: 518, 1967.
Vitaliano P P, Maivro R D, Russo J, Mitchell E S, Carr J E, Van Citters R L: A biopsychosocial model of medical student distress. J Behav Med *11*: 311, 1988.

# Relational Problems

Relationships form the matrix within which most people live their lives. Relationships are the sources of comfort, connection, and happiness for people; they are also the sources of obligation, responsibility, and friction. Psychological problems affect the way people function in a variety of relationships. External events (illness, war, natural disaster, economic crises, and social change) can also stress relationships. The lack of relationships or the loss of relationships can lead to feelings of isolation and depression.

The fourth edition of *Diagnostic and Statistical Manual of Mental Disorders* (DSM-IV) considers relational problems in a variety of relationships in which the focus of attention is a pattern of interaction that results in clinically significant impairment in one or more persons involved in those relationships.

## RELATIONAL PROBLEM RELATED TO A MENTAL DISORDER OR GENERAL MEDICAL CONDITION

According to DSM-IV, this category should be used when the focus of clinical attention is a pattern of impaired interaction associated with a mental disorder or a general medical condition in a family member.

Adults often assume the responsibility of caring for aging parents while they are still caring for their children. That dual obligation often creates stress. Also, caring for elderly parents involves the adaptation of both parties to a reversal of their former roles, facing the potential loss of the parent, and coping with evidence of one's own mortality.

A problem that is now receiving attention is the abuse of the elderly by some caretaking children. The problem is most likely to occur when the abusing offspring have substance abuse problems, are under economic stress, and have no relief from their caretaking duties and when the elderly parent is bedridden or has a chronic illness that requires constant nursing attention. More elderly women are abused than are elderly men, and most abuse occurs in the elderly over age 75.

The development of a chronic illness in a family member stresses the family system. It requires adaptation on the part of the sick person and other family members. The sick person frequently deals with some loss of autonomy, an increased sense of vulnerability, and sometimes a taxing medical regimen. Other family members also experience the loss of the person as he or she was before the illness and usually have substantial caretaking responsibility—for example, in debilitating neurological diseases, including dementia of the Alzheimer's type, and with such diseases as acquired immune deficiency syndrome (AIDS) and cancer. In those cases the whole family has to deal with the stress of both prospective death and the current illness. Some families use the anger engendered by such situations to create support organizations, increase public awareness of the disease, and rally the family around the sick member. However, chronic illness frequently causes depression in family members and may cause them to withdraw from one another or to attack one another. The burden of caring for ill family members falls disproportionately on the women in a family—mothers, daughters, and daughters-in-law.

Chronic emotional illness also requires major adaptations by families. For instance, family members may react with chaos or fear to the psychotic productions of a schizophrenic family member. Family systems are stressed by the schizophrenic member's regression, exaggerated emotions, frequent hospitalizations, and economic and social dependence. Family members may react with hostile feelings (referred to as expressed emotion) that are associated with poor prognoses in the sick patients. Similarly, families are stressed when a family member has bipolar I disorder, particularly during manic episodes.

Illness devastates a family when it suddenly strikes a previously healthy family member, when it occurs earlier than expected in the life cycle (some impairment of physical capacities is expected in old age, although many elderly people are healthy), when the economic stability of the family is affected by the illness, and when little can be done to improve or ease the condition of the sick family member.

## PARENT-CHILD RELATIONAL PROBLEM

Parent-child problems apply to the parent or to the child or to both and are often conflicts that fall within the range of the normal developmental stages or crises of each. According to DSM-IV, this category should be used when the focus of clinical attention is a pattern of interaction between parent and child (for example, impaired communication, overprotection, inadequate discipline) associated with clinically significant impairment in individual or family functioning or clinically significant symptoms.

Difficulties arise in a variety of situations that stress the usual parent-child interaction. For instance, in a family in which the parents are divorced, parent-child problems may arise in the relationship with either the custodial or the noncustodial parent. The remarriage of a divorced or widowed parent can also lead to a parent-child problem. The resentment of a stepparent and the favoring of a natural child are usual in the initial phases of adjustment of a new family. The birth of a second child is an occasion for both familial stress and happiness. The birth of a child can also be troublesome if the parents had adopted a child in the belief that they were infertile.

Other situations that may cause a parent-child problem are the development, in either a parent or a child, of a fatal, crippling, or chronic illness—such as leukemia, epilepsy, sickle-cell anemia, or a spinal cord injury—or the birth of a child with congenital defects (for example, cerebral palsy, blindness, and deafness). Although those situations are not rare, they challenge the emotional resources of the people involved. The parents and the child have to face present and potential loss and must adjust their day-to-day lives physically, economically, and emotionally. Those situations can try the healthiest families and produce parent-child problems not just with the sick child but also with the unaffected siblings. Those siblings may be resented, preferred, or neglected because the ill child requires so much time and attention.

## PARTNER RELATIONAL PROBLEM

According to DSM-IV, this category should be used when the focus of clinical attention is a pattern of interaction between the spouses or the partners characterized by negative communication (for example, criticisms), distorted communication (for example, unrealistic expectations), or noncommunication (for example, withdrawal) associated with clinically significant impairment in individual or family functioning or symptoms in one or both partners.

When a person presents with a partner relational problem, the psychiatrist must assess whether the patient's distress arises from the relationship or whether it is part of a mental disorder. Mental disorders are more common among single people—the never married, widowed, separated, and divorced—than among married people. The developmental, sexual, and occupational histories and the relationship history of the patients are necessary for purposes of diagnosis.

Divorce is discussed in Section 2.5 and marital therapy in Section 32.4.

### Demands of Marriage

Marriage demands a sustained level of adaptation from both partners. Areas to be explored in a troubled marriage include the extent of communication between the partners, their ways of solving disputes, their attitudes toward childbearing and child rearing, their relationships with their in-laws, their attitudes toward social life, their handling of finances, and the couple's sexual interaction. Stressful periods in the relationship may be precipitated by the birth of a child, abortion or miscarriage, economic stresses,

moves to new areas, episodes of illness, major career changes, and any situations that involve a significant change in marital roles. Illness in a child exerts the greatest strain on a marriage, and marriages in which a child has died through illness or an accident end in divorce more often than not. Complaints of primary anorgasmia or impotence by marital partners are usually indicative of intrapsychic problems, although sexual dissatisfaction is involved in many cases of marital maladjustment.

Adjustment to marital roles can be a problem if the partners are of different backgrounds and have been raised with different value systems. For example, members of low socioeconomic status (SES) groups perceive the wife as making most of the decisions regarding the family and accept physical punishment as a way to discipline children. Middle-class persons perceive the decision-making process as shared, the husband often being the final arbiter, and they prefer to discipline children by verbal chastisement.

Problems involving conflicts in values, adjustment to new roles, and poor communication are most effectively handled when the relationship between the partners is examined, as in marital therapy.

A 30-year-old male chemist was referred to a psychiatrist by his internist because the patient wanted to talk to someone about his shaky marriage. During five years of courtship and two years of marriage, the couple had had numerous separations, usually precipitated by the patient's dissatisfaction. Although he and his wife shared many interests and, until recently, had had a satisfactory sexual relationship, he thought that his wife was basically a cold and self-centered person who had no real concern about his career or feelings. His dissatisfactions periodically built up to fights, which often resulted in temporary separations. He then felt lonely and came "crawling back" to her. Their relationship was currently one of "icy separateness," and the patient seemed to be seeking support to make a permanent break. Although he was in distress because of his marital situation, frequently choking back tears, he showed no evidence that he had difficulties with his other interpersonal relationships. He had many good friends, functioned well in his job, and denied symptoms other than distress about his marital situation.

## SIBLING RELATIONAL PROBLEM

According to DSM-IV, this category should be used when the focus of clinical attention is a pattern of interaction between siblings associated with clinically significant impairment in individual or family functioning or symptoms in one or more of the siblings.

Problems arising from sibling rivalry can occur with the birth of a child and can recur as the children grow up. Competition among children for the attention, affection, and esteem of their parents is a fact of family life. That rivalry can extend to others who are not siblings and remains a factor in normal and abnormal competitiveness throughout life. In some families, children receive labels early in life, such as "the good child" or "the black sheep," and may turn those labels into self-fulfilling prophesies. In good sibling relationships the pleasures of companionship and the bonds created by kinship and shared experiences outweigh feelings of rivalry.

## RELATIONAL PROBLEM
## NOT OTHERWISE SPECIFIED

According to DSM-IV, this category should be used when the focus of clinical attention is on relational problems not classifiable by any of the specific problems listed above—for example, difficulties with coworkers.

Problems causing sufficient strain to bring a person into contact with the mental health care system may arise in relationships with romantic partners, coworkers, neighbors, teachers, students, friends, and social groups.

Racial and religious prejudices cause problems in interpersonal relationships. Some social scientists believe that racism and religious bigotry do not have a strong psychological base, and they emphasize social and class factors as causative. Other investigators view prejudice as a learned attitude and consider it a cultural variant. A number of psychiatrists believe that people are motivated to change their prejudices only if they see them as part of a mental disorder. Prejudice may be a maladaptive defense erected to protect the prejudiced person from profound feelings of inadequacy. It involves the projection of unwanted and devalued attributes onto the scapegoated group.

### References

Barth J M, Parke R D: Parent-child relationship influences on children's transition to school. Merrill Palmer Q *39*: 173, 1993.

Brody G H, Stoneman Z, McCoy J K, Forehand R: Contemporaneous and longitudinal associations of sibling conflict with family relationship assessments and family discussions about siblings problems. Child Dev *63*: 391, 1992.

Cook W L: Interdependence and the interpersonal sense of control: An analysis of family relationships. J Pers Soc Psychol *64*: 587, 1993.

Dwyer J W, Henretta J C, Coward R T, Barton A J: Changes in the helping behaviors of adult children as caregivers. Res Aging *14*: 351, 1992.

Galambos N L: Parent-adolescent relations. Curr Direct Psychol Sci *1*: 146, 1992.

Hetherington E M, Clingempeel W G: Coping with marital transitions: A family systems perspective. Monogr Soc Res Child Dev *57*: 1, 1992.

Hibbs E D, Hamburger S D, Kruesi M J, Lenane M: Factors affecting expressed emotion in parents of ill and normal children. Am J Orthopsychiatry *63*: 103, 1993.

Innocenti M S, Huh K, Boyce G C: Families of children with disabilities: Normative data and other considerations on parenting stress. Top Early Child Spec Educ *12*: 403, 1992.

Jacob T, Leonard K: Sequential analysis of marital interactions involving alcoholic, depressed, and nondistressed men. J Abnorm Psychol *101*: 647, 1992.

Jouriles E N, Farris A M: Effects of marital conflict on subsequent parent-son interactions. Behav Ther *23*: 355, 1992.

Katz I: Gordon Allport's *The Nature of Prejudice*. Polit Psychol *12*: 125, 1991.

Krauss M W: Child-related and parenting stress: Similarities and differences between mothers and fathers of children with disabilities. Am J Ment Retard *97*: 393, 1993.

Maccoby E E: The role of parents in the socialization of children: An historical overview. Dev Psychol *28*: 1006, 1992.

Manne S L, Jacobsen P B, Gorfinkle K, Gerstein F: Treatment adherence difficulties among children with cancer: The role of parenting style. J Pediatr Psychol *18*: 47, 1993.

Oliver J M, Berger L S: Depression, parent-offspring relationships, and cognitive vulnerability. J Soc Behav Pers *7*: 415, 1992.

Pruchno R, Kleban M H: Caring for an institutionalized parent: The role of coping strategies. Psychol Aging *8*: 18, 1993.

Sternberg K J, Lamb M E, Greenbaum C, Cicchetti D: Effects of domestic violence on children's behavior problems and depression. Dev Psychol *29*: 44, 1993.

Takigiku S K, Brubaker T H, Hennon C B: A contextual model of stress among parent caregivers of gay sons with AIDS. AIDS Educ Prev *5*: 25, 1993.

Tuttle D H, Cornell D G: Maternal labeling of gifted children: Effects on the sibling relationship. Except Child *59*: 402, 1993.

Volling B L, Belsky J: The contribution of mother-child and father-child relationships to the quality of sibling interaction: A longitudinal study. Child Dev *63*: 1209, 1992.

# Problems Related to Abuse or Neglect

The fourth edition of *Diagnostic and Statistical Manual of Mental Disorders* (DSM-IV) specifies five problems related to abuse or neglect: (1) physical abuse of child, (2) sexual abuse of child, (3) neglect of child, (4) physical abuse of adult, and (5) sexual abuse of adult (Table 29–1).

## CHILD ABUSE AND NEGLECT

Child abuse and neglect occur in girls and boys of all ages, in all ethnic groups, and at all socioeconomic levels. Abuse and neglect occur at alarmingly high rates and are associated with a wide range of emotional problems and psychiatric symptoms. Children who are beaten or burned, repeatedly sexually assaulted, or deprived of food, clothing, and shelter may perish or survive to struggle with the consequences. In most cases of persistent incest, sexually abused children are threatened with further abuse or abandonment if they disclose the family secrets, leaving them in the irreconcilable position of silently enduring continued abuse or risking the total loss of their families.

Children who have been physically or sexually abused present with a multitude of psychiatric disturbances, including anxiety, aggressive behavior, paranoid ideation, posttraumatic stress disorder, depressive disorders, and an increased risk of suicidal behavior. Abuse appears to increase the risk of psychiatric disturbances in already vulnerable children. Abused children of parents with psychopathology are more likely to experience a mental disorder than are nonabused children of psychiatrically disturbed parents. Children who have been sexually abused reportedly have an increased frequency of poor self-esteem, depression, dissociative disorders, and substance abuse. Chronic maltreatment appears to promote aggressive and violent behavior in vulnerable children.

### Epidemiology

According to the National Committee for the Prevention of Child Abuse, in 1992 about 3 million cases of child abuse and neglect were reported to public social service agencies; of that number, about 1 million cases were substantiated. Each year in the United States, 2,000 to 4,000 deaths are caused by child abuse and neglect. Each year 150,000 to 200,000 new cases of sexual abuse are reported. An estimated one of every three to four girls will be sexually assaulted by the age of 18 years, and an estimated one of every seven to eight boys will be sexually assaulted

by the age of 18 years. The actual occurrence rates are likely to be higher than those estimates, because many maltreated children go unrecognized, and many are reluctant to report the abuse. Of those children physically abused, 32 percent are under 5 years of age; 27 percent are between 5 and 9 years; 27 percent are between 10 and 14 years; and 14 percent are between 15 and 18 years. More than 50 percent of all abused and neglected children were born prematurely or had low birth weights.

Recently, sexual attacks on children by groups of other children have increased. Of 1,600 young sex abusers whose cases were analyzed by a university abuse-prevention center, more than 25 percent started abusing other children before the age of 12 years. The group leaders have often been abused themselves, but the followers seem to succumb to peer pressure and to a society that glamorizes violence and links violence with sex.

### Etiology

Many factors contribute to the development of child abuse and neglect. Many abusive parents have themselves been victims of physical and sexual abuse and of long-term exposure to violent home lives. A powerful promoter of aggression is long-term exposure to pain and physical torment. Thus, parents who were brought up with harsh corporal punishment and cruel treatment by their own families may continue the abuse tradition with their children. In some cases, the adults believe that their methods are acceptable ways of teaching discipline. In other cases, parents are ambivalent about their methods of abusive parenting but find themselves without coping mechanisms, so they fall into behaviors similar to their own parents' behaviors.

Stressful living conditions, including overcrowding and poverty, are associated with aggressive behavior and may contribute to physical abuse toward children.

Social isolation, the lack of a support system, and parental substance abuse increase the potential for abusive and neglectful treatment of children. Such environmental crises as lack of finances, unemployment, and housing problems may increase the stress levels in vulnerable families, and neglect or abuse may ensue.

Mental disorders may play a role in child abuse and neglect insofar as a parent's judgment and thought processes may be impaired. Parents who are depressed or psychotic or have severe personality disorders may view their children as bad or as trying to drive them crazy.

Certain childhood characteristics may increase a child's vulnerability to neglect and physical and sexual abuse.

**Table 29–1**
**Problems Related to Abuse or Neglect**

**Physical Abuse of Child**

This category should be used when the focus of clinical attention is physical abuse of a child.

**Sexual Abuse of Child**

This category should be used when the focus of clinical attention is sexual abuse of a child.

**Neglect of Child**

This category should be used when the focus of clinical attention is child neglect.

**Physical Abuse of Adult**

This category should be used when the focus of clinical attention is physical abuse of an adult (e.g., spouse beating, abuse of elderly parent).

**Sexual Abuse of Adult**

This category should be used when the focus of clinical attention is sexual abuse of an adult (e.g., sexual coercion, rape).

Table from DSM-IV, *Diagnostic and Statistical Manual of Mental Disorders*, ed 4. Copyright American Psychiatric Association, Washington, 1994. Used with permission.

Children who are premature, mentally retarded, or physically handicapped and those who cry excessively or are unusually demanding may be at high risk for being abused or neglected.

Many abused children are perceived by their parents as being different, slow in development, bad, selfish, or hard to discipline. Children who are hyperactive are particularly vulnerable to abuse, especially if they were born to parents with limited capacities for nurturant behavior.

The perpetrator of the battered child syndrome (that is, physical abuse) is more often the mother than the father. One parent is usually the active batterer, and the other passively accepts the battering. Of the perpetrators studied, 80 percent were regularly living in the homes of the children they abused. More than 80 percent of the children studied were living with married parents, and about 20 percent were living with a single parent. The average age of the mother who abused her children is reported to be around 26 years; the average age of the father is 30 years. Many abused children come from poor homes, and the families tend to be socially isolated.

The abusive parents have inappropriate expectations of their children, with a reversal of dependence needs. The parent deals with the child as if the child were older than the parent. The parent often turns to the child for reassurance, nurturing, comfort, and protection and expects a loving response. Ninety percent of such parents were severely physically abused by their own mothers or fathers.

Sexual abuse is usually by men, although women acting in concert with men or alone have also been involved, especially in child pornography. Sexual abuse is usually perpetrated by someone known to the child. Males are the perpetrators in about 95 percent of the cases of sexual abuse of girls and about 80 percent of the cases of sexual abuse of boys. In many cases the perpetrator of sexual abuse has been a victim of physical or sexual abuse. In

some circumstances, pedophilia is a factor; the adult perpetrator is more aroused by children than by adult partners. In other cases the sexual abuse may be mixed with physical abuse. In many instances the perpetrator shows no specific preference for child sexual partners.

## Diagnosis and Clinical Features

**Physical abuse of child.** Physical abuse must always be considered when a child presents with bruises or injuries that cannot be adequately explained or that are not compatible with the history given by the parent. Suspicious physical indicators include bruises and marks that form symmetrical patterns, such as injuries to both sides of the face, and regular patterns on the back, the buttocks, and the thighs. Accidental injuries are not likely to result in symmetrical patterns. Bruises may have the shape of the instrument used to make them, such as a belt buckle or a cord. Burns by cigarettes may result in symmetrical round scars, and immersions in boiling water result in burns that look like socks or gloves or that are doughnut-shaped. Multiple and spiral fractures, especially in a young baby, may be the result of physical aggression; retinal hemorrhages in an infant may be due to shaking.

Children who are repeatedly brought to hospitals for treatment of peculiar or puzzling problems by parents who at first appear to be overly cooperative may be victims of Munchausen syndrome by proxy. In that abuse scenario a parent repeatedly inflicts illness or injury on a child—by injecting toxins or inducing the child to ingest drugs or toxins so as to cause diarrhea, dehydration, or other symptoms—and then eagerly seeks medical attention. Since the pathological parents are sneaky and on the surface compliant, the diagnosis is difficult to make.

Severely abused children are seen in hospital emergency rooms with external evidences of body trauma, bruises, abrasions, cuts, lacerations, burns, soft tissue swellings, and hematomas (Figures 29–1 and 29–2). Hypernatremic dehydration, after periodic water deprivation by psychotic mothers, has been reported as a form of child abuse. Inability to move certain extremities, because of dislocations and fractures associated with neurological signs of intracranial damage, can also indicate inflicted trauma. Other clinical signs and symptoms attributed to inflicted abuse may include injury to the viscera. Abdominal trauma may result in unexplained ruptures of the stomach, the bowel, the liver, or the pancreas, with manifestations of an injured abdomen. Those children with the most severe maltreatment injuries arrive at the hospital or physician's office in a coma or convulsions, and some arrive dead.

Behaviorally, abused children may appear withdrawn and frightened or may present with aggressive behavior and labile mood. They often exhibit depression, poor self-esteem, and anxiety. They may try to physically cover up injuries and are usually reticent to disclose the abuse for fear of retaliation. They may show some delay in developmental milestones, often have difficulties with peer relationships, and may engage in self-destructive or suicidal behaviors.

**Sexual abuse of child.** The majority of child sexual abuse is perpetrated by adults within the immediate or

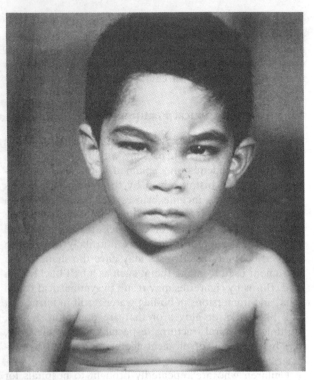

**Figure 29–1.** A 5-year-old boy was admitted with abrasions and bruises in various stages of healing and evidence of recent trauma to his right eye and face. A history of periodic beatings by his sadistic, mentally retarded mother facilitated the diagnosis of physical abuse of child.

extended family of the child. Thus, most sexual abusers are known to their child victims and are often highly trusted members of the family who have wide access to the child and are in a position of authority (Table 29–2). Most cases of sexual abuse involving children are never revealed because of the victim's guilt feelings, shame, ignorance, and tolerance, compounded by some physicians' reluctance to recognize and report sexual abuse, the court's insistence on strict rules of evidence, and the families' fears of dissolution if the sexual abuse is discovered. Despite the familial roles of the sexual abusers, many sexually abused children are threatened with being hurt, killed or abandoned if the events are disclosed.

Sexual abuse has been reported in schools, day-care centers, and group homes, where adult caretakers have been found to be the major offenders. The incidence of sexual abuse and child pornography is much higher than was previously assumed. Children may be sexually abused as early as infancy and through adolescence.

Identifying sexual abuse in children is complicated by the overwhelming fear, shame, and guilt that contributes to a child's reticence to disclose the abuse. Most often, no definitive physical evidence proves that sexual abuse is occurring. Physical indicators of sexual abuse include bruises, pain, and itching in the genital region. Genital or rectal bleeding may be a sign of sexual molestation. Recurrent urinary tract infections and vaginal discharges may be related to abuse. Difficulty in walking and sitting and sexually transmitted diseases raise suspicions of sexual abuse.

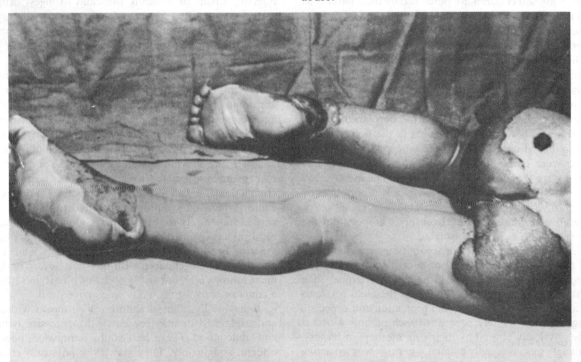

**Figure 29–2.** A 3½-year-old boy, brought into an emergency room by his mother, had second-degree burns of his buttocks, perineum, hands, and feet. His mother related that the child accidentally fell into a tub of hot water while preparing to take a bath. Physical examination revealed burns of his buttocks, hands, and feet without any evidence of burns along the body area. The location of the burns led physicians to suspect that the child's buttocks were forced into boiling water, and, in an attempt to keep himself from being submerged, he extended his feet and hands into the water. Scalding injury to his feet, perineum, and buttocks caused burn areas corresponding to the child's posture on dunking. His mother later admitted to the child's placement into a tub of hot water by a boyfriend while she was out shopping.

**Table 29–2**
**Sexual Abuse of Children**

| | |
|---|---|
| Reported cases in U.S., 1985* | 123,000 |
| Prevalence of male abuse | 3–31 percent |
| Prevalence of female abuse | 6–62 percent |
| Perpetrators | |
|   Father or stepfather | 7–8 percent |
|   Uncles or older siblings | 16–42 percent |
|   Friends | 32–60 percent |
|   Strangers | 1 percent |
| Sexual activity | |
|   Coitus | 16–29 percent |
|   Oral sex and intercourse | 3–11 percent |
|   Touching genitals | 13–33 percent |
| Age | Peak between ages 9 and 12 25 percent below age 8 |
| High-risk factors | Child living in single-parent home Marital conflict History of physical abuse Increase in sexual abuse |
| Reported motivation of abuser | Pedophilic impulses No other sexual object Inability to delay gratification |

*Current estimates are 150,000 to 200,000 new cases each year.
Table data from D Finklehor: The sexual abuse of children: Current research reviewed. Psychiatr Ann *17*: 4, 1987. Figures may total more than 100 percent because of overlapping studies.

No specific behavioral manifestations prove that sexual abuse has taken place, but children may exhibit many behaviors that raise suspicions. Young children who present a detailed knowledge of sexual acts have usually witnessed or participated in sexual behavior. Young sexually abused children often exhibit their sexual knowledge through play and may initiate sexual behaviors with their peers. Aggressive behavior is common among abused children. Children who are extremely fearful of adults, particularly men, may have been subjected to sexual abuse.

Children who report sexual assaults should be listened to carefully, even when parts of their stories are not consistent. Typically, when a child begins to disclose information about sexual assaults, retractions and contradictions are typical, and anxiety may prevent full disclosure.

The diagnosis of sexual abuse in children is full of pitfalls. An estimated 2 to 8 percent of the allegations of sexual abuse are false. A much higher percentage of reports cannot be substantiated. Many investigations are done hastily or by inexperienced evaluators. In custody cases an allegation of sexual abuse can be used as a maneuver to limit a parent's visitation rights. Alleged sexual abuse of a preschool-age child is particularly difficult to evaluate because of the child's immature cognitive and language development. The use of anatomically correct dolls has grown in popularity, but the use of such dolls is controversial. Patient and careful evaluations by experienced objective professionals are necessary; leading questions must be avoided. Children under the age of 3 years are unlikely to produce a verbal memory of past trauma or abuses; however, their experiences may be reflected in their play or fantasies. Some abused children meet the

DSM-IV diagnostic criteria for posttraumatic stress disorder.

No specific psychiatric symptom universally results from sexual abuse. Vulnerability to the sequelae of sexual abuse depends on the type of abuse, the chronicity of the abuse, the age of the child, and the overall relationship of the victim and the abuser.

The psychological and physical effects of sexual abuse can be devastating and long-lasting. Children who are sexually stimulated by an adult feel anxiety and overexcitement, lose confidence in themselves, and become mistrustful of adults. Seduction, incest, and rape are important predisposing factors to later symptom formations, such as phobias, anxiety, and depression. The abused children tend to be hyperalert to external aggression, as shown by an inability to deal with their own aggressive impulses toward others or with others' hostility directed toward them.

Depressive symptoms are commonly reported among children who have been sexually abused. The depressive feelings are usually combined with shame, guilt, and a sense that the victim has been permanently damaged. Poor impulse control and self-destructive and suicidal behaviors are reported to be high among adolescents who have been sexually abused. Posttraumatic stress disorder and dissociative disorders are seen in some patients who have been sexually abused. Sexual abuse is a common preexisting factor in the development of dissociative identity disorder (also known as multiple personality disorder). Signs of dissociation are described as periods in which the children are amnestic, do not feel the pain, or feel that they are somewhere else. Borderline personality disorder has been reported in some patients with histories of sexual abuse. Substance abuse has also been reported with high frequency among adolescents and adults who were sexually abused as children.

INCEST. *Incest* is defined as the occurrence of sexual relations between close blood relatives. A broader definition describes incest as intercourse between participants who are related to one another by some formal or informal bond of kinship that is culturally regarded as a bar to sexual relations. For example, sexual relations between stepparents and stepchildren or among stepsiblings are usually considered incestuous, even though no blood relationship exists.

The most common abuse is by fathers, stepfathers, uncles, and older siblings. Features of father-daughter incest that have been described as common in many homes include a passive, sick, absent, or in some other way incapacitated mother; a daughter who takes on the maternal role in the family; alcohol abuse in the father; and overcrowding.

The strongest and most universal taboo exists against mother-son incest. It occurs much less frequently than any other form of incest. Such behavior is usually indicative of more severe psychopathology in the participants than are father-daughter and sibling incest.

Sociologists have underlined the role of incest prohibitions as socialization factors. Biological factors also support the taboo. Groups that inbreed risk the unmasking of lethal or detrimental recessive genes, and the progeny of inbreeding groups are generally less fit than are other progeny. Anthropologists have observed that the particular form of the incest taboo is culturally determined. In *Totem and Taboo* Sigmund Freud developed the concept of primal horde, in which the young men collectively murdered the group's patriarch, who had kept all the women of the tribe to himself. The incest taboo arose both out of guilt after the murder and to prevent a repetition of the act, further rivalry after the murder, and subsequent disintegration of the horde.

Accurate figures on the incidence of incest are difficult to obtain because of the general shame and embarrassment of the entire family. Girls are victims more often than are boys. About 15 million women in the United States have been the objects of incestuous attention, and one third of all sexually abused persons have been molested before the age of 9.

Incestuous behavior is reported much more frequently among families of low socioeconomic status than among other families. The difference may be due to greater contact with reporting officials—such as welfare workers, public health personnel, and law enforcement agents—and is not a true reflection of a higher incidence in families of low socioeconomic status. Incest is more easily hidden by economically stable families than by the poor.

Social, cultural, physiological, and psychological factors—all contribute to the breakdown of the incest taboo. Incestuous behavior has been associated with alcohol abuse, overcrowding, increased physical proximity, and rural isolation that prevents adequate extrafamilial contacts. Some communities may be more tolerant of incestuous behavior than is society in general. Major mental disorders and intellectual deficiencies have been described in some cases of clinical incest. Some family therapists view incest as a defense designed to maintain a dysfunctional family unit. The older and stronger participant in incestuous behavior is usually male. Thus, incest may be viewed as a form of child abuse, as a pedophilia, or as a variant of rape.

About 75 percent of reported cases involve father-daughter incest. However, many cases of sibling incest are denied by parents or involve nearly normal interaction if the activity is prepubertal sexual play and exploration.

The daughter in father-daughter incest has frequently had a close relationship with her father throughout her childhood and may be pleased at first when he approaches her sexually. The onset of incestuous behavior usually occurs when the daughter is 10 years old. As the behavior continues, however, the abused daughter becomes bewildered, confused, and frightened. As she nears adolescence, she undergoes physiological changes that add to her confusion. She never knows whether her father will be parental or sexual. Her mother may be alternately caring and competitive; the mother often refuses to believe her daughter's reports or refuses to confront her husband with her suspicions. The daughter's relationships with her siblings are also affected as they sense her special position with her father and treat her as an outsider. The father, fearful that his daughter may expose their relationship and often jealousy possessive of her, interferes with her development of normal peer relationships.

The physician must be aware of the possibility of intrafamilial sexual abuse as the cause of a wide variety of emotional and physical symptoms, including abdominal pain, genital irritations, separation anxiety disorder, phobias, nightmares, and school problems. When incest is suspected, the clinician must interview the child apart from the rest of the family.

*Homosexual incest.* The family in which father-son incest occurs is usually highly disturbed, with a violent, alcohol-dependent, or psychopathic father; a dependent or disabled mother who is unable to protect her children; and an absence of the usual family roles and individual identities. Father-son and mother-daughter incest are rarely reported. The son in father-son incest is frequently the eldest child, and, if he has a sister, she is often sexually abused by the father as well. The father does not necessarily have any other history of homosexual behavior. The sons in the situation may experience homicidal or suicidal ideation and may first present to a psychiatrist with self-destructive behavior.

STATUTORY RAPE. Intercourse is unlawful between a male more than 16 years of age and a female under the age of consent, which varies from 14 to 21 years, depending on the jurisdiction. Thus, a man of 18 and a girl of 15 may have consensual intercourse, yet the man may be held for statutory rape. Statutory rape may vary dramatically from other types of rape in being nonassaultive, not a violent act. Nor is it a deviant act, unless the age discrepancy is sufficient for the man to be defined as a pedophile—that is, when the girl is less than 13 years old. Charges of statutory rape are rarely pressed by the consenting girl; they are brought by her parents.

**Neglect of child.** A maltreated child often presents no obvious signs of being battered but has multiple minor physical evidences of emotional and, at times, nutritional deprivation, neglect, and abuse. The maltreated child is often taken to a hospital or a private physician and has a history of failure to thrive, malnutrition, poor skin hygiene, irritability, withdrawal, and other signs of psychological and physical neglect.

Children who have been neglected may show overt failure to thrive at less than 1 year of age; their physical and emotional development is drastically impaired. The children may be physically small and not able to show appropriate social interaction. Hunger, chronic infections, poor hygiene, and inappropriate dress may be present. Malnutrition may eventually be evident. Behaviorally, children who are chronically neglected may be indiscriminately affectionate, even with strangers, or they may be socially unresponsive, even in familiar social situations. Neglected children may present as runaways or with conduct disorder.

An extreme form of failure to thrive in children of 5 years or older is psychosocial dwarfism, in which a chronically deprived child does not grow and develop, even when adequate amounts of food are present. Such children have normal proportions but are exceedingly small for their age. They often have reversible endocrinological changes resulting in decreased growth hormone, and they cease to grow for a time. Behaviorally, children with the disorder exhibit bizarre eating behaviors and disturbed social relationships. Binge eating, the ingestion of garbage or nonedible substances, the drinking of toilet water, and induced vomiting have been reported.

Parents who neglect their children are often overwhelmed, depressed, isolated, and impoverished. Unemployment, the lack of a two-parent family, and substance abuse may exacerbate the situation. Several prototypes of neglectful mothers have been suggested. Some mothers are young, inexperienced, socially isolated, and ignorant, leading to a temporary period of inability to care for their children. Other neglectful mothers are chronically passive and withdrawn women who may have been raised in chaotic, abusive, and neglectful homes. In those cases, once the situation comes to the attention of a child protective agency, the mother often accepts help. Mothers with major mental disorders who view their children as evil or as purposely driving them crazy are difficult to help.

**Pathology and laboratory examination.** Although no definitive laboratory tests are available to help the clinician make a diagnosis of child physical or sexual abuse or neglect, a physical examination is indicated when abuse is suspected to identify physical stigmata. In cases of failure to thrive, endocrinological screening is indicated. An external genital examination is indicated in cases of suspected child sexual abuse to identify scars, tears, and genital infections.

X-ray evidences of fractures may be present in various stages of reparative changes; however, if no fractures or dislocations are apparent on examination, bone injury may remain obscure during the first few days after inflicted trauma. In those cases, bone repair may become evident within weeks after the specific bone trauma.

Roentgenological examinations of unrecognized traumatic fractures reveal several unusual bone changes (Figure 29–3). Metaphyseal fragmentation is caused by twisting or pulling of the afflicted extremity. There may be squaring of the long bones secondary to the new bone formation on the metaphyseal fragments. Periosteal hemorrhages are frequently noted because the periosteum of infants is not securely attached to the underlying bone. That hemorrhaging is followed by periosteal calcification, which begins to become apparent from five to seven days after the inflicted trauma. That layer of calcification around the shaft of the bone should cause suspicion of inflicted abuse. Epiphyseal separations and periosteal shearing usually result from traction and torsion of the affected extremity. The X-ray findings of reparative changes involving excessive new bone formation or previously healed fractures with periosteal reactions may be diagnostic when correlated with the other manifestations of child abuse.

## Differential Diagnosis

Factors that complicate the identification and the substantiation of abuse and neglect situations include parental feuding and custody disputes. When the marital discord is severe or the separated parents are in conflict, children are often caught in the line of fire. For example, a mother who is overwhelmingly hostile toward a separated father may be convinced and may convince a child that the father is abusive. In some cases, parents have gone so far as to fabricate entire abuse scenarios and to coach children to repeat them. In other cases a parent may refuse to accept the possibility that a spouse or a close relative is the per-

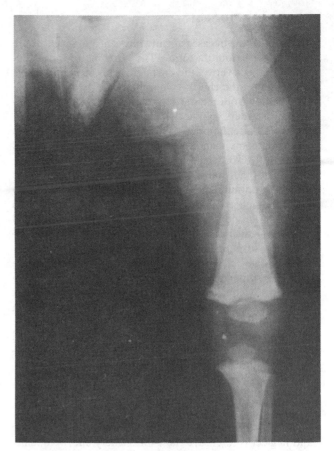

**Figure 29–3.** Follow-up X-ray of a maltreated 6-month-old infant taken four weeks after inflicted trauma to the upper thigh. Extensive reparative changes are noted in association with new bone formation, external cortical thickening, and squaring of the metaphysis—diagnostic evidence of bone changes after trauma. The layer of calcification around the shaft of the bone and the presence of bone fragments at the ends of the bone should be evidence for suspicion of inflicted trauma and should prompt further investigations into the causes of the X-ray findings. The X-ray changes may be diagnostic when correlated with other manifestations of physical abuse of child.

petrator of abuse, may repeatedly insist that a child stop telling lies, and may coerce a child into retracting the disclosures. In either scenario the child suffers profoundly, and the alleged abuse situation is never disentangled. Factors that support the veracity of abuse allegations are the use of phrases by the child that are consistent with the child's language development and that do not sound like rehearsed adult phrasing. Distress, the display of precocious sexual behavior, and a knowledge of or a preoccupation with sexual material also support the possibility of sexual abuse. A child who is not being abused but who is being coached to report sexual or physical abuse is also being placed under unbearable duress. Therefore, the clinician must recognize that severe chronic discord between the parents in which a child is caught in the crossfire can be as abusive as physical and sexual abuse. Controversies are arising in the courts because children are accusing caretakers and teachers of sexual abuse and the children's veracity is being challenged.

## Course and Prognosis

The outcome of cases of child physical and sexual abuse and neglect is multifactorial. The outcome of a case depends on the severity, the duration, and the nature of the abuse and on the child's vulnerabilities. Children who already suffer from mental retardation, pervasive developmental disorders, physical handicaps, and disruptive behavior and attention-deficit disorders are likely to have a poorer outcome than are children unhampered by mental or physical disorders. Children who are abused for long periods of time, starting when they are babies or toddlers and going on into adolescence, are likely to be more profoundly damaged than are those who have experienced only brief episodes of abuse. The development of mental disorders—such as major depressive disorder, suicidal behavior, posttraumatic stress disorder, dissociative identity disorder, and substance abuse—further complicates the long-term prognosis. The nature of the relationship between the victim and the abuser and the adult support figures available to the child after the disclosure also affect the prognosis. The best outcomes are expected when the children are intact cognitively, the abuse is recognized and interrupted in an early phase, and the entire family is capable of participating in treatment.

## Treatment

**Child.** The first part of the treatment of child abuse and neglect is to ensure the child's safety and well-being. The child may need to be removed from an abusive or neglectful family to ensure protection, yet, on an emotional level, the child may feel additionally vulnerable in an unfamiliar setting. Because of the high risk for psychiatric symptoms in abused and neglected children, a comprehensive psychiatric evaluation is in order. Next, along with providing specific treatments for any mental disorders present, the therapist may have to deal with the immediate situation and the long-term implications of the abuse or neglect. Psychotherapeutic issues to be addressed with an abused child include dealing with the child's fears, anxieties, and self-esteem; building a trusting relationship with an adult (the therapist) in which the child will not be exploited or betrayed; and gaining a beneficial perspective over time of the factors that contributed to the child's victimization at home.

Ideally, each abused and neglected child should be given the benefit of an intervention plan based on the assessment of (1) the factors responsible for the parent's psychopathology; (2) the overall prognosis for the parents' achieving adequate parenting skills; (3) the time estimated to achieve meaningful change in the parent's ability to parent; (4) an estimate of whether the parent's dysfunction is confined to this child or involves other children; (5) the extent to which the parent's overall malfunctioning, if that is the case, is short-term or long-term (reflecting a lifelong pattern); (6) the extent to which the mother's malfunctioning is confined to infants, as opposed to older children (that is, the incidence of abuse is inversely related to the child's age); (7) the parent's willingness to participate in the intervention plan; (8) the availability of personnel and

physical resources to implement the various intervention strategies; and (9) the risk of the child's sustaining additional physical or sexual abuse by remaining in the home.

**Parents.** On the basis of the information obtained, several options can be selected to improve the parents' functioning: (1) eliminate or diminish the social or environmental stresses; (2) lessen the adverse psychological effects of the social factors on the parents; (3) reduce the demands on the mother to a level that is within her capacity through day-care placement of the child or the provision of a housekeeper or baby-sitter; (4) provide emotional support, encouragement, sympathy, stimulation, instruction in maternal care, and aid in learning to plan for, assess, and meet the needs of the infant (supportive casework); and (5) resolve or diminish the parents' inner psychic conflicts (psychotherapy).

INCESTUOUS BEHAVIOR. The first step in the treatment of incestuous behavior is its disclosure. Once a breakthrough of the denial and the collusion or fear by the family members has been achieved, incest is not likely to recur. When the participants suffer from severe psychopathology, treatment must be directed toward the underlying illness. Family therapy is useful to reestablish the group as a functioning unit and to develop healthier role definitions for each member. While the participants are learning to develop internal restraints and appropriate ways to gratify their needs, the external control provided by therapy helps prevent further incestuous behavior. At times, legal agencies are involved to help enforce external controls.

**Reporting.** In cases of suspected child abuse and neglect, the physician should diagnose the suspected maltreatment; secure the child's safety by admitting the child to a hospital or by arranging out-of-home placement; report the case to the appropriate social service department, child protection unit, or central registry; make an assessment with the help of a history, a physical examination, a skeletal survey, and photographs; request a social worker's report and appropriate surgical and medical consultations; confer within 72 hours with members of a child abuse committee; arrange a program of care for the child and the parents; and arrange for social service follow-up.

Among those generally included as mandated child-abuse reporters are physicians, psychologists, school officials, police officers, hospital personnel engaged in the treatment of patients, district attorneys, and providers of child day care and foster care.

**Prevention.** To prevent child abuse and neglect, the clinician must identify those families who are at high risk and intervene before a child becomes a victim. Once high-risk families have been identified, a comprehensive program should include psychiatric monitoring of the families, including the identified high-risk child. Families can be educated to recognize when they are being neglectful or abusive, and alternative coping strategies can be suggested.

In general, child abuse and neglect prevention and treatment programs should try to (1) prevent the separation of parents and children if possible, (2) prevent the placement of children in institutions, (3) encourage the parents' attainment of self-care status, and (4) encourage the family's attainment of self-sufficiency. As a last resort and to prevent further abuse and neglect, children may have to be removed from families who are unwilling or unable to profit from the treatment program. In cases of sexual abuse, the licensing of day-care centers and the psychological screening of those persons who work in them should be mandatory to prevent further abuses. Education of the medical profession, members of allied health fields, and all who come in contact with children will aid in early detection. And providing support services to stressed families will aid in preventing the problem in the first place.

## PHYSICAL ABUSE OF ADULT

### Spouse Abuse

Spouse abuse is estimated to occur in 2 million to 12 million families in the United States. That aspect of domestic violence has been recognized as a severe problem, largely as a result of recent cultural emphasis on civil rights and the work of feminist groups. However, the problem itself is one of long standing.

The major problem in spouse abuse is wife abuse. One study estimated that there are 1.8 million battered wives in the United States, excluding divorced women and girls battered on dates. Wife beating occurs in families of every racial and religious background and in all socioeconomic strata. It is most frequent in families with problems of substance abuse, particularly alcohol abuse and crack abuse.

Behavioral, cultural, intrapsychic, and interpersonal factors—all contribute to the development of the problem. Abusive men are likely to have come from violent homes where they witnessed wife beating or were abused themselves as children. The act itself is reinforcing; once a man has beaten his wife, he is likely to do so again. Abusive husbands tend to be immature, dependent, and nonassertive and to suffer from strong feelings of inadequacy.

The husbands' aggression is bullying behavior, designed to humiliate their wives to build up their own low self-esteem. The abuse is most likely to occur when the man feels threatened or frustrated at home, at work, or with his peers. The Surgeon General's office has identified pregnancy as a high-risk period for battering; 15 to 25 percent of pregnant women are physically abused while pregnant, and the abuse often results in birth defects.

Impatient and impulsive, abusive husbands physically displace aggression provoked by others onto their wives. The dynamics include identification with an aggressor (father, boss), testing behavior (Will she stay with me, no matter how I treat her?), distorted desires to express manhood, and dehumanization of the woman. As in rape, aggression is deemed permissible when the woman is perceived as property. About 50 percent of battered wives grew up in violent homes. The trait most commonly found in abused wives is dependence.

Recently, hot lines, emergency shelters for women, and other organizations (such as the National Coalition Against Domestic Violence) have been developed to aid battered wives and to educate the public. A presidential commission was established to investigate spouse abuse. A major problem for abused women has been where to find a place to go when they leave home, frequently in fear of their lives. Battering is often severe, involving broken limbs, broken ribs, internal bleeding, and brain damage. When an abused wife tries to leave her husband, he often becomes doubly intimidating and threatens, "I'll get you." If the woman has small children to care for, her problem is compounded. The abusive husband wages a conscious campaign to isolate his wife and to make her feel worthless.

The woman faces a risk in leaving an abusive husband; women who leave their batterers are at a 75 percent greater risk for being killed by their batterers than are women who stay. In 1990 California passed the first antistalking law, making stalking a crime. In 1992 a total of 28 states passed similar laws.

Some men feel remorse and guilt after an episode of violent behavior and become particularly loving. That behavior gives the wife hope, and she remains until the next cycle of violence, which inevitably occurs.

Change is initiated when the man is convinced that the woman will not tolerate the situation and when she begins to exert control over his behavior. She can do so by leaving for a prolonged period—if she is physically and economically able to do so—with therapy for the man as a condition of return. Family therapy is effective in treating the problem, usually in conjunction with social and legal agencies. With relatively less impulsive men, external controls, such as calling the neighbors or the police, may be sufficient to stop the behavior.

Some beatings of husbands are also reported. In those cases the husbands complain of fear of ridicule if they expose the problem, fear of charges of counterassault, and inability to leave the situation because of financial difficulties. Husband abuse has also been reported when a frail elderly man is married to a much younger woman.

### Elder Abuse

Elder abuse is discussed in Chapter 50.

## SEXUAL ABUSE OF ADULT

### Rape

The problem of rape is most appropriately discussed under the heading of aggression. Rape is an act of violence and humiliation that happens to be expressed through sexual means. Rape is used to express power or anger. Rapes in which sex is the dominant issue are rare; sexuality is usually used in the service of nonsexual needs.

Rape is the perpetration of an act of sexual intercourse with a female, against her will and consent, whether her will is overcome by force or fear resulting from the threat of force or by drugs or intoxicants; or when because of mental deficiency she is incapable of exercising rational judgment, or when she is below an arbitrary age of consent. Rape can occur between married persons and same sex persons.

The crime of rape requires only slight penile penetration of the victim's outer vulva. Full erection and ejaculation are not necessary. Forced acts of fellatio and anal penetration, although they frequently accompany rape, are legally considered sodomy.

**Rape of women.** Recent research has categorized male rapists into separate groups: sexual sadists, who are aroused by the pain of their victims; exploitive predators, who use their victims as objects for their gratification in an impulsive way; inadequate men, who believe that no woman would voluntarily sleep with them and who are obsessed with fantasies about sex; and men for whom rape is a displaced expression of anger and rage. Some workers believe that the anger was originally directed toward a wife or mother. Feminist theory, however, proposes that the woman serves as an object for the displacement of aggression that the rapist cannot express directly toward other men. The woman is considered men's property or vulnerable possession and is the rapist's instrument for revenge against other men.

Rape often occurs as an accompaniment to another crime. The rapist always threatens his victim with fists, a gun, or a knife and frequently harms her in nonsexual ways, as well as in sexual ways. The victim may be beaten, wounded, and sometimes killed.

Statistics show that most men who commit rapes are between 25 and 44 years of age; 51 percent are white and tend to rape white victims, 47 percent are black and tend to rape black victims, and the remaining 2 percent come from all other races. Alcohol is involved in 34 percent of all forcible rapes. A composite characterization of the archetypical rapist drawn from police statistics portrays a single 19-year-old man from the low socioeconomic groups who has a police record of acquisitive offenses.

According to the Federal Bureau of Investigation (FBI) Uniform Crime Reports, 106,590 rapes were reported in the United States in 1991. However, rape is a highly underreported crime. An estimated 1 out of 4 to 1 out of 10 rapes is reported. The underreporting is attributed to feelings of shame on the part of the victim and to the belief that she has no recourse through the legal system.

Victims of rape can be of any age. Cases have been reported in which the victims were as young as 15 months and as old as 82 years. The greatest danger exists for women age 16 to 24. Rape most commonly occurs in a woman's own neighborhood, frequently inside or near her own home. Most rapes are premeditated. About half are committed by strangers and half by men known, to varying degrees, by the victims; 7 percent of all rapes are perpetrated by close relatives of the victim; 10 percent of rapes involve more than one attacker.

The woman being raped is frequently in a life-threatening situation. During the rape she experiences shock and fright approaching panic. Her prime motivation is to stay alive. In most cases, rapists choose victims slightly smaller than themselves. The rapist may urinate or defecate on his victim, ejaculate into her face and hair, force anal intercourse, and insert foreign objects into her vagina and rectum.

After the rape the woman may experience shame, humiliation, confusion, fear, and rage. The type and the duration of the reaction are variable, but women report that the effects last for a year or longer. Many women experience the symptoms of posttraumatic stress disorder.

Some women are able to resume sexual relations with men, particularly if they have always felt sexually adequate. Other women become phobic about sexual interaction or have such symptoms as vaginismus. Few women emerge from the assault completely unscathed. The manifestations and the degree of damage depend on the violence of the attack itself, the vulnerability of the woman, and the support systems available to her immediately after the attack.

The victim fares best when she receives immediate support and is able to ventilate her fear and rage to loving family members and to sympathetic physicians and law enforcement officials. She is helped when she knows that she has socially acceptable means of recourse, such as the arrest and conviction of the rapist.

Therapy is usually supportive in approach unless the woman has a severe underlying disorder. Therapy focuses on restoring the victim's sense of adequacy and control over her life and relieving the feelings of helplessness, dependence, and obsession with the assault that frequently follow rape. Group therapy with homogeneous groups composed of rape victims is a particularly effective form of treatment.

The rape victim experiences a physical and psychological trauma when she is assaulted. Until recently, she also faced frequent skepticism from those to whom she reported the crime (if she had sufficient strength to do so) or accusations of having provoked or desired the assault. In reality, the National Commission on the Causes and Prevention of Violence found discernible victim precipitation of rape in only 4.4 percent of all cases. That statistic is lower than in any other crime of violence. The education of police officers and the assignment of policewomen to deal with rape victims have helped increase the reporting of the crime. Rape crisis centers and telephone hot lines are available for immediate aid and information for victims. Volunteer groups work in emergency rooms in hospitals and with physician education programs to assist in the treatment of victims.

Legally, women no longer have to prove in court that they actively struggled against the rapist. Testimony regarding the victim's prior sexual history has recently been declared inadmissible as evidence in a number of states. Also, penalties for first-time rapists have been reduced, making juries likely to consider a conviction. In some states, wives can now prosecute husbands for rape.

DATE RAPE. Date or acquaintance rape is a term applied to rapes in which the rapist is known to the victim. The assault can occur on a first date or after the man and the woman have known each other for many months. Considerable data on date rape have been gathered from college populations. In one study, 38 percent of male students said that they would commit rape if they thought they could get away with it, and 11 percent stated that they had committed rape; 16 percent of the female students said that they had been raped by men they knew or were dating.

In addition to suffering the symptoms of all rape survivors, victims of date rape berate themselves for exercising poor judgment in their choice of male friends and are more likely to blame themselves for provoking the rapist than are other victims. Many schools have set up programs for rape prevention and for counseling those who have been assaulted.

**Rape of men.** In some states the definition of rape is being changed to substitute the word "person" for "female." In most states, male rape is legally defined as sodomy. Homosexual rape is much more frequent among men than among women, and it occurs frequently in closed institutions, such as prisons and maximum-security hospitals.

The dynamics are identical to those of heterosexual rape. The crime enables the rapist to discharge aggression and to aggrandize himself. The victim is usually smaller than the rapist, is always perceived as passive and unmanly (weaker), and is used as an object. The rapist selecting a male victim may be heterosexual, bisexual, or homosexual. The most common act is anal penetration of the victim; the second most common act is fellatio.

Homosexual-rape victims often feel, as do raped women, that they have been ruined. In addition, some fear that they will become homosexual because of the attack.

## Sexual Coercion

Sexual coercion is a term used in DSM-IV for incidents in which one person dominates another by force or compels the other person to perform a sexual act.

## References

American Academy of Child and Adolescent Psychiatry: Guidelines for the clinical evaluation of child and adolescent sexual abuse. J Am Acad Child Adolesc Psychiatry 27: 655, 1988.

Becker J V, Skinner L J, Abel G G, Treacy E C: Incidence and types of sexual dysfunctions in rape and incest victims. J Sex Marital Ther 8: 65, 1982.

Benedek E P, Schetsky D H: Problems in validating allegations of sexual abuse: Part 1. Factors affecting perception and recall of events. J Am Acad Child Adolesc Psychiatry 26: 912, 1987.

Benedek E P, Schetsky D H: Problems in validating allegations of sexual abuse: Part 2. Clinical evaluation. J Am Acad Child Adolesc Psychiatry 26: 916, 1987.

Brownmiller S: *Against Our Will: Men, Women and Rape.* Simon & Schuster, New York, 1975.

Campbell J C, Poland M L, Waller J B, Ager J: Correlates of battering during pregnancy. Res Nurs Health 15: 219, 1992.

Everson M D, Boat B W: False allegations of sexual abuse by children and adolescents. Am J Psychiatry 28: 230, 1989.

Fitzpatrick K M, Boldizar J P: The prevalence and consequences of exposure to violence among African-American youth. J Am Acad Child Adolesc Psychiatry 32: 424, 1993.

Foa E B, Rothbaum B O, Steketee G S: Treatment of rape victims. J Interpers Violence 8: 256, 1993.

Fontana V J: *The Maltreated Child: The Maltreatment Syndrome in Children,* ed 4. Thomas, Springfield, Ill, 1979.

Frazier P A: A comparative study of male and female rape victims seen at a hospital-based rape crisis program. J Interpers Violence 8: 64, 1993.

Freud S: Totem and taboo. In *Standard Edition of the Complete Psychological Works of Sigmund Freud,* vol 13, p 1. Hogarth Press, London, 1953.

Henderson D J: Incest. In *The Sexual Experience,* B J Sadock, H I Kaplan, A M Freedman, editors, p 415. Williams & Wilkins, Baltimore, 1976.

Herman J L, Hirschman L: Families at risk for father-daughter incest. Am J Psychiatry 138: 967, 1981.

Herman J L, Perry C, Van der Kolk B A: Childhood trauma in borderline personality disorder. Am J Psychiatry 146: 490, 1989.

Lewis D O: From abuse to violence: Psychophysiological consequences of maltreatment. J Am Acad Child Adolesc Psychiatry 31: 383, 1992.

McCall G J: Risk factors and sexual assault prevention. J Interpers Violence 8: 277, 1993.

McLear S V, Deblinger E, Atkins M S, Foa E B, Raphe D L: Posttraumatic stress disorder in sexually abused children. J Am Acad Child Adoles Psychiatry 27: 650, 1988.

O'Brien J D: The effects of incest on female adolescent development. J Am Acad Psychoanal 15: 83, 1987.

Ogletree R J: Sexual coercion experience and help-seeking behavior of college women. J Am Coll Health 41: 149, 1993.

Resick P A: The psychological impact of rape. J Interpers Violence 8: 223, 1993.

Rubinstein M, Yeager C A, Goodstein C, Lewis D O: Sexually assaultive male juveniles: A follow-up. Am J Psychiatry 150: 262, 1993.

Salzinger S, Feldman, R S, Hammer M, Rosario M: The effects of physical abuse on children's social relationships. Child Dev 64: 169, 1993.

Sarrel P M, Masters W H: Sexual molestation of men by women. Arch Sex Behav 11: 117, 1982.

Sternberg K J, Lamb M E, Greenbaum C, Cicchetti D, et al: Effects of domestic violence on children's behavior problems and depression. Dev Psychol 29: 44, 1993.

Stewart B D, Hughes C, Frank E. Andersen B, Kendall K, West D: The aftermath of rape: Profiles of immediate and delayed treatment seekers. J Nerv Ment Dis 175: 90, 1987.

Terr L: What happens to early memories of trauma? A study of twenty children under age 5 at time of documented traumatic events. J Am Acad Child Adolesc Psychiatry 27: 96, 1988.

True W R, Rice J, Eisen S A, Heath A C, Goldberg J, Lyons M J, Nowak J: A twin study of genetic and environmental contributions to liability for posttraumatic stress symptoms. Arch Gen Psychiatry 50: 257, 1993.

Ullman S E, Knight R A: The efficacy of women's resistance strategies in rape situations. Psychol Women 17: 23, 1993.

# 30 |||||

# Additional Conditions That May Be a Focus of Clinical Attention

The fourth edition of *Diagnostic and Statistical Manual of Mental Disorders* (DSM-IV) lists 13 conditions that make up the category of additional conditions that may be a focus of clinical attention. They include the following: bereavement, occupational problem, adult antisocial behavior, malingering, phase of life problem, noncompliance with treatment for a mental disorder, religious or spiritual problem, acculturation problem, and age-associated memory decline, each of which is discussed in this chapter. Borderline intellectual functioning, academic problem, childhood or adolescent antisocial behavior, and identity problem are discussed in Chapter 48.

The additional conditions that may be a focus of clinical attention are not true mental disorders and are not considered as such by DSM-IV. Rather, they are conditions that have led to contact with the mental health care system. Once in the system, a person with an additional condition that may be a focus of clinical attention should have a thorough neuropsychiatric evaluation, which may or may not uncover a mental disorder. The categories listed above are of clinical interest to psychiatrists because they may accompany mental illness or, in some cases, be early harbingers of underlying mental disorders. For recording purposes in DSM-IV, the disorders are coded on Axis I.

According to DSM-IV, even if a person has a mental disorder, the focus of attention or treatment may be on a condition that is not due to the mental disorder. For example, the treatment of a person with social phobia who has an occupational problem not directly related to the phobia may focus on the occupational problem. At times, however, the distinction is not clear-cut, and it behooves the clinician to do as thorough a workup as possible so as not to overlook a diagnosable mental disorder.

## BEREAVEMENT

Immediately after or within a few months of the loss of a loved one, a normal period of bereavement begins. Feelings of sadness, preoccupation with thoughts about the deceased, tearfulness, irritability, insomnia, and difficulties in concentrating and carrying out one's daily activities are some of the signs and symptoms. The bereavement is limited to a varying period of time, based on one's cultural group (usually no longer than six months). Normal bereavement, however, may lead to a full depressive disor-

der, which requires treatment. Section 2.7 presents a further discussion of bereavement.

In DSM-IV the following statement about bereavement appears:

This category can be used when the focus of clinical attention is a reaction to the death of a loved one. As part of their reaction to the loss, some grieving individuals present with symptoms characteristic of a major depressive episode (e.g., feelings of sadness and associated symptoms such as insomnia, poor appetite, and weight loss). The bereaved individual typically regards the depressed mood as "normal," although the person may seek professional help for relief of associated symptoms such as insomnia or anorexia. The duration and expression of "normal" bereavement vary considerably among different cultural groups. The diagnosis of major depressive disorder is generally not given unless the symptoms are still present 2 months after the loss. However, the presence of certain symptoms that are not characteristic of a "normal" grief reaction may be helpful in differentiating bereavement from a major depressive episode. These include 1) guilt about things other than actions taken or not taken by the survivor at the time of the death; 2) thoughts of death other than the survivor feeling that he or she would be better off dead or should have died with the deceased person; 3) morbid preoccupation with worthlessness; 4) marked psychomotor retardation; 5) prolonged and marked functional impairment; and 6) hallucinatory experiences other than thinking that he or she hears the voice of, or transiently sees the image of the deceased person.

## OCCUPATIONAL PROBLEM

Occupational or industrial psychiatry is that area of psychiatry specifically concerned with the psychiatric aspects of problems at work and with vocational maladjustment. The practical symptoms of job dissatisfaction are mistakes at work, accident-proneness, absenteeism, and sabotage. The psychiatric symptoms include insecurity, reduced self-esteem, anger, and resentment at having to work.

In DSM-IV the following statement about occupational problem appears:

This category can be used when the focus of clinical attention is an occupational problem that is not due to a mental disorder, or if it is due to a mental disorder, is sufficiently severe to warrant independent clinical attention. Examples include job dissatisfaction and uncertainty about career choices.

People are particularly vulnerable to occupational problems at several points in their working lives—on entry into the working world, at times of promotion or transfer, during periods of unemployment, and at retirement. Specific situations—such as having too much or too little to do, being subjected to conflicting demands, feeling distracted by family problems, having responsibility without authority, and working for demanding and unhelpful managers—also create occupational distress.

## Career Choices and Changes

The choice of a career is a major life decision. A significant number of young people follow in their parents' footsteps, but many are unsure of what to do and try several jobs before settling on an occupation. Disadvantaged youngsters frequently have little choice about a career. When young adults have a poor education and lack training and skills, even overwhelming ambition rarely leads them out of poverty or into occupational satisfaction. When the disadvantaged are women or members of minority groups, they have even less chance of occupational success. In discussing career choices with a patient, a psychiatrist should explore special talents and interests, childhood goals, the patient's models, family influences, future expectations, work and academic histories, and motivation to work.

Distress about work is readily understood when an employee has been fired, demoted, or passed over for promotion. Minorities and those in low socioeconomic groups are particularly vulnerable to losing their jobs. In one five-year period, 11.5 million persons in the United States age 20 or over lost their jobs as a result of industrial plant closings and cutbacks. Some left the labor force altogether. Others moved to lower-paying, low-skill jobs with fewer benefits than their former jobs. Some worked intermittently.

Women are specifically at risk for stress when they leave outside employment for homemaking, a transition that researchers have found to be extremely stressful.

Some people have problems after receiving professional advancement. Reasons for that reaction include anxiety about assuming new responsibilities and the fact that people are sometimes promoted to jobs that are beyond their capacities to perform.

Adjusting to retirement is most difficult for people who are unprepared for it. Adverse reactions occur when a person is forced to retire prematurely or because of illness. Retirement is also a problem for the person whose identity is based primarily on occupational status and income. Women have been reported to be able to adjust faster to retirement than are men. Some workers, however, feel that retirement poses a greater hardship for women than for men; women face a longer retirement period owing to their greater life expectancy, are more likely to be alone (widowed) during their retirement years, and are usually poorer and have lower retirement incomes than men.

## Psychological Problems and the Workplace

Maladaptation at work may arise from psychodynamic conflicts. Those conflicts can be reflected in the person's

fill infantile needs. People with unresolved conflicts about their competitive and aggressive impulses may experience great difficulties in the work area. They may suffer from a pathological envy of the success of others or fear success for themselves because of their inability to tolerate envy from others. Those conflicts are also manifest in other areas of the patient's life, and the maladaptation is not limited to the patient's occupation.

## Career Problems of Women

A number of changes have occurred in the business world in the United States during the past 25 years. A significant number of women have entered the work force; many corporations are now willing to employ a husband and wife in the same firm; and teenagers have entered the work force, on a part-time basis, on a large scale.

Ninety percent of all females alive today in the United States will have to work to support themselves and probably one or two other people. Economic necessity now prompts the homemaker to enter the labor force. Rejection by employers on the basis of age, lack of recent experience, or insufficient training can cause dysphoria and depression. That is particularly true for the recently divorced woman in her 40s or 50s who has spent most of her adult life in the occupations of wife and mother.

The young woman has different stresses, primarily related to the conflicting demands of work and family responsibilities. More than 50 percent of all mothers in the work force have children 1 year old or younger. But women's organizations and other critics charge that few corporations are removing barriers to women's advancement or are concerned about reducing the tension that arises when job and family demands conflict. Specific issues that need to be addressed are provisions for child care or for the care of elderly parents, the option of flexible work hours, and the availability and use of unpaid parental leaves. Studies reveal that, when those leaves are made available to both parents, fathers rarely take them; that managers are more sensitive to crises in men's lives than to crises in the lives of female employees; and that managers respond to such major events as divorce and the death of a family member but ignore the stress placed on a worker by the illness of a child or a school closing because of a snow day. A few socially conscious corporations are holding workshops to address the changes arising from the influx of women into the work force and such issues as family responsibilities, sexual harrassment in the workplace, personal safety during business travel, and rape prevention.

Dual-career families (in which both the husband and the wife have jobs) now constitute more than 40 percent of all families. A problem arises if the employer wants one partner to make a geographic move to a new post. Even if the transfer is a promotion, it can result in lower total income for the family because of the spouse's loss of job or disruption of career. Some corporations offer new jobs to both spouses when one is asked to relocate; however, such approaches are rare. A more common advance is the acceptance of couples, married or unmarried, as employees of the same corporation. Formerly, the employment inability to accept the authority of competent superiors or, conversely, in overdependence on authority figures to ful- of a husband and a wife by the same firm was considered taboo by many businesses. Couples employed by the same firm seem to suffer only if they are competitive with each other. The couples who fare best treat their spouses dif- ferently at the office than at home. Resentment from co- workers occurs if one spouse reports directly to the other. Otherwise, no adverse responses from other employees have been noted.

## ADULT ANTISOCIAL BEHAVIOR

Antisocial behavior is a pattern that usually begins in childhood and often persists throughout life. It is charac- terized by activities that are illegal or immoral or both and that violate the society's legal system.

In DSM-IV the following statement about adult anti- social behavior appears:

This category can be used when the focus of clinical at- tention is adult antisocial behavior that is not due to a mental disorder (e.g., Conduct Disorder, Antisocial Personality Dis- order, or an Impulse Control Disorder). Examples include the behavior of some professional thieves, racketeers, or dealers in illegal substances.

The term "antisocial behavior" is sometimes confusing because it refers both to behavior by persons whose be- havior is not due to a mental disorder and to behavior by persons who have never received an adequate neuropsy- chiatric workup to determine the presence or the absence of a mental disorder. As Dorothy Lewis noted, the term can apply to behavior by normal persons who "struggle to make a dishonest living."

### Epidemiology

Estimates of the prevalence of adult antisocial behavior range from 5 to 15 percent of the population, depending on the criteria and the sampling. Within the prison pop- ulation, investigators report prevalence figures of between 20 and 80 percent. Men account for more adult antisocial behavior than do women.

### Etiology

Antisocial behaviors in adulthood are characteristic of a variety of persons, ranging from those with no demon- strable psychopathology to those who are severely im- paired, suffering from psychotic disorders, cognitive dis- orders, and retardation, among other conditions. A comprehensive neuropsychiatric assessment of antisocial adults usually reveals a myriad of potentially treatable psy- chiatric and neurological impairments that can easily be overshadowed by offensive behaviors and thus be over- looked. But only in the absence of mental disorders should patients be categorized as displaying adult antisocial be- havior.

Adult antisocial behavior may be influenced by genetic and social factors.

**Genetic factors.** Data supporting the genetic trans- mission of antisocial behavior are based on studies that find a 60 percent concordance rate in monozygotic twins and about a 30 percent concordance rate in dizygotic twins. Adoption studies show a high rate of antisocial behavior in the biological relatives of adoptees identified with an- tisocial behavior and a high incidence of antisocial behavior in the adopted-away offspring of those with antisocial be- havior. A high incidence of abnormalities are seen during the prenatal and perinatal periods of those who subse- quently display antisocial behavior.

**Social factors.** Studies note that in neighborhoods in which low socioeconomic status (SES) families predomi- nate, the sons of unskilled workers are more likely to com- mit more numerous and more serious criminal offenses than are the sons of middle-class and skilled workers, at least during adolescence and early adulthood. Those data are not as clear for women, but the findings are generally similar in studies from many countries. Areas of family training that have been particularly cited as differing by SES group are the use in middle-SES parents of love-oriented techniques in discipline, the withdrawal of affection versus physical punishment, negative parental at- titudes toward aggressive behavior, attempts to curb ag- gressive behavior, and the verbal ability to communicate the various reasons for the parents' values and proscrip- tions of such behavior.

Adult antisocial behavior is associated with the use and the abuse of alcohol and other substances. Violent anti- social acts are also associated with the easy availability of handguns.

## Diagnosis and Clinical Features

The diagnosis of adult antisocial behavior is one of ex- clusion. Substance dependence in such behavior often makes it difficult to separate the antisocial behavior related primarily to substance dependence from disordered be- haviors that occurred either before substance use or during episodes unrelated to substance dependence.

During the manic phases of bipolar I disorder, certain aspects of behavior can be similar to adult antisocial be- havior, such as wanderlust, sexual promiscuity, and finan- cial difficulties. Schizophrenic patients may have episodes of adult antisocial behavior, but the symptom picture is usually clear, especially with regard to thought disorder, delusions, and hallucinations on the mental status exam- ination.

Neurological conditions may be associated with adult antisocial behavior, and so electroencephalograms (EEGs), computed tomography (CT) scans, magnetic res- onance imaging (MRI), and a complete neurological ex- amination should be done. Temporal lobe epilepsy is often considered in the differential diagnosis. When a clear-cut diagnosis of temporal lobe epilepsy or encephalitis can be made, that may contribute to the adult antisocial behavior. Abnormal EEG findings are prevalent among violent of- fenders. An estimated 50 percent of aggressive criminals have abnormal EEG findings.

Persons with adult antisocial behavior have difficulties in work, marriage, and money matters and conflicts with

**Table 30–1**
**Symptoms of Adult Antisocial Behavior**

| Life Area | Antisocial Patients with Significant Problems in Area (%) |
| --- | --- |
| Work problems | 85 |
| Marital problems | 81 |
| Financial dependence | 79 |
| Arrests | 75 |
| Alcohol abuse | 72 |
| School problems | 71 |
| Impulsiveness | 67 |
| Sexual behavior | 64 |
| Wild adolescence | 62 |
| Vagrancy | 60 |
| Belligerence | 58 |
| Social isolation | 56 |
| Military record (of those serving) | 53 |
| Lack of guilt | 40 |
| Somatic complaints | 31 |
| Use of aliases | 29 |
| Pathological lying | 16 |
| Drug abuse | 15 |
| Suicide attempts | 11 |

Data from L Robins: *Deviant Children Grown Up: A Sociological and Psychiatric Study of Sociopathic Personality*. Williams & Wilkins, Baltimore, 1966. Used with permission.

various authorities. The symptoms of adult antisocial behavior are summarized in Table 30–1.

Antisocial personality disorder is discussed in Chapter 26.

## Treatment

In general, adult antisocial behavior provokes therapeutic pessimism. That is, therapists have little hope of changing a pattern of behavior that has been present almost continuously throughout the patient's life. Psychotherapy has not been effective, and there have been no major breakthroughs with biological treatments, including the use of medications.

More enthusiasm is found for the use of therapeutic communities and other forms of group treatment, even though the data provide little basis for enthusiasm. Many adult criminals who are incarcerated and in institutional settings have shown some response to group therapy approaches. The history of violence, criminality, and antisocial behavior has shown that such behaviors seem to decrease after age 40. Recidivism in criminals, which can reach 90 percent in some studies, also decreases in middle age.

**Prevention.** Because antisocial behavior often begins during childhood, one must focus on delinquency prevention. Any measures that improve the physical and mental health of socioeconomically disadvantaged children and their families are likely to reduce delinquency and violent crime. Since many recurrently violent persons have sustained many insults to the central nervous system (CNS), starting prenatally and continuing through childhood and adolescence, programs need to be developed to educate parents of the dangers to their children of CNS injury, including the effects of psychoactive substances on the

brain of the growing fetus. Public education regarding the releasing effect of alcohol on violent behaviors (not to mention its contribution to vehicular homicide) may also reduce crime.

In the Surgeon General's Report on Violence and Public Health of 1985, the committee on the prevention of assault and homicide emphasized the importance of discouraging corporal punishment in the home, forbidding it in the schools, and even abolishing capital punishment by the state, saying that all are models and sanctions for violence.

Although people disagree about the contribution of violence in the media to violent crime, there is universal recognition that the media have propaganda potential. The extent to which the media, such as television, can be used to transmit positive social values has not yet been realized.

The most successful preventive measures within the field of medicine have come from community-wide public health programs (such as the campaign against smoking) and from programs that detect individual vulnerabilities (such as individual monitoring of blood pressure). Studies of adult antisocial behavior reveal the contribution of broad cultural factors and constellations of individual biopsychosocial vulnerabilities. Prevention programs must recognize and address both kinds of factors.

## MALINGERING

Malingering is characterized by the voluntary production and presentation of false or grossly exaggerated physical or psychological symptoms. The patient always has an external motivation, which falls into one of three categories: (1) to avoid difficult or dangerous situations, responsibilities, or punishment; (2) to receive compensation, free hospital room and board, a source of drugs, or haven from the police; and (3) to retaliate when the patient feels guilt or suffers a financial loss, legal penalty, or job loss. The presence of a clearly definable goal is the main factor that differentiates malingering from factitious disorders.

### Epidemiology

The incidence of malingering is unknown, but it is common. It occurs most frequently in settings with a preponderance of men—the military, prisons, factories, and other industrial settings—although the condition also occurs in women.

### Diagnosis and Clinical Features

In DSM-IV the following statement about malingering appears:

The essential feature of Malingering is the intentional production of false or grossly exaggerated physical or psychological symptoms, motivated by external incentives such as avoiding military duty, avoiding work, obtaining financial compensation, evading criminal prosecution, or obtaining drugs. Under some circumstances Malingering may represent adaptive behavior, for example, feigning illness while a captive of the enemy during wartime.

Malingering should be strongly suspected if any combination of the following is noted:

(1) medicolegal context of presentation (e.g., the person is referred by an attorney to the clinician for examination)
(2) marked discrepancy between the person's claimed stress or disability and the objective findings
(3) lack of cooperation during the diagnostic evaluation and in complying with the prescribed treatment regimen
(4) the presence of Antisocial Personality Disorder

Many malingerers express mostly subjective, vague, ill-defined symptoms—for example, headache; pains in the patient's neck, lower back, chest, or abdomen; dizziness; vertigo; amnesia; anxiety; and depression—and the symptoms often have a family history, in all likelihood not organically based but incredibly difficult to refute. Malingerers may complain bitterly, describing how much the symptoms impair their normal function and how much they dislike the symptoms. The patients may use the best doctors who are the most trusted (and perhaps most easily fooled) and promptly and willingly pay all their bills, even if excessive, to impress the doctors with their integrity. To seem credible, malingerers must report the symptoms but tell their physicians as little as possible. But often they complain of misery without objective signs or other symptoms congruent with recognized diseases and syndromes; if they do describe all the symptoms of a disease, the symptoms are said to come and go. Malingerers are often preoccupied with cash, rather than cure, and have a knowledge of the law and precedents relative to their claims.

Objective tests—such as audiometry, brainstem audiometry, auditory and visually evoked potentials, galvanic skin response, electromyography, and nerve conduction studies—may be helpful in sorting out auditory, labyrinthine, ophthalmological, neurological, and other problems.

## Differential Diagnosis

As DSM-IV notes:

Malingering differs from Factitious Disorder in that the motivation for the symptom production in Malingering is an external incentive, whereas in Factitious Disorder external incentives are absent. Evidence of an intrapsychic need to maintain the sick role suggests Factitious Disorder.

Malingering is differentiated from Conversion and other Somatoform Disorders by the intentional production of symptoms and by the obvious, external incentives associated with it. In Malingering (in contrast to Conversion Disorder), symptom relief is not often obtained by suggestion or hypnosis.

Table 30–2 lists features that differentiate malingering from genuine illness.

## Treatment

A patient suspected of malingering should be thoroughly and objectively evaluated, and the physician should refrain from showing any suspicion. If the clinician becomes angry (a common response to malingerers), a confrontation may occur, with two consequences: (1) The doctor–patient relationship is disrupted, and no further positive intervention is possible. (2) The patient will be

**Table 30–2**
**Malingering Features Usually Not Found in Genuine Illness**

Symptoms are vague, ill-defined, overdramatized, and not in conformity with known clinical conditions.
The patient seeks addicting drugs, financial gain, the avoidance of onerous (e.g., jail) or other unwanted conditions.
History, examination, and evaluative data do not elucidate complaints.
The patient is uncooperative and refuses to accept a clean bill of health or an encouraging prognosis.
The findings appear compatible with self-inflicted injuries.
History or records reveal multiple past episodes of injury or undiagnosed illness.
Records or test data appear to have been tampered with (e.g., erasures, unprescribed substances in urine).

Table by Arthur T. Meyerson, M.D.

even more on guard, and proof of deception may become virtually impossible. If the patient is accepted and not discredited, subsequent observation, while the patient is hospitalized or an outpatient, may reveal the versatility of the symptoms, which are consistently present only when patients know that they are being observed. Preserving the doctor-patient relationship is often essential to the diagnosis and long-term treatment of the patient. Careful evaluation usually reveals the relevant issue without the need for a confrontation. It is usually best to use an intensive treatment approach, as though the symptoms were real. The symptoms can then be given up in response to treatment, without the patient's losing face.

## PHASE OF LIFE PROBLEM

In DSM-IV the following statement about phase of life problem appears:

This category can be used when the focus of clinical attention is a problem associated with a particular developmental phase or some other life circumstance that is not due to a mental disorder, or if it is due to a mental disorder, is sufficiently severe to warrant independent clinical attention. Examples include problems associated with entering school, leaving parental control, starting a new career, and changes involved in marriage, divorce, and retirement.

External events are most likely to overwhelm a person's adaptive capacities if they are unexpected, if they are numerous—that is, a number of stresses occurring within a short time—if the strain is chronic and unremitting, or if one loss heralds a myriad of concomitant adjustments that strain a person's recuperative powers.

The strains most likely to produce anxiety and depression relate to major life-cycle changes: marriage, occupation, and parenthood changes. Those events affect both men and women, but women, the poor, and minority groups seem particularly vulnerable to adverse reactions. Again, the change creates significant strain when it is unexpected and when it involves not only adjustment to a loss (a spouse or a job) but also the need to adjust to a new status that entails further hardships and problems.

In general, people are able to adjust to life changes if they have mature defense mechanisms, such as altruism, humor, and a capacity for sublimation. Flexibility, reliability, strong family ties, regular employment, adequate income, job satisfaction, a pattern of regular recreation and social participation, realistic goals, and a history of adequate performance—in short, a full and satisfying life—create resilience to deal with life changes.

## NONCOMPLIANCE WITH TREATMENT

In DSM-IV the following statement appears:

This category can be used when the focus of clinical attention is noncompliance with an important aspect of the treatment for a mental disorder or a general medical condition. The reasons for noncompliance may include discomfort resulting from treatment (e.g., medication side effects), expense of treatment, decisions based on personal value judgments or religious or cultural beliefs about the advantages and disadvantages of the proposed treatment, maladaptive personality traits or coping styles (e.g., denial of illness), or the presence of a mental disorder (e.g., Schizophrenia, Avoidant Personality Disorder). This category should be used only when the problem is sufficiently severe to warrant independent clinical attention.

Further discussion of compliance appears in Chapter 1.

## RELIGIOUS OR SPIRITUAL PROBLEM

In DSM-IV the following statement appears:

This category can be used when the focus of clinical attention is a religious or spiritual problem. Examples include distressing experiences that involve loss or questioning of faith, problems associated with conversion to a new faith, or questioning of other spiritual values which may not necessarily be related to an organized church or religious institution.

### Cults

Cults are charismatic groups that can affect participants in adverse ways, which may eventually bring them into contact with the mental health care system. Cults are characterized by an intensely held belief system and ideology that are imposed on their members, by a high level of group cohesion that tries to prevent members' freedom of choice to leave the group, and by a profound influence on the members' behavior that may include frank psychiatric symptoms, including psychotic disorders.

Most potential cult members are in their adolescence or otherwise struggling with establishing their own identities. They are drawn to the cult, which holds out the false promise of emotional well-being and purports to offer the sense of direction for which the persons are searching. Cult members are encouraged to proselytize and to draw new members into the group. They are often encouraged to break with family members and friends and to socialize only with other group members. Cults are invariably led by charismatic personalities, who are often ruthless in their quest for financial, sexual, and power gains and in their insistence on conformity to the cult's ideological belief system, which may have strong religious or quasireligious overtones. Exit therapy has been developed to guide cult members out of the group, provided their lingering emotional ties to persons outside the cult can be mobilized.

## ACCULTURATION PROBLEM

In DSM-IV the following statement about acculturation problem appears:

This category can be used when the focus of clinical attention is a problem involving adjustment to a different culture (e.g., following migration).

Periods of cultural transition, with changing mores and fluidity of role definition, may increase a person's vulnerability to life strain. Extreme cultural transition can create a condition of severe distress. The problem, also called culture shock, occurs when a person is suddenly thrust into an alien culture or has divided loyalties to two different cultures. In a less extreme form, culture shock occurs when young men or women enter the army, when people change jobs, when families move or undergo a significant change in income, when children have their first day in school, and when black ghetto children are bused to white middle-class schools.

Further discussion of culture change and culture shock appears in Section 4.6.

### Brainwashing

First practiced by the Chinese Communists on American prisoners in the Korean war, brainwashing is the deliberate creation of culture shock. A condition of isolation, alienation, and intimidation is developed for the express purpose of assaulting ego strengths and leaving the person to be brainwashed vulnerable to the imposition of alien ideas and behavior that would usually be rejected. Brainwashing relies on both mental and physical coercion. All people are vulnerable to brainwashing if they are exposed to it for a sufficient length of time, if they are alone and without support, and if they are without hope of escape from the situation. Help from the mental health care system is usually necessary to help brainwashed persons readjust to their usual environments after the brainwashing experience, a process known as deprogramming. Supportive therapy is offered, with emphasis on reeducation, restitution of ego strengths that existed before the trauma, and alleviation of the guilt and depression that are remnants of the frightening experience and the lost confidence and confusion in identity that results from it.

## AGE-RELATED COGNITIVE DECLINE

In DSM-IV the following statement appears:

This category can be used when the focus of clinical attention is an objectively identified decline in cognitive functioning consequent to the aging process that is within normal limits given the person's age. Individuals with this condition may report problems remembering names or appointments or may experience difficulty in solving complex problems. This category should be considered only after it has been determined that the cognitive impairment is not attributable to a specific mental disorder or neurological condition.

### References

Albert S, Fox H M, Kahn M W: Faking psychosis on the Rorschach: Can expert judges detect malingering? J Pers Assess *44:* 115, 1980.
Bash I Y, Alpert M: The determination of malingering. Ann N Y Acad Sci *347:* 86, 1980.

Bernard L C, Houston W, Natoli L: Malingering on neuropsychological memory tests: Potential objective indicators. J Clin Psychol *49*: 45, 1993.

Blazer D, Hughes D, George L: Stressful life events and the onset of a generalized anxiety syndrome. Am J Psychiatry *144:* 1178, 1987.

Caine E D: Should aging-associated cognitive decline be included in DSM-IV? J Neuropsychiatry Clin Neurosci *5*: 1, 1993.

Holmes T: Life situations, emotions, and disease. Psychosomatics *19:* 747, 1978.

Lehman D R, Davis C G, DeLongis A, Wortman C B: Positive and negative life changes following bereavement and their relations to adjustment. J Soc Clin Psychol *12*: 90, 1993.

Lewis D O, Pincus J H, Feldman M, Jackson L, Bard B: Psychiatric, neurological, and psychoeducational characteristics of 15 death row inmates in the United States. Am J Psychiatry *143:* 7, 1986.

Lidz T: *The Person*. Basic Books, New York, 1968.

Martinson R, Palmer T, Adams S: *Rehabilitation, Recidivism, and Research*. National Council on Crime and Delinquency, Hackensack, N J, 1976.

Meyerson A T: Malingering. In *Comprehensive Textbook of Psychiatry,* ed 5, H I Kaplan, B J Sadock, editors, p 1396. Williams & Wilkins, Baltimore, 1989.

Neugarten B L: Time, age and the life cycle. Am J Psychiatry *136:* 887, 1979.

Repetti R L: Short-term effects of occupational stressors on daily mood and health complaints. Health Psychol *12*: 125, 1993.

Rogler L H, Cortes D E, Malgady R G: Acculturation and mental health status among Hispanics: Convergence and new directions for research. Am Psychol *46*: 585, 1991.

Sadock V A: Other conditions not attributable to a mental disorder. In *Comprehensive Textbook of Psychiatry,* ed 5, H I Kaplan, B J Sadock, editors, p 1408. Williams & Wilkins, Baltimore, 1989.

Yalom I D, Lieberman M A: Bereavement and heightened existential awareness. Psychiatry *54*: 334, 1991.

# 31 ||||||

# Psychiatric Emergencies

## 31.1 / Suicide

Suicide is intentional self-inflicted death. Edwin Schneidman defined suicide as "the conscious act of self-induced annihilation, best understood as a multidimensional malaise in a needful individual who defines an issue for which the act is perceived as the best solution." Suicide is not a random or pointless act. On the contrary, it is a way out of a problem or a crisis that is invariably causing intense suffering. Suicide is associated with thwarted or unfulfilled needs, feelings of hopelessness and helplessness, ambivalent conflicts between survival and unbearable stress, a narrowing of perceived options, and a need for escape; the suicidal person sends out signals of distress.

Suicide in children and adolescents is discussed in Chapter 46.

### EPIDEMIOLOGY

#### Incidence and Prevalence

Each year about 30,000 deaths are attributed to suicide in the United States (30,232 deaths in 1989). That figure is for successful suicides; the number of attempted suicides is estimated to be 8 to 10 times that number. Lost in the reporting are intentional misclassifications of the cause of death, accidents of undetermined cause, and the so-called chronic suicides—for example, deaths through alcohol and other substance abuse and consciously poor adherence to medical regimens for diabetes, obesity, and hypertension.

Between 1970 and 1980 more than 230,000 people committed suicide in the United States—about one every 20 minutes, 75 suicides a day. The total suicide rate has remained fairly constant over the years. The current rate is 12.5 suicide deaths per 100,000. In 1977 suicide was at a peak of 13.3 per 100,000. Since then, there has been a slight decline. Currently, suicide is ranked as the eighth overall cause of death in this country, after heart disease, cancer, cerebrovascular disease, accidents, pneumonia, diabetes mellitus, and cirrhosis.

Suicide rates in the United States are at the midpoint of the national rates reported to the United Nations by the industrialized countries. Internationally, suicide rates range from highs of more than 25 per 100,000 people in Scandinavia, Switzerland, Germany, Austria, the eastern European countries (the suicide belt), and Japan to fewer than 10 per 100,000 in Spain, Italy, Ireland, Egypt, and the Netherlands.

A state-by-state analysis of suicides from 1979 to 1981 among those aged 15 to 44 revealed that New Jersey had the nation's lowest suicide rates for both sexes. Nevada and New Mexico had the highest rates for men, and Nevada and Wyoming had the highest rates for women. Women in Nevada killed themselves at a higher frequency than did men in New Jersey. The number-one suicide site in the world is the Golden Gate Bridge in San Francisco, with more than 800 suicides since it opened in 1937.

### Associated Factors

**Sex.** Men commit suicide more than three times as often as do women, a rate that is stable over all ages. Women, however, are four times as likely to attempt suicide as are men.

**Methods.** The higher rate of successful suicide for men is related to the methods they use. Men use firearms, hanging, or jumping from high places. Women are more likely to take an overdose of psychoactive substances or a poison, but they are beginning to use firearms more often than previously. The use of guns has decreased as a method of suicide in those states with gun control laws.

**Age.** Suicide rates increase with age. The significance of the mid-life crisis is underscored by suicide rates. Among men, suicides peak after age 45; among women, the greatest number of completed suicides occurs after age 55. Rates of 40 per 100,000 population are found in men aged 65 and older. The elderly attempt suicide less often than do younger people but are successful more often. The elderly account for 25 percent of the suicides, although they make up only 10 percent of the total population. The rate for those 75 or older is more than three times the rate among the young.

The suicide rate is rising most rapidly in young people. For males 15 to 24 years old, the rate increased 40 percent between 1970 and 1980, and the rate is still rising. The suicide rate for females in the same age group showed only a slight increase. Among men 25 to 34 years old, the suicide rate increased almost 30 percent. Suicide is the third leading cause of death in the 15-to-24-year-old age group after accidents and homicides. Attempted suicides in that age group number between 1 million and 2 million annually. The majority of suicides now occur among those 15 to 44.

**Race.** The rate of suicide among whites is nearly twice that among nonwhites, but the figures are being questioned, as the suicide rate among blacks is increasing. In 1989 the suicide rate for white males (19.6 per 100,000 persons) was 1.6 times that for black males (12.5), 4 times that for white females (4.8), and 8.2 times that for black females (2.4) (Figure 31.1–1). Among ghetto youth and certain Native American and Alaskan Indian groups, suicide rates have greatly exceeded the national rate. Suicide among immigrants is higher than in the native-born population. Two out of every three suicides are white males.

**Religion.** Historically, suicide rates among Catholic populations have been lower than the rates among Protestants and Jews. It may be that a religion's degree of orthodoxy and integration is a more accurate measure of risk in this category than is simple institutional religious affiliation.

**Marital status.** Marriage reinforced by children seems to significantly lessen the risk of suicide. Among married persons the rate is 11 per 100,000. Single, never-married persons register an overall rate of nearly double the rate for married persons. However, previously married persons show sharply higher rates than do never-married persons: 24 per 100,000 among the widowed; 40 per 100,000 among divorced persons, with divorced men registering 69 suicides per 100,000, as compared with 18 per 100,000 for divorced women. Suicide is more common than usual in persons who have a history of suicide (attempted or real) in the family and who are socially isolated. So-called anniversary suicides are suicides by persons who take their lives on the same day as did a member of their families.

**Occupation.** The higher a person's social status is, the greater is the suicide risk, but a fall in social status also increases the risk. Work, in general, protects against suicide.

Among occupational rankings, professionals, particularly physicians, have traditionally been considered to be at the greatest risk for suicide. However, the best recent studies have found no increased suicide risk for male physicians in the United States. Their annual suicide rate is about 36 per 100,000, which is the same as that for white men over 25. Recent British and Scandinavian data, by contrast, show that the suicide rate for male physicians is two to three times the rate found in the general male population of the same age.

Studies agree that female physicians have a higher risk of suicide than do other women. In the United States the annual suicide rate for female physicians is about 41 per 100,000, compared with the rate of 12 per 100,000 among all white women over 25 years of age. Similarly, in England and Wales the suicide rate for unmarried female physicians is 2.5 times greater than the rate among unmarried women in the general population, although it is comparable to that found among other groups of professional women.

Studies show that the physician who commits suicide has a mental disorder. The most common mental disorders found among physicians and among physician suicide victims are depressive disorders and substance dependence. Often, the physician who commits suicide has experienced recent professional, personal, or family difficulties. Both male and female physicians commit suicide significantly more often by substance overdoses and less often by firearms than do persons in the general population; drug availability and knowledge about toxicity are important factors in physician suicides. Some evidence indicates that female physicians have an unusually high lifetime risk for mood disorders, which may be the major determinant of the elevated suicide risk.

Among physicians, psychiatrists are considered to be at greatest risk, followed by ophthalmologists and anesthesiologists, but the trend is toward an equalization among all specialties. Special at-risk populations are musicians, dentists, law enforcement officers, lawyers, and insurance agents. Suicide is higher among unemployed persons than among employed persons. During economic recessions and depressions and times of high unemployment, the suicide rate increases. During times of high employment and during war, the rate decreases.

**Climate.** No seasonal correlation with suicide has been found. The spring and the fall see a slight increase in suicides, but, contrary to popular belief, suicides do not increase during December and holiday periods.

**Physical health.** The relation of physical health and illness to suicide is significant. Prior medical care appears to be a positively correlated risk indicator of suicide: 32 percent of all people who commit suicide have had medical attention within six months of death. Postmortem studies show that a physical illness is present in some 25 to 75 percent of all suicide victims; a physical illness is estimated to be an important contributing factor in 11 to 51 percent of all suicides. In each instance the percentage increases with age.

For example, 50 percent of men with cancer who commit suicide do so within a year of receiving the diagnosis. Cancer of the breast or the genitals is found in 70 percent of all women with cancer who commit suicide. Seven diseases of the central nervous system (CNS) increase the risk for suicide: epilepsy, multiple sclerosis, head injury, cardiovascular disease, Huntington's disease, dementia, and acquired immune deficiency syndrome (AIDS). All are diseases in which an associated mood disorder is known to occur. Epileptic patients have avail-

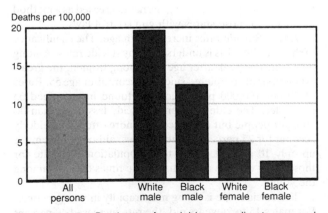

Deaths per 100,000

**Figure 31.1–1.** Death rates for suicide, according to race and sex: United States, 1989. Death rates are age-adjusted. (Figure from National Center for Health Statistics: *Health, United States, 1991.* Public Health Service, Hyattsville, Md, 1992.)

able barbiturates and other medications with which to kill themselves.

Some endocrine conditions are associated with increased suicide risk: Cushing's disease, Klinefelter's syndrome, and porphyria. Mood disorders also attend those disorders. The two gastrointestinal disorders with an increased suicide risk are peptic ulcer and cirrhosis, both physical disorders found among alcohol-dependent persons. The two urogenital problems with an increased suicide risk are prostatic hypertrophy and renal disease treated with hemodialysis, both problems in which changes in mood occur.

Factors associated with illness and contributing to both suicides and suicide attempts are loss of mobility among persons to whom physical activity is occupationally or recreationally important; disfigurement, particularly among women; and chronic, intractable pain. In addition to the direct effects of illness, the secondary effects of illness—for example, disruption of relationships and loss of occupational status—are prognostic factors.

Certain drugs can produce depression, which may lead to suicide in some cases. Among those drugs are reserpine (Serpasil), corticosteroids, antihypertensives (for example, propranolol [Inderal], and some anticancer agents.

**Mental health.** Highly significant psychiatric factors in suicide include substance abuse, depressive disorders, schizophrenia, and other mental disorders. Almost 95 percent of all patients who commit or attempt suicide have a diagnosed mental disorder. Depressive disorders account for 80 percent of that figure, schizophrenia accounts for 10 percent, and dementia or delirium for 5 percent. Among all mentally disordered persons, 25 percent are also alcohol-dependent and have dual diagnoses. Patients who suffer from delusional depression are at the highest risk for suicide. The risk of suicide in patients with depressive disorders is about 15 percent. Twenty-five percent of all patients who have a history of impulsive behavior or violent acts are also at high risk for suicide. Previous psychiatric hospitalization for any reason increases the risk for suicide.

Among adult suicide victims, significant differences are seen between the young and the old for both psychiatric diagnoses and antecedent stressors. A study in San Diego showed that diagnoses of substance abuse and antisocial personality disorder were found most often among suicide victims under 30 years of age, and diagnoses of mood disorders and cognitive disorders were found most often among suicides aged 30 and over. Stressors associated with suicide in those under 30 were separation, rejection, unemployment, and legal troubles; illness stressors were found most often among suicide victims over 30.

**Psychiatric patients.** Psychiatric patients' risk for suicide is 3 to 12 times greater than that of nonpatients. The degree of risk varies according to age, sex, diagnosis, and inpatient or outpatient status. After adjustment for age, male and female psychiatric patients who have at some time been inpatients have 5 and 10 times higher suicide risks, respectively, than do their counterparts in the general population. For male and female outpatients who have never been admitted to a hospital for psychiatric treatment, the suicide risks are three and four times greater, respectively, than are those of their counterparts in the general population. The higher suicide risk for psychiatric patients who have been inpatients reflects the fact that patients with severe mental disorders tend to be hospitalized—for

example, depressive disorder patients requiring electroconvulsive therapy (ECT). The psychiatric diagnosis that carries the greatest risk for suicide in both sexes is a mood disorder.

Persons in the general population who commit suicide tend to be middle-aged or elderly; however, increasingly, studies report that psychiatric patients who commit suicide tend to be relatively young. In one study the mean age of male suicide victims was 29.5 years and that of women 38.4 years. The relative youthfulness of those suicide victims was due partly to the fact that two early-onset, chronic mental disorders—schizophrenia and recurrent major depressive disorder—accounted for just over half of all those suicides, reflecting an age and diagnostic pattern found in most studies of psychiatric patient suicides.

A small but significant percentage of psychiatric patients who commit suicide do so while they are inpatients. The majority of inpatients who commit suicide do not kill themselves in the psychiatric ward itself but do so on the hospital grounds, while on a pass or weekend leave, or when absent without leave.

The suicide risk is highest for both sexes in the first week of the psychiatric admission; after three to five weeks, inpatients have a risk no greater than the risk in the general population. Also, the inpatient rates of suicide do not rise uniformly with age, as they do in the general population. In fact, the rates for female psychiatric patients fall with advancing age. That difference is due mainly to the fact that suicidal elderly persons do not present themselves to medical services. Times of staff rotation, particularly of the psychiatric residents, are periods associated with inpatient suicides. Epidemics of inpatient suicides tend to be associated with periods of ideological change on the ward, staff disorganization, and staff demoralization.

Among psychiatric outpatients the period after discharge is a period of increased suicide risk. A follow-up study of 5,000 patients discharged from an Iowa psychiatric hospital showed that, in the first three months after discharge, the rate of suicide for female patients was 275 times higher than that of all Iowa females; the rate of suicide for male patients was 70 times higher than that of all Iowa males.

Patients attending emergency services, especially those with panic disorder, also have an increased suicide risk. One study reported that such patients have a suicide rate more than seven times the age-adjusted and sex-adjusted rate for the general population (but the rate is similar to that of other clinical psychiatric populations). There are two main risk groups: patients with depressive disorders, schizophrenia, and substance abuse and patients who make repeated visits to the emergency room. Thus, mental health professionals working in the emergency services must be well-trained in the taking of the patient's psychiatric history, the examination of the patient's mental state, the assessment of the patient's suicidal risk, and the making of appropriate dispositions and must be aware of the need to contact patients at risk who fail to keep follow-up appointments.

DEPRESSIVE DISORDERS. Mood disorders are the diagnoses most commonly associated with suicide. As the suicide risk in depressive disorders is raised mainly when the patient is depressed, the psychopharmacological advances of the past 25 years may have reduced the suicide risk among depressive disorder patients. Nevertheless, the age-adjusted suicide rates for patients suffering from mood disorders has been estimated to be 400 per 100,000 for male patients and 180 per 100,000 for female patients.

More depressive disorder patients commit suicide early in

the course of the illness than later in the illness; more males than females commit suicide; and the chance of depressed persons' killing themselves is increased by their being single, separated, divorced, widowed, or recently bereaved. Depressive disorder patients in the community who commit suicide tend to be middle-aged or elderly.

A few studies have investigated which mood disorder patients have an increased suicide risk. Those studies indicate that, among depressed patients, social isolation enhances a suicidal tendency. That finding is in accord with the data from epidemiological studies showing that persons who commit suicide tend to be poorly integrated into society.

Suicide among depressed patients is likely at the onset or the end of a depressive episode. As among other psychiatric patients, the months after discharge from a hospital are a time of high risk. Studies show that one third or more of depressed patients who commit suicide do so within six months of leaving a hospital, presumably having relapsed.

SCHIZOPHRENIA. The suicide risk is high among schizophrenic patients: up to 10 percent die by committing suicide. In the United States an estimated 4,000 schizophrenic patients commit suicide each year. The age of onset of schizophrenia is typically in adolescence or early adulthood, and most schizophrenic patients who commit suicide do so during the first few years of their illness; therefore, schizophrenic patients who commit suicide tend to be relatively young.

About 75 percent of all schizophrenic suicide victims are unmarried males. About 50 percent have made a previous suicide attempt. Depressive symptoms are closely associated with their suicides. Hospital-based studies have reported that depressive symptoms were present during the last period of contact in at least two thirds of all the schizophrenic patients who committed suicide; only a small percentage committed suicide because of hallucinated instructions or to escape persecutory delusions. Up to 50 percent of suicides among schizophrenic patients occur during the first few weeks and months after discharge from a hospital; only a minority commit suicide while inpatients.

Thus, the risk factors for suicide among schizophrenic patients are young age, male sex, single marital status, a previous suicide attempt, a vulnerability to depressive symptoms, and a recent discharge from a hospital. Having three or four hospitalizations during their 20s probably undermines the social, occupational, and sexual adjustment of schizophrenic potential suicides. Consequently, potential suicide victims are likely to be male, unmarried, unemployed, socially isolated, and living alone—perhaps in a single room. After discharge from their last hospitalization, they may experience some new adversity or return to ongoing difficulties. Consequently, they become dejected, experience feelings of helplessness and hopelessness, go on to a depressed mood, and, in that state, have suicidal ideas that are eventually acted on.

ALCOHOL DEPENDENCE. Up to 15 percent of all alcohol-dependent persons commit suicide. The suicide rate for alcoholics is estimated to be about 270 per 100,000 a year; in the United States, between 7,000 and 13,000 alcohol-dependent persons are suicide victims each year.

About 80 percent of all alcohol-dependent suicide victims are male, largely reflecting the sex ratio for alcohol dependence. Alcohol-dependent suicide victims tend to be white, middle-aged, unmarried, friendless, socially isolated, and currently drinking. Up to 40 percent have made a previous suicide attempt. Up to 40 percent of all suicides by alcohol-dependent patients occur within a year of the patient's last hospitalization; elderly alcohol-dependent patients are at particular risk during the postdischarge period.

Studies show that many alcohol-dependent patients who eventually commit suicide are rated as being depressed during hospitalization and that up to two thirds are assessed as having mood disorder symptoms during the period in which they commit suicide. As many as 50 percent of all alcohol-dependent suicide victims have experienced the loss of a close affectionate relationship during the previous year. Such interpersonal losses and other types of undesirable life events are probably brought about by the alcohol dependence and contribute to the development of the mood disorder symptoms, which are often present in the weeks and months before the suicide.

The largest group of male alcohol-dependent patients are those with an associated antisocial personality disorder. Studies show that such patients are particularly likely to attempt suicide; to abuse other substances; to exhibit impulsive, aggressive, and criminal behaviors; and to be found among alcohol-dependent suicide victims.

OTHER SUBSTANCE DEPENDENCE. Studies in various countries have found an increased suicide risk among substance abusers. The suicide rate for heroin-dependent persons is about 20 times greater than the rate for the general population. Adolescent girls who use intravenous substances also have a high suicide rate. The availability of a lethal amount of substances, intravenous use, associated antisocial personality disorder, a chaotic life-style, and impulsivity are some of the factors that predispose substance-dependent persons to suicidal behavior, particularly when they are dysphoric, depressed, or intoxicated.

PERSONALITY DISORDERS. A high proportion of suicide victims have various associated personality difficulties or disorders. Having a personality disorder may be a determinant of suicidal behavior in several ways: by predisposing to major mental disorders like depressive disorders or alcohol dependence, by leading to difficulties in relationships and social adjustment, by precipitating undesirable life events, by impairing the ability to cope with a mental or physical disorder, and by drawing persons into conflicts with those around them, including family members, physicians, and hospital staff members.

An estimated 5 percent of patients with antisocial personality disorder commit suicide. Suicide is three times more common among prisoners than among the general population. More than one third of prisoner suicides have had past psychiatric treatment, and half have made a previous suicide threat or attempt, often in the previous six months.

**Previous suicidal behavior.** A past suicide attempt is perhaps the best indicator that a patient is at increased risk for suicide. Studies show that about 40 percent of depressed patients who commit suicide have made a previous attempt. The risk of a patient's making a second suicide attempt is highest within three months of the first attempt. The relation between a mood disorder, completed suicide, and attempts at suicide is shown in Figure 31.1–2.

Depression is associated not only with completed suicide but also with serious attempts at suicide. Studies that relate the clinical characteristics of those who attempt suicide with various measures of the medical seriousness of the attempt or of the intent to die show that the clinical feature most often associated with the seriousness of the intent to die is a diagnosis of a depressive disorder. Also, intent-to-die scores correlate significantly with both suicide risk scores and the number and the severity of depressive symptoms. When the attempters rated as having high suicide intent are compared with those with low intent, they are significantly more often male, older, single or separated, and living alone. The inference from that correlation

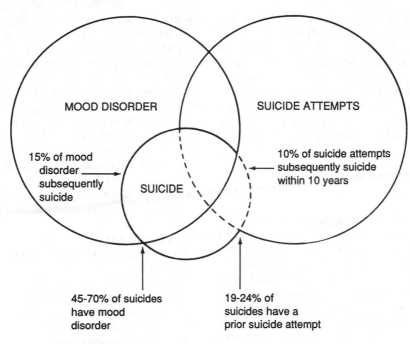

**Figure 31.1–2.** Venn diagram summarizing data concerning suicide and its relation to mood disorder and suicide attempts. (Figure by Alec Roy, M.D.)

is that depressed patients who make a serious suicide attempt more closely resemble suicide victims than they do suicide attempters.

## ETIOLOGY

### Sociological Factors

**Durkheim's theory.** The first major contribution to the study of the social and cultural influences on suicide was made at the end of the last century by the French sociologist Emile Durkheim. In an attempt to explain statistical patterns, Durkheim divided suicides into three social categories: egoistic, altruistic, and anomic. Egoistic suicide applies to those who are not strongly integrated into any social group. The lack of family integration can be used to explain why the unmarried are more vulnerable to suicide than are the married and why couples with children are the best-protected group of all. Rural communities have more social integration than do urban areas and, thus, less suicide. Protestantism is a less-cohesive religion than Catholicism is, and so Protestants have a higher suicide rate than do Catholics.

Altruistic suicide applies to those whose proneness to suicide stems from their excessive integration into a group, with suicide being the outgrowth of that integration—for example, the Japanese soldier who sacrifices his life in battle.

Anomic suicide applies to those persons whose integration into society is disturbed, thereby depriving them of the customary norms of behavior. Anomie can explain why those whose economic situation has changed drastically are more vulnerable than they were before their change in fortune. Anomie also refers to social instability, with a breakdown of society's standards and values.

### Psychological Factors

**Freud's theory.** The first important psychological insight into suicide came from Sigmund Freud. He described only one patient who made a suicide attempt, but he saw many depressed patients.

In his paper, "Mourning and Melancholia," Freud stated his belief that suicide represents aggression turned inward against an introjected, ambivalently cathected love object. Freud doubted that there would be a suicide without the earlier repressed desire to kill someone else.

**Menninger's theory.** Building on Freud's concepts, Karl Menninger in *Man Against Himself* conceived of suicide as a retroflexed murder, inverted homicide as a result of the patient's anger toward another person, which is either turned inward or used as an excuse for punishment. He also described a self-directed death instinct (Freud's concept of Thanatos). He described three components of hostility in suicide: the wish to kill, the wish to be killed, and the wish to die.

**Recent theories.** Contemporary suicidologists are not persuaded that a specific psychodynamic or personality structure is associated with suicide. However, they have written that much can be learned about the psychodynamics of suicidal patients from their fantasies as to what would happen and what the consequences would be if they were to commit suicide. Such fantasies often include wishes for revenge, power, control, or punishment; for atonement, sacrifice, or restitution; for escape or sleep; or for rescue, rebirth, reunion with the dead, or a new life. The suicidal patients who are most likely to act out suicidal fantasies may be those who have suffered the loss of a love object or had a narcissistic injury, who experience overwhelming affects like rage and guilt, or who identify with a suicide victim. Group dynamics underlie mass suicides like those at Masada and Jonestown.

Depressed persons may attempt suicide just as they appear to be recovering from their depression. And a suicide attempt can cause a long-standing depression to disappear, especially if it fulfills the patient's need for punishment. Of equal relevance, many suicide patients use a preoccupation with suicide as a way of fighting off intolerable depression and a sense of hopelessness. In fact, hopelessness was found, in a study by Aaron Beck, to be one of the most accurate indicators of long-term suicidal risks.

## Physiological Factors

**Genetics.** A genetic factor in suicide has been suggested. Studies show that suicide tends to run in families. For example, at all stages of the life cycle, a family history of suicide has been noted to be present significantly more often among persons who have attempted suicide than among those who have not. One major study found that the suicide risk for first-degree relatives of psychiatric patients was almost eight times greater than that for the relatives of controls. Furthermore, the suicide risk among the first-degree relatives of the psychiatric patients who had committed suicide was four times greater than that found among the relatives of patients who had not committed suicide. In some situations, particularly among adolescents, the family member who has committed suicide may serve as a role model with whom to identify when the option of committing suicide becomes one possible solution to intolerable psychological pain.

One study of 51 monozygotic twin pairs found nine cases of suicide; no dizygotic twins were concordant for suicide. A longitudinal study of an Amish community found 26 suicides committed in just four families, all of whom exhibited heavy genetic loading for major depressive disorder, bipolar I disorder, and other mood disorders.

There may be genetic factors in suicide, primarily those factors involved in the transmission of bipolar I disorder, schizophrenia, and alcohol dependence—the mental disorders most commonly associated with suicide. However, a genetic factor for suicide may be independent of or in addition to the genetic transmission of a mental disorder. It may be a genetic factor for impulsivity, which may be related to an abnormality in the central serotonin system.

**Neurochemistry.** A serotonin deficiency, measured as a decrease in the metabolism of 5-hydroxyindoleacetic acid (5-HIAA), was found in a group of depressed patients who attempted suicide. Those patients who attempted suicide by violent means (for example, guns or jumping) had a lower 5-HIAA level in the cerebrospinal fluid (CSF) than did those depressed patients who were not suicidal or who attempted suicide in a less violent manner (for example, a substance overdose).

Some animal and human studies have indicated an association between a deficiency in the central serotonin system and poor impulse control. Some workers have viewed suicide as one type of impulsive behavior. Furthermore, a significant negative correlation between CSF 5-HIAA levels and lifetime aggression scores has been reported among personality disorder patients. Other patient groups thought to have problems with impulse control include violent offenders, arsonists, and those with alcohol dependence, groups who have also been noted to have lower CSF 5-HIAA levels than do controls.

Possible peripheral markers of suicidal behavior have also been examined. High outputs of urinary free cortisol, nonsuppression of plasma cortisol after the administration of dexamethasone, an exaggerated plasma cortisol response to the infusion of 5-hydroxytryptophan, a blunted plasma thyroid-stimulating hormone (TSH) response to the infusion of thyrotropin-releasing hormone (TRH), skin conductance abnormalities, altered urinary catechol ratios, decreases in platelet serotonin uptake or titrated imipramine (Tofranil) binding number have all been reported to be associated with suicidal behavior among depressed patients.

A few studies have found ventricular enlargement and abnormal electroencephalograms (EEGs) in some suicidal patients.

Blood samples analyzed for platelet monoamine oxidase (MAO) from a group of normal volunteers revealed that those persons with the lowest level of the enzyme in their platelets had eight times the prevalence of suicide in their families, compared with persons with high levels of the enzyme. There is strong evidence for an alteration of platelet MAO activity in depressive disorders.

## SELF-INJURY

Studies show that about 4 percent of all patients in psychiatric hospitals have cut themselves; the female-to-male ratio is almost 3 to 1. The incidence of self-injury in psychiatric patients is estimated to be more than 50 times greater than in the general population. Cutters presenting to psychiatrists tend to have cut chronically over several years. Self-injury is found in about 30 percent of all abusers of oral substances and 10 percent of all intravenous users admitted to substance-treatment units.

The patients are usually in their 20s and may be single or married. Most cut delicately, not coarsely. Cutting is usually done in private with a razor blade, a knife, broken glass, or a mirror. The wrists, arms, thighs, and legs are the most common sites cut; the face, breasts, and abdomen are cut infrequently. Most cutters claim to experience no pain. The reasons given include anger at themselves or others, relief of tension, and the wish to die. The great majority of cutters are classified as those with personality disorders and are significantly more introverted, neurotic, and hostile than are controls. Alcohol abuse and other substance abuse are common, and the majority of cutters have attempted suicide.

Self-mutilation has been viewed as localized self-destruction, with mishandling of aggressive impulses caused by an unconscious wish to punish either oneself or an introjected object. Some have referred to cutters as pseudosuicidal.

## PREDICTION

The clinician must assess an individual patient's risk for suicide on the basis of the clinical examination. The most predictive items associated with suicide risk are listed in Table 31.1–1. Among the high-risk characteristics are age over 45, male sex, alcohol dependence (the suicide rate is 50 times higher in alcohol dependent persons than in those who are not alcohol-dependent), violent behavior, prior suicidal behavior, and previous psychiatric hospitalization. Suicide is grouped into high-risk-related and low-risk-related factors (Table 31.1–2).

The clinician should always ask about suicide ideation as part of every mental status examination, especially if the patient is depressed. The patient should be asked directly: "Are you or have you ever been suicidal? Do you want to die?" Eight out of 10 persons who eventually kill themselves give warnings of their intent. Fifty percent say openly that they want to die. If the patient admits to a plan of action, that is a particularly dangerous sign. Also, if a patient who has been threatening suicide becomes quiet and less agitated than in the past, that may be an ominous sign. The clinician should be especially concerned with the factors listed in Table 31.1–3.

## TREATMENT

The great majority of suicides among psychiatric patients are preventable. Some patients experience suffering so great and intense or so chronic and unresponsive to treatment that their eventual suicides may be perceived as inevitable; fortunately, such patients are relatively uncommon. Some other patients have severe personality disor-

**Table 31.1–1**
**Factors Associated with Suicide Risk**

| Rank Order | Factor |
|---|---|
| 1 | Age (45 and older) |
| 2 | Alcohol dependence |
| 3 | Irritation, rage, violence |
| 4 | Prior suicidal behavior |
| 5 | Male· |
| 6 | Unwilling to accept help |
| 7 | Longer than usual duration of current episode of depression |
| 8 | Prior inpatient psychiatric treatment |
| 9 | Recent loss or separation |
| 10 | Depression |
| 11 | Loss of physical health |
| 12 | Unemployed or retired |
| 13 | Single, widowed, or divorced |

Table modified from R E Litman, N L Faberow, C I Wold, T R Brown: Prediction models of suicidal behaviors. In *The Prediction of Suicide*, H Beck, L P Resnik, D J Lettieri, editors, p 141. Charles Press, Bowie, Md, 1974. Used with permission.

**Table 31.1–2**
**Evaluation of Suicide Risk**

| Variable | High Risk | Low Risk |
|---|---|---|
| Demographic and social profile | | |
| Age | Over 45 years | Below 45 years |
| Sex | Male | Female |
| Marital status | Divorced or widowed | Married |
| Employment | Unemployed | Employed |
| Interpersonal relationship | Conflictual | Stable |
| Family background | Chaotic or conflictual | Stable |
| Health | | |
| Physical | Chronic illness | Good health |
| | Hypochondriac | Feels healthy |
| | Excessive substance intake | Low substance use |
| Mental | Severe depression | Mild depression |
| | Psychosis | Neurosis |
| | Severe personality disorder | Normal personality |
| | Substance abuse | Social drinker |
| | Hopelessness | Optimism |
| Suicidal activity | | |
| Suicidal ideation | Frequent, intense, prolonged | Infrequent, low intensity, transient |
| Suicide attempt | Multiple attempts | First attempt |
| | Planned | Impulsive |
| | Rescue unlikely | Rescue inevitable |
| | Unambiguous wish to die | Primary wish for change |
| | Communication internalized (self-blame) | Communication externalized (anger) |
| | Method lethal and available | Method of low lethality or not readily available |
| Resources | | |
| Personal | Poor achievement | Good achievement |
| | Poor insight | Insightful |
| | Affect unavailable or poorly controlled | Affect available and appropriately controlled |
| Social | Poor rapport | Good rapport |
| | Socially isolated | Socially integrated |
| | Unresponsive family | Concerned family |

Table from K Adam: Attempted suicide. Psychiatr Clin North Am 8: 183, 1985. Used with permission.

**Table 31.1–3
History, Signs, and Symptoms of Suicidal Risk**

1. Previous attempt or fantasized suicide
2. Anxiety, depression, exhaustion
3. Availability of means of suicide
4. Concern for effect of suicide on family members
5. Verbalized suicidal ideation
6. Preparation of a will, resignation after agitated depression
7. Proximal life crisis, such as mourning or impending surgery
8. Family history of suicide
9. Pervasive pessimism or hopelessness

ders, are highly impulsive, and commit suicide apparently in an impulsive manner, often when dysphoric or intoxicated or both. The evidence that inadequate assessment or treatment is associated with suicide indicates that the great majority of suicides of psychiatric patients are probably preventable.

The evaluation for suicide potential involves a complete psychiatric history; a thorough examination of the patient's mental state; and inquiry about depressive symptoms, suicidal thoughts, intents, plans, and attempts. A lack of future plans, giving away personal property, making a will, and having recently experienced a loss imply increased risk for suicide. The decision to hospitalize the patient depends on the diagnosis, the severity of the depression and the suicidal ideation, the patient's and the family's ability to cope, the patient's living situation, the availability of social support, and the absence or the presence of risk factors for suicide.

## Inpatient versus Outpatient Treatment

Whether to hospitalize patients with suicidal ideation is the most important clinical decision to be made. Not all such patients require hospitalization; some may be treated on an outpatient basis. But the absence of a strong social support system, a history of impulsive behavior, and a suicidal plan of action are indications for hospitalization. To determine whether outpatient treatment is feasible, the clinician should use a straightforward clinical approach—asking patients considered suicidal to agree to call when reaching a point beyond which they are uncertain of their ability to control their suicidal impulses. Patients who can make such an agreement reaffirm the belief that they have sufficient strength to control such impulses and to seek help.

In return for the patient's commitment, the clinician should be available to the patient 24 hours a day. If a patient who is considered seriously suicidal cannot make the commitment, immediate emergency hospitalization is indicated, and both the patient and the patient's family should be so advised. If, however, the patient is to be treated on an outpatient basis, the therapist should note the patient's home and work telephone numbers for emergency reference; occasionally, a patient hangs up unexpectedly during a late night call or gives only a name to the answering service. If the patient refuses hospitalization, the family must take the responsibility to be with the patient 24 hours a day.

According to Schneidman, the clinician has several practical preventive measures for dealing with a suicidal person: (1) reduce the psychological pain by modifying the patient's stressful environment, enlisting the aid of the spouse, the employer, or a friend; (2) build realistic support by recognizing that the patient may have a legitimate complaint; and (3) offer alternatives to suicide.

Many psychiatrists believe that any patient who has made a suicidal attempt, regardless of its lethality, should be hospitalized. Although most of those patients voluntarily enter the hospital, a danger to self is one of the few clear-cut indications currently acceptable in all states for involuntary hospitalization.

In the hospital the patient can receive antidepressant or antipsychotic medications as indicated; individual therapy, group therapy, and family therapy are available; and the patient receives the hospital's social support and sense of security. Other therapeutic measures depend on the patient's underlying diagnosis. For example, if alcohol dependence is an associated problem, treatment must be directed toward alleviating that condition.

Although patients classified as acutely suicidal may have favorable prognoses, chronically suicidal patients are difficult to treat, and they exhaust the caretakers. Constant observation by special nurses, seclusion, and restraints cannot prevent suicide if the patient is resolute. Electroconvulsive therapy (ECT) may be necessary for some severely depressed patients, who may require several treatment courses.

Useful measures for the treatment of the depressed suicidal inpatient include searching the patient's belongings and person on arrival in the ward for objects that may be used for suicide and repeating the search at times of exacerbation of the suicidal ideation. Ideally, the suicidal depressed inpatient should be treated on a locked ward where the windows are shatterproof, and the patient's room should be located near the nursing station to maximize observation by the nursing staff. The treating team has to assess how much to restrict the patient and whether to make regular checks or continued direct observation. Vigorous treatment with antidepressant medication should be initiated.

Supportive psychotherapy by the psychiatrist shows concern and may alleviate some of the patient's intense suffering. Some patients may be able to accept the idea that they are suffering from a recognized illness and that they will probably make a complete recovery. Patients should be dissuaded from making major life decisions while they are suicidally depressed, because such decisions are often morbidly determined and may be irrevocable. The consequences of such bad decisions can cause further anguish and misery when the patient has recovered.

Patients recovering from a suicidal depression are at particular risk. As the depression lifts, patients become energized and are thus able to put their suicidal plans into action. Sometimes depressed patients, with or without treatment, suddenly appear to be at peace with themselves, because they have reached a secret decision to commit suicide. The clinician should be especially suspicious of such a dramatic clinical change, which may portend a suicidal attempt.

A patient may commit suicide even when in the hospital. According to one survey, about 1 percent of all suicides were committed by patients who were being treated in general medical-surgical or psychiatric hospitals; however, the annual suicide rate in psychiatric hospitals is only 0.003 percent.

**Legal and ethical considerations.** Liability issues stemming from suicides in psychiatric hospitals frequently involve questions about the patient's rate of deterioration, the presence during hospitalization of clinical signs indicating risk, and the psychiatrist's and the staff members' awareness of and response to those clinical signs.

In about half the cases in which suicide occurs while the patient is on a psychiatric unit, a lawsuit results. What the courts require is not that suicide never occur but that the patient be periodically evaluated for suicidal risk, that a treatment plan with a high level of security be formulated, and that the staff members follow that treatment plan.

At present, suicide and attempted suicide are variously viewed as a felony and a misdemeanor, respectively; in some states the acts are considered not crimes but unlawful under common law and statutes. The role of an aider and abettor in suicide adds another dimension to the legal morass; some court decision have held that, although neither suicide nor attempted suicide is punishable, anyone who assists in the act may be punished.

Doctor-assisted suicide is discussed in Section 2.7.

### Community Organizations

Community organizations seem to have fewer problems than do individual therapists with the ethics and the legalities of helping suicidal people. Prevention centers, crisis listening posts, and so-called suicide telephone hot lines are clear attempts to intervene and diminish the isolation, withdrawal, and loneliness of the suicidal patient. Outreach programs enable highly motivated laypersons to respond to cries for help in a variety of ways. But such responses do no more than just diminish an acute crisis; highly suicidal people place fewer than 10 percent of such calls. Two studies in the United States have failed to find that suicide prevention centers had an effect on suicide rates. Nevertheless, suicide prevention centers are important mental health resources for persons in distress.

### References

Asnis G M, Friedman T A, Sanderson W C, Kaplan M L: Suicidal behaviors in adult psychiatric outpatients: I. Description and prevalence. Am J Psychiatry *150*: 108, 1993.
Barraclough B, Bunch J, Nelson B, Sainsbury P: A hundred cases of suicide. Br J Psychiatry *125*: 355, 1974.
Beskow J: Depression and suicide. Pharmacopsychiatry *23* (Suppl 1): 3, 1990.
Duberstein P R, Conwell Y, Caine E D: Interpersonal stressors, substance abuse, and suicide. J Nerv Ment Dis *181*: 80, 1993.
Dublin L: *Suicide: A Sociological and Statistical Study.* Ronald, New York, 1963.
Durkheim E: *Suicide.* Free Press, Glencove, Ill, 1951.
Farmer R, Hirsch S, editors: *The Suicide Syndrome.* Croom Helm, London, 1980.
Griffith E E, Bell C C: Recent trends in suicide and homicide among blacks. JAMA *262*: 2265, 1989.
Hawton K, Catalan J, editors: *Attempted Suicide.* Oxford University Press, Oxford, 1982.
Kastenbaum R: Death, suicide and the older adult. Suicide Life Threat Behav *22*: 1, 1992.
Kreitman N, editor: *Parasuicide.* Wiley, New York, 1977.

Kreitman N, editor: Suicide, age and marital status. Psychol Med *18*: 121, 1988.
Mann J, Stanley M, editors: *Psychobiology of Suicidal Behavior.* New York Academy of Sciences, New York, 1986.
Murphy G E, Wetzel R D, Robins E, McEvoy L: Multiple risk factors predict suicide in alcoholism. Arch Gen Psychiatry *49*: 459, 1992.
Osgood N J: Suicide in the elderly: Etiology and assessment. Int Rev Psychiatry *4*: 217, 1992.
Perlin S, editor: *A Handbook for the Study of Suicide.* Oxford University Press, Oxford, 1975.
Robins E: *The Final Months: A Study of the Lives of 134 Persons Who Committed Suicide.* Oxford University Press, New York, 1981.
Roy A: Are there genetic factors in suicide? Int Rev Psychiatry *4*: 169, 1992.
Roy A: Family history of suicide. Arch Gen Psychiatry *40*: 971, 1983.
Roy A: Risk factors for suicide in psychiatric patients. Arch Gen Psychiatry *39*: 1089, 1982.
Roy A, editor: Self-destructive behavior. Psychiatr Clin North Am *8*: 215, 1985.
Roy A, editor: *Suicide.* Williams & Wilkins, Baltimore, 1986.
Roy A: Suicide. In *Comprehensive Textbook of Psychiatry,* ed 5, H I Kaplan, B J Sadock, editors, p 1414. Williams & Wilkins, Baltimore, 1989.
Roy A: Suicide in chronic schizophrenia. Br J Psychiatry *141*: 171, 1982.
Roy A, Segal N, Centerwall B, Robinette D: Suicide in twins. Arch Gen Psychiatry *48*: 29, 1991.
Shneidman E: *Definition of Suicide.* Wiley, New York, 1985.
Tsuang M T, Simpson J C, Fleming J A: Epidemiology of suicide. Int Rev Psychiatry *4*: 117, 1992.
Weishaar M E, Beck A T: Hopelessness and suicide. Int Rev Psychiatry *4*: 177, 1992.

# 31.2 / Other Psychiatric Emergencies

A psychiatric emergency is any disturbance in thoughts, feelings, or actions for which immediate therapeutic intervention is necessary. For a variety of reasons—such as the growing incidence of violence, the increased appreciation of the role of organic disease in altered mental status, and the epidemic of alcohol dependence and other substance-related disorders—the number of emergency patients is on the rise. Physicians, including psychiatrists, are performing an expanded role as the primary clinician or consultant as part of integrated emergency medicine services. The widening scope of emergency psychiatry goes beyond general psychiatric practice to include such specialized problems as the abuse of substances, children, and spouses; violence in the form of suicide, homicide, and rape; and such social issues as homelessness, aging, competence, and acquired immune deficiency syndrome (AIDS). The emergency psychiatrist must be up-to-date on medicolegal issues and managed care.

## EPIDEMIOLOGY

Psychiatric emergency rooms are used equally by men and women and more by single persons than by married persons. About 20 percent of patients are suicidal, and about 10 percent are violent. The most common diagnoses are mood disorders (including depressive disorders and manic episodes), schizophrenia, and alcohol dependence. About 40 percent of all patients seen in psychiatric emergency rooms require hospitalization. Most visits occur during the night hours, but there is no utilization difference based on the day of the week or the month of the year. Contrary to popular belief, studies have not found a higher than usual use of psychiatric emergency rooms during a full moon or during the Christmas season.

# EMERGENCY PSYCHIATRIC INTERVIEW

The emergency interview is similar to the standard psychiatric interview except for the time limitation imposed by the other patients waiting to be seen and by the potential sense of urgency in assessing the risk to the patient or others. In general, the physician focuses on the presenting complaint and the reasons that the patient has come to the emergency room at that time. The time constraint requires that the clinician structure the interview, particularly with patients who may respond with long, rambling accounts of their illnesses. If friends, relatives, or the police accompany the patient, a supplemental history should be obtained from them, especially if the patient is mute, negativistic, uncooperative, or otherwise unable to give a coherent history.

Patients may be highly motivated to reveal themselves to gain relief from suffering, but they may also be both consciously and unconsciously motivated to conceal innermost feelings that they perceive to be shameful or threatening. If the patient has been brought to the hospital involuntarily, willingness or ability to cooperate may be impaired for that reason. The psychiatrist's relationship with the patient strongly influences what the patient does and does not say, even within the context of a first interview in an emergency room; therefore, a large portion of the psychiatric emergency interview involves the specific and sophisticated techniques of listening, observation, and interpretation that provide the foundation of psychiatric training in general. Being straightforward, honest, calm, and nonthreatening is of utmost importance, as is the ability to convey to patients the idea that the clinician is in control and will act decisively to protect them from hurting themselves or others.

Table 31.2–1 summarizes a number of necessary initial factors in the evaluation of a psychiatric emergency.

Sometimes the contact with the emergency room is by telephone. In such cases the psychiatrist should obtain the number from which the call is made and the exact address. Those items are important in case the call is interrupted; they allow the psychiatrist to direct help to the patient. If the patient is alone and the psychiatrist ascertains that the patient is in danger, the police should be alerted. If possible, an assistant should call the police on another line while the psychiatrist keeps the patient engaged until help arrives. The patient should not be told to drive alone to the hospital. Rather, an emergency medical team should be dispatched to bring the patient to the hospital.

The greatest potential error in emergency room psychiatry is overlooking a physical illness as the cause of the emotional illness. Head traumas, medical illnesses, substance abuse (including alcohol), cerebrovascular diseases, metabolic abnormalities, and medications may all cause

**Table 31.2–1**
**General Strategy in Evaluating Patients**

**I. Self-protection**
A. Know as much as possible about the patients before meeting them.
B. Leave physical restraint procedures to those who are trained to handle them.
C. Be alert to risks for impending violence.
D. Attend to the safety of the physical surroundings (e.g., door access, room objects).
E. Have others present during the assessment if needed.
F. Have others in the vicinity.
G. Attend to developing an alliance with the patient (e.g., do not confront or threaten patients with paranoid psychoses).

**II. Prevent harm**
A. Prevent self-injury and suicide. Use whatever methods are necessary to prevent patients from hurting themselves during the evaluation.
B. Prevent violence toward others. During the evaluation, briefly assess the patient for the risk of violence. If the risk is deemed significant, consider the following options:
1. Inform the patient that violence is not acceptable.
2. Approach the patient in a nonthreatening manner.
3. Reassure and calm the patient or assist in reality testing.
4. Offer medication.
5. Inform the patient that restraint or seclusion will be used if necessary.
6. Have teams ready to restrain the patient.
7. When patients are restrained, always closely observe them, and frequently check their vital signs. Isolate restrained patients from agitating stimuli. Immediately plan a further approach—medication, reassurance, medical evaluation.

**III. Rule out cognitive disorders caused by a general medical condition.**

**IV. Rule out impending psychosis.**

abnormal behavior, and the psychiatrist should take a concise medical history that concentrates on those areas.

## Violence and Assaultive Behavior

The first task in evaluating violent behavior is to ascertain its cause. Cause directs treatment. Patients with thought disorders characterized by hallucinations commanding them to kill someone require psychiatric hospitalization and antipsychotic medication. If they are unwilling to accept treatment, certification is necessary to protect the intended victim and the patient. Those who take an extreme civil libertarian perspective fail to recognize that medical certification has evolved legally not only to protect society from the violent patient but also to protect patients from the consequences of their uncontrollable behavior. Patients who, while psychotic, destroy families' and friends' property or threaten to commit or do commit violent assaults destroy social supports that they need to help them function after the aberrant mood or delusional ideation is corrected.

Violence and assaultive behavior are difficult to predict (Table 31.2–2). However, the fear with which some people regard all psychiatric patients is completely out of pro-

**Table 31.2–2**
**Assessing and Predicting Violent Behavior**

Signs of impending violence
    Recent acts of violence, including property violence
    Verbal or physical threats (menacing)
    Carrying weapons or other objects that may be used as
      weapons (e.g., forks, ashtrays)
    Progressive psychomotor agitation
    Alcohol or other substance intoxication
    Paranoid features in a psychotic patient
    Command violent auditory hallucinations—some but not all
      patients are at high risk
    Brain diseases, global or with frontal lobe findings; less
      commonly with temporal lobe findings (controversial)
    Catatonic excitement
    Certain manic episodes
    Certain agitated depressive episodes
    Personality disorders (rage, violence, or impulse dyscontrol)

Assess the risk for violence
    Consider violent ideation, wish, intention, plan, availability of
      means, implementation of plan, wish for help
    Consider demographics—sex (male), age (15–24),
      socioeconomic status (low), social supports (few)
    Consider the patient's history: violence, nonviolent antisocial
      acts, impulse dyscontrol (e.g., gambling, substance
      abuse, suicide or self-injury, psychosis)
    Consider overt stressors (e.g., marital conflict, real or
      symbolic loss)

**Table 31.2–3**
**Differential Diagnosis of Anxiety**

Alcohol delirium and withdrawal
Amphetamine (or related substance) intoxication and
    withdrawal
Anxiety disorders
Bipolar I disorder
Borderline personality disorder
Caffeine intoxication
Cerebral arteriosclerosis
Cocaine intoxication
Encephalitis
Essential hypertension
Hyperthyroidism
Hyperventilation syndrome
Hypocalcemia
Hypoglycemia
Hypokalemia
Impending myocardial infarction
Internal hemorrhage
Major depressive disorder
Mitral valve prolapse
Normal anxiety
Other temporal lobe diseases
Panic disorder
Paroxysmal atrial tachycardia and other cardiac arrhythmias
Pheochromocytoma
Phobias
Postconcussion syndrome
Psychomotor epilepsy
Psychotic disorders
Pulmonary embolism
Schizophrenia
Sedative, hypnotic, or anxiolytic withdrawal and delirium
Sexual disorders
Subacute bacterial endocarditis

Table adapted from Andrew Edmund Slaby, M.D., Ph.D.

portion to the small group who are an authentic danger to others. The best predictors of potential violent behavior are (1) excessive alcohol intake, (2) a history of violent acts with arrests or criminal activity, and (3) a history of childhood abuse. Although violent patients can arouse a realistic fear in the psychiatrist, they can also touch off irrational fears that impair clinical judgment and that may lead to the premature and excessive use of sedation or physical restraint. Violent patients are usually frightened by their own hostile impulses and desperately seek help to prevent loss of control. Nevertheless, restraints should be applied if there is a reasonable risk of violence.

## DIFFERENTIAL DIAGNOSIS

The emergency psychiatrist must consider a wide range of conditions that may account for the presenting signs and symptoms. The most common complaints fall within the categories of anxiety, depression, mania, and thought disorder. Those conditions may overlap and have multiple causes.

The differential diagnoses of anxiety, depressive episodes, manic episodes, and thought disorders are listed in Tables 31.2–3 through 31.2–6. Anxiety is different from depression, mania, and thought disorder in that a number of the illnesses that can cause anxiety are life threatening. Incipient myocardial infarctions, pulmonary emboli, cardiac arrhythmias, and internal hemorrhages cause acute anxiety to the degree of panic. Untreated congestive heart failure secondary to a silent myocardial infarction or malignant cardiac arrhythmia may be fatal. Elderly people and those who have just suffered a loss may be perceived

as having depressive or nihilistic ideation when, in fact, age or stress has propelled them into a life-threatening illness manifested by anxiety and a sense of impending doom. Persons who experience depression as a side effect of antihypertensive medication—for example, propranolol (Inderal)—may perceive spouse, children, friends, or work in a negative light that changes on cessation of the medication.

Table 31.2–7 outlines features that should make the emergency room clinician consider an organic condition as the cause of the complaint.

Table 31.2–8 lists the central nervous system (CNS) disorders that require immediate treatment. Table 31.2–9 lists the CNS disorders with behavioral features that may cause the patient to be brought to the psychiatric emergency room.

The differential diagnosis of violent behavior includes substance-induced persisting dementia, antisocial personality disorder, catatonic schizophrenia, cerebral infection, cerebral neoplasm, obsessive-compulsive personality disorder, dissociative disorders, impulse control disorders, sexual disorders, idiosyncratic alcohol intoxication, delusional disorder, paranoid personality disorder, schizophrenia, social maladjustment without mental disorder, temporal lobe epilepsy, bipolar I disorder, and uncontrollable violence secondary to interpersonal stress.

**Table 31.2–4**
**Differential Diagnosis of Depressive Episodes**

Adjustment disorder with depressed mood
Dysthymic disorder
Schizoaffective disorder
Schizophrenia
Major depressive disorder
Bipolar I disorder
Borderline personality disorder
Hypokalemia
Brief psychotic disorder
Cyclothymic disorder
Antihypertensive toxicity
Steroid psychotic disorder
Hypothyroidism
Cerebral neoplasm
General paresis
Amphetamine use disorders
Cocaine use disorders
Carcinoma of pancreas
Hepatitis
Postviral infection syndrome
Dementia of the Alzheimer's type
Vascular dementia
Dementia of the Alzheimer's type with late onset
Dementia of the Alzheimer's type with early onset
Cirrhosis of the liver
Arteriosclerosis
Infectious mononucleosis
Hyperthyroidism
Occult malignancy
AIDS
Schizoid personality disorder
Schizotypal personality disorder

Table adapted from Andrew Edmund Slaby, M.D., Ph.D.

**Table 31.2–5**
**Differential Diagnosis of Manic Episodes**

Bipolar I disorder
Schizoaffective disorder
Alcohol intoxication
Catatonic schizophrenia
Delirium
Hyperthyroidism
Postencephalitic syndrome
Steroid-induced mania
Antidepressant-induced mania
Decongestant-induced mania
Amphetamine-induced mania
Cocaine-induced mania
L-Dopa-induced mania
Bronchodilator-induced mania
Phencyclidine-induced mania
AIDS
Atypical psychosis

Table by Andrew Edmund Slaby, M.D., Ph.D.

# TREATMENT

Patients in the grip of a violent episode pay no attention to the rational intercessions of others and probably do not even hear them. When armed, they are particularly dangerous and capable of murder. Such patients should be disarmed by trained law enforcement personnel without their harming the patients if at all possible. If unarmed,

**Table 31.2–6**
**Differential Diagnosis of Thought Disorders**

Schizophrenia
Bipolar I disorder
Major depressive disorder
Alcohol psychotic disorder with hallucinations
Dementia of the Alzheimer's type with early onset
Frontal lobe neoplasm
Alcohol intoxication
Adjustment disorder
Dissociative disorders
Delusional disorder
Substance-induced (e.g., PCP, amphetamine) psychotic
    disorder
Steroid psychotic disorder
Syphilis
Endocrine diseases
Pernicious anemia
Temporal lobe epilepsy
Migraine equivalent
Cimetidine psychotic disorder
AIDS
Brief psychotic disorder
Schizophreniform disorder
Shared psychotic disorder
Atypical psychosis
Dementia of the Alzheimer's type
Vascular dementia
Dementia of the Alzheimer's type with late onset

Table adapted from Andrew Edmund Slaby, M.D., Ph.D.

**Table 31.2–7**
**Features That Point to a Medical Cause**
**of a Mental Disorder**

Acute onset (within hours or minutes, with prevailing
    symptoms)
First episode
Geriatric age
Current medical illness or injury
Significant substance abuse
Nonauditory disturbances of perception
Neurological symptoms—loss of consciousness, seizures,
    head injury, change in headache pattern, change in vision
Classic mental status signs—diminished alertness,
    disorientation, memory impairment, impairment in
    concentration and attention, dyscalculia, concreteness
Other mental status signs—speech, movement, or gait
    disorders
Constructional apraxia—difficulties in drawing clock, cube,
    intersecting pentagons, Bender gestalt design
Catatonic features—nudity, negativism, combativeness,
    rigidity, posturing, waxy flexibility, echopraxia, echolalia,
    grimacing, muteness

**Table 31.2–8**
**Common Global Central Nervous System Disorders**
**That Require Immediate Treatment**

Hypoglycemia—dextrose 50% IV or juice orally, immediately;
    give to all diabetics
Wernicke's encephalopathy—thiamine, 100 mg IV,
    immediately
Opioid intoxication—nalaxone (Narcan), 4 mg IV, immediately

**Table 31.2–9**
**Common Focal Central Nervous System Disorders with Behavioral Features**

Aphasias—fluent or receptive aphasia results in patients' not understanding spoken word, although they have fluent but incoherent speech

Frontal lobe syndromes—changes in motor behavior, ability to concentrate, reasoning, thinking, social judgment, and impulse control

Temporal lobe syndromes—psychosis, seizure, personality and Klüver-Bucy features

Parietal lobe syndromes—right lesion with denial and hypomania

Occipital lobe syndromes—Anton's syndrome (cortical blindness with denial)

such patients should be approached with sufficient help and with overwhelming strength, so that there is, in effect, no contest. In the emergency room, armed police should always remove bullets from their weapons. In numerous instances, disturbed patients grabbed a loaded gun and randomly killed others.

Patients must be placed in a safe setting. Some need to be transferred to a forensic unit because of the magnitude of their violent potential. Medication specific to a disorder is administered when indicated, unless a nonspecific measure is required to modify behavior until the cause is ascertained and specific therapy can be initiated.

The use of medication is contraindicated in acutely agitated patients who have suffered a head injury, because medication can confuse the clinical picture. In general, intramuscular (IM) haloperidol is one of the most useful emergency treatments for violent psychotic patients.

Electroconvulsive therapy (ECT) had also been used in emergencies to control psychotic violence. One or several ECT sessions within several hours usually ends an episode of psychotic violence.

## Psychotherapy

In an emergency psychiatric intervention, all attempts are made to help patients maintain self-esteem. Empathy is critical to healing in a psychiatric emergency. The acquired knowledge of how biogenetic, situational, developmental, and existential forces converge at one point in history to create a psychiatric emergency is tantamount to the maturation of skill in emergency psychiatry.

Adjustment disorder in all age groups may result in tantrumlike outbursts of rage. Those outbursts are seen particularly in marital quarrels. Police are often summoned by neighbors distressed by the sounds of a violent altercation. Such family quarrels should be approached with caution, because they may be complicated by the use of alcohol and the presence of dangerous weapons. The warring couple frequently turn their combined fury on the unwary outsider. Wounded self-esteem is a big issue. Therefore, patronizing or contemptuous attitudes must be avoided, and an effort must be made to communicate an attitude of respect and an authentic peacemaking concern.

In family violence the psychiatrist should note the special vulnerability of selected close relatives. A wife or a husband may have a curious masochistic attachment to the spouse and provoke violence by taunting and otherwise undermining the partner's self-esteem. Such relationships often end in the murder of the provoking partner and sometimes in the suicide of the other partner, the dynamics behind most so-called suicide pacts.

As in the case of many suicidal patients, many violent patients require hospitalization and usually accept the offer of inpatient care with a sense of relief.

More than one psychotherapist or psychotherapy is frequently used in emergency therapy. For example, a 28-year-old man, depressed and suicidal after a colostomy for intractable colitis, whose wife was threatening to leave him because of his irritability and their constant altercations, may be referred to a psychiatrist for supportive psychotherapy and antidepressants, to a marital therapist with his wife to improve their marital functioning, and to a colostomy support group to learn ways of coping with a colostomy. Emergency psychiatric clinicians are pragmatic. They use every necessary mode of therapeutic intervention available to enhance the resolution of the crisis and to facilitate value exploration and growth. There is less concern than usual about the dilution of a therapeutic relationship. Emphasis is on how various psychiatric modalities act synergistically to enhance recovery.

No one word is appropriate for all people in similar situations. What does one say to a patient and family experiencing a psychiatric emergency, such as a suicide attempt or a schizophrenic break? For some a genetic rationale helps. The information that an illness has a strong biological component relieves some people. For others it underlines lack of control and increases depression and anxiety; they feel helpless because neither the family nor the patient can alter the behavior to minimize the likelihood of recurrence. Others may benefit from an explanation of family or individual dynamics. Still others only want someone to listen; in time, they will reach their own understanding.

In the emergency situation, as in any other psychiatric situation, when a clinician does not know what to say, the best approach is to listen. People in crisis reveal how much they need support, denial, ventilation, and words to conceptualize the meaning of their crisis and to discover paths to resolution.

## Pharmacotherapy

The major indications for the use of psychotropic medication in the emergency room include violent or assaultive behavior, massive anxiety or panic, and extrapyramidal reactions, such as dystonia and akathisia as side effects of psychiatric drugs. A rare form of dystonia is laryngospasm, and the psychiatrist should be prepared to maintain an open airway with intubation if necessary.

Persons who are paranoid or in a state of catatonic excitement require tranquilization. Episodic outbursts of violence respond to lithium (Eskalith), β-blockers, and carbamazepine (Tegretol). If the history suggests a seizure disorder, clinical studies are performed to confirm the diagnosis, and an evaluation is performed to ascertain the cause. If the findings are positive, anticonvulsants are commenced, or appropriate surgery is provided (for example, in the instance of a cerebral mass). For intoxication from recreational substances, conservative measures may be adequate. In some instances, drugs such as thiothixene (Navane) and haloperidol (Haldol), 5 to 10 mg every half hour to an hour, are needed until a patient is stabilized. Benzodiazepines are used instead of or in addition to antipsychotics (to reduce the antipsychotic dosage). If a recreational drug has strong anticholinergic properties, benzodiazepines are more appropriate than antipsychotics. Persons with allergic or aberrant responses to antipsychotics and benzodiazepines are treated with sodium amobarbital (Amytal) (for example, 130 mg orally or IM, paraldehyde, or diphenhydramine (Benadryl, 50 to 100 mg orally or IM).

Violent, struggling patients are most effectively subdued with an appropriate sedative or antipsychotic. Diazepam (Valium), 5 to 10 mg, or lorazepam (Ativan), 2 to 4 mg, may be given slowly intravenously (IV) over two minutes. The clinician must give the IV medication with great care, so that respiratory arrest does not occur. Patients who require IM medication can be sedated with haloperidol, 5 to 10 mg IM, or with chlorpromazine (Thorazine), 25 mg IM. If the furor is due to alcohol or is part of a postseizure psychomotor disturbance, the sleep produced by a relatively small amount of an IV medication may go on for hours. On awakening, the patients are often entirely alert and rational and typically have a complete amnesia for the violent episode.

If the furor is part of an ongoing psychotic process and returns as soon as the IV medication wears off, continuous medication may be given. It is sometimes better to use small IM or oral doses at half-hour to one-hour intervals—for example, haloperidol, 2 to 5 mg, or diazepam, 10 mg—until the patient is controlled than to use large dosages initially and end up with an overmedicated patient. As the patient's disturbed behavior is brought under control, successively smaller and less frequent doses should be used. During the preliminary treatment, the patient's blood pressure and other vital signs should be monitored.

**Rapid tranquilization.** Antipsychotic medication can be given in a rapid manner at 30-to-60-minute intervals to achieve a therapeutic result as quickly as possible. The procedure is useful in agitated patients and those in excited states. The drugs of choice for rapid tranquilization are haloperidol and other high-potency antipsychotics. In adults 5 to 10 mg of haloperidol can be given orally or IM and repeated in 20 to 30 minutes until the patient becomes calm. Some patients may experience mild extrapyramidal symptoms within the first 24 hours after rapid tranquilization; although the side effects are rare, the psychiatrist should not overlook them. In general, most patients respond before a total dose of 50 mg is given. The goal is not to produce sedation or somnolence; rather, the patient should be able to cooperate in the assessment process and, ideally, be able to provide some explanation of the agitated behavior. Agitated or panic-stricken patients can be treated with small doses of lorazepam, 2 to 4 mg IV or IM, which can be repeated if necessary in 20 to 30 minutes until the patient has quieted down.

The extrapyramidal emergencies respond to benztropine (Cogentin), 2 mg orally or IM, or diphenhydramine,

50 mg IM or IV. Some patients respond to diazepam, 5 to 10 mg orally or IV.

## Restraints

Restraints are used when patients are so dangerous to themselves or others that they pose a severe threat that cannot be controlled in any other way. Patients may be restrained temporarily to receive medication or for long periods if medication cannot be used. Most often, patients in restraints quiet down after some time has elapsed. On a psychodynamic level, such patients may even welcome the control of their impulses that restraints provide. Table 31.2–10 lists the guidelines for the use of the restraints.

**Table 31.2–10**
**Use of Restraints**

Preferably five or a minimum of four persons should be used to restrain the patient. Leather restraints are the safest and surest type of restraints.

Explain to the patient why he or she is going into restraints.

A staff member should always be visible and reassuring the patient who is being restrained. Reassurance helps alleviate the patient's fear of helplessness, impotence, and loss of control.

Patients should be restrained with legs spread-eagled and one arm restrained to one side and the other arm restrained over the patient's head.

Restraints should be placed so that intravenous fluids can be given if necessary.

The patient's head is raised slightly to decrease the patient's feelings of vulnerability and to reduce the possibility of aspiration.

The restraints should be checked periodically for safety and comfort.

After the patient is in restraints, the clinician begins treatment, using verbal intervention.

Even in restraints, a majority of patients still take antipsychotic medication in concentrated form.

After the patient is under control, one restraint at a time should be removed at five-minute intervals until the patient has only two restraints on. Both of the remaining restraints should be removed at the same time, because it is inadvisable to keep a patient in only one restraint.

Always thoroughly document the reason for the restraints, the course of treatment, and the patient's response to treatment while in restraints.

Table data from W R Dubin, K J Weiss: Emergency psychiatry. In *Psychiatry*, vol 2, R Michaels, A Cooper, S B Guze, L L Judd, G L Klerman, A J Solnit, A J Sunkard, P J Wilner, editors. Lippincott, Philadelphia, 1991. Used with permission.

## SPECIFIC PSYCHIATRIC EMERGENCIES

Table 31.2–11 outlines in alphabetical order common psychiatric emergencies. The reader is referred to the index and to specific chapters of this textbook for a thorough discussion of each disorder.

**References**

Barbee J G, Clark P D, Crapanzano M S, Heintz G C, Kehoe C E: Alcohol and substance abuse among schizophrenic patients presenting to an emergency psychiatric service. J Nerv Ment Dis *177*: 400, 1989.

**Table 31.2–11**
**Common Psychiatric Emergencies**

| Syndrome | Emergency Manifestations | Treatment Issues |
|---|---|---|
| Abuse of child or adult | Signs of physical trauma | Management of medical problems; psychiatric evaluation |
| Acquired immune deficiency syndrome (AIDS) | Changes in behavior secondary to organic causes; changes in behavior secondary to fear and anxiety; suicidal behavior | Management of neurological illness; management of psychological concomitants; reinforcement of social support |
| Adolescent crises | Suicidal attempts and ideation; substance abuse, truancy, trouble with law, pregnancy, running away; eating disorders; psychosis | Evaluation of suicidal potential, extent of substance abuse, family dynamics; crisis-oriented family and individual therapy; hospitalization if necessary; consultation with appropriate extrafamilial authorities |
| Agoraphobia | Panic; depression | Alprazolam (Xanax), 0.25 mg to 2 mg; propranolol (Inderal); antidepressant medication |
| Agranulocytosis (Clozapine [Clozaril]-induced) | High fever, pharyngitis, oral and perianal ulcerations | Discontinue medication immediately; administer granulocyte-colony stimulating factor |
| Akathisia | Agitation, restlessness, muscle discomfort; dysphoria | Reduce antipsychotic dosage; propranolol (30 to 120 mg a day); benzodiazepines; diphenhydramine (Benadryl) orally or IV; benztropine (Cogentin) IM |
| Alcohol-related emergencies | | |
| Alcohol delirium | Confusion, disorientation, fluctuating consciousness and perception, autonomic hyperactivity; may be fatal | Chlordiazepoxide; haloperidol (Haldol) for psychotic symptoms may be added if necessary |
| Alcohol intoxication | Disinhibited behavior, sedation at high doses | With time and protective environment, symptoms abate |
| Alcohol persisting amnestic disorder | Confusion, loss of memory even for all personal identification data | Hospitalization; hypnosis; amobarbital (Amytal) interview; rule out organic cause |
| Alcohol persisting dementia | Confusion, agitation, impulsivity | Rule out other causes for dementia; no effective treatment; hospitalization if necessary |
| Alcohol psychotic disorder with hallucinations | Vivid auditory (at times visual) hallucinations with affect appropriate to content (often fearful); clear sensorium | Haloperidol for psychotic symptoms |
| Alcohol seizures | Grand mal seizures; rarely status epilepticus | Diazepam (Valium), phenytoin (Dilantin); prevent by using chlordiazepoxide (Librium) during detoxification |
| Alcohol withdrawal | Irritability, nausea, vomiting, insomnia, malaise, autonomic hyperactivity, shakiness | Fluid and electrolytes maintained; sedation with benzodiazepines; restraints; monitoring of vital signs; 100 mg thiamine IM |
| Idiosyncratic alcohol intoxication | Marked aggressive or assaultive behavior | Generally no treatment required other than protective environment |
| Korsakoff's syndrome | Alcohol stigmata, amnesia, confabulation | No effective treatment; institutionalization often needed. |
| Wernicke's encephalopathy | Oculomotor disturbances, cerebellar ataxia; mental confusion | Thiamine, 100 mg IV or IM, with $MgSO_4$ given before glucose loading |
| Amphetamine (or related substance) intoxication | Delusions, paranoia; violence; depression (from withdrawal); anxiety, delirium | Antipsychotics; restraints; hospitalization if necessary; no need for gradual withdrawal; antidepressants may be necessary |
| Anorexia nervosa | Loss of 25 percent of body weight of the norm for age and sex | Hospitalization; electrocardiogram (ECG), fluid and electrolytes; neuroendocrine evaluation |
| Anticholinergic intoxication | Psychotic symptoms, dry skin and mouth, hyperpyrexia, midriasis, tachycardia, restlessness, visual hallucinations | Discontinue drug, IV physostigmine (Antilirium), 0.5 to 2 mg, for severe agitation or fever, benzodiazepines; antipsychotics contraindicated |
| Anticonvulsant intoxication | Psychosis; delirium | Dosage of anticonvulsant is reduced |

**Table 31.2–11**
*Continued*

| Syndrome | Emergency Manifestations | Treatment Issues |
|---|---|---|
| Benzodiazepine intoxication | Sedation, somnolence, and ataxia | Supportive measures; midazolam (Versed), 7.5 to 45 mg a day, titrated as needed, should be used only by skilled personnel with resuscitative equipment available |
| Bereavement | Guilt feelings; irritability; insomnia; somatic complaints | Must be differentiated from major depressive disorder; antidepressants not indicated; benzodiazepines for sleep; encouragement of ventilation |
| Borderline personality disorder | Suicidal ideation and gestures; homicidal ideations and gestures; substance abuse; micropsychotic episodes; burns, cut marks on body | Suicidal and homicidal evaluation (if great, hospitalization); small dosages of antipsychotics; clear follow-up plan |
| Brief psychotic disorder | Emotional turmoil, extreme lability; acutely impaired reality testing after obvious psychosocial stress | Hospitalization often necessary; low dosage of antipsychotics may be necessary but often resolves spontaneously |
| Bromide intoxication | Delirium; mania; depression; psychosis | Serum levels obtained (>50 mg a day); bromide intake discontinued; large quantities of sodium chloride IV or orally; if agitation, paraldehyde or antipsychotic is used |
| Caffeine intoxication | Severe anxiety, resembling panic disorder; mania; delirium; agitated depression; sleep disturbance | Cessation of caffeine-containing substances; benzodiazepines |
| Cannabis intoxication | Delusions; panic; dysphoria; cognitive impairment | Benzodiazepines and antipsychotics as needed; evaluation of suicidal or homicidal risk; symptoms usually abate with time and reassurance |
| Catatonic schizophrenia | Marked psychomotor disturbance (either excitement or stupor); exhaustion, can be fatal | Rapid tranquilization with antipsychotics; monitor vital signs; amobarbital may release patient from catatonic mutism or stupor but can precipitate violent behavior |
| Cimetidine psychotic disorder | Delirium; delusions | Reduce dosage or discontinue drug |
| Clonidine withdrawal | Irritability; psychosis; violence; seizures | Symptoms abate with time, but antipsychotics may be necessary; gradual lowering of dosage |
| Cocaine intoxication and withdrawal | Paranoia and violence; severe anxiety; manic state; delirium; schizophreniform psychosis; tachycardia, hypertension, myocardial infarction, cerebrovascular disease; depression and suicidal ideation | Antipsychotics and benzodiazepines; antidepressants or ECT for withdrawal depression if persistent; hospitalization |
| Delirium | Fluctuating sensorium; suicidal and homicidal risk; cognitive clouding; visual, tactile, and auditory hallucinations; paranoia | Evaluate all potential contributing factors and treat each accordingly; reassurance, structure, clues to orientation; benzodiazepines and low-dosage, high-potency antipsychotics must be used with extreme care because of their potential to act paradoxically and increase agitation |
| Delusional disorder | Most often brought in to emergency room involuntarily; threats directed toward others | Antipsychotics if patient will comply (IM if necessary); intensive family intervention; hospitalization if necessary |
| Dementia | Unable to care for self; violent outbursts; psychosis; depression and suicidal ideation; confusion | Small dosages of high-potency antipsychotics; clues to orientation; organic evaluation, including medication use; family intervention |
| Depressive disorders | Suicidal ideation and attempts; self-neglect; substance abuse | Assessment of danger to self; hospitalization if necessary; nonpsychiatric causes of depression must be evaluated |
| L-Dopa intoxication | Mania; depression; schizophreniform disorder; may induce rapid cycling in patients with bipolar I disorder | Lower dosage or discontinue drug |

**Table 31.2–11**
*Continued*

| Syndrome | Emergency Manifestations | Treatment Issues |
|---|---|---|
| Dystonia, acute | Intense involuntary spasm of muscles of neck, tongue, face, jaw, eyes, or trunk | Decrease dosage of antipsychotic; benztropine or diphenhydramine IM |
| Group hysteria | Groups of people exhibit extremes of grief or other disruptive behavior | Group is dispersed with help of other health care workers; ventilation, crisis-oriented therapy; if necessary, small dosages of benzodiazepines |
| Hallucinogen psychotic disorder with hallucinations | Symptom picture is result of interaction of type of substance, dose taken, duration of action, user's premorbid personality, setting; panic; agitation; atropine psychosis | Serum and urine screens; rule out underlying medical or mental disorder; benzodiazepines (2 to 20 mg) orally; reassurance and orientation; rapid tranquilization; often responds spontaneously |
| Homicidal and assaultive behavior | Marked agitation with verbal threats. | Seclusion, restraints, medication |
| Homosexual panic | Not seen with men or women who are comfortable with their sexual orientation; occurs in those who adamantly deny having any homoerotic impulses; impulses are aroused by talk, a physical overture, or play among same-sex friends, such as wrestling, sleeping together, or touching each other in a shower or hot tub; panicked person sees others as sexually interested in him or her and defends against them | Ventilation, environmental structuring, and, in some instances, medication for acute panic (e.g., alprazolam, 0.25 to 2 mg) or antipsychotics may be required; opposite-sex clinician should evaluate the patient whenever possible, and the patient should not be touched save for the routine examination; patients have attacked physicians who were examining an abdomen or performing a rectal examination (e.g., on a man who harbors thinly veiled unintegrated homosexual impulses) |
| Hypertensive crisis | Life-threatening hypertensive reaction secondary to ingestion of tyramine-containing foods in combination with MAOIs; headache, stiff neck, sweating, nausea, vomiting | α-Adrenergic blockers (e.g., phentolamine [Regitine]); nifedipine (Procardia) 10 mg orally; chlorpromazine (Thorazine); make sure symptoms are not secondary to hypotension (side effect of monoamine oxidase inhibitors [MAOIs] alone) |
| Hyperthermia | Extreme excitement or catatonic stupor or both; extremely elevated temperature; violent hyperagitation | Hydrate and cool; may be drug reaction, so discontinue any drug; rule out infection |
| Hyperventilation | Anxiety, terror, clouded consciousness; giddiness, faintness; blurring vision | Shift alkalosis by having patient breathe into paper bag; patient education; antianxiety agents |
| Hypothermia | Confusion; lethargy; combativeness; low body temperature and shivering; paradoxical feeling of warmth | IV fluids and rewarming; cardiac status must be carefully monitored; avoidance of alcohol |
| Incest and sexual abuse of a child | Suicidal behavior; adolescent crises; substance abuse | Corroboration of charge; protection of victim; contact social services; medical and psychiatric evaluation; crisis intervention |
| Insomnia | Depression and irritability; early morning agitation; frightening dreams; fatigue | Hypnotics only in short term; e.g., triazolam (Halcion), 0.25 to 0.5 mg, at bedtime; treat any underlying mental disorder; rules of sleep hygiene (Table 23.2–7) |
| Intermittent explosive disorder | Brief outbursts of violence; periodic episodes of suicide attempts | Benzodiazepines or antipsychotics for short term; long-term evaluation with computed tomography (CT) scan, sleep-deprived electroencephalogram (EEG), glucose tolerance curve |
| Jaundice | Uncommon complication of low-potency phenothiazine use (e.g., chlorpromazine) | Change drug to low dosage of a low-potency agent in a different class |
| Leukopenia and agranulocytosis | Side effects within the first two months of treatment with antipsychotics | Patient should call immediately for sore throat, fever, etc., and obtain immediate blood count; discontinue drug; hospitalize if necessary |
| Lithium toxicity | Vomiting; abdominal pain; profuse diarrhea; severe tremor, ataxia; coma; seizures; confusion; dysarthria; focal neurological signs | Lavage with wide-bore tube; osmotic diuresis; medical consultation; may require ICU treatment |

**Table 31.2–11**
*Continued*

| Syndrome | Emergency Manifestations | Treatment Issues |
|---|---|---|
| Major depressive episode with psychotic features | Major depressive episode symptoms with delusions; agitation, severe guilt; ideas of reference; suicide and homicide risk | Antipsychotics plus antidepressants; evaluation of suicide and homicide risk; hospitalization and ECT if necessary |
| Manic episode | Violent, impulsive behavior; indiscriminate sexual or spending behavior; psychosis; substance abuse | Hospitalization; restraints if necessary; rapid tranquilization with antipsychotics; restoration of lithium levels |
| Marital crises | Precipitant may be discovery of an extramarital affair, onset of serious illness, announcement of intent to divorce, or problems with children or work; one or both members of the couple may be in therapy or may be psychiatrically ill; one spouse may be seeking hospitalization for the other | Each should be questioned alone regarding extramarital affairs, consultations with lawyers regarding divorce, and willingness to work in crisis-oriented or long-term therapy to resolve the problem; sexual, financial, and psychiatric treatment histories from both, psychiatric evaluation at the time of presentation; may be precipitated by onset of untreated mood disorder or affective symptoms caused by medical illness or insidious-onset dementia; referral for management of the illness reduces immediate stress and enhances the healthier spouse's coping capacity; children may give insights available only to someone intimately involved in the social system |
| Migraine | Throbbing, unilateral headache | Sumatriptan (Imitrex) 6 mg IM |
| Mitral valve prolapse | Associated with panic disorder; dyspnea and palpitations; fear and anxiety | Echocardiogram; alprazolam or propranolol |
| Neuroleptic malignant syndrome | Hyperthermia; muscle rigidity; autonomic instability; parkinsonian symptoms; catatonic stupor; neurological signs; 10 to 30 percent fatality; elevated creatine phosphokinase | Discontinue antipsychotic; IV dantrolene (Dantrium); bromocriptine (Parlodel) orally; hydration and cooling; monitor CPK levels |
| Nitrous oxide toxicity | Euphoria and light-headedness | Symptoms abate without treatment within hours of use |
| Nutmeg intoxication | Agitation; hallucinations; severe headaches; numbness in extremities | Symptoms abate within hours of use without treatment |
| Opioid intoxication and withdrawal | Intoxication can lead to coma and death; withdrawal is not life-threatening | IV naloxone, narcotic antagonist; urine and serum screens; psychiatric and medical illnesses (e.g., AIDS) may complicate picture |
| Panic disorder | Panic, terror; acute onset | Must differentiate from other anxiety-producing disorders, both medical and psychiatric; ECG to rule out mitral valve prolapse; propranolol (10 to 30 mg); alprazolam (0.25 to 2.0 mg); long-term management may include an antidepressant |
| Paranoid schizophrenia | Command hallucinations; threat to others or themselves | Rapid tranquilization; hospitalization; long-acting depot medication; threatened persons must be notified and protected |
| Parkinsonism | Stiffness, tremor, bradykinesia, flattened affect, shuffling gait, salivation, secondary to antipsychotic medication | Oral antiparkinsonian drug for four weeks to three months; decrease dosage of the antipsychotic |
| Perioral (rabbit) tremor | Perioral tremor (rabbitlike facial grimacing) usually appearing after long-term therapy with antipsychotics | Decrease dosage or change to a medication in another class |
| Phencyclidine (or related substance) intoxication | Paranoid psychosis; can lead to death; acute danger to self and others | Serum and urine assay; benzodiazepines may interfere with excretion; antipsychotics may worsen symptoms because of anticholinergic side effects; medical monitoring and hospitalization for severe intoxication |
| Phenelzine psychotic disorder | Psychosis and mania in predisposed people | Reduce dosage or discontinue drug |

**Table 31.2–11**
*Continued*

| Syndrome | Emergency Manifestations | Treatment Issues |
|---|---|---|
| Phenylpropanolamine toxicity | Psychosis; paranoia; insomnia; restlessness; nervousness; headache | Symptoms abate with dosage reduction or discontinuation (found in over-the-counter diet aids and oral and nasal decongestants) |
| Phobias | Panic, anxiety; fear | Treatment same as for panic disorder |
| Photosensitivity | Easy sunburning secondary to use of antipsychotic medication | Patient should avoid strong sunlight and use high-level sunscreens |
| Pigmentary retinopathy | Reported with dosages of thioridazine (Mellaril) equal to or greater than 800 mg a day | Remain below 800 mg a day of thioridazine |
| Postpartum psychosis | Childbirth can precipitate schizophrenia, depression, reactive psychoses, mania, and depression; affective symptoms are most common; suicide risk is reduced during pregnancy but increased in the postpartum period | Danger to self and others (including infant) must be evaluated and proper precautions taken; medical illness presenting with behavioral aberrations is included in the differential diagnosis and must be sought and treated; care must be paid to the effects on father, infant, grandparents, and other children |
| Posttraumatic stress disorder | Panic, terror; suicidal ideation; flashbacks | Reassurance; encouragement of return to responsibilities; avoid hospitalization if possible to prevent chronic invalidism; monitor suicidal ideation |
| Priapism (trazodone [Desyrel]-induced) | Persistent penile erection accompanied by severe pain | Intracorporeal epinephrine; mechanical or surgical drainage |
| Propranolol toxicity | Profound depression; confusional states | Reduce dosage or discontinue drug; monitor suicidality |
| Rape | Not all sexual violations are reported; silent rape reaction is characterized by loss of appetite, sleep disturbance, anxiety, and, sometimes, agoraphobia; long periods of silence, mounting anxiety, stuttering, blocking, and physical symptoms during the interview when the sexual history is taken; fear of violence and death and of contracting a sexually transmitted disease or being pregnant | Rape is a major psychiatric emergency; victim may have enduring patterns of sexual dysfunction; crisis-oriented therapy, social support, ventilation, reinforcement of healthy traits, and encouragement to return to the previous level of functioning as rapidly as possible; legal counsel; thorough medical examination and tests to identify the assailant (e.g., obtaining samples of pubic hairs with a pubic hair comb, vaginal smear to identify blood antigens in semen); if a woman, methoxyprogesterone or diethylstilbestrol orally for five days to prevent pregnancy; if menstruation does not commence within one week of cessation of the estrogen, all alternatives to pregnancy, including abortion, should be offered; if the victim has contracted a venereal disease, appropriate antibiotics; witnessed written permission is required for the physician to examine, photograph, collect specimens, and release information to the authorities; obtain consent, record the history in the patient's own words, obtain required tests, record the results of the examination, save all clothing, defer diagnosis, and provide protection against disease, psychic trauma, and pregnancy; men's and women's responses to rape affectively are reported similarly, although men are more hesitant to talk about the assault, particularly if it was homosexual, for fear they will be assumed to have consented |
| Reserpine intoxication | Major depressive episode; suicidal ideation; nightmares | Evaluation of suicidal ideation; lower dosage or change drug; antidepressants or ECT may be indicated |

**Table 31.2–11**
*Continued*

| Syndrome | Emergency Manifestations | Treatment Issues |
|---|---|---|
| Schizoaffective disorder | Severe depression; manic symptoms; paranoia | Evaluation of dangerousness to self or others; rapid tranquilization if necessary; treatment of depression (antidepressants alone can enhance schizophrenic symptoms); use of antimanic agents |
| Schizophrenia | Extreme self-neglect; severe paranoia; suicidal ideation or assaultiveness; extreme psychotic symptoms | Evaluation of suicidal and homicidal potential; identification of any illness other than schizophrenia; rapid tranquilization |
| Schizophrenia in exacerbation | Withdrawn; agitation; suicidal and homicidal risk | Suicide and homicide evaluation; screen for medical illness; restraints and rapid tranquilization if necessary; hospitalization if necessary; reevaluation of medication regimen |
| Sedative, hypnotic, or anxiolytic intoxication and withdrawal | Alterations in mood, behavior, thought—delirium; derealization and depersonalization; untreated, can be fatal; seizures | Naloxone (Narcan) to differentiate from opioid intoxication; slow withdrawal with phenobarbital (Luminal) or sodium thiopental or benzodiazepine; hospitalization |
| Seizure disorder | Confusion; anxiety; derealization and depersonalization; feelings of impending doom; gustatory or olfactory hallucinations; fugue-like state | Immediate EEG; admission and sleep-deprived and 24-hour EEG; rule out pseudoseizures; anticonvulsants |
| Substance withdrawal | Abdominal pain; insomnia, drowsiness; delirium; seizures; symptoms of tardive dyskinesia may emerge; eruption of manic or schizophrenic symptoms | Symptoms of psychotropic drug withdrawal disappear with time and disappear with reinstitution of the substance; symptoms of antidepressant withdrawal can be successfully treated with anticholinergic agents, such as atropine; gradual withdrawal of psychotropic substances over two to four weeks generally obviates development of symptoms |
| Sudden death associated with antipsychotic medication | Seizures; asphyxiation; cardiovascular causes; postural hypotension; laryngeal-pharyngeal dystonia; suppression of gag reflex | Specific medical treatments |
| Sudden death of psychogenic origin | Myocardial infarction after sudden psychic stress; voodoo and hexes; hopelessness, especially associated with serious physical illness | Specific medical treatments; folk healers |
| Suicide | Suicidal ideation; hopelessness | Hospitalization, antidepressants |
| Sympathomimetic withdrawal | Paranoia; confessional states; depression | Most symptoms abate without treatment; antipsychotics; antidepressants if necessary |
| Tardive dyskinesia | Dyskinesia of mouth, tongue, face, neck, and trunk; choreoathetoid movements of extremities; usually but not always appearing after long-term treatment with antipsychotics, especially after a reduction in dosage; incidence highest in the elderly and brain-damaged; symptoms are intensified by antiparkinsonian drugs and masked but not cured by increased dosages of antipsychotic | No effective treatment reported; may be prevented by prescribing the least amount of drug possible for as little time as is clinically feasible and using drug-free holidays for patients who need to continue taking the drug; decrease or discontinue drug at first sign of dyskinetic movements |
| Thyrotoxicosis | Tachycardia; gastrointestinal dysfunction; hyperthermia; panic, anxiety, agitation; mania; dementia; psychosis | Thyroid function test ($T_3$, $T_4$, thyroid-stimulating hormone [TSH]); medical consultation |
| Toluene abuse | Anxiety; confusion; cognitive impairment | Neurological damage is nonprogressive and reversible if toluene use is discontinued early |
| Vitamin $B_{12}$ deficiency | Confusion; mood and behavior changes; ataxia | Treatment with vitamin $B_{12}$ |
| Volatile nitrates | Alternations of mood and behavior; light-headedness; pulsating headache | Symptoms abate with cessation of use |

Bassuk E L, Birk A W, editors: *Emergency Psychiatry: Concepts, Methods, and Practices.* Plenum, New York, 1984.

Bellack L, Siegel H: *The Handbook of Intensive Brief and Emergency Psychiatry.* C.R.S., Larchmont, N Y, 1983.

Boyer W F, Bakalar N H, Lake C R: Anticholinergic prophylaxis of acute haloperidol-induced acute dystonic reactions. J Clin Psychopharmacol 7: 264, 1987.

Brown G L, Linnoila M I: CSF serotonin metabolite (5-HIAA) studies in depression, impulsivity, and violence. J Clin Psychiatry *51* (4, Suppl): 31, 1990.

Dubin W R, Stolberg R: *Emergency Psychiatry for the House Officer.* SP Medical & Scientific, New York, 1981.

Ellison J M, Blum N R, Barsky A J: Frequent repeaters in a psychiatric emergency service. Hosp Community Psychiatry *40*: 958, 1989.

Ellison J M, Hughes D H, White K A: An emergency psychiatry update. Hosp Community Psychiatry *40*: 250, 1989.

Emery R E: Family violence. Am Psychol *44*: 321, 1989.

Faulstick, M E: Psychiatric aspects of AIDS. Am J Psychiatry *144*: 511, 1987.

Fauman B J, Fauman M A: *Emergency Psychiatry for the House Officer.* Williams & Wilkins, Baltimore, 1981.

Frommer D A, Kulig K W, Mark J A, Rumack B: Tricyclic antidepressant overdose: A review. JAMA *257*: 521, 1987.

Hanke N: *Handbook of Emergency Psychiatry.* Health, Lexington, Mass, 1984.

Hillard J R, editor: *Manual of Clinical Emergency Psychiatry.* American Psychiatric Press, Washington, 1990.

Hyman S E, editor: *Manual of Psychiatric Emergencies,* ed 2. Little, Brown, Boston, 1988.

Marson D C, McGovern M P, Pomp H C: Psychiatric decision making in the emergency room: A research overview. Am J Psychiatry *145*: 918, 1988.

Monahan J, Shah S A: Dangerousness and commitment of the mentally disordered in the United States. Schizophr Bull *15*: 541, 1989.

Nicholi A M: The nontherapeutic use of psychoactive drugs. N Engl J Med *108*: 925, 1983.

Puryear D A, Lovitt R, Miller D A: Characteristics of elderly persons seen in an urban psychiatric emergency room. Hosp Community Psychiatry *42*: 802, 1991.

Rosenberg R C, Kesselman M: The therapeutic alliance and the psychiatric emergency room. Hosp Community Psychiatry *44*: 78, 1993.

Sanguineti V R, Brooks M O: Factors related to emergency commitment of chronically mentally ill patients who are substance abusers. Hosp Community Psychiatry *43*: 237, 1992.

Slaby A E: Other psychiatric emergencies. In *Comprehensive Textbook of Psychiatry,* ed 5, H I Kaplan, B J Sadock, editors, p 1427. Williams & Wilkins, Baltimore, 1989.

Szuster R R, Schanbacher B L, McCann S C: Characteristics of psychiatric emergency room patients with alcohol- or drug-induced disorders. Hosp Community Psychiatry *41*: 1342, 1990.

Tancredi L R: Emergency psychiatry and crisis intervention: Some legal and ethical issues. Psychiatr Ann *12*: 799, 1982.

Thienhaus O J: Rational physical evaluation in the emergency room. Hosp Community Psychiatry *43*: 311, 1992.

Thienhaus O J, Rowe C, Woellert P, Hillard J R: Geropsychiatric emergency services: Utilization and outcome predictors. Hosp Community Psychiatry *39*: 1301, 1988.

Waller F S: Hospital and room security: The next decade. J Health Prot Manage *7*: 43, 1991.

Weissberg M: Chained in the emergency department: The new asylum for the poor. Hosp Community Psychiatry *42*: 317, 1991.

# Psychotherapies

## 32.1 / Psychoanalysis and Psychoanalytic Psychotherapy

The problems that take people to psychiatrists for treatment are of two kinds: those that seem to have their origins largely in the remote past of patients' lives and those that seem to arise largely from current stresses and pressures that seem beyond the patients' conscious control. However, current external stresses may occur in combination with older problems, and some patients who have old but still active and unsolved problems may arrange their lives in such a way that they appear to be the victims of current life situations.

When a patient's problem stems mainly from the past with relatively little contribution from the present, psychoanalysis may well be the treatment of choice. During classic psychoanalysis, regressive patterns often appear in the patient's feelings and fantasies toward the psychoanalyst. Those patterns provide the necessary ingress into the past.

Psychoanalytic therapy uses the theoretical framework provided by psychoanalysis, but its therapeutic goals are less extensive than the goals of psychoanalysis, and it uses some techniques that are not part of the analytic model. Current interpersonal and intrapsychic dynamics are likely to receive the greatest emphasis in psychoanalytic therapy, and there is less concern with detailed reconstructions of the patient's past life. The contrast, however, between the historical and the current loses its sharp outline in the treatment of the individual patient.

Psychoanalysis and the analytic psychotherapies, uniquely among the available therapies, provide a theoretical and clinical framework for investigating the richly complex and multidetermined psychological forces (psychodynamics) that shape human development—from motivation, impulse, and conflict to attachment, intimacy, and the nature of self-esteem. Table 32.1–1 summarizes the steps involved in formulating a psychodynamic assessment of a patient.

Tables 32.1–2 and 32.1–3 briefly outline the differences between classic psychoanalysis and psychoanalytically oriented psychotherapy.

## PSYCHOANALYSIS

Psychoanalysis began with the treatment of patients by hypnosis. In 1881 Anna O, a neurotic young woman who suffered from multiple visual and motor disturbances and alterations of consciousness, was treated by the Viennese internist Josef Breuer. He observed that the patient's symptoms disappeared when she expressed them verbally while hypnotized. Sigmund Freud used the technique with Breuer, and they reported their findings in 1895 in *Studies on Hysteria*. They explained hysteria (now called conversion disorder) as the result of a traumatic experience, which was usually sexual in nature and associated with a large quantity of affect, that was barred from consciousness and that expressed itself in a disguised form through various symptoms. Freud eventually gave up placing his patients in a hypnotic trance; instead, he urged them to recline on a couch and concentrate with their eyes closed on past memories related to their symptoms. That concentration method eventually became the technique of free association. Freud instructed his patients to say whatever came into their minds, without censoring any of their thoughts. That method is still used today and is one of the hallmarks of psychoanalysis, through which thoughts and feelings that are kept in the unconscious are brought into consciousness.

In *The Interpretation of Dreams* Freud described the topographical model of the mind as consisting of a conscious, preconscious, and unconscious. The conscious mind was conceptualized as awareness; the preconscious, as thoughts and feelings that are easily available to consciousness; and the unconscious, as thoughts and feelings that cannot be made conscious without overcoming strong resistances. The unconscious contains nonverbal forms of thought function and gives rise to dreams, parapraxes (slips of the tongue), and psychological symptoms. Psychoanalysis emphasizes the conflict between unconscious drives and moral judgments that patients may make about their impulses. That conflict accounts for the phenomenon of repression, which is regarded as pathological. Free association allows repressed memories to be recovered and thereby contributes to cure.

In 1923 Freud described his structural theory of the mind in *The Ego and the Id*. He saw the ego as a group of functions accessible to consciousness that mediate among the demands of the id, the superego, and the environment. He viewed anxiety as the ego's reaction to the threatened breakthrough of forbidden impulses. Figure 32.1–1 is a schematic rendering of Freud's structural model.

Modern advances in psychoanalysis have focused on the increased understanding of the ego's functions (ego psychol-

**Table 32.1–1**
**Psychodynamic Assessment**

Historical data
  Present illness with attention to associative linkages and
    Axis IV stressors
History with emphasis on how the past is repeating itself in the
  present
  Developmental history
  Family history
  Cultural-religious background
Mental status examination
  Orientation and perception
  Cognition
  Affect
  Action
Projective psychological testing (if necessary)
Physical and neurological examination
Psychodynamic diagnosis
  Descriptive DSM-IV diagnosis
  Interactions among Axes I–V
  Characteristics of the ego
    Strengths and weaknesses
    Defense mechanisms and conflicts
    Relation to superego
  Quality of object relations
    Family relationships
    Transference-countertransference patterns
    Inferences about internal object relations
  Characteristics of the self
    Self-esteem and self-cohesiveness
    Self-continuity
    Self-boundaries
    Mind-body relation
  Explanatory formulation using above data

Table from G O Gabbard: *Psychodynamic Psychiatry in Clinical Practice*, p 67. American Psychiatric Press, Washington, 1990. Used with permission.

**Table 32.1–2**
**Psychoanalysis**

| | |
|---|---|
| Goal | Resolution of the childhood neurosis as it presents itself in the transference neurosis |
| Selection criteria | Primarily oedipal conflict |
| | Experiences internal conflict |
| | Obtains symptom relief through understanding |
| | Psychologically minded |
| | Able to experience and observe strong affects without acting out |
| | Supportive relationships available in both the present and the past |
| Duration | Four or five sessions a week |
| | Three to six years, average duration |
| Techniques | Free association |
| | Therapeutic alliance |
| | Neutrality |
| | Abstinence |
| | Defense analysis |
| | Interpretation of transference |

Table from R J Ursano, E K Silberman: Individual psychotherapies. In *The American Psychiatric Press Textbook of Psychiatry*, J A Talbott, R E Hales, S C Yudofsky, editors, p 858. American Psychiatric Press, Washington, 1988. Used with permission.

ogy), the role of early relationships (object relations), and the relationship between the analyst and the patient (transference and countertransference).

**Table 32.1–3**
**Intensive (Long-Term) Psychoanalytically Oriented Psychotherapy**

| | |
|---|---|
| Goal | Defense and transference analysis with limited reconstruction of the past |
| Selection criteria | When a narrower focus and less comprehensive outcome is acceptable, the same selection criteria as in psychoanalysis are used |
| | Seriously disturbed patients who can use understanding to resolve symptoms when some supportive elements are available in the treatment |
| Duration | Two or three sessions a week for one to six years on average |
| Techniques | Therapeutic alliance |
| | Face-to-face |
| | Free association |
| | Defense and transference interpretation |
| | More use of clarification, suggestion, and learning through experience than in psychoanalysis |
| | Medications |

Table from R J Ursano, E K Silberman: Individual psychotherapies. In *The American Psychiatric Press Textbook of Psychiatry*, J A Talbott, R E Hales, S C Yudofsky, editors, p 860. American Psychiatric Press, Washington, 1988. Used with permission.

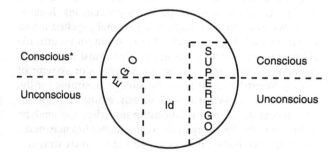

**Figure 32.1–1.** Freud's structural model. (Figure from G O Gabbard: *Psychodynamic Psychiatry in Clinical Practice*, p 21. American Psychiatric Press, Washington, 1990. Used with permission.)

## Goal

The chief requirement of psychoanalysis is the gradual integration of the previously repressed material into the total structure of the personality. It is a slow process, requiring the analyst to maintain a balance between the interpretation of unconscious material and the patient's ability to deal with increased awareness. If the work proceeds too rapidly, the patient may experience the analysis as a new trauma. The work of analysis initially is preparing the patient to deal with the anxiety-producing material that has been uncovered. The patient is taught to be aware of innermost thoughts and feelings and to recognize the natural resistances to the mind's willingness or ability to deal directly with noxious psychic material. The patient and the analyst seldom follow a straight path to insight. Instead, the process of analysis is more like putting together pieces of an immense and complicated jigsaw puzzle.

## Analytic Setting

The usual analytic setting is for the patient to lie on a couch or sofa and the analyst to sit behind, partially or totally outside the patient's field of vision. The couch helps the analyst produce the controlled regression that favors the emergence of repressed material. The patient's reclining position in the presence of an attentive analyst almost re-creates symbolically the early parent-child situation, which varies from patient to patient. The position also helps the patient focus on inner thoughts, feelings, and fantasies, which can then become the focus of free associations. Moreover, the use of the couch introduces an element of sensory deprivation because the patient's visual stimuli are limited and the analyst's verbalizations are relatively few. That state promotes regression. There has been some disagreement, however, about the use of the couch as always characteristic of psychoanalysis. Otto Fenichel stated that whether the patient lies down or sits and whether certain rituals of procedure are used do not matter. The best condition is the one most appropriate to the analytic task.

## Role of the Analyst

For the most part, the analyst's activity is limited to timely interpretation of the patient's associations. Ideally, analysts—who have undergone a personal psychoanalysis as part of their training—are able to maintain an attitude of benevolent objectivity or neutrality toward the patient, trying not to impose their own personalities or systems of values. Nevertheless, it is not possible or desirable for the analyst to be a so-called blank screen, *tabula rasa*, or analyst incognito. A real relationship underlies the analytic setting, and the handling of the real relationship may make the difference between success and failure in treatment.

## Duration of Treatment

The patient and the psychoanalyst must be prepared to persevere in the process for an indefinite period. Psychoanalysis takes time—between three and six years, sometimes even longer. Sessions are usually held four or more times a week for 45 to 50 minutes each. Some analyses are conducted with less frequency and with the sessions varying from 20 to 30 minutes. The French psychoanalyst Jacques Lacan introduced sessions of variable length (3 to 45 minutes), which he believed to be equally effective.

## Treatment Methods

**Fundamental rule of psychoanalysis.** The fundamental or basic rule is that the patient agrees to be completely honest with the analyst and to tell everything without selection. Freud referred to the technique that allowed for such honesty as free association.

**Free association.** In free association, patients say everything that comes to mind without any censoring, regardless of whether they believe the thought to be unacceptable, unimportant, or embarrassing. Associations are directed by three kinds of unconscious forces: the patho-genic conflicts of the neurosis, the wish to get well, and the wish to please the analyst. The interplay among those factors becomes complex. For example, a thought or an impulse that is unacceptable to patients and that is a part of their neuroses may conflict with their wishes to please the analyst, who, they assume, also finds the impulse unacceptable. But if patients follow the fundamental rule, they overcome the resistance.

**Free-floating attention.** The analysts' counterpart to the patients' free association is a special way of listening called free-floating attention. Analysts allow the patients' associations to stimulate their own associations and are thereby able to discern a theme in the patients' free associations that may be reflected back to the patients then or at some later time. Analysts' careful attention to their own subjective experiences is an indispensable part of analysis.

**Rule of abstinence.** By following the rule of abstinence, the patient is able to delay gratifying any instinctual wishes so as to talk about them in treatment. The tension thus engendered produces relevant associations that the analyst uses to increase the patient's awareness. The rule does not refer to sexual abstinence but, rather, to not allowing the treatment setting to gratify the patient's infantile longing for love and affection.

## Analytic Process

**Transference.** A major criterion by which psychoanalysis can be differentiated in principle from other forms of psychotherapy is the management of the transference. Indeed, psychoanalysis has been defined as the analysis of transference.

Transference was first described by Freud and concerns the patient's feelings and behavior toward the analyst that are based on infantile wishes the patient has toward parents or parental figures. Those feelings are unconscious but are revealed in the transference neurosis, in which patients struggle to gratify their unconscious infantile wishes through the analyst. The transference may be positive, in which the analyst needs to be seen as a person of exceptional worth, ability, and character; or it may be negative, in which the analyst becomes the embodiment of what the patient experienced or feared from parental figures in the past. Negative transferences can be expressed and experienced in highly labile and volatile ways, especially in patients whose personalities are described as borderline or narcissistic. Both situations reflect the patient's need to repeat unresolved childhood conflicts.

The analyst's role is to help the patient gain true insight into the distortions of transference and, through insight, to increase the patient's capacity for gratifying relationships based on mature and realistic expectations, rather than on irrational, childhood-derived fantasies.

**Interpretation.** In psychoanalysis the analyst provides the patient with interpretations about psychological events that were neither previously understood by the patient nor meaningful to the patient. The transference constitutes a major frame of reference for interpretation. A complete psychoanalytic interpretation includes meaningful statements of current conflicts and the historical factors that influenced them. However, complete interpretations of that kind constitute a relatively small part of the analysis. Most interpretations are limited in scope and deal with matters of immediate concern.

Interpretations must be well-timed. The analyst may have a formulation in mind, but the patient may not be prepared to deal with it directly because of a variety of factors, such as anxiety level, negative transference, and external life stress. The analyst may decide to wait until the patient can fully understand the interpretation. The proper timing of interpretations requires great clinical skill.

DREAM INTERPRETATION. In his classic work *The Interpretation of Dreams,* Freud referred to the dream as the "royal road to the unconscious." The *manifest content* of a dream is what the dreamer reports. The *latent content* is the unconscious meaning of the dream after the condensations, substitutions, and symbols are analyzed. The dream arises from what Freud referred to as the *day's residue* (that is, the events of the preceding day that stimulated the patient's unconscious mind). Dreams may serve as a wish-fulfillment mechanism and as a way of mastering anxiety about a life event.

Freud outlined several technical procedures to use in dream interpretation: (1) have the patient associate to elements of the dream in the order in which they occurred; (2) have the patient associate to a particular dream element that the patient or the therapist chooses; (3) disregard the content of the dream, and ask the patient what events of the previous day could be associated with the dream (the day's residue); and (4) avoid giving any instructions, and leave it to the dreamer to begin. The analyst uses the patient's associations to find a clue to the workings of the unconscious mind.

**Countertransference.** Just as the term "transference" is used to encompass the patient's total range of feelings for and against the analyst, "countertransference" encompasses a broad spectrum of the analyst's reactions to the patient. Countertransference has unconscious components based on conflicts of which the analyst is not aware. Ideally, the analyst ought to be aware of countertransference issues, which may interfere with the analyst's ability to remain detached and objective. The analyst should remove such impediments by either further analysis or self-analysis. However, with some patients or groups of patients, a particular analyst does not work well, and the experienced clinician, recognizing that fact, refers such patients to a colleague.

**Therapeutic alliance.** In addition to transferential and countertransferential issues, a real relationship between the analyst and the patient involves two adults entering into a joint venture, referred to as the therapeutic or working alliance. Both commit themselves to exploring the patient's problems, to establishing mutual trust, and to cooperating with each other to achieve a realistic goal of cure or the amelioration of symptoms.

**Resistance.** Freud believed that unconscious ideas or impulses are repressed and prevented from reaching awareness because they are unacceptable to consciousness for some reason. He referred to that phenomenon as resistance, which has to be overcome if the analysis is to proceed. Resistance may sometimes be a conscious process manifested by withholding relevant information. Other examples of resistance are remaining silent for a long time, being late or missing appointments, and paying bills late

or not at all. The signs of resistance are legion, and almost any feature of the analytic situation can be used in resistance. Freud once said that any treatment can be considered psychoanalysis that works by undoing resistance and interpreting transferences.

## Indications for Treatment

The primary indications for psychoanalysis are long-standing psychological conflicts that have produced a symptom or disorder. The connection between the conflict and the symptom may be direct or indirect. Psychoanalysis is considered effective in treating certain anxiety disorders, such as phobias and obsessive-compulsive disorder, mild depressive disorders (dysthymic disorder), some personality disorders, and some impulse control and sexual disorders. More important than diagnosis, however, is the patient's ability to form an analytic pact and to maintain a commitment to a progressively deepening analytic process that brings about internal change through increasing self-awareness. Freud believed that the patient also has to be able to form a strong transference attachment to the analyst (termed *transference neurosis*), without which analysis is not possible. That excluded most psychotic patients because of the difficulty they have in forming the affective and realistic bonds that are essential to the development and the resolution of the transference neurosis. The ego of a patient in analysis must be able to tolerate frustration without responding with some serious form of acting out or shifting from one pathological pattern to another. That excludes most substance-dependent patients, who are regarded as unsuitable because their egos are unable to tolerate the frustrations and the emotional demands of psychoanalysis.

## Contraindications for Treatment

The various contraindications to psychoanalysis are relative, but each must be considered before embarking on a course of treatment.

**Age.** Traditionally, many analysts believed that most adults over age 40 lack sufficient flexibility for major personality changes. However, most analysts now believe that more important than age is the patient's individual capacity for thoughtful introspection and desire for change. The ideal candidates are generally young adults. Children are unable to follow the rule of free association, but, with modifications of technique (for example, play therapy), they have been successfully analyzed.

**Intelligence.** Patients must be intelligent enough to be able to understand the procedure and to cooperate in the process.

**Life circumstances.** If the patient's life situation cannot be modified, analysis may only make it worse. For example, it can be hazardous to create goals for patients who are unable to fulfill them because of external limitations.

**Antisocial personality disorder.** Clinicians and researchers seem to agree that the absence of relatedness to others is the single most negative predictor of psychotherapy response. The true antisocial personality is a person who may benefit from certain types of therapy, such as group therapy with other antisocial personalities, but who is not suited for analytically oriented psychotherapy. J. R. Meloy defined five clinical features that contraindicate any attempt at psychotherapy. Table 32.1–4 summarizes those features.

Meloy believed that sadistic cruelty to others, total absence of remorse, and lack of emotional attachment are the key distinguishing features that lead to an inability to engage in therapy. Also, countertransference fears often paralyze therapists, making therapy impossible. An extremely intelligent person with antisocial personality disorder can be expert at sabotaging therapy; and a mildly retarded antisocial personality may not have the cognitive ability to engage in the psychoanalysis.

**Time constraints.** Unless the patient has time to participate and to wait for change, another type of therapy should be considered. The constraint applies especially to emergency symptoms and to those that the patient can no longer tolerate, including those that are dangerous (for example, strong suicidal impulses).

**Nature of the relationship.** The analysis of friends, relatives, and acquaintances is contraindicated because it distorts the transference and the analyst's objectivity.

**Other contraindications.** Some patients work better with some analysts than with others. Sometimes that determination can be made after a single consultation, but often a trial analysis of several sessions may be necessary. That time also allows patients to see whether they wish to continue. Experience has shown that it does not matter whether the analyst is a man or a woman, although some patients may initially prefer to see one or the other, a preference that is eventually understood as the analysis proceeds.

### Dynamics of Therapeutic Results

The process of cure or improvement involves the release of repression safely and effectively. The structural apparatus of the mind—id, ego, and superego—are modified. The ego is able to deal with repressed impulses and is finally in a position to accept or renounce them.

---

**Table 32.1–4**
**Clinical Features That Contraindicate Psychotherapy of Any Kind**

---

1. A history of sadistic, violent behavior toward others that resulted in serious injury or death
2. A total absence of remorse or rationalization for such behavior
3. Intelligence that is in either the very superior or the mildly mentally retarded range
4. A historical incapacity to develop emotional attachments to others
5. An intense countertransference fear of predation on the part of experienced clinicians even without clear precipitating behavior on the part of the patient

---

Table based on J R Meloy: *The Psychopathic Mind: Origins, Dynamics and Treatment*. Aronson, Northvale, N J, 1988.
Table from G O Gabbard: *Psychodynamic Psychiatry in Clinical Practice*, p 417. American Psychiatric Press, Washington, 1990. Used with permission.

Analysis helps reduce the intensity of the conflicts and helps find acceptable ways of handling impulses that cannot be reduced. Instead of an acceptable method of channeling unmodified infantile strivings, the drives' primary-process quality itself is lessened, and they become adapted to reality. The ultimate goal is the elimination of symptoms, thereby increasing the patient's capacity for work, enjoyment, and self-understanding.

Few long-term outcome studies of psychoanalysis have been conducted because of the complex patient-therapist variables. Nevertheless, psychoanalysis is thought to be effective under some circumstances for many disorders.

## PSYCHOANALYTIC PSYCHOTHERAPY

Psychoanalytic psychotherapy is therapy based on psychoanalytic formulations that have been modified conceptually and technically. Unlike psychoanalysis, which has as its ultimate concern the uncovering and the subsequent working through of infantile conflicts as they arise in the transference neurosis, psychoanalytic psychotherapy takes as its focus the patients' current conflicts and current dynamic patterns—that is, the analysis of the patients' problems with other persons and with themselves. Also unlike psychoanalysis, which has as its technique the use of free association and the analysis of the transference neurosis, psychoanalytic psychotherapy is characterized by interviewing and discussion techniques that infrequently use free association. And again unlike psychoanalysis, psychoanalytic psychotherapy usually limits its work on transference to a discussion of the patient's reactions to the psychiatrist and others. The reaction to the psychiatrist is not interpreted to as great a degree as it is in psychoanalysis. Nevertheless, transference attitudes and responses to the therapist may arise from time to time and can be used productively. For example, spontaneous transferences in the therapeutic situation may give valuable clues to patients' behavior in extratherapeutic situations and, at times, to their childhood. Those transferences may tell the therapist the probable focus for the patient at any given time, inside or outside the treatment relationship.

### Treatment Techniques

One way in which psychoanalytic psychotherapy differs from classical psychoanalysis is that the former does not usually use a couch. The stimulation of temporary regressive patterns of feeling and thinking, which is valuable to psychoanalysis, is much less necessary in psychoanalytic psychotherapy, with its focus on current dynamic patterns. In psychoanalytic psychotherapy the patient and the therapist are usually in full view of each other, which may make the therapist seem real and not a composite of projected fantasies. That type of therapy is much more flexible than psychoanalysis, and it may be used in conjunction with psychotropic medication more often than is psychoanalysis.

Psychoanalytic psychotherapy can range from a single supportive interview, centering on a current but pressing problem, to many years of treatment, with one to three interviews a week of varying length. In contrast to psychoanalysis, psychoanalytic psychotherapy treats most of the disorders in the field of psychopathology.

## Types

Many clinicians and researchers have conceptualized the types of psychotherapies as occurring along a spectrum, with expressive (insight-oriented) therapies, such as psychoanalysis and analytically oriented therapies, at one end of the spectrum and supportive therapies at the other end. The Menninger Clinic Treatment Intervention Project has indicated that therapist intervention can be placed in seven categories along an expressive (insight-oriented)-support-ive continuum. Figure 32.1–2 summarizes that intervention continuum. Table 32.1–5 summarizes the Menninger group's definitions of the terms.

**Insight-oriented psychotherapy.** Insight is patients' understanding of their psychological functioning and personalities. The clinician should specify the area or the level of understanding or experience into which the patient is to achieve insight. The psychiatrist's emphasis in insight-oriented therapy (also called expressive therapy and intensive psychoanalytic psychotherapy) is on the value to patients of gaining a number of new insights into the current dynamics of their feelings, responses, behavior, and, especially, current relationships with other persons. To a smaller extent the emphasis is on the value of developing

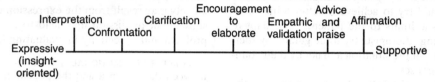

**Figure 32.1–2.** An expressive (insight-oriented)-supportive continuum of interventions. (Figure from G O Gabbard: *Psycho-dynamic Psychiatry in Clinical Practice*, p 78. American Psychiatric Press, Washington, 1990. Used with permission.)

**Table 32.1–5**
**Psychotherapeutic Interventions Defined**

1. *Interpretation.* In the most expressive forms of treatment, interpretation is regarded as the therapist's ultimate decisive instrument. In its simplest form, interpretation involves making something conscious that was previously unconscious. An interpretation is an explanatory statement that links a feeling, thought, behavior, or symptom to its unconscious meaning or origin. For example, the therapist might say to a patient who is late, "Perhaps the reason you are late is that you were afraid I would react to the success you are now having the way your father reacted." Depending on the point in therapy and the patient's readiness to hear the interpretation, interpretations may focus on the transference (as in that example), extratransference issues, the patient's past or present situation, or the patient's resistances or fantasies. As a general rule, the therapist does not address unconscious content by interpretation until the material is almost conscious and, therefore, relatively accessible to the patient's awareness.

2. *Confrontation.* The next most expressive intervention is confrontation, which addresses something the patient does not want to accept or identifies the patient's avoidance or minimization. A confrontation may be geared to clarifying how the patient's behavior affects others or to reflecting back to the patient a denied or suppressed feeling. Confrontation, which is often gentle, carries the unfortunate connotation in common parlance of being aggressive or blunt. The following example illustrates that confrontation is not necessarily forceful or hostile. In the last session of a long-term therapy process, one patient talked at great length about car problems he encountered on the way to the session. The therapist commented, "I think you'd rather talk about your car than face the sadness you're feeling about our last session."

3. *Clarification.* Further along the continuum from expressive to supportive interventions, clarification involves a reformulation or pulling together of the patient's verbalizations to convey a coherent view of what is being communicated. Clarification differs from confrontation because it lacks the element of denial or minimization. A clarification is aimed at helping the patient articulate something that is difficult to put into words.

4. *Encouragement to elaborate.* Closer to the center of the continuum come interventions that are neither supportive nor expressive in and of themselves. Encouragement to elaborate may be broadly defined as a request for information about a topic brought up by the patient. It may be an open-ended question, such as, "What comes to mind about that?" or a more specific request, as in, "Tell me more about your father." Such interventions are commonly used in both the most expressive and the most supportive treatments.

5. *Empathic validation.* This intervention is a demonstration of the therapist's empathic attunement with the patient's internal state. A typically validating comment is, "I can understand why you feel depressed about that," or "It hurts when you're treated that way." In the view of the self psychologists, empathic immersion in the patient's internal experience is essential, regardless of the location of the therapy on the expressive-supportive continuum. When patients feel that the therapist understands their subjective experiences, they are likely to accept interpretations.

6. *Advice and praise.* This category really includes two interventions that are linked by the fact that they both prescribe and reinforce certain activities. Advice involves direct suggestions to the patient regarding how to behave; praise reinforces certain patient behaviors by expressing overt approval of them. An example of the former is, "I think you should stop going out with that man immediately." An example of the latter is, "I'm very pleased that you were able to tell him that you would not see him anymore." Those comments are on the opposite end of the continuum from traditional psychoanalytic interventions because they are departures from neutrality and to some extent compromise the patient's autonomy in making decisions.

7. *Affirmation.* This simple intervention involves succinct comments in support of the patient's comments or behaviors, such as "Uh-huh," and "Yes, I see what you mean."

Table adapted from G O Gabbard: *Psychodynamic Psychiatry in Clinical Practice*, p 78. American Psychiatric Press, Washington, 1990. Used with permission.

some insight into patients' responses to the therapist and responses in childhood.

Insight-oriented therapy is the treatment of choice for a patient who has adequate ego strength but who, for one reason or another, should not or cannot undergo psychoanalysis.

The therapy's effectiveness does not depend solely on the insights developed or used. The patient's therapeutic response is also based on such factors as the ventilation of feelings in a nonjudgmental but limit-setting atmosphere, identification with the therapist, and other relationship factors. A therapeutic relationship does not require an indiscriminate acceptance of all that a patient says and does. At times, the therapist must intervene on the side of a relatively weak ego by giving unmistakable evidence that the patient could try to achieve a better adjustment or by setting realistic limits to the patients' maladaptive behavior. In so doing, therapists try to be guided by their dynamic assessments of the situation and not by their countertransference responses.

Inevitably, the therapists' attitudes and responses to the patient are different from those of important figures in the patient's childhood. At times, the therapist discusses those differences. Patients may come to see that they have generalized their parents' attitudes as being universal and have generalized their own responses, so that they have become automatic responses to all parental or significant figures.

Insight-oriented psychotherapy is frequently complicated by spontaneous strong transferences to the therapist that at times threaten to disrupt the treatment. The insight-oriented therapist must decide, on the basis of an understanding of each individual patient, how to respond to those transference reactions. If the patient is highly introspective and psychologically minded, the therapist may choose to make relatively deep transference interpretations (for example, relating the reactions to significant childhood fantasies). If the patient is fragile and not capable of tolerating an interpretation that is perceived as emotionally threatening, the therapist may choose to remain relatively superficial in approach (for example, relating the reactions to current, reality-based feelings).

**Supportive psychotherapy.** Supportive psychotherapy (also called relationship-oriented psychotherapy) offers the patient support by an authority figure during a period of illness, turmoil, or temporary decompensation. It also has the goal of restoring and strengthening the patient's defenses and integrating capacities that have been impaired. It provides a period of acceptance and dependence for a patient who is in need of help in dealing with guilt, shame, and anxiety and in meeting the frustrations or the external pressures that may be too great to handle.

Supportive therapy uses a number of methods, either singly or in combination, including (1) warm, friendly, strong leadership; (2) gratification of dependence needs; (3) support in the ultimate development of legitimate independence; (4) help in the development of pleasurable sublimations (for example, hobbies); (5) adequate rest and diversion; (6) the removal of excessive external strain if possible; (7) hospitalization when indicated; (8) medication to alleviate symptoms; and (9) guidance and advice in dealing with current issues. It uses the techniques that help the patient feel secure, accepted, protected, encouraged, and safe and not anxious.

One of the greatest dangers lies in the possibility of fostering too great a regression and too strong a dependence. From the beginning, the psychiatrist must plan to work persistently to enable the patient to assume independence. But some patients require supportive therapy indefinitely, often with just the goal of maintaining a marginal adjustment that enables them to function in society.

The expression of emotion is an important part of supportive psychotherapy. The verbalization of unexpressed strong emotions may bring considerable relief. The goal of such talking out is not primarily to gain insight into the unconscious dynamic patterns that may be intensifying current responses. Rather, the reduction of inner tension and anxiety may result from the expression of emotion, and its subsequent discussion may lead to insight into a current problem and objectivity in evaluating it.

CORRECTIVE EMOTIONAL EXPERIENCE. The relationship between the therapist and the patient gives the therapist an opportunity to display behavior different from the destructive or unproductive behavior of the patient's parents. At times, such experiences seem to neutralize or reverse some of the effects of the parents' mistakes. If the patient had overly authoritarian parents, the therapist's friendly, flexible, nonjudgmental, nonauthoritarian—but at times firm and limit-setting—attitude means that the patient has an opportunity to adjust to, be led by, and identify with a new type of parent figure. Franz Alexander called that process a corrective emotional experience.

Supportive psychotherapy is suitable for a variety of psychogenic illnesses. For example, it may be useful when a patient resists an expressive psychotherapy or is considered too emotionally disturbed for such a procedure. Supportive therapy may be chosen when the diagnostic assessment indicates that a gradual maturing process, based on the elaboration of new foci for identification, is the most promising path toward improvement. Table 32.1–6 summarizes important features of supportive psychotherapy. Table 32.1–7 summarizes the in-

**Table 32.1–6**
**Supportive Psychotherapy**

| | |
|---|---|
| Goal | Support reality testing |
| | Provide ego support |
| | Maintain or reestablish usual level of functioning |
| Selection criteria | Very healthy patient faced with overwhelming crises |
| | Patient with ego deficits |
| Duration | Days, months, or years—as needed |
| Technique | Therapist predictably available |
| | Interpretation used to strengthen defenses |
| | Therapist maintains working, reality-based relationship based on support, concern, and problem solving |
| | Suggestion, reinforcement, advice, reality testing, cognitive restructuring, and reassurance |
| | Psychodynamic life narrative |
| | Medication |

Table from R J Ursano, E K Silberman: Individual psychotherapies. In *The American Psychiatric Press Textbook of Psychiatry*, J A Talbott, R E Hales, S C Yudofsky, editors, p 878. American Psychiatric Press, Washington, 1988. Used with permission.

**Table 32.1–7**
**Indications for Expressive or Supportive Emphasis in Psychotherapy**

| Insight-Oriented (Expressive) | Supportive |
|---|---|
| Strong motivation to understand | Significant ego defects of a long-term nature |
| Significant suffering | Severe life crisis |
| Ability to regress in the service of the ego | |
| Tolerance for frustration | Poor frustration tolerance |
| Capacity for insight (psychological-mindedness) | Lack of psychological-mindedness |
| Intact reality testing | Poor reality testing |
| Meaningful object relations | Severely impaired object relations |
| Good impulse control | Poor impulse control |
| Ability to sustain work | Low intelligence |
| Capacity to think in terms of analogy and metaphor | Little capacity for self-observation |
| Reflective responses to trial interpretations | Organically based cognitive dysfunction |
| | Tenuous ability to form a therapeutic alliance |

Table from G O Gabbard: *Psychodynamic Psychotherapy in Clinical Practice*, p 88. American Psychiatric Press, Washington, 1990. Used with permission.

dications for insight-oriented (expressive) therapy versus supportive therapy. Table 32.1–8 outlines a comparison and description of the types of therapies discussed in this section.

## REFERRAL BY A NONPSYCHIATRIC PHYSICIAN

Nonpsychiatric physicians often treat psychiatric patients in their practices. Those patients may require referral to a psychiatrist for more in-depth evaluation and treatment than can be provided in the nonpsychiatric setting. Or nonpsychiatric physicians may think that some of their patients would benefit from psychotherapy. Those patients may or may not carry an Axis I or Axis II diagnosis. Table 32.1–9 summarizes a few key features involved in effectively referring a patient for psychotherapy.

## CURRENT PROBLEMS

With the advent of managed care, increasing pressure is put on psychiatrists to provide psychotherapy that is short-term and thus, theoretically, low in cost. Short-term therapies—enthusiastically promoted by private insurance companies, health maintenance organizations, and a number of psychiatric residency programs—have parameters that are explicitly delineated with regard to such issues as the number of sessions, concrete goals, and outcome eval-

**Table 32.1–8**
**Scope of Psychoanalytic Practice: A Clinical Continuum***

| Feature | Psychoanalysis | Psychoanalytic Psychotherapy | |
|---|---|---|---|
| | | Expressive Mode | Supportive Mode |
| Frequency | Regular four to five times a week: 50-minute hour | Regular one to three times a week: half to full hour | Flexible one time a week or less; or as needed, half to full hour |
| Duration | Long-term: usually three to five + years | Short-term or long-term: several sessions to months or years | Short-term or intermittent long-term; single session to lifetime |
| Setting | Patient primarily on couch with analyst out of view | Patient and therapist face-to-face; occasional use of couch | Patient and therapist face-to-face; couch contraindicated |
| Modus operandi | Systematic analysis of all (positive and negative) transference and resistance; primary focus on analyst and intrasession events; transference neurosis facilitated; regression encouraged | Partial analysis of dynamics and defenses; focus on current interpersonal events and transference to others outside sessions; analysis of negative transference; positive transference left unexplored unless it impedes progress; limited regression encouraged | Formation of therapeutic alliance and real object relationship; analysis of transference contraindicated wit rare exceptions; focus on conscious external events; regression discouraged |
| Analyst-therapist role | Absolute neutrality; frustration of patient; reflector-mirror role | Modified neutrality; implicit gratification of patient and great activity | Neutrality suspended; limited explicit gratification, direction, and disclosure |
| Mutative change agents | Insight predominates within relatively deprived environment | Insight within empathic environment; identification with benevolent object | Auxiliary or surrogate ego as temporary substitute; holding environment; insight to degree possible |
| Patient population | Neuroses; mild character psychopathology | Neuroses; mild to moderate character psychopathology, especially narcissistic and borderline personality disorders | Severe character disorders; latent or manifest psychoses; acute crises; physical illness |

**Table 32.1–8**
*Continued*

| Feature | Psychoanalysis | Psychoanalytic Psychotherapy | |
| --- | --- | --- | --- |
| | | **Expressive Mode** | **Supportive Mode** |
| Patient requisites | High motivation; psychological-mindedness; good previous object relationships; ability to maintain transference neurosis; good frustration tolerance | High to moderate motivation and psychological-mindedness; ability to form therapeutic alliance; some frustration tolerance | Some degree of motivation and ability to form therapeutic alliance |
| Basic goals | Structural reorganization of personality; resolution of unconscious conflicts; insight into intrapsychic events; symptom relief an indirect result | Partial reorganization of personality and defenses; resolution of preconscious and conscious derivatives of conflicts; insight into current interpersonal events; improved object relations; symptom relief a goal or prelude to further exploration | Reintegration of self and ability to cope; stabilization or restoration of preexisting equilibrium; strengthening of defenses; better adjustment or acceptance of pathology; symptom relief and environmental restructuring as primary goals |
| Major techniques | Free association method predominates; fully dynamic interpretation (including confrontation, clarification, and working through), with emphasis on genetic reconstruction | Limited free association; confrontation, clarification, and partial interpretation predominate, with emphasis on here-and-now interpretation and limited genetic interpretation | Free association method contraindicated; suggestion (advice) predominates; abreaction useful; confrontation, clarification, and interpretation in the here and now secondary; genetic interpretation contraindicated |
| Adjunct treatment | Primarily avoided; if applied, all negative and positive meanings and implications thoroughly analyzed | May be necessary (e.g., psychotropic drugs as temporary measure); if applied, negative implications explored and diffused | Often necessary (e.g., psychotropic drugs, family therapy, rehabilitative therapy, or hospitalization); if applied, positive implications are emphasized |

*This division is not categorical; all practice resides on a clinical continuum.
Table by Toksoz Byram Karasu, M.D.

**Table 32.1–9**
**Guidelines for Patient Referral**

It is important to exhibit confidence and enthusiasm when making a referral for psychiatric evaluation or psychotherapy. Patients will detect ambivalence and skepticism on the physician's part about the need for such treatment. It is usually helpful to recommend a psychiatrist or other mental health professional who is known *personally* by the physician.

Always present the psychiatric referral as part of the patient's ongoing medical care. Some patents view a psychiatric referral as a means to dump them onto another doctor or as a rejection. Patients should be reassured that any psychiatric treatment will be in parallel with their ongoing medical care.

Have the name and telephone number of your referral source readily available to give to the patient.

Call the psychiatrist to personally explain the reason and need for the referral and what role you would like to continue to play in the patient's care.

Make the appointment for the psychiatric evaluation while the patient is still in the office or clinic.

Be sure to schedule a follow-up appointment after the date of the psychiatric evaluation to check on the patient's reaction to the referral and his or her response to the initial treatment.

Table from A Stoudemire: *Clinical Psychiatry for Medical Students*, p 457. Lippincott, Philadelphia, 1990. Used with permission.

uation criteria. They are largely designed so that the techniques involved can be learned quickly and performed with the aid of instructional manuals by a variety of practitioners other than psychiatrists.

Although the pressure to develop less expensive, less training-intensive, and less time-involving therapies than psychoanalysis stems from some legitimate concerns about the accessibility of the traditional insight-oriented approaches typical of psychoanalysis and analytically oriented psychotherapy, the rush to relegate such powerfully effective treatments to the periphery of the mainstream seems short-sighted and ultimately impoverishing to the field.

**References**

Abend S M: Countertransference and psychoanalytic technique. Psychoanal Q *58*: 374, 1989.

Blechner J: Psychoanalysis and HIV disease. Contemp Psychoanal *29*: 61, 1993.

Bowden C L: Implications of psychopharmacological studies for the practice of psychoanalysis. J Am Acad Psychoanal *20*: 477, 1992.

Brenner C: *Psychoanalytic Technique and Psychic Conflict*. International Universities Press, New York, 1976.

Fenichel O: *Problems of Psychoanalytic Technique*. Psychoanalytic Q *10*; 84, 1941.

Freud A: *The Ego and Mechanisms of Defense*. International Universities Press, New York, 1966.

Gabbard G O: *Psychodynamic Psychiatry in Clinical Practice*. American Psychiatric Press, Washington, 1990.

Hartmann H: *Ego Psychology and the Problem of Adaptation*. International Universities Press, New York, 1959.

Hirsch I: An interpersonal perspective: The analyst's unwitting participation in the patient's change. Psychoanal Psychol 9: 299, 1992.

Holinser P C: A developmental perspective on psychotherapy and psychoanalysis. Am J Psychiatry 146: 1494, 1989.

Jones E: *The Life and Work of Sigmund Freud*, vols 1–3. Basic Books, New York, 1953–1957.

Karasu T B: Psychoanalysis and psychoanalytic psychotherapy. In *Comprehensive Textbook of Psychiatry*, ed 5, H I Kaplan, B J Sadock, editors, p 1442. Williams & Wilkins, Baltimore, 1989.

Karasu T B: *Treatments of Psychiatric Disorders: A Task Force Report of the American Psychiatric Association*. American Psychiatric Press, Washington, 1989.

Kernberg O F: The current status of psychoanalysis. J Am Psychoanal Assoc 41: 45, 1993.

Kernberg O F: *Object Relations Therapy and Clinical Psychoanalysis*. Aronson, New York, 1976.

Klein M: *Contributions of Psychoanalysis, 1921–45*. Hogarth Press, London, 1948.

Kohut H H: *The Analysis of the Self*. International Universities Press, New York, 1984.

Mahler M: *On Human Symbiosis and the Vicissitudes of Individuation*. International Universities Press, New York, 1968.

May R, Angel E, Ellenberger H: *Existence: A New Dimension in Psychiatry and Psychology*. Basic Books, New York, 1958.

Reich W: *Character Analysis*. Touchstone, New York, 1974.

Shafer R: *A New Language for Psychoanalysis*. Yale University Press, New Haven, 1976.

Sullivan H S: *Interpersonal Theory of Psychiatry*. Norton, New York, 1953.

Wallerstein R S: Followup in psychoanalysis: What happens to treatment gains? J Am Psychoanal Assoc 40: 665, 1992.

Yorke V: Boundaries, psychic structure, and time. J Anal Psychol 38: 57, 1993.

# 32.2 / Brief Psychotherapy and Crisis Intervention

Brief dynamic psychotherapies are short-term therapies based on psychoanalytic concepts. Most of those therapies have specific patient selection criteria and treatment techniques that are designed problems. The therapies have become increasingly popular over the past decade, as numerous clinical reports have indicated their effectiveness with select groups of patients. With the renewed emphasis on primary care and cost containment in the health care delivery system, a good deal of worldwide interest has been aroused by the treatment modalities. Although time limitation is an essential and obvious feature of all short-term therapies, their adherents share no clear consensus about exactly what is meant by the concept. Thus, a number of therapies are subsumed under the category of "brief psychotherapies."

Crisis intervention, by definition, is a therapy limited by the parameters of whatever crisis has led the patient to be seen. Crisis intervention is based on crisis theory, which emphasizes not only immediate responses to an immediate situation but also long-term development of psychological adaptation aimed at preventing future problems.

## BRIEF PSYCHOTHERAPY

### History

Most of the basic characteristics of brief psychotherapy were identified by Franz Alexander and Thomas French in 1946. They described a therapeutic experience that puts the patient at ease, manipulates the transference, and uses trial interpretations in a flexible manner. The emphasis was on developing a corrective emotional experience capable of repairing traumatic events of the past and convincing the patient that new ways of thinking, feeling, and behaving are possible.

At about the same time Eric Lindemann established a consultation service at the Massachusetts General Hospital for persons experiencing a crisis. New treatment methods were developed to deal with those situations and were eventually applied to persons who were not in crisis but who were experiencing emotional distress from a variety of sources.

### Selection Criteria

The most valuable predictor of a successful outcome is the patients' motivation for treatment. In addition, patients must be able to deal with psychological concepts, to respond to interpretation, and to concentrate on and resolve the conflict around the central issue or focus that underlies their basic problems. Patients must also be able to develop a therapeutic alliance and work with the therapist toward achieving emotional health.

### Types

**Brief focal psychotherapy (Tavistock-Malan).** Brief focal psychotherapy was originally developed by the Michael Balint team at the Tavistock Clinic in London in the 1950s. Daniel Malan, a member of that team, reported the results of the therapy. Malan's selection criteria for treatment are eliminating absolute contraindications; rejecting patients for whom certain dangers seem inevitable; clearly assessing the patient's psychopathology; and determining the patient's capacity to consider problems in emotional terms, face disturbing material, respond to interpretations, and endure the stress of the treatment. Malan found that high motivation invariably correlated with successful outcome.

Contraindications to treatment are serious suicidal attempts, substance dependence, chronic alcohol abuse, incapacitating chronic obsessional symptoms, incapacitating chronic phobic symptoms, and gross destructive or self-destructive acting out.

**Requirements and techniques.** Malan emphasized using the following routine: Identify the transference early and interpret it. Interpret also the negative transference. Link transferences to patients' relationships to their parents. Both patient and therapist must be willing to become deeply involved and to bear the ensuing tension. A circumscribed focus is formulated, and a termination date is set in advance. Grief and anger about termination are worked through.

About 20 sessions is suggested as an average length for the therapy for an experienced therapist and about 30 sessions for a trainee. However, Malan did not go beyond 40 interviews.

Tables 32.2-1 and 32.2-2 summarize Malan's techniques and exclusion criteria.

**Time-limited psychotherapy (Boston University-Mann).** A psychotherapeutic model of exactly 12 interviews focusing on a specified central issue was developed at Boston University by James Mann and his colleagues in the early 1970s. In contrast with Malan's emphasis on clear-cut selection and rejection criteria, Mann has not been as explicit as to who is a good candidate to receive time-limited psychotherapy.

The main points that Mann considers importants are the determination of a reasonably correct central conflict in the patient and, in young people, maturational crises with many psychological and somatic complaints.

Mann also mentioned a few exceptions, which are similar to Mann's rejection criteria. Those exceptions are major depressive disorder that interferes with the treatment agreement, an acute psychotic state, and a desperate patient who needs but is incapable of tolerating object relations.

REQUIREMENTS AND TECHNIQUES. The following are Mann's technical requirements: strict limitation to 12 sessions; positive transference predomianting early; specification and strict adherence to a central issue involving transference; positive identification; making separation a maturational event for the patient; absolute prospect of termination, avoiding development of dependence; clarification of present and past experiences and resistances; an active therapist who supports and encourages the patient; and education of the patient through direct information, reeducation, and manipulation.

The conflicts likely to be encountered include independence versus dependence, activity versus passitivity, unresolved or delayed grief, and adquate versis inadequate self-esteem.

Table 32.2-3 summarizes the features of Mann's time-limited psychotherapy.

**Short-term dynamic psychotherapy (McGill University-Davanloo).** As conducted by Habib Davanloo at McGill University, short-term dynamic psychotherapy encompass all the varieties of brief psychotherapy and crisis intervention. Patients treated in Davanloo's series are classified as those whose psychological conflicts are predominantly oedipal, those whose conflicts are not oedipal, and those whose conflicts have more than one focus.

In addition, Davanloo devised a specific psychotherapeutic technique for patients suffering from severe, long-standing neurotic problems, specifically those suffering from incapacitating obsessive-compulsive disorders and phobias.

Davanloo's selection criteria emphasize the evaluation of those ego functions that are of primary importance to the psychotherapeutic work: the establishment of a psychotherapeutic focus; the psychodynamic formulation of the patient's psychological problem; the ability to get involved in emotional interaction with the evaluator; the history of a give-and-take relationship with a significant person in the patient's life; the extent to which the patient's

**Table 32.2–1**
**Malan and the Tavistock Group: Brief Focal Psychotherapy**

| | |
|---|---|
| Goal | Clarify the nature of the defense, the anxiety, and the impulse<br>Link the present, the past, and the transference |
| Selection criteria | Patient able to think in feeling terms<br>High motivation<br>Good response to trial interpretation |
| Duration | Up to one year<br>Mean, 20 sessions |
| Focus | Internal conflict present since childhood |
| Termination | Set definite date at beginning of treatment |

Table from R J Ursano, E K Silberman: Individual psychotherapies. In *The American Psychiatric Press Textbook of Psychiatry*, J A Talbott, R E Hales, S C Yudofsky, editors, p 861. American Psychiatric Press, Washington, 1988. Used with permission.

**Table 32.2–2**
**Malan and the Tavistock Group's Exclusion Criteria for Brief Focal Psychotherapy**

1. Patient is unavailable to therapeutic contact.

2. Therapist anticipates that prolonged work will be needed
   - to generate motivation
   - to penetrate rigid defenses
   - to deal with complex or deep-seated issues
   - to resolve unfavorable, intense transference, dependent or other, that may develop

3. Depressive or psychotic disturbance may intensify

Table from R J Ursano, E K Silberman: Individual psychotherapies. In *The American Psychiatric Press Textbook of Psychiatry*, J A Talbott, R E Hales, S C Yudofsky, editors, p 861. American Psychiatric Press, Washington, 1988. Used with permission.

**Table 32.2–3**
**Mann: Time-Limited Psychotherapy**

| | |
|---|---|
| Goal | Resolution of the present and chronically endured pain and the patient's negative self-image |
| Selection criteria | High ego strength<br>Able to engage and disengage<br>Therapist quickly able to identify a central issue<br>Excludes major depressive disorder, acute psychosis, and borderline personality disorder |
| Duration | 12 treatment hours |
| Focus | Present and chronically endured pain<br>Particular image of the self |
| Termination | Specific last session set at beginning of treatment<br>Termination a major focus of the therapy work |

Table from R J Ursano, E K Silberman: Individual psychotherapies. In *The American Psychiatric Press Textbook of Psychiatry*, J A Talbott, R E Hales, S C Yudofsky, editors, p 864. American Psychiatric Press, Washington, 1988. Used with permission.

ability to experience and tolerate anxiety, guilt, and depression; the patient's motivation for change; the patient's psychological-mindedness; and the patient's ability to respond to interpretation and to link the evaluator with people in the present and in the past.

Both Malan and Davanloo emphasize the patient's response to interpretation and consider it both an important selection criterion and a prognostic criterion.

REQUIREMENTS AND TECHNIQUES. The highlights of Davanloo's psychotherapeutic approach are flexibility (the therapist should adapt the technique to the patient's needs); control of the patient's regressive tendencies; active intervention, so as not to allow the development of overdependence on the therapist; and intellectual insight and emotional experiences by the patient in the transference. Those emotional experiences become corrective as a result of the interpretation.

Table 32.2-4 summarizes the features of Davanloo's short-term dynamic psychotherapy.

**Short-term anxiety-provoking psychotherapy (Harvard University-Sifneos).** Short-term anxiety-provoking psychotherapy was first developed at the Massachusetts General Hospital by Peter Sifneos during the 1950s. The following criteria for selection are used: circumscribed chief complaint (implying an ability to select one out of a variety of problems to which the patient assigns top priority and that the patient wants to resolve in treatment); one meaningful or give-and-take relationship during early childhood; the ability to interact flexibly with the evaluator and to express feelings appropriately; above-average psychological sophistication (implying not only an above-average intelligence but also an ability to respond to interpretations); a specific psychodynamic formulation (usually a set of psychological conflicts underlying the patient's difficulties and centering on an oedipal focus); a contract between the therapist and the patient to work on the specified focus and the formulation of minimal expectations of outcome; and good-to-excellent motivation for change and not just for symptom relief.

REQUIREMENTS AND TECHNIQUES. The treatment can be divided into four major phases; patient–therapist encoun-

ter, early therapy, height of the treatment, and evidence of change and termination. The therapist uses the following techniques during the four phases:

*Patient–therapist encounter.* The therapist establishes a working alliance by using the quick rapport and the positive feelings for the therapist that appear in this phase. Judicious use of open-ended and forced-choice questions enables the therapist to outline and concentrate on a therapeutic focus. The therapist specifies the minimum expectations of outcome to be achieved by the therapy.

*Early therapy.* In transference, feelings for the therapist are clarified as soon as they appear, leading to the establishment of a true therapeutic alliance.

*Height of the treatment.* This phase emphasizes active concentration on the oedipal conflicts that have been chosen as the therapeutic focus for the therapy; repeated use of anxiety-provoking questions and confrontations; avoidance of pregenital characterological issues, which the patient uses defensively to avoid dealing with the therapist's anxiety-provoking techniques; avoidance at all costs of a transference neurosis; repetitive demonstration of the patient's neurotic ways or maladaptive patterns of behavior; concentration on the anxiety-laden material, even before the defense mechanisms have been clarified; repeated demonstrations of parent–transference links by the use of properly timed interpretations based on material given by the patient; establishment of a corrective emotional experience; encouragement and support of the patient, who becomes anxious while struggling to understand the conflicts; new learning and problem-solving patterns; and repeated presentations and recapitulations of the patient's psychodynamics until the defense mechanisms used in dealing with oedipal conflicts are understood.

*Evidence of change and termination of psychotherapy.* This phase emphasizes the tangible demonstration of change in the patient's behavior outside the therapy; evidence that adaptive patterns of behavior are being used, and initiation of talk about terminating the treatment.

Table 32.2-5 summarizes features of the Sifneos short-term anxiety-provoking psychotherapy.

**Interpersonal psychotherapy.** A specific type of short-term psychotherapy called interpersonal psychotherapy

**Table 32.2–4
Davanloo: Short-Term Dynamic Psychotherapy**

| | |
|---|---|
| Goal | Resolution of oedipal conflict, loss focus, or multiple foci |
| Selection criteria | Psychological-mindedness<br>At least one past meaningful relationship<br>Able to tolerate affect<br>Good response to trial transference interpretation<br>High motivation<br>Flexible defenses<br>Lack of projection, splitting, and denial |
| Duration | 5–40 sessions, usually 5–25<br>Longer durations for seriously ill |
| Termination | No specific termination date<br>Patient is told that treatment will be short |

Table from R J Ursano, E K Silberman: Individual psychotherapies. In *The American Psychiatric Press Textbook of Psychiatry*, J A Talbott, R E Hales, S C Yudofsky, editors, p 865. American Psychiatric Press, Washington, 1988. Used with permission.

**Table 32.2–5
Sifneos: Short-Term Anxiety-Provoking Psychotherapy**

| | |
|---|---|
| Goal | Resolution of oedipal conflict |
| Selection criteria | Above-average intelligence<br>At least one past meaningful relationship<br>High motivation<br>Specific chief complaint<br>Able to interact with evaluator<br>Able to express feelings<br>Flexible |
| Duration | A few months<br>Average 12–16 sessions |
| Focus | Oedipal (triangular) conflict |
| Termination | No specific date given |

Table from R J Ursano, E K Silberman: Individual psychotherapies. In *The American Psychiatric Press Textbook of Psychiatry*, J A Talbott, R E Hales, S C Yudofsky, editors, p 863. American Psychiatric Press, Washington, 1988. Used with permission.

(IPT), described by Myrna Weissman and Gerald Klerman, is used to treat depressive disorders. Therapy consists of 45-to-50-minute sessions held weekly over a three-to-four-month period. Interpersonal behavior is emphasized as a cause of depressive disorders and as a method of cure. Patients are taught to evaluate realistically their interactions with others and to become aware of how they isolate themselves, which contributes to or aggravates the depression about which they complain. The therapist offers direct advice, aids the patient in making decisions, and helps clarify areas of conflict. Little or no attention is given to the transference. The therapist attempts to be consistently supportive, empathic, and flexible. Studies of interpersonal psychotherapy have shown that, in selected cases of depressive disorders, it compares favorably with drug therapy with antidepressant agents.

Table 32.2-6 summarizes the features of interpersonal psychotherapy.

## Outcome

The shared techniques of all those kinds of brief psychotherapy (except interpersonal psychotherapy) far outdistance their differences. They include the therapeutic alliance or dynamic interaction between the therapist and the patient, the use of transference, the active interpretation of a therapeutic focus or central issue, the repetitive links between parental and transference issues, and the early termination of the therapy.

More than in any other form of psychotherapy, the outcomes of those brief treatments have been investigated extensively. Contrary to prevailing ideas that the therapeutic factors in psychotherapy are nonspecific, controlled studies and other assessment methods (for example, interviews with unbiased evaluators, patients' self-evaluations) point to the importance of the specific techniques used. Malan summarized the results in five major generalizations: (1) The capacity for genuine recovery in certain patients is far greater than was thought. (2) A certain type of patient receiving brief psychotherapy can benefit greatly from a practical working through of his or her nuclear conflict in the transference. (3) Such patients can be rec-

ognized in advance through a process of dynamic interaction, because they are responsive and motivated and able to face disturbing feelings and a circumscribed focus can be formulated for them. (4) The more radical the technique is in terms of transference, depth of interpretation, and the link to childhood, the more radical the therapeutic effects will be. (5) For some disturbed patients a carefully chosen partial focus can be therapeutically effective.

## CRISIS INTERVENTION

### Theory

A crisis is a response to hazardous events and is experienced as a painful state. Consequently, it tends to mobilize powerful reactions to help the person alleviate the discomfort and return to the state of emotional equilibrium that existed before its onset. If that takes place, the crisis can be overcome, but, in addition, the person learns how to use adaptive reactions. Furthermore, by resolving the crisis, the patient may be in a better state of mind, superior to that before the onset of psychological difficulties. If, however, the patient uses maladaptive reactions, the painful state will intensify, the crisis will deepen, and a regressive deterioration will take place, producing psychiatric symptoms. Those symptoms, in turn, may crystallize into a neurotic pattern of behavior that restricts the patient's ability to function freely. At times, however, the situation cannot be stabilized; new maladaptive reactions are introduced; and the consequences can be of catastrophic proportions, leading at times to death by suicide. In that sense, psychological crises are painful and may be viewed as turning points for better or for worse.

A crisis is self-limited and can last anywhere from a few hours to weeks. The crisis as such is characterized by an initial phase, in which anxiety and tension rise. That phase is followed by a phase in which problem-solving mechanisms are set in motion. Those mechanisms may be successful, depending on whether they are adaptive or maladaptive.

Patients during a period of turmoil are receptive to minimal help and obtain meaningful results. All sorts of services, therefore, have been devised for such purposes. Some are open-ended; others limit the time available or the number of sessions.

Crisis theory helps one understand healthy normal people in crisis and develop therapeutic tools aimed at preventing future psychological difficulties.

Crisis intervention is offered to persons who are incapacitated or severely disturbed by a crisis.

### Criteria for Selection

The criteria used to select patients are a history of a specific hazardous situation of recent origin that produced the anxiety, a precipitating event that intensified the anxiety, clear-cut evidence that the patient is in a state of psychological crisis as previously defined, high motivation to overcome the crisis, a potential for making a psychological adjustment equal or superior to the one that existed

**Table 32.2–6**
**Interpersonal Psychotherapy**

| | |
|---|---|
| Goal | Improvement in current interpersonal skills |
| Selection criteria | Outpatient, nonbipolar disorder, nonpsychotic depressive disorder |
| Duration | 12–16 weeks, usually once-weekly meetings |
| Technique | Reassurance<br>Clarification of feeling states<br>Improvement of interpersonal communication<br>Testing perceptions<br>Development of interpersonal skills<br>Medication |

Table from R J Ursano, E K Silberman: Individual psychotherapies. In *The American Psychiatric Press Textbook of Psychiatry*, J A Talbott, R E Hales, S C Yudofsky, editors, p 868. American Psychiatric Press, Washington, 1988. Used with permission.

before the development of the crisis, and a certain degree of psychological sophistication—an ability to recognize psychological reasons for the present predicament.

## Requirements and Techniques

Crisis intervention deals with persons in the midst of a crisis in which rapidity is of the essense. Therapy requires a joint understanding of the psychodynamics involved and an awareness of how they are responsible for the crisis. The participants work together, aiming at resolving the crisis. In addition, the patient, as well as the therapist, actively participates in the treatment.

Techniques include reassurance, suggestion, environmental manipulation, and psychotropic medications. Brief hospitalization may be added as part of the treatment plan. All those therapeutic maneuvers are aimed at decreasing the patient's anxiety. The length of crisis intervention varies from one or two sessions to several interviews over a period of one or two months. The technical requirements for crisis intervention involve rapidly establishing a rapport with the patient that is aimed at creating a therapeutic alliance; review the steps that have led to the crisis; understanding the maladaptive reactions that the patient is using to deal with the crisis; focusing only on the crisis; learning to use adaptive ways to deal with crises; avoiding the development of symptoms; using the predominating positive transference feelings for the therapist, so as to transform the work into a learning experience; teaching the patient how to avoid hazardous situations that are likely to produce future crises; and ending the intervention as soon as evidence indicates that the crisis has been resolved and that the patient clearly understands all the steps that led to its development and its resolution.

## Outcome

The most striking result of crisis therapy pertains to the patient's ability to become better equipped to avoid or, if necessary, to deal with future hazards. In addition, on the basis of some patients' objective observations, the therapeutic experience has enabled them to attain a level of emotional functioning that is superior to that before the onset of the crisis. In that sense, therefore, crisis intervention is not only therapeutic but also preventive.

## References

Brom D, Kleber R J, Defares P B: Brief psychotherapy for posttraumatic stress disorders. J Consult Clin Psychol 57: 607, 1989.
Davanloo H: Basic Principles and Technique of Short Term Dynamic Psychotherapy. Spectrum, New York, 1978.
Flesenheimer W V, Pollack J: The time limit in brief psychotherapy. Bull Menninger Clin 53: 44, 1989.
Gillieron E: Setting and motivation in brief psychotherapy. Psychother Psychosom 47: 194, 1987.
Hirschowitz R: Crisis theory: A formulation. Psychiatr Ann 3: 33, 1973.
Horowitz M. Personality Styles and Brief Psychotherapy. Basic Books, New York, 1984.
MacKenzie K R: Recent developments in brief psychotherapy. Hosp Community Psychiatry 39: 742, 1988.
Malan D: The Frontier of Brief Psychotherapy. Plenum, New York, 1976.
Malan D: A Study of Brief Psychotherapy. Plenum, New York, 1976.
Mann J: Time Limited Psychotherapy. Harvard University Press, Cambridge, 1973.

Maxim R E, Hunt D D: Appraisal and coping in the process of patient change during short-term psychotherapy. J Nerv Ment Dis 178: 235, 1990.
Porter R: The Role of Learning in Psychotherapy. Churchill, London, 1968.
Schram P C, Burti, L: Crisis intervention techniques designed to prevent hospitalization. Bull Menninger Clin 50: 194, 1986.
Sifneos P E: Brief dynamic and crisis therapy. In Comprehensive Textbook of Psychiatry, ed 5, H I Kaplan, B J Sadock, editors, p 1562. Williams & Wilkins, Baltimore, 1989.
Sifneos P E: The current status of individual short-term dynamic psychotherapy and its future. Am J Psychother 38: 234, 1984.
Sifneos P E: A historical account of preventive psychiatry in the greater Boston area, 1942–1979. Bibl Psychiatr 160: 251, 1981.
Sifneos P E: Learning to solve emotional problems: A controlled study of short-term anxiety provoking psychotherapy. In The Role of Learning is Psychotherapy, R Porter, editor, p 37. Churchill, London, 1968.
Sifneos P E: Short-Term Dynamic Psychotherapy Evaluation and Technique, ed 2. Plenum, New York, 1987.
Sifneos P E: Short-Term Psychotherapy and Emotional-Crisis. Harvard University Press, Cambridge, 1972.
Sifneos P E, Greenberg W E: Patient management. In The New Harvard Guide to Psychiatry, p 589. Harvard University Press, Cambridge, 1988.
Sloane R B: Psychotherapy versus Behavior Therapy. Harvard University Press, Cambridge, 1975.
Swinson R P, Soulios C, Cox B J, Kuch K: Brief treatment of emergency room patients with panic attacks. Am J Psychiatry 149: 944, 1992.

---

# 32.3 / Group Psychotherapy, Combined Individual and Group Psychotherapy, and Psychodrama

---

## GROUP PSYCHOTHERAPY

Group psychotherapy is a treatment in which carefully selected emotionally ill persons are placed into a group guided by a trained therapist to help one another effect personality change. By using a variety of technical maneuvers and theoretical constructs, the leader uses the group members' interactions to make that change.

Group psychotherapy encompasses the theoretical spectrum of therapies in psychiatry: supportive, structured, limit-setting (for example, groups with chronically psychotic people), cognitive-behavioral, interpersonal, family, and analytically oriented groups. Two of the main strengths of group therapy, when compared with individual therapies, are (1) the opportunity for immediate feedback from the patient's peers and (2) the opportunity for both the patient and the therapist to observe the patient's psychological, emotional, and behavioral responses to a variety of persons, eliciting a variety of transferences. Table 32.3–1 outlines some of the key features of group therapies.

## Classification

At the present time, many approaches are used in the group method of treatment. Many clinicians work within a psychoanalytic frame of reference. Other therapy techniques include transactional group therapy, which was devised by Eric Berne and which emphasizes the here-and-

**Table 32.3–1**
**Group Therapies**

| | |
|---|---|
| Goal | Alleviation of symptoms |
| | Change interpersonal relations |
| | Alter specific family-couple dynamics |
| Selection | Varies greatly based on type of group |
| | Homogeneous groups target specific disorders |
| | Adolescents and patients with personality disorders may especially benefit |
| | Families and couples where the system needs change |
| | Contraindications: substantial suicide risk, sadomasochistic acting out in family or couple |
| Types | Directive-supportive group psychotherapy |
| | Psychodynamic-interpersonal group psychotherapy |
| | Psychoanalytic group psychotherapy |
| | Family therapy |
| | Couples therapy |
| Duration | Weeks to years; time limited and open-ended |

Table from A Stoudemire: *Clinical Psychiatry for Medical Students*, p 449. Lippincott, Philadelphia, 1990. Used with permission.

now interactions among group members; behavioral group therapy, which relies on conditioning techniques based on learning theory; Gestalt group therapy, which was created from the theories of Frederick Perls and enables patients to abreact and express themselves fully; and client-centered group psychotherapy, which was developed by Carl Rogers and is based on the nonjudgmental expression of feelings among group members. Table 32.3-2 outlines the major group psychotherapy approaches.

## Patient Selection

To determine a patient's suitability for group psychotherapy, the therapist needs a great deal of information, which is gathered in a screening interview. The psychiatrist should take a psychiatric history and perform a mental status examination to obtain certain dynamic, behavioral, and diagnostic information.

Table 32.3–3 outlines the general criteria for the selection of patients for group therapy.

**Authority anxiety.** Those patients whose primary problem is their relationship to authority and who are extremely anxious in the presence of authority figures may or may not do well in group therapy. However, they often do better in a group setting than in a dyadic (one-to-one) setting, because they are more comfortable in a group. Patients with a great deal of authority anxiety may be blocked, anxious, resistant, and unwilling to verbalize thoughts and feelings in an individual setting, generally for fear of censure or disapproval from the therapist. Thus, they may welcome the suggestion of group psychotherapy so as to avoid the scrutiny of the dyadic situation. Conversely, if the patient reacts negatively to the suggestion of group psychotherapy or is openly resistant to the idea, the therapist should consider the possibility of a high degree of peer anxiety.

**Peer anxiety.** Patients, such as those with borderline and schizoid personality disorders, who have destructive relationships with their peer groups or who have been extremely isolated from peer group contact generally react negatively or anxiously when placed in a group setting. If such patients can

work through their anxiety, however, group therapy can be beneficial.

**Diagnosis.** The diagnosis of patients' disorders is important in determining the best therapeutic approach and in evaluating patients' motivations for treatment, capacities for change, and personality structure strengths and weaknesses.

There are few contraindications to group therapy. Antisocial patients generally do poorly in a heterogeneous group setting because they cannot adhere to group standards. However, if the group is composed of other antisocial patients they may respond better to peers than to perceived authority figures. Depressed patients do well after they have established a trusting relationship with the therapist. Actively suicidal or severely depressed patients should not be treated solely in a group setting. Manic patients are disruptive, but, once under pharmacological control, they do well in the group setting. Patients who are delusional and who may incorporate the group into their delusional system should be excluded, as should patients who pose a physical threat to other members because of uncontrollable aggressive outbursts.

## Preparation

Patients who are prepared by the therapist for a group experience tend to continue in treatment longer and report less initial anxiety than do those who are not so prepared. The preparation consists of the therapist's explaining, before the first session, the procedure in as much detail as possible and answering any questions the patient may have.

## Structural Organization

Table 32.3–4 summarizes some of the critical tasks that a group therapist must face when organizing a group.

**Size.** Group therapy has been successful with as few as 3 members and as many as 15, but most therapists consider 8 to 10 members the optimal size. With fewer members there may not be enough interaction unless the members are especially verbal. But with more than 10 members the interaction may be too great for the members or the therapist to follow.

**Frequency of sessions.** Most group psychotherapists conduct group sessions once a week. Maintaining continuity in sessions is important. When alternate sessions are used, the group meets twice a week, once with the therapist and once without the therapist.

**Length of sessions.** In general, group sessions last anywhere from one to two hours, but the time limit set should be constant.

Time-extended therapy (marathon group therapy) is a method in which the group meets continuously for 12 to 72 hours. Enforced interactional proximity and, during the longest time-extended sessions, sleep deprivation break down certain ego defenses, release affective processes, and theoretically promote open communication. However, time-extended sessions may be dangerous for patients with weak ego structures, such as schizophrenic and borderline personality disorder patients. Marathon groups were most popular in the 1970s but are much less often used today.

**Homogeneous versus heterogeneous groups.** In general, most therapists believe that the group should be as heterogeneous as possible to ensure maximum interaction. Thus, the group should be composed of members from different diagnostic categories and with varied behavioral patterns;

**Table 32.3–2**
**Comparison of Types of Group Psychotherapy**

| Parameters | Supportive Group Therapy | Analytically Oriented Group Therapy | Psychoanalysis of Groups | Transactional Group Therapy | Behavioral Group Therapy |
|---|---|---|---|---|---|
| Frequency | Once a week | 1 to 3 times a week | 1 to 5 times a week | 1 to 3 times a week | 1 to 3 times a week |
| Duration | Up to 6 months | 1 to 3+ years | 1 to 3+ years | 1 to 3 years | Up to 6 months |
| Primary indications | Psychotic and anxiety disorders | Anxiety disorders, borderline states, personality disorders | Anxiety disorders, personality disorders | Anxiety and psychotic disorders | Phobias, passivity, sexual problems |
| Individual screening interview | Usually | Always | Always | Usually | Usually |
| Communication content | Primarily environmental factors | Present and past life situations, intragroup and extragroup relationships | Primarily past life experiences, intragroup relationships | Primarily intragroup relationships; rarely, history; here and now stressed | Specific symptoms without focus on causality |
| Transference | Positive transference encouraged to promote improved functioning | Positive and negative transference evoked and analyzed | Transference neurosis evoked and analyzed | Positive relationships fostered, negative feelings analyzed | Positive relationships fostered, no examination of transference |
| Dreams | Not analyzed | Analyzed frequently | Always analyzed and encouraged | Analyzed rarely | Not used |
| Dependence | Intragroup dependence encouraged, members rely on leader to great extent | Intragroup dependence encouraged, dependence on leader variable | Intragroup dependence not encouraged, dependence on leader variable | Intragroup dependence encouraged, dependence on leader not encouraged | Intragroup dependence not encouraged; reliance on leader is high |
| Therapist activity | Strengthen existing defenses, active, give advice | Challenge defenses, active, give advice or personal response | Challenge defenses, passive, give no advice or personal response | Challenge defenses, active, give personal response, rather than advice | Create new defenses, active and directive |
| Interpretation | No interpretation of unconscious conflict | Interpretation of unconscious conflict | Interpretation of unconscious conflict extensive | Interpretation of current behavioral patterns in the here and now | Not used |
| Major group processes | Universalization, reality testing | Cohesion, transference, reality testing | Transference, ventilation, catharsis, reality testing | Abreaction, reality testing | Cohesion, reinforcement, conditioning |
| Socialization outside of group | Encouraged | Generally discouraged | Discouraged | Variable | Discouraged |
| Goals | Improved adaptation to environment | Moderate reconstruction of personality dynamics | Extensive reconstruction of personality dynamics | Alteration of behavior through mechanism of conscious control | Relief of specific psychiatric symptoms |

from all races, social levels, and educational backgrounds; and of varying ages and both sexes.

In general, patients between ages 20 and 65 can be effectively included in the same group. Age differences aid in the development of parent–child and brother–sister models. Moreover, patients have the opportunity to relive and rectify interpersonal difficulties that may have appeared insurmountable.

Both children and adolescents are best treated in groups composed mostly of patients of their own age group. Some adolescent patients are capable of assimilating the material of an adult group, regardless of content, but they should not be deprived of a constructive peer experience that they may otherwise not have.

**Open versus closed groups.** Some groups have a set number and composition of patients. If members leave, no

**Table 32.3–3**
**General Membership Criteria for Group Therapy**

Inclusion criteria
    Ability to perform the group task
    Problem areas compatible with goals of group
    Motivation to change

Exclusion criteria
    Marked incompatibility with group norms for acceptable
      behavior
    Inability to tolerate group setting
    Severe incompatibility with one or more of the other
      members
    Tendency to assume deviant role

Table from S Vinogradov, I D Yalom: Group therapy. In *The American Psychiatric Press Textbook of Psychiatry*, J A Talbott, R E Hales, S C Yudofsky, editors, p 956. American Psychiatric Press, Washington, 1988. Used with permission.

**Table 32.3–4**
**Therapist's Basic Tasks in Group Therapy**

1. The decision to establish a therapy group:
    Determine setting and size of the group
    Choose frequency and length of group sessions
    Decide on open versus closed group
    Select a cotherapist for the group
    Formulate policy on group therapy with other therapeutic
      modalities

2. The act of creating a therapy group:
    Formulate appropriate goals
    Select patients who can perform the group task
    Prepare patients for group therapy

3. The construction and maintenance of a therapeutic
    environment:
    Build the culture of the group explicitly and implicitly
    Identify and resolve common problems (membership
      turnover, subgrouping, conflict)

Table from S Vinogradov, I D Yalom: Group therapy. In *The American Psychiatric Press Textbook of Psychiatry*, J A Talbott, R E Hales, S C Yudofsky, editors, p 964. American Psychiatric Press, Washington, 1988. Used with permission.

new members are taken on; that is termed a closed group. An open group is one in which there is more fluidity of membership; new members are taken on whenever old members leave.

## Mechanisms

**Group formation.** Each patient approaches the group differently, and in that sense the group is a microcosm. Patients use typical adaptive abilities, defense mechanisms, and ways of relating, which are ultimately reflected back to them by the group, thus allowing them to become introspective about their personality functioning. But a process inherent in group formation requires that the patients suspend their previous ways of coping. In entering the group, they allow their executive ego functions—reality testing, adaptation to and mastery of the environment, and perception—to be assumed to some degree by the collective assessment provided by the total membership, including the leader.

**Therapeutic factors.** Table 32.3-5 outlines 20 significant therapeutic factors that account for change in group psychotherapy. Table 32.3-6 summarizes the forces that shape learn-

ing and change secondary to the nature of the group as a social microcosm.

## Role of the Therapist

Although opinions differ regarding how active or passive the therapist should be, the consensus is that the therapist's role is primarily a facilitative one. Ideally, the group members themselves are the primary source of cure and change.

The climate produced by the therapist's personality is a potent agent of change. The therapist is more than an expert applying techniques; the therapist exerts a personal influence that taps such variables as empathy, warmth, and respect.

## Inpatient Group Psychotherapy

Group therapy is an important part of the hospitalized patient's therapeutic experience. Groups may be organized on a ward in a variety of ways: in a community meeting, an entire inpatient unit meets with all the staff members (for example, psychiatrists, psychologists, and nurses); in a team meeting, 15 to 20 patients and staff members meet; and a regular or small group composed of 8 to 10 patients may meet with one or two therapists, as in traditional group therapy. Although the goals of each type of group vary, they all have common purposes: (1) to increase the patients' awareness of themselves through their interactions with the other group members, who provide feedback about their behavior; (2) to provide patients with improved interpersonal and social skills; (3) to help the members adapt to the inpatient setting; and (4) to improve communication between the patients and the staff. In addition, one type of group meeting is composed of only the inpatient hospital staff; it is used to improve communication among the staff members and to provide mutual support and encouragement in their day-to-day work with the patients. The community meeting and the team meeting are more helpful in dealing with patient treatment problems than they are for providing insight-oriented therapy, which is the province of the small-group therapy meeting.

Tables 32.3-7 and 32.3-8 summarize the goals and the techniques for short-term inpatient therapy groups.

**Group composition.** Two key factors of the inpatient group, common to all short-term therapies, are the heterogeneity of its members and the rapid turnover of patients. Outside the hospital, the therapist has a large caseload from which to select patients for group therapy. On the ward, the therapist has a limited number of patients from which to draw and is restricted further to those patients who are both willing to participate in and suitable for a small-group experience. In certain settings, group participation may be mandatory (for example, in substance abuse and alcohol dependence units). But that is not usually true for a general psychiatry unit; in fact, most group experiences are better when the patients themselves choose to enter them.

More sessions are preferable to fewer sessions. During a patient's hospital stay, groups may meet daily, allowing for interactional continuity and the carryover of themes from one session to the next. A new member of the group can quickly be brought up-to-date, either by the therapist in an orientation meeting or by one of the members. A newly admitted patient

**Table 32.3–5**
**Twenty Therapeutic Factors in Group Psychotherapy**

| Factor | Definition |
|---|---|
| Abreaction | A process by which repressed material, particularly a painful experience or conflict, is brought back to consciousness. In the process, the person not only recalls but relives the material, which is accompanied by the appropriate emotional response; insight usually results from the experience. |
| Acceptance | The feeling of being accepted by other members of the group; differences of opinion are tolerated, and there is an absence of censure. |
| Altruism | The act of one member's being of help to another; putting another person's need before one's own and learning that there is value in giving to others. The term was originated by Auguste Comte (1798–1857), and Sigmund Freud believed it was a major factor in establishing group cohesion and community feeling. |
| Catharsis | The expression of ideas, thoughts, and suppressed material that is accompanied by an emotional response that produces a state of relief in the patient. |
| Cohesion | The sense that the group is working together toward a common goal; also referred to as a sense of "we-ness"; believed to be the most important factor related to positive therapeutic effects. |
| Consensual validation | Confirmation of reality by comparing one's own conceptualizations with those of other group members; interpersonal distortions are thereby corrected. The term was introduced by Harry Stack Sullivan; Trigant Burrow had used the phrase "consensual observation" to refer to the same phenomenon. |
| Contagion | The process in which the expression of emotion by one member stimulates the awareness of a similar emotion in another member. |
| Corrective familial experience | The group re-creates the family of origin for some members who can work through original conflicts psychologically through group interaction (e.g., sibling rivalry, anger toward parents). |
| Empathy | The capacity of a group member to put himself or herself into the psychological frame of reference of another group member and thereby understand his or her thinking, feeling, or behavior. |
| Identification | An unconscious defense mechanism in which the person incorporates the characteristics and the qualities of another person or object into his or her ego system |
| Imitation | The conscious emulation or modeling of one's behavior after that of another (also called role modeling); also known as spectator therapy, as one patient learns from another. |
| Insight | Conscious awareness and understanding of one's own psychodynamics and symptoms of maladaptive behavior. Most therapists distinguish two types: (1) intellectual insight—knowledge and awareness without any changes in maladaptive behavior; (2) emotional insight—awareness and understanding leading to positive changes in personality and behavior. |
| Inspiration | The process of imparting a sense of optimism to group members; the ability to recognize that one has the capacity to overcome problems; also known as instillation of hope. |
| Interaction | The free and open exchange of ideas and feelings among group members; effective interaction is emotionally charged. |
| Interpretation | The process during which the group leader formulates the meaning or significance of a patient's resistance, defenses, and symbols; the result is that the patient has a cognitive framework within which to understand his or her behavior. |
| Learning | Patients acquire knowledge about new areas, such as social skills and sexual behavior; they receive advice, obtain guidance, and attempt to influence and are influenced by other group members. |
| Reality testing | Ability of the person to evaluate objectively the world outside the self; includes the capacity to perceive oneself and other group members accurately. *See also* Consensual validation. |
| Transference | Projection of feelings, thoughts, and wishes onto the therapist, who has come to represent an object from the patient's past. Such reactions, while perhaps appropriate for the condition prevailing in the patient's earlier life, are inappropriate and anachronistic when applied to the therapist in the present. Patients in the group may also direct such feelings toward one another, a process called multiple transferences. |
| Universalization | The awareness of the patient that he or she is not alone in having problems; others share similar complaints or difficulties in learning; the patient is not unique. |
| Ventilation | The expression of suppressed feelings, ideas, or events to other group members; the sharing of personal secrets that ameliorate a sense of sin or guilt (also referred to as self-disclosure). |

Table by Benjamin J. Sadock, M.D.

**Table 32.3–6**
**Learning from Behavioral Patterns in the Social Microcosm of the Therapy Group**

Display of interpersonal pathology
↓
Feedback and self-observation
↓
Sharing reactions
↓
Examining the results of sharing reactions
↓
Understanding one's opinion of self
↓
Developing a sense of responsibility
↓
Realizing one's power to effect change
↓
High affect potentiates change

Table from S Vinogradov, I D Yalom: Group therapy. In *The American Psychiatric Press Textbook of Psychiatry*, J A Talbott, R E Hales, S C Yudofsky, editors, p 962. American Psychiatric Press, Washington, 1988. Used with permission.

**Table 32.3–7**
**Goals for Short-Term Inpatient Therapy Groups**

Engaging patients in the therapeutic process
Teaching patients that talking helps
Problem spotting
Decreasing isolation
Allowing patients to be helpful
Alleviating hospital-related anxiety

Table from S Vinogradov, I D Yalom: Group therapy. In *The American Psychiatric Press Textbook of Psychiatry*, J A Talbott, R E Hales, S C Yudofsky, editors, p 980. American Psychiatric Press, Washington, 1988. Used with permission.

**Table 32.3–8**
**Techniques for Short-Term Inpatient Therapy Groups**

Use a shortened time frame.
Show direct support.
Emphasize the here and now.
Provide structure.

Table from S Vinogradov, I D Yalom: Group therapy. In *The American Psychiatric Press Textbook of Psychiatry*, J A Talbott, R E Hales, S C Yudofsky, editors, p 981. American Psychiatric Press, Washington, 1988. Used with permission.

has often learned many details about the small-group program from another patient before actually attending the first session. The less frequently the group sessions are held, the greater is the need for the therapist to structure the group and be active.

**Inpatient versus outpatient groups.** Although the therapeutic factors that account for change in the small inpatient group are similar to those in the outpatient setting, there are qualitative differences. For example, the relatively high turnover of patients in the inpatient group complicates the process of cohesion. But the fact that all the members of the group are together in the hospital aids the cohesion, as do efforts by the therapist to foster the process, emphasizing other similarities. Sharing of information, universalization, and catharsis are the main therapeutic factors at work in inpatient groups.

Although insight is more likely to occur in outpatient groups because of their long-term nature, within the confines of a single group session, some patients can obtain a new understanding of their psychological makeup. A unique quality of the inpatient group is the patients' extragroup contact, which is extensive, as they live together on the same ward. Verbalizing their thoughts and feelings about such contacts in the therapy sessions encourages interpersonal learning. In addition, conflicts between patients or between patients and staff members can be anticipated and resolved. Table 32.3-9 lists the differences between inpatient groups and outpatient groups.

## Self-Help Groups

Self-help groups are composed of persons who want to cope with a specific problem or life crisis. Usually organized with a particular task in mind, such groups do not attempt to explore individual psychodynamics in great depth or to change personality functioning significantly. But self-help groups have improved the emotional health and well-being of many people.

A distinguishing characteristic of the self-help group is its homogeneity. The members suffer from the same dis-

**Table 32.3–9**
**Differences Between Outpatient Groups and Inpatient Groups**

| Outpatient Groups | Inpatient Groups |
|---|---|
| Stable composition | Rarely the same group for more than one or two meetings |
| Patients well selected and prepared | Patients admitted to the group with little prior selection or preparation |
| Group is homogeneous regarding ego function, although conflicts and issues differ | Heterogeneous level of ego functioning |
| Motivated, self-referred patients; growth-oriented | Ambivalent, often compulsory patients in crisis; relief-oriented |
| Treatment proceeds as long as required; 1 to 2 years; 50 to 100 meetings | Treatment limited to the hospitalization period; 1 to 3 weeks, with rapid patient turnover |
| Boundary of group well maintained with few external influences | Continuous boundary interface with the milieu |
| Group cohesion develops normally, given sufficient time in treatment | No time for cohesion to develop spontaneously; group development aborted in early phases |
| Therapy is private and unexposed | Exposed, open to observation and scrutiny by the milieu |
| Leader allows the process to unfold; there is ample time to set group norms | Group leader's structuring of the group is critical; passive analytic approaches lead to group disintegration |
| No extra group contact encouraged | Patients sleep, eat, and live together outside the group; extragroup contact endorsed |

Table from M Leszcz: Inpatient groups, Ann Rev Psychiatry 5: 729, 1986. Used with permission.

orders, and they share their experiences—good and bad, successful and unsuccessful—with one another. By so doing, they educate one another, provide mutual support, and alleviate the sense of alienation that is usually felt by the person drawn to that type of group.

Self-help groups emphasize cohesion, which is exceptionally strong in those groups. Because of the group members' similar problems and symptoms, a strong emotional bond and the group's own characteristics develop, to which the members may attribute magical qualities of healing. Examples of self-help groups are Alcoholics Anonymous (AA), Gamblers Anonymous (GA), and Overeaters Anonymous (OA).

The self-help group movement is in its ascendency. The groups meet their members' needs by providing acceptance, mutual support, and help in overcoming maladaptive patterns of behavior or states of feeling with which traditional mental health and medical professionals have not been generally successful. Self-help groups and therapy groups have begun to converge: the self-help groups have enabled their members to give up a pattern of unwanted behavior; the therapy groups help their members understand why and how they got to be the way they were or are.

## COMBINED INDIVIDUAL AND GROUP PSYCHOTHERAPY

In combined individual and group psychotherapy, patients are seen individually by the therapist and also take part in group sessions. The therapist for the group and for the individual sessions is usually the same person.

Groups can vary in size from 3 to 15 members, but the best size is 8 to 10. Patients must attend all group sessions. Attendance at individual sessions is also important, and the failure to attend either group or individual sessions should be examined as part of the therapeutic process.

Combined therapy is a particular treatment modality. It is not a system by which individual therapy is augmented by an occasional group session, nor does it mean that a participant in group therapy meets alone with the therapist from time to time. Rather, it is an ongoing plan in which the group experience interacts meaningfully with the individual sessions and in which reciprocal feedback helps form an integrated therapeutic experience. Although the one-to-one doctor-patient relationship makes possible a deep examination of the transference reaction for some patients, it may not provide the corrective emotional experiences necessary for therapeutic change for other patients. The group gives patients a variety of persons with whom they can have transferential reactions. In the microcosm of the group, patients can relive and work through familial and other important influences.

### Techniques

Various techniques based on varying theoretical frameworks have been used in the combined therapy format. Some clinicians increase the frequency of the individual sessions to encourage the emergence of the transference

neurosis. In the behavioral model, individual sessions are regularly scheduled but tend to be less frequent than in other approaches. Depending on the therapist's orientation, during the individual sessions the patient may use a couch or a chair. Techniques such as alternate meetings may be used in the group setting. Harold Kaplan and Benjamin Sadock developed a combined therapy approach called structured interactional group psychotherapy, in which a different member is the focus at each weekly group session and is discussed in some depth by the other members.

### Results

Most workers in the field believe that combined therapy has the advantages of both the dyadic setting and the group setting, without sacrificing the qualities of either. Generally, the dropout rate in combined therapy is lower than that in group therapy alone. In many cases, combined therapy appears to bring problems to the surface and to resolve them more quickly than may be possible with either method alone.

## PSYCHODRAMA

Psychodrama is a method of group psychotherapy originated by the Viennese-born psychiatrist Jacob Moreno in which personality makeup, interpersonal relationships, conflicts, and emotional problems are explored by means of special dramatic methods. The therapeutic dramatization of emotional problems includes (1) the protagonist or patient, the person who acts out problems with the help of (2) auxiliary egos, persons who enact varying aspects of the patient, and (3) the director, psychodramatist, or therapist, the person who guides those in the drama toward the acquisition of insight.

### Roles

**Director.** The director is the leader or therapist and so must be active and participating. He or she encourages the members of the group to be spontaneous and so has a catalytic function. The director must also be available to meet the group's needs and not superimpose his or her values on it. Of all the group psychotherapies, psychodrama requires of the therapist the most participation and ability to lead.

**Protagonist.** The protagonist is the patient in conflict. The patient chooses the situation to portray in the dramatic scene, or the therapist may choose it if the patient so desires.

**Auxiliary ego.** An auxiliary ego is another group member who represents something or someone in the protagonist's experience. The auxiliary egos help account for the great range of therapeutic effects available in psychodrama.

**Group.** The members of the psychodrama and the audience make up the group. Some are participants, and others are observers, but all benefit from the experience to the extent that they can identify with the ongoing events. The concept of spontaneity in psychodrama refers to the ability of each member of the group, especially the protagonist, to experience the thoughts and feelings of the moment and to communicate emotion as authentically as possible.

## Techniques

The psychodrama may focus on any special area of functioning (a dream, a family, or a community situation), a symbolic role, an unconscious attitude, or an imagined future situation. Such symptoms as delusions and hallucinations can also be acted out in the group. Techniques to advance the therapeutic process, productivity, and creativity include the soliloquy (a recital of overt and hidden thoughts and feelings), role reversal (the exchange of the patient's role for the role of a significant person), the double (an auxiliary ego acting as the patient), the multiple double (several egos acting as the patient did on varying occasions), and the mirror technique (an ego imitating the patient and speaking for him or her). Other techniques include the use of hypnosis and psychoactive drugs to modify the acting behavior in various ways.

## References

Amaranto E A, Bender S S: Individual psychotherapy as an adjunct to group psychotherapy. Int J Group Psychother *40*: 91, 1990.
American Psychiatric Association: *Task Force Report on Encounter Groups and Psychiatry*. American Psychiatric Association, Washington, 1970.
Bloch S, Crouch E: *Therapeutic Factors in Group Psychotherapy*. Oxford University Press, New York, 1985.
Cartwright D, Zander A, editors: *Group Dynamics and Research Theory*. Harper & Row, New York, 1960.
Dies R R: The future of group therapy. Psychotherapy *29*: 58, 1992.
Erickson R C: *Inpatient Small Group Psychotherapy*. Thomas, Springfield, Ill, 1984.
Freud S: Group psychology and analysis of the ego. In *Standard Edition of the Complete Psychological Works of Sigmund Freud*, vol 18, p 67. Hogarth Press, London, 1962.
Grotjohn M, Freedman C T H, editors: *Handbook of Group Therapy*. Van Nostrand Reinhold, New York, 1983.
Kaplan H I, Sadock B J, editors: *Comprehensive Group Psychotherapy*, ed 3. Williams & Wilkins, Baltimore, 1993.
Karterud S W: Reflections on group-analytic research. Group Analysis *25*: 353, 1992.
Leszcz M: In inpatient groups. In *Psychiatry Update*, vol 5, A J Frances, R E Aoles, editors, p 729. American Psychiatric Press, Washington, 1986.
Leszcz M: The interpersonal approach to group psychotherapy. Int J Group Psychother *42*: 37, 1992.
Lieberman M A: Effects of large group awareness training on participants' psychiatric status. Am J Psychiatry *144*: 460, 1987.
Lieberman M A, Berman L: *Self-Help Groups for Coping with Crisis: Origins, Members, Processes and Import*. Jossey-Bass, San Francisco, 1979.
Lieberman M A, Yalom I: Brief group psychotherapy for the spousally bereaved: A controlled study. Int J Group Psychother *42*: 117, 1992.
Moreno J L: *Psychodrama*. Beacon Press, Beacon, N Y, 1947.
Olsen P A, Barth P A: New uses of psychodrama. Operational Psychiatry *14*: 95, 1983.
Ormont L R: Subjective countertransference in the group setting: The modern analytic experience. Mod Psychoanal *17*: 3, 1992.
Pilkonis P A, Imber S D, Lewis P, Rubinsky P: A comparative outcome study of individual, group and conjoint psychotherapy. Arch Gen Psychiatry *41*: 431, 1984.
Piper W E, Perrault E L: Pretherapy preparation for group members. Int J Group Psychother *39*: 17, 1989.
Rutan J S: Psychodynamic group psychotherapy. Int J Group Psychother *42*: 19, 1992.
Sadock B J: Group psychotherapy, combined individual and group psychotherapy, and psychodrama. In *Comprehensive Textbook of Psychiatry*, ed 5, H I Kaplan, B J Sadock, editors, p 1517. Williams & Wilkins, Baltimore, 1989.
Sigrell B: The long-term effects of group psychotherapy: A thirteen-year follow-up study. Group Anal *25*: 333, 1992.
Soldz S, Budman S, Demby A, Feldstein M: Patient activity and outcome in group psychotherapy: New findings. Int J Group Psychother *40*: 53, 1990.
Stone W N: The place of self psychology in group psychotherapy: A status report. Int J Group Psychother *42*: 335, 1992.
Weiner M F: Group therapy reduces medical and psychiatric hospitalization. Int J Group Psychother *42*: 267, 1992.
Weiner M F: *Techniques of Group Psychotherapy*. American Psychiatric Press, Washington, 1984.
Wolf A, Schwartz M: *Psychoanalysis in Groups*. Grune & Stratton, New York, 1962.
Yalom I D: *The Theory and Practice of Group Psychotherapy*, ed 3. Basic Books, New York, 1985.

# 32.4 / Family Therapy and Marital Therapy

Family systems theory states that a family behaves as if it were a unit with a particular homeostasis of relating that is maintained regardless of how maladaptive it is. The goals of family therapy are to recognize and acknowledge the often covert pattern of maintaining balance within a family and to help the family understand the pattern's meaning and purpose.

Family therapists generally believe that one member of the family has been labeled the identified patient. That person is identified by the family as "the one who is the problem, is to blame, needs help." The family therapist's goal is to help the family understand that the identified patient's symptoms are, in fact, serving a crucial function in maintaining the family's homeostasis. The process of family therapy helps reveal a family's repetitious and ultimately predictable communication patterns that are sustaining and reflecting the identified patient's behavior.

Inherent in family systems theory is the belief, to one degree or another, that the marital relationship strongly influences the nature of a family's system and homeostasis. One influential family therapist has described that concept as the marital dyad's being the "architects of the family."

## FAMILY THERAPY

### Initial Consultation

Family therapy is well-enough known that families with a high level of conflict may request it specifically. When the initial complaint is about an individual family member, however, pretreatment work may be necessary. Typical fears underlying resistance to a family approach are fears (1) by parents that they will be blamed for their child's difficulties, (2) that the entire family will be pronounced sick, (3) that a spouse will object, and (4) that open discussion of one child's misbehavior will have a negative influence on younger siblings. Refusal by an adolescent or young adult patient to participate in family therapy is frequently a disguised collusion with the fears of one or both parents.

## Interview Technique

The special quality of the family interview proceeds from two important facts: (1) The family comes to treatment with its history and dynamics firmly in place. To the family therapist, it is the established nature of the group, more than the symptoms, that constitutes the clinical problem. (2) Family members usually live together and, at some level, depend on one another for their physical and emotional well-being. Whatever transpires in the therapy session is known to all. Central principles of technique derive from those facts. For example, the catharsis of anger by one family member toward another must be carefully channeled by the therapist. The person who is the object of the anger is present and will react to the attack, running the danger of escalation toward violence, fractured relationships, and withdrawal from therapy. Free association is likewise not appropriate, because it would encourage one person to dominate the session. For those reasons the therapist must always control and direct the family interview.

Virginia Satir recommended initiating at least the first two sessions of family therapy with a family-life chronology. The technique reflects many family therapy precepts. Figure 32.4–1 summarizes the key features of the family-life chronology, and Table 32.4–1 summarizes Satir's reasoning behind its use, reflecting many family therapy paradigms.

## Frequency and Length of Treatment

Unless an emergency arises, sessions are usually held no more than once a week. Each session, however, may require as much as two hours. Long sessions can include an intermission to give the therapist time to organize the material and plan a response. A flexible schedule is necessary when geography or personal circumstances make it physically difficult for the family to get together. The length of treatment depends not only on the nature of the problem but also on the therapeutic model. Therapists who use problem-solving models exclusively may accomplish their goals in a few sessions; therapists using growth-oriented models may work with a family for years, with sessions at long intervals

Table 32.4–2 summarizes one model for treatment termination.

## Models of Intervention

An overview of family therapy models, techniques, and goals is given in Table 32.4–3.

**Psychodynamic-experiential models.** Psychodynamic-experiential models emphasize individual maturation in the context of the family system, free from unconscious patterns of anxiety and projection rooted in the past. Therapists seek to establish an intimate bond with each family member, alternating between the therapist's exchanges with the members and the members' exchanges with one another. Clarity of communication and honestly admitted feelings are given high priority; toward that end, family members may be encouraged to change their seats, to touch one another, and to make direct eye contact. Their use of metaphor, body language, and para-

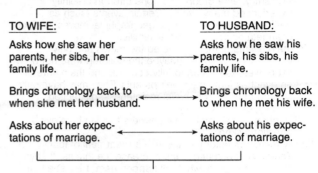

**Figure 32.4–1** Main flow of family-life chronology to family as a whole. (Figure from V Satir: *Conjoint Family Therapy,* p 55. Science and Behavior, Palo Alto, 1967. Used with permission.)

**Table 32.4–1**
**Rationale for Family-Life Chronology**

The family therapist enters a session knowing little or nothing about the family.
The therapist may know who the identified patient is and what symptoms the patient manifests, but that is usually all. So the therapist must get clues about the meaning of the symptom.
The therapist may know that pain exists in the marital relationship but needs to get clues about how the pain shows itself.
The therapist needs to get clues about how the pain shows itself.
The therapist needs to know how the mates have tried to cope with their problems.
The therapist may know that the mates both operate from models (from what they saw going on between their own parents) but needs to find out how those models have influenced each mate's expectations about how to be a mate and how to be a parent.

**Table 32.4–1**
*Continued*

The family therapist enters a session knowing that the family has, in fact, had a history, but that is usually all.

Every family, as a group, has gone through or jointly experienced many events. Certain events (such as deaths, childbirth, sickness, geographical moves, and job changes) occur in almost all families.

Certain events primarily affected the mates and only indirectly the children. (Maybe the children were not born yet or were too young to fully comprehend the nature of an event as it affected their parents. They may have only sensed periods of parental remoteness, distraction, anxiety, or annoyance.)

The therapist can profit from answers to just about every question asked.

Family members enter therapy with a great deal of fear.

Therapist structuring helps decrease the threats. It says: "I am in charge of what will happen here. I will see to it that nothing catastrophic happens here."

All members are covertly feeling to blame for the fact that nothing seems to have turned out right (even though they may overtly blame the identified patient or the other mate).

Parents, especially, need to feel that they did the best they could as parents. They need to tell the therapist: "This is why I did what I did. This is what happened to me."

A family-life chronology that deals with such facts as names, dates, labeled relationships, and moves seems to appeal to the family. It asks questions that members can answer, questions that are relatively nonthreatening. It deals with life as the family understands it.

Family members enter therapy with a great deal of despair. Therapist structuring helps stimulate hope.

As far as family members are concerned, past events are part of them. They now can tell the therapist, "I existed." And they can also say: "I am not just a big blob of pathology. I succeeded in overcoming many handicaps."

If the family knew what questions needed asking, they would not need to be in therapy. So the therapist does not say, "Tell me what you want to tell me." Family members will simply tell the therapist what they have been telling themselves for years. The therapist's questions say: "I know what to ask. I take responsibility for understanding you. We are going to go somewhere."

The family therapist also knows that, to some degree, the family has focused on the identified patient to relieve marital pain. The therapist also knows that, to some degree, the family will resist any effort to change that focus. A family-life chronology is an effective, nonthreatening way to change from an emphasis on the "sick" or "bad" family member to an emphasis on the marital relationship.

The family-life chronology serves other useful therapy purposes, such as providing the framework within which a reeducation process can take place. The therapist serves as a model in checking out information or correcting communication techniques and placing questions and eliciting answers to begin the process. In addition, when taking the chronology, the therapist can introduce in a relatively nonfrightening way some of the crucial concepts to induce change.

Table adapted from V Satir: *Conjoint Family Therapy,* p 57. Science and Behavior, Palo Alto, 1967. Used with permission.

**Table 32.4–2**
**Criteria for Treatment Termination**

Treatment is completed:

When family members can complete transactions, check, ask.

When they can interpret hostility.

When they can see how others see them.

When they can see how they see themselves.

When one member can tell others how they manifest themselves.

When one member can tell others what is hoped, feared, and expected from them.

When they can disagree.

When they can make choices.

When they can learn through practice.

When they can free themselves from the harmful effects of past models.

When they can give a clear message—that is, be congruent in their behavior—with a minimum of difference between feelings and communication and with a minimum of hidden messages.

Table adapted from V Satir: *Conjoint Family Therapy,* p 133. Science and Behavior, Palo Alto, 1967. Used with permission.

praxes helps reveal the unconscious pattern of family relationships. The therapist may also use *family sculpting,* in which family members physically arrange one another in tableaus depicting their personal view of relationships, past or present. The therapist both interprets the sculpture and modifies it in a way to suggest new relationships. In addition, the therapist's subjective responses to the family are given great importance. At appropriate moments the responses are expressed to the family to form yet another feedback loop of self-observation and change.

**Bowen model.** Murray Bowen called his model simply "family systems," but in the field it has rightly been given the name of its originator. Its hallmark is personal differentiation from the family of origin, the ability to be one's true self in the face of the familial or other pressures that threaten the loss of love or social position. The problem family is assessed on two levels: (1) the degree of their enmeshment versus the degree of their ability to differentiate and (2) the analysis of emotional triangles in the presenting problem. An *emotional triangle* is defined as a three-party system (of which there can be many within a family) arranged so that the closeness of two members tends to exclude a third. The closeness may be expressed as either love or repetitive conflict. In either case, emotional cross-currents are activated when the excluded third party attempts to join with one of the others or when one of the involved parties shifts in the direction of the excluded one. The role of the therapist is, first, to stabilize or shift the hot triangle—the one that relates to the presenting symptoms—and, second, to work with the most psychologically available family members, individually if necessary, on achieving enough personal differentiation so that the hot triangle does not recur. To stay neutral in their triangles, the therapist minimizes emotional contact with family members. Bowen originated the *genogram,* which is a historical survey of the family going back several generations.

**Structural model.** In a structural model the family is viewed as a single interrelated system assessed along the following lines: (1) significant alliances and splits among family members, (2) hierarchy of power (that is, the parents in charge of the children), (3) the clarity and firmness of boundaries between the generations, and (4) the family's tolerance of one another. The structural model uses concurrent individual and family therapy.

**General systems model.** Based on general systems theory, a general systems model holds that the family is a system and that every action in the family produces a reaction in one or more of its members. Every member is presumed to play a role (for example, spokesperson, persecutor, victim, rescuer,

**Table 32.4–3**
**Major Models of Family Therapy: Normality, Dysfunction, and Therapeutic Goals**

| Model of Family Therapy | View of Normal Family Functioning | View of Dysfunction and Symptoms | Goals of Therapy |
|---|---|---|---|
| **Structural**<br>Minuchcin<br>Montaivo<br>Aponte | Boundaries clear and firm<br>Hierarchy with strong parental subsystem<br>Flexibility of system for autonomy and interdependence, individual growth and system maintenance, continuity and adaptive restructuring in response to changing internal (developmental) and external (environmental) demands | Symptoms result from current family structural imbalance: malfunctioning hierarchical arrangement, boundaries maladaptive reaction to changing requirements (developmental, environmental) | Reorganize family structure:<br>shift members' relative positions to disrupt malfunctioning pattern and strengthen parental hierarchy<br>create clear, flexible boundaries mobilize more adaptive alternative patterns |
| **Strategic**<br>Haley<br>Milan team<br>Palo Alto group | Flexibility<br>Large behavioral repertoire for problem resolution and life-cycle passage<br>Clear rules governing hierarchy (Haley) | Multiple origins of problems; symptoms maintained by family's unsuccessful problem-solving attempts; inability to adjust the life-cycle transitions (Haley), malfunctioning hierarchy: triangle or coalition across hierarchy (Haley)<br>Symptom is a communicative act embedded in interaction pattern | Resolve presenting problem only: specific behaviorally defined objectives<br>Interrupt rigid feedback cycle: change symptom-maintaining sequence to new outcome<br>Define clearer hierarchy (Haley) |
| **Behavioral-social exchange**<br>Liberman<br>Patterson<br>Alexander | Maladaptive behavior is not reinforced<br>Adaptive behavior is rewarded<br>Exchange of benefits outweighs costs<br>Long-term reciprocity | Maladaptive symptomatic behavior reinforced by family attention and reward, deficient reward exchanges (e.g., coercive), and communication deficit | Concrete, observable behavioral goals: change contingencies of social reinforcement (interpersonal consequences of behavior):<br>rewards for adaptive behavior no rewards for maladaptive behavior |
| **Psychodynamic**<br>Ackerman<br>Boszormenyl-Nagy<br>Framo<br>Lidz<br>Meissner<br>Paul<br>Stierlin | Parental personalities and relationships well-differentiated<br>Relationship perceptions based on current realities, not projections from past<br>Boszormenyl-Nagy: relational equitability<br>Lidz: family task requisites: parenteral coalition; generation boundaries, and sex-linked parental roles | Symptoms caused by family projection process stemming from unresolved conflicts and losses in family of origin | Insight and resolution of family of origin conflict and losses<br>Family projection processes<br>Relationship reconstruction and reunion<br>Individual and family growth |
| **Family systems therapy**<br>Bowen | Differentiation of self<br>Intellectual-emotional balance | Functioning impaired by relationships with family of origin: poor differentiation, anxiety (reactivity), family projection process, and triangulation | Differentiation<br>Cognitive functioning<br>Emotional reactivity<br>Modification of relationships in family system: detriangulation repair cutoffs |
| **Experiential**<br>Satir<br>Whitaker | Satir:<br>Self-worth: high<br>Communication: clear, specific, honest<br>Family rules: flexible, human, appropriate<br>Linkage to society: open, hopeful<br>Whitaker: multiple aspects of family structure and shared experience | Symptoms are nonverbal messages in reaction to current communication dysfunction in system | Direct, clear communication<br>Individual and family growth through immediate shared experience |

Table from F Walsh: Conceptualizations of normal family functioning. In *Normal Family Processes*, F Walsh, editor, p 133. Guilford, New York, 1982. Used with permission.

symptom bearer, nurturer), which is relatively stable; however, the member who fills each role may change. Some families try to scapegoat one member by blaming him or her for the family's problems (the identified patient). If the identified patient improves, another family member may become the scapegoat. The family is defined as having external boundaries and internal rules. The general systems model overlaps with some of the other models presented, particularly the Bowen and structural models.

## Techniques

**Family group therapy.** Family group therapy combines several families into a single group. Mutual problems are shared, and families compare their interactions with those of the other families in the group. Multiple family groups have been used effectively in the treatment of schizophrenia. Parents of disturbed children may also be gathered together to share their situations.

**Social network therapy.** Social network therapy gathers together the social community or network of a disturbed patient, all of whom meet in group sessions with the patient. The network includes those persons with whom the patient comes into contact in daily life, not only the immediate family but also relatives, friends, tradespeople, teachers, and coworkers.

**Paradoxical therapy.** This approach, which evolved from the work of Gregory Bateson, consists of suggesting that the patient intentionally engage in the unwanted behavior (called the paradoxical injunction), such as avoiding the phobic object or performing the compulsive ritual. Although paradoxical therapy and the use of paradoxical injunctions are relatively new, the therapy may create new insights for some patients. The danger of the approach is that it may be used in an arbitrary or routinized fashion.

**Positive connotation.** Positive connotation or reframing is a relabeling of all negatively expressed feelings or behavior as positive. The therapist attempts to get family members to view behavior from a new frame of reference—for example, "This child is impossible" becomes "This child is desperately trying to distract and protect you from what he or she perceives as an unhappy marriage."

## Goals

The goals of treatment are (1) to resolve or reduce pathogenic conflict and anxiety within the matrix of interpersonal relationships, (2) to enhance the perception and fulfillment by family members of one another's emotional needs, (3) to promote appropriate role relationships between the sexes and between the generations, (4) to strengthen the capacity of individual members and the family as a whole to cope with destructive forces inside and outside the surrounding environment, and (5) to influence family identity and values so that members are oriented toward health and growth.

A final goal is to integrate the family into the large systems in the society, which include not only the extended family but also society—as represented by such systems as schools, medical facilities, and social, recreational, and welfare agencies—so that the family is not isolated.

## MARITAL THERAPY

Marital therapy is a form psychotherapy designed to psychologically modify the interaction of two people who are in conflict with each other over one parameter or a variety of parameters—social, emotional, sexual, economic. In marital therapy a trained person establishes a therapeutic contract with the patient-couple and, through definite types of communication, attempts to alleviate the disturbance, to reverse or change maladaptive patterns of behavior, and to encourage personality growth and development.

Marriage counseling may be considered more limited in scope than marital therapy in that only a particular familial conflict is discussed. Marriage counseling may also be primarily task-oriented, geared to solving a specific problem, such as child rearing. Marriage therapy emphasizes restructuring the interaction between the couple, sometimes exploring the psychodynamics of each partner. Both therapy and counseling stress helping the marital partners cope effectively with their problems. Most important is the definition of appropriate and realistic goals, which may involve extensive reconstruction of the union or problem-solving approaches or a combination of both.

### Types of Therapy

**Individual therapy.** In individual therapy the marital partners may be seen by different therapists, who may not necessarily communicate with each other. Indeed, they may not even know each other. The goal of the treatment is to strengthen each partner's adaptive capacities. At times, only one of the partners is in treatment; in such cases, a visit by the spouse who is not in treatment with the therapist may be helpful. The visiting partner may give the therapist data about the patient that may otherwise be overlooked; overt or covert anxiety in the visiting partner as a result of change in the patient can be identified and dealt with; irrational beliefs about treatment events can be corrected; and conscious or unconscious attempts by the partner to sabotage the patient's treatment can be examined.

**Individual marital therapy.** In individual marital therapy each of the marriage partners is in therapy. When the same therapist conducts the treatment, it is called concurrent therapy; when the partners are seen by different therapists, it is called collaborative therapy.

**Conjoint therapy.** Conjoint therapy is the treatment of partners in joint sessions conducted by either one or two therapists; it is the treatment method most frequently used in marital therapy. Cotherapy with therapists of both sexes prevents a particular patient from feeling ganged up on when confronted by two members of the opposite sex.

**Four-way session.** In a four-way session each partner is seen by a different therapist, with regular joint sessions in which all four persons participate. A variation of the four-way session is the roundtable interview, developed by William Masters and Virginia Johnson for the rapid treatment of sexually dysfunctional couples. Two patients and two opposite-sex therapists meet regularly.

**Group psychotherapy.** Therapy for married couples placed in a group allows a variety of group dynamics to affect the couples. The group usually consists of three to four couples and one or two therapists. The couples identify with one another and recognize that others have similar problems; each gains support and empathy from fellow group members of the same or opposite sex; they explore sexual attitudes and have an opportunity to gain new information from their peer groups, and each receives specific feedback about his or her behavior, either negative or positive, that may have more meaning and be better assimilated coming from a neutral non-spouse member than from the spouse or the therapist.

When only one partner is in a therapy group, the spouse may occasionally visit the group, so as to allow the members to test reality. At times, a group may be so organized that only one married couple is part of the large group.

**Combined therapy.** Combined therapy refers to all or any of the preceding techniques used concurrently or in combination. Thus, a particular patient-couple may begin treatment with one or both partners in individual psychotherapy, continue to conjoint therapy with the partner, and terminate therapy after a course of treatment in a married couples group. The rationale for combined therapy is that no single approach to marital problems has been shown to be superior to another. A familiarity with a variety of approaches thus allows the therapist a degree of flexibility that provides maximum benefit for the couple in distress.

## Indications

Regardless of the specific therapeutic technique used, certain indications for initiating marital therapy have been agreed on: (1) when individual therapy has failed to resolve the marital difficulties, (2) when the onset of distress in one or both partners is clearly related to marital events, and (3) when marital therapy is requested by a couple in conflict. Problems in communication between partners are a prime indication for marital therapy. In such instances one spouse may be intimidated by the other, may become anxious when attempting to tell the other about thoughts or feelings, or may project unconscious expectations onto the other. The therapy is geared toward enabling each of the partners to see the other realistically.

Conflicts in one or several areas, such as the partners' sexual life, are also indications for treatment. Similarly, difficulty in establishing satisfactory social, economic, parental, or emotional roles is an indication for help. The clinician should evaluate all aspects of the marital relationship before attempting to treat only one problem, as it may be a symptom of a pervasive marital disorder.

## Contraindications

Contraindications for marital therapy include patients with severe forms of psychosis, particularly patients with paranoid elements and those in whom the marriage's homeostatic mechanism is a protection against psychosis; one or both of the partners really wants to divorce; or one spouse refuses to participate because of anxiety or fear.

## Goals

Nathan Ackerman defined the aims of marital therapy as follows: The goals of therapy for marital disorders are to alleviate emotional distress and disability and to promote the levels of well-being of both partners together and each as an individual. In a general way, the therapist moves toward those goals by strengthening the shared resources for problem solving, by encouraging the substitution of adequate controls and defenses for pathogenic ones, by enhancing both the immunity against the disintegrative effects of emotional upset and the complementarity of the relationship, and by promoting the growth of the relationship and each partner.

Part of the therapeutic task is to persuade each partner in the marriage to take responsibility in understanding the psychodynamic makeup of his or her personality. Accountability for the effects of behavior on one's own life, the life of the spouse, and the lives of others in the environment is emphasized, which often results in a deep understanding of the problems that created the marital discord.

Marital therapy does not ensure the maintenance of any marriage. Indeed, in certain instances it may show the partners that they are in a nonviable union that should be dissolved. In those cases the couple may continue to meet with the therapist to work through the difficult process of separating and obtaining a divorce. That has been called divorce therapy.

## References

Babcock J C, Waltz J, Jacobson N S, Gottman J M: Power and violence: The relation between communication patterns, power discrepancies, and domestic violence. J Consult Clin Psychol *61*: 40, 1993.

Berkowitz D: An overview of the psychodynamics of couples: Bridging concepts. In *Marriage and Divorce: A Contemporary Perspective*, C C Nadelson, D C Polonsky, editors, p 83. Guilford, New York, 1984.

Bowen M: *Family Theory in Clinical Practice*. Aronson, New York, 1978.

Brody S: Simultaneous psychotherapy of married couples in current psychiatric therapy. In *Current Psychiatric Therapy*, J Masserman, editor, p 524. Grune & Stratton, New York, 1961.

Coyne J C: Strategic therapy with married depressed persons: Initial agenda, themes and interventions. J Mar Fam Ther *10*: 153, 1984.

Crago M A: Psychopathology in married couples. Psychol Bull *77*: 114, 1972.

Framo J: Family of origin as a therapeutic response for adults in marital and family therapy: You can and should go home again. Fam Pract *15*: 193, 1976.

Goldstein M, editor: *New Developments in Interventions with Families of Schizophrenics*. Jossey-Bass, San Francisco, 1981.

Green R J, Framo J L, editors: *Family Therapy: Major Contributions*. International Universities Press, New York, 1981.

Greene B L, Broadhurst B P, Lustig N: Treatment of marital disharmony. In *Psychotherapy of Marital Disharmony*, B Greene, editor, p 317. Free Press, New York, 1965.

Guerin P J, Pendagast E: Evaluation of family systems and genogram. In *Family Therapy Theory and Practice*, P J Guerin, editor, p 450. Gardner, New York, 1976.

Houlihan M M, Jackson J, Rogers T R: Decision making of satisfied and dissatisfied married couples. J Soc Psychol *130*: 89, 1990.

Lansky M R: Family therapy. In *Comprehensive Textbook of Psychiatry*, ed 5, H I Kaplan, B J Sadock, editors, p 1535. Williiams & Wilkins, Baltimore, 1989.

Lansky M R, editor: *Family Therapy and Major Psychopathology*. Grune & Stratton, New York, 1981.

Lidz T, Fleck S, Cornelison A: *Schizophrenia and the Family*. International Universities Press, New York, 1965.

Main T F: Mutual projection in marriage. Compr Psychiatry *7*: 432, 1966.

Markman H J, Hahlweg K: The prediction and prevention of marital distress: An international perspective. Clin Psychol Rev *13*: 29, 1993.

Minuchin S: *Families and Family Therapy*. Harvard University Press, Cambridge, 1974.

Mittleman B: Complementary neurotic reactions in intimate relationships. Psychoanal Q *13*: 479, 1944.

Nadelson C, Polonsky D C: Couples therapy. In *Comprehensive Textbook of Psychiatry*, ed 5, H I Kaplan, B J Sadock, editors, p 1550. Williams & Wilkins, Baltimore, 1989.

Nadelson C C, Polonsky D C, Mathews M A: Marriage as a developmental process. In *Marriage and Divorce: A Contemporary Perspective*, C C Nadelson, D C Polonsky, editors, p 137. Guilford, New York, 1983.

O'Leary K D, Beach S R: Marital therapy: A viable treatment for depression and marital discord. Am J Psychiatry *147*: 183, 1990.

Paul N, Grosser G: Operational mourning and its role in conjoint family therapy. Community Ment Health J *1*: 339, 1965.

Pinsof W M: A conceptual framework and methodological criteria for family therapy process research. J Consult Clin Psychol *57*: 53, 1989.

Polonsky D, Nadelson C C: An integrative approach to couples therapy. In *New Clinical Concepts in Marital Therapy,* O J W Bjorksten, editor, p 201. American Psychiatric Press, Washington, 1985.

Satir V: *Conjoint Family Therapy.* Science & Behavior, Palo Alto, 1967.

Scharff N, Scharff J: *Object Relations Family Therapy.* Aronson, New York, 1987.

Snyder D K, Wills R M: Behavioral versus insight-oriented marital therapy: Effects on individual and interspousal functioning. J Consult Clin Psychol *57*: 39, 1989.

Tarrier N: Effect of treating the family to reduce relapse in schizophrenia: A review. J R Soc Med *82*: 423, 1989.

# 32.5 / Biofeedback

Biofeedback provides information to a person regarding one or more physiological processes in an effort to enable the person to gain some element of voluntary control over bodily functions that normally operate outside consciousness. Biofeedback is based on the concept that autonomic responses can be controlled through the process of operant or instrumental conditioning. Physiological manifestations of anxiety or tension (for example, headaches, tachycardia, and pain) can be reduced by teaching the patient to be aware of the physiological differences between tension and relaxation. The teaching involves immediate feedback to the patient through concrete, visible or audible recordings of the patient's biological functioning during anxiety versus relaxation states; the procedure reinforces the patient's awareness of which state is present and helps the patient control it.

## THEORY

Neal Miller demonstrated the medical potential of biofeedback by showing that the normally involuntary autonomic nervous system can be operantly conditioned, using appropriate feedback. By means of instruments, the patient is given information about the status of certain involuntary biological functions, such as skin temperature and electrical conductivity, muscle tension, blood pressure, heart rate, and brain wave activity. The patient is then taught to regulate one or more of those biological states, which affect symptoms. For example, the ability to raise the temperature of one's hands may be used to reduce the frequency of migraines, palpitations, or angina pectoris. A presumptive mechanism is a lowering of sympathetic activation and a voluntary self-regulation of arterial smooth muscle vasoconstrictive tendencies in predisposed persons. Section 27.3 discusses biofeedback further.

## METHODS

The type of feedback instrument used depends on the patient and the specific problem. The most effective instruments are the electromyogram (EMG), which measures the electrical potentials of muscle fibers; the electroencephalogram (EEG), which measures alpha waves that occur in relaxed states; the galvanic skin response gauge (GSR), which shows decreased skin conductivity during a relaxed state; and the thermistor, which measures skin temperature, which drops during tension because of peripheral vasoconstriction. The patient is attached to one of the measuring instruments, which measures a physiological function and translates the impulse into an audible or visual signal that the patient uses to gauge his or her responses. For example, in the treatment of bruxism, an EMG is attached to the masseter muscle. The EMG emits a high tone when the muscle is contracted and a low tone when at rest. The patient can learn to alter the tone to indicate relaxation. The patient receives feedback about the masseter muscle; the tone reinforces the learning; and the condition ameliorates—all those events interacting synergistically.

Table 32.5-1 outlines some of the important clinical applications of biofeedback. As can be seen in the table, a wide variety of biofeedback modalities have been used to treat numerous conditions. Many less specific clinical applications—such as treating insomnia, dysmenorrhea, and speech problems; improving athletic performance; treating volitional disorders; achieving altered states of consciousness; managing stress; and using biofeedback as

**Table 32.5–1**
**Biofeedback Applications**

| Condition | Effects |
|---|---|
| Asthma | Both frontal EMG and airway resistance biofeedback have been reported as producing relaxation from the panic associated with asthma, as well as improving air flow rate. |
| Cardiac arrhythmias | Specific biofeedback of the electrocardiogram has permitted patients to lower the frequency of premature ventricular contractions. |
| Fecal incontinence and enuresis | The timing sequence of internal and external anal sphincters has been measured, using triple lumen rectal catheters providing feedback to incontinent patients in order for them to reestablish normal bowel habits in a relatively small number of biofeedback sessions. An actual precursor of biofeedback dating to 1938 was the sounding of a buzzer for sleeping enuretic children at the first sign of moisture (the pad and bell). |

**Table 32.5–1**
*Continued*

| Condition | Effects |
| --- | --- |
| Grand mal epilepsy | A number of EEG biofeedback procedures have been used experimentally to suppress seizure activity prophylactically in patients not responsive to anticonvulsant medication. The procedures permit patients to enhance the sensorimotor brain wave rhythm or to normalize brain activity as computed in real-time power spectrum displays. |
| Hyperactivity | EEG biofeedback procedures have been used on children with attention-deficit/hyperactivity disorder to train them to reduce their motor restlessness. |
| Idiopathic hypertension and orthostatic hypotension | A variety of specific (direct) and nonspecific biofeedback procedures—including blood pressure feedback, galvanic skin response, and foot-hand thermal feedback combined with relaxation procedures—have been used to teach patients to increase or decrease their blood pressure. Some follow-up data indicate that the changes may persist for years and often permit the reduction or elimination of antihypertensive medications. |
| Migraine | The most common biofeedback strategy with classic or common vascular headaches has been thermal biofeedback from a digit accompanied by autogenic self-suggestive phrases encouraging hand warming and head cooling. The mechanism is thought to help prevent excessive cerebral artery vasoconstriction, often accompanied by an ischemic prodromal symptom, such as scintillating scotomata, followed by rebound engorgement of arteries and stretching of vessel wall pain receptors. |
| Myofacial and temporomandibular joint (TMJ) pain | High levels of EMG activity over the powerful muscles associated with bilateral temporomandibular joints have been decreased, using biofeedback in patients who are jaw clenchers or have bruxism. |
| Neuromuscular rehabilitation | Mechanical devices or an EMG measurement of muscle activity displayed to a patient increases the effectiveness of traditional therapies, as documented by relatively long clinical histories in peripheral nerve-muscle damage, spasmodic torticollis, selected cases of tardive dyskinesia, cerebral palsy, and upper motor neuron hemiplegias. |
| Raynaud's syndrome | Cold hands and cold feet are frequent concomitants of anxiety and also occur in Raynaud's syndrome, caused by vasospasm of arterial smooth muscle. A number of studies report that thermal feedback from the hand, an inexpensive and benign procedure compared with surgical sympathectomy, is effective in about 70 percent of cases of Raynaud's syndrome. |
| Tension headaches | Muscle contraction headaches are most frequently treated with two large active electrodes spaced on the forehead to provide visual or auditory information about the levels of muscle tension. The frontal electrode placement is sensitive to EMG activity regarding the frontalis and occipital muscles, which the patient learns to relax. |

an adjunct to psychotherapy for anxiety associated with somatoform disorders—use a model in which frontalis muscle EMG biofeedback is combined with thermal biofeedback and verbal instructions in progressive relaxation.

**References**

Basmajian J V, editor: *Biofeedback: Principles and Practice for Clinicians.* Williams & Wilkins, Baltimore, 1983.

Burgio K L, Engel B T: Biofeedback-assisted behavioral training for elderly men and women. J Am Geriatr Soc *38*: 338, 1990.

Burish T G, Jenkins R A: Effectiveness of biofeedback and relaxation training in reducing the side effects of cancer chemotherapy. Health Psychol *11*: 17, 1992.

Butler F: *Biofeedback: A Survey of the Literature.* Plenum, New York, 1978.

Elton D: Combined use of hypnosis and EMG biofeedback in the treatment of stress-induced conditions. Stress Med *9*: 25, 1993.

Gaarder K R, Montgomery S: *Clinical Biofeedback: A Procedural Manual for Behavioral Medicine.* Williams & Wilkins, Baltimore, 1981.

Hatch J P, Fisher J G, Rugh J D, editors: *Biofeedback: Studies in Clinical Efficacy.* Plenum, New York, 1987.

Lisspers J, Ost L G: BVP-biofeedback in the treatment of migraine: The effects of constriction and dilatation during different phases of the migraine attack. Behav Modif *14*: 200, 1990.

McGrady A, Conran P, Dickey D, Garman D, et al: The effects of biofeedback-assisted relaxation on cell-mediated immunity, cortisol, and white blood cell count in healthy adult subjects. J Behav Med *15*: 343, 1992.

Olton D S, Noonberg A R: *Biofeedback: Clinical Applications in Behavioral Medicine.* Prentice-Hall, Englewood Cliffs, N J, 1980.

Orne M T, editor: *Task Force Report No. 19: Biofeedback.* American Psychiatric Association, Washington, 1980.

Peper E, Ancoli S, Quinn M, editors: *Mind-Body Integration: Essential Readings in Biofeedback.* Plenum, New York, 1979.

Runck B: *Biofeedback: Issues and Treatment Assessment.* National Institute of Mental Health (DDHS Pub. No. ADM 80-1032), Rockville, Md, 1980.

Stroebel C F, editor: Biofeedback and behavioral medicine and biofeedback in clinical practice. Psychiatr Ann *11*: 331, 1981.

Whitehead W E: Biofeedback treatment of gastrointestinal disorders. Biofeedback Self Regul *17*: 59, 1992.

## 32.6 / Behavior Therapy

Behavior therapists focus on overt behavior, emphasizing the removal of overt symptoms, without regard for the patient's private experiences or inner conflicts. The behaviorist's therapeutic goal is straightforward and concrete: the extinction of maladaptive habits or attitudes and the substitution of new, appropriate, nonanxiety-provoking patterns of behavior. The methods inherent to behavior therapies are based on the fundamental belief that persistent maladaptive behaviors and anxieties have been conditioned (or learned); therefore, successful treatment consists of various forms of deconditioning (or unlearning)—that is, whatever bad behavior has been learned can be unlearned.

Behavior therapy is based on the principles of learning theory—in particular, operant and classical conditioning. Behavior therapy is most often used when it is directed at specific, delineated habits of reacting with anxiety to objectively nondangerous stimuli (for example, phobias, compulsions, psychophysiological reactions, and sexual dysfunctions).

Clinicians who wish to embrace the behavioral approach must answer the four questions in Table 32.6–1 in conjunction with the patient, relatives, and other caretakers. The questions are raised repeatedly throughout the course of treatment in recurring cycles—first tentatively and later definitively as information accrues and progress occurs.

### HISTORY

As early as the 1920s, scattered reports began to appear on the application of learning principles to the treatment of behavioral disorders. Those reports, however, had little effect on the mainstream of psychiatry and clinical psychology. Not until the 1960s did behavior therapy emerge as a systematic and comprehensive approach to psychiatric (behavioral) disorders. Those developments arose independently of one another on three continents. Joseph Wolpe and his colleagues in Johannesburg, South Africa, used largely Pavlovian techniques to produce and eliminate experimental neuroses in cats. From that research Wolpe developed systematic desensitization, the prototype of many current behavioral procedures for the treatment of maladaptive anxiety that is produced by identifiable stimuli in the environment. At about the same time a group at the Institute of Psychiatry of the University of London, particularly Hans Jurgen Eysenck and M. B. Shapiro, stressed the importance of an empirical, experimental approach to the understanding and treatment of the individual patient, using own-control, single-case experimental paradigms and modern learning theory. The third origin of behavior therapy was work inspired by the research of Harvard psychologist B. F. Skinner. Skinner's students began to apply

**Table 32.6–1**
**Behavior Analysis of Clinical Problems Requires Answers to These Questions**

1. What are the problems and goals for therapy?
   This question addresses the patient's assets, as well as deficits of adaptive behavior and the excesses of maladaptive behavior. Often, the patient's problems are related to inappropriate timing or context of behavioral responses. The assessment of problems and the formulation of goals must consider the full range of objective, subjective, affective, social, and cognitive responses.

2. How can progress be measured and monitored?
   Each problem and goal requires behavioral specification and ongoing monitoring in terms of frequency, duration, form, latency, or context of occurrence. Operationalizing the goals of therapy enables the therapist to determine whether selected interventions are effective and provides the empirical basis for behavior therapy.

3. What environmental contingencies are maintaining the problem?
   A behavior analysis considers the functional relations between clinical problems and their environmental antecedents (precipitants or triggering stimuli) and consequences (reinforcers). Before formulating a treatment plan, the therapist must understand the current social and instrumental contingencies that may have to be modified for a successful outcome.

4. Which interventions are likely to be effective?
   This final question addresses the specific techniques that can be used in the treatment plan. Only after the first three questions are answered can a rational selection of interventions be made. Often, a combination of learning principles is packaged to maximize treatment effects.

Table by Robert Paul Liberman, M.D., and Jeffery Bedell, Ph.D.

his operant-conditioning technology, which was developed in animal-conditioning laboratories, to human beings in clinical settings.

### SYSTEMATIC DESENSITIZATION

Systematic desensitization was developed by Joseph Wolpe and is based on the behavioral principle of counterconditioning, which states that a person can overcome maladaptive anxiety elicited by a situation or object by approaching the feared situation gradually and in a psychophysiological state that inhibits anxiety.

In systematic desensitization the patient attains a state of complete relaxation and is then exposed to the stimulus that elicits the anxiety response. The negative reaction of anxiety is then inhibited by the relaxed state, a process called *reciprocal inhibition.*

Rather than use actual situations or objects that elicit fear, the patient and the therapist prepare a graded list or hierarchy of anxiety-provoking scenes associated with the patient's fears. The learned relaxation state and the anxiety-provoking scenes are systematically paired in the treatment. Thus, systematic desensitization consists of three steps: relaxation training, hierarchy construction, and the desensitization of the stimulus.

## Relaxation Training

Relaxation produces physiological effects that are opposite to those of anxiety—that is, slow heart rate, increased peripheral blood flow, and neuromuscular stability. A variety of relaxation methods have been developed, although some, such as yoga and Zen, have been known for centuries.

Most methods of achieving relaxation are based on a method called progressive relaxation. The patient relaxes major muscle groups in a fixed order, beginning with the small muscle groups of the feet and working cephalad or vice versa. Some clinicians use hypnosis to facilitate relaxation or use tape-recorded procedures to allow patients to practice relaxation on their own.

Mental imagery is a relaxation method in which patients are instructed to imagine themselves in a place associated with pleasant relaxed memories. Such images allow the patients to enter a relaxed state or experience or, as H. Benson termed it, the relaxation response.

## Hierarchy Construction

When constructing the hierarchy, the clinician determines all the conditions that elicit anxiety and then has the patient create a list or hierarchy of 10 to 12 scenes in order of increasing anxiety. For example, the acrophobic hierarchy may begin with the patient's imagining standing near a window on the second floor and end with being on the roof of a 20-story building, leaning on a guard rail and looking straight down. Table 32.6–2 provides two examples of hierarchy constructions described by the British psychiatrist Thomas Kraft.

## Desensitization of the Stimulus

Desensitization is done systematically by having the patient proceed through the list from the least anxiety-provoking scene to the most anxiety-provoking one while in a deeply relaxed state. The rate at which patients progress through the list is determined by their responses to the stimuli. When patients can vividly imagine the most anxiety-provoking scene of the hierarchy with equanimity, they experience little anxiety in the corresponding real-life situation.

## Adjunctive Use of Drugs

Various drugs have been used to hasten desensitization, but they should be used with caution and only by clinicians trained and experienced in potential adverse effects. The widest experience is with the ultrarapidly acting barbiturate sodium methohexital (Brevital), which is given intravenously in subanesthetic doses. Usually, up to 60 mg of the drug is given in divided doses in a session. Intravenous diazepam (Valium) may also be used cautiously. If the procedural details are carefully followed, almost all patients find the procedure pleasant, with few unpleasant side effects. The advantages of pharmacological desensitization are that preliminary training in relaxation can be shortened, almost all patients are able to become adequately

**Table 32.6–2**
**Two Examples of Hierarchy Constructions**

**Dog Phobia**
1. Looking at a picture of a dog in a children's picture book.
2. Cuddling the children's toy dog.
3. Seeing a poodle on a lead (a) 10 yards away.
   (b) 5 yards away.
   (c) passing by.
4. Touching a puppy behind a wire mesh in the market.
5. Looking at the neighbor's spaniel, Kim, held in the arms of its mistress.
6. Touching Kim when the dog is quiet and held in the arms of its mistress.
7. Touching Kim when the dog is quiet.
8. Stroking Kim.
9. Kim putting up her paws.
10. Looking at an Alsatian dog.
11. Watching Kim jumping on the road when the patient is indoors and the windows are closed.
12. Watching Kim walk around the room.
13. Feeding Kim a biscuit.
14. Kim held by its mistress and then jumping onto the ground.
15. Kim running.
16. Kim jumping from a chair onto the floor.
17. Kim jumping onto the floor and then putting up her paw.
18. Kim wagging her tail.
19. Kim wagging her tail and then putting her paw up.
20. Kim running down the corridor.
21. Kim running away from the patient.
22. Kim running toward the patient.
23. Kim roaming around the house without a lead.
24. Knocking on the door of the neighbor, and Kim running toward her, barking.
25. Dogs fighting.

**Fear of Water and Heights**
1. Taking a bath at home.
2. Taking a shower at home.
3. Going into the shallow end of the swimming pool.
4. Starting to swim at the shallow end of the swimming pool, breaststroke only.
5. Swimming at the shallow end, doing the crawl.
6. Jumping into the swimming pool at the shallow end.
7. Jumping into the pool and then doing the crawl.
8. Swimming at the shallow end, first breaststroke, then the crawl.
9. Pushing away from the bars and causing a splash.
10. Swimming in the middle of the pool at a depth of 5 feet 3 inches.
11. Swimming at the shallow end and then at the deep end (10 feet 3 inches).
12. Going into the deep end of the swimming pool.
13. Watching people jump from the diving boards.
14. Standing on a step at the deep end of the pool and making a little jump into the water.
15. Backstroke at the shallow end of the pool.
16. Jumping into the water at the shallow end of the pool (belly-flop dive).
17. Belly-flop dive at the deep end of the pool.
18. Racing dive at the shallow end of the pool.
19. Racing dive at the deep end of the pool.
20. Swimming three times across the deep end of the pool without stopping
    (a) breaststroke
    (b) crawl
    (c) backstroke
21. Jumping into the pool at a depth of:
    (a) 5 feet 3 inches
    (b) 6 feet
    (c) 7 feet
22. Several jumps at 6 feet and 7 feet, alternating them, and then remaining at the 7-foot depth.

*Continued*

**Table 32.6–2**
*Continued*

23. Going onto the first diving board and jumping into the water.
24. Jumping off the first diving board, then diving from the first board.
25. Diving off the first board.
26. Jumping from the first diving board, jumping from the second diving board, then diving from the first diving board.
27. Jumping off the first, second, and third diving boards, then diving from the first diving board.
28. Jumping off the first, second, and third diving boards, then diving from the first and then the second diving board.
29. Jumping off the fourth diving board, then diving off the second diving board.
30. Jumping off the fifth diving board, then diving off the third diving board.
31. Jumping off the fifth diving board, then diving off the fourth diving board.
32. Jumping off the top board, then diving off the fourth diving board.
33. Jumping off the top board, then diving off the fifth diving board.
34. Diving off the top diving board.
35. Random stimuli.
36. Looking around before jumping off the third diving board.
37. Looking around before jumping off the fourth diving board.
38. Looking around before jumping off the fifth diving board.
39. Diving from the fifth diving board and looking around before diving.
40. Diving from the top board and looking around before diving.

Table from T Kraft: The use of behavior therapy in a psychotherapeutic context. In *Clinical Behavior Therapy*, A A Lazarus, editor, p 222. Brunner/Mazel, New York, 1972. Used with permission.

relaxed, and the treatment itself seems to proceed more rapidly than without the drugs.

**Indications**

Systematic desensitization works best when there is a clearly identifiable anxiety-provoking stimulus. Phobias, obsessions, compulsions, and certain sexual disorders have been successfully treated with the technique.

## GRADED EXPOSURE

Graded exposure is similar to systematic desensitization except that relaxation training is not involved and treatment is usually carried out in a real-life context.

## FLOODING

Flooding is based on the premise that escaping from an anxiety-provoking experience reinforces the anxiety through conditioning. Thus, by not allowing the person to escape, the clinician can extinguish the anxiety and prevent the conditioned avoidance behavior.

The technique is to encourage the patient to confront the feared situation directly, without a gradual build-up as in systematic densensitization or graded exposure. No relaxation exercises are used, as in systematic desensitization. The patient experiences fear, which gradually subsides after a time. The success of the procedure depends on patients' remaining in the fear-generating situation until they are calm and feeling a sense of mastery. Prematurely withdrawing from the situation or prematurely terminating the fantasized scene is equivalent to an escape, and then both the conditioned anxiety and the avoidance behavior are reinforced, the opposite of what was intended. A variant of flooding is called *implosion*, in which the feared object or situation is confronted only in the imagination, rather than in real life. Many patients refuse flooding because of the psychological discomfort involved. It is also contraindicated in patients for whom intense anxiety would be hazardous (for example, patients with heart disease or fragile psychological adaptation). The technique works best with specific phobias.

## PARTICIPANT MODELING

In participant modeling the patient learns by imitation. The patient learns a new behavior primarily by observation, without having to perform the behavior until the patient feels ready. Just as irrational fears may be acquired by learning, they can be unlearned by observing a fearless model confront the feared object. The technique has been useful with phobic children who are placed with other children of their own age and sex who approach the feared object or situation. With adults a therapist may describe the feared activity in a calm manner with which the patient can identify, or the therapist may act out with the patient the process of mastering the feared activity. Sometimes a hierarchy of activities is established, with the least anxiety-provoking activity being dealt with first. The participant-modeling technique has been used successfully with agoraphobia by having a therapist accompany the patient into the feared situation. A variant of the procedure is called *behavior rehearsal*, in which real-life problems are acted out under the therapist's observation or direction. The technique is useful for complex behavioral patterns, such as job interviews and shyness.

## ASSERTIVENESS AND SOCIAL SKILLS TRAINING

To be assertive requires that persons have confidence in their judgment and sufficient self-esteem to express their opinions. Assertiveness and social skills training teaches people how to respond appropriately in social situations, to express their opinions in acceptable ways, and to achieve their goals. A variety of techniques—including role modeling, desensitization, and positive reinforcement (reward of desired behavior)—are used to increase assertiveness. Social skills training deals with assertiveness but also attends to a variety of real-life tasks, such as food shopping, looking for work, interacting with other people, and overcoming shyness.

## AVERSION THERAPY

When a noxious stimulus (punishment) is presented immediately after a specific behavioral response, theoretically the response is eventually inhibited and extinguished. Many types of noxious stimuli are used: electric shocks, substances that induce vomiting, corporal punishment, and social disapproval. The negative stimulus is paired with the behavior, which is thereby suppressed. The unwanted behavior usually disappears after a series of such sequences. Aversion therapy has been used for alcohol abuse, paraphilias, and other behaviors with impulsive or compulsive qualities. Aversion therapy is controversial for many reasons. For example, punishment does not always lead to the expected decrease in response and can sometimes be positively reinforcing.

## POSITIVE REINFORCEMENT

If a behavioral response is followed by a generally rewarding event—for example, food, avoidance of pain, or praise—it tends to be strengthened and to occur more frequently than before the reward. That principle has been applied in a variety of situations. On inpatient hospital wards, mental disorder patients have been rewarded for performing a desired behavior with tokens that they may use to purchase luxury items or certain privileges. The process has been successful in altering behavior and is known as a *token economy*. Some workers have suggested that psychotherapy is effective, in part, because patients want to please the therapist and so change their behavior to receive the therapist's praise. Sigmund Freud stated that, in treating phobias, the doctor needs to encourage the patient to face the phobia at some point determined by the positive relationship between the doctor and the patient.

## RESULTS

Behavior therapy has been successful in a variety of disorders (Table 32.6–3) and can be easily taught (Table 32.6–4). It requires less time than other therapies and is less expensive to administer. A limitation of the method is that it is useful for circumscribed behavioral symptoms, rather than for global areas of dysfunction (for example, neurotic conflicts, personality disorders). Analytically oriented theorists have criticized behavior therapy by saying that simple symptom removal may lead to symptom substitution. In other words, if symptoms are not viewed as consequences of inner conflicts and if the core cause of the symptoms is not addressed or altered, the result is the production of new symptoms. One interpretation of behavior theory is epitomized by Eysenck's controversial statement: "Learning theory regards neurotic symptoms as simply learned habits; there is no neurosis underlying the symptoms, but merely the symptom itself. Get rid of the symptom and you have eliminated the neurosis." Some therapists believe that behavior therapy is an oversimplified approach to psychopathology and the complex interaction between therapist and patient. Symptom substitu-

**Table 32.6–3**
**Some Common Clinical Applications of Behavior Therapy**

| Disorder | Comments |
|---|---|
| Agoraphobia | Graded exposure and flooding can reduce the fear of being in crowded places. About 60 percent of patients so treated are improved. In some cases the spouse can serve as the model while accompanying the patient into the fear situation; however, the patient cannot get a secondary gain by keeping the spouse nearby and displaying symptoms. |
| Alcohol dependence | Aversion therapy in which the alcohol-dependent patient is made to vomit (by adding an emetic to the alcohol) every time a drink is ingested is effective in treating alcohol dependence. Disulfiram (Antabuse) can be given to alcohol-dependent patients when they are alcohol-free. Such patients are warned of the severe physiological consequences of drinking (e.g., nausea, vomiting, hypotension, collapse) with disulfiram in the system. |
| Anorexia nervosa | Observe eating behavior; contingency management; record weight. |
| Bulimia nervosa | Record bulimic episodes; log moods |
| Hyper-ventilation | Hyperventilation test; controlled breathing; direct observation. |
| Other phobias | Systematic desensitization has been effective in treating phobias, such as fears of heights, animals, and flying. Social skills training has also been used for shyness and fear of other people. |
| Paraphilias | Electric shocks or other noxious stimuli can be applied at the time of a paraphilic impulse, and eventually the impulse subsides. Shocks can be administered by either the therapist or the patient. The results are satisfactory but must be reinforced at regular intervals. |
| Schizophrenia | The token economy procedure, in which tokens are awarded for desirable behavior and can be used to buy ward privileges, has been useful in treating inpatient schizophrenic patients. Social skills training teaches schizophrenic patients how to interact with others in a socially acceptable way so that negative feedback is eliminated. In addition, the aggressive behavior of some schizophrenic patients can be diminished through those methods. |
| Sexual dysfunctions | Dual-sex therapy, developed by William Masters and Virginia Johnson, is a behavior therapy technique used for various sexual dysfunctions, especially male erectile disorder, orgasm disorders, and premature ejaculation. It uses relaxation, desensitization, and graded exposure as the primary techniques. |
| Shy bladder | Inability to void in a public bathroom; relaxation exercises. |
| Type A behavior | Physiological assessment; muscle relaxation, biofeedback (on EMG) |

**Table 32.6–4**
**Social Skills Competence Checklist of Therapist-Trainer Behaviors**

1. Actively helps the patient in setting and eliciting specific interpersonal goals.

2. Promotes favorable expectations, a therapeutic orientation, and motivation before role playing begins.

3. Assists the patient in building possible scenes in terms of: "What emotion or communication?" "Who is the interpersonal target?" "Where and when?"

4. Structures the role playing by setting the scene and assigning roles to the patient and surrogates.

5. Engages the patient in behavioral rehearsal—getting the patient to role-play with others.

6. Uses self or other group members in modeling appropriate alternatives for the patient.

7. Prompts and cues the patient during the role playing.

8. Uses an active style of training through coaching, shadowing, being physically out of a seat, and closely monitoring and supporting the patient.

9. Gives the patient positive feedback for specific verbal and nonverbal behavioral skills.

10. Identifies the patient's specific verbal and nonverbal behavioral deficits or excesses and suggests constructive alternatives.

11. Ignores or suppresses inappropriate and interfering behavior.

12. Shapes behavioral improvements in small, attainable increments.

13. Solicits from the patient or suggests an alternative behavior for a problem situation that can be used and practiced during the behavioral rehearsal or role playing.

14. Evaluates deficits in social perception and problem solving and remedies them.

15. Gives specific attainable and functional homework assignments.

Table by Robert Paul Liberman, M.D., and Jeffrey Bedell, Ph.D.

---

tion may not be inevitable, but its possibility is an important consideration in the evaluation of behavior therapy's efficacy.

As with other forms of treatment, an evaluation of the patient's problems, motivation, and psychological strengths should be made before instituting any behavior therapy approach.

Table 32.6–5 gives a summary of behavior therapy.

### References

Achenbach T M: Implications of multiaxial empirically based assessment for behavior therapy with children. Behav Ther *24*: 91, 1993.

Agras W S, Kazdin A E, Wilson G T: *Behavior Therapy: Toward an Applied Clinical Science*. Freeman, San Francisco, 1979.

Antonuccio D O, Ward C H, Tearnan B H: The behavioral treatment of unipolar depression in adult outpatients. Prog Behav Modif *24*: 152, 1989.

Barlow D, editor: *Clinical Handbook of Psychological Disorders*. Guilford, New York, 1985.

Baum M: Contributions of animal studies of response prevention (flooding) to human exposure therapy. Psychol Rep *63*: 421, 1988.

Becker R E, Heimberg R G, Bellack A S: *Social Skills Training Treatment for Depression*. Pergamon, New York, 1987.

Black J L, Bruce B K: Behavior therapy: A clinical update. Hosp Community Psychiatry *40*: 1152, 1989.

---

**Table 32.6–5**
**Behavior Therapy**

| | |
|---|---|
| Goal | Modify learned maladaptive behavior patterns that lead to pathological symptoms |
| Selection criteria | Specific, well-delineated, circumscribed, easily identified maladaptive behaviors (e.g., phobias, overeating, sexual dysfunctions) Psychophysiological disorders in which manifestations of symptoms are affected by stress (e.g., asthma, pain, hypertension) |
| Duration | Generally time-limited, specific to specific behavior |
| Techniques | Based on learning theory principles (e.g., operant and classical conditioning) Relaxation training Reinforcements Aversive therapy Systematic desensitization Flooding Participant modeling Token economies |

Table by Rebecca Jones, M.D.

---

Ciminero A R, Calhoun K S, Adams H E, editors.: *Handbook of Behavioral Assessment*, ed 2. Wiley, New York, 1986.

Collins F L, Thompson J K: The integration of empirically derived personality assessment data into a behavioral conceptualization and treatment plan: Rationale, guidelines, and caveats. Behav Modif *17*: 58, 1993.

Council on Scientific Affairs: Aversion therapy. JAMA *13*: 2562, 1987.

Forehand R, Wierson M: The role of developmental factors in planning behavioral interventions for children: Disruptive behavior as an example. Behav Ther *24*: 117, 1993.

Frawley P J, Smith J W: Chemical aversion therapy in the treatment of cocaine dependence as part of a multimodal treatment program: Treatment outcome. J Subst Abuse Treat *7*: 21, 1990.

Hersen M, editor: *Pharmacological and Behavioral Treatment: An Integrative Approach*. Wiley, New York, 1986.

Hersen M, Bellack A S, editors: *Behavioral Assessment: A Practical Handbook*. Pergamon, New York, 1988.

Hersen M, Eisler R M, Miller P M, editors: *Progress in Behavior Modification*, vols 1–19. Academic Press, New York, 1975–87.

Kellner R, Neidhardt J, Krakow B, Pathak D: Changes in chronic nightmares after one session of desensitization or rehearsal instructions. Am J Psychiatry *149*: 659, 1992.

Liberman R P: *A Guide to Behavioral Analysis and Therapy*. Pergamon, New York, 1972.

Liberman R P, Bedell J R: Behavior therapy. In *Comprehensive Textbook of Psychiatry*, ed 5, H L Kaplan, B J Sadock, editors, p 1462. Williams & Wilkins, Baltimore, 1989.

Liberman R P, Mueser K, DeRisi W J: *Social Skills Training for Psychiatric Disorders*. Pergamon, New York, 1988.

Marks I M: *Fears, Phobias and Rituals*. Oxford University Press, New York, 1987.

McKee M G: Behavioral techniques in pain modification. Cleve Clin J Med *56*: 502, 1989.

Wadden T A, Foster G D, Letizia K A: Response of obese binge eaters to treatment by behavior therapy combined with very low calorie diet. J Consult Clin Psychol *60*: 808, 1992.

---

# 32.7 / Hypnosis

---

A pioneer in the field of clinical hypnotic induction, Milton Erickson, described the process of a clinical trance as "a free period in which individuality can flourish." Martin Orne defined hypnosis as that state or condition in which a person is able to respond to appropriate suggestions by experiencing alterations of perceptions, memory, or mood. The essential feature of hypnosis is the subjective experiential change.

Hypnotherapists generally believe that clinical hypnosis and therapeutic trance are extensions of common processes inherent in everyday life. The experiences of daydreaming and inner preoccupation during which one goes through the motions of one's daily routine, seemingly automatically, are typical examples. During those periods, attention is spontaneously focused inward, just as in the clinical use of a trance state a patient is induced to be receptive to inner experiences. The primary view that hypnotherapists share with other psychotherapists is an appreciation and understanding of the dynamics of unconscious processes in behavior.

Hypnosis is a complex mental phenomenon that has been defined as a state of heightened focal concentration and receptivity to the suggestions of another person. It has also been called an altered state of consciousness, a dissociated state, and a stage of repression. However, there is no known psychophysiological basis for hypnosis, as there is for sleep, in which characteristic electroencephalogram (EEG) changes appear.

## HISTORY

Modern hypnosis originated with the Austrian physician Friedrich Anton Mesmer (1734–1815), who believed the phenomenon, known as mesmerism, to be the result of animal magnetism or an invisible fluid that passes between the subject and the hypnotist. The term "hypnosis" originated in the 1840s with a Scottish physician, James Braid (1795–1860), who believed the subject to be in a particular state of sleep (*hypnos* is the Greek word for sleep). In the late 19th century the French neurologist Jean-Martin Charcot (1825–1893) thought hypnotism to be a special physiological state, and his contemporary Hippolyte-Marie Bernheim (1840–1919) believed it to be a psychological state of heightened suggestibility.

Sigmund Freud, who studied with Charcot, used hypnosis early in his career to help patients recover repressed memories. He noted that patients would relive traumatic events while under hypnosis, a process known as abreaction. Freud later replaced hypnosis with the technique of free association.

Today, hypnosis is a method that is used as a form of therapy (hypnotherapy), a method of investigation to recover lost memories, and a research tool.

## HYPNOTIC CAPACITY AND INDUCTION

The therapist can use a number of specific procedures to help the patient be hypnotized and respond to suggestion. Those procedures involve capitalizing on some naturally occurring hypnosislike phenomena that have probably occurred in the life experiences of most patients. However, those experiences are rarely talked about; consequently, patients find them fascinating. For example, when discussing what hypnosis is like with a patient, the therapist may say: "Have you ever had the experience of driving home while thinking about an issue that preoccu-

pies you and suddenly realize that, although you have arrived safe and sound, you can't recall having driven past familiar landmarks? It's as if you had been asleep, and yet you stopped at all the red lights, and you avoided collisions. You were somehow traveling on automatic pilot." Most people resonate to that experience and are usually happy to describe similar personal experiences.

A discussion about experiences of that kind gives patients examples of hypnosislike episodes that they have probably had; thus, the patients realize that they have the capacity to use the hypnotic mode, as it is merely an extension of that kind of episode. Although the episodes were not necessarily hypnotic states, the extent to which a person experiences them is correlated with hypnotizability. Table 32.7–1 lists a variety of naturally occurring trancelike experiences that can be discussed with patients and that point to the capacity to be hypnotized. Table 32.7–2 sum-

**Table 32.7–1**
**Naturally Occurring Hypnoticlike Experiences and the Percentage of Persons Indicating That They Have Had Such Experiences**

| | |
|---|---|
| Have you ever been in a room full of people, ostensibly taking part in the group yet mentally being far away from it? | 90% |
| Have you ever been unsure whether you did something or just thought about having to do it (e.g., not knowing whether you either mailed a certain letter or just thought about mailing it)? | 87% |
| Have you ever been able to block out sounds from your mind so that they were no longer important to you? Or so that they seemed very far away? Or so that you no longer understood them? Or so that you did not hear them at all? | 87% |
| Have you ever been so lost in thought that you did not understand what people said to you, even when they were talking directly to you and even when you nodded token agreement? | 84% |
| Have you ever been staring off into space, actually thinking of nothing and hardly been aware of the passage of time? | 81% |
| Have you ever had the experience of recollecting a past experience in your life with such clarity and vitality that it was almost like living it again? Or so that it actually seemed identical with living it again? | 78% |
| Have you ever been able to shut out your surroundings from your mind by concentrating very hard on something else? | 77% |
| Have you ever had the experience of reading a novel (or watching a play) and, while doing so, actually forget yourself, your surroundings, and live the story with such great reality and vividness that it became temporarily almost reality for you? Or actually seemed to become reality for you? | 76% |
| Have you ever been lulled into a groggy state or put to sleep by a lecture or a concert, even though you were not otherwise fatigued or tired? | 73% |
| Have you ever wandered off in your own thoughts while doing a routine task so that you actually forgot you were doing the task and then found, a few minutes later, that you had completed it without even being aware that you were doing it? | 70% |

Table by Martin Orne, M.D., Ph.D., and David Dinges, Ph.D.

**Table 32.7–2
Purposes of Trance Induction**

To reduce the foci of attention (usually to a few inner realities)

To facilitate alterations in the habitual patterns of direction and control

To facilitate patients' receptivity to their own inner associations and mental skills that can be integrated into therapeutic responses

Table from M Erickson, E L Rossi, S I Rossi: *Hypnotic Realities: The Induction of Clinical Hypnosis and Forms of Indirect Suggestion*, p 97. Irvington, New York, 1976. Used with permission.

marizes the three key purposes of trance induction, as set forth by Erickson.

The following is a typical induction protocol (courtesy of William Holt, M.D.) that is used to induce the trance state. There are many variations of the protocol, some less directive than this one. The one presented here is most likely to be effective in those persons with a high hypnotizability potential.

Take a long, deep, breath—inhale and exhale; now close your eyes and relax. Pay particular attention to the muscles in and about your eyes—relax them to the point that they just won't work. Are you trying to do that? Good. If you really have them relaxed, right at this very moment, no matter how hard you try, they just won't open. Test them. The harder you try, the faster they stick together, just as if they were glued together. That's fine!

Now you can open your eyes; that's good. When I tell you to and not before, open and close your eyes once more, and, when you close them this time, you will be 10 times as relaxed as you are right now. Go ahead, open and close, and feel that surge of relaxation go through your whole body, from the top of your head to the tip of your toes. Very good!

Now once again, open and close your eyes, and this time, when you close them, you will double the relaxation that you now have. Fine.

If you have followed my suggestions, right at this very moment, when I lift your hand and let it drop into your lap, it will drop like a wet cloth, heavy and limp. That's very, very good.

You now have good physical relaxation, but medical relaxation consists of two phases: physical, which you now have, and mental, which I will now show you how to achieve.

When I ask you to and not before, I want you to start counting backward from 100. I know you can count; that is not what we're after. I just want you to relax mentally. As you say each number, pause momentarily until you feel a wave of relaxation cover your whole body, from the top of your head to the tip of your toes. When you feel this wave of relaxation, then say the next number, and each time you say a number, you will double the relaxation you had before you said the number. If you do this properly, an interesting thing will happen—as you say the numbers and relax, the succeeding numbers will start to disappear and vanish from your mind. Command your mind to dispel these numbers. Now, aloud and slowly, start counting backward from 100.

Patient: One hundred.
Doctor: Very good.
Patient: Ninety-nine.
Doctor: Make them start to disappear now.
Patient: Ninety-eight.

Doctor: Now they're fading away, and after the next number they'll all be gone. Make them disappear. Let the numbers go.
Patient: Ninety-seven.
Doctor: And now they're all gone. Are they gone? Fine. If there are any numbers still lurking in your mind, when I lift your hand and drop it, they will all disappear.

## TRANCE STATE

Persons under hypnosis are said to be in a trance state, which may be light, medium, or heavy (deep). In a light trance there are changes in motor activity such that the person's muscles can feel relaxed, the hands can levitate, and paresthesia can be induced. A medium trance is characterized by diminished pain sensation and partial or complete amnesia. A deep trance is associated with induced visual or auditory experiences and deep anesthesia. Time distortion occurs at all trance levels but is most profound in the deep trance. Table 32.7–3 summarizes a number of the indicators of a developing and deepening of the trance state. Patients manifest the indications in differing degrees and combinations.

Posthypnotic suggestion is characterized by the person's being instructed to perform a simple act or to experience a particular sensation after awakening from the trance state. It may be used to give a bad taste to cigarettes or a particular food, thus aiding in the treatment of nicotine dependence or obesity. Posthypnotic suggestions are associated with deep trance states.

## HYPNOTHERAPY

The patient in a hypnotic trance can recall memories that are not available to consciousness in the nonhypnotic state. Such memories can be used in therapy to corroborate

**Table 32.7–3
Indicators of Trance Development**

| | |
|---|---|
| Autonomous ideation | Retardation of reflexes: |
| Balanced tonicity (catalepsy) | Swallowing |
| | Blinking |
| Changed voice quality | Sensory, muscular, and |
| Comfort, relaxation | body changes |
| Economy of movement | Slowing and loss of |
| Eye changes and closure | blink reflex |
| Facial features ironed out | Slowing pulse |
| Feeling distant | Slowing respiration |
| Feeling good after trance | Spontaneous hypnotic |
| Lack of body movement | phenomena: |
| Lack of startle response | Amnesia |
| Literalism | Anesthesia |
| Objective and impersonal ideation | Catalepsy |
| | Regression |
| Pupillary changes | Time distortion |
| Response attentiveness | Time lag in motor and conceptual behavior |

Table from M Erickson, E L Rossi, S I Rossi: *Hypnotic Realities: The Induction of Clinical Hypnosis and Forms of Indirect Suggestion*, p. 98. Irvington, New York, 1976. Used with permission.

psychoanalytic hypotheses regarding the patient's dynamics or to enable the patient to use such memories as a catalyst for new associations. Some patients can induce age regression, during which they reexperience events that occurred at an earlier time in life. Whether the patient experiences the events as they actually occurred is controversial; however, the material elicited can be used to further the therapy. Patients in a trance state may describe an event with an intensity similar to that when it occurred (abreaction) and experience a sense of relief as a result. The trance state plays a role in the treatment of amnestic disorders and dissociative fugue, although the clinician should be aware that it may be hazardous to bring the repressed memory into consciousness quickly, as the patient may be overwhelmed by anxiety.

### Indications and Uses

Hypnosis has been used, with varying degrees of success, to control obesity and substance-related disorders, such as alcohol abuse and nicotine dependence. It has been used to induce anesthesia, and major surgery has been performed with no anesthetic except hypnosis. It has also been used to manage chronic pain disorder, asthma, warts, pruritis, aphonia, and conversion disorder.

Relaxation can be achieved easily with hypnosis, so that patients may deal with phobias by controlling their anxiety. It has also been used to induce relaxation in systematic desensitization.

### Contraindications

Hypnotized patients are in a state of atypical dependence on the therapist, and so a strong transference may develop, characterized by a positive attachment that must be respected and interpreted. In other instances a negative transference may erupt in patients who are fragile or who have difficulty in testing reality. Patients who have difficulty with basic trust, such as paranoid patients, or who have problems giving up control, such as obsessive-compulsive patients, are not good candidates for hypnosis. A secure ethical value system is important to all therapy and particularly to hypnotherapy, in which patients (especially those in a deep trance) are extremely suggestible and malleable. There is controversy about whether patients will perform acts during a trance state that they otherwise find repugnant or that run contrary to their moral code.

### References

Barnier A J, McConkey K M: Reports of real and false memories: The relevance of hypnosis, hypnotizability, and context of memory test. J Abnorm Psychol *101*: 521, 1992.

Benson H: Hypnosis and the relaxation response. Gastroenterology *96*: 1609, 1989.

Bowers K: *Hypnosis for the Seriously Curious*. Norton, New York, 1976.

Crasilneck H, Hall J: *Clinical Hypnosis: Principles and Applications*, ed 2. Grune & Stratton, Orlando, 1985.

Erickson M, Rossi E L, Rossi S I: *Hypnotic Realities: The Induction of Clinical Hypnosis and Forms of Indirect Suggestion*. Irvington, New York, 1976.

Frankel F: *Hypnosis: Trance as a Coping Mechanism*. Plenum, New York, 1976.

Fromm E, Shor E: *Hypnosis: Developments in Research and New Perspectives*, ed 2. Aldine, New York, 1979.

Gabel S: The right hemisphere in imagery, hypnosis, rapid eye movement sleep and dreaming: Empirical studies and tentative conclusions. J Nerv Ment Dis *176*: 323, 1988.

Hilgard E: *The Experience of Hypnosis: A Shorter Version of Hypnotic Susceptibility*. Harcourt, Brace & World, New York, 1968.

Hilgard E, Hilgard J: *Hypnosis in the Relief of Pain*. Kaufmann, Los Altos, Calif, 1983.

Kingsbury S J: Brief hypnotic treatment of repetitive nightmares. Am J Clin Hypn *35*: 161, 1993.

Kroger W: *Clinical and Experimental Hypnosis*, ed 2. Lippincott, Philadelphia, 1977.

Laurence J-R, Perry C: *Hypnosis, Will and Memory: A Psycho-Legal History*. Guilford, New York, 1988.

MacHovec F: Hypnosis complications, risk factors, and prevention. Am J Clin Hypn *31*: 40, 1988.

Meares A: *A System of Medical Hypnosis*. Julian, New York, 1960.

Miller M E, Bowers K S: Hypnotic analgesia: Dissociated experience or dissociated control? J Abnorm Psychol *102*: 29, 1993.

Orne M: The construct of hypnosis: Implications of the definition for research and practice. Ann N Y Acad Sci *296*: 14, 1977.

Orne M, Dinges D: Hypnosis. In *Textbook of Pain*, P Wall, R Melzack, editors, p 806. Churchill Livingston, New York, 1984.

Orne M T, Dinges D F: Hypnosis. In *Comprehensive Textbook of Psychiatry*, ed 5, H I Kaplan, B J Sadock, editors, p 1501. Williams & Wilkins, Baltimore, 1989.

Patterson D R, Everett J J, Burns G L, Marvin J A: Hypnosis for the treatment of burn pain. J Consult Clin Psychol *60*: 713, 1992.

Silva C E, Kirsch I: Interpretive sets, expectancy, fantasy proneness, and dissociation as predictors of hypnotic response. J Pers Soc Psychol *63*: 847, 1992.

Syrjala K L, Cummings C, Donaldson G W: Hypnosis or cognitive behavioral training for the reduction of pain and nausea during cancer treatment: A controlled clinical trial. Pain *48*: 137, 1992.

---

# 32.8 / Cognitive Therapy

Cognitive therapy—according to its originator, Aaron Beck—is "based on an underlying theoretical rationale that an individual's affect and behavior are largely determined by the way in which he structures the world." A person's structuring of the world is based on cognitions (verbal or pictorial ideas available to consciousness), which are based on assumptions (schemas developed from previous experiences). According to Beck,

if a person interprets all his experiences in terms of whether he is competent and adequate, his thinking may be dominated by the schema, "Unless I do everything perfectly, I'm a failure." Consequently, he reacts to situations in terms of adequacy even when they are unrelated to whether or not he is personally competent.

Table 32.8–1 summarizes the general assumptions underlying cognitive therapy.

## GENERAL CONSIDERATIONS

Cognitive therapy is a short-term structured therapy that uses active collaboration between the patient and the therapist to achieve the therapeutic goals. It is oriented

**Table 32.8–1**
**General Assumptions of Cognitive Therapy**

Perception and experiencing in general are active processes that involve both inspective and introspective data.

The patient's cognitions represent a synthesis of internal and external stimuli.

How persons appraise a situation is generally evident in their cognitions (thoughts and visual images).

Those cognitions constitute their stream of consciousness or phenomenal field, which reflects their configuration of themselves, their world, their past and future.

Alterations in the content of their underlying cognitive structures affect their affective state and behavioral pattern.

Through psychological therapy, patients can become aware of their cognitive distortions.

Correction of those faulty dysfunctional constructs can lead to clinical improvement.

Table adapted from A T Beck, A J Rush, B F Shaw, G Emery: *Cognitive Therapy of Depression*, p 47. Guilford, New York, 1979. Used with permission.

**Table 32.8–2**
**Primitive versus Mature Thinking**

| Primitive Thinking | Mature Thinking |
|---|---|
| Nondimensional and global: I am fearful | Multidimensional: I am moderately fearful, quite generous, and fairly intelligent. |
| Absolutistic and moralistic: I am a despicable coward. | Relativistic and nonjudgmental: I am more fearful than most people I know. |
| Invariant: I always have been and always will be a coward. | Variable: My fears vary from time to time and from situation to situation. |
| Character diagnosis: I have a defect in my character | Behavioral diagnosis: I avoid situations too much, and I have many fears. |
| Irreversibility: Since I am basically weak, there's nothing that can be done about it. | Reversibility: I can learn ways of facing situations and fighting my fears. |

Table from A T Beck, A J Rush, B F Shaw, G Emery: *Cognitive Therapy of Depression*, p 31. Guilford, New York, 1979. Used with permission.

toward current problems and their resolution. Therapy is usually conducted on an individual basis, although group methods are also used. Therapy may also be used in conjunction with drugs.

Cognitive therapy has been applied mainly to depressive disorders (with or without suicidal ideation); however, it is also used with other conditions, such as panic disorder, obsessive-compulsive disorder, paranoid personality disorder, and somatoform disorders. The treatment of depression can serve as a paradigm of the cognitive approach.

## COGNITIVE THEORY OF DEPRESSION

The cognitive theory of depression holds that cognitive dysfunctions are the core of depression and that affective and physical changes and other associated features of depression are consequences of the cognitive dysfunctions. For example, apathy and low energy are results of a person's expectation of failure in all areas. Similarly, paralysis of will stems from a person's pessimism and feelings of hopelessness.

The cognitive triad of depression consists of (1) a negative self-percept that sees oneself as defective, inadequate, deprived, worthless, and undesirable; (2) a tendency to experience the world as a negative, demanding, and self-defeating place and to expect failure and punishment; and (3) the expectation of continued hardship, suffering, deprivation, and failure.

The goal of therapy is to alleviate depression and to prevent its recurrence by helping the patient (1) to identify and test negative cognitions, (2) to develop alternative and more flexible schemas, and (3) to rehearse both new cognitive responses and new behavioral responses. The goal is to change the way a person thinks and, subsequently, to alleviate the depressive disorder. Table 32.8–2 gives examples of typical depressive thinking (termed primitive thinking by Beck), contrasted with the adaptive (mature) thinking that cognitive therapy attempts to foster.

## STRATEGIES AND TECHNIQUES

Overall, therapy is relatively short, lasting up to about 25 weeks. If the patient does not improve in that time, the diagnosis should be reevaluated. Maintenance therapy can be carried out over a period of years.

As with other psychotherapies, the therapists' attributes are important to successful therapy. The therapists must be able to exude warmth, understand the life experience of each patient, and be truly genuine and honest with themselves and with their patients. Therapists must be able to relate skillfully and interactively with their patients.

The cognitive therapist sets the agenda at the beginning of each session, assigns homework to be performed between sessions, and teaches new skills. The therapist and the patient actively collaborate (Table 32.8–3). Cognitive therapy has three components: didactic aspects, cognitive techniques, and behavioral techniques.

**Table 32.8–3**
**Cognitive Psychotherapy**

| | |
|---|---|
| Goal | Identify and alter cognitive distortions that maintain symptoms |
| Selection criteria | Primarily used in dysthymic disorder |
| | Nonendogenous depressive disorders |
| | Symptoms not sustained by pathological family |
| Duration | Time-limited, usually 15–25 weeks, once-weekly meetings |
| Techniques | Collaborative empiricism |
| | Structured and directive |
| | Assigned readings |
| | Homework and behavioral techniques |
| | Identification of irrational beliefs and automatic thoughts |
| | Identification of attitudes and assumptions underlying negatively biased thoughts |

Table from R J Ursano, E K Silberman: Individual psychotherapies. In *The American Psychiatric Press Textbook of Psychiatry*, J A Talbott, R E Hales, S C Yudofsky, editors, p 872. American Psychiatric Press, Washington, 1988. Used with permission.

## Didactic Aspects

The didactic aspects include explaining to the patient the cognitive triad, schemas, and faulty logic. The therapist must tell the patient that they will formulate hypotheses together and test them over the course of the treatment. Cognitive therapy requires a full explanation of the relationship between depression and thinking, affect, and behavior, as well as the rationale for all aspects of the treatment. The explanation contrasts with the psychoanalytically oriented therapies, which require little explanation.

## Cognitive Techniques

The cognitive approach includes four processes: (1) eliciting automatic thoughts, (2) testing automatic thoughts, (3) identifying maladaptive underlying assumptions, and (4) testing the validity of maladaptive assumptions.

**Eliciting automatic thoughts.** Automatic thoughts are cognitions that intervene between external events and the person's emotional reaction to the event. An example of an automatic thought is the belief that "everyone is going to laugh at me when they see how badly I bowl"—a thought that occurs to someone who has been asked to go bowling and responds negatively. Another example is a person's thought that "she doesn't like me" if someone passes the person in the hall without saying hello.

Automatic thoughts are also termed cognitive distortions. Every psychopathological disorder has its own specific cognitive profile of distorted thought, which, if known, provides a framework for specific cognitive interventions (Table 32.8–4).

**Testing automatic thoughts.** Acting as a teacher, the therapist helps the patient test the validity of automatic thoughts. The goal is to encourage patients to reject in-

accurate or exaggerated automatic thoughts after careful examination.

Patients often blame themselves for things that go wrong that may well have been outside their control. The therapist reviews with the patient the entire situation and helps reattribute the blame or the cause of the unpleasant events. Generating alternative explanations for events is another way of undermining inaccurate and distorted automatic thoughts.

**Identifying maladaptive assumptions.** As the patient and the therapist continue to identify automatic thoughts, patterns usually become apparent. The patterns represent rules or maladaptive general assumptions that guide the patient's life. Samples of such rules are "In order to be happy, I must be perfect" and "If anyone doesn't like me, I'm not lovable." Such rules inevitably lead to disappointments and failure and then to depression (Figure 32.8–1).

**Testing the validity of maladaptive assumptions.** Similar to the testing of the validity of automatic thoughts is the testing of the accuracy of maladaptive assumptions. One particularly effective test is for the therapist to ask the patient to defend the validity of an assumption. For example, if a patient stated that he should always work up to his potential, the therapist might ask, "Why is that so important to you?"

Table 32.8–5 gives examples of some of the interventions designed to elicit, identify, test, and correct the cognitive distortions that lead to depressive and other painful affects.

**Table 32.8–4**
**Cognitive Profile of Psychiatric Disorders**

| Disorder | Specific Cognitive Content |
|---|---|
| Depressive disorder | Negative view of self, experience, and future |
| Hypomanic episode | Inflated view of self, experience, and future |
| Anxiety disorders | Fear of physical or psychological danger |
| Panic disorder | Catastrophic misinterpretation of bodily and mental experiences |
| Phobias | Danger in specific, avoidable situations |
| Paranoid personality disorder | Negative bias, interference, and so forth by others |
| Conversion disorder | Concept of motor or sensory abnormality |
| Obsessive-compulsive disorder | Repeated warning or doubting about safety and repetitive acts to ward off threat |
| Suicidal behavior | Hopelessness and deficit in problem solving |
| Anorexia nervosa | Fear of being fat or unshapely |
| Hypochondriasis | Attribution of serious medical disorder |

Table adapted from Aaron Beck, M.D., and A. John Rush, M.D.

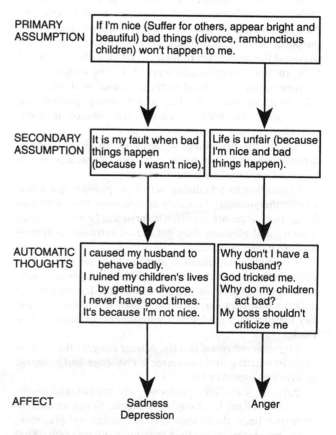

**Figure 32.8–1.** Cognition-affect flowchart. (Figure from A T Beck, A J Rush, B F Shaw, G Emery: *Cognitive Therapy of Depression,* p 33. Guilford, New York, 1979. Used with permission.)

**Table 32.8–5**
**Cognitive Errors Derived from Assumptions**

| Cognitive Error | Assumption | Intervention |
|---|---|---|
| Overgeneralizing | If it's true in one case, it applies to any case that is even slightly similar. | Exposure of faulty logic. Establish criteria of which cases are similar and to what degree. |
| Selective abstraction | The only events that matter are failures, deprivation, etc. Should measure self by errors, weaknesses, etc. | Use log to identify successes patient forgot. |
| Excessive responsibility (assuming personal casualty) | I am responsible for all bad things, failures, etc. | Disattribution technique. |
| Assuming temporal causality (predicting without sufficient evidence) | If it has been true in the past, it's always going to be true. | Expose faulty logic. Specify factors that could influence outcome other than past events. |
| Self-references | I am the center of everyone's attention—especially my bad performances. I am the cause of misfortunes. | Establish criteria to determine when patient is the focus of attention and also the probable facts that cause bad experiences. |
| Catastrophizing | Always think of the worst. It's most likely to happen to you. | Calculate real probabilities. Focus on evidence that the worst did not happen. |
| Dichotomous thinking | Everything is either one extreme or another (black or white, good or bad). | Demonstrate that events may be evaluated on a continuum. |

Table from A T Beck, A J Rush, B F Shaw, G Emery: *Cognitive Therapy of Depression,* p 48. Guilford, New York, 1979. Used with permission.

## Behavioral Techniques

Behavioral techniques go hand in hand with cognitive techniques: Behavioral techniques are used to test and change maladaptive and inaccurate cognitions. The overall purposes of such techniques are to help the patients understand the inaccuracy of their cognitive assumptions and to learn new strategies and ways of dealing with issues.

Among the behavioral techniques used in therapy are scheduling activities, mastery and pleasure, graded task assignments, cognitive rehearsal, self-reliance training, role playing, and diversion techniques.

Among the first things done in therapy is to *schedule activities* on an hourly basis. A record of the activities is kept and reviewed with the therapist.

In addition to scheduling activities, patients are asked to rate the amount of *mastery and pleasure* their activities bring them. Patients are often surprised at how much more mastery and pleasure they get out of activities than they had otherwise believed.

To simplify the situation and to allow for miniaccomplishments, therapists often break tasks down into subtasks, as in *graded task assignments,* to demonstrate to patients that they can succeed. Table 32.8–6 outlines the key features of a graded task assignment, as described by Beck.

*Cognitive rehearsal* has the patient imagine the various steps in meeting and mastering a challenge and rehearse the various aspects of it.

Patients, especially inpatients, are encouraged to become self-reliant by doing such simple things as making their own beds, doing their own shopping, and preparing their own meals, rather than relying on other people. That is known as *self-reliance training.*

*Role playing* is a particularly powerful and useful tech-

**Table 32.8–6**
**Key Features of Graded Task Assignment**

Problem definition—for example, patients' beliefs that they are not capable of attaining goals that are important to them.

Formulation of a project. Stepwise assignment of tasks (or activities) from simple to complex.

Immediate and direct observation by patients that they are successful in reaching a specific objective (carrying out an assigned task). The continual concrete feedback provides patients with new corrective information regarding their functional capacity.

Ventilation of patients' doubts, cynical reactions, and belittling of their achievements.

Encouragement of realistic evaluation by patients of their actual performance.

Emphasis on the fact that patients reached goals as a result of their own efforts and skill.

Devising new, complex assignments in collaboration with the patients.

Table adapted from A T Beck, A J Rush, B F Shaw, G Emery: *Cognitive Therapy of Depression,* p 39. Guilford, New York, 1979. Used with permission.

nique to elicit automatic thoughts and to learn new behaviors.

*Diversion techniques* are useful in helping patients get through particularly difficult times and include physical activity, social contact, work, play, and visual imagery.

**Imagery.** Imagery is a phenomenon that affects behavior, as first discussed by Paul Schilder in his book *The Image and Appearance of the Human Body,* in which he described images as having physiological components. According to Schilder, *visualizing* oneself running activates subliminally the same muscles used in running, which can be measured with electromyography. That phenomenon is used in sports training, in which athletes visualize every conceivable event in a performance and develop a muscle memory for the activity. It can also be used to master anxiety or to deal with feared situations by combining behavioral and cognitive theories.

Impulsive or obsessive behavior has been treated with *thought stoppage.* For instance, patients imagine a stop sign with a police officer nearby or another image that evokes inhibition at the same time that they recognize an impulse or obsession that is alien to the ego. Similarly, obesity can be treated by having patients visualize themselves as thin, athletic, trim, and well-muscled and then training them to evoke that image whenever they have an urge to eat. Such imagery can be enhanced with hypnosis or autogenic training. In a technique called *guided imagery,* patients are encouraged to have fantasies that can be interpreted as wish fulfillments or attempts to master disturbing affects or impulses.

# EFFICACY

Cognitive therapy can be used alone in the treatment of mild to moderate depressive disorders or in conjunction with antidepressant medication for major depressive disorder. Studies have clearly shown that cognitive therapy is effective and in some cases is superior or equal to medication alone. It is one of the most useful psychotherapeutic interventions currently available for depressive disorders and shows promise in the treatment of other disorders.

Cognitive therapy has also been studied in relation to increasing compliance with lithium (Eskalith) in bipolar I disorder patients and as an adjunct in treating withdrawal from heroin.

Table 32.8–7 summarizes a number of negative cognitions that are common in producing noncompliance with medications.

Table 32.8–8 outlines Beck's criteria for determining when cognitive therapy is and is not indicated.

Table 32.8–9 summarizes and contrasts the major features of three of the most commonly used psychotherapeutic approaches to the treatment of depression, including the cognitive approach.

**Table 32.8–7**
**Cognitions Contributing to Poor Adherence to Medication Prescription**

Cognitions about the medication (before taking it):
It's addicting.
I am stronger if I don't need medicine.
I am weak to need it (a crutch).
It won't work for me.
If I don't take medication, I'm not crazy.
I can't stand side effects.
I'll never get off medication once I start.
There's nothing I need to do except take medicine.
I only need to take medication on bad days.
Cognitions about medication (while taking it):
Since I'm not perfectly well (any better) after days or weeks, the medicine isn't working.
I should feel good right away.
The medicine will solve all my problems.
The medicine won't solve problems, so how can it help?
I can't stand the dizziness (or fuzziness) or other side effects.
It makes me into a zombie.
Cognitions about depression:
I am not ill (I don't need help).
Only weak people get depressed.
I deserve to be depressed, since I am a burden to everybody.
Isn't depression a normal reaction to the bad state of things?
Depression is incurable.
I am one of the small percentage who do not respond to any treatment.
Life isn't worth living, so why should I try to get over my depression?

Table from A T Beck, A J Rush, B F Shaw, G Emery: *Cognitive Therapy of Depression*, p 72. Guilford, New York, 1979. Used with permission.

**Table 32.8–8**
**Indications for Cognitive Therapy**

Criteria that justify the administration of cognitive therapy alone:
Failure to respond to adequate trials of two antidepressants
Partial response to adequate dosages of antidepressants
Failure to respond or only a partial response to other psychotherapies
Diagnosis of dysthymic disorder
Variable mood reactive to environmental events
Variable mood that correlates with negative cognitions
Mild somatoform disorders (sleep, appetite, weight, libidinal)
Adequate reality testing (i.e., no hallucinations or delusions), span of concentration, and memory function
Inability to tolerate medication side effects or evidence that excessive risk is associated with pharmacotherapy
Features that suggest cognitive therapy alone is not indicated:
Evidence of coexisting schizophrenia, dementia, substance-related disorders, mental retardation
Patient has medical illness or is taking medication that is likely to cause depression
Obvious memory impairment or poor reality testing (hallucinations, delusions)
History of manic episode (bipolar I disorder)
History of family member who responded to antidepressant
History of family member with bipolar I disorder
Absence of precipitating or exacerbating environmental stresses
Little evidence of cognitive distortions
Presence of severe somatoform disorders (e.g., pain disorder)
Indications for combined therapies (medication plus cognitive therapy):
Partial or no response to trial of cognitive therapy alone
Partial but incomplete response to adequate pharmacotherapy alone
Poor compliance with medication regimen
Historical evidence of chronic maladaptive functioning with depressive syndrome on intermittent basis
Presence of severe somatoform disorders and marked cognitive distortions (e.g., hopelessness)
Impaired memory and concentration and marked psychomotor difficulty
Major depressive disorder with suicidal danger
History of first-degree relative who responded to antidepressants
History of manic episode in relative or patient

Table adapted from A T Beck, A J Rush, B F Shaw, G Emery: *Cognitive Therapy of Depression*, p 42. Guilford, New York, 1979. Used with permission.

**Table 32.8–9**
**Major Features of Three Psychotherapeutic Approaches to Depression**

| Feature | Psychodynamic Approach | Cognitive Approach | Interpersonal Approach |
|---|---|---|---|
| Major theorists | Freud, Abraham, Jacobson, Kohut | Plato, Adler, Beck, Rush | Meyer, Sullivan, Klerman, Weissman |
| Concepts of pathology and causes | Ego regression: damaged self-esteem and unresolved conflict caused by childhood object loss and disappointment | Distorted thinking: dysphoria caused by learned negative views of self, others, and the world | Impaired interpersonal relationships: absent or unsatisfactory significant social bonds |
| Major goals and mechanisms of change | To promote personality change through understanding of past conflicts; to achieve insight into defenses, ego distortions, and superego defects; to provide a role model; to permit cathartic release of aggression | To provide symptomatic relief through alteration of target thoughts; to identify self-destructive cognitions; to modify specific erroneous assumptions; to promote self-control over thinking patterns | To provide symptomatic relief through solution of current interpersonal problems; to reduce stress involving family or work; to improve interpersonal communication skills |
| Primary techniques and practices | Expressive, empathic; fully or partially analyzing transference and resistance; confronting defenses; clarifying ego and superego distortions | Behavioral cognitive: recording and monitoring cognitions; correcting distorted themes with logic and experimental testing; providing alternative thought content; homework | Communicative, environmental: clarifying and managing maladaptive relationships and learning new ones through communication and social skills training; providing information on illness |
| Therapist role, therapeutic relationship | Interpreter, reflector: establishment and exploration of transference; therapeutic alliance for benign dependence and empathic understanding | Educator, shaper: positive relationship instead of transference; collaborative empiricism as basis for joint scientific (logical) task | Explorer, prescriber: positive relationship, transference without interpretation; active therapist role for influence and advocacy |
| Marital, family role | Full individual confidentiality; exclusion of significant others except in life-threatening situations | Use of spouse as objective reporter; couples therapy for disturbed cognitions sustained in marital relationship | Integral role of spouse in treatment; examination of spouse's role in patient's predisposition to depression and effect of illness on marriage |

Table from T B Karasu: Psychotherapy for depression. Am J Psychiatry *147*: 2, 1990. Used with permission.

## References

Barlow D H: Cognitive-behavioral approaches to panic disorder and social phobia. Bull Menninger Clin 56 (2, Suppl A): *14*, 1992.

Beck A T: *Cognitive Therapy and the Emotional Disorders*. International Universities Press, New York, 1976.

Beck A T: *Depression: Clinical Experimental, and Theoretical Aspects*. Harper & Row, New York, 1970.

Beck A T, Emery G: *Anxiety Disorders and Phobias: A Cognitive Perspective*. Basic Books, New York, 1985.

Beck A T, Greenberg R L: Cognitive therapy of panic disorders. In *American Psychiatric Press Review of Psychiatry*, A J Frances, R E Hales, editors, vol. 7, p 571. American Psychiatric Press, Washington, 1988.

Beck A T, Rush A J: Cognitive therapy. In *Comprehensive Textbook of Psychiatry*, ed 5, H I Kaplan, B J Sadock, editors, p 1541. Williams & Wilkins, Baltimore, 1989.

Beck A T, Rush A J, Shaw B F, Emery G: *Cognitive Therapy of Depression*. Guilford, New York, 1979.

Covi L, Primakoff L: Cognitive group therapy. In *American Psychiatric Press Review of Psychiatry*, A J Frances, R E Hales, editors, vol 7, p 608. American Psychiatric Press, Washington, 1988.

Elliott C H, Adams R L, Hodge G K: Cognitive therapy: Possible strategies for optimizing outcome. Psychiatr Ann 22: 459, 1992.

Epstein N, Baucom D H, Rankin L A: Treatment of marital conflict: A cognitive-behavioral approach. Clin Psychol Rev *13*: 45, 1993.

Garner D M, Rockert W, Davis R, Garner M V, et al: Comparison of cognitive-behavioral and supportive-expressive therapy for bulimia nervosa. Am J Psychiatry *150*: 37, 1993.

Hoffart A: Cognitive treatments of agoraphobia: A critical evaluation of theoretical basis and outcome evidence. J Anx Disord 7: 75, 1993.

Hollon S D, Bedrosian R, editors: *New Directions in Cognitive Therapy: A Casebook*. Guilford, New York, 1981.

Hollon S D, Najavits L: Review of empirical studies on cognitive therapy. In *American Psychiatric Press Review of Psychiatry*, A J Frances, R E Hales, editors, vol 7, p 643. American Psychiatric Press, Washington, 1988.

Jarrett R B, Rush A J: Psychotherapeutic approaches for depression. In *Psychiatry*, vol 1, p 1173. Lippincott, Philadelphia, 1985.

Liberman R P, Green M F: Whither cognitive-behavioral therapy for schizophrenia? Schizophr Bull *18*: 27, 1992.

Mahoney M J: *Cognition and Behavior Modification*. Ballinger, Cambridge, 1974.

Meichenbaum D H: *Cognitive Behavior Modification: An Integrative Approach*. Plenum, New York, 1977.

Pruitt D: Cognitive therapy: Efficacy of current applications. Psychiatr Ann 22: 474, 1992.

Rush A J: Cognitive therapy in combination with antidepressant medication. In *Combining Psychotherapy and Drug Therapy in Clinical Practice*, B D Beitman, G L Klerman, editors, p 121. Spectrum, New York, 1984.

Shaw B, Segal Z V: Introduction to cognitive theory and therapy. In *American Psychiatric Press Review of Psychiatry*, vol 7, A J Frances, R E Hales, editors, p 538. American Psychiatric Press, Washington, 1988.

Trautman P D, Rotheram-Borum M J: Cognitive therapy with children and adolescents. In *American Psychiatric Press Review of Psychiatry*, vol 7, A J Frances, R E Hales, editors, p 584. American Psychiatric Press, Washington, 1988.

# Biological Therapies

## 33.1 / General Principles of Psychopharmacology

Because the pharmacotherapy for mental disorders is one of the most rapidly evolving areas of clinical medicine, any practitioner who prescribes such drugs must remain current with the research literature. The key areas for regular update are the emergence of new agents—for example, risperidone (Risperdal), tacrine (Cognex), venlafaxine (Effexor)—new indications for existing agents—for example, valproate (Depakene)—the clinical usefulness of plasma concentrations, and the identification and treatment of drug-related adverse effects.

Drug therapy and other organic treatments of mental disorders may be defined as attempts to modify or correct pathological behaviors, thoughts, or moods by chemical or other physical means. The relations between, on the one hand, the physical state of the brain and, on the other hand, its functional manifestations (behaviors, thoughts, and moods) are highly complex, imperfectly understood, and at the frontier of biological knowledge. However, the various parameters of normal and abnormal behavior—such as perception, affect, and cognition—may be profoundly affected by physical changes in the central nervous system (for example, by cerebrovascular diseases, epilepsy, and legal and illicit drugs).

Because of incomplete knowledge regarding the brain and the disorders that affect it, the drug treatment of mental disorders is empirical. Nevertheless, many organic therapies have proved to be highly effective and constitute the treatment of choice for certain psychopathological conditions. Organic therapies form a key part of the armamentarium for the treatment of mental disorders.

The practice of pharmacotherapy in psychiatry should not be oversimplified—for example, a one diagnosis-one pill approach. Many variables impinge on the practice of psychopharmacology, including drug selection, prescription, administration, psychodynamic meaning to the patient, and family and environmental influences. Some patients may view a drug as a panacea, and other patients may view a drug as an assault. The nursing staff and relatives, as well as the patient, must be instructed regarding the reasons, the expected benefits, and the potential risks of pharmacotherapy. In addition, the clinician often finds it useful to explain the theoretical basis for pharmacotherapy to the patient, the patient's caretakers, and psychiatric staff members. Moreover, the theoretical biases of the treating psychiatrist are critical to the success of drug treatment, since psychiatrists prescribe pharmacotherapeutic drugs as a function of their theoretical beliefs about such treatments.

Drugs must be used in effective dosages for sufficient time periods, as determined by previous clinical investigations and personal experience. Subtherapeutic dosages and incomplete trials should not be given to a patient because the psychiatrist is excessively concerned about the development of adverse effects. The prescription of drugs for mental disorders must be made by a qualified practitioner and requires continuous clinical observation. Treatment response and the emergence of adverse effects must be monitored closely. The dosage of the drug should be adjusted accordingly, and appropriate treatments for emergent adverse effects must be instituted as quickly as possible.

### HISTORY

The history of the development of organic therapies in psychiatry extends from the mid 1800s to the present, although by 1960 the psychiatric drug armamentarium was essentially as it is known today (Table 33.1–1). Organic therapies such as electroconvulsive therapy (ECT) (pioneered by Ugo Cerletti and Lucio Bini), insulin coma therapy (developed by Manfred Sakel), and psychosurgery (introduced by Antonio Egas Moniz) all began in the first half of the 20th century and heralded the biological revolution in psychiatry. In 1917 Julius Wagner-Jauregg introduced malaria toxin to treat syphilis and is the only psychiatrist to have won a Nobel prize.

In the second half of the 20th century, chemotherapy as a treatment for mental disorders became a major field of research and practice. Almost immediately after the introduction of chlorpromazine (Thorazine) in the early 1950s, psychotherapeutic drugs became a mainstay of psychiatric treatment, particularly for seriously mentally ill patients.

In 1949 the Australian psychiatrist John Cade described the treatment of manic excitement with lithium (Eskalith). While conducting animal experiments, Cade noted that lithium carbonate made the animals lethargic, thus prompting him to administer the drug to several agitated psychiatric patients, who received therapeutic benefit from the drug.

In 1950 Charpentier synthesized chlorpromazine (an aliphatic phenothiazine antipsychotic) in an attempt to develop

**Table 33.1–1**
**Some Historical Events in Psychopharmacology, 1845–1960**

---

1845—Hashish intoxication proposed as a model of insanity (Moreau)

1869—Chloral hydrate introduced as a treatment for melancholia and mania

1875—Cocaine proposed as a treatment in psychiatry (Freud)

1882—Paraldehyde introduced

1892—Research with morphine, alcohol, ether, and paraldehyde in normal persons (Kraepelin)

1903—Barbiturates introduced

1917—Psychosis of syphilis treated with malaria fever therapy (Julius Wagner-Jauregg)

1922—Barbiturate-induced coma (Jaboe Klaesi)

1927—Insulin shock for schizophrenia (Manfred Sakel)

1931—*Rauwolfia serpentina* (reserpine) introduced (Sen and Bose) (confirmed as a treatment of schizophrenia in 1953 by Nathan Kline)

1934—Pentylenetetrazol-induced convulsions (Ladislas von Meduna)

1936—Frontal lobotomies (Egas Moniz)

1938—Electroconvulsive therapy (Ugo Cerletti and Lucio Bini)

1940—Phenytoin introduced as anticonvulsant (Tracy Putnam)

1943—Lysergic acid diethylamide (LSD) synthesized (Albert Hofmann)

1949—Lithium introduced

1952—Chlorpromazine introduced

1955–1958—Tricyclic drugs and monoamine oxidase inhibitors introduced

1960—Chlordiazepoxide introduced

---

a histaminergic drug that would serve as an adjuvant to anesthetics. Laborit reported the ability of the drug to induce an artificial hibernation. Reports by Paraire and Sigwald, John Delay and Pierre Deniker, and Heinz Lehmann and Hanrahan described the effectiveness of chlorpromazine in treating severe agitation and psychosis. Chlorpromazine was quickly introduced into American psychiatry, and many similarly effective drugs have since been synthesized, including haloperidol (Haldol) (a butyrophenone antipsychotic) in 1958 by Paul Janssen.

Imipramine (Tofranil) (a tricyclic drug) is structurally related to the phenothiazine antipsychotics. While carrying out clinical research on chlorpromazinelike drugs, Thomas Kuhn found that, although imipramine was not effective in reducing agitation, it did seem to reduce depression in some patients. The introduction of monoamine oxidase inhibitors (MAOIs) to treat depression evolved from the observation that the antituberculosis agent iproniazid had mood-elevating effects in some patients. In 1958 Nathan Kline was one of the first investigators to report the efficacy of MAOI treatment in depressed psychiatric patients.

By 1960, with the introduction of chlordiazepoxide (Librium) (a benzodiazepine antianxiety agent synthesized by Richard Sternbach at Roche Laboratories in the late 1950s), the psychiatric armamentarium of drugs included antipsychotics (for example, chlorpromazine), tricyclic drugs for depression (for example, imipramine), monoamine oxidase inhibitors for depression (for example, tranylcypromine [Parnate]), lithium for the treatment of mania, and the benzodiazepines, as well as the barbiturates, for the treatment of anxiety and insomnia. The next 30 years were devoted primarily to clinical studies demonstrating the efficacy of those drugs and to the development of related drugs in each category. The efficacy of each class of drugs for treating relatively specific psychiatric syndromes and the elucidation of their

pharmacodynamic effects provided the impetus to develop the various neurotransmitter hypotheses of mental disorders (for example, the dopamine hypothesis of schizophrenia and the biogenic amine hypothesis of mood disorders).

Since 1960 the major additions to the psychotherapeutic drugs have been the anticonvulsants, particularly carbamazepine (Tegretol) and valproate, which are effective in the treatment of bipolar I disorder. Buspirone (BuSpar), a nonbenzodiazepine anxiolytic, was introduced for clinical use in the United States in 1986. Several serotonin-specific reuptake inhibitors—for example fluoxetine (Prozac)—and the serotonergic-specific tricyclic drug clomipramine (Anafranil) are effective in the treatment of depression and some anxiety disorders, including obsessive-compulsive disorder. The most recently introduced drugs include a dopamine receptor antagonist that may be associated with few neurological adverse effects (risperidone), the first drug for the treatment of cognitive decline in dementia of the Alzheimer's type (tacrine), and two new antidepressants, venlafaxine and nefazodone, that may eventually be shown to have some therapeutic advantage over currently available drugs.

## PHARMACOLOGICAL ACTIONS

Pharmacokinetic interactions concern how the body handles a drug; pharmacodynamic interactions concern the effects of the drug on the body. In a parallel fashion, pharmacokinetic drug interactions concern the effects of drugs on the plasma concentrations of each other, and pharmacodynamic drug interactions concern the effects of drugs on the receptor activities of each other.

### Pharmacokinetics

**Absorption.**  A psychotherapeutic drug must first reach the blood on its way to the brain, unless it is directly administered into the cerebrospinal fluid or the brain. Orally administered drugs must dissolve in the fluid of the gastrointestinal (GI) tract before the body can absorb them. Drug tablets can be designed to disintegrate quickly or slowly, the absorption depending on the drug's concentration and lipid solubility and the GI tract's local pH, motility, and surface area. Depending on the drug's $pK_a$ and the GI tract's pH, the drug may be present in an ionized form that limits its lipid solubility. If the pharmacokinetic absorption factors are favorable, the drug may reach therapeutic blood concentrations quickly if it is administered intramuscularly. If a drug is coupled with an appropriate carrier molecule, intramuscular administration can sustain the drug's release over a long period of time. Some antipsychotic drugs are available in depot forms that allow the drug to be administered only once every one to four weeks. Even though intravenous administration is the quickest route to achieve therapeutic blood levels, it also carries the highest risk of sudden and life-threatening adverse effects.

**Distribution.**  Drugs can be freely dissolved in the blood plasma, bound to dissolved plasma proteins (primarily albumin), or dissolved within the blood cells. If a drug is bound too tightly to plasma proteins, it may have to be metabolized before it can leave the bloodstream, thus greatly reducing the amount of active drug reaching the brain. The lithium ion is an example of a water-soluble drug that is not bound to plasma proteins. The distribution of a drug to the brain is determined by the blood-brain barrier, the brain's regional blood flow, and the drug's affinity with its receptors in the brain. Both high blood flow and high affinity favor the distribution of the drug to the brain. Drugs may also reach the brain after passively diffusing into the cerebrospinal fluid from the bloodstream. The volume of distribution is a measure of the apparent space in the body available to contain the drug. The volume distribution can also vary with the patient's age, sex, and disease state.

**Metabolism and excretion.** Metabolism is synonymous with the term "biotransformation." The four major metabolic routes for drugs are oxidation, reduction, hydrolysis, and conjugation. Although the usual result of metabolism is to produce inactive metabolites that are more readily excreted than are the parent compounds, many examples of active metabolites are produced from psychoactive drugs. The liver is the principal site of metabolism, and bile, feces, and urine are the major routes of excretion. Psychoactive drugs are also excreted in sweat, saliva, tears, and breast milk; therefore, mothers who are taking psychotherapeutic drugs should not breastfeed their children. Disease states and coadministered drugs can both raise and lower the blood concentrations of a psychoactive drug.

Four concepts regarding metabolism and excretion are time of peak plasma level, half-life, first-pass effect, and clearance. The time between the administration of a drug and the appearance of peak concentrations of the drug in the plasma varies primarily according to the route of administration and absorption. A drug's half-life is defined as the amount of time it takes for half of the drug's peak plasma level to be metabolized and excreted from the body. A general guideline is that, if a drug is administered repeatedly in doses separated by time intervals shorter than its half-life, the drug will reach 97 percent of its steady-state plasma concentrations in a time equal to five times its half-life. The first-pass effects concern the extensive initial metabolism of some drugs within the portal circulation of the liver, thereby reducing the amount of unmetabolized drug that reaches the systemic circulation. Clearance is a measure of the amount of the drug excreted in each unit of time. If some disease process or other drug interferes with the clearance of a psychoactive drug, the drug accumulates in the patient and may reach toxic plasma concentrations.

An increasingly important area of consideration is the specific isoform of the hepatic cytochrome $P_{450}$ (CYP) enzyme that is involved in the metabolism of any drug. In particular, there is a genetic heterogeneity in CYP2D6 that puts some individuals at risk for developing high drug levels of drugs that are metabolized by the enzyme, especially when two drugs metabolized in CYP2D6 are taken concurrently by a person with genetically low CYP2D6 activity.

## Pharmacodynamics

The major pharmacodynamic considerations include receptor mechanisms; the dose-response curve; the therapeutic index; and the development of tolerance, dependence, and withdrawal phenomena. The receptor for a drug can be defined generally as the cellular component that binds to the drug and initiates the drug's pharmacodynamic effects. A drug can be an agonist for its receptor, thereby stimulating a physiological effect; conversely, a drug can be an antagonist for the receptor, most often by blocking the receptor so that an endogenous agonist cannot affect the receptor. The receptor site for most psychotherapeutic drugs is also a receptor site for an endogenous neurotransmitter. For example, the primary receptor site for chlorpromazine is the dopamine type 2 receptor. How-

ever, for other psychotherapeutic drugs, that may not be the case. The receptor for lithium may be the enzyme inositol-1-phosphatase, and the receptor for verapamil (Calan) is a calcium channel.

The dose-response curve plots the drug concentration against the effects of the drug (Figure 33.1–1). The potency of a drug is the relative dose required to achieve a certain effect. Haloperidol, for example, is more potent than is chlorpromazine because about 5 mg of haloperidol is required to achieve the same therapeutic effect as 100 mg of chlorpromazine. However, haloperidol and chlorpromazine are equal in their clinical efficacy—that is, the maximum clinical response achievable by the administration of a drug.

The side effects of most drugs are often direct results of their primary pharmacodynamic effects and are conceptualized as adverse effects. The therapeutic index is a relative measure of a drug's toxicity or safety. It is defined as the ratio of the median toxic dose ($TD_{50}$) to the median effective dose ($ED_{50}$). The $TD_{50}$ is the dose at which 50 percent of patients experience toxic effects, and the $ED_{50}$ is the dose at which 50 percent of patients experience therapeutic effects. Haloperidol, for example, has a high therapeutic index, as evidenced by the wide range of dosages in which it is prescribed. Conversely, lithium has a low therapeutic index, thereby requiring the monitoring of serum lithium levels. Both interindividual and intraindividual variation can be present in the response to a specific drug. An individual patient may be hyporeactive, normally reactive, or hyperreactive to a particular drug. For example, some patients require 150 mg a day of imipramine, whereas other patients require 300 mg a day. Idiosyncratic drug responses occur when a patient experiences a particularly unusual effect from a drug. For example, some patients become agitated when given benzodiazepines, such as diazepam (Valium).

A patient may become less responsive to a particular drug as it is administered over time, which is referred to as tolerance. The development of tolerance can be associated with the appearance of physical dependence, which

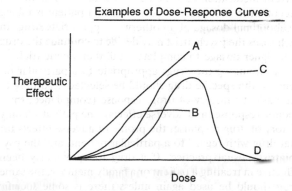

**Figure 33.1–1.** These dose-response curves plot the therapeutic effect as a function of increasing the dose, often calculated as the log of the dose. Drug A has a linear dose response; drugs B and C have sigmoidal curves; and drug D has a curvilinear dose-response curve. Although doses of drug B are more potent than are equal doses of drug C, drug C has a higher maximum efficacy than does drug B. Drug D has a therapeutic window, such that both low and high doses are less effective than are midrange doses.

may be defined as the necessity to continue administering the drug to prevent the appearance of withdrawal symptoms.

## CLINICAL GUIDELINES

The practice of clinical psychopharmacology requires skill as both a diagnostician and a psychotherapist, knowledge of the available drugs, and the ability to plan a pharmacotherapeutic regimen. The selection and the initiation of drug treatment should be based on the patient's history, the patient's current clinical state, and the treatment plan. The psychiatrist should know the purpose or the goal of a drug trial, the length of time that the drug needs to be administered to assess its efficacy, the approach to be taken to reduce any adverse effects that may occur, alternative drug strategies should the current one fail, and whether long-term maintenance of the patient on the drug is indicated. In almost all cases the psychiatrist should explain the treatment plan to the patient and often to the family and other caretakers. The patient's reaction to and ideas about a proposed drug trial should be considered. However, if the psychiatrist believes that accommodating the patient's wishes would hinder treatment, that should also be explained to the patient.

### Choice of Drug

The first two steps in selecting drug treatment, the diagnosis and the identification of the target symptoms, should ideally be carried out when the patient has been in a drug-free state for one to two weeks. The drug-free state should include the absence of medications for sleep, such as hypnotics, as the quality of sleep can be both an important diagnostic guide and a target symptom. However, if a patient is hospitalized, insurance guidelines may make a drug-free period difficult or even impossible to obtain. Psychiatrists often evaluate symptomatic patients who are already receiving one or more psychoactive medications, and so it is usually necessary to wean the patient from the current medication and then to make an assessment. An exception to that practice occurs when a patient is taking a suboptimal dosage of an otherwise appropriate drug. In such cases the psychiatrist may decide to continue the drug at a higher dosage to complete a full therapeutic trial.

From among the drugs appropriate to a particular diagnosis, the specific drug should be selected according to the patient's history of drug response (compliance, therapeutic response, and adverse effects), the patient's family history of drug response, the profile of adverse effects for that drug with regard to a particular patient, and the psychiatrist's usual practice. If a drug has previously been effective in treating a patient or a family member, the same drug should be used again unless there is some specific reason not to use the drug. A history of severe adverse effects from a specific drug is a strong indicator that the patient would not be compliant with that drug regimen. Patients and their families are often ignorant about what drugs have been used before, in what dosages, and for how long. That ignorance may reflect the tendency of psychiatrists not to explain drug trials to their patients. Psychi-

atrists should consider giving their patients written records of drug trials for their personal medical records. A caveat to obtaining a history of drug response from patients is that, because of their mental disorders, they may inaccurately report the effects of a previous drug trial. If possible, therefore, the patients' medical records should be obtained to confirm their reports. Most psychotherapeutic drugs of a single class are equally efficacious; however, the drugs do differ in their adverse effects on individual patients. A drug should be selected that minimally exacerbates any preexisting medical problems that a particular patient has.

**Nonapproved dosages and uses.** Under the federal Food, Drug, and Cosmetic (FDC) Act, the Food and Drug Administration (FDA) has authority to control the initial availability of a drug by approving only those new drugs that demonstrate both safety and effectiveness and then to ensure that the drug's proposed labeling is truthful and contains all pertinent information for the safe and effective use of that drug. An additional level of government regulation is directed by the Drug Enforcement Agency (DEA), which has classified drugs according to their abuse potential (Table 33.1–2). Clinicians are advised to exercise increased caution when prescribing controlled substances.

Before a new drug can be approved by the FDA, it must be studied in humans. For the drug ultimately to be approved for commercial use, the sponsor must justify the safety and effectiveness of the drug by submitting a New Drug Application (NDA) to the FDA. The NDA is approved or disapproved, depending on the clinical data accumulated. For approval, the FDA requires that adequate tests be conducted showing that the drug is "safe for use under the conditions prescribed, recommended, or suggested." There must also be "substantial evidence that the drug will have the effect it purports under the conditions of use prescribed, recommended, or suggested in the proposed labeling."

According to Medical Liability Mutual Insurance Company, once a drug is approved for commercial use, the physician may, as part of the practice of medicine, lawfully prescribe a different dosage for a patient or otherwise vary the conditions of use from what is approved in the package labeling without notifying the FDA or obtaining its approval. Specifically, the FDC Act does not limit the manner in which a physician may use an approved drug. However, although physicians may treat patients with an approved drug for unapproved purposes—that is, indications not included on the drug's official labeling—without violating the FDC Act, the patient's right to redress for possible medical malpractice remains. That is a significant concern, because the failure to follow the FDA-approved label may create an inference that the physician was varying from the prevailing standard of care. Although the failure to follow the contents of the drug label does not impose liability per se and should not preclude a physician from using good clinical judgment in the interest of the patient, the physician should be aware that the drug label presents important information regarding the safe and effective use of the drug.

In summary, psychiatrists may prescribe medication for any reason that they believe to be medically indicated for the welfare of the patient. That clarification is important in view of the increasing regulation of physicians by federal, state, and local government agencies and the intimidation being experienced by many physicians in exercising their best medical judgment. When using a drug for an unapproved indication or in a dosage outside the usual range, the physician should document the reasons for those treatment decisions in the patient's chart. If clinicians are in doubt about a treatment

**Table 33.1–2**
**Characteristics of Drugs at Each DEA Level**

| DEA Control Level (Schedule) | Characteristics of Drug at Each Control Level | Examples of Drugs at Each Control Level |
|---|---|---|
| I | High abuse potential<br>No accepted use in medical treament in the United States at the present time and, therefore, not for prescription use<br>Can be used for research | LSD, heroin, marijuana, peyote, PCP, mescaline, psilocybin, tetrahydrocannabinols, nicocodeine, nicomorphine |
| II | High abuse potential<br>Severe physical dependence liability<br>Severe psychological dependence liability<br>No refills; no telephone prescriptions | Amphetamine, opium, morphine, codeine, hydromorphine, phenmetrazine, amobarbital, secobarbital, pentobarbital, methylphenidate |
| III | Abuse potential less than levels I and II<br>Moderate or low physical dependence liability<br>High psychological liability<br>Prescriptions must be rewritten after six months or five refills | Glutethimide, methyprylon, nalorphine, sulfonmethane, benzphetamine, phendimetrazine, mazindol, chlorphentermine; compounds containing codeine, morphine, opium, hydrocodone, dihydrocodeine, naltrexone, diethylpropion |
| IV | Low abuse potential<br>Limited physical dependence liability<br>Limited psychological dependence liability<br>Prescriptions must be rewritten after six months or five refills | Phenobarbital, benzodiazepines,* chloral hydrate, ethchlorvynol, ethinamate, meprobamate, paraldehyde |
| V | Lowest abuse potential of all controlled substances | Narcotic preparations containing limited amounts of nonnarcotic active medicinal ingredients |

*In New York State, benzodiazepines are treated as schedule II substances, which require a triplicate prescription for a maximum of one month's supply.

plan, they should consult a colleague or suggest that the patient obtain a second opinion.

**Therapeutic trials.** A drug's therapeutic trial should last for a previously determined length of time. Because behavioral symptoms are more difficult to assess than are other physiological symptoms, such as hypertension, it is particularly important for specific target symptoms to be identified at the initiation of a drug trial. The psychiatrist and the patient can then assess the target symptom over the course of the drug trial to help determine whether the drug has been effective. A number of objective rating scales, such as the Brief Psychiatric Rating Scale (BPRS) and the Hamilton Rating Scale for Depression (HAM-D), are available to help assess a patient's progress over the course of a drug trial. If a drug has not been effective in reducing target symptoms within the specified length of time and if other reasons for the lack of response can be eliminated, the drug should be tapered and stopped. The brain is not a group of on-off neurochemical switches; rather, it is an interactive network of neurons in a complex homeostasis. Thus, the abrupt discontinuation of virtually any psychoactive drug is likely to disrupt the brain's functioning. Another common clinical mistake is the routine addition of medications without the discontinuation of a prior drug. Although that practice is indicated in specific circumstances, such as lithium potentiation of an unsuccessful trial of antidepressants, it often results in increased noncompliance and adverse effects and the clinician's not knowing whether it was the second drug alone or the combination of drugs that resulted in a therapeutic success or adverse effect.

**Therapeutic failures.** The failure of a specific drug trial should prompt the clinician to reconsider a number of possibilities. First, was the original diagnosis correct? That reconsideration should include the possibility of an undiagnosed cognitive disorder, including illicit drug abuse. Second, are the observed remaining symptoms the drug's adverse effects and not related to the original disease? Antipsychotic drugs, for example, can produce akinesia, which resembles psychotic withdrawal; akathisia and neuroleptic malignant syndrome resemble increased psychotic agitation. Third, was the drug administered in sufficient dosage for an appropriate period of time? Patients can have varying drug absorption and metabolic rates for the same drug, and plasma drug levels should be obtained to assess that variable. Fourth, did a pharmacokinetic or pharmacodynamic interaction with another drug the patient was taking reduce the efficacy of the psychotherapeutic drug? Fifth, did the patient take the drug as directed? Drug noncompliance is a common clinical problem. The reasons for drug noncompliance include complicated drug regimens (more than one drug in more than one daily dose), adverse side effects (especially if unnoticed by the clinician), and poor patient education about the drug treatment plan (Table 33.1–3).

## COMBINED PSYCHOTHERAPY AND PHARMACOTHERAPY

Using drugs that affect the brain in combination with psychotherapy is one of the fastest growing practices in contemporary psychiatry. In that therapeutic approach, individual or group therapy is combined with pharmacological therapy. It should not be a system in which the therapist meets with the patient on an occasional or irregular basis to monitor the effects of medication or to make notations on a rating scale to assess progress and side effects; rather, it should be a system in which both therapies are integrated and synergistic (Table 33.1–4). In many cases the results of combined therapy are superior to either

**Table 33.1–3**
**Conditions That May Reduce Adherence to Recommended Treatment**

Excessively complex regimen (multiple agents, multiple small doses)
Early onset and persistence of side effects
Slow onset of beneficial effects
Low apparent relapse risk experienced if treatment is interrupted
Psychosis, confusion, dementia, pseudodementia, low intelligence, impaired hearing or vision, illiteracy
Simple lack of information, need for patient education
Financial hardship, conflicting obligations of time or money
Resentment, lack of confidence or trust
Specific psychopathology: paranoid delusions, hopelessness, masochism, anxiety and fear, ambivalence, control, splitting, passive aggression, passive dependence, denial, sociopathy, substance abuse
Involvement of multiple clinicians
Poor clinician-patient relationship
Inevitable human error

Adapted from R J Baldessarini, J O Cole: Chemotherapy. In *The New Harvard Guide to Psychiatry*, A M Nicholi, editor, p 530. Belknap, Cambridge, Mass, 1988. Used with permission.

type of therapy used alone. The term "pharmacotherapy-oriented psychotherapy" is used by some practitioners for the combined approach. The methods of psychotherapy used can vary, and all can be combined with pharmacotherapy.

## Countertransference

As in all types of psychotherapy, psychiatrists must be aware of their conscious and unconscious feelings toward their patients, known as countertransference. Similarly, psychiatrists must be aware of their own psychological attitudes toward drugs. Medications cannot replace the therapeutic alliance. They are not a shortcut to cure and are no substitute for the intense concentration and involvement on the part of the psychiatrist who is conducting psychotherapy. Therapists who are pessimistic about the value of psychotherapy or who misjudge the patient's motivation may prescribe medications out of their own nihilistic beliefs. Others may withhold medication if they overvalue psychotherapy or devalue pharmacological agents. Withholding medication is most likely to occur with borderline personality disorder patients, suicidal patients, and patients with a history of substance abuse. Each case must be evaluated individually, and the risk-benefit ratio must be carefully assessed so that the patient is not punished, deprived, or mistreated.

## Combined Therapy in Specific Disorders

**Depressive disorders.** Some patients and clinicians fear that medications will cover the depression and that psychotherapy will be impeded. Medications should be viewed as facilitators in overcoming the anergia that may

**Table 33.1–4**
**Stages of Individual Psychotherapy: A Medication Emphasis**

| Stage | Engagement | Pattern Search | Change | Termination |
|---|---|---|---|---|
| Goals | Trust<br>Credibility<br>Self-observer alliance | To define problem patterns that, if changed, would lead to a desirable outcome | 1. Relinquish old pattern(s)<br>2. Initiate new pattern(s)<br>3. Practice new pattern(s) | To separate efficiently |
| Techniques | Convey empathic understanding<br>Effective suggestions<br>Effective medications | Questionnaires<br>Homework— idiosyncratic meanings ascribed to medication | Interpretation<br>Reframing<br>Behavioral suggestion<br>Medication-induced change | Mutually agreed<br>Patient initiates<br>Therapist initiates<br>Medication-influenced |
| Content | Medication responsive<br>Diagnosis | Does response to medication reflect a problem pattern? | Medication effects or insight around medication use accelerates change | Medications may prolong termination |
| Resistance | Are excessive side effects resistance to treatment? | Does pattern of nonadherence to medication regimen reflect a problem pattern? | Do new side effects suggest resistance to change? | Symptom reoccurrence not necessarily indication for medication change |
| Transference | Physician seen as malevolent or all-powerful | Is key interpersonal pattern reflected in meaning of medication? | Unresolved distortions may be signaled by a new medication issue inhibiting change | Desire for new or more medication reflects desire to hold therapist |
| Countertransference | Physician failure to prescribe appropriately | Medication prescription reflects distorted response to patient | Sudden change in regimen reflects an attempt to undermine change | New medication reflects desire to keep contact |

Table by B D Beitman. In *Integrating Pharmacotherapy and Psychotherapy*, B D Beitman, G L Klerman, editors, p 22. American Psychiatric Press, Washington, 1991. Used with permission.

inhibit a communication process between doctor and patient. The psychiatrist should also explain to the patient that depression interferes with interpersonal activity in a variety of ways. For example, depression produces withdrawal and irritability, which alienates significant others who may otherwise gratify the patient's strong dependence needs that make up much of depressive disorders' psychodynamics.

The psychiatrist should be alert for signs and symptoms of recurrent major depressive disorder. Medication may have to be reinstituted. Before doing so, however, the psychiatrist should review any stress, especially rejections, that may have precipitated recurrent major depressive disorder. A major depressive episode may occur because the patient is in a stage of negative transference, and the psychiatrist must try to elicit negative feelings. In many cases the ventilation of angry feelings toward the therapist without an angry response can serve as a corrective emotional experience, and a major depressive episode necessitating medication can thereby be forestalled. Depressed patients are generally maintained on their medication for six months or longer after clinical improvement. The cessation of pharmacotherapy before that time is likely to result in a relapse.

**Suicidal behavior.** The possibility of suicide must be considered in treating patients with schizophrenia, bipolar I disorder, depressive disorders, and anxiety disorders (especially those with panic attacks). If the psychiatrist decides that the patient is in imminent risk for suicidal behavior, hospitalization is always indicated. If the patient can be managed outside a hospital, medication should be given to a responsible family member who can monitor the dosage and the frequency of the prescribed medication. As a further precaution, the psychiatrist may treat the patient with a drug known to have little or no lethal potential when taken in an overdose attempt. Medication is almost always indicated in suicidally depressed patients.

**Bipolar I disorder.** Patients taking lithium or other treatments for bipolar I disorder are usually medicated for an indefinite period of time for recent episodes of either mania or depression. Most psychotherapists insist that patients with bipolar I disorder be medicated before starting any insight-oriented therapy. Without such premedication, most bipolar I disorder patients are unable to make the necessary therapeutic alliance. When those patients are depressed, their abulia seriously disrupts their flow of thoughts, and the sessions are nonproductive. When they are manic, their flow of associations can be rapid and their speech so pressured that the therapist may be flooded with material and unable to make appropriate interpretations or unable to assimilate the material into the patient's disrupted cognitive framework.

**Anxiety disorders.** Anxiety disorders encompass obsessive-compulsive disorder, posttraumatic stress disorder, generalized anxiety disorder, phobias, and panic disorder with or without agoraphobia. Many drugs are effective in managing distressing signs and symptoms associated with those disorders. As the symptoms are controlled by medication, patients are reassured and develop confidence that they will not be incapacitated by the disorder. That effect is particularly strong in panic disorder, which is often associated with anticipatory anxiety about the attack. Depression may complicate the symptom picture in patients with anxiety disorders and has to be addressed both pharmacologically and psychotherapeutically.

**Schizophrenia and other psychotic disorders.** Included in this group of disorders are schizophrenia, delusional disorder, schizoaffective disorder, schizophreniform disorder, and brief psychotic disorder. Drug treatment for those disorders is always indicated, and hospitalization is often necessary for diagnostic purposes, to stabilize medication, to prevent danger to self or others, and to establish a psychosocial treatment program that may include individual psychotherapy. In attempting individual psychotherapy, the therapist must establish a treatment relationship and a therapeutic alliance with the patient. The schizophrenic patient defends against closeness and trust and often becomes suspicious, anxious, hostile, or regressed in therapy.

**Substance abuse.** Patients who abuse alcohol or other substances present the most difficult challenge in combined therapy. The patients are often impulsive and, even though they promise not to abuse a substance, they may do so repeatedly. In addition, they frequently withhold information from the psychiatrist about episodes of abuse. For that reason, some psychiatrists do not prescribe medications to such patients, especially not medications with a high abuse potential, such as benzodiazepines, barbiturates, and amphetamines. Drugs with no abuse potential—such as thioridazine (Mellaril), amitriptyline (Elavil), and fluoxetine—have an important role in the treatment of the anxiety or depression or both that almost always accompanies substance-related disorders. The psychiatrist conducting psychotherapy with such patients should have no reservations about sending the patient to a laboratory for random urine toxicological tests. As in all forms of insight-oriented psychotherapy, the psychological significance of such tests should be examined.

## SPECIAL TREATMENT CONSIDERATIONS

### Children

Special care must be given when administering psychotherapeutic drugs to children. Although the small volume of distribution suggests the use of lower dosages than in adults, children's higher rate of metabolism indicates that higher ratios of milligrams of drug to kilograms of body weight should be used. In practice, it is best to begin with a small dose and to increase the dosage until clinical effects are observed (Table 49.4–2). The clinician, however, should not hesitate to use adult dosages in children if the dosages are effective and the side effects are acceptable.

### Geriatric Patients

The two major concerns when treating geriatric patients with psychotherapeutic drugs are that elderly persons may be especially susceptible to adverse effects (particularly cardiac effects) and may metabolize drugs slowly (Table 33.1–5), thus requiring low dosages of medication (Tables 50–3, 50–4, 50–5, 50–6, 50–7, and 50–8). Another concern

**Table 33.1–5**
**Pharmacokinetics and Aging**

| Phase | Change | Effect |
|---|---|---|
| Absorption | Gastric pH increases<br>Decreased surface villi<br>Decreased gastric motility and delayed gastric emptying<br>Intestinal perfusion decreases | Little overall change<br>Absorption is slowed but just as complete |
| Distribution | Total body water and lean body mass decrease<br>Increased total body fat, more marked in women than in men<br>Albumin decreases, gamma globulin increases, alpha₁ acid glycoprotein unchanged | Volume of distribution (Vd) increases for lipid-soluble drugs, decreases for water-soluble drugs<br>The free or unbound percentage of albumin-bound drugs increases |
| Metabolism | Renal: renal blood flow and glomerular filtration rates decrease<br>Hepatic: decreased enzyme activity and perfusion | Decreased metabolism leads to prolonged half-lives, if Vd remains the same |
| Total body weight | Decreases | Think on a mg-per-kg basis |
| Receptor sensitivity | May increase | Increased effect |

Table from L B Guttmacher: *Concise Guide to Somatic Therapies in Psychiatry*, p 126. American Psychiatric Press, Washington, 1988. Used with permission.

is that geriatric patients are often taking other medications, thereby requiring the psychiatrist to consider the possible drug interactions. In practice, psychiatrists should begin treating geriatric patients with a small dose, usually about one half the usual dose. The dosage should be raised in small amounts more slowly than in middle-aged adults until either a clinical benefit is achieved or unacceptable adverse effects appear. Although many geriatric patients require a small dosage of medication, many others require the usual adult dosage.

## Pregnant and Nursing Women

The basic rule is to avoid administering any drug to a woman who is pregnant (particularly during the first trimester) or who is breast-feeding a child. That rule, however, occasionally needs to be broken when the mother's mental disorder is severe. If psychotherapeutic medications need to be administered during a pregnancy, the possibility of therapeutic abortion should be discussed. The two most teratogenic drugs in the psychopharmacopeia are lithium and anticonvulsants. Lithium administration during pregnancy is associated with a high incidence of birth abnormalities, including Ebstein's anomaly, a serious abnormality in cardiac development. Other psychoactive

drugs (antidepressants, antipsychotics, and anxiolytics), although less clearly associated with birth defects, should also be avoided during pregnancy if at all possible. The most common clinical situation occurs when a pregnant woman becomes psychotic. If a decision is made not to terminate the pregnancy, antipsychotics or electroconvulsive therapy (ECT) are preferable to lithium.

The administration of psychotherapeutic drugs at or near delivery may cause the baby to be overly sedated at delivery, requiring a respirator, or to be physically dependent on the drug, requiring detoxification and the treatment of a withdrawal syndrome. Virtually all psychotropic drugs are secreted in the milk of a nursing mother; therefore, mothers taking those agents should not breast-feed their infants.

## Medically Ill Patients

Considerations in administering psychotropic drugs to medically ill patients include a potentially increased sensitivity to the drug's side effects, either increased or decreased metabolism and excretion of the drug, and interactions with other medications. As with children and geriatric patients, the most reasonable clinical practice is to begin with a small dose, increase it slowly, and watch for both clinical and adverse effects. The testing of plasma drug levels may be particularly helpful in those patients.

## ADVERSE EFFECTS

Most psychotherapeutic drugs do not affect a single neurotransmitter system, nor are their effects localized to the brain. Psychotherapeutic drugs result in a wide range of adverse effects on neurotransmitter systems. For example, some of the most common adverse effects of psychotherapeutic drugs are caused by the blockade of muscarinic acetylcholine receptors (Table 33.1–6). Many psychotherapeutic drugs antagonize dopaminergic, histaminergic, and adrenergic neurons, resulting in the adverse effects listed in Table 33.1–7. There are also several commonly observed adverse effects for which the neurotransmitters involved have not been specifically identified.

Patients generally have decreased trouble with adverse effects if they have been told to expect them. The psy-

**Table 33.1–6**
**Potential Adverse Effects Caused by Blockade of Muscarinic Acetylcholine Receptors**

Blurred vision
Constipation
Decreased salivation
Decreased sweating
Delayed or retrograde ejaculation
Delirium
Exacerbation of asthma (through decreased bronchial secretions)
Hyperthermia (through decreased sweating)
Memory problems
Narrow-angle glaucoma
Photophobia
Sinus tachycardia
Urinary retention

**Table 33.1–7**
**Potential Adverse Effects of Psychotherapeutic Drugs and Associated Neurotransmitter Systems**

Antidopaminergic
  Endocrine dysfunction
    Hyperprolactinemia
    Menstrual dysfunction
    Sexual dysfunction
  Movement disorders
    Akathisia
    Dystonia
    Parkinsonism
    Tardive dyskinesia
Antiadrenergic (primarily $\alpha_1$)
  Dizziness
  Postural hypotension
  Reflex tachycardia
Antihistaminergic
  Hypotension
  Sedation
  Weight gain
Multiple neurotransmitter systems
  Agranulocytosis (and other blood dyscrasias)
  Allergic reactions
  Anorexia
  Cardiac conduction abnormalities
  Nausea and vomiting
  Seizures

chiatrist can explain the appearance of adverse effects as evidence that the drug is working. But clinicians should distinguish between probable or expected adverse effects and rare or unexpected adverse effects.

## Treatment of Common Adverse Effects

Many adverse effects are seen with psychotherapeutic drugs. The management of the adverse effects is similar, regardless of which psychotherapeutic drug the patient is taking.

**Dry mouth.** Dry mouth is caused by the blockade of muscarinic acetylcholine receptors. When patients attempt to relieve the dry mouth by constantly sucking on sugar-containing hard candies, they increase their risk for dental caries. They can avoid the problem by chewing sugarless gum or sucking on sugarless hard candies. Some clinicians recommend the use of a 1 percent solution of pilocarpine, a cholinergic agonist, as a mouth wash three times daily. Other clinicians suggest bethanechol (Urecholine, Myotonachol) tablets, another cholinergic agonist, 10 to 30 mg, once or twice daily. It is best to start with 10 mg once a day and to increase the dosage slowly. Adverse effects of cholinomimetic drugs, such as bethanechol, include tremor, diarrhea, abdominal cramps, and excessive eye watering.

**Blurred vision.** The blockage of muscarinic acetylcholine receptors causes mydriasis (pupillary dilation) and cycloplegia (ciliary muscle paresis), resulting in presbyopia (blurred near vision). The symptom can be relieved by cholinomimetic eyedrops. A 1 percent solution of pilocarpine can be prescribed as one drop four times daily. As an alternative, bethanechol can be used as it is used for dry mouth.

**Urinary retention.** The anticholinergic activity of many psychotropic drugs can lead to urinary hesitation, dribbling, urinary retention, and increased urinary tract infections. Elderly persons with enlarged prostates are at increased risk for those adverse effects. Ten to 30 mg of bethanechol three to four times daily is usually effective in the treatment of the adverse effects.

**Constipation.** The anticholinergic activity of psychotropic drugs can result in the particularly disturbing adverse effect of constipation. The first line of treatment involves the prescribing of bulk laxatives, such as Metamucil and Fiberall. If that treatment fails, cathartic laxatives, such as milk of magnesia, can be tried. Prolonged use of cathartic laxatives can result in a loss of their effectiveness. Bethanechol, 10 to 30 mg three to four times daily, can also be used.

**Orthostatic hypotension.** Orthostatic hypotension is caused by the blockade of $\alpha_1$-adrenergic receptors. The psychiatrist should warn patients of that possible adverse effect, particularly if the patient is elderly. The risk of hip fractures from falls is significantly elevated in patients who are taking psychotropic drugs. With patients at high risk for orthostatic hypotension, the clinician should choose a drug with low $\alpha_1$-adrenergic activity. Most simply, the patient can be instructed to get up slowly and to sit down immediately if dizziness is experienced. The patient can also try support hose to help reduce venous pooling. Specific adjuvant medications have been recommended for specific pharmacotherapeutic drugs.

**Sexual dysfunction.** Psychotropic drug use can be associated with sexual dysfunctions—decreased libido, impaired ejaculation and erection, and inhibition of female orgasm. Warning a patient about those adverse effects may increase the patient's concern. Alternatively, patients are not likely to report adverse sexual effects spontaneously to the physician. Also, some sexual dysfunctions may be related to the primary mental disorder. Nevertheless, if sexual dysfunctions emerge after pharmacotherapy has begun, it may be worthwhile to treat them. Neostigmine (Prostigmin), 7.5 to 15 mg orally 30 minutes before sexual intercourse, may help alleviate impaired ejaculation. Impaired erectile function may be helped with bethanechol given regularly or possibly yohimbine (Yocon). Cyproheptadine (Periactin), 4 mg every morning, can be used for the treatment of inhibited female orgasm; 4 to 8 mg orally can be taken one to two hours before anticipated sexual activity for the treatment of inhibited male orgasm secondary to serotonergic agents.

**Weight gain.** Weight gain accompanies the use of many psychotropic drugs. The weight gain can be the result of retained fluid, increased caloric intake, or decreased exercise. Edema can be treated by elevating the affected body parts or by administering a thiazide diuretic. If the patient is taking lithium or cardiac medications, the clinician must monitor blood levels, blood chemistries, and vital signs. The patient should also be instructed to minimize the intake of fats and carbohydrates and to exercise regularly. However, if the patient has not been exercising, the clinician should recommend that the patient start an exercise program at a modest level of exertion.

## Overdoses

An extreme adverse effect of drug treatment is an attempt by a patient to commit suicide by overdosing on a psychotherapeutic drug. One psychodynamic theory of such behavior is that the patients are angry at their therapists for not having been able to help them. Whatever the motivation, psychiatrists should be aware of the risk and attempt to prescribe the safest possible drugs. It is good clinical practice to write nonrefillable prescriptions for small quantities of drugs when suicide is a consideration. In extreme cases, an attempt should be made to verify that patients are taking the medication and not hoarding the pills for a later overdose attempt. Patents may attempt suicide just as they are beginning to get better. Clinicians, therefore, should continue to be careful about prescribing large quantities of medication until the patient is almost completely recovered. Another consideration for psychiatrists is the possibility of an accidental overdose, particularly by children in the household. Patients should be advised to keep psychotherapeutic medications in a safe place. A guide to the signs and symptoms and the treatment of overdoses with psychotherapeutic drugs is contained in Table 33.1–8.

# DRUG INTERACTIONS

Drug interactions may be either pharmacokinetic or pharmacodynamic, and they vary greatly in their potential to cause serious problems. An additional consideration is one of phantom drug interactions. The patient may be taking only drug A and then later receive both drug A and drug B. The clinician may notice some effect and attribute it to the induction of metabolism. What may have gone on is that the patient was more compliant at one point in the observation period than in another, or there may have been some other effect of which the clinician was unaware. The clinical literature may contain reports of phantom drug interactions that are rare or nonexistent.

Other interactions are true but unproved, although reasonably plausible. Still other interactions have some modest effects and are well-documented. And some clinically important drug interactions are well-studied and well-proved. However, clinicians must remember that (1) animal pharmacokinetic data are not always readily generalizable to humans; (2) in vitro data do not necessarily replicate the results obtained under in vivo conditions; (3) single-case reports can contain misleading information; and (4) studies of acute conditions should not be uncritically regarded as relevant to chronic, steady-state conditions.

**Table 33.1–8**
**Intoxication and Overdose with Psychotherapeutic Drugs**

| Drug | Toxic or Lethal Dose* | Signs and Symptoms | Treatment† |
|---|---|---|---|
| β-Adrenergic receptor antagonists | Propranolol 1 g | Hypotension, bradycardia, seizures, loss of consciousness, bronchospasm, cardiac failure | Supportive care; emesis or gastric lavage after ingestion. If needed (comatose, seizures, absent gag), lavage with endotracheal tube with inflated cuff in place; intravenous (IV) atropine for symptomatic bradycardia, IV isoproterenol for persistent cases, a pacemaker if refractory; norepinephrine or dopamine for severe hypotension; IV diazepam for seizures; glucagon may be useful for hypotension and myocardial depression, theophylline or β₂-agonist for bronchospasm, a diuretic or cardiac glycoside for heart failure |
| Amantadine | 2.5 g | Disorientation, visual hallucinations, confusion, aggressive behavior, minimally reactive and slightly dilated pupils, urinary retention, acid-base disturbances, coma | Induce emesis or use gastric lavage in recent overdose; supportive measures, including airway maintenance, cardiovascular monitoring, control of respiration and oxygen administration: monitoring urine pH, urinary output, serum electrolytes; acidifying agents can increase the rate of excretion, force fluids (IV if needed); observe for hypotension, seizures, psychosis, urinary retention, arrhythmias, hyperactivity, which should be treated appropriately; physostigmine may be useful in treating central nervous system (CNS) toxicity; chlorpromazine may be useful for toxic psychosis; adrenergic agents may predispose the patient to ventricular arrhythmias |
| Amphetamine | 100 mg | Elation, irritability, hyperactivity, rapid speech, anorexia, hyperreflexia, insomnia, dry mouth, chest pain, arrhythmia, heart block, poor concentration, restlessness, psychotic symptoms | Emesis or lavage can be effective long after ingestion because of recycling through gastric mucosa; reduce external stimuli; treat cerebral edema and hyperthermia; peritoneal dialysis; sedate with chlorpromazine 0.5–1 mg/kg intramuscular (IM) or by mouth every 30 minutes as needed; use ½ the dose for mixed amphetamine-barbiturate overdose |

**Table 33.1–8**
*Continued*

| Drug | Toxic or Lethal Dose* | Signs and Symptoms | Treatment† |
|------|----------------------|--------------------|------------|
| Anticholinergics | 700 mg–7 g, (doses vary, depending on agent involved) | Hot, dry, flushed skin; unreactive dilated pupils; blurred vision; dry mucous membranes; foul breath; difficulty in swallowing; urinary retention; decreased bowel sounds; tachycardia; nausea; vomiting; rash; anticholinergic delirium with delusions, hallucinations, disorientation | Supportive and symptomatic therapy; continuous electrocardiograph (ECG) monitoring; empty stomach immediately by inducing emesis if patient is conscious, has gag reflex and no seizures; otherwise, gastric lavage and activated charcoal can be used with endotracheal tube with inflated cuff in place; saline cathartics may be used; exchange transfusions can be considered in extreme cases; fluid therapy should be used for shock; cold packs, mechanical cooling devices, or sponging with tepid water can be used for hyperthermia; diazepam can be used for agitation; 1 mg can reverse adverse effects of physostigmine; IV propranolol may be useful for supraventricular tachyarrhythmias; avoid dopamine receptor antagonists |
| Antihistamines | 2.8 g (diphenhydramine), 1,750–17,500 mg (hydroxyzine) | Disorientation, drowsiness, excitation or depression, hallucinations, anxiety, delirium, hyperthermia, tachycardia, arrhythmias, seizures | Empty stomach with ipecac emesis or gastric lavage; support cardiorespiratory function; physostigmine may be useful for anticholinergic effects, diazepam for seizures; sponge baths with tepid water (not alcohol) or cold packs for hyperthermia |
| Barbiturates | 10 times the daily therapeutic dose (e.g., 1–2 g of secobarbital) | Delirium, confusion, excitement, headache, CNS and respiratory depression from somnolence to coma, areflexia, circulatory collapse | Supportive treatment, including maintaining airway and respiration and treating shock as needed; within 30 minutes of ingestion, use activated charcoal; gastric lavage and aspiration can be used within 4 hours of ingestion; nasogastric administration of charcoal in multiple doses can shorten coma; maintain vital signs, fluid balance; alkalinizing the urine increases the excretion of mephobarbital, aprobarbital, phenobarbital; forced diuresis may be of use if renal function is normal; hemodialysis or peritoneal dialysis may be useful in severe cases |
| Benzodiazepines | Toxic dose: diazepam: 2 g; chlordiazepoxide: 6 g | Slurred speech, incoordination, somnolence, confusion, coma, hyporeflexia, hypotension | General supportive care; induce emesis for recent ingestions in fully conscious patients; gastric lavage with endotracheal tube with inflated cuff if comatose; after above, use a saline cathartic and activated charcoal; maintain airway, monitor vital signs, give IV fluids; norepinephrine or metaraminol can be used for hypotension; flumazenil can be used with extreme caution |
| Bromocriptine | Survival of 225 mg dose reported | Severe hypotension, nausea, vomiting, psychosis | Empty stomach by lavage and aspiration, IV fluids for hypotension |
| Bupropion | Ingestions of 850–4,200 mg have been survived; deaths have been reported in massive overdoses | Seizures, loss of consciousness, hallucinations, tachycardia | Ipecac emesis if conscious; gastric lavage with endotracheal tube in place with inflated cuff if there are seizures or a decreased level of consciousness; during first 12 hours after ingestion, use activated charcoal every 6 hours, provide fluids; electroencephalogram (EEG) and ECG monitoring for 48 hours; seizures can be treated with IV benzodiazepines |

**Table 33.1–8**
**Continued**

| Drug | Toxic or Lethal Dose* | Signs and Symptoms | Treatment† |
|---|---|---|---|
| Buspirone | Toxic dose of 375 mg (used in studies); lethal dose unknown | Dizziness, drowsiness, nausea, vomiting, miosis, gastric distention | Symptomatic and supportive care; empty stomach with emesis or lavage in large ingestions; if needed, perform lavage with endotracheal tube in place with cuff inflated; monitor vital signs |
| Calcium channel inhibitors | 9.6 g of verapamil has resulted in death; patients have survived ingestion of 8 to 10 g of diltiazem and 9 g of nifedipine (case reports) | Confusion, headache, nausea, vomiting, seizures, flushing, constipation, bradycardia, hypotension, atrioventricular block, hyperglycemia, metabolic acidosis | Emesis followed by gastric lavage with activated charcoal; calcium gluconate or calcium chloride 10–20 mg/kg in 10% solution with normal saline IV given over 30 minutes and repeated as needed; atropine or isoproterenol for atrioventricular block; a pacemaker may be needed |
| Carbamazepine | Lowest known lethal dose in adults: 60 g; highest doses survived: children 10 g, adults 30 g | Drowsiness, stupor, dizziness, restlessness, ataxia, agitation, nausea, vomiting, involuntary movements, abnormal reflexes, adiadochokinesis, nystagmus, mydriasis, flushing, cyanosis, urinary retention, hypotension or hypertension, coma, cardiac arrhythmias | Induce emesis or gastric lavage; supportive measures; ECG monitoring |
| Carisoprodol | Patients have recovered from 3.4 g and 9.45 g ingestions | Stupor, shock, coma, respiratory depression, headache, diplopia, dizziness, drowsiness, nystagmus | Supportive treatment; induce emesis or use gastric lavage with endotracheal tube in place with cuff inflated if clinically indicated; activated charcoal after emptying stomach; maintain airway, respiration, and blood pressure; pressor agents can be used with caution if necessary; elimination may be enhanced by forced diuresis with hemodialysis, peritoneal dialysis, or osmotic diuresis; avoid overhydration; monitor neurological status, electrolytes, and vital signs; continue monitoring for relapse secondary to delayed absorption and incomplete gastric emptying |
| Chloral hydrate | 4–10 g | Coma, confusion, drowsiness, respiratory depression, hypotension, hypothermia, vomiting, miosis, gastric necrosis and perforation, esophageal stricture, hepatic injury, renal injury | General supportive measures; gastric lavage with endotracheal tube with inflated cuff in place; maintain airway, oxygenation, cardiorespiratory function, and body temperature; hemodialysis or peritoneal dialysis may be of use; saline enema if drug was administered rectally |
| Clonidine | No known deaths from overdoses of clonidine alone; 100 mg is the largest known overdose survived; 2 known deaths from mixed overdoses that included clonidine | Hypotension, hyporeflexia or areflexia, vomiting, weakness, irritability, sedation, coma, lethargy, hypothermia, constricted pupils, dry mouth, hypoventilation, seizures, arrhythmia, cardiac conduction defects | Induce emesis or lavage followed by activated charcoal and a saline cathartic; lavage is preferred in patients with decreased levels of consciousness and should be used with endotracheal tube with inflated cuff in place if patient is comatose, has seizures, or lacks gag reflex; supportive and symptomatic measures; establish airway, IV fluids, and Trendelenburg's position for hypotension; if persistent, use dopamine; atropine IV for symptomatic bradycardia; tolazoline 10 mg IV every 30 minutes may reverse cardiovascular effects of clonidine; IV furosemide, α-blockers, or diazoxide for hypertension; IV benzodiazepines can be used for seizures |

**Table 33.1–8**
*Continued*

| Drug | Toxic or Lethal Dose* | Signs and Symptoms | Treatment[†] |
|---|---|---|---|
| Clozapine | Lethal dose: >2.5 g, although patients have survived ingestions of >4 g | Delirium, drowsiness, coma, respiratory depression, tachycardia, arrhythmias, hypotension, hypersalivation, seizures | Symptomatic and supportive care; establish and maintain airway, ventilation, and oxygenation; activated charcoal with sorbitol (may be as effective as or more effective than lavage or emesis); monitor and adjust acid-base and electrolyte balance; physostigmine may be a useful adjunct for anticholinergic toxicity but is not for routine use; epinephrine, quinidine, procainamide are to be avoided; patient should be observed for several days for delayed effects |
| Dantrolene | No data available | Speech and visual disturbances, gastrointestinal (GI) upset or bleeding, liver damage, nausea, vomiting, CNS depression | Supportive measures; immediate gastric lavage; ECG monitoring; large quantities of IV fluids; maintain airway; have artificial respiratory measures available; observe patient |
| Disulfiram | 6 or more fatilities have occurred with ingestions of 0.5–1 g of disulfiram with blood alcohol levels of 1 mg/mL; a 30 g ingestion would produce serious toxicity | Headache, rash, peripheral or optic neuropathy, mucous membrane injury, psychotic behavior | Supportive treatment, gastric lavage or aspiration |
| L-Dopa | Dose should not exceed 8 g a day in therapeutic use | Palpitations, arrhythmias, spasm or closing of eyes, psychosis | Symptomatic treatment; maintain airway, lavage; ECG monitoring; IV fluids; treat arrhythmias as necessary |
| Dopamine receptor antagonists | Fatal doses reported: chlorpromazine: 26 g (in an adult), 350 mg in a child; thiothixene: 2.5–4 g; phenothiazines: 1,050 mg–10.5 g | Sedation, hypotension, severe extrapyramidal symptoms, confusion, excitement, CNS depression, coma, arrhythmias, miosis, tremor, spasm, rigidity, seizures, dry mouth, ileus, difficulty in swallowing, muscular hypotonia, difficulty in breathing, hypothermia, vasomotor or respiratory collapse, sudden apnea | Symptomatic and supportive care; if clinically indicated, lavage may be performed with endotracheal tube with inflated cuff in place; emesis should not be induced; saline cathartic may be helpful; hypotension should be treated as necessary (avoid epinephrine); anticholinergics may be useful for extrapyramidal symptoms; exchange transfusions may be useful; oversedation and hypothermia should be treated as appropriate |
| Ethchlorvynol | 6 g has been lethal; overdoses of 50 g and in one case 100 g have been survived | Hypotension, hypothermia, severe respiratory depression, apnea, deep coma (can last days to weeks), areflexia, mydriasis, bradycardia | Supportive treatment; gastric lavage with endotracheal tube with inflated cuff in place; maintain airway; give oxygen; maintain cardiorespiratory function and body temperature; monitor blood gases; provide pulmonary care; hemoperfusion with Amberlite XAD-4 resin hastens drug elimination; hemodialysis or peritoneal dialysis may be beneficial |
| Fenfluramine | 2 g (460 mg in a child) was lowest reported fatal dose; 1.8 g in an adult is the highest reported nonfatal dose | Drowsiness, agitation, flushing, tremor, confusion, shivering, hyperventilation, dilated nonreactive pupils, tachycardia, hyperpyrexia, coma, seizures, cardiac arrest | Symptomatic and supportive care; gastric lavage; activated charcoal; endotracheal tube placement in consultation with an anesthesiologist is needed if trismus is present and lavage is to be performed; maintain cardiorespiratory function; cardiac monitoring; defibrillation, cardioversion, ventilatory support if needed; phenobarbital or diazepam for seizures or muscle hyperactivity; propranolol for severe tachycardia; |

**Table 33.1–8**
**Continued**

| Drug | Toxic or Lethal Dose* | Signs and Symptoms | Treatment† |
|---|---|---|---|
| | | | lidocaine for ventricular extrasystoles; chlorpromazine may be useful for hyperthermia; forced acid diuresis with ammonium chloride may increase excretion rate |
| Fluoxetine | Lethal dose unknown (one death reported) | Restlessness, insomnia, agitation, tremor, hypomania, tachycardia, seizures, nausea, vomiting, hypertension, drowsiness, coma, nystagmus | Supportive and symptomatic care; keep airway open; maintain oxygenation and ventilation; monitor ECG and vital signs; gastric lavage (if clinically indicated, have endotracheal tube with cuff inflated during lavage) or emesis in recent ingestion, or use activated charcoal; IV diazepam for ongoing seizures; consider phenobarbital or phenytoin if refractory to diazepam |
| Glutethimide | 5 g: severe intoxication; 10–20 g: often lethal | Hypotension, prolonged coma (up to days), shock, respiratory depression, hypothermia, fever, inadequate ventilation, apnea, cyanosis, fixed and dilated pupils, ileus, bladder atony, dry mouth, hyporeflexia, areflexia, intermittent spasticity or flaccidity | Supportive treatment; gastric lavage using 1 to 1 mixture of castor oil and water (may be more effective than aqueous lavage); perform with endotracheal tube in place with inflated cuff; leave 50 mL castor oil in stomach as a cathartic; activated charcoal may be of use; maintain airway and cardiorespiratory function; hemodialysis may be useful in severe cases (particularly with activated charcoal or soybean dialysate); hemoperfusion with Amberlite XAD-2 resin may be more effective than hemodialysis; charcoal hemoperfusion may be useful; continue drug removal procedures for at least 2 hours after the patient regains consciousness; maintain urinary output but avoid overhydration |
| Lithium | Lethal dose produces serum levels of >3.5 mEq/L 12 hours after ingestion | Diarrhea, vomiting, confusion, drowsiness, tremor, apathy, giddiness, nausea, ataxia, muscle rigidity, vertical nystagmus, impaired consciousness, cogwheel rigidity, coma, seizures, cardiovascular collapse | Induce emesis or lavage (lavage with endotracheal tube in place with cuff inflated if indicated); infuse 0.9% sodium chloride IV if toxicity is due to sodium depletion; hemodialysis for 8–12 hours if fluid and electrolyte imbalance does not respond to supportive measures; if level is >3 mEq/L or if level is 2–3 mEq/L and patient is deteriorating or if level has not decreased 20% in 6 hours, repeated courses of dialysis are often needed; goal is level of <1 mEq/L 8 hours after dialysis is completed |
| Meprobamate | 12 g is usually lethal; 40 g overdoses have been survived | Stupor, drowsiness, lethargy, ataxia, coma, respiratory depression, hypotension | Supportive treatment; induce emesis or use gastric lavage with endotracheal tube in place with cuff inflated if clinically indicated; use activated charcoal after emptying stomach; maintain airway, respiration, and blood pressure; pressor agents can be used with caution if necessary; elimination may be enhanced by forced diuresis with hemodialysis, peritoneal dialysis, or osmotic diuresis |
| Methadone | Lethal dose: 40–60 mg in nontolerant persons | CNS depression (stupor to coma), pinpoint pupils, shallow respiration, bradycardia, hypotension, hypothermia, cold and clammy skin, apnea, cardiac arrest, mydriasis in severe hypoxia or terminal narcosis | Establish and maintain airway and respiration; gastric lavage; supportive care with IV fluids; naloxone may be used to treat respiratory depression; initial adult dose is 0.4–2 mg IV every 2–3 minutes if needed; if there is no response after a total of 10 mg has |

**Table 33.1–8**
*Continued*

| Drug | Toxic or Lethal Dose* | Signs and Symptoms | Treatment† |
|------|----------------------|--------------------|-----------|
| | | | been given, other diagnoses should be considered; repeated doses of naloxone may be needed, as narcotic-induced respiratory depression may return as the effects of naloxone diminish; dosage regimens for continuous naloxone infusions are not well established and should be titrated to the patient's response; patients should be observed for sustained improvement after treatment |
| Methylphenidate hydrochloride | 2 g | Delirium, confusion, psychosis, agitation, hallucinations, palpitations, arrhythmias, hypertension, vomiting, hyperpyrexia, mydriasis, sweating, tremors, muscle twitching, seizures, coma | Emesis or lavage in mild cases; if patient is conscious, careful use of a short-acting barbiturate may be required before lavage in severe cases; supportive measures, including maintenance of respiratory and circulatory function; isolation to reduce external stimuli; protection against self-harm; external cooling procedures for hyperpyrexia |
| Methyprylon | Toxic blood concentration: 30 μg/mL | Confusion, somnolence, hypotension, tachycardia, edema, coma, shock, respiratory depression | Induce emesis or gastric lavage with endotracheal tube in place with cuff inflated if clinically indicated; support cardiorespiratory function; barbiturates can be used with caution to control seizures and agitation |
| Monoamine oxidase inhibitors (MAOIs) | Single doses of 1.75–7 g have been fatal | Dizziness, drowsiness, irritability, ataxia, restlessness, insomnia, headache, tachycardia, hypotension, arrhythmia, confusion, fever, diaphoresis, hyporeflexia or hyperreflexia, respiratory depression, chest pain, shock, hypertension (rare) | Symptomatic and supportive care; induce emesis or use gastric lavage with endotracheal tube in place with inflated cuff if clinically indicated; maintain normal vital signs; correct fluid and electrolyte abnormalities with conservative measures; volume expansion for hypotension (pressor amines may be potentiated by MAOIs and may be of limited value); evaluate liver function immediately and 4–6 weeks later; barbiturates may relieve myoclonic reactions, but MAOIs may prolong their effect; phenothiazines can be used for agitation; hypertensive crisis mainly occurs in conjunction with tyramine; discontinue MAOIs and treat with phentolamine (5 to 10 mg by slow IV injection) |
| Pemoline | 2 g | Excitement, agitation, restlessness, hallucinations, tachycardia, rhabdomyolysis, choreoathetosis | Gastric lavage in mild cases; symptomatic treatment, maintain respiratory and circulatory function; monitor cardiac function; reduce stimulation; haloperidol or chlorpromazine for psychosis and agitation; IV benzodiazepines can control choreoathetosis; hemodialysis may be of value |
| Sertraline | 3 known overdoses at 750–2,1000 mg; no deaths reported | Possible symptoms include confusion, ataxia, incoordination, hypotension, hypertension, seizures, arrhythmias, serotonin syndrome, coma, mydriasis | General symptomatic and supportive measures; establish and maintain airway; ensure adequate oxygenation and ventilation; use activated charcoal with sorbitol; monitor vital signs and cardiac function |
| Thyroid hormones | 0.3 g per kg desiccated thyroid has caused severe | Nervousness, sweating, palpitations, abdominal cramps, diarrhea, tachycardia, hypertension, headache, arrhythmias, tremors, cardiac failure | Symptomatic and supportive treatment; induce emesis or use gastric lavage with endotracheal tube in place with cuff inflated if clinically indicated; |

**Table 33.1–8**
**Continued**

| Drug | Toxic or Lethal Dose* | Signs and Symptoms | Treatment† |
|---|---|---|---|
| | toxicity (with recovery) | | control fluid loss, fever, hypoglycemia; give oxygen and maintain ventilation; β-adrenergic receptor antagonists can be used to counteract increased sympathetic activity |
| Trazodone | Patients have survived overdoses of 7.5 g and 9.2 g | Lethargy, vomiting, drowsiness, headache, orthostasis, dizziness, dyspnea, tinnitus, myalgias, tachycardia, incontinence, shivering, coma | Symptomatic and supportive treatment; induce emesis or use gastric lavage; forced diuresis may enhance elimination; treat hypotension and sedation as appropriate |
| Tricyclics and tetracyclics | 700–1,400 mg: moderate to severe toxicity; 2.1–2.8 g: often fatal; one patient survived ingestion of 10 g amitriptyline; lowest known fatal dose of amitriptyline: 500 mg; average lethal dose of imipramine: 30 mg per kg (fatalities occurred with 500 mg) | Initial CNS stimulation, confusion, agitation, hallucinations, hyperpyrexia, hypertension, nystagmus, hyperreflexia, parkinsonian symptoms, mydriasis, ileus, constipation, seizures, CNS depression (follows stimulation), hyperthermia, areflexia, respiratory depression, cyanosis, hypotension, coma, cardiac conduction abnormalities, tachycardia, quinidinelike effects (QRS prolongation, the degree of which may be the best indication of the severity of the overdose) | Symptomatic and supportive care; monitor ECG and vital signs; support vital functions; establish and maintain airway; treat and correct fluid, electrolyte, acid-base, and temperature abnormalities; minimize stimulation; gastric lavage with activated charcoal or ipecac emesis if gag reflex is present and patient is awake; treat hypotension supportively: IV diazepam (with caution) for seizures; lidocaine, phenytoin, propranolol for life-threatening arrhythmias, sodium bicarbonate IV to achieve pH of 7.4–7.5 to help treat arrhythmias and hypotension; use of multiple antiarrhythmics or pacemaker may be needed in some cases; physostigmine has been used for anticholinergic symptoms, but its use is controversial because of serious adverse effects, and it should be used only for life-threatening treatment-refractory anticholinergic toxicity |
| Valproic acid | One adult survived an ingestion of 36 g valproic acid as part of a polydrug overdose | Somnolence, coma | Supportive measures; lavage may be of limited value because of drug's rapid absorption; the value of emesis or lavage varies with time since ingestion if delayed-release preparations are ingested; maintain adequate urinary output; naloxone may reverse CNS depressant effects of overdose but may also reverse anticonvulsant effects and should be used with caution |

*The toxic dose is the amount of the drug capable of producing signs and symptoms of an overdose. The same dose may also have lethal effects, depending on such factors as the rate of administration, the rate of absorption, and the age and general health of the patient. A toxic dose for one patient may be lethal for another. The ranges given in this table are approximate, based on available scientific literature.

The clinician should always consult Physician's Desk Reference *(PDR)* or contact the manufacturer of the drug for the latest information on toxicity and lethality.

†A patient may have ingested more than one substance, and the signs and symptoms may represent polysubstance abuse or overdose. Treatment must be adjusted accordingly, and a history (from other persons, if necessary) and an inspection of all drugs should be obtained.

The informed clinician needs to keep those considerations in mind and to focus on the clinically important interactions, not on the ones that may be mild, unproved, or entirely phantom. At the same time, the clinician should maintain an open and receptive attitude toward the possibility of pharmacokinetic and pharmacodynamic drug interactions.

## DEVELOPMENT OF NEW DRUGS

The first stage in the development of a new drug involves the identification of a compound that for theoretical reasons may be effective in treating some disorder. The compound is then studied in a wide variety of in vitro and in vivo tests that may predict the clinical drug effects.

Compounds found to be of potential importance in those tests then undergo studies of their toxicity and pharmacokinetics in animals. If those preliminary preclinical tests are thought to merit the costs of further drug development, a pharmaceutical company in the United States can file an Investigational New Drug (IND) application with the FDA. If the application is granted, the compound can then be used in humans for research purposes.

The first such experiments are called phase I experiments, in which the drug is administered to normal persons to assess its pharmacokinetics and its potential to cause adverse effects. Phase I studies are conducted primarily to determine the safety and the tolerability of a new compound. The information from the phase I trials is then used to help decide on a dosage of the new drug in phase II trials, which involve the use of the new compound in a patient population. The primary purpose of phase II trials is to assess the efficacy of the new drug in the treatment of specific disorders. If the phase II trials indicate that a drug is efficacious, safe, and well-tolerated, much larger phase III trials are conducted to validate the findings of the phase II studies. Phase III studies also gather detailed information regarding the optimum dosage schedules and the use of the drug in elderly and young populations and in persons with impaired hepatic or renal function. After the completion of the phase III trials, the pharmaceutical company can apply to the FDA for a New Drug Application (NDA), which, if granted, allows the drug company to market the drug commercially.

## Drugs under Development

Ten years from now the psychopharmacotherapy armamentarium will probably be very different from the one available today. For a variety of reasons, however, it is difficult to predict which new drugs will come to market in the United States. First, for commercial reasons, pharmaceutical companies are secretive about their drugs under development. Second, a candidate drug may be well into phase III development before its association with a particularly severe adverse effect is noted, resulting in the termination of the compound's development. Third, a candidate drug may be well into phase II or even phase III development before an assessment of its efficacy results in a determination that it is not significantly better than competing compounds to merit the cost of introducing the drug commercially.

## References

Beitman B D, Klerman G L, editors: *Integrating Pharmacotherapy and Psychotherapy.* American Psychiatric Press, Washington, 1991.
Dahl M L, Bertilsson L: Genetically variable metabolism of antidepressants and neuroleptic drugs in man. Pharmacogenetics *3*: 61, 1993.
Fisher S, Greenburg R P: How sound is the double-blind design for evaluating psychotropic drugs? J Nerv Ment Dis *181*: 345, 1993.
Gabbard G O: *Psychodynamic Psychiatry in Clinical Practice.* American Psychiatric Press, Washington, 1990.
Krishna D R, Klotz U: *Clinical Pharmacokinetics: A Short Introduction.* Springer, Berlin, 1990.
Rowland M, Tozer T N: *Clinical Pharmacokinetics: Concepts and Applications,* ed 2. Lea & Febiger, Philadelphia, 1989.
Tallarida R J, Raffa R B, McGonigle P: *Principles in General Pharmacology,* Springer, Berlin, 1988.
Welling P G, Tse F L S, Dighe S V, editors: *Pharmaceutical Bioequivalence.* Dekker, New York, 1991.

# 33.2 / Medication-Induced Movement Disorders

The fourth edition of *Diagnostic and Statistical Manual of Mental Disorders* (DSM-IV) introduces a new diagnostic category, "medication-induced movement disorders." In reality, however, the category includes not only medication-induced movement disorders but also any medication-induced adverse effect that becomes a focus of clinical attention. When one of the diagnoses is made and included as a focus of treatment, the movement disorder or adverse effect diagnosis should be listed on Axis I of the DSM-IV multiaxial diagnostic formulation.

The advent of the diagnostic category recognizes the fact that many, if not most, of the pharmacological therapies available to treat mental disorders can cause adverse effects that themselves may require the formulation of a specific treatment plan. The most common of the adverse effects are the movement disorders related to the dopamine receptor antagonists, which are also referred to as neuroleptics and antipsychotics. However, the term "antipsychotics" also includes drugs that are seldom associated with the production of movement disorders—for example, clozapine (Clozaril).

In addition to providing a systematized and standardized diagnosis for the drug-induced movement disorders and adverse effects, the formalization of the diagnoses encourages the clinician to consider the differential diagnoses for those symptoms. For example, anxiety needs to be distinguished from akathisia, catatonia from neuroleptic malignant syndrome, parkinsonism from depression, and tardive dyskinesia from other basal ganglia-related movement disorders.

The extrapyramidal system is that part of the central nervous system (CNS) motor control system that is outside the pyramidal system, which includes the cortical motor areas and the spinal pyramidal tracts. The major component of the extrapyramidal system is the group of nuclei collectively known as the basal ganglia. The key symptoms of medication-induced movement disorders are those of parkinsonism (tremor, rigidity, and bradykinesia), dystonia, akathisia, and tardive dyskinesia. The pathophysiology of neuroleptic malignant syndrome is not completely understood, but it may involve the basal ganglia, although its symptoms also involve nonmotor symptoms (for example, autonomic instability). The common mechanism of many of the disorders includes some involvement with the dopamine type 2 ($D_2$) receptor antagonism by that class of antipsychotic drugs. The association between $D_2$ blockade and the extrapyramidal system is not straightforward, as indicated by the lack of an immediate and direct temporal association between the administration of the drugs and the appearance of the various symptom patterns, which occur at different times after the administration of dopamine receptor antagonists (Figure 33.2–1).

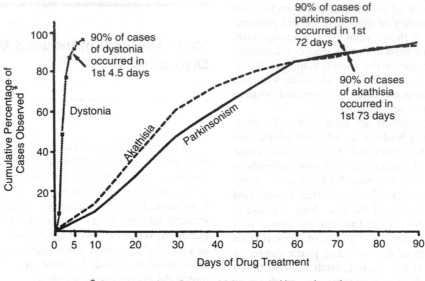

**Figure 33.2–1.** Drug-induced extrapyramidal reactions: time for onset. (Figure from J H Friedman: Drug-induced parkinsonism. In *Drug-Induced Movement Disorders*, A F Lang, W J Weiner, editors, p 49. Futura, Mount Kisco, N Y, 1992. Used with permission.)

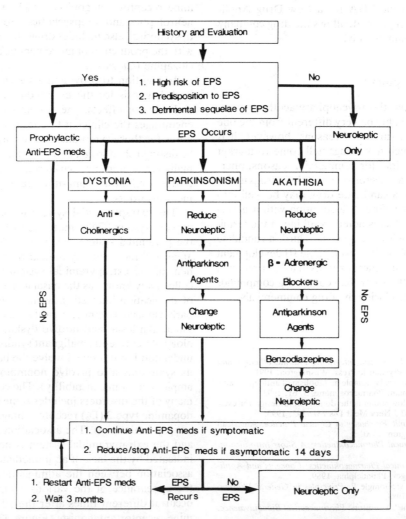

**Figure 33.2–2.** Outline of the treatment approach for major extrapyramidal system disorders. (Figure from D E Casey: Neuroleptic drug-induced extrapyramidal syndromes and tardive dyskinesia. Schizophr Res *4*: 109, 1991. Used with permission.)

# NEUROLEPTIC-INDUCED MOVEMENT DISORDERS

The most common neuroleptic-related movement disorders are parkinsonism, acute dystonia, and acute akathisia. The general outline of the treatment approach for those three disorders is shown in Figure 33.2–2. Neuroleptic malignant syndrome is a life-threatening and often misdiagnosed condition. Neuroleptic-induced tardive dyskinesia is a late-appearing adverse effect of neuroleptic drugs and can be irreversible; however, recent data indicate that the syndrome, although still serious and potentially disabling, is less pernicious than was previously thought.

## Neuroleptic-Induced Parkinsonism

Neuroleptic-induced parkinsonism is characterized principally by the triad of a tremor that is most pronounced at rest, rigidity, and bradykinesia (Table 33.2–1). Rigidity is a disorder of muscle tone—that is, the degree of tension present in the muscles. Disorders of tone can result in

**Table 33.2–1**
**Diagnostic and Research Criteria for Neuroleptic-Induced Parkinsonism**

Parkinsonian tremor, muscular rigidity or akinesia developing within a few weeks of starting or raising the dose of a neuroleptic medication (or after reducing a medication used to treat extrapyramidal symptoms).

A. One (or more) of the following signs or symptoms has developed in association with the use of neuroleptic medication:

  (1) parkinsonian tremor (i.e., a coarse, rhythmic, resting tremor with a frequency between 3 and 6 cycles per second, affecting the limbs, head, mouth, or tongue)
  (2) parkinsonian muscular rigidity (i.e., cogwheel rigidity or continuous "lead-pipe" rigidity)
  (3) akinesia (i.e., a decrease in spontaneous facial expressions, gestures, speech, or body movements)

B. The symptoms in criterion A developed within a few weeks of starting or raising the dose of a neuroleptic medication, or of reducing medication used to treat (or prevent) acute extrapyramidal symptoms (e.g., anticholinergic agents).

C. The symptoms in criterion A are not better accounted for by a mental disorder (e.g., catatonic or negative symptoms in schizophrenia, psychomotor retardation in a major depressive episode). Evidence that the symptoms are better accounted for by a mental disorder might include the following: the symptoms precede the exposure to neuroleptic medication or are not compatible with the pattern of pharmacologic intervention (e.g., no improvement after lowering the neuroleptic dose or administering anticholinergic medication).

D. The symptoms in criterion A are not due to a nonneuroleptic substance or to a neurological or other general medical condition (e.g., Parkinson's disease, Wilson's disease). Evidence that the symptoms are due to a general medical condition might include the following: the symptoms precede exposure to neuroleptic medication, unexplained focal neurological signs are present, or the symptoms progress despite a stable medication regimen.

Table from DSM-IV, *Diagnostic and Statistical Manual of Mental Disorders*, ed 4. Copyright American Psychiatric Association, Washington, 1994. Used with permission.

either hypertonia (that is, rigidity) or hypotonia. The hypertonia associated with neuroleptic-induced parkinsonism is of either the lead-pipe type or the cogwheel type, two terms that are descriptive of the subjective impression of the affected limbs or joints. The syndrome of bradykinesia can include the masklike facial appearance of the patient, the decreased accessory arm movements while the patient is walking, and a characteristic difficulty in initiating movement. The so-called rabbit syndrome is a tremor affecting the lips and the perioral muscles; it is most commonly thought to be part of the syndrome of neuroleptic-induced parkinsonism, although it often appears later in treatment than do other symptoms. The pathophysiology of neuroleptic-induced parkinsonism involves the blockade of $D_2$ receptors in the caudate at the termination of the nigrostriatal dopamine neurons, the same neurons that degenerate in idiopathic Parkinson's disease. Patients who are elderly (Figure 33.2–3) and female are at the highest risk for neuroleptic-induced parkinsonism.

**Treatment.** The benefits and the risks of prophylactic treatment with anti-extrapyramidal system medications—for example, anticholinergics and amantadine (Symmetrel) or antihistamines—continues to be debated. However, once parkinsonian symptoms do appear, the three steps in treatment are to reduce the dosage of the neuroleptic, institute anti-extrapyramidal system medications, and possibly change the neuroleptic. A poorly understood phenomenon is the common development of tolerance to the parkinsonian adverse effects of those drugs. Once treatment is initiated, therefore, the clinician should attempt to reduce or stop the anti-extrapyramidal system medications after 14 to 21 days of treatment to assess whether the medications continue to be necessary.

## Neuroleptic Malignant Syndrome

Neuroleptic malignant syndrome is a life-threatening complication of antipsychotic treatment and can occur anytime during the course of treatment (Table 33.2–2). The symptoms include muscular rigidity and dystonia (hence the classification of the disorder as a movement disorder), akinesia, mutism, obtundation, and agitation. The autonomic symptoms include high fever, sweating, and increased blood pressure and heart rate. In addition to supportive medical treatment, the most commonly used medications for the condition are dantrolene (Dantrium) and bromocriptine (Parlodel), although amantadine is sometimes used.

## Neuroleptic-Induced Acute Dystonia

Dystonias are brief or prolonged contractions of muscles, usually resulting in obviously abnormal movements or postures, including oculogyric crises, tongue protrusion, trismus, torticollis, laryngeal-pharyngeal dystonias, and dystonic postures of the limbs and the trunk (Table 33.2–3). The development of dystonic symptoms is characterized by their early onset during the course of treatment with neuroleptics (Figure 33.2–1) and their high incidence in men, in patients under age 30, and in patients given high dosages of high-potency medications. The pathophysiological mechanism for dystonias is not clearly understood, although changes in neuroleptic concentrations and

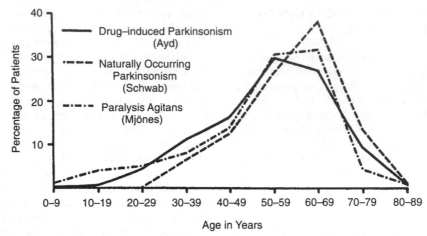

**Figure 33.2–3.** Parkinsonism: age distribution. (Figure from J H Friedman: Drug-induced parkinsonism. In *Drug-Induced* *Movement Disorders*, A F Lang, W J Weiner, editors, p 54. Futura, Mount Kisco, N Y, 1992. Used with permission.)

**Table 33.2–2**
**Diagnostic and Research Criteria for Neuroleptic Malignant Syndrome**

Severe muscle rigidity, elevated temperature, and other related findings (e.g., diaphoresis, dysphagia, incontinence, changes in level of consciousness ranging from confusion to coma, mutism, elevated or labile blood pressure, elevated creatine phosphokinase [CPK]) developing in association with the use of neuroleptic medication.

A. The development of severe muscle rigidity and elevated temperature associated with the use of neuroleptic medication.

B. Two (or more) of the following:

   (1) diaphoresis
   (2) dysphagia
   (3) tremor
   (4) incontinence
   (5) changes in level of consciousness ranging from confusion to coma
   (6) mutism
   (7) tachycardia
   (8) elevated or labile blood pressure
   (9) leucocytosis
  (10) laboratory evidence of muscle injury (e.g., elevated CPK)

C. The symptoms in criteria A and B are not due to another substance (e.g., phencyclidine) or a neurological or other general medical condition (e.g., viral encephalitis).

D. The symptoms in criteria A and B are not better accounted for by a mental disorder (e.g., mood disorder with catatonic features).

the resulting changes in homeostatic mechanisms within the basal ganglia may be the major causes of dystonias.

**Treatment.** Treatment of dystonias should be immediate, most commonly with anticholinergic or antihistaminergic drugs. If a patient fails to respond to three doses of those drugs within two hours, the clinician should consider a cause of the dystonic movements other than neuroleptic medications.

**Table 33.2–3**
**Diagnostic and Research Criteria for Neuroleptic-Induced Acute Dystonia**

Abnormal positioning or spasm of the muscles of the head, neck, limbs, or trunk developing within a few days of starting or raising the dose of a neuroleptic medication (or after reducing a medication used to treat extrapyramidal symptoms).

A. One (or more) of the following signs or symptoms has developed in association with the use of neuroleptic medication:

   (1) abnormal positioning of the head and neck in relation to the body (e.g., retrocollis, torticollis)
   (2) spasms of the jaw muscles (trismus, gaping, grimacing)
   (3) impaired swallowing (dysphagia), speaking, or breathing (laryngeal-pharyngeal spasm, dysphonia)
   (4) thickened or slurred speech due to hypertonic or enlarged tongue (dysarthria, macroglossia)
   (5) tongue protrusion or tongue dysfunction
   (6) eyes deviated up, down, or sideward (oculogyric crisis)
   (7) abnormal positioning of the distal limbs or trunk

B. The signs or symptoms in criterion A developed within seven days of starting or rapidly raising the dose of neuroleptic medication, or of reducing a medication used to treat (or prevent) acute extrapyramidal symptoms (e.g., anticholinergic agents).

C. The symptoms in criterion A are not better accounted for by a mental disorder (e.g., catatonic symptoms in schizophrenia). Evidence that the symptoms are better accounted for by a mental disorder might include the following: the symptoms precede the exposure to neuroleptic medication or are not compatible with the pattern of pharmacologic intervention (e.g., no improvement after neuroleptic lowering or anticholinergic administration).

D. The symptoms in criterion A are not due to a nonneuroleptic substance or to a neurological or other general medical condition. Evidence that the symptoms are due to general medical condition might include the following: the symptoms precede the exposure to the neuroleptic medication, unexplained focal neurological signs are present, or the symptoms progress in the absence of change in medication.

**Table 33.2–4**
**Diagnostic and Research Criteria for Neuroleptic-Induced Acute Akathisia**

Subjective complaints of restlessness accompanied by observed movements (e.g., fidgety movements of the legs, rocking from foot to foot, pacing, or inability to sit or stand still) developing within a few weeks of starting or raising the dose of a neuroleptic medication (or reducing medication used to treat extrapyramidal symptoms).

A. The development of subjective complaints of restlessness after exposure to a neuroleptic medication.

B. At least one of the following is observed:

(1) fidgety movements or swinging of the legs
(2) rocking from foot to foot while standing
(3) pacing to relieve restlessness
(4) inability to sit or stand for at least several minutes

C. The onset of the symptoms in criteria A and B occur within four weeks of initiating or increasing the dose of the neuroleptic, or of reducing medication used to treat (or prevent) acute extrapyramidal symptoms (e.g., anticholinergic agents).

D. The symptoms in criterion A are not better accounted for by a mental disorder (e.g., schizophrenia, substance withdrawal, agitation from a major depressive or manic episode, hyperactivity in attention-deficit/hyperactivity disorder). Evidence that symptoms may be better accounted for by a mental disorder might include the following: the onset of symptoms preceding the exposure to the neuroleptics, the absence of increasing restlessness with increasing neuroleptic doses, and the absence of relief with pharmacological interventions (e.g., no improvement after decreasing the neuroleptic dose or treatment with medication intended to treat the akathisia).

E. The symptoms in criterion A are not due to a nonneuroleptic substance or to a neurological or other general medical condition. Evidence that symptoms are due to a general medical condition might include the onset of the symptoms preceding the exposure to neuroleptics or the progression of symptoms in the absence of a change in medication.

Table from DSM-IV, *Diagnostic and Statistical Manual of Mental Disorders*, ed 4. Copyright American Psychiatric Association, Washington, 1994. Used with permission.

## Neuroleptic-Induced Acute Akathisia

Akathisia is characterized by the subjective feelings of restlessness or the objective signs of restlessness or both. Examples include a sense of anxiety, an inability to relax, jitteriness, pacing, rocking motions while sitting, and the rapid alternation of sitting and standing (Table 33.2–4). Akathisia can often be misdiagnosed as anxiety or as increased psychotic agitation. Middle-aged women are at increased risk for akathisia, and the time course of akathisia is similar to that for neuroleptic-induced parkinsonism (Figure 33.2–1).

**Treatment.** The three basic steps in the treatment of akathisia are to reduce the neuroleptic medication dosage, to attempt treatment with appropriate drugs, and to consider changing the neuroleptic. The most efficacious drugs in the treatment of akathisia are the β-adrenergic receptor antagonists, although the anticholinergic drugs and the benzodiazepines may also be useful in some cases. Patients may be less likely to experience akathisia on low-potency

neuroleptics—for example, thioridazine (Mellaril)—than on high-potency neuroleptics—for example, haloperidol (Haldol)—and some of the new antipsychotics (for example, risperidone and remoxipride) may be associated with a low incidence of akathisia.

## Neuroleptic-Induced Tardive Dyskinesia

Neuroleptic-induced tardive dyskinesia is a late-appearing disorder of involuntary, choreoathetoid movements (Table 33.2–5). The most common movements involve the orofacial region and choreoathetoid movements of the fingers and the toes. Athetoid movements of the head, the neck, and the hips are also present in seriously affected patients. In the most serious cases the patients may have irregularities in breathing and swallowing, resulting in aerophagia, belching, and grunting. The risk factors for tardive dyskinesia include long-term treatment with neuroleptics, increasing age, female sex, the presence of a mood disorder, and the presence of a cognitive disorder. Although various treatments for tardive dyskinesia have not been successful, the course of tardive dyskinesia

**Table 33.2–5**
**Diagnostic and Research Criteria for Neuroleptic-Induced Tardive Dyskinesia**

Involuntary choreiform, athetoid, or rhythmic movements (lasting at least a few weeks) of the tongue, jaw, or extremities developing in association with the use of neuroleptic medication for at least a few months (may be for a shorter period of time in elderly persons).

A. Involuntary movements of the tongue, jaw, trunk, or extremities have developed in association with the use of neuroleptic medication.

B. The involuntary movements are present over a period of at least four weeks, and occur in any of the following patterns:

(1) chloreiform movements (i.e., rapid, jerky, nonrepetitive)
(2) athetoid movements (i.e., slow, sinuous, continual)
(3) rhythmic movements (i.e., stereotypies)

C. The signs or symptoms in criteria A and B develop during exposure to a neuroleptic medication or within 4 weeks of withdrawal from an oral (or within 8 weeks of withdrawal from a depot) neuroleptic medication.

D. There has been exposure to neuroleptic medication for at least three months (one month if age 60 or older).

E. The symptoms are not due to a neurological or general medical condition (e.g., Huntington's disease, Sydenham's chorea, spontaneous dyskinesia, hyperthyroidism, Wilson's disease); ill-fitting dentures; or exposure to other medications that cause acute reversible dyskinesia (e.g., L-dopa, bromocriptine). Evidence that the symptoms are due to one of these etiologies might include the following: the symptoms precede the exposure to the neuroleptic medication or unexplained focal neurological signs are present.

F. The symptoms are not better accounted for by a neuroleptic-induced acute movement disorder (e.g., neuroleptic-induced acute dystonia, neuroleptic-induced acute akathisia).

Table from DSM-IV, *Diagnostic and Statistical Manual of Mental Disorders*, ed 4. Copyright American Psychiatric Association, Washington, 1994. Used with permission.

is considered less relentless than was previously thought. A recent alternative for such patients is to be treated with one of the new antipsychotics that may be little associated with the development of tardive dyskinesia (for example, clozapine, remoxipride, and risperidone).

## MEDICATION-INDUCED POSTURAL TREMOR

Tremor is defined as a rhythmical alteration in movement that is usually faster than one beat a second (Table 33.2–6). Typically, tremors decrease during periods of relaxation and sleep and increase during periods of anger and increased tension. Those characteristics sometimes mistakenly lead inexperienced clinicians to assume that the patient is faking the tremor. Whereas all the above DSM-IV diagnoses specifically include an association with neuroleptics, DSM-IV acknowledges that a range of psychiatric medications can produce tremor—most notably lithium (Eskalith), antidepressants, and valproate (Depakene)— although still other psychiatric medications are associated with the induction of tremor.

The treatment of tremor involves four general steps. First, the lowest possible dosage of the psychiatric drug should be used. Second, patients should minimize their caffeine consumption. Third, the psychiatric drug should be taken at bedtime to minimize the amount of daytime tremor. Fourth, β-adrenergic receptor antagonists can be given in the treatment of drug-induced tremors.

## MEDICATION-INDUCED MOVEMENT DISORDER NOT OTHERWISE SPECIFIED

Although neuroleptics are the psychiatric drugs most commonly associated with movement disorders, almost all the most commonly used psychiatric drugs can produce

**Table 33.2–6**
**Diagnostic and Research Criteria for Medication-Induced Postural Tremor**

Fine tremor occurring during attempts to maintain a posture and developing in association with the use of medication (e.g., lithium, antidepressants, valproate).

A. A fine postural tremor that has developed in association with the use of a medication (e.g., lithium, antidepressants, valproic acid).

B. The tremor (i.e., a regular, rhythmic oscillation of the limbs, head, mouth, or tongue) has a frequency between 8 and 12 cycles per second.

C. The symptoms are not due to a pre-existing nonpharmacologically-induced tremor. Evidence that the symptoms are due to a pre-existing tremor might include the following: the tremor was present prior to the introduction of the medication, the tremor does not correlate with serum levels of the medication, and the tremor persists after discontinuation of the medication.

D. The symptoms are not better accounted for by neuroleptic-induced parkinsonism.

Table from DSM-IV, *Diagnostic and Statistical Manual of Mental Disorders*, ed 4. Copyright American Psychiatric Association, Washington, 1994. Used with permission.

movement disorders in some patients (Table 33.2–7). Furthermore, many nonpsychiatric drugs can also produce movement disorders, and patients who are treated with both psychiatric and nonpsychiatric drugs may experience the additive effects of those medications with movement disorders. DSM-IV also defines the diagnostic category as including movement disorders other than those specified above. Such movement disorders include tardive dystonia and tardive parkinsonism. Table 33.2–8 lists a number of movement disorders and the drugs that induce them.

## ADVERSE EFFECTS OF MEDICATION NOT OTHERWISE SPECIFIED

This category allows clinicians to record the adverse effects of medications, other than movement symptoms, that become a focus of treatment (Table 33.2–9). Examples of such adverse effects include priapism, severe hypotension, and cardiac abnormalities.

**Table 33.2–7**
**Diagnostic Criteria for Medication-Induced Movement Disorder Not Otherwise Specified**

This category is for medication-induced movement disorders not classified by any of the specific disorders listed above. Examples include 1) parkinsonism, acute akathisia, acute dystonia, or dyskinetic movement that is associated with a medication other than a neuroleptic; 2) a presentation that resembles neuroleptic malignant syndrome that is associated with a medication other than a neuroleptic; or 3) tardive dystonia.

Table from DSM-IV, *Diagnostic and Statistical Manual of Mental Disorders*, ed 4. Copyright American Psychiatric Association, Washington, 1994. Used with permission.

**Table 33.2–8**
**Drug-Induced Movement Disorders**

| Syndrome | Drugs Responsible | |
|---|---|---|
| Postural tremor | Sympathomimetics | + + |
| | Levodopa | + + |
| | Amphetamines | + + |
| | Bronchodilators | + + |
| | Tricyclic drugs | + + |
| | Lithium carbonate | + + |
| | Caffeine | + + |
| | Thyroid hormone | + + |
| | Sodium valproate | + + |
| | APDs | + + |
| | Hypoglycemic agents | + + |
| | Adrenocorticosteroids | + + |
| | Alcohol withdrawal | + + |
| | Amiodarone | + |
| | Cyclosporin A | + |
| | MAOIs | + + |
| Acute dystonic reactions | APDs | + + |
| | Metoclopramide | + + |
| | Antimalarial agents | + |
| | Tetrabenazine | +/− |
| | Diphenhydramine | +/− |
| | Mefenamic acid | +/− |
| | Oxatomide | +/− |
| | Tricyclic drugs | +/− |
| | Flunarizone and cinnarizine | +/− |

**Table 33.2–8**
*Continued*

| Syndrome | Drugs Responsible | |
|---|---|---|
| Akathisia | APDs | + + |
| | Metoclopramide | + + |
| | Reserpine | + + |
| | Tetrabenazine | + + |
| | Levodopa and dopamine agonists†‡ | + |
| | Flunarizine and cinnarizine | +/− |
| | Ethosuximide | +/− |
| | Methysergide | +/− |
| | Amoxapine | +/− |
| Parkinsonism, including rabbit syndrome | APDs | + + |
| | Metoclopramide | + + |
| | Reserpine | + + |
| | Tetrabenazine | + + |
| | Methyldopa | + |
| | Flunarizine and cinnarizine | +/− |
| | Fluoxetine | +/− |
| | Lithium | +/− |
| | Phenelzine | +/− |
| | Phenytoin | +/− |
| | Captopril | +/− |
| | Alcohol withdrawal | + |
| | MPTP | + |
| | Other toxins (manganese, carbon disulfide, cyanide) | + |
| | Cytosine arabinoside | +/− |
| Chorea, including tardive dyskinesia and orofacial dyskinesia | APDs | + + |
| | Metoclopramide | + + |
| | Levodopa | + + |
| | Direct dopamine agonists | + + |
| | Indirect dopamine agonists and other catecholaminergic drugs† | + + |
| | Anticholinergics | + |
| | Antihistaminics | + |
| | Oral contraceptives | + |
| | Phenytoin (T) | + |
| | Carbamazepine (T) | +/− |
| | Ethosuximide | +/− |
| | Phenobarbital (T) | +/− |
| | Lithium carbonate (T) | +/− |
| | Benzodiazepines | +/− |
| | MAOIs | +/− |
| | Tricyclic drugs | +/− |
| | Methyldopa | +/− |
| | Methadone | +/− |
| | Digoxin | +/− |
| | Alcohol withdrawal | +/− |
| | Toluene (glue) sniffing | +/− |
| | Flunarizine and cinnarizine | +/− |
| Dystonia, including tardive dystonia (excluding acute dystonic reactions) | APDs | + + |
| | Metoclopramide | + + |
| | Levodopa | + + |
| | Direct dopamide agonists† | + |
| | Phenytoin (T) | + |
| | Carbamazepine (T) | +/− |
| | Flunarizine and cinnarizine | +/− |
| | Trazodone | +/− |
| | Lithium | +/− |
| Neuroleptic malignant syndrome | APDs | + |
| | Tetrabenazine with AMPT | +/− |
| Tics (simple and complex), including aggravation of preexisting tic | Withdrawal of antiparkinsonian drugs in Parkinson's disease | +/− |
| | Levodopa | + |
| | Direct dopamine agonists | + |
| | Indirect dopamine agonists | + + |

**Table 33.2–8**
*Continued*

| Syndrome | Drugs Responsible | |
|---|---|---|
| disorders | APDs | + |
| | Carbamazepine | +/− |
| Myoclonus | Levodopa | + + |
| | Anticonvulsants§(T) | + + |
| | MAOIs | + + |
| | Lithium | + + |
| | Tricyclic drugs | + + |
| | APDs | +/− |
| Asterixis | Anticonvulsants§(T) | + + |
| | Levodopa | +/− |
| | Hepatotoxins (T) | + + |
| | Respiratory depressants (T) | + + |

+ +—Well documented; common or not infrequent; +—relatively well documented; uncommon; +/−—not well documented or only small number of cases in literature; AMPT—α-methyl-paratyrosine; APD—antipsychotic drug; MAOI—monoamine oxidase inhibitor; MPTP—1-methyl-4-phenyl-1,2,3,6-tetrahydropyridine; T—usually evidence of drug toxicity present (including serum drug levels).
†Includes apomorphine, bromocriptine, lisuride, pergolide.
‡Includes amphetamines, methylphenidate, amantadine, pemoline, fenfluramine.
§Includes most categories of anticonvulsant drugs.
Table adapted from O S Gershanik: Drug-induced movement disorders. Curr Opin Neurol Neurosurg 6: 369, 1993. Used with permission.

**Table 33.2–9**
**Diagnostic Criteria for Adverse Effects of Medication Not Otherwise Specified**

This category is available for optional use by clinicians to code side effects of medication (other than movement symptoms) when these adverse effects become a main focus of clinical attention. Examples include severe hypotension, cardiac arrhythmias, and priapism.

Table from DSM-IV, *Diagnostic and Statistical Manual of Mental Disorders*, ed 4. Copyright American Psychiatric Association, Washington, 1994. Used with permission.

**References**

Adler L A, Angrist B, Reiter S, Rotrosen J: Neuroleptic-induced akathisia: A review. Psychopharmacology 97: 1, 1989.
Casey D E: Neuroleptic drug-induced extrapyramidal syndromes and tardive dyskinesia. Schizophr Res 4: 109, 1991.
Fleischhacker W W, Roth S D, Kane J M: The pharmacologic treatment of neuroleptic-induced akathisia. J Clin Psychopharmacol 10: 12, 1990.
Gerlach J, Casey D E: Tardive dyskinesia. Acta Psychiatr Scand 77: 369, 1988.
Gershanik O S: Drug-induced movement disorders. Curr Opin Neurol Neurosurg 6: 369, 1993.
Glazer W M, Morgenstern H, Doucette J T: Predicting long-term risk of tardive dyskinesia in outpatients maintained on neuroleptic medications. J Clin Psychiatry 54: 133, 1993.
Lang A E, Weiner W J: *Drug-Induced Movement Disorders*. Futura, Mount Kisco, N Y, 1992.
Lipinski J F, Mallya G, Zimmerman P, Pope H G Jr: Fluoxetine-induced akathisia: Clinical and theoretical implications. J Clin Psychiatry 50: 339, 1989.
Owens D G C: Dystonia: A potential psychiatric pitfall. Br J Psychiatry 156: 620, 1990.
Weiner W J, Lang A E: *Movement Disorders: A Comprehensive Survey*. Futura, Mount Kisco, N Y, 1989.
Zubenko G S, Cohen B M, Lipinski J F: Antidepressant-related akathisia. J Clin Psychopharmacol 7: 254, 1987.

# 33.3 / Psychotherapeutic Drugs

The numerous pharmacological agents used to treat mental disorders are referred to by three general terms that are used interchangeably: psychotropic drugs, psychoactive drugs, and psychotherapeutic drugs. Traditionally, the agents were divided into four categories: (1) antipsychotic or neuroleptic drugs used to treat psychosis, (2) antidepressant drugs used to treat depression, (3) an-timanic drugs used to treat bipolar disorder, and (4) antianxiety or anxiolytic drugs used to treat anxious states, although those drugs were also effective as hypnotics in high dosages. That division, however, is less valid now than it was in the past for the following reasons: (1) Many drugs of one class are used to treat disorders previously assigned to another class. For example, many antidepressant drugs are used to treat anxiety disorders; and some antianxiety drugs are used to treat psychoses, depressive disorders, and bipolar disorders. (2) Drugs from all four categories are used to treat disorders not previously treatable by drugs—for example, eating disorders, panic disorder, and impulse control disorders. (3) Drugs such as clonidine (Catapres), propranolol (Inderal), and verapamil (Isoptin) can effectively treat a variety of mental disorders and do not fit easily into the traditional classification of

**Table 33.3–1**
**Index by Generic Name of Drug**

| Generic Name | Trade Name | Subsection Title | Subsection Number |
|---|---|---|---|
| Acetophenazine | Tindal | Dopamine Receptor Antagonists (Antipsychotics) | 17 |
| Alprazolam | Xanax | Benzodiazepine Receptor Agonists and Antagonists | 5 |
| Amantadine | Symmetrel | Anticholinergics and Amantadine | 2 |
| Amitriptyline | Elavil | Tricyclic and Tetracyclic Drugs (Antidepressants) | 27 |
| Amobarbital | Amytal | Barbiturates and Similarly Acting Drugs | 4 |
| Amoxapine | Asendin | Tricyclic and Tetracyclic Drugs (Antidepressants) | 27 |
| Atenolol | Tenormin | β-Adrenergic Receptor Antagonists | 1 |
| Benztropine | Cogentin | Anticholinergics and Amantadine | 2 |
| Biperiden | Akineton | Anticholinergics and Amantadine | 2 |
| Brofaromine | Consonar (not sold in U.S.) | Monoamine Oxidase Inhibitors | 21 |
| Bromocriptine | Parlodel | Bromocriptine | 6 |
| Bupropion | Wellbutrin | Bupropion | 7 |
| Buspirone | BuSpar | Buspirone | 8 |
| Butabarbital | Butisol | Barbiturates and Similarly Acting Drugs | 4 |
| Butaperazine | Repoise (not sold in U.S.) | Dopamine Receptor Antagonists (Antipsychotics) | 17 |
| Carbamazepine | Tegretol | Carbamazepine | 10 |
| Carphenazine | Proketazine (not sold in U.S.) | Dopamine Receptor Antagonists (Antipsychotics) | 17 |
| Chloral hydrate | Noctec | Chloral Hydrate | 11 |
| Chlordiazepoxide | Librium | Benzodiazepine Receptor Agonists and Antagonists | 5 |
| Chlorpromazine | Thorazine | Dopamine Receptor Antagonists (Antipsychotics) | 17 |
| Chlorprothixene | Taractan | Dopamine Receptor Antagonists (Antipsychotics) | 17 |
| Citalopram | (not sold in U.S.) | Serotonin-Specific Reuptake Inhibitors | 22 |
| Clomipramine | Anafranil | Tricyclic and Tetracyclic Drugs (Antidepressants) | 27 |
| Clonazepam | Klonopin | Benzodiazepine Receptor Agonists and Antagonists | 5 |
| Clonidine | Catapres | Clonidine | 12 |
| Clorazepate | Tranxene | Benzodiazepine Receptor Agonists and Antagonists | 5 |
| Clorgyline | — | Monoamine Oxidase Inhibitors | 21 |
| Clozapine | Clozaril | Clozapine | 13 |
| Cyproheptadine | Periactin | Antihistamines | 3 |
| Dantrolene | Dantrium | Dantrolene | 14 |
| Desipramine | Norpramine, Pertofane | Tricyclic and Tetracyclic Drugs (Antidepressants) | 27 |
| Dextroamphet-amine | Dexedrine | Sympathomimetics | 23 |
| Diazepam | Valium | Benzodiazepine Receptor Agonists and Antagonists | 5 |
| Diltiazem | Cardizem | Calcium Channel Inhibitors | 9 |
| Diphenhydramine | Benadryl | Antihistamines | 3 |
| Disulfiram | Antabuse | Disulfiram | 15 |
| L-Dopa | Larodopa | L-Dopa | 16 |
| Doxepin | Adapin, Sinequan | Tricyclic and Tetracyclic Drugs (Antidepressants) | 27 |
| Droperidol | Inapsine | Dopamine Receptor Antagonists | 17 |
| Estazolam | ProSom | Benzodiazepine Receptor Agonists and Antagonists | 5 |
| Ethopropazine | Parsidol | Anticholinergics and Amantadine | 2 |
| Fenfluramine | Pondimin | Fenfluramine | 18 |
| Flumazenil | Romazicon | Benzodiazepine Receptor Agonists and Antagonists | 5 |
| Fluoxetine | Prozac | Serotonin-Specific Reuptake Inhibitors | 22 |
| Fluphenazine | Permitil, Prolixin | Dopamine Receptor Antagonists (Antipsychotics) | 17 |
| Flurazepam | Dalmane | Benzodiazepine Receptor Agonists and Antagonists | 5 |

**Table 33.3–1**
*Continued*

| Generic Name | Trade Name | Subsection Title | Subsection Number |
|---|---|---|---|
| Fluvoxamine | Luvox | Serotonin-Specific Reuptake Inhibitors | 22 |
| Halazepam | Paxipam | Benzodiazepine Receptor Agonists and Antagonists | 5 |
| Haloperidol | Haldol | Dopamine Receptor Antagonists (Antipsychotics) | 17 |
| Hydroxyzine | Atarax, Vistaril | Antihistamines | 3 |
| Imipramine | Tofranil | Tricyclic and Tetracyclic Drugs (Antidepressants) | 27 |
| Isocarboxazid | Marplan | Monoamine Oxidase Inhibitors | 21 |
| Lithium | Eskalith, Lithobid | Lithium | 19 |
| Lorazepam | Ativan | Benzodiazepine Receptor Agonists and Antagonists | 5 |
| Loxapine | Loxitane | Dopamine Receptor Antagonists (Antipsychotics) | 17 |
| Maprotiline | Ludiomil | Tricyclic and Tetracyclic Drugs (Antidepressants) | 27 |
| Mephobarbital | Mebaral | Barbiturates and Similarly Acting Drugs | 4 |
| Mesoridazine | Serentil | Dopamine Receptor Antagonists (Antipsychotics) | 17 |
| Methadone | Dolophine, Methadose | Methadone | 20 |
| Methylphenidate | Ritalin | Sympathomimetics | 23 |
| Metoprolol | Lopressor | β-Adrenergic Receptor Antagonists | 1 |
| Midazolam | Versed | Benzodiazepine Receptor Agonists and Antagonists | 5 |
| Moclobemide | Aurorix (not sold in U.S.) | Monoamine Oxidase Inhibitors | 21 |
| Molindone | Lidone, Moban | Dopamine Receptor Antagonists (Antipsychotics) | 17 |
| Nadolol | Corgard | β-Adrenergic Receptor Antagonists | 1 |
| Nefazodone | Serzone | Trazodone and Nefazodone | 26 |
| Nifedipine | Adalat, Procardia | Calcium Channel Inhibitors | 9 |
| Nimodipine | Nimotop | Calcium Channel Inhibitors | 9 |
| Nortriptyline | Aventyl, Pamelor | Tricyclic and Tetracyclic Drugs (Antidepressants) | 27 |
| Orphenadrine | Dispal, Norflex | Anticholinergics and Amantadine | 2 |
| Oxazepam | Serax | Benzodiazepine Receptor Agonists and Antagonists | 5 |
| Pargyline | Eutonyl | Monoamine Oxidase Inhibitors | 21 |
| Paroxetine | Paxil | Serotonin-Specific Reuptake Inhibitors | 22 |
| Pemoline | Cylert | Sympathomimetics | 23 |
| Pentobarbital | Nembutal | Barbiturates and Similarly Acting Drugs | 4 |
| Perphenazine | Trilafon | Dopamine Receptor Antagonists (Antipsychotics) | 17 |
| Phenelzine | Nardil | Monoamine Oxidase Inhibitors | 21 |
| Phenobarbital | Luminal | Barbiturates and Similarly Acting Drugs | 4 |
| Pimozide | Orap | Dopamine Receptor Antagonists (Antipsychotics) | 17 |
| Piperacetazine | Quide (not sold in U.S.) | Dopamine Receptor Antagonists (Antipsychotics) | 17 |
| Prazepam | Centrax | Benzodiazepine Receptor Agonists and Antagonists | 5 |
| Prochlorperazine | Compazine | Dopamine Receptor Antagonists (Antipsychotics) | 17 |
| Procyclidine | Kemadrin | Anticholinergics and Amantadine | 2 |
| Promazine | Sparine | Dopamine Receptor Antagonists (Antipsychotics) | 17 |
| Propranolol | Inderal | β-Adrenergic Receptor Antagonists | 1 |
| Protriptyline | Vivactil | Tricyclic and Tetracyclic Drugs (Antidepressants) | 27 |
| Quazepam | Doral | Benzodiazepine Receptor Agonists and Antagonists | 5 |
| Remoxipride | Roxiam (not sold in U.S.) | Dopamine Receptor Antagonists (Antipsychotics) | 17 |
| Risperidone | Risperdal | Dopamine Receptor Antagonists (Antipsychotics) | 17 |
| Secobarbital | Seconal | Barbiturates and Similarly Acting Drugs | 4 |
| Selegiline | Eldepryl | Monoamine Oxidase Inhibitors | 21 |
| Sertraline | Zoloft | Serotonin-Specific Reuptake Inhibitors | 22 |
| Tacrine | Cognex | Tacrine | 24 |
| Temazepam | Restoril | Benzodiazepine Receptor Agonists and Antagonists | 5 |
| Thioridazine | Mellaril | Dopamine Receptor Antagonists (Antipsychotics) | 17 |
| Thiothixene | Navane | Dopamine Receptor Antagonists (Antipsychotics) | 17 |
| Thyroxine | Levothroid, Levoxine, Synthroid | Thyroid Hormones | 25 |
| Tranylcypromine | Parnate | Monoamine Oxidase Inhibitors | 21 |
| Trazodone | Desyrel | Trazodone and Nefazodone | 26 |
| Triazolam | Halcion | Benzodiazepine Receptor Agonists and Antagonists | 5 |
| Trifluoperazine | Stelazine | Dopamine Receptor Antagonists (Antipsychotics) | 17 |
| Triflupromazine | Vesprin | Dopamine Receptor Antagonists (Antipsychotics) | 17 |
| Trihexyphenidyl | Artane, Tremin, Trihex-ane, Trihexy-5 | Anticholinergics and Amantadine | 2 |
| L-Triiodothyronine | Cytomel | Thyroid Hormones | 25 |
| Trimipramine | Surmontil | Tricyclic and Tetracyclic Drugs (Antidepressants) | 27 |
| L-Tryptophan | — | L-Tryptophan | 28 |
| Valproate | Depakene, Depakote | Valproate | 29 |
| Velnacrine | Mentane | Tacrine | 24 |
| Venlafaxine | Effexor | Venlafaxine | 30 |
| Verapamil | Calan, Isoptin | Calcium Channel Inhibitors | 9 |
| Yohimbine | Yocon | Yohimbine | 31 |
| Zolpidem | Ambien | Benzodiazepine Receptor Agonists and Antagonists | 5 |

**Table 33.3–2**
**Major Mental Disorders and the Drugs and Classes of Drugs Used in Their Treatment**

| | Subsection Number | | Subsection Number |
|---|---|---|---|
| Aggression and agitation (see Intermittent explosive disorder) | | Intermittent explosive disorder | |
| Akathisia (see Medication-induced movement disorders) | | β-Adrenergic receptor antagonists | 1 |
| | | Barbiturates (primarily for acute agitation) | 4 |
| Alcohol use disorders | | Buspirone | 8 |
| β-Adrenergic receptor antagonists | 1 | Carbamazepine | 10 |
| Benzodiazepines | 5 | Dopamine receptor antagonists | 17 |
| Carbamazepine | 10 | Lithium | 19 |
| Disulfiram | 15 | Valproate | 29 |
| Lithium | 19 | Medication-induced movement disorders (see also Neuroleptic malignant syndrome) | |
| Anorexia nervosa (see Eating disorders) | | β-Adrenergic receptor antagonists | 1 |
| Anxiety (see also specific anxiety disorders) | | Amantadine | 2 |
| Antihistamines | 3 | Anticholinergics | 2 |
| Barbiturates and similarly acting drugs | 4 | Antihistamines | 3 |
| Benzodiazepines | 5 | Benzodiazepines | 5 |
| Buspirone | 8 | L-Dopa | 16 |
| Bipolar disorders | | Neuroleptic malignant syndrome | |
| Benzodiazepines (especially clonazepam) | 5 | Bromocriptine | 6 |
| Calcium channel inhibitors | 9 | Dantrolene | 14 |
| Carbamazepine | 10 | Obsessive-compulsive disorder | |
| Clozapine | 13 | Serotonin-specific reuptake inhibitors | 22 |
| Dopamine receptor antagonists | 17 | Tricyclic and tetracyclic drugs (especially clomipramine) | 27 |
| Lithium | 19 | | |
| L-Tryptophan | 28 | Opioid use disorders | |
| Valproate | 29 | Clonidine | 12 |
| Bulimia nervosa (see Eating disorders) | | Methadone | 20 |
| Catatonic disorder due to a general medical condition | | Panic disorder (with and without agoraphobia) | |
| Barbiturates | 4 | β-Adrenergic receptor antagonists | 1 |
| Benzodiazepines | 5 | Benzodiazepines (especially alprazolam and clonazepam) | 5 |
| Clozapine | 13 | Monoamine oxidase inhibitors | 21 |
| Dopamine receptor antagonists | 17 | Serotonin-specific reuptake inhibitors | 22 |
| Cyclothymic disorder (see Bipolar disorders) | | Tricyclic and tetracyclic drugs (antidepressants) | 27 |
| Delusional disorder (see Schizophrenia) | | | |
| Dementia of the Alzheimer's type (cognitive symptoms) | | Parkinsonism (see Medication-induced movement disorders) | |
| Tacrine | 24 | Phobias (see also Panic disorder) | |
| Depressive disorders | | β-Adrenergic receptor antagonists | 1 |
| Benzodiazepines (especially alprazolam) | 5 | Benzodiazepines | 5 |
| Bromocriptine | 6 | Monoamine oxidase inhibitors | 21 |
| Bupropion | 7 | Posttraumatic stress disorder | |
| Carbamazepine | 10 | Monoamine oxidase inhibitors | 21 |
| Lithium | 19 | Serotonin-specific reuptake inhibitors | 22 |
| Monoamine oxidase inhibitors | 21 | Tricyclic and tetracyclic drugs (antidepressants) | 27 |
| Serotonin-specific reuptake inhibitors | 22 | | |
| Sympathomimetics | 23 | Psychosis (see Schizophrenia) | |
| Thyroid hormones | 25 | Rabbit syndrome (see Medication-induced movement disorders) | |
| Trazodone (and nefazodone) | 26 | | |
| Tricyclic and tetracyclic drugs (antidepressants) | 27 | Schizoaffective disorder (see Depressive disorders, Bipolar disorders, and Schizophrenia) | |
| L-Tryptophan | 28 | | |
| Venlafaxine | 30 | Schizophrenia | |
| Dysthymic disorder (see Depressive disorders) | | Benzodiazepines | 5 |
| Dystonia (see Medication-induced movement disorders) | | Carbamazepine | 10 |
| | | Clozapine | 13 |
| Eating disorders | | Dopamine receptor antagonists | 17 |
| Fenfluramine | 18 | Lithium | 19 |
| Lithium | 19 | Sexual dysfunctions | |
| Monoamine oxidase inhibitors | 21 | Antihistamines (cyproheptadine) | 3 |
| Serotonin-specific reuptake inhibitors | 22 | Yohimbine | 31 |
| Tricyclic and tetracyclic drugs (antidepressants) | 27 | Sleep disorders | |
| | | Antihistamines | 3 |
| Generalized anxiety disorder | | Barbiturates and similarly acting drugs | 4 |
| β-Adrenergic receptor antagonists | 1 | Benzodiazepines | 5 |
| Barbiturates and similarly acting drugs | 4 | Chloral hydrate | 11 |
| Benzodiazepines | 5 | Sympathomimetics | 23 |
| Buspirone | 8 | Trazodone | 26 |
| Tricyclic and tetracyclic drugs (antidepressants) | 27 | L-Tryptophan | 28 |
| | | Violence (see Intermittent explosive disorder) | |

**Table 33.3–3**
**Combination Drugs Used in Psychiatry**

| Ingredients | Preparation | Manufacturer | Amount of Each Ingredient | Recommended Dosage | Indications | D.E.A.* Con-trol |
|---|---|---|---|---|---|---|
| Perphenazine and amitriptyline | Triavil | Merck, Sharp & Dohme | Tablet—2:25, 4:25, 4:50, 2:10, 4:10 | Initial therapy: tablet of 2:25 or 4:25 q.i.d. | Depression and associated anxiety | 0 |
| | Etrafon | Schering | | Maintenance therapy: tablet 2:25 or 4:25 b.i.d. or q.i.d. | | |
| Meprobamate and benactyzine | Deprol | Wallace | Tablet—400:1 | Initial therapy: one tablet q.i.d. Maintenance therapy: initial dosage may be increased to six tablets a day, then gradually reduced to the lowest levels that provide relief | Depression and associated anxiety | IV |
| Dextroamphetamine and amphetamine | Biphetamine† | Fisons | Sustained release capsule—6.25:6.24 | One capsule in the morning | Exogenous obesity Attention-deficit/ hyperactivity disorder (ADHD) | II |
| Chlordiazepoxide and clidinium bromide | Librax | Roche | Capsule—5:25 | One or two capsules t.i.d. or q.i.d. before meals and at bedtime | Peptic ulcer, gastritis, duodenitis, irritable bowel syndrome, spastic colitis, and mild ulcerative colitis | O |
| Chlordiazepoxide and amitriptyline | Limbitrol | Roche | Tablet—5:12.5, 10:25 | Tablet of 5:12.5 t.i.d. or q.i.d. Tablet of 10:25 t.i.d. or q.i.d. initially, then may increase to six tablets daily as required | Depression and associated anxiety | IV |

*DEA, Drug Enforcement Administration.
†The U.S. Food and Drug Administration recommends the use of amphetamine only for weight reduction and ADHD.

drugs. (4) Some descriptive psychopharmacological terms overlap in meaning. For example, anxiolytics decrease anxiety, sedatives produce a calming or relaxing effect, and hypnotics induce sleep. However, most anxiolytics function as sedatives and at high dosages can be used as hypnotics, and all hypnotics at low dosages can be used for daytime sedation. For those reasons this book uses a classification in which each drug is discussed according to its pharmacological category.

## GUIDE TO USE

The table of contents lists the 31 groups into which the drugs used in psychiatry have been divided for discussion within this textbook. An alphabetical list of generic drug names discussed in this book is presented in Table 33.3–1, with cross-references to the subsection in which they are discussed. A list of therapeutic indications and the drugs commonly used for those indications is presented in Table 33.3–2, with cross-references to the appropriate subsection.

## COMBINATION DRUGS

In addition to the drugs that contain a single active component, a small number of combination drugs are available in the United States (Table 33.3–3). The use of such drugs may increase patient compliance by simplifying the drug regimen. However, a problem with combination drugs is that the clinician has little flexibility in adjusting the dosage of one of the components; that is, the use of combination drugs may cause two drugs to be administered when only one drug continues to be necessary for therapeutic efficacy.

## 33.3.1 / β-Adrenergic Receptor Antagonists

The β-adrenergic receptor antagonists, which are variously referred to as β-blockers and β-antagonists, are commonly used in medical practice for the treatment of hypertension, angina, and certain cardiac arrhythmias, but the drugs are also used for the treatment of glaucoma, migraine, and the symptoms of hyperthyroidism. Although the drugs are not officially approved for use in psychiatric indications, their effectiveness has been well demonstrated for social phobia (for example, performance anxiety), lithium-induced postural tremor, and neuroleptic-induced acute akathisia. Preliminary research regarding their use in other psychiatric conditions has also been reported and is described below.

## CHEMISTRY

The four β-adrenergic receptor antagonists most commonly studied for psychiatric indications in the United States are atenolol (Tenormin), metoprolol (Lopressor), nadolol (Corgard), and propranolol (Inderal). The molecular structures of those drugs are shown in Figure 33.3.1–1. A comparison of the properties of those four drugs is presented in Table 33.3.1–1.

## PHARMACOLOGICAL ACTIONS

### Pharmacokinetics

The four β-adrenergic receptor antagonists listed in Table 33.3.1–1 and the other available drugs of that class differ with regard to lipophilicities, metabolic routes, β-adrenergic receptor selectivity, and half-lives (Table 33.3.1–1). The absorption of the four β-adrenergic receptor antagonists from the gastrointestinal tract varies, but the absorption is good enough to permit oral formulations of all four drugs. Two of the drugs, metoprolol and propranolol, are metabolized by the liver; the other two drugs, atenolol and nadolol, are excreted largely unmetabolized by the kidneys. The half-lives of atenolol and nadolol are such that once-daily dosing is possible, but metoprolol and propranolol require at least twice-daily dosing. The agents that are most soluble in lipids (that is, are lipophilic) are likely to cross the blood-brain barrier and enter the brain; those agents that are least lipophilic are not likely to enter the brain in significant concentrations.

### Pharmacodynamics

Although three subtypes of the β-adrenergic receptor have been reported, significant data are currently available on only two of those subtypes, the $\beta_1$ and $\beta_2$ receptors. Antagonist activity of peripheral β-adrenergic receptors blocks the activation of those receptors by peripheral epinephrine and norepinephrine, the primary neurotransmitters of the sympathetic nervous system. Thus, when acting peripherally, the β-adrenergic receptor antagonists act as sympatholytic drugs. In the central nervous system (CNS), the locus ceruleus contains the majority of the noradrenergic and adrenergic neurons, which project widely throughout the brain. Within the brain, β-adrenergic receptors are located primarily postsynaptically, and those receptors are blocked by the β-adrenergic receptor antagonists.

Some of the available β-adrenergic receptor antagonists (for example, nadolol and propranolol) have essentially equal potency at both the $\beta_1$ and $\beta_2$ receptors, whereas other β-adrenergic receptor antagonists (for example, atenolol and metoprolol) have greater affinity for the $\beta_1$ receptor than for the $\beta_2$ receptor. That relative $\beta_1$ selectivity confers few pulmonary and vascular effects on those drugs, although their use in asthmatic patients must be undertaken with caution, because the drugs retain some activity at the $\beta_2$ receptors.

## EFFECTS ON SPECIFIC ORGANS AND SYSTEMS

The relative importance of $\beta_1$ and $\beta_2$ receptor activity in the central nervous system is uncertain regarding the effects of β-adrenergic receptor antagonists in the treatment of mental disorders (for example, social phobia) and medication-induced movement disorders (for example, lithium-induced postural tremor). Studies of the least lipophilic β-adrenergic receptor drugs, which are not likely to cross the blood-brain barrier, indicate that blocking peripheral $\beta_1$ receptors may be enough to obtain certain desired clinical benefits in psychiatry (for example, the re-

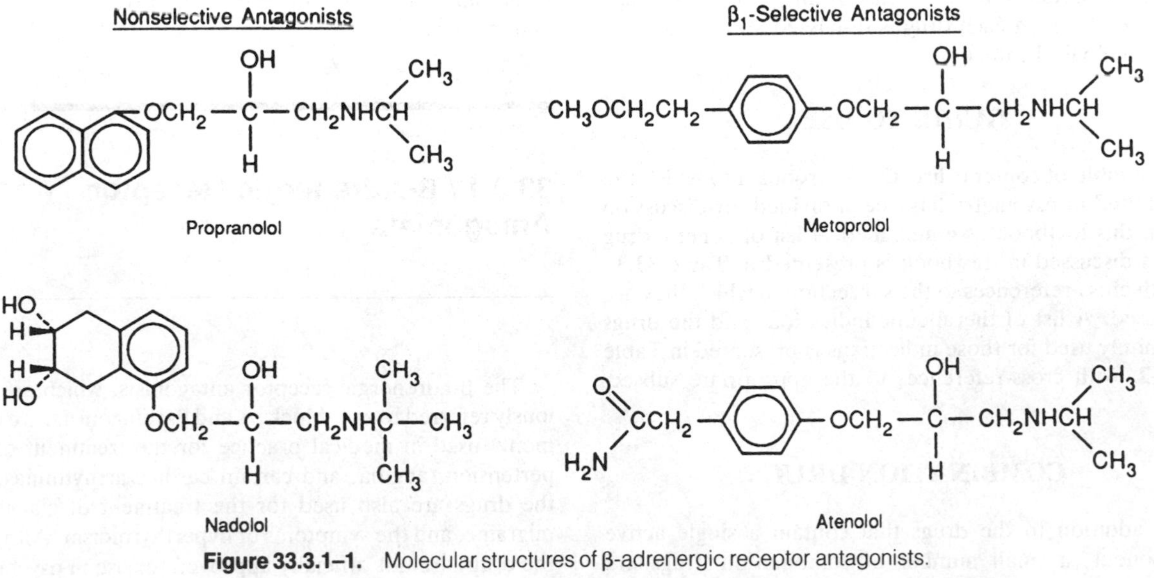

**Figure 33.3.1–1.** Molecular structures of β-adrenergic receptor antagonists.

**Table 33.3.1–1**
**β-Adrenergic Drugs Used in Psychiatry**

| Generic Name | Trade Name | Lipophilic | Metabolism | Receptor Selectivity | Half-Life (hrs) | Usual Starting Dosage (mg) | Usual Maximal Dosage (mg) |
|---|---|---|---|---|---|---|---|
| Atenolol | Tenormin | No | Renal | $\beta_1 > \beta_2$ | 6–9 | 50 once a day | 50–100 once a day |
| Metoprolol | Lopressor | Yes | Hepatic | $\beta_1 > \beta_2$ | 3–4 | 50 twice a day | 75–150 twice a day |
| Nadolol | Corgard | No | Renal | $\beta_1 = \beta_2$ | 14–24 | 40 once a day | 80–240 once a day |
| Propranolol | Inderal | Yes | Hepatic | $\beta_1 = \beta_2$ | 3–6 | 10–20 two or three times a day | 80–140 three times a day |

duction of lithium-induced postural tremor), although whether central β-adrenergic receptor activity or peripheral $\beta_2$-adrenergic receptor activity increases the efficacy of those drugs for those indications is not certain.

With regard to nonneural organs and systems, peripheral $\beta_1$-adrenergic receptors modulate chronotropic and inotropic cardiac functions. Peripheral $\beta_2$-adrenergic receptors modulate bronchodilatation and vasodilation. For that reason, $\beta_1$-selective drugs are preferable in the treatment of patients with asthma and other obstructive pulmonary diseases, since the blockade of the pulmonary $\beta_2$ receptors blocks the bronchodilating effects of epinephrine.

## THERAPEUTIC INDICATIONS

Although the β-adrenergic receptor antagonists have been studied for use in many mental disorders and medication-induced movement disorders (Table 33.3.1–2), the use of the β-adrenergic receptor antagonists is best supported for social phobia, lithium-induced postural tremor, and neuroleptic-induced acute akathisia. The data on the use of those drugs as adjuncts to benzodiazepines for alcohol withdrawal and for the control of impulsive aggression or violence are also promising.

### Social Phobia

Propranolol has been well-studied for the treatment of social phobia, primarily of the performance type (for ex-

**Table 33.3.1–2**
**Indications for β-Adrenergic Receptor Antagonists in Psychiatric Practice**

Effective
  Social phobia (especially of the performance type)
  Lithium-induced postural tremor
  Neuroleptic-induced acute akathisia

Probably effective
  Control of impulsive aggression or violence
  Adjunct to benzodiazepines in the treatment of alcohol
    withdrawal

Possibly effective
  Generalized anxiety disorder
  Schizophrenia

ample, disabling anxiety before a musical performance). Although the beneficial effects probably result primarily from the reduction of the sympathetic peripheral manifestations of anxiety (for example, tremor, sweating, and tachycardia), the blocking of central nervous system β-adrenergic receptors may be of some additional benefit. However, studies of the least lipophilic β-adrenergic receptor antagonists have also shown them to be of benefit for that indication. A common treatment approach is to have the patient take 10 to 40 mg of propranolol 20 to 30 minutes before the anxiety-provoking situation. Patients may try a test run of the β-adrenergic antagonist before using it before an anxiety-provoking situation to be sure that they do not experience any adverse effects from the drug or the dosage.

### Lithium-Induced Postural Temor

Lithium-induced postural tremor is perhaps the most common of the medication-induced postural tremors. Although most of the studies of the β-adrenergic receptor antagonists for medication-induced postural tremor have been conducted for lithium-induced postural tremor, a β-adrenergic receptor antagonist would probably also be beneficial in other medication-induced postural tremors—for example, induced by tricyclic drugs and valproate (Depakene). Propranolol in the range of 20 to 160 mg a day, given two or three times daily, is generally effective for the treatment of lithium-induced postural tremor. Some studies have found that the least lipophilic β-adrenergic receptor antagonists are also effective, although other studies have reported that those drugs are not as effective as propranolol.

### Neuroleptic-Induced Acute Akathisia

Neuroleptic-induced acute akathisia is recognized in the fourth edition of *Diagnostic and Statistical Manual of Mental Disorders* (DSM-IV) as one of the medication-induced movement disorders. Many studies have shown that β-adrenergic receptor antagonists can be effective in the treatment of neuroleptic-induced acute akathisia. The majority of clinicians and researchers believe that β-adrenergic receptor antagonists are more effective for that indication than are anticholinergics and benzodiazepines, although the relative efficacy of those agents may vary among patients. However, the clinician must realize that the β-adrenergic receptor antagonists are not effective in the treatment of such neuroleptic-induced movement disorders as acute dystonia and parkinsonism. Propranolol is the drug that has been most studied for neuroleptic-induced acute akathisia, and at least one study has reported that a less lipophilic compound was not effective in the treatment of the disorder.

## Aggression and Violent Behavior

A number of studies have shown that β-adrenergic receptor antagonists may be effective in reducing the number of aggressive and violent outbursts in patients with impulse disorders, schizophrenia, and aggression associated with brain injuries, such as trauma, tumors, anoxic injury, encephalitis, alcohol dependence, and degenerative disorders (for example, Huntington's disease). Many of those studies have added a β-adrenergic receptor antagonist to the ongoing therapy (for example, antipsychotics, anticonvulsants, lithium); therefore, it is difficult to distinguish additive effects from independent effects. Nevertheless, about 50 percent of all patients studied in various trials showed a clinically significant reduction in their aggressive and violent symptoms after the addition of a β-adrenergic receptor antagonist. Many controlled and anecdotal reports indicate that high doses of β-adrenergic receptor antagonists, sometimes up to a gram of propranolol, were used.

## Alcohol Withdrawal

Propranolol has been reported to be useful as an adjuvant to benzodiazepines but not as a sole agent in the treatment of alcohol withdrawal. One study used the following dose schedule: no propranolol for a pulse less than 50; 50 mg propranolol for a pulse between 50 and 79; and 100 mg propranolol for a pulse equal to or greater than 80. The patients who received propranolol and benzodiazepines had less severe withdrawal symptoms, more stable vital signs, and a shorter hospital stay than did the patients who received only benzodiazepines.

## Other Disorders

A number of case reports and controlled studies have reported data indicating that β-adrenergic receptor antagonists may be of benefit for patients with generalized anxiety disorder, schizophrenia, and manic symptoms. The efficacy of β-adrenergic receptor antagonists in generalized anxiety disorder may be due to their reducing the autonomic symptoms that are associated with the disorder. The clinician must be cognizant of the possibility that the β-adrenergic receptor antagonists induce depression in some patients. The data regarding the effectiveness of β-adrenergic receptor antagonists in schizophrenia and mania are not robust, although a trial of the medications may be warranted under extreme or research situations.

## PRECAUTIONS AND ADVERSE REACTIONS

The β-adrenergic receptor antagonists are contraindicated for use in patients with asthma, insulin-dependent diabetes, congestive heart failure, significant vascular disease, persistent angina, and hyperthyroidism. The contraindication in diabetic patients is due to the drugs' antagonizing the normal physiological response to hypoglycemia. The β-adrenergic receptor antagonists can worsen atrioventricular (A-V) conduction defects and lead to complete A-V heart block and death. If the clinician decides that the risk-benefit ratio warrants a trial of a β-adrenergic receptor antagonist in a patient with one of those coexisting medical conditions, a β₁-selective agent should probably be the first choice.

The most common adverse effects of β-adrenergic receptor antagonists are hypotension and bradycardia (Table 33.3.1–3). In patients at risk for those adverse effects, a test dosage of 20 mg a day of propranolol can be given to assess the patient's reaction to the drug. Depression has been associated with lipophilic β-adrenergic receptor antagonists, such as propranolol, but it is probably rare. Nausea, vomiting, diarrhea, and constipation may also be caused by treatment with those agents. Serious CNS adverse effects (for example, agitation, confusion, and hallucinations) are rare.

**Table 33.3.1–3**
**Side Effects and Toxicity of β-Blockers**

Cardiovascular
  Hypotension
  Bradycardia
  Dizziness
  Congestive failure (in patients with compromised myocardial function)

Respiratory
  Asthma (less risk with β₁-selective drugs)

Metabolic
  Worsened hypoglycemia in diabetic patients receiving insulin or oral agents

Gastrointestinal
  Nausea
  Diarrhea
  Abdominal pain

Sexual function
  Impotence

Neuropsychiatric
  Lassitude
  Fatigue
  Dysphoria
  Insomnia
  Vivid nightmares
  Depression (possible)
  Psychosis (rare)

Other (rare)
  Raynaud's phenomenon
  Peyronie's disease

Withdrawal syndrome
  Rebound worsening of preexisting angina pectoris when β-blockers are discontinued

Table from G W Arana, S E Hyman: *Handbook of Psychiatric Drug Therapy*, ed 2, p 176. Little Brown, Boston, 1991. Used with permission.

**Table 33.3.1–4**
**β-Adrenergic Receptor Antagonist Preparations**

| | Tablets | Capsules (Extended Release) | Solution | Parenteral |
|---|---|---|---|---|
| Atenolol | 50, 100 mg | — | — | 50 mg/10 mL ampules |
| Metoprolol | 50, 100 mg | — | — | 1 mg/mL |
| Nadolol | 20, 40, 80, 120, 160 mg | — | — | — |
| Propranolol | 10, 20, 40, 60, 80, 90 mg | 60, 80, 120, 160 mg | 20 mg/5 mL, 40 mg/5 mL, 80 mg/mL (concentrate) | 1 mg/mL |

## DRUG INTERACTIONS

A number of studies have found that concomitant administration of propranolol has resulted in increases in plasma concentrations of antipsychotics, theophylline (Primatene), and thyroxine. The plasma concentrations of antiepileptics would probably be affected similarly. Other β-adrenergic receptor antagonists possibly have similar effects. The β-adrenergic receptor antagonists that are eliminated by the kidneys may have similar effects on drugs that are also eliminated by the renal route. When there is a possibility of a drug-drug interaction, the plasma concentrations of the involved drugs should be monitored whenever possible. Barbiturates increase the elimination of β-adrenergic receptor antagonists that are metabolized by the liver. Several reports have associated hypertensive crises and bradycardia with the coadministration of β-adrenergic receptor antagonists and monoamine oxidase inhibitors. Patients on those two types of drugs should be treated with low dosages of both drugs and should have their blood pressure and pulse rates monitored regularly.

## LABORATORY INTERFERENCES

The β-adrenergic receptor antagonists have no known interferences with standard laboratory tests.

## DOSAGE AND ADMINISTRATION

Since some β-adrenergic receptor antagonists act peripherally and others act both peripherally and centrally, peripherally acting drugs may be safer than the drugs that act both centrally and peripherally, especially with regard to such CNS side effects as depression, lassitude, and changes in sleep patterns. The problem with the data is that for most indications it remains unclear whether the peripherally acting drugs (that is, those that are least lipophilic) are as effective as the most lipophilic drugs.

For the treatment of chronic disorders, propranolol is usually initiated at 10 mg by mouth three times a day or 20 mg by mouth twice daily (Table 33.3.1–4). The dosage can be raised by 20 to 30 mg a day until a therapeutic effect begins to emerge. The dosage should be leveled off at the appropriate range for the disorder under treatment. The treatment of aggressive behavior sometimes requires dosages up to 800 mg a day, and therapeutic effects may not be seen until the patient has been receiving the maximal dosage for four to eight weeks.

The patient's pulse and blood pressure readings should be taken regularly, and the drug should be withheld if the patient's pulse is less than 50 or the patient's systolic blood pressure is less than 90. The drug should be temporarily withheld if the patient has severe dizziness, ataxia, or wheezing. Treatment with β-adrenergic receptor antagonists should never be discontinued abruptly. Propranolol should be tapered by 60 mg a day until a dosage of 60 mg a day is reached, after which the drug should be tapered by 10 to 20 mg a day every three or four days.

### References

Bright R A, Everitt D E: β-Blockers and depression. JAMA *267*: 1783, 1992.

Dimsdale J E, Newton R P, Joist T: Neuropsychological side effects of beta-blockers. Arch Intern Med *149*: 514, 1989.

Kraus M L, Gottlieb L D, Horwitz R I, Anscher M: Randomized clinical trial of atenolol in patients with alcohol withdrawal. N Engl J Med *313*: 905, 1985.

Lader M: β-Adrenoceptor antagonists in neuropsychiatry: An update. J Clin Psychiatry *49*: 213, 1988.

Lipinski J F, Keck P E, McElroy S L: β-Adrenergic antagonists in psychosis: Is improvement due to treatment of neuroleptic-induced akathisia? J Clin Psychopharmacol 8: 409, 1988.

Mattes J A: Comparative effectiveness of carbamazepine and propranolol for rage outbursts. J Neuropsychiatry Clin Neurosci 2: 159, 1990.

Ratey J J, Sorgi P, O'Driscoll G A, Sands S, Daehler M L, Fletcher J R, Kadish W, Spruiell G, Polakoff S, Lindem K J, Bemporad J R, Richardson L, Rosenfeld B: Nadolol to treat aggression and psychiatric symptomatology in chronic psychiatric inpatients: A double-blind, placebo-controlled study. J Clin Psychiatry 53: 41, 1992.

Silver J M, Yudofsky S C, Kogan M: Elevation of thioridazine levels by propranolol. Am J Psychiatry *143*: 1290, 1986.

Sorgi P, Ratey J, Knoedler D, Arnold W, Cole L: Depression during treatment with beta-blockers: Results from a double-blind placebo-controlled study. J Neuropsychiatry Clin Neurosci 4: 187, 1992.

Tryer P: Current status of β-blocking drugs in the treatment of anxiety disorder. Drugs 36: 773, 1988.

Volavka J: Can aggressive behavior in humans be modified by beta-blockers? Postgrad Med 29: 163, 1988.

Wells B G, Cold J A, Marken P A, Brown C S, Chu C-C, Johnson R P, Nasdahl C S, Ayubi M A, Knott D H, Arheart K I: A placebo-controlled trial of nadolol in the treatment of neuroleptic-induced akathisia. J Clin Psychiatry 52: 255, 1991.

# 33.3.2 / Anticholinergics and Amantadine

**Figure 33.3.2–1.** Molecular structures of selected anticholinergic drugs and amantadine.

In the clinical practice of psychiatry, the anticholinergic drugs and amantadine (Symmetrel), like the antihistamines, have their primary use as treatments for medication-induced movement disorders, particularly neuroleptic-induced parkinsonism, neuroleptic-induced acute dystonia, and medication-induced postural tremor. The anticholinergic drugs and amantadine may also be of limited use in the treatment of neuroleptic-induced acute akathisia. Before the introduction of levodopa (Larodopa), the anticholinergic drugs were commonly used in the treatment of idiopathic Parkinson's disease. The antiparkinsonian effects of amantadine, which was initially developed as an antiviral compound, were initially discovered when its use improved the parkinsonian symptoms of a patient who was being treated with amantadine for influenza A2.

The common use of the term "anticholinergic drugs" is misleading. There are two general types of acetylcholine receptors, the muscarinic receptors and the nicotinic receptors. The muscarinic receptors are G protein-linked receptors, and the nicotinic receptors are ligand-gated ion channels. The anticholinergic drugs discussed in this subsection are specific for the muscarinic receptors and, therefore, are also referred to as antimuscarinic drugs. Another name used for the general class of drugs (that is, the antimuscarinic drugs, amantadine, and the antihistamines) used to treat the symptoms of medication-induced movement disorders is antiparkinsonian drugs.

## CHEMISTRY

The molecular structures of representative anticholinergic drugs and amantadine are shown in Figure 33.3.2–1. The two most commonly used anticholinergic drugs, benztropine (Cogentin) and trihexyphenidyl (Artane), are tertiary amines. Benztropine is similar to both atropine, the classic anticholinergic compound, and diphenhydramine (Benadryl), the classic antihistaminergic compound, and, in fact, possesses antihistaminergic activity.

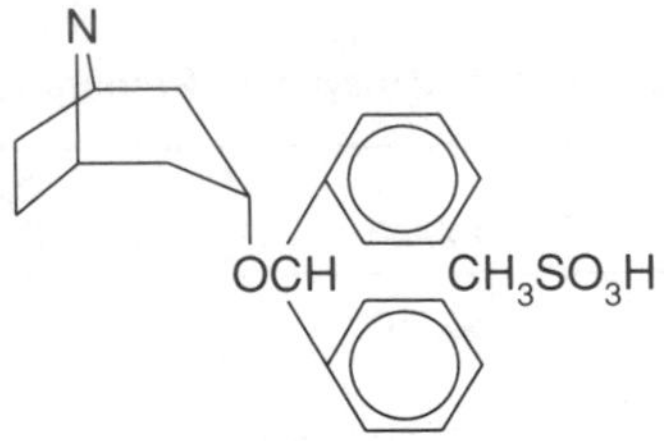

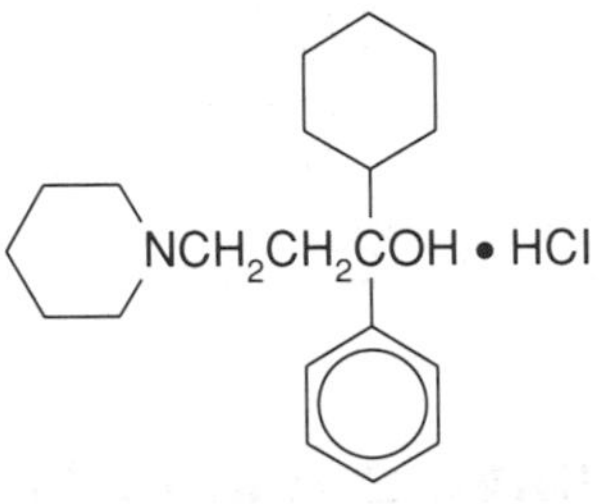

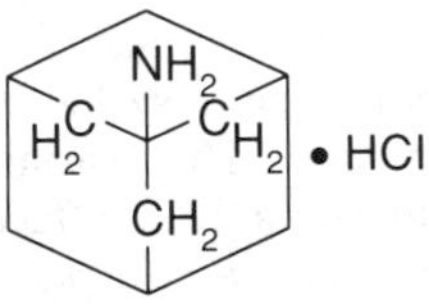

## PHARMACOLOGICAL ACTIONS

### Pharmacokinetics

Six anticholinergic drugs are available in the United States (Table 33.3.2–1). The pharmacokinetics of the anticholinergics are not well-studied, but all are well-absorbed from the gastrointestinal (GI) tract after oral administration, and all are lipophilic enough to enter the central nervous system (CNS). Trihexyphenidyl reaches peak plasma concentrations in two to three hours after oral administration and has a duration of action of 1 to 12 hours. Benztropine probably has similar pharmacokinetic properties. Only three of the marketed anticholinergics are available in parenteral forms. Benztropine is probably the most commonly used parenteral anticholinergic. Benztropine is absorbed equally rapidly by intramuscular (IM) and intravenous (IV) administration; therefore, IM is preferred because of its low risk for adverse effects.

Amantadine is well-absorbed from the GI tract, reaches peak plasma levels in about two to three hours, has a half-life of 16 to 24 hours, and attains steady-state plasma levels after about four or five days of administration. Amantadine is excreted unmetabolized in the urine. Amantadine plasma concentrations can be as much as twice as high in elderly persons as in nonelderly adults because of decreased renal function in the elderly, although other patients with renal failure accumulate administered amantadine in their bodies.

### Pharmacodynamics

Although all six available anticholinergics have their primary effects through the blockade of muscarinic acetylcholine receptors, benztropine and ethopropazine (Parsidol) also have some antihistaminergic effects. None of the available anticholinergic drugs discussed in this subsection has any effects on the nicotinic acetylcholine receptors. Of the six drugs, trihexyphenidyl is the most stimulating agent, perhaps acting through dopaminergic neurons, and benztropine may be the least stimulating and, thus, is least associated with abuse potential.

Amantadine augments dopaminergic neurotransmission in the CNS; however, the precise mechanism for that effect is unknown. The mechanism may involve increasing the release

**Table 33.3.2–1**
**Anticholinergic (Antimuscarinic) Drugs and Amantadine**

| Generic Name | Trade Name | Average Daily Dosage (Oral) | Short-Term Dose (IM or IV) |
|---|---|---|---|
| Amantadine | Symmetrel, Symadine | 100 mg bid or tid | |
| Benztropine | Cogentin | 1–3 mg bid | 1–2 mg |
| Biperiden | Akineton | 1–3 mg bid | 2 mg |
| Ethopropazine | Parsidol | 50–100 mg bid | |
| Orphenadrine citrate | Norflex, Dispal | 50–100 mg tid | 60 mg IV given over 5 min. |
| Procyclidine | Kemadrin | 2.5–5 mg tid | |
| Trihexyphenidyl | Artane, Tremin, Trihexane, Trihexy-5 | 2–5 mg tid | |

of dopamine from presynaptic vesicles, blocking the reuptake of dopamine into presynaptic nerve terminals, or exerting an agonist effect on postsynaptic dopamine receptors.

## EFFECTS ON SPECIFIC ORGANS AND SYSTEMS

The antimuscarinic activity of the anticholinergic drugs discussed here affects the functioning of the autonomic ganglia, most commonly affecting the gastrointestinal tract, the heart, the bladder, and other parasympathetic functions. Amantadine is generally better tolerated than the anticholinergics, although it is associated with CNS adverse effects at high dosages, as are the anticholinergic compounds.

## THERAPEUTIC INDICATIONS

### Neuroleptic-Induced Parkinsonism

The primary indication for the use of anticholinergics or amantadine in psychiatric practice is for the treatment of neuroleptic-induced parkinsonism, which, in the full clinical syndrome, is characterized by tremor, rigidity, cogwheeling, bradykinesia, sialorrhea, stooped posture, and festination. Akinesia and the so-called rabbit syndrome may be related to the characteristic parkinsonian symptoms. Neuroleptic-induced akinesia can sometimes be confused clinically with catatonic symptoms. Rabbit syndrome is characterized by a rhythmic, involuntary, approximately 5 Hz perioral tremor that resembles the masticatory movements of a rabbit. Neuroleptic-induced parkinsonism is most common in the elderly and is most frequently seen with high-potency antipsychotics—for example, haloperidol (Haldol). The onset of symptoms usually occurs after two or three weeks of treatment.

All the available anticholinergics and amantadine are equally effective in the treatment of parkinsonian symptoms, although the efficacy of amantadine may diminish in some patients within the first month of treatment. Amantadine may be more effective than the anticholinergics in the treatment of rigidity and tremor. Amantadine may also be the drug of choice if a clinician does not want to add additional anticholinergic drugs to a patient's treatment regimen, particularly if a patient is taking an antipsychotic or an antidepressant with high anticholinergic activity—for example, chlorpromazine (Thorazine) or amitriptyline (Elavil)—or is elderly and, therefore, at risk for anticholinergic adverse effects.

### Neuroleptic-Induced Acute Dystonia

Neuroleptic-induced acute dystonia is most common in young men. The syndrome often occurs early in the course of treatment and is commonly associated with high-potency antipsychotics (for example, haloperidol). The dystonia most commonly affects the muscles of the neck, the tongue, the face, and the back. Opisthotonos (involving the entire body) and oculogyric crises (involving the muscles of the eyes) are examples of specific dystonias. Dystonias are uncomfortable, sometimes painful, and often frightening to the patient. Although the onset is often sudden, onset in three to six hours may occur, often resulting in patients' complaining about having a thick tongue or difficulty in swallowing. Dystonic contractions can be powerful enough to dislocate joints, and laryngeal dystonias can result in suffocation if the patient is not treated immediately.

Anticholinergic drugs are effective both in the short-term treatment of dystonias and in prophylaxis against neuroleptic-induced acute dystonias. Prophylactic treatment may, in fact, be indicated in the treatment of young patients, particularly men. If anticholinergics are not effective or if a patient cannot tolerate anticholinergics, treatment with antihistamines (for example, diphenhydramine) or benzodiazepines (for example, lorazepam [Ativan]) may be effective. Amantadine is not generally considered as effective as the anticholinergics for the treatment of acute dystonias.

### Neuroleptic-Induced Acute Akathisia

Akathisia is characterized by a subjective and objective sense of restlessness, anxiety, and agitation. Although a trial of anticholinergics or amantadine for the treatment of neuroleptic-induced acute akathisia is reasonable, those drugs are not generally considered the first drugs of choice for the syndrome. The β-adrenergic receptor antagonists and perhaps the benzodiazepines and clonidine (Catapres) are preferable as the drugs to try initially.

## PRECAUTIONS AND ADVERSE REACTIONS

The adverse effects of the anticholinergic drugs are those resulting from the blockade of muscarinic acetylcholine receptors (Table 33.3.2–2). Anticholinergic drugs should be given cautiously, if at all, to patients with prostatic hypertrophy, urinary retention, and narrow-angle glaucoma because the antimuscarinic activity exacerbates those problems. The anticholinergics are occasionally used as drugs of abuse on the street and by patients. Their abuse potential is related to their mild mood-elevating properties.

Amantadine is generally well tolerated, especially in dosages below 200 mg a day; dosages above 400 mg a day should be avoided. Amantadine is generally better tolerated than the anticholinergics, and preliminary data indicate that amantadine is associated with less memory impairment than are the anticholinergics. The most common CNS effects of amantadine are mild dizziness, insomnia, and impaired concentration, which occur in 5 to 10 percent of all patients. Irritability, depression, anxiety, and ataxia occur in 1 to 5 percent of all patients. Severe CNS adverse effects, including seizures, have been reported. Nausea is the most common peripheral adverse effect of amantadine. Livedo reticularis, usually affecting the lower extremities, is seen in a few patients who are treated with amantadine for a long time. Amantadine is relatively contraindicated in patients with renal disease and seizure disorders. Some evidence indicates that amantadine is teratogenic and, therefore, should not be given to pregnant women. Because amantadine is excreted in breast milk, women who are breast-feeding should not be given the drug. Suicide attempts with amantadine overdoses are life-threatening. The symptoms can include toxic psychoses (confusion, hallucinations, and aggressiveness) and cardiopulmonary arrest. Emergency treatment beginning with gastric lavage or the induction of emesis is indicated.

### Anticholinergic Intoxication

The most serious adverse effect associated with anticholinergic toxicity is anticholinergic intoxication, which can be characterized by delirium, coma, seizures, agita-

tion, hallucinations, severe hypotension, supraventricular tachycardia, and the usual peripheral manifestations—flushing, mydriasis, dry skin, hyperthermia, and decreased bowel sounds. Treatment should begin with the immediate discontinuation of all anticholinergic drugs. The syndrome of anticholinergic intoxication can be diagnosed and treated with physostigmine (Antilirium, Eserine), an inhibitor of anticholinesterase, 1 to 2 mg IV (1 mg every two minutes) or IM every 30 to 60 minutes, although the absorption of IM physostigmine can be erratic. The first dose should be repeated in 15 to 20 minutes if no improvement is seen. Benzodiazepines can be used to treat agitation. Treatment with physostigmine should be used only when emergency cardiac monitoring and life-support services are available, because physostigmine can lead to severe hypotension and bronchial constriction. Those effects of physostigmine can be reversed with rapid IV administration of atropine, 0.5 mg per each milligram of physostigmine administered. Physostigmine is also contraindicated in patients with unstable vital signs, asthma, or a history of cardiac abnormalities. In general, physostigmine should be used only to confirm a diagnosis of anticholinergic activity or to treat the most serious symptoms of anticholinergic intoxication—seizures, severe hypotension, and delirium.

## DRUG INTERACTIONS

The most common drug-drug interactions with the anticholinergics occur when they are coadministered with psychotropics that also have high anticholinergic activity, such as most antipsychotics, tricyclic and tetracyclic drugs, and monoamine oxidase inhibitors (MAOIs). Elderly patients may be taking other medications that may also contribute significant anticholinergic activity (Table 33.3.2–3). Many over-the-counter cold preparations also induce significant anticholinergic activity. The coadministration of those drugs can result in a life-threatening anticholinergic intoxication syndrome. Anticholinergic drugs can also delay gastric emptying, thereby decreasing the absorption of drugs that are broken down in the stomach and usually absorbed in the duodenum (for example, levodopa and antipsychotics). Coadministration of amantadine with anticholinergics may result in an increased incidence of cognitive impairment, confusion, nightmares, and psychotic symptoms (for example, hallucinations). That combination of drugs, therefore, should be used cautiously, especially in elderly patients.

In one case report, amantadine coadministered with phenelzine (Nardil) resulted in a significant increase in resting blood pressure. Because of the dopaminergic activity of amantadine, the drug may augment the stimulatory effects of CNS stimulant substances, such as cocaine and other symphomimetics (for example, amphetamine).

**Table 33.3.2–2**
**Potential Adverse Effects Caused by Blockade of Muscarinic Acetylcholine Receptors**

Blurred vision
Constipation
Decreased salivation
Decreased sweating
Delayed or retrograde ejaculation
Delirium
Exacerbation of asthma (because of decreased bronchial secretions)
Exacerbation of narrow-angle glaucoma
Hyperthermia (through decreased sweating)
Memory problems
Photophobia
Sinus tachycardia
Urinary retention

## LABORATORY INTERFERENCES

No known laboratory interferences have been associated with either anticholinergics or amantadine.

**Table 33.3.2–3**
**Anticholinergic Drug Levels in 25 Medications Ranked by the Frequency of Their Prescription for Elderly Patients**

| Medication* | Anticholinergic Drug Level (ng/mL of Atropine Equivalents)‡ |
|---|---|
| 1. Forosemide | 0.22 |
| 2. Digoxin | 0.25 |
| 3. Dyazido† | 0.08 |
| 4. Lanoxin | 0.25 |
| 5. Hydrochlorothiazide | 0.00 |
| 6. Propranolol | 0.00 |
| 7. Salicyclic acid | 0.00 |
| 8. Dipyridamole | 0.11 |
| 9. Theophylline anhydrous | 0.44 |
| 10. Nitroglycerin | 0.00 |
| 11. Insulin | 0.00 |
| 12. Warfarin | 0.12 |
| 13. Prednisolone | 0.55 |
| 14. α-Methyldopa | 0.00 |
| 15. Nifedipine | 0.22 |
| 16. Isosorbide dimitrate | 0.15 |
| 17. Ibuprofen | 0.00 |
| 18. Codeine | 0.11 |
| 19. Cimetidine | 0.86 |
| 20. Diltiazem hydrochloride | 0.00 |
| 21. Captopril | 0.02 |
| 22. Atenolol | 0.00 |
| 23. Metoprolol | 0.00 |
| 24. Timolol | 0.00 |
| 25. Ranitidine | 0.22 |

★ At a $10^8$M concentration.
† A digoxin compound.
‡ Drugs above 0.1 can contribute significant anticholinergic effects in patients.
Table from L Tune, S Carr, E Hoag, T Cooper: Anticholinergic effects of drugs commonly prescribed for the elderly: Potential means for assessing risk of delirium. Am J Psychiatry *149*: 1393, 1992. Used with permission.

**Table 33.3.2–4**
**Anticholinergic Drugs**

| Name | Tablet Size | Injectable |
|---|---|---|
| Benztropine mesylate | 0.5, 1.2 mg | 1 mg per mL. |
| Biperiden hydrochloride (tab) luctate (inj) | 2 mg | 5 mg per mL. |
| Ethopropazine hydrochloride | 10, 50 mg | -- |
| Procyclidine hydrochloride | 5 mg | |
| Trihexyphenidyl hydrochloride | 2, 5 mg elixir 2 mg per 5 mL | -- |
| Orphenadrine citrate | 100 mg | 30 mg per mL |

## DOSAGE AND ADMINISTRATION

Although the anticholinergic drugs and amantadine are the most commonly used drugs for the treatment of neuroleptic-induced parkinsonism and neuroleptic-induced acute dystonia, antihistamines and benzodiazepines are also effective. Amantadine and the six anticholinergic drugs discussed in this subsection are available in a range of preparations (Table 33.3.2–4).

### Neuroleptic-Induced Parkinsonism

In addition to the use of antiparkinsonian drugs, the treatment of neuroleptic-induced parkinsonism can involve the reduction of the antipsychotic dosage or switching to a less potent antipsychotic. Both anticholinergics and amantadine are effective, as are antihistaminergic drugs. For the treatment of neuroleptic-induced parkinsonism, the equivalent of 1 to 4 mg benztropine should be given one to four times daily. Patients usually respond to that dosage of benztropine in one or two days. When amantadine is used for the treatment of neuroleptic-induced parkinsonism, the starting dosage is usually 100 mg orally twice a day, although that dosage can be cautiously increased up to 200 mg orally twice a day if indicated. The anticholinergic drug or amantadine should be administered

for four to eight weeks; then it should be discontinued to assess whether the patient still requires the drug. Anticholinergic drugs and amantadine should be tapered over a period of one to two weeks.

Treatment with anticholinergics or amantadine as prophylaxis against the development of neuroleptic-induced parkinsonism is usually not indicated, since the symptoms of neuroleptic-induced parkinsonism are usually mild enough and gradual enough in onset to allow the clinician to initiate treatment only after it is clearly indicated. However, in young men, prophylaxis may be indicated, especially if a high-potency antipsychotic is being used. The clinician should attempt to discontinue the antiparkinsonian agent in four to six weeks to assess whether its continued use is necessary.

### Neuroleptic-Induced Acute Dystonia

Although anticholinergics are indicated for the short-term treatment and prophylaxis of neuroleptic-induced acute dystonia, amantadine is not considered effective. For the treatment of neuroleptic-induced acute dystonia, 1 to 2 mg benztropine or its equivalent in another drug should be given IM. If that dose is not effective in 20 to 30 minutes, the drug should be administered again. If the patient still does not improve in another 20 to 30 minutes, a benzodiazepine (for example, 1 mg IM or IV lorazepam) should be given. Laryngeal dystonia is a medical emergency and should be treated with benztropine, up to 4 mg in a 10-minute period, followed by 1 to 2 mg of lorazepam, administered slowly by the IV route.

Prophylaxis against dystonias is indicated in patients who have had one episode or in patients at high risk (young men taking high-potency antipsychotics). The clinician should continue prophylactic treatment for four to eight weeks and then gradually taper the drug over a period of one to two weeks to allow an assessment regarding the continued need for the prophylactic treatment. Whether prophylaxis with anticholinergics is indicated when first giving a patient an antipsychotic continues to be debated. Clinicians in favor of prophylaxis argue that patient compliance is hindered if uncomfortable neurological adverse effects occur. Clinicians opposed to prophylactic treatment cite the increased risk of anticholinergic toxicity. Studies have shown that prophylactic treatment with anticholinergic drugs does reduce the incidence of acute dystonias.

**References**

Arana G W, Goff D C, Baldessarini R J, Keepers G A: Efficacy of anticholinergic prophylaxis for neuroleptic-induced acute dystonia. Am J Psychiatry *145*: 993, 1988.

Dilsaver S C: Antimuscarinic agents as substances of abuse: A review. J Clin Psychopharmacol *8*: 14, 1988.

Fayen M, Goldman M B, Molthrop M A, Luchins D J: Differential memory function with dopaminergic versus anticholinergic treatment of drug-induced extrapyramidal symptoms. Am J Psychiatry *145*: 483, 1988.

Goff D C, Arana G W, Greenblatt D J, DuPont R, Ornsteen M J, Harmatz J S, Shader R I: The effect of benztropine on haloperidol-induced dystonia, clinical efficacy and pharmacokinetics: A prospective, double-blind trial. J Clin Psychopharmacol *11*: 106, 1991.

Johnson A L, Hollister L E, Berger P A: The anticholinergic intoxication syndrome: Diagnosis and treatment. J Clin Psychiatry *42*: 313, 1981.

Modell J G, Tandon R, Beresford T P: Dopaminergic activity of the antimuscarinic antiparkinsonian agents. J Clin Psychopharmacol *9*: 347, 1989.

Spina E, Sturiale V, Valvo S, Ancione M, Di Rosa A E, Meduri M, Caputi A P: Prevalance of acute dystonic reactions associated with neuroleptic treatment with and without anticholinergic prophylaxis. Int Clin Psychopharmacol *8*: 21, 1993.

Stenson R L, Donlon P T, Meyer J E: Comparison of benztropine mesylate and amantadine HCl in neuroleptic-induced extrapyramidal symptoms. Compr Psychiatry *17*: 763, 1976.

Tune L, Carr S, Hoag E, Cooper T: Anticholinergic effects of drugs commonly prescribed for the elderly: Potential means for assessing risk of delirium. Am J Psychiatry *149*: 1393, 1992.

Wada Y, Yamaguchi N: The rabbit syndrome and antiparkinsonian medication in schizophrenic patients. Neuropsychobiology *25*: 149, 1992.

Wells B G, Marken P A, Rickman L A, Brown C S, Hamann G, Grimmig J: Characterizing anticholinergic abuse in community mental health. J Clin Psychopharmacol *9*: 431, 1989.

# 33.3.3 / Antihistamines

A group of drugs that block the histamine type 1 ($H_1$) receptor are used in clinical psychiatry for the treatment of neuroleptic-induced parkinsonism and neuroleptic-induced acute dystonia and as hypnotics and anxiolytics. Although the drugs are generally referred to as antihistamines, another class of antihistamines that block the histamine type 2 ($H_2$) receptor—for example, cimetidine (Tagamet)—are used for the treatment of gastric ulcer. Diphenhydramine (Benadryl) is used for the treatment of neuroleptic-induced parkinsonism and neuroleptic-induced acute dystonia and sometimes as a hypnotic. Hydroxyzine hydrochloride (Atarax) and hydroxyzine pamoate (Vistaril) are used as anxiolytics. Cyproheptadine (Periactin) has been used for the treatment of inhibited male and female orgasm caused by serotonergic agents, such as fluoxetine (Prozac).

The use of antihistamines in the treatment of mental disorders began in the 1940s, when the drugs were first introduced. Histamine $H_1$ antagonists are found in a variety of over-the-counter hypnotic drugs. Because the antihis-

tamines have been in clinical use for a long time, their use in specific clinical situations has not been well-studied in well-controlled, double-blind clinical trials. Therefore, comparative data regarding the use of antihistamines are limited.

## CHEMISTRY

The molecular structures of representative antihistamines are shown in Figure 33.3.3–1.

## PHARMACOLOGICAL ACTIONS

### Pharmacokinetics

Both diphenhydramine and hydroxyzine are well-absorbed from the gastrointestinal (GI) tract. About 50 percent of diphenhydramine is metabolized in a first-pass effect by the liver, and the metabolites are excreted in the urine. The antiparkinsonian effects of intramuscular (IM) diphenhydramine have their onset in 15 to 30 minutes; the sedative effects of diphenhydramine peak in one to three hours. Hydroxyzine is also metabolized by the liver, but its metabolites are excreted in the feces. The sedative effects begin between 30 and 60

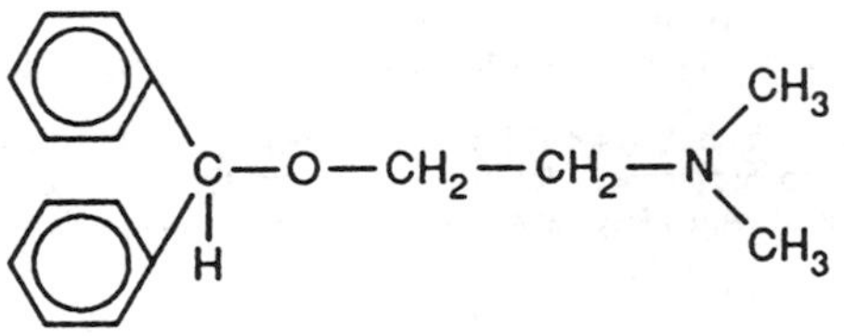

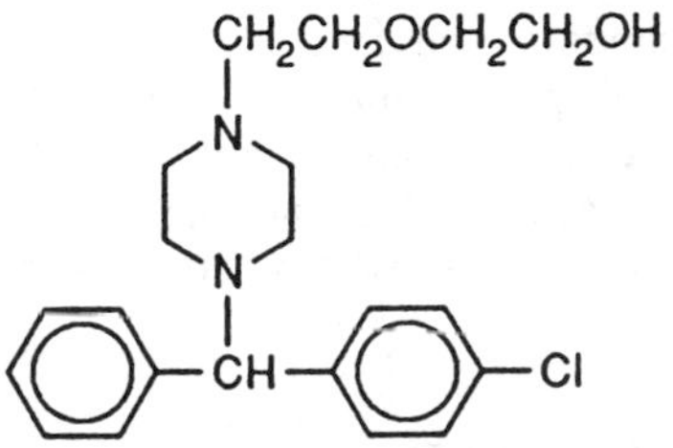

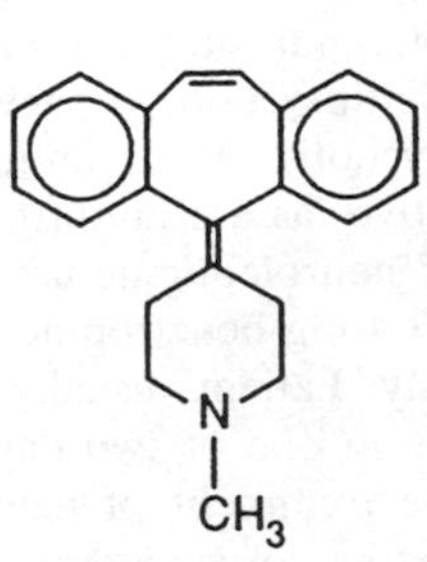

**Figure 33.3.3–1.** Molecular structures of selected antihistamines.

minutes after administration and last four to six hours. Because both drugs are metabolized in the liver, patients with hepatic disease, such as cirrhosis, may attain high plasma concentrations with long-term administration. Cyproheptadine is well-absorbed after oral administration, and its metabolites are excreted in the urine.

## Pharmacodynamics

All the drugs share the blockade of $H_1$ receptors as a common mechanism of action. However, diphenhydramine and hydroxyzine also possess some antimuscarinic cholinergic activity. Cyproheptadine is unique among the drugs, since it has potent activity both as a serotonin antagonist and as a histamine antagonist.

## EFFECTS ON SPECIFIC ORGANS AND SYSTEMS

The central nervous system (CNS) effects of the antihistamines include sedation and antagonism of dopamine type 2 ($D_2$) receptor blockade-induced movement disorders. The antihistamines may also reduce the symptoms of motion sickness in some patients. The peripheral effects of the antihistamines are mediated by the autonomic nervous system and include effects on the respiratory system (for example, bronchodilatation) and the cardiovascular system (for example, tachycardia).

## THERAPEUTIC INDICATIONS

The most justified indication for the use of the antihistamines is as a treatment for neuroleptic-induced parkinsonism and neuroleptic-induced acute dystonia. The use of cyproheptadine for impaired orgasms is also reasonable. The availability of carefully investigated drugs (for example, benzodiazepines) for use as hypnotics and anxiolytics makes the routine use of antihistamines for those indications a questionable practice.

### Neuroleptic-Induced Parkinsonism and Neuroleptic-Induced Acute Dystonia

The use of diphenhydramine is a reasonable alternative to anticholinergics and amantadine for neuroleptic-induced parkinsonism and neuroleptic-induced acute dystonia, especially in patients who are particularly sensitive to the adverse effects of the other drugs.

### Hypnotic and Anxiolytic Applications

The antihistamines are relatively safe hypnotics, but they are not superior to the benzodiazepines, which are a much-better-studied class of drugs in terms of efficacy and safety. The antihistamines have not been proved to be effective as long-term anxiolytic therapy; therefore, either the benzodiazepines or buspirone (BuSpar) is preferable for such treatment.

### Other Indications

A number of case reports have asserted that cyproheptadine (4 to 8 mg before coitus) is efficacious in the treatment of abnormal orgasm, especially abnormal orgasm resulting from treatment with serotonergic drugs (for example, fluoxetine). A number of case reports and small studies have also reported that cyproheptadine may be of some use in the treatment of eating disorders, such as anorexia nervosa.

## PRECAUTIONS AND ADVERSE REACTIONS

Antihistamines are commonly associated with sedation, dizziness, and hypotension, all of which can be severe in elderly patients, who are also likely to suffer from the anticholinergic effects of those drugs. Paradoxical excitement and agitation is an adverse effect that is seen in a small proportion of patients. Poor motor coordination can result in accidents; therefore, patients should be warned about driving and operating dangerous machinery. Other common adverse effects include epigastric distress, nausea, vomiting, diarrhea, and constipation. Because of the drugs' mild anticholinergic activity, some patients experience dry mouth, urinary retention, blurred vision, and constipation. The use of cyproheptadine in some patients has been associated with weight gain, which may contribute to its reported efficacy in some patients with anorexia nervosa.

In addition to the above adverse effects, antihistamines have some potential for abuse by susceptible patients. The coadministration of antihistamines and opioids can increase the rush experienced by persons with substance dependence. Also, overdoses of antihistamines can be fatal. Antihistamines are excreted in breast milk, so their use should be avoided by nursing mothers. Because of some potential for teratogenicity, the use of antihistamines should also be avoided by pregnant women.

## DRUG INTERACTIONS

The sedative property of antihistamines can be additive with other CNS depressants, such as alcohol, other sedative-hypnotic drugs, and many psychotropic drugs, including tricyclic drugs and monoamine oxidase inhibitors. The anticholinergic activity can also be additive with other drugs producing anticholinergic effects, sometimes resulting in severe anticholinergic symptoms or intoxication.

## LABORATORY INTERFERENCES

Hydroxyzine has been reported to falsely elevate the values of urinary 17-hydroxycorticosteroids when assayed

**Table 33.3.3–1**
**Antihistamine Preparations**

| | Tablets (mg) | Capsules (mg) | Elixir[1] (mg/5 mL) | Solution[2] (mg/5 mL) | Parenteral (mg/mL) | Suspension[3] (mg/5 mL) |
|---|---|---|---|---|---|---|
| Diphenhydramine | 25, 50 | 25, 50 | 12.5 | 8.3, 12.5 | 10, 50 | — |
| Hydroxyzine | 10, 25, 50, 100 | 25, 50, 100 | — | 10 | 25, 50 | 25 |
| Cyproheptadine | 4 | — | — | 2 | — | — |

1—A sweetened hydroalcoholic liquid intended for oral use.
2—A drug incorporated into an aqueous or alcoholic solution.
3—Undissolved drug dispersed in a liquid for oral or parenteral use.

with either the Porter-Silber chromogens test or the Glenn-Nelson test.

## DOSAGE AND ADMINISTRATION

The antihistamines are available in a variety of preparations (Table 33.3.3–1). Diphenhydramine is used in the short-term and the long-term treatment of neuroleptic-induced parkinsonism and neuroleptic-induced acute dystonia. When the drug is used for intramuscular (IM) injections, it should be given deep, since superficial administration can cause local irritation. Short-term intravenous (IV) administration of 25 to 50 mg is an effective treatment for neuroleptic-induced acute dystonia. Treatment with 25 mg three times a day—up to 50 mg four times a day if necessary—can be used to treat neuroleptic-induced parkinsonism, akinesia, and rabbit syndrome. When used as a hypnotic, doses of 50 mg are recommended, since doses of 100 mg have not been shown to be superior to 50 mg.

Hydroxyzine is most commonly used as a short-term anxiolytic, although the data supporting that indication are limited. Dosages of 50 to 100 mg orally four times a day for long-term treatment or 50 to 100 mg every four to six hours for short-term treatment are usually recommended. However, recent studies have indicated that 150 mg a day is ineffective as an anxiolytic, although 400 mg a day may be as effective as chlordiazepoxide (Librium). Other studies have indicated that hydroxyzine is not useful as an anxiolytic in children and that it should be used for that indication with some caution.

### References

Avorn J, Soumerai S B, Everitt D E, Ross-Degnan D, Beers M H, Sherman D, Salem-Schatz S R, Fields D: A randomized trial of a program to reduce the use of psychoactive drugs in nursing homes. N Engl J Med *327*: 168, 1992.
Carruthers S G, Shoeman D W, Hignite C E, Azarnoff D L: Correlation between plasma diphenhydramine level and sedative and antihistamine effects. Clin Pharmacol Ther *23*: 375, 1978.
Gengo F M, Gabos C, Mechtler L: Quantitative effects of diphenhydramine on mental performance measured using an automobile driving simulator. Ann Allergy *64*: 520, 1990.
Goldbloom D S, Kennedy S H: Adverse interaction of fluoxetine and cyproheptadine in two patients with bulimia nervosa. J Clin Psychiatry *52*: 261, 1991.
Kutcher S P, Reiter S, Gardner D M, Klein R G: The pharmacotherapy of anxiety disorders in children and adolescents. Psychiatr Clin North Am *15*: 41, 1992.

# 33.3.4 / Barbiturates and Similarly Acting Drugs

## BARBITURATES

The barbiturates were first introduced into clinical psychiatry in 1903 and were the sedative-hypnotic drugs of first choice until chlordiazepoxide (Librium) and other benzodiazepines were introduced in the early 1960s. The introduction of the benzodiazepines and other anxiolytics—for example, buspirone (BuSpar)—and hypnotics—for example, zolpidem (Ambien)—has practically eliminated the use of the barbiturates and other prebenzodiazepine-era compounds—for example, meprobamate (Miltown)—because of the lower abuse potential, higher therapeutic index, and lack of hepatic enzyme induction by the new compounds.

### Chemistry

The various clinically available barbiturates are derived from the same barbituric acid substrate and differ primarily in their substitutions at the $C_5$ position of the parent molecule (Figure 33.3.4–1). Those $C_5$ molecular substitutions are the primary basis for the differing lipid solubilities and half-lives of the various resulting molecules.

### Pharmacological Actions

**Pharmacokinetics.** The barbiturates vary in their degree of absorption after oral administration, and their absorption is delayed when taken with food. The binding of the barbiturates to plasma proteins ranges from 20 to 70 percent, and their degree of lipid solubility varies, although all are lipophilic enough to cross the blood-brain barrier. The barbiturates are metabolized by the hepatic microsomal enzyme (P450) system, and the metabolites are largely excreted by the kidneys. Barbiturates are associated with an induction of hepatic enzymes, thereby reducing the levels of both the barbiturates and other concurrently administered drugs that are also metabolized by the liver. The half-lives of the various barbiturates range from

| Barbiturate | $R_{5a}$ | $R_{5b}$ |
|---|---|---|
| Amobarbital | Ethyl | Isopentyl |
| Aprobarbital | Allyl | Isopropyl |
| Butabarbital | Ethyl | *Sec*-Butyl |
| Butalbital | Allyl | Isobutyl |
| Mephobarbital* | Ethyl | Phenyl |
| Metharbital* | Ethyl | Ethyl |
| Methohexital* | Allyl | 1-Methyl-2-Pentynyl |
| Pentobarbital | Ethyl | 1-Methylbutyl |
| Phenobarbital | Ethyl | Phenyl |
| Secobarbital | Allyl | 1-Methylbutyl |
| Talbutal | Allyl | *Sec*-Butyl |
| Thiamylal[†] | Allyl | 1-Methylbutyl |
| Thiopental[†] | Ethyl | 1-Methylbutyl |

*$R_3$ = $H_1$ except in mephobarbital, metharbital, and methohexital, where it is replaced by $CH_3$.

[†]O, except in thiamylal and thiopental, where it is replaced by S. (Figure from T W Rall: Hypnotics and sedatives: Ethanol. In *Goodman and Gilman's The Pharmacological Basis of Therapeutics*, ed 8, A Goodman Gilman, T W Rall, A S Nies, P Taylor, editors, p 358. McGraw-Hill, New York, 1990. Used with permission.)

General Formula:

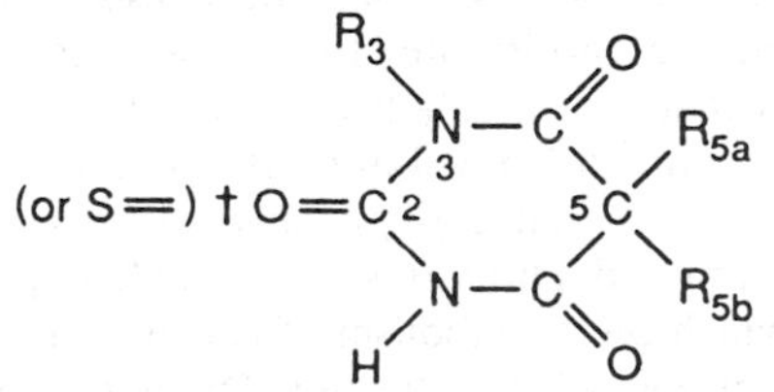

**Figure 33.3.4–1.** Molecular structures and names of barbiturates currently available in the United States.

1 to 120 hours. Increasing age, hepatic disease, and renal disease (in the case of phenobarbital [Luminal]) can be associated with an increase in the half-lives of barbiturates.

**Pharmacodynamics.** The mechanism of action for the barbiturates appears to involve the γ-aminobutyric acid (GABA) receptor-benzodiazepine receptor-chloride ion channel complex. Current data are consistent with the hypothesis that barbiturates enhance the activity of GABA on the $GABA_A$ receptor complex, thus increasing the inhibitory actions of that neurotransmitter. Some preliminary data indicate that barbiturates may inhibit the entry of calcium ions into presynaptic nerve terminals, thus potentially reducing neurotransmitter release.

## Effects on Specific Organs and Systems

The barbiturates have their major effects on the central nervous system (CNS), although significant effects also occur in the liver and can occur in the cardiovascular system. Within the CNS, barbiturates are associated with the inhibition of the reticular activating system, resulting in respiratory depression, which can be additive with other respiratory depressants (for example, alcohol). Within the liver, barbiturate use can cause a twofold induction of metabolic liver enzymes, thus causing a lowering of the plasma levels of both the barbiturates and other drugs metabolized in the liver. Although at low dosages barbiturates have a relatively safe cardiovascular profile, at high dosages they may impair cardiac contractility or result in

cardiac arrhythmias. Barbiturate administration rarely causes potentially fatal laryngospasm, a potential adverse event that may guide the clinician to use benzodiazepines, rather than barbiturates, in most situations (for example, drug-assisted interviewing).

## Therapeutic Indications

All the barbiturates were approved by the Food and Drug Administration (FDA) before the current rigorous guidelines for drug approval were instituted. Therefore, the FDA-approved indications for those drugs should be viewed with some caution. Nevertheless, the FDA has approved the use of amobarbital (Amytal), aprobarbital (Alurate), butabarbital (Butisol), mephobarbital (Mebaral), pentobarbital (Nembutal), phenobarbital, and secobarbital (Seconal) for the treatment of anxiety and apprehension. However, there have been no carefully conducted clinical trials of those agents for diagnoses of anxiety specified by the revised third edition of *Diagnostic and Statistical Manual of Mental Disorders* (DSM-III-R) or the fourth edition (DSM-IV). The FDA has approved the use of amobarbital, aprobarbital, butabarbital, pentobarbital, phenobarbital, and secobarbital for the treatment of insomnia. Methohexital (Brevital) is aproved for use as an anesthetic agent for electroconvulsive therapy (ECT), and amobarbital is approved for use in narcoanalysis, which includes the concept of drug-assisted interviewing.

Although the FDA guidelines approve of the wide application of the barbiturates, the availability of newer, safer, better-studied drugs reduced the number of reasonable applications of the barbiturates to nine circumstances: (1) Amobarbital (50–250 mg intramuscular [IM]) may be used in emergency settings to control agitation. However, the use of IM lorazepam (Ativan) or intravenous (IV) diazepam (Valium) is replacing that usage because of the risk of laryngospasm and respiratory depression associated with the barbiturates. (2) Amobarbital interviews are sometimes used for diagnostic purposes. However, several studies have reported that other sedative drugs, particularly the benzodiazepines, are as effective as the barbiturates. (3) Several reports indicate that barbiturates can activate some catatonic patients, although benzodiazepines may also have that effect. (4) Barbiturate use may be indicated for patients who have serious adverse effects associated with the use of benzodiazepines or buspirone. (5) Some patients who do not respond adequately to benzodiazepines or buspirone may respond to barbiturates. (6) Some patients, particularly elderly patients, may have received barbiturates in the past and may insist on taking barbiturates currently, rather than switching to a benzodiazepine or buspirone. (7) Methohexital is a safe and effective anesthetic agent to use during ECT. (8) The pentobarbital challenge test (Table 33.3.4–1) is a safe and effective way to assess the degree of CNS tolerance for barbiturates once a patient's period of initial barbiturate intoxication has resolved. That test is particularly useful when the patient's history regarding the previously used daily dosage of barbiturates is unreliable. (9) Phenobarbital is the barbiturate of choice to be used when detoxifying a patient from barbiturate dependence.

**Table 33.3.4–1**
**Pentobarbital Challenge Test**

1. Give pentobarbital 200 mg orally.
2. Observe for intoxication after one hour (e.g., sleepiness, slurred speech, or nystagmus).
3. If patient is not intoxicated, give another 100 mg of pentobarbital every two hours (maximum 500 mg over six hours).
4. Total dose given to produce mild intoxication is equivalent to daily abuse level of barbiturates.
5. Substitute phenobarbital 30 mg (longer half-life) for each 100 mg of pentobarbital.
6. Decrease by about 10 percent a day.
7. Adjust rate if signs of intoxication or withdrawal are present.

## Precautions and Adverse Reactions

Some of the adverse effects of the barbiturates are similar to those of the benzodiazepines, including paradoxical dysphoria, hyperactivity, and cognitive disorganization. Rare side effects associated with barbiturate use include the development of Stevens-Johnson syndrome (exfoliative dermatitis), megaloblastic anemia, and osteopenia.

A major difference between the barbiturates and the benzodiazepines is the low therapeutic index of the barbiturates, an overdose of which can easily prove fatal. In addition to narrow therapeutic indexes, the barbiturates are associated with a significant risk of abuse potential and the development of tolerance and dependence. That increased risk is reflected by the fact that the Drug Enforcement Agency (DEA) has classified most of the barbiturates as schedule II drugs; the benzodiazepines are classified as schedule IV drugs. Barbiturate intoxication is manifested by confusion, drowsiness, irritability, hyporeflexia or areflexia, ataxia, and nystagmus. The symptoms of barbiturate withdrawal are similar to those of benzodiazepine withdrawal but are more marked.

Because of some evidence of teratogenicity, barbiturates should not be used by pregnant women or nursing women. Barbiturates should be used with caution in patients with a history of substance abuse, depression, diabetes, hepatic impairment, renal disease, severe anemia, pain, hyperthyroidism, or hypoadrenalism. Barbiturates are also contraindicated in patients with acute intermittent porphyria, impaired respiratory drive, or limited respiratory reserve.

## Drug Interactions

The primary area for concern regarding drug interactions is the potentially additive effects of respiratory depression. Barbiturates should be used with great caution with other prescribed CNS drugs (including antipsychotic and antidepressant drugs) and nonprescribed CNS agents (for example, alcohol). Caution must also be exercised when prescribing barbiturates to patients who are taking other drugs that are metabolized in the liver, especially cardiac drugs and anticonvulsants. Because individual patients have a wide range of sensitivities to barbiturate-induced enzyme induction, it is not possible to predict the degree to which the metabolism of concurrently administered medications will be affected. Drugs that may have their metabolism enhanced by barbiturate administration include narcotic analgesics, antiarrhythmic agents, antibiotics, anticoagulants, anticonvulsants, antidepressants, β-adrenergic receptor antagonists, contraceptives, and immunosuppressants.

**Table 33.3.4–2**
**Selected Barbiturates**

| Generic Name | DEA Control Level | Trade Name | Half-Life (hrs) | Sedative Adult Dosage Range (mg per day) | Sedative Adult Single Dose Range (mg) | Hypnotic Dose Range (mg) |
|---|---|---|---|---|---|---|
| Amobarbital | II | Amytal | 8–42 | 65–400 | 65–100 | 100–200 |
| Butabarbital | III | Butisol | 34–42 | 15–120 | 15–30 | 50–100 |
| Mephobarbital | IV | Mebaral | 11–67 | 32–400 | 32–100 | — |
| Pentobarbital | II | Nembutal | 15–48 | 32–120 | 30–40 | 100–200 |
| Phenobarbital | IV | Luminal | 80–120 | 15–600 | 15–60 | 100–200 |
| Secobarbital | II | Seconal | 15–40 | — | — | 100–300 |

**Table 33.3.4–3**
**Barbiturate Preparations**

| | Tablets | Capsules | Elixir | Parenteral | Rectal Suppositories |
|---|---|---|---|---|---|
| Amobarbital | 30 mg | 200 mg | — | 250, 500 mg | — |
| Butabarbital | 15, 30, 50, 100 mg | — | 30 mg/5 L, 33.3 mg/5mL | — | — |
| Mephobarbital | 32, 50, 100 mg | — | — | — | — |
| Pentobarbital | — | 50, 100 mg | 18.2 mg/5 mL | 50 mg/mL | 30, 60, 120, 200 mg |
| Phenobarbital | 15, 16, 30, 32, 60, 65, 100 mg | 16 mg | 15 mg/5 mL, 20 mg/5 mL | 30 mg/mL, 60 mg/mL, 65 mg/mL, 130 mg/mL | — |
| Secobarbital | — | 50, 100 mg | — | 50 mg/mL | — |

## Laboratory Interferences

No known laboratory interferences are associated with the administration of barbiturates.

## Dosage and Administration

The dosages of barbiturates vary (Table 33.3.4–2), and treatment should begin with low dosages that are increased to achieve a clinical effect. Children and the elderly are more sensitive than are young adults to the effects of the barbiturates. The most commonly used barbiturates are available in a variety of dose forms (Table 33.3.4–3). Barbiturates with half-lives in the 15-to-40-hour range are preferable, because long–acting drugs tend to accumulate in the body. The clinician should clearly instruct the patient about the adverse effects and the potential for dependence associated with barbiturates.

Although plasma levels of barbiturates are rarely necessary in psychiatry, plasma monitoring of phenobarbital levels is standard practice when the drug is used as an anticonvulsant. The therapeutic blood concentrations for phenobarbital in that indication range from 15 to 40 mg/L, although some patients may experience significant adverse effects within that range.

## OTHER SEDATIVE-HYPNOTICS

Four other classes of drugs—carbamates, piperidinediones, cyclic ethers, and tertiary carbinols—are still available for use as sedatives and hypnotics (Figure 33.3.4–2). Those drugs are even more rarely used than are barbiturates, because of their high abuse potential and additional toxic effects.

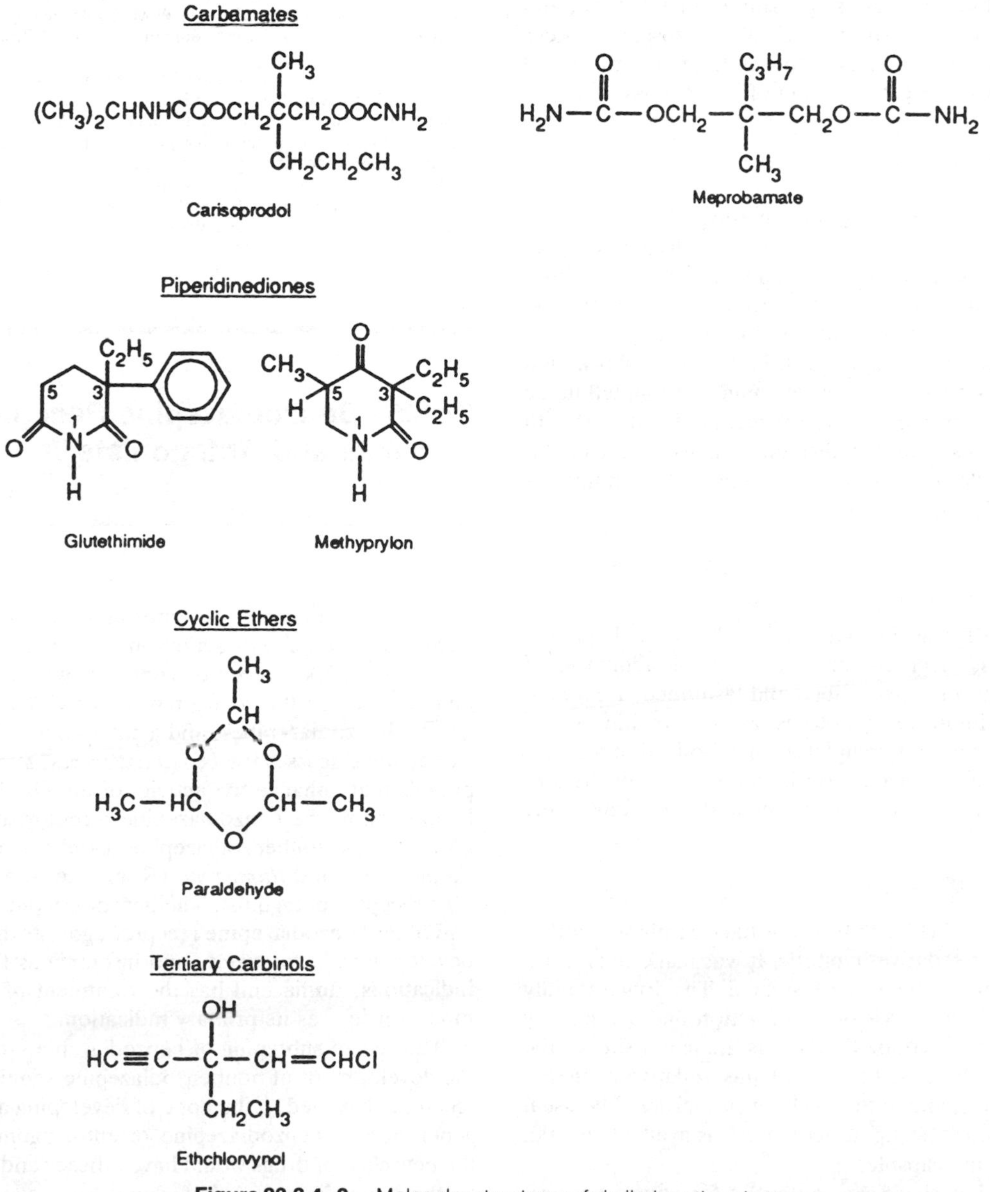

**Figure 33.3.4–2.** Molecular structures of similarly acting drugs.

## Carbamates

Meprobamate (Miltown, Equanil), ethinamate (Valmid), and carisoprodol (Soma) are carbamates that are effective as anxiolytics, sedatives, hypnotics, and muscle relaxants. Those drugs have a lower therapeutic index and a higher abuse potential than do the benzodiazepines, and their use is indicated only if the previously described drugs are not options. The carbamates have even more abuse potential and may be more dependence-inducing than the barbiturates.

The usual dosage of meprobamate is 400 mg, three or four times daily. Meprobamate is available in 200, 400, and 600 mg tablets and 200 and 400 mg extended-release capsules. Drowsiness is a common adverse effect, and patients should be warned about the additive effects of sedative drugs. Sudden withdrawal may cause anxiety, restlessness, weakness, delirium, and seizures. Adverse effects can include urticarial or erythematous rashes, anaphylactoid and other allergic reactions, angioneurotic edema, dermatitis, blood dyscrasias, gastrointestinal distress, and extraocular muscular paralysis. Fatal overdoses can occur with meprobamate in doses as low as 12 grams (thirty 400 mg tablets) without the ingestion of other sedatives.

## Piperidinediones

Glutethimide (Doriden) and methyprylon (Noludar) are piperidinediones that are effective as hypnotics, sedatives, and anxiolytics but are even more subject to abuse and more lethal in overdose than are the barbiturates and carbamates. Glutethimide has a slow and unpredictable absorption after oral administration. Seizures, shock, and anticholinergic toxicity are more common in glutethimide overdoses than in barbiturate overdoses. Treatment with piperidinediones is rarely indicated. The usual dose of glutethimide is 250 to 500 mg at bedtime. Glutethimide is available in 500 mg tablets.

## Cyclic Ethers

Paraldehyde was introduced in 1882 as a hypnotic. When 5 mL is given IM or 5 to 10 mL is administered orally, it is an effective, albeit old-fashioned, treatment for alcohol withdrawal symptoms, anxiety, and insomnia. Paraldehyde is almost completely metabolized, but its excretion in unmetabolized form by the lungs limits its usefulness because of its offensive taste and ubiquitous odor.

## Tertiary Carbinols

Ethchlorvynol (Placidyl) is a tertiary carbinol, another nonbarbiturate sedative-hypnotic. It was marketed for use as a short-term treatment for insomnia. The drug is rapidly absorbed and has a fast onset of action and a relatively short duration of action. The liver is the major site for the drug's metabolism. Ethchlorvynol has sedative-hypnotic, muscle relaxant, and anticonvulsant properties. The usual hypnotic dose is 500 mg at bedtime. It is available in 200, 500, and 750 mg capsules.

The drug has significant potential for abuse, physical

dependence, and tolerance. It is particularly dangerous in overdose. The lethal dose range is 10 to 25 grams, although death has been reported as low as 3 grams. There is little to recommend the drug, especially in view of the much safer alternatives that are available. It is cross-tolerant with other sedative-hypnotics, and detoxification can be achieved with barbiturates by using the pentobarbital challenge test (Table 33.3.4–1) to establish an appropriate dose of barbiturates.

### References

Ator N A, Griffiths R R: Self-administration of barbiturates and benzodiazepines: A review. Pharmacol Biochem Behav 27: 391, 1987.
Berger F M: The similarities and differences between meprobamate and barbiturates. Clin Pharmacol Ther 4: 209, 1963.
Goodman R A, Mercy J A, Rosenberg M L: Drug use and interpersonal violence: Barbiturates detected in homicide victims. Am J Epidemiol 124: 851, 1986.
Harris R A: Distinct actions of alcohols, barbiturates and benzodiazepines on GABA-activated chloride channels. Alcohol 7: 273, 1990.
Jensen C F, Cowley D S, Walker R D: Drug preferences of alcoholic polydrug abusers with and without panic. J Clin Psychiatry 51: 189, 1990.
McCall W V, Shelp F E, McDonald W M: Controlled investigation of the amobarbital interview for catatonic mutism. Am J Psychiatry 149: 202, 1992.
Sullivan J T, Sellers E M: Treatment of the barbiturate abstinence syndrome. Med J Aust 145: 456, 1986.
Taberber P V: The GABA system in functional tolerance and dependence following barbiturates, benzodiazepines, or ethanol: Correlation or causality? Comp Biochem Physiol 93: 241, 1989.
Yu S, Ho I K: Effects of acute barbiturate administration, tolerance and dependence on brain GABA system: Comparison to alcohol and benzodiazepines. Alcohol 7: 261, 1990.

## 33.3.5 / Benzodiazepine Receptor Agonists and Antagonists

The benzodiazepine receptor agonists and antagonists have a common site of action on the γ-aminobutyric acid type A (GABA$_A$) receptor complex, which consists of a binding site for the neurotransmitter GABA, a binding site for benzodiazepines, and a chloride ion channel. This subsection discusses the *benzodiazepines*, a group of compounds that enhance the activity of the GABA$_A$ receptor by binding to the benzodiazepine receptor site; *zolpidem* (Ambien), a nonbenzodiazepine agonist at the benzodiazepine site; and *flumazenil* (Romazicon), a benzodiazepine receptor antagonist. The benzodiazepines, zolpidem, and other benzodiazepine receptor agonists that are under development have anxiety and insomnia as their primary indications; flumazenil has the treatment of benzodiazepine overdose as its primary indication.

The recent subtyping of benzodiazepine receptors and the development of nonbenzodiazepine agonists for those receptors have led to the hope of developing an even safer generation of benzodiazepine receptor agonists. Ideally, the new class of drugs would have efficacy and safety equal to the benzodiazepines but would have even less abuse potential and less rebound anxiety or insomnia. Zolpidem is the first nonbenzodiazepine benzodiazepine receptor agonist available in the United States, and preliminary data indicate that it may have some limited benefits over some of the benzodiazepine hypnotics. Because benzodiazepines can be fatal in overdoses when combined with other central nervous system (CNS) depressants, the introduction of flumazenil has greatly improved the ability of physicians to treat such a medical emergency.

## BENZODIAZEPINES

The benzodiazepine-type benzodiazepine receptor agonists are commonly referred to simply as the benzodiazepines. Benzodiazepines are also variously referred to as antianxiety agents, anxiolytics, and minor tranquilizers. All those terms are misleading, since the benzodiazepines have multiple nonanxiety-related indications. Furthermore, the use of the term "minor tranquilizer" may cause confusion between this class of drugs and the major tranquilizers, another faulty but commonly used term for the antipsychotic drugs.

Benzodiazepines are sometimes classified as sedative-hypnotics, although other drugs can also be classified in that group (for example, barbiturates). A *sedative drug* reduces daytime anxiety, tempers excessive excitement, and generally quiets or calms the patient. Although a distinction is sometimes drawn between sedatives and anxiolytics, stating that sedatives treat less pathological conditions than do anxiolytics, that is a poorly defined distinction that should be avoided. A *hypnotic drug* is one that produces drowsiness and facilitates the onset and the maintenance of sleep. In general, benzodiazepines act as hypnotics in high doses and as anxiolytics or sedatives in low doses.

In addition to their use as sedatives and hypnotics, some benzodiazepines are useful in other psychiatric indications, including panic disorder, phobias, and agitation associated with bipolar I disorder. In addition, the benzodiazepines are used as anesthetics, anticonvulsants, and muscle relaxants.

The benzodiazepines have become the sedative-hypnotic drugs of first choice because they have a higher therapeutic index and significantly less abuse potential than do many of the other sedative hypnotics (for example, barbiturates). One exception is buspirone (BuSpar), which is also a safe and effective anxiolytic drug.

### Chemistry

The benzodiazepine nucleus consists of a benzene ring fused to the seven-sided diazepine ring (Figure 33.3.5–1). All clinically important benzodiazepines also have a second benzene ring attached to the carbon atom at position 5 on the diazepine ring (Table 33.3.5–1). The benzodiazepines can be classified according to the substitution on the diazepine ring. The 2-keto benzodiazepines have a keto group off the carbon atom in position 2 on the diazepine ring. Although chlordiazepoxide (Librium) has a different substitution at the $C_2$ site, a -$NHCH_3$ group, it is useful to classify it along with the 2-keto derivatives. The 3-hydroxy benzodiazepines have a hy-

droxy (OH) group on the carbon atom at position 3 of the diazepine ring. The triazolo benzodiazepines have a triazolo ring fused to the nitrogen atom at position 1 and to the carbon atom at position 2 of the diazepine ring. Although clonazepam (Klonopin) has a 2-keto group, it is classified separately as a nitroderivative because of the nitrous group ($NO_2$) off the benzene ring. Quazepam (Doral) is also classified separately as a 2-thione derivative because of the sulfur atom at the $C_2$ site of the diazepine ring.

### Pharmacological Actions

**Pharmacokinetics.** With the exception of clorazepate (Tranxene), all the benzodiazepines are completely absorbed unchanged from the gastrointestinal (GI) tract. Clorazepate is converted to desmethyldiazepam in the GI tract and is absorbed in that form. Absorption, the attainment of peak levels, and the onset of action are quickest for diazepam (Valium), lorazepam (Ativan), alprazolam (Xanax), triazolam (Halcion), and estazolam (ProSom). The rapid onset of effects is important to patients who take a single dose of a benzodiazepine to calm an episodic burst of anxiety or to fall asleep rapidly. The drugs' rapid onset of effects can be partly attributed to their high lipid solubility, a characteristic that varies fivefold among the benzodiazepines. The range of time to peak plasma level is one to three hours, although prazepam (Centrax) may take up to six hours. There may also be a secondary peak plasma level at 6 to 10 hours because of enterohepatic recirculation. Although several benzodiazepines are available in parenteral forms for intramuscular (IM) administration, only lorazepam has rapid and reliable absorption from that route, a fact that is behind the gradual replacement of intravenous (IV) diazepam by IM lorazepam in psychiatric emergency settings.

The metabolism of the benzodiazepines differs for the drugs' various classes. Chlordiazepoxide is metabolized to diazepam, then to desmethyldiazepam (nordiazepam), then to oxazepam, and finally to a glucuronide form; all those metabolites have some degree of agonist activity at the benzodiazepine receptor. Diazepam, clorazepate, prazepam, and halazepam (Paxipam) are metabolized first to desmethyldiazepam and then follow the same route as chlordiazepoxide takes. Flurazepam (Dalmane) follows similar biochemical steps. As a result of the slow metabolism of desmethyldiazepam, all the 2-keto benzodiazepines have plasma half-lives of 30 to more than 100 hours and are, therefore, the longest-acting benzodiazepines. The plasma half life can be as high as 200 hours in persons who are genetically slow metabolizers of those compounds. Quazepam, a 2-thione benzodiazepine, follows the same metabolic pathway as 2-keto benzodiazepines and, thus, has metabolites with long half-lives. Because the attainment of steady-state plasma levels of the drugs can take up to two weeks, patients may experience symptoms and signs of toxicity after only 7 to 10 days of treatment with a dosage that may have seemed to be in the therapeutic range at the initiation of treatment.

The 3-hydroxy benzodiazepines have short half lives (10 to 30 hours) because they are directly metabolized by glucuronidation and, thus, have no active metabolites. The triazolo benzodiazepines are hydroxylated before they undergo glucuronidation. Alprazolam has a half-life of 10 to 15 hours; estazolam has a half-life of 10 to 24 hours; and triazolam has the shortest half-life (two to three hours) of all the orally administered benzodiazepines.

Midazolam (Versed), an imidazobenzodiazepine, is available only in an injectable form. It is used for sedation during medical procedures and has no clinical use in psychiatry. It

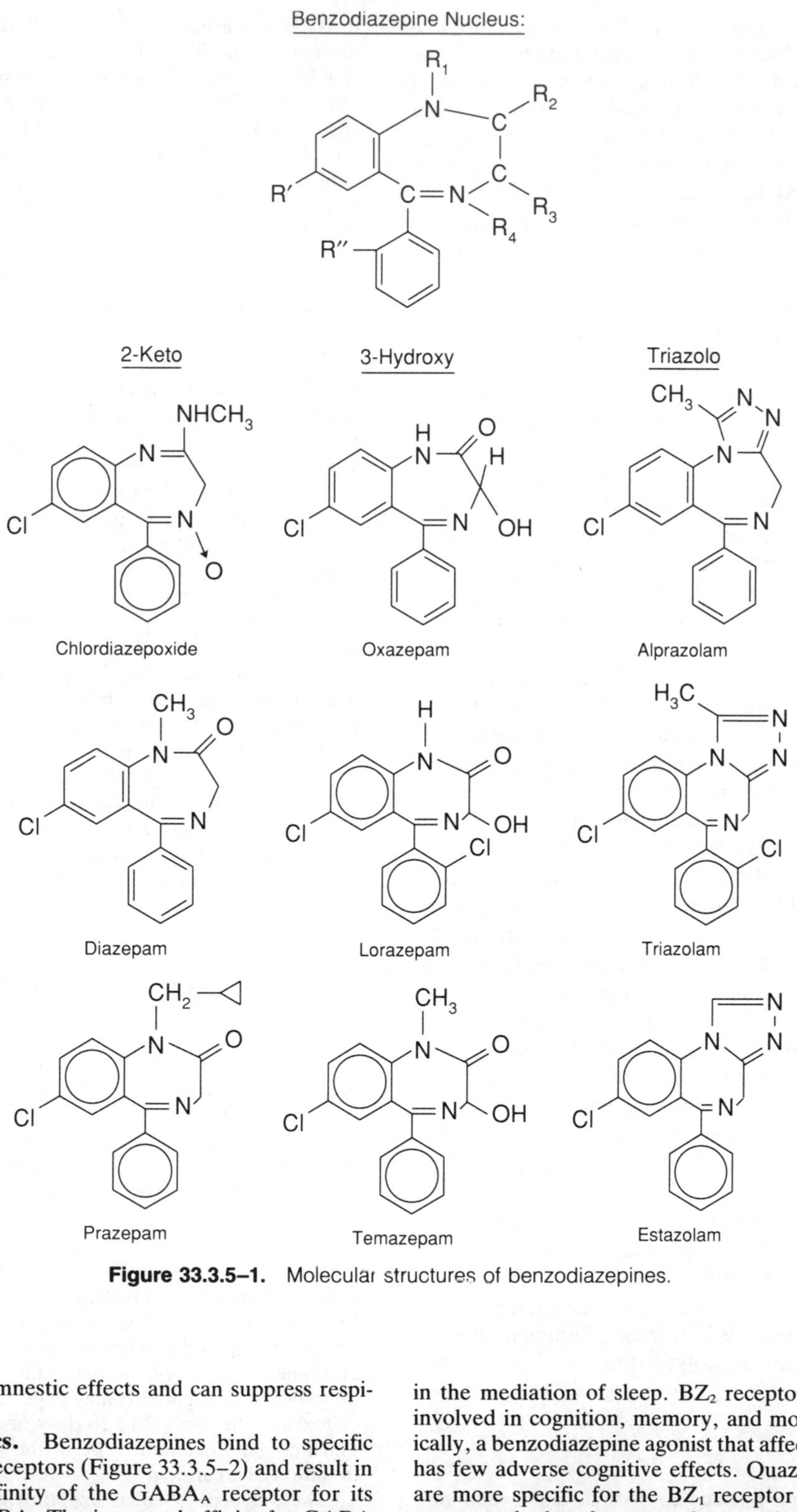

Benzodiazepine Nucleus:

**Figure 33.3.5–1.** Molecular structures of benzodiazepines.

produces significant amnestic effects and can suppress respiration.

**Pharmacodynamics.** Benzodiazepines bind to specific sites on the GABA$_A$ receptors (Figure 33.3.5–2) and result in an increase in the affinity of the GABA$_A$ receptor for its neurotransmitter, GABA. The increased affinity for GABA results in sustained activation of the ion channel and, thus, the passage of increased chloride ions into the neuron. One preliminary study of the other effects of alprazolam reported a global decrease in cerebral blood flow and decreases in plasma epinephrine concentrations. Recently, basic neuroscience research has found evidence for two subtypes of CNS benzodiazepine (BZ) receptors (also called omega receptors)—BZ$_1$ (also called omega$_1$) receptors and BZ$_2$ (also called omega$_2$) receptors. BZ$_1$ receptors are believed to be involved

in the mediation of sleep. BZ$_2$ receptors are believed to be involved in cognition, memory, and motor control. Theoretically, a benzodiazepine agonist that affects only BZ$_1$ receptors has few adverse cognitive effects. Quazepam and halazepam are more specific for the BZ$_1$ receptor than for the BZ$_2$ receptor and, therefore, may be associated with less amnesia and other cognitive impairments than are other currently available benzodiazepines.

## Effects on Specific Organs and Systems

In addition to the CNS effects on anxiety and sleep, the benzodiazepines are effective anticonvulsants. In addition to those CNS effects, benzodiazepines are effective

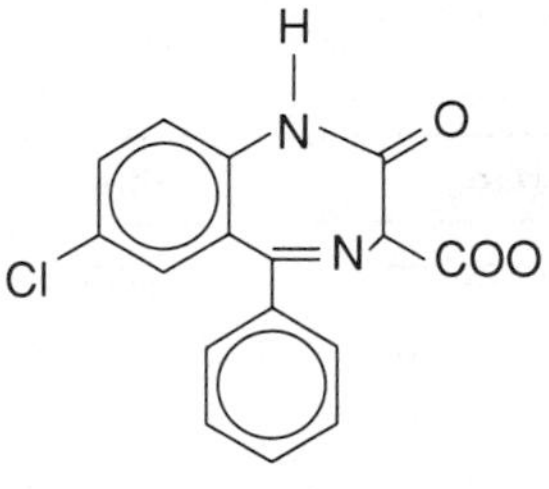

Clorazepate

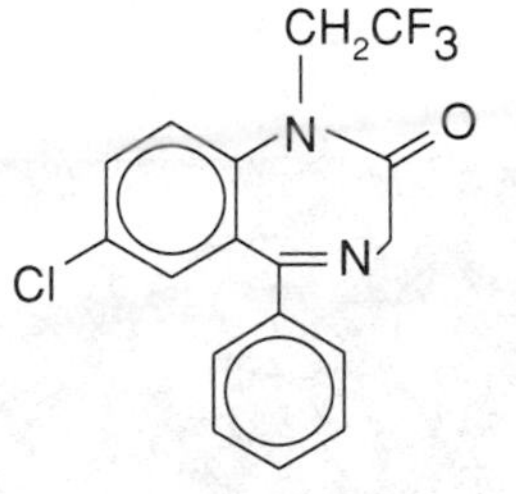

Halazepam

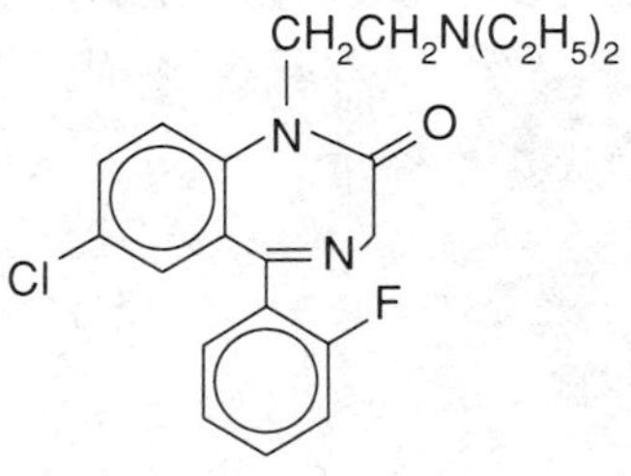

Flurazepam

Imidazo 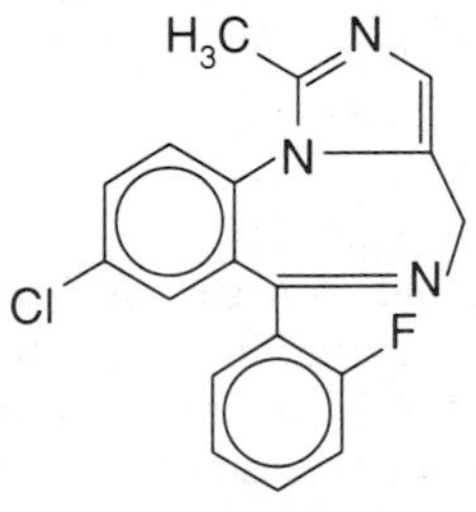
Midazolam

Nitro 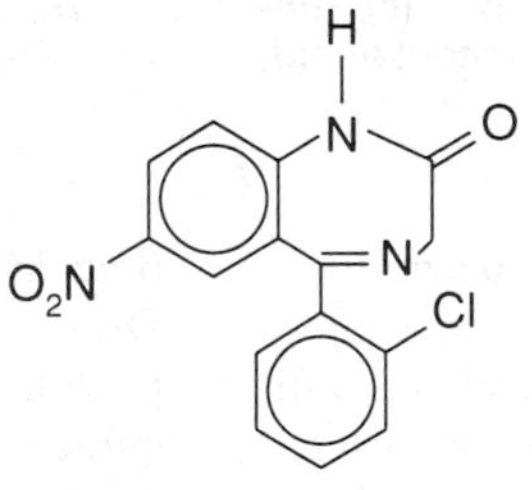
Clonazepam

2-Thione 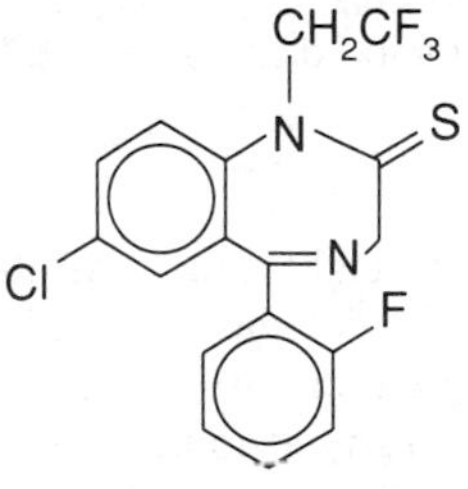
Quazepam

**Figure 33.3.5–1.** *Continued*

as skeletal muscle relaxants, primarily through their ability to inhibit spinal polysynaptic afferent pathways, although monosynaptic afferent pathways may also be affected.

## Therapeutic Indications

**Anxiety.** Generalized anxiety disorder, adjustment disorder with anxiety, and not necessarily pathological anxiety associated with life events (for example, after an accident) are the major clinical applications for benzodiazepines in psychiatry and general medical practice. Most patients should be treated for a predetermined, specific, and relatively brief period. Some patients with generalized anxiety disorder may warrant maintenance treatment with benzodiazepines.

**Insomnia.** Flurazepam, temazepam (Restoril), quazepam, estazolam, and triazolam are the benzodiazepines approved for use as hypnotics. The benzodiazepine hypnotics differ principally in their half-lives; flurazepam has the longest half-life, and triazolam has the shortest half-life. Flurazepam may be associated with minor cognitive impairment on the day after its administration, and triazolam may be associated with mild rebound anxiety. Temazepam or estazolam may be a reasonable compromise for the usual adult patient. Because of its high specificity for the $BZ_1$ receptor, quazepam may be associated with few adverse cognitive effects; however, quazepam shares the final metabolite with flurazepam—desakylflurazepam (half-life of about 100 hours)—and, therefore, may be associated with daytime impairment when used for a long time. Estazolam produces a rapid onset of sleep and a

**Table 33.3.5–1**
**Classification of Benzodiazepines**

| 2-Keto | 3-Hydroxy | Triazolo | Imidazo | Nitro | 2-Thione |
|--------|-----------|----------|---------|-------|----------|
| Chlordiazepoxide | Oxazepam | Alprazolam | Midazolam | Clonazepam | Quazepam |
| Diazepam | Lorazepam | Triazolam | | | |
| Prazepam | Temazepam | Estazolam | | | |
| Clorazepate | | | | | |
| Halazepam | | | | | |
| Flurazepam | | | | | |

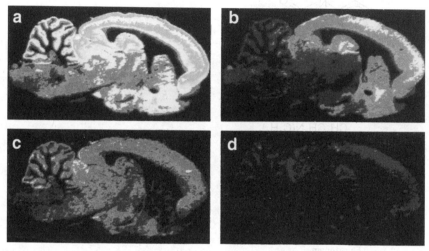

**Figure 33.3.5–2.** Distribution of BZ$_1$ and BZ$_2$ receptors determined by autoradiography. Binding of [H$^3$] suriclone (1.5 nM) to sagittal sections of rat brain. (a) Total binding. (b) Binding in the presence of alpidem (300 nM) shows BZ$_2$ receptors. (c) Subtracting (b) from (a) gives the distribution of BZ$_1$ receptors. (d) Nonspecific binding in presence of flumazenil (1 μM). From C. Malgouris. (Figure from A Doble, I L Martin: Multiple benzodiazepine receptors: No reason for anxiety. Trends Pharmacol Sci *13*: 76, 1992.) Used with permission.

hypnotic effect for six to eight hours. All the benzodiazepines produce a moderate decrease in rapid eye movement (REM) sleep, although their use is not associated with REM rebound. The benzodiazepines are also associated with a decrease in stage 3 and stage 4 sleep, although the significance is not known.

**Depression.** Unique among the benzodiazepines, alprazolam has antidepressant effects equal to those of the tricyclic drugs, but alprazolam is not effective in seriously depressed inpatients. The efficacy of alprazolam in depressive disorders may be a reflection of its high potency; the antidepressant effects of other benzodiazepines may be evident only at doses that also induce sedation or sleep. The starting dosage of alprazolam for the treatment of depression should be 1 to 1.5 mg a day and should be raised in 0.5 mg a day intervals every three or four days. The maximal dosage is usually 4 to 5 mg a day, although some investigators and clinicians have used dosages as high as 10 mg a day. The use of high dosages is controversial because of the possibility of withdrawal symptoms. The clinician must taper alprazolam, rather than abruptly stop, usually at the rate of 0.5 mg a day every three to four days.

**Panic disorder and social phobia.** For two anxiety disorders, panic disorder with or without agoraphobia and social phobia, the two high-potency benzodiazepines, al-

prazolam and clonazepam, are effective. The Food and Drug Administration (FDA) has approved the use of alprazolam for the treatment of panic disorder. The dosage guidelines for the use of alprazolam in panic disorder are similar to those for depression, discussed above.

**Bipolar I disorder.** Clonazepam is effective in the management of manic episodes and as an adjuvant to lithium (Eskalith) therapy in lieu of antipsychotics. As an adjuvant to lithium, clonazepam may result in an increased time between cycles and fewer than usual depressive episodes. The other high-potency benzodiazepine, alprazolam, may be as effective as clonazepam for that indication, which is not recognized by the FDA, and alprazolam should be considered a second-line treatment.

**Akathisia.** Standard anticholinergic drugs—for example, benztropine (Cogentin)—are often ineffective in treating neuroleptic-induced acute akathisia. The first-line drug for akathisia is most commonly a β-adrenergic receptor antagonist—for example, propranolol (Inderal). However, several studies have found that benzodiazepines are also effective in treating some cases of akathisia.

**Other psychiatric indications.** Chlordiazepoxide is used to manage the symptoms of alcohol withdrawal. The benzodiazepines (especially IM lorazepam) are used to manage both substance-induced (except amphetamine) and psychotic agitation in the emergency room. A few studies report the use of high dosages of benzodiazepines in patients with schizophrenia who had not responded to antipsychotics or who were unable to take the traditional drugs because of adverse effects. The use of intramuscular lorazepam for the treatment of catatonia has been reported. And benzodiazepines have been used instead of amobarbital (Amytal) for drug-assisted interviewing.

## Precautions and Adverse Reactions

The most common adverse effect of benzodiazepines is drowsiness, which occurs in about 10 percent of all patients. Because of that adverse effect, patients should be advised to be careful while driving or using dangerous machinery when taking the drugs. Drowsiness can be present during the day after the use of a benzodiazepine for insomnia the previous night, so-called residual daytime sedation. Some patients also experience dizziness (less than 1 percent) and ataxia (less than 2 percent). Those symptoms can result in falls and hip fractures, especially in elderly patients. The most serious adverse effects of benzodiazepines occur when other sedative substances, such as alcohol, are taken concurrently. The combinations can result in marked drowsiness, disinhibition, or even respiratory depression. Other relatively rare adverse effects have been mild cognitive deficits that may impair job performance in patients who are taking benzodiazepines. Anterograde amnesia has also been associated with benzodiazepines, particularly high-potency benzodiazepines. A rare, paradoxical increase in aggression has been reported in patients given benzodiazepines, although that effect may be most common in patients with brain damage. Allergic reactions to the drugs are also rare, but a few studies report maculopapular rashes and generalized itching. The symptoms of benzodiazepine intoxication include confusion, slurred speech, ataxia, drowsiness, dyspnea, and hyporeflexia.

Triazolam has received significant attention in the media because of an alleged association with serious aggressive behavioral manifestations. Although little evidence supports the association, the Upjohn Company, which manufactures triazolam, has issued a statement emphasizing that the drug is best used as a short-term (fewer than 10 days) treatment of insomnia and that physicians should carefully evaluate the emergence of any abnormal thinking or behavioral changes in patients treated with triazolam, giving appropriate consideration to all potential causes.

Patients with hepatic disease and elderly patients are particularly likely to have adverse effects and toxicity from the benzodiazepines, especially when the drugs are administered in repeated or high doses, because of the patients' impairment in the metabolism of the compounds. Benzodiazepines can produce clinically significant impairment of respiration in patients with chronic obstructive pulmonary disease and sleep apnea. Benzodiazepines should be used with caution in patients with a history of substance abuse, cognitive disorders, renal disease, hepatic disease, porphyria, CNS depression, and myasthenia gravis.

Some data indicate that benzodiazepines are teratogenic; therefore, their use during pregnancy is not advised. Moreover, the use of benzodiazepines in the third trimester can precipitate a withdrawal syndrome in the newborn. The drugs are secreted in the breast milk in sufficient concentrations to affect the newborn. Benzodiazepines may cause dyspnea, bradycardia, and drowsiness in nursing babies.

**Tolerance, dependence, and withdrawal.** When benzodiazepines are used for short periods of time (one to two weeks) in moderate dosages, they usually cause no significant tolerance, dependence, or withdrawal effects. The short-acting benzodiazepines (for example, triazolam) may be an exception to that rule, as some patients have reported increased anxiety the day after taking a single dose of the drug. Some patients also report a tolerance for the anxiolytic effects of benzodiazepines and require increased dosages to maintain the clinical remission of symptoms. There is also a cross-tolerance among most of the classes of antianxiety drugs, with the notable exception of buspirone.

The appearance of a withdrawal syndrome, also called a discontinuation syndrome (Table 33.3.5–2), depends on the length of time the patient has taken a benzodiazepine, the dosage the patient has been taking, the rate at which the drug is tapered, and the half-life of the compound. Abrupt discontinuation of benzodiazepines, particularly those with short half-lives, is associated with severe withdrawal symptoms. Serious symptoms may include depression, paranoia, delirium, and seizures. The incidence of the syndrome is controversial; however, some features of the syndrome may occur in as many as 50 percent of the patients treated with the drugs. The development of a severe withdrawal syndrome is seen only in patients who have taken high dosages for long periods. The appearance of the syndrome may be delayed for one to two weeks in patients who had been taking 2-keto benzodiazepines with long half-lives. Alprazolam seems to be particularly as-

**Table 33.3.5–2**
**Commonly Observed Withdrawal Symptoms**
**(Benzodiazepine Withdrawal Syndrome)**

Anxiety
Irritability
Insomnia
Fatigue
Headache
Muscle twitching or aching
Tremor, shakiness
Sweating
Dizziness
Concentration difficulties
*Nausea, loss of appetite
Observable depression
*Depersonalization, derealization
*Increased sensory perception (smell, sight, taste, touch)
*Abnormal perception or sensation of movement

---

*Symptoms likely to represent true withdrawal, rather than an exacerbation or return of original anxiety.
Table from P P Roy-Byrne, D Hommer: Benzodiazepine withdrawal: Overview and implications for the treatment of anxiety. Am J Med *84*: 1041, 1988. Used with permission.

sociated with an immediate and severe withdrawal syndrome and should be tapered gradually.

**Overdoses.** Overdoses with benzodiazepines alone have a predictably favorable outcome. When the overdose involves drugs in addition to the benzodiazepines, however, respiratory depression, coma, seizures, and death are likely. Drugs that are commonly taken with benzodiazepines in fatal overdoses include alcohol, antipsychotics, and antidepressants. The availability of flumazenil (Romazicon) has facilitated the medical management of benzodiazepine overdoses.

## Drug Interactions

Because benzodiazepines are widely used, clinicians must be aware of the possible interactions of benzodiazepines and other drugs (Table 33.3.5–3). Cimetidine (Tagamet), disulfiram (Antabuse), isoniazid (Nydrazid), and estrogen increase the plasma levels of 2-keto benzodiazepines. Antacids and food may decrease the plasma levels of benzodiazepines, and smoking may increase the metabolism of benzodiazepines. The benzodiazepines may increase the plasma levels of phenytoin (Dilantin) and digoxin (Lanoxin). All benzodiazepines have additive CNS effects with other sedative drugs. Ataxia and dysarthria may be likely to occur when lithium, antipsychotics, and clonazepam are combined.

## Laboratory Interferences

No known laboratory interferences are associated with the use of benzodiazepines.

## Dosage and Administration

The clinical decision to treat an anxious patient with a benzodiazepine should be carefully considered. Medical causes of anxiety (for example, thyroid dysfunction, caffeinism, and medications) should be ruled out. The ben-

**Table 33.3.5–3**
**Interactions of Benzodiazepines with Other Drugs**

Decrease absorption
  Antacids
Increase central nervous system depression
  Antihistamines
  Barbiturates and similarly acting drugs
  Cyclic antidepressants
  Ethanol
Increase benzodiazepine levels (compete for microsomal
    enzymes; probably little or no effect on lorazepam,
    oxazepam, temazepam)
  Cimetidine
  Disulfirarn
  Erythromycin
  Estrogens
  Fluoxetine
  Isoniazid
Decrease benzodiazepine levels
  Carbamazepine (possibly other anticonvulsants)

zodiazepine should be started at a low dosage, and the patient should be instructed regarding the drug's sedative properties and abuse potential. An estimated length of therapy should be decided at the beginning of therapy, and the need for continued therapy should be reevaluated at least monthly because of the problems associated with long-term use.

**Duration of treatment.** Benzodiazepines can be used to treat illnesses other than anxiety disorders. In such cases the duration of treatment should generally be similar to that for the standard drugs used to treat those disorders. The use of benzodiazepines over a long period for the chronically anxious patient is often valuable, although controversial. In his 1980 textbook on drug treatment in psychiatry, Donald Klein stated, "There are many reports of patients maintained on benzodiazepines for years with apparent benefit and without the development of tolerance. Nonetheless, it is dubious practice to prescribe such medications indefinitely without accompanying psychotherapy."

**Discontinuation of therapy.** Benzodiazepine withdrawal syndrome occurs when patients discontinue benzodiazepines abruptly; 90 percent of patients after long-term use experience some symptoms of withdrawal on discontinuation, even if the drug is tapered slowly. Benzodiazepine withdrawal syndrome consists of anxiety, nervousness, diaphoresis, restlessness, irritability, fatigue, light-headedness, tremor, insomnia, and weakness. The higher the dose and the shorter the half-life, the more severe the withdrawal symptoms can be.

When the medication is to be discontinued, the drug must be tapered slowly (25 percent a week); otherwise, recurrence or rebound of symptoms is likely to occur. Monitoring of any withdrawal symptoms (possibly with a standardized rating scale) and psychological support of the patient are helpful in the successful accomplishment of benzodiazepine discontinuation. Concurrent use of carbamazepine (Tegretol) during benzodiazepine discontinuation has been reported to permit a more rapid and better-tolerated withdrawal than does a gradual taper alone. The dosage range of carbamazepine used to facilitate withdrawal is 400 to 500 mg a day. Some clinicians report particular difficulty in tapering and discontinuing alprazolam, particularly in patients who have been receiving high dosages for long periods. There have been reports of successful discontinuation of alprazolam by switching to clonazepam, which is then gradually withdrawn.

**Choice of drug and potency.** The wide range of benzodiazepines are available in an equally wide range of formulations (Table 33.3.5–4). The drugs differ primarily in their half-lives. Another difference is in the rate of onset of their potency and anxiolytic effects. Potency is a general term used to express the pharmacological activity of a drug. Some benzodiazepines are more potent than others in that one compound requires a relatively smaller dose than another compound to achieve the same effect. For example, clonazepam requires 0.25 mg to achieve the same effect as 5 mg of diazepam; thus, clonazepam is considered a high-potency benzodiazepine. Conversely, oxazepam (Serax) has an approximate dose equivalence of 15 mg and is a low-potency drug. The four high-potency benzodiazepines—alprazolam, triazolam, estazolam, and clonaze-

**Table 33.3.5–4**
**Benzodiazepines**

| Drug | Approximate Dose Equivalents[1] | Dose Forms | Benzodiazepines Rate of Absorption | Major Active Metabolites | Average Half-Life of Metabolites (hrs) | Short-Acting/ Long-Acting[3] | Usual Adult Dosage Range (mg per day) |
|---|---|---|---|---|---|---|---|
| Alprazolam (Xanax) | 0.25 | 0.25, 0.5, 1, 2 mg tablets | Medium | α-Hydroxyalprazolam, 4-hydroxyalprazolam | 12 | Short | 0.5–6 |
| Chlordiazepoxide (Librium) | 10 | 5, 10, 25 mg tablets: 5, 10, 25 mg capsules; 100 mg parenteral | Medium | Desmethylchlordiazepoxide, demoxopam, desmethyldiazepam, oxazepam | 100 | Long | 15–100 |
| Clonazepam (Klonopin) | 0.5 | 0.5, 1, 2 mg tablets | Rapid | None | 34 | Long | 0.5–10 |
| Clorazepate (Tranxene) | 7.5 | 3.75, 7.5, 11.25, 15, 22.5 mg tablets; 3.75, 7.5, 15 mg capsules | Rapid | Desmethyldiazepam, oxazepam | 100 | Long | 7.5–60 |
| Diazepam (Valium) | 5 | 2, 5, 10 mg tablets; 15 mg capsules (extended release); 5 mg/mL parenteral; 5 mg/5 mL, 5 mg/mL solution | Rapid | Desmethyldiazepam, oxazepam | 100 | Long | 2–60 |
| Estazolam (ProSom) | 0.33 | 1, 2 mg tablets | Rapid | 4-Hydroxy estazolam, 1-oxo estazolam | 17 | Short | 1–2 |
| Flurazepam (Dalmane) | 5 | 15, 30 mg tablets | Rapid | Desalkylflurazepam, N-l-hydroxyethylflurazepam | 100 | Long | 15–30 |
| Halazepam (Paxipam) | 20 | 20, 40 mg tablets | Medium | Desmethyldiazepam, oxazepam | 100 | Long | 60–160 |
| Lorazepam (Ativan) | 1 | 0.5, 1, 2 mg tablets; 2 mg/mL, 4 mg/mL parenteral | Medium | None | 15 | Short | 2–6 |
| Midazolam (Versed)[2] | 1.25–1.7 | 1 mg/mL, 5 mg/mL parenteral | N/A | l-Hydroxymethylmidazolam | 2.5 | Short | Parenteral form only; 7.5–45 |
| Oxazepam (Serax) | 15 | 15 mg tablets; 10, 15, 30 mg capsules | Slow | None | 8 | Short | 30–120 |
| Prazepam (Centrax) | 10 | 10 mg tablets; 5, 10, 20 mg capsules | Slow | Desmethyldiazepam, oxazepam | 100 | Long | 20–60 |
| Quazepam (Doral) | 5 | 7.5, 15 mg tablets | Rapid | 2 oxoquazepam, N-desalkyl-2-oxoquazepam, and 3-hydroxy-2-oxoquazepam glucoronide | 100 | Long | 7.5–30 |
| Temazepam (Restoril) | 5 | 15, 30 mg tablets | Medium | None | 11 | Short | 15–30 |
| Triazolam (Halcion) | 0.1 | 0.125, 0.25 mg tablets | Rapid | None | 2 | Short | 0.125–0.25 |

[1]High-potency drugs have an approximage dose equivalent of under 1.0; 1.0–10-medium potency; over 10, low potency.
[2]Used only by anesthesiologists.
[3]Short-acting benzodiazepines have a half-life of under 25 hrs.

pam—are the drugs most likely to be effective for the new applications, such as depression, bipolar I disorder, panic disorder, and the phobias.

The advantages of the long-half-life drugs over the short-half-life drugs include less frequent dosing, less variation in plasma concentration, and less severe withdrawal phenomena. The disadvantages include drug accumulation, increased risk of daytime psychomotor impairment, and increased daytime sedation. The advantages of the short-half-life drugs over the long-half-life drugs include no drug accumulation and less daytime sedation. The disadvantages include more frequent dosing and earlier and more severe withdrawal syndromes. Rebound insomnia and anterograde amnesia are thought to be more of a problem with the short-half-life drugs than with the long-half-life drugs.

**Drug combinations.** The most common drug combinations with benzodiazepines involve the antipsychotics and the antidepressants, in addition to the benzodiazepines' obvious use as adjuvant hypnotics. The combination of a benzodiazepine and an antidepressant may be indicated in the treatment of markedly anxious depressed patients and patients with panic disorder. Several reports indicate that the combined use of alprazolam and an antipsychotic may further reduce psychotic symptoms in patients who did not respond adequately to the antipsychotic alone. The combined use of benzodiazepines and tricyclic drugs may improve compliance by reducing the subjective side effects and producing an immediate reduction in anxiety and insomnia. However, the combination may also cause excessive sedation, cognitive impairment, and even exacerbations of the depression, and it significantly adds to the lethality of an overdose.

## ZOLPIDEM

Zolpidem (Ambien) is a new hypnotic that acts at the γ-aminobutyric acid (GABA)-benzodiazepine complex as the benzodiazepines do, but it is not itself a benzodiazepine. The only indication for zolpidem at this time is as a hypnotic. The drug lacks the muscle-relaxant effects that are common to the benzodiazepines.

### Chemistry

Zolpidem is an imidazopyridine, and its chemical structure is shown in Figure 33.3.5–3.

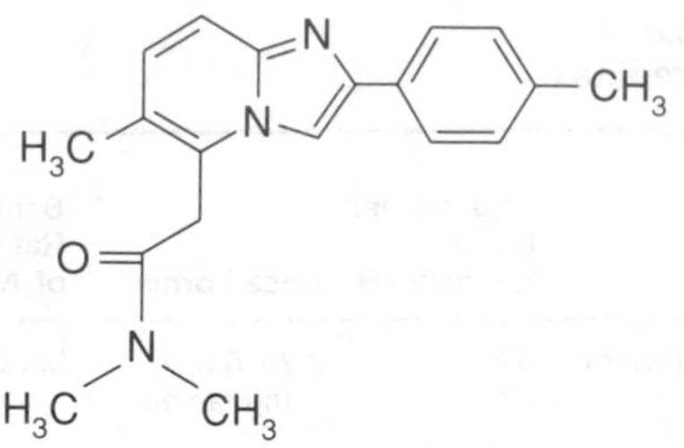

### Pharmacological Actions

**Pharmacokinetics.** Zolpidem is rapidly and well absorbed after oral administration, and it reaches peak plasma levels in about two to three hours. Zolpidem has a half-life of about two to three hours and is metabolized primarily by conjugation. Zolpidem does not have any active metabolites.

**Pharmacodynamics.** Zolpidem has a much higher affinity for $BZ_1$ receptors than for $BZ_2$ receptors. Zolpidem is also more specific for the CNS benzodiazepine receptors than for the peripheral benzodiazepine receptors. Those pharmacodynamic properties are consistent with the drug's efficacy as a hypnotic in the absence of significant muscle-relaxant prop-

**Figure 33.3.5–3.** Molecular structure of zolpidem.

erties. The binding site of zolpidem is likely to be similar to that of the benzodiazepines, since the effects of zolpidem can be prevented or reversed by the benzodiazepine receptor antagonist flumazenil.

### Therapeutic Indications

The sole indication at this time for zolpidem is as a hypnotic. Several studies have found an absence of rebound REM after the use of the compound for the induction of sleep. The comparatively few data available indicate that zolpidem may not be associated with rebound insomnia after the discontinuation of its use for short periods.

### Precautions and Adverse Reactions

Because of the short half-life of zolpidem, the clinician may reasonably evaluate the patient for the possibility of anterograde amnesia and anxiety the day after its administration, although neither of those adverse effects has been reported. Emesis and dysphoric reactions have been reported as adverse effects. Although tolerance and dependence have not been demonstrated or reported, that may be due to the still limited experience with the drug. Patients taking zolpidem should be advised to exercise additional caution when driving or operating dangerous machinery. Zolpidem is secreted in breast milk and is, therefore, contraindicated for use by nursing mothers. The dosage of zolpidem should be reduced in patients with renal and hepatic impairment. Preliminary data indicate that zolpidem has a longer than usual half-life in the elderly and a shorter than usual half-life in children.

### Drug Interactions and Laboratory Interferences

Information on drug interactions and laboratory interferences is limited. Therefore, the clinician should consider the possibility of such an interaction or interference in a patient who is being treated with zolpidem.

### Dosage and Administration

Zolpidem is available in 5, 10, 15, and 20 mg tablets, and a single 10 mg dose is the usual dose for the treatment of insomnia. For patients under age 65, the initial dose of 10 mg can be increased to 15 or 20 mg if necessary. For patients over age 65, an initial dose of 5 mg may be advised. Prolonged use of zolpidem or any hypnotic is not recommended.

# FLUMAZENIL

Flumazenil (Mazicon) is a benzodiazepine receptor antagonist. It reverses the psychophysiological effects of the benzodiazepine agonists (for example, diazepam). The use of flumazenil is limited to emergency rooms and other emergency settings.

## Chemistry

The molecular structure of flumazenil is based on a benzodiazepine nucleus (Figure 33.3.5–4).

## Pharmacological Actions

**Pharmacokinetics.**　After IV administration, flumazenil has a half-life of 7 to 15 minutes. Protein binding is about 50 percent. Clearance of flumazenil occurs primarily by hepatic metabolism. The major metabolites of flumazenil are the deethylated free acid and its glucuronide conjugate, which are excreted in the urine. Elimination of the drug is essentially complete within 72 hours. The pharmacokinetics of flumazenil are not significantly affected by gender, age, renal failure, or hemodialysis but are affected by hepatic impairment, which prolongs the half-life.

**Pharmacodynamics.**　Flumazenil can both block and reverse the CNS effects of currently available benzodiazepine receptor agonists (for example, diazepam and zolpidem). Specifically, intravenous flumazenil antagonizes sedation, impairment of recall, and psychomotor retardation produced by benzodiazepine receptor agonists. However, flumazenil does not reverse the effects of other CNS depressants, even if they also act partly on the $GABA_A$ receptor (for example, ethanol and barbiturates). Flumazenil is also ineffective in reversing the effects of opioids and opiates.

## Therapeutic Indications

Flumazenil is used to reverse the effects of benzodiazepine receptor agonists that have been used for clinical indications (for example, sedation and anesthesia) or in overdose.

## Precautions and Adverse Reactions

The most common adverse effects of flumazenil are nausea, vomiting, dizziness, agitation, emotional lability, cutaneous vasodilation, injection-site pain, fatigue, impaired vision, and headache.

## Drug Interactions and Laboratory Interferences

No deleterious drug interactions have been noted when flumazenil is administered after narcotics, inhalation anesthetics, muscle relaxants, and muscle-relaxant antagonists administered in conjunction with sedation or anesthesia. In mixed-drug overdose the toxic effects (for example, seizures and cardiac arrhythmias) of other drugs (for example, tricyclic drugs) may emerge with the reversal of the benzodiazepine effects of flumazenil. For example, seizures caused by an overdose of tricyclic drugs may have been partially treated in a patient who had also taken an overdose of benzodiazepines. With flumazenil treatment, the tricyclic-induced seizures or cardiac arrhythmias may present themselves and may result in a fatal outcome.

No laboratory interferences have been associated with the use of flumazenil.

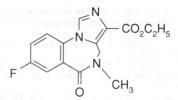

**Figure 33.3.5–4.**　Molecular structure of flumazenil.

## Dosage and Administration

For the initial management of a known or suspected benzodiazepine overdose, the recommended initial dose of flumazenil is 0.2 mg (2 mL) administered intravenously over 30 seconds. If the desired level of consciousness is not obtained after waiting 30 seconds, a further dose of 0.3 (3 mL) can be administered over 30 seconds. Further doses of 0.5 mg (5 mL) can be administered over 30 seconds at one-minute intervals up to a cumulative dose of 3.0 mg. The clinician should not rush the administration of flumazenil. A secure airway and intravenous access should be established before the administration of the drug. Patients should be awakened gradually.

Most patients with a benzodiazepine overdose respond to a cumulative dose of 1 to 3 mg of flumazenil; doses beyond 3 mg of flumazenil do not reliably produce additional effects. If a patient has not responded five minutes after receiving a cumulative dose of 5 mg flumazenil, the major cause of sedation is probably not due to benzodiazepine receptor agonists, and additional flumazenil is likely to have no effect.

**Return of sedation.**　The return of sedation can occur in 1 to 3 percent of patients. It can be prevented or treated by giving repeated doses of flumazenil at 20-minute intervals. For repeat treatment, no more than 1 mg (given as 0.5 mg a minute) should be given at any one time, and no more than 3 mg should be given in any one hour.

## References

Ankier S I, Goa K L: Quazepam: A preliminary review of its pharmacodynamic and pharmacokinetic properties, and therapeutic efficacy in insomnia. Drugs 35: 42, 1988.

Balkin T J, O'Donnell V M, Wesenten N, McCann U, Belenky G: Comparison of the daytime sleep and performance effects of zolpidem versus triazolam. Psychopharmacology 107: 83, 1992.

Busto U E, Sykora K, Sellers E M: A clinical scale to assess benzodiazepine withdrawal. J Clin Psychopharmacol 9: 412, 1989.

Curran H V, Birch B: Differentiating the sedative, psychomotor and amnesic effects of benzodiazepines: A study with midazolam and the benzodiazepine antagonist flumazenil. Psychopharmacology 103: 519, 1991.

Doble A, Martin I L: Multiple benzodiazepine receptors: No reason for anxiety. Trends Pharmacol Sci 13: 76, 1992.

Dubin W R: Rapid tranquilization: Antipsychotics or benzodiazepines? J Clin Psychiatry 49 (12, Suppl): 5, 1988.

Journal of Clinical Psychiatry: High-potency benzodiazepines: Emerging uses in psychiatry. J Clin Psychiatry 51 (5, Suppl): 2, 1990.

Journal of Clinical Psychiatry: Pharmacokinetic and clinical considerations in selecting appropriate benzodiazepine hypnotic therapy. J Clin Psychiatry 52 (9, Suppl): 2, 1991.

Journal of Clinical Psychiatry: The use of benzodiazepine hypnotics: A scientific examination of a clinical controversy. J Clin Psychiatry *53* (12, Suppl): 2, 1992.

Klein D: *Diagnostic and Drug Treatment for Psychiatry*, ed 2. Williams & Wilkins, Baltimore, 1980.

Kryger M H, Steljes D, Pouliot Z, Neufeld H, Odynski T: Subjective versus objective evaluation of hypnotic efficacy: Experience with zolpidem. Sleep *14*: 399, 1991.

Lader M: Rebound insomnia and newer hypnotics. Psychopharmacology *108*: 248, 1992.

Langry H D, Benfield P: Zolpidem: A review of its pharmacodynamic and pharmacokinetic properties and therapeutic potential. Drugs *40*: 291, 1990.

Lenox R H, Newhouse P A, Creelman W L, Whitaker T M: Adjunctive treatment of manic agitation with lorazepam versus haloperidol: A double-blind study. J Clin Psychiatry *53*: 47, 1992.

Noyes R, Garvey M J, Cook B L, Perry P J: Benzodiazepine withdrawal: A review of the evidence. J Clin Psychiatry *49*: 382, 1988.

Rickels K, Schweizer E, Case G, Greenblatt D J: Long-term therapeutic use of benzodiazepines: I. Effects of abrupt discontinuation. Arch Gen Psychiatry *47*: 899, 1990.

Romach M K, Somer G R, Sobell L C, Sobell M B, Kaplan H L, Seller E M: Characteristics of long-term alprazolam users in the community. J Clin Psychopharmacol *12*: 316, 1992.

Roy-Byrne P, Fleishaker J, Arnett C, Dubach M, Steward J, Radant A, Veith R, Graham M: Effects of acute and chronic alprazolam treatment on cerebral blood flow, memory, sedation, and plasma catecholamines. Neuropsychopharmacology *8*: 161, 1993.

Schlich D, L'Heritier C, Coquelin J P, Attali P: Long-term treatment of insomnia with zolpidem: A multicentre general practioner study of 107 patients. J Int Med Res *19*: 271, 1991.

Schweizer E, Rickels K, Case G, Greenblatt D J: Long-term therapeutic use of benzodiazepines. Arch Gen Psychiatry *47*: 908, 1990.

Shaw S H, Curson H, Coquelin J P: A double-blind, comparative study of zolpidem and placebo in the treatment of insomnia in elderly psychiatric in-patients. J Int Med Res *20*: 150, 1992.

Tiller J W G, Schweitzer I: Benzodiazepines: Depressants or antidepressants? Drugs *44*: 165, 1992.

Woods S W, Charney D S, Silver J M, Krystal J H: Behavioral, biochemical, and cardiovascular responses to the benzodiazepine receptor antagonist flumazenil in panic disorder. Psychiatry Res *36*: 115, 1991.

Zorumski C F, Isenberg K E: Insights into the structure and function of GABA-benzodiazepine receptors: Ion channels and psychiatry. Am J Psychiatry *148*: 162, 1991.

# 33.3.6 / Bromocriptine

Bromocriptine (Parlodel) has been studied as a potential therapeutic agent in a number of psychiatric conditions. Those studies have been conducted because of interest in the mixed dopamine agonist-antagonist properties of bromocriptine, which is available in the United States as an approved treatment for Parkinson's disease. The most robust data are in support of the therapeutic benefit of bromocriptine in the treatment of antipsychotic-induced hyperprolactinemia and galactorrhea and in the treatment of neuroleptic malignant syndrome. Increasing data also support the use of bromocriptine for the treatment of cocaine withdrawal and depression, although the latter indication should be considered only after standard therapies have failed. The use of bromocriptine for any psychiatric indication should be undertaken only after a review of the recent literature about those novel applications, which remain controversial.

## CHEMISTRY

The molecular structure of bromocriptine is shown in Figure 33.3.6–1.

## PHARMACOLOGICAL ACTIONS

### Pharmacokinetics

Bromocriptine is rapidly but only partially (about 30 percent) absorbed from the gastrointestinal (GI) tract. Peak concentrations are achieved $1\frac{1}{2}$ to 3 hours after oral administration. Bromocriptine is metabolized in the liver and is excreted in the bile. No active metabolites have been identified.

### Pharmacodynamics

Depending on dosage, bromocriptine has two effects on dopamine function. At low dosages, bromocriptine affects primarily presynaptic dopamine type 2 ($D_2$) receptors as an agonist, thus inhibiting the release of dopamine and thereby effectively acting as an antagonist to the dopamine system. At high dosages, bromocriptine acts directly on postsynaptic dopamine receptors, thus acting as a direct dopamine agonist. That differential activity is due to the increased sensitivity of presynaptic $D_2$ receptors to dopamine agonist compounds.

## EFFECTS ON SPECIFIC ORGANS AND SYSTEMS

Bromocriptine has effects on many organ systems in addition to the central nervous system (CNS) because of its dopaminergic activity. Because of the role of dopamine in the maintenance of blood pressure, bromocriptine use is commonly associated with hypotension, although hypertension has also been reported in some patients treated with the drug. The dopaminergic activity of bromocriptine can also affect heart rate and rhythm. The GI system is also sensitive to dopaminergic drugs, and bromocriptine administration is frequently associated with symptoms of GI distress, especially nausea.

## THERAPEUTIC INDICATIONS

### Antipsychotic-Induced Hyperprolactinemia

Because most antipsychotic drugs act as potent antagonists of $D_2$ receptors, they cause an increase in prolactin release by blocking the inhibitory effects of endogenous dopamine in the pituitary. The increase in serum prolactin can result in amenorrhea and galactorrhea in women. Bromocriptine is an effective treatment because its dopamine agonist activity stimulates the $D_2$ receptors in the pituitary and inhibits prolactin release. In spite of the dopamine agonist activity of bromocriptine, its use does not appear to be associated with an exacerbation of psychotic symptoms. Bromocriptine is used in a dosage range of 5 to 15 mg a day for that indication.

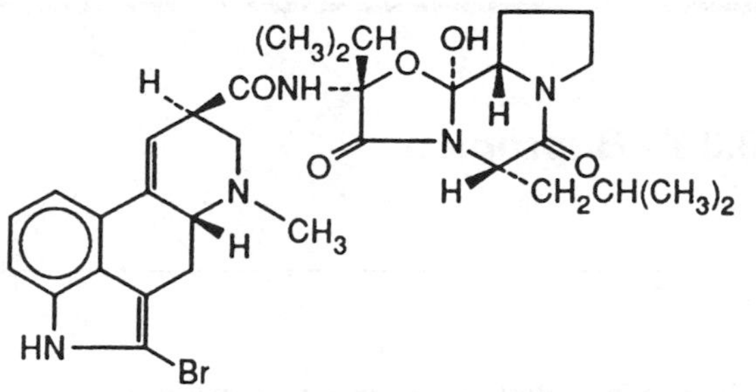

**Figure 33.3.6–1.** Molecular structure of bromocriptine.

## Neuroleptic Malignant Syndrome

Neuroleptic malignant syndrome is a potentially fatal syndrome of autonomic instability associated with the use of antipsychotics—for example, haloperidol (Haldol). Because of the sporadic, unpredictable nature of neuroleptic malignant syndrome, most of the data regarding the effectiveness of bromocriptine in the condition come from case reports. Bromocriptine may be effective in neuroleptic malignant syndrome because its dopamine agonist activity reverses the effects of the dopamine antagonists on hypothalamic thermoregulatory function and peripheral muscle contraction.

The first and most crucial step in the treatment of neuroleptic malignant syndrome is the recognition that the syndrome is present in a patient. The first steps in the management of the syndrome are discontinuation of the antipsychotic drug and the initiation of supportive care. If bromocriptine or other drugs are used to treat neuroleptic malignant syndrome, the earlier they are begun, the greater benefit they are likely to be to the patient. Amantadine (Symmetrel), another dopamine agonist, and dantrolene (Dantrium), a direct-acting skeletal muscle relaxant, are also of benefit in the treatment of neuroleptic malignant syndrome.

Treatment usually begins with 2.5 to 5.0 mg orally three times daily. The dosage can then be increased gradually up to 60 mg a day in divided doses to control fever, rigidity, and autonomic instability. In the available case reports published in the literature, the length of treatment has ranged from less than one week to two months.

## Cocaine Withdrawal

The data in support of the use of bromocriptine in cocaine withdrawal come primarily from case reports and not well-controlled studies. Nevertheless, since there is no clearly superior treatment for cocaine withdrawal, a clinical trial of bromocriptine may be warranted in some patients. Bromocriptine has been used to treat both the withdrawal symptoms of cocaine and the long-term craving for cocaine. Dosages for the treatment of cocaine use disorders have ranged from 0.625 to 12.5 mg a day.

## Depressive Disorders

The data in support of the use of bromocriptine in depressive disorders come primarily from case reports that

have described its use in patients who have not responded to conventional antidepressant drugs. Although the neurotransmitters serotonin and norepinephrine have been emphasized in theories regarding depressive disorders, dopamine has also been hypothesized to be involved in the pathophysiology of mood disorders. Specifically, mania may be associated with dopaminergic hyperactivity, and depression may be associated with dopaminergic hypoactivity. In the studies of bromocriptine in depressive disorders, the daily dosages have ranged from 10 to 200 mg, with a mean dosage around 40 mg a day. Response to bromocriptine treatment has been reported to occur usually within two weeks, although it may take up to four weeks. Some investigators have suggested that bromocriptine is especially effective in the treatment of bipolar I disorder depressed patients and is particularly safe in elderly depressed patients because of its low sedative and anticholinergic activities. However, the use of bromocriptine in depressive disorders should be considered an experimental treatment that is used only after other treatments have failed.

## Other Psychiatric Indications

Some reports support the use of bromocriptine in the treatment of antipsychotic-induced parkinsonism, antipsychotic-induced tardive dyskinesia, and alcohol withdrawal. Since bromocriptine is used to treat idiopathic Parkinson's disease, it may be effective in the treatment of antipsychotic-induced parkinsonism; however, the availability of other, probably safer, drugs—for example, benztropine (Cogentin)—should limit the use of bromocriptine for that indication. In several studies, bromocriptine, in dosages ranging from 0.75 to 7.5 mg a day, has been reported to be effective in reducing tardive dyskinesia symptoms by about 50 percent in about 20 percent of the patients treated. Several case studies have reported that bromocriptine may be effective in the treatment of alcohol withdrawal.

On an experimental basis, bromocriptine has been reported to be effective in the treatment of anxiety disorders (including obsessive-compulsive disorder), mania, and schizophrenia. Bromocriptine should not be used for the treatment of those disorders unless many other drug trials have failed and the clinician has undertaken a complete review of the available literature regarding the use of bromocriptine in the particular disorder.

## PRECAUTIONS AND ADVERSE REACTIONS

The side effects of bromocriptine tend to be severe at the initiation of treatment and with dosages of more than 20 mg a day. The most common side effects are nausea, headache, and dizziness. Less common GI side effects include vomiting, abdominal cramps, and constipation. About 1 percent of patients have syncopal episodes 15 to 60 minutes after the first dose of the drug, although they can tolerate subsequent doses and dosage increases without syncope. Other patients, however, experience symptomatic orthostatic hypotension, for which they do not have tolerance with continued treatment. Other cardiovascular symptoms can include cardiac arrhythmias and an exacerbation of underlying angina. Rare psychiatric side effects can include hallucinations, delusions, confusion, and other behavioral changes, although those symptoms are most common after long-term usage and in elderly patients. Bromocriptine should be used with caution in patients with hypertension, cardiovascular disease, and hepatic disease. Bromocriptine is not recommended for pregnant or breast-feeding patients.

## DRUG INTERACTIONS

Although the concurrent use of bromocriptine and drugs that have dopamine antagonist activity (for example, phenothiazines) may theoretically decrease the activity of each of the drugs, the interaction has not proved to be of major clinical importance. The use of bromocriptine in conjunction with antihypertensive agents may produce additive hypotensive effects. Ergot alkaloids and bromocriptine should not be used concurrently, as they may cause hypertension and myocardial infarction. Progestins, estrogens, and oral contraceptives may interfere with the effets of bromocriptine.

## LABORATORY INTERFERENCES

No laboratory interferences are known to be associated with the administration of bromocriptine.

## DOSAGE AND ADMINISTRATION

Bromocriptine is available in 2.5 mg scored tablets and 5 mg capsules. The dosage of bromocriptine for mental disorders is uncertain, although it seems prudent to begin with low dosages (1.25 mg twice daily) and to increase the dosage gradually. Bromocriptine is usually taken with meals to help reduce the likelihood of nausea.

## References

Borg V: Bromocriptine in the treatment of the alcohol withdrawal syndrome. Acta Psychiatr Scand *65*: 101, 1982.
Colonna L, Petit M, Lepine J P: Bromocriptine in affective disorders. J Affect Disord *1*: 173, 1979.
Dackis C A, Gold M S, Davis R K: Bromocriptine treatment for cocaine abuse: The dopamine depletion hypothesis. Int J Psychiatry Med *15*: 125, 1972.
Giannini A J, Baumgartel P, DiMarzio L R: Bromocriptine therapy in cocaine withdrawal. J Clin Pharmacol *27*: 267, 1987.
Mueller P S, Vester J W, Fermaglich J: Neuroleptic malignant syndrome: Successful treatment with bromocriptine. JAMA *249*: 386, 1983.
Nordin C, Siwers B, Bertillson L: Bromocriptine treatment of depressive disorders: Clinical and biochemical effects. Acta Psychiatr Scand *64*: 25, 1981.
Perovich R M, Lieberman J A, Fleischhacker W W, Alvir J: The behavioral toxicity of bromocriptine in patients with psychiatric illness. J Clin Psychopharmcol *9*: 417, 1989.
Shenoy R S, Ettigi P, Johnson C H: Bromocriptine in the treatment of galactorrhea caused by haloperidol: A case study. J Clin Psychopharmacol *3*: 187, 1983.
Sitland-Marken P A, Wells B G, Froemming J H, Chu C-C, Brown C S: Psychiatric applications of bromocriptine therapy. J Clin Psychiatry *51*: 68, 1990.
Wang G, Lam K S L, Ma J T C: Long-term treatment of hyperprolactinemia with bromocriptine: Effect of drug withdrawal. Clin Endocrinol *27*: 363, 1987.

# 33.3.7 / Bupropion

Bupropion (Wellbutrin) was first synthesized in 1966 and approved by the Food and Drug Administration (FDA) for use in depression in 1985. Shortly after its approval, however, a study of bupropion in nondepressed bulimic patients found an increased incidence of drug-induced seizures, thereby causing the drug company to suspend marketing activities while the incidence of seizures was reevaluated. Subsequent studies of depressed patients found that the incidence of drug-induced seizures did not differ from that for traditional antidepressants when bupropion was used in its usual therapeutic dosage range (300 to 450 mg a day), and the drug was reintroduced into the United States in 1989.

Bupropion is a unique antidepressant in the available armamentarium of drugs, and it is unfortunate that its past inaccurate association with seizure liability has limited its use in the United States. Bupropion is a unicyclic antidepressant that is unrelated to any other antidepressant available in the United States. Bupropion has been shown to be as effective as any other antidepressant and has been proved to be safe and well-tolerated. The established safety and efficacy of bupropion should make it an option for the first-line treatment of depressive disorders.

## CHEMISTRY

Bupropion is an aminoketone that resembles amphetamine in its molecular structure (Figure 33.3.7–1).

## PHARMACOLOGICAL ACTIONS

### Pharmacokinetics

Bupropion is well-absorbed from the gastrointestinal (GI) tract and is metabolized by the liver, with its metabolites excreted by the kidneys. Peak plasma levels of bupropion are usually reached within two hours of oral administration. The mean half-life of the compound during the postdistributional phase is 12 hours, although its half-life ranges from 8 to 40 hours. Bupropion has two major active metabolites, hydroxybupropion and threohydrobupropion, which may be associated with the drug's therapeutic and adverse effects. Both of those metabolites have about a twofold longer half-life than

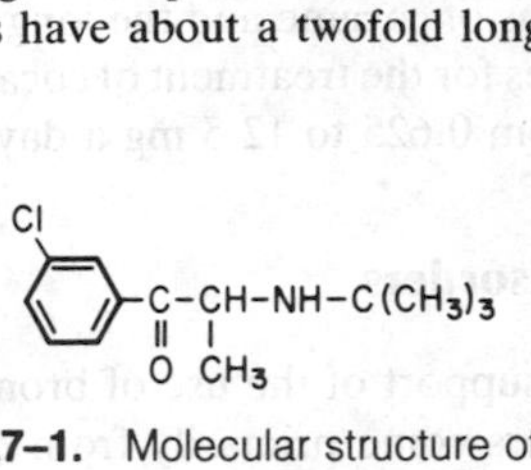

**Figure 33.3.7–1.** Molecular structure of bupropion.

does the parent compound; therefore, it may take up to 10 days to reach steady-state concentrations of those metabolites. The rate of metabolism is regulated by the liver, although about 90 percent of the drug and its metabolites are excreted in the urine.

### Pharmacodynamics

The mechanism of action for the antidepressant effects of bupropion are unknown. Although it was initially thought that bupropion acts through the blockade of dopamine reuptake, one study found that an increase in homovanillic acid (a metabolite of dopamine) was associated with a lack of clinical response. Furthermore, central nervous system (CNS) concentrations of bupropion are probably not sufficient to result in significant dopamine reuptake inhibition. Bupropion is also associated with low activity either as an uptake inhibitor of norepinephrine and serotonin or as an agonist or an antagonist of biogenic amine receptors. Nonetheless, some data indicate that bupropion exerts its antidepressant effects by acting on the noradrenergic system. Those data include the observation that bupropion can reduce the firing rate of noradrenergic neurons in the locus ceruleus of animals that are being studied in animal behavioral models of depression.

## EFFECTS ON SPECIFIC ORGANS AND SYSTEMS

Except for its CNS effects, bupropion is devoid of activity in human organs. No evidence has been found for significant effects of bupropion on liver, cardiac, or renal function, although the dosage of bupropion should be adjusted downward in patients with liver and renal impairment. Rare cases of lymphadenopathy, anemia, and pancytopenia have been reported, although their association with bupropion use is uncertain, and routine monitoring of blood is not indicated. Bupropion does not affect sexual functioning, and it has not been associated with changes in weight.

## THERAPEUTIC INDICATIONS

The therapeutic efficacy of bupropion in depression has been established in four well-controlled trials with depressed inpatients and outpatients. In comparison studies, bupropion has shown efficacy equal to fluoxetine (Prozac), nortriptyline (Aventyl), trazodone (Desyrel), doxepin (Adapin), amitriptyline (Elavil), and imipramine (Tofranil), although patients treated with bupropion may have less improvement in their sleep early in the course of treatment because of the lack of sedative effects.

Single reports have appeared about the use of bupropion in winter depression (that is, recurrent major depressive disorder with seasonal pattern) and in both childhood and adult attention-deficit/hyperactivity disorders. The use of bupropion in attention-deficit/hyperactivity disorder should be considered experimental at this time. Additional preliminary reports concern the use of bupropion in the treatment of cocaine abuse and chronic fatigue.

## PRECAUTIONS AND ADVERSE REACTIONS

The side-effect profile of bupropion in placebo-controlled studies did not differ significantly from that for placebo-treated patients (Table 33.3.7–1). No significant cardiovascular or clinical laboratory changes were reported in those placebo-controlled studies. A major advantage of bupropion over serotonin-specific reuptake inhibitors (SSRIs) is that bupropion is virtually devoid of any adverse effects on sexual functioning, whereas the SSRIs are associated with the occurrence of such effects in perhaps 25 to 50 percent of all patients.

The most common adverse effects are headache, insomnia, upper respiratory complaints, and nausea. Restlessness, agitation, and irritability may also occur. Most notable about bupropion is the absence of significant drug-induced orthostatic hypotension, weight gain, daytime drowsiness, and anticholinergic effects; however, some patients may experience dry mouth or constipation. In fact, weight loss may occur in about 25 percent of all patients. Bupropion may be a drug to consider early in the treatment of depressed patients with preexisting cardiovascular disease.

At dosages less than 450 mg a day, the incidence of seizures is about 0.4 percent, which is comparable to the incidence of seizures with tricyclic drugs. The risk of seizures increases to about 5 percent in dosages from 450 to 600 mg a day. Bupropion may be less likely than tricyclic drugs to cause a switch into mania or rapid cycling in bipolar I disorder patients; however, the drug can cause mania in some patients.

Overdoses with bupropion are associated with a generally favorable outcome, except in the cases of huge doses and mixed-drug overdoses. Seizures occur in about a third of all overdoses, and fatalities can involve uncontrollable seizures, bradycardia, and cardiac arrest. In general, however, bupropion is safer in overdose cases than are other antidepressants, except perhaps for the SSRIs.

The use of bupropion is contraindicated in patients with histories of head trauma, brain tumors, and other organic brain diseases because the drug may reduce the patient's seizure threshold. The presence of electroencephalographic abnormalities and the recent withdrawal of the patient from alcohol or a sedative-hypnotic may also increase the risk of having a bupropion-induced seizure. Because high dosages (more than 450 mg a day) of bupropion may be associated with a euphoric feeling, bupropion may be relatively contraindicated in patients with histories of substance abuse. The use of bupropion by pregnant women has not been studied and is not recommended. Because bupropion is secreted in breast milk, the use of bupropion in nursing women is not recommended.

## DRUG INTERACTIONS

Bupropion should not be used concurrently with monoamine oxidase inhibitors (MAOIs) because of the possibility of inducing a hypertensive crisis, and at least 14 days should pass after the discontinuation of an MAOI before initiating treatment with bupropion. Delirium, psychotic symptoms, and dyskinetic movements may be associated

Table 33.3.7–1
**Adverse Events Associated with Treatment***

| Body System | Adverse Event | Bupropion (N = 110) | | Placebo (N = 109) | |
|---|---|---|---|---|---|
| | | N | % | N | % |
| Cardiovascular | Palpitations | 5 | 4.6 | 7 | 6.4 |
| Gastrointestinal | Abdominal pain | 6 | 5.5 | 3 | 2.8 |
| | Anorexia | 6 | 5.5 | 5 | 4.6 |
| | Constipation | 11 | 10.0 | 6 | 5.5 |
| | Dyspepsia | 7 | 6.4 | 8 | 7.3 |
| | Nausea | 14 | 12.7 | 11 | 10.1 |
| Genitourinary | Dysmenorrhea[†] | 3 | 4.2 | 6 | 8.5 |
| | Impotence[‡] | 2 | 5.1 | 0 | 0.0 |
| Musculoskeletal | Back pain | 9 | 8.2 | 8 | 7.3 |
| | Muscle spasms | 2 | 1.8 | 6 | 5.5 |
| Neurological | Dizziness | 16 | 14.6 | 6 | 5.5 |
| | Headache | 42 | 38.2 | 28 | 25.7 |
| | Insomnia | 25 | 22.7 | 8 | 7.3 |
| | Tremor | 8 | 7.3 | 3 | 2.8 |
| Psychiatric | Agitation | 12 | 10.9 | 8 | 7.3 |
| | Anxiety | 10 | 9.1 | 5 | 4.6 |
| | Irritability | 6 | 5.5 | 6 | 5.5 |
| Nonspecific | Fatigue | 6 | 5.5 | 2 | 1.8 |
| | Flulike symptoms | 7 | 6.4 | 3 | 2.8 |
| Oral complaints | Dry mouth | 8 | 7.3 | 9 | 8.3 |
| Respiratory | Upper respiratory complaints | 21 | 19.1 | 36 | 33.0 |
| Special senses | Blurred vision | 6 | 5.5 | 1 | 0.9 |
| | Tinnitus | 7 | 6.4 | 2 | 1.8 |

*Those events reported at greater than a 5 percent incidence in either group.
[†]Percentages are based on number of female patients only (placebo, N = 71; bupropion, N = 71).
[‡]Percentages are based on number of male patients only (placebo, N = 38; bupropion, N = 39).
Table from C G Lineberry, J A Johnston, R N Raymond, B Samara, J P Feighner, N E Harto, R P Granacher, R H Weisler, J S Carman, W F Boyer: A fixed-dose (300 mg) efficacy study of bupropion and placebo in depressed outpatients. J Clin Psychiatry *51*: 194, 1990.

with the coadministration of bupropion and dopamine agonists, such as amantadine (Symmetrel), L-dopa (Larodopa), and bromocriptine (Parlodel). There have also been case reports of CNS toxicity with the combination of lithium (Eskalith) and bupropion, although there have also been case reports that the combination is effective and well-tolerated in some patients with refractory depression. A few case reports indicate that delirium or seizures are associated with the combination of bupropion and fluoxetine. When bupropion is coadministered with drugs that are also metabolized in the liver, particular clinical attention should be given to the possibility of affecting the blood levels of the other drugs. Examples of other drugs metabolized in the liver are carbamazepine (Tegretol), cimetidine (Tagamet), barbiturates, and phenytoin (Dilantin).

## LABORATORY INTERFERENCES

No reports have appeared of laboratory interferences clearly associated with bupropion treatment. Clinically nonsignificant changes in the electrocardiogram (ECG) (premature beats and nonspecific ST-T changes) and decreases in the white blood cell count (by about 10 percent) have been reported in a small number of patients.

## DOSAGE AND ADMINISTRATION

Bupropion is available in 75 and 100 mg tablets. Initiation of treatment in the average adult patient should be at 100 mg orally twice a day. On the fourth day of treatment, the dosage can be raised to 100 mg orally three times a day. Because 300 mg is the recommended dosage, the patient should be maintained on that dosage for several weeks before further increasing the dosage. Because of the risk of seizures, increases in dosage should never exceed 100 mg in a three-day period; a single dose of bupropion should never exceed 150 mg; and the total daily dose should not exceed 450 mg.

One study of bupropion efficacy found that patients with trough blood levels of 10 to 29 ng per mL were more likely to respond to bupropion than were patients with trough blood levels of 30 ng per mL or more. That report was based on a small number of patients and needs to be replicated in a larger series before its accuracy can be assessed.

### References

Davidson J: Seizures and bupropion: A review. J Clin Psychiatry *50*: 256, 1989.
Feighner J P, Gardner E A, Johnston J A, Batey S R, Khayrallah M A,

Ascher J A, Lineberry C G: Double-blind comparison of bupropion and fluoxetine in depressed outpatients. J Clin Psychiatry *52*: 329, 1991.

Golden R N, Rudorfer M V, Sherer M A, Linnoila M, Potter W Z: Bupropion in depression: I. Biochemical effects and clinical response. Arch Gen Psychiatry *45*: 139, 1988.

Goodnick P J: Blood levels and acute response to bupropion. Am J Psychiatry *149*: 399, 1992.

Goodnick P J: Pharmacokinetics of second generation antidepressants: Bupropion. Psychopharmacol Bull *27*: 513, 1991.

Johnston J A, Lineberry C G, Ascher J A, Davidson J, Khayrallah M A, Feighner J P, Stark P: A 102-center prospective study of seizure in association with bupropion. J Clin Psychiatry *52*: 450, 1991.

Lineberry C G, Johnston J A, Raymond R N, Samara B, Feighner J P, Harto N E, Granacher R P, Weisler R H, Carman J S, Boyer W F: A fixed-dose (300 mg) efficacy study of bupropion and placebo in depressed outpatients. J Clin Psychiatry *51*: 194, 1990.

Roose S P, Dalack G W, Glassman A H, Woodring S, Walsh B T, Giardina E G V: Cardiovascular effects of bupropion in depressed patients with heart disease. Am J Psychiatry *148*: 512, 1991.

# 33.3.8 / Buspirone

Buspirone (BuSpar) is the first clinically available azaspirone drug in the United States. It is approved for the treatment of anxiety disorders. Buspirone is unrelated to the benzodiazepines or the barbiturates, and it does not directly affect the γ-aminobutyric acid (GABA) neurotransmitter system. Also unlike the benzodiazepines and the barbiturates, buspirone does not have sedative, hypnotic, muscle-relaxant, or anticonvulsant effects. In further contrast to those other drugs, buspirone carries a low potential for abuse and is not associated with withdrawal phenomena or cognitive impairment.

## CHEMISTRY

The molecular structure of buspirone is shown in Figure 33.3.8–1. It is chemically distinct from currently available benzodiazepines, barbiturates, and antidepressants.

## PHARMACOLOGICAL ACTIONS

### Pharmacokinetics

Buspirone is well-absorbed from the gastrointestinal (GI) tract and is unaffected by food intake. Buspirone is metabolized by the liver and excreted by the kidneys. Oxidative dealkylation produces an active metabolite, which, although less

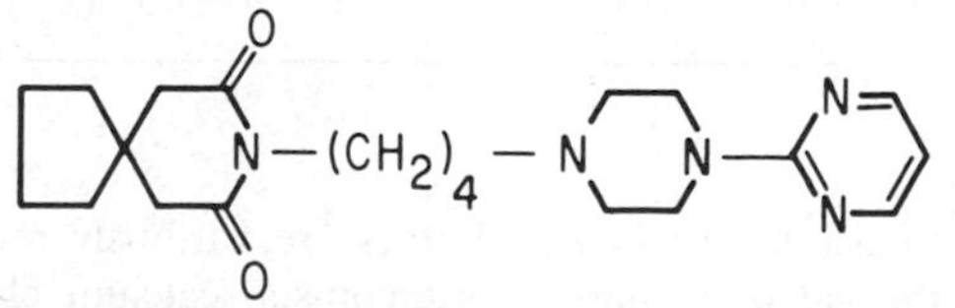

**Figure 33.3.8–1.** Molecular structure of buspirone.

potent than the parent compound, is present in higher concentrations. The drug reaches peak plasma levels in 60 to 90 minutes after oral administration. The short half-life (2 to 11 hours) necessitates three-times-daily dosing, although the active metabolite has a twofold longer half-life than does the parent compound.

### Pharmacodynamics

In contrast to benzodiazepines and barbiturates, which act on the GABA-associated chloride ion channel, buspirone has no effect on that receptor mechanism. Rather, buspirone acts as an agonist or partial agonist on serotonin type $1_A$ (5-$HT_{1A}$) receptors. In animal models, buspirone decreases the firing rates of serotonergic neurons located in the median raphe nuclei and reduces the release of serotonin in the hippocampus, which has a high concentration of 5-$HT_{1A}$ receptors. Buspirone also has activity at 5-$HT_2$ and dopamine type 2 ($D_2$) receptors, although the significance of the effects at those receptors is unknown. At $D_2$ receptors, it has properties of both an agonist and an antagonist, and buspirone treatment may lead to a decrease in the firing rate of the mesolimbic dopaminergic neurons. The mechanism of action for buspirone is incompletely understood at this time. The fact that buspirone takes two to three weeks to exert its therapeutic effects implies that, whatever its initial effects, the therapeutic effects may involve the modulation of several neurotransmitters and intraneuronal mechanisms.

## EFFECTS ON SPECIFIC ORGANS AND SYSTEMS

The effects of buspirone on organs other than the brain are minimal. The drug has no significant effects on the respiratory system, the heart, the vascular system, the blood, smooth muscles, or the autonomic nervous system.

## THERAPEUTIC INDICATIONS

The efficacy and the safety of buspirone in the treatment of generalized anxiety disorder have been demonstrated in at least 10 placebo-controlled trials. Most of those trials have found that the efficacy of buspirone did not differ from the efficacy of the benzodiazepines tested—diazepam (Valium), lorazepam (Ativan), clorazepate (Tranxene), and alprazolam (Xanax). However, all those studies used criteria in the third edition of *Diagnostic and Statistical Manual of Mental Disordes* (DSM-III) for generalized anxiety disorder, which differ from the criteria in the fourth edition (DSM-IV) by requiring only one month of symptoms, compared with the six months required in DSM-IV. Many clinicians are not convinced of the efficacy of buspirone, probably because of its delayed onset of action in comparison with the benzodiazepines and its lack of the mild euphoric effect or sense of well-being that can be associated with benzodiazepine use.

Both the benzodiazepines and buspirone have advantages and disadvantages. The beneficial effects of benzodiazepines are felt the same day the drug is started, and the full clinical response takes only days, whereas buspirone has no immediate effects, and the full clinical response may take two to four weeks. Sometimes the sedative effects of benzodiazepines, which are not found with buspirone, are desirable; however, those sedative effects are also associated with impaired motor performance and cognitive deficits. The major disadvantages of benzodiazepine treatment are its addictive potential and the development of withdrawal phenomena on its discontinuation. Buspirone is not associated with any abuse potential, even in groups of patients who are at high risk for addictive behavior.

Buspirone has been studied in patient populations with symptoms in addition to anxiety. The studies produced mixed results regarding the efficacy of buspirone in depressive disorders and obsessive-compulsive disorder. The use of buspirone for those disorders should be considered experimental and should be undertaken only after traditional therapies have proved to be ineffective. The data indicate that buspirone is not effective in the treatment of panic disorder or social phobia of the performance type. Because buspirone does not act on the GABA-chloride ion channel complex, the drug is not recommended for the treatment of withdrawal from benzodiazepines, alcohol, or sedative-hypnotic drugs.

## PRECAUTIONS AND ADVERSE REACTIONS

The most common adverse effects of buspirone are headache, nausea, dizziness, and, rarely, insomnia. No sedation is associated with buspirone. Some patients may report a minor feeling of restlessness, although that symptom may reflect an incompletely treated anxiety disorder. No deaths have been reported from overdoses of buspirone, and the median lethal dose ($LD_{50}$) is estimated to be 160 to 550 times the recommended daily dose. Buspirone should be used with caution in patients with hepatic and renal impairment, in pregnant women, and in nursing mothers. Buspirone can be used safely for the elderly; however, no specific information is available about its use for children.

## DRUG INTERACTIONS

One study reported that the coadministration of buspirone and haloperidol (Haldol) resulted in increased blood concentrations of haloperidol. Buspirone should not be used with monoamine oxidase inhibitors (MAOIs), and a two-week washout period should pass between the discontinuation of an MAOI and the initiation of treatment with buspirone.

## LABORATORY INTERFERENCES

Single doses of buspirone can cause transient elevations in growth hormone, prolactin, and cortisol concentrations, although the effects are not clinically significant.

## DOSAGE AND ADMINISTRATION

Buspirone is available in 5 and 10 mg tablets, and treatment is usually initiated with 5 mg orally three times daily. The dosage can be raised 5 mg every two to three days to the usual dosage range of 15 to 30 mg a day. The maximum dosage is 60 mg a day.

Buspirone is as effective as the benzodiazepines in the treatment of anxiety in patients who have not received benzodiazepines in the past. However, buspirone does not cause the same response in patients who have received benzodiazepines in the past. The reason is probably buspirone's absence of the immediate mildly euphoric and sedative effects of the benzodiazepines. The most common clinical problem, therefore, is how to initiate buspirone therapy in a patient who is currently taking benzodiazepines. There are two alternatives: First, the clinician can start buspirone treatment gradually while the benzodiazepine is being withdrawn. Second, the clinician can start buspirone treatment and bring the patient up to a therapeutic dosage for two to three weeks while the patient is still receiving the regular dosage of the benzodiazepine; at that point the benzodiazepine can be slowly tapered. A few initial reports indicate that the coadministration of buspirone and benzodiazepines may be effective in the treatment of anxiety disorders that have not responded to treatment with either drug alone.

### References

Allman B J C, Domantay A, Schoeman H S: Antidepressant activity of buspirone in anxiety. Curr Ther Res 52: 406, 1992.
Feighner J P, Cohn J B: Analysis of individual symptoms in generalized anxiety: A pooled, multistudy, double-blind evaluation of buspirone. Neuropsychobiology 21: 124, 1989.
Gammans R E, Stringfellow J C, Hvizdos A J, Seidehamel R J, Cohn J B, Wilcox C S, Fabre L F, Pecknold J C, Smith W T, Rickels K: Use of buspirone in patients with generalized anxiety disorder and coexisting depressive symptoms. Pharmacopsychiatry 25: 193, 1992.
Goff D C, Midha K K, Brotman A W, McCormick S, Waites M, Amico E T: An open trial of buspirone added to neuroleptics in schizophrenic patients. J Clin Psychopharmacol 11: 193, 1991.
Jacobsen F M: Possible augmentation of antidepressant response by buspirone. J Clin Psychiatry 52: 217, 1991.
Jacobson A F, Dominguez R A, Goldstein B J, Steinbook R M: Comparison of buspirone and diazepam in generalized anxiety disorder. Pharmacotherapy 5: 290, 1985.
Joffe R T, Schuller D R: An open study of buspirone augmentation of serotonin reuptake inhibitors in refractory depression. J Clin Psychiatry 54: 269, 1993.
Journal of Clinical Psychiatry: Serotonin partial agonists in the treatment of anxiety and depression. J Clin Psychiatry 51 (9, Suppl): 30, 1990.
Journal of Clinical Psychopharmacology: Azaspirones: A novel class of broad-spectrum psychotropic agents. J Clin Psychopharmacol 10 (3, Suppl): 2, 1990.
Manfredi R L, Kales A, Vgontzas A N, Bixler E O, Isaac M A, Falcone C M: Buspirone: Sedative or stimulant effect? Am J Psychiatry 148: 1213, 1991.
Mitsukini M, Miura S: The future of 5-HT$_{1A}$ receptor agonists (arylpiperazine derivatives). Prog Neuropsychopharmacol Biol Psychiatry 16: 833, 1992.
Sheehan D V, Raj A B, Sheehan K H, Soto S: Is buspirone effective for panic disorder? J Clin Psychopharmacol 10: 3, 1990.

# 33.3.9 / Calcium Channel Inhibitors

The calcium channel inhibitors are variously referred to as the calcium channel antagonists, calcium channel blockers, and organic calcium channel inhibitors. The calcium channel inhibitors were first developed as cardiac drugs for the treatment of hypertension, angina, and specific types of cardiac arrhythmias—indications that remain important in general medical practice. Although about a dozen calcium channel inhibitors are now available in the United States, most of the studies of calcium channel inhibitors in psychiatric disorders have been conducted with verapamil (Calan, Isoptin) and, recently, nimodipine (Nimotop). Diltiazem (Cardizem) and nifedipine (Adalat, Procardia) have also been used in a few clinical trials of psychiatric patients.

## CHEMISTRY

The molecular structures of the four calcium channel inhibitors that are most relevant to psychiatry are shown in Figure 33.3.9–1. Three chemical classes are represented by the four compounds. Nifedipine and nimodipine are dihydropyridine calcium channel inhibitors; verapamil and diltiazem are referred to as nondihydropyridines, but they are chemically distinct from each other.

## PHARMACOLOGICAL ACTIONS

### Pharmacokinetics

The calcium channel inhibitors are well-absorbed from the gastrointestinal (GI) tract, but all four drugs are substantially metabolized by the liver in a first-pass effect. Considerable intraindividual and interindividual variations are seen in the plasma concentrations of the drugs after a single dose. The half-life of verapamil after the first dose is two to eight hours; the half-life increases to 5 to 12 hours after the first few days of therapy. According to some studies, verapamil does pass the blood-brain barrier and reaches the cerebrospinal fluid (CSF) in concentrations about 0.05 percent of the plasma concentrations.

### Pharmacodynamics

The calcium ion is a major intracellular second messenger. Intraneuronal calcium has many functions, including the activation of calcium-dependent protein kinases. The calcium channel inhibitors inhibit the influx of calcium into neurons through one type of voltage-dependent calcium channel called the L-type calcium channel. The calcium channel inhibitors bind to the channel and inhibit its opening. Nifedipine and nimodipine bind to a different part of the channel than do verapamil and diltiazem.

## EFFECTS ON SPECIFIC ORGANS AND SYSTEMS

The major effects of calcium channel inhibitors are on the vasculature, which responds with vasodilation to the calcium channel inhibitors. Diuresis has also been associated with the use of calcium channel inhibitors. The calcium channel inhibitors interfere with atrioventricular (AV) conduction and can lead to AV heart block, especially in elderly patients.

## THERAPEUTIC INDICATIONS

### Bipolar I Disorder

Case reports describing the efficacy of verapamil in bipolar I disorder first appeared in the early 1980s, and subsequent placebo-controlled and lithium-controlled studies have generally supported the initial finding of efficacy for that indication. Available data support the use of verapamil for both the short-term and maintenance treatment of bipolar I disorder, although verapamil should be considered a fourth-line drug, following trials of lithium (Eskalith), carbamazepine (Tegretol), and valproate (Depakene). Because of potential drug interactions, valproate should be coadministered with lithium or carbamazepine with caution. Some patients who are treated with lithium and calcium channel inhibitors concurrently may be at increased risk for the signs and symptoms of neurotoxicity.

Preliminary data indicate that nimodipine may be particularly effective in the treatment of rapid-cycling bipolar I disorder. Since nimodipine is currently an expensive drug and those data are preliminary, the use of nimodipine for bipolar I disorder is best limited to research settings at this time.

### Hypertensive Crisis Associated with Monoamine Oxidase Inhibitors

One controversial use of a calcium channel inhibitor in psychiatry is the use of nifedipine to treat monoamine oxidase inhibitor (MAOI)-induced hypertensive crises. When patients begin to experience the symptoms of a hypertensive crisis, they are instructed to bite into a 20 mg capsule of nifedipine, to swallow the contents with water, to contact their physician, and to go to an emergency room. The concern is that patients may misidentify minor symptoms as hypertensive symptoms and take nifedipine unnecessarily, possibly resulting in a hypotensive episode or syncope.

### Other Psychiatric Indications

Perhaps the most hopeful of the other indications studied with calcium channel inhibitors are the use of nimodipine for dementia and the use of a range of calcium channel inhibitors for tardive dyskinesia. Using nimodipine for dementia is strictly experimental at this time, but using a calcium channel inhibitor for tardive dyskinesia may be worth a therapeutic trial in severely affected patients. Case reports and small studies provide preliminary evidence of the efficacy of calcium channel inhibitors in Tourette's disorder, Huntington's disease, panic disorder, premenstrual dysphoric disorder, and intermittent explosive disorder. Well-controlled studies have found a lack of efficacy for calcium channel inhibitors in schizophrenia and depressive disorders.

## PRECAUTIONS AND ADVERSE REACTIONS

The most common adverse effects associated with calcium channel inhibitors are hypotension, bradycardia, and

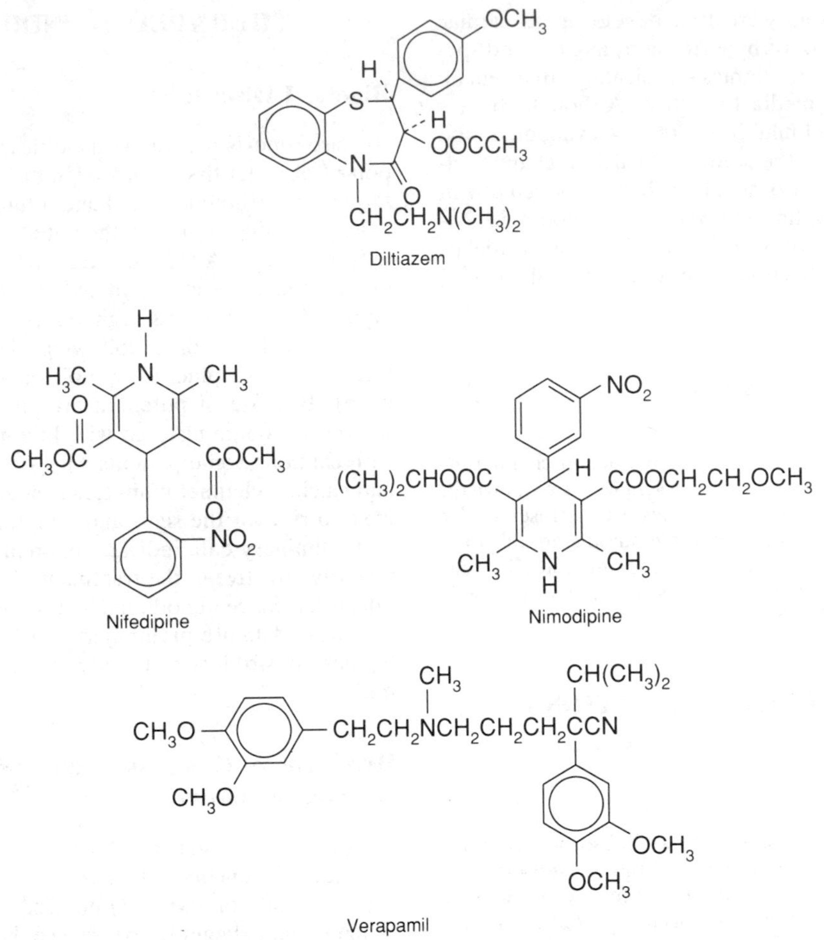

**Figure 33.3.9–1.** Molecular structures of calcium channel inhibitors.

AV heart block, which sometimes necessitate discontinuing the drug. In all patients with cardiovascular disease, the drugs should be used with caution. Common GI symptoms include constipation, nausea, and occasionally dry mouth, GI distress, and diarrhea. Adverse effects on the central nervous system include dizziness, headache, and fatigue. Adverse effects noted in case reports with diltiazem include hyperactivity, akathisia, and parkinsonism; with verapamil, delirium, hyperprolactinemia, and galactorrhea have been noted. The drugs have not been evaluated for safety in pregnant women and are best avoided. Because the drugs are secreted in breast milk, nursing mothers should also avoid the drugs. The elderly are more sensitive to the calcium channel inhibitors than are younger adults. No specific information is available regarding the use of the agents for children.

## DRUG INTERACTIONS

Calcium channel inhibitors should not be prescribed for patients taking β-adrenergic receptor antagonists, hypotensives (for example, diuretics, vasodilators, and angiotensin-converting enzyme inhibitors), or antiarrhythmic drugs (for example, quinidine and digoxin) without consultation with the patient's internist or cardiologist. Verapamil and diltiazem but not nifedipine have been reported to precipitate carbamazepine-induced neurotoxicity. Cimetidine (Tagamet) has been reported to increase plasma concentrations of nifedipine and diltiazem.

## LABORATORY INTERFERENCES

No known laboratory interferences are associated with the use of calcium channel inhibitors.

## DOSAGE AND ADMINISTRATION

Verapamil is available in 40, 80, and 120 mg tablets; 180 and 240 mg extended-release tablets; and 120 and 240 mg capsules. The starting dosage is 40 mg orally three times a day and can be raised in increments every four to five days up to 80 to 120 mg three times a day. The patient's blood pressure, pulse, and electrocardiogram (ECG) (in patients more than 40 years old or with a history of cardiac illness) should be routinely monitored. Diltiazem is available in 30, 60, 90, and 120 mg tablets and 60, 90, and 120 mg capsules. It should be started at 30 mg orally four times a day and can be increased up to a maximum of 360 mg a day. Nifedipine is available in 10 and 20 mg capsules and 30, 60, and 90 mg tablets. It should be started at 10 mg orally three or four times a day and can be increased up to a maximum dosage of 180 mg a day.

### References

Duncan E, Adler L, Angrist B, Rotrosen J: Nifedipine in the treatment of tardive dyskinesia. J Clin Psychopharmacol *10*: 414, 1990.

Freeman T W, Clothier J L, Pazzaglia P, Lesem M D, Swann A C: A double-blind comparison of valproate and lithium in the treatment of acute mania. Am J Psychiatry *149*: 108, 1992.

Garza-Trevino E S, Overall J E, Hollister L E: Verapamil versus lithium in acute mania. Am J Psychiatry *149*: 121, 1992.

Grebb J A, Shelton R C, Taylor E H, Bigelow L B: A negative, double-blind, placebo-controlled, clinical trial of verapamil in chronic schizophrenia. Biol Psychiatry *21*: 691, 1986.

Pickar D, Wolkowitz O M, Doran A R, Labarca R, Roy A, Breier A, Narang P K: Clinical and biochemical effects of verapamil administration to schizophrenic patients. Arch Gen Psychiatry *44*: 113, 1987.

Pollack M H, Rosenbaum J F, Hyman S E: Calcium channel blockers in psychiatry. Psychosomatics *28*: 356, 1987.

Pucilowski O: Psychopharmacological properties of calcium channel inhibitors. Psychopharmacology *109*: 12, 1992.

Tollefson G D: Short-term effects of the calcium channel blocker nimodipine (Bay-e-9736) in the management of primary degenerative dementia. Biol Psychiatry *27*: 1133, 1990.

# 33.3.10 / Carbamazepine

Carbamazepine (Tegretol) is an iminodiabenzyl drug, structurally similar to imipramine (Tofranil) and approved for use in the United States for the treatment of temporal lobe epilepsy and trigeminal neuralgia. A large body of data supports the use of carbamazepine for the treatment of acute mania and for the prophylactic treatment of bipolar I disorder.

## CHEMISTRY

The molecular structure of carbamazepine, shown in Figure 33.3.10–1, is similar to the tricyclic structure of imipramine.

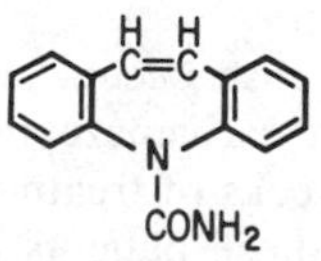

## PHARMACOLOGICAL ACTIONS

### Pharmacokinetics

Carbamazepine is absorbed slowly and erratically from the gastrointestinal (GI) tract; absorption is enhanced when the drug is taken with meals. Peak plasma levels are reached two to eight hours after a single dose; steady-state levels are

**Figure 33.3.10–1.** Molecular structure of carbamazepine.

reached after two to four days on a steady dosage. The half-life of carbamazepine at the initiation of treatment has a wide range; during long-term administration the half-life decreases to a range from 12 to 17 hours because of the induction of hepatic enzymes. The induction of hepatic enzymes reaches its maximum level after about one month of therapy. Carbamazepine is metabolized in the liver and is excreted by the kidneys. The 10-,11-epoxide metabolite is active as an anticonvulsant; its activity in the treatment of bipolar I disorder is unknown. Recent reports have indicated that carbamazepine can lose one third of its potency when stored in a humid environment. Manufacturers are now advising consumers not to store the drug in such environments as bathrooms.

### Pharmacodynamics

Although it is parsimonious to hypothesize that the antimanic properties of carbamazepine result from the same biochemical effects as its anticonvulsant properties, that assumption could be inaccurate. Arguing against that hypothesis is the observation that, although the anticonvulsant and antinociceptive effects of carbamazepine have a rapid onset, the antimanic effects take longer to develop. The anticonvulsant effects of carbamazepine may be mediated through so-called peripheral benzodiazepine receptors located in the brain, the potentiation of $\alpha_2$-adrenergic receptors, or the stabilization of sodium channels on neurons. Central benzodiazepine receptors are more or less the same as the $\gamma$-aminobutyric acid (GABA) type A receptor and are the site of action for the benzodiazepines. $GABA_A$ receptors are essentially GABA-gated ion channels. Peripheral benzodiazepine receptors, which exist in both the periphery and the central nervous system (CNS), are thought to be regulators of calcium channel function. The potential effect of carbamazepine on calcium channels is interesting theoretically in the light of the increasing use of calcium channel inhibitors for the treatment of bipolar I disorder.

Theoretically, another basis for the antimanic effect of carbamazepine involves the concept of kindling. *Kindling* is the electrophysiological process in which repeated subthreshold stimulations of a neuron eventually generate an action potential. Bipolar I disorder may represent a covert form of limbic epilepsy, which is responsive to carbamazepine; however, electroencephalograms (EEGs) are normal in the majority of bipolar I disorder patients who respond to carbamazepine.

## EFFECTS ON SPECIFIC ORGANS AND SYSTEMS

Besides the effects on the CNS, carbamazepine has its most significant effects on the hematopoietic system. Carbamazepine is associated with a benign decrease in the white blood cell count, with values always remaining above 3,000. The decrease is thought to be due to the inhibition of the colony-stimulating factor in the bone marrow, an effect that can be reversed by the coadministration of lithium (Eskalith), which stimulates the colony-stimulating factor. The benign suppression of white blood cell production must be differentiated from the potentially fatal adverse effects of agranulocytosis, pancytopenia, and aplastic anemia.

As reflected by its use to treat diabetes insipidus, carbamazepine apparently has a vasopressinlike effect on the vasopressin receptor, sometimes causing the development of water intoxication or hyponatremia, particularly in elderly patients. That side effect can be treated with dem-eclomycin (Declomycin) or lithium. Another endocrine effect associated with carbamazepine is an increase in urinary free cortisol.

The effects of carbamazepine on the cardiovascular system are minimal. It does decrease atrioventricular (A-V) conduction, thus the use of carbamazepine is contraindicated in patients with A-V heart blocks.

## THERAPEUTIC INDICATIONS

### Bipolar I Disorder

Almost two dozen well-controlled studies have shown that carbamazepine is effective in the treatment of acute mania, with efficacy comparable to lithium and antipsychotics. About 10 studies have also shown that carbamazepine is effective in the prophylaxis of both manic and depressive episodes in bipolar I disorder when it is used for prophylactic treatment. Carbamazepine is an effective antimanic agent in 50 to 70 percent of all patients. Additional evidence from those studies indicates that carbamazepine may be effective in some patients who are not responsive to lithium, such as patients with dysphoric mania, rapid cycling, or a negative family history of mood disorders. However, a few clinical and basic science data indicate that some patients may experience a tolerance for the antimanic effects of carbamazepine.

### Schizophrenia and Schizoaffective Disorder

Several well-controlled studies have produced data indicating that carbamazepine is effective in the treatment of schizophrenia and schizoaffective disorder. Patients with positive symptoms (for example, hallucinations) and few negative symptoms (for example, anhedonia) may be likely to respond, as are patients who have impulsive aggressive outbursts as a symptom.

### Depressive Disorders

The available data indicate that carbamazepine is an effective treatment for depression in some patients. About 25 to 33 percent of depressed patients respond to carbamazepine. That percentage is significantly smaller than the 60 to 70 percent response rate for standard antidepressants. Nevertheless, carbamazepine is an alternative drug for depressed patients who have not responded to conventional treatments, including electroconvulsive therapy (ECT), or who have a marked or rapid periodicity in their depressive episodes.

### Impulse Control Disorders

Several studies have reported that carbamazepine is effective in controlling impulsive, aggressive behavior in nonpsychotic patients. Other drugs for impulse control disorders, particularly intermittent explosive disorder, include lithium, propranolol (Inderal), and antipsychotics. Because of the risk of serious adverse effects with carbam-

azepine, clinical trials with those other agents are warranted before initiating a trial with carbamazepine.

Carbamazepine is also effective in controlling nonacute agitation and aggressive behavior in schizophrenic patients. Diagnoses to be ruled out before treatment with carbamazepine is begun include akathisia and neuroleptic malignant syndrome. Lorazepam (Ativan) is more effective than carbamazepine for the control of acute agitation.

**Alcohol withdrawal.** According to several studies, carbamazepine is as effective as the benzodiazepines in the control of symptoms associated with alcohol withdrawal. However, the lack of any advantage of carbamazepine over the benzodiazepines and the potential risk of adverse effects with carbamazepine limit the clinical usefulness of that application.

## PRECAUTIONS AND ADVERSE REACTIONS

Although the drug's benign hematological effects are not dose-related, most of the adverse effects of carbamazepine are correlated with plasma concentrations above 9 µg per mL. A comparison of the adverse effects of lithium and carbamazepine is presented in Table 33.3.10–1. The rarest but most serious adverse effects of carbamazepine are blood dyscrasias, hepatitis, and exfoliative dermatitis. Otherwise, carbamazepine is relatively well-tolerated by patients except for mild GI and CNS effects that can be significantly reduced if the dosage is increased slowly and minimal effective plasma concentrations are maintained.

### Blood Dyscrasias

Severe blood dyscrasias (aplastic anemia, agranulocytosis) occur in about 1 in 20,000 patients treated with carbamazepine. There does not appear to be a correlation between the degree of benign white blood cell suppression and the emergence of life-threatening blood dyscrasias. Patients should be warned that the emergence of such symptoms as fever, sore throat, rash, petechiae, bruising, and easy bleeding are potentially symptoms of a serious dyscrasia and should cause the patient to seek medical evaluation immediately. The benefit of routine hematological monitoring in carbamazepine-treated patients is uncertain.

### Hepatitis

Within the first few weeks of therapy, carbamazepine can cause both a hypersensitivity hepatitis associated with increases in liver enzymes and a cholestasis associated with elevated bilirubin and alkaline phosphatase. Hepatitis will recur if the drug is reintroduced to the patient and can result in the death of the patient.

### Exfoliative Dermatitis

A benign pruritic rash occurs in 10 to 15 percent of patients treated with carbamazepine, usually occurring within the first few weeks of treatment. Unfortunately, a small percentage of those patients may then experience life-threatening dermatological syndromes, including ex-

**Table 33.3.10–1**
**Comparative and Differential Side-Effects Profiles of Lithium Carbonate and Carbamazepine**

| Side Effects | Lithium Carbonate | Carbamazepine | Lithium and Carbamazepine Combination |
|---|---|---|---|
| White blood count | ↑ | ↓ | ↑, —, Li* |
| Diabetes insipidus | ↑ | | ↑, Li* |
| Thyroid hormones $T_3$, $T_4$ | ↓ | ↓ | ↓ ↓ |
| TSH | ↑ | (−) | ↑, Li* |
| Serum calcium | (↑) | ↓ | (↑), (Li*) |
| Weight gain | (↑) | (−) | |
| Tremor | (↑) | (−) | |
| Memory disturbances | (↑) | ? | |
| Diarrhea | (↑) | | |
| Teratogenic effects | (↑) | − | |
| Psoriasis | (↑) | (−) | |
| Pruritic rash (allergy) | − | ↑ | |
| Agranulocytosis | − | (↑) | |
| Hepatitis | − | (↑) | |
| Hyponatremia, water intoxication | − | (↑) | |
| Dizziness, ataxia, diplopia | − | ↑ | |
| Hypercortisolism, escape from dexamethasone suppression | − | ↑ | |

↑ : Increase
↓ : Decrease
( ): Inconsistent or rare
− : Absent
↓ ↓ : Potentiation
Li*: Effect of lithium predominates
Table adapted from Robert M. Post, M.D. Used with permission.

foliative dermatitis, erythema multiforme, Stevens-Johnson syndrome, and toxic epidermal necrolysis. The possible emergence of those serious dermatological problems causes most clinicians to discontinue carbamazepine use if any type of rash develops in a patient. If carbamazepine seems to be the only effective drug for a patient who has a benign rash with carbamazepine treatment, a retrial of the drug can be undertaken with pretreatment of the patient with prednisone (40 mg a day) in an attempt to treat the rash, although other symptoms of an allergic reaction (for example, fever and pneumonitis) may develop, even with steroid pretreatment.

## Gastrointestinal Effects

The most common adverse effects of carbamazepine are nausea, vomiting, gastric distress, constipation, diarrhea, and anorexia. The severity of the adverse effects is reduced if the dosage of carbamazepine is increased slowly and kept at the minimal effective plasma concentration.

## Central Nervous System Effects

Acute confusional states can occur with carbamazepine alone but occur most often in combination with lithium or antipsychotic drugs. The symptoms of CNS toxicity include drowsiness, confusion, ataxia, hyperreflexia, clonus, and tremor. Elderly patients and patients with cognitive disorders are at increased risk for CNS toxicity from carbamazepine. The common CNS effects of dizziness, ataxia, clumsiness, and sedation are often associated with carbamazepine treatment, although they are reduced by a slow upward titration of the dosage.

## Other Adverse Effects

Carbamazepine decreases cardiac conduction (although less than the tricyclic drugs do) and can, thus, exacerbate preexisting cardiac disease. Carbamazepine should be used with caution in patients with glaucoma, prostatic hypertrophy, diabetes, or a history of alcohol abuse. Some evidence indicates that minor cranial facial abnormalities and spina bifida in infants may be associated with the maternal use of carbamazepine during pregnancy. Therefore, pregnant women should not use carbamazepine unless absolutely necessary. Carbamazepine is secreted in breast milk, so women taking carbamazepine should not nurse their babies.

## Overdoses

Overdoses of carbamazepine, when taken alone, have a generally favorable outcome. Symptoms associated with an overdose include drowsiness, stupor, coma, sinus tachycardia, hypotension or hypertension, A-V conduction block, seizures, nystagmus, hypothermia, facial dyskinesias, and respiratory depression. Gastric lavage and the use of activated charcoal (50 to 100 grams, followed by 12.5 grams an hour until the patient has recovered) early in the course of emergency treatment are recommended. Some investigators have recommended the use of flumazenil (Mazicon) to block the effects of carbamazepine on central-type benzodiazepine receptors.

## DRUG INTERACTIONS

The mechanisms for drug interactions with carbamazepine are many (Table 33.3.10–2) and result in many po-

**Table 33.3.10–2**
**Carbamazepine (CBZ) Properties**
**Relevant to Pharmacokinetics and Drug Interactions**

| Property | Relevance |
|---|---|
| Induces catabolic enzymes | ↓ Levels of CBZ and other drugs<br>↓ Thyroid hormones*, and androgens*<br>↓ Effects of mild inducers on CBZ (induction ceiling ?)<br>↑ 6-β-Hydroxycortisol excretion<br>↑ Pseudocholinesterase |
| Exclusively hepatic metabolism | ↑ CBZ levels with certain enzyme inhibitors<br>↓ CBZ levels with certain robust inducers (phenytoin, phenobarbital, primidone)<br>No kinetic interactions with lithium |
| Active (CBZ-E) metabolite | Occult ↑ therapeutic and side effects with inducers of CBZ metabolism and inhibitors of CBZ-E metabolism |
| Induces anabolic enzymes | ↑ HDL cholesterol, ↑ cortisol*<br>↑ Sex hormone binding globulin<br>↑ $\alpha_1$-Acid glycoprotein |
| Antidiuretic hormone agonist | Hyponatremia (↑ with diuretics)*<br>↑ Antidiuretic drug effects*<br>↓ Diuretic drug effects* |
| Plasma protein binding not extensive | Few binding interactions in general |
| Primary albumin binding | ↑ Free CBZ with valproate (displaced) |
| Secondary $\alpha_1$-acid glycoprotein binding | ↑ Bound CBZ and other drugs (in CBZ induction and acute disease)<br>Interindividual variations in free CBZ |

*Entirely or partially pharmacodynamic mechanism hypothesized.
Table from T A Ketter, R M Post, K Worthington: Principles of clinically important drug interactions with carbamazepine: Part I. J Clin Psychopharmacol *11*: 199, 1991. Used with permission.

**Table 33.3.10–3**
**Clinically Important Interactions**
**Between Carbamazepine and Other Drugs**

**Influences of Other Drugs on Carbamazepine**

| | |
|---|---|
| Increased carbamazepine levels and toxicity produced by<br>Danazol<br>Diltiazen (not nifedipine)<br>Erythromycin (and analogues)<br>Influenza vaccine<br>Isoniazid (not tranylcypromine)<br>Nafimidone<br>Triacetyloleandomycin<br>Verapamil<br>Viloxazine<br>Decreased carbamazepine levels produced by<br>Phenobarbital<br>Phenytoin<br>Primidone<br>Theophylline<br>Tricyclic drugs | Increased carbamazepine levels not associated with marked toxicity<br>Cimetidine (mild acute increases; none after one week)<br>Josamycin<br>Nicotinamide<br>Propoxyphene<br>Valproate (increases epoxide only) |

**Influences of Carbamazepine on Other Drugs**

Carbamazepine decreases levels or effects of
Clonazepam
Cyclosporine
Dexamethasone
Dicoumarol
Doxycycline
Ethosuximide
Haloperidol
Pregnancy tests
Theophylline
Tricyclic drugs
Valproate
Warfarin

thyronine [$T_3$]) without an associated increase in thyroid-stimulating hormone (TSH). Carbamazepine is also associated with an increase in total serum cholesterol, primarily by increasing high-density lipoproteins. The thyroid and cholesterol effects are not clinically significant. Carbamazepine may also cause a false-positive result in a pregnancy test.

tentially relevant drug interactions (Table 33.3.10–3). Coadministration with lithium, antipsychotic drugs, verapamil (Calan), or nifedipine (Procardia) can precipitate carbamazepine-induced CNS adverse effects. Carbamazepine can decrease the blood concentrations of oral contraceptives, resulting in breakthrough bleeding and uncertain prophylaxis against pregnancy. Carbamazepine should not be administered with monoamine oxidase inhibitors (MAOIs), which should be discontinued for at least two weeks before initiating treatment with carbamazepine.

## LABORATORY INTERFERENCES

Carbamazepine treatment is associated with a decrease in thyroid hormones (thyroxine [$T_4$], free $T_4$, and triiodo-

## DOSAGE AND ADMINISTRATION

Carbamazepine can be used alone or with an antipsychotic drug for the treatment of manic episodes, although carbamazepine-induced CNS adverse effects (drowsiness, dizziness, ataxia) are likely to occur with that combination of drugs. Patients who do not respond to lithium alone may respond when carbamazepine is added to the lithium treatment. If patients then respond, an attempt should be made to withdraw the lithium to assess whether the patient can be treated successfully with carbamazepine alone. When lithium and carbamazepine are used together, the clinician should minimize or discontinue any antipsychotics, sedatives, or anticholinergic drugs the patient may be taking to reduce the risks for adverse effects associated with taking multiple drugs. The lithium and the carbamazepine should both be used at standard therapeutic plasma concentrations before a trial of combined therapy is considered to have been a therapeutic failure. A three-week trial of carbamazepine at therapeutic plasma concentrations is usually sufficient to determine whether the drug will be effective in the treatment of acute mania; a longer trial is necessary to assess efficacy in the treatment of depression. Carbamazepine is also used in combination with valproate (Depakene), another anticonvulsant that is effective in bipolar I disorder. When carbamazepine and valproate are used in combination, the dosage of carbamazepine should be decreased, because valproate displaces carbamazepine binding on proteins, and the dosage of valproate may need to be increased.

## Pretreatment Medical Evaluation

The patient's medical history should include information about preexisting hematological, hepatic, and cardiac diseases, because all three can be relative contraindications for carbamazepine treatment. Patients with hepatic disease require only one third to one half the usual dosage; the clinician should be cautious about raising the dosage in such patients and should do so only slowly and gradually. The laboratory examination should include a complete blood count with platelet count, liver function tests, serum electrolytes, and an electrocardiogram in patients more than 40 years of age or with a preexisting cardiac disease. An electroencephalogram (EEG) is not necessary before the initiation of treatment, but it may be helpful in some cases for the documentation of objective changes correlated with clinical improvement.

## Initiation of Treatment

Carbamazepine is available in 100 and 200 mg tablets and as a 100 mg per 5 mL suspension. The usual starting dosage is 200 mg orally two times a day. Carbamazepine should be taken with meals, and the drug should be stored in a cool, dry place. Carbamazepine stored in a bathroom medicine cabinet can lose up to one third of its activity. In an inpatient setting with seriously ill patients, the dosage can be raised by not more than 200 mg a day until a dosage of 600 to 1,000 mg a day is reached. That relatively rapid titration, however, is often associated with adverse effects and may adversely affect compliance with the drug. In less ill patients and in outpatients, the dosage should be raised no more quickly than 200 mg every two to four days to minimize the occurrence of minor adverse effects, such as nausea, vomiting, drowsiness, and dizziness. When discontinuing treatment with carbamazepine, the clinician need not taper the dosage.

## Blood Levels

The anticonvulsant blood level range for carbamazepine is 4 to 12 μg per mL, and that range should be reached before determining that carbamazepine is not effective in the treatment of a mood disorder. It is clinically prudent to come up to that range gradually, since the patient is likely to tolerate a gradual increase of carbamazepine bet-

ter than a rapid increase. The clinician should titrate carbamazepine up to the highest well-tolerated dosage before deciding that the drug is ineffective. Plasma concentrations should be obtained when a patient has been receiving a steady dosage for at least five days. Blood for the determination of plasma levels is drawn in the morning before the first daily dose of carbamazepine is given. The total daily dosage necessary to achieve plasma concentrations in the usual therapeutic range varies from 400 to 1,600 mg a day, with a mean around 1,000 mg a day.

## Routine Laboratory Monitoring

The most serious potential effects of carbamazepine are agranulocytosis and aplastic anemia. Although it has been suggested that complete laboratory blood assessments be performed every two weeks for the first two months of treatment and quarterly thereafter, that conservative approach may not be justified by a cost-benefit analysis and may not detect a serious blood dyscrasia before it occurs. The Food and Drug Administration (FDA) has revised the package insert for carbamazepine to suggest that blood monitoring be performed at the discretion of the physician. Patient education about the signs and the symptoms of a developing hematological problem is probably more effective than is frequent blood monitoring in protecting against that adverse event. It has also been suggested that liver and renal function tests be conducted quarterly, although the benefit of conducting those tests that frequently has been questioned. It seems reasonable, however, to assess hematological status, along with liver and renal functions, whenever a routine examination of the patient is being conducted.

The following laboratory values should prompt the physician to discontinue carbamazepine treatment and to consult a hematologist: total white blood cell count less than 3,000 mm$^3$, erythrocytes less than $4.0 \times 10^6$ per mm$^3$, neutrophils less than 1,500 per mm$^3$, hematocrit less than 32 percent, hemoglobin less than 11 grams per 100 mL, platelet count less than 100,000 per mm$^3$, reticulocyte count less than 0.3 percent, and serum iron level less than 150 mg per 100 mL.

## References

Adamec R E: Does kindling model anything clinically relevant? Biol Psychiatry 27: 249, 1990.
Cullen M, Mitchell P, Brodaty H, Boyce P, Parker G, Hickie I, Wilhelm K: Carbamazepine for treatment-resistant melancholia. J Clin Psychiatry 52: 472, 1991.
Elphick M, Yang J-D, Cowen P J: Effects of carbamazepine on dopamine- and serotonin-mediated neuroendocrine responses. Arch Gen Psychiatry 47: 135, 1990.
Ketter T A, Post R M, Worthington K: Principles of clinically important drug interactions with carbamazepine: Part I. J Clin Psychopharmacol 11: 198, 1991.
Ketter T A, Post R M, Worthington K: Principles of clinically important drug interactions with carbamazepine: Part II. J Clin Psychopharmacol 11: 306, 1991.
Kramlinger K G, Post R M: Addition of lithium carbonate to carbamazepine: Hematological and thyroid effects. Am J Psychiatry 147: 615, 1990.
Kramlinger K G, Post R M: The addition of lithium to carbamazepine: Antidepressant efficacy in treatment-resistant depression. Arch Gen Psychiatry 46: 794, 1989.
Leinonen E, Lillsunde P, Laukkanen V, Ylitalo P: Effects of carbamazepine on serum antidepressant concentrations in psychiatric patients. J Clin Psychopharmacol 11: 313, 1991.
Lerer B, Moore N, Meyendorff E, Cho S-R, Gershorn S: Carbamazepine

versus lithium in mania: A double-blind study. J Clin Psychiatry *48*: 89, 1987.

Malcolm R, Ballenger J C, Sturgis E T, Anton R: Double-blind controlled trial comparing carbamazepine to oxazepam treatment of alcohol withdrawal. Am J Psychiatry *146*: 617, 1989.

Neppe W M, editor: Carbamazepine use in neuropsychiatry. J Clin Psychiatry *49* (4, Suppl): 2, 1988.

Post R M, Leverich G S, Rosoff A S, Altshuler L L: Carbamazepine prophylaxis in refractory affective disorders: A focus on long-term follow-up. J Clin Psychopharmacol *10*: 318, 1990.

Stuppaeck C, Barbas C, Miller C, Schwitzer J, Fleischhacker W W: Carbamazepine in the prophylaxis of mood disorders. J Clin Psychopharmacol *10*: 39, 1990.

Tohen M, Castillo J, Cole J O, Miller M G, de los Heros R, Farrer R J: Thrombocytopenia associated with carbamazepine: A case series. J Clin Psychiatry *52*: 496, 1991.

VanValkenburg C, Kluznik J C, Merrill R: New uses of anticonvulsant drugs in psychosis. Drugs *44*: 326, 1992.

# 33.3.11 / Chloral Hydrate

Chloral hydrate (Noctec) is one of the oldest sedative-hypnotic drugs still in use, having been used since 1869. Because of the introduction of many compounds since that time, chloral hydrate is now used only as a short-term (two- or three-day) hypnotic.

## CHEMISTRY

Its chemical formula is $CCl_3CH(OH)_2$.

## PHARMACOLOGICAL ACTIONS

### Pharmacokinetics

Chloral hydrate is well-absorbed from the gastrointestinal (GI) tract. The parent compound is metabolized within minutes by the liver and red blood cells and is excreted by the kidneys. An active metabolite, trichloroethanol, has a half-life of 8 to 11 hours. A dose of chloral hydrate induces sleep in about 30 to 60 minutes and maintains sleep for four to eight hours.

### Pharmacodynamics

The pharmacodynamic basis for the hypnotic effect of chloral hydrate is not known, although some investigators have hypothesized that the metabolite trichloroethanol is the active agent involved in producing hypnosis.

## EFFECTS ON SPECIFIC ORGANS AND SYSTEMS

In addition to its central nervous system (CNS) effects, chloral hydrate has effects on the GI system and the skin. The GI effects include nonspecific irritation, nausea, vomiting, flatulence, and an unpleasant taste. The dermatological effects, although not common, include rashes, urticaria, purpura, eczema, and erythema multiforme. The dermatological lesions are sometimes accompanied by fever.

## THERAPEUTIC INDICATIONS

The major indication for chloral hydrate is insomnia. Whether chloral hydrate affects rapid eye movement (REM) sleep is controversial; however, the patient experiences no REM rebound after discontinuation of chloral hydrate therapy. Long-term treatment with chloral hydrate is associated with an increased incidence and severity of adverse effects. Tolerance develops to the hypnotic effects of chloral hydrate after two weeks of treatment.

## PRECAUTIONS AND ADVERSE REACTIONS

The most common GI adverse effects are nausea, vomiting, and diarrhea. Patients should be warned that they may experience residual daytime sedation and impaired motor coordination. Chloral hydrate should be avoided in patients with severe renal, cardiac, or hepatic disease or with porphyria. The drug may aggravate GI inflammatory conditions. Chloral hydrate should not be used during pregnancy or by nursing women. It is not expected to cause particular difficulties in children or the elderly; however, no specific information is available for chloral hydrate use in those populations.

In addition to the development of tolerance, dependence on chloral hydrate can occur, with symptoms similar to those of alcohol dependence. The symptoms of intoxication include confusion, ataxia, dysarthria, bradycardia, arrhythmia, and severe drowsiness. The lethal dose of chloral hydrate is between 5,000 and 10,000 mg, thus making chloral hydrate a particularly poor choice for potentially suicidal patients. The lethality of the drug is potentiated by other CNS depressants, including alcohol. With long-term use and with overdose, gastritis and gastric ulceration can develop. Hepatic and renal damage can follow overdose attempts, resulting in jaundice and albuminuria.

## DRUG INTERACTIONS

Patients who have received chloral hydrate less than 24 hours before receiving intravenous furosemide (Lasix) can have diaphoresis, flushes, and an unsteady blood pressure. Reports are somewhat controversial concerning the potentiation of warfarin (Coumadin) when coadministered with chloral hydrate.

## LABORATORY INTERFERENCES

Chloral hydrate administration can lead to false-positive results for urine glucose determinations that use cupric sulfate in the determination (for example, Clinitest) but not in tests that use glucose oxidase (for example, Clinistix and Tes-Tape). Chloral hydrate may also interfere with the determination of urinary catecholamines and 17-hydroxycorticosteroids.

## DOSAGE AND ADMINISTRATION

Chloral hydrate is available in 250 and 500 mg capsules, 250 and 500 mg per 5 mL solutions, and 325, 500, and 650 mg rectal suppositories. The standard dose of chloral hydrate is 500 to 2,000 mg at bedtime. Because the drug is a GI irritant, it should be administered with excess water, milk, other liquids, or antacids to decrease the gastric irritation.

### References

Graham S R, Day R O, Lee R, Fulde G W: Overdose with chloral hydrate: A pharmacological and therapeutic review. Med J Aust *149*: 686, 1988.
Keeter S, Benator R M, Weinberg S M, Hartenburg M A: Sedation in pediatric CT: National survey of current practice. Radiology *175*: 745, 1990.
Schuler M E: Augmentation of chloral hydrate induced sleep by centrally acting hypertensive agents. Proc West Pharmacol Soc *25*: 347, 1982.

# 33.3.12 / Clonidine

Clonidine (Catapres) is an $\alpha_2$-adrenergic receptor agonist used primarily as a hypotensive agent. Its major indications in psychiatry are the control of the withdrawal symptoms from opiates and opioids and the treatment of Tourette's disorder.

## CHEMISTRY

The molecular structure of clonidine is shown in Figure 33.3.12–1.

## PHARMACOLOGICAL ACTIONS

### Pharmacokinetics

Clonidine is well-absorbed from the gastrointestinal (GI) tract and reaches peak plasma levels one to three hours after

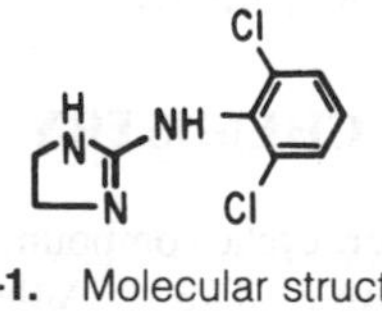

**Figure 33.3.12–1.** Molecular structure of clonidine.

oral administration. About 35 percent of the drug is metabolized by the liver, and 65 percent is excreted in both unchanged and metabolized forms by the kidneys. The half-life of the parent compound is 6 to 20 hours, and there are no active metabolites.

### Pharmacodynamics

The agonist effects of clonidine on presynaptic $\alpha_2$-adrenergic receptors result in a decrease in the amount of neurotransmitter released from the presynaptic nerve terminals. Both the hypotensive and the psychiatric effects of clonidine are mediated by central nervous system (CNS) $\alpha_2$-adrenergic receptors, rather than by peripheral receptors.

## EFFECTS ON SPECIFIC ORGANS AND SYSTEMS

Clonidine exerts its hypotensive effects by stimulating $\alpha_2$-adrenergic receptors in the medulla oblongata, thus causing the inhibition of sympathetic vasomotor centers. Those central effects result in reduced peripheral sympathetic tone, the reduction of diastolic and systolic blood pressure, and bradycardia. Clonidine administration also results in sedation and the release of growth hormone. The effects of clonidine on the gastrointestinal tract and the kidneys are minimal.

## THERAPEUTIC INDICATIONS

### Opiate and Opioid Withdrawal

Clonidine is effective in reducing the autonomic symptoms of opiate and opioid withdrawal (for example, hypertension, tachycardia, dilated pupils, sweating, lacrimation, and rhinorrhea) but not the associated subjective sensations. Clonidine can be used in withdrawing a patient from methadone. Usually, dosages of 0.15 mg twice a day are sufficient for that purpose. The efficacy of clonidine in treating opiate and opioid withdrawal may reflect its activity on the noradrenergic neurons of the locus ceruleus.

### Tourette's Disorder

Some clinicians use clonidine as a first-line drug for the treatment of Tourette's disorder instead of the standard drugs, haloperiodol (Haldol) and pimozide (Orap), because of the serious adverse effects associated with those antipsychotics. The starting child dosage is 0.05 mg a day; it can be raised to 0.3 mg a day in divided doses. Three months are needed before the beneficial effects of clonidine can be seen in Tourette's disorder.

### Other Disorders

Other potential indications for clonidine include the anxiety disorders (panic disorder, phobias, obsessive-compulsive disorder, posttraumatic stress disorder, and generalized anxiety disorder) and mania, in which it may be synergistic with lithium (Eskalith) or carbamazepine (Tegretol). Anecdotal reports have noted the efficacy of clonidine in schizophrenia, tardive dyskinesia, and smoking cessation.

## PRECAUTIONS AND ADVERSE REACTIONS

The most common adverse effects associated with clonidine are dry mouth and eyes, fatigue, sedation, dizziness, nausea, hypotension, and constipation, which result in the discontinuation from therapy of about 10 percent of all patients taking the drug. Some patients also experience sexual dysfunction. Uncommon CNS adverse effects include insomnia, anxiety, and depression; rare CNS adverse effects include vivid dreams, nightmares, and hallucinations. Fluid retention associated with clonidine treatment can be treated with diuretics.

Patients who overdose on clonidine can present with coma and constricted pupils, symptoms similar to an opioid overdose. Other symptoms of overdose are decreased blood pressure, pulse, and respiratory rates. Clonidine should be used with caution in patients with heart disease, renal disease, Raynaud's syndrome, or a history of depression. Clonidine should be avoided during pregnancy and by nursing mothers. The elderly are more sensitive to the drug than are younger adults. Children are susceptible to the same side effects as are adults.

## DRUG INTERACTIONS

The most relevant drug interaction is that the coadministration of clonidine and tricyclic drugs can inhibit the hypotensive effects of clonidine. Clonidine may also enhance the CNS depressive effects of barbiturates, alcohol, and other sedative-hypnotics. The concomitant use of β-adrenergic receptor antagonists can increase the severity of rebound phenomena when clonidine is discontinued.

## LABORATORY INTERFERENCES

No known laboratory interferences are associated with the use of clonidine.

## DOSAGE AND ADMINISTRATION

Clonidine is available in 0.1, 0.2, and 0.3 mg tablets. The usual starting dosage is 0.1 mg orally twice a day; the dosage can be raised by 0.1 mg a day to an appropriate level. Clonidine must always be tapered when it is discontinued to avoid rebound hypertension, which occurs about 20 hours after the last clonidine dose. Regardless of the indication for which clonidine is being used, the drug should be withheld if a patient becomes hypotensive (blood pressure less than 90/60).

**References**

Charney D C, Heninger G R, Kleber H D: The combined use of clonidine and naltrexone as a rapid, safe, and effective treatment of abrupt withdrawal from methadone. Am J Psychiatry *143*: 831, 1986.

Cuthill J D, Baroniada V, Salvatori V A, Viguie F: Evaluation of clonidine suppression of opiate withdrawal reactions: A multidisciplinary approach. Can J Psychiatry *35*: 377, 1990.
Fankhauser M P, Karumanchi V C, German M L, Yates A, Karumanchi S D: A double-blind, placebo-controlled study of the efficacy of transdermal clonidine in autism. J Clin Psychiatry *53*: 77, 1992.
Giannini A J, Pascarzi G A, Loiselle R H, Price W A, Giannini M C: Comparison of clonidine and lithium in the treatment of mania. Am J Psychiatry *143*: 1608, 1986.
Hardy M-C, Lecrubier Y, Widlöcher D: Efficacy of clonidine in 24 patients with acute mania. Am J Psychiatry *143*: 1450, 1986.
Heidemann S M, Sarnaik A P: Clonidine poisoning in children. Crit Care Med *18*: 618, 1990.
Leckman J F, Hardin M T, Riddle M A, Stevenson J, Ort S I, Cohen D J: Clonidine treatment of Gilles de la Tourette's syndrome. Arch Gen Psychiatry *48*: 324, 1991.
Ornish S A, Zisook S, McAdams L A: Effects of transdermal clonidine treatment on withdrawal symptoms associated with smoking cessation: A randomized, controlled trial. Arch Intern Med *148*: 2027, 1988.
Sandyk R, Gillman M A, Iacono R P, Bamford C R: Clonidine in neuropsychiatric disorders: A review. Int J Neurosci *35*: 205, 1987.
Tulen J H M, van de Wetering B J M, Kruijk M P C W, von Saher R A, Moleman P, Boomsma F, van Steenis H G, Man in 't Veld A J: Cardiovascular, neuroendocrine, and sedative responses to four graded doses of clonidine in a placebo-controlled study. Biol Psychiatry *32*: 485, 1992.

# 33.3.13 / Clozapine

Clozapine (Clozaril) is an effective antipsychotic drug that is associated with significantly fewer parkinsonianlike side effects than are the conventional antipsychotics, which act primarily by their antagonist activity at dopamine type 2 ($D_2$) receptors. In addition, clozapine may be more effective in the treatment of the negative symptoms of schizophrenia than are the conventional antipsychotics and in the treatment of schizophrenic patients who have not responded to the traditional antipsychotic drugs. However, treatment with clozapine is associated with specific adverse events, the most serious of which is the occurrence of agranulocytosis in about 1 to 2 percent of all patients, an adverse event that necessitates the weekly hematological monitoring of patients who are being treated with clozapine.

Clozapine was approved in 1990 by the U.S. Food and Drug Administration (FDA) for use by treatment-resistant schizophrenic patients. The drug had been discovered in 1958, and its therapeutic antipsychotic effects in the absence of extrapyramidal effects was noted soon after it was used in clinical trials. By 1975 the association between clozapine and agranulocytosis had been recognized; however, the uniqueness of the therapeutic and side-effect profiles of clozapine spurred researchers to continue carefully monitored studies with the drug. A series of studies in Europe and the United States eventually showed that clozapine can be used safely if weekly hematological monitoring is performed, thus leading to the approval of the drug by the FDA.

## CHEMISTRY

Clozapine is a heterocyclic compound; its molecular structure is shown in Figure 33.3.13–1. Although some other an-

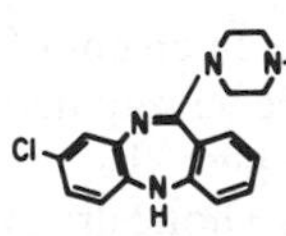

**Figure 33.3.13–1.** Molecular structure of clozapine.

tipsychotic compounds are structurally similar to clozapine— for example, loxapine (Loxitane)—clozapine remains a unique compound pharmacologically and therapeutically.

## PHARMACOLOGICAL ACTIONS

### Pharmacokinetics

Clozapine is rapidly absorbed from the gastrointestinal (GI) tract, and peak plasma levels are reached in one to four hours (mean, two hours). The drug is completely metabolized, with a half-life between 10 and 16 hours (mean, 12 hours); steady-state levels are usually reached in three to four days if twice-daily dosing is used. The two major metabolites have minimal pharmacological activity and have a shorter half-life than does the parent compound. The metabolites are excreted in both the urine and the feces.

### Pharmacodynamics

The unique efficacy and safety profiles of clozapine have prompted intensive study of its pharmacodynamic and pharmacological properties. Although clozapine is effective in at least one animal model used to test antipsychotic drugs, the conditioned avoidance test, the drug is inactive in three other commonly used animal models—the ability to induce catalepsy in rats, the ability to block the effects of amphetamine in rodents, and the ability to block the effects of apomorphine in animals. The lack of effects in those animal models is consistent with the low potency of clozapine as a $D_2$ receptor antagonist. Clozapine has a much higher potency as an antagonist at $D_1$, serotonin type 2 (5-$HT_2$), and noradrenergic alpha receptors (especially $\alpha_1$). Clozapine also has antagonist activity at muscarinic and histamine type 1 ($H_1$) receptors. Recently, it was reported that clozapine has a high affinity for the dopamine type 4 ($D_4$) receptor. The diversity of receptor effects has led to three major hypotheses regarding the pharmacological basis for the efficacy of clozapine and to new hypotheses regarding the pathophysiology of schizophrenia. First, it has been hypothesized that the diversity and the multiplicity of receptor activities lead to the unique properties of clozapine, thus questioning the common pharmaceutical development approach of developing drugs that are receptor-specific. Second, it has been hypothesized that the mix of serotonin and dopamine activities is important, a hypothesis that has led to research on several new antipsychotics, including risperidone. Third, the discovery that clozapine has a high binding affinity for the $D_4$ receptor has led to the hypothesis that a non-$D_2$ dopamine receptor may be the most effective target for antipsychotic drugs, thus leading to research on additional $D_4$ and $D_3$ antagonist drugs. One or more of those hypotheses may help explain the experimental observation in animal models that clozapine is more potent in affecting dopamine neurons that project to the limbic system (that is, mesolimbic neurons) than it is in affecting dopamine neurons that project to the basal ganglia (that is, nigrostriatal neurons).

## EFFECTS ON SPECIFIC ORGANS AND SYSTEMS

In addition to its antipsychotic effects, clozapine is associated with an increased risk for seizures. The most significant effects outside the central nervous system (CNS) are on the hematopoietic system and the cardiovascular system.

## THERAPEUTIC INDICATIONS

### Treatment-Resistant Schizophrenia

The only FDA-approved indication for clozapine is as a therapy for treatment-resistant schizophrenia. Many studies suggested that indication; the most carefully conducted United States trial compared about 250 schizophrenic patients who had been defined as treatment-resistant because they had failed to improve during at least three adequate trials of various antipsychotic drugs. One group of patients were treated with clozapine, the others with both chlorpromazine (Thorazine) and benztropine (Cogentin). The treatment response of the clozapine group was clearly superior to the response of the chlorpromazine-benztropine group; only 4 percent of patients in the chlorpromazine-benztropine group showed significant improvement, compared with 30 percent in the clozapine group.

A challenge to day's clinician is to define the meaning of "treatment-resistant," since many patients have minimal responses to conventional antipsychotic drugs, resulting in minimally productive and rewarding lives. As clinicians become comfortable with the hematological monitoring necessary with clozapine treatment, clozapine may be used in a broad range of patients, since it may be a more effective treatment than the conventional antipsychotic drugs.

### Other Indications

Many clinicians are using clozapine in patients who are seriously ill or who have severe tardive dyskinesia or a particular sensitivity to the extrapyramidal side effects of standard antipsychotic drugs. Clozapine treatment suppresses the abnormal movements of tardive dyskinesia, as does treatment with conventional antipsychotics; but, in contrast to conventional antipsychotics, clozapine may treat the movement disorder. Anecdotal reports and small, uncontrolled studies note the use of clozapine in schizoaffective disorder patients, severely ill bipolar I disorder patients, patients with borderline personality disorder, and patients with Parkinson's disease.

## PRECAUTIONS AND ADVERSE REACTIONS

The feature of clozapine that distinguishes it from standard antipsychotics is its absence of extrapyramidal adverse effects (Table 33.3.13–1). Clozapine does not cause acute dystonia, and it is associated with low incidences of parkinsonism (less than 5 percent), rabbit syndrome, and

**Table 33.3.13–1**
**Adverse Reactions Reported with Clozapine**

| | |
|---|---:|
| Drowsiness or sedation | 39 |
| Salivation | 31 |
| Tachycardia | 25 |
| Dizziness | 19 |
| Constipation | 14 |
| Nausea and vomiting | 11 |
| Hypotension | 9 |
| Sweating | 6 |
| Dry mouth | 6 |
| Urinary problems | 6 |
| Tremor | 6 |
| Visual disturbance | 5 |
| Fever | 5 |
| Hypertension | 4 |
| Weight gain | 4 |
| Seizures | 3 |
| Akathisia | 3 |
| Rigidity | 3 |
| Agranulocytosis | 1 |

akinesia, although there are reports that clozapine may be associated with akathisia. Clozapine may be associated with a much lower incidence of tardive dyskinesia than are other antipsychotics, although a few case reports do note that association. Because of its weak effects on $D_2$ receptors, clozapine does not affect prolactin secretion; thus, clozapine does not cause galactorrhea. The two most serious adverse effects associated with clozapine are agranulocytosis and seizures.

**Agranulocytosis**

*Agranulocytosis* is defined as a decrease in the number of white blood cells, with a specific decrease in the number of polymorphonuclear leukocytes. The erythrocyte and platelet concentrations are unaffected. Agranulocytosis occurs in 1 to 2 percent of all patients treated with clozapine; that percentage contrasts with an incidence of 0.04 to 0.5 percent of patients treated with standard antipsychotics. Early studies showed that a third of the patients who experienced agranulocytosis from clozapine died; however, careful clinical monitoring of the hematological status of clozapine-treated patients can virtually prevent fatalities by the early recognition of hematological problems and the cessation of clozapine use. Agranulocytosis can appear precipitously or gradually; it most often develops in the first six months of treatment, although it can appear much later than that. Increased age and female sex are additional risk factors for the development of clozapine-induced agranulocytosis. However, some undetermined genetic factor probably puts specific patients at risk for agranulocytosis.

Clozapine is also associated with the development of benign cases of leukocytosis (0.6 percent of patients), leukopenia (3 percent), eosinophilia (1 percent), and elevated erythrocyte sedimentation rates.

**Seizures**

About 5 percent of patients taking more than 600 mg a day of clozapine, 3 to 4 percent of patients taking 300

to 600 mg a day, and 1 to 2 percent of patients taking less than 300 mg a day have clozapine-associated seizures. Those percentages are higher than those associated with the use of standard antipsychotic drugs. If seizures develop in a patient, clozapine should be temporarily stopped. Phenobarbital (Luminal) treatment can be initiated, and clozapine can be restarted at about 50 percent of the previous dosage, then gradually raised again. Carbamazepine (Tegretol) should not be used in combination with clozapine because of its association with agranulocytosis. The plasma concentrations of other antiepileptics must be monitored carefully because of the possibility of pharmacokinetic interactions with clozapine.

**Cardiovascular Effects**

Tachycardia, hypotension, and electrocardiographic (ECG) changes are associated with clozapine treatment. The tachycardia is due to vagal inhibition and can be treated with peripherally acting β-adrenergic antagonists, such as atenolol (Tenormin), although that treatment may aggravate the hypotensive effects of the clozapine. The hypotensive effects of clozapine may be severe enough to result in syncopal episodes, especially whenever the initial dosage exceed 75 mg a day. Syncopal episodes can usually be avoided if the starting dosage is low (25 mg a day) and the dosage is raised gradually, thus allowing tolerance for the hypotensive effects of the drug to develop. Additional treatment measures for hypotension include support stockings, increased sodium intake, and, possibly, fludrocortisone treatment. In addition to tachycardia, potential ECG changes with clozapine include nonspecific ST-T wave changes, T wave flattening, or T wave inversions, although those changes are usually not clinically significant.

**Other Adverse Effects**

The most common other adverse effects associated with clozapine treatment are sedation, fatigue, sialorrhea, weight gain, various GI symptoms (most commonly constipation), anticholinergic effects, and fever. Sedation and sialorrhea can often be the most troubling of those adverse effects to the patient. Sedation is most common early in the course of treatment, and the effects of daytime sedation can be reduced by giving most of the clozapine dosage at night. Sialorrhea can be a disturbing adverse effect, and it is often most severe at night, resulting in the complaint by patients that their pillows are wet when they awake in the morning. Because of the potentially additive effects of anticholinergic drugs and the anticholinergic activity of clozapine, treatment of sialorrhea with anticholinergic drugs is not advised; however, there have been reports of successful treatment with clonidine (Catapres) patches (0.1 mg weekly) and low doses of amitriptyline (Elavil) at bedtime. Although mild hypothermia is commonly associated with clozapine, fevers of 1° to 2°F above normal may develop, usually during the first month of treatment, often causing concern regarding the development of an infection because of agranulocytosis. Clozapine should be withheld in those cases; if the white blood cell count (WBC) is normal, clozapine can be reinstituted slowly and at a low dosage. Because neuroleptic malignant syndrome has been reportedly associated with clozapine, the clinician must also consider that possibility in the differential diagnosis of fever in a clozapine-treated patient.

## Precautions

Clozapine use by pregnant women has not been studied; because the drug can be excreted in breast milk, it should not be taken by nursing mothers. Clozapine should also not be used in patients with WBCs below 3,500, a history of a bone marrow disorder, or a history of clozapine-induced agranulocytosis. Because of the variety of cardiovascular changes associated with clozapine use, the drug should be used with caution by patients with preexisting cardiac disease. Patients with preexisting seizure disorders or histories of significant head trauma are at greater risk for seizures while taking clozapine.

## DRUG INTERACTIONS

Clozapine should not be used with any other drug that is associated with the development of agranulocytosis or bone marrow suppression. Such drugs include carbamazepine, propylthiouracil, sulfonamides, and captopril (Capoten). Central nervous system depressants, alcohol, or tricyclic drugs coadministered with clozapine may increase the risk for seizures, sedation, and cardiac effects. The coadministration of benzodiazepines and clozapine may be associated with an increased incidence of orthostasis and syncope. There have been rare case reports of respiratory depression after the coadministration of benzodiazepines and clozapine at the initiation of clozapine treatment. Lithium (Eskalith) combined with clozapine may increase the risk of seizures, confusion, and movement disorders. A few case reports suggest that lithium not be used in combination with clozapine by patients who have experienced an episode of neuroleptic malignant syndrome.

## LABORATORY INTERFERENCES

No known laboratory interferences are associated with clozapine use.

## DOSAGE AND ADMINISTRATION

### Pretreatment Assessment

Once a physician has determined that a trial of clozapine is warranted for a particular patient, the risks and the benefits of clozapine treatment must be explained to the patient and the family. The informed consent procedure should be documented in the patient's chart. The patient's history should include information about blood disorders, epilepsy, cardiovascular disease, and hepatic and renal diseases. The presence of a hepatic or renal disease necessitates the use of low starting dosages of the drug. The laboratory examination should include an electrocardio-

gram (ECG), several complete blood counts (CBCs) with white blood cell counts (WBCs), which can then be averaged, and liver and renal function tests.

### Titration and Dosage

Clozapine is available in 25 and 100 mg tablets; 1 mg of clozapine is equivalent to about 1½ to 2 mg of chlorpromazine. The initial dosage is usually 25 mg one or two times daily, although a conservative initial dosage is 12.5 mg twice daily. The dosage can then be raised gradually (25 mg a day every two or three days) to 300 mg a day in divided doses, usually two or three times daily. The gradual increase in dosage is necessitated by the potential development of hypotension, syncope, and sedation, which are adverse effects for which the patient can usually develop tolerance if the dose titration is gradual enough. The usual effective treatment range is 400 to 500 mg a day, although dosages up to 600 mg a day can be used. If a patient stops taking clozapine for more than a 36-hour period, the clinician should restart the drug at 12.5 to 25 mg twice daily and then titrate the dosage upward to the previous dosage level. After the decision to terminate the drug, clozapine treatment should be tapered whenever possible to avoid cholinergic rebound symptoms, such as diaphoresis, flushing, diarrhea, and hyperactivity.

### Plasma Concentrations

Data on the relation between plasma concentrations of clozapine and clinical efficacy are still limited, and many of the available data indicate a lack of any clear correlation. Nevertheless, for cases in which it seems indicated and possible to check plasma concentrations, the average range of plasma concentrations is 200 to 400 ng per mL, with concentrations below 100 ng per mL considered to be low and those above 500 ng per mL to be high, although one study indicated that concentrations above 500 ng per mL are associated with improved response.

### Laboratory Monitoring

Weekly WBCs are indicated to monitor the patient for the development of agranulocytosis. Although monitoring is expensive, early indication of agranulocytosis can prevent a fatal outcome. If the WBC is less than 2,000 cells per mm³ or the granulocyte count is less than 1,000 per mm³, clozapine should be discontinued, a hematological consultation should be obtained, and the obtaining of a bone marrow sample should be considered. Patients with agranulocytosis should not be reexposed to the drug. Physicians can monitor the WBC through any laboratory. Proof of monitoring must be presented to the pharmacist to obtain the medication.

### References

Alphs L D, Lee H S: Comparison of withdrawal of typical and atypical antipsychotic drugs: A case study. J Clin Psychiatry *52*: 346, 1991.
British Journal of Psychiatry: Clozapine: The atypical antipsychotic. Br J Psychiatry *160* (Suppl 17): 2, 1992.

Cohen B M, Keck P E, Satlin A, Cole J O: Prevalence and severity of akathisia in patients on clozapine. Biol Psychiatry 29: 1215, 1991.

Farde L, Nordström A-L, Wiesel F-A, Pauli S, Halldin C, Sedvall G: Positron emission tomographic analysis of central D₁ and D₂ receptor occupancy in patients treated with classical neuroleptics and clozapine. Arch Gen Psychiatry 49: 538, 1992.

Goldberg T E, Greenberg R D, Griffin S J, Gold J M, Kleinman J E, Pickar D, Schulz S C, Weinberger D R: The effect of clozapine on cognition and psychiatric symptoms in patients with schizophrenia. Br J Psychiatry 162: 43, 1993.

Haller E, Binder R L: Clozapine and seizures. Am J Psychiatry 147: 1069, 1990.

Haring C, Fleischhacker W W, Schett P, Humpel C, Barbas C, Saria A: Influence of patient-related variables on clozapine plasma levels. Am J Psychiatry 147: 1471, 1990.

Jann M W: Clozapine. Pharmacotherapy 11: 179, 1991.

Kahn R S, Davidson M, Siever L, Gabriel S, Apter S, Davis K L: Serotonin function and treatment response to clozapine in schizophrenic patients. Am J Psychiatry 150: 9, 1993.

Kane J, Honigfeld G, Singer J, Meltzer H, Clozaril Collaborative Study Group: Clozapine for the treatment-resistant schizophrenic. Arch Gen Psychiatry 45: 789, 1988.

Leadbetter R, Shutty M, Pavalonis D, Vieweg V, Higgins P, Downs M: Clozapine-induced weight gain: Prevalence and clinical relevance. Am J Psychiatry 149: 68, 1992.

McElroy S L, Dessain E C, Pope H G Jr, Cole J O, Keck P E, Frankenberg F R, Aizley H G, O'Brien S: Clozapine in the treatment of psychotic mood disorders, schizoaffective disorder, and schizophrenia. J Clin Psychiatry 52: 411, 1991.

Merchant K M, Dorsa D M: Differential induction of neurotensin and c-fos gene expression by typical versus atypical antipsychotics. Proc Natl Acad Sci U S A 90: 3447, 1993.

Miller D D, Sharafuddin M J A, Kathol R G: A case of clozapine-induced neuroleptic malignant syndrome. J Clin Psychiatry 52: 99, 1991.

Pickar D, Owen R R, Litman R E, Koniski E, Gutierrez R, Rapaport M H: Clinical and biologic response to clozapine in patients with schizophrenia: Crossover comparison with fluphenazine. Arch Gen Psychiatry 49: 345, 1992.

Safferman A, Lieberman J A, Kane J M, Szymanski S, Kinon B: Update on the clinical efficacy and side effects of clozapine. Schizophr Bull 17: 247, 1991.

Seeman P: Dopamine receptor sequences: Therapeutic levels of neuroleptics occupy D₂-receptors, clozapine occupies D₄. Neuropsychopharmacology 7: 261, 1992.

# 33.3.14 / Dantrolene

Dantrolene (Dantrium) is a direct-acting skeletal muscle relaxant. The only indication for dantrolene in contemporary clinical psychiatry is as one of the potentially effective treatments for neuroleptic malignant syndrome.

## CHEMISTRY

Dantrolene is derived from hydantoin, as indicated in its molecular structure (Figure 33.3.14–1). Dantrolene is structurally and pharmacologically unrelated to other skeletal muscle relaxants.

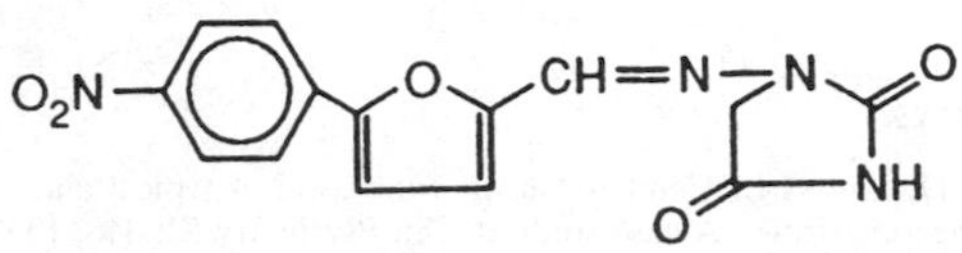

**Figure 33.3.14–1.** Molecular structure of dantrolene.

## PHARMACOLOGICAL ACTIONS

### Pharmacokinetics

About one third of orally administered dantrolene is slowly absorbed from the gastrointestinal (GI) tract. At sufficient dosages, consistent plasma concentrations can be maintained. Peak blood concentrations are seen about five hours after oral administration. The elimination half-life of dantrolene is about nine hours. Dantrolene is largely protein-bound, metabolized by the liver, and excreted in the urine.

### Pharmacodynamics

Dantrolene produces skeletal muscle relaxation by directly affecting the contractile response of the muscle at a site beyond the myoneural junction. Specifically, dantrolene dissociates excitation-contraction coupling by interfering with the release of calcium from the sarcoplasmic reticulum. The skeletal muscle relaxant effect is the basis of its efficacy in reducing the muscle destruction and hyperthermia associated with neuroleptic malignant syndrome.

## EFFECTS ON SPECIFIC ORGANS AND SYSTEMS

The skeletal muscle relaxant effect of dantrolene can cause muscle weakness and such symptoms as slurring of speech and drooling. Dantrolene also has effects on the GI system (for example, diarrhea) and the nervous system (for example, headache and depression) and possibly toxic effects on hepatocytes, as indicated by an association with elevated liver function test results.

## THERAPEUTIC INDICATIONS

The primary psychiatric indication for intravenous (IV) dantrolene is spasticity in neuroleptic malignant syndrome. Dantrolene is almost always used in conjunction with appropriate supportive measures and a dopamine receptor agonist—for example, bromocriptine (Parlodel). If all available case reports and studies are summarized, about 80 percent of all patients with neuroleptic malignant syndrome who received dantrolene apparently benefited clinically from the drug. Muscle relaxation and a general and dramatic improvement in symptoms can appear within minutes of IV administration, although in most cases the beneficial effects can take several hours to appear. Some evidence indicates that dantrolene treatment must be continued for some time, perhaps days to a week or more, to minimize the risk of the recurrence of symptoms, although the data for that clinical opinion are limited.

## PRECAUTIONS AND ADVERSE REACTIONS

Muscle weakness, drowsiness, dizziness, light-headedness, nausea, diarrhea, malaise, and fatigue are the most common adverse effects of dantrolene. Those effects are generally transient. The central nervous system (CNS) effects of dantrolene can include speech disturbances (which may also reflect its effects on the muscles of speech), headache, visual disturbances, alteration of taste, depression, confusion, hallucinations, nervousness, and insomnia. Many of the serious adverse effects of dantrolene are associated with long-term treatment, rather than short-term use for the treatment of neuroleptic malignant syndrome. The potential serious side effects include hepatitis, seizures, and pleural effusion with pericarditis. Because of its potential for severe side effects, dantrolene should not be used by psychiatric patients for any long-term treatment. The effects are not associated with short-term IV use. Dantrolene should be used with caution by patients with hepatic, renal, and chronic lung diseases. Dantrolene can cross the placenta and is, thus, contraindicated for pregnant women and should not be used by nursing mothers except in emergency situations, such as neuroleptic malignant syndrome. Data are not available regarding the use of dantrolene by the elderly, and no unique problems have been associated with its use by children.

## DRUG INTERACTIONS

The risk of liver toxicity may be increased in patients who are also taking estrogens. Dantrolene should be used with caution by patients who are using other drugs that produce drowsiness, most notably the benzodiazepines. In the case of neuroleptic malignant syndrome, however, the general guidelines regarding dantrolene must be weighed against the severity of the syndrome. Dantrolene should not be given IV in combination with calcium channel blockers.

## LABORATORY INTERFERENCES

No known laboratory interferences are associated with dantrolene, although experience with its use in patients with neuroleptic malignant syndrome is still limited.

## DOSAGE AND ADMINISTRATION

In addition to the immediate discontinuation of antipsychotic drugs, medical support to cool the patient, and the monitoring of vital signs and renal output, dantrolene in dosages of 1 mg per kg can be given orally four times daily, or 1 to 5 mg per kg can be given IV to reduce muscle spasms in patients with neuroleptic malignant syndrome. Although some clinicians have recommended low dosages because of the side effects, other clinicians indicate that dosages of 10 mg per kg a day are most likely to be effective. Dantrolene is supplied as 25 mg, 50 mg, and 100 mg capsules and in a 20 mg parenteral preparation

**References**

Coons D K, Hillman E F, Marshall R W: Treatment of neuroleptic malignant syndrome with dantrolene sodium: Case report. Am J Psychiatry *139*: 944, 1982.
Granato J E, Stern B J, Ringel A: Neuroleptic malignant syndrome: Successful treatment with dantrolene and bromocriptine. Ann Neurol *14*: 89, 1983.

Khan A, Jaffe J H, Nelson W H, Morrison B: Resolution of neuroleptic malignant syndrome with dantrolene sodium: Case report. J Clin Psychiatry *46*: 244, 1985.
May D C, Norris S W, Stewart R M: Neuroleptic malignant syndrome: Response to dantrolene sodium. Ann Intern Med *98*: 183, 1983.
Pennati A, Sacchetti E, Calzeroni A: Dantrolene in lethal catatonia. Am J Psychiatry *148*: 268, 1991.

# 33.3.15 / Disulfiram

Disulfiram (Antabuse) is used in the treatment of alcohol dependence. Its main effect is to produce an unpleasant reaction in a person who ingests even a small amount of alcohol while taking disulfiram. However, because of the risk of severe and even fatal disulfiram-alcohol reactions, disulfiram therapy is used less often today than previously.

## CHEMISTRY

The molecular structure of disulfiram is presented in Figure 33.3.15–1.

## PHARMACOLOGICAL ACTIONS

### Pharmacokinetics

Disulfiram is almost completely absorbed from the gastrointestinal (GI) tract after oral administration. It is metabolized in the liver and excreted in the urine. It is lipid-soluble and has a half-life estimated at 60 to 120 hours. One or two weeks may be needed before disulfiram is totally eliminated from the body after the last dose has been taken.

### Pharmacodynamics

Disulfiram is an aldehyde dehydrogenase inhibitor that interferes with the metabolism of alcohol by producing a marked increase in blood acetaldehyde levels. The accumulation of acetaldehyde (to a level up to 10 times higher than occurs in the normal metabolism of alcohol) produces a wide array of unpleasant reactions called the disulfiram-alcohol reaction, characterized by the following signs and symptoms: nausea, throbbing headache, vomiting, hypertension, flushing, sweat-

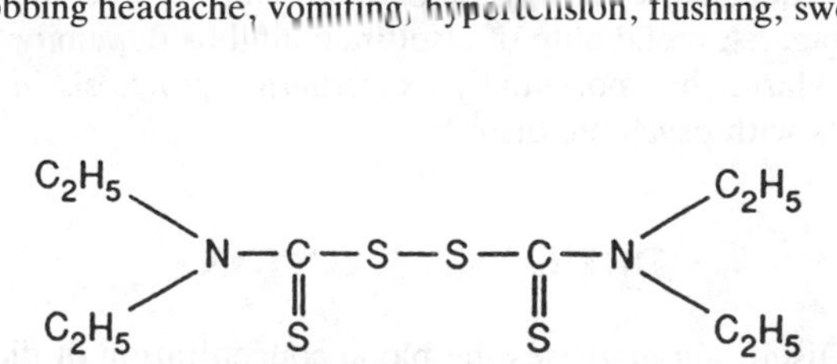

**Figure 33.3.15–1.** Molecular structure of disulfiram.

ing, thirst, dyspnea, tachycardia, chest pain, vertigo, and blurred vision. The reaction occurs almost immediately after the ingestion of one alcoholic drink and may last up to 30 minutes.

## THERAPEUTIC INDICATIONS

The primary indication for disulfiram use is as an aversive conditioning treatment for alcohol dependence. Either the fear of having a disulfiram-alcohol reaction or the memory of having had one is meant to condition the patient not to use alcohol. Some clinicians induce a disulfiram-alcohol reaction in patients at the beginning of therapy to convince the patients of the severe unpleasantness of the symptoms. However, that practice is not recommended, since a disulfiram-alcohol reaction can lead to cardiovascular collapse. It is usually sufficient to describe the severity and the unpleasantness of the disulfiram-alcohol reaction graphically enough to discourage the patient from imbibing alcohol. Disulfiram treatment should be combined with such treatments as psychotherapy, group therapy, and support groups like Alcoholic Anonymous (AA). The treatment of alcohol dependence requires careful monitoring; since a patient can simply decide not to take the disulfiram, compliance with the medication should be monitored if possible.

## PRECAUTIONS AND ADVERSE REACTIONS

### With Alcohol Consumption

The intensity of the disulfiram-alcohol reaction varies with each patient. In extreme cases it is marked by respiratory depression, cardiovascular collapse, myocardial infarction, convulsions, and death. Therefore, disulfiram is contraindicated for a patient with a significant pulmonary or cardiovascular disease. In addition, disulfiram should be used with caution, if at all, by a patient with nephritis, brain damage, hypothyroidism, diabetes, hepatic disease, seizures, polydrug dependence, or an abnormal electroencephalogram (EEG). Most fatal reactions occur in patients who are taking more than 500 mg a day of disulfiram and who consume more than three ounces of alcohol. The treatment of a severe disulfiram-alcohol reaction is primarily supportive to prevent shock.

### Without Alcohol Consumption

The adverse effects of disulfiram in the absence of alcohol consumption include fatigue, dermatitis, impotence, optic neuritis, a variety of mental changes, and hepatic damage. A metabolite of disulfiram inhibits dopamine hydroxylase, thus potentially exacerbating psychosis in patients with psychotic disorders.

## DRUG INTERACTIONS

Disulfiram increases the blood concentration of diazepam (Valium), paraldehyde, phenytoin (Dilantin), caf-

feine, tetrahydrocannabinol (the active ingredient in marijuana), barbiturates, anticoagulants, isoniazid, and tricyclic drugs.

## LABORATORY INTERFERENCES

In rare instances, disulfiram has been reported to decrease the uptake of iodine-131 ($I^{131}$) and protein-bound iodine test results. In research settings, disulfiram may reduce urinary concentrations of homovanillic acid, the major metabolite of dopamine, because of its inhibition of dopamine hydroxylase.

## DOSAGE AND ADMINISTRATION

Disulfiram is supplied in tablets of 250 mg and 500 mg. The usual initial dosage is 500 mg a day taken by mouth for the first one or two weeks, followed by a maintenance dosage of 250 mg a day. The dosage should not exceed 500 mg a day. The maintenance dosage range is 125 to 500 mg a day.

The patient must be instructed that the ingestion of even the smallest amount of alcohol will bring on a disulfiram-alcohol reaction, with all its unpleasant effects. In addition, the patient should be warned against ingesting any alcohol-containing preparations, such as cough drops, tonics of any kind, and alcohol-containing foods and sauces. Some reactions have occurred in men who used alcohol-based after-shave lotions and inhaled the fumes; therefore, precautions must be explicit and should include any topically applied preparations containing alcohol, such as perfume.

Disulfiram should not be administered until the patient has abstained from alcohol for at least 12 hours. Patients should be warned that the disulfiram-alcohol reaction may occur as long as one or two weeks after the last dose of disulfiram. Patients should carry identification cards describing the disulfiram-alcohol reaction and listing the name and the telephone number of the physician to be called.

**References**

Banys P: The clinical use of disulfiram (Antabuse): A review. J Psychoactive Drugs *20*: 243, 1988.
Elder I R, Voris J C, Sebastian P S, Acevedo A G: Disulfiram compliance as a function of patient motivation, program philosophy and side effects. J Alcohol Drug Educ *34*: 23, 1988.
Friedman T C, Fulop G: Disulfiram use at hospital-based and free-standing alcoholism treatment centers. J Subst Abuse Treat *5*: 139, 1988.
Fuller R K: Current status of alcoholism treatment outcome research. NIDA Res Monogr *95*: 85, 1989.
Kingsbury S J, Salzman C: Disulfiram in the treatment of alcoholic patients with schizophrenia. Hosp Community Psychiatry *41*: 133, 1990.
Kranzler H R, Dolinsky Z, Kaplan R F: Giving ethanol to alcoholics in a research setting: Its effect on compliance with disulfiram treatment. Br Addic *85*: 119, 1990.
Larson E W, Olincy A, Rummans T A, Morse R M: Disulfiram treatment of patients with both alcohol dependence and other psychiatric disorders: A review. Alcoholism *16*: 125, 1992.
Liskow B, Nickel E, Tunley N, Powell B J: Alcoholics' attitudes toward and experiences with disulfiram. Am J Drug Alcohol Abuse *16*: 147, 1990.

# 33.3.16 / L-Dopa

L-Dopa, also known as levodopa (Larodopa), is an indirectly acting dopamine agonist. L-Dopa, given in combination with a peripheral inhibitor of L-dopa decarboxylase (for example, carbidopa), is the most commonly used treatment for idiopathic Parkinson's disease. A commonly used commercially available combination of L-dopa and carbidopa is Sinemet. Within the field of clinical psychiatry, L-dopa is not a primary therapy for any single indication; rather, L-dopa is used as a second-line or third-line treatment for antipsychotic-induced parkinsonism.

## CHEMISTRY

The molecular structure of L-dopa is shown in Figure 33.3.16–1.

## PHARMACOLOGICAL ACTIONS

### Pharmacokinetics

L-Dopa is rapidly absorbed after oral administration, and peak plasma levels are reached after 30 to 120 minutes. The half-life of L-dopa is one to three hours. Absorption of L-dopa can be significantly reduced by changes in gastric pH and by injection with meals. L-Dopa is almost entirely decarboxylated in the periphery by L-amino acid decarboxylase. Dopamine, the decarboxylated form of L-dopa, is pharmacologically active. However, dopamine, in contrast to L-dopa, cannot cross the blood-brain barrier. Clinically, L-dopa is given in combination with a peripherally active inhibitor of L-dopa decarboxylase, such as carbidopa, thus resulting in the efficient delivery of L-dopa into the central nervous system (CNS).

### Pharmacodynamics

Once L-dopa enters the CNS, it is available to be converted into dopamine by CNS L-amino acid decarboxylase. The dopamine can then act as a neurotransmitter at dopamine receptor sites.

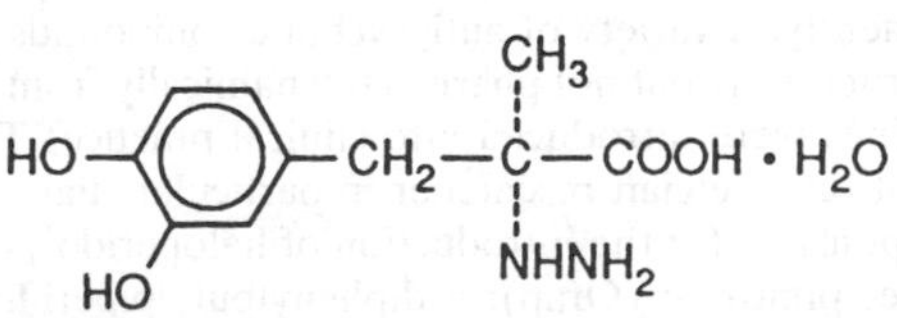

**Figure 33.3.16–1.** Molecular structure of L-dopa.

## THERAPEUTIC INDICATIONS

In psychiatry, L-dopa is used for the treatment of antipsychotic-induced parkinsonism, although anticholinergics, amantadine (Symmetrel), antihistamines, and bromocriptine (Parlodel) are more frequently used. L-Dopa is the least often used because the other drugs are equally effective and are associated with fewer side effects. Nonetheless, L-dopa can be used in patients to treat extrapyramidal symptoms, akinesia, and focal perioral tremors (sometimes called rabbit syndrome). Additional evidence, based on case reports and small studies, indicates that L-dopa may be effective in the treatment of restless legs syndrome and tardive dyskinesia. Preliminary data indicate that L-dopa may be effective in the treatment of the negative symptoms of schizophrenia, although that indication should be considered only in research settings.

## PRECAUTIONS AND ADVERSE REACTIONS

Side effects commonly occur with L-dopa therapy, thus limiting its usefulness in general psychiatric practice. Most side effects are dose-related or associated with withdrawal from the drug. Some side effects are seen early in treatment and include nausea, vomiting, orthostatic hypotension, and cardiac arrhythmias. After long-term use, patients may experience abnormal involuntary movements and psychiatric disturbances, including psychosis, depression, and mania. Anecdotal reports indicate that the abrupt discontinuation of L-dopa can precipitate a syndrome similar to neuroleptic malignant syndrome, especially if the patient is concomitantly receiving an antipsychotic. L-Dopa is contraindicated during pregnancy and is contraindicated for nursing mothers, especially since it inhibits lactation.

## DRUG INTERACTIONS

Drugs that block dopamine type 2 ($D_2$) receptors—for example, haloperiodol (Haldol)—are capable of reversing the effects of L-dopa. The concurrent use of tricyclic drugs and L-dopa has been reported to cause symptoms of neurotoxicity, such as rigidity, agitation, and tremor. L-Dopa is also capable of potentiating the hypotensive effects of diuretics and other antihypertensive medications. L-Dopa should not be used in conjunction with monoamine oxidase inhibitors (MAOIs), including selegiline (Eldepryl). MAOIs should be discontinued at least two weeks before the initiation of L-dopa therapy. Benzodiazepines, phenytoin (Dilantin), and pyridoxine may interfere with the therapeutic effects of L-dopa.

## LABORATORY INTERFERENCES

L-Dopa administration has been associated with false reports of elevated serum and urinary uric acid concentrations, urinary glucose tests, urinary ketone tests, and urinary catecholamine concentrations. Whether L-dopa results in a false-positive result in those tests depends on the specific test method used, since some test methods are not affected by L-dopa.

## DOSAGE AND ADMINISTRATION

Dosages of L-dopa for the treatment of antipsychotic-induced parkinsonism should be similar to the dosages used for idiopathic parkinsonism. Starting dosages of 100 mg three times a day may be increased until the patient is functionally improved. Hyperkinesias, in the form of choreiform and dystonic movements, are dose-related side effects. Particularly after prolonged therapy, periods of profound bradykinesia may alternate with periods during which the patient can move well or is hyperkinetic (on-off phenomenon). The addition of other antiparkinsonian medications, usually such dopamine agonists as bromocriptine, may ameliorate the problem, although the on-off phenomenon may eventually require the cessation of L-dopa therapy. L-Dopa is available in 100 mg, 250 mg, and 500 mg tablets and capsules.

**References**

Fayen M, Goldman M B, Moulthrop M A, Luchins D J: Differential memory function with dopaminergic versus anticholinergic treatment of drug-induced extrapyramidal symptoms. Am J Psychiatry *145*: 483, 1988.
Geminiani G, Cesana B M, Scigliano G, Soliveri P: Variation of therapeutic response in Parkinson's disease: A retrospective study. Acta Neurol Scand *81*: 397, 1990.
Kaplan B, Mason N A: Levodopa in restless legs syndrome. Ann Pharmacother *26*: 214, 1992.
Ludatscher J I: Stable remission of tardive dyskinesia by L-dopa. J Clin Psychopharmacol *9*: 39, 1989.
Ray S R, Opler L A: L-Dopa in the treatment of negative schizophrenic symptoms: A single-subject experimental study. Int J Psychiatry Med *15*: 293, 1986.

# 33.3.17 / Dopamine Receptor Antagonists (Antipsychotics)

A diverse group of drugs that blockade the dopamine type 2 ($D_2$) receptor are commonly referred to as antipsychotic drugs. The major indication for the use of the drugs is the treatment of schizophrenia and other psychotic disorders. The antipsychotic drug class includes chlorpromazine (Thorazine), thioridazine (Mellaril), fluphenazine (Prolixin), and haloperidol (Haldol). One new antipsychotic drug, risperidone (Risperdal), has been introduced in the United States. Although risperidone is a potent antagonist of $D_2$ receptors, it has additional pharmacological features that may confer therapeutic advantages and improved side-effect profile, compared with previously available dopamine receptor antagonists. The introduction of another antipsychotic, remoxipride, has been delayed or aborted because of a possible association between the use of remoxipride and the development of aplastic anemia.

"Antipsychotics" and "dopamine receptor antagonists" are not necessarily synonymous. Clozapine (Clozaril) is an effective antipsychotic but differs from all the drugs discussed here in that it has comparatively little activity at $D_2$ receptors. The drugs discussed here have also been referred to as neuroleptics and major tranquilizers. The term "neuroleptic" denotes the neurological or motor effects of most of the drugs. The development of new compounds, such as risperidone and remoxipride, that are associated with few neurological effects makes the continued use of the term "neuroleptic" inaccurate as an overall label for the compounds. The term "major tranquilizer" inaccurately implies that the primary effect of the drugs is to sedate patients and confounds the drugs with the so-called minor tranquilizers, such as the benzodiazepines. An additional confusion in the nomenclature of the drugs is the common misuse of the term "phenothiazine" as a synonym for the term "antipsychotic." That use is inaccurate because the phenothiazines, such as chlorpromazine, are only one type of antipsychotic drug.

## HISTORY

Reserpine (Serpasil) is not a dopamine receptor antagonist; rather, it depletes presynaptic biogenic amine neurotransmitter stores, including those of dopamine. Nevertheless, reserpine is historically the first effective antipsychotic drug. Reserpine is a constituent of the shrub rauwolfia, which is native to areas of India, Africa, and South America and which has been used as an ingredient in folk medicines for centuries. In 1931 Sen and Bose published the first paper reporting the effectiveness of rauwolfia in hypertension and mania. In 1953 the active ingredient, reserpine, was identified and quickly entered into the then limited pharmacological approaches to psychosis.

Chlorpromazine, a phenothiazine derivative that was later shown to be a dopamine receptor antagonist, was the first so-called classic or typical antipsychotic to be synthesized in the early 1950s and to enter widespread clinical use. Chlorpromazine was initially used as an adjuvant to anesthetics; but two clinically astute anesthesiologists in France, Henri Laborit and Huguenard, observed the unusual psychic properties of the compound. Two French psychiatrists, Jean Delay and Pierre Deniker, tried the drug in schizophrenic patients and reported their success in 1952. Compared with reserpine, chlorpromazine was more effective and had a more rapid onset. In addition, the use of reserpine was associated with a high incidence of depression and suicide, side effects that are now understood to be consistent with reserpine's generalized depletion of biogenic amine neurotransmitters. Word of the clinical results with chlorpromazine quickly spread throughout Europe and then to North America, where a number of investigators were instrumental in its rapid introduction in American psychiatry.

The clinical introduction of chlorpromazine was quickly followed by the introduction of other phenothiazine compounds, such as perphenazine (Trilafon) and fluphenazine. Subsequently, a variety of antipsychotic compounds that differed structurally but not pharmacodynamically from the phenothiazines were introduced into clinical practice. The laboratory of one Belgian researcher in particular, Paul Janssen, was responsible for the introduction of haloperidol, a butyrophenone; pimozide (Orap), a diphenylbutylpiperidine; and, most recently, risperidone, a benzisoxazole. Risperidone and remoxipride reflect the continuing efforts of clinicians, researchers, and pharmaceutical companies to develop effective antipsychotic drugs that are associated with few adverse effects, particularly neurological adverse effects, such as parkinsonism, dystonias, akathisia, and tardive dyskinesia.

In contrast to the so-called typical antipsychotics (for example, chlorpromazine and haloperidol), the three most extensively studied new antipsychotic drugs—clozapine, risperidone, and remoxipride—are often referred to as atypical antipsychotics, although there is no generally agreed-on definition regarding the distinctions between typical and atypical antipsychotics. The label "atypical" is variably meant to imply all or any of the following characteristics: associated with less risk of neurological side effects; less potent at causing increases in prolactin secretion; lacking dopamine antagonism as a primary mechanism of action; possessing significant activity at specific, nondopaminergic receptors (for example, serotonin and sigma receptors); allegedly possessing greater efficacy in the treatment of schizophrenia's negative symptoms (for example, anhedonia). An alternative to the vague subtyping of antipsychotics into typical and atypical drugs is to recognize antipsychotic drugs as being structurally or pharmacologically distinct from one another and not to generalize regarding those distinctions.

The introduction of antipsychotic drugs revolutionized the treatment of schizophrenic patients and other seriously ill psychotic patients. The use of the typical antipsychotics results in significant clinical improvement in 50 to 75 percent of psychotic patients, and almost 90 percent of psychotic patients receive some clinical benefit from the drugs. Nevertheless, the introduction of the antipsychotics, in combination with a poorly planned and executed program of deinstitutionalization, has led over the past 40 years to a situation in which many schizophrenic patients receive inadequate treatment that does not address the full extent of their illness-related problems. Among the issues that are poorly addressed by many mental health care delivery systems are community and family support, adequate living arrangements, quality-of-life factors, the reduction of environmental and family stressors, and compliance with medication regimens. Even the most appropriate and effective use of typical antipsychotics is not consistently applied in treatment programs, especially in the use of the lowest effective dosage, the appropriate monitoring of blood levels, the recognition and the treatment of side effects, and the treatment of residual and negative symptoms. In fact, some evidence indicates that—although there has been a general trend toward the use of high-potency antipsychotics, which may have few side effects, and a reduction in the unwarranted use of many antipsychotic drugs simultaneously (polypharmacy)—there is also a trend toward using unnecessarily high dosages of antipsychotics and thus causing more frequent and more severe adverse effects in patients than is necessary to obtain the optimal clinical benefits.

One additional result of the introduction of the antipsychotic drugs was the eventual appreciation of the fact that all the typical antipsychotic drugs act by blocking the effects of dopamine at $D_2$ receptors. Specifically, there is an impressive negative correlation between the affinities of those drugs for $D_2$ receptors and their clinical potency. Thus, haloperidol, which has a high affinity for $D_2$ receptors, is used clinically in low dosages, but chlorpromazine, which has a comparatively low affinity for $D_2$ receptors, is used clinically in high dosages. That observation—in addition to the observation that dopamine agonists, such as amphetamine, can induce psychotic symptoms—led to the development of the dopamine hypothesis of schizophrenia. The introduction of new antipsychotic drugs—such as clozapine and risperidone—has continued to provide basic and clinical data that have allowed for the steady evolution of the dopamine hypothesis from one involving only dopamine receptors to one that includes interactions with many dopamine receptor subtypes (for example, $D_3$ and $D_4$) and other neurotransmitter receptors (for example, serotonin and sigma receptors).

## CLASSIFICATION AND CHEMISTRY

Not counting reserpine (which is relevant only historically) and clozapine (which is classified in this textbook separately from the dopamine receptor antagonists), eight classes of drugs are generally grouped together as the dopamine receptor antagonist antipsychotics (Figure 33.3.17–1). Seven of those classes contain drugs that are generally considered typical antipsychotics: phenothiazine, thioxanthene, dibenzoxazepine, dihydroindole, butyrophenone, diphenylbutylpiperidine, and benzamide. The benzamide class also contains a drug that is considered atypical, remoxipride. Some clinicians and researchers also consider thioridazine, a piperidine phenothiazine, to be atypical, because it may be associated with fewer neurological side effects than are other antipsychotics. The eighth class, benzisoxazole, currently contains only one drug, risperidone.

### Phenothiazine

All the phenothiazines have the same three-ring phenothiazine nucleus but differ in the side chains joined to the nitrogen atom of the middle ring. The phenothiazines are typed according to the nature of the side chain: aliphatic (for example, chlorpromazine), piperazine (for example, fluphenazine), or piperidine (for example, thioridazine).

### Thioxanthene

The thioxanthene three-ring nucleus differs from the phenothiazine nucleus by the substitution of a carbon atom for the nitrogen atom in the middle ring. The two available thioxanthenes have either an aliphatic (chlorprothixene [Taractan]) or a piperazine (thiothixene [Navane]) side chain.

### Dibenzoxazepine

The dibenzoxazepines are based on another modification of the three-ring phenothiazine nucleus. The only dibenzoxazepine available in the United Stated is loxapine (Loxitane), which has a piperazine side chain. Although loxapine is similar in structure to clozapine, the two compounds have dramatically different pharmacodynamic properties, and loxapine is clearly classifiable with the dopamine receptor antagonists, whereas clozapine is not.

### Dihydroindole

The only dihydroindole available in the United States, molindone (Moban, Lidone), has unusual clinical properties, such as not inducing weight gain and perhaps being less epileptogenic than are the other dopamine receptor antagonist antipsychotics.

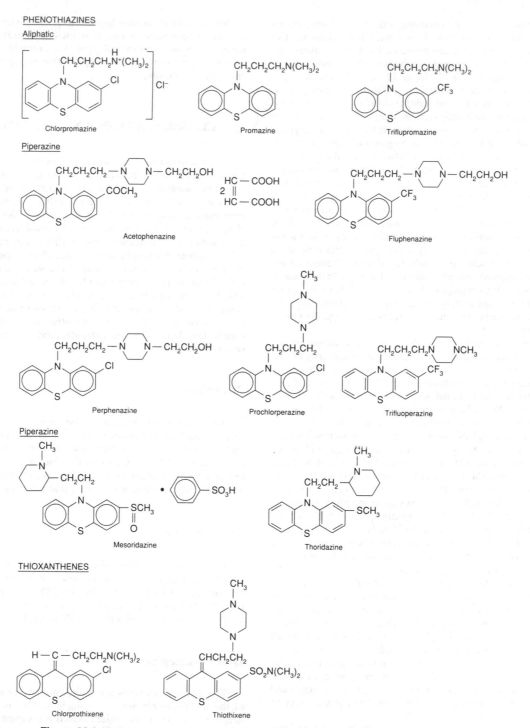

**Figure 33.3.17–1.** Molecular structures of dopamine receptor antagonists and reserpine.

## Butyrophenone

The two butyrophenones available in the United States are haloperidol and droperidol (Inapsine). Haloperidol is perhaps the most widely used antipsychotic. Although droperidol is approved only for use as an adjuvant to anesthetics, some researchers and clinicians have used droperidol as an intravenous (IV) antipsychotic drug in emergency settings. Spiroperidol, also called spiperone, is a butyrophenone compound that can be labeled with a radioactive atom and used

in basic and clinical research studies (for example, positron emission tomography [PET]) to label dopamine receptors.

## Diphenylbutylpiperidine

Diphenylbutylpiperidines are structurally similar to the butyrophenones. Only one diphenylbutylpiperidine, pimozide, is available in the United States; it is approved for the treatment of Tourette's disorder. In Europe, however, pimozide

Dibenzoxazepine

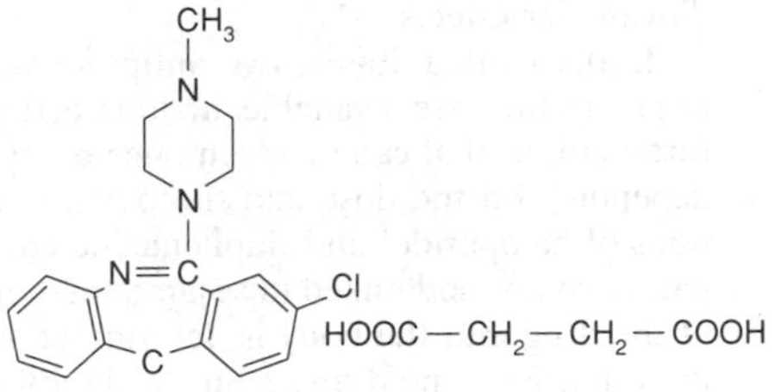

Loxapine

Dihydroindole

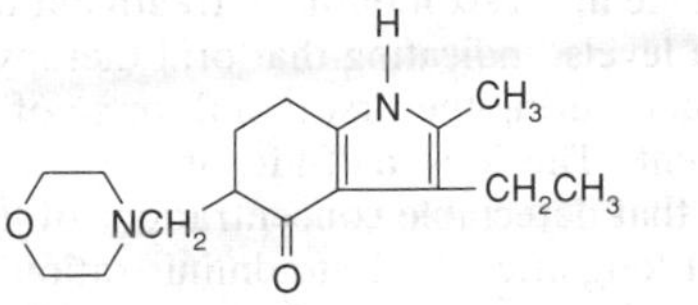

Molindone

Butyrophenones

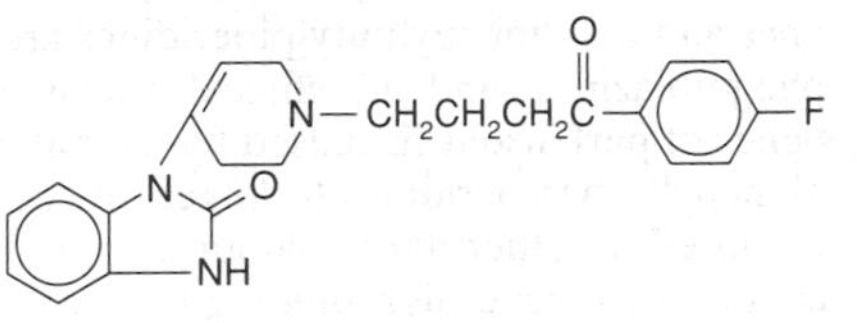

Droperidol

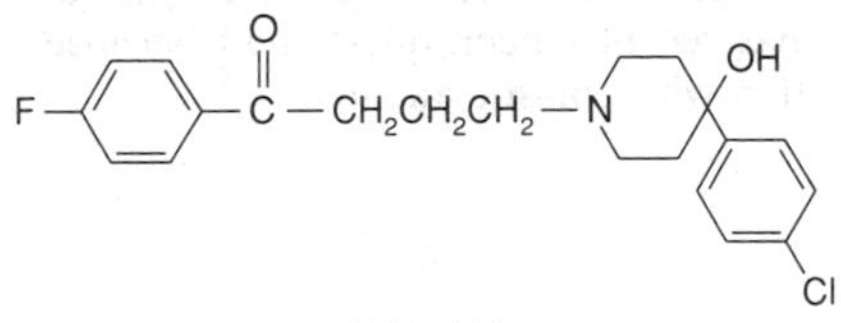

Haloperidol

Diphenylbutylpiperidine

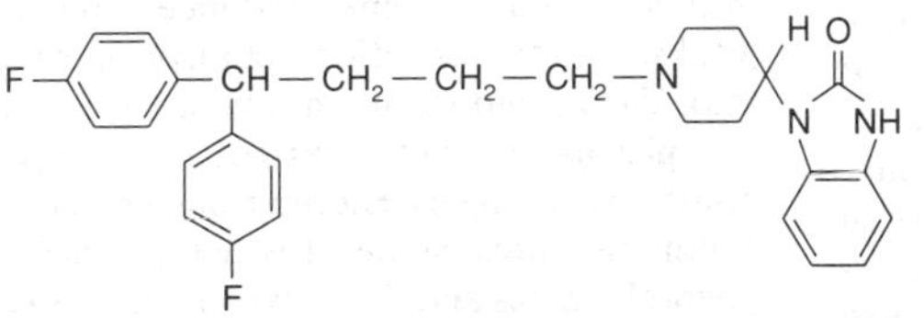

Pimozide

Benzamides

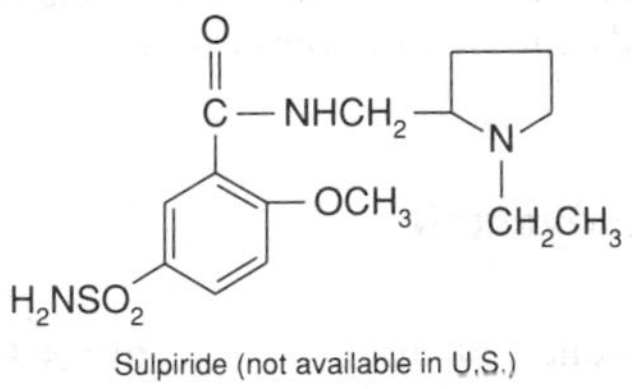

Sulpiride (not available in U.S.)

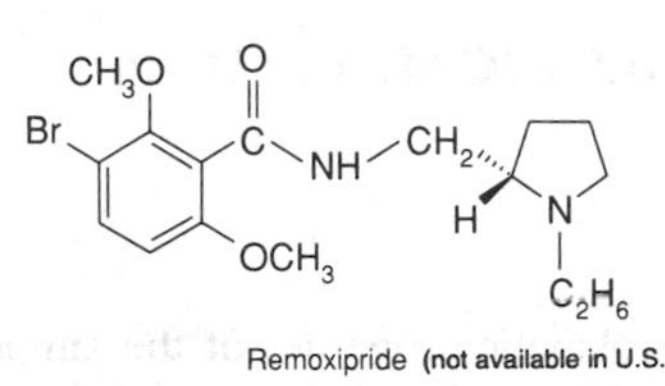

Remoxipride (not available in U.S.)

Benzisoxazole

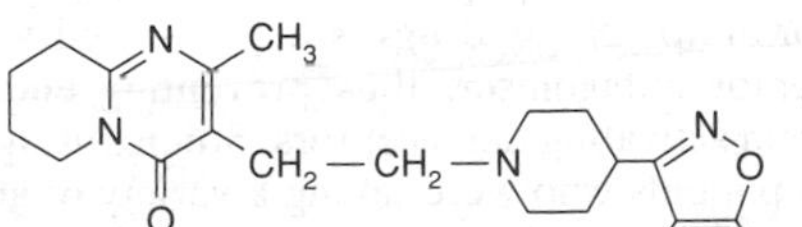

Risperidone

Rauwolfia Alkaloid

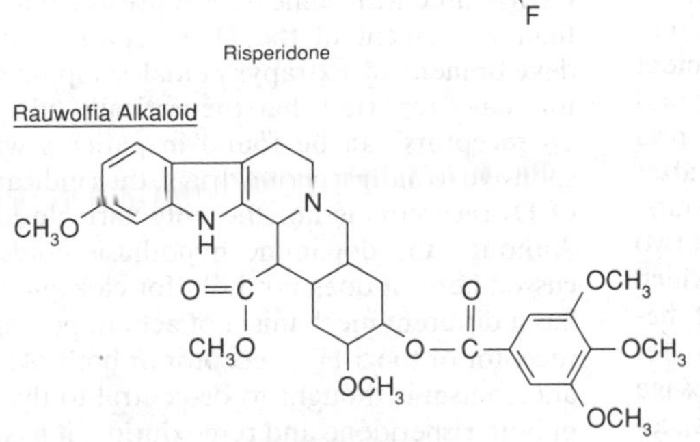

Reserpine

**Figure 33.3.17–1.** *Continued*

has been shown to be an effective antipsychotic agent. A controversial clinical and research observation about pimozide is that it may be more effective than the other antipsychotics in reducing the deficit or negative symptoms of schizophrenia, although strongly supportive data for that impression are lacking.

## Benzamide

Sulpiride (Dogmatil) and raclopride are available in some countries outside the United States and have been found to be effective antipsychotic drugs. Similar to spiperone, raclopride has been used as a radio-labeled ligand in research studies, particularly in PET studies of schizophrenic patients, because of its specific labeling of $D_2$ receptors. Remoxipride is a benzamide derivative that has specific receptor activity at $D_2$ receptors and at sigma receptors. Available research data on remoxipride support its use as an effective antipsychotic that may be associated with fewer neurological side effects than are most other antipsychotics. However, the general safety of remoxipride has recently been questioned because of the possible association with aplastic anemia.

## Benzisoxazole

Risperidone is the first benzisoxazole to be introduced in the United States for the treatment of schizophrenia. It is chemically distinct from all other antipsychotics. In addition to its significant affinity for the $D_2$ receptor, a property it shares with other antipsychotics, risperidone is a potent antagonist at serotonin type 2 (5-$HT_2$) receptors. Available published data indicate that risperidone may be more effective in the treatment of negative symptoms than is haloperidol; risperidone is also associated with fewer neurological adverse effects than are other drugs in its class.

# PHARMACOLOGICAL ACTIONS

## Pharmacokinetics

Although the pharmacokinetic properties of the antipsychotics vary widely (for example, their half-lives range from 10 to 20 hours), the most important clinical generalization is that all the antipsychotics currently available in the United States (with the exception of clozapine) can be given in one daily oral dose once the patient is in a stable condition and has adjusted to any adverse effects. Most antipsychotics are incompletely absorbed after oral administration, although liquid preparations are absorbed more efficiently than are other forms. Many antipsychotics are also available in parenteral forms that can be given intramuscularly in emergency situations, resulting in a more rapid and more reliable attainment of therapeutic plasma concentrations than is possible with oral administration. Risperidone is rapidly absorbed after oral administration, reaches peak levels about one hour after administration, and has a plasma half-life of about 24 hours. Steady-state levels of remoxipride are reached after about two days of dosing; in contrast to other antipsychotics, in which hepatic impairment can have a clinically significant effect, hepatic impairment has little effect on the elimination of remoxipride. Because of that pattern of metabolism, the dosage of remoxipride should be reduced for elderly patients, although the drug may turn out to be particularly useful in the

elderly because of its apparently minimal cognitive and cardiovascular effects.

In the United States, two antipsychotics, haloperidol and fluphenazine, are available in long-acting depot parenteral formulations that can be given once every one to four weeks, depending on the dose and the patient. The depot formulations of haloperidol and fluphenazine consist of esters of the parent compound mixed in sesame seed oil. The rate of entry of the drug into the body is determined by the rate at which the esterified drug diffuses out of the oil into the body; then the esterified drug is rapidly hydrolyzed, releasing the active compound. Because of the long half-life of that formulation, it can take up to six months of treatment to reach steady-state plasma levels, indicating that oral therapy should perhaps be continued during the first month or so of depot antipsychotic treatment. The long half-life of the depot formulation also means that detectable concentrations of the antipsychotic are present long after the last administration of the drug.

Peak plasma concentrations are usually reached one to four hours after oral administration and 30 to 60 minutes after parenteral administration. The half-lives of the butyrophenones and the diphenylbutylpiperidines are longer than for the phenothiazines, and the clinical effects are seen in the tendency of parkinsonism caused by the butyrophenones and the diphenylbutylpiperidines to linger longer when parkinsonism is caused by other antipsychotics. In addition, most antipsychotic drugs have high binding to plasma proteins, volumes of distribution, and lipid solubilities. Antipsychotic drugs are metabolized in the liver and reach steady-state plasma levels in 5 to 10 days. Some evidence indicates that, after a few weeks of administration, chlorpromazine, thiothixene, and thioridazine induce metabolic enzymes, thereby resulting in low plasma concentrations of the drugs. Chlorpromazine is notorious among psychopharmacologists for having more than 150 metabolites, some of which are active. The nonaliphatic phenothiazines and the butyrophenones have few metabolites, and whether those metabolites are active remains controversial. The potential presence of active metabolites complicates the interpretation of plasma drug levels that report the presence of only the parent compound.

## Pharmacodynamics

The potency of antipsychotic drugs to reduce psychotic symptoms is most closely correlated with the affinity of those drugs with $D_2$ receptors. The mechanism of therapeutic action for antipsychotic drugs is hypothesized to be through $D_2$ receptor antagonism, thus preventing endogenous dopamine from activating the receptors. Studies using the PET technique in patients who were taking a variety of antipsychotics in different dosages have produced data indicating that occupancy of about 60 percent of the $D_2$ receptors in the caudate-putamen is correlated with clinical response and that occupancy of more than 70 percent of the $D_2$ receptors is correlated with the development of extrapyramidal symptoms. Other investigators have reported that theoretically adequate occupancy of $D_2$ receptors can be found in patients who are still nonresponsive to antipsychotic drugs, thus indicating that occupancy of $D_2$ receptors is not the only variable in clinical response. Although the dopamine hypothesis holds for all drugs discussed here, it does not hold for clozapine, which apparently has a different mechanism of action, perhaps involving the $D_4$ receptor or the 5-$HT_2$ receptor or both. Although $D_2$ receptor antagonism is thought to be central to the therapeutic effects of both risperidone and remoxipride, it has been hypothesized that the additional antagonist activities of those drugs at the

5-HT₂ receptor for risperidone and the sigma receptor for remoxipride explain, at least in part, their favorable side-effect profiles.

There are two major caveats to the dopamine hypothesis of schizophrenia as it evolved out of the mechanism of action for the antipsychotics: First, although the dopamine receptor blocking effect occurs immediately, the full antipsychotic effects of the drugs may take weeks to develop. That observation indicates that some slowly developing, still unknown homeostatic change in the brain is the mechanism of action for the antipsychotic effects of the drugs. An example of such a delayed effect is the observation that dopaminergic neurons significantly decrease their firing rates after long-term administration but not after short-term administration of $D_2$ antagonist drugs, an effect referred to as depolarization blockade. Second, although the correlation of dopamine blocking effects and clinical potency has led to the dopamine hypothesis of schizophrenia, it is also true that the antipsychotic drugs reduce psychotic symptoms regardless of diagnosis. The therapeutic effects of dopamine receptor blockade, therefore, are not unique to the pathophysiology of schizophrenia. Another positive association between the clinical efficacy of antipsychotics and their dopamine receptor activity is suggested by the effects of the drugs on the plasma concentrations of homovanillic acid, the major metabolite of dopamine. Several studies have reported that high pretreatment concentrations of plasma homovanillic acid are positively correlated with an increased likelihood of a favorable clinical response. Furthermore, a decrease in plasma homovanillic acid concentrations early in the course of treatment is correlated with a favorable clinical response.

Most of the neurological and endocrinological adverse effects of antipsychotics can also be explained by their blockade of dopamine receptors. However, various antipsychotics also block noradrenergic, cholinergic, and histaminergic receptors, thus accounting for the variation in adverse-effect profiles seen among the drugs.

## EFFECTS ON SPECIFIC ORGANS AND SYSTEMS

Although some of the antipsychotic drugs are relatively specific in their effects on dopamine receptors (for example, remoxipride), most have significant effects on other receptors, including adrenergic, cholinergic, and histaminergic receptors. The other receptor effects result in a variety of effects on organs and systems in addition to the effect on the brain. Perhaps the most significant effects involve the heart and the vascular system. Many antipsychotic drugs, particularly the low-potency drugs, decrease cardiac contractility, increase atrial and ventricular conduction times, and increase the length of refractory periods. The $\alpha_1$-adrenergic antagonist activity of many of the antipsychotics, including clozapine and to some extent risperidone, can result in vasodilation and orthostatic (postural) hypotension. The major effects on the gastrointestinal system is mediated by the drugs' blockade of muscarinic cholinergic receptors, resulting in dry mouth and constipation, especially for clozapine and the low-potency drugs. The antipsychotic drugs as a class can have a variety of effects on the skin (for example, rashes, photosensitivities, and discoloring), although those effects are not common. A transient decrease in leukopoiesis is seen as a common result of antipsychotic treatment. Chlor-

promazine has weak diuretic effects, but the predominant genitourinary effects are those affecting sexual function. The effects on sexual function are mediated primarily through the resulting imbalances in adrenergic and cholinergic activities, decreases in catecholamine activity, and endocrine effects of the antipsychotics (for example, increased prolactin).

## THERAPEUTIC INDICATIONS

The controlled clinical trials that were conducted to demonstrate the efficacy of antipsychotic drugs set a high standard of design for clinical trials in general. From the earliest trials in the 1950s and the 1960s, the trials were conducted by using double-blind, placebo-controlled, parallel-group, randomized designs. Those design features usually result in the most compelling data regarding the efficacy or the lack of efficacy of a compound, and literally hundreds of such well-controlled studies have demonstrated the efficacy of antipsychotic compounds for the treatment of schizophrenia and other psychotic conditions.

### Idiopathic Psychoses

The idiopathic psychoses include those in the fourth edition of *Diagnostic and Statistical Manual of Mental Disorders* (DSM-IV) that have no known cause. Those disorders include schizophrenia, schizophreniform disorder, schizoaffective disorder, delusional disorder, brief psychotic disorder, manic episodes, and major depressive disorder with psychotic features. Antipsychotic drugs are effective in both the short-term and the long-term management of those conditions; that is, antipsychotics both reduce acute symptoms and prevent future exacerbations.

**Schizophrenia.** The short-term efficacy of antipsychotics in the treatment of schizophrenia has been demonstrated in hundreds of trials. The comparatively small number of trials that failed to demonstrate the superiority of the antipsychotics over a placebo almost always used dosages of an antipsychotic that were too low (less than 300 mg chlorpromazine equivalence) or were not rigorously designed studies in the first place. Similarly, dozens of well-controlled studies have demonstrated the efficacy of antipsychotic drugs in the maintenance treatment of psychotic patients. One survey of those studies found that about 75 percent of all schizophrenic patients relapse over the course of one year if treated with a placebo, in comparison with only 15 to 25 percent of patients who relapse after being treated with antipsychotic drugs. Furthermore, the severity of the symptoms during the relapses are less severe in the patients receiving maintenance treatment than in those patients not receiving antipsychotic treatment.

In general, the antipsychotics are thought to be more effective in the treatment of the positive symptoms (for example, hallucinations, delusions, and agitation) than in the treatment of the negative symptoms (for example, emotional withdrawal and ambivalence). A debate continues about that belief, since the antipsychotic drugs themselves may contribute to the negative symptoms. It is also generally believed that paranoid patients are more responsive than nonparanoid patients, that so-called reactive psychoses are more responsive than so-called process psychoses, and that female patients are more responsive than male patients. Some patients do not respond to any of the old antipsychotic drugs, and those patients are often referred to as treatment-resistant patients. Clozapine has been approved by the Food and Drug Administration (FDA) for the treatment of such patients. Although large-scale studies of the use of risperidone and remoxipride for that patient population have not yet been conducted, clinical trials of those drugs for treatment-resistant patients are warranted.

RISPERIDONE.   At least two large, multicenter, well-controlled clinical trials have shown that risperidone is superior in efficacy to a placebo and may be superior to haloperidol in the treatment of schizophrenia and related psychotic disorders. Those studies used dosages ranging from 2 to 16 mg a day of risperidone in comparison with a placebo and 10 mg a day of haloperidol in one study and in comparison with a placebo and 20 mg a day of haloperidol in another study. Dosages of 4, 6, and 8 mg a day of risperidone were the most effective and were reported to be more effective than haloperidol in reducing the negative symptoms of schizophrenia. Dosages of risperidone in that range were also reported to be associated with fewer extrapyramidal side effects than was haloperidol treatment. Additional studies of risperidone have shown that the drug is safe and generally well-tolerated, even with long-term treatment for periods of up to 12 months; longer periods of treatment are also likely to be safe and well-tolerated.

REMOXIPRIDE.   Remoxipride has also been shown to be an effective treatment of schizophrenia and related psychotic disorders. Remoxipride has been studied in dosages ranging from 100 to 600 mg a day in comparison with a placebo and a range of haloperidol dosages. The studies found that haloperidol and remoxipride are equally effective and that remoxipride is associated with fewer and less severe extrapyramidal symptoms, less drowsiness and fatigue, and fewer autonomic and endocrine side effects than is haloperidol. Studies have also found that remoxipride is generally well-tolerated for treatment periods of at least 12 months. The possible association between remoxipride and aplastic anemia may limit the use of the drug if it is approved by the Food and Drug Administration (FDA).

**Other idiopathic psychoses.**   Antipsychotics are often used in combination with antimanic drugs to treat psychosis or manic excitement in bipolar I disorder. Although lithium (Eskalith), carbamazepine (Tegretol), and valproate (Depakene) are the drugs of choice for that condition, those drugs generally have a slower onset of action than do antipsychotics in the treatment of the acute symptoms. Thus, the general practice is to use combination therapy at the initiation of treatment and to gradually withdraw the antipsychotic after the antimanic agent has reached its onset of activity.

Combination treatment with an antipsychotic and an antidepressant is the treatment of choice for major depressive disorder with psychotic features, although electroconvulsive therapy (ECT) is also likely to be effective. Because of the potential adverse effects of long-term administration of the old antipsychotics (for example, tardive dyskinesia with long-term treatment), maintenance

treatment with those drugs is indicated primarily for schizophrenia and not for the mood disorders. However, the introduction of such new antipsychotics as risperidone may make the long-term treatment of mood disorder patients with those drugs a clinically warranted treatment.

Schizoaffective disorder patients and delusional disorder patients often respond favorably to treatment with antipsychotic drugs. Some patients with borderline personality disorder who have marked psychotic symptoms as part of their disorder are also at least partially responsive to antipsychotic drugs, although those patients in particular also require psychotherapeutic treatment.

## Secondary Psychoses

Secondary psychoses are psychotic syndromes that are associated with an identified organic cause, such as a brain tumor, a dementing disorder (for example, dementia of the Alzheimer's type), or substance abuse. The antipsychotic drugs are generally effective in the treatment of psychotic symptoms that are associated with those syndromes. The high-potency antipsychotics are usually safer than the low-potency antipsychotics in such patients because of the high-potency drugs' lower cardiotoxic, epileptogenic, and anticholinergic activities. However, antipsychotic drugs should not be used to treat withdrawal symptoms associated with ethanol or barbiturates because of the risk that such treatment will facilitate the development of withdrawal seizures. The drug of choice in such cases is usually a benzodiazepine. Because of the antagonist activity of remoxipride at the sigma receptors, that drug may be particularly effective in the treatment of psychosis associated with phencyclidine (PCP) use, although that possibility has not yet been demonstrated clinically. Agitation and psychosis associated with such neurological conditions as dementia of the Alzheimer's type are responsive to antipsychotic treatment; high-potency drugs and low dosages are generally preferable. Even with high-potency drugs, as many as 25 percent of elderly patients may experience episodes of hypotension. Risperidone may have a superior side-effect profile in those patients, although that has not been shown in well-controlled studies at this time. Low dosages of high-potency drugs, such as 0.5 to 5 mg a day of haloperidol, are usually sufficient for the treatment of those patients, although thioridazine 10 to 50 mg a day is also used because of its particularly potent sedative properties.

## Severe Agitation and Violent Behavior

Antipsychotic drugs are commonly used for the treatment of patients who are severely agitated and violent, although other drugs, such as benzodiazepines and barbiturates, are also usually effective for the immediate control of such behavior. Symptoms such as extreme irritability, lack of impulse control, severe hostility, gross hyperactivity, and agitation are responsive to short-term antipsychotic treatment. The long-term use of antipsychotic drugs for those indications must be weighed against the risk for neurological side effects (for example, tardive dyskinesia), although the advent of new antipsychotic drugs (for example, risperidone) may affect the risk-benefit consideration in some instances. Mentally handicapped children, especially those with profound mental retardation and autistic disorder, often have associated episodes of violence, aggression, and agitation, which are responsive to treatment with antipsychotic drugs. Again, the risk of the old antipsychotic drugs must be considered before instituting long-term treatment, and the potentially low risk of the new antipsychotic drugs will have to be evaluated in subsequent clinical trials. In general, the use of the high-potency antipsychotics, which cause little sedation, is preferred to the use of the more sedating low-potency drugs. Also, especially for long-term treatment, drugs such as lithium, the anticonvulsants (carbamazepine and valproate), the β-adrenergic receptor antagonists, and even serotonergic drugs should be considered before long-term treatment with antipsychotic drugs is undertaken.

### Movement Disorders

Both the psychosis and the movement disorder of Huntington's disease are responsive to treatment with dopamine receptor antagonists, such as haloperidol. Clinical trials of risperidone, remoxipride, and clozapine in Huntington's disease patients have not yet been conducted, although such trials may show those drugs' superior efficacy, safety, or tolerability in the condition.

One of the antipsychotic drugs, pimozide, is specifically approved in the United States for the treatment of the motor and vocal tics of Tourette's disorder, although other dopamine receptor antagonists are likely to be equally effective. Pimozide is used for Tourette's disorder because of its alleged association with few extrapyramidal effects, although pimozide has its own side effects, such as marked prolongation of the QT interval of the electrocardiogram (ECG) in dosages over 10 mg a day and an increased risk for drug-induced seizures in dosages of 20 mg a day.

The rare neurological disorders ballismus and hemiballismus (which affects only one side of the body) are characterized by propulsive movements of the limbs away from the body. They are also responsive to treatment with dopamine receptor antagonists.

### Other Psychiatric and Nonpsychiatric Indications

The use of thioridazine for the treatment of depression with marked anxiety or agitation has been approved in the United States, although that is an outdated indication for the drug because of the availability of drugs with superior efficacy and safety profiles. Nevertheless, some clinicians use small dosages of antipsychotic drugs (0.5 mg of haloperidol or 25 mg of chlorpromazine two or three times daily) to treat severe anxiety. The risk of inducing neurological side effects must be carefully weighed against the potential therapeutic benefits in such cases. The dopamine receptor antagonists are also sometimes used as adjuvants to treatment regimens for chronic pain disorder, although the use of the drugs for that indication should generally be done only by specialists in the treatment of chronic pain. Miscellaneous indications for the use of dopamine receptor

antagonists include the treatment of nausea, emesis, hiccups, and pruritus.

## PRECAUTIONS AND ADVERSE REACTIONS

One generalization about the adverse effects of antipsychotics is that low-potency drugs cause most nonneurological adverse effects and high-potency drugs cause most neurological (EPS) adverse events (Table 33.3.17–1).

### Nonneurological Adverse Effects

**Cardiac effects.** Low-potency antipsychotics are more cardiotoxic than are high-potency antipsychotics. Chlorpromazine causes prolongation of the QT and PR intervals, blunting of the T waves, and depression of the ST segment. Thioridazine, in particular, has marked effects on the T wave and is associated with malignant arrhythmias, such as torsade de pointes, perhaps explaining why overdoses of piperidine phenothiazines may be the most lethal of this group of drugs. When QT intervals exceed 0.44 msec, there is some correlation with an increased risk for sudden death, possibly secondary to ventricular tachycardia or ventricular fibrillation. Although risperidone is associated with some increase in the QT interval, that is not clinically significant in the limited clinical data currently available. The early reports of remoxipride indicate that it may be a particularly safe antipsychotic from a cardiac standpoint.

**Sudden death.** The cardiac effects of antipsychotics have been hypothesized to be related to sudden death in patients treated with the drugs. However, careful evaluation of the literature indicates that it is premature to attribute the sudden deaths to the antipsychotic drugs. Supporting that view is the observation that the introduction of antipsychotics had no effect on the incidence of sudden death in schizophrenic patients. In addition, both low-potency and high-potency drugs were involved in the reported cases. Furthermore, many reports were of patients with other medical problems who were also treated with several other drugs.

**Orthostatic (postural) hypotension.** Orthostatic (postural) hypotension is mediated by adrenergic blockade and is most common with low-potency antipsychotics, particularly chlorpromazine, thioridazine, chlorprothixene, and clozapine. It occurs most frequently during the first few days of treatment, and tolerance is rapidly developed for the adverse effects. The chief dangers of orthostatic hypotension are that the patients may faint, fall, and injure themselves, although such occurrences are not common.

When using intramuscular (IM) low-potency antipsychotics, the clinician should measure the patient's blood pressure (lying and standing) before and after the first dose and during the first few days of treatment. When appropriate, patients should be warned of the possibility of fainting and should be given the usual instructions to rise from bed gradually, sit at first with their legs dangling, wait for a minute, and sit or lie down if they feel faint. Support hose may help some patients.

If hypotension does occur in patients receiving the medications, the symptoms can usually be managed by having

**Table 33.3.17–1**
**Relative Adverse Effects of Antipsychotics**

| | Sedation | Anticholinergic | Hypotension | Extrapyramidal |
|---|---|---|---|---|
| Acetophenazine | Low | Low | Low | Medium |
| Chlorpromazine | High | High | High | Low |
| Chlorprothixene | High | High | High | Low |
| Fluphenazine | Medium | Low | Low | High |
| Haloperidol | Low | Low | Low | High |
| Loxapine | Medium | Medium | Medium | High |
| Mesoridazine | Medium | High | Medium | Medium |
| Molindone | Medium | Medium | Low | High |
| Perphenazine | Low | Low | Low | High |
| Pimozide | Low | Low | Low | High |
| Remoxipride | Low | Low | Low | Low |
| Risperidone | Low | Low | Low–Medium | Low |
| Thioridazine | High | High | High | Low |
| Thiothixene | Low | Low | Low | High |
| Trifluoperazine | Medium | Low | Low | High |
| Triflupromazine | High | Medium | High | Medium |

the patients lie down with the feet higher than the head. On rare occasions, volume expansion or vasopressor agents, such as norepinephrine (Levophed), may be indicated. Because hypotension is produced by α-adrenergic blockade, the drugs also block the α-adrenergic stimulating properties of epinephrine, leaving the β-adrenergic stimulating effects untouched. Therefore, the administration of epinephrine results in a paradoxical worsening of hypotension and is contraindicated in cases of antipsychotic-induced hypotension. Pure α-adrenergic pressor agents, such as metaraminol (Aramine) and norepinephrine, are the drugs of choice in the treatment of the disorder.

**Hematological effects.** An often transient leukopenia with a white blood cell (WBC) count around 3,500 is a common but not serious problem. A life-threatening hematological problem is agranulocytosis, which occurs most often with chlorpromazine and thioridazine use but is seen with almost all antipsychotics. Agranulocytosis occurs most frequently during the first three months of treatment and with an incidence of around 5 in 10,000 patients treated with antipsychotics. Routine complete blood counts (CBCs) are not indicated; however, if a patient reports a sore throat and fever, a CBC should be done immediately to check for the possibility. If the blood indexes are low, the antipsychotic should be stopped, and the patient should be transferred to a medical facility. The mortality rate for the complication may be as high as 30 percent. Thrombocytopenic or nonthrombocytopenic purpura, hemolytic anemias, and pancytopenia may occur rarely in patients treated with antipsychotics. If remoxipride is approved for use in the United States, hematological monitoring may be required because of the possible association of the drug with aplastic anemia.

**Peripheral anticholinergic effects.** Peripheral anticholinergic effects are common and consist of dry mouth and nose, blurred vision, constipation, urinary retention, and mydriasis. Some patients also have nausea and vomiting. Chlorpromazine, thioridazine, mesoridazine (Serantil), and trifluoperazine (Stelazine) are potent anticholinergics (Table 33.3.17–1). Anticholinergic effects can be particularly severe if a low-potency antipsychotic is used with a tricyclic drug and an anticholinergic drug; such a practice

is seldom warranted. In contrast to the dry nose of old antipsychotics, risperidone may be associated with nasal congestion or rhinitis, possibly a result of α₁-adrenergic blockade.

Dry mouth can be a troubling symptom for some patients and can endanger continued compliance. The patients can be advised to rinse out their mouths frequently with water and not to chew gum or candy containing sugar, as that can result in fungal infections of the mouth or an increased incidence of dental caries. Constipation should be treated with the usual laxative preparations, but the condition can still progress to paralytic ileus in some patients. A decrease in the antipsychotic dosage or a change to another less anticholinergic drug is warranted in such a case. Pilocarpine may be used to treat paralytic ileus, although the relief is only transitory. Bethanechol (Urecholine) (20 to 40 mg a day) may be useful in some patients with urinary retention.

**Endocrine effects.** Blockade of the dopamine receptors in the tuberoinfundibular tract results in the increased secretion of prolactin, which can result in breast enlargement, galactorrhea, impotence in men, and amenorrhea and inhibited orgasm in women. In spite of the specificity of remoxipride for the $D_2$ receptor, the drug is not particularly associated with an increase in prolactin levels and may be the drug of choice for patients in whom increased prolactin release results in disturbing side effects.

**Sexual side effects.** Psychiatrists may not find out about the disturbing sexual effects of an antipsychotic if they do not ask about the effects specifically. The incidence of those effects is believed to be significantly underestimated. As many as 50 percent of men taking antipsychotics may experience impotence. Several reports have stated that treatment of the condition with bromocriptine (Parlodel), or yohimbine (Yocon) is successful in some patients, although the risk of exacerbating the underlying psychosis must be considered with both drugs. Both men and women taking antipsychotics can experience anorgasmia and decreased libido. Thioridazine is particularly associated with decreased libido and retrograde ejaculation in men. Other antipsychotics have been associated with both delayed and retrograde ejaculation, although some therapeutic success has been reported after treatment with brompheniramine (Bromfed), ephedrine (Primatene), phenylpropanolamine (Comtrex), midrione, and imipramine (Tofranil) for the condition. Priapism and reports of painful orgasms have also been described, both possibly resulting from $\alpha_1$-adrenergic antagonist activity.

**Weight gain.** A common adverse effect of treatment with antipsychotics is weight gain, which can be significant in some cases. Molindone and, perhaps, loxapine are not associated with the symptom and may be indicated in patients for whom weight gain is a serious health hazard or a reason for noncompliance.

**Dermatological effects.** Allergic dermatitis and photosensitivity occur in a small percentage of patients, most commonly those taking low-potency drugs, particularly chlorpromazine. A variety of skin eruptions—urticarial, maculopapular, petechial, and edematous eruptions—have been reported. The eruptions occur early in treatment, generally in the first few weeks, and remit spontaneously. A photosensitivity reaction that resembles a severe sunburn also occurs in some patients taking chlorpromazine. Patients should be warned of that adverse effect, should spend no more than 30 to 60 minutes in the sun, and should use sun screens. Chlorpromazine is also associated with some cases of a blue-gray discoloration of the skin over areas exposed to sunlight. The skin changes often begin with a tan or golden brown color and progress to such colors as slate gray, metallic blue, and purple.

**Ophthalmological effects.** Thioridazine is associated with irreversible pigmentation of the retina when given in dosages of more than 800 mg a day. An early symptom of the side effect can sometimes be nocturnal confusion related to difficulty with night vision. The pigmentation is similar to that seen in retinitis pigmentosa, and it can progress even after the thioridazine is stopped, finally resulting in blindness. The pigmentation is not reversible.

In contrast, chlorpromazine is associated with a relatively benign pigmentation of the eyes, characterized by whitish-brown granular deposits concentrated in the anterior lens and posterior cornea and visible only by slit-lens examination. The deposits can progress to opaque white and yellow-brown granules, often stellate. Occasionally, the conjunctiva is discolored by a brown pigment. Retinal damage is not seen in the patients, and their vision is almost never impaired. The majority of patients who show the deposits are those who have ingested 1 to 3 kg of chlorpromazine throughout their lives.

**Jaundice.** Obstructive or cholestatic jaundice is associated as a rare side effect with antipsychotic treatment. The adverse effect usually occurs in the first month of treatment and is heralded by symptoms of upper abdominal pain, nausea and vomiting, a flulike syndrome, fever, rash, eosinophilia, bilirubin in the urine, and increases in serum bilirubin, alkaline phosphatase, and hepatic transaminases. In the early days of chlorpromazine treatment, jaundice was not unusual, occurring in about 1 out of every 100 patients treated. For the past decade, the incidence has hovered around 1 in 1,000. The drop in the incidence is perhaps due to a reduction in impurities in the manufacturing of the compound, although the definitive reason for the drop in incidence is unknown.

If jaundice occurs, the clinician generally discontinues the medication, although the value of that practice has never been proved. Indeed, patients have continued to receive chlorpromazine throughout the illness without adverse effects, although that approach does not seem to be warranted, given the wide range of alternative treatments available. Jaundice has also been reported to occur with promazine (Sparine), thioridazine, mepazine (Pacalal), and prochlorperazine (Compazine) and very rarely with fluphenazine and trifluoperazine. No convincing evidence indicates that haloperidol or many of the other nonphenothiazine antipsychotics can produce jaundice. Remoxipride may be particularly unlikely to produce liver toxicity. The hepatotoxicity of risperidone is not known at this time; no particular evidence indicates that it is associated with jaundice, but risperidone does have nausea, vomiting, and abdominal pain as common side effects.

**Overdoses of antipsychotics.** The symptoms of antipsychotic overdose include extrapyramidal symptoms, mydriasis, decreased deep tendon reflexes, tachycardia, and hypotension. With the exception of overdoses of thioridazine and mesoridazine, the outcome of antipsychotic overdose is generally favorable unless the patient has also ingested other central nervous system (CNS) depressants, such as alcohol and benzodiazepines. The severe symptoms of overdose include delirium, coma, respiratory depression, and seizures. Haloperidol and possibly remoxipride may be among the safest antipsychotics in overdose. After an overdose, the electroencephalogram (EEG) shows diffuse slowing and low voltage. The piperazine phenothiazines (for example, thioridazine) can lead to heart block and ventricular fibrillation, resulting in death.

The treatment of antipsychotic overdose should include the use of activated charcoal, if possible, and gastric lavage. The use of emetics is not indicated, since the antiemetic actions of the antipsychotics inhibit their efficacy. Seizures can be treated with IV diazepam (Valium) or phenytoin (Dilantin). Hypotension can be treated with either norepinephrine or dopamine (Dopastat) but not epinephrine (Adrenalin).

## Neurological Adverse Effects

The antipsychotic drugs, especially the typical or old ones, are associated with a number of uncomfortable neurological adverse effects and several potentially serious neurological adverse effects. Many of the neurological adverse effects are severe enough to warrant attention as separate problems that require their own treatment plans. The recognition that the treatment-emergent adverse effects are of significant clinical importance is reflected in DSM-IV by the inclusion of a separate group of medication-induced movement disorders (Table 33.3.17–2). The common occurrence of uncomfortable neurological adverse effects—particularly parkinsonism, tremor, akathisia, and dystonia—prompted the search for new antipsychotic drugs that are not likely to cause medication-induced movement disorders. Clozapine, remoxipride, and risperidone are antipsychotic drugs that are less likely than the typical or old antipsychotic drugs to cause those movement disorders.

**Neuroleptic-induced parkinsonism.** Parkinsonian adverse effects occur in about 15 percent of patients who are

**Table 33.3.17–2**
**DSM-IV Medication-Induced Movement Disorders**

Neuroleptic-induced parkinsonism
Neuroleptic malignant syndrome
Neuroleptic-induced acute dystonia
Neuroleptic-induced acute akathisia
Neuroleptic-induced tardive dyskinesia
Medication-induced postural tremor
Medication-induced movement disorder not otherwise
 specified

treated with antipsychotics, usually in 5 to 90 days of the initiation of treatment. Symptoms include muscle stiffness (lead-pipe rigidity), cogwheel rigidity, shuffling gait, stooped posture, and drooling. The pill-rolling tremor of idiopathic parkinsonism is rare, but a regular, coarse tremor similar to essential tremor may be present and is referred to as medication-induced postural tremor in DSM-IV. A focal, perioral tremor, sometimes referred to as rabbit syndrome (a term that is best avoided because of its insensitive comparison between the movement disorder and the masticatory movements of a rabbit), is another parkinsonian effect seen with antipsychotics, although perioral tremor is more likely than other tremors to occur late in the course of treatment. A physical sign of parkinsonism is a positive glabella tap reflex. The glabella tap reflex is elicited by tapping the forehead between the eyebrows. The failure of the orbicularis oculi to habituate to repeated taps constitutes a positive glabella tap reflex. The masklike facies, bradykinesia, akinesia (lack of initiative), and ataraxia (indifference toward the environment) that are also symptoms of the parkinsonian syndrome are often misdiagnosed as being part of the negative or deficit symptom picture of schizophrenia. That misdiagnosis results in the incorrect clinical decision not to attempt to treat the symptoms with anticholinergic drugs or similarly effective drugs for the treatment of neuroleptic-induced movement disorders.

Women are affected by neuroleptic-induced parkinsonism about twice as often as men, and the disorder can occur at all ages, although it is most common after age 40. All antipsychotics can cause the symptoms, especially high-potency drugs with low anticholinergic activity. Chlorpromazine and thioridazine are not likely to be involved. The blockade of dopaminergic transmission in the nigrostriatal tract is the cause of neuroleptic-induced parkinsonism. The differential diagnosis of the parkinsonian symptoms should include idiopathic parkinsonism, other organic causes of parkinsonism, and depression, which can also be associated with parkinsonian symptoms.

The disorder can be treated with anticholinergic agents, amantadine (Symadine, Symmetrel), or diphenhydramine (Benadryl). Although amantadine may have fewer side effects than anticholinergics, it may be less effective at reducing muscular rigidity. Anticholinergics should be withdrawn after four to six weeks to assess whether the patient has developed a tolerance for the parkinsonian effects; about 50 percent of patients with neuroleptic-induced parkinsonism need continued treatment. Even after the antipsychotics are withdrawn, parkinsonian symptoms may last up to two weeks and even up to three months in

elderly patients. With such patients the clinician may continue the anticholinergic drug after stopping the antipsychotic until the parkinsonian symptoms have completely resolved.

**Neuroleptic-induced acute dystonia.** About 10 percent of all patients experience dystonia as an adverse effect of antipsychotics, usually in the first few hours or days of treatment. Dystonic movements result from a slow, sustained muscular contraction or spasm that can result in an involuntary movement. Dystonia can involve the neck (spasmodic torticollis or retrocollis), the jaw (forced opening resulting in a dislocation of the jaw or trismus), the tongue (protrusions, twisting), and the entire body (opisthotonos). Involvement of the eyes can result in an oculogyric crisis, characterized by the eyes' upward lateral movement. Unlike other types of dystonia, an oculogyric crisis may also occur late in treatment. Other dystonias include blepharospasm and glossopharyngeal dystonia, resulting in dysarthria, dysphagia, and even trouble in breathing, which can cause cyanosis. Children are particularly likely to evidence opisthotonos, scoliosis, lordosis, and writhing movements. Dystonia can be painful and frightening and often results in noncompliance with the drug treatment regimen.

Dystonia is most common in young men (less than 40 years old) but can occur at any age in either sex. Although it is most common with IM dosages of high-potency antipsychotics, dystonia can occur with any antipsychotic; it is least common with thioridazine and will probably be uncommon with risperidone and remoxipride. The mechanism of action is thought to be the dopaminergic hyperactivity in the basal ganglia that occurs when the CNS levels of the antipsychotic drug begin to fall between doses. Dystonia can fluctuate spontaneously, responding to reassurance and resulting in the clinician's false impression that the movement is hysterical or completely under conscious control. The differential diagnosis of a dystonic movement should include seizures and tardive dyskinesia.

Prophylaxis with anticholinergics or related drugs (Table 33.3.17–3) usually prevents the development of dystonia, although the risks of prophylactic treatment weigh against that benefit. Treatment with IM anticholinergics or IV or IM diphenhydramine (50 mg) almost always relieves the symptoms. Diazepam (10 mg IV), amobarbital (Amytal), caffeine sodium benzoate, and hypnosis have also been reported to be effective. Although tolerance for the adverse effect usually develops, it is sometimes prudent to change the antipsychotic if the patient is particularly concerned that the reaction may recur.

**Neuroleptic-induced acute akathisia.** Akathisia is a subjective feeling of muscular discomfort that can cause the patient to be agitated, pace relentlessly, alternately sit and stand in rapid succession, and feel generally dysphoric. The symptoms are primarily motor and cannot be controlled by the patient's will. Akathisia can appear at any time during treatment. The disorder is probably underdiagnosed because the symptoms are mistakenly attributed to psychosis, agitation, or lack of cooperation. The mechanism underlying akathisia is poorly understood, although the disorder may represent some imbalance between the noradrenergic and dopaminergic systems caused by the antipsychotics.

**Table 33.3.17–3**
**Drug Treatment of Extrapyramidal Disorders**

| Generic Name | Trade Name | Usual Daily Dosage | Indications |
|---|---|---|---|
| Anticholinergic | | | |
| Benztropine | Cogentin | PO 0.5–2 mg tid; IM or IV 1–2 mg | Acute dystonic |
| Biperiden | Akineton | PO 2–6 mg tid; IM or IV 2 mg | reaction, |
| Procyclidine | Kemadrin | PO 2.5–5 mg bid-qid | parkinsonism, |
| Trihexyphenidyl | Artane, Tremin, Pipanol | PO 2–5 mg tid | akinesia, akathisia, |
| Ethopropazine | Parsidol | PO 50–100 mg bid-qid | rabbit syndrome |
| Orphenadrine | Norflex, Disipal | PO 50–100 mg bid-qid; IV 60 mg | |
| Antihistaminergic | | | |
| Diphenhydramine | Benadryl | PO 25 mg qid; IM or IV 25 mg | Acute dystonic reaction, parkinsonism, akinesia, rabbit syndrome |
| Dopamine agonists | | | |
| Amantadine | Symmetrel | PO 100–200 mg bid | Parkinsonism, akinesia, rabbit syndrome |
| β-Adrenergic antagonists | | | |
| Propranolol | Inderal | PO 20–40 mg tid | Akathisia, tremor |
| α-Adrenergic antagonists | | | |
| Clonidine | Catapres | PO 0.1 mg tid | Akathisia |
| Benzodiazepines | | | |
| Clonazepam | Klonopin | PO 1 mg bid | Akathisia, acute |
| Lorazepam | Ativan | PO 1 mg tid | dystonic reactions |

Once akathisia is recognized and diagnosed, the antipsychotic dosage should be reduced to the minimal effective level. Treatment can be attempted with anticholinergics or amantadine, although those drugs are not particularly effective for akathisia. Drugs that may be more effective include propranolol (Inderal) (30 to 120 mg a day), benzodiazepines, and clonidine (Catapres). In some cases of akathisia, no treatment seems to be effective.

**Neuroleptic-induced tardive dyskinesia.** Tardive dyskinesia is a delayed effect of antipsychotics; it rarely occurs until after six months of treatment. The disorder consists of abnormal, involuntary, irregular choreoathetoid movements of the muscles of the head, the limbs, and the trunk. The severity of the movements ranges from minimal— often missed by patients and their families—to grossly incapacitating. Perioral movements are the most common and include darting, twisting, and protruding movements of the tongue; chewing and lateral jaw movements; lip puckering; and facial grimacing. Finger movements and hand clenching are also common. Torticollis, retrocollis, trunk twisting, and pelvic thrusting are seen in severe cases. Respiratory dyskinesia has also been reported. Dyskinesia is exacerbated by stress and disappears during sleep. Other late-appearing movement disorders have been noted and have been referred to, depending on the symptoms, as tardive dystonia, tardive parkinsonism, and tardive Tourette's disorder.

All the old dopamine receptor antagonists have been associated with tardive dyskinesia. Some data indicate that thioridazine is less associated with tardive dyskinesia than are the other antipsychotics, and insufficient data are available to make conclusions regarding risperidone and remoxipride. The longer patients take antipsychotics, the more likely they are to experience tardive dyskinesia.

About 10 to 20 percent of patients who are treated for more than a year have tardive dyskinesia. About 15 to 20 percent of long-term hospital patients have tardive dyskinesia. Women are more likely to be affected than are men, and patients more than 50 years of age, patients with brain damage, children, and patients with mood disorders are also at high risk. Before the introduction of antipsychotics in the early 1950s, 1 to 5 percent of schizophrenic patients had similar abnormal movements, indicating that the pattern of movement disorders is related to the underlying pathophysiology of schizophrenia itself. Tardive dyskinesia may be caused by dopaminergic receptor supersensitivity in the basal ganglia resulting from chronic blockade of dopamine receptors by antipsychotics.

The three basic approaches to tardive dyskinesia are prevention, diagnosis, and management. Prevention is best achieved by using antipsychotic medications only when clearly indicated and in the lowest effective dosages. Long-term data may eventually show that the new antipsychotics (for example, risperidone and remoxipride) are associated with less tardive dyskinesia than the old antipsychotics. Patients who are receiving antipsychotics should be examined regularly for the appearance of abnormal movements, preferably by using a standardized rating scale (Table 33.3.17–4). When abnormal movements are detected, a differential diagnosis should be considered (Table 33.3.17–5).

Once a diagnosis of tardive dyskinesia is made, the clinician must regularly conduct objective ratings of the movement disorder. Although tardive dyskinesia often emerges while the patient is taking a steady dosage of medication, it is even more likely to emerge when the dosage is reduced, which some investigators have referred to as withdrawal dyskinesia, although differentiating with-

**Table 33.3.17–4**
**Abnormal Involuntary Movement Scale (AIMS) Examination Procedure**

| Patient Identification | Date |
|---|---|

Rated by

Either before or after completing the examination procedure, observe the patient unobtrusively at rest (e.g., in waiting room).

The chair to be used in this examination should be a hard, firm one without arms.

After observing the patient, rate him or her on a scale of 0 (none), 1 (minimal), 2 (mild), 3 (moderate), and 4 (severe) according to the severity of the symptoms.

Ask the patient whether there is anything in his or her mouth (i.e., gum, candy, etc.) and, if so, to remove it.

Ask the patient about the *current* condition of his or her teeth. Ask patient if he or she wears dentures. Do teeth or dentures bother patient *now*.

Ask patient whether he or she notices any movement in mouth, face, hands, or feet. If yes, ask patient to describe and indicate to what extent they *currently* bother patient or interfere with his or her activities.

0 1 2 3 4  Have patient sit in chair with hands on knees, legs slightly apart, and feet flat on floor. (Look at entire body for movements while in this position.)

0 1 2 3 4  Ask patient to sit with hands hanging unsupported. If male, between legs, if female and wearing a dress, hanging over knees. (Observe hands and other body areas.)

0 1 2 3 4  Ask patient to open mouth. (Observe tongue at rest within mouth.) Do this twice.

0 1 2 3 4  Ask patient to protrude tongue. (Observe abnormalities of tongue movement.) Do this twice.

0 1 2 3 4  Ask the patient to tap thumb, with each finger, as rapidly as possible for 10 to 15 seconds; separately with right hand, then with left hand. (Observe facial and leg movements.)

0 1 2 3 4  Flex and extend patient's left and right arms. (One at a time.)

0 1 2 3 4  Ask patient to stand up. (Observe in profile. Observe all body areas again, hips included.)

0 1 2 3 4  *Ask patient to extend both arms outstretched in front with palms down. (Observe trunk, legs, and mouth.)

0 1 2 3 4  *Have patient walk a few paces, turn and walk back to chair. (Observe hands and gait.) Do this twice.

*Activated movements.

**Table 33.3.17–5**
**Differential Diagnosis for Tardive Dyskinesialike Movements**

Common: Schizophrenic mannerisms and stereotypies
  Dental problems (e.g., ill-fitting dentures)
  Meige's syndrome and other senile dyskinesias

Drug-induced: Antidepressants
  Antihistamines
  Antimalarials
  Antipsychotics
  Diphenylhydantoin
  Heavy metals
  Levodopa
  Sympathomimetics

CNS: Anoxia-induced
  Hepatic failure
  Huntington's disease
  Parathyroid hypoactivity
  Postencephalitic
  Pregnancy (chorea gravidarum)
  Renal failure
  Sydenham's chorea
  Systemic lupus erythematosus
  Thyroid hyperactivity
  Torsion dystonia
  Tumors
  Wilson's disease

drawal dyskinesia from tardive dyskinesia is impossible. Once tardive dyskinesia is recognized, the clinician should consider reducing the dosage of the antipsychotic or even stopping the medication altogether. Alternatively, the clinician may switch the patient to clozapine or to one of the new dopamine receptor antagonists, such as risperidone.

When tardive dyskinesia was first recognized and until recently, the movement disorder was believed to be chronic and progressive. Recent surveys conclude that tardive dyskinesia develops rapidly, stabilizes, and then often remits, sometimes even when the patient continues the same drug treatment. Nonetheless, continuing the same drug does not seem necessary when potentially better drugs are available. Between 5 and 40 percent of all cases of tardive dyskinesia eventually remit, and between 50 and 90 percent of all mild cases remit. However, tardive dyskinesia is less likely to remit in elderly patients than in young patients.

Tardive dyskinesia has no single effective treatment. Lowering the dosage of the antipsychotic and switching to a new antipsychotic, including clozapine, are the primary treatment strategies. In patients who cannot continue taking any antipsychotic medication, lithium, carbamazepine, or benzodiazepines may be effective in reducing both the movement disorder symptoms and the psychotic symptoms, although those drugs are less effective than the antipsychotics in treating the psychiatric symptoms. Various small studies have reported that cholinergic agonists and antagonists, dopaminergic agonists, and γ-aminobutyric acid (GABA)-ergic drugs—for example, valproic acid (Depakene)—may be useful, although the use of those drugs should be considered experimental and should be started only after a review of the most recent literature.

**Neuroleptic malignant syndrome.**  Neuroleptic malignant syndrome is a life-threatening complication that can occur anytime during the course of antipsychotic treatment. The motor and behavioral symptoms include muscular rigidity and dystonia, akinesia, mutism, obtundation, and agitation. The autonomic symptoms include hyperpyrexia (up to 107°F), sweating, and increased pulse and blood pressure. Laboratory findings include increased white blood cell count, creatinine phosphokinase, liver enzymes, plasma myoglobin, and myoglobinuria, occasionally associated with renal failure. The symptoms usually evolve over 24 to 72 hours, and the untreated syndrome lasts 10 to 14 days. The diagnosis is often missed in the early stages, and the withdrawal or agitation may mistakenly be considered to reflect increased psychosis. Men are affected more frequently than are women, and young patients are affected more commonly than elderly patients. The mortality rate can reach 20 to 30 percent or even higher when depot antipsychotic medications are involved. The pathophysiology is unknown.

The first step in treatment is the immediate discontinuation of antipsychotic drugs, medical support to cool the patient, and the monitoring of vital signs, electrolytes, fluid balance, and renal output and the symptomatic treatment of fevers. Antiparkinsonian medications may reduce some of the muscle rigidity. Dantrolene (Dantrium), a skeletal muscle relaxant (0.8 to 2.5 mg per kg every six hours, up to a total dosage of 10 mg a day), may be useful in the treatment of the disorder. Once the patient can take oral medications, the dantrolene can be given in doses of 100 to 200 mg a day. Bromocriptine (20 to 30 mg a day in four divided doses) or perhaps amantadine can be added to the regimen. Treatment should usually be continued for 5 to 10 days. When antipsychotic treatment is restarted, the clinician should consider switching to a low-potency drug or to clozapine, although neuroleptic malignant syndrome has also been reported to be associated with clozapine treatment.

**Epileptogenic effects.**  Antipsychotic administration is associated with a slowing and an increased synchronization of the EEG. That effect may be the mechanism by which some antipsychotics decrease the seizure threshold. Chlorpromazine, loxapine, and other low-potency antipsychotics are thought to be more epileptogenic than are high-potency drugs. Animal data and in vitro experimental data indicate that molindone may be the least epileptogenic of the old antipsychotic drugs. The epileptogenicity of remoxipride and risperidone is not known. The risk of inducing a seizure by drug administration warrants consideration when the patient already has a seizure disorder or an organic brain lesion.

**Sedation.**  Sedation is primarily a result of the blockade of histamine type 1 receptors. Chlorpromazine is the most sedating antipsychotic; thioridazine, chlorprothixene, and loxapine are also sedating; the high-potency an-

tipsychotics are much less sedating than those drugs (Table 33.3.17–1). When first treated with antipsychotics, patients should be warned about driving and operating machinery. Giving the entire daily antipsychotic dose at bedtime usually eliminates any problems from sedation, and tolerance for that adverse effect often develops.

**Central anticholinergic effects.**  The symptoms of central anticholinergic activity include severe agitation; disorientation to time, person, and place; hallucinations; seizures; high fever; and dilated pupils. Stupor and coma may ensue. The treatment of anticholinergic toxicity consists of discontinuing the causal agent or agents, close medical supervision, and physostigmine (Antilirium, Eserine), 2 mg by slow IV infusion, repeated within one hour as necessary. Too much physostigmine is dangerous, and symptoms of physostigmine toxicity induce hypersalivation and sweating. Atropine sulfate (0.5 mg) can reverse the effects of physostigmine toxicity.

**Prevention and treatment of some neuroleptic-induced movement disorders.**  A variety of drugs (Table 33.3.17–3) may be used to prevent and treat medication-induced movement disorders, particularly neuroleptic-induced parkinsonism and neuroleptic-induced acute dystonia. The drugs include anticholinergics, amantadine, antihistamines, benzodiazepines, β-adrenergic receptor antagonists, and clonidine. Most acute dystonia and parkinsonism symptoms are effectively treated by those drugs, and acute akathisia may also respond in some cases.

It remains controversial whether prophylactic treatment with those drugs is warranted when starting a patient on antipsychotic medications. The proponents of prophylactic treatment argue that the increased likelihood of avoiding adverse neurological effects is humane to the patient and increases the possibility of future compliance. The opponents of the practice argue that a large proportion (30 to 50 percent) of patient do not need antiparkinsonian drugs, that their use may increase the likelihood of tardive dyskinesia, autonomic side effects, cognitive impairment, hyperthermia, and anticholinergic toxicity. Many of the drugs used to treat parkinsonian symptoms also have some abuse liability and may be associated with changes in the plasma concentrations of the antipsychotics. A reasonable compromise is to use the drugs prophylactically in patients under the age of 45 who are at risk for adverse effects, particularly dystonia, and not to use the drugs prophylactically in patients over 45 who are at increased risk for anticholinergic toxicity.

Once patients start taking drugs to treat a movement disorder, they should be treated for four to six weeks. Then the clinician should attempt to taper and stop the medication over a one-month period. Many patients become tolerant for the neurological adverse effects and no longer require treatment for the neuroleptic induced movement disorder. Some patients experience the return of neurological symptoms and should be restarted on the appropriate drugs.

Most clinicians use one of the anticholinergic drugs or diphenhydramine to provide prophylaxis or treatment of neurological adverse effects. Of those drugs, diphenhydramine is the most sedating; biperiden (Akineton) is neither sedating nor stimulating; and trihexyphenidyl (Artane) may be slightly stimulating. Amantadine is most often used when one of the anticholinergic drugs is ineffective. Although amantadine does not typically exacerbate the psychosis of schizophrenia, some patients become tolerant for its antiparkinsonian effects. Amantadine is also a sedating drug for some patients.

### Pregnancy and Lactation

If possible, antipsychotics should be avoided during pregnancy, particularly in the first trimester, unless the benefit outweighs the risk. In fact, however, very few data indicate a correlation between the presence of congenital malformations in the infant and the use of antipsychotics during pregnancy, except perhaps for chlorpromazine. Some data do indicate that the use of antipsychotics during pregnancy may result in decreased dopamine receptors in the neonate, increased cholesterol, and perhaps behavioral disturbances. Nevertheless, antipsychotic use in the second and third trimesters is probably relatively safe. High-potency antipsychotics are preferable to low-potency drugs, since the low-potency drugs are associated with hypotension. Although animal data indicate that risperidone and remoxipride are relatively safe for pregnant women, no clinical data support those basic science data.

Haloperidol and phenothiazines pass into breast milk. Whether loxapine, molindone, and pimozide pass into breast milk is not known, although they probably do. Women who are taking antipsychotics should not breast-feed their infants, since the available data do not prove that the practice is safe.

## DRUG INTERACTIONS

Because of their many receptor effects and because of the metabolism of most of the dopamine receptor antagonists in the liver, many pharmacokinetic and pharmacodynamic drug interactions are associated with the drugs (Table 33.3.17–6). However, remoxipride, because of its simple metabolic route and specific $D_2$ activity, may have the fewest drug interactions of this group of drugs.

### Antacids

Antacids and cimetidine (Tagamet), administered within two hours of antipsychotic administration, can reduce the absorption of antipsychotic drugs.

### Anticholinergics

Anticholinergics may decrease the absorption of antipsychotics. The additive anticholinergic activity of antipsychotics, anticholinergics, and tricyclic drugs may result in anticholinergic toxicity.

### Anticonvulsants

Phenothiazines, especially thioridazine, may decrease the metabolism of diphenylhydantoin, resulting in toxic levels of diphenylhydantoin. Barbiturates may increase the metabolism of antipsychotics, and the antipsychotics may lower the patient's seizure threshold.

### Antidepressants

Tricyclic drugs and antipsychotics may decrease each other's metabolism, resulting in increased plasma concentrations of both drugs. The anticholinergic, sedative, and hypotensive effects of the drugs may also be additive.

### Antihypertensives

Antipsychotics may inhibit the uptake of guanethidine (Esimil, Ismelin) in the synapse and may also inhibit the hypotensive effects of clonidine and α-methyldopa (Aldomet). Conversely, antipsychotics may have an additive effect on some hypotensive drugs. Antipsychotic drugs have a variable effect on the hypotensive effects of clonidine. Propranolol coadministration with antipsychotics increases the blood concentrations of both drugs.

### CNS Depressants

Antipsychotics potentiate the CNS depressant effects of sedatives, antihistamines, opiates, opioids, and alcohol, particularly in patients with impaired respiratory status. When those agents are taken with alcohol, the risk for heat stroke may be increased.

### Other Substances

Cigarette smoking may decrease the plasma levels of antipsychotic drugs. Epinephrine has a paradoxical hypotensive effect in patients taking antipsychotics. Antipsychotic drugs may decrease the blood concentration of warfarin (Coumadin), resulting in decreased bleeding time. Phenothiazines and pimozide should not be coadministered with other agents that prolong the QT interval.

## LABORATORY INTERFERENCES

Antipsychotic drugs have been reported to interfere with some laboratory tests. Chlorpromazine and perphenazine have been reported to cause both false-positive results and false-negative results in immunological pregnancy tests and falsely elevated bilirubin (with reagent test strips) and urobilinogen (with Ehrlich's reagent test) values. Antipsychotic drugs have also been associated with an abnormal shift in the glucose tolerance test, although that shift may reflect the effects of the drugs on the glucose-regulating system. Phenothiazines have been reported to interfere with the measurement of 17-ketosteroids (with the Haltorff-Koch modification of the Zimmerman reaction) and 17-hydroxycorticosteroids (with the modified Glenn-Nelson reaction).

## DOSAGE AND ADMINISTRATION

Antipsychotic drugs are remarkably safe in short-term use, and, if necessary, a clinician can administer the drugs without conducting a physical or laboratory examination of the patient. The major contraindications for antipsychotics are (1) a history of a serious allergic response, (2) the possibility that the patient has ingested a substance

**Table 33.3.17–6**
**Important Drug Interactions with Dopamine Receptor Anatagonist Medications**[*]

| Agent | Possible Effects |
|---|---|
| Anesthetics | Potentiate hypotension |
| Antacid | Decrease absorption of antipsychotic |
| Anticholinergics | Decrease absorption |
| Anticoagulants | Increase bleeding time |
| Anticonvulsants | Increase anticonvulsant levels, effect on seizures variable; decrease antipsychotic levels |
| Antidepressants | Increase tricyclic and antipsychotic levels, additive hypotension effects |
| Antihypertensives | Generally potentiate hypotension |
| β-Blockers (propranolol) | Potentiate hypotension |
| Clonidine | Variable |
| Diuretics and smooth-muscle blockers | May potentiate hypotension |
| Guanethidine | Antagonize antihypertensive effect |
| α-Methyldopa | May potentiate hypotension; ? neurological brain condition with haloperidol |
| Barbiturates | |
| Long-term use | Decrease antipsychotic level |
| Short-term use | Increase CNS depressant effect |
| Carbamazepine | Decrease plasma levels of haloperidol and possibly all antipsychotics |
| Digitalis | Thioridazine may nullify inotropic effect |
| Estrogens | May increase antipsychotic blood level |
| Levodopa | Mutual antagonism |
| Lithium | Possible toxic synergism, ? decrease chlorpromazine levels |
| Narcotics | Potentiate analgesia, increase respiratory depression |
| Oral hypoglycemics | Variable |
| Pressor agents | |
| α-Agonists (norepinephrine) | Antagonize pressor effect |
| β-Agonists (isoproterenol) | Marked hypotension |
| Quinidine | May potentiate cardiac effect |
| Sedative-hypnotics | Additive CNS depressant effects |

*Adapted from R B Lydiard, J S Carman, M S Gold: Antipsychotics: Predicting effect/maximizing efficacy. In *Advances in Psychopharmacology: Predicting and Improving Treatment Response*, M S Gold, R B Lydiard, J S Carman, editors, p 134. CRC Press. Boca Raton, Fla., 1964.
Table adapted from A Beebee, G Bartzokis: Neuroleptic antipsychotic medications. In *The Handbook of Psychiatry*, Residents of the UCLA Department of Psychiatry, p 366. Year Book Medical, Chicago, 1990. Used with permission.

that will interact with the antipsychotic to induce CNS depression (for example, alcohol, opiates, opioids, barbiturates, and benzodiazepines) or anticholinergic delirium (for example, scopolamine [Donnatal] and possibly PCP), (3) the presence of a severe cardiac abnormality, (4) a high risk for seizures from organic and idiopathic causes, (5) the presence of narrow-angle glaucoma or prostatic hypertrophy if an antipsychotic with high anticholinergic activity is to be used, and (6) the presence or a history of tardive dyskinesia. Antipsychotics should be administered with caution in patients with hepatic disease, since impaired hepatic metabolism may result in high plasma concentrations of the antipsychotics. In the usual assessment, the clinician should obtain a complete blood count (CBC) with white blood cell indexes, liver function tests, and an electrocardiogram, especially in women over 40 and men over 30. The elderly and children are more sensitive to side effects than are young adults; therefore, the dosage of the drug should be adjusted accordingly.

**Choice of Drug**

Although the potencies of the antipsychotics vary widely (Table 33.3.17–7), all available typical antipsychotics are equally efficacious in the treatment of schizophrenia. The antipsychotics are available in a wide range

of formulations and dose sizes (Table 33.3.17–8). Data support the conclusion that clozapine and risperidone may be more effective than other antipsychotic drugs for the treatment of the negative symptoms of schizophrenia. With the old antipsychotic drugs, no type of schizophrenia and no particular symptoms are most effectively treated by any single class of antipsychotics. However, risperidone may become the drug of first choice in the treatment of schizophrenia if its possibly superior efficacies with negative symptoms and its superior safety profiles are confirmed in wide clinical testing.

The general guidelines for choosing a particular psychotherapeutic drug should be followed when choosing an antipsychotic drug (Section 33.3.1). If no other rationale prevails, the choice should be based on adverse-effect profiles and the clinician's preference. Although high-potency antipsychotics are associated with increased neurological adverse effects, current clinical practice favors using them because of the high incidence of other adverse effects (for example, cardiac, hypotensive, epileptogenic, sexual, and allergic) with the low-potency drugs. A myth in psychiatry is that hyperexcitable patients respond best to chlorpromazine because it is highly sedating, whereas withdrawn patients respond best to high-potency antipsychotics, such as fluphenazine. That myth has never been proved; if sedation is a desired goal, either the antipsychotic can be given

**Table 33.3.17–7**
Dopamine Receptor Antagonist Drugs, Trade Names, Potencies, and Dosages

| Generic Name | Trade Name | Potency* (mg of drug equivalent to 100 mg chlorpromazine) | Usual Adult Dosage Range (mg per day) | Usual Single IM Dose (mg) |
|---|---|---|---|---|
| Phenothiazines | | | | |
| Aliphatic | | | | |
| Chlorpromazine | Thorazine | 100—low | 300–800 | 25–50 |
| Triflupromazine | Vesprin | 25–50—low | 100–150 | 20–60 |
| Promazine | Sparine | 40—low | 40–800 | 50–150 |
| Piperazine | | | | |
| Prochlorperazine | Compazine | 15—medium | 40–150 | 10–20 |
| Perphenazine | Trilafon | 10—medium | 8–40 | 5–10 |
| Trifluoperazine | Stelazine | 3–5—high | 6–20 | 1–2 |
| Fluphenazine | Prolixin, Permitil | 1.5–3—high | 1–20 | 2–5 |
| Acetophenazine | Tindal | 25—medium | 60–120 | — |
| Butaperazine | Repoise (not sold in U.S.) | 10—medium | — | — |
| Carphenazine | Proketazine (not sold in U.S.) | 25—medium | — | — |
| Piperidine | | | | |
| Thioridazine | Mellaril | 100—low | 200–700[1] | — |
| Mesoridazine | Serentil | 50—low | 75–300 | 25 |
| Piperacetazine | Quide (not sold in U.S.) | 10—medium | — | — |
| Thioxanthenes | | | | |
| Chlorprothixene | Taractan | 50—low | 50–400 | 25–50 |
| Thiothixene | Navane | 2–5—high | 6–30 | 2–4 |
| Dibenzoxazepine | | | | |
| Loxapine | Loxitane | 10–15—medium | 60–100 | 12.5–50 |
| Dihydroindole | | | | |
| Molindone | Moban, Lidone | 6–10—medium | 50–100 | — |
| Butyrophenones | | | | |
| Haloperidol | Haldol | 2–5—high | 6–20 | 2–5 |
| Droperidol | Inapsine | 10—medium | — | — |
| Diphenylbutylpiperidine | | | | |
| Pimozide | Orap | 1—high | 1–10[2] | — |
| Benzamide | | | | |
| Remoxipride[3] | Roxiam (not sold in U.S.) | 50–75—low | 200–400 | — |
| Benzisoxasole | | | | |
| Risperidone | Risperdal | 2–3—low | 4–8 | — |

*Recommended adult dosages are 200 to 400 mg a day of chlorpromazine or an equivalent amount of another drug.
[1]Maximum 800 mg.
[2]Second-line drug because of cardiotoxicity.
[3]Not currently available in the United States; possible association with hematological toxicity.

in divided doses or a sedative drug, such as a benzodiazepine, can also be administered.

A clinical observation supported by some research is than an unpleasant reaction by the patient to the first dose of an antipsychotic drug correlates highly with future poor response and noncompliance. Such experiences include a subjective negative feeling, oversedation, and acute dystonia. If a patient reports such a reaction, the clinician may be well-advised to switch the patient to a different antipsychotic. Similarly, if patients say that they did not feel well while taking a particular drug in the past, the clinician is well-advised not to initiate treatment with that drug again.

## Dosage and Schedule

The therapeutic index for antipsychotics is favorable and has contributed to the unfortunate practice of routinely using high dosages of the drugs. Nevertheless, because of that common practice, physicians may be pressured by staff members to use very high dosages. Recent investigations of the dose-response curve for antipsychotics indicate that the equivalent of 10 to 20 mg of haloperidol is usually

efficacious for either the short-term or the long-term treatment of schizophrenia. Some clinicians and researchers recommend that dosages equivalent to 5 to 10 mg of haloperidol be used before going to higher dosages. Antipsychotic drugs may have a bell-shaped dose-response curve. In general, the dosage of an antipsychotic drug should be evaluated over a six-week period before increasing the dosage or switching to another antipsychotic drug. Overly high dosages of antipsychotics may lead to neurological side effects, such as akinesia and akathisia, which are difficult to distinguish from exacerbations of psychosis.

Although patients can build up a tolerance for most of the adverse effects caused by antipsychotics, patients do not build up a tolerance for the antipsychotic effect. Nevertheless, the clinician should taper the dosage when a drug is being discontinued, as the patient may experience rebound effects from the other neurotransmitter systems that the drug may have blocked. Cholinergic rebound, for example, can produce a flulike syndrome in patients.

**Short-term treatment.** The equivalent of 5 to 10 mg of haloperidol is a reasonable dose for an adult patient in an acute state. A geriatric patient may benefit from as little as 1 mg of haloperidol. The administration of more than

**Table 33.3.17–8**
**Dopamine Receptor Antagonist Preparations**

| | Tablets | Capsules | Solution | Parenteral | Rectal Suppositories |
|---|---|---|---|---|---|
| Acetophenazine | 20 mg | — | — | — | — |
| Chlorpromazine | 10, 25, 50, 100, 200 mg | 30, 75, 150, 200, 300 mg | 10 mg/5mL, 30 mg/mL, 100 mg/mL | 25 mg/mL | 25, 100 mg |
| Chlorprothixene | 10, 25, 50, 100 mg | — | 100 mg/5 mL (suspension) | 12.5 mg/mL | — |
| Droperidol | — | — | — | 2.5 mg/mL | — |
| Fluphenazine | 1, 2.5, 5, 10 mg | — | 2.5 mg/5 mL, 5 mg/mL | 2.5 mg/mL (IM only) | — |
| Fluphenazine decanoate | — | — | — | 25 mg/mL | — |
| Fluphenazine enanthate | — | — | — | 25 mg/mL | — |
| Haloperidol | 0.5, 1, 2, 3, 10, 20 mg | — | 2 mg/mL | 5 mg/mL (IM only) | — |
| Haloperidol decanoate | — | — | — | 50 mg/mL, 100 mg/mL (IM only) | — |
| Loxapine | — | 5, 10, 25, 50 mg | 25 mg/mL | 50 mg/mL | — |
| Mexonidazine | 10, 25, 50, 100 mg | — | 25 mg/mL | 25 mg/mL | — |
| Molindone | 5, 10, 75, 50, 100 mg | — | 20 mg/mL | — | — |
| Perphenazine | 2, 4, 8, 16 mg | — | 16 mg/5 mL | 5 mg/mL | — |
| Pimozide | 2 mg | — | — | — | — |
| Prochlorperazine | 5, 10, 25 mg | 10, 15, 30 mg | 5 mg/mL | 5 mg/mL | 2.5, 5, 25 mg |
| Promazine | 25, 50, 100 mg | — | — | 25 mg/mL, 50 mg/mL | — |
| Remoxipride | ? | ? | ? | ? | ? |
| Risperidone | ? | ? | ? | — | — |
| Thioridazine | 10, 15, 25, 50, 100, 150, 200 mg | — | 25 mg/5 mL, 100 mg/5 mL, 30 mg/mL, 100 mg/mL | — | — |
| Thiothixene | — | 1, 2, 5, 10, 20 mg | 5 mg/mL | 10 mg (IM only), 2 mg/mL (IM only) | — |
| Trifluoperazine | 1, 2, 5, 10 mg | — | — | — | — |
| Triflupromazine | — | — | — | 10 mg/mL, 20 mg/mL | — |

50 mg of chlorpromazine in one injection may result in serious hypotension. IM administration of the antipsychotic results in peak plasma levels in about 30 minutes versus 90 minutes with the oral route. Doses of antipsychotics for IM administration are about half the doses given by the oral route. In a short-term treatment setting, the patient should be observed for one hour after the first dose of antipsychotic medication. After that time, most clinicians administer a second dose of an antipsychotic or a sedative agent (for example, a benzodiazepine) to achieve effective behavioral control. Possible sedatives include lorazepam (Ativan) (2 mg IM) and amobarbital (50 to 250 mg IM).

RAPID NEUROLEPTIZATION. Rapid neuroleptization (also called psychotolysis and digitalization) is the practice of administering hourly IM doses of antipsychotic medications until marked sedation of the patient is achieved. However, several research studies have shown that merely waiting several more hours after one dose of an antipsychotic results in the same clinical improvement as that seen with repeated doses of antipsychotics. Nevertheless, clinicians must be careful to keep patients from becoming violent while they are psychotic. Clinicians can help prevent violent episodes by the use of adjuvant sedatives or by temporarily using physical restraints until the patients can control their behavior.

**Early treatment.** Agitation and excitement are usually the first symptoms to improve with antipsychotic treatment. In patients with a short history of illness, about 75 percent of them have significant improvement in their psychosis. In patients with a long history of illness, a full six weeks may be necessary to evaluate the extent of the improvement in psychotic symptoms. Data indicate that psychotic symptoms, both positive and negative, continue to improve 3 to 12 months after the initiation of treatment.

The equivalent of 10 to 20 mg of haloperidol or 400 mg of chlorpromazine a day is adequate treatment for most patients with schizophrenia. Some research studies indicate that, in a significant proportion of patients, 5 mg of haloperidol or 200 mg of chlorpromazine may, in fact, be just as effective as higher doses. It is a reasonable practice to give antipsychotic drugs in divided doses when initiating treatment to minimize the peak plasma levels and reduce the incidence of side effects. The total daily dose can subsequently be consolidated into a single daily dose after the first week or two of treatment. The single daily dose is usually given at bedtime to help induce sleep and to reduce the incidence of adverse effects. However, in elderly patients that practice may increase the risk of their falling if they get out of bed during the night. The sedative effects of antipsychotics last only a few hours, in contrast to the antipsychotic effects, which last for one to three days.

PRN MEDICATIONS. It is common clinical practice to order medications to be given as needed (PRN). Although that practice may be reasonable during the first few days that a patient is hospitalized, the amount of time the patient takes antipsychotic drugs, rather than an increase in dosage, is what produces therapeutic improvement. Clinicians may feel pressured by their staff members to write PRN antipsychotic orders. Such orders for PRN medications should include specific symptoms, how often the drugs should be given, and how many doses can be given each day. Clinicians may choose to use small doses for the PRN doses (for example, 2 mg haloperidol) or use a benzodiazepine instead (for example, 2 mg lorazepam IM). If PRN doses of an antipsychotic are necessary after the first week of treatment, the clinician may want to consider increasing the standing daily dosage of the drug.

**Maintenance treatment.** The first three to six months after a psychotic episode is usually considered a period of stabilization for the patient. After that time, the dosage of the antipsychotic can be decreased about 20 percent every six months until the minimum effective dosage is found. A patient is usually maintained on antipsychotic medications for one to two years after the first psychotic episode. Antipsychotic treatment is often continued for five years after a second psychotic episode, and lifetime maintenance is considered after the third psychotic episode, although attempts to reduce the daily dosage can be made every 6 to 12 months.

Antipsychotic drugs are effective in controlling psychotic symptoms, but patients may report that they prefer being off the drugs, because they feel better without them. That problem may be less common with the new antipsychotic drugs, such as risperidone and remoxipride. Normal persons who have taken antipsychotic drugs report a sense of dysphoria. The clinician must discuss maintenance medication with the patients and take into account the patients' wishes, the severity of their illnesses, and the quality of their support systems.

**Alternative maintenance regimens.** Alternative maintenance regimens have been designed to reduce both the risk of long-term adverse effects and any unpleasantness associated with taking antipsychotic medications. Intermittent medication is the use of antipsychotics only when patients require them. That arrangement requires that the patients or their caretakers be both willing and able to watch carefully for early signs of clinical exacerbations. At the earliest signs of such problems, antipsychotic medications should be reinstituted for a reasonable period, usually one to three months. Although that treatment approach is not indicated for the majority of patients, it is a safe and effective treatment approach for some patients.

Drug holidays are regular two-to-seven-day periods during which the patient is not given antipsychotic medications. Currently, no evidence indicates that drug holidays reduce the risk of long-term adverse effects from antipsychotics, and drug holidays may increase the incidence of noncompliance.

**Long-acting depot medications.** Because some patients with schizophrenia do not comply with oral antipsychotic regimens, long-acting depot preparations may be needed (Table 33.3.17–9). A clinician usually administers the IM preparations once every one to four weeks. Therefore, the clinician immediately knows if a patient has missed a dose of medication. Depot antipsychotics may be associated with increased adverse effects, including tardive dyskinesia, although the data for that increased association is controversial. Some researchers and clinicians limit their use of depot antipsychotics to those patients who are not compliant with oral medications; other researchers and clinicians, particularly in Europe, consider depot antipsychotics the formulation of choice for the treatment of schizophrenia.

Two depot preparations (a decanoate and an enanthate) of fluphenazine and a decanoate preparation of haloperidol are available in the United States. The preparations are injected IM into an area of large muscle tissue, from

**Table 33.3.17–9**
**Use of Long-Acting Dopamine Receptor Antagonists**

**Dosage**
a. Stabilize patient on lowest effective dose of oral preparation.
b. Usual dosage conversion:
   10 mg/day oral fluphenazine = 12.5–25 mg/2 weeks fluphenazine decanoate
   10 mg/day oral haloperidol = 100–200 mg/4 weeks haloperidol decanoate
c. As with all other antipsychotic medications, the lowest effective dose should be used. Note that patients with long-term schizophrenia have been adequately maintained on dosages of fluphenazine decanoate as low as 5 mg/2 weeks.
d. Supplementation with oral medication may be necessary for the first several months until the optimum dosage regimen has been determined.

**Techniques of Injection**
a. Using a 2-inch needle, inject no more than 3 cc of medication per injection into upper quadrant of buttock (to inject more than 3 cc, use alternate buttocks and vary injection sites).
b. After drawing up medication, draw a small air bubble of 0.1 cc into syringe and change needle for injection.
c. Wipe injection site with alcohol swab and allow to dry before giving injection, otherwise alcohol may infiltrate subcutaneous tissue and cause local irritation.
d. Stretch the skin over the injection site to one side and hold firmly.
e. Inject medication slowly, including air bubble, which forces last drop from needle into the muscle and prevents any medication from being deposited in subcutaneous tissue as needle is withdrawn.
f. Wait about 10 seconds before withdrawing needle, then do so quickly and release skin.
g. Do not massage injection site, as that may force medication to ooze from muscle and infiltrate subcutaneous tissue.
h. Precautions should also be taken with glass ampules to avoid injection of glass particles.

Table from J M Silver, S C Yudofsky: Psychopharmacology and electroconvulsive therapy. In *The American Psychiatric Press Textbook of Psychiatry*, J A Talbott, R E Hales, S C Yudofsky, p 782. American Psychiatric Press, Washington, 1988.
Adapted from M C Belanger, G Chouinard: Technique for injecting long-acting neuroleptics. Br J Psychiatry *141*: 316, 1982. Used with permission.

which they are absorbed slowly into the blood. Decanoate preparations can be given less frequently than are enanthate preparations because they are absorbed more slowly. Although stabilizing a patient on the oral preparation of the specific drug is not necessary before initiating the depot form, it is good practice to give at least one oral dose of the drug to assess the possibility of an adverse effect, such as severe extrapyramidal symptoms or an allergic reaction.

The correct dosage and the time interval for depot preparations are difficult to predict. It is reasonable to begin with 12.5 mg (0.5 cc) of either fluphenazine preparation or 25 mg (0.5 cc) of haloperidol decanoate. If symptoms emerge in the next two to four weeks, the patient can be treated temporarily with additional oral medications or with additional small depot injections. After three to four weeks the depot injection can be increased to include the supplemental doses given during the initial period.

A good reason to initiate depot treatment with low doses is that the absorption of the preparations may be faster than usual at the onset of treatment, resulting in frightening episodes of dystonia that eventually discourage compliance with the medication. Some clinicians keep patients drug-free for three to seven days before initiating depot treatment and give very small doses of the depot preparations (3.125 mg fluphenazine or 6.25 mg haloperidol) every few days to avoid those initial problems. Because the major indication for depot medication is poor compliance with oral forms, the clinician should go slowly with what is practically the last method of achieving compliance.

**Plasma concentrations.** Interindividual variation in the metabolism of the antipsychotics is significant, resulting in part from genetic differences among patients and from pharmacokinetic interactions with other drugs. In patients who have not improved after four to six weeks of antipsychotic treatment, a plasma concentration of the drug should be obtained if such a test is available. Other possible indications for obtaining a plasma concentration are questions regarding compliance, concern regarding pharmacokinetic interactions, and the development of significant akathisia or akinesia.

The blood sample must be obtained after the patient has been taking a particular dosage for at least five times the half-life of the drug, so as to approach steady-state concentrations. It is also standard practice to obtain plasma samples at trough levels—that is, just before the daily dose is given, usually at least 12 hours after the previous dose and most commonly 20 to 24 hours after the previous dose. Unfortunately, the quality of the laboratories that perform the analyses varies significantly; therefore, the clinician must obtain the normal ranges for a particular laboratory and must test the laboratory with multiple plasma samples from well-controlled patients. Having taken all those precautions, the clinician is still left with the reality that most antipsychotics have no well-defined dose-response curve. The best-studied drug is haloperidol, which may have a therapeutic window ranging from 2 to 15 ng/mL. Other therapeutic ranges that have been reasonably well-documented are 30 to 100 ng/mL for chlorpromazine and 0.8 to 2.4 ng/mL for perphenazine.

**Treatment-resistant patients and adjuvant medications.** Various estimates have ranged from 10 to 35 percent for the proportion of schizophrenic patients who fail to obtain significant benefit from the old antipsychotic drugs (that is, all the drugs except clozapine, risperidone, and remoxipride). Patients are often defined as being treatment-resistant if they have failed at least two adequate trials of antipsychotics from two classes. Adequate trials are usually defined as lasting at least six weeks, and using daily dosages equivalent to 20 mg of haloperidol or 1,000 mg of chlorpromazine. It is useful to obtain plasma concentrations for such patients, since one possibility is that they are slow metabolizers and are grossly overmedicated with the antipsychotic drugs. More likely, however, they are simply nonresponsive to those typical antipsychotic drugs.

ADJUVANT TREATMENTS. Before the introduction of the new antipsychotics, the only approach to treatment-resistant schizophrenic patients was the use of adjuvant medications. Medications that have been reported to be useful as adjuvants to antipsychotics include lithium, carbamazepine, β-adrenergic receptor antagonists, antidepressants, and benzodiazepines. Of those medications, the most robust data support the use of lithium as an adjuvant to antipsychotic medications. When using the combination of lithium and antipsychotics, the clinician may want to use slightly lower dosages of each initially to avoid the development of delirium or neurotoxicity that has been reported in a few cases, with the combination. The use of carbamazepine has also been reported to be effective as an addition to antipsychotic drugs, although the coadministration of carbamazepine and an antipsychotic can lower the plasma concentrations of the antipsychotic as much as 50 percent because of the induction of hepatic enzymes. Although benzodiazepines have been reported to be effective as adjuvant treatments, their withdrawal can precipitate a significant worsening of symptoms. An increasing body of data supports the use of antidepressants in schizophrenic patients who have significant depressive symptoms.

NEW ANTIPSYCHOTICS. Clozapine has been shown to be effective in treating at least 30 percent of patients who are nonresponsive to typical antipsychotic drugs. Although other new antipsychotic drugs, such as risperidone and remoxipride, may also be effective in a proportion of treatment-resistant schizophrenic patients, that has yet to be demonstrated in large, well-controlled clinical trials.

### References

Acta Psychiatrica Scandinavica: Remoxipride. Acta Psychiatr Scand 82 (Suppl 358): 2, 1990.
Berger J, Kitchin R, Berry G: Predictors of the course of tardive dyskinesia in patients receiving neuroleptics. Biol Psychiatry 32: 580, 1992.
Bilder R M, Turkel E, Lipschutz-Broch L, Lieberman J A: Antipsychotic medication effects on neuropsychological functions. Psychopharmacol Bull 28: 353, 1992.
Borison R L, Diamond B I, Pathiraja A, Meibach R C: Clinical overview of risperidone. In Novel Antipsychotic Drugs, H Y Meltzer, editor, p 223. Raven, New York, 1992.
Caroff S N, editor: Neuroleptic malignant syndrome. Psychiatr Ann 21 (3): 2, 1991.
Chouinard G, Jones B, Remington G, Bloom D, Addington D, MacEwan G W, Labelle A, Beauclair L, Arnott W: A Canadian multicenter placebo-controlled study of fixed doses of risperidone and haloperidol in the treatment of chronic schizophrenic patients. J Clin Psychopharmacol 13: 25, 1993.
Claus A, Bollen J, De Cuyper H, Eneman M, Malfroid M, Peuskens J, Heylen S: Risperidone versus haloperidol in the treatment of chronic schizophrenic inpatients: A multicentre double-blind comparative study. Acta Psychiatr Scand 85: 295, 1992.
Dilsaver S C: Antipsychotic agents: A review. Am Fam Physician 47: 199, 1993.

Druckenbrod R W, Rosen J, Cluxton R J: As-needed dosing of antipsychotic drugs: limitations and guidelines for use in the elderly agitated patient. Ann Pharmacotherapy 27: 645, 1993.

Gardos G, Teicher M H, Lipinski J F, Matthews J D, Morrison L, Conley C, Cole J O: Quantitative assessment of psychomotor activity in patients with neuroleptic-induced akathisia. Prog Neuropsychopharmacol Biol Psychiatry 16: 27, 1992.

Glazer W M, Morgenstern H, Doucette J T: Predicting the long-term risk of tardive dyskinesia in outpatients maintained on neuroleptic medications. J Clin Psychiatry 54: 133, 1993.

Guerrera R J, Chang S S, Romero J A: A comparison of diagnostic criteria for neuroleptic malignant syndrome. J Clin Psychiatry 53: 56, 1992.

Hansen T E, Weigel R M, Brown W L, Hoffman W F, Casey D E: A longitudinal study of correlations among tardive dyskinesia, drug-induced parkinsonism, and psychosis. J Neuropsychiatry Clin Neurosci 4: 29, 1992.

Hermesh H, Aizenberg D, Weizman A, Lapidot M, Mayor C, Munitz H: Risk for definite neuroleptic malignant syndrome: A prospective study of 223 consecutive in-patients. Br J Psychiatry 161: 254, 1992.

Huang M L, Van Peer A, Woestenborghs R, De Coster R, Heykants J, Jansen A A I, Zylicz Z, Visscher H W, Jonkman J H G: Pharmacokinetics of the novel antipsychotic agent risperidone and the prolacting response in healthy subjects. Clin Pharmacol Ther 54: 257, 1993.

Khot V, Wyatt R J: Not all that moves is tardive dyskinesia. Am J Psychiatry 148: 661, 1991.

King D J: The effects of neuroleptics on cognitive and psychomotor function. Br J Psychiatry 157: 799, 1990.

King D J, Blomqvist M, Cooper S J, Doherty M M, Mitchell M J, Montgomery R C: A placebo controlled trial of remoxipride in the prevention of relapse in chronic schizophrenia. Psychopharmacology 107: 175, 1992.

Levinson D F, Singh H, Simpson G M: Timing of acute clinical response to fluphenazine. Br J Psychiatry 160: 365, 1992.

Leysen J E, Gommeren W, Eens A, de Chaffoy de Courcelles D, Stoof J C, Janssen P A J: Biochemical profile of risperidone, a new antipsychotic. J Pharmacol Exp Ther 247: 661, 1988.

Marken P A, Kaykal R F, Fisher J N: Management of psychotropic-induced hyperprolactinemia. Clin Pharm 11: 851, 1992.

McCreadie R G, Robertson L J, Wiles D H: The Nithsdale schizophrenia surveys: IV. Akathisia, parkinsonism, tardive dyskinesia and plasma neuroleptic levels. Br J Psychiatry 161: 793, 1992.

McEvoy J P, Hogarty G E, Steingard S: Optimal dose of neuroleptic in acute schizophrenia: A controlled study of the neuroleptic threshold and higher haloperidol dose. Arch Gen Psychiatry 48: 739, 1991.

Meltzer H Y: Serotonin-dopamine interactions and atypical antpsychotic drugs. Psychiatr Ann 23: 193, 1993.

Opler L A, Feinberg S S: The role of pimozide in clinical psychiatry: A review. J Clin Psychiatry 52: 221, 1991.

Rifkin A, Doddi S, Karajgi B, Borenstein M, Wachspress M: Dosage of haloperidol for schizophrenia. Arch Gen Psychiatry 48: 166, 1991.

Schwartz J T, Brotman A W: A clinical guide to antipsychotic drugs. Drugs 44: 981, 1992.

Sewell D D, Jeste D V: Distinguishing neuroleptic malignant syndrome (NMS) from NMS-like acute medical illnesses: A study of 34 cases. J Neuropsychiatry Clin Neurosci 4: 265, 1992.

Shriqui C L, Bradwejn J, Annable L, Jones B D: Vitamin E in the treatment of tardive dyskinesia: A double-blind placebo-controlled study. Am J Psychiatry 149: 391, 1992.

Stern R G, Kahn R S, Harvey P D, Amin F, Apter S H, Hirschowitz J: Early response to haloperidol treatment in chronic schizophrenia. Schizophr Res 10: 165, 1993.

Szymanski S, Munne R, Gordon M F, Lieberman J: A selective review of recent advances in the management of tardive dyskinesia. Psychiatr Ann 23: 209, 1993.

Teicher M H, Barber N I, Gelbard H A, Gallitano A L, Campbell A, Marsh E, Baldessarini R J: Developmental differences in acute nigro-striatal and mesocorticolimbic system response to haloperidol. Neuropsychopharmacology 9: 147, 1993.

Vanden Borre R, Ermote R, Buttiëns M, Thiry P, Dierick G, Geutjens J, Sieben G, Heylen S: Risperidone as add-on therapy in behavioral disturbances in mental retardation: A double-blind placebo-controlled cross-over study. Acta Psychiatr Scand 87: 167, 1993.

Van Putten T, Marder S R, Mintz J, Poland R E: Haloperidol plasma levels and clinical response: A therapeutic window relationship. Am J Psychiatry 149: 500, 1992.

Vartiainen H, Leinonen E, Putkonen A, Lang S, Hagert U, Tolvanen U: A long-term study of remoxipride in chronic schizophrenic patients. Acta Psychiatr Scand 87: 114, 1993.

Verghese C, Kessel J B, Simpson G M: Pharmacokinetics of neuroleptics. Psychopharmacol Bull 27: 551, 1991.

Volavka J, Cooper T, Czobor P, Bitter I, Meisner M, Laska E, Gastanaga P, Krakowski M, Chou J C, Crowner M, Douyon R: Haloperidol blood levels and clinical effects. Arch Gen Psychiatry 49: 354, 1992.

Wadsworth A N, Heel R C: Remoxipride: A review of its pharmacodynamic and pharmacokinetic properties, and therapeutic potential in schizophrenia. Drugs 40: 863, 1990.

# 33.3.18 / Fenfluramine

In psychiatry, fenfluramine (Pondimin) has been studied and used as a treatment for autistic disorder. Because of its anorectic effect, it has also been studied and used in the treatment of obesity.

## CHEMISTRY

Fenfluramine is a congener of amphetamine, with which it shares some effects. Its molecular structure is shown in Figure 33.3.18–1.

## PHARMACOLOGICAL ACTIONS

### Pharmacokinetics

Fenfluramine is well-absorbed from the gastrointestinal tract. Maximal anorectic effect is seen after two to four hours, although the effect may decrease with time. The half-life of fenfluramine is about 20 hours. Fenfluramine is a lipid-soluble compound that can cross the placenta.

### Pharmacodynamics

The major short-term effect of fenfluramine is to release neuronal stores of serotonin. Some data indicate that fenfluramine is also an inhibitor of serotonin reuptake. Perhaps because of its relation to amphetamine, fenfluramine may also be associated with a facilitation of dopamine release from neurons.

## EFFECTS ON SPECIFIC ORGANS AND SYSTEMS

Some data indicate that fenfluramine has a stimulatory effect on the ventromedial nucleus of the hypothalamus, perhaps explaining the appetite suppressive effects of the drug. Fenfluramine may also decrease the absorption of dietary fat, increase fat mobilization, and increase cellular

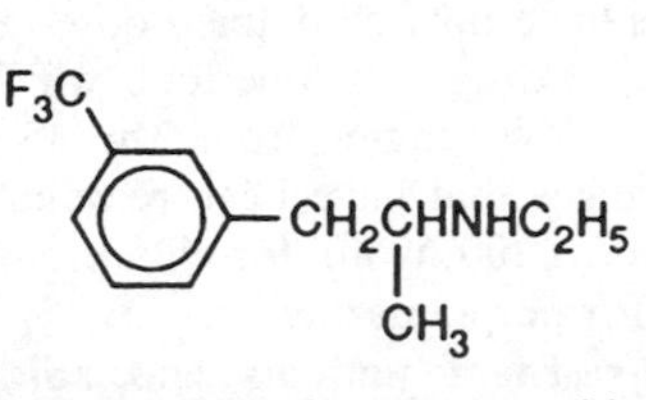

**Figure 33.3.18–1.** Molecular structure of fenfluramine.

glucose uptake. The cardiovascular and autonomic effects of fenfluramine are similar to those of amphetamine, although fenfluramine is a much less potent pressor agent than is amphetamine.

## THERAPEUTIC INDICATIONS

Fenfluramine has been studied primarily as a treatment for autistic disorder. Although several reports note that some patients have improved while taking the drug, fenfluramine is not an effective drug for that condition. Some data indicate that autistic disorder children with significant agitation and an intelligence quotient (I.Q.) above 40 are likely to benefit from treatment with the drug. The use of fenfluramine for weight reduction is controversial. Data indicate that tolerance develops for that effect. The advantage of fenfluramine over amphetamine as an anorectic agent is that fenfluramine does not produce euphoria.

## PRECAUTIONS AND ADVERSE REACTIONS

Drowsiness, diarrhea, and dry mouth are the most common adverse effects of fenfluramine. Other adverse effects include dizziness, confusion, incoordination, headache, elevated mood, depressed mood, anxiety, nervousness, tension, insomnia, weakness, fatigue, agitation, dysarthria, and altered libido. Fenfluramine has not been studied in pregnant women and should be avoided during pregnancy. Whether fenfluramine passes into breast milk is not known.

## DRUG INTERACTIONS

Patients should be advised to avoid alcoholic beverages during fenfluramine treatment. The drug may have additive effects when used with central nervous system (CNS) depressants. Fenfluramine may increase the efficacy of some antihypertensives. Coadministration of fenfluramine with serotonergic antidepressants—for example, fluoxetine (Prozac)—and monoamine oxidase inhibitors (MAOIs) should be avoided.

## LABORATORY INTERFERENCES

Fenfluramine has no known laboratory interferences.

## DOSAGE AND ADMINISTRATION

In autistic disorder the dosage should be increased gradually to 1.0 to 1.5 mg per kg a day in divided doses. The reported therapeutic effects of fenfluramine include improved sleep, improved interpersonal skills, and a decrease in aggression, tantrums, irritability, self-mutilation, and hyperactivity. Fenfluramine is supplied in 20 mg tablets.

### References

Du Verglas G, Banks S R, Guyer K E: Clinical effects of fenfluramine on children with autism: A review of the research. Ann Prog Child Psychiatry Child Dev 22: 471, 1989.

Ekman G, Miranda-Linne F, Gillberg C, Garle M: Fenfluramine treatment of twenty children with autism. J Autism Dev Disord 19: 511, 1989.

Lichtenberg P, Shapira B, Blacker M, Gropp C, Calev A, Larer B: Effect of fenfluramine on mood: A double-blind placebo-controlled trial. Biol Psychiatry 31: 351, 1992.

McBride P A, Anderson G M, Hertzig M E, Sweeny J A, Kream J, Cohen D J, Mann J J: Serotonergic responsivity in male young adults with autistic disorder: Results of a pilot study. Arch Gen Psychiatry 46: 213, 1989.

Sherman J, Factor D C, Swinson R, Darjes R W: The effects of fenfluramine (hydrochloride) on the behaviors of fifteen autistic children. J Autism Dev Disord 19: 533, 1989.

Stern L M, Walker M K, Sawyer M G, Oades R D: A controlled crossover trial of fenfluramine in autism. J Child Psychol Psychiatry 31: 569, 1990.

Varley C K, Holm V A: A two-year follow-up of autistic children treated with fenfluramine. J Am Acad Child Adolesc Psychiatry 29: 137, 1990.

# 33.3.19 / Lithium

Lithium (Eskalith, Lithobid) is the most commonly used short-term and prophylactic treatment for bipolar I disorder.

## HISTORY

Building on the discoveries of others, Humphrey Davy isolated the lithium metal in 1818. Lithium was introduced into medicine in the 1840s by Alexander Ure for the treatment of bladder stones and by Alfred Garrod for the treatment of gout. In 1873, in the United States, William Hammond described the use of lithium bromide for the treatment of manic episodes, although the bromide was considered the active ingredient. In 1886, in Denmark, Carl Lange and Fritz Lange described the prophylactic and short-term effects of lithium for depression. In the late 1880s and early 1900s the general public in the United States were enthusiastically endorsing the taking of the waters, the use of mineral spring waters that supposedly contained lithium. The waters were misleadingly advertised as being beneficial for a wide variety of aches, pains, and ills. In the United States in the 1940s, lithium chloride was used as a replacement for sodium chloride in hypertensive patients with low-salt diets, resulting in lithium toxicity and death for some patients and causing lithium-related products to be withdrawn from the marketplace. In 1949 an Australian, John F. J. Cade, noticed that lithium urate caused lethargy when injected into animals; he later reported the successful therapeutic effects of lithium in a patient with manic episodes. In the 1950s and the 1960s Mogens Schou conducted the critical experiments demonstrating the short-term and prophylactic efficacy of lithium for bipolar I disorder, which eventually resulted in the approval of lithium for the treatment of bipolar I disorder by the U.S. Food and Drug Administration (FDA) in 1970.

## CHEMISTRY

Lithium (Li), a monovalent ion, is an element and the lightest of the alkali metals (group IA of the periodic table), similar to sodium, potassium, and rubidium. Lithium exists as both $Li^6$ and $Li^7$. The latter isotope allows the imaging of lithium by magnetic resonance spectroscopy.

## PHARMACOLOGICAL ACTIONS

### Pharmacokinetics

After ingestion, lithium is completely absorbed by the gastrointestinal tract. Serum levels peak in 1 to 1 ½ hours for standard preparations and in 4 to 4 ½ hours for controlled-release preparations. Lithium does not bind to plasma proteins, is not metabolized, and is distributed nonuniformly throughout body water. Lithium does not cross the blood-brain barrier rapidly, perhaps explaining why an overdose is not usually a problem and why long-term lithium intoxication takes times to resolve completely. The half-life of lithium is about 20 hours, and equilibrium is reached after five to seven days of regular intake. Lithium is almost entirely eliminated by the kidneys. Because lithium is absorbed by the proximal tubules, lithium clearance is about one fifth of creatinine clearance. Renal clearance of lithium is decreased with renal insufficiency (common in the elderly) and in the puerperium and is increased during pregnancy. Lithium is excreted in breast milk and in insignificant amounts in the feces and sweat.

### Pharmacodynamics

The therapeutic mechanism of action for lithium remains uncertain. The similarity of the lithium ion to the sodium, potassium, calcium, and magnesium ions may be related to its therapeutic effects. The mechanism of action for lithium may involve various neurotransmitter systems and the membrane structure. One theory, which has mixed support in the literature, is that lithium works by blocking inositol phosphatases within the neurons. That inhibition results in decreased cellular responses to neurotransmitters that are linked to the phosphatidylinositol second-messenger system (Figure 33.3.19–1).

## EFFECTS ON SPECIFIC ORGANS AND SYSTEMS

The most common effects of lithium are on the thyroid, heart, kidneys, and hematopoietic system. Lithium impedes the release of thyroid hormone from the thyroid and can result in hypothyroidism or goiter; the disorder affects women more than men. Lithium also impairs sinus node function, which can result in heart block in susceptible persons. Lithium reduces the ability of the kidneys to concentrate urine. Although that effects is usually not clinically significant, the effect is not always reversible after the discontinuation of lithium. Pathological nonspecific interstitial fibrosis has been reported as a postmortem finding in some persons who had been treated for a long time with lithium. The major effect of lithium on the hematopoietic

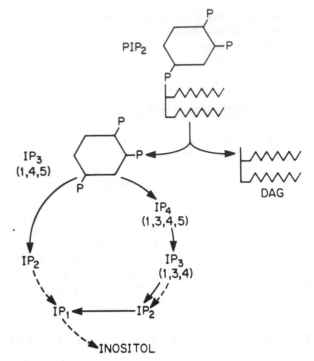

**Figure 33.3.19–1.** Inositol phosphate metabolism. Phosphatidylinositol-bis-phosphate ($PIP_2$) is hydrolyzed by phospholipase C, generating diacylglycerol (DAG) and inositol 1,4,5-triphosphate ($IP_3[1,4,5]$). $IP_3(1,4,5)$ is acted on by either a kinase or a phosphatase, generating 1,3,4,5-tetrakisphosphate ($IP_4[1,3,4,5]$) or inositol 1,4-bis-phosphate ($IP_2[1,4]$), respectively. $IP_4(1,3,4,5)$ is hydrolyzed to $IP_3(1,3,4)$ and then to $IP_2$. Specific phosphatases hydrolyze the various $IP_2$ isomers to inositol. Several inositol phosphatases are inhibited by lithium. Those are shown as dotted arrows. In some steps both lithium-sensitive and lithium-insensitive enzymes are involved, so both solid and dotted arrows are shown. (Figure from J M Baraban, P F Worley, S H Snyder: Second messenger systems and psychoactive drug action: Focus on the phosphoinositide system and lithium. Am J Psychiatry *146*: 1254, 1989.)

system is a clinically nonsignificant increase in leukocyte production.

## THERAPEUTIC INDICATIONS

### Bipolar I Disorder

Lithium has proved to be effective in both the short-term treatment and the prophylaxis of bipolar I disorder in about 70 to 80 percent of patients. Both manic and depressive episodes respond to lithium treatment alone. Lithium should also be considered as a potential treatment in patients with severe cyclothymic disorder.

**Manic episodes.** About 80 percent of manic patients respond to lithium treatment, although the response to lithium alone can take one to three weeks of treatment at therapeutic concentrations. Because of the delay in response to lithium alone, benzodiazepines—for example, clonazepam (Klonopin) and lorazepam (Ativan)—or antipsychotics are used for the first one to three weeks to obtain immediate relief from the mania. Predictors of a poor response to lithium in the treatment of manic episodes include mixed and dysphoric manic episodes (which may occur in as many as 40 percent of patients), rapid cycling, and coexisting substance-related disorders.

**Depressive episodes.** Although not approved by the Food and Drug Administration, lithium is effective in the treatment of bipolar I disorder depression. About 80 percent of bipolar I disorder depressive patients respond to lithium treatment alone, thereby eliminating the risk of an antidepressant-induced manic episode. When a depressive episode occurs in a patient already receiving maintenance lithium, the differential diagnosis should include lithium-induced hypothyroidism, substance abuse, and the lack of compliance with the lithium therapy. Possible treatment approaches include increasing the lithium concentration (up to 1.2 mEq per L), adding supplemental thyroid hormone (for example, 25 μg a day L-iodothyronine) even in the presence of normal findings on thyroid function tests, the judicious use of antidepressants, and electroconvulsive therapy (before which lithium should be discontinued to avoid complicating the cognitive assessment of the patient).

**Maintenance.** Maintenance treatment with lithium markedly decreases the frequency, the severity, and the duration of manic and depressive episodes in bipolar I disorder patients. Compared with placebo treatment, during which about 80 percent of bipolar I disorder patients relapse, only about 35 percent of lithium-treated patients relapse. Lithium maintenance is almost always indicated after the second episode of bipolar I disorder depression or mania. Lithium maintenance should be seriously considered after the first episode in patients who are adolescents, have a family history of bipolar I disorder, have poor support systems, had no precipitating factors for the first episode, had a serious first episode, have a high suicide risk, are 30 years old or older, had a sudden onset of their first episode, had a first episode of mania, or are male. Increased interest in initiating maintenance after the first episode is motivated by several observations: First, subsequent episodes may be increasingly likely after each additional episode. Second, some data indicate that relapses increase after lithium is discontinued. Third, case reports describe patients who were initially responsive to lithium but who lost their lithium-responsiveness with subsequent episodes. The treatment response to lithium is such that continued maintenance treatment may be associated with increasing efficacy. It is not necessarily representative of treatment failure, therefore, if an episode of depression or mania occurs after a relatively short time of lithium maintenance. If lithium treatment alone loses its effectiveness, the clinician should consider supplemental treatment with carbamazepine (Tegretol) or valproate (Depakene).

## Schizoaffective Disorder

The use of lithium for schizoaffective disorder (bipolar type) is certainly indicated. If a patient has schizoaffective disorder (depressive type) with a particularly cyclic nature, a lithium trial may be warranted. In general, the more a schizoaffective disorder patient resembles a mood disorder patient, the more likely lithium is to be effective; the more

a schizoaffective disorder patient resembles a schizophrenia patient, the less likely lithium is to be effective.

## Major Depressive Disorder

The primary indication for lithium in major depressive disorder is as an adjuvant treatment to antidepressants in patients who have failed to respond to the antidepressants alone. Many studies have shown that about 50 percent of antidepressant nonresponders do respond when lithium 300 mg given three times daily is added to the antidepressant regimen. In some patients the response is dramatically rapid, occurring in days; in most patients, several weeks are required to assess the efficacy of the regimen. Lithium alone may be an effective treatment of depressed patients who are actually bipolar I disorder patients who have not yet had their first manic episode. Moreover, lithium has been reported to be effective in major depressive disorder patients whose disorder has a particularly marked cyclicity.

## Schizophrenia

The symptoms of one fifth to one half of all schizophrenic patients are further reduced when lithium is coadministered with their antipsychotic drug. The therapeutic benefit of lithium does not seem to be correlated with the absence or the presence of affective symptoms in those patients. Some schizophrenic patients who cannot take antipsychotic drugs may benefit from lithium treatment alone. The intermittent aggressive outbursts of some schizophrenic patients may also be reduced by lithium treatment.

## Aggression

Lithium has been used to treat aggressive outbursts in schizophrenic patients, prison inmates, and mentally retarded patients. Less success has been reported in the treatment of aggressiveness associated with head trauma and epilepsy. Other drugs for the treatment of aggression include anticonvulsants, β-adrenergic receptor antagonists, and antipsychotics. The treatment of aggressive patients requires a flexible approach to the use of those drugs and the use of psychosocial and behavioral treatment strategies.

## Other Disorders

A few studies have reported that the episodic disorder characterizing premenstrual dysphoric disorder, the intermittent behaviors seen in borderline personality disorder, bulimia nervosa, and episodes of binge drinking respond to lithium treatment. Animal models of alcohol dependence have shown that lithium intake can reduce the intake of alcohol. In spite of those basic data, at least one large study has not shown any benefit of lithium treatment in alcohol dependence, although anecdotal case reports and small studies in the literature are hopeful.

## PRECAUTIONS AND ADVERSE REACTIONS

The most common adverse effects of lithium treatment are gastric distress, weight gain, tremor, fatigue, and mild cognitive impairment (Table 33.3.19–1). Gastrointestinal symptoms can include nausea, decreased appetite, vomiting, and diarrhea and can often be reduced by dividing the dosage, administering the lithium with food, or switching to another lithium preparation. Weight gain results from a poorly understood effect of lithium on carbohydrate metabolism. Weight gain can also result from lithium-induced edema. The only reasonable approach to weight gain is to encourage the patient to eat wisely and to engage in moderate exercise.

### Tremor

The significance of drug-induced tremors is recognized in the fourth edition of *Diagnostic and Statistical Manual of Mental Disorders* (DSM-IV) by the inclusion of the diagnosis medication-induced postural tremor. The tremor is usually a 8–10 Hz tremor and is most notable in outstretched hands, especially in the fingers. The tremor is sometimes worse during times of peak drug levels. The tremor can be reduced by dividing the daily dosage and reducing caffeine intake. Propranolol (Inderal) (30 to 160 mg a day in divided doses) is usually effective in reducing the tremor in most patients. When a lithium-treated patient has a severe tremor, the possibility of lithium toxicity should be suspected and evaluated.

### Cognitive Effects

Lithium use has been associated with dysphoria, lack of spontaneity, slowed reaction times, and impaired memory. The differential diagnosis for such symptoms should include depressive disorders, hypothyroidism, other illnesses, and other drugs. Some patients have reported that fatigue and mild cognitive impairment decrease with time.

### Renal Effects

The most common adverse renal effect of lithium is polyuria with secondary polydipsia. The symptom is particularly a problem in 25 to 35 percent of patients who may have a urine output of $\geq$ 3 liters a day (normal 1 to 2 liters a day). The polyuria is a result of the lithium antagonism to the effects of antidiuretic hormone, thus decreasing the resorption of fluid from the distal tubules of the kidneys. Polyuria may be significant enough to result in problems at work and in social settings, with associated insomnia, weight gain, and dehydration. When polyuria is a significant problem, the patient's renal function should be evaluated and followed up with 24-hour urine collections for creatinine clearance and with consultation with a nephrologist. Treatment consists of fluid replacement, the use of the lowest effective dosage of lithium, and single daily dosing of lithium. Treatment can also involve the use of a thiazide or potassium-sparing diuretic—for example, amiloride (Midamor) or amiloride-hydrochlorothiazide (Moduretic). If treatment with a diuretic is initiated, the lithium dosage should be halved, and the diuretic should not be started for five days, because the diuretic is likely to increase the retention of lithium.

The most serious renal adverse effects, which are rarely associated with lithium administration, are minimal change glomerulonephritis, interstitial nephritis, and renal failure. The incidence of those severe renal complications is now thought to be lower than was originally thought; however, the clinician should consider such complications if the clinical picture warrants it.

**Table 33.3.19–1**
**Side Effects of Lithium and Their Management**

| Side Effect | Management |
|---|---|
| Gastrointestinal complaints | Give lithium after meals, give smaller doses more often, try slow-release preparation, lower the dosage |
| Tremor | Lower the dosage, give propranolol (40–100 mg/day), consider adding a benzodiazepine |
| Polyuria-diabetes insipidus | Try slow-release preparation, lower the dosage, add amiloride (5–10 mg/day), careful monitoring of lithium levels |
| Acne | Benzoyl peroxide (5–10%) topical solution, erythromycin (1.5–2%) topical solution |
| Muscular weakness, fasciculations, headaches | Usually resolve with first few weeks of treatment |
| Hypothyroidism | Levothyroxine (0.05 mg qd), follow TSH level and increase to 0.2 mg qd as needed |
| T wave inversion | Benign, no treatment needed |
| Cardiac dysrhythmias | Usually must discontinue lithium |
| Psoriasis, alopecia areata | Dermatology consult, reversible if lithium stopped |
| Weight gain | Difficult to treat, diet, may be partially reversible if lithium stopped |
| Edema | Consider spironolactone (50 mg orally qd); if severe, monitor lithium levels; resolves when lithium stopped |
| Leukocytosis | Benign, no treatment needed |

qd—every day.
Table from A Doupe, M Szuba: Lithium and other antimanic agents. In *The Handbook of Psychiatry*, Residents of the UCLA Department of Psychiatry, p 386. Year Book Medical, Chicago, 1990. Used with permission.

## Thyroid Effects

Lithium affects thyroid function, causing a generally benign and often transient diminution in the concentrations of circulating thyroid hormones. Reports have attributed goiter (5 percent of patients), benign reversible exophthalmos, and hypothyroidism (7 to 9 percent of patients) to lithium treatment. About 50 percent of patients receiving long-term lithium treatment have an abnormal thyrotropin-releasing hormone (TRH) response, and about 30 percent have elevated levels of thyroid-stimulating hormone (TSH). If symptoms of hypothyroidism are present, treatment with levothyroxine (Synthroid) is indicated. Even in the absence of hypothyroid symptoms, some clinicians treat patients with elevated TSH levels with levothyroxine. In lithium-treated patients, TSH levels should be measured every 6 to 12 months. Lithium-induced hypothyroidism should be considered when evaluating depressive episodes that emerge during lithium therapy.

## Cardiac Effects

The cardiac effects of lithium, which resemble those of hypokalemia on the electrocardiogram (ECG), are caused by the displacement of intracellular potassium by the lithium ion. The most common changes on the ECG are T wave flattening or inversion. The changes are benign and disappear after the lithium is excreted from the body. Nevertheless, baseline ECGs are essential and should be repeated annually.

Because lithium also depresses the pacemaking activity of the sinus node, lithium treatment can result in sinus dysrhythmias and episodes of syncope. Lithium treatment, therefore, is contraindicated in patients with sick sinus syndrome. In rare cases, ventricular arrhythmias and congestive heart failure have been associated with lithium therapy.

## Dermatological Effects

Several cutaneous adverse effects, which may be dose-dependent, have been associated with lithium treatment. The most prevalent effects include acneiform, follicular, and maculopapular eruptions; pretibial ulcerations; and worsening of psoriasis. Alopecia has also been reported. Many of those conditions respond favorably to changing to another lithium preparation and the usual dermatological measures. Lithium levels should be monitored if tetracycline is used for the treatment of acne because of several reports of its increasing the retention of lithium. Occasionally, aggravated psoriasis or acneiform eruptions may force the discontinuation of lithium treatment.

## Lithium Toxicity and Overdoses

The early signs and symptoms of lithium toxicity include coarse tremor, dysarthria, and ataxia; the later signs and symptoms include impaired consciousness, muscular fasciculations, myoclonus, seizures, and coma (Table 33.3.19–2). The higher the lithium levels and the longer the lithium levels have been high, the worse the symptoms

**Table 33.3.19–2**
**Signs and Symptoms of Lithium Toxicity**

**Mild to moderate intoxication**
(lithium level, 1.5–2.0 mEq per L)
Gastrointestinal:
   Vomiting
   Abdominal pain
   Dryness of mouth
Neurological:
   Ataxia
   Dizziness
   Slurred speech
   Nystagmus
   Lethargy or excitement
   Muscle weakness

**Moderate to severe intoxication**
(lithium level, 2.0–2.5 mEq per L)
Gastrointestinal:
   Anorexia nervosa
   Persistent nausea and vomiting
Neurological:
   Blurred vision
   Muscle fasciculations
   Clonic limb movements
   Hyperactive deep tendon reflexes
   Choreoathetoid movements
   Convulsions
   Delirium
   Syncope
   Electroencephalographic changes
   Stupor
   Coma
Circulatory failure (lowered blood pressure, cardiac arrhythmias, and conduction abnormalities)

**Severe intoxication**
(lithium level, > 2.5 mEq per L)
Generalized convulsions
Oliguria and renal failure
Death

Table from J M Silver, S C Yudofsky: Psychopharmacology and electroconvulsive therapy. In *The American Psychiatric Press Textbook of Psychiatry*, J A Talbott, R E Hales, S C Yudofsky, editors, p 826. American Psychiatric Association Press, Washington, 1988. Used with permission.

of lithium toxicity are. Lithium toxicity is a medical emergency, since it can result in permanent neuronal damage and death. The treatment of lithium toxicity involves discontinuing the lithium and treating the dehydration. The value of forced diuresis has been disputed. In the most serious cases, hemodialysis is an effective means by which lithium can be removed from the body (Table 33.3.19–3).

**Overdoses.** Overdoses of lithium result in symptoms of severe lithium toxicity. Treatment should be similar to that for lithium toxicity in general but can also include gastric lavage with a wide-bore tube because of the tendency of the drug to form large clumps in the stomach.

## Adolescents

The serum lithium levels for adolescents is similar to that used for adults. Although the side-effect profile is similar in adolescents and adults, the weight gain and the acne associated with lithium use can be particularly troublesome to an adolescent.

**Table 33.3.19–3
Management of Lithium Toxicity**

1. The patient should immediately contact his or her personal physician or go to a hospital emergency room.
2. Lithium should be discontinued and the patient instructed to ingest fluids, if possible.
3. Physical examination, including vital signs, and a neurological examination with complete formal mental status examination should be completed.
4. Lithium level, serum electrolytes, renal function tests, and electrocardiogram should be obtained as soon as possible.
5. For significant short-term ingestions, residual gastric contents should be removed by induction of emesis, gastric lavage, and absorption with activated charcoal.
6. Vigorous hydration and maintenance of electrolyte balance are essential.
7. For any patient with a serum lithium level greater than 4.0 mEq per L within six hours of ingestion or for any patient with serious manifestations of lithium toxicity, hemodialysis should be initiated.
8. Repeat dialysis may be required every 6 to 10 hours until the lithium level is within nontoxic range and the patient has no signs or symptoms of lithium toxicity.

Table from J M Silver, S C Yudofsky: Psychopharmacology and electroconvulsive therapy. In *The American Psychiatric Press Textbook of Psychiatry*, J A Talbott, R E Hales, S C Yudofsky, editors, p 827. American Psychiatric Association Press, Washington, 1988. Used with permission.

### Geriatric Patients

Lithium is a safe and effective drug for the elderly. However, the treatment of elderly lithium-treated patients is complicated by the presence of other medical illnesses, decreased renal function, special diets that affect lithium clearance, and generally increased sensitivity to lithium-induced side effects. Because of that increased sensitivity, many elderly patients must be maintained on lower lithium concentrations than are younger adults. Elderly patients should be started on low dosages, their dosages should be switched less frequently than are dosages in younger patients, and a longer time must be allowed before assuming that their lithium concentrations are at steady-state levels because of possibly decreased renal function.

### Pregnant Women

Early studies reported that about 10 percent of newborns who were exposed to lithium in the first trimester of pregnancy had major congenital malformations. The most common malformations involve the cardiovascular system, most commonly Ebstein's anomaly of the tricuspid valves. Recent epidemiological studies have found that the early studies may have significantly overestimated the risk. Although, ideally, a woman should not take any drug during pregnancy, the continuation of lithium therapy by a pregnant woman should not be considered out of the question. The possibility of fetal anomalies can be evaluated with fetal echocardiography. If a woman continues taking lithium during pregnancy, the lowest effective dosage should be used. Also, the maternal lithium level must be monitored closely during pregnancy and especially after pregnancy, because of the significant change in renal function that occurs over that time period. Lithium should be

discontinued shortly before delivery, and the drug should be restarted after an assessment of the usually high risk of a postpartum mood disorder and the mother's desire to breast-feed her infant. Lithium should not be administered to a woman who is breast-feeding. Signs of lithium toxicity in infants include lethargy, cyanosis, abnormal reflexes, and sometimes hepatomegaly.

### Miscellaneous Effects

Rare neurological adverse effects include symptoms of mild parkinsonism, ataxia, and dysarthria, although those last two symptoms are usually symptoms of lithium intoxication. Lithium should be used with caution in diabetic patients, who should monitor their blood glucose levels carefully. Leukocytosis is a common benign effect of lithium treatment. Dehydrated, debilitated, and mentally ill patients are susceptible to side effects and toxicity.

## DRUG INTERACTIONS

Because of the possibility of lithium toxicity on the one hand and the need to maintain therapeutic lithium on the other hand, the clinician must be aware of the many drug interactions that can involve lithium (Table 33.3.19–4). In lithium-treated patients who are about to undergo electroconvulsive therapy (ECT), the lithium should be discontinued two days before beginning ECT to reduce the risk of delirium resulting from the coadministration of the two treatments.

Most diuretics (for example, thiazides, potassium-sparing, and loop) can increase lithium levels; when treatment with such a diuretic is stopped, the clinician may need to increase the patient's daily lithium dosage. Osmotic diuretics, carbonic anhydrase inhibitors, and xanthines (including caffeine) may reduce lithium levels to below therapeutic levels. Increasing reports indicate that angiotensin-converting enzyme inhibitors cause an increase in lithium concentrations. A wide range of nonsteroidal anti-inflammatory drugs can decrease lithium clearance, thereby increasing lithium concentrations; those drugs include indomethacin (Indocin), phenylbutazone (Azolid), diclofenac (Voltaren), ketoprofen (Orudis), oxyphenbutazone (Oxalid), ibuprofen (Motrin), piroxicam (Feldene), and naproxan (Naprosyn). Aspirin and sulindac do not affect lithium concentrations.

When coadministered, antipsychotics and lithium may result in a synergistic increase in the symptoms of lithium-induced neurological adverse effects. That interaction is not, as was initially thought, specifically associated with the coadministration of lithium and haloperidol (Haldol). Although the validity of the clinical observation has been questioned, the clinician should probably avoid the coadministration of high dosages of antipsychotics in the presence of high serum concentrations of lithium.

The coadministration of lithium and anticonvulsants—including carbamazepine, valproate, and clonazepam—may increase lithium levels and aggravate lithium-induced neurological adverse effects. As with antipsychotic medications, the clinician should probably avoid the administration of high dosages of anticonvulsants in patients with high lithium concentrations. However, the coadministration of lithium and anticonvulsants can be therapeutically beneficial to some patients. Treatment with the combination should be initiated at slightly lower dosages than usual, and the dosages should be increased gradually. Lithium may have some protective effect against the granulocytopenia induced by carbamazepine, although no data indicate that the lithium reduces the risk of the serious carbamazepine-induced problems with agranulocytosis.

## LABORATORY INTERFERENCES

Lithium is not known to interfere with any laboratory tests. However, lithium treatment does affect a number of commonly obtained laboratory values (Table 33.3.19–5).

## DOSAGE AND ADMINISTRATION

Lithium is a monovalent ion and is available as a carbonate (for example, Lithane) ($Li_2CO_3$) for oral use in both rapidly acting and slow-release tablets and capsules. Lithium citrate (Cibalith) is available in a liquid form for oral administration (Table 33.3.19–6). Regular-release capsules or tablets are usually used first, and the syrup or slow-release preparations are used if noncompliance, nau-

sea, or other adverse effects occur and may improve with a different formulation.

### Initial Medical Workup

Before the clinician administers lithium, a physician other than a psychiatrist should conduct a routine laboratory and physical examination. The laboratory examination should include a serum creatinine level (or a 24-hour urine creatinine if the clinician has any reason to be concerned about renal function), an electrolyte screen, thyroid function tests ($T_4$, $T_3RU$, $FT_4I$, and TSH), a complete blood count (CBC), an ECG, and a pregnancy test if there is any possibility that the patient is pregnant.

### Plasma Concentrations

Serum and plasma concentrations of lithium are the standard methods of assessing lithium concentrations, and they serve as the basis by which to titrate the dosages. Although reports have noted the measurement of lithium concentrations in saliva, tears, and red blood cells, those methods have no clinical superiority to the standard methods. The patient must be at steady state (usually after five days of constant dosing), and the blood sample must be drawn 12 hours (plus or minus 30 minutes) after the last dose in a twice-or-thrice-daily dosing regimen. Because available data are based on those standards, the clinician should initiate lithium treatment with regular-releas for-

**Table 33.3.19–4**
**Drug Interactions with Lithium**

| Class and Generic Name | Effect on Plasma Lithium Concentration | Significance |
|---|---|---|
| Antibiotics | | |
|   Tetracycline | Possible increase | Case reports; possibly from nephrotoxic |
|   Spectinomycin | Possible increase |   effect of antibiotics; tetracycline may be safe |
| Tricyclic drugs | Unknown | May cause switch to mania; increase in tremors |
| Anti-inflammatory agents | | |
|   Ibuprofen | Increase | Case reports of piroxicam and diclofenac |
|   Indomethacin | Increase |   sodium increasing lithium concentrations; |
|   Naproxen | Increase |   sulindac may have minimal effect |
|   Phenylbutazone | Increase | |
| Antipsychotics | | |
|   Chlorpromazine | Possibly increase in red blood cell (RBC) lithium | All antipsychotics may increase lithium's neurotoxicity |
|   Fluphenazine | Possibly increase RBC lithium | |
|   Haloperidol | Possibly increase plasma lithium | |
|   Perphenazine | Possibly increase RBC lithium | |
|   Thioridazine | Possibly increase RBC lithium | |
| Cardiovascular drugs | | |
|   Digoxin | Unknown | Case report of CNS confusion and bradycardia |
|   ACE inhibitors | Increase | Case reports of toxicity, renal insufficiency |
|   Methyldopa | Unknown | Case reports of neurological toxicity |
|   Diltiazem | Unknown | Case report of neurological toxicity |
|   Verapamil | Unknown | Case report of neurological toxicity |
| Diuretics | | |
|   Carbonic anhydrase inhibitors | Decrease | Increase lithium excretion |
|   Acetazolamide | Decrease | |

**Table 33.3.19–4**
*Continued*

| Class and Generic Name | Effect on Plasma Lithium Concentration | Significance |
|---|---|---|
| Loop diuretics | | |
|   Furosemide | Unclear | May increase lithium concentrations |
|   Ethacrynic acid | Unclear | |
| Distal tubule diuretics | | |
|   Thiazides | Increase | Well-documented interaction with increase in lithium concentrations |
|   Metolazone | Increase | |
|   Chlorthalidone | Increase | |
| Osmotic diuretics | | |
|   Mannitol | Decrease | Increase lithium excretion |
|   Urea | Decrease | |
| Potassium-sparing diuretics | | |
|   Triamterene | Increase | May increase lithium concentrations |
|   Spironolactone | Increase | |
|   Amiloride | Unclear | May be used to treat lithium-induced polyuria |
| Xanthines | | |
|   Theophylline | Decrease | Increase lithium excretion |
|   Caffeine | Decrease | |
| Neuromuscular blocking drugs | | |
|   Succinylcholine | Unknown | May prolong neuromuscular blockade |
|   Pancuronium bromide | Unknown | |
| Miscellaneous | | |
|   Sodium chloride | Decrease | Increase lithium excretion |
|   Sodium bicarbonate | Decrease | Alkalinization of urine increases lithium excretion |
|   Metronidazole | Increase | Reports of toxicity, renal damage |
|   Metoclopramide | Unknown | Case report of extrapyramidal symptoms |
|   Carbamazepine | Unknown | May have synergistic effect in treating mania and depression; case reports of neurotoxicity |
|   Iodides | Unknown | May have additive or synergistic hypothyroid effect |
|   Alcohol | Unknown | Increased lithium toxicity in animals; acute alcohol ingestion may increase peak lithium concentration |
|   Phenytoin | Possible increase | Case reports of lithium toxicity and changes in phenytoin concentrations |

Table adapted from J L Kinney-Parker, M P Fankhauser: Bipolar disorder. In *Pharmacotherapy : A Pathophysiologic Approach,* J T DiPiro, R L Talbert, P E Hayes, G C Yee, L M Posey, editors, p 741. Elsevier, New York, 1989. Used with permission.

**Table 33.3.19–5**
**Possible Effects of Lithium on Laboratory Values**

| Laboratory Value | Possible Effect |
|---|---|
| White blood cells (WBCs) | Increased count |
| Serum glucose | Increased level |
| Serum magnesium | Increased level |
| Serum potassium | Decreased level |
| Serum uric acid | Decreased level |
| Serum thyroxine | Decreased |
| Serum cortisol | Decreased AM levels |
| Serum parathyroid hormone | Increased level due to adenoma |
| Serum calcium | Increased level due to increased parathyroid hormone level |
| Serum phosphorus | Decreased level due to increased parathyroid hormone level |

Table from A Doupe, M Szuba: Lithium and other antimanic agents. In *The Handbook of Psychiatry,* Residents of the UCLA Department of Psychiatry, p 386. Year Book Medical, Chicago, 1990. Used with permission.

**Table 33.3.19–6**
**Lithium Carbonate Preparations**

Regular-release capsules 150, 300, 600 mg (Eskalith, Lithotabs, generic)
  Regular-release tablets 300 mg (Eskalith, Lithane, Lithobid)
  Slow-release tablets 300, 450 mg (Eskalith, Lithobid)
  Syrup 8 mEq per 5 mL (lithium citrate) (Cibalith-S, generic)

mulations of lithium given at least twice daily. Once the dosage has been adjusted, changing the formulation of the dosing schedule is reasonable. Lithium levels in patients treated with slow-release preparations are about 30 percent higher than the levels obtained with the normal-release preparations.

The most common guidelines are for 1.0 to 1.5 mEq per L for the treatment of acute mania and 0.6 to 1.2 mEq per L for maintenance treatment. It is almost never necessary to exceed 1.5 mEq per L, since patients with higher lithium levels are at much higher risk for lithium toxicity. If, in a very few patients, maximal therapeutic benefit has not been obtained and if side effects are absent, titration of the patient above 1.5 mEq per L may be warranted. One recent study found that patients with lithium concentrations in the range of 0.8 to 1.0 mEq per L are 2.6 times less likely to relapse than are patients with lithium concentrations in the range of 0.4 to 0.6 mEq per L. That study led some researchers and clinicians to consider 0.8 to 1.0 mEq per L as the most effective range for maintenance lithium concentrations.

**Lithium dose prediction.** A number of researchers and clinicians have proposed various lithium dose prediction protocols. The protocols are generally based on the administration of a single dose of lithium, followed by the assessment of lithium concentrations at 12- or 24-hour time points. Those concentrations are then used to predict the final dose of lithium that a patient will require. Most clinicians and researchers have not adopted lithium dose prediction protocols for two reasons: First, the upward titration of lithium in patients is relatively straightforward and quick without the use of such a protocol. Second, the rapid dose increase associated with the use of a dose prediction protocol often results in adverse effects, especially gastrointestinal effects, that may adversely affect the patient's subsequent compliance with the medication regimen.

## Dosage

If a patient has previously been treated with lithium and the previous dosage is known, the clinician should probably use that dosage for the current episode unless changes in the patient's pharmacokinetic parameters have affected lithium clearance. For most adult patients, the clinician should start lithium at 300 mg three times daily. The starting dosage in patients who are elderly or who have renal impairment should be 300 mg once or twice daily. The usual eventual dosage if between 900 and 1,800 mg a day, given in two or three divided doses.

The use of divided doses reduces gastric upset and avoids single high-peak lithium levels. A current debate concerns whether multiple small daily peaks are less likely than a single high daily peak to cause adverse effects. Single daily dosing is not considered standard practice at this time. Slow-release lithium preparations can be given two or three times daily; they result in low peak levels of lithium, but that procedure has not been proved to be of special value.

## Patient Education

The clinician should advise the patient that changes in the body's water and salt content can affect the amount of lithium excreted, resulting in either increases or decreases in lithium levels. Excessive sodium intake (for example, a dramatic dietary change) lowers lithium levels. Conversely, too little sodium (for example, fad diets) can lead to potentially toxic levels of lithium. Decreases in body fluid (for example, excessive sweating) can lead to dehydration and lithium intoxication.

## Failure of Drug Treatment

If the drug produces no clinical response after four weeks at therapeutic levels, slightly higher serum levels (up to 1.5 mEq per L) may be tried if there are no limiting adverse effects. If, after two weeks at a high serum concentration, the drugs is still ineffective, the patient should be tapered off the drug over one to two weeks. Other drugs should be given therapeutic trials at that point.

**Rapid cycling.** Rapid cycling is defined as the presence of four or more episodes of illness during the year; some patients experience many more than four episodes. Rapid-cycling bipolar I disorder is present in as many as 20 percent of all patients and is associated with antidepressant treatment, thyroid abnormalities, and neurological disorders. If lithium treatment is ineffective in a rapid-cycling patient, thyroid hormones, carbamazepine, valproate, electroconvulsive therapy, calcium channel inhibitors, monoamine oxidase inhibitors, and clozapine are all potential treatment options for the clinician to consider.

## References

Baraban J M, Worley P F, Snyder S H: Second messenger systems and psychoactive drug action: Focus on the phosphoinositide system and lithium. Am J Psychiatry *146*: 1251, 1989.

Bouman T K, de Vries J, Koopmans I H: Lithium prophylaxis and interepisode mood: A prospective longitudinal comparison of euthymic bipolars and non-patient controls. J Affect Disord *24*: 199, 1992.

Crabtree B L, Mack J E, Johnson C D, Amyx B C: Comparison of the effects of hydrochlorothiazide and furosemide on lithium disposition. Am J Psychiatry *148*: 1060, 1991.

Garland E J, Remick R A, Zis A P: Weight gain with antidepressants and lithium. J Clin Psychopharmacol *8*: 323, 1988.

Gitlin M J, Cochran S D, Jamison K R: Maintenance lithium treatment: Side effects and compliance. J Clin Psychiatry *50*: 127, 1989.

Jefferson J W: Lithium: A therapeutic magic wand. J Clin Psychiatry *50*: 81, 1989.

Jefferson J W: Lithium: The present and the future. J Clin Psychiatry *51* (9, Suppl): 4, 1990.

Manji H K, Hsiao J K, Risby E D, Oliver J, Rudorfer M V, Potter W Z: The mechanisms of action of lithium: I. Effects on serotonergic and noradrenergic systems in normal subjects. Arch Gen Psychiatry *48*: 505, 1991.

Markott R A, King M Jr: Does lithium dose prediction improve treatment efficiency? Prospective evaluation of a mathematical method. J Clin Psychopharmacol *12*: 305, 1992.

Müller-Oerlinghausen B, Ahrens B, Grof E, Grof P, Lenz G, Shou M, Simhandl C, Thau K, Volk J, Wolf R, Wolf T: The effect of long-term lithium treatment on the mortality of patients with manic-depressive and schizoaffective illness. Acta Psychiatr Scand *86*: 218, 1992.

Pert M, Pratt J P: Lithium: Current status in psychiatric disorders. Drugs *46*: 7, 1993.

Risby E D, Hsiao J K, Manji H K, Bitran J, Moses F, Zhou D F, Potter W Z: The mechanisms of action of lithium: II. Effects on adenylate cyclase activity and β-adrenergic receptor binding in normal subjects. Arch Gen Psychiatry *48*: 513, 1991.

Schou M: Effects of long-term lithium treatment on kidney function: An overview. J Psychiatr Res *22*: 287, 1988.

Schou M: Lithium prophylaxis: Myths and realities. Am J Psychiatry *146*: 573, 1989.

Schou M: Lithium treatment during pregnancy, delivery, and lactation: An update. J Clin Psychiatry *51*: 410, 1990.

Stein G, Bernadt M: Lithium augmentation therapy in tricyclic-resistant depression: A controlled trial using lithium in low and normal doses. Br J Psychiatry *162*: 634, 1993.

Vestergaard P, Schou M: Prospective studies on a lithium cohort: 1. General features. Acta Psychiatr Scand *78*: 421, 1988.

# 33.3.20 / Methadone

Methadone hydrochloride (Dolophine, Methadose) is used in psychiatry primarily for the detoxification and maintenance therapy for patients who are addicted to opiates and opioids. The treatment was introduced by Vincent Dole and Marie Nyswander in 1965.

## CHEMISTRY

Methadone is a synthetic diphenylheptane derivative. Its molecular structure is shown in Figure 33.3.20–1.

## PHARMACOLOGICAL ACTIONS

### Pharmacokinetics

Methadone is well-absorbed from the gastrointestinal tract and has an initial duration of action of four to six hours. The duration of action increases to 22 to 48 hours with repeated administration and is elevated in persons who have been abusing opiate agonists. Methadone is metabolized by the liver and is excreted by the kidneys.

### Pharmacodynamics

Methadone is an opiate receptor agonist. It has activity at mu, kappa, and, probably, delta opiate receptors. The agonist effects of methadone on those receptors blocks the withdrawal symptoms caused by the cessation of heroin abuse.

## EFFECTS ON SPECIFIC ORGANS AND SYSTEMS

The most significant effects of methadone are on the gastrointestinal, genitourinary, and autonomic systems. Within the gastrointestinal system, methadone can cause biliary spasm, colic, and constipation. Within the genitourinary system, methadone is associated with urinary retention and oliguria. Autonomic activation by methadone can cause sweating, flushing, pruritus, and urticaria.

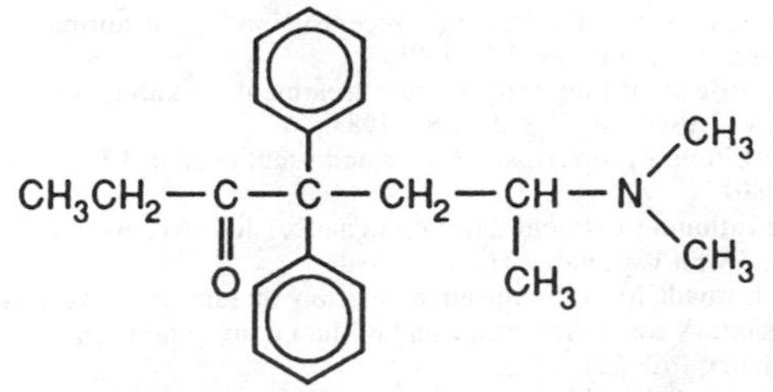

**Figure 33.3.20–1.** Molecular structure of methadone.

## THERAPEUTIC INDICATIONS

Methadone is used for the short-term detoxification (30 days), long-term detoxification (180 days), and maintenance of opiate and opioid addicts. Methadone is a schedule II drug; its administration is governed by specific federal laws and regulations. Those regulations are currently in a state of flux because of the increase in efforts to place intravenous drug abusers in methadone programs. The aim of such renewed efforts is to reduce the spread of acquired immune deficiency syndrome (AIDS), which can be contracted by the use of contaminated needles.

## PRECAUTIONS AND ADVERSE REACTIONS

An overdose of methadone can cause respiratory and circulatory depression, leading to respiratory arrest, cardiac arrest, and death. Methadone is also capable of inducing tolerance, psychological dependence, and physical dependence. Other adverse effects on the central nervous system include dizziness, depression, sedation, euphoria, dysphoria, agitation, and seizures. Delirium and insomnia have also been reported in rare cases. Methadone should be used with caution in patients with respiratory disease, hepatic or renal dysfunction, and seizure disorders.

### Pregnancy

Methadone should be administered to pregnant women only if the potential benefits outweigh the possible risks. Detoxification is not recommended for pregnant women; maintenance methadone may be appropriate in some circumstances. Whether methadone treatment is harmful to the fetus is not known. A significant number of infants born to mothers receiving methadone show withdrawal symptoms. Women should not breast-feed their babies if they are taking methadone.

## DRUG INTERACTIONS

Methadone can potentiate the central nervous system (CNS) depressant effects of other opiate agonists, barbiturates, benzodiazepines, and alcohol. Antipsychotics, especially low-potency agents, tricyclic and tetracyclic drugs, and monoamine oxidase inhibitors (MAOIs) should be used cautiously with methadone. Two other opiate agonists, meperidine (Demerol) and fentanyl (Duragesic), have been associated with fatal drug-drug interactions with the MAOIs.

## LABORATORY INTERFERENCES

No known laboratory interferences are associated with methadone treatment.

## DOSAGE AND ADMINISTRATION

Methadone is supplied in tablets of 5, 10, and 40 mg; solutions of 5 mg per 5 mL, 10 mg per 5 mL, and 10 mg per mL; and a parenteral form of 10 mg per mL.

In maintenance programs, methadone is usually administered dissolved in water or fruit juice. For short-term detoxification, an initial dose of 15 to 20 mg usually suppresses withdrawal symptoms; additional doses can be given if the initial dose is insufficient. A dosage of 40 mg a day in single or divided doses is usually sufficient to control withdrawal symptoms in most patients. After stabilization, the methadone dosage is tapered at a rate that depends on the type of program, whether the patient is an inpatient or an outpatient, and the patient's level of tolerance for the withdrawal symptoms. If withdrawal takes more than 180 days, the treatment program is officially described as methadone maintenance. Maintenance should be at the lowest possible dosage of methadone, and, generally, the patient should eventually be withdrawn completely from methadone. The administration of methadone for both withdrawal and maintenance must follow strict federal guidelines, which generally require that patients receive the methadone in person to avoid its abuse by persons other than the patient.

### References

Ball J C, Corty E: Basic issues pertaining to the effectiveness of methadone maintenance treatment. NIDA Res Monogr *86*: 178, 1988.

Cooper J R: Methadone treatment and acquired immunodeficiency syndrome. JAMA *262*: 1664, 1989.

Goehl L, Nunes E, Quitkin F, Hilton I: Social networks and methadone treatment outcome: The costs and benefits of social ties. Am J Drug Alcohol Abuse *19*: 251, 1993.

Gossop M, Strang J: A comparison of the withdrawal responses of heroin and methadone addicts during detoxification. Br J Psychiatry *158*: 697, 1991.

Greif G L, Drechsler M: Common issues for parents in a methadone maintenance group. J Subst Abuse Treat *10*: 339, 1993.

Ladewig D: Opiate maintenance and abstinence: Attitudes, treatment modalities and outcome. Drug Alcohol Depend *25*: 245, 1990.

Liappas J A, Jenner F A, Vincente B: Literature on methadone maintenance clinics. Int J Addict *23*: 927, 1988.

Loimer N, Lenz K, Schmid R, Presslich O: Technique for greatly shortening the transition from methadone to naltrexone maintenance of patients addicted to opiates. Am J Psychiatry *148*: 933, 1991.

Longshore D, Hsieh S-C, Danila B, Anglin M D: Methadone maintenance and needle/syringe sharing. Int J Addict (USA), *28*, 983, 1993.

Maddux J F, Desmond D P: Methadone maintenance and recovery from opioid dependence. Am Drug Alcohol Abuse *18*: 63, 1992.

Nunes E V, Quitkin F M, Brady R, Stewart J W: Imipramine treatment of methadone maintenance patients with affective disorder and illicit drug use. Am J Psychiatry *148*: 667, 1991.

Segest E, Mygind O, Bay H: The influence of prolonged stable methadone maintenance treatment on mortality and employment: An 8-year follow-up. Int J Addict *25*: 53, 1990.

Wolff K, Hay A, Raistrick D, Calvert R, Feely M: Measuring compliance in methadone maintenance patients: Use of a pharmacologic indicator to estimate methadone plasma levels. Clin Pharmacol Ther *50*: 199, 1991.

# 33.3.21 / Monoamine Oxidase Inhibitors

The monoamine oxidase inhibitors (MAOIs) have the treatment of depressive disorders as their primary indication and are generally accepted as being equal in efficacy to other antidepressant drugs (for example, tricyclic drugs and serotonin-specific reuptake inhibitors). The MAOIs are currently used less frequently than other antidepressants because of the dietary precautions that must be followed to avoid tyramine-induced hypertensive crises. That clinical practice may change in the near future after the introduction of MAOIs that are less likely to cause tyramine-induced hypertensive crises.

Two advances in neurochemistry and pharmacology will probably affect the use of MAOIs in the future. First, two types of the monoamine oxidase (MAO) enzyme have been characterized, $MAO_A$ and $MAO_B$. Inhibitors that are specific for $MAO_B$ are not associated with tyramine-induced hypertensive crises, although those inhibitors are probably not effective in the treatment of depression. Second, a new class of MAOIs are the reversible inhibitors of monoamine oxidase (RIMAs). Currently available MAOIs irreversibly inactivate and destroy the MAO that is present in a patient, and a period of at least two weeks must follow the last dose of an MAOI before a patient can safely ingest tyramine-containing foods. Drugs of the RIMA class have a reversible binding to MAO and require that only an average of two to five days pass before tyramine-containing foodstuffs can be safely ingested.

## HISTORY

Iproniazid (Marsilid), which was a derivative of the antituberculosis drug isoniazid (INH) (Cotinazin), was abandoned as a potential treatment for tuberculosis and introduced as a treatment for depression in 1952, when its stimulatory effects in tubercular patients were noted. That discovery led to the development of several MAOIs that were effective in the treatment of depression. In 1962, however, a case report described the death from a hypertensive crisis of a patient who was being treated with an MAOI and had ingested a tyramine-rich cheese. That report led to the brief withdrawal in the United States of the MAOIs. After the drugs were reintroduced, they had a long period of minimal use and negative image. The lack of use of MAOIs was driven further by the introduction of the tricyclic drugs, which were judged to have a more favorable side-effect profile, a judgment that many clinicians and researchers think is not entirely accurate. The use of MAOIs has increased in the past decade, because several research groups observed that MAOIs may have superior efficacy in the treatment of specific groups of patients—for example, depressed patients with marked anxiety or phobic symptoms. In addition, clinicians now realize that the dietary restrictions that must be followed by patients taking MAOIs are not as difficult or as extensive as was previously thought and that, in general, large amounts of tyramine-containing foods must be consumed to induce a serious hypertensive crisis.

## CHEMISTRY

Four MAOIs are commonly used in the United States (Figure 33.3.21–1). Phenelzine (Nardil) and isocarboxazid (Marplan) are derivatives of hydrazine (-CNN is the hydrazine moiety). Tranylcypromine (Parnate) is a cyclopropylamine that is structurally related to amphetamine. Whereas those three drugs are nonspecific inhibitors of $MAO_A$ and $MAO_B$ and are approved for the treatment of depression in the United

States, selegiline (Eldepryl, Deprenyl), which is also a cyclo-propylamine, is a specific inhibitor of MAO$_B$ and is approved only for use in the treatment of Parkinson's disease. Clorgyline is a specific inhibitor of MAO$_A$ and has been reported to be useful in the treatment of rapid-cycling bipolar I disorder, but it is not available for clinical use in the United States. Two RIMAs that are currently under development and that may be introduced in the United States for the treatment of depressive disorders in the near future are moclobemide (Aurorix) and brofaromine (Consonar) (Figure 33.3.21–1).

## PHARMACOLOGICAL ACTIONS

### Pharmacokinetics

The currently available MAOIs are readily absorbed when administered orally. The hydrazine MAOIs are metabolized by acetylation. About half of all North Americans and Europeans and an even higher proportion of Asians are slow acetylators, which may explain why, when given a hydrazine MAOI, some patients have more adverse effects than do others. Tranylcypromine reaches peak plasma concentrations in about two hours and has a half-life of two to three hours. Unlike the hydrazine MAOIs, the plasma concentrations of tranylcypromine are correlated with its hypotensive effects. Therefore, a clinician can administer tranylcypromine in multiple small daily doses to reduce its hypotensive effects. That approach to administration does not reduce the hypotensive effects of the hydrazine MAOIs.

### Pharmacodynamics

Monoamine oxidase (MAO) is a widely distributed enzyme in the body and is located primarily intracellularly, where it is usually bound to the external side of the mitochondrial membrane. MAO concentrations are highest in the liver, the gastrointestinal tract, the central nervous system, and the sympathetic nervous system. The MAO$_A$ in the gastrointestinal tract is responsible for the metabolism of dietary tyramine; when MAO$_A$ is inhibited by an MAOI, dietary tyramine can enter the circulation directly and unmetabolized and can then act as a pressor, resulting in a hypertensive crisis.

As previously mentioned, MAO has two types (Table 33.3.21–1). MAO$_A$ is relatively specific for the metabolism of norepinephrine and serotonin; MAO$_B$ is relatively specific for the metabolism of phenylethylamine; both MAO$_A$ and MAO$_B$ are involved in the metabolism of dopamine. Phenelzine, isocarboxazid, and tranylcypromine are nonselective in their effects on the MAO types. Selegiline is selective (at low doses) for MAO$_B$, and clorgyline is selective for MAO$_A$. The two RIMAs under development, moclobemide and brofaromine, are known to inhibit MAO$_A$, and their effects on MAO$_B$ have not yet been fully characterized. Moclobemide and brofaromine differ from the other MAOIs mentioned in that their interaction with MAO is reversible. Specifically, the binding of those two drugs to MAO can be displaced by tyramine, thus contributing significantly to the safety profile of the new drugs.

The measurement of MAO activity in platelets has been used in research and some clinical settings to assess the degree of MAO inhibition that has been obtained. Platelets contain only MAO$_B$ and, therefore, are not necessarily accurate indicators of the degree of inhibition of MAO$_A$ that is perhaps more closely associated with antidepressant effects in the brain. Nevertheless, platelet MAO activity needs to be reduced to at least 80 percent to achieve a therapeutic response when phenelzine is being used. The measurement of platelet MAO activity is not useful when treating a patient with tranylcypromine, which is more potent at inhibiting MAO$_A$ than at inhibiting MAO$_B$. When the irreversible MAOIs are used to treat a patient, a period of at least two weeks must pass after the last dose of the drug before the patient can safely eat tyramine-containing foods, because the body takes about two weeks to resynthesize enough MAO to replace the MAO that had been irreversibly inhibited and destroyed by the irreversible MAOI.

Although inhibition of monoamine oxidase is hypothesized to be the primary mechanism of action for the drugs, the MAOIs have additional neurochemical effects. Tranylcypromine, in particular, has significant activity as an inhibitor of catecholamine and serotonin reuptake. Tranylcypromine—because of its similarity to amphetamine, to which it may be metabolized in part—also has some activity on receptors as an indirectly acting sympathomimetic. Brofaromine is also active as an inhibitor of serotonin reuptake. Recent neuroscience studies have shown additional roles for MAO in the central nervous system. One of the additional roles is as an enzymatic pathway for the production of so-called free radicals, a molecular species that may be involved in cell death. The inhibition of free radical production has been hypothesized to be a factor in the efficacy of selegiline in the treatment of Parkinson's disease.

## EFFECTS ON SPECIFIC ORGANS AND SYSTEMS

The primary effects of the MAOIs in psychiatry are on the central nervous system, discussed above. In addition to their effects on depressed mood, the MAOIs are associated with potentially clinically significant disturbances in sleep and sleep architecture. Use of the MAOIs is frequently associated with decreased sleep and insomnia, sometimes resulting in daytime drowsiness in MAOI-treated patients. Furthermore, the sleep of MAOI-treated patients is characterized by significantly decreased amounts of rapid eye movement (REM) sleep.

The other principal concerns when treating patients with MAOIs are the cardiovascular system and the liver. MAOIs are commonly associated with hypotension because of their effects on vascular tone, which may be mediated both centrally and peripherally. In rare cases, MAOI use alone (without tyramine) is associated with episodes of acute hypertension. With regard to the liver, phenelzine and isocarboxazid are associated with a significant liability for hepatotoxicity.

## THERAPEUTIC INDICATIONS

The indications for MAOIs are similar to those for tricyclic and tetracyclic drugs. MAOIs may be particularly effective in panic disorder with agoraphobia, posttraumatic stress disorder, eating disorders, social phobia, and pain disorder. Some investigators have reported that MAOIs may be preferable to tricyclic drugs in the treatment of atypical depression characterized by hypersomnia, hyperphagia, anxiety, and the absence of vegetative symptoms.

| Generic | Trade | Usual Adult Dose Range (mg/day) | How Supplied (mg) |
|---|---|---|---|
| Isocarboxazid 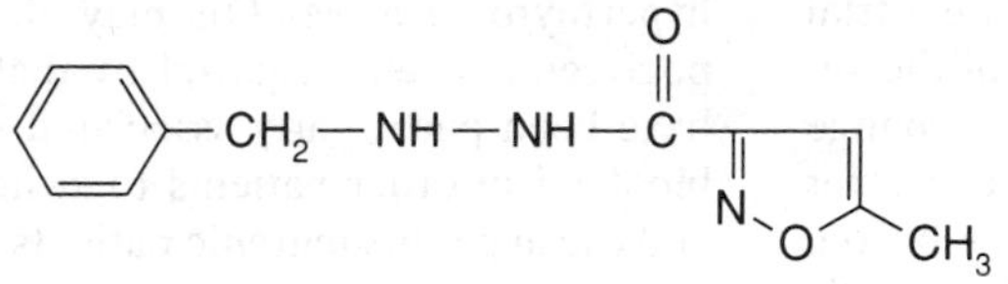 | Marplan | 10 – 30 | 10 |

| Phenelzine 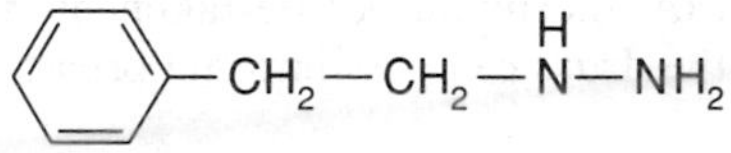 | Nardil | 15 – 90 | 15 |

| Tranylcypromine 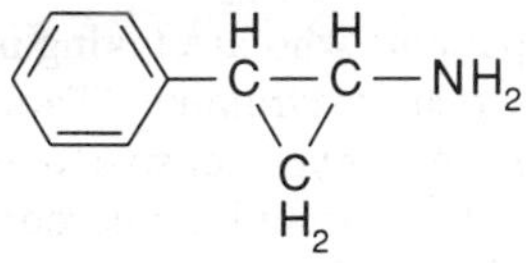 | Parnate | 10 – 30 | 10 |

| Selegiline 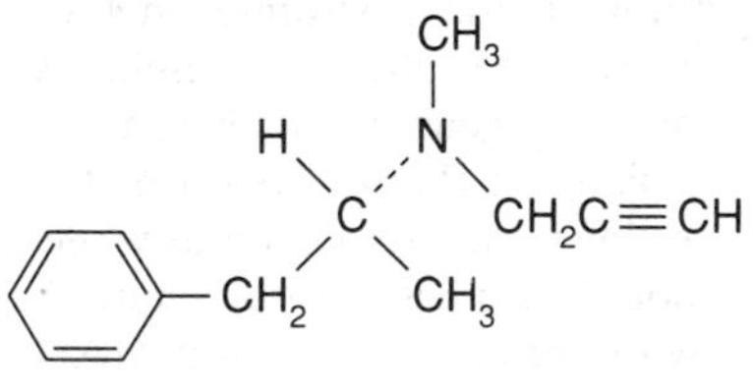 | Eldepryl, Deprenyl | 10* | 5 |

| Moclobemide† 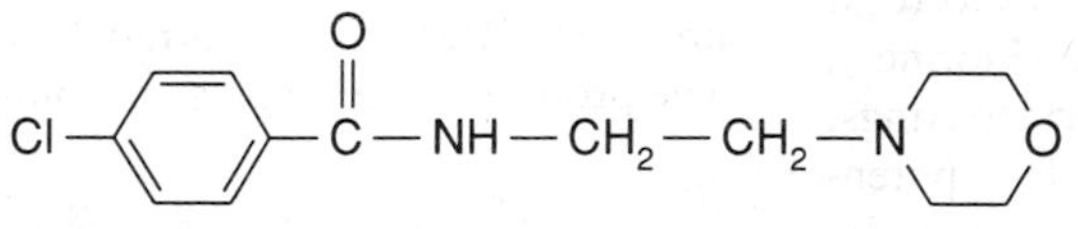 | Aurorix | — | — |

| Brofaromine† 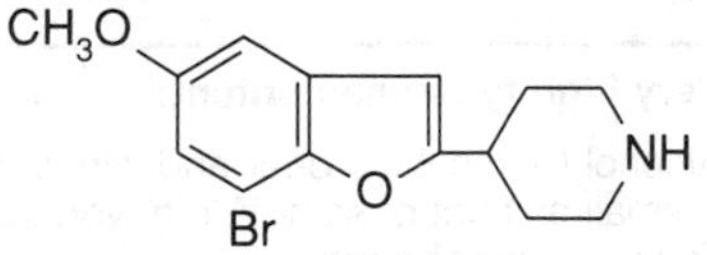 | Consonar | — | — |

**Figure 33.3.21–1.** Molecular structures of the monoamine oxidase inhibitors. *Therapeutic dosage for the treatment of par- kinsonism. †Not available in the United States as of December 1993.

**Table 33.3.21–1**
**Comparison of Monoamine Oxidase A and B**

| Type | Location | Preferred Substrates | Selective Inhibitors |
|---|---|---|---|
| A | Central nervous system, sympathetic terminals, liver, gut, skin | Norepinephrine, serotonin, dopamine, tyramine, octopamine, tryptamine | Clorgyline |
| B | Central nervous system, liver, platelets | Dopamine, tyramine, tryptamine, phenylethylamine, benzylamine, N-methylhistamine | *Selegiline (Deprenyl) |

*Selectivity lost at higher doses (≥ 10 mg a day)
Table from G W Arana, S E Hyman: *Handbook of Psychiatric Drug Therapy*, ed 2, p 68. Little, Brown, Boston, 1991. Used with permission.

Patients with that symptom pattern are often less severely depressed than are patients with classic symptoms of depression, which is often evidenced by less functional impairment. For those patients, many clinicians and researchers recommend a trial with an MAOI before a trial with a tricyclic drug, although the introduction of the serotonin-selective reuptake inhibitors (SSRIs) may change that practice. The failure of a patient to improve after treatment with a tricyclic or tetracyclic drug may be the most common reason why a patient is given a therapeutic trial of an MAOI.

Although depression is not an approved indication for selegiline, some positive results have been reported. A possible advantage of selegiline is that its primary effect in low dosages is on $MAO_B$, thus lessening the risk of an $MAO_A$-associated tyramine-induced hypertensive crisis. Unfortunately, many of the positive results with selegiline for depression have been at higher dosages (20 to 60 mg a day) than the dosages used to treat Parkinson's disease (10 mg a day). At those higher dosages, selegiline loses a significant amount of its specificity for $MAO_A$ and requires that patients follow the guidelines for a restricted tyramine diet.

## PRECAUTIONS AND ADVERSE REACTIONS

The most frequent adverse effects of MAOIs are orthostatic hypotension, weight gain, edema, sexual dysfunction, and insomnia. If the orthostatic hypotension associated with phenelzine or isocarboxazid use is severe, it may respond to treatment with fludrocortisone (Florinef), a mineralocorticoid, 0.1 to 0.2 mg a day; support stockings; hydration; and increased salt intake. Orthostatic hypotension associated with tranylcypromine use can usually be relieved by dividing the daily dose. A rare adverse effect of MAOIs, most commonly of tranylcypromine, is a spontaneous hypertensive crisis that occurs after the first exposure to the drug and that is not associated with tyramine ingestion. The mechanism for that rare event is not understood, but tolerance for the hypertensive response does not develop, and patients should not be rechallenged with the drug. Weight gain, edema, and sexual dysfunction are often not responsive to any treatment and may warrant switching from a hydrazine to a nonhydrazine MAOI or vice versa. When switching from one MAOI to another, the clinician should taper and stop the first drug for 10 to 14 days before beginning the second drug. Insomnia and behavioral activation can be treated by dividing the dose, not giving the medication after dinner, and using a benzodiazepine hypnotic if necessary.

Myoclonus, muscle pains, and parathesias are occasionally seen in patients treated with MAOIs. Parathesias may be secondary to MAOI-induced pyridoxine deficiency, which may respond to supplementation with pyridoxine, 50 to 150 mg orally each day. Occasionally, patients complain of feeling drunk or confused, perhaps indicating that the dosage should be reduced and then increased gradually. Reports that the hydrazine MAOIs are associated with hepatotoxic effects are relatively uncommon. MAOIs are less cardiotoxic and less epilepto-

genic than are the tricyclic and tetracyclic drugs that are used to treat depression.

MAOIs should be used with caution by patients with renal disease, seizure disorders, cardiovascular disease, or hyperthyroidism. MAOIs may alter the dosage of a hypoglycemic agent required by diabetic patients. MAOIs have been particularly associated with causing depressed bipolar I disorder patients to switch into manic episodes and causing schizophrenic patients to have a psychotic decompensation. MAOIs are contraindicated during pregnancy, although data on their teratogenic risk are minimal. MAOIs should not be taken by nursing women because the drugs can pass into the breast milk.

### Tyramine-Induced Hypertensive Crisis

When patients who are taking nonselective MAOIs ingest foods rich in tyramine (Table 33.3.21–2), they are likely to have a hypertensive reaction that can be life-threatening (for example, a cerebrovascular disease). Patients should also be warned that bee stings may cause a hypertensive crisis. The mechanism involves $MAO_A$ inhibition in the gastrointestinal tract, resulting in the increased absorption of tyramine, which then acts as a pressor in the general circulation.

Patients should be warned about the dangers of ingesting tyramine-rich foods while taking MAOIs, and they should be advised to continue the dietary restrictions for two weeks after they stop MAOI treatment to allow the body to resynthesize the enzyme. The risk of tyramine-induced hypertensive crises is decreased in patients who are taking RIMAs, such as moclobemide and brofaromine. The prodromal signs and symptoms of a hypertensive crisis

**Table 33.3.21–2**
**Tyramine-Rich Foods to Be Avoided while Taking MAOIs**

**Very high tyramine content:**

Alcohol (particularly beer and wines, especially Chianti; a small amount of scotch, gin, vodka, or sherry is permissible)
Fava or broad beans
Aged cheese (e.g., Camembert, Liederkranz, Edam, and cheddar; cream cheese and cottage cheeses are permitted)
Beef or chicken liver
Orange pulp
Pickled or smoked fish, poultry, and meats
Soups (packaged)
Yeast vitamin supplements
Meat extracts (e.g., Marmite, Bovril)
Summer (dry) sausage

**Moderately high tyramine content (no more than one or two servings a day):**

Soy sauce
Sour cream
Bananas (green bananas can be included only if cooked in their skins; ordinary peeled bananas are fine)
Avocados
Eggplant
Plums
Raisins
Spinach
Tomatoes
Yogurt

may include headache, stiff neck, sweating, nausea, and vomiting. If those signs and symptoms occur, a patient should seek immediate medical treatment. An MAOI-induced hypertensive crisis can be treated with nifedipine (Procardia); however, some controversy exists regarding that practice because nifedipine produces a rapid drop in arterial pressure. That drop is a concern if a patient mistakes a headache resulting from the rebound of MAOI-induced orthostatic hypotension for a hypertensive-related headache. When nifedipine is used, the patient should bite into a 10 mg nifedipine capsule and swallow its contents with water. Additional treatment can include the use of α-adrenergic antagonists—for example, phentolamine (Regitine) or chlorpromazine (Thorazine).

## Overdose Attempts

In general, intoxication caused by MAOIs is characterized by agitation that progresses to coma with hyperthermia, hypertension, tachypnea, tachycardia, dilated pupils, and hyperactive deep tendon reflexes. Involuntary movements may be present, particularly in the face and the jaw. There is often an asymptomatic period of one to six hours after the ingestion of the drugs before the occurrence of the symptoms of toxicity. Acidification of the urine markedly hastens the excretion of MAOIs, and dialysis can be of some use. Nifedipine, phentolamine, or chlorpromazine may be useful if hypertension is a problem.

## DRUG INTERACTIONS

The inhibition of MAO can cause severe and even fatal interactions with various other drugs (Table 33.3.21–3). Patients should be instructed to tell any other physicians who are treating them that they are taking an MAOI. MAOIs may potentiate the action or be additive with cen-

**Table 33.3.21–3**
**Drugs to Be Avoided during MAOI Treatment**

**Never use:**

Anesthetic—never spinal anesthetic or local anesthetic containing epinephrine (lidocaine and procaine are safe)
Antiasthmatic medications
Antihypertensives (α-methyldopa, guanethidine, reserpine, pargyline)
L-Dopa, L-tryptophan
Narcotics (especially meperidine [Demerol]; morphine or codeine may be less dangerous)
Over-the-counter cold, hay fever, and sinus medications, especially those containing dextromethorphan (aspirin, acetaminophen, and menthol lozenges are safe)
Sympathomimetics (amphetamine, cocaine, methylphenidate, dopamine, metaraminol, epinephrine, norepinephrine, isoproterenol)
Serotonin-specific reuptake inhibitors, clomipramine

**Use carefully:**

Antihistamines
Hydralazine (Apresoline)
Propranolol (Inderal)
Terpin hydrate with codeine
Tricyclic and tetracyclic drugs

tral nervous system depressants, including alcohol and barbiturates. A serotonergic syndrome has been described when MAOIs are coadministered with serotonergic drugs, such as serotonin-specific reuptake inhibitors and clomipramine (Anafranil), thus resulting in the recommendation that those combinations be avoided. The initial symptoms of a serotonin syndrome can include tremor, hypertonicity, myoclonus, and autonomic signs, which can then progress to hallucinosis, hyperthermia, and even death.

## LABORATORY INTERFERENCES

The MAOIs are associated with the lowering of blood glucose levels, which are accurately reflected by laboratory analysis. However, MAOIs have been reported to be associated with a minimal false elevation in thyroid function tests.

## DOSAGE AND ADMINISTRATION

There is no definitive rationale for choosing one MAOI over another, although some clinicians recommend tranylcypromine because of its activating qualities, possibly associated with a fast onset of action, and its low hepatotoxic potential. Phenelzine should be started with a test dose of 15 mg on the first day. On an outpatient basis, the dosage can be increased to 45 mg a day during the first week and increased by 15 mg a day each week thereafter until the dosage of 90 mg a day is reached by the end of the fourth week. Tranylcypromine and isocarboxazid should begin with a test dose of 10 mg and may be increased to 30 mg a day by the end of the first week. Many clinicians and researchers have recommended upper limits of 50 mg a day for isocarboxazid and 40 mg a day for tranylcypromine. If an MAOI trial is not successful after six weeks, lithium (Eskalith) or L-triiodothyronine (T₃ or liothyronine [Cytomel]) augmentation is warranted. The combined treatment of depressive disorders with MAOIs and tricyclic drugs is described in Section 33.3.27.

Liver functions tests should be monitored periodically because of the potential of hepatotoxicity, especially with phenelzine and isocarboxazid. The elderly may be more sensitive to MAOI side effects than are younger adults, although, because MAO activity increases with age, the usual dosages of MAOIs are required to treat elderly patients. The use of MAOIs for children has been minimally studied.

## References

Amrein R, Hetzel W, Stabl M, Schmid-Burgk W: RIMA: A new concept in the treatment of depression with moclobemide. Int Clin Psychopharmacol 7: 123, 1993.
Clary C, Mandos L A, Schweizer E: Results of a brief survey on the prescribing practices for monoamine oxidase inhibitor antidepressants. J Clin Psychiatry 51: 226, 1990.
Fitton A, Faulds D, Goa K L: Moclobemide: A review of its pharmacological properties and therapeutic use in depressive illness. Drugs 43: 561, 1992.
Georgotas A, McCue R E, Cooper T B: A placebo-controlled comparison of nortriptyline and phenelzine in maintenance therapy of elderly depressed patients. Arch Gen Psychiatry 46: 783, 1989.
Kahn D, Silver J M, Opler L A: The safety of switching rapidly from

tricyclic antidepressants to monoamine oxidase inhibitors. J Clin Psychopharmacol 9: 198, 1989.

Keck P E Jr, Vuvkovic A, Pope H G, Nierenberg A, Gribble G W, White K: Acute cardiovascular response to monoamine oxidase inhibitors: A prospective assessment. J Clin Psychopharmacol 9: 203, 1989.

Mallinger A G, Himmelhoch J M, Thase M E, Edwards D J, Knopf S: Plasma tranylcypromine: Relationship to pharmacokinetic variables and clinical antidepressant actions. J Clin Psychopharmacol 10: 176, 1990.

Quitkin F M, McGrath P J, Stewart J W, Harrison W M, Wager S G, Nunes E, Rabkin J G, Tricamo E, Markowitz J S, Klein D F: Phenelzine and imipramine in mood reactive depressives. Arch Gen Psychiatry 46: 787, 1989.

Quitkin F M, Steward J W, McGrath P J, Liebowitz M R, Harrison W M, Tricamo E, Klein D F, Rabkin J G, Markowitz J S, Wager S G: Phenelzine versus imipramine in the treatment of probably atypical depression: Defining syndrome boundaries of selective MAOI responders. Am J Psychiatry 145: 306, 1988.

Teicher M H, Cohen B M, Baldessarini R J, Cole J O: Severe daytime somnolence in patients treated with an MAOI. Am J Psychiatry 145: 1552, 1988.

Thase M E, Mallinger A G, McKnight D, Himmelhoch J M: Treatment of imipramine-resistant recurrent depression: IV. A double-blind crossover study of tranylcypromine for anergic bipolar depression. Am J Psychiatry 149: 195, 1992.

# 33.3.22 / Serotonin-Specific Reuptake Inhibitors

The group of drugs discussed here are widely known as antidepressants. The drugs, along with the tricyclic and tetracyclic drugs and the monoamine oxidase inhibitors (MAOIs), are often considered the major antidepressant drugs. Although depressive disorders were the initial indications for the drugs, they are effective in a wide range of disorders, including eating disorders, panic disorder, obsessive-compulsive disorder, and borderline personality disorder. Therefore, it is misleading to call the drugs antidepressants. In this textbook they are referred to as the serotonin-specific reuptake inhibitors (SSRIs) because they share the pharmacodynamic property that they are specific inhibitors of serotonin reuptake by presynaptic neurons.

Fluoxetine, the SSRI first introduced for clinical use in the United States in 1988, was discovered in the early 1970s. Currently, three SSRIs are available in the United States and approved for the treatment of depression: fluoxetine (Prozac), paroxetine (Paxil), and sertraline (Zoloft). A fourth SSRI, fluvoxamine, is likely to be approved by the Food and Drug Administration (FDA) in the near future. Both fluvoxamine and a fifth SSRI, citalopram, are in widespread clinical use in Europe. Clomipramine (Anafranil) is another drug that is specific in its actions as an inhibitor of serotonin reuptake, but, because it is structurally similar to the tricyclic drugs used to treat depression, it is classified along with the tricyclic and tetracyclic drugs (antidepressants). The SSRIs have dramatically changed the treatment approach to depression because they are as effective as the old antidepressants yet are associated with a generally more favorable side-effect profile. Since its introduction in 1988, fluoxetine has become the most widely prescribed antidepressant in the United States.

## CHEMISTRY

The molecular structures of fluoxetine, fluvoxamine, sertraline, and paroxetine are shown in Figure 33.3.22–1.

## PHARMACOLOGICAL ACTIONS

### Pharmacokinetics

The major differences among the available SSRIs lie primarily in their pharmacokinetic profiles (Table 33.3.22–1), specifically their half-lives. Fluoxetine has the longest half-life, two to three days; its active metabolite has a half-life of seven to nine days. The half-lives of the other SSRIs are much shorter, about 20 hours, and those SSRIs have no major active metabolites. All SSRIs are well-absorbed after oral administration and have their peak effects in the range of four to eight hours. All SSRIs are metabolized in the liver. Paroxetine and fluoxetine are metabolized in the liver by $P_{450}IID6$, a specific subtype of the enzyme, which may indicate that clinicians should be careful in the coadministration of other drugs that are also metabolized by $P_{450}IID6$. In general, food does not have a large effect on the absorption of the SSRIs; in fact, the administration of the SSRIs with food often reduces the incidence of the common symptoms of nausea and diarrhea associated with SSRI use.

### Pharmacodynamics

The SSRIs share two common features: First, they have specific activity regarding the inhibition of serotonin reuptake without effects on norepinephrine and dopamine reuptake. Although the available compounds differ in their specific potencies (Table 33.3.22–2), the differences do not result in any meaningful clinical differences. Second, the SSRIs are essentially devoid of agonist and antagonist activities on any neurotransmitter receptor. The lack of anticholinergic, antihistaminergic, and anti-$\alpha_1$-adrenergic receptor activities is the pharmacodynamic basis for the low incidence of side effects seen with SSRI administration.

## EFFECTS ON SPECIFIC ORGANS AND SYSTEMS

Besides their effects on the central nervous system, the SSRIs have minimal effects on other organs and systems. Specifically, the SSRIs have minimal effects on blood pressure and cardiac function, as reflected by electrocardiograms. The major system affected by the SSRIs is the gastrointestinal tract, and symptoms of nausea, anorexia, and diarrhea are common with SSRI administration. Weight loss has also been reported to be associated with fluoxetine.

## THERAPEUTIC INDICATIONS

### Depression

The major indication for SSRI use is major depressive disorder; studies with fluoxetine have also shown that it is

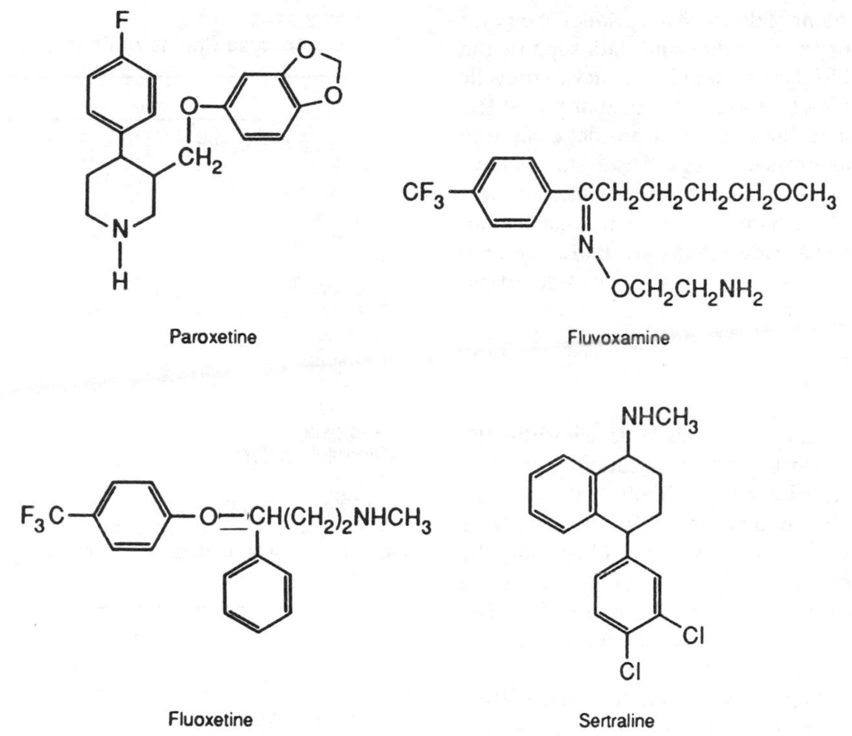

**Figure 33.3.22–1.** Molecular structures of serotonin-specific reuptake inhibitors.

Table 33.3.22–1
**Mean (Range) Pharmacokinetic Parameters of 5-HT Reuptake Inhibitors Estimated in Healthy Subjects**

| Parameter | FLX | FLV | PAR | SERT |
|---|---|---|---|---|
| Time of peak plasma concentration from initial dose (hours) | 4–8 | 2–8 | 3–8 | 6–10 |
| Elimination half-life (hours) | 84[a] | 15 | 21 | 26 |
| | (26–220) | (13–19) | (4–65) | (NA) |
| Protein binding (%) | 95 | 77 | 95 | >97[b] |
| Time for steady-state plasma concentration (days) | 14–28 | 10 | 4–14 | 10–14 |
| Volume of distribution (L/kg) | 25 | >5 | 13 | 25[b] |
| | (12–42) | (NA) | (3–28) | (NA) |
| Plasma clearance (L/hr/kg) | 0.29 | NA | 0.76 | NA |
| | (0.09–0.53) | | (0.21–1.31) | |
| Active metabolites | NORFLX | None | None | DMSERT |

DMSERT—dexmethylsertraline, FLV—fluvoxamine, FLX—fluoxetine, NA—not available, NORFLX—norfluoxetine, PAR—paroxetine, SERT—sertraline.
[a]Elimination half-life for norfluoxetine is 146 hours (range 77–235).
[b]Value from animal studies.
Table from C L DeVane: Pharmacokinetics of the selective serotonin reuptake inhibitors. J Clin Psychiatry 53 (2, Suppl): 14, 1992.

Table 33.3.22–2
**Approximate Potency of Inhibition of $H^3$ Biogenic Amine Uptake***

| Compound | Serotonin | $K_i$ (nM) Norepinephrine | Dopamine |
|---|---|---|---|
| Fluoxetine | 6 | 1,100 | >10,000 |
| Fluvoxamine | 25 | 500 | 4,200 |
| Paroxetine | 1 | 350 | 2,000 |
| Sertraline | 7 | 1,400 | 230 |

*In in vitro rat brain tissue preparation. Lower $K_i$ values indicate higher potency. All four compounds are potent inhibitors of serotonin reuptake.

effective for the treatment of depressive episodes in bipolar I disorder. The majority of studies and data support the conclusions that the SSRIs are equal in efficacy to tricyclic drugs in the treatment of depression and that the SSRIs have a significantly superior side-effect profile, compared with those other antidepressant drugs. Those studies have also consistently shown that some degree of nervousness or agitation, sleep disturbances, gastrointestinal symptoms, and perhaps sexual side effects are more common in SSRI-treated patients than in tricyclic drug-treated patients.

## Other Indications

Because fluoxetine has been available clinically the longest, most studies regarding other indications have been done with fluoxetine, although it is likely that the other SSRIs are similar to fluoxetine in their efficacies for those additional indications. In particular, it is likely that the FDA will approve the use of fluoxetine and fluvoxamine for the treatment of obsessive-compulsive disorder. The most data on other indications involve bulimia nervosa and obesity. In several well-controlled studies, fluoxetine has been effective in reducing the vomiting and binge-eating symptoms of bulimia nervosa, in promoting weight loss in overweight persons, and in reducing the symptoms of obsessive-compulsive disorder. However, whereas the most commonly effective dosage of fluoxetine in the treatment of depression is 20 mg a day, the effective dosage of fluoxetine for those other indications appears to be 60 mg a day.

Other indications for which there is preliminary evidence of efficacy for the SSRIs are dysthymic disorder, borderline personality disorder, and panic disorder. In contrast to the higher dosages of fluoxetine for some disorders, panic disorder patients are best started on lower dosages of fluoxetine, around 5 mg a day. That variation in dosages for fluoxetine among the indications suggests that it may not be wise to use nonfluoxetine SSRIs for nondepression indications without knowing the approximate dosage range in which a patient is likely to respond.

## PRECAUTIONS AND ADVERSE REACTIONS

### Fluoxetine

Because fluoxetine has been available the longest time and has been used in the most patients, the available data on its side effects are the most complete of the SSRIs. The side-effect profile of fluoxetine shows that it is a well-tolerated drug. The most common adverse effects of fluoxetine involve the central nervous system and the gastrointestinal system (Table 33.3.22–3). The most common central nervous system effects include headache, nervousness, insomnia, drowsiness, and anxiety. Seizures have been reported in 0.2 percent of all patients treated with the drug, an incidence that is comparable to the incidence reported with other antidepressants. The most common gastrointestinal complaints are nausea, diarrhea, anorexia, and dyspepsia. Data indicate that the nausea is dose-re-

**Table 33.3.22–3**
**Common Adverse Effects of Fluoxetine**

| | Patients (%) |
|---|---|
| Central nervous system | |
| Headache | 20 |
| Nervousness | 15 |
| Insomnia | 14 |
| Drowsiness | 12 |
| Anxiety | 9 |
| Tremor | 8 |
| Dizziness | 6 |
| Gastrointestinal system | |
| Nausea | 21 |
| Diarrhea | 12 |
| Dry mouth | 10 |
| Anorexia | 9 |
| Stomach upset | 6 |
| Other | |
| Excessive sweating | 8 |
| Weight loss >5% body weight | 13 |
| Increase in suicidal ideation or violent behavior (six cases reported) | |

lated and is an adverse effect for which patients apparently develop tolerance.

Other adverse effects involve sexual functioning and the skin. Anorgasmia, delayed ejaculation, and impotence apparently affect at least 5 percent of all patients treated. Those sexual side effects may respond to yohimbine (Yocon) or to cyproheptadine (Periactin). Various types of rashes may appear in about 4 percent of all patients; in a small subset of those patients, the allergic reaction may generalize and involve the pulmonary system, resulting rarely in fibrotic damage and dyspnea. Fluoxetine treatment may have to be discontinued in patients with drug-related rashes. Fluoxetine is associated with a decrease in glucose concentrations; therefore, diabetic patients should be carefully monitored regarding the possibility of decreasing the dosage of their hypoglycemic drug. Rare cases of fluoxetine-associated hyponatremia have been seen in patients treated with diuretics who are also water-deprived.

Fluoxetine, compared with non-SSRI antidepressants, is a safe drug when taken in overdoses. Only one report has noted a lethal overdose of fluoxetine taken by itself and only a small number of lethal overdoses when fluoxetine was taken with other drugs. The symptoms of overdose include agitation, restlessness, insomnia, tremor, nausea, vomiting, tachycardia, and seizures. The clinician should ascertain whether other drugs were taken with the fluoxetine. The first steps in the treatment of overdose are gastric lavage and emesis. In the late 1980s a widely publicized report suggested an association between fluoxetine administration and violent acts, including suicide, but many subsequent reviews have clearly proved no increased likelihood of such an association with fluoxetine. However, a few patients become especially anxious and agitated, almost in an akathisialike fashion, when given fluoxetine, and the appearance of those symptoms in an already-suicidal patient may aggravate the seriousness of the suicidal ideation.

Because of the large number of patients who have taken fluoxetine, it is possible to state that the number of birth defects and birth complications when the mothers took fluoxetine during pregnancy is not significantly different from those seen when mothers did not take fluoxetine during pregnancy. Nevertheless, the general rule of avoiding all drugs during pregnancy should be adhered to unless there is a compelling reason to treat a pregnant woman with an antidepressant drug. Fluoxetine is excreted in breast milk; therefore, nursing mothers should not take fluoxetine. Fluoxetine should also be used with caution by patients with hepatic disease.

## Other SSRIs

The adverse effects associated with other SSRIs are similar to those seen with fluoxetine (Table 33.3.22–4), although the fact that the other drugs have been given to fewer patients increases the possibility that some rare adverse effects are not fully recognized. The data on paroxetine, sertraline, and fluvoxamine are too limited at this point to differentiate them from fluoxetine, although their use in medically ill patients should be carried out with the appreciation that the new compounds have had relatively limited clinical exposure.

## DRUG INTERACTIONS

The clinician must be informed about a number of potential drug interactions with the SSRIs (Table 33.3.22–5). No SSRI should be administered with L-tryptophan or a monoamine oxidase inhibitor (MAOI) because of the possibility of inducing a potentially fatal serotonin syndrome. Fluoxetine can be administered with tricyclic drugs, but the clinician should use low dosages of the tricyclic drug. Possibly significant drug interactions have been described for fluoxetine with benzodiazepines, antipsychotics, and lithium (Eskalith). Fluoxetine has no interactions with warfarin (Coumadin), tolbutamide (Orinase), or chlorthiazide (Diuril). The drug interaction data on sertraline support a generally similar profile, although sertraline does not interact with the hepatic $P_{450}IID6$ enzyme. Paroxetine has a higher risk for drug interactions than does either fluoxetine or sertraline because of its metabolic pathway through the $P_{450}IID6$ hepatic enzyme. Cimetidine (Tagamet) can increase the concentration of paroxetine,

and phenobarbital (Luminal) and phenytoin (Dilantin) can decrease the concentrations of paroxetine. The coadministration of paroxetine with other antidepressants and antiarrhythmic drugs should be undertaken with caution.

## LABORATORY INTERFERENCES

No laboratory interferences have been shown as yet with the available SSRI drugs.

## DOSAGE AND ADMINISTRATION

### Fluoxetine

Fluoxetine is available in 10 mg and 20 mg pulvules (that is, capsules) and as a liquid (20 mg per 5 mL). Fluoxetine may be available in 60 mg preparations in the near future. For depression, the initial dosage is usually 20 mg orally each day, usually given in the morning, because insomnia is a potential adverse effect of the drug. Fluoxetine should be taken with food to minimize the possible nausea. The long half-lives of the drug and its metabolite contribute to a four-week period to reach steady-state concentrations. As with all available antidepressants, the antidepressant effects of fluoxetine may be seen in the first one to three weeks, but the clinician should wait until the patient has been taking the drug for four to six weeks before evaluating its antidepressant activity. Several studies indicate that 20 mg is as effective as higher doses. The maximum daily dosage recommended by the manufacturer is 80 mg a day. A reasonable strategy is to maintain a patient with 20 mg a day for three weeks. If the patient shows no signs of clinical improvement at that time, an increase to 20 mg twice a day may be warranted, although at least one study has found that keeping a patient on the 20 mg a day dosage longer is as effective as increasing the dosage.

To minimize the early side effects of anxiety and restlessness, some clinicians initiate fluoxetine at 5 to 10 mg a day either by instructing the patient to dissolve the contents of a capsule in water or juice or by using the liquid preparation. If a patient mixes the contents of a capsule with a liquid, the mixture should be kept refrigerated. Alternatively, because of the long half-life of fluoxetine,

**Table 33.3.22–4**
**Side Effects with an Incidence of ≥19 Percent Reported for Selected Serotonin Reuptake Inhibitors, Imipramine, and Placebo**

| Side Effect | Sertraline N = 1,568 | Placebo N = 851 | Fluoxetine N = 1,378 | Fluvoxamine N = 222 | Paroxetine N = 1,387 | Imipramine N = 599 |
|---|---|---|---|---|---|---|
| Nausea and vomiting | 21% | — | 25% | 37% | 29% | — |
| Headache | — | 20% | — | 22 | 20 | 19% |
| Dry mouth | — | — | — | 26 | 20 | 76 |
| Sedation | — | — | — | 26 | 24 | 30 |
| Nervousness, restlessness, and anxiety | — | — | 21 | — | — | — |
| Dizziness | — | — | — | — | — | 27 |
| Insomnia | — | — | 19 | — | — | — |
| Sweating | — | — | — | — | — | 21 |

Table adapted from K Rickels, E Schweizer: Clinical overview of serotonin reuptake inhibitors. J Clin Psychiatry 51: 10, 1990. Used with permission.

**Table 33.3.22–5**
**Interactions of Drugs with the SSRIs Fluoxetine, Fluvoxamine, Paroxetine, and Sertraline**

| SSRI | Other Drugs | Effect | Clinical Importance |
|---|---|---|---|
| Fluoxetine | Desipramine | Inhibits metabolism | Possible |
| | Carbamazepine | Inhibits metabolism | Possible |
| | Diazepam | Inhibits metabolism | Not important |
| | Haloperidol | Inhibits metabolism | Possible |
| | Warfarin | No interaction | |
| | Tolbutamide | No interaction | |
| Fluvoxamine | Antipyrine | Inhibits metabolism | Not important |
| | Propranolol | Inhibits metabolism | Unlikely |
| | Tricyclics | Inhibits metabolism | Unlikely |
| | Warfarin | Inhibits metabolism | Possible |
| | Atenolol | No interaction | |
| | Digoxin | No interaction | |
| Paroxetine | Phenytoin | AUC increases by 12% | Possible |
| | Procyclidine | AUC increases by 39% | Possible |
| | Cimetidine | Paroxetine AUC increased by 50% | Possible |
| | Antipyrine | No interaction | |
| | Digoxin | No interaction | |
| | Propranolol | No interaction | |
| | Tranylcypromine | No interaction | Caution with combined treatment |
| | Warfarin | No interaction | |
| Sertraline | Antipyrine | Increased clearance | Not important |
| | Diazepam | 13% decreased clearance | Not important |
| | Tolbutamide | 16% decreased clearance | Not important |
| | Digoxin | No interaction | |
| | Lithium | No pharmacokinetic interaction | Caution with combined treatment |
| | Desipramine | No interaction | |
| | Atenolol | No pharmacodynamic interaction | |

Table from S J Warrington: Clinical implications of the pharmacology of serotonin reuptake inhibitors. Int Clin Psychopharmacol 7 (Suppl 2): 13, 1992. Used with permission.

the drug can be initiated with an every-other-day administration schedule.

With depressed patients who do not respond to fluoxetine treatment, the clinician can augment fluoxetine with other drugs, including tricyclic drugs (for example, desipramine [Norpramin]), sympathomimetics (for example, pemoline [Cylert]), buspirone (BuSpar), and lithium. Adding those drugs when a patient has been nonresponsive to fluoxetine alone has resulted in a significant proportion of patients' converting to treatment-responders. At least two weeks should elapse between the discontinuation of MAOIs and the initiation of fluoxetine. Fluoxetine must be discontinued for at least five weeks before the initiation of MAOI treatment.

The dosage of fluoxetine that is effective in other indications may differ from the 20 mg a day that is generally used for depression. A dosage of 60 mg a day has been reported to be the most efficacious dosage for obsessive-compulsive disorder, obesity, and bulimia nervosa. In contrast, a starting dosage of 5 mg a day with minimal increases has been reported to be effective in the treatment of panic disorder.

## Fluvoxamine

Fluvoxamine is available in Europe in 50 and 100 mg tablets but has not been approved by the Food and Drug Administration (FDA) for use in the United States. The effective daily dosage range is from 50 mg a day to 300 mg a day. A usual starting dosage is 100 mg a day for the first

week, after which the dosage can be adjusted according to the adverse effects and the patient's response. A tapered reduction of the dosage may be necessary if nausea develops over the first two weeks of therapy. Fluvoxamine can be administered as a single evening dose to minimize its adverse effects. Tablets should be swallowed with water and, preferably, food without chewing the tablet.

## Paroxetine

Paroxetine is available in scored 20 mg and 30 mg unscored tablets. Paroxetine is usually initiated for the treatment of depression at a dosage of 20 mg a day. An increase in the dosage should be considered when patients do not show an adequate response in one to three weeks. At that point, the clinician can initiate upward dose titration in 10 mg increments at weekly intervals to a maximum of 50 mg a day. Patients who experience gastrointestinal upsets may benefit by taking the drug with food. Paroxetine should be taken as a single daily dose in the morning. Patients with melancholic features may require dosages greater than 20 mg a day. The suggested therapeutic dosage range for elderly patients is 20 to 40 mg a day, as the elderly have been found to have higher mean plasma concentrations than do younger adults.

## Sertraline

For the initial treatment of depression, sertraline should be initiated with a dosage of 50 mg once daily. Patients who do not respond after one to three weeks may benefit from dosage increases of 50 mg every week up to a maximum of 200 mg given once daily. Sertraline can be administered in the morning or the evening without regard for meals.

### References

American College of Neuropsychopharmacology Council: Suicidal behavior and psychotropic medication. Neuropsychopharmacology *8*: 177, 1993.

Beasley C M, Masica D N, Potvin J H: Fluoxetine: A review of receptor and functional effects and their clinical implications. Psychopharmacology *107*: 1, 1992.

Boyer W F: Potential indications for the selective serotonin reuptake inhibitors. Int Clin Psychopharmacol *6* (Suppl 5): 5, 1992.

Burton S W: A review of fluvoxamine and its uses in depression. Int Clin Psychopharmacol *6* (Suppl 3): 1, 1991.

Ciraulo D A, Shader R I: Fluoxetine drug-drug interactions: II. J Clin Psychopharmacol *10*: 213, 1990.

De Wilde J, Spieres R, Mertens C, Bartholomé F, Schotte G, Leyman S: A double-blind, comparative, multicentre study comparing paroxetine with fluoxetine in depressed patients. Acta Psychiatr Scand *87*: 141, 1993.

Doogan D P, Caillard V: Sertraline in the prevention of depression. Br J Psychiatry *160*: 217, 1992.

Jacobsen F M: Fluoxetine-induced sexual dysfunction and an open trial of yohimbine. J Clin Psychiatry *53*: 119, 1992.

Journal of Clinical Psychiatry: A clinical profile of paroxetine: A novel selective serotonin reuptake inhibitor (SSRI). *53* (2, Suppl): 2, 1992.

Kuhs H, Schlake H-P, Rolf L H, Rudolf G A E: Relationship between parameters of serotonin transport and antidepressant plasma levels on therapeutic response in depressive patients treated with paroxetine and amitriptyline. Acta Psychiatr Scand *85*: 364, 1992.

Laird L K, Lydiard R B, Morton W A, Steede T E, Kellner C, Thompson N M, Ballenger J C: Cardiovascular effects of imipramine, fluoxamine, and placebo in depressed outpatients. J Clin Psychiatry *54*: 224, 1993.

Milne R J, Goa K L: Citalopram: A review of its pharmacodynamic and pharmacokinetic properties, and therapeutic potential in depressive illness. Drugs *3*: 450, 1991.

Murdoch D, McTavish D: Sertraline: A review of its pharmacodynamic and pharmacokinetic propertics, and therapeutic potential in depression and obsessive-compulsive disorder. Drugs *4*: 604, 1992.

Nyth A L, Gottfries C G: The clinical efficacy of citalopram in treatment of emotional disturbances in dementia disorders: A Nordic multicentre study. Br J Psychiatry *157*: 894, 1990.

Power A C, Cowen P J: Fluoxetine and suicidal behavior: Some clinical and theoretical aspects of a controversy. Br J Psychiatry *161*: 735, 1992.

Song F, Freemantle N, Sheldon T A, House A, Watson P, Long A, Mason J: Selective serotonin reuptake inhibitors: Meta-analysis of efficacy and acceptability. Br J Med *306*: 683, 1993.

Warrington S J: Clinical implications of the pharmacology of serotonin reuptake inhibitors. Int Clin Psychopharmacol *7* (Suppl 2): 13, 1992.

# 33.3.23 / Sympathomimetics

The sympathomimetics are a class of drugs that act primarily by stimulating the release of dopamine from presynaptic terminals. The drugs are also referred to as stimulants, psychostimulants, and analeptics. The first sympathomimetic, amphetamine (Benzedrine), was synthesized in 1935 and was recognized as efficacious in the treatment of narcolepsy, depressive disorders, and hyperactive children shortly thereafter. The use of amphetamine was soon replaced by the use of dextroamphetamine (Dexedrine), which was then joined by the two other currently

available sympathomimetics, methylphenidate (Ritalin) and pemoline (Cylert). The Food and Drug Administration (FDA)-approved indications for dextroamphetamine and methylphenidate are narcolepsy and attention-deficit/hyperactivity disorder, and the approved indication for pemoline is attention-deficit/hyperactivity disorder. The drugs are also effective in the treatment of depressive disorders in special populations (for example, the medically ill).

## CHEMISTRY

Dextroamphetamine and methylphenidate are structurally similar to each other and to amphetamine, and all three drugs are similar in structure to the catecholamines (for example, dopamine) (Figure 33.3.23–1). Pemoline has a different structure from the other three compounds and differs in its speed of onset.

## PHARMACOLOGICAL ACTIONS

### Pharmacokinetics

All three sympathomimetics are well-absorbed from the gastrointestinal tract. Dextroamphetamine reaches peak plasma concentrations in two to three hours and has a half-life of about six hours, thereby necessitating multiple-daily dosing. Dextroamphetamine is partially metabolized in the liver and is partially excreted unchanged by the kidneys. Methylphenidate reaches peak plasma levels in one to two hours and has a short half-life of two to three hours, thereby necessitating multiple-daily dosing. Methylphenidate is completely metabolized by the liver. Pemoline reaches peak plasma concentrations in two to four hours and has a half-life of about 12 hours, thereby allowing once-daily dosing. Pemoline is metabolized by the liver and is excreted unchanged by the kidneys.

### Pharmacodynamics

Dextroamphetamine and methylphenidate are indirectly acting sympathomimetics, with the primary effect of causing

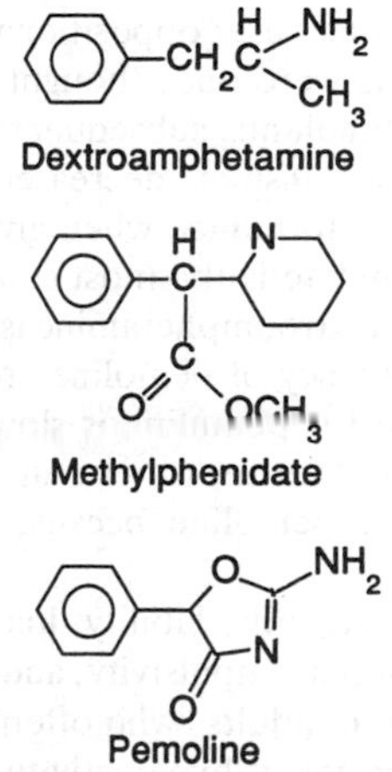

**Figure 33.3.23–1.** Molecular structures of sympathomimetics.

the release of catecholamines from presynaptic neurons. The release of dopamine may be of primary importance in the sympathomimetics' clinical effects, although recent data indicate that the release of norepinephrine may be more involved with the clinical effects than was previously thought. Dextroamphetamine and methylphenidate are also inhibitors of catecholamine reuptake and inhibitors of monoamine oxidase. The net result of those activities is believed to be the stimulation of several brain regions, particularly the ascending reticular activating system and areas of the striatum, which have recently been implicated in the pathophysiology of attention-deficit/hyperactivity disorder. The pharmacodynamics of pemoline are less well-understood than are the pharmacodynamics of dextroamphetamine and methylphenidate.

The short-term use of the sympathomimetics induces a euphoric feeling; however, tolerance develops for both the euphoric feeling and the sympathomimetic activity. Tolerance does not develop for the therapeutic effects in attention-deficit/hyperactivity disorder.

## EFFECTS ON SPECIFIC ORGANS AND SYSTEMS

In addition to the effects of the sympathomimetics on the central nervous system, the drugs have significant effects on the cardiovascular and endocrine systems. At regular clinical dosages the cardiovascular effects are minimal, but at high dosages the sympathomimetics can cause increases in the blood pressure, either increases in the heart rate or reflex decreases in the heart rate, and cardiac arrhythmias at still higher dosages. Studies have indicated that sympathomimetics, particularly amphetamine, affect the endocrine system, as indicated by a decreased growth rate in children during the first year of treatment.

## THERAPEUTIC INDICATIONS

### Attention-Deficit/Hyperactivity Disorder

The major indication for the sympathomimetics is attention-deficit/hyperactivity disorder in children. The sympathomimetics are effective in about 75 percent of those patients. Many well-controlled studies have shown that the drugs increase the attention span, increase the ability to concentrate, and decrease oppositional behaviors. Although those effects were once thought of as paradoxical effects for psychostimulants, subsequent studies found that normal children also display decreased activity and increased cognitive performance when given the drugs. Although methylphenidate is the most commonly used drug for the indication, dextroamphetamine is equally effective. The data on the efficacy of pemoline are less robust, and the onset of action for pemoline is slower (three to four weeks) than the onset for the other drugs. Some clinicians, nevertheless, prefer pemoline because of its low abuse potential.

A syndrome of affective lability, inability to complete tasks, explosive temper, impulsivity, and stress intolerance has been described in adults, who often have a history of childhood attention-deficit/hyperactivity disorder. Data indicate that the sympathomimetics are effective in the treatment of those adults. Amphetamines (5 to 60 mg a day) or methylphenidate (5 to 60 mg a day) may be efficacious, and psychopharmacological therapy may need to be continued indefinitely.

### Narcolepsy

Narcolepsy is the second approved use of sympathomimetics in the United States. The symptoms of narcolepsy include excessive daytime sleepiness and transient, irresistible attacks of daytime sleep. Unfortunately, patients with narcolepsy, unlike patients with attention-deficit/hyperactivity disorder, develop tolerance for the therapeutic effects of the sympathomimetics.

### Depressive Disorders

Sympathomimetics may be used to treat depressive disorders. Possible indications for their use include treatment-resistant depressive disorders; depression in the elderly, who are at increased risk for adverse effects from tricyclic and tetracyclic drugs and monoamine oxidase inhibitors; depression in medically ill patients—especially acquired immune deficiency (AIDS) patients—and clinical situations in which a rapid response is important but for which electroconvulsive therapy (ECT) is contraindicated.

Dextroamphetamine may be useful in differentiating pseudodementia of depression from dementia. A depressed patient generally responds to a 5 mg dose with increased alertness and improved cognition. Sympathomimetics are thought to provide only short-term benefit (two to four weeks) for depression, because tolerance for the antidepressant effects of the drugs develops rapidly in most patients. However, some research data and some clinicians report that long-term treatment of patients with sympathomimetics can be of benefit in some cases. Certainly, long-term treatment must be monitored to assess the continuing benefit of the drugs and to assess the patient's abuse of the drugs.

### Obesity

Sympathomimetics were previously used in the treatment of obesity because of their anorexia-inducing effects. Because tolerance develops for the anorectic effects and because of the drugs' high abuse potential, that indication is no longer considered justified.

## PRECAUTIONS AND ADVERSE REACTIONS

The most common adverse effects associated with sympathomimetics are anxiety, irritability, insomnia, and dysphoria. Sympathomimetics cause a decreased appetite, although tolerance develops for that effect. The treatment of common adverse effects in children with attention-deficit/hyperactivity disorder is usually straightforward (Table 33.3.23–1). The drugs can also cause increases in the heart rate and the blood pressure and may cause palpitations. Less common adverse effects include the induction of movement disorders, such as tics, Tourette's disorderlike

**Table 33.3.23–1**
**Management of Common Stimulant-Induced Adverse Effects in Attention-Deficit/Hyperactivity Disorder**

| Adverse Effect | Management |
| --- | --- |
| Anorexia, nausea, weight loss | Administer stimulant with meals. Use caloric-enhanced supplements. Discourage forcing meals. If using pemoline, check liver function tests. |
| Insomnia, nightmares | Administer stimulants earlier in day. Change to short-acting preparations. Discontinue afternoon or evening dosing. Consider adjunctive treatment (e.g., antihistamines, clonidine, antidepressants). |
| Dizziness | Monitor blood pressure. Encourage fluid intake. Change to long-acting form. |
| Rebound phenomena | Overlap stimulant dosing. Change to long-acting preparation or combine long-acting and short-acting preparations. Consider adjunctive or alternative treatment (e.g., clonidine, antidepressants). |
| Irritability | Assess timing of phenomena (during peak or withdrawal phase). Evaluate comorbid symptoms. Reduce dosage. Consider adjunctive or alternative treatment (e.g., lithium, antidepressants, anticonvulsants). |
| Growth impairment | Attempt weekend and vacation holidays. If severe, consider nonstimulant treatment. |
| Dysphoria, moodiness, agitation | Consider comorbid diagnosis (e.g., mood disorder). Reduce dosage or change to long-acting preparation. Consider adjunctive or alternative treatment (e.g., lithium, anticonvulsants, antidepressants). |

Table from T E Wilens, J Biederman: The stimulants. In *The Psychiatric Clinics of North America: Pediatric Psychopharmacology*, D Shaffer, editor, p 172. Saunders, Philadelphia, 1992. Used with permission.

symptoms, and dyskinesia. In children, sympathomimetics may cause a transient suppression of growth. The most limiting adverse effect of sympathomimetics is their association with psychological and physical dependence. Sympathomimetics may exacerbate glaucoma, hypertension, cardiovascular disorders, hyperthyroidism, anxiety disorders, psychotic disorders, and seizure disorders.

High dosages of sympathomimetics can cause dry mouth, pupillary dilation, bruxism, formication, and emotional lability. Long-term use of high dosages can cause a delusional disorder that is indistinguishable from paranoid schizophrenia. Overdosages of sympathomimetics present with hypertension, tachycardia, hyperthermia, toxic psychosis, delirium, and occasionally seizures. Overdosages of sympathomimetics can also result in death, often due to cardiac arrhythmias. Seizures can be treated with benzodiazepines, cardiac effects with β-adrenergic receptor antagonists, fever with cooling blankets, and delirium with dopamine receptor antagonists.

There is virtually no justifiable indication for the use of sympathomimetics during pregnancy. Dextroamphetamine and methylphenidate pass into the breast milk, and it is not known whether pemoline does.

## DRUG INTERACTIONS

The coadministration of sympathomimetics and tricyclic or tetracyclic drugs used for the treatment of depressive disorders, warfarin (Coumadin), primidone (Mysoline), phenobarbital (Luminal), phenytoin (Dilantin), or phenylbutazone (Butazolidin) decreases the metabolism of those compounds, resulting in increased plasma levels.

Sympathomimetics decrease the therapeutic efficacy of many hypertensives, especially guanethidine (Esimil, Ismelin). The sympathomimetics should be used with extreme caution with monoamine oxidase inhibitors.

## LABORATORY INTERFERENCES

Dextroamphetamine may elevate plasma corticosteroid levels and interfere falsely with some assay methods for urinary corticosteroids.

## DOSAGE AND ADMINISTRATION

The dosage ranges and the available preparations for sympathomimetics are presented in Table 33.3.23–2. Sympathomimetics are schedule II drugs and in some states require triplicate prescriptions. Many clinicians initiate treatment with pemoline, because it is associated with less abuse potential than either dextroamphetamine or methylphenidate. Pretreatment evaluation should include an evaluation of the patient's cardiac function, with particular attention to the presence of hypertension or tachyarrhythmias. The clinician should also examine the patient for the presence of movement disorders, such as tics and dyskinesia, because those conditions can be exacerbated by the administration of sympathomimetics. Liver function and renal function should be assessed, and dosages of sympathomimetics should be reduced if the patient's metabolism is impaired.

When treating children for attention-deficit/hyperactivity disorder, the clinician can give dextroamphetamine or

**Table 33.3.23–2**
**Sympathomimetics**

| Generic Name | Trade Name | Preparations | Adult Starting Dose (mg a day) | Adult Average Daily Dose (mg) | Adult Maximum Daily Dose (mg) |
|---|---|---|---|---|---|
| Dextroamphetamine | Dexedrine | 5, 10 mg tablets<br>5 mg per 5 mL elixir<br>5, 10, 15 mg sustained-release capsules | 2.5–10 | 10–20 | 60 |
| Methylphenidate | Ritalin | 5, 10, 20 mg tablets<br>20 mg sustained-release tablets | 5–10 | 20–30 | 60–80 |
| Pemoline | Cylert | 18.75, 37.5, 75 mg tablets | 18.75–37.5 | 56.25–75 | 112.5 |

methylphenidate at 8 AM and 12 noon. Pemoline is given at 8 AM. The dosage of dextroamphetamine is 2.5 to 40 mg a day up to 0.5 mg per kg a day. Pemoline is given in dosages of 18.75 to 112.5 mg a day. Liver function tests should be monitored when using pemoline. Children are generally more sensitive to side effects than are adults.

Many psychiatrists believe that amphetamine use has been overly regulated by governmental authorities. Amphetamines and narcotics are listed as schedule II drugs by the U.S. Drug Enforcement Agency (DEA). In addition, in New York State, for example, physicians must use triplicate prescriptions for such drugs; one copy is filed with a state government agency. Such mandates worry both patients and physicians about breaches in confidentiality, and physicians are concerned that their prescribing practices may be misinterpreted by official agencies. Consequently, some physicians may withhold sympathomimetics, even from patients who may benefit from the medications.

The outstanding psychopharmacologist Donald Klein and associates in their 1980 book *Diagnosis and Drug Treatment of Psychiatric Disorders* (and reaffirmed in a personal communication [1990]) summarized the use of stimulant medication in the practice of psychiatry as follows:

The use of stimulant medication, e.g., dextroamphetamine, methylphenidate, and magnesium pemoline, has been energetically discouraged in our present social climate, the reason being that such drugs may be abused, in common with cocaine, their illegal relative. In addition, there is the frightening possibility that prolonged use of stimulants in high doses may result in a paranoid psychosis or the exacerbation of a schizophrenic disorder. In view of these two considerations, it is not surprising that the prescription of these agents is attended by considerable anxiety and that many doctors simply refuse to use them. In certain jurisdictions, e.g., Sweden, they are outlawed.

. . . Short-term use of stimulant medication is often of marked value in helping demoralized people to get going by overcoming their hampering appetitive inhibition. A daily dose of dextroamphetamine (5 to 15 mg) may enable a patient to start constructive activity, such as searching for a job or becoming socially active. . . .

A much more difficult question is whether chronic administration of stimulant medication is ever justified, in view of the risks of addiction and psychosis.

We have treated a number of patients who seem in chronically "low gear," have difficulty mustering energy and initiative, have a variety of neurasthenic complaints and, despite high intelligence, are underachievers, with chronic small doses of dextroamphetamine (5 to 15 mg) daily. The potential development of tolerance and dependence and the conceivable psychotogenic effects are thoroughly discussed with these patients, and the utilization of the medication is closely monitored. Strikingly, some have been able to maintain the use of amphetamines, at a level that has never exceeded 15 mg daily, for years. During this period their mood has remained consistently improved and their ability to muster energy and function effectively has been clearly benefited. They have been able to cease taking the medication on numerous occasions, such as during vacations, when a high level of focused attention was not necessary and the circumstances were rewarding, so that the mood-elevating effects were superfluous. Several of these patients have been switched from dextroamphetamine to a MAOI with good results.

The controversial use of triplicate prescriptions is discussed further in Section 12.12.

### References

Breitbart W, Mermelstein H: Pemoline: An alternative psychostimulant for the management of depressive disorders in cancer patients. Psychosomatics 33: 352, 1992.

Chiarello R J, Cole J O: The use of psychostimulants in general psychiatry: A reconsideration. Arch Gen Psychiatry 44: 286, 1987.

Fawcett J, Kravitz H M, Zajecka J M, Schaff M R: CNS stimulant potentiation of monoamine oxidase inhibitors in treatment-refractory depression. J Clin Psychopharmacol 11: 127, 1991.

Kraus M F, Burch E A: Methylphenidate hydrochloride as an antidepressant: Controversy, case studies and review. South Med J 85: 985, 1992.

Lazarus L W, Winemiller D R, Lingam V R, Neyman I, Hartman C, Abassian M, Kartan U, Groves L, Fawcett J: Efficacy and side effects of methylphenidate for poststroke depression. J Clin Psychiatry 53: 447, 1992.

Masand P, Murray G B, Pickett P: Psychostimulants in post-stroke depression. J Neuropsychiatry Clin Neurosci 3: 23, 1991.

Rosenberg P B, Ahmed I, Hurwitz S: Methylphenidate in depressed medically ill patients. J Clin Psychiatry 52: 263, 1991.

Satel S L, Nelson J C: Stimulants in the treatment of depression: A critical overview. J Clin Psychiatry 50: 241, 1989.

Wroblewski B A, Leary J M, Phelan A M, Whyte J, Manning K: Methylphenidate and seizure frequency in brain injured patients with seizure disorders. J Clin Psychiatry 53: 86, 1992.

# 33.3.24 / Tacrine

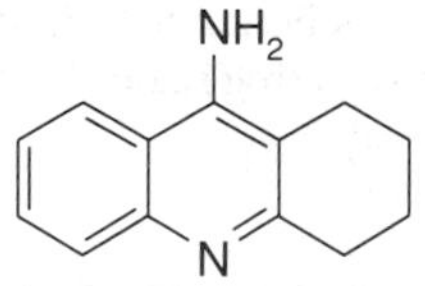

**Figure 33.3.24–1.** Molecular structure of tacrine.

Tacrine (tetrahydroaminoacridine, THA) (Cognex) is the first drug approved in the United States for the treatment of cognitive impairment in dementia of the Alzheimer's type. Tacrine has inhibition of acetylcholinesterase, the enzyme that catabolizes acetylcholine, as its primary mechanism of action. A deficit in acetylcholine function may be involved in the pathophysiology of dementia of the Alzheimer's type for at least a decade. Several pharmacological approaches to address the deficit have been studied. In addition to the inhibition of acetylcholinesterase, the approaches include the administration of acetylcholine precursors (that is, lecithin and choline) and the direct stimulation of acetylcholine receptors (both muscarinic and nicotinic). Preliminary studies suggested the efficacy of physostigmine, an old acetylcholinesterase inhibitor; however, tacrine has a longer half-life and a wider therapeutic window than the old drug possesses.

Tacrine was first synthesized in 1945 by Albert and Gledhill, although its inhibition of acetylcholinesterase was not recognized and demonstrated until 1953. In the late 1940s, tacrine was found to antagonize morphine-induced narcosis in dogs, thus leading to its use as an adjuvant to morphine treatment of severe pain in cancer patients. The first small pilot studies of the use of tacrine in the treatment of dementia of the Alzheimer's type were conducted in the early 1980s, although a small study by Summers and his colleagues, published in 1986, stimulated the development of a much larger research program regarding the use of tacrine in the treatment of dementia of the Alzheimer's type. Although the strikingly positive effects of tacrine reported by Summers and his colleagues have not been replicated in larger studies, the larger studies have replicated the basic finding that tacrine is a safe and therapeutic treatment of the cognitive symptoms of dementia of the Alzheimer's type.

The approval of tacrine is an important first step; it indicates that clinically important treatment effects can be attained through the manipulation of the central nervous system (CNS) cholinergic system. Second-generation anticholinesterases and selective muscarinic and nicotinic receptor agonists will receive increasing attention as potential therapeutic approaches over the next decade. Other treatment approaches are also beginning to be evaluated (for example, agents affecting amyloid deposition directly).

## CHEMISTRY

The molecular structure of tacrine is shown in Figure 33.3.24–1. Tacrine is metabolized to a number of hydroxylated products, including 1-OH-tacrine, which is being developed

as velnacrine (Mentane) for the treatment of dementia of the Alzheimer's type.

## PHARMACOLOGICAL ACTIONS

### Pharmacokinetics

Tacrine is absorbed rapidly from the gastrointestinal tract. Peak plasma concentrations are reached about 90 minutes after oral dosing. Tacrine is rapidly metabolized and is cleared by the hepatic route. The half-life of tacrine is about three to four hours, thereby necessitating three-times-daily dosing.

### Pharmacodynamics

The primary mechanism of action of tacrine is reversible, nonacylating inhibition of acetylcholinesterase, the enzyme that catabolizes acetylcholine. The inhibition of the enzyme results in high concentrations of acetylcholine in the synaptic clefts. Some data indicate that tacrine also affects excitatory amino acids (for example, glutamate and aspartate), potassium channels, and biogenic amine systems, although the contribution of those pharmacodynamic effects to the clinical effects of tacrine is not known.

## EFFECTS ON SPECIFIC ORGANS AND SYSTEMS

In addition to its effects on cognitive performance, tacrine affects the liver and the parasympathetic nervous system. Tacrine is associated with an increase in hepatic enzymes—serum glutamic-oxaloacetic transaminase (SGOT) and serum glutamic-pyruvic transaminase (SGPT)—in 25 to 30 percent of all patients. Because of its cholinomimetic properties, tacrine causes activation of the parasympathetic nervous system, resulting in all the usual signs and symptoms of muscarinic activity: nausea, vomiting, diarrhea, and other autonomic symptoms.

## THERAPEUTIC INDICATIONS

The only indication for tacrine at this time is the treatment of mildly to moderately demented patients with dementia of the Alzheimer's type. The efficacy of tacrine in mildly demented patients and in patients with other forms of dementia has not been studied at this time. Tacrine was approved for clinical use primarily on the basis of two large multicenter placebo-controlled studies, although a number of other studies with various designs have also demonstrated the clinical efficacy of tacrine. The two studies demonstrated tacrine's beneficial effect as measured both by a specific cognitive rating scale and by a clinically based global impression scale.

## PRECAUTIONS AND ADVERSE REACTIONS

The data presented here are based on studies of about 10,000 patients given tacrine. The safety data base for tacrine will expand quickly now that it has been introduced into clinical practice. On the basis of the available studies, researchers believe that about 70 percent of all patients started on tacrine will be able to tolerate long-term treatment with the drug. The most troublesome and common side effects are potentially significant elevations in hepatic transaminase levels in 25 to 30 percent of the patients, nausea and vomiting in about 20 percent of the patients, and diarrhea and other cholinergic symptoms in about 11 percent of the patients. Aside from elevations in transaminase levels, the most common specific adverse effects associated with tacrine treatment are nausea, vomiting, myalgia, anorexia, and rash, but only nausea, vomiting, and anorexia have been found to have a clear relation to the dosage. Decreases in weight, eructation, and increased sweating may also be caused by tacrine treatment, but those effects occur in less than 2 percent of tacrine-treated patients. Transaminase elevations characteristically develop during the first 6 to 12 weeks of treatment, and cholinergically mediated events are dosage-related. No significant effects of tacrine treatment have been seen in vital signs, cardiac function as indicated by electrocardiograms (ECGs), or laboratory measures of anything other than transaminases. Although a low incidence of white blood cell dyscrasias (for example, neutropenia, leukopenia, and agranulocytosis) has been associated with a metabolite of tacrine (1-hydroxytacrine, velnacrine), there is no evidence at this time that such blood dyscrasias are associated with tacrine treatment.

### Hepatoxicity

Tacrine is clearly associated with increases in the plasma concentrations of alanine aminotransferase (ALT) and aspartate aminotransferase (AST). The ALT measurement is the more sensitive indicator for the hepatic effects of tacrine. About 50 percent of tacrine-treated patients show ALT concentrations higher than the upper limit of normal (>ULN), about 25 to 30 percent of the patients show ALT concentrations higher than three times the upper limit of normal (>3× ULN); and about 2 percent of the patients have ALT concentrations higher than 20 times the upper limit of normal (>20×ULN). Women are more likely than men to have elevated ALT concentrations, as evidenced by 54 percent of women with ALT values >ULN, compared with 43 percent of men with ALT values >ULN. The development of elevated ALT concentrations is not correlated with age or weight. About 95 percent of tacrine-treated patients who show elevated ALT concentrations evidence that effect in the first 18 weeks of treatment. The mean time to the development of ALT concentrations >3×ULN is nine weeks, but patients with higher elevations show those elevations sooner than do patients with lower elevations. For example, the mean time to the development of ALT concentrations >10×ULN is six

weeks. The average length of time for elevated ALT concentrations to return to normal after stopping tacrine treatment is four weeks.

The development of elevated ALT concentrations does not necessarily indicate that tacrine treatment must be stopped or, if stopped, that tacrine treatment cannot be restarted once the ALT concentrations have returned to normal. Specific guidelines for the treatment of patients with elevated ALT concentrations are suggested in the discussion of dosage and administration. Virtually all tacrine-treated patients with elevations in ALT concentrations have been asymptomatic, although jaundice has been associated with rare cases. Currently available clinical data indicate that all patients have recovered from their tacrine-associated ALT concentration elevations, and no cases of hepatic failure or death have been reported. However, the possibility of such extreme outcomes remains possible, thus warranting monitoring of the hepatic enzymes during tacrine treatment.

## DRUG INTERACTIONS

Data on drug interactions with tacrine are not available at this time, but tacrine should be used cautiously with drugs that also possess cholinomimetic activity. The coadministration of tacrine and drugs that have cholinergic antagonist activity (for example, tricyclic drugs) is probably counterproductive.

## LABORATORY INTERFERENCES

No information is currently available on laboratory interferences associated with tacrine administration.

## DOSAGE AND ADMINISTRATION

Before the initiation of tacrine treatment, a complete physical and laboratory examination should be conducted, with special attention to liver function tests and baseline hematological indexes. Treatment should be initiated at 40 mg a day and then raised by 40 mg a day increments every six weeks up to 160 mg a day; the patient's tolerance of each dosage is indicated by the absence of unacceptable side effects and elevated ALT concentrations. Some small studies and case reports have used dosages up to 200 mg a day, but those higher dosages should probably be avoided at this time. Tacrine should be given three or four times daily—ideally one hour before meals, since the absorption of tacrine is reduced by about 25 percent when it is taken with meals or within two hours after meals.

### Management of ALT Concentration Elevations

Although experience regarding the management of ALT concentration elevations is based only on the research populations, specific guidelines have been proposed. For routine monitoring of hepatic enzymes, AST and ALT concentrations should be measured weekly for the first 18 weeks, every month for the second four months, and every three months thereafter. Weekly assessments of the AST and ALT concentrations should be performed for at least six weeks after any increase in dosage. For patients with elevated

ALT concentrations between $3 \times$ ULN and $5 \times$ ULN, their ALT concentrations should be monitored weekly, and the tacrine dosage should not be increased until the ALT concentration drops to below $3 \times$ ULN. For patients with ALT concentrations $\geq 5 \times$ ULN, the clinician should stop tacrine immediately, monitor ALT concentrations weekly, and not rechallenge the patients with tacrine until the ALT concentrations return to the normal range. When tacrine treatment is reinitiated, the same upward titration schedule can be followed, but ALT concentrations should be assessed weekly. For patients with ALT concentrations greater than $10 \times$ ULN, the clinician should stop tacrine and monitor the patients until their ALT concentrations return to normal; the decision to rechallenge the patients should be based on a careful assessment of the risk-benefit ratio for each patient. For any patient with elevated ALT concentrations and jaundice, tacrine treatment should be stopped, and the patients should not be given the drug again.

## References

Chatellier G, Lacomblez L, Groupe Francais d'Etude de la Tetrahydroaminoacridine: Tacrine (tetrahydroaminoacridine; THA) and lecithin in senile dementia of the Alzheimer's type: A multicentre trial. Br J Med *300*: 495, 1990.

Davis K L, Thal L J, Gamzu E R, Davis C S, Woolson R F, Gracon S I, Drachman D A, Schneider L S, Whitehouse P J, Hoover T M, Morris J C, Kawas C H, Knopman D S, Earl N I, Kumar V, Doody R S, Tacrine Collaborative Study Group: A double-blind, placebo-controlled multicenter study of tacrine for Alzheimer's disease. N Engl J Med *327*: 1253, 1992.

Eager S, Levy R, Sahakian B J: Tacrine in Alzheimer's disease. Lancet *337*: 989, 1991.

Eager S, Morant N, Levy R, Sahakian B: Tacrine in Alzheimer's disease: Time course of changes in cognitive function and practice effects. Br J Psychiatry *160*: 36, 1992.

Ebmeier K P, Hunter R, Curran S M, Dougal N J, Murray C L, Wyper D J, Patterson J, Hanson M T, Siegfried K, Goodwin G M: Effects of a single dose of the acetylcholinesterase inhibitor velnacrine on recognition memory and regional cerebral blood flow in Alzheimer's disease. Psychopharmacology *108*: 103, 1992.

Farlow M, Gracon S I, Hershey L A, Lewis K W, Sadowsky C H, Dolan-Ureno J, Tacrine Study Group: A controlled trial of tacrine in Alzheimer's disease. JAMA *268*: 2523, 1992.

Ford J M, Truman C A, Wilcock G K, Roberts C J C: Serum concentrations of tacrine hydrochloride predict its adverse effects in Alzheimer's disease. Clin Pharmacol Ther *53*: 691, 1993.

Freeman S E, Dawson R M: Tacrine: A pharmacological review. Prog Neurobiol *36*: 257, 1991.

Gauthier S, Bouchard R, Lamontagne A, Bailey P, Bergman H, Ratner J, Tesfaye Y, Saint-Martin M, Bacher Y, Carrier L, Charbonneau R, Clarfield A M, Germain M, Kissel C, Krieger M, Suchnir S, Masson H, Morin J, Nair V, Neirinck L, Suissa S: Tetrahydroaminoacridine-lecithin combination treatment in patients with intermediate-stage Alzheimer's disease: Results of a Canadian double-blind, crossover, multicenter study. N Engl J Med *322*: 1272, 1990.

Jaen J C, Davis R E: Cholinergic therapies for Alzheimer's disease: Acetylcholinesterase inhibitors of current clinical interest. Curr Opin Invest Drugs *2*: 363, 1993.

Jenike M A, Albert M S, Heller H, Gunther J, Goff D: Oral physostigmine treatment for patients with presenile and senile dementia of the Alzheimer's type: A double-blind placebo-controlled trial. J Clin Psychiatry *51*: 3, 1990.

Miller S W, Mahoney J M, Jann M W: Therapeutic frontiers in Alzheimer's disease. Pharmacotherapy *12*: 217, 1992.

Minthon L, Gustafson L, Dalfelt G, Hagberg B, Nilsson K, Risberg J, Rosen I, Seiving B, Wendt P E: Oral tetrahydroaminoacridine treatment of Alzheimer's disease evaluated clinically and by regional cerebral blood flow and EEG. Dementia *4*: 32, 1993.

Puri S K, Ho I, Hsu R, Lassman H B: Multiple dose pharmacokinetics, safety, and tolerance of velnacrine (HP 029) in healthy elderly subjects: A potential therapeutic agent for Alzheimer's disease. J Clin Pharmacol *30*: 948, 1990.

Rupniak N M J: Profile of cholinomimetic drugs in primates: Status of screens for potential Alzheimer therapies. Drug Dev Res *27*: 77, 1992.

Williams M: Tacrine-recommendation for approval. Curr Opin Invest Drugs *2*: 541, 1993.

# 33.3.25 / Thyroid Hormones

Thyroid hormones are used in psychiatry as adjuvants to antidepressants, often in an attempt to convert an antidepressant-nonresponsive patient into an antidepressant-responsive patient. Thyroid hormones have also been used in the treatment rapid-cycling bipolar I disorder patients. The most commonly used thyroid hormone is L-triiodothyronine ($T_3$, liothyronine) (Cytomel). Thyroxine ($T_4$, levothyroxine) (Levoxine, Levothroid, Synthroid) is sometimes used for the same indications.

## CHEMISTRY

The molecular structures of thyroxine and L-triiodothyronine are shown in Figure 33.3.25–1. Both endogenous thyroxine and exogenous thyroxine are converted into triiodothyronine in the body.

## PHARMACOLOGICAL ACTIONS

### Pharmacokinetics

Thyroid hormones are administered orally, and their absorption from the gastrointestinal tract is variable. Absorption is increased if the drug is administered while the patient's stomach is empty. The half-life of thyroxine is six to seven days, and the half-life of L-triiodothyronine is one to two days.

### Pharmacodynamics

The mechanism of action for thyroid hormone effects on antidepressant efficacy is unknown, but interactions with the β-adrenergic receptors may be involved.

## EFFECTS ON SPECIFIC ORGANS AND SYSTEMS

The effects of the drugs thyroxine and L-triiodothyronine on specific organs and systems are the same as the effects of endogenous thyroid hormones, and the symptoms of toxicity and overdose are the symptoms of hyperthyroidism. Thyroid hormones affect most of the body's organs and systems, especially the cardiovascular system.

## THERAPEUTIC INDICATIONS

The major indication for thyroid hormones in psychiatry is as adjuvants to antidepressants. There is no correlation between the laboratory measures of thyroid function

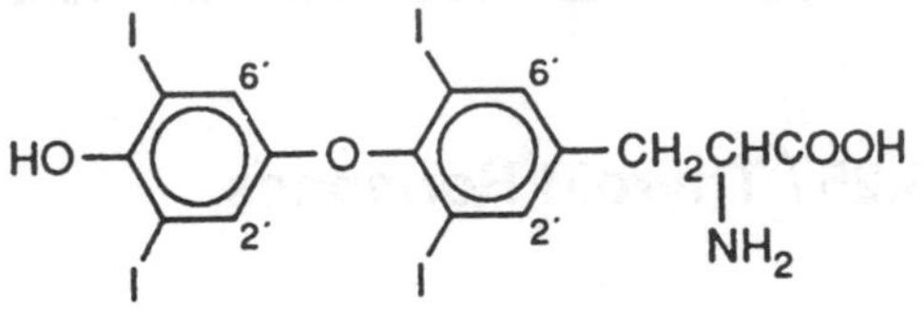

**Figure 33.3.25–1.** Molecular structures of the thyroid hormones.

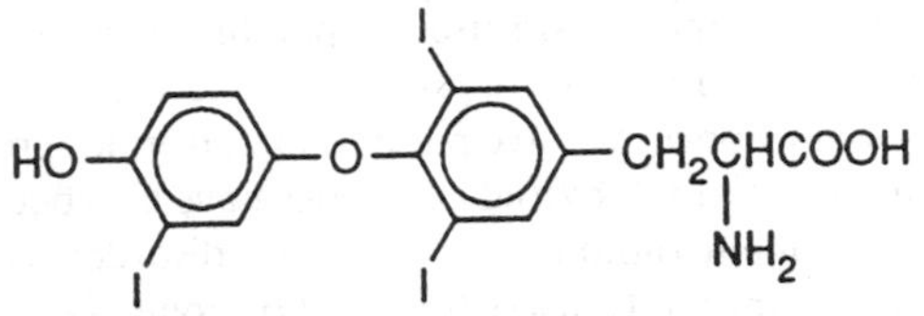

and the response to thyroid hormone supplementation of antidepressants. If a patient has been nonresponsive to a six-week course of an antidepressant at an appropriate dosage, adjuvant therapy with either lithium (Eskalith) or a thyroid hormone is an alternative. Most clinicians use adjuvant lithium before trying a thyroid hormone. The available clinical data indicate that L-triiodothyronine is more effective than thyroxine. Although several controlled trials have indicated that the use of L-triiodothyronine converts 33 to 75 percent of antidepressant nonresponders to responders, several other studies have failed to support that finding.

## PRECAUTIONS AND ADVERSE REACTIONS

The most common adverse effects associated with thyroid hormones are weight loss, palpitations, nervousness, diarrhea, abdominal cramps, sweating, tachycardia, increased blood pressure, tremors, headache, and insomnia. Osteoporosis may also occur with long-term treatment. Overdoses of thyroid hormones can lead to cardiac failure and death.

Thyroid hormones should not be administered to patients with cardiac disease, angina, or hypertension. The hormones are contraindicated in thyrotoxicosis and uncorrected adrenal insufficiency and in patients with acute myocardial infarctions. Thyroid hormones can be administered safely to pregnant women, because the thyroid hormones do not cross the placenta. Thyroid hormones are minimally excreted in the breast milk and have not been shown to cause problems in nursing babies.

## DRUG INTERACTIONS

Thyroid hormones can potentiate the effects of warfarin (Coumadin) and other anticoagulants by increasing the catabolism of clotting factors. Thyroid hormones may increase the insulin requirement for diabetic patients. Sympathomimetics and thyroid hormones should not be coadministered because of the risk of cardiac decompensation.

## LABORATORY INTERFERENCES

Thyroxine has not been reported to interfere with any laboratory test. L-Triiodothyronine, however, causes a suppression in the release of endogenous $T_4$, thereby lowering the value of any thyroid function test dependent on the measure of $T_4$. The value for thyroid-stimulating hormone (TSH) is not affected by either thyroxine or L-triiodothyronine administration.

## DOSAGE AND ADMINISTRATION

L-Triiodothyronine is available in 5, 25, and 50 μg tablets. Thyroxine is available in 12.5, 25, 50, 75, 88, 100, 112, 125, 150, 175, 200, and 300 μg tablets; it is also available in a 200 and 500 μg parenteral form. The dosage of L-triiodothyronine is 25 or 50 μg a day added to the patient's antidepressant regimen. L-Triiodothyronine has been used as an adjuvant for all the available antidepressant drugs. An adequate trial of L-triiodothyronine supplementation should last 7 to 14 days. If L-triiodothyronine supplementation is successful, it should be continued for two months and then tapered at the rate of 12.5 μg a day every three to seven days.

### References

Bauer M S, Whybrow P P: Rapid cycling bipolar affective disorder: II. Treatment of refractory rapid cycling with high-dose levothyroxine: A preliminary study. Arch Gen Psychiatry *47*: 435, 1990.
Joffe R T: Triiodothyronine potentiation of fluoxetine in depressed patients. Can J Psychiatry *37*: 48, 1992.
Joffe R T: Triiodothyronine potentiation of the antidepressant effect of phenelzine. J Clin Psychiatry *49*: 409, 1988.
Joffe R T, Singer W: A comparison of triiodothyronine and thyroxine in the potentiation of tricyclic antidepressants. Psychiatry Res *32*: 241, 1990.
Stein D, Anvi A: Thyroid hormones in the treatment of affective disorders. Acta Psychiatr Scand *77*: 623, 1988.
Thase M E, Kupfer D K, Jarrett D B: Treatment of imipramine-resistant recurrent depression: I. An open clinical trial of adjunctive L-triiodothyronine. J Clin Psychiatry *50*: 385, 1989.

# 33.3.26 / Trazodone and Nefazodone

Trazodone (Desyrel) and nefazodone are effective in the treatment of depressive disorders. Trazodone and nefazodone are structurally unrelated to the tricyclic and tetracyclic drugs used to treat depressive disorders, the monoamine oxidase inhibitors (MAOIs), serotonin-specific reuptake inhibitors, and other currently available antidepressant drugs.

Trazodone differs from tricyclic and tetracyclic drugs and from monoamine oxidase inhibitors in having almost no anticholinergic adverse effects. Trazodone is also distinctive in having more marked sedative effects than those found with other antidepressants.

Nefazodone is distinct from trazodone in its pharmacological effects and its adverse-effect profile, especially its lack of sedation. Nefazodone has not yet been approved by the U.S. Food and Drug Administration (FDA), but approval is likely in the near future.

# TRAZODONE

## Chemistry

Trazodone is a triazolopyridine derivative, which shares the triazolo ring structure with alprazolam (Xanax), a benzodiazepine with possible antidepressant effects (Figure 33.3.26–1).

## Pharmacological Actions

**Pharmacokinetics.** Trazodone is readily absorbed from the gastrointestinal tract, reaches peak plasma levels in one to two hours, and has a half-life of 6 to 11 hours. Trazodone is metabolized in the liver, and 75 percent of its metabolites are excreted in the urine.

**Pharmacodynamics.** Trazodone has its therapeutic effects as a relatively specific inhibitor of serotonin reuptake. One active metabolite of trazodone, *m*-chloropheny-piperazine, also possesses some postsynaptic serotonin activity. The adverse effects of trazodone are partially mediated by $\alpha_1$-adrenergic antagonisms and antihistaminergic activity.

## Effects on Specific Organs and Systems

Besides its effects on the central nervous system, trazodone has relatively few effects on organs and systems. The effects it does have are primarily the result of its $\alpha_1$-adrenergic antagonism, which can affect vascular tone and result in orthostatic hypotension. The drug is also associated with gastric irritation. Relatively rare among the antidepressants is trazodone's association with priapism, which is also probably a result of its $\alpha_1$-adrenergic antagonist activity.

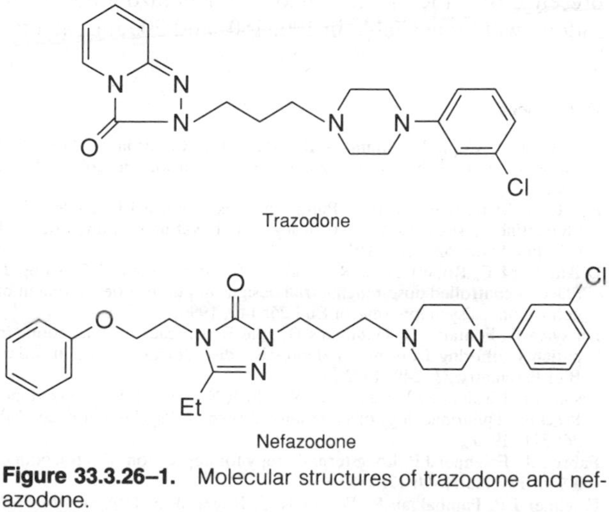

**Figure 33.3.26–1.** Molecular structures of trazodone and nefazodone.

## Therapeutic Indications

**Depressive disorders.** The primary indication for the use of trazodone is major depressive disorder. Trazodone is as effective as the standard antidepressants in the short-term and long-term treatment of major depressive disorder. The drug is particularly effective at improving sleep quality—increasing total sleep time, decreasing the number and the duration of nighttime awakenings, and decreasing the amount of rapid eye movement (REM) sleep. Unlike tricyclic drugs, trazodone does not decrease stage 4 sleep.

**Insomnia.** The marked sedative qualities of trazodone and its favorable effects on sleep architecture have suggested to many clinicians that it would be effective as a hypnotic, and a number of clinicians have used trazodone effectively as a hypnotic. It has also been used effectively as a hypnotic in combination with less sedating psychotropic drugs. Trazodone has been reported to be useful in treating fluoxetine (Prozac)-induced insomnia. The usual dosage is 50 to 100 mg at bedtime.

**Other indications.** Some data indicate that trazodone may be useful in low dosages for controlling severe agitation in elderly patients. A few case reports and uncontrolled trials of trazodone have indicated its usefulness for the treatment of depression with marked anxiety symptoms and for panic disorder with agoraphobia. The final evaluation of the use of trazodone for those disorders requires further research.

## Precautions and Adverse Reactions

The most common adverse effects associated with trazodone are sedation, orthostatic hypotension, dizziness, headache, and nausea. As a result of $\alpha_1$-adrenergic blockade, dry mouth is present in some patients. Trazodone may also cause gastric irritation in some patients. The drug is not associated with the usual anticholinergic adverse effects, such as urinary retention and constipation. A few case reports have noted an association between trazodone and arrhythmias in patients with preexisting premature ventricular contractions or mitral valve prolapse.

Trazodone is relatively safe in overdose attempts. No fatalities from trazodone overdoses have been reported when the drug was taken alone; however, there have been fatalities when trazodone was taken with other drugs. The symptoms of an overdose include the loss of muscle coordination, nausea and vomiting, and drowsiness. Trazodone does not have the quinidinelike antiarrhythmic effects of imipramine (Tofranil).

Trazodone is associated with the rare occurrence of priapism, prolonged erection in the absence of sexual stimuli. Patients should be advised to tell their clinicians if erections are gradually becoming frequent or prolonged. In such cases, physicians should consider switching the patients to another antidepressant medication. Untreated priapism can lead to impotence. A patient who experiences priapism while taking trazodone should stop taking the drug and consult a physician immediately. One effective treatment for priapism involves the intracavernosal injection of a 1 µg per mL solution of epinephrine (an α-adrenergic agonist). Other forms of sexual dysfunction may also occur with trazodone treatment.

The use of trazodone is contraindicated in pregnant and nursing women. Trazodone should be used with caution in patients with hepatic and renal diseases.

### Drug Interactions

Trazodone potentiates the central nervous system depressant effects of other centrally acting drugs and alcohol. The combination of MAOIs and trazodone should be avoided. Concurrent use of trazodone and antihypertensives may cause hypotension. Electroconvulsive therapy (ECT) concurrent with trazodone administration should also be avoided.

### Laboratory Interferences

No known laboratory interferences are associated with the administration of trazodone.

### Dosage and Administration

Trazodone is available in tablets that can be divided into 50, 100, 150, and 300 mg amounts. The usual starting dose is 50 mg orally the first day. The dosage can be increased to 50 mg orally twice daily on the second day and possibly 50 mg orally three times daily on the third and fourth days if sedation or orthostatic hypotension does not become a problem. The therapeutic range for trazodone is 200 to 600 mg a day in divided doses. Some reports indicate that dosages of 400 to 600 mg a day are required for maximal therapeutic effects; other reports indicate that 300 to 400 mg a day is sufficient. The dosage may be titrated up to 300 mg a day; then the patient can be evaluated for the need for further dosage increases on the basis of the presence or the absence of signs of clinical improvement.

## NEFAZODONE

### Chemistry

Nefazodone is a phenylpiperazine analogue of trazodone. Its molecular structure is shown in Figure 33.3.26–1.

### Pharmacological Actions

**Pharmacokinetics.** The pharmacokinetic parameters for nefazodone have not yet been reported. However, nefazodone does have two active metabolites. Hydroxynefazodone has a pharmacodynamic profile similar to the parent compound. The second metabolite, which is also a metabolite of trazodone, is *m*-chlorophenylpiperazine, which possesses some postsynaptic serotonin activity.

**Pharmacodynamics.** The primary pharmacodynamic effects of nefazodone are antagonism of the serotonin type 2 (5-HT$_2$) receptor and its effects as a weak inhibitor of serotonin reuptake. That combination of serotonergic effects may also result in a sensitization of 5-HT$_{1A}$ receptors. Although nefazodone has some mild short-term norepinephrine reuptake

blocking activity, that effect does not seem to be relevant to its long-term effects. In contrast to trazodone, nefazodone lacks antagonist activity at α-adrenergic and histaminergic receptors. Thus, nefazodone will probably have a much more favorable side-effect profile than does trazodone; specifically, nefazodone is not likely to be associated with sedation or orthostatic hypotension.

### Therapeutic Indications

Nefazodone has not yet been approved by the FDA for use in the United States. However, the drug will probably receive FDA approval as a safe and effective treatment for depressive disorders on the basis of the positive results of several well-controlled efficacy studies. Preliminary clinical reports indicate that nefazodone may also be an effective treatment for premenstrual dysphoric disorder, and preliminary preclinical reports indicate that nefazodone may be effective in the management of chronic pain disorder.

### Precautions and Adverse Reactions

The adverse-effect profile for nefazodone has not yet been reported in the literature, but its relatively specific effects on the serotonin system indicate that the side-effect profile will be fairly benign. Nefazodone will probably not produce the sedation, orthostatic hypotension, and priapism that have been associated with trazodone use.

### Drug Interactions and Laboratory Interferences

The presence or the absence of drug interactions and laboratory interferences with nefazodone has not yet been reported in the literature.

### Dosage and Administration

On the basis of the clinical studies to date, the recommended dosage of nefazodone will probably be in the range of 300 to 500 mg a day; some data indicate that dosages of less than 300 mg a day and dosages of more than 500 mg a day are less effective, thus suggesting the presence of a therapeutic window for nefazodone. Nefazodone will be available in 100, 150, and 200 mg tablets.

### References

Archibald D, Copp J, Gammans R, Hardy D, Robinson D: Dose and antidepressant response to nefazodone. Clin Neuropharmacol *15*: 327B, 1992.

Beasley C M Jr, Dornseif B E, Pultz J A, Bosomworth J C, Sayler M E: Fluoxetine versus trazodone: Efficacy and activating-sedating effects. J Clin Psychiatry *52*: 294, 1991.

D'Amico M F, Robert D L, Robinson D S, Schwiderski U E, Copp J: Placebo-controlled dose-ranging trial designs in phase II development of nefazodone. Psychopharmacol Bull *26*: 147, 1990.

Dassylva B, Fontaine R, Gammans D, Elie R: Efficacy of nefazodone in patients suffering from major depressive disorder and panic disorder. Biol Psychiatry *31*: 249, 1992.

Eison A S, Eison M S, Torrente J R, Wright R N, Yocca F D: Nefazodone: Preclinical pharmacology of a new antidepressant. Psychopharmacol Bull *26*: 311, 1990.

Fabre L F, Feighner J P: Long-term therapy for depression with trazodone. J Clin Psychiatry *44*: 17, 1983.

Feighner J P, Pambakian R, Fowler R C, Boyer W F, D'Amico M F: A comparison of nefazodone, imipramine, and placebo in patients with moderate to severe depression. Psychopharmacol Bull *25*: 219, 1989.

Gammans R, Breuel H, Roberts D, Kensler T, Ecker J, Robinson D: Cardiovascular effects of nefazodone and imipramine in elderly volunteers. Clin Neuropharmacol *15*: 332B, 1992.

Greenblatt D J, Friedman H, Burstein E S, Scavone J M, Blyden G T, Ochs H R, Miller I G, Harmatz J S, Shader R I: Trazodone kinetics: Effects of age, gender, obesity. Clin Pharmacol Ther *42*: 193, 1987.

Himmelhoch J M: Cardiovascular effects of trazodone in humans. J Clin Psychopharmacol *1* (6, Suppl): 76S, 1981.

Mouret J, Lemoine P, Minuit M P, Benkelfat C, Renardet M: Effects of trazodone on the sleep of depressed subjects: A polygraphic study. Psychopharmacology *95*: S37, 1988.

Sharpley A L, Walsh A E, Cowen P J: Nefazodone, a novel antidepressant, may increase REM sleep. Biol Psychiatry *31*: 1070, 1992.

Thompson J W Jr, Ware M R, Blashfield R K: Psychotropic medication and priapism: A comprehensive review. J Clin Psychiatry *51*: 430, 1990.

## 33.3.27 / Tricyclic and Tetracyclic Drugs (Antidepressants)

The group of drugs discussed here are widely known as the tricyclic antidepressants and the tetracyclic antidepressants (both commonly abbreviated as the TCAs). The drugs, along with the monoamine oxidase inhibitors (MAOIs), are often considered the classic antidepressant drugs. Although depressive disorders were the initial indications for the drugs, they are effective in a wide range of disorders, including panic disorder, generalized anxiety disorder, posttraumatic stress disorder, obsessive-compulsive disorder, eating disorders, and pain disorder. Therefore, it seems at least misleading, if not incorrect, to call the drugs antidepressants. For that reason, in this textbook they are referred to as the tricyclic and tetracyclic drugs.

The tricyclic drugs share many pharmacokinetic and pharmacodynamic properties and possess similar adverse reaction profiles. Three tetracyclic drugs were initially introduced as being significantly different from the tricyclics; however, further study and clinical use have shown that the tetracyclic drugs and the tricyclic drugs can best be conceptualized as constituting one large family of drugs. They are sometimes referred to as the heterocyclic drugs, which potentially include monocyclic, dicyclic, tricyclic, and tetracyclic drugs. That term is not used in this textbook because it is an overinclusive classification of a diverse group of drugs with no single side-effect or therapeutic profile.

### CHEMISTRY

All tricyclics have a three-ring nucleus in their molecular structures (Figure 33.3.27–1). Imipramine (Tofranil), amitriptyline (Elavil), clomipramine (Anafranil), trimipramine (Surmontil), and doxepin (Adapin, Sinequan) are called tertiary amines because two methyl groups are on the nitrogen atom of the side chain. Desipramine (Norpramin, Pertofrane), nortriptyline (Pamelor, Aventyl), and protriptyline (Vivactil) are called secondary amines because only one methyl group is in that position. The tertiary amines are metabolized into their corresponding secondary amines in the body.

The classification of tetracyclic drugs is arbitrarily based on a gross count of the number of rings in their molecular structures. Amoxapine (Asendin), a dibenzoxazepine, is a derivative of the antipsychotic drug loxapine (Loxitane) and has a cyclic side chain off the three-ring nucleus, for a total of four rings. Maprotiline (Ludiomil) is a tetracyclic with the same side chain as desipramine; its fourth ring bridges the center of the standard tricyclic nucleus. Mianserin is a tetra-

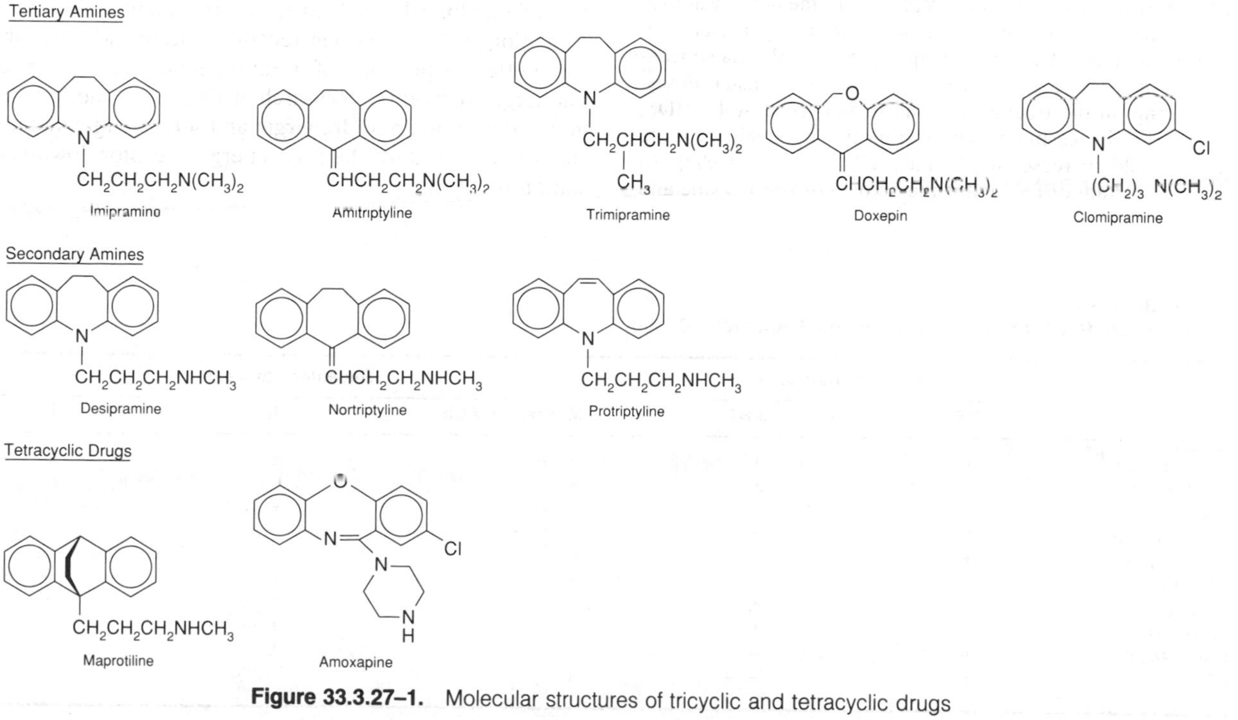

**Figure 33.3.27–1.** Molecular structures of tricyclic and tetracyclic drugs

cyclic drug whose side chain has been cyclized to form a fourth ring; mianserin is not currently available for clinical use in the United States.

## PHARMACOLOGICAL ACTIONS

### Pharmacokinetics

Absorption from oral administration of most tricyclics and tetracyclics is incomplete, and there is significant metabolism from the first-pass effect. Imipramine pamoate is a depot form of the drug for intramuscular (IM) administration; indications for the use of that preparation are limited. Protein binding is usually more than 75 percent, the lipid solubility is high, and the volume of distribution ranges from 10 to 30 L per kg for tertiary amines to 20 to 60 L per kg for secondary amines. The tertiary amines are demethylated to form the related secondary amines. The ratio of methylated to demethylated forms varies widely from person to person. The tricyclic nucleus is oxidized in the liver, conjugated with glucuronic acid, and excreted. The 7-hydroxymetabolite of amoxapine has potent dopamine-blocking activity, thus causing the antipsychoticlike neurological and endocrinological adverse effects that are seen with the drug. The half-lives of the tricyclic and tetracyclic drugs vary from 10 to 70 hours, but nortriptyline, maprotiline, and particularly protriptyline can have longer half-lives. The long half-lives allow all the compounds to be given once daily; five to seven days are needed to reach steady-state plasma levels.

Because it has been recognized that many tricyclic drugs are metabolized by the hepatic enzyme $P_{450}IID6$ (CYP2D6) the Food and Drug Administration (FDA) has recommended including the following precaution for prescribing physicians:

The biochemical activity of the drug metabolizing enzyme cytochrome $P_{450}IID6$ (debrisoquin hydroxylase) is reduced in a subset of the caucasian population (about 7–10% of caucasians are so called "poor metabolizers"); reliable estimates of the prevalence of reduced CYP2D6 enzyme activity among Asian, African and other populations are not yet available. Poor metabolizers have higher than expected plasma concentrations of tricyclic antidepressants when given usual doses. Depending on the fraction of drug metabolized by $P_{450}IID6$, the increase in plasma concentration may be small, or quite large (8 fold increase in plasma AUC of the tricyclic). In addition, certain drugs inhibit the activity of this enzyme and make normal metabolizers resemble poor metabolizers. An individual who is stable on a given dose of tricyclic may become abruptly toxic when given one of these inhibiting drugs as concomitant therapy. The drugs that inhibit cytochrome $P_{450}IID6$, include some that are not metabolized by the enzyme (quinidine; cimetidine) and many that are substrates for $P_{450}IID6$ (most other antidepressants, including fluoxetine, sertraline, and paroxetine; phenothiazines, carbamazepine, and the Type IC antiarrhythmics propafenone and flecainide).

Concomitant use of tricyclic antidepressants with drugs that can inhibit cytochrome $P_{450}IID6$ may require lower doses than usually prescribed for either the tricyclic antidepressant or the other drug. Furthermore, whenever one of these other drugs is withdrawn from co-therapy, an increased dose of tricyclic antidepressants may be required.

### Pharmacodynamics

The short-term effects of tricyclics and tetracyclics are to reduce the reuptake of norepinephrine and serotonin and to block the muscarinic acetylcholine and histamine receptors. The tricyclics and tetracyclics vary in their pharmacodynamic effects (Table 33.3.27–1). Amoxapine, nortriptyline, desipramine, and maprotiline have the least anticholinergic activity; doxepin has the most antihistaminergic activity; clomipramine is the most serotonin-selective of the tricyclics and tetracyclics and is often included with the serotonin-specific reuptake inhibitors (SSRIs), such as fluoxetine (Prozac).

The reuptake blockade of norepinephrine and serotonin by the drugs and the monoamine oxidase inhibition by the MAOIs led to the development of the monoamine hypothesis of mood disorders. Long-term administration of tricyclic and tetracyclic drugs results in a decrease in the number of β-adrenergic receptors and, perhaps, a similar decrease in the number of serotonin type 2 (5-$HT_2$) receptors. The down-regulation of receptors after repeated administration most closely correlates with the time needed for clinical effects to appear in patients. The down-regulation of β-adrenergic receptors occurs whether the initial effect is blocking of noradrenergic receptors or serotonergic receptors. Research with animal models has shown that intact noradrenergic and serotonergic systems are both required for the β-adrenergic receptor down-regulation to occur.

**Table 33.3.27–1**
**Neurotransmitter Effects of Tricyclic and Tetracyclic Drugs**

| Drug | Reuptake Blockade | | Receptor Blockade | | |
|------|------|------|------|------|------|
| | NE | 5-HT | Muscarinic ACh | H₁ | H₂ |
| Imipramine | + | + | + + | ± | ± |
| Desipramine | + + + | ± | ± | − | − |
| Trimipramine | ± | ± | + + | + + | ? |
| Amitriptyline | ± | + + | + + + | + + | + + |
| Nortriptyline | + + | ± | + | ± | ± |
| Protriptyline | + + + | ± | + | + + + | − |
| Amoxapine | + + | ± | + | ± | ? |
| Doxepin | + | ± | + + | + + + | + |
| Maprotiline | + + + | − | + | ± | ? |
| Clomipramine | ± | + + | + | ? | ? |

## EFFECTS ON SPECIFIC ORGANS AND SYSTEMS

The major effects of the tricyclic and tetracyclic drugs are on the central nervous system, although the anticholinergic effects of the drugs produce a diverse range of adverse effects mediated by the autonomic nervous system. In addition to those effects, the tricyclic and tetracyclic drugs have significant effects on the cardiovascular system. In therapeutic dosages the drugs are classified as type 1A antiarrhythmic drugs, since they terminate ventricular fibrillation and can increase the collateral blood supply to an ischemic heart. However, in overdoses the drugs are highly cardiotoxic and cause decreased contractility, increased myocardial irritability, hypotension, and tachycardia.

## THERAPEUTIC INDICATIONS

### Major Depressive Disorder

The treatment of a major depressive episode and the prophylactic treatment of major depressive disorder are the principal indications for using tricyclic and tetracyclic drugs. The drugs are also effective in the treatment of depression in bipolar I disorder patients. Melancholic features, prior major depressive episodes, and a family history of depressive disorders increase the likelihood of a therapeutic response. The treatment of a major depressive episode with psychotic features almost always requires the coadministration of an antipsychotic drug and an antidepressant.

### Mood Disorder Due to a General Medical Condition with Depressive Features

Depression associated with a general medical condition (secondary depression) may respond to tricyclic and tetracyclic drug treatment. The depression may occur after cerebrovascular diseases and central nervous system (CNS) trauma. Depression can also be associated with dementias and movement disorders, such as Parkinson's disease. Depression associated with acquired immune deficiency syndrome (AIDS) may also respond to the drugs.

### Panic Disorder with Agoraphobia

Imipramine is the tricyclic most studied for panic disorder with agoraphobia, but other tricyclic and tetracyclics are also effective. Early reports indicated that small dosages of imipramine (50 mg a day) were often effective; however, recent studies indicate that the usual antidepressant dosages are usually required.

### Generalized Anxiety Disorder

The use of doxepin for the treatment of anxiety disorders is approved by the Food and Drug Administration (FDA). Some research data show that imipramine may also be useful, and some clinicians use a drug containing a combination of chlordiazepoxide and amitriptyline (marketed as Limbitrol) for mixed anxiety and depressive disorders.

### Obsessive-Compulsive Disorder

In the fourth edition of *Diagnostic and Statistical Manual of Mental Disorders* (DSM-IV), obsessive-compulsive disorder is classified under the anxiety disorders. The disorder appears to respond specifically to clomipramine and the serotonin-specific reuptake inhibitors (SSRIs). None of the other tricyclic and tetracyclic drugs appears to be nearly as effective as clomipramine for the disorder.

### Eating Disorders

Both anorexia nervosa and bulimia nervosa have been successfully treated with imipramine and desipramine, although other tricyclics and tetracyclics may also be effective.

### Pain Disorder

Chronic pain disorder, including headache (such as migrane), is often treated with tricyclics and tetracyclics.

### Other Disorders

Childhood enuresis is often treated with imipramine. Peptic ulcer disease can be treated with doxepin, which has marked antihistaminergic effects. Other indications for tricyclics and tetracyclics are narcolepsy, nightmare disorder, and posttraumatic stress disorder. The drugs are sometimes used for children and adolescents with attention-deficit/hyperactivity disorder, sleepwalking disorder, separation anxiety disorder, and sleep terror disorder.

## PRECAUTIONS AND ADVERSE REACTIONS

### Psychiatric Effects

A major adverse effect of all tricyclic and tetracyclic drugs and other antidepressants is the possibility of inducing a manic episode in both bipolar I disorder patients and in patients without a history of bipolar I disorder. Clinicians should watch for that effect in bipolar I disorder patients, especially if substance-induced mania has been a problem in the past. It is prudent to use low dosages of tricyclic and tetracyclic drugs in such patients or to use an agent such as fluoxetine (Prozac) or bupropion (Wellbutrin), which may be less likely to induce a manic episode. Tricyclic and tetracyclic drugs have also been reported to exacerbate psychotic disorders in susceptible patients.

### Anticholinergic Effects

Clinicians should warn patients that anticholinergic effects are common but that the patient may develop a tolerance for them with continued treatment. Amitriptyline, imipramine, trimipramine, and doxepin are the most anticholinergic drugs; amoxapine, nortriptyline, and maprotiline are less anticholinergic; and desipramine may be the least anticholinergic. Anticholinergic effects include dry mouth, constipation, blurred vision, and urinary retention. Sugarless gum, candy, or fluoride lozenges can alleviate the dry mouth. Bethanechol (Urecholine), 25 to 50 mg three or four times a day, may reduce urinary hesitancy and may be helpful in cases of impotence when the drug is taken 30 minutes before sexual intercourse. Narrow-angle glaucoma can also be aggravated by anticholinergic drugs, and the precipitation of glaucoma requires emergency treatment with a miotic agent. Tricyclic and tetracyclic drugs can be used in patients with glaucoma, provided pilocarpine eye drops are administered concurrently. Severe anticholinergic effects can lead to a CNS anticholinergic syndrome with confusion and delirium, especially if tricyclic and tetracyclic drugs are administered with antipsychotics or anticholinergic drugs. Some clinicians have used IM or intravenous (IV) physostigmine (Antilirium, Eserine) as a diagnostic tool to confirm the presence of anticholinergic delirium.

## Sedation

Sedation is a common effect of tricyclic and tetracyclic drugs and may be welcomed if sleeplessness has been a problem. The sedative effect of tricyclic and tetracyclic drugs is a result of serotonergic, cholinergic, and histaminergic ($H_1$) activities. Amitriptyline, trimipramine, and doxepin are the most sedating agents; imipramine, amoxapine, nortriptyline, and maprotiline have some sedating effects; and desipramine and protriptyline are the least sedating agents.

## Autonomic Effects

The most common autonomic effect, partly because of $\alpha_1$-adrenergic blockade, is orthostatic hypotension, which can result in falls and injuries in affected patients. Nortriptyline may be the drug least likely to cause the problem, and some patients respond to fludrocortisone (Florinef), 0.02 to 0.05 mg twice a day. Other possible autonomic effects are profuse sweating, palpitations, and increased blood pressure.

## Cardiac Effects

When administered in their usual therapeutic dosages, the tricyclic and tetracyclic drugs may cause tachycardia, flattened T waves, prolonged QT intervals, and depressed ST segments in the electrocardiographic (ECG) recording. Imipramine has a quinidinelike effect at therapeutic plasma levels and may reduce the number of premature ventricular contractions. Because the drugs prolong conduction time, their use in patients with preexisting conduction defects is contraindicated. In patients with cardiac histories, tricyclic and tetracyclic drugs should be initiated at low dosages, with gradual increases in dosage and monitoring of cardiac functions. At high plasma levels, as seen

in overdoses, the drugs become arrhythmogenic. The agents should be discontinued several days before elective surgery because of the occurrence of hypertensive episodes during surgery in patients receiving tricyclic and tetracyclic drugs.

## Neurological Effects

In addition to the sedation induced by tricyclics and tetracyclics and the possibility of anticholinergic-induced delirium, two tricyclics—desipramine and protriptyline—are associated with psychomotor stimulation. Myoclonic twitches and tremors of the tongue and the upper extremities are common. Rare effects include speech blockage, paresthesia, peroneal palsies, and ataxia.

Amoxapine is unique in causing parkinsonian symptoms, akathisia, and even dyskinesia because of the dopaminergic blocking activity of one of its metabolites. Amoxapine may also cause neuroleptic malignant syndrome in rare cases. Maprotiline may cause seizures when the dosage is increased too quickly or is kept at high levels for too long. Clomipramine and amoxapine may lower the seizure threshold more than do other drugs in the class. As a class, however, the tricyclic and tetracyclic drugs have a relatively low risk for inducing seizures, except in patients who are at risk for seizures (for example, epileptic patients and patients with brain lesions). Although tricyclics and tetracyclics can still be used in such patients, the initial dosages should be lower than usual, and subsequent dosage increases should be gradual.

## Allergic and Hematological Effects

Exanthematous skin rashes are seen in 4 to 5 percent of all patients treated with maprotiline. Jaundice is rare. Agranulocytosis, leukocytosis, leukopenia, and eosinophilia are rare complications of tetracyclic drug treatment. However, a patient who has a sore throat or a fever during the first few months of tricyclic and tetracyclic drug treatment should have a complete blood count (CBC) done immediately.

## Other Adverse Effects

Weight gain, primarily an effect of the blockade of histamine type 2 ($H_2$) receptors, is common. If it is a major problem, changing to a different class of antidepressants may help. Impotence, an occasional problem, is perhaps most often associated with amoxapine because of the drug's blockade of dopamine receptors in the tuberoinfundibular tract. Amoxapine can also cause hyperprolactinemia, galactorrhea, anorgasmia, and ejaculatory disturbances. Other tricyclic and tetracyclic drugs have also been associated with gynecomastia and amenorrhea. Inappropriate secretion of antidiuretic hormone has also been reported with tricyclic and tetracyclic drugs. Other effects include nausea, vomiting, and hepatitis.

## Precautions

The tricyclic and tetracyclic drugs should be avoided during pregnancy. The drugs pass into breast milk and have the potential to cause serious adverse reactions in nursing infants. The drugs should be used with caution in patients with hepatic and renal diseases.

Tricyclics and tetracyclics should not be administered during a course of electroconvulsive therapy (ECT), primarily because of the risk of serious adverse cardiac effects.

## Overdoses

Overdoses with tricyclic and tetracyclic drugs are serious and can often be fatal. Prescriptions for the drugs should be nonrefillable and for no longer than a week at a time for patients who are at risk for suicide attempts. Amoxapine may be more likely than are other tricyclic and tetracyclic drugs to result in death when taken in an overdose, but all drugs in the class can be lethal in an overdose.

Symptoms of an overdose include agitation, delirium, convulsions, hyperactive deep tendon reflexes, bowel and bladder paralysis, dysregulation of the blood pressure and the temperature, and mydriasis. The patient then progresses to coma and perhaps respiratory depression. Cardiac arrhythmias may not respond to treatment. Because of the long half-lives of tricyclic and tetracyclic drugs, patients are at risk for cardiac arrhythmias for three to four days after the overdose, so they should be monitored in an intensive care medical setting.

## DRUG INTERACTIONS

### Antihypertensives

Tricyclic and tetracyclic drugs block the neuronal reuptake of guanethidine (Esimil, Ismelin), which is required for antihypertensive activity. The antihypertensive effects of β-adrenergic receptor antagonists—for example, propranolol (Inderal)— and clonidine (Catapres) may also be blocked by tricyclic and tetracyclic drugs. The coadministration of a tricyclic or tetracyclic drug and α-methyldopa (Aldomet) may cause behavioral agitation.

### Antipsychotics

The plasma levels of tricyclic and tetracyclic drugs and antipsychotics are increased by their coadministration. Antipsychotics also add to the anticholinergic and sedative effects of the tricyclic and tetracyclic drugs.

### CNS Depressants

Opiates, opioids, alcohol, anxiolytics, hypnotics, and over-the-counter cold medications have additive effects by causing CNS depression when coadministered with tricyclic or tetracyclic drugs.

### Sympathomimetics

Tricyclic drug use with sympathomimetic drugs may cause serious cardiovascular effects.

### Oral Contraceptives

Birth control pills may decrease tricyclic and tetracyclic drug plasma levels through the induction of hepatic enzymes.

### Other Interactions

Tricyclic and tetracyclic drug plasma levels may also be increased by acetazolamide (Diamox), acetylsalicylic acid, cimetidine (Tagamet), thiazide diuretics, fluoxetine, and sodium bicarbonate. Decreased plasma levels may be caused by ascorbic acid, ammonium chloride, barbiturates, cigarette smoking, chloral hydrate, lithium (Eskalith), and primidone (Mysoline). Tricyclic drugs that are metabolized by CYP2D6 may interfere with the metabolism of other drugs metabolized by the hepatic enzyme.

## LABORATORY INTERFERENCES

Laboratory interferences with the tricyclic and tetracyclic drugs have not been reported.

## DOSAGE AND ADMINISTRATION

### Choice of Drug

The choice of which tricyclic or tetracyclic to use should be based on the general guidelines outlined in Subsection 33.3.1. All available tricyclic and tetracyclic drugs are equally effective in the treatment of depressive disorders. In the case of an individual patient, however, one tricyclic or tetracyclic may be effective, whereas another one may be ineffective. The adverse effects among the tricyclic and tetracyclic drugs differ (Table 33.3.27–2). The tertiary amine tricyclics tend to produce more adverse effects—including sedation, orthostatic hypotension, and such anticholinergic effects as dry mouth—than do the secondary amines. Among the secondary amine tricyclics, nortriptyline is associated with the least orthostatic hypotension, and desipramine is associated with the least anticholinergic activity. Among the tetracyclic drugs, amoxapine is sometimes recommended for the treatment of a major depressive episode with psychotic features because of the drug's antidopaminergic activity.

Researchers have found differences among the tricyclics and the tetracyclics in their relative abilities to block either serotonin reuptake or norepinephrine reuptake. No study has found that the serotonin-to-norepinephrine ratio for each of the drugs can be used to help choose a specific drug to treat a particular patient. Switching from a strongly serotonergic to a strongly noradrenergic drug or vice versa may be reasonable if the first drug is ineffective in relieving the patient's symptoms.

**Clomipramine.** Clomipramine is an effective antidepressant that is also the first-line drug in the treatment of obsessive-compulsive disorder and, therefore, may be the drug of choice for depressed patients with marked obsessive features. Clomipramine has its major effect as an in-

**Table 33.3.27–2**
**Side-Effect Profile of Tricyclic and Tetracyclic Drugs**

| Drug | Anticholinergic Effects | Sedation | Orthostatic Hypotension | Seizures | Conduction-Abnormalities |
|------|------------------------|----------|-------------------------|----------|--------------------------|
| Tertiary amines | | | | | |
| Amitriptyline | + + + + | + + + + | + + + | + + + | + + + + |
| Doxepin | + + + | + + + + | + + | + + + | + + |
| Imipramine | + + + | + + + | + + + + | + + + | + + + + |
| Trimipramine | + + + + | + + + + | + + + | + + + | + + + + |
| Secondary amines | | | | | |
| Desipramine | + + | + + | + + + | + + | + + + |
| Nortriptyline | + + + | + + + | + | + + | + + + |
| Protriptyline | + + + | + | + + | + + | + + + + |
| Tetracyclics | | | | | |
| Amoxapine | + + + | + + | + | + + + | + + |
| Maprotiline | + + + | + + + | + + | + + + + | + + + |

+ + + +, high; + + +, moderate; + +, low; +, very low

hibitor of serotonin reuptake but may also affect dopaminergic neurotransmission. Clomipramine is more effective than a placebo, amitriptyline, imipramine, and doxepin in the treatment of obsessive-compulsive disorder, although the serotonin-specific reuptake inhibitors (SSRIs) may also be effective. Improvement is usually seen in two to four weeks, but a gradual improvement may continue for the first four to five months of treatment. Like the standard tricyclic and tetracyclic drugs, clomipramine may also be effective in the treatment of panic disorder, phobias, and pain disorder.

## Initiation of Treatment

A routine physical and laboratory examination of a patient to be administered a tricyclic or a tetracyclic should be conducted. The routine laboratory tests should include a complete blood count (CBC), a white blood cell (WBC) count with differential, and serum electrolytes (sequential multichannel autoanalyzer [SMA]-6) with liver function tests (SMA-12). An electrocardiogram (ECG) should probably be obtained for all patients, especially women over 40 and men over 30. The initial dose should be small and should be raised gradually. The clinician can raise the dosage for inpatients more quickly than for outpatients because of the inpatients' close clinical supervision.

The clinician should explain to patients that, although

sleep and appetite may improve in one to two weeks, tricyclics and tetracyclics usually take three to four weeks to have significant antidepressant effects, and a complete trial should last six weeks. The clinician may also explain to patients exactly what the drug treatment plan is if no clinical response is seen after six weeks.

The elderly and children are more sensitive to antidepressant side effects than are young adults. In children, ECG monitoring is needed. A baseline electroencephalogram (EEG) is recommended, as children are sensitive to the epileptogenic effects of antidepressants and are prone to medication-induced constipation.

## Dosage

The available preparations of tricyclic and tetracyclic drugs are presented in Table 33.3.27–3.

**Depressive disorders.** The dosage schedule for the tricyclics and tetracyclics varies among the drugs (Table 33.3.27–4). Imipramine, amitriptyline, doxepin, desipramine, clomipramine, and trimipramine can be started at 75 mg a day. Divided doses at first reduce the severity of the side effects, although most of the dosage should be given at night to help induce sleep if a sedating drug, such as amitriptyline, is used. Eventually, the entire daily dose can be given at bedtime. Protriptyline and less-sedating drugs should be given at least two to three hours before a

**Table 33.3.27–3**
**Tricyclic and Tetracyclic Drug Preparations**

| Drug | Tablets | Capsules | Parenteral | Solution |
|------|---------|----------|------------|----------|
| Imipramine | 10, 25, 50 mg | 75, 100, 125, 150 mg | 12.5 mg/mL | — |
| Desipramine | 10, 25, 50, 75, 100, 150 mg | 25, 50 mg | — | — |
| Trimipramine | — | 25, 50, 100 mg | — | — |
| Amitriptyline | 10, 25, 50, 75, 100, 150 mg | — | 10 mg/mL | — |
| Nortriptyline | — | 10, 25, 50, 75 mg | — | 10 mg/5 mL |
| Protriptyline | 5, 10 mg | — | — | — |
| Amoxapine | 25, 50, 100, 150 mg | — | — | — |
| Doxepin | — | 10, 25, 50, 75, 100, 150 mg | — | 10 mg/mL |
| Maprotiline | 25, 50, 75 mg | — | — | — |
| Clomipramine | — | 25, 50, 75 mg | — | — |

**Table 33.3.27–4**
**Clinical Information for the Tricyclic and Tetracyclic Drugs**

| Generic Name | Trade Name | Usual Adult Dosage Range (mg a day) | Therapeutic Plasma Levels* (ng per mL) |
|---|---|---|---|
| Imipramine | Tofranil | 150–300† | 150–300 |
| Desipramine | Norpramin, Pertofrane | 150–300† | 150–300 |
| Trimipramine | Surmontil | 150–300† | ? |
| Amitriptyline | Elavil | 150–300† | 100–250† |
| Nortriptyline | Pamelor, Aventyl | 50–150 | 50–150 (maximum) |
| Protriptyline | Vivactil | 15–60 | 75–250 |
| Amoxapine | Asendin | 150–400 | ? |
| Doxepin | Adapin, Sinequan | 150–400† | 100–250 |
| Maprotiline | Ludiomil | 150–225 | 150–300 |
| Clomipramine | Anafranil | 150–250 | ? |

*Exact range may vary among laboratories.
†Includes parent compound and desmethyl metabolite.

patient goes to sleep. For outpatients the dosage can be raised to 150 mg a day the second week, 225 mg a day the third week, and 300 mg a day the fourth week. A common clinical mistake is to stop increasing the dosage when the patient is taking less than 250 mg a day and does not show clinical improvement. Doing so can result in a further delay in obtaining a therapeutic response, disenchantment with the treatment, and premature discontinuation of the drug. The clinician should routinely assess the patient's pulse and orthostatic changes in blood pressure while the dosage is being increased.

Nortriptyline should be started at 50 mg a day and raised to 150 mg a day over three or four weeks unless a response occurs at a lower dosage, such as 100 mg a day. Amoxapine should be started at 150 mg a day and raised to 400 mg a day. Protriptyline should be started at 15 mg a day and raised to 60 mg a day. Maprotiline has been associated with an increased incidence of seizures if the dosage is raised too quickly or is maintained at too high a level. Maprotiline should be started at 75 mg a day and maintained at that level for two weeks. The dosage can be increased over four weeks to 225 mg a day but should be kept at that level for only six weeks and then reduced to 175 to 200 mg a day.

**Pain disorder.** Pain disorder patients may be particularly sensitive to side effects when tricyclics or tetracyclics are started. Therefore, it may be prudent to begin with low dosages that are raised in small increments. Some clinicians coadminister benzodiazepines until the patients are stabilized on an antidepressant.

**Children.** In children, imipramine can be initiated at 1.5 mg per kg a day. The dosage can be titrated to no more than 5 mg per kg a day. In enuresis the dosage is usually 50 to 100 mg a day taken at bedtime. Clomipramine can be initiated at 50 mg a day and increased to no more than 3 mg per kg a day or 200 mg a day.

## Failure of Drug Trial and Treatment-Resistant Depression

If a tricyclic or a tetracyclic has been used for four weeks at maximal dosages without a therapeutic effect, the clinician should obtain a plasma level and adjust the dosage

accordingly. If plasma levels are adequate, supplementation with lithium or L-triiodothyronine ($T_3$) (Cytomel) should be considered.

**Lithium.** Lithium (900 to 1,200 mg a day, serum level between 0.6 and 0.8 mEq per L) can be added to the tricyclic or tetracyclic dosage for 7 to 14 days. That approach converts a significant number of nonresponders into responders. The mechanism of action is not known, but the lithium may potentiate the serotonergic neuronal system.

**L-Triiodothyronine.** The addition of 25 to 50 μg a day of $T_3$ to the regimen for 7 to 14 days may convert a tricyclic or tetracyclic nonresponder into a responder. The mechanism of action for $T_3$ augmentation is not known. Empirical data indicate that $T_3$ is more effective than thyroxine ($T_4$) as an adjunct to tricyclic and tetracyclic drugs. If $T_3$ augmentation is successful, the $T_3$ should be continued for two months and then tapered at the rate of 12.5 μg a day every three to seven days.

**MAOIs.** MAOIs should be discontinued for two weeks before initiating treatment with a tricyclic or a tetracyclic. A minimum of a one-week washout is needed when switching from a tricyclic or tetracyclic to an MAOI. The two classes of drugs are sometimes used in combination for resistant depressions. Certain precautions must be taken to avoid hypertensive crises. Desipramine, imipramine, clomipramine, and tranylcypromine (Parnate) should be avoided in combination with MAOIs. A low dosage of a tricyclic should be initiated after at least a one-week washout of the tricyclics. The MAOI is then added, also in a low dosage. Every few days, each of the medications is alternately increased in dosage while the patient is monitored.

## Termination of Short-Term Treatment

Tricyclics and tetracyclics effectively resolve the acute symptoms of depression. If treatment is stopped prematurely, symptom reemergence is likely to occur. To minimize the risk for recurrence or relapse, the clinician should continue the tricyclic or the tetracyclic at the same treatment dosage throughout the course of treatment. When treatment is discontinued, the clinician may reasonably reduce the dosage to three fourths the maximal dosage for another month. At that time, if no symptoms are present, the drug can be tapered by 25 mg (5 mg for protriptyline) every two to three days. The slow tapering process is indicated for most psychotherapeutic drugs; in the case of most tricyclics and tetracyclics, slow tapering avoids a cholinergic rebound syndrome, consisting of nausea, upset stomach, sweating, headache, neck pain, and vomiting. The appearance of that syndrome can be treated by reinstituting a small dosage of the drug and tapering more slowly than before. Several case reports note the appearance of rebound mania or hypomania after the abrupt discontinuation of tricyclic and tetracyclic drugs. If a patient has been treated with lithium augmentation, the clinician should probably taper and stop the lithium first and then the tricyclic or tetracyclic drug. However, clinical studies supporting that approach are lacking, and the guidelines may change as more physicians report their experience with the drug combination.

### Maintenance

Tricyclics and tetracyclics are effective in preventing the recurrence of major depressive episodes. The decision to institute prophylactic treatment is based on the severity and the nature of the disorder in a particular patient. However, increasing data argue for prophylactic treatment in patients with major depressive disorder. Conversely, some data indicate that the long-term use of antidepressants may induce a rapid-cycling bipolar I disorder. Lithium prophylaxis, therefore, has been suggested as an alternative treatment in selected patients who have frequent, episodic, and serious depressive episodes.

Several investigators have noted that neuroendocrine tests may be a guide for deciding when to maintain the use of tricyclics, tetracyclics, and other antidepressant drugs. Specifically, the investigators note that the normalization of a previously abnormal result in a dexamethasone-suppression test or a thyrotropin-releasing hormone (TRH) stimulation test may indicate that a patient can safely discontinue drug treatment. That use of neuroendocrine testing and monitoring is still in the research phases of development.

### Plasma Levels

Research has defined the dose-response curves for a number of the tricyclic and tetracyclic drugs when given to treat depressive disorders. Clinical determinations of plasma levels should be conducted 8 to 12 hours after the last dose and after five to seven days on the same dosage of medication. Because of variations in absorption and metabolism, there is a 30-to-50-fold difference in the plasma levels in humans given the same dosage of a tricyclic or tetracyclic drug. The therapeutic ranges for plasma levels have been determined (Table 33.3.27–4). Nortriptyline is unique in its association with a therapeutic window; that is, plasma levels of more than 150 ng per mL may reduce its efficacy. Clinicians must follow the directions for collection from the testing laboratory and have confidence in the assay procedure used at a particular laboratory.

The use of plasma levels in clinical practice is still an evolving skill. Plasma levels may be useful in confirming compliance, assessing reasons for drug failures, and documenting effective plasma levels for future treatment. Clinicians should always treat the patient and never the plasma level. Some patients have adequate clinical responses with seemingly subtherapeutic plasma levels, and other patients have responses only at supratherapeutic plasma levels without experiencing adverse effects. The latter situation, however, should alert the clinician to monitor the patient's condition with, for example, serial ECG recordings.

### References

Dietch J T, Fine M: The effect of nortriptyline in elderly patients with cardiac conduction disease. J Clin Psychiatry *51*: 65, 1990.
Frank E, Kupfer D J, Perel J M, Cornes C, Jarrett D B, Mallinger A G, Thase M E, McEachran A B, Grochocinski V J: Three-year outcomes for maintenance therapies in recurrent depression. Arch Gen Psychiatry *47*: 1093, 1990.
Haddad L M: Managing tricyclic antidepressant overdose. Am Fam Physician *46*: 153, 1992.
Jick S S, Jick H, Knauss T A, Dean A D: Antidepressants and convulsions. J Clin Psychopharmacol *12*: 241, 1992.
Lejoyeyx M, Rouillon F, Ades J, Gorwood P: Neural symptoms induced by tricyclic antidepressants: Phenomenology and pathophysiology. Acta Psychiatr Scand *85*: 249, 1992.
Levin G M, DeVane C L: A review of cyclic antidepressant-induced blood dyscrasias. Ann Pharmacother *26*: 378, 1992.
Misri S, Sivertz K: Tricyclic drugs in pregnancy and lactation: A preliminary report. Int J Psychiatry Med *21*: 157, 1991.
Nelson J C: Current status of tricyclic antidepressants in psychiatry: Their pharmacology and clinical applications. J Clin Psychiatry *52*: 193, 1991.
Nierenberg A A, Cole J O: Antidepressant adverse drug reactions. J Clin Psychiatry *52*: 40, 1991.
Norman T R: Pharmacokinetic aspects of antidepressant treatment in the elderly. Prog Neuropsychopharmacol Biol Psychiatry *17*: 329, 1993.
Peselow E D, Dunner D L, Fieve R R, Difiglia C: The prophylactic efficacy of tricyclic antidepressants: A five year followup. Prog Neuropsychopharmacol Biol Psychiatry *15*: 71, 1991.
Pohl R, Pandey G N, Yeragani V K, Balon R, Davis J M, Berchou R: β-Receptor responsiveness after desipramine treatment. Psychopharmacology *110*: 37, 1993.
Pollack M H, Rosenbaum J F: Management of antidepressant-induced side effects: A practical guide for the clinician. J Clin Psychiatry *48*: 3, 1987.
Potter W Z, Manji H K: Antidepressants, metabolites, and apparent drug resistance. Clin Neuropharamacol *13*: 545, 1990.
Preskorn S H, Gast G A: Tricyclic antidepressant-induced seizures and plasma drug concentration. J Clin Psychiatry *53*: 160, 1992.
Rouillon F, Serrurier D, Miller H D, Gerard M-J: Prophylactic efficacy of maprotiline on unipolar depression relapse. J Clin Psychiatry *52*: 423, 1991.
Trimble M R: Worldwide use of clomipramine. J Clin Psychiatry *51* (8, Suppl): 51, 1990.
Warnock J K, Knesevich J W: Adverse cutaneous reactions to antidepressants. Am J Psychiatry *145*: 425, 1988.

## 33.3.28 / L-Tryptophan

L-Tryptophan is the amino acid precursor of the neurotransmitter serotonin. L-Tryptophan administration to humans results in increased concentrations of serotonin in the central nervous system. That pharmacological effect led to the use of orally administered L-tryptophan as a hypnotic and as an adjuvant to antidepressant treatment.

In 1989 L-tryptophan and L-tryptophan-containing products were recalled in the United States because of an outbreak of eosinophilia-myalgia syndrome associated with those products. However, those drugs will probably be reintroduced in the United States.

## CHEMISTRY

The molecular structure of L-tryptophan is shown in Figure 33.3.28–1.

## PHARMACOLOGICAL ACTIONS

### Pharmacokinetics

L-Tryptophan is erratically absorbed from the gastrointestinal tract. A significant portion of the drug is metabolized by the liver in a first-pass effect. Absorption of L-tryptophan can be enhanced by taking the drug with a low-protein, high-carbohydrate meal. The half-life of L-tryptophan may be as little as one to two hours; therefore, unless the drug is used as a hypnotic, four-times-daily dosing is necessary to maintain plasma levels.

### Pharmacodynamics

L-Tryptophan has its effects because a portion of the ingested dose crosses the blood-brain barrier, is taken up by serotonergic neurons, and is converted into serotonin, thus raising serotonin concentrations in the central nervous system (CNS).

## EFFECTS ON SPECIFIC ORGANS AND SYSTEMS

Other than the CNS, the major organ system affected by L-tryptophan is the gastrointestinal system, which also contains a high concentration of serotonin. The effects of L-tryptophan on the gastrointestinal system are usually limited to mild gastrointestinal distress.

## THERAPEUTIC INDICATIONS

### Primary Insomnia

The most common indication for L-tryptophan is insomnia, although that indication does not have the approval of the Food and Drug Administration (FDA).

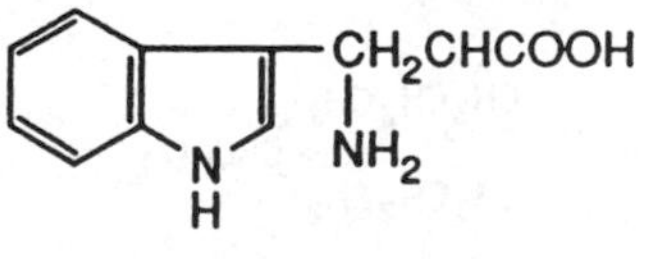

**Figure 33.3.28–1.** Molecular structure of L-tryptophan.

Whether the hypnotic effects of L-tryptophan persist with long-term treatment is not certain. L-Tryptophan is not associated with visuospatial, cognitive, or memory deficits the day after drug ingestion, as are many of the standard hypnotic agents. Low doses of L-tryptophan are not associated with any change in the sleep electroencephalogram (EEG) other than earlier than usual sleep onset; high doses of L-tryptophan are associated with increases in slow-wave sleep.

### Antidepressant Adjuvant Treatment

L-Tryptophan has been used as an adjuvant to tricyclic and tetracyclic drug administration for depressed patients who have not responded to the tricyclic or tetracyclic drug alone. The use of either lithium (Eskalith) or L-triiodothyronine (T₃) (Cytomel) adjuvant therapy with antidepressant nonresponders was more commonly used than was L-tryptophan supplementation when L-tryptophan was still available. L-Tryptophan has also been used as an adjuvant to lithium treatment for bipolar I disorder patients who had incomplete symptom remission with lithium treatment alone.

## PRECAUTIONS AND ADVERSE REACTIONS

Except for experiencing eosinophilia-myalgia syndrome, most patients tolerate moderate doses of L-tryptophan. The only significant adverse effect reported is nausea, which is sometimes compared to the nausea associated with pregnancy. L-Tryptophan has also been associated with hepatotoxicity in rare cases.

### Eosinophilia-Myalgia Syndrome

The symptoms of eosinophilia-myalgia syndrome include fatigue, myalgia, shortness of breath, rashes, and swelling of the extremities. Congestive heart failure and death can occur. The syndrome was related to a contaminant in a single manufacturing plant. Remaining concerns about protecting against that contaminant have slowed the reintroduction of L-tryptophan in the United States market.

## DRUG INTERACTIONS

L-Tryptophan should not be coadministered with serotonin-specific reuptake inhibitors (SSRIs)—for example, fluoxetine (Prozac) and clomipramine (Anafranil)—or monoamine oxidase inhibitors (MAOIs). Those combinations can result in a syndrome related to serotonin excess and characterized by diarrhea, insomnia, nausea, headaches, chills, agitation, and poor concentration.

## LABORATORY INTERFERENCES

No laboratory interferences have been associated with the administration of L-tryptophan.

## DOSAGE AND ADMINISTRATION

L-Tryptophan is currently not available in the United States. When it was used as a hypnotic, the dosage ranged from 1 to 15 grams taken at bedtime. The use of L-tryptophan as an adjuvant to antidepressant treatment was often in the range of 5 to 10 mg a day in divided doses.

### References

Adachi J, Naito T, Ueno Y, Ogawa Y, Ninomiya I, Tatsuno Y: Metabolism and distribution in the rat of peak-E substance, a constituent in L-tryptophan product implicated in eosinophilia-myalgia-syndrome. Journal Arch Toxicol *67*: 284, 1993.
Brewerton T D, Reus V I: Lithium carbonate and L-tryptophan in the treatment of bipolar and schizoaffective disorders. Am J Psychiatry *140*: 757, 1983.
Flannery M T, Wallach P M, Espinoza L R, Dohrenwend M P, Moscisnski L C: A case of eosinophilia-myalgia syndrome associated with the use of an L-tryptophan product. Ann Intern Med *112*: 300, 1990.
Hajak G, Huenther G, Blanke J, Blomer M, Freyer C, Poeggeler B, Reimer A, Rodenbeck A, Schulz-Varszegi M, Ruther E: The influence of intravenous L-tryptophan on plasma melatonin and sleep in men. Pharmacopsychiatry *24*: 17, 1991.
Hedaya R J: Pharmacokinetic factors in the clinical use of tryptophan. J Clin Psychopharmacol *4*: 347, 1984.
Kamb M L, Murphy J J, Jones J L, Caston J L: Eosinophilia-myalgia syndrome in L-tryptophan-exposed patients. JAMA *267*: 77, 1992.
Maes M, Vandewoude M, Schotte C, Martin M, D'Hondt P, Scharpe S, Block P: The decreased availability of L-tryptophan in depressed females: Clinical and biological correlates. Prog Neuropsychopharmacol Biol Psychiatry *14*: 903, 1990.
Schneider-Helmert D, Spinwebere C L: Evaluation of L-tryptophan for treatment of insomnia: A review. Psychopharmacology *89*: 1, 1986.
Steiner W, Fontaine R: Toxic reaction following the combined administration of fluoxetine and L-tryptophan: Five case reports. Biol Psychiatry *21*: 1067, 1986.
Thomas J M, Rubin E H: Case report of a toxic reaction from a combination of tryptophan and phenelzine. Am J Psychiatry *141*: 281, 1984.
Villanova M, Declerck L S, Cras P, Ceuterick C, Vanmarck E, Guazzi G C, Martin J J: Eosinophilia-myalgia-syndrome—a clinicopathological study of 4 patients. Clin Neuropathol *12*: 201, 1993.
Zajecka J M, Fawcett J: Antidepressant combination and potentiation. Psychiatr Med *9*: 55, 1991.

---

# 33.3.29 / Valproate

---

Valproate (Depakene), also called valproic acid (because it is rapidly converted to the acid form in the stomach), was first recognized as an effective antiepileptic drug in 1963 in France and was approved for use in certain types of epilepsy in the United States in 1978. Since that time, valproate has been shown to be effective in a range of epileptic conditions. In addition, valproate and two other anticonvulsant drugs, carbamazepine (Tegretol) and clonazepam (Klonopin), have been shown to be effective in the treatment of bipolar I disorder. Although lithium (Eskalith) is still widely considered the first-line drug in the treatment of bipolar I disorder, many clinicians consider valproate at least equal in efficacy and safety to carbamazepine as a second-line drug. Unlike carbamazepine, valproate may shortly receive official approval by the Food and Drug Administration (FDA) as a safe and effective treatment for bipolar I disorder.

## CHEMISTRY

The molecular structure of valproic acid is shown in Figure 33.3.29–1. Valproic acid is a simple, branched-chain, carboxylic, *n*-dipropylacetic acid.

## PHARMACOLOGICAL ACTIONS

### Pharmacokinetics

When a formulation containing sodium valproate is ingested, the drug is converted into valproic acid in the stomach. Some formulations contain valproic acid itself, which is readily and almost completely absorbed from the gastrointestinal tract. Peak plasma levels vary, depending on the preparation (Table 33.3.29–1) and whether food is ingested with the drug. The ingestion of food with the drug delays the absorption of the drug but does not affect the ultimate amount of drug absorbed. The half-life of valproate is about 8 to 17 hours, commonly making three-times-daily dosing necessary to maintain stable plasma concentrations, although sustained-release preparations are now available (for example, divalproex sodium [Depakote]). Valproate is metabolized by the liver, and some of its metabolites are also effective as antiepileptic agents.

### Pharmacodynamics

The therapeutic effects of valproate in both epilepsy and bipolar I disorder may be mediated by the effects of the drug on γ-aminobutyric acid (GABA), an inhibitory amino acid neurotransmitter. In preclinical studies, valproate has both increased and decreased the synthesis of GABA. Valproate may also enhance the postsynaptic effects of GABA through poorly understood mechanisms. Although a precise role for GABA in the pathophysiology of mood disorders has not been defined, GABA may act directly or by regulating the activities of the biogenic amine neurotransmitters (for example, serotonin) or by affecting other central nervous system (CNS) mechanisms (for example, the control of circadian rhythms).

## EFFECTS ON SPECIFIC ORGANS AND SYSTEMS

Although the principal effects of valproate are on the central nervous system, the drug also affects the gastrointestinal and hematopoietic systems. The effects on the gastrointestinal system lead both to common adverse effects (for example, nausea) and to serious but rare effects (for example, fatal hepatotoxicity).

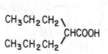

$$CH_3CH_2CH_2 \diagdown$$
$$CHCOOH$$
$$CH_3CH_2CH_2 \diagup$$

**Figure 33.3.29–1.** Molecular structure of valproic acid.

**Table 33.3.29–1**
**Valproate Preparations Available in the United States**

| Generic Name | Trade Name, Form (doses) | Time to Peak Serum Concentration |
| --- | --- | --- |
| Valproic acid | Depakene, capsules (250 mg) | 1–2 hrs |
| Sodium valproate | Depakene, syrup (250 mg/5 mL) | 1–2 hrs |
| Divalproex sodium | Depakote, delayed-release tablets (125, 250, 500 mg) | 3–8 hrs |
| Divalproex sodium coated particles in capsules | Depakote, sprinkle capsules (125 mg) | Compared with divalproex tablets, divalproex sprinkle has earlier onset and slower rate of absorption, with slightly lower peak plasma concentrations |

## THERAPEUTIC INDICATIONS

### Bipolar I Disorder

About a half-dozen well-controlled but small studies have shown that valproate is effective in the treatment of acute mania. Data from uncontrolled studies support the hypothesis that valproate is effective in the prophylactic treatment of bipolar I disorder. Specifically, the patients who were treated with valproate had fewer, less severe, and shorter manic episodes while taking valproate than when they were not taking the drug prophylatically. Some of the available data from both uncontrolled and controlled studies have reported that valproate may be particularly effective in patients with rapid-cycling bipolar I disorder, dysphoric or mixed mania, and mania due to a general medical condition and in patients who have not had complete favorable responses to lithium treatment. Additional data from case reports indicate that valproate can be used effectively in combination with lithium or carbamazepine in patients who do not respond sufficiently to a treatment regimen with a single drug. The data are less supportive of the use of valproate alone for the short-term treatment of depressive episodes in bipolar I disorder, although the data from open-label studies support the conclusion that valproate is effective in the prophylactic treatment of depressive episodes in bipolar I disorder patients.

### Schizoaffective Disorder

Although no controlled studies of valproate in schizoaffective disorder have been conducted, data from uncontrolled studies and case reports support the conclusion that valproate is effective in treating the short-term phase of the bipolar type of schizoaffective disorder. However, some data indicate that valproate is less effective in schizoaffective disorder than in bipolar I disorder.

### Other Mental Disorders

Preliminary reports note the therapeutic efficacy of valproate in other mental disorders, including major depressive disorder; panic disorder; posttraumatic stress disorder; bulimia nervosa; alcohol and sedative, hypnotic, or anxiolytic withdrawal; and intermittent explosive disorder. Although the data for those indications are limited, the use of valproate for patients who have not responded to other treatments may be indicated, although its use should be undertaken only after a thorough review of the most recent literature. The available data have led many researchers to conclude that valproate is not effective in the treatment of schizophrenia.

## PRECAUTIONS AND ADVERSE REACTIONS

Valproate treatment is generally well-tolerated and safe, although a range of common mild adverse effects and serious and rare adverse effects have been associated with valproate treatment. The common adverse effects associated with valproate are those affecting the gastrointestinal system, such as nausea (25 percent of all patients treated), vomiting (5 percent of patients), and diarrhea. The gastrointestinal effects are generally most common in the first month of treatment but are also common when the treatment is with valproic acid or sodium valproate, rather than enteric-coated divalproex sodium (Depakote), especially the sprinkle formulation. Some clinicians have also treated gastrointestinal symptoms with histamine type 2 ($H_2$) receptor antagonists, such as cimetidine (Tagamet). Other common adverse effects involve the nervous system, such as sedation, ataxia, dysarthria, and tremor. Valproate-induced tremor has been reported to respond well to treatment with β-adrenergic receptor antagonists. Treatment of the other neurological adverse effects usually requires lowering of the valproate dosage. Weight gain is a common adverse effect, especially in long-term treatment, and can best be treated by recommending a combination of a reasonable diet and moderate exercise. Hair loss has been reported to occur in 5 to 10 percent of all patients treated; rare cases of complete loss of body hair have been reported. Some clinicians have recommended treatment of valproate-associated hair loss with vitamin supplements that contain zinc and selenium. Another adverse effect that may occur in 5 to 40 percent of patients is a persistent elevation in liver transaminases, which is usually asymptomatic and resolves after discontinuation of the drug. Other rare adverse events include effects on the hematopoietic system, including thrombocytopenia and platelet dysfunction, occurring most commonly at high dosages and resulting in the prolongation of bleeding times. Overdoses of valproate can lead to coma and death. There are reports that valproate-induced coma can be successfully treated with naloxone (Narcan) and reports that hemodialysis and hemoperfusion can be useful in the treatment of valproate overdoses.

The two most serious adverse effects of valproate treatment involve the pancreas and the liver. Rare cases of pancreatitis have been reported; they occur most often in the first six months of treatment, and the condition occasionally results in death. The most attention has been paid to an association between valproate and fatal hepatotoxicity. A result of that focus has been the identification of risk factors, including young age (less than 2 years), the use of multiple anticonvulsants, and the presence of neurological disorders in addition to epilepsy. The rate of fatal hepatotoxicity in patients who have been treated with only valproate is 0.85 per 100,000 patients; no patients over the age of 10 years are reported to have died from fatal hepatotoxicity. Therefore, the risk of that adverse reaction in adult psychiatric patients seems to be extremely low. Nevertheless, if symptoms of malaise, anorexia, nausea and vomiting, edema, and abdominal pain occur in a patient treated with valproate, the clinician must consider the possibility of severe hepatotoxicity. However, a modest increase in liver function test results does not correlate with the development of serious hepatotoxicity.

Valproate should not be used by pregnant or nursing women. The drug has been associated with neural tube defects (for example, spinal bifida) in about 1 to 2 percent of all women who took valproate during the first trimester of the pregnancy. Valproate is contraindicated in nursing mothers because it is excreted in breast milk. Clinicians should not administer the drug to patients with hepatic diseases.

## DRUG INTERACTIONS

Valproate is commonly coadministered with lithium and the antipsychotics. The only consistent drug interaction with lithium is the exacerbation of drug-induced tremors, which can usually be treated with β-adrenergic receptor antagonists. The combination of valproate and antipsychotics may result in increased sedation, as can be seen when valproate is added to any CNS depressant (for example, alcohol), and increased severity of extrapyramidal symptoms, which usually respond to treatment with the usual antiparkinsonian drugs. The plasma concentrations of diazepam (Valium) and phenobarbital (Luminal) may be increased when those drugs are coadministered with valproate, and the plasma concentrations of phenytoin (Dilantin) may be decreased when phenytoin is combined with valproate. The plasma concentrations of valproate may be decreased when the drug is coadministered with carbamazepine and may be increased when coadministered with amitriptyline (Elavil) or fluoxetine (Prozac). Patients who are treated with anticoagulants—for example, aspirin and warfarin (Coumadin)—should also be monitored when valproate is initiated to assess the development of any undesired augmentation of the anticoagulation effects.

## LABORATORY INTERFERENCES

Valproate has been reported to cause an overestimation of serum free fatty acids in almost half of the patients tested. Valproate has also been reported to elevate urinary ketone estimations falsely and to result in falsely abnormal thyroid function test results.

## DOSAGE AND ADMINISTRATION

Valproate is available in a number of formulations and dosages (Table 33.3.29–1). It is best to initiate drug treatment gradually, so as to minimize the common adverse effects of nausea, vomiting, and sedation. The dose on the first day should be 250 mg administered with a meal. The dosage can be raised up to 250 mg orally three times daily over the course of three to six days. Plasma levels can be assessed in the morning before the first daily dose of the drug is administered. Therapeutic plasma levels for the control of seizures range between 50 and 100 mg per mL, although some physicians use 125 or even 150 mg per mL if the drug is well-tolerated. It is reasonable to use the same range for the treatment of mental disorders; most of the controlled studies have used 50 to 100 mg per mL. Most patients attain therapeutic plasma levels on a dosage between 1,200 and 1,500 mg a day in divided doses.

**References**

Calabrese J R, Delucchi G A: Spectrum of efficacy of valproate in 55 patients with rapid-cycling bipolar disorder. Am J Psychiatry *147*: 431, 1990.
Emrich H M, Wolf R: Valproate treatment of mania. Prog Neuropsychopharmacol Biol Psychiatry *16*: 691, 1992.
Jacobsen F M: Low-dose valproate: A new treatment for cyclothyma, mild rapid cycling disorders, and premenstrual syndrome. J Clin Psychiatry *54*: 229, 1993.
Journal of Clinical Psychiatry: Emerging perspectives on valproate in affective disorders. J Clin Psychiatry *50* (3, Suppl): 2, 1989.
Journal of Clinical Psychopharmacology: Valproate and mood disorders: Perspectives. J Clin Psychopharmacol *12* (2, Suppl): 2, 1992.
Kastner T, Friedman D L: Verapamil and valproic acid. J Am Acad Child Adolesc Psychiatry 31: 271, 1992.
Keck P E, McElroy S L, Tugrul K C, Bennett J A: Valproate oral loading in the treatment of acute mania. J Clin Psychiatry *54*: 305, 1993.
Ketter T A, Passaglia P J, Post R M: Synergy of carbamazepine and valproic acid in affective illness: Case report and review of the literature. J Clin Psychopharmacol *12*: 276, 1992.
Mazure C M, Druss B G, Cellar J S: Valproate treatment of older psychotic patients with organic mental syndromes and behavioral dyscontrol. J Am Geriatr Soc *40*: 914, 1992.
McFarland B H, Miller M R, Starumfjorf A A: Valproate use in the older manic patient. J Clin Psychiatry *51*: 479, 1990.

## 33.3.30 / Venlafaxine

Venlafaxine (Effexor) is an effective antidepressant drug that is chemically distinct from other antidepressants, possesses a slightly different mechanism of action, and may have unique efficacy properties. Those efficacy properties may include a faster than usual onset of action and demonstrated efficacy in seriously depressed patients (for example, patients with melancholic features), although the data in support of those properties are limited at this time.

## CHEMISTRY

Venlafaxine is a novel phenylethylamine that is structurally distinct from existing antidepressant drugs (Figure 33.3.30–1).

## PHARMACOLOGICAL ACTIONS

### Pharmacokinetics

Venlafaxine is absorbed from the gastrointestinal tract and has a half-life of about five hours, thereby necessitating two-to-three-times-daily dosing of the drug. Venlafaxine is metabolized by the liver and possesses at least one active metabolite.

### Pharmacodynamics

Venlafaxine is a nonselective inhibitor of the reuptake of three biogenic amines—serotonin, norepinephrine, and dopamine. It is most potent as a reuptake inhibitor of serotonin (IC50 = 0.21 mmol), but its potency as a norepinephrine reuptake inhibitor is also high (IC50 = 0.64 mmol), and its potency as a dopamine reuptake inhibitor is significant (IC50 = 2.8 mmol). Venlafaxine does not have activity at muscarinic, histaminergic, or adrenergic receptors, and it is not active as a monoamine oxidase inhibitor.

## EFFECTS ON SPECIFIC ORGANS AND SYSTEMS

The effects of venlafaxine on specific organs and systems have not yet been reported in the literature.

## THERAPEUTIC INDICATIONS

The available data support the use of venlafaxine in the treatment of major depressive disorder. A number of well-controlled studies with a sufficient number of patients have shown the efficacy of venlafaxine for that indication. Some of the data from those studies have indicated that venlafaxine may be associated with a faster onset of action of antidepressant effects than are currently available antidepressants. However, the methods for demonstrating a faster onset of effect have not been carefully worked out,

and subsequent studies may not support the initial findings. Another study with venlafaxine included 93 depressed inpatients with melancholic features. Those patients also responded to venlafaxine in a relatively short time period, indicating that venlafaxine may become a preferred drug to use for seriously ill patients. Again, the data require replication before they are considered to be well-proved.

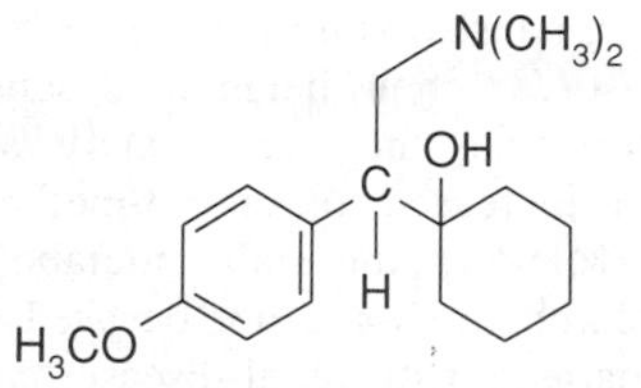

## PRECAUTIONS AND ADVERSE REACTIONS

In the published clinical reports, venlafaxine has generally been reported to be well-tolerated. However, caution is warranted with the use of all newly introduced drugs until a sufficient number of patients have been treated with the drug under usual clinical conditions. The following were the most common adverse reactions reported in the placebo-controlled studies: nausea (37 percent of all patients treated), somnolence (23 percent), dry mouth (22 percent), dizziness (19 percent), nervousness (13 percent), constipation (15 percent), asthenia (12 percent), anxiety (6 percent), anorexia (11 percent), blurred vision (6 percent), abnormal ejaculation or orgasm (12 percent), and impotence (6 percent). Nausea, somnolence, and insomnia were the three most common adverse reactions associated with patient discontinuation of venlafaxine.

The most potentially worrisome adverse effect associated with venlafaxine is an increase in blood pressure in some patients, particularly in patients who are treated with more than 300 mg a day. In clinical trials a mean increase of 1.2 mm Hg was observed in diastolic blood pressure in patients who were receiving venlafaxine, in contrast to a mean increase of 1.3 mm Hg in patients who were receiving imipramine (Tofranil) and a mean decrease of 1.6 mm Hg in patients who were receiving a placebo. In one study, sustained elevations of blood pressure higher than 140/90 were experienced by 1 percent of the patients who received a placebo, by no patients who received 75 mg a day of venlafaxine, by 1 percent of the patients who received 225 mg a day of venlafaxine, and by 3 percent of the patients who received 375 mg a day of venlafaxine. That adverse effect may lead the Food and Drug Administration to suggest that the drug be used cautiously in patients with preexisting hypertension. The clinical significance of the side effect may be less worrisome if low dosages of venlafaxine are found to be as efficacious as high dosages.

Information concerning use of venlafaxine by pregnant and nursing women is not available at this time. However, clinicians should avoid the use of all newly introduced drugs by pregnant and nursing women until more clinical experience has been gained.

## DRUG INTERACTIONS

Data are not currently available on drug interactions with venlafaxine.

## LABORATORY INTERFERENCES

Data are not currently available on laboratory interferences with venlafaxine.

**Figure 33.3.30–1.** Molecular structure of venlafaxine.

## DOSAGE AND ADMINISTRATION

Venlafaxine is available in 37.5 and 75 mg tablets. The usual starting dose in depressed outpatients is 75 mg a day, given in two to three divided doses. In that patient population the dose can be raised to 150 mg a day, given in two or three divided doses after an appropriate period of clinical assessment at the lower dose (usually two to three weeks). The dose can be raised in 75 mg a day increments. Doses of venlafaxine that are over 300 mg a day should be given in three divided doses. The maximum dose of venlafaxine is 375 mg a day. The dose of venlafaxine should be halfed in patients with significant diminished renal function. In those patients the drug can be administered in one daily dosing. The clinician should be guided by the reports yet to be published and by the manufacturer's product insert.

### References

Goldberg H L, Finnerty R: An open-label, variable-dose study of WY-45,030 (venlafaxine) in depressed outpatients. Psychopharmacol Bull *24*: 198, 1988.
Montgomery S A (chairperson): Venlafaxine: A new dimension in antidepressant pharmacotherapy. J Clin Psychiatry *54*: 119, 1993.
Saletu B, Grunberger J, Anderer P, Linzmayer L, Semlitsch H V, Magni G: Pharmacodynamics of venlafaxine evaluated by EEG brain mapping, psychometry, and psychophysiology. Br J Clin Pharmacol *33*: 589, 1992.
Schweizer E, Weise C, Clary C, Fox I, Rickels K: Placebo-controlled trial of venlafaxine for the treatment of major depression. J Clin Psychopharmacol *11*: 233, 1991.

# 33.3.31 / Yohimbine

Yohimbine (Yocon) is an $\alpha_2$-adrenergic receptor antagonist that has been used as a treatment for both idiopathic and drug-induced male sexual dysfunction. The efficacy of the drug for that indication remains controversial.

## CHEMISTRY

The molecular structure of yohimbine is shown in Figure 33.3.31–1. Yohimbine is derived from an alkaloid found in *Rubaceae* and related trees and in the *Rauwolfia serpentina* plant.

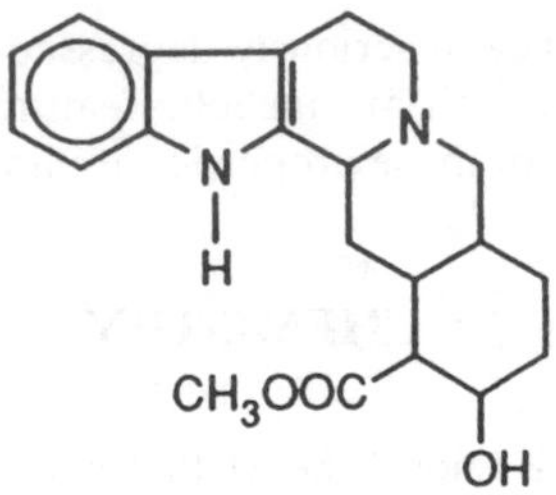

## PHARMACOLOGICAL ACTIONS

### Pharmacokinetics

Data on the pharmacokinetic parameters of yohimbine are not available.

**Figure 33.3.31–1.** Molecular structure of yohimbine.

### Pharmacodynamics

Yohimbine is an antagonist of $\alpha_2$-adrenergic receptors, which are located both presynaptically and postsynaptically on noradrenergic neurons. $\alpha_2$-Adrenergic receptors are also located on the synaptic terminals of some serotonergic neurons. Stimulation of presynaptic $\alpha_2$-adrenergic receptors results in a decrease in the release of neurotransmitters from that neuron; therefore, blockade of the receptors results in an increase in the release of neurotransmitters. Both norepinephrine and serotonin are involved in the physiology of the male sexual response.

## EFFECTS ON SPECIFIC ORGANS AND SYSTEMS

The primary effects of yohimbine are on the peripheral nervous system through its effects on adrenergic neurotransmission. The effects on the peripheral nervous system affect vascular, cardiac, and gastrointestinal functions.

## THERAPEUTIC INDICATIONS

In psychiatry, yohimbine has been used experimentally as a possible treatment for organic, psychogenic, and substance-induced erectile impotence and other male sexual dysfunctions. Its effects on male sexual performance are possibly related to its peripheral autonomic nervous system effects, although it is not possible to rule out central nervous system effects completely. Urologists have also used yohimbine for the diagnostic classification of certain types of male impotence.

## PRECAUTIONS AND ADVERSE REACTIONS

The side effects of yohimbine include elevated blood pressure and heart rate, increased psychomotor activity, irritability, tremor, headache, skin flushing, dizziness, urinary frequency, nausea, vomiting, and sweating. Patients with panic disorder show heightened sensitivity to yohimbine, experiencing increased anxiety, a rise in blood pressure, and increased plasma 3-methoxy-4-hydroxyphenylglycol (MHPG), the major metabolite of norepinephrine. Yohimbine should not be used by female patients or by patients with renal disease, cardiac disease, glaucoma, or a history of gastric or duodenal ulcers.

## DRUG INTERACTIONS

Yohimbine should not be used with clonidine (Catapres), an $\alpha_2$-adrenergic receptor agonist, because the two drugs have mutually canceling pharmacodynamic effects.

## LABORATORY INTERFERENCES

No known laboratory interferences are associated with the use of yohimbine.

## DOSAGE AND ADMINISTRATION

The dosage of yohimbine in the treatment of impotence is about 18 mg a day. The dosage range is 4 to 7.5 mg three times a day. In the event of significant adverse effects, the dosage should first be reduced and then gradually increased. Yohimbine is available in 5.4 mg tablets.

### References

Clark J, Smieth E R, Davidson J M: Enhancement of sexual motivation in male rats with yohimbine. Science *225*: 847, 1984.
Hollander E, McCarley A: Yohimbine treatment of sexual side effects induced by serotonin reuptake blockers. J Clin Psychiatry *53*: 207, 1992.
Price J, Grunhaus L J: Treatment of clomipramine-induced anorgasmia with yohimbine: A case report. J Clin Psychiatry *51*: 32, 1990.
Reid K, Morales A, Harris C: Double-blind trial of yohimbine in treatment of psychogenic impotence. Lancet *2*: 421, 1987.

# 33.4 / Electroconvulsive Therapy

Electroconvulsive therapy (ECT) is a safe and effective treatment of patients with major depressive disorder, manic episodes, and other serious mental disorders. Many clinicians and researchers believe that ECT is grossly underused as a treatment. The major reason for the underuse is hypothesized to be misconceptions and biases about ECT, at least partly fueled be widespread misinformation and inflammatory articles in the lay press. Because ECT requires the use of electricity and the production of a seizure, many laypersons, patients, and patients' families are understandably frightened by ECT. Many inaccurate reports have appeared in both professional and lay literature about alleged permanent brain damage resulting from ECT. Although those reports have been largely disproved, the specter of ECT-induced brain damage remains.

The decision to suggest ECT to a patient, like all treatment recommendations, should be based on both the treatment options available to the patient and the risk-benefit considerations. The major alternatives to ECT are usually pharmacotherapy and psychotherapy; both have their own risks and benefits. ECT has been shown to be a safe and effective treatment; clinicians should not allow their biases to deprive patients of the effective treatment.

## HISTORY

Although camphor-induced seizures were used as early as the 16th century as a treatment of psychosis, most histories of ECT start in 1934, when Ladislas J. von Meduna reported the successful treatment of catatonia and other schizophrenic symptoms with pharmacologically induced seizures. Von Meduna began by using intramuscular injections of camphor suspended in oil but quickly switched to intravenously administered pentylenetetrazol (Metrazol). Von Meduna attempted the treatment method on the basis of two observations: First, schizophrenic symptoms often decrease after a seizure; seizures were often accidentally or iatrogenically induced in psychiatric patients secondary to withdrawal from medications (for example, barbiturates). Second, schizophrenia and epilepsy, it was incorrectly believed, cannot coexist in the same patient; therefore, the induction of seizures might rid the patient of schizophrenia. Pentylenetetrazol-induced seizures were used as an effective treatment for four years before the introduction of electrically induced seizures. Primarily on the basis of the work of von Meduna, Ugo Cerletti and Lucio Bini administered the first electroconvulsive treatment in April 1938 in Rome. Initially, the treatment was referred to as electroshock therapy (EST), but it later became known as electroconvulsive therapy.

The major problems associated with ECT were the patients' discomfort caused by the procedure and the bone fractures resulting from the motor activity of the seizure. Those problems were eventually eliminated by the use of general anesthetics and pharmacological muscle relaxation during the treatment. An American psychiatrist, Abram E. Bennett, helped develop the method for extracting pure curare from plant material. Bennett suggested the use of spinal anesthetics during ECT and the use of curare to paralyze the muscles to prevent fractures. In 1951 succinylcholine (Anectine) was introduced and became the most widely used muscle relaxant for ECT. In 1957 hexafluorinated diethylether (Indokolon) was introduced as a new pharmacological means of inducing seizures by administering the compound as a gas. The lack of its superiority to ECT, together with the introduction of antidepressant drugs in the 1950s, led to the removal of hexafluorinated diethylether from the market and to a decline in the number of patients who were given ECT. Currently, about 50,000 to 100,000 patients receive ECT annually in the United States.

## OHM'S LAW

The qualities of the electricity used in ECT can be described by Ohm's law $E = IR$ or $I = E/R$, in which $E$ is voltage, $I$ is current, and $R$ is resistance. The intensity or dose of electricity in ECT is measured in terms of charge (milliampere-seconds or millicoulombs) or energy (watt-seconds or joules). Resistance is synonymous with impedance; in the case of ECT, the contact of the electrode with the body and the nature of the bodily tissues are the major determinants of resistance. The skull has a high impedance; the brain has a low impedance. The ECT machines that are now widely used can be adjusted to administer the electricity under conditions of constant current, voltage, or energy.

## MECHANISM OF ACTION

The induction of a bilateral generalized seizure is necessary for both the beneficial effects and the adverse effects of ECT. Although a seizure superficially seems like an all-or-none event, some data indicate that not all generalized seizures involve all the neurons in deep brain structures (for example, the basal ganglia and the thalamus); recruitment of those deep neurons may be necessary for full therapeutic benefit. After the generalized seizure, the electroencephalogram (EEG) shows a period of about 60 to 90 seconds of postictal suppression. That period is followed by the appearance of high-voltage delta and theta waves and a return of the EEG to preseizure appearances in about 30 minutes. During the course of a series of ECT treatments, the interictal EEG is generally slower and of greater amplitude than usual, but the EEG returns to pretreatment appearances between one month and one year after the end of the course of treatment.

One research approach to the mechanism of action for ECT has been to study the neurophysiological effects of treatment. Positron emission tomography (PET) studies of both cerebral blood flow and glucose use have been reported. Those studies have shown that during seizures cerebral blood flow, use of glucose and oxygen, and permeability of the blood-brain barrier increase. After the seizure, blood flow and glucose metabolism are decreased, perhaps most markedly in the frontal lobes. Some research indicates that the degree of decrease in cerebral metabolism is correlated with therapeutic response. Seizure foci in idiopathic epilepsy are hypometabolic during interictal periods; ECT itself acts as an anticonvulsant, since its administration is associated with an increase in the seizure threshold as treatment progresses.

Neurochemical research regarding the mechanisms of action of ECT has focused on changes in neurotransmitter receptors and, recently, changes in second-messenger systems. Virtually every neurotransmitter system is affected by ECT. However, a series of ECT sessions result in a down-regulation of postsynaptic β-adrenergic receptors, the same receptor change observed with virtually all antidepressant treatments. The effects of ECT on serotonergic neurons remains a controversial area of research. Various research reports have found an increase in postsynaptic serotonin receptors, no change in serotonin receptors, and a change in the presynaptic regulation of serotonin release. ECT has also been reported to affect changes in the muscarinic, cholinergic, and dopaminergic neuronal systems. On second-messenger systems, ECT has been reported to affect the coupling of G-proteins to receptors, the activity of adenylyl cyclase and phospholipase C, and the regulation of calcium entry into neurons.

## INDICATIONS

Patients with bipolar I disorder account for about 70 percent of the patients who receive ECT; patients with schizophrenia account for about 17 percent. The three clearest indications for ECT are major depressive disorder, manic episodes, and, in some instances, schizophrenia.

### Major Depressive Disorder

The most common indication for ECT is major depressive disorder. ECT should be considered as a treatment for patients who have failed medication trials, have not tolerated medications, have severe or psychotic symptoms, are acutely suicidal or homicidal, or have marked symptoms of agitation or stupor. Most clinicians believe that ECT results in at least the same degree of clinical improvement as does standard treatment with antidepressant drugs. Recently, the old studies that reported those comparisons have been questioned because of their use of low dosages of antidepressant drugs. In spite of that controversy, few clinicians doubt that ECT and pharmacotherapy are at least equal in their efficacy and response times.

ECT is effective for depression in both major depressive disorder and bipolar I disorder. Delusional or psychotic depression has long been thought to be particularly responsive to ECT; however, recent studies have indicated that major depressive episodes with psychotic features are no more responsive to ECT than are nonpsychotic depressive disorders. Nevertheless, since major depressive episodes with psychotic features are poorly responsive to antidepressant pharmacotherapy alone, ECT should be considered much more often as the first-line treatment for patients with the disorder. Major depressive disorder with melancholic features (such as markedly severe symptoms, psychomotor retardation, early morning awakening, diurnal variation, decreased appetite and weight, and agitation) is thought to be likely to respond to ECT. Elderly patients tend to respond to ECT more slowly than do young patients. However, ECT is a treatment for major depressive episode and does not provide prophylaxis unless it is administered on a long-term maintenance basis.

### Manic Episodes

ECT is at least equal to and perhaps superior to lithium (Eskalith) in the treatment of acute manic episodes. Some data indicate that bilateral placement of electrodes during ECT is more effective than unilateral placement in the treatment of manic episodes. However, the pharmacological treatment of manic episodes is so effective in the short-term and for prophylaxis that the use of ECT for the treatment of manic episodes is generally limited to those situations with specific contraindications to all available pharmacological approaches.

### Schizophrenia

ECT is an effective treatment for the symptoms of acute schizophrenia and not for the symptoms of chronic schizophrenia. Schizophrenic patients with marked positive symptoms, catatonia, or affective symptoms are thought to be most likely to respond to ECT. The efficacy of ECT in such patients is about equal to that of antipsychotics.

### Other Indications

Small studies have found ECT to be effective in the treatment of catatonia, a symptom associated with mood disorders, schizophrenia, and medical and neurological disorders. ECT has also been reported to be useful in the treatment of episodic psychoses, atypical psychoses, obsessive-compulsive disorder, and delirium and such medical conditions as neuroleptic malignant syndrome, hypopituitarism, intractable seizure disorders, and the on-off phenomenon of Parkinson's disease. ECT may also be the treatment of choice for depressed pregnant women who require treatment and cannot take medication, geriatric and medically ill patients who cannot take antidepressant drugs safely, and perhaps even depressed children and adolescents who may be less likely to respond to antidepressant drugs than are adults.

## CLINICAL GUIDELINES

Patients and their families are often apprehensive about ECT; therefore, the clinician must explain its beneficial and adverse effects and alternative treatment approaches to them. That informed-consent process should be documented in the patient's medical record. The informed-consent process should include a discussion of the disorder, its natural course, and the option of receiving no treatment. Printed literature and videotapes about ECT may be useful in attempting to obtain a truly informed consent. The use of involuntary ECT is rare today and should be reserved for patients for whom the treatment is urgent and for whom a legally appointed guardian has agreed to its use. The clinician must know the local, state, and federal laws about the use of ECT.

### Pretreatment Evaluation

The pretreatment evaluation should include standard physical, neurological, and preanesthesia examinations and a complete medical history. Laboratory evaluations should include blood and urine chemistries, a chest X-ray, and an electrocardiogram (ECG). A dental examination to assess the state of the patient's dentition is advisable in elderly patients and patients who have had inadequate dental care. An X-ray of the spine is needed if there is other evidence of a spinal disorder. Computed tomography (CT) or magnetic resonance imaging (MRI) should be performed if the clinician suspects the presence of a seizure disorder or a space-occupying lesion.

**Concomitant medications.** The patient's ongoing medications should be assessed for possible interactions with the induction of a seizure and for drug interactions with the medications used during ECT. The presence of tricyclic and tetracyclic drugs, monoamine oxidase inhibitors, and antipsychotics are generally thought to be acceptable. Benzodiazepines should be withdrawn, because of their anticonvulsant activity; lithium should be withdrawn, because it can result in increased postictal delirium and prolonged seizure activity, and clozapine (Clozaril) should be withdrawn, because it is associated with the development of late-appearing seizures. Lidocaine (Xylocaine) should not be administered during ECT, because it markedly increases the seizure threshold, and theophylline (Theodur) is also contraindicated, because it increases the duration of the seizures. Reserpine (Serpasil) is also contraindicated, because it is associated with further

compromise of the respiratory and cardiovascular systems during ECT.

### Premedications, Anesthetics, and Muscle Relaxants

Patients should not be given anything orally for six hours before treatment. Just before the procedure, the patient's mouth should be checked for dentures and other foreign objects, and an intravenous (IV) line should be established. A bite block is inserted in the mouth just before the treatment is administered to protect the patient's teeth and tongue during the seizure. Except for the brief interval of electrical stimulation, 100 percent oxygen is administered at a rate of 5 L a minute during the procedure until spontaneous respiration returns. Emergency equipment for the establishment of an airway should be immediately available in case it is needed.

**Muscarinic anticholinergic drugs.** Muscarinic anticholinergic drugs are administered before ECT to minimize oral and respiratory secretions and to block bradycardias and asystoles. Some ECT centers have stopped the routine use of anticholinergics as premedications, although their use is still indicated for patients talking β-adrenergic receptor antagonists and for patients with ventricular ectopic beats. The most commonly used drug is atropine, which can be administered 0.3 to 0.6 mg intramuscularly (IM) or subcutaneously 30 to 60 minutes before the anesthetic or 0.4 to 1.0 mg IV two to three minutes before the anesthetic. An option is to use glycopyrrolate (Robinul) (0.2 to 0.4 mg IM, IV, or subcutaneously), which is less likely to cross the blood-brain barrier and less likely to cause cognitive dysfunction and nausea, although it is thought to have less cardiovascular protective activity than does atropine.

**General anesthetics.** The administration of ECT requires general anesthesia and oxygenation. The depth of anesthesia should be as light as possible, not only to minimize the adverse effects but also to avoid elevating the seizure threshold associated with many anesthetics. Methohexital (Brevital) (0.75 to 1.0 mg per kg IV bolus) is the most commonly used anesthetic because of its short duration of action and lower association with postictal arrhythmias than is seen with thiopental (Pentothal) (usual dose 2 to 3 mg per kg IV), although that difference in cardiac effects is not universally accepted. Three other anesthetic alternatives are etomidate, ketamine (Ketalar), and alfentanil (Alfenta). Etomidate (0.15 to 0.3 mg per kg IV) is sometimes used because it does not increase the seizure threshold, which can particularly useful in elderly patients, because the seizure threshold increases with age. Ketamine (6 to 10 mg per kg IM) is sometimes used because it does not increase the seizure threshold, although its use is limited by the frequent association of psychotic symptoms with emergence from anesthesia seen with the drug. Alfentanil (2 to 9 mg per kg IV) is sometimes coadministered with barbiturates to allow the use of low doses of the barbiturate anesthetics and thus to reduce the seizure threshold less than usual, although its use may be associated with an increased incidence of nausea.

**Muscle relaxants.** After the onset of the anesthetic effect, usually within a minute, a muscle relaxant is administered to minimize the risk of bone fractures and other injuries resulting from motor activity during the seizure. The goal is to produce a profound relaxation of the muscles, not necessarily to paralyze the muscles, unless the patient has a history of osteoporosis or spinal injury or has a pacemaker and is, therefore, at risk for injury related to the motor activity during the seizure. Succinylcholine (Anectine), an ultrafast-acting depolarizing blocking agent, has gained virtually universal acceptance for the purpose. Succinylcholine is usually administered in a dose of 0.5 to 1.0 mg per kg as an IV bolus or IV drip. Because succinylcholine is a depolarizing agent, its action is marked by the presence of muscle fasciculations, which move in a rostrocaudal progression. The disappearance of those movements in the feet or the absence of muscle contractions after peripheral nerve stimulation indicates that maximal muscle relaxation has been achieved. In some patients, tubocurare (3 mg IV) is administered to prevent myoclonus and increases in potassium and muscle enzymes, which may be a problem in patients with musculoskeletal disease or cardiac disease.

If the patient has a known history of pseudocholinesterase deficiency, atracurium (Tracrium) (0.5 to 1.0 mg per kg IV) or curare can be used instead of succinylcholine. In such a patient, the metabolism of succinylcholine is disrupted, and a prolonged apnea may occur, thus necessitating emergency airway management. In general, however, because of the short half-life of succinylcholine, the duration of apnea after its administration is generally shorter than the delay in regaining consciousness caused by the anesthetic and the postictal state.

### Stimulus Electrode Placement

ECT can be conducted with either bilaterally or unilaterally placed electrodes. In general, bilateral placement results in a more rapid therapeutic response, and unilateral placement results in less marked cognitive adverse effects in the first week or weeks after treatment, although that difference between placements is absent two months after treatment. In bilateral placement, which was introduced first, one stimulating electrode is placed over each hemisphere of the brain. In unilateral ECT, both electrodes are placed over the nondominant hemisphere, almost always the right hemisphere. Some attempts have been made to vary the location of the electrodes in unilateral ECT; however, those attempts have not been successful in obtaining the rapidity of response seen with bilateral ECT or in further reducing the cognitive adverse effects. The most common approach is to initiate treatment with unilateral ECT because of its more favorable side-effect profile. However, if the patient does not improve after four to six unilateral treatments, the technique is switched to the bilateral placement. Initial bilateral placement of the electrodes may be indicated in the following situations: severe depressive symptoms, marked agitation, immediate suicide risk, manic symptoms, catatonic stupor, and treatment-resistant schizophrenia. Some patients are particularly at risk for anesthetic-related adverse effects, and those patients may also be treated with bilateral placement from the beginning to minimize the number of treatments and exposures to anesthetics.

Traditional bilateral ECT places electrodes bifrontotemporally; each electrode has its center about one inch above the midpoint of an imaginary line drawn from the tragus to the external canthus. With unilateral ECT, one stimulus electrode is typically placed over the nondominant frontotemporal area. Although several locations for the second stimulus electrode have been proposed, placement on the nondominant centroparietal scalp, just lateral to the midline vertex, appears to provide the most effective configuration.

Which cerebral hemisphere is dominant can generally be determined by a simple series of performance tasks (for example, for handedness and footedness) and stated preference. Right body responses correlate highly with left brain dominance. If the responses are mixed or if they clearly indicate left body dominance, clinicians should alternate the polarity of unilateral stimulation during successive treatments. Clinicians should also monitor the time that it takes for patients to recover consciousness and to answer simple orientation and naming questions. The side of stimulation associated with less rapid recovery and return of function is considered dominant. The left hemisphere is dominant in the vast majority of persons; therefore, unilateral electrode placement is almost always over the right hemisphere.

### Electrical Stimulus

The electrical stimulus must be sufficiently strong to reach the seizure threshold (the level of intensity needed to produce a seizure). The electrical stimulus is given in cycles, each cycle containing a positive wave and a negative wave. Old machines used a sine wave; however, that type of machine is now considered obsolete because of the inefficiency of that wave shape. When a sine wave is delivered, the electrical stimulus in the sine wave before the seizure threshold is reached and after the seizure is activated is unnecessary and excessive. Modern ECT machines use a brief pulse wave form, which administers the electrical stimulus usually in a 1 to 2 msec time period. Machines that use an ultrabrief pulse (0.5 msec) are not as effective as brief pulse machines.

The establishment of a patient's seizure threshold is not straightforward. A 40-fold variability in seizure thresholds is seen among patients. In addition, during the course of ECT treatment, a patient's seizure threshold may increase 25 to 200 percent. Also, the seizure threshold is higher in men than in women, and higher in elderly patients than in younger adults. A common technique is to initiate treatment at an electrical stimulus that is thought to be lower than the seizure threshold for a particular patient and then to increase that intensity by 100 percent for unilateral placement and by 50 percent for bilateral placement until the seizure threshold is reached. A debate in the literature concerns the question of whether a minimally superthreshold dose, a moderately superthreshold dose (1½ times the threshold), or a high superthreshold dose (three times the threshold) is preferable. The debate about stimulus intensity is like the debate regarding electrode placement. Essentially, the data support the conclusion that doses of three times the threshold are the most rapidly effective and that minimal superthreshold doses are associated with the fewest and least severe cognitive adverse effects.

### Induced Seizures

A brief muscular contraction, usually strongest in the patient's jaw and facial muscles, is seen concurrently with the flow of stimulus current, regardless of whether a seizure occurs. The first behavioral sign of the seizure is often a plantar extension, which lasts 10 to 20 seconds and marks the tonic phase. That phase is followed by rhythmic (that is, clonic) contractions that decrease in frequency and finally disappear. The tonic phase is marked by high-frequency, sharp EEG activity on which may be superimposed an even higher-frequency muscle artifact. During the clonic phase, bursts of polyspike activity occur simultaneously with the muscular contractions but usually persist for at least a few seconds after the clonic movements stop.

**Monitoring seizures.** The physician must have an objective measure that a bilateral generalized seizure has occurred after the stimulation. The physician should be able to observe either some evidence of tonic-clonic movements or electrophysiological evidence of seizure activity from the EEG or electromyogram (EMG). Seizures with unilateral ECT are asymmetrical, with higher ictal EEG amplitudes over the stimulated hemisphere than over the nonstimulated hemisphere. Occasionally, unilateral seizures are induced; for that reason, at least a single pair of EEG electrodes should be placed over the contralateral hemisphere when using unilateral ECT. For a seizure to be effective in the course of ECT, the seizure should have a duration of at least 25 seconds.

**Missed seizures.** If a particular stimulus fails to cause a seizure of sufficient duration, up to four attempts at seizure induction can be tried during a course of treatment. However, the onset of seizure activity is sometimes delayed as long as 20 to 40 seconds after the stimulus administration. If a stimulus fails to result in a seizure, the contact between the electrodes and the skin should be checked, and the intensity of the stimulus should be increased by 25 to 100 percent. The clinician can also change the anesthetic agent to minimize increases in the seizure threshold caused by the anesthetic. Additional procedures to lower the seizure threshold include hyperventilation, the administration of 500 to 2000 mg IV of caffeine sodium benzoate 5 to 10 minutes before the stimulus, and the administration of 500 to 800 mg IV of pentylenetetrazol 60 to 90 seconds before the stimulus.

**Prolonged and tardive seizures.** Prolonged seizures (seizures lasting more than 180 seconds) and status epilepticus can be terminated either with additional doses of the barbiturate anesthetic agent or with intravenous diazepam (Valium) (5 to 10 mg). Management of such complications should be accompanied by intubation, because the oral airway is insufficient to maintain adequate ventilation over an extended apneic period. Tardive seizures— that is, additional seizures appearing some time after the

ECT treatment—may develop in patients with preexisting seizure disorders. In rare patients, ECT precipitates the development of an epileptic disorder. Such situations should be managed clinically as if they were pure epileptic disorders.

### Number and Spacing of ECT Treatments

ECT treatments are usually administered two to three times a week; two-times-weekly treatments are associated with less memory impairment than are three-times-weekly treatments. In general, the course of treatment of major depressive disorder can take 6 to 12 treatments (although up to 20 sessions is possible), the treatment of manic episodes can take 8 to 20 treatments, the treatment of schizophrenia can take more than 15 treatments, and the treatment of catatonia and delirium can take as few as one to four treatments. Treatment should continue until the patient achieves what is thought to be the maximum therapeutic response. Treatment past that point does not result in any therapeutic benefit but increases the severity and the duration of the side effects. The point of maximal improvement is usually thought to be that point at which a patient fails to continue to improve after two consecutive treatments. If a patient is not improving after 6 to 10 sessions, bilateral placement and high-intensity treatment (three times the seizure threshold) should be attempted before ECT is abandoned.

**Multiple monitored ECT.** Multiple monitored ECT (MMECT) involves giving multiple ECT stimuli during a single session, most commonly two bilateral stimuli within two minutes. That approach may be warranted in severely ill patients and in patients who are at especially high risk from the anesthetic procedures. MMECT is associated with the most frequent occurrences of serious cognitive side effects.

### Maintenance Treatment

A short-term course of ECT induces a remission in symptoms but does not, in itself, prevent a relapse. Post-ECT maintenance treatment should always be considered. Generally, the maintenance therapy is pharmacological, but maintenance ECT treatments (weekly, biweekly, or monthly) have been reported to be effective relapse prevention treatments, although data from large studies are lacking. Indications for maintenance ECT treatments may include a rapid relapse after initial ECT, severe symptoms, psychotic symptoms, and the inability to tolerate medications.

### Failure of ECT Trial

If a patient fails to improve after a trial of ECT, the patient should again be treated with the pharmacological agents that failed in the past. Although the data are primarily anecdotal, many reports indicate that patients who had previously failed to improve while taking an antidepressant drug do improve while taking the same drug after receiving a course of ECT treatments, even if the ECT seemed to be a therapeutic failure.

## ADVERSE EFFECTS

### Contraindications

ECT has no absolute contraindications, only situations in which the patient is at increased risk and has an increased need for close monitoring. Pregnancy is not a contraindication for ECT, and fetal monitoring is generally thought to be unnecessary unless the pregnancy is high-risk or complicated. Patients with space-occupying central nervous system (CNS) lesions are at increased risk for edema and brain herniation after ECT. However, if the lesion is small, pretreatment with dexamethasone is given, and hypertension is controlled during the seizure, the risk of serious complications can be minimized in those patients. Patients who have increased intracerebral pressure or are at risk for cerebral bleeding (for example, with cerebrovascular diseases and aneurysms) are at risk during ECT because of the increased cerebral blood flow during the seizure. That risk can be lessened, although not eliminated, by control of the patient's blood pressure during the treatment. Patients with recent myocardial infarctions are another high-risk group, although the risk is greatly diminished two weeks after the myocardial infarction and is even further reduced three months after the myocardial infarction. Patients with hypertension should be stabilized on their antihypertensive medications before ECT is administered. Propranolol (Inderal), sublingual nifedipine (Procardia), and sublingual nitroglycerin can also be used to protect such patients during treatment.

### Mortality

The mortality rate with ECT is about 0.002 percent per treatment and 0.01 percent for each patient. Those numbers compare favorably with the risks associated with general anesthesia and childbirth. ECT death is usually from cardiovascular complications and is most likely to occur in patients whose cardiac status is already compromised.

### Central Nervous System Effects

Common side effects associated with ECT are confusion and delirium shortly after the seizure while the patient is coming out of anesthesia. Marked confusion may occur in up to 10 percent of patients within 30 minutes of the seizure and can be treated with barbiturates and benzodiazepines. Delirium is usually most pronounced after the first few treatments and in patients who receive bilateral ECT or who have coexisting neurological disorders. The delirium characteristically clears within days or a few weeks at the longest.

**Memory.** The greatest concern regarding ECT is the association between ECT and memory loss. About 75 percent of all patients given ECT say that the memory impairment is the worst side effect of the treatment. Although memory impairment during a course of treatment is almost the rule, follow-up data indicate that almost all patients are back to their cognitive baselines after six months. However, some patients do complain of persistent memory difficulties. For example, a patient may not remember the

events leading up to the hospitalization and ECT, and such autobiographical memories may never be recalled. The degree of cognitive impairment during treatment and the time it takes to return to baseline are related in part to the amount of electrical stimulation used during treatment. Memory impairment is most reported by patients who have experienced little improvement with ECT. In spite of the memory impairment, which usually resolves, there is no evidence of brain damage caused by ECT. The subject has been the focus of a number of brain imaging studies, using a variety of modalities; virtually all concluded that permanent brain damage is not a side effect of ECT.

### Systemic Effects

Occasional usually mild transient cardiac arrhythmias occur during ECT, particularly in patients with existing cardiac disease. The arrhythmias are usually a by-product of the brief postictal bradycardia and, therefore, can often be prevented by increasing the dosage of anticholinergic premedication. Other arrhythmias are secondary to a tachycardia during the seizure and may occur as the patient returns to consciousness. The prophylactic administration of a β-adrenergic receptor antagonist can be useful in such cases. As mentioned above, an apneic state may be prolonged if the metabolism of succinylcholine is impaired. Toxic and allergic reactions to the pharmacological agents used in ECT have rarely been reported. Sore muscles resulting from the seizure motor activity can be generally alleviated by pretreatment with curare or atracorium or by increasing the succinylcholine dose by 10 to 25 percent.

### References

Abrams R, Swartz C M, Vedak C: Antidepressant effects of high-dose right unilateral electroconvulsive therapy. Arch Gen Psychiatry *48*: 746, 1991.

Black D W, Winokur G, Nasrallah A: Treatment of mania: A naturalistic study of electroconvulsive therapy versus lithium in 438 patients. J Clin Psychiatry *48*: 132, 1987.

Buchan H, Johnstone E, McPherson K, Palmer R L, Crow T J, Brandon S: Who benefits from electroconvulsive therapy? Combined results of the Leicester and Northwick Park trials. Br J Psychiatry *160*: 355, 1992.

Coffey C E, Weiner R D, Djang W T, Figiel G S, Soady S A R, Patterson L J, Holt P D, Spritzer C E, Wilkinson W E: Brain anatomic effects of electroconvulsive therapy: A prospective magnetic resonance imaging study. Arch Gen Psychiatry *48*: 1013, 1991.

King B H, Liston E H: Proposals for the mechanism of action of convulsive therapy: A synthesis. Biol Psychiatry *27*: 76, 1990.

Klein D F (editor): Review and commentaries: ECT. Neuropsychopharmacology *3*: 73, 1990.

Milstein V, Small J G, Miller M J, Sharpley P H, Small I F: Mechanisms of action of ECT: Schizophrenia and schizoaffective disorder. Biol Psychiatry *27*: 1282, 1990.

O'Connor M K, Rummans T A (editors): Updating ECT. Psychiatr Ann *23* (1): 2, 1993.

Potter W Z, Rudorfer M V: Electroconvulsive therapy: A modern medical procedure. N Engl J Med *328*: 882, 1993.

Prudic J, Sackheim H A, Devanand D P, Kiersky J E: The efficacy of ECT in double depression. Depression *1*: 38, 1993.

Rifkin A: ECT versus tricyclic antidepressants in depression: A review of the evidence. J Clin Psychiatry *49*: 3, 1988.

Sackheim H A, Prudic J, Devanand D P, Kiersky J E, Fitzsimmons L, Moody B J, McElhiney M C, Coleman E A, Settembrino J M: Effects of stimulus intensity and electrode placement on the efficacy and cognitive effects of electroconvulsive therapy. N Engl J Med *328*: 839, 1993.

Scott A I F, Rodger C R, Stocks R H, Shering A P: Is old-fashioned electroconvulsive therapy more efficacious? A randomized comparative study of bilateral brief-pulse and bilateral sine-wave treatments. Br J Psychiatry *160*: 360, 1992.

Solan W J, Khan A, Avery D H, Cohen S: Psychotic and nonpsychotic depression: Comparison of response to ECT. J Clin Psychiatry *49*: 97, 1988.

Thienhaus O J, Margletta S, Bennett J A: A study of the clinical efficacy of maintenance ECT. J Clin Psychiatry *51*: 141, 1990.

Thompson J W, Blaine J D: Use of ECT in the United States in 1975 and 1980. Am J Psychiatry *144*: 557, 1987.

Zielinski R J, Roose S P, Devanand D P, Woodring S, Sackeim H A: Cardiovascular complications of ECT in depressed patients with cardiac disease. Am J Psychiatry *150*: 904, 1993.

# 33.5 / Other Biological Therapies

## LIGHT THERAPY

The major indication for light therapy is major depressive disorder with seasonal pattern, a disorder characterized by symptoms that appear on a seasonal basis, usually in the fall and the winter. In light therapy, also called phototherapy, the patient is exposed to a bright artificial light source on a daily basis during the treatment.

### Mechanism of Action

**Phase-response curves.** Human circadian rhythms result from the entrainment of endogenous pacemakers by exogenous zeitgebers. The suprachiasmatic nucleus of the hypothalamus is thought to be the major endogenous pacemaker; the light-dark cycle is thought to be the major exogenous zeitgeber. The rhythms of the body exhibit a biological feature called a phase-response curve, which is based on a 24-hour unit. Perturbations, such as exposure to light, have a differential effect on bodily rhythms (for example, sleep and hormone secretion), depending on the time of day—hence, the location on the phase-response curve. Exposure to light in the morning results in a phase advance— that is, rhythms are shifted to an earlier time; exposure to light in the evening results in a phase delay— that is, rhythms are shifted to a later time. Therefore, the entrainment of the endogenous pacemakers by light is the result of a phase advance at dawn and a phase delay at dusk. Melatonin is secreted by the pineal gland during the night. Secretion is stopped by exposure to light during the night but is not stimulated by exposure to darkness during the day.

**Effects of light exposure.** More than 50 controlled studies have shown that light therapy is effective, although its mechanism of action is still uncertain. The most accepted theory is that exposure to bright artificial light in the morning causes a phase advance of biological rhythms that effectively treats the delayed circadian rhythms associated with major depressive disorder with seasonal pattern. That hypothesis is supported by the observations of several investigators that other types of depressive disorders do not respond to phototherapy. The initial theory that light exposure works by affecting melatonin secretion has not been supported by subsequent experiments. A high intensity of light was thought to be required for therapeutic effects, but that hypothesis has been disputed by recent studies. Most studies support the idea that two hours of exposure is more effective than 30 minutes of exposure. Whether light should be administered in the morning or the evening or at both times to obtain maximal benefit is undetermined, but the majority of studies support the administration of light in the morning. Full-spectrum light is effective, and some studies have found that narrow-spectrum light is ineffective. Whether an intermediate spectrum of light would be effective is not known.

### Indications

The major indication for light therapy is major depressive disorder with seasonal pattern, seen predominantly (80 percent) in women. The mean age of presentation is 40, although the mean age may decrease with better recognition of the disorder. The symptoms usually appear during the winter and remit spontaneously in the spring, but sometimes the symptoms appear in the summer. The most common symptoms include depression, fatigue, hypersomnia, hyperphagia, carbohydrate craving, irritability, and interpersonal difficulties. One third to one half of all patients with the disorder have not previously sought psychiatric help. The remainder have most often been previously classified as having a mood disorder. More than 50 percent of the patients with the disorder have a first-degree relative with a mood disorder. Some recent evidence indicates that persons with mild, subsyndromal symptoms of a seasonal pattern disorder may also experience some relief with phototherapy.

### Clinical Guidelines

The treatment requires exposure to bright light (2,500 lux) that is about 200 times brighter than the usual indoor lighting. The initial experiments exposed patients to the light for two to three hours before dawn and sometimes an additional two to three hours after dusk every day. The patients were instructed not to look directly into the light but to glance at it only occasionally. Patients usually responded after two to four days of treatment and relapsed two to four days after the treatment was stopped. Recent studies have indicated that only morning exposure may be necessary and that one hour of daily exposure may be sufficient. A debate remains about the required intensity of the light.

The most commonly reported adverse effects are headache, eyestrain, and feeling wired or irritable. Those adverse effects can usually be managed by reducing the length of time that the patient is exposed to the light.

## SLEEP DEPRIVATION AND ALTERATIONS OF SLEEP SCHEDULES

Sleep deprivation has been suggested as a short-term treatment of depressive disorders, as an adjuvant to antidepressant drugs to facilitate improvement, and as a treatment for premenstrual dysphoric disorder. One night's sleep deprivation results in a dramatic reduction of depressive symptoms in about 60 percent of all patients with depressive disorders. Unfortunately, the beneficial effects last only one day. The depressive disorder symptoms are often brought back quickly if the patient takes even a short nap after the night of sleep deprivation. That finding caused some researchers to hypothesize that some sleep-related depressogenic process may be temporarily aborted by the sleep deprivation. Some studies have reported that preventing only rapid eye movement (REM) sleep has the same effects as preventing all sleep, causing some researchers to hypothesize that a REM-related process may be related to maintaining or even causing depressive disorders.

Phase-advancing the sleep cycle—that is, going to bed early and waking up early—may have antidepressant effects in some depressed patients, especially when used as an adjuvant to pharmacotherapy. In contrast to the single-day improvement associated with sleep deprivation, the beneficial effects of sleep phase advance sometimes last for a week.

## DRUG-ASSISTED INTERVIEWING

To facilitate gathering information during a psychiatric interview, some psychiatrists advocate drug-assisted interviewing. The common use of an intravenous injection of sodium amobarbital (Amytal) led to the popular name of "Amytal interview" for the technique. Narcotherapy or narcoanalysis consists of a series of drug-assisted psychotherapy sessions. Both sedatives (for example, barbiturates and benzodiazepines) and stimulants—for example, methylphenidate (Ritalin)—have been used. Narcotherapy was thought to benefit patients by allowing them to experience the catharsis of having a repressed memory or thought brought to conscious awareness. Although narcotherapy is rarely used in modern psychiatry, there has been some renewed interest in it. Some noted psychiatrists have proposed that 3, 4-methylenedioxymethamphetamine (MDMA, ecstasy) may be beneficial when used as an agent for drug-assisted psychotherapy. That suggestion has been extremely controversial.

### Indications

Although much has been written about drug-assisted interviewing, the literature consists mainly of uncontrolled studies and anecdotal reports, thus making it difficult to determine a definitive statement about its indications. Furthermore, several controlled trials have shown that the use of drugs does not guarantee that patients will tell the truth, in spite of the popular misconception that sodium amobarbital is a truth serum. A few studies have shown, in fact, that drug-assisted interviews are no better at eliciting information than an empathic interviewer, hypnosis, or the administration of a placebo.

The most common reasons for drug-assisted interviews in modern practice are the presentation of uninformative

or mute patients, catatonia, and supposed conversion disorder. Although drug-assisted interviews often elicit information sooner than interviews without the drug, no evidence indicates that the technique has a positive effect on the therapeutic outcome. Patients may be silent because of excessive anxiety about recounting a traumatic event (for example, a rape or an accident), and drug-assisted interviews have been used successfully in such cases. But hypnosis, daytime sedation, empathic and supportive approaches, and time also help elicit information and do not have the risks of drug-assisted interviewing.

Mute patients with a mental disorder may have catatonic schizophrenia or conversion disorder or may be malingering. Barbiturates or benzodiazepines help in temporarily activating catatonic patients; therefore, catatonic schizophrenia may be a reasonable indication for using drug-assisted interviewing. Patients with conversion disorder or malingering may or may not improve during a drug-assisted interview. The commonly held but controversial belief is that a functional or psychological disorder improves during a drug-assisted interview, whereas an organic or medical disorder does not improve or even worsens. If patients do improve, there is no indication that the drug-assisted interview facilitated their improvement; if they do not improve or even worsen, the information gained from the interview is of little help in guiding the patients' treatment.

Another indication for drug-assisted interviewing is the differential diagnosis of confusion; the assumption is that functional confusion will clear during the procedure and that organic confusion will not. False positives occur when a confused patient is withdrawing from alcohol or barbiturates and when a patient has an epileptic disorder. False-negative results occur when the interviewer uses too much drug and sometimes when the patient has conversion disorder or is a malingerer. Another proposed indication for drug-assisted interviewing is to differentiate between schizophrenia and a depressive disorder. When given sodium amobarbital, schizophrenic patients, it was once thought, would recall bizarre material, and depressed patients would recall depressive material. That hypothesis has not been confirmed in controlled studies. Sodium amobarbital has also been suggested as an adjuvant in supportive therapy; the drug is used to reinforce a therapeutic suggestion (for example, to stop smoking). Furthermore, muscle relaxation is more powerful than sodium amobarbital as an adjuvant in behavior therapy.

### Clinical Guidelines

A 10 percent solution of sodium amobarbital is administered at a rate of about 0.5 to 1.0 mL a minute. The rate and the total dose should be adjusted for each patient. The total dose may vary between 0.25 and 0.5 grams, although some patients need up to 1 gram. The end point is a state of mild sedation but not sleep. The benzodiazepines—for example, diazepam (Valium)—are just as effective as the barbiturates and less dangerous.

Barbiturates should not be given to patients with liver, renal, or cardiopulmonary diseases or to patients with porphyria or a history of sedative abuse. Patients may have allergic reactions or respiratory suppression during barbiturate interviews, and the clinician must be prepared for both those possibilities. Furthermore, the use of what patients may perceive as a truth serum may increase their paranoia and interfere with the development of a psychotherapuetic transference.

## PSYCHOSURGERY

Psychosurgery involves surgical modification of the brain with the goal of reducing the symptoms of the most severely ill psychiatric patients who have not responded adequately to less radical treatments. Psychosurgical procedures lesion specific brain regions (for example, in lobotomies and cingulotomies) or their connecting tract (for example, in tractotomies and leukotomies). Psychosurgical techniques are also used in the treatment of neurological disorders, such as epilepsy and chronic pain disorder.

The interest in psychosurgical approaches to mental disorders has only recently been rekindled. The renewed interest is based on a number of factors, including much-improved techniques that allow the neurosurgeon to make exact stereotactically placed lesions, improved preoperative diagnoses, comprehensive preoperative and postoperative psychological assessments, complete follow-up data, and a growing understanding regarding the neuroanatomical basis of some mental disorders.

### History

In 1935, after the demonstration by C. F. Jacobsen and John F. Fulton at Yale University that frontal lobe ablation in a monkey had a calming effect, Antonio Egas Moniz and Almidia, working in Portugal, severed frontal lobe white matter in 20 psychotic patients and reported a decrease in their tension and psychotic symptoms. In 1936 Walter Freeman and James Watts at George Washington University introduced the psychosurgical technique of prefrontal lobotomy to the United States. Although early procedures required burr holes or other exposure of the brain, Freeman eventually developed the technique of transorbital leukotomy, which involved the introduction and lateral movement of a sharp instrument (actually an ice pick) through the eye socket as a method of sectioning the white matter of the frontal lobes. By the late 1940s psychosurgery was being performed worldwide, and an estimated 5,000 patients were being operated on each year. In 1949 Egas Moniz won the Nobel Prize for his work in developing psychosurgical techniques. Shortly thereafter, the introduction of antipsychotic drugs and the increasing public concern about the ethics of psychosurgery led to a near abandonment of those techniques for the treatment of psychiatric patients, although psychosurgical procedures for pain control and epilepsy continued to be used.

### Modern Psychosurgical Techniques

Stereotactic neurosurgical equipment now allows the neurosurgeon to place discrete lesions in the brain. Radioactive implants, cryoprobes, electrical coagulation, proton beams, and ultrasonic waves are used to make the actual lesions.

### Indications

The major indication for psychosurgery is the presence of a debilitating, chronic mental disorder that has not responded to any other treatment. A reasonable guideline is that the disorder should have been present for five years, during which a wide variety of alternative treatment approaches were attempted. Chronic intractable major depressive disorder and obsessive-compulsive disorder are the two disorders reportedly most responsive to psychosurgery. The presence of vegetative symptoms and marked anxiety further increases the likelihood of a successful therapeutic outcome. Whether psychosurgery is a reasonable treatment for intractable and extreme aggression is still controversial. Psychosurgery is not indicated for the treatment of schizophrenia, and data regarding manic episodes are controversial.

### Therapeutic and Adverse Effects

When patients are carefully selected, between 50 and 70 percent have significant therapeutic improvement with psychosurgery. Fewer than 3 percent become worse. Continued improvement is often noted from one to two years after surgery, and patients are often more responsive than they were before psychosurgery to traditional pharmacological and behavioral treatment approaches. Postoperative seizures are present in fewer than 1 percent of patients, and those seizures are usually controlled with phenytoin (Dilantin). As measured by intelligence quotient (I.Q.) scores, cognitive abilities improve after surgery, probably because of the patient's increased ability to attend to cognitive tasks. Undesired changes in personality have not been noted with the modern limited procedures.

## PLACEBOS

Placebos are substances that have no known pharmacological activity. Although it is usually thought that placebos act through suggestion, rather than biological action, that idea is based on the artificial distinction between the mind and the body. Virtually every treatment modality is accompanied by poorly understood factors affecting its outcome (for example, the taste of a medicine and the patient's emotional response to a physician). Indeed, those poorly understood factors and the effects of placebos are better called nonspecific therapeutic factors. For example, at least one study has shown that naloxone (Narcan), an opiate antagonist, can block the analgesic effects of a placebo, thus indicating that a release of an endogenous opiate may explain some placebo effects.

Long-term treatment with placebos should never be undertaken when patients have clearly stated an objection to such a treatment. Furthermore, deceptive treatment with placebos seriously undermines patients' confidence in their physicians. And placebos should never be used when an effective therapy is available, as placebos can lead to both a dependence on pills and various adverse effects.

## ACUPUNCTURE AND ACUPRESSURE

An ancient Chinese treatment, acupuncture is the stimulation of specific points of the body with electrical stimulation or the twisting of a needle. Acupressure is the stimulation of those same points with pressure; however, acupressure was not a part of traditional Chinese medicine. The stimulation of specific points is associated with the relief of certain symptoms and is identified with particular organs. Many Chinese doctors have reported therapeutic success with those treatments in combination with herbal treatment (given orally, topically, or intradermally) for a variety of disorders, including mental disorders. Several American investigators have reported that acupuncture is an effective treatment for some patients with depressive disorders and substance dependence (for example, to nicotine, caffeine, cocaine, and heroin). Although it is difficult to approach Eastern treatments with a Western mind, it is also true that history has shown that many ancient remedies have a firm biological basis.

## ORTHOMOLECULAR THERAPY

Megavitamin therapy is treatment with large dosages of niacin, ascorbic acid, pyridoxine, folic acid, vitamin $B_{12}$, and various minerals. Special diets and hormone treatments are often part of those treatment protocols. Uncontrolled reports of the successful treatment of schizophrenia with niacin have not been replicated in controlled collaborative studies. Despite claims to the contrary, megavitamin and diet therapies currently have no proved clinical use in psychiatry. However, a balanced diet reasonably supplemented with vitamins is a good prescription for all patients and physicians.

## HISTORICAL TREATMENTS

A variety of treatments were used before the introduction of effective pharmacological agents. Although most of the treatments never underwent controlled therapeutic trials, many clinicians report that the treatments were, in fact, effective. But because most of them were associated with unpleasant or dangerous adverse effects, they have been virtually supplanted by pharmacotherapy.

### Subcoma Insulin Therapy

Psychiatrists used to inject small doses of insulin to induce mild hypoglycemia and the resultant sedative effects. Because of the possible complications of the treatment and the introduction of sedating drugs, the treatment has been abandoned.

### Coma Therapy

Insulin coma therapy was introduced in 1933 by Manfred Sakel after his observation that schizophrenic patients who went into coma appeared to have decreased psychiatric symptoms after the coma. Insulin was used to induce a comatose state lasting 15 to 60 minutes. The risk of death or cognitive impairment and the introduction of antipsychotic drugs led to the abandonment of the treatment in the United States.

Atropine sulfate was first used in 1950 to induce coma in psychiatric patients. The atropine-induced comas lasted six to eight hours, and the patients took warm and cold showers after awakening. Atropine coma is no longer used in the United States.

### Carbon Dioxide Therapy

Carbon dioxide therapy, first used in 1929, involved having the patients inhale carbon dioxide, resulting in an abreaction with severe motor excitement after removing the breathing mask. The treatment was used principally for neurotic patients, and there was doubt, even when it was in use, that the treatment was effective. Carbon dioxide therapy is no longer used in the United States.

### Electrosleep Therapy

Electrosleep therapy involves applying a low level of current through electrodes applied to the patient's head. The patient usually feels a tingling sensation at the sites of the electrodes, but sleep is not necessarily induced. The treatment is applied to a wide variety of disorders, with mixed reports of efficacy, but it is not used in the United States.

### Continuous Sleep Treatment

Continuous sleep treatment is a symptomatic method of treatment in which the patient is sedated with any of a variety of drugs to induce 20 hours of sleep a day, sometimes for as long as three weeks in severely agitated patients. Klaesi introduced the name in 1922 and used barbiturates to obtain deep narcosis. The treatment is not used in the United States.

### References

Avery D H, Bolte M A P, Cohen S, Millet M S: Gradual versus rapid dawn simulation treatment of winter depression. J Clin Psychiatry 53: 359, 1992.

Avery D H, Khan A, Dager S R, Cohen S, Cox G B, Dunner D L: Morning or evening bright light treatment of winter depression? The significance of hypersomnia. Biol Psychiatry 29: 117, 1991.

Ballantine H T, Bouckoms A J, Thomas E K, Giriunas I E: Treatment of psychiatric illness by stereotactic cingulotomy. Biol Psychiatry 22: 807, 1987.

Blehar M C, Rosenthal N E: Seasonal affective disorders and phototherapy: Report of a National Institute of Mental Health-sponsored workshop. Arch Gen Psychiatry 46: 469, 1989.

Bridges P: Psychosurgery revisited. J Neuropsychiatry 2: 326, 1990.

Brody H: The lie that heals: The ethics of giving placebos. Ann Intern Med 97: 112, 1982.

Dysken M W, Chang S S, Casper R C: Barbiturate-facilitated interviewing. Biol Psychiatry 14: 421, 1979.

Eastman C I, Lahmeyer H W, Watell L G, Good G D, Young M A: A placebo-controlled trial of light treatment for winter depression. J Affect Disord 26: 211, 1992.

Giedke H, Geilenkirchen R, Hauser M: The timing of partial sleep deprivation in depression. J Affect Disord 25: 117, 1992.

Hay P J, Sachdev P S: The present status of psychosurgery in Australia and New Zealand. Med J Aust 157: 17, 1992.

Hay P, Sachdev P, Cumming S, Smith J S, Lee T, Kitchener P, Matheson J: Treatment of obsessive-compulsive disorder by psychosurgery. Acta Psychiatr Scand 87: 197, 1993.

Jenike M A, Baer L, Ballantine T, Martuza R L, Tynes S, Giriunas I, Buttolph M L, Cassem N H: Cingulotomy for refractory obsessive-compulsive disorder. Arch Gen Psychiatry 48: 548, 1991.

Kasper S, Rogers S L B, Yancey A, Schulz P M, Skwerer R G, Rosenthal N E: Phototherapy in individuals with and without subsyndromal seasonal affective disorder. Arch Gen Psychiatry 46: 837, 1989.

Leibenluft E, Wehr T A: Is sleep deprivation useful in the treatment of depression? Am J Psychiatry 149: 159, 1992.

Levitt A J, Joffe R T, Kennedy S H: Bright light augmentation in antidepressant nonresponders. J Clin Psychiatry 52: 236, 1991.

Levitt A J, Joffe R T, Moul D E, Lam R W, Teicher M H, Lebegue B, Murray M G, Oren D A, Schwartz P, Buchanan A, Glod C A, Brown J: Side effects of light therapy in seasonal affective disorder. Am J Psychiatry *150*: 650, 1993.

Mackert A, Volz H-P, Stieglitz R-D, Muller-Oerlinghausen B: Phototherapy in nonseasonal depression. Biol Psychiatry *30*: 257, 1991.

Mindus P, Jenike M A: Neurosurgical treatment of malignant obsessive compulsive disorder. Psychiatr Clin North Am *15*: 921, 1992.

Pangalos M N, Malizia A L, Francis P T, Lowe S L, Bertolucci P H F, Procter A W, Bridges P K, Bartlett J R, Bowen D M: Effect of psychotropic drugs on excitatory amino acids in patients undergoing psychosurgery for depression. Br J Psychiatry *160*: 638, 1992.

Quitkin F M, McGrath P J, Rabkin J G, Stewart J W, Harrison W, Ross D C, Tricamo E, Fleiss J, Markowitz J, Klein D F: Different types of placebo response in patients receiving antidepressants. Am J Psychiatry *148*: 197, 1991.

Quitkin F M, Rabkin J G, Stewart J W, McGrath, P J, Harrison W, Ross D C, Tricamo E, Fleiss J, Markowitz J, Klein D F: Heterogeneity of clinical response during placebo treatment. Am J Psychiatry *148*: 193, 1991.

Reynolds C F, Buysse D J, Kupfer D J, Hoch C C, Houck P R, Matzzie J, George C J: Rapid eye movement sleep deprivation as a probe in elderly subjects. Arch Gen Psychiatry *47*: 1128, 1990.

Rosenthal N E, Moul D E, Hellekson C J, Oren D A, Frank A, Brainard G C, Murray M G, Wehr T A: A multicenter study of the light visor for seasonal affective disorder: No difference in efficacy found between two different intensities. Neuropsychopharmacology *8*: 151, 1993.

Sachdev P, Smith J S, Matheson J: Is psychosurgery antimanic? Biol Psychiatry *27*: 363, 1990.

Sack R L, Lewy A J, White D M, Singer C M, Fireman M J, Vandiver R: Morning vs evening light treatment for winter depression: Evidence that the therapeutic effects of light are mediated by circadian phase shifts. Arch Gen Psychiatry *47*: 343, 1990.

Southmayd S E, David M M, Cairns J, Delva N J, Letemendia F J, Waldron J J: Sleep deprivation in depression: Pattern of relapse and characteristics of preceding sleep. Biol Psychiatry *28*: 979, 1990.

Wu J C, Bunney W E: The biological basis of an antidepressant response to sleep deprivation and relapse: Review and hypothesis. Am J Psychiatry *147*: 14, 1990.

# Child Psychiatry: Assessment, Examination, and Psychological Testing

A comprehensive evaluation of a child includes clinical interviews with the parents, the child, and the family; information regarding the child's current school functioning; and a standardized assessment of the child's intellectual level and academic achievement. In some cases, developmental tests and neuropsychological assessments are useful. Since psychiatric evaluations of children are rarely initiated by the child, the clinican must obtain information from the family, the school, and any involved community agencies to understand the reasons for the referral. Although children can be excellent informants about symptoms related to mood and inner experiences—such as psychotic phenomena, sadness, fears, and anxiety—they often have difficulty with the chronology of symptoms and are sometimes reticent to report behaviors that have gotten them into trouble. Very young children often cannot articulate their experiences verbally and are better at showing their feelings and preoccupations in a play situation.

The first step in the comprehensive evaluation of a child is to meet with the parents to obtain a full description of the current concerns and a history of the child's psychiatric and medical status. An interview and observation of the child is the next step. Then psychological testing should be done.

Clinical interviews allow for the most flexibility in understanding the evolution of problems over time and in establishing the role of environmental stressors, but clinical interviews may not systematically cover every clinical area. To increase the amount of information generated, the clinican may use semistructured or structured interviews—such as the Kiddie Schedule for Affective Disorders and Schizophrenia (K-SADS) and the Diagnostic Interview Schedule for Children-Revised (DISC-R)—and rating scales. Rating scales such as the Child Behavior Checklist and the Teacher Questionnaire can also help the clinician systematically collect clinical information.

Sources often disagree about a variety of symptoms and behaviors during a comprehensive assessment of a child. When faced with contradictory information, the clinician must realize that those differences may reflect an accurate picture of the child's presentation in different settings. Once a full history is obtained from the parents, the child is examined, the child's current functioning at home and at school is assessed, and psychological testing is completed, the clinician can make a best-estimate diagnosis by using all the available information and can make recommendations.

## CLINICAL INTERVIEWS

To conduct a useful interview with a child of any age, the clinician must be familiar with normal development, so that the child's responses can be put in the proper perspective. For example, a young child's discomfort on separation from a parent and the lack of clarity regarding the purpose of the interview in a school-age child are perfectly normal and should not be misconstrued as psychiatric symptoms. Furthermore, behavior that is normal in a child of one age, such as temper tantrums in a 2-year-old, takes on a different meaning if present, for example, in a 17-year-old.

The first task of the interviewer is to engage the child and develop a rapport, so that the child is comfortable. The interviewer should find out the child's concept of the purpose of the interview and should ask what a parent has told the child. The interviewer can then briefly describe the reason the interview is taking place in a way that the child understands and that is supportive of the child. During the course of the interview, the clinician should learn about the child's relationships with family members and peers, how well the child is functioning academically and behaviorally in school, and what the child enjoys doing. A general sense of the child's cognitive functioning is a part of the mental status examination.

The level of confidentiality in a child assessment is correlated with the age of the child—that is, just about all specific information is shared with the parents of a very young child and more privacy is reasonable with an adolescent. School-age and older children may be told that, if the clinician becomes concerned that the children are dangers to themselves or to others, that information must be shared with other adults. However, the clinician must determine whether the children are safe in their environments and make clinical judgments about whether the children are victims of abuse or neglect.

Toward the end of the interview, children may be asked in an open-ended manner whether they would like to bring up anything else. Every child should be complimented for his or her cooperation and thanked for participating in the interview, and the interview should end on a positive note.

### Infants and Young Children

Assessments of infants usually begin with their parents present, since very young children may be frightened by the interview situation; also, the interview with the parents present provides the best way for the clinician to assess the parent-infant interaction. Infants may be referred for a variety of reasons, including high levels of irritability, difficulty in being consoled, disturbances of eating, poor weight gain, sleep disturbances, withdrawn behavior, lack of engagement in play, and developmental delay. Areas of functioning to be assessed include motor development, activity level, verbal communication, ability to engage in play, problem-solving skills, adaptation to daily routines, relationships, and social responsivity. The parents' ability to provide a nurturing, safe, and stimulating environment for the child is assessed through observation and discussions with the parents. The child's developmental level of functioning is determined by combining observations made during the interview with standardized developmental measures. Observations of play reveal a child's developmental level and reflect the child's emotional state and preoccupations. The examiner can interact with an infant of 18 months or less in a playful manner by using such games as peekaboo. Children between the ages of 18 months and 3 years can be observed in a playroom. Children over 2 years old may exhibit symbolic play with toys and may reveal more in that mode than through conversation. The use of puppets and dolls with children under 6 years is often an effective way to elicit information, especially if questions are directed to the dolls, rather than to the child.

## School-Age Children

Some school-age children are comfortable while conversing with an adult; others are hampered by fear, anxiety, poor verbal skills, or oppositionalism. School-age children can usually tolerate a 45 minute session. The room should be spacious enough for the child to be able to move around but not so large as to reduce intimate contact between the examiner and the child. Part of the interview can be reserved for unstructured play, and a variety of toys can be made available to capture the child's interest and to elicit themes and feelings.

The initial part of the interview should explore the child's understanding of the reasons for the meeting and should confirm the fact that the interview was not set up because the child did something wrong. Techniques that can facilitate the disclosure of feelings include asking the child to draw a person, family members, and a house and then questioning the child about the drawings. Children may be asked to reveal three wishes, to describe the best and worst events of their lives, and who would be a favorite person to be stranded with on a desert island. Games such as Donald Winnicott's squiggle, in which the examiner draws a curved line and then the examiner and the child take turns continuing the drawing, may open lines of communication.

Questions that are partially open-ended with some multiple choices may elicit the most complete answers in school-age children. Simple, closed (yes-no) questions may not elicit enough information, and completely open-ended questions can overwhelm a school-age child who is not able to construct a chronological narrative, resulting in a

shrugging of the child's shoulders. The use of indirect commentary—such as, "I once knew a child who felt very sad when he moved away from all his friends. . ."—is helpful, although the clinician must be careful not to lead the child into confirming what the child thinks the clinician wants to hear. School-age children respond well to a clinician who helps them compare moods or feelings by asking them to rate feelings on a scale of 1 to 10.

## Adolescents

Adolescents can usually give a chronological account of the events leading to the evaluation, although some may disagree with the need for the evaluation. The clinician should communicate the value of hearing the story from the adolescent's point of view and must be careful to reserve judgment and not assign blame. Adolescents may be concerned about confidentiality, and the clinician can assure them that permission will be requested from them before any specific information is shared with parents, except for situations involving danger to the adolescents or others, in which case confidentiality must be sacrificed. Adolescents can be approached in an open-ended manner, but, when silences occur during the interview, the clinician should break the ice and attempt to reengage them. The clinician can explore what the adolescents believe the outcomes of the evaluation will be (change of school, hospitalization, removal from home, removal of privileges).

Some adolescents approach the interview with apprehension or outright hostility but open up when the clinician is neither punitive nor judgmental. Clinicians must be aware of their own responses to an adolescent's behavior (countertransference), so as to remain therapeutic, even in the face of a defiant, angry, or difficult adolescent. Clinicians should set appropriate limits and should postpone or discontinue the interview if they feel threatened or if patients become destructive to property or to themselves. The interview should always include an exploration of suicidal thoughts, assaultive behavior, psychotic phenomena, substance use, and sexual relationships. Once rapport has been established, many adolescents appreciate the opportunity to tell their side of the story and may reveal things that have not been disclosed to anyone else.

## Family Interview

An interview with the parents and the patient together may be done first or as a later part of the evaluation. Sometimes an interview with the entire family, including the parents' other children, can be enlightening. The purpose is to observe the attitudes of the parents toward the patient and the affective responses of the children to their parents. The clinician's job is to maintain a nonthreatening atmosphere in which each member of the family can speak freely without feeling that the clinician is taking sides with any particular member. Although child psychiatrists generally function as advocates for the child, the clinician must validate each family member's feelings in the setting, because a lack of communication within the family often contributes to their problems.

## Parents

The interview with the patient's parents or caretakers is necessary to get a chronological picture of the child's growth and development. A thorough developmental history and details of any stressors or important events that have influenced the child's development must be elicited. The parents' view of the family dynamics, their marital history, and their own emotional adjustment are also elicited. The family's psychiatric history and the parenting styles of the grandparents are pertinent. Parents can be the best informants about the child's previous psychiatric and medical illnesses, evaluations, and treatments and about the time frame and severity of any preexisting problems. The clinician should question the parents about their understanding of the causes and the nature of their child's problems and about their expectations in regard to the assessment and potential treatments.

## STRUCTURED AND SEMISTRUCTURED INTERVIEWS

The advantage of using a structured interview is that information that might otherwise be overlooked or minimized is collected in a comprehensive way. Structured interviews, however, cannot take the place of clinical interviews, since structured interviews do not adequately address the chronology of symptoms, the interplay between environmental stressors and emotional responses, and developmental issues. Nevertheless, the clinician may find it helpful to have the data from a structured interview to combine with other materials in a comprehensive evaluation.

## Kiddie Schedule for Affective Disorders and Schizophrenia (K-SADS)

This semistructured interview presents multiple items with some space for further clarification of symptoms that are keyed to many diagnoses in the third edition of *Diagnostic and Statistical Manual of Mental Disorders* (DSM-III). It comes in a form for parents about their child and a version to be used with the child directly. It takes about 1 to 1 ½ hours to administer and is applicable for children between the ages of 6 and 17 years. The interviewer should have some training in the field of child psychiatry but need not be a psychiatrist.

## Diagnostic Interview Schedule for Children-Revised (DISC-R)

This structured interview was designed to be administered by trained lay people. It is available in parallel child and parent forms and is applicable for a multitude of diagnoses keyed to the revised third edition of DSM (DSM-III-R); computer scoring algorithm is available. Since it is a fully structured interview, the instructions serve as a complete guide for the questions, and the examiner need not have any knowledge of child psychiatry to administer the interview correctly. It is applicable to children between the ages of 8 and 17 years of age. The interview assesses symptoms over the previous six months and, thus, may be useful adjunctively in the evaluation process.

## RATING SCALES

### Child Behavior Checklist

The parent and teacher versions of this checklist were developed to cover a broad range of symptoms and several positive attributes related to academic and social competence. It presents items related to mood, frustration tolerance, hyperactivity, oppositional behavior, anxiety, and a variety of other behaviors. The parent version consists of 118 items that are rated on a scale of 0 (not true), 1 (sometimes true), and 2 (very true). The teacher version is similar but without the items that apply only to home life. Profiles were developed that are based on normal children of three different age groups (4 to 5, 6 to 11, and 12 to 16).

Such a checklist identifies specific problem areas that would otherwise be overlooked, and it may point out areas in which the child's behavior is deviant, compared with normal children of the same age group, although the checklist is not used specifically to make diagnoses.

### Revised Behavior Problem Checklist

This scale consists of 150 items that cover a variety of childhood behavioral and emotional symptoms. It discriminates between clinic-referred and nonreferred children. Separate subscales have been found to correlate in the appropriate direction with other measures of intelligence, academic achievement, clinical observations, and peer popularity. As with the other broad rating scales, such an instrument can be helpful in gaining a comprehensive view of a multitude of behavioral areas, yet it is not designed to make psychiatric diagnoses.

## CHILD PSYCHIATRIC EVALUATION

The child psychiatric evaluation should include a description of the reason for the referral, the child's past and present functioning, and any test results. An outline of the evaluation is given in Table 34–1.

**Table 34–1**
**Child Psychiatric Evaluation**

Identifying data
    Identified patient and family members
    Source of referral
    Informants
History
    Chief complaint
    History of present illness
    Developmental history and milestones
    Psychiatric history
    Medical history, including immunizations
    Family social history and parents' marital status
    Educational history and current school functioning
    Peer relationship history
    Current family functioning
    Family psychiatric and medical histories
    Current physical examination
Mental status examination
Neuropsychiatric examination (when applicable)
Developmental, psychological, and educational testing
Formulation and summary
DSM-IV diagnosis
Recommendations and treatment plan

## Identifying Data

To understand the clinical problems to be evaluated, the clinician must first identify the patient and keep in mind the family constellation surrounding the child. The clinician must also pay attention to the source of the referral—that is, whether it is the child's family, school, or some other agency, since that influences the family's attitude toward the evaluation. Finally, many informants contribute to the child's evaluation, so identifying each of them is important in gaining insight into the functioning of the child in different settings.

## History

A comprehensive history comprises information about the child's current and past functioning, based on the reports of the parents from clinical and structured interviews and on the reports of teachers and previous medical and psychiatric physicians and therapists. The chief complaint, the history of the present illness, and the child's developmental history are usually obtained from the parents. Psychiatric and medical histories, current physical examination findings, and immunization histories are usually obtained from the psychiatrists and pediatricians who treated the child in the past. The child is helpful in reporting the current situation with regard to peer relationships, adjustment to school, and family functioning. The family's psychiatric and social histories are best obtained from the parents.

## Mental Status Examination

A detailed description of the child's current mental functioning can be obtained through observation and specific questioning. An outline of the mental status examination is presented in Table 34–2.

**Physical appearance.** The examiner should note and document the child's size, grooming, nutritional state, bruising, head circumference, physical signs of anxiety, facial expressions, and mannerisms.

**Parent-child interaction.** The examiner can observe the interactions between the parents and the child in the waiting area before the interview and in the family session. The manner in which the parents and the child converse and the emotional overtones are pertinent.

**Table 34–2**
**Mental Status Examination for Children**

1. Physical appearance
2. Parent-child interaction
3. Separation and reunion
4. Orientation to time, place, and person
5. Speech and language
6. Mood
7. Affect
8. Thought process and content
9. Social relatedness
10. Motor behavior
11. Cognition
12. Memory
13. Judgment and insight

**Separation and reunion.** The examiner should note both the manner in which the child responds to the separation from a parent for an individual interview and the reunion behavior. Either lack of affect at separation and reunion or severe distress on separation or reunion can indicate the presence of problems in the parent-child relationship or other psychiatric disturbances.

**Orientation to time, place, and person.** Impairments in orientation can reflect organic damage, low intelligence, or a thought disorder; however, the age of the child must be kept in mind, since very young children are not expected to know the date, other chronological information, or the name of the interview site.

**Speech and language.** The examiner should note the presence of an appropriate level of speech and language acquisition for the child's age. An observable disparity between expressive language usage and receptive language is notable. The examiner should note the child's rate of speech, rhythm, latency to answer, spontancity of speech, intonation, articulation of words, and prosody. Echolalia, repetitive stereotypical phrases, and unusual syntax are important psychiatric findings. Children who do not use words by 18 months or who do not use phrases by 2 ½ to 3 years but who have a history of normal babbling and responding appropriately to nonverbal cues are probably developing normally. The examiner should consider the possibility that a hearing loss is contributing to a speech and language deficit.

**Mood.** A child's sad expression, lack of appropriate smiling, tearfulness, anxiety, euphoria, and anger are valid indicators of mood, as are verbal admissions of feelings. Persistent themes in play and fantasy also reflect the child's mood.

**Affect.** The examiner should note the child's range of emotional expressivity, appropriateness of affect to the content of thought, ability to move smoothly from one affect to another, and sudden labile emotional shifts.

**Thought process and content.** In evaluating a thought disorder in a child, the clinician must always consider what is developmentally expected for the child's age and what is deviant for any age group. The evaluation of the form of thought considers loosening of associations, excessive magical thinking, perseveration, echolalia, the child's ability to distinguish fantasy from reality, coherence of sentences, and the ability to reason logically. The evaluation of the content of thought considers delusions, obsessions, themes, fears, wishes, preoccupations, and interests.

Suicidal ideation is always a part of the mental status examination in children who are verbal enough to understand the questions and old enough to understand the concept. Children of average intelligence over 4 years of age usually have some understanding of what is real and what is make believe and may be asked about suicidal ideation, although a firm concept of the permanence of death may not be present until several years later.

Aggressive thoughts and homicidal ideation are assessed here. Perceptual disturbances, such as hallucinations, are also assessed. Very young children are expected to have short attention spans and may change the topic of conversation abruptly without exhibiting a symptomatic flight of ideas. Transient visual and auditory hallucinations in very young children do not necessarily represent major psychotic illnesses, but they do deserve further investigation.

**Social relatedness.** The examiner assesses the child's appropriateness of response to the interviewer, general level of social skills, eye contact, and degree of familiarity or withdrawal to the interview process. Overly friendly or familiar behavior may be as troublesome as extremely retiring and withdrawn presentations. The examiner assesses the child's self-esteem, general and specific areas of confidence, and success with family and peer relationships.

**Motor behavior.** This part of the mental status examination includes observations regarding the child's activity level, ability to pay attention and carry out developmentally appropriate tasks, coordination, involuntary movements, tremors, motor overflow, and any unusual focal asymmetries of muscle movement.

**Cognition.** The examiner assesses the child's intellectual functioning, problem-solving abilities, and memory. An approximate level of intelligence can be estimated by the child's general information, vocabulary, and comprehension. For a specific assessment of the child's cognitive abilities, the examiner can use a standardized test.

**Memory.** School-age children should be able to remember three objects after five minutes and to repeat five digits forward and three digits backward. Anxiety may interfere with the child's performance, but an obvious inability to repeat digits or to add simple numbers together may reflect brain damage, mental retardation, or learning disabilities.

**Judgment and insight.** The child's view of the problems, the reactions to them, and the potential solutions suggested by the child may give the clinician a good idea of the child's judgment and insight. In addition, the child's understanding of what is realistic for the child to do to help and what the clinician can do adds to the assessment of the child's judgment.

## Neuropsychiatric Assessment

A neuropsychiatric assessment is appropriate for children who are suspected of having a neurological disorder, a psychiatric impairment that coexists with neurological signs, or psychiatric symptoms that may be due to neuropathology. The neuropsychiatric evaluation combines information from a neurological examination, a physical examination, and the mental status examination. The neurological examination can identify asymmetrical abnormal signs (hard signs) that may indicate lesions in the brain. A physical examination can evaluate the presence of physical stigmata of particular syndromes in which neuropsychiatric symptoms or developmental aberrations play a role (for example, fetal alcohol syndrome, Down's syndrome).

Part of the neuropsychiatric examination is the assessment of neurological soft signs and minor physical anomalies. The term "neurological soft signs" was first noted by Loretta Bender in the 1940s in reference to nondiagnostic abnormalities in the neurological examinations of schizophrenic children. Soft signs are not indicative of focal neurological disorders, but they are associated with a wide variety of developmental disabilities and are seen frequently in children with low intelligence, learning disabilities, and behavioral disturbances. Soft signs may refer to both behavioral symptoms (which are sometimes associated with brain damage, such as severe impulsivity and hyperactivity), physical findings (including contralateral overflow movements), and a variety of nonfocal signs (such as mild choreiform movements, poor balance, mild incoordination, asymmetry of gait, nystagmus, and the persistence of infantile reflexes). Soft signs can be divided into (1) those that are normal in a young child but become abnormal when they persist in an older child and (2) those that are abnormal at any age. The Physical and Neurological Examination for Soft Signs (PANESS) is an instrument that is used with children up to age 15 years. It consists of 15 questions regarding general physical status and medical history and 43 physical tasks (for example, touch your finger to your nose, hop on one foot to the end of the line, tap this fast with your finger). Neurological soft signs are important to note but are not specific in making a psychiatric diagnosis.

Minor physical anomalies or dysmorphic features occur with a higher than usual frequency in children with developmental disabilities, learning disabilities, speech and language disorders, and hyperactivity. As with soft signs, the documentation of minor physical anomalies is part of the neuropsychiatric assessment, but they are rarely helpful in the diagnostic process, nor do they imply a good or bad prognosis. Minor physical anomalies include a high-arched palate, epicanthus folds, hypertelorism, low-set ears, transverse palmar creases, multiple hair whorls, a large head, a furrowed tongue, and partial syndactyly of several toes.

When a seizure disorder is being considered in the differential diagnosis or a structural abnormality in the brain is suspected, an electroencephalogram (EEG), computed tomography (CT), or magnetic resonance imaging (MRI) may be indicated.

## Developmental, Psychological, and Educational Testing

Psychological tests are not always required to assess psychiatric symptoms, but they are valuable in determining a child's developmental level, intellectual functioning, and academic difficulties. A measure of adaptive functioning (including the child's competence in communication, daily living skills, socialization, and motor skills) is a prerequisite when a diagnosis of mental retardation is being considered. Table 34–3 outlines the general categories of psychological tests.

**Development tests for infants and preschoolers.** The Gesell Infant Scale, the Cattell Infant Scale, the Bayley Infant Scale of Development, and the Denver Developmental Screening Test include developmental assessments of infants as young as 2 months of age. When used with very young infants, the tests focus on sensorimotor and social responses to a variety of objects and interactions. When those instruments are used with older infants and preschoolers, emphasis is placed on language acquisition. The Gesell Infant Scale measures development in four areas: motor, adaptive functioning, language, and social. The Cattell Infant Scale was developed as a downward extension of the Stanford-Binet

**Table 34–3**
**Commonly Used Child and Adolescent Psychological Assessment Instruments**

| Test | Ages or Grades | Comments and Data Generated |
|------|----------------|------------------------------|
| **Intellectual Ability** | | |
| Wechsler Intelligence Scale for Children-Revised (WISC-R) (Psychological Corporation) | 6–16 | Standard scores: verbal, performance, and full-scale I.Q.; scaled subtest scores permitting specific skill assessment |
| Wechsler Adult Intelligence Scale-Revised (WAIS-R) (Psychological Corporation) | 16–adult | Same as WISC-R |
| Wechsler Preschool and Primary Scale of Intelligence (WPPSI) (Psychological Corporation) | 4–6 | Same as WISC-R |
| McCarthy Scales of Children's Abilities (MSCA) (Psychological Corporation) | 2.6–8 | Scores: general cognitive index (I.Q. equivalent), language, perceptual performance, quantitative memory and motor domain scores; percentiles |
| Kaufman Assessment Battery for Children (K-ABC) (American Guidance Service) | 2.6–12.6 | Well-grounded in theories of cognitive psychology and neuropsychology. Allows immediate comparison of intellectual capacity with acquired knowledge. Scores: mental processing composite (I.Q. equivalent); sequential and simultaneous processing and achievement standard scores; scaled mental processing and achievement subtest scores; age equivalents, percentiles |
| Stanford-Binet, 4th edition (SB:FE) (Riverside Publishing Company) | 2–23 | Scores: I.Q., verbal, abstract-visual, and quantitative reasoning; short-term memory; standard age |
| Peabody Picture Vocabulary Test-Revised (PPVT-R) (American Guidance Service) | 4–adult | Measures receptive vocabulary acquisition. Standard scores, percentiles, age equivalents |
| **Development** | | |
| Gesell Infant Scale | 8 wk–3½ yr | Mostly motor development in the first year, with some social and language assessment |
| Bayley Infant Scale of Development | 8 wk–2½ yr | Motor and social |
| Denver Developmental Screening Test | 2 mo–6 yr | Screening |
| Yale Revised Developmental Schedule | 4 wk–6 yr | Gross motor, fine motor, adaptive, personal-social, language |
| **Achievement** | | |
| Woodcock-Johnson Psycho-Educational Battery (DLM/ Teaching Resources) | K–12 | Scores: reading and mathematics (mechanics and comprehension), written language, other academic achievement; grade and age scores, standard scores, percentiles |
| Wide-Range Achievement Test-Revised, Levels 1 and 2 (WRAT-R) (Jastak Associates) | Level 1: 5–11 Level 2: 12–75 | Permits screening for deficits in reading, spelling, and arithmetic; grade levels, percentiles, stanines, standard scores |
| Kaufman Test of Educational Achievement, Brief and Comprehensive Forms (K-TEA) (American Guidance Service) | 1–12 | Standard scores: reading, mathematics, and spelling; grade and age equivalents, percentiles, stanines. Brief form sufficient for most clinical applications; comprehensive form allows error analysis and more detailed curriculum planning |
| **Adaptive Behavior** | | |
| Vineland Adaptive Behavior Scales (American Guidance Service) | Normal: 0–19 Retarded: all ages | Standard scores: adaptive behavior composite and communication, daily living skills, socialization and motor domains; percentiles, age equivalents, developmental age scores. Separate standardization groups for normal, visually handicapped, hearing-impaired, emotionally disturbed, and retarded |
| Scales of Independent Behavior (DLM Teaching Resources) | Newborn–adult | Standard scores: four adaptive (motor, social interaction and communication, personal living, community living) and three maladaptive (internalized, asocial, and externalized) areas; general maladaptive index and broad independence cluster |

**Table 34–3**
*Continued*

| Test | Ages or Grades | Comments and Data Generated |
|------|----------------|------------------------------|
| **Projective** | | |
| Rorschach Inkblots (Huber, Haus; U.S. Distrib.: Grune & Stratton) | 3–adult | Special scoring systems. Most recently developed and increasingly universally accepted is Exner's (1974) Comprehensive System. Assesses perceptual accuracy, integration of affective and intellectual functioning, reality testing, and other psychological processes |
| Thematic Apperception Test (TAT) (Harvard University Press) | 6–adult | Generates stories that are analyzed qualitatively. Assumed to provide especially rich data regarding interpersonal functioning |
| Machover Draw-A-Person Test (DAP) (Charles C Thomas) | 3–adult | Qualitative analysis and hypothesis generation, especially regarding subject's feelings about self and significant others |
| Kinetic Family Drawing (KFD) (Brunner/Mazel) | 3–adult | Qualitative analysis and hypothesis generation regarding a person's perception of family structure and sentient environment. Some objective scoring systems in existence |
| Rotter Incomplete Sentences Blank (Psychological Corporation) | Child, adolescent, and adult forms | Primarily qualitative analysis, although some objective scoring systems have been developed |
| **Personality** | | |
| Minnesota Multiphasic Personality Inventory (MMPI) (University of Minnesota Press) | 16–adult | Most widely used personality inventory. Standard scores: 3 validity scales and 14 clinical scales |
| Millon Adolescent Personality Inventory (MAPI) (National Computer Systems) | 13–18 | Standard scores for 20 scales grouped into three categories: personality styles, expressed concerns, behavioral correlates. Normed on adolescent population. Focuses on broad functional spectrum, not just problem areas |
| Children's Personality Questionnaire (Institute for Personality and Ability Testing) | 8–12 | Measures 14 primary personality traits, including emotional stability, self-concept level, excitability, and self-assurance. Generates combined broad trait patterns, including extraversion and anxiety |
| **Neuropsychological** | | |
| Beery-Buktenika Developmental Test of Visual-Motor Integration (VMI) (Modern Curriculum Press) | 2–16 | Screening instrument for visual-motor deficits. Standard scores, age equivalents, percentiles |
| Benton Visual Retention Test (Psychological Corporation) | 6–adult | Assesses presence of deficits in visual-figural memory. Mean scores by age |
| Bender Visual-Motor Gestalt Test (American Orthopsychiatric Association) | 5–adult | Assesses visual-motor deficits and visual-figural retention. Age equivalents |
| Reitan-Indiana Neuropsychological Test Battery for Children (Neuropsychology Press) | 5–8 | Cognitive and perceptual-motor tests for children with suspected brain damage |
| Halstead-Reitan Neuropsychological Test Battery for Older Children (Neuropsychology Press) | 9–14 | Same as Reitan-Indiana |
| Luria-Nebraska Neuropsychological Battery: Children's Revision (LNNB-C) (Western Psychological Services) | 8–12 | Sensory-motor, perceptual, and cognitive tests measuring 11 clinical and 2 additional domains of neuropsychological functioning. Provides standard scores |

Table from G R Racusin, N E Moss: Psychological assessment of children and adolescents. In *Child and Adolescent Psychiatry: A Comprehensive Textbook*, M Lewis, editor, p 475. Williams & Wilkins, Baltimore, 1991. Used with permission. Adapted by Melvin Lewis, M.B.

Intelligence Scale and is administered in a test-oriented fashion.

An infant's score on one of the above developmental assessments is not a reliable way to predict a child's future intelligence quotient (I.Q.) in most cases. Infant assessments are valuable, however, in detecting developmental deviation and mental retardation and in raising suspicions of a developmental disorder. Whereas infant assessments rely heavily on sensorimotor functions, intelligence testing in older children and adolescents comprises later-developing functions, including verbal, social, and abstract cognitive abilities.

**Intelligence tests for school-age children and adolescents.** The most widely used test of intelligence for school-age children and adolescents is the Wechsler Intelligence Scale for Children-III (WISC-III). It can be given to children from 6 to 17 years old, yields a verbal I.Q., a performance I.Q., and a combined full-scale I.Q. The verbal subtests consist of vocabulary, information, arithmetic, similarities, comprehension, and digit span (supplemental) categories. The performance subtests include block design, picture completion, picture arrangement, object assembly, coding, mazes (supplemental), and symbol search (supplemental). The scores of the supplemental subtests are not included in the computation of the intelligence quotient.

Each of the subcategories is scored from 1 to 19, with 10 being the average score. An average full-scale I.Q. is 100, with 70 to 80 representing borderline intellectual function, 80 to 90 being in the low average range, 90 to 109 being average, 110 to 119 being high average, and above 120 being in the superior or very superior range. The multiple breakdowns of the performance and verbal subscales allow a great deal of flexibility in identifying specific areas of deficit and scatter in intellectual abilities. Since a large part of intelligence testing measures abilities that are used in academic settings, the breakdown of the WISC-III can also be helpful in pointing out skills in which a child is weak and may benefit from remedial education.

The Stanford-Binet Intelligence Scale covers an age range that extends from 2 to 24 years. It relies on pictures, drawings, and objects for very young children and on verbal performance in older children and adolescents. The Stanford-Binet Intelligence Scale, the earliest version of an intelligence test of its kind, leads to a mental age score, as well as an intelligence quotient.

The McCarthy Scales of Children's Abilities and the Kaufman Assessment Battery for Children are two other tests of intelligence that are available for preschool and school-age children. They do not cover the adolescent age group.

LONG-TERM STABILITY OF INTELLIGENCE. Although a child's intelligence is relatively stable throughout the school-age years and adolescence, some factors can influence intelligence and a child's score on an intelligence test. The intellectual functions of children with severe mental illnesses and of those from socioeconomically deprived environments may decrease over time, whereas the intelligence quotients of children whose environments have been enriched may increase over time. Factors that influence a child's score on a given test of intellectual functioning and thus affect the accuracy of the test are motivation, emotional state, anxiety, and cultural milieu.

**Perceptual and perceptual motor tests.** The Bender Visual-Motor Gestalt test can be given to children between the ages of 4 and 12 years. It consists of a set of spatially related figures that the child is asked to copy. The scores are based on the child's number of errors. Although not a diagnostic test, it is useful in identifying developmentally age-inappropriate perceptual performances.

**Personality tests.** Personality tests are not of much use in making diagnoses, and they are less satisfactory than intelligence tests in regard to norms, reliability, and validity. However, they can be helpful in eliciting themes and fantasies.

The Rorschach test is a projective technique in which ambiguous stimuli—a set of bilaterally symmetrical inkblots—are shown to a child, who is then asked to describe what he or she sees in each one. The hypothesis is that the child's interpretation of the vague and ambiguous stimuli reflects basic characteristics of the child's personality. The examiner notes the themes and patterns. Two sets of norms have been established for the Rorschach test, one for children between 2 and 10 years and one for adolescents between 10 and 17 years.

A more structured projective test is the Children's Apperception Test (CAT), which is an adaptation of the Thematic Apperception Test (TAT). The CAT consists of cards with pictures of animals in situations that are somewhat ambiguous but that show scenes related to parent-child and sibling issues, caretaking, and other relationships. The child is asked to describe what is happening and to tell a story about what happens. Animals are used because it was hypothesized that children may respond more readily to the animal images than to human figures.

Drawings, toys, and play are also applications of projective techniques that can be used during the evaluation of a child. Doll houses, dolls, and puppets have been especially helpful in allowing the child a nonconversational mode in which to express a variety of attitudes and feelings. Play materials that reflect household situations are likely to elicit the child's fears, hopes, and conflicts about the family.

Projective techniques have not fared well as standardized instruments. Rather than being considered tests, projective techniques are best considered as additional clinical modalities.

**Educational tests.** Achievement tests measure the attainment of knowledge and skills based on a particular academic curriculum. The Wide-Range Achievement Test-Revised (WRAT-R) consists of tests of knowledge and skills and timed performances of reading, spelling, and mathematics. It is used with children ranging from 5 years to adulthood. The test yields a score that is compared with the average expected score for the child's chronological age and grade level.

The Peabody Individual Achievement Test (PIAT) includes word identification, spelling, mathematics, and reading comprehension.

The Kaufman Test of Educational Achievement, the Gray Oral Reading Test-Revised (GORT R), and the Sequential Tests of Educational Progress (STEP) are achievement tests that determine whether a child has achieved the level expected for the child's grade level. Children with an average I.Q. whose achievement is significantly lower than expected for their grade level in one or more subjects are considered to be learning-disabled. Thus, achievement testing, combined with a measure of intellectual function, can identify specific learning disabilities for which remediation is recommended. Children who do not reach their grade level according to their chronological age but who function intellectually in the borderline range or lower are not necessarily learning-disabled unless there is a disparity between their I.Q.s and their levels of achievement.

## Formulation and Summary

Once all the information is available, the clinician must put all the pieces together in a formulation that includes the psychodynamic summary, family environmental stressors, the psychiatric symptoms and any disorders that they constitute, and the specific physical, neuromotor, or developmental abnormalities that are causing the impairment. The clinician should also use the information from standardized psychological and developmental assessments in the summary. Since children are pervasively influenced by their environments, the psychiatric formulation includes not only the child's impairments but also the manner in which the family functions and affects the child's impairments. The clinician should also comment on the appropriateness of the child's educational setting and the issue of the child's general well-being with respect to abuse and neglect.

## Diagnosis

At the close of the evaluation process, the clinician should make a diagnosis. A child whose daily function is significantly impaired either in a school setting or at home is likely to meet the criteria for one or more psychiatric disorders. The fourth edition of DSM (DSM-IV) provides a guideline for psychiatric diagnosis that reflects a consensus of current expertise in the field; other clinical situations may not fall within DSM-IV's categories, but they require psychiatric attention and treatment. When dealing with children who are an integral part of a family and who are vulnerable to environmental stressors, the clinician must consider interventions that go beyond the DSM-IV diagnoses.

## Recommendations and Treatment Plan

Along with recommending appropriate courses of treatment for psychiatric disorders, the clinician must consider the family's level of functioning and the need for family and environmental interventions that are likely to ameliorate the child's condition. The clinician's decisions in those areas may range from determining that a child's entire family is in need of psychotherapy to recommending that a child's school setting be changed to recommending that the child live outside the family setting. The clinician must communicate the recommendations and proposed treatment plan to the parents and the child; without the parents' cooperation, treatment may not be obtained.

In many cases the child was referred by an outside agency, such as a school, a therapist, or a protective service agency. Therefore, with the family's permission, the clinician needs to communicate the recommendations to the referring source.

## References

Bender L: Childhood schizophrenia: Clinical study of 100 schizophrenic children. Am J Orthopsychiatry *17*: 40, 1947.

Caplan R, Guthrie D, Fish B, Tanguay P E, David-Lando G: The kiddie formal thought disorder rating scale: Clinical assessment, reliability, and validity. J Am Acad Child Adolesc Psychiatry *28*: 408, 1989.

Chandler M C, Gualtieri C T, Barnhill L J: The neuropsychiatric examination of the child. In *Handbook of Studies on Child Psychiatry*, B J Tonge, G D Burrows, J C Werry, editors, p 91. Elsevier, Amsterdam, 1990.

Gittleman R: The role of psychological tests for differential diagnosis in child psychiatry. J Am Acad Child Adolesc Psychiatry *19*: 413, 1980.

Gutterman E M, O'Brien J D, Young J G: Structured diagnostic interviews for children and adolescents: Current status and future directions. J Am Acad Child Psychiatry *26*: 621, 1987.

Guy W: Physical and Neurological Examination for Soft Signs (PANESS). In *ECDEU Assessment Manual for Psychopharmacology*, W Guy, editor, p 186. National Institute of Mental Health, Rockville, Md, 1976.

Herjanic B, Reich W: Development of a structured psychiatric interview for children: Agreement between child and parent on individual symptoms. J Abnorm Child Psychol *10*: 307, 1982.

Kaufman A S, Kaufman N L: *Kaufman Assessment Battery for Children: Interpretive Manual*. American Guidance Service, Circle Pines, Minn, 1983.

Lewis M: Psychiatric examination of the infant, child, and adolescent. In *Comprehensive Textbook of Psychiatry*, ed 5, H I Kaplan, B J Sadock, editors, p 1716. Williams & Wilkins, Baltimore, 1989.

Ollendick T H, Hersen M, editors: *Handbook of Child and Adolescent Assessment*. Allyn & Bacon, Boston, 1993.

Parrott R, Burgoon M, Ross C: Parents and pediatricians talk: Compliance-gaining strategies' use during well-child exams. Health Commun *4*: 57, 1992.

Puig-Antich J, Chambers W J, Tabrizi M A: The clinical assessment of current depressive episodes in children and adolescents: Interviews with parents and children. In *Affective Disorders in Childhood and Adolescence: An Update*, D P Cantwell, G A Carlson, editors, p 157. SP Medical & Scientific, New York, 1983.

Rating scales and assessment instruments for use in pediatric psychopharmacology research. Psychopharmacol Bull *21*: 205, 1985.

Shaffer D: Introduction and overview. In *Comprehensive Textbook of Psychiatry*, ed 5, H I Kaplan, B J Sadock, editors, p 1689. Williams & Wilkins, Baltimore, 1989.

Winnicott D W: *Therapeutic Consultations in Child Psychiatry*. Hogarth Press, London, 1971.

Young J G, O'Brien J B, Gutterman E M, Cohen P: Research on the clinical interview. J Am Acad Child Adolesc Psychiatry *26*: 613, 1987.

# 35 ||||||

# Mental Retardation

Mental retardation is a heterogeneous disorder consisting of below-average intellectual functioning and impairment in adaptive skills that is present before the person is 18 years of age. The impairments are influenced by genetic, environmental, and psychosocial factors. During the past decade, increased recognition has been given to subtle biological factors, including small chromosomal abnormalities, genetic syndromes, subclinical lead intoxication, and various prenatal toxic exposures in persons with mild mental retardation (up to 85 percent of the mentally retarded population). In past years the development of mild mental retardation had traditionally been attributed mainly to psychosocial deprivation.

A developmental approach to mental retardation includes investigation into environmental influences on rates of development. Social and moral behavior seems to be shaped by environmental factors to a larger degree than is cognition. However, increasing evidence indicates that specific groups of mentally retarded persons, such as those with fragile X syndrome and Down's syndrome, have characteristic patterns of social, linguistic, and cognitive development and typical behavioral manifestations.

The American Association of Mental Deficiency (AAMD) and the fourth edition of *Diagnostic and Statistical Manual of Mental Disorders* (DSM-IV) define mental retardation as significantly subaverage general intellectual functioning resulting in or associated with concurrent impairments in adaptive behavior and manifested during the developmental period—that is, before the age of 18. The diagnosis is made regardless of whether the patient has a coexisting physical disorder or other mental disorder. Table 35–1 presents an overview of developmental levels in communication, academic functioning, and vocational skills expected of persons with various degrees of mental retardation. Table 35–2 presents the DSM-IV diagnostic criteria for mental retardation.

General intellectual functioning is determined by the use of standardized tests of intelligence, and the term "significantly subaverage" is defined as an intelligence quotient (I.Q.) of approximately 70 or below or two standard deviations below the mean for the particular test. Adaptive functioning can be measured by using a standardized scale, such as the Vineland Adaptive Behavior Scale. In that scale, communication, daily living skills, socialization, and motor skills (up to 4 years, 11 months) are scored and generate an adaptive behavior composite that is correlated with the expected skills at a given age.

## NOMENCLATURE

The term "mental deficiency" was used interchangeably with "mental retardation" until recently, when the Association for Mental Retardation chose "mental retardation" as the preferred term. The World Health Organization (WHO) has recommended the term "mental subnormality," which includes two categories: mental retardation (subnormal functioning secondary to identifiable underlying pathological causes) and mental deficiency (I.Q. of less than 70), which is often used as a legal term.

The tenth revision of the International Classification of Diseases (ICD-10) uses the term "mental retardation" but defines it slightly differently than does DSM-IV. According to ICD-10, "Mental retardation is a condition of arrested or incomplete development of the mind, which is especially characterized by impairment of skills manifested during the developmental period, which contribute to the overall level of intelligence, i.e., cognitive, language, motor, and social abilities."

The term "feeble-mindedness" was used in the past in the American literature and in Great Britain, where the term "mental handicap" was also used until recently to denote a mild form of mental retardation. The term "oligophrenia" has been used in Russia, Scandinavia, and other European countries. "Amentia" is no longer used in modern psychiatry except occasionally to refer to a terminal stage of a degenerative disease.

## CLASSIFICATION

The degrees or levels of mental retardation are expressed in various terms. DSM-IV presents four types of mental retardation, reflecting the degree of intellectual impairment: mild mental retardation, moderate mental retardation, severe mental retardation, and profound mental retardation. The degrees of mental retardation by I.Q. range are indicated in Table 35–2. The category of borderline mental retardation (between one and two standard deviations below the test mean) was eliminated in 1973. Borderline intellectual functioning, according to DSM-IV, is not within the category of mental retardation but refers to an I.Q. in the 71 to 84 range and may be a focus of psychiatric attention.

In addition, DSM-IV lists mental retardation, severity unspecified, as a type reserved for those persons who are

**Table 35–1**
**Developmental Characteristics of Mentally Retarded Persons**

| Degree of Mental Retardation | Preschool Age (0–5) Maturation and Development | School Age (6–20) Training and Education | Adult (21 and Over) Social and Vocational Adequacy |
|---|---|---|---|
| Profound | Gross retardation; minimal capacity for functioning in sensorimotor areas; needs nursing care; constant aid and supervision required | Some motor development present; may respond to minimal or limited training in self-help | Some motor and speech development; may achieve very limited self-care; needs nursing care |
| Severe | Poor motor development; speech minimal; generally unable to profit from training in self-help; little or no communication skills | Can talk or learn to communicate; can be trained in elemental health habits; profits from systematic habit training; unable to profit from vocational training | May contribute partially to self-maintenance under complete supervision; can develop self-protection skills to a minimal useful level in controlled environment |
| Moderate | Can talk or learn to communicate; poor social awareness; fair motor development; profits from training in self-help; can be managed with moderate supervision | Can profit from training in social and occupational skills; unlikely to progress beyond second-grade level in academic subjects; may learn to travel alone in familiar places | May achieve self-maintenance in unskilled or semiskilled work under sheltered conditions; needs supervision and guidance when under mild social or economic stress |
| Mild | Can develop social and communication skills; minimal retardation in sensorimotor areas; often not distinguished from normal until later age | Can learn academic skills up to approximately sixth-grade level by late teens; can be guided toward social conformity | Can usually achieve social and vocational skills adequate to minimum self-support but may need guidance and assistance when under unusual social or economic stress |

Table adapted from *Mental Retardation Activities of the U.S. Department of Health, Education and Welfare*, p 2. U S Government Printing Office, Washington, 1983. Used with permission. DSM-IV criteria are adapted essentially from this chart.

**Table 35–2**
**Diagnostic Criteria for Mental Retardation**

A. Significantly subaverage intellectual functioning: an I.Q. of approximately 70 or below on an individually administered I.Q. test (for infants, a clinical judgment of significantly subaverage intellectual functioning).

B. Concurrent deficits or impairments in present adaptive functioning (i.e., the person's effectiveness in meeting the standards expected for his or her age by his or her cultural group) in at least two of the following areas: communication, self-care, home living, social/interpersonal skills, use of community resources, self-direction, functional academic skills, work, leisure, health and safety.

C. The onset is before age 18 years.

*Code* based on degree of severity reflecting level of intellectual impairment:

   **Mild mental retardation:** IQ level 50–55 to approximately 70
   **Moderate retardation:** IQ level 35–40 to 50–55
   **Severe mental retardation:** IQ level 20–25 to 35–40
   **Profound mental retardation:** IQ level below 20 or 25
   **Mental retardation, severity unspecified:** when there is a strong presumption of mental retardation but the person's intelligence is untestable by standard tests

Table from DSM-IV, *Diagnostic and Statistical Manual of Mental Disorders*, ed 4. Copyright American Psychiatric Association, Washington, 1994. Used with permission.

strongly suspected of having mental retardation but cannot be tested by standard intelligence tests or are too impaired or uncooperative to be tested. That type may be applicable to infants whose significantly subaverage intellectual func-

tioning is clinically judged but for whom the available tests (for example, Bayley Infant Scale of Development and Cattell Infant Scale) do not yield numerical I.Q. values. That type should not be used when the intellectual level is presumed to be above 70.

## EPIDEMIOLOGY

The prevalence of mental retardation at any one time is estimated to be about 1 percent of the population. The incidence of mental retardation is difficult to calculate because of the difficulty of identifying its onset. In many cases, retardation may be latent for a long time before the person's limitations are recognized, or, because of good adaptation, the formal diagnosis cannot be made at a particular point in the person's life. The highest incidence is in school-age children, with the peak at ages 10 to 14. Mental retardation is about 1½ times more common among men than among women. In the elderly, prevalence is less, as those with severe or profound mental retardation have high mortality rates resulting from the complications of associated physical disorders.

## ETIOLOGY

Causative factors in mental retardation include genetic (chromosomal and inherited) conditions, prenatal exposure to infections and toxins, perinatal trauma (such as prematurity), acquired conditions, and sociocultural factors. The severity of the resulting mental retardation is related to the timing and the duration of the trauma or exposure to the central nervous system. The more severe the mental retardation, the more likely it is that the cause is evident. In about three fourths of the persons with severe mental retardation, the cause is known, whereas the cause is apparent in only half of the persons with mild mental retardation. No cause is known for three fourths of the persons with borderline intellectual functioning. Overall, in up to two thirds of all mentally retarded persons, the probable cause can be identified.

Among chromosomal and metabolic disorders, Down's syndrome, fragile X syndrome, and phenylketonuria (PKU) are the most common disorders, usually producing at least moderate mental retardation. Those with mild mental retardation sometimes have a familial pattern in their parents and siblings.

Low socioeconomic groups seem to be overrepresented in cases of mild mental retardation, the significance of which is not clear. Current knowledge suggests that genetic factors, environmental biological factors, and psychosocial factors work additively in mental retardation.

## Chromosomal Abnormalities

Abnormalities in autosomal chromosomes are associated with mental retardation, although aberrations in sex chromosomes are not always associated with mental retardation (such as Turner's syndrome with XO and Klinefelter's syndrome with XXY, XXXY, and XXYY variations). Some children with Turner's syndrome have normal to superior intelligence.

**Down's syndrome.** Down's syndrome was first described by the English physician Langdon Down in 1866 and was based on the physical characteristics associated with subnormal mental functioning. Since then, Down's syndrome has remained the most investigated and the most discussed syndrome in mental retardation. The children with the syndrome were originally called "mongoloid" because of their physical characteristics of slanted eyes, epicanthal folds, and flat nose.

Despite a plethora of theories and hypotheses advanced in the past 100 years, the cause of Down's syndrome is still unknown. There is agreement on a few predisposing factors in chromosomal disorders—among them, the increased age of the mother, possibly the increased age of the father, and X-ray radiation. The problem of cause is complicated even further by the recent recognition of three types of chromosomal aberrations in Down's syndrome:

1. Patients with trisomy 21 (three of chromosome 21, instead of the usual two) represent the overwhelming majority; they have 47 chromosomes, with an extra chromosome 21. The mothers' karyotypes are normal. A nondisjunction during meiosis, occurring for unknown reasons, is held responsible for the disorder.
2. Nondisjunction occurring after fertilization in any cell division results in mosaicism, a condition in which both normal and trisomic cells are found in various tissues.
3. In translocation there is a fusion of two chromosomes, mostly 21 and 15, resulting in a total of 46 chromosomes, despite the presence of an extra chromosome

21. The disorder, unlike trisomy 21, is usually inherited, and the translocated chromosome may be found in unaffected parents and siblings. Those asymptomatic carriers have only 45 chromosomes.

The incidence of Down's syndrome in the United States is about 1 in every 700 births. In his original description, Down mentioned the frequency of 10 percent among all mentally retarded patients. Today, around 10 percent of patients with Down's syndrome are in institutions for the mentally retarded. For a middle-aged mother (more than 32 years old), the risk of having a Down's syndrome child with trisomy 21 is about 1 in 100 births, but, when translocation is present, the risk is about one in three. Those facts assume special importance in genetic counseling.

Mental retardation is the overriding feature of Down's syndrome. The majority of patients belong to the moderately and severely retarded groups, with only a minority having an I.Q. above 50. Mental development seems to progress normally from birth to 6 months of age. I.Q. scores gradually decrease from near normal at 1 year of age to about 30 at older ages. The decline in intelligence may be real or apparent. It could be that infantile tests do not reveal the full extent of the defect, which may become manifest when sophisticated tests are used in early childhood. According to many sources, patients with Down's syndrome are placid, cheerful, and cooperative, which facilitates their adjustment at home. The picture seems to change in adolescents who may experience various emotional difficulties, behavior disorders, and (rarely) psychotic disorders.

The diagnosis of Down's syndrome is made with relative ease in an older child but is often difficult in newborn infants. The most important signs in a newborn include general hypotonia, oblique palpebral fissues, abundant neck skin, a small flattened skull, high cheekbones, and a protruding tongue. The hands are broad and thick, with a single palmar transversal crease, and the little fingers are short and curved inward. Moro reflex is weak or absent. More than 100 signs or stigmata are described in Down's syndrome, but rarely are all found in one person.

Life expectancy used to be about 12 years. With the advent of antibiotics, few young patients succumb to infections, but many of them do not live beyond the age of 40.

Persons with Down's syndrome tend to show a marked deterioration in language, memory, self-care skills, and problem solving in their 30s. Postmortem studies of those with Down's syndrome over 40 have shown a high incidence of senile plaques and neurofibrillary tangles, as seen in Alzheimer's disease. Neurofibrillary tangles are known to occur in a variety of degenerative diseases, whereas senile plaques seem to be found most often in Alzheimer's disease and in Down's syndrome, suggesting that the two disorders share some degree of pathophysiology.

**Fragile X syndrome.** Fragile X syndrome is the second most common single cause of mental retardation. The syndrome results from a mutation on the X chromosome at what is known as the fragile site (Xq27.3). The fragile site is expressed in only some cells, and it may be absent in asymptomatic males and female carriers. Much variability is present in both genetic and phenotypic expression. Fragile X syndrome is believed to occur in about 1 in every 1,000 males and 1 in every 2,000 females. The typical phenotype includes a large long head and ears, short stature, hyperextensible joints, and postpubertal macro-orchidism. The degree of mental retardation ranges from mild to severe. The behavioral profile of persons with the syndrome includes a high rate of attention-deficit/hyperactivity disorder, learning disorders, and pervasive developmental disorders, such as autistic disorder. Deficits in language function include rapid perseverative speech with abnormalities in combining words into phrases and sentences. Persons with fragile X syndrome seem to have relatively strong skills in communication and socialization, and their intellectual functions seem to decline in the pubertal period. Female carriers are often less impaired than are males with fragile X syndrome, but females can manifest the typical physical characteristics and can be mildly retarded.

**Prader-Willi syndrome.** Prader-Willi syndrome is postulated to be the result of a small deletion involving chromosome 15, usually occurring sporadically. Its prevalence is less than 1 in 10,000. Persons with the syndrome exhibit compulsive eating behavior and often obesity, mental retardation, hypogonadism, small stature, hypotonia, and small hands and feet. Children with the syndrome often have oppositional and defiant behavior.

**Cat-cry (cri-du-chat) syndrome.** Children with cat-cry syndrome are missing part of chromosome 5. They are severely retarded and show many stigmata often associated with chromosomal aberrations, such as microcephaly, low-set ears, oblique palpebral fissues, hypertelorism, and micrognathia. The characteristic catlike cry—caused by laryngeal abnormalities—that gave the syndrome its name gradually changes and disappears with increasing age.

**Other chromosomal abnormalities.** Other syndromes of autosomal aberrations associated with mental retardation are much less prevalent than is Down's syndrome. Various types of autosomal and sex chromosome aberration syndromes are included in Table 35–3.

## Other Genetic Factors

**Phenylketonuria.** Phenylketonuria (PKU) was first described by Ivar Asbjörn Fölling in 1934 as the paradigmatic inborn error of metabolism. PKU is transmitted as a simple recessive autosomal Mendelian trait and occurs in about 1 in every 10,000 to 15,000 live births. To the parents who have already had a child with PKU, the chance of having another child with PKU is one in every four to five successive pregnancies. Although the disease is reported predominantly in people of north European origin, a few cases have been described in blacks, Yemenite Jews, and Asians. The frequency among institutionalized retarded patients is about 1 percent.

The basic metabolic defect in PKU is an inability to convert phenylalanine, an essential amino acid, to paratyrosine because of the absence or the inactivity of the liver enzyme phenylalanine hydroxylase, which catalyzes the conversion. Two other types of hyperphenylalaninemia have recently been described. One is due to a deficiency of an enzyme, dihydroperidine reductase, and the other to a deficiency of a cofactor, biopterin. The first defect

can be detected in fibroblasts, and biopterin can be measured in body fluids. Both of those rare disorders carry a high risk of fatality.

The majority of patients with PKU are severely retarded, but some are reported to have borderline or normal intelligence. Eczema, vomiting, and convulsions are present in about a third of all cases. Although the clinical picture varies, typical PKU children are hyperactive and exhibit erratic, unpredictable behavior, which makes them difficult to manage. They frequently have temper tantrums and often display bizarre movements of their bodies and upper extremities and twisting hand mannerisms, and their behavior sometimes resembles that of autistic or schizophrenic children. Verbal and nonverbal communication is usually severely impaired or nonexistent. The children's coordination is poor, and they have many perceptual difficulties.

The disease was previously diagnosed on the basis of a urine test: phenylpyruvic acid in the urine reacts with ferric chloride solution to yield a vivid green color. However, that test has its limitations, as it may not detect the presence of phenylpyruvic acid in urine before the baby is 5 or 6 weeks old and it may give positive responses with other aminoacidurias. Currently, a more reliable screening test that is widely used is the Guthrie inhibition assay, which uses a bacteriological procedure to detect blood phenylalanine.

Early diagnosis is important, as a low phenylalanine diet, in use since 1955, significantly improves both behavior and developmental progress. The best results seem to be obtained with early diagnosis and the start of dietary treatment before the child is 6 months of age.

Dietary treatment, however, is not without risk. Phenylalanine is an essential amino acid, and its omission from the diet may lead to such severe complications as anemia, hypoglycemia, edema, and even death. Dietary treatment of PKU should be continued indefinitely. Children who receive a diagnosis before the age of 3 months and are placed on an optimal dietary regimen may have normal intelligence. For untreated older children and adolescents with PKU, a low phenylalanine diet does not influence the level of mental retardation. However, the diet does decrease their irritability and abnormal EEG changes and does increase their social responsiveness and attention span.

The parents of PKU children and some of the children's normal siblings are heterozygous carriers. The disease can be detected by a phenylalanine tolerance test, which may be important in the genetic counseling of the people.

**Rett's disorder.** Rett's disorder is hypothesized to be an X-linked dominant mental retardation syndrome that is degenerative and affects only females. Andreas Rett reported on 22 girls with serious progressive neurological disability in 1966. Deterioration in communications skills, motor behavior, and social functioning starts at 1½ years of age. Autisticlike symptoms are common, as are ataxia, facial grimacing, teeth grinding, and loss of speech. Intermittent hyperventilation and a disorganized breathing pattern are characteristic while the child is awake. Stereotypical hand movements, including handwringing, are typical. Progressive gait disturbance, scoliosis, and seizures occur. Severe spasticity is usually present by middle childhood.

**Table 35–3**
**Thirty-Five Important Syndromes with Multiple Handicaps**

| Syndrome | Diagnostic Manifestations | | | Mental Retardation | Short Stature | Genetic Transmission |
|---|---|---|---|---|---|---|
| | Craniofacial | Skeletal | Other | | | |
| Aarskog-Scott syndrome | Hypertelorism; broad nasal bridge, anteverted nostrils, long philtrum | Small hands and feet; mild interdigital webbing; short stature | Scrotal shawl above penis | | + | X-linked semidominant |
| Apert's syndrome (acrocephalosyndactyly) | Craniosynostosis; irregular midfacial hypoplasia; hypertelorism | Syndactyly; broad distal thumb and toe | | ± | | Autosomal dominant |
| Cerebral gigantism (Sotos syndrome) | Large head; prominent forehead; narrow anterior mandible | Large hands and feet | Large size in early life; poor coordination | ± | | ? |
| Cockayne's syndrome | Pinched facies; sunken eyes; thin nose prognathism; retinal degeneration | Long limbs, with large hands and feet; flexion deformities | Hypotrichosis; photosensitivity; thin skin; diminished subcutaneous fat; impaired hearing | + | + | Autosomal recessive |
| Cohen syndrome | Maxillary hypoplasia with prominent central incisors | Narrow hands and feet | Hypotonia; obesity | + | ± | ? Autosomal recessive |
| Cornelia de Lange syndrome | Synophrys (continuous eyebrows); thin down-turning upper lip; long philtrum; anteverted nostrils; microcephaly | Small or malformed hands and feet; proximal thumb | Hirsutism | + | + | ? |
| Cri-du-chat syndrome | Epicanthic folds, slanting palpebral fissures; round facial contour; hypertelorism; microcephaly | Short metacarpals or metatarsals; four-finger line in palm | Catlike cry in infancy | + | + | ? |
| Crouzon's syndrome (craniofacial dysostosis) | Proptosis with shallow orbits; maxillary hypoplasia; craniosynostosis | | | | | Autosomal dominant |
| Down's syndrome | Upward slant to palpebral fissures; midface depression; epicanthic folds; Brushfield spots; brachycephaly | Short hands; clinodactyly of fifth finger; four-finger line in palm | Hypotonia; loose skin on back of neck | + | + | Trisomy 21 |
| Dubowitz syndrome | Small facies; lateral displacement of inner canthi; ptosis; broad nasal bridge; sparse hair; microcephaly | | Infantile eczema; high-pitched hoarse voice | ± | + + | ? Autosomal recessive |
| Fetal alcohol syndrome | Short palpebral fissures; mid-facial hypoplasia; microcephaly | | ± Cardiac defect; fine motor dysfunction | + | + | |
| Fetal hydantoin syndrome (phenytoin) | Hypertelorism; short nose; occasional cleft lip | Hypoplastic nails, especially fifth | Cardiac defect | ± | ± | |

**Table 35–3**
**Continued**

| Syndrome | Diagnostic Manifestations | | | Mental Retardation | Short Stature | Genetic Transmission |
|---|---|---|---|---|---|---|
| | Craniofacial | Skeletal | Other | | | |
| Goldenhar's syndrome | Malar hypoplasia; macrostomia; micrognathia; epibulbar dermoid, lipodermoid; malformed ear with preauricular tags | ± Vertebral anomalies | | | | ? |
| Incontinentia pigmenti | ± Dental defect; deformities of ears; ± patchy alopecia | | Irregular skin pigmentation in fleck, whorl, or spidery form | ± | | ? Dominant, X-linked ? Lethal in males |
| Laurence-Moon-Bardet-Biedl syndrome | Retinal pigmentation | Polydactyly; syndactyly | Obesity; seizures; hypogenitalism | + | ± | Autosomal recessive |
| Linear nevus sebaceus syndrome | Nevus sebaceus, face or neck | | +/− Seizures | + | ± | ? |
| Lowe's syndrome (oculocerebrorenal syndrome) | Cataract | Renal tubular dysfunction | Hypotonia | + | + | X-linked recessive |
| Möbius' syndrome (congenital facial diplegia) | Expressionless facies; ocular palsy | ± Clubfoot; syndactyly | | ± | ± | ? |
| Neurofibromatosis | ± Optic gliomas; acoustic neuromas | ± Bone lesions; pseudarthroses | Neurofibromas; café-au-lait spots; seizures | ± | | Autosomal dominant |
| Noonan's syndrome | Webbing of posterior neck; malformed ears; hypertelorism | Pectus excavatum; cubitus valgus | Cryptorchidism; pulmonic stenosis | ± | + | ? |
| Prader-Willi syndrome | ± Upward slant to palpebral fissures | Small hands and feet | Hypotonia, especially in early infancy; then polyphagia and obesity; hypogenitalism | + | + | ? |
| Robin's syndrome | Micrognathia; glossoptosis; cleft palate, U-shaped | | ± Cardiac anomalies | | | ? |
| Rubella | Cataract; retinal pigmentation; ocular malformations | | Sensorineural deafness; patent ductus arteriosus | ± | ± | ? |
| Rubinstein-Taybi syndrome | Slanting palpebral fissures; maxillary hypoplasia; microcephaly | Broad thumbs and toes | Abnormal gait | + | + | ? |
| Seckel syndrome | Facial hypoplasia; prominent nose; microcephaly | Multiple minor joint and skeletal abnormalities | | + | + | Autosomal recessive |
| Sjögren-Larsson syndrome | | Spasticity, especially of legs | Ichthyosis | + | + | Autosomal recessive |
| Smith-Lemli-Opitz syndrome | Anteverted nostrils, ptosis of eyelid | Syndactyly of second and third toes | Hypospadias; cryptorchidism | + | + | Autosomal recessive |
| Sturge-Weber syndrome | Flat hemangioma of face, most commonly trigeminal in distribution | | Hemangiomas of meninges with seizures | ± | | ? |

| Syndrome | Features | | | | Etiology |
|---|---|---|---|---|---|
| Treacher Collins' syndrome (mandibulofacial dysostosis) | Malar and mandibular hypoplasia; downslanting palpebral fissures; defect of lower eyelid; malformed ears | | | | Autosomal dominant |
| Trisomy 18 | Microstomia; short palpebral fissures; malformed ears; elongated skull | Clenched hand, second finger over third; low arches on fingertips; short sternum | Cryptorchidism; congenital heart disease | + | Trisomy 18 |
| Trisomy 13 | Defects of eyes, nose, lips, ears, and forebrain of holoprosencephaly type | Polydactyly; narrow hyperconvex fingernails | Skin defects, posterior scalp | + | Trisomy 13 |
| Tuberous sclerosis | Hamartomatous pink to brownish facial skin nodules | ± Bone lesions | Seizures; intracranial calcification | ± | Autosomal dominant |
| Waardenburg syndrome | Lateral displacement of inner canthi and puncta | | Partial albinism; white forelock; heterochromia of iris; vitiligo; +/– deafness | | Autosomal dominant |
| Williams syndrome | Full lips; small nose with anteverted nostrils; iris dysplasia | Mild hypoplasia of nails | ± Hypercalcemia in infancy; supravalvular aortic stenosis | + | ? |
| Zellweger syndrome (cerebrohepatorenal syndrome) | High forehead; flat facies | | Hypotonia; hepatomegaly; death in early infancy | | |

Table from L. Syzmanski, A Crocker and adapted from D W Smith: Patterns of malformation. In *Nelson Textbook of Pediatrics*, ed 11, V C Vaughan III, R J McKay, R E Behrman, editors, p 2035. Saunders, Philadelphia, 1979. Used with permission.

Cerebral atrophy occurs with decreased pigmentation of the substantia nigra, suggesting abnormalities of the dopaminergic nigrostriatal system. Chapter 38 discusses the disorder further.

**Neurofibromatosis.** Also called von Recklinghausen's disease, neurofibromatosis is the most common of the neurocutaneous syndromes caused by a single dominant gene. It may be inherited, or it may be a new mutation. It occurs in about 1 in 5,000 births. The disorder is characterized by café-au-lait spots on the skin and neurofibromas, including optic gliomas and acoustic neuromas, caused by abnormal cell migration. Mild mental retardation is present in up to one third of the persons with the disease.

**Tuberous sclerosis.** Tuberous sclerosis is the second most common of the neurocutaneous syndromes; a progressive mental retardation is present in up to two thirds of all affected persons. It occurs in about 1 in 15,000 persons and is caused by autosomal dominant transmission. Seizures are present in all the patients who are mentally retarded and in two thirds of those who are not mentally retarded. Infantile spasms may occur as early as 6 months. The phenotypic presentation includes adenoma sebaceum and ash-leaf spots that can be identified with a slit lamp. The rate of autism is higher than the intellectual impairment would lead one to expect.

**Lesch-Nyhan syndrome.** Lesch-Nyhan syndrome is a rare disorder caused by a deficiency of an enzyme involved in purine metabolism. It is associated with severe compulsive self-mutilation by biting of the mouth and the fingers. It is an X-linked disorder and presents with mental retardation, microcephaly, seizures, choreoathetosis, and spasticity. The disorder is another example of a genetically determined syndrome in which a specific behavioral pattern is predictable.

**Adrenoleukodystrophy.** The most common of several disorders of sudanophilic cerebral sclerosis, adrenoleuko-dystrophy is characterized by diffuse demyelination of the cerebral white matter, resulting in visual and intellectual impairment, seizures, spasticity, and progression to death. The cerebral degeneration in adrenoleukodystrophy is accompanied by adrenocortical insufficiency. The disorder is transmitted by a sex-linked gene located on the distal end of the long arm of the X chromosome. The clinical onset is generally between 5 and 8 years, with early seizures, disturbances in gait, and mild intellectual impairment. Abnormal pigmentation reflecting adrenal insufficiency sometimes precedes the neurological symptoms, and attacks of crying are common. Spastic contractures, ataxia, and disturbances of swallowing are common. Although the course is often rapidly progressive, some patients may have a relapsing and remitting course. The disorder was presented in the 1992 film *Lorenzo's Oil.*

**Maple syrup urine disease.** The clinical symptoms of maple syrup urine disease appear during the first week of life. The infant deteriorates rapidly and has decerebrate rigidity, seizures, respiratory irregularity, and hypoglycemia. If untreated, most patients die in the first months of life, and the survivors are severely retarded. Some variants have been reported with transient ataxia and only mild retardation.

Treatment follows the general principles established for PKU and consists of a diet very low in the three involved amino acids—leucine, isoleucine, and valine.

**Other enzyme deficiency disorders.** Several enzyme deficiency disorders associated with mental retardation have been identified, and still more diseases are being added as new discoveries are made. Some of them include Hartnup disease, galactosemia, and glycogen-storage disease. Thirty important disorders with inborn errors of metabolism, hereditary transmission patterns, defective enzymes, clinical signs, and relation to mental retardation are listed in Table 35–4.

**Table 35–4**
**Thirty Important Disorders with Inborn Errors of Metabolism**

| Disorder | Hereditary Transmission* | Enzyme Defect | Prenatal Diagnosis | Mental Retardation | Clinical Signs |
|---|---|---|---|---|---|
| | | I. LIPID METABOLISM | | | |
| Niemann-Pick disease Group A, infantile Group B, adult | A.R. | Sphingomyelinase | + | ± | Hepatosplenomegaly |
| Groups C and D, intermediate | | Unknown | – | + | Pulmonary infiltration |
| Infantile Gaucher's disease | A.R. | β-Glucosidase | + | ± | Hepatosplenomegaly, pseudobulbar palsy |
| Tay-Sachs disease | A.R. | Hexosaminidase A | + | + | Macular changes, seizures, spasticity |
| Generalized gangliosidosis | A.R. | β-Galactosidase | + | + | Hepatosplenomegaly, bone changes |
| Krabbe's disease | A.R. | Galactocerebroside β-Galactosidase | + | + | Stiffness, seizures |
| Metachromatic leukodystrophy | A.R. | Cerebroside sulfatase | + | + | Stiffness, developmental failure |
| Wolman's disease | A.R. | Acid lipase | + | – | Hepatosplenomegaly, adrenal calcification, vomiting, diarrhea |

**Table 35-4**
**Continued**

| Disorder | Hereditary Transmission* | Enzyme Defect | Prenatal Diagnosis | Mental Retardation | Clinical Signs |
|---|---|---|---|---|---|
| Farber's lipogranulomatosis | A.R. | Acid ceramidase | + | + | Hoarseness, arthropathy, subcutaneous nodules |
| Fabry's disease | X.R. | α-Galactosidase | + | − | Angiokeratomas, renal failure |
| II. MUCOPOLYSACCHARIDE METABOLISM | | | | | |
| Hurler's syndrome MPS I | A.R. | Iduronidase | + | + | |
| Hunter's disease II | X.R. | Iduronate sulfatase | + | + | |
| Sanfilippo's syndrome III | A.R. | Various sulfatases (types A–D) | + | + | Varying degrees of bone changes, hepatosplenomegaly, joint restriction, etc. |
| Morquio's disease IV | A.R. | N-Acetylgalactosamine-6-sulfate sulfatase | + | − | |
| Maroteaux-Lamy syndrome VI | A.R. | Arylsulfatase B | + | ± | |
| III. OLIGOSACCHARIDE AND GLYCOPROTEIN METABOLISM | | | | | |
| I-cell disease | A.R. | Glycoprotein N-acetylglucosaminyl-phosphotransferase | + | + | Hepatomegaly, bone changes, swollen gingivae |
| Mannosidosis | A.R. | Mannosidase | + | + | Hepatomegaly, bone changes, facial coarsening |
| Fucosidosis | A.R. | Fucosidase | + | + | Same as above |
| IV. AMINO ACID METABOLISM | | | | | |
| Phenylketonuria | A.R. | Phenylalanine hydroxylase | − | + | Eczema, blonde hair, musty odor |
| Homocystinuria | A.R. | Cystathionine β-synthetase | + | + | Ectopia lentis, Marfanlike phenotype, cardiovascular anomalies |
| Tyrosinosis | A.R. | Tyrosine amine transaminase | − | + | Hyperkeratotic skin lesions, conjunctivitis |
| Maple syrup urine disease | A.R. | Branched chain ketoacid decarboxylase | + | + | Recurrent ketoacidosis |
| Methylmalonic acidemia | A.R. | Methylmalonyl-CoA mutase | + | + | Recurrent ketoacidosis, hepatomegaly, growth retardation |
| Propionicacidemia | A.R. | Propionyl-CoA carboxylase | + | + | Same as above |
| Nonketotic hyperglycinemia | A.R. | Glycine cleavage enzyme | + | + | Seizures |
| Urea cycle disorders | Mostly A.R. | Urea cycle enzymes | + | + | Recurrent acute encephalopathy, vomiting |
| Hartnup disease | A.R. | Renal transport disorder | − | | None consistent |
| V. OTHERS | | | | | |
| Galactosemia | A.R. | Galactose-1-phosphate uridyltransferase | + | + | Hepatomegaly, cataracts, ovarian failure |
| Wilson's hepatolenticular degeneration | A.R. | Unknown factor in copper metabolism | − | ± | Liver disease, Kayser-Fleischer ring, neurological problems |
| Menkes's kinky-hair disease | X.R. | Same as above | + | − | Abnormal hair, cerebral degeneration |
| Lesch-Nyhan syndrome | A.R. | Hypoxanthine guanine phosphoribosyltransferase | + | + | Behavioral abnormalities |

*A.R. = autosomal recessive transmission. X.R. = X-linked recessive transmission.
Table by L Dyzilianski, A Crocker and adapted from J G Leroy: Heredity, development, and behavior. In *Developmental-Behavioral Pediatrics*, M D Levine, W B Carey, A C Crocker, editors, p 315. Saunders, Philadelphia, 1983. Used with permission.

## Prenatal Factors

Important prerequisites for the overall development of the fetus include the mother's physical, psychological, and nutritional health during pregnancy. Maternal chronic illnesses and conditions affecting the normal development of the fetus's central nervous system include uncontrolled diabetes, anemia, emphysema, hypertension, and long-term use of alcohol and narcotic substances. Maternal infections during pregnancy, especially viral infections, have been known to cause fetal damage and mental retardation. The degree of fetal damage depends on such variables as the type of viral infection, the gestational age of the fetus, and the severity of the illness. Although numerous infectious diseases have been reported to affect the fetus's central nervous system, the following medical disorders have been definitely identified as high-risk conditions for mental retardation.

**Rubella (German measles).** Rubella has replaced syphilis as the major cause of congenital malformations and mental retardation caused by maternal infection. The children of affected mothers may present a number of abnormalities, including congenital heart disease, mental retardation, cataracts, deafness, microcephaly, and microphthalmia. Timing is crucial, as the extent and the frequency of the complications are inversely related to the duration of the pregnancy at the time of the maternal infection. When mothers are infected in the first trimester of pregnancy, 10 to 15 percent of the children are affected, but the incidence rises to almost 50 percent when the infection occurs in the first month of pregnancy. The situation is often complicated by subclinical forms of maternal infection, which often go undetected. Maternal rubella can be prevented by immunization.

**Cytomegalic inclusion disease.** In many cases, cytomegalic inclusion disease remains dormant in the mother. Some children are stillborn, and others have jaundice, microcephaly, hepatosplenomegaly, and radiographic findings of intracerebral calcification. Children with mental retardation from the disease frequently have cerebral calcification, microcephaly, or hydrocephalus. The diagnosis is confirmed by positive findings on throat and urine cultures of the virus and by the recovery of inclusion-bearing cells in the urine.

**Syphilis.** Syphilis in pregnant women used to be the main cause of various neuropathological changes in their offspring, including mental retardation. Today, the incidence of syphilitic complications of pregnancy fluctuates with the incidence of syphilis in the general population. Some recent alarming statistics from several major cities in the United States indicate that there is still no room for complacency.

**Toxoplasmosis.** Toxoplasmosis can be transmitted by the mother to the fetus. It causes mild or severe mental retardation and, in severe cases, hydrocephalus, seizures, microcephaly, and chorioretinitis.

**Herpes simplex.** The herpes simplex virus can be transmitted transplacentally, although the most common mode of infection is during birth. Microcephaly, mental retardation, intracranial calcification, and ocular abnormalities may result.

**Acquired immune deficiency syndrome (AIDS).** Many fetuses of mothers with AIDS never come to term because of stillbirth or spontaneous abortion. In those who are born infected with the human immunodeficiency virus (HIV) up to half have progressive encephalopathy, mental retardation, and seizures within the first year of life. Children born infected with HIV often live only a few years.

**Fetal alcohol syndrome.** Fetal alcohol syndrome consists of mental retardation and a typical phenotypic picture of facial dysmorphism that includes hypertelorism, microcephaly, short palpebral fissures, inner epicanthal folds, and a short turned-up nose. Often, the affected children have learning disorders and attention-deficit/hyperactivity disorder. Cardiac defects are also frequent. The entire syndrome occurs in up to 15 percent of babies born to women who regularly ingest large amounts of alcohol. Babies born to women who consume alcohol regularly during pregnancy have a high incidence of attention-deficit hyperactivity disorder, learning disorders, and mental retardation without the facial dysmorphism.

**Prenatal substance exposure.** Prenatal exposure to opiates, such as heroin, often results in an infant who is small for its gestational age, with a head circumference below the 10th percentile and withdrawal symptoms that are manifest within the first two days of life. The withdrawal symptoms in the infant include irritability, hypertonia, tremor, vomiting, a high-pitched cry, and an abnormal sleep pattern. Seizures are unusual, but the withdrawal syndrome can be life-threatening to the infant if it is untreated. Diazepam (Valium), phenobarbital (Luminal), chlorpromazine (Thorazine), and paregoric have been used to treat neonatal opiate withdrawal. The long-term sequelae of prenatal opiate exposure are not fully known; the children's developmental milestones and intellectual functions may be within the normal range, but they have an increased risk for impulsivity and behavioral problems.

Infants exposed to cocaine prenatally are at high risk for low birth weight and premature delivery. In the early neonatal period, they may have transient neurological and behavioral abnormalities, including abnormal results on electroencephalograms (EEGs), tachycardia, poor feeding patterns, irritability, and excessive drowsiness. The physiological and behavioral abnormalities are a response to the cocaine, rather than a withdrawal reaction, since the cocaine may be excreted for up to a week postnatally.

**Complications of pregnancy.** Toxemia of pregnancy and uncontrolled maternal diabetes present hazards to the fetus and sometimes result in mental retardation. Maternal malnutrition during pregnancy often results in prematurity and other obstetrical complications. Vaginal hemorrhage, placenta previa, premature separation of the placenta, and prolapse of the cord may damage the fetal brain by causing anoxia.

The potential teratogenic effect of pharmacological agents administered during pregnancy was widely publicized after the thalidomide tragedy (the drug produced a high percentage of deformed babies when given to pregnant women). So far, with the exception of metabolites used in cancer chemotherapy, no usual dosages are known to damage the fetus's central nervous system, but caution and restraint in prescribing drugs to pregnant women are certainly indicated. The use of lithium during pregnancy was recently implicated in some congenital malformations, especially of the cardiovascular system (for example, Ebstein's anomaly).

## Perinatal Factors

Some evidence indicates that premature infants and infants with low birth weight are at high risk for neurological and intellectual impairments that are manifest during their school years. Those infants who sustain intracranial hemorrhages or evidence of cerebral ischemia are especially vulnerable to cognitive abnormalities. The degree of neurodevelopmental impairment generally correlates to the severity of the intracranial hemorrhage. Socioeconomic deprivation can also affect the adaptive function of those vulnerable infants. Early intervention may improve their cognitive, language, and perceptual abilities.

## Acquired Childhood Disorders

Occasionally, a child's developmental status changes dramatically as a result of a specific disease or physical trauma. In retrospect, it is sometimes difficult to ascertain the full picture of the child's developmental progress before the insult, but the adverse effects on the child's development or skills are apparent after the insult.

**Infection.** The most serious infections affecting cerebral integrity are encephalitis and meningitis. Measles encephalitis has been virtually eliminated by the universal use of measles vaccine, and the incidences of other bacterial infections of the central nervous system have been markedly reduced with antibacterial agents. Most episodes of encephalitis are caused by viral organisms. Sometimes a clinician must retrospectively consider a probable encephalitic component in a past obscure illness with high fever and lasting encephalopathy. Meningitis that was diagnosed late, even when followed by antibiotic treatment, can seriously affect a child's cognitive development. Thrombotic and purulent intracranial phenomena secondary to septicemia are rarely seen today except in small infants.

**Head trauma.** The best-known causes of head injury in children that produce developmental handicaps, including seizures, are motor vehicle accidents. However, more head injuries are caused by household accidents, such as falls from tables, from open windows, and on stairways. Child abuse is also a cause of head injury.

**Other issues.** Brain damage from cardiac arrest during anesthesia is rare. One cause of complete or partial brain damage is asphyxia associated with near drowning. Long-term exposure to lead is a well-established cause of compromised intelligence and learning skills. Intracranial tumors of various types and origins, surgery, and chemotherapy can also adversely affect brain function.

## Environmental and Sociocultural Factors

Mild retardation is significantly prevalent among persons of culturally deprived, low socioeconomic groups, and many of their relatives are affected with similar degrees of mental retardation. No biological causes have been identified in those cases.

Children in poor, socioculturally deprived families are subjected to potentially pathogenic and developmentally adverse conditions. The prenatal environment is compromised by poor medical care and poor maternal nutrition. Teenage pregnancies are frequent and are associated with obstetrical complications, prematurity, and low birth weight. Poor postnatal medical care, malnutrition, exposure to such toxic substances as lead, and physical traumata are frequent. Family instability, frequent moves, and multiple but inadequate caretakers are common. Furthermore, the mothers in such families are often poorly educated and ill-equipped to give the child appropriate stimulation.

Another unresolved issue is the influence of severe parental mental disorders. Such disorders may adversely affect the child's care and stimulation and other aspects of the environment, thus putting the child at a developmental risk. Children of parents with mood disorders and schizophrenia are known to be at risk for those and related disorders. Recent studies indicate a high prevalence of motor skills disorder and other developmental disorders among the children but not necessarily mental retardation.

## DIAGNOSIS

The diagnosis of mental retardation can be made after the history, a standardized intellectual assessment, and a measure of adaptive function indicate that the child's current behavior is significantly below the expected level (Tables 35–1 and 35–2). The diagnosis itself does not specify either the cause or the prognosis. A history and a psychiatric interview are useful in obtaining a longitudinal picture of the child's development and functioning, and examination of physical stigmata, neurological abnormalities, and laboratory tests can be used to ascertain the cause and the prognosis.

### History

The history is most often taken from the parents or the caretaker, with particular attention to the mother's pregnancy, labor, and delivery; the presence of a family history of mental retardation; consanguinity of the parents; and hereditary disorders. As part of the history, the clinician assesses the parents' sociocultural background, the home's emotional climate, and the parents' intellectual functioning.

### Psychiatric Interview

Two factors are of paramount importance when interviewing the patient: the interviewer's attitude and the manner of communication with the patient. The interviewer should not be guided by the patient's mental age, as it cannot fully characterize the person. A mildly retarded adult with a mental age of 10 is not a 10-year-old child. When addressed as if they were children, some retarded persons become justifiably insulted, angry, and uncooperative. Passive and dependent persons, alternatively, may assume the child's role that they think is expected of them. In both cases, no valid diagnostic data can be obtained.

The patient's verbal abilities, including receptive and expressive language, should be assessed as soon as possible by observing the verbal and nonverbal communication between the caretakers and the patient and from the history. The clinician often finds it helpful to see the patient and the caretakers together. If the patient uses sign language, the caretaker may have to stay during the interview as an interpreter.

Retarded persons have the lifelong experience of failing in many areas, and they may be anxious before seeing an interviewer. The interviewer and the caretaker should attempt to give such patients a clear, supportive, and concrete explanation of the diagnostic process, particularly those patients with sufficient receptive language. Giving patients the impression that their bad behavior is the cause of the referral should be avoided. Support and praise should be offered in language appropriate to the patient's age and understanding. Leading questions should be avoided, as retarded persons may be suggestible and wish to please others. Subtle directiveness, structure, and reinforcements may be necessary to keep them on the task or topic.

The patient's control over motility patterns should be ascertained, and clinical evidence of distractibility and distortions in perception and memory may be evaluated. The use of speech, reality testing, and the ability to generalize from experiences are important to note.

The nature and the maturity of the patient's defenses—particularly exaggerated or self-defeating uses of avoidance, repression, denial, introjection, and isolation—should be observed. Sublimation potential, frustration tolerance, and impulse control—especially over motor, aggressive, and sexual drives—should be assessed. Also important are self-image and its role in the development of self-confidence, as well as the assessment of tenacity, persistence, curiosity, and the willingness to explore the unknown.

In general, the psychiatric examination of the retarded patient should reveal how the patient has coped with the stages of development. In regard to failure or regression, the clinician can develop a personality profile that allows the logical planning of management and remedial approaches.

## Physical Examination

Various parts of the body may have certain characteristics that are commonly found in mentally retarded persons and have prenatal causes. For example, the configuration and the size of the head offer clues to a variety of conditions, such as microcephaly, hydrocephalus, and Down's syndrome. The patient's face may have some of the stigmata of mental retardation, which greatly facilitate the diagnosis. Such facial signs are hypertelorism, a flat nasal bridge, prominent eyebrows, epicanthal folds, corneal opacities, retinal changes, low-set and small or misshapen ears, a protruding tongue, and a disturbance in dentition. Facial expression, such as a dull appearance, may be misleading and should not be relied on without

other supporting evidence. The color and the texture of the skin and the hair, a high-arched palate, the size of the thyroid gland, and the size of the child and his or her trunk and extremities are further areas to be explored. The circumference of the head should be measured as part of the clinical investigation. The clinician should bear in mind during the examination that mentally retarded children, particularly those with associated behavioral problems, are at increased risk for child abuse.

Dermatoglyphics may offer another diagnostic tool, as uncommon ridge patterns and flexion creases are often found in retarded persons. Abnormal dermatoglyphics may be found in chromosomal disorders and in patients who were infected prenatally with rubella. Table 35–3 lists the multiple handicaps associated with the syndromes discussed.

## Neurological Examination

Sensory impairments occur frequently among mentally retarded persons; for example, up to 10 percent of mentally retarded persons are hearing-impaired at a rate that is four times that of the general population. A variety of other neurological impairments are also high in mentally retarded persons; seizure disorders occur in about 10 percent of all mentally retarded persons and in one third of persons with severe mental retardation.

When neurological abnormalities are present, their incidence and severity generally rise in direct proportion to the degree of retardation. However, many severely retarded children have no neurological abnormalities; conversely, about 25 percent of all children with cerebral palsy have normal intelligence.

Disturbances in motor areas are manifested in abnormalities of muscle tone (spasticity or hypotonia), reflexes (hyperreflexia), and involuntary movements (choreoathetosis). A smaller degree of disability is revealed in clumsiness and poor coordination.

Sensory disturbances may include hearing difficulties, ranging from cortical deafness to mild hearing deficits. Visual disturbances may range from blindness to disturbances of spatial concepts, design recognition, and concept of body image.

The infants with the poorest prognoses are those who manifest a combination of inactivity, general hypotonia, and exaggerated response to stimuli. In older children, hyperactivity, short attention span, distractibility, and a low frustration tolerance are often signs of brain damage.

In general, the younger the child is at the time of investigation, the more caution is indicated in predicting future ability, as the recovery potential of the infantile brain is very good. Observing the child's development at regular intervals is probably the most reliable approach.

Skull X-rays are usually taken routinely but are illuminating only in a relatively few conditions, such as craniosynostosis, hydrocephalus, and others that result in intracranial calcifications (for example, toxoplasmosis, tuberous sclerosis, cerebral angiomatosis, and hypoparathyroidism). Computed tomography (CT) scans and magnetic resonance imaging (MRI) have become important tools for uncovering central nervous system pathology associated with mental retardation. The occasional findings of internal hydrocephalus, cortical atrophy, or porencephaly in a severely retarded, brain-damaged child are not considered important to the general picture.

An electroencephalogram (EEG) is best interpreted with caution in cases of mental retardation. The exceptions are patients with hypsarhythmia and grand mal seizures, in whom the EEG may help establish the diagnosis and suggest treatment. In most other conditions a diffuse cerebral disorder produces nonspecific EEG changes, characterized by slow frequencies with bursts of spikes and sharp or blunt wave complexes. The confusion over the significance of the EEG in the diagnosis of mental retardation is best illustrated by the reports of frequent EEG abnormalities in Down's syndrome, which range from 25 percent to the majority of patients examined.

## Laboratory Tests

Laboratory tests used in cases of mental retardation include examination of the urine and the blood for metabolic disorders. Enzymatic abnormalities in chromosomal disorders, particularly Down's syndrome, promise to become useful diagnostic tools. The determination of the karyotype in a suitable genetic laboratory is indicated whenever a chromosomal disorder is suspected.

Amniocentesis, in which a small amount of amniotic fluid is removed from the amniotic cavity transabdominally between the 14th and the 16th weeks of gestation, has been useful in diagnosing various infant chromosomal abnormalities, especially Down's syndrome. Amniotic fluid cells, mostly fetal in origin, are cultured for cytogenetic and biochemical studies. Many serious hereditary disorders can be predicted with amniocentesis, and therapeutic abortion is the only method of prevention. Amniocentesis is recommended for all pregnant women over the age of 35. Fortunately, most chromosomal anomalies occur only once in a family.

Chronic villi sampling (CVS) is a new screening technique to determine fetal abnormalities. It is done at 8 to 10 weeks of gestation, which is six weeks earlier than amniocentesis is done. The results are available in a short time (hours or days), and, if the result is abnormal, the decision to terminate the pregnancy can be made within the first trimester. The procedure has a miscarriage risk of between 2 and 5 percent.

## Hearing and Speech Evaluations

Hearing and speech evaluations should be done routinely. The development of speech may be the most reliable criterion in investigating mental retardation. Various hearing impairments are often present in mentally retarded persons; however, in some instances the impairments simulate mental retardation. Unfortunately, the commonly used methods of hearing and speech evaluation require the patient's cooperation and, thus, are often unreliable in severely retarded persons.

## Psychological Assessment

Examining clinicians may use several screening instruments for infants and toddlers. As in many areas of mental retardation, the controversy over the predictive value of infant psychological tests is heated. Some report the correlation of abnormalities during infancy with later abnormal functioning as very low, and others report it as very high. However, the correlation rises in direct proportion to the age of the child at the time of the developmental examination.

Copying geometric figures, the Goodenough Draw-a-Person Test, the Kohs Block Test, and geometric puzzles—all may be used as quick screening tests of visual-motor coordination.

Psychological testing, performed by an experienced psychologist, is a standard part of an evaluation for mental retardation. The Gesell, Bayley, and Cattell tests are most commonly used with infants. For children the Stanford–Binet and the Wechsler Intelligence Scale for Children-Revised (WISC-R, WISC-3) are the most widely used in this country. Both tests have been criticized for penalizing the culturally deprived child, for being culturally biased, for testing mainly the potential for academic achievement and not for adequate social functioning, and for their unreliability in children with I.Q.s of less than 50. Some people have tried to overcome the language barrier of mentally retarded patients by devising picture vocabulary tests, of which the Peabody Vocabulary Test is the most widely used.

The tests often found useful in detecting brain damage are the Bender Gestalt and the Benton Visual Retention tests (Figures 5.2–1 and 5.2–2). Those tests are also useful for mildly retarded children. In addition, a psychological evaluation should assess perceptual, motor, linguistic, and cognitive abilities. Information about motivational, emotional, and interpersonal factors is also important.

Todd, a 13-year-old boy, was referred to a psychiatrist by his special education teacher because she could no longer handle his irritability and his sudden physical outbursts. Although he had always had a short attention span and occasional temper tantrums in school and at home, his recent growth spurt had made him increasingly difficult to subdue. Todd's psychiatric history was significant for mild mental retardation, diagnosed in the first grade, and significant poor attention span and hyperactivity since age 6. He had been placed in special education in the middle of the first grade, after he was unable stay on tasks or grasp the concepts being taught. At that time, placement in a small structured classroom with increased individual attention was sufficient to control his behavior problems. At that age, Todd was congenial, although he had a tendency to get frustrated easily. He was socially well-related, and he had no problems with asking for help when he needed it. Beginning in the third grade, he was treated with methylphenidate (Ritalin), 20 mg in the morning and at noon, which seemed to help him pay attention and remain on tasks in the classroom. At home, he had never been considered a behavior problem until the present time.

Todd's family history was remarkable for one first cousin on his mother's side who was mildly mentally retarded; his two older brothers and younger sister were of average intelligence and free of mental disorders. Neither parent reported a psychiatric history. Interviews with his parents made it clear that Todd had enjoyed a warm relationship with his parents and all three siblings, and only recently had he become irritable and intermittently physically aggressive toward his 10-year-old sister.

Over the past two months, since school began, Todd had become increasingly defiant and explosive with minimal provocation. He had just gone through puberty, had grown several inches, and looked older than his age. A physical examination by his pediatrician revealed no remarkable results, and a laboratory examination also revealed a healthy profile. Todd was remorseful after he hit his sister or threw a chair at school, but he could not control his intermittent rage. He knew that what he had done was wrong and that he was much too old for that sort of behavior, and he always apologized after the incidents. Nevertheless, his sister was frightened of him, and he was in danger of being expelled from school.

In consultation with the psychiatrist, Todd was able to admit how inferior he felt, since he had to remain in special education classes, and how devastated he was that both of his older brothers now had girlfriends; he said that he would probably "never get a girl to like me." He was aware that he was losing his temper, but he could not seem to interrupt the process. Although Todd expressed some sadness and misery, he did not meet the criteria for a depressive disorder, and his primary problem seemed to be controlling his rage.

Todd's regimen of methylphenidate was stopped, and a trial of propranolol (Inderal) was started. The school nurse monitored his blood pressure in the morning and in the afternoon. His blood pressure remained stable, and he began to feel a slight improvement in his lability when he reached a dosage of 10 mg three times a day. He was also referred for weekly psychotherapy to discuss his negative feelings about himself and his future. A recommendation was also made for him to be treated in group therapy with other adolescents with similar problems. Although the group therapy was not immediately available, he was placed on a waiting list for an appropriate group. His parents were also counseled about his overwhelming fears regarding his ability to become independent and someday function in the world autonomously. They were supportive and agreed to work with Todd in gradually increasing his responsibilities and privileges at home and to encourage him to socialize with other boys and with girls.

## CLINICAL FEATURES

### Mild Mental Retardation

Mild mental retardation may not be diagnosed until the affected children enter school, since their social skills and communication may be adequate in the preschool years. As they get older, however, such cognitive deficits as poor ability to abstract and egocentric thinking may distinguish them from others of their age. Although mildly retarded persons are capable of academic functions at the high elementary level and their vocational skills are sufficient to support themselves in some cases, social assimilation may be difficult. Communication deficits, poor self-esteem, and dependence may contribute to their relative lack of social spontaneity. Some mildly retarded persons may fall into relationships with peers who exploit their shortcomings. In most cases, persons with mild mental retardation can achieve some degree of social and vocational success in a supportive environment.

### Moderate Mental Retardation

Moderate mental retardation is likely to be diagnosed at a younger age than is mild mental retardation because communication skills develop more slowly in moderately retarded persons, and their social isolation may begin in the elementary school years. Although academic achievement is usually limited to the mid-elementary level, mod-

erately retarded children benefit from individual attention focused on the development of self-help skills. Children with moderate mental retardation are aware of their deficits and often feel alienated from their peers and frustrated by their limitations. They continue to require a relatively high level of supervision but can become competent at occupational tasks set in supportive conditions.

### Severe Mental Retardation

Severe mental retardation is generally obvious in the preschool years, since the affected children's speech is minimal, and their motor development is poor. Some language development may occur in the school-age years; by adolescence, if language is poor, nonverbal forms of communication have evolved. The inability to fully articulate needs may reinforce the physical means of communicating. Behavioral approaches can help promote some degree of self-care, although persons with severe mental retardation generally need extensive supervision.

### Profound Mental Retardation

Children with profound mental retardation require constant supervision and are severely limited in communication and motor skills. By adulthood, some speech development may be present, and simple self-help skills may be acquired. Even in adulthood, nursing care is needed.

### Other Features

Surveys have identified a number of clinical features that occur with greater frequency in mentally retarded persons than in the general population. The features, which may occur in isolation or as part of a mental disorder, include hyperactivity, low frustration tolerance, aggression, affective instability, repetitive stereotypic motor behaviors, and self-injurious behaviors of various kinds. Self-injurious behaviors seem to be more frequent and more intense with increasingly severe mental retardation. It is often difficult to decide whether the above clinical features are comorbid mental disorders or direct sequelae of the developmental limitations imposed by mental retardation.

## COMORBID PSYCHOPATHOLOGY

### Prevalence

Over the past decade, several epidemiological surveys indicated that the rates of other mental disorders in children and adults with mental retardation range between one third and two thirds, rates that are several times higher than those in nonmentally retarded community samples. The prevalence of psychopathology seems to be correlated with the degree of mental retardation; the more severe the mental retardation, the higher is the risk for other mental disorders.

The types of mental disorders appear to run the gamut of those seen in nonmentally retarded persons, including mood disorders, schizophrenia, attention-deficit/hyperactivity disorder, and conduct disorder. Persons with severe mental retardation have a particularly high rate of autistic disorder and pervasive developmental disorders. About 2 to 3 percent of mentally retarded persons meet the criteria for schizophrenia; that is several times higher than the rate for the general population. Up to 50 percent of mentally retarded children and adults had a mood disorder when such instruments as the Kiddie Schedule for Affective Disorders and Schizophrenia, the Beck Depression Inventory, and the Children's Depression Inventory were used in pilot studies. Since the above instruments have not been standardized within the mentally retarded population, those findings must be considered preliminary.

Highly prevalent psychiatric symptoms that can occur in mentally retarded persons outside the context of a mental disorder include hyperactivity and short attention span, self-injurious behaviors (for example, head banging and self-biting), and repetitive stereotypical behaviors (hand flapping and toe walking).

Personality styles and traits in mentally retarded persons are not unique to them. However, negative self-image, low self-esteem, poor frustration tolerance, interpersonal dependence, and a rigid problem-solving style are overrepresented in mentally retarded persons. Specific causal syndromes seen in mental retardation may also predispose the affected persons to various types of psychopathology.

### Risk Factors

**Neurological impairment.** Reports indicate that the risk for psychopathology increases in a variety of neurological conditions, such as seizure disorders. Rates of psychopathology increase with the severity of mental retardation, indicating an increase in neurological impairment as intellectual impairment increases.

**Genetic syndromes.** Some evidence indicates that genetically based syndromes—such as fragile X syndrome, Prader-Willi syndrome, and Down's syndrome—are associated with specific behavioral manifestations.

Persons with fragile X syndrome are known to have extremely high rates (up to three fourths of those studied) of attention-deficit/hyperactivity disorders. High rates of aberrant interpersonal behavior and language function often meet the criteria for autistic disorder and avoidant personality disorder.

Prader-Willi syndrome is almost always associated with compulsive eating disturbances, hyperphagia, and obesity. Children with the syndrome have been described as oppositional and defiant. Socialization is an area of weakness, especially in coping skills. Externalizing behavior problems—such as temper tantrums, irritability, and arguing—seem to be heightened in adolescence.

In Down's syndrome, language function is a relative weakness, whereas sociability and social skills, such as interpersonal cooperation and conformity with social conventions, are relative strengths. Most studies have noted muted affect in children with Down's syndrome relative to nonretarded children of the same mental age. Persons with Down's syndrome also manifest deficiencies in scanning the environment and are likely to focus on a single stimulus, making it difficult for them to notice environmental changes and to communicate. A variety of mental disorders occur in persons with Down's syndrome, but the rates appear to be lower than those in other mental retardation syndromes, especially of autistic disorder.

**Psychosocial factors.** A negative self-image and poor self-esteem are common features of mildly and moderately mentally retarded persons, who are well aware of being different from others. They experience repeated failure and disappointment in not meeting their parents' and society's expectations and of progressively falling behind their peers and even their younger siblings. Communication difficulties further increase their vulnerability to feelings of ineptness and frustration. Inappropriate behaviors, such as withdrawal, are common. The perpetual sense of isolation and inadequacy has been linked to feelings of anxiety, anger, dysphoria, and depression.

## DIFFERENTIAL DIAGNOSIS

By definition, mental retardation must begin before the age of 18. A mentally retarded child has to cope with so many difficult social and academic situations that maladaptive patterns often form, complicating the diagnostic process. However, vulnerable children who are exposed to perpetual environmental stressors may not develop at the expected rate.

Children who come from deprived homes that provide inadequate stimulation may manifest motor and mental retardation that can be reversed if an enriched, stimulating environment is provided in early childhood. A number of sensory handicaps, especially deafness and blindness, may be mistaken for mental retardation if, during testing, no compensation for the handicap is allowed. Speech deficits and cerebral palsy often make a child seem retarded, even in the presence of borderline or normal intelligence.

Chronic, debilitating diseases of any kind may depress the child's functioning in all areas. Convulsive disorders may give an impression of mental retardation, especially in the presence of uncontrolled seizures.

Chronic brain syndromes may result in isolated handicaps—failure to read (alexia), failure to write (agraphia), failure to communicate (aphasia), and several other handicaps—that may exist in a person of normal and even superior intelligence.

Children with learning disorders, which can coexist with mental retardation, experience a delay or a failure of development in a specific area, such as reading or mathematics, but the children develop normally in other areas. In contrast, children with mental retardation show general delays in most areas of development.

Mental retardation and pervasive developmental disorders often coexist; 70 to 75 percent of those with pervasive developmental disorders have an I.Q. of less than 70. A pervasive developmental disorder results in the distortion of the timing, the rate, and the sequence of many basic psychological functions necessary for social development. Because of their general level of functioning, children with pervasive developmental disorders have more problems with social relatedness and have more deviant language than do those with mental retardation. In mental retardation, generalized delays in development are present, and mentally retarded children behave in some ways as though they were passing through an earlier normal developmental stage, rather than with completely aberrant behavior.

A most difficult differential diagnostic problem concerns children with severe mental retardation, brain damage, autistic disorder, schizophrenia with childhood onset, or, according to some, Heller's disease. The confusion stems from the fact that details of the child's early history are often unavailable or unreliable. In addition, when the children are evaluated, many with those conditions display similar bizarre and stereotyped behavior—mutism, echolalia, or functioning on a retarded level. By the time the children are usually seen, it does not matter from a practical point of view whether the child's retardation is secondary to a primary early infantile autistic disorder or schizophrenia or whether the personality and behavioral distortions are secondary to brain damage or mental retardation. When ego functions are delayed in development or are atrophic because of other reasons, the physician must first concentrate on overcoming the child's unrelatedness. A relationship with the child must be established before remedial education measures can be successful.

Children under the age of 18 years who meet the diagnostic criteria for dementia and who manifest an I.Q. of less than 70 are given the diagnosis of dementia and mental retardation. Persons whose I.Q.s drop to less than 70 after the age of 18 years and who have new onsets of cognitive disorders are not given the diagnosis of mental retardation but receive only the diagnosis of dementia.

## COURSE AND PROGNOSIS

In most cases of mental retardation, the underlying intellectual impairment does not improve, yet the affected person's level of adaptation can be positively influenced by an enriched and supportive environment. As in persons who are not mentally retarded, the more comorbid mental disorders occur, the more guarded is the overall prognosis. When clear-cut mental disorders are superimposed on mental retardation, standard treatments for the comorbid mental disorders are often beneficial. However, there is still a lack of clarity about the classification of such aberrant behaviors as hyperactivity, emotional lability, and social dysfunction; are they additional psychiatric symptoms or direct sequelae of the mental retardation? In general, persons with mild and moderate mental retardation have the most flexibility in adapting to various environmental conditions.

## TREATMENT

Mental retardation is associated with several heterogeneous groups of disorders and a multitude of psychosocial factors. The best treatment of mental retardation is primary, secondary, and tertiary prevention.

### Primary Prevention

Primary prevention concerns actions taken to eliminate or reduce the conditions that lead to the development of the disorders associated with mental retardation. Such measures include (1) education to increase the general public's knowledge and awareness of mental retardation, (2) continuing efforts of health professionals to ensure and upgrade public health policies, (3) legislation to provide optimal maternal and child health care, and (4) the eradication of the known disorders associated with central nervous system damage. Family and genetic counseling helps reduce the incidence of mental retardation in a family with a history of a genetic disorder associated with mental retardation. For the children and the mothers of low socioeconomic status, proper prenatal and postnatal medical care and various supplementary enrichment programs and social service assistance may help minimize the medical and psychosocial complications.

### Secondary and Tertiary Prevention

Once a disorder associated with mental retardation has been identified, the disorder should be treated to shorten the course of the illness (secondary prevention) and to minimize the sequelae or consequent handicaps (tertiary prevention).

Hereditary metabolic and endocrine disorders, such as PKU and hypothyroidism, can be effectively treated in an early stage by dietary control or hormone replacement therapy.

Mentally retarded children frequently have emotional and behavioral difficulties requiring psychiatric treatment. Those children's limited cognitive and social capabilities require modified psychiatric treatment modalities based on the children's level of intelligence.

**Education for the child.** Educational settings for mentally retarded children should include a comprehensive program that addresses adaptive skills training, social skills training, and vocational training. Particular attention should be focused on communication and efforts to improve the quality of life. Group therapy has often been a successful format in which mentally retarded children can learn and practice hypothetical real-life situations and receive supportive feedback.

**Behavior, cognitive, and psychodynamic therapies.** The difficulties in adaptation among mentally retarded persons are widespread and so varied that a number of interventions alone or in combination may be beneficial.

Behavior therapy has been used for many years to shape and enhance social behaviors and to control and minimize the patient's aggressive and destructive behaviors. Positive reinforcement for desired behaviors and benign punishment (such as loss of privileges) for objectionable behaviors have been helpful.

Cognitive therapy, such as dispelling false beliefs and relaxation exercises with self-instruction, has also been recommended for those mentally retarded patients who are able to follow the instructions.

Psychodynamic therapy has been used with mentally retarded patients and their families to decrease conflicts regarding expectations that result in persistent anxiety, rage, and depression.

**Family education.** One of the most important areas that can be addressed by a clinician is that of educating the family of a mentally retarded patient regarding ways to enhance competence and self-esteem while maintaining realistic expectations for the patient. The family often finds it difficult to balance the fostering of independence and the providing of a nurturing and supportive environment for the mentally retarded child, who is likely to experience some degree of rejection and failure outside the family context.

The parents may benefit from continuous counseling or family therapy. The parents should be allowed opportunities to express their feelings of guilt, despair, anguish, recurring denial, and anger regarding the child's disorder and future. The psychiatrist should be prepared to give the parents all the basic and current medical information regarding causes, treatment, and other pertinent areas (such as special training and the correction of sensory defects).

**Pharmacological intervention.** Pharmacological approaches to the treatment of comorbid mental disorders in mentally retarded patients is much the same as it is for patients who are not mentally retarded. Increasing data support the use of a variety of medications for patients with mental disorders who are not mentally retarded. Some studies have focused on the use of medications for the following behavioral syndromes that are frequent among the mentally retarded:

AGGRESSION AND SELF-INJURIOUS BEHAVIOR. Some evidence from controlled and uncontrolled studies indicate that lithium (Eskalith) has been useful in decreasing aggression and self-injurious behavior. Narcotic antagonists such as naltrexone (Trexan) have been reported to decrease self-injurious behaviors in mentally retarded patients who also meet the diagnostic criteria for infantile autistic disorder. One hypothesis proposed as the mechanism of naltrexone treatment is that it interferes with the release of endogenous opioids that are presumed to be associated with self-injury. Carbamazepine (Tegretol) and valproic acid (Depakene) are medications that have also been beneficial in some cases of self-injurious behavior.

STEREOTYPICAL MOTOR MOVEMENTS. Antipsychotic medications, such as haloperidol (Haldol) and chlorpromazine (Thorazine), decrease repetitive self-stimulatory behaviors in mentally retarded patients, but those medications have not increased adaptive behavior. Some mentally retarded children and adults (up to one third) face a high risk for tardive dyskinesia with the continued use of antipsychotic medications.

EXPLOSIVE RAGE BEHAVIOR. β-Blockers, such as propranolol and buspirone (BuSpar), have been reported to result in a decrease in explosive rages among patients with mental retardation and autistic disorder. Systematic study is necessary before those drugs can be confirmed as efficacious.

ATTENTION-DEFICIT/HYPERACTIVITY DISORDER. Studies of methylphenidate treatment in mildly retarded patients with attention-deficit/hyperactivity disorder have shown a significant improvement in the ability to maintain attention and to stay on tasks. Methylphenidate treatment studies have not shown evidence of long-term improvement in social skills or learning.

**References**

Aman M G, Teehan C J, White A J, Turbott S H, Vaithianathan C: Haloperidol treatment with chronically medicated residents: Dose effects on clinical behavior and contingencies. Am J Ment Retard 4: 452, 1989.

Bregman J D: Current developments in the understanding of mental retardation: Part II. Psychopathology. J Am Acad Child Adolesc Psychiatry 30: 861, 1991.

Bregman J D, Hodapp R M: Current developments in the understanding of mental retardation: Part I. Biological and phenomenological perspectives. J Am Acad Child Adolesc Psychiatry 30: 707, 1991.

Brown W T: The fragile X syndrome. Neurol Clin 7: 107, 1989.

Burd L, Martsolf J T: Fetal alcohol syndrome: Diagnosis and syndromal variability. Physiol Behav 46: 39, 1989.

Campbell M G, Anderson L T, Small A M, Locasio J J, Lynch N S, Choroco M C: Naltrexone in autistic children: A double blind and placebo-controlled study. Psychopharmacol Bull 26: 130, 1990.

Craft M J, Ismail I A, Krishnamurti D, Matthews J, Regan A, Seth R V, North P M: Lithium in the treatment of aggression in mentally handicapped patients: A double blind trial. Br J Psychiatry 150: 685, 1987.

Crocker A C: The causes of mental retardation. Pediatr Ann 18: 623, 1989.

Davis E, Fennoy I: Growth and development in infants of cocaine abusing mothers. Am J Dis Child 144: 426, 1990.

Diamond G W: Developmental problems in children with HIV infection. Ment Retard 27: 213, 1989.

Dosen A: Diagnosis and treatment of mental illness in mentally retarded children: A developmental model. Child Psychiatry Hum Dev 20: 73, 1989.

Dykens E M, Hodapp R M, Walsh K, Nash L J: Adaptive and maladaptive behavior in Prader-Willi syndrome. J Am Acad Child Adolesc Psychiatry 31: 1131, 1992.

Hagberg B A: Rett syndrome: Clinical peculiarities, diagnostic approach, and possible cause. Pediatr Neurol 5: 75, 1989.

Handen B L, Breaux A M, Janosky J, McAuliffe S, Feldman H, Gosling A: Effects and noneffects of methylphenidate in children with mental retardation and ADHD. J Am Acad Child Adolesc Psychiatry 31: 455, 1992.

Hurley A D: Individual psychotherapy with mentally retarded individuals: A review and call for research. Res Dev Disabil 10: 261, 1989.

Menkes J H: Heredodegenerative diseases: In Textbook of Child Neurology, p 139. Lea & Febiger, Philadelphia, 1990.

Ratey J, Sovner R, Mikkelsen E, Chmielinski H E: Buspirone therapy for maladaptive behavior and anxiety in developmentally disabled persons. J Clin Psychiatry 50: 382, 1989.

Spreat S, Behar D, Reneski B, Miazzo P: Lithium carbonate for aggression in mentally retarded persons. Compr Psychiatry 30: 505, 1989.

Sturmey P: The use of DSM and ICD diagnostic criteria in people with mental retardation: A review of empirical studies. J Nerv Ment Dis 181: 38, 1993.

Szymanski L S, Crocker A C: Mental retardation. In Comprehensive Textbook of Psychiatry, ed 5, H I Kaplan, B J Sadock, editors, p 1728. Williams & Wilkins, Baltimore, 1989.

Williams D T, Mehl R, Yudofsky S, Adams D, Roseman B: The effects of propranolol on uncontrolled rage outbursts in children and adolescents with organic brain dysfunction. J Am Acad Child Psychiatry 21: 129, 1982.

# Learning Disorders

## 36.1 / Reading Disorder

Reading disorder is characterized by an impaired ability to recognize words, slow and inaccurate reading, and poor comprehension in the absence of low intelligence or significant sensory deficits. The relatively common school-age childhood disorder seems to run in families and is often associated with disorder of written expression, mathematics disorder, or one of the communication disorders. In addition, children with attention-deficit/hyperactivity disorder have a high risk for reading disorder. Over the years, a variety of labels have been used to describe reading disabilities, including "dyslexia," "reading backwards," "learning disability," "alexia," and "developmental word blindness." The term "dyslexia" was used extensively for a number of years to describe a reading disability syndrome that often included speech and language deficits and right-left confusion. When it became evident that reading disorder is frequently accompanied by disabilities in other academic skills, the use of the term "dyslexia" diminished, and general terms, such as "learning disorder," began to be used.

Although the nomenclature of the category within which reading disorder falls has been modified from specific developmental disorders in the revised third edition of *Diagnostic and Statistical Manual of Mental Disorders* (DSM-III-R) to learning disorders (academic skills disorders) in the fourth edition of *Diagnostic and Statistical Manual of Mental Disorders* (DSM-IV), the definition of reading disorder has remained the same. Essentially, reading achievement is below the expected level for the child's age, education, and intelligence, and the impairment significantly interferes with academic success or the daily activities that involve reading. According to DSM-IV, if a neurological condition or sensory disturbance is present, the degree of reading disability exhibited exceeds that usually associated with it.

The DSM-IV definition of reading disorder differs from that in the 10th revision of the International Classification of Diseases (ICD-10). According to ICD-10, children with specific reading disorder frequently have a history of impaired speech, language, and spelling.

## EPIDEMIOLOGY

An estimated 4 percent of school-age children in the United States have reading disorder; prevalence studies find rates ranging between 2 and 8 percent. Three to four times as many boys as girls are reported to have reading disability in school and clinically referred samples. The rate for boys may be inflated, since boys with reading disorder are apt to be picked up because of their increased behavioral difficulties. Adults with reading backwardness or reading retardation reportedly show no sex difference in the frequency of the disorder.

## ETIOLOGY

No unitary cause is known for reading disorder; given the many associated learning disorders and language difficulties, reading disorder is probably multifactorial. One recent study found an association between dyslexia and birth in the months of May, June, and July, suggesting that prenatal exposure to a maternal infectious illness, such as influenza, in the winter months may contribute to reading disorder.

Reading disorder tends to be more prevalent among family members of persons affected by the disorder than in the general population, leading to the speculation that the disorder may have a genetic origin. However, family and twin studies have not supplied definitive evidence to support that theory.

Studies in the 1930s attempted to explain reading disorder with the cerebral hemispheric function model, which suggested positive correlations of reading disorder with left-handedness, left-eyedness, or mixed laterality. But subsequent epidemiological studies did not find any consistent association between reading disorder and laterality of handedness or eyedness. However, right-left confusion has been shown to be associated with reading difficulties. The reversal of cerebral asymmetry may result in the transference of language lateralization to a cerebral hemisphere that is less differentiated to accommodate language function, thereby leading to reading disorder. A few recent studies (computed tomography [CT] scan, magnetic resonance imaging [MRI], and on autopsy) have shown abnormal symmetries in the temporal or parietal lobes of persons with reading disorder.

Many attribute reading disorder to subtle deficits that are either visual or verbal (that is, auditory). There is more evidence for verbal deficits than for visual deficits; thus, reading disorder is considered to be part of an oral language disorder.

Reading requires a brain that is mature enough and sufficiently intact to integrate information arriving through various processing systems and to relegate disturbing stimuli to the background. In addition, reading requires sufficient freedom from conflict to permit the investment of energy in the task and a sociocultural value system that views reading as basic to survival.

A high incidence of reading disorder tends to be found among children with cerebral palsy who are of normal intelligence. A slightly increased incidence of reading disorder is seen among epileptic children. Complications during pregnancy; prenatal and perinatal difficulties, including prematurity; and low birth weight are common in the histories of children with reading disorder.

Secondary reading disorder may be seen in children with postnatal brain lesions in the left occipital lobe resulting in right visual field blindness. The disorder may also be seen in children with lesions in the splenum of the corpus callosum that block the transmission of visual information from the intact right hemisphere to the language areas of the left hemisphere.

Reading disorder may be one manifestation of developmental delay or maturational lag. Temperamental attributes have been reported to be closely associated with reading disorder. Compared with nonreading-disordered children, children with reading disorder often have more difficulty in concentrating and a shorter attention span.

Some studies suggest an association between malnutrition and cognitive function. Children who were malnourished for a long time during early childhood show subaverage performances in various cognitive tests. Their cognitive performances are lower than those of their siblings who grew up in the same family environment but who were not subjected to the same degree of malnutrition.

Severe reading disorder is often associated with psychiatric problems. Reading disorder may be the result of a preexisting psychiatric disorder or the cause of emotional and behavior disorders; however, it is not always easy to ascertain the causal relation between reading disorder and a coexisting psychiatric disorder.

## DIAGNOSIS

The main diagnostic feature of reading disorder is reading achievement markedly below the person's intellectual capacity (Table 36.1–1). Other characteristic features include difficulties with the recall, evocation, and sequencing of printed letters and words; with the processing of sophisticated grammatical constructions; and with the making of inferences. Clinically, the observer is impressed by the interaction between emotional and specific features. The experience of school failure seems to confirm preexisting doubts that some children have about themselves. The energy of some children is so bound to their psycho-

**Table 36.1–1**
**Diagnostic Criteria for Reading Disorder**

A. Reading achievement, as measured by individually administered standardized tests of reading accuracy or comprehension, is substantially below that expected given the person's chronological age, measured intelligence, and age-appropriate education.

B. The disturbance in criterion A significantly interferes with academic achievement or activities of daily living that require reading skills.

C. If a sensory deficit is present, the reading difficulties are in excess of those usually associated with it.

**Coding note:** if a general medical (e.g., neurological) condition or sensory deficit is present, code the condition on Axis III.

Table from DSM-IV, *Diagnostic and Statistical Manual of Mental Disorders*, ed 4. Copyright American Psychiatric Association, Washington, 1994. Used with permission.

logical conflicts that they are unable to use their assets. The psychiatric evaluation should assess the need for psychiatric intervention and decide on the appropriate treatment.

The diagnosis of reading disorder cannot be established without confirmation by a standardized reading achievement test, and pervasive developmental disorders and mental retardation must be ruled out.

### Psychoeducational Tests

In addition to standardized intelligence tests, psychoeducational diagnostic tests should be administered. The diagnostic battery may include a standardized spelling test, the writing of a composition, the processing and the use of oral language, and design copying, a judgment of the adequacy of pencil use. A screening projective battery may include human-figure drawings, picture-story tests, and sentence completion. The evaluation should also include a systematic observation of behavior variables.

## CLINICAL FEATURES

Reading disorder is usually apparent by age 7 (second grade). In severe cases, evidence of reading difficulty may be apparent as early as age 6 (first grade). Sometimes reading disorder is compensated for in the early elementary grades, particularly when it is associated with high scores on intelligence tests. In those cases the disorder may not be apparent until age 9 (fourth grade) or later.

Reading-disordered children make many errors in their oral reading. The faulty reading is characterized by omissions, additions, and distortions of words. Such children have difficulty in distinguishing between printed letter characters and sizes, especially those that differ only in spatial orientation and length of line. The problems in managing printed or written language may pertain to individual letters, sentences, and even a whole page. The children's reading speed is slow, often with minimal comprehension. Most children with reading disorder have an age-appropriate ability to copy from a written or printed text, but nearly all are poor spellers.

Associated problems include language difficulties, shown often as impaired sound discrimination and difficulties in properly sequencing words. The reading-disordered child may start a word in the middle or at the end of a printed or written sentence. At times, such children transpose letters that are to be read because of a poorly established left-to-right tracking sequence. Failures in both memory recall and sustained elicitation result in the poor recall of letter names and sounds.

Most children with reading disorder dislike reading and writing and avoid them. Their anxiety is heightened when they are confronted with demands that involve printed language.

Most reading-disordered children who do not receive remedial education have a sense of shame and humiliation because of their continuing failure and subsequent frustration. Those feelings become more intense as time progresses. Older children tend to be angry and depressed, and they exhibit poor self-esteem.

## DIFFERENTIAL DIAGNOSIS

Deficits in expressive language and speech discrimination are usually present in reading disorder and may be severe enough to warrant the additional diagnosis of expressive language disorder or mixed receptive/expressive language disorder. Disorder of written expression is often present. In some cases there is a discrepancy between verbal and performance intelligence scores. Visual perceptual deficits are seen in only about 10 percent of cases.

Reading difficulties may be caused primarily by the generalized impairment in intellectual functioning seen in mental retardation, which can be checked by administering a standardized intelligence test.

Inadequate schooling resulting in poor reading skills can be determined by finding out whether other children in the same school have similarly poor reading performances on standardized reading tests.

Hearing and visual impairments should be ruled out with screening tests.

Reading disorder often accompanies other emotional and behavioral disorders, especially attention-deficit/hyperactivity disorder, conduct disorder, and depressive disorders, particularly in older children and adolescents.

## COURSE AND PROGNOSIS

Even without any remedial assistance, many reading-disordered children acquire a little information about printed language during their first two years in grade school. By the end of the first grade, some have learned how to read a few words. However, if no remedial educational intervention is given by the third grade, the children remain reading-impaired. Under the best circumstances, a child is classified as being at risk for a reading disorder during the kindergarten year or early in the first grade.

When remediation is instituted early, it can sometimes be discontinued by the end of the first or second grade. In severe cases and depending on the pattern of deficits and strengths, remediation may be continued into the middle and high school years. Children who have either compensated satisfactorily or recovered from early reading disorder are overrepresented in families with socioeconomically advantaged backgrounds.

## TREATMENT

The treatment of choice for reading disorder is a remedial educational approach; however, the relative efficacy of various remedial teaching strategies is controversial.

One frequently used method, developed by Samuel Orton, urges therapeutic attention to the mastery of simple phonetic units, followed by the blending of those units into words and sentences. An approach that systematically engages several senses is recommended. The rationale for that and similar methods is that children's difficulties in managing letters and syllables are basic to their failures to learn to read; therefore, if they are taught to cope with graphemes, they will learn to read.

As in psychotherapy, the therapist–patient relationship is important to a successful treatment outcome in remedial educational therapy.

Reading-disordered children should be placed in a grade as close as possible to their social functional level and given special remedial work in reading. Coexisting emotional and behavioral problems should be treated by appropriate psychotherapeutic means. Parental counseling may also be helpful.

### References

Badian N A: The prediction of good and poor reading before kindergarten entry: A nine-year follow-up. J Learn Disabil *21*: 88, 1988.

Duane D D: Neurobiological correlates of learning disorders. J Am Acad Child Adolesc Psychiatry *28*: 314, 1989.

Duffy F H, Geschwind N: *Dyslexia: A Neuroscientific Approach to Clinical Evaluation*. Little, Brown, Boston, 1985.

Fellon R H, Wood F B: Cognitive deficits in reading disability and attention deficit disorder. J Learn Disabil *22*: 3, 1989.

Galaburda A M: Learning disability: Biological, societal or both? A response to Gerald Coles. J Learn Disabil *22*: 238, 1989.

Geschwind N: Asymmetries of the brain: New development. Bull Orton Soc *29*: 67, 1979.

Hyrid G W, Semrod-Clikeman E: Dyslexia and neurodevelopmental pathology: Relationships to cognition, intelligence, and reading skill acquisition. J Learn Disabil *22*: 204, 1989.

LaBuda M C, DeFries J C: Cognitive abilities in children with reading disabilities and controls: A follow-up study. J Learn Disabil *21*: 562, 1988.

Lerner J W: Educational interventions in learning disabilities. J Am Acad Child Adolesc Psychiatry *28*: 326, 1989.

Livingston R, Adam B S, Bracha H S: Season of birth and neurodevelopmental disorder: Summer birth is associated with dyslexia. J Am Acad Child Adolesc Psychiatry *32*: 612, 1993.

Semrod-Clikeman E, Biederman J, Sprich-Buckminster S, Lehman B K, Faraone S V, Norman D: Comorbidity between ADDH and learning disability: A review and report in a clinically referred sample. J Am Acad Child Adolesc Psychiatry *31*: 439, 1992.

Shepherd M J, Charnow D A, Silver L B: Developmental reading disorder. In *Comprehensive Textbook of Psychiatry*, ed 5, H I Kaplan, B J Sadock, editors, p 1790. Williams & Wilkins, Baltimore, 1989.

Silver A A, Hagin R A: *A Scanning Instrument for the Identification of Learning Disability*. Walker Educational, New York, 1980.

Smith S D, Pennington B F, Kimberling W J, Ing P S: Familial dyslexia: Use of genetic linkage data to define subtypes. J Am Acad Child Adolesc Psychiatry *29*: 204, 1990.

# 36.2 / Mathematics Disorder

Mathematics disorder is essentially a disability in performing arithmetic skills that are expected for a person's intellectual capacity and educational level. Arithmetic skills are measured by standardized, individually administered tests. The lack of expected mathematics ability interferes with school performance or daily life activities, and the difficulties are in excess of impairments associated with any existing neurological or sensory deficits.

Mathematics disorder has been around for many decades, as evidenced by the many terms that have been applied to it, but it was not recognized as a psychiatric disorder until 1980 in the third edition of *Diagnostic and Statistical Manual of Mental Disorders* (DSM-III). Past terminology for the disorder includes "Gerstmann syndrome," "dyscalculia," "congenital arithmetic disorder," "acalculia," and "developmental arithmetic disorder."

According to the fourth edition of *Diagnostic and Statistical Manual for Mental Disorders* (DSM-IV), mathematics disorder is one of the learning disorders. Impairment in four groups of skills have been identified in mathematics disorder: linguistic skills (those related to understanding mathematical terms and to converting written problems into mathematical symbols), perceptual skills (the ability to recognize and understand symbols and to order clusters of numbers), mathematical skills (basic addition, subtraction, multiplication, and division and following sequences of basic operations), and attentional skills (copying figures correctly and observing operational symbols correctly).

Other disorders often accompany mathematics disorder, including reading disorder, developmental coordination disorder, and mixed receptive/expressive language disorder. Unlike DSM-IV, the equivalent disorder in the 10th revision of the International Classification of Diseases (1CD–10) excludes reading and spelling disabilities.

## EPIDEMIOLOGY

The prevalence of mathematics disorder has not been well studied and can be only roughly estimated to be 6 percent of school-age children who are not mentally retarded. The extent to which educational limitations influence that number is not clear. Data do suggest that children with mathematics disorder are likely to exhibit another learning disorder or language disability. The sex ratio of mathematics disorder is still under investigation. The disorder may be more common in girls than in boys.

## ETIOLOGY

The cause of mathematics disorder is not known. An early theory proposed a neurological deficit in the right cerebral hemisphere, particularly in the occipital lobe areas. Those regions are responsible for processing visual-spatial stimuli that, in turn, are responsible for mathematical skills. However, the validity of that theory has received little support in subsequent neuropsychiatric studies.

The current view is that the cause is multifactorial. Maturational, cognitive, emotional, educational, and socioeconomic factors account in varying degrees and combinations for mathematics disorder. Compared with reading, arithmetic abilities seem to be more dependent on the amount and the quality of instruction.

## DIAGNOSIS

In a typical case of mathematics disorder, a careful inquiry into the child's school performance history reveals early difficulties with arithmetic subjects. The definitive diagnosis can be made only after the child takes an individually administered standardized arithmetic test and scores markedly below the expected level, considering the child's schooling and intellectual capacity as measured by a standardized intelligence test. A pervasive developmental disorder and mental retardation should also be ruled out before confirming the diagnosis of mathematics disorder. The diagnostic criteria for mathematics disorder are given in Table 36.2–1.

## CLINICAL FEATURES

Most children with mathematics disorder can be classified during the second and third grades in elementary school. The affected child's performance in handling basic number concepts, such as counting and adding even one-digit numbers, is significantly below the age-expected norms, but the child shows normal intellectual skills in other areas.

During the first two or three years of elementary school, a child with mathematics disorder may appear to make some progress in mathematics by relying on rote memory. But soon, as arithmetic progresses into complex levels re-

**Table 36.2–1**
**Diagnostic Criteria for Mathematics Disorder**

A. Mathematical ability, as measured by individually administered standardized tests, is substantially below that expected given the person's chronological age, measured intelligence, and age-appropriate education.

B. The disturbance in criterion A significantly interferes with academic achievement or activities of daily living that require mathematical ability.

C. If a sensory deficit is present, the difficulties in mathematical ability are in excess of those usually associated with it.

**Coding note:** if a general medical (e.g., neurological) condition or sensory deficit is present, code the condition on Axis III.

Table from DSM-IV, *Diagnostic and Statistical Manual of Mental Disorders*, ed 4. Copyright American Psychiatric Association, Washington, 1994. Used with permission.

quiring discrimination and manipulation of spatial and numerical relations, the presence of the disorder becomes conspicuous.

Some investigators have classified mathematics disorder into several categories: (1) difficulty in learning to count meaningfully, (2) difficulty in mastering cardinal and ordinal systems, (3) difficulty in performing arithmetic operations, and (4) difficulty in envisioning clusters of objects as groups. In addition, affected children may have difficulties in associating auditory and visual symbols, understanding the conservation of quantity, remembering sequences of arithmetic steps, and choosing principles for problem-solving activities. Children with those problems are presumed to have good auditory and verbal abilities.

Mathematics disorder often coexists with other disorders affecting the following skills: reading, expressive writing, coordination, and expressive and receptive language. Spelling problems, deficits in memory or attention, and emotional or behavioral problems may be present. Young grade-school children often present first with other learning disorders and should be checked for mathematics disorder. Children with cerebral palsy may have mathematics disorder with normal overall intelligence.

The relation between mathematics disorder and other communication and learning disorders is not yet clear. Although children with mixed receptive/expressive language disorder and expressive language disorder are not necessarily affected by mathematics disorder, the conditions often coexist, as they are associated with impairments in both decoding and encoding processes.

## DIFFERENTIAL DIAGNOSIS

Arithmetic difficulties seen in mental retardation are accompanied by a generalized impairment in overall intellectual functioning. In unusual cases of mild mental retardation, arithmetic skills may be significantly below the expected level, given the persons' schooling and level of mental retardation. In such cases the additional diagnosis of mathematics disorder should be made, as treatment of the arithmetic difficulties can be particularly helpful to the child's chances for employment in adulthood.

Inadequate schooling can often cause the child's poor arithmetic performance on a standardized arithmetic test. If so, most of the other children in the same class probably have similarly poor arithmetic performances.

Conduct disorder and attention-deficit/hyperactivity disorder may be present with mathematics disorder, and in those cases both diagnoses should be made.

## COURSE AND PROGNOSIS

Mathematics disorder is usually apparent by the time the child is 8 years old (third grade). In some children the disorder is apparent as early as 6 years (first grade), and in others it may not occur until age 10 (fifth grade) or later. Thus far few longitudinal study data are available to predict clear patterns of developmental and academic progress of children classified as having mathematics disorder in early school grades. However, untreated children with a moderate mathematics disorder and those children whose arithmetic difficulties cannot be resolved by intensive remedial interventions may have complications, including continuing academic difficulties, poor self-concept, depression, and frustration. Those complications may then lead to a reluctance to attend school, truancy, or conduct disturbance.

## TREATMENT

The currently most effective treatment of mathematics disorder is remedial education. Controversy continues as to the comparative effectiveness of various remedial educational treatments. However, the current consensus is that the treatment methods and materials are useful only when they fit the particular child, the disorder, and the severity and feasibility of the teaching plans. Project MATH, a multimedia self-instructional or group-instructional in-service training program, has been successful for some children with mathematics disorder. Computer programs can be helpful and can increase compliance with remediation efforts. Poor coordination may accompany the disorder, so physical therapy and sensory integration activities may be helpful.

### References

Badian N A: Dyscalculia and nonverbal disorders of learning. In *Progress in Learning Disabilities*, vol 5, H R Myklebust, editor, p 235. Grune & Stratton, New York, 1983.

Fleischner J E, Garnett K, Silver L B: Developmental arithmetic disorder. In *Comprehensive Textbook of Psychiatry*, ed 5, H I Kaplan, B J Sadock, editors, p 1800. Williams & Wilkins, Baltimore, 1989.

Grant M L, Ilai D, Nussbaum N L, Bigler E D: The relationship between continuous performance tasks and neuropsychological tests in children with attention-deficit hyperactivity disorder. Percept Mot Skills *70:* 435, 1990.

Johnson D, Myklebust H: *Learning Disabilities: Educational Principles and Practices.* Grune & Stratton, New York, 1967.

Kose L: Neuropsychological implications of diagnoses and treatment of mathematical learning disabilities. Top Lang Learn Disord *1:* 19, 1981.

Lerner J W: Educational intervention in learning disabilities. J Am Acad Child Adolesc Psychiatry *28:* 326, 1989.

McCleod T M, Crump W D: The relationship of visuospatial skills and verbal ability to learning disabilities in mathematics. J Learn Disabil *11:* 237, 1978.

Nussbaum N L, Grant M L, Roman M J, Poole J H, Bigler E D: Attention-deficit disorder and the mediating effect of age on academic and behavioral variables. J Dev Behav Pediatr *11:* 22, 1990.

Rourke B P, Strang J D: Subtypes of reading and arithmetic disabilities: A neuropsychological analysis. In *Developmental Neuropsychiatry*, M Rutter, editor, p 473. Guilford, New York, 1983.

Share D L, Moffitt T E, Silva P A: Factors associated with arithmetic and reading disability and specific arithmetic disability. J Learn Disabil *21:* 313, 1988.

Vogel S A: Gender differences in intelligence, language, visual motor abilities, and academic achievement in students with learning disabilities: A review of the literature. J Learn Disabil *23:* 44, 1990.

Yule W, Lansdown R, Urbanowicz M: Predicting educational attainment for WISC-R in a primary school sample. Br J Psychol *21:* 43, 1982.

# 36.3 / Disorder of Written Expression

## DISORDER OF WRITTEN EXPRESSION

Disorder of written expression is characterized by writing skills that are significantly below the expected level for a person's age, intellectual capacity, and education as measured by a standardized test. The impairment interferes with the person's school performance and with the demands for writing in everyday life, and the disorder is not due to a neurological or sensory deficit. The components of writing disability include poor spelling, errors in grammar and punctuation, and poor handwriting.

Disorder of written expression was first recognized in the psychiatric diagnostic system in the revised third edition of *Diagnostic and Statistical Manual of Mental Disorders* (DSM-III-R) as developmental expressive writing disorder, and the definition of the disorder has remained essentially the same in the fourth edition of DSM (DSM-IV). Several decades ago the prevailing view was that writing disabilities did not develop in the absence of a reading disorder, but it has become known that disorder of written expression can occur on its own. Terms used in the past to describe writing disability included "spelling disorder" and "spelling dyslexia."

Writing disabilities are often associated with other learning disorders but may be diagnosed later than others, since expressive writing is acquired later than language and reading.

In addition to a disorder similar to the DSM-IV disorder of written expression, the 10th revision of the International Classification of Diseases (ICD-10) also includes a separate specific spelling disorder.

### Epidemiology

The prevalence of disorder of written expression is not known but has been estimated at 3 to 10 percent of school-age children. The male-to-female ratio is also unknown. Some evidence indicates that affected children are frequently from families with a history of the disorder.

### Etiology

One hypothesis holds that disorder of written expression results from the combined effects of one or more of the following disorders: expressive language disorder, mixed receptive/expressive language disorder, and reading disorder. That view suggests the possible existence of neurological and cognitive defects or malfunctions somewhere in the central information-processing areas of the brain.

Hereditary predisposition to the disorder has been suggested by empirical findings that most children with disorder of written expression have relatives with the disorder.

Temperamental characteristics may play some role in disorder of written expression, especially such characteristics as short attention span and easy distractibility.

### Diagnosis

The diagnosis of disorder of written expression is made on the basis of the person's consistently poor performance on the composition of written text. Performance is markedly below the person's intellectual capacity, as confirmed by an individually administered standardized expressive writing test (Table 36.3–1). The presence of a major disorder, such as a pervasive developmental disorder or mental retardation, may obviate the diagnosis of disorder of written expression. Other disorders to be differentiated from disorder of written expression are communication disorders, reading disorder, and impaired vision and hearing.

Dyslexia is characterized by an inability to read and dysgraphia by an inability to write. Any person suspected of having disorder of written expression should first be given a standardized intelligence test, such as the Revised Wechsler Intelligence Scale for Children (WISC-R, WISC-3) or the Revised Weschsler Adult Intelligence Scale (WAIS-R) to determine the person's intellectual capacity before administering a standardized expressive writing test.

### Clinical Features

Children with disorder of written expression present difficulties early in grade school in spelling words and expressing their thoughts according to age-appropriate grammatical norms. Their spoken and written sentences contain an unusually large number of grammatical errors and poor paragraph organization. During and after the second grade, the children commonly make simple grammatical

**Table 36.3–1**
**Diagnostic Criteria for Disorder of Written Expression**

A. Writing skills, as measured by individually administered standardized tests (or functional assessments of writing skills), are substantially below those expected given the person's chronological age, measured intelligence, and age-appropriate education.

B. The disturbance in criterion A significantly interferes with academic achievement or activities of daily living that require the composition of written texts (e.g., writing grammatically correct sentences and organized paragraphs).

C. If a sensory deficit is present, the difficulties in writing skills are in excess of those usually associated with it.

**Coding note:** if a general medical (e.g., neurological) condition or sensory deficit is present, code the condition on Axis III.

Table from DSM-IV, *Diagnostic and Statistical Manual of Mental Disorders*, ed 4. Copyright American Psychiatric Association, Washington, 1994. Used with permission.

errors in writing a short sentence. For example, they frequently fail, despite constant reminders, to start the first letter of the first word in a sentence with a capital letter and to end a sentence with a period.

As they grow older and progress into higher grades in school, such children's spoken and written sentences become more conspicuously primitive, odd, and inferior to what is expected of students at their grade level. Their word choices are erroneous and inappropriate; their paragraphs are disorganized and not in proper sequence; and spelling correctly becomes increasingly difficult as their vocabulary becomes more abstract and larger in number and characters.

Associated features of disorder of written expression include refusal or reluctance to go to school and to do assigned written homework, poor academic performance in other areas (such as mathematics), general disinterest in school work, truancy, attention-deficit, and conduct disturbance.

Most children with disorder of written expression become frustrated and angry because of their feelings of inadequacy and failure in their academic performance. They may have a chronic depressive disorder as a result of their growing sense of isolation, estrangement, and despair.

Adults with disorder of written expression who do not receive remedial intervention continue to have difficulties in social adaptation involving writing skills and a continuing sense of incompetence, inferiority, isolation, and estrangement. Some of them even try to avoid or procrastinate writing a response letter or a simple greeting card for fear that their writing incompetence will be exposed. When their coping mechanisms fail, the severity of their psychopathology is likely to be increased. Most adults with the disorder choose occupations that require minimal writing skills, such as in trade, custodianship, and other menial work; seldom do they achieve or hold a socially desirable occupational position requiring a high level of expressive writing. Common associated disorders are reading disorder, mixed receptive/expressive language disorder, expressive language disorder, mathematics disorder, developmental coordination disorder, and disruptive behavior and attention-deficit disorders.

## Course and Prognosis

Because writing, language, and reading disorders often coexist and because a child normally speaks well before learning to read and learns to read well before writing well, a child with all three disorders has expressive language disorder diagnosed first and disorder of written expression diagnosed last. In severe cases a disorder of written expression is apparent by age 7 (second grade); in less severe cases the disorder may not be apparent until age 10 (fifth grade) or later. Most persons with mild and moderate disorder of written expression fare well if they receive timely remedial education early in grade school. Severe disorder of written expression requires continual extensive remedial treatment through the late part of high school and even into college.

The prognosis depends on the severity of the disorder, the age or grade when the remedial intervention is started, the length and the continuity of treatment, and the presence or the absence of associated or secondary emotional or behavioral problems.

Those persons who later become well compensated or who recover from disorder of written expression are often from families with high socioeconomic backgrounds.

## Treatment

Disorder of written expression responds to treatment. The best treatment to date is remedial education. Although controversy continues as to the effectiveness of various remedial expressive writing modalities, an intensive and continuous administration of individually tailored one-to-one expressive and creative writing therapy appears to show the most favorable treatment outcomes. Teachers in some special schools devote as much as two hours a day to such writing instruction.

The treatment of the disorder requires an optimal patient-therapist relationship, as in psychotherapy. Success or failure in sustaining the patient's motivation greatly affects the treatment's long-term efficacy.

Associated and secondary emotional and behavioral problems should be given prompt attention, with appropriate psychiatric treatment and parental counseling.

## LEARNING DISORDER NOS

Learning disorder not otherwise specified (NOS) is a new category in DSM-IV for disorders that do not meet the criteria for any specific learning disorder but that cause impairment and reflect learning abilities below those expected for a person's intelligence, education, and age. An example of a disability that could be placed in the category is a spelling skills deficit (Table 36.3–2).

The DSM-III-R category specific developmental disorder not otherwise specified covered residual disorders of language, speech, academic, and motor skills; the category has been divided in DSM-IV into learning disorder not otherwise specified and communication disorder not otherwise specified.

**Table 36.3–2**
**Diagnostic Criteria for Learning Disorder Not Otherwise Specified**

This category is for disorders in learning that do not meet criteria for any specific learning disorder. This category might include problems in all three areas (reading, mathematics, written expression) that together significantly interfere with academic achievement even though performance on tests measuring each individual skill is not substantially below that expected given the person's chronological age, measured intelligence, and age-appropriate education.

Table from DSM-IV, *Diagnostic and Statistical Manual of Mental Disorders*, ed 4. Copyright American Psychiatric Association, Washington, 1994. Used with permission.

## References

Friedland J: Development and breakdown of written language. J Commun Disord *23:* 171, 1990.
Houck C K, Billingsley B S: Written expression of students with and without learning disabilities: Differences across the grades. J Learn Disabil *22:* 561, 1989.

Johnson D, Myklebust H: *Learning Disabilities: Educational Principles and Practices.* Grune & Stratton, New York, 1967.

Oliver C E: A sensorimotor program for improving writing readiness skills in elementary-age children. Am J Occup Ther *44:* 111, 1990.

Orton S: *Reading, Writing, and Speech Problems in Children.* Norton, New York, 1937.

Outhred: Word processing: Its impact on children's writing. J Learn Disabil *22:* 262, 1989.

Persell C H: *Education and Inequality: A Theoretical and Empirical Synthesis.* Free Press, New York, 1977.

Shepherd M J, Charnow D A, Silver L B: Developmental expressive writing disorder. In *Comprehensive Textbook of Psychiatry*, ed 5, H I Kaplan, B J Sadock, editors, p 1796. Williams & Wilkins, Baltimore, 1989.

Weiss C E, Lillywhite H S: *Communicative Disorders: Prevention and Early Intervention*, Mosby, St. Louis, 1981.

# 37

# Developmental Coordination Disorder

Developmental coordination disorder is currently the only disorder in the category of motor skills disorder, according to the fourth edition of *Diagnostic and Statistical Manual of Mental Disorders* (DSM-IV). It was first included as a psychiatric disorder in the revised third edition of *Diagnostic and Statistical Manual of Mental Disorders* (DSM-III-R).

The disorder is characterized by markedly lower than expected performance in activities requiring motor coordination. The child may have delays in achieving motor milestones, such as sitting up, crawling, and walking. The patient is usually clumsy in gross and fine motor skills but is not globally impaired. Developmental coordination disorder may also include deficits in handwriting and in the frequency of dropping things. Children with the disorder may motorically resemble children of a younger age. The deficits are significantly poor for the child's chronological and mental age, and they interfere with daily functioning or school performance. Motor impairment in the disorder cannot be explained on the basis of a medical condition, such as cerebral palsy, muscular dystrophy, or any other neuromuscular disorder.

Clumsiness in children has been associated with learning disorders, communication disorders, and disruptive behavior and attention-deficit disorders, such as attention-deficit/hyperactivity disorder. Children who are clumsy are often poor in sports and may be socially ostracized.

DSM-IV makes no provision for motor coordination deficits that do not meet the criteria for developmental coordination disorder. In DSM-III-R such deficits fell into the category of specific developmental disorder not otherwise specified.

## EPIDEMIOLOGY

The prevalence of developmental coordination disorder is not known but has been estimated at about 6 percent of school-age children. The male-to-female ratio is also not known, but more boys than girls have developmental coordination disorder. Reports in the literature of the male-to-female ratio have ranged from 2 to 1 to as much as 4 to 1.

## ETIOLOGY

The causes of developmental coordination disorder are unknown, but hypotheses include both organic and developmental causes. Risk factors postulated in the disorder include prematurity, hypoxia, perinatal malnutrition, and low birth weight. Neurochemical abnormalities and parietal lobe lesions have also been suggested as contributors to coordination deficits.

Developmental coordination disorder and communication disorders have strong associations, although the specific causative agents are unknown for both. Coordination problems are also more than usually frequent in children with impulsive behavior and a variety of learning disorders. Developmental coordination disorder probably has a multifactorial cause.

## DIAGNOSIS

The diagnosis of developmental coordination disorder requires a history of the child's early motor behavior, including the direct observation of motor activities. Informal screening for developmental coordination disorder can be done by asking the child to perform tasks involving gross motor coordination (for example, hopping, jumping, and standing on one foot), fine motor coordination (for example, finger tapping and shoelace tying), and hand-eye coordination (for example, catching a ball and copying letters). The diagnosis is supported by below-normal scores on the performance subtests of standardized intelligence tests and by normal or above-normal scores on the verbal subtests. Specialized tests of motor coordination can be useful, such as the Bender Gestalt Visual Motor test, the Frostig Movement Skills Test Battery, and the Bruininks-Oseretsky Test of Motor Development. The child's chronological age and intellectual capacity must be taken into account, and the disorder cannot be caused by a neurological or neuromuscular condition. However, slight reflex abnormalities and other soft neurological signs may occasionally be found on examination. The DSM-IV diagnostic criteria are given in Table 37-1.

## CLINICAL FEATURES

The clinical signs suggesting the existence of developmental coordination disorder are evident as early as infancy, when the affected child begins to attempt tasks requiring motor coordination. The essential clinical feature is the child's markedly impaired performance in motor coordination. The difficulties in motor coordination may vary with the child's age and developmental stage.

In infancy and early childhood the disorder may be manifested as delays in normal developmental milestones, such as turning over, crawling, sitting, standing, walking, buttoning shirts, and zipping up pants. Between the ages of 2 and 4 years, clumsiness appears in almost all activities requiring motor coordination. The affected children can-

**Table 37–1**
**Diagnostic Criteria for Developmental Coordination Disorder**

A. Performance in daily activities that require motor coordination is substantially below that expected given the person's chronological age and measured intelligence. This may be manifested by marked delays in achieving motor milestones (e.g., walking, crawling, sitting), dropping things, "clumsiness," poor performance in sports, or poor handwriting.

B. The disturbance in criterion A significantly interferes with academic achievement or activities of daily living.

C. The disturbance is not due to a general medical condition (e.g., cerebral palsy, hemiplegia, or muscular dystrophy) and does not meet criteria for a pervasive developmental disorder.

D. If mental retardation is present, the motor difficulties are in excess of those usually associated with it.

**Coding note:** If a general medical (e.g., neurological) condition or sensory deficit is present, code the condition on Axis III.

Table from DSM-IV, *Diagnostic and Statistical Manual of Mental Disorders*, ed 4. Copyright American Psychiatric Association, Washington, 1994. Used with permission.

not hold objects, and they drop them easily; their gait is unsteady; they often trip over their own feet; and they may bump into other children while attempting to go around them.

In older children the impaired motor coordination may be shown in table games, such as putting together puzzles or building blocks, and in any type of ball game. Although no specific features are pathognomonic of developmental coordination disorder, developmental milestones are frequently delayed. Many children with the disorder also have a speech disorder. Older children may also have secondary problems of school difficulties, including behavioral and emotional problems, that require appropriate therapeutic interventions.

## DIFFERENTIAL DIAGNOSIS

The differential diagnosis includes medical disorders that produce coordination difficulties (such as cerebral palsy and muscular dystrophy), pervasive developmental disorders, and mental retardation. In mental retardation and in the pervasive developmental disorders, coordination usualy does not stand out as a deficit compared with other skills. Children with neuromuscular disorders may exhibit more global muscle impairment than clumsiness and delayed motor milestones. In those cases, neurological workups usually reveal more extensive deficits than are present in developmental coordination disorder. Extremely hyperactive and impulsive children may be physically careless because of their high levels of motor activity. Clumsy motor behavior and attention-deficit/hyperactivity disorder seem to be associated.

## COURSE AND PROGNOSIS

No reliable data are available on the prospective longitudinal outcomes of both treated and untreated children with developmental coordination disorder. Some studies suggest a favorable outcome for those children who have an average or above-average intellectual capacity, because they are able to learn to compensate for their coordination deficits. In general, the clumsiness persists into adolescence and adult life.

In severe cases that remain untreated, the patient may have a number of secondary complications, such as repeated failures in both nonacademic and academic school tasks, repeated problems in attempting to integrate with a peer group, and inability to play games and sports. Those problems may lead to low self-esteem, unhappiness, withdrawal, and, in some cases, increasingly severe behavioral problems as a reaction to the frustration engendered by the disorder. All levels of adaptive functioning can be expected in the children. Commonly associated features include delays in nonmotor milestones, expressive language disorder, and mixed receptive/expressive language disorder.

## TREATMENT

The treatments of developmental coordination disorder include perceptual motor training, neurophysiological techniques of exercise for motor dysfunction, and modified physical education. The Montessori technique (developed by Maria Montessori) may be useful with many preschool children, as it emphasizes the development of motor skills. No single exercise or training method seems to be more advantageous or effective than another. Secondary behavioral or emotional problems and coexisting communication disorders must be managed by appropriate treatment methods.

No large-scale controlled studies have reported on the effects of treatment, although small studies have suggested that exercises in rhythmic coordination, practicing motor movements, and learning to use typewriters are all helpful.

Parental counseling helps reduce the parents' anxiety and guilt over the child's impairment and increases their awareness, giving them confidence to cope with the child.

**References**

Arnheim D D, Sinclair W A: *The Clumsy Child.* Mosby, St. Louis, 1975.
Baker L: Developmental coordination disorder. In *Comprehensive Textbook of Psychiatry*, ed 5, H I Kaplan, B J Sadock, editors, p 1818. Williams & Wilkins, Baltimore, 1989.
Breaner M W, Gillman S, Zangwill O L, Farrell M: Visuo-motor disability in school children. Br Med J 4: 259, 1967.
Drillien C M: Etiology and outcome in low-birth-weight infants. Dev Med Child Neurol 14: 563, 1972.
Gordon N: *Pediatric Neurology for the Clinician.* Heinemann, Philadelphia, 1976.
Losse A, Henderson S E, Elliman D, Hall D, Knight E, Jongmans M: Clumsiness in children: Do they grow out of it? A ten-year follow-up study. Dev Med Child Neurol 33: 55, 1991.
Prechtl H F, Stemmer C J: The choreiform syndrome in children. Dev Med Child Neurol 4: 119, 1962.
Robinson R J: Causes and associations of severe and persistent specific speech and language disorders in children. Dev Med Child Neurol 33: 943, 1991.
Roussounis S H, Gaussen T H, Stratton P: A 2-year follow-up study of children with motor coordination problems identified at school entry age. Child Care Health Dev 13: 377, 1987.
Smyth T R: Abnormal clumsiness in children: A defect of motor programming? Child Care Health Dev 17: 283, 1991.
Stott D H: A general test of motor impairment for children. Dev Med Child Neurol 8: 523, 1966.

# 38 ||||| Pervasive Developmental Disorders

The pervasive developmental disorders are a group of psychiatric conditions in which expected social skills, language development, and behavioral repetoire either do not develop appropriately or are lost in early childhood. In general, the disorders affect multiple areas of development, are manifested early in life, and cause persistent dysfunction.

Autistic disorder (also known as infantile autism), best-known of the disorders, is characterized by sustained impairments in reciprocal social interactions, communication deviance, and restricted, stereotypical behavioral patterns. According to the fourth edition of *Diagnostic and Statistical Manual of Mental Disorders* (DSM-IV), abnormal functioning in the above areas must be present by age 3. More than two thirds of the persons with autistic disorder have mental retardation, but that is not required for the diagnosis.

Infantile autism was described by Leo Kanner in 1943, but it was not until 1980, in the third edition of DSM (DSM-III), that autistic disorder was recognized as a distinct clinical entity. Before 1980, children with any of the pervasive developmental disorders were classified as having a type of childhood schizophrenia.

DSM-IV maintains the category of pervasive developmental disorder not otherwise specified for patients who show a qualitative impairment in reciprocal social interactions and verbal and nonverbal communication but who do not meet the full criteria for autistic disorder.

DSM-IV includes several other disorders in the category of pervasive developmental disorders: Rett's disorder, childhood disintegrative disorder, and Asperger's disorder. Rett's disorder appears to occur exclusively in girls; it is characterized by normal development for at least six months, followed by a degenerating developmental course. Typically, the child begins to show stereotyped hand movements, a loss of purposeful motions, diminishing social engagement, poor coordination, and decreasing language use. In childhood disintegrative disorder, development progresses normally for the first two years, after which the child shows a loss of previously acquired skills in two or more of the following areas: language use, social responsiveness, play, motor skills, and bladder or bowel control. Asperger's disorder is a condition in which the child shows a marked impairment in social relatedness and repetitive and stereotyped patterns of behavior without a delay in language development. The child's cognitive abilities and adaptive skills are normal.

## AUTISTIC DISORDER

### History

In 1867 Henry Maudsley was the first psychiatrist to pay serious attention to very young children with severe mental disorders involving a marked deviation, delay, and distortion in the developmental processes. Initially, all such disorders were considered psychoses. In 1943 Leo Kanner, in his classic paper "Autistic Disturbances of Affective Contact," coined the term "infantile autism" and provided a clear and comprehensive account of the early childhood syndrome. He described children who exhibited extreme autistic aloneness, failure to assume an anticipatory posture, delayed or deviant language development with echolalia and pronominal reversal (using "you" for "I"), monotonous repetitions of noises or verbal utterances, excellent rote memory, limited range in the variety of spontaneous activities, stereotypies and mannerisms, anxiously obsessive desire for the maintenance of sameness and a dread of change, poor eye contact and abnormal relationships with people and a preference for pictures and inanimate objects. Kanner suspected the syndrome to be more frequent than it seemed and suggested that some children had been misclassified as mentally retarded or schizophrenic.

There has been confusion about whether autistic disorder is an early manifestation of schizophrenia or a discrete clinical entity, but the evidence points toward autistic disorder and schizophrenia as separate entities.

### Epidemiology

**Prevalence.** Autistic disorder occurs at a rate of 2 to 5 cases per 10,000 children (0.02 to 0.05 percent) under age 12. If severe mental retardation with some autistic features is included, the rate can rise as high as 20 per 10,000. In most cases autism begins before 36 months but may not be evident to parents, depending on their awareness and the severity of the disorder.

**Sex distribution.** Autistic disorder is found more frequently in boys than in girls. Three to five times more boys than girls have autistic disorder. But autistic girls tend to be more seriously affected and more likely to have family histories of cognitive impairment than are boys.

**Socioeconomic status.** Early studies suggested that a high socioeconomic status was common in families with autistic children; however, those findings were probably based on referral biases. Over the past 25 years, an increasing proportion of cases has been found in the low socioeconomic groups. That finding may well be due to an increased awareness of the disorder and the increased availability of child mental health workers for poor children.

## Etiology and Pathogenesis

Autistic disorder is a developmental behavioral disorder. Although autistic disorder was first considered to be psychosocial or psychodynamic in origin, much evidence has accumulated to support a biological substrate.

**Psychodynamic and family factors.** In his initial report Kanner noted that few parents of autistic children were really warmhearted and that, for the most part, the parents and other family members were preoccupied with intellectual abstractions and tended to express little genuine interest in their children. That finding, however, has not been replicated over the past 50 years. Other theories, such as parental rage and rejection and parental reinforcement of autistic symptoms, have also not been substantiated. Recent studies comparing parents of autistic children with parents of normal children have not shown significant differences in child-rearing skills. No satisfactory evidence indicates that any particular kind of deviant family functioning or psychodynamic constellation of factors leads to the development of autistic disorder. Nevertheless, some autistic children respond to psychosocial stressors, such as the birth of a sibling or the move to a new home, with an exacerbation of symptoms.

**Organic-neurological-biological abnormalities.** Autistic disorder and autistic symptoms are associated with conditions that have neurological lesions, notably congenital rubella, phenylketonuria (PKU), tuberous sclerosis, and Rett's disorder. Autistic children show more evidence of perinatal complications than do comparison groups of normal children and those with other disorders.

The finding that autistic children have significantly more minor congenital physical anomalies than do their siblings and normal controls suggests that complications of pregnancy in the first trimester are significant. Four to 32 percent of autistic persons have grand mal seizures at some point in life, and about 20 to 25 percent of autistic persons show ventricular enlargement on computed tomography scans. Various electroencephalogram (EEG) abnormalities are found in 10 to 83 percent of autistic children, and, although no EEG finding is specific to autistic disorder, there is some indication of failed cerebral lateralization. Recently, one magnetic resonance imaging (MRI) study revealed hypoplasia of cerebellar vermal lobules VI and VII, and another MRI study revealed cortical abnormalities, particularly polymicrogyria, in some autistic patients. Those abnormalities may reflect abnormal cell migrations in the first six months of gestation. An autopsy study revealed decreased Purkinje's cell counts, and in another study there was increased diffuse cortical metabolism during positron emission tomography (PET) scanning.

**Genetic factors.** In several surveys, between 2 and 4 percent of siblings of autistic persons have been found to be afflicted with autistic disorder, a rate 50 times greater than in the general population. The concordance rate of autistic disorder in the two largest twin studies was 36 percent in monozygotic pairs versus 0 percent in dizygotic

pairs in one study and about 96 percent in monozygotic pairs versus about 27 percent in dizygotic pairs in the second study. In the second study, however, zygosity was confirmed in only about half of the sample. Clinical reports and studies suggest that the nonautistic members of the families share various language or other cognitive problems with the autistic person but have them in a less severe form. Fragile X syndrome appears to be associated with autistic disorder, but the number of persons with both autistic disorder and fragile X syndrome is unclear.

**Immunological factors.** Some evidence indicates that immunological incompatibility between the mother and the embryo or fetus may contribute to autistic disorder. The lymphocytes of some autistic children react with maternal antibodies, raising the possibility that embryonic neural or extraembryonic tissues may be damaged during gestation.

**Perinatal factors.** A high incidence of various perinatal complications seems to occur in children with autistic disorder, although no complication has been directly implicated as causative. During gestation, maternal bleeding after the first trimester and meconium in the amniotic fluid have been reported in autistic children more often than in the general population. In the neonatal period, autistic children have a high incidence of respiratory distress syndrome and neonatal anemia. Some evidence indicates a high incidence of medication usage during pregnancy in the mothers of autistic children.

**Neuroanatomical findings.** The temporal lobe has been suggested as a critical part of the brain that may be abnormal in autistic disorder. That suggestion is based on reports of autisticlike syndromes in some persons who have temporal lobe damage. When the temporal region of animals is damaged, expected social behavior is lost, and restlessness, repetitive motor behavior, and a limited behavioral repertoire are seen. Other findings in autistic disorder include decreased Purkinje's cells in the cerebellum, potentially resulting in abnormalities of attention, arousal, and sensory processes.

**Biochemical findings.** At least one third of autistic disorder patients have elevated plasma serotonin. That finding is not specific to autistic disorder, since persons with mental retardation without autistic disorder also have that trait. Autistic disorder patients without mental retardation also have a high incidence of hyperserotonemia.

In some autistic children, increased cerebrospinal fluid (CSF) homovanillic acid (the major dopamine metabolite) is associated with increased withdrawal and stereotypies. Some evidence indicates that symptom severity decreases as the ratio of CSF 5-hydroxyindoleacetic acid (5-HIAA, metabolite of serotonin) to CSF homovanillic acid increases. CSF-5-HIAA may be inversely proportional to blood serotonin levels; those levels are increased in one third of autistic disorder patients, a nonspecific finding that is also found in mentally retarded persons.

## Diagnosis and Clinical Features

The DSM-IV diagnostic criteria for autistic disorder are given in Table 38–1.

**Physical characteristics**

APPEARANCE. Kanner was struck by autistic children's

**Table 38–1**
**Diagnostic Criteria for Autistic Disorder**

A. A total of six (or more) items from (1), (2), and (3), with at least two from (1), and one each from (2) and (3):

(1) Qualitative impairment in social interaction, as manifested by at least two of the following:
  (a) marked impairment in the use of multiple nonverbal behaviors such as eye-to-eye gaze, facial expression, body postures, and gestures to regulate social interaction
  (b) failure to develop peer relationships appropriate to developmental level
  (c) a lack of spontaneous seeking to share enjoyment, interests, or achievements with other people (e.g., by a lack of showing, bringing, or pointing out objects of interest)
  (d) lack of social or emotional reciprocity

(2) Qualitative impairments in communication as manifested by at least one of the following:
  (a) delay in, or total lack of, the development of spoken language (not accompanied by an attempt to compensate through alternative modes of communication such as gesture or mime)
  (b) in individuals with adequate speech, marked impairment in the ability to initiate or sustain a conversation with others
  (c) stereotyped and repetitive use of language or idiosyncratic language
  (d) lack of varied spontaneous make-believe play or social imitative play appropriate to developmental level

(3) Restricted repetitive and stereotyped patterns of behavior, interests, and activities, as manifested by at least one of the following:
  (a) encompassing preoccupation with one or more stereotyped and restricted patterns of interest that is abnormal either in intensity or focus
  (b) apparently inflexible adherence to specific, nonfunctional routines or rituals
  (c) stereotyped and repetitive motor mannerisms (e.g., hand or finger flapping or twisting, or complex whole body movements)
  (d) persistent preoccupation with parts of objects

B. Delays or abnormal functioning in at least one of the following areas, with onset prior to age 3 years: (1) social interaction, (2) language as used in social communication, or (3) symbolic or imaginative play.

C. The disturbance is not better accounted for by Rett's disorder or childhood disintegrative disorder.

Table from DSM-IV, *Diagnostic and Statistical Manual of Mental Disorders*, ed 4. Copyright American Psychiatric Association, Washington, 1994. Used with permission.

intelligent and attractive appearance. Between the ages of 2 and 7, they also tend to be shorter than the normal population.

HANDEDNESS. Many autistic children have a failure of lateralization. That is, they remain ambidextrous at an age when cerebral dominance is established in normal children. Autistic children also have a higher incidence of abnormal dermatoglyphics (for example, fingerprints) than do the general population, which may suggest a disturbance in neuroectodermal development.

INTERCURRENT PHYSICAL ILLNESS. Young autistic disorder children have a higher incidence of upper respiratory infections, excessive burping, febrile seizures, constipation, and loose bowel movements than do controls. Many autistic children react differently to illness than do normal children, which may reflect an immature or abnormal autonomic nervous system. Autistic children may not have elevated temperatures with infectious illnesses, may not complain of pain either verbally or by gesture, and may not show the malaise of ill children. Their behavior and relatedness may improve to a noticeable degree when they are ill, and in some cases that is a clue to physical illness.

**Behavioral characteristics**

QUALITATIVE IMPAIRMENTS IN SOCIAL INTERACTION. All autistic children fail to show the usual relatedness to their parents and other people. As infants, many lack a social smile and anticipatory posture for being picked up as an adult approaches. Abnormal eye contact is a common finding. The social development of autistic children is characterized by a lack (but not always a total absence) of attachment behavior and a relatively early failure of person-specific bonding. Autistic children often do not seem to recognize or differentiate the most important people in their lives—parents, siblings, and teachers. And they may show virtually no separation anxiety on being left in an unfamiliar environment with strangers.

When autistic children have reached school age, their withdrawal may have diminished or not be as obvious, particularly in better-functioning children. Instead, their failure to play with peers and to make friends, their social awkwardness and inappropriateness, and, particularly, their failure to develop empathy are observed.

In late adolescence, those autistic persons who make the most progress often have a desire for friendships. However, their ineptness of approach and their inability to respond to another's interests, emotions, and feelings are major obstacles in developing friendships. Autistic adolescents and adults have sexual feelings, but their lack of social competence and skills prevents most of them from developing a sexual relationship. It is extremely rare for autistic persons to marry.

DISTURBANCES OF COMMUNICATION AND LANGUAGE. Gross deficits and deviances in language development are among the principal criteria for diagnosing autistic disorder. Autistic children are not simply reluctant to speak, and their speech abnormalities are not due to lack of motivation. Language deviance, as much as language delay, is characteristic of autistic disorder. In contrast to normal and mentally retarded children, autistic children make little use of meaning in their memory and thought processes. When autistic persons do learn to converse fluently, they lack social competence, and their conversations are not characterized by reciprocal responsive interchanges.

In the first year of life, the autistic child's amount and pattern of babbling may be reduced or abnormal. Some children emit noises—clicks, sounds, screeches, and nonsense syllables—in a stereotyped fashion with no seeming intent at communication.

Unlike normal young children, who always have better receptive language skills and understand much before they can speak, verbal autistic children may say more than they understand. Words and even entire sentences may drop in and out of a child's vocabulary. Autistic children may use a word once and then not use it again for a week, a month, or years. Their speech contains echolalia, both immediate and delayed, or stereotyped phrases out of context. Those abnormalities are often associated with pronominal reversal; that is, a girl asks, "Do you want the toy?" when she means she wants it. Difficulties in articulation are also noted. The use of peculiar voice quality and rhythm is observed clinically in many cases. About 50 percent of all autistic children never have useful speech. Some of the brightest children show a particular fascination with letters and numbers. A few literally teach themselves to read at a preschool age (hyperlexia), often astonishingly well. In virtually all cases, however, the children read without any comprehension whatsoever.

STEREOTYPED BEHAVIOR. In the first years of an autistic child's life, much of the normal child's exploratory play is absent or minimal. Toys and objects are often manipulated in a way that was not intended, with little variety, creativity, and imagination and few symbolic features. Autistic children cannot imitate or use abstract pantomime. The activities and play, if any, of the autistic child are rigid, repetitive, and monotonous. Ritualistic and compulsive phenomena are common in early and middle childhood. The autistic children often spin, bang, and line up objects and become attached to inanimate objects. In addition, many autistic children, particularly those who are the most intellectually impaired, exhibit various abnormalities of movements. Stereotypies, mannerisms, and grimacing are most frequent when the child is left alone and may decrease in a structured situation. Autistic children are resistant to transition and change. Moving to a new house, moving furniture in a room, and having breakfast before a bath when the reverse was the routine may result in panic or temper tantrums.

INSTABILITY OF MOOD AND AFFECT. Some children with autistic disorder exhibit sudden mood changes, with bursts of laughing or crying for no apparent reason and without expressing thoughts congruent to the affect.

RESPONSE TO SENSORY STIMULI. Autistic children may be overresponsive or underresponsive to sensory stimuli (for example, to sound and pain). They may selectively ignore spoken language directed at them, and so they are often thought to be deaf. However, they may show unusual interest in the sound of a wristwatch. Many have a heightened pain threshold or an altered response to pain. Indeed, autistic children may injure themselves severely and not cry.

Many autistic children seem to enjoy music. They frequently hum a tune or sing a song or commercial jingle before saying words or using speech. Some particularly enjoy vestibular stimulation—spinning, swinging, and up-and-down movements.

OTHER BEHAVIORAL SYMPTOMS. Hyperkinesis is a common behavior problem in young autistic children. Hypokinesis is less frequent; when present, it often alternates with hyperactivity. Aggressiveness and temper tantrums are observed, often for no apparent reason, or they are prompted by change or demands. Self-injurious behavior includes head banging, biting, scratching, and hair pulling. Short attention span, a complete inability to focus on a task, insomnia, feeding and eating problems, enuresis, and encopresis are also frequent.

Seth, a 3½-year-old boy, was brought to a psychiatrist be-

cause of his inability to speak in sentences, his idiosyncratic use of language, and his hyperactive and at times uncontrollable behavior.

Seth was the product of a pregnancy complicated by second-trimester bleeding and delivery four weeks early. At birth, Seth had a mild respiratory distress syndrome and remained in the hospital for two weeks after delivery, but he went home with a clean bill of health. He was a baby who had chronic ear infections, and he seemed to always be on antibiotics until the age of 2 years. Other than his infections, Seth was an easy baby to care for; he hardly ever cried, and he did not demand much attention.

Seth's parents began to worry slightly when he did not seem to be able to coordinate himself to walk by 16 months. They brought him to their pediatrician, who examined him and assured the parents that some babies develop slowly and that they should come back if he was not walking by 18 months. At just 18 months Seth did start to walk. Although he was clumsy, his parents felt that the clumsiness was normal for his age.

One of the things that his parents had noted since he was 6 months old was that Seth rarely made eye contact, did not seem to smile when they played with him, and seemed to prefer being left on the floor with a favorite spinning toy, rather than being held.

At age 2 years, he was a handsome toddler who was growing well and had no special health problems. His mother did notice that he seemed to have poor coordination when swallowing, and he liked only one or two foods. Although he had several words then, they were his own made-up words for various household items. His parents could not understand why he had a fascination with certain things, such as the vacuum cleaner, the sprinkler, and the dryer. He did not say "Mama" or "Daddy," and he seemed relatively unconcerned with his mother's proximity most of the time. Occasionally, he started crying hysterically for up to an hour, and his mother was unable to console him. His development, especially his lack of social interest, was different from his older sister's, but his mother felt that perhaps the difference was due to gender difference.

Not until Seth was enrolled in preschool at 3 years of age did his parents realize how different he was from other children. Seth was able to speak in short sentences, but, rather than responding to questions, he seemed to repeat the exact phrases that were spoken to him. He had noticeable problems with pronouns and frequently said "you" when he meant "I." He was still fascinated by the vacuum cleaner, the sprinkler, and the dryer; he would stand in front of the dryer and look in the window at the clothes spinning around for as long as his mother would allow him to remain. He seemed unable to turn from one activity to another in school, and he ignored all the other children and the teacher. When he got excited, he would begin to flap his arms up and down repetitively. He was also too clumsy to climb on the outdoor toys. When he fell down, he showed no reaction to pain and never sought comfort from his teachers. He seemed to most enjoy twirling himself around and around in a circle. In addition to his inability to play with the other children, Seth was unable to sit still during quiet activities, and he refused to eat snacks in school. His teachers contacted his parents and requested that he be evaluated for his poor social skills and unmanageable behavior.

Seth was first seen by a pediatrician, who found him to be in excellent health. The findings of the laboratory workup were normal. A neurological examination revealed a number of soft signs, including poor fine motor coordination and a high-arched palate.

A psychiatric examination showed a well-developed boy

who made no eye contact and showed no interest in the examiner. Seth answered a few questions with one-word answers but, for the most part, did not acknowledge the presence of his mother or the examiner.

Seth's communication was characterized by echolalia and delayed language. He also had a limited range of interests. Intellectual testing found an intelligence quotient (I.Q.) of 68, with mild impairment in adaptive function. Language evaluation showed a marked idiosyncratic use of language and frequent echolalia. The diagnosis was autistic disorder and mild mental retardation.

*Discussion.* A recommendation was made for a specialized preschool that could concentrate on communication skills and help Seth during transitions from one activity to the next. A small class setting was suggested in the hope of improving his restlessness and hyperactivity. Seth's parents were referred to a support group for the parents of children with developmental disorders.

**Intellectual functioning.** About 40 percent of the children with infantile autism have intelligence quotient (I.Q.) scores below 50 to 55 (moderate, severe, or profound mental retardation); 30 percent have scores of 50 to approximately 70 (mild mental retardation); and 30 percent have scores of 70 or more. Epidemiological and clinical studies show that the risk for autistic disorder increases as the I.Q. decreases. About one fifth of all autistic children have a normal nonverbal intelligence. The I.Q. scores of autistic children tend to reflect problems with verbal sequencing and abstraction skills, rather than with visuospatial or rote memory skills, suggesting the importance of defects in language-related functions.

Unusual or precocious cognitive or visuomotor abilities are present in some autistic children. The abilities may exist even within the overall retarded functioning and are referred to as splinter functions or islets of precocity. Perhaps the most striking examples are the idiot savants who have prodigious rote memories or calculating abilities. Their specific abilities usually remain beyond the capabilities of normal peers. Other precocious abilities in young autistic children include hyperlexia, an early ability to read well (although they are not able to understand what they read), memorizing and reciting, and muscial abilities (singing tunes or recognizing musical pieces).

## Differential Diagnosis

The major differential diagnoses are schizophrenia with childhood onset, mental retardation with behavioral symptoms, mixed receptive/expressive language disorder, congential deafness or severe hearing disorder, psychosocial deprivation, and disintegrative (regressive) psychoses.

Because children with a pervasive developmental disorder usually have many concurrent problems, Michael Rutter suggested a stepwise approach to use in the differential diagnosis (Table 38–2).

**Schizophrenia with childhood onset.** Whereas a wealth of literature on autistic disorder is available, there are few data on children under age 12 who meet the diagnostic criteria for schizophrenia. Schizophrenia is rare in children under the age of 5. It is accompanied by hallucinations or delusions, with a lower incidence of seizures

**Table 38–2**
**Procedure for Differential Diagnosis on a Multiaxial System**

1. Determine intellectual level.
2. Determine level of language development.
3. Consider whether child's behavior is appropriate for
   (i) chronological age
   (ii) mental age
   (iii) language age
4. If not appropriate, consider differential diagnosis of psychiatric disorder according to
   (i) pattern of social interaction
   (ii) pattern of language
   (iii) pattern of play
   (iv) other behaviors
5. Identify any relevant medical conditions
6. Consider whether there are any relevant psychosocial factors.

Table from M Rutter, L Hersov: *Child and Adolescent Psychiatry: Modern Approaches*, ed 2, p 73. Blackwell, Oxford, England, 1985. Used with permission.

and mental retardation and a more even I.Q. than in autistic children. Table 38–3 compares autistic disorder and schizophrenia with childhood onset.

**Mental retardation with behavioral symptoms.** About 40 percent of autistic children are moderately, severely, or profoundly retarded, and retarded children may have behavior symptoms that include autistic features. When both disorders are present, both should be diagnosed. The main differentiating features between autistic disorder and mental retardation are that (1) mentally retarded children usually relate to adults and other children in accordance with their mental age; (2) they use the language they do have to communicate with others; and (3) they have a relatively even profile of impairments without splinter functions.

**Mixed receptive/expressive language disorder.** A group of children with mixed receptive/expressive language disorder have autisticlike features and may present a diagnostic problem. Table 38–4 summarizes the major differences between autistic disorder and mixed receptive/expressive language disorder.

**Acquired aphasia with convulsion.** Acquired aphasia with convulsion is a rare condition and is sometimes difficult to differentiate from autistic disorder and childhood disintegrative disorder. Children with the condition are normal for several years before losing both their receptive and their expressive language over a period of weeks or months. Most of them have a few seizures and generalized EEG abnormalities at the onset, but those signs usually do not persist. A profound disorder of language comprehension then follows, characterized by a deviant speech pattern and speech impairment. Some children recover but with considerable residual language impairment.

**Congenital deafness or severe hearing impairment.** Because autistic children are often mute or show a selective disinterest in spoken language, they are often thought to be deaf. The following may be differentiating features: Autistic infants may babble only infrequently, whereas deaf infants have a history of relatively normal babbling that then gradually tapers and may stop from 6 months to 1 year of age. Deaf children respond only to loud sounds, whereas autistic children may ignore loud or

**Table 38-3**
**Autistic Disorder versus Schizophrenia with Childhood Onset**

| Criteria | Autistic Disorder | Schizophrenia (with Onset before Puberty) |
|---|---|---|
| Age of onset | Before 36 months | Not under 5 years of age |
| Incidence | 2–5 in 10,000 | Unknown, possibly same or even rarer |
| Sex ratio (M:F) | 3–4:1 | 1.67:1 (nearly equal, or slight preponderance of males) |
| Family history of schizophrenia | Not raised or probably not raised | Raised |
| Socioeconomic status (SES) | Overrepresentation of upper SES groups (artifact) | More common in lower SES groups |
| Prenatal and perinatal complications and cerebral dysfunction | More common in autistic disorder | Less common in schizophrenia |
| Behavioral characteristics | Failure to develop relatedness; absence of speech or echolalia; stereotyped phrases; language comprehension absent or poor; insistence on sameness and stereotypies | Hallucinations and delusions; thought disorder |
| Adaptive functioning | Usually always impaired | Deterioration in functioning |
| Level of intelligence | In majority of cases subnormal, frequently severely impaired (70 percent ≤ 70) | Usually within normal range, mostly dull normal (15 percent ≤ 70) |
| Pattern of I.Q. | Marked unevenness | More even |
| Grand mal seizures | 4–32 percent | Absent or lower incidence |

Table by Magda Campbell, M.D., and Wayne Green, M.D.

**Table 38-4**
**Autistic Disorder versus Mixed Receptive/Expressive Language Disorder**

| Criteria | Autistic Disorder | Mixed Receptive/Expressive Language Disorder |
|---|---|---|
| Incidence | 2–5 in 10,000 | 5 in 10,000 |
| Sex ratio (M:F) | 3–4:1 | Equal or almost equal sex ratio |
| Family history of speech delay or language problems | Present in about 25 percent of cases | Present in about 25 percent of cases |
| Associated deafness | Very infrequent | Not infrequent |
| Nonverbal communication (gestures, etc.) | Absent or rudimentary | Present |
| Language abnormalities (e.g., echolalia, stereotyped phrases out of context) | More common | Less common |
| Articulatory problems | Less frequent | More frequent |
| Level of Intelligence | Often severely impaired | Though may be impaired, less frequently severe |
| Patterns of I.Q. tests | Uneven, lower on verbal scores than dysphasic patients, lower on comprehension subtest than dysphasic patients | More even, though verbal I.Q. lower than performance I.Q. |
| Autistic behaviors, impaired social life, stereotypies and ritualistic activities | More common and more severe | Absent or, if present, less severe |
| Imaginative play | Absent or rudimentary | Usually present |

Table adapted from M Campbell, W H Green: Pervasive developmental disorders of childhood. In *Comprehensive Textbook of Psychiatry*, ed 4, H I Kaplan, B J Sadock, editors, p 1681. Williams & Wilkins, Baltimore, 1985.

normal sounds and respond to soft or low sounds. Most important, audiogram or auditory evoked potentials indicate significant hearing loss in deaf children. Unlike autistic children, deaf children usually relate to their parents, seek their affection, and, as infants, enjoy being held.

**Psychosocial deprivation.** Severe disturbances in the physical and emotional environment (such as maternal deprivation, psychosocial dwarfism, hospitalism, and failure to thrive) can cause children to appear apathetic, withdrawn, and alienated. Language and motor skills can be delayed. Children with those signs almost always rapidly improve when placed in a favorable and enriched psychosocial environment, which is not the case with autistic children.

## Course and Prognosis

Autistic disorder has a long course and a guarded prognosis. Some autistic children suffer a loss of all or some of their preexisting speech. That occurs most often between 12 and 24 months of age. As a general rule, the autistic children with I.Q.s above 70 and those who use communicative language by ages 5 to 7 have the best prognoses. Adult outcome studies indicate that about two thirds of autistic adults remain severely handicapped and live in complete dependence or semidependence, either with their relatives or in long-term institutions. Only 1 or 2 percent acquire a normal and independent status with gainful employment, and 5 to 20 percent achieve a borderline normal status. The prognosis is improved if the environment or the home is supportive and capable of meeting the extensive needs of such a child.

Although a decrease of symptoms is noted in many cases, severe self-mutilation or aggressiveness and regression may develop in others. About 4 to 32 percent have grand mal seizures in late childhood or adolescence, and the seizures adversely affect the prognosis.

## Treatment

The goals of treatment are to decrease the behavioral symptoms and to aid in the development of delayed, rudimentary, or nonexistent functions, such as language and self-care skills. In addition, the parents, often distraught, need support and counseling.

Insight-oriented individual psychotherapy has proved to be ineffective. Educational and behavioral methods are currently considered the treatments of choice.

Structured classroom training in combination with behavioral methods is the most effective treatment method for many autistic children and is superior to other types of behavioral approaches. Well-controlled studies indicate that gains in the areas of language and cognition and decreases in maladaptive behaviors are achieved by consistent behavioral programs. Careful training of parents in the concepts and the skills of behavior modification and the resolution of the parents' concerns may yield considerable gains in the child's language, cognitive, and social areas of behavior. However, the training programs are rigorous and require a great deal of the parents' time. The autistic child requires as much structure as possible, and a daily program for as many hours as feasible is desirable.

Although no drug has been found to be specific for autistic disorder, psychopharmacotherapy is a valuable adjunct in comprehensive treatment programs. The administration of haloperidol (Haldol) both reduces behavioral symptoms and accelerates learning. The drug decreases hyperactivity, stereotypies, withdrawal, fidgetiness, abnormal object relations, irritability, and labile affect. Supportive evidence indicates that, when used judiciously, haloperidol remains an effective long-term drug. Although

tardive and withdrawal dyskinesias can occur with haloperidol treatment in autistic children, evidence indicates that those dyskinesias can resolve when haloperidol is discontinued. Fenfluramine (Pondimin), which reduces blood serotonin levels, is effective in a few autistic children. Improvement does not seem to be associated with a reduction in blood serotonin level. Naltrexone (Trexan), an opiate antagonist, is currently being investigated in the hope that blocking endogenous opioids will reduce autistic symptoms. Lithium (Eskalith) can be tried for aggressive or self-injurious behaviors when other medications fail.

## RETT'S DISORDER

In 1965 Andreas Rett, an Austrian physician, identified a syndrome in 22 girls who appeared to have had normal development for a period of at least six months, followed by a devastating developmental deterioration. Although few surveys have been done, the ones available indicate a prevalence of 6 to 7 cases of Rett's disorder per 100,000 girls.

## Etiology

The cause of Rett's disorder is unknown, although the progressive deteriorating course after an initial normal period is compatible with a metabolic disorder. In some patients with Rett's disorder, hyperammonemia has been found, leading to the postulation that an enzyme that metabolizes ammonia is deficient. However, hyperammonemia has not been found in the majority of Rett's disorder patients. It is likely that Rett's disorder has a genetic basis, since it has been seen only in girls, and case reports so far indicate complete concordance in monozygotic twins.

## Diagnosis and Clinical Features

During the first five months after birth, the infant has age-appropriate motor skills, a normal head circumference, and normal growth. Social interactions show the expected reciprocal quality. At 6 months to 2 years of age, the child has a progressive encephalopathy, with a number of characteristic features. The signs often include the loss of purposeful hand movements, which are replaced by stereotypic motions, such as handwringing, the loss of previously acquired speech, psychomotor retardation, and ataxia. Other stereotypical movements of the hands may occur, such as licking or biting the fingers and tapping or slapping movements. The head-circumference growth decelerates, resulting in microcephaly. All language skills are lost, and both receptive and expressive communicative and social skills seem to plateau at developmental levels between 6 months and 1 year. Poor muscle coordination and an apraxic gait develop; the gait has an unsteady and stiff quality. All the above clinical features are diagnostic criteria for the disorder (Table 38–5).

Associated features include seizures in up to 75 percent of affected children and disorganized EEGs with some epileptiform discharges in almost all young children with Rett's disorder, even in the absence of clinical seizures.

**Table 38–5**
**Diagnostic Criteria for Rett's Disorder**

A. All of the following:
  (1) apparently normal prenatal and perinatal development
  (2) apparently normal psychomotor development through the first five months after birth
  (3) normal head circumference at birth

B. Onset of all of the following after the period of normal development:
  (1) deceleration of head growth between ages 5 and 48 months
  (2) loss of previously acquired purposeful hand skills between ages 5 and 30 months with the subsequent development of stereotyped hand movements (e.g., handwringing or handwashing)
  (3) loss of social engagement early in the course (although often social interaction develops later)
  (4) appearance of poorly coordinated gait or trunk movements
  (5) severely impaired expressive and receptive language development with severe psychomotor retardation

Table from DSM-IV, *Diagnostic and Statistical Manual of Mental Disorders*, ed 4. Copyright American Psychiatric Association, Washington, 1994. Used with permission.

An additional associated feature is irregular respiration, with episodes of hyperventilation, apnea, and breath holding. The disorganized breathing occurs in most patients while they are awake; during sleep the breathing usually normalizes. Many patients with Rett's disorder also have scoliosis. As the disorder progresses, muscle tone seems to increase from an initial hypotonic condition to spasticity to rigidity. Although children with Rett's disorder may live for well over a decade from the onset of the disorder, after 10 years of the disorder, many patients are wheelchair-bound, with muscle wasting, rigidity, and virtually no language ability. Long-term receptive and expressive communication and socialization abilities remain at a developmental level of less than 1 year.

## Differential Diagnosis

Some children with Rett's disorder receive initial diagnoses of autistic disorder because of the marked disability in social interactions in both disorders. However, the two disorders have some predictable differences. In Rett's disorder, the child shows a deterioration of developmental milestones, head circumference, and overall growth; in autistic disorder, aberrant development in the majority of cases is present from early on. In Rett's disorder, specific and characteristic hand motions are always present; in autistic disorder, a variety of hand mannerisms may or may not occur. Poor coordination, ataxia, and apraxia are predictably part of Rett's disorder; many persons with autistic disorder have unremarkable gross motor function. In Rett's disorder, verbal abilities are usually lost completely; in autistic disorder, the patient uses characteristic aberrant language. Respiratory irregularity is characteristic of Rett's disorder, and seizures often appear early on; in autistic disorder, no respiratory disorganization is seen, and seizures do not develop in the majority of patients; when seizures do develop, they are more likely in adolescence than in childhood.

## Course and Prognosis

Rett's disorder is progressive. The prognosis is not fully known, but those patients who live into adulthood remain at a cognitive and social level equivalent to that in the first year of life.

## Treatment

Treatment is aimed at symptomatic intervention. Physiotherapy has been beneficial for the muscular dysfunction, and anticonvulsant treatment is usually necessary to control the seizures. Behavior therapy is useful to control self-injurious behaviors, as it is in the treatment of autistic disorder, and may help regulate the breathing disorganization.

## CHILDHOOD DISINTEGRATIVE DISORDER

Childhood disintegrative disorder, also known as Heller's syndrome and disintegrative psychosis, was described in 1908 as a deterioration over several months of intellectual, social, and language function occurring in 3- and 4-year-olds with previously normal functions. After the deterioration the children closely resembled children with autistic disorder.

### Epidemiology

Epidemiological data have been complicated by the variable diagnostic criteria used, but childhood disintegrative disorder is estimated to be at least one tenth as common as autistic disorder, and the prevalence has been estimated to be about one case in 100,000 boys. The ratio of boys to girls seems to be between 4 and 8 boys to 1 girl.

### Etiology

The cause is unknown, but the disorder has been associated with other neurological conditions, including seizure disorders, tuberous sclerosis, and various metabolic disorders.

### Diagnosis and Clinical Features

The diagnosis is made on the basis of features that fit a characteristic age of onset, clinical picture, and course. Cases reported have ranged in onset from ages 1 to 9 years, but in the vast majority the onset is between 3 and 4 years; according to DSM-IV, the minimum age of onset is 2 years (Table 38–6). The onset may be insidious over several months, or it may be relatively abrupt, with diminishing abilities occurring in days or weeks. In some cases, the child displayed restlessness, increased activity level, and anxiety before the loss of function.

The core features of the disorder include a loss of communication skills, marked regression of reciprocal interactions, and the onset of stereotyped movements and compulsive behavior. Affective symptoms are common, particularly anxiety, as is the regression of self-help skills,

**Table 38–6**
**Diagnostic Criteria for Childhood Disintegrative Disorder**

A. Apparently normal development for at least the first two years after birth as manifested by the presence of age-appropriate verbal and nonverbal communication, social relationships, play, and adaptive behavior.

B. Clinically significant loss of previously acquired skills (before age 10 years) in at least two of the following areas:
  (1) expressive or receptive language
  (2) social skills or adaptive behavior
  (3) bowel or bladder control
  (4) play
  (5) motor skills

C. Abnormalities of functioning in at least two of the following areas:
  (1) qualitative impairment in social interaction (e.g., impairment in nonverbal behaviors, failure to develop peer relationships, lack of social or emotional reciprocity)
  (2) qualitative impairments in communication (e.g., delay or lack of spoken language, inability to initiate or sustain a conversation, stereotyped and repetitive use of language, lack of varied make-believe play)
  (3) restricted, repetitive, and stereotyped patterns of behavior, interests, and activities, including motor stereotypies and mannerisms

D. The disturbance is not better accounted for by another specific pervasive developmental disorder or by schizophrenia.

Table from DSM-IV, *Diagnostic and Statistical Manual of Mental Disorders*, ed 4. Copyright American Psychiatric Association, Washington, 1994. Used with permission.

such as bowel and bladder control. To receive the diagnosis, the child must exhibit a loss of skills in two of the following areas: language, social or adaptive behavior, bowel or bladder control, play, and motor skills. Abnormalities must be present in at least two of the following categories: reciprocal social interaction, communication skills, and stereotyped or restricted behavior. The main neurological associated feature is seizure disorder.

### Differential Diagnosis

The differential diagnosis of childhood disintegrative disorder includes autistic disorder and Rett's disorder. In many cases the clinical features overlap with autistic disorder, but childhood disintegrative disorder is distinguished from autistic disorder by the loss of previously acquired development. Before the onset of childhood disintegrative disorder (occurring at 2 years or older), language has usually progressed to sentence formation. That skill is strikingly different from the premorbid history of even high-functioning autistic disorder patients, in whom language generally does not exceed single words or phrases before the diagnosis of the disorder. Once the disorder occurs, however, those with childhood disintegrative disorder are more likely to have no language abilities than are high-functioning autistic disorder patients.

In Rett's disorder, the deterioration occurs much earlier than in childhood disintegrative disorder, and the char-

acteristic hand stereotypies of Rett's disorder do not occur in childhood disintegrative disorder.

### Course and Prognosis

The course of childhood disintegrative disorder is variable, with a plateau reached in most cases, a progressive deteriorating course in rare cases, and some improvement in occasional cases to the point of regaining the ability to speak in sentences. Most patients are left with at least moderate mental retardation.

### Treatment

Because of the clinical similarity to autistic disorder, the treatment of childhood disintegrative disorder is the same as that for autistic disorder.

## ASPERGER'S DISORDER

In 1944 Hans Asperger, an Austrian physician, described a syndrome that he named "autistic psychopathy." His original description was of persons with normal intelligence who exhibit a qualitative impairment in reciprocal social interaction and behavioral oddities without delays in language development. Since that time, persons with mental retardation but without language delay have received diagnoses of Asperger's disorder, and persons with language delay but without mental retardation have been given the diagnosis.

In the 10th revision of the International Classification of Diseases (ICD-10), Asperger's disorder is called Asperger's sydnrome and is characterized by qualitative social impairment, a lack of significant language and cognitive delays, and the presence of restricted interests and behavior.

Assessing the prevalence of the disorder is difficult because of the lack of stability in the diagnostic criteria.

### Etiology

The cause of Asperger's disorder is unknown, but family studies suggest a possible relation to autistic disorder. The similarity of Asperger's disorder to autistic disorder leads to genetic, metabolic, infectious, and perinatal hypotheses.

### Diagnosis and Clinical Features

The clinical features include at least two of the following indications of qualitative social impairment: markedly abnormal nonverbal communicative gestures, the failure to develop peer relationships, the lack of social or emotional reciprocity, and an impaired ability to express pleasure in other people's happiness. Restricted interests and patterns of behavior are always present. According to DSM-IV, the patient shows no language delay, clinically significant cognitive delay, or adaptive impairment (Table 38–7).

**Table 38–7**
**Diagnostic Criteria for Asperger's Disorder**

A. Qualitative impairment in social interaction, as manifested by at least two of the following:
   (1) marked impairment in the use of multiple nonverbal behaviors such as eye-to-eye gaze, facial expression, body postures, and gestures to regulate social interaction
   (2) failure to develop peer relationships appropriate to developmental level
   (3) a lack of spontaneous seeking to share enjoyment, interests, or achievements with other people (e.g., by a lack of showing, bringing, or pointing out objects of interest to other people)
   (4) lack of social or emotional reciprocity

B. Restricted, repetitive, and stereotyped patterns of behavior, interests, and activities, as manifested by at least one of the following:
   (1) encompassing preoccupation with one or more stereotyped and restricted patterns of interest that is abnormal either in intensity or focus
   (2) apparently inflexible adherence to specific, nonfunctional routines or rituals
   (3) stereotyped and repetitive motor mannerisms (e.g., hand or finger flapping or twisting, or complex whole-body movements)
   (4) persistent preoccupation with parts of objects

C. The disturbance causes clinically significant impairment in social, occupational, or other important areas of functioning.

D. There is no clinically significant general delay in language (e.g., single words used by age 2 years, communicative phrases used by age 3 years).

E. There is no clinically significant delay in cognitive development or in the development of age-appropriate self-help skills, adaptive behavior (other than in social interaction), and curiosity about the environment in childhood.

F. Criteria are not met for another specific pervasive developmental disorder or schizophrenia.

Table from DSM-IV, *Diagnostic and Statistical Manual of Mental Disorders*, ed 4. Copyright American Psychiatric Association, Washington, 1994. Used with permission.

## Differential Diagnosis

The differential diagnosis includes autistic disorder, pervasive developmental disorder not otherwise specified, and, in patients approaching adulthood, schizoid personality disorder. According to DSM-IV, the most obvious distinctions between Asperger's disorder and autistic disorder are the criteria regarding language delay and dysfunction. The lack of language delay is a requirement for Asperger's disorder, but language impairment is a core feature in autistic disorder.

## Course and Prognosis

Although little is known about the cohort described by the DSM-IV diagnostic criteria, past case reports have shown variable courses and prognoses for patients who have received diagnoses of Asperger's disorder. The factors associated with a good prognosis are a normal I.Q. and high-level social skills.

## Treatment

Treatment depends on the patient's level of adaptive function. For those patients with severe social impairment, some of the same techniques used for autistic disorder are likely to be beneficial in the treatment of Asperger's disorder.

# PERVASIVE DEVELOPMENTAL DISORDER NOT OTHERWISE SPECIFIED

Pervasive developmental disorder not otherwise specified should be diagnosed when a child manifests a qualitative impairment in the development of reciprocal social interaction and verbal and nonverbal communication skills but does not meet the criteria for other pervasive developmental disorders, schizophrenia, or schizotypal or avoidant personality disorder (Table 38–8).

Some children who receive the diagnosis exhibit a markedly restricted repertoire of activities and interests. The condition usually shows a better outcome than does autistic disorder.

## Treatment

The treatment approach is basically the same as in autistic disorder. Mainstreaming in school may be possible. Compared with autistic children, those with pervasive developmental disorder not otherwise specified generally have better language skills and more self-awareness, so they are better candidates for psychotherapy.

**Table 38–8**
**Diagnostic Criteria for Pervasive Developmental Disorder Not Otherwise Specified**

This category should be used when there is a severe and pervasive impairment in the development of reciprocal social interaction or verbal and nonverbal communication skills, or when stereotyped behavior, interests, and activities are present, but the criteria are not met for a specific pervasive developmental disorder, schizophrenia, schizotypal personality disorder, or avoidant personality disorder. For example, this category includes "atypical autism"—presentations that do not meet the criteria for autistic disorder because of late age at onset, atypical symptomatology, or subthreshold symptomatology, or all of these.

Table from DSM-IV, *Diagnostic and Statistical Manual of Mental Disorders*, ed 4. Copyright American Psychiatric Association, Washington, 1994. Used with permission.

### References

Anderson L T, Campbell M, Adams P, Small A M, Perry R, Shell J: The effects of haloperidol on discrimination learning, and behavioral symptoms in autistic children. J Autism Dev Disord *19*: 227, 1989.

Balottin V, Bejor M, Cecchini A, Martelli A, Polazzi S, Lanzi G: Infantile autism and CT brain-scan findings: Specific versus nonspecific abnormalities. J Autism Dev Disord *19*: 109, 1989.

Burd L, Fisher W, Kerbeshian J: A prevalence study of pervasive developmental disorders in North America. J Am Acad Child Psychiatry *26*: 700, 1987.

Cook E H: Autism: Review of neurochemical investigation. Synapse *6*: 292, 1990.

Folstein S E, Rutter M L: Autism: Familial aggregation and genetic implications. J Autism Dev Disord *18*: 3, 1988.

Ghaziuddin M, Tsai L Y, Ghaziuddin N: Brief report: A comparison of the diagnostic criteria for Asperger's syndrome. J Autism Dev Disord *22*: 643, 1992.

Kazdin A E: Replication and extension of behavioral treatment of autistic disorder. Am J Ment Retard *97*: 377, 1993.

Lovaas O I: Behavioral treatment and normal educational and intellectual functioning in young autistic children. J Consult Clin Psychol *55*: 3, 1987.

McEachin J J, Smith T, Lovaas O I: Long-term outcome for children with autism who received early intensive behavioral treatment. Am J Ment Retard *97*: 359, 1993.

Mesibov E B, Schopler E, editors: *Neurobiological Issues in Autism.* Plenum, New York, 1987.

Mundy P: Normal versus high-functioning status in children with autism. Am J Ment Retard *97*: 381, 1993.

Payton J B, Steele M W, Wenger S L, Minshew N J: The fragile X marker and autism in perspective. J Am Acad Child Adolesc Psychiatry *28*: 417, 1989.

Perry A: Rett's syndrome: A comprehensive review of the literature. Am J Ment Retard *96*: 275, 1991.

Petty L, Ornitz E M, Michelman J D, Zimmerman E G: Autistic children who become schizophrenic. Arch Gen Psychiatry *41*: 129, 1984.

Pisen J, Berthier M L, Sharkstein S E, Nehme E, Pearlson G, Folstein S: Magnetic resonance imaging: Evidence for a defect of cerebral cortical development in autism. Am J Psychiatry *147*: 734, 1990.

Reiss A L, Freund L: Fragile X syndrome, DSM-III-R, and autism. J Am Acad Child Adolesc Psychiatry *29*: 885, 1990.

Rogers S J, Di Lalla D L: Age of symptom onset in young children with pervasive developmental disorders. J Am Acad Child Adolesc Psychiatry *29*: 863, 1990.

Rutter M: Infantile autism and other pervasive developmental disorders. In *Child and Adolescent Psychiatry: Modern Approaches*, ed 2. M Rutter, L Hersov, editors, p 545. Blackwell, Oxford, England, 1985.

Tsai L Y: Is Rett's syndrome a subtype of pervasive developmental disorders? J Autism Dev Disord *22*: 551, 1992.

Volkmar F R: Childhood disintegrative disorder: Issues for DSM-IV. J Autism Dev Disord *22*: 625, 1992.

Warren R P, Cole P, Odell D, Pingree C B, Warren W L, White E, Yonk J, Singh V K: Detection of maternal antibodies in infantile autism. J Am Acad Child Adolesc Psychiatry *29*: 873, 1990.

Young J G, Newcorn J H, Leven L I: Pervasive developmental disorders. In *Comprehensive Textbook of Psychiatry*, ed 5, H I Kaplan, B J Sadock, editors, p 1772. Williams & Wilkins, Baltimore, 1989.

# Attention-Deficit Disorders

## ATTENTION-DEFICIT/HYPERACTIVITY DISORDER

Attention-deficit/hyperactivity disorder (ADHD) is characterized by a developmentally inappropriate poor attention span or age-inappropriate features of hyperactivity and impulsivity or both. To meet the diagnostic criteria the disorder must be present for at least six months, cause impairment in academic or social functioning, and occur before the age of 7 years. According to the fourth edition of *Diagnostic and Statistical Manual of Mental Disorders* (DSM-IV), the diagnosis is made by confirming numerous symptoms in the inattention domain or the hyperactivity-impulsivity domain or both. Thus, a child may qualify for the disorder with symptoms of inattention only or with symptoms of hyperactivity and impulsivity but not inattention. Some children exhibit multiple symptoms along both dimensions. Accordingly, DSM-IV lists three subtypes of attention-deficit/hyperactivity disorder: predominantly inattentive type, predominantly hyperactive-impulsive type, and combined type. An additional criterion in DSM-IV that was not present in the revised third edition of DSM (DSM-III-R) is the presence of symptoms in two or more situations, such as at school, home, and work.

Attention-deficit/hyperactivity disorder has been identified in the literature for many years under a variety of terms. In the early 1900s impulsive, disinhibited, and hyperactive children—many of whom had neurological damage caused by encephalitis—were grouped under the label "hyperactive syndrome." In the 1960s a heterogeneous group of children with poor coordination, learning disabilities, and emotional lability but without specific neurological damage were described as having minimal brain damage. Since that time other hypotheses have been put forth to explain the origin of the disorder, such as a genetically based condition reflecting an abnormal level of arousal and poor ability to modulate emotions. That theory was initially supported by the observation that stimulant medications help produce sustained attention and improve the child's ability to focus on a given task. Currently, no single factor is believed to cause the disorder, although many environmental variables may contribute to it and many predictable clinical features are associated with it.

### Epidemiology

Reports on the incidence of ADHD in the United States have varied from 2 to 20 percent of grade-school children. A conservative figure is about 3 to 5 percent of prepubertal elementary school children. In Great Britain the incidence is reported to be lower than in the United States, less than 1 percent. Boys have a greater incidence than do girls, with the ratio being from 3 to 1 to as much as 5 to 1. The disorder is most common in firstborn boys. The parents of children with ADHD show an increased incidence of hyperkinesis, sociopathy, alcohol use disorders, and conversion disorder. Although the onset is usually by the age of 3, the diagnosis is generally not made until the child is in elementary school and the formal learning situation requires structured behavior patterns, including developmentally appropriate attention span and concentration.

### Etiology

The causes of attention-deficit/hyperactivity disorders are not known. The majority of children with ADHD do not show evidence of gross structural damage in the central nervous system (CNS). Conversely, most children with known neurological disorders caused by brain injuries do not display attention deficits and hyperactivity. Despite the lack of a specific neurophysiological or neurochemical basis for the disorder, it is predictably associated with a variety of other disorders that affect brain function, such as learning disorders. The suggested contributing factors for ADHD include prenatal toxic exposures, prematurity, and prenatal mechanical insult to the fetal nervous system.

Food additives, colorings, preservatives, and sugar have also been suggested as possible causes of hyperactive behavior. No scientific evidence indicates that those factors cause attention-deficit/hyperactivity disorder.

**Genetic factors.** Evidence for a genetic basis for attention-deficit/hyperactivity disorder includes the greater concordance in monozygotic twins than in dizygotic twins. Also, siblings of hyperactive children have about twice the risk of having the disorder as does the general population. One sibling may have predominantly hyperactivity symptoms, and the others may have predominantly inattention.

Biological parents of children with the disorder have a higher risk for attention-deficit/hyperactivity disorder than do adoptive parents. When attention-deficit/hyperactivity disorder coexists with conduct disorder in the child, alcohol use disorders and antisocial personality disorder are more common in the parents than in the general population.

**Brain damage.** It has long been speculated that some children affected by ADHD received minimal and subtle brain damage to the CNS during their fetal and perinatal periods. Or the brain damage may have been caused by adverse circulatory, toxic, metabolic, mechanical, and other effects and by stress and physical insult to the brain during early infancy caused by infection, inflammation, and trauma. Minimal, subtle, and subclinical brain damage may be responsible for the genesis of learning disorders and ADHD. Nonfocal (soft) neurological signs are frequent.

Computed tomographic (CT) head scans in children with attention-deficit/hyperactivity disorder show no consistent findings. Studies using positron emission tomography (PET) have found decreased cerebral blood flow and metabolic rates in the frontal lobe areas of children with attention-deficit/hyperactivity disorder compared with controls. One theory is that the frontal lobes in children with attention-deficit/hyperactivity disorder are not adequately performing their inhibitory mechanism on lower structures, leading to disinhibition.

**Neurochemical factors.** Many neurotransmitters have been associated with attention-deficit and hyperactivity symptoms. In part, the findings have come out of the use of many medications that exert some positive effect on the disorder. The most widely studied drugs in the treatment of attention-deficit/hyperactivity disorder, the stimulants, affect both dopamine and norepinephrine, leading to neurotransmitter hypotheses that include possible dysfunction in both the adrenergic and the dopaminergic systems. Stimulants increase catecholamines by promoting their release and by blocking their uptake. Stimulants and some tricyclic drugs—for example, desipramine (Norpramine)—reduce urinary 3-methoxy-4-hydroxyphenylglycol (MHPG), which is a metabolite of norepinephrine. Clonidine (Catapres), a norepinephrine agonist, has been helpful in treating hyperactivity. Other drugs that have reduced hyperactivity include tricyclic drugs and monoamine oxidase inhibitors (MAOIs). Overall, no clear-cut evidence implicates a single neurotransmitter in the development of attention-deficit/hyperactivity disorder, but many neurotransmitters may be involved in the process.

**Neurophysiological factors.** The human brain normally undergoes major growth spurts at several ages: 3 to 10 months, 2 to 4 years, 6 to 8 years, 10 to 12 years, and 14 to 16 years. Some children have a maturational delay in the sequence and manifest symptoms of ADHD that appear to be temporary. A physiological correlate is the presence of a variety of nonspecific abnormal electroencephalogram (EEG) patterns that are disorganized and characteristic of young children. In some cases the EEG findings normalize over time.

**Psychosocial factors.** Children in institutions are frequently overactive and have poor attention spans. Those signs result from prolonged emotional deprivation, and they disappear when deprivational factors are removed, such as through adoption or placement in a foster home. Stressful psychic events, a disruption of the family equilibrium, and other anxiety-inducing factors contribute to the initiation or the perpetuation of ADHD. Predisposing factors may include the child's temperament, genetic-familial factors, and the demands of society to adhere to a routinized way of behaving and performing. Socioeconomic status does not seem to be a predisposing factor.

## Diagnosis

The principal sign of hyperactivity should alert clinicians to the possibility of ADHD. A detailed prenatal history of the child's early developmental patterns and direct observation usually reveal excessive motor activity. Hyperactivity may be seen in some situations (for example, school) but not in others (for example, one-to-one interviews and watching television), and it may be less obvious in structured situations than in unstructured situations. However, the hyperactivity should not be an isolated, brief, and transient behavioral manifestation under stress but should have been present over a long time. According to DSM-IV, symptoms must be present in at least two settings (for example, school, home) to meet the diagnostic criteria for attention-deficit/hyperactivity disorder (Table 39–1).

**Table 39–1**
**Diagnostic Criteria for Attention-Deficit/Hyperactivity Disorder**

A. Either (1) or (2):

  (1) Inattention: six (or more) of the following symptoms of inattention have persisted for at least six months to a degree that is maladaptive and inconsistent with developmental level:

    (a) often fails to give close attention to details or makes careless mistakes in schoolwork, work, or other activities

    (b) often has difficulty sustaining attention in tasks or play activities

    (c) often does not seem to listen when spoken to directly

    (d) often does not follow through on instructions and fails to finish schoolwork, chores, or duties in the workplace (not due to oppositional behavior or failure to understand instructions)

    (e) often has difficulties organizing tasks and activities

    (f) often avoids, dislikes, or is reluctant to engage in tasks that require sustained mental effort (such as schoolwork or homework)

    (g) often loses things necessary for tasks or activities (e.g., school assignments, pencils, books, or tools)

    (h) is often easily distracted by extraneous stimuli

    (i) is often forgetful in daily activities

  (2) Hyperactivity-impulsivity: Six (or more) of the following symptoms of hyperactivity-impulsivity have persisted for at least six months to a degree that is maladaptive and inconsistent with developmental level:

**Hyperactivity**

    (a) often fidgets with hands or feet or squirms in seat

    (b) often leaves seat in classroom or in other situations in which remaining seated is expected

    (c) often runs about or climbs excessively in situations in which it is inappropriate (in adolescents or adults, may be limited to subjective feelings of restlessness)

    (d) often has difficulty playing or engaging in leisure activities quietly

    (e) is often "on the go" or often acts as if "driven by a motor"

    (f) often talks excessively

**Impulsivity**

    (g) often blurts out answers to questions before the questions have been completed

    (h) often has difficulty awaiting turn

**Table 39–1**
*Continued*

    (i)  often interrupts or intrudes on others (e.g., butts into conversations or games)

B. Some hyperactive-impulsive or inattentive symptoms that caused impairment were present before age 7 years.

C. Some impairment from the symptoms is present in two or more settings (e.g., at school [or work] and at home).

D. There must be clear evidence of clinically significant impairment in social, academic, or occupational functioning.

E. The symptoms do not occur exclusively during the course of a pervasive developmental disorder, schizophrenia, or other psychotic disorder, and are not better accounted for by another mental disorder (e.g., mood disorder, anxiety disorder, dissociative disorder, or a personality disorder).

*Code* based on type:

**Attention-deficit/hyperactivity disorder, combined type:** if both criteria A1 and A2 are met for the past 6 months

**Attention-deficit/hyperactivity disorder, predominantly inattentive type:** if criterion A1 is met but criterion A2 is not met for the past 6 months

**Attention-deficit/hyperactivity disorder, predominantly hyperactive-impulsive type:** if criterion A2 is met but criterion A1 is not met for the past 6 months

**Coding note:** For individuals (especially adolescents and adults) who currently have symptoms that no longer meet full criteria, "in partial remission" should be specified.

Table from DSM-IV, *Diagnostic and Statistical Manual of Mental Disorders*, ed 4. Copyright American Psychiatric Association, Washington, 1994. Used with permission.

---

Other distinguishing features of ADHD are short attention span and easy distractibility. In school, children with ADHD cannot follow instructions and often demand extra attention from their teachers. At home, they often do not follow through on their parents' requests. They act impulsively, show emotional lability, and are explosive and irritable. The DSM-IV diagnostic criteria for attention-deficit/hyperactivity disorder are given in Table 39–1.

Children who have hyperactivity as a predominant feature are more likely to be referred for treatment than are children with primarily symptoms of attention deficit. Children with the predominantly hyperactive-impulsive type of ADHD are more likely to have a stable diagnosis over time and are more likely to have concurrent conduct disorder than are children with the predominantly inattentive type without hyperactivity.

Disorders involving reading, arithmetic, language, and coordination may be found in association with ADHD. The child's history may give clues to prenatal (including genetic), natal, and postnatal factors that may have affected the CNS structure or function. Rates of development, deviations in development, and parental reactions to significant or stressful behavioral transitions should be ascertained, as they may help the clinician determine the degree to which parents have contributed to or reacted to the child's inefficiencies and dysfunctions.

School history and teachers' reports are important in evaluating whether children's difficulties in learning and school behavior are primarily due to their attitudinal or maturational problems or to their poor self-image because of felt inadequacies. Those reports may also reveal how the children have handled those problems. How they have related to siblings, to peers, to adults, and to free and structured activities gives valuable diagnostic clues to the presence of ADHD and helps identify the complications of the disorder.

The mental status examination may show a secondarily depressed mood but no thought disturbance, impaired reality testing, or inappropriate affect. The child may show great distractibility, perseveration, and a concrete and literal mode of thinking. Indications of visual-perceptual, auditory-perceptual, language, or cognition problems may be present. Occasionally, evidence appears of a basic, pervasive, organically based anxiety, often referred to as body anxiety.

A neurological examination may reveal visual-motor-perceptual or auditory-discriminatory immaturity or impairments without overt signs of disorders of visual or auditory acuity. Children may show problems with motor coordination and difficulties in copying age-appropriate figures, rapid alternating movements, right-left discrimination, ambidexterity, reflex asymmetries, and a variety of subtle nonfocal neurological signs (soft signs). The clinician should obtain an EEG to recognize the child with frequent bilaterally synchronous discharges resulting in short absence spells. Such a child may react in school with hyperactivity out of sheer frustration. The child with an unrecognized temporal lobe seizure focus can present a secondary behavior disorder. In those instances, several features of ADHD are often present. Identification of the focus requires an EEG obtained during drowsiness and during sleep.

## Clinical Features

ADHD may have its onset in infancy. Infants with ADHD are unduly sensitive to stimuli and are easily upset by noise, light, temperature, and other environmental changes. At times, the reverse occurs, and the children are placid and limp, sleep much of the time, and appear to develop slowly in the first months of life. It is more common, though, for infants with ADHD to be active in the crib, sleep little, and cry a great deal. ADHD children are far less likely than are normal children to reduce their locomotor activity when their environment is structured by social limits. In school, ADHD children may rapidly attack a test but answer only the first two questions. They may be unable to wait to be called on in school and may respond for everyone else. At home, they cannot be put off for even a minute.

Children with ADHD are often explosively irritable. The irritability may be set off by relatively minor stimuli, which may puzzle and dismay the children. They are frequently emotionally labile, easily set off to laughter or to tears, and their mood and performance are apt to be variable and unpredictable. Impulsiveness and an inability to delay gratification are characteristic. They are often accident-prone.

Concomitant emotional difficulties are frequent. The fact that other children grow out of that kind of behavior but ADHD children do not grow out of it at the same time and rate may lead to adults' dissatisfaction and pressure. The resulting negative self-concept and reactive hostility are worsened by the children's recognition that they have problems.

The characteristics of children with ADHD most often cited are, in order of frequency, (1) hyperactivity, (2) perceptual motor impairment, (3) emotional lability, (4) general coordination deficit, (5) disorders of attention (short attention span, distractibility, perseveration, failure to finish things, inattention, poor concentration), (6) impulsivity (action before thought, abrupt shifts in activity, lack of organization, jumping up in class), (7) disorders of memory and thinking, (8) specific learning disabilities, (9) disorders of speech and hearing, and (10) equivocal neurological signs and EEG irregularities.

About 75 percent of children with ADHD fairly consistently show behavioral symptoms of aggression and defiance. But, whereas defiance and aggression are generally associated with adverse intrafamily relationships, hyperactivity is more closely related to impaired performance on cognitive tests requiring concentration. Some studies claim that some relatives of hyperactive children show features of antisocial personality disorder.

School difficulties, both learning and behavorial, are common, sometimes coming from concomitant communication disorders or learning disorders or from the children's distractibility and fluctuating attention, which hamper their acquisition, retention, and display of knowledge. Those difficulties are noted especially on group tests. The adverse reactions of school personnel to the behavior characteristic of ADHD and the lowering of self-regard because of felt inadequacies may combine with the adverse comments of peers to make school a place of unhappy defeat, which may lead to acting-out antisocial behavior and self-defeating, self-punitive behaviors.

A 9-year-old boy was referred to a child psychiatrist at the request of his school because of the difficulties he created in class. He had twice been suspended for a day in the school year. His teacher complained that he was so restless that the other students were unable to concentrate. He was hardly ever in his seat but roamed around the class, talking to other children while they were working. He never seemed to know what he was going to do next and sometimes suddenly did something outrageous. His most recent suspension had been for swinging from the fluorescent light fixture over the blackboard, where he had climbed in the transition from one class to the next; since he had been unable to climb down again, the class was in an uproar.

His mother said that the boy's behavior had been difficult since he was a toddler and that, as a 3-year-old, he had been unbearably restless and demanding. He had always required little sleep and was awake before anyone else. When he was small, "he got into everything," particularly in the early morning, when he would awaken at 4:30 or 5:00 AM and go downstairs by himself. His parents would awaken to find the living room or kitchen "demolished." When he was 4, he managed to unlock the door of the apartment and wander off into a busy main street; fortunately, he was rescued from oncoming traffic by a passerby. He was rejected by a preschool program because of his difficult behavior; eventually, after a difficult year in kindergarten, he was placed in a special behavioral program for first- and second-graders. He was in a regular class for most subjects but spent a lot of time in a resource room with a special teacher.

Psychological testing had shown the boy to be of average ability, and his achievements were only slightly below the expected level. His attention span was described by the psychologist as "virtually nonexistent." He had no interest in TV and disliked games and toys that required any concentration or patience on his part. He was not popular with other children, and at home he preferred to be outdoors, playing with his dog or riding his bike. If he did play with toys, his games were messy and destructive, and his mother could not get him to keep his things in any order.

He was also disobedient and in the preceding year or so had been provocative and defiant at school and, to some extent, at home. He had stolen small sums of money from home and school, and other children had complained because he had taken small toys that they had brought to school.

The boy had been treated with a stimulant, methylphenidate (Ritalin), in a small dosage (5 to 10 mg a day); but that medication had been discontinued in the previous year, apparently because it was having no effect on his defiance and conduct problems. When he was taking the drug, he was much easier to manage at school; he was less restless and possibly more attentive than before, even though other aspects of his behavior were unsatisfactory.

*Discussion.* The boy's behavior graphically showed the characteristic inattention, impulsivity, and hyperactivity of attention-deficit/hyperactivity disorder. He had difficulty in remaining seated, fidgeted, could not follow through on instructions, could not sustain attention, often did not seem to listen to what was being said to him, shifted from one activity to another, had difficulty in playing quietly, and often engaged in physically dangerous activities without considering the consequences. Because he almost certainly had the other symptoms of attention-deficit/hyperactivity disorder (such as difficulty in waiting his turn, blurting out answers to questions, talking excessively, and interrupting others) and because his symptoms significantly interfered with his functioning at home and at school, it was noted that the disorder was severe.

**Pathology and laboratory examination.** No specific laboratory measures are pathognomonic of attention-deficit/hyperactivity disorder. Several laboratory measures often yield nonspecific abnormal results in hyperactive children, such as a disorganized, immature result on an EEG, and positron emission tomography (PET) may show decreased cerebral blood flow in the frontal regions.

Cognitive testing that is helpful in confirming the child's inattention and impulsivity includes the continuous performance task, in which the child is asked to press a button each time a particular sequence of letters or numbers is flashed on a screen. Children with poor attention make errors of omission—that is, they fail to press the button, even when the sequence has flashed. Impulsivity is manifested by errors of commission, in which they are unable to resist pushing the button, even though the desired sequence has not yet appeared on the screen.

## Differential Diagnosis

A temperamental constellation consisting of high activity level and short attention span should be first considered. Differentiating those temperamental characteristics from the cardinal symptoms of ADHD before age 3 is difficult, mainly because of the overlapping features of a normally immature nervous system and the emerging signs of visual-motor-perceptual impairments frequently seen in ADHD.

Anxiety in the child needs to be evaluated. Anxiety may accompany ADHD as a secondary feature, and anxiety by itself may be manifested by overactivity and easy distractibility.

Many children with ADHD have secondary depression in reaction to their continuing frustration over their failure to learn and their consequent low self-esteem. That condition must be distinguished from a primary depressive disorder, which is likely to be distinguished by hypoactivity and withdrawal.

Frequently, conduct disorder and ADHD coexist, and so both must be diagnosed.

Learning disorders of various kinds must also be distinguished from ADHD, since a child may be unable to read or do mathematics because of a learning disorder, rather than inattention. However, attention-deficit/hyperactivity disorder often coexists with one or more learning disorders, including reading disorder, mathematics disorder, and disorder of written expression.

## Course and Prognosis

The course of ADHD is highly variable. Symptoms may persist into adolescence or adult life, they may remit at puberty, or the hyperactivity may disappear, but the decreased attention span and impulse-control problems may persist.

The overactivity is usually the first symptom to remit and distractibility the last. Remission is not likely before the age of 12. If remission does occur, it usually occurs between the ages of 12 and 20. Remission may be accompanied by a productive adolescence and adult life, satisfying interpersonal relationships, and few significant sequelae. The majority of patients with ADHD, however, undergo partial remission and are vulnerable to antisocial and other personality disorders and mood disorders. Learning problems often continue.

In about 15 to 20 percent of cases, the symptoms of ADHD persist into adulthood. Those with the disorder may show diminished hyperactivity but remain impulsive and accident-prone. Although their educational attainments are lower than those of persons without ADHD, their early employment histories are not different from those of persons with similar educations.

Children with ADHD whose symptoms persist into adolescence are at high risk for developing conduct disorder. Approximately 50 percent of children with conduct disorder will develop antisocial personality disorder in adulthood. Children with both ADHD and conduct disorder are also at risk for developing a substance-related disorder.

Overall, the outcome of ADHD in childhood seems to be related to the amount of persistent conduct disorder and chaotic family factors. Optimal outcomes may be promoted by ameliorating the children's aggression and by improving family functions as early as possible.

## Treatment

**Pharmacotherapy.** The pharmacological agents for ADHD are the CNS stimulants, primarily dextroamphetamine (Dexedrine), methylphenidate, and pemoline (Cylert). The Food and Drug Administration (FDA) approves of dextroamphetamine in children 3 years and older and methylphenidate in those 6 years and older; those two are the most commonly used drugs.

The precise mechanism of action of the stimulants remains unknown. The idea of a paradoxical response by hyperactive children is no longer accepted. Methylphenidate has been shown to be highly effective in up to three quarters of all children with ADHD and to have relatively few side effects. Methylphenidate is a short-acting medication that is generally used to be effective during school hours, so that children with the disorder can attend to tasks and remain in the classroom. The drug's most common side effects include headaches, stomachaches, nausea, and insomnia. Some children experience a rebound effect, in which they become mildly irritable and appear to be slightly hyperactive for a brief period when the medication wears off. In children with a history of motor tics, some caution must be used, since, in some cases, methylphenidate may cause an exacerbation of the tic disorder. Another common concern about methylphenidate is whether it will cause some suppression of growth. During periods of use, methylphenidate is associated with growth suppression, but children tend to make up the growth when they are given drug holidays in the summer or on weekends. An important question regarding the use of methylphenidate is how much it normalizes school performance. A recent study found that about 75 percent of a group of hyperactive children exhibited a significant improvement in their ability to pay attention in class and on measures of academic efficiency when treated with methylphenidate. The drug has been shown to improve hyperactive children's scores on tasks of vigilance, such as the continuous performance task and paired associations.

Antidepressants—including imipramine (Tofranil), desipramine, and nortriptyline (Pamelor)—have been used to treat ADHD with some success. In children with comorbid anxiety disorders or depressive disorders and in children in whom tic disorders preclude the use of stimulants, the antidepressants may be beneficial, although, for hyperactivity itself, the stimulants are more efficacious. The antidepressants require careful monitoring of cardiac function. Several studies have reported sudden death in children with ADHD who were being treated with desipramine. Why the deaths occurred is not clear, but the deaths reinforce the need for close follow-up of any child receiving a tricyclic drug.

A recent study of children with ADHD and depressive symptoms who were taking methylphenidate and desipramine simultaneously found that the combination enhanced the children's abilities to use visual search strategies on such cognitive tasks as comparing several pictures with subtle differences—for example, the matching familiar faces task.

Clonidine has also been used in the treatment of ADHD with some degree of success. It may be especially helpful in cases in which the patients also have tic disorders.

Overall, stimulants remain the first drug of choice in the pharmacological treatment of ADHD.

EVALUATION OF THERAPEUTIC PROGRESS. Monitoring starts with the initiation of the medication. Because school performance is most markedly affected, special attention and effort should be given to establishing and maintaining a close collaborative working relation with the child's school.

In most patients, stimulants reduce overactivity, distractibility, impulsiveness, explosiveness, and irritability.

No evidence indicates that the medications directly improve any existing impairments in learning, although, when the attention deficits diminish, the children can learn more effectively than in the past. In addition, the medication can improve self-esteem when the ADHD children are no longer constantly reprimanded for their behavior.

**Psychotherapy.** Medication alone rarely satisfies the comprehensive therapeutic needs of ADHD children and is usually but one facet of a multimodality regimen. Individual psychotherapy, behavior modification, parent counseling, and the treatment of any coexisting learning disorder may be necessary.

When taking medication, ADHD children should be given the opportunity to explore the meaning of the medication to them. Doing so helps dispel misconceptions (such as, "I'm crazy") about medication use and makes it clear that the medication is only an adjuvant. The children have to understand that they need not always be perfect.

When ADHD children are helped to structure their environment, their anxiety diminishes. Therefore, their parents and teachers should set up a predictable structure of reward and punishment, using a behavior therapy model and applying it to the physical, temporal, and interpersonal environment. An almost universal requirement of therapy is to help the parents recognize that permissiveness is not helpful to their children. The parents should also be helped to recognize that, in spite of their children's deficiencies in some areas, they face the normal tasks of maturation, including the need to take responsibility for their actions. Therefore, children with ADHD do not benefit from being exempted from the requirements, expectations, and planning applicable to other children.

## ATTENTION-DEFICIT/HYPERACTIVITY DISORDER NOT OTHERWISE SPECIFIED

DSM-IV includes attention-deficit/hyperactivity disorder not otherwise specified (NOS) as a residual category for disturbances with prominent symptoms of inattention or hyperactivity that do not meet the criteria for ADHD (Table 39–2). The incidence of adult manifestations of ADHD is unknown; however, there are many more cases than were previously thought or diagnosed. This category of illness will be more frequently diagnosed and will require much greater attention and study.

In adults, residual signs of the disorder include impulsivity and attention deficit (for example, difficulty in organizing and completing work, inability to concentrate, increased distractibility, and sudden decision making without a thought of the consequences). Many patients with

**Table 39–2**
**Diagnostic Criteria for Attention-Deficit/Hyperactivity Disorder Not Otherwise Specified**

This category is for disorders with prominent symptoms of attention-inattention or hyperactivity-impulsivity that do not meet criteria for attention-deficit/hyperactivity disorder.

Table from DSM-IV, *Diagnostic and Statistical Manual of Mental Disorders*, ed 4. Copyright American Psychiatric Association, Washington, 1994. Used with permission.

the disorder suffer from a secondary depressive disorder that is associated with low self-esteem related to their impaired performance and that affects both occupational and social functioning. The treatment of the disorder involves the use of amphetamines (5 to 60 mg a day) or methylphenidate (5 to 60 mg a day). Signs of a positive response are an increased attention span, decreased impulsiveness, and improved mood. Psychopharmacological therapy may need to be continued indefinitely. Because of the abuse potential of the drugs, clinicians should monitor drug response and patient compliance.

### References

Biederman J, Baldessarini R J, Wright V, Keenan K, Faraone S: A double-blind placebo controlled study of desipramine in the treatment of ADD: III. Lack of impact of comorbidity and family history factors on clinical response. J Am Acad Child Adolesc Psychiatry 32: 199, 1993.

Biederman J, Munir K, Knee D, Armentano M, Auter S, Waternaux C, Tsuang M: High rate of affective disorders in probands with attention deficit disorder and in their relatives: A controlled family study. Am J Psychiatry 144: 330, 1987.

Cantwell D P, Baker L: Attention deficit disorder with and without hyperactivity: A review and comparison of matched controls. J Am Acad Child Adolesc Psychiatry 31: 432, 1992.

DuPaul G J, Rapport M D: Does methylphenidate normalize the classroom performance of children with attention deficit disorders? J Am Acad Child Adolesc Psychiatry 32: 190, 1993.

Fischer M, Barkley R A, Fletcher K E, Smallish L: The adolescent outcome of hyperactive children: Predictors of psychiatric, academic, social and emotional adjustment. J Am Acad Child Adolesc Psychiatry 32: 324, 1993.

Garfinkel B D, Wender P H: Attention-deficit hyperactivity disorder. In *Comprehensive Textbook of Psychiatry*, ed 5, H I Kaplan, B J Sadock, editors, p 1828. Williams & Wilkins, Baltimore, 1989.

Hechtman L: Attention-deficit hyperactivity disorder in adolescence and adulthood: An updated follow-up. Psychiatr Ann 19: 597, 1989.

Hechtman, L: Developmental, neurobiological, and psychosocial aspects of hyperactivity, impulsivity, and inattention. In *Child and Adolescent Psychiatry: A Comprehensive Textbook*, M Lewis, editor, p 318. Williams & Wilkins, Baltimore, 1991.

Jacobvitz D, Sroufe L A, Stewart M, Leffert N: Treatment of attentional and hyperactivity problems in children with sympathicomimetic drugs: A comprehensive review. J Am Acad Child Adolesc Psychiatry 29: 677, 1990.

Klein R G, Landa B, Mattes J A, Klein D: Methylphenidate and growth in hyperactive children. Arch Gen Psychiatry 45: 1127, 1988.

Klorman R, Brumaghim J T, Fitzpatrick P A, Borgstedt A D: Clinical effects of a controlled trial of methylphenidate on adolescents with attention deficit disorder. J Am Acad Child Adolesc Psychiatry 29: 702, 1990.

Loge D V, Staton D, Beatty W W: Performance of children with ADHD on tests sensitive to frontal lobe dysfunction. J Am Acad Child Adolesc Psychiatry 29: 540, 1990.

Loncy J, Kramer J, Milich R: The hyperkinetic child grows up: Predictors of symptoms, delinquency, and achievement at follow-up. In *Psychosocial Aspects of Drug Treatment for Hyperactivity*, K D Gadow, J Loney, editors, p 381. Westview Press, Boulder, Colo, 1981.

Rapport M D, Carlson G A, Kelly K L, Pataki C: Methylphenidate and desipramine in hospitalized children: I. Separate and combined effects on cognitive function. J Am Acad Child Adolesc Psychiatry 32: 333, 1993.

Steingard R, Biederman J, Spencer T, Wilens T, Gonzalez A: Comparison of clonidine response in the treatment of attention-deficit hyperactivity disorder with and without comorbid tic disorders. J Am Acad Child Adolesc Psychiatry 3: 350, 1993.

Taylor E: Syndromes of overactivity and attention deficit. In *Child and Adolescent Psychiatry: Modern Approaches*, ed 2, M Rutter, L Hersov, editors, p 424. Blackwell, Oxford, England, 1985.

Vincent J, Varley C K, Leger P: Effects of methylphenidate on early adolescent growth. Am J Psychiatry 147: 501, 1990.

Wender P H, Garfinkel B D: Attention-deficit hyperactivity disorder: Adult manifestations. In *Comprehensive Textbook of Psychiatry*, ed 5, H I Kaplan, B J Sadock, editors, p 1837. Williams & Wilkins, Baltimore, 1989.

Wilens T E, Biederman J, Geist D E, Steingard R, Spencer T: Nortriptyline in the treatment of ADHD: A chart review of 58 cases. J Am Acad Child Adolesc Psychiatry 32: 343, 1993.

# Disruptive Behavior Disorders

## 40.1 / Oppositional Defiant Disorder

Oppositional defiant disorder is an enduring pattern of negativistic, hostile, and defiant behaviors in the absence of serious violations of social norms or the rights of others. The fourth edition of *Diagnostic and Statistical Manual of Mental Disorders* (DSM-IV) defines the disorder as the revised third edition of DSM (DSM-III-R) did, with the following minor modifications. In DSM-IV, one diagnostic criterion has been removed (often swears or uses obscene language), and only four, instead of five, symptoms are required for the diagnosis. The disorder cannot be diagnosed if the criteria for conduct disorder are met. Unlike conduct disorder, oppositional defiant disorder cannot be diagnosed if the symptoms emerge exclusively during a mood disorder or a psychotic disorder. The most common symptoms of oppositional defiant disorder include the following: often loses temper, often argues with adults, often actively defies or refuses to comply with adults' requests or rules, often deliberately does things that annoy other people, and often blames others for his or her mistakes or misbehavior.

### EPIDEMIOLOGY

Oppositional, negativistic behavior may be developmentally normal in early childhood. Epidemiological studies of negativistic traits in nonclinical populations found them in between 16 and 22 percent of school-age children. Although oppositional defiant disorder can begin as early as 3 years of age, it typically begins by 8 years of age and usually not later than adolescence.

The disorder is more prevalent in boys than in girls before puberty, and the sex ratio is probably equal after puberty. One authority suggests that girls are classified as having oppositional disorder more frequently than boys, as boys are more often given the diagnosis of conduct disorder.

There are no distinct family patterns, but almost all parents of oppositional defiant disorder children are themselves overconcerned with issues of power, control, and autonomy. Some families contain several obstinate children, controlling and depressed mothers, and passive-aggressive fathers. In many cases the patients were unwanted children.

### ETIOLOGY

Asserting one's own will and opposing that of others is crucial to normal development. It is related to establishing one's autonomy, forming an identity, and setting inner standards and controls. The most dramatic example of normal oppositional behavior peaks between 18 and 24 months, the terrible twos, when the toddler behaves negativistically as an expression of growing autonomy. Pathology begins when that developmental phase persists abnormally, authority figures overreact, or oppositional behavior recurs considerably more frequently than in most children of the same mental age.

Children may have constitutional or temperamental predispositions to strong will, strong preferences, or great assertiveness. If power and control are issues for the parents or if they exercise authority for their own needs, a struggle can ensue that sets the stage for the development of oppositional defiant disorder. What begins for the infant as an effort to establish self-determination becomes transformed into a defense against overdependence on the mother and a protective device against intrusion into the ego's autonomy. In late childhood, environmental traumata, illness, or chronic incapacity, such as mental retardation, may trigger oppositionalism as a defense against helplessness, anxiety, and loss of self-esteem. Another normative oppositional stage occurs in adolescence as an expression of the need to separate from the parents and to establish an autonomous identity.

Classic psychoanalytic theory implicates unresolved conflicts that developed during the anal period. Behaviorists have suggested that oppositionalism is a reinforced, learned behavior through which the child exerts control over authority figures—for example, by having a temper tantrum when some undesired act is requested, the child coerces the parents to withdraw their request. In addition, increased parental attention—for example, long discussions about the behavior—many reinforce the behavior.

### DIAGNOSIS AND CLINICAL FEATURES

Children with oppositional defiant disorder often argue with adults, lose their temper, and are angry, resentful, and easily annoyed by others. They frequently actively defy adults' requests or rules and deliberately annoy other people. They tend to blame others for their own mistakes and misbehavior. Manifestations of the disorder are almost invariably present in the home but may not be present at school or with other adults or peers. In some cases, features of the disorder from the beginning of the disturbance are displayed outside the home; in other cases, they start in the home but are later displayed outside the home. Typically, symptoms of the disorder are most evident in interactions with adults or peers whom the child knows well. Thus, children with the disorder are likely to show little or no sign of the disorder when examined clinically. Usually, they do not regard themselves as oppositional or defiant but justify their behavior as a response to unreasonable circumstances. The disorder appears to cause more distress to those around the children than to the children themselves. The DSM-IV diagnostic criteria for oppositional defiant disorder are given in Table 40.1–1.

Chronic oppositional defiant disorder almost always interferes with interpersonal relationships and school performance. The children are often friendless and perceive human relationships as unsatisfactory. Despite adequate intelligence, they do poorly or fail in school, as they withhold participation, resist external demands, and insist on solving problems without others' help.

Secondary to those difficulties are low self-esteem, poor frustration tolerance, depressed mood, and temper outbursts. Adolescents may abuse alcohol and illegal substances. Often, the disturbance evolves into a conduct disorder or a mood disorder.

### Pathology and Laboratory Examination

No specific laboratory tests or pathological findings help diagnose oppositional defiant disorder. Since some chil-

---

**Table 40.1–1**
**Diagnostic Criteria for Oppositional Defiant Disorder**

A. A pattern of negativistic, hostile, and defiant behavior lasting at least 6 months, during which four (or more) of the following are present:

  (1) often loses temper
  (2) often argues with adults
  (3) often actively defies or refuses to comply with adults' requests or rules
  (4) often deliberately annoys people
  (5) often blames others for his or her mistakes or misbehavior
  (6) is often touchy or easily annoyed by others
  (7) is often angry and resentful
  (8) is often spiteful or vindictive

  **Note:** Consider a criterion met only if the behavior occurs more frequently than is typically observed in individuals of comparable age and developmental level.

B. The disturbance in behavior causes significant impairment in social, academic or occupational functioning.

C. The behaviors do not occur exclusively during the course of a psychotic or mood disorder.

D. Criteria are not met for conduct disorder and, if individual is age 18 years or older, criteria are not met for antisocial personality disorder.

---

dren with the disorder become physically aggressive and do violate the rights of others as they get older, they may share some of the same characteristics that are being investigated in violent persons, such as decreased central nervous system serotonin.

## DIFFERENTIAL DIAGNOSIS

Because oppositional behavior is both normal and adaptive at specific developmental stages, those periods of negativism must be distinguished from oppositional defiant disorder. Developmental-stage oppositional behavior is of shorter duration than oppositional defiant disorder and is not considerably more frequent or more intense than that seen in other children of the same mental age.

Oppositional defiant behavior that occurs temporarily in reaction to a severe stress should be diagnosed as an adjustment disorder.

When features of oppositional defiant disorder appear during the course of conduct disorder, schizophrenia, or a mood disorder, the diagnosis of oppositional defiant disorder should not be made.

Oppositional and negativistic behaviors may also be present in attention-deficit/hyperactivity disorder, cognitive disorders, and mental retardation. Whether a concomitant diagnosis of oppositional defiant disorder should be given depends on the severity, pervasiveness, and duration of such behavior.

Some young children who receive a diagnosis of oppositional defiant disorder go on in several years to meet the criteria for conduct disorder. Some investigators believe that the two disorders may be developmental variants of each other, with conduct disorder being the natural progression of oppositional defiant disorder when the child matures. However, the majority of children with oppositional defiant disorder do not later meet the criteria for conduct disorder, and up to one quarter of children with oppositional defiant disorder may not meet the diagnosis for either disorder several years later. Overall, the current consensus indicates that, although certain symptoms of conduct disorder (for example, fighting and bullying) seem to occur in children with oppositional defiant disorder, the two disorders remain distinct on the basis of the children's overall impairment, with oppositional defiant disorder producing less dysfunction than does conduct disorder.

## COURSE AND PROGNOSIS

The course and the prognosis of children with oppositional defiant disorder depend on many variables, including the severity of the disorder, its stability over time, the likelihood of comorbid (dual-diagnosis) disorders (such as conduct disorder, learning disorders, mood disorders, and substance use disorders), and the degree of the family's intactness.

About one quarter of all the children who receive the diagnosis of oppositional defiant disorder may no longer qualify for it within the next several years. It is not clear in those cases whether the criteria captured children whose behavior was not developmentally abnormal or whether the disorder spontaneously remitted Such patients have the best prognosis.

Patients in whom the diagnosis persists may remain stable or may go on to violate the rights of others, leading to conduct disorder. Such patients should receive guarded prognoses. Parental psychopathology, such as antisocial personality disorder and substance abuse, appears to be more common in families with children with oppositional defiant disorder than in the general population, creating additional risks for chaotic and troubled home environments. The prognosis of a child with oppositional defiant disorder depends somewhat on the degree of functioning within the family and on the development of comorbid psychopathology.

## TREATMENT

The primary treatment of oppositional defiant disorder is individual psychotherapy for the child with counseling and direct training of the parents in child management skills.

Behavior therapists emphasize teaching parents how to alter their behavior to discourage their child's oppositional behavior and to encourage appropriate behavior. Behavior therapy focuses on selectively reinforcing and praising appropriate behavior and ignoring or not reinforcing undesired behavior.

Clinicians who treat patients with individual psychotherapy note that family patterns are rigid and difficult to alter unless the children themselves have a new type of object relationship with the therapist. Within the therapeutic relationship, the children can relive the autonomy-threatening experiences that produced their defenses. In the safety of a noncontrolling relationship, they can understand the self-destructive nature of their behavior and risk expressing themselves directly. Their self-esteem must be restored before their defenses against external control can be relinquished. In that way, independence may replace habitual defenses against intrusion and control. Once a therapeutic relationship has been formed on the basis of respect for the patient's separateness, the patient is ready to understand the source of the defenses and to try new coping behavior.

**References**

Cantwell D P: Oppositional defiant disorder. In *Comprehensive Textbook of Psychiatry*, ed 5, H I Kaplan, B J Sadock, editors, p 1842. Williams & Wilkins, Baltimore, 1989.
Doke L A, Flippo J R: Aggressive and oppositional behavior. In *Handbook of Child Psychopathology*, T Ollendick, editor p 222. Plenum, New York, 1982.
Farrington D P: The family backgrounds of aggressive youths. In *Aggression and Antisocial Behavior in Childhood and Adolescence*, L Herzov, M Berger, D Shaffer, editors, p 68. Pergamon, Oxford, England, 1978.
Glueck S, Glueck E: *Unraveling Juvenile Delinquency*. Commonwealth Fund, New York, 1950.
Group for the Advancement of Psychiatry: *Psychopathological Disorders in Childhood. Theoretical Considerations and a Proposed Classification*. Group for the Advancement of Psychiatry, New York, 1966.
Lahey B B, Loeber R, Quay H C, Frick P J, Grimm J: Oppositional defiant disorders: Issues to be resolved for DSM-IV. J Am Acad Child Adolesc Psychiatry *31:* 539, 1992.
Levy D M: Oppositional syndromes and oppositional behavior. In *Psychopathology of Childhood*, P Hoch, J Zubin, editors, p 204. Grune & Stratton, New York, 1955.
Lewis D O, Shanok S S, Grant M, Ritvo E: Homicidally aggressive young children: Neuropsychiatric and experiential correlates. Am J Psychiatry *140:* 148, 1983.
Lewis D O, Shanok S S, Lewis M L, Unger L, Goldman C: Conduct

disorder and its synonyms: Diagnosis of dubious validity and usefulness. Am J Psychiatry *141:* 514, 1984.
Rey J M, Bashir M R, Schwartz M, Richards I N, Plapp J M, Stewart A W: Oppositional disorder: Fact or fiction. J Am Acad Child Adolesc Psychiatry *27:* 157, 1988.
Robins L: *Deviant Children Grown Up*. Williams & Wilkins, Baltimore, 1966.

# 40.2 / Conduct Disorder and Disruptive Behavior Disorder NOS

## CONDUCT DISORDER

The essential feature of conduct disorder is a repetitive and persistent pattern of behavior in which either the basic rights of others or major age-appropriate societal norms or rules are violated. The behaviors must be present for at least six months to qualify for the diagnosis. The criteria in the fourth edition of *Diagnostic and Statistical Manual of Mental Disorders* (DSM-IV) are similar to those in the revised third edition (DSM-III-R) in that three specific behaviors are required for the diagnosis, but DSM-IV has enlarged the list of potential symptoms from 13 to 15. The two new symptoms that appear in DSM-IV but not in DSM-III-R are "often bullies, threatens, or intimidates others" and "often stays out at night despite parental prohibitions, beginning before 13 years of age." DSM-IV also specifies that truancy from school must begin before 13 years of age to be considered a symptom of conduct disorder. The disorder can be diagnosed in a person more than 18 years old only if the criteria for antisocial personality disorder are not met.

DSM-III-R divided conduct disorder into three subtypes: group type, solitary aggressive type, and undifferentiated type. DSM-IV divides conduct disorder into two types with respect to age of onset: childhood-onset type and adolescent-onset type. In the childhood-onset type, at least one conduct problem must have its onset before the age of 10 years. In adolescent-onset type, no conduct problems were present before the age of 10 years. DSM-IV also labels severity, ranging from mild (few if any conduct problems in excess of those needed to make the diagnosis and conduct problems cause only minor harm to others), moderate (intermediate between mild and severe), and severe (many conduct problems in excess of the minimal diagnostic criteria or conduct problems cause considerable harm to others).

### Epidemiology

Conduct disorder is common during childhood and adolescence. An estimated 6 to 16 percent of boys and 2 to 9 percent of girls under the age of 18 years have the disorder. The disorder is more common among boys than among girls, and the ratio ranges from 4 to 1 to as much as 12 to 1. Conduct disorder is more common in the children of parents with antisocial personality disorder and alcohol dependence than it is in the general population. The prevalence of conduct disorder and antisocial behavior is significantly related to socioeconomic factors.

## Etiology

No single factor can account for children's antisocial behavior and conduct disorder. Rather, a variety of biopsychosocial factors contribute to the development of the disorder.

**Parental factors.** Some parental attitudes and faulty child-rearing practices influence the development of children's maladaptive behaviors. Chaotic home conditions are associated with conduct disorder and delinquency. However, broken homes per se are not causatively significant; it is the strife between the parents that contributes to conduct disorder. Parental psychopathology, child abuse, and negligence often contribute to conduct disorder. Sociopathy, alcohol dependence, and substance abuse in the parents are associated with conduct disorder in their children. Parents may be so negligent that care of the child is shared by relatives or assumed by foster parents. Many such parents were scarred by their own upbringing and tend to be abusive, negligent, or engrossed in getting their own personal needs met. In the 1980s, particularly in urban areas, cocaine abuse and acquired immune deficiency syndrome (AIDS) increased family dysfunction. Recent studies suggest that many parents of conduct disorder children suffer from serious psychopathology, including psychotic disorders. Psychodynamic hypotheses suggest that children with conduct disorder unconsciously act out their parent's antisocial wishes.

**Sociocultural factors.** Current theories suggest that socioeconomically deprived children, unable to achieve status and obtain material goods through legitimate routes, are forced to resort to socially unacceptable means to reach those goals and that such behavior is normal and acceptable under circumstances of socioeconomic deprivation, as the children are adhering to the values of their own subculture.

**Psychological factors.** Children brought up in chaotic, negligent conditions generally become angry, disruptive, demanding, and unable to progressively develop the tolerance for frustration necessary for mature relationships. As their role models are poor and often frequently changing, the basis for developing both an ego-ideal and a conscience is lacking. The children are left with little motivation to follow societal norms and are relatively remorseless.

**Neurobiological factors.** Neurobiological factors in conduct disorder have been little studied. However, research in attention-deficit/hyperactivity disorder (ADHD) yields some important findings, and conduct disorder and ADHD often coexist. In some conduct-disordered children a low level of plasma dopamine β-hydroxylase, an enzyme that converts dopamine to norepinephrine, has been found. That finding supports a theory of decreased noradrenergic functioning in conduct disorder. Some conduct-disordered juvenile offenders have increased blood serotonin (5-hydroxytryptamine [(5-HT]) levels. Some evidence indicates that blood 5-HT levels correlate negatively with levels of the 5-HT metabolite 5-hydroxyindoleacetic

acid (5-HIAA) in the cerebrospinal fluid (CSF) and that low CSF 5-HIAA correlates with aggression and violence.

**Child abuse and maltreatment.** Children who are exposed to violence for long periods, especially those who endure physically abusive treatment, often behave in aggressive ways. Such children may have difficulty in verbalizing their feelings, and that difficulty increases their tendency to express themselves physically. In addition, severely abused children and adolescents tend to be hypervigilant; in some cases they misperceive benign situations and respond with violence. Not all physical behavior is synonymous with conduct disorder, but children with a pattern of hypervigilance and violent responses are likely to violate the rights of others.

**Other factors.** ADHD, central nervous system (CNS) dysfunction or damage, and early extremes of temperament can predispose a child to conduct disorder. Propensity to violence correlates with CNS dysfunction and signs of severe psychopathology, such as delusional tendencies. Longitudinal temperament studies suggest that many behavioral deviations are initially a straightforward response to a poor fit between, on the one hand, a child's temperament and emotional needs and, on the other hand, parental attitudes and child-rearing practices.

## Diagnosis and Clinical Features

Conduct disorder does not develop overnight; instead, a variety of symptoms evolve over time until a consistent pattern violates the right of others. Very young children are unlikely to meet the criteria for the disorder, since they are not developmentally able to exhibit the symptoms typical of older children with conduct disorder. A 3-year-old does not break into someone's home, steal with confrontation, force someone into sexual activity, or deliberately use a weapon that can cause serious harm. However, school-age children may become bullies, initiate physical fights, destroy property, or set fires. The DSM-IV diagnostic criteria for conduct disorder are given in Table 40.2–1.

The average age of onset of conduct disorder is younger in boys than in girls. Boys most commonly meet the diagnostic criteria by 10 to 12 years of age, whereas girls

**Table 40.2–1**
**Diagnostic Criteria for Conduct Disorder**

A. A repetitive and persistent pattern of behavior in which either the basic rights of others or major age-appropriate societal norms or rules are violated, as manifested by the presence of three (or more) of the following criteria in the past 12 months, with at least one criterion present in the past 6 months:

**Aggression to people and animals**
(1) often bullies, threatens, or intimidates others
(2) often initiates physical fights
(3) has used a weapon that can cause serious physical harm to others (e.g., a bat, brick, broken bottle, knife, gun)
(4) has been physically cruel to people
(5) has been physically cruel to animals
(6) has stolen while confronting a victim (e.g., mugging, purse snatching, extortion, armed robbery)
(7) has forced someone into sexual activity

**Table 40.2–1**
*Continued*

**Destruction of property**
  (8) has deliberately engaged in fire setting with the intention of causing serious damage
  (9) has deliberately destroyed others' property (other than by fire setting)

**Deceitfulness or theft**
  (10) has broken into someone else's house, building, or car
  (11) often lies to obtain goods or favors or to avoid obligations (i.e., "cons" others)
  (12) has stolen items of nontrivial value without confronting a victim (e.g., shoplifting, but without breaking and entering; forgery)

**Serious violations of rules**
  (13) often stays out at night despite parental prohibitions, beginning before 13 years
  (14) has run away from home overnight at least twice while living in parental or parental surrogate home (or once without returning for a lengthy period)
  (15) often truant from school, beginning before age 13 years

B. The disturbance in behavior causes clinically significant impairment in social, academic, or occupational functioning.

C. If the individual is age 18 years or older, criteria are not met for antisocial personality disorder.

*Specify* type based on age of onset:

**Childhood-onset type:** onset of at least one criterion characteristic of conduct disorder prior to age 10 years
**Adolescent-onset type:** absence of any criteria characteristic of conduct disorder prior to age 10 years

*Specify* severity:

**Mild:** few if any conduct problems in excess of those required to make the diagnosis **and** conduct problems cause only minor harm to others

**Moderate:** number of conduct problems and effect on others intermediate between "mild" and "severe"

**Severe:** many conduct problems in excess of those required to make the diagnosis **or** conduct problems cause considerable harm to others

Table from DSM-IV, *Diagnostic and Statistical Manual of Mental Disorders*, ed 4. Copyright American Psychiatric Association, Washington, 1994. Used with permission.

often reach 14 to 16 years of age before the criteria are met.

Children who meet the criteria for conduct disorder express their overt aggressive behavior in various forms. The aggressive antisocial behavior may take the form of bullying, physical aggression, and cruel behavior toward peers. The children may be hostile, verbally abusive, impudent, defiant, and negativistic toward adults. Persistent lying, frequent truancy, and vandalism are common. In severe cases there is often destructiveness, stealing, and physical violence. The children usually make little attempt to conceal their antisocial behavior. Sexual behavior and the regular use of tobacco, liquor, or nonprescribed psychoactive substances begin unusually early for such children and adolescents. Suicidal thoughts, gestures, and acts are frequent.

Many of the children with aggressive behaviors fail to develop social attachments, as manifested by their difficulty in peer relationships or their lack of sustained normal peer relationships. Such children are often socially withdrawn or isolated. Some of them may befriend a much older or younger person or have superficial relationships with other antisocial youngsters. Most of them have low self-esteem, although they may project an image of toughness. Characteristically, they do not put themselves out for others, even if doing so would have an obvious immediate advantage. Their egocentrism is shown by their readily manipulating others for favors without any effort to reciprocate. They lack concern for the feelings, wishes, and welfare of others. They seldom have feelings of guilt or remorse for their callous behavior and try to blame others.

Not only have the children frequently encountered unusual frustrations, particularly of their dependency needs, but they also have escaped any consistent pattern of discipline. Their deficient socialization is revealed in their excessive aggressiveness and in their lack of sexual inhibition. Their general behavior is unacceptable in almost any social setting. Unfortunately, severe punishment almost invariably increases their maladaptive expression of rage and frustration, rather than ameliorating the problem.

In evaluation interviews, aggressive conduct-disordered children are typically uncooperative, hostile, and provocative. Some have a superficial charm and compliance until they are urged to talk about their problem behaviors. Then they may angrily deny any problems. If the interviewer persists, conduct-disordered children may attempt to justify their misbehavior or become suspicious and angry about the source of the examiner's information and perhaps bolt from the room. Most often, they become angry at the examiner and express their resentment of the examination with open belligerence or sullen withdrawal. Their hostility is not limited to adult authority figures but is expressed with equal venom toward their age-mates and younger children. In fact, they often bully those who are smaller and weaker than they. By boasting, lying, and expressing little interest in the listener's responses, such children reveal their profoundly narcissistic orientation.

Evaluation of the family situation often reveals severe marital disharmony, which initially may center on disagreements concerning management of the child. Because of a tendency toward family instability, parent surrogates are often in the picture. Many children with conduct disorder are only children of unplanned or unwanted pregnancies. The parents, especially the father, often have antisocial personality disorder or alcohol dependence.

The aggressive child and the child's family show a stereotyped pattern of impulsive and unpredictable verbal and physical hostility. The child's aggressive behavior rarely seems directed toward any definable goal and offers little pleasure, success, or even sustained advantages with peers or authority figures.

In other cases, conduct disorder includes repeated truancy, vandalism, and serious physical aggression or assault against others by a gang, such as mugging, gang fighting, and beating.

Children who become part of a gang usually have age-appropriate friendships. They are likely to show concern for the welfare of their friends or their own gang members and are unlikely to blame them or inform on them.

In most cases, gang members have a history of adequate or even excessive conformity during early childhood that ended when the youngster became a member of the delinquent peer group, usually in preadolescence or during adolescence. Also present in the history is some evidence of early problems, such as marginal or poor school performance, mild behavior problems, anxiety, and depressive symptoms.

Some degree of family social or psychological pathology is usually evident. Patterns of paternal discipline are rarely ideal and may vary from harshness and excessive strictness to inconsistency or relative absence of supervision and control. The mother has often protected the child from the consequences of early mild misbehavior but does not seem to actively encourage delinquency. Delinquency, also called juvenile delinquency, is most often associated with conduct disorder but may also be the result of other psychological or neurological disorders.

**Pathology and laboratory examination.** No specific laboratory test or neurological pathology helps make the diagnosis of conduct disorder. Some evidence indicates that certain neurotransmitters, such as serotonin in the central nervous system, are low in some persons with a history of violent or aggressive behavior toward others or themselves. Whether that association is related to the cause or is the effect of violence or is unrelated to the violence is not clear.

## Differential Diagnosis

Disturbances of conduct may be part of many childhood psychiatric conditions, ranging from mood disorders to psychotic disorders to learning disorders. Therefore, the clinician must obtain a history of the chronology of the symptoms to determine whether the conduct disturbance is a transient or reactive phenomenon. Isolated acts of antisocial behavior do not justify a diagnosis of conduct disorder; an enduring pattern must be present.

The relation of conduct disorder to oppositional defiant disorder is still under debate. Historically, oppositional defiant disorder has been conceptualized as a mild precursor of conduct disorder that is likely to be diagnosed in young children at risk for conduct disorder. Children who progress from oppositional defiant disorder to conduct disorder do maintain their oppositional characteristics, but some evidence indicates that the two disorders are independent. Many children with oppositional defiant disorder never go on to have conduct disorder, and, when conduct disorder first appears in adolescence, it may be unrelated to oppositional defiant disorder. The main distinguishing clinical feature of the two disorders is that, in conduct disorder, the basic rights of others are violated, whereas, in oppositional defiant disorder, hostility and negativism fall short of seriously violating the rights of others.

Mood disorders are often present in children with some degree of irritability and aggressive behavior. Both major depressive disorder and bipolar disorders must be ruled out. However, the full syndrome of conduct disorder may occur and be diagnosed during the onset of a mood disorder. That is not the case for oppositional defiant disorder, which cannot be diagnosed if it occurs exclusively during a mood disorder.

Attention-deficit/hyperactivity disorder and learning disorders are commonly associated with conduct disorder. Usually, the symptoms of those disorders predate the diagnosis of conduct disorder.

All the above disorders should be noted when they co-occur. Children with attention-deficit/hyperactivity disorder often exhibit impulsive and aggressive behaviors that may not meet the full criteria for conduct disorder.

## Course and Prognosis

In general, children who have conduct disorder symptoms at a young age, exhibit the greatest number of symptoms, and express them most frequently have the poorest prognoses. That is true partly because those with severe conduct disorder seem to be the most vulnerable to another disorder later in life, such as a mood disorder. Conduct disorder is also associated with substance-related disorders later in life. It stands to reason that, the more concurrent mental disorders a person suffers from, the more troublesome life will be. A recent report found that, although assaultive behavior in childhood and parental criminality predict a high risk for incarceration later in life, the diagnosis of conduct disorder per se was not correlated with imprisonment.

A good prognosis is predicted by mild conduct disorder, the absence of coexisting psychopathology, and normal intellectual functioning. Although assessing treatment strategies is difficult because of the many symptoms involved in conduct disorder, it appears to be more difficult to design effective treatment programs for the covert symptoms of conduct disorder than for overt aggression.

## Treatment

Multimodality treatment programs that use all the available family and community resources are likely to bring about the best results in efforts to control conduct-disordered behavior. No treatment is considered curative for the entire spectrum of behaviors that contribute to conduct disorder. A variety of treatments may be helpful for certain components of the chronic disorder.

An environmental structure with consistent rules and expected consequences can help control a variety of problem behaviors. The structure can be applied to family life in some cases, so that the parents become aware of behavioral techniques and proficient at using them to foster appropriate behaviors. Families in which psychopathology or environmental stressors prevent the parents' grasping the techniques may require parental psychiatric evaluation and treatment before making such an endeavor. When the family is abusive or chaotic, the child may have to be removed from the home to benefit from a consistent and structured environment.

School settings can also use behavioral techniques to promote socially acceptable behavior toward peers and to discourage covert antisocial incidents.

Individual psychotherapy oriented toward improving problem-solving skills can be useful, since children with

**Table 40.2–2**
**Diagnostic Criteria for Disruptive Behavior Disorder**
**Not Otherwise Specified**

---

This category is for disorders characterized by conduct or oppositional-defiant behaviors that do not meet the criteria for conduct disorder or oppositional defiant disorder. For example, include clinical presentations that do not meet full criteria either for oppositional defiant disorder or conduct disorder, but in which there is clinically significant impairment.

---

Table from DSM-IV, *Diagnostic and Statistical Manual of Mental Disorders*, ed 4. Copyright American Psychiatric Association, Washington, 1994. Used with permission.

conduct disorder may have a long-standing pattern of maladaptive responses to daily situations. The age at which treatment begins is important, since, the longer the maladaptive behaviors continue, the more entrenched they become.

Medication can be a useful adjunctive treatment for a number of symptoms that often contribute to conduct disorder. Overt explosive aggression responds to several medications. Antipsychotics, most notably haloperidol (Haldol), decreases aggressive and assaultive behaviors that may be present in various disorders. Lithium (Eskalith) also has some benefit in the treatment of aggression within or outside the context of bipolar disorders. Some trials suggest that carbamazepine (Tegretol) may help control aggression. A recent pilot study found that clonidine (Catapres) may decrease aggression.

Since conduct disorder frequently coexists with attention-deficit/hyperactivity disorder, learning disorders, and, over time, mood disorders and substance-related disorders, the treatment of any concurrent disorders must also be addressed.

## DISRUPTIVE BEHAVIOR DISORDER NOT OTHERWISE SPECIFIED

Disruptive behavior disorder not otherwise specified (NOS) can be used for disorders of conduct or oppositional-defiant behaviors that do not meet the diagnostic criteria for either conduct disorder or oppositional defiant disorder but in which there is notable impairment (Table 40.2–2).

**References**

Apter A, Bleich A, Plutchik R, Mendelsohn S, Tyano S: Suicidal behavior, depression and conduct disorder in hospitalized adolescents. J Am Acad Child Adolesc Psychiatry 27: 696, 1988.

Berger M: Personality development and temperament. In *Temperamental Differences in Infants and Young Children*, R Porter, G M Collins, editors, p 176. Pitmann, London, 1982.

Cantwell D P: Conduct disorder. In *Comprehensive Textbook of Psychiatry*, ed 5, H I Kaplan, B J Sadock, editors, p 1821. Williams & Wilkins, Baltimore, 1989.

Farrington D P: The family backgrounds of aggressive youths. In *Aggression and Antisocial Behavior in Childhood and Adolescence*, L Herzov, M Berger, D Shaffer, editors, p 27. Oxford University Press, Oxford, England, 1978.

Kemph J P, DeVane C L, Levin G M, Jarecke R, Miller R L: Treatment of aggressive children with clonidine: Results of an open pilot study. J Am Acad Child Adolesc Psychiatry 32: 577, 1993.

Lahey B B, Loeber R, Quay H C, Frick P J, Grimm J: Oppositional defiant disorder and conduct disorders: Issues to be resolved for DSM-IV. J Am Acad Child Adolesc Psychiatry 31: 539, 1992.

Lamb M E: Parental influences on early socioemotional development. J Child Psychol Psychiatry 23: 185, 1982.

Lewis D O: From abuse to violence: Psychophysiological consequences of maltreatment. J Am Acad Child Adolesc Psychiatry 31: 383, 1992.

Lewis D O, editor: *Vulnerabilities to Delinquency*, Spectrum, New York, 1981.

Lewis D O, Lovely R, Yeager C, Ferguson G, Friedman M, Sloane G, Friedman H, Pincus J H: Intrinsic and environmental characteristics of juvenile murderers. J Am Acad Child Adolesc Psychiatry 27: 582, 1988.

Lewis D O, Shanok S S, Lewis M L, Unger L, Goldman C: Conduct disorder and its synonyms: Diagnosis of dubious validity and usefulness. Am J Psychiatry 141: 514, 1984.

Lundy M S, Pfohl B M, Kuperman S: Adult criminality among formerly hospitalized psychiatric patients. J Am Acad Child Adolesc Psychiatry 32: 568, 1993.

Maziade M, Caron C, Côté R, Boutin P, Thivierge J: Extreme temperament and diagnoses. Arch Gen Psychiatry 47: 477, 1990.

McAuley R: Annotation: Training parents to modify conduct problems in their children. J Child Psychol Psychiatry 23: 335, 1982.

Pliszka S R, Rogness G A, Renner P, Sherman J, Broussard T: Plasma neurochemistry in juvenile offenders. J Am Acad Child Adolesc Psychiatry 27: 588, 1988.

Robins L: *Deviant Children Grown Up*. Williams & Wilkins, Baltimore, 1966.

Stewart J T, Myers W C, Burket R C, Lyles W B: A review of the pharmacotherapy of aggression in children and adolescents. J Am Acad Child Adolesc Psychiatry 29: 269, 1990.

Szatmari P, Boyle M, Offord D R: ADDH and conduct disorder: Degree of diagnostic overlap and differences among correlates. J Am Acad Child Adolesc Psychiatry 28: 865, 1989.

Zoccolillo M: Co-occurrence of conduct disorder and its adult outcomes with depressive and anxiety disorders: A review. J Am Acad Child Adolesc Psychiatry 31: 547, 1992.

# Feeding and Eating Disorders of Infancy or Early Childhood

## 41.1 / Pica

Pica is a pattern of eating nonnutritive substances for at least one month. According to the fourth edition of *Diagnostic and Statistical Manual of Mental Disorders* (DSM-IV), the ingestion of nonnutritive substances must be inappropriate to the child's developmental level. In addition, the eating behavior is not part of a culturally sanctioned practice. The exclusionary criteria in the revised third edition of DSM (DSM-III-R) (does not meet the criteria for either autistic disorder, schizophrenia, or Kleine-Levin syndrome) have been removed from the DSM-IV diagnostic criteria.

Pica is seen much more frequently in young children than in adults. It also occurs in mentally retarded persons. Among adults, certain forms of pica, including geophagia (clay eating) and amylophagia (starch eating), have been reported to occur in pregnant women. In certain regions of the world and among certain cultures, such as the Australian aborigines, rates of pica in pregnant women have been reported to be high. According to DSM-IV, however, if the practices are culturally determined, the diagnostic criteria for pica are not met.

### EPIDEMIOLOGY

Pica is estimated to occur in 10 to 32 percent of children between 1 and 6 years of age. In children more than 10 years old, reports of pica have indicated a rate of about 10 percent. In older children and adolescents with normal intelligence, the frequency of pica diminishes. Among institutionalized mentally retarded children and adolescents, pica has been reported to occur in up to one fourth of older school-age children and adolescents. The presence of pica appears to affect both sexes equally.

### ETIOLOGY

A number of theories have been proposed to explain the phenomenon of pica, but none has been universally accepted. A higher than expected incidence of pica seems to occur in the relatives of persons with the symptoms.

Nutritional deficiencies have been postulated as causes of pica, since in particular circumstances cravings for nonedible substances have been produced by deficiencies. For example, cravings for dirt and ice are sometimes associated with iron and zinc deficiencies and are eliminated by their administration.

A high incidence of parental neglect and deprivation has been associated with cases of pica. Theories relating the child's psychological deprivation and subsequent ingestion of inedible substances have been suggested as compensatory mechanisms to satisfy oral needs.

An important contributing factor is the influence of widely accepted cultural rituals and practices in promoting such behaviors as geophagia and the eating of starch. Those influences can be compelling, and they disqualify the diagnosis of pica, according to DSM-IV.

### DIAGNOSIS AND CLINICAL FEATURES

Eating nonedible substances after 18 months of age is usually considered abnormal. The onset of pica is usually between ages 12 and 24 months, and the incidence declines with age. The specific substances ingested vary with their accessibility, and they increase with the child's mastery of locomotion and the resultant increased independence and decreased parental supervision. Typically, young children ingest paint, plaster, string, hair, and cloth; older children have access to dirt, animal feces, stones, and paper.

The clinical implications may be benign or life-threatening, according to the objects ingested. Among the most serious complications are lead poisoning, usually from lead-based paint; intestinal parasites after the ingestion of soil or feces; anemia and zinc deficiency after the ingestion of clay; severe iron deficiency after the ingestion of large quantities of starch; and intestinal obstruction from the ingestion of hair balls, stones, or gravel.

Except in the case of mentally retarded persons, pica usually remits by adolescence. Pica associated with pregnancy is usually limited to the pregnancy itself. The DSM-IV diagnostic criteria for pica are given in Table 41.1–1.

### Pathology and Laboratory Examination

No single laboratory test confirms or rules out a diagnosis of pica. However, several laboratory tests are useful, since pica has frequently been associated with abnormal

**Table 41.1–1**
**Diagnostic Criteria for Pica**

A. Persistent eating of nonnutritive substances for a period of at least 1 month.

B. The eating of nonnutritive substances is inappropriate to developmental level.

C. The eating behavior is not part of a culturally sanctioned practice.

D. If the eating behavior occurs exclusively during the course of another mental disorder (e.g., mental retardation, pervasive developmental disorder, schizophrenia), it is sufficiently severe to warrant independent clinical attention.

Table from DSM-IV, *Diagnostic and Statistical Manual of Mental Disorders*, ed 4. Copyright American Psychiatirc Association, Washington, 1994. Used with permission.

indexes. Serum levels of iron and zinc should always be obtained; in many cases of pica, those levels are low and may contribute to the development of pica. Pica may disappear when oral iron and zinc are administered. The patient's hemoglobin level should be obtained, since it may be reduced, resulting in anemia. In children with pica, the serum lead level should be obtained if the physician has any concern that the child is ingesting lead, which can lead to lead poisoning. The child's lead level may be increased; if so, that condition must be treated.

## DIFFERENTIAL DIAGNOSIS

The differential diagnosis of pica includes iron and zinc deficiencies. Pica may also occur in conjunction with failure to thrive and several other mental and medical disorders, including schizophrenia, autistic disorder, anorexia nervosa, and Kleine-Levin syndrome. In psychosocial dwarfism, a dramatic but reversible endocrinological and behavioral form of failure to thrive, children often present with bizarre behaviors, including the ingestion of toilet water, garbage, and other nonnutritive substances. A small minority of children with autistic disorder and schizophrenia may have pica. In children who exhibit pica along with another mental disorder, both disorders should be coded, according to DSM-IV.

## COURSE AND PROGNOSIS

The prognosis for pica is variable. In children, pica usually resolves with increasing age; in pregnant women, pica is usually limited to the term of the pregnancy. However, in some adults, especially in the mentally retarded, pica may continue for years. Follow-up data on those populations are too limited to permit conclusions.

## TREATMENT

There is no definitive treatment for pica. Treatments basically emphasize psychosocial, environmental, behavioral, and family guidance approaches.

An effort should be made to ameliorate any significant psychosocial stressors that are present. When lead is present in the surroundings, it must be eliminated or rendered inaccessible, or the child must be moved to new surroundings.

Several behavioral techniques have been used with some effect. The most rapidly successful seems to be mild aversion therapy or negative reinforcement (for example, a mild electric shock, an unpleasant noise, or an emetic drug). Positive reinforcement, modeling, behavioral shaping, and overcorrection treatment have also been used.

Increasing parental attention, stimulation, and emotional nurturance may have positive results. One study found that pica was negatively correlated with involvement with play materials and occurred most frequently in impoverished environments.

In some patients, the correction of an iron or zinc deficiency has resulted in the elimination of pica.

Medical complications (for example, lead poisoning) that develop secondarily to the pica must also be treated.

**References**

Blinder B J, Chaitin B, Goldstein R, editors: *The Eating Disorders*. Pergamon, New York, 1987.
Connors M E, Morse W: Sexual abuse and eating disorders: A review. Int J Eating Disord 13: 1, 1993.
Cooper M: *Pica*. Thomas, Springfield, Ill, 1957.
Danford D E, Smith C J, Huber A M: Pica and mineral status in the mentally retarded. Am J Clin Nutr 35: 958, 1982.
Lourie R S, Millican F K: Pica. In *Modern Perspectives in International Child Psychiatry*, J G Howells, editor, p 445. Brunner/Mazel, New York, 1971.
Millican F K, Dublin C C, Lourie R S: Pica. In *Basic Handbook of Child Psychiatry*, J D Noshpitz, editor, vol 2, p 660. Basic Books, New York, 1979.
Millican F K, Lourie R S, Laymen E M: Emotional factors in the etiology and treatment of lead poisoning. Am J Dis Child 91: 144, 1956.
Provence S, Lipton R C: *Infants and Institutions*. International Universities Press, New York, 1962.
Vanderlinden J, Vandereycken W, van Dyck R, Vertommen H: Dissociative experiences and trauma in eating disorders. Int J Eating Disord 13: 187, 1993.

# 41.2 / Rumination Disorder and Feeding Disorder of Infancy or Early Childhood

## RUMINATION DISORDER

Rumination disorder is the repeated regurgitation of food, usually in infants. Its onset generally occurs after 3 months of age; once the regurgitation occurs, the food may be swallowed or spit out. The disorder is rare in older children, adolescents, and adults. It varies in its severity, and it is sometimes associated with medical conditions, such as hiatus hernia, that results in esophageal reflux. In its most severe form, the disorder can be fatal. The fourth edition of *Diagnostic and Statistical Manual of Mental Disorders* (DSM-IV) removes one of the diagnostic criteria (weight loss or failure to make expected weight gain) that was present in the revised third edition (DSM-III-R). According to DSM-IV, the disorder must be present for at least one month after a period of normal functioning, and it is not associated with gastrointestinal illness or other general medical conditions.

Rumination has been recognized for hundreds of years. An awareness of the disorder is important, so that it is correctly diagnosed and so that unnecessary surgical procedures and inappropriate treatment are avoided.

"Rumination" is derived from the Latin word *ruminare,* meaning to chew the cud. The Greek equivalent is *merycism,* the act of regurgitating food from the stomach into the mouth, rechewing the food, and reswallowing it.

## Epidemiology

Rumination is a rare disorder. It seems to be most common among infants between 3 months and 1 year of age and among mentally retarded children and adults. Adults with rumination usually maintain a normal weight. The disorder is apparently equally common in boys and girls. No reliable figures on predisposing factors or familial patterns are available. The disorder may be seen in up to 10 percent of persons with bulimia nervosa.

## Etiology

Several causes of rumination have been proposed. In mentally retarded ruminators, the disorder may simply be self-stimulatory behavior. In nonretarded ruminators, psychodynamic theories hypothesize various disturbances in the mother-child relationship. The mothers of infants with the disorder are usually immature, involved in a marital conflict, and unable to give much attention to the baby. Those factors result in insufficient emotional gratification and stimulation for the infant, who seeks gratification from within. The rumination is interpreted as the infant's attempt to re-create the feeding process and provide gratification that the mother does not provide. Overstimulation and tension have also been suggested as causes of rumination.

A dysfunctional autonomic nervous system may be implicated. As sophisticated and accurate investigative techniques are refined, a substantial number of children classified as ruminators are shown to have gastroesophageal reflux or hiatal hernia.

Behaviorists attribute rumination to the positive reinforcement of the pleasurable self-stimulation and to the attention the baby receives from others as a consequence of the disorder.

## Diagnosis and Clinical Features

The DSM-IV diagnostic criteria for rumination disorder are given in Table 41.2–1. DSM-IV notes that the essential feature of the disorder is repeated regurgitation and rechewing of food for a period of at least one month after a period of normal functioning. Partially digested food is brought up into the mouth without nausea, retching, disgust, or associated gastrointestinal disorder. The food is then ejected from the mouth or reswallowed. A characteristic position of straining and arching of the back, with the head held back, is observed. The infant makes sucking movements with the tongue and gives the impression of gaining considerable satisfaction from the activity. An as-

**Table 41.2–1**
**Diagnostic Criteria for Rumination Disorder**

A. Repeated regurgitation and rechewing of food for a period of at least 1 month following a period of normal functioning.

B. The behavior is not due to an associated gastrointestinal or other general medical condition (e.g., esophageal reflux).

C. The behavior does not occur exclusively during the course of anorexia nervosa or bulimia nervosa. If the symptoms occur exclusively during the course of mental retardation or a pervasive developmental disorder, they are sufficiently severe to warrant independent clinical attention.

Table from DSM-IV, *Diagnostic and Statistical Manual of Mental Disorders*, ed 4. Copyright American Psychiatric Association, Washington, 1994. Used with permission.

sociated feature that is usually present is that the infant is generally irritable and hungry between episodes of rumination.

Initially, rumination may be difficult to distinguish from the regurgitation that frequently occurs in normal infants. In the fully developed case, however, the diagnosis is obvious. Food or milk is regurgitated without nausea, retching, or disgust and is subjected to what appears to be innumerable pleasurable sucking and chewing movements. The food is then reswallowed or ejected from the mouth.

Although spontaneous remissions are common, severe secondary complications may develop, such as progressive malnutrition, dehydration, and lowered resistance to disease. Failure to thrive, with growth failure and developmental delays in all areas, may occur. Mortality as high as 25 percent has been reported in severe cases.

An additional complication is that the mother or caretaker is often discouraged by the failure to feed the infant successfully and may become alienated, if not already so. Further alienation often occurs as the noxious odor of the regurgitated material leads to avoidance of the infant.

**Pathology and laboratory examination.** No specific laboratory examination is pathognomonic of rumination disorder. The clinician must rule out physical causes of vomiting, such as pyloric stenosis and hiatal hernia, before making the diagnosis of rumination disorder. Rumination disorder can be associated with failure to thrive and varying degrees of starvation. Thus, laboratory measures of endocrinological function (thyroid function tests, dexamethasone-suppression test), serum electrolytes, and a hematological workup help determine the severity of the effects of rumination disorder.

## Differential Diagnosis

To make the diagnosis of rumination disorder, the clinician must rule out gastrointestinal congenital anomalies, infections, and other medical illnesses. Pyloric stenosis is usually associated with projectile vomiting and is generally evident before 3 months of age, when rumination has its onset. Rumination has been associated with various mental retardation syndromes in which other stereotypic behaviors and eating disturbances, such as pica, have been present. Rumination disorder may occur in patients with other eating disorders, such as bulimia nervosa.

## Course and Prognosis

Rumination disorder is believed to have a high rate of spontaneous remission. Indeed, many cases of rumination disorder may develop and remit without ever being diagnosed. Only limited data are available regarding the prognosis of rumination disorder in adults.

## Treatment

The effectiveness of treatments is difficult to evaluate, as most reports are single-case studies and patients are not randomly assigned to controlled studies. Any concomitant medical complications must also be treated.

Treatments include improvement of the child's psychosocial environment, increased tender loving care from the mother or caretakers, and psychotherapy for the mother or both parents.

When anatomical abnormalities such as hiatal hernia are present, surgical repair may be necessary.

Behavioral techniques have been used effectively. Aversive conditioning involves administering a mild electric shock or squirting an unpleasant substance (such as lemon juice) in the child's mouth whenever rumination occurs. That practice appears to be the most rapidly effective treatment; rumination is eliminated in three to five days. In the aversive-conditioning reports on rumination disorder, the infants were doing well at 9- or 12-month follow-ups, with no recurrence of the rumination and with weight gains, increased activity levels, and increased responsiveness to people.

One study showed that, if the infants were allowed to eat as much as they wanted, the rate of rumination decreased.

## FEEDING DISORDER OF INFANCY OR EARLY CHILDHOOD

According to DSM-IV, this diagnosis is used for feeding disturbances manifested by persistent failure to eat adequately, resulting in failure to gain expected weight or in significant weight loss over at least one month (Table 41.2–

**Table 41.2–2**
**Diagnostic Criteria for Feeding Disorder of Infancy or Early Childhood**

A. Feeding disturbance as manifested by persistent failure to eat adequately with significant failure to gain weight or significant loss of weight over at least 1 month.

B. The disturbance is not due to an associated gastrointestinal or other general medical condition (e.g., esophageal reflux).

C. The disturbance is not better accounted for by another mental disorder (e.g., rumination disorder) or by lack of available food.

D. The onset is before age 6 years.

Table from DSM-IV, *Diagnostic and Statistical Manual of Mental Disorders*, ed 4. Copyright American Psychiatric Association, Washington, 1994. Used with permission.

2). The disorder is not due to any gastrointestinal illness or other medical illness. It is not due to a lack of available food, and it cannot be better accounted for by another mental disorder. The disorder must have its onset before age 6 years.

**References**

Blinder B J, Chaitin B, Goldstein R, editors: *The Eating Disorders*. Pergamon, New York, 1987.
Davis P K, Cuvo A J: Chronic vomiting and rumination in intellectually normal and retarded individuals: Review and evaluation of behavioral research. Behav Res Severe Dev Disabil *1*: 31, 1980.
Flanagan C H: Rumination in infancy: Past and present: With a case report. J Am Acad Child Psychiatry *16*: 40, 1977.
Hodes M, Le Grange D: Expressed emotion in the investigation of eating disorders: A review. Int J Eating Disord *13*: 279, 1993.
Humphrey F J, Mayes S D, Bixler E O: Variables associated with frequency of rumination in a boy with profound mental retardation. J Autism Dev Disord *19*: 435, 1989.
Linscheid T R, Cunningham C E: A controlled demonstration of the effectiveness of electric shock in the elimination of chronic infant rumination. J Appl Behav Anal *10*: 500, 1977.
Mayes S D, Humphrey F J, Handford H A, Mitchell J F: Rumination disorder: Differential diagnosis. J Am Acad Child Adolesc Psychiatry *27*: 300, 1988.
Nasser M: A prescription of vomiting; Historical footnotes. Int J Eating Disord *13*: 129, 1993.
Rast J, Johnston J M, Drum C, Conrin J: The relation of food quantity to rumination behavior. J Appl Behav Anal *14*: 221, 1981.
Stunkard A J, Stellar E, editors: *Eating and Its Disorders*. Raven, New York, 1984.

# Tic Disorders

Tics are involuntary, sudden, rapid, recurrent, non-rhythmic, stereotyped motor movements or vocalizations. Motor and vocal tics are divided into those that are simple and those that are complex. Simple motor tics are those composed of repetitive, rapid contractions of functionally similar muscle groups—for example, eye blinking, neck jerking, shoulder shrugging, and facial grimacing. Common simple vocal tics include coughing, throat clearing, grunting, sniffing, snorting, and barking. Complex motor tics appear to be more purposeful and ritualistic than are simple motor tics. Common complex motor tics include grooming behaviors, the smelling of objects, jumping, touching behaviors, echopraxia (the imitation of observed behavior), and copropraxia (the display of obscene gestures). Complex vocal tics include repeating words or phrases out of context, coprolalia (the use of obscene words or phrases), palilalia (the repetition of one's own words), and echolalia (the repetition of the last-heard words of others).

Tic disorders include a number of transient and chronic conditions severe enough to cause impairment. The fourth edition of *Diagnostic and Statistical Manual of Mental Disorders* (DSM-IV) contains four tic disorders: Tourette's disorder, chronic motor or vocal tic disorder, transient tic disorder, and tic disorder not otherwise specified. In contrast to the revised third edition of DSM (DSM-III-R), DSM-IV provides the definition of a tic parenthetically within the criteria of each tic disorder except tic disorder not otherwise specified.

In all the tic disorders, stressful situations and anxiety may result in an exacerbation of tics. Some persons with tic disorders have the ability to suppress the tics for minutes or hours, but other persons, especially young children, either are not cognizant of their tics or experience their tics as irresistible. Tics may be attenuated by sleep, relaxation, or absorption in an activity. Tics often disappear during sleep, but tics do occur while some persons are asleep.

## TOURETTE'S DISORDER

Georges Gilles de la Tourette first described a patient with what came to be known as Tourette's disorder in 1885, while he was studying with Jean-Martin Charcot in France. He noted a syndrome among several patients that included multiple motor tics, coprolalia, and echolalia.

## Epidemiology

The lifetime prevalence of Tourette's disorder is estimated to be 4 to 5 per 10,000. The onset of the motor component of the disorder generally occurs by age 7 years; vocal tics emerge on average by age 11 years. Tourette's disorder occurs about three times more often in boys than in girls.

## Etiology

**Genetic factors.**   Increasing evidence indicates that genetic factors play a role in the development of Tourette's disorder. Twin studies have indicated that concordance for the disorder in monozygotic twins is significantly greater than in dizygotic twins. The fact that Tourette's disorder and chronic motor or vocal tic disorder are likely to occur in the same families lends support to the view that the disorders are part of a genetically determined spectrum. The sons of mothers with Tourette's disorder seem to be at the highest risk for the disorder. Evidence in some families indicates that Tourette's disorder is transmitted in an autosomal dominant fashion. There is a relation between Tourett's disorder and attention-deficit/hyperactivity disorder; up to half of all Tourett's disorder patients also have attention-deficit/hyperactivity disorder. A relation has also been found between Tourette's disorder and obsessive-compulsive disorder; up to 40 percent of all Tourette's disorder patients also have obsessive-compulsive disorder. In addition, first-degree relatives of persons with Tourette's disorder are at high risk for the development of Tourette's disorder, chronic motor or vocal tic disorder, and obsessive-compulsive disorder. In view of the presence of symptoms of attention-deficit/hyperactivity disorder in more than half of the patients with Tourette's disorder, questions arise regarding a genetic relation between those two disorders.

**Neurochemical and neuroanatomical factors.**   Compelling evidence of dopamine system involvement in tic disorders includes the observations that pharmacological agents that antagonize dopamine—haloperidol (Haldol), pimozide (Orap), and fluphenazine (Prolixin)—suppress tics and that agents that increase central dopaminergic activity—methylphenidate (Ritalin), amphetamines, pemoline (Cylert), and cocaine—tend to exacerbate tics. However, the relation of tics to the dopamine system is not simple, since in some cases antipsychotic medications, such as haloperidol, are not effective in the reduction of tics and the effect of stimulants on tic disorders has been reported as variable. In some cases, Tourette's disorder has emerged during treatment with antipsychotic medications, leading to a term "tardive Tourette's disorder" because of that disorder's similarity to tardive dyskinesia. Endogenous opiates may be involved in tic disorders and obsessive-compulsive disorder. Some evidence indicates that pharmacological agents that antagonize endogenous opiates—for example, naltrexone (Trexan)—reduce tics and attention deficits in Tourette's disorder patients.

Abnormalities in the noradrenergic system have been implicated by the reduction of tics in some cases by clonidine (Catapres), an α-adrenergic agonist that reduces the release of norepinephrine in the central nervous system, which may reduce activity in the dopaminergic system.

Abnormalities in the basal ganglia result in various movement disorders, such as in Huntington's disease, and are implicated as possible sites of disturbance in Tourette's disorder, obsessive-compulsive disorder, and attention-deficit/hyperactivity disorder.

## Diagnosis and Clinical Features

To make a diagnosis of Tourette's disorder, the clinician must obtain a history of multiple motor tics and the emergence of at least one vocal tic at some point in the disorder. According to DSM-IV, the tics must occur many times a day nearly every day or intermittently for more than one year. The average age of onset of tics is 7 years, but the tics may occur as early as age 2 years. The onset must occur before age 18 years. According to DSM-IV, the tics may not be the direct result of a substance (such as stimulants) or a medical condition (Table 42–1). In Tourette's disorder, the initial tics are in the face and the neck. Over time, the tics tend to occur in a downward progression.

The most commonly described tics are those affecting (1) the face and the head: grimacing; puckering of the forehead; raising of the eyebrows: blinking eyelids: winking: wrinkling of the nose; trembling nostrils; twitching mouth; displaying of the teeth; biting of the lips and other parts; extruding the tongue; protracting the lower jaw; nodding, jerking, or shaking the head; twisting the neck; looking sideways; and head rolling; (2) the arms and the hands: jerking of the hands, jerking of the arms, plucking fingers, writhing fingers, and clenching fists; (3) the body

and the lower extremities: shrugging of the shoulders; shaking a foot, a knee, or a toe; peculiarities of gait; body writhing; and jumping; and (4) the respiratory and alimentary systems: hiccuping, sighing, yawning, snuffing, blowing through the nostrils, whistling inspiration, exaggerated breathing, belching, sucking or smacking sounds, and clearing the throat.

Typically, prodromal behavioral symptoms—such as irritability, attention difficulties, and poor frustration tolerance—are evident before or coincide with the onset of tics. More than 25 percent of the persons in some studies received stimulants for a diagnosis of attention-deficit/hyperactivity disorder before receiving a diagnosis of Tourette's disorder.

The most frequent initial symptom is an eye-blink tic, followed by a head tic or a facial grimace. Most of the complex motor and vocal symptoms emerge several years after the initial symptoms. Coprolalia usually begins in early adolescence and occurs in about one third of all cases. Mental coprolalia—in which the patient thinks a sudden, intrusive, socially unacceptable thought or obscene word—may also occur. In some severe cases, physical injuries, including retinal detachment and orthopedic problems, have resulted from severe tics.

Obsessions, compulsions, attention difficulties, impulsivity, and personality problems have been associated with Tourette's disorder. Attention difficulties often precede the onset of tics, whereas obsessive-compulsive symptoms often occur after the onset of tics. It is still being debated whether those problems usually develop secondarily to the patient's tics or are caused primarily by the same underlying pathobiological condition.

Many tics have an aggressive or sexual component, which may result in serious social consequences for the patient. Phenomenologically, the tics resemble a failure of censorship, both conscious and unconscious, with increased impulsivity and a too-ready transformation of thought into action.

A 46-year-old married man was referred for psychiatric evaluation in 1966 because of unremitting tics. At age 13 he had a persistent eye blink, soon followed by lip smacking, head shaking, and barkinglike noises. In spite of those symptoms, he functioned well academically and eventually graduated from high school with honors. He was drafted during World War II. In the army his tics subsided significantly but were still troublesome and eventually resulted in a medical discharge. He married, had two children, and worked as a semiskilled laborer and foreman. At the age of 30, his symptoms included tics of the head, neck, and shoulders; hitting his forehead with his hand and various objects; repeated throat clearing; spitting; and shouting out, "Hey, hey, hey; la, la, la." Six years later, noisy coprolalia started; he would emit a string of profanities—such as "Fuck you, you cocksucking bastard"—in the middle of a sentence and then resume his conversation.

From 1951 to 1957, various treatments, all without benefit, were tried: insulin shock therapy, electroshock treatment, and the administration of various phenothiazines and antidepressants. The patient's social life became increasingly constricted because of his symptoms. He was unable to go to church or to the movies because of his cursing and noises. He worked at night to avoid social embarrassment. His family and friends became increasingly intolerant of his symptoms, and his daughters refused to bring friends home. He was depressed

---

**Table 42–1**
**Diagnostic Criteria for Tourette's Disorder**

A. Both multiple motor and one or more vocal tics have been present at some time during the illness, although not necessarily concurrently. (A *tic* is a sudden, rapid, recurrent, nonrhythmic, stereotyped motor movement or vocalization.)

B. The tics occur many times a day (usually in bouts), nearly every day or intermittently throughout a period of more than 1 year, and during this period there was never a tic-free period of more than 3 consecutive months.

C. The disturbance causes marked distress or significant impairment in social, occupational, or other important areas of functioning.

D. The onset is before age 18 years.

E. The disturbance is not due to the direct physiological effects of a substance (e.g., stimulants) or a general medical condition (e.g., Huntington's disease or postviral encephalitis).

Table from DSM-IV, *Diagnostic and Statistical Manual of Mental Disorders*, ed 4. Copyright American Psychiatric Association, Washington, 1994. Used with permission.

because of his enforced isolation and the seeming hopelessness of finding effective treatment. At the age of 46, he sought a prefrontal lobotomy; but, after psychiatric evaluation, his request was denied. That led to the 1966 psychiatric referral.

*Discussion.* The patient had the characteristic features of Tourette's disorder: onset before age 18, multiple motor and one or more vocal tics (involuntary cursing or shouting), and the tics' occurring many times a day (usually in bouts) nearly every day or intermittently throughout a period of more than one year.

Largely for historical reasons is the disorder classified as a mental disorder, rather than a neurological disorder. Originally, the coprolalia and the other bizarre symptoms were thought to be pregenital conversion symptoms. Now most investigators believe that the cause of the disorder is organic and that whatever psychological disturbance may be present is best understood as a reaction to the chronic, incapacitating symptoms. In this case, when the symptoms of Tourette's disorder were brought under control, the patient was no longer depressed.

When the patient was evaluated, he was described as being "depressed because of his enforced isolation and the seeming hopelessness of finding effective treatment." That description raised the question of adjustment disorder with depressed mood or of major depressive disorder. Adjustment disorder generally does not include situations in which patients are distressed because of the consequences of the symptoms of their mental disorder or the reactions of others to the disorder. Such distress is commonplace in chronic illnesses and is better thought of as an associated feature of the illness, rather than an adjustment disorder. However, if the depression is severe enough to meet the criteria for major depressive disorder, the additional diagnosis of major depressive disorder is appropriate. In this case, no information about the other features of a depressive disorder made such a diagnosis necessary.

**Pathology and laboratory examination.** There is no specific laboratory diagnostic test for Tourette's disorder. However, many patients with Tourette's disorder have non-specific abnormal electroencephalogram (EEG) findings. Computed tomography (CT) and magnetic resonance imaging (MRI) scans have not revealed specific structural lesions, although about 10 percent of all Tourette's disorder patients show some nonspecific abnormality on CT scans.

## Differential Diagnosis

Tics must be differentiated from other disordered movements (for example, dystonic, choreiform, athetoid, myoclonic, and hemiballismic movements) and the neurological diseases of which they are characteristic (for example, Huntington's disease, parkinsonism, Sydenham's chorea, and Wilson's disease), as listed in Table 42-2. Tremors, mannerisms, and stereotypic movement disorder (for example, head banging or body rocking) must also be distinguished from tic disorders. The voluntary nature of stereotypic movement disorder and the fact that such movements do not cause subjective distress differentiate it from tic disorders. Compulsions are also intentional behaviors.

Both autistic and mentally retarded children may exhibit symptoms similar to those seen in tic disorders, including Tourette's disorder. Tardive dyskinesia must also be considered in those patients who are receiving or have received medications that may cause that untoward effect. Before instituting antipsychotic medication, the clinician must make a baseline evaluation of preexisting abnormal movements, as such medication can mask abnormal movements. If the movements occur later, they can be mistaken for tardive dyskinesia.

Stimulant medications (such as methylphenidate, amphetamines, and pemoline) have been reported to exacerbate preexisting tics in some cases. Those effects have been reported primarily in some children and adolescents being treated for attention-deficit/hyperactivity disorder. In most but not all cases, after the drug was discontinued, the tics remitted or returned to premedication levels. Most experts suggest that children and adolescents who experience tics while receiving stimulants are probably predisposed genetically and would have experienced tics regardless of their treatment with stimulants. Until the situation is clarified, clinicians should use great caution and should frequently monitor the children at risk for tics who are given stimulants.

## Course and Prognosis

Untreated, Tourette's disorder is usually a chronic, life-long disease with relative remissions and exacerbations. Initial symptoms may decrease, persist, or increase, and old symptoms may be replaced by new ones. Severely afflicted persons may have serious emotional problems, including major depressive disorder. Some of those difficulties appear to be associated with Tourette's disorder, whereas others result from severe social, academic, and vocational consequences, which are frequent sequelae of the disorder. In some cases, despair over the disruption of social and occupational functioning is so severe that the persons contemplate and attempt suicide. But some children with Tourette's disorder have satisfactory peer relationships, function well in school, and have adequate self-esteem; they may need no treatment and can be monitored by their pediatricians.

## Treatment

Pharmacological treatments are most effective for Tourette's disorder, but patients with mild cases may not require medication. Psychotherapy is usually ineffective as a primary treatment modality, although it may help the patient cope with the symptoms of the disorder and any concomitant personality and behavioral difficulties that arise.

Several behavioral techniques—including massed (negative) practice, self-monitoring, incompatible response training, presentation and removal of positive reinforcement, and habit reversal treatment—were reviewed by Stanley A. Hobbs. He reported that tic frequency was reduced in many cases, particularly with habit reversal treatment, but relatively few studies have reported clinically significant changes. In general, behavioral treatments were most effective in treating transient and chronic motor or vocal tic disorders, but relatively few cases of Tourette's disorder responded favorably. Behavior therapy currently seems to be most useful in reducing stresses that may aggravate Tourette's disorder. Whether behavior therapy and pharmacotherapy together have a synergistic effect has not been sufficiently investigated.

**Table 42–2**
**Differential Diagnosis of Tic Disorders**

| Disease or Syndrome | Age at Onset | Associated Features | Course | Predominant Type of Movement |
|---|---|---|---|---|
| Hallervorden-Spatz | Childhood–adolescence | May be associated with optic atrophy, club feet, retinitis pigmentosa, dysarthria, dementia, ataxia, emotional lability, spasticity, autosomal recessive inheritance | Progressive to death in 5 to 20 years | Choreic, athetoid, myoclonic |
| Dystonia musculorum deformans | Childhood–adolescence | Autosomal recessive inheritance commonly, primarily among Ashkenazi Jews; a more benign autosomal dominant form also occurs | Variable course, often progressive but with rare remissions | Dystonia |
| Sydenham's chorea | Childhood, usually 5–15 years | More common in females, usually associated with rheumatic fever (carditis elevated ASLO titers) | Usually self-limited | Choreiform |
| Huntington's disease | Usually 30–50 years, but childhood forms are known | Autosomal dominant inheritance, dementia, caudate atrophy on CT scan | Progressive to death in 10 to 15 years after onset | Choreiform |
| Wilson's disease (hepatolenticular degeneration) | Usually 10–25 years | Kayser-Fleischer rings, liver dysfunction, inborn error of copper metabolism; autosomal recessive inheritance | Progressive to death without chelating therapy | Wing-beating tremor, dystonia |
| Hyperreflexias (including latah, myriachit, jumper disease of Maine) | Generally in childhood (dominant inheritance) | Familial; may have generalized rigidity and autosomal inheritance | Nonprogressive | Excessive startle response; may have echolalia, coprolalia, and forced obedience |
| Myoclonic disorders | Any age | Numerous causes, some familial, usually no vocalizations | Variable, depending on cause | Myoclonus |
| Myoclonic dystonia | 5–47 years | Nonfamilial, no vocalizations | Nonprogressive | Torsion dystonia with myoclonic jerks |
| Paroxysmal myoclonic dystonia with vocalization | Childhood | Attention, hyperactive, and learning disorders; movements interfere with ongoing activity | Nonprogressive | Bursts of regular, repetitive clonic (less tonic) movements and vocalizations |
| Tardive Tourette's disorder syndromes | Variable (after antipsychotic medication use) | Reported to be precipitated by discontinuation or reduction of medication | May terminate after increase or decrease of dosage | Orofacial dyskinesias, choreoathetosis, tics, vocalization |
| Neuroacanthocytosis | Third or fourth decade | Acanthocytosis, muscle wasting, parkinsonism, autosomal recessive inheritance | Variable | Orofacial dyskinesia and limb chorea, tics, vocalization |
| Encephalitis lethargica | Variable | Shouting fits, bizarre behavior, psychosis, Parkinson's disease | Variable | Simple and complex motor and vocal tics, coprolalia, echolalia, echopraxia, palilalia |

*Continued*

**Table 42–2**
*Continued*

| Disease or Syndrome | Age at Onset | Associated Features | Course | Predominant Type of Movement |
|---|---|---|---|---|
| Gasoline inhalation | Variable | Abnormal EEG; symmetrical theta and theta bursts frontocentrally | Variable | Simple motor and vocal tics |
| Postangiographic complications | Variable | Emotional lability, amnestic syndrome | Variable | Simple motor and complex vocal tics, palilalia |
| Postinfectious | Variable | EEG: occasional asymmetrical theta bursts before movements, elevated ASLO titers | Variable | Simple motor and vocal tics, echopraxia |
| Posttraumatic | Variable | Asymmetrical tic distribution | Variable | Complex motor tics |
| Carbon monoxide poisoning | Variable | Inappropriate sexual behavior | Variable | Simple and complex motor and vocal tics, coprolalia, echolalia, palilialia |
| XYY genetic disorder | Infancy | Aggressive behavior | Static | Simple motor and vocal tics |
| XXY and 9ₚ mosaicism | Infancy | Multiple physical anomalies, mental retardation | Static | Simple motor and vocal tics |
| Duchenne's muscular dystrophy (X-linked recessive) | Childhood | Mild mental retardation | Progressive | Motor and vocal tics |
| Fragile X syndrome | Childhood | Mental retardation, facial dysmorphism, seizures, autistic features | Static | Simple motor and vocal tics, coprolalia |
| Developmental and perinatal disorders | Infancy, childhood | Seizures, EEG and CT abnormalities, psychosis, agressivity, hyperactivity, Ganser's syndrome, compulsivity, torticollis | Variable | Motor and vocal tics, echolalia |

Table adapted from A K Shapiro, E Shapiro, J G Young, T E Feinberg: *Gilles de la Tourette Syndrome*, ed 2. Raven, New York, 1987. Used with permission.

**Pharmacotherapy.** Haloperidol is the most frequently prescribed drug for Tourette's disorder. Up to 80 percent of the patients have a favorable response; their symptoms decrease by as much as 70 to 90 percent of baseline frequency. Follow-up studies, however, indicate that only 20 to 30 percent of those patients continue to take long-term maintenance therapy. Discontinuation is often based on the drug's adverse effects.

Haloperidol appears to be most effective at relatively low dosages. The initial daily dosage for adolescents and adults is usually between 0.25 and 0.5 mg of haloperidol. Haloperidol is not approved for use in children under 3 years of age. For children between 3 and 12, the recommended total daily dosage is between 0.05 and 0.075 mg per kg, administered in divided doses either two or three times a day. That dosage imposes a daily limit of 3 mg of haloperidol for a 40-kg child. The dosage for all patients should be increased slowly, to minimize the likelihood of an acute dystonic reaction. The maximum effective dosage in adolescents and adults is often in the range of 3 to 4 mg a day, but some patients require dosages of up to 10 to 15 mg a day.

Patients and their parents, when appropriate, must be made aware of the drug's possible immediate and long-term adverse effects. The clinician must forewarn them of the possibilities of acute dystonic reactions and parkinsonian symptoms. Although the prophylactic use of an anticholinergic agent is not recommended, it is appropriate to prescribe diphenhydramine (Benadryl) or benztropine (Cogentin) to the patient, so that it is available should an acute dystonic reaction or parkinsonian effects occur at home or on vacation. Other effects of special concern are cognitive dulling, which can impair school performance and learning, and the risk of tardive dyskinesia. School phobias in children and disabling social phobias in adults have been reported during the early phase of treatment, but the phobias usually remit within a few weeks after discontinuing haloperidol.

Pimozide, an inhibitor of postsynaptic dopamine receptors, is also effective in treating Tourette's disorder. In a recent large study, haloperidol was more effective than pimozide. Pimozide, like haloperidol, should not be used to treat simple tics. Pimozide is an antipsychotic and has adverse effects similar to those of other antipsychotics. Furthermore, adverse cardiac effects are unusually frequent, and deaths have occurred at high dosages. Notwithstanding that, pimozide appears to be safe at recommended dosages, with cardiotoxicity limited to prolonged QT wave intervals. Electrocardiograms must be performed at baseline and periodically during treatment. There is little experience in administering pimozide to children under age 12 years.

The initial dosage of pimozide is usually 1 to 2 mg daily in divided doses; the dosage may be increased every other day. Most patients are maintained at less than 0.2 mg per kg a day or 10 mg a day, whichever is less. A dosage of 0.3 mg per kg a day or 20 mg a day should never be exceeded.

Although not presently approved for use in Tourette's disorder, clonidine, a noradrenergic antagonist, has been reported in several studies to be efficacious; 40 to 70 percent of patients benefited from the medication. Some clinicians have used it after they have considered its risks and benefits and fully informed the patient and, when appropriate, the parents. Clonidine has a slower onset of action than does haloperidol, and improvement may continue for more than a year in some cases. In addition to the improvement in tic symptoms, patients may experience less tension, a greater sense of well-being, and a longer attention span than before receiving clonidine.

Children suffering from tics and severe attention-deficit/hyperactivity disorder can be treated with desipramine (Norpramin) for their attention problems. The benzodiazepines may be useful in diminishing anxiety in some patients, but they do not appear to significantly reduce the frequency of tics.

Other tricyclic drugs, such as nortriptyline (Aventyl), have also been used to treat children with attention-deficit/hyperactivity disorder and Tourette's disorder with some degree of success. Although clinicians must weigh the risks versus the benefits of using stimulants in cases of severe hyperactivity and comorbid tics, a recent study reported that methylphenidate reduced the occurrence of vocal tics in some children with hyperactivity and tic disorders. Another recent case report indicated that bupropion (Wellbutrin), an antidepressant of the aminoketone class, resulted in increased tic behavior in several children being treated for Tourette's disorder and attention-deficit/hyperactivity disorder.

## CHRONIC MOTOR OR VOCAL TIC DISORDER

In chronic motor or vocal tic disorder, motor or vocal tics but not both have been present intermittently or nearly every day for more than one year. According to DSM-IV criteria, the disorder must have its onset before the age of 18 years, and it is not diagnosed if the criteria for Tourette's disorder have ever been met.

### Epidemiology

The rate of chronic motor or vocal tic disorder has been estimated to be from 100 to 1,000 times greater than that of Tourette's disorder. School-age boys are at highest risk, but the incidence is not known. Although the disorder was once believed to be rare, current estimates of the prevalence of chronic motor or vocal tic disorder range from 1 to 2 percent.

### Etiology

Both Tourette's disorder and chronic motor or vocal tic disorder aggregate within the same families. Twin studies have found a high concordance for either Tourette's disorder or chronic motor tics in monozygotic twins. That finding lends support to the importance of hereditary factors in the transmission of at least some tic disorders.

### Diagnosis and Clinical Features

The onset of chronic motor or vocal tic disorder appears to be in early childhood. The types of tics and their locations are similar to those in transient tic disorder. Chronic vocal tics are considerably rarer than chronic motor tics. The chronic vocal tics are usually much less conspicuous than those in Tourette's disorder. The vocal tics are usually not loud or intense; they consist of grunts or other noises caused by thoracic, abdominal, or diaphragmatic contractions; the tics are not primarily from the vocal cords. The DSM-IV diagnostic criteria are given in Table 42–3.

**Table 42–3**
**Diagnostic Criteria for Chronic Motor or Vocal Tic Disorder**

A. Single or multiple motor or vocal tics (i.e., sudden, rapid, recurrent, nonrhythmic, stereotyped motor movements or vocalizations), but not both, have been present at some time during the illness.

B. The tics occur many times a day nearly every day or intermittently throughout a period of more than 1 year, and during this period there was never a tic-free period of more than 3 consecutive months.

C. The disturbance causes marked distress or significant impairment in social, occupational, or other important areas of functioning.

D. The onset is before 18 years.

E. The disturbance is not due to the direct physiological effects of a substance (e.g., stimulants) or a general medical condition (e.g., Huntington's disease or postviral encephalitis)

F. Criteria have never been met for Tourette's disorder.

Table from DSM-IV, *Diagnostic and Statistical Manual of Mental Disorders*, ed 4. Copyright American Psychiatric Association, Washington, 1994. Used with permission.

## Differential Diagnosis

Chronic motor tics must be differentiated from a variety of other motor movements, including choreiform movements, myoclonus, restless legs syndrome, akathisia, and dystonias. Involuntary vocal utterances can occur in certain neurological disorders, such as Huntington's disease and Parkinson's disease.

## Course and Prognosis

Children whose tics start between the ages of 6 and 8 years seem to have the best outcomes. Symptoms usually last for four to six years and stop in early adolescence. Those children whose tics involve the limbs or the trunk tend to do less well than those with only facial tics.

## Treatment

The treatment of chronic motor or vocal tic disorder depends on the severity and the frequency of the tics; the patient's subjective distress; the effects of the tics on school or work, job performance, and socialization; and the presence of any other concomitant mental disorder.

Psychotherapy may be indicated to minimize the secondary emotional problems caused by the tics. Several studies have found that behavioral techniques, particularly habit reversal treatments, have been effective in treating chronic motor or vocal tic disorder. Antianxiety agents have not been successful. Haloperidol has been helpful in some cases, but the risks must be weighed against the possible clinical benefits because of the drug's adverse effects, including the development of tardive dyskinesia.

## TRANSIENT TIC DISORDER

Transient tic disorder consists of single or multiple motor or vocal tics that occur many times a day nearly every day for at least four weeks but for no longer than 12 consecutive months. According to DSM-IV, the disorder must have its onset before age 18 years; it is not diagnosed if either Tourette's disorder or chronic motor or vocal tic disorder has ever been diagnosed.

### Epidemiology

Transient, ticlike habit movements and nervous muscular twitches are common in children. From 5 to 24 percent of all school-age children have a history of tics. The prevalence of tics as defined here is unknown.

### Etiology

Transient tic disorder probably has either organic or psychogenic origins, with some tics combining elements of both. Organic tics are probably most likely to progress to Tourette's disorder and have an increased family history of tics, whereas psychogenic tics are most likely to remit spontaneously. Those tics that progress to chronic motor or vocal tic disorder are most likely to have components

of both. Tics of all sorts are exacerbated by stress and anxiety, but no evidence is available that tics are caused by stress or anxiety.

## Diagnosis and Clinical Features

The DSM-IV criteria for establishing the diagnosis of transient tic disorder are as follows: (1) The tics are single or multiple motor or vocal tics. (2) The tics occur many times a day nearly every day for at least four weeks but for no longer than 12 consecutive months. (3) The patient has no history of Tourette's disorder or chronic motor or vocal tic disorder. (4) The onset is before age 18. (5) The tics do not occur exclusively during substance intoxication or a general medical condition. The diagnosis should specify whether a single episode or recurrent episodes are present (Table 42-4).

Transient tic disorder can be distinguished from chronic motor or vocal tic disorder and Tourette's disorder only by observing the symptoms' progression over time.

## Course and Prognosis

Most persons with transient tic disorder do not progress to a more serious tic disorder. Their tics either disappear permanently or recur during periods of special stress. Only a small percentage go on to chronic motor or vocal tic disorder or Tourette's disorder.

## Treatment

Whether the tics will disappear spontaneously, progress, or become chronic is unclear in the beginning. Focusing attention on tics may exacerbate them, so the clinician often recommends that, at first, the family disregard the tics as much as possible. But if the tics are so severe

**Table 42–4**
**Diagnostic Criteria for Transient Tic Disorder**

A. Single or multiple motor and/or vocal tics (i.e., sudden, rapid, recurrent, nonrhythmic, stereotyped motor movements or vocalizations)

B. The tics occur many times a day, nearly every day for at least four weeks but for no longer than 12 consecutive months.

C. The disturbance causes marked distress or significant impairment in social, occupational, or other important areas of functioning.

D. The onset is before age 18 years.

E. The disturbance is not due to the direct physiological effects of a substance (e.g., stimulants) or a general medical condition (e.g., Huntington's disease or postviral encephalitis).

F. Criteria have never been met for Tourette's disorder or chronic motor or vocal tic disorder.

*Specify* if: **Single episode** or **recurrent.**

Table from DSM-IV, *Diagnostic and Statistical Manual of Mental Disorders*, ed 4. Copyright American Psychiatric Association, Washington, 1994. Used with permission.

**Table 42–5**
**Diagnostic Criteria for Tic Disorder**
**Not Otherwise Specified**

This category is for disorders characterized by tics that do not meet criteria for a specific tic disorder. Examples include tics lasting less than 4 weeks or tics with an onset after age 18 years.

Table from DSM-IV, *Diagnostic and Statistical Manual of Mental Disorders*, ed 4. Copyright American Psychiatric Association, Washington, 1994. Used with permission.

that they impair the patient or if they are accompanied by significant emotional disturbances, complete psychiatric and pediatric neurological examinations are recommended. Treatment depends on the results of the evaluations. Psychopharmacology is not recommended unless the symptoms are unusually severe and disabling. Several studies have found that behavioral techniques, particularly habit reversal treatment, have been effective in treating transient tics.

## TIC DISORDER NOT OTHERWISE SPECIFIED

The DSM-IV category of tic disorder not otherwise specified is used for tic disorders that do not meet the criteria for any of the above disorders (Table 42–5).

**References**

Caine E D, McBride M C, Chiverton P, Bamford K A, Rediess S, Shiao J: Tourette's syndrome in Monroe County school children. Neurology *38*: 472, 1988.

Cohen D J, Leckman J F, Shaywitz B A: The Tourette's syndrome and other tics. In *The Clinical Guide to Child Psychiatry,* D Shaffer, A A Ehrandt, L L Greenhill, editors, p 3. Free Press, New York, 1985.

Friedhoff A J, Chase T N, editors: *Gilles de la Tourette Syndrome.* Raven, New York, 1982.

Gadow K D, Nolan E E, Sverd J: Methylphenidate in hyperactive boys with comorbid tic disorder: II. Short-term behavioral effects in school settings. J Am Acad Child Adolesc Psychiatry *31*: 462, 1992.

Hobbs S A, Dorsett P G, Dahlquist L M: Tic disorders. In *Behavior Therapy with Children and Adolescents: A Clinical Approach,* M Hersen, V B Van Hasselt, editors, p 241. Wiley, New York, 1987.

Leckman J F, Walkup J T, Riddle M A, Toubin K E, Cohen D J: Tic disorders. In *Psychopharmocology: The Third Generation of Progress,* H Y Meltzer, editor, p 102. Raven, New York, 1987.

Price R A, Kidd K K, Cohen D J, Pauls D L, Leckman J F: A twin study of Tourette's syndrome Arch Gen Psychiatry *43*: 815, 1985.

Segal N L, Dysken M W, Bouchard T J, Petersen N L, Eckert E D, Heston L L: Tourette's disorder in a set of reared-apart triplets: Genetic and environmental influences. Am J Psychiatry *147*: 196, 1990.

Shapiro A K, Shapiro E: Tic disorders. In *Comprehensive Textbook of Psychiatry,* ed 5, H I Kaplan, B J Sadock, editors, p 1865. Williams & Wilkins, Baltimore, 1989.

Shapiro E, Shapiro A K, Fulop G, Hubbard M, Mendell J, Nordie J, Phillips R: Controlled study of haloperidol, pimozide and placebo for the treatment of Gilles de la Tourette's syndrome. Arch Gen Psychiatry *46*: 722, 1989.

Spencer T, Biederman J, Steingard R, Wilens T: Bupropion exacerbates tics in children with attention-deficit hyperactivity disorder and Tourette's syndrome. J Am Acad Child Adolesc Psychiatry *32*: 211, 1993.

Spencer T, Biederman J, Wilens T, Steingard R, Geist D: Nortriptyline treatment of children with attention-deficit hyperactivity disorder and tic disorder or Tourette's syndrome. J Am Acad Child Adolesc Psychiatry *32*: 205, 1993.

Steingard R, Biederman J, Spencer T, Wilens T, Gonzalez A: Comparison of clonidine response in the treatment of attention-deficit hyperactivity disorder with and without comorbid tic disorders. J Am Acad Child Adolesc Psychiatry *32*: 350, 1993.

# Communication Disorders

## 43.1 / Expressive Language Disorder

With expressive language disorder the child is below the expected ability in vocabulary, the use of correct tenses, the production of complex sentences, and the recall of words. Language disability can be acquired at any time during childhood (for example, secondary to a trauma or a neurological disorder), or it can be developmental and is usually congenital without an obvious cause. The majority of childhood language disorders fall within the developmental category. In either case, deficits in receptive skills (comprehension of language) or in expressive skills (ability to express language) can occur. Expressive language disturbance often occurs in the absence of comprehension difficulties, whereas receptive dysfunction generally also affects the expression of language.

Children with only expressive language disorder have courses, prognoses, and comorbid diagnoses that are different from those of children with mixed receptive/expressive language disorder. In the revised third edition of *Diagnostic and Statistical Manual of Mental Disorders* (DSM-III-R), developmental expressive language disorder and developmental receptive language disorder were listed separately, although in most cases, when receptive disorder occurs, expressive disorder co-occurs. In the fourth edition (DSM-IV) the diagnosis of expressive language disorder still exists but not receptive language disorder. In DSM-IV, mixed receptive/expressive language disorder is diagnosed when both receptive and expressive language syndromes are present and mixed receptive/expressive language disorder is an exclusionary criterion for expressive language disorder. Thus, in DSM-IV, receptive language disorder can be diagnosed only if the full syndrome of expressive disorder is also present.

In DSM-IV, expressive language disorder and mixed receptive/expressive language disorder are not limited to developmental language disabilities; the acquired forms of language disturbances are included.

To meet the criteria for expressive language disorder, the patient must have scores from standardized measures of expressive language that are markedly below those of standardized nonverbal I.Q. subtests and standardized tests of receptive language.

## EPIDEMIOLOGY

The prevalence of expressive language disorder ranges from 3 to 10 percent of all school-age children, with most estimates between 3 and 5 percent. The disorder is two to three times more common in boys than in girls. The disorder is also most prevalent among children whose relatives have a family history of phonological disorder or other communication disorders.

## ETIOLOGY

The cause of expressive language disorder is not known. Subtle cerebral damage and maturational lags in cerebral development have been postulated as being the underlying causes, but no evidence supports those theories. Left-handedness or ambilaterality appears to increase the risk.

Unknown genetic factors have been suspected to have a role, because the relatives of children with learning disorders have a relatively high incidence of expressive language disorder.

## DIAGNOSIS

The presence of markedly below-age-level verbal or sign language, accompanied by a low score on standardized expressive verbal tests, is diagnostic of expressive language disorder (Table 43.1–1). The disorder is not caused by a pervasive developmental disorder, as the child shows a desire to communicate. If the child uses any language, it is severely retarded, vocabulary is limited, grammar is simple, and articulation is variable. Inner language or the appropriate use of toys and household objects is present.

To confirm the diagnosis, the clinician should have the child tested with standardized expressive language and nonverbal intellectual tests. Observations of the child's verbal and sign language patterns in various settings (for example, in the school yard, the classroom, the home, and the playroom) and during interactions with other children help ascertain the severity and the specific areas of the child's impairment and aid in the early detection of behavioral and emotional complications.

The family history should include the presence or the absence of expressive language disorder among relatives.

An audiogram is indicated for very young children and for those children whose hearing acuity appears to be impaired.

**Table 43.1–1**
**Diagnostic Criteria for Expressive Language Disorder**

A. The scores obtained from standardized individually administered measures of expressive language development are substantially below those obtained from standardized measures of both nonverbal intellectual capacity and receptive language development. The disturbance may be manifest clinically by symptoms that include having a markedly limited vocabulary, making errors in tense, or having difficulty recalling words or producing sentences with developmentally appropriate length or complexity.

B. The difficulties with expressive language interfere with academic or occupational achievement or with social communication.

C. Criteria are not met for mixed receptive-expressive language disorder or a pervasive developmental disorder.

D. If mental retardation, a speech-motor or sensory deficit, or environmental deprivation is present, the language difficulties are in excess of those usually associated with these problems.

**Coding note:** if a speech-motor or sensory deficit or a neurological condition is present, code the condition on Axis III.

Table from DSM-IV, *Diagnostic and Statistical Manual of Mental Disorders*, ed 4. Copyright American Psychiatric Association, Washington, 1994. Used with permission.

## CLINICAL FEATURES

Severe forms of the disorder are evident before the age of 3 years. Less severe forms may not occur until early adolescence, when language ordinarily becomes complex. The essential feature of the child with expressive language disorder is a marked impairment in the development of age-appropriate expressive language, which results in the use of verbal or sign language that is markedly below the expected level, considering the child's nonverbal intellectual capacity. The child's language understanding (decoding) skills remain relatively intact.

The disorder becomes conspicuous by about the age of 18 months, when the child fails to utter spontaneously or even to echo single words or sounds. Even simple words, such as "mama" and "dada," are absent from the child's active vocabulary, and the child points or uses gestures to indicate desires. The child seems to want to communicate, maintains eye contact, relates well to the mother, and enjoys games such as pat-a-cake and peekaboo.

The child's repertoire of vocabulary is severely limited. At 18 months the child can, at most, comprehend simple commands and can point to common objects when they are named. When the child finally begins to speak, the language deficit becomes apparent. Articulation is usually immature. Numerous articulation errors are present but are inconsistent, particularly with such sounds as *th*, *r*, *s*, *z*, *y*, and *l*, which are either omitted or are substituted for other sounds.

By the age of 4, most children with expressive language disorder can speak in short phrases, but they appear to forget old words as they learn new ones. After beginning to speak, they acquire language more slowly than do normal children. Their use of various grammatical structures is also markedly lower than the age-expected level. Their developmental milestones may also be slightly delayed. Phonological disorder is often present. Developmental coordination disorder and enuresis are common associated disorders.

## Complications

Emotional problems involving poor self-image, frustration, and depression may develop in school-age children. Children with expressive language disorder may also have a learning disorder, manifested by reading retardation, that may result in serious difficulties in various academic subjects. The major learning difficulties are in perceptual skills and skills of recognizing and processing symbols in the proper sequence.

Other behavioral symptoms and problems that may appear in children with expressive language disorder include hyperactivity, short attention span, withdrawing behavior, thumb sucking, temper tantrums, bed-wetting, disobedience, accident-proneness, and conduct disorder. Neurological abnormalities have been reported in a number of children, including soft neurological signs, depressed vestibular responses, and electroencephalogram (EEG) abnormalities.

Many disorders—such as reading disorder, developmental coordination disorder, and other communication disorders—are associated with expressive language disorder. Children with expressive language disorder often have some degree of receptive impairment, although not always significant enough for the diagnosis of mixed receptive/expressive language disorder. Delayed motor milestones and a history of enuresis are common in children with expressive language disorder. Phonological disorder is commonly found in young children with the disorder.

A large study of children at a community speech and language clinic found that half of those with expressive language disorder met the criteria for another mental disorder, most commonly attention-deficit/hyperactivity disorder. Another recent study found that more than a third of the children referred to a psychiatric outpatient clinic had a language impairment.

## DIFFERENTIAL DIAGNOSIS

In mental retardation, the patient has an overall impairment in intellectual functioning, as shown by below-normal intelligence test scores in all areas. The nonverbal intellectual capacity and functioning of children with expressive language disorder are within normal limits.

In mixed receptive/expressive language disorder, comprehension of language (decoding) is markedly below the expected age-appropriate level, whereas, in expressive language disorder, language comprehension remains within normal limits.

In pervasive developmental disorders the affected children have, in addition to the cardinal cognitive characteristics, no inner language, symbolic or imagery play, appropriate use of gesture, or capacity to form warm and meaningful social relationships. Moreover, the children show little or no frustration with the inability to communicate verbally. In contrast, all those characteristics are present in children with expressive language disorder.

Children with acquired aphasia or dysphasia have a history of early normal language development, and the disordered language had its onset after a head trauma or another neurological disorder (for example, a seizure disorder).

Children with selective mutism have a history of normal language development, and their speech is limited to certain family members (for example, mother, father, and siblings). More girls than boys are affected by selective mutism, and the affected children are mostly shy and withdrawn outside the family.

## COURSE AND PROGNOSIS

In general, the prognosis for expressive language disorder is favorable. The rapidity and the degree of recovery depend on the severity of the disorder, the child's motivation to participate in therapies, and the timely institution of speech and other therapeutic interventions. The presence or the absence of other factors—such as moderate to severe hearing loss, mild mental retardation, and severe emotional problems—also affects the prognosis for recovery. As many as 50 percent of children with mild expressive language disorder recover spontaneously without any sign of language impairment, but children with severe expressive language disorder may later display the features of mild to moderate language impairment.

## TREATMENT

Language therapy should be started immediately after the diagnosis of expressive language disorder. Such therapy consists of behaviorally reinforced exercises and practice with phonemes (sound units), vocabulary, and sentence construction. The goal is to increase the number of phrases by using block-building methods and conventional speech therapies.

Psychotherapy is not usually indicated unless the language-disordered child shows signs of concurrent or secondary behavioral or emotional difficulties.

Supportive parental counseling may be indicated in some cases. The parents may need help to reduce intrafamilial tensions arising from difficulties in rearing the language-disordered child and to increase their awareness and understanding of the child's disorder.

### References

Baker L, Cantwell D P: Specific language and learning disorders. In *Handbook of Child Psychopathology*, ed 2, T H Ollendick, M Herson, editors, p 93. Plenum, New York, 1989.
Beitchman J H, Nair R, Clegg M, Ferguson B, Patel P G: Prevalence of psychiatric disorders in children with speech and language disorders. J Am Acad Child Psychiatry 25: 528, 1986.
Bishop D V M, Edmundson A: Language impaired 4-year-olds: Distinguishing transient from persistent impairment. J Speech Hear Disord 52: 156, 1987.
Campbell T F, Dollaghan C A: Expressive language recovery in severely brain-injured children and adolescents. J Speech Hear Disord 55: 567, 1990.
Cantwell D P, Baker L: *Developmental Speech and Language Disorders.* Guilford, New York, 1987.
Cantwell D P, Baker L: *Psychiatric and Developmental Disorders in Children with Communication Disorders*, American Psychiatric Association Press, Washington, 1991.
Caulfield M B, Fischel J E, DeBaryshe B D, Whitehurst G J: Behavioral correlates of developmental expressive language disorder. J Abnorm Child Psychol 17: 187, 1989.
Cohen N J, Davine M, Horodezky N, Lipsett L, Isaacson L: Unsuspected language impairment in psychiatrically disturbed children: Prevalence and language and behavioral characteristics. J Am Acad Child Adolesc Psychiatry 32: 595, 1993.
Fischel J E, Whitehurst G J, Caulfield M B, DeBaryshe B D: Language growth in children with expressive language delay. Pediatrics 83: 218, 1989.
Fundudis T, Kolvin I, Garside R: *Speech Retarded and Deaf Children: Their Psychological Development.* Academic, New York, 1987.
Hall P, Tomblin J: A follow-up study of children with articulation and language disorders. J Speech Hear Disord 43: 227, 1987.
Johnston J R: Specific language disorders in the child. In *Handbook of Speech-Language Pathology*, N J Lass, L V McReynolds, J L Northern, D E Yoder, editors, p 685. Decker, New York, 1988.
McCauley R J, Demetras M J: The identification of language impairment in the selection of specifically language-impaired subjects. J Speech Hear Disord 55: 468, 1990.
O'Donnell J P, Romero J J, Leicht D J: A comparison of language deficits in learning-disabled, head-injured, and nondisabled young adults. J Clin Psychol 46: 310, 1990.
Trantham C R, Pedersen J K: *Normal Language Development: The Key to Diagnosis and Therapy for Language Disordered Children.* Williams & Wilkins, Baltimore, 1976.
Wiig E H, Semel E M: *Language Assessment and Intervention for the Learning Disabled.* Merrill, Columbus, Ohio, 1980.

# 43.2 / Mixed Receptive/Expressive Language Disorder

In mixed receptive/expressive language disorder the child is impaired in both the understanding and the expression of language. The fourth edition of *Diagnostic and Statistical Manual of Mental Disorders* (DSM-IV) is the first diagnostic manual to combine receptive language disorder with expressive language disorder. The implication is that clinically significant receptive language impairment is always accompanied by expressive language dysfunction. With DSM-IV, it is not possible to code receptive language disorder in the absence of expressive language disorder. In the revised third edition of DSM (DSM-III-R), the category developmental receptive language disorder was limited to receptive dysfunction of a developmental nature. DSM-IV allows for receptive and expressive disorders that are acquired, as well as those that are congenital or developmental.

The essential features of mixed receptive/expressive language disorder require that scores from standardized tests of both receptive (comprehension) and expressive language development fall substantially below those obtained from standardized measures of nonverbal intellectual capacity. The language difficulties must be severe enough to impair academic achievement or daily social communication. The patient may not meet the criteria for a pervasive developmental disorder, and the language dysfunctions must be in excess of those usually associated with mental retardation and other neurological and sensory-deficit syndromes.

## EPIDEMIOLOGY

Prevalence estimates range from 1 to 13 percent for either receptive or expressive language disorder. Expressive language disorder alone is thought to be much more common than receptive language disorder alone. Both disorders are believed to be more common in boys than in girls.

No studies have examined the prevalence of the DSM-IV category of mixed receptive/expressive language disorder, but prevalence estimates of children who possess both receptive and expressive language disorders are in the 3 to 5 percent range.

## ETIOLOGY

The cause of mixed receptive/expressive language disorder is not known. Early theories listed perceptual dysfunction, subtle cerebral damage, maturational lag, and genetic factors as probable causative factors, but no definitive evidence supports those theories. Several studies suggest the presence of underlying impairment of auditory discrimination, as most children with the disorder are more responsive to environmental sounds than to speech sounds. As with expressive language disorder, left-handedness and ambilaterality seem to increase the risk.

## DIAGNOSIS

The presence of a markedly below-age-appropriate level of comprehension of verbal sign language with intact age-appropriate nonverbal intellectual capacity, the confirmation of the language difficulties by standardized receptive language tests, and the absence of pervasive developmental disorders confirm the diagnosis of mixed receptive/expressive language disorder (Table 43.2–1). In mixed receptive/expressive language disorder, receptive dysfunction coexists with expressive dysfunction. Therefore, standardized tests for both receptive and expressive language abilities must be given to any child suspected of having mixed receptive/expressive language disorder.

An audiogram is indicated in all suspected mixed receptive/expressive language-disordered children to rule out or to confirm the presence of deafness and to determine the types of auditory deficits.

A history of the child and the family and observation of the child in various settings help clarify the diagnosis.

## CLINICAL FEATURES

The essential clinical feature of the disorder is significant impairment in both language comprehension and language expression. In the mixed disorder, the expressive impairments are similar to those seen in expressive language disorder but can be more severe.

**Table 43.2–1**
**Diagnostic Criteria for Mixed Receptive/Expressive Language Disorder**

A. The scores obtained from a battery of standardized individually administered measures of both receptive and expressive language development are substantially below those obtained from standardized measures of nonverbal intellectual capacity. Symptoms include those for expressive language disorder as well as difficulty understanding words, sentences, or specific types of words, such as spatial terms.

B. The difficulties with receptive and expressive language significantly interfere with academic or occupational achievement or with social communication.

C. Criteria are not met for a pervasive developmental disorder.

D. If mental retardation, a speech-motor or sensory deficit, or environmental deprivation is present, the language difficulties are in excess of those usually associated with these problems.

**Coding note:** if a speech-motor or sensory deficit or a neurological condition is present, code the condition on Axis III.

Table from DSM-IV, *Diagnostic and Statistical Manual of Mental Disorders*, ed 4. Copyright American Psychiatric Association, Washington, 1994. Used with permission.

The clinical features of the receptive component of the disorder typically appear before the age of 4 years. Severe forms are apparent by age 2; mild forms may not become evident until age 7 (second grade) or older, when language becomes complex. Children with mixed receptive/expressive language disorder show markedly delayed and below-normal ability to comprehend (decode) verbal or sign language, although they do have age-appropriate nonverbal intellectual capacity. In most cases of receptive dysfunction, verbal or sign expression (encoding) of language is also impaired. The clinical features of mixed receptive/expressive language disorder in children between the ages of 18 and 24 months are the results of the child's failure to make spontaneous utterances of a single phoneme (sound unit) or to mimic another person's words.

Many children with mixed receptive/expressive language disorder have auditory sensory difficulties or are unable to process visual symbols, such as the meaning of a picture. They have deficits in integrating both auditory and visual symbols—for example, recognizing the basic common attributes of a toy truck and a toy passenger car. Whereas a child with expressive language disorder only at 18 months can comprehend simple commands and can point to familiar household objects when told to do so, the child of the same age with mixed receptive/expressive language disorder is not able either to point to common objects or to obey simple commands. A child with mixed receptive/expressive language disorder usually appears to be deaf; however, the child does hear and responds normally to nonlanguage sounds from the environment but not to spoken language. If the child starts to speak at a later time, the speech contains numerous articulation errors, such as omissions, distortions, and substitutions of phonemes. Language acquisition is much slower for the children with mixed receptive/expressive language disorder than for normal children.

Children with mixed receptive/expressive language disorder also have difficulty in recalling early visual and auditory memories and recognizing and reproducing symbols in proper sequence. In some cases bilateral electroencephalogram (EEG) abnormalities are seen. Some children with mixed receptive/expressive language disorder have a partial hearing defect for true tones, an increased threshold of auditory arousal, and an inability to localize sound sources. Seizure disorders and reading disorder are more common among the relatives of children with mixed receptive/expressive language disorder than they are in the general population.

Associated comorbid disorders with mixed receptive/expressive language disorder include reading disorder, mathematics disorder, and disorder of written expression. In a large study of children with communication disorders, more than half of the children who met the criteria for mixed receptive/expressive language disorder also had a learning disorder. More than 70 percent in the same study had other mental disorders, especially attention-deficit/hyperactivity disorder, anxiety disorders, and depressive disorders.

## DIFFERENTIAL DIAGNOSIS

In expressive language disorder alone, comprehension of spoken language (decoding) remains within age norms. Children with phonological disorder or stuttering have normal expressive and receptive language competence, despite their having speech impairments. Hearing impairment should be ruled out. Most children with mixed receptive/expressive language disorder have a history of variable and inconsistent responses to sounds; they respond more often to environmental sounds than to speech sounds (Table 43.2–2).

Mental retardation, acquired aphasia, and pervasive developmental disorders should also be ruled out.

## COURSE AND PROGNOSIS

The overall prognosis for mixed receptive/expressive language disorder is less favorable than for expressive language disorder alone. When the mixed disorder is identified in a young child, it is usually severe, and the short-term prognosis is poor, since early childhood is a time when language develops at a rapid rate. Young children with the disorder may appear to be falling behind. In view of the likelihood of comorbid learning disorders and other mental disorders, the prognosis is guarded. Young children with severe mixed receptive/expressive language disorder are likely to have learning disorders in the future. In children with mild versions of the mixed disorder, it may not be identified for several years, and the disruption in everyday life may be less overwhelming than that seen in severe forms of the disorder. Over the long run, some children with mixed receptive/expressive language disorder achieve close to normal language functions.

The prognosis for children who acquire mixed receptive/expressive language disorder is widely variable and depends on the nature and the severity of the damage.

## TREATMENT

A comprehensive speech and language evaluation, leading to speech and language therapy, is usually recommended for children with mixed receptive/expressive language disorder, despite the lack of controlled treatment

**Table 43.2–2**
**Differential Diagnosis of Language Disorders***

| | Hearing Impairment | Mental Retardation | Infantile Autism | Expressive Language Disorder | Mixed Receptive/ Expressive Language Disorder | Selective Mutism | Phonological Disorder |
|---|---|---|---|---|---|---|---|
| Language comprehension | – | – | – | + | – | + | + |
| Expressive language | – | – | – | – | – | Variable | + |
| Audiogram | – | + | + | + | Variable | + | + |
| Articulation | – | – | (Variable) | (Variable) | – (Variable) | + | – |
| Inner language | + | + (Limited) | – | + | + (Slightly limited) | + | + |
| Uses gestures | + | + (Limited) | – | + | + | + (Variable) | + |
| Echoes | – | + | + (Inappropriate) | + | + | + | + |
| Attends to sounds | Loud or low frequency only | + | – | + | Variable | + | + |
| Watches faces | + | + | – | + | + | + | + |
| Performance I.Q. | + | – | + | + | + | + | + |

*+ = normal; – = abnormal.
Table adapted from Lorian Baker, Ph.D., and Dennis Cantwell, M.D.

studies for the disorder. Some language therapists favor a low-stimuli setting, in which children are given individual linguistic instruction. Others recommend that speech and language instruction be integrated into a varied setting with a group of children who are taught several language structures simultaneously. Many symptoms are involved in the disorder, so a small specialized educational setting may be beneficial in maximizing the results.

Psychotherapy is often necessary because children with the mixed disorder frequently have emotional and behavioral problems. Particular attention should be paid to improving the child's self-image and social skills. Family counseling in which the parents are taught appropriate patterns of interaction with the child can also be helpful.

### References

Baker L, Cantwell D P: The association between emotional/behavioral disorders and learning disorders in a sample of speech/language impaired children. Adv Learn Behav Disord 6: 27, 1990.
Baker L, Cantwell D P: A prospective psychiatric follow-up of children with speech/language disorders. J Am Acad Child Adolesc Psychiatry 26: 546, 1987.
Baker L, Cantwell D P: Specific language and learning disorders. In Handbook of Child Psychopathology, ed 2, T H Ollendick, M Herson, editors, p 93. Plenum, New York, 1989.
Beitchman J H, Nair R, Clegg M, Ferguson B, Patel P G: Prevalence of psychiatric disorders in children with speech and language disorders. J Am Acad Child Adolesc Psychiatry 25: 528, 1986.
Benaisich A A, Curtiss S, Tallal P: Language, learning and behavioral disturbances in childhood: A longitudinal perspective. J Am Acad Child Adolesc Psychiatry 32: 585, 1993.
Bishop D V M: The causes of specific developmental language disorders. J Child Psychol Psychiatry 28: 1, 1987.
Bliss L S: A symptom approach to the intervention of childhood language disorders. J Commun Disord 18: 91, 1985.
Cantwell D P, Baker L: Developmental Speech and Language Disorders. Guilford, New York, 1987.
Cantwell D P, Baker L: Psychiatric and Developmental Disorders in Children with Communication Disorders. American Psychiatric Association Press, Washington, 1991.
Fundudis T, Kolvin I, Garside R: Speech Retarded and Deaf Children: Their Psychological Development. Academic, New York, 1987.
Geschwind N, Galaburda A: Cerebral Lateralization. MIT Press, Cambridge, 1987.
Gibbs D P, Cooper E B: Prevalence of communication disorders in students with learning disabilities. J Learn Disord 22: 60, 1989.
Lucas E: Semantic and Pragmatic Language Disorders. Aspen, Rockville, Colo, 1980.
Miller J F, Campbell T F, Chapman R S, Weismer S E: Language behavior in acquired childhood asphasia. In Language Disorders in Children, A Holland, editor, p 57. College Hill, San Diego, 1984.
Njiokiktjien C: Developmental dysphasia: Clinical importance and underlying neurological causes. Acta Paedopsychiat 53: 126, 1990.
O'Donnell J P, Romero J J, Leicht D J: A comparison of language deficits in learning-disabled, head-injured, and nondisabled young adults. J Clin Psychol 46: 310, 1990.
Orton S T: Reading, Writing, and Speech Problems in Children. Norton, New York, 1937.
Plante E, Swisher L, Vance R: Anatomical correlates of normal and impaired language in a set of dizygotic twins. Brain Lang 37: 643, 1989.
Richardson S O: Developmental language disorder. In Comprehensive Textbook of Psychiatry, ed 5, H I Kaplan, B J Sadock, editors, p 1812. Williams & Wilkins, Baltimore, 1989.
Robinson R J: Causes and associations of severe and persistent specific speech and language disorders in children. Dev Med Child Neurol 33: 943, 1991.
Rosenberg S: Disorders of first-language development: Trends in research and theory. In Malformations in Development: Biological and Psychological Sources and Consequences, E Gollin, editor, p 195. Academic, New York, 1984.
Tomblin J B, Hardy J C, Hein H A: Predicting poor communication status in preschool children using risk factors present at birth. J Speech Hear Res 34: 1096, 1991.
Trantham C R, Pedersen J K: Normal Language Development: The Key to Diagnosis and Therapy for Language Disordered Children. Williams & Wilkins, Baltimore, 1976.
Zirkelbach T, Blakesley K: The language deficient child in the classroom. Acad Ther 20: 605, 1985.

# 43.3 / Phonological Disorder

Phonological disorder includes many disorders in which developmentally expected speech sounds for the patient's age and intelligence are incorrect or delayed. The disorder can consist of errors in sound production, substitutions of one sound for another, and omissions of such sounds as final consonants. The difficulties interfere with academic achievement or social communication. According to the fourth edition of Diagnostic and Statistical Manual of Mental Disorders (DSM-IV), if mental retardation, a speech-motor or sensory deficit, or environmental deprivation is present, the language dysfunction is in excess of that associated with those problems.

Phonological disorder is a broader category than developmental articulation disorder, which was listed in the revised third edition of DSM (DSM-III-R). Developmental articulation disorder is the most common phonological disorder in children and is the prototype of the disorders defined by the DSM-IV category of phonological disorder. Phonological disorder is characterized by frequent misarticulations, sound substitutions, and omissions of speech sounds, giving the impression of baby talk. It is not caused by any anatomical, structural, physiological, auditory, or neurological abnormalities. It varies from mild to severe and results in speech that ranges from completely intelligible to unintelligible.

## EPIDEMIOLOGY

The prevalence of all phonological dysfunctions in children is unknown, and estimates vary widely with the diagnostic criteria used. The prevalence of phonological disorder is conservatively estimated to be 10 percent of children below 8 years of age and 5 percent of children 8 years of age and above. The disorder is two to three times more common in boys than in girls. It is also more common among the first-degree relatives of patients with the disorder than in the general population. DSM-IV reports 2 to 3 percent of 6 to 7 year olds have the disorder.

## ETIOLOGY

The causes of phonological disturbance are variable and range from perinatal problems to hearing impairment to structural abnormalities related to speech. Phonological disorder in children has an unknown cause. A simple developmental lag or maturational delay in the neurological process underlying speech, rather than an organic dysfunction, is at fault.

A disproportionately high frequency of phonological disorder has been found among children from large families and from low socioeconomic status families, suggesting the possible causal effects of inadequate speech stimulation and reinforcement in those families.

Constitutional factors, rather than environmental factors, seem to be of major importance in determining whether a child has phonological disorder. The high proportion of children with the disorder who have relatives with a similar disorder suggests that the disorder may have a genetic component.

Poor motor coordination, laterality, and handedness do not contribute to phonological disorder.

## DIAGNOSIS

The essential feature of phonological disorder is an articulation defect characterized by the child's consistent failure to use developmentally expected speech sounds of certain consonants, including omissions, substitutions, and distortions of phonemes, which are generally late-learned phonemes. The disorder cannot be attributed to structural or neurological abnormalities and is accompanied by normal language development. The DSM-IV diagnostic criteria for phonological disorder are given in Table 43.3–1.

## CLINICAL FEATURES

The essential clinical feature of phonological disorder is a variety of developmentally inappropriate speech sounds. The sounds are often substitutions—for example, the use of "t" instead of "k"—and omissions, such as leaving off the final consonants of words.

Phonological disorder is recognized in early childhood. In severe cases the disorder is first recognized at about 3 years of age. In less severe cases the disorder may not be apparent until the age of 6 years. Articulation is judged to be defective when compared with the speech of children at the same age level, and the differences cannot be attributed to abnormalities in intelligence, hearing, or the physiology of the patient's speech mechanism. In very mild cases only one phoneme may be affected. Single phonemes are usually affected, most commonly those acquired late in the normal language acquisition process.

In phonological disorder the speech sounds that are most frequently misarticulated are those acquired late in the developmental sequence (*r, sh, th, f, z, l,* and *ch*). But in severe cases and in young children, sounds such as *b, m, t, d, n,* and *h* may be mispronounced. One or many speech sounds may be affected, but vowel sounds are not among them.

The child with phonological disorder is not able to articulate certain phonemes correctly and may distort, substitute, or even omit the affected phonemes. With omissions, the phonemes are absent entirely—for example, "bu" for "blue," "ca" for "car," or "whaa?" for "what's that?" With substitutions, difficult phonemes are replaced with incorrect ones—for example, "wabbit" for "rabbit," "fum" for "thumb," or "whath dat?" for "what's that?" With distortions, the correct phoneme is approximated but is articulated incorrectly. Rarely do additions, usually of

**Table 43.3–1**
**Diagnostic Criteria for Phonological Disorder**

A. Failure to use developmentally expected speech sounds that are appropriate for age and dialect (e.g., errors in sound production, use, representation or organization such as, but not limited to, substitutions of one sound for another [use of /t/ for target /k/ sound] or omissions of sounds such as final consonants).

B. The difficulties in speech sound production interfere with academic or occupational achievement or with social communication.

C. If mental retardation, a speech-motor or sensory deficit, or environmental deprivation is present, the speech difficulties are in excess of those usually associated with these problems.

**Coding note:** if a speech-motor or sensory deficit or a neurological condition is present, code the condition on Axis III.

Table from DSM-IV, *Diagnostic and Statistical Manual of Mental Disorders*, ed 4. Copyright American Psychiatric Association, Washington, 1994. Used with permission.

the vowel "schwa" or "uh," occur—for example, "puhretty" for "pretty," "what's uh that uh?" for "what's that?"

Omissions are thought to be the most serious type of misarticulation, with substitutions the next most serious type, and distortion the least serious type. Omissions are most frequently found in the speech of young children and usually occur at the end of words or in clusters of consonants ("ka" for "car," "scisso" for "scissors"). Distortions, which are found mainly in the speech of older children, result in a sound that is not part of the speaker's dialect. Distortions may be the last type of misarticulation remaining in the speech of children whose articulation problems have mostly remitted. The most common types of distortions are the *lateral slip*—in which the child pronounces "s" sounds with the air stream going across the tongue, producing a whistling effect—and the *palatal lisp*—in which the "s" sound is formed with the tongue too close to the palate, producing a "shh" sound effect. The misarticulations of children with phonological disorder are often inconsistent and random. A phoneme may be pronounced correctly in one situation and incorrectly another time. Misarticulations are most common at the ends of words, in long and syntactically complex sentences, and during rapid speech.

Omissions, distortions, and substitutions also occur normally in the speech of young children learning to talk. However, whereas young normal children soon replace those misarticulations, children with phonological disorder do not. Even as children with phonological disorder grow and finally acquire the correct phoneme, they may use it only in newly acquired words and may not correct earlier learned words that they have been mispronouncing for some time.

Most children eventually outgrow phonological disorder, usually by the third grade. After the fourth grade, however, spontaneous recovery is unlikely, and so it is important to try to remediate the disorder before the development of complications.

In most mild cases, recovery from phonological disorder is spontaneous, and often the child's beginning kindergarten or school precipitates the improvement. Speech therapy is clearly indicated for those children who have not shown a spontaneous improvement by the third or fourth grade. For those children whose articulation is significantly unintelligible and are clearly troubled by their inability to speak clearly, speech therapy should be initiated at an early age.

Other disorders are commonly present with phonological disorder, including expressive language disorder, mixed receptive/expressive language disorder, reading disorder, and developmental coordination disorder. Enuresis may also be present.

A delay in reaching speech milestones (such as first word and first sentence) has been reported in some children with phonological disorder, but most children with the disorder begin speaking at the appropriate age.

Children with phonological disorder may have various concomitant social, emotional, and behavioral problems. About a third of the children with the condition have a psychiatric disorder, such as attention-deficit/hyperactivity disorder, separation anxiety disorder, adjustment disorders, and depressive disorders. Those children with a severe degree of articulation impairment or whose disorder is chronic and nonremitting are the ones most likely to suffer from psychiatric problems.

## DIFFERENTIAL DIAGNOSIS

The differential diagnostic process for phonological disorder involves three steps: First, the clinician must determine that the misarticulations are severe enough to be considered abnormal and must rule out the normal misarticulations of young children. Second, the clinician must determine that no physical abnormalities account for the articulation errors and must rule out dysarthria, hearing impairment, and mental retardation. And third, the clinician must establish that expressive language is within normal limits and must rule out expressive language disorder, mixed receptive/expressive language disorder, and pervasive developmental disorders.

A rough guideline for a clinical assessment of children's articulation is that normal 3-year-olds correctly articulate *m, n, ng, b, p, h, t, k, q,* and *d;* normal 4-year-olds correctly articulate *f, y, ch, sh,* and *z;* and normal 5-year-olds correctly articulate *th, s,* and *r.*

Neurological, oral structural, and audiometric examinations may be necessary to rule out physical factors that may cause certain types of articulation abnormalities.

Children with dysarthria, a disorder caused by structural or neurological abnormalities, differ from children with phonological disorder in that dysarthria is difficult and sometimes impossible to remedy. Drooling, slow or uncoordinated motor behavior, abnormal chewing or swallowing, and awkward or slow protrusion and retraction of the tongue are indications of dysarthria. A slow rate of speech is another indication of dysarthria (Table 43.3–2).

## COURSE AND PROGNOSIS

Recovery is frequently spontaneous, particularly in children whose misarticulations involve only a few phonemes. Spontaneous recovery is rare after the age of 8 years.

**Table 43.3–2**
**Differential Diagnosis of Phonological Dysfunctions**

| Criteria | Phonological Dysfunction Due to Structural or Neurological Abnormalities (Dysarthria) | Phonological Dysfunction Due to Hearing Impairment | Phonologial Disorder | Phonological Dysfunction Associated with Mental Retardation, Infantile Autism, Developmental Dysphasia, Acquired Aphasia, or Deafness |
|---|---|---|---|---|
| Language development | Within normal limits | Within normal limits unless hearing impairment is serious | Within normal limits | Not within normal limits |
| Examination | Possible abnormalities of lips, tongue, or palate; muscular weakness, incoordination, or disturbance of vegetative functions, such as sucking or chewing | Hearing impairment shown on audiometric testing | Normal | |
| Rate of speech | Slow; marked deterioration of articulation with increased rate | Normal | Normal; possible deterioration of articulation with increased rate | |
| Phonemes affected | Any phonemes, even vowels | *F, th, sh,* and *s* | *R, sh, th, ch, dg, j, f, v, s,* and *z* are most commonly affected | |

Table adapted from Lorian Baker, Ph.D., and Dennis Cantwell, M.D.

## TREATMENT

Speech therapy is considered the most successful treatment for most phonological errors. Speech therapy is indicated when the child's articulation intelligibility is poor; when the affected child is over 8 years of age; when the speech problem is apparently causing problems with peers, learning, and self-image; when the disorder is so severe that many consonants are misarticulated; and when errors involve omissions and substitutions of phonemes, rather than distortions.

Monitoring of the child's peer relationships, school behavior, and parental counseling may be necessary for the timely implementation of psychiatric treatment when the need arises.

### References

Bernthal J E, Bankson N W: *Articulation and Phonological Disorders*, ed 2. Prentice-Hall, Englewood Cliffs, N J, 1988.
Cantwell D P, Baker L: *Developmental Speech and Language Disorders*. Guilford, New York, 1987.
Cantwell D P, Baker L: *Psychiatric and Developmental Disorders in Children with Communication Disorder*. American Psychiatric Association Press, Washington, 1991.
Coplan J, Gleason J R: Unclear speech: Recognition and significance of unintelligible speech in preschool children. Pediatrics *82*: 447, 1988.
Freeman F J, Silver L B: Developmental articulation disorder. In *Comprehensive Textbook of Psychiatry*, ed 5, H I Kaplan, B J Sadock, editors, p 1804. Williams & Wilkins, Baltimore, 1989.
Johnson J P: *Nature and Treatment of Articulation Disorders*. Thomas, Springfield, Ill, 1980.
Leonard L: Unusual and subtle behavior in the speech of phonologically disordered children. J Speech Hear Disord *50*: 4, 1985.
Lewis B A: Familial phonological disorders: Four pedigrees. J Speech Hear Disord *55*: 160, 1990.
Shriberg L D, Kwiatkowski J: A follow-up study of children with phonologic disorders of unknown origin. J Speech Hear Disord *53*: 144, 1988.
Stoel-Gamon C: Evaluation of phonological skills in preschool children. Semin Speech Lang *9*: 15, 1988.
Weiss C, Gordon M, Lillywhite H: *Articulatory and Phonologic Disorders*. Williams & Wilkins, Baltimore, 1987.

# 43.4 / Stuttering and Communication Disorder NOS

## STUTTERING

In the fourth edition of *Diagnostic and Statistical Manual of Mental Disorders* (DSM-IV), stuttering is classified under communication disorders and is defined by a disturbance in the normal fluency and time patterning of speech that is inappropriate for the patient's age and that consists of one or more of the following: sound repetitions, prolongations, interjections, pauses within words, observable word substitutions to avoid blocking, and audible or silent blocking. The disturbance in fluency is severe enough to interfere with academic or occupational achievement or social communication. In most cases the disorder originates in childhood. The degree of stuttering may vary with situations and with particular words. The revised third edition of DSM (DSM-III-R) included stuttering under the category of speech disorders not elsewhere classified. The term "stammering" has been used synonymously with "stuttering."

### Epidemiology

Within the general population the prevalence of stuttering is about 1 percent, but the incidence is estimated at close to 3 percent. Stuttering tends to be most common in young children and to resolve in older children and in adults. Stuttering affects about three to four males for every female. The disorder is more common among family members of the affected child than in the general population.

### Etiology

The precise cause of stuttering is unknown, but a variety of theories have been proposed. In the past it was hypothesized that stuttering occurs as a response to conflicts, fears, or neurosis. No evidence indicates that conflicts or anxiety causes stuttering or that persons who stutter have more psychiatric disturbances than do persons with other forms of speech and language disorders. However, stuttering may be exacerbated by certain stressful situations.

Other theories about the cause of stuttering include organic models and learning models. The organic models include those that focus on incomplete lateralization or abnormal cerebral dominance. Several studies using electroencephalography (EEG) found that stuttering males had right-hemispheric alpha suppression across stimulus words and tasks; nonstutters had left-hemispheric suppression. An overrepresentation of left-handedness and ambidexterity is found in stutterers. The theory of abnormal cerebral dominance essentially hypothesizes a conflict between the two halves of the cerebrum for control of language functions. The striking gender differences in stuttering and twin studies indicate that stuttering has some genetic basis.

The learning theories about the cause of stuttering include the semantogenic theory, in which stuttering is basically a learned response to normative early childhood dysfluencies. Another learning model focuses on classical conditioning, in which the stuttering becomes conditioned to environmental factors. In the cybernetic model, speech is viewed as a process that depends on appropriate feedback for regulation; stuttering is hypothesized to occur because of a breakdown in the feedback loop. The observations that stuttering is reduced by white noise and that delayed auditory feedback produces stuttering in normal speakers increase the potential validity of the above theory.

Stuttering is probably caused by a set of interacting variables that include genetic and environmental factors.

### Diagnosis

The diagnosis of stuttering is not difficult when the clinical features are apparent and well-developed and each of the four phases, as described below, can be readily recognized. Diagnostic difficulties may arise when trying to determine the existence of stuttering in young children, as some preschool children experience a period of transient dysfluency. It may not be clear whether the nonfluent pattern is part of normal speech and language development or whether it represents the initial stage in the development of stuttering. If incipient stuttering is suspected, referral to a speech pathologist is indicated. Table 43.4–1 presents the DSM-IV diagnostic criteria for stuttering.

## Clinical Features

Stuttering usually appears before the age of 12 years, in most cases between 18 months and 9 years, with two sharp peaks of onset between the ages of 2 to 3½ and 5 to 7 years. Some but not all stutterers have other speech and language problems, such as phonological disorder and expressive language disorder. Stuttering does not suddenly begin; it typically occurs over a period of weeks or months with a repetition of initial consonants, whole words that are usually the first words of a phrase, or long words. As the disorder progresses, the repetitions become more frequent, with consistent stuttering on the most important words or phrases. Even after it develops, stuttering may be absent during oral readings, singing, and talking to pets or inanimate objects.

Four gradually evolving phases in the development of stuttering have been identified.

**Table 43.4–1**
**Diagnostic Criteria for Stuttering**

A. Disturbance in the normal fluency and time patterning of speech (inappropriate for the individual's age), characterized by frequent occurrences of one or more of the following:

(1) sound and syllable repetitions

(2) sound prolongations

(3) interjections

(4) broken words (e.g., pauses within a word)

(5) audible or silent blocking (filled or unfilled pauses in speech)

(6) circumlocutions (word substitutions to avoid problematic words)

(7) words produced with an excess of physical tension

(8) monosyllabic whole-word repetitions (e.g., "I-I-I-I-see him.")

B. The disturbance in fluency interferes with academic or occupational achievement, or with social communication.

C. If a speech-motor or sensory deficit is present, the speech difficulties are in excess of those usually associated with these problems.

**Coding note:** If a speech-motor or sensory deficit or a neurological condition is present, code the condition on Axis III.

Phase 1 occurs during the preschool period. Initially, the difficulty tends to be episodic, appearing for periods of weeks or months between long interludes of normal speech. There is a high percentage of recovery from those periods of stuttering. During phase 1, children stutter most often when excited or upset, when they seem to have a great deal to say, and under other conditions of communicative pressure.

Phase 2 usually occurs in the elementary school years. The disorder is chronic, with few if any intervals of normal speech. Affected children become aware of their speech difficulties and regard themselves as stutterers. In phase 2 the stuttering occurs mainly on the major parts of speech—nouns, verbs, adjectives, and adverbs.

Phase 3 is usually seen after age 8 and up to adulthood. It occurs most often in late childhood and early adolescence. During phase 3 the stuttering comes and goes largely in response to specific situations, such as reciting in class, speaking to strangers, making purchases in stores, and using the telephone. Some words and sounds are regarded as more difficult than others.

Phase 4 is typically seen in late adolescence and adulthood. Stutterers show a vivid, fearful anticipation of stuttering. They fear words, sounds, and situations. Word substitutions and circumlocutions are common. Stutterers avoid situations requiring speech and show other evidence of fear and embarrassment.

Stutterers may have associated clinical features: vivid, fearful anticipation of stuttering, with avoidance of particular words, sounds, or situations in which stuttering is anticipated; eye blinks; tics; and tremors of the lips or the jaw. Frustration, anxiety, and depression are common among those with chronic stuttering. Other disorders that coexist with stuttering include phonological disorder, expressive language disorder, mixed receptive/expressive language disorder, and attention-deficit/hyperactivity disorder.

## Differential Diagnosis

Normal speech dysfluency in the preschool years is difficult to differentiate from incipient stuttering. In stuttering there are more nonfluencies, part-word repetitions, sound prolongations, and disruptions in voice airflow through the vocal track.

Spastic dysphonia is a stutteringlike speech disorder and is distinguished from stuttering by the presence of an abnormal pattern of breathing.

Cluttering is a speech disorder characterized by erratic and dysrhythmic speech patterns of rapid and jerky spurts of words and phrases. In cluttering, the affected persons are usually unaware of the disturbance, whereas, after the initial phase of the disorder, stutterers are aware of their speech difficulties.

## Course and Prognosis

The course of stuttering is usually long-term, with some periods of partial remission lasting for weeks or months and exacerbations occurring most frequently when the stutterer is under pressure to communicate. Fifty to 80 percent of all children with stuttering, most with mild cases, recover spontaneously.

In chronic stuttering by school-age children, impairment in peer relationships may be a result of teasing and social ostracism. The children may face academic difficulties if they avoid speaking in class. Later major complications include the affected person's limitations in occupational choice and advancement.

## Treatment

Until the end of the 19th century, the most common treatments for stuttering were distraction, suggestion, and relaxation. Recent approaches using distraction include teaching stutterers to talk in time to rhythmic movements of the arm, the hand, or the fingers. Stutterers are also advised to speak slowly in a sing-song or monotone. Those approaches, however, remove the stuttering only temporarily. Suggestion techniques, such as hypnosis, also stop stuttering but, again, only temporarily. Relaxation techniques are based on the premise that it is almost impossible to be relaxed and at the same time to stutter in the usual manner. Because of their lack of long-term benefits, distraction, suggestion, and relaxation approaches as such are not currently used.

Classic psychoanalysis, insight-oriented psychotherapy, group therapy, and other psychotherapeutic modalities have not been successful in treating stuttering. However, if stutterers have a poor self-image, are anxious or depressed, or show evidence of an established emotional disorder, individual psychotherapy is indicated and effective for the associated condition. In one study the reaction of nonstuttering listeners to stutterers who acknowledged their stuttering was much more positive than to stutterers who did not acknowledge their stuttering.

Family therapy should also be considered if there is evidence of family dysfunction, family contribution to the stutterer's symptoms, or family stress caused by trying to cope with or to help the stutterer.

Most of the modern treatments of stuttering are based on the view that stuttering is essentially a learned form of behavior that is not necessarily associated with a basic mental disorder or neurological abnormality. The approaches work directly with the speech difficulty to minimize the issues that maintain and strengthen the stuttering, to modify or decrease the severity of the stuttering by eliminating the secondary symptoms, and to encourage the stutterer to speak, even if stuttering, in a relatively easy and effortless fashion, thereby avoiding fears and blocks.

One example of that approach is the self-therapy proposed by the Speech Foundation of America. Self-therapy is based on the premise that stuttering is not a symptom but a behavior that can be modified. Stutterers are told that they can learn to control their difficulty partly by modifying their feelings about stuttering and attitudes toward it and partly by modifying the deviant behaviors associated with their stuttering blocks. The approach includes desensitization, reducing the emotional reaction to and fears of stuttering, and substituting positive action to control the moment of stuttering. The basic principle is that stuttering is something one is doing and that stutterers can learn to change what they are doing.

**Table 43.4–2**
**Diagnostic Criteria for Communication Disorder Not Otherwise Specified**

This category is for disorders in communication that do not meet criteria for any specific communication disorder; for example, a voice disorder (i.e., an abnormality of vocal pitch, loudness, quality, tone, or resonance).

Table from DSM-IV, *Diagnostic and Statistical Manual of Mental Disorders*, ed 4. Copyright American Psychiatric Association, Washington, 1994. Used with permission.

Recently developed therapies focus on the restructuring of fluency. The entire pattern of speech production is reshaped, with emphasis on a variety of target behaviors, including rate reduction, easy or gentle onset of voicing, and smooth transitions between sounds, syllables, and words. With adults, the approaches have met with substantial success in establishing perceptually fluent speech. However, the maintenance of fluency over long periods of time and relapses remain problems for all involved in adult-stuttering treatment.

Whichever therapeutic approach is used, individual and family assessments and supportive interventions may be helpful. A team assessment of the child or the adolescent and his or her family should be made before any approaches to treatment are begun.

## COMMUNICATION DISORDER NOT OTHERWISE SPECIFIED

This category is used for disorders that do not meet the diagnostic criteria for any specific communication disorder. An example is voice disorder, in which the patient has an abnormality in pitch, loudness, quality, tone, or resonance. To be coded as a disorder, the voice abnormality must be severe enough to cause an impairment in academic achievement or social communication (Table 43.4–2).

A speech disorder that was listed in DSM-III-R but that is omitted from DSM-IV is cluttering. Cluttering was defined in DSM-III-R as a disorder in which the rate and the rhythm of speech is disturbed, resulting in impaired speech intelligibility. Speech is erratic and dysrhythmic, consisting of rapid and jerky spurts that are inconsistent with normal phrasing patterns. The disorder usually occurs in children between 2 and 8 years of age; in two thirds of the cases, the patient has a spontaneous recovery by early adolescence. Cluttering is associated with learning disorders and other communication disorders.

### References

Andrew G, Craig A, Feyer A M, Hoddinot S, Howie P, Neilson M: Stuttering: A review of research findings and theories circa 1982. J Speech Hear Disord 48: 226, 1983.
Andrew G, Guitar B, Howie P: Meta-analysis of the effects of stuttering treatment. J Speech Hear Disord 45: 287, 1980.
Cantwell D P, Baker L: *Developmental Speech and Language Disorders.* Guildord, New York, 1987.
Cantwell D P, Baker L: *Psychiatric and Developmental Disorders in Children with Communication Disorder.* American Psychiatric Press, Washington, 1991.
Collins C R, Blood G W: Acknowledgement and severity of stuttering as factors influencing nonstutterers' perceptions of stutterers. J Speech Hear Disord 55: 75, 1990.

Conture E G: *Stuttering*, ed 2. Prentice-Hall, Englewood Cliffs, N J, 1990.

Cullata R, Leeper L: Dysfluency isn't always stuttering. J Speech Hear Disord *53*: 486, 1988.

Freeman F J, Silver L B: Speech disorders not elsewhere classified. In *Comprehensive Textbook of Psychiatry,* ed 5, H I Kaplan, B J Sadock, editors, p 1810. Williams & Wilkins, Baltimore, 1989.

Homzie M J, Lindsay J S: Language and the young stutterer. Brain Lang *22*: 232, 1984.

Kidd K K: Genetic models of stuttering. J Fluen Disorder *5*: 187, 1980.

Nippold M A: Concomitant speech and language disorders in stuttering children: A critique of the literature. J Speech Hear Disord *55*: 51, 1990.

Perkins W H: What is stuttering. J Speech Disord *55*: 370, 1990.

Pool K D, Devous M D, Freeman F J, Watson B, Flinitzo T: Regional cerebral blood flow in developmental stutterers. Arch Neurol *48*: 509, 1991.

Rosenfield D B, Derman H S: Physician referral patterns for stutterers. J Otolaryngol *19*: 19, 1990.

St. Louis K O: *The Atypical Stutterer*. Academic, Orlando, 1986.

Schwartz H D, Conture E G: Subgrouping young stutterers: Preliminary behavioral observations. J Speech Hear Res *31*: 62, 1988.

# Elimination Disorders

Bowel and bladder control develop gradually over a period of time. Toilet training is affected by many factors, such as the child's intellectual capacity and social maturity, cultural determinants, and the psychological interactions between the child and the parents. The fourth edition of *Diagnostic and Statistical Manual of Mental Disorders* (DSM-IV) includes two elimination disorders, encopresis and enuresis. Encopresis is defined in DSM-IV as a pattern of passing feces into inappropriate places, whether the passage is involuntary or intentional. The pattern must be present for at least three months, and the child's chronological age must be at least 4 years, or the child must have the developmental level of a 4-year-old. Enuresis is defined in DSM-IV by the repeated voiding of urine into clothes or bed, whether the voiding is involuntary or intentional. The behavior must occur twice weekly for at least three months or must cause clinically significant distress or impairment socially or academically. The child's chronological or developmental age must be at least 5 years.

The normal sequence of developing control over bowel and bladder functions is (1) the development of nocturnal fecal continence, (2) the development of diurnal fecal continence, (3) the development of diurnal bladder control, and (4) the development of nocturnal bladder control.

## ENCOPRESIS

### Epidemiology

In Western culture, bowel control is established in more than 95 percent of children by the fourth birthday and in 99 percent by the fifth birthday. Thereafter, frequency decreases to virtual absence by age 16. After age 4, encopresis at all ages is three to four times as common in boys as in girls. At ages 7 to 8, frequency is about 1.5 percent in boys and about 0.5 percent in girls. By ages 10 to 12, once-a-month soiling occurs in 1.3 percent of boys and in 0.3 percent of girls.

### Etiology

The lack of appropriate toilet training or inadequate training may delay the child's attainment of continence. Evidence indicates that some encopretic children suffer from lifelong inefficient and ineffective sphincter control. Either of those factors alone but especially the two in combination offer an opportunity for a power struggle be-tween the child and the parent over issues of autonomy and control; such battles often aggravate the disorder, frequently causing secondary behavioral difficulties. Many encopretic children, however, do not have behavioral problems. When behavioral problems do occur, they are the social consequences of soiling.

Encopretic children who are clearly able to control their bowel function adequately and who deposit feces of relatively normal consistency in abnormal places usually have a psychiatric difficulty.

Encopresis may be associated with other neurodevelopmental problems, including easy distractibility, short attention span, low frustration tolerance, hyperactivity, and poor coordination. Occasionally, the child has a special fear of using the toilet. Encopresis may also be precipitated by life events, such as the birth of a sibling or a move to a new home.

Encopresis after a long period of fecal continence sometimes appears to be a regression after such stresses as a parental separation, a change in domicile, or the start of school.

**Psychogenic megacolon.** Many encopretic children also retain feces and become constipated either voluntarily or secondary to painful defecation. In those cases no clear evidence indicates that preexisting anorectal dysfunction contributes to the constipation. The resulting chronic rectal distention from large, hard fecal masses may cause loss of tone in the rectal wall and desensitization to pressure. Thus, many children become unaware of the need to defecate, and overflow encopresis occurs, usually with relatively small amounts of liquid or soft stool leaking out. Olfactory accommodation may diminish or eliminate sensory cues.

### Diagnosis and Clinical Features

Encopresis is diagnosed when feces are passed into inappropriate places on a regular basis (at least once a month) for three months. Encopresis may be present in children who have bowel control and intentionally deposit feces in their clothes or other places for a variety of emotional reasons. Some children engage in the inappropriate behavior when angry at parental figures or as part of a pattern of oppositional defiant disorder. The children often develop repetitive behaviors that seem to seek negative attention. In other children, sporadic episodes of encopresis may occur during times of stress—for example, proximal to the birth of a new sibling—but in such cases the behavior is usually transient and does not fulfill the diagnostic criteria for the disorder. Encopresis may also be present on an involuntary basis in the absence of physiological abnormalities. In those cases the child may not exhibit adequate control over the sphincter muscles, either because the child is absorbed in another activity or because the child lacks an awareness of the process. The feces may be of normal, near-normal, or liquid consistency. Some involuntary soiling is due to the chronic retaining of stool, resulting in liquid overflow. In rare cases the involuntary overflow of stool results from psychological causes of diarrhea or anxiety disorder symptoms. DSM-IV breaks down the types of encopresis into (1) with constipation and overflow incontinence and (2) without constipation and overflow incontinence. To receive a diagnosis of encopresis, a child must have a developmental or chronological level of at least 4 years. If the fecal incontinence is directly related to a medical condition, encopresis is not diagnosed (Table 44–1). Whereas the revised third edition of DSM (DSM-III-R) designated primary type when the child had not exhibited fecal continence for a year before encopresis and secondary type when the child had at least one year of fecal continence, DSM-IV removes those types.

Studies have indicated that children with encopresis who do not have gastrointestinal illnesses have high rates of abnormal anal sphincter contractions. That finding is particularly prevalent among children with encopresis with constipation and overflow incontinence. Those children have difficulty in relaxing their anal sphincter muscles when trying to defecate. Children with constipation who have difficulties with sphincter relaxation are not likely to be good responders to laxatives in the treatment of their encopresis. Encopretic children without abnormal sphincter tone are likely to improve over a short period.

**Pathology and laboratory examination.** Although no specific test indicates a diagnosis of encopresis, the clinician must rule out medical illnesses, such as Hirschsprung's disease, before making a diagnosis. If it is unclear whether fecal retention is responsible for encopresis with constipation and overflow incontinence, a physical examination of the abdomen is indicated, and an abdominal X-ray can be helpful in determining the degree of constipation present. Sophisticated tests to determine whether sphincter tone is abnormal are generally not conducted in simple cases of encopresis.

**Table 44–1**
**Diagnostic Criteria for Encopresis**

A. Repeated passage of feces into inappropriate places (e.g., clothing or floor) whether involuntary or intentional.

B. At least one such event a month for at least 3 months.

C. Chronological age of at least 4 years (or equivalent developmental level).

D. The behavior is not due exclusively to the direct physiological effects of a substance (e.g., laxatives) or a general medical condition except through a mechanism involving constipation.

Code as follows:
**with constipation and overflow incontinence**
**without constipation and overflow incontinence**

## Differential Diagnosis

In encopresis with constipation and overflow incontinence, constipation can begin as early as the child's first year, peaking between the second and fourth years. Soiling usually begins at age 4. Frequent liquid stools and hard fecal masses are found in the colon and the rectum on abdominal palpation and rectal examination. Complications include impaction, megacolon, and anal fissures.

Encopresis with constipation and overflow incontinence can be caused by faulty nutrition; structural disease of the anus, the rectum, and the colon; medicinal side effects; or nongastrointestinal medical (endocrine or neurological) disorders. The chief differential problem is aganglionic megacolon or Hirschsprung's disease, in which the patient may have an empty rectum and no desire to defecate but may still have an overflow of feces. The disease occurs in 1 in 5,000 children; signs appear shortly after birth.

## Course and Prognosis

The outcome of encopresis depends on the cause, the chronicity of the symptoms, and coexisting behavioral problems. In many cases, encopresis is self-limiting, and it rarely continues beyond middle adolescence.

Children who have contributing physiological factors, such as poor gastric motility and an inability to relax the anal sphincter muscles, are more difficult to treat than are those with constipation but normal sphincter tone.

Encopresis is a particularly repugnant disorder to most people, including family members; thus, family tension is often high. The child's peers are also sensitive to the developmentally inappropriate behavior and often ostracize the child. An encopretic child is often scapegoated by peers and shunned by adults. Many encopretic children have abysmally low self-esteem and are aware of their constant rejection. Psychologically, the children may appear blunted regarding the symptoms, or they may be entrenched in a pattern of encopresis as a mode of expressing anger.

The outcome of cases of encopresis is affected by the family's willingness and ability to participate in treatment without being overly punitive and by the child's awareness of when the passage of feces is about to occur.

## Treatment

By the time a child is brought in for treatment, considerable family discord and distress are common. Family tensions regarding the symptom must be reduced, and a nonpunitive atmosphere must be created. Similar efforts should be made to reduce the child's embarrassment at school. Many changes of underwear with a minimum of fuss should be arranged.

Psychotherapy is useful for easing family tensions, for treating the encopretic children's reactions to their symptoms (such as low self-esteem and social isolation), for addressing the psychodynamic causes present in those children who have bowel control but continue to deposit their feces in inappropriate locations, and for treating those cases of encopresis after a long period of fecal continence that are reactions to psychological stressors. A good outcome occurs when the child feels in control of life events. Coexisting behavior problems predict a poor outcome.

Behavioral techniques have been used with great success, including such behavior reinforcers as star charts, in which the child places a star on a chart for dry or continent nights.

A pediatrician should be consulted in cases of encopresis with constipation and overflow incontinence. First, the child's bowel must be cleared, and then stool movements must be maintained with stool softeners or laxatives. Proper bowel habits should be taught. Biofeedback techniques can be of help.

# ENURESIS

## Epidemiology

The prevalence of enuresis decreases with increasing age. Thus, 82 percent of 2-year-olds, 49 percent of 3-year-olds, 26 percent of 4-year-olds, and 7 percent of 5-year-olds have been reported to be enuretic on a regular basis. However, prevalence rates vary, depending on the population studied and the tolerance for the symptoms in various cultures and socioeconomic groups.

The Isle of Wight study reported that 15.2 percent of 7-year-old boys were enuretic occasionally and that 6.7 percent of boys were enuretic at least once a week. The study reported that 3.3 percent of girls at age 7 years were enuretic at least once a week. By age 10 the overall prevalence of enuresis has been reported to be 3 percent. The rate drastically drops for teenagers, in whom a prevalence of 1.5 percent has been reported for 14-year-olds. In adults, enuresis affects about 1 percent.

Mental disorders are present in only about 20 percent of enuretic children and are most common in enuretic girls, in children with symptoms during the day and the night, and in children who maintain the symptoms into older childhood.

## Etiology

Normal bladder control is acquired gradually and is influenced by neuromuscular and cognitive development, socioemotional factors, toilet training, and, possibly, genetic factors. Difficulties in one or more of those areas may delay urinary continence. Although an organic cause precludes a diagnosis of enuresis, the correction of an anatomical defect or the cure of an infection does not always cure the enuresis, indicating that the cause may be unrelated to organic abnormality in some cases.

In a longitudinal study of child development, those children who were enuretic were about twice as likely to have concomitant developmental delays as were dry children.

About 75 percent of enuretic children have a first-degree relative who is or was enuretic. The concordance rate is higher in monozygotic twins than in dizygotic twins. Although there may be a genetic component, much can be accounted for by tolerance for enuresis in those families and by other psychosocial factors.

Some studies report that enuretic children have a bladder with a normal anatomical capacity when anesthetized but a functionally small bladder, so that the child feels an urge to void with little urine in the bladder. Other studies report that bed-wetting occurs because the bladder is full and there is an absence of the high levels of a nighttime antidiuretic hormone. Those factors allow for a higher than usual urine output. Enuresis does not appear to be related to a specific stage of sleep or time of night; rather, bed-wetting appears randomly. In most cases the quality of sleep is normal. Little evidence indicates that enuretic children sleep more soundly than do other children.

Psychosocial stressors appear to precipitate some cases of enuresis. In young children the disorder has been particularly associated with the birth of a sibling, hospitalization between the ages of 2 and 4, the start of school, the breakup of a family because of divorce or death, and a move to an new domicile.

## Diagnosis and Clinical Features

Enuresis is the repeated voiding of urine into the patient's clothes or bed; the voiding may be involuntary or intentional. For the diagnosis to be made, the child must exhibit a developmental or chronological age of at least 5 years. According to DSM-IV, the behavior must occur twice weekly for a period of at least three months or must cause distress and impairment in functioning to meet the diagnostic criteria. Enuresis is diagnosed only if the behavior is not due to a medical condition. DSM-IV breaks down the disorder into three types: (1) nocturnal only, (2) diurnal only, and (3) nocturnal and diurnal (Table 44–2). The DSM-III-R types primary and secondary, depending on whether the disturbance was preceded by a yearlong period of urinary continence, have been removed from the DSM-IV diagnostic criteria.

**Pathology and laboratory examination.** No single laboratory finding is pathognomonic of enuresis. However, the clinician must rule out organic factors, such as the presence of urinary tract infections that may predispose a child to enuresis. Structural obstructive abnormalities may

**Table 44–2**
**Diagnostic Criteria for Enuresis**

A. Repeated voiding of urine into bed or clothes (whether involuntary or intentional).

B. The behavior is clinically significant as manifested by either a frequency of twice a week for at least 3 consecutive months or the presence of clinically significant distress or impairment in social, academic (occupational), or other important areas of functioning.

C. Chronological age is at least 5 years (or equivalent developmental level).

D. The behavior is not due to the direct physiological effect of a substance (e.g., a diuretic) or a general medical condition (e.g., diabetes, spina bifida, a seizure disorder).

*Specify* type:
**Nocturnal only**
**Diurnal only**
**Nocturnal and diurnal**

Table from DSM-IV, *Diagnostic and Statistical Manual of Mental Disorders*, ed 4. Copyright American Psychiatric Association, Washington, 1994. Used with permission.

be present in up to 3 percent of children who present with apparent enuresis. Sophisticated radiographic studies are usually deferred in simple cases of enuresis with no signs of repeated infections or other medical problems.

## Differential Diagnosis

Possible organic causes of bed-wetting must be ruled out. Organic features are found most often in children with both nocturnal and diurnal enuresis combined with urinary frequency and urgency. The organic features include (1) genitourinary pathology—structural, neurological, and infectious—such as obstructive uropathy, spina bifida occulta, and cystitis; (2) other organic disorders that may cause polyuria and enuresis, such as diabetes mellitus and diabetes insipidus; (3) disturbances of consciousness and sleep, such as seizures, intoxication, and sleepwalking disorder, during which the patient urinates; and (4) side effects from treatment with antipsychotics—for example, thioridazine (Mellaril).

## Course and Prognosis

Enuresis is usually self-limited. The child can eventually remain dry without psychiatric sequelae. Most enuretic children find their symptom ego-dystonic and have enhanced self-esteem and improved social confidence when they become continent.

About 80 percent of affected children never achieved a yearlong period of dryness. Enuresis after at least one dry year usually begins between ages 5 and 8 years; if it occurs much later, especially during adulthood, organic causes must be investigated. Some evidence indicates that late onset of enuresis in children is more frequently associated with a concomitant psychiatric difficulty than is enuresis without at least one dry year. Relapses occur in enuretics who are becoming dry spontaneously and in those who are being treated.

The significant emotional and social difficulties of enuretic children usually include poor self-image, decreased self-esteem, social embarrassment and restriction, and intrafamilial conflict.

## Treatment

Because there is usually no identifiable cause of enuresis and because the disorder tends to remit spontaneously, even if not treated, some success has been achieved by a number of methods.

**Appropriate toilet training.** Appropriate toilet training with parental reinforcement should have been attempted, especially in enuresis in which the disturbance was not preceded by a period of urinary continence. If toilet training was not attempted, the parents and the patient should be guided in that undertaking. Record keeping is helpful in determining a baseline and following the child's progress and may itself be a reinforcer. A star chart may be particularly helpful. Other useful techniques include restricting fluids before bed and night lifting to toilet train the child.

**Behavior therapy.** Classic conditioning with the bell (or buzzer) and pad apparatus is generally the most effective treatment for enuresis. Dryness results in more than 50 percent of all cases. The treatment is equally effective in children with and without concomitant mental disorders, and there is no evidence of symptom substitution. Difficulties may include child and family noncompliance, improper use of the apparatus, and relapse.

Bladder training—encouragement or reward for delaying micturition for increasing lengths of time during waking hours—has also been used. Although sometimes effective, the method is decidedly inferior to the bell and pad.

**Pharmacotherapy.** Drugs should rarely be used to treat enuresis and then only as a last resort in intractable cases causing serious socioemotional difficulties for the sufferer. Imipramine (Tofranil) is efficacious and has been approved for use in treating childhood enuresis, primarily on a short-term basis. Initially, up to 30 percent of enuretic patients stay dry, and up to 85 percent wet less frequently than before treatment. The success, however, does not often last. Tolerance often develops after six weeks of therapy. Once the drug is discontinued, relapse and enuresis at former frequencies usually occur within a few months. A serious problem is the drug's adverse effects, which include cardiotoxicity. Desmopressin (DDAVP), an antidiuretic compound that is available as an intranasal spray, has shown some initial success in reducing enuresis.

**Psychotherapy.** Although many psychological and psychoanalytic theories regarding enuresis have been advanced, controlled studies have found that psychotherapy alone is not an effective treatment of enuresis. Psychotherapy, however, may be useful in dealing with the co-existing psychiatric problems and the emotional and family difficulties that arise secondary to the disorder.

## References

Fournier J-P, Garfinkel B D, Bond A, Becuchesne H, Shapiro S K: Pharmacological and behavioral management of enuresis. J Am Acad Child Adolesc Psychiatry 26: 849, 1987.

Friman P C, Matthews J R, Finney J W, Christophersen E R, Leibowitz J M: Do encopretic children have clinically significant behavior problems? Pediatrics 82: 407, 1988.

Hatch T F: Encopresis and constipation in children. Pediatr Clin North Am 35: 257, 1988.

Hersov L: Faecal soiling. In *Child and Adolescent Psychiatry: Modern Approaches,* ed 2, M Rutter, L Hersov, editors, p 482. Blackwell, Oxford, England, 1985.

Kisch E H, Pfeffer C R: Functional encopresis: Psychiatric inpatient treatment. Am J Psychother 38: 264, 1984.

Landman G B: Locus of control and self-esteem in children with encopresis. J Dev Behav Pediatr 7: 11, 1986.

LaVietes R L: Functional enuresis. In *Comprehensive Textbook of Psychiatry,* ed 5, H I Kaplan, B J Sadock, editors, p 1883. Williams & Wilkins, Baltimore, 1989.

Loening-Baucke V: Modulation of abnormal defecation dynamics by biofeedback treatment in chronically constipated children with encopresis. J Pediatr 116: 214, 1990.

Mikkelsen E J: Modern approaches to enuresis and encopresis. In *Child and Adolescent Psychiatry: A Comprehensive Textbook,* M Lewis, editor, p 583. Williams & Wilkins, Baltimore, 1991.

Nørgaard J P, Rittig S, Djurkuus J C: Nocturnal enuresis: An approach to treatment based on pathogenesis. J Pediatr 114: 705, 1989.

Rew D A, Rundle J S: Assessment of the safety of regular DDVAP therapy in primary nocturnal enuresis: BRG. Urology 63: 352, 1989.

Rushton H G: Nocturnal enuresis: Epidemiology, evaluation, and currently available treatment options. J Pediatr 114: 691, 1989.

Rutter M: Isle of Wight revisited: Twenty-five years of child psychiatric epidemiology. J Am Acad Child Adolesc Psychiatry 28: 633, 1989.

Shaffer D: Enuresis. In *Child and Adolescent Psychiatry: Modern Approaches,* ed 2, M Rutter, L Hersov, editors, p 465. Blackwell, Oxford, England, 1985.

Steinhausen H-C, Göbel D: Enuresis in child psychiatric clinic patients. J Am Acad Child Adolesc Psychiatry 28: 279, 1989.

# Other Disorders of Infancy, Childhood, or Adolescence

## 45.1 / Separation Anxiety Disorder

Some degree of separation anxiety is a universal phenomenon, and it is an expected part of a child's normal development. Infants exhibit separation anxiety in the form of stranger anxiety at less than 1 year of age when the infant and the mother are separated. Some separation anxiety is also normal in young children who are entering school for the first time. Separation anxiety disorder, however, is present when developmentally inappropriate and excessive anxiety emerges concerning separation from the major attachment figure. School avoidance may occur. According to the fourth edition of *Diagnostic and Statistical Manual of Mental Disorders* (DSM-IV), separation anxiety disorder requires the presence of at least three symptoms related to excessive worry regarding separation from the major attachment figures. The worries may take the form of refusal to go to school, fears and distress on separation, repeated complaints of such physical symptoms as headaches and stomachaches when separation is anticipated, and nightmares related to separation issues. The DSM-IV diagnostic criteria include a duration of at least four weeks and an onset before the age of 18 years.

Separation anxiety disorder is the only anxiety disorder currently contained in the child and adolescent section of DSM-IV. In contrast, the child and adolescent section of the revised third edition of DSM (DSM-III-R) included overanxious disorder and avoidant disorder of childhood or adolescence in addition to separation anxiety disorder. In DSM-III-R, overanxious disorder was marked by excessive anxiety unrelated to separation issues. Children with symptoms consistent with overanxious disorder are currently covered by the DSM-IV adult category of generalized anxiety disorder. In the DSM-III-R category of avoidant disorder of childhood or adolescence, a child exhibited warm and satisfying relationships with family members but avoided contact with unfamiliar people; no parallel diagnostic category appears in the childhood section of DSM-IV. Children with symptoms of avoidant disorder meet the DSM-IV diagnostic criteria for social phobia, which is also used for adults. Children and adolescents may also present with anxiety disorders described in the adult section of DSM-IV, including specific phobia, panic disorder, obsessive-compulsive disorder, and posttraumatic stress disorder.

## EPIDEMIOLOGY

Separation anxiety disorder is more common in young children than in adolescents and has been reported to occur equally in boys and girls. The onset may occur in preschool years but is most commonly seen in 7-to-8-year-olds. The prevalence of separation anxiety disorder has been estimated at 3 to 4 percent of all school-age children and 1 percent of all adolescents.

## ETIOLOGY

### Psychosocial Factors

Young children, immature and dependent on a mothering figure, are particularly prone to anxiety related to separation. Because children undergo a series of developmental fears—fear of losing the mother, fear of losing the mother's love, fear of bodily damage, fear of their impulses, and fear of the punishing anxiety of the superego and of guilt—most have transient experiences of separation anxiety based on one or another of those fears. However, separation anxiety disorder occurs when the child has a disproportionate fear of mother-loss. A frequent dynamic is the child's disavowal and displacement of angry feelings toward the parents onto the environment, which then becomes overly threatening. Fears of personal harm and of danger to one's parents are persistent preoccupations; the child can feel safe and secure only in the parent's presence. The syndrome is common in childhood, especially in mild forms that do not reach the physician's office. Only when the symptoms have become established and disturb the child's general adaptation to family life, peers, and school do they come to the attention of professionals.

The character structure pattern in many children with the disorder includes conscientiousness, eagerness to please, and a tendency toward conformity. Families tend to be close-knit and caring, and the children often seem to be spoiled or the objects of parental overconcern.

External life stresses often coincide with the development of the disorder. The death of a relative, illness in the child, a change in the child's environment, or a move to a new neighborhood or a new school is frequently noted in the histories of children with the disorder.

## Learning Factors

Phobic anxiety may be communicated from parents to children by direct modeling. If a parent is fearful, the child will probably have a phobic adaptation to new situations, especially to the school environment. Some parents appear to teach their children to be anxious by overprotecting them from expected dangers or by exaggerating the dangers. For example, the parent who cringes in a room during a lightning storm teaches a child to do the same. The parent who is frightened of mice or insects conveys the affect of fright to the child. Conversely, the parent who becomes angry at a child during an incipient phobic concern about animals may inculcate a phobic concern in the child by the very intensity of the anger expressed.

## Genetic Factors

The intensity with which separation anxiety is experienced by individual children probably has a genetic basis. Family studies have shown that the biological offspring of adults with anxiety disorders are prone to suffer in childhood from separation anxiety disorder. Parents who have panic disorder with agoraphobia appear to have an increased risk of having a child with separation anxiety disorder. Separation anxiety disorder and depression in children overlap, and some clinicians view separation anxiety disorder as a variant of depressive disorders.

## DIAGNOSIS AND CLINICAL FEATURES

Separation anxiety disorder is the most common anxiety disorder in childhood. To meet the diagnostic criteria, according to DSM-IV, the disorder must be characterized by three of the following symptoms for at least four weeks: (1) persistent and excessive worry about losing or possible harm befalling major attachment figures; (2) persistent and excessive worry that an untoward event will lead to separation from a major attachment figure; (3) persistent reluctance or refusal to go to school or elsewhere because of fear of separation; (4) persistent and excessive fear or reluctance to be alone or without major attachment figures at home or without significant adults in other settings; (5) persistent reluctance or refusal to go to sleep without being near a major attachment figure or to sleep away from home; (6) repeated nightmares involving the theme of separation; (7) repeated complaints of physical symptoms, including headaches and stomachaches, when separation from major attachment figures is anticipated; and (8) recurrent excessive distress when separation from home or major attachment figures is anticipated or involved. According to DSM-IV, the disturbance must also cause significant distress or impairment in functioning (Table 45.1–1)

The patient's history may reveal important episodes of separation in the child's life, particularly because of illness and hospitalization, illness of a parent, loss of a parent, or geographic relocation. The clinician should scrutinize the period of infancy for evidence of separation-individuation disorders or lack of an adequate mothering figure.

**Table 45.1–1**
**Diagnostic Criteria for Separation Anxiety Disorder**

A. Developmentally inappropriate and excessive anxiety concerning separation from home or from those to whom the individual is attached, as evidenced by three (or more) of the following:

(1) recurrent excessive distress when separation from home or major attachment figures occurs or is anticipated
(2) persistent and excessive worry about losing, or about possible harm befalling, major attachment figures
(3) persistent and excessive worry that an untoward event will lead to separation from a major attachment figure (e.g., getting lost or being kidnapped)
(4) persistent reluctance or refusal to go to school or elsewhere because of fear of separation
(5) persistently and excessively fearful or reluctant to be alone or without major attachment figures at home or without significant adults in other settings
(6) persistent reluctance or refusal to go to sleep without being near a major attachment figure or to sleep away from home
(7) repeated nightmares involving the theme of separation
(8) repeated complaints of physical symptoms (such as headaches, stomachaches, nausea, or vomiting) when separation from major attachment figures occurs or is anticipated

B. The duration of the disturbance is at least 4 weeks.

C. The onset is before age 18 years.

D. The disturbance causes clinically significant distress or impairment in social, academic (occupational), or other important areas of functioning.

E. The disturbance does not occur exclusively during the course of a pervasive developmental disorder, schizophrenia, or other psychotic disorder and, in adolescents and adults, is not better accounted for by panic disorder with agoraphobia.

*Specify* if:
**Early onset:** if onset occurs before age 6 years

Table from DSM-IV, *Diagnostic and Statistical Manual of Mental Disorders*, ed 4. Copyright American Psychiatric Association, Washington, 1994. Used with permission.

The use of fantasies, dreams, and play materials and the observation of the child are of great help in making the diagnosis. The clinician should examine not only the content of thought but also the way in which thoughts are expressed. For example, children may express fears that their parents will die, even when their behavior does not show evidence of motor anxiety. Similarly, their difficulty in describing events or their bland denial of obviously anxiety-provoking events may indicate the presence of separation anxiety disorder. Difficulty with memory in expressing separation themes and patent distortions in the recital of such themes may give clues to the disorder's presence.

The essential feature of separation anxiety disorder is extreme anxiety precipitated by separation from parents, home, or other familiar surroundings. The child's anxiety may approach terror or panic. The distress is greater than that normally expected for the child's developmental level and cannot be explained by any other disorder. In many cases the disorder is a kind of phobia, although the phobic concern is a general one and not directed to a particular symbolic object. Because the disorder is associated with childhood, it is not included among the phobias of adulthood, which imply a much greater structuralization of the personality.

Morbid fears, preoccupations, and ruminations are characteristic of separation anxiety disorder. Children with the disorder become fearful that someone close to them will be hurt or that something terrible will happen to them when they are away from important caring figures. Many children worry that they or their parents will have an accident or become ill. Fears about getting lost and about being kidnapped and never again finding their parents are common.

Adolescents may not directly express any anxious concern about separation from a mothering figure. Yet their behavior patterns often reflect a separation anxiety in that they express discomfort about leaving home, engage in solitary activities, and continue to use the mothering figure as a helper in buying clothes and entering social and recreational activities.

Separation anxiety disorder in children is often manifested at the thought of travel or in the course of travel away from home. The children may refuse to go to camp, a new school, or even a friend's house. Frequently, a continuum exists between mild anticipatory anxiety before separation from an important figure and pervasive anxiety after the separation has occurred. Premonitory signs include irritability, difficulty in eating, whining, staying in a room alone, clinging to parents, and following a parent everywhere. Often, when a family moves, the child displays separation anxiety by intense clinging to the mother figure. Sometimes geographic relocation anxiety is expressed in feelings of acute homesickness or psychophysiological symptoms that break out when the child is away from home or is going to a new country. The child yearns to return home and becomes preoccupied with fantasies of how much better the old home was. Integration into the new life situation may become extremely difficult.

Sleep difficulties are frequent and may require that someone remain with the children until they fall asleep. Children often go to their parents' bed or even sleep at the parents' door when the bedroom is barred to them. Nightmares and morbid fears are other expressions of anxiety.

Associated features include fear of the dark and imaginary, bizarre worries. Children may see eyes staring at them and become preoccupied with mythical figures or monsters reaching out for them in their bedrooms.

Many children are demanding and intrusive in adult affairs and require constant attention to allay their anxieties. Symptoms emerge when separation from an important parent figure becomes necessary. If separation is threatened, many children with the disorder do not experience interpersonal difficulties. They may, however, look sad and may cry easily. They sometimes complain that they are not loved, express a wish to die, or complain that siblings are favored over them. They frequently experience gastrointestinal symptoms of nausea, vomiting, and stomachaches and have pains in various parts of the body, sore throats, and flulike symptoms. In older children, typical cardiovascular and respiratory symptoms of palpitations, dizziness, faintness, and strangulation are reported.

The most common anxiety disorder that coexists with separation anxiety disorder is specific phobia, which occurs in about one third of all referred separation anxiety disorder cases.

## Pathology and Laboratory Examination

No specific laboratory measures are helpful in the diagnosis of separation anxiety disorder.

## DIFFERENTIAL DIAGNOSIS

Some degree of separation anxiety is a normal phenomenon, and clinical judgment must be used in distinguishing that normal anxiety from separation anxiety disorder. In generalized anxiety disorder, anxiety is not focused on separation. In pervasive developmental disorders and schizophrenia, anxiety about separation may occur but is viewed as caused by those conditions, rather than as a separate disorder. In depressive disorders occurring in children, the diagnosis of separation anxiety disorder should also be made when the criteria for both disorders are met; the two diagnoses often coexist. Panic disorder with agoraphobia is uncommon before age 18, and the fear is of being incapacitated by a panic attack, rather than of separation from parental figures; in some adult cases, however, many of the symptoms of separation anxiety disorder may be present. In conduct disorder, truancy is common, but the child stays away from home and does not have anxiety about separation. School refusal is a frequent symptom in separation anxiety disorder but is not pathognomonic of it. Children with other diagnoses, such as phobias, can present with school refusal; in those disorders, the age of onset may be later and the school refusal more severe than in separation anxiety disorder. Table 45.1–2 presents common characteristics of selected anxiety disorders that occur in children.

## COURSE AND PROGNOSIS

The course and the prognosis of separation anxiety disorder are variable and are related to the age of onset, the duration of the symptoms, and the development of comorbid anxiety and depressive disorders. Young children who experience the disorder but are able to maintain attendance in school generally have a better prognosis than do adolescents with the disorder who refuse to attend school for long periods. Reports have indicated a significant overlap of separation anxiety disorder and depressive disorders. In those complicated cases, the prognosis is guarded.

Most follow-up studies have methodological problems and are of hospitalized, school-phobic children, not of children with separation anxiety disorder per se. Little is reported about the outcome of mild cases, whether the children are seen in outpatient treatment or receive no treatment. Notwithstanding the limitations of the studies, they indicate that some children with severe school phobia continue to resist attending school for many years.

During the 1970s it was reported that many adult agoraphobic women suffered separation anxiety disorder in childhood. Although research indicates that many children with an anxiety disorder are at increased risk for an adult

**Table 45.1–2**
**Common Characteristics of Selected Anxiety Disorders that Occur in Children**

| Criteria | Separation Anxiety Disorder | Social Phobia | Generalized Anxiety Disorder |
|---|---|---|---|
| Minimum duration to establish diagnosis | At least four weeks | No minimum | At least six months |
| Age of onset | Preschool to 18 years | Not specified | Not specified |
| Precipitating stresses | Separation from significant parental figures, other losses, travel | Pressure for social participation with peers | Unusual pressure for performance, damage to self-esteem, feelings of lack of competence |
| Peer relationships | Good when no separation is involved | Tentative, overly inhibited | Overly eager to please, peers sought out and dependent relationships established |
| Sleep | Reluctance or refusal to go to sleep, fear of dark, nightmares | Difficulty in falling asleep at times | Difficulty in falling asleep |
| Psychophysiological symptoms | Complaints of stomachaches, nausea, vomiting, flulike symptoms, headaches, palpitations, dizziness, faintness | Blushing, body tension | Stomachaches, nausea, vomiting, lump in the throat, shortness of breath, dizziness, palpitations |
| Differential diagnosis | Generalized anxiety disorder, schizophrenia, depressive disorders, conduct disorder, pervasive developmental disorders, major depressive disorder, panic disorder with agoraphobia | Adjustment disorder with depressed mood, generalized anxiety disorder, separation anxiety disorder, major depressive disorder, dysthymic disorder, avoidant personality disorder, borderline personality disorder | Separation anxiety disorder, attention-deficit/hyperactivity disorder, social phobia, adjustment disorder with anxiety, obsessive-compulsive disorder, psychotic disorders, mood disorders |

Table adapted from Sidney Werkman, M.D.

anxiety disorder, the specific link between separation anxiety disorder in childhood and agoraphobia in adulthood has not been clearly established. Studies do indicate that anxious parents are at increased risk to have children with anxiety disorders. In addition, in recent years some cases have been reported of children presenting with both panic disorder and separation anxiety disorder.

## TREATMENT

A multimodal treatment approach—including individual psychotherapy, family education, and family therapy—is recommended for separation anxiety disorder. Family therapy helps the parents understand the need for consistent, supportive love and the importance of preparing for any important change in life, such as illness, surgery, or geographic relocation. Specific cognitive strategies and relaxation exercises may help the child control the anxiety. Pharmacotherapy is also useful when psychotherapy alone is not sufficient.

School refusal associated with separation anxiety disorder may be viewed as a psychiatric emergency. A comprehensive treatment plan involves the child, the parents, and the child's peers and school. The child should be encouraged to attend school, but, if a return to a full school day is overwhelming, a program should be arranged for the child to progressively increase his or her time spent at school. Graded contact with an object of anxiety is a form of behavior modification that can be applied to any type

of separation anxiety. In some severe cases of school refusal, hospitalization is required.

Pharmacotherapy is useful for separation anxiety disorder. The tricyclic and tetracyclic drugs, such as the tricyclic imipramine (Tofranil), are usually begun in dosages of 25 mg daily, increased by additional 25 mg doses up to a total of 150 to 200 mg daily until a therapeutic effect is noted. If no effect is noted with 200 mg daily, the plasma levels of imipramine and its active metabolite, desmethylimipramine, should be studied to determine whether a therapeutic blood level has been attained. Aside from its antidepressant effect, imipramine has been postulated to yield results that reduce panic and fear related to separation. Diphenhydramine (Benadryl) can be used to break a dangerous cycle of sleep disturbances.

### References

Alessi N E, Magen D R: Panic disorder in psychiatrically hospitalized children. Am J Psychiatry *145*: 1450, 1988.

Bell-Dolan D J, Last C G, Strauss C C: Symptoms of anxiety disorders in normal children. J Am Acad Child Adolesc Psychiatry *29*: 759, 1990.

Bernstein G A, Garfinkel B D, Borchardt C M: Comparative studies of pharmacotherapy for school refusal. J Am Acad Child Adolesc Psychiatry *29*: 773, 1990.

Black B, Robbins D R: Case study: Panic disorder in children and adolescents. J Am Acad Child Adolesc Psychiatry *29*: 36, 1990.

Bowlby J: *Attachment and Loss*, 3 vols. Basic Books, New York, 1969, 1973, 1980.

Bradley S J, Hood L: Psychiatrically referred adolescents with panic attacks: Presenting symptoms, stressors, and comorbidity. J Am Acad Child Adolesc Psychiatry *32*: 826, 1993.

Francis G, Last C G, Strauss C C: Avoidant disorder and social phobia in children and adolescents. J Am Acad Child Adolesc Psychiatry *31*: 1086, 1992.

Freud S: Introductory lectures on psychoanalysis. In *Standard Edition of the Complete Psychological Works of Sigmund Freud*, vol 16, p 393. Hogarth Press, London, 1963.

Gittelman R, editor: *Anxiety Disorders of Children*. Guilford, New York, 1986.

Kashani J H, Orveschel H: A community study of anxiety in children and adolescents. Am J Psychiatry *147*: 313, 1990.

Kranzler H R: Use of buspirone in an adolescent with overanxious disorder. J Am Acad Child Adolesc Psychiatry 27: 789, 1988.

Last C G, Perrin S, Hersen M, Kazdin A E: DSM-III-R anxiety disorders in children: Sociodemographic and clinical characteristics. J Am Acad Child Adolesc Psychiatry *31*: 1070, 1992.

Last C G, Strauss C C: School refusal in anxiety-disordered children and adolescents. J Am Acad Child Adolesc Psychiatry *29*: 31, 1990.

Rosenbaum J F, Biederman J, Gersten M, Hirshfeld D R, Meminger S R, Herman J B, Kagan J, Reznick J S, Snidman N: Behavioral inhibition in children of parents with panic disorder and agoraphobia. Arch Gen Psychiatry *45*: 463, 1988.

Sheehan K H, Sheehan D N, Shaw K R: Diagnosis and treatment of anxiety disorders in children and adolescents. Psychiatr Ann *18*: 146, 1988.

Silverman W K, Cerny J A, Welles W B, Burke A E: Behavior problems in children of parents with anxiety disorders. J Am Acad Child Adolesc Psychiatry 27: 779, 1988.

# 45.2 / Selective Mutism

Selective mutism is an uncommon childhood condition in which a child who is fluent with language consistently fails to speak in specific social situations, such as school, in which language is expected. Most children with the disorder are silent in their mute situations, but some whisper or use single-syllable words. Despite the absence of speech, some children communicate with eye contact or nonverbal gestures. Those children speak fluently in other situations, such as at home and in certain familiar settings. According to the fourth edition of *Diagnostic and Statistical Manual of Mental Disorders* (DSM-IV), the symptoms must be present for at least one month but are not limited to the first month of school, and the disturbance must interfere with educational or occupational achievement or social communication. The disorder is diagnosed only if the condition is not better accounted for by a communication disorder, such as stuttering, or by a lack of knowledge of appropriate language skills.

## EPIDEMIOLOGY

The prevalence of selective mutism is estimated to range between 3 and 8 per 10,000. Young children are more vulnerable than older children to the disorder. Although still under investigation, selective mutism appears to be more common in girls than in boys.

## ETIOLOGY

Selective mutism is a psychologically determined inhibition or refusal to speak. However, many children with selective mutism have histories of the delayed onset of speech or speech abnormalities that may be contributory. Parental discord, maternal depression, and heightened de-

pendence needs are noted in many of the families. Those factors result in maternal overprotection and an overly close but ambivalent relationship between the mother and her selectively mute child. Children with selective mutism usually speak freely at home; they have no significant biological disability. Some children seem predisposed to selective mutism after early emotional or physical trauma; therefore, some clinicians refer to the phenomenon as traumatic mutism, rather than selective mutism.

## DIAGNOSIS AND CLINICAL FEATURES

The diagnosis of selective mutism is not difficult to make once it is clear that the child has adequate language skills in some environments but not in others (Table 45.2–1). The mutism may develop gradually or suddenly after a disturbing experience. The age of onset can range from 4 to 8 years, and it is usually noticed in the school setting. Mute periods are most commonly manifested in school or outside the home; in rare cases a child is mute at home but not in school. Children who exhibit selective mutism may also have symptoms of separation anxiety disorder, school refusal, and delayed language acquisition. Since social anxiety is almost always present in children with selective mutism, some investigators have suggested that selective mutism is a symptom of social phobia. Behavioral disturbances, such as temper tantrums and oppositional behaviors, may also occur in the home.

### Pathology and Laboratory Examination

No specific laboratory measures are useful in the diagnosis or treatment of selective mutism.

## DIFFERENTIAL DIAGNOSIS

Shy children may exhibit a transient muteness in new, anxiety-provoking situations. Those children often have histories of not speaking in the presence of strangers and of clinging to their mothers. Most of the children who are

**Table 45.2–1**
**Diagnostic Criteria for Selective Mutism**

A. Consistent failure to speak in specific social situations (in which there is an expectation for speaking, e.g., at school) despite speaking in other situations.

B. The disturbance interferes with educational or occupational achievement or with social communication.

C. The duration of the disturbance is at least 1 month (not limited to the first month of school).

D. The failure to speak is not due to a lack of knowledge of, or comfort with, the spoken language required in the social situation.

E. The disturbance is not better accounted for by a communication disorder (e.g., stuttering) and does not occur exclusively during the course of a pervasive developmental disorder, schizophrenia, or other psychotic disorder.

Table from DSM-IV, *Diagnostic and Statistical Manual of Mental Disorders*, ed 4. Copyright American Psychiatric Association, Washington, 1994. Used with permission.

mute on entering school improve spontaneously and may be described as having transient adaptational shyness.

Selective mutism must also be distinguished from mental retardation, pervasive developmental disorders, and expressive language disorder. In those disorders, however, the symptoms are widespread, and there is not one situation in which the child communicates normally; the child may have an inability to speak, rather than a refusal to speak. In mutism secondary to conversion disorder, the mutism is pervasive.

Children introduced into an environment where a different language is spoken may be reticent to begin using the new language. Selective mutism should be diagnosed only when children also refuse to converse in their native language and when they have gained communicative competence in the new language.

## COURSE AND PROGNOSIS

Although children with selective mutism are often abnormally shy in the preschool years, the onset of the disorder is usually at age 5 or 6. The most common pattern is that the children speak almost exclusively at home with the nuclear family but not elsewhere, especially not at school. Consequently, they may have significant academic difficulties and even failure. Children with selective mutism are generally shy, anxious, and depressed. They may not form social relationships, and teasing and scapegoating by peers may cause them to refuse to go to school. Frequently, the children display at home compulsive traits, negativism, temper tantrums, and oppositional and aggressive behavior.

Some children with selective mutism communicate with gestures, such as nodding and shaking the head and saying "umm-hum" or "no." Most cases last only a few weeks or months, but some may persist for years. In one follow-up study, about half the children improved within 5 to 10 years. Children who do not improve by age 10 appear to have a long-term course and a worse prognosis than do children who do improve by age 10.

Some mute children appear to have negativistic and sadistic relationships with adults and use their defiant muteness to punish them. That behavior seems to improve concomitantly with increasing speech in the environments where the child had previously been mute.

## TREATMENT

A multimodal approach using individual, behavioral, and family interventions is most likely to be successful. In the preschool years, counseling or psychotherapy for the parents may be indicated. The preschool child may also benefit from a therapeutic nursery. For the school-age child, individual psychotherapy or behavior therapy may be indicated. When a child's independence is being thwarted, marital counseling or psychotherapy for the parents is paramount.

Some reports suggest the use of pharmacological agents as adjunctive treatments for selective mutism. Those suggestions are based on the observation that children with the disorder often exhibit symptoms consistent with social phobia. Therefore, such medications as phenelzine (Nardil) may be helpful. No data confirm the efficacy of such treatment, although case reports have been published. Further investigation is needed to determine the usefulness of pharmacological interventions for selective mutism.

**References**

Atoynatan T H: Elective mutism: Involvement of the mother in the treatment of the child. Child Psychiatry Hum Dev *17*: 15, 1986.
Black B, Uhde T W: Elective mutism as a variant of social phobia. J Am Acad Child Adolesc Psychiatry *31*: 1090, 1991.
Golwyn D H, Weinstock R C: Phenelzine treatment of elective mutism: A case report. J Clin Psychiatry *51*: 384, 1990.
Hasselman S: Elective mutism in children 1877–1981. A literary summary. Acta Paedopsychiatry *49*: 297, 1983.
Hayden T L: Classification of elective mutism. J Am Acad Child Psychiatry *19*: 18, 1980.
Klin A, Volkmar F R: Elective mutism and mental retardation. J Am Acad Child Adolesc Psychiatry *32*: 860, 1993.
Kolvin I, Fundudis T: Elective mute children: Psychological development and background factors. J Child Psychol Psychiatry *22*: 219, 1981.
Lesser-Katz M: Stranger reaction and elective mutism in young children. Am J Orthopsychiatry *56*: 458, 1986.
Wilkins R: A comparison of elective mutism and emotional disorders in children. Br J Psychiatry *146*: 198, 1985.
Wright H L: A clinical study of children who refuse to talk in school. J Am Acad Child Psychiatry *7*: 603, 1968.
Wright H L, Miller M D, Cook M A, Littman J R: Early identification and intervention with children who refuse to speak. J Am Acad Child Psychiatry *24*: 739, 1985.

# 45.3 / Reactive Attachment Disorder of Infancy or Early Childhood

Reactive attachment disorder of infancy or early childhood is a disturbance of social interaction and relatedness based on grossly inappropriate caretaking—that is, neglect of the child's basic physical or emotional needs or multiple changes in caretakers, preventing appropriate bonds. The fourth edition of *Diagnostic and Statistical Manual of Mental Disorders* (DSM-IV) specifies that before the age of 5 years, one of the following two patterns of inappropriate behavior is exhibited: (1) persistent failure to initiate or respond appropriately to most social interactions as manifested by excessively inhibited, hypervigilant, or ambivalent responses; (2) indiscriminate expressions of familiarity with relative strangers and diffuse attachments. Those developmentally inappropriate behaviors are presumed to be due to a large degree to pathogenic caretaking, but less severe disturbances in parenting may also be associated with infants who exhibit the disorder. In DSM-IV, the disturbance cannot be accounted for solely on the basis of developmental delay, such as in mental retardation, and is not a symptom of a pervasive developmental disorder. In the revised third edition of DSM (DSM-III-R), the disorder could not be a symptom of mental retardation or a pervasive developmental disorder. The disorder may result in a picture of failure to thrive, in which the infant shows physical signs of malnourishment and does not exhibit the expected developmental motor and verbal milestones. When that is the case, the failure to thrive is coded on Axis III.

## EPIDEMIOLOGY

No specific data on the prevalence, sex ratio, or familial pattern are available at this time. Although patients with reactive attachment disorder of infancy or early childhood come from all socioeconomic (SES) groups, studies of some patients (such as infants with failure to thrive) indicate an increased vulnerability among the low SES groups. That finding is congruent with the likelihood of psychosocial deprivation, single-parent households, family disorganization, and economic difficulties in families in low SES groups.

A caretaker may be fully satisfactory for one child, but another child under the same care may have a reactive attachment disorder of infancy or early childhood.

## ETIOLOGY

The cause of reactive attachment disorder of infancy or early childhood is included in the disorder's definition. Grossly pathogenic care of the infant or young child by the caretaker presumably causes the markedly disturbed social relatedness usually evident. The emphasis is on the unidirectional cause; that is, the caretaker does something inimical or neglects to do something essential for the infant or child. However, in evaluating a patient for whom such a diagnosis is appropriate, the clinician should consider the contributions of each member of the caretaker-child dyad and their interactions. The clinician should weigh such things as infant or child temperament, deficient or defective bonding, a developmentally disabled or sensorially impaired child, and a particular caretaker-child mismatch. The likelihood of neglect increases with parental mental retardation; lack of parenting skills because of personal upbringing, social isolation, or deprivation and lack of opportunities to learn about caretaking behavior; and premature parenthood (during early and middle adolescence), in which the parents are unable to respond to and care for the infant's needs and in which the parents' own needs take precedence over their infant's or child's needs.

Frequent changes of the primary caretaker—as may occur in institutionalization, repeated lengthy hospitalizations, and multiple foster home placements—may also cause a reactive attachment disorder of infancy or early childhood.

## DIAGNOSIS AND CLINICAL FEATURES

Children with reactive attachment disorder of infancy or early childhood often first come to the attention of their pediatrician. The clinical picture varies greatly according to the child's chronological and mental ages. Perhaps the most typical clinical picture of the infant with the disorder is the nonorganic failure to thrive. In such infants, hypo-

kinesis, dullness, listlessness, and apathy with a poverty of spontaneous activity are usually seen. The infants look sad, unhappy, joyless, and miserable. Some infants also appear frightened and watchful, with a radarlike gaze. In spite of that, the infants may exhibit delayed responsiveness to a stimulus that would elicit fright or withdrawal in a normal infant (Table 45.3–1). DSM-IV specifies two types: inhibited and disinhibited.

Most of the infants appear significantly malnourished, and many have protruding abdomens (Figures 45.3–1 and 45.3–2). Occasionally, foul-smelling, celiaclike stools are reported. In unusually severe cases a clinical picture of marasmus appears. The infant's weight is often below the third percentile and markedly below the appropriate weight for the infant's height. If serial weights are available, the weight percentiles may have progressively decreased because of an actual weight loss or a failure to gain weight as height increases. Head circumference is usually normal for the infant's age. Muscle tone may be poor. The skin may be colder and paler or more mottled than the normal child's skin. Laboratory findings are usually within normal limits except for those abnormal findings

**Table 45.3–1**
**Diagnostic Criteria for Reactive Attachment Disorder of Infancy or Early Childhood**

A. Markedly disturbed and developmentally inappropriate social relatedness in most contexts, beginning before age 5 years, as evidenced by either (1) or (2):

  (1) persistent failure to initiate or respond in a developmentally appropriate fashion to most social interactions, as manifest by excessively inhibited, hypervigilant, or highly ambivalent and contradictory responses (e.g., the child may respond to caregivers with a mixture of approach, avoidance, and resistance to comforting, or may exhibit frozen watchfulness)

  (2) diffuse attachments as manifested by indiscriminate sociability with marked inability to exhibit appropriate selective attachments (e.g., excessive familiarity with relative strangers or lack of selectivity in choice of attachment figures)

B. The disturbance in criterion A is not accounted for solely by developmental delay (as in mental retardation) and does not meet criteria for a pervasive developmental disorder.

C. Pathogenic care as evidenced by at least one of the following:

  (1) persistent disregard of the child's basic emotional needs for comfort, stimulation, and affection

  (2) persistent disregard of the child's basic physical needs

  (3) repeated changes of primary caregiver that prevent formation of stable attachments (e.g., frequent changes in foster care)

D. There is a presumption that the care in criterion C is responsible for the disturbed behavior in A (e.g., the disturbances in criterion A began following the pathogenic care in criterion C).

*Specify* type:
  **Inhibited Type:** if criterion A1 predominates in the clinical presentation.
  **Disinhibited Type:** if criterion A2 predominates in the clinical presentation.

Table from DSM-IV, *Diagnostic and Statistical Manual of Mental Disorders*, ed 4. Copyright American Psychiatric Association, Washington, 1994. Used with permission.

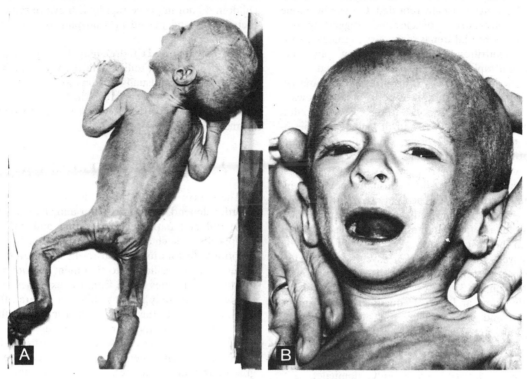

**Figure 45.3–1.** Three-month-old baby boy suffering from failure to thrive secondary to caloric deprivation. Weight is only 1 ounce over birth weight. (Figure courtesy of Barton Schmitt, M.D., Children's Hospital, Denver, Colo.)

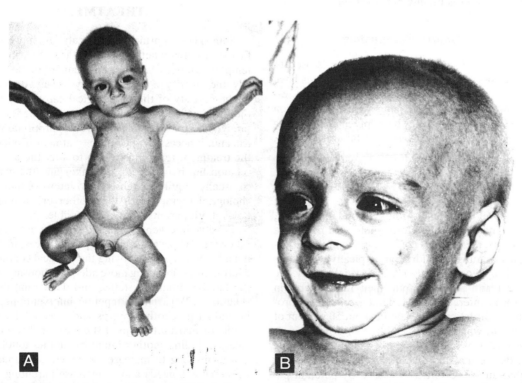

**Figure 45.3–2.** The same infant as in Figure 45.3–1, three weeks later, after hospitalization. (Figure courtesy of Barton Schmitt, M.D., Children's Hospital, Denver, Colo.)

coincident with any malnutrition, dehydration, or concurrent illness. Bone age is usually retarded. Growth hormone levels are usually normal or elevated, suggesting that growth failure in the children is secondary to caloric deprivation and malnutrition. The children improve physically and gain weight rapidly after they are hospitalized.

Socially, the infants usually show little spontaneous activity and a marked diminution of both initiative toward others and reciprocity in response to the caretaking adult or examiner. Both the mother and the infant may be indifferent to their separation on hospitalization or the termination of subsequent hospital visits. The infants frequently show none of the normal upset, fretting, or protest about hospitalization. Older infants usually show little interest in their environment. They may have little interest in playing with toys, even if encouraged. However, they rapidly or gradually take an interest in and relate to their caretakers in the hospital.

Classic psychosocial dwarfism or psychosocially determined short stature is a syndrome that is usually first manifested in children 2 to 3 years of age. The children typically are unusually short and have frequent growth hormone abnormalities and severe behavioral disturbances. All those symptoms are the result of an inimical caretaker-child relationship, and the symptoms resolve without any medical or psychiatric treatment after the child is removed from the home and placed in a favorable domicile.

The affectionless character may appear when there is a failure or lack of opportunity to form attachments before age 2 to 3 years. The child is unable to form lasting relationships, and that inability is sometimes accompanied by a lack of guilt, an inability to obey rules, and a need for attention and affection. Some children are indiscriminately friendly. The disorder is usually not reversible.

### Pathology and Laboratory Examination

Although no single specific laboratory test is used to make a diagnosis, many children with the disorder have disturbances of growth and development. Therefore, establishing a growth curve and examining the progression of developmental milestones may be helpful in determining whether associated phenomena, such as failure to thrive, are present.

## DIFFERENTIAL DIAGNOSIS

Pervasive developmental disorders, mental retardation, various severe neurological abnormalities, and psychosocial dwarfism are the primary considerations in the differential diagnosis. Autistic children are typically well-nourished and of age-appropriate size and weight; they are generally alert and active, despite their impairments in reciprocal social interactions. Moderate, severe, or profound mental retardation is present in about 50 percent of autistic children, whereas most children with reactive attachment disorder of infancy or early childhood are only mildly retarded or have normal intelligence. No evidence indicates that autistic disorder is caused by parental pathology, and most parents of autistic children do not differ significantly from the parents of normal children. Unlike most children with reactive attachment disorder, autistic children do not improve rapidly if they are removed from their homes and placed in a hospital or other favorable environment.

Mentally retarded children may show delays in all social skills. Such children, unlike children with reactive attachment disorder, are usually adequately nourished, their social relatedness is appropriate to their mental age, and they show a sequence of development similar to that seen in normal children.

## COURSE AND PROGNOSIS

The course and the prognosis of reactive attachment disorder depend on the duration and the severity of the neglectful and pathogenic parenting and on associated complications, such as failure to thrive. Constitutional and nutritional factors interact to result in children who may either respond resiliently to treatment or continue to fail to thrive. Outcomes range from the extremes of death to the developmentally healthy child. In general, the longer a child remains in the adverse environment without adequate intervention, the more physical and emotional damage is done, and the worse the prognosis is. Once the pathological environmental situation is recognized, the degree of treatment and rehabilitation that the family receives affects the child returning to that family. For children who have multiple problems stemming from the pathogenic caretaking, their physical recovery may be faster and more complete than is their emotional well-being.

## TREATMENT

Some general principles of treatment apply. Often, the first decision is whether to hospitalize the child or to attempt treatment while the child remains in the home. Usually, the severity of the child's physical and emotional state or the severity of the pathological caretaking determines the strategy. The overriding choice must be for the child's safety. The patient must be given appropriate psychological and, if necessary, pediatric treatment. Concomitantly, the treatment team must begin to alter the unsatisfactory relationship between the caretaker and the child. Doing so usually requires extensive and intensive long-term psychological therapy with the mother or, in intact households, both parents whenever possible.

Possible interventions include but are not limited to the following: (1) psychosocial support services, including hiring a homemaker, improving the physical condition of the apartment or obtaining more adequate housing, improving the family's financial status, and decreasing the family's isolation; (2) psychotherapeutic interventions, including individual psychotherapy, psychotropic medications, and family or marital therapy; (3) educational-counseling services, including mother-infant or mother-toddler groups, and counseling to increase awareness and understanding of the child's needs and to increase parenting skills; and (4) provisions for close monitoring of the progression of the patient's emotional and physical well-being. Should those interventions be unfeasible, be inadequate, or fail, placement with relatives or in foster care, adoption, or a group home or residential treatment facility must be considered.

### References

Ainsworth M D S: The development of infant-mother attachment. In *Review of Child Development Research*, vol 3, B M Caldwen, H N Ricciuhi, editors, p 1. University of Chicago Press, Chicago, 1973.
Bowlby J: *Attachment and Loss*, 3 vols. Basic Books, New York, 1969, 1973, 1980.
Campbell M, Green W H, Caplon R, David R: Psychiatry and endocrinology in children: Early infantile autism and psychosocial dwarfism. In *Handbook of Psychiatry and Endocrinology*, P J V Beumont, G D Burrows, editors, p 15. Elsevier, Amsterdam, 1982.
Ferholt J B: A psychodynamic study of psychosomatic dwarfism. J Am Acad Child Psychiatry *14*: 49, 1985.
Green W H, Campbell M, David R: Psychosocial dwarfism: A critical review of the evidence. J Am Acad Child Psychiatry *23*: 39, 1984.
Greenspan S I: *Psychopathology and Adaptation in Infancy and Early Childhood: Principles of Clinical Diagnosis and Preventive Intervention.* International Universities Press, New York, 1981.
Klaus M H, Kennell J M: *Parent-Infant Bonding*, ed 2. Mosby, St. Louis, 1982.
Lamb M E: Social development. Pediatr Ann *18*: 292, 1989.
Rutter M: *Maternal Deprivation Reassessed*, ed 2. Penguin, Middlesex, England, 1981.
Terwogt M M, Schene J, Koops W: Concepts of emotion in institutionalized children. J Child Psychol Psychiatry *31*: 1131, 1990.
Zeanah C H, Zeanah P D: Intergenerational transmission of maltreatment: Insights from attachment theory and research. Psychiatry *52*: 177, 1989.

# 45.4 / Stereotypic Movement Disorder and Disorder of Infancy, Childhood, or Adolescence NOS

## STEREOTYPIC MOVEMENT DISORDER

Stereotypic movement disorder is defined in the fourth edition of *Diagnostic and Statistical Manual of Mental Disorders* (DSM-IV) by repetitive, seemingly driven, and nonfunctional motor behavior—such as rocking, head banging, self-biting, picking, and waving—for at least four weeks. The behaviors markedly interfere with normal activities or would result in injury if preventive measures were not used. If the behaviors coexist with mental retardation or a pervasive developmental disorder, they must be sufficiently severe to be a focus of treatment. The disorder is diagnosed only if the symptoms are not better accounted for by a compulsion or a tic and are not restricted to hair pulling (as in trichotillomania).

According to DSM-IV, stereotypic movement disorder can be diagnosed with mental retardation or a pervasive developmental disorder when the stereotypic behaviors are severe enough to warrant treatment. In the revised third edition of DSM (DSM-III-R), stereotypic movement disorder could not be diagnosed if a pervasive developmental disorder or a tic disorder was not present. Stereotypic behaviors are not specified as intentional in DSM-IV, as they were in DSM-III-R, since it is not clear to what extent the patients maintain voluntary control over the behaviors. In DSM-IV, self-injurious behavior is specified if bodily damage requires medical treatment.

### Epidemiology

The prevalence of stereotypic movement disorder is not known. Behaviors such as nail biting are common, affecting up to half of all school-age children; behaviors such as thumb sucking and rocking are normal in young children but are often maladaptive in older children and adolescents. In most cases, those behaviors do not constitute a stereotypic movement disorder, since the majority of children who bite their nails function in daily activities without impairment or self-injury. In one pediatric clinic up to 20 percent of the children had a history of rocking, head banging, or swaying in one form or another. Deciding which cases are severe enough to confirm a diagnosis of stereotypic movement disorder may be difficult.

The diagnosis is a compilation of many symptoms, and various behaviors have to be studied separately to obtain data concerning prevalence, sex ratio, and familial patterns. It is clear, however, that stereotypic movement disorder is more prevalent in boys than in girls. Stereotypic behaviors are common among the mentally retarded, affecting 10 to 20 percent. Self-injurious behaviors are seen in some genetic syndromes, such as Lesch-Nyhan syndrome, and are also present in some patients with Tourette's disorder. Self-injurious stereotypic behaviors are increasingly common in persons with severe mental retardation. Stereotypic behaviors are also common in children with sensory impairments, such as blindness and deafness.

### Etiology

The causes of stereotypic movement disorder are essentially unknown, but several theories have been advanced. Many of the behaviors may be associated with normal development. For example, up to 80 percent of all normal children show rhythmic activities that phase out by the age of 4 years. Those rhythmic patterns seem to be purposeful, to provide sensorimotor stimulation and tension release, and to be satisfying and pleasurable to the children. The movements may increase at times of frustration, boredom, and tension.

The progression from what are perhaps viscissitudes of normal development to stereotypic movement disorder is thought to reflect disordered development, as in mental retardation or a pervasive developmental disorder, or psychological conflict. Such behaviors as head banging may result from maternal neglect or abuse and the lack of psychosocial and physical stimulation.

Stereotypic movements appear to be associated with dopamine activity. Dopamine agonists induce or increase stereotypic behaviors, whereas dopamine antagonists decrease them. In one report four children with attention-deficit/hyperactivity disorder were treated with a stimulant medication and began to bite their nails and fingertips. The nail biting ceased when the medication was eliminated. Endogenous opiates have also been implicated in the production of self-injurious behaviors.

## Diagnosis and Clinical Features

Affected persons may suffer from one or more symptoms of stereotypic movement disorder; thus, the clinical picture varies considerably. Most commonly, one symptom predominates. The presence of several severe symptoms tends to occur among the most severely afflicted persons with mental retardation or a pervasive developmental disorder. Those persons frequently have other significant mental disorders, especially disruptive behavior disorders.

In extreme cases, severe mutilation and life-threatening injuries may result, and secondary infection and septicemia may follow self-inflicted trauma.

The DSM-IV diagnostic criteria for stereotypic movement disorder are given in Table 45.4–1.

**Head banging.** Head banging is an example of a stereotypic movement disorder that can result in functional impairment. The reported incidence varies between 3.3 and 19 percent. Typically, head banging begins during infancy, between 6 and 12 months of age. Infants strike their heads with a definite rhythmic and monotonous continuity against the crib or other hard surface. Infants appear to be absorbed in the activity, which may persist until they become exhausted and fall asleep. The head banging is transitory in many children, but in some cases it persists into middle childhood.

Head banging that is a component of temper tantrums is different from stereotypic head banging and ceases once the tantrums and their secondary gains are controlled.

**Nail biting.** Nail biting may begin as early as 1 year of age and increase in incidence until age 12. Usually, all the nails are bitten. Most cases are not sufficiently severe

to meet the DSM-IV diagnostic criteria. The other cases are those that cause physical damage to the fingers themselves, usually by associated biting of the cuticles and by secondary infections of the fingers and nail beds. Nail biting seems to occur or increase in intensity when the person is either anxious or bored. Some of the most severe nail biting occurs in the severely and profoundly mentally retarded and in some paranoid schizophrenic patients. Some nail biters, however, have no obvious emotional disturbance.

**Pathology and laboratory examination.** No specific laboratory measures are helpful in the diagnosis of stereotypic movement disorder.

## Differential Diagnosis

The differential diagnosis of stereotypic movement disorder includes obsessive-compulsive disorder and tic disorders, both of which are exclusionary criteria in DSM-IV. Although stereotypic movements are not spasmodic and are voluntary, the clinician may find it difficult to differentiate those features from tics in all cases. Stereotypic movements are likely to be comforting, whereas tics are often associated with distress. In obsessive-compulsive disorder, the compulsions must be ego-dystonic, although that, too, is difficult to discern in young children.

Differentiating dyskinetic movements from stereotypic movements can be difficult. Because antipsychotic medications can suppress stereotypic movements, the clinician must note any stereotypic movements before initiating treatment with an antipsychotic.

Stereotypic movement disorder may be diagnosed concurrently with substance-related disorders (for example, amphetamine use disorders), severe sensory impairments, central nervous system and degenerative disorders (for example, Lesch-Nyhan syndrome), and severe schizophrenia.

## Course and Prognosis

The duration and the course of stereotypic movement disorder are variable, and the symptoms may wax and wane. The disorder ranges from brief episodes occurring under stress or with transient mental conditions to an ongoing pattern in the context of a chronic disorder, such as mental retardation or a pervasive developmental disorder. Even in chronic conditions the emergence of stereotypic behaviors may come and go. In some cases, stereotypic movements are prominent in early childhood and diminish as the child gets older.

The severity of the dysfunction caused by stereotypic movements also ranges with the associated frequency, quantity, and degree of self-injury. Persons who exhibit frequent, severe self-injurious stereotypic behaviors have the poorest prognoses. Repetitive episodes of head banging, biting oneself, and eye poking may be difficult to control without physical restraints.

Most nail biting is benign and often does not meet the diagnostic criteria for stereotypic movement disorder. In severe cases in which the nail beds are repetitively damaged, bacterial and fungal infections can occur.

Although chronic stereotypic movement disorders can

---

**Table 45.4–1**
**Diagnostic Criteria for Stereotypic Movement Disorder**

A. Repetitive, seemingly driven, and nonfunctional motor behavior (e.g., hand shaking or waving, body rocking, head banging, mouthing of objects, self-biting, picking at skin or bodily orifices, hitting own body).

B. The behavior markedly interferes with normal activities or results in self-inflicted bodily injury that requires medical treatment (or would result in an injury if preventive measures were not used).

C. If mental retardation is present, the stereotypic or self-injurious behavior is of sufficient severity to become a focus of treatment.

D. The behavior is not better accounted for by a compulsion (as in obsessive-compulsive disorder) a tic (as in tic disorder), a stereotypy that is part of a pervasive developmental disorder, or hair pulling (as in trichotillomania).

E. The behavior is not due to the direct physiological effects of a substance or a general medical condition.

F. The behavior persists for 4 weeks or longer.

*Specify* if:
  **with Self-Injurious Behavior:** if the behavior results in bodily damage that requires specific treatment (or that would result in bodily damage if protective measures were not used)

Table from DSM-IV, *Diagnostic and Statistical Manual of Mental Disorders*, ed 4. Copyright American Psychiatric Association, Washington, 1994. Used with permission.

severely impair daily functioning, a number of treatments help control the symptoms.

## Treatment

Treatment should be related to the specific symptom or symptoms being treated, their causes, and the patient's mental age.

The psychosocial environment should be changed for those infants, young children, and mentally retarded persons for whom lack of adequate caretaking, little opportunity for physical expression, boring inactivity, and self-stimulation seem to be important causes. In those cases, increased nurturance and stimulation may be helpful. Such measures as padding hard surfaces may be important for head bangers.

Behavioral techniques, including reinforcement and behavioral shaping, are successful in some cases. A large, specialized literature addresses the problems in the seriously retarded.

Psychotherapy has been used primarily in older, mentally normal persons in whom intrapsychic conflict or interpersonal difficulties seem to be prominent.

For those cases in which severe physical damage occurs, especially in the severely retarded, psychopharmacology must be considered. Phenothiazines have been the most frequently used drugs; however, the psychiatrist must be particularly aware of adverse effects, including tardive dyskinesia and impairment of cognition. Opiate antagonists have reduced self-injurious behaviors in some patients without exposing them to tardive dyskinesia or impaired cognition.

Additional pharmacological agents that have been tried in the treatment of stereotypic movement disorder include fenfluramine (Pondimin), clomipramine (Anafranil), and fluoxetine (Prozac). In some reports, fenfluramine diminished stereotypic behaviors in children with autistic disorder; in other studies, the results were less encouraging. Open trials indicate that both clomipramine and fluoxetine may decrease self-injurious behaviors and other stereotypic movements in some patients.

# DISORDER OF INFANCY, CHILDHOOD, OR ADOLESCENCE NOT OTHERWISE SPECIFIED

This residual category is for disorders with an onset in infancy, childhood, or adolescence that do not meet the diagnostic criteria for any specific disorder in the DSM-IV classification (Table 45.4–2).

**Table 45.4–2**
**Diagnostic Criteria for Disorder of Infancy, Childhood, or Adolescence Not Otherwise Specified**

This category is a residual category for disorders with onset in infancy, childhood, or adolescence that do not meet criteria for any specific disorder in the classification.

Table from DSM-IV, *Diagnostic and Statistical Manual of Mental Disorder*, ed 4. Copyright American Psychiatric Association, Washington, 1994. Used with permission.

## References

Barrett R P, Feinstein C, Hole W T: Effects of naloxone and nalotrexone on self-injury: A double-blind, placebo controlled analysis. Am J Ment Retard *93*: 644, 1989.

Cerny R: Thumb and finger sucking. Aust Dent J *26*: 167, 1981.

Coid J, Allolio B, Rees L H: Raised plasma metenkephalin in patients who habitually mutilate themselves. Lancet *2*: 545, 1983.

Evans J: Rocking at night. J Child Psychol Psychiatry *2*: 71, 1961.

Green W H: Stereotypy and habit disorder. In *Comprehensive Textbook of Psychiatry*, ed 5, H I Kaplan, B J Sadock, editors, p 1903. Williams & Wilkins, Baltimore, 1989.

Leonard H L, Lenane M C, Swedo S E, Rettew D C, Rapoport J L: A double-blind comparison of clomipramine and desipramine treatment of severe onychophagia (nail biting). Arch Gen Psychiatry *48*: 821, 1992.

Matthews L H, Leibowitz J M, Matthews J R: Tics, habits and mannerisms. In *Handbook of Clinical Child Psychology*, C E Walker, M C Roberts, editors, p 406. Wiley, New York, 1983.

Meiselas K D, Spencer E K, Oberfield R, Peselow E D, Angrist B, Campbell M: Differentiation of stereotypies from neuroleptic-related dyskinesias in autistic children. J Clin Psychopharmacol *9*: 207, 1989.

Ratey J J: *Mental Retardation: Developing Pharmacotherapies.* American Psychiatric Press, Washington, 1991.

Ricketts R W, Goza A B, Ellis C R, Singh Y N, Singh N N, Cooke J C III: Fluoxetine treatment of severe self-injury in young adults with mental retardation. J Am Acad Child Adolesc Psychiatry *32*: 865, 1993.

Schroeder S R, Schroeder C S, Rojahn J, Mulick J A: Self-injurious behavior: An analysis of behavior management techniques. In *Handbook of Behavior Modification with the Mentally Retarded*, p 61. Plenum, New York, 1981.

Silberstein R M, Blackman S, Mandell W: Autoerotic head banging: A reflection of the opportunism of infants. J Am Acad Child Psychiatry *5*: 235, 1966.

Sokol M S, Campbell M, Goldstein M, Kriechman A M: Attention deficit disorder with hyperactivity and the dopamine hypothesis: Case presentations with theoretical background. J Am Acad Child Adolesc Psychiatry *26*: 428, 1987.

Werry J, Corlielle J, Fitzpatrick J: Rhythmic motor activities in children under five: Etiology and prevalence. J Am Acad Child Psychiatry *22*: 329, 1983.

# Mood Disorders and Suicide

## MOOD DISORDERS

Mood disorders in children and adolescents have received increasing recognition and attention over the past few decades. For many generations, sadness and despair have been known to occur in children and adolescents, yet the concept of enduring disorders of mood has taken longer to be generally accepted. A criterion for mood disorders in childhood and adolescence is a disturbance of mood, such as depression or elation. In addition, irritability can be a sign of a mood disorder in children and adolescents. Mood disorders in adults are reviewed in detail in Chapter 15. Only those issues that pertain specifically to children and adolescents are considered here.

The diagnostic criteria in the fourth edition of *Diagnostic and Statistical Manual of Mental Disorders* (DSM-IV) for major depressive disorder, dysthymic disorder, and bipolar I disorder are the same for children and adolescents as they are for adults with some minor modifications. The modifications in the criteria for childhood and adolescent major depressive disorder include the following: can be irritable mood, instead of depressed mood, and failure to make expected weight gains, instead of significant weight loss or weight gain. In dysthymic disorder, irritable mood may replace depressed mood, and the duration criterion in children and adolescents has been modified to one year, instead of the obligatory two years in adults. The criteria for bipolar I disorder are the same for children and adolescents as for adults.

Although the DSM-IV diagnostic criteria used for mood disorders are almost identical across all age groups, the expression of disturbed mood varies in children according to their ages. Symptoms commonly seen in young depressed children and less often as their ages increase are mood-congruent auditory hallucinations, somatic complaints, withdrawn and sad appearance, and poor self-esteem. Other symptoms more common in depressed late adolescence than in young childhood are pervasive anhedonia, severe psychomotor retardation, delusions, and a sense of hopelessness. Symptoms that appear with the same frequency regardless of age and developmental status include suicidal ideation, depressed or irritable mood, insomnia, and diminished ability to concentrate. However, developmental issues do influence the expression of all the symptoms. For example, miserable young children who exhibit recurrent suicidal ideation are generally unable to

come up with a realistic suicide plan or to put their ideas into action.

Children's moods are especially vulnerable to the influences of severe social stressors, such as chronic family discord, abuse and neglect, and academic failure. The vast majority of young children with major depressive disorder have histories of abuse or neglect. Children with depressive disorders in the midst of toxic environments may have remission of some or much of their depressive symptoms when the stressors diminish or when the children are removed from the stressful environment. Bereavement often becomes a focus of psychiatric treatment when children have lost a loved one, even when a depressive disorder is not present.

Depressive disorders and bipolar I disorder are generally episodic, although their onset may be insidious. Manic episodes are rare in prepubertal children but fairly common in adolescents. Attention-deficit/hyperactivity disorder, oppositional defiant disorder, and conduct disorder may occur in children who later experience depression. In some cases, conduct disturbances or full disorders may occur within the context of a major depressive episode and resolve with the resolution of the depressive episode. The clinician must clarify the chronology of the symptoms to determine whether a given behavior (such as poor concentration, defiance, or temper tantrums) was present before the depressive episode and is unrelated to it or whether the behavior is occurring for the first time and is directly related to the depressive episode.

### Epidemiology

Mood disorders increase with increasing age, and prevalence in any age group is drastically higher within psychiatrically referred groups than in the general population. Mood disorders in preschool-age children are extremely rare. The rate of major depressive disorder in preschoolers has been estimated to be about 0.3 percent in the community, compared with 0.9 percent in a clinic setting. Among school-age children in the community, about 2 percent have major depressive disorder. Depression is more common in boys than in girls in school-age children. Some bias may be present in the clinic reports, since boys outnumber girls in psychiatric clinics. Among adolescents, about 5 percent in the community have major depressive disorder. Among hospitalized children and adolescents, the rates of major depressive disorder are much higher than in the general community; up to 20 percent of children and 40 percent of adolescents are depressed.

Dysthymic disorder is estimated to be more common than major depressive disorder in school-age children, with rates up to 2.5 percent, compared with 2 percent for major depressive disorder. School-age children with dysthymic disorder have a high likelihood that major depressive disorder will develop at some point after one year of the dysthymic disorder. In adolescents, as in adults, dysthymic disorder is less common than major depressive disorder, with a rate of about 3.3 percent for dysthymic disorder, compared with about 5 percent for major depressive disorder.

The rate of bipolar I disorder is exceedingly low in prepubertal children and may take years to be diagnosed, since mania typically presents for the first time in adolescence. The lifetime rate of bipolar I disorder has been estimated to be 0.6 percent in a community study of adolescents. Adolescents with clinical variants of mania—that is, with some manic symptoms but without the full diagnostic criteria (bipolar II disorder)—have rates of up to about 10 percent, according to some studies.

## Etiology

Considerable evidence indicates that the mood disorders are the same fundamental disease or disease group, regardless of the age of onset.

**Genetic factors.** Mood disorders in children, adolescents, and adult patients tend to cluster in the same families. An increased incidence of mood disorders is generally found in the children of mood-disordered parents and in the relatives of mood-disordered children. However, in one study, depression was equally increased in the parents of both depressed and nondepressed children and adolescent inpatients and outpatients. However, having one depressed parent probably doubles the risk for the offspring. Having both parents depressed probably quadruples the risk of a child's having a mood disorder before age 18 when compared with the risk for children with two unaffected parents.

Some evidence indicates that the number of recurrences of parental depression does increase the likelihood that their children will be affected, but that increase may be related, at least in part, to the affective loading of that parent's own family tree. Similarly, children with the most severe episodes of major depressive disorder have shown much evidence of dense and deep familial aggregation for major depressive disorder.

**Other biological factors.** Studies of prepubertal major depressive disorder and adolescent mood disorders have revealed biological abnormalities.

Prepubertal children in an episode of major depressive disorder secrete significantly more growth hormone during sleep than do normal children and those with nondepressed mental disorders. They also secrete significantly less growth hormone in response to insulin-induced hypoglycemia than do nondepressed patients. Both abnormalities have been found to remain abnormal and basically unchanged after at least four months of full, sustained clinical response, the last month in a drug-free state.

In contrast, the data conflict about cortisol hypersecretion during major depressive disorder. Some workers report hypersecretion, and some report normal secretion. The dexamethasone-suppression test is used in childhood and adolescence but not as frequently or as reliably as in adults.

Sleep studies are inconclusive in depressed children and adolescents. Polysomnography shows either no change or changes characteristic of adults with major depressive disorder: reduced rapid eye movement (REM) latency and an increased number of REM periods.

**Social factors.** The finding that identical twins do not have a 100 percent concordance rate suggests a role for nongenetic factors. So far, little evidence indicates that parental marital status, the number of siblings, the family's socioeconomic status, parental separation, divorce, marital functioning, or the familial constellation or structure plays much of a role in causing depressive disorders in children. However, some evidence indicates that boys whose fathers died before they were 13 years old are more likely than are controls to have depression.

The psychosocial deficits found in depressed children improve after sustained recovery from the depression. Those deficits' appear to be secondary to the depression itself and to be compounded by the long duration of most dysthymic or depressive episodes, during which poorly accomplished or unaccomplished developmental tasks accumulated. Among preschoolers in whom depressive clinical presentations are described, the role of environmental influences will probably receive experimental support in the future.

## Diagnosis and Clinical Features

**Major depressive disorder.** Major depressive disorder in children is most easily diagnosed when it is acute and occurs in a child without previous psychiatric symptoms. In many cases, however, the onset is insidious and presents in a child who has had several years of difficulties with hyperactivity, separation anxiety disorder, or intermittent depressive symptoms.

According to the DSM-IV diagnostic criteria for major depressive disorder, at least five symptoms must be present for a period of two weeks and must be a change from previous functioning (Table 15.1–3). Among the necessary symptoms are either (1) a depressed or irritable mood or (2) a loss of interest or pleasure. Other symptoms from which the other four diagnostic criteria are drawn include the child's failure to make expected weight gains, daily insomnia or hypersomnia, psychomotor agitation or retardation, daily fatigue or loss of energy, feelings of worthlessness or inappropriate guilt, diminished ability to think or concentrate, and recurrent thoughts of death. Those symptoms must produce social or academic impairment. To meet the diagnostic criteria for major depressive disorder, the symptoms cannot be the direct effects of a substance (for example, alcohol) or a general medical condition. A diagnosis of major depressive disorder is not made within two months of the loss of a loved one except when marked functional impairment, morbid preoccupation with worthlessness, suicidal ideation, psychotic symptoms, or psychomotor retardation is present.

A major depressive episode in a prepubertal child is likely to be manifested by somatic complaints, psychomotor agitation, and mood-congruent hallucinations. Anhedonia is also frequent, but anhedonia, hopelessness, psychomotor retardation, and delusions are more common in adolescent and adult major depressive episodes than in young children. Adults have more problems with sleep and appetite than do depressed children and adolescents. In adolescence, negativistic or frankly antisocial behavior and the use of alcohol or illicit substances may be present and justify the additional diagnoses of oppositional defiant disorder, conduct disorder, and substance abuse or dependence. Feelings of restlessness, grouchiness, aggression, sulkiness, reluctance to cooperate in family ventures, withdrawal from social activities, and a desire to leave home are all common in adolescent depression. School difficulties are likely. The adolescent may be inattentive to personal appearance and show increased emotionality, with particular sensitivity to rejection in love relationships.

Children can be reliable reporters about their own behavior, emotions, relationships, and difficulties in psychosocial functions. They may, however, refer to their feelings by many names. Thus, the clinician must ask about feeling sad, empty, low, down, blue, very unhappy, or like crying or having a bad feeling inside that is there most of the time. Depressed children usually identify one or more of those terms as the persistent feeling they have had. The clinician should assess the duration and the periodicity of the depressive mood to differentiate relatively universal, short-lived, and sometimes frequent periods of sadness, usually after a frustrating event, from a true, persistent depressive mood. The younger the children, the more imprecise their time estimates are likely to be.

Mood disorders tend to be chronic if they begin early. Childhood onset may be the most severe form of a mood disorder and tends to appear in families with a high incidence of mood disorders and alcohol abuse. The children are likely to have such secondary complications as conduct disorder, alcohol and other substance abuse, and antisocial behavior.

Functional impairment associated with a depressive disorder in childhood extends to practically all areas of the child's psychosocial world; school performance and behavior, peer relationships, and family relationships—all suffer. Only highly intelligent and academically oriented children with no more than a moderate depression can compensate for their difficulties in learning by substantially increasing their time and effort. Otherwise, school performance is invariably affected by a combination of difficulty in concentrating, slowed-down thinking, lack of interest and motivation, fatigue, sleepiness, depressive ruminations, and preoccupations. Depression in a child may be misdiagnosed as a learning disorder. Learning problems secondary to depression, even when long-standing, correct themselves rapidly after the child's recovery from the depressive episode.

Children and adolescents with major depressive disorder may have hallucinations and delusions. In most cases those psychotic symptoms are thematically consistent with the depressed mood, occur with the depressive episode (usually at its worst), and do not include certain types of hallucinations, such as conversing voices and a commenting voice, which are specific to schizophrenia. Depressive hallucinations usually consist of a single voice speaking to the person from outside his or her head, with derogatory or suicidal content. Depressive delusions center on themes of guilt, physical disease, death, nihilism, deserved punishment, personal inadequacy, and sometimes persecution. Those delusions are rare in prepuberty, probably because of cognitive immaturity, but are present in about half of all psychotically depressed adolescents.

Adolescent onset of a mood disorder may be difficult to diagnose when first seen if the adolescent has attempted self-medication with alcohol or other illicit substances. In a recent study 17 percent of the youngsters with a mood disorder first presented to medical attention as substance abusers. Only after detoxification could the psychiatric symptoms be properly assessed and the correct mood disorder diagnosis be made.

**Dysthymic disorder.** Dysthymic disorder in children and adolescents consists of a depressed or irritable mood for most of the day, for more days than not, over a period of at least one year. DSM-IV notes that, in children and adolescents, irritable mood can replace the depressed mood criterion for adults and that the duration criterion is not two years but one year for children and adolescents. According to the DSM-IV diagnostic criteria, at least three of the following symptoms must accompany the depressed or irritable mood: poor self-esteem, pessimism or hopelessness, loss of interest, social withdrawal, chronic fatigue, feelings of guilt or brooding about the past, irritability or excessive anger, decreased activity or productivity, and poor concentration or memory. During the year of the disturbance, the above symptoms have never resolved for more than two months at a time. In addition, no major depressive episode was present during the first year of the disturbance. To meet the DSM-IV diagnostic criteria for dysthymic disorder, the child must not have a history of a manic or hypomanic episode. Also, dysthymic disorder is not diagnosed if the symptoms occur exclusively during a chronic psychotic disorder or if they are the direct effects of a substance or a general medical condition. DSM-IV provides for the specification of early onset (before age 21 years) or late onset (after 21 years) (Table 15.2–1).

A child or an adolescent with dysthymic disorder may have had a previous major depressive episode before the onset of dysthymic disorder, but it is much more common for a child with dysthymic disorder for more than one year to have major depressive disorder. In that case, both depressive diagnoses are given (double depression).

Dysthymic disorder in children is known to have an average age of onset that is several years earlier than the age of onset of major depressive disorder. Clinicians disagree about whether dysthymic disorder is a chronic and insidious version of major depressive disorder or a separate disorder.

Occasionally, youngsters fulfill the criteria for dysthymic disorder except that their episodes last only two weeks to several months, with symptom-free intervals lasting for two to three months. Those minor mood presentations in children are likely to indicate severe mood disorder episodes in the future. Current knowledge suggests that the longer, the more recurrent, the more frequent, and perhaps the less related to social stress those episodes are, the greater is the likelihood of a severe mood disorder in the future.

However, when minor depressive episodes follow a significant stressful life event by less than three months, they do not indicate future mood disorder episodes, and so they should be diagnosed as adjustment disorder with depressed mood or bereavement.

**Bipolar I disorder.** Bipolar I disorder is rarely diagnosed in prepubertal children, since manic episodes are uncommon in that age group, even when depressive symptoms have already appeared. In general, a major depressive episode precedes a manic episode in an adolescent who experiences bipolar I disorder. However, when a classic manic episode appears in an adolescent, it is recognized as a definitive change from a preexisting state and often presents with grandiose and paranoid delusions and hallucinatory phenomena. According to DSM-IV, the diagnostic criteria for a manic episode remain the same for children and adolescents as for adults (Table 15.1–7). The diagnostic criteria for a manic episode include a distinct period of an abnormally elevated, expansive, or irritable mood that lasts at least one week or for any duration if hospitalization is necessary. In addition, during the period of mood disturbance, at least three of the following significant and persistent symptoms must be present: inflated self-esteem or grandiosity, decreased need for sleep, pressure to talk, flight of ideas or racing thoughts, distractibility, an increase in goal-directed activity, and excessive involvement in pleasurable activities that may result in painful consequences. The mood disturbance is sufficient to cause marked impairment, and it is not due to the direct effect of a substance or a general medical condition. Thus, manic states precipitated by somatic medications (for example, antidepressants) cannot be counted as indicating a diagnosis of bipolar I disorder.

In contrast to the classic manic episode, childhood manic episodes may be variants but have a relation to bipolar I disorder. The atypical manic episodes are sometimes observed in children with family histories of classic bipolar I disorder; the atypical manic episodes consist of extreme mood variability, cyclic aggressive behavior, high levels of distractibility, and poor attention span. Those episodes are not likely to be clearly episodic, and they may be less treatment-responsive than are classic manic episodes. Children with atypical hypomanic episodes must be differentiated from children with severe attention-deficit/hyperactivity disorder, who share some features of mania but exhibit their behaviors on a long-term basis, rather than on an episodic basis. In attention-deficit/hyperactivity disorder, family histories of bipolar I disorder are uncommon.

In general when manic episodes appear in an adolescent, they are often accompanied by psychotic features, and hospitalization is often necessary. Adolescents' delusions and hallucinations may involve grandiose notions about their power, worth, knowledge, family, or relationships. Persecutory delusions and flight of ideas are common. Overall, gross impairment of reality testing is common in adolescent manic episodes. In adolescents with

major depressive disorder destined for bipolar I disorder, those at highest risk have family histories of bipolar I disorder and exhibit acute severe depressive episodes with psychosis, hypersomnia, and psychomotor retardation.

**Cyclothymic disorder.** The only difference in the DSM-IV diagnostic criteria for child or adolescent cyclothymic disorder is that a period of one year of numerous mood swings is necessary, instead of the adult criterion of two years. Some cyclothymic adolescents probably go on to bipolar I disorder.

**Schizoaffective disorder.** The criteria for schizoaffective disorder in children and adolescents are identical to those in adults. Although some adolescents and probably some children do fit the criteria for schizoaffective disorder, little is now known about the natural course of their illness, family history, psychobiology, and treatment. In DSM-IV schizoaffective disorder in children is classified as a psychotic disorder.

**Bereavement** Bereavement is a state of grief related to the death of a loved one that may present with symptoms characteristic of a major depressive episode. Typical depressive symptoms associated with bereavement include feelings of sadness, insomnia, diminished appetite, and in some cases weight loss. Grieving children may become withdrawn and appear sad, and they are not easily drawn into even favorite activities. In DSM-IV bereavement is not a mental disorder but is in the category of additional conditions that may be a focus of clinical attention. Persons in the midst of a typical bereavement period may also meet the criteria for a major depressive disorder when the symptoms persist longer than two months after the loss. In some instances, severe depressive symptoms within two months of the loss are considered to be beyond the scope of normal grieving, and a diagnosis of major depressive disorder is warranted. Symptoms indicative of major depressive disorder exceeding usual bereavement include guilt related to issues beyond those surrounding the death of the loved one, preoccupation with death other than thoughts of being dead to be with the deceased person, morbid preoccupation with worthlessness, marked psychomotor retardation, prolonged serious functional impairment, and hallucinations other than transient perceptions of the voice of the deceased person.

The duration of a normal period of bereavement varies; in children the duration may depend partly on the support system in place. For example, a child who must be removed from home because of the death of the only parent in the home may feel devastated and abandoned for a long time. Children who lose loved ones may feel that the death occurred because they were bad or did not perform as expected. The reaction to the loss of a loved one may be partly influenced by being prepared for the death in cases of chronic illness.

Chapter 30 and Section 2.7 also discuss bereavement.

**Pathology and laboratory examination.** No single laboratory test is useful in making a diagnosis of a mood disorder. A screening test for thyroid function can rule out the possibility of an endocrinological contribution to a mood disorder. Dexamethasone-suppression tests may be done serially in cases of major depressive disorder to document whether an initial nonsuppressor becomes a suppressor with treatment or with resolution of the symptoms.

## Differential Diagnosis

Psychotic forms of depressive and manic episodes must be differentiated from schizophrenia. Substance-induced mood disorder can sometimes be differentiated from other mood disorders only after detoxification. Anxiety symptoms and conduct-disordered behavior can coexist with depressive disorders and can frequently pose problems in differentiating those disorders from nondepressed emotional and conduct disorders.

Of particular importance is the distinction between agitated depressive or manic episodes and attention-deficit/hyperactivity disorder, in which the persistent excessive activity and restlessness can cause confusion. Prepubertal children do not present with classic forms of agitated depression, such as hand wringing and pacing. Instead, their inability to sit still and their frequent temper tantrums are the most common symptoms. Sometimes the correct answer becomes evident only after the depressive episode has remitted. If the child has no difficulty in concentrating and is not hyperactive while recovered from the depressive episode in a drug-free state, attention-deficit/hyperactivity disorder was probably not present.

### Course and Prognosis

The course and the prognosis of mood disorders in children and adolescents depend on the age of onset, the severity of the episode, and the presence of comorbid disorders, with a young age of onset and multiple disorders predicting a bad prognosis.

Depressive disorders are likely to recur and, if not successfully treated, produce considerable short-term and long-term difficulties and complications: poor academic achievement, arrest or delay in psychosocial development patterns, suicide, substance abuse as a means of self-medication, and conduct disorder. Follow-up studies to date indicate a continued risk for mood disorders.

### Treatment

**Hospitalization.** The important immediate consideration is often whether hospitalization is indicated. When the patient is suicidal, hospitalization is indicated to provide maximum protection against the patient's own self-destructive impulses and behavior. Hospitalization may also be needed when the child or adolescent has coexisting substance abuse or dependence.

**Psychotherapy.** Few data confirm the superiority of one kind of psychotherapeutic approach over another in the treatment of childhood and adolescent mood disorders. However, family therapy is needed to educate families about serious mood disorders that occur in children at times of overwhelming family stress. Psychotherapeutic approaches for depressed children include cognitive approaches and a more directed and structured approach than that usually used with adults. Since depressed children's psychosocial functions may remain impaired for long periods, even after the depressive episode has remitted, long-term social skills interventions are needed. In some treatment programs, modeling and role playing can help establish good problem-solving skills.

**Pharmacotherapy.** No clear evidence from double-blind, placebo-controlled studies indicates that antidepressants are of benefit in child and adolescent depressive disorders. Moreover, antidepressants have yet to receive

Food and Drug Administration (FDA) approval for use in depressed children. Nonetheless, if a trial of antidepressants is indicated, the following should be kept in mind: The use of antidepressants requires baseline studies, gradual titration of the drug, and monitoring of electrocardiogram (ECG) changes, blood pressure, side effects, and, whenever possible, serum levels. Because toxicity produces serious cardiac arrhythmias, seizures, coma, and death, monitoring is essential. The clinical response may be correlated with plasma level. In one uncontrolled study using imipramine (Tofranil) to treat prepubertal major depressive disorder, good responses were seen when blood levels were about 140 to 150 ng per mL. Because antidepressants have not yet been approved for use by depressed children and because of their potentially serious side effects and toxicity, clinicians should use antidepressants for children only after study or consultation with a clinician experienced in their use.

Fluoxetine (Prozac) has been used with some success in adolescents with major depressive disorder. Since some children and adolescents who have depressive episodes go on to experience bipolar II disorder, the clinician must note hypomanic symptoms that may occur during the use of fluoxetine and other antidepressants. In those cases the medication should be discontinued to determine if the hypomanic episode then resolves. However, hypomanic responses to antidepressants do not necessarily predict that bipolar II disorder has developed.

Bipolar I disorder and bipolar II disorder in childhood and adolescence are treated with lithium (Eskalith) with good results. However, children who have preexisting disruptive behavior disorders (for example, conduct disorder and attention-deficit/hyperactivity disorder) and then experience bipolar disorders early in adolescence are less likely to respond well to lithium than are those without the behavior disorders.

## SUICIDE

Suicidal ideation, gestures, and attempts are frequently associated with depressive disorders, and those suicidal phenomena, particularly in adolescence, are a growing public mental health problem. Suicidal ideation occurs with greatest frequency when the depressive disorder is severe. More than 12,000 children and adolescents are hospitalized in the United States each year because of suicidal threats or behavior. However, completed suicide is rare under the age of 12 years. A young child is little able to design and carry out a realistic suicide plan. Cognitive immaturity seems to play a protective role in preventing even children who wish they were dead from committing suicide. Completed suicide occurs about five times more often in adolescent boys than in girls, although the rate of suicide attempts is at least three times higher among adolescent girls than among boys.

Suicidal ideation is not a static phenomenon; it may wax and wane with time. The decision to engage in suicidal behavior may be impulsive, without a great deal of forethought, or it may be the culmination of prolonged rumination. The method of the suicide attempt influences the morbidity and the completion rate independent of the severity of the intent to die at the time of the suicidal behavior. Thus, the most common method of completed suicide in children and adolescents is through the use of firearms, which account for about two thirds of all suicides in boys and almost half of the suicides in girls. The second most common method of suicide in boys, occurring in about a fourth of all cases, is by hanging; in girls about a fourth commit suicide through the ingestion of toxic substances. Carbon monoxide poisoning is the next most common method for suicide in boys but occurs in less than 10 percent; suicide by hanging and carbon monoxide poisoning are equally frequent among girls, accounting for about 10 percent each.

## Epidemiology

In recent years the suicide rate among adolescents in the United States has risen dramatically, although in some other countries it has not. There has been a steady increase in suicide rate for Americans 15 to 19 years of age. It is now 13.6 per 100,000 for boys and 3.6 per 100,000 for girls. More than 5,000 adolescents commit suicide each year in the United States, one every 90 minutes. The increased suicide rates are thought to reflect changes in the social environment, changing attitudes toward suicide, and the increasing availability of the means to commit suicide; for example, in the United States 66 percent of adolescent suicides in boys are committed by firearms, compared with 6 percent in the United Kingdom. Suicide is the third leading cause of death in the United States for persons aged 15 to 24 years and is second among white males in that age group.

The rates for suicide depend on age, and they increase significantly after puberty. Whereas less than 1 completed suicide per 100,000 occurs under 14 years of age, about 10 per 100,000 completed suicides occur in adolescents between 15 and 19 years of age. Under 14 years of age, suicide attempts are at least 50 times more common than are suicide completions. Between 15 and 19 years, however, the rate of suicide attempts is about 15 times greater than suicide completions. The number of adolescent suicides over the past several decades has increased three- or fourfold.

## Etiology

Universal features in suicidal adolescents are their inability to synthesize solutions to problems and their lack of coping strategies to deal with immediate stressors. Thus, a narrow view of the options available to deal with recurrent family discord, rejection, or failure contributes to a decision to commit suicide.

**Genetic factors.** Evidence for a genetic contribution to suicidal behavior is based on family suicide risk studies and the higher concordance for suicide among monozygotic twins compared with dizygotic twins. Although the risk for suicide is high in persons with mental disorders—including schizophrenia, major depressive disorder, and bipolar I disorder—the risk for suicide is much higher in the relatives of those with mood disorders than in the relatives of persons with schizophrenia.

**Other biological factors.** Neurochemical findings show some overlap between persons with aggressive, impulsive behaviors and those who complete suicide. Low levels of serotonin (5-HT) and its major metabolite, 5-hydroxyindoleacetic acid (5-HIAA), have been found postmortem in the brains of suicide completers. Low levels of 5-HIAA have been found in the cerebrospinal fluid of depressed persons who attempted suicide by violent methods. Alcohol and other psychoactive substances may lower 5-HIAA, perhaps increasing the vulnerability to suicidal behavior in an already predisposed person. The mechanism linking decreased serotonergic function and aggressive or suicidal behavior is unknown, and low serotonin may turn out to be a marker, rather than a cause, of aggression and suicidal propensity.

The dexamethasone-suppression test has produced less reliable findings in depressed children and adolescents than in adults. However, some studies of children and adolescents indicate an association of nonsuppression on the dexamethasone-suppression test and potentially lethal suicide attempts. In children and adolescents the association between suicidality and nonsuppression is not necessarily in the context of a major mood disorder.

**Social factors.** Children and adolescents are vulnerable to overwhelmingly chaotic, abusive, and neglectful environments. A wide range of psychopathological symptoms may occur secondary to exposure to violent and abusive homes. Aggressive, self-destructive, and suicidal behaviors seem to occur with greatest frequency in persons who have endured chronically stressful family lives.

## Diagnosis and Clinical Features

Direct questioning of children and adolescents about suicidal thoughts is necessary, because studies have consistently shown that parents are frequently unaware of such ideas in their children. Suicidal thoughts (that is, children's talk about wanting to harm themselves) and suicidal threats (that is, children's statements that they want to jump in front of a car) are more common than is suicide completion.

The characteristics of adolescents who attempt suicide and those who complete suicide are similar, and about one third of those who complete suicide made prior attempts. Mental disorders present in some suicide attempters and completers include major depressive disorder, manic episodes, and psychotic disorders. Persons with mood disorders in combination with substance abuse and a history of aggressive behavior are particularly high-risk adolescents. Those without mood disorders who are violent, aggressive, and impulsive may be prone to suicide during family or peer conflicts. High levels of hopelessness, poor problem-solving skills, and a history of aggressive behavior are risk factors for suicide. Depression alone is a more serious risk factor for suicide in girls than in boys, but boys often have more severe psychopathology than do girls who commit suicide. The profile of an adolescent who commits suicide is occasionally one of high achievement and perfectionistic character traits; such an adolescent may have recently been humiliated by a perceived failure, such as diminished academic performance.

In psychiatrically disturbed and vulnerable adolescents, suicide attempts are often related to recent stressors. The precipitants of suicidal behavior include conflicts and arguments with family members and boyfriends or girlfriends. Alcohol and other substance use may further predispose an already vulnerable adolescent to suicidal behavior. In other cases, an adolescent attempts suicide in anticipation of punishment after being caught by the police or other authority figures for a forbidden behavior.

About 40 percent of youthful suicide completers had previous psychiatric treatment, and about 40 percent made a previous suicide attempt. A child who has lost a parent by any means before the age of 13 has a high risk for mood disorders and suicide. The precipitating factors include loss of face with peers, a broken romance, school difficulties, unemployment, bereavement, separation, and rejection.

Clusters of suicides among adolescents who know one another and go to the same school have been reported. Suicidal behavior may precipitate other such attempts within a peer group through identification—so-called copycat suicides. Some studies have found an increase in adolescent suicide after television programs were shown whose main theme was the suicide of a teenager. In general, however, many other factors are involved, including a necessary substrate of psychopathology. One recent study investigated two clusters of teenage suicide in Texas. The researchers found that indirect exposure to suicide through the media was not significantly associated with suicide. Factors that were associated included previous suicidal threats or attempts, self-injury, exposure to someone who had died violently, recent romantic breakups, and a high frequency of moves, schools attended, and parental figures lived with.

The tendency of disturbed young persons to imitate highly publicized suicides has been called the Werther syndrome, after the protagonist in Johann Wolfgang von Goethe's novel *The Sorrows of Young Werther*. The novel, in which the hero kills himself, was banned in some European countries after its publication more than 200 years ago because of a rash of suicides by young men who had read it; some, when they killed themselves, dressed like Werther or left the book open to the passage describing his death. In general, although imitation may play a role in the timing of suicide attempts by vulnerable adolescents, the overall suicide rate does not seem to increase when media exposure increases.

## Treatment

Adolescent suicide attempters must be evaluated before the decision is made to hospitalize them or return them home. Those who fall into high-risk groups should be hospitalized until the suicidality is no longer present. High-risk persons include those who have made previous suicide attempts; boys more than 12 years old with histories of aggressive behavior or substance abuse; those who have made an attempt with a lethal method, such as a gun or a toxic ingested substance; those with major depressive dis-

order characterized by social withdrawal, hopelessness, and a lack of energy; girls who have run away from home, are pregnant, or have made an attempt with a method other than ingesting a toxic substance; and any person who exhibits persistent suicidal ideation. A child or an adolescent with suicidal ideation must be hospitalized if the clinician has any doubts about the family's ability to supervise the child or cooperate with treatment in an outpatient setting. In such a situation, child protective services must be involved before the child can be discharged.

When adolescents with suicidal ideation report that they are no longer suicidal, discharge can be considered only after a complete discharge plan is in place. The plan must include psychotherapy, pharmacotherapy, and family therapy as indicated. A written contract with the adolescent, outlining the adolescent's agreement not to engage in suicidal behavior and providing an alternative if suicidal ideation re-occurs, should be in place. In addition, a follow-up outpatient appointment should be made before the discharge, and a telephone hot-line number should be provided to the adolescent and the family in case suicidal ideation reappears before treatment begins.

## Reference

Blumenthal S J: Youth suicide: Risk factors, assessment, and treatment of adolescent and young adult suicidal patients. Psychiatr Clin North Am *13*: 511, 1990.

Casat C D, Arana G W, Powell K: The DST in children and adolescents with major depressive disorder. Am J Psychiatry *146*: 505, 1989.

Emslie G J, Rush A J, Weinberg W A, Rintelmann J W, Roffwarg H P: Children with major depression show reduced rapid eye movement latencies. Arch Gen Psychiatry *47*: 199, 1990.

Garland A F, Zigler E: Adolescent suicide prevention: Current research and social policy implications. Am Psychol *48*: 169, 1993.

Harrington R C: Depressive disorder in children and adolescents. Br J Hosp Med *43*: 108, 1990.

Hendin H: Psychodynamics of suicide, with particular reference to the young. Am J Psychiatry *48* 1150, 1991.

Kazdin A E: Childhood depression. J Child Psychol Psychiatry *31*: 121, 1990.

Kovacs M, Goldston D, Gatsonis C: Suicidal behaviors and childhood-onset depressive disorders: A longitudinal investigation. J Am Acad Child Adolesc Psychiatry *32*: 8, 1993.

Lewinsohn P M, Rohde P, Seeley J R: Psychosocial characteristics of adolescents with a history of suicide attempt. J Am Acad Child Adolesc Psychiatry *32*: 60, 1993.

Mann J J, Arango V, Underwood M D: Serotonin and suicidal behavior. In *The Neuropharmacology of Serotonin,* P Whitaker-Azmitia, S Peroutka, editors, p. 476. Annals of the New York Academy of Sciences, New York, 1990.

Marttunen M J, Aro H M, Henriksson M M, Lonnqvist J K: Mental disorders in adolescent suicide. Arch Gen Psychiatry *48*: 834, 1991.

Mitchell J, McCauley E, Burke P, Calderon R, Schloredt K: Psychopathy in parents of depressed children and adolescents. J Am Acad Child Adolesc Psychiatry *28*: 352, 1989.

Mitchell J, McCauley E, Burke P, Moss S J: Phenomenology of depression in children and adolescents. J Am Acad Child Adolesc Psychiatry *27*: 12, 1988.

Pataki C S, Carlson G A: Affective disorders in children and adolescents. In *Handbook on Studies on Child Psychiatry*, B Tonge, G D Burrows, J S Werry, editors, p. 137. Elsevier, Amsterdam, 1990.

Pataki C S, Carlson G A: Bipolar disorder in children and adolescents. In *Clinical Guide to Depression in Children and Adolescents*, M Shafii, S Shafii, editors, p. 269. American Psychiatric Press, Washington, 1992.

Pfeffer C R, Klerman G L, Hurt S W, Kakuma T, et al: Suicidal children grow up: Rates and psychosocial risk factors for suicide attempts during follow-up. J Am Acad Child Adolesc Psychiatry *32*: 106, 1993.

Puig-Antich J, Dahl R, Ryan N, Novacento H, Goetz D, Goetz R, Tworrey J, Klepper T: Cortisol secretion in prepubertal children with major depressive disorder. Arch Gen Psychiatry *46*: 801, 1989.

Puig-Antich J, Perel J M, Lupatkin W, Chambers W, Tabrizi M A, King

J, Goetz R, Davies M, Stiller R L: Imipramine in prepubertal major depressive disorders. Arch Gen Psychiatry 44: 81, 1987.

Rotheram-Borus M J: Suicidal behavior and risk factors among runaway youths. Am J Psychiatry 150: 103, 1993.

Ryland D H, Kruesi M J: Suicide among adolescents, Int Rev Psychiatry 4: 185, 1992.

Shaffer D, Garland A, Gould M, Fisher P, Trautman P: Preventing teenage suicide: A critical review. J Am Acad Child Adolesc Psychiatry 27: 675, 1988.

Varanka T M, Weller R A, Weller E B, Fristad M A: Lithium treatment of manic episodes with psychotic features in prepubertal children. Am J Psychiatry 145: 1557, 1988.

Walker M, Moreau D, Weissman M M: Parents' awareness of children's suicide attempts. Am J Psychiatry 147: 1364, 1990.

Zahn-Waxler C, Mayfield A, Radke-Yarrow M, McKnew D H. Cytryn L, Davenport Y B: A follow-up investigation of offspring of parents with bipolar disorder. Am J Psychiatry 145: 506, 1988.

# Schizophrenia with Childhood Onset

Schizophrenia with childhood onset is conceptually the same as schizophrenia in adolescence and adulthood. Although rare, schizophrenia in prepubertal children includes the presence of at least two of the following: hallucinations, delusions, grossly disorganized speech or behavior, and severe withdrawal for at least one month. Social or academic dysfunction must be present, and continuous signs of the disturbance must persist for at least six months. The diagnostic criteria for schizophrenia in children are identical to the criteria for the adult form except that children may fail to achieve their expected levels of social and academic functioning, instead of having their functioning deteriorate.

Prior to the 1960s the term "childhood psychosis" was applied to a heterogeneous group that included a variety of pervasive developmental disorders without hallucinations and delusions. In the 1960s and the 1970s the observation was made that children who had evidence of a profound psychotic disturbance early in life tended to be mentally retarded, had severe communication and language impairments, were socially dysfunctional, and had no family history of schizophrenia. But children whose psychoses emerged after the age of 5 years manifested auditory hallucinations, delusions, inappropriate affects, thought disorder, and normal intelligence, and they often had a family history of schizophrenia; they were viewed as exhibiting schizophrenia, whereas the younger children were identified as evidencing an entirely different disorder, either autistic disorder or a pervasive developmental disorder.

Beginning with the third edition of *Diagnostic and Statistical Manual of Mental Disorders* (DSM-III), schizophrenia with childhood onset was formally separated from autistic disorder. That change reflected evidence accrued during the 1960s and the 1970s that the clinical picture, the family history, the age of onset, and the course of the two disorders are different. After the separation of the disorders, two controversies ensued. In the first, a minority of researchers remained of the opinion that a group of autistic children go on to have schizophrenia. Evidence is available that a few autistic children do experience schizophrenia, but assertions that those children constitute a large group are unsubstantiated. In general, schizophrenia is easily differentiated from autistic disorder (Table 38–3). The majority of autistic children are impaired in all areas of adaptive functioning from early life onward. The onset is almost always before the age of 3 years, whereas the onset of schizophrenia is usually in adolescence or young adulthood. There are practically no reports of an onset of schizophrenia before the age of 5 years. In the revised third edition of DSM (DSM-III-R), schizophrenia could be diagnosed in autistic children only if hallucinations or delusions developed and became a prominent clinical feature. According to the fourth edition of DSM (DSM-IV), schizophrenia can be diagnosed in the presence of autistic disorder.

The second controversy concerned the application of basic adult criteria for schizophrenia to children. Several reports indicate that some children present with hallucinations, delusions, and thought disorders typical of schizophrenia. However, normal developmental immaturities in language development and in separating reality from fantasy sometimes make it difficult to diagnose schizophrenia in children ages 5 to 7 years.

## EPIDEMIOLOGY

Schizophrenia in prepubertal children is exceedingly rare; it is estimated to occur less frequently than autistic disorder. In adolescents the prevalence of schizophrenia is estimated to be 50 times greater than in younger children, with probable rates of 1 to 2 per 1,000. Boys seem to have a slight preponderance among schizophrenic children, with an estimated ratio of about 1.67 boys to 1 girl. Boys often become symptomatic at a younger age than do girls. Schizophrenia is rarely diagnosed in children less than 5 years of age; it is commonly diagnosed in adolescents over 15 years. The symptoms usually emerge insidiously, and the diagnostic criteria are met gradually over time. Occasionally, the onset of schizophrenia is sudden and occurs in a previously well-functioning child. Schizophrenia may also be diagnosed in a child who has had chronic difficulties and then experiences a significant exacerbation.

The prevalence of schizophrenia among the parents of schizophrenic children is about 8 percent, which is close to double the prevalence in the parents of adult-onset schizophrenic patients.

Schizotypal personality disorder is similar to schizophrenia in its inappropriate affects, excessive magical thinking, odd beliefs, social isolation, ideas of reference, and unusual perceptual experiences, such as illusions. However, schizotypal personality disorder does not have psychotic features; still, the disorder seems to aggregate in families with adult-onset schizophrenia, leading to an unclear relation between the two disorders.

## ETIOLOGY

Although family and genetic studies provide substantial evidence of a biological contribution to the development of schizophrenia, no specific biological markers have been identified, and the precise mechanisms of transmission of schizophrenia are not understood.

Schizophrenia is significantly more prevalent among first-degree relatives of those with schizophrenia than in the general population. Adoption studies of adult-onset schizophrenic patients have shown that schizophrenia occurs in the biological relatives, not the adoptive relatives. Additional genetic evidence is supported by the higher concordance rates for schizophrenia in monozygotic twins than in dizygotic twins. The genetic transmission pattern of schizophrenia remains unknown; however, more genetic loading is seen in the relatives of those with childhood-onset schizophrenia than in the relatives of those with adult-onset schizophrenia.

Currently, no reliable way is available to identify those persons who are at the highest risk for schizophrenia in a given family. However, higher than expected rates of neurological soft signs and impairments in sustaining attention and in strategies for information processing are seen among high-risk groups of children.

Increased rates of disturbed communication styles are found in families with a schizophrenic patient. High expressed emotion, characterized by overly reactive and critical responses in families, negatively affect the prognosis of schizophrenic patients.

A variety of abnormal, nonspecific results on computed tomography (CT) scans and electroencephalograms (EEGs) have been noted in schizophrenic patients.

Children and adolescents with schizophrenia are more apt to have a premorbid history of social rejection, poor peer relationships, clingy withdrawn behavior, and academic trouble than are those with adult-onset schizophrenia. Some children whose schizophrenia is first seen in middle childhood have early histories of delayed motor milestones and delayed language acquisition that are similar to some symptoms of autistic disorder.

The mechanism of biological vulnerability and environmental influences resulting in the manifestations of schizophrenia remains under investigation.

## DIAGNOSIS AND CLINICAL FEATURES

All the symptoms included in adult-onset schizophrenia may be manifested by children with the disorder. The onset is frequently insidious; after first exhibiting inappropriate affects or unusual behavior, a child may take months or years to meet all the diagnostic criteria for schizophrenia. Children who eventually meet the criteria are often socially rejected and clingy and have limited social skills. They may have histories of delayed motor and verbal milestones and do poorly in school in spite of normal intelligence. Although schizophrenic children and autistic children may be similar in their early histories, schizophrenic children have normal intelligence and do not meet the criteria for a pervasive developmental disorder. According to DSM-IV, a schizophrenic child may experience a deterioration of function, along with the emergence of psychotic symptoms, or the child may never achieve the expected level of functioning (Table 13–3).

Auditory hallucinations are commonly manifested by children with schizophrenia. They may hear several voices making an ongoing critical commentary about the child, or command hallucinations may tell the children to kill themselves or others. The voices may be of a bizarre nature, identified as a "computer in my head" or Martians or the voice of someone familiar, such as a relative.

Visual hallucinations are experienced by a significant number of children with schizophrenia and are often frightening; the children may see the devil, skeletons, scary faces, or space creatures. Transient phobic visual hallucinations also occur in traumatized children who do not go on to have a major psychotic disorder.

Delusions are present in more than half of all schizophrenic children; the delusions take various forms, including persecutory, grandiose, and religious. Delusions increase in frequency with increased age.

Blunted or inappropriate affects are almost universally present in children with schizophrenia. Schizophrenic children may giggle inappropriately or cry without being able to explain why.

Formal thought disorders, including loosening of associations and thought blocking, are common features among children with schizophrenia. Illogical thinking and poverty of thought are also often present. Schizophrenic children speak less than do other children of the same intelligence, and schizophrenic children are ambiguous in the way they refer to people, objects, and events.

The core phenomena for schizophrenia appear to be the same among various age groups, but the child's developmental level influences the presentation of the symptoms. Thus, delusions present in young children are less complex than are those in older children. Age-appropriate content, such as animal imagery and monsters, are likely to be a source of delusional fear in children.

Other features that seem to be present with a high frequency in schizophrenic children are poor motor functioning, visuospatial impairments, and attention deficits.

DSM-IV delineates five types of schizophrenia: paranoid, disorganized, catatonic, undifferentiated, and residual.

Dan, a 9-year-old boy, was referred for a psychiatric evaluation by his special education schoolteacher, who reported that his schoolwork was deteriorating, he appeared to be dysphoric, and he refused to listen to her. He occasionally mentioned that ghosts were in his basement and that he and his mother had both heard the ghosts' voices. Dan was an isolated boy who looked younger than his age. He was functioning several years below his grade level, although his intelligence quotient (I.Q.) test revealed a normal intelligence. He had been in special education since kindergarten, when he showed poor expressive language ability and an inability to sit still. Dan's mother was at her wit's end, reporting that in the house he was difficult to handle, he would not do anything that she asked, and she would often find him wandering outside.

Dan was born after a full-term pregnancy, and he went home from the hospital with his mother without any neonatal problems. His mother began to feel that something was wrong when he did not learn to walk until he was 18 months old, and he did not speak any words until he was 2 years of age.

Her pediatrician told her that some children develop more slowly than others. When he was 3½ years old, Dan's mother became more concerned, since he did not seem to be able to follow rules at his preschool, and he seemed to be disinterested in his peers. His teachers told his mother that Dan seemed to have a short attention span, a difficult time sitting still, and poor language abilities.

Dan was placed in special education in kindergarten, and things seemed to be under control for the next two years. He did not make any friends, and he seemed to be unable to fit in with the other children, but the teachers were able to handle him in the classroom. He always seemed to be one or two years younger than his age.

Six months before the psychiatric evaluation, Dan began to become frightened at night, stating that he saw scary faces in his window and that skeletons and ghosts were after him. His mother also believed in ghosts, but she realized that he was hearing voices and seeing things that were not there. She felt that he was just stressed and that the visions and voices would probably go away. By the time Dan came for his psychiatric evaluation, he was involved with a number of characters that he believed were invisible to others but that contacted him. Some friendly characters, such as a dog and a policeman, tried to help him, but he generally felt frightened and overwhelmed, and he kept looking over his shoulder. Ultimately, he believed that the devil was after him, and that belief scared and upset him.

Dan was admitted to the psychiatric inpatient unit for observation and to be given a trial of antipsychotic medication if the voices and faces continued to plague him. On the unit, Dan conversed coherently and participated in activities, but he continued to feel uneasy and upset, and he expressed fears about his hallucinations. He spoke about the characters to staff members, believing that the characters were real but that others could not see them because the characters chose to show themselves only to him. He was given a trial of haloperidol (Haldol), which he reported made some of the voices get lower. At times, he continued to hear multiple voices arguing with each other and saying negative things about him. They told him to hurt his mother's new baby, but he never listened to that.

Dan was conversing with hallucinatory characters and maintaining the delusion that the devil was showing himself in various forms. His stories were not simply imaginative, since he was frightened and suspicious. The psychiatrists gave Dan a diagnosis of schizophrenia.

Dan's symptoms were moderately improved after taking the antipsychotic medication, and he was then referred to a day treatment special education school, so that he could be monitored and educated in a therapeutic milieu. On discharge from the psychiatric unit, he continued to believe that invisible characters appeared only to him and spoke with him frequently.

## Pathology and Laboratory Examination

No specific laboratory tests are helpful in the diagnosis of schizophrenia with childhood onset. High incidences of pregnancy and birth complications have been reported among schizophrenic children, but at the present time no specificity has been found in those risks for childhood schizophrenia. EEG studies have also not been helpful in distinguishing schizophrenic children from other children.

## DIFFERENTIAL DIAGNOSIS

Children with schizotypal personality disorder and children with schizophrenia have many similarities. Blunted affect, social isolation, eccentric thoughts, ideas of reference, and bizarre behavior may be seen in both disorders; however, in schizophrenia, overt psychotic symptoms—such as hallucinations, delusions, and incoherence—must be present at some point; when they are present, they exclude a diagnosis of schizotypal personality disorder.

However, hallucinations alone are not evidence of schizophrenia, since the patient must show either a deterioration of function or an inability to meet the expected developmental level to warrant the diagnosis of schizophrenia. Auditory and visual hallucinations can appear as self-limited events in nonpsychotic young children who are faced with extreme psychosocial stressors, such as the breakup of their parents, and in children experiencing a major loss or a significant change in life-style.

Psychotic phenomena are common among children with major depressive disorder, in which both hallucinations and, less commonly, delusions may occur. The congruence of mood with the psychotic features is most pronounced in depressed children, although schizophrenic children may also appear sad. The hallucinations and the delusions of schizophrenia are more likely to have a bizarre quality than are those of children with depressive disorders. In children and adolescents with bipolar I disorder, it is often difficult to distinguish a first episode of mania with psychotic features from schizophrenia if the child has no history of prior depressions. Grandiose delusions and hallucinations are typical of manic episodes, but often the clinician must follow the natural history of the disorder to confirm the presence of a mood disorder.

Pervasive developmental disorders, including autistic disorder with normal intelligence, may share some features with schizophrenia. Most notably, difficulty with social relationships, an early history of delayed language acquisition, and ongoing communication deviance are manifested in both disorders; however, hallucinations, delusions, and formal thought disorder are core features of schizophrenia and are not expected features of pervasive developmental disorders. Pervasive developmental disorders are usually diagnosed by the age of 3 years, but schizophrenia with childhood onset is rarely diagnosable before the age of 5 years.

The abuse of alcohol and other substances can sometimes result in a deterioration of function, psychotic symptoms, and paranoid delusions. Amphetamines, lysergic acid diethylamide (LSD), and phencyclidine (PCP) may lead to a psychotic state. A sudden, flagrant onset of paranoid psychosis is more suspicious of drug-induced psychoses than is an insidious onset.

Medical conditions that may induce psychotic features include thyroid disease, systemic lupus erythematosus, and temporal lobe disease.

## COURSE AND PROGNOSIS

Important predictors of the course and the outcome of childhood-onset schizophrenia include the child's level of functioning before the onset of schizophrenia, the age of onset, the child's degree of functioning regained after the first episode, and the degree of support available from the family.

Children who have developmental delays and premorbid behavioral disorders, such as attention-deficit/hyperactivity disorder and conduct disorder, and learning disorders seem to be poor responders to medication treatment of schizophrenia and are likely to have the most guarded prognoses. In a long-term outcome study of schizophrenic patients with onset before age 14 years, the worst prognoses occurred in children whose schizophrenia was diagnosed before they were 10 years of age and who had preexisting personality disorders.

An additional issue in outcome studies is the stability of the diagnosis of schizophrenia. Up to a third of all children who receive a diagnosis of schizophrenia may end up with a diagnosis of a mood disorder (instead of schizophrenia) in adolescence. Children and adolescents with bipolar I disorder may have a better long-term prognosis than do children and adolescents with schizophrenia.

In adult-onset schizophrenia, family interactions, such as high expressed emotion, may be associated with increased relapse rates. No clear-cut data are available in childhood schizophrenia, but the degree of supportiveness, as opposed to critical and overinvolved family responses, probably influences the prognosis.

In general, schizophrenia with childhood onset appears to be less medication-responsive than is adult-onset and adolescent-onset schizophrenia, and the prognosis may be poorer. The positive symptoms—that is, hallucinations and delusions—are likely to be more responsive to medication than are negative symptoms, such as withdrawal. In a recent report of 38 schizophrenic children who had been hospitalized, two thirds required placement in residential facilities, and only one third were improved enough to return home.

## TREATMENT

The treatment of schizophrenia with childhood onset includes a multimodality approach. Antipsychotic medications are indicated and may be effective, although many patients show little or no response. In addition, family education and ongoing supportive family meetings are needed to maximize the level of support that the family can give the patient. The proper educational setting for the child is also important, since social skills deficits, attention deficits, and academic difficulties often accompany childhood schizophrenia.

Few studies document the efficacy of antipsychotic medications in children and adolescents with schizophrenia. The medications appear to be helpful, and high-potency medications, such as haloperidol and trifluoperazine (Stelazine), are favored because of their decreased sedative side effects. The dosages for haloperidol range from about 1 to 10 mg a day in divided doses. Acute dystonic reactions do occur in children, and 1 to 2 mg a day of benztropine (Cogentin) is usually enough to treat the extrapyramidal side effects. Children and adolescents who are treated with antipsychotic medications are at risk for

withdrawal dyskinesias when the medication is withdrawn. The long-term side effects, including tardive dyskinesia, are perpetual risks for any patients who are treated with an antipsychotic medication.

A new antipsychotic medication, clozapine (Clozaril) has been used with some success in schizophrenic adults who are resistant to treatment with multiple conventional antipsychotics. Clozapine has the advantage that it generally does not induce extrapyramidal side effects and is not likely to cause tardive dyskinesia. However, because of its serious, potentially fatal side effect, agranulocytosis, the patient's white blood cell count must be monitored before treatment and frequently while the medication is being used. Agranulocytosis occurs in 1 to 2 percent of all patients. Other side effects associated with clozapine include somnolence, tachycardia, postural hypotension, hypersalivation, hyperthermia, and seizures. No available data evaluate its efficacy in treatment-resistant children and adolescents with schizophrenia. One published case study has reported on three successfully treated schizophrenic adolescents who were resistent to traditional antipsychotic treatment. The adolescents treated with clozapine reported sedation and increased salivation but were able to tolerate the medication. However, because of the serious nature of agranulocytosis, patients and families should be counseled extensively, and clinicians should record that the families understand the risks and the need for close monitoring.

Psychotherapy with schizophrenic children must take into account the child's developmental level, must continually support the child's good reality testing, and must include sensitivity to the child's sense of self.

## References

Asarnow J R, Goldstein M J, Ben-Meir S: Parental communication deviance in childhood onset schizophrenia spectrum and depressive disorders. J Child Psychol Psychiatry 29: 825, 1988.

Beitchman J H: Childhood schizophrenia: A review and comparison with adult onset schizophrenia. Psychiatr J Ottawa 8: 25, 1983.

Birmaher B, Baker R, Kapur S, Quinatana H, Ganguli R: Clozapine for the treatment of adolescents with schizophrenia. J Am Acad Child Adolesc Psychiatry 31: 160, 1992.

Burd L, Kerbeshian J: A North Dakota prevalence study of schizophrenia presenting in childhood. J Am Acad Child Adolesc Psychiatry 26: 347, 1987.

Burke P, DelBeccaro M, McCauley E, Clark C: Hallucinations in children. J Am Acad Child Adolesc Psychiatry 24: 71, 1985.

Campbell M, Grega D M, Green W H, Bennett W G: Neuroleptic-induced dyskinesias in children. Clin Neuropharmacol 6: 207, 1983.

Cantor S, Kestenbaum C: Psychotherapy with schizophrenic children. J Am Acad Child Adolesc Psychiatry 25: 623, 1986.

Caplan R, Guthrie D, Foy J G: Communication deficits and formal thought disorder in schizophrenic children. J Am Acad Child Adolesc Psychiatry 31: 151, 1992.

Eggers C: Course and prognosis of childhood schizophrenia. J Autism Child Schizophr 8: 21, 1978.

Fish B: Antecedents of a schizophrenic break. J Am Acad Child Psychiatry 25: 595, 1986.

Green W H, Padron-Gayol M, Hardesty A S, Bassiri M: Schizophrenia with childhood onset: A phenomenological study of 38 cases. J Am Acad Child Adolesc Psychiatry 31: 968, 1992.

Hellgren L, Gillberg C, Enerskog I: Antecedents of adolescent psychoses: A population-based study of school health problems in children who develop psychosis in adolescence. J Am Acad Child Adolesc Psychiatry 26: 351, 1987.

Kemph J: Hallucinations in psychotic children. J Am Acad Child Adolesc Psychiatry 26: 556, 1987.

Kydd R R, Werry J S: Schizophrenia in children under 16 years. J Autism Dev Disord 12: 343, 1982.

Petty L P, Ornitz E M, Michelman J D, Zimmerman E G: Autistic children who became schizophrenic. Arch Gen Psychiatry *41:* 129, 1984.

Schreier H A, Libow J A: Acute phobic hallucinations in very young children. J Am Acad Child Adolesc Psychiatry *25:* 574, 1986.

Towbin K E, Dykens E M, Pearson G S, Cohen D J: Conceptualizing "borderline syndrome of childhood" and "childhood schizophrenia" as a developmental disorder. J Am Acad Child Adolesc Psychiatry *32:* 775, 1993.

Watkins J, Asarnow J R, Tanguay P: Symptoms development in childhood onset schizophrenia. J Child Psychol Psychiatry *29:* 865, 1988.

Welner A, Welner Z, Fishman R: Psychiatric adolescent inpatients: Eight to ten year follow-up. Arch Gen Psychiatry *36:* 698, 1979.

Werry J S, McClellan J M: Predicting outcome in child and adolescent (early onset) schizophrenia and bipolar disorder. J Am Acad Child Adolesc Psychiatry *31:* 147, 1992.

# Child Psychiatry: Additional Conditions That May Be a Focus of Clinical Attention

## BORDERLINE INTELLECTUAL FUNCTIONING

Borderline intellectual functioning is defined by the presence of an intelligence quotient (I.Q.) within the range of 71 to 84. According to the fourth edition of *Diagnostic and Statistical Manual of Mental Disorders* (DSM-IV), a diagnosis of borderline intellectual functioning is made when issues pertaining to that level of cognition become the focus of clinical attention.

The clinician must assess the patient's intellectual level and current and past levels of adaptive functioning to diagnose borderline intellectual functioning. In cases of major mental disorders in which the current level of adaptive functioning has deteriorated, the diagnosis of borderline intellectual functioning may not be clearly evident. In such situations the clinician must evaluate the patient's chronological history to determine whether a compromised level of adaptive functioning was present even before the onset of the mental disorder.

Only about 6 to 7 percent of the population are found to have a borderline I.Q., as determined by the Stanford-Binet test or the Wechsler scales. The premise behind the inclusion of borderline intellectual functioning in DSM-IV is that persons at that level may experience difficulties in their adaptive capacities, which may ultimately become a focus of treatment. Thus, in the absence of specific intrapsychic conflicts, developmental traumas, biochemical abnormalities, and other factors linked to a mental disorder, such persons may experience severe emotional distress. Frustration and embarrassment over their difficulties may shape their life choices and lead to circumstances warranting psychiatric intervention.

### Etiology

Heritable factors and environmental conditions can contribute to a variety of cognitive impairments. Twin and adoption studies support hypotheses that many genes contribute to the development of a particular intelligence quotient. Specific infectious processes (such as congenital rubella), prenatal exposures (such as fetal alcohol syndrome), and specific chromosomal abnormalities (such as fragile X syndrome) result in mental retardation, but such causal factors probably do not lead to borderline intellectual functioning.

### Diagnosis

In DSM-IV the following statement about borderline intellectual functioning appears:

This category can be used when the focus of clinical attention is associated with borderline intellectual functioning, that is, an IQ in the 71–84 range. Differential diagnosis between Borderline Intellectual Functioning and Mental Retardation (an IQ of 70 or below) is especially difficult when the coexistence of certain mental disorders (e.g., Schizophrenia) is involved.
*Coding note: This is coded on Axis II.*

### Treatment

Once the underlying problem is known to the therapist, psychiatric treatment can be useful. Many persons with borderline intellectual functioning are able to function at a superior level in some areas while being markedly deficient in other areas. By directing such persons to appropriate areas of endeavor, by pointing out socially acceptable behavior, and by teaching them living skills, the therapist can help improve their self-esteem.

## ACADEMIC PROBLEM

In DSM-IV, academic problem is a condition that is not due to a mental disorder, such as a learning disorder or a communication disorder, or, if it is due to a mental disorder, it is severe enough to warrant independent clinical attention. Thus, a child or an adolescent who is of normal intelligence and is free of a learning disorder or a communication disorder but is failing in school or doing poorly falls into this category.

### Etiology

An academic problem may result from a variety of contributing factors and may arise at any time during a child's school years. School is the major occupation of children and adolescents and is their main social and educational instrument. Adjustment and success in the school setting depend on the child's physical, cognitive, social, and emotional adjustment. Children's general coping mechanisms in a variety of developmental tasks are usually reflected in their academic and social success in school. Boys and girls must cope with the process of separation from parents, adjustments to new environments, adaptation to social contacts, competition, assertion, intimacy, and exposure to unfamiliar attitudes. A corresponding relation often exists between school performance and how well those tasks are mastered.

Anxiety may play a major role in interfering with children's academic performances. Anxiety may hamper children's abilities to perform well on tests, to speak in public, and to ask questions when they do not understand something. Some children are so concerned about the way others view them that they are unable to attend to their academic tasks. In some children, conflicts regarding success and fears regarding the consequences that are imagined to accompany the attainment of success may hamper academic success. Sigmund Freud described persons with such conflicts as "those wrecked by success." An example is an adolescent girl whose inability to succeed in school is linked to her fear of social rejection or the loss of femiity or both, since she perceives success as being involved with aggressivity and competition with boys.

Depressed children may also withdraw from academic pursuits; they require specific interventions to improve their academic performances and to treat their depression. Children who do not have major depressive disorder but who are consumed by family problems—such as financial troubles, marital discord in their parents, and mental illness in family members—may be distracted and unable to attend to academic tasks.

Children who receive mixed messages from their parents about accepting criticism and redirection from their teachers may become confused and unable to perform well in school. The loss of the parents as the primary and predominant teachers in the child's life may result in identity conflicts for some children. Some students lack a stable sense of self and are unable to identify goals for themselves, leading to a sense of boredom or futility as students.

The cultural and economic background can play a role in how well accepted a child feels in school and can affect the child's academic achievement. Familial socioeconomic level, parental education, race, religion, and family functioning can influence a child's sense of fitting in and can affect a child's preparation to meet school demands. Schools, teachers, and clinicians can share insights about how to foster productive and cooperative environments for all students in a classroom.

The teachers' expectations concerning their students' performances influence those performances. Teachers serve as causal agents whose varying expectations can shape the differential development of students' skills and abilities. Such conditioning early in school, especially if negative, can disturb academic performance. Thus, a teacher's affective response to a child can prompt the appearance of academic problem. Most important is the teacher's humane approach to the student at all levels of education, including medical school.

## Diagnosis

In DSM-IV the following statement about academic problem appears:

This category can be used when the focus of clinical attention is an academic problem that is not due to a mental disorder, or if due to a mental disorder, is sufficiently severe to warrant independent clinical attention. An example is a pattern of failing grades or of significant underachievement in a person with adequate intellectual capacity in the absence of a Learning or Communication Disorder or any other mental disorder that would account for the problem.

## Treatment

Although not considered a mental disorder, academic problem can often be alleviated by psychological means. Psychotherapeutic techniques can be used successfully for scholastic difficulties related to poor motivation, poor self-concept, and underachievement.

Early efforts to relieve the problem are critical, as sustained problems in learning and school performance are frequently compounded and precipitate severe difficulties. Feelings of anger, frustration, shame, loss of self-respect, and helplessness—emotions that most often accompany school failures—emotionally and cognitively damage self-esteem, disabling future performance and clouding expectations for success.

Tutoring is an effective technique in dealing with academic problems and should be considered in most cases. Tutoring is of proved value in preparing for objective multiple-choice examinations, such as the Scholastic Aptitude Test (SAT), Medical College Aptitude Test (MCAT), and national boards. Taking such examinations repetitively and using relaxation skills are two behavioral techniques of great value to diminish anxiety.

## CHILDHOOD OR ADOLESCENT ANTISOCIAL BEHAVIOR

Antisocial behavior in children and adolescents covers many acts that violate the rights of others, including overt acts of aggression and violence and such covert acts as lying, stealing, truancy, and running away from home. The DSM-IV definition of conduct disorder requires a repetitive pattern of at least three antisocial behaviors for at least six months, but childhood or adolescent antisocial behavior may consist of isolated events that do not constitute a mental disorder but do become the focus of clinical attention. The emergence of occasional antisocial symptoms is common among children who have a variety of mental disorders, including psychotic disorders, depressive disorders, impulse control disorders, and disruptive behavior and attention-deficit disorders, such as attention-deficit/hyperactivity disorder and oppositional defiant disorder.

The child's age and developmental level play roles in the manifestations of disturbed conduct and influence the child's likelihood to meet the diagnostic criteria for a conduct disorder, as opposed to childhood antisocial behavior. Thus, a child of 5 or 6 years is not likely to meet the criteria for three antisocial symptoms—for example, physical confrontations, the use of weapons, and forcing someone into sexual activity—but a single symptom, like initiating fights, is common in that age group.

The term "juvenile delinquent" is defined by the legal system as a youth who has violated the law in some way, but it does not mean that the youth meets the criteria for a mental disorder.

## Epidemiology

Estimates of antisocial behavior range from 5 to 15 percent of the general population and somewhat less among children and adolescents. Reports have documented the increased frequency of antisocial behaviors in urban settings, compared with rural areas. In one report, the risk of coming into contact with the police for an antisocial behavior was estimated to be 20 percent for teenage boys and 4 percent for teenage girls.

## Etiology

Antisocial behaviors may occur within the context of a mental disorder or in its absence. Antisocial behavior is multidetermined, occurring most frequently in children or adolescents with many risk factors. Among the most common risk factors are harsh and physically abusive parenting, parental criminality, and impulsive and hyperactive behavior in the child. Additional associated features of children and adolescents with antisocial behavior are low I.Q., academic failure, and low levels of adult supervision.

Chapter 30 discusses genetic and social factors as causes of adult antisocial behavior.

**Psychological factors.** If the parenting experience is poor, children experience emotional deprivation, which leads to low self-esteem and unconscious anger. They are not given any limits, and their consequences are deficient because they have not internalized parental prohibitions that account for superego formation. Therefore, they have so-called superego lacunae, which allow them to commit antisocial acts without guilt. At times, such children's antisocial behavior is a vicarious source of pleasure and gratification for parents who act out through the children their own forbidden wishes and impulses. A consistent finding in persons with repeated acts of violent behavior is a history of physical abuse.

## Diagnosis and Clinical Features

In DSM-IV the following statement about childhood or adolescent antisocial behavior appears:

This category can be used when the focus of clinical attention is antisocial behavior in a child or adolescent that is not due to a mental disorder (e.g., Conduct Disorder or an Impulse Control Disorder). Examples include isolated antisocial acts of children or adolescents (not a pattern of antisocial behavior).

The childhood behaviors most associated with antisocial behavior are theft, incorrigibility, arrests, school problems, impulsiveness, promiscuity, oppositional behavior, lying,

suicide attempts, substance abuse, truancy, running away, associating with undesirable persons, and staying out late at night. The greater the number of symptoms present in childhood, the greater is the probability of adult antisocial behavior; however, the presence of many symptoms also indicates the development of other mental disorders in adult life.

## Differential Diagnosis

Substance-related disorders—including alcohol, cannabis, and cocaine use disorders—bipolar I disorder, and schizophrenia in childhood often manifest themselves as antisocial behavior.

## Treatment

The first step in determining the appropriate treatment for a child or an adolescent who is manifesting antisocial behavior is to evaluate the need to treat any coexisting mental disorder, such as bipolar I disorder, a psychotic disorder, or a depressive disorder that may be contributing to the antisocial behavior.

The treatment of antisocial behavior usually involves behavioral management, which is most effective when the patient is in a controlled environment or when the child's family members cooperate in maintaining the behavioral program. Schools can help modify antisocial behavior within classrooms. Rewards for prosocial behaviors and positive reinforcement for the control of unwanted behaviors have merit.

In cases of aggressive and violent behavior, medications have been used with some success. Lithium (Eskalith), haloperidol (Haldol), and methylphenidate (Ritalin) can decrease aggression in some cases.

It is more difficult to treat children and adolescents with long-term patterns of antisocial behavior—particularly covert behaviors, such as stealing and lying. Group therapy has been used to treat those behaviors, and cognitive problem-solving approaches are potentially helpful.

## IDENTITY PROBLEM

Identity problem is related to severe distress about one's sense of self as it pertains to long-term goals, friendships, moral values, career aspirations, sexual orientation, and group loyalties. It is not a mental disorder in DSM-IV. In the revised third edition of DSM (DSM-III-R), the disturbance was considered a mental disorder, identity disorder. Identity problem is sometimes manifested in the context of such mental disorders as mood disorders, psychotic disorders, and borderline personality disorder.

## Epidemiology

No reliable information is available on predisposing factors, familial pattern, sex ratio, or prevalence. However, problems with identity formation appear to be a result of life in modern society. Today, children and adolescents experience great instability of family life, increased problems with identity formation, increased conflicts between adolescent peer values and the values of parents and society, and increased exposure through the media and education to a variety of moral, behavioral, and life-style possibilities.

### Etiology

The causes of identity problem are often multifactorial and include the pressures of a highly dysfunctional family and the influences of coexisting mental disorders. In general, adolescents who suffer from major depressive disorder, psychotic disorders, and other mental disorders report feeling alienated from family members and experience a degree of turmoil.

Children who have had difficulties in mastering expected developmental tasks all along are likely to have difficulties with the pressure to establish a well-defined identity during adolescence.

Erik Erikson used the term "identity versus role diffusion" to describe the developmental and psychosocial tasks challenging adolescents to incorporate past experiences and present goals into a coherent sense of self.

### Diagnosis and Clinical Features

In DSM-IV the following statement about identity problem appears:

This category can be used when the focus of clinical attention is uncertainty about multiple issues relating to identity such as long-term goals, career choice, friendship patterns, sexual orientation and behavior, moral values, and group loyalties.

The essential features of identity problem seem to revolve around the question "Who am I?" Conflicts are experienced as irreconcilable aspects of the self that the adolescent is unable to integrate into a coherent identity. If the symptoms are not recognized and resolved, a full-blown identity crisis may develop. As Erikson described, youth manifests severe doubting and an inability to make decisions (abulia), a sense of isolation and inner emptiness, a growing inability to relate to others, disturbed sexual functioning, a distorted time perspective, a sense of urgency, and the assumption of a negative identity.

The associated features frequently include marked discrepancy between the adolescent's self-perception and the views that others have of the adolescent; moderate anxiety and depression that are usually related to inner preoccupation, rather than external realities; and self-doubt and uncertainty about the future, with either difficulty in making choices or impulsive experiments in an attempt to establish an independent identity. Some persons with identity problem join cultlike groups.

### Differential Diagnosis

Identity problem must be differentiated from a mental disorder (such as borderline personality disorder, schizophreniform disorder, schizophrenia, or a mood disorder). At times, what initially appears to be identity problem may be the prodromal manifestations of one of those disorders.

Intense but normal conflicts associated with maturing, such as adolescent turmoil and mid-life crisis, may be confusing, but they are usually not associated with marked deterioration in school, vocational, or social functioning or with severe subjective distress. However, considerable evidence indicates that adolescent turmoil is often not a phase that is outgrown but indicates true psychopathology.

### Course and Prognosis

The onset of identity problem is most frequently in late adolescence, as the teenager separates from the nuclear family and attempts to establish an independent identity and value system. The onset is usually manifested by a gradual increase in anxiety, depression, regressive phenomena—such as loss of interest in friends, school, and activities—irritability, sleep difficulties, and changes in eating habits.

The course is usually relatively brief, as developmental lags are responsive to support, acceptance, and the provision of a psychosocial moratorium. An extensive prolongation of adolescence with continued identity problem may lead to the chronic state of role diffusion that may indicate a disturbance of early developmental stages and the presence of borderline personality disorder, a mood disorder, or schizophrenia. Identity problem usually resolves by the mid-20s. If it persists, the person with identity problem may be unable to make career commitments or lasting attachments.

### Treatment

Individual psychotherapy directed toward encouraging growth and development is usually considered the therapy of choice. Adolescents with identity problem often react as do borderline personality disorder patients to the psychotherapeutic technique in which the transference is permitted to develop in the context of a controlled regression without gratifying or infantilizing the patient. The patients' feelings and wishes are recognized, and the patients are encouraged to examine their longings and feelings of deprivation and to try to understand, with the empathic help of the therapist, what is happening to them.

### References

Anderson J C: The conduct disorders. In *Handbook of Studies on Child Psychiatry*, B J Tonge, G D Burrows, J S Werry, editors, p 283. Elsevier Science, New York, 1990.

Benasich A A, Curtiss S, Tallal P: Language, learning and behavioral disturbances in childhood. J Am Acad Child Adolesc Psychiatry *32:* 585, 1993.

Blos P: *On Adolescence.* Free Press, Glen Cove, N Y, 1962.

Bow J N: A comparison of intellectually superior male reading achievers and underachievers from a neuropsychological perspective. J Learn Disabil *21:* 118, 1988.

Brent D A, Johnson B, Bartles S, Bridge J, Rather C, Matta J, Connolly J, Constantine D: Personality disorder, tendency to impulsive violence and suicidal behavior in adolescents. J Am Acad Child Adolesc Psychiatry *32:* 69, 1993.

DuPaul G, Rapport M: Does methylphenidate normalize the classroom performance of children with attention deficit disorder. J Am Acad Child Adolesc Psychiatry *32:* 190, 1993.

Egan J: Etiology and treatment of borderline personality disorder in adolescents. Hosp Community Psychiatry *37:* 6, 1986.

Eiserman W D: Three types of peer tutoring: Effects on the attitudes of students with learning disabilities and their regular class peers. J Learn Disabil *21:* 249, 1988.

Erikson E H: The problems of ego identity. J Am Psychoanal Assoc *4:* 428, 1956.

Galanter M: Cults and zealous self-help movements: A psychiatric perspective. Am J Psychiatry *147:* 543, 1990.

Keogh B K: Improving services for problem learners: Rethinking and restructuring. J Learn Disabil *21:* 19, 1988.

Lewis D O: *Vulnerabilities to Delinquency.* Spectrum, New York, 1981.

Lundy M S, Pfohl B, Kuperman S: Adult criminality among formerly hospitalized child psychiatric patients. J Am Acad Child Adolesc Psychiatry *32:* 568, 1993.

Masterson J F: *The Psychiatric Dilemma of Adolescence.* Little, Brown, Boston, 1967.

Petti T A, Vela R M: Borderline disorders of childhood: An overview. J Am Acad Child Adolesc Psychiatry *29:* 327, 1990.

Rende R D: Longitudinal relations between temperamental traits and behavioral syndromes in middle childhood. J Am Acad Child Adolesc Psychiatry *32:* 287, 1993.

Robson K S: *The Borderline Child: Approaches to Etiology, Diagnosis, and Treatment.* McGraw-Hill, New York, 1983.

Sadock V A: Other conditions not attributable to a mental disorder. In *Comprehensive Textbook of Psychiatry,* ed 5, H I Kaplan, B J Sadock, editors, p 1408. Williams & Wilkins, Baltimore, 1989.

Soloff P H, George A, Nathan R S, Schulz P M: Progress in pharmacotherapy of borderline disorders. Arch Gen Psychiatry *43:* 7, 1986.

Stone M H: *The Borderline Syndromes.* McGraw-Hill, New York, 1980.

Tremblay R E, Masse B, Perron D, Leblanc M, et al: Early disruptive behavior, poor school achievement, delinquent behavior, and delinquent personality: Longitudinal analyses. J Consult Clin Psychol *60:* 64, 1992.

Verhulst I C, Eussen M L J M, Berden G F M G, Sanders-Woodstra J, van der Ende J: Pathways of problem behaviors from childhood to adolescence. J Am Acad Child Adolesc Psychiatry *32:* 388, 1993.

Zahner G E D, Jacobs J H, Freeman D H, Trainor K F: Rural-urban child psychopathology in a northeastern U.S. state: 1986–1989. J Am Acad Child Adolesc Psychiatry *32:* 378, 1993.

# 49 ||||||

# Psychiatric Treatment of Children and Adolescents

## 49.1 / Individual Psychotherapy

Individual psychotherapy with children must reflect an understanding of the child's developmental level and sensitivity toward the family and the environment in which the child lives. Most children do not seek psychiatric treatment; they are brought to a psychotherapist because of a disturbance that is noted by a family member, a schoolteacher, or a pediatrician. Children often believe that they are being brought for treatment because of their misbehavior or as a punishment for some wrongdoing. Children are able to disclose their own thoughts, feelings, moods, and perceptual experiences better than are others; but, even when external behavior problems have been identified by others, the child's internal experience may be largely unknown.

Child psychotherapists also function as advocates for their child patients in interactions with schools, legal agencies, and community organizations. Child psychotherapists may be called on to make recommendations that affect various aspects of a child's life.

### THEORIES

Clinicians should have a working knowledge of several psychotherapeutic theories and their applications in children, since a combination of therapeutic interventions is often used in a child's treatment. Psychodynamic approaches are at times mixed with supportive components and behavioral management techniques to build a comprehensive treatment plan for a child. Individual psychotherapy with children is frequently done in conjunction with family therapy, group therapy, and, when indicated, psychopharmacology.

A number of theoretical systems underlie psychotherapeutic approaches with children, including (1) psychoanalytic theories, (2) behavioral theories, (3) family systems theories, and (4) developmental theories.

### Psychoanalytic Theories

Classic psychoanalytic theory conceives of exploratory psychotherapy's working, with patients of all ages, by reversing the evolution of psychopathological processes. A principal difference noted with advancing age is a sharpening distinction between psychogenetic and psychodynamic factors. The younger the child, the more the genetic and dynamic forces are intertwined.

The development of those pathological processes is generally thought to begin with experiences that have proved to be particularly significant to the patients and have affected them adversely. Although in one sense the experiences were real, in another sense they may have been misinterpreted or imagined. In any event, for the patients they were traumatic experiences that caused unconscious complexes. Being inaccessible to conscious awareness, the unconscious elements readily escape rational adaptive maneuvers and are subject to pathological misuse of adaptive and defensive mechanisms. The end result is the development of conflicts leading to distressing symptoms, character attitudes, or patterns of behavior that constitute the emotional disturbance.

Increasingly, the psychoanalytic view of emotional disturbances in children has assumed a developmental orientation. Thus, the maladaptive defensive functioning is directed against conflicts between impulses that are characteristic of a specific developmental phase and environmental influences or the child's internalized representations of the environment. In that framework the disorders are the result of environmental interferences with maturational timetables or conflicts with the environment engendered by developmental progress. The result is difficulty in achieving or resolving developmental tasks and achieving the capacities specific to later phases of development, which can be expressed in various ways, such as Anna Freud's lines of development and Erik Erikson's concept of sequential psychosocial capacities.

The goal of therapy is to help develop good conflict-resolution skills in the child, so that the child can function at the appropriate developmental level. Therapy may again be necessary as the child faces the challenges of subsequent developmental periods.

Psychoanalytic psychotherapy is a modified form of psychotherapy that is expressive and exploratory and that endeavors to reverse the evolution of emotional disturbance through a reenactment and desensitization of the traumatic events by the free expression of thoughts and feelings in an interview-play situation. Ultimately, the therapist helps patients understand the warded-off feelings, fears, and wishes that have beset them.

Whereas the psychoanalytic psychotherapeutic approach seeks improvement by exposure and resolution of buried conflicts, suppressive-supportive-educative psychotherapy works in an opposite fashion. It aims to facilitate repression. The therapist, capitalizing on the patient's desire to please, encourages the patient to substitute new adaptive and defensive mechanisms. In that type of therapy, the therapist uses interpretations minimally; instead, the therapist emphasizes suggestion, persuasion, exhortation, operant reinforcement, counseling, education, direction, advice, abreaction, environmental manipulation, intellectual review, gratification of the patient's current dependent needs, and similar techniques.

## Behavioral Theories

All behavior, regardless of whether it is adaptive or maladaptive, is a consequence of the same basic principles of behavior acquisition and maintenance. Behavior is either learned or unlearned, and what renders behavior abnormal or disturbed is its social significance.

Although the theories and their derivative therapeutic intervention techniques have become increasingly complex over the years, all learning can be subsumed within two global basic mechanisms. One is classic respondent conditioning, akin to Ivan Pavlov's famous experiments, and the second is operant instrumental learning, which is associated with B. F. Skinner, even though it is basic to both Edward Thorndike's law of effect regarding the influence of reinforcing consequences of behavior and to Sigmund Freud's pain-pleasure principle. Both of those basic mechanisms assign the highest priority to the immediate precipitants of behavior, deemphasizing those remote underlying causal determinants that are important in the psychoanalytic tradition. The theory asserts that there are but two types of abnormal behavior: behavioral deficits that result from a failure to learn and deviant maladaptive behaviors that are a consequence of learning inappropriate things.

Such concepts have always been an implicit part of the rationale underlying all child psychotherapy. Intervention strategies derive much of their success, particularly with children, from rewarding previously unnoticed good behavior, thereby highlighting it and making it more frequent than in the past.

## Family Systems Theories

Although families have long been an interest of child psychotherapists, the understanding of transactional family processes has been greatly enhanced by conceptual contributions from cybernetics, systems theory, communications theory, object relations theory, social role theory, ethology, and ecology.

The bedrock premise entails the family's functioning as a self-regulating open system that possesses its own unique history and structure. Its structure is constantly evolving

as a consequence of the dynamic interaction between the family's mutually interdependent systems and persons who share a complementarity of needs. From that conceptual foundation, a wealth of ideas has emerged under rubrics such as the family's development, life cycle, homeostasis, functions, identity, values, goals, congruence, symmetry, myths, rules, roles (spokesperson, symptom bearer, scapegoat, affect barometer, pet, persecutor, victim, arbitrator, distractor, saboteur, rescuer, breadwinner, disciplinarian, nurturer), structure (boundaries, splits, pairings, alliances, coalitions, enmeshed, disengaged), double bind, scapegoating, pseudomutuality, and mystification. Increasingly, appreciation of the family system sometimes explains why a minute therapeutic input at a critical junction may result in far-reaching changes, whereas in other situations huge quantities of therapeutic effort appear to be absorbed with minimal evidence of change.

## Developmental Theories

Underlying child psychotherapy is the assumption that, in the absence of unusual interferences, children mature in basically orderly, predictable ways that are codifiable in a variety of interrelated psychosociobiological sequential systematizations. The central and overriding role of a developmental frame of reference in child psychotherapy distinguishes it from adult psychotherapy. The therapist's orientation should entail something more than a knowledge of age-appropriate behavior derived from such studies as Arnold Gesell's descriptions of the morphology of behavior. It should encompass more than psychosexual development with ego-psychological and sociocultural amendments, exemplified by Erikson's epigenetic schema. It extends beyond familiarity with Jean Piaget's sequence of intellectual evolution as a basis for acquaintance with the level of abstraction at which children of various ages may be expected to function or for assessing their capacities for a moral orientation.

## TYPES OF PSYCHOTHERAPY

Among the common bases for the classification of child therapy is the identification of the element presumed to be helpful for the young patient. Isolating a single therapeutic element as the basis for classification tends to be artificial, because most, if not all, of the factors are present in varying degrees in every child psychotherapeutic undertaking. For example, in every psychotherapy the relationship between the therapist and the patient is a vital factor; nevertheless, child psychotherapists commonly talk of relationship therapy to describe a form of treatment in which a positive, friendly, helpful relationship is viewed as the primary, if not the sole, therapeutic ingredient. Probably one of the best examples of pure relationship therapy is found outside a clinical setting in the work of the Big Brother Organization.

Remedial, educational, and patterning psychotherapy endeavors to teach new attitudes and patterns of behavior to children who persist in using immature and inefficient patterns, which are often presumed to be due to a maturational lag.

Supportive psychotherapy is particularly helpful in enabling a well-adjusted youngster to cope with the emotional turmoil engendered by a crisis. It is also used with disturbed youngsters whose less than adequate ego functioning may be seriously disrupted by an expressive-exploratory mode or by other forms of therapeutic intervention. At the beginning of most psychotherapy, regardless of the patient's age and the nature of the therapeutic interventions, the principal therapeutic elements perceived by the patient tend to be the supportive ones, a consequence of therapists' universal efforts to be reliably and sensitively responsive. In fact, some therapy may never proceed beyond the supportive level, whereas others develop an expressive-exploratory or behavioral modification flavor on top of the supportive foundation.

Release therapy, described initially by David Levy, facilitates the abreaction of pent-up emotions. Although abreaction is an aspect of many therapeutic undertakings, in release therapy the treatment situation is structured to encourage only that factor. It is indicated primarily for preschool-age children who are suffering from a distorted emotional reaction to an isolated trauma.

Preschool-age children are sometimes treated through the parents, a process called filial therapy. The therapist using the strategy should be alert to the possibility that apparently successful filial treatment can obscure a significant diagnosis because the patient is not directly seen. The first case of filial therapy was that of Little Hans, reported by Sigmund Freud in 1905. Hans was a 5-year-old phobic child who was treated by Hans's father under Freud's supervision.

Psychotherapy with children is often psychoanalytically oriented, which means that it endeavors through the vehicle of self-understanding to enable the child's potential to develop further. That development is accomplished by liberating for constructive use the psychic energy that is presumed to be expended in defending against fantasied dangers. Children are generally unaware of those unreal dangers, their fear of them, and the psychological defenses they use to avoid both the danger and the fear. With the awareness that is facilitated, patients can evaluate the usefulness of their defensive maneuvers and can relinquish the unnecessary maneuvers that constitute the symptoms of their emotional disturbance.

Child psychoanalysis—an intensive, uncommon form of psychoanalytic psychotherapy—works on unconscious resistance and defenses during three to four sessions a week. Under those circumstances the therapist anticipates unconscious resistance and allows transference manifestations to mature to a full transference neurosis, through which neurotic conflicts are resolved.

Interpretations of dynamically relevant conflicts are emphasized in psychoanalytic descriptions. However, that does not imply the absence of elements that are predominant in other types of psychotherapies. Indeed, in all psychotherapy the child should derive support from the consistently understanding and accepting relationship with the therapist. Remedial educational guidance is provided when necessary.

Probably the most vivid examples of the integration of psychodynamic and behavioral approaches, even though they are not always explicitly conceptualized as such, are to be found in the milieu therapy of child and adolescent psychiatric inpatient, residential, and day treatment facilities. Behavioral change is initiated in those settings, and its repercussions are explored concurrently in individual psychotherapeutic sessions, so that the action in one arena and the information stemming from it augment and illuminate what transpires in the other arena.

Cognitive therapy has been used with children, adolescents, and adults. The approach attempts to correct cognitive distortions, particularly negative conceptions of oneself, and is used mainly in depressive disorders.

## DIFFERENCES BETWEEN CHILDREN AND ADULTS

Logic suggests that psychotherapy with children, who are generally more flexible than adults and have simpler defenses and other mental mechanisms, should consume less time than comparable treatment of adults. Experience does not usually confirm that expectation, because of the relative absence in children of some elements that contribute to successful treatment.

A child, for example, typically does not seek help. As a consequence, one of the first tasks for the therapist is to stimulate the child's motivation for treatment. Children commonly begin therapy involuntarily, often without the benefit of true parental support. Although the parents may want their child helped or changed, that desire is often generated by frustrated anger with the child. Typically, the anger is accompanied by relative insensitivity to what the therapist perceives as the child's need and the basis for a therapeutic alliance. Thus, whereas adult patients frequently perceive advantages in getting well, children may envision therapeutic change as nothing more than conforming to a disagreeable reality, which heightens the likelihood of perceiving the therapist as the parent's punitive agent. That is hardly the most fertile soil in which to nurture a therapeutic alliance.

Children tend to externalize internal conflicts in search of alloplastic adaptations, and they find it difficult to conceive of problem resolution except by altering an obstructing environment. The passive, masochistic boy who is the constant butt of his schoolmates' teasing finds it inconceivable that the situation can be rectified by altering his mode of handling his aggressive impulses, rather than by someone's controlling his tormentors, a view that may be reinforced by significant adults in his environment.

The tendency of children to reenact their feelings in new situations facilitates the early appearance of spontaneous and global transference reactions that may be troublesome. Concurrently, the eagerness that children have for new experiences, coupled with their natural developmental fluidity, tends to limit the intensity and the therapeutic usefulness of subsequent transference developments.

Children have a limited capacity for self-observation, with the notable exception of some obsessive children who resemble adults in that ability. Such obsessive children, however, usually isolate the vital emotional components. In the exploratory-interpretative psychotherapies, the development of a capacity for ego splitting—that is, simultaneous emotional involvement and self-observation—is most helpful. Only by means of identification with a trusted adult and in alliance with that adult are children able to approach such an ideal. The therapist's sex and the relatively superficial aspects of the therapist's demeanor may be important elements in the development of a trusting relationship with a child.

Regressive behavioral and communicative modes can be wearing on child therapists. Typically motor-minded, even when they do not require external controls, children may demand a degree of physical stamina that is not of consequence in therapy with adults. The age appropriateness of such primitive mechanisms as denial, projection, and isolation hinders the process of working through, which relies on a patient's synthesizing and integrating capacities, both of which are immature in children. Also, environmental pressures on the therapist are generally greater in psychotherapeutic work with children than in work with adults.

Although children compare unfavorably with adults in many of the qualities that are generally considered desirable in therapy, children have the advantage of active maturational and developmental forces. The history of psychotherapy for children is punctuated by efforts to harness those assets and to overcome the liabilities. Recognition of the importance of play constituted a major forward stride in those efforts.

## PLAYROOM

The playroom's structure, design, and furnishing are most important. Some therapists say that the toys should be few, simple, and carefully selected to facilitate the communication of fantasy. Other therapists suggest that a wide variety of playthings be available to increase the range of feelings the child may express. Those contrasting recommendations have been attributed to differences in therapeutic methods. Some therapists tend to avoid interpretation, even of conscious ideas, whereas others recommend the interpretation of unconsicous content directly and quickly. Therapists tend to change their preferences in equipment as they accumulate experience and develop confidence in their abilities.

Although special equipment—such as genital dolls, amputation dolls, and see-through anatomically complete (except for genitalia) models—have been used in therapy, many therapists have observed that the unusual nature of such items risks making children wary and suspicious of the therapist's motives. Until the dolls available to the children in their own homes include genitalia, the psychic content that special dolls are designed to elicit may be more available at the appropriate time with conventional dolls.

Although the choices of play materials vary from therapist to therapist, the following equipment can constitute a well-balanced playroom or play area: multigenerational families of flexible but sturdy dolls of various races; additional dolls repressenting special roles and feelings, such as police officer, doctor, and soldier; dollhouse furnishings with or without a dollhouse; toy animals; puppets; paper, crayons, paint, and blunt-ended scissors; a spongelike ball; clay or something comparable; tools like rubber hammers,

rubber knives, and guns; building blocks, cars, trucks, and airplanes; and eating utensils. The toys should enable children to communicate through play. The therapist should avoid toys and materials that are fragile or break easily, which can result in physical injury to the child or can increase the child's guilt.

A special drawer or box should be available to each child, space permitting, in which to store items the child brings to the therapy session or to store projects, such as drawings and stories, for future retrieval. Limits have to be set, so that the private storage area is not used to hoard communal play equipment, depriving the therapist's other patients. Some therapists assert that an absence of such arrangements evokes material about sibling rivalry; however, others think that assertion is a rationalization for not respecting the child's privacy, inasmuch as such feelings can be expressed in other ways.

## INITIAL APPROACH

A variety of approaches can be derived from the therapist's individual style and perception of the child's needs. The range extends from those in which the therapist endeavors to direct the child's thought content and activity— as in release therapy, some behavior therapy, and certain educational patterning techniques—to those exploratory methods in which the therapist endeavors to follow the child's lead. Even though the child determines the focus, the therapist structures the situation. Encouraging children to say whatever they wish and to play freely, as in exploratory psychotherapy, establishes a definite structure. The therapist creates an atmosphere in which to get to know all about the child—the good side, as well as the bad side, as children would put it. The therapist may communicate to the child that the child's response will not elicit either anger or pleasure, only understanding from the therapist. Such an assertion does not imply that therapists do not have emotions, but it assures the young patient that the therapist's personal feelings and standards are subordinate to understanding the youngster.

## THERAPEUTIC INTERVENTIONS

Therapeutic interventions with children encompass a range comparable to those used with adults in psychotherapy. If the amount of therapist activity is used as the basis for a classificatory continuum of interventions, at the least active end are the questions posed by the therapist requesting an elaboration of patients' statements or behavior. Next on the continuum of therapeutic activity are the exclamations and confrontations in which the therapist directs attention to some data of which the patients are cognizant. Then the therapist uses interpretations, designed to expand patients' conscious awareness of themselves by making explicit those elements that have previously been implicitly expressed in their thoughts, feelings, and behavior. Beyond interpretation, the therapist may educatively offer information that is new because the patients have not been exposed to it previously. At the most active end of the continuum are advising, counseling, and directing, designed to help patients adopt a course of action or a conscious attitude.

Nurturing and maintaining a therapeutic alliance may require some education of children regarding the process of therapy. Another educational intervention may entail assigning labels to affects that have not been part of the youngsters' past experience. Rarely does therapy have to compensate for a real absence of education regarding acceptable decorum and playing games. Usually, children are in therapy not because of the absence of educational efforts but because repeated educational efforts have failed. Therefore, therapy generally does not need to include additional teaching efforts, despite the frequent temptation to offer them.

Adults' natural educational fervor with children is often accompanied by a paradoxical tendency to protect them from learning about some of life's realities. In the past, that tendency contributed to the stork's role in childbirth, the dead having taken a long trip, and similar fairy-tale explanations for natural phenomena about which adults were uncomfortable in communicating with children. Although adults are more honest with children today, therapists can find themselves in a situation in which their overwhelming urge to protect the hurt child may be as disadvantageous to the child as was the stork myth. Alternatively, information given to the child must take into account individual problems and developmental levels.

The temptation to offer oneself as a model for identification may stem also from helpful educational attitudes toward children. Although that may sometimes be an appropriate therapeutic strategy, therapists should not lose sight of the pitfalls in that apparently innocuous strategy.

## PARENTS

Psychotherapy with children is characterized by the need for parental involvement. The involvement does not necessarily reflect parental culpability for the youngster's emotional difficulties but is a reality of the child's dependent state. That fact cannot be stressed too much because of what can be considered an occupational hazard shared by many who work with children. That hazard is the urge to rescue children from the negative influences of their parents, sometimes related to an unconscious competitive desire to be a better parent than the child's or one's own parents.

Parents are involved to varying degrees in child psychotherapy. With preschool-age children the entire therapeutic effort may be directed toward the parents, without any direct treatment of the child. At the other extreme, children can be seen in psychotherapy without any parental involvement beyond the payment of fees and perhaps transporting the child to the therapy sessions. However, the majority of practitioners prefer to maintain an informative alliance with the parents for the purpose of obtaining additional information about the child.

Probably the most frequent arrangements are those that were developed in child guidance clinics—that is, parent guidance focused on the child or on the parent-child interaction and therapy for the parents' own individual needs concurrent with the child's therapy. The parents may be

seen by the child's therapist or by someone else. In recent years increasing efforts have been made to shift the focus from the child as the primary patient to the child as the family's emissary to the clinic. In such family therapy, all or selected members of the family are treated simultaneously as a family group. Although the preferences of specific clinics and practitioners for either an individual or a family therapeutic approach may be unavoidable, the final decision as to which therapeutic strategy or combination to use should be derived from the clinical assessment.

## CONFIDENTIALITY

Consideration of parental involvement highlights the question of confidentiality in psychotherapy with children. There are advantages to creating an atmosphere in which the child can feel that all words and actions will be viewed by the therapist as simultaneously both serious and tentative. In other words, the child's communications do not bind the therapist to a commitment; nevertheless, they are too important to be communicated to a third party without the patient's permission. Although such an attitude may be conveyed implicitly, sometimes the therapist should explicitly discuss confidentiality with the child. Promising a child not to tell the parents what transpires in therapeutic sessions can be risky. Although the therapist has no intention of disclosing such data to the parents, the bulk of what children do and say in psychotherapy is common knowledge to the parents. Therefore, a child so motivated can easily manipulate the situation so as to produce circumstantial evidence that the therapist has betrayed a confidence. Accordingly, if confidentiality requires specific discussion during treatment, the therapist may not want to go beyond indicating that the therapist is not in the business of telling parents what goes on in therapy, as the therapist's role is to understand and help children.

The therapist should try to enlist the parents' cooperation in respecting the privacy of the child's therapeutic sessions. That respect is not always readily honored, as parents are naturally curious about what transpires and may be threatened by the therapist's apparently privileged position.

Routinely reporting to the child the essence of the communications with the third parties regarding the child underscores the therapist's reliability and respect for the child's autonomy. In certain types of treatment, the report may be combined with soliciting the child's guesses about those transactions. Also, the therapist may find it fruitful to invite children, particularly older children, to participate in discussions about them with third parties.

## INDICATIONS AND CONTRAINDICATIONS

The present level of knowledge does not permit the compilation of a meaningful list of the multifaceted indications for child psychotherapy. Existing diagnostic classifications cannot serve as the basis for such a list because of invariable deficiencies in nosological specificity and comprehensiveness. In general, psychotherapy is indicated for children with emotional disorders that appear to be permanent enough to impede maturational and developmental forces. Psychotherapy may also be indicated when the child's development is not impeded but is inducing reactions in the environment that are considered pathogenic. Ordinarily, such disharmonies are dealt with by the child with parental assistance, but, when those efforts are persistently inadequate, psychotherapeutic interventions may be indicated.

Psychotherapy should be limited to those instances in which positive indicators point to its potential usefulness. For the child to benefit from psychotherapy, the home situation must provide a certain amount of nurturance, stability, and motivation for therapy. The child must have adequate cognitive resources to participate in the process and profit from it. If psychotherapy, despite contraindications, is invariably recommended after every child psychiatric evaluation by a particular therapist or clinic, that fact suggests not only unsatisfactory professional practice and a disservice to patients but also an indiscriminate use of psychotherapy.

Psychotherapy is contraindicated if the emotional disturbance is judged to be an intractable one that will not respond to treatment. That is a difficult judgment but one that is essential, considering the excess of the demand for psychotherapy over its supply. Because the potential for error in such prognostic assessments is great, therapists should bring to them both professional humility and a readiness to offer a trial of therapy. Sometimes the essential factor in intractability is the therapist. Certain patients may elicit a reaction from one therapist that is a contraindication for psychotherapy with that therapist but not necessarily with another.

Another contraindication is evidence that the therapeutic process will interfere with reparative forces. A difficult question is posed by suggestions that the forces mobilized as a consequence of psychotherapy may have dire social or somatic effects. For example, psychotherapy may upset a precarious family equilibrium, thereby causing more difficulty than the original problem posed.

## References

Abrams S: The psychoanalytic process in adults and children. Psychoanal Study Child *43:* 245, 1988.
Adams P L: *A Primer of Child Psychotherapy.* Little, Brown, Boston, 1982.
Beardslee W R, Salt P, Porterfield K, Rothberg P C, van de Velde P, Swatling S, Hoke L, Moilanen D L, Wheelock I: Comparison of preventive interventions for families with parental affective disorder. J Am Acad Child Adolesc Psychiatry *32:* 254, 1993.
Berlin L N: Some transference and countertransference issues in the playroom. J Am Acad Child Adolesc Psychiatry *26:* 101, 1987.
Cohen J A, Mannarino A P: A treatment model for sexually abused preschoolers. J Interpers Violence *8:* 115, 1993.
Dulcan M K: Brief psychotherapy with children and their families: The state of the art. J Am Acad Child Adolesc Psychiatry *23:* 544, 1984.
Eyberg S M: Assessing therapy outcome with preschool children: Progress and problems. J Clin Child Psychol *21:* 306, 1992.
Forehand R, Wierson M: The role of developmental factors in planning behavioral interventions for children: Disruptive behavior as an example. Behav Ther *24:* 117, 1993.
Glenn J, editor: *Child Analysis and Therapy.* Aronson, New York, 1978.
Kazdin A E: Effectiveness of psychotherapy with children and adolescents. J Consult Clin Psychol *59:* 785, 1991.
Kendall P C, Morris R J: Child therapy: Issues and recommendations. J Consult Clin Psychol *59:* 777, 1991.
Kernberg P F: A reevaluation of estimates of child therapy effectiveness: Discussion. J Am Acad Child Adolesc Psychiatry *31:* 710, 1992.
Kernberg P F, Chazan S E, Frankel A, Hariton J R, Kruger R S, Scholl

H: *Children with Conduct Disorders: A Psychotherapy Manual.* Basic Books, New York, 1991.
Leichtman M: Psychotherapeutic interventions with brain-injured children and their families: II. Psychotherapy. Bull Menninger Clin *56:* 338, 1992.
Looney J G: Treatment planning in child psychiatry. J Am Acad Child Psychiatry *23:* 529, 1984.
Mullins L L, Olson R A, Chaney J M: A social learning/family systems approach to the treatment of somatoform disorders in children and adolescents. Fam Syst Med *10:* 201, 1992.
Ronen T: Cognitive therapy with young children. Child Psychiatry Hum Dev *23:* 19, 1992.
Rutter M: Psychological therapies in child psychiatry: Issues and prospects. Psychol Med *12:* 723, 1982.
Shapiro T, Esman A: Psychoanalysis and child and adolescent psychiatry. J Am Acad Child Adolesc Psychiatry *31:* 6, 1992.
Shapiro T, Esman A H: Psychotherapy with children and adolescents. Psychiatr Clin North Am *8:* 909, 1985.
Shirk S R, Phillips J S: Child therapy training: Closing the gaps with research and practice. J Consult Clin Psychol *59:* 766, 1991.
Shirk S R, Russell R L: A reevaluation of estimates of child therapy effectiveness. J Am Acad Child Adolesc Psychiatry *31:* 703, 1992.
Shirk S R, Saiz C C: Clinical, empirical, and developmental perspectives on the therapeutic relationship in child psychotherapy. Dev Psychopathol *4:* 713, 1992.
Sholevar G P, Burland J A, Frank J L, Etezady M H, Goldstein J: Psychoanalytic treatment of children and adolescents, J Am Acad Child Adolesc Psychiatry *28:* 685, 1989.
Weisz J R, Weiss B, Donenberg G R: The lab versus the clinic: Effects of child and adolescent psychotherapy. Am Psychol *47:* 1578, 1992.
Werry J S, Wollerheim J P: Behavior therapy with children and adolescents: A twenty-year overview. J Am Acad Child Adolesc Psychiatry *28:* 1, 1989.

# 49.2 / Group Psychotherapy

Group psychotherapy can be modified to suit groups of children in various age groups and can focus on behavioral, educational, social skills, and psychodynamic issues. The mode in which the group functions depends on the children's developmental levels, intelligence, and problems to be addressed. In behaviorally oriented groups, the group leader is directive and an active participant, facilitating prosocial interactions and desired behaviors. In groups using psychodynamic approaches, the leader may monitor interpersonal interactions less actively than in behavior therapy groups.

Groups are highly effective in providing peer feedback and support to children who are either socially isolated or unaware of their effects on their peers.

Groups with very young children are generally highly structured by the leader and use imagination and play to foster socially acceptable peer relationships and positive behavior. The therapist must be keenly aware of the level of the children's attention span and the need for consistency and limit setting. Leaders of preschool-age groups can model supportive adult behavior in meaningful ways to children who have been deprived or neglected.

School-age children's groups may be single-sex groups or include both boys and girls. Children of school age are more sophisticated in verbalizing their feelings than are preschoolers, but they also benefit from structured therapeutic games. Children of school age need frequent reminders about rules, and they are quick to point out infractions of the rules to each other. Interpersonal skills can be addressed nicely in group settings with school-age children.

Among early adolescents, same-sex groups are often used. In early adolescence, physiological changes and the new demands of high school lead to stress that may be ameliorated when groups of same-age peers compare and share. In older adolescence, groups more often include both boys and girls. Even with older adolescents, the leader often uses structure and direct intervention to maximize the therapeutic value of the group. Adolescents who are feeling dejected or alienated may find a special sense of belonging in a therapy group.

## PRESCHOOL-AGE AND EARLY-SCHOOL-AGE GROUPS

Work with a preschool-age group is usually structured by the therapist through the use of a particular technique, such as puppets or artworks, or is couched in terms of a permissive play atmosphere. In therapy with puppets, the children project their fantasies onto the puppets in a way not unlike ordinary play. The main value lies in the cathexis afforded the children, especially if they show difficulty in expressing their feelings. Here the group aids the child less by interaction with other members than by action with the puppets.

In play group therapy the emphasis rests on the interactional qualities of the children with each other and with the therapist in the permissive playroom setting. The therapist should be a person who can allow the children to produce fantasies verbally and in play but who can also use active restraint when the children undergo excessive tension. The toys are the traditional ones used in individual play therapy. The children use the toys to act out aggressive impulses and to relive with the group members and with the therapist their home difficulties. The children catalyze each other and obtain libido-activating stimulation from the catalysis and from their play materials. The therapist interpets a child to the group in the context of the transference to the therapist and to other group members.

The children selected for group treatment show in common a social hunger, the need to be like their peers and to be accepted by them. Usually, the therapist excludes the children who have never realized a primary relationship, as with their mothers, inasmuch as individual psychotherapy can better help those children. The children selected for group psychotherapy usually include those with phobias, effeminate boys, shy and withdrawn children, and children with disruptive behavior disorders.

Modifications of those criteria have been used in group psychotherapy for autistic children, parent group therapy, and art therapy.

A modification of group psychotherapy has been used for physically handicapped toddlers who show speech and language delays. The experience of twice-a-week group activities involves the mothers and their children in a mutual teaching-learning setting. The experience has proved effective for the mothers, who received supportive psy-

chotherapy in the group experience; their formerly hidden fantasies about the children emerged, to be dealt with therapeutically.

## LATENCY-AGE GROUPS

Activity group psychotherapy assumes that poor and divergent experiences have led to deficits in appropriate personality development in the behavior of children; therefore, corrective experiences in a therapeutically conditioned environment will modify them. Because some latency-age children present deep disturbances involving fears, high anxiety levels, and guilt, an activity-interview group psychotherapy modification has evolved. The format uses interview techniques, verbal explanations of fantasies, group play, work, and other communications.

In that type of group psychotherapy, the children verbalize in a problem-oriented manner, with the awareness that problems brought them together and that the group aims to change them. They report dreams, fantasies, daydreams, and traumatic and unpleasant experiences. Both the experiences and the group behavior undergo open discussion.

Therapists vary in their use of time, cotherapists, food, and materials. Most groups meet after school and last at least one hour, although some group leaders prefer 90 minutes. Some therapists serve food in the last 10 minutes, and others prefer serving times when the children are more together for talking. Food, however, does not become a major feature, never becoming central to the group's activities.

## PUBERTAL AND ADOLESCENT GROUPS

Group therapy methods similar to those used in latency-age groups can be used with pubertal children, who are often grouped monosexually, rather than mixed. Their problems resemble those of late latency-age children, but they are also beginning, especially the girls, to feel the effects and the pressures of early adolescence. In a way the groups offer help during a transitional period. The group appears to satisfy the social appetite of preadolescents, who compensate for feelings of inferiority and self-doubt by the formation of groups. That form of therapy puts to advantage the influence of the process of socialization during those years. Because pubertal children experience difficulties in conceptualizing, pubertal therapy groups tend to use play, drawing, psychodrama, and other nonverbal modes of expression. The therapist's role is active and directive.

Activity group psychotherapy has been the recommended type of group therapy for pubertal children who do not have significantly disturbed personality patterns. The children, usually of the same sex and in groups of not more than eight, freely engage in activities in a setting especially designed and planned for its physical and milieu characteristics.

Samuel Slavson, one of the pioneers in group psychotherapy, pictured the group as a substitute family in which the passive, neutral therapist becomes the surrogate for the parents. The therapist assumes various roles, mostly in a nonverbal manner, as each child interacts with the therapist and with other group members. Recent therapists, however, tend to see the group as a form of peer group, with its attendant socializing processes, rather than as a reenactment of the family.

Late adolescents, 16 years of age and up, may be included in groups of adults when indicated. Group therapy has been useful in the treatment of substance-related disorders. Combined therapy (the use of group and individual therapy) has also been used successfully with adolescents.

## OTHER GROUP SITUATIONS

Some residential and day treatment units frequently use group psychotherapy techniques in their work. Group psychotherapy in schools for underachievers and for the underprivileged has relied on reinforcement and on modeling theory, in addition to traditional techniques, and has been supplemented by parent groups.

In controlled conditions, residential treatment units have been used for specific studies in group psychotherapy, such as behavioral contracting. Behavioral contracting with reward-punishment reinforcement provides positive reinforcements among preadolescent boys with severe concerns in basic trust, low self-esteem, and dependence conflicts. Somewhat akin to formal residential treatment units are social group work homes. The children undergo many psychological assaults before placement, so that supportive group psychotherapy offers ventilation and catharsis, but more often it succeeds in letting the children become aware of the enjoyment of sharing activities and developing skills.

Public schools—also a structured environment, although usually not considered the best site for group psychotherapy—have been used by a number of workers. Group psychotherapy as group counseling readily lends itself to school settings. One such group used gender- and problem-homogeneous selection for groups of six to eight students, who met once a week during school hours over two to three years.

## INDICATIONS

There are many indications for the use of group psychotherapy as a treatment modality. Some indications are situational; the therapist may work in a reformatory setting, where group psychotherapy seems to reach the adolescents better than does individual treatment. Another indication is time economics; more patients can be reached within a given time by the use of groups than by individual therapy. Using groups best helps the child at a given age and developmental stage and with a given type of problem. In the young age group the children's social hunger and their potential need for peer acceptance help to determine their suitability for group therapy. Criteria for unsuitability are controversial and have been progressively loosened.

## PARENT GROUPS

In group psychotherapy, as in most treatment procedures for children, parental difficulties present obstacles.

Sometimes uncooperative parents refuse to bring a child or to participate in their own therapy. The extreme of that situation reveals itself when severely disturbed parents use the child as their channel of communication in working out their own needs. In such circumstances the child is in an intolerable position of receiving positive group experiences that seem to create havoc at home.

Parent groups, therefore, can be a valuable aid to the group psychotherapy for their children. The parent of a child in therapy often has difficulty in understanding the nature of the child's ailment, in discerning the line of demarcation between normal and pathological behavior, in relating to the medical establishment, and in coping with feelings of guilt. A parent group assists them in those areas and helps the members formulate guidelines for action.

### References

Abramowitz C V: The effectiveness of group psychotherapy with children. Arch Gen Psychiatry 33: 320, 1976.
Blotcky M, Sheinbein M, Wiggins K, Forgotson J: A verbal group technique for ego-disturbed children: Action to words. Int J Psychoanal Psychother 8: 203, 1980.
Bromfield R, Pfeifer G: Combining group and individual psychotherapy: Impact on the individual treatment experience. J Am Acad Child Adolesc Psychiatry 27: 220, 1988.
Cerda R A, Nemiroff H W, Richmond A H: Therapeutic group approaches in an inpatient facility for children and adolescents: A 15-year perspective. Group 15: 71, 1991.
Chase J L: Inpatient adolescent and latency-age children's perspectives on the curative factors in group psychotherapy. Group 15: 95, 1991.
Clifford M W: A model for group therapy with latency-age boys. Group 15: 116, 1991.
Garland J A: The establishment of individual and collective competency in children's groups as a prelude to entry into intimacy, disclosure, and bonding. Int J Group Psychother 42: 395, 1992.
Kraft I A: Group therapy. In *Basic Handbook of Child Psychiatry,* J D Noshpitz, editor, vol 3, p 159. Basic Books, New York, 1979.
Kraft I A: Some special considerations in adolescent group psychotherapy. Int J Group Psychother 11: 196, 1961.
Kymissis P, Licamele W L, Boots S, Kessler E: Training in child and adolescent group therapy: Two surveys and a model. Group 15: 163, 1991.
Schamess G: Reflections on a developing body of group-as-a-whole theory for children's therapy groups: An introduction. Int J Group Psychother 42: 351, 1992.
Scheidlinger S: Group treatment of adolescents. Am J Orthopsychiatry 55: 102, 1985.
Scheidinger S: Short-term group psychotherapy for children: An overview. Int J Group Psychother 34: 573, 1984.
Slavson S R, Schiffer M: *Group Psychotherapies for Children.* International Universities Press, New York, 1985.
Yalom I D. *Inpatient Group Psychotherapy.* Basic Books, New York, 1983.
Zimpfer D G: Group work with juvenile delinquents. J Spec Group Work 17. 116, 1992.

# 49.3 / Residential, Day, and Hospital Treatment

Residential treatment centers and facilities are appropriate settings for children and adolescents with mental disorders who require a highly structured and supervised setting over a substantial period. Such settings have the advantage of being able to provide a stable and consistent environment with a high level of psychiatric monitoring but one that is less intensive than a hospital. Many treatments are offered in residential settings, including behavioral management, the therapeutic milieu itself, psychotherapy, medication, and special education. Children and adolescents who benefit from residential settings have a wide variety of psychiatric problems and commonly have difficulties with impulse control and structuring their own time. Many residents of such programs also have families with serious psychiatric, financial, and parenting difficulties.

Day treatment programs are excellent alternatives for children and adolescents who require more intensive support, monitoring, and supervision than is available in the community but are able to live successfully at home, given the right level of intervention. In most cases, children and adolescents who attend day hospital programs have serious mental disorders and may warrant psychiatric hospitalization without the support of the program. Family therapy, group and individual psychotherapy, psychopharmacology, behavioral management programs, and special education are integral parts of the programs.

Psychiatric hospitalization is needed when a child or an adolescent exhibits dangerous behavior, is contemplating suicide, or is experiencing an exacerbation of a psychotic disorder or another serious mental disorder. Safety, stabilization, and efficacious treatment are the goals of hospitalization. In recent years the length of stay of child and adolescent psychiatric patients has decreased because of financial pressures and the increased availability of day treatment programs. Psychiatric hospitalization may be the first opportunity for some children to experience a stable and safe environment. The hospital is often the most appropriate place to start new medications, and it provides a round-the-clock setting in which to observe a child's behavior. Children may show a remission of some symptoms by virtue of their removal from a stressful or abusive environment. Once the child has been observed for several weeks, the best treatment and disposition may become clear.

## RESIDENTIAL TREATMENT

More than 20,000 emotionally disturbed children are in residential treatment centers in the United States, and that number is increasing. Deteriorating social conditions, particularly in cities, often make it impossible for a child with a serious mental disorder to live at home. In those cases, residential treatment centers serve a real need. They provide a structured living environment where children may form strong attachments to and receive commitments from the staff members. The purpose of the centers is to provide treatment and special education for the children and treatment of their families.

### Staff and Setting

Staffing patterns include various combinations of child care workers, teachers, social workers, psychiatrists, pediatricians, nurses, and psychologists, making the cost of residential treatment very high.

The Joint Commission on the Mental Health of Children made the following structural and setting recommendations:

In addition to space for therapy programs, there should be facilities for a first-rate school and a rich evening activity program, and there should be ample space for play, both indoors and out. Facilities should be small, seldom exceeding 60 in capacity, with 100 a maximum limit, and should make provision for children to live in small groups. The centers should be located near the families they serve and be readily accessible by public transportation. They should be located for ready access to special medical and educational services and to various community resources, including consultants. They should be open institutions whenever possible; locked buildings, wards, or rooms should only rarely be required. In designing residential programs, the guiding principle should be this: Children should be removed the least possible distance—in space, in time, and in the psychological texture of the experience—from their normal life setting.

### Indications

Most children who are referred for residential treatment have already been seen by one or more professional persons, such as a school psychologist, a pediatrician, and members of a child guidance clinic, juvenile court, or state welfare agency. Attempts at outpatient treatment and foster home placement usually precede residential treatment. Sometimes the severity of the child's problems or the inability of the family to provide for the child's needs prohibits sending a child home. Many children sent to residential treatment centers have conduct disorder. The age range of the children varies from institution to institution, but most children are between 5 and 15 years of age. Boys are referred more frequency than are girls.

An initial review of the data enables the intake staff to determine whether a particular child is likely to benefit from their treatment program. Often, for every one child accepted for admission, three are rejected. The next step is usually interviews with the child and the parents by various staff members, such as a therapist, a group living worker, and a teacher. Psychological testing and neurological examinations are given when indicated if they have not already been done. The child and the parents should be prepared for those interviews.

### Group Living

Most of the children's time in a residential treatment setting is spent in group living. The group living staff consists of child care workers who offer a structured environment that constitutes a therapeutic milieu. The environment places boundaries and limitations on the children. Tasks are defined within the limits of the children's abilities; incentives, such as additional privileges, encourage them to progress, rather than regress. In milieu therapy the environment is structured, limits are set, and a therapeutic atmosphere is maintained.

The children often select one or more staff members with whom to form a relationship through which they express, consciously and unconsciously, many of their feelings about their parents. The child care staff should be trained to recognize such transference reactions and to respond to them in a way that is different from the children's expectations, based on their previous or even current relationships with their parents.

To maintain consistency and balance, the group living staff members must communicate freely and regularly with one another and with the other professional and administrative staff members of the residential setting, particularly the children's teachers and therapists. The child care staff members must recognize any tendency toward becoming the good (or bad) parent in response to a child's splitting behavior. That tendency may be manifested as a pattern of blaming other staff members for a child's disruptive behavior. Similarly, the child care staff must recognize and avoid such individual and group countertransference reactions as sadomasochistic and punitive behavior toward a child.

The structured setting should offer a corrective emotional experience and opportunities for facilitating and improving the children's adaptive behavior, particularly when such deficiencies as speech and language deficits, intellectual retardation, inadequate peer relationships, bed-wetting, poor feeding habits, and attention deficits are present. Some of those deficits are the basis of the children's poor school academic performance and unsocialized behavior, including temper tantrums, fighting, and withdrawal.

Behavior modification principles have also been used, particularly in group work with children. Behavior therapy is part of the residential center's total therapeutic effort.

## Education

Children in residential treatment frequently have severe learning disorders and disruptive behavior and attention-deficit disorders. Usually, the children cannot function in a regular community school and, consequently, need a special on-grounds school. A major goal of the on-grounds school is to motivate the children to learn.

The educational process in residential treatment is complex, and Table 49.3–1 shows some of its components.

## Therapy

Traditional modes of psychotherapy have a place in residential treatment, including intensive, individual psychotherapy with the child; group therapy with selected children; individual therapy or group therapy or both for the parents; and, in some cases, family therapy. However, several modifications need to be kept in mind.

The child relates to the total staff of the setting and, therefore, needs to know that what transpires in the therapist's office is shared with all professional staff members. The therapist informs the child that what they discuss and do in individual therapy will not be revealed to other family members or to other children in the residential center but will be shared with the professional staff members within the setting itself.

## Parents

Concomitant work with the parents is essential. The child usually has a strong tie to at least one parent, no matter how disturbed the parent is. Sometimes the child idealizes the parent, who repeatedly fails the child. Sometimes the parent has an ambivalent or unrealistic expectation that the child will return home. In some instances the parent must be helped to enable the child to live in another setting when that is in the child's best interests.

**Table 49.3–1**
**Education Process in Residential Treatment**

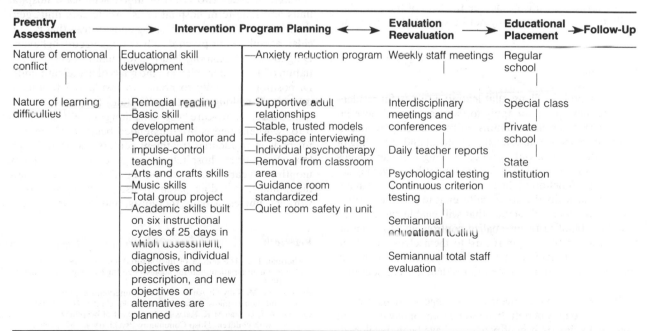

| Preentry Assessment | Intervention Program Planning | | Evaluation Reevaluation | Educational Placement | Follow-Up |
|---|---|---|---|---|---|
| Nature of emotional conflict | Educational skill development | —Anxiety reduction program | Weekly staff meetings | Regular school | |
| Nature of learning difficulties | — Remedial reading<br>—Basic skill development<br>—Perceptual motor and impulse-control teaching<br>—Arts and crafts skills<br>—Music skills<br>—Total group project<br>—Academic skills built on six instructional cycles of 25 days in which assessment, diagnosis, individual objectives and prescription, and new objectives or alternatives are planned | —Supportive adult relationships<br>—Stable, trusted models<br>—Life-space interviewing<br>—Individual psychotherapy<br>—Removal from classroom area<br>—Guidance room standardized<br>—Quiet room safety in unit | Interdisciplinary meetings and conferences<br><br>Daily teacher reports<br><br>Psychological testing<br>Continuous criterion testing<br><br>Semiannual educational testing<br><br>Semiannual total staff evaluation | Special class<br><br>Private school<br><br>State institution | |

Table by Melvin Lewis, M.B., B.S. (London), F.R.C. Psych, D.C.H.

Most residential treatment centers offer individual or group therapy for the parents, couples or marital therapy, and in some cases conjoint family therapy.

## DAY TREATMENT

The concept of daily comprehensive therapeutic experiences without removing the children from their homes or families derived in part from experiences with a therapeutic nursery school. The development of day hospital programs for children followed, and the number of programs continues to grow.

The main advantage of day treatment is that the children remain with their families, and so the families can be more involved in day treatment than in residential treatment or hospital treatment. Day treatment is also much less expensive than is residential treatment. At the same time, the risks of day treatment are the child's social isolation and confinement to a narrow band of social contacts within the program's disturbed peer population.

### Indications

The primary indication for day treatment is the need for a more structured, intensive, and specialized treatment program than can be provided on an outpatient basis. At the same time, the home in which the child is living should be able to provide an environment that is at least not destructive to the child's development. Children who are likely to benefit from day treatment may have a wide range of diagnoses, including autistic disorder, conduct disorder, attention-deficit/hyperactivity disorder, and mental retardation. Exclusion symptoms include behavior that is likely to be destructive to the children themselves or to others under the treatment conditions. Thus, some children who threaten to run away, set fires, attempt suicide, hurt others, or disrupt to a significant degree the lives of their families while they are at home may not be suitable for day treatment.

### Programs

The same ingredients that lead to a successful residential treatment program apply to day treatment. Those ingredients include clear administrative leadership, team collaboration, open communication, and an understanding of the children's behavior. Indeed, having a single agency offer both residential and day treatment has advantages.

A major function of the child care staff in day treatment for psychiatrically disturbed children is to provide positive experiences and a structure that will enable the children and their families to internalize controls and to function better than in the past in regard to themselves and to the outside world. Again, the methods used are essentially similar to those found in the full residential treatment program.

Because the ages, needs, and range of diagnoses of children who may benefit from some form of day treatment vary, many day treatment programs have been developed. Some programs specialize in the special educational and structured environmental needs of mentally retarded children. Others offer the special therapeutic efforts required to treat autistic and schizophrenic children. Still other programs provide the total spectrum of treatment usually found in full residential treatment, of which they may be a part. The children may then move from one part of the program to another and may be in residential treatment or day treatment according to their needs. The school program is always a major component of day treatment, and the psychiatric treatment varies according to the child's needs and diagnosis.

### Results

The results of day treatment have not yet been adequately evaluated. The assessment of the long-term effectiveness of day treatment is fraught with difficulties, whether one is making the assessment from the point of view of the child's maintenance of gains, the therapist's view of what has been accomplished, or society's concerns for such matters as cost-benefit ratios.

At the same time, the advantage of day treatment has encouraged further development of the programs. Moreover, the lessons learned from day treatment programs have moved the mental health disciplines toward having the services follow the children, rather than perpetuating discontinuities of care. The experiences of day treatment for the psychiatric conditions of children and adolescents have also encouraged pediatric hospitals and departments to adapt that model for the medical nursing care of children with physical disorders, particularly those with chronic physical illnesses.

## HOSPITAL TREATMENT

Begun in the 1920s, inpatient psychiatric treatment of children includes two types of units: acute-care hospital units and long-term hospital units. Acute-care units generally accept children manifesting dangerous—that is, suicidal, assaultive, or psychotically disorganized—behavior. Diagnosis, stabilization, and the formulation and the initiation of a treatment plan are the goals of acute-care units. Disposition is usually to home, to residential treatment centers, or to long-term (usually state) hospitals for continued care. Acute-care hospitalization generally lasts from 6 to 12 weeks and is often extended because of the wait for beds in residential treatment centers and state hospitals. Long-term hospitalization generally lasts many months to years. The staffs on inpatient units are interdisciplinary, including psychiatrists, psychologists, social workers, nurses, activity therapists, and teachers.

### References

Ascherman L I: The impact of unstructured games of fantasy and role playing on an inpatient unit for adolescents. Int J Group Psychother *43:* 335, 1993.
Bishop E G, McNally G: An in-home crisis intervention program for children and their families. Hosp Community Psychiatry *44:* 182, 1993.
Costello A J, Dulcan M K, Kalas R: A checklist of hospitalization criteria for use with children. Hosp Community Psychiatry *42:* 823, 1991.
Evangelakis M G: *A Manual for Residential and Day Treatment of Children.* Thomas, Springfield, Ill, 1974.

Gold J, Shera D, Clarkson B: Private psychiatric hospitalization of children: Predictors of length of stay. J Am Acad Child Adolesc Psychiatry *32:* 135, 1993.

Grizenko N, Papineau D, Sayegh L: Effectiveness of a multimodal day treatment program for children with disruptive behavior problems. J Am Acad Child Adolesc Psychiatry *32:* 127, 1993.

Hunger D S, Webster C D, Konstantareas M M, Sloman L: Ten years later: What becomes of the psychiatrically disturbed child in day treatment. J Child Care *1:* 45, 1982.

Kiser L J, Heston J D, Millsap P A, Pruitt D B: Testing the limits: Special treatment procedures for child and adolescent partial hospitalization. Int J Partial Hosp *7:* 37, 1991.

Lewis M, Brown T E: Child care in the residential treatment of the borderline child. Child Care Q *9:* 41, 1980.

Lewis M, Lewis D O, Shanok S S, Klatskin E, Osborn J R: The undoing of residential treatment. J Am Acad Child Adolesc Psychiatry *19:* 160, 1980.

Lyman R D, Prentice-Dunn S, Gabel S, editors: *Residential and Inpatient Treatment of Children and Adolescents.* Plenum, New York, 1989.

Mikkelsen E J, Bereika G M, McKenzie J C: Short-term family-based residential treatment: An alternative to psychiatric hospitalization for children. Am J Orthopsychiatry *63:* 28, 1993.

Nurcombe B: Goal-directed treatment planning and the principles of brief hospitalization. J Am Acad Child Adolesc Psychiatry *28:* 26, 1989.

Perrin E C: Children in hospitals. J Dev Behav Pediatr *14:* 50, 1993.

Pfeiffer S I, Strzelecki S C: Inpatient psychiatric treatment of children and adolescents: A review of outcome studies. J Am Acad Child Adolesc Psychiatry *29:* 847, 1990.

Prentice-Dunn S, Wilson D R, Lyman R D: Client factors related to outcome in a residential and day treatment program for children. J Clin Child Psychol *10:* 188, 1981.

Zang L D: The antisocial aggressive school-age child: Day hospitals. In *Handbook of Treatment of Mental Disorders and Adolescence,* B Wolman, J Egan, A Ross, editors, p 317. Prentice-Hall, Englewood Cliffs, N J, 1978.

Zimet S G, Farley G K: Academic achievement of children with emotional disorders treated in a day hospital program: An outcome study. Child Psychiatry Hum Dev *23:* 183, 1993.

# 49.4 / Biological Therapies

## PHARMACOTHERAPY

In the 1990s, several interests and concerns about child and adolescent psychopharmacotherapy are particularly important, including the use of serotonin-specific reuptake inhibitors (SSRIs) in almost every childhood mental disorder. For example, will early-onset major depressive disorder respond better to SSRIs than to tricyclic drugs? Researchers are still trying to determine why tricyclic drugs seem to be ineffective in early-onset major depressive disorder. Another concern is the safety of medications, particularly tricyclic drugs, whose cardiotoxicity may have contributed to the mysterious deaths of four children who were taking desipramine (Norpramin, Pertofane). In addition, the management of disruptive behavior and attention-deficit disorders is a challenge. Multiple drugs are sometimes used in those cases, although few studies attest to the efficacy or the safety of the drug combinations used.

The goals of pediatric psychopharmacotherapy have not changed. One aim is to decrease maladaptive behaviors and promote adaptive behaviors in such areas as school performance. To accomplish that end, the clinician must try to avoid cognitive dulling. The medications used in pediatric psychopharmacotherapy are often associated with a specific disorder or target symptoms that appear in several disorders. For example, haloperidol (Haldol) is used to treat Tourette's disorder and also severe aggression, which may occur in many disorders.

### Therapeutic Considerations

The evaluation for psychopharmacotherapy must first include an assessment of the child's psychopathology and physical condition to rule out any predisposition for side effects (Table 49.4–1). An assessment of the child's caretakers focuses on their ability to provide a safe and consistent environment in which the clinician can conduct a drug trial. The physician must consider the benefit-risk ratio and must explain it to the patient, if old enough, and to the child's caretakers and for others (for example, child welfare workers) who may be involved in the decision to medicate.

The clinician must obtain baseline ratings before medicating. Behavioral rating scales help objectify the child's response to medication. The physician generally starts at a low dosage and titrates upward on the basis of the child's response and the appearance of side effects. Optimal drug trials cannot be rushed (for example, by insurance-imposed inadequately short hospital stays or infrequent outpatient visits), nor can drug trials be prolonged by insufficient contact of the physician with the patient and the caretakers. The success of drug trials often hinges on the daily accessibility of the physician.

### Childhood Pharmacokinetics

Children, compared with adults, have greater hepatic capacity, more glomerular filtration, and less fatty tissue. Therefore, stimulants, antipsychotics, and tricyclic drugs are eliminated more rapidly by children than by adults; lithium (Eskalith) may be eliminated more rapidly, and children may have less ability to store drugs in their fat. Because of children's quick elimination, the half-lives of many medications may be shorter in children than in adults.

Little evidence indicates that the clinician can predict a child's blood level from the dosage or predict a child's treatment response from the plasma level. Relatively low serum levels of haloperidol appear to be adequate to treat Tourette's disorder in children. No correlation is seen between methylphenidate (Ritalin) serum level and the child's response. The data are incomplete and conflicting about major depressive disorder and serum levels of tri-

**Table 49.4–1**
**Stepwise Process of Biological Therapy**

1. Diagnostic evaluation
2. Symptom measurement
3. Risk-benefit ratio analysis
4. Establishment of a contract for therapy
5. Periodic reevaluation
6. Termination and tapered drug withdrawal

cyclic drugs. A serum-level-to-response relation has been found for tricyclic drugs in the treatment of enuresis.

With lithium therapy, a saliva-to-serum-lithium ratio can be established for a child by averaging three to four individual ratios. The average ratio can then be used to convert subsequent saliva levels to serum levels and thus avoid some venupunctures in children who are stressed by blood tests. As with serum levels, regular clinical monitoring for side effects is necessary.

Table 49.4–2 lists representative drugs and their indications, dosages, adverse reactions, and monitoring requirements.

## Indications

**Mental retardation.** The psychopharmacotherapy for mental retardation most often addresses behavioral problems, especially aggression, and the coexistence of other mental disorders. Medications are overused to control the behavior of institutionalized retarded children because other therapies and services are not available. For severe

aggression, antipsychotics are most commonly used, and cognitive dulling can best be avoided with high-potency drugs. β-Adrenergic receptor antagonists have reduced aggression in uncontrolled studies of adults and children with mental retardation. Lithium and anticonvulsants such as carbamazepine (Tegretol) may also be tried.

Antipsychotics have the advantage of a fast onset of action and little need for laboratory monitoring of their side effects. However, the use of other drugs eliminates the risk for tardive dyskinesia.

The endogenous opiate antagonists, such as naltrexone (Trexan), and the serotonin-specific reuptake inhibitors, such as fluoxetine (Prozac), reduce self-injurious behavior in some patients with mental retardation. When attention-deficit/hyperactivity disorder coexists with mental retardation, methylphenidate is often effective, and a small study showed behavioral improvements with fenfluramine (Pondimin).

Recent attempts have been made to treat the behavioral problems associated with fragile X syndrome with folic acid supplements. Some prepubescent children experienced less active or less aggressive behavior and concentrated

**Table 49.4–2**
**Common Psychoactive Drugs in Childhood and Adolescence**

| Drugs | Indications | Dosage | Adverse Reactions and Monitoring |
|---|---|---|---|
| Antipsychotics—also known as major tranquilizers, neuroleptics<br>Divided into (1) high-potency, low-dosage, e.g. haloperidol (Haldol), trifluoperazine (Stelazine), Thiothixene (Navane); (2) low-potency, high-dosage (more sedating), e.g., chlorpromazine (Thorazine), thioridazine (Mellaril); and (3) clozapine (Clozaril) | In general, for agitated, aggressive, self-injurious behaviors in mental retardation (MR), pervasive developmental disorders (PDD), conduct disorder (CD), and schizophrenia<br>Studies support following specific indications: haloperidol–PDD, CD with severe aggression, Tourette's disorder | All can be given in two to four divided doses or combined into one dose after gradual buildup<br>Haloperidol—child 0.5–6 mg a day, adolescent 0.5–16 mg a day<br>Thiothixene—5–42 mg a day<br>Chlorpromazine and thioridazine—child 10–200 mg a day, adolescent 50–600 mg a day, over 16 years of age 100–700 mg a day | Sedation, weight gain, hypotension, lowered seizure threshold, constipation, extrapyramidal symptoms, jaundice, agranulocytosis, dystonic reaction, tardive dyskinesia; with clozapine, no extrapyramidal adverse effects<br>Monitor: blood pressure, complete blood count (CBC), liver function tests (LFTs), electroencephalogram, if indicated; with thioridazine, pigmentary retinopathy is rare but dictates ceiling of 800 mg in adults and proportionately lower in children; with clozapine, weekly white blood counts (WBCs) for development of agranulocytosis |
| Stimulants<br>Dextroamphetamine (Dexedrine)<br>FDA-approved for children 3 years and older<br>Methylphenidate (Ritalin) and pemoline (Cylert)<br>FDA-approved for children 6 years and older | In attention-deficit/hyperactivity disorder (ADHD) for hyperactivity, impulsivity, and inattentiveness | Dextroamphetamine and methylphenidate are generally given at 8 AM and noon (the usefulness of sustained-release preparations is not proved)<br>Dextroamphetamine—2.5–40 mg a day up to 0.5 mg per kg a day<br>Methylphenidate—10–60 mg a day or up to 1.0 mg per kg a day<br>Pemoline—37.5–112.5 mg given at 8 AM | Insomnia, anorexia, weight loss (and possibly growth delay), headache, tachycardia, precipitation or exacerbation of tic disorders<br>With pemoline, monitor LFTs, as hepatoxicity is possible |

**Table 49.4–2**
*Continued*

| Drugs | Indications | Dosage | Adverse Reactions and Monitoring |
|---|---|---|---|
| Lithium—considered an antipsychotic drug, also has antiaggression properties | Studies support use in MR and CD for aggressive and self-injurious behaviors; can be used for same in PDD; also indicated for early-onset bipolar I disorder | 600–2,100 mg in two or three divided doses; keep blood levels to 0.4–1.2 mEq per L | Nausea, vomiting, enuresis, headache, tremor, weight gain, hypothyroidism Experience with adults suggests renal function monitoring |
| Tricyclic drugs Imipramine (Tofranil) has been used in most child studies Nortriptyline (Pamelor) has been studied in children Clomipramine (Anafranil) is effective in child obsessive-compulsive disorder (OCD) | Major depressive disorder, separation anxiety disorder, bulimia nervosa, enuresis; sometimes used in ADHD, anorexia nervosa, sleepwalking disorder, and sleep terror disorder | Imipramine—start with dosage of about 1.5 mg per kg a day; can build up to not more than 5 mg per kg a day Start with two or three divided doses; eventually combine in one dose Not FDA-approved for children except for enuresis; dosage is usually 50–100 mg before sleep; clomipramine—start at 50 mg a day; can raise to not more than 3 mg per kg a day or 200 mg a day | Dry mouth, constipation, tachycardia, drowsiness, postural hypotension, hypertension, mania Electrocardiogram (ECG) monitoring is needed because of risk for cardiac conduction slowing; consider lowering dosage if PR interval >0.20 seconds or QRS interval >0.12 seconds; baseline EEG is advised, as it can lower seizure threshold; blood levels of drug are sometimes useful |
| Fluoxetine (Prozac)—a serotonin-specific reuptake inhibitor | OCD, major depressive disorder; may be useful in anorexia nervosa, bulimia nervosa | Fluoxetine dosage not established in children | Nausea, headache, nervousness, insomnia, dry mouth, diarrhea, anorexia nervosa, drowsiness |
| Carbamazepine (Tegretol)—an anticonvulsant | Aggression or dyscontrol in MR or CD | Start with 10 mg per kg a day; can build to 20–30 mg per kg a day; therapeutic blood level range appears to be 4–12 mg per L | Drowsiness, nausea, rash, vertigo, irritability Monitor: CBC and LFTs for possible blood dyscrasias and hepatotoxicity; blood levels are necessary |
| Benzodiazepines—have been insufficiently studied in childhood and adolescence | Sometimes effective in parasomnias: sleepwalking disorder or sleep terror disorder; can be tried in generalized anxiety disorder Clonazepam (Klonopin) can be tried in separation anxiety disorder Alprazolam (Xanax) can be tried in separation anxiety disorder | Parasomnias: diazepam (Valium) 2–10 mg before bedtime | Can cause drowsiness, ataxia, tremor, dyscontrol; can be abused |
| Fenfluramine (Pondimin)—an amphetamine congener | Well-studied in autistic disorder; generally ineffective, but some patients show improvement | Gradually increase to 1.0–1.5 mg per kg a day in divided doses | Weight loss, drowsiness, irritability, loose bowel movements |
| Propranolol (Inderal)—a β-adrenergic blocker | Aggression in MR, PDD, and cognitive disorder; awaits controlled studies | Effective dosage in children and adolescents is not yet established; range is probably 40–320 mg a day | Bradycardia, hypotension, nausea, hypoglycemia, depression; avoid in asthma |
| Clonidine (Catapres)—a presynaptic α-adrenergic blocking agent | Tourette's disorder; some success in ADHD | 0.1–0.3 mg a day; 3–5.5 µg per kg a day | Orthostatic hypotension, nausea, vomiting, sedation, elevated blood glucose |
| Cyproheptadine (Periactin) | Anorexia nervosa | Dosages up to 8 mg four times a day | Antihistaminic side effects, including sedation and dryness of the mouth |
| Naltrexone (Trexan) | Self-injurious behaviors in MR and PDD; currently being studied in PDD | 0.5–2.0 mg per kg a day | Sleepiness, aggressivity Monitor LFTs, as hepatotoxicity has been reported in adults at high dosages |

Table by Richard Perry, M.D.

better when they took folic acid than they did before treatment.

**Learning disorders.** No pharmacological agent significantly improves any learning disorder. However, many children with other mental disorders also have learning disorders, and many who have learning disorders also have behavioral problems. Those associations and the importance of school and learning in children's lives raise questions about the cognitive effects of psychotropics. Table 49.4–3 summarizes the effects of drugs on cognitive tests of learning functions.

In children with learning disorders but no other mental disorder, methylphenidate facilitates performance on several standard cognitive, psycholinguistic, memory, and vigilance tests but does not improve the child's academic achievement ratings or teacher ratings. Cognitive impairment from psychotropic drugs, especially antipsychotics, may be an even greater problem in mentally retarded persons than in those with learning disorders.

**Autistic disorder.** The behavioral problems of children with autistic disorder can be extreme. In short-term and long-term studies, haloperidol, often in nonsedating dosages, has proved to be efficacious in reducing temper tantrums, aggression, stereotypies, self-injurious behavior, hyperactivity, and withdrawal. However, dyskinesia is a risk. In recent years the serotonin-specific reuptake inhibitors have been studied in autistic disorder as researchers posited an association between the compulsive behaviors in obsessive-compulsive disorder and the stereotypic behaviors common in autistic children. To date, clomipramine (Anafranil) and fluoxetine have shown promise in ending stereotypies and other behaviors in autistic children and adults.

The opiate antagonists naloxone (Narcan) and naltrexone are effective in reducing self-injurious behavior in some autistic children. However, to what degree other behaviors are benefited is not yet clear. Improvements appear to be modest.

The behavioral difficulties of autistic children can be difficult to manage. Much effort, firmness, and consistency are required from caretakers. The psychiatrist may need to try many medications. β-Blockers, lithium, or anticonvulsants may be helpful. Polypharmacy is not unusual but has not been formally studied. Stimulants can be tried to reduce hyperactivity and inattentiveness in relatively manageable autistic children.

**Attention-deficit/hyperactivity disorder.** Studies in recent years continue to support the use of stimulants in the treatment of attention-deficit/hyperactivity disorder. The most frequently researched and used stimulant is methylphenidate. Dextroamphetamine (Dexedrine) is of comparable efficacy and, unlike methylphenidate, is approved by the Food and Drug Administration (FDA) for children 3 years and older, whereas the starting age for methylphenidate is 6 years. Pemoline (Cylert) is a less effective but longer-acting stimulant that carries a small risk for hepatotoxicity. Stimulants reduce the hyperactivity, inattentiveness, and impulsivity in about 75 percent of children with attention-deficit/hyperactivity disorder. The effects are not paradoxical, as normal children respond similarly. The dose-related side effects of stimulants are listed in Table 49.4–4.

Attention-deficit/hyperactivity disorder often coexists with oppositional defiant disorder or conduct disorder. With those added disorders comes aggression; in some cases stimulants appear to reduce aggression. However, a common mistake is to prolong stimulant trials when the aggression is not subsiding and when a switch to or the addition of a more specifically antiaggression drug is indicated.

In those children with attention-deficit/hyperactivity disorder in which stimulants are ineffective and in children with preexisting tic disorders, antidepressants can be tried. Desipramine has proved to be effective in studies, but its use is limited because four children who took desipramine died suddenly. Other tricyclic drugs, including nortriptyline (Pamelor) and clomipramine, have been tried successfully. The response of children with attention-deficit/hyperactivity disorder to antidepressants can occur within days of the beginning of treatment.

Clonidine (Catapres) has also been tried with some success in attention-deficit/hyperactivity disorder in a few studies. Antipsychotics can be used to treat attention-deficit/hyperactivity disorder but only after other treatments have failed because of the risks for sedation and tardive dyskinesia.

Attention-deficit/hyperactivity disorder often precedes and then coexists with tic disorders. Chapter 42 discusses the pharmacotherapy for the child who has the two conditions.

The dietary management of hyperactivity has received a great amount of public attention, but controlled studies

**Table 49.4–3**
**Effects of Psychotropic Drugs on Cognitive Tests of Learning Functions***

| Drug Class | Continuous Performance Test (Attention) | Matching Familiar Figures (Impulsivity) | Paired Associates (Verbal Learning) | Porteus Maze (Planning Capacity) | Short-Term Memory* | WISC (Intelligence) |
|---|---|---|---|---|---|---|
| | | | **Test Function** | | | |
| Stimulant | ↑ | ↑ | ↑ | ↑ | ↑ | ↑ |
| Antidepressant | ↑ | 0 | | 0 | 0 | 0 |
| Antipsychotic | ↑↓ | | ↓ | ↓ | ↓ | 0 |

↑ Improved, ↑↓ inconsistent, ↓ worse, 0 no effect.
*Various tests; digit span, word recall, etc.
Table adapted from M G Aman: Drugs, learning and the psychotherapies. In *Pediatric Psychopharmacology: The Use of Behavior Modifying Drugs in Children*, J S Werry, editor, p 355. Brunner/Mazel, New York, 1978. Used with permission.

**Table 49.4–4**
**Common Dose-Related Side Effects of Stimulants**

Insomnia
Decreased appetite
Irritability or nervousness
Weight loss

have not substantiated its benefit. Similarly, in most controlled studies, caffeine was not found superior to a placebo for attention-deficit/hyperactivity disorder.

**Conduct disorder.** The assaultiveness that is frequently associated with conduct disorder is targeted by pharmacotherapy. Antipsychotics such as haloperidol can quell aggression, but sedation and the risk of tardive dyskinesia are major drawbacks. Lithium has reduced aggression in conduct disorder, and propranolol (Inderal) and carbamazepine have been effective in open studies.

When conduct disorder is associated with attention-deficit/hyperactivity disorder and when the aggression is mild, a trial of a stimulant may be indicated, as stimulants are faster acting and easier to monitor than the drugs noted above. Clonidine may be effective and deserves further study.

The aggression associated with conduct disorder is often difficult to get under control, leading to the use of polypharmacy. No studies have demonstrated the benefits of that approach.

**Tourette's disorder.** The strongly antidopaminergic antipsychotics haloperidol and pimozide (Orap) remain the most effective medications for Tourette's disorder. Pimozide prolongs the QT interval, necessitating electrocardiographic monitoring. Clonidine, a presynaptic α-adrenergic blocking agent, is less effective than the two antipsychotics but avoids the risk for tardive dyskinesia; sedation is a frequent side effect of clonidine.

Tic disorders often coexist with attention-deficit/hyperactivity disorder in children and adolescents. Stimulants, which can precipitate tics, should be avoided in those cases, although recent studies indicate that the prohibition may not be totally warranted. Clonidine reduces tics in both attention-deficit/hyperactivity disorder and the comorbid cases. A small study supports the use of nortriptyline.

**Enuresis.** Before initating psychopharmacotherapy in the treatment of enuresis, the clinician has to consider the merits of waiting for a possible spontaneous remission and of using behavioral techniques; bell-and-pad conditioning (a bell awakens the child when the mattress becomes wet) is perhaps the most elaborate behavioral treatment and seems to be more successful than are medications.

Tricyclic drugs are effective in reducing enuresis in about 60 percent of enuretic patients, and desmopressin (DDAVP) is effective in about 50 percent of enuretic patients. Improvement ranges from complete cessation of wetting to continued wetting but with less urine volume. Tricyclic drugs are given about one hour before bedtime. The starting dosage is usually 25 mg a day, a lower dosage than that used in trials for depression. One can increase the dosage to 75 mg a day for an adolescent, but the dosage should not exceed 2 mg per kg a day. The child usually responds within days. Desmopressin is taken intranasally

in dosages of 10 to 40 mg a day. When used over months, nasal discomfort can occur. Water retention is potentially a problem. Those patients who respond with full dryness should continue to take the medication for several months to prevent relapses.

**Separation anxiety disorder.** Few studies support the use of anxiolytics in pediatric psychopharmacology. A recent double-blind, placebo-controlled study did not replicate a similar study done by the same workers 20 years before, when imipramine (Tofranil) was shown to be effective for school refusal. Alprazolam (Xanax) may be helpful in separation anxiety disorder, but the data are conflicting.

**Schizophrenia.** Antipsychotics are commonly used for schizophrenia in childhood and adolescence. However, only two double-blind studies showed a modest effectiveness of antipsychotics in adolescent schizophrenia and only one of those studies was placebo-controlled. In the only double-blind placebo-controlled study of childhood schizophrenia, haloperidol was significantly superior to the placebo. Schizophrenia with onset in late adolescence is treated like adult-onset schizophrenia.

**Mood disorders.** Tricyclic drugs have not been shown to be superior to a placebo in double-blind, placebo-controlled studies of children and adolescents with major depressive disorder. In children, developmental differences in neurotransmitters and neuroendocrine systems may be associated with responses to antidepressants. In any case, the 1990s will undoubtedly see a number of studies of serotonin-specific reuptake inhibitors in the treatment of early-onset major depressive disorder.

Most researchers still advocate a trial of antidepressant medication in severe, prolonged major depressive disorder. However, because of their potential cardiotoxic effects, tricyclic drugs require a knowledge of appropriate dosing, electrocardiographic monitoring, and circumspection about prescribing the drugs to those at risk for suicide.

Manic episodes in childhood and adolescence are treated as they are in adults. No double-blind, placebo-controlled studies have demonstrated the effectiveness of lithium in treating adolescent mania.

**Obsessive-compulsive disorder.** In a growing number of studies, clomipramine has proved to be effective in diminishing obsessions and compulsions in children and adolescents. Fluoxetine has been studied less than clomipramine but also appears to be effective. Clomipramine is generally well-tolerated. The side effects of fluoxetine appear to be more frequent, bothersome, and dramatic than the side effects of clomipramine. Other serotonin-specific reuptake inhibitors will probably be studied for their use in the treatment of early-onset obsessive-compulsive disorder.

**Eating disorders.** Pharmacotherapy has little to offer in the treatment of anorexia nervosa. Cyproheptadine (Periactin) benefits some anorectic patients, and antidepressants may benefit those with comorbid depressive disorders. However, the compromised metabolism of many anorectic patients can put them at a high risk for cardiac arrhythmias if tricyclic drugs are administered.

Many antidepressants—imipramine, desipramine, trazodone (Desyrel), fluoxetine, and monoamine oxidase inhibitors (MAOIs)—reduce the binge eating and purging in bulimia nervosa. Bupropion (Wellbutrin) in one large study of bulimic nervosa patients was associated with a dramatic incidence of seizures.

**Sleep terror disorder and sleepwalking disorder.** Sleep terror disorder and sleepwalking disorder occur in the transition from deep delta-wave sleep (stages 3 and 4) to light sleep. Benzodiazepines and tricyclic drugs are effective in those disorders. They work by reducing both delta-wave sleep and the arousals between sleep stages. The medications should be used temporarily and in only severe cases, because tolerance to the medications develops, cessation of the medications can lead to severe rebound worsening of the disorders, and reducing delta sleep in chlidren may have deleterious effects. Therefore, behavioral approaches are preferred in the disorders.

**Other disorders.** Buspirone (BuSpar) has been effective in an open trial of adolescents suffering from generalized anxiety disorder. Patients with early-onset panic disorder and panic attacks have benefited from clonazepam (Klonopin) in several open trials.

## Side Effects and Complications

**Antidepressants.** The side effects of antidepressants in children are usually similar to those in adults and result from the antidepressant's anticholinergic properties. The side effects include dry mouth, constipation, palpitations, tachycardia, loss of accommodation, and sweating. The most serious side effects are cardiovascular, although, in children, diastolic hypertension is more common, and postural hypotension occurs more rarely than in adults. Electrocardiographic (ECG) changes are most apt to be seen in children receiving high dosages. Slowed cardiac conduction (PR interval >0.20 seconds or QRS interval >0.12) may necessitate lowering the dosage. FDA guidelines limit dosages to a maximum of 5 mg per kg a day. The drug can be toxic in an overdose, and, in small children, ingestions of 200 to 400 mg can be fatal. When the dosage is lowered too rapidly, withdrawal effects are manifested mainly by gastrointestinal symptoms: cramping, nausea, vomiting, and sometimes apathy and weakness. The treatment is a slower tapering of the dosage.

**Antipsychotics.** The best studied of the antipsychotics given to pediatric-age groups are chlorpromazine (Thorazine), thioridazine (Mellaril), and haloperidol. High-potency and low-potency antipsychotics are believed to differ in their side-effect profiles. The phenothiazine derivatives (chlorpromazine and thioridazine) have the most pronounced sedative and atropinic actions, whereas the high-potency antipsychotics are commonly thought to be associated with extrapyramidal reactions, such as parkinsonian symptoms, akathisia, and acute dystonias. Caution is warranted in assuming that those things are also true in children. In particular, when comparisons are made at low-dosage levels of equivalent potency, differences may not be detected.

Even if the frequency of the side effects differs among the medications, they are always caused by antipsychotics. Evidence in children of impaired cognitive function and, most important, of tardive dyskinesia calls for great caution in the use of drugs. Tardive dyskinesia—which is char-

acterized by persistent abnormal involuntary movements of the tongue, the face, the mouth, or the jaw and which may also involve the extremities—is a known hazard when giving antipsychotics to patients of all age groups. No known treatment is effective. Tardive dyskinesia has not been reported in patients taking less than 375 to 400 grams of chlorpromazine equivalents. Because nonpersistent choreiform movements of the extremities and the trunk are common after an abrupt discontinuation of antipsychotics, the clinician must distinguiush those symptoms from persistent dyskinesias.

Whenever clinically feasible, children receiving antipsychotics should be periodically withdrawn from the medication, so that the clinician can assess the patient's current clinical need and the possible development of tardive dyskinesia.

**Stimulants.** Problems with retarded growth associated with taking stimulants have been reported, although little evidence for the problems is available. The current thinking is that any growth suppression is temporary and that children taking stimulants will eventually reach their normal height.

## OTHER BIOLOGICAL THERAPIES

Electroconvulsive therapy (ECT) is not indicated in childhood or adolescence. Psychosurgery for severe and intransigent obsessive-compulsive disorder should probably be delayed until adulthood, after all attempts at less drastic treatment have failed and when the patient can participate fully in the process of informed consent.

Little evidence indicates that food allergies or sensitivities play a role in childhood mental disorders. Diets that eliminate food additives, colorings, and sugar are difficult to maintain and usually have no effect. Megavitamin therapy is usually ineffective (unless the child has a frank vitamin deficiency) and can cause bad side effects.

## Refrences

Aman M G, Kern R A, McGhee O E, Arnold L E A: Fenfluramine and methylphenidate in children with mental retardation and ADHD: Clinical and side effects. J Am Acad Child Adolesc Psychiatry *32:* 851, 1993.

American Psychiatric Association: Practice guidelines for eating disorders. Am J Psychiatry *150:* 212, 1993.

Biederman J, Baldessarini R J, Goldblatt A, Lapey K A, Doyle A, Hesslein P S: A naturalistic study of 24-hour electrocardiographic recordings and echocardiographic findings in children and adolescents treated with desipramine. J Am Acad Child Adolesc Psychiatry *32:* 805, 1993.

Campbell M, Small A M, Green W H, Jennings S J, Perry R, Bennett W G, Anderson L: Behavioral efficacy of haloperidol and lithium carbonite: A comparison in hospitalized aggressive children with conduct disorder. Arch Gen Psychiatry *41:* 650, 1984.

Geller B: Psychopharmacology of children and adolescents: Pharmacokinetics and relationships of plasma/serum levels to response. Psychopharmacol Bull *27:* 401, 1991.

Geller B, Cooper T B, Graham D L, Fetner H H, Marsteller F A, Wells J M: Pharmacokinetically designed double-blind placebo-controlled study of nortriptyline in 6- to 12-year olds with major depressive disorder. J Am Acad Child Adolesc Psychiatry *31:* 34, 1992.

Gordon C T, State R C, Nelson J E, Hamburger S D, Rapoport J L: A double-blind comparison of clomipramine, desipramine, and placebo in the treatment of autistic disorder. Arch Gen Psychiatry *50:* 441, 1993.

Green W H: *Child and Adolescent Clnical Psychopharmacology.* Williams & Wilkins, Baltimore, 1991.

Green W H: Nonstimulant drugs in the treatment of attention-deficit hyperactivity disorder. Child Adolesc Psychiatr Clin North Am *1:* 449, 1992.

Greenhill L: Pharmacotherapy: Stimulants. Child Adolesc Clin North Am *1*: 411, 1992.

Jensen P S, Ryan W D, Prien R: Psychopharmacology of child and adolescent major depression: Present status and future directions. J Child Adolesc Psychopharmacol *2*: 31, 1992.

Ratey J J, Gordon A: The psychopharmacology of aggression: Toward a new day. Psychopharmacol Bull *29*: 65, 1993.

Riddle M A, Geller B, Rayn N: Another sudden death in a child treated with desipramine. J Am Acad Child Adolesc Psychiatry *32*: 792, 1993.

Spencer T, Biederman J, Wilens T, Steingard R, Geist D: Nortriptyline treatment of children with attention-deficit hyperactivity disorder and tic disorder or Tourette's syndrome. J Am Acad Child Adolesc Psychiatry *32*: 205, 1993.

Steingard R, Biederman J, Spencer T, Wilens T, Gonzalez A: Comparison of clonidine response in the treatment of attention-deficit hyperactivity disorder with and without comorbid tic disorders. J Am Acad Child Adolesc Psychiatry *32*: 350, 1993.

# 49.5 / Psychiatric Treatment of Adolescents

Adolescence is a time when environmental demands increase and many serious mental disorders have their onset. Schizophrenia, bipolar I disorder, and the risk for completed suicide—all drastically increase during adolescence. Although some degree of stress is virtually universal during adolescence, most teenagers without mental disorders are able to cope well with the environmental demands. Those teenagers with preexisting mental disorders may have exacerbations during adolescence and become frustrated, alienated, and demoralized.

One must be sensitive to adolescents' perceptions of themselves, since a range of emotional maturity exists within a group of same-aged teenagers. Issues that are specific to adolescents are related to their new evolving identities, the development of sexual activities, and their plans to meet future life goals.

## DIAGNOSIS

Adolescents can be assessed in both their specific stage-appropriate functions and their general progress in accomplishing the tasks of adolescence. For almost all adolescents in today's culture, at least until their late teens, school performance is the prime barometer of healthy functioning. Intellectually normal adolescents who are not functioning satisfactorily in some form of schooling have significant psychological problems whose nature and causes should be identified.

Questions to be asked in regard to adolescents' stage-specific tasks are the following: What degree of separation from their parents have the adolescents achieved? What sort of identities are evolving? How do they perceive their past? Do they perceive themselves as being responsible for their own development or as being only the passive recipients of their parents' influences? How do they perceive themselves with regard to the future, and how do they anticipate their future responsibilities for themselves

and others? Can they think about the varying consequences of various ways of living? How do they express their sexual and affectionate interests? Those tasks occupy all adolescents and normally are performed at varying times.

Adolescents' object relations must be evaluated. Do they perceive and accept both the good and the bad qualities in their parents? Do they see their peers and boyfriends or girlfriends as separate persons with needs and identities of their own, or do they exist only for the patients' own needs?

A respect for and, if possible, some actual understanding of the adolescent's subcultural and ethnic background are essential. For example, in some groups, depression is acceptable; in other groups, overt depression is a sign of weakness and is masked by antisocial acts, substance misuse, and self-destructive risks. However, a psychiatrist need not be of the same race or group identity as the adolescent to be effective. Respect and knowledgeable concern are human qualities, not group-restricted qualities.

## INTERVIEWS

Whenever circumstances permit, both the adolescent patient and the parents should be interviewed. Other family members may also have to be included, depending on their degree of involvement in the youngster's life and difficulties. However, the clinician should see the adolescent first; that preferential treatment helps avoid the appearance of being the parents' agent.

In psychotherapy for an older adolescent, the therapist and the parents usually have little contact after the initial part of the therapy, because ongoing contact inhibits the adolescent's desire to open up.

### Interview Techniques

All patients test and mistrust the therapist, but in adolescents those manifestations are likely to be crude, intense, provocative, and prolonged. Clinicians must establish themselves as trustworthy and helpful adults, so as to promote a therapeutic alliance. They should have the adolescents tell their own stories, without interrupting to check out discrepancies, as that will sound like correcting and disbelief. Clinicians should obtain explanations and theories from the patients about what happened, why those behaviors or feelings occurred, when things changed, and what caused the identified problems to begin when they did.

Sessions with adolescents generally follow the adult model of the therapist's sitting across from the patient. However, in early adolescence board games (for example, checkers) may be helpful in stimulating conversation in an otherwise quiet, anxious patient.

Language is crucial. Even when a teenager and a clinician come from the same socioeconomic group, their languages are seldom the same. Psychiatrists should use their own language, explain any specialized terms or concepts, and ask for an explanation of unfamiliar in-group jargon or slang.

Many adolescents do not talk spontaneously about illicit

substances and suicidal tendencies but do respond honestly to the therapist's questions. The therapist may need to ask specifically about each substance and the amount and the frequency of its use.

Adolescents' sexual histories and current sexual activities are increasingly important pieces of information for adequate evaluation. The nature of adolescents' sexual behaviors is often a vignette of their whole personality structures and ego development. However, a long time in therapy may pass before adolescents begin to talk about their sexual behavior.

## TREATMENT

Usually, no single therapy modality is specific to a particular disorder. The best choice, then, is often what best fits the characteristics of the individual adolescent and the family or social milieu. Adolescents' real dependence needs may press clinicians to strive to maintain even the sickest youngster in a satisfactory home. But for the same reason, clinicians may be forced to remove adolescents from pathogenic homes, even when the severity of the illness alone does not dictate it, because the youngsters are not developmentally capable of handling the double burden of working to overcome their illness and being traumatized at home. Also, adolescents' striving for autonomy may so complicate problems of compliance with therapy that they force involuntary inpatient treatment of difficulties for which such treatment may not be necessary at a different stage of life. Thus, the following discussion is less a set of guidelines than a brief summary of what each treatment modality can or should offer.

### Individual Psychotherapy

Few, if any, adolescent patients are trusting or open without considerable time and testing, and so it is helpful to anticipate the testing period by letting the patients know that it is to be expected and is natural and healthy. Pointing out the likelihood of therapeutic problems—for instance, impatience and disappointment with the psychiatrist, with the therapy, with the time required, and with the often-intangible results—may help keep the problems under control. Therapeutic goals should be stated in terms that adolescents understand and value. Although they may not see the point in exercising self-control, enduring dysphoric emotions, or forgoing impulsive gratification, they may value feeling more confident than in the past and gaining more control over their lives and the events that affect them.

Typical adolescent patients need a real relationship with a therapist whom they can perceive as a real person. The therapist becomes another parent, because adolescents still need appropriate parenting or reparenting. Thus, the professional who is impersonal and anonymous is a less useful model than is one who can accept and respond rationally to an angry challenge or confrontation without fear or false conciliation, can impose limits and controls when the adolescents cannot, can admit mistakes and ignorance, and can openly express the gamut of human emotions. The failure to take a stand regarding self-damaging and self-

destructive behavior or a passive response to manipulative and dishonest behavior is perceived as indifference or collusion.

Countertransference reactions can be intense in psychotherapeutic work with an adolescent, and the therapist must be aware of them. The adolescent often expresses hostile feelings toward adults, such as parents and teachers. The therapist may react with an overidentification with the adolescent or with the parents. Such reactions are determined, at least in part, by the therapist's own experiences during adolescence or, when applicable, by the therapist's own experiences as a parent.

Individual outpatient therapy is appropriate for adolescents whose problems are manifested in conflicted emotions and nondangerous behavior, who are not too disorganized to be maintained outside a structured setting, and whose families or other living environments are not so disturbed as to negate the influence of therapy. Such therapy characteristically focuses on intrapsychic conflicts and inhibitions; on the meanings of emotions, attitudes, and behavior; and on the influence of the past and the present.

Antianxiety agents can be considered in adolescents whose anxiety may be high at certain times during psychotherapy. However, the adolescent's potential for abusing those drugs must be carefully weighed.

### Group Psychotherapy

In many ways group psychotherapy is a natural setting for adolescents. Most teenagers are more comfortable with peers than with adults. A group diminishes the sense of unequal power between the adult therapist and the adolescent patient. Participation varies, depending on the adolescent's readiness. Not all interpretations and confrontations need come from the parent-figure therapist; group members are often adept at picking up symptomatic behavior in one another, and adolescents may find it easier to hear and consider critical or challenging comments from their peers.

Group psychotherapy usually addresses interpersonal and present life issues. But some adolescents are too fragile for group psychotherapy or have symptoms or social traits too likely to elicit peer group ridicule, and so they need individual therapy to attain enough ego strength to struggle with peer relationships. Conversely, other adolescents need to resolve interpersonal issues in a group before they can tackle intrapsychic issues in the intensity of one-to-one therapy.

### Family Therapy

Family therapy is the primary modality when the adolescent's difficulties are mainly a reflection of a dysfunctional family (for example, teenagers with simple school phobia, runaways). The same may be true when developmental issues, such as adolescent sexuality and striving for autonomy, trigger family conflicts. Or the family pathology may be severe, as in cases of incest and child abuse. In those instances the adolescent usually needs individual therapy as well, but family therapy is mandatory if the adolescent is to remain in the home or return to it. Serious character pathology, such as that underlying antisocial and borderline personality disorders, often develops out of highly pathogenic early parenting. Family therapy is strongly indicated whenever possible in such disorders, but most authorities consider it adjunctive to intensive individual psychotherapy when individual psychopathology has become so internalized that it persists regardless of the current family status.

## Inpatient Treatment

Residential treatment schools are often preferable for long-term therapy, but hospitals are more suitable for emergencies, although some adolescent inpatient hospital units also provide educational, recreational, and occupational facilities for long-term patients. Adolescents whose families are too disturbed or incompetent, who are dangerous to themselves or others, who are out of control in ways that preclude further healthy development, or who are seriously disorganized require, at least temporarily, the external controls of a structured environment.

Long-term inpatient therapy is the treatment of choice for those severe disorders that are considered wholly or largely psychogenic in origin, such as major ego deficits that are caused by early massive deprivation and that respond poorly or not at all to medication. Severe borderline personality disorder, for example, regardless of the behavioral symptoms, requires a full-time corrective environment in which regression is possible and safe and in which ego development can take place. Psychotic disorders in adolescence often require hospitalization, but psychotic adolescents often respond to appropriate medication, so that therapy is usually feasible in an outpatient setting except during exacerbations. Schizophrenic adolescents who show a long-term deteriorating course may require hospitalization periodically.

## Day Hospitals

In day hospitals, which have become increasingly popular, the adolescent spends the day in class, individual and group psychotherapy, and other programs but goes home in the evenings. Compared with full hospitalization, day hospitals are less expensive and are usually preferred by the patient.

## CLINICAL PROBLEMS

## Atypical Puberty

Pubertal changes that occur 2½ years earlier or later than the average age are within the normal range. But body image is so important to adolescents that extremes of the norm may be distressing to some, either because markedly early maturation subjects them to social and sexual pressures for which they are unready or because late maturation makes them feel inferior and excludes them from some peer activities. Medical reassurance, even if

based on examination and testing to rule out pathophysiology, may be insufficient. The adolescent's distress may show as sexual or delinquent acting out, withdrawal, or problems at school of such a degree as to warrant therapeutic intervention. Therapy may also be prompted by similar disturbances in some adolescents who fail to achieve the peer-valued stereotypes of physical development, despite normal pubertal physiology.

## Substance-Related Disorders

Some experimentation with psychoactive substances is almost ubiquitous among adolescents, especially if one includes alcohol. But the majority of adolescents do not become abusers, particularly of prescription drugs and illegal substances.

Regular substance abuse of any degree represents disturbance. Substance abuse is sometimes self-medication against depression or schizophrenic deterioration and is sometimes a sign of characterological disorder in teenagers whose ego deficits render them unequal to the stresses of puberty and the tasks of adolescence. However, many substances, especially cocaine, have a physiologically reinforcing action that acts independently of preexisting psychopathology. Regardless of why the abuse developed, it becomes a problem in itself. Ego development depends on confronting and learning to cope adaptively with reality. The substances become both a substitute for reality and an avoidance of it, thus impairing ego development and perpetuating substance abuse to conceal poor coping skills.

When substance abuse covers an underlying illness or is a maladaptive response to current stresses or disturbed family dynamics, treatment of the underlying cause may take care of the substance abuse. Outpatient psychotherapy, however, is generally useless with long-term abusers, who require a structured setting where the substances are not available.

## Suicide

Suicide is now the second leading cause of death among adolescents. Many hospital admissions of adolescents result from suicidal ideation or behavior. Suicide is the final common pathway for a number of disorders, and its high incidence reflects grave psychopathology. Some authorities think that in adolescence, in contrast to adulthood, schizophrenia more often underlies suicide than do major mood disorders. Among adolescents who are not psychotic, the highest suicidal risks occur in those adolescents who have a history of parental suicide, who are unable to form stable attachments, who display impulsive behavior or episodic dyscontrol, and who abuse alcohol or other substances. Many adolescent suicides show a common pattern of long-standing family and social problems throughout childhood and the escalation of subjective distress under the pressures and stresses of puberty and adolescence, followed by a suicide attempt precipitated by the sudden real or perceived loss of some person or social support felt to be the one source of meaning or closeness.

Normal developmental losses—of childhood dependence, of the parents, of childhood—can also cause psychogenic depression in adolescents. The rapid and extreme mood swings in adolescence, coupled with the adolescent's difficulty in seeing beyond the intensity of the moment, contribute to catastrophic despair and impulsive suicide attempts over losses that adults could weather. Moreover, alcohol and other substances can decrease the resistance to suicidal impulses. Normally persistent magical thinking may impair the sense of permanence of one's own death, allowing adolescents to contemplate suicide more lightly than do adults.

During both evaluation and treatment, suicidal thoughts, plans, and past attempts must be discussed directly when the concern arises and information is not volunteered. Long-term or recurring thoughts should be taken seriously, and an agreement or contract should be negotiated with the adolescent not to attempt suicide without first calling and talking about it with the psychiatrist. Adolescents are usually honest about making and keeping, or refusing, such agreements; if they refuse, closed hospitalization is indicated. Hospitalization is a sign of serious, protective concern and may be as therapeutic as the opportunity to conduct or plan further treatment in a safe environment.

**References**

Blos P: *On Adolescence.* Free Press, New York, 1962.
Davis M, Raffe I H: The holding environment in the inpatient treatment of adolescents. Adolesc Psychiatry *12:* 434, 1985.
Erikson E H: The problem of ego identity, J Am Psychoanal Assoc *4:* 56, 1966.
Feldman L B: Integrating individual and family therapy in the treatment of symptomatic children and adolescents. Am J Psychother *42:* 272, 1988.
Freud A: Adolescence, Psychoanal Study Child *16:* 225, 1958.
Gartner A F: Countertransference issues in the psychotherapy of adolescents. J Child Adolesc Psychother *2:* 187, 1985.
Group for the Advancement of Psychiatry: *Normal Adolescence,* vol 6, Report 68. Group for the Advancement of Psychiatry, New York, 1968.
Kazdin A E: Psychotherapy for children and adolescents. Annu Res Psychol *41:* 21, 1990.
Lyman R D, Prentice-Dunn S, Gabel S: *Residential and Inpatient Treatment of Children and Adolescents.* Plenum, New York, 1989.
Moreau D, Mufson L, Weissman M M, Klerman G L: Interpersonal psychotherapy for adolescent depression: Description of modification and preliminary application J Am Acad Child Adolesc Psychiatry *30:* 642, 1991.
O'Brien J D: Current prevention concepts in child and adolescent psychiatry. Am J Psychother *45:* 261, 1991.
Peterson A C, Taylor B: The biological approach to adolescence. In *Handbook of Adolescent Development,* J Adelson, editor, p 68. Wiley, New York, 1980.
Schowalter J E, Anyan W R: *The Family Handbook of Adolescence.* Knopf, New York, 1979.
Shaffer D, Garland A, Vieland V, Underwood M, Busner C: The impact of curriculum-based suicide prevention programs for teenagers. J Am Acad Child Adolesc Psychiatry *30:* 588, 1991.
Sholevar G P, Burland A, Frank J L, Etezady M H, Goldstein J: Psychoanalytic treatment of children and adolescents. J Am Acad Child Adolesc Psychiatry *28:* 685, 1989.

# Geriatric Psychiatry

Geriatric psychiatry is the branch of medicine concerned with the prevention, diagnosis, and treatment of physical and psychological disorders in the elderly and with the promotion of longevity. Because Americans are living longer than in the past, the number and the relative percentage of elderly persons in the general population are markedly increased. According to the 1990 United States census, the oldest old—people at least 85 years old—are the fastest-growing group of the elderly population. Although the oldest old constitute only 1.2 percent of the total population, they have increased 232 percent since 1960. People at least 85 years old now constitute 10 percent of those 65 and older. Since 1960 the elderly population has grown 89 percent; the total population has increased 39 percent. There are 39 men for every 100 women 85 years old or older.

Geriatric psychiatry is the fastest growing field in psychiatry. The diagnosis and the treatment of mental disorders in the elderly require special knowledge because of possible differences in clinical manifestations, pathogenesis, and pathophysiology of mental disorders between young adults and the elderly. Complicating factors in elderly patients also need to be considered; the factors include the frequent presence of coexisting chronic medical diseases and disabilities, the use of many medications, and the increased susceptibility to cognitive impairment.

Geriatric psychiatry was declared an official subspecialty by the American Board of Psychiatry and Neurology (ABPN) in 1989. The first examination for certification was given in 1991 and resulted in the first group of certified geropsychiatrists.

The term "geriatric" stems from the Greek *geras,* meaning old age, and *iatros,* meaning physician, and so "geriatric" means the medical treatment or healing of the aged.

## PSYCHIATRIC ASSESSMENT

Psychiatric history taking and the mental status examination of an elderly patient should follow the same format that applies to young adults. Because of the high prevalence of cognitive disorders in elderly patients, the psychiatrist should determine whether the patient understands the nature and the purpose of the examination. If the patient is cognitively impaired, an independent history should be obtained from a family member or caretaker. The patient should still be seen alone—even if there is clear evidence of impairment—to preserve the privacy of the doctor-patient relationship and to elicit the patient's

suicidal thoughts or paranoid ideation, which may not be voiced in the presence of a relative or a nurse.

### Laboratory Studies

Laboratory and imaging studies can help the clinician establish a diagnosis and detect treatable conditions, especially disorders that might otherwise be regarded as part of normal aging. Computed tomography, magnetic resonance imaging, or single photon emission computed tomography scans are probably indicated whenever a notable change in mental status occurs.

### Psychiatric History

A complete psychiatric history includes the preliminary identification (name, age, sex, marital status), chief complaint, history of the present illness, history of previous illnesses, personal history, and family history. A review of the medications (including over-the-counter medications) that the patient is currently using or has used in the recent past is also important.

Patients over age 65 often have subjective complaints of minor memory impairments, such as not remembering the names of persons and misplacing objects. Those age-associated memory impairments are of no significance. Minor cognitive problems may also occur because of anxiety in the interview situation. The term "benign senescent forgetfulness" has been used to describe those phenomena.

The patient's medical history should note all major illnesses, especially seizure disorders, loss of consciousness, headaches, visual problems, and hearing loss. A history of alcohol use should be ascertained. Although substance abuse is less of a problem in the aged than in young adults, a history of prolonged substance abuse may account for current deficits.

The patient's childhood and adolescent history can provide information about personality organization and give important clues about coping strategies and defense mechanisms that the aged person may use under stress. A history of learning disability or minimal cerebral dysfunction is significant.

The psychiatrist should inquire about friends, sports, hobbies, social activity, and work. The occupational history should include the patient's feeling about work, relationships with peers, problems with authority, and attitudes toward retirement. The patient should also be questioned about plans for the future. What are the patient's hopes and fears?

The family history should include the patient's description of parents' attitudes and adaptation to their old age and, if applicable, information about the causes of their deaths. Alzheimer's disease is transmitted as an autosomal dominant trait in 10 to 30 percent of the offspring of parents with Alzheimer's disease; depression and alcohol dependence also run in families. The patient's current social situation should be evaluated: Who cares for the patient? Does the patient have children? What are the characteristics of the parent-child relationships? A financial history helps the psychiatrist evaluate the role of economic hardship in the patient's illness and make realistic treatment recommendations.

The marital history includes a description of the spouse and the characteristics of the relationship. If the patient is a widow or a widower, the psychiatrist should explore how grieving was handled. If the loss of the spouse occurred within the past year, the patient is at high risk for an adverse physical or psychological event.

The patient's sex history includes sexual activity, orientation, libido, masturbation, extramarital affairs, and sexual symptoms (such as impotence and anorgasmia). Young clinicians may have to overcome their own biases about taking a sex history in the aged; however, sex is an important area of concern for many geriatric patients, who welcome the chance to talk about their sexual feelings and attitudes.

## Mental Status Examination

The mental status examination is a cross-sectional view of how the patient thinks, feels, and behaves during the examination. In the aged patient, the psychiatrist may not be able to rely on a single examination to answer all the diagnostic questions. Repeat mental status examinations may have to be performed because of fluctuating changes in the patient's mental status. The longitudinal history from the patient or the patient's family is important.

**General description.** A general description of the patient includes appearance, psychomotor activity, attitude toward the examiner, and speech activity.

Motor disturbances—such as shuffling gait, stooped posture, pill-rolling movements of the fingers, tremors, and body asymmetry—should be noted. Involuntary movements of the mouth or the tongue may be side effects of phenothiazine medication. Many depressed patients appear to be slow in speech and movement. A masklike facies occurs in Parkinson's disease.

The patient's speech may be pressured in agitated, manic, and anxious states. Tearfulness and overt crying are seen in depressive disorders and cognitive disorders, especially if the patient feels frustrated about being unable to answer one of the examiner's questions. The presence of a hearing aid or some other indication that the patient has a hearing problem, such as requesting the repetition of questions, should be noted.

The patient's attitude toward the examiner—cooperative, suspicious, guarded, ingratiating—can give clues about possible transference reactions. Elderly patients can react to younger physicians as if the physicians were parent figures, in spite of the age difference, because of transference distortions.

**Functional assessment.** Elderly patients should be evaluated for their capacity to maintain independence and to perform the activities of daily life. Those activities include toileting, preparing meals, dressing, grooming, and eating. The degree of functional competence in their everyday behaviors is an important consideration in formulating a plan of treatment for elderly patients.

**Mood, feelings, and affect.** Suicide is a leading cause of death in the elderly, and an evaluation of the patient's suicidal ideation is essential. Feelings of loneliness, worthlessness, helplessness, and hopelessness are symptoms of depression. Loneliness is the most common reason cited by elderly persons who consider suicide. Depression carries a high risk for suicide. Nearly 75 percent of all suicide victims suffer from depression or alcohol abuse or both. The examiner should specifically ask the patient about any thoughts of suicide, whether the patient feels life is no longer worth living, whether one is better off dead or, when dead, is no longer a burden to others. Such thoughts—especially when associated with alcohol abuse, living alone, the recent death of the spouse, physical illness, and somatic pain—are indicative of a high suicidal risk.

Disturbances in mood states, most notably depression and anxiety, may interfere with memory functioning. An expansive or euphoric mood may indicate a manic episode or may be part of a dementing disorder. Frontal lobe dysfunction often produces *witzelsucht,* which is the tendency to make puns and jokes and then laugh aloud at them.

The patient's affect may be flat, blunted, constricted, shallow, or inappropriate, which can indicate a depressive disorder, schizophrenia, or brain dysfunction. Such an affect is an important abnormal finding, even though it is not pathognomonic of a specific disorder. Dominant lobe dysfunction causes dysprosody, an inability to express emotional feelings through speech intonation.

**Perceptual disturbances.** Hallucinations and illusions in the elderly may be transitory phenomena resulting from decreased sensory acuity. The examiner should note whether the patient is confused about time or place during the hallucinatory episode; confusion points to an organic condition. Distorted perceptions of the body are particularly important to ask about in the elderly. Since hallucinations may be caused by brain tumors and other focal pathology, a diagnostic workup may be indicated. Brain diseases cause perceptive impairments.

Agnosia (the inability to recognize and interpret the significance of sensory impressions) is associated with organic brain diseases. The examiner should note the type of agnosia—the denial of illness (anosognosia), the denial of a body part (autopagnosia), or the inability to recognize objects (visual agnosia) or faces (prosopagnosia).

**Language output.** This category of the geriatric mental status examination covers the aphasias, which are disorders of language output related to organic lesions of the brain. The best described are (1) nonfluent or Broca's aphasia, (2) fluent or Wernicke's aphasia, and (3) global aphasia, a combination of fluent and nonfluent aphasias.

In nonfluent or Broca's aphasia, the patient's understanding remains intact, but the ability to speak is impaired. The patient is unable to pronounce "Methodist Episcopalian." Speech is generally mispronounced and may be telegraphic in nature.

A simple test for Wernicke's aphasia is to point to some common objects—such as a pen or a pencil, a doorknob, and a light switch—and ask the patient to name them. The patient may be unable to demonstrate the use of simple objects, such as a key and a match (ideomotor apraxia).

**Visuospatial functioning.** Some decline in visuospatial capability is normal with aging. Asking a patient to copy figures or a drawing may be helpful in assessing the function. A neuropsychological assessment should be performed when visuospatial functioning is obviously impaired.

**Thought.** Disturbances in thinking include neologisms, word salad, circumstantiality, tangentiality, loosening of associations, flight of ideas, clang associations, and blocking. The loss of the ability to appreciate nuances of meaning (abstract thinking) may be an early sign of dementia. Thinking is then described as concrete or literal.

Thought content should be examined for phobias, obsessions, somatic preoccupations, and compulsions. Ideas about suicide or homicide should be discussed. The examiner should determine if delusions are present and how such delusions affect the patient's life. Delusions may be present in nursing home patients and may be a reason for admission. Patients who are hard of hearing may be mistakenly classified as paranoid or suspicious. Ideas of reference or of influence should be described.

**Sensorium and cognition.** Sensorium concerns the functioning of the special senses; cognition concerns information processing and intellect. The survey of both areas is known as the neuropsychiatric examination and consists of the assessment done by the clinician and a comprehensive battery of psychological tests.

CONSCIOUSNESS. A sensitive indicator of brain dysfunction is an altered state of consciousness in which the patient does not appear to be alert, shows fluctuations in levels of awareness, or appears to be lethargic. In severe cases the patient is somnolescent or stuporous.

ORIENTATION. Impairment in orientation to time, place, and person is associated with cognitive disorders. Cognitive impairment is often observed in mood disorders, anxiety disorders, factitious disorders, conversion disorder, and personality disorders, especially during periods of severe physical or environmental stress.

The examiner should test for orientation to place by asking the patient to describe the present location. Orientation to person may be approached in two ways: does the patient know his or her own name, and are nurses and doctors identified as such? Time is tested by asking the patient the date, the year, the month, and the day of the week. The patient should also be asked about the length of time spent in a hospital, during what season of the year, and how the patient knows those facts. Greater significance is given to difficulties concerning person than to difficulties of time and place, and more significance is given to orientation to place than to orientation to time.

MEMORY. Memory is usually evaluated in terms of immediate, recent, and remote memory. Immediate retention and recall are tested by giving the patient six digits to repeat forward and backward. The examiner should record the result of the patient's capacity to remember. Patients with unimpaired memory can usually recall six digits forward and five or six digits backward. The clinician should be aware that the ability to do well on digit-span tests is impaired in extremely anxious patients. Remote memory can be tested by asking for the patient's location and date of birth, mother's name before she was married, and names and birthdays of the patient's children.

Recent memory deteriorates first in cognitive disorders. Recent memory assessment can be approached in a number of ways. Some examiners give the patient the names of three items early in the interview and ask for recall later. Others prefer to tell a brief story and ask the patient to repeat it verbatim. Memory of the recent past can also be tested by asking for the patient's place of residence, including the street number; the method of transportation to the hospital; and some current events.

If the patient has a deficit in memory, such as amnesia, careful testing should be done to see if it is retrograde amnesia (loss of memory before an event) or anterograde amnesia (loss of memory after the event). Retention and recall can also be tested by having the patient retell a simple story. Patients who confabulate make up new material in the retelling of the story.

INTELLECTUAL TASKS, INFORMATION, AND INTELLIGENCE. A number of intellectual tasks may be presented to estimate the patient's general fund of knowledge and intellectual functioning.

Counting and calculation can be tested by asking the patient to subtract 7 from 100 and to continue subtracting 7 from he result until the number 2 is reached. The examiner records the responses as a baseline for future testing. The examiner can also ask the patient to count backward from 20 to 1, recording the time necessary to complete the exercise. The patient can also be asked to do simple arithmetic—for example, to state the number of nickels in $1.35.

The patient's general fund of knowledge is related to intelligence. The patient can be asked to name the President of the United States, to name the three largest cities in the United States, to give the population of the United States, and to give the distance from New York to Paris. The examiner must take into account the patient's educational level, socioeconomic status, and general life experience in assessing the results of some of those tests.

READING AND WRITING. It may be important for the clinician to examine the patient's reading and writing and to determine whether the patient has a specific speech deficit. The examiner may have the patient read a simple story aloud or write a short sentence to test for a reading or writing disorder. Whether the patient is right-handed or left-handed should be noted.

**Judgment.** Judgment is the capacity to act appropriately in various situations: Does the patient show impaired judgment? What would the patient do if a stamped, sealed, addressed envelope was found in the street? What would the patient do if smoke was smelled in a theater? Can the patient discriminate? What is the difference between a dwarf and a boy? Why are persons required to get a marriage license?

### Neuropsychological Assessment

A thorough neuropsychological examination includes a comprehensive battery of tests that can be replicated by various examiners and can be repeated over time to assess the course of a specific illness. The mose widely used test of current cognitive functioning is the Mini-Mental State Examination (MMSE), which assesses orientation, attention, calculation, immediate and short-term recall, language, and the ability to follow simple commands (Table 10.1–2). The MMSE is used to detect impairments, follow the course of an illness, and monitor the patient's treatment responses. It is not used to make a formal diagnosis.

The maximum MMSE score is 30. Age and educational level influence cognitive performance as measured by the MMSE. It is useful to compare an individual patient's score with a population reference group (Figures 50–1 and 50–2).

The assessment of intellectual abilities is performed with the Wechsler Adult Intelligence Scale—Revised (WAIS-R), which gives verbal, performance, and full scale intelligence quotient (I.Q.) scores. Some tests, such as vocabulary tests, hold up as aging progresses; others, such as tests of similarities and digit-symbol substitution, do not. The performance part of the WAIS-R is a more sensitive indicator of brain damage than is the verbal part.

Visuospatial functions are sensitive to the normal aging process. The Bender gestalt test is one of a large number of instruments used to test visuospatial functions; another is the Halstead-Reitan battery, the most complex battery

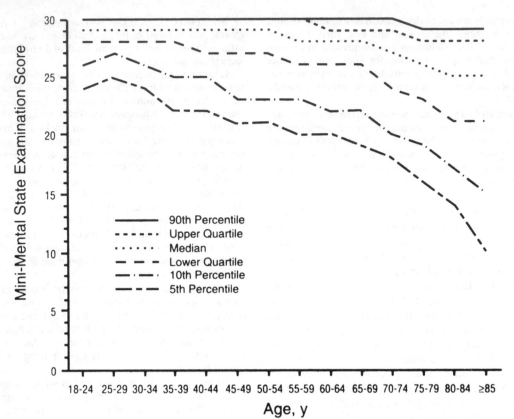

**Figure 50–1.** Mini-Mental State Examination score by age and selected percentiles. Data from the Epidemiologic Catchment Area surveys, 1980 to 1984, with weights based on the 1980 U.S. population distributions for age, sex, and race. (Figure from R M Crum, J C Anthony, S S Bassett, M F Folstein: Population-based norms for the Mini-Mental State Examination by age and educational level. JAMA *269*: 2388, 1993. Used with permission.)

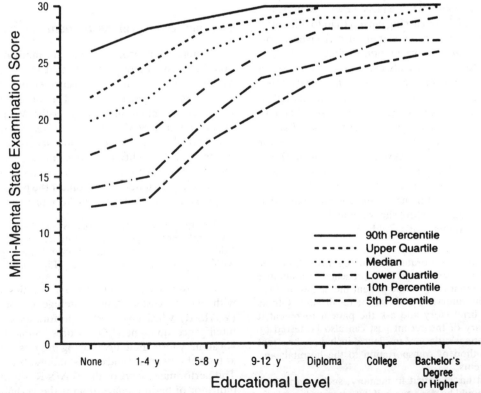

**Figure 50–2.** Mini-Mental State Examination score by educational level and selected percentiles. Data from the Epidemiologic Catchment Area surveys, 1980 to 1984, with weights based on the 1980 U.S. population distributions for age, sex, and race. (Figure from R M Crum, J C Anthony, S S Bassett, M F Folstein: Population-based norms for the Mini-Mental State Examination by age and educational level. JAMA *269*: 2388, 1993. Used with permission.)

of tests covering the entire spectrum of information processing and cognition.

Depression, even in the absence of dementia, often impairs psychomotor performance, especially visuospatial functioning and timed motor performance. The Geriatric Depression Scale is a useful screening instrument that excludes somatic complaints from its list of items. The presence of somatic complaints on a rating scale tends to confound the diagnosis of a depressive disorder.

## Current Medications Used

Elderly patients are susceptible to the adverse behavioral and cognitive effects of drugs. The most commonly used class of psychoactive drugs among the elderly, the benzodiazepines, can cause sedation, behavioral disinhibition, depression, and memory impairment as side effects. Benzodiazepine discontinuation can cause insomnia and anxiety. Many antidepressant drugs cause nervousness and insomnia. Medications used to treat cardiovascular, pulmonary, and endocrine disorders are known to cause psychiatric side effects. The clinician must obtain a complete list of all current medications used by the patient.

## MENTAL DISORDERS OF OLD AGE

The National Institute of Mental Health's Epidemiologic Catchment Area (ECA) program has found that the most common mental disorders of old age are depressive disorders, cognitive disorders, phobias, and alcohol use disorders. The elderly also have a high risk for suicide and drug-induced psychiatric symptoms. Many mental disorders of old age can be prevented, ameliorated, or even reversed. Of special importance are the reversible causes of delirium and dementia. If not diagnosed accurately and treated in a timely fashion, those conditions can progress to an irreversible state requiring institutionalization of the patient.

A number of psychosocial risk factors also predispose the elderly to mental disorders. Those risk factors include loss of social roles, loss of autonomy, the deaths of friends and relatives, declining health, increased isolation, financial constraints, and decreased cognitive functioning.

Many drugs can cause psychiatric symptoms in the elderly. Those symptoms occur as a result of age-related alterations in drug absorption, prescribing the drug in too large a dosage, the patient's not following the instructions for the drug's use and taking too much, the patient's sensitivity to the medication, and conflicting regimens presented by several physicians. Almost the entire spectrum of mental disorders can be caused by drugs.

## Dementing Disorders

Dementia, a generally progressive and irreversible impairment of the intellect, increases in prevalence with age. Of Americans over the age of 65, about 5 percent have severe dementia, and 15 percent have mild dementia. Of Americans over the age of 80, about 20 percent have severe dementia. Only arthritis is a more common cause of disability among the elderly than dementia. Known risk factors for dementia are age, family history, and female sex.

In contrast to mental retardation, the intellectual impairment in dementia develops over time—that is, previously achieved mental functions are gradually lost. The characteristic changes of dementia involve cognition, memory, language, and visuospatial functions, but behavioral disturbances are common. The behavioral disturbances include agitation, restlessness, wandering, rage, violence, shouting, social and sexual disinhibition, impulsiveness, sleep disturbances, and delusions. Delusions and hallucinations occur during the course of the dementias in nearly 75 percent of all patients.

Many conditions impair cognition. The conditions include brain injuries, cerebral tumors, acquired immune deficiency syndrome (AIDS), alcohol, medications, infections, chronic pulmonary diseases, and inflammatory diseases. Although dementias associated with advanced age are typically caused by primary degenerative central nervous system (CNS) disease and vascular disease, many factors contribute to cognitive impairment; in the elderly, mixed causes of dementia are common.

About 10 to 15 percent of all patients who exhibit symptoms of dementia have potentially treatable conditions. The treatable conditions include systemic disorders, such as heart disease, renal disease, and congestive heart failure; endocrine disorders, such as hypothyroidism; vitamin deficiency; medications; and primary mental disorders—most notably, depressive disorders.

Dementias have been classified as cortical and subcortical, depending on the site of the cerebral lesion. A subcortical dementia is seen in Huntington's disease, Parkinson's disease, normal pressure hydrocephalus, multi-infarct dementia, and Wilson's disease. The subcortical dementias are associated with movement disorders, gait apraxia, psychomotor retardation, apathy, and akinetic mutism that can be confused with catatonia. The cortical dementias are seen in dementias of the Alzheimer's type, Creutzfeldt-Jakob disease, and Pick's disease, which frequently manifest aphasia, agnosia, and apraxia. In clinical practice the two types of dementia overlap, and in most cases an accurate diagnosis can be made only by autopsy.

Further information on dementia is contained in Section 10.3.

**Dementia of the Alzheimer's type.** Of all patients with dementia, 50 to 60 percent have dementia of the Alzheimer's type, the most common type of dementia. About 5 percent of all persons who reach age 65 have dementia of the Alzheimer's type, compared with 15 to 25 percent of all persons age 85 or older. The prevalence of dementia of the Alzheimer's type is higher in women than in men. Patients with dementia of the Alzheimer's type occupy more than 50 percent of all the nursing home beds.

Dementia of the Alzheimer's type is characterized by the gradual onset and progressive decline of cognitive functions. Memory is impaired, and at least one of the following is seen: aphasia, apraxia, agnosia, and disturbances in executive functioning. The general sequence of deficits is memory, language, and visuospatial functions. Initially, the patient may have an inability to learn and recall new information, then impaired naming, then an inability to copy figures. Early dementia of the Alzheimer's type may be difficult to diagnose, since the patient's I.Q. may be normal.

Personality changes—such as depression, obsessiveness, and suspiciousness—occur. Outbursts of anger are common, and violent acts are a risk. Disorientation leads to wandering, and the patient may be found far from home in a dazed condition. Loss of initiative is common. Neurological defects—such as gait disturbances, aphasia, apraxia, and agnosia—eventually appear.

The dementia has an insidious onset and is progressive. The mean survival for patients with dementia of the Alzheimer's type is about 8 years, with a range of 1 to 20 years. The diagnosis is made on the basis of the patient's history and a mental status examination. Brain-imaging techniques may also be useful.

ETIOLOGY. The cause of Alzheimer's disease is unknown, although postmortem neuropathological and biochemical studies have found a selective loss of cholinergic neurons. Structural and functional changes occur. Gross anatomical findings include reduced gyral volume in the frontal and temporal lobes, with relative sparing of the primary motor and sensory cortex. Typical microscopic alterations include senile plaques and neurofibrillary tangles (Figures 50–3 and 10.3-1). Those tangles are derived from tau proteins. Blocking the aberrant phosphorylation of tau proteins is being explored as a possible therapeutic intervention in dementia of the Alzheimer's type.

TREATMENT. Dementia of the Alzheimer's type has no known prevention or cure. Treatment is palliative, consisting of proper nutrition, exercise, and supervision of daily activity. Medication may be helpful in managing agitation and behavioral disturbances. Propranolol (Inderal), pindolol (Visken), buspirone (BuSpar), and valprotate (Depakene) have all been reported to help reduce agitation and aggression. Haloperidol (Haldol) and other high-potency dopamine blocking agents may be used to control acute behavior disturbances. A subgroup of patients with dementia of the Alzheimer's type show improvement in cognitive and functional measures when treated with tacrine hydrochloride (Cognex), a potent centrally active, reversible acetylcholinesterase inhibitor.

**Vascular dementia.** Vascular dementia is the second most common type of dementia. It is characterized by the same cognitive deficits as dementia of the Alzheimer's type, but it has focal neurological signs and symptoms, such as an exaggeration of deep tendon reflexes, extensor plantar response, pseudobulbar palsy, gait abnormalities, and weakness of an extremity. Compared with dementia of the Alzheimer's type, vascular dementia has an abrupt onset and a stepwise deteriorating cause. Vascular dementia may be prevented through the reduction of known risk factors, such as hypertension, diabetes, cigarette smoking, and arrhythmias. Diagnosis can be confirmed with magnetic reasonance imaging (MRI) and cerebral blood flow studies.

**Dementia due to Pick's disease.** Pick's disease causes a slowly progressing dementia. It is associated with focal cortical lesions, primarily of the frontal lobe, producing aphasia, apraxia, and agnosia. The disease lasts from 2 to 10 years, with an average duration of 5 years. Clinically, Pick's disease is difficult to distinguish from Alzheimer's disease. On autopsy, however, the brain reveals intraneuronal inclusions called Pick bodies, which are different from the neurofibrillary tangles of Alzheimer's dementia. Pick's disease is much rarer than Alzheimer's dementia, and no treatment is available.

**Dementia due to Creutzfeldt-Jakob disease.** Creutzfeldt-Jakob disease is a diffuse degenerative disease that affects the pyramidal and extrapyramidal systems. Creutzfeldt-Jakob disease usually affects people in their 50s, and the usual course is about one year. Creutzfeldt-Jakob disease is not associated with aging. Its incidence actually decreases after age 60. The terminal stage is characterized by severe dementia, generalized hypertonicity, and profound speech disturbances. It is caused by a slow-growing infectious virus. Some cases have been traced to the transplantation of the cornea of an infected person to a previously noninfected person.

**Dementia due to Huntington's disease.** Huntington's disease is a hereditary disease associated with progressive degeneration of the basal ganglia and the cerebral cortex. Huntington's disease is transmitted as an autosomal dominant gene (traced to the G8 fragment of chromosome 4); each offspring of an affected parent has a 50 percent chance of getting the disease. Everyone with the gene eventually has the disease.

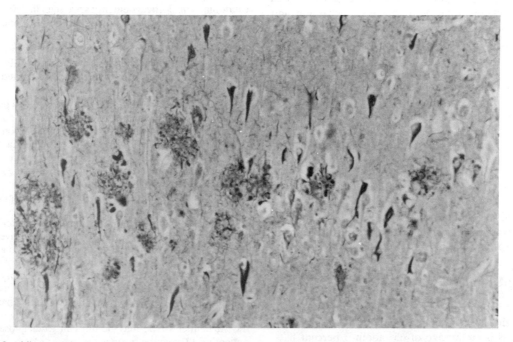

**Figure 50–3.** Microscopic appearance of the hippocampus from a patient with Alzheimer's disease, showing large numbers of neurofibrillary tangles and senile plaques (modified Biel-schowsky's stain, original magnification x 190. (Figure courtesy of Daniel Perl, M.D.)

A genetic screening test for the disorder is now available. Currently 25,000 Americans have Huntington's disease, and about 125,000 children are at risk. The onset of Huntington's disease occurs between 35 and 50 years of age, but the disease may begin later than that in rare cases. It is characterized by progressive dementia, muscular hypertonicity, and bizarre choreiform movements; death usually occurs 15 to 20 years after the onset of the disease. No treatment is available.

**Dementia due to normal pressure hydrocephalus.** In the elderly, normal pressure hydrocephalus causes gait disturbances (unstable or shuffling gait), urinary incontinence, and dementia. Enlargement of the ventricles with increased cerebrospinal fluid (CSF) pressure is found.

**Dementia due to Parkinson's disease.** Parkinson's disease is characterized primarily by motor dysfunction, but cognitive disturbances, including dementia, may be part of the disorder. Frontal lobe symptoms and memory deficits are common. Nearly half of all affected patients are depressed, making depression the most common mental disturbance in Parkinson's disease. Patients are also at increased risk for anxiety.

Medications used to treat Parkinson's disease—particularly drugs that facilitate dopaminergic neurotransmission, such as L-dopa, amantadine (Symmetrel), and bromocriptine (Parlodel)—may cause psychosis and delirium.

## Depressive Disorders

Depressive symptoms are present in about 15 percent of all elderly community residents and nursing home patients. Age itself is not a risk factor for the development of depression, but being widowed and having a chronic medical illness are associated with vulnerability to depressive disorders. Late-onset depression is characterized by high rates of recurrence.

The common signs and symptoms of depressive disorders include reduced energy and concentration, sleep problems (especially early morning awakening and multiple awakenings), decreased appetite, weight loss, and somatic complaints. The presenting symptoms may be different in elderly depressed patients from those seen in younger adults because of an increased emphasis on somatic complaints in the elderly. The elderly are particularly vulnerable to major depressive episodes with melancholic features, characterized by depression, hypochondriasis, low self-esteem, feelings of worthlessness, and self-accusatory trends (especially about sex and sinfulness), with paranoid and suicidal ideation.

Cognitive impairment in depressed geriatric patients is referred to as the dementia syndrome of depression (pseudodementia), which can easily be confused with true dementia. In true dementia, intellectual performance is usually global in nature, and impairment is consistently poor; in pseudodementia, deficits in attention and concentration are variable. Distinguishing between the two disorders is difficult. Compared with patients who have true dementia, patients with pseudodementia are less likely to have language impairment and to confabulate; when uncertain, they are more likely to say "I don't know"; memory difficulties are more limited to free recall, as compared with recognition on cued recall tests. Pseudodementia occurs in about 15 percent of depressed elderly patients, and 25 to 50 percent of patients with dementia are depressed. Table 10.3–10 compares dementia and pseudodementia.

Depression may be associated with physical illness and with the medications used for treating illness. The clinician needs to be aware of the many pharmacological agents that are common causes of depression (Table 15.1–22).

## Bipolar I Disorder

Bipolar I disorder usually begins in middle adulthood, although the lifetime prevalence of 1 percent remains steady throughout life. A vulnerability to recurrences remains, so the patient with a history of bipolar I disorder may present with a manic episode in late life. In most instances a first episode of manic behavior after age 65 should alert the clinician to search for an associated physiological or organic cause, such as the side effects of medication or an early dementia.

The signs and symptoms of mania in the elderly are similar to those in younger adults and include an elevated, expansive, or irritable mood; a decreased need for sleep; distractibility; impulsivity; and, often, excessive alcohol intake. Hostile or paranoid behavior is usually present. The presence of cognitive impairment, disorientation, or fluctuating levels of awareness should make the clinician suspicious of an organic cause.

Lithium (Eskalith) remains the treatment of choice for mania; however, its use by elderly patients must be carefully monitored, because their reduced renal clearance makes lithium toxicity a significant risk. Neurotoxic effects are also more common in the elderly than in younger adults.

## Schizophrenia

Schizophrenia usually begins in late adolescence or young adulthood and persists throughout life. Although first episodes diagnosed after age 65 are rare, a late-onset type beginning after age 45 has been described. Women are more likely to have a late onset of schizophrenia than are men. Another difference between early-onset and late-onset schizophrenia is the greater prevalence of paranoid schizophrenia in the late-onset type.

About 20 percent of schizophrenic persons show no active symptoms by age 65; 80 percent show varying degrees of impairment. Psychopathology becomes less marked as the patient ages.

The residual type of schizophrenia occurs in about 30 percent of all schizophrenic persons. Its signs and symptoms include emotional blunting, social withdrawal, eccentric behavior, and illogical thinking. Delusions and hallucinations are not common. Since most residual schizophrenic persons are unable to care for themselves, long-term hospitalization is required.

Aged persons with schizophrenic symptoms respond well to antipsychotic drugs. Medication must be judiciously administered. Lower than usual dosages are often effective in the elderly.

## Delusional Disorder

The age of onset of delusional disorder is usually between 40 and 55; however, it can occur at any time in the geriatric period. Delusions can take many forms, the most common being persecutory in nature—patients believe that they are being spied on, followed, poisoned, or harassed in some way. Delusional disorder persons may become violent against their supposed persecutors. In some cases they lock themselves in their rooms and live reclusive lives. Somatic delusions, in which the persons believe they have a fatal illness, may also occur in the elderly. In one study of persons over 65, pervasive persecutory ideation was present in 4 percent of those sampled.

Delusional disorder occurs under physical or psychological stress in vulnerable persons and may be precipitated by the death of the spouse, loss of a job, retirement, social isolation, adverse financial circumstances, debilitating medical illness or surgery, visual impairment, and deafness. Delusions may also accompany other disorders—such as dementia of the Alzheimer's type, alcohol use disorders, schizophrenia, depressive disorders, and bipolar I disorder—which need to be ruled out. Delusional syndromes may also result from prescribed medications or from early signs of a brain tumor.

The prognosis is fair to good in most cases, with best results achieved through a combination of psychotherapy and pharmacotherapy.

A late-onset delusional disorder called paraphrenia is characterized by persecutory delusions. It develops over several years and is not associated with dementia. Some workers believe the disorder to be a variant of schizophrenia that first becomes manifest after age 60. Patients with a family history of schizophrenia show an increase in paraphrenia.

## Anxiety Disorders

The anxiety disorders include panic disorder, phobias, obsessive-compulsive disorder, generalized anxiety disorder, acute stress disorder, and posttraumatic stress disorder. The ECA study has found that the one-month prevalence of anxiety disorders in persons aged 65 years and older is 5.5 percent. By far, the most common disorders are phobias (4 to 8 percent). The rate for panic disorder is 1 percent. Anxiety disorders begin in early or middle adulthood, but some appear for the first time after age 60. An initial onset of panic disorder in the elderly is rare but can occur.

The signs and symptoms of phobias in the elderly are less severe than those that occur in younger persons, but the effects as equally, if not more, debilitating in aged patients.

Existential theories help explain anxiety when there is no specifically identifiable stimulus for a chronically anxious feeling. The aged person has to come to grips with death. The person may deal with the thought of death with a sense of despair and anxiety, rather than with equanimity and Erik Erikson's sense of integrity.

The fragility of the autonomic nervous system in the aged may account for the development of anxiety after a major stressor. Posttraumatic stress disorder is often more severe in the elderly than in younger persons because of concurrent physical disability in the aged.

Obsessions and compulsions may appear for the first time in the aged person, although one usually finds signs of obsessive-compulsive disorder in the personalities of patients who,

when younger, were orderly, perfectionistic, punctual, and parsimonious. When symptomatic, the patients become excessive in their desire for orderliness, rituals, and sameness. They may also have compulsions to check things over and over, becoming generally inflexible and rigid. Obsessive-compulsive disorder, in contrast to obsessive-compulsive personality disorder, is characterized by ego-dystonic rituals and obsessions and may begin late in life.

Treatment of anxiety disorders must be individually tailored to the patient, taking into account the biopsychosocial interplay producing the disorder. Both pharmacotherapy and psychotherapy are required.

## Somatoform Disorders

Somatoform disorders, characterized by physical symptoms resembling medical diseases, are relevant to geriatric psychiatry because somatic complaints are common among the aged. More than 80 percent of the aged have at least one chronic disease—usually arthritis or cardiovascular problems. After the age of 75 years, 20 percent have diabetes and an average of four diagnosable chronic illnesses that require medical attention.

Hypocondriasis is common in patients over 60, although the peak incidence is in the 40-to-50-year-old age group. The disorder is usually chronic, and the prognosis is guarded. Repeated physical examinations are useful in reassuring patients that they do not have a fatal illness; however, invasive and high-risk diagnostic procedures should be avoided unless medically indicated.

Telling patients that their symptoms are imaginary usually meets with resentment and is counterproductive. The clinician should acknowledge that the complaint is real, that the pain is really there and perceived as such by the patient, and that a psychological or pharmacological approach to the problem is indicated.

## Alcohol and Other Substance Use Disorders

Aged patients with alcohol dependence usually give a history of excessive drinking that began in young or middle adulthood. They are usually medically ill, primarily with liver disease, and are either divorced, widowers, or men who never married. Many have arrest records and are numbered among the homeless poor. A large number have chronic dementing illnesses, such as Wernicke's encephalopathy and Korsakoff's syndrome. Twenty percent of nursing home patients have alcohol dependence.

Overall, alcohol and other substance use disorders account for 10 percent of all emotional problems in the aged, and dependence on such substances as hypnotics, anxiolytics, and narcotics is more common in old age than is generally recognized. Substance-seeking behavior—characterized by crime, manipulativeness, and antisocial behavior—is relatively rare in the elderly, compared with younger adults. Elderly patients may abuse anxiolytics to allay chronic anxiety or to ensure sleep. The maintenance of the chronically ill cancer patient with narcotics prescribed by a physician produces dependence; however, the need to provide pain relief takes precedence over the possibility of narcotic dependence and is entirely justified.

The clinical presentation of elderly patients with alcohol

and other substance use disorders and is varied. It includes falls, confusion, poor personal hygiene, depression, malnutrition, and the effects of exposure. The sudden onset of delirium in elderly persons hospitalized for medical illness is most often caused by alcohol withdrawal. Alcohol abuse should be considered in elderly patients with chronic gastrointestinal problems.

Over-the-counter substances, including nicotine and caffeine, may also be misused by the elderly. Over-the-counter analgesics are the most common offenders (used by 35 percent), followed by laxatives (used by 30 percent). Unexplained gastrointestinal, psychological, and metabolic problems should alert the clinician to over-the-counter substance abuse.

## Sleep Disorders

Advanced age is the single most important factor associated with the increased prevalence of sleep disorders. Sleep-related phenomena that are more frequently reported by the elderly than by younger adults are trouble sleeping, daytime sleepiness, daytime napping, and the use of hypnotic drugs. Clinically, the elderly experience higher rates of breathing-related sleep disorder and medication-induced movement disorders than do younger adults.

In addition to altered regulatory and physiological systems, the causes of sleep disturbances in the elderly include primary sleep disorders, other mental disorders, general medical disorders, and social and environmental factors. Among the primary sleep disorders, dyssomnias are the most frequent, especially primary insomnia, nocturnal myoclonus, restless legs syndrome, and sleep apnea. Of the parasomnias, REM sleep behavior disorder occurs almost exclusively among elderly men. The conditions that commonly interfere with sleep in the elderly include pain, nocturia, dyspnea, and heartburn. The lack of a daily structure and of social or vocational responsibilities contributes to poor sleep.

As a result of the decreased length of the daily sleep-wake cycle in the elderly, those without daily routines, especially patients in nursing homes, may experience an advanced sleep phase, in which they go to sleep early and awaken during the night.

Even modest amounts of alcohol can interfere with the quality of sleep, causing sleep fragmentation and early morning awakening. Alcohol may also precipitate or aggravate obstructive sleep apnea. Many elderly patients use alcohol, hypnotics, and other central nervous system depressants to help them fall asleep. However, data show that most elderly patients experience more early morning awakening than trouble in falling asleep. When prescribing sedative-hypnotic drugs for the elderly, clinicians must monitor the patients for unwanted cognitive, behavioral, and psychomotor effects, including memory impairment (anterograde amnesia), residual sedation, rebound insomnia, daytime withdrawal, and unsteady gait.

Dementia may be associated with sundowning, an increase in confusion and agitation after nightfall. Dementia is associated with an increased frequency of arousals, increased stage 1 sleep, and decreased stages 3 and 4 sleep.

Many demented patients, however, have no sleep disturbance.

Changes in sleep structure among the elderly involve both rapid eye movement (REM) sleep and nonrapid eye movement (NREM) sleep. The REM changes include the redistribution of REM sleep throughout the night, an increased number of REM episodes, the decreased length of REM episodes, and reduced total REM sleep. The NREM changes include the decreased amplitude of delta waves, a decreased percentage of stages 3 and 4 sleep, and an increased percentage of stages 1 and 2 sleep. In addition, the elderly experience increased awakening after sleep onset.

Much of the observed deterioration in the quality of sleep in the elderly is due to the altered timing and consolidation of sleep. For example, with advanced age, people have a lower amplitude of circadian rhythms, a circasemidian (12-hour) sleep-propensity rhythm, and a decreased length of circadian cycles.

# OTHER DISORDERS OF OLD AGE

## Vertigo

Feelings of vertigo or dizziness, a common complaint in the elderly, cause many elderly persons to become inactive because they fear falling. The causes of vertigo are varied and include anemia, hypotension, cardiac arrhythmia, cerebrovascular disease, basilar artery insufficiency, middle ear disease, acoustic neuroma, and Ménière's disease. Most cases of vertigo have a strong psychological component, and the clinician should ascertain any secondary gain from the symptom. The overuse of anxiolytics can cause dizziness and daytime somnolence. Treatment with meclizine (Antivert), 25 to 100 mg daily, has been successful in many cases of vertigo.

## Syncope

The sudden loss of consciousness associated with syncope results from a reduction of cerebral blood flow and brain hypoxia. A thorough medical workup is required to rule out the various causes listed in Table 50–1.

**Table 50–1**
**Common Causes of Syncope**

Epilepsy
Cerebral ischemia
Coronary artery insufficiency; valvular disease
Anemia
Carotid sinus syndrome
Cardiac arrhythmia
Stokes-Adams conduction defect
Hyperventilation
Hypoglycemia
Anxiety attack
Cerebrovascular disease; vertebral-basilar insufficiency

## ELDER ABUSE

An estimated 10 percent of those more than 65 years old are abused. Elder abuse is defined by the American Medical Association as "an act or omission which results in harm or threatened harm to the health or welfare of an elderly person." Mistreatment includes abuse and neglect—physically, psychologically, financially, and materially. Sexual abuse does occur. Acts of omission include the withholding of food, medicine, clothing, and other necessities. Table 50–2 lists the types of elder abuse.

Family conflicts and other problems often underlie elder abuse. The victims tend to be very old and frail. They often live with their assailants, who are often financially dependent on the victims. Both the victim and the perpetrator tend to deny or minimize the presence of abuse. Interventions include providing legal services, housing, and medical, psychiatric, and social services.

## PSYCHOPHARMACOLOGICAL TREATMENT OF GERIATRIC DISORDERS

In the elderly, certain guidelines should be followed regarding the use of all drugs. A pretreatment medical evaluation is essential, including an electrocardiogram (ECG). It is especially useful to have the elderly patient or the family bring in all currently used medications, be-

cause multiple drug use may be contributing to the symptoms.

Most psychotropic drugs should be given in equally divided doses three or four times over a 24-hour period. Elderly patients may not be able to tolerate a sudden rise in drug blood level resulting from one large daily dose. Any changes in blood pressure and pulse rate and other side effects should be watched. For patients with insomnia, however, giving the major portion of an antipsychotic or antidepressant at bedtime takes advantage of its sedating and soporific effects. Liquid preparations are useful for elderly patients who cannot or who refuse to swallow tablets. Clinicians should frequently reassess all patients to determine the need for maintenance medication, changes in dosage, and the development of side effects.

If the patient is taking psychotropic drugs at the time of the evaluation, the clinician should, if possible, discontinue those medications and, after a washout period, reevaluate the patient during a drug-free baseline state.

The elderly use the greatest number of medications of any age group, with 25 percent of all prescriptions written for those over age 65. Adverse drug reactions caused by medications result in the hospitalization of nearly 250,000 persons in the United States each year. Psychotropic drugs are among the most commonly prescribed, along with cardiovascular and diuretic medications; 40 percent of all hypnotics dispensed in the United States each year are to those over age 65, and 70 percent of elderly patients use over-

---

**Table 50–2**
**Types of Elder Abuse**

**Physical or Sexual Abuse**
    Bruises (bilateral and at various stages of healing)
    Welts
    Lacerations
    Punctures
    Fractures
    Evidence of excessive drugging
    Burns
    Physical constraints (tying to beds, etc.)
    Malnutrition and dehydration
    Lack of personal care
    Inadequate heating
    Lack of food and water
    Unclean clothes or bedding
    Lack of needed medication
    Lack of eyeglasses, hearing aids, false teeth
    Difficulty in walking or sitting
    Venereal disease
    Pain or itching, bruises, or bleeding of external genitalia, vaginal area, or anal area

**Psychological Abuse** (vulnerable adults react by exhibiting resignation, fear, depression, mental confusion, anger, ambivalence, insomnia)
    Threats
    Insults
    Harassment
    Withholding of security and affection
    Harsh orders
    Refusal on the part of the family or those caring for the adult

to allow travel, visits by friends or other family members, attendance at church

**Exploitation**
    Misuse of vulnerable adult's income or other financial resources (victim is best source of information but in most cases has turned management of financial affairs over to another person; as a result, there may be some confusion about finances)

**Medical Abuse**
    Withholding or improper administration of medications or necessary medical treatments for a condition or the withholding of aids the person would medically require, such as false teeth, glasses, hearing aids
    May be a cause of
        Confusion
        Disorientation
        Memory impairment
        Agitation
        Lethargy
        Self-neglect

**Neglect**
    Conduct of vulnerable adult or others that results in deprivation of care necessary to maintain physical and mental health
    May be manifested by
        Malnutrition
        Poor personal hygiene
        Any of the indicators for medical abuse

---

Table from Washington State Medical Association: *Elder Abuse: Guidelines for Intervention by Physicians and Other Service Providers.* Washington State Medical Association, Seattle, 1985.

the-counter medications, compared with only 10 percent of young adults.

Chapter 33 presents a comprehensive survey of the psychopharmacological agents, including a detailed discussion of their dosages.

## Principles

The major goals of the pharmacological treatment of the elderly are to improve the quality of life, maintain them in the community, and delay or avoid their placement in nursing homes. Individualization of dosage is the basic tenet of geriatric psychopharmacology.

Alterations of drug dosages are required because of the physiological changes that occur as the person ages. Renal disease is associated with decreased renal clearance of drugs; liver disease results in a decreased ability to metabolize drugs; cardiovascular disease and reduced cardiac output can affect both renal and hepatic drug clearance; and gastrointestinal disease and decreased gastric acid secretion influence drug absorption. As a person ages, the ratio of lean-to-fat body mass also changes. With normal aging, lean body mass decreases, and body fat increases. Changes in the lean-to-fat body mass ratio that accompany aging affect the distribution of drugs. Many lipid-soluble psychotropic drugs are more widely distributed in fat tissue than in lean tissue, thus prolonging the drug action more than expected. Similarly, changes in end-organ or receptor-site sensitivity need to be taken into account. The increased risk of orthostatic hypotension in the elderly from psychotropic drugs is related to reduced functioning of blood-pressure regulating mechanisms.

As a general rule, the lowest possible dosage should be used to achieve the desired therapeutic response. The clinician must know the pharmacodynamics, pharmacokinetics, and biotransformation of each drug prescribed and the effects of the interaction of the drug with other drugs that the patient is taking.

## Antidepressants

All antidepressant drugs are equally effective in treating depression, making the dominant consideration in selecting a drug that of side effects. Elderly patients are often more susceptible to some antidepressant side effects than are younger adults. Table 50–3 lists the geriatric dosages of commonly used antidepressants. The consequences of adverse drug reactions in the elderly are also potentially more severe than in younger adults. Among the factors that contribute to side-effect prevalence and severity in the elderly are altered drug metabolism, compromised physiological functions, altered body composition, and drug interactions.

Tricyclic drugs are among the oldest psychopharmacological agents. When used by elderly patients, the secondary amine agents desipramine (Norpramin) and nortriptyline (Aventyl, Pamelor) are preferred because of their low propensity to cause anticholinergic, orthostatic, and sedative side effects. Nortriptyline is less likely than are other tricyclic agents to cause orthostatic hypotension in patients with congestive heart failure. Because of the

quinidinelike effect of all tricyclics, a pretreatment electroencephalogram (EEG) is essential to determine if the patient has a preexisting cardiac conduction defect.

Monoamine oxidase inhibitors (MAOIs) are also useful in treating depression because monoamine oxidase (MAO) decreases in the aging brain and may account for diminished catecholamines and a resultant depression. MAOIs may be used with caution in elderly patients. Orthostatic hypotension is common and severe with MAOIs. Patients need to adhere to a tyramine-free diet to avoid hypertensive crises. The potential for serious drug interactions involving certain analgesics, such as meperidine (Demerol) and sympathomimetics, also requires that patients understand what food and drugs they may use. Tranylcypromine (Parnate) and phenelzine (Nardil) are representative drugs that should be used cautiously in patients prone to hypertension. Table 50–4 lists the geriatric dosages of the MAOIs. Any kind of cognitive impairment precludes MAOI therapy.

Major side-effect considerations with some other antidepressants are as follows: for trazodone (Desyrel), sedation and orthostatic hypotension; for amoxapine (Asendin), extrapyramidal effects; and for maprotiline (Ludiomil), seizures. With the exception of the risk of seizures at high

**Table 50–3**
**Geriatric Dosages of Commonly Used Antidepressants**

| Generic Name | Trade Name | Geriatric Dosage Range (mg a day) |
|---|---|---|
| Imipramine | Tofranil | 25–300 |
| Desipramine | Norpramin, Pertofrane | 10–300 |
| Trimipramine | Surmontil | 25–300 |
| Amitriptyline | Elavil | 25–300 |
| Nortriptyline | Aventyl, Pamelor | 10–150 |
| Protriptyline | Vivactil | 10–40 |
| Doxepin | Adapin, Sinequan | 10–300 |
| Maprotiline | Ludiomil | 25–150 |
| Trazodone | Desyrel | 100–500 |
| Amoxapine | Asendin | 25–200 |
| Bupropion | Wellbutrin | 75–450 |
| Fluoxetine | Prozac | 10–60 |
| Sertraline | Zoloft | 50–200 |
| Paroxetine | Paxil | 10–50 |

**Table 50–4**
**Geriatric Dosages of Monoamine Oxidase Inhibitors (MAOIs)\***

| Generic Name | Trade Name | Geriatric Dosage Range (mg a day) |
|---|---|---|
| Isocarboxid | Marplan | 10–30 |
| Phenelzine | Nardil | 15–45 |
| Tranylcypromine[†] | Parnate | 10–20 |

\*Persons taking MAOIs should be on a tyramine-free diet.
[†]Not recommended in persons over 60 because of pressor effects.

dosages, bupropion (Wellbutrin) is generally well-tolerated; it is nonsedating and does not produce orthostasis; it should be given in three divided doses.

In general, the serotonin-specific reuptake inhibitors (SSRIs)—such as fluoxetine (Prozac), sertraline (Zoloft), and paroxetine (Paxil)—are safe and well-tolerated by elderly patients. As a group, those drugs may cause nausea and other gastrointestinal symptoms, nervousness, agitation, headache, and insomnia, most often to mild degrees. Fluoxetine is the drug most likely to cause nervousness, insomnia, and loss of appetite, particularly early in treatment. Sertraline is the drug most likely to produce nausea and diarrhea. Paroxetine causes some anticholinergic effects. The SSRIs do not cause the characteristic side effects of the tricyclic agents. The absence of orthostatic hypotension is a clinically significant factor in the use of SSRIs by the elderly.

## Psychostimulants

The psychostimulants, which are also called analeptics, include amphetamines (for example, dextroamphetamine [Dexedrine]), methylphenidate (Ritalin), and pemoline (Cylert). In selected cases they can improve the mood, apathy, and anhedonia of the depressed elderly patient, especially when those symptoms are caused by some associated chronic medical illness, such as rheumatoid arthritis or multiple sclerosis. Amphetamines may also augment analgesia in patients who require pain medication. The use of psychostimulants is controversial because of the risk of abuse; however, when prescribed judiciously in small dosages, they are of value. Table 50–5 lists the geriatric dosages of the psychostimulants.

## Lithium and Drugs Used to Treat Bipolar I Disorder

The use of lithium in aged patients is more hazardous than its use in young patients because of the common occurrence of age-related morbidity and physiological changes of the heart, the thyroid, and the kidneys. Lithium is excreted by the kidneys, and decreased renal clearance and renal disease can increase the risk of toxicity. Thiazide diuretics decrease the renal clearance of lithium; consequently, the concomitant use of those medications can necessitate adjustments in lithium dosage. Other medications may also interfere with lithium clearance. Lithium may cause CNS effects to which the elderly may be especially sensitive. Because of those factors, frequent serum mon-

**Table 50–5**
**Geriatric Dosages of Psychostimulants**

| Generic Name | Trade Name | Geriatric Dosage Range (mg a day) |
|---|---|---|
| Dextroamphetamine | Dexedrine | 2.5–10 |
| Pemoline | Cylert | 18.75–37 |
| Methylphenidate | Ritalin | 2.5–20 |

itoring of lithium levels is recommended for the elderly. In addition, cardiac, kidney, and thyroid workups are essential before initiating therapy. Table 50–6 lists the geriatric dosages of drugs used in bipolar I disorder.

## Antipsychotics

In addition to treating overt signs of psychosis, such as hallucinations and delusions, antipsychotics have been used to deal effectively with violent, agitated, and abusive geriatric patients.

In general, psychosis in the elderly frequently responds to much lower dosages of medication than those used for young patients. The elderly are also much more sensitive to many of the side effects of antipsychotic medications than are young patients, specifically to the extrapyramidal (parkinsonian) side effects. Elderly patients have been known to stop speaking, ambulating, and swallowing as a result of those side effects. The same dosages of medication are not likely to produce significant problems for young patients.

**Neurological side effects.** The most common side effects of antipsychotic drugs are extrapyramidal signs, such as akathisia and acute dystonia. Akathisia may be misinterpreted as psychotic agitation, and the acute dyskinesias (especially of the face, the tongue, and the neck) may simulate the bizarre movements of schizophrenia. Parkinsonian symptoms are a late complication of drug therapy. The dyskinesias, manifested mainly by buccolingual movements, are noted late in the course of high-dosage antipsychotic therapy, especially in the elderly. Autonomic side effects are particularly troublesome because they may upset the homeostasis of organs innervated by the autonomic nervous system, such as the bladder, the gastrointestinal tract, and the cardiovascular system. Alterations in sleep—such as insomnia, bizarre dreams, and sleepwalking—can occur. The toxic confusional state may occur

**Table 50–6**
**Geriatric Dosages of Drugs Commonly Used to Treat Bipolar I Disorder**

| Class | Generic Name | Trade Name | Geriatric Dosage Range (mg a day) |
|---|---|---|---|
| Lithium salts | Lithium carbonate | Eskalith, Lithane, Lithotabs | 75–900 |
| Anticonvulsants | Carbamazepine | Tegretol | 200–1,200 |
| | Valproate | Depakene, Depakote | 250–1,000 |
| | Clonazepam (a benzodiazepine) | Klonopin | 0.5–1.5 |

with all drugs with anticholinergic properties, which may also cause mydriasis and blurring of vision. Other drugs have adrenergic properties causing miosis.

Hip fracture resulting from falls, in part associated with medication use, is a major cause of morbidity in the elderly and can be a proximal or distal factor associated with demise. Consequently, to minimize the potential deleterious and even life-threatening side effects, the clinician should monitor drug use. Hip fractures are least often associated with short half-life anxiolytics and most often associated with antipsychotics.

Clinical experience indicates that the therapeutic effects of antipsychotic medications in the elderly may not become evident on a given dosage of medication for four weeks or longer. Because of the therapeutic factors and risks, the dictum in treating psychosis in the elderly is to start low and go slow. As in younger patients, side-effect profiles should help determine the choice of medication; however, no consensus exists regarding the choice or the dosage level of antipsychotics for the elderly. There is no need to administer prophylactic antiparkinsonian agents on a regular basis when prescribing antipsychotics. The anticholinergic aspects of those drugs can create unwanted side effects, especially memory impairment. Table 50–7 lists the geriatric dosages for commonly used antipsychotic agents.

## Anxiolytics

The population over age 65 constitutes less than 12 percent of the total population but includes 15 percent of long-term-anxiolytic drug users. Their rate of regular use is five times that seen in the general population. Furthermore, among men with equivalent degrees of high emotional distress, those over the age of 60 are four times more likely to use an antianxiety drug than are men between the ages of 18 and 29.

**Table 50–7**
**Geriatric Dosages of Commonly Used Antipsychotics**

| Generic Name | Trade Name | Geriatric Dosage Range (mg a day) |
|---|---|---|
| Phenothiazines | | |
| Aliphatic | | |
| Chlorpromazine | Thorazine | 30–300 |
| Triflupromazine | Vesprin | 1–15 |
| Piperazine | | |
| Perphenazine | Trilafon | 8–32 |
| Trifluoperazine | Stelazine | 1–15 |
| Fluphenazine | Permitil, Prolixin | 1–10 |
| Piperidine | | |
| Thioridazine | Mellaril | 25–300 |
| Mesoridazine | Serentil | 50–400 |
| Thioxanthenes | | |
| Chlorprothixene | Taractan | 30–300 |
| Thiothixene | Navane | 2–20 |
| Dibenzoxazepine | | |
| Loxapine | Loxitane | 50–250 |
| Dihydroindole | | |
| Molindone | Moban | 50–225 |
| Butyrophenone | | |
| Haloperidol | Haldol | 2–20 |

The geriatric patient with mild or moderate anxiety can benefit from anxiolytics. The benzodiazepines are the most widely used anxiolytics. Most patients are treated for brief periods, although some may have to be maintained on small dosages for long periods. The long-term use of benzodiazepines is controversial, because they are controlled substances with a potential for abuse. Benzodiazepines with short or intermediate half-lives are preferable for use as hypnotics. The benzodiazepines may cause short periods of memory impairment, such as anterograde amnesia, which may aggravate an already existing cognitive disorder in the elderly patient. Elderly patients accumulate the long-acting benzodiazepines (such as diazepam [Valium]) in adipose tissues, increasing such unwanted effects as ataxia, insomnia, and confusion (sundowner syndrome). That effect can be avoided if the smallest possible dosage is prescribed and if intake is monitored until a therapeutic response is achieved.

Barbiturates may be substituted for the benzodiazepines in the few patients who do not respond to benzodiazepines. The geriatric patient is particularly prone to paradoxical dysphoria and cognitive disorganization, which can result from barbiturates. The barbiturates have a higher abuse potential, compared with the benzodiazepines. Barbiturates are controlled substances (schedule II), and the Drug Enforcement Agency (DEA) imposes constraints on their use.

Buspirone (BuSpar) is an anxiolytic drug without sedative properties. It has a longer onset of action—up to three weeks—than either the benzodiazepines or the barbiturates and does not cause cognitive impairment. Moreover, it does not have any potential for abuse. A summary of the geriatric dosages of drugs used to treat anxiety and insomnia is presented in Table 50–8.

## Pharmacological Management of Agitation and Aggression in Dementia

A common issue in the treatment of elderly patients with dementia is the management of agitation and aggression. The use of antipsychotics is generally unsatisfactory because of their limited efficacy and their parkinsonian side effects. Benzodiazepines, although frequently used to treat behavior disturbances, may produce cognitive impairment, sedation, and paradoxical worsening of the patient's behavior. Some β-adrenergic antagonists, such as propranolal and pindolol, the partial 5-HT$_{1A}$ agonist buspirone, and the 5-HT$_2$ antagonist trazodone have been reported to reduce agitation, aggression, and impulsivity in patients with dementia and other cognitive disorders.

## PSYCHOTHERAPY FOR THE AGED

The standard psychotherapeutic interventions—such as insight-oriented psychotherapy, supportive psychotherapy, cognitive therapy, group therapy, and family therapy—should be available to the geriatric patient. According to Sigmund Freud, persons more than 50 years of age are not suited for psychoanalysis because they lack elasticity of the mental processes. But in the view of many

**Table 50–8**
**Geriatric Dosages of Drugs Commonly Used to Treat Anxiety and Insomnia**

| Generic Name | Trade Name | Geriatric Dosage Range (mg a day) |
|---|---|---|
| Benzodiazepines | | |
| Alprazolam | Xanax | 0.5–6 |
| Chlordiazepoxide | Librium | 15–100 |
| Clorazepate | Tranxene | 7.5–60 |
| Diazepam | Valium | 2–60 |
| Estazolam | ProSom | 1–2 |
| Flurazepam | Dalmane | 15–30 |
| Halazepam | Paxipam | 60–160 |
| Lorazepam | Ativan | 2–6 |
| Oxazepam | Serax | 30–120 |
| Prazepam | Centrax | 20–60 |
| Quazepam | Doral | 10–20 |
| Temazepam | Restoril | 7.5–30 |
| Triazolam | Halcion | 0.125–0.25 |
| Nonbenzodiazepines | | |
| Zolpidem | Ambien | 5–10 |
| Buspirone | BuSpar | 5–60 |
| Secobarbital | Seconal | 50–300 |
| Meprobamate | Miltown | 400–800 |
| Chloral hydrate | Noctec | 500–1,000 |
| β-Adrenergic blocking agents | | |
| Propranolol | Inderal | 40–160 |
| Atenolol | Tenormin | 25–100 |

who followed Freud, psychoanalysis is possible after that age. Advanced age certainly limits the plasticity of the personality, but, as Otto Fenichel stated: "It does so in varying degrees and at very different ages so that no general rule can be given." Insight-oriented psychotherapy may be tried for removing a specific symptom, even with old persons. It is of most benefit if the patient has possibilities for libidinal and narcissistic gratification, but it is contraindicated if it would bring only the insight that life has been a failure and that the patient has no opportunity to make up for it.

Common age-related issues in therapy involve the need to adapt to recurrent and diverse losses (such as the deaths of friends and loved ones), the need to assume new roles (such as the adjustment to retirement and the disengagement from previously defined roles), and the need to accept one's mortality.

Psychotherapy helps the aged deal with those issues and the emotional problems surrounding them and to understand their behavior and the effects of their behavior on others. In addition to improving interpersonal relationships, psychotherapy increases self-esteem and self-confidence, decreases feelings of helplessness and anger, and improves the quality of life. As described by Alvin Goldfarb, psychotherapy for the aged has the general aim of assisting the elderly to have minimal complaints, to help them make and keep friends of both sexes, and to have sexual relations when they have interest and capacity. Psychotherapy helps relieve tensions of biological and cultural origins and helps old persons work and play within the limits of their functional status and as determined by their past training, activities, and self-concept in society. In patients with impaired cognition, psychotherapy can produce remarkable gains in both physical and mental

symptoms. In one study conducted in an old-age home, 43 percent of the patients receiving psychotherapy showed decreased urinary incontinence, improved gait, greater mental alterness, improved memory, and better hearing than before psychotherapy.

In general, the therapist is more active, supportive, and flexible in conducting therapy with the aged person than with the young adult. The therapist must be prepared to act decisively at the first sign of an incapacity that requires the active involvement of another physician, such as an internist, or the need to consult or enlist the aid of a family member.

The aged person comes to therapy wanting the therapist's unqualified and unlimited support, reassurance, and approval. The most important irrational attitude the patient brings to the therapeutic situation is the expectation that the therapist is all-powerful, all-knowing, and able to effect a magical cure. Most patients eventualy learn to recognize that the therapist is human and that they are engaged in a collaborative effort. In some cases, however, the therapist may have to assume the idealized role, especially when the patient is unable or unwilling to test reality effectively. With the help of the therapist, the patient deals with problems that were previously avoided. Direct encouragement, reassurance, and advice can be offered, increasing the patient's self-confidence as conflicts are resolved.

### Transference

In most cases the elderly patient parentifies the younger psychiatrist and transfers the infantile responses from the past relationship with the parent to the present relationship with the physician. A childlike dependence can then develop, or, conversely, a childlike defiance and disobedience may appear. The patient can be shown how the infantile behavior is at work now in relation to the psychiatrist and to others in the patient's life. Other transferential reactions include the patient's reacting to the therapist as a brother, sister, uncle, or even grandparent.

### Group Therapy

Group therapy with the aged provides an opportunity for mutual support and is an aid in helping patients deal with the stresses of adapting to declining resources. Group members provide new friendships at a time when there has been a loss of old friends by death. Patients have the opportunity to be of help to one another, increasing their self-esteem. Even patients with mild to moderate dementia can be helped to remain stimulated, active, and oriented through group interaction.

### Family Therapy

Engaging the patient's family in treatment is frequently desirable and often necessary. Issues in family therapy are myriad. They include the distribution of family resources in providing care for the patient, the attitudes of the children toward their parent and their parent's need for therapy, the grandparenting role, and the examination of family conflicts.

### Brief Therapy

Short-term therapy approaches, such as cognitive therapy, help the aged by correcting distortions in thinking, especially self-induced prejudices about the aging process. Persons who think they are too old for sports, sex, learning new things, acquiring new skills, helping others, and working at new jobs can have those cognitive distortions modified by direct therapeutic interventions. Patients can learn to use adaptive defense mechanisms and can be persuaded to make an effort to fight phobic avoidances and other inhibitions.

## INSTITUTIONAL CARE OF THE AGED

The placement of the aged person in an institution is often viewed as a failure in management. It is, however, often a carefully thought out and executed treatment option that improves the person's quality of life. Several types of institutions are available.

Old-age homes and board-and-care homes are voluntary nonprofit institutions in which old persons are expected to live together for the rest of their lives, with no attempt to rehabilitate them for discharge. Instead, they are helped to adjust to the protective setting and to have a better social life than they could have in their own homes.

Nursing homes and extended-care facilities are institutions for the long-term care of chronically ill or permanently impaired persons. Those institutions emphasize the admission of short-term convalescent patients and persons with the potential for rehabilitation to community life. However, only 50 percent stay less than three months, and 50 percent stay on as permanent residents. The government divides nursing homes into skilled nursing facilities and intermediate-care facilities. Seventy percent are proprietary, and 30 percent are nonproprietary or governmental. In 1988 the average cost to stay in a nursing home was $22,000 a year. The cost is now more than $30,000 a year. A total of $38 billion is spent annually on nursing home care; half of that is paid by the government (through Medicaid). An increasing number of private insurance companies now offer long-term care insurance to help cover nursing home costs.

Day-care centers and community centers for the aged are places for elderly persons to congregate, to enjoy socializing experiences, and to deal with feelings of depression, anxiety, boredom, and loneliness.

The state psychiatric hospitals used to have a large geriatric population with various cognitive disorders. Today those hospitals exclude aged persons with dementia unless the dementia is mild or reversible and the patient is not likely to become a permanent resident. As a result, both old-age homes and nursing homes have received patients who are similar to the disorganized, bizarre, and violent patients formerly in mental hospitals. The likelihood that those brain-damaged old persons will ever be discharged from those long-term care facilities is slim, because even willing and effective families cannot cope with the many around-the-clock need of those patients.

A new trend to help avoid institutionalization is the so-called retirement community composed of relatively healthy old persons who live and work together. The communities are usually run on a nonprofit basis and may have an associated medical facility for the treatment of medical problems. Increasingly, profit-making companies are establishing retirement communities.

### Restraints

Restraints are belts and vests that keep patients from falling out of bed and wheelchairs or from wandering away. For some patients (such as patients who would pull out feeding or oxygen tubes) such restraints are necessary, but for most patients they are used excessively. Some federal surveys have found that about 40 percent of all nursing home residents are put in restraints each year. The alternatives include tilted recliners, safe wandering paths, and floor alarms. Patients without restraints have better muscle tone from the exercise of walking and, psychologically, have less rage and a greater sense of mastery than do patients in restraints.

### Psychosocial Therapy

Institutions can provide a total-push approach to the patient that involves a variety of professional staff members, including psychologists; social workers; psychiatric aides; occupational, vocational, and activity therapists; nutritionists; and exercise therapists. Each has skills that, when brought to bear on the institutionalized resident either individually or in a group, can markedly improve the patient's quality of life.

Psychiatrists who work with the aged must be especially aware of their own attitudes toward the aging process and aged persons, particularly their own parents and grandparents. If the psychiatrists have unresolved resentments or unconscious anger toward the aged in their own lives, they are likely to have countertransference problems that interfere with their ability to do good psychotherapy. Similarly, if they have unresolved fears of death, dying, or chronic illness, they may have blind spots that interfere with therapy. Psychiatrists must have an optimistic view of the last stage of the life cycle and a genuine belief that aged persons have a rightful place in society and a reservoir of wisdom from their accumulated years of experience that enables them to change.

### References

Addonizio G, Alexopoulos G S: Affective disorders in the elderly. Int J Geriatr Psychiatry 8: 41, 1993.

American Association for Geriatric Psychiatry Board of Directors, American Geriatrics Society Clinical Practice Committee: Psychotherapeutic medications in the nursing home. J Am Geriatr Soc 40: 946, 1992.

Coyne A C, Reichman W E, Berbig L J: The relationship between dementia and elder abuse. Am J Psychiatry 150: 643, 1993.

Francis J, Kapoor W N: Delirium in hospitalized elderly. J Gen Intern Med 5: 65, 1990.

Francis J, Kapoor W N: Prognosis after hospital discharge of older medical patients with delirium. J Am Geriatr Soc 40: 601, 1992.

Goldberg R: Geriatric consultation/liaison psychiatry. Adv Psychosom Med 19: 138, 1989.

Jenike M A: Treatment of affective illness in the elderly with drugs and electroconvulsive therapy. J Geriatr Psychiatry 22: 77, 1989.

Koenig H G, Breitner J C: Use of antidepressants in medically ill older patients. Psychosomatics 31: 22, 1990.

Kohn R R: Cause of death in very old people. JAMA 247: 2703, 1982.

Onofrij M, Gambi D, Malatesta G, Ferracci F, Fulgente T: Electrophysiological techniques in the assessment of aging brain: Lacunar state and differential diagnosis. Eur Neurol 29: 44, 1989.

Ramsdell J W, Rothrock J F, Ward H W, Volk D M: Evaluation of cognitive impairment in the elderly. J Gen Intern Med 5: 55, 1990.

Rosenberg D R, Wright B, Gershon S: Depression in the elderly. Dementia 3: 157, 1992.

Rovner B W, Katz I R: Psychiatric disorders in the nursing home: A selective review of studies related to clinical care. Int J Geriatr Psychiatry 8: 75, 1993.

Salzman C: Practical considerations in the pharmacologic treatment of depression and anxiety in the elderly. J Clin Psychiatry 51: 40, 1990.

Solomon K, Manepalli J, Ireland G A, Mahon G M: Alcoholism and prescription drug abuse in the elderly: St. Louis University grand rounds. J Am Geriatr Soc 41: 57, 1993.

Thomas C, Kelman H R, Kennedy G J, Ahn C et al: Depressive symptoms and mortality in elderly persons. J Gerontol 47: S80, 1992.

Ulhmann R, Larson E: Relationship of hearing impairment to dementia and cognitive dysfunction in older adults. JAMA 261: 1916, 1989.

Weiss L J, Lazarus L W: Psychosocial treatment of the geropsychiatric patient. Int J Geriatr Psychiatry 8: 95, 1993.

Williams G. O: Management of depression in the elderly. Prim Care 16: 451, 1989.

Forensic psychiatry is the branch of medicine that deals with disorders of the mind and their relation to legal principles. The word "forensic" means belonging to the courts of law. At various stages in their historical development, psychiatry and the law have converged. Today, the two disciplines often intersect when dealing with the social deviant who, by violating the rules of society secondary to some presumed or proposed mental disorder, adversely affects the functioning of the community. Traditionally, the psychiatrist's efforts are directed toward elucidation of the causes and, through prevention and treatment, reduction of the self-destructive elements of harmful behavior. The lawyer, as the agent of society, is concerned with the fact that the social deviant is a potential threat to the safety and the security of other people. Both psychiatry and the law seek to implement their respective goals through the application of pragmatic techniques based on empirical observations.

The "legalization" of psychiatry has had a major serious side effect—the increasing practice of defensive medicine. Defensive practice converts patients into adversaries against whom clinicians must defend themselves. Patients readily sense the shift from the clinician's interest in the patient to the clinician's self-protection. The patient's feeling may trigger litigation and also negates the most important element the clinician has in avoiding lawsuits: the therapeutic alliance.

The interface between psychiatry and the law is complex and has the potential for gross misunderstandings.

During a routine outpatient psychotherapy appointment, a male middle-level manager began to complain to his therapist about his boss. Feeling the freedom of expression that the therapeutic situation is intended to foster, the man worked himself up to a higher pitch than usual, and, in the emotional intensity of the moment, he stated that he would like to kill his boss. He then calmed down, somewhat relieved by having let off steam, went on to discuss other subjects, and departed at the end of the session.

The therapist did not believe that the patient was anywhere near the point of seriously acting on the feelings that were expressed. However, the therapist had heard of a case in which the therapist got into trouble for not warning third parties, so he decided to take action.

On a sheet with his letterhead, he typed a warning to the employer that his patient, John Jones, had expressed the desire to kill him. He sent the letter by first-class mail—not express or registered—and he addressed it not to the employer but to the personnel department of the company.

The resulting uproar, although perhaps predictable, surprised the therapist. During the subsequent liability suit for breach of confidentiality, he was heard to sputter, "But I was only doing what the law requires of me!"

Another patient, on a psychiatric inpatient ward, was totally out of control and was holding his therapist by the lapels, slamming him repeatedly against the office door frame. Ward staff members were about to intervene when a new attendant cried: "Wait! Laying hands on the patient may not be legally justified!" That remark momentarily paralyzed the staff members until reason reasserted itself, and the patient was contained but not before a few additional slams had taken place.

## PSYCHIATRISTS AND THE COURTS

Most psychiatric work with patients is based on the therapeutic alliance between the clinician and the patient, but the legal model works from an adversarial position. The complexity of medicolegal matters is inevitably divided (or, more often, polarized) into two sides, which pull against each other in an effort to place the truth in the hands of the fact finder (the judge or the jury). For the clinician exposed to merciless cross-examination scenes in all media, that fundamental element of the American legal system is apt to evoke fear, revulsion, and dismay. But those feelings may be tempered somewhat by insights into the process. From the clinician's viewpoint an important distinction must first be made regarding the clinician's role as witness. The earliest point to establish in sorting out the clinician's role is what kind of witness the psychiatrist will be.

### Witness of Fact

The first type of witness is the witness of fact (also called an ordinary witness). As a witness of fact, the psychiatrist functions no differently from laypersons generally—for example, as observers of an accident on the street. The witness's input—the facts—are direct observations and material from direct scrutiny. A witness of fact may be a psychiatrist who reads portions of the medical record aloud to bring it into the legal record and thus make it available for testimony. In theory, any psychiatrist at any level of training can fulfill that role.

### Expert Witness

In contrast, a psychiatrist under certain circumstances may be qualified as an expert. The qualifying process, however, consists not of popular recognition in one's clinical field but of being accepted by the court and both sides of the case as suitable to perform expert functions. Thus, the term "expert" has particular legal meaning and is independent of any actual or presumed expertise the clinician may have in a given area. The clinician's expertise is elucidated during direct examination and cross-examination of the clinician's education, publications, and certifications. In the context of the courtroom, an expert witness is one who may draw conclusions from data and thereby render an opinion—for example, that a patient meets the required criteria for commitment or for an insanity defense under the standards of a jurisdiction. Expert witnesses play a role in determining the standard of care and what constitutes the average practice of psychiatry.

The most common role of a psychiatrist in court proceedings is as an expert. When psychiatrists are asked to serve as experts, they are usually asked to do so for one of the sides in the case; rarely are clinicians independent examiners reporting directly to the court. That can lead to a scenario known as the battle of the experts, in which each side hires an expert witness and the two experts give opposing opinions. The battle of the experts can leave the jury in a quandary and can result in the jury's discounting the testimony of each expert and deciding the case on other evidence and testimony. Testimony is brought out by the hiring attorney in that part of the presentation known as the direct examination. The opposing attorney then draws out additional material through the cross-examination.

**Direct examination.** Direct examination is the first questioning of a witness by the attorney for the party on whose behalf the witness is called. Direct examination generally consists of open-ended questions that require narrative-type answers. It is a friendly interrogation that is routinely rehearsed with one's attorney before the trial.

**Cross-examination.** Cross-examination is the questioning of a witness by the attorney for the opposing party. Cross-examination usually involves long, possibly leading questions that demand a yes or no answer. Few experiences can be as demoralizing for the clinician as cross-examination by an eager, aggressive, and sarcastic attorney for the opposing side. That segment of the total experience, more than any other, makes many clinicians leery of appearing in the courtroom in any role. For the clinician in that situation, certain principles may be helpful to keep in mind.

First, the clinician should listen closely to the question being asked and always pause a moment before answering, not only to replay the question mentally for clarity but to allow the other side to object. Then, the clinician should answer only the question asked. The expert witness should stop talking the moment the judge begins to speak.

Second, the clinician should keep in mind the limits of his or her field and should be particularly careful about words like "always" and "never," as those words identify predictions the clinician is asked to make. If pressed to give a yes or no answer to a complex question, the clinician should recall that he or she is permitted to answer, "That question cannot be answered with a yes or a no."

Third, the clinician should not be afraid or reluctant to say, "I don't know" when that is the true response; not all questions that attorneys ask have answers.

Fourth, the clinician should insist on pretrial preparation by the hiring attorney. Few situations are as needlessly traumatic as being sent into court unprepared. The clinician should speak simply, avoid jargon, and be tactful. And the clinician should be careful about accepting professional literature as authoritative and should ask to see or hear relevant sections before conceding that an entire work is an authority.

Expert witnesses have several rights in court. If they are uncertain how to answer a question or whether they must answer the question posed, they may ask the judge for guidance. They may ask the judge whether the material asked for is privileged. They may refuse to answer questions they do not understand. They may ask the examining counsel to clarify or repeat the question. They may state that they do not know the answer to the question. They may ask the judge whether they can qualify the answer when a yes or no answer is requested. They have a right to complete their answers and should protest if they are interrrupted. They may refer to written records to refresh their recollection or memory.

In general, the attorneys in a case guide the psychiatrist in proper courtroom procedure and the admissibility of various sorts of testimony. Attorneys are free to object at any point in the examination if they think that certain lines of inquiry, types of evidence, or content are inappropriate for the court's consideration.

**Court-mandated evaluations.** In several legal situations the judge asks clinicians to be consultants to the court, which raises the issue of for whom the clinicians work. Because clinical information may have to be revealed to the court, clinicians may not enjoy the same confidential relationship with their patients in those situations that they have in private practice. Clinicians who make such court-ordered evaluations are under an ethical obligation and, in some states, a legal obligation to so inform the patients at the outset of the examinations and to make sure that the patients understand that condition. Such court-mandated evaluations were supported by the Supreme Court of the United States in *Ake v. Oklahoma*. The Court held that, when a state allows a defense of sanity, it must provide funds for a psychiatric expert for an indigent defendant. Such an expert may be part of the defense if appropriate.

**Evaluation of witnesses' credibility.** It is up to the trial judge to grant a psychiatric examination requested by one of the parties to the action. Before ordering such an examination, the trial judge asks for evidence showing that such an examination is necessary to determine the merits of the case and that the imposition on or inconvenience to the witness does not outweigh the examination's value. Many courts limit psychiatric examinations to complaining witnesses in rape and other sex-offense cases, in which corroborative proof is nearly always circumstantial. In incest cases, for example, the father and the daughter may jointly deny the incest that the mother persistently alleges; or the father may steadfastly deny the act, and the mother may support his denial; or, after accusing her father, the daughter may retract her accusation. Psychiatrists say that only a thorough psychiatric examination of the family can eliminate the confusion. Recognizing that false sex charges may stem from the psychodynamics of a victim who appears to be normal to a layperson, the courts permit psychiatrists to expose mental processes and defenses in complaining witnesses. The liberal attitude in that area is probably caused by the gravity of the charge or by the general lack of corroborating evidence.

## PRIVILEGE AND CONFIDENTIALITY

### Privilege

Privilege is the right to maintain secrecy or confidentiality in the face of a subpoena. Privileged communications are those statements made by certain persons within a relationship—such as husband-wife, priest-penitent, or doctor-patient—that the law protects from forced disclosure on the witness stand. Privilege is a right that belongs to the patient, not to the physician, and so the right can be waived by the patient. Psychiatrists, who are licensed to practice medicine, may claim medical privilege, but they have found that the privilege is so riddled with qualifications that it is practically meaningless. Purely federal cases have no psychotherapist-patient privilege. Moreover, the privilege does not exist at all in military courts, regardless of whether the physician is military or civilian and whether the privilege is recognized in the state where the court-martial takes place. The privilege has numerous exceptions, which are often viewed as implied waivers. In the most common exception, patients are said to waive the privilege by injecting their condition into the litigation, thereby making their condition an element of their claim or defense. Another exception involves proceedings for hospitalization, in which the interests of both the patient and the public are said to call for a departure from confidentiality. In a number of contexts, clinicians may be ordered to give the court information that is ordinarily considered privileged. Yet another exception is made in child-custody and child-protection proceedings in regard to the best interest of the child. Furthermore, the privilege does not apply to actions between a therapist and a patient. Thus, in a fee dispute or a malpractice claim, the complainant's lawyer can obtain the necessary therapy records to resolve the dispute.

Psychiatrists and other physicians do not legally have the same privilege that exists between client and attorney, priest and churchgoer, and husband and wife. Most physicians are not aware of that fact.

## Confidentiality

A long-held premise of medical ethics binds the physician to hold secret all information given by a patient. That professional obligation is what is meant by confidentiality. Understanding confidentiality requires an awareness that it applies to certain populations and not to others. That is, one can identify a group that is within the circle of confidentiality, meaning that sharing information with the members of that group does not require specific permission from the patient. Within that circle are other staff members treating the patient, clinical supervisors, and consultants. Parties outside the circle include the patient's family, attorney, and previous therapist; sharing information with such people requires the patient's permission. Nevertheless, in numerous instances the psychiatrist may be asked to divulge information imparted by the patient. Although a court demand for information worries psychiatrists the most, the most frequent demand is by someone, such as an insurer, who cannot compel disclosure but who can withhold a benefit without it. Generally, the patient makes disclosures or authorizes the psychiatrist to make disclosures in order to receive a benefit, such as employment, welfare benefits, or insurance.

A psychiatrist can be forced to breach confidentiality by a subpoena. The law could not function adequately if courts did not have the right to compel witnesses to testify. A subpoena (meaning "under penalty") is an order to appear as a witness in court or at a deposition. Physicians are usually served with a *subpoena duces tecum*, which requires that they also produce their relevant records and documents. Although the power to issue subpoenas belongs to a judge, they are routinely issued at the request of an attorney representing a party to an action.

In bona fide emergencies, information may be released in as limited a way as feasible to carry out emergency interventions. Sound clinical practice holds that efforts should be made, time allowing, to obtain the patient's permission anyway. After the emergency the clinician should debrief the patient.

As a rule, clinical information may be shared with the patient's permission—preferably written permission, although oral permission suffices with proper documentation. Each release is good for only one bolus of information, and permission should be reobtained for each subsequent release, even to the same party. Permission overcomes only the legal barrier, not the clinical one; the release is permission, not obligation. If the clinician believes that the information may be destructive, the matter should be discussed, and the release may be refused with some exceptions.

**Third-party payers and supervision.** Increased insurance coverage for health care is precipitating a concern about confidentiality and the conceptual model of psychiatric practice. Today, insurance covers about 70 percent of all health care bills; to provide coverage, an insurance carrier must be able to obtain information with which it can assess the administration and the cost of various programs.

Quality control of care necessitates that confidentiality not be absolute; it also requires a review of individual patients and therapists. The therapist in training must breach a patient's confidence by discussing the case with a supervisor. Also, institutionalized patients who have been ordered by a court to get treatment must have their individualized treatment programs submitted to a mental health board.

**Discussions about patients.** In general, psychiatrists have multiple loyalties: to patients, to society, and to the profession. Through their writings, teaching, and seminars, they can share their acquired knowledge and experience, providing information that may be valuable to other professionals and to the public. But it is not easy to write or talk about a psychiatric patient without breaching the confidentiality of the relationship. Unlike physical ailments, which can be discussed without anyone's recognizing the patient, a psychiatric history usually entails a discussion of distinguishing characteristics. Psychiatrists have an obligation not to disclose identifiable patient information (and, perhaps, any descriptive patient information) without appropriate informed consent. Failure to obtain informed consent may result in claims based on breach of privacy or defamation or both.

**Child abuse.** In New York all physicians are legally required to take a course on child abuse for medical licensure. All states now legally require that psychiatrists, among others, who have reason to believe that a child has been the victim of physical or sexual abuse make an immediate report to an appropriate agency. In that situation, confidentiality is decisively limited by legal statute on the ground that potential or actual harm to vulnerable children outweighs the value of confidentiality in a psychiatric setting. Although many complex psychodynamic nuances accompany the required reporting of suspected child abuse, such reports are generally considered ethically justified.

**Disclosure to safeguard.** In some situations the physician must report to the authorities, as specifically required by law. The classic example of mandatory reporting involves a patient with epilepsy who operates a motor vehicle. Another example of mandatory reporting—one in which penalties are imposed for failing to report—involves child abuse. Expanded definitions of what constitutes child abuse under the law have been amended in some jurisdictions to include both emotional and physical child abuse. Under the legislation, practitioners who learn that a patient is engaged in sexual activity with a child are obliged to report it. In the absence of a specific statute that mandates reporting, a report is optional. As a general principle, a person has no duty to come to the aid of another unless a special relationship mandates that duty. However, once a person does come to the aid of another, a relationship is established, and a duty may be imposed.

TARASOFF I. Does the establishment of a therapist-patient relationship obligate the therapist to care for the safety of not only the patient but also others? The issue was raised in the case of *Tarasoff v. Regents of University of California* in 1976 (now known as *Tarasoff I*). In that case, Prosenjit Poddar, a student and a voluntary outpatient at the mental health clinic of the University of California, told his therapist that he intended to kill a student readily identified as Tatiana Tarasoff. Realizing the seriousness of the intention, the therapist, with the concurrence of a colleague, concluded that Poddar should be committed for observation under a 72-hour emergency psychiatric detention provision of the California commitment law. The therapist notified the campus police both orally and in writing that Poddar was dangerous and should be committed.

Concerned about the breach of confidentiality, the therapist's supervisor vetoed the recommendation and ordered all records relating to Poddar's treatment destroyed. At the same time the campus police temporarily detained Poddar but released him on his assurance that he would "stay away from that girl." Poddar stopped going to the clinic when he learned from the police of his therapist's recommendation to commit him. Two months later, he carried out his previously announced threat to kill Tatiana. The young woman's parents thereupon sued the university for negligence.

As a consequence, the California Supreme Court, which deliberated the case for the unprecedented time of some 14 months, ruled that a physician or a psychotherapist who has reason to believe that a patient may injure or kill someone must notify the potential victim, the victim's relatives or friends, or the authorities.

The discharge of the duty imposed on the therapist to warn intended victims against danger may take one or more various steps, depending on the case. Thus, said the court, it may call for the therapist to notify the intended victim or others likely to notify the victim of the danger, to notify the police, or to take whatever other steps are reasonably necessary under the circumstances.

The *Tarasoff I* decision has not drastically affected psychiatrists, as it has long been their practice to warn the appropriate persons or law enforcement authorities when a patient presents a distinct and immediate threat to someone. According to the American Psychiatric Association,

confidentiality may, with careful judgment, be broken in the following ways: (1) A patient will probably commit murder, and the act can be stopped only by the psychiatrist's notification of the police. (2) A patient will probably commit suicide, and the act can be stopped only by the psychiatrist's notification of the police. (3) A patient, such as a bus driver or an airline pilot who has potentially life-threatening responsibilities, shows marked impairment of judgment.

The *Tarasoff I* ruling does not require therapists to report fantasies; rather, it requires a therapist to report an intended homicide; it is the therapist's duty to exercise good judgment.

TARASOFF II. In 1982 the California Supreme Court issued a second ruling in the case of *Tarasoff v. Regents of University of California* (now known as *Tarasoff II*), which broadened its earlier ruling, the duty to *warn*, to include the duty to *protect* (Figure 51–1).

The *Tarasoff II* ruling has stimulated intense debates in the medicolegal field. Lawyers, judges, and expert witnesses argue the definition of protection, the nature of the relationship between the therapist and the patient, and the balance between public safety and individual privacy.

Clinicians argue that the duty to protect hinders treatment because the patient may not trust the doctor if confidentiality is not maintained. Furthermore, because it is not easy to determine if a patient is dangerous enough to justify long-term incarceration, unnecessary involuntary hospitalization because of defensive practices may occur.

As a result of such debates in the medicolegal field, since 1976 the state courts have not made a uniform interpretation of the *Tarasoff II* ruling (the duty to protect). Generally, one should note whether a specific identifiable victim appears to be in imminent and probable danger from the threat of an action contemplated by a mentally ill patient; the harm, in addition to being imminent, should be potentially serious or severe. Usually, the patient must be a danger to another person and not to property. And the therapist should take clinically reasonable actions.

Claims have already been advanced in a few cases (none successful so far) that a *Tarasoff*-like duty applies to the infection of partners with human immunodeficiency virus (HIV) by patients under mental health treatment. The breach of confidentiality in *Tarasoff* cases is justified only by the threat of violence. Laws vary confusingly by jurisdiction. The ideal solution is to persuade the patient to make the disclosure and report the matter to the public health authorities.

## HOSPITALIZATION

All states, as part of their police power, provide for some form of involuntary hospitalization. Such action is usually taken when psychiatric patients present a danger to themselves or to others in their environment to the degree that their urgent need for treatment in a closed institution is evident. Certain states allow for involuntary hospitalization if patients are unable to care for themselves adequately.

The doctrine of *parens patriae* allows the state to intervene and to act as a surrogate parent for those unable

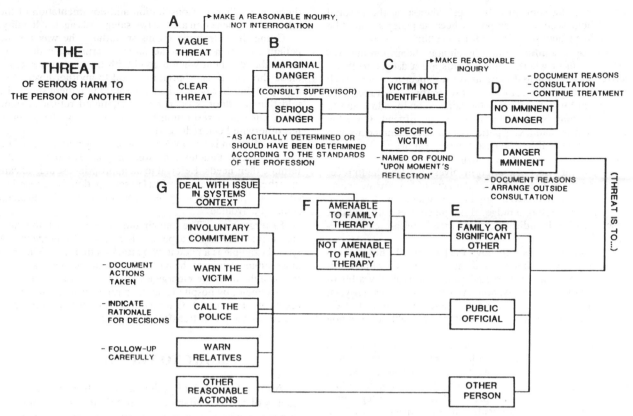

**Figure 51–1.** Tarasoff II decision chart. (Figure from B H Gross, L E Weiberjer, editors: *The Mental Health Professional and the Legal System*, p 98. Jossey-Bass, San Francisco, 1982. Used with permission.)

to care for themselves or who may harm themselves. *Parens patriae* ("father of his country") in common law goes back to Edward I of England and derives from English common law. It was transformed into American common law to mean paternalism in which the state acts for its mentally ill and its minors.

The statutes governing hospitalization of the mentally ill have generally been designated commitment laws. However, psychiatrists have long considered the term an undesirable one, because commitment legally means a warrant for imprisonment. The American Bar Association and the American Psychiatric Association have recommended that the term "commitment" be replaced by the less offensive and more accurate term "hospitalization," which has been adopted by most states. Although that change in terminology does not correct the attitudes of the past, the emphasis on hospitalization is in keeping with psychiatrists' views of treatment over punishment.

"False imprisonment" is the name of the legal action that arises from the claim that a patient has been negligently hospitalized. It is an uncommon basis for malpractice litigation and is rarely successful when invoked, at present, society tends to emphasize social protection more than individual rights. The clinician's guidelines are to (1) obtain an emergency or involuntary hospitalization in good faith, for reasonable cause, with data obtained from personal examination or a reliable report of danger; (2) seclude the patient for proper indications according to local regulations; and (3) obtain consultation on ambiguous cases.

## Procedures of Admission

Four procedures of admission to psychiatric facilities have been endorsed by the American Bar Association to safeguard civil liberties and to make sure that no person is railroaded into a mental hospital. Although each of the 50 states has the power to enact its own laws regarding psychiatric hospitalization, the procedures outlined here are gaining much acceptance.

**Informal admission.** Informal admission operates on the general hospital model, in which the patient is admitted to a psychiatric unit of a general hospital in the same way that a medical or surgical patient is admitted. Under such circumstances the ordinary doctor-patient relationship applies, with the patient free to enter and to leave, even against medical advice.

**Voluntary admission.** In cases of voluntary admission, patients apply in writing for admission to a psychiatric hospital. They may come to the hospital on the advice of their personal physician, or they may seek help on their own. In either case the patients are examined by a psychiatrist on the hospital staff and are admitted if that examination reveals the need for hospital treatment.

**Temporary admission.** Temporary admission is used for patients who are so senile or so confused that they require hospitalization and are not able to make decisions of their own and for patients who are so acutely disturbed that they must be immediately admitted to a psychiatric hospital on an emergency basis. Under the procedure a person is admitted to the hospital on the written recommendation of one physician. Once the patient has been admitted, the need for hospitalization must be confirmed by a psychiatrist on the hospital staff. The procedure is temporary because patients cannot be hospitalized against their will for more than 15 days.

**Involuntary admission.** Involuntary admission involves the question of whether the patients are a danger to themselves, such as suicidal patients, or a danger to others, such as homicidal patients. Because those persons do not recognize their need for hospital care, the application for admission to a hospital may be made by a relative or a friend. Once the application is made, the patients must be examined by two physicians, and, if both physicians confirm the need for hospitalization, the patients can then be admitted.

Involuntary hospitalization involves an established procedure for written notification of the next of kin. Furthermore, the patients have access at any time to legal counsel, who can bring the case before a judge. If the judge does not think that hospitalization is indicated, the patient's release can be ordered.

Involuntary admission allows the patient to be hospitalized for 60 days. After that time, if the patient is to remain hospitalized, the case must be reviewed periodically by a board consisting of psychiatrists, nonpsychiatric physicians, lawyers, and other citizens not connected with the institution. In New York State the board is called the Mental Health Information Service.

Persons who have been hospitalized involuntarily and who believe that they should be released have the right to file a petition for a writ of habeas corpus. Under law, a writ of habeas corpus may be proclaimed by those who believe that they have been illegally deprived of liberty. The legal procedure asks a court to decide whether a patient has been hospitalized without due process of law. The case must be heard by a court at once, regardless of the manner or the form in which the motion is filed. Hospitals are obligated to submit the petitions to the court immediately.

## Involuntary Discharge

Under a variety of circumstances, patients may have to be discharged from a hospital against their will—if they have intentionally broken a major hospital rule (for example, smuggled drugs or assaulted another patient), refused treatment, or been restored to health but still wish to remain hospitalized. Some people may wonder why many patients wish to remain in a psychiatric hospital. For some patients, such a protective environment is preferable to the streets, jail, or the family's home. Although the focus here is on discharge from an inpatient unit, similar issues are involved in unilateral termination with an outpatient.

**Abandonment as cause of action.** For the clinician the potential pitfall of involuntary discharge or involuntary termination is the charge of abandonment. That claim can be a particularly fertile ground for malpractice litigation when inevitable bad feelings are combined with a bad result. The clinician's vulnerability in that context is augmented by the jury's tendency to project a prejudicial distaste for the mentally ill person onto the physician, viewing the physician as someone who probably wants to get rid of the patient and be free to play golf. That popular perception places an additional onus on the clinician to exercise special care in that charged situation.

**Ending the relationship.** An involuntary discharge entails all the pain of the usual therapy termination process with far less opportunity for perspective, healing, and growth. Most important, in that situation the clinician directly opposes the patient's proclaimed wishes, thereby severely straining the therapeutic alliance. Consultation and documentation of the rationale for the action are the two safeguards against liability.

Going the extra mile means smoothing the way for the patient to obtain care in the future. Termination does not mean abandonment when a good-faith transfer of services is made through an appropriate referral to another hospital or therapist. Furthermore, when possible, the patient should be told that the door is open for a negotiated return at some future time after restitution has been made or the problem has otherwise been redressed.

The clinician is not obliged to accept any patient back into full treatment. Patients are owed only an evaluation to determine their needs. Referral to an appropriate source of care may then follow. Blanket refusal to see a patient is a dangerous course and, short of serious risk of bodily harm to the clinician, should be avoided.

**Emergencies.** The one circumstance in which the clinician cannot terminate a patient is a state of emergency. A typical example is a patient who attacks a therapist. The therapist cannot terminate the patient's care, no matter how severe the assault, until the emergency situation has been resolved (for example, by hospitalizing the patient or by arranging for seclusion or restraint). Only then can the therapist terminate the relationship and transfer the patient.

## RIGHT TO TREATMENT

Among the rights of patients, the right to the standard quality of care is fundamental. That right has been litigated in much-publicized cases in recent years under the slogan of "right to treatment."

In 1966, Judge David Bazelon, speaking for the District of Columbia Court of Appeals in *Rouse v. Cameron*, noted that the purpose of involuntary hospitalization is treatment and concluded that the absence of treatment draws into question the constitutionality of the confinement. Treatment in exchange for liberty is the logic of the ruling. In that case the patient was discharged on a writ of habeas corpus, the basic legal remedy to ensure liberty. Judge Bazelon further held that, if alternative treatments that infringe less on personal liberty are available, involuntary hospitalization cannot take place.

Alabama Federal District Court Judge Frank Johnson was more venturesome in the decree he rendered in 1971 in *Wyatt v. Stickney*. The *Wyatt* case was a class-action proceeding, brought under newly developed rules that sought not release but treatment. Judge Johnson ruled that persons civilly committed to a mental institution have a constitutional right to receive such individual treatment as will give them a reasonable opportunity to be cured or to have their mental condition improved. Judge Johnson set out minimum requirements for staffing, specified physical facilities and nutritional standards, and required individualized treatment plans.

The new codes, more detailed than the old ones, include the right to be free from excessive or unnecessary medication; the right to privacy and dignity; the right to the least restrictive environment; the unrestricted right to be visited by attorneys, clergy, and private physicians; and the right not to be subjected to lobotomies, electroconvulsive treatments, and other procedures without fully informed consent. Patients can be required to perform therapeutic tasks but not hospital chores unless they volunteer for them and are paid the federal minimum wage. That requirement is an attempt to eliminate the practice of peonage, in which psychiatric patients were forced to work at menial tasks, without payment, for the benefit of the state.

In a number of states today, medication or electroconvulsive therapy cannot be forcibly administered to a patient without first obtaining court approval, which may take as long as 10 days. The right to refuse treatment is a legal doctrine that holds that persons cannot be forced to have treatment against their will unless it is an emergency. An emergency is a condition in clinical practice that requires immediate intervention to prevent death or serious harm to the patient or others or deterioration of the patient's clinical state.

In the 1976 case of *O'Connor v. Donaldson*, the Supreme Court of the United States ruled that harmless mentally ill patients cannot be confined against their will without treatment if they can survive outside. According to the Court, a finding of mental illness alone cannot justify a state's confining persons in a hospital against their will. Instead, involuntarily confined patients must be considered dangerous to themselves or others or possibly so unable to care for themselves that they cannot survive outside. As a result of the 1979 case of *Rennie v. Klein*, patients have the right to refuse treatment and to use an appeal process. As a result of the 1981 case of *Roger v. Oken*, patients have an absolute right to refuse treatment, but a guardian may authorize treatment.

Questions have been raised about psychiatrists' ability to accurately predict dangerousness and about the risk to psychiatrists, who may be sued for monetary damages if persons are thereby deprived of their civil rights.

The ethical controversy over applications of the law to psychiatric patients came to the fore through Thomas Szasz, a professor of psychiatry at the State University of New York. In his book *The Myth of Mental Illness*, Szasz argued that the various psychiatric diagnoses are totally devoid of significance and contended that psychiatrists have no place in the courts of law and that all forced confinements because of mental illness are unjust. Szasz's opposition to suicide prevention and the imposition of treatment, with or without confinement, is interesting but is viewed by the psychiatric community with strong misgivings.

## CIVIL RIGHTS OF PATIENTS

Thanks to several clinical, public, and legal movements certain civil rights of the mentally ill, apart from their rights as patients, have been both established and affirmed.

### Least Restrictive Alternative

Clinicians are often puzzled by this right, which is perhaps the most legalistic of the group, as nothing in clinical work or training prepares one to think in terms of restrictiveness. Instead, clinical interventions are undertaken according to their effectiveness, positive benefit-risk ratio, and other operational criteria. A series of legal decisions on state intervention in organizations maneuvered the concept of the least restrictive alternative into mental health law, where it has taken solid root.

The principle holds that patients have the right to receive the least restrictive means of treatment for the requisite clinical effect. Thus, if a patient can be treated as an outpatient, commitment should not be used; if a patient can be treated on an open ward, seclusion should not be used.

Although apparently fairly straightforward on first reading, difficulty arises when attempts are made to apply the concept in choosing among involuntary medication, seclusion, and restraint as the intervention of choice. Distinguishing among those interventions on the basis of restrictiveness proves to be a purely subjective exercise fraught with personal bias. Moreover, each of those three interventions is both more and less restrictive than each of the other two. Nevertheless, the effort should be made to think in terms of restrictiveness when deciding how to treat patients.

### Visitation Rights

Patients have the right to receive visitors and to do so at reasonable hours (customary hospital visiting hours). Allowance must be made for the possibility that, at certain times, the patient's clinical condition may not permit visits. That fact should be clearly documented, however, as such rights must not be suspended without good reason.

Certain categories of visitors are not limited to the regular visiting hours, including the patient's attorney, private physician, and members of the clergy—all of whom have, broadly speaking, unrestricted access to the patient, including the right to privacy in their discussions. Even here, a bona fide emergency may delay such visits. Again, the patient's needs come first. Under similar reasoning, certain noxious visits may be curtailed (for example, a patient's relative bringing drugs into the ward).

### Communication Rights

Patients should, in general, have free and open communication with the outside world by the telephone or mail, but the right varies regionally to some degree. Some jurisdictions charge the hospital administration with a responsibility for monitoring the communications of patients. In some areas, hospitals are expected to make available reasonable supplies of paper, envelopes, and stamps for patients' use.

Specific circumstances affect communication rights. The patient who is hospitalized in relation to a criminal charge of making harassing or threatening phone calls should not be given unrestricted access to the telephone, and similar considerations apply to mail. As a rule, however, patients should be allowed private telephone calls, and their incoming and outgoing mail should not be opened by hospital staff members.

### Private Rights

Patients have several rights to privacy. In addition to confidentiality, they are allowed private bathroom and shower space, secure storage space for clothing and other belongings, and adequate floor space per person. They also have the right to wear their own clothes, and carry their own money.

## Economic Rights

Apart from special considerations related to incompetence, psychiatric patients are generally permited to manage their own financial affairs. One feature of that fiscal right is the requirement that patients be paid if they do work in the institution, such as gardening or preparing food. The right often creates tension between the valid therapeutic need for activity, including jobs, and exploitative labor. A consequence of that tension is that valuable occupational, vocational, and rehabilitative therapeutic programs may have to be eliminated because of the failure of legislatures to supply the funding to pay wages to patients who participate in those programs.

## SECLUSION AND RESTRAINT

Seclusion is the placement and retention of an inpatient in a bare room for the purpose of containing a clinical situation that may result in a state of emergency. Restraint involves measures designed to confine a patient's bodily movements, such as the use of leather cuffs and anklets or straitjackets. The use of seclusion and restraint raises issues of safety. The American Psychiatric Association's *Task Force Report on Seclusion and Restraint* provides standards for the use of those interventions. Clinicians practicing in institutions that use such measures should be familiar with that report and with local statutes. In most areas the doctrine of the least restrictive alternative is invoked. According to that concept, commitment should be used only when no less restrictive alternative is available. However, clinicians facing a genuine emergency should act conservatively. A patient can always be released from restraints or seclusion, whereas the harm caused by uncontained violence may be irreversible.

## INFORMED CONSENT

Lawyers representing an injured claimant now invariably add to a claim of negligent performance of procedures (malpractice) an informed consent claim as another possible area of liability. Ironically, it is one claim under which the requirement of expert testimony may be avoided. The usual claim of medical malpractice requires the litigant to produce an expert to establish that the defendant physician departed from accepted medical practice. But in a case in which the physician did not obtain informed consent, the fact that the treatment was technically well performed, in accord with the generally accepted standard of care, and effected a complete cure is immaterial. However, as a practical matter, unless the treatment had adverse consequences, a complainant will not get far with a jury in an action based solely on an allegation that the treatment was performed without consent.

In classic tort theory (a *tort* is a civil wrongful act other than a breach of contract) an intentional touching to which one has not given consent is *battery*. Thus, the administration of electroconvulsive therapy or chemotherapy, though it may be therapeutic, is a battery when done without consent. Indeed, any unauthorized touching outside conventional social intercourse constitutes a battery. It is

an offense to the dignity of the person, an invasion of the person's right of self-determination, for which punitive and actual damages may be imposed. Justice Benjamin Cardozo wrote: "Every human being of adult years and sound mind has a right to determine what shall be done with his own body; and a surgeon who performs an operation without his patient's consent commits [a battery] for which he is liable in damages." In addition to battery, a procedure performed without informed consent may be malpractice, as informed consent has become a broadly recognized part of the standard of care.

According to Justice Cardozo, it is not the effectiveness or the timeliness of the treatment that allows taking care of another but the consent to it. Thus, a mentally competent adult may refuse treatment, even though it is effective and involves little risk. But, for example, when gangrene sets in and the patient is psychotic, treatment—even of such momentous proportions as amputation—may be ordered to save the patient's life. The state is also said to have a compelling interest in preventing its citizens from committing suicide, thus allowing for treatment without consent in that situation as well.

In the case of minors, the parent or the guardian is the person legally empowered to consent to medical treatment. However, most states by statute list specific diseases and conditions that a minor can consent to have treated—including venereal disease, pregnancy, substance dependence, alcohol abuse, and contagious diseases. And in an emergency a physician can treat a minor without parental consent. The trend is to adopt what is referred to as the mature minor rule, allowing minors to consent to treatment under ordinary circumstances. As a result of the Supreme Court's 1967 *Gault* decision, all juveniles must now be represented by counsel, must be able to confront witnesses, and must be given proper notice of any charges. Emancipated minors have the rights of an adult when it can be shown that they are living as adults with control over their own lives.

In the past, to obviate a claim of battery, physicians only needed to relate what they proposed to do and obtain the patient's consent thereto. However, simultaneously with the growth of product liability and consumer law, the courts began to require that physicians also relate sufficient information to allow the patient to decide whether such a procedure is acceptable in the light of the risks and the benefits and the available alternatives, including no treatment at all. In general, informed consent requires that there be (1) an understanding of the nature and the foreseeable risks and benefits of a procedure, (2) a knowledge of alternative procedures, (3) awareness of the consequences of withholding consent, and (4) the recognition that the consent is voluntary. The physician must convey to the patient a readiness to listen and to discuss anything the patient may fear as a risk, a side effect, or a concern about the proposed treatment.

### Consent Form

The consent form is a written document outlining the patient's informed consent to a proposed procedure. The use of the consent form followed revelations of harm done to patients during clinical experimentation. Consent forms are usually designed by attorneys whose aim is to protect the institution from liability. Therefore, such forms are often exhaustive and require a level of reading comprehension that is beyond that of many patients. Paradoxically, if such a form truly covered all possible eventualities, it would probably be too long to be comprehensible, and, if it were short enough to be comprehensible, it might be incomplete. Some theorists have recommended that the form be replaced by a standardized discussion and a progress note. The basic elements of a consent form should include a fair explanation of the procedures to be followed and their purposes, including identification of any procedures that are experimental: a description of any attendant discomforts and risks reasonably to be expected; a description of any benefits reasonably to be expected; a disclosure of any appropriate alternative procedures that may be advantageous to the patient; an offer to answer any inquiries concerning the procedures; and an instruction that the patient is free to withdraw patient consent and to discontinue participation in the project or activity at any time without prejudice. The patient has the right to refuse treatment.

## CHILD CUSTODY

The action of a court in a child-custody dispute is now predicated on the best interests of the child. That maxim reflects the idea that a natural parent does not have an inherent right to be named as the custodial parent, but the presumption, although a bit eroded, remains in favor of the mother in the case of young children. By a rule of thumb, the courts presume that the welfare of a child of tender years is generally best served by maternal custody when the mother is a good and fit parent. The best interest of the mother may be served by naming her as the custodial parent, as a mother may never resolve the effects of the loss of a child, but her best interest is not to be equated ipso facto with the best interest of the child. Care and protection proceedings are the court's interventions in the welfare of a child when the parents are unable to care for the child.

More and more fathers are asserting custodial claims. In about 5 percent of all cases, fathers are named custodians. The movement supporting women's rights is also enhancing the chances of paternal custody. With more and more women going outside the home to work, the traditional rationale for maternal custody has less force today than it did in the past.

Every state today has a statute allowing a court, usually a juvenile court, to assume jurisdiction over a neglected or abused child and to remove the child from parental custody. Most states provide several grounds for assuming jurisdiction, such as parental abuse and an injurious living environment. If the court removes the child from parental custody, it usually orders that the care and custody of the child be supervised by the welfare or probation department.

## TESTAMENTARY AND CONTRACTUAL CAPACITY AND COMPETENCE

Psychiatrists may be asked to evaluate patients' testamentary capacity—that is, their competence to make a will. Three psychological abilities are necessary to prove that competence. Patients must know (1) the nature and the extent of their bounty (property), (2) that they are making a bequest, and (3) who their natural beneficiaries are—that is, the spouse, their children, and other relatives.

When a will is being probated, one of the heirs or some other person often challenges its validity. A judgment in such cases must be based on a reconstruction of what the testator's mental state was at the time the will was written, using data from documents and from expert psychiatric testimony.

When one is unable or does not exercise one's right to make a will, the law in all states provides for the distribution of one's property to the heirs; if there are no heirs, the estate goes to the public treasury.

Witnesses at the signing of the will, which may include a psychiatrist, may attest that the testator was rational at the time the will was executed. In unusual cases the lawyer may videotape the signing to safeguard the will from attack. Ideally, persons thinking of making a will who believe that questions may be raised about their testamentary competence hire a forensic psychiatrist to perform a dispassionate examination antemortem to validate and record that capacity.

An incompetence proceeding and the appointment of a guardian may be considered necessary when a member of the family is spending the family's assets. The guardianship process may be used when property is in danger of dissipation, as in the case of aged, retarded, alcohol-dependent, and psychotic persons. The issue is whether such persons are capable of managing their own affairs. However, a guardian appointed to take control of the property of one deemed incompetent cannot make a will for the ward (the incompetent patient).

Competence is determined on the basis of a person's ability to make a sound judgment—that is, to weigh, to reason, and to make reasonable decisions. There is no such thing as general competence; competence is task-specific. The capacity to weigh decision-making factors (competence) is often best demonstrated by the patient's asking pertinent and knowledgeable questions after the risks and the benefits have been explained. Although physicians (especially psychiatrists) often give opinions on competence, only a judge's ruling converts the opinion into a finding; a patient is not competent or incompetent until the court says so. The diagnosis of a mental disorder is not, in itself, sufficient to warrant a finding of incompetence. Rather, the mental disorder must cause an impairment in judgment regarding the specific issues involved. Once declared incompetent, persons are deprived of certain rights: they cannot make contracts, marry, start a divorce action, drive a vehicle, handle their own property, or practice their profession. Incompetence is decided at a formal courtroom proceeding, and the court usually appoints a guardian who will best serve the patient's interests. Another hearing is necessary to declare the patient competent. Admission to a mental hospital does not automatically mean the person is incompetent.

Competence is also essential in contracts, as a contract is an agreement between parties to do some specific act. The contract is declared invalid if, when it was signed, one of the parties was unable to comprehend the nature and the effect of his or her act. The marriage contract is subject to the same standard and, thus, can be voided if either party did not understand the nature, duties, obligations, and other characteristics entailed at the time they were married. In general, however, the courts are unwilling to declare a marriage void on the basis of incompetence.

Whether the competence is related to wills, contracts, or the making or breaking of marriages, the fundamental concern is the person's state of awareness and capacity to comprehend the significance of the particular commitment made.

## Durable Power of Attorney

A modern development that permits persons to make provisions for their own anticipated loss of decision-making capacity is called a durable power of attorney. The document permits the advance selection of a substitute decision maker who can act without the necessity of court proceedings when the signatory becomes incompetent through illness, progressive dementia, or perhaps a relapse of bipolar I disorder.

## Competence to Inform

Competence to inform is a relatively new concept involving the patient's interaction with the clinician; it is useful in ambiguous situations that may have a poor outcome. The clinician first explains to the patient the value of being honest with the clinician and then attempts to determine whether the patient is competent to weigh the risks and the benefits of withholding information about suicidal or homicidal intent. The process must be documented.

## CRIMINAL LAW

### Competence to Stand Trial

The Supreme Court of the United States stated that the prohibition against trying someone who is mentally incompetent is fundamental to the United States system of justice. Accordingly, the Court, in *Dusky v. United States*, approved a test of competence that seeks to ascertain whether a criminal defendant "has sufficient present ability to consult with his lawyer with a reasonable degree of rational understanding—and whether he has a rational as well as factual understanding of the proceedings against him."

One of the most useful clinical guides for determining a patient's competence to stand trial is the McGarry instrument, which identifies 13 areas of functioning:

1. Ability to appraise the legal defenses available
2. Level of unmanageable behavior
3. Quality of relating to the attorney
4. Ability to plan legal strategy
5. Ability to appraise the roles of various participants in the courtroom proceedings
6. Understanding of court procedure
7. Appreciation of the charges
8. Appreciation of the range and the nature of the possible penalties
9. Ability to appraise the likely outcome
10. Capacity to disclose to the attorney available pertinent facts surrounding the offense
11. Capacity to challenge prosecution witnesses realistically
12. Capacity to testify relevantly
13. Manifestation of self-serving versus self-defeating motivation

An apparent strength of such a guide is that it helps the clinician picture the effects of the familiar forms of psychopathology on those parameters, even without courtroom experience.

Clinicians must remember that they merely offer opinions about competence. The judge is free to honor, modify, or disregard those opinions. A patient is not competent or incompetent until the judge says so. One would do well to refrain from protesting a competence judgment that contradicts one's clinical opinion—which is a matter for appeals courts, not clinical objections.

## Competence to Be Executed

One of the new areas of competence to emerge in the interface between psychiatry and the law is the question of the patient's competence to be executed. That requirement for competence is thought to rest on three general principles: First, the patient's awareness of what is happening is supposed to heighten the retributive element of the punishment. Punishment is held as meaningless unless the patient is aware of what it is and to what it is a response. The second element is a religious one; competent persons about to be executed are thought to be in the best position to make whatever peace is appropriate with their religious beliefs, including confession and absolution. Third, the competent person about to be executed preserves until the end the possibility (admittedly slight) of recalling some forgotten detail of the events or the crime that may prove exonerating.

The need to preserve competence was recently supported in the Supreme Court case of *Ford v. Wainwright*. But no matter how the courts struggle with the question, most medical bodies have gravitated toward the position that it is unethical for any clinician to participate, no matter how remotely, in state-mandated executions, as the physician's duty to preserve life transcends all other competing requirements. Thus, the average psychiatrist has ethical guidance on the point. However, ethical dilemmas are readily predictable. A psychiatrist who examines a patient slated for execution may find the person incompetent on the basis of a mental disorder but may incur a medical obligation to recommend a treatment plan, which, if implemented, would ensure that person's fitness to be executed. There is room for a difference of opinion as to whether treatment under those circumstances is humane or inhumane.

### Criminal Responsibility

According to criminal law, a socially harmful act is not the sole criterion of a crime. Rather, the objectionable act must have two components: voluntary conduct (*actus reus*) and evil intent (*mens rea*). There cannot be an evil intent if the offender's mental status is so deficient, so abnormal, or so diseased as to have deprived the offender of the capacity for rational intent. The law can be invoked only when an illegal intent is implemented. Neither behavior, however harmful, nor the intent to do harm is, in itself, a ground for criminal action.

Until recently, in most American jurisdictions, persons

could be found not guilty by reason of insanity if they suffered from a mental illness, did not know the difference between right and wrong, and did not know the nature and the consequences of their acts.

The tenacity of the insanity defense appears to derive from two profound medicolegal forces. One is the moral imperative; the insanity defense is perhaps more nearly a moral issue than either a clinical issue or a legal issue. The moral dimension speaks to the reluctance to hold blameworthy or culpable those persons in society who do not appear to merit those labels because of their psychological or neurological condition—what the law calls mental disease or defect. Children and severely retarded persons have traditionally occupied that moral niche; the mentally ill have always been in an ambiguous position.

The second force is the perception of fairness. Society's sense of the fairness of its courts is undermined when, as one judge put it, "drooling idiots are treated as if they were responsible defendants." Ultimately, the legal system requires a class of nonculpable persons and a system and standards for defining that class—in short, the theory and practice of an insanity defense.

The main problem with the insanity defense, from a societal point of view, is that it generates two common misconceptions that make it unpopular. The first misconception is that many hardened criminals use the loophole in the law to escape conviction. In reality, the insanity defense is used in only a tiny fraction of cases, and it prevails in a tiny fraction of that fraction—precisely because of its unpopularity.

The second misconception is that the insanity defense allows psychiatrists to get criminals off by acting as apologists for their evil actions. That view fails because the adversarial system requires two psychiatric opinions and also because no psychiatrist ever decides a case.

**M'Naghten rule.** The precedent for determining legal responsibility was established in the British courts in 1843. The so-called M'Naghten rule, which has until recently determined responsibility in most of the United States, holds that people are not guilty by reason of insanity if they labored under a mental disease such that they were unaware of the nature, the quality, and the consequences of their acts or if they were incapable of realizing that their acts were wrong. Moreover, to absolve people from punishment, a delusion has to be one that, if true, would be an adequate defense. If the deluded idea does not justify the crime, such persons are presumably held responsible, guilty, and punishable. The M'Naghten rule is known commonly as the right-wrong test.

The M'Naghten rule derives from the famous M'Naghten case dating back to 1843 (Figure 51–2). At that time Edward Drummond, the private secretary of Robert Peel, was murdered by Daniel M'Naghten. M'Naghten had been suffering from delusions of persecution for several years. He had complained to many people about his "persecutors," and finally he decided to correct the situation by murdering Robert Peel. When Drummond came out of Peel's home, M'Naghten shot Drummond, mistaking him for Peel. The jury, as instructed under the prevailing law, found M'Naghten not guilty by reason of insanity. M'Naghten was later committed to a hospital for the insane. The case aroused great interest, causing the House of Lords to

**Figure 51–2.** Daniel M'Naghten. His 1843 murder trial led to the establishment of rules still generally observed in legal insanity pleas. (Figure courtesy of Culver Pictures.)

debate the problems of criminality and insanity. In response to questions about what guidelines could be used to determine whether a person could plead insanity as a defense against criminal responsibility, the English chief judge wrote:

1. To establish a defense on the ground of insanity it must be clearly proved that, at the time of committing the act, the party accused was laboring under such a defect of reason, from disease of the mind, as not to know the nature and quality of the act he was doing, or if he did know it, he did not know he was doing what was wrong.

2. Where a person labors under partial delusions only and is not in other respects insane and as a result commits an offense he must be considered in the same situation as to responsibility as if the facts with respect to which the delusion exists were real.

The M'Naghten rule does not ask whether the accused knows the difference in general between right and wrong; it asks whether the defendant understood the nature and the quality of the act and if the defendant knew the difference between right and wrong with respect to the act. It asks specifically whether the defendant knew the act was wrong or, perhaps, thought the act was correct—that is, was a delusion causing the defendant to act in legitimate self-defense.

**Irresistible impulse.** In 1922 a committee of jurists in England reexamined the M'Naghten rule and suggested broadening the concept of insanity in criminal cases to include the concept of the irresistible impulse. That concept holds that a person charged with a criminal offense is not responsible for an act if the act was committed under an impulse that the person was unable to resist because of mental disease. The courts have chosen to interpret the law in such a way that it has been called the policeman-at-the-elbow law. In other words, the court grants the impulse to be irresistible only if it determines that the accused would have gone ahead with the act even if a policeman had been at the accused's elbow. To most psychiatrists the law is unsatisfactory because it covers only a small special group of those who are mentally ill.

**Durham rule.** In 1954 in the case of *Durham v. United States*, a decision was handed down by Judge David Bazelon in the District of Columbia Court of Appeals that resulted in the product rule of criminal responsibility: an accused is not criminally responsible if his or her unlawful act was the product of mental disease or mental defect.

In the *Durham* case, Judge Bazelon expressly stated that the purpose of the rule was to get good and complete psychiatric testimony. He sought to release the criminal law from the theoretical straitjacket of the M'Naghten rule. However, judges and juries in cases using the *Durham* rule became mired in confusion over the terms "product," "disease," and "defect." In 1972, some 18 years after the rule's adoption, the Court of Appeals for the District of Columbia, in *United States v. Brawner*, discarded the rule. The court—all nine members, including Judge Bazelon—decided in a 143-page opinion to throw out its *Durham* rule and to adopt in its place the test recommended in 1962 by the American Law Institute in its model penal code, which is the law in the federal courts today.

**Model penal code.** In its model penal code the American Law Institute recommended the following test of criminal responsibility: (1) Persons are not responsible for criminal conduct if at the time of such conduct, as a result of mental disease or defect, they lacked substantial capacity either to appreciate the criminality (wrongfulness) of their conduct or to conform their conduct to the requirement of the law. (2) The term "mental disease or defect" does not include an abnormality manifested only by repeated criminal or otherwise antisocial conduct.

Subsection 1 of the American Law Institute rule contains five operative concepts: (1) mental disease or defect, (2) lack of substantial capacity, (3) appreciation, (4) wrongfulness, and (5) conformity of conduct to the requirements of law. The rule's second subsection, stating that repeated criminal or antisocial conduct is not of itself to be taken as mental disease or defect, aims to keep the sociopath or psychopath within the scope of criminal responsibility.

**Other tests.** The test of criminal responsibility and other tests of criminal liability refer to the time of the offense's commission, whereas the test of competence to stand trial refers to the time of the trial.

The 1982 verdict of a District of Columbia jury—finding John W. Hinckley, Jr., the would-be assassin of President Ronald Reagan, not guilty by reason of insanity—ignited moves to limit or abolish the special plea (Figure 51–3). Hinckley's trial by jury also turned out to be a trial of law and psychiatry. The psychiatrists and the law that allows their testimony were made the culprits for the unpopular verdict. "The psychiatrists spun sticky webs of pseudo-scientific jargon," wrote a prominent columnist, "and in these webs the concept of justice, like a moth, fluttered feebly and was trapped." The American Bar Association and the American Psychiatric Association quickly issued statements calling for a change in the law. More than 40

**Figure 51–3.** John Hinkley, Jr. In 1980 he tried to shoot President Ronald Reagan, but instead hit Secretary John Brady. Hinkley was found guilty by reason of insanity in 1982. The Brady Bill, a gun control bill, became law in 1993. (Figure courtesy of Wide World Photos.)

bills were introduced in Congress to amend the law, but none was passed. However, the bills helped defuse the public criticism. At present, Hinckley is hospitalized indefinitely at the federal St. Elizabeth's Hospital in Washington, D.C.

Attempts at reform have included the plea of guilty but mentally ill, which is already used in some jurisdictions. That standard has the advantage of identifying guilt while allowing some adaptation to psychiatric conditions. For example, it allows for treatment in restricted settings while permitting the courts to maintain an active role. "Guilty but insane" is a contradiction in terms. Insanity has no legal meaning except the exculpation of guilt. The defense of diminished capacity is based on the claim that the defendant suffered some impairment (usually but not always because of mental illness) sufficient to interfere with the ability to formulate a specific element (such as forethought) of the particular crime charged. Hence, the defense finds its most common use with so-called specific-intent crimes, such as first-degree murder.

Under that concept, Dan White, who had killed two city officials of San Francisco, had his crime reduced from murder to manslaughter (Figure 51–4). White's "Twinkie defense" involved psychiatrists who testified that he was depressed and that his compulsive eating of junk foods was a symptom of depression. His depression led to a manslaughter conviction, rather than a first-degree murder

**Figure 51–4.** Dan White. The former San Francisco supervisor killed San Francisco mayor George Moscone and supervisor Harvey Milk at City Hall in 1978. White's "Twinkie defense" helped reduce his crime from murder to manslaughter, for which he served five years. White committed suicide a few days after he was released from prison. (Figure courtesy of Wide World Photos.)

conviction. After he was released from prison, White committed suicide.

The American Medical Association has proposed yet another reform: limiting the insanity exculpation to cases in which the person is so ill as to lack the necessary criminal intent (*mens rea*). That approach would all but eliminate the insanity defense and place a burden on the prisons to accept large numbers of mentally ill persons.

The American Bar Association and the American Psychiatric Association in their 1982 statements recommended a defense of nonresponsibility, which focuses solely on whether defendants, as a result of mental disease or defect, are unable to appreciate the wrongfulness of their conduct. Those proposals would limit the evidence of mental illness to cognition and would exclude control, but apparently a defense would still be available under a not-guilty plea—such as extreme emotional disturbance, automatism, provocation, or self-defense—that would be established without psychiatric testimony about mental illness. The American Psychiatric Association also urged that "mental illness" be limited to severely abnormal mental conditions. Those proposals remain controversial, and the issue will probably rise again with each sensational case in which the insanity defense is used.

Figures 51–5, 51–6, 51–7, 51–8, and 51–9 represent a variety of cases in which mental illness was a factor.

## MALPRACTICE

"Malpractice" is the term commonly used to refer to professional negligence. Legally, negligence is defined by what a reasonably prudent person would or would not do in the same or similar circumstances. An action based on negligence, whatever the specific situation, involves basic problems of the relationship among the parties, the risk, and the reason. A negligence action is often precipitated by a bad outcome and resultant bad feelings.

The usual claim of malpractice requires the litigant to produce an expert to establish the four D's of malpractice: that there was the Dereliction (negligent performance or omission) of a Duty that Directly led to Damages. In negligence (1) a standard of care requisite under the particular circumstances must exist, (2) a duty must have been owed by the defendant or by someone for whose conduct the defendant is answerable, (3) the duty must have been owed

**Figure 51–5.** Jack Ruby. He was convicted of slaying President Kennedy's assassin, Lee Harvey Oswald, in 1964. He appealed his death sentence in a sanity hearing on the basis of his suffering from psychomotor epilepsy which prevented him from determining right from wrong. He was found legally sane and eventually died in prison. (Figure courtesy of Wide World Photos.)

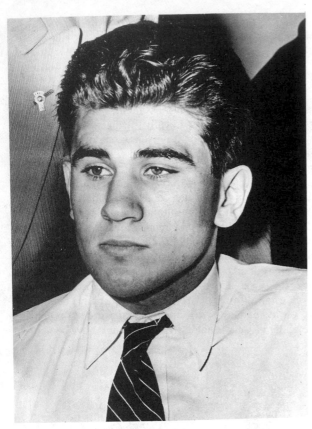

**Figure 51–6.** William Heirens. The 17-year-old University of Chicago student who pleaded guilty to three murders in 1946 was ruled legally insane by Joliet prison psychiatrists and moved to a state mental institution. (Figure courtesy of Wide World-Photos.)

**Figure 51–7.** Winnie Ruth Judd. Known as the "trunk murderess" of the early 1930s, Judd was saved from execution by a sanity hearing. She was committed in an Arizona state hospital from which she made her seventh escape in 1962. She was found in 1969 working as a receptionist. An Arizona Board of Pardons and Parole recommended her freedom. (Figure courtesy of Wide World Photos.)

to the plaintiff, and (4) a breach of the duty must be the legal cause of the plaintiff's asserted damage or injury.

The requisite standard of care under the circumstances may be established in the federal or state constitution, statutes, administrative regulations, court decisions, or the custom of the community. However, the law, with few exceptions, does not specifically define the particular duties. And it is not possible to define the way in which a person ought to act under various circumstances and conditions. As a general rule, professionals have the duty to exercise the degree of skill ordinarily used under similar circumstances by similar professionals.

Complainants in a malpractice action must prove their allegations by a preponderance of evidence. To sustain the burden of proof, the plaintiff must show (1) an act or omission on the part of the defendant or of someone for whose conduct the defendant is answerable, (2) a causal relation between the conduct and the damage or injury allegedly suffered by the plaintiff, and (3) the negligent quality of the conduct. Because most professional conduct is not within the common knowledge of the layperson, expert testimony must usually provide such information.

In relative frequency of malpractice suits, psychiatry ranks eighth among the medical specialties; in almost every suit for psychiatric malpractice in which liability was imposed, tangible physical injury was proved. The number of suits against psychiatrists is said to be small because of

the patient's reluctance to expose a psychiatric history, the skill of the psychiatrist in dealing with the patient's negative feelings, and the difficulty in linking injury with treatment. Psychiatrists have been sued for malpractice for faulty diagnosis and screening, improper certification in hospitalization, suicide, harmful effects of electroconvulsive treatments and psychotropic drugs, improper divulgence of information, and sexual intimacy with patients (Figure 51–10).

## Respondeat Superior

The Latin phrase *respondeat superior* expresses the axiom, "Let the master answer for the deeds of the servant." That doctrine holds that a person occupying a high position in a chain or hierarchy of responsibility is liable for the actions of a person in a lower position. A typical example is the psychiatric attending physician who supervises a resident. By the same reasoning, when a state hospital, say, is named in a lawsuit, the list of cited defendants may extend upward to include the commissioner of mental health and the governor of the state. After that traditional first response, the attorneys usually weed out the irrelevant defendants.

A few critical issues should be noted here: First, consultation from outside the line of clinical responsibility often does

**Figure 51–8.** Sirhan Bishara Sirhan. Sirhan shot Senator Robert F. Kennedy, after celebrating presidental primary victories in 1968. He is presently incarcerated. (Figure courtesy of Wide World Photos.)

**Figure 51–9.** Richard Speck. He was convicted in 1966 of slaying eight nurses in Chicago by stabbing and strangulation. He was sentenced to death in the electric chair. His legal defense was based on his genetic makeup which was "XYY." Individuals with these genes have been reported to be tall, be mentally retarded, have acne, and show aggressive behavior. (Figure courtesy of Wide World Photos.)

not fit the model. The consultant is an adviser, not a superior. Second, the question of the particular defendant's authority (whether that person can hire and fire, censure, or control subordinates in the system) is relevant to the assignment of blame. Third, as a rule, psychiatrists should remove themselves from situations in which they bear responsibility (liability) for the practice of other professionals but cannot control the activities of those persons or perform their own assess-

ments of the patients. In addition, psychiatrists should clarify ambiguities of responsibility at the point of entry into a system.

### Sexual Relations with Patients

Although sexual relations with patients is not a common form of malpractice, it is not rare enough. The most com-

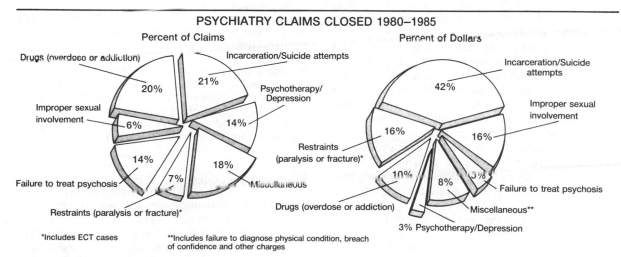

**Figure 51–10.** Psychiatry claims closed 1980–1985. (Figure from American Psychiatric Association: Psychiatric News 22: 12, 1987. Used with permission.)

mon form is heterosexual relations occurring in an out-patient context between a male therapist and a female patient, but all other permutations have come to light and to litigation.

Sexual relations with a patient is considered a breach of the fiduciary (trust-based) relationship of physician to patient and a negligent failure by the physician to work correctly with transference and countertransference issues in a manner consistent with the standard of care. The usual harms identified are the failure to provide treatment during the affair, the misuse of time that might be spent in treatment elsewhere, the creation of severe difficulties for future therapy, and the direct emotional harms of guilt, depression, anxiety, shame, humiliation, and suicidal intent.

As a ground for malpractice, engagement in sexual relations with patients poses many complex conundrums about the nature of adult consent, transference and transference love, countertransference, confidentiality, mutuality, and exploitation. Such situations may represent neurotic acting out by a therapist whose marriage is in difficulty, successful seduction by a patient, exploitive or psychopathic manipulation of a vulnerable patient by the therapist, the development of true love, or false (groundless) accusations by a vengeful borderline personality disorder patient expressing sadistic transference.

The consensus, drawn from the case law and the codes of practice espoused by national professional organizations, clearly dictates that sexual relations with a patient under any circumstances (usually including ex-patients) is unethical, a deviation from the standard of care, and, therefore, proscribed. Numerous social activities that are not overtly sexual are highly suspect (one famous case involved a therapist's taking tea with a patient). As a form of liability prevention, such activities should also be avoided.

Several questions are often raised on the subject. First, does some rule of limitations specify that, after a certain period of time has elapsed, an ex-patient can properly be dated? Although some states have defined time limits, the short answer is "probably not." Once a patient, always a patient, as far as that issue is concerned. The judgment calls are more difficult in the case of a colleague's patient or a patient seen for a one-time evaluation, but a conservative approach is recommended.

Second, what counts as sexual relations? Hugging? Hand holding? There is no way to tell what a court of law may consider sexual activity, but handshakes under appropriate circumstances should probably be the limit of physical contact between parties. Clinicians who perform physical examinations of their patients should have them chaperoned, just as in medical practice.

Third, can a therapist refer and then date a patient, so that the patient's clinical needs are addressed and the therapist is not pretending to offer treatment while being paid and leaving the patient without psychiatric care? At that point in malpractice law, the answer must again be "no." The transference relationship with the original therapist is still thought to cloud the autonomy of the patient's consent. However, the therapist whose feelings of love (or hate, for that matter) toward the patient become unmanageable and do not respond to the usual means of countertransference

resolution should terminate and refer the patient elsewhere in the interests of sound, objective care.

The problem of sexual relations with patients is such a serious issue that some governmental authorities require that psychotherapists give a publication that explains patient rights to those patients who report having been involved in sexual relations with a previous therapist (Figure 51–11).

## Suicide and Suicidal Attempts by Patients

Suicide and suicidal attempts are the most frequent causes for lawsuits against psychiatrists. An estimated one out of every two suicides leads to a malpractice action. Psychiatrists may be charged with negligence because they did not properly control a patient under treatment; such negligence causes injury, and the suicidal behavior must have been predictable. The psychiatrist may be judged with malpractice, in decreasing order of culpability, during the patient's hospitalization, while the patient is out of the hospital on a pass, during outpatient treatment. Supervision is greatest during hospitalization, and supervision is least during outpatient treatment.

## Misdiagnosis

For the clinician still grappling with the often counterintuitive complexities of the various editions of the *Diagnostic and Statistical Manual of Mental Disorders*, the idea that misdiagnosis can result in litigation may precipitate needless anxiety. Cases on that point are not concerned with whether a patient unambiguously suffered from schizophrenia or bipolar I disorder. Rather, the imputation is that the clinician negligently missed some diagnostic point. Typical examples include failures to discover a patient's suicidal or homicidal intent, a concomitant or underlying medical condition, or a side effect of consequence. The diagnoses, by inference, are diagnoses that would be detected by the average practitioner.

A patient was evaluated by a psychiatrist, who recommended that the patient receive a skull X-ray. The patient refused. Years later, the patient sued the psychiatrist for missing the diagnosis of a pituitary tumor, which had been discovered during an examination for another problem. In court, the expert witness for the defense brought out the fact that, as such tumors are "silent" at that point of growth, the average practitioner could detect them only by accident. Moreover, the patient's refusal of an X-ray—a legitimate right—prevented even the adventitious discovery at an earlier point. The jury agreed and found for the psychiatrist.

## Negligent Treatment

After diagnosis comes treatment, which may be claimed to be negligent in various ways, perhaps most succinctly summarized as "too much, too little, or wrong." Typical claims allege inadequate or insufficient treatment (undertreatment), excessive or overly aggressive treatment (overtreatment), and variations on the theme of improper treat-

**A**

# PROFESSIONAL THERAPY NEVER

# INCLUDES SEX!

This brochure was developed pursuant to Senate Bill 1004 (Senator Diane Watson). Under this law, psychotherapists are required to provide a copy to any patient who has been the victim of sexual exploitation by another psychotherapist.

### STATE OF CALIFORNIA
### DEPARTMENT OF CONSUMER AFFAIRS

George Deukmejian, Governor

Shirley Chilton
Secretary, State and Consumer Services Agency

Michael A. Kelley
Director, Department of Consumer Affairs

John C. Lungren, Jr.
Deputy Director, Division of Consumer Services

1990

**B**

**Table of contents**

*I foolishly put my trust in him. I assumed he was the professional. He told me that a body massage, touching me in intimate areas, was a legitimate part of therapy and that it helped release deep feelings and emotions. When I felt uneasy about it, I told myself that it was my hangup getting in the way of therapy.*

**Figure 51–11.** Title page (A) and table of contents (B) of a booklet that must be given to any patient in California who reports a history of sexual involvement with a therapist. A new edition of this booklet was published in 1992. (Produced by the State of California Department of Consumer Affairs. Used with permission.)

---

ment, such as using the wrong medication, failing to anticipate or respond to side effects appropriately, and creating iatrogenic harms or addictions.

Clinicians often worry about being sued for harm caused by a drug that is detected years after the drug was introduced, such as unsuspected, late-appearing side effects; but here the law is logical. The relevant standard is information available to the average practitioner at the time of the event. In court, for example, the latest edition of an appropriate textbook that was available at the time of the alleged negligence may be referred to in order to illuminate the issue.

Among the treatment modalities that are a source of professional liability are various antipsychotic medications associated with the development of tardive dyskinesia. Accordingly, psychiatrists should monitor their patients receiving such medications after warning the patients and their guardians of the risk. Documented evidence of informed consent should be in the patients' medical records. Other risks—such as retinopathy, teratogenicity, and kidney failure—should be noted when appropriate. Informed consent should be obtained before initiating electroconvulsive therapy. Recently, a hospital was judged liable for

withholding antipsychiatric medication in a case of depression when psychotherapy was the sole treatment used.

## Preventing Liability

Although eliminating malpractice is impossible, some preventive approaches have proved valuable in clinical practice: (1) Clinicians should provide only those kinds of care that they are qualified to offer. They should not overload their practices or overstretch their abilities; they should take reasonable care of themselves; and they should treat their patients with respect. (2) The documentation of good care is a strong deterrent to liability. Such documentation should include the decision-making process, the clinician's rationale for treatment, and an evaluation of the costs and the benefits. (3) A consultation affords protection against liability, because it allows the clinician to obtain information about the peer group's standard of practice. It also provides a second opinion, enabling the clinician to submit any judgment to the scrutiny of a peer. A clinician who takes the trouble to obtain a consultation in a difficult and complex case is unlikely to be viewed by a jury as careless or negligent. (4) The informed-consent process involves a discussion of the inherent uncertainty of psychiatric practice. Such a dialogue helps prevent a liability suit.

## OTHER AREAS OF FORENSIC PSYCHIATRY

### Emotional Damage and Distress

There has been a rapidly rising trend to sue for psychological and emotional damage in recent years, both secondary to physical injury or as a consequence of witnessing a stressful act and from the suffering endured under the stress of such circumstances as concentration camp experiences. The West German government heard many of those claims from persons detained in Nazi camps during World War II. In the United States the courts have moved from a conservative to a liberal position in awarding damages for such claims. Psychiatric examinations and testimony are sought in those cases, often by both the plaintiffs and the defendants.

### Workmen's Compensation

The stresses of employment may cause or accentuate mental illness. Patients are entitled to be compensated for their job-related disabilities or to receive disability retirement benefits. A psychiatrist is often called on to evaluate such situations.

## References

Adler G, Beckett A: Psychotherapy of the patient with an HIV infection: Some ethical and therapeutic dilemmas. Psychosomatics *30*: 202, 1989.
Conte H R, Plutchik R, Picard S, Karasu T B: Ethics in the practice of psychotherapy: A survey. Am J Psychother *43*: 32, 1989.
Fink P J: On being ethical in an unethical world. Am J Psychiatry *146*: 1097, 1989.
Gutheil T G: Approaches to forensic assessment of false claims of sexual misconduct by therapists. Bull Am Acad Psychiatry Law *20*: 289, 1992.
Jobes D A, Berman A L: Suicide and malpractice liability: Assessing and revising policies, procedures, and practice in outpatient settings. Prof Psychol Res Pract *24*: 91, 1993.
Jonsen A R, Siegler M, Winslade W J: *Clinical Ethics*, ed 2. Macmillan, New York, 1986.
Kant I: *Foundations of the Metaphysics of Morals*. Bobbs-Merrill, Indianapolis, 1959.
Kantor J E: *Medical Ethics for Physicians-in-Training*. Plenum, New York, 1989.
Kluft R P: Treating the patient who has been sexually exploited by a previous therapist. Psychiatr Clin North Am *12*: 1483, 1989.
Kunjukrishnan R, Varan L R: Major affective disorders and forensic psychiatry. Psychiatr Clin North Am *15*: 569, 1992.
Mill J S: *Essential Works of John Stuart Mill*, M Lerner, editor. Bantam, New York, 1961.
Miller R D: Need-for-treatment criteria for involuntary civil commitment: Impact in practice. Am J Psychiatry *149*: 1380, 1992.
Oppenheimer K, Swanson G: Duty to warn: When should confidentiality be breached? J Fam Pract *30*: 179, 1990.
Perlin M L: Tarasoff and the dilemma of the dangerous patient: New directions for the 1990's. Law Psychol Rev *16*: 29, 1992.
Reid W H, Wise M, Sutton B: The use and reliability of psychiatric diagnosis in forensic settings. Psychiatr Clin North Am *15*: 529, 1992.
Schwartz I M: Hospitalization of adolescents for psychiatric and substance abuse treatment: Legal and ethical issues. J Adolesc Health Care *10*: 473, 1989.
Serban G: Multiple personality: An issue for forensic psychiatry. Am J Psychother *46*: 269, 1992.
Stone A: *Law, Psychiatry and Morality*. American Psychiatric Press, Washington, 1984.
Weiner I B: On competence and ethicality in psychodiagnostic assessment. J Pers Assess *53*: 827, 1989.
Werner P D, Meloy J R: Decision making about dangerousness in releasing patients from long-term psychiatric hospitalization. J Psychiatry Law *20*: 35, 1992.
Winslade W J: Ethics in psychiatry. In *Comprehensive Textbook of Psychiatry*, ed 5, H I Kaplan, B J Sadock, editors, p 2124. Williams & Wilkins, Baltimore, 1989.

# Ethics in Psychiatry

Ethical principles underlie the practice of medicine, providing a foundation and a direction for complex and often painful decisions about the most fundamental of human behaviors. That fact is perhaps most explicitly and overtly true in the field of psychiatry, in which the practice of treating patients routinely involves confrontations with basic ethical dilemmas, such as restricting individual freedom through involuntary commitment and administering medicine to patients deemed not competent to refuse intervention. Hospitalizing patients and treating them against their will are common practices in psychiatry, as is the debate about the limits and the extent of rights of people who are mentally ill.

Since ethics involves a set of principles guiding a person in deciding what is right or wrong, good or bad, physicians are often tempted to seek answers in the law or in professional codes of ethics. However, those approaches to the problems they encounter do not necessarily solve the problems. Laws may change, as they have in regard to involuntary hospitalization and treatment, or they may be ambiguous, as they are in regard to the limits of patient confidentiality. Codes of ethics are also subject to change and are often ambiguous. For example, does the rule "do no harm" help when trying to decide whether to force hospitalization on a patient in order to protect society? Does the rule mean no harm to the patient or no harm to society?

As stated in the third edition of *American College of Physicians Ethics Manual*, the law does not always establish positive duties (what one should do) to the extent that professional (especially medical) ethical standards do. The physician's positive duties are based on specific ethical principles, including *beneficence* or nonmalfeasance (the duty to do no harm) and *autonomy* (the duty to protect a patient's freedom to choose). Other ethical principles are derived from the specific underlying principles, including those shaping the parameters of truth telling, disclosure, informed consent, involuntary hospitalization, the right to receive and refuse treatment, and duties to third parties.

Because of the unique nature of the disorders suffered by mentally ill people, the principles of beneficence and autonomy in psychiatry may be interpreted in many conflicting ways, leading to potential or actual conflicts in values and beliefs about appropriate care. To understand the ethical dilemmas inherent in the practice of psychiatry, one must first understand the theories that are the source of most ethical issues.

## ETHICAL PRINCIPLES

Many forces in today's society create an implicit demand on physicians. Those forces include advances in scientific research, the civil rights and consumer movements, increased public education, the effects of law on medicine, the pressure of the economy on health care delivery, and the complex moral, ethical, cultural, and religious heterogeneity of American society. The implicit demands provided by those interlocking forces create a need for physicians to be clear and precise about the ethical principles that guide their practice of medicine.

Most ethical issues find their source in two major ethical theories: utilitarian theory and autonomy theory.

### Utilitarian Theory

Utilitarian theory holds that one's fundamental obligation when making decisions is to try to produce the greatest possible happiness for the greatest number of people. When one is considering which decisions to make, laws to enact, or policies to follow, utilitarian theory requires that one (1) consider all the available evidence relevant to decisions about the consequences of alternative courses of action and (2), on the basis of that evidence, make the decision, law, or policy most likely to produce the greatest happiness in society. When alternative courses of action are dismal, one acts in ways that produce the least amount of pain. Sometimes the predictions about consequences are difficult to make and are controversial. For example, part of the debates about mandatory human immunodeficiency virus (HIV) testing and reporting and about mandatory substance testing center on the question of whether mandatory policies discourage persons from seeking medical treatment and, thus, have counterproductive consequences. Utilitarian theory recognizes no fundamental rights to truth, to informed consent, and to confidentiality. Truth telling, confidentiality, and informed consent are recognized only when and if they result in the most happiness or the least pain. Utilitarianism has also been used to justify medical paternalism, which is discussed below.

Utilitarian approaches to the physician-patient relationship are being replaced by approaches based on the second of the important ethical theories—autonomy theory. However, utilitarian theory is still used as the basis for making macro decisions about the allocation of society's resources for treatment and medical research.

**Paternalism.** Paternalism may be defined as performing actions for someone's benefit without that person's consent. Paternalism in medicine takes two forms: state paternalism and individual paternalism. Requirements that patients go to licensed practitioners for treatment and that certain drugs be given only through prescriptions are examples of state paternalism. Individual paternalism has been the traditional model for the physician-patient relationship. In that model the physician is supposed to treat the patient as a caring parent would treat a young child. The physician has a duty of beneficence to the patient, just as a parent has a duty of beneficence toward a child. The physician or the parent is presumed to know what is best for the patient or the child and has no obligation to explain each decision or to ask permission to perform actions that may benefit the patient or the child. The physician, like a parent, is presumed to have knowledge that the patient may be incapable of understanding or, in the physician's judgment, is better off not knowing.

## Autonomy Theory

Based on the writings of Immanuel Kant, autonomy theory conceives of the relationship between the physician and the normal adult patient as a relationship between two responsible persons, rather than as one between a parent and a child. The relationship is deontological, implying a moral obligation between the two parties.

The normal adult patient is presumed to have the ability and the right to make rational and responsible life decisions. The patient is autonomous (self-governing) and has rights to self-determination that must be respected, even if the physician believes that a decision will work against the patient's best interests. The law's assumption of adults' competence, the right to informed consent in treatment and research, the right to refuse treatment, and the limitations on the ability of psychiatrists to involuntarily hospitalize and involuntarily treat persons may all be seen as examples of the law's growing recognition of adults' fundamental rights to self-determination in medical decision making.

Autonomy theory accepts the idea that there are obligations to produce happiness and diminish pain. However, unlike utilitarian theory, autonomy theory prohibits using persons to achieve those goals without their consent. For example, to lie to normal adults, even for their benefit, is to show a lack of respect for their ability to be responsible self-determined beings. For another example, autonomy theory claims that to use persons as research subjects without their consent is to treat them as things, rather than as persons, and is absolutely wrong. Utilitarian theory permits such research if it produces happiness in society.

Autonomy theory also holds that paternalistic treatment of persons is justified only when those persons lack the capacity to be autonomous—for example, young children, profoundly retarded persons, and some psychotic persons.

## Further Ethical Principles

Ethical principles can both support and further the goals of psychiatric practice and research. In particular situations, awareness of the relevance and conscious application of those principles can help clarify treatment options and justify particular decisions.

**Justice.**   An ethical principle that is especially relevant to the ethics of mental health policy is *justice*, understood in this context as a fair distribution and application of psychiatric services. Justice in the sense of fair procedures enters into the involuntary hospitalization and treatment of persons who, as a result of mental illness, are dangerous to themselves or oth-

ers. The rules of procedural justice are central in that context because involuntary treatment restricts both the liberty and the choices of such persons.

**Respect.**   An additional ethical principle is respect for persons, displayed through efforts to restore or maximize patients' competence or other capacities. The more that psychiatric treatment moves toward the restoration of a patient's capacity to function, the more the treatment approximates the ethical ideal of respect for persons. That task is difficult, however, when patients suffer from enduring or permanent disabilities. Dealing with adult autistic persons whose capacity for insight, motivation, and judgment is permanently impaired is difficult. It is tempting to institutionalize such persons, to control their behavior by forcing them to function within a highly structured and sheltered environment. For some persons that may be the best treatment option. For others, despite their autistic tendencies and habits, a living situation may be possible that combines therapy and behavioral management with those preferences of the patient that, although eccentric, are socially permissible. Treatments that maximize patients' capacities and choices are ethically preferable to treatments that are designed primarily for the convenience of caretakers.

## PROFESSIONAL CODES

Most professional organizations and many business groups have codes of ethics. Such codes reflect a consensus about the general standards of appropriate professional conduct. The American Medical Association's *Principles of Medical Ethics* with annotations especially applicable to psychiatry, the *American College of Physicians Ethics Manual*, and the American Psychiatric Association's *Principles of Ethics for Psychoanalysts* articulate ideal standards of practice and professional virtues of practitioners. They include exhortations to use skillful and scientific techniques, self-regulation of misconduct within the profession, and respect for the rights and needs of patients, families, colleagues, and society. Such exhortations are reinforced by ethical principles, such as beneficence, utility, autonomy, respect for the persons, and justice.

In recent years there has been increased interest in the use of professional codes of ethics as a standard of criticism and as a means to regulate professional misconduct. Local chapters of psychiatric societies and psychoanalytic institutes have strengthened their enforcement mechanisms for dealing with complaints against their members. For example, much attention has been given to complaints against psychiatrists who have allegedly exploited their patients, especially through sexual contact. That behavior is both unethical and illegal. The action of professional ethics committees does not prevent patients' pursuing legal actions against their psychiatrists, and some patients have done so successfully.

Many critics of professional ethics note that professional ethics codes, in psychiatry and in other professions, have little effect on education, on advanced training, and on routine professional practice. And others question the efficacy of the enforcement mechanism for the codes because of the lack of sanctions and the lack of public disclosure about psychiatrists who have acted unethically. At the same time, psychiatrists who are brought before ethics committees sometimes feel badly treated by their colleagues, especially if they have already been legally penalized for misconduct.

The third edition of the *American College of Physicians Ethics Manual* provides a useful and comprehensive example of a professional code. Table 52–1 summarizes the areas covered in the manual. The manual is addressed to all physicians, not just psychiatrists; therefore, some of the ethical issues presented are not ones commonly confronted in psychiatry. However, a number of the issues are universal to the practice of medicine, regardless of specialty.

# PATIENT-THERAPIST SEXUAL RELATIONS

For a psychiatrist to engage a patient in a sexual relationship is clearly unethical. Furthermore, legal sanctions against such behavior make the ethical question moot. Various criminal law statutes have been used against psychiatrists who violate the ethical principle; rape charges may be and have been brought against such psychiatrists; sexual assault and battery charges have also been used to convict psychiatrists.

In addition, patients who have been sexually victimized by psychiatrists and other physicians have won damages in malpractice suits. Insurance carriers for the American Psychiatric Association and the American Psychological Association no longer insure against patient-therapist sexual relations, and the carriers exclude liability for any such sexual activity.

Finally, professional boards and associations have formulated procedures to review charges made by patients and are able to censure or suspend physicians. Ultimately, licenses to practice medicine may be revoked. In one case involving patient-therapist sexual relations, the court stated: "There is a public policy to protect the patient from the deliberate and malicious abuse of power and breach of trust by a psychiatrist when the patient entrusts to him her body and mind in the hope that he will use his best efforts to find a cure."

The issue of whether sexual relations between an ex-patient and a therapist violate any ethical principle remains an area of controversy. Proponents of the view "once a patient always a patient" maintain that any involvement with an ex-patient—even one that leads to marriage—should be prohibited. Such proponents maintain that a transferential reaction always exists between the patient and the therapist that prevents a rational decision about their emotional or sexual union. Others insist that, if a transferential reaction still exists, the therapy is not complete. They hold that an ex-patient is an autonomous human being who should not be subjected to paternalistic moralizing by physicians. Accordingly, they believe that no sanctions should prohibit emotional or sexual involvements by ex-patients and their psychiatrists. Some psychiatrists maintain that a reasonable time period should elapse before such a liaison, but the amount of time remains controversial. Some have suggested two years. Other psychiatrists maintain that any period of prohibited involvement with an ex-patient is an unnecessary restriction. However, *The Principles of Medical Ethics* with Annotations Especially Applicable to Psychiatry, published by the American Medical Association, states: "Sexual ac-

**Table 52–1**
**Outline of Physicians' Professional Code**

A. *The Physician and the Patient*
 1. Initiating and discontinuing the treatment relationship
 2. Confidentiality
 3. The patient and the medical record
 4. Consent
 5. Disclosure
 6. Decisions about reproduction
 7. Medical risk to the physician and patient
 8. The physician and unorthodox treatments
 9. Care of the physician's family
 10. Sexual contact between physician and patient
 11. Financial arrangements
 12. Conflicts of interest
 13. Advertising
 14. Fee splitting

B. *Decisions near the End of Life*
 1. Who should make the decision?
 2. Criteria for decisions
 3. Dilemmas regarding life-sustaining treatments
  a. Withdrawing or withholding treatment
  b. Do-not-resuscitate orders
  c. Terminally ill patients
  d. Determination of death
  e. Irreversible loss of consciousness
  f. Intravenous fluids and artificial feedings
 4. Physician-assisted suicide and euthanasia

C. *The Physician's Relationship to Other Physicians*
 1. Teaching
 2. Physicians in training
 3. Consultation
 4. The impaired physician
 5. Peer review

D. *The Physician and Society*
 1. Obligations of physicians to society
 2. Resource allocation
 3. Relationship of the physician to government
 4. Relationship of physicians to other health professionals
 5. Ethics committees and ethics consultants
 6. Medicine and the law
  a. Expert witnesses
 7. Strikes by physicians

E. *Research*
 1. Clinical investigation
 2. Innovative medical therapies
 3. Scientific publication
 4. Public announcement of research discoveries

Table from American College of Physicians: American College of Physicians Ethics Manual, third edition. Ann Intern Med *117:* 947, 1992. Used with permission.

tivity with a current or *former* [italics added] patient is unethical."

# INFORMED CONSENT

Informed consent is the cornerstone of autonomy theory. Adult patients are assumed to have the right to consent or refuse to consent to treatment. United States law reflects strong popular beliefs about deep cultural commitments to self-determination. To permit competent adults to make important personal choices about lifestyles, careers, relationships, and other values is one way to demonstrate respect for persons. However, the disabling effects of illness, especially mental illness, confuse the issue. How is it possible for psychiatrists to show respect for persons whose capacity to choose is compromised by the very condition for which the treatment is offered?

A document of informed consent serves only as a record of the completion of a process. That process should include enough uncoerced time and information to make an informed choice about treatment. Information about the diagnosis, the prognosis, and the risks and benefits of accepting or rejecting alternative courses of treatment enables patients to make informed choices.

As physicians, psychiatrists are educated to respond to persons in need of help, often in emergency or crisis situations. Often, persons in need of medical care do not want to make choices; they want physicians to take care of them and to tell them what to do to get well. The psychological authority of psychiatrists, in particular, is well documented. Patients often regress in response to mental and physical illness and may become especially vulnerable to influence and exploitation. Psychiatrists must guard against the tendency to dominate their patients' decision making.

The legal doctrine of informed consent is a reminder that psychiatrists must respect the rights of patients, including their right to be informed and to make treatment choices. However, the law does not provide guidance about the complex and subtle ethical responsibility to show respect for one's patients, especially when their competence is, to some degree, compromised by their illness. The psychiatrist's first ethical task relates to the manner in which the patient is treated. To show respect is to listen, to try to understand, and to avoid stereotyping and a premature diagnosis. Respect is further conveyed by the way the psychiatrist talks, tries to explain, and seeks to provide realistic options to patients, even questionably competent ones.

Physicians must take precautions against presuming that patients are incompetent to decide for themselves until proved otherwise or protected by courts. Respect for patients is achieved by reciprocity, communication, and concern, not domination. Respect can be shown for severely mentally disordered and disorganized patients, as illustrated in the case reports of the British neurologist Oliver Sacks, through painstaking assessments of fragmentary communications. Even with patients with minimal mental disorders who are undergoing psychotherapy, it is not primarily informed consent that displays respect for them; instead, respect is manifested most in the attentive and sensitive responses of psychiatrists to the nuances of their patients' verbal and nonverbal behavior.

## RIGHT TO DIE

The patient's right to refuse treatment is part of the rationale used to support seriously ill patients' right to forgo life-sustaining treatment. That is, patients who believe that their quality of life would be compromised by continued treatment have the right to demand that such treatment be withheld or withdrawn. Patients who are expected to lose their capacity to make decisions may express their wishes on a prospective basis, usually through the use of an advanced directive or living will. Those directives have full legal standing in some states and may be used as evidence about a patient's wishes in the states that do not recognize the directives. However, living wills present problems because they are often too general, making it impossible to cover all the eventualities in the course of a serious illness.

On June 25, 1990, the Supreme Court of the United States made a determination in the right to die issue raised by *Cruzan v. Missouri Board of Health*. The Court upheld the right of a competent person to have "a constitutionally protected liberty interest in refusing unwanted medical treatment." The Supreme Court applied that principle to all patients who have made their wishes clearly known, whether or not they ever regain consciousness.

In the case of *Cruzan v. Missouri Board of Health*, the issue under dispute was who has the right to determine the care of an unconscious person who has not previously made his or her wishes known. The Supreme Court found that, when a permanently unconscious person has left no clear instructions, a state may carry out its interest in "the protection and preservation of human life" by denying a request by others, including family members, to withhold treatment. However, it was later determined that Cruzan had indicated to family and friends that she did not want life support, and she died in December 1990 after the withdrawal of treatment.

That ruling makes it possible for each state to decide the rigor of the evidentiary standards it wishes to apply when asked to withhold or withdraw treatment from a person in a persistent vegetative state who has not previously stated his or her wishes. Physicians are encouraged to consider the laws pertaining to the preservation of life in the states in which they practice before advising patients about writing a living will. The lack of clear documentation of a patient's wishes may cause those wishes to be set aside by surrogate decision makers or by the state.

## SURROGATE DECISION MAKING

Sometimes a surrogate is designated to make treatment decisions for patients who have lost decisional capabilities. The surrogate may be designated by the patient before losing capacity or may be chosen by a court. Sometimes states allow surrogates to be designated by the hospital. The designated surrogate is usually a next of kin, although next of kin may not always be the appropriate decision makers. Relatives may have psychological and other agendas that interfere with their ability to make just decisions. In the past, surrogates made decisions for patients on a best-interests principle. The surrogate was supposed to decide which treatments could be reasonably expected to be in the patient's best interests. Present autonomy-based legal approaches require surrogates to decide on the basis of what the patient would have wished, known as substituted judgment. The surrogate should be familiar with the patient's values and attitudes. Substituted judgments present problems because it may be difficult to determine whether a surrogate is really able to determine what the patient would have wished. If a substituted judgment cannot be made, the surrogate is to use the best-interests approach.

## INVOLUNTARY TREATMENT

The principle of beneficence is invoked to justify the treatment of some persons against their will. If a person has a mental disorder that is dangerous to self or others, the law permits involuntary treatment. The legal ground for the treatment of persons dangerous to others is to protect public safety; the legal basis for the treatment of suicidal and gravely disabled persons is to protect their lives and safety. In both cases the ethical basis is to benefit the patient by treating the mental disorder.

There are legal and ethical limits to involuntary hospitalization. Involuntarily hospitalized patients have a right to a judicial review of the grounds for their confinement and treatment. Because involuntary treatment restricts a person's liberty and personal choice, the law requires that it be done for good reasons. Moreover, the hospitalization may not be indefinite, as it was before the late 1960s. From an ethical perspective, involuntary treatment is permitted on a time-limited trial basis to determine if the treatment is beneficial. The law usually permits a longer duration of involuntary treatment for persons dangerous to others than it does for patients who are dangerous only to themselves. In both cases the benefits of treatment must accrue within a finite time. However, a voluntary and consenting patient can be treated as long as it is deemed medically necessary.

Some mentally disordered, disruptive, and dangerous patients cannot benefit from treatment unless their behavior and the underlying psychoses can be brought under control. Sedation or restraint may be unavoidable. At the same time, behavior control alone is not a sufficient goal of ethical psychiatric care. It may, in some instances, be all that can be achieved; sometimes mental illness defies psychiatry's best efforts to control it. But treating the mental illness, restoring competence and ability to function, and helping the mentally ill person cope with or even conquer mental illness are the ultimate goals of psychiatric intervention. Issues involved in psychiatric hospitalization are discussed in greater detail in Chapter 51.

## LIAISON PSYCHIATRY

Liaison psychiatrists are often called on to evaluate a patient's ability to make decisions about medical care. A physician may request a psychiatric consultation because a patient is refusing to consent to a procedure. Such evaluations often present ethical and conceptual problems. Under law, adult persons are considered competent until proved otherwise. That presumption of competence is reflected in the law's recognition that patients have the right to consent or refuse to consent to medical treatment. Incompetence is a legal concept and can be established only by the courts, but psychiatrists are often given leeway to establish whether a patient has decisional capacity. If a psychiatrist evaluates a patient as decisionally incapable, the burden of disproof effectively rests with the patient.

The patient must then ask a patient advocate or a lawyer to request a competence hearing before a court.

In such cases the autonomy ethic, backed by both the law and contemporary psychiatric diagnosis, is clear: No matter how beneficial a physician believes a treatment will be and no matter how dangerous the probable consequences of rejecting that treatment, a patient has a presumptive right to reject that treatment. Refusal of treatment is not sufficient justification for claiming that the patient is decisionally incapacitated. What is at question in that evaluation is the patient's ability to give informed consent. That is, can the patient understand and appreciate the diagnosis, the prognosis, and the risks and benefits of accepting or rejecting the offered treatment? If the patient can do so, the patient has the right to refuse treatment.

## MEDICAL RISKS

Although psychiatry is among the least physically invasive of the medical specialities, a physician's right to refuse treatment to a patient on the basis of a perceived medical risk to the physician is a current issue because of the reality of acquired immune deficiency syndrome (AIDS) and all the fears attached to that disease. Bluntly stated, professional codes are clear on the subject: it is unethical for a physician to refuse to treat a patient solely because of a perceived medical risk to the physician.

The transmission of HIV from physician to patient can occur (as evidenced by the case of the dentist in Florida), but the risk is deemed extraordinarily low. The idea of mandatory testing of physicians, as well as patients, for HIV is controversial and appears to be based largely on irrational fear, rather than on scientific realities. However, the *American College of Physicians Ethics Manual* does state that physicians who may have been exposed to HIV have an ethical obligation to be tested for HIV and should do so voluntarily. The manual suggests that seropositive physicians place themselves "under the guidance of a local expert review panel, which will determine in a confidential manner whether practice restrictions are appropriate based on the physician's compliance with infection control precautions and physical and mental fitness to work." The manual goes on to state, in agreement with all medically informed and responsible parties, that infection with HIV "does not in itself justify restrictions on the practice of an otherwise competent health care worker."

### Impaired Physicians

The *American College of Physicians Ethics Manual* states, "Every physician is responsible for protecting patients from an impaired physician and for assisting a colleague whose professional capability is impaired."

Impairment in a physician may occur as the result of psychiatric or medical disorders or the use of mind-altering and habit-forming substances (for example, alcohol and drugs). A number of organic illnesses may interfere with the cognitive and motor skills required to provide medical care competently. Although the legal responsibility to report an impaired physician varies, depending on the state, the ethical responsibility remains universal. An incapacitated physician should be reported to an appropriate authority, and the reporting physician is required to follow specific hospital, state, and legal procedures. The physician who treats an impaired physician should not be required to monitor the impaired physician's progress or fitness to return to work. The monitoring should be done by an independent physician or group of physicians who have no conflicts of interest.

### Physicians in Training

It is unethical to delegate authority for patient care to anyone who is not appropriately qualified and experienced, such as a medical student or a resident, without adequate supervision from an attending physician. Residents are physicians in training and, as such, must provide a good deal of patient care. Within a healthy, ethical teaching environment, residents and medical students may be involved with and responsible for the day-to-day care of many ill patients, but they are supervised, supported, and directed by highly trained and experienced physicians. Patients have the right to know the level of training of their care providers and should be made aware of the resident's or medical student's level of training. Residents and medical students should know and acknowledge their limitations and should ask for supervision from experienced colleagues as necessary.

## PUBLIC HEALTH POLICY

### Right to Health Care

After years of debate about the right to health care, public and professional opinions remain divided. Some believe that health care is a right to which all persons are equally entitled. Others think that health care is a privilege that must be privately purchased. Still others believe that some amount of health care should be provided for those with significant health care needs who are unable to obtain them with their own resources—if not as a matter of right, as an act of benevolence. Various proposals for national health insurance, catastropic health insurance, and managed competition, among others, have been considered, and some coverage for certain categories of needy persons in the United States is made available through Medicare, Medicaid, and other special programs. However, many persons' medical and psychiatric needs are covered inadequately or not at all.

Managed competition proposes to organize people and most employers into large purchasing groups in the hope that the large groups will create competition and drive down costs to consumers. Critics of the proposal argue that only large insurance providers could handle the volume of those large purchasing groups; small providers would be driven out of business, eventually creating less competition and higher insurance costs than at present.

How managed competition would affect psychiatric services is not known, but current political trends may not be moving toward better provision of psychiatric services for underserved populations or even the middle class. Psychiatric services, both inpatient and outpatient, are currently restricted by federal and state programs. Private insurance also seems to be moving toward reductions of psychiatric coverage. The trends are toward little outpatient coverage, few visits, and reduced long-term care.

Most commentators on the ethics of the allocation of psychiatric services are critical of the injustice of mental health policies and pessimistic about the prospect of much improvement. Many indigent persons and even people with moderate financial resources who have serious and long-term psychiatric needs will go untreated. Only patients with substantial private wealth will have ready access to psychiatric care. The economics of health care and health care policy including President Bill Clinton's American Health Security Bill is discussed in detail in Section 4.9.

### Abortion

Abortion is among the most controversial ethical issues confronting physicians, lawmakers, and the general public.

In *Roe v. Wade* the Supreme Court of the United States, basing its decision on common law precedents that gave no legal standing to early-stage fetuses, ruled that there are no legal obligations toward fetuses in the early stages of development. Early abortions, therefore, can be regulated only for the purpose of ensuring the safety of the pregnant woman. The Court ruled that common law precedents give limited obligations to the fetus once it becomes viable. Therefore, states are permitted to regulate late-stage abortions.

Since *Roe v. Wade*, antiabortion advocates have tried various ways to limit abortions. In the case of *Missouri v. Reproductive Services*, the Supreme Court ruled that, because states have no constitutional obligation to provide any health care at all, they can choose not to provide publicly funded abortions.

The Supreme Court of the United States in 1990 upheld two state laws requiring an unmarried minor to give her parents advance notice of her intention to have an abortion. An Ohio law, debated in *Ohio v. Akron Center for Reproductive Health*, requires that a parent be notified 24 hours before an abortion. A Minnesota law, debated in *Hodgson v. Minnesota*, requires that both biological parents be given 48 hours notice of a minor's proposed abortion. It also provides that the minor may petition the court for permission to have an abortion without telling her parents, a provision known as judicial bypass.

In *Planned Parenthood of Southeastern Pennsylvania v. Casey*, the Supreme Court ruled in 1992 that states can impose restrictions on abortions as long as such restrictions are not a substantial obstacle to obtaining an abortion and do not unduly burden a woman's right to an abortion. That ruling upheld Pennsylvania's requirements that a woman be presented with antiabortion material during family-planning counseling and that she wait at least 24 hours between family-planning counseling and an abortion.

In 1993 President Bill Clinton overturned the gag rule that prohibited the use of public funds by clinics that included abortion as a family-planning option. He also lifted the ban on federal funding of research involving tissue from aborted fetuses. Many researchers consider fetal-tissue transplants to be a promising treatment for Parkinson's disease and dementia of the Alzheimer's type.

The Freedom of Choice Act is still before the Congress; this act would restore most of the protections of *Roe v. Wade* that have been overturned by the Supreme Court since 1973. Congress also passed laws in 1993 that impose harsh penalties on persons blockading or physically obstructing access to facilities that perform abortions.

## References

Adler G, Beckett A: Psychotherapy of the patient with an HIV infection: Some ethical and therapeutic dilemmas. Psychosomatics *30*: 202, 1989.
American College of Physicians: American College of Physicians Ethics Manual, third edition. Ann Intern Med *117:* 947, 1992.
Conte H R, Plutchik R, Picard S, Karasu T B: Ethics in the practice of psychotherapy: A survey. Am J Psychother *43*: 32, 1989.
Fink P J: On being ethical in an unethical world. Am J Psychiatry *146*: 1097, 1989.
Fitten L J: The ethics of conducting research with older psychiatric patients. Int J Geriatr Psychiatry *8* (1, Suppl): 33, 1993.
Gutheil T G, Gabbard G O: Obstacles to the dynamic understanding of therapist-patient sexual relations. Am J Psychother *46:* 515, 1992.
Jonsen A R, Siegler M, Winslade W J: *Clinical Ethics*, ed 2. Macmillan, New York, 1986.
Hartmann L: Presidential address: Reflections on humane values and bio-psychosocial integration. Am J Psychiatry *149:* 1135, 1992.
Hendin H, Klerman G: Physician-assisted suicide: The dangers of legalization. Am J Psychiatry *150:* 143, 1993.
Kant I: *Foundations of the Metaphysics of Morals*. Bobbs-Merrill, Indianapolis. 1959.
Kantor J E: *Medical Ethics for Physicians-in-Training*. Plenum, New York, 1989.
Kluft R P: Treating the patient who has been sexually exploited by a previous therapist. Psychiatr Clin North Am *12*: 1483, 1989.
Mill J S: *Essential Works of John Stuart Mill*, M Lerner, editor. Bantam, New York, 1961.
Oppenheimer K, Swanson G: Duty to warn: When should confidentiality be breached? J Fam Pract *30*: 179, 1990.
Redden K, Frankel C: Liability of psychiatrists for sexual relations with patients. Psychiatry Digest *3*: 89, 1977.
Schwartz I M: Hospitalization of adolescents for psychiatric and substance abuse treatment: Legal and ethical issues. J Adolesc Health Care *10*: 473, 1989.
Stone A: *Law, Psychiatry and Morality*. American Psychiatric Press, Washington, 1984.
Thoreson R W, Shaughnessy P, Heppner P P, Cook S W: Sexual contact during and after the professional relationship: Attitudes and practices of male counselors. J Counsel Dev *71:* 429, 1993.
Weiner I B: On competence and ethicality in psychodiagnostic assessment. J Pers Assess *53*: 827, 1989.
Winslade W J: Ethics in psychiatry. In *Comprehensive Textbook of Psychiatry*, ed 5, H I Kaplan, B J Sadock, editors, p 2124. Williams & Wilkins, Baltimore, 1989.

# Index

Page numbers followed by *t* and *f* indicate tables and figures, respectively.
Page numbers in **boldface** indicate main discussions.

differential diagnosis of, 558
Minor tranquilizer(s), 907. *See also* Benzodiazepine(s)
  definition of, 450
Mirror stage, 257
Mirror transference, 257
Miscarriage, **29–30**
Misdiagnosis, legal aspects of, 1186
*Missouri v. Reproductive Services*, 1194
Mitosis, definition of, 149*t*
Mitral valve prolapse
  emergency manifestations of, 820*t*
  and panic disorder, 584
Mixed anxiety-depressive disorder, 326, **581**
  clinical features of, 581
  course of, 582
  diagnosis of, 581
  differential diagnosis of, 581
  epidemiology of, 581
  etiology of, 581
  treatment of, 582
Mixed receptive-expressive language disorder, **1090–1093**
  clinical features of, 1091–1092
  course of, 1092
  diagnosis of, 1091
  diagnostic criteria for, 1091*t*
  differential diagnosis of, 1056, 1057*t*, 1092, 1092*t*
  DSM-IV classification of, 1090
  epidemiology of, 1091
  etiology of, 1091
  prognosis for, 1092
  treatment of, 1092–1093
MMDA. *See* 2,5-Dimethoxy-4-methylamphetamine
MMSE. *See* Mini-Mental State Examination
M'Naghten, Daniel, 1181, 1181*f*
M'Naghten rule, **1181**
Moban. *See* Molindone
Moclobemide, 972
  structure of, 973*f*
Modafinil, for narcolepsy, 708
Mode, definition of, 197
Modeling, 169
Mode of inheritance, definition of, 149*t*
Molecular behavioral genetics, 154–155
Molindone
  dosage and administration, 956*t*
    for elderly, 1161*t*
  potency, 956*t*
  preparations, 957*t*
  structure of, 943*f*
Money, John, 677
Money-Kryle, R.E., concept of normality, 19*t*
Moniz, Antonio Egas, 865, 1013
Monkey(s)
  behavior, individual differences in, 184
  catecholamine depletion, and social interaction, 181
  chronic stress experiments with, 181, 182*f*
  isolate-reared, rehabilitation of, 183–184
  social isolation studies with, 162, 182, 183*f*
Monoamine oxidase, 135, 137*f*, 139
  platelet
    and suicide, 808
    testing for, 291*t*

types of, 971–972, 973*t*
Monoamine oxidase inhibitors, 866, **971–976.** *See also* Isocarboxazid; Phenelzine; Selegiline; Tranylcypromine
  adverse effects of, 547–548, 551*t*, 974–975
  chemistry of, 971–972
  and cyclic antidepressants, combination therapy with, 551, **553**
  dosage and administration, 975
    in elderly, 1165*t*, 1165–1166
  drug interactions, 975, 975*t*
  effects on specific organs and systems, 972
  features of, 549*t*–550*t*
  historical perspective on, 971
  indications for, 546–548, 560, 971, **972–974, 997**
  intoxication/overdose, 879*t*
  laboratory interferences with, 975
  laboratory testing with, 286
  mechanism of action, 139
  for obsessive-compulsive disorder, 605
  overdose attempts, 975
  for panic disorder, 589–590
  patient education about, 545–546
  pharmacodynamics of, 972
  pharmacokinetics of, 972
  pharmacological actions of, 972
  for posttraumatic stress disorder, 610
  precautions with, 974
  side effects of, 548
  for social phobia, 598
  tyramine-induced hypertensive crisis with, 548, 971, **974–975**
  pharmacotherapy for, **923**
Monomania, 504
  definition of, 306
Monozygotic (monozygous) twin(s), 154
  definition of, 149*t*
Monroe County (NY) study, 193
Mood
  in autistic disorder, 1055
  definition of, 276, 303
  in delirium, 343
  depressed, 516. *See also* Depression
  of depressed patient, 534
  diurnal variation, definition of, 303
  dysphoric, definition of, 303
  elevated, 516. *See also* Mania
    definition of, 303
  euthymic, definition of, 303
  expansive, definition of, 303
  of geriatric patient, 1156
  irritable, definition of, 303
  of manic patient, 534
  in mental status examination, 276
  normal, 516
  physiological disturbances associated with, definition of, 303–304
  in schizophrenia, 476–477
Mood disorder(s), **516–572.** *See also* Schizoaffective disorder
  acetylcholine in, 141
  adoption studies of, 522
  and alcohol dependence, 532
  with alcohol use disorders, 397
  and anxiety, 532
  with atypical features, 528–529, 529*t*
  biogenic amine hypothesis of, 139

biogenic amines in, 518*t*, 518–519, 519*t*
biological factors in, 518–522
brain imaging in, 521, 521*f*
in cancer patient, 767, 767*t*
with catatonic features, 529, 529*t*
in children and adolescents, **1116–1120**
  biological factors in, 1117
  clinical features of, 1117–1119
  course of, 1120
  diagnosis of, 1117–1119
  differential diagnosis of, 1119–1120
  DSM-IV classification of, 1116
  epidemiology of, 1116–1117
  etiology of, 1117
  genetic factors in, 1117
  hospitalization for, 1120
  pharmacotherapy for, 1120, 1149
  prognosis for, 1120
  psychotherapy for, 1120
  social factors in, 1117
  treatment of, 1120
circadian rhythm disturbance in, 521
clinical features of, **530–532**
coexisting disorders in, 532
cognitive therapy for, 541*t*–544*t*, **541–545**
course of, **538–539**
course specifiers, 530, 530*t*
cross-sectional symptom features, 526–530
diagnosis of, **523–530**
differential diagnosis of, 480, **535–538**
  decision tree for, 329*f*
DSM-IV classification of, 516, 562, 568
due to a general medical condition, 516, 535–536, 562, **568–569**
  with depressive features, pharmacotherapy for, **993**
  diagnostic criteria for, 569, 569*t*
  treatment of, 569
electroconvulsive therapy in, 546
endogenous-reactive continuum of, 529
and environmental stress, 522–523
etiology of, **518–523**
and family functioning, 523
family studies in, 522
genetic factors in, 522
hospitalization for, 540
immunologic abnormalities and, 521
interpersonal therapy for, 541*t*–544*t*, **545**
kindling in, 520–521
and life events, 522–523
life events and, 538, 538*t*
linkage studies (molecular biology) of, 522
longitudinal course specifiers, 530, 530*t*–531*t*
and medical illness, 532
with melancholic features, 527–528, 528*t*
mental status examination in, 532–535
neuroanatomical considerations in, 521–522
neurochemistry of, 518–520
neuroendocrine regulation in, 520
non-DSM-IV types, 529–530
not otherwise specified, 516, 571
  diagnostic criteria for, 571, 571*t*
pathophysiology of, 138, 144
pharmacotherapy for, **546–555**
phototherapy for, 546
with postpartum onset, 530, 530*t*

Venereal Disease Research Laboratory test, 284, 293*t*
Venlafaxine, 866, **1002–1004**
  adverse effects of, 1003
  chemistry of, 1003
  dosage and administration, 1004
  indications for, **1003**
  pharmacodynamics of, 1003
  pharmacokinetics of, 1003
  pharmacological actions of, 1003
  precautions with, 1003
  structure of, 1003, 1003*f*
Ventilation, definition of, 841*t*
Ventral tegmental area, 135, 136*f*
Ventricle(s), cerebral, 92, 93*f*
  enlarged, 92
Ventricular system, cerebral, 92, 93*f*
Veraguth's fold, 533*f*
Verapamil, **922–925.** *See also* Calcium channel inhibitors
  indications for, 554
  receptor, 867
  structure of, 924*f*
Verbigeration
  definition of, 305
  in schizophrenia, 478
Veronal. *See* Barbital
*Verrücktheit,* 504
Versed. *See* Midazolam
Vertigo, in elderly, **1163**
Vesprin. *See* Triflupromazine
Vineland Adaptive Behavior Scales, 1021*t*, 1025
Violence. *See also* Domestic violence; Intermittent explosive disorder
  biological factors in, 717–718
  differential diagnosis, 178*t*
  DSM-IV disorders associated with, 171, 171*t*
  in epilepsy, 366–367
  incidence of, 172
  and limbic system, 107
  mechanisms of, 171, 171*f*
  pharmacotherapy for, **894**
  prediction of, 812–813, 813*t*
  predictors of, 171, 172*t*
  prevention of, 176–177, 799
  and previous abuse, 174
  as psychiatric emergency, initial evaluation of patient, 812–813
  psychopharmacological interventions for, 177, 178*t*
  and steroid abuse, 394
  televised, and violent behavior, 175, 175*t*
  victims of, 177, 179*t*
Violent behavior
  differential diagnosis of, 813
  pharmacotherapy for, 815–816
  severe, pharmacotherapy for, **946–947**
  treatment of, 814–816
Violent patient
  interviewing, 269–270
  treatment, dos and don'ts of, 270*t*
Virilizing adrenal hyperplasia, 654*t*
Vision
  blurred, as drug side effect, treatment, 873
  medical assessment of, 294–295
Visitation rights, **1177**
Vistaril. *See* Hydroxyzine

Visual agnosia, 103–104
Visual discrimination, complex, assessment of, 232–233
Visual evoked potentials, 124
Visuoconstructive capacity, assessment of, 232
Visuoperceptive capacity, assessment of, 232
Visuospatial ability, assessment of, in mental status examination, 279
Visuospatial functioning, in geriatric patient, 1156
Vitamin A, serum, testing for, 293*t*
Vitamin B₁₂
  deficiency, 372
    emergency manifestations of, 822*t*
    psychiatric symptoms in, 774*t*
  serum, testing for, 293*t*
Vitamin deficiency, psychiatric symptoms in, 774*t*
Vivactil. *See* Protriptyline
VNTRs. *See* Variable number of tandem repeats
Vogt, Cecile and Oskar, 95
Vogt syndrome, 176
Volatile hydrocarbons, use disorders, 385*t*
Volatile nitrate(s), abuse, emergency manifestations of, 822*t*
Volubility, definition of, 306
von Economo, Constantin, 95
von Frisch, Karl, 179, **180–181**
von Meduna, Ladislas J., 1005
Voodoo, 191
Voyeurism
  diagnosis of, 677
  diagnostic criteria for, 677*t*
  epidemiology of, 674, 675*t*
  etiology of, 675
Vulnerability theory, 200

**W**

Waardenburg syndrome, 1031*t*
Wagner-Jauregg, Julius, 865
WAIS. *See* Wechsler Adult Intelligence Scale
WAIS-R. *See* Wechsler Adult Intelligence Scale-Revised
Warfarin, drug interactions, with antipsychotics, 954
Watson, John B., 166, 593
Watts, James, 1013
Waxy flexibility, definition of, 304
WBC. *See* White blood cell count
WCST. *See* Wisconsin Card Sorting Test
Wechsler Adult Intelligence Scale, 222*f*, **222–223,** 230, 234
Wechsler Adult Intelligence Scale-Revised, 1021*t*, 1157
Wechsler Intelligence Scale for Children, 234
Wechsler Intelligence Scale for Children-III, 1023
Wechsler Intelligence Scale for Children-Revised, 1021*t*, 1037
Wechsler Memory Scale, 231
Wechsler Preschool and Primary Scale of Intelligence, 234, 1021*t*
Weight gain
  with antipsychotics, 949
  as drug side effect, treatment, 873
  medication-induced, 994

Weiner, Herbert, 753
Weissman, Myrna, 836
Wellbutrin. *See* Bupropion
Wernicke, Karl, 170
Wernicke-Korsakoff syndrome, 372
Wernicke's aphasia, **102,** 102*t*, 104, 1156
Wernicke's encephalopathy, 359
  emergency manifestations of, 817*t*
Wernicke's syndrome, 407
Werther syndrome, 1122
Western blot assay, for HIV, 376
Westheimer, Max, 258
White, Dan, 1182–1183, 1183*f*
White blood cell count, 293*t*
  with antipsychotic drug therapy, 285, 286*t*
White matter, 91
WHO. *See* World Health Organization
Wide-Range Achievement Test-Revised, 1021*t*, 1023
Wihtigo, **494**
William Alanson White Institute for Psychiatry, 255
Williams syndrome, 1031*t*
Will therapy, 259
Wilson's disease, **111,** 363, 1033*t*, 1083*t*
  psychiatric symptoms in, 774*t*
Windigo, 190*t*
Windigo psychosis, **494**
Winnicott, Donald W., 44, 162, 248, **259–260,** 717
Winokur, George, 470
WISC-III. *See* Wechsler Intelligence Scale for Children-III
Wisconsin Card Sorting Test, 100, **231**
Wish fulfillment, 240, 242
Witness. *See also* Expert witness
  credibility of, examining, 1172
  cross-examination of, 1172
  direct examination of, 1172
  of fact, 1171
Witzelsucht, 100
*Witzelsucht,* 1156
WMS. *See* Wechsler Memory Scale
Wolf-Man, 626
Wolman's disease, 1032*t*
Wolpe, Joseph, 168, 597, 852
Women
  career problems of, 797–798
  climacterium, 61
  elderly
    number living alone, 73, 75*f*
    socioeconomic status of, 72, 72*f*
  as head of household, 60
  life expectancy of, 67, 68*f*
  in middle adulthood, 60
  in midlife, 61–62
  and psychiatric help seeking, 200–201
  sexual functioning, in midlife, 61
  suicide of, 803–804
  use of physician services, 211
  and work, 58
Woodcock-Johnson Psycho-Educational Battery, 1021*t*
Word-association technique, 229
Word deafness, 104
Word production, assessment of, 297
Word salad, 278
  definition of, 305
  in schizophrenia, 478